CASES AND MATERIALS

TRADE REGULATION

FIFTH EDITION

by

ROBERT PITOFSKY
Sheehy Professor of Law,
Georgetown University Law Center

HARVEY J. GOLDSCHMID
Dwight Professor of Law,
Columbia University School of Law
(on leave during government service)

DIANE P. WOOD
Circuit Judge, U.S. Court of Appeals,
Seventh Circuit;
Senior Lecturer in Law
University of Chicago Law School

FOUNDATION PRESS

NEW YORK, NEW YORK

2003

© 1975, 1983, 1990, 1997 FOUNDATION PRESS

© 2003 By FOUNDATION PRESS

       395 Hudson Street

       New York, NY 10014

       Phone Toll Free 1–877–888–1330

       Fax (212) 367–6799

       fdpress.com

Printed in the United States of America

ISBN 1–58778–545–5

 TEXT IS PRINTED ON 10% POST CONSUMER RECYCLED PAPER

1st Reprint—2004

This book is dedicated to

MILTON HANDLER

*Our teacher and guiding spirit in all aspects of Trade
Regulation*

*

PREFACE

In a Preface to the fourth edition of this casebook, published in 1997, we noted the increased willingness of courts, academics, enforcement officials and the bar to reconsider almost all aspects of competition policy in the United States. Much of the need to reconcile doctrine emerged out of the exceptionally divergent attitudes toward appropriate objectives, and levels of enforcement, during the second half of the 20th Century.

We also noted that the aggressive enforcement of antitrust in the 1960s (many today would say unduly aggressive) and the minimalist enforcement of the 1980s (many today would say unjustifiably permissive) have led to efforts across the ideological spectrum to find a middle way that respected the role of antitrust in protecting free markets as well as traditional non-economic values, but also was sensitive to preserving and encouraging efficiencies and protecting incentives to innovate.

Reconciliation of competing ideologies, in our view, made debate about antitrust all the more fascinating to teach and to study. It is now six years and one edition later. Those early trends, and particularly a search for an enforcement posture that is durable and stable – and most importantly beyond the reach of political ideology – continues.

There are several noteworthy changes in the approach of this edition to the study of antitrust.

First, the tradition of this casebook, going back to Milton Handler's earliest treatment of the subject, was to concentrate on Supreme Court case law. In recent decades, the Supreme Court has only rarely addressed major substantive antitrust issues. As a result, much law is made in the Courts of Appeals, in federal and state guidelines, and in consent orders, especially at the federal level, elaborated by Federal Trade Commission and Antitrust Division explanations of the terms of particular settlements. Non-Supreme Court materials have always been included in prior editions, but their proportion has notably increased.

Second, as the American economy grows increasingly high-tech, difficult issues at the intersection of antitrust and protection of intellectual property frequently arise. These issues are particularly important because products that are the embodiment of ideas, and therefore candidates for intellectual property protection, are found in the most dynamic and fastest growing sectors of the U.S. economy. There has been an increase in the number of antitrust cases that require reconciliation of antitrust policy on the one hand and patent, copyright and trade secret protection on the other

– Microsoft, of course, Kodak, and the settlement of the FTC's complaint against Intel among many others. Differences between intellectual property and other forms of property are examined in a new note in Chapter 8 along with illustrative cases demonstrating the difficulty of reconciling legitimate but sometimes conflicting values reflected in antitrust enforcement and IP protection.

Third, we commented previously that it is no longer enough to address competition questions in the United States without some knowledge of the antitrust systems of other countries. Comparative insights may lead to policy adjustments and are increasingly important in lawyering major transactions. The volume of comparative materials (mostly from the European Union) has been expanded in this edition in the form of extensive notes – due in large part to the special knowledge and experience of our colleague Diane Wood. We realize these materials are no substitute for a full analysis of foreign law, but expect that many teachers will find them useful in the way they expose first principles and offer alternatives to accepted ways of regulating competition in the United States.

This edition of the casebook retains the fundamental approach of its predecessors. It has been written and edited to be used as a teaching tool. The cases are supplemented with materials from the related fields of economics, history, political science and even law. A continuing feature of this edition is a series of notes prepared in collaboration with Professor Steven C. Salop of Georgetown University Law Center.

The casebook again includes hypothetical problems, spaced frequently throughout the chapters. A principal virtue of the problem method – optional, of course, for teachers – is the opportunity afforded students to "synthesize" particular assignments in the context of focused, structured discussion. An additional virtue is the opportunity provided to students to sharpen their lawyering skills with respect to concrete issues of fact and law. Many teachers assign two, four or more students in advance to address each problem, asking them to prepare to argue in class as counsel for defendant, plaintiff or, for example, a government intervenor. In an advanced class, which describes antitrust in virtually every law school, the problems demand all the reconciliation of doctrine, and all the policy scrutiny, of more traditional teaching methods.

Finally, we gratefully acknowledge the valuable assistance of the following individuals who participated in the preparation of this edition: Michael Carlson, Kerin Coughlin, Hwang Lee, Zsuzsanna Belenyessy, Richard S. Snyder and Macrui Dosturian. In addition we would like to express our very special thanks to Linda Newsome, Hilda Daniels and Shirley Newsome who worked with enormous skill in the preparation of this manuscript.

ROBERT PITOFSKY
HARVEY J. GOLDSCHMID
DIANE P. WOOD

September 2003

EDITORIAL NOTE

Throughout the casebook omissions are generally indicated by ellipses. However, (i) some footnotes from judicial opinions and secondary sources, (ii) repetitive or unnecessary citations in the text of opinions and secondary sources, and (iii) most parallel citations have been omitted without ellipses or other warnings to the reader. Parallel citations appear only for main cases, important note (as opposed to footnote) cases, and in a few other instances where it appeared likely that students might go to the original opinion. Footnotes that have been retained, whether in judicial opinions or secondary sources, have been renumbered. Unless the context clearly indicates otherwise or an "Ed." has been inserted, a footnote found in an opinion or secondary source is the work of the indicated court or commentator.

*

SUMMARY OF CONTENTS

TABLE OF CONTENTS

*

TABLE OF CASES

Principal cases are in bold type. Non-principal cases are in roman type. References are to Pages.

*

TRADE REGULATION

*

CHAPTER 1

THE OBJECTIVES AND ORIGINS OF ANTITRUST LAW

SECTION 1. THE GOALS OF ANTITRUST POLICY

A. THE ROLE OF COMPETITION AND ALTERNATIVES TO COMPETITIVE MARKETS

F.M. Scherer & David Ross, Industrial Market Structure and Economic Performance[1]

1, 18–19 (3d ed. 1990).

Any economy, whatever its cultural and political traditions may be, must decide what products to supply and how much of each to produce, how scarce resources will be apportioned in producing each, and how the end products will be divided up or distributed among the various members of society. There are three alternative methods to solve this bundle of problems. First, decisions can be made to conform with *tradition*. The economic organization of manors in Europe during feudal times and the caste system of occupational selection in India are prominent examples. Second, the problem can be solved through *central planning*. Illustrations include output and input planning for most industries in the [former] Soviet Union and the elaborate controls the U.S. Department of Defense imposes over its contractors. Finally, there is the *market system* approach, under which consumers and producers act in response to price signals generated by the interplay of supply and demand in more or less freely operating markets. . . .

We proceed now to the principal questions on our agenda. Why is a competitive market system held in such high esteem by statesmen and economists alike? Why is competition the ideal in a market economy, and what is wrong with monopoly?

We begin with the political arguments, not merely because they are sufficiently transparent to be treated briefly, but also because when all is said and done, they, and not the economists' abstruse models, have tipped the balance of social consensus toward competition. One of the most important arguments is that the atomistic structure of buyers and sellers required for competition decentralizes and disperses power. The resource

---

1. Reprinted by permission of Houghton Mifflin Company.

allocation and income distribution problem is solved through the almost mechanical interaction of supply and demand forces on the market, and not through the conscious exercise of power held in private hands (for example, under monopoly) or government hands (that is, under state enterprise or government regulation). Limiting the power of both government bodies and private individuals to make decisions that shape people's lives and fortunes was a fundamental goal of the men who wrote the U.S. Constitution, which in turn has served as a model for many other nations. As James Madison wrote (under the pseudonym Publius) in Federalist Paper No. 10, nothing was more important to a well-constructed union than avoiding the imposition on all citizens of measures favored by narrow factions.[2] Factions, continued Madison, arise most frequently from the unequal distribution of property, pitting the wishes of "a landed interest, a manufacturing interest, a mercantile interest, a moneyed interest, with many lesser interests" against the common good. The best way to avoid faction-dominated outcomes, said Madison, was to keep the individual factions so small and diverse that they would be "unable to concert and carry into effect schemes of oppression."

A closely related benefit is the fact that competitive market processes solve the economic problem *impersonally,* and not through the personal control of entrepreneurs and bureaucrats. There is nothing more galling than to have the achievement of some desired objective frustrated by the decisions of an identifiable individual or group. Who, on the other hand, can work up much outrage about a setback administered by the impersonal interplay of competitive market forces?

A third political merit of a competitive market is its freedom of opportunity. When the no-barriers-to-entry condition of perfect competition is satisfied, individuals are free to choose whatever trade or profession they prefer, limited only by their own talent and skill and by their ability to raise the (presumably modest) amount of capital required.

Lawrence A. Sullivan & Warren S. Grimes, The Law of Antitrust: An Integrated Handbook[3]

11–15, 19 (2000).

As a protector of the market mechanism, antitrust's primary goal is in maintaining a system of economic allocation that decentralizes power while leaving decisions, as much as possible, in the hands of individual firms. A decentralized market system promotes progress and efficiency, reduces risks of mistakes, minimizes opportunities and reduces incentives for corruption of government officials, and generally increases public confidence in the fairness and equity of the allocation of available resources. . . .

---

2. *The Federalist Papers,* Mentor Book edition (New York: New American Library, 1961), pp. 77–84.

3. By permission of West Group.

In addition to maintaining public confidence in the market system, reasonably precise goals delimit American antitrust policy in the late twentieth century. These goals generally fall into four categories: (1) consumer welfare goals, including the efficient allocation of existing resources and avoiding wealth transfers to participants with market power; (2) fostering innovation and technological progress; (3) protecting individual firms through fairness and equity goals; and (4) maintaining decentralized economic power.

If there is universal agreement on one antitrust goal, it is that antitrust should strive for the *efficient allocation of society's available goods and services*. One of the costs of monopoly is the loss to consumers that would have purchased the monopolized product or service at a competitive price, but switch to a less desired substitute to avoid the monopoly price. When compared to competition, the monopolist's output is limited and fewer desired goods or services are distributed (economists call this a deadweight loss). What makes monopoly pricing lucrative for the monopolist are those consumers who continue to buy at the monopoly price. These consumers suffer loss in the form of a wealth transfer to the monopolist. This wealth transfer loss can be, and probably is, more substantial than any deadweight loss. Thus, a second widely recognized and important goal of antitrust policy is to ensure that sellers (or buyers that are monopsonists) do not use market power to shift wealth from consumers to themselves at levels above those that would be possible in competitive conditions.

Taken together, the goals of efficient allocation and avoidance of wealth transfer are consistent with the framers' original goal of protecting consumers against high prices associated with market power. All theorists recognize that avoiding or reducing the deadweight loss caused by monopoly is a proper goal of antitrust policy. Traditionalists and post-Chicagoans have regarded avoiding or reducing wealth transfers as an appropriate, consumer-oriented antitrust goal. Many Chicago theorists, however, dispute whether a wealth transfer loss is a legitimate concern. Wealth distribution, in the view of these theorists, ought to be addressed through tax policy, or through other means than antitrust law.... The dominant view, and certainly the one more attuned to the original goals of the Sherman Act, is that antitrust laws properly aim at avoiding both deadweight and wealth transfer losses....

Another widely accepted goal of antitrust policy is to promote innovation, or what the economists sometimes refer to as the *dynamic efficiency* of the economy. For economists, allocative efficiency means producing and distributing more efficiently through the use of existing technology. Dynamic efficiency refers to improvements in the technology: improving the product, producing it more efficiently, or perhaps replacing it with an entirely different product that outperforms the old one. Economists believe that society benefits far more (real income rates grow faster) from dynamic efficiency than from allocative efficiency....

There is agreement that the market fosters innovation by rewarding those who bring new and better products into the market. A diverse market with multiple players competing to be the first to introduce meaningful innovation should increase the pace and variety of innovation—both the development of new processes or products and their use and commercialization. A monopolist has a reduced incentive to innovate; if it does innovate, it may be motivated to suppress or delay commercialization. Indeed, to protect its monopoly, a firm may even attempt to suppress or discourage others from marketing available innovation. . . .

Another goal of the framers of the Sherman Act was to protect the right of any person to enter and pursue a line of work or business. Today, that goal has been rejected by some theorists and courts, and given low priority by others. Competition is a dispassionate mechanism that will cause many business failures. The Supreme Court has said that "[i]t is competition, not competitors, which the Act protects. . . ."[4] By the end of the twentieth century, there was no longer (if there ever was) a right of a displaced competitor to claim that the displacement in and of itself was grounds for antitrust relief. But given allocative or wealth transfer effects, evidence of such injury (and perhaps the unfairness associated with it) may weigh in favor of finding an antitrust violation.

[Finally, the] populist goal of preventing the growth of big business motivated many supporters of the Sherman Act and still had some force during the activist period of antitrust enforcement that lasted into the 1960s. . . . As allocative efficiency became a more dominant goal of antitrust, the goal of maintaining a decentralized economy lost force. The internationalization of markets has reenforced this change. As major U.S. industries lost ground in competition with foreign rivals, it became clear that the efficiency of American firms should be a priority in crafting antitrust policy. A second consideration was the difficulty in formulating a workable test for pursuit of a decentralization goal: unless all moves toward concentration were to be condemned, courts were faced with an impossibly subjective balancing of how much lost efficiency should be tolerated in order to maintain dispersed economic power.

Robert H. Bork, The Antitrust Paradox: A Policy at War With Itself

10–11, 20–21 (1978).

The language of the statute, which is singularly opaque, was chosen not merely because it employed familiar common law terminology but also to allay fears that the law might go beyond the then narrowly conceived commerce power of Congress. The act's reach would be coextensive with the Supreme Court's demarcation of commerce. This common law phraseology has caused no end of confusion, however, since there was no unitary body of common law doctrine that could give meaning to the statute. The common law of restraints of trade and monopolies has been a variable growth, composed of diverse and contradictory strains, many of them

4. Brown Shoe Co. v. United States, 370 U.S. 294, 344 (1962).

obviously irrelevant or even hostile to the policy of fostering competition. Yet Sherman and many of his colleagues repeatedly assured the Senate, without objection by anyone, that they proposed merely to enact the common law.

There is no mystery, for Sherman and the others also repeatedly stated what their version of the common law was. The statute's ultimate use of common law terms thus carried with it the substantive rules that Sherman and others thought appropriate to the policy they sought to enact. The cases discussed by Sherman as representative of the common law held illegal the predatory extraction of railroad rebates by the Standard Oil Co., cartel agreements, and monopolistic horizontal mergers. Cases going the other way he simply ignored. The fact that the statements of Sherman and his colleagues did not accurately portray the actual confusion of common law precedent at the time does not obscure what they intended to accomplish. It is clear from the debates that the "common law" relevant to the Sherman Act is an artificial construct, made up for the occasion out of a careful selection of a few recent decisions from different jurisdictions, plus a liberal admixture of the senators' own policy prescriptions. It is to this "common law," holding full sway nowhere but in the debates of the Fifty-first Congress, that one must look to understand the Sherman Act.

The statute was intended to strike at cartels, horizontal mergers of monopolistic proportions, and predatory business tactics. Wide discretion was delegated to the courts to frame subsidiary rules, but it was also clear ... that the delegation was confined by the policy of advancing consumer welfare. Sherman's draft of the statute outlawed arrangements "designed, or which tend, to advance the cost to the consumer." And in the debates Sherman demonstrated his understanding that higher prices were brought about by what an economist today would call a restriction of output, as when he asked whether Congress had not the power to "protect commerce, nullify contracts that restrain commerce, turn it from its natural courses, increase the price of articles, and thereby diminish the amount of commerce?" The wide variety of other policy goals that have since been attributed to the framers of the Sherman Act is not to be found in the legislative history. . . .

Antitrust is, first and most obviously, law, and law made primarily by judges. We are right to be concerned about the integrity and legitimacy of that lawmaking process, both for its own sake and because ideas about the power and discretion proper to courts in one field of law will inevitably affect their performance elsewhere. At issue is the question central to democratic society: Who governs?

Antitrust is also a set of continually evolving theories about the economics of industrial organization. These theories affect the thought of laymen about business and its behavior, of course, but it is nothing short of extraordinary to see how powerfully the enshrinement of an economic theory in a Supreme Court opinion affects the thought even of economists. For this and other reasons the political fate of the competitive, free-market ideal is heavily involved with developments in antitrust. The capture of the field by anti-free-market theories will have an impact far beyond the confines of antitrust itself.

The struggle between economic freedom and regulation also reflects and reacts upon the tension in our society between the ideals of liberty and equality. Neither of these can be an absolute, of course, but the balance between them and the movement of that balance are crucial.

Within the limited frame for observation provided by antitrust, therefore, it is worth noting that the general movement has been away from legislative decision by Congress and toward political choice by courts, away from the ideal of competition and toward the older idea of protected status for each producer, away from concern for general welfare and toward concern for interest groups, and away from the ideal of liberty toward the ideal of enforced equality. No one can know how far these trends may go, but if, as I believe, they have already gone much too far in antitrust as elsewhere in our polity, they should be recognized and reversed, for they are ultimately incompatible with the preservation of a liberal capitalist social order. Antitrust should not be permitted to remain an unknown policy.

Richard A. Posner, Antitrust Law

1–2 (2d ed. 2001).

To the layperson a "law" is a rule written down in a book somewhere. The lawyer realizes that the matter is often a good deal more complicated. There are federal antitrust statutes, and they are brief and readable compared to the Internal Revenue Code. But their operative terms— "restraint of trade," "substantially to lessen competition," "monopolize"— are opaque; and the congressional debates and reports that preceded their enactment, and other relevant historical materials, cast only a dim light on the intended meaning of the key terms. The courts have spent many years interpreting, or perhaps more accurately supplying, that meaning. But the course of judicial interpretation has not always run true. And the rules of law as they are articulated and as they are applied to alter behavior are often and in this instance two different things. The result of the "common-law" (that is, judge-made) character of antitrust law, despite its statutory foundations, and of the practical complications of its enforcement, is a considerable fluidity in the meaning and application of the law, and uncertainty about its effects.

One thing that has long been clear, however, is that antitrust deals with what are at root economic phenomena. The basic phenomenon is that of monopoly or monopolizing, broadly defined to include collusion between competing firms aimed at jacking up the market price above the competitive level, and also practices, such as certain mergers, that create a danger rather than a certainty of monopoly. . . .

[E]conomic theory provides a solid basis for the belief that monopoly pricing, which results when firms create an artificial scarcity of their product and thereby drive price above its level under competition, is presumptively inefficient in the sense most commonly used by economists in discussing issues of monopoly and competition (the Kaldor–Hicks, or potential Pareto, sense of efficiency). Since efficiency is an important social value, this conclusion establishes a prima facie case for having an antitrust policy. It also implies the limitations of that policy: to the extent that efficiency is the goal of antitrust enforcement, there is no justification for carrying enforcement into areas where competition is less efficient than monopoly because the costs of monopoly pricing are outweighed by the economies of centralizing production in one or a very few firms.[5] That is why I referred to monopoly pricing as "presumptively" inefficient and as creating merely a "prima facie" case for having an antitrust policy. Nor is there any justification for using the antitrust laws to attain goals unrelated or antithetical to efficiency. . . .

Robert Pitofsky, The Political Content of Antitrust

127 U.Pa.L.Rev. 1051–66 (1979).

Although the political forces that produced the major antitrust statutes—in 1890, 1914, 1936, and 1950—varied widely, those statutes once enacted have almost always been enforced and interpreted so that economic considerations were paramount. The issue among most serious people has never been whether non-economic considerations should outweigh significant long-term economies of scale, but rather whether they had any role to play at all, and, if so, how they should be defined and measured.

There probably has never been a period comparable to the last decade, however, when antitrust economists and lawyers have had such success in persuading the courts to adopt an *exclusively* economic approach to antitrust questions. . . . I will urge a different view. It is bad history, bad policy, and bad law to exclude certain political values in interpreting the antitrust laws. By "political values," I mean, first, a fear that excessive concentration of economic power will breed antidemocratic political pressures, and second, a desire to enhance individual and business freedom by reducing the range within which private discretion by a few in the economic sphere controls the welfare of all. A third and overriding political concern is that if the free-market sector of the economy is allowed to develop under antitrust rules that are blind to all but economic concerns, the likely result will be an economy so dominated by a few corporate giants that it will be impossible for the state not to play a more intrusive role in economic affairs. . . .

It can be argued that the political considerations discussed here are ill-defined and incapable of exact or even meaningful definition. Also, it will be difficult to balance vague concepts such as a fear of economic conditions conducive to totalitarianism against the efficiency loss of an industry

---

5. It might be possible to have one's cake and eat it by limiting the price charged by the efficient monopolist. That is the premise of public utility regulation, but, as I believe all competent students of antitrust agree, it is not a feasible project for antitrust law.

structure that is disassembled or a series of business transactions that are disallowed. Finally, it may be that when such vague and controversial factors are introduced into antitrust considerations, some enforcement officials and judges will lose sight of the secondary role of these political factors and will distort and misinterpret antitrust policy. There is merit to each of these concerns. But despite the inconvenience, lack of predictability, and general mess introduced into the economists' allegedly cohesive and tidy world of exclusively micro-economic analysis, an antitrust policy that failed to take political concerns into account would be unresponsive to the will of Congress and out of touch with the rough political consensus that has supported antitrust enforcement for almost a century. . . .

But putting aside the Sherman Act and its admittedly obscure legislative history, can we discern anything with respect to legislative intent from subsequent antitrust statutes? If we can, it seems clear that those subsequent statutes must be interpreted to incorporate political concerns, and it appears arguable that these subsequent expressions define Congress' vague intentions in earlier enactments. Specifically, can fair-minded commentators read the legislative history of amended section 7—the most recent major substantive revision of general antitrust policy—and conclude that Congress intended to regulate mergers and joint ventures without taking into account the political consequences of what it perceived to be an ongoing merger movement? . . .

Some of the key passages of section 7's legislative history reveal strong congressional concern with the political implications of mergers; in this era of augmented influence by economists and economically sophisticated lawyers, we seem to have lost sight of these attitudes. . . . A striking feature of the legislative history of amended section 7 was the widely shared perception of danger to the political well-being of the country and its citizens stemming from the merger movement. . . .[6] Virtually all proponents of the bill who spoke asserted that the merger trend must be blocked because concentrated economic power would lead to increased government control, because freedom would corrode and totalitarianism prosper, and because absentee ownership by large corporations would diminish local initiative and civic responsibility.[7] Of course, that kind of language is not helpful in deciding whether a merger between two companies of given size in specific markets is legal. Congress in 1950 left those questions to the courts much as it did in 1890. But to proceed from that starting point to the conclusion that Congress in 1950 would be satisfied with a judicial interpretation that excluded all non-economic concerns—a position advocated largely by scholars who would not themselves regard the merger movement as a serious threat to political values—reflects a striking disregard for the political process.

6. Bok, Section 7 of the Clayton Act and the Merging of Law and Economics, 74 Harv.L.Rev. 226, 234–37 (1960).

7. Id. 235–36. The Supreme Court has ratified the view that Congress was intent on stemming a rising tide of concentration because of a threat to non-economic values. *See* Brown Shoe Co. v. United States, 370 U.S. 294 (1962).

Suppose a political component were to be included in an antitrust enforcement equation. Would that introduce chaos into what otherwise would be an orderly, reliable, and predictable regulatory process? Such a result is unlikely. Those opposed to the inclusion of political factors exaggerate the precision of an enforcement approach that incorporates solely economic concerns, and overstate the administrative difficulties and enforcement costs of taking noneconomic concerns into account. It has been argued that if political concerns are to be satisfied, there is no clear stopping place short of atomistic competition.[8] That position overstates the difficulties of introducing political values to leaven what would otherwise be an exclusively economic analysis of antitrust problems.

Political concerns ought to be treated as limited factors that influence the way in which prospective rules are designed to accomplish antitrust objectives. If the rules themselves are clear, introduction of a political dimension will not generate undue uncertainty in enforcement. Moreover, because these political concerns are clearly and expressly secondary, major dislocations in competitive policy will be avoided.

Herbert Hovenkamp, Antitrust Policy After Chicago

84 Mich.L.Rev. 213, 215–16, 226, 249–51, 283–84 (1985).

If one hundred years of federal antitrust policy have taught us anything, it is that antitrust is both political and cyclical. Almost every political generation has abandoned the policy of its predecessors in favor of something new. . . .

The Chicago School model of antitrust policy dictates that allocative efficiency as defined by the market should be the only goal of the antitrust laws.[9] Within that paradigm even evidence derived from the legislative history of the antitrust laws is unimportant, unless to show that the legislative history supports or undermines the model. If the latter, the preservation of the model requires that the legislative history of the antitrust laws be deemed irrelevant to their current interpretation.

The market efficiency model for antitrust policy is very powerful, and is as appealing intellectually as any of its predecessors. One of the strongest elements in its appeal has been its advocacy of expertise outside the legal profession. Today more than ever antitrust decisionmakers have been forced to submit their views to another group of specialists—economists—for evaluation. Antitrust academia, the antitrust bar, and the federal judiciary are filled with people who have made serious efforts to learn about price theory and industrial organization. . . . [Today, however,] the cutting edge of antitrust scholarship is coming, not from protagonists of the Chicago School, but rather from its critics. . . .[10]

8. *See* Bork, The Rule of Reason and the *Per Se* Concept: Price Fixing and Market Division, 74 Yale L.J. 775, 831–32 (1965).

9. *See* R. Bork, at 91; R. Posner, Antitrust Law: An Economic Perspective 4 (1976).

10. *See* Dixit, A Model of Duopoly Suggesting a Theory of Entry Barriers, 10 Bell J.

Orthodox Chicago School antitrust policy is predicated on two assumptions about the goals of the federal antitrust laws: (1) the best policy tool currently available for maximizing economic efficiency in the real world is the neoclassical price theory model; and (2) the pursuit of economic efficiency should be the exclusive goal of antitrust enforcement policy.

Both of these statements are controversial. The first one raises several economic questions about the internal integrity of the neoclassical price theory model, as well as questions about the ability of *any* economic model to identify efficient policies in the real world. The second statement is probably contrary to the intent of the Congresses that drafted the various antitrust laws. . . .

The legislative histories of the various antitrust laws fail to exhibit anything resembling a dominant concern for economic efficiency. Dozens of scholars have scrutinized these legislative histories in order to determine what Congress had in mind. . . . The strongest argument that Congress was motivated by concerns of efficiency when it passed an antitrust law has been made by Professor . . . Bork, and is concerned largely with the Sherman Act. However, Bork's work has been called into question by subsequent scholarship showing that in 1890 Congress had no real concept of efficiency and was really concerned with protecting consumers from unfavorable wealth transfers.

Of course, Congress could rewrite the antitrust laws and make concerns for efficiency express, but it has not done so. In fact, the widely proclaimed Chicago School "revolution" has pretty much passed Congress by. Historically, liberals have been fairly successful in getting Congress to write liability-expanding antitrust statutes.[11] However, with only a few trivial exceptions, free marketers have had no such luck.[12] Leaders in

Econ. 20 (1979); Kaplow, Extension of Monopoly Power Through Leverage, 85 Colum.L.Rev. 515 (1985); Markovits, The Limits to Simplifying Antitrust: A Reply to Professor Easterbrook, 63 Texas L.Rev. 41 (1984); Salop, Strategic Entry Deterrence, Am.Econ. Rev., May 1979, at 335; Salop & Scheffman, Raising Rivals' Costs, Am.Econ.Rev., May 1983, at 267; Scherer, The Economics of Vertical Restraints, 52 Antitrust L.J. 687 (1983); Wentz, Mobility Factors in Antitrust Cases: Assessing Market Power in Light of Conditions Affecting Entry and Fringe Expansion, 80 Mich.L.Rev. 1545 (1982); Williamson, Antitrust Enforcement: Where It's Been, Where It's Going, 27 St. Louis U.L.J. 289 (1983).

11. For example, the Clayton Act, ch. 323, 38 Stat. 730 (1914) (codified as amended in scattered sections of 15 U.S.C. and 29 U.S.C. (1982)), passed in 1914 during the Wilson administration; the Robinson–Patman Act, ch. 592, 49 Stat. 1526–28 (1936) (codified at 15 U.S.C. §§ 13–13b, 21a (1982)), passed

during the Franklin D. Roosevelt administration; the Celler–Kefauver amendments to § 7 (relating to mergers) of the Clayton Act, ch. 1184, 64 Stat. 1125 (1950) (codified at 15 U.S.C. § 18 (1982)), passed during the Truman administration.

Perhaps the one notable exception is the Consumer Goods Pricing Act of 1975, Pub.L. 94–145, 89 Stat. 801 (amending 15 U.S.C. §§ 1, 45a (1968)), which abolished "fair trade" and arguably restored the *per se* rule for resale price maintenance. That statute was passed during the Nixon administration. However, given the controversial nature of resale price maintenance, it is difficult to characterize the statute as either liberal or conservative.

12. The liability-restricting statutes that have been passed are generally either jurisdictional, or else nibble away at economic areas that cover a relatively small percentage of antitrust activity. Examples are the

conservative administrations have asked for legislation weakening the merger laws or abolishing treble damages, but Congress has generally resisted these requests.[13] ...

The Chicago School of antitrust analysis has made an important and lasting contribution to antitrust policy. The School has placed an emphasis on economic analysis in antitrust jurisprudence that will likely never disappear. At the same time, however, the Chicago School's approach to antitrust is defective for two important reasons. First of all, the notion that public policymaking should be guided exclusively by a notion of efficiency based on the neoclassical market efficiency model is naive. That notion both overstates the ability of the policymaker to apply such a model to real world affairs and understates the complexity of the process by which the policymaker must select among competing policy values. Second, the neoclassical market efficiency model is itself too simple to account for or to predict business firm behavior in the real world.

John E. Kwoka, Jr. & Lawrence J. White, The Antitrust Revolution: Economics, Competition, and Policy

3–4 (3d ed. 1999).

Chicago School economics permanently altered the debate over the purposes and methods of antitrust. Regardless of how much of it one agreed with, the Chicago School view raised a series of fundamental questions, provided its answers to those questions, and made clear that any other answers would be held to an intellectually rigorous standard. And there *were*, and are, other answers. . . .

Apart from those who never accepted this new [Chicago School] learning, theorists and applied economists have more recently been drawn to the intellectual challenges of antitrust economics. They have revisited traditional issues and put Chicago School formulations under the same intense scrutiny as that school gave earlier views. Those formulations have not always held up. The new analyses have involved more powerful theory,

Local Government Antitrust Act of 1984, 15 U.S.C. §§ 35, 36 (Supp. II 1984), which abolished treble damages for antitrust violations by municipalities; the Export Trading Company Act of 1982, 15 U.S.C. §§ 4001–4021 (1982), which gives a limited antitrust exemption to qualified export trade associations and companies; and the National Cooperative Research Act of 1984, 15 U.S.C. §§ 4301–05 (Supp. II 1984), which gives an exemption from the *per se* rule to qualified research joint ventures. All three of these statutes were passed during the Reagan administration.

13. For example, *see* Commerce Secretary Malcolm Baldridge's proposal to repeal

§ 7 of the Clayton Act, 48 Antitrust & Trade Reg.Rep. (BNA) 385 (Feb. 28, 1985); and *see* the Reagan administration proposal to abolish treble damages for rule of reason violations, Draft Reagan Administration Legislation on Antitrust, Patents, and Joint Research and Development Ventures, 44 Antitrust & Trade Reg.Rep. (BNA) No. 1121, at 1272 (June 30, 1983). *See also* the comprehensive administration package of antitrust proposals, intended to reduce damages, narrow the coverage of § 7 of the Clayton Act, and reduce the extraterritorial jurisdiction of the antitrust laws. Administration's Antitrust Law Package, [Current] Trade Reg. Rep. (CCH) No. 744, pt. 2 (Feb. 24, 1986).

which is better adapted to specific issues and more capable of identifying conditions under which various practices might have procompetitive versus anticompetitive effects. The result has been demonstrations of the potential competitive harm from actions that the Chicago School exonerated. In addition, techniques of empirical analysis have become much more sophisticated, with data better suited to its task, models well grounded in theory, and superior econometric tools. The return to empirical inquiry has helped counterbalance the near-exclusive reliance on theory that characterizes the Chicago approach.

Out of this has emerged an alternative approach to antitrust economics. Sometimes called "post-Chicago economics," it argues that many formulations of the past twenty years are *too* reliant on theory—and simplistic theory at that—with the result that important issues are overlooked and incorrect conclusions are drawn. It contends that many practices must be evaluated in light of facts specific to the case, rather than being pigeonholed into some tidy theoretical box. And it is far more skeptical of the ability of the market to discipline firms and thereby negate the anticompetitive potential of mergers and various practices.

Post–Chicago economics is not—or at least not yet—a unified alternative paradigm. It certainly has not displaced the Chicago approach in many quarters. And some have expressed concern that its more fact-based approach will make determinations of antitrust violations more difficult. But it has gained acceptance as an intellectually rigorous alternative approach to antitrust. It represents a significant counterweight to the views that have dominated the past twenty years, with fundamentally different policy implications and with increasing impact on antitrust enforcement and court decisions.

And significantly, post-Chicago antitrust economics is very much a part of the "antitrust revolution." Economics constitutes its foundation just as much as economics did for the new learning—indeed, its advocates would argue, more so. These new views simply represent another step in that revolution. And there will be many more such steps, as economics strives to clarify the effects of structural changes and various business practices on market performance.

NOTES

1. NORTHERN PACIFIC RAILWAY CO. v. UNITED STATES, 356 U.S. 1, 4–5, 78 S.Ct. 514, 517–18, 2 L.Ed.2d 545, 549 (1958). "The Sherman Act was designed to be a comprehensive charter of economic liberty aimed at preserving free and unfettered competition as the rule of trade. It rests on the premise that the unrestrained interaction of competitive forces will yield the best allocation of our economic resources, the lowest prices, the highest quality and the greatest material progress, while at the same time providing an environment conducive to the preservation of our democratic political and social institutions." (Black, J.)

2. BROWN SHOE CO. v. UNITED STATES, 370 U.S. 294, 344, 82 S.Ct. 1502, 1534, 8 L.Ed.2d 510, 547 (1962). " ... [W]e cannot fail to recognize Congress' desire to promote competition through the protection of viable, small, locally owned businesses. Congress appreciated that occasional higher costs and prices might result from the maintenance of fragmented industries and markets. It resolved these competing considerations in favor of decentralization. We must give effect to that decision." (Warren, C.J.)

3. UNITED STATES v. ALUMINUM CO. OF AMERICA, 148 F.2d 416, 427 (2d Cir.1945).

"[I]t is no excuse for 'monopolizing' a market that the monopoly has not been used to extract from the consumer more than a 'fair' profit. The Act has wider purposes. Indeed, even though we disregarded all but economic considerations, it would by no means follow that such concentration of producing power is to be desired, when it has not been used extortionately. Many people believe that possession of unchallenged economic power deadens initiative, discourages thrift and depresses energy; that immunity from competition is a narcotic, and rivalry is a stimulant, to industrial progress; that the spur of constant stress is necessary to counteract an inevitable disposition to let well enough alone. Such people believe that competitors, versed in the craft as no consumer can be, will be quick to detect opportunities for saving and new shifts in production, and be eager to profit by them. In any event the mere fact that a producer, having command of the domestic market, has not been able to make more than a 'fair' profit, is no evidence that a 'fair' profit could not have been made at lower prices. True, it might have been thought adequate to condemn only those monopolies which could not show that they had exercised the highest possible ingenuity, had adopted every possible economy, had anticipated every conceivable improvement, stimulated every possible demand. No doubt, that would be one way of dealing with the matter, although it would imply constant scrutiny and constant supervision, such as courts are unable to provide. Be that as it may, that was not the way that Congress chose; it did not condone 'good trusts' and condemn 'bad' ones; it forbad all. Moreover, in so doing it was not necessarily actuated by economic motives alone. It is possible, because of its indirect social or moral effect, to prefer a system of small producers, each dependent for his success upon his own skill and character, to one in which the great mass of those engaged must accept the direction of a few." (L. Hand, J.)

4. NATIONAL SOCIETY OF PROFESSIONAL ENGINEERS v. UNITED STATES, 435 U.S. 679, 688, 695, 98 S.Ct. 1355, 1363, 1367, 55 L.Ed.2d 637, 648, 652 (1978).

"Congress ... did not intend the text of the Sherman Act to delineate the full meaning of the statute or its application in concrete situations. The legislative history makes it perfectly clear that it expected the courts to give shape to the statute's broad mandate by drawing on common-law tradition. The Rule of Reason, with its origins in common-law precedents long antedating the Sherman Act, has served that purpose. It has been used to give the Act both flexibility and definition, and its central principle of antitrust analysis has remained constant. Contrary to its name, the Rule does not open the field of antitrust inquiry to any argument in favor of a challenged restraint that may fall within the realm of reason. Instead ... it focuses directly on the challenged restraint's impact on competitive conditions.

"The Sherman Act reflects a legislative judgment that ultimately competition will not only produce lower prices, but also better goods and services.... The assumption that competition is the best method of allocating resources in a free market recognizes that all elements of a bargain—quality, service, safety, and durability—and not just the immediate cost, are favorably affected by the free opportunity to select among alternative offers. Even assuming occasional exceptions to the presumed consequences of competition, the statutory policy precludes inquiry into the question whether competition is good or bad." (Stevens, J.)

5. BERKEY PHOTO, INC. v. EASTMAN KODAK CO., 603 F.2d 263, 273 (2d Cir.1979), cert. denied, 444 U.S. 1093, 100 S.Ct. 1061, 62 L.Ed.2d 783 (1980).

"Because, like all power, it is laden with the possibility of abuse; because it encourages sloth rather than the active quest for excellence; and because it tends to damage the very fabric of our economy and our society, monopoly power is 'inherently evil....' [W]hile proclaiming vigorously that monopoly power is the evil at which § 2 is aimed, courts have declined to take what would have appeared to be the next logical step—declaring monopolies unlawful *per se* unless specifically authorized by law....

"The conundrum was indicated in characteristically striking prose by Judge Hand, who was not able to resolve it. Having stated that Congress 'did not condone' 'good trusts' and condemn 'bad' ones; it forbad all," he declared with equal force, 'The successful competitor, having been urged to compete, must not be turned upon when he wins.' Hand, therefore, told us that it would be inherently unfair to condemn success when the Sherman Act itself mandates competition. Such a wooden rule, it was feared, might also deprive the leading firm in an industry of the incentive to exert its best efforts. Further success would yield not rewards but legal castigation. The antitrust laws would thus compel the very sloth they were intended to prevent. We must always be mindful lest the Sherman Act be invoked perversely in favor of those who seek protection against the rigors of competition." (Kaufman, C.J.)

6. EASTMAN KODAK CO. v. IMAGE TECHNICAL SERVICES, INC., 504 U.S. 451, 112 S.Ct. 2072, 119 L.Ed.2d 265 (1992).

"The second element of a § 2 claim is the use of monopoly power 'to foreclose competition, to gain a competitive advantage, or to destroy a competitor....' [R]espondents have presented evidence that Kodak took exclusionary action to maintain its parts monopoly and used its control over parts to strengthen its monopoly share of the Kodak service market. Liability turns, then, on whether 'valid business reasons' can explain Kodak's action."

B. THE SHERMAN ACT AND COMPARATIVE LEGISLATION

Sherman Act[14]

Act of July 2, 1890, ch. 647, 26 Stat. 209.

An Act To Protect Trade and Commerce Against Unlawful Restraints and Monopolies

Section 1. Every contract, combination in the form of trust or otherwise, or conspiracy, in restraint of trade or commerce among the several States, or with foreign nations, is declared to be illegal. Every person who shall make any contract or engage in any combination or con-

---

14. The Sherman Act, as amended, appears at 15 U.S.C.A. §§ 1–7. Only the first   two sections are set out above.

spiracy hereby declared to be illegal shall be deemed guilty of a felony, and, on conviction thereof, shall be punished by fine not exceeding $10,000,000 if a corporation, or, if any other person, $350,000,[15] or by imprisonment not exceeding three years, or by both said punishments, in the discretion of the court.

Section 2. Every person who shall monopolize, or attempt to monopolize, or combine or conspire with any other person or persons, to monopolize any part of the trade or commerce among the several States, or with foreign nations, shall be deemed guilty of a felony, and, on conviction thereof, shall be punished by fine not exceeding $10,000,000 if a corporation, or, if any other person, $350,000, or by imprisonment not exceeding three years, or by both said punishments, in the discretion of the court.

COMPARATIVE NOTE ON COMPETITION LAW IN OTHER NATIONS AND REGIONS

Although there was a time when antitrust, or competition law as it is more commonly called in international circles, was regarded as a peculiarity of United States legislation, those days are long since past. Today, more than ninety[16] countries have competition laws, and more are considering enacting such laws every year. In fact, the popularity of competition law has become so great that many scholars and public officials have called for some kind of world competition code to be negotiated under the auspices of the World Trade Organization, to ensure that companies in all countries operate under the same set of rules and to guard against the possibility that private restraints of trade might undo the great strides in global trade liberalization that have taken place during the fifty years after World War II.[17] Although the momentum to launch such an ambitious undertaking seems to

15. The ceiling on fines was set at $5,000 in 1890, increased to $50,000 in 1955, and then raised to $1,000,000 for corporations in 1974. Most recently, in 1990, the fine was raised to $10,000,000 for corporations and $350,000 for individuals. Pub.L. 101–588, 104 Stat. 2880. Much greater fines than are available under the Sherman Act may be imposed under the Criminal Fines Improvements Act of 1987, which is applicable to federal felonies, 18 U.S.C.A. § 3571. The Criminal Fines Improvements Act and private treble damage actions under the Sherman Act are discussed in Chapter 2 infra. The maximum term of imprisonment, originally set at one year in 1890, was increased to three years in 1974, and the status of an offense was changed from misdemeanor to felony.

16. *See* William J. Kolasky, Deputy Assistant Attorney General, Antitrust Division, US Department of Justice, "International Convergence Efforts: A U.S. Perspective," Speech before the International Dimensions of Competition Law Conference, Toronto, Ontario, Canada, March 22, 2002, available at http://www.internationalcompetitionnetwork.org/speech_wkolasky.html

17. Fox, Competition Law and the Agenda for the WTO: Forging the Links of Competition and Trade, 4 Pacific Rim Law & Policy J. 1 (1995); Petersmann, Proposals for Negotiating International Competition Rules in the GATT–WTO World Trade and Legal System, 49 Aussenwirtschaft 231 (1994); Chu, Towards the Establishment of an Order of Competition for the International Economy: With References to the Draft Interna-

have faded, those efforts have been replaced with concrete steps to improve international coordination of competition law enforcement. The possibility of the eventual international harmonization of competition law and the current trend toward more effective cooperation both put a premium on understanding how competition law is viewed in other countries and how it differs from or is similar to the law in the United States.

The reasons why competition laws exist vary just as much as the laws themselves do in their scope and the vigor of their enforcement. Something as fundamental as the purpose of competition law is still a matter of debate. Over the years, a consensus has developed in the United States that the purpose of the antitrust laws is principally (if not exclusively) to promote consumer welfare, by banning economically inefficient transactions and practices. Other countries, however, take additional considerations into account, such as the development of the national economy, expansion of opportunities for cross-border trade, or protection of small and medium-sized enterprises. Some countries add a broader "public interest" dimension to antitrust enforcement: South Africa, for example, specifically includes among the purposes of its antitrust law the promotion of employment and the increase of the ownership stakes of historically disadvantaged persons.

Considering the different purposes reflected in these different laws, it is not surprising that this diverse set of legal regimes might not always work harmoniously together. One solution to that problem could be some kind of binding agreement, perhaps among the parties to the World Trade Organization, but as noted above, that is something only on the distant horizon. For now, the trend is toward "soft" harmonization of national and regional laws: discussion of specific cases, sharing of expertise, and mutual education about the ways antitrust laws operate, under the auspices of a variety of global fora. The work of groups such as the new multilateral International Competition Network, or the Global Competition Forum sponsored by the Organisation for Economic Co-operation and Development, may in time create a solid foundation for eventual formal harmonization.

Before World War II, competition laws were quite rare. Aside from the United States, there was a narrow law in Canada, passed in 1889, which established such stringent requirements for liability it was rarely invoked. Isolated instances of anti-cartel rules appeared elsewhere, but again they had little real impact. For example, the 1917 Mexican Constitution and the 1934 Mexican Monopolies Law proscribed monopolies and restraints of trade, with exceptions for labor unions, certain export cartels, intellectual property, and specified strategic activities reserved to the government.[18] Some of the Scandinavian countries also had similar laws. But it is fair to say that competition law as a global phenomenon was born in the years following World War II.

In some cases, the United States simply imposed antitrust laws on the vanquished nations. Thus, the occupational authorities put competition laws into effect in both Germany and Japan. However, interest in competition law was growing more generally. The draft Charter for an International Trade Organization (known as the Havana Charter) included an entire chapter on restrictive business practices that would have required each member country to take steps to prevent such

---

tional Antitrust Code, the Parallel Imports Problem, and the Experience of Taiwan, ROC, in International Harmonization of Competition Laws (eds.), Wang, Cheng & Liu (1995); Brittan, Europe: The Europe We Need 163 (1994).

18. Constitution of Mexico, art. 28; Ley Organica del Articulo 28 Constitucional en Material de Monopolios, D.O. Aug. 31, 1934; *see generally* Report of the Task Force of the ABA Section of Antitrust Law on the Competition Dimension of NAFTA 47 (1994).

practices when they would have harmful effects on international trade.[19] The European Coal and Steel Treaty of 1952 included competition provisions for the six-nation community it created.[20] In the United Kingdom, in sharp contrast to the rather pro-cartel attitude that had prevailed prior to the war, the post-war government accepted the proposition that monopolies and restrictive practices could have a deleterious effect on output and employment, and it thus sponsored the Monopolies and Restrictive Practices (Inquiry and Control) Act of 1948.[21] Norway enacted its Price Act on June 26, 1953, which established a system of control and supervision of restrictive business practices and dominant enterprises. These examples indicate that competition law was gaining a foothold even in countries that were not in the unusual position of post-war Germany and Japan.

Why this was so is harder to explain. One important factor, which led to the inclusion of provisions relating to restrictive business practices in the unsuccessful Havana Charter, was a general consensus among the founding members of the GATT that the pre-war cartels in Germany and Japan had contributed to the strength of the fascist or monarchist systems of government. Second, the rampant inflation after the war experienced by so many countries naturally led to a strong interest in any economic policy that focused on lowering prices. Third, the performance of the American economy excited admiration. Antitrust was in its heyday in the United States; the U.S. government was bringing actions to bring down numerous global cartels,[22] and other countries could not help but be impressed by the competitive vigor of the U.S. market.

Without a doubt, the most important emulator of American-style antitrust laws proved to be the European Community. The Community itself is now part of the broader European Union, which was inaugurated when the Maastricht Treaty on European Union established a framework for closer cooperation of the Member States of the European Community.[23] The Maastricht Treaty renamed the European Community the European Union and outlined what are now known as the three pillars of the EU: European Community, Common Foreign and Security Policy, and Justice and Home Affairs. The first pillar is responsible for economic and monetary union and relies on a vast body of competition law as one of the primary tools to integrate European markets. Recognizing that the EC is currently only one of the three "pillars" of the EU, we will generally use the term European Union (EU); occasionally, however, we will call it European Community (EC) to refer to historical facts or to emphasize the economic aspect of the cooperation.

In order to understand the nature of EC competition law, it is helpful to look at the broad outline of the European Union's system of governance. There are now five principal institutions in the Union: a European Parliament, a Council, a

---

19. Havana Charter for an International Trade Organization, Ch. V, March 24, 1948, U.S. Dept. of State Publ. No. 3206, Commercial Policy Series 114 (Sept. 1948).

20. Treaty Establishing the European Coal and Steel Community, Articles 65–66, April 18, 1951, 261 UNTS 140.

21. *See generally* Whish, Competition Law 60–61 (3d ed. 1993).

22. *See, e.g.,* United States v. General Electric Co., 82 F.Supp. 753 (D.N.J.1949) (*Incandescent Lamp*); United States v. National Lead Co., 332 U.S. 319 (1947); Timken Roller Bearing Co. v. United States, 341 U.S. 593 (1951); United States v. United States Alkali Export Ass'n, 86 F.Supp. 59 (S.D.N.Y.1949); United States v. Standard Oil (N.J.), Civ. No. 86–27 (S.D.N.Y.1953) (complaint); 1963 Trade Cas. (CCH) ¶ 70,819 (consent judgt), 1969 Trade Cas. (CCH) ¶ ¶ 72, 742, 72,743 (superseding consent judgts).

23. Treaty on European Union, signed at Maastricht on February 7, 1992. Published by the EC Office for Official Publications; reprinted in part at CCH Common Market Law Rept. [1992] 1 CMLR 719.

Commission, a Court of Justice, and a Court of Auditors. Most important is the Council, or the Council of Ministers as it is often called. The Council, according to Article 203 (ex Article 146) of the Rome Treaty,[24] is composed of ministers representing each Member State.[25] If the question before the Council is a general one, it is usually composed of the foreign ministers of the fifteen Member States, but if it is a specialized question, such as agriculture or finance, the ministers with the relevant portfolios will be in attendance. So constituted, the Council functions both as a head of state for the Union and as its chief legislative body.

The Commission in Brussels is the Union's administrative and executive arm. It now has 20 members, which, according to Article 213 (ex Article 157) of the Treaty of Rome, are chosen on the grounds of general competence and independence (although in practice are also allocated carefully among Member States). The Commission is divided into various Directorates–General with responsibility for substantive areas within the Union's competence. The Competition Directorate General, or DG Comp, is responsible for competition policy and enforcement.

The European Court of Justice (ECJ) and the Court of First Instance (CFI), both located in Luxembourg, constitute the Union's judicial branch. The ECJ's function is to review formal decisions of the Commission and to review questions of EC law referred to it by the national courts of the Member States. Since 1988, the ECJ has been assisted by the Court of First Instance, which was established by the Council pursuant to authority granted under Article 225 (ex Article 168a) of the Treaty of Rome.[26] The CFI has always had jurisdiction over competition cases. Over time, its authority has expanded. It currently also has jurisdiction to rule in the first instance on (1) all actions for annulment, for failure to act, and for damages brought by natural or legal persons against the Community, (2) actions brought against the Commission under the ECSC Treaty by business firms or associations, and (3) disputes between the Community and its officials and employees. The Treaty of Amsterdam, which entered into force on May 1, 1999, contemplates that the Court of First Instance may eventually have jurisdiction over all categories of cases now within the jurisdiction of the Court of Justice except for preliminary references from the national courts made pursuant to Article 234 (ex Article 177) of the Treaty.

24. The European Economic Community was established by the Rome Treaty in 1957. The Rome Treaty has been amended several times since then, and the subsequent amendments, along with the initial text, have now been consolidated into a continuously updated version. The current version of the Rome Treaty is referred to as the "Treaty Establishing the European Community." Following a major amendment by the 1997 Treaty of Amsterdam, the previously used numbering of treaty provisions has been changed as well. To avoid confusion, we will refer to both the former and the new article references, as is customarily done.

25. *See* Treaty of Rome, 298 UNTS 11, as amended. There are now fifteen Member States of the European Union: Austria, Belgium, Denmark, Finland, France, Germany, Greece, Ireland, Italy, Luxembourg, the Netherlands, Portugal, Spain, Sweden, and the United Kingdom. Thirteen more countries are on the list of candidates to join: Czech Republic, Estonia, Cyprus, Latvia, Lithuania, Hungary, Malta, Poland, Slovenia, Slovakia, Bulgaria, Romania, and Turkey. The first ten of these candidates are scheduled to join the EU in time for the next elections to the European Parliament in June 2004. Bulgaria, Romania, and Turkey are on a slower timetable. *See* http://europa.eu.int/comm/enlargement/enlargement.htm.

26. Article 225 (ex Article 168a) was added by the Single European Act of 1987, which amended the Rome Treaty in a number of significant respects.

Two principles developed by the ECJ make EC competition law of particular importance: first, the Court has held that it has "direct effect" on individuals and companies, which means that violations can be prosecuted without regard to any measures in national law that may apply; second, the Court has developed an equivalent to the Supremacy Clause of the U.S. Constitution, under which EC competition law has primacy over conflicting Member State legislation.

The European Parliament has been gaining power over the years, but it is still misleading to think of it as the counterpart to the British Parliament, the French Assemblé Nationale, or the German Bundestag. Since 1979, members of the Parliament have been elected directly by European voters. The Parliament sits in Strasbourg. Its most important role now is to review legislative proposals from the Council and the Commission. If it approves such a proposal, the Council may act by qualified majority; if it does not, or if it is not consulted, then the Council must act unanimously. The Parliament also has the power to put questions to the Commission, which must be answered, and it reviews the Commission's annual general report.

The last institution, the Court of Auditors, was introduced by the Maastricht Treaty. It is responsible for examining the accounts of all revenue and expenditure of the Union and its various constituent bodies, and reporting to both the Parliament and the Council.

Through this elaborate set of institutions, the Union has developed one of the most sophisticated bodies of competition law in the world. When the original Treaty of Rome, which established the European Economic Community, was signed on March 25, 1957, it included as one of its fundamental goals "the institution of a system ensuring that competition in the common market is not distorted."[27] Part Three, Title I, Chapter 1 of the Treaty implemented that goal by setting forth rules on competition that would apply both to "undertakings" (Eurospeak for companies or business entities) and to States. Article 81 (ex Article 85–a point not repeated further in this note) of the Rome Treaty prohibits agreements and other concerted practices that have as their object or effect the prevention, restriction, or distortion of competition, unless the European Commission finds that the particular agreement should be exempted from the prohibition because of its beneficial effects. (You should note that the extent to which the beneficial effects must relate to efficiencies, as contrasted with effects on employment, regional development, or other industrial policy goals, has been debated for years within European circles.) Article 82 (ex Article 86) of the Treaty prohibits abuses of a dominant position. Article 86 (ex Article 90) seeks to place state operated monopolies or enterprises with special privileges under the competition regime, to the greatest extent possible. Finally, Article 87 (ex Article 92) declares that governmental subsidies that distort or threaten to distort competition within the common market are incompatible with it. The Commission is responsible for reviewing state aids, as they are called, and it has the power to require that incompatible aids must be discontinued. Finally, a review of EC competition law would not be complete without reference to the Merger Regulation, which the Council adopted after seventeen years of debate, in 1989, and which establishes a system of merger regulation at the Community level for very large transactions.[28]

27. 298 UNTS 11.

28. *See* Council Reg. 4064/89, (1990 O.J. (L257) 14). In general, transactions that involve a worldwide turnover of 5 billion Eu- ros, which in 2002 dollars represents about $5 billion, and for which the intra-community turnover is 250 million Euros for each of at least two participants, as long as more than

The Commission has extensive powers that it can bring to bear on companies that violate the EC's competition rules. Until the reorganization plan described below enters into force, on May 1, 2004, the Commission will continue to receive extensive information from the business community, through "notifications" filed pursuant to Article 81(1) and Council Regulation 17, through complaints, and through more informal letters seeking "negative clearances."[29] Article 81(2) provides that a failure to notify an agreement that the Commission later concludes is unlawful under Article 81 means that the agreement is void. In addition, the Commission can and does impose significant fines, sometimes in the millions of dollars, for violations of Articles 81 or 82.

Important changes in the way that European competition law is administered have recently been enacted. On November 26, 2002, the member states of the EU agreed on fundamental reforms of Regulation 17. Under the new system, which as noted will take effect on May 1, 2004, agreements and other arrangements falling under article 81(1) will no longer need to be notified, and there will be no more article 81(3) exemption decisions. Instead, article 81(3) will operate automatically to exempt from article 81(1) all agreements falling within the scope of subpart (3), without the need for any official decision to that effect. This paves the way for the other significant aspect of the new system: decentralized enforcement. With the Commission's monopoly over the conferral of article 81(3) exemptions abolished, national authorities and courts will have substantially greater responsibility for the enforcement of both article 81 and article 82. To ensure that all national institutions are applying the EU law in a consistent way, there will be a new network of competition authorities through which the Commission and those authorities will exchange information, consult with one another, and to the extent possible, cooperate in their enforcement efforts. Finally, there will be a rule adopted to the effect that when an agreement or practice affects trade between member states, the national authorities and courts will be obliged to apply EU law (*i.e.* articles 81 and 82), even if they also apply national law (which cannot in any event be inconsistent with EU law).[30] These changes are far-reaching and are expected to have a profound effect on the way European competition law is enforced.

The near-explosive spread of competition laws around the world in more recent years reflects both the success and the strong influence of the European Union's competition laws, both taken alone and in combination with those in the Americas and the Asia–Pacific region. Throughout Central and Eastern Europe, countries

two-thirds of the intra-Community turnover is not in one and the same Member State, fall within the Merger Regulation. Other "concentrations" are regulated only at the Member State level. This was the Community's effort to establish a "one stop shopping" system, under which it would be clear which regulator had jurisdiction over the case. On the whole, it has worked well, although occasionally cases arise where the rules for calculating turnover are unclear, or where it may be possible for a Member State to refer the case to Brussels or vice versa.

29. *See* Council Reg. 17/62. *See generally* Barry Hawk, Common Market and International Antitrust—A Comparative Guide

(ed.); Richard Whish, Competition Law, ch. 9 (3d ed. 1993); Leonard Ritter, Francis Rawlinson, and W. David Braun, EC Competition Law—A Practitioner's Guide (Kluwer 1991).

30. For background on these new rules, *see* Proposal for a Council Regulation on the implementation of the rules on competition laid down in Articles 81 and 82 (ex Articles 85 and 86) of the Treaty and amending Regulations (EEC) No 1017/68, (EEC) No 2988/74, (EEC) No 4056/86 and (EEC) No 3975/87, Brussels, September 17, 2000, COM(2000) 582 final, available on the website of the Competition Directorate. That website is now found at http://www.europa.eu.int/comm/com petition.

eager to join the EU one day have modeled their new competition laws on those of the EU, in recognition of the fact that accession would mean the acceptance of the full *acquis communautaire* of competition laws, regulations, and court precedents. In addition, the administrative approach taken by the EC appeals to countries that do not share the Anglo–American common-law tradition. For that reason, we allude from time to time throughout this casebook to European rules, both by way of comparison and contrast. The extent to which European law follows efficiency principles, the extent to which it continues to reflect its roots by giving primacy to intra-European market integration goals, and the extent to which it displays more concern for equitable market behavior, all provide a useful perspective for our consideration of U.S. law.

As noted above, the central competition provisions of EC law are Articles 81 and 82 of the Rome Treaty. These provisions are set forth below. At this point, please compare Articles 81 and 82 with the provisions of Sections 1 and 2 of the Sherman Act, pp. [14–15] supra.

Treaty Establishing the European Community (Rome Treaty)

Article 81

1. The following shall be prohibited as incompatible with the Common Market: all agreements between undertakings, decisions by associations of undertakings and concerted practices which may affect trade between Member States and which have as their object or effect the prevention, restriction or distortion of competition within the Common Market, and in particular those which:

(a) directly or indirectly fix purchase or selling prices or any other trading conditions;

(b) limit or control production, markets, technical development, or investment;

(c) share markets or sources of supply;

(d) apply dissimilar conditions to equivalent transactions with other trading parties, thereby placing them at a competitive disadvantage;

(e) make the conclusion of contracts subject to acceptance by the other parties of supplementary obligations which, by their nature or according to commercial usage, have no connection with the subject of such contracts.

2. Any agreements or decisions prohibited pursuant to this Article shall be automatically void.

3. The provisions of paragraph 1 may, however, be declared inapplicable in the case of:

—any agreement or category of agreements between undertakings;

—any decision or category of decisions by associations of undertakings;

—any concerted practice or category of concerted practices;

which contributes to improving the production or distribution of goods or to promoting technical or economic progress, while allowing consumers a fair share of the resulting benefit, and which does not:

(a) impose on the undertakings concerned restrictions which are not indispensable to the attainment of these objectives;

(b) afford such undertakings the possibility of eliminating competition in respect of a substantial part of the products in question.

Article 82

Any abuse by one or more undertakings of a dominant position within the Common Market or in a substantial part of it shall be prohibited as incompatible with the Common Market in so far as it may affect trade between Member States.

Such abuse may, in particular, consist in:

(a) directly or indirectly imposing unfair purchase or selling prices or other unfair trading conditions;

(b) limiting production, markets or technical development to the prejudice of consumers;

(c) applying dissimilar conditions to equivalent transactions with other trading parties, thereby placing them at a competitive disadvantage;

(d) making the conclusion of contracts subject to acceptance by the other parties of supplementary obligations which, by their nature or according to commercial usage, have no connection with the subject of such contracts.[31]

QUESTIONS

1. What are the key substantive words of the Sherman Act and the EC Treaty? What, if any, are the differences between the concepts of "restraint of trade" and "monopolization," on the one hand, and "prevention, restriction, or distortion of competition" and "abuse of a dominant position," on the other?

2. What does the Sherman Act mean when it refers to "every ... restraint of trade"? Should this be read literally as meaning without exception? Does Article 81(1) really prohibit *all* agreements setting trading conditions, or controlling technical development, or sharing sources of supply? Is there any room in Section 1

---

31. Consolidated version of the Rome Treaty (Treaty Establishing the European Community), March 25, 1957, Arts. 81 and 82 (ex Articles 85 and 86), 298 UNTS 11, 48.

of the Sherman Act or Article 81(1) for a "rule of reason"? If Article 81(1) incorporates a rule of reason, what function is left for Article 81(3)?

3.   Compare Article 82 with Section 2 of the Sherman Act. What, if any, is the relation between a "dominant position" and "monopolization"? Does Article 82 forbid "dominance" as such? Does Sherman Act Section 2 forbid "monopoly" as such? What is the significance of conduct under both systems of law? Must a dominant firm justify its prices, production policies, and discriminatory treatment of customers to the Commission, or to the European courts? How would you determine what an unfair selling price was, or what constituted prejudice to consumers? How can you tell the difference between vigorous competition that might harm other trading partners and abusive practices that place them at a competitive disadvantage?

SECTION 2.   THE HISTORICAL SOURCES OF ANTITRUST, LEGISLATIVE HISTORY, AND EARLY DEVELOPMENTS

A.   THE EARLY LAW ON MONOPOLY AND CONTRACTS IN RESTRAINT OF TRADE

William L. Letwin, The English Common Law Concerning Monopolies[32]

21 U.Chi.L.Rev. 355 (1954).

It has been widely believed that the common law always favored freedom of trade. When English and American judges during the eighteenth and nineteenth centuries decided cases against monopolists, engrossers, or restrainers of trade, they thought they were continuing a tradition that reached back into "time of which no man hath memory." The congressmen who drafted and passed the Sherman Antitrust Law thought they were merely declaring illegal offenses that the common law had always prohibited. Those judges and legislators, like other lawyers, must have known, or at least would not have doubted, that the common law rules on these subjects had changed in the course of time, for it is taken as axiomatic that the common law "grows." But it is not always recognized that the common law can change its direction, and without much warning begin to prohibit practices it had formerly endorsed, or to protect arrangements it had earlier condemned. Lawyers do not so readily see that the common law at any given time reflects the economic theories and policies then favored by the community, and may change as radically as those theories and policies. As a result they have too easily accepted the mistaken view that the attitude of the common law toward freedom of trade was essentially the same throughout its history.

32.   Reprinted by permission of the University of Chicago Law Review, University of Chicago Law School.

But the common law did not always defend freedom of trade and abhor monopoly. For a long time it did quite the opposite: it supported an economic order in which the individual's getting and spending were closely controlled by kings, parliaments, and mayors, statutes and customs, and his opportunities limited by the exclusive powers of guilds, chartered companies, and patentees. The common law first began to oppose this system of regulation and privilege at the end of the sixteenth century; it did not do so wholeheartedly until the eighteenth century; and by the middle of the nineteenth century, it had again lost its enthusiasm for the task. It would have been surprising if the pattern of development had been different. Changes in the common law are changes in the attitudes of judges and of lawyers; it would have been remarkable if they had persistently opposed monopoly when the rest of the community did not know the word and considered the phenomenon natural or desirable. It would have been strange if lawyers had upheld laissez-faire policies centuries before any statesman or economist had advocated or stated them, and had continued following them long after they had been abandoned or denied by the rest of the community. In fact, English laws governing monopoly and English policies for the economic organization of society changed together, except for minor differences in timing. The English law of monopoly traditionally includes four branches: the law on monopoly proper, whether by patent, charter, or custom; on forestalling, engrossing, and regrating; on contracts in restraint of trade; and on combinations in restraint of trade. These branches, distinct in form and based on more or less independent bodies of precedent, nevertheless show the same development from an active support of monopolies in the earliest period, through active opposition during an interlude of less than two centuries, to the leniency and indifference which characterized them in 1890.

The idea that the common law opposed monopolies from the earliest time onward was invented largely by Sir Edward Coke, who argued that monopoly was forbidden by the Civil Law,[33] and implicitly by Magna Carta as well as by certain statutes of Edward III's reign.[34] But the earliest common-law precedent he could mention was a case that arose during the fourteenth century,[35] and the modern lawyers and historians who follow his authority continue to cite that case as evidence of the ancient antagonism of common law to monopolies.[36] Yet the case gives at least equally good evidence to the contrary. . . .

The great movement against the granting of monopolies by letter-patent began only at the end of the sixteenth century, although it was so strongly supported that within less than a hundred years the principle had

---

33. *See* Coke's argument in Davenant v. Hurdis, Moore *576, *580 (K.B., 1599).

34. 2 Coke, Institutes 47, 62–63; 3 ibid., at c. 85.

35. Ed. Pecche's Case, Rot.Parl., 50 Edw. 3, No. 33 (1376).

36. 3 Coke Institutes, 47, 181; 11 Co. Rep. *53, *88a, b. Cf. 4 Holdsworth, History 344, n. 6 (1924). The case was cited in the same sense by Laurence Hyde during the parliamentary debate on monopolies in 1601. Tawney and Power, 2 Tudor Economic Documents 275 (1924).

been established that Parliament alone could grant a monopoly, and that generally even it could not, as the King had regularly done, sell a patent or award it on a whim or as a friendly gesture. By the end of the seventeenth century the royal letter-patent had been converted into a more or less modern version of the patent, justifiable only by a solid contribution to economic development. The process was not, however, moved by coherent opposition to monopoly; it was brought about mainly by disturbances within the monopolistic system administered largely by the guilds, and by objections not to the broad economic effect of monopolies but to the political power which the crown exercised in granting them....

... [P]erhaps the greatest single [step] in creating the modern common law on monopolies was Darcy v. Allen, or *The Case of Monopolies,*[37] decided in 1603.... [It] laid down the principle that even a royal grant by patent would be invalid if it [created a monopoly].... In short, Darcy's patent was held void on the argument that it violated the right of others to carry on their trade.

... The common-law right to work was predicated on an economic system that would protect the established trades from competition, whether from foreign workmen, improperly qualified English workmen, overly aggressive guilds, or domestic monopolists. The right to work was protected by giving each guild a monopoly, and Darcy's grant was condemned not because it was a monopoly and therefore necessarily bad, but because it was a bad monopoly....

... The fact is that the monopolistic powers of guilds, which Coke insisted repeatedly were always void at common law, had really been supported by law. That support first began to be withdrawn in the beginning of the seventeenth century, under the pressure of, among other things, Coke's powerful but inaccurate polemics.

There is no doubt that the series of cases at the turn of the seventeenth century radically changed the attitude of the common law toward monopolies. But it must be borne in mind that this change was also a consequence of the decay of the monopolistic system from within.... Darcy v. Allen was not the action of a solitary champion bravely contesting the monopoly of a powerful courtier; it has been shown instead that Allen was supported in the case by the Mayor and Aldermen of London, who, regarding Darcy's patent as an attack on all the trades and privileges of the City, "comforted and animated [Allen] to continue his selling of cards" and promised to pay the costs of any legal action that might follow....

Moreover, the mercantilist system of private and corporate monopolies, though very much weakened by 1600, was still too widespread to be destroyed by the application of common-law remedies in specific cases. It was seriously limited, and in the end destroyed, by legislation. The first important law contributing to that result was the Statute of Monopolies of 1624, which, however, has a deceptive ring. For though it was certainly

---

37. 11 Co.Rep. *84, Moore *671 (K.B., 1599), Noy *173. These reports are collated   in Gordon, Monopolies by Patents 193–232 (1897).

directed against monopolies, it was based not on a preference for competition, but on constitutional objections to the power which the Crown presumed in granting monopolies and to the arbitrary reasons for which it had granted them. Parliament did not at this period oppose monopolies in themselves.... [In] the final irony in the case of Darcy v. Allen: only a few years after Darcy's monopoly of playing cards was judged void at common law, the same monopoly was given, under authority of the Statute of Monopolies, to the Company of Card Makers.

The Statute of Monopolies soon put an end to the arbitrary granting of private monopolies. But it was not intended to abolish customary monopoly privileges of corporations. Cities and boroughs, guilds, and chartered trading companies continued to exercise their monopoly powers to exclude strangers from various trades. The common law continued to protect them, though with lessening fervor as the influence of economic liberalism grew, and some of these monopolistic controls were finally abolished only by legislation in the nineteenth century.

Throughout these early monopoly cases the complaint is made that practices are objectionable because they tend to raise prices. But even this complaint did not arise from opposition to monopolies. It did not mean that the common law early in the seventeenth century favored competition or endorsed the determination of prices by the free play of the market. The common law favored "low" prices rather than free prices, and accepted as a matter of course that all important prices would be set by political or corporate authorities. The complaint meant only that Englishmen objected to private efforts to raise prices, and that they readily attributed a rise in prices to the evil machinations of profiteers....

The body of law concerning these crimes has been thought to be an integral part of the law on monopolies because forestalling and the associated offenses seem at first sight to be older names for the modern monopolistic tactic known as "cornering the market...." The basic legal difference is that the monopolist had a legal warrant for his activity, whereas the forestaller was justified by no custom, grant, or statute whatsoever.... [T]he first statute prohibiting it defined forestallers as those "that buy anything before the due hour, or that pass out of the town to meet such things as come to the market...."

The major objective of laws against forestalling was to keep food prices low. Such laws fit very neatly into the more general price-fixing program administered by medieval and, later, mercantilist governments. Local authorities of manors, cities, and guilds had customary rights to control food prices; kings issued proclamations and parliaments passed statutes for the same end; all these are implicitly confirmed in a statute of 1533 which gave certain members of the Privy Council as well the right to set "reasonable prices" of "cheese, butter, capons, hens, chickens, and other victuals necessary for man's sustenance."[38] The work of surveillance would be much easier if all sales were made publicly in the market, and so forestall-

---

38. 25 Hen. VIII, c. 2, § 1 (1533).

ing and engrossing, means of evading the market, were seen as attempts to evade price-controls.

But to maintain low food prices was not the sole objective of the laws against forestalling. Just as monopolies by patent were attacked by those who feared to lose their own monopoly powers, so forestalling was abhorred not only by a public which hated high prices but also by those who saw in it an infringement of their privileges as owners of markets. Rights to hold markets were granted or confirmed by the Crown, and established local but powerful monopolies. What was given was not the mere right to hold a market, but an exclusive right....

The objectives of statesmen and the interest of owners of markets coincided with the prejudices of the public. They considered forestalling, engrossing, and regrating the typical tricks of middlemen and speculators, and were convinced that merchants who used such tactics were parasites profiting by the distress of others.... The practices described show no sign of being, properly speaking, monopolistic; they appear on the contrary to have been acts of speculation, arbitrage, or wholesaling; but most men continued to identify the two phenomena until the new economic theory in the eighteenth century taught a few of them at least ... that the community had as much to gain as the merchant from free trade.

The development of laissez-faire economic theory accounted for the abolition of the laws against forestalling.... Parliament in 1844 passed a law repealing all the remaining statutes against it, and utterly abolishing the common-law crimes of forestalling, engrossing, and regrating.

Clearly, then, the laws against forestalling and engrossing, which some have tried to identify as a fount of modern antitrust law, did not have the required character. They were of narrow scope, applying almost exclusively to trade in foodstuffs; they were part of a program to regulate all economic activities; like the common law against monopolies by patent, they were supported by monopolists—in this case, the owners of markets—who found them useful protection; and they were finally repealed by the supporters of free trade and in the name of free trade....

By 1890, what there had been of English common law against monopolies had become quite weak. The common law against monopoly proper had been superseded by the Statute of Monopolies. The common law against forestalling had been abolished by the statute of 1844. The common law against combinations of workmen and of masters had been overruled by the Trade Union Acts. The common law against contracts and combinations in restraint of trade alone remained in force....

Anonymous—"Dyer's Case"

Y.B., 2 Hen. V, vol. 5, pl. 26 (1415).

A writ of debt was brought on an obligation by one John Dyer wherein the defendant alleged, by Lod, that, according to a certain indenture which he put forth and on condition that the defendant should not use his art of a dyer's craft within the town where the plaintiff, etc. for a certain time, viz., for half a year, the obligation was to lose its force; and he said that he did not use his art of a dyer's craft within the time limited, which matter he offered to prove and demanded judgment whether the action, etc.

HULL. To my mind you might have demurred on him since the obligation is void because the condition is against the common law, and per Dieu, if the plaintiff were here, he should go to prison till he paid a fine to the king.[39]

Anonymous—"The Schoolmaster Case"

Court of Common Pleas, Hilary Term, 1410.
Y.B., 11 Hen. IV, f. 47, pl. 21.

Two masters of a grammar school at Gloucester brought a writ of trespass against another master, and counted that the defendant had started a school in the same town, so that whereas the plaintiffs had formerly received 40*d.* or two shillings a quarter from each child, now they got only 12*d.*, to their damage, & c.

TILDESLEY. His writ is worthless.

SKRENE. It is a good action on the case, and the plaintiffs have shown well enough how they are damaged; wherefore, & c.

HANKFORD, J. There may be damnum absque injuria. As if I have a mill, and my neighbor builds another mill, whereby the profit of mine is diminished, I shall have no action against him; still I am damaged, quod Thirning, C.J., concessit, and said that the instruction of children is a spiritual matter; and if one retains a master in his house to teach his children, it is a damage to the common master of the town, yet, I think, he will have no action.

SKRENE. The masters of Paul's claim that there shall be no other masters in all London except themselves.

HORTON demurred because the action was not maintainable.

HILL, J. There is no ground to maintain this action, since the plaintiffs have no estate, but a ministry for the time; and though another equally competent with the plaintiffs comes to teach the children, this is a virtuous and charitable thing, and an ease to the people, for which he cannot be punished by our law.

SKRENE. If a market is erected to the nuisance of my market I shall have an assize of nuisance; and in a common case, if those coming to my

---

39. Ed. *See* Blake, Employee Agreements Not to Compete, 73 Harv.L.Rev. 625, 632–37 (1960). Consider the plight of an apprentice or journeyman, bound by a covenant not to exercise the only craft for which he had been trained. On the possibility of migration to other towns, consider the conditions of travel during this period, Day, History of Commerce 54–55 (4th ed. 1938), and the position of strangers. On the legislative prohibition of guild exactions of covenants not to engage in trade from apprentices or journeymen, *see* 28 Hen. VIII, c. 5 (1536).

market be disturbed or beaten, whereby I lose my toll, I shall have a good action on my case; so here.

HANKFORD, J. Not the same case, because in the case put you have a freehold and inheritance in the market; but here the plaintiffs have no estate in the schoolmastership, & c., but for an uncertain time, and it would be against reason for a master to be hindered from keeping school where he pleases, unless where a university was incorporated or a school founded in ancient times.

And the opinion of the court was that the writ would not lie. Wherefore it was awarded that they should take nothing, & c.

Case of Monopolies

Court of King's Bench, 1602.
11 Coke 84, 77 Eng.Rep. 1260.[40]

Edward Darcy, Esq., a groom of the Privy Chamber to Queen Elizabeth, brought an action on the case against T. Allein, Haberdasher of London, and declared that Queen Elizabeth by her letters patent in 30 Eliz. granted to Ralph Bowes power to buy playing cards overseas and import them, he to enjoy the whole trade, and that Bowes and none other should have the making of playing cards within the realm for twelve years. In 40 Eliz., the grant was extended for 21 years after the end of the former term, he rendering to the Queen 100 marks per annum; and further declared that the defendant, knowing of plaintiff's grant, made and sold cards, to the plaintiff's damage, 200 pounds, whereby the plaintiff was unable to pay his farm to the crown. Defendant, except as to one half gross, pleaded not guilty and as to that pleaded that he is a member of the society of Haberdashers of London, and that by custom all members of that society could freely sell all manner of goods. The plaintiff demurred.

DYER and CROKE argued against the patent that the Queen could not grant a patent to restrain any from their usual trades and that no occupation can be put in monopoly but only such a thing as is newly invented.

FULLER: The Judges in the exposition of the Kings Letters Patents are to be guided not by the precise words of the Patents, but by the Laws of the Realm.

Before, cards were and ought to be sold at reasonable prices, or else be punished as inhauncers of merchandize, now Darcy may sell cards for his most advantage, as he doth, viz., one gross for 35s. where the Haberdashers have offered to sell better for 20s. the gross; this is malum in se against the Common Law that cannot be dispensed with by patent as malum prohibitum may be.

---

40. Abridged from the combined reports in Gordon, Monopolies by Patents 199– 232 (1897).

Before a person might have reaped the fruits of his skill; now Darcy hath devised a means to take away a man's skill from him, which was never heard of before.

The condition in the *Dyer's* Case, not to use his trade for half a year in the town of Dale, was void; much more so this Patent, restraining men from their trade 21 years throughout the whole realm.

There is no wrong done to the plaintiff by the defendant's selling cards cheaper than the Plaintiff would, though he received losse, and therefore no cause of action lies, as in the *Schoolmaster's* Case. When a miller loses some of his trade to a new mill, this is no wrong though it be damage, and therefore no cause of action.

I.S. hath a pasture where the tenants sometimes put their cattle; another person makes a good pasture where the tenants have cattle cheaper to the damage of I.S. & yet no cause of action, being neither wrong to I.S. nor hurt to the commonwealth.

The Attorney General contra argued that the King can prohibit or license mala prohibita and can restrain matters of pleasure and it is for the public good although it may involve damage to private persons.

Judgment.

Resolved by Popham Chief Justice & per totam curiam that the grant to the plaintiff of the sole making of cards within the realm was utterly void and that for two reasons: 1. That it is a monopoly and against the common law. 2. That it is against divers acts of Parliament. Against the common law for four reasons:

1. All trades which prevent idleness and keep men in labour are profitable to the commonwealth and therefore the grant to the plaintiff to have the sole making is against the common law and the benefit and liberty of the subject.

2. Any monopoly is not only a damage to those that exercise the same trade but also to others, for the end of all these monopolies is the private gain of the patentees. There are three inseparable incidents to every monopoly: (1) That the price will be raised. (2) After the monopoly grant, the commodity is not so good as it was before. (3) It tends to the impoverishment of divers artificers and others who before by their labour had maintained themselves and their families, who now will of necessity be constrained to live in idleness and beggary.

3. The Queen was deceived in her grant.

4. This grant is primae impressionis, for no such was ever seen to pass by letters patent before, and therefore it is a dangerous innovation.

Also such charter of monopoly, against the freedom of trade and traffic, is against divers acts of Parliament, sc. 9 E. 3 c. 1 & 2, which for the advancement of the freedom of trade and traffic extends to all things vendible, notwithstanding any charter to the contrary or usage or custom, which charters are adjudged to be of no force and effect.

Also, the licence to have the sole importation and merchandizing is utterly against law, since Parliament pro bono publico has prohibited the importation of foreign manufactures to the intent that subjects might apply themselves to the making of the said manufactures, and for a private gain to grant the sole importation is a monopoly against the common law, for this is not to maintain the card-makers but to take away their trade, and that without any reason.

And admitting that such grant was valid, yet the plaintiff cannot maintain an action on the case against those who import any foreign goods, but the remedy which the act of 3 Eliz. 4 gives ought to be pursued.[41] And judgment was given, quod querens nihil caperet per billam.[42]

NOTE

The Statute of Monopolies, 21 Jac. I, ch. 3 (1623–34), provided that, with certain exceptions—including one for patents and grants of privileges for "true inventors"—"all monopolies ... are and shall be utterly void ..." unless granted or confirmed by an act of Parliament.

Mitchel v. Reynolds

1 P.Wms. 181, 24 Eng.Rep. 347 (K.B.1711).

■ PARKER, C.J. ...

41. *I.e.*, forfeiture of the goods, imported in breach of the statute, half to the king, the other half to him who will first seize them for the king.

42. "Allein was not an independent, unsupported protagonist on behalf of the liberty of the subject to pursue lawful and established trades, but rather a freeman of the City actively instigated to resistance to the monopolist by the most influential authorities of the City of London." Davies, Further Light on the Case of Monopolies, 48 L.Q.Rev. 394, 395 (1932).

The practice of granting special monopoly privileges as a means of revenue to the crown or as a reward for services "reached its climax while Elizabeth was in power. A list of her grants includes patents giving the sole rights to sell or manufacture currants, salt, iron, powder, cards, calf-skins, fells, pouldavies, ox-shin bones, train-oil, lists of cloth, potashes, aniseseed, vinegar, sea-coals, steel, aquavitae, brushes, pots, saltpetre, bottles, lead, accidences, oil, calamine-stone, oil-of-blubber, glasses, paper, starch, tin, sulphur,

new drapery, dried pilchards, beer, horn, leather, Irish yarn, importation of Spanish wool, and transportation of iron-ordinance." Miller, The Case of the Monopolies, 6 Mich. L.Rev. 1, 2 (1907).

Prior to 1601, grants of monopoly had been sustained in Privy Council and Star Chamber as a valid expression of the royal prerogative. In 1601, however, popular opposition to these privileges forced Elizabeth to concede that in the future the validity of such grants was to be determined according to the common law. *See* 4 Holdsworth, History of English Law 346 (1924). For accounts of the Tudor patents and monopolies, *see* Price, English Patents of Monopoly (1906); 3 Lipson, Economic History of England 352–86 (6th ed. 1935); Thorelli, Federal Antitrust Policy 20 (1954); Letwin, English Common Law Concerning Monopolies, 21 U.Chi.L.Rev. 355 (1954); Churchill, Monopolies, 41 L.Q.Rev. 275 (1925); Hulme, Early History of the English Patent System, in 3 Select Essays in Anglo–American Legal History 117–47 (1909).

Debt upon a bond. The condition recited that the defendant had assigned to the plaintiff a bakehouse in the parish of St. Andrews Holborn for the term of five years, and that if he did not exercise the trade of baker within that parish during that term, or if he did and paid fifty pounds to the plaintiff within three days after proof thereof, the obligation was to be void. Defendant pleaded that he was a baker by trade and the obligation was void in law. Plaintiff demurred. *Held,* for plaintiff. The general question upon this record is, whether this bond being made in restraint of trade, be good? The resolutions of the books seeming to disagree, I will endeavor to reconcile the jarring opinions. The cases are either of involuntary contracts, or voluntary restraints by agreement of the parties. Voluntary restraints are general or particular, as to places or persons. General restraints are all void. Particular restraints are either without consideration, all of which are void, or upon a good and adequate consideration so as to make it a proper and useful contract. A man may, upon a valuable consideration, by his own consent, and for his own profit, give over his trade, and part with it to another in a particular place. All the books, when carefully examined, seem to concur in the distinctions of restraints general and particular, and with or without consideration, which stand upon very good foundation. *Volenti non fit injuria.* Some observations which may be useful in understanding these cases are: First, that to obtain the sole exercise of any known trade throughout England is a complete monopoly, and against the policy of the law. Secondly, that when restrained to particular places or persons, the same is not a monopoly. Thirdly, that since these restraints may be by custom, and custom must have a good foundation, the thing is not absolutely and in itself unlawful. Fourthly, that it is lawful upon good consideration for a man to part with his trade. Fifthly, that actions on the case will lie for a man's using a trade contrary to custom, or to his own agreement; for there he uses it injuriously. Sixthly, that where the law allows a restraint of trade, it is not unlawful to enforce it with a penalty. Seventhly, that no man can contract not to use his trade at all. Eighthly, that a particular restraint is not good without just reason and consideration. The true reasons for the distinctions in the cases of voluntary restraints are founded on the mischief which may arise from them, to the party by the loss of his livelihood, and to the public by depriving it of an useful member. Another reason is the great abuses they are liable to; from corporations who are perpetually laboring for exclusive advantages in trade, from masters who are apt to give their apprentices much vexation on this account. In a great many instances they can be of no use to the obligee, which holds in all cases of general restraint throughout England; for what does it signify to a tradesman in London what another does at Newcastle? A reason in favour of these contracts is that there may happen instances wherein they may be useful and beneficial, as to prevent a town being overstocked with any particular trade; or in case an old man is likely to be a loser by continuing his trade. The law is not so unreasonable, as to set aside a man's own agreement for fear of an uncertain injury to him, and fix a certain damage upon another; as it must do, if contracts with a consideration were made void. Wherever such a contract *stat indifferenter,* and for ought appears, may be either good or bad, the law presumes it bad. For there plainly appears a mischief, but the benefit (if any) can only be presumed. There is a sort of presumption, that it is not of any benefit to the obligee himself, it being a general mischief to the publick, everybody is affected thereby. The presumption answers all the difficulties that are to be found in the books. All contracts where there is a bare restraint of trade and no more, must be void; where special matter appears so as to make it a reasonable and useful contract, the presumption is excluded. This shews why promises in restraint of trade have been held good, but the contracts are governed by the special matter shown. The application of this to the case at bar is very plain. The true distinction of this case is, not between promises and bonds, but between contracts with and without consideration. The plaintiff took a baker's house and the question is whether he or the defendant shall have the trade of this neighborhood; the concern of the public is the same on both sides. What makes this the more reasonable is, that the restraint is exactly proportioned to the consideration, viz., the term of five years. To conclude: In all restraints of trade, where nothing more appears, the law presumes them bad; but if the circumstances are set forth, that presumption is excluded, and the court is to judge of those circumstances, and determine accordingly; and if upon them it appears to be a just and honest contract it ought to be maintained.[43]

NOTES AND QUESTIONS

1. The leading decisions between *Dyer's* Case of 1415 and Mitchel v. Reynolds in 1711 are set forth in full in Oliphant, Cases on Trade Regulation 34–42 (1923).

2. The "rule of reason" originates with Mitchel v. Reynolds. What are the standards by which the reasonableness of an agreement not to compete may be measured? Should the same test be applicable to the restrictions in contracts of employment and contracts of sale? Contracts ancillary to purchases of property? Naked restrictions which are not ancillary to any major transaction? In general it is desirable to consider the purposes served by the agreements not to engage in a trade or exercise a craft, the reasons why they were exacted from the covenantors, and the factors that might condition their reasonableness. Can the judicial impairment of the voluntary arrangements of the parties be reconciled with the basic tenets of laissez faire?

---

43. Ed. For discussions of the early common-law cases, *see* Letwin, English Common Law Concerning Monopolies, 21 U.Chi. L.Rev. 355 (1954); Thorelli, Federal Antitrust Policy, Ch. I (1954); Blake, Employee Covenants Not to Compete, 73 Harv.L.Rev. 625, 629 (1960); Sanderson, Restraint of Trade in English Law, Ch. I (1926); Dewey, Common Law Background of Antitrust Policy, 41 Va. L.Rev. 759 (1955); Jones, Historical Development of the Law of Business Competition, 35 Yale L.J. 905 (1926); Carpenter, Validity of Contracts Not to Compete, 76 U.Pa.L.Rev. 244 (1928); Herbruck, Forestalling, Regrating and Engrossing, 27 Mich.L.Rev. 365 (1928); Schueller, The New Antitrust Illegality *Per Se*: Forestalling and Patent Misuse, 50 Colum.L.Rev. 170 (1950). Cf. Schiller, Restraint of Trade in Classical Roman Law (1934).

3. The English courts considered a different kind of restrictive agreement in Mogul Steamship Co., Ltd. v. McGregor, Gow & Co., Ltd. (1889) 23 Q.B.D. 598, aff'd, A.C. 25 (1892). *Mogul Steamship* involved a combination of steamship companies that had fixed rates and divided cargoes among them. When one member of the association attempted to sue for a breach of the agreement, the court concluded that the contract was invalid, because it was in restraint of trade. The court therefore found that the agreement was unenforceable. Third parties, however, could not complain about the agreement, and the court thought that it would not subject the parties to criminal liability. Compare the court's decision to find the agreement void and unenforceable to the consequences of entering into an anticompetitive agreement in the EU, as specified in Article 81.

4. During the late eighteenth and nineteenth centuries, a flood of restrictive covenant cases reached English and American courts.[44] Judges struggled with whether "general restraints" (*e.g.*, covenants not to carry on a given trade anywhere in England), as opposed to "particular restraints" (such as those limited in time and space), could ever be reasonable.[45] They further refined the reasonableness test.[46] Mitchel v. Reynolds, however, remained the starting place for all analyses; cases which failed to cite it are difficult to find. National Society of Professional Engineers v. United States, p. 230 infra, is a relatively recent (1978) example of its continuing vitality. The Supreme Court cited Mitchel v. Reynolds in

44. *See, e.g.*, Morse Twist Drill & Mach. Co. v. Morse, 103 Mass. 73 (1869); Diamond Match Co. v. Roeber, 106 N.Y. 473, 13 N.E. 419 (1887); Dunlop v. Gregory, 10 N.Y. 241 (1851); Horner v. Graves, 7 Bing. 735, 131 Eng.Rep. 284 (C.P.1831); N. Moller, Voluntary Covenants in Restraint of Trade 6–14 (1925).

45. The distinction between "general" and "particular" restraints was rejected in a series of cases that took cognizance of industrial and technological change. *See, e.g.*, Diamond Match Co. v. Roeber, 106 N.Y. 473, 13 N.E. 419 (1887); Rousillon v. Rousillon, 14 Ch.D. 351 (1880). General restraints have been upheld if no broader than the business sold. *See, e.g.*, Ace Tackless Corp. v. American Tackless Corp., 3 A.D.2d 672, 158 N.Y.S.2d 635 (1957) (United States); Burton, Parsons & Co. v. Parsons, 146 F.Supp. 114 (D.D.C.1956) (unlimited area interpreted to include only the United States, the area in which the company was doing business); Peterson v. Johnson Nut Co., 204 Minn. 300, 283 N.W. 561 (1939) (eastern United States and eastern Canada); Voices, Inc. v. Metal Tone Mfg. Co., 119 N.J.Eq. 324, 182 A. 880 (1936), affirmed, 120 N.J.Eq. 618, 187 A. 370, cert. denied, 300 U.S. 656 (1937) (United States and territories). General employment restraints have also been enforced. *See, e.g.*, Hulsenbusch v. Davidson Rubber Co., 344 F.2d 730 (8th Cir.1965), cert. denied, 382

U.S. 977 (1966) (United States); De Long Corp. v. Lucas, 278 F.2d 804 (2d Cir.1960), cert. denied, 364 U.S. 833 (1960) (worldwide); World Wide Pharmacal Distributing Co. v. Kolkey, 5 Ill.App.2d 201, 125 N.E.2d 309 (1955) (United States); Wiegand Glass Co. v. Wiegand, 105 N.J.Eq. 434, 148 A. 174 (1930) (United States). *See generally* Unitel Corp. v. Decker, 731 S.W.2d 636 (Tex.App.1987); Beckman v. Cox Broadcasting Corp., 250 Ga. 127, 296 S.E.2d 566 (1982); 14 Williston, Contracts § 1638 (3d ed. 1972).

46. In Horner v. Graves, 7 Bing. 735, 743, 131 Eng.Rep. 284, 287 (C.P.1831), for example, the court clarified Mitchel v. Reynolds by ruling that the standard of reasonableness applied not only to the consideration stated in the contract, but also to the question of "whether the restraint is such only as to afford a fair protection to the interests of the party in favour of whom it is given, and not so large as to interfere with the interests of the public." The court held that a restraint upon a dentist's assistant not to practice dentistry within 100 miles of his employer's town was unreasonably broad. *See* James C. Greene Co. v. Kelley, 261 N.C. 166, 134 S.E.2d 166 (1964) (employee's promise, made after employment began, held unenforceable because no consideration given by employer).

On the sufficiency of the consideration for the covenant, *see* 6A Corbin, Contracts § 1395 (1962).

the *Professional Engineers* case for the proposition that the rule of reason is not open ended but "focuses directly on the challenged restraint's impact on competition." Later in that case, Justice Stevens states that "the inquiry mandated by the Rule of Reason is whether the challenged agreement is one that promotes competition or one that suppresses competition." Other social values may be irrelevant. Is all this explicit or implicit in Mitchel v. Reynolds?

5. By 1890, when Section 1 of the Sherman Act was adopted to prohibit restraints illegal at common law or "those which are comparable to restraints deemed illegal at common law,"[47] the validity of restrictive covenants was clearly to be measured by a "rule of reason" test.

6. "The true view at the present time I think, is this: The public have an interest in every person's carrying on his trade freely: so has the individual. All interference with individual liberty of action in trading, and all restraints of trade of themselves, if there is nothing more, are contrary to public policy, and therefore void. That is the general rule. But there are exceptions: restraints of trade and interference with individual liberty of action may be justified by the special circumstances of a particular case. It is a sufficient justification, and indeed it is the only justification, if the restriction is reasonable—reasonable, that is, in reference to the interests of the parties concerned and reasonable in reference to the interests of the public, so framed and so guarded as to afford adequate protection to the party in whose favour it is imposed, while at the same time it is in no way injurious to the public." Lord MacNaghten, in Nordenfelt v. Maxim Nordenfelt Guns and Ammunition Co. [1894] A.C. 535, 565.[48]

B. THE SHERMAN ACT—SOME LEGISLATIVE HISTORY

William L. Letwin, Congress and the Sherman Antitrust Law: 1887–1890[49]

23 U.Chi.L.Rev. 221 et seq. (1956).

The deceptive simplicity of the Sherman Act has led many historians to believe that the intention of Congress was equally simple. Although they

---

47. Apex Hosiery Co. v. Leader, 310 U.S. 469, 498 (1940); *see* Standard Oil Co. v. United States, 221 U.S. 1, 58–59 (1911); United States v. Addyston Pipe & Steel Co., 85 F. 271, 279, 282–83 (6th Cir.1898), affirmed, 175 U.S. 211 (1899).

48. In some cases, covenants broader than the business sold have been sustained without being pared down. *See e.g.*, Hall Mfg. Co. v. Western Steel & Iron Works, 227 F. 588 (7th Cir.1915) (upholding unlimited covenant although existing business covered 34 states and two Canadian provinces); Diamond Match Co. v. Roeber, 106 N.Y. 473, 13 N.E. 419 (1887) (upholding covenant covering the United States, except Nevada and Montana, and territories, although business sold reached ten states). It has been intimated

that the covenant may embrace the area of probable expansion of the business sold. *See e.g.*, Knapp v. S. Jarvis Adams Co., 135 F. 1008, 1012 (6th Cir.1905); Swingle & Co. v. Reynolds, 140 Neb. 693, 1 N.W.2d 307 (1941); Schultz v. Johnson, 110 N.J.Eq. 566, 160 A. 379 (1932); cf., Rubel & Jensen Corp. v. Rubel, 85 N.J.Super. 27, 37–38, 203 A.2d 625, 630 (1964) (employee); Budget Rent–A–Car Corp. v. Fein, 342 F.2d 509, 518 (5th Cir. 1965) (prospective franchise); *but see* Martin v. Hawley, 50 S.W.2d 1105 (Tex.Civ.App. 1932). *See generally* 14 Williston, Contracts § 1638 (3d ed.1972).

49. Reprinted by permission of The University of Chicago Law Review, University of Chicago Law School.

have not agreed on what the intention was.... Some suppose that the congressmen of 1890 were committed to a policy of laissez-faire, interpret that policy as a dogmatic faith in competition, and regard the Sherman Act as an effort to enforce that orthodoxy. Others less trustful maintain that the Act was a fraud, contrived to soothe the public without injuring the trusts, and they insist that no other result was possible because the Republican Party, in control of the 51st Congress, was "itself dominated at the time by many of the very industrial magnates most vulnerable to real antitrust legislation."[50] Both these schools can draw support from distinguished men who lived while the Act was being passed.[51] ...

I

No one denies that Congress passed the Sherman Act in response to real public feeling against the trusts, but at this distance it is difficult to be sure how hostile the public was and why. The intensity of public opposition, difficult though it may be to assess, is of some importance in explaining what Congress did. If public hatred of trusts was violent, or if congressmen thought it was, then they might have felt so pressed to pass the law, whatever their own judgments, as to have done the work hastily and perhaps spitefully. If, on the other hand, the public opposition was firm but calm, then Congress may have felt free to pass the best law it could devise. In fact, though the public sentiment may not have been so intense as some believed, yet it was more deeply rooted than many have noticed, and sufficient in any event to persuade Congress that something had to be done; but since the public, despite its hostility, did not and could not suggest any specific solution for the problem, Congress was left very much to its own devices in deciding what was to be done.

In the years immediately before the Sherman Act, between 1888 and 1890, there were few who doubted that the public hated the trusts fervently. Those who fanned the prejudice and those who hoped to smother it agreed that the fire was already blazing. Radical agitators and polite reformers spoke admiringly of the "people's wrath." Apologists for the trust did not deny its unpopularity....

These impressions of the state of public opinion were supported by more nearly impartial contemporaries, including the judges who, with William Howard Taft, took it quite for granted that the Act "was a step taken by Congress to meet what the public had found to be a growing and intolerable evil."[52] Here and there a few doubts were expressed about the

---

50. Fainsod and Gordon, Government and the American Economy 450 (1941). Cochran and Miller, The Age of Enterprise 171–2 (1942). *See also*, Papandreou and Wheeler, Competition and Its Regulation 213 (1954) in which the Sherman Act is described as a measure of "appeasement."

51. Senator Platt said that his colleagues were interested in only one thing, "to get some bill headed: 'A Bill to Punish Trusts' with which to go to the country." Coolidge, An Old–Fashioned Senator: Orville H. Platt 444 (1910). Justice Holmes thought that the Act was "a humbug based on economic ignorance and incompetence." 1 Holmes–Pollock Letters 163 (Howe ed., 1941).

52. Taft, The Anti–Trust Act and the Supreme Court 2 (1914).

public's determination. Some extremists said that the people could solve the trust problem—by establishing government ownership of all industry—if it would only awake and "prove itself worthy to be free."[53] Some free-traders said that trusts could be eradicated by abolishing protective tariffs, if the people would only "open their eyes."[54] A skeptic has since held that government would have destroyed the trusts, if the people had really cared.[55] But these irregular views have not received much notice, and most later commentators have been satisfied to believe that there was a "great public outcry" against the trusts. . . .

Between 1887 and 1890 the tariff question had priority in the newspapers, party platforms, and, as Senator Sherman himself said, in the work of the 51st Congress.[56] But the pre-eminence of the tariff question did not detract from the trust problem, and if the tariff constantly intruded in congressional debate on trusts, so did the trust problem regularly infiltrate discussion of tariffs. . . .

The pervasive antitrust sentiment did not spring up overnight. Hatred of monopoly is one of the oldest American political habits and, like most profound traditions, it consisted of an essentially permanent idea expressed at different times. "Monopoly," as the word was used in America, meant at first a special legal privilege granted by the state; later it came more often to mean exclusive control that a few persons achieved by their own efforts; but it always meant some sort of unjustified power, especially one that raised obstacles to equality of opportunity. The trust was popularly regarded as nothing but a new form of monopoly, and the whole force of the tradition was focused against it immediately.

The principle that government should create no monopolies was one of those deep political convictions that the colonists had brought with them from England. There the matter had been settled in 1624 by the Statute of Monopolies, which closely limited the King's power to grant exclusive privileges. In America the same attitude was expressed when the colonial legislature of Massachusetts decreed that "there shall be no monopolies granted or allowed among us but of such new inventions as are profitable to the country, and that for a short time."[57] Soon after the Revolution several states included in their bills of rights rather more philosophic statements, similar to that adopted by Virginia: "No man, or set of men, are entitled to exclusive or separate emoluments or privileges from the community. . . ."[58] Jefferson thought that a prohibition to the same effect

53. Lewis, A Talk About "Trusts" 13 (1889).

54. N.Y. Times, p. 4, col. 3 (Dec. 28, 1887) (editorial).

55. Wollman, The Mortality of Trusts, 67 Alb.L.J. 227 (1905).

56. Sen. Sherman to Gen. W.T. Sherman, Nov. 9, 1889, The Sherman Letters 379 (Thorndike ed., 1894).

57. C. 71 (1641); Charters and General Laws of the Colony and Province of Massachusetts Bay 170 (1814).

58. Va. Bill of Rights § 4 (1776); Mass. Const. Part I, Art. 6 (1780); Conn. Const. Art. I, § 1 (1818).

should appear in the federal Bill of Rights,[59] and there are signs that his opinion was widely supported. Several of the states, having agreed to ratify the Constitution although they were not satisfied that it sufficiently guaranteed the people's rights, proposed amendments which they submitted with their acts of ratification. Among these were proposals offered by New York, "that the Congress do not grant monopolies,"[60] and by Massachusetts, New Hampshire, and Rhode Island, "that the Congress erect no company of merchants with exclusive advantages of commerce."[61] In the end, however, no specific prohibition of monopoly was included in the federal Bill of Rights. Some afterwards maintained that since the power of creating monopolies had not been explicitly denied to Congress, it had been implicitly conceded;[62] others said that a legislature could not grant monopolies unless the Constitution expressly authorized it;[63] but no one argued that the prohibition was omitted because the public favored or was even indifferent to monopolies.

In spite of this hostility, the federal government after the Revolution did from time to time create private monopolies, but these did more to renew and deepen the public sentiment than to dilute it. The most numerous were patent monopolies granted to inventors, but the patent system was generally tolerated as a traditional exception to the traditional principle. Other monopolies, such as the two Banks of the United States, were not tolerated so quietly....

There were other institutions more numerous and permanent than the central banks, against which public opposition to monopoly was more regularly expressed. Chief among these was the corporation.... The chief attacks on monopolies after the Civil War became more specific. They were no longer directed at incorporation itself or corporations in the mass, but more particularly against certain practices, above all economic abuses, that were attributed to some corporations. No one could by this time reasonably want or hope to solve the problem by abolishing corporations or by making it easier to establish more of them. The idea began, therefore, to spread that the power and injurious behavior of monopolistic corporations should be controlled by government regulation.

Agitation for anti-monopoly laws was first led by the Grangers or Patrons of Husbandry. Founded two years after the Civil War and at first intended to serve the social and educational needs of farmers, it soon became involved in economic and political activities. By 1871, its founder reported that " 'Cooperation' and 'Down with monopolies' were proving

59. Jefferson, 5 Works 371 (Ford ed., 1904) (Jefferson to Madison, Dec. 20, 1787).

60. I Elliot, Debates in the Several State Conventions 330 (2d ed., 1854).

61. Ibid., at 323, 326, 337.

62. Rep. Lawrence, in congressional debate on the first Bank of the United States, Feb. 4, 1791. 2 Debates and Proceedings in Congress of United States 1915 (Gales, comp., 1834).

63. As Attorney General of the United States, Taney gave this opinion in 1833 concerning the monopoly granted the Camden and Amboy Railroad by the New Jersey legislature. Dodd, American Business Corporations 125 (1954).

popular watchwords"[64]—indeed by 1875, when the Grange reached its peak, it had brought within its ranks at least one of every ten American farmers. "Cooperation" meant organization of farmers' cooperatives, while "Down with monopolies" meant principally regulation of railroads. Granger opposition to railroads and monopolies was expressed in a host of manifestos, declarations, petitions and statements, of which the resolutions adopted by an Illinois Farmers' Convention in 1873 were fairly typical. The first two stated "that all chartered monopolies, not regulated and controlled by law, have proved detrimental to the public prosperity, corrupting in their management, and dangerous to republican institutions," and "that the railways of the world, except in those countries where they have been held under the strict regulation and supervision of the government, have proved themselves arbitrary, extortionate and as opposed to free institutions and free commerce between states as were the feudal barons of the middle ages."[65] The traditional theme, that monopolies are dangerous to liberty, was there as always, but with it a contemporary variation: the only cure is regulation by law....

Reformers with rather broader interests succeeded the Grange as leading anti-monopolists during the early 1880's, and in their hands "monopoly" was a brush that could tar many rich or exclusive institutions. One crusader condemned as monopolistic not only railroads, banks, and public utility companies, but also speculative dealing in grains, restrictive licensing of businesses and professions, laws limiting the ballot to males, and "those nurseries of caste"—West Point and Annapolis.[66] ...

Many other companies and institutions were attacked as monopolies during the years after 1880, but more and more attention was devoted to combinations of industrial firms, all of which, however organized, came by the end of the decade to be called trusts. Public prominence was achieved first by the Standard Oil Company, which by 1880 controlled much of the country's petroleum refining. Thereafter it became a favorite butt of the anti-monopolists.... In 1882, Standard Oil adopted the trust device, and the effectiveness of this method for making combinations permanently cohesive and easily manageable recommended it to others....

Trust-building did not begin in earnest until 1887, but then it took hold quickly. That year saw the formation of the Sugar and Whisky Trusts, which until the end of the century contended for unpopularity only with Standard Oil. Others, affecting lesser industries or smaller markets, added to the list....

The greater fervor against trusts in 1888, which bursts so unexpectedly on an historian like Clark, was for the people living at the time nothing so sudden or strange. It was simply a familiar feeling raised to a high pitch, intense because the speed with which new trusts were being hatched made

64. Buck, The Granger Movement 52–53 (1913).

65. Periam, The Groundswell 286 (1874).

66. Bland, The Reign of Monopoly (1881).

it seem that they would overrun everything unless some remedy were found soon. The general disposition of the public was not in doubt. There were numerous objections to the trusts—complaints of a traditional sort as well as newer ones suited to the character of these particular monopolies. Trusts, it was said, threatened liberty, because they corrupted civil servants and bribed legislators; they enjoyed privileges such as protection by tariffs; they drove out competitors by lowering prices; victimized consumers by raising prices; defrauded investors by watering stocks; put laborers out of work by closing down plants; and somehow or other abused everyone. The kind of remedy that the public desired was also clear enough: it wanted a law to destroy the power of the trusts. The alternative suggestion that government should take over the trusts and operate them as public property seems to have had scant support. But the desire was not, and, in the nature of public opinion, could not be expressed in much greater detail. Any law might be acceptable if it really suppressed the worst abuses of the trusts, especially of those like the Standard Oil, Sugar, and Whisky Trusts, that were most noticeable and most important in the everyday life of many people. The public's mandate was clear, but so broad that Congress had to look elsewhere for advice on how to implement it.

II

Expert judgment on how to solve the trust problem would naturally be expected from the two professions most closely concerned with it, the economists and the lawyers. . . .

Although they differed as to the exact action government should take, nearly all the economists were convinced that any attempt to prohibit combinations would be either unnecessary or futile. Since many of the trusts were "natural," the law could not destroy them. . . . Moreover, some economists argued, any combination that was not justified by the underlying conditions of its industry would decay of its own accord or be controlled by what came to be called "the active influence of the potential competitor."[67]

The legal profession was more apt to suggest means that Congress might use in solving the trust problem, since most lawyers believed that laws could prohibit monopolies. Indeed they thought that the common law already did so, although their conviction rested on a somewhat tenuous basis. . . .

To say that monopolies were illegal at common law was one thing, to destroy them by using the common law was another. . . . Active prosecution of trusts was needed, and indeed a few public officials managed to do it. If they could not sue monopolies in any other way, they could and did use the legal weapons provided by their power over corporations. Between 1887 and 1890 the attorneys-general of five states more or less enthusiastically initiated suits to dissolve corporations that exceeded their chartered pow-

67. Gunton, The Economic and Social Aspects of Trusts, 3 Pol.Sci.Q. 385, 403 (1888); Clark, The "Trust," 52 New Englander 223 (1890).

ers, or to destroy associations that exercised corporate powers without having charters. Most of the lawyers who insisted on the legality of trusts argued that they were either unincorporated joint-stock companies or partnerships of shareholders, both perfectly lawful forms of organization. The public prosecutors set out to prove the opposite, and in every case they won. . . . But in any case, few monopolies had been destroyed in this way by 1890.

Still, these few recent attacks on monopolies, together with the current view that the common law expressed a public policy hostile to monopolies, made lawyers confident that the common law went in the right direction. Some of them thought it went far enough. . . .

Few of the lawyers who believed that statutes were needed—at least few who wrote in legal periodicals—suggested how the statutes should be framed. One of the rare proposals was that laws be passed to subject the trust to corporation law, and to prohibit any corporation from holding stock in any other.[68] This second hint was rather far-sighted, for the author understood, as few others yet did, that the corporate holding-company or merged corporation might be a much safer method of organizing monopolies than the trust. But there was a serious flaw in this scheme, as in all antitrust laws proposed or passed by the states (the Missouri antitrust law, for instance, had already encountered it by March of 1890):[69] the states lacked authority to regulate corporations engaged in interstate commerce. It seemed therefore that if antitrust legislation were needed and if it were to be effective against the largest and most powerful trusts, it must be passed by Congress.

The lawyers and the economists offered Congress little specific help and much conflicting advice. Yet, although the economists advocated some sort of public regulation while the lawyers suggested nothing but prohibitory laws, their underlying views were well adapted to each other. The economists thought that both competition and combination should play their parts in the economy. The lawyers saw that the common law permitted combination in some instances and prohibited it in others. Congressmen seized on this hidden agreement, and set out to construct a statute which by the use of common law principles would eliminate excesses but allow "healthy" competition and combination to flourish side by side.

III

The political parties officially recognized the trust problem soon after it arose. The third parties needed no urging; . . .

The major parties were anything but anxious to appear as champions of the trusts. The Democrats had made the appropriate general statements against monopoly in 1880 and 1884, but they had especially good reasons for carrying these further in 1888. For one thing, they could cite the new offense as additional evidence against their old enemy, protection. Presi-

68. Stimson, Trusts, 1 Harv.L.Rev. 132 (1887).

69. Consult, 30 Cen.L.J. 1 (1890); 7 Ry. & Corp.L.J. 241 (1890).

dent Cleveland, in his annual message to Congress at the end of 1887, said it was "notorious" that the "combinations quite prevalent at this time, and frequently called trusts," strangled competition; he urged that action be taken against them, and suggested that Congress reduce the customs duties protecting them against foreign competitors.[70] Moreover, the trust issue was especially useful for appealing to farmers and laborers who might shift their vote to the third party....

The Republican Party had even more compelling need to condemn the trusts. They had since 1880 achieved the reputation of being the party of the rich, and in 1884 Ben Butler began calling them the "Party of Monopolists." This label became especially current after their presidential candidate was given a banquet by a group of businessmen, among them Gould, Vanderbilt, and Astor, which the New York World titled "The Royal Feast of Belshazzar Blaine and the Money Kings," and during which, it said, the "Millionaires and Monopolists" sealed their allegiance to the party. A party whose policies were subject to so crudely cynical an interpretation and which was undoubtedly supported—as were the others—by some millionaires, must have condemned the trusts in self-defense even if it had not objected to them in principle. In their convention of 1888, the Republicans accordingly condemned "all combinations of capital, organized in trusts or otherwise, to control arbitrarily the conditions of trade among our citizens," and recommended "such legislation as will prevent the execution of all schemes to oppress the people by undue charges on their supplies, or by unjust rates for the transportation of their products to market." Because they elected President Harrison and won decisive control of Congress in the following election, responsibility for carrying out the recommendation became theirs.

Congress began to concern itself with the trust problem in January of 1888. The antitrust bill was brought to the floor of Congress by Senator John Sherman because he wanted to leave one more monument to himself. By 1888 he was aging, at times impatient and confused, but still the most prominent and esteemed Republican in Congress. He had served as representative for eight years, senator for over twenty-five, and had been Secretary of the Treasury under Hayes. He had been a candidate for the presidential nomination since 1880, and seemed finally to be winning it at the convention of 1888 until Harrison took the lead during the seventh ballot. Soon after this defeat he began to take serious interest in the trust question. His seniority and experience gave him great authority on financial questions and his recent disappointment gave him the urge to do something memorable. He began by establishing personal jurisdiction over the antitrust problem. The antitrust bills introduced earlier in the year[71]

70. 8 Richardson, Messages and Papers of the Presidents 588 (1900) (Message of Dec. 6, 1887).

71. Sen. 2,906; H.R. 6,113, 6,117, 8,036, 8,054, 9,449, 10,049, 50th Cong. 1st Sess. (1888). The bills, as well as debates directly concerned with them, are conveniently gathered in Sen.Doc. No. 147, Bills and Debates in Congress Relating to Trusts, 57th Cong. 2d Sess. (1903), from which, however, some relevant matter is omitted, e.g., H.R. 4,406, 50th Cong. 1st Sess. (1888).

had been referred to committees, but none had yet been debated, when, on July 10, Sherman successfully introduced a resolution directing the Senate Committee on Finance, of which he was a ranking member, to investigate all antitrust bills. He maintained that the Committee would investigate antitrust bills "in connection with" tariff bills, which were undoubtedly its proper province; but this argument had its danger as well, for by stressing the connection between trusts and tariffs he was playing into the hands of the Democrats. He had already made this blunder when, in replying to Cleveland's annual message, he agreed that the trusts might be fought by reducing duties that protected them—though he then added that he knew of no trusts which had such protection. Now he was a little more on guard, and argued that the trusts not only prevented "freedom of trade and production" but also subverted the tariff system; they undermined "the policy of the Government to protect and encourage American industries by levying duties on imported goods."

The effect of Sherman's maneuver became evident a month later, when Senator John Reagan, a Democrat from Texas, introduced an antitrust bill which was read and about to be referred to committee. At this point Sherman rose to insist that according to the resolution the bill should be sent to the Finance Committee. He maintained that this was appropriate because the only constitutional provision enabling Congress to legislate against trusts was the power to levy taxes: though the federal government might not be able to attack trusts like Standard Oil, it could certainly use the taxing power to control monopolies like the Sugar Trust, which were aided by tariffs. But this doctrine was far from congenial to him, and, when Senator Ransom replied that Congress derived its jurisdiction over trusts from its constitutional power to regulate commerce, Sherman was ready to shift ground. He answered: "I always take the revenue laws as commercial laws. They always go together, interchangeably." Though this may have been an accurate interpretation of the Constitution, it was less than an adequate reason for referring trust bills to the Finance Committee rather than the Commerce Committee, but the Senate was impressed by Sherman's determination and agreed to send Reagan's bill to his committee. Sherman immediately capped the day's work by introducing an antitrust bill of his own.[72]

His bill, unlike Reagan's, was returned in short order to the Senate floor, where it was briefly debated and considerably amended in January, 1889.[73] By now it had begun to look like a serious effort, and was honored with a long attack by Senator James George of Mississippi, formerly a Confederate general and Chief Justice of the state supreme court, a Democrat and fervent upholder of states' rights. George questioned both its effectiveness and constitutionality. He declared that although he firmly opposed the trusts and was eager to destroy them, he saw no hope that the bill could do so. It declared illegal "all arrangements, contracts, agreements, trusts, or combinations between persons or corporations made with

72. 19 Cong.Rec. 7,512 (1888).   **73.** 20 Cong.Rec. 1,167–69 (1889).

a view, or which tend, to prevent full and free competition" in certain goods, or "to advance the cost to the consumer;"[74] yet these words, George said, would condemn not only the trusts and combinations but also arrangements made "for moral and defensive purposes."[75]

These preliminary skirmishes were continued during the early months of the 51st Congress. The moment the session began Sherman introduced a bill that, except for changes in detail, contained the words and principles of his previous drafts. It declared unlawful and void all combinations preventing competition in foreign and interstate commerce; it authorized any person injured by such combinations to recover damages; and it subjected all members and agents of such combinations to fine and imprisonment.[76] The bill, introduced on December 4, 1889, and very slightly amended by the Finance Committee, was brought to the floor of the Senate in February 1890, whereupon Senator George once again made a full-scale attack on it. He repeated his previous objections, and as before concluded that the bill was "utterly unconstitutional, and even if constitutional, utterly worthless."[77] The matter was left there, and it began to look as though antitrust legislation was a dim prospect. More than two years had passed since the first bills had been put before Congress, and as yet only one had been briefly considered. The machinery seemed to have come to a standstill. . . .

Suddenly the situation changed, and in the last weeks of March 1890, the serious work of preparing an antitrust law was begun. The burst of energy may have come because the Republican congressmen gave up the idea, supposing they ever had it, of treating the trust problem in the McKinley Tariff Bill. To have done so would have given the impression that they agreed with the Democrats about the causes of trusts and the constitutional powers available to destroy them. They may have felt that the public was becoming impatient, for congressmen were receiving an increasing number of petitions advocating antitrust legislation. Or the new activity may have come at Sherman's insistence. He announced a few days before it began that he had revised his bill to meet George's objections, having deleted the provisions George had criticized because they would make the law a criminal one and thus oblige the courts to interpret it narrowly. In any case, by the time Sherman submitted his new bill on March 21, the Senate was prepared to concentrate on it and spent the next five days doing little else.

The great debate opened with a long, formal address in which Sherman praised his bill. He began by explaining its political and legal theory. It was intended, he said, to destroy combinations, not all combinations, but all those which the common law had always condemned as unlawful. It was not intended to outlaw all partnerships and corporations, though they were by nature combinations. The corporations had demonstrated their usefulness by the vast development of railroads and industry, and Sherman added—bearing in mind the lingering prejudice against them—that as long

74. Ibid., at 1,459–61.

75. Ibid.

76. Sen. 1, 51st Cong. 1st Sess. (1889).

77. 21 Cong.Rec. 1,765–72 (1890).

as every man had the right under general laws to form corporations, they were "not in any sense a monopoly."[78] But any combination which sought to restrain trade, any combination of the leading corporations in an industry, organized in a trust to stifle competition, dictate terms to railroads, command the price of labor, and raise prices to consumers, was a "substantial monopoly." It smacked of tyranny, "of kingly prerogative," and a nation that "would not submit to an emperor ... should not submit to an autocrat of trade." Sherman went on to say that all such combinations in restraint of trade were prohibited by the common law, wherever it was in force; it had always applied in the states, and the "courts in different States have declared this thing, when it exists in a State, to be unlawful and void." Senator Cullom interrupted to ask, "Everywhere?" "In every case, everywhere,"[79] Sherman replied, and went on to list the recent decisions supporting his view. . . . Once again, he insisted that Congress was authorized alike by the commerce and revenue clauses of the Constitution to regulate combinations affecting interstate and foreign commerce; and he concluded that his bill, based on this constitutional power and declaring the common law rule, would effectively destroy the power of the trusts.

The debate which occupied much of the following week was untidy but not without pattern. Many senators delivered great orations, but few were heard to say that the trusts were desirable or an antitrust law unnecessary. George repeatedly questioned the bill's constitutionality; certain of his Democratic colleagues took occasion to avow their opposition to tariffs. A number of senators tried to substitute their own bills for Sherman's and failing this they attached them to his as amendments. By the end of the third day, the bill before the Senate consisted of sixteen sections. Sherman's bill now had tailing after it: Reagan's bill, which, instead of relying on common-law formulas, gave a long explicit definition of the term "trust;"[80] Ingall's bill, which was a more or less independent effort to prohibit speculation in farm products; and George's clause, which exempted labor unions and farmers' organizations from the general prohibitions. Moreover, the constitutional issue was still confused, and George suggested that the bill be referred to the Judiciary Committee, who, chosen for their legal wisdom, might be able to restore order to the law. Sherman, piqued and impatient, objected that it was most unusual to transfer a bill from one committee to another; Reagan, whose original bill had never yet been reported to the floor by the Judiciary Committee, was equally adamant; and Vance called the Judiciary Committee a "grand mausoleum of Senatorial literature" in which this bill would be buried.[81] But after two more days in

78. Cong.Rec. 2,456 (1890).

79. Ibid.

80. Reagan defined a trust as a "combination of capital, skill, or acts" by two or more persons or associations for any of the following purposes: to restrict trade, to limit production, to increase or reduce price, to prevent competition, to fix prices, to "create a monopoly," to make any agreement to set minimum prices, to agree to "pool, combine, or unite" so as to affect prices. Sen. 62, 51st Cong. 1st Sess. (1889).

81. 21 Cong.Rec. 2,600 et seq., 2,604, 2,610 (1890).

which further amendments were added and further profound doubts expressed, the matter had become so tangled that little alternative remained, and the bill was referred to the Judiciary Committee with instructions to report within twenty days.

The Judiciary Committee took the matter out of Sherman's hands, much to his regret and anger. But within a week, surprising everyone, the Committee produced a bill of its own. The work was done largely by its chairman, George Edmunds of Vermont. He disposed of the constitutional question very quickly: when the Committee first met to consider the bill, he proposed to his colleagues "that it is competent for Congress to pass laws preventing and punishing contracts etc. in restraint of commerce between the states." And they, including George, who had raised objections to this theory all along, unanimously agreed.[82] Edmunds then presented drafts of the critical sections of the Act, that made it a misdemeanor to engage in any combination in restraint of trade or to "monopolize" trade, and these were agreed to by all the committeemen present. Two of the remaining sections were written by others: George prepared the section authorizing the Attorney General to sue for injunctions against violators, and Hoar wrote the section authorizing private persons to sue violators for triple damages.[83] The Committee's draft was in broad outline the same as Sherman's original bill, yet Sherman was not pleased. He immediately denounced it as "totally ineffective in dealing with combinations and trusts. All corporations can ride through it or over it without fear of punishment or detection."[84] His reaction was particularly ungenerous, since aside from the fact that the new bill was simpler than his, it differed mainly in providing a greater number of more severe penalties. But when the time came, he voted for it, and as a matter of courtesy it bears his name. The Senate as a whole seemed well satisfied, and after hearing Edmunds' plea that they "pass a bill that is clear in its terms, is definite in its definitions, and is broad in its comprehension, without winding it up into infinite details,"[85] they passed it by fifty-two votes to one.

The action of the House was less systematic. Representative Culberson, who was in charge of the debate, tried to limit it to one hour. His colleagues, who had not until now considered any antitrust bill, complained that they could not get printed copies of the one before them. A strong group insisted that a section should be added to the bill specifically aimed at outlawing railroad and meat-packing pools. After a rather desultory debate, the House passed the bill with one amendment, on May 1. During the next two months, conferences were held between the two chambers,

82. Senate, Committee on the Judiciary, Minute Book 226 (March 31, 1890) (Ms. in U.S. Archives).

83. The Committee Minute Book, ibid., at 227–33, shows that sections 1, 2, 5, and 6 were drafted by Edmunds, section 4 by George, section 7 by Hoar, and the phrase "in the form of a trust or otherwise" by Evarts. It does not indicate who drafted sections 3 and 8. There is a strong presumption, but no proof, to support Walker's assertion that Edmunds did; consult Walker, Who Wrote the Sherman Law, 73 Cen.L.J. 257, 258 (1911).

84. N.Y. Times p. 4, col. 4 (April 8, 1890).

85. 21 Cong.Rec. 3,148 (April 8, 1890).

and the House was eventually prevailed on to withdraw its amendment.[86] President Harrison signed the bill, and it became law on July 2, 1890.

Hans B. Thorelli, The Federal Antitrust Policy[87]

180–85, 226–29 (1955).

March 21, 1890. Sherman's Defense of Bill. Debate Begun

... Senator Sherman stated that no intelligent person could question, in good faith, the need for some form of congressional action against the trusts:

> The popular mind is agitated with problems that may disturb social order, and among them all none is more threatening than the inequality of condition, of wealth, and opportunity that has grown within a single generation out of the concentration of capital into vast combinations to control production and trade and to break down competition. These combinations already defy or control powerful transportation corporations and reach State authorities. They reach out their Briarean arms to every part of our country. They are imported from abroad. Congress alone can deal with them, and if we are unwilling or unable there will soon be a trust for every production and a master to fix the price for every necessity of life....

And again:

> The sole subject of such a combination (of "the controlling corporations, partnerships, and individuals engaged in the same business") is to make competition impossible. It can control the market, raise or lower prices, as will best promote its selfish interests, reduce prices in a particular locality and break down competition and advance prices at will where competition does not exist.... The law of selfishness, uncontrolled by competition, compels it to disregard the interest of the consumer. It dictates terms to transportation companies, it commands the price of labor without fear of strikes, for in its field it allows no competitors.... It is this kind of a combination we have to deal with now.
>
> If we will not endure a king as a political power we should not endure a king over the production, transportation, and sale of any of the necessaries of life. If we would not submit to an emperor we should not submit to an autocrat of trade, with power to prevent competition and to fix the price of any commodity....

Before closing his speech Sherman once more returned to this subject. Calling the proposed measure a "bill of rights" and a "charter of liberty," he said, "Now, Mr. President, what is this bill? A remedial statute to

---

86. Bills and Debates 327–402 (1890).

87. Reprinted by permission of the publisher, the Johns Hopkins Press and the author.

enforce by civil process in the courts of the United States the common law
against monopolies. . . ."

Turning to the problem of intent, which had occupied such a large part
of the critical argumentation of Senator George, Sherman continued:

> In providing a remedy the intention of the combination is immate-
> rial. The intention of a corporation can not be proven. If the
> natural effects of its acts are injurious, if they tend to produce evil
> results, if their policy is denounced by the law as against the
> common good, it may be restrained, be punished with a penalty or
> with damages, and in a proper case it may be deprived of its
> corporate powers and franchises. It is the tendency of a corpora-
> tion, and not its intention, that the courts can deal with. . . .

The second section offered relief to private parties injured by unlawful
combination. Such a party could

> . . . sue for and recover in any court of the United States of
> competent jurisdiction, of any person or corporation a party to
> such a combination, all damages sustained by him. The measure of
> damages, whether merely compensatory, punitive, or vindictive, is
> a matter of detail depending upon the judgment of Congress. My
> own opinion is that the damages should be commensurate with the
> difficulty of maintaining a private suit against a combination such
> as is described.

The bill did not declare unlawful *all* restraints of trade. An individual
or a firm achieving a position of full-fledged monopoly in some line of trade
without having made any arrangements with competitors on the way would
not be affected by it. Combinations in intrastate trade made by citizens or
corporations all belonging to the same state, and not relating to commodities competing with articles imported into the United States, were also
excluded. And despite the sweeping language of the bill it could not
conceivably be directed even against all other combinations. If this were the
case two small coffee importers (out of a possible thousand), for instance,
would be unable to join in a partnership. Sherman recognized that the
coverage of the bill would be narrower than its wording. He has already
been quoted as saying that the courts would "distinguish between lawful
combinations in aid of production and unlawful combinations to prevent
competition and in restraint of trade." This and similar statements by
Sherman have been used, or rather abused, by numerous authors, including some judges, to write almost any pet interpretation into the language of
the bill as well as the final Sherman Act.[88] Thus, it becomes imperative to
examine just what Sherman said. He stated on several occasions that the
object of the bill was to make the common law against monopolies and
restraint of trade applicable on the federal level. The common law as it had
been applied in Britain and in the several states was to be the main guide

88. Clark, Federal Trust Policy 45
(1931), cites Felix H. Levy as but one example.

of the national courts in drawing the line of demarcation between lawful and unlawful combinations.

What was, then, a representative contemporary concept of the common law on the subject? Sherman tried to illustrate his ideas by reviewing several court decisions. . . . In all these cases the combination was held void or unlawful. Milton Handler also maintains "that in all the cited cases, the combination controlled the market in which it operated."[89]

Be that as it may, the fact remains that Sherman did not consider only these cases as illustrative:

> I might add to the cases cited innumerable cases in nearly all the States and in England, and in all of them it will appear that while the law in respect to contracts in restraint of trade and combinations to prevent competition and to advance the price of necessaries of life has varied somewhat, but in all of them, whether the combinations are by individuals, partnerships, or corporations, when the purpose of the combination or its plain tendency is to prevent competition, the courts have enforced the rule of the common law and have vigorously used the judicial power in subverting them.

That Sherman wanted the bill to cover the great industrial trusts proper as well as mergers and other tight combinations when of a monopolistic nature there can be no doubt. With regard to simple agreements, pools and similar loose associations no equally emphatic statement can be made. Only one or two of the cases referred to . . . belong to this category. . . . By implication the bill intended to leave the task of drawing these lines of demarcation to the courts. This brings us back to the common law and the observation that Sherman's general concept of the common law on monopolies and restraint of trade as evidenced in his speech was quite "radical." Thus, either line of reasoning would seem to suggest that Sherman wanted to give the bill a broad coverage with respect to all kinds of combinations "made with a view or which tend to prevent full and free competition."

. . . There can be no doubt that Sherman's views were typical in the sense that the vast majority of congressmen were sincere proponents of a private enterprise system founded on the principle of "full and free competition." Most of the legislators sponsoring bills or participating in debates with speeches relating to the principal issues involved made vigorous statements to this effect. But, generally speaking, little need was felt to attempt penetrating analyses of the underlying economic theory or to support the prevalent belief by extended argument—the members of Congress proclaimed "the norm of a free competition too self-evident to be debated, too obvious to be asserted." . . .

There can be no doubt that the Congress felt that the ultimate beneficiary in this whole process was the consumer, enjoying a continuous

89. Milton Handler, Cases and Materials on Trade Regulation (1937), 215, note 27.

increase in production and commodity quality at progressively lowered prices. The immediate beneficiary legislators had in mind, however, was in all probability the small business proprietor or tradesman whose opportunities were to be safeguarded from the dangers emanating from those recently-evolving elements of business that seemed so strange, gigantic, ruthless and awe-inspiring. This is one reason why it was natural to adopt the old doctrines of the common law, doctrines whose meaning had been established largely in cases brought by business or professional people dissatisfied with the behavior of competitors. Perhaps we are even justified in saying that the Sherman Act is not to be viewed exclusively as an expression of economic policy. In safeguarding rights of the "common man" in business "equal" to those of the evolving more "ruthless" and impersonal forms of enterprise the Sherman Act embodies what is to be characterized as an eminently "social" purpose. A moderate limitation of the freedom of contract was expected to yield a maximization of the freedom of enterprise. Sherman himself, furthermore, expressed the idea probably in the minds of many of his colleagues that the legislation contemplated constituted an important means of achieving freedom from corruption and maintaining freedom of independent thinking in political life, a treasured cornerstone of democratic government....

It seems futile and superfluous to discuss whether the Sherman Act was intended to bring the body of common law on the subject within reach of the United States courts. Authors questioning that this was the intent of Congress manifest a striking lack of familiarity with the records of legislative proceedings. There is ample evidence that not only the bills reported by Sherman in the 51st Congress but also the bill finally passed were intended by their sponsors primarily to be federal codifications of the common law of England and the several states....

While available evidence suggests that those members of Congress who had given the matter special consideration felt that the common law was slightly more "radical," generally speaking, than it actually may have been, that evidence also indicates that legislators realized that the doctrines of the common law were far from "perfection" in the sense of clarity and unambiguousness. This may be derived, in part at least, from the recurrent references in the debates to the courts as instrumentalities for the clarification of the law. Moreover, there can be no reasonable doubt that legislators realized that the current meaning of the doctrines might undergo some changes with the evolution of the economy and its institutions. Thus, we are led to agree with Albert M. Kales in his conclusion (not based on the records of congressional proceedings) that in adopting the standard of the common law Congress expected the courts not only to apply a set of somewhat vague doctrines but also in doing so to make use of that "certain technique of judicial reasoning" characteristic of common law courts.[90]

90. Albert M. Kales, Contracts and Combinations in Restraint of Trade (1918), 106f.

It must be said that the "solution" of the trust problem represented by the Sherman Act was an elegant one. The complexities of the problem were enormous. Under the circumstances two radically different types of legislation would theoretically have been equally plausible. Congress could have tried to define every type of behavior or practice it found reprehensible. This would have necessitated a multitude of detailed provisions. Or it could have gone to what may almost be called the other extreme, enacting a few fundamental principles in the light of which the courts would evaluate the multifarious types of business combinations and methods with which they would be confronted. The former solution might conceivably—not necessarily—have the advantage of great certainty of the meaning of the law in individual cases. On the other hand, available information would hardly allow legislation spelled out in great detail. And, equally important, detailed legislation would run a serious risk of becoming obsolete in a very short time in the dynamics of economic life and its institutions. Congress wanted the law to be flexible to a certain extent. Restrainers of trade were not to be able to find subterfuge behind new forms of combinations or methods. What mattered was whether trade *was restrained* (or monopolized) or not. Thus the second line of action was chosen. And in this realm the evolved doctrines and the "philosophy" of evolution of the common law most nearly met the requirements of the legislator. . . .

C.   EARLY DEVELOPMENT OF LEGAL DOCTRINE

1.   THE FIRST CARTEL CASES

United States v. Trans–Missouri Freight Association

Supreme Court of the United States, 1897.
166 U.S. 290, 17 S.Ct. 540, 41 L.Ed. 1007.

[Suit in equity by the United States to dissolve the Trans–Missouri Freight Association, and to set aside and to have declared illegal and void the articles of agreement by which the association was formed on March 15, 1889. The association includes among its members eighteen carriers whose lines extend from the Mississippi River to the west coast and which, according to the bill, control the freight traffic in this region. The defendants are charged with fixing rates, and establishing rules and regulations for the traffic which they carry. Under the articles of the association, rates are set by a committee, and the members are required to observe the rates thus fixed, with the privilege of withdrawal from the association on thirty days' notice. Members may, in order to meet the competition of non-member roads, change their rates, subject, however, to penalty if the association finds that the change was not actually necessary. Any proposed change in rates must be submitted to the vote of the association, and members must abide by the association's decision unless at least ten days' written notice shall have been given of an intention to make such change notwithstanding the vote of the association. The case was heard on the pleadings and the bill was dismissed by the District Court. The dismissal was affirmed by the Circuit Court of Appeals. Motion is made in the Supreme Court to dismiss the appeal on the ground that the association was dissolved on November 18, 1892.]

■ PECKHAM, J. . . .

[T]he results of trusts, or combinations of that nature, may be different in different kinds of corporations, and yet they all have an essential similarity, and have been induced by motives of individual or corporate aggrandizement as against the public interest. In business or trading combinations they may even temporarily, or perhaps permanently, reduce the price of the article traded in or manufactured, by reducing the expense inseparable from the running of many different companies for the same purpose. Trade or commerce under those circumstances may nevertheless be badly and unfortunately restrained by driving out of business the small dealers and worthy men whose lives have been spent therein, and who might be unable to readjust themselves to their altered surroundings. Mere reduction in the price of the commodity dealt in might be dearly paid for by the ruin of such a class, and the absorption of control over one commodity by an all-powerful combination of capital. In any great and extended change in the manner or method of doing business it seems to be an inevitable necessity that distress and, perhaps, ruin shall be its accompaniment in regard to some of those who were engaged in the old methods. . . .

It takes time to effect a readjustment of industrial life so that those who are thrown out of their old employment, by reason of such changes as we have spoken of, may find opportunities for labor in other departments than those to which they have been accustomed. It is a misfortune, but yet in such cases it seems to be the inevitable accompaniment of change and improvement.

It is wholly different, however, when such changes are effected by combinations of capital, whose purpose in combining is to control the production or manufacture of any particular article in the market, and by such control dictate the price at which the article shall be sold, the effect being to drive out of business all the small dealers in the commodity and to render the public subject to the decision of the combination as to what price shall be paid for the article. In this light it is not material that the price of an article may be lowered. It is in the power of the combination to raise it, and the result in any event is unfortunate for the country by depriving it of the services of a large number of small but independent dealers who were familiar with the business and who had spent their lives in it, and who supported themselves and their families from the small profits realized therein. Whether they be able to find other avenues to earn their livelihood is not so material, because it is not for the real prosperity of any country that such changes should occur which result in transferring an independent business man, the head of his establishment, small though it might be, into a mere servant or agent of a corporation for selling the commodities which he once manufactured or dealt in, having no voice in shaping the business policy of the company and bound to obey orders issued by others. Nor is it for the substantial interests of the country that any one commodity should be within the sole power and subject to the sole will of one powerful combination of capital. Congress has, so far as its jurisdiction extends, prohibited all contracts or combinations in the form of trusts entered into for the purpose of restraining trade and commerce. The results naturally flowing from a contract or combination in restraint of trade or commerce, when entered into by a manufacturing or trading company such as above stated, while differing somewhat from those which may follow a contract to keep up transportation rates by railroads, are nevertheless of the same nature and kind, and the contracts themselves do not so far differ in their nature that they may not all be treated alike and be condemned in common.

... [T]he next question to be discussed is as to what is the true construction of the statute, assuming that it applies to common carriers by railroad.... Is it confined to a contract or combination which is only in unreasonable restraint of trade or commerce, or does it include what the language of the act plainly and in terms covers, all contracts of that nature?

We are asked to regard the title of this act as indicative of its purpose to include only those contracts which were unlawful at common law, but which require the sanction of a Federal statute in order to be dealt with in a Federal court. It is said that when terms which are known to the common law are used in a Federal statute those terms are to be given the same meaning that they received at common law, and that when the language of the title is "to protect trade and commerce against unlawful restraints and monopolies," it means those restraints and monopolies which the common law regarded as unlawful, and which were to be prohibited by the Federal statute. We are of opinion that the language used in the title refers to and includes and was intended to include those restraints and monopolies which are made unlawful in the body of the statute. It is to the statute itself that resort must be had to learn the meaning thereof, though a resort to the title here creates no doubt about the meaning of and does not alter the plain language contained in its text.

It is now with much amplification of argument urged that the statute, in declaring illegal every combination in the form of trust or otherwise, or conspiracy in restraint of trade or commerce, does not mean what the language used therein plainly imports, but that it only means to declare illegal any such contract which is in unreasonable restraint of trade, while leaving all others unaffected by the provisions of the act; that the common law meaning of the term "contract in restraint of trade" includes only such contracts as are in unreasonable restraint of trade, and when that term is used in the Federal statute it is not intended to include all contracts in restraint of trade, but only those which are in unreasonable restraint thereof.

The term is not of such limited signification. Contracts in restraint of trade have been known and spoken of for hundreds of years both in England and in this country, and the term includes all kinds of those contracts which in fact restrain or may restrain trade. Some of such contracts have been held void and unenforceable in the courts by reason of their restraint being unreasonable, while others have been held valid because they were not of that nature. A contract may be in restraint of trade and still be valid at common law. Although valid, it is nevertheless a contract in restraint of trade, and would be so described either at common law or elsewhere. By the simple use of the term "contract in restraint of trade," all contracts of that nature, whether valid or otherwise, would be included, and not alone that kind of contract which was invalid and unenforceable as being in unreasonable restraint of trade. When, therefore, the body of an act pronounces as illegal every contract or combination in restraint of trade or commerce among the several States, etc., the plain and ordinary meaning of such language is not limited to that kind of contract alone which is in unreasonable restraint of trade, but all contracts are included in such language, and no exception or limitation can be added without placing in the act that which has been omitted by Congress.

Proceeding, however, upon the theory that the statute did not mean what its plain language imported, and that it intended in its prohibition to denounce as illegal only those contracts which were in unreasonable restraint of trade, the courts below have made an exhaustive investigation as to the general rules which guide courts in declaring contracts to be void as being in restraint of trade, and therefore against the public policy of the country. In the course of their discussion of that subject they have shown that there has been a gradual though great alteration in the extent of the liberty granted to the vendor of property in agreeing, as part consideration for his sale, not to enter into the same kind of business for a certain time or within a certain territory. So long as the sale was the bona fide consideration for the promise and was not made a mere excuse for an evasion of the rule itself, the later authorities, both in England and in this country, exhibit a strong tendency towards enabling the parties to make such a contract in relation to the sale of property, including an agreement not to enter into the same kind of business, as they may think proper, and this with the view to granting to a vendor the freest opportunity to obtain the largest consideration for the sale of that which is his own. A contract which is the mere accompaniment of the sale of property, and thus entered into for the purpose of enhancing the price at which the vendor sells it, which in effect is collateral to such sale, and where the main purpose of the whole contract is accomplished by such sale, might not be included, within the letter or spirit of the statute in question. But we cannot see how the statute can be limited, as it has been by the courts below, without reading into its text an exception which alters the natural meaning of the language used, and that, too, upon a most material point, and where no sufficient reason is shown for believing that such alteration would make the statute more in accord with the intent of the law-making body that enacted it. . . .

The plaintiffs are, however, under no obligation in order to maintain this action to show that by the common law all agreements among competing railroad companies to keep up rates to such as are reasonable were void as in restraint of trade or commerce. There are many cases which look in that direction if they do not precisely decide that point. . . . But assuming that agreements of this nature are not void at common law and that the various cases cited by the learned courts below show it, the answer to the statement of their validity now is to be found in the terms of the statute under consideration. . . .

Reversed, and the case remanded to the Circuit Court for further proceedings in conformity with this opinion.[91]

NOTE

1. The trial court in *Trans–Missouri* had held that the combination was lawful in that its activities served to prevent "unhealthy competition . . . and furnish the public with adequate facilities at . . . reasonable prices." 53 F. 440, 451 (D.Kan. 1892). The Circuit Court of Appeals affirmed, finding "fair, open, and healthy" competition to be necessary, thus rejecting the "plain meaning" approach. 58 F. 58, 69 (8th Cir.1893).

2. UNITED STATES v. JOINT TRAFFIC ASSOCIATION, 171 U.S. 505, 567–568, 19 S.Ct. 25, 30–31, 43 L.Ed. 259, 287 (1898). Justice Peckham retreated from his earlier literal interpretation of the Sherman Act and recognized exceptions for ordinary contracts which might arguably restrain trade including traditional ancillary restraints. He rejected counsel's contention that the statute as construed in *Trans–Missouri* invalidates such agreements, stating: "We are not aware that it has ever been claimed that a lease or purchase by a farmer, manufacturer, or merchant of an additional farm, manufactory or shop, or the withdrawal from business of any farmer, merchant or manufacturer, restrained commerce or trade within any legal definition of that term; and the sale of a good will of a business with an accompanying agreement not to engage in a similar business was instanced in the *Trans–Missouri* case as a contract not within the meaning of the act; and it was said that such a contract was collateral to the main contract of sale and was entered into for the purpose of enhancing the price at which the vendor sells his business. . . . An agreement entered into for the purpose of promoting the legitimate business of an individual or corporation, with no purpose to thereby affect or restrain interstate commerce, and which does not directly restrain such commerce, is not, as we think, covered by the act, although the agreement may indirectly and remotely affect that commerce. We also repeat what is said in the case above cited,

---

91. The dissenting opinion of White, J., with whom Field, Gray and Shiras, JJ., concurred, is omitted. In his dissent, Justice White expressed the view that:

"If these obvious rules of interpretation be applied, it seems to me they render it impossible to construe the words 'every restraint of trade' used in the act in any other sense than as excluding reasonable contracts, as the fact that such contracts were not considered to be within the rule of contracts in restraint of trade, was thoroughly established both in England and in this country at the time the act was adopted. It is, I submit, not to be doubted that the interpretation of the words 'every contract in restraint of trade,' so as to embrace within its purview every contract, however reasonable, would certainly work an enormous injustice and operate to the undue restraint of the liberties of the citizen. But there is no canon of interpretation which requires that the letter be followed, when by so doing an unreasonable result is accomplished. On the contrary, the rule is the other way, and exacts that the spirit which vivifies, and not the letter which killeth, is the proper guide, by which to correctly interpret a statute." 166 U.S. at 354.

that 'the act of Congress must have a reasonable construction, or else there would scarcely be an agreement or contract among business men that could not be said to have, indirectly or remotely, some bearing upon interstate commerce, and possibly to restrain it.' "

3. HOPKINS v. UNITED STATES, 171 U.S. 578, 19 S.Ct. 40, 43 L.Ed. 290 (1898), referred to by Justice Peckham in *Joint Traffic,* involved a voluntary association of livestock commission merchants. The rules of the association forbade members from buying from non-members in Kansas City, fixed the commission for selling livestock, prohibited the employment of agents to solicit consignments except upon a stipulated salary, and forbade the sending of prepaid telegrams or telephone messages with information as to the condition of the markets.

Justice Peckham found that the defendants "entered into a voluntary association for the purpose of . . . better conducting their business, and that after they entered into such association they still continued their individual business in full competition with each other, and that the association itself . . . is simply a means by and through which the individual members who have become thus associated are the better enabled to transact their business; to maintain and uphold a proper way of doing it; and to create the means for preserving business integrity. . . .

To treat as condemned by the act all agreements under which as a result, the cost of conducting an interstate commercial business may be increased would enlarge the application of the act far beyond the fair meaning of the language used. There must be some direct and immediate effect upon interstate commerce in order to come within the act."

4. ANDERSON v. UNITED STATES, 171 U.S. 604, 19 S.Ct. 50, 43 L.Ed. 300 (1898), dealt with a livestock exchange similar to that in *Hopkins,* except that exchange members in *Anderson* were purchasers of cattle for their own account. The *Anderson* court followed *Hopkins,* holding that the defendants were not in restraint of interstate commerce, since "the purpose of the agreement was not to regulate, obstruct or restrain that commerce, but . . . it was entered into with the object of properly and fairly regulating the transaction of the business in which the parties to the agreement were engaged . . . and . . . the effect of its formation and enforcement upon interstate trade or commerce is in any event but indirect and incidental, and not its purpose or object."

United States v. Addyston Pipe & Steel Co.

Circuit Court of Appeals of the United States, Sixth Circuit, 1898.
85 F. 271, affirmed, 175 U.S. 211, 20 S.Ct. 96, 44 L.Ed. 136 (1899).

[Suit in equity by the United States against six corporations engaged in the manufacture of cast iron pipe, charging a combination and conspiracy in violation of the Sherman Act. The bill sought a forfeiture of all pipe shipped by the defendants pursuant to the conspiracy and for an injunction against the continuance of the combination. The case was heard upon the pleadings and affidavits. The Circuit Court dismissed the petition on the merits. The government appeals.

The defendants on December 31, 1896, entered into an agreement of two years' duration. A large part of their business consisted of selling pipes to gas and water works. Under this agreement, the gas and water works in designated cities in the southern and central parts of the United States were assigned to each defendant. The price at which pipe was sold in the reserved territories was determined by the association and the member to whom the business was assigned paid a fixed bonus to the association. The other members submitted fictitious bids to the customers in the reserved cities in order to create the appearance of competition. A secret auction pool was conducted for the allocation of business arising outside the reserved cities. The price was determined by the association and the business was assigned to the member who offered the largest bonus to the association. The unsuccessful bidders in the auction pool submitted padded bids to the purchaser to maintain the pretense of competitive bidding. The bonuses were distributed to members in proportion to their respective tonnage capacities. The total tonnage capacity of all the defendants was 220,000 tons annually. In territories in which there was considerable outside competition, members were permitted to sell without restriction and without payment of any bonus to the association. Such territory was called "free" territory as contrasted with "pay" territory, on the sales in which a bonus was paid. Sales in free territory to customers situated more than 500 miles from defendants' foundries were made at lower prices than sales in reserved cities near their mills. The capacity of nonmember mills in pay territory was 170,500 tons, and in free territory 348,000 tons. The evidence was scanty as to rates of freight upon iron pipes, but enough appeared to show that the advantage in freight rates which the defendants had over the large pipe foundries in New York, eastern Pennsylvania, and New Jersey in bidding on contracts to deliver pipe in almost all of the pay territory varied from $2 to $6 a ton, according to the location. The defendants filed the affidavits of their managing officers, in which they stated that the object of their association was not to raise prices beyond what was reasonable, but only to prevent ruinous competition among defendants, which would have carried prices far below a reasonable point; that the bonuses charged were not exorbitant profits and additions to a reasonable price, but they were deductions from a reasonable price, in the nature of a penalty or burden intended to curb the natural disposition of each member to get all the business possible, and more than his due proportion; that the prices fixed by the association were always reasonable, and were always fixed, as they must have been, with reference to the very active competition of other pipe manufacturers for every job; that the reason why they sold pipe at cheaper rates in the free territory than in the pay territory was that they were willing to sell at a loss to keep their mills going rather than to shut them down; that the prices in a city such as St. Louis, in which the specifications were detailed and precise, were higher because pipe had to be made specially for the job, and stock on hand could not be used.]

■ Before HARLAN, CIRCUIT JUSTICE, and TAFT and LURTON, CIRCUIT JUDGES.

■ TAFT, J. . . . Two questions are presented in this case for our decision: First. Was the association of the defendants a contract, combination, or conspiracy in restraint of trade, as the terms are to be understood in the act? Second. Was the trade thus restrained trade between the states?

The contention on behalf of defendants is that the association would have been valid at common law, and that the federal antitrust law was not intended to reach any agreements that were not void and unenforceable at common law. It might be a sufficient answer to this contention to point to the decision of the Supreme Court of the United States in U.S. v. Trans–Missouri Freight Ass'n, 166 U.S. 290, in which it was held that contracts in restraint of interstate transportation were within the statute, whether the restraints would be regarded as reasonable at common law or not. It is suggested, however, that that case related to a quasi public employment necessarily under public control, and affecting public interests, and that a less stringent rule of construction applies to contracts restricting parties in sales of merchandise, which is purely a private business, having in it no element of a public or quasi public character. Whether or not there is substance in such a distinction—a question we do not decide—it is certain that, if the contract of association which bound the defendants was void and unenforceable at the common law because in restraint of trade, it is within the inhibition of the statute if the trade it restrained was interstate. Contracts that were in unreasonable restraint of trade at common law were not unlawful in the sense of being criminal, or giving rise to a civil action for damages in favor of one prejudicially affected thereby, but were simply void, and were not enforced by the courts. The effect of the act of 1890 is to render such contracts unlawful in an affirmative or positive sense, and punishable as a misdemeanor, and to create a right of civil action for damages in favor of those injured thereby, and a civil remedy by injunction in favor of both private persons and the public against the execution of such contracts and the maintenance of such trade restraints.

The argument for defendants is that their contract of association was not, and could not be, a monopoly, because their aggregate tonnage capacity did not exceed 30 per cent of the total tonnage capacity of the country; that the restraints upon the members of the association, if restraints they could be called, did not embrace all the states, and were not unlimited in space; that such partial restraints were justified and upheld at common law if reasonable, and only proportioned to the necessary protection of the parties; that in this case the partial restraints were reasonable, because without them each member would be subjected to ruinous competition by the other, and did not exceed in degree of stringency or scope what was necessary to protect the parties in securing prices for their product that were fair and reasonable to themselves and the public; that competition was not stifled by the association because the prices fixed by it had to be fixed with reference to the very active competition of pipe companies which were not members of the association, and which had more than double the defendants' capacity; that in this way the association only modified and restrained the evils of ruinous competition, while the public had all the benefit from competition which public policy demanded.

From early times it was the policy of Englishmen to encourage trade in England, and to discourage those voluntary restraints which tradesmen were often induced to impose on themselves by contract. Courts recognized this public policy by refusing to enforce stipulations of this character. The objections to such restraints were mainly two. One was that by such contracts a man disabled himself from earning a livelihood with the risk of becoming a public charge, and deprived the community of the benefit of his labor. The other was that such restraints tended to give to the covenantee, the beneficiary of such restraints, a monopoly of the trade, from which he had thus excluded one competitor, and by the same means might exclude others. . . .

Much has been said in regard to the relaxing of the original strictness of the common law in declaring contracts in restraint of trade void as conditions of civilization and public policy have changed, and the argument drawn therefrom is that the law now recognizes that competition may be so ruinous as to injure the public, and, therefore, that contracts made with a view to check such ruinous competition and regulate prices, though in restraint of trade, and having no other purpose, will be upheld. We think this conclusion is unwarranted by the authorities when all of them are considered. It is true that certain rules for determining whether a covenant in restraint of trade ancillary to the main purpose of a contract was reasonably adapted and limited to the necessary protection of a party in the carrying out of such purpose have been somewhat modified by modern authorities. . . . But these cases all involved contracts in which the covenant in restraint of trade was ancillary to the main and lawful purpose of the contract, and was necessary to the protection of the covenantee in the carrying out of that main purpose. They do not manifest any general disposition on the part of the courts to be more liberal in supporting contracts having for their sole object the restraint of trade than did the courts of an earlier time. It is true that there are some cases in which the courts, mistaking, as we conceive, the proper limits of the relaxation of the rules for determining the unreasonableness of restraints of trade, have set sail on a sea of doubt, and have assumed the power to say, in respect to contracts which have no other purpose and no other consideration on either side than the mutual restraint of the parties, how much restraint of competition is in the public interest, and how much is not.

The manifest danger in the administration of justice according to so shifting, vague, and indeterminate a standard would seem to be a strong reason against adopting it. . . .

Upon this review of the law and the authorities, we can have no doubt that the association of the defendants, however reasonable the prices they fixed, however great the competition they had to encounter, and however great the necessity for curbing themselves by joint agreement from committing financial suicide by ill-advised competition, was void at common law, because in restraint of trade, and tending to a monopoly. But the facts of the case do not require us to go so far as this, for they show that the attempted justification of this association on the grounds stated is without foundation. . . .[92]

92. The court then analyzes the facts and concludes that the members of the combination were not subject to substantial out-

NOTE

1. The Supreme Court had first given its attention to the Sherman Act in United States v. E.C. Knight Co., 156 U.S. 1 (1895). In that case, the defendant, which refined and manufactured 65% of the nation's sugar, had completed its monopoly by acquiring four smaller independent manufacturers. Defendant and the acquired firms were all located in the same state, indeed, in the same city, Philadelphia. The government's petition sought cancellation of the contracts by which the consolidation had taken place. The Court affirmed the decisions of the lower courts denying relief, asserting that the monopoly of manufacture only "incidentally and indirectly" affected commerce, and that the Constitution's commerce clause did not reach so far. The Court found nothing to indicate "any intention to put a restraint on trade...."

2. In *Addyston Pipe,* the trial court had dismissed the government's petition on the basis of the *E.C. Knight* decision. On appeal, Judge Taft read the *Knight* decision as drawing "the distinction between a restraint upon the business of manufacturing and a restraint upon the trade or commerce between the states in the articles after manufacture, with the manifest purpose of showing that the regulating power of congress under the Constitution could affect only the latter...." 85 F. 271, 297 (1898). In the Supreme Court, Justice Peckham affirmed:

> The direct purpose of the combination of the *Knight* case was the control of the manufacture of sugar. There was no combination or agreement, in terms, regarding the future disposition of the manufactured article; nothing looking to a transaction in the nature of interstate commerce. The probable intention on the part of the manufacturer of the sugar to thereafter dispose of it by sending it to some market in another State, was held to be immaterial and not to alter the character of the combination.... [T]he case was decided upon the principle that a combination simply to control manufacture was not a violation of the act of Congress, because such a contract or combination did not directly control or affect interstate commerce....

175 U.S. 211, 240 (1899).

3. In SWIFT & CO. v. UNITED STATES, 196 U.S. 375, 25 S.Ct. 276, 49 L.Ed. 518 (1905), the Court severely undercut any remaining force of the distinction between "direct" and "indirect" effects by holding that price fixing in livestock markets could be reached since the markets, although themselves each located in a single state, were part of "a current of commerce among the States...." Id. at 399. Thus, although the *Knight* decision temporarily placed manufacturing beyond the purview of direct national regulation, it did not substantially impede antitrust enforcement. The narrow view of the reach of the "commerce clause" which gave rise to these early problems has, of course, long since given way to an expansive view, and the

side competition in the territories in which they operated.

For a discussion of the *Addyston Pipe* case, *see* Ripley, Trusts, Pools and Corporations Ch. IV (rev. ed. 1916); Jones, The Trust Problem in the United States 12–13 (1921); Seager & Gulick, Trust and Corporation Problems Ch. VII (1929); 2 Whitney, Antitrust Policies 4 (1958); Kauper, The Sullivan

Approach to Horizontal Restraints, 75 Cal. L.Rev. 893 (1987).

On the early pools, *see* Craft v. McConoughy, 79 Ill. 346 (1875); Burns, The Decline of Competition 146–51 (1936); Belcher, Industrial Pooling Agreements, 19 Quar. J.Econ. 111 (1904); Edgerton, Wire Nail Association of 1895–1896, 12 Pol.Sci.Q. 246 (1897).

reach of the Sherman Act, understood to be as broad as the Constitution permits, has grown accordingly.

NOTE ON RESTRICTIVE COVENANTS UNDER STATE AND FEDERAL LAW

After passage of the Sherman Act, both state and federal courts adopted the principal approaches set forth in *Mitchel v. Reynolds* (p. 31 supra) and *Addyston Pipe* with respect to restrictive covenants. The Restatement (Second) Contracts § 187 (1981), for example, adopted Judge Taft's ancillary/non-ancillary theme by concluding: "A promise to refrain from competition that imposes a restraint that is not ancillary to an otherwise valid transaction or relationship is unreasonably in restraint of trade."

Section 188 of the Restatement (Second) Contracts (1981), which is consistent with the great bulk of state law, explains how to judge the reasonableness of a restrictive covenant:

(1) A promise to refrain from competition that imposes a restraint that is ancillary to an otherwise valid transaction or relationship is unreasonably in restraint of trade if

(a) the restraint is greater than is needed to protect the promisee's legitimate interest, or

(b) the promisee's need is outweighed by the hardship to the promisor and the likely injury to the public.

(2) Promises imposing restraints that are ancillary to a valid transaction or relationship include the following:

(a) a promise by the seller of a business not to compete with the buyer in such a way as to injure the value of the business sold;

(b) a promise by an employee or other agent not to compete with his employer or other principal;

(c) a promise by a partner not to compete with the partnership.

Generally, courts have looked at three dimensions in evaluating whether a restrictive covenant is unnecessarily burdensome. First, they have considered the geographic area covered by the restraint; second, they have reviewed the duration of the covenant; and third, they have considered whether the scope of the restraint is unreasonably broad. *See, e.g.*, Karpinski v. Ingrasci, 28 N.Y.2d 45, 320 N.Y.S.2d 1, 268 N.E.2d 751 (1971).

Courts have tended to apply a more stringent requirement of reasonableness to covenants appearing in contracts of employment, than to contracts for the sale of a business or formation of a partnership, which are more likely to have been fully negotiated. The social policy underlying enforceable post-employment covenants is that they permit an employer greater freedom to use employees' services and to make available to them confidential information; they may increase efficiency. On the other hand, the employer's justifiably protectable interests are apt to be fewer and less broad with respect to employees having less access to trade secrets, customer lists, and the like. As Professor Blake put it:

From the point of view of the employer, postemployment restraints are regarded as perhaps the only effective method of preventing unscrupulous competitors or employees from appropriating valuable trade information and customer relationships for their own benefit.... The opposite view is that postemployment restraints reduce both the economic mobility of employees and their personal freedom to follow their own interests. These restraints also diminish competition by intimidating potential competitors and by slowing down the dissemination of ideas, processes, and methods. Blake, Employee Agreements Not to Compete, 73 Harv.L.Rev. 625, 627, 638 (1960); *see* Purchasing Associates, Inc. v. Weitz, 13 N.Y.2d 267, 246 N.Y.S.2d 600, 196 N.E.2d 245 (1963).

Today, almost all restrictive covenant cases are handled under state law. But the enforcement, for example, of an overly restrictive covenant by a dominant firm, which prevents a likely innovative new entrant from coming into a concentrated market, may give rise to a Sherman Act violation. *See* Lektro–Vend Corp. v. Vendo Co., 660 F.2d 255 (7th Cir.1981), cert. denied, 455 U.S. 921 (1982). Such normally privileged conduct will be much more likely to run afoul of the antitrust laws if it is part of a pattern of repetitive litigation or seen to involve intentional harassment. The Seventh Circuit concluded that the restrictive covenant in issue was not unreasonably broad, at least as enforced against the conduct of the plaintiff. In an earlier stage of that litigation, the Supreme Court did not reach the issue. Vendo Co. v. Lektro–Vend Corp., 433 U.S. 623 (1977).

In Newburger, Loeb & Co., Inc. v. Gross, 563 F.2d 1057 (2d Cir.1977), cert. denied, 434 U.S. 1035 (1978), the Second Circuit indicated some concern about applying the Sherman Act to "employer-employee controversies which individually have only a small impact on commerce and which have traditionally been handled in state courts." But many large employers use "form" restrictive covenants across-the-board with numerous employees, and other businesses have used restrictive covenants in ways that significantly impact commerce. For example, various types of restrictive covenants, most often inserted at the insistence of large department stores or other major tenants, have appeared in the leasing arrangements of major shopping centers. These include: (i) "exclusivity" clauses that insure that the lessee will have limited (or no) competition within the center; (ii) clauses that prevent the lessor from leasing to discount stores or houses; and (iii) "veto" clauses that grant the lessee discretion to disapprove prospective tenants and to limit their floor space and general business operations.[93] Should such covenants receive scrutiny under the Sherman Act? Would state judges be as likely as federal judges to take account of competitive market values? *See* Goldschmid, Antitrust's Neglected Stepchild: A Proposal for Dealing with Restrictive Covenants Under Federal Law, 73 Colum.L.Rev. 1193 (1973); cf. Consultants & Designers, Inc. v. Butler Service Group, Inc., 720 F.2d 1553, 1562–64 (11th Cir.1983) (restrictive covenant survived a rule of reason analysis under the Sherman Act because covenant did "not have a sufficiently adverse impact on competition").

2. EARLY MERGERS AND THE DEVELOPMENT OF THE "RULE OF REASON"

The early wave of industrial consolidations, which gave rise to the political pressures leading to the Sherman Act, was renewed and intensified

---

93. *See* Dalmo Sales Co. v. Tysons Corner Regional Shopping Center, 308 F.Supp. 988, 993 (D.D.C.), affirmed, 429 F.2d 206 (D.C.Cir.1970); FTC Complaint, Proposed Order § I, Gimbel Brothers, Inc., Docket No. 8885 (filed May 8, 1972); FTC Complaint ¶ 11, Tysons Corner Regional Shopping Center, Docket No. 8886 (filed May 8, 1972), 3 Trade Reg.Rep. ¶ 20,003. The FTC decision in *Tysons Corner* is summarized at p. 402 infra.

after 1890. By 1899, the number of major firms absorbed annually by merger had risen to more than one thousand. DuPont, United States Steel, American Tobacco, and International Harvester were products of this wave, which abated only with the government's more vigorous antitrust enforcement activities in the first decade of the new century. *See, e.g., Northern Securities Co. v. United States,* 193 U.S. 197 (1904); United States v. Union Pacific Railroad Co., 226 U.S. 61 (1912); United States v. Reading Co., 253 U.S. 26 (1920); United States v. Southern Pacific Co., 259 U.S. 214 (1922).

The *Northern Securities* case was one of the most important antitrust cases historically. The government's prosecution of the Northern Securities Company was filed in a politically charged atmosphere involving famous defendants, powerful newspaper editors, and the "trust busting" rhetoric of President Theodore Roosevelt.

The company was formed during a period of large railroad consolidations, and competition by various financial groups to bring together attractive systems of connecting long distance routes. The Northern Pacific Railway Company, controlled by associates of defendant J.P. Morgan, and Great Northern Railway Company, controlled by defendant James J. Hill, were parallel and competing lines connecting St. Paul and other points in Minnesota with the northwest. The two companies jointly acquired the Burlington line, which connected Chicago and St. Paul with Billings, Montana, where it connected with the Northern Pacific. E.H. Harriman, president of the Union Pacific, which also wanted access to the Burlington connections, sought access to the Burlington routes by purchasing large amounts of Northern Pacific stock. In response, the Morgan interests and the Hill interests created Northern Securities Company, a holding company for their stock. Northern Securities almost immediately became a target for action under the Sherman Act. The President and the nation's newspapers held the holding company up as a prototype of the giant "trusts," at which the Sherman Act had been directed.

The trial court ruled that the defendants, in creating the company, had entered into an unlawful combination for the restraint of trade. By a 5–4 margin, the Supreme Court, in an opinion often criticized for leaving important questions unanswered, affirmed the lower court's ruling. Justice Harlan, writing for the majority, listed a number of "propositions" of the Sherman Act, including that the Act "embraces *all* direct *restraints,*" that "Congress . . . has prescribed the rule of free competition," and that "*every* combination or conspiracy which would extinguish competition between otherwise competing railroads engaged in *interstate trade or commerce,* and which would *in that way* restrain *such* trade or commerce, is made illegal by the act."

Justice Brewer, who delivered a concurring opinion in *Northern Securities,* expressed the view that Congress intended only to prohibit those contracts which were in "direct restraint of trade, unreasonable and against public policy." Nevertheless, he condemned the combination effected in *Northern Securities,* which, he declared, might be extended until a single corporation would be in control of the whole transportation system of the country.

Justice Holmes' dissent in *Northern Securities* began with the famous language:

> Great cases like hard cases make bad law. For great cases are called great, not by reason of their real importance in shaping the law of the future, but because of some accident of immediate overwhelming interest which appeals to the feelings and distorts the judgment.

Justice Holmes was referring to the extensive public interest in the *Northern Securities* decision which was a result of the notoriety of the defendants and Roosevelt's behind-the-scenes participation in the prosecution.[94]

Holmes felt that the plain meaning of § 1 of the Sherman Act did not prohibit "partnerships" such as in *Northern Securities* whose effect is to suppress competition.

> The law ... says nothing about competition, and only prevents its suppression by contracts or combinations in restraint of trade, and such contracts or combinations derive their character as restraining trade from other features than the suppression of competition alone. . . .

The *Union Pacific* and *Southern Pacific* cases illustrate the Supreme Court's receptivity to the government's more rigorous antitrust approach. In the *Union Pacific* case, the Supreme Court struck down Union Pacific's acquisition of a controlling interest in Southern Pacific, holding:

> The consolidation of two great competing systems of railroad engaged in interstate commerce by a transfer to one of a dominating stock interest in the other creates a combination which restrains interstate commerce within the meaning of the statute, because, in destroying or greatly abridging the free operation of competition theretofore existing, it tends to higher rates. It directly tends to less activity in furnishing the public with prompt and efficient service in carrying and handling freight and in carrying passengers, and in attention to and prompt adjustment of the demands of patrons for losses, and in these respects puts interstate commerce under restraint. Nor does it make any difference that rates for the time being may not be raised and much money be spent in improvements after the combination is effected. It is the scope of such combinations and their power to suppress or stifle competition or create monopoly which determines the applicability of the act. 226 U.S. at 88.

94. *See* Letwin, Law and Economic Policy in America: The Evolution of the Sherman Antitrust Act (Phoenix ed. 1981).

In the *Southern Pacific* case, the Southern Pacific's acquisition of the stock of the Central Pacific was held to violate the Sherman Act. Relying on the earlier railroad cases, the Supreme Court said:

> These cases, collectively, establish that one system of railroad transportation cannot acquire another, nor a substantial and vital part thereof, when the effect of such acquisition is to suppress, or materially reduce the free and normal flow of competition in the channels of interstate trade. 259 U.S. at 230.

In Standard Oil Co. of New Jersey v. United States, 221 U.S. 1 (1911), the government charged that defendants (including John D. and William Rockefeller and 71 corporate defendants) were conspiring to monopolize and restrain domestic and foreign trade in crude oil, refined oil, and other petroleum products. Chief Justice White found unreasonable restraints, including the "slow but resistless methods" by which means of transportation and other aspects of the petroleum business "were absorbed and brought under control." The Supreme Court described the "evils which led to the public outcry against monopolies and to the final denial of the power to make them" as follows:

> (1) The power which the monopoly gave to the one who enjoyed it to fix the price and thereby injure the public; (2) The power which it engendered of enabling a limitation on production; and, (3) The danger of deterioration in quality of the monopolized article which it was deemed was the inevitable resultant of the monopolistic control over its production and sale.

The Supreme Court ordered the dissolution of Standard Oil.

But a renewal of the incidence of large consolidations followed World War I. The Supreme Court's 4–3 decision, in 1920, upholding the organization of United States Steel encouraged this round of mergers. United States Steel had 80% to 90% of the output of iron and steel products when it was established in 1901, but its market share had fallen to roughly 50% by the time the Supreme Court addressed the consolidation in 1920. *See* United States v. United States Steel Corp., 251 U.S. 417 (1920).

As we will see in Chapters 6 and 9 infra, it is difficult to reconcile the *United States Steel* case with the *Standard Oil* and the *Railroad* cases. In general, however, it should be recognized that consolidations—unlike price-fixing agreements—may have underlying business purposes and effects (*e.g.*, the closing of inefficient plants, the attainment of manufacturing or distributional efficiencies) that are economically desirable and which must be balanced against the likelihood of public injury arising from an increase of market power. Note also that as a matter of judicial administration, a merger or consolidation is a discrete event that has to be passed upon only once, in contrast with the continuing surveillance of cartels which would be necessary to determine whether or not their prices remain "reasonable" in terms of ever-changing economic conditions.

Also, in the *Standard Oil* case, the Supreme Court—noting that the sweeping language of Section 1 of the Sherman Act was "broad enough to embrace every conceivable contract or combination"—rejected such an interpretation in favor of a reasonableness approach. Justice White concluded that Congress "intended that the standard of reason which had been applied at the common law ... was intended to be the measure used...." 221 U.S. at 60.

In the majority opinion of United States v. American Tobacco Co., 221 U.S. 106, 179 (1911), Chief Justice White affirmed the Court's adoption of the rule of reason and acknowledged its departure from the across-the-board *per se* approach: "[T]he doctrine thus stated [in *Standard Oil*] was in accord with all the previous decisions of this court.... That such a view [of Section 1 as expressed in *Trans–Missouri*] was a mistaken one was fully pointed out in the *Standard Oil Case*...." In the *American Tobacco* case, five firms that together were responsible for 95% of the cigarettes sold in the United States had merged into the American Tobacco Company. The merged entity purchased forty going tobacco concerns and required those concerns' stockholders and managers to bind themselves not to compete with American Tobacco in the future. The combination not only maintained its control of the cigarette market, but also achieved dominance in the manufacture of other tobacco-related products. Upon applying a rule of reason analysis, the Court determined that the defendant combination had in fact violated Section 1, and remanded the case to the lower court to develop a means of "dissolving the combination and of recreating ... a new condition which shall be honestly in harmony with and not repugnant to the law." 221 U.S. at 187.

Although the rule of reason approach to Section 1 analysis continues to be used by courts today, some behavior is considered so plainly anticompetitive that it warrants invocation of the *per se* rule. As we will see in Chapters 4 and 5 infra, among the most common examples of such conduct are horizontal agreements among firms to fix prices, divide territories, or to refuse to deal. Generally, however, agreements that do not fall into one of these so-called *per se* categories are evaluated according to the rule of reason.

NOTES AND QUESTIONS

1. Can the "rule of reason" announced by Chief Justice White be reconciled with the view of Justice Peckham or of Judge (later Chief Justice) Taft? Chief Justice Taft attempted a reconciliation in Cline v. Frink Dairy Co., 274 U.S. 445, 460 (1927). *See also* Taft, The Antitrust Act and the Supreme Court (1914).

2. In 1913, the Supreme Court largely put to rest the question of whether the criminal provisions of the Sherman Act could be declared void for vagueness. In Nash v. United States, 229 U.S. 373 (1913), the American Naval Stores Company was engaged in buying, selling, shipping and exporting turpentine in interstate and foreign commerce, and the National Transportation & Terminal Company had warehouses and terminal facilities for handling turpentine and other naval stores in a number of southern states. Of the six officers of American Naval Stores named in

the opinion, three were also officers of National Transportation & Terminal. The two corporations and six officers were indicted in two counts for conspiracy to restrain trade and to monopolize in violation of Sections 1 and 2 of the Sherman Act.

It was alleged that the corporations and individual defendants conspired to restrain commerce in turpentine and naval stores by the following means: (1) bidding down turpentine and rosin so that competitors could sell them only at ruinous prices; (2) causing naval stores receipts to go to ports other than those to which they would normally go; (3) refraining from purchasing supplies at Savannah, the primary market in the United States for naval stores, because purchases there would tend to strengthen prices in the market; (4) refusing to purchase from factors and brokers unless they entered into contracts for the storage and purchase of defendants' receipts, thereby coercing the factors and brokers into such contracts; (5) circulating false statements as to production and stocks of naval stores; (6) issuing fraudulent warehouse receipts; (7) fraudulently grading rosin and gauging turpentine; (8) attempting to bribe rivals' employees to gain information as to their business and stocks; (9) inducing consumers by payments and threats of boycott to delay dates of delivery of contract supplies, enabling defendants to avoid making purchases at times when such purchases would tend to strengthen the market; (10) offering large amounts of naval stores to depress the market, accepting contracts only for small amounts, and purchasing when the market had been depressed by the offers; (11) selling far below cost to compel competitors to meet prices ruinous to everybody; and (12) fixing the price of turpentine below the cost of production—all for the purpose of driving competitors out of business and restraining and monopolizing trade. A jury found five of the individual defendants guilty, one of them not guilty, and rendered no verdict as to the two corporations.

The defendants had demurred to the indictment on the grounds, among others, that the statute was so vague as to be inoperative on its criminal side; that neither count alleged an overt act; and that the contemplated acts would not have constituted an offense if they had been done. With respect to the first issue raised by the demurrer, the Court (per Holmes, J.) rejected the contention that the Sherman Act was too vague, stating that "the law is full of instances where a man's fate depends on his estimating rightly, that is, as the jury subsequently estimates it, some matter of degree. If his judgment is wrong, not only may he incur a fine or a short imprisonment, as here; he may incur the penalty of death." As to the objection that no overt act was alleged, the Court said that "the Sherman Act punishes the conspiracies at which it is aimed on the common law footing—that is to say, it does not make the doing of any act other than the act of conspiring a condition of liability." Then "as to the suggestion that the matters alleged to have been contemplated would not have constituted an offense if they had been done, it is enough to say that some of them conceivably might have been adequate to accomplish the result, and that the intent alleged would convert what on their face might be no more than ordinary acts of competition or the small dishonesties of trade into a conspiracy of wide scope...." But, after upholding the indictment against claims raised by the demurrer, the Court went on to reverse the verdict because of errors in the charge.

SELECTIVE BIBLIOGRAPHY

1. Antitrust Law and Policy

Posner, Antitrust Law (2d ed. 2001). (Antitrust policy as viewed by a distinguished jurist and leading member of the so-called Chicago School).

Areeda & Hovenkamp, Antitrust Law: An Analysis of Antitrust Principles and Their Application (18 Vol. 1980–2000 & Supp. 2002). (Highly influential and comprehensive treatise).

Sullivan & Grimes, The Law of Antitrust: An Integrated Handbook (2000). (Thoughtful and forceful analysis of antitrust cases and policy.)

Scherer (ed.), Competition Policy, Domestic and International (2000).

Gellhorn & Kovacic, Antitrust Law and Economics in a Nutshell (5th ed. 2003).

Hovenkamp, Federal Antitrust Policy: The Law of Competition and Its Practice (2d ed. 1999). (Both the Gellhorn & Kovacic and Hovenkamp works clearly explain the essentials of antitrust law and microeconomics).

FTC Staff, Anticipating the 21st Century: Competition Policy in the New High–Tech, Global Marketplace (1996).

Ross, Principles of Antitrust Law (1993).

Bork, The Antitrust Paradox (1978). (A statement on antitrust policy as viewed by a leading member of the so-called Chicago School).

Elzinga & Breit, The Antitrust Penalties: A Study in Law and Economics (1976).

Goldschmid, Mann & Weston (eds.), Industrial Concentration: The New Learning (1974).

Kaysen & Turner, Antitrust Policy (1959). (A classic integration of economic and legal analysis with respect to antitrust law and policy).

Report of the Attorney General's National Committee to Study the Antitrust Laws (1955). (Updated through 2001 in ABA volumes.)

Symposium (consisting of numerous leading commentators), Anticipating Antitrust's Centennial, 75 Cal.L.Rev. 787 (1987) (Part I) and 4 Cardozo L.Rev. 1135 (1988) (Part II).

Pitofsky, The Political Content of Antitrust, 127 U.Pa.L.Rev. 105 (1979).

Students should learn to use the Trade Regulation Reporter, published by Commerce Clearing House, as a research tool and particularly for current developments. Note also the related, bound Trade Case volumes for each year and, for Federal Trade Commission materials, the Transfer Binders. Antitrust and Trade Regulation Reporter ("ATRR"), a weekly newsletter published by the Bureau of National Affairs, provides a particularly helpful summary of current judicial, administrative, and legislative developments.

2. Primarily Economic Studies

A number of the works noted in the previous section are by economists or contain substantial doses of descriptive or analytical economics. All, however, deal primarily with antitrust policy and cases. Students who care to refresh or repair their education in economics should read one or more of the following works:

Kwoka & White (eds.), The Antitrust Revolution (3d ed. 1999).

Scherer & Ross, Industrial Market Structure and Economic Performance (3d ed. 1990). (Recommended as the most comprehensive and analytically useful book for law students.)

Porter, The Competitive Advantage of Nations (1990).

Calvani & Siegfried (eds.), Economic Analysis and Antitrust Law (2d ed. 1988).

Williamson, Markets and Hierarchies: Analysis and Antitrust Implications (1983).

3. **Origins and History of U.S. Antitrust Policy**

Peritz, Competition Policy in America: History, Rhetoric, Law (Rev. Ed. 2001).

Letwin, Law and Economic Policy in America: The Evolution of the Sherman Antitrust Act (Phoenix ed. 1981).

Hofstadter, What Happened to the Antitrust Movement, in The Paranoid Style in American Politics and Other Essays (Phoenix ed. 1979).

Thorelli, The Federal Antitrust Policy (1954).

Nevins, John D. Rockefeller 338–574 (1941).

Jones, The Trust Problem in the United States (1921).

Ripley (ed.), Trusts, Pools and Corporations (1916).

Walker, History of the Sherman Law of the United States of America (1910).

4. **General Comparative Materials**

Atwood, Brewster & Waller, Antitrust and American Business Abroad (3d ed. 1996).

Comanor, et al., Competition Policy in Europe and North America: Economic Issues and Institutions (1990).

Goyder, EC Competition law (3d ed. 1998).

Hawk, United States, Common Market and International Antitrust: A Comparative Guide (2d ed., 3 vol., 1985 & Supp. 1996).

Scherer, Competition Policies for an Integrated World Economy (1994).

Wang, et al., International Harmonization of Competition Laws (1995).

Whish, Competition Law (3d ed. 1993).

The OECD Journal of Competition Law and Policy.

The competition page of the Organisation for Economic Co-operation and Development (OECD) at http://www.oecd.org.

The website of the International Competition Network at http://www.internationalcompetitionnetwork.org.

The website of DG–Comp, the European Commission's directorate responsible for antitrust issues at http://www.europa.eu.int/comm/competition.

CHAPTER 2

Institutional Framework of Antitrust Policy

Section 1. The Three-Level Antitrust Enforcement Pattern

The antitrust laws are administered and enforced by the Antitrust Division of the Department of Justice and by the Federal Trade Commission. Either agency may proceed against violations of the Clayton Act, while the Justice Department alone is charged with enforcement of the Sherman Act. But the FTC may, in effect, enforce the Sherman Act since under Section 5 of the Federal Trade Commission Act it acts against "unfair methods of competition," a phrase which has been interpreted broadly to encompass practices contravening public policy as declared in the Sherman Act and other antitrust laws.

As an addition to governmental proceedings, a third level of antitrust enforcement has assumed increased importance in recent decades—the enforcement of the antitrust laws by state attorneys general and private parties. State attorneys general, usually acting as representatives of those injured as a result of antitrust violations,[1] and private parties can seek not only equitable relief but also treble damages, the cost of suit, and a reasonable attorney's fee.

This section will profile the two principal federal enforcement agencies. It will summarize briefly the nature and extent of antitrust enforcement by state attorneys general and private claimants, and then discuss a variety of procedural and process problems relating to antitrust enforcement. Antitrust administration and enforcement each year generate an increasingly wide range of complex procedural and process problems. Most of these, for example, the proper scope of pretrial discovery in antitrust cases and the limits on proof at trial, are related principally to the fields of civil procedure and judicial administration, or are of marginal significance, and therefore do not merit separate treatment in an antitrust course. Other problem areas, discussed here, are so intimately connected with fundamental questions of antitrust policy that they must be more fully considered.

1. See discussion, pp. 80–84 infra.

A.   SOURCES OF ANTITRUST LITIGATION

1.   DEPARTMENT OF JUSTICE

Statutory Responsibilities. Within the Department of Justice is the Antitrust Division, headed by an Assistant Attorney General. The Antitrust Division is responsible for enforcing the Sherman and Clayton Acts, and is required or permitted to intervene in some proceedings before federal administrative agencies involving considerations of public policy with respect to competition and monopoly.[2]

Violations of Sections 1 and 2 of the Sherman Act can be enforced in both civil and criminal proceedings. Today, under the Antitrust Procedures and Penalties Act (enacted in 1974), criminal proceedings can result in imprisonment of individuals for up to three years.[3] A criminal fine of up to $350,000 is available against individuals, and a fine of up to $10 million is available against corporations. In addition, under the Criminal Fine Improvements Act of 1987, fines as high as $500 million have been imposed. The Improvements Act, which is applicable to all felonies, reads as follows:

(d) Alternative fine based on gain or loss.

If any person derives pecuniary gain from the offense, or if the offense results in pecuniary loss to a person other than the defendant, the defendant may be fined not more than the greater of twice the gross gain or twice the gross loss, unless imposition of a fine under this subsection would unduly complicate or prolong the sentencing process.[4]

As applied to a Sherman Act offense, this fine is an *alternative* to what would otherwise be the maximum statutory fine. Thus, for example, in a price-fixing case, the alternative fine would be twice the excess profit derived (*i.e.*, the difference between the fixed price and the price under normal conditions) by each defendant from a conspiracy, which could total hundreds of millions or even billions of dollars. In fiscal 2001, for example, the Antitrust Division obtained fines of over $280 million, which is more than ten times the average that was being collected a decade earlier.

---

2. For example, the Antitrust Division has responsibility to intervene before administrative agencies, functioning wholly or in part under regulatory statutes which require an accommodation between their purposes and those of the antitrust laws, such as the Commodities Futures Trading Commission, Federal Reserve Board, FCC, International Trade Commission, and the SEC. In the past few decades, the Antitrust Division has become much more active in this sort of intervention, generally advocating a policy of free competition before these regulatory agencies.

3. Antitrust Procedures and Penalties Act—Expediting Act, 15 U.S.C.A. § 1.

4. 18 U.S.C.A. § 3571(d). A dramatic use of this provision was first made in a price-fixing case against Archer Daniels Midland, where a "$100 million criminal fine—the largest criminal antitrust fine ever"—was collected. Department of Justice, Press Release (Oct. 15, 1996). Since 1996, five other antitrust defendants have been fined $100 million or more, including a $500 million fine imposed in 1999 on F. Hoffman–La Roche for its leadership role in an international price-fixing cartel involving vitamins.

When the Sherman Act was enacted in 1890, the criminal sanctions were imprisonment "not to exceed one year" for a misdemeanor and a $5,000 fine. From 1890 until relatively recently, criminal prosecution followed by imprisonment of individuals was rare; fines were seldom large enough to constitute much of a deterrent. This fact frequently was cited by critics of the antitrust system as an instance of weak law enforcement against "white collar" crime.

Beginning in the mid 1970's, the Antitrust Division put new emphasis on criminal prosecutions. In "Guidelines for Sentencing Recommendations in Felony Cases Under the Sherman Act," issued in 1977, the Antitrust Division explained that an antitrust offender "has a clear option to engage or not to engage in criminal activity." Prison sentences for hard-core offenses (*e.g.*, horizontal price fixing or market allocations), therefore,

> are uniquely effective in deterring antitrust violators (who are generally white collar businessmen) who may view a fine as a "license fee" for fixing prices but who view the threat of a substantial prison term more seriously.[5]

This theme has been consistently repeated by Antitrust Division officials through 2002. The significant issues raised by this emphasis on criminal prosecutions are discussed at pages 90–94 infra.

Violations of the Clayton Act, including its Robinson–Patman Act amendments, are not treated criminally.[6] Since 1990, the United States has had a right to recover treble damages for injuries resulting from antitrust violations (*e.g.*, because of government purchasing). Not only are defendants in criminal prosecutions entitled to a jury trial, but either party in a civil treble damage action may demand a jury trial as well.

Budget and Personnel. After a period of growth in the mid 1970's, the resources available to the Antitrust Division stabilized through 1980, and then dramatically decreased throughout the rest of the decade. During the 1990's and early years of the new century, the resources increased, but did not reach the level of the late 1970's. In fiscal 1972, the Antitrust Division had about 325 attorneys and a budget of approximately $12 million. In fiscal 1977, the Antitrust Division had about 421 attorneys and a budget of almost $27 million. In fiscal 1989, the Antitrust Division's budget was only about $45 million, and because inflation had taken a toll, the number of attorneys was down to 229.[7] For fiscal 2002, the Antitrust Division was authorized to employ about 400 attorneys and had a budget of about $141 million. The resources available to the Antitrust Division in fiscal 2003 will be roughly the same as in 2002.

5. 803 ATRR p. F–1 (1977).

6. Two minor exceptions are § 10 of the Clayton Act which imposes criminal penalties for certain transactions among common carriers, and § 3 of the Robinson–Patman Act which contains criminal penalties for certain price discrimination activities. These sections give rise to almost no enforcement activity.

7. These figures are taken from data prepared in 1989 by the Department of Justice for the Subcommittee on Antitrust, Monopolies and Business Restraints of the Senate Judiciary Committee.

Given the continued growth of the national economy, the increased need for vigilance created by newly deregulated corporations and foreign companies (with different traditions) doing business in the United States in the shrinking global market,[8] the breadth of responsibilities imposed on the Antitrust Division, the technical complexity of the products and services produced by the so-called "new economy," and the economic strength of many antitrust defendants, thoughtful observers worry about whether the resources available to the Antitrust Division in the early years of the 21st century are adequate. A consensus developed that the resources available in the late 1980's were inadequate. In 1989, a blue ribbon ABA "Task Force on the Antitrust Division" reported as follows:

> [T]he Task Force has concluded that the core mission of the Antitrust Division—to preserve competitive markets—cannot be carried out at current reduced levels of resources and morale.... Likelihood of apprehension is a key variable in deterring antitrust violations. Without sufficient antitrust enforcement resources available, the prospects of being caught are reduced substantially. The Task Force does not believe that, at the present time, the Division's enforcement resources and the public perception of the Division's ability and determination to enforce the laws are adequate to achieve antitrust policy objectives.[9]

In 2001, an ABA Task Force on the Federal Antitrust Agencies concluded:

> The Task Force believes that more resources should be devoted to the full range of tasks that are inherent in the broad mission responsibilities of the federal antitrust agencies.... [T]he performance of the U.S. competition policy system today suffers from the failure of budgets to keep pace with legitimate enforcement and policymaking functions assigned to the two federal enforcement agencies.[10]

2. FEDERAL TRADE COMMISSION

Origins of the FTC and Statutory Responsibilities. The FTC is an independent regulatory agency established in 1914 under the Federal Trade Commission Act. That statute together with the Clayton Act was the culmination of several years of congressional debate and represented compromise positions among the provisions in a series of proposed bills. In a general sense, these statutes constituted a response to the *Standard Oil* decision of 1911,[11] where the Supreme Court first enunciated a "rule of

---

8. *See* Goldschmid, Horizontal Restraints in Antitrust: Current Treatment and Future Needs, 75 Cal.L.Rev. 925, 929–30 (1987).

9. Report of the American Bar Association Section of Antitrust Law Task Force on the Antitrust Division of the U.S. Department of Justice 19–20 (1989) (hereinafter ABA 1989 Task Force Report).

10. ABA Section of Antitrust Law, The State of Federal Antitrust Enforcement—2001: Report of the Task Force on the Federal Antitrust Agencies 14–15 (2001) (hereinafter ABA 2001 Task Force Report).

11. Standard Oil Co. of New Jersey v. United States, 221 U.S. 1 (1911).

reason" approach to antitrust violations. Advocates of a vigorous antitrust policy felt that this flexible approach gave undesirable and unreviewable power over the nation's economic development to the judiciary. On the other hand, businessmen worried about how to stay within the confines of this vague standard.

One result was a series of statutory provisions in the Clayton Act which outlawed specific business practices such as creation of certain holding companies, price discrimination, and tie-in sales. Of course, specificity in describing illegal practices generated the danger that businessmen might skirt the edges of practices declared illegal. To deal with this problem, Congress enacted Section 5 of the FTC Act which declared unlawful "unfair methods of competition"—an exceptionally broad and vague grant of authority to supervise the functioning of the economy. Congress also created a new agency to enforce these laws. The FTC was given concurrent jurisdiction with the Department of Justice to enforce the provisions of the Clayton Act, and exclusive jurisdiction to enforce the FTC Act. Subsequently, Section 5 of the latter Act has been interpreted not only to cover trade practices which violate a particular provision of the antitrust laws but also those "which conflict with the basic policies of the Sherman and Clayton Acts even though such practices may not actually violate these laws."[12] In a classic work on the origins of the FTC, Gerard C. Henderson summarized the 1914 legislation as follows:

> This apparently widespread demand for a new administrative agency to carry out the anti-trust laws concealed, however, two radically divergent policies. Especially among the business interests, support of a federal trade commission rested not only upon the expectation that such a commission would administer a policy more tolerant toward large aggregations of capital, but on the belief that it could give to a group of business men, in advance, authoritative advice as to the legality of a contemplated undertaking.... Plans presented to the Senate Committee on Interstate Commerce by Mr. E.H. Gary, Mr. Francis Lynde Stetson, Mr. Victor Morawetz, and Mr. George W. Perkins all had in common this theory of "advice in advance"—in the nature of an administrative "declaratory judgment," to obviate uncertainty and litigation. In general these proposals embodied the theory advocated by President Roosevelt, that combinations and consolidations were not of themselves an evil; that there were good as well as bad trusts; and that rather than pursue a policy of indiscriminate warfare against big business, it was the part of wisdom to license big business under competent regulation in the public interest.
>
> Very different were the grounds upon which such men as Senator Newlands, Senator Cummins, and later President Wilson supported a federal trade commission. In their view of the matter

---

12. FTC v. Brown Shoe Co., 384 U.S. 316, 321 (1966); *see* FTC v. Sperry & Hutchinson Co., 405 U.S. 233 (1972).

such a commission was to be merely a more effective agency for the enforcement of the anti-trust laws. The purpose of the anti-trust laws was to maintain competitive conditions—a field free to all upon equal terms—and this purpose was not to be abandoned. The only object was to eliminate the delays and uncertainties incident to judicial enforcement. . . .

. . . [I]t was the Congressional intention to confer on the Commission, subject to court review, the duty of giving a detailed content to the general principle embodied in the phrase ["unfair methods of competition"], and to employ, in fulfilling this duty, not only the rules and precedents established by the courts at common law and under previous statutes, but the technique of reasoning by analogy and upon principle, with which jurists are familiar. . . .

It will be apparent from this review of the legislation of 1914, that in so far as the proponents of supplemental antitrust legislation had hoped to clarify the law of restraints and monopolies by substituting specific rules of conduct for general principles, they had largely failed. The draftsmen of the Federal Trade Commission Act avowedly chose a phrase embodying a general principle, while the unlawfulness of the practices somewhat inaptly described in the Clayton Act is made to depend upon the construction of a phrase at least as indefinite as the standard of the Sherman Law under the rule of reason. Both statutes were rather a victory for those who doubted the efficacy of legislative codification, and placed their reliance instead upon the development of rules and precedents by the gradual process of interpretation and decision of controversies by administrative and judicial tribunals.[13]

The FTC also has been empowered by legislation subsequent to the Clayton and FTC Acts to enforce laws with respect to a broad variety of other statutes including, for example, fair packaging and labeling legislation,[14] consumer credit statutes,[15] and laws regulating debt collection.[16] Far more important, however, are those provisions of Section 5 which in effect make the agency the principal regulatory force at the federal level dealing with unfair and deceptive advertising and general consumer exploitation and abuse.[17] Partly in response to the consumer movement of the 1970's, FTC activities in the consumer protection area have increased to the point where, in terms of budget and total personnel, they now exceed the agency's antitrust efforts. The FTC also has certain rulemaking powers, regulatory intervention responsibilities, and information gathering functions.

---

13. Henderson, The Federal Trade Commission: A Study in Administrative Law and Procedure 21, 48 (1924).

14. 15 U.S.C.A. §§ 1451–61.

15. 15 U.S.C.A. §§ 1601–65.

16. 15 U.S.C.A. § 1692.

17. 15 U.S.C.A. § 45(a)(1).

Organization. The FTC is headed by a chair and four other commissioners who are appointed by the President, with the advice and consent of the Senate, for staggered terms of seven years. No more than three members of the Commission may be of the same political party.

Commission proceedings are initiated by an administrative complaint which is then tried before an "administrative law judge." The findings of the administrative law judge are reviewed by the Commission which may dismiss the complaint or issue a cease and desist order. Much criticism has been directed to the fact that the commissioners both issue the complaint and later pass upon the alleged violation of law—a combination of prosecutorial and judicial functions present in many administrative agencies.

Appeal from a Commission order may be taken directly to a Court of Appeals. The Court of Appeals must uphold Commission orders that are in accord with governing law and supported by substantial evidence. This means that a Court of Appeals must approach the Commission's findings of fact with considerable deference.

Budget and Personnel. The budget and personnel trends at the FTC have been similar to those at the Antitrust Division, but the enhanced resources made available to the Antitrust Division during the 1990's for antitrust enforcement were not paralleled at the FTC. In fiscal 1972, the budget for the FTC was somewhat above $25 million; it employed 1,386 persons. In fiscal 1977, the budget for the FTC was $54.7 million; it employed 1,712 persons. In fiscal 1989, the FTC's budget was about $67 million and it employed fewer than 900 persons. The Bush Administration has requested about $171 million for the FTC in fiscal 2003, but the bulk of this appropriation (*i.e.*, $94 million) would go to the Commission's consumer protection mission, and the FTC will be able to employ only slightly over 1,000 persons. The ABA 2001 Task Force observed:

> Measured by full-time equivalent work years, from 1981 to 1989 outlays for the Antitrust Division and the FTC's competition mission fell by approximately 50 percent. In the 1990s, Congress restored the budget for the Antitrust Division to nearly 80 percent of its level in 1980. The FTC's competition-related activities, however, continued to receive funding at roughly 50 percent of the budget they received in 1980.

The Task Force concluded that by "almost any measure, the resources allocated the federal antitrust agencies in recent years have not kept up with the increasing scope and complexity of their mission responsibilities."[18]

3.   NATURE AND SCOPE OF ANTITRUST ENFORCEMENT EFFORTS BY THE TWO FEDERAL AGENCIES

Over the years, there has been a substantial increase in the number of actions brought by the Antitrust Division and the FTC. From 1890 to 1925,

18.   ABA 2001 Task Force Report at 4, 14.

for example, the Antitrust Division brought an average of about 8 cases a year. Between 1926 and 1937, the average number of new actions rose to about 11; for the years 1938 to 1950, the average was about 50. The following chart indicates the situation in more recent years:

FISCAL YEAR*	PRICE FIXING CRIMINAL	MERGER CIVIL	MONOPOLY CIVIL
1952	6	0	8
1962	31	10	9
1972	14	19	13
1977	34	4	2
1983	92	4	1
1993	78	5	0
1998	57	15	3
2000	52	21	1
2001	37	8	0

* Sources: Annual Hearings Before the Subcommittee of the House Committee on Appropriations and the Annual Reports of the Attorney General.

Although merger reviews and negotiations (*i.e.*, where no case is actually filed) and unreasonable restraint cases are time-consuming, important, and not reflected on the foregoing chart, it is obvious that criminal price-fixing cases have played a large role in the Antitrust Division's enforcement effort in recent decades, and this role increased sharply during the Reagan years. Indeed, from 1981 to 1989, with the exception of price-fixing cases and a relatively few challenges to very large horizontal mergers, enforcement activity by the Antitrust Division was virtually nonexistent:

> [T]he Reagan enforcement agencies largely removed the government from the business of scrutinizing exclusionary or abusive conduct by dominant firms. From 1981 through 1988, the Justice Department and the Federal Trade Commission initiated three cases enforcing the Sherman Act's ban on monopolization and attempted monopolization. This level of federal enforcement activity was the lowest in any eight-year period since 1900.

> [T]he focus of Reagan non-merger enforcement activity shifted heavily to smaller firms. From 1973 through the arrival of Reagan appointees in 1981, the federal antitrust agencies brought a total of 108 non-merger cases involving Fortune 500 companies. From 1981 through 1988, the number fell to 11.... Critics argue that the Reagan administration pursued an aggressive campaign to collar a hapless, economically trivial parade of asphalt suppliers, lawyers for indigent criminal defendants, moving and storage firms, bakeries, individual physicians, obscure trade associations and a host of other commercial pygmies.[19]

---

19. Kovacic, Steady Reliever at Antitrust, Wall St.J., Oct. 10, 1989, at A14, col. 4; *see* Handler, Antitrust Review—1988, 115 N.Y.L.J., Dec. 15, 1988, at 1, col. 1.

Since 1914, a succession of independent investigations and reports have concluded that the performance of the FTC has not measured up to its potential.[20] During the late 1970's and early 1980's the FTC received heavy criticism for "excessive activism" from business groups, segments of the bar, and members of the Reagan Administration.[21] During most of 1980's, critiques of the FTC contained terms like "passivity" and "timidity."[22] Both the Antitrust Division and the FTC began more vigorous enforcement programs during the first Bush Administration, and grew even more rigorous and enforcement-oriented during the Clinton Administration.[23] The ABA 2001 Task Force concluded that the Clinton Administration's antitrust policy was "within the broad mainstream of American antitrust thinking, albeit at the more activist end of the spectrum."[24] It is too early to accurately describe the antitrust policy of the second Bush Administration.

4. PRIVATE ACTIONS AND STATE ATTORNEYS GENERAL

Statutory Authority and Profile of Private Actions. The key legislative provisions authorizing and controlling private treble damage actions are Sections 4 and 5(a) of the Clayton Act which read as follows:[25]

> **Sec. 4. Any person who shall be injured in his business or property by reason of anything forbidden in the antitrust laws may sue therefor in any district court of the United States in the district in which the defendant resides, or is found, or has an agent, without respect to the amount in controversy, and shall recover threefold the damages by him sustained, and the cost of suit, including a reasonable attorney's fee....**

> **Sec. 5. (a) A final judgment or decree heretofore or hereafter rendered in any civil or criminal proceeding**

---

20. *See* Henderson, The Federal Trade Commission: A Study in Administrative Law and Procedure (1924). Compare Henderson to the strikingly similar criticisms 45 years later in Cox, Fellmeth, & Schultz, The Nader Report on the Federal Trade Commission (1969) and in the ABA Report on the Federal Trade Commission (1969).

21. For example, David Stockman, President Reagan's first Director of the Office of Management and Budget, referred to the FTC as a "passel of ideologues who are hostile to the business system." Impact of OMB–Proposed Budget Cuts for the Federal Trade Commission, Hearing before a Subcommittee of the House Committee on Government Operations, 97th Cong. 1st Sess. 265 (1981).

22. *See, e.g.*, Correia & Rothbard, Consumer Protection: The Federal Trade Commission, in Green & Pinsky (ed.), America's Transition: Blueprints for the 1990's 247–67 (1989).

23. Anne K. Bingaman and Joel I. Klein, who headed the Antitrust Division during the Clinton Administration, were described as "most aggressive trustbusters," and Robert Pitofsky, who became Chairman of the FTC in 1995, received high praise because he "revived an agency whose influence had waned for more than a decade." Bencivenga, Invigorating the FTC, N.Y.L.J., Feb. 1, 1996, at 5.

24. ABA 2001 Task Force Report at 2.

25. 15 U.S.C.A. §§ 15, 16.

brought by or on behalf of the United States under the antitrust laws to the effect that a defendant has violated said laws shall be prima facie evidence against such defendant in any action or proceeding brought by any other party against such defendant under said laws as to all matters respecting which said judgment or decree would be an estoppel as between the parties thereto: Provided, That this section shall not apply to consent judgments or decrees entered before any testimony has been taken.

Until the 1960's, very few private plaintiffs were successful. During the period 1890 to 1940, 175 private damage suits proceeded to final adjudication and plaintiffs prevailed in only 13.[26] Between 1952 and 1958, plaintiffs recovered in only 20 of 144 reported cases.[27] In addition, plaintiffs were able to achieve an advantageous settlement in only about 25% of all private suits filed.

The lack of successful private litigation during the first 70 years of antitrust enforcement was particularly remarkable in light of the fact that so many litigants relied on prior government judgments. It has been estimated that approximately 75% of private treble damage suits prior to 1960 were initiated after government suit, and in reliance on prior judgments against defendants.[28] Since 1960, however, the situation has changed, probably largely as a result of a number of Supreme Court decisions easing procedural hurdles and damage standards, and changing substantive norms.[29]

A comparison of U.S. government cases and private antitrust cases filed since 1941 indicates that private suits have been the predominant form of antitrust litigation—at least in terms of number of cases filed—for more than 40 years. Professors Salop and White explained:

> Until 1965, with the exception of a "spike" in 1962 due to the electrical conspiracy follow-on cases, the ratio of private to government cases tended to be 6 to 1 or less. From the mid 1960's until the late 1970's the absolute and relative number of private antitrust cases grew, reaching a peak of 1,611 cases in 1977, while the ratio of private to public cases exceeded 20 to 1. In the 1980's, however, both the absolute and relative numbers of antitrust cases have declined, and the private to public ratio has fallen to the 10 to 1 range.[30]

26. *See* Att'y Gen. Rep. on the Antitrust Laws 378 (1955).

27. Bicks, The Department of Justice and Private Treble Damage Actions, 4 Antitrust Bull. 5, 11 (1959).

28. Stedman, Consent Decrees and Private Action: An Antitrust Dilemma, 53 Cal. L.Rev. 627, 628 n. 7 (1965).

29. *See* discussion of the "Policy Issues Related to Actions by Private Parties and State Attorneys General," pp. 81–84 *infra*.

30. Commentary by Salop & White, in White (ed.), Private Antitrust Litigation: New Evidence, New Learning 3 (1988).

This pattern of private and governmental enforcement appears to have continued throughout the 1990's and into the new century.

Statutory Authority and Profile of Enforcement by State Attorneys General. Private actions are also available to states.[31] A state may show damages caused, for example, by overcharges to it resulting from price fixing or other cartel activity or, in its capacity as *parens patriae,* may seek injunctive relief without the need to show damage to its "business or property."[32]

In addition, in September, 1976, Congress enacted the Hart–Scott–Rodino Act which contained new *parens patriae* provisions.[33] These permit state attorneys general to bring Sherman Act cases on behalf of natural persons (as opposed to business entities) residing in their states. The attorneys general may seek treble damages, costs, and attorney's fees in addition to injunctive relief. Most importantly, in any action in which it has been determined that a defendant fixed prices in violation of the Sherman Act:

> damages may be proved and assessed in the aggregate by statistical or sampling methods, by the computation of illegal overcharges, or by such other reasonable system of estimating aggregate damages as the court in its discretion may permit without the necessity of separately proving the individual claim of, or amount of damage to, persons on whose behalf the suit was brought.

Where price fixing has been found the Act provides, in essence, for "fluid recoveries." Once aggregate damages have been awarded, each person in the attorney general's class may come forward and prove the extent of his or her injury. Monies not claimed by individuals:

> Shall (1) be distributed in such manner as the district court in its discretion may authorize; or (2) be deemed a civil penalty by the court and deposited with the State as general revenues.

Critics contended that the *parens patriae* provisions improperly focus on "ill-gotten gains rather than on consumer compensation," and would result in unmanageable classes and ruinous exposures. The report of the Senate Judiciary Committee responded:

> The economic burden of most antitrust violations is borne by the consumer in the form of higher prices for goods and services.... When everyday consumer purchases are involved (*e.g.,* bread, dairy products, gasoline, etc.), the individual dollar amounts are so small

---

31. Under certain circumstances, foreign governments may also recover in treble damage actions. *See* Antitrust Reciprocity Amendment, Pub.L. No. 97–393, 96 Stat. 1964 (1982); Pfizer, Inc. v. Government of India, 434 U.S. 308 (1978).

32. *See* Georgia v. Pennsylvania Railroad Co., 324 U.S. 439 (1945). States, however, may not bring treble damage actions for general injury to their economies. *See* Hawaii v. Standard Oil Co., 405 U.S. 251 (1972) (The Court focused on the danger of double recovery by both a state and individual citizens for the same injury).

33. Hart–Scott–Rodino Antitrust Improvements Act of 1976, Pub.L. No. 94–435, 90 Stat. 1383; 15 U.S.C.A. §§ 15, 1311–1314.

that, as a practical matter, an individual antitrust lawsuit is out of the question. Similarly, consumers have found little relief under the class action provisions of the Federal Rules. . . .

The Committee believes that this title provides a practical remedy for consumers, and that it is necessary to deter antitrust violations, to take the profit out of white collar crime, and to dispense equal justice to the rich and poor alike. The predictions of ruinous liability made by opponents . . . [are unproven and must be rejected].[34]

The *parens patriae* provisions of the Hart–Scott–Rodino Act and the general contractions of antitrust enforcement at the federal level led, as the National Association of Attorneys General describe it, to "a revolution in the patterns of enforcement" during the 1980's. In this decade, state attorney general enforcement:

experienced first renaissance and then an explosive increase in cases, investigations, and legislative and other policy initiatives. To the traditional attorney general role of *parens patriae* in local cases involving price-fixing and bid-rigging was added a concern with the entire spectrum of competition law and policy.[35]

During the 1990's and early 2000's, with more aggressive enforcement by the Antitrust Division and the FTC, the antitrust activity of state attorneys general somewhat receded. But, often through a Multistate Antitrust Task Force (which coordinates the activities of state attorneys general), state antitrust enforcement remains vigorous by any historic measure. Also, particularly in the late 1990's, state attorneys general worked effectively with the federal enforcement agencies through cooperation agreements and joint proceedings (*e.g.*, state attorneys general joined with the Antitrust Division in the Microsoft case[36] and with the FTC in a merger proceeding against Exxon and Mobil).

Policy Issues Related to Actions by Private Parties and State Attorneys General. One result of the surge of antitrust enforcement activity by private parties and state attorneys general has been to change the balance of potential profit and risk for businessmen contemplating questionable conduct under the antitrust laws. Since the Antitrust Division and the FTC have limited resources, allowing them to bring perhaps 100 to 150 cases even in well-funded years, the question of whether a particular new distribution policy, or other practice questionable under the antitrust laws,

34. S.Rep. No. 803, 94th Cong., 2d Sess. 7 (1976).

35. National Association of Attorneys General, State Attorney General Antitrust Enforcement (i) (1989). The *parens patriae* role of state attorneys general must be viewed in the light of the Supreme Court's decisions in Illinois Brick Co. v. Illinois, 431 U.S. 720 (1977), which may prevent consum-

ers (often indirect purchasers) from proving antitrust damage, and California v. ARC America Corp., 490 U.S. 93 (1989), which acknowledges the right of indirect purchasers to recover under state antitrust statutes. *See* pp. 104–06 infra. In general, state antitrust statutes, which usually parallel the federal antitrust laws, are beyond the purview of this casebook.

36. *See* Section 1 of Chapter 8 infra.

will be attempted often comes down to an inquiry about whether or not there is a potential litigant (or a class of litigants) who has the resources and staying power to take its claim to the courts.

In 1982, in several cases, the Supreme Court reemphasized its long-standing recognition of the important role played by private treble damage actions:

> Congress sought to create a private enforcement mechanism that would deter violators and deprive them of the fruits of their illegal actions, and would provide ample compensation to the victims of antitrust violations. . . . Consistent with the congressional purpose, we have refused to engraft artificial limitations on the § 4 remedy. . . . [W]e have applied § 4 in accordance with its plain language and its broad remedial and deterrent objectives.

Blue Shield of Virginia v. McCready, 457 U.S. 465 (1982); *see* American Society of Mechanical Engineers, Inc. v. Hydrolevel Corp., 456 U.S. 556, 571 (1982).

On the other hand, many commentators agree that some private damage claimants, attracted by the possibility of a treble damage "bonanza," have instituted suits with little merit in the hope of at least extracting a settlement. Defendants are often hesitant to go to trial when faced with large damage exposures in complex antitrust litigation. Also, as the Supreme Court noted in Blue Chip Stamps v. Manor Drug Stores, 421 U.S. 723, 742–43 (1975), in the context of securities litigation:

> [I]n this type of litigation . . . the mere existence of an unresolved lawsuit has settlement value to the plaintiff not only because of the possibility that he may prevail on the merits, an entirely legitimate component of settlement value, but because of the threat of extensive discovery and disruption of normal business activities which may accompany a lawsuit which is groundless in any event, but cannot be proved so before trial. . . .

Additional problems may be caused by the fact that competitors will sometimes have perverse (anticompetitive) reasons for challenging a practice or opposing a merger, and in antitrust class actions, the plaintiffs' attorney is often the engine (with a large financial stake in the result) of the litigation. These problems create the danger of overenforcement and, in comparison to a government action, leave little room for prosecutorial discretion in the public interest.

Similarly, actions by state attorneys general have been challenged as involving heavy political components or undue concern for special local interests. Nevertheless, during the past twenty years or so, a broad consensus appears to have developed in support of vigorous state attorney general action. For example, Charles F. Rule, the last Assistant Attorney in charge of the Antitrust Division during the Reagan years, stated:

> In the ten years since the *parens patriae* remedy was enacted, state antitrust activity has increased greatly. Consumers likely

have benefited from having their antitrust damage concerns addressed by those best able to identify and respond to them.

State attorneys general, being closer to their citizens injured by antitrust violations, have a greater incentive to bring consumer-based damage actions than would the federal government. State attorneys general have been steadily accumulating the expertise needed successfully to pursue complex antitrust damages actions, and are free to hire outside counsel when additional assistance is required. Furthermore, the state attorneys general have shown in several instances that, by coordinating their efforts, they can pursue antitrust actions of multi-state scope that approach the limits on the size of such consumer damage actions that successfully can be litigated.[37]

The ABA 1989 Task Force recommended striking the balance between federal and state activities in the following way:

Much of the increased enforcement by the states and the increased activism of NAAG [National Association of Attorneys General] is a reaction to the perception of lax federal enforcement. Yet the present overlap of state and federal enforcement responsibilities does not reflect the most efficient use of scarce enforcement resources. Moreover, the specter of multiple enforcement by entities applying different standards can create a real problem for businesses engaged in interstate commerce.

Therefore, the Task Force majority believes that the Antitrust Division should once again be recognized as the national policy maker to the businesses that must interpret and comply with the law, and recommends that the Division strive to improve relations with the State Attorneys General and to engage in a program of cooperative enforcement. In recognition that the State Attorneys General are an important source of expertise and enforcement capability, the Division should attempt to foster a "cross-deputizing" relationship with the State Attorneys General in which the Division refers localized cases to the states and the State Attorneys General refer national cases to the Division. Such a move would harmonize Division and state enforcement while saving budgetary and staff resources at both the federal and state levels. . . .

Specifically . . . the Antitrust Division should consider working more closely with State Attorneys General on localized price-fixing investigations as a means of freeing Division resources to pursue cases of more national significance. . . . Although substantive issues of merger policy are national in scope, the states do have a legitimate interest in regulating local and regional mergers.[38]

---

37. Rule, Remarks at an ALI–ABA Course of Study 30 (May 6, 1988).

38. ABA 1989 Task Force Report at 49–51.

The ABA 2001 Task Force observed that [t]here "are many enforcers of the American antitrust laws-federal antitrust agencies, state attorneys general, and multiple private attorneys general," and that "our system generates large administrative costs, large legal fees, and haphazard results in terms of victim compensation." It urged careful study of the problem.[39] Throughout the course consider the costs and benefits—including the deterrent, resource enhancement, and compensation advantages—of antitrust's three-level enforcement pattern. In response to the important role in antitrust enforcement that is played by private actions and to the potential for abuse of such actions, the procedural and process rules discussed in Section C infra have been developed.

B.   SPECIAL ISSUES RELATED TO ENFORCEMENT BY THE FEDERAL AGENCIES

1.   COORDINATION BETWEEN THE DEPARTMENT OF JUSTICE AND THE FTC AND THE ISSUE OF DUAL ENFORCEMENT

The Antitrust Division has left to the FTC virtually all enforcement of the price discrimination provisions of the Robinson–Patman Act. The FTC, of course, brings no action of a criminal nature. In other areas of antitrust enforcement, there is a substantial overlap in jurisdiction, and as a result, the two agencies have developed a "liaison" system to avoid duplication of effort and unnecessary harassment of businesses. Investigations are cleared between the two agencies. Some particular antitrust practices appear to fall within the special province of the Antitrust Division, such as "hard-core" price fixing, and some industries, such as data processing and basic metals, also seem to devolve upon the Antitrust Division rather than the FTC. On the other hand, pharmaceutical and food distribution problems are regularly handled by the FTC. There are exceptions to these generalizations. In March 2002, the heads of the Antitrust Division and FTC worked out an agreement to formally allocate industries between the two agencies in order to provide transparency, and to reduce the controversy and delay that can occur when both agencies wish to investigate the same matter. The plan was dropped because of opposition in Congress. Arguably, there are advantages to the overlapping responsibilities; Congress had consciously created the agencies' concurrent jurisdiction. In any event, most former heads of the Antitrust Division and FTC believe the system works well. John H. Shenefield, for example, who was in charge of the Antitrust Division during the Carter Administration, testified as follows:

> The liaison arrangement gives weight to several factors in resolving conflicts between the two agencies. First, the existence within an agency of special industry expertise or a prior case or past investigation concerning the same companies or products should operate presumptively to give that same agency responsibility for any new case. In addition the availability of resources is

39.   ABA 2001 Task Force Report at 4–
5.

relevant to the necessity for immediate action. The type of conduct involved may suggest that one or another agency is the more suitable. Finally, the existence within an agency of an investigation or decree that would be interfered with should another agency proceed would be taken into account.

In general, the liaison arrangement has worked extremely well. In only four or five cases during the two and two-thirds years that I was in charge of the Antitrust Division were liaison disagreements referred to me.... [I was] able easily to resolve the disputes without delay. Such disputes only seem to arise in cases involving significant mergers, particularly in the conglomerate area where both agencies can legitimately claim involvement or familiarity with one of the merging firms.[40]

Neither the Antitrust Division nor the FTC has been able to resist all outside pressures seeking to influence enforcement policies. The Antitrust Division, as a part of the executive branch, is necessarily somewhat more responsive to pressures exerted by way of the White House. The FTC, as an independent agency relying in the last analysis on Congressional appropriations, is apt to feel more strongly pressures from crucial legislators. In a field where private financial stakes are often high, there is real danger that the public interest will be inadequately represented. In this context, many argue that any inefficiencies arising from overlapping enforcement responsibilities are more than offset by the advantage provided by the different positions of the two agencies in the political and administrative structures. In many ways, the two agencies—with somewhat different focuses and expertise—stimulate and complement each other. For many, the existence of two agencies, with different appointment processes and somewhat different institutional loyalties, provides an important safety valve in so sensitive an area of national policy.

2. INVESTIGATIVE AUTHORITY AND REQUIRED REPORTING

Most antitrust investigations proceed through informal interviews and questionnaires, with voluntary compliance by the person or firm being investigated. The Antitrust Division may also convene a grand jury with subpoena powers, although the Supreme Court, in United States v. Procter & Gamble Co., 356 U.S. 677 (1958), made it clear that a grand jury may not be used if the Antitrust Division's principal intent is eventually to bring a civil action. Partly in response to that decision, in 1962, the Antitrust Division obtained from Congress broad civil investigatory powers under the Antitrust Civil Process Act.[41] The Act enabled the Antitrust Division to issue a civil investigative demand ("CID") to obtain documentary evidence from non-natural persons (*e.g.*, corporations) suspected of committing a violation.

---

40. Impact of OMB–Proposed Budget Cuts for the Federal Trade Commission, Hearing before a Subcommittee of the House Committee on Government Operations, 97th Cong., 1st Sess. 245–46 (1981).

41. 15 U.S.C.A. §§ 1311–14.

In 1976, in the Hart–Scott–Rodino Act,[42] the Antitrust Division was empowered to issue a demand (i) for oral testimony or written interrogatories (*i.e.*, in addition to documentary evidence), (ii) to all persons (*i.e.*, non-natural and natural), (iii) including "non-target" third parties, such as competitors, suppliers, customers, and employees, with relevant information. In addition to the authority to investigate past or present violations, the Act also gives investigators authority to inquire into "activities in preparation for a merger, acquisition, joint venture, or similar transaction, which, if consummated, may result in an antitrust violation." Additional amendments to the Act in 1980 further strengthened the Antitrust Division's CID power. The FTC has similar investigative powers.[43] Once an action has been instituted, in general, the usual civil discovery procedures are available, and extensive use of interrogatories and depositions is customary.

The Hart–Scott–Rodino Act also required pre-merger notification. Parties, including foreign interests, involved in a merger must file a pre-merger notification form with the FTC and Antitrust Division. Under a 2000 amendment to the Hart–Scott–Rodino Act and FTC implementing regulations, filings must involve a "size-of-transaction" threshold of $50 million (up from $15 million) for the Act to be applicable. The amendment did away with prior "size-of-person" tests for transactions valued in excess of $200 million, and put into effect a graduated scale for filing fees based on the size of a transaction. An automatic waiting period, prior to the consummation of a merger, is mandated, and the waiting period runs for 15 to at least 50 days, depending on circumstances and the type of merger.

3.   CASE SELECTION AND PROSECUTORIAL DISCRETION

In the past, thoughtful critics of governmental antitrust enforcement have focused on deficiencies in policy planning and case selection at both the Antitrust Division and FTC. Many have urged more systematic policy planning. Effective planning would, for example, involve consideration of available enforcement techniques (*e.g.*, case-by-case litigation, rulemaking, guides, stimulation of industry self-regulation), and selection of cases and litigating theories that would achieve maximum deterrence of anticompetitive activities.

There is evidence that a good deal of public antitrust enforcement in the past has been triggered by complaints by businessmen who felt they were losing out in the competitive battle. When those complaints had the benefit of political support—*e.g.*, suggestions for investigation of particular practices by the administration or powerful legislators—there seems to have been a tendency to satisfy the complainants. A major effort to do the type of policy planning being advocated was carried out by the FTC in 1995–96. After two months of hearings during the fall of 1995, the FTC released a report, dated May 1996, that "analyzes and makes recommenda-

---

42. Hart–Scott–Rodino Antitrust Improvements Act of 1976, Pub.L. No. 94–435, 90 Stat. 1383; 15 U.S.C.A. §§ 15, 1311–1314.

43. 15 U.S.C.A. §§ 46, 49.

tions on how to continue the FTC's mission in light of increased global and innovation-based competition." The report, among other topics, deals with: "competition at the close of the century"; efficiencies; "innovation, intellectual property, and competition"; joint ventures; and "themes for the future."[44]

There remains, however, a concern that enforcement priorities shift too sharply with each new Assistant Attorney General in charge of the Antitrust Division, Chair of the FTC, and, of course, with each new administration. Although shifts in emphasis may reflect desirable flexibility and a healthy concern about new developments, serious questions may be raised about *ad hoc* case selection and sharply shifting priorities.

In addition, as discussed earlier, the 1980's saw a significant issue arise as to the proper boundaries of prosecutorial discretion. Particularly in the area of vertical restraints, but in other areas also, enforcement officials stated that they would not enforce certain antitrust rules (supported by recent Supreme Court opinions) with which they disagreed. While some prosecutorial discretion is both necessary and desirable, the scope of discretion asserted by recalcitrant officials reemphasized, at least for some observers, the importance of the antitrust roles played by private parties and state attorneys general.

4. LITIGATION OR SETTLEMENT

The vast majority (*i.e.*, 80% or more) of government cases never go to trial but rather are settled through some sort of voluntary agreement. The Antitrust Division and the FTC both accept "consent" decrees or orders, respectively, which, in effect, are negotiated settlements between the staff of the agency and counsel for the litigants, approved by a federal district court in Antitrust Division proceedings or by the commissioners in FTC matters. In addition, the FTC occasionally will accept assurances of voluntary compliance and informal corrective actions which are written commitments by respondents to discontinue objectionable practices. These have no legal effect, except that the FTC is more likely to take vigorous enforcement action against a company that continues a violation after voluntary compliance has been assured.

Given the great expense and length of many antitrust actions (*see* Section D infra), consent agreements often offer advantages to all parties. Defendants can usually avoid the government obtaining its maximum relief, avoid any *prima facie* effect of a pretrial consent decree (*see* pp. 94–96 infra), and avoid significant business disruption. The Antitrust Division and FTC may be able to obtain expeditious relief while husbanding scarce enforcement resources.

---

44. FTC Staff, Anticipating the 21st Century: Competition Policy in the New High–Tech, Global Marketplace (1996). More than 200 business and consumer representatives, practitioners, government officials, and academicians participated in the FTC's hearings.

During the 1960's and early 1970's observers of the antitrust scene increasingly came to realize that major questions of antitrust policy were being resolved in the context of consent negotiations. This led Congress in 1974 to enact the Antitrust Procedures and Penalties Act, known as the Tunney Act, which subjects antitrust settlements made by the Antitrust Division to greater court and public scrutiny.[45] The Act required the Department of Justice to file a detailed "competitive impact statement" with respect to any proposed consent decree and creates a 60–day waiting period (which allows for public comment) between the filing of a proposed consent judgment and the effective date of the decree. The "competitive impact statement" must include descriptions of the nature and purposes of the proceeding and an explanation of the proposed consent decree. The sponsors of the Act suggested these statements would: (i) increase public understanding of, and participation in, consent decree proceedings; (ii) focus government attorneys on the public impact of their case; and (iii) encourage district judges more carefully to review consent decrees in appropriate instances.

Under the Act, a district judge is not to enter a proposed consent judgment unless he or she determines that it is "in the public interest." Congress contemplated that district judges would be more deeply involved in evaluating consent judgments than had previously been the practice, and evidence suggests that district judges are respecting this Congressional mandate.

District judges can, however, carry their mandate too far. In a recent celebrated case, United States v. Microsoft Corp., 56 F.3d 1448 (D.C.Cir. 1995), the district court had refused to enter a proposed consent decree between the Antitrust Division and Microsoft. The Circuit Court concluded that the district court exceeded its authority and reasoned:

> At the heart of this case, then, is the proper scope of the district court's inquiry into the "public interest." Is the district judge entitled to seize hold of the matter—the investigation into the putative defendant's business practices—and decide for himself the appropriate combined response of the executive and judicial branches to those practices? With respect to the specific allegations in the government's complaint, may the court interpose its own views of the appropriate remedy over those the government seeks as a part of its overall settlement? To be sure, Congress, in passing the Tunney Act, intended to prevent "judicial rubber stamping" of the Justice Department's proposed consent decree. . . .
>
> [Nevertheless, although] the language of section 16(e) is not precise, we think the government is correct in contending that section 16(e)(1)'s reference to the alleged violations suggests that Congress did not mean for a district judge to construct his own

---

45. Antitrust Procedures and Penalties Act—Expediting Act, Pub.L. No. 93–528, 88   Stat. 1706; 15 U.S.C.A. § 16.

hypothetical case and then evaluate the decree against that case. Moreover, in section 16(e)(2), the court is authorized to consider "the public benefit ... of the determination of the issues at trial." Putting aside the perplexing question of how the district judge could insure a trial if the government did not wish one, "the issues" referred to must be those formulated in the complaint. Congress surely did not contemplate that the district judge would, by reformulating the issues, effectively redraft the complaint himself.[46]

Either the government or a defendant may petition for court modification of a previously entered consent decree, but consent decrees have seldom been modified absent the agreement of the original parties. Both the Antitrust Division and the FTC now have active programs for reviewing past consent decrees to determine whether or not they continue to effectuate antitrust objectives.

5.   INTERVENTION

Business conduct at issue in a particular government (or private) antitrust action may have ramifications far beyond the interests of the particular litigants. Accordingly, parties may attempt to intervene, either "of right" under Rule 24(a) or as a matter of discretion under Rule 24(b) of the Federal Rules of Civil Procedure.

Rule 24(a)(2) was amended in 1966 to permit intervention of right when the applicant claims an interest such that disposition of the action as a practical matter may "impair or impede his ability to protect that interest ..." unless that interest "is adequately represented by existing parties." Prior to 1966, intervention was rarely granted, particularly in government antitrust litigation. Arguably, the Supreme Court might have signaled a change in attitude in this area in Cascade Natural Gas Corp. v. El Paso Natural Gas Co., 386 U.S. 129 (1967), where the Court sustained the right of California, Southern California Edison (a large industrial user of natural gas), and Cascade Natural Gas (a distributor whose sole supplier had been one of the companies in the challenged merger) to intervene in a divestiture proceeding looking toward the breakup of El Paso and Pacific Northwest, two natural gas companies that previously had been held to have merged illegally. Noting that "the United States knuckled under to El Paso," the Court found inadequacy of representation in the divestiture proceedings.

Though many expected the *Cascade* decision would lead to expanded opportunities for intervention in government antitrust litigation,[47] subsequent cases have not borne this out. For example, intervention was denied in United States v. Automobile Manufacturers Ass'n,[48] where the City of New York and others attempted to intervene in proposed consent proceed-

46.   56 F.3d 1448, 1458–59 (D.C.Cir. 1995).

47.   *See* 3B J. Moore, Federal Practice, ¶ 24.08[6] at 24–198 (2d ed. 1975).

48.   307 F.Supp. 617 (C.D.Cal.1969), affirmed per curiam sub nom., City of New York v. United States, 397 U.S. 248 (1970).

ings to dispose of a pollution conspiracy case against the big four automobile manufacturers. Similarly, Ralph Nader's attempt to intervene to challenge an *ITT–Hartford* consent decree was denied in United States v. International Telephone & Telegraph Corp.[49]

The judicial tendency to construe *Cascade* narrowly reflects a reluctance to assume that plaintiffs—particularly in government litigation—will inadequately represent the public interest. The current test in determining intervention of right is probably close to the standard announced in United States v. Ciba Corp., 50 F.R.D. 507, 513 (S.D.N.Y.1970), where *Cascade* was distinguished and the district court announced a standard which includes requirements that: (1) the interest justifying intervention be substantial; (2) it "lie at the center" of the controversy; and (3) there be a clear showing that the interest is less than "adequately represented."[50]

Under Rule 24(b), permissive intervention may be granted when there are common questions of law or fact and where the court determines that intervention will not unduly delay or prejudice the adjudication of the rights of individual parties. Requests for permissive intervention are rarely granted in antitrust cases.

Intervention in an adjudicative proceeding at the FTC is at the Commission's discretion. In the past, in several consumer protection cases, intervention by public interest law groups has been permitted.

6. GOVERNMENT ANTITRUST REMEDIES AND THE EMPHASIS ON CRIMINAL PROSECUTIONS

As previously indicated, the Antitrust Division may seek either criminal or civil remedies when challenging anticompetitive activity. Section 4 of the Sherman Act and Section 15 of the Clayton Act confer jurisdiction on the federal courts to "prevent and restrain" violations.[51] The FTC is empowered to issue "cease and desist" orders and may thereby undo or prevent unlawful activity. In fashioning relief, courts and the FTC have considerable discretion and are entitled to enjoin a broad range of possible future violations. The classic statement is found in International Salt Co. v. United States, 332 U.S. 392, 400 (1947):

> The District Court is not obliged to assume, contrary to common experience, that a violator of the antitrust laws will relinquish the fruits of his violation more completely than the court requires him to do. . . . When the purpose to restrain trade appears from a clear

---

49. 349 F.Supp. 22 (D.Conn.1972), affirmed mem. sub nom., Nader v. United States, 410 U.S. 919 (1973). *See generally* Note, The ITT Dividend: Reform of Department of Justice Consent Decree Procedures, 73 Colum.L.Rev. 594 (1973).

50. *See* United States v. Associated Milk Producers, Inc., 534 F.2d 113 (8th Cir. 1976), cert. denied, 429 U.S. 940 (1976); cf. United States v. AT & T, 1981–2 Trade Cas. (CCH) ¶ 64,979 at 73,142 (D.D.C.1982)(intervention permitted).

51. 15 U.S.C.A. §§ 4, 25.

violation of law, it is not necessary that all the untraveled roads to that end be left open and that only the worn one be closed.[52]

Until recently, injunctive sanctions, damage claims, and criminal fines were the principal remedies available to the government. Particularly for "hard-core" anticompetitive offenses, these remedies have been inadequate. Indeed, from 1890 to about 20 years ago, private treble damage actions constituted the most significant antitrust sanction. Prison sentences were almost never imposed.

Since the mid 1970's, Congress has played an active role in broadening and strengthening antitrust remedies. Presently, violation of the Sherman Act is a felony for which individuals may be sentenced to a prison term of up to three years, and a fine of no more than $350,000. Corporations face a fine of up to $10 million. Even more important in monetary terms, the Criminal Fine Improvements Act of 1987[53] provides for an alternative maximum fine, for both individual and corporate antitrust offenders, of twice the gross pecuniary gain or loss resulting from the violation. Until fiscal 1992, the largest corporate fine ever imposed in an antitrust prosecution was $2 million, and during the late 1980's and early 1990's, annual fines collected by the Antitrust Division averaged about $27 million. By contrast, since the Improvements Act was applied to antitrust (by way of a $100 million fine in a price-fixing case against Archer Daniels Midland in 1996), six defendants have been fined $100 million or more (including a $500 million fine), and in fiscal 2001, the Antitrust Division obtained fines of over $280 million.[54] On the civil side, the FTC recently obtained a $100 million settlement in an action seeking disgorgement of illicit profits. In FTC v. Mylan, the Commission persuaded a district court, relying on equitable powers in a disgorgement settlement, to require repayment of the $100 million to exploited consumers.[55]

Since the mid 1970's, there has been increasing recognition of the significance of imprisonment as a uniquely important antitrust sanction. Until 1977, the most notable instance of the imposition of prison sentences involved 30–day sentences for General Electric and Westinghouse executives after they pleaded guilty to price fixing on electrical equipment in the early 1960's. But this in no way established a trend. No one convicted of an antitrust violation—no matter how egregious or hard-core—received a prison sentence from fiscal 1962 through 1968. From 1969 to 1977, fewer than a dozen individuals received prison sentences of more than 30 days.[60] Even in the GE–Westinghouse price-fixing cases, most observers concluded that although the 30–day sentences may have made a few executives

---

52. *See, e.g.,* Atlantic Refining Co. v. FTC, 381 U.S. 357 (1965); FTC v. Henry Broch & Co., 368 U.S. 360, 364 (1962).

53. *See* discussion p. 71 supra.

54. *See* Hammond, A Review of Recent Cases and Developments in the Antitrust Division's Criminal Enforcement Program (Conference Board program March 7, 2002).

55. *See* FTC v. Mylan Laboratories, FTC File No. X990015 (2000); FTC v. Mylan Laboratories, Civil 1:98CV03114 (TFH) (D.D.C.2000).

60. Baker and Reeves, The Paper Label Sentences: Critiques, 86 Yale L.J. 619, 623 n. 16 (1977).

contrite, the real bite came from the approximately 1,800 private lawsuits which cost GE and other companies upwards of $350 million to litigate and settle.

In 1974, however, in the Antitrust Procedures and Penalties Act, Congress attempted to alter the antitrust sanctions equation. Congress, in effect, mandated heavier prison sentences for antitrust violators by increasing the maximum prison term to three years and by making violations felonies.[61] A cynical wag suggested that: "Congress decided on three years by adding up all of the time spent in prison by antitrust violators since 1890." There is, of course, truth in the statement, but it misses the point. Congress was really saying that criminal fines, treble damages, and injunctive provisions were not enough; to make antitrust enforcement work, what was needed was the general deterrence created by the threat of imprisonment for meaningful periods of time.

In 1977, the Department of Justice issued sentencing guidelines for felony cases under the Sherman Act. The guidelines indicate that the Antitrust Division had taken Congress' hint. The Antitrust Division said that it would recommend to district judges that antitrust violators—at least where hard-core offenses were involved—should go to jail. The guidelines also indicated that fines were "poor alternatives" to imprisonment and would be recommended only where prison sentences were inappropriate.

Although Nash v. United States, 229 U.S. 373 (1913), largely put to rest the question of whether or not the criminal provisions of the Sherman Act would be declared void for vagueness, critics of criminal enforcement still raise the "vagueness" policy issue: "Is it fair," they ask, "to prosecute a defendant who was understandably confused about the state of the law?" The Antitrust Division's answer is that criminal prosecutions will take place only where hard-core offenses—for example, horizontal price fixing, bid-rigging schemes, and market allocations—are involved. Even in these areas, it is unlikely that criminal cases will be brought if a potential defendant was understandably confused about the state of the law or otherwise acted reasonably and in good faith.

The most significant recent development with respect to sentencing for antitrust offenses came in the Sentencing Guidelines, which took effect on November 1, 1987, are amended annually by the United States Sentencing Commission, and apply to all crimes that occur after November 1, 1987.[62] The Guidelines are too complicated to explain in any great detail here, but in broad outline, they operate as follows. Chapter 5, Part A, of the Guidelines sets forth a Sentencing Table, which is a matrix expressing

61. *See* p. 72 supra.

62. The Sentencing Reform Act of 1984 (Title II of the Comprehensive Crime Control Act of 1984) established the United States Sentencing Commission in the Judicial Branch. It charged the Commission with developing a set of guidelines that would, while reducing the variance in sentences imposed for similar offenses, also meet the goals of criminal sentencing: respect for the law, deterrence, incapacitation, and rehabilitation. It is important to bear in mind that antitrust offenses are only the smallest part of the overall Sentencing Guidelines, which cover virtually all federal crimes.

sentences in terms of ranges of months that are required for particular "offense levels," in light of the defendant's "criminal history category." Within a given sentencing range, the district court has discretion to select a sentence. It begins by calculating the appropriate offense level and criminal history category. While the latter calculation is fairly straightforward, ascertaining the offense level is far more complicated. The final offense level reflects, among other things, all relevant conduct (including certain uncharged conduct), specific characteristics of the offense, the defendant's role in the offense, whether the defendant has accepted responsibility for the offense, and whether the defendant obstructed the investigation of the offense.

In limited circumstances, the court may "depart" from the Guidelines range. For example, the court may conclude that the sentence range does not reflect the likelihood that the defendant would commit this same crime again upon release and for that reason it may depart upward and impose a harsher sentence. Alternatively, the court may believe that the Guidelines sentence is too severe and decide to depart downward.[63] Any such departure must be generally consistent with the structure of the Guidelines.

The background notes to the antitrust Guideline predicted that prison terms for antitrust offenders will become more common, and usually longer, than was the case under pre-Guidelines practice. Although sentences are still not particularly long, this prediction has been verified. From 1984 to 1988, the average sentence for an antitrust felony was 5 months. In the five-year period ending in February 1993, the average sentence was 10 months for offenses under the Sentencing Guidelines (where judges have more limited discretion) and 7.5 months for non-Guideline offenses.[64] During fiscal 2001, the average prison term had increased to nearly 15 months.[65]

In thinking about sentencing issues, consider the following:

a.   Do you agree with the Antitrust Division that prison sentences are uniquely effective in deterring antitrust violators? There is almost no empirical evidence available to support or refute this view.[66] What about "certainty of punishment"?[67] Are the two mutually exclusive? Since price fixing is a crime that involves rational choice, are not both substantial enforcement efforts and meaningful punishments necessary to create viable deterrence?

b.   Sentencing for the purpose of "general deterrence" makes the character of the offense—rather than the offender—the central focus in the sentencing decision. A defendant's background and peculiar characteristics

---

63. *See, e.g.,* Koon v. United States, 518 U.S. 81 (1996).

64. *See* 60 Minutes with Anne K. Bingaman, Assistant Attorney General Antitrust, 63 Antitrust L.J. 323, 329 (1994).

65. *See* Hammond, A Review of Recent Cases and Developments in the Antitrust Division's Criminal Enforcement Program (Conference Board program March 7, 2002).

66. Compare Baker and Reeves, The Paper Label Sentences: Critiques, 86 Yale L.J. 619, 622 (1977) with Wheeler, Critique, 86 Yale L.J. 836 (1977).

67. *See* United States v. Alton Box Co., ATRR No. 805, P.E.–1 (N.D. Ill. 1977).

are given little weight since he or she is not being imprisoned for the purpose of self-improvement. Thus, tailoring sentences to take account of community service, family needs, etc., may actually undermine general deterrence. But what about fairness to the offender and the flexibility that individual tailoring provides? This question is important today because the Sentencing Guidelines allow for "downward departures" for individual defendants who meet specified criteria.[68]

c.   Evaluate the following view of Judge Renfrew:

> Despite the seriousness of antitrust violations, I find a blanket comparison between these crimes and other felonies inappropriate. I believe that crimes of violence are, in general, much more destructive of the fabric of society than are nonviolent commercial crimes.... While the two kinds of crime may have a similar economic impact, and may both instill some apprehension in the public, the psychological effect of violent crime is clearly more pernicious.[69]

Consider the impact on public confidence in the legal system if the perception grows that blue-collar criminals go to jail but white-collar criminals do not.

d.   Are "alternative sentences" (*e.g.*, to provide community service) sufficiently unpleasant or stigmatizing to create general deterrence? What other sanctions (*e.g.*, suspensions or forced resignations of corporate offenders, civil money penalties) might be made available?

e.   There has been no study of the level of recidivism among individuals convicted of price fixing.[70] Is it unreasonable to assume that a corporate officer, who is convicted of price fixing and returns to the job after little punishment, may be tempted to engage in price fixing again?

f.   Although the United States is not the only country in the world to use criminal sanctions for antitrust offenders, this system is more the exception than the rule. Of our two NAFTA partners, Canada also criminalizes certain conduct, and Mexico does not. The European Union relies exclusively on a system of injunctions and administrative fines, some of which can run into the hundreds of millions of dollars. In light of this, do you regard criminal penalties (fines and imprisonment) as (i) necessary, (ii) desirable, (iii) one optional way to achieve deterrence, on a par with others, or (iv) affirmatively undesirable? Why?[71]

7.   INTERFACES BETWEEN GOVERNMENT LITIGATION AND PRIVATE ACTIONS: AFTEREFFECTS AND TOLLING THE STATUTE OF LIMITATIONS

Much private antitrust litigation follows in the wake of victories by the government. Under Section 5(a) of the Clayton Act, a private litigant may

---

68.   18 U.S.C.A. § 3553(b).

69.   Renfrew, The Paper Label Sentences: An Evaluation, 86 Yale L.J. 590, 593 n.8 (1977).

70.   Baker and Reeves, supra at 619 n. 1.

71.   Price fixing and other hard-core antitrust offenses are considered in Chapter 4 infra.

use a judgment or decree in a prior civil or criminal action brought by the government as *"prima facie* evidence against such defendant . . . as to all matters respecting which said judgment or decree would be an estoppel as between the parties thereto." A proviso to this statute, however, excludes "consent judgments or decrees entered before any testimony has been taken."[72]

The exact scope of Section 5(a) has been the subject of some controversy. It clearly permits a private litigant to utilize a final judgment in favor of the government in a prior criminal suit or civil suit for an injunction that proceeded to trial. On the other hand, an action brought by the government under Section 4(a) of the Clayton Act[73] for damages resulting from an antitrust violation may not be used in a subsequent private action. A suit by the government that is terminated by a consent decree before any testimony has been taken is expressly inadmissible in subsequent private litigation. Pleas of *nolo contendere* to criminal indictments, although not specifically mentioned in the statute, also have been deemed unavailable to a private plaintiff. The reasoning is that a *nolo* plea, although an implied confession of guilt upon which criminal penalties can be imposed, is equivalent to a consent decree and is governed by the proviso. There is no doubt that many defendants accept consent decrees or enter *nolo* pleas mainly to avoid the *prima facie* effect risk under Section 5(a).

The courts have not been unanimous in their treatment of guilty pleas. A majority have treated them as *prima facie* evidence under Section 5,[74] but others have rejected that approach on grounds that the overriding purpose of Section 5 was to encourage the quick capitulation of the defendant, and that this policy would be frustrated by permitting subsequent litigants to make use of guilty pleas entered before the taking of testimony.[75]

For many years, FTC orders had been held to be unavailable to private litigants under Section 5(a), but that approach was abandoned by the First Circuit in 1969, when an FTC administrative judgment under the price discrimination provisions of the Robinson–Patman Act was given 5(a) effect.[76] It now appears possible that FTC orders, when based on findings that the Clayton Act or one of the other antitrust laws has been violated, could be given *prima facie* effect.[77]

These "aftereffect" aspects have generated much controversy. Occasionally, the government has succeeded in negotiating special admissions on consent judgments for the benefit of subsequent private litigants.

---

72. 15 U.S.C.A. § 16(a).

73. 15 U.S.C.A. § 15(a).

74. *See* City of Burbank v. General Electric Co., 329 F.2d 825 (9th Cir.1964).

75. *See* Twin Ports Oil Co. v. Pure Oil Co., 26 F.Supp. 366, 374–6 (D.Minn.1939), aff'd, 119 F.2d 747 (8th Cir.), cert. denied, 314 U.S. 644 (1941). On the question of issues as to which a judgment will have *prima facie* effect, see Emich Motors Corp. v. General Motors Corp., 340 U.S. 558 (1951).

76. Farmington Dowel Products Co. v. Forster Manufacturing Co., 421 F.2d 61 (1st Cir.1969). But see Proper v. John Bene & Sons, 295 F. 729 (E.D.N.Y.1923).

77. See Purex Corp. v. Procter & Gamble Co., 453 F.2d 288 (9th Cir.1971), cert. denied, 405 U.S. 1065 (1972); cf. Sullivan & Grimes, The Law of Antitrust: An Integrated Handbook 963 (2000).

Prior to 1955, there was no federal statute of limitations for private antitrust actions. The federal courts simply borrowed state rules. In 1955, the Clayton Act was amended to provide for a four-year statute of limitations in both private and government damage actions.[78] Section 5(i) of the Clayton Act provides that where there is pending a civil or criminal proceeding instituted by the government to enforce the "antitrust laws," any private action based in whole or part on any matter complained of in the proceeding shall not be barred until one year after the conclusion of the government's case. Although Section 5(i) speaks of enforcement of the "antitrust laws," the Supreme Court has held that FTC proceedings trigger the section's tolling provisions.[79]

8. INTERNATIONAL COOPERATION

While the United States had relatively little company in the world of antitrust at the mid-point of the twentieth century, today the field of countries with antitrust laws is quite crowded, with more than 90 participants. As the world is moving steadily toward a more integrated global economy, and the number of countries with competition laws increases, some degree of international cooperation seems to be essential.

Initially, the United States was almost alone in its view that enforcement of its domestic antitrust law to arrangements outside its territory with an effect within the country (so-called extraterritorial enforcement) was an appropriate response to global competition issues. This policy led to a significant number of conflicts with other countries. As time went on, however, more and more countries and regions adopted competition laws, and as they did, they began to accept variants of the effects principle. While on one level this was a philosophical victory for the United States, on a more pragmatic level it created a more urgent need for more effective coordination and cooperation. A task force of the American Bar Association expressed its concern in 2001 about the complexity, costs, and delays of the present system:

> In today's global economy, American companies are affected not only by domestic antitrust enforcement but also by the actions of a growing number of foreign competition agencies and regimes. This proliferation of competition policy throughout the world is highly desirable in concept, but it matters greatly how those policies are defined and enforced.... The burdens of complying with a growing number of antitrust regimes, particularly in the

---

78. 15 U.S.C.A. § 15b. Although the four-year limitations period applies only to damage actions under Section 4 of the Clayton Act, and not to private actions for equitable relief under Section 16 of the Clayton Act, the defense of laches is applicable to Section 16 claims. See ITT Corp. v. GTE Corp., 518 F.2d 913, 926–29 (9th Cir.1975) (equitable defense of laches may be available in an action under Section 16 of the Clayton Act, and the four-year statutory limitations period should be used as a guideline in determining whether the action was brought within a reasonable time).

79. Minnesota Mining and Manufacturing Co. v. New Jersey Wood Finishing Co., 381 U.S. 311, 317–18 (1965).

case of cross-border transactions, are significant and growing; a high priority effort of the U.S. antitrust agencies should be an attempt to find procedural common ground with (at least) the most significant international antitrust regimes.[80]

The earliest and most informal options to accomplish the goal of coordination are commonly known as "soft" measures, while those that would be legally binding on signatories are called "hard" agreements. For the most part, "soft" cooperation has been the chosen form for most countries thus far. This has occurred on two fronts: multilaterally, largely under the auspices of the Organisation for Economic Co-operation and Development (OECD), and bilaterally. The OECD has served as a gathering place for discussion and exchange of expertise about the enforcement of competition laws, and the new International Competition Network promises to accomplish the same goals more broadly. Speaking about the ICN, Chairman Timothy Muris of the FTC reported as follows:

> International Competition Network will provide a venue where senior antitrust officials from developed and developing countries will work to reach consensus on concrete proposals for procedural and substantive convergence in antitrust enforcement. We hope to make international antitrust enforcement more efficient and effective, to the benefit of consumers and companies around the world. The ICN also will assist developing countries in building a competition culture based on sound economic principles. One of the ICN's first topics is merger review in a multi-jurisdictional context, and includes projects focusing on merger notification and procedures, the framework for analyzing mergers, and merger investigation techniques.[81]

Even without the new ICN, bilateral cooperation agreements have grown in number, ambition and importance over the years. Many of the early Friendship, Commerce, and Navigation treaties concluded by the United States contain language committing both treaty partners to prevent anticompetitive and monopolistic practices. In the 1960's, more specific antitrust cooperation agreements began to appear. They offered a framework for conflict management, some general form of cooperation, and regular consultations. (See, for example, the agreements concluded with Germany, Australia and Canada that entered into force in the seventies and eighties.)

In 1991 the United States and the European Community signed an antitrust cooperation agreement that broke new ground. (This agreement was temporarily derailed by the European Court of Justice for technical reasons relating to EU law, but the agreement later was reaffirmed and is effective today.) In that agreement, the two parties undertook a new kind of commitment to one another. This came to be known as "positive

---

80. ABA 2001 Task Force Report at 5.

81. Muris, Prepared Remarks before Brookings Institution Roundtable on Trade and Investment Policy 15 (December 21, 2001).

comity," under which each party promised to consider using its own competition laws to address practices within its territory that were harming the other. If a positive comity request is made and it is legally possible for the requested party to take action, the requesting party no longer has any reason to resort to extraterritorial measures. Similar agreements that commit both parties to the principle of positive comity and cooperation now exist between the United States and Brazil, Canada, Israel, Japan, and Mexico.

Another important breakthrough occurred in 1994, when Congress passed the International Antitrust Enforcement Assistance Act (IAEAA). That statute empowers the U.S. Department of Justice and Federal Trade Commission to enter into binding international agreements that authorize information sharing between the United States and a foreign competition agency, with strict protection of any confidential information that may be exchanged. Joint investigations and prosecutions are also made possible. At present, one such agreement exists, between the United States and Australia. Similar cooperation exists between the United States and Canada with respect to criminal antitrust matters, which fall under the general U.S.-Canadian Mutual Legal Assistance Treaty.

Finally, the U.S. antitrust agencies have been working with foreign antitrust authorities in recent years to facilitate parallel investigations, to conduct operations jointly where legally possible, and to create effective leniency programs (to encourage the reporting of cartel activities). The leniency programs have brought results. From 1987–1990, the Antitrust Division did not bring a single case against foreign-based companies or foreign individuals. By 2001, "nearly 70 percent of the companies charged by the Division . . . were foreign-based firms, and roughly 33 percent of the individual defendants were foreign nationals."[82] The Division prosecuted international cartels affecting more than $10 billion in U.S. commerce from 1997 through 2001. These prosecutions "dwarfed the domestic and regional conspiracies that the Division had traditionally prosecuted over the years."[83]

C.   SPECIAL ISSUES RELATED TO PRIVATE ENFORCEMENT

Private treble damage actions can be big business. For example, as indicated earlier, GE and other companies paid upwards of $350 million, in the early 1960's, to litigate and settle price-fixing cases. Although the Department of Justice stipulated to the dismissal of its monopolization case against IBM in 1982, in 1973 Control Data settled its private monopolization action against IBM for upwards of $100 million (including $15 million to reimburse legal fees and expenses); senior officers of Control Data boasted that the lawsuit had been the best investment the company had

---

82. Hammond, A Review of Recent Cases and Developments in the Antitrust Division's Criminal Enforcement Program 2 (Conference Board program March 7, 2002).

83. Id.

ever made. A number of private monopolization cases against Microsoft are now being litigated. In the early 1980's, private antitrust actions shook the paper industry to its economic foundations; as the result of this series of private actions (through settlements and judgments), over $1 billion changed hands. Similarly, in the 1990's and early 2000's, large litigations and settlements involved actions against pharmaceutical manufacturers, Sotheby's and Christie's auction houses, and an international vitamin cartel.

In general, as Section A supra demonstrates, private antitrust enforcement now dwarfs government enforcement in the number of cases brought, and in many areas, because of treble damage provisions, in economic impact. In older cases, the courts often were reluctant to authorize massive recoveries, partly because of the vague line between legal and illegal conduct in many areas of antitrust. In the last forty years or so, however, a recognition of the importance of the contribution of these "private attorneys general" to an effective national antitrust policy has led the courts to clear many obstacles—procedural, substantive, and related to damages— from the path of private actions. Discussed below are procedural and process issues related to private enforcement that have special antitrust significance.

1.   STANDING, CAUSATION, AND ANTITRUST INJURY

Section 4 of the Clayton Act requires that a private treble damage plaintiff be a "person" (defined in the Act to include corporations and associations) who was "injured in his business or property." The Supreme Court noted in Reiter v. Sonotone Corp., 442 U.S. 330, 337 (1979), that Section 4 "contains little in the way of restrictive language." Nevertheless, numerous lower court decisions have restricted the class of plaintiffs who may claim damages under Section 4. For example, a shareholder may not sue in his own right (as opposed to derivatively for his corporation) for a reduction in the value of his stock.[84] Neither a trade association nor a nonprofit institution may maintain private actions to recover damages allegedly inflicted on members,[85] nor according to most cases, may a landlord sue even though it has leased property under terms which include payment of a percentage of the profits.[86] As previously indicated, a state or municipality can sue for treble damages for injuries to its property, but a

---

84. See Lovett v. General Motors Corp., 975 F.2d 518, 521 (8th Cir.1992); Peter v. Western Newspaper Union, 200 F.2d 867 (5th Cir.1953).

85. See Buckley Towers Condominium, Inc. v. Buchwald, 533 F.2d 934 (5th Cir. 1976), cert. denied, 429 U.S. 1121 (1977); Northern California Monument Dealers Association v. Interment Association, 120 F.Supp. 93 (D.Cal.1954).

86. See Calderone Enterprises Corp. v. United Artists Theatre Circuit, Inc., 454 F.2d 1292 (2d Cir.1971), cert. denied, 406 U.S. 930 (1972); Harrison v. Paramount Pictures, 115 F.Supp. 312 (E.D.Pa.1953), aff'd, 211 F.2d 405 (3d Cir.), cert. denied, 348 U.S. 828 (1954); cf. G.K.A. Beverage Corp. v. Honickman, 55 F.3d 762 (2d Cir.), cert. denied, 516 U.S. 944 (1995). But see Congress Building Corp. v. Loew's, Inc., 246 F.2d 587 (7th Cir. 1957).

state may not sue in a *parens patriae* capacity on behalf of its citizens to recover for general damages to the state's economy.[87]

The theory underlying standing cases has often been stated elliptically and without analytical precision. Many of the cases cannot be reconciled. The language of standing cases—*e.g.*, was the injury "direct" or "indirect," was plaintiff within the "target area" of the offense—often obscures underlying policy issues. In general, what courts should be doing in this area is analyzing the purposes of the antitrust laws and the probable costs and benefits to the antitrust system of allowing a particular plaintiff to vindicate its claim to protection against antitrust injuries. At issue will be a series of discrete policy questions such as: Are the injuries to this particular plaintiff too speculative or remote to make it an appropriate antitrust enforcer? Is the injury of a type with which the antitrust laws should be concerned? Is there an excessive risk of duplicative recovery? Would affording standing create unmanageable complexity, and on balance, discourage vigorous private enforcement? A precise analysis of the answers to these questions is what is desirable. In recent years, the Supreme Court has moved in this direction.

Blue Shield of Virginia v. McCready, 457 U.S. 465 (1982), in which the justices split 5–4, illustrates the Supreme Court's approach and the difficult policy issues that lie at the heart of standing cases. Careful note should be taken of the Court's sympathetic attitude towards private enforcement and of its analytical framework for resolving standing issues. McCready's antitrust complaint alleged that Blue Shield's practice of refusing to reimburse subscribers for psychotherapy performed by *psychologists,* while providing reimbursement for comparable treatment by *psychiatrists,* was in furtherance of an unlawful conspiracy to restrain competition in the psychotherapy market. The question presented was "whether a subscriber who employed the services of a psychologist has standing to maintain an action under § 4 of the Clayton Act based upon the plan's failure to provide reimbursement for the costs of that treatment." The Supreme Court held that McCready had standing. Justice Brennan, writing for the majority, emphasized the "broad remedial and deterrent objectives" of Section 4 of the Clayton Act. Nevertheless, he "acknowledged two types of limitation on the availability of the § 4 remedy."

For the first type of limitation Justice Brennan cited Hawaii v. Standard Oil Co., 405 U.S. 251 (1972) (discussed supra), and Illinois Brick Co. v. Illinois, 431 U.S. 720 (1977) (discussed infra), and explained these cases as "focused on the risk of duplicative recovery" not present in the *McCready* case. Id. at 474. The Court noted that a subordinate theme in the *Hawaii* and *Illinois Brick* cases involved a concern about "burdening § 4 actions with damages issues giving rise to the need for 'massive evidence and complicated theories,' where the consequence would be to discourage vigorous enforcement." The Court concluded, however, that "our cautious

---

87. Hawaii v. Standard Oil Co., 405 U.S. 251 (1972).

approach to speculative, abstract, or impractical damages theories has no application to McCready's suit." Id. at 475 n.11.

The second type of limitation related to the "conceptually more difficult question 'of which persons have sustained injuries *too remote* . . . to give them standing to sue.' " As to this issue, the Court reasoned:

> An antitrust violation may be expected to cause ripples of harm to flow through the Nation's economy; but "despite the broad wording of § 4 there is a point beyond which the wrongdoer should not be held liable." . . . It is reasonable to assume that Congress did not intend to allow every person tangentially affected by an antitrust violation to maintain an action to recover threefold damages for the injury to his business or property. Of course, neither the statutory language nor the legislative history of § 4 offers any focused guidance on the question of which injuries are too remote from the violation and the purposes of the antitrust laws to form the predicate for a suit under § 4; indeed, the unrestrictive language of the section, and the avowed breadth of the congressional purpose, cautions us not to cabin § 4 in ways that will defeat its broad remedial objective. But the potency of the remedy implies the need for some care in its application. In the absence of direct guidance from Congress, and faced with the claim that a particular injury is too remote from the alleged violation to warrant § 4 standing, the courts are thus forced to resort to an analysis no less elusive than that employed traditionally by courts at common law with respect to the matter of "proximate cause." . . . In applying that elusive concept to this statutory action, we look (1) to the physical and economic nexus between the alleged violation and the harm to the plaintiff, and, (2) more particularly, to the relationship of the injury alleged with those forms of injury about which Congress was likely to have been concerned in making defendant's conduct unlawful and in providing a private remedy under § 4. Id. at 476–78.

In answer to item (1), the "physical and economic nexus," the Court concluded:

> We do not think that because the goal of the conspirators was to halt encroachment by psychologists into a market that physicians and psychiatrists sought to preserve for themselves, McCready's injury is rendered "remote." The availability of the § 4 remedy to some person who claims its benefit is not a question of the specific intent of the conspirators. Here the remedy cannot reasonably be restricted to those competitors whom the conspirators hoped to eliminate from the market. McCready claims that she has been the victim of a concerted refusal to pay on the part of Blue Shield, motivated by a desire to deprive psychologists of the patronage of Blue Shield subscribers. Denying reimbursement to subscribers for the cost of treatment was the very means by which it is alleged that Blue Shield sought to achieve its illegal ends. The

harm to McCready and her class was clearly foreseeable; indeed, it was a necessary step in effecting the ends of the illegal conspiracy. Id. at 478–79.

In answer to item (2), the "relationship of the injury" to Congress' antitrust concern, the Court concluded:

> Relying on ... [language in Brunswick Corp. v. Pueblo Bowl–O–Mat, Inc., 429 U.S. 477, 489 (1977), as to the need to "prove antitrust injury"], petitioners reason that McCready can maintain no action under § 4 because her injury "did not reflect the anticompetitive effect" of the alleged violation.
>
> *Brunswick* is not so limiting. Indeed, as we made clear in a footnote to the relied-upon passage, a § 4 plaintiff need not "prove an actual lessening of competition in order to recover. ...[C]ompetitors may be able to prove antitrust injury before they actually are driven from the market and competition is thereby lessened." ... Thus while an increase in price resulting from a dampening of competitive market forces is assuredly one type of injury for which § 4 potentially offers redress, see Reiter v. Sonotone, supra, that is not the only form of injury remediable under § 4. We think it plain that McCready's injury was of a type that Congress sought to redress in providing a private remedy for violations of the antitrust laws.
>
> ... [W]e think that McCready's injury "flows from that which makes defendants' acts unlawful" within the meaning of *Brunswick,* and falls within the area of congressional concern. Id. at 482–84.

Two dissenting opinions found no " 'antitrust injury' within the meaning of *Brunswick*"(Justices Burger, Rehnquist, and O'Connor) and no injury to plaintiff's "property by reason of the alleged antitrust violation" (Justice Stevens).

The "causality" and "antitrust injury"[88] cases referred to in the *McCready* opinions also use "direct-indirect" and "target area" terminology. These cases appear to have the same conceptual and policy underpinnings as do the standing cases.

In Associated General Contractors v. California State Council of Carpenters, 459 U.S. 519, 537–46 (1983), the Supreme Court decided that the plaintiff union was not a proper party to bring a private antitrust action. The Court focused principally on whether the harm to plaintiff was: (i) the sort that the Sherman Act was designed to protect; (ii) direct or indirect; (iii) intended; (iv) speculative; (v) likely to lead to duplicative recoveries, difficulties of apportionment, or burdensome complex trials; and (vi) likely

---

88. For a discussion of "antitrust injury" in the merger context, see p. 1024 infra. See Atlantic Richfield Co. v. USA Petroleum Co., 495 U.S. 328 (1990) ("Although a vertical maximum price-fixing agreement ... [was then (but not now, see Chapter 7 infra) *per se*] unlawful under § 1 of the Sherman Act, it does not cause a competitor injury unless it results in predatory pricing").

to be vindicated by more direct victims of the alleged wrongful acts or whether harm was likely to go undetected or unremedied. Cf. Cargill, Inc. v. Monfort of Colorado, Inc., 479 U.S. 104 (1986).

Circuit court opinions, reaching opposite or varying conclusions, illustrate both the interplay among the "standing," "causation," and "antitrust injury" concepts, and the difficult policy judgments that must be made. In Ostrofe v. H.S. Crocker Co., Inc., 670 F.2d 1378, 1382 (9th Cir.1982) (*Ostrofe I*), the Ninth Circuit ruled that an employee who was forced to resign because he refused to participate in an alleged price-fixing and market-allocation scheme by his employer, and others, had standing to bring a treble damage action against his employer.

The Supreme Court vacated the Ninth Circuit's judgment in *Ostrofe I*[89] and directed that on remand the lower court review its decision in light of the Supreme Court's *Associated General Contractors* case, supra. In *Ostrofe II*, the Ninth Circuit reaffirmed plaintiff's standing and focused on the fact that he was an "essential participant" in the price-fixing scheme, which "could not succeed without his active cooperation"; moreover, no one had as strong an interest as the discharged employee in vindicating the public interest in effective antitrust enforcement. 740 F.2d 739, 745–47 (9th Cir.1984), cert. dismissed, 469 U.S. 1200 (1985). Recently, the Ninth Circuit dismissed a terminated employee's claim because the "loss of a job is not the type of injury that the antitrust laws were designed to prevent." *Ostrofe II* was distinguished as involving a limited exception for an "essential participant" whose dismissal was a "necessary means" to accomplish the anticompetitive scheme.[90]

Other circuit courts have rejected *Ostrofe I and II*. The Seventh Circuit, for example, in Bichan v. Chemetron Corp., 681 F.2d 514, 519 (7th Cir.1982), concluded that plaintiff had not established "antitrust injury" since he was "not the target of the alleged anticompetitive practices:"

> [A] determination of antitrust standing should focus not only on whether there has been an "antitrust injury," but also on whether the particular plaintiff is the appropriate antitrust enforcer. Thus, the conflicting interests of deterrence through private antitrust enforcement and redress for injury must be balanced against the avoidance of excessive treble damages litigation. An appropriate balance is achieved by granting standing only to those who, as consumers or competitors, suffer immediate injuries with respect to their business or property, while excluding persons whose injuries were more indirectly caused by the antitrust conduct.[91]

---

89. 460 U.S. 1007 (1983).

90. Vinci v. Waste Management Inc., 80 F.3d 1372 (9th Cir.1996).

91. *See, e.g.,* Adams v. Pan American World Airways, Inc., 828 F.2d 24 (D.C.Cir. 1987) (employees of defunct airline denied standing); Gregory Marketing Corp. v. Wakefern Food Corp., 787 F.2d 92 (3d Cir.), cert. denied, 479 U.S. 821 (1986). But see Ashmore v. Northeast Petroleum, 843 F.Supp. 759, 767 n. 15 (D.Me.1994) ("providing standing to employees who are coerced to violate the

In thinking about these employee cases, consider the following: Was not the deterrence of anticompetitive acts a fundamental Congressional concern? Who is in a better position than an employee to prevent—or alleviate *early* the consequences of—unlawful acts? How much danger is there here of duplicative recovery or of any of the other concerns articulated in the Supreme Court's *McCready* and *Associated General Contractors* opinions? There is, of course, real danger of increased litigation (true or untrue allegations of this type may be made by disgruntled present or former employees), and treble damage exposure could lead to unwarranted settlements. How would you draw the policy balance? Is the Ninth Circuit on the right track in concluding that all employees or agents need not be treated alike?

The *Illinois Brick* case,[92] discussed in the *McCready* opinion supra, is of large practical importance. *Illinois Brick,* at least as the Supreme Court majority saw it, built upon Hanover Shoe, Inc. v. United Shoe Machinery Corp., 392 U.S. 481 (1968), where a plaintiff's claim that it paid illegally high prices could not be defeated by proof that it recaptured part or all of the extra cost by charging higher prices to its customers, *i.e.,* by "passing-on" the higher prices. In reaching its result in *Hanover Shoe,* the Court took into account that it would be unlikely that large numbers of ultimate consumers would have the economic interest to sue for the relatively small damages each might have suffered.

In *Illinois Brick,* Justice White, writing for the majority, held that pass-on theory could not be used offensively by an indirect purchasing plaintiff (*i.e.,* further down the distribution line) against price-fixing manufacturers. Illinois Brick had sold concrete block to masonry contractors who were employed as subcontractors by general contractors working on construction projects for the plaintiffs, local government entities. The Court saw the plaintiffs' action as an *offensive* use of the passing-on theory rejected as a defense in *Hanover Shoe.*

In rejecting the offensive use of pass-on theory, the Court concluded that whatever rule was applied, it should be applied equally to both defendants and plaintiffs since concerns about "evidentiary complexities and uncertainties" were similar in each instance. The Court feared that the offensive use of pass-on theory might create the possibility of multiple recoveries against a single defendant. Justice White stated:

> Permitting the use of pass-on theories under § 4 essentially would transform treble-damage actions into massive efforts to apportion the recovery among all potential plaintiffs ... [and] would add whole new dimensions of complexity to treble-damage suits and seriously undermine their effectiveness.[93]

The Court also indicated its hesitancy to involve the judiciary in measuring market elasticities and pricing policies (*i.e.,* to measure how much, if any, of

---

antitrust laws is more likely to provide efficient enforcement").

92. 431 U.S. 720 (1977).

93. 431 U.S. at 737.

price increases were passed on), and repeated the concerns expressed in *Hanover Shoe* about a plaintiff's reduced incentive to sue since apportionment would diminish each plaintiff's recovery. The Court concluded that plaintiffs had not sustained legally cognizable "antitrust injury" under Section 4.

Justice Brennan dissented in *Illinois Brick* and argued that the "broad objectives" of Section 4, to "compensate victims of antitrust violations and to deter future violations," were sufficient to allow the plaintiff and defendant to be treated differently:

> [T]he same policies [outlined in *Hanover Shoe*] of insuring the continued effectiveness of the treble-damages action and preventing wrongdoers from retaining the spoils of their misdeeds favor allowing indirect purchasers to prove that overcharges were passed on to them.[94]

Justice Brennan was unconvinced that the complexities of the offensive use of pass-on theory were any different from issues regularly decided in antitrust cases, and was convinced that "existing procedural mechanisms" could largely eliminate the danger of multiple recoveries. He was particularly concerned that "direct purchasers, acting as middlemen, and ordinarily reluctant to sue their suppliers, [would] pass on the bulk of their increased cost to consumers farther along the chain of distribution."

In *Illinois Brick* the majority indicated two possible special circumstances in which an indirect purchaser might be permitted to recover: first, where a "pre-existing cost-plus contract" existed, and second, "where the direct purchaser is owned or controlled by its customer." The first possibility was narrowly construed in Kansas v. UtiliCorp United, Inc., 497 U.S. 199 (1990), where states (asserting *parens patriae* claims under the Hart–Scott–Rodino Act[95]) argued that public utilities (direct buyers) had passed on 100% of inflated prices to their customers.

In a 5–4 decision, the Supreme Court held that no exception to the *Hanover Shoe/Illinois Brick* rulings would be made. Continuing the focus on judicial resources and evidentiary complexities, Justice Kennedy, writing for the majority, was not convinced that proof of the passage of 100% of the overcharge on to utility customers was easily ascertainable under a system of regulated rates:

> [S]tate regulation does not simplify the problem but instead imports an additional level of complexity.... [A] court would have to consider not only the extent to which market conditions would have allowed the utility to raise its rates prior to the overcharge, as in the case of an unregulated business, but also what the state regulators would have allowed.... Proof ... would turn upon the intricacies of state laws.... To the extent that the [utility] could have sought and gained permission to raise its rates in the absence

94. 431 U.S. at 753.   **95.** See discussion p. 80 supra.

of an overcharge, at least some portion of the overcharge is being borne by it.[96]

Justice Kennedy went on to reject the contention that the situation of a regulated utility was identical to the exception for cost-plus contracts:

> [W]e might allow indirect purchasers to sue only when, by hypothesis, the direct purchaser will bear no portion of the overcharge and otherwise suffer no injury. That certainty does not exist here.... [T]he need to inquire into the precise operation of market forces [in the context of a public utility's market] would negate the simplicity and certainty that could justify a cost-plus contract exception.[97]

The Court also concluded that the Hart–Scott–Rodino Act did not create any new substantive liabilities when it provided for *parens patriae* claims. Claims by state attorneys general may only be brought on behalf of customers who themselves have incurred a Section 4 injury.

Justice White, the author of the majority opinions in *Hanover Shoe* and *Illinois Brick,* dissented on the basis that the difficulties relied upon by the majority were "speculative" and that state regulation made this a case "in which it would be easy to prove the extent to which the overcharge was passed on."[98]

Although the Supreme Court has refused to allow pass-on theory to be used offensively or defensively in federal antitrust cases, California v. ARC America Corp., 490 U.S. 93 (1989), presented the Court with the question of whether state antitrust laws were similarly limited. Justice White, writing for a unanimous Court, held that the federal policies outlined in *Hanover Shoe* and *Illinois Brick* for federal antitrust laws did not preempt the states from allowing indirect purchasers to recover under state antitrust laws. The Court found that "Congress intended the federal antitrust laws to supplement, not displace, state antitrust remedies."[99] In the early 2000's, more than half the states allowed indirect purchasers to sue for antitrust violations under state law.[1]

2. CLASS ACTIONS

Antitrust violations frequently cause relatively modest damages to a large number of victims. For example, price fixing on consumer products may raise the price of a commodity only a few cents on each purchase, and only a few dollars per year for individual consumers. In those circumstances, no individual plaintiff ordinarily suffers sufficient damages to justify the expense and inconvenience of private litigation, even where

---

96. 497 U.S. at 209–10.

97. 497 U.S. at 218.

98. 497 U.S. at 220.

99. 409 U.S. at 102.

1. For recent lower court cases dealing with still complex and difficult *Illinois Brick* issues in special circumstances under the fed-

eral antitrust laws, *see, e.g.*, Blue Cross & Blue Shield United of Wisc. v. Marshfield Clinic, 65 F.3d 1406 (7th Cir.1995); Three Crown Limited Partnership v. Salomon Bros., 1995 WL 422467, 1995–2 Trade Cases ¶ 71,-076 (S.D.N.Y.1995).

damages may be trebled and attorney's fees and costs returned to the victorious plaintiff.[2]

Under Rule 23(a) of the Federal Rules, plaintiffs may aggregate their claims in a "class action" if (1) the class is so numerous that joinder of all members is impractical, (2) there are common questions of law or fact, (3) claims or defenses of the representative parties are typical, and (4) the representative parties will fairly and adequately protect the interests of the class. In addition, those seeking to maintain class actions must satisfy one of the provisions of 23(b), the most important of which is subsection (3), which requires that common questions of law and fact predominate and that a class action is superior to other available methods of adjudication. All sorts of complicated questions of "manageability" arise under that provision, including requirements of notice to the class, possible opting out of those who do not want to participate in the class action but would rather enforce individual rights, computation of damages, and distribution of any eventual recovery. Class actions in antitrust have increased dramatically in recent years along with complex procedural disputes as to their enforcement and management.

3.   POSSIBLE DISQUALIFICATION—UNCLEAN HANDS

Under the doctrines of *in pari delicto* and unclean hands, the courts for many years dismissed private antitrust actions where the plaintiff could be shown either to have participated in the challenged antitrust practice or to have been engaged in some other violation of the antitrust laws. These related doctrines were narrowed, and perhaps almost eliminated, by the Supreme Court in Perma Life Mufflers, Inc. v. International Parts Corp.— at least where the plaintiff did not "aggressively support and further the monopolistic scheme."[3] Justice Black reasoned that while a "plaintiff who reaps the reward of treble damages may be no less morally reprehensible than the defendant," the purposes of the antitrust statutes are best served by insuring that the private action will be an ever-present threat to deter anyone contemplating anticompetitive behavior. The Court did not reach the question whether "truly complete involvement" could be a basis for barring a plaintiff's cause of action. The Court was probably influenced in *Perma Life* by the fact that plaintiff was a franchisee—much smaller in terms of assets and market power than defendant—and may have been coerced into accepting otherwise undesirable contractual provisions. Where the plaintiff has the capacity to resist a proffered anticompetitive arrangement but does not do so, the result might be different.[4]

2.   Antitrust plaintiffs may sue under 28 U.S.C.A. § 1337 and 15 U.S.C.A. § 15.

3.   392 U.S. 134 (1968); *see, e.g.,* Sullivan v. NFL, 34 F.3d 1091 (1st Cir.1994); Southwest Marine, Inc. v. Campbell Indus., 732 F.2d 744 (9th Cir.), cert. denied, 469 U.S. 1072 (1984); Memorex Corp. v. IBM Corp., 555 F.2d 1379 (9th Cir.1977).

4.   For the distinction between *in pari delicto* and the equitable doctrine of unclean hands, and an attempt to reconcile the cases in this area, see Handler & Sacks, The Continued Vitality of In Pari Delicto as an Antitrust Defense, 70 Geo.L.J. 1123 (1982).

A related situation arises where a defendant resists a non-antitrust action—for example, an effort to collect monies due on a contract—on grounds that the cause of action was tainted with antitrust illegality. For example, in Kelly v. Kosuga,[5] the Court would not prevent collection of the purchase price for onions where the alleged antitrust agreement was independent of the particular purchase-sale transaction. The courts have made clear that they will recognize a defense based on antitrust in those circumstances where failure to do so would in effect make the court a party to implementing the unlawful restraint.

4. DAMAGES AND EQUITABLE RELIEF

Enormous time and effort in private antitrust litigation is devoted to proof of the fact and amount of damages. Bigelow v. RKO Radio Pictures, Inc.[6] is a landmark case and generally adopted a liberal posture toward plaintiffs' claims. Plaintiffs, owners of a motion picture theater, had alleged that the defendants had discriminated against them in distribution of motion pictures pursuant to a conspiracy, and as a result profits were reduced. To support the damage claim, plaintiffs introduced evidence comparing their profits with those of a competing theater, and also comparing profits during the period of the alleged conspiracy with corresponding receipts for the years immediately preceding. Noting that defendant "by his own wrong has prevented a more precise computation," the Supreme Court affirmed a jury verdict based on those two categories of evidence. "Any other rule would enable the wrongdoer to profit by his wrongdoing at the expense of his victim. It would be an inducement to make wrongdoing so effective and complete in every case as to preclude any recovery, by rendering the measure of damages uncertain."[7]

Today, questions related to damages generally arise after threshold issues are resolved concerning standing, causation, and antitrust injury.[8] Once these hurdles have been cleared, *Bigelow* remains good law, and proof of the actual amount of damage is treated liberally and realistically.

Particularly difficult damage questions arise where the plaintiff is a party who claims he was prevented from starting a business by the anticompetitive activities of the defendant,[9] since the plaintiff has had no actual experience in the market to use as a basis for assessing what profits might have been earned absent the challenged conduct. The Supreme Court has said the following on the topic of future profits:

> [E]ach separate action that so accrues entitles a plaintiff to recover not only those damages which he has suffered at the date of accrual, but also those which he will suffer in the future from

---

5. 358 U.S. 516 (1959).
6. 327 U.S. 251 (1946).
7. 327 U.S. at 264.
8. See p. 99 supra.
9. *See, e.g.*, Dominicus Americana Bohio v. Gulf & Western Industries, Inc., 473 F.Supp. 680 (S.D.N.Y.1979); William Goldman Theatres, Inc. v. Loew's, Inc., 69 F.Supp. 103 (E.D.Pa.1946), aff'd per curiam, 164 F.2d 1021 (3d Cir.), cert. denied, 334 U.S. 811 (1948).

particular invasion.... On the other hand, it is hornbook law, in antitrust actions as in others, that even if injury and a cause of action have accrued as of a certain date, future damages that might arise from the conduct sued on are unrecoverable if the fact of their accrual is speculative or their amount and nature unprovable.[10]

In general, however, if the jury is presented with evidence somewhat beyond pure guesswork, a damage award is likely to be sustained.

Since 1914, Section 16 of the Clayton Act has permitted private plaintiffs to obtain injunctive relief. As in damage actions, plaintiffs asking for injunctive relief must allege "threatened loss or damage 'of the type the antitrust laws were designed to prevent and that flows from that which makes defendant's acts unlawful.' "[11] The Supreme Court has observed: "Section 16 should be construed and applied ... with the knowledge that the remedy it affords, like other equitable remedies, is flexible and capable of nice 'adjustments and reconciliation between the public interest and private needs....' "[12] In general, the courts have exercised their injunctive powers flexibly and appear to grant injunctive relief more readily to the government than to private plaintiffs. The issue of the availability of divestiture as a remedy in private actions and actions by state attorneys general under Section 7 of the Clayton Act (*i.e.*, where a merger or an acquisition is involved), which the Supreme Court has recently resolved in favor of such relief, is discussed in Chapter 9 infra.

5. THE TREBLE DAMAGE BONANZA, REASONABLE ATTORNEY'S FEES, AND PROPOSED PROCEDURAL REFORMS

In American Society of Mechanical Engineers, Inc. v. Hydrolevel Corp., 456 U.S. 556, 574 (1982), the Supreme Court said the following about treble damages:

> It is true that antitrust treble damages were designed in part to punish past violations of the antitrust laws.... But treble damages were also designed to deter future antitrust violations. Moreover, the antitrust private action was created primarily as a remedy for the victims of antitrust violations.... Treble damages "make the remedy meaningful by counter-balancing 'the difficulty of maintaining a private suit' " under the antitrust laws. *Brunswick Corp.*, supra, at 486, n. 10, quoting 21 Cong.Rec. 2456 (1890) (remarks of Sen. Sherman).

While private treble damage actions undoubtedly have an important role to play in overall antitrust enforcement, they still have some questionable aspects. Some antitrust rules are vague, and a single misstep by a company can subject it to liability of disastrous proportions.

10. Zenith Radio Corp. v. Hazeltine Research Inc., 401 U.S. 321, 338–39 (1971).

11. Cargill, Inc. v. Monfort of Colorado, Inc., 479 U.S. 104, 113 (1986).

12. Zenith Radio Corp. v. Hazeltine Research, Inc., 395 U.S. 100, 131 (1969).

During the past twenty-five years there has been considerable controversy about antitrust remedies in general and the so-called "treble damage bonanza" in particular. It was claimed that many private lawsuits:

> were of little merit and were instigated in the hopes of generous settlements and generous attorneys' fee awards. Further many critics claimed that the fear of private treble damage actions deterred companies from taking risks in areas near the uncertain line defining legal behavior, for fear of becoming the targets of enormous private actions. As a result innovative manufacturing, organizational, and distributional techniques were not adopted.[13]

Responding in part to such claims, three times during the 1980's Congress adjusted antitrust damage rules for specific types of cases. The Export Trading Company Act of 1982[14] and the National Cooperative Research Act of 1984[15] basically limited specific types of claims to actual damages. The Local Government Antitrust Act of 1984,[16] in certain circumstances entirely eliminated antitrust damage recoveries. Numerous general legislative proposals to "detreble" antitrust damages were made.[17]

A broad consensus developed around the proposition that while there was "no lack of debate" on treble damage policy issues and on antitrust remedies generally, "there was a striking absence of hard empirical data about the cost and benefits of the present system."[18] After extensive empirical study, however, a Georgetown private treble damage project provided no definitive policy guidance. The "policy session," at the end of a conference in 1985, was summarized as follows:

> In the policy session ... several participants expounded the view that the private treble damage system is not out of control. Private antitrust litigation generally does not appear to be excessively expensive, to consume a large amount of judicial resources, or to result in inappropriate recoveries. They argued that any significant reform proposals would damage a system that is fair and useful, particularly during periods when government antitrust enforcement is lax and pro-business. But other participants in the policy session thought that the present system unduly encourages frivolous suits and deters efficient behavior, and they suggested a variety of ways to reform private enforcement.[19]

13. Pitofsky & Salop, Foreword, in White (ed.), Private Antitrust Litigation xi (1988).

14. Pub.L. No. 97–290, 96 Stat. 1233 (1982).

15. Pub.L. No. 98–462, 98 Stat. 1815 (1984).

16. Pub.L. No. 98–544, 98 Stat. 2750 (1984); see discussion p. 470 infra.

17. For a comprehensive review of these proposals, see Cavanagh, Detrebling Antitrust Damages: An Idea Whose Time Has Come?, 61 Tul.L.Rev. 777 (1987).

18. Pitofsky & Salop, Foreword, in White (ed.), Private Antitrust Litigation xi (1988).

19. Id. at xiii. See Lande, Are Antitrust "Treble" Damages Really Single Damages?, 54 Ohio St.L.J. 1151 (1993).

The data produced by the Georgetown study did not provide clear answers to basic questions such as: Do mandatory treble damages create excessive deterrence? Are a significant number of weak cases brought, containing large damage claims, which lead to unwarranted, large settlements? How do the considerable advantages of the deterrence associated with treble damages balance against perceived failings in the system? There is, however, substantial evidence that judges are increasingly using summary disposition motions to weed out meritless cases before unwarranted settlements are made.[20] This evidence is examined more fully at pp. 518–20 infra.

The debate on treble damages and other remedial issues will clearly continue through the early 2000's. One ameliorating technique with respect to treble damages would be to eliminate mandatory trebling of damages and confer authority on trial courts to award single, double, or triple damages depending on the circumstances of the antitrust violation.[21]

Another approach would be to eliminate mandatory trebling (and permit judicial discretion to award single, double, or triple damages)—in non-*per se* cases—when a defendant can show that it "reasonably believed" that a given act or transaction would not violate the antitrust laws.[22] This second approach would encourage antitrust counseling (in order to be in a position to establish a "reasonable belief") and promote self-policing compliance programs.

Congress' decision to supplement treble-damage recovery with the award of reasonable attorney's fees also provides litigation incentives to potential plaintiffs. The Second Circuit, for example, held that the plaintiffs, including the United States Football League, who were awarded only $3 in treble damages, should be awarded $5.5 million in attorney's fees and $62,221 in costs.[23] The Second Circuit reasoned:

> In the instant case, the jury found that the NFL's monopolization of the United States major league professional football market injured the USFL. An injury having been found, the awarding of attorney's fees to the USFL was compulsory. . . . That the USFL only received nominal damages is relevant in determining the amount of fees allowed and may be a factor used in reducing a fee award, but it does not affect the entitlement to an award. See Home Placement Serv., 819 F.2d at 1210.

20. See Calkins, Equilibrating Tendencies in the Antitrust System, With Special Attention to Summary Judgment and to Motions to Dismiss, in White (ed.), Private Antitrust Litigation 185–239 (1988).

21. See Cavanagh, Detrebling Antitrust Damages: An Idea Whose Time Has Come?, 61 Tul.L.Rev. 777 (1987).

22. Goldschmid, Comment on the Policy Implications of the Georgetown Study, in White (ed.), Private Antitrust Litigation 412–15 (1988).

23. United States Football League v. National Football League, 887 F.2d 408 (2d Cir.1989), cert. denied, 493 U.S. 1071 (1990); Gulfstream III Associates, Inc. v. Gulfstream Aerospace Corp., 995 F.2d 414 (3d Cir.1993); see generally Cavanagh, Attorneys' Fees in Antitrust Litigation: Making the System Fairer, 57 Fordham L.Rev. 51 (1988).

As the First Circuit has stated, the purpose behind mandatory attorney's fees in antitrust cases is "to encourage private prosecution of antitrust violations by insulating plaintiff's treble damage recoveries from the expense of legal fees." Id. What is important is encouraging the detection and cessation of anticompetitive behavior, not the amount of damages found. Because of the importance of the policy of encouraging private parties to bring antitrust actions, recovery of their reasonable attorney's fees must be sustained regardless of the amount of damages awarded.... [T]here is no requirement in section 4 of the Clayton Act that an antitrust plaintiff be a "prevailing party" to recover attorney's fees. The term "prevailing party" appears nowhere in section 4 of the Clayton Act. All that is required is an injury. As stated supra, an injury was found, therefore the award of attorney's fees was automatic.[24]

6.　CONTRIBUTION AND CLAIM REDUCTION

In Texas Industries, Inc. v. Radcliff Materials, Inc., 451 U.S. 630 (1981), the Supreme Court held that defendant, against whom damages had been assessed, had no right of contribution from other participants in an unlawful conspiracy under the federal antitrust laws. Since liability for antitrust damage is joint and several, the absence of contribution means that when, for example, a plaintiff releases a defendant in a price-fixing case from liability for damages in a settlement, only the actual amount paid for the release is deducted from the plaintiff's claim against the remaining defendants. Thus, if a plaintiff enters into a settlement with a defendant for an amount that is less than the share of the injury caused by the settling defendant, responsibility for the difference is shifted to the remaining defendants.

The term "whipsaw" settlement has come to be applied to settlements that build a plaintiff's "war chest" for litigation and raise the perceived liability of nonsettling defendants to the point where they may be forced to abandon meritorious defenses and settle out of fear of facing ruinous liability should they litigate and lose. Since about 1979, Congress has been struggling with the question of whether it should legislatively provide for a right of contribution or a right to claim reduction.

In 1987, the arguments for and against contribution were effectively summarized in a Senate report as follows:

The ultimate result of this restructuring of the defendants relationship to their liability will assure that: (1) every defendant pays an equitable share of the liability; (2) no defendant will be able to get out of the suit so cheaply as to weaken deterrence; and (3) those defendants who wish to defend the suit will not be left with a disproportionately large part of the liability and will be able to

---

24. The district court had reduced the request for attorney's fees from about $7.7 million to $5.5 million in light of the nominal damage award and this conclusion was sustained by the Second Circuit.

put their claim of innocence to the test of the trial.... [T]he counter arguments ... are that [the contribution bill:] (1) will dilute deterrence, (2) will deter settlements, and (3) will unfairly burden the plaintiff's case (and the courts) with unnecessary complexities.[25]

How can it be that both the proponents and opponents of contribution legislation cite improved deterrence as a reason for their positions? If there is no right of contribution, might not some defendants settle early at relatively modest expense, and by helping to finance the plaintiff's lawsuit, also enhance deterrence? Is this fair? Contribution is permitted in the admiralty area, and the Supreme Court there had the following to say about the argument that a contribution right would deter settlement:

> [A]t bottom, [this argument] asks us to continue the operation of an archaic rule because its facile application out of court yields quick, though inequitable, settlements, and relieves the court of some litigation. Congestion in the courts cannot justify a legal rule that produces unjust results in litigation simply to encourage speedy out-of-court accommodations.[26]

After almost a decade of hearings, Congress flirted with passing claim reduction legislation for price-fixing cases in the late 1980's. Claim reduction differs from contribution in that it requires automatic deduction from a plaintiff's remaining claim for the share of damages attributable to the acts of any person released by the plaintiff from liability. Contribution permits liable defendants who have paid more than their share of a plaintiff's damages to sue other liable defendants who have not. Claim reduction would, of course, alleviate "whipsaw" pressures, but would potentially reduce recoveries and, to a degree, deterrence. The difficulty of calculating how much of the loss of a class of plaintiffs is attributable to the acts of a given defendant has led some to question the wisdom of either contribution or claim reduction legislation and others to suggest that any legislation should deal only with horizontal price fixing.[27] Some defendants have created claim reduction agreements among themselves.[28]

D.   SPECIAL ISSUES RELATED TO THE "BIG CASE"

In approaching antitrust policy questions, it is essential to have some appreciation of the size, duration, and complexity of antitrust litigation. In both government and private actions, it is not uncommon for discovery, trial, and appeal to take ten or more years and to involve a vast number of documents. Scores of attorneys often represent the parties to an antitrust

---

25. Senate Comm. on the Judiciary, Antitrust Equal Enforcement Act of 1979, S.Rep. No. 96–428, 96th Cong., 1st Sess. (1979).

26. United States v. Reliable Transfer Co., 421 U.S. 397, 408 (1975).

27. For a comprehensive review of this area, see Cavanagh, Contribution, Claim Re-

duction and Individual Treble Damage Responsibility: Which Path to Reform of Antitrust Remedies?, 40 Vand.L.Rev. 1277 (1987).

28. Kenny & Bassett, Private Enforcement of the Antitrust Laws, in Scher (ed.), Antitrust Adviser ch. 10 (4th ed.1995).

litigation. This "big case" problem has always been part of the antitrust scene. In 1953, in the *United Shoe Machinery* case,[29] for example, the government offered 4,600 exhibits at one time; the *Alcoa* case[30] (p. 130 infra) involved 15,000 pages of record.

Although there were relatively few large government cases brought during the past thirty years, the combined experience of the 1970's through the early 2000's indicates that the "big case" in antitrust has grown even bigger and more unmanageable. The most "horrible" recent example is the government's monopolization case against IBM. After several years of investigation, the case was filed in 1969. In January 1982, the government stipulated to the dismissal of the case. During the intervening 13 years (including about 6 years of trial) more than 66 million pages of documents were produced; the government's trial presentation took 104,000 pages of transcript; IBM called 856 witnesses and cited 12,280 exhibits. IBM is conservatively estimated to have spent well over $150 million on its defense; the cost to the government is estimated to have been about $20 million.[31] Former Assistant Attorney General Baker analyzed the problem as follows:

> From our experience with *IBM* and other such cases, we can draw several conclusions. One of these is that the Division itself shares some of the responsibility for the current state of affairs. First, there is an obvious tendency to broaden and overtry these complicated cases. In such high stakes cases, both parties will naturally attempt to introduce every shred of even marginally probative evidence in the trial of every conceivable theory of antitrust violation.

> Second, it is difficult to manage litigation in the context of budget limitations and bureaucratic requirements. Private parties in big cases draw on mammoth litigation budgets, retain several law firms and multitudes of paralegal assistants and technical advisors, and are able to utilize every form of litigation support system that current technology can make available. By contrast, the Government must rely on fewer resources spread over a wide front as it attempts a trial. . . .

> The Antitrust Division often finds itself in a big case with fewer, more overworked and less experienced staff than its private opponents. This inevitably makes the hard-pressed Government attorneys more willing to accede in suggestions of delay. . . . The defendant, who benefits from stringing out litigation in order to preserve the status quo and put off the day on which remedial relief will produce an impact, sees no advantage in litigation efficiency. Delays are thus frequently sought by the parties on

29. United States v. United Shoe Machinery Corp., 110 F.Supp. 295 (D.Mass. 1953), affirmed per curiam, 347 U.S. 521 (1954).

30. United States v. Aluminum Co. of America, 148 F.2d 416 (2d Cir.1945).

31. See ATRR No. 1051, 310–11 (1982); N.Y. Times, Jan. 18, 1982, at D 1, col. 5.

both sides, and are acquiesced in by courts that are themselves overworked and reluctant to become mired in swamps of difficult, inaccessible, economic evidence, without adequate assistance to deal with the massive record, multiple witnesses and mammoth briefs.[32]

Similar illustrations are all too evident. In 1990, the FTC began investigating Microsoft's alleged acquisition and maintenance of monopoly power in the market for operating systems. After an extensive investigation, the FTC deadlocked 2–2 on the decision whether to file a complaint. The Antitrust Division then initiated its own investigation using the FTC's extensive investigative files as a starting point. The Antitrust Division reviewed one million pages of documents, conducted over 100 interviews, and deposed 22 persons, including Microsoft Chairman Bill Gates. In July 1994, the Antitrust Division filed a complaint and a settlement with Microsoft. As indicated earlier, the district judge reviewing the settlement under the Tunney Act rejected it because its scope was too narrow, and it did not deal with "certain anticompetitive practices." In 1995, the Circuit Court for the District of Columbia concluded that the district court exceeded its authority; the Circuit Court implicitly suggested that the Antitrust Division should not be forced to take on a huge litigation burden that it wished to avoid.[33]

Litigation between Microsoft and the Antitrust Division continued in 1997–98 when the government filed a civil contempt action against Microsoft for violating a consent decree resulting from 1994 action. The government's claim, however, was rejected by the Circuit Court.[34] Finally, in May 1998, the Antitrust Division and a group of states (represented by state attorneys general) took on the "huge litigation burden" (which the government had avoided in 1994–95) by filing broad monopolization suits against Microsoft; the suits were consolidated. The district court scheduled the case on a "fast track," and a bench trial commenced less than four months after the complaints had been filed. Each side was limited to a maximum of 12 trial witnesses, and two rebuttal witnesses, and the trial was completed in 76 days. The D.C. Circuit, when the case was on appeal, said "it is noteworthy that a case of this magnitude and complexity has proceeded from the filing of complaints through trial to appellate decision in a mere three years."[35] The Circuit Court held that district courts have "extraordinarily broad discretion to determine the manner in which they will conduct trials," and "easily disposed" of Microsoft's challenges to the "fast track" process.

---

32. Oversight of Antitrust Enforcement, Hearings before the Subcommittee on Antitrust and Monopoly of the Senate Committee on the Judiciary, 95th Cong., 1st Sess. 345 (May 5, 1977) (statement of Donald I. Baker).

33. United States v. Microsoft Corp., 56 F.3d 1448 (D.C.Cir.1995). For a discussion of Tunney Act issues, see p. 88 supra.

34. See United States v. Microsoft Corp., 147 F.3d 935 (D.C.Cir.1998).

35. For a discussion of the substantive issues resolved in the *Microsoft* case, see p. 765 infra.

Nevertheless, despite the innovative and relatively speedy "fast track" process, the D.C. Circuit observed that in technologically dynamic markets remedies for anticompetitive conduct may not be available "because innovation to a large degree has already rendered the anticompetitive conduct obsolete (although by no means harmless)."[36] In early 2003, various remedial issues related to the *Microsoft* case were still being litigated.

The FTC's "shared monopoly" case against the ready-to-eat cereal manufacturers was commenced in 1972, and after more than two years of trial before an administrative law judge, was dismissed with prejudice by the Commission in 1982.[37] The FTC's case against the oil industry, filed in 1973, was abandoned in 1981 without even progressing beyond the early stages of discovery.[38] A private action, Zenith Radio Corp. v. Matsushita Electric Industrial Co., Ltd., 513 F.Supp. 1100 (E.D.Pa.1981), was filed in 1970; defendants' motions for summary judgment were granted in 1981. In the interim, nearly 30 million pages of documents were exchanged, and in 1980 alone, the parties filed 114 briefs or memoranda estimated to total 7,500 pages.[39] In 1986, in sustaining the grant of defendants' motion for summary judgment, the Supreme Court observed:

> Stating the facts of this case is a daunting task. The opinion of the Court of Appeals for the Third Circuit runs to 69 pages; the primary opinion of the District Court is more than three times as long. 732 F.2d 238 (CA3 1983); 513 F.Supp. 110 (ED Pa. 1981). Two respected District Judges each have authored a number of opinions in this case; the published ones alone would fill an entire volume for the Federal Supplement. In addition, the parties have filed a forty-volume appendix in this Court that is said to contain the essence of the evidence on which the District Court and the Court of Appeals based their respective decisions.[40]

Vast amounts of time and energy of government officials, judges, lawyers, court administrators, and scholars have been devoted to analyzing techniques to bring these massive proceedings under control. President Carter, for example, in June 1978, appointed a National Commission for the Review of Antitrust Laws and Procedures (the "National Commission"). This twenty-two member National Commission (composed of ten members of Congress, seven public members, and various government officials) proposed managerial and procedural approaches to: (i) limit and speed discovery; (ii) lead to the early refinement of issues; and (iii) encourage aggressive judicial participation in the shaping of complex antitrust cases. See National Commission, Report to the President and the

---

36. United States v. Microsoft Corp., 253 F.3d 34, 49 (D.C.Cir.), cert. denied, 534 U.S. 952 (2001).

37. ATRR No. 1048, pp. 154–182 (1982).

38. ATRR No. 1031, p. A–28 (1981).

39. See Judge Becker Cuts 11–Year Monster Down to Size, Legal Times of Washington, May 11, 1981, at 1.

40. Matsushita Electric Industrial Co. v. Zenith Radio Corp., 475 U.S. 574, 576 (1986).

Attorney General 111–112 (1979).[41] The trial judge in the *Microsoft* case made contributions along these lines. How to gain control of these "big cases"—through new procedural, process and/or substantive rules—remains one of the principal antitrust problems of our time.

In reading substantive chapters of this casebook, ask yourself whether courts have taken (or should take) into account this "big case" problem in fashioning substantive rules defining legal or illegal behavior. Should, for example, "shortcut" approaches to proof, or to the definition of an offense, be adopted because full exploration of economic cause and effect would produce unwieldy or unmanageable litigation?

SECTION 2.   THE LIMITS OF ANTITRUST

The free-market model assumes that key economic decisions—(1) what commodities shall be produced and in what quantities, (2) who will produce goods, with what resources, and in what technological manner, and (3) how goods will be distributed among different individuals or factions within a society—will be determined in the competitive market place. In a broad sense, most of antitrust represents a system of rules designed to prevent individuals or groups from interfering unduly in the operations of these market forces. For example, supply and demand factors theoretically determine the prices and amounts of particular commodities to be produced; antitrust laws prohibit conspiracies to increase price or limit production. Antitrust laws limiting mergers and consolidations are designed to prevent the creation or growth of excessive market power which would result in private interference with these economic determinations.

American political rhetoric tends to exaggerate somewhat the extent to which the free market governs economic decisionmaking in the United States. In certain sectors of the economy, antitrust has been replaced by more intrusive systems of government regulation, while in other segments—for example, organized baseball and insurance—it has been displaced with no other federal government regulation being substituted in its place.

A.   GOVERNMENT OWNERSHIP OF THE MEANS OF PRODUCTION

The most intrusive form of government presence occurs where, as in the former Soviet Union, the government owns outright the principal means of production and makes all relevant economic decisions in those sectors of the economy. Again, political rhetoric in the United States is somewhat deceptive in tending to focus upon delivery of the mails and generating of electric power (*e.g.*, TVA) as prime domestic examples of this

---

41. The National Commission's Report is reprinted at 80 F.R.D. 509 (1979); *see, e.g.*, Judicial Conference of the United States, Report on Procedure in Antitrust and Other Protracted Cases, 13 F.R.D. 62 (1951); McAllister, The Big Case: Procedural Problems in Antitrust Litigation, 64 Harv.L.Rev. 27 (1950).

approach, but these areas have never been of great significance economically.

More significant instances of federal and state enterprise include the development of major weapons systems within the national defense program, providing public education, and operating a large portion of local urban transit. The federal government also participates in the health care and insurance businesses through programs it operates relating to veterans affairs and agricultural commodities. In these markets, economic decisions are made through the political process. Measured against the total economy, these federal and state enterprises are relatively insignificant, accounting for well less than 2% of the total.

B. REGULATED INDUSTRIES

Displacement of antitrust can also occur through extensive government regulation falling short of outright ownership of the means of production. Regulatory systems vary widely in the scope and intensity of government intrusion. A useful but arbitrary guideline in distinguishing "free market" sectors from "regulated industries" focuses on entry and price. When both of these are controlled by government processes, the industry often is categorized as "regulated."

The theory underlying government intrusion is that free-market forces will discipline inadequately or will produce otherwise unacceptable results. The beneficiary of a natural monopoly—for example, the owner of a ferry landing at the only point where a river can conveniently be crossed—will neither be permitted to take advantage of that geographic good fortune by charging whatever the market will bear nor be allowed to discriminate among potential customers. As Professor W.K. Jones has noted:

> The unifying characteristic of natural monopoly industries is the ability of a single firm to provide the most economical service to a given area. Within the area reached by the physical facilities of the firm, the introduction of additional suppliers requires a wasteful duplication of plant and a significant increase in cost not normally justified by any benefits to users of the service. Under such circumstances, monopoly is accepted as the most appropriate industry structure and the industry is subjected to regulation as a "public utility."[42]

However, federal and state legislatures have sometimes been persuaded to displace competition with regulation in markets that are neither natural monopolies nor even highly concentrated. The statute which until relatively recently gave the Interstate Commerce Commission (which no longer exists) extensive authority to regulate the otherwise highly competitive interstate trucking industry was one example of many at the federal level. Since it passed the Interstate Commerce Act in 1887, Congress has established numerous regulatory agencies charged with supervision of the eco-

---

42. Jones, Government Price Controls and Inflation: A Prognosis Based on the Impact of Controls in the Regulated Industries, 65 Cornell L.Rev. 303, 304 (1980).

nomic activities of particular industries engaged in interstate commerce. The FCC, FERC, CFTC, and SEC, as well as the Secretary of Agriculture, the Board of Governors of the Federal Reserve System, the Comptroller of the Currency, the Secretary of the Interior, and the Secretary of Transportation, among other agencies and administrators, have been given broad grants of regulatory authority in areas of economic activity related to their broader duties.

In general, each of these regulatory bodies operates under a separate statute, the regulatory criteria of which may or may not include provisions analogous to the proscriptions of the antitrust laws. In some, Congress has incorporated language from the Sherman or Clayton Acts; several of the regulatory bodies are given specific authority to enforce Sections 3, 7, and 8 of the Clayton Act. Some statutes, however, clearly express Congressional acquiescence in activity which would otherwise be subject to antitrust sanction, usually subject to the regulator's review or approval. Thus, the regulatory body may have authority (by its own action or by approval of private transactions) to fix rates or prices, control market entry, or eliminate existing or potential competition.

Some statutes confer an express antitrust exemption. More frequently, no express immunity is granted but the nature of the regulation is such that the courts have implied a limited immunity for certain activities. *See, e.g.*, Gordon v. NYSE, 422 U.S. 659 (1975) (active agency regulation, pursuant to a Congressional directive, implied immunity); United States v. NASD, 422 U.S. 694 (1975) (regulatory scheme so pervasive that immunity assumed). However, the Supreme Court has held that immunity from the antitrust laws "is not lightly implied." California v. FPC, 369 U.S. 482, 485 (1962). The Court has also stated that repeal of antitrust "is to be regarded as implied only if necessary to make . . . [the regulatory scheme] work, and even then only to the minimum extent necessary." Silver v. New York Stock Exchange, 373 U.S. 341, 357 (1963).

An increasingly significant activity of the Antitrust Division and the FTC has been to appear in federal regulatory proceedings as an advocate for competitive policy. In addition, Congress, during the past three decades, has entered into a far-reaching program of deregulation. Significant steps have been taken, for example, with respect to railroads, airlines, trucking, telecommunications, and financial institutions. Deregulation has usually been accompanied by some limitation of the existing scope of antitrust immunity.

At the state level, laws by the thousands assist such professionals or businessmen as lawyers, doctors, druggists, liquor dealers, funeral home operators, barbers, optometrists—an endless list—in combatting the forces of competition, by implementing self-regulation of "ethical standards" or other forms of cartelization. Local ordinances perform similar functions for other business groups, seldom overlooking the "desirability" of providing a city commission to keep taxis from crowding the streets and to keep their rates at non-competitive (high) levels.[43]

Major regulated industries in the United States are banking, public transportation, provision of gas and electric services, local telephone services, television broadcasting, and portions of agricultural production. In each instance the regulated industry has felt the winds of deregulation during the 1970's, 1980's, 1990's, and early 2000's. A primary policy concern underlying the deregulation movement is that regulation may be less efficient economically than the operation of market forces. Many of these regulatory regimes were instituted during the New Deal, and were designed as a liberal alternative to Marxism. After more than 60 years of experience, however, the conviction has come to be widely shared that many regulatory agencies, particularly those regulating entry and price, no longer serve adequately the public interest and some have, in fact, become captives of the industries they were designed to regulate.[44] As indicated earlier, during the past three decades "deregulation" advocacy has become an increasingly important activity of both the Antitrust Division and the FTC. In the mid 1990's and early 2000's a major new area of competition advocacy involves intellectual property protection for new technologies. In 1996, an important FTC staff report concluded:

> As the Supreme Court has recognized many times, there is a need to balance intellectual property and competition values.... Accordingly, in light of testimony and literature on this topic, we believe that the FTC should act to ensure that intellectual property policy and decision makers, including the courts, the PTO [U.S. Patent and Trademark Office], the Registrar of Copyrights, and the legislature, are aware of the potential competitive consequences of intellectual property policy for new technologies such as biotechnology and computer software.[45]

Government regulation of industries is obviously too vast a topic to be treated in an antitrust course. However, Section 3 of Chapter 5 examines the increasingly complex and important interface between federal antitrust policy and state and local business regulation; Section 1 of Chapter 8 deals with the current tension between intellectual property protection and antitrust.

C.   Interstate and Foreign Commerce

1.   INTERSTATE COMMERCE

The Sherman Act prohibits only "restraints of trade or commerce among the several States." During the past sixty-five years, this language

---

43. For a discussion of efforts to influence government action and the so-called "state action" doctrine, see Chapter 5 infra.

44. *See, e.g.*, Jones, supra note 42, at 313–18; Breyer & MacAvoy, Energy Regulation by the Federal Power Commission 72–88 (1974); Green & Nader, Economic Regulation vs. Competition: Uncle Sam the Monopoly Man, 82 Yale L.J. 871 (1973); Winter, Economic Regulation vs. Competition: Ralph Nader and Creeping Capitalism, 82 Yale L.J. 890 (1973).

45. FTC Staff, Anticipating the 21st Century: Competition Policy in the New High–Tech, Global Marketplace Ch. 8 at 22 (1996).

has been interpreted very broadly. In general, today it is unlikely that economic activity of sufficient significance to attract the attention of federal enforcement agencies, or justify private litigation, will not directly involve interstate commerce. Even where involvement is not direct, the courts have developed an expansive "effect on commerce" test to justify federal jurisdiction. In Burke v. Ford, 389 U.S. 320 (1967), a group of Oklahoma liquor dealers sued under Section 1 of the Sherman Act to enjoin an alleged statewide division of markets by all Oklahoma liquor wholesalers. The Supreme Court, without hearing argument, summarily reversed the finding below that the interstate commerce prerequisite of the Sherman Act had not been satisfied, noting that anticompetitive arrangements are likely to lead to increased prices and, therefore, lower unit sales. Accordingly, territorial market division almost certainly resulted in fewer sales to retailers and hence fewer purchases of out-of-state liquor by wholesalers than would have occurred but for the anticompetitive arrangements.

In Goldfarb v. Virginia State Bar, 421 U.S. 773 (1975), the Supreme Court continued its expansive reading of the Sherman Act's commerce clause.[46] The Court of Appeals (Fourth Circuit) had held that real estate title examinations (which had to be performed by lawyers) "are performed wholly intrastate, are essentially local in nature and therefore a restraint with respect to them can never substantially affect interstate commerce." Id. at 783. The Supreme Court reversed, pointing out that a significant portion of the funds for purchasing homes in Fairfax County (a suburb of Washington, D.C.) came from out of state and that significant amounts of loans were guaranteed by the Veterans Administration and HUD, both headquartered in the District of Columbia.

Chief Justice Burger's opinion noted that the "necessary connection between the interstate transactions and the restraint of trade provided by the minimum-fee schedule is present because, in a practical sense, title examinations are necessary in real estate transactions." The Chief Justice continued:

> The fact that there was no showing that home buyers were discouraged by the challenged activities [*i.e.*, price fixing] does not mean that interstate commerce was not affected. Otherwise, the magnitude of the effect would control, and our cases have shown that, once an effect is shown, no specific magnitude need be proved. Nor was it necessary for petitioners to prove that the fee schedule raised fees. Petitioners clearly proved that the fee schedule fixed fees and thus "deprive[d] purchasers or consumers of the advantages which they derive from free competition." Apex Hosiery Co. v. Leader, 310 U.S. 469, 501 (1940).

> Where, as a matter of law or practical necessity, legal services are an integral part of an interstate transaction, a restraint on

---

46. For portions of the *Goldfarb* opinion setting forth the facts of the case and discussing other issues, see Chapter 4 infra.

those services may substantially affect commerce for Sherman Act purposes. Id. at 785.[47]

In McLain v. Real Estate Board of New Orleans, Inc., 444 U.S. 232 (1980), in which a class of private plaintiffs alleged a price-fixing conspiracy among real estate brokers in Greater New Orleans, the Supreme Court reversed a dismissal and reasoned:

> The broad authority of Congress under the Commerce Clause has, of course, long been interpreted to extend beyond activities actually *in* interstate commerce to reach other activities that, while wholly local in nature, nevertheless substantially *affect* interstate commerce....
>
> To establish the jurisdictional element of a Sherman Act violation it would be sufficient for petitioners to demonstrate a substantial effect on interstate commerce generated by respondents' brokerage activity. Petitioners need not make the more particularized showing of an effect on interstate commerce caused by the alleged conspiracy to fix commission rates, or by those other aspects of respondents' activity that are alleged to be unlawful. The validity of this approach is confirmed by an examination of the case law. If establishing jurisdiction required a showing that the unlawful conduct itself had an effect on interstate commerce, jurisdiction would be defeated by a demonstration that the alleged restraint failed to have its intended anticompetitive effect. This is not the rule of our cases....
>
> Nor is jurisdiction defeated in a case relying on anticompetitive effects by plaintiff's failure to quantify the adverse impact of defendant's conduct.... Even where there is an inability to prove that concerted activity has resulted in legally cognizable damages, jurisdiction need not be impaired, though such a failure may confine the available remedies to injunctive relief....
>
> ... Brokerage activities necessarily affect both the frequency and the terms of residential sales transactions. Ultimately, whatever stimulates or retards the volume of residential sales, or has an impact on the purchase price, affects the demand for financing and title insurance, those two commercial activities that on this record are shown to have occurred in interstate commerce. Where, as here, the services of respondent real estate brokers are often employed in transactions in the relevant market, petitioners at trial may be able to show that respondents' activities have a not insubstantial effect on interstate commerce.

Recently, in Summit Health, Ltd. v. Pinhas, 500 U.S. 322 (1991), an ophthalmologist sued members of a medical center and the hospital itself for revoking his staff privileges and conspiring to prevent him from finding employment in the Los Angeles area. A 5–4 majority of the Supreme Court

47. See Hospital Building Co. v. Trustees of Rex Hospital, 425 U.S. 738 (1976).

stated that the Sherman Act was intended to "go as far as the Constitution permits Congress to go." 500 U.S. at 328 n.7. Pointing to general activities of the hospital, the Court noted that as "a 'matter of practical economics' ... the effect of such a conspiracy on the hospital's 'purchase of out-of-state medicines and supplies as well as its revenues from out-of-state insurance companies' ... would establish the necessary interstate nexus." 500 U.S. at 329.

The Court rejected the hospital's argument that the elimination of one physician's practice could not affect interstate commerce. First, the Court indicated that a violation of the Sherman Act is not found by looking at the "actual consequences" of the action, but by consideration of the "potential harm that would ensue if the conspiracy were successful." Second, the change in the make-up of the Los Angeles market was stated to have a "market-wide impact and therefore an effect on interstate commerce." The Court reasoned:

> The competitive significance of [plaintiff's] exclusion from the market must be measured, not just by a particularized evaluation of his own practice, but rather, by a general evaluation of the impact of the restraint on other participants and potential partici-pants in the market from which he has been excluded. 500 U.S. at 332.

Justices Scalia, O'Connor, Kennedy, and Souter dissented. First, they disagreed with the proposition that the Sherman Act extended to the reach of the Commerce Clause: "[T]he question before us is not whether Congress *could* reach the activity before us here if it wanted to, but whether it *has done* so via the Sherman Act." 500 U.S. at 333 (emphasis in original). The dissent then noted a circuit split on the issue of whether the unlawful activities or merely the general business activities of a defendant need to affect interstate commerce. The dissent stated:

> Today the Court could have cleared up the confusion created by *McLain,* refocused the inquiry along the lines marked by our previous cases (and still adhered to by most Circuits), and [found that there was no jurisdiction under the Sherman Act in this case]. Instead, it compounds the confusion by rejecting the two compet-ing interpretations of *McLain* and adding yet a third candidate to the field.... To determine Sherman Act jurisdiction it looks *neither* to the effect on commerce of the restraint, *nor* to the effect on commerce of the defendants' infected activity, but rather, it seems, to the effect on commerce of the activity from which the plaintiff has been excluded.... This analysis tell us nothing about the substantiality of the impact on interstate commerce generated by the particular conduct at issue here. 500 U.S. at 336.

After *McLain* and *Summit Health* how much room is left for a jurisdictional defense given the Court's willingness to focus on "brokerage activity," or non-litigating "participants and potential participants in the market," as opposed to the "effect on interstate commerce caused by the alleged conspiracy"?

Unlike the Sherman Act, the Clayton Act and the Robinson–Patman Act apply to persons and conduct "in commerce." In two cases, in 1974 and 1975,[48] the Supreme Court limited the jurisdictional reach of this "in commerce" language. In Gulf Oil Corp. v. Copp Paving Co., 419 U.S. 186, 194–195 (1974), the Court said:

> The jurisdictional reach of § 1 [of the Sherman Act] thus is keyed directly to effects on interstate markets and the interstate flow of goods. Moreover, our cases have recognized that in enacting § 1 Congress "wanted to go to the utmost extent of its Constitutional power in restraining trust and monopoly agreements." . . .

> In contrast to § 1, the distinct "in commerce" language of the Clayton and Robinson–Patman Act provisions with which we are concerned here appears to denote only persons or activities within the flow of interstate commerce—the practical, economic continuity in the generation of goods and services for interstate markets and their transport and distribution to the consumer. If this is so, the jurisdictional requirements of these provisions cannot be satisfied merely by showing that allegedly anticompetitive acquisitions and activities *affect* commerce.

In 1980, however, Congress amended Section 7 of the Clayton Act to reach mergers involving companies engaged "in any activity affecting commerce."[49] Similarly, in 1975, Congress amended Section 5 of the Federal Trade Commission Act as follows:

> Section 5 [also Sections 6 and 12] of the Federal Trade Commission Act (15 U.S.C. § 45) is amended by striking out "in commerce" wherever it appears and inserting in lieu thereof "in or affecting commerce."[50]

Of course, cases occasionally do arise, particularly in large states like New York, Texas, or California, or physically isolated states like Alaska and Hawaii, where interstate commerce cannot be demonstrated. In those situations, state antitrust statutes or common-law "restraint of trade" provisions may serve objectives parallel to those of the federal laws.

2. FOREIGN COMMERCE

The Sherman Act and other antitrust laws also apply to foreign trade or commerce. Chapter 10 deals with the complex jurisdictional issues presented in the context of foreign trade or commerce, and with the

---

48. See United States v. American Building Maintenance Industries, 422 U.S. 271 (1975); Gulf Oil Corp. v. Copp Paving Co., Inc., 419 U.S. 186 (1974). For recent Robinson–Patman cases, *see, e.g.*, Godfrey v. Pulitzer Pub. Co., 161 F.3d 1137 (8th Cir. 1998); McCallum v. City of Athens, 976 F.2d 649 (11th Cir.1992).

49. 15 U.S.C.A. § 18.

50. Magnuson–Moss Warranty–Federal Trade Commission Improvement Act § 201, Pub.L. 93–637, 88 Stat. 2183; 15 U.S.C.A. § 45. This amendment legislatively overruled FTC v. Bunte Brothers, Inc., 312 U.S. 349 (1941).

application of United States antitrust laws to the acts and instrumentalities of foreign sovereigns. Various substantive sections of the casebook deal with the subtle and increasingly significant issues related to whether or not antitrust rules should be modified when they are applied to foreign activities.

D. ADDITIONAL EXEMPTIONS, EXCLUSIONS, AND OTHER ASPECTS OF ECONOMIC CONTROL

As indicated, the United States relies only in part on competition to regulate its markets. In addition to government ownership and regulation (see A and B supra), numerous exemptions and exclusions from the antitrust laws exist, and the influences of various governmental policies and controls on the free-market sector are so varied and widespread as to be impossible to summarize. For example, government policies designed to increase productivity or control inflation—including tax policies, control of monetary supply, intellectual property policy, and spending—powerfully influence free-market economic determinations. Some government programs stimulate arguably desirable economic activity (*e.g.*, housing allowances), while others intervene in order to prevent undesirable social consequences (*e.g.*, pollution control). Collaboration between competitors can be authorized by the President and Department of Defense in the name of national defense,[51] or by the Small Business Administration to assist small entrepreneurs.[52]

The most important legislative exemption from the antitrust laws is in the labor market where national policy—recognized in a statutory exemption and a nonstatutory exemption—permits collective bargaining by employees when negotiating wages and other terms of their employment.[53] The collective bargaining process can produce effects in product markets which would otherwise be impermissible under the antitrust laws—for example, where negotiations result in a combination between labor and some employers to advance mutual interests at the expense of other employer groups. While the labor exemption is not intended to cover these practices,[54] there will be relatively few situations in which unacceptable anticompetitive consequences occurring in the product market could not be justified by some arguably legitimate and allegedly "unilaterally sought" union objective. The labor exemption is applicable to a collective bargaining

51. Defense Production Act of 1950, 50 U.S.C.A. app. § 2158.

52. 15 U.S.C.A. §§ 638, 640.

53. Section 6 of the Clayton Act (15 U.S.C.A. § 17) provides that: "The labor of a human being is not a commodity or article of commerce." And Section 20 (29 U.S.C.A. § 52) prohibits issuance of injunctions to prevent peaceful activities by employees growing out of a labor dispute except under special circumstances.

54. The various Supreme Court opinions in United Mine Workers v. Pennington, 381 U.S. 657 (1965), and Local Union No. 189, Amalgamated Meat Cutters v. Jewel Tea Co., 381 U.S. 676 (1965), demonstrate what a complicated matter it is to draw meaningful distinctions in this area. See generally Connell Construction Co. v. Plumbers and Steamfitters Local Union No. 100, 421 U.S. 616 (1975); Gifford, Redefining the Antitrust Labor Exemption, 72 Minn.L.Rev. 1379 (1988).

agreement, and to negotiation-impasse situations involving wages and working conditions.[55]

Another area of antitrust exemption involves agricultural cooperatives. Section 6 of the Clayton Act and the Capper–Volstead Act,[56] in effect, allow farmers organized into agricultural cooperatives to fix prices at which farm produce will be sold without antitrust consequences. Maryland & Virginia Milk Producers Association v. United States, 362 U.S. 458 (1960), contains a useful review of the history and purpose of this statutory scheme. The exemption of most efforts by competitors to influence public officials or engage in "political activities," under the so-called Noerr–Pennington doctrine, is discussed at pp. 410–50 infra.

Finally, there are a number of "rifle-shot exceptions" which usually reflect successful petitioning by particular groups to Congress for relief from allegedly onerous aspects of antitrust rules or decisions. Although increasingly subject to question, the McCarran–Ferguson Act exempts insurance activities (other than practices involving boycott, coercion, and intimidation) from the antitrust laws to the extent those activities are regulated by state law.[57] Another example is the Newspaper Preservation Act, discussed at p. 1012 infra, which under certain conditions permits newspaper publishers to engage in otherwise illegal joint publishing ventures.

SELECTIVE BIBLIOGRAPHY

1. The Three–Level Enforcement Pattern

ABA Section of Antitrust Law, The State of Federal Antitrust Enforcement—2001: Report of the Task Force on the Federal Antitrust Agencies (2001).

Sullivan & Grimes, The Law of Antitrust: An Integrated Handbook 887–967 (2000).

FTC Staff, Anticipating the 21st Century: Competition Policy in the New High–Tech, Global Marketplace (1996).

1–2 Areeda & Hovenkamp, Antitrust Law: An Analysis of Antitrust Principles and Their Application (2d ed. 2000 & Supp. 2002).

Report of the American Bar Association Section of Antitrust Law Task Force on the Antitrust Division of the U.S. Department of Justice (1989).

Report of the American Bar Association Section of Antitrust Law, Special Committee to Study the Role of the Federal Trade Commission, 56 ATRR S–1–53 (1989).

55. *See, e.g.,* Brown v. Pro Football, Inc., 518 U.S. 231 (1996) (permitting use of the nonstatutory exemption in a negotiation-impasse situation). For a further discussion of the labor exemption, see pp. 300–03, infra.

56. 7 U.S.C.A. §§ 291–92.

57. 15 U.S.C.A. §§ 1011–1015. As to what constitutes the business of insurance, see Union Labor Life Insur. Co. v. Pireno, 458 U.S. 119 (1982); Group Life & Health Insurance Co. v. Royal Drug Co., 440 U.S. 205 (1979). On the question of what constitutes sufficient state regulation to oust federal jurisdiction, see FTC v. Travelers Health Association, 362 U.S. 293 (1960); FTC v. National Casualty Co., 357 U.S. 560 (1958). On the boundaries of the "boycott" non-exemption, see Hartford Fire Insur. Co. v. California, 509 U.S. 764 (1993).

White (ed.), Private Antitrust Litigation: New Evidence, New Learning (1988).

National Commission for the Review of Antitrust Laws and Procedures, Report to the President and the Attorney General, 80 F.R.D. 509 (1979).

Elzinga & Breit, The Antitrust Penalties: A Study in Law and Economics (1976).

Report of the ABA Commission to Study the Federal Trade Commission (1969).

2.   The Limits of Antitrust

1A Areeda & Hovenkamp, Antitrust Law: An Analysis of Antitrust Principles and Their Application (2d ed. 2000 & Supp. 2002).

Sullivan & Grimes, The Law of Antitrust: An Integrated Handbook 697–886 (2000).

Green & Nader, Economic Regulation vs. Competition: Uncle Sam the Monopoly Man, 82 Yale L.J. 871 (1973).

Kaysen & Turner, Antitrust Policy Chs. 6–7 (1959).

Turner, The Scope of Antitrust and Other Economic Regulatory Policies, 82 Harv. L. Rev. 1207 (1969).

CHAPTER 3

MARKET STRUCTURE AND A FIRST LOOK AT THE PROBLEM OF MONOPOLY POWER

SECTION 1. MONOPOLIZATION AND THE PROBLEM OF MARKET DEFINITION

SCOPE NOTE

The Sherman Act is a composite of two major concepts—restraint of trade and monopoly. The cases in this section are concerned with single firm monopolies. At issue are three interrelated antitrust questions: (i) what is the proper technique for measuring market shares, usually phrased as the problem of "defining relevant market;" (ii) at what point and in what circumstances do large market shares give rise to market power of monopoly dimensions; and (iii) given monopoly power, what kinds of business conduct on the part of the firm will the antitrust laws tolerate?[1]

The measurement problem is best addressed by considering at the outset the purposes of antitrust. With respect to a single firm, one chief evil with which antitrust policy is concerned is power to curtail output and thereby raise prices above the levels that would exist under competitive conditions. A firm's power to raise prices is limited primarily by the existence of other producers who, by failing similarly to raise prices, would take over enough of its business to make a price rise unprofitable. The principal problem in any given case is to determine which existing firms and potential competitors have sufficient restraining influence on the defendant's power over price to warrant their inclusion in the "relevant market."

Three considerations are of primary importance in distinguishing the relevant firms from the irrelevant. Two of these pertain to the "demand" side of the analysis. The first is the nature of the product and the ability or willingness of its users to substitute other products for it. As alternative products become generally less "substitutable," their influence on defendant's price diminishes.

Consider three competitive situations. In the first, we are concerned with a single farmer who produces wheat that is completely fungible with the wheat produced by a large number of other producers. In that situation, the price the

---

1. In this chapter, we will examine some "simple" aspects of the conduct question, and then discuss those issues again in detail in Chapter 8. The remainder of the chapter will address questions (i) and (ii)— related to market definition and the identification of market power of monopoly dimen-

sions. Problems of market definition and market power cut across every area of antitrust. They arise, for example, in many Sherman Act "restraint of trade" cases and are often a decisive factor in merger enforcement.

seller charges will be determined entirely by the market and will not be significantly affected by any individual farmer's decision to expand or curtail his production. Thus, if the market is working perfectly and purchasers are fully informed, the farmer will find that he can sell no wheat at all if he charges even a penny more than the going market price. On the other hand, since the farmer can sell his full supply at the market price, it would be senseless to sell for even a penny less. By contrast, consider the market position of the manufacturer of a patented drug that is far more effective in treating a serious disease than any alternative course of treatment. At least during the period of the patent, the seller can curtail production and raise price considerably in the expectation that consumers will prefer its product to very imperfect existing substitutes.

The common situation is neither of these two—that is, neither perfect competition nor monopoly—but rather one in which a seller or group of sellers offers a product for which there are many close but not perfect substitutes.[2] Coca Cola could be viewed as a monopolist if in the minds of buyers it is completely different from any other liquid beverage. Its market power would be less if as a result of slight changes in price buyers quickly were willing to switch to other carbonated cola beverages, and its market power would be still less if they would be similarly willing to switch to non-cola carbonated beverages or even to coffee, tea, or milk. A threshold problem in any given case is to determine which existing firms and potential competitors have sufficient restraining influence on the seller's power over price to warrant their inclusion as effective competitors. The process of resolving that set of questions is called "defining the relevant market."

The second consideration is spatial or geographic. One obvious matter that bears on the substitutability of alternatives is their location. If X owns every shoe store in a particular city, his prices are still limited by the presence of independent stores in the suburbs or in shopping centers located on highways leading into the city and by mail-order possibilities. But he may nevertheless be able to raise his prices above the going rate—by a dollar, let us say—on the assumption that relatively few customers would take the trouble to buy elsewhere in order to save so small an amount. Note, however, that this might not be the case if he owned wholesale rather than retail outlets. Even a dollar's difference would cause retail stores to turn to more remote sources since such a differential becomes important to anyone buying in quantity.

The "supply" side of the equation has received less attention in the cases. A firm may not be limited in its power over price solely by the alternative sources of supply (of its product or widely acceptable substitutes) that are at present in existence. It may also be limited by the desire to forestall possible competition that would enter the field if its profits were to rise too high. Any firm with market power approaching monopoly dimensions could be expected to take account of potential competition of this sort. The importance of this factor is hard to assess, however, and will differ from industry to industry. A steel rolling mill may be able to move from one product market (sheets for automobile manufacturers) to another (sheets for metal containers) by a simple adjustment in its processing. At the other extreme, entry into a new market may require construction of completely new production facilities. In either case, the likelihood of a new firm entering a market depends on the expense to the newcomer of obtaining and operating a plant, the availability of raw materials, skilled personnel and production processes, the cost of obtaining a satisfactory share of the market (advertising, sales network, etc.), and

---

2. An early and extremely influential analysis of these various structural conditions is found in Bain, Industrial Organization, 27–31 (1959).

so forth—in other words, the cost and other barriers to entry. As these barriers become more imposing, the likelihood of new competition declines and its influence over the pricing policy of an existing firm diminishes correspondingly.

We start our examination of questions of "monopoly power" by examining the *Alcoa* case—one of the landmark opinions in antitrust. While there are some interesting relevant market definition issues in the case, it is principally concerned with the question of limits on permissible behavior by a company that has achieved or is in the process of achieving monopoly power.

Alcoa will be followed by United States v. E.I. du Pont (the "Cellophane Case") and then United States v. Grinnell. While the notes in this chapter demonstrate that the approach and holdings of these three cases may have been modified, the cases nevertheless raise the central questions under American law of how to measure and deal with substantial instances of market power.

Sherman Act, Section 2

[Reprinted p. 15 supra.]

Treaty of Rome, Article 82 (ex. Article 86)

[Reprinted pp. 21–22 supra.]

United States v. Aluminum Co. of America

United States Court of Appeals, Second Circuit, 1945.
148 F.2d 416.

■ Before L. HAND, SWAN and AUGUSTUS N. HAND, CIRCUIT JUDGES.

L. Hand, J. This appeal comes to us by virtue of a certificate of the Supreme Court, under the amendment of 1944 to § 29 of 15 U.S.C.A. The action was brought under § 4 of that title, praying the district court to adjudge that the defendant, Aluminum Company of America, was monopolizing interstate and foreign commerce, particularly in the manufacture and sale of "virgin" aluminum ingot, and that it be dissolved; and further to adjudge that that company and the defendant, Aluminum Limited, had entered into a conspiracy in restraint of such commerce. It also asked incidental relief.... The action came to trial on June 1, 1938, and proceeded without much interruption until August 14, 1940, when the case was closed after more than 40,000 pages of testimony had been taken. The judge ... entered final judgment dismissing the complaint on July 23, [1942].... On June 12, 1944, the Supreme Court, declaring that a quorum of six justices qualified to hear the case was wanting, referred the appeal to this court under § 29 of Title 15, already mentioned....

"Alcoa" is a corporation, organized under the laws of Pennsylvania on September 18, 1888; its original name, "Pittsburgh Reduction Company," was changed to its present one on January 1, 1907. It has always been engaged in the production and sale of "ingot" aluminum, and since 1895 also in the fabrication of the metal into many finished and semi-finished articles. It has proliferated into a great number of subsidiaries, created at various times between the years 1900 and 1929, as the business expanded. Aluminum is a chemical element; it is never found in a free state, being always in chemical combination with oxygen. One form of this combination is known as alumina; and for practical purposes the most available material from which alumina can be extracted is an ore called "bauxite." Aluminum was isolated as a metal more than a century ago, but not until about 1886 did it become commercially practicable to eliminate the oxygen, so that it could be exploited industrially. One, Hall, discovered a process by which this could be done in that year, and got a patent on April 2, 1889, which he assigned to "Alcoa," which thus secured a legal monopoly of the manufacture of the pure aluminum until on April 2, 1906, when this patent expired. Meanwhile Bradley had invented a process by which the smelting could be carried on without the use of external heat, as had theretofore been thought necessary; and for this improvement he too got a patent on February 2, 1892. Bradley's improvement resulted in great economy in manufacture, so that, although after April 2, 1906, anyone could manufacture aluminum by the Hall process, for practical purposes no one could compete with Bradley or with his licensees until February 2, 1909, when Bradley's patent also expired. On October 31, 1903, "Alcoa" and the assignee of the Bradley patent entered into a contract by which "Alcoa" was granted an exclusive license under that patent, in exchange for "Alcoa's" promise to sell to the assignee a stated amount of aluminum at a discount of ten percent below "Alcoa's" published list price, and always to sell at a discount of five per cent greater than that which "Alcoa" gave to any other jobber. Thus until February 2, 1909, "Alcoa" had either a monopoly of the manufacture of "virgin" aluminum ingot, or the monopoly of the process which eliminated all competition.

The extraction of aluminum from alumina requires a very large amount of electrical energy, which is ordinarily, though not always, most cheaply obtained from waterpower. Beginning at least as early as 1895, "Alcoa" secured such power from several companies by contracts, containing in at least three instances, covenants binding the power companies not to sell or let power to anyone else for the manufacture of aluminum. "Alcoa"—either itself or by a subsidiary—also entered into four successive "cartels" with foreign manufacturers of aluminum by which, in exchange for certain limitations upon its import into foreign countries, it secured covenants from the foreign producers, either not to import into the United States at all, or to do so under restrictions, which in some cases involved the fixing of prices. These "cartels" and restrictive covenants and certain other practices were the subject of a suit filed by the United States against "Alcoa" on May 16, 1912, in which a decree was entered by consent on June 7, 1912, declaring several of these covenants unlawful and enjoining their performance; and also declaring invalid other restrictive covenants obtained before 1903 relating to the sale of alumina. ("Alcoa" failed at this time to inform the United States of several restrictive covenants in water-power contracts; its justification—which the judge accepted—being that they had been forgotten.) "Alcoa" did not begin to manufacture alumina on its own behalf until the expiration of a dominant patent in 1903. In that year it built a very large alumina plant at East St. Louis, where all of its alumina was made until 1939, when it opened another plant in Mobile, Alabama.

None of the foregoing facts are in dispute, and the most important question in the case is whether the monopoly in "Alcoa's" production of "virgin" ingot, secured by the two patents until 1909, and in part perpetuated between 1909 and 1912 by the unlawful practices, forbidden by the decree of 1912, continued for the ensuing twenty-eight years; and whether, if it did, it was unlawful under § 2 of the Sherman Act. It is undisputed that throughout this period "Alcoa" continued to be the single producer of "virgin" ingot in the United States; and the plaintiff argues that this without more was enough to make it an unlawful monopoly. It also takes an alternative position: that in any event during this period "Alcoa" consistently pursued unlawful exclusionary practices, which made its dominant position certainly unlawful, even though it would not have been, had it been retained only by "natural growth." Finally, it asserts that many of these practices were of themselves unlawful, as contracts in restraint of trade under § 1 of the Act. "Alcoa's" position is that the fact that it alone continued to make "virgin" ingot in this country did not, and does not, give it a monopoly of the market; that it was always subject to the competition of imported "virgin" ingot, and of what is called "secondary" ingot; and that even if it had not been, its monopoly would not have been retained by unlawful means, but would have been the result of a growth which the Act does not forbid, even when it results in a monopoly. We shall first consider the amount and character of this competition; next, how far it established a monopoly; and finally, if it did, whether that monopoly was unlawful under § 2 of the Act.

From 1902 onward until 1928 "Alcoa" was making ingot in Canada through a wholly owned subsidiary; so much of this as it imported into the United States it is proper to include with what it produced here. In the year 1912 the sum of these two items represented nearly ninety-one per cent of the total amount of "virgin" ingot available for sale in this country. This percentage varied year by year up to and including 1938: in 1913 it was about seventy-two per cent; in 1921 about sixty-eight per cent; in 1922 about seventy-two; with these exceptions it was always over eighty per cent of the total and for the last five years 1934–1938 inclusive it averaged over ninety per cent. The effect of such a proportion of the production upon the market we reserve for the time being, for it will be necessary first to consider the nature and uses of "secondary" ingot, the name by which the industry knows ingot made from aluminum scrap. . . .

. . . [The court went on to hold that ingot fabricated by "Alcoa" should be included and "secondary" ingot should be excluded[3] in determining "Alcoa's" control of the aluminum market.[4]]

We conclude therefore that "Alcoa's" control over the ingot market must be reckoned at over ninety per cent; that being the proportion which its production bears to imported "virgin" ingot. If the fraction that it did not supply were the produce of domestic manufacture, there could be no doubt that this percentage gave it a monopoly—lawful or unlawful, as the case might be. The producer of so large a proportion of the supply has complete control within certain limits. It is true that if by raising the price he reduces the amount which can be marketed—as always, or almost always, happens—he may invite the expansion of the small producers who will try to fill the place left open; nevertheless, not only is there an inevitable lag in this, but the large producer is in a strong position to check such competition; and, indeed, if he has retained his old plant and personnel, he can inevitably do so. There are indeed limits to his power; substitutes are available for almost all commodities, and to raise the price enough is to evoke them. [Citing cases.] Moreover, it is difficult and expensive to keep idle any part of a plant or of personnel; and any drastic contraction of the market will offer increasing temptation to the small producers to expand. But these limitations also exist when a single producer occupies the whole market: even then, his hold will depend upon his moderation in exerting his immediate power.

The case at bar is however different, because, for aught that appears, there may well have been a practically unlimited supply of imports as the price of ingot rose. Assuming that there was no agreement between "Alcoa" and foreign producers not to import, they sold what could bear the handicap of the tariff and the cost of transportation. For the period of eighteen years–1920–1937—they sold at times a little above "Alcoa's" prices, at times a little under; but there was substantially no gross difference between what they received and what they would have received, had they sold uniformly at "Alcoa's" prices. While the record is silent, we may therefore assume—the plaintiff having the burden—that, had "Alcoa" raised its prices, more ingot would have been imported. Thus there is a distinction between domestic and foreign competition: the first is limited in quantity, and can increase only by an increase in plant and personnel; the

---

3. Ed. Ingot fabricated by "Alcoa" was included because it had a direct effect upon the ingot market by virtue of the fact that the intermediate or end products fabricated by "Alcoa" *"pro tanto* reduce the demand for ingot itself." Secondary ingot was excluded because "Alcoa" had originally produced all of the secondary ingot as virgin ingot and it could, therefore, regulate the future return of secondary ingot to the market by controlling the production of virgin ingot. Judge Knox, when he fashioned the decree in 1950, found

that, since scrap aluminum no longer necessarily originated with "Alcoa," secondary aluminum would not be excluded from the market. United States v. Aluminum Co. of America, 91 F.Supp. 333, 358 (S.D.N.Y.1950).

4. Ed. In the course of this discussion, Judge Hand asserts: "That percentage [over ninety] is enough to constitute a monopoly; it is doubtful whether sixty or sixty-four per cent would be enough; and certainly thirty-three per cent is not."

second is of producers who, we must assume, produce much more than they import, and who a rise in price will presumably induce immediately to divert to the American market what they have been selling elsewhere. It is entirely consistent with the evidence that it was the threat of greater foreign imports which kept "Alcoa's" prices where they were, and prevented it from exploiting its advantage as sole domestic producer; indeed, it is hard to resist the conclusion that potential imports did put a "ceiling" upon those prices. Nevertheless, within the limits afforded by the tariff and the cost of transportation, "Alcoa" was free to raise its prices as it chose, since it was free from domestic competition, save as it drew other metals into the market as substitutes. Was this a monopoly within the meaning of § 2? The judge found that, over the whole half century of its existence, "Alcoa's" profits upon capital invested, after payment of income taxes, had been only about ten per cent, and, although the plaintiff puts this figure a little higher, the difference is negligible. The plaintiff does indeed challenge the propriety of computing profits upon a capital base which included past earnings that have been allowed to remain in the business; but as to that it is plainly wrong. An argument is indeed often made in the case of a public utility, that the "rate-base" should not include earnings reinvested which were greater than a fair profit upon the actual investment outstanding at the time. That argument depends, however, upon the premise that at common law—even in the absence of any commission or other authority empowered to enforce a "reasonable" rate—it is the duty of a public utility to charge no more than such a rate, and that any excess is unlawfully collected. Perhaps one might properly use the same argument in the case of a monopolist; but it would be a condition that one should show what part of the past earnings were extortionate, for not all that even a monopolist may earn is *caput lupinum*. The plaintiff made no such attempt, and its distinction between capital, "contributed by consumers", and capital, "contributed by shareholders," has no basis in law. "Alcoa's" earnings belonged to its shareholders, they were free to withdraw them and spend them, or to leave them in the business. If they chose to leave them, it was no different from contributing new capital out of their pockets. This assumed, it would be hard to say that "Alcoa" had made exorbitant profits on ingot, if it is proper to allocate the profit upon the whole business proportionately among all its products—ingot, and fabrications from ingot. A profit of ten per cent in such an industry, dependent, in part at any rate, upon continued tariff protection, and subject to the vicissitudes of new demands, to the obsolescence of plant and process—which can never be accurately gauged in advance—to the chance that substitutes may at any moment be discovered which will reduce the demand, and to the other hazards which attend all industry: a profit of ten per cent, so conditioned, could hardly be considered extortionate.

There are however, two answers to any such excuse; and the first is that the profit on ingot was not necessarily the same as the profit of the business as a whole, and that we have no means of allocating its proper share to ingot. It is true that the mill cost appears; but obviously it would be unfair to "Alcoa" to take, as the measure of its profit on ingot, the difference between selling price and mill cost; and yet we have nothing else. It may be retorted that it was for the plaintiff to prove what was the profit upon ingot in accordance with the general burden of proof. We think not. Having proved that "Alcoa" had a monopoly of the domestic ingot market, the plaintiff had gone far enough; if it was an excuse, that "Alcoa" had not abused its power, it lay upon "Alcoa" to prove that it had not. But the whole issue is irrelevant anyway, for it is no excuse for "monopolizing" a market that the monopoly has not been used to extract from the consumer more than a "fair" profit. The Act has wider purposes. Indeed, even though we disregarded all but economic considerations, it would by no means follow that such concentration of producing power is to be desired, when it has not been used extortionately. Many people believe that possession of unchallenged economic power deadens initiative, discourages thrift and depresses energy; that immunity from competition is a narcotic, and rivalry is a stimulant, to industrial progress; that the spur of constant stress is necessary to counteract an inevitable disposition to let well enough alone. Such people believe that competitors, versed in the craft as no consumer can be, will be quick to detect opportunities for saving and new shifts in production, and be eager to profit by them. In any event the mere fact that a producer, having command of the domestic market, has not been able to make more than a "fair" profit, is no evidence that a "fair" profit could not have been made at lower prices. United States v. Corn Products Refining Co., [234 F.] 1014, 1015. True, it might have been thought adequate to condemn only those monopolies which could not show that they had exercised the highest possible ingenuity, had adopted every possible economy, had anticipated every conceivable improvement, stimulated every possible demand. No doubt, that would be one way of dealing with the matter, although it would imply constant scrutiny and constant supervision, such as courts are unable to provide. Be that as it may, that was not the way that Congress chose; it did not condone "good trusts" and condemn "bad" ones; it forbade all. Moreover, in so doing it was not necessarily actuated by economic motives alone. It is possible, because of its indirect social or moral effect, to prefer a system of small producers, each dependent for his success upon his own skill and character, to one in which the great mass of those engaged must accept the direction of a few. These considerations, which we have suggested only as possible purposes of the Act, we think the decisions prove to have been in fact its purposes.

It is settled, at least as to § 1, that there are some contracts restricting competition which are unlawful, no matter how beneficent they may be; no industrial exigency will justify them; they are absolutely forbidden. Chief Justice Taft said as much of contracts dividing a territory among producers, in the often quoted passage of his opinion in the Circuit Court of Appeals in United States v. Addyston Pipe and Steel Co., 6 Cir., 85 F. 271, 291. The Supreme Court unconditionally condemned all contracts fixing prices in United States v. Trenton Potteries Company, 273 U.S. 392, 397, 398, and whatever doubts may have arisen as to that decision from Appalachian Coals Inc. v. United States, 288 U.S. 344; they were laid aside United States v. Socony–Vacuum Co., 310 U.S. 150, 220–224. It will now scarcely be denied that the same notion originally extended to all contracts—"reasonable," or "unreasonable"—which restrict competition. United States v. Trans–Missouri Freight Association, 166 U.S. 290, 327, 328; United States v. Joint Traffic Association, 171 U.S. 505, 575–577. The decisions in Standard Oil Co. v. United States, 221 U.S. 1, and American Tobacco Company v. United States, 221 U.S. 106, certainly did change this, and since then it has been accepted law that not all contracts which in fact put an end to existing competition are unlawful. Starting, however, with the authoritative premise that all contracts fixing prices are unconditionally prohibited, the only possible difference between them and a monopoly is that while a monopoly necessarily involves an equal, or even greater, power to fix prices, its mere existence might be thought not to constitute an exercise of that power. That distinction is nevertheless purely formal; it would be valid only so long as the monopoly remained wholly inert; it would disappear as soon as the monopoly began to operate; for, when it did—that is, as soon as it began to sell at all—it must sell at some price and the only price at which it could sell is a price which it itself fixed. (Thereafter the power and its exercise must needs coalesce.) Indeed it would be absurd to condemn such contracts unconditionally, and not to extend the condemnation to monopolies; for the contracts are only steps toward that entire control which monopoly confers: they are really partial monopolies.

But we are not left to deductive reasoning. Although in many settings it may be proper to weigh the extent and effect of restrictions in a contract against its industrial or commercial advantages, this is never to be done when the contract is made with intent to set up a monopoly. As much was plainly implied in Swift & Co. v. United States, 196 U.S. 375, 396, where the court spoke of monopoly as being the "result" which the law seeks to prevent; and, although the language on pages 60 and 61 of Standard Oil Co. v. United States, 221 U.S. 1, is not altogether clear, it seems to presuppose as a premise that a monopoly is always an "unreasonable restraint of trade." Again, the opinion in Sugar Institute v. United States, 297 U.S. 553, 598—borrowing from Appalachian Coals Inc. v. United States, supra, 288 U.S. 344, 374—said: "Accordingly, we have held that a cooperative enterprise otherwise free from objection which carries with it no monopolistic menace" need not always be condemned. These were indeed only thrown out as steps in the argument; but Fashion Originators' Guild v. Federal Trade Commission, 312 U.S. 457, was a ruling. That concerned a combination of dressmakers who set up a boycott against all retailers who should deal in dresses copied—"pirated"—from the dressmakers' designs. Before the Commission the dressmakers had offered to prove that "the practices of FOGA were reasonable and necessary to protect the manufacturer, laborer, retailer and consumer against devastating evils growing from the pirating of original designs and had in fact benefited all four." (P. 467.) All such evidence the Commission refused to hear, raising as sharply as possible the issue whether the combination could excuse itself as "reasonable" because of the benefits it conferred upon the industry. The court sustained the Commission because "the purpose and object of this combination, its potential power, its tendency to monopoly, the coercion it could and did practice upon a rival method of competition, all brought it within the policy of the prohibition." (P. 467.) Moreover, the Clayton Act itself (§§ 14 and 18, Title 15, U.S.C.) shows that practices harmless in themselves will not be tolerated when they "tend to create a monopoly." Perhaps, it has been idle to labor the point at length; there can be no doubt that the vice of restrictive contracts and of monopoly is really one, it is the denial to commerce of the supposed protection of competition. To repeat, if the earlier stages are proscribed, when they are parts of a plan, the mere projecting of which condemns them unconditionally, the realization of the plan itself must also be proscribed.

We have been speaking only of the economic reasons which forbid monopoly; but, as we have already implied, there are others, based upon the belief that great industrial consolidations are inherently undesirable, regardless of their economic results. In the debates in Congress Senator Sherman himself ... showed that among the purposes of Congress in 1890 was a desire to put an end to great aggregations of capital because of the helplessness of the individual before them. Another aspect of the same notion may be found in the language of Mr. Justice Peckham in United States v. Trans–Missouri Freight Association, supra, 323 (166 U.S. 290). That Congress is still of the same mind appears in the Surplus Property Act of 1944, and the Small Business Mobilization Act. Not only does § 2(d) of the first declare it to be one aim of that statute "to preserve the competitive position of small business concerns," but § 18 is given over to directions designed to "preserve and strengthen" their position.... Throughout the history of these statutes it has been constantly assumed that one of their purposes was to perpetuate and preserve, for its own sake and in spite of possible cost, an organization of industry in small units which can effectively compete with each other. We hold that "Alcoa's" monopoly of ingot was of the kind covered by § 2.

It does not follow because "Alcoa" had such a monopoly, that it "monopolized" the ingot market; it may not have achieved monopoly; monopoly may have been thrust upon it. If it had been a combination of existing smelters that united the whole industry and controlled the production of all aluminum ingot, it would certainly have "monopolized" the market. In several decisions the Supreme Court has decreed the dissolution of such combinations, although they had engaged in no unlawful trade practices. Perhaps we should not count among these Northern Securities Co. v. United States, 193 U.S. 197, 327; because it was decided under the old dispensation which ended with Standard Oil Co. v. United States, supra (221 U.S. 1); but the following cases were later. United States v. Union Pacific R.R. Co., 226 U.S. 61, 88; International Harvester v. Missouri, 234 U.S. 199, 209; United States v. Reading Company, 253 U.S. 26, 57–59; United States v. Southern Pacific Company, 259 U.S. 214, 230, 231. We may start therefore with the premise that to have combined ninety per cent of the producers of ingot would have been to "monopolize" the ingot market; and, so far as concerns the public interest, it can make no difference whether an existing competition is put an end to, or whether prospective competition is prevented. The Clayton Act itself speaks in that alternative: "to injure, destroy or prevent competition." (§ 13(a) Title 15, U.S.C.) Nevertheless, it is unquestionably true that from the very outset the courts have at least kept in reserve the possibility that the origin of a monopoly may be critical in determining its legality; and for this they had warrant in some of the congressional debates which accompanied the passage of the Act. [Citing cases.] This notion has usually been expressed by saying that size does not determine guilt; that there must be some "exclusion" of competitors; that the growth must be something else than "natural" or "normal;" that there must be a "wrongful intent," or some other specific intent; or that some "unduly" coercive means must be used. At times there has been emphasis upon the use of the active verb, "monopolize," as the judge noted in the case at bar. [Citing cases.] What engendered these compunctions is reasonably plain; persons may unwittingly find themselves in possession of a monopoly, automatically so to say: that is, without having intended either to put an end to existing competition, or to prevent competition from arising when none had existed; they may become monopolists by force of accident. Since the Act makes "monopolizing" a crime, as well as a civil wrong, it would be not only unfair, but presumably contrary to the intent of Congress, to include such instances. A market may, for example, be so limited that it is impossible to produce at all and meet the cost of production except by a plant large enough to supply the whole demand. Or there may be changes in taste or in cost which drive out all but one purveyor. A single producer may be the survivor out of a group of active competitors, merely by virtue of his superior skill, foresight and industry. In such cases a strong argument can be made that, although the result may expose the public to the evils of monopoly, the Act does not mean to condemn the resultant of those very forces which it is its prime object to foster: *finis opus coronat*. The successful competitor, having been urged to compete, must not be turned upon when he wins. The most extreme expression of this view is in United States v. United States Steel Corporation, 251 U.S. 417, from which we quote in the margin[5] and which Sanford, J. in part repeated in United States v. International Harvester Corp., 274 U.S. 693, 708. It so chances that in both instances the corporation had less than two-thirds of the production in its hands, and the language quoted was not necessary to the decision; so that even if it had

---

5. Justice McKenna for the majority said, 251 U.S. 417, at page 451: "The Corporation is undoubtedly of impressive size and it takes an effort of resolution not to be affected by it or to exaggerate its influence. But we must adhere to the law and the law does not make mere size an offence or the existence of unexerted power an offence. It, we repeat, requires overt acts and trusts to its prohibition of them and its power to repress or punish them. It does not compel competition nor require all that is possible." The minority through Day, J. agreed, 215 U.S. 417, at page 460: "the act offers no objection to the mere size of a corporation nor to the continued exertion of its lawful power, when that size and power have been obtained by lawful means and developed by natural growth, although its resources, capital and strength may give to such corporation a dominating place in the business and industry with which it is concerned. It is entitled to maintain its size and the power that legitimately goes with it, provided no law has been transgressed in obtaining it."

not later been modified, it has not the authority of an actual decision. But, whatever authority it does have was modified by the gloss of Cardozo, J. in Swift & Company v. United States, 286 U.S. 106, when he said, at 116: "Mere size . . . is not an offense against the Sherman Act unless magnified to the point at which it amounts to a monopoly . . . but size carries with it an opportunity for abuse that is not to be ignored when the opportunity is proved to have been utilized in the past." "Alcoa's" size was "magnified" to make it a "monopoly;" indeed, it has never been anything else; and its size, not only offered it an "opportunity for abuse," but it "utilized" its size for "abuse," as can easily be shown.

It would completely misconstrue "Alcoa's" position in 1940 to hold that it was the passive beneficiary of a monopoly, following upon an involuntary elimination of competitors by automatically operative economic forces. Already in 1909, when its last lawful monopoly ended, it sought to strengthen its position by unlawful practices, and these concededly continued until 1912. In that year it had two plants in New York, at which it produced less than 42 million pounds of ingot; in 1934 it had five plants (the original two, enlarged; one in Tennessee; one in North Carolina; one in Washington), and its production had risen to about 327 million pounds, an increase of almost eight-fold. Meanwhile not a pound of ingot had been produced by anyone else in the United States. This increase and this continued and undisturbed control did not fall undesigned into "Alcoa's" lap; obviously it could not have done so. It could only have resulted, as it did result, from a persistent determination to maintain the control, with which it found itself vested in 1912. There were at least one or two abortive attempts to enter the industry, but "Alcoa" effectively anticipated and forestalled all competition, and succeeded in holding the field alone. True, it stimulated demand and opened new uses for the metal, but not without making sure that it could supply what it had evoked. There is no dispute as to this; "Alcoa" avows it as evidence of the skill, energy and initiative with which it has always conducted its business; as a reason why, having won its way by fair means, it should be commended, and not dismembered. We need charge it with no moral derelictions after 1912; we may assume that all it claims for itself is true. The only question is whether it falls within the exception established in favor of those who do not seek, but cannot avoid, the control of a market. It seems to us that that question scarcely survives its statement. It was not inevitable that it should always anticipate increases in the demand for ingot and be prepared to supply them. Nothing compelled it to keep doubling and redoubling its capacity before others entered the field. It insists that it never excluded competitors; but we can think of no more effective exclusion than progressively to embrace each new opportunity as it opened, and to face every newcomer with new capacity already geared into a great organization, having the advantage of experience, trade connections and the elite of personnel. Only in case we interpret "exclusion" as limited to maneuvers not honestly industrial, but actuated solely by a desire to prevent competition, can such a course indefatigably pursued, be deemed not "exclusionary." So to limit it would in our judgment emasculate the Act; would permit just such consolidations as it was designed to prevent.

"Alcoa" answers that it positively assisted competitors, instead of discouraging them. That may be true as to fabricators of ingot; but what of that? They were its market for ingot, and it is charged only with a monopoly of ingot. We can find no instance of its helping prospective ingot manufacturers. . . .

We disregard any question of "intent." Relatively early in the history of the Act–1905—Holmes, J. in Swift & Company v. United States, supra (196 U.S. 375, 396), explained this aspect of the Act in a passage often quoted. Although the primary evil was monopoly, the Act also covered preliminary steps, which, if not contained, would lead to it. These may do no harm of themselves; but, if they are initial moves in a plan or scheme which, carried out, will result in monopoly, they are dangerous and the law will nip them in the bud. For this reason conduct falling short of monopoly, is not illegal unless it is part of a plan to monopolize, or to gain such other control of a market as is equally forbidden. To make it so, the plaintiff must prove what in the criminal law is known as a "specific intent;" an intent which goes beyond the mere intent to do the act. By far the greatest part of the fabulous record piled up in the case at bar, was concerned with proving such an intent. The plaintiff was seeking to show that many transactions, neutral on their face, were not in fact necessary to the development of "Alcoa's" business, and had no motive except to exclude others and perpetuate its hold upon the ingot market. Upon that effort success depended in case the plaintiff failed to satisfy the court that it was unnecessary under § 2 to convict "Alcoa" of practices unlawful of them-selves. The plaintiff has so satisfied us, and the issue of intent ceases to have any importance; no intent is relevant except that which is relevant to any liability, criminal or civil: *i.e.*, an intent to bring about the forbidden act. Note 59 on page 226 of United States v. Socony–Vacuum Oil Co., supra (310 U.S. 150, on page 226), on which "Alcoa" appears so much to rely, is in no sense to the contrary. Douglas, J. was answering the defendants' argument that, assuming that a combination had attempted to fix prices, it had never had the power to do so, for there was too much competing oil. His answer was that the plan was unlawful, even if the parties did not have the power to fix prices, provided that they intended to do so; and it was to drive home this that he contrasted the case then before the court with monopoly, where power was a necessary element. In so doing he said: "An intent and a power . . . are then necessary," which he at once followed by quoting the passage we have just mentioned from Swift & Co. v. United States, supra (196 U.S. 375). In order to fall within § 2, the monopolist must have both the power to monopolize, and the intent to monopolize. To read the passage as demanding any "specific" intent, makes nonsense of it, for no monopolist monopolizes unconscious of what he is doing. So here, "Alcoa" meant to keep, and did keep, that complete and exclusive hold upon the ingot market with which it started. That was to "monopolize" that market, however innocently it otherwise proceeded. So far as the judgment held that it was not within § 2, it must be reversed.

Judgment reversed, and cause remanded for further proceedings not inconsistent with the foregoing.[6]

NOTES AND QUESTIONS

1. Despite Judge Hand's pronouncement in *Alcoa* on the market share required to sustain the charge of monopolization (see note 4, supra), no fixed percentages have been established under Section 2. The Supreme Court has expressly stated that the "relative effect of percentage command of the market varies with the setting in which that factor is placed." United States v. Columbia Steel Co., 334 U.S. 495, 528 (1948). In Domed Stadium Hotel, Inc. v. Holiday Inns, Inc., 732 F.2d 480, 489–90 (5th Cir.1984), the Fifth Circuit handled the market share issue as follows:

> The precise market share a defendant must control, absent supporting evidence of monopoly power before he is guilty of monopolization, remains undefined.... Supreme Court cases, as well as cases from this court, suggest that absent special circumstances, a defendant must have a market share of at least fifty percent before he can be guilty of monopolization. Further, undisputed evidence of low market share may make monopolization an impossibility as a matter of law. *Dimmitt,* 679 F.2d 516, 529. Recent cases by this court hold that market shares of between seventeen and twenty-five percent are legally insufficient to uphold a finding of monopolization, at least absent other compelling evidence that the defendant had monopoly power.

See Syufy Enterprises v. American Multicinema, Inc., 793 F.2d 990 (9th Cir.1986), cert. denied, 479 U.S. 1031 (1987) (market share of 60–69% is sufficient to show monopoly power when coupled with other factors, including the fragmentation of competition and the presence of entry barriers).

What factors other than market share *should* be considered in determining the presence of market power? How much weight should a court place on the presence or absence of entry barriers, abnormal profits, historical trend, fragmented competition, corporate conduct, and other such factors? Could Alcoa have held down its market share by charging exorbitant prices? Would a 49% market share in such circumstances indicate a lack of monopoly power? See Broadway Delivery Corp. v. United Parcel Service of America, Inc., 651 F.2d 122 (2d Cir.), cert. denied, 454 U.S. 968 (1981) (trial court instruction precluding a finding of monopoly power where defendant's market share was less than 50% was in error but was harmless in the circumstances). Conversely, should a corporation with a very large market share *always* be considered a company with monopoly power? In Ball Memorial Hospital,

---

6. On remand, Judge Knox denied the government's prayer for divestiture and ordered that stockholders with shares in both Alcoa and Aluminum Limited, the Canadian producer, sell their interest in one of the companies and that certain patent practices be terminated. United States v. Aluminum Co. of America, 91 F.Supp. 333 (S.D.N.Y. 1950). And see Judge Cashin's opinion, finding that during the five-year period set by Judge Knox to determine if further relief was warranted, such competitive conditions had been established that a further extension of time to request relief should be denied. United States v. Aluminum Co. of America, 153 F.Supp. 132 (S.D.N.Y.1957).

On the Alcoa decree, see 2 Whitney, Antitrust Policies 98 (1958); Comment, Vertical Integration in Aluminum: A Bar to "Effective Competition," 60 Yale L.J. 294 (1951).

Inc. v. Mutual Hospital Insurance, Inc., 784 F.2d 1325, 1335 (7th Cir.1986), the Court of Appeals opined as follows:

> Market power comes from the ability to cut back the market's total output and so raise price; consumers bid more in competing against one another to obtain the smaller quantity available. When a firm (or group of firms) controls a significant percentage of the productive assets in the market, the remaining firms may not have the capacity to increase their sales quickly to make up for any reduction by the dominant firm or group of firms. In other cases, however, a firm's share of current sales does not reflect an ability to reduce the total output in the market, and therefore it does not convey power over price. Other firms may be able, for example, to divert production into the market from outside. They may be able to convert productive capacity to the product in question or import the product from out of the area. If firms are able to enter, expand, or import sufficiently quickly, that may counteract a reduction in output by existing firms. And if current sales are not based on the ownership of productive assets—so that entrants do not need to build new plants or otherwise take a long time to supply consumers' wants—the existing firms may have no power at all to cut back the market's output. To put these points a little differently, the lower the barriers to entry, and the shorter the lags of new entry, the less power existing firms have. When the supply is highly elastic, existing market share does not signify power.

These issues will again be considered in United States v. Grinnell Corp., 384 U.S. 563 (1966), p. 172 infra, and Chapter 8, Section 1.

2. If Judge Hand in *Alcoa* had excluded the ingot processed by Alcoa's subsidiaries, its share of the market would have been reduced to about 60%. Why was Alcoa's captive production included in the market? Do you agree with the Court's reasoning?

3. Judge Hand apparently assumed that secondary aluminum ingot competed effectively with primary aluminum ingot, but excluded secondary ingot from the relevant market on grounds that Alcoa, in the past, had controlled the commodity. In Judge Hand's view, the monopolist would have been guided "not alone by [the] effect [of its production] at that time upon the market, but by his knowledge that some part of it was likely to be reclaimed and seek the future market. That consideration will to some extent affect its production ... and, if it was as far-sighted as it proclaimed itself, that consideration must have had its share in determining how much to produce." See note 3, p. 133, supra.

How could Alcoa's prior control over production give it the capacity to influence competition during any relevant subsequent period? Suppose Alcoa knew in 1927 that 25% of a given year's production would re-enter the market in the form of secondary aluminum about 10 years later. Would Alcoa really be likely to leave demand unsatisfied in 1927, beyond levels that would prevail if aluminum were a fully consumed product, in order to protect its predicted market position in 1937? Would even a far-sighted monopolist have sufficiently reliable information about market conditions a decade later to make that judgment?

4. What exactly did Alcoa do wrong? What must a firm with monopoly power do—or not do—in order to avoid violating Section 2? Were Alcoa's profits too high? Does Judge Hand's opinion provide the answer? Should high profits matter? What if potentially high profits were lost because of what economists call X-inefficiencies—

i.e., monopoly power acted as a "narcotic," depressed energy, led to luxurious management perks, and created slack throughout the operation?

Under the *Alcoa* conduct standard, must a firm with monopoly power avoid hiring too many scientists for its research and development department, so as not to exclude competitors through consistently successful product innovation? Must a firm with monopoly power disclose trade secrets or avoid the use of restrictive covenants?

Suppose a monopolist engages in deceptive advertising or some other kind of business tort; would that constitute illegal behavior under Section 2 regardless of whether the conduct bears a direct or significant relationship to the acquisition or maintenance of monopoly power? In other words, does every sort of illegality taint monopoly power?

What if a firm with monopoly power charged relatively low prices and made only a reasonable profit, but, in doing so, drove its few weak competitors from the market? Must a firm with monopoly power price its products in such a way as not to drive out its few remaining competitors or not to discourage new entry?

These questions are meant to raise broad policy issues about the permissible behavior of a firm with monopoly power. The issues are considered again, and in more depth, in Chapter 8, Sections 1–5. For present purposes, however, consider the following decisions, which should help you analyze the *Alcoa* decision and its sweeping language.

(a) BERKEY PHOTO, INC. v. EASTMAN KODAK CO., 603 F.2d 263 (2d Cir.1979), cert. denied, 444 U.S. 1093 (1980). In 1972, Kodak introduced its immensely successful pocket Instamatic 110, a much smaller version of its successful Instamatic line, along with a specially designed film called Kodacolor II. Even before these new developments, Kodak had a monopoly in the sale of "amateur conventional still cameras" and in camera film. The pocket Instamatic was dramatically successful, improving and solidifying its monopoly position, and Berkey's market position, along with all other Kodak competitors, was adversely affected.

Berkey had begun to sell amateur still cameras in 1968 and from 1970 to 1977 accounted for 8.2% of U.S. camera sales. In 1978, Berkey sold its camera division and abandoned the market. Several years earlier Berkey had sued Kodak for treble damages, charging among other things that Kodak had acquired and maintained its monopoly position in camera and films in violation of Section 2 of the Sherman Act.

Among many charges of monopolization and attempt to monopolize leveled by Berkey, one of special interest contended that it was a violation of Section 2 for Kodak to fail to predisclose "sufficient advance information to enable [competitors] to enter the market with copies of the new product on the day of Kodak's introduction." Berkey did not contend that every monopolist had to predisclose innovations but rather that Kodak's related monopolies in camera and film created a special obligation. In fact, Kodak had notified competitors in January 1972 that it would introduce a new camera and offered to sell further information to all camera makers describing the new products, indicating anticipated dates of announcement and commercial introduction, and providing specifications and technical notes about the product. Berkey paid the fee but as a result obtained only about two months' advance knowledge of information needed to compete on the new product.

The Court of Appeals held as a matter of law that Kodak, for policy and practical reasons, did not have a duty to predisclose information about the pocket Instamatic or its new film to competing camera manufacturers. It concluded that even a monopolist has a right to the lead time that follows from success in innovation, and that Kodak's related monopoly position in film, and the simultaneous introduction of a new film type, did not create any additional obligations. If the result were otherwise, the Court observed, aggressive competition in innovation would be discouraged.

The Second Circuit was also concerned about the difficulty of fashioning a workable rule describing where and under what circumstances a monopolist had a duty to disclose:

> But it is difficult to comprehend how a major corporation ... could possess the omniscience to anticipate all the instances in which a jury might one day in the future retrospectively conclude that predisclosure was warranted. And it is equally difficult to discern workable guidelines that a court might set forth to aid the firm's decision. For example, how detailed must the information conveyed be? And how far must research have progressed before it is "ripe" for disclosure? These inherent uncertainties would have an inevitable chilling effect on innovation. They go far, we believe, towards explaining why no court has ever imposed the duty Berkey seeks to create here.

Can you imagine any circumstances in which a monopolist might have some duty to disclose? How does *Berkey's* holding affect Judge Hand's comment in *Alcoa* that "We can find no instance of [Alcoa] helping prospective ingot manufacturers...." Did Judge Hand mean to rely on the failure to assist as a basis for his finding of monopolization?

(b) IN RE E.I. DUPONT DE NEMOURS & CO., 3 Trade Reg.Rep. (CCH) ¶ 21,770 (FTC Oct. 20, 1980). In the early 1970s, duPont found itself with about a 25% cost advantage in the production of titanium dioxide pigments (TiO2), a chemical used in the manufacture of paint and paper. DuPont had concentrated on a "chloride process" and had constructed two plants in the 1950s based on that technology; all its competitors had built plants based on a competing "sulfate process." In the 1950s and 60s, the sulfate process was equally or more efficient, but in about 1970, a worldwide shortage drove up the price of raw materials used in the sulfate process while environmental regulations imposed costly pollution abatement requirements on sulfate but not chloride manufacturing facilities.

In 1972, duPont accounted for about 30% of TiO2 sales. Recognizing its substantial cost advantage, duPont embarked on a growth strategy that incorporated three elements. First, it expanded its two existing plants and planned to construct a new large-scale facility. Its acknowledged goal was to expand capacity to serve all the expected increase in marketwide demand for TiO2 from the late 1970s into the mid–1980s, but not, according to its expectations, to take much market share away from existing competitors. Second, it priced its TiO2 products high enough to finance its own expansion of capacity, yet low enough to discourage existing rivals from expanding and to discourage new domestic or foreign entry. DuPont earned at all times a reasonable profit on its TiO2 sales. Third, it refused to license its cost-saving chloride technology (patents and know-how) to rivals.

DuPont's market share increased from 30% in 1972 to 42% in 1977, and it anticipated in 1977 that it would achieve 55% by 1985. (At an earlier date in the 1970s, duPont thought its expansion program might achieve for it a 65% market share by 1985.) While not part of its expressed aim, duPont's expansion was to some extent at the expense of existing rivals. Its expansion and construction program produced plants of optimally efficient scale, and there was no evidence of an intention to build excess capacity for strategic competitive reasons. DuPont anticipated that the prices it would charge in the period 1972 to 1980 would be somewhat lower than would be the case if it were not pursuing an expansion strategy, but that profits after 1984 and through 1992 would be higher under the expansion plan.

The FTC's staff counsel argued that duPont's construction program, though not illegal in itself, became illegal when viewed in conjunction with the pricing and non-licensing policies. They argued that duPont's willingness to forego available short-term profits and invest in expansion of capacity would only make sense if non-competitive profits would become available at a later date, and the combination of duPont's construction/pricing/non-licensing policies therefore constituted an "attempt to monopolize" under Section 2 of the Sherman Act and an unfair practice under Section 5 of the Federal Trade Commission Act.

The full Commission unanimously rejected these staff arguments, emphasizing that duPont's expansion program grew out of legally obtained efficiencies and that its pricing program was rational, earning substantial profits for the company through the entire period of expansion, without regard to any ability to extract monopoly profits in the future. Moreover, the Commission noted there simply is no duty under the antitrust laws for a firm that develops superior products or processes to license or disclose its technology to rivals.

The Commission observed that a different conclusion would have required that the firm with the most efficient process not expand its capacity, or not lower its prices, in order to provide market opportunities or funds to less efficient rivals. The opinion concluded:

> Antitrust policy wisely disfavors monopoly, but it also seeks to promote vigorous competitive behavior. Indeed, the essence of the competitive process is to induce firms to become more efficient and to pass the benefits of the efficiency along to consumers. That process would be ill-served by using antitrust to block hard, aggressive competition that is solidly based on efficiencies and growth opportunities, even if monopoly is a possible result. Such a view, we believe, is entirely consistent with the "superior skill, foresight and industry" exception in *Alcoa* and subsequent cases, for those decisions clearly indicate that monopolies may be lawfully created by superior competitive ability.

(c) Olympia Equipment Leasing Co. v. Western Union Telegraph, 797 F.2d 370, 375–76 (7th Cir.1986), cert. denied, 480 U.S. 934 (1987). Judge Posner, writing for a panel of the Seventh Circuit, had the following to say about monopoly conduct:

> Opinion about the offense of monopolization has undergone an evolution. Forty years ago it was thought that even a firm with a lawful monopoly (there is no suggestion that Western Union's monopoly of telex service is unlawful) could not be allowed to defend its monopoly against would-be competitors by tactics otherwise legitimate; it had to exercise special restraint—perhaps, indeed, had to hold its prices high, to encourage new entry. So Alcoa was condemned as a monopolist because it had assiduously created enough productive capacity to supply all new increments of demand for aluminum.... Later, as the emphasis of antitrust policy shifted from the protection of competition as a process of rivalry to the protection of competition as a means of promoting economic efficiency ... it became recognized that the lawful monopolist should be free to compete like everyone else; otherwise the antitrust laws would be holding an umbrella over inefficient competitors. "A monopolist, no less than any other competitor, is permitted and indeed encouraged to compete aggres-

sively on the merits...." Foremost Pro Color, Inc. v. Eastman Kodak Co., 703 F.2d 534, 544 (9th Cir.1983). With Judge Hand's opinion in *Alcoa* compare the approach of his successors in Berkey Photo, Inc. v. Eastman Kodak Co., 603 F.2d 263, 274, 276, 287 (2d Cir.1979).

Today it is clear that a firm with lawful monopoly power has no general duty to help its competitors, whether by holding a price umbrella over their heads or by otherwise pulling its competitive punches. *See, e.g.,* MCI Communications Corp. v. AT & T, 708 F.2d 1081, 1149 (7th Cir.1983); Catlin v. Washington Energy Co., 791 F.2d 1343 (9th Cir.1986). "There is a difference between positive and negative duties, and the antitrust laws, like other legal doctrines sounding in tort, have generally been understood to impose only the latter." USM Corp. v. SPS Technologies, Inc., 694 F.2d 505, 512–13 (7th Cir.1982). So if a firm went to a monopolist and said, "Please—for the sake of competition—give me a loan so I can compete with you and make this a competitive market," and it was turned down, it could not invoke the Sherman Act. A monopolist has no duty to reduce its prices in order to help consumers—and no duty to extend a helping hand to new entrants; thus IBM "was under no duty to help CalComp or other peripheral equipment manufacturers survive or expand. IBM need not have provided its rivals with disk products to examine and copy...." California Computer Products, Inc. v. IBM, 613 F.2d 727, 744 (9th Cir.1979) (citation omitted). *Berkey, Foremost* and other cases make clear that a monopolist has no duty to disclose its plans to rivals in order to help the rivals compete with it.

If a monopolist does extend a helping hand, though not required to do so, and later withdraws it as happened in this case, does he incur antitrust liability? We think not.

(d) IN RE INTEL CORPORATION, FTC Dkt No. 9288 (1999). In 1998, the Federal Trade Commission filed a complaint charging that Intel had monopoly power in the microprocessor product market (it was alleged to have approximately an 80% market share in dollar sales), and had violated Section 2 by denying advance technical information about new microprocessor products, product samples and related technical assistance to customers so that they could perform system testing and debugging on new generations of microprocessors. Microprocessors are sometimes described as the "brains" of computers because they perform major data processing functions.

Intel followed a policy of providing technical data and samples to a group of about a dozen preferred customers. Three of those customers—Digital Equipment, Intergraph and Compaq—became involved in intellectual property (IP) disputes with Intel, essentially complaining that Intel's new microprocessors infringed upon each company's patents. After negotiations proved fruitless, two of the companies sued Intel, and one threatened to sue, for patent infringement. Intel retaliated by cutting each of the three off from product information and samples, allegedly essential to compete effectively in design and sale of new computer systems. The FTC charged that Intel's actions had several anticompetitive effects, the most significant being that coercion by a monopolist that forces customers to license away IP rights on unfavorable terms tends to diminish the customers' incentives to develop new technologies, and thus is likely to harm competition by reducing innovation. Intel defended on grounds that it had the right not to deal with companies that sued it. The Commission's response was that a refusal to continue to do business by a monopolist was unreasonably exclusionary behavior under

Section 2 and that IP controversies should be addressed in court rather than by self-help.

The case was settled in 1999 with an agreed-upon consent order acknowledging that Intel was free to decide in the first instance whether to provide or not provide information to customers, and could discontinue business relations on many grounds such as that the customer did not protect the confidentiality of Intel's IP. But it could not discriminate among customers once business arrangements were initiated on grounds that it found itself in an IP dispute. One interesting exception to Intel's obligation to continue providing information and product related to the remedy that the customer sought in court. Customers were free to seek a wide range of legal and equitable remedies, including damages (trebled or otherwise increased in appropriate cases), reasonable royalties and attorneys' fees and costs. On the other hand, if the customer sought a preliminary or permanent injunction to put Intel out of the business of selling microprocessors, then Intel was free to deny the customer information and products. The rationale appears to be that neither party should deny ultimate consumers the benefits of innovation while the parties litigate over their respective views in court.

Digital and Compaq had settled their quarrels with Intel before completion of the FTC action. Intergraph pursued its remedies and, in November 1999, the Court of Appeals for the Federal Circuit found in favor of Intel. The Circuit Court concluded:

> "The remedy of compulsory disclosure of proprietary information and provision of pre-production chips and other commercial and intellectual property is a dramatic remedy for antitrust illegality, and requires violation of antitrust law or the likelihood that such violation would be established. In the proceedings whose record is before us, Intergraph has not shown a substantial likelihood of success in establishing that Intel violated the antitrust laws...." See Intergraph Corp. v. Intel Corp., 195 F.3d 1346 (Fed.Cir.1999).

Should a monopolist that finds itself in legal controversies with other companies that depend on its essential product or services be entitled to use self-help? If self-help is permitted, will it turn out that the monopolist will prevail every time?

Should a monopolist be free to compete like everyone else? What if it controls a facility essential to competitors and refuses them access? What if a monopolist who is a supplier retaliates against a customer—*e.g.*, by refusing to deal—who has the temerity to try to compete with it? Think about other instances where a firm with monopoly power should be treated differently than a company with 4% of a competitive market. In general, see Aspen Skiing Co. v. Aspen Highlands Skiing Corp., 472 U.S. 585 (1985), p. 736 infra, and other materials in Chapter 8, Section 1A. For a discussion of "attempt to monopolize," see Chapter 8, Section 1B.

United States v. E.I. du Pont de Nemours & Co.

Supreme Court of the United States, 1956.
351 U.S. 377, 76 S.Ct. 994, 100 L.Ed. 1264.

■ REED, J. The United States brought this civil action under § 4 of the Sherman Act against E.I. du Pont de Nemours and Company. The complaint ... charged du Pont with monopolizing, attempting to monopolize and conspiracy to monopolize interstate commerce in cellophane and cellulosic caps and bands in violation of § 2 of the Sherman Act. Relief by injunction was sought against defendant and its officers, forbidding monopolizing or attempting to monopolize interstate trade in cellophane. The prayer also sought action to dissipate the effect of the monopolization by divestiture or other steps.... After a lengthy trial, judgment was entered for du Pont on all issues.

The Government's direct appeal here does not contest the findings that relate to caps and bands, nor does it raise any issue concerning the alleged attempt to monopolize or conspiracy to monopolize interstate commerce in cellophane. The appeal, as specifically stated by the Government, "attacks only the ruling that du Pont has not monopolized trade in cellophane." At issue for determination is only this alleged violation by du Pont of § 2 of the Sherman Act.

During the period that is relevant to this action, du Pont produced almost 75% of the cellophane sold in the United States, and cellophane constituted less than 20% of all "flexible packaging material" sales....

The Government contends that, by so dominating cellophane production, du Pont monopolized a "part of the trade or commerce" in violation of § 2. Respondent agrees that cellophane is a product which constitutes "a 'part' of commerce within the meaning of Section 2." But it contends that the prohibition of § 2 against monopolization is not violated because it does not have the power to control the price of cellophane or to exclude competitors from the market in which cellophane is sold. The court below found that the "relevant market for determining the extent of du Pont's market control is the market for flexible packaging materials," and that competition from those other materials prevented du Pont from possessing monopoly powers in its sales of cellophane.

The Government asserts that cellophane and other wrapping materials are neither substantially fungible nor like priced. For these reasons, it argues that the market for other wrappings is distinct from the market for cellophane and that the competition afforded cellophane by other wrappings is not strong enough to be considered in determining whether du Pont has monopoly powers. Market delimitation is necessary under du Pont's theory to determine whether an alleged monopolist violates § 2. The ultimate consideration in such a determination is whether the defendants control the price and competition in the market for such part of trade or commerce as they are charged with monopolizing. Every manufacturer is the sole producer of the particular commodity it makes but its control in the above sense of the relevant market depends upon the availability of alternative commodities for buyers: *i.e.*, whether there is a cross-elasticity of demand between cellophane and the other wrappings. This interchangeability is largely gauged by the purchase of competing products for similar uses considering the price, characteristics and adaptability of the competing commodities. The court below found that the flexible wrappings afforded such alternatives. This Court must determine whether the trial court erred in its estimate of the competition afforded cellophane by other materials.

The burden of proof, of course, was upon the Government to establish monopoly. See United States v. Aluminum Co. of America, 2 Cir., 148 F.2d 416, 423, 427. This the trial court held the Government failed to do, upon findings of fact and law stated at length by that court. For the United States to succeed in this Court now, it must show that erroneous legal tests were applied to essential findings of fact or that the findings themselves were "clearly erroneous." . . .

Factual Background.— For consideration of the issue as to monopolization, a general summary of the development of cellophane is useful.

In the early 1900s Jacques Brandenberger, a Swiss chemist, attempted to make tablecloths impervious to dirt by spraying them with liquid viscose (a cellulose solution available in quantity from wood pulp) and by coagulating this coating. His idea failed, but he noted that the coating peeled off in a transparent film. This first "cellophane" was thick, hard, and not perfectly transparent, but Brandenberger apparently foresaw commercial possibilities in his discovery. By 1908 he developed the first machine for the manufacture of transparent sheets of regenerated cellulose. The 1908 product was not satisfactory, but by 1912 Brandenberger was making a saleable thin flexible film used in gas masks. He obtained patents to cover the machinery and the essential ideas of his process.

It seems to be agreed, however, that the disclosures of these early patents were not sufficient to make possible the manufacture of commercial cellophane. The inadequacy of the patents is partially attributed to the fact that the essential machine (the Hopper) was improved after it was patented. But more significant was the failure of these patents to disclose the actual technique of the process. This technique included the operational data acquired by experimentation.

In 1917 Brandenberger assigned his patents to La Cellophane Societe Anonyme and joined that organization. Thereafter developments in the production of cellophane somewhat paralleled those taking place in artificial textiles. Chemical science furnished the knowledge for perfecting the new products. The success of the artificial products has been enormous. Du Pont was an American leader in the field of synthetics and learned of cellophane's successes through an associate, Comptoir des Textiles Artificiel.

In 1923 du Pont organized with La Cellophane an American company for the manufacture of plain cellophane. The undisputed findings are that:

> "On December 26, 1923, an agreement was executed between duPont Cellophane Company and La Cellophane by which La Cellophane licensed duPont Cellophane Company exclusively under its United States cellophane patents, and granted duPont Cellophane Company the exclusive right to make and sell in North and Central America under La Cellophane's secret processes for cellophane manufacture. DuPont Cellophane Company granted to La Cellophane exclusive rights for the rest of the world under any

cellophane patents or processes duPont Cellophane Company might develop."

Finding 24.

Subsequently du Pont and La Cellophane licensed several foreign companies, allowing them to manufacture and vend cellophane in limited areas. Finding 601. Technical exchange agreements with these companies were entered into at the same time. However, in 1940, du Pont notified these foreign companies that sales might be made in any country, and by 1948 all the technical exchange agreements were canceled.

Sylvania, an American affiliate of a Belgian producer of cellophane not covered by the license agreements above referred to, began the manufacture of cellophane in the United States in 1930. Litigation between the French and Belgian companies resulted in a settlement whereby La Cellophane came to have a stock interest in Sylvania, contrary to the La Cellophane-du Pont agreement. This resulted in adjustments as compensation for the intrusion into United States of La Cellophane that extended du Pont's limited territory. The details do not here seem important. Since 1934 Sylvania has produced about 25% of United States cellophane.

An important factor in the growth of cellophane production and sales was the perfection of moistureproof cellophane, a superior product of du Pont research and patented by that company through a 1927 application. Plain cellophane has little resistance to the passage of moisture vapor. Moistureproof cellophane has a composition added which keeps moisture in and out of the packed commodity. This patented type of cellophane has had a demand with much more rapid growth than the plain.

In 1931 Sylvania began the manufacture of moistureproof cellophane under its own patents. After negotiations over patent rights, du Pont in 1933 licensed Sylvania to manufacture and sell moistureproof cellophane produced under the du Pont patents at a royalty of 2% of sales. These licenses with the plain cellophane licenses from the Belgian company, made Sylvania a full cellophane competitor, limited on moistureproof sales by the terms of the licenses to 20% of the combined sales of the two companies of that type by the payment of a prohibitive royalty on the excess. There was never an excess production. The limiting clause was dropped on January 1, 1945, and Sylvania was acquired in 1946 by the American Viscose Corporation with assets of over two hundred million dollars.

Between 1928 and 1950, du Pont's sales of plain cellophane increased from $3,131,608 to $9,330,776. Moistureproof sales increased from $603,222 to $89,850,416, although prices were continuously reduced. It could not be said that this immense increase in use was solely or even largely attributable to the superior quality of cellophane or to the technique or business acumen of du Pont, though doubtless those factors were important. The growth was a part of the expansion of the commodity-packaging habits of business, a by-product of general efficient competitive merchandising to meet modern demands. The profits, which were large, apparently arose from this trend in marketing, the development of the industrial use of chemical research and production of synthetics, rather than from elimination of other producers from the relevant market....

The Sherman Act, § 2—Monopolization.— The only statutory language of § 2 pertinent on this review is: "Every person who shall monopolize ... shall be deemed guilty.... This Court has pointed out that monopoly at common law was a grant by the sovereign to any person for the sole making or handling of anything so that others were restrained or hindered in their lawful trade.... However, as in England, it came to be recognized here that acts bringing the evils of authorized monopoly—unduly diminishing competition and enhancing prices—were undesirable ... and were declared illegal by § 2. Our cases determine that a party has monopoly power if it has, over 'any part of the trade or commerce among the several states,' a power of controlling prices or unreasonably restricting competition."

Senator Hoar, in discussing § 2, pointed out that monopoly involved something more than extraordinary commercial success, "that it involved something like the use of means which made it impossible for other persons to engage in fair competition."[7] This exception to the Sherman Act prohibi-

7. 21 Cong.Rec. 3151:

"Mr. Kenna. Mr. President, I have no disposition to delay a vote on the bill, but I would like to ask, with his permission, the Senator from Vermont a question touching the second section:

" 'Every person who shall monopolize, or attempt to monopolize or combine or conspire with any other person or persons, to monopolize any part of the trade, etc.'

"Is it intended by the committee, as the section seems to indicate, that if an individual engaged in trade between States or between States and Territories, or between States or Territories and the District of Columbia, or between a State and a foreign country, by his own skill and energy, by the propriety of his conduct generally, shall pursue his calling in such a way as to monopolize a trade, his action shall be a crime under this proposed act? To make myself understood, if I am not clear—

"Mr. Edmunds. I think I understand the Senator.

"Mr. Kenna. Suppose a citizen of Kentucky is dealing in shorthorn cattle and by virtue of his superior skill in that particular product it turns out that he is the only one in the United States to whom an order comes from Mexico for cattle of that stock for a considerable period, so that he is conceded to have a monopoly of that trade with Mexico; is it intended by the committee that the bill shall make that man a culprit?

"Mr. Edmunds. It is not intended by it and the bill does not do it. Anybody who knows the meaning of the word 'monopoly,' as the courts apply it, would not apply it to such a person at all; and I am sure my friend must understand that."

Id., at 3152:

"Mr. Hoar. I put in the committee, if I may be permitted to say so (I suppose there is no impropriety in it), the precise question which has been put by the Senator from West Virginia, and I had that precise difficulty in the first place with this bill, but I was answered, and I think all the other members of the committee agreed in the answer, that 'monopoly' is a technical term known to the common law, and that it signifies—I do not mean to say that they stated what the signification was, but I became satisfied that they were right and that the word 'monopoly' is a merely technical term which has a clear and legal signification, and it is this: It is the sole engrossing to a man's self by means which prevent other men from engaging in fair competition with him.

"Of course a monopoly granted by the King was a direct inhibition of all other per-

tions of monopoly power is perhaps the monopoly "thrust upon" one of United States v. Aluminum Co. of America, 2 Cir., 148 F.2d 416, 429, left as an undecided possibility by American Tobacco Co. v. United States, 328 U.S. 781. Compare United States v. United Shoe Machinery Corp., D.C., 110 F.Supp. 295, 342.

If cellophane is the "market" that du Pont is found to dominate, it may be assumed it does have monopoly power over that "market." Monopoly power is the power to control prices or exclude competition. It seems apparent that du Pont's power to set the price of cellophane has been limited only by the competition afforded by other flexible packaging materials. Moreover, it may be practically impossible for anyone to commence manufacturing cellophane without full access to du Pont's technique. However, du Pont has no power to prevent competition from other wrapping materials. The trial court consequently had to determine whether competition from the other wrappings prevented du Pont from possessing monopoly power in violation of § 2. Price and competition are so intimately entwined that any discussion of theory must treat them as one. It is inconceivable that price could be controlled without power over competition or vice versa. This approach to the determination of monopoly power is strengthened by this Court's conclusion in prior cases that, when an alleged monopolist has power over price and competition, an intention to monopolize in a proper case may be assumed.

If a large number of buyers and sellers deal freely in a standardized product, such as salt or wheat, we have complete or pure competition. Patents, on the other hand, furnish the most familiar type of classic monopoly. As the producers of a standardized product bring about significant differentiations of quality, design, or packaging in the product that permit differences of use, competition becomes to a greater or less degree incomplete and the producer's power over price and competition greater over his article and its use, according to the differentiation he is able to create and maintain. A retail seller may have in one sense a monopoly on certain trade because of location, as an isolated country store or filling station, or because no one else makes a product of just the quality or attractiveness of his product, as for example in cigarettes. Thus one can theorize that we have monopolistic competition in every nonstandardized commodity with each manufacturer having power over the price and production of his own product.[8] However, this power that, let us say, automobile or soft-drink manufacturers have over their trademarked prod-

---

sons to engage in that business or calling or to acquire that particular article, except the man who had a monopoly granted him by the sovereign power. I suppose, therefore, that the courts of the United States would say in the case put by the Senator from West Virginia that a man who merely by superior skill and intelligence, a breeder of horses or raiser of cattle, or manufacturer or artisan of any kind, got the whole business because nobody could do it as well as he could was not a monopolist, but that it involved something like the use of means which made it impossible for other persons to engage in fair competition, like the engrossing, the buying up of all other persons engaged in the same business."

8. See Chamberlin, Theory of Monopolistic Competition, c. IV.

ucts is not the power that makes an illegal monopoly. Illegal power must be appraised in terms of the competitive market for the product.

Determination of the competitive market for commodities depends on how different from one another are the offered commodities in character or use, how far buyers will go to substitute one commodity for another. For example, one can think of building materials as in commodity competition but one could hardly say that brick competed with steel or wood or cement or stone in the meaning of Sherman Act litigation; the products are too different. This is the interindustry competition emphasized by some economists. See Lilienthal, Big Business, c. 5. On the other hand, there are certain differences in the formulae for soft drinks but one can hardly say that each one is an illegal monopoly. Whatever the market may be, we hold that control of price or competition establishes the existence of monopoly power under § 2. Section 2 requires the application of a reasonable approach in determining the existence of monopoly power just as surely as did § 1. This of course does not mean that there can be a reasonable monopoly. Our next step is to determine whether du Pont has monopoly power over cellophane: that is, power over its price in relation to or competition with other commodities. The charge was monopolization of cellophane. The defense, that cellophane was merely a part of the relevant market for flexible packaging materials.

The Relevant Market.—When a product is controlled by one interest, without substitutes available in the market, there is monopoly power. Because most products have possible substitutes, we cannot, as we said in Times–Picayune Pub. Co. v. United States, 345 U.S. 594, 612, give "that infinite range" to the definition of substitutes. Nor is it a proper interpretation of the Sherman Act to require that products be fungible to be considered in the relevant market.

The Government argues:

"We do not here urge that in *no* circumstances may competition of substitutes negative possession of monopolistic power over trade in a product. The decisions make it clear at the least that the courts will not consider substitutes other than those which are substantially fungible with the monopolized product and sell at substantially the same price."

But where there are market alternatives that buyers may readily use for their purposes, illegal monopoly does not exist merely because the product said to be monopolized differs from others. If it were not so, only physically identical products would be a part of the market. To accept the Government's argument, we would have to conclude that the manufacturers of plain as well as moistureproof cellophane were monopolists, and so with films such as Pliofilm, foil, glassine, polyethylene, and Saran, for each of these wrapping materials is distinguishable. These were all exhibits in the case. New wrappings appear, generally similar to cellophane: is each a monopoly? What is called for is an appraisal of the "cross-elasticity" of demand in the trade. See Note, 54 Col.L.Rev. 580. The varying circumstances of each case determine the result. In considering what is the relevant market for determining the control of price and competition, no more definite rule can be declared than that commodities reasonably interchangeable by consumers for the same purposes make up that "part of the trade or commerce," monopolization of which may be illegal. As respects flexible packaging materials, the market geographically is nation-wide.

Industrial activities cannot be confined to trim categories. Illegal monopolies under § 2 may well exist over limited products in narrow fields where competition is eliminated.[9] That does not settle the issue here. In determining the market under the Sherman Act, it is the use or uses to which the commodity is put that control. The selling price between commodities with similar uses and different characteristics may vary, so that the cheaper product can drive out the more expensive. Or, the superior quality of higher priced articles may make dominant the more desirable. Cellophane costs more than many competing products and less than a few. But whatever the price, there are various flexible wrapping materials that are bought by manufacturers for packaging their goods in their own plants or are sold to converters who shape and print them for use in the packaging of the commodities to be wrapped.

9. The Government notes that the prohibitions of § 2 of the Sherman Act have often been extended to producers of single products and to businesses of limited scope. But the cases to which the Government refers us were not concerned with the problem that is now before the Court. In Story Parchment Co. v. Paterson Parchment Paper Co., 282 U.S. 555, a conspiracy to monopolize trade in vegetable parchment was held to be a violation of § 2. Parchment paper is obviously no larger a part of commerce than cellophane. Recovery, however, was based on proven allegations of combination and conspiracy to monopolize, and the scope of the market was not in issue. 282 U.S. at page 560. Similarly, Indiana Farmer's Guide Pub. Co. v. Prairie Farmer Publishing Co., 293 U.S. 268, ruled that a combination or conspiracy for the purpose of monopolizing the farm-paper business in the north central part of the Nation would be illegal by reason of the second section of the Sherman Act. Lorain Journal Co. v. United States, 342 U.S. 143, a case not cited by the Government, was concerned with even a smaller geographical area (dissemination of news in a community and surrounding territory). But the Court held only that defendant had attempted to monopolize, not that he had in fact monopolized. Also, this Court found in United States v. Columbia Steel Co., 334 U.S. 495, that the "relevant competitive market" for determin-

ing whether there had been an unreasonable restraint of trade (or an attempt to monopolize) was the market for "rolled steel" products in an 11-state area. Women's dresses of "original design," Fashion Originators' Guild of America v. Federal Trade Comm., 312 U.S. 457; "first run" motion pictures, United States v. Paramount Pictures, 334 U.S. 131; the news services of one news agency, United States v. Associated Press, 52 F.Supp. 362 (S.D.N.Y.), aff'd, 326 U.S. 1; and newspaper advertising as distinguished from other means of news dissemination, Times-Picayune Pub. Co. v. United States, 345 U.S. 594, have all been designated as parts of commerce. All four were concerned only with the question of whether there had been an attempt to monopolize. United States v. Aluminum Co. of America, 2 Cir., 148 F.2d 416, did involve the question of monopolization. Judge Hand found that the relevant market for measuring Alcoa's power was the market for "virgin" aluminum; he refused to consider the close competition offered by "secondary" (used) aluminum. The reason for the narrow definition was that Alcoa's control over virgin aluminum permitted it to regulate the supply of used aluminum even though the latter should be actually sold by a competitor. Consequently, the case is not particularly helpful in the problem of market definition now before the Court.

Cellophane differs from other flexible packaging materials. From some it differs more than from others. The basic materials from which the wrappings are made and the advantages and disadvantages of the products to the packaging industry are summarized in Findings 62 and 63. They are aluminum, cellulose acetate, chlorides, wood pulp, rubber hydrochloride, and ethylene gas. It will adequately illustrate the similarity in characteristics of the various products by noting here Finding 62 as to glassine.[10] Its use is almost as extensive as cellophane and many of its characteristics equally or more satisfactory to users.[11]

It may be admitted that cellophane combines the desirable elements of transparency, strength and cheapness more definitely than any of the others. Comparative characteristics have been noted thus:

"Moistureproof cellophane is highly transparent, tears readily but has high bursting strength, is highly impervious to moisture and gases, and is resistant to grease and oils. Heat sealable, printable, and adapted to use on wrapping machines, it makes an excellent packaging material for both display and protection of commodities.

"Other flexible wrapping materials fall into four major categories: (1) opaque nonmoistureproof wrapping *paper* designed primarily for convenience and protection in handling packages; (2) moistureproof *films* of varying degrees of transparency designed primarily either to protect, or to display and protect, the products they encompass; (3) nonmoistureproof transparent *films* designed primarily to display and to some extent protect, but which obvious-

---

10. "62. *Greaseproof paper* is made by beating wood pulp in a vat filled with water until the fibers become saturated and gelatinous in texture. Resulting product is translucent and resistant to oil and grease.

"*Glassine* is produced by finishing greaseproof paper between highly polished metal rollers under heat and at pressure. This process develops the transparency and surface gloss which are characteristic of glassine. It is greaseproof and can be sealed by heat, if coated. It is made moistureproof by coating and with appropriate lacquers or waxes and may be printed."

11. "63. There are respects in which other flexible packaging materials are as satisfactory as cellophane:

"Glassine

"Glassine is, in some types, about 90% transparent, so printing is legible through it.

"Glassine affords low cost transparency.

"Moisture protection afforded by waxed or lacquered glassine is as good as that of moistureproof cellophane.

"Glassine has greater resistance to tearing and breakage than cellophane.

"Glassine runs on packaging machinery with ease equal to that of cellophane.

"Glassine can be printed faster than cellophane, and can be run faster than moistureproof cellophane on bag machines.

"Glassine has greater resistance than cellophane to rancidity-inducing ultraviolet rays.

"Glassine has dimensional stability superior to cellophane.

"Glassine is more durable in cold weather than cellophane.

"Printed glassine can be sold against cellophane on the basis of appearance.

"Glassine may be more easily laminated than cellophane.

"Glassine is cheaper than cellophane in some types, comparable in others."

ly do a poor protecting job where exclusion or retention of moisture is important; and (4) moistureproof *materials* other than films of varying degrees of transparency (foils and paper products) designed to protect and display."[12]

But, despite cellophane's advantages, it has to meet competition from other materials in every one of its uses.... Food products are the chief outlet, with cigarettes next. The Government makes no challenge to Finding 283 that cellophane furnishes less than 7% of wrappings for bakery products, 25% for candy, 32% for snacks, 35% for meats and poultry, 27% for crackers and biscuits, 47% for fresh produce, and 34% for frozen foods. Seventy-five to eighty per cent of cigarettes are wrapped in cellophane. Thus, cellophane shares the packaging market with others. The over-all result is that cellophane accounts for 17.9% of flexible wrapping materials, measured by the wrapping surface.

Moreover a very considerable degree of functional interchangeability exists between these products.[13] ... It will be noted, that except as to permeability to gases, cellophane has no qualities that are not possessed by a number of other materials. Meat will do as an example of interchangeability. Although du Pont's sales to the meat industry have reached 19,000,000 pounds annually, nearly 35%, this volume is attributed "to the rise of self-service retailing of fresh meat." In fact, since the popularity of self-service meats, du Pont has lost "a considerable proportion" of this packaging business to Pliofilm. Pliofilm is more expensive than cellophane, but its superior physical characteristics apparently offset cellophane's price advantage. While retailers shift continually between the two, the trial court found that Pliofilm is increasing its share of the business. One further example is worth noting. Before World War II, du Pont cellophane wrapped between 5 and 10% of baked and smoked meats. The peak year was 1933. Thereafter du Pont was unable to meet the competition of Sylvania and of greaseproof paper. Its sales declined and the 1933 volume was not reached again until 1947. It will be noted that greaseproof paper, glassine, waxed paper, foil and Pliofilm are used as well as cellophane. Findings 209–210 show the competition and 215–216 the advantages that have caused the more expensive Pliofilm to increase its proportion of the business.

An element for consideration as to cross-elasticity of demand between products is the responsiveness of the sales of one product to price changes of the other.[14] If a slight decrease in the price of cellophane causes a considerable number of customers of other flexible wrappings to switch to cellophane, it would be an indication that a high cross-elasticity of demand exists between them; that the products compete in the same market. The

12. Stocking and Mueller, The Cellophane Case, XLV Amer.Economic Rev. 29, 48–49.

13. There are eighteen classifications: White Bread; Specialty Breads; Cake and Sweet Goods; Meat; Candy; Crackers and Biscuits; Frozen Foods; Potato Chips; Pop Corn and Snacks; Cereals; Fresh Produce; Paper Goods and Textiles; Cigarettes; Butter; Chewing Gum; Other Food Products; Other Tobacco Products; Cheese; Oleomargarine.

14. Scitovsky, Welfare and Competition (1951), 396; Bain, Pricing, Distribution, and Employment (1953 rev. ed.), 52.

court below held that the "[g]reat sensitivity of customers in the flexible packaging markets to price or quality changes" prevented du Pont from possessing monopoly control over price. . . .

We conclude that cellophane's interchangeability with the other materials mentioned suffices to make it a part of this flexible packaging material market.

The Government stresses the fact that the variation in price between cellophane and other materials demonstrates they are noncompetitive. As these products are all flexible wrapping materials, it seems reasonable to consider, as was done at the trial, their comparative cost to the consumer in terms of square area. . . . Findings as to price competition are set out in the margin.[15] Cellophane costs two or three times as much, surface measure, as its chief competitors for the flexible wrapping market, glassine and greaseproof papers. Other forms of cellulose wrappings and those from other chemical or mineral substances, with the exception of aluminum foil, are more expensive. The uses of these materials . . . are largely to wrap small packages for retail distribution. The wrapping is a relatively small proportion of the entire cost of the article. Different producers need different qualities in wrappings and their need may vary from time to time as their products undergo change. But the necessity for flexible wrappings is the central and unchanging demand. We cannot say that these differences in cost gave du Pont monopoly power over prices in view of the findings of fact on that subject.[16]

15. "132. The price of cellophane is today an obstacle to its sales in competition with other flexible packaging materials.

"133. Cellophane has always been higher priced than the two largest selling flexible packaging materials, wax paper and glassine, and this has represented a disadvantage to sales of cellophane.

"134. DuPont considered as a factor in the determination of its prices, the prices of waxed paper, glassine, greaseproof, vegetable parchment, and other flexible packaging materials.

"135. DuPont, in reducing its prices, intended to narrow price differential between cellophane and packaging papers, particularly glassine and waxed paper. The objective of this effort has been to increase the use of cellophane. Each price reduction was intended to open up new uses for cellophane, and to attract new customers who had not used cellophane because of its price."

16. "140. Some users are sensitive to the cost of flexible packaging materials; others are not. Users to whom cost is important include substantial business: for example, General Foods, Armour, Curtiss Candy Co.,

and smaller users in the bread industry, cracker industry, and frozen food industry. These customers are unwilling to use more cellophane because of its relatively high price, would use more if the price were reduced, and have increased their use as the price of cellophane has been reduced.

"141. The cost factor slips accounts away from cellophane. This hits at the precarious users, whose profit margins on their products are low, and has been put in motion by competitive developments in the user's trade. Examples include the losses of business to glassine in candy bar wraps in the 30's, frozen food business to waxed paper in the late 40's, and recent losses to glassine in cracker packaging.

"142. The price of cellophane was reduced to expand the market for cellophane. DuPont did not reduce prices for cellophane with intent of monopolizing manufacture or with intent of suppressing competitors.

"143. DuPont reduced cellophane prices to enable sales to be made for new uses from which higher prices had excluded cellophane, and to expand sales. Reductions were made as sales volume and market conditions war-

It is the variable characteristics of the different flexible wrappings and the energy and ability with which the manufacturers push their wares that determine choice. A glance at "Modern Packaging," a trade journal, will give, by its various advertisements, examples of the competition among manufacturers for the flexible packaging market. The trial judge visited the 1952 Annual Packaging Show at Atlantic City, with the consent of counsel. He observed exhibits offered by "machinery manufacturers, converters and manufacturers of flexible packaging materials." He states that these personal observations confirmed his estimate of the competition between cellophane and other packaging materials. From this wide variety of evidence, the Court reached the conclusion expressed in Finding 838:

> "The record establishes plain cellophane and moistureproof cellophane are each flexible packaging materials which are functionally interchangeable with other flexible packaging materials and sold at same time to same customers for same purpose at competitive prices; there is no cellophane market distinct and separate from the market for flexible packaging materials; the market for flexible packaging materials is the relevant market for determining nature and extent of duPont's market control; and duPont has at all times competed with other cellophane producers and manufacturers of other flexible packaging materials in all aspects of its cellophane business."

The facts above considered dispose also of any contention that competitors have been excluded by du Pont from the packaging material market. That market has many producers and there is no proof du Pont ever has possessed power to exclude any of them from the rapidly expanding flexible packaging market. The Government apparently concedes as much, for it states that "lack of power to inhibit entry into this so-called market [*i.e.,* flexible packaging materials], comprising widely disparate products, is no indicium of absence of power to exclude competition in the manufacture and sale of cellophane." The record shows the multiplicity of competitors and the financial strength of some with individual assets running to the hundreds of millions. Indeed, the trial court found that du Pont could not exclude competitors even from the manufacture of cellophane, an immaterial matter if the market is flexible packaging material. Nor can we say that du Pont's profits, while liberal (according to the Government 15.9% net after taxes on the 1937–1947 average), demonstrate the existence of a

ranted. In determining price reductions, duPont considered relationship between its manufacturing costs and proposed prices, possible additional volume that might be gained by the price reduction, effect of price reduction upon the return duPont would obtain on its investment. It considered the effect its lowered price might have on the manufacture by others, but this possible result of a price reduction was never a motive for the reduction.

"144. DuPont never lowered cellophane prices below cost, and never dropped cellophane prices temporarily to gain a competitive advantage.

"145. As duPont's manufacturing costs declined, 1924 to 1935, duPont reduced prices for cellophane. When costs of raw materials increased subsequent to 1935, it postponed reductions until 1938 and 1939. Subsequent increases in cost of raw material and labor brought about price increases after 1947."

monopoly without proof of lack of comparable profits during those years in other prosperous industries. Cellophane was a leader, over 17%, in the flexible packaging materials market. There is no showing that du Pont's rate of return was greater or less than that of other producers of flexible packaging materials.

The "market" which one must study to determine when a producer has monopoly power will vary with the part of commerce under consideration. The tests are constant. That market is composed of products that have reasonable interchangeability for the purposes for which they are produced—price, use and qualities considered. While the application of the tests remains uncertain, it seems to us that du Pont should not be found to monopolize cellophane when that product has the competition and interchangeability with other wrappings that this record shows.

On the findings of the District Court, its judgment is affirmed.

■ CLARK and HARLAN, JJ., took no part in the consideration or decision of this case.

■ WARREN, C.J., with whom BLACK and DOUGLAS, JJ., join, dissenting.

This case, like many under the Sherman Act, turns upon the proper definition of the market. In defining the market in which du Pont's economic power is to be measured, the majority virtually emasculate § 2 of the Sherman Act. They admit that "cellophane combines the desirable elements of transparency, strength and cheapness more definitely than any of" a host of other packaging materials. Yet they hold that all of those materials are so indistinguishable from cellophane as to warrant their inclusion in the market. We cannot agree that cellophane, in the language of Times–Picayune Publishing Co. v. United States, 345 U.S. 594, 613, is "the self-same product" as glassine, greaseproof and vegetable parchment papers, waxed papers, sulphite papers, aluminum foil, cellulose acetate, and Pliofilm and other films.[17]

The majority opinion states that "[I]t will adequately illustrate the similarity in characteristics of the various products by noting here Finding 62 as to glassine." But Finding 62 merely states the respects in which the selected flexible packaging materials are as satisfactory as cellophane; it does not compare all the physical properties of cellophane and other materials. The Table incorporated in Finding 59 does make such a comparison, and enables us to note cellophane's unique combination of qualities lacking among less expensive materials in varying degrees.[18] A glance at

---

17. In Times–Picayune Publishing Co. v. United States, 345 U.S. 594, 612, note 31, the Court said:

"For every product, substitutes exist. But a relevant market cannot meaningfully encompass that infinite range. The circle must be drawn narrowly to exclude any other product to which, within reasonable variations in price,

only a limited number of buyers will turn; in technical terms, products whose 'cross-elasticities of demand' are small."

18. See 118 F.Supp. at page 64. The majority opinion quotes at length from Stocking and Mueller, The Cellophane Case, XLV Amer.Economic Rev. 29, 48–49, in noting the comparative characteristics of cellophane and other products. Unfortunately, the opinion

this Table reveals that cellophane has a high bursting strength while glassine's is low; that cellophane's permeability to gases is lower than that of glassine; and that both its transparency and its resistance to grease and oils are greater than glassine's. Similarly, we see that waxed paper's bursting strength is less than cellophane's and that it is highly permeable to gases and offers no resistance whatsoever to grease and oils. With respect to the two other major products held to be close substitutes for cellophane, Finding 59 makes the majority's market definition more dubious. In contrast to cellophane, aluminum foil is actually opaque and has a low bursting strength. And sulphite papers, in addition to being opaque, are highly permeable to both moisture and gases, have no resistance to grease and oils, have a lower bursting strength than cellophane, and are not even heat sealable. Indeed, the majority go further than placing cellophane in the same market with such products. They also include the transparent films, which are more expensive than cellophane. These bear even less resemblance to the lower priced packaging materials than does cellophane. The juxtaposition of one of these films, Cry–O–Rap, with sulphite in the Table facilitates a comparison which shows that Cry–O–Rap is markedly different and far superior.

If the conduct of buyers indicated that glassine, waxed and sulphite papers and aluminum foil were actually "the self-same products" as cellophane, the qualitative differences demonstrated by the comparison of physical properties in Finding 59 would not be conclusive. But the record provides convincing proof that businessmen did not so regard these products. During the period covered by the complaint (1923–1947) cellophane enjoyed phenomenal growth. Du Pont's 1924 production was 361,249 pounds, which sold for $1,306,662. Its 1947 production was 133,502,858 pounds, which sold for $55,339,626. Findings 297 and 337. Yet throughout this period the price of cellophane was far greater than that of glassine, waxed paper or sulphite paper. Finding 136 states that in 1929 cellophane's price was seven times that of glassine; in 1934, four times, and in 1949 still more than twice glassine's price. Reference to DX–994, the graph upon which Finding 136 is based, shows that cellophane had a similar price relation to waxed paper and that sulphite paper sold at even less than glassine and waxed paper. We cannot believe that buyers, practical businessmen, would have bought cellophane in increasing amounts over a quarter of a century if close substitutes were available at from one-seventh to one-half cellophane's price. That they did so is testimony to cellophane's distinctiveness.

The inference yielded by the conduct of cellophane buyers is reinforced by the conduct of sellers other than du Pont. Finding 587 states that Sylvania, the only other cellophane producer, absolutely and immediately

fails to quote the conclusion reached by these economists. They state: "The [trial] court to the contrary notwithstanding, the market in which cellophane meets the 'competition' of other wrappers is narrower than the market for all flexible packaging materials." Id., at 52. And they conclude that "... cellophane is so differentiated from other flexible wrapping materials that its cross elasticity of demand gives du Pont significant and continuing monopoly power." Id., at 63.

followed every du Pont price change, even dating back its price list to the effective date of du Pont's change. Producers of glassine and waxed paper, on the other hand, displayed apparent indifference to du Pont's repeated and substantial price cuts. DX–994 shows that from 1924 to 1932 du Pont dropped the price of plain cellophane 84%, while the price of glassine remained constant. And during the period 1933–1946 the prices for glassine and waxed paper actually increased in the face of a further 21% decline in the price of cellophane. If "shifts of business" due to "price sensitivity" had been substantial, glassine and waxed paper producers who wanted to stay in business would have been compelled by market forces to meet du Pont's price challenge just as Sylvania was. The majority correctly point out that:

> "An element for consideration as to cross-elasticity of demand between products is the responsiveness of the sales of one product to price changes of the other. If a slight decrease in the price of cellophane causes a considerable number of customers of other flexible wrappings to switch to cellophane, it would be an indication that a high cross-elasticity of demand exists between them; that the products compete in the same market."

Surely there was more than "a slight decrease in the price of cellophane" during the period covered by the complaint. That producers of glassine and waxed paper remained dominant in the flexible packaging materials market without meeting cellophane's tremendous price cuts convinces us that cellophane was not in effective competition with their products.

Certainly du Pont itself shared our view. From the first, du Pont recognized that it need not concern itself with competition from other packaging materials. For example, when du Pont was contemplating entry into cellophane production, its Development Department reported that glassine "is so inferior that it belongs in an entirely different class and has hardly to be considered as a competitor of cellophane." This was still du Pont's view in 1950 when its survey of competitive prospects wholly omitted reference to glassine, waxed paper or sulphite paper and stated that "Competition for du Pont cellophane will come from competitive cellophane and from non-cellophane films made by us or by others."

Du Pont's every action was directed toward maintaining dominance over cellophane. Its 1923 agreements with La Cellophane, the French concern which first produced commercial cellophane, gave du Pont exclusive North and Central American rights to cellophane's technology, manufacture and sale, and provided, without any limitation in time, that all existing and future information pertaining to the cellophane process be considered "secret and confidential," and be held in an exclusive common pool. In its subsequent agreements with foreign licensees, du Pont was careful to preserve its continental market inviolate. In 1929, while it was still the sole domestic producer of cellophane, du Pont won its long struggle to raise the tariff from 25% to 60%, ad valorem, on cellophane imports, substantially foreclosing foreign competition. When Sylvania became the second American cellophane producer the following year and du Pont filed suit claiming infringement of its moistureproof patents, they settled the suit by entering into a cross-licensing agreement. Under this agreement, du Pont obtained the right to exclude third persons from use of any patentable moistureproof invention made during the next 15 years by the sole other domestic cellophane producer, and, by a prohibitive royalty provision, it limited Sylvania's moistureproof production to approximately 20% of the industry's moistureproof sales. The record shows that du Pont and Sylvania were aware that, by settling the infringement suit, they avoided the possibility that the courts might hold the patent claims invalid and thereby open cellophane manufacture to additional competition. If close substitutes for cellophane had been commercially available, du Pont, an enlightened enterprise, would not have gone to such lengths to control cellophane.

As predicted by its 1923 market analysis, du Pont's dominance in cellophane proved enormously profitable from the outset. After only five years of production, when du Pont bought out the minority stock interests in its cellophane subsidiary, it had to pay more than fifteen times the original price of the stock. But such success was not limited to the period of innovation, limited sales and complete domestic monopoly. A confidential du Pont report shows that during the period 1937–1947, despite great expansion of sales, du Pont's "operative return" (before taxes) averaged 31%, while its average "net return" (after deduction of taxes, bonuses, and fundamental research expenditures) was 15.9%. Such profits provide a powerful incentive for the entry of competitors.[19]

Yet from 1924 to 1951 only one new firm, Sylvania, was able to begin cellophane production. And Sylvania could not have entered if La Cellophane's secret process had not been stolen. It is significant that for 15 years Olin Industries, a substantial firm, was unsuccessful in its attempt to produce cellophane, finally abandoning the project in 1944 after having spent about $1,000,000. When the Government brought this suit, du Pont, "to reduce the hazard of being judged to have a monopoly of the U.S. cellophane business," decided to let Olin enter the industry. Despite this demonstration of the control achieved by du Pont through its exclusive dominion over the cellophane process, the District Court found that du Pont could not exclude competitors from the manufacture of cellophane. Finding 727. This finding is "clearly erroneous." The majority avoid passing upon Finding 727 by stating that it is "immaterial ... if the market is flexible packaging material." They do not appear to disagree with

---

19. See Stocking and Mueller, The Cellophane Case, XLV Amer.Economic Rev. 29, 60–63, where the authors compare the domestic economic history of rayon with that of cellophane. The first American rayon producer earned 64.2% on its investment in 1920, thereby attracting du Pont. After a loss in 1921, du Pont's average return for the next four years was roughly 32%. As more firms began rayon production, du Pont's and the industry's return on investment began to drop. When 6 new firms entered the industry in 1930, bringing the number of producers to 20, average industry earnings for that year declined to 5% and du Pont suffered a net loss. "From the beginning of the depression in 1929 through the succeeding recovery and the 1938 recession du Pont averaged 29.6 per cent before taxes on its cellophane investment. On its rayon investment it averaged only 6.3 per cent." Id., at 62–63.

our conclusion, however, since they concede that ... "it may be practically impossible for anyone to commence manufacturing cellophane without full access to du Pont's technique."

The trial court found that:

> "Du Pont has no power to set cellophane prices arbitrarily. If prices for cellophane increase in relation to prices of other flexible packaging materials it will lose business to manufacturers of such materials in varying amounts for each of du Pont cellophane's major end uses."

This further reveals its misconception of the antitrust laws. A monopolist seeking to maximize profits cannot raise prices "arbitrarily." Higher prices of course mean smaller sales, but they also mean higher per-unit profit. Lower prices will increase sales but reduce per-unit profit. Within these limits a monopolist has a considerable degree of latitude in determining which course to pursue in attempting to maximize profits. The trial judge thought that, if du Pont raised its price, the market would "penalize" it with smaller profits as well as lower sales. Du Pont proved him wrong. When 1947 operating earnings dropped below 26% for the first time in 10 years, it increased cellophane's price 7% and boosted its earnings in 1948....

The majority opinion purports to reject the theory of "interindustry competition." Brick, steel, wood, cement and stone, it says, are "too different" to be placed in the same market. But cellophane, glassine, wax papers, sulphite papers, greaseproof and vegetable parchment papers, aluminum foil, cellulose, acetate, Pliofilm and other films are not "too different," the opinion concludes. The majority approach would apparently enable a monopolist of motion picture exhibition to avoid Sherman Act consequences by showing that motion pictures compete in substantial measure with legitimate theater, television, radio, sporting events and other forms of entertainment. Here, too, "shifts of business" undoubtedly accompany fluctuations in price and "there are market alternatives that buyers may readily use for their purposes." Yet, in United States v. Paramount Pictures, 334 U.S. 131, where the District Court had confined the relevant market to that for nationwide movie exhibition, this Court remanded the case to the District Court with directions to determine whether there was a monopoly on the part of the five major distributors "in the *first-run* field for the entire country, in the *first-run* field in the 92 largest cities of the country, or in the *first-run* field in separate localities." 334 U.S. at 172. Similarly, it is difficult to square the majority view with United States v. Aluminum Co. of America, 2 Cir., 148 F.2d 416, a landmark § 2 case. There Judge Learned Hand, reversing a district court, held that the close competition which "secondary" (used) aluminum offered to "virgin" aluminum did not justify including the former within the relevant market for measuring Alcoa's economic power. Against these and other precedents, which the Court's opinion approves but does not follow, the formula of "reasonable interchangeability," as applied by the majority, appears indistinguishable from the theory of "interindustry competition."

The danger in it is that, as demonstrated in this case, it is "perfectly compatible with a fully monopolized economy."

The majority hold in effect that, because cellophane meets competition for many end uses, those buyers for other uses who need or want only cellophane are not entitled to the benefits of competition within the cellophane industry. For example, Finding 282 shows that the largest single use of cellophane in 1951 was for wrapping cigarettes, and Finding 292 shows that 75 to 80% of all cigarettes are wrapped with cellophane. As the recent report of the Attorney General's National Committee to Study the Antitrust Laws states: "In the interest of rivalry that extends to *all* buyers and *all* uses, competition among rivals within the industry is always important." (Emphasis added.) Furthermore, those buyers who have "reasonable alternatives" between cellophane and other products are also entitled to competition within the cellophane industry, for such competition may lead to lower prices and improved quality.

The foregoing analysis of the record shows conclusively that cellophane is the relevant market. Since du Pont has the lion's share of that market, it must have monopoly power, as the majority concede.[20] This being so, we think it clear that, in the circumstances of this case, du Pont is guilty of "monopolization." The briefest sketch of du Pont's business history precludes it from falling within the "exception to the Sherman Act prohibitions of monopoly power" (majority opinion, 76 S.Ct. 1004) by successfully asserting that monopoly was "thrust upon" it. Du Pont was not "the passive beneficiary of a monopoly" within the meaning of United States v. Aluminum Co. of America, supra, 148 F.2d at pages 429–430. It sought and maintained dominance through illegal agreements dividing the world market, concealing and suppressing technological information, and restricting its licensee's production by prohibitive royalties, and through numerous maneuvers which might have been "honestly industrial" but whose necessary effect was nevertheless exclusionary.[21] Du Pont cannot bear "the burden of proving that it owes its monopoly *solely* to superior skill. . . ." (Emphasis supplied.) United States v. United Shoe Machinery Corp., D.C., 110 F.Supp. 295, 342, affirmed per curiam 347 U.S. 521. . . .

If competition is at the core of the Sherman Act, we cannot agree that it was consistent with that Act for the enormously lucrative cellophane industry to have no more than two sellers from 1924 to 1951. The conduct of du Pont and Sylvania illustrates that a few sellers tend to act like one and that an industry which does not have a competitive structure will not have competitive behavior. The public should not be left to rely upon the

20. "If cellophane is the 'market' that du Pont is found to dominate, it may be assumed it does have monopoly power over that 'market.' Monopoly power is the power to control prices or exclude competition. It seems apparent that du Pont's power to set the price of cellophane has only been limited by the competition afforded by other flexible packaging materials. Moreover, it may be practically impossible for anyone to commence manufacturing cellophane without full access to du Pont's technique." Majority opinion, 76 S.Ct. 1005.

21. See United States v. Aluminum Co. of America, 2 Cir., 148 F.2d 416, 431.

dispensations of management in order to obtain the benefits that normally accompany competition. Such beneficence is of uncertain tenure. Only actual competition can assure long-run enjoyment of the goals of a free economy.

We would reverse the decision below and remand the cause to the District Court with directions to determine the relief that should be granted against du Pont.

■ The concurring opinion of Frankfurter, J., is omitted.

NOTES AND QUESTIONS

1.   In International Boxing Club v. United States, 358 U.S. 242 (1959), the Supreme Court purported to apply the *Cellophane* reasoning where not only actual monopolization but conspiracy to monopolize had been found by the district court.

The complaint alleged, *inter alia,* that Norris and Wirtz, owners of controlling interests in important sports arenas in Chicago, Detroit, and St. Louis, conspired with the management of Madison Square Garden, the foremost sports arena in New York City, to control the promotion, broadcasting and televising of championship boxing contests in the United States. The complaint further alleged that defendants effectuated their conspiracy chiefly by using their control of arenas to coerce contenders for boxing titles into granting exclusive promotional contracts for championship fights, including film and broadcasting rights, for a period of from three to five years.

In the Supreme Court, defendants' chief attack on the findings turned on the contention that the proper relevant market should not have been the promotion of professional championship boxing contests, as found by the district court, but the promotion of all professional boxing contests. Defendants' control of championship boxing contests in the four years immediately succeeding their first championship promotion was approximately 81% of the field, but was much less if all professional boxing contests were considered. With respect to the relevant market issue, the Supreme Court, per Clark, J., wrote:

> Appellants . . . rely primarily on United States v. du Pont & Co. That case, involving an alleged monopoly of the market in cellophane, held that the relevant market was not cellophane alone but the entire field of flexible packaging materials. . . . The appellants argue that the "physical identity of the products here would seem necessarily to put them in one and the same market." They say that any boxing contest, whether championship or not, always includes one ring, two boxers and one referee, fighting under the same rules before a greater or lesser number of spectators either present at ringside or through the facilities of television, radio, or moving pictures.

> We do not feel that this conclusion follows. . . . [T]he lower court in the instant case found that there exists a "separate, identifiable market" for championship boxing contests. This general finding is supported by detailed findings to the effect that the average revenue from all sources for appellants' championship bouts was $154,000, compared to $40,000 for their nonchampionship programs; that television rights to one champion-

ship fight brought $100,000, in contrast to $45,000 for a nontitle fight seven months later between the same two fighters; that the average "Nielsen" ratings over a two-and-one-half year period were 74.9% for appellants' championship contests, and 57.7% for their nonchampionship programs (reflecting a difference of several million viewers between the two types of fights); that although the revenues from movie rights for six of appellants' championship bouts totaled over $600,000 no full-length motion picture rights were sold for a nonchampionship contest; and that spectators pay "substantially more" for tickets to championship fights than for nontitle fights. In addition, numerous representatives of the broadcasting, motion picture and advertising industries testified to the general effect that a "particular and special demand exists among radio broadcasting and telecasting [and motion picture] companies for the rights to broadcast and telecast [and make and distribute films of] championship contests in contradistinction to similar rights to non-championship contests."[22]

In view of these findings, we cannot say that the lower court was "clearly erroneous" in concluding that nonchampionship fights are not "reasonably interchangeable for the same purpose" as championship contests....

... [C]hampionship boxing is the "cream" of the boxing business, and, as has been shown above ... is a sufficiently separate part of the trade or commerce to constitute the relevant market for Sherman Act purposes.

2. IN SYUFY ENTERPRISES V. AMERICAN MULTICINEMA, INC., 793 F.2d 990 (9th Cir.1986), cert. denied, 479 U.S. 1031 (1987), Syufy was charged with having a monopoly in the exhibition of certain motion pictures in the area of San Jose, California. The following excerpt from the Ninth Circuit decision illustrates the difficulties inherent in the market definition task:

AMC defined the relevant market as the market for exhibition of industry anticipated top-grossing motion pictures in the San Jose area. Syufy does not dispute the geographic component of this definition—the San Jose area. Nor does it dispute limiting the product market definition to hardtop theaters. The only aspect of AMC's market definition that Syufy disputes is the limitation of the relevant product market to the exhibition of major films, more specifically to industry-anticipated top-grossing films. Syufy argues that this market definition is ex post facto and ad hoc, and that all first run films are in substantial competition with each other.

In evaluating Syufy's challenge, we begin with the principle that assessment of a product market definition must take into account whether products excluded from the definition are "interchangeab[le] in use" with those included in the market and whether there is "cross-elasticity of demand" between excluded and included products. United States v. E.I. duPont de Nemours & Co., 351 U.S. 377, 394–95 (1956). In economic terms, we might recharacterize Syufy's argument as follows: all first run films are interchangeable in use and the price and availability of any one film will affect the demand for all other films. Top-grossing films, Syufy argues, are simply those films that prove to be highly successful in the market place, but they possess no special characteristics that differentiate

---

22. Approximately 25% of the revenue produced by the appellants' championship fights during the period covered by the com- plaint was derived through the sale of radio, television and motion picture rights.

them from less successful films from an ex ante perspective. Syufy also argues that limiting the product definition to top-grossing films has the effect of irrationally and unfairly penalizing the exhibitor with the prescience to book films that later prove to be big hits with the movie-going public.

AMC's rejoinder is that Syufy's argument mischaracterizes the product market definition. AMC points out that it did not define the market as simply top-grossing films, but as *industry anticipated* top-grossing films. AMC argues that these films can be differentiated from other first run films from an ex ante perspective because they have larger budgets, "name" stars and directors, larger advertising budgets, command large guarantees, and possess other distinctive characteristics which can be identified before the film is released. In economic terms, the viability of AMC's product market definition depends on the proposition that anticipated top-grossing films are not interchangeable with other films in the eyes of consumers and that price increases or supply constrictions for such films do not result in a shift in consumption patterns to other films. In legal terms, the question is whether the films excluded from the definition are "interchangeab[le] in use" with those included in the market and whether there is "cross-elasticity of demand" between excluded and included products. United States v. E.I. duPont de Nemours & Co., 351 U.S. 377, 394–95 (1956). In more colloquial terms, the viability of the proposed definition depends on the argument that if the price for admission to *E.T.* goes up, audiences will not flock to *My Dinner with Andre.*

We conclude that there is sufficient evidence in the record to permit a rational jury to conclude that industry anticipated top-grossing films constitute a distinct product market. The evidence indicates that approximately thirty pictures a year are identifiable as "anticipated top grossing films" on the basis of such criteria as national advertising support, longer playtimes, guaranteed rentals, famous stars, directors and producers, booking in first class theatres, and lucrative terms offered for the pictures by exhibitors. AMC compiled a list of the industry anticipated top-grossing films based on bidding materials submitted by both Syufy and AMC. Although AMC did not present direct evidence going to the "cross-elasticity of demand" between this limited class of pictures and other films, the jury could reasonably have concluded from the evidence presented that the industry anticipated top-grossing films were not in substantial competition with other films.

3.   United States v. Microsoft Corp., 253 F.3d 34 (D.C.Cir. 2001), one of the most widely discussed antitrust cases in recent decades, will be considered at length in Chapter 8. We pause here only to explore briefly the question of definition of relevant market, which turned out not to be a central issue in the proceeding.

The Department of Justice and several state attorneys general had brought suit charging Microsoft, along with other antitrust violations, with illegally maintaining a monopoly in the market for personal computer ("PC") operating systems and attempting to monopolize the market for web browsers–both allegedly illegal under Section 2 of the Sherman Act. The court defined the market as "the licensing of all Intel-compatible PC operating systems worldwide." and concluded that Microsoft had 95% of that market. Microsoft argued that this definition was too narrow and failed to include three product categories: (1) non-Intel PC operating systems (such as Apple computers); (2) operating systems for non-PC devices, such as handheld computers or personal digital assistants; and (3) "middleware" products. Middleware is a software product that exposes other application programs ("APIs") and had the potential to incorporate a consistent set of APIs while running on a variety of operating systems, allowing programs to more easily "port" applications from one system to another. Netscape Navigator and the Java programming language, the most well-known of middleware products, were at issue in the case and had been targets of conduct by Microsoft that formed the basis of liability for monopoly maintenance.

In a unanimous *per curiam* opinion, the Court of Appeals easily dismissed non-Intel PC operating systems and non-PC devices from the market. Other systems like the Apple system cost more, supported fewer applications, and involved considerable effort in transferring files to its format. As to other information appliances like handheld devices, the Court found that they fell short of performing all the functions of a PC, and therefore most consumers would buy them only as a supplement.

The decision of the lower court to exclude "middleware" from the relevant product market raised more serious questions, addressed by the Court of Appeals as follows:

> "This brings us to Microsoft's main challenge to the District Court's market definition: the inclusion of middleware.... Microsoft argues that, because middleware could usurp the operating system's platform function and might eventually take over other operating system functions (for instance, by controlling peripherals), the District Court erred in excluding Navigator and Java from the relevant market. The District Court found, however, that neither Navigator, Java, nor any other middleware product could now, or would soon, expose enough APIs to serve as a platform for popular applications, much less take over all operating system functions. Again, Microsoft fails to challenge these findings, instead simply asserting middleware's "potential" as a competitor.

> "The test of reasonable interchangeability, however, required the District Court to consider only substitutes that constrain pricing in the reasonably foreseeable future, and only products that can enter the market in a relatively short time can perform this function. Whatever middleware's ultimate potential, the District Court found that consumers could not now abandon their operating systems and switch to middleware in response to a sustained price for Windows above the competitive level. Nor is middleware likely to overtake the operating system as the primary platform for software development at any time in the near future.... Because market definition is meant to identify products "reasonably interchangeable by consumers," *du Pont*, 351 U.S. at 395, 76 S.Ct. 994, and because middleware is not now interchangeable with Windows, the District Court had good reason for excluding middleware from the relevant market."

By contrast, the D.C. Circuit found Microsoft was not liable for attempting to monopolize the market for web browsers because the government had failed to define a relevant market. The D.C. Circuit chastised the District Court for "never engag[ing] in an ... analysis [of the browser market] nor enter[ing] detailed findings defining what a browser is or what products might constitute substitutes." Essentially, the D.C. Circuit rejected out of hand the government's effort to define a market for web browsers.

NOTE ON MARKET POWER AND CONSUMER LOSS[23]

The following note explores some economic concepts about the value of competition, and the injuries to competition and to consumers that can result from monopoly or cartel behavior.

Market power is the ability to profitably reduce output below the competitive level of production, and the corresponding power to raise or maintain prices above the competitive level when consumers bid up the price of the constricted supply. Market power can be achieved and exercised either by a "monopolist" (*i.e.*, a single firm) or by a "cartel" (*i.e.*, a group of competitors) directly restricting output and raising price.[24]

Antitrust law is premised on the general principle that competition, as opposed to monopolization or cartelization, tends to maximize the economic performance of a market. Economic performance refers to the economic achievements of the market. Performance involves *economic efficiency,* the degree to which (i) enough output is produced to satisfy all the demand of consumers who value the product in excess of its cost of production ("allocative efficiency") and (ii) output is produced at minimum cost ("productive efficiency"). Performance also involves *wealth distribution,* the degree to which consumers do or do not pay a market price for the product that equals the cost of production. Over time, market performance also involves the speed of innovation in the market ("dynamic efficiency"), the degree to which sellers reduce their costs and design new and superior products to satisfy consumer preferences.[25]

When a monopolist or cartel restricts output and raises price, this exercise of market power injures consumers (as a group) in two separate ways. First, the higher price creates a monopoly overcharge on the quantity sold by the monopolist. This monopoly overcharge involves a transfer of wealth from consumers to the shareholders (or persons) who own the monopoly firm. Second, the higher price chokes off demand somewhat, creating a loss of potential consumption benefits. Although the consumer values units of the commodity in excess of their production cost, the units are not produced and consumed. This "deadweight loss," a term used by economists, is not gained by the shareholders. It is a reduction in the economic efficiency of the market.

A. *Monopoly Overcharge*

Consider the case of a monopoly or cartel taking over an initially perfectly competitive market, restricting output, and raising price. If a particular consumer continues to purchase the product at the higher, monopoly price, this creates a transfer of wealth from that purchaser to the monopolist or cartel. This wealth transfer takes place as the consumer now pays the higher monopoly price for the same product previously purchased at the competitive price. The monopoly overcharge may be compared to theft. Relative to the competitive price, the cartel or

---

23. This note was written in collaboration with Professor Steven C. Salop.

24. Market power also can be achieved and exercised by exclusionary conduct that raises rivals' costs and erects barriers to entry. This is discussed in more detail in Chapter 8, Section 4.

25. *See, e.g.,* Lande, Wealth Transfers as the Original and Primary Concern of Antitrust: The Efficiency Interpretation Challenged, 34 Hastings L.J. 65 (1982).

monopolist simply expropriates more of the purchaser's money without providing any additional goods or services.

B. *Deadweight Loss*

Some consumers will react to the higher price by purchasing less of the product or eliminating purchases entirely. Pricing above the competitive level thereby reduces economic efficiency by restricting consumption below the efficient level achieved in a perfectly competitive market. The higher prices eliminate consumption by those consumers who value units of the product at more than the (marginal) cost of production but at less than the monopoly price. Those consumers lose the "benefit of the bargain" they might have received on those units no longer purchased. This consumer loss amounts to the difference in the dollar value the consumer places on those foregone units ("willingness to pay") less the competitive price paid for them; this excess of value over price is referred to by economists as "consumer surplus." The loss in consumer surplus is called a "deadweight loss" to denote the fact that the consumer loss is not gained by the monopolist. It is not a wealth transfer, but rather represents wasted resources—that is, a loss in economic efficiency.

An analogous loss in "producer surplus" is borne by the cartel or monopolist when output is restricted below the efficient, competitive level. The sellers lose the incremental profit (or "surplus") they earned by selling some units of output at the competitive price that were produced at a lower "marginal" cost. This reduction in producer surplus harms the seller as well as society. For the seller, of course, this loss is more than counterbalanced by the gains from the monopoly overcharge.

For those students who are interested in a more technical explanation, the monopoly overcharge to consumers and deadweight loss can be seen diagrammatically:

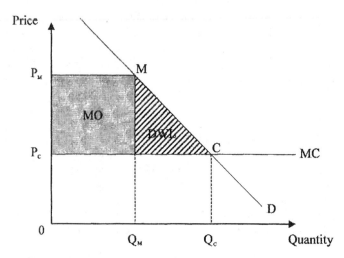

The competitive price and quantity are given by the point C (price P_c and quantity Q_c) and the monopoly price and quantity are given by point M (price P_m and quantity Q_m). The diagram assumes that the competitive price P_c equals marginal cost MC, so that there is no producer surplus. The monopoly overcharge consists of the price overcharge over and above the competitive level paid by consumers on the output they purchase. Diagrammatically, it is illustrated by the "rectangle" labelled MO. (The height of this rectangle is the price overcharge P_m $-P_c$. The base of the rectangle is the quantity purchased by consumers at the monopoly price Q_m. Thus, the area of the rectangle is the product of the price overcharge times the quantity, or $(P_m-P_c)Q_m$.) The deadweight loss in consumer surplus is the loss in surplus resulting from the monopoly output restriction over and above the monopoly overcharge. The deadweight loss is illustrated by the triangle labelled DWL. (The height of this triangle is the price overcharge P_m-P_c. The base of the triangle is the reduction in quantity purchased by consumers resulting from the monopoly, or Q_c-Q_m. Thus, the area of the rectangle is the product of the price overcharge times the quantity reduction, or (*i.e.*, area = $\frac{1}{2}(P_m$ $-P_c)(Q_c-Q_m)$). For example, suppose the monopolist raised price from the competitive level of $100 to the monopoly level of $140 (*i.e.*, a price increase of $40) and restricted output from the competitive level of 1,000 units to the monopoly level of 700 (*i.e.*, a reduction of 300 units). In this case, the monopoly overcharge equals $28,000 (*i.e.*, 700 units $\times$ $40) and the deadweight loss in consumer surplus equals $6,000 (*i.e.*, $\frac{1}{2} \times 300 \times$ $40). If the original cost curve were rising, then there also would be a deadweight loss in producer surplus from the output reduction.

C. Comparing the Harms

From the point of view of a single consumer, the per unit wealth transfer from the monopoly overcharge on each unit he or she continues to buy necessarily exceeds the deadweight loss on each unit he or she stops purchasing. This is because the consumer *voluntarily* chooses to forego purchasing those units, implying that reducing consumption necessarily dominates paying the higher price. In effect, the consumer mitigates the damages from the monopoly price by reducing consumption.

However, some argue that, from the point of view of the economy as a whole, the monopoly overcharge is *less* significant than the deadweight loss. This result follows if it is recognized that the cartel or monopolist actually consists of stockholders who are themselves members of society. From this broader vantage point, the monopoly overcharge is "just" a transfer of wealth from one group of society to another. A policymaker not allied with any particular segment of society may have little if any interest in this redistribution of wealth. In contrast, the deadweight efficiency losses represent unrecoverable reductions in social wealth, rather than "simply" a wealth transfer. As a result, some commentators argue that antitrust should be concerned purely with efficiency, not consumer welfare and wealth distribution.[26] Thus, minimization of the deadweight losses, and indifference to the wealth transfer resulting from the monopoly overcharge, should provide the exclusive focus of antitrust policy.[27]

26. This is a view advocated by Judge Robert Bork in his book, The Antitrust Paradox, Chapter 5 (1978). Bork actually refers to his pure efficiency view as a "consumer welfare" approach, thereby treating the owners of firms, in effect, as consumers. According to this view, income redistribution should be the concern of tax and expenditure statutes, not antitrust. In contrast, the pure consumer welfare standard would be concerned with the distribution of wealth. In particular, it evaluates conduct on the basis of the impact on consumers, not the owners of the firms.

27. As discussed below, analysis of the long run implications of monopoly pricing is more complex. On the one hand, the monopoly overcharge may be converted into a deadweight loss in the long run as the monopolist expends some of his monopoly profits in order to erect barriers to entry to protect the monopoly. Posner, The Social Costs of Monopoly and Regulation, 83 Journal of Political Economy 807 (1975). On the other hand, the prospect of large monopoly profits provides an added incentive for firms to innovate, in order to achieve the monopoly, with the ultimate effect of providing better or less expensive products that benefit consumers. Schumpeter, Capitalism, Socialism and Democracy (1942). But once the monopoly is achieved,

Price fixing both reduces efficiency and harms consumers. The analysis becomes more complicated when a merger or other conduct reduces costs at the same time that it reduces competition. In such cases, the pure efficiency and consumer welfare standards may lead to opposing recommendations.[28]

Are wealth transfers—earlier analogized to theft—a legitimate concern of antitrust policy? From your reading of Chapter 1, what would Congress in 1890 have thought?

United States v. Grinnell Corp.

Supreme Court of the United States, 1966.
384 U.S. 563, 86 S.Ct. 1698, 16 L.Ed.2d 778.

■ DOUGLAS, J. This case presents an important question under § 2 of the Sherman Act, which makes it an offense for any person to "monopolize . . . any part of the trade or commerce among the several States." This is a civil suit brought by the United States against Grinnell Corporation (Grinnell), American District Telegraph Co. (ADT), Holmes Electric Protective Co. (Holmes) and Automatic Fire Alarm Co. of Delaware (AFA). The District Court held for the Government and entered a decree. . . . All parties appeal, the United States because it deems the relief inadequate and the defendants both on the merits and on the relief and on the ground that the District Court denied them a fair trial. We noted probable jurisdiction. 381 U.S. 910, 85 S.Ct. 1538, 14 L.Ed.2d 432.

Grinnell manufactures plumbing supplies and fire sprinkler systems. It also owns 76% of the stock of ADT, 89% of the stock of AFA, and 100% of the stock of Holmes. ADT provides both burglary and fire protection services; Holmes provides burglary services alone; AFA supplies only fire protection service. Each offers a central station service under which hazard-detecting devices installed on the protected premises automatically transmit an electric signal to a central station.[29] The central station is manned 24 hours a day. Upon receipt of a signal, the central station, where appropriate, dispatches guards to the protected premises and notifies the police or fire department direct. There are other forms of protective services. But the record shows that subscribers to accredited central station

and the monopolist is free of competitive pressures, the monopolist may feel less need to innovate. Scherer & Ross, Industrial Market Structure and Economic Performance, Ch. 17 (3d ed. 1990).

28. For the general framework, see Williamson, Economics as an Antitrust Defense: The Welfare Tradeoffs, 58 American Economic Review 18 (1968); Williamson, Economics as an Antitrust Defense Revisited, 125 U.Pa. L.Rev. 699 (1977).

29. Among the various central station services offered are the following:

(1) *automatic burglar alarms.*

(2) *automatic fire alarms.*

(3) *sprinkler supervisory service:* any malfunctions in the fire sprinkler system (*e.g.*, changes in water pressure, dangerously low water temperatures, etc.) are reported to the central station.

(4) *watch signal service:* night watchmen, by operating a key-triggered device on the protected premises, indicate to the central station that they are making their rounds and that all is well; the failure of a watchman to make his electrical report alerts the central station that something may be amiss.

service (*i.e.*, that approved by the insurance underwriters) receive reductions in their insurance premiums that are substantially greater than the reduction received by the users of other kinds of protection service. In 1961 accredited companies in the central station service business grossed $65,000,000. ADT, Holmes, and AFA are the three largest companies in the business in terms of revenue: ADT (with 121 central stations in 115 cities) has 73% of the business; Holmes (with 12 central stations in three large cities) has 12.5%; AFA (with three central stations in three large cities) has 2%. Thus the three companies that Grinnell controls have over 87% of the business.

Over the years ADT purchased the stock or assets of 27 companies engaged in the business of providing burglar or fire alarm services. Holmes acquired the stock or assets of three burglar alarm companies in New York City using a central station. Of these 30, the officials of seven agreed not to engage in the protective service business in the area for periods ranging from five years to permanently. After Grinnell acquired control of the other defendants, the latter continued in their attempts to acquire central station companies—offers being made to at least eight companies between the years 1955 and 1961, including four of the five largest nondefendant companies in the business. When the present suit was filed, each of those defendants had outstanding an offer to purchase one of the four largest nondefendant companies.

In 1906, prior to the affiliation of ADT and Holmes, they made a written agreement whereby ADT transferred to Holmes its burglar alarm business in a major part of the Middle Atlantic States and agreed to refrain forever from engaging in that business in that area, while Holmes transferred to ADT its watch signal business and agreed to limit its activities to burglar alarm service and night watch service for financial institutions. While this agreement was modified several times and terminated in 1947, in 1961 Holmes still restricted its business to burglar alarm service and operated only in those areas which had been allocated to it under the 1906 agreement. Similarly, ADT continued to refrain from supplying burglar alarm service in those areas earlier allocated to Holmes.

In 1907 Grinnell entered into a series of agreements with the other defendant companies and with Automatic Fire Protection Co. to the following effect:

AFA received the exclusive right to provide central station sprinkler supervisory and waterflow alarm and automatic fire alarm service in New York City, Boston and Philadelphia, and agreed not to provide burglar alarm service in those cities or central station service elsewhere in the United States.

Automatic Fire Protection Co. obtained the exclusive right to provide central station sprinkler supervisory and waterflow alarm service everywhere else in the United States except for the three cities in which AFA received that exclusive right, and agreed not to engage in burglar alarm service.

ADT received the exclusive right to render burglar alarm and night-watch service throughout the United States. (Under ADT's 1906 agreement with Holmes, however, it could not provide burglar alarm services in the areas for which it had given Holmes the exclusive right to do so.) It agreed not to furnish sprinkler supervisory and waterflow alarm service anywhere in the country and not to furnish automatic fire alarm service in New York City, Boston or Philadelphia (the three cities allocated to AFA). ADT agreed to connect to its central stations the systems installed by AFA and Automatic.

Grinnell agreed to furnish and install all sprinkler supervisory and waterflow alarm actuating devices used in systems that AFA and Automatic would install, and otherwise not to engage in the central station protection business.

AFA and Automatic received 25% of the revenue produced by the sprinkler supervisory waterflow alarm service which they provided in their respective territories; ADT and Grinnell received 50% and 25%, respectively, of the revenue which resulted from such service. The agreements were to continue until February 1954.

The agreements remained substantially unchanged until 1949 when ADT purchased all of Automatic Fire Protection Co.'s rights under it for $13,500,000. After these 1907 agreements expired in 1954, AFA continued to honor the prior division of territories; and ADT and AFA entered into a new contract providing for the continued sharing of revenues on substantially the same basis as before.[30] In 1954 Grinnell and ADT renewed an agreement with a Rhode Island company which received the exclusive right to render central station service within Rhode Island at prices no lower than those of ADT and which agreed to use certain equipment supplied by Grinnell and ADT and to share its revenues with those companies. ADT had an informal agreement with a competing central station company in Washington, D.C., "that we should not solicit each other's accounts."

ADT over the years reduced its minimum basic rates to meet competition and renewed contracts at substantially increased rates in cities where it had a monopoly of accredited central station service. ADT threatened retaliation against firms that contemplated inaugurating central station service. And the record indicates that, in contemplating opening a new central station, ADT officials frequently stressed that such action would deter their competitors from opening a new station in that area.

30. In 1959, ADT complained that AFA's share of the revenues was excessive. AFA replied, in a letter to the president of Grinnell (which by that time controlled both ADT and AFA), that its share was just compensation for its continued observance of the service and territorial restrictions: "[T]he geographic restrictions placed upon us plus *the requirement that we confine our activities to sprinkler and fire alarm services exclusively,* since 1907 and presumably into the future, has definitely retarded our expansion in the past to the benefit of ADT growth.... [AFA's] contribution must also include the many things that helped make ADT big." (Emphasis added.)

The District Court found that the defendant companies had committed *per se* violations of § 1 of the Sherman Act as well as § 2 and entered a decree. 236 F.Supp. 244.

The offense of monopoly under § 2 of the Sherman Act has two elements: (1) the possession of monopoly power in the relevant market and (2) the willful acquisition or maintenance of that power as distinguished from growth or development as a consequence of a superior product, business acumen, or historic accident. We shall see that this second ingredient presents no major problem here, as what was done in building the empire was done plainly and explicitly for a single purpose. In United States v. E.I. du Pont De Nemours & Co., 351 U.S. 377, 391, we defined monopoly power as "the power to control prices or exclude competition." The existence of such power ordinarily may be inferred from the predominant share of the market. In American Tobacco Co. v. United States, 328 U.S. 781, 797, we said that "over two-thirds of the entire domestic field of cigarettes and ... over 80 per cent of the field of comparable cigarettes" constituted "a substantial monopoly." In United States v. Aluminum Co. of America, 2 Cir., 148 F.2d 416, 429, 90% of the market constituted monopoly power. In the present case, 87% of the accredited central station service business leaves no doubt that the congeries of these defendants have monopoly power—power which, as our discussion of the record indicates, they did not hesitate to wield—if that business is the relevant market. The only remaining question therefore is, what is the relevant market?

In case of a product it may be of such a character that substitute products must also be considered, as customers may turn to them if there is a slight increase in the price of the main product. That is the teaching of the *du Pont* case, (supra, 351 U.S. at 395, 404) viz., that commodities reasonably interchangeable make up that "part" of trade or commerce which § 2 protects against monopoly power.

The District Court treated the entire accredited central station service business as a single market and we think it was justified in so doing. Defendants argue that the different central station services offered are so diverse that they cannot under *du Pont* be lumped together to make up the relevant market. For example, burglar alarm services are not interchangeable with fire alarm services. They further urge that *du Pont* requires that protective services other than those of the central station variety be included in the market definition.

But there is here a single use, *i.e.*, the protection of property, through a central station that receives signals. It is that service, accredited, that is unique and that competes with all the other forms of property protection. We see no barrier to combining in a single market a number of different products or services where that combination reflects commercial realities. To repeat, there is here a single basic service—the protection of property through use of a central service station—that must be compared with all other forms of property protection.

In § 2 cases under the Sherman Act, as in § 7 cases under the Clayton Act (Brown Shoe Co. v. United States, 370 U.S. 294, 325), there may be submarkets that are separate economic entities. We do not pursue that question here. First we deal with services, not with products, and second, we conclude that the accredited central station is a type of service that makes up a relevant market and that domination or control of it makes out a monopoly of a "part" of trade or commerce within the meaning of § 2 of the Sherman Act. The defendants have not made out a case for fragmentizing the types of services into lesser units.

Burglar alarm service is in a sense different from fire alarm service; from waterflow alarms; and so on. But it would be unrealistic on this record to break down the market into the various kinds of central station protective services that are available. Central station companies recognize that to compete effectively, they must offer all or nearly all types of service.[31] The different forms of accredited central station service are provided from a single office and customers utilize different services in combination. We held in United States v. Philadelphia Nat'l Bank, 374 U.S. 321, 356, that "the cluster" of services denoted by the term "commercial banking" is "a distinct line of commerce." ... There is, in our view, a comparable cluster of services here. Those bank cases arose under § 7 of the Clayton Act where the question was whether the effect of a merger "in any line of commerce" may be "substantially to lessen competition." We see no reason to differentiate between "line" of commerce in the context of the Clayton Act and "part" of commerce for purposes of the Sherman Act. In the § 7 national bank case just mentioned, *services,* not *products* in the mercantile sense, were involved. In our view the lumping of various kinds of *services* makes for the appropriate market here as it did in the § 7 case.

There are, to be sure, substitutes for the accredited central station service. But none of them appears to operate on the same level as the central station service so as to meet the interchangeability test of the *du Pont* case. Nonautomatic and automatic local alarm systems appear on this record to have marked differences, not the low degree of differentiation required of substitute services as well as substitute articles.

Watchman service is far more costly and less reliable. Systems that set off an audible alarm at the site of a fire or burglary are cheaper but often less reliable. They may be inoperable without anyone knowing it. Moreover, there is a risk that the local ringing of an alarm will not attract the needed attention and help. Proprietary systems that a customer purchases and operates are available; but they can be used only by a very large business or by government and are not realistic alternatives for most concerns. There are also protective services connected directly to a municipal police or fire

---

31. Thus, of the 38 nondefendant firms operating a central service station protective service in the United States in 1961, 24 offered all of the following services: automatic fire alarm; waterflow alarm and sprinkler supervision; watchman's reporting and manual fire alarm; and burglar alarm. Of the other firms, 11 provided no watchman's reporting and manual fire alarm service; six provided no automatic fire alarm service; and two offered no sprinkler supervisory and waterflow alarm service. Moreover, of the 14 firms not providing the full panoply of services, 10 lacked only *one* of the above-described services. Appellant ADT's assertion that "very few accredited central stations furnish the full variety of services" is flatly contradicted by the record.

department. But most cities with an accredited central station do not permit direct, connected service for private businesses. These alternate services and devices differ, we are told, in utility, efficiency, reliability, responsiveness, and continuity, and the record sustains that position. And, as noted, insurance companies generally allow a greater reduction in premiums for accredited central station service than for other types of protection.

Defendants earnestly urge that despite these differences, they face competition from these other modes of protection. They seem to us seriously to overstate the degree of competition, but we recognize that (as the District Court found) they "do not have unfettered power to control the price of their services . . . due to the fringe competition of other alarm or watchmen services." 236 F.Supp., at 254. What defendants overlook is that the high degree of differentiation between central station protection and the other forms means that for many customers, only central station protection will do. Though some customers may be willing to accept higher insurance rates in favor of cheaper forms of protection, others will not be willing or able to risk serious interruption to their businesses, even though covered by insurance, and will thus be unwilling to consider anything but central station protection.

The accredited, as distinguished from nonaccredited, service is a relevant part of commerce. Virtually the only central station companies in the status of the nonaccredited are those that have not yet been able to meet the standards of the rating bureau. The accredited ones are indeed those that have achieved, in the eyes of underwriters, superiorities that other central stations do not have. The accredited central station is located in a building of approved design, provided with an emergency lighting system and two alternate main power sources, manned constantly by at least a required minimum of operators, provided with a direct line to fire headquarters and, where possible, a direct line to a police station; and equipped with all the devices, circuits and equipment meeting the requirements of the underwriters. These standards are important as insurance carriers often require accredited central station service as a condition to writing insurance. There is indeed evidence that customers consider the unaccredited service as inferior.

We also agree with the District Court that the geographic market for the accredited central station service is national. The activities of an individual station are in a sense local as it serves, ordinarily, only that area which is within a radius of 25 miles. But the record amply supports the conclusion that the business of providing such a service is operated on a national level. There is national planning. The agreements we have discussed covered activities in many States. The inspection, certification and rate-making is largely by national insurers. The defendant ADT has a national schedule of prices, rates, and terms, though the rates may be varied to meet local conditions. It deals with multi-state businesses on the basis of nationwide contracts. The manufacturing business of ADT is interstate. The fact that Holmes is more nearly local than the others does not save it, for it is part and parcel of the combine presided over and controlled by Grinnell.

As the District Court found, the relevant market for determining whether the defendants have monopoly power is not the several local areas which the individual stations serve, but the broader national market that reflects the reality of the way in which they built and conduct their business.

We have said enough about the great hold that the defendants have on this market. The percentage is so high as to justify the finding of monopoly. And, as the facts already related indicate, this monopoly was achieved in large part by unlawful and exclusionary practices. The restrictive agreements that preempted for each company a segment of the market where it was free of competition of the others were one device. Pricing practices that contained competitors were another. The acquisition by Grinnell of ADT, AFA, and Holmes were still another. Grinnell long faced a problem of competing with ADT. That was one reason it acquired AFA and Holmes. Prior to settlement of its dispute and controversy with ADT, Grinnell prepared to go into the central station service business. By acquiring ADT in 1953, Grinnell eliminated that alternative. Its control of the three other defendants eliminated any possibility of an outbreak of competition that might have occurred when the 1907 agreements terminated. By those acquisitions it perfected the monopoly power to exclude competitors and fix prices. . . .

The final decree enjoins the defendants in general terms from restraining trade or attempting or conspiring to restrain trade in this particular market, from further monopolizing, and attempting or conspiring to monopolize. The court ordered the alarm companies to file with the Department of Justice standard lists of prices and terms and every quotation to customers that deviated from those lists and enjoined the defendants from acquiring stock, assets, or business of any enterprise in the market. Grinnell was ordered to file, not later than April 1, 1966, a plan of divestiture of its stock in each of the other defendant companies. It was given the option either to sell the stock or distribute it to its stockholders or combine or vary those methods. The court further enjoined any of the defendants from employing in any capacity the President and Chairman of the Board of Grinnell, James D. Fleming. Both the Government and the defendants challenge aspects of the decree.

We start from the premise that adequate relief in a monopolization case should put an end to the combination and deprive the defendants of any of the benefits of the illegal conduct, and break up or render impotent the monopoly power found to be in violation of the Act. That is the teaching of our cases, notably Schine Theatres v. United States, 334 U.S. 110, 128–129.

We largely agree with the Government's views on the relief aspect of the case. We start with ADT, which presently does 73% of the business done by accredited central stations throughout the country. It is indeed the keystone of the defendants' monopoly power. The mere dissolution of the combination through the divestiture by Grinnell of its interests in the other companies does not reach the root of the evil. In 92 of the 115 cities in which ADT operates there are no other accredited central stations. Perhaps some cities could not support more than one. Defendants recognized prior to trial that at least 13 cities can; the Government urged divestiture in 48 cities. That there should be some divestiture on the part of ADT seems clear; but the details of such divestiture must be determined by the District Court as the matter cannot be resolved on this record.

Two of the means by which ADT acquired and maintained its large share of the market are the requirement that subscribers sign five-year contracts and the retention by ADT of title to the protective services equipment installed on a subscriber's premises. On this record it appears that these practices constitute substantial barriers to competition and that relief against them is appropriate. The *pros* and *cons* are argued with considerable vehemence here.[32] Again, we cannot resolve them on this record. The various aspects of this controversy must be explored by the District Court and suitable protective provisions included in the decree that deprive these two devices of the coercive power that they apparently have had towards restraining competition and creating a monopoly.

The Government proposed that the defendants be required to sell, on nondiscriminatory terms, any devices manufactured by them for use in furnishing central station service. It seems clear that if the competitors are to be able to compete effectively for the existing customers of the defendants when the present service contracts expire, they must be assured of replacement parts to maintain those systems.

. . .

Defendants urge and the Government concedes that the barring of Mr. Fleming from the employment of any of the defendants is unduly harsh and quite unnecessary on this record. While relief of that kind may be appropriate where the predatory conduct is conspicuous, we cannot see that any such case was made out on this record.

. . .

The defendants object to the requirements that Grinnell divest itself of its holdings in the three alarm company defendants, but we think that provision is wholly justified. Dissolution of the combination is essential as indicated by many of our cases, starting with Standard Oil Co. v. United States, 221 U.S. 1, 78. The defendants object to that portion of the decree

---

32. Specifically, the areas of disagreement are: (1) Defendants urge that barring them from offering five-year contracts would put them at a competitive disadvantage *vis-à-vis* nondefendant firms; the Government responds that since they violated the law, they may properly be subjected to restrictions not borne by others. See United States v. Bausch & Lomb Co., 321 U.S. 707, 723–724. (2) Some customers of defendants may wish to have long-term contracts; the Government responds that this may be explored on remand. (3) There is some dispute as to whether, if the central station company cannot retain title to the equipment it installs, the insurance companies will accredit the system. This, too, is a proper subject for inquiry on remand.

that bars them from acquiring interests in firms in the accredited central station business. But since acquisition was one of the methods by which the defendants acquired their market power and was the method by which Grinnell put the combination together, an injunction against the repetition of the practice seems fully warranted....

The judgment below is affirmed except as to the decree. We remand for further hearings on the nature of the relief....

■ MR. JUSTICE FORTAS, with whom MR. JUSTICE STEWART, joins, dissenting. I agree that the judgment below should be reversed, but I do not agree that the remand should be limited to reshaping the decree. Because I believe that the definition of the relevant market here cannot be sustained, I would reverse and remand for a new determination of this basic issue, subject to proper standards.

We have here a case under both § 1 and § 2 of the Sherman Act, which proscribe combinations in restraint of trade, and monopolies and attempts to monopolize. The judicial task is not difficult to state: Does the record show a combination in restraint of trade or a monopoly or attempt to monopolize? If so, what are its characteristics, scope and effect? And, finally, what is the appropriate remedy for a court of equity to decree?

Each of these inquiries depends upon two basic referents: definition of the geographical area of trade or commerce restrained or monopolized, and of the products or services involved. In § 1 cases this problem ordinarily presents little difficulty because the combination in restraint of trade itself delineates the "market" with sufficient clarity to support the usual injunctive form of relief in those cases. *See, e.g.,* United States v. Griffith, 334 U.S. 100. In the present case, however, the essence of the offense is monopolization, achieved or attempted, and the major relief is divestiture. For these purposes, "market" definition is of the essence, just as in § 7 cases the kindred definition of the "line of commerce" is fundamental. We must define the area of commerce that is allegedly engrossed before we can determine its engrossment; and we must define it before a decree can be shaped to deal with the consequences of the monopoly, and to restore or produce competition. [Citing cases.]

In § 2 cases, the search for "the relevant market" must be undertaken and pursued with relentless clarity. It is, in essence, an economic task put to the uses of the law. Unless this task is well done, the results will be distorted in terms of the conclusion as to whether the law has been violated and what the decree should contain.

In this case, the relevant geographical and product markets have not been defined on the basis of the economic facts of the industry concerned. They have been tailored precisely to fit defendants' business. The Government proposed and the trial court concluded that the relevant market is not the business of fire protection, or burglary protection, or protection against waterflow, etc., or all of these together. It is not even the business of furnishing these from a central location. It is the business, viewed nationally, of supplying "insurance accredited central station protection services." (CSPS)—that is, fire, burglary and other kinds of protection furnished from a central station that is accredited by insurance companies. The business of defendants fits neatly into the product and geographic market so defined. In fact, it comes close to filling the market so defined. This Court has now approved this Procrustean definition.

The geographical market is defined as nationwide. But the need and the service are intensely local—more local by far, for example, than the market which this Court found to be local in United States v. Philadelphia Nat. Bank, 374 U.S. 321, 357–362. The premises protected do not travel. They are fixed locations. They must be protected where they are. Protection must be provided on the spot. It must be furnished by local personnel able to bring help to the scene within minutes. Even the central stations can provide service only within a 25–mile radius. Where the tenants of the premises turn to central stations for this service, they must make their contracts locally with the central station and purchase their services from it on the basis of local conditions.

But because these defendants, the trial court found, are connected by stock ownership, interlocking management and some degree of national corporate direction, and because there is some national participation in selling as well as national financing, advertising, purchasing of equipment, and the like,[33] the court concluded that the competitive area to be considered is national. This Court now affirms that conclusion.

This is a nonsequitur. It is not permissible to seize upon the nation-wide scope of defendants' operation and to bootstrap a geographical definition of the market from this. The purpose of the search for the relevant geographical market is to find the area or areas to which a potential buyer may rationally look for the goods or services that he seeks. The test, as this Court said in United States v. Philadelphia Nat. Bank, is "the geographic structure of supplier-customer relations," 374 U.S. 321, 357, quoting Kaysen and Turner, Antitrust Policy 102 (1959). And as Mr. Justice Clark put it in Tampa Electric Co. v. Nashville Coal Co., 365 U.S. 320, 327, the definition of the relevant market requires "careful selection of the market area in which the seller operates, and to which the purchaser can practicably turn for supplies." The central issue is where does a potential buyer look for potential suppliers of the service—what is the geographical area in which the buyer has, or, in the absence of monopoly, would have, a real choice as to price and alternative facilities? This depends upon the facts of the market place, taking into account such economic factors as the distance over which supplies and services may be feasibly furnished, consistently with cost and functional efficiency.

The incidental aspects of defendants' business which the court uses cannot control the outcome of this inquiry. They do not measure the

33. There is a danger that this Court's opinion will be read as somewhat overstating the case. There is neither finding or record to support the implication that rates are to any substantial extent fixed on a nationwide ba-sis, or that there are nationwide contracts with multi-state businesses in any significant degree, or that insurers inspect or certify central stations on a nationwide basis.

market area in which buyer and sellers meet. They have little impact upon the ascertainment of the geographical areas in which the economic and legal questions must be answered: have defendants "monopolized" or "restrained" trade; have they eliminated or can they eliminate competitors or prevent or obstruct new entries into the business; have they controlled or can they control price for the services? These are the issues; and, in defendants' business, a finding that the "relevant market" is national is nothing less than a studied failure to assess the effect of defendants' position and practices in the light of the competition which exists, or could exist, in economically defined areas—in the real world.

Here, there can be no doubt that the correct geographic market is local. The services at issue are intensely local: they can be furnished only locally. The business as it is done is local—not nationwide. If, as might well be the case on this record, defendants were found to have violated the Sherman Act in a number of these local areas, a proper decree, directed to those markets, as well as to general corporate features relevant to the condemned practices, could be fashioned. On the other hand, a gross definition of the market as nationwide leads to a gross, nationwide decree which does not address itself to the realities of the market place. This is what happened here: The District Court's finding that the market was *nationwide* logically led it to a decree which operated on the only *national* aspect of the situation, the parent company nexus, instead of on the economically realistic areas—the local situations. This Court now directs the trial court to require "some [unspecified] divestiture" locally by the alarm companies. This is a recognition of the economic reality that the relevant competitive areas are local. In plain terms, the Court's direction to the trial court means a "market-by-market" analysis for the purpose of breaking up defendants' monopoly position and creating competitors and competition wherever feasible in particular cities. In my view, however, by so directing, the Court implies that which it does not command: that the case should be reconsidered at the trial court level because of the improper standard it used to define the relevant geographic markets.

The trial court's definition of the "product" market even more dramatically demonstrates that its action has been Procrustean—that it has tailored the market to the dimensions of the defendants. It recognizes that a person seeking protective services has many alternative sources. It lists "watchmen, watchdogs, automatic proprietary systems confined to one site (often, but not always), alarm systems connected with some local police or fire station, often unaccredited CSPS [central station protective services], and often accredited CSPS." The court finds that even in the same city a single customer seeking protection for several premises may "exercise its option" differently for different locations. It may choose accredited CSPS for one of its locations and a different type of service for another.

But the court isolates from all of these alternatives only those services in which defendants engage. It eliminates all of the alternative sources despite its conscientious enumeration of them. Its definition of the "relevant market" is not merely confined to "central station" protective services, but to those central station protective services which are "accredited" by insurance companies.

There is no pretense that these furnish peculiar services for which there is no alternative in the market place, on either a price or a functional basis. The court relies solely upon its finding that the services offered by accredited central stations are of better quality, and upon its conclusion that the insurance companies tend to give "noticeably larger" discounts to policyholders who are accredited central station protective services. This Court now approved this strange red-haired, bearded, one-eyed man-with-a-limp classification....

. . .

I do not suggest that wide disparities in quality, price and customer appeal could never affect the definition of the market. But this follows only where the disparities are so great that they create separate and distinct categories of buyers and sellers. The record here and the findings do not approach this standard. They fall far short of justifying the narrowing of the market as practiced here. I need refer only to the exclusion of non-accredited central stations, which the court seeks to justify by reference to differentials in insurance discounts. This differential may indeed affect the relative cost to the consumer of the competing modes of protection. But, in the absence of proof that it results in eliminating the competing services from the category of those to which the purchaser "can practically turn" for supplies, it does not justify their total exclusion. This sort of exclusion of the supposedly not-quite-so-attractive service from the basic definition of the kinds of business and service against which defendants' activity will be measured, is entirely unjustified on this record....[34]

---

34. The dissenting opinion of Harlan, J., is omitted.

The opinion of Wyzanski, J., below, 236 F.Supp. 244, 247–48 (D.R.I.1964), contained the following observations:

With regard to § 2 of the Sherman Act ... in the two decades since the opinion of Judge Learned Hand in United States v. Aluminum Co. of America, 2nd Cir., 148 F.2d 416 (1945), most of the cognoscenti have expected that a day would come when the Supreme Court would announce that where one or more persons acting jointly had acquired so clear a dominance in a market as to have the power to exclude competition therefrom, there was a *rebuttable* presumption that such power had been criminally acquired and was a monopolizing punishable under § 2. To be sure, the putative offender would be allowed to avoid or defeat this presumption if he bore the burden of proving that this share of the market was the result of superior skill, superior products, natural advantages, technological or economic efficiency, scientific research, low margins of profit maintained permanently and without discrimination, legal licenses, or the like. Cf. United States v. United Shoe Machinery Corp., D.Mass., 110 F.Supp. 295, aff'd 347 U.S. 521. Such a shifting of the burden not merely of going forward, but of proof, such a rebuttable presumption rests on the by-now dozens of court records which make it quite clear that it is the highly exceptional case, a *rara avis* more often found in academic groves than in the thickets of business, where monopoly power was thrust upon an enterprise by the economic character of the industry and by what Judge L. Hand in *Aluminum* called "superior skill, foresight and industry." More than 7 decades of Sherman Act enforcement leave the informed observer with the abiding conviction that durable non-statutory

NOTES AND QUESTIONS

1. In *Grinnell,* the majority said a violation of Section 2 occurs when a company with monopoly power willfully acquires or maintains that power, "as distinguished from growth or development as a consequence of a superior product, business acumen or historic accident." That language, if read as an acceptance of the *Alcoa* approach, would, of course, make it difficult for any company to obtain a dominant position in any market without violating Section 2.

Why not go the next step and explicitly eliminate the "conduct" element in Section 2 cases? In 1979, the National Commission for the Review of Antitrust Laws and Procedures (NCRALP), a group of antitrust experts under the leadership of the Assistant Attorney General for Antitrust, recommended that Congress conduct hearings to explore the advisability of an amendment to Section 2 to cover "no-fault" violations. No-fault proposals usually provide that substantial, persistent single-firm monopoly power will violate Section 2 regardless of whether it was achieved or maintained by objectionable conduct. The essential point is that monopoly is undesirable in a free market system regardless of how it was achieved, and that enormous time and resources are expended in Section 2 litigation—up to 40% in discovery and trial time according to recent studies—to explore "conduct" issues. Almost all no-fault proposals are limited to government civil suits, have minimum trigger figures (the FTC's submission to NCRALP suggested $500 million in sales in the relevant market), and require a finding of persistent or durable monopoly power (*e.g.,* 5 or 10 years). No-fault proposals usually provide exemptions for natural monopoly (*i.e.,* situations where there is not sufficient demand to support two efficiently operated firms), and some create a defense where it can be shown that the monopoly power derives solely from production and distribution efficiencies.

What's wrong with the concept of a no-fault violation of Section 2? Would such an amendment create undesirable disincentives for aggressive competition; specifically, would large companies avoid aggressive competitive action out of fear that they would become a no-fault monopolist and then be summarily dismembered? Would the cost to society of this kind of anticipatory avoidance be greater than the current cost of monopoly profits? Is the proposal "unfair" to corporate managers and shareholders? Or should those two groups welcome the new career and profit

monopolies (ones created without patents or licenses or lasting beyond their term) are, to a moral certainty, due to acquisitions of competitors or restraints of trade prohibited by § 1. They are the achievement of the quiet life after the enemy's capitulation or his defeat in inglorious battle.

To this Court it appears that the day has come for it, and more important for counsel, to proceed on the acknowledged principle that once the Government has borne the burden of proving what is the relevant market and how predominant a share of that market defendant has, it follows that there are rebuttable presumptions that defendant has monopoly power and has monopolized in violation of § 2. The Government need not prove,

and in a well-conducted trial ought not to be allowed to consume time in needlessly proving, defendant's predatory tactics, if any, or defendant's pricing, or production, or selling, or leasing, or marketing, or financial policies while in this predominant role. If defendant does wish to go forward, it is free to do so and to maintain the burden of showing that its eminence is traceable to such highly respectable causes as superiority in means and methods which are "honestly industrial," as Judge Hand characterized the supposititious socially desirable monopolizer.

Compare Judge Wyzanski's conduct approach with the Supreme Court's approach in *Grinnell* and with the discussions at pp. 142–147 supra and in Chapter 8, Section 1.

opportunities that could result if a giant company were split into five aggressive competitors?

NCRALP's suggestion that Congress hold hearings on the no-fault issue has been studiously ignored, and the concept is no longer being pursued.

2. Are you satisfied with the majority view that Grinnell operated in a national geographic market? Could individual users rationally seek CSPS protection from suppliers located throughout the country? Are you satisfied that the factors cited by the court at p. 177 overcome the otherwise local nature of the market, or might the court have been influenced to choose a national market in order to justify the relief it imposed?

KEY ISSUES RAISED BY *CELLOPHANE* AND *GRINNELL* AND CURRENT VIEWS ON RELEVANT MARKET

As we have seen, definition of relevant market is an analytical tool to assist in estimating the market power of a firm or group of firms. Essentially, it is an attempt to identify those firms that would at once be looked to as offering alternatives if one or more sellers of a product raises its price.

In theory and practice, relevant market definition is as difficult an undertaking as any in antitrust. How do we decide whether Coca Cola or the New York Times should be regarded as monopolies? The sellers of each of these products have some discretion in setting price—partly because each is in some degree different from all possible substitutes, and partly because buyers perceive the products to be different. But when the sellers of these products seek to exercise that discretion—raising prices and curtailing output—competition from substitutes will soon be encountered.

There is, of course, no such thing as pure monopoly, in the sense of absolute discretion over price, because at some point a further price increase will lead some consumers to switch to less satisfactory products, or to withdraw from the market.

Between the poles of absolute market power and zero market power are an infinite array of market possibilities, on both the demand and supply sides. Thus, market definition involves matters of degree, approximation, and judgment. The Supreme Court's decisions in the *Cellophane* and *Grinnell* cases provide the framework for market analysis under Section 2 of the Sherman Act. The problem, of course, is that the market approaches in the two cases differ and each case—for different reasons—raises significant analytical questions. Added complexity comes by way of market definition precedents from other areas of antitrust (*e.g.*, merger precedents) and developing views on market definition and power articulated by leading economists. Set forth below are critiques of the *Cellophane* and *Grinnell* opinions and appraisals of the adequacy and practicality of various approaches to the task of defining relevant market.

1. **The *Cellophane* and *Grinnell* cases.** In its *Cellophane* decision, the Supreme Court found that cellophane competed with Pliofilm, Saran Wrap, wax paper, and other flexible wrapping materials for a wide range of end uses. It found that if du Pont raised the price of cellophane even slightly, it would lose substantial sales to these other materials. If prices of the other materials changed, cellophane sales would be affected. This competitive feature it denominated "cross-elasticity of demand," borrowing a technical concept of economic analysis.[35] The Court found

---

35. "Elasticity of demand" is the percentage change in the quantity of a product   sold resulting from a percentage change in price. If a small percentage change leads to

that even though cellophane costs "two or three times as much, surface measure, as its chief competitors," p. 157 supra, and even though there were pronounced differences from the other wrapping materials in functional characteristics, the cross-elasticity of demand between cellophane and the other products was nevertheless sufficient to warrant including them in the same product market. By defining the relevant product market as "flexible wrapping materials," rather than "cellophane," the Court was able to conclude that du Pont had less than 20% rather than about 75% of the relevant market.

One problem with the *Cellophane* approach is that it involves circular reasoning. A firm with significant market power will normally set a price just high enough so that if it raised the price another notch, the price increase would not increase profits because of the business that would be lost. Thus, the fact that du Pont would lose business to other flexible wraps if it raised the current price slightly is entirely consistent with its possessing market power. Du Pont's current price could include an abnormally high profit level.

As we will see in Chapter 9, which deals with mergers, during the 1980s, the Department of Justice adopted merger guidelines which set forth an analytical framework for defining relevant markets and then elaborated a methodology for applying that definition to given cases.[36] Those guidelines have the same failing as the *Cellophane* case when dealing with *exercised* market power. As one group of commentators put it:

> The Justice Department's merger guidelines begin by taking the product of one of the merging firms and asking whether a coordinated, significant price increase above the current level by all the firms making the product would be profitable. The hypothesized increase usually is a five percent price rise lasting one year. If the hypothesized increase would be profitable, those firms constitute a relevant market.
>
> The most obvious problem with this approach ... is that the guidelines will not identify as a relevant market the product of a profit-maximizing monopolist.... A single firm that already is maximizing profits cannot, by definition, increase profits by raising its price further. Thus, this single firm cannot constitute a relevant market under the Justice Department's approach. Consider, for example, the case of a firm charged with monopolization for excluding all other producers of a particular product, but which faces a competitive fringe comprised of a large number of small producers of a substitute product, each of which can produce an

great increases or decreases in the volume of sale, demand is said to be elastic; if it results in only slight changes in volume, demand is said to be inelastic.

Economists attach numbers to these concepts. If the price of product A is increased two per cent and a four per cent decrease in sales results, an economist would describe the elasticity of demand as 2. If a two per cent increase in the price of a product resulted in only a one per cent decrease in demand, the elasticity would be ½.

Cross-elasticity—the concept cited by the Supreme Court in *Cellophane*- concerns the relative demand of one product compared to another. If product A is an excellent substitute for product B, then a slight increase in the price of B should lead to a substantial increase in volume of sales of product A at the expense of product B. That situation would be described as one of high cross-elasticity of demand. The Supreme Court in *Cellophane* apparently believed that all products with high cross-elasticities of demand belong in the same relevant product market. As we shall see, that is an incomplete analysis of the market definition issue.

36. See Chapter 9, p. 964 infra.

unlimited amount at some constant unit cost level. That firm might set its price at the level just below the value consumers place on the substitute, such that any further price increase would eliminate virtually all of its sales. As a result, under the Justice Department's test, the relevant market would include the substitute products. If the firm's share of capacity in that broader market was small, the Justice Department would conclude that it had no market power. Because a finding of market power is a prerequisite to a section 2 violation, that firm's exclusionary conduct would be immunized.[37]

In the monopoly context, one way of avoiding the *Cellophane* fallacy is to focus on the degree of cross-elasticity of demand at the price that would provide only normal competitive profits. If current prices are used, the relevant cross-elasticities would be those among alternative products, if any, with price structures that have the same relationship to cost, *i.e.*, whose cost/price ratios are the same.

In *Grinnell* the Supreme Court noted that some buyers had a special preference for accredited central station protective service (CSPS)—for many customers "only central station protection will do," p. 177 supra. It defined CSPS as a separate product market, using the concept of "submarket." A Fifth Circuit decision described the submarket concept as follows:

> Antitrust law recognizes that economically significant submarkets may exist which themselves constitute relevant product markets. The fact finder may determine a submarket exists by "examining such practical indicia as industry or public recognition of the sub-market as a separate economic entity, the product's peculiar characteristics and uses, unique production facilities, distinct customers, distinct prices, sensitivity to price changes, and specialized vendors." *Brown Shoe,* 370 U.S. at 325.[38]

In *Grinnell* the Supreme Court focused on the existence of a vulnerable group of buyers. Would it be appropriate to carve out a separate market (*i.e.*, decide that a seller is a monopolist) every time there is a class of purchasers that has a decided preference for a seller's particular product? With almost any consumer product—consider Coca Cola and the New York Times again—there will be a class of customers who greatly prefer the product. Should the criterion be how large the class? How strong the preference? There was no finding in *Grinnell* as to what percentage of purchasers had a preference for CSPS, or how much more they were being charged or would be willing to pay.

While neither the *Cellophane* nor the *Grinnell* approach is entirely satisfactory, there is an important difference between the market situations in the two cases that may partially explain their outcomes. Most cellophane users did have acceptable alternatives, since most categories of purchasers (produce packers, bakers, etc.) used or could use other wrappings than cellophane. Users for whom substitutes were poor—such as the cigarette manufacturers, reluctant to market their product in Saran Wrap or wax paper—were protected to some extent by the fact that, if need be, they could arrange to buy cellophane from the channels of supply to those other users or in "arbitrage" transactions. For example, if du Pont were to attempt to double the price of cellophane to the cigarette companies ("captive users," because for them there were no reasonable substitutes) while maintaining the price

37. Krattenmaker, Lande & Salop, Monopoly Power and Market Power in Antitrust Law, 76 Geo.L.J. 241, 256 (1987).

38. Domed Stadium Hotel, Inc. v. Holiday Inns, Inc., 732 F.2d 480, 487–88 (5th Cir.1984).

to bakers ("precarious users," because they would shift to other wraps if even a slight price increase were announced), the bakers or their suppliers could offer cellophane at a slight profit to the cigarette companies. Since cigarette companies constituted only a fairly small part of total sales, this possibility would offer them important protection, unless du Pont could prevent such sales by policing channels of distribution.

In *Grinnell,* in contrast, customers were buyers of "services," as the Court notes, p. 176 supra, and each protection service contract was presumably independently negotiated. If the seller of CSPS could identify users who were strongly attracted to its product, it could raise price to such users without concern that they might be able to protect their position by buying from others who paid a lower price. Since arbitrage in services is usually impossible, it may be necessary to define the market narrowly in such cases if captive users are to be protected against discretionary market power.

2. **Standardized vs. differentiated products.** When products are identical or regarded as perfect substitutes, the real test of market power derives from the relative efficiency (*i.e.*, unit costs of production) of each producer. Suppose there are five producers of identical products, and each has 20% of the market and essentially similar costs. No one seller can significantly increase its market share without being checked by the competitive response of the others. But suppose further, given the same market structure, that unit costs of one of the sellers are 30% below the others. Assuming the low-cost producer has unused capacity, it might lower its price to a point where none of its rivals could respond, and take as much of the market as it chose (unless and until its increased volume resulted in costs increased to a level comparable to those of its rivals). In terms of market power, it is a matter of indifference whether a company earns (or dissipates) a 30% profit on a 20% market share, or a 15% profit on a 90% market share. In the first instance, it is a "latent monopolist" with the power to exclude its competitors; in the latter, it has exercised that power in order to obtain an overwhelming market share.

Where products differ—in physical characteristics or perceived desirability—the problem of market definition is more difficult. A common situation involves a set of producers of competing products that are more or less valued for different attributes by different groups of buyers. For example, cellophane was recognized as having physical properties (transparency, bursting strength, impermeability, etc.) which resulted in its being preferred in different degrees by different classes of purchasers. Du Pont, as the sole producer of cellophane, had some degree of market power with respect to each group of purchasers; its overall market power at any given price level would depend upon: (1) the size of each such group; (2) the strength of each group's preference for cellophane; (3) the relative costs of each substitute product; (4) whether new entrants were expected to appear at a higher price level for cellophane; and (5) the ability of du Pont to discriminate in price among various groups of users.

With data providing answers to all five questions, it would be possible to make at least a preliminary estimate of du Pont's market power. Unfortunately, the kind of information necessary to make such judgments will almost never be available, to say nothing of its being amenable to the judicial process. First, cost of production and profit data are difficult to ascertain and exist, if at all, in the books of defendant companies. Companies tend to resist disclosure efforts and, even when outsiders can obtain access, they must worry about the accuracy of the information. Second, information as to how different groups of purchasers will react at a given time to a price increase at a range of price levels is never available, and estimates are unlikely to be very reliable. If the price of cellophane were raised from $1.00 per surface unit to $1.10, what would tobacco companies, fresh fruit packers, candy companies, frozen food packers, and bakers do? Some would switch immediately to substitutes, others would regard cellophane as a bargain at an even higher price, and a third group might hedge its bets while awaiting future price developments. Since a comparable price rise usually will not actually have occurred, estimates will necessarily be speculative. In any event, the amount and complexity of information necessary to measure market power with a high degree of accuracy would swamp any trial court. This may be the most important reason why the courts, in *Cellophane, Grinnell*, and other cases, have sought more manageable shortcut approaches to relevant market questions.

3. **Added complications.** Even if the cost, price, and customer preference data were adequate to produce some tentative conclusion about market share, there would be other important factors to be taken into account.

(a) *Time.* The foregoing information would provide a somewhat fuzzy snapshot at some point in time of a seller's market power, but markets are dynamic and that position may well be expanding or eroding. New products or production processes may appear at any moment to undercut a dominant market position, or a patent or other temporary advantage may be expiring. Hence, current market power may predictably be transitory. It has occasionally been suggested that monopoly antitrust cases take so long to litigate that market power that may have existed when the complaint was filed will have been dissipated by the time trial is over and appeals exhausted. On the other hand, a superior product or process may be in the early stages of eliminating all rivals so that present market share bears little relationship to reasonably predictable future market power.

(b) *Barriers to entry of potential competition.* The existence of potential entrants may constrain market power; thus they should somehow be encompassed within the definition of relevant market, although they have no current market share. Put another way, if there are significant or no barriers to new entry, so that if a seller raised price even a fraction of a cent, it would be swamped by new competition, that seller regardless of its current market share has no market power. For example, suppose a seller dominates the current supply of a specialized kind of unpatented microfilm. Suppose further that three large film manufacturers do not currently make such microfilm but could do so by minor changes in existing machinery or the addition of an inexpensive chemical ingredient. The current market for microfilm might appear to be monopolized, using all the demand and cost data described above, but the existence of substantial potential entrants, capable of cheaply and promptly increasing the availability of the product, sharply limits the market power of the microfilm "monopolist."

Potential competition can derive from a number of sources. As in the example discussed above, existing manufacturers who make a slightly different product can modify their manufacturing process to compete in an adjacent product market (often referred to as "supply substitutability"). Similarly, manufacturers currently serving a remote market can divert their production into the monopolist's market ("geographic diversion"). Firms actively competing in the market but operating at less than full capacity can expand their operations. Finally, companies entirely outside the product and geographic market may be able to invest quickly in new facilities and become competitors ("new entrants") if a current monopolist attempts to exploit its market position by charging excessive prices.

(c) *Countervailing buyer power.* The dominant supplier of a particular ingredient may be a small company whose only customer is an industrial giant. The large company may have bargaining resources that limit the market power of the supplier, regardless of current market share. For example, it might be able to induce small competitors of the dominant firm to deviate from the monopoly price by offering a very large contract. It might also enter into the manufacture of its own supply of the ingredient in question or break down the monopoly price with a credible threat of entry, or it might encourage other firms to enter the market with the offer of a substantial, long-term contract.

(d) *Conduct evidence.* Often an indication of a firm's market power can be obtained inferentially from the way it behaves in the marketplace. A firm may raise prices in a period of declining demand with no loss of sales volume, engage in effective price discrimination, or drive competitors out of the market through product innovation, distribution methods or advertising, even though it enjoys no apparent cost advantage. It may raise or maintain price above competitive levels by raising the costs of its rivals by, for example, exclusionary conduct.[39] In such cases, the behavior itself may demonstrate market power and properly be taken into account. On the other hand, there can be many explanations for an apparent ability to control market price or exclude competitors, and such "conduct" evidence of market power must be handled with a high degree of care.

4. **Conclusion.** Courts often do face extremely close relevant market questions. For example, does domestic sherry compete with imported sauternes? Does a department store at a shopping mall with good public transportation compete with downtown stores three miles away? Does bus transportation compete with subways? Do sales of soft drinks through vending machines compete with sales of the same soft drinks in supermarkets? Do industry anticipated top-grossing motion pictures compete with other first-run films? In these cases it is important for courts to remember that market definition is no more than a tool for estimating market power, not a scientific test that produces precise results.

Difficulties arise in two main ways. First, a trial court, perhaps considering itself required to do so by Supreme Court opinions, permits or requires the parties to exhaust enormous resources, energies, and litigation efforts in an essentially fruitless search for some ideal of relevant market. The case may go on almost endlessly, or the party with fewest resources for pretrial proceedings, expert witnesses, market research, and such paraphernalia, eventually collapses. Second, having invested heavily, often with less than satisfying results, in this unusual fact-finding venture, the court feels impelled to make use of the results in its findings and opinion, perhaps making it appear more cogent and relevant to the decision than it in fact was. The worst outcome is when—as might appear to be the case in *Cellophane*—the market *share* figure thus produced is treated as dispositive and the proceeding is terminated without the ultimate question of market *power* having been adequately dealt with. Having made a close call on market definition, the court usually proceeds to count (or not to count) percentage market shares on an all-or-nothing basis, forgetting the number of difficult judgments involved and the approximate nature of the underlying market decision. This kind of mechanical jurisprudence, more frequently than the application of "wrong" relevant market rules, is what produces so much costly wasted effort in the courtroom and error and confusion in the cases.

39. See Krattenmaker, Lande & Salop,   trust Law, 76 Geo.L.J. 241 (1987).
Monopoly Power and Market Power in Anti-

Given the difficulties of proof and the dangers of trying to seem more "scientific" than the process warrants, it probably would make more sense in close cases for trial courts (at least where bench trials are involved) to select tentatively a plausible market definition as to which some usable market data are available, and then investigate to determine whether existing or potential substitutes, cost differences among producers, entry conditions, and dynamic factors in the marketplace indicate the existence of durable and significant market power. An important consideration in taking any line of evidence into account is the practical one of assessing the quality of the data available and the nature of problems that will be encountered in introducing such evidence into a legal proceeding. This first-cut approach would allow trials to proceed without committing judges or the parties to final judgments about the market before all the relevant evidence is in.

PROBLEM 1

THE BATTLE FOR SAWVILLE

For a number of years there have been three "regular" motion picture theaters and one "art" house in Sawville, New York, a suburb of New York City about a 40–minute drive from Times Square. The "art" house—the Frolic—has a policy of showing foreign films and more esoteric films of independent domestic producers not regularly handled by national distributors; the films are almost always "X-rated" or have not been submitted for classification. There has only been sufficient demand for "art films" in Sawville to permit profitable operations by one theater, but the management of the Frolic has noticed that its theater is increasingly filled to capacity and sometimes patrons must be turned away.

The Frolic is locally owned. It charges more than the three regular theaters for general evening admission ($12 as compared to $9), and, unlike the other three, is open every weekday evening for a midnight show. The Frolic is closed all day Sunday. A study for a local newspaper showed that almost all patrons of the Frolic have visited the other three movie theaters at least once in the previous six months, and about 30% of the patrons of the three regular theaters have attended the Frolic at least once in the last six months.

The closest art houses to Sawville are in mid-town New York and they charge, on the average, an admission price of $10. Sawville's local cable company, which is owned by a non-profit corporation with strong moral and ethical commitments, has refused to show "X-rated" films, but such films are available on DVD (at an average rental of $5 per day), for home video use, in Sawville.

The Frolic has earned about 30% on its investment in each of the last three years, while the three regular theaters have earned about 10% on investment. One reason for the difference in profitability is that the Frolic spends little on advertising, new equipment, decor, and maintenance.

There is one empty building in Sawville—an auditorium once used for club meetings and amateur theater productions—that could be converted promptly and without great expense to a movie theater. About six months ago there were rumors that Read Theaters, a large East Coast chain of art houses, was negotiating to purchase the building and convert it into an art house. Whether the rumors were true or not, the Frolic's owners purchased the empty building announcing that they believed demand in Sawville would soon be sufficiently great to support a second profitable art theater operation. To date, however, the building remains dark and the Frolic remains the only art theater in Sawville.

Does the Frolic have monopoly power? Has it violated Section 2 of the Sherman Act?

COMPARATIVE NOTE ON ARTICLE 82 (EX ARTICLE 86) AND THE "ABUSE OF DOMINANT POSITION" IN THE EC

Article 82 of the Treaty of Rome provides that any "abuse by one or more undertakings of a dominant position within the Common Market or in a substantial part of it" is prohibited if it may affect trade between member states. See Article 82, page 22 supra. A "dominant position" for purposes of Article 82 is the analogue to the possession of monopoly power for purposes of section 2 of the Sherman Act. The European Court of Justice explained the concept of "dominant position" in the early case of Hoffmann–LaRoche v. Commission, 1979 ECR 461, [1978–1979 Transfer Binder] Comm. Mkt. Rep. (CCH) ¶ 8527. at 7542–43 (ECJ 1979):

> Article 86 [now 82] is an application of the general objective of the activities of the Community laid down in Article 3(f) [now Article 3] of the Treaty, namely, the institution of a system ensuring that competition in the Common Market is not distorted. Article 86 prohibits any abuse by an undertaking of a dominant position in a substantial part of the Common Market in so far as it may affect trade between Member States. The dominant position thus referred to related to a position of economic strength enjoyed by an undertaking which enables it to prevent effective competition being maintained in the relevant market by affording it the power to behave to an appreciable extent independently of its competitors, its customers and ultimately of the consumers.

> Such a position does not preclude some competition, which it does where there is a monopoly or a quasi-monopoly, but enables the undertaking which profits by it, if not to determine at least to have an appreciable influence on the conditions under which that competition will develop, and in any case to act largely in disregard of it so long as such conduct does not operate to its detriment.

More recently, the Court of First Instance had the following to say about the way that a dominant position can be demonstrated, in the case of Amministrazione Autonoma dei Monopoli di Stato (AAMS) v. EC Commission, Case No. T–139/98, [2002] 4 CMLR 10 (CFI 5th Chamber 2001):

> It is settled case law that very large market shares are in themselves, and save in exceptional circumstances, evidence of the existence of a dominant position. An undertaking which has a very large market share and holds it for some time, by means of the volume of production and the scale of the supply for which it stands—without holders of much smaller market shares being able to meet rapidly the demand from those who would like to break away from the undertaking which has the largest market share—is by virtue of that share in a position of strength which makes it an unavoidable trading partner and which, because of this alone, secures for it, at the very least during relatively long periods, that freedom of action which is the special feature of a dominant position. Moreover, a dominant position is a position of economic strength enjoyed by an undertaking which enables it to prevent effective competition being maintained on the relevant market by giving it the power to behave to an appreciable extent independently of its competitors, customers and ultimately of its consumers.

It is also possible for companies collectively to hold a position of dominance. The European Court of Justice noted in Irish Sugar Plc v. EC Commission, Case C–497/99, [2001] CMLR 29 (ECJ 5th Chamber 2001), that

> in order to establish whether the undertakings concerned together constitute a collective entity on a given market, it is necessary to examine the economic links or factors which give rise to a connection between them, and, in particular, whether economic links exist between them which enable them to act together independently of their competitors, their customers and consumers.

See also the Italian Flat Glass case, Societe Italiano Vetro SpA (SIV) v. Commission, Case T–68, 77 & 78/89 (March 10, 1992). See also Chapter 6, section 2, infra, comparing the European doctrine of collective dominance to the idea of shared monopoly or tacit collusion in U.S. law.

Whether the dominant position is held by a single firm or a group of firms, it appears that the emphasis of Article 82 is primarily on the abusive nature of the conduct in question when undertaken by the powerful firm or group, rather than on acquisition or maintenance of that power. The Court of Justice defined "abuse" in Hoffmann–LaRoche as follows:

> The concept of abuse is an objective concept relating to the behavior of an undertaking in a dominant position which is such as to influence the structure of a market where, as a result of the very presence of the undertaking in question, the degree of competition is weakened and which, through recourse to methods different from those which condition normal competition in products or services on the basis of the transactions of commercial operators, has the effect of hindering the maintenance of the degree of competition still existing in the market or the growth of that competition. [At page 7541.]

An Article 82 proceeding begins, much like a case under Sherman Act § 2, with the definition of the relevant market. In the earliest case on this subject from the Court of Justice, Europemballage Corp. v. Commission, Case 6/72, [1973] ECR 215, the Court rejected the Commission's effort to define separate markets for light containers for canned meat products, light containers for canned seafood, and metal closures for the food packing industry. It held that the Commission should have considered not only the separate uses to which the products were put, but also production characteristics, possibility of production substitution, and interchangeability of use. See also L'Oreal, ECJ Dec. 11, 1980, 1980 ECR 3775, 1981–2 CMLR 235. Although this result looks familiar to U.S. eyes, there are other examples where the Commission and the European courts have taken a narrower approach to relevant markets. In their book on EC Competition law[40], Ritter, Braun & Rawlinson offer the following examples of that point:

Natural sugar as distinct from sugar substitutes

Cola as distinct from other soft drinks

Bananas, not other fresh fruit

Advance weekly television listings different from daily listings

Spare parts for particular makes of cash registers or particular car models

In its recent decision in Tetra Laval BV v. EC Commission, Case No. T–5/02, CFI 25 October 2002 (a merger case), the Court of First Instance apparently did not find

---

40. See Ritter. Braun & Rawlinson, EC Competition Law 274–75 (Kluwer 1991).

fault with the idea that there is no single "liquid food packaging industry," but instead different technologies must be regarded separately. (The ultimate result of that case was to reject the Commission's decision to block the merger in question, but the point about relevant market is unaffected by the ultimate outcome of the case.)

Article 82 sweeps more broadly than Sherman Act section 2 in a second way: the degree of market power that suffices to make a firm "dominant" is distinctly less than the degree required for monopolization. One Commission official noted that, in the absence of special circumstances, market shares between 40 and 65% are considered strong evidence of dominance, citing Hoffmann–LaRoche (47–66%), United Brands, 1978 ECR 267 (40–45%), ECS/Akzo II, Comm. Dec. 15.12.1985, O.J. L 374/1, p. 18 (50%), and Sabena, Com. Dec. 4.11.1988, O.J. L 317, 47, p. 52 (50%). Nacke, Abuse of Dominant Positions: Recent Developments (Taipei, April 19, 1995).

Once the Commission has determined that a firm is dominant within a given market, it must decide whether the conduct amounts to an abuse. It is important to recall in this context that dominance might arise because the firm has been given special privileges by a public body. *See, e.g.,* Re Landing Fees at Portuguese Airports: Portugal v. EC Commission, Case C–163/99, [2002] 4 CMLR 31 (ECJ 6th Chamber 2001). The European courts have made it clear that such firms are equally subject to the rules of Article 82, unless the alleged abuse is an inevitable consequence of the public responsibility. The concept of abuse is elastic, encompassing almost any kind of behavior that would allow the dominant firm to put its rivals at a competitive disadvantage. For example, in the Portuguese Landing Fees case just mentioned, the Commission argued that the dominant carriers were abusing their dominant position through certain discounts. The Court had the following to say in response:

> Nonetheless, where as a result of the thresholds of the various discount bands, and the levels of discount offered, discounts (or additional discounts) are enjoyed by only some trading parties, giving them an economic advantage which is not justified by the volume of business they bring or by any economies of scale they allow the supplier to make compared with their competitors, a system of quantity discounts leads to the application of dissimilar conditions to equivalent transactions.

Thus, in European law some kind of objective justification for the dominant firm's conduct is required. It is not enough to say that all firms are entitled to compete. Recall that Article 82 itself specifies that abuse may consist in imposing "unfair" purchase or selling prices, limiting production or technical development to the detriment of consumers, applying dissimilar conditions to "equivalent" transactions, and requiring supplemental obligations unconnected to the subject of the contract.

The net result of the EU's approach to market definition, the concept of dominance, and the idea of abuse, is a body of law that reaches more deeply into the internal affairs of companies than Sherman Act § 2. At first blush, this may seem paradoxical, because Europe has generally had a more hospitable attitude toward larger companies than the United States has historically held. On closer examination, however, the differences are more understandable. In part, the European approach has been possible because the Commission controls which cases will be brought for the most part, and what penalty will be imposed. (It is theoretically possible now to bring Article 82 cases in the national courts, and there may be much more of this kind of litigation once the reforms that have been proposed enter into force, but up until the present there has been little private enforcement of the competition laws in Europe.) Thus, the actual field for application of Article 82 is far smaller than the potential field. Second, the European approach here as elsewhere reflects the overall goal of the Treaty to integrate the separate national markets into one. Practices that tend to divide member states from one another are a matter of great concern, and the Community institutions as a whole tend to mobilize against them. Finally, it may be that the Europeans have more experience with the administrative state, and thus more confidence in its operation, than their American counterparts. See generally Fox, Monopolization and Dominance in the United States and the European Community: Efficiency, Opportunity, and Fairness, 61 Notre Dame L. Rev. 981 (1986).

SELECTIVE BIBLIOGRAPHY

1. General

Areeda, Antitrust Law Chs. 4–6 (2000 & Supp. 2002).

Posner, Antitrust Law: An Economic Perspective (2001).

Hovenkamp, Federal Antitrust Policy: The Law of Competition and its Practice Ch. 3 (1999).

Bork, The Antitrust Paradox (1978).

Sullivan, Handbook of the Law of Antitrust Ch. 2 (1977).

Goldschmid, Mann & Weston (eds.), Industrial Concentration: The New Learning (1974).

Pitofsky, New Definitions of Relevant Market and the Assault on Antitrust, 90 Colum.L.Rev. 1805 (1990).

Krattenmaker, Lande & Salop, Monopoly Power and Market Power in Antitrust Law, 76 Geo.L.J. 241 (1987).

Fox, Monopolization and Dominance in the United States and the European Community: Efficiency, Opportunity, and Fairness, 61 Notre Dame L.Rev. 981 (1986).

Harris & Jorde, Antitrust Market Definition: An Integrated Approach, 72 Cal.L.Rev. 1 (1984).

Kaplow, The Accuracy of Traditional Market Power Analysis and a Direct Adjustment Alternative, 95 Harv.L.Rev. 1817 (1982).

Landes & Posner, Market Power in Antitrust Cases, 94 Harv.L.Rev. 937 (1981).

Pitofsky, The Political Content of Antitrust, 127 U.Pa.L.Rev. 1051 (1979).

2. Economic Materials

Adams (ed.), The Structure of American Industry (10 ed. 2001)

Scherer & Ross, Industrial Market Structure and Economic Performance (3d ed. 1990).

Shepherd, The Economics of Industrial Organization (3rd ed. 1990).

Kaysen & Turner, Antitrust Policy Ch. 2 (1959).

Dewey, Monopoly in Economics and Law Chs. 1, 5–8 (1959).

See the Selective Bibliographies of Chapters 1, 8, and 9 for additional relevant materials.

3. Comparative Materials

Berry, The Uncertainty of Monopolistic Conduct: A Comparative Review of Three Jurisdictions, 32 Law & Policy in Int'l Bus. 263 (2001)

Jebsen, Assumptions, Goals and Dominant Undertakings: The Regulation of Competition Under Article 86, 64 Antitrust L.J. 443 (1996).

Rodger, The Oligopoly Problem and the Concept of Collective Dominance: EC Developments in Light of US Trends in Antitrust and Policy, 2 Colum. J.Eur. L. 25 (1996).

CHAPTER 4

COMPETITOR COLLABORATION ON PRICE FIXING AND DIVISION OF MARKETS

SECTION 1.   CONSPIRACY IN THEORY AND ACTION

John S. McGee, Cartels: Organization and Functions[1]
27 U.Chi.L.Rev. 191, 201 (1960).

A.   CONDITIONS FAVORING CARTELIZATION

A cartel is an association of firms cooperating to fix price or other terms of trade. To the extent that a cartel is successful, it suppresses competition in those terms about which there is agreement. From the standpoint of any industry, it is desirable to suppress competition entirely, or at least to mitigate it. Such a task is not equally easy or attractive everywhere. Both to predict where cartels are most likely to appear and to understand them better wherever they are found, it would be useful to draw up a brief list of conditions that favor cartelization. First, the costs of organizing and maintaining the cartel should be small; ideally, zero. The number of independent firms to be coordinated will probably influence such costs. On this account alone, a plan to cartelize all of, say, retail trade is more likely to be a vainglorious dream than a scheme to be relied upon. If, however, some smaller portion of the market can be carved out and insulated, there is hope.

Second, it is highly desirable that there not be burdensome size or other diseconomies to plague the cartel once it is organized.[2]

Third, the price elasticity of demand for the product should ideally be very low at the competitive price. The lower it is, the further the cartel can advance prices without suffering a disastrous loss of custom. Put simply, any cartel can make greater profits if, under competition, buyers were not

---

1. This is an excerpt from the article, Ocean Freight Rate Conferences and the American Merchant Marine, reprinted by permission of The University of Chicago Law Review, University of Chicago Law School.

2. This is much to be hoped for, not only for the obvious reason that any produc-

er, competitor or cartelist will fare better if he can produce any output at lower cost, but also because if entrants of a more efficient size arise, the cartel would face a somber long run.

197

very sensitive to a price increase. This may be roughly equivalent to saying that there is no very good substitute for the service or product, a condition that often appears to be met in the real world.

Fourth, it would be of slight comfort to construct a cartel that scarcely survives its creation. A durable one is what is wanted. Durability will be lessened by centrifugal forces within the combination itself and by the easy creation or expansion of outside supplies. In cartels the first problem is that of defection; the second, of entry and the growth of existing outsiders. Though both are influenced by technological and other natural conditions, both may, nevertheless, be subject to a considerable degree of control, as we shall see.

As the number of participants in a loose confederation rises, the problem of coordination grows, even if all concerned honestly and earnestly seek to preserve that solidarity which is the central object of the coalition. Furthermore, with greater numbers, it becomes somewhat easier for an individual member to defect without appearing to have done so. The difficulties of policing the agreement multiply; the attractiveness of a unilateral policy grows. In sum, large numbers encourage a separation of group and individual interests. In addition is the problem of heterogeneity within the group, which is sometimes a function of the numbers of participants. Cartels are much concerned with these problems, which are multiplied by the uncertainty and wavering confidence that are inherent in human affairs....

Important though these internal problems are, there are also dangers from outside. Entry is the nemesis of cartels. Cartels could rest much more securely if there were natural barriers to entry. These might include scarce resources or a very long gestation period for those resources that must be committed for successful entry. Still another might be economies of size, of various kinds, that compel entry on a scale so large relative to the market that no entry will occur. Every cartel would welcome some check on entry, and some of them have devised policies and institutions to accomplish that objective....

The more subject cartels are to problems of the sort just discussed, the more likely it is that they will require meticulous centralized administration to achieve the desired coordination. Because of the very nature of cartels, we should expect that they will seldom function quite so precisely or reliably as would a single firm operating under like circumstances....

Where cartels operate in a hostile legal climate, which has generally been the case in the United States since the Sherman Law of 1890, it is to be expected that their organizations will be less formal and tight. As a consequence it would not be surprising to find that departures from the "ideal" behavior expected of cartels in theory will be greater than when the law is neutral or promotive. This hypothesis is broadly confirmed by American experience. Before the law intruded, cartels in the United States were often tightly organized, with pools, penalties and other devices to assure precision and solidarity. After the Sherman Law was passed and was found to have some force, it was only natural that a successful cartel would have to function as well as could be, taking into account the need to minimize discovery and punishment.

NOTE ON BARRIERS TO ENTRY AND POTENTIAL COMPETITION[3]

Consideration of conditions of entry is essential to any appraisal of market power[4]—including whatever market power may be created by the organization of a cartel. If entry were completely unimpeded, it would make no sense for companies in a particular market to go to the trouble of setting up a cartel. As soon as the cartel members curtailed output and raised price, potential entrants rapidly would enter the market (and non-members of the cartel in that market would expand existing production) to seek profits by pricing below the cartel price but above the competitive price. Under these conditions of a "perfect contestable market," established sellers would have no market power (to raise price) even though over long intervals actual entry seldom, if ever, took place. See Bain, Barriers to New Competition 1–14 (1962); Baumol, Contestable Markets: An Uprising in the Theory of Industry Structure (1982).

Some commentators have questioned the need for Sherman Act enforcement against cartels, arguing that they are inherently unstable and would break down eventually without government intervention (primarily because members of the cartel will offer secret discounts), and because new entry will restore competitive conditions as soon as the cartel attempts to extract monopoly profits.[5]

We have seen that cartel "chiseling" is indeed a destabilizing factor, but can often be suppressed over the short run. See McGee, p. 197 supra. As to new entry, it can be delayed or prevented entirely by "barriers" of various kinds. If the cartel price is high enough, almost all barriers to entry eventually can be overcome. But given delays in entry, there can be short-run monopoly profit and misallocation of resources that make cartel behavior inviting and cartel profits significant.

It is important to recognize that not every economic condition which delays entry or makes it more difficult is a "barrier" in the same sense of the word. Some "barriers" simply reflect costs that existing companies must assume in order to be competitive. If higher-than-competitive prices are being charged (*i.e.*, prices substantially above marginal costs plus a fair return on investment) and potential entrants recognize that fact, they can incur the same costs and eventually compete with the incumbents on roughly equal terms. Other economic conditions are more extreme "barriers" in that they either require the potential entrant to bear *higher* costs than established sellers in the industry or in other ways deter entry by equally efficient competitors. These barriers may be "structural," meaning that they tend to disappear only over a long-run period, or when legal protection is withdrawn. When "barriers" in the strict sense are present, the incumbent can charge a higher-than-competitive price, up to or beyond the level of the challenger's costs, without seeing its sales threatened by a challenger.

3. This note was revised by Professor Steven C. Salop from materials appearing in earlier editions of the casebook.

4. For a further discussion of barriers to entry, see U.S. Department of Justice and FTC Joint Horizontal Merger Guidelines, § 3, p. 1052 infra.

5. *See, e.g.*, Dewey, Industrial Concentration and the Rate of Profit, 19 J. Law & Econ. 67 (1976).

The point can be illustrated in connection with capital costs of entry. Suppose it would take a capital investment of $100 million to establish an efficient plant in a particular industry. In one sense, that condition impedes entry. First, it certainly is true that more entry would occur if the necessary investment were smaller. Second, not everyone has access to $100 million to compete in that market. On the other hand, that entry requires investment is a fact of life. It does not reflect lack of competition in any meaningful sense. Moreover, if an established company in another industry or a group of experienced entrepreneurs can show that they have the managerial talent, access to raw materials, potential for a distribution network, and know-how, they may well be able to obtain financing from a bank or from venture capitalists. If they build a plant, they will amortize its costs over the useful life of the facility—say $10 million per year for ten years. A comparable $100 million expense for plant construction is a cost that the incumbent has already paid. In addition, companies ordinarily intend to replace their plants at the end of their useful lives, and put aside an amount annually—in this illustration, the incumbent and the entrant each might reasonably put aside $10 million per year for ten years—to pay the cost of that replacement.

In this case, if established firms tried to price non-competitively, by raising prices above their costs, these "barriers" would not deter entry. In this sense, they are not true barriers to entry.

A more significant type of "barrier to entry" arises where the new entrant must pay more to obtain capital to build a new plant than the incumbent must pay to replace the existing plant. That might be the case because banks or venture capitalists charge most new entrants a higher rate of interest (a "risk premium"), reflecting the fact that the entrant may not have the technical or managerial capacity to be successful, entry requires expensive price promotions to induce consumers to try the new product, or simply because the new entrant or the new product lacks a record of success and achievement.[6] Suppose as a result of different costs of capital (and perhaps other factors), the new entrant's average costs of producing a product are $10.00, while the incumbents have average costs of only $8.00. The difference between the cost of the incumbents and the entrant is a more intractable barrier to entry—allowing the incumbents to charge more than their average cost without attracting new entry.

The principal barriers to entry that permit non-competitive pricing are slow speed of entry, cost and demand disadvantages, economies of scale, and sunk costs. These are discussed below.

1. **Slow Speed of Entry.** If entry takes a long time or if new producers are unable to gain sales rapidly after initially entering a market, the fear of potential entry provides less of a competitive check on that market. There are two reasons for this. First, if entry takes a long time, it may not be worthwhile for established firms to reduce their prices before entry actually occurs. In this case, only after actual entry occurred would prices fall back to the competitive level, as opposed to the fear of potential entry keeping prices at competitive levels before any entry occurred. Thus, consumers would pay higher prices in the interim until entry occurred. Second, if entry takes a long time, established firms have ample time to react to a planned entry (unless secrecy could be maintained by the entrant). Thus, the

---

6. Of course, if the "new entrant" is Procter & Gamble or General Electric initiating a new line, any risk premium is not likely to be as substantial. In contrast, if the expansion is internally financed, from retained earnings, management may tend to underestimate its own limitations, and include a smaller risk premium.

entrant would be unable to get a jump on the competition before it responds. This will deter entry. In short, if established firms do not fear the loss of significant sales to potential entrants, potential entry will not constrain them from raising prices.

2. **Cost and Demand Disadvantages.** If entrants face significant cost or demand disadvantages relative to established firms, potential entry will not constrain price increases, at least increases up to a level roughly equal to the cost or demand disadvantage. This is illustrated by the capital cost example discussed earlier. For example, if entrants' costs are 10% above the costs of established firms, or if later entrants must sell at a permanent 10% price discount below the prices of firms that entered earlier, they obviously would be unable to prevent established firms from raising prices by 5% above costs.

Significant cost disadvantages can arise when the established firms have patents or other legal licenses or when incumbents have superior access to scarce or low cost resources.

a. *Patents and Other Legal Licenses.* Entry might be impossible because a governmental unit has decided to franchise only one competitor—for example, a single cable TV outlet in a given city. In other industries regulated by federal or state bodies, entry is possible only after a license has been obtained. Similarly, we confer on inventors an exclusive right (usually for 20 years) in the form of patent protection. Common-law protection of trade secrets or know-how may also make it impossible for potential rivals to compete on equal terms in a given market.

The magnitude of the barrier will vary according to the circumstances. A true "monopoly" franchise means the incumbent need fear no competition for the duration of the legal privilege. The significance of patent protection as a barrier to entry varies according to the strength of the patent and scope of the invention. If a potential entrant can develop a comparable product that does not infringe on the patent, then the entry barrier—in the strict sense—is no greater than the costs of avoiding the patent. Similarly, trade information and know-how often can be purchased or developed independently; in either case, the barrier may only be the cost of acquiring the additional information and the cost may be comparable to the expenditure previously made by the incumbent.

Suppose there is extensive research and development activity continuously taking place in the drug industry, eventually leading to the securing of patents. Is the research and development activity itself a barrier to entry? In what sense?

b. *Scarce Resources.* Incumbents in a market can sometimes earn large profits because they control all or most of an essential raw material, a unique or superior locational advantage, or an existing distribution network that is impossible or extremely costly to duplicate. A classic example would be a situation in which a factory is located near an essential raw material or power source and other factories cannot be located nearby. If the resource is unique, entry is fully blockaded; this is a "bottleneck" case. Where it is not, the barrier—again in the strict sense—consists of the amount it would cost the entrant to obtain access to the resource in excess of the amount it costs the incumbent.

c. *Product Differentiation.* Particularly in consumer product markets, a potential entrant may find that the most serious barrier to entry is established consumer loyalty to an existing brand or brands. Thus, sellers with a high degree of product acceptance can charge considerably more than their costs—even including their cost of establishing consumer loyalty—confident that they will not quickly or easily lose sales to a newcomer.

Product loyalty can be based on a combination of several factors. It may reflect the cumulative impact of many years of successful and effective advertising. Studies show that any particular message—even an emphatic and repeated sales theme—will soon be forgotten by consumers, but the cumulative impression that a company makes reliable and reasonably priced products may persist. That impression may be reinforced by favorable experiences with its products (perhaps during an early period in which few or no other comparable products were on the market) and by special product characteristics.

A new entrant may find that it is necessary to charge a significantly lower price in order to overcome such established consumer loyalty, or it may have to spend greater sums in advertising and promotion than did the incumbent. The magnitude of those differences constitutes a barrier to entry in the strict sense described above.

On the other hand, promotional price discounts and temporary cost disadvantages may reflect necessary investments by all entrants, costs that the established firms also needed to bear when they entered. Competition must allow these costs to be recovered. Thus, if all firms must invest equal amounts and recover these costs on an equal basis after entry, a barrier is not created automatically. However, as discussed below, these costs also can have other effects: they increase effective scale economies and increase entrants' financial exposure. These effects of the entry costs and pricing discounts can serve to deter entry even if established firms had to bear similar costs when they entered.

3. **Economies of Scale.** If only large scale entry is possible or if entrants suffer significant cost disadvantages from small scale entry, established firms may be able to raise their prices above the competitive level without attracting entry. Minimum viable scale (MVS) is the smallest annual level of sales that an entrant must persistently achieve to make entry profitable.

If MVS is large, entry is less likely for two reasons. First, the entrant is less likely to achieve the MVS sales level, and so is less likely to enter. Second, when MVS is high, an entrant attempting to reach MVS is more likely to induce a competitive price reaction by incumbent firms, a price reaction that will reduce the profitability of the entry (*i.e.*, at a lower price MVS is higher).[7] Suppose, for example, there are five companies in an industry, each accounting for 20% of the market, and that a plant of a size efficient enough to produce at costs comparable to the incumbents must produce the equivalent of 20% of current sales. Since the incumbents have sufficient productive capacity to satisfy current demand, any effort to challenge them is likely to create significant excess capacity in the industry, leading to a price war and diminished profits for all. If no incumbent goes out of business, the industry will have so much capacity after the new entrant builds its

7. MVS is a function of expected revenues and expected costs associated with entry, including an appropriate rate of return on invested capital. The appropriate rate of return, often called the "hurdle rate," depends on the degree of risk and the magnitude of sunk costs that would be lost if entry fails. For a further discussion of MVS, see U.S. Department of Justice and FTC Joint Horizontal Merger Guidelines § 3.3, p. 1054 infra.

plant to assure that all participants will find competition in that market less profitable. Since potential entrants will understand this, the incumbents will be able to charge a higher-than-competitive price without triggering entry, even if the entrants can produce as efficiently as incumbents.

Thus, the effect on consumers is ambiguous. Although *post-entry* competition increases the consumer benefits from *successful* entry, the fear of setting off a round of matching price reductions after entry may deter a potential entrant from attempting entry to begin with.

4. **Sunk Costs**. Successful entry is not a sure thing. Entry may fail because the entrant's costs are relatively high, its products prove to be unpopular, the economy enters a serious recession or the entry sets off a price war. Entry is a financially risky proposition to the extent that entry costs cannot be recovered if entry fails and the entrant must exit from the market. If entry costs are irreversible (or "sunk," in the jargon of economists), the entrant's financial exposure is greater and entry less likely to be attempted.

Some but not all capital costs are sunk. Promotional and design expenses usually cannot be used for other products if exit occurs. In addition, many new products must be sold at a loss until consumer goodwill is achieved. Because a significant portion of its capital costs of entry are sunk in the case of differentiated consumer products, the resulting lower likelihood of attempted entry permits established firms to earn monopoly profits without inducing entry.

It is by focusing only on costs that differentially affect new entrants, as opposed to established sellers, that some critics of antitrust policy have been led to argue that collusion will rarely be attempted and will frequently be unsuccessful. They conclude that anticompetitive effects are too infrequent and insignificant to justify a costly antitrust enforcement program against price-fixing or other cartel activities. Consider the following questions in connection with that policy issue:

1. Are "strict" barriers to entry so unusual and insignificant as to justify a policy of indifference toward explicit or tacit cartels?

2. With respect to the broader definition of barriers to entry, will they protect cartel profits where the capital market does not operate perfectly or where a significant lag time will occur before effective new entry can make itself felt?

3. With respect to lag time, how long is it likely to be before fringe companies or outsiders detect the existence of persistent higher-than-competitive profits, assemble the staff and prepare plans for entry or expansion, obtain necessary capital, and construct and put into operation, new production facilities? Might the incumbents use strategic ploys—for example, reducing their prices or threatening to reduce prices in the face of entry—to discourage new challengers? Might such conduct extend the lag time before entry sufficiently to give competitors an incentive to work out a price-fixing arrangement or settle into a price-leadership relationship?

4. What are the social costs of a vigorous anti-cartel policy that does not differentiate between various kinds of barriers to entry? How likely is it to deter efficient or otherwise desirable business conduct?

NOTE ON PRICE FIXING IN ACTION

1. **Auction Houses.** As indicated in Chapter 2, price-fixing conspiracies— domestic and increasingly international—have been a major concern of the antitrust

enforcement agencies for many years. Criminal sanctions, imprisonment and heavy fines are usually imposed for hard-core price fixing. A sense of the new concern about international cartels is shown by the following comparison: for the five years from fiscal 1987 through 1991, the Antitrust Division brought only two cases against foreign corporations and no foreign individuals were charged; in fiscal 2001, however, about 70% of the companies prosecuted for price fixing by the Antitrust Division were foreign-based, and about 33% of the individual defendants were foreign citizens. Foreign executives from, for example, Canada, Germany, Japan, Mexico, South Korean, Sweden, Switzerland, and the United Kingdom were convicted, and a number of the executives served prison sentences in the United States for their parts in price-fixing conspiracies.

An auction house price-fixing scheme between Sotheby's and Christie's, the world's two dominant auction firms with more than 90% of the market, illustrates how modern price fixing may work in practice. For generations, Sotheby's and Christie's were known as archrivals and competed vigorously on commissions. But for much of the 1990's the most senior executives of the two firms colluded in order to take higher commissions from sellers of art, antiques, and other collectibles.

In the excerpt that follows, Diana D. Brooks, the CEO of Sotheby's, is testifying at the price-fixing trial of Alfred Taubman, the chairman of Sotheby's board during the conspiracy and the firm's dominant shareholder. Taubman was convicted in December 2001, and after an unsuccessful appeal, began serving a one-year prison term (at age 78) in 2002. Sotheby's was sentenced to pay a $45 million fine. Ms. Brooks was sentenced to three years of probation, including six months of home detention, and a $350,000 fine. The sentencing judge acknowledged her "substantial assistance in the investigation and prosecution of the price-fixing conspiracy," but concluded that she had "traded [her] title of CEO to be branded a thief," and blinded "by ambition, you substituted shame for fame." In private litigations, Sotheby's, Christie's, and Taubman reportedly paid over $500 million in settlements.

Q. While you were in London at the board meeting [in 1993], did you have a discussion with Alfred Taubman?

A. Brooks. Yes, I did.

Q. What did you say to him and what did he say to you at this meeting?

A. Mr. Taubman told me that he had just met with Sir Anthony Tennant, who was the chairman of Christie's, that they had had a very good meeting.... He told me that he and Mr. Tennant agreed that the business was—this is now in 1993, that we were both killing each other on the bottom line and that, you know, it was time to do something about it. He said that he and Mr. Tennant had gotten along very well and he could see working with him.

Q. Did Mr. Taubman show you anything?

A. Yes, he did. He showed me a piece of paper, a small piece of paper.

Q. What was on the paper?

A. There were a number of topics on the paper that started with pricing....

Q. Would you tell the jury what Mr. Taubman told you with respect to the subjects on the paper and any other subjects that you mentioned?

A. Mr. Taubman told me that he and Mr. Tennant had agreed on a number of subjects and that they wanted Christopher Davidge [of Christie's] and I to meet and to go forward and implement them, some of the agreements that they had reached, and in some cases to actually work out the details.

He asked me not to talk to anyone else about this and it was left and I was to call Mr. Davidge. And on each of the topics, the first topic being pricing, Mr. Taubman told me that he and Mr. Tennant felt that it was time to increase pricing and he told me that he had told Mr. Tennant that it was their turn to go first.... He told me that they had agreed that we were no longer going to do interest free or single lot advances. He also told me that they had agreed that we were no longer going to let our people bad-mouth each other out in the public....

And he told me that they had talked about not poaching each other's staff. They also had covered several other topics that they wanted us to work on, one being introductory commissions, which were commissions that were paid to third parties for delivering business, and the idea was that they were paying more and more out and they wanted us, Christopher Davidge and I, to work out an implementation of a maximum that we would pay, and they also had talked about charitable contributions that were more and more being used to obtain business....

Q. After this did you in fact meet with Christopher Davidge?

A. Yes. I did....

Q. You told Mr. Taubman beforehand?

A. Yes, I did.

Q. What did Mr. Taubman say about that?

A. He was pleased that we were finally going to meet....

Q. [At the meeting, what] did Mr. Davidge say about ... changing pricing?

A. He said that his view was that we had to be careful as to when we did it because we had done the buyer's premium only a year before, which was the first time the buyer's premium had been changed in many, many years, the first time we had actually increased pricing. And that he wanted to work with me on coming up with what he thought would be the best way to change or increase pricing.

But all of us were concerned about the bottom line and the fact that we were killing each other and we were going to try to come up with a way that we were paid fairly for what we did and that we provided a decent return to our shareholders....

Q. Did you tell anybody about your conversation [on February 8, 1995] with Mr. Davidge at Kennedy Airport?

A. Yes, I did.

Q. Who did you tell?

A. I told Mr. Taubman....

Q. This was a face-to-face meeting?

A. Yes.

Q. What did Mr. Taubman say to you?

A. I don't remember what his words were. I think he was just pleased it was happening.

Q. When did you first see Christie's March 9, 1995 price announcement?

A. My first recollection of seeing this is on March 9, 1995.

Q. What did you do when you saw the Christie's price announcement?

A. I was thrilled. I was delighted that it actually had happened?

2. **The Airlines.** In 1982, American Airlines and Braniff, two leading airlines serving the Dallas–Fort Worth airport, were engaged in a price war. The Department of Justice obtained a tape of a phone conversation between Robert L. Crandall, President of American Airlines, and Howard Putnam, President of Braniff. According to the Fifth Circuit of Appeals' opinion,[8] the following conversation occurred.

Crandall: I think it's dumb as hell for Christ's sake, all right, to sit here and pound the ... out of each other and neither one of us making a ... dime.

Putnam: Well—

Crandall: I mean, you know, goddamn, what the ... is the point of it?

Putnam: Nobody asked American to serve Harlingen. Nobody asked American to serve Kansas City, and there were low fares in there, you know, before. So—

Crandall: You better believe it, Howard. But, you, you, you know, the complex is here—ain't gonna change a goddamn thing, all right. We can, we can both live here and there ain't no room for Delta. But there's, ah, no reason that I can see, all right, to put both companies out of business.

Putnam: But if you're going to overlay every route of American's ... on top of every route that Braniff has—I can't just sit here and allow you to bury us without giving our best effort.

Crandall: Oh sure, but Eastern and Delta do the same thing in Atlanta and have for years.

Putnam: Do you have a suggestion for me?

Crandall: Yes. I have a suggestion for you. Raise your goddamn fares twenty percent. I'll raise mine the next morning.

Putnam: Robert, we—

Crandall: You'll make more money and I will too.

Putnam: We can't talk about pricing.

Crandall: Oh Bull ..., Howard. We can talk about any goddamn thing we want to talk about.

Putnam turned the tape recording of the conversation over to the Government. American Airlines and Crandall were proceeded against successfully by the Government, which charged an attempt to monopolize under Section 2 of the Sherman Act.

---

8. United States v. American Airlines,   474 U.S. 1001 (1985).
743 F.2d 1114 (5th Cir.1984), cert. dismissed,

SECTION 2.   DEVELOPMENT OF THE *"PER SE"* RULE ON PRICE FIXING

United States v. Addyston Pipe & Steel Co.

Circuit Court of Appeals of the United States, Sixth Circuit, 1898.
85 F. 271, affirmed, 175 U.S. 211, 20 S.Ct. 96, 44 L.Ed. 136 (1899).

[Reprinted p. 56 supra].

Chicago Board of Trade v. United States

Supreme Court of the United States, 1918.
246 U.S. 231, 38 S.Ct. 242, 62 L.Ed. 683.

■ BRANDEIS, J. Chicago is the leading grain market in the world. Its Board of Trade is the commercial center through which most of the trading in grain is done. The character of the organization is described in Board of Trade v. Christie Grain & Stock Co., 198 U.S. 236. Its 1600 members include brokers, commission merchants, dealers, millers, maltsters, manufacturers of corn products and proprietors of elevators. Grains there dealt in are graded according to kind and quality and are sold usually "Chicago weight, inspection and delivery." The standard forms of trading are: (a) Spot sales; that is, sales of grain already in Chicago in railroad cars or elevators for immediate delivery by order on carrier or transfer of warehouse receipt. (b) Future sales; that is, agreements for delivery later in the current or in some future month. (c) Sales "to arrive;" that is, agreements to deliver on arrival grain which is already in transit to Chicago or is to be shipped there within a time specified. On every business day sessions of the Board are held at which all bids and sales are publicly made. Spot sales and future sales are made at the regular sessions of the Board from 9:30 A.M. to 1:15 P.M., except on Saturdays, when the session closes at 12 A.M. Special sessions, termed the "Call," are held immediately after the close of the regular session, at which sales "to arrive" are made. These sessions are not limited as to duration, but last usually about half an hour. At all these sessions transactions are between members only; but they may trade either for themselves or on behalf of others. Members may also trade privately with one another at any place, either during the sessions or after, and they may trade with non-members at any time except on the premises occupied by the Board.

Purchases of grain "to arrive" are made largely from country dealers and farmers throughout the whole territory tributary to Chicago, which includes besides Illinois and Iowa, Indiana, Ohio, Wisconsin, Minnesota, Missouri, Kansas, Nebraska, and even South and North Dakota. The purchases are sometimes the result of bids to individual country dealers made by telegraph or telephone either during the sessions or after; but most purchases are made by the sending out from Chicago by the afternoon mails to hundreds of country dealers offers to buy, at the prices named, any number of carloads, subject to acceptance before 9:30 A.M. on the next business day.

In 1906 the Board adopted what is known as the "Call" rule. By it members were prohibited from purchasing or offering to purchase, during the period between the close of the Call and the opening of the session on the next business day, any wheat, corn, oats or rye "to arrive" at a price other than the closing bid at the Call. The Call was over, with rare exceptions, by two o'clock. The change effected was this: Before the adoption of the rule, members fixed their bids throughout the day at such prices as they respectively saw fit; after the adoption of the rule, the bids had to be fixed at the day's closing bid on the Call until the opening of the next session.

In 1913 the United States filed in the District Court for the Northern District of Illinois this suit against the Board and its executive officers and directors, to enjoin the enforcement of the Call rule, alleging it to be in violation of the Antitrust Law. The defendants admitted the adoption and enforcement of the Call rule, and averred that its purpose was not to prevent competition or to control prices, but to promote the convenience of members by restricting their hours of business and to break up a monopoly in that branch of the grain trade acquired by four or five warehousemen in Chicago. On motion of the Government the allegations concerning the purpose of establishing the regulation were stricken from the record. The case was then heard upon evidence; and a decree was entered which declared that defendants became parties to a combination or conspiracy to restrain interstate and foreign trade and commerce "by adopting, acting upon and enforcing" the Call rule; and enjoined them from acting upon the same or from adopting or acting upon any similar rule.

No opinion was delivered by the District Judge. The Government proved the existence of the rule and described its application and the change in business practice involved. It made no attempt to show that the rule was designed to or that it had the effect of limiting the amount of grain shipped to Chicago; or of retarding or accelerating shipment; or of raising or depressing prices; or of discriminating against any part of the public; or that it resulted in hardship to anyone. The case was rested upon the bald proposition, that a rule or agreement by which men occupying positions of strength in any branch of trade, fixed prices at which they would buy or sell during an important part of the business day, is an illegal restraint of trade under the Antitrust Law. But the legality of an agreement or regulation cannot be determined by so simple a test, as whether it restrains competition. Every agreement concerning trade, every regulation of trade, restrains. To bind, to restrain, is of their very essence. The true test of legality is whether the restraint imposed is such as merely regulates and perhaps thereby promotes competition or whether it is such as may suppress or even destroy competition. To determine that question the court must ordinarily consider the facts peculiar to the business to which the restraint is applied; its condition before and after the restraint was imposed; the nature of the restraint and its effect, actual or probable. The history of the restraint, the evil believed to exist, the reason for adopting the particular remedy, the purpose or end sought to be attained, are all relevant facts. This is not because a good intention will save an otherwise objectionable regulation or the reverse; but because knowledge of intent may help the court to interpret facts and to predict consequences. The District Court erred, therefore, in striking from the answer allegations concerning the history and purpose of the Call rule and in later excluding evidence on that subject. But the evidence admitted makes it clear that the rule was a reasonable regulation of business consistent with the provisions of the Antitrust Law.

First: The nature of the rule: The restriction was upon the period of price-making. It required members to desist from further price-making after the close of the Call until 9:30 A.M. the next business day: but there was no restriction upon the sending out of bids after close of the Call. Thus it required members who desired to buy grain "to arrive" to make up their minds before the close of the Call how much they were willing to pay during the interval before the next session of the Board. The rule made it to their interest to attend the Call; and if they did not fill their wants by purchases there, to make the final bid high enough to enable them to purchase from country dealers.

Second: The scope of the rule: It is restricted in operation to grain "to arrive." It applies only to a small part of the grain shipped from day to day to Chicago, and to an even smaller part of the day's sales; members were left free to purchase grain already in Chicago from anyone at any price throughout the day. It applies only during a small part of the business day; members were left free to purchase during the sessions of the Board grain "to arrive," at any price, from members anywhere and from nonmembers anywhere except on the premises of the Board. It applied only to grain shipped to Chicago: members were left free to purchase at any price throughout the day from either members or nonmembers, grain "to arrive" at any other market. Country dealers and farmers had available in practically every part of the territory called tributary to Chicago some other market for grain "to arrive." Thus Missouri, Kansas, Nebraska, and parts of Illinois are also tributary to St. Louis; Nebraska and Iowa, to Omaha; Minnesota, Iowa, South and North Dakota, to Minneapolis or Duluth; Wisconsin and parts of Iowa and of Illinois, to Milwaukee; Ohio, Indiana and parts of Illinois, to Cincinnati; Indiana and parts of Illinois, to Louisville.

Third: The effects of the rule: As it applies to only a small part of the grain shipped to Chicago and to that only during a part of the business day and does not apply at all to grain shipped to other markets, the rule had no appreciable effect on general market prices; nor did it materially affect the total volume of grain coming to Chicago. But within the narrow limits of its operation the rule helped to improve market conditions thus:

(a) It created a public market for grain "to arrive." Before its adoption, bids were made privately. Men had to buy and sell without adequate knowledge of actual market conditions. This was disadvantageous to all concerned, but particularly so to country dealers and farmers.

(b) It brought into the regular market hours of the Board sessions more of the trading in grain "to arrive."

(c) It brought buyers and sellers into more direct relations; because on the Call they gathered together for a free and open interchange of bids and offers.

(d) It distributed the business in grain "to arrive" among a far larger number of Chicago receivers and commission merchants than had been the case there before.

(e) It increased the number of country dealers engaging in this branch of the business; supplied them more regularly with bids from Chicago; and also increased the number of bids received by them from competing markets.

(f) It eliminated risks necessarily incident to a private market, and thus enabled country dealers to do business on a smaller margin. In that way the rule made it possible for them to pay more to farmers without raising the price to consumers.

(g) It enabled country dealers to sell some grain to arrive which they would otherwise have been obliged either to ship to Chicago commission merchants or to sell for "future delivery."

(h) It enabled those grain merchants of Chicago who sell to millers and exporters to trade on a smaller margin and, by paying more for grain or selling it for less, to make the Chicago market more attractive for both shippers and buyers of grain.

(i) Incidentally it facilitated trading "to arrive" by enabling those engaged in these transactions to fulfill their contracts by tendering grain arriving at Chicago on any railroad, whereas formerly shipments had to be made over the particular railroad designated by the buyer.

The restraint imposed by the rule is less severe than that sustained in Anderson v. United States, 171 U.S. 604. Every board of trade and nearly every trade organization imposes some restraint upon the conduct of business by its members. Those relating to the hours in which business may be done are common; and they make a special appeal where, as here, they tend to shorten the working day or, at least, limit the period of most exacting activity. The decree of the District Court is reversed with directions to dismiss the bill.

■ McREYNOLDS, J., took no part in the consideration or decision of this case.[9]

---

9. Justice Brandeis' opinion was quoted by the Court in Continental T.V., Inc. v. GTE Sylvania, Inc., 433 U.S. 36 (1977), printed p. 657 n. 27 infra. The views of Justice Brandeis

APPALACHIAN COALS, INC. v. UNITED STATES, 288 U.S. 344, 53 S.Ct. 471, 77 L.Ed. 825 (1933). In 1932, Appalachian Coals, Inc., was organized as the exclusive selling agent for 137 producers of bituminous coal in the so-called Appalachian territory (*i.e.*, eight coal districts lying in Virginia, West Virginia, Kentucky and Tennessee). The company's capital stock was owned solely by the producers in proportion to their production.

For a commission of 10%, Appalachian Coals was to sell the entire production of its 137 shareholders. The coal was to be sold at prices to be fixed by the officers of the company. These were to be the best prices obtainable. It was insisted that the primary purpose of the formation of the selling agency was to increase the sale and production of Appalachian coal through better methods of distribution, intensive advertising and research, and the achievement of economies in marketing; the company was also to "eliminate abnormal deceptive and destructive trade practices."

The company was formed in response to depressed conditions in the coal industry. Circumstances during and after World War I had led to the development of over 700,000,000 tons capacity to meet a demand of less than 500,000,000 tons, which was being further eroded by oil, water power, and natural gas substitutes and the more efficient use of coal itself.

The unfavorable industry condition was further aggravated by alleged "destructive trade practices." "Distress coal," dumped on the market because a given buyer did not want certain grades or sizes and storage facilities were not available, pushed prices down. To make matters worse, producers often offered the same coal for sale through different agents, and this "pyramiding of coal" artificially inflated the supply and drove down prices as agents bid against each other.

In 1929, the 137 producers mined less than 12% of the bituminous coal east of the Mississippi River. But deducting the output of "captive" mines (those producing for the consumption of owners), the 137 producers mined 64% of the coal in the Appalachian territory and immediately surrounding area and 74.4% of coal in the Appalachian territory.

The serious economic condition of the industry led to discussions among coal operators and state and national officials. Finally, in December, 1931 a meeting of producers, sales agents, and attorneys recommended the creation of Appalachian Coals.

The coal producers owned all of the voting stock in Appalachian Coals, divided among them in proportion to their production. Seventeen members owned the majority of the stock. The Company was by common agreement to serve as exclusive sales representative, selling all coal at the best price available, with prices tentatively set by the officers of the Company; if the entire production of members could not be sold, orders would be apportioned among members. The Company was paid a 10% commission on sales.

It was agreed that a minimum of 70% and a maximum of 80% of the commercial tonnage of a territory should be secured before the plan would become effective. Approximately 73% was actually obtained. The 80% maximum figure was adopted, according to the coal producers, because they felt that an organization with a greater percentage control of production would unduly restrict competition in the

on antitrust are discussed in Handler, Antitrust in Perspective 17 (1957); Comment, Mr. Justice Brandeis, Competition and Smallness: A Dilemma Reexamined, 66 Yale L.J. 69 (1956).

local markets. It was expected that similar agencies would be established in other districts, but the formation of Appalachian Coals was not dependent on that development.

The plan for Appalachian Coals was submitted to the Department of Justice for approval just prior to the commencement of operations. At the Government's request, a district court enjoined the plan under Section 1 of the Sherman Act because the concerted action would eliminate competition and would have a "tendency to stabilize prices and to raise prices to a higher level than would prevail under conditions of free competition."

The Supreme Court (per Hughes, C.J.) reversed, reasoning as follows:

> The restrictions the Act imposes are not mechanical or artificial. Its general phrases, interpreted to attain its fundamental objects, set up the essential standard of reasonableness. They call for vigilance in the detection and frustration of all efforts unduly to restrain the free course of interstate commerce, but they do not seek to establish a mere delusive liberty either by making impossible the normal and fair expansion of that commerce or the adoption of reasonable measures to protect it from injurious and destructive practices and to promote competition upon a sound basis. . . .

> In applying this test, a close and objective scrutiny of particular conditions and purposes is necessary in each case. Realities must dominate the judgment. The mere fact that the parties to an agreement eliminate competition between themselves is not enough to condemn it. . . . The question of the application of the statute is one of intent and effect, and is not to be determined by arbitrary assumptions. It is therefore necessary in this instance to consider the economic conditions peculiar to the coal industry, the practices which have obtained, the nature of defendants' plan of making sales, the reasons which led to its adoption, and the probable consequences of the carrying out of that plan in relation to market prices and other matters affecting the public interest in interstate commerce in bituminous coal.

> With respect to defendants' purposes, we find no warrant for determining that they were other than those they declared. Good intentions will not save a plan otherwise objectionable, but knowledge of actual intent is an aid in the interpretation of facts and prediction of consequences. . . . The industry was in distress. It suffered from over-expansion and from a serious relative decline through the growing use of substitute fuels. It was afflicted by injurious practices within itself—practices which demanded correction. If evil conditions could not be entirely cured, they at least might be alleviated. The unfortunate state of the industry would not justify any attempt unduly to restrain competition or to monopolize, but the existing situation prompted defendants to make, and the statute did not preclude them from making, an honest effort to remove abuses, to make competition fairer, and thus to promote the essential interests of commerce. . . .

> The evidence as to the conditions of the production and distribution of bituminous coal, the available facilities for its transportation, the extent of developed mining capacity, and the vast potential undeveloped capacity, makes it impossible to conclude that defendants through the operation of their plan will be able to fix the price of coal in the consuming markets. . . . While conditions are more favorable to the position of defendants' group in

some markets than in others, we think that the proof clearly shows that, wherever their selling agency operates, it will find itself confronted by effective competition backed by virtually inexhaustible sources of supply, and will also be compelled to cope with the organized buying power of large consumers. The plan cannot be said either to contemplate or to involve the fixing of market prices.

The contention is, and the court below found, that while defendants could not fix market prices, the concerted action would "affect" them, that is, that it would have a tendency to stabilize market prices and to raise them to a higher level than would otherwise obtain.... A cooperative enterprise, otherwise free from objection, which carries with it no monopolistic menace, is not to be condemned as an undue restraint merely because it may effect a change in market conditions, where the change would be in mitigation of recognized evils and would not impair, but rather foster, fair competitive opportunities. Voluntary action to rescue and preserve these opportunities, and thus to aid in relieving a depressed industry and in reviving commerce by placing competition upon a sounder basis, may be more efficacious than an attempt to provide remedies through legal processes.... Defendants insist that on the evidence adduced as to their competitive position in the consuming markets, and in the absence of proof of actual operations showing an injurious effect upon competition, either through possession or abuse of power, no valid objection could have been interposed under the Sherman Act if the defendants had eliminated competition between themselves by a complete integration of their mining properties in a single ownership. United States v. U.S. Steel Corp., 251 U.S. 417.... We agree that there is no ground for holding defendants' plan illegal merely because they have not integrated their properties and have chosen to maintain their independent plants, seeking not to limit but rather to facilitate production....

We think that the Government has failed to show adequate grounds for an injunction in this case. We recognize, however, that the case has been tried in advance of the operation of defendants' plan, and that it has been necessary to test that plan with reference to purposes and anticipated consequences without the advantage of the demonstrations of experience. If in actual operation it should prove to be an undue restraint upon interstate commerce, if it should appear that the plan is used to the impairment of fair competitive opportunities, the decision upon the present record should not preclude the Government from seeking the remedy which would be suited to such a state of facts....

————

In appraising the effect of the *Appalachian Coals* case as a precedent, what weight should be given to the disorganized and distressed condition of the coal industry? Paragraph 3 of Article 81 (ex Article 85) of the Treaty of Rome, p. 21 supra, provides that the EU's prohibition against price fixing is "inapplicable" to agreements that contribute to "improving the production or distribution of goods or to promoting technical or economic progress, while allowing consumers a fair share of the resulting benefit." When, if at all, should this provision be read to protect price-fixing arrangements in distressed industries? See Comparative Note on Crisis Cartels, p. 325 infra. In *Appalachian Coals*, were there less onerous alternatives, from an antitrust standpoint, available to the coal producers? Could, for example, joint ventures as to storage facilities have mitigated the problem of "distress coal"? Chief Justice Hughes suggests that the 137 coal producers could have merged. That is doubtful under present law, as you will see when examining merger policy in Chapter 9 infra.[10]

United States v. Socony–Vacuum Oil Co.

Supreme Court of the United States, 1940.
310 U.S. 150, 60 S.Ct. 811, 84 L.Ed. 1129.

[Respondents were major oil companies operating in the Mid–Western States. They were integrated firms, engaged in every branch of the petroleum industry—owning and operating oil wells, pipelines, refineries, bulk storage plants and service stations—and they accounted for 83% of all gasoline sold in their market in 1935.

The course of conduct condemned in the indictment consisted of two concerted gasoline buying programs, one in the East Texas and the other in the Mid–Continent oil fields, for the purchase in spot transactions of large quantities of gasoline, in tank-car lots, by each respondent from independent refiners. This "distress" gasoline amounted to about 17% of the gasoline marketed in the territory but, as will be discussed below, the prices at which it was sold had an important effect on jobber and retail prices in the entire Mid–Western market. The purchases involved surplus gasoline that the independents could not dispose of except at distress prices.

All but one of the respondents sold large quantities of gasoline to jobbers in the Mid–Western area under long-term contracts, with the price to the jobbers in 80% of the agreements dependent, pursuant to a formula, on the spot market price. Jobbers in the area distributed about 50% of all gasoline sold to retail service stations. When respondents sold direct to retailers, they customarily sold at a standard margin of two cents a gallon above the jobber price. At the retail level a system of price leadership was customarily adhered to by both independent retailers and outlets owned or controlled by major companies. As thus formulated and executed, the alleged conspiracy enabled the major companies through the concerted purchase of a very small percentage of the total available gasoline to raise the spot market, tank-car price to artificial levels, and in turn indirectly to raise and maintain prices to jobbers and consumers throughout the Mid–Western area.

Certain market journals—including Chicago Journal of Commerce and Platt's Oilgram—were made defendants and charged with printing the prices which these buying programs effected, as though they were bona fide sales of gasoline by independent refiners in the two fields to their independent jobbers and consumers. The vulnerability of the spot market prices to

---

10. For a recent discussion of distressed industries in the merger context, see FTC Staff, Anticipating the 21st Century: Competition Policy in the New High–Tech, Global Marketplace Ch. 3 (1996).

manipulation was emphasized by the allegation that spot market prices published in the journals were the result of spot sales made chiefly by independent refiners of less than 5 per cent of the gasoline sold in the Mid–Western area. The prices paid by respondents themselves were not reported in the trade journals.

The history of depressed conditions in the petroleum industry, mainly relevant to certain defenses raised by respondents (including removal of competitive evils and acquiescence by the federal government), revealed a background of overproduction in the '20s and '30s, with prices often falling below costs of production. States had little success in enforcing proration laws aimed at limiting production. Unlawfully produced "hot oil" and "hot gasoline" were marketed for substantially lower prices than those posted for legal oil and gasoline. Moreover, as a result of inadequate storage facilities at the disposal of independent refiners, the market was further flooded with legally manufactured "distress" gasoline which had to be sold for whatever price it would bring.

As an outgrowth of the N.R.A., a Tank Car Stabilization Committee was established by respondents to consider methods of dealing with problems created by sale of distress gasoline. The Committee decided that the major companies would select one or more of the independent refiners having distress gasoline as its "dancing partner," and would assume responsibility for purchasing the distress supply. These were informal gentlemen's agreements lacking any specific coercive element. At monthly meetings each member indicated how much distress gasoline his company would buy and from whom, relying on surveys and recommendations compiled by the Stabilization Committee. As contacts between respondent buyers and their dancing partners became well established, the buying program worked almost automatically.

Since the sale of gasoline to jobbers was for the most part computed pursuant to a formula dependent on the spot market price, the entire retail price structure throughout the Mid–Western area during the indictment period was based on the Mid–Continent spot market quotations.

The essence of the charge against respondents was that through regular purchases at the going market price they eliminated a part of the supply of distress gasoline which in the absence of the buying programs would have been a factor in determining prices of the spot market. Control over prices was not accomplished directly, but rather indirectly by maintaining a floor under the spot market through the removal of the depressing distress gasoline. It was not alleged that respondents concertedly bid up the spot market price in order to profit from the sale of their own products on the price chargeable under their jobbers' contracts. All purchases of distress gasoline were at prices determined by the forces of competition. Nevertheless, during the operation of the program, retail prices rose in close step with rising Mid–Continent spot market prices during 1935 and 1936. In March, 1935, before the buying program was instituted, the low Mid–Continent spot market price for regular gasoline was 4⅜ cents. In

December, 1935, after the buying program, the price was 5⅝ cents. The retail price rose from 12.56 cents to 13.41 cents.]

■ DOUGLAS, J. . . . The court charged the jury that it was a violation of the Sherman Act for a group of individuals or corporations to act together to raise the prices to be charged for the commodity which they manufactured where they controlled a substantial part of the interstate trade and commerce in that commodity. The court stated that where the members of a combination had the power to raise prices and acted together for that purpose, the combination was illegal; and that it was immaterial how reasonable or unreasonable those prices were or to what extent they had been affected by the combination. It further charged that if such illegal combination existed, it did not matter that there may also have been other factors which contributed to the raising of the prices. In that connection, it referred specifically to the economic factors which we have previously discussed and which respondents contended were primarily responsible for the price rise and the spot markets' stability in 1935 and 1936, viz. control of production, the Connally Act, the price of crude oil, an increase in consumptive demand, control of inventories and manufacturing quotas, and improved business conditions. The court then charged that, unless the jury found beyond a reasonable doubt that the price rise and its continuance were "caused" by the combination and not caused by those other factors, verdicts of "not guilty" should be returned. It also charged that there was no evidence of governmental approval which would exempt the buying programs from the prohibitions of the Sherman Act; and that knowledge or acquiescence of officers of the government or the good intentions of the members of the combination would not give immunity from prosecution under that Act.

The Circuit Court of Appeals held this charge to be reversible error, since it was based upon the theory that such a combination was illegal *per se*. In its view respondents' activities were not unlawful unless they constituted an unreasonable restraint of trade. Hence, since that issue had not been submitted to the jury and since evidence bearing on it had been excluded, that court reversed and remanded for a new trial so that the character of those activities and their effect on competition could be determined. In answer to the government's petition respondents here contend that the judgment of the Circuit Court of Appeals was correct, since there was evidence that they had affected prices only in the sense that the removal of the competitive evil of distress gasoline by the buying programs had permitted prices to rise to a normal competitive level; that their activities promoted rather than impaired fair competitive opportunities; and therefore that their activities had not unduly or unreasonably restrained trade. And they also contend that certain evidence which was offered should have been admitted as bearing on the purpose and end sought to be attained, the evil believed to exist, and the nature of the restraint and its effect. By their cross-petition respondents contend that the record contains no substantial competent evidence that the combination, either in purpose or effect, unreasonably restrained trade within the meaning of the Sherman Act, and therefore that the Circuit Court of

Appeals erred in holding that they were not entitled to directed verdicts of acquittal.

[The Court then reviews United States v. Trenton Potteries Co., 273 U.S. 392]. . . .

But respondents claim that other decisions of this Court afford them adequate defenses to the indictment. Among those on which they place reliance are Appalachian Coals, Inc. v. United States, 288 U.S. 344; Sugar Institute, Inc. v. United States, 297 U.S. 553; Maple Flooring Mfrs. Association v. United States, 268 U.S. 563; Cement Mfrs. Protective Association v. United States, 268 U.S. 588; Chicago Board of Trade v. United States, 246 U.S. 231; and the *American Tobacco* and *Standard Oil* cases [221 U.S. 1; 221 U.S. 106].

But we do not think that line of cases is apposite. As clearly indicated in the *Trenton Potteries* case, the *American Tobacco* and *Standard Oil* cases have no application to combinations operating directly on prices or price structures.

And we are of the opinion that Appalachian Coals, Inc. v. United States, supra, is not in point. . . .

Thus in reality the only essential thing in common between the instant case and the *Appalachian Coals* case is the presence in each of so-called demoralizing or injurious practices. The methods of dealing with them were quite divergent. In the instant case there were buying programs of distress gasoline which had as their direct purpose and aim the raising and maintenance of spot market prices and of prices to jobbers and consumers in the Mid–Western area, by the elimination of distress gasoline as a market factor. The increase in the spot market prices was to be accomplished by a well organized buying program on that market: regular ascertainment of the amounts of surplus gasoline; assignment of sellers among the buyers; regular purchases at prices which would place and keep a floor under the market. Unlike the plan in the instant case, the plan in the *Appalachian Coals* case was not designed to operate vis-à-vis the general consuming market and to fix the prices on that market. Furthermore, the effect, if any, of that plan on prices was not only wholly incidental but also highly conjectural. For the plan had not then been put into operation. Hence this Court expressly reserved jurisdiction in the District Court to take further proceedings if, inter alia, in "actual operation" the plan proved to be "an undue restraint upon interstate commerce." And as we have seen it would *per se* constitute such a restraint if price-fixing were involved. . . .

Nor can respondents find sanction in Chicago Board of Trade v. United States, supra, for the buying programs here under attack. That case involved a prohibition on the members of the Chicago Board of Trade from purchasing or offering to purchase between the closing of the session and its opening the next day grains (under a special class of contracts) at a price other than the closing bid. The rule was somewhat akin to rules of an exchange limiting the period of trading, for as stated by this Court the "restriction was upon the period of price-making" [246 U.S. 231, 239]. No attempt was made to show that the purpose or effect of the rule was to raise or depress prices. The rule affected only a small proportion of the commerce in question. And among its effects was the creation of a public market for grains under that special contract class, where prices were determined competitively and openly. Since it was not aimed at price manipulation or the control of the market prices and since it had "no appreciable effect on general market prices," the rule survived as a reasonable restraint of trade.

There was no deviation from the principle of the *Trenton Potteries* case in Sugar Institute, Inc. v. United States, supra. For in that case so-called competitive abuses were not permitted as defenses to violations of the Sherman Act bottomed on a trade association's efforts to create and maintain a uniform price structure.

Thus for over forty years this Court has consistently and without deviation adhered to the principle that price-fixing agreements are unlawful *per se* under the Sherman Act and that no showing of so-called competitive abuses or evils which those agreements were designed to eliminate or alleviate may be interposed as a defense. . . .

Therefore the sole remaining question on this phase of the case is the applicability of the rule of the *Trenton Potteries* case to these facts.

Respondents seek to distinguish the *Trenton Potteries* case from the instant one. They assert that in that case the parties substituted an agreed-on price for one determined by competition; that the defendants there had the power and purpose to suppress the play of competition in the determination of the market price; and therefore that the controlling factor in that decision was the destruction of market competition, not whether prices were higher or lower, reasonable or unreasonable. Respondents contend that in the instant case there was no elimination in the spot tank car market of competition which prevented the prices in that market from being made by the play of competition in sales between independent refiners and their jobber and consumer customers; that during the buying programs those prices were in fact determined by such competition; that the purchases under those programs were closely related to or dependent on the spot market prices; that there was no evidence that the purchases of distress gasoline under those programs had any effect on the competitive market price beyond that flowing from the removal of a competitive evil; and that if respondents had tried to do more than free competition from the effect of distress gasoline and to set an arbitrary non-competitive price through their purchases, they would have been without power to do so.

But we do not deem those distinctions material.

In the first place, there was abundant evidence that the combination had the purpose to raise prices. And likewise, there was ample evidence that the buying programs at least contributed to the price rise and the stability of the spot markets, and to increases in the price of gasoline sold in the Mid–Western area during the indictment period. That other factors also may have contributed to that rise and stability of the markets is immaterial. For in any such market movement, forces other than the purchasing power of the buyers normally would contribute to the price rise and the market stability. So far as cause and effect are concerned it is sufficient in this type of case if the buying programs of the combination resulted in a price rise and market stability which but for them would not have happened. For this reason the charge to the jury that the buying programs must have "caused" the price rise and its continuance was more favorable to respondents than they could have required. Proof that there was a conspiracy, that its purpose was to raise prices, and that it caused or contributed to a price rise is proof of the actual consummation or execution of a conspiracy under § 1 of the Sherman Act [15 U.S.C.A. § 1.]

Secondly, the fact that sales on the spot markets were still governed by some competition is of no consequence. For it is indisputable that that competition was restricted through the removal by respondents of a part of the supply which but for the buying programs would have been a factor in determining the going prices on those markets. But the vice of the conspiracy was not merely the restriction of supply of gasoline by removal of a surplus. As we have said, this was a well organized program. The timing and strategic placement of the buying orders for distress gasoline played an important and significant role. Buying orders were carefully placed so as to remove the distress gasoline from weak hands. Purchases were timed. Sellers were assigned to the buyers so that regular outlets for distress gasoline would be available. The whole scheme was carefully planned and executed to the end that distress gasoline would not overhang the markets and depress them at any time. And as a result of the payment of fair going market prices a floor was placed and kept under the spot markets. Prices rose and jobbers and consumers in the Mid–Western area paid more for their gasoline than they would have paid but for the conspiracy. Competition was not eliminated from the markets; but it was clearly curtailed, since restriction of the supply of gasoline, the timing and placement of the purchases under the buying programs and the placing of a floor under the spot markets obviously reduced the play of the forces of supply and demand.

The elimination of so-called competitive evils is no legal justification for such buying programs. The elimination of such conditions was sought primarily for its effect on the price structures. Fairer competitive prices, it is claimed, resulted when distress gasoline was removed from the market. But such defense is typical of the protestations usually made in price-fixing cases. Ruinous competition, financial disaster, evils of price cutting and the like appear throughout our history as ostensible justifications for price-fixing. If the so-called competitive abuses were to be appraised here, the reasonableness of prices would necessarily become an issue in every price-fixing case. In that event the Sherman Act would soon be emasculated; its philosophy would be supplanted by one which is wholly alien to a system of free competition; it would not be the charter of freedom which its framers intended.

The reasonableness of prices has no constancy due to the dynamic quality of the business facts underlying price structures. Those who fixed reasonable prices today would perpetuate unreasonable prices tomorrow, since those prices would not be subject to continuous administrative supervision and readjustment in light of changed conditions. Those who controlled the prices would control or effectively dominate the market. And those who were in that strategic position would have it in their power to destroy or drastically impair the competitive system. But the thrust of the rule is deeper and reaches more than monopoly power. Any combination which tampers with price structures is engaged in an unlawful activity. Even though the members of the price-fixing group were in no position to control the market, to the extent that they raised, lowered, or stabilized prices they would be directly interfering with the free play of market forces. The Act places all such schemes beyond the pale and protects that vital part of our economy against any degree of interference. Congress has not left with us the determination of whether or not particular price-fixing schemes are wise or unwise, healthy or destructive. It has not permitted the age-old cry of ruinous competition and competitive evils to be a defense to price-fixing conspiracies. It has no more allowed genuine or fancied competitive abuses as a legal justification for such schemes than it has the good intentions of the members of the combination. If such a shift is to be made, it must be done by the Congress. Certainly Congress has not left us with any such choice. Nor has the Act created or authorized the creation of any special exception in favor of the oil industry. Whatever may be its peculiar problems and characteristics, the Sherman Act, so far as price-fixing agreements are concerned, establishes one uniform rule applicable to all industries alike. There was accordingly no error in the refusal to charge that in order to convict the jury must find that the resultant prices were raised and maintained at "high, arbitrary and non-competitive levels." The charge in the indictment to that effect was surplusage.

Nor is it important that the prices paid by the combination were not fixed in the sense that they were uniform and inflexible. Price-fixing as used in the *Trenton Potteries* case has no such limited meaning. An agreement to pay or charge rigid, uniform prices would be an illegal agreement under the Sherman Act. But so would agreements to raise or lower prices whatever machinery for price-fixing was used. That price-fixing includes more than the mere establishment of uniform prices is clearly evident from the *Trenton Potteries* case itself, where this Court noted with approval Swift & Co. v. United States, 196 U.S. 375, in which a decree was affirmed which restrained a combination from "raising or lowering prices or fixing uniform prices" at which meats will be sold. Hence prices are fixed within the meaning of the *Trenton Potteries* case if the range within which purchases or sales will be made is agreed upon, if the prices paid or charged are to be at a certain level or on ascending or descending scales, if they are to be uniform, or if by various formulae they are related to the market prices. They are fixed because they are agreed upon. And the fact that, as here, they are fixed at the fair going market price is immaterial. For purchases at or under the market are one species of price-fixing. In this case, the result was to place a floor under the market—a floor which served the function of increasing the stability and firmness of market prices. That was repeatedly characterized in this case as stabilization. But in terms of market operations stabilization is but one form of manipulation. And market manipulation in its various manifestations is implicitly an artificial stimulus applied to (or at times a brake on) market prices, a force which distorts those prices, a factor which prevents the determination of those prices by free competition alone. Respondents, however, argue that there was no correlation between the amount of gasoline which the major companies were buying and the trend of prices on the spot markets. They point to the fact that such purchasing was lightest during the period of the market rise in the spring of 1935, and heaviest in the summer and early fall of 1936 when the prices declined; and that it decreased later in 1936 when the prices rose. But those facts do not militate against the conclusion that these buying programs were a species of price-fixing or manipulation. Rather they are wholly consistent with the maintenance of a floor under the market or a stabilization operation of this type, since the need for purchases under such a program might well decrease as prices rose and increase as prices declined.

As we have indicated, the machinery employed by a combination for price-fixing is immaterial.

Under the Sherman Act a combination formed for the purpose and with the effect of raising, depressing, fixing, pegging, or stabilizing the price of a commodity in interstate or foreign commerce is illegal *per se.* Where the machinery for price-fixing is an agreement on the prices to be charged or paid for the commodity in the interstate or foreign channels of trade, the power to fix prices exists if the combination has control of a substantial part of the commerce in that commodity. Where the means for price-fixing are purchases or sales of the commodity in a market operation or, as here, purchases of a part of the supply of the commodity for the purpose of keeping it from having a depressive effect on the markets, such power may be found to exist though the combination does not control a substantial part of the commodity. In such a case that power may be established if as a result of market conditions, the resources available to the combinations, the timing and the strategic placement of orders and the like, effective means are at hand to accomplish the desired objective. But there may be effective influence over the market though the group in question does not control it. Price-fixing agreements may have utility to members of the group though the power possessed or exerted falls far short of domination and control. Monopoly power (United States v. Patten, 226 U.S. 525) is not the only power which the Act strikes down, as we have said. Proof that a combination was formed for the purpose of fixing prices and that it caused them to be fixed or contributed to that result is proof of the completion of a price-fixing conspiracy under § 1 of the Act.[11] The indictment in this case charged that this combination had that purpose and

11. [The following is the often-discussed footnote 59 to the Court's opinion—Ed.] Under this indictment proof that prices in the Mid–Western area were raised as a result of the activities of the combination was essential, since sales of gasoline by respon-

effect. And there was abundant evidence to support it. Hence the existence of power on the part of members of the combination to fix prices was but a conclusion from the finding that the buying programs caused or contributed to the rise and stability of prices. . . .

dents at the increased prices in that area were necessary in order to establish jurisdiction in the Western District of Wisconsin. Hence we have necessarily treated the case as one where exertion of the power to fix prices (*i.e.*, the actual fixing of prices) was an ingredient of the offense. But that does not mean that both a purpose and a power to fix prices are necessary for the establishment of a conspiracy under § 1 of the Sherman Act. That would be true if power or ability to commit an offense was necessary in order to convict a person of conspiring to commit it. But it is well established that a person "may be guilty of conspiring, although incapable of committing the objective offense." United States v. Rabinowich, 238 U.S. 78, 86. And it is likewise well settled that conspiracies under the Sherman Act are not dependent on any overt act other than the act of conspiring. Nash v. United States, 229 U.S. 373, 378. It is the "contract, combination . . . or conspiracy in restraint of trade or commerce" which § 1 of the Act strikes down, whether the concerted activity be wholly nascent or abortive on the one hand, or successful on the other. See United States v. Trenton Potteries Co., 273 U.S. 392, 402. Cf. Retail Lumber Dealers' Ass'n v. State, 95 Miss. 337, 48 So. 1021. And the amount of interstate or foreign trade involved is not material (Montague & Co. v. Lowry, 193 U.S. 38), since § 1 of the Act brands as illegal the character of the restraint not the amount of commerce affected. Steers v. United States, 6 Cir., 192 F. 1, 5; Patterson v. United States, 6 Cir., 222 F. 599, 618, 619. In view of these considerations a conspiracy to fix prices violates § 1 of the Act though no overt act is shown, though it is not established that the conspirators had the means available for accomplishment of their objective, and though the conspiracy embraced but a part of the interstate or foreign commerce in the commodity. Whatever may have been the status of price-fixing agreements at common law (Allen, Criminal Conspiracies in Restraint of Trade at Common Law, 23 Harv.L.Rev. 531) the Sherman Act has a broader application to them than the common law prohibitions or sanctions. See United States v. Trans–Missouri Freight Ass'n, 166 U.S. 290, 328. Price-fixing agreements may or may not be aimed at complete elimination of price competition. The group making those agreements may or may not have power to control the market. But the fact that the group cannot control the market prices does not necessarily mean that the agreement as to prices has no utility to the members of the combination. The effectiveness of price-fixing agreements is dependent on many factors, such as competitive tactics, position in the industry, the formula underlying price policies. Whatever economic justification particular price-fixing agreements may be thought to have, the law does not permit an inquiry into their reasonableness. They are all banned because of their actual or potential threat to the central nervous system of the economy. See Handler, Federal Antitrust Laws—A Symposium (1931), pp. 91 et seq.

The existence or exertion of power to accomplish the desired objective (United States v. United States Steel Corp., 251 U.S. 417, 444–451; United States v. International Harvester Co., 274 U.S. 693, 708, 709), becomes important only in cases where the offense charged is the actual monopolizing of any part of trade or commerce in violation of § 2 of the Act. An intent and a power to produce the result which the law condemns are then necessary. As stated in Swift & Co. v. United States, 196 U.S. 375, 396, " . . . when that intent and the consequent dangerous probability exist, this statute, like many others and like the common law in some cases, directs itself against that dangerous probability as well as against the completed result." But the crime under § 1 is legally distinct from that under § 2 (United States v. MacAndrews & Forbes Co., 149 F. 836; United States v. Buchalter, 2 Cir., 88 F.2d 625) though the two sections overlap in the sense that a monopoly under § 2 is a species of restraint of trade under § 1. Standard Oil Co. v. United States, 221 U.S. 1, 59–61. Only a confusion between the nature of the offenses under those two sections . . . would lead to the conclusion that power to fix prices was necessary for proof of a price-fixing conspiracy under § 1.

Accordingly we conclude that the Circuit Court of Appeals erred in reversing the judgments on this ground. *A fortiori* the position taken by respondents in their cross petition that they were entitled to directed verdicts of acquittal is untenable. . . .[12]

NOTES AND QUESTIONS

1. Antitrust enforcement against agreements that affect price usually involve conspiracies among competitors to fix minimum prices on sales through channels of distribution toward consumers. For a recent case, see JTC Petroleum Co. v. Piasa Motor Fuels, Inc., 179 F.3d 1073 (7th Cir.1999).

But suppose the agreement among competitors relates to the purchase of products or of a raw material that is incorporated in products that they sell. In National Macaroni Manufacturers Association v. FTC, 345 F.2d 421 (7th Cir.1965), the FTC charged that the Association and its members had entered into an agreement fixing the composition of macaroni products. Members of the Association constituted 84 of 125 commercially important domestic manufacturers of macaroni and macaroni products, accounting for about 70% of sales in the United States.

Macaroni products are manufactured from dough and flour mainly derived from "durum wheat" and farina flour which is a hard wheat other than durum. Durum wheat improves the quality of macaroni products, and products containing 100% durum enjoy the best consumer acceptance.

Early in 1961, it became apparent that there would be a short crop of durum wheat in the 1961–62 harvest year as a result of a drought. Association members saw as their alternatives continued production of 100% durum products which would gradually lead to the payment of "astronomical prices" to suppliers, discontinuance in the use of durum wheat with resulting sales loss because of consumer preferences, or an industry switch to 50–50 durum and non-durum wheat blends. Manufacturer-members of the Association adopted a resolution supporting the 50–50 blend alternative "to maintain the highest quality possible to best utilize the available supply of durum during the current crop year." Most manufacturers followed the course proposed in the resolution although a few did not, and sales of 100% durum products were negligible after the resolution was adopted.

The Commission found that "the agreement was intended to ward off price competition for durum wheat in short supply by lowering total industry demand to the level of available supply ... and concluded that 'where all or the dominant firms in the market combined to fix the composition of their product with the design and result of depressing the price of an essential raw material, they violate

---

12. Hughes, C.J., and Murphy, J., did not participate. The dissenting opinion of Roberts, J., in which McReynolds, J., joined, is omitted.

Concerning the significance of the depressed status of an industry, compare Socony–Vacuum and Fashion Originators' Guild v. FTC, 312 U.S. 457, 467 (1941), with Appalachian Coals, Inc. v. United States, p. 211 supra and National Ass'n of Window Glass Mfrs. v. United States, 263 U.S. 403 (1923), p. 298 infra. See FTC Staff, Anticipating the 21st Century: Competition Policy in the New High–Tech, Global Marketplace Ch. 3 (1996); First, Structural Antitrust Rules and International Competition: The Case of Distressed Industries, 62 N.Y.U.L.Rev. 1054 (1987); Pitofsky, Antitrust and Problems of Adjustment in Distressed Industries, 55 Antitrust L.J. 21 (1986).

the rule against price fixing agreements....'" The Court of Appeals affirmed, noting that the Commission decision did not hold illegal all efforts at product standardization, or all buying agencies[13] or other cooperative agreements, or all attempts to cope with scarcity or other conditions of economic dislocation.

What kinds of agreements affecting components would be legal? For example, there is evidence that children suffer serious health risks when they chew or swallow chipped paint containing lead. Would the same result follow if all manufacturers of toys agreed they would exclude paint containing lead from their toy products? Suppose the major automobile manufacturers agreed to add a special safety device on no more than one model per year for three years to test statistically the advantages and disadvantages of the new safety device?

2. An agreement among competitors may relate to a term of sale only indirectly connected with price. In Catalano, Inc. v. Target Sales, Inc., 446 U.S. 643 (1980), a group of beer retailers charged that wholesalers had conspired to eliminate short-term credit in violation of § 1 of the Sherman Act. The retailers alleged that prior to the agreement, the wholesalers had extended credit without interest up to the 30 and 42-day limits permitted by state law, and wholesalers had competed with each other in offering favorable credit terms. The District Court concluded that the allegations did not constitute a *per se* violation; the Court of Appeals affirmed, suggesting that the agreement might enhance competition by removing a barrier to entry to some sellers and by increasing visibility of price.

In a *per curiam* opinion, the Supreme Court reversed:

> It is virtually self-evident that extending interest-free credit for a period of time is equivalent to giving a discount equal to the value of the use of the purchase price for that period of time.... While it may be that the elimination of a practice of giving variable discounts will ultimately lead in a competitive market to corresponding decreases in the invoice price, that is surely not necessarily to be anticipated. It is more realistic to view an agreement to eliminate credit sales as extinguishing one form of competition among the sellers. In any event, when a particular concerted activity entails an obvious risk of anti-competitive impact with no apparent potentially redeeming value, the fact that a practice may turn out to be harmless in a particular set of circumstances will not prevent its being declared unlawful *per se*.

> The majority of the panel of the Court of Appeals suggested, however, that a horizontal agreement to eliminate credit sales may remove a barrier to other sellers who may wish to enter the market. But in any case in which competitors are able to increase the price level or to curtail production by agreement, it could be argued that the agreement has the effect of making the market more attractive to potential new entrants....

> Nor can the informing function of the agreement, the increased price visibility, justify its restraint on the individual wholesaler's freedom to select his own prices and terms of sale. For, again, it is obvious that any

13. Ed. National Macaroni was distinguished by the First and Third Circuits as a case in which the buyer was "a 'sham' organization seeking only to combine otherwise independent buyers in order to suppress their otherwise competitive instinct to bid up price." Tennessean Truckstop, Inc. v. NTS, Inc., 875 F.2d 86, 89 (6th Cir.1989), quoting Kartell v. Blue Shield of Mass., 749 F.2d 922, 925 (1st Cir.1984). When would a buying agency pass antitrust muster? See Northwest Wholesale, p. 354 infra.

industrywide agreement on prices will result in a more accurate understanding of the terms offered by all parties to the agreement.

3. In ARIZONA v. MARICOPA COUNTY MEDICAL SOCIETY, 457 U.S. 332, 102 S.Ct. 2466, 73 L.Ed.2d 48 (1982), the Supreme Court considered whether Section 1 of the Sherman Act was violated by an agreement among competing physicians that set, by majority vote, maximum fees. The maximum fees were for health services provided to policyholders of specified insurance plans. The Ninth Circuit had held that the issue could not be decided without evaluating the purpose and effect of the agreement at a full trial. Justice Stevens, writing for a 4–3 majority, concluded that the agreement constituted *per se* price fixing. The Supreme Court reasoned as follows:

> Our decisions foreclose the argument that the agreements at issue escape *per se* condemnation because they are horizontal and fix maximum prices.... In this case the rule is violated by a price restraint that tends to provide the same economic rewards to all practitioners regardless of their skill, their experience, their training, or their willingness to employ innovative and difficult procedures in individual cases. Such a restraint also may discourage entry into the market and may deter experimentation and new developments by individual entrepreneurs. It may be a masquerade for an agreement to fix uniform prices, or it may in the future take on that character.

> Nor does the fact that doctors—rather than nonprofessionals—are the parties to the price fixing agreements support the respondents' position. In Goldfarb v. Virginia State Bar, 421 U.S. 773, 788 n. 17 (1975), we stated that the "public service aspect, and other features of the professions, may require that a particular practice, which could properly be viewed as a violation of the Sherman Act in another context, be treated differently." See National Society of Professional Engineers v. United States, 435 U.S. 679, 696 (1978). The price fixing agreements in this case, however, are not premised on public service or ethical norms. The respondents do not argue, as did the defendants in *Goldfarb* and *Professional Engineers,* that the quality of the professional service that their members provide is enhanced by the price restraint. The respondents' claim for relief from the *per se* rule is simply that the doctors' agreement not to charge certain insureds more than a fixed price facilitates the successful marketing of an attractive insurance plan. But the claim that the price restraint will make it easier for customers to pay does not distinguish the medical profession from any other provider of goods or services.

> We are equally unpersuaded by the argument that we should not apply the *per se* rule in this case because the judiciary has little antitrust experience in the health care industry. The argument quite obviously is inconsistent with *Socony–Vacuum.* In unequivocal terms, we stated that, "[w]hatever may be its peculiar problems and characteristics, the Sherman Act, so far as price-fixing agreements are concerned, establishes one uniform rule applicable to all industries alike." 310 U.S., at 222. We also stated that "[t]he elimination of so-called competitive evils [in an industry] is no legal justification" for price fixing agreements, id., at 220, yet the Court of Appeals refused to apply the *per se* rule in this case in part because the health care industry was so far removed from the competitive model. Consistent with our prediction in *Socony–Vacuum,* id., at 221, the result of this reasoning was the adoption by the Court of Appeals of a legal

standard based on the reasonableness of the fixed prices, an inquiry we have so often condemned. Finally, the argument that the *per se* rule must be rejustified for every industry that has not been subject to significant antitrust litigation ignores the rationale for *per se* rules, which in part is to avoid "the necessity for an incredibly complicated and prolonged economic investigation into the entire history of the industry involved, as well as related industries, in an effort to determine at large whether a particular restraint has been unreasonable—an inquiry so often wholly fruitless when undertaken." Northern Pac. R. Co. v. United States.

The respondents' principal argument is that the *per se* rule is inapplicable because their agreements are alleged to have procompetitive justifications. The argument indicates a misunderstanding of the *per se* concept. The anticompetitive potential inherent in all price fixing agreements justifies their facial invalidation even if procompetitive justifications are offered for some. Those claims of enhanced competition are so unlikely to prove significant in any particular case that we adhere to the rule of law that is justified in its general application. Even when the respondents are given every benefit of the doubt, the limited record in this case is not inconsistent with the presumption that the respondents' agreements will not significantly enhance competition. . . .

Even if a fee schedule is therefore desirable, it is not necessary that the doctors do the price fixing. The record indicates that the Arizona Comprehensive Medical/Dental Program for Foster Children is administered by the Maricopa foundation pursuant to a contract under which the maximum fee schedule is prescribed by a state agency rather than by the doctors. This program and the Blue Shield plan challenged in Group Life & Health Insurance Co. v. Royal Drug Co., 440 U.S. 205 (1979), indicate that insurers are capable not only of fixing maximum reimbursable prices but also of obtaining binding agreements with providers guaranteeing the insured full reimbursement of a participating provider's fee. In light of these examples, it is not surprising that nothing in the record even arguably supports the conclusion that this type of insurance program could not function if the fee schedules were set in a different way. . . .

The foundations are not analogous to partnerships or other joint arrangements in which persons who would otherwise be competitors pool their capital and share the risks of loss as well as the opportunities for profit. In such joint ventures, the partnership is regarded as a single firm competing with other sellers in the market. The agreement under attack is an agreement among hundreds of competing doctors concerning the price at which each will offer his own services to a substantial number of consumers. It is true that some are surgeons, some anesthesiologists, and some psychiatrists, but the doctors do not sell a package of three kinds of services. If a clinic offered complete medical coverage for a flat fee, the cooperating doctors would have the type of partnership arrangement in which a price fixing agreement among the doctors would be perfectly proper. But the fee agreements disclosed by the record in this case are among independent competing entrepreneurs. They fit squarely into the horizontal price fixing mold.

Did the doctors in *Maricopa* have a real incentive to achieve cost containment as they voted on prices? What if some of the doctors in *Maricopa* had negotiated as individuals—directly or through an organization—with health insurers to accept maximum fees? Recently, in Levine v. Central Florida Medical Affiliates, Inc., 72 F.3d 1538 (11th Cir.1996), the Eleventh Circuit awarded summary judgment to defendant Healthchoice, Inc., a preferred provider organization, that negotiated "health care coverage [agreements] in which physicians agree to accept no more than a maximum allowable fee for services rendered to plan enrollees." The Court reasoned:

> Providers must either accept not more than the maximum reimbursement negotiated by Healthchoice with the payors and not charge the patient for any difference between their fee and the reimbursement, or else opt out of the plan. The result is that the providers' actual fees are not set. The only figure that is set is the maximum allowable fee that they will be reimbursed by Healthchoice. Nothing prevents the physician from dropping his fees even further in order to compete should he choose to do so.

> This method of negotiating fees, in which the payors decide the maximum amount they are willing to reimburse providers for medical services and providers decide whether they are willing to accept that limitation on the reimbursement they receive, is a kind of "price fixing," but it is a kind that the antitrust laws do not prohibit. . . . Dr. Levine's section 1 claim against these defendants, to the extent that it alleges illegal price fixing, fails.

> Our decision that Healthchoice's method of negotiating with payors the fees it pays providers does not violate the Sherman Act as a matter of law is supported by the Department of Justice and the Federal Trade Commission's recently issued "Statements of Enforcement Policy and Analytical Principles Relating to Health Care and Antitrust" ("DOJ Enforcement Policy" or "the policy"), available in WESTLAW, 1994 WL 642477 [*1549] (F.T.C.). The DOJ Enforcement Policy separates those multiprovider networks wherein competitors agree with one another regarding prices or market allocation, from those networks wherein such decisions are handled unilaterally by each competitor or through a third party "messenger." The policy defines the "messenger model" as involving "an agent or third party conveying to purchasers information obtained individually from providers in the network about prices the network participants are willing to accept, and conveying to providers any contract offers made by purchasers." The latter will "rarely present substantial antitrust concerns." The policy states that "the critical antitrust issue is whether the arrangement creates or facilitates agreements that restrict price or other significant terms of competition among the provider members of the network." In this case, there is no evidence that the Healthchoice method of negotiating maximum fee reimbursement facilitates any agreements among its provider panel members to restrict price or any other forms of competition.

PROBLEM 2

PRICING PLAN OF THE SNORKA CAR DEALERS

Japan's popular front wheel drive compact car, the Snorka, sold in the San Francisco area last year for about $14,000. In that area, Snorka sales equal 3% of all passenger car sales; 10% of all compact car sales; and 15% of all low-price compact car sales (sales at less than $15,000). All Snorka dealers in the area belong to the Snorka Car Dealers' Protective Association.

Intensive price competition among Snorka dealers last year led to public dissatisfaction with pricing practices. Each dealer posted the manufacturer's list price (about $13,500) on the car windows according to federal law but, because demand for the product exceeded supply, the dealers charged a "dealer's add-on" that ranged up to $1,000. Purchasers from one dealer complained bitterly when they discovered that lower "dealer add-ons" were being quoted by other dealers for the exact model they had just purchased. To overcome public animosity, the dealers agreed that henceforth the announced "dealer add-on" of a Snorka with standard accessories, prominently posted on the car window, would be $1,000, and that each dealer would make adjustments in individual cases by giving overly generous trade-in allowances and comparable discounts for "cash" (*i.e.*, non-trade-in transactions). Following the institution of this plan, vigorous competition continued; net prices remained in the vicinity of $14,000, no sales were recorded at the full list plus dealer add-on price, and competition from other car models forced downward revision, and ultimately abandonment, of the fixed "dealer add-on" price.

On an indictment for violation of the antitrust laws, the Snorka dealers moved to dismiss at the end of the government's case after the foregoing facts had been shown. What result?

SECTION 3. CHARACTERIZATION QUESTIONS AND OTHER ISSUES

In its most sweeping formulation, *Socony–Vacuum* held that any combination which "tampers with price structures" is illegal *per se*. In effect, illegality would be determined without regard to the traditional criteria for ascertaining unreasonable restraints—market power of the parties to the agreement, purpose, anticompetitive effect, and consideration of justifications. (Note, however, that the arrangement in *Socony–Vacuum* systematically removed a portion of the supply of oil from the market, at least temporarily, and thus it can be said that it had the "necessary effect" of altering the forces of price-formation.)

This abbreviated approach to illegality stands in contrast to the "rule of reason," one formulation of which was announced by Justice Brandeis in *Chicago Board of Trade* (p. 207 supra). That approach calls for examination, analysis, and ultimately the balancing of a wide range of factors before any practice is condemned.

The rationale for a *per se* rule covering horizontal price fixing was touched upon in *Socony–Vacuum,* but has been formulated more explicitly in Supreme Court opinions that we will deal with later in the casebook. (See Northwest Wholesale Stationers, Inc. v. Pacific Stationery & Printing Co., 472 U.S. 284 (1985) and FTC v. Superior Court Trial Lawyers Association, 493 U.S. 411 (1990) in Chapter 5 and Continental TV, Inc. v. GTE Sylvania Inc., 433 U.S. 36 (1977) in Chapter 7.) Those decisions make it clear that where a practice usually results in significant adverse competitive effects, rarely is justified by significant redeeming virtues, and when there are often less restrictive alternatives available, there is no reason for an extended trial before such practices will be condemned.

The *per se* rule against outright horizontal price fixing satisfies those tests. Price-fixing cartels tend to misallocate society's resources, rarely achieve efficiencies that could not occur through less objectionable means, and seldom pass any benefits on to consumers. The *per se* rule itself is relatively clear and thus can be made effective through the self-policing of businessmen and their legal counsellors. (In later chapters, we will see examples of *per se* rules, covering other sorts of practices, made less precise by exceptions which impair clarity and predictability.) Also, the alternative to a simple *per se* rule of illegality would involve continuing supervision of price by enforcement agencies and the judiciary—a "public utility" type rate regulation which is contrary to the central idea of a free-market economy and well beyond judicial competence. Note finally that defense of a *per se* rule does not require demonstrating that every transaction or form of conduct to which it applies is on balance anticompetitive. Rather, the point is that in the overwhelming majority of instances, full exploration or analysis of all relevant factors would show anticompetitive effects, and the few instances in which "errors" occur constitute a price worth paying to have an effective legal rule.

While a *per se* rule works well enough in simple price-fixing situations, there are many other arrangements that have some relatively less substantial effect on price—though they arguably "tamper" with price structure in some sense—or where efficiency claims are more plausible. In this situation, it is simply impossible to conclude without full analysis—or at least a fuller analysis than a *per se* rule would afford—that the type of restraint is socially undesirable. Actually, we have already seen examples of that in *Chicago Board of Trade,* and the multiprovider networks discussed after *Maricopa.* In *Chicago Board of Trade* the plausible argument was raised that the restrictions on the hours of bidding in effect "made a market," that is, facilitated effective competition during the hours in which the exchange operated. (Can you think of any less anticompetitive way in which that result could have been achieved?)

In this section, we will examine cases raising a series of "characterization" issues. In such cases, there is common ground that price fixing is illegal *per se,* but questions are raised as to what constitutes "price fixing" and how that determination is to be made. In the following cases, keep in mind how the courts deal, or fail to deal, with the following questions:

  1. Is the conduct involved likely to have a substantial and direct effect on price; is that effect one which "necessarily" results from the arrangement?

  2. Are there likely to be substantial redeeming virtues flowing from the practice or conduct?

  3. Could the same or similar redeeming virtues be achieved through reasonably available and less harmful alternatives?

  4. How difficult would it be to explore relevant considerations? In other words, what will the costs be in terms of transaction costs and future uncertainty with respect to the legality of

certain categories of business behavior and thus the effectiveness of the rule?

Federal Trade Commission v. Superior Court Trial Lawyers Association

Supreme Court of the United States, 1990.
493 U.S. 411, 110 S.Ct. 768, 107 L.Ed.2d 851.

[Reprinted p. 372 infra].

NOTE ON REGULATION OF THE PROFESSIONS

1. NATIONAL SOCIETY OF PROFESSIONAL ENGINEERS v. UNITED STATES, 435 U.S. 679, 98 S.Ct. 1355, 55 L.Ed.2d 637 (1978). The National Society of Professional Engineers ("Society") was an organization of 69,000 professional engineers who performed services in connection with the study, design, and construction of various kinds of improvements (buildings, bridges, factories, etc.) on real property. As a condition of membership, individual engineers were required to agree to refuse to negotiate or discuss the question of fees with a prospective client until the client had selected engineers for a particular project. This rule was embodied in Section 11(c) of the Society's Code of Ethics, which provided:

> Section 11—The Engineer will not compete unfairly with another engineer by attempting to obtain employment or advancement or professional engagements by competitive bidding . . .

> (c) He shall not solicit or submit engineering proposals on the basis of competitive bidding. Competitive bidding for professional engineering services is defined as the formal or informal submission, or receipt, of verbal or written estimates of cost or proposals . . . whereby the prospective client may compare engineering services on a price basis prior to the time that one engineer, or one engineering organization, has been selected for negotiations. . . . An Engineer requested to submit a proposal or bid prior to the selection of an engineer or firm subject to the negotiation of a satisfactory contract, shall attempt to have the procedure changed to conform to ethical practices, but if not successful he shall withdraw from consideration for the proposed work.

The United States challenged the Code on the ground that it constituted an agreement to suppress price competition and sought an injunction. The Society's principal defense was that competitive pressure to offer engineering services at low prices would be dangerous to the public health, safety, and welfare and therefore that the ethical provision was reasonable in the circumstances. The District Court rejected that defense, making no findings on the question of whether free competition would lead to inferior engineering, but concluded rather that any such inquiry was unnecessary. The Court of Appeals affirmed.

In the Supreme Court, the Society relied on Goldfarb v. Virginia State Bar, 421 U.S. 773 (1975), indicating that certain practices by members of a "learned profession" might be reasonable even though viewed as a violation in some other context. The rule of reason itself, the Court noted, can be traced to origins in the common law, and specifically to Mitchel v. Reynolds, 24 Eng.Rep. 347 (1711) (p. 31 supra). The Court described *Mitchel* as follows:

> *Mitchel* involved the enforceability of a promise by the seller of a bakery that he would not compete with the purchaser of his business. The covenant was for a limited time and applied only to the area in which the bakery had operated. It was therefore upheld as reasonable, even though it deprived the public of the benefit of potential competition. The long-run benefit of enhancing the marketability of the business itself—and thereby providing incentives to develop such an enterprise—outweighed the temporary and limited loss of competition.

The Court noted that subsequent rule of reason cases, such as *Trans–Missouri, Standard Oil,* and *Chicago Board of Trade,* developed the position that the inquiry mandated by the rule of reason is "whether the challenged agreement is one that promotes competition or one that suppresses competition":

> There are, thus, two complementary categories of antitrust analysis. In the first category are agreements whose nature and necessary effect are so plainly anticompetitive that no elaborate study of the industry is needed to establish their illegality—they are "illegal *per se.*" In the second category are agreements whose competitive effect can only be evaluated by analyzing the facts peculiar to the business, the history of the restraint, and the reasons why it was imposed. In either event, the purpose of the analysis is to form a judgment about the competitive significance of the restraint; it is not to decide whether a policy of favoring competition is in the public interest ...

As to the ethical rule itself, the Court concluded that it should be judged as illegal on its face because it operated as an absolute ban on competitive bidding, applying with equal force to all kinds of transactions. The Society had argued that because the engineer and customer could bargain about price after selection of an engineer had occurred, the arrangement could be justified under *Chicago Board of Trade* as relating only to the timing of competition. The Court distinguished *Chicago Board of Trade* on two grounds; first, that negotiation between a single seller and single buyer is not the equivalent of competition among competing sellers, and second, because there was absent here any suggestion that the regulation of price information had "a positive effect on competition." The Sherman Act, the Court continued, reflects a legislative judgment that competition will produce not only lower prices but better goods and services, and any claim, with respect to particular products or markets, that competition will not produce such results should be addressed to the legislature.

As to the "learned profession" defense, the Court concluded:

> We adhere to the view expressed in *Goldfarb* that, by their nature, professional services may differ significantly from other business services, and accordingly, the nature of the competition in such services may vary.... But the Society's argument in this case is a far cry from such a position. We are faced with a contention that a total ban on competitive bidding is necessary because otherwise engineers will be tempted to submit deceptively low bids. Certainly, the problem of professional deception is a proper subject of an ethical canon. But once again, the equation of competition with deception, like the similar equation with safety hazards, is simply too broad; we may assume that competition is not entirely conducive to ethical behavior, but that is not a reason, cognizable under the Sherman Act, for doing away with competition.

> In sum, the Rule of Reason does not support a defense based on the assumption that competition is itself unreasonable.

Finally, the Court concluded that the injunction entered below, prohibiting the Society "from adopting any official opinion, policy statement or guideline stating or implying that competitive bidding is unethical" was not an abridgement of the Society's First Amendment rights but rather a reasonable method of eliminating the consequences of illegal conduct.

Blackmun, J., with whom Rehnquist, J., joined, concurred in the conclusion that the Society's ethical rules were overly broad in preventing any dissemination of competitive price information, but declined to concur in the conclusion that professional society rules "which have a more-than-*de minimis* anticompetitive effect" are illegal unless they produce the benefit of increased competition. The concurring Justices noted that it was necessary to leave "elbow room" for such regulations as a bar association restriction of "permissible forms of price advertising for non-routine legal services or a limitation of in-person solicitations...." Should there be special "elbow room" for noneconomic justifications of allegedly anticompetitive conduct by nonprofit institutions? See United States v. Brown University, 5 F.3d 658 (3d Cir.1993), p. 265 infra.

Chief Justice Burger dissented from the portion of the opinion which prohibited the Society from stating in its Code the view that competitive bidding is unethical, regarding that as a right of expression protected by the First Amendment.

2.   AMERICAN MEDICAL ASSOCIATION v. FTC, 638 F.2d 443 (2d Cir.1980), affirmed by an equally divided Court, 455 U.S. 676 (1982). The American Medical Association (AMA) is a not-for-profit corporation whose membership includes over 50% of all licensed physicians in the United States. Its legislative body is an elected House of Delegates which in 1957 approved some ethical canons called the "Principles of Medical Ethics." These principles in turn are interpreted by the Association's Judicial Council. In 1975 the FTC charged the AMA and its constituent state and local groups with restricting the ability of the members to advertise or solicit patients and with restricting their ability to engage in non-traditional forms of medical practice (*e.g.*, group practice) through interpretations and enforcement of its ethical canons.

The canons themselves were vague and sweeping; for example, Section 6 of the Principles provided that "a physician should not dispose of his services under terms or conditions which tend to interfere with or impair the free and complete exercise of his medical skill and judgment...." The Commission found that, in the AMA's interpretations and enforcement actions, it restricted the ability of members to advertise (permitting only the furnishing of name, type of practice, location of office, and office hours) to "accepted local media" such as telephone listings, office signs, and professional cards. In effect, all price advertising, including the price of routine services such as a physical exam or blood test, was prevented in radio, newspapers, and other broadly disseminated publications. Similarly, ethical opinions of the AMA described as "unfair or unethical," among other practices, providing medical services at compensation so low as to make it impossible for competent service to be rendered, or underbidding by physicians in order to secure medical contracts.

The Federal Trade Commission rejected a *per se* approach to the AMA's restrictions—noting that regulation of professional services may justify differences in treatment under the antitrust laws—but found the arrangements illegal under a rule of reason. The Court of Appeals affirmed.

In its discussion of remedy, the FTC had noted that "the AMA has a valuable and unique role to play with respect to deceptive advertising and oppressive forms of solicitation by physicians." As a result, it incorporated in its Order the following paragraph:

Nothing contained in this part shall prohibit respondents from . . . enforcing reasonable ethical guidelines governing the conduct of its members with respect to representations, including unsubstantiated representations, that would be false or deceptive within the meaning of § 5 of the Federal Trade Commission Act . . .

The Court of Appeals approved the proviso, adding however that AMA guidelines would not violate the order if "respondent reasonably believes" that any medical advertising or solicitation was false or deceptive.[14]

3. With respect to advertising rules, see CALIFORNIA DENTAL ASSN. v. FEDERAL TRADE COMMISSION, 526 U.S. 756, 119 S.Ct. 1604, 143 L.Ed.2d 935 (1999), p. 276 infra.

4. VOGEL v. AMERICAN SOCIETY OF APPRAISERS, 744 F.2d 598 (7th Cir.1984). Vogel, a gem appraiser, attempted to charge a flat 1% fee for his work, subject to a minimum fee of $10. As a result, he was expelled from the American Society of Appraisers on grounds that it was "unprofessional and unethical for [an] appraiser to do work for a fixed percentage of the amount of value . . . which he determines at the conclusion of his work." Vogel claimed he lost referrals from members of the society as a result of his expulsion.

On a request for a preliminary injunction, the Court of Appeals, per Posner J., declined to treat the Association bylaw as either a boycott or price fixing that was illegal *per se*. Although in the broadest sense the bylaw may have had the effect of "tampering" with price, its purpose or likely effect was not to raise price above competitive levels. On the contrary, it seemed designed to outlaw a method of fee setting that could lead to fraud on customers; thus, the appraiser might have an incentive to over-appraise items in order to maximize his fee. Moreover, there was no evidence that the society's outlawing of fixed percentage of fees was designed as a subterfuge to somehow maintain or stabilize cartel pricing. It remained open to Vogel, on a full trial and under a rule of reason, to demonstrate any anticompetitive purpose or effect of the society bylaw.

5. Regulation of competition within the professions, even when imposed as a result of state legislation, can be challenged under the First Amendment as well as the antitrust laws. For example, in Virginia State Board of Pharmacy v. Virginia Citizens Consumer Council, Inc., 425 U.S. 748 (1976), a Virginia statute providing that a licensed pharmacist was guilty of unprofessional conduct if he advertised or published price information about prescription drugs was struck down as a violation of the First Amendment. Similarly, in Bates v. State Bar of Arizona, 433 U.S. 350 (1977), state disciplinary rules prohibiting a lawyer from engaging in price advertising were condemned as violations of the First Amendment. These and similar cases are examined in Chapter 5 infra in connection with the "state action" doctrine.

Broadcast Music, Inc. v. Columbia Broadcasting System, Inc.

Supreme Court of the United States, 1979.
441 U.S. 1, 99 S.Ct. 1551, 60 L.Ed.2d 1.

■ WHITE, J. This case involves an action under the antitrust and copyright laws brought by respondent Columbia Broadcasting System, Inc. (CBS),

---

14. Mansfield, J., dissented on grounds that the AMA had amended its ethical Principles and interpretations so as to eliminate any prior restraints that may have existed on advertising or solicitation.

against petitioners, American Society of Composers, Authors and Publishers (ASCAP) and Broadcast Music, Inc. (BMI), and their members and affiliates. The basic question presented is whether the issuance by ASCAP and BMI to CBS of blanket licenses to copyrighted musical compositions at fees negotiated by them is price fixing *per se* unlawful under the antitrust laws.

I

CBS operates one of three national commercial television networks, supplying programs to approximately 200 affiliated stations and telecasting approximately 7,500 network programs per year. Many, but not all, of these programs make use of copyrighted music recorded on the soundtrack. CBS also owns television and radio stations in various cities. It is "the giant of the world in the use of music rights," the "No. 1 outlet in the history of entertainment."

Since 1897 the copyright laws have vested in the owner of a copyrighted musical composition the exclusive right to perform the work publicly for profit, but the legal right is not self-enforcing. In 1914 Victor Herbert and a handful of other composers organized ASCAP because those who performed copyrighted music for profits were so numerous and widespread, and most performances so fleeting, that as a practical matter it was impossible for the many individual copyright owners to negotiate with and license the users and to detect unauthorized uses. "ASCAP was organized as a 'clearing-house' for copyright owners and users to solve these problems" associated with the licensing of music. CBS, Inc. v. ASCAP, 400 F.Supp. 737, 741 (S.D.N.Y.1975). As ASCAP operates today, its 22,000 members grant it nonexclusive rights to license nondramatic performances of their works, and ASCAP issues licenses and distributes royalties to copyright owners in accordance with a schedule reflecting the nature and amount of the use of their music and other factors.

BMI, a nonprofit corporation owned by members of the broadcasting industry, was organized in 1939, is affiliated with or represents some 10,000 publishing companies and 20,000 authors and composers, and operates in much the same manner as ASCAP. Almost every domestic copyrighted composition is in the repertory either of ASCAP, with a total of three million compositions, or of BMI, with one million.

Both organizations operate primarily through blanket licenses, which give the licensees the right to perform any and all of the compositions owned by the members or affiliates as often as the licensees desire for a stated term. Fees for blanket licenses are ordinarily a percentage of total revenues or a flat dollar amount, and do not directly depend on the amount or type of music used. Radio and television broadcasters are the largest users of music, and almost all of them hold blanket licenses from both ASCAP and BMI. Until this litigation, CBS held blanket licenses from both organizations for its television network on a continuous basis since the late

1940's and had never attempted to secure any other form of license from either ASCAP[15] or any of its members. 400 F.Supp., at 752–754.

The complaint filed by CBS charged various violations of the Sherman Act and the copyright laws. . . . After an eight-week trial, limited to the issue of liability, the court dismissed the complaint, rejecting . . . the claim that the blanket license was price fixing and a *per se* violation of § 1 of the Sherman Act, and holding that since direct negotiation with individual copyright owners is available and feasible there is no undue restraint of trade, illegal tying, misuse of copyrights, or monopolization. 400 F.Supp., at 781–783.

Though agreeing with the District Court's factfinding and not disturbing its legal conclusions on the other antitrust theories of liability,[16] the Court of Appeals held that the blanket license issued to television networks was a form of price fixing illegal *per se* under the Sherman Act. CBS, Inc. v. ASCAP, 562 F.2d 130, 140 (C.A.2 1977). This conclusion, without more, settled the issue of liability under the Sherman Act, . . . and required reversal of the District Court's judgment, as well as a remand to consider the appropriate remedy.[17]

. . . Because we disagree with the Court of Appeals' conclusions with respect to the *per se* illegality of the blanket license, we reverse its judgment and remand the cause for further appropriate proceedings.

II

. . . [The *per*] *se* rule is a valid and useful tool of antitrust policy and enforcement. And agreements among competitors to fix prices on their

---

15. Unless the context indicates otherwise, references to ASCAP alone in this opinion usually apply to BMI as well. . . .

16. The Court of Appeals affirmed the District Court's rejection of CBS's monopolization and tying contentions but did not rule on the District Court's conclusion that the blanket license was not an unreasonable restraint of trade.

17. The Court of Appeals went on to suggest some guidelines as to remedy, indicating that despite its conclusion on liability the blanket license was not totally forbidden. The Court of Appeals said:

"Normally, after a finding of price-fixing, the remedy is an injunction against the price-fixing—in this case, the blanket license. We think, however, that if on remand a remedy can be fashioned which will ensure that the blanket license will not affect the price or negotiations for direct licenses, the blanket license need not be prohibited in all circumstances. The blanket license is not

simply a "naked restraint" ineluctably doomed to extinction. There is not enough evidence in the present record to compel a finding that the blanket license does not serve a market need for those who wish full protection against infringement suits or who, for some other business reason, deem the blanket license desirable. The blanket license includes a practical covenant not to sue for infringement of any ASCAP copyright as well as an indemnification against suits by others.

"Our objection to the blanket license is that it reduces price competition among the members and provides a disinclination to compete. We think that these objections may be removed if AS-CAP itself is required to provide some form of per use licensing which will ensure competition among the individual members with respect to those networks which wish to engage in per use licensing." 562 F.2d, at 140 (footnotes omitted).

individual goods or services are among those concerted activities that the Court has held to be within the *per se* category. But easy labels do not always supply ready answers.

A

To the Court of Appeals and CBS, the blanket license involves "price fixing" in the literal sense: the composers and publishing houses have joined together into an organization that sets its price for the blanket license it sells. But this is not a question simply of determining whether two or more potential competitors have literally "fixed" a "price." As generally used in the antitrust field, "price fixing" is a shorthand way of describing certain categories of business behavior to which the *per se* rule has been held applicable. The Court of Appeals' literal approach does not alone establish that this particular practice is one of those types or that it is "plainly anticompetitive" and very likely without "redeeming virtue." Literalness is overly simplistic and often overbroad. When two partners set the price of their goods or services they are literally "price fixing," but they are not *per se* in violation of the Sherman Act. See United States v. Addyston Pipe & Steel Co., 85 F. 271, 280 (C.A.6 1898), aff'd, 175 U.S. 211 (1899). Thus, it is necessary to characterize the challenged conduct as falling within or without that category of behavior to which we apply the label *"per se* price fixing." That will often, but not always, be a simple matter.[18]

Consequently, as we recognized in United States v. Topco Associates, Inc., 405 U.S. 596, 607–608 (1972), "[i]t is only after considerable experience with certain business relationships that courts classify them as *per se* violations".... See White Motor Co. v. United States, 372 U.S. 253, 263 (1963). We have never examined a practice like this one before; indeed, the Court of Appeals recognized that "[i]n dealing with performing rights in the music industry we confront conditions both in copyright law and in antitrust law which are *sui generis*." 562 F.2d, at 132. And though there has been rather intensive antitrust scrutiny of ASCAP and its blanket licenses, that experience hardly counsels that we should outlaw the blanket license as a *per se* restraint of trade.

B

This and other cases involving ASCAP and its licensing practices have arisen out of the efforts of the creators of copyrighted musical compositions to collect for the public performance of their works, as they are entitled to do under the Copyright Act. As already indicated, ASCAP and BMI originated to make possible and to facilitate dealings between copyright owners

---

18. *Cf., e.g.,* United States v. McKesson & Robbins, Inc., 351 U.S. 305 (1956) (manufacturer/wholesaler agreed with independent wholesalers on prices to be charged on products it manufactured); United States v. Socony–Vacuum Oil Co., 310 U.S. 150 (1940) (firms controlling a substantial part of an industry agreed to purchase "surplus" gasoline with the intent and necessary effect of increasing the price); United States v. Trenton Potteries Co., 273 U.S. 392 (1927) (manufacturers and distributors of 82% of certain vitreous pottery fixtures agreed to sell at uniform prices).

and those who desire to use their music. Both organizations plainly involve concerted action in a large and active line of commerce, and it is not surprising that, as the District Court found, "[n]either ASCAP nor BMI is a stranger to antitrust litigation."

The Department of Justice first investigated allegations of anticompetitive conduct by ASCAP over 50 years ago.... In separate complaints in 1941, the United States charged that the blanket license, which was then the only license offered by ASCAP and BMI, was an illegal restraint of trade and that arbitrary prices were being charged as the result of an illegal copyright pool. The Government sought to enjoin ASCAP's exclusive licensing powers and to require a different form of licensing by that organization. The case was settled by a consent decree that imposed tight restrictions on ASCAP's operations. Following complaints relating to the television industry, successful private litigation against ASCAP by movie theaters, and a Government challenge to ASCAP's arrangements with similar foreign organizations, the 1941 decree was reopened and extensively amended in 1950.[19]

Under the amended decree, which still substantially controls the activities of ASCAP, members may grant ASCAP only nonexclusive rights to license their works for public performance. Members, therefore, retain the rights individually to license public performances, along with the rights to license the use of their compositions for other purposes. ASCAP itself is forbidden to grant any license to perform one or more specified compositions in the ASCAP repertory unless both the user and the owner have requested it in writing to do so. ASCAP is required to grant to any user making written application a nonexclusive license to perform all ASCAP compositions either for a period of time or on a per program basis. ASCAP may not insist on the blanket license, and the fee for the per program license, which is to be based on the revenues for the program on which ASCAP music is played, must offer the applicant a genuine economic choice between the per program license and the more common blanket license. If ASCAP and a putative licensee are unable to agree on a fee within 60 days, the applicant may apply to the District Court for a determination of a reasonable fee, with ASCAP having the burden of proving reasonableness.[20]

The 1950 decree, as amended from time to time, continues in effect, and the blanket license continues to be the primary instrument through which ASCAP conducts its business under the decree. The courts have twice construed the decree not to require ASCAP to issue licenses for selected portions of its repertory. It also remains true that the decree guarantees the legal availability of direct licensing of performance rights by ASCAP members; and the District Court found, and in this respect the Court of Appeals agreed, that there are no practical impediments preventing direct dealing by the television networks if they so desire. Historically, they have not done so. Since 1946, CBS and other television networks have

---

19. United States v. ASCAP, 1950–1951 Trade Cas. ¶ 62,595 (S.D.N.Y.1950).

20. BMI is in a similar situation....

taken blanket licenses from ASCAP and BMI. It was not until this suit arose that the CBS network demanded any other kind of license.

Of course, a consent judgment, even one entered at the behest of the Antitrust Division, does not immunize the defendant from liability for actions, including those contemplated by the decree, that violate the rights of nonparties.... But it cannot be ignored that the Federal Executive and Judiciary have carefully scrutinized ASCAP and the challenged conduct, have imposed restrictions on various of ASCAP's practices, and, by the terms of the decree, stand ready to provide further consideration, supervision, and perhaps invalidation of asserted anticompetitive practices. In these circumstances, we have a unique indicator that the challenged practice may have redeeming competitive virtues and that the search for those values is not almost sure to be in vain.[21] Thus, although CBS is not bound by the Antitrust Division's actions, the decree is a fact of economic and legal life in this industry, and the Court of Appeals should not have ignored it completely in analyzing the practice. That fact alone might not remove a naked price-fixing scheme from the ambit of the *per se* rule, but, as discussed infra, Part III, here we are uncertain whether the practice on its face has the effect, or could have been spurred by the purpose, of restraining competition among the individual composers....

... [T]he United States disagrees with the Court of Appeals in this case and urges that the blanket licenses, which the consent decree authorizes ASCAP to issue to television networks, are not *per se* violations of the Sherman Act. It takes no position, however, on whether the practice is an unreasonable restraint of trade in the context of the network television industry.

Finally, we note that Congress, in the new Copyright Act, has itself chosen to employ the blanket license and similar practices.... Though these provisions are not directly controlling, they do reflect an opinion that the blanket license, and ASCAP, are economically beneficial in at least some circumstances.

There have been District Court cases holding various ASCAP practices, including its licensing practices, to be violative of the Sherman Act,[22] but even so, there is no nearly universal view that either the blanket or the per-program licenses issued by ASCAP at prices negotiated by it are a form of price fixing subject to automatic condemnation under the Sherman Act, rather than to a careful assessment under the rule of reason.

---

21. Cf. Continental TV, Inc. v. GTE Sylvania Inc., 433 U.S. 36, 50 n. 16 (1977). Moreover, unthinking application of the *per se* rule might upset the balancing of economic power and of pro-and anticompetitive effects presumably worked out in the decree.

22. Those cases involved licenses sold to individual movie theaters to "perform" compositions already on the motion pictures' soundtracks. ASCAP had barred its members from assigning performing rights to movie producers at the same time recording rights were licensed, and the theaters were effectively unable to engage in direct transactions for performing rights with individual copyright owners.

III

Of course, we are no more bound than is CBS by the views of the Department of Justice, the results in the prior lower court cases, or the opinions of various experts about the merits of the blanket license. But while we must independently examine this practice, all those should caution us against too easily finding blanket licensing subject to *per se* invalidation.

A

As a preliminary matter, we are mindful that the Court of Appeals' holding would appear to be quite difficult to contain. If, as the court held, there is *per se* antitrust violation whenever ASCAP issues a blanket license to a television network for a single fee, why would it not also be automatically illegal for ASCAP to negotiate and issue blanket licenses to individual radio or television stations or to other users who perform copyrighted music for profit? Likewise, if the present network licenses issued through ASCAP on behalf of its members are *per se* violations, why would it not be equally illegal for the members to authorize ASCAP to issue licenses establishing various categories of uses that a network might have for copyrighted music and setting a standard fee for each described use?

Although the Court of Appeals apparently thought the blanket license could be saved in some or even many applications, it seems to us that the *per se* rule does not accommodate itself to such flexibility and that the observations of the Court of Appeals with respect to remedy tend to impeach the *per se* basis for the holding of liability.[23]

CBS would prefer that ASCAP be authorized, indeed directed, to make all its compositions available at standard per-use rates within negotiated categories of use. 400 F.Supp., at 747 n. 7.[24] But if this in itself or in

---

23. See n. 17, supra. The Court of Appeals would apparently not outlaw the blanket license across the board but would permit it in various circumstances where it is deemed necessary or sufficiently desirable. It did not even enjoin blanket licensing with the television networks, the relief it realized would normally follow a finding of *per se* illegality of the license in that context. Instead, as requested by CBS, it remanded to the District Court to require ASCAP to offer in addition to blanket licensing some competitive form of per-use licensing. But per-use licensing by ASCAP, as recognized in the consent decrees, might be even more susceptible to the *per se* rule than blanket licensing.

The rationale for this unusual relief in a *per se* case was that "[t]he blanket license is not simply a 'naked restraint' ineluctably doomed for extinction." 562 F.2d, at 140. To the contrary, the Court of Appeals found that

the blanket license might well "serve a market need" for some. Ibid. This, it seems to us is not the *per se* approach, which does not yield so readily to circumstances, but in effect is a rather bobtailed application of the rule of reason, bobtailed in the sense that it is unaccompanied by the necessary analysis demonstrating why the particular licensing system is an undue competitive restraint.

24. Surely, if ASCAP abandoned the issuance of all licenses and confined its activities to policing the market and suing infringers, it could hardly be said that member copyright owners would be in violation of the antitrust laws by not having a common agent issue per-use licenses. Under the copyright laws, those who publicly performed copyrighted music have the burden of obtaining prior consent. Cf. Zenith Radio Corp. v. Hazeltine Research, Inc., 395 U.S. 100, 139–140 (1969).

conjunction with blanket licensing constitutes illegal price fixing by copyright owners, CBS urges that an injunction issue forbidding ASCAP to issue any blanket license or to negotiate any fee except on behalf of an individual member for the use of his own copyrighted work or works. Thus, we are called upon to determine that blanket licensing is unlawful across the board. We are quite sure, however, that the *per se* rule does not require any such holding.

B

In the first place, the line of commerce allegedly being restrained, the performing rights to copyrighted music, exists at all only because of the copyright laws. Those who would use copyrighted music in public performances must secure consent from the copyright owner or be liable at least for the statutory damages for each infringement and, if the conduct is willful and for the purpose of financial gain, to criminal penalties. Furthermore, nothing in the Copyright Act of 1976 indicates in the slightest that Congress intended to weaken the rights of copyright owners to control the public performance of musical compositions. Quite the contrary is true. Although the copyright law confers no rights on copyright owners to fix prices among themselves or otherwise to violate the antitrust laws, we would not expect that any market arrangements reasonably necessary to effectuate the rights that are granted would be deemed a *per se* violation of the Sherman Act. Otherwise, the commerce anticipated by the Copyright Act and protected against restraint by the Sherman Act would not exist at all or would exist only as a pale reminder of what Congress envisioned.

C

More generally, in characterizing this conduct under the *per se* rule,[25] our inquiry must focus on whether the effect and, here because it tends to show effect, see United States v. United States Gypsum Co., 438 U.S. 422, 436 n. 13 (1978), the purpose of the practice is to threaten the proper operation of our predominantly free market economy—that is, whether the practice facially appears to be one that would always or almost always tend to restrict competition and decrease output, and in what portion of the market, or instead one designed to "increase economic efficiency and render markets more rather than less competitive." Id., at 441 n. 16; see National Society of Professional Engineers v. United States, 435 U.S. 679, 688....

The blanket license, as we see it, is not a "naked restraint of trade with no purpose except stifling of competition," White Motor Co. v. United States, 372 U.S. 253, 263 (1963), but rather accompanies the integration of sales, monitoring, and enforcement against unauthorized copyright use. See

---

25. The scrutiny occasionally required must not merely subsume the burdensome analysis required under the rule of reason, see National Society of Professional Engineers v. United States, 435 U.S. 679 (1978), or else we should apply the rule of reason from the start. That is why the *per se* rule is not employed until after considerable experience with the type of challenged restraint.

L. Sullivan, Antitrust, § 59, at 154 (1977). As we have already indicated, ASCAP and the blanket license developed together out of the practical situation in the market place: thousands of users, thousands of copyright owners, and millions of compositions. Most users want unplanned, rapid and indemnified access to any and all of the repertory of compositions, and the owners want a reliable method of collecting for the use of their copyrights. Individual sales transactions in this industry are quite expensive, as would be individual monitoring and enforcement, especially in light of the resources of single composers. Indeed, as both the Court of Appeals and CBS recognize, the costs are prohibitive for licenses with individual radio stations, night clubs, and restaurants, 562 F.2d, at 136–137, n. 26, and it was in that milieu that the blanket license arose.

A middleman with a blanket license was an obvious necessity if the thousands of individual negotiations, a virtual impossibility, were to be avoided. Also, individual fees for the use of individual compositions would presuppose an intricate schedule of fees and uses, as well as a difficult and expensive reporting problem for the user and policing task for the copyright owner. Historically, the market for public performance rights organized itself largely around the single-fee blanket license, which gave unlimited access to the repertory and reliable protection against infringement. When ASCAP's major and user-created competitor, BMI, came on the scene, it also turned to the blanket license.

With the advent of radio and television networks, market conditions changed, and the necessity for and advantages of a blanket license for those users may be far less obvious than is the case when the potential users are individual television or radio stations, or the thousands of other individuals and organizations performing copyrighted compositions in public.[26] But even for television network licenses, ASCAP reduces costs absolutely by creating a blanket license that is sold only a few, instead of thousands, of times, and that obviates the need for closely monitoring the networks to see that they do not use more than they pay for. ASCAP also provides the necessary resources for blanket sales and enforcement, resources unavailable to the vast majority of composers and publishing houses. Moreover, a bulk license of some type is a necessary consequence of the integration necessary to achieve these efficiencies, and a necessary consequence of an aggregate license is that its price must be established.

D

This substantial lowering of costs, which is of course potentially beneficial to both sellers and buyers, differentiates the blanket license from individual use licenses. The blanket license is composed of the individual compositions plus the aggregating service. Here, the whole is truly greater than the sum of its parts; it is, to some extent, a different product. The blanket license has certain unique characteristics: It allows the licensee immediate use of covered compositions, without the delay of prior individu-

---

26. And of course changes brought about by new technology or new marketing techniques might also undercut the justification for the practice.

al negotiations and great flexibility in the choice of musical material. Many consumers clearly prefer the characteristics and cost advantages of this marketable package, and even small performing rights societies that have occasionally arisen to compete with ASCAP and BMI have offered blanket licenses. Thus, to the extent the blanket license is a different product, ASCAP is not really a joint sales agency offering the individual goods of many sellers, but is a separate seller offering its blanket license, of which the individual compositions are raw material.[27] ASCAP, in short, made a market in which individual composers are inherently unable to fully effectively compete.[28]

E

Finally, we have some doubt—enough to counsel against application of the *per se* rule—about the extent to which this practice threatens the "central nervous system of the economy," United States v. Socony–Vacuum Oil Co., 310 U.S. 150, 226 n. 59 (1940), that is, competitive pricing as the free market's means of allocating resources. Not all arrangements among actual or potential competitors that have an impact on price are *per se* violations of the Sherman Act or even unreasonable restraints. Mergers among competitors eliminate competition, including price competition, but they are not *per se* illegal and many of them withstand attack under any existing antitrust standard. Joint ventures and other cooperative arrangements are also not usually unlawful, at least not as price-fixing schemes, where the agreement on price is necessary to market the product at all.

Here, the blanket license fee is not set by competition among individual copyright owners, and it is a fee for the use of any of the compositions covered by the license. But the blanket license cannot be wholly equated with a simple horizontal arrangement among competitors. ASCAP does set the price for its blanket license, but that license is quite different from anything any individual owner could issue. The individual composers and authors have neither agreed not to sell individually in any other market nor use the blanket license to mask price fixing in such other markets. Moreover, the substantial restraints placed on ASCAP and its members by the consent decree must not be ignored. The District Court found that there was no legal, practical, or conspiratorial impediment to CBS obtaining individual licenses; CBS, in short, had a real choice.

---

27. Moreover, because of the nature of the product—a composition can be simultaneously "consumed" by many users—composers have numerous markets and numerous incentives to produce, so the blanket license is unlikely to cause decreased output, one of the normal undesirable effects of a cartel. And since popular songs get an increased share of ASCAP's revenue distributions, composers compete even within the blanket license in terms of productivity and consumer satisfaction.

28. Cf. United States v. Socony–Vacuum Oil Co., 310 U.S. 150, 217 (1940) (distinguishing Chicago Bd. of Trade v. United States, 246 U.S. 231 (1918), on the ground that among the effects of the challenged rule there "was the creation of a public market"); United States v. Trenton Potteries Co., 273 U.S. 392, 401 (1927) (distinguishing Chicago Bd. of Trade on the ground that it did not involve "a price agreement among competitors in an open market").

With this background in mind, which plainly enough indicates that over the years, and in the face of available alternatives, the blanket license has provided an acceptable mechanism for at least a large part of the market for the performing rights to copyrighted musical compositions, we cannot agree that it should automatically be declared illegal in all of its many manifestations. Rather, when attacked, it should be subjected to a more discriminating examination under the rule of reason. It may not ultimately survive that attack, but that is not the issue before us today.

IV

As we have noted, supra, the enigmatic remarks of the Court of Appeals with respect to remedy appear to have departed from the court's strict, *per se* approach and to have invited a more careful analysis. But this left the general import of its judgment that the licensing practices of ASCAP and BMI under the consent decree are *per se* violations of the Sherman Act. We reverse that judgment, and the copyright misuse judgment dependent upon it, and remand for further proceedings to consider any unresolved issues that CBS may have properly brought to the Court of Appeals.[29] Of course, this will include an assessment under the rule of reason of the blanket license as employed in the television industry, if that issue was preserved by CBS in the Court of Appeals.[30]

The judgment of the Court of Appeals is reversed and the case is remanded to that court for further proceedings consistent with this opinion.

■ Stevens, J., dissenting. The Court holds that ASCAP's blanket license is not a species of price fixing categorically forbidden by the Sherman Act. I agree with that holding. The Court remands the case to the Court of Appeals, leaving open the question whether the blanket license as employed by ASCAP and BMI is unlawful under a rule of reason inquiry. I think that question is properly before us now and should be answered affirmatively. . . .

. . . It is the refusal to license anything less than the entire repertoire—rather than the decision to offer blanket licenses themselves—that raises the serious antitrust questions in this case. . . .

---

29. It is argued that the judgment of the Court of Appeals should nevertheless be affirmed on the ground that the blanket license is a tying arrangement in violation of § 1 of the Sherman Act or on the ground that ASCAP and BMI have monopolized the relevant market contrary to § 2. The District Court and the Court of Appeals rejected both submissions, and we do not disturb the latter's judgment in these respects, particularly since CBS did not file its own petition for certiorari challenging the Court of Appeals'

failure to sustain its tying and monopolization claims.

30. The Court of Appeals did not address the rule-of-reason issue, and BMI insists that CBS did not preserve the question in that court. In any event, if the issue is open in the Court of Appeals, we prefer that court first to address the matter. Because of the United States' interest in the enforcement of the consent decree, we assume it will continue to play a role in this litigation on remand.

The market for music at issue here is wholly dominated by ASCAP-issued blanket licenses. Virtually every domestic copyrighted composition is in the repertoire of either ASCAP or BMI. And again, virtually without exception, the only means that has been used to secure authority to perform such compositions is the blanket license.

The blanket all-or-nothing license is patently discriminatory. The user purchases full access to ASCAP's entire repertoire, even though his needs could be satisfied by a far more limited selection. The price he pays for this access is unrelated either to the quantity or the quality of the music he actually uses, or, indeed to what he would probably use in a competitive system. Rather, in this unique all-or-nothing system, the price is based on a percentage of the user's advertising revenues, a measure that reflects the customer's ability to pay but is totally unrelated to factors—such as the cost, quality, or quantity of the product—that normally affect price in a competitive market. The ASCAP system requires users to buy more music than they want at a price which, while not beyond their ability to pay and perhaps not even beyond what is "reasonable" for the access they are getting, may well be far higher than what they would choose to spend for music in a competitive system. It is a classic example of economic discrimination.

The record plainly establishes that there is no price competition between separate musical compositions. Under a blanket license, it is no more expensive for a network to play the most popular current hit in prime time than it is to use an unknown composition as background music in a soap opera. Because the cost to the user is unaffected by the amount used on any program or on all programs, the user has no incentive to economize by, for example, substituting what would otherwise be less expensive songs for established favorites or by reducing the quantity of music used on a program. The blanket license thereby tends to encourage the use of more music, and also of a larger share of what is really more valuable music, than would be expected in a competitive system characterized by separate licenses. And since revenues are passed on to composers on a basis reflecting the character and frequency of the use of their music, the tendency is to increase the rewards of the established composers at the expense of those less well known. Perhaps the prospect is in any event unlikely, but the blanket license does not present a new songwriter with any opportunity to try to break into the market by offering his product for sale at an unusually low price. The absence of that opportunity, however unlikely it may be, is characteristic of a cartelized rather than a competitive market.

The current state of the market cannot be explained on the ground that it could not operate competitively, or that issuance of more limited—and thus less restrictive—licenses by ASCAP is not feasible. The District Court's findings disclose no reason why music performing rights could not be negotiated on a per-composition or per-use basis, either with the composer or publisher directly or with an agent such as ASCAP. In fact, ASCAP now compensates composers and publishers on precisely those bases. If distributions of royalties can be calculated on a per-use and per-composition basis, it is difficult to see why royalties could not also be collected in the same way. Moreover, the record also shows that where ASCAP's blanket license scheme does not govern, competitive markets do. A competitive market for "synch rights" exists,[31] and after the use of blanket licenses in the motion picture industry was discontinued, such a market promptly developed in that industry. In sum, the record demonstrates that the market at issue here is one that could be highly competitive, but is not competitive at all.

Since the record describes a market that could be competitive and is not, and since that market is dominated by two firms engaged in a single, blanket method of dealing, it surely seems logical to conclude that trade has been restrained unreasonably. ASCAP argues, however, that at least as to CBS, there has been no restraint at all since the network is free to deal directly with copyright holders....

... Despite its size, CBS itself may not obtain music on a competitive basis without incurring unprecedented costs and risks. The fear of unpredictable consequences, coupled with the certain and predictable costs and delays associated with a change in its method of purchasing music, unquestionably inhibits any CBS management decision to embark on a competitive crusade. Even if ASCAP offered CBS a special bargain to forestall any such crusade, that special arrangement would not cure the marketwide restraint....

Antitrust policy requires that great aggregations of economic power be closely scrutinized. That duty is especially important when the aggregation is composed of statutory monopoly privileges. Our cases have repeatedly stressed the need to limit the privileges conferred by patent and copyright strictly to the scope of the statutory grant. The record in this case plainly discloses that the limits have been exceeded and that ASCAP and BMI exercise monopoly powers that far exceed the sum of the privileges of the individual copyright holders. Indeed, ASCAP itself argues that its blanket license constitutes a product that is significantly different from the sum of its component parts. I agree with that premise, but I conclude that the aggregate is a monopolistic restraint of trade proscribed by the Sherman Act.

NOTES AND QUESTIONS

1. On remand in *BMI*, the Second Circuit affirmed the District Court decision, holding that its findings of fact "demonstrate that the blanket license has no anticompetitive effect at all," since CBS had always had a "realistic opportunity" to

---

31. The "synch" right is the right to record a copyrighted song in synchronization with the film or videotape, and is obtained separately from the right to perform the mu-sic. It is the latter which is controlled by ASCAP and BMI. See CBS, Inc. v. ASCAP, *supra*, 400 F.Supp., at 743.

obtain performance rights from individual copyright holders, 620 F.2d 930 (2d Cir.1980), cert. denied, 450 U.S. 970 (1981). "An antitrust plaintiff is not obligated to pursue any imaginable alternative, regardless of cost or efficiency, before it can complain that a practice has restrained competition." But in this case, CBS had not even offered to buy from competing sellers, arguing that it had not done so because (1) there would have inevitably been a period of double payment—both to individual copyright owners and under the license, and (2) no machinery existed to handle the numerous individual negotiations. The Court of Appeals rejected these arguments: "CBS cannot expect the antitrust laws to assure it that a changeover to direct licensing can be accomplished instantly or at no expense."

2. In BUFFALO BROADCASTING CO. V. ASCAP, 744 F.2d 917, 924–32 (2d Cir.1984), cert. denied, 469 U.S. 1211 (1985), the Court of Appeals reversed a district court finding against BMI and ASCAP, concluding that even for small local TV stations, there were realistic alternative ways to obtain performance rights other than those being offered by the joint ventures.

3. Reconsider *Socony–Vacuum* in light of *BMI*. In *Socony–Vacuum,* the problem the major oil companies were trying to address was that independent refiners were producing more gasoline than the market could absorb, and these same independents had inadequate storage facilities. As a result, they occasionally flooded the market with "distress" gasoline which created "disorderly marketing conditions." Suppose that the majors, instead of the "dancing partner" scheme they adopted, set up an industry-wide joint venture for transportation and storage of gasoline with access available to all sellers, including the independents, on fair and reasonable terms. Suppose further that membership in the joint venture was voluntary for all parties, some efficiencies of scale from joint warehousing could be demonstrated, and that the warehousing plan did "stabilize" market conditions. Would that joint venture be legal under *BMI*? Why is it different from the dancing partner scheme which the court in *BMI* apparently assumed was properly declared illegal in *Socony–Vacuum*?

4. In UNITED STATES V. UNITED STATES GYPSUM CO., 438 U.S. 422 (1978), six major manufacturers of gypsum board were indicted for engaging in a program of interseller price verification. Under the program, sellers telephoned competing producers to determine the price currently being offered on gypsum board to specific customers. Defendants claimed that the information was being exchanged for the purpose of perfecting a "meeting competition" defense under Section 2(b) of the Robinson–Patman Act.

We will examine the Robinson–Patman Act in detail in Chapter 11. For the time being, simply note that the Act prohibits a seller from discriminating in price between competing customers where there is an injury to competition, but allows an absolute defense where the lower price is offered to a customer "in good faith to meet an equally low price of a competitor. . . ." The Supreme Court had concluded in FTC v. A.E. Staley Manufacturing Co., 324 U.S. 746 (1945), that the seller must "show the existence of facts which would lead a reasonable and prudent person to believe that the granting of a lower price would in fact meet the equally low price of a competitor." Thus, the gypsum manufacturers argued with some plausibility that *Staley* required that they not simply accept the word of their customers about receipt of lower prices, but rather that they investigate and verify these reports by checking with competing sellers.

The jury had returned criminal verdicts against defendants, but the Supreme Court reversed. It held that in criminal cases it was necessary for the government to prove both anticompetitive effect and intent (*i.e.,* "knowledge of . . . probable consequences" of an act), and that the requisite intent could not be inferred, as a matter of law, from a finding that the exchange of price information had an impact on prices:

> Although an effect on prices may well support an inference that the defendant had knowledge of the probability of such a consequence at the time he acted, the jury must remain free to consider additional evidence before accepting or rejecting the inference. Therefore, although it would be correct to instruct the jury that it may infer intent from an effect on prices, ultimately the decision on the issue of intent must be left to the trier of fact alone.

The conduct alleged in *Gypsum* was judged against a rule of reason. Would the "effects and intent" rule discussed above be applied in cases where *per se* violations are alleged? In *Gypsum,* the Supreme Court noted that its "knowledge of the probable consequences" intent formulation was not meant to "suggest that conduct undertaken with the purpose of producing anticompetitive effects would not also support criminal liability, even if such effects did not come to pass." *See, e.g.,* United States v. Alston, 974 F.2d 1206, 1212 (9th Cir.1992) (the government need not prove specific intent to produce anticompetitive effects where a *per se* violation is alleged); United States v. Brown, 925 F.2d 1182, 1187 (9th Cir.1991) (the intent requirement of *Gypsum* "does not apply to charges of *per se* violations"; a finding of intent to conspire to commit the offense is sufficient); United States v. Brighton Building and Maintenance Co., 598 F.2d 1101 (7th Cir.1979) (only if the conduct "directly proved" is not illegal *per se* are defendants entitled to an instruction that the government must prove intent); United States v. Gillen, 599 F.2d 541 (3d Cir.1979) (*Gypsum* directed at "borderline violations," not price-fixing conspiracies which are illegal *per se*). The *Gypsum* opinion will be examined in Chapter 11 in connection with consideration of policy questions in enforcement of the Robinson–Patman Act.

5. In his memoirs, William S. Paley, founder and long-time Chairman of the Columbia Broadcasting System, reported that he had proposed to the presidents of NBC and ABC an arrangement whereby each network could broadcast cultural, educational, and high-quality programs without fear of adverse ratings. Paley said he proposed that "representatives of the three major networks meet to work out the feasibility and the details in setting aside a given period of time—say, two hours a week in prime time—for special, high-quality programs that would appeal to educated, sophisticated tastes more than to the mass audience. Each network would take different nights of the week, thus offering the public six hours of high-quality programming each week." NBC and ABC were not interested. W. Paley, As It Happened 275–76 (1979).

Paley pointed out that no one network could schedule quality programs alone since it would not only derive small revenues from the hour devoted to quality broadcasting, but would forfeit revenues for the whole evening through the adverse effect on later scheduled programs. Should Paley's proposal be characterized as price-fixing? If not, would its social and cultural virtues constitute a justification? Would such considerations be relevant under *Professional Engineers*? Consider these issues when reading United States v. Brown University, p. 265 infra.

VIRGINIA EXCELSIOR MILLS, INC. v. FTC, 256 F.2d 538 (4th Cir.1958). Excelsior is a shredded wood product used principally to package fragile materials. A group of small producers in Northern Virginia found that competition among them was extremely keen and they therefore organized a corporate sales agency, Virginia Excelsior Mills, which they appointed as exclusive sales agent for each of them. Orders were to be allocated among producers on the basis of their relative productive capacity, and the producers agreed not to increase that capacity. The contracts also contemplated that prices would be established by the Board of Directors of the sales corporation elected by the producer members. Prices after establishment of the joint sales agency were uniform, and increased across the board in response to rising costs.

The Federal Trade Commission found the agreement illegal *per se* under § 1 of the Sherman Act, and the Court of Appeals affirmed:

> Price fixing through such an arrangement is a violation, *per se,* of § 1 of the Sherman Act. Though the needs and problems of the producers, which stimulated the creation of the arrangement, may have seemed pressing, they cannot lend a cloak of legality to conduct which, whatever the supposed justification, the Act condemns.... What contrary suggestion may be found in Appalachian Coals, Inc. v. United States, 288 U.S. 344, has not survived the strong and consistent course of subsequent decision....

In commenting on the Order entered by the FTC, the Court of Appeals noted that there would be nothing unlawful in an arrangement whereby each producer appoints a common sales agent, but reserves and exercises independence in pricing, acceptance of orders, production, and other similar decisions.

NOTE ON JOINT VENTURES

1. *Virginia Excelsior* is only one of many cases finding that price fixing occurring as a result of the activities of a joint sales agency can be illegal *per se*. *See, e.g.*, United States v. American Smelting and Refining Co., 182 F.Supp. 834 (S.D.N.Y.1960) (two competitors agree that one will serve as exclusive sales agent for the other in the eastern part of the United States, but that the agent would not sell on its own behalf in the western part of the United States); United States v. Columbia Pictures Industries, Inc., 507 F.Supp. 412 (S.D.N.Y.1980), affirmed without opinion, 659 F.2d 1063 (2d Cir.1981) (joint venture to market films of various production companies to cable TV systems). In most of these cases, the joint venture accounted for a substantial share of the market.

In another line of cases, joint buying and selling ventures, usually involving small companies joining together to reduce costs and compete more effectively with larger rivals, have been upheld under a rule of reason. *See, e.g.*, Webster County Memorial Hospital, Inc. v. United Mine Workers of America Welfare and Retirement Fund of 1950, 536 F.2d 419, 420 (D.C.Cir.1976) (joint negotiation on behalf of fund beneficiaries with a hospital regarded as reasonable); Instant Delivery Corp. v. City Stores Co., 284 F.Supp. 941 (E.D.Pa.1968) (joint purchasing arrangement designed to reduce costs found to be reasonable).

Is it a satisfactory resolution to declare joint buying and selling co-ops legal or illegal solely on grounds of the share of the market accounted for by the members of the co-op? Would *per se* treatment be avoided in a cartel which accounts for only a small share of the market? If not, why the difference here?

2. As Levine v. Central Florida Medical Affiliates, Inc., 72 F.3d 1538 (11th Cir.1996), p. 227 supra, indicates, joint ventures of various types have become particularly important in the fast-changing health care field. The Department of Justice and FTC "Statements of Enforcement Policy and Analytical Principles Relating to Health Care and Antitrust," cited in the *Levine* case, draws distinctions among ventures that should be treated as *per se,* scrutinized under a rule of reason, and treated as benign. Where would you draw the lines? These issues are raised continually in cases forthcoming in this chapter, again in Chapter 5, and still again in Chapter 9.

National Collegiate Athletic Association v. Board Of Regents of University of Oklahoma

Supreme Court of the United States, 1984.
468 U.S. 85, 104 S.Ct. 2948, 82 L.Ed.2d 70.

■ STEVENS, J. The University of Oklahoma and the University of Georgia contend that the National Collegiate Athletic Association has unreasonably restrained trade in the televising of college football games. After an extended trial, the District Court found that the NCAA had violated § 1 of the Sherman Act and granted injunctive relief. 546 F.Supp. 1276 (W.D.Okla.1982). The Court of Appeals agreed that the Statute had been violated but modified the remedy in some respects. 707 F.2d 1147 (C.A.10 1983). We granted certiorari, 464 U.S. 913 (1983), and now affirm.

I

The NCAA

Since its inception in 1905, the NCAA has played an important role in the regulation of amateur collegiate sports. It has adopted and promulgated playing rules, standards of amateurism, standards for academic eligibility, regulations concerning recruitment of athletes, and rules governing the size of athletic squads and coaching staffs. In some sports, such as baseball, swimming, basketball, wrestling and track, it has sponsored and conducted national tournaments. It has not done so in the sport of football, however. With the exception of football, the NCAA has not undertaken any regulation of the televising of athletic events.[32]

The NCAA has approximately 850 voting members. The regular members are classified into separate divisions to reflect differences in size and scope of their athletic programs. Division I includes 276 colleges with major athletic programs; in this group only 187 play intercollegiate football. Divisions II and III include approximately 500 colleges with less extensive athletic programs. Division I has been subdivided into Divisions I–A and I–AA for football.

Some years ago, five major conferences together with major football-playing independent institutions organized the College Football Association

32. Presumably, however, it sells the television rights to events that the NCAA itself conducts.

(CFA). The original purpose of the CFA was to promote the interests of major football—playing schools within the NCAA structure. The Universities of Oklahoma and Georgia, respondents in this Court, are members of the CFA. . . .

The Current Plan

The plan adopted in 1981 for the 1982–1985 seasons is at issue in this case.[33] This plan, like each of its predecessors, recites that it is intended to reduce, insofar as possible, the adverse effects of live television upon football game attendance.[34] It provides that "all forms of television of the football games of NCAA member institutions during the Plan control periods shall be in accordance with this Plan." The plan recites that the television committee has awarded rights to negotiate and contract for the telecasting of college football games of members of the NCAA to two "carrying networks." In addition to the principal award of rights to the carrying networks, the plan also describes rights for a "supplementary series" that had been awarded for the 1982 and 1983 seasons,[35] as well as a procedure for permitting specific "exception telecasts."[36]

In separate agreements with each of the carrying networks, ABC and the Columbia Broadcasting System (CBS), the NCAA granted each the right to telecast the 14 live "exposures" described in the plan, in accordance with the "ground rules" set forth therein.[37] Each of the networks agreed to pay a specified "minimum aggregate compensation to the participating NCAA member institutions" during the 4–year period in an amount

33. Because respondents sought and obtained only injunctive relief against future violations of § 1 in the District Court, we do not consider previous NCAA television plans except to the extent that they shed light on the purpose and effect of the current plan.

34. "The purposes of this Plan shall be to reduce, insofar as possible, the adverse effects of live television upon football game attendance and, in turn, upon the athletic and related educational programs dependent upon the proceeds therefrom; to spread football television participation among as many colleges as practicable; to reflect properly the image of universities as educational institutions; to promote college football through the use of television, to advance the overall interests of intercollegiate athletics, and to provide college football television to the public to the extent compatible with these other objectives." Id., at 35 (parenthetical omitted).

35. The supplementary series is described in a separate article of the plan. It is to consist of no more than 36 exposures in each of the first two years and no more than 40 exposures in the third and fourth years of

the plan. Those exposures are to be scheduled on Saturday evenings or at other times that do not conflict with the principal football series that is scheduled for Saturday afternoons.

36. An "exception" telecast is permitted in the home team's market of games that are sold out and in the visiting team's market of games played more than 400 miles from the visiting team's campus, but in both cases only if the broadcast would not be shown in an area where another college football game is to be played. Also, Division II and Division III institutions are allowed complete freedom to televise their games, except that the games may not appear on a network of more than five stations without the permission of the NCAA.

37. In addition to its contracts with the carrying networks, the NCAA has contracted with Turner Broadcasting System, Inc. (TBS), for the exclusive right to cablecast NCAA football games. The minimum aggregate fee for the initial two-year period of the TBS contract is $17,696,000. 546 F.Supp., at 1291–1292.

that totaled $131,750,000. In essence the agreement authorized each network to negotiate directly with member schools for the right to televise their games. The agreement itself does not describe the method of computing the compensation for each game, but the practice that has developed over the years and that the District Court found would be followed under the current agreement involved the setting of a recommended fee by a representative of the NCAA for different types of telecasts, with national telecasts being the most valuable, regional telecasts being less valuable, and Division II or Division III games commanding a still lower price.[38] The aggregate of all these payments presumably equals the total minimum aggregate compensation set forth in the basic agreement. Except for differences in payment between national and regional telecasts, and with respect to Division II and Division III games, the amount that any team receives does not change with the size of the viewing audience, the number of markets in which the game is telecast, or the particular characteristic of the game or the participating teams. Instead, the "ground rules" provide that the carrying networks make alternate selections of those games they wish to televise, and thereby obtain the exclusive right to submit a bid at an essentially fixed price to the institutions involved. See 546 F.Supp., at 1289–1293.[39]

The plan also contains "appearance requirements" and "appearance limitations" which pertain to each of the 2–year periods that the plan is in effect. The basic requirement imposed on each of the two networks is that it must schedule appearances for at least 82 different member institutions during each 2–year period. Under the appearance limitations no member institution is eligible to appear on television more than a total of six times and more than four times nationally, with the appearances to be divided equally between the two carrying networks. See id., at 1293. The number of exposures specified in the contracts also sets an absolute maximum on the number of games that can be broadcast.

38. The football television committee's briefing book for 1981 recites that a fee of $600,000 was paid for each of the 12 national games telecast by ABC during the regular fall season and $426,779 was paid for each of the 46 regional telecasts in 1980. The report further recites that "Division I members received $27,842,185 from 1980 football television revenue, 89.8 percent of the total. Division II's share was $625,195 (2.0 percent), while Division III received $385,195 (1.3 percent) and the NCAA $2,147,425 (6.9 percent)."

39. The District Court explained how the agreement eliminates competition for broadcasting rights:

"First, the networks have no intention to engage in bidding. Second, once the network holding first choice for any given date has made its choice and agreed to a rights fee for that game with the two teams involved, the other network is then in a monopsony position. The schools cannot threaten to sell the broadcast rights to any other network. They cannot sell to NBC without committing a violation of NCAA rules. They cannot sell to the network which had first choice over that particular date because, again, they would be in violation of NCAA rules, and the network would be in violation of its agreement with NCAA. Thus, NCAA creates a single eligible buyer for the product of all but the two schools selected by the network having first choice. Free market competition is thus destroyed under the new plan." 546 F.Supp., at 1292–1293.

Thus, although the current plan is more elaborate than any of its predecessors, it retains the essential features of each of them. It limits the total amount of televised intercollegiate football and the number of games that any one team may televise. No member is permitted to make any sale of television rights except in accordance with the basic plan.

Background of this Controversy

Beginning in 1979 CFA members began to advocate that colleges with major football programs should have a greater voice in the formulation of football television policy than they had in the NCAA. CFA therefore investigated the possibility of negotiating a television agreement of its own, developed an independent plan, and obtained a contract offer from the National Broadcasting Co. (NBC). This contract, which it signed in August 1981, would have allowed a more liberal number of appearances for each institution, and would have increased the overall revenues realized by CFA members.

In response the NCAA publicly announced that it would take disciplinary action against any CFA member that complied with the CFA–NBC contract. The NCAA made it clear that sanctions would not be limited to the football programs of CFA members, but would apply to other sports as well. On September 8, 1981, respondents commenced this action in the United States District Court for the Western District of Oklahoma and obtained a preliminary injunction preventing the NCAA from initiating disciplinary proceedings or otherwise interfering with CFA's efforts to perform its agreement with NBC. Notwithstanding the entry of the injunction, most CFA members were unwilling to commit themselves to the new contractual arrangement with NBC in the face of the threatened sanctions and therefore the agreement was never consummated.

[The District Court and the Court of Appeals found the *NCAA* television plan illegal *per se,* primarily on grounds that it constituted price fixing and a limitation on output. The Court of Appeals considered, but rejected on the facts, arguments by the NCAA that the plan promoted live attendance, and also rejected as illegitimate the NCAA's purpose of promoting an athletically balanced competition on grounds that such a consideration was inconsistent with the policy of the Sherman Act.]

II

There can be no doubt that the challenged practices of the NCAA constitute a "restraint of trade" in the sense that they limit members' freedom to negotiate and enter into their own television contracts. In that sense, however, every contract is a restraint of trade, and as we have repeatedly recognized, the Sherman Act was intended to prohibit only unreasonable restraints of trade.

It is also undeniable that these practices share characteristics of restraints we have previously held unreasonable. The NCAA is an association of schools which compete against each other to attract television revenues, not to mention fans and athletes. As the District Court found, the policies of the NCAA with respect to television rights are ultimately controlled by the vote of member institutions. By participating in an association which prevents member institutions from competing against each other on the basis of price or kind of television rights that can be offered to broadcasters, the NCAA member institutions have created a horizontal restraint—an agreement among competitors on the way in which they will compete with one another. A restraint of this type has often been held to be unreasonable as a matter of law. Because it places a ceiling on the number of games member institutions may televise, the horizontal agreement places an artificial limit on the quantity of televised football that is available to broadcasters and consumers. By restraining the quantity of television rights available for sale, the challenged practices create a limitation on output; our cases have held that such limitations are unreasonable restraints of trade.[40] Moreover, the District Court found that the minimum aggregate price in fact operates to preclude any price negotiation between broadcasters and institutions, thereby constituting horizontal price fixing, perhaps the paradigm of an unreasonable restraint of trade.[41]

Horizontal price-fixing and output limitation are ordinarily condemned as a matter of law under an "illegal *per se*" approach because the probability that these practices are anticompetitive is so high; a *per se* rule is applied when "the practice facially appears to be one that would always or almost always tend to restrict competition and decrease output." Broadcast Music, Inc. v. CBS, 441 U.S. 1, 19–20 (1979). In such circumstances a restraint is presumed unreasonable without inquiry into the particular market context in which it is found. Nevertheless, we have decided that it would be inappropriate to apply a *per se* rule to this case. This decision is not based on a lack of judicial experience with this type of arrangement,[42] on the fact that the NCAA is organized as a nonprofit entity,[43] or on our respect for

40. *See, e.g.,* United States v. Topco Associates, Inc., 405 U.S. 596, 608–609 (1972); United States v. Sealy, Inc., 388 U.S. 350 (1967); United States v. American Linseed Oil Co., 262 U.S. 371, 388–390 (1923); American Column & Lumber Co. v. United States, 257 U.S. 377, 410–412 (1921).

41. *See, e.g.,* Arizona v. Maricopa County Medical Society, 457 U.S. 332, 344–348 (1982); Catalano, Inc. v. Target Sales, Inc., 446 U.S. 643, 646–647 (1980) (per curiam); Kiefer–Stewart Co. v. Joseph E. Seagram & Sons, Inc., 340 U.S. 211, 213 (1951); United States v. Socony–Vacuum Oil Co., 310 U.S. 150, 212–214 (1940); United States v. Trenton Potteries Co., 273 U.S. 392, 396–398 (1927).

42. While judicial inexperience with a particular arrangement counsels against extending the reach of *per se* rules, see Broadcast Music, 441 U.S., at 9–10; United States v. Topco Associates, Inc., 405 U.S. 596, 607–

608 (1972); White Motor Co. v. United States, 372 U.S. 253, 263 (1963); the likelihood that horizontal price and output restrictions are anticompetitive is generally sufficient to justify application of the *per se* rule without inquiry into the special characteristics of a particular industry. See Arizona v. Maricopa County Medical Society, 457 U.S. 332, 349–351 (1982); National Society of Professional Engineers v. United States, 435 U.S. 679, 689–690 (1978).

43. There is no doubt that the sweeping language of § 1 applies to nonprofit entities, Goldfarb v. Virginia State Bar, 421 U.S. 773, 786–787 (1975), and in the past we have imposed antitrust liability on non-profit entities which have engaged in anticompetitive conduct, American Society of Mechanical Engineers, Inc. v. Hydrolevel Corp., 456 U.S. 556, 576 (1982). Moreover, the economic significance of the NCAA's nonprofit character is questionable at best. Since the District

the NCAA's historic role in the preservation and encouragement of inter-collegiate amateur athletics.[44] Rather, what is critical is that this case involves an industry in which horizontal restraints on competition are essential if the product is to be available at all.

As Judge Bork has noted: "[S]ome activities can only be carried out jointly. Perhaps the leading example is league sports. When a league of professional lacrosse teams is formed, it would be pointless to declare their cooperation illegal on the ground that there are no other professional lacrosse teams." R. Bork, The Antitrust Paradox 278 (1978). What the NCAA and its member institutions market in this case is competition itself—contests between competing institutions. Of course, this would be completely ineffective if there were no rules on which the competitors agreed to create and define the competition to be marketed. A myriad of rules affecting such matters as the size of the field, the number of players on a team, and the extent to which physical violence is to be encouraged or proscribed, all must be agreed upon, and all restrain the manner in which institutions compete. Moreover, the NCAA seeks to market a particular brand of football—college football. The identification of this "product" with an academic tradition differentiates college football from and makes it more popular than professional sports to which it might otherwise be compara-ble, such as, for example, minor league baseball. In order to preserve the character and quality of the "product," athletes must not be paid, must be required to attend class, and the like. And the integrity of the "product" cannot be preserved except by mutual agreement; if an institution adopted such restrictions unilaterally, its effectiveness as a competitor on the playing field might soon be destroyed. Thus, the NCAA plays a vital role in enabling college football to preserve its character, and as a result enables a product to be marketed which might otherwise be unavailable. In perform-ing this role, its actions widen consumer choice—not only the choices available to sports fans but also those available to athletes—and hence can be viewed as procompetitive.[45]

Broadcast Music squarely holds that a joint selling arrangement may be so efficient that it will increase sellers' aggregate output and thus be procompetitive. See 441 U.S., at 18–23. Similarly, as we indicated in Continental T.V., Inc. v. GTE Sylvania Inc., 433 U.S. 36, 51–57 (1977), a

---

Court found that the NCAA and its member institutions are in fact organized to maximize revenues, see 546 F.Supp., at 1288–1289, it is unclear why petitioner is less likely to re-strict output in order to raise revenues above those that could be realized in a competitive market than would be a for-profit entity. Petitioner does not rely on its nonprofit char-acter as a basis for reversal. Tr. of Oral Arg. 24.

44. While as the guardian of an impor-tant American tradition, the NCAA's motives must be accorded a respectful presumption of validity, it is nevertheless well-settled that good motives will not validate an otherwise anticompetitive practice. See United States v. Griffith, 334 U.S. 100, 105–106 (1948); Asso-ciated Press v. United States, 326 U.S. 1, 16, n. 15 (1945); Chicago Board of Trade v. Unit-ed States, 246 U.S. 231, 238 (1918); Standard Sanitary Manufacturing Co. v. United States, 226 U.S. 20, 49 (1912); United States v. Trans–Missouri Freight Assn., 166 U.S. 290, 342 (1897).

45. See Justice v. NCAA, 577 F.Supp. 356, 379–383 (Ariz.1983); Jones v. NCAA, 392 F.Supp. 295, 304 (Mass.1975); College Athletic Placement Service, Inc. v. NCAA, 1975–1 Trade Cases ¶ 60,117 (NJ), aff'd mem., 506 F.2d 1050 (CA3 1974)....

restraint in a limited aspect of a market may actually enhance marketwide competition. Respondents concede that the great majority of the NCAA's regulations enhance competition among member institutions. Thus, despite the fact that this case involves restraints on the ability of member institutions to compete in terms of price and output, a fair evaluation of their competitive character requires consideration of the NCAA's justifications for the restraints.

Our analysis of this case under the Rule of Reason, of course, does not change the ultimate focus of our inquiry. Both *per se* rules and the Rule of Reason are employed "to form a judgment about the competitive significance of the restraint." National Society of Professional Engineers v. United States, 435 U.S. 679, 692 (1978). A conclusion that a restraint of trade is unreasonable may be

> "based either (1) on the nature or character of the contracts, or (2) on surrounding circumstances giving rise to the inference or presumption that they were intended to restrain trade and enhance prices. Under either branch of the test, the inquiry is confined to a consideration of impact on competitive conditions." Id., at 690 (footnotes omitted).

Per se rules are invoked when surrounding circumstances make the likelihood of anticompetitive conduct so great as to render unjustified further examination of the challenged conduct.[46] But whether the ultimate finding is the product of a presumption or actual market analysis, the essential inquiry remains the same—whether or not the challenged restraint enhances competition.[47] Under the Sherman Act the criterion to be used in judging the validity of a restraint on trade is its impact on competition.[48]

III

Because it restrains price and output, the NCAA's television plan has a significant potential for anticompetitive effects.[49] The findings of the District Court indicate that this potential has been realized. The District Court found that if member institutions were free to sell television rights, many

---

46. See Jefferson Parish Hosp. Dist. No. 2 v. Hyde, 466 U.S. 2, 15 n. 25 (1984); Arizona v. Maricopa County Medical Society, 457 U.S. 332, 350–351 (1982); Continental T.V., Inc., 433 U.S., at 50, n. 16.

47. Indeed, there is often no bright line separating *per se* from Rule of Reason analysis. *Per se* rules may require considerable inquiry into market conditions before the evidence justifies a presumption of anticompetitive conduct. For example, while the Court has spoken of a "per se" rule against tying arrangements, it has also recognized that tying may have procompetitive justifications that make it inappropriate to condemn without considerable market analysis. See Jeffer-

son Parish Hosp. Dist. No. 2 v. Hyde, 466 U.S. 2, 16 (1984).

48. "The Sherman Act was designed to be a comprehensive charter of economic liberty aimed at preserving free and unfettered competition as the rule of trade...." Northern Pacific R. Co. v. United States, 356 U.S. 1, 4–5 (1958).

49. In this connection, it is not without significance that Congress felt the need to grant professional sports an exemption from the antitrust laws for joint marketing of television rights. See 15 U.S.C. §§ 1291–1295. The legislative history of this exemption demonstrates Congress' recognition that agreements among league members to sell televi-

more games would be shown on television, and that the NCAA's output restriction has the effect of raising the price the networks pay for television rights.[50] Moreover, the court found that by fixing a price for television rights to all games, the NCAA creates a price structure that is unresponsive to viewer demand and unrelated to the prices that would prevail in a competitive market.[51] And, of course, since as a practical matter all member institutions need NCAA approval, members have no real choice but to adhere to the NCAA's television controls.[52]

The anticompetitive consequences of this arrangement are apparent. Individual competitors lose their freedom to compete. Price is higher and

sion rights in a cooperative fashion could run afoul of the Sherman Act, and in particular reflects its awareness of the decision in United States v. National Football League, 116 F.Supp. 319 (E.D.Pa.1953), which held that an agreement between the teams of the National Football League that each team would not permit stations within 75 miles of the home city of another team to telecast its games on a day when that team was playing at home violated § 1 of the Sherman Act. . . .

50. "It is clear from the evidence that were it not for the NCAA controls, many more college football games would be televised. This is particularly true at the local level. Because of NCAA controls, local stations are often unable to televise games which they would like to, even when the games are not being televised at the network level. The circumstances which would allow so-called exception telecasts arise infrequently for many schools, and the evidence is clear that local broadcasts of college football would occur far more frequently were it not for the NCAA controls. This is not a surprising result. Indeed, this horizontal agreement to limit the availability of games to potential broadcasters is the very essence of NCAA's agreements with the networks. The evidence establishes the fact that the networks are actually paying the large fees because the NCAA agrees to limit production. If the NCAA would not agree to limit production, the networks would not pay so large a fee. Because NCAA limits production, the networks need not fear that their broadcasts will have to compete head-to-head with other college football telecasts, either on the other networks or on various local stations. Therefore, the Court concludes that the membership of NCAA has agreed to limit production to a level far below that which would occur in a free market situation." 546 F.Supp., at 1294.

51. Turning to the price paid for the product, it is clear that the NCAA controls utterly destroy free market competition. NCAA has commandeered the rights of its members and sold those rights for a sum certain. In so doing, it has fixed the minimum, maximum and actual price which will be paid to the schools appearing on ABC, CBS and TBS. NCAA has created the mechanism which produces a uniform price for each national telecast, and a uniform price for each regional telecast. Because of the NCAA controls, the price which is paid for the right to televise any particular game is responsive neither to the relative quality of the teams playing the game nor to viewer preference.

"In a competitive market, each college fielding a football team would be free to sell the right to televise its games for whatever price it could get. The prices would vary for the games, with games between prominent schools drawing a larger price than games between less prominent schools. Games between the more prominent schools would draw a larger audience than other games. Advertisers would pay higher rates for commercial time because of the larger audience. The telecaster would then be willing to pay larger rights fees due to the increased prices paid by the advertisers. Thus, the price which the telecaster would pay for a particular game would be dependent on the expected size of the viewing audience. Clearly, the NCAA controls grossly distort the prices actually paid for an individual game from that to be expected in a free market." 546 F.Supp., at 1318.

52. Since, as the District Court found, NCAA approval is necessary for any institution that wishes to compete in intercollegiate sports, the NCAA has a potent tool at its disposal for restraining institutions which require its approval. See Silver v. New York

output lower than they would otherwise be, and both are unresponsive to consumer preference.[53] This latter point is perhaps the most significant, since "Congress designed the Sherman Act as a 'consumer welfare prescription.'" Reiter v. Sonotone Corp., 442 U.S. 330, 343 (1979). A restraint that has the effect of reducing the importance of consumer preference in setting price and output is not consistent with this fundamental goal of antitrust law.[54] Restrictions on price and output are the paradigmatic examples of restraints of trade that the Sherman Act was intended to prohibit. See Standard Oil Co. v. United States, 221 U.S. 1, 52–60 (1911). At the same time, the television plan eliminates competitors from the market, since only those broadcasters able to bid on television rights covering the entire NCAA can compete.[55] Thus, as the District Court found, many telecasts that would occur in a competitive market are foreclosed by the NCAA's plan.

Petitioner argues, however, that its television plan can have no significant anticompetitive effect since the record indicates that it has no market power—no ability to alter the interaction of supply and demand in the market.[56] We must reject this argument for two reasons—one legal, one factual.

Stock Exchange, 373 U.S. 341, 347–349 and n. 5 (1963); Associated Press v. United States, 326 U.S. 1, 17–18 (1945).

53. In this case the rule is violated by a price restraint that tends to provide the same economic rewards to all practitioners regardless of their skill, their experience, their training, or their willingness to employ innovative and difficult procedures. Arizona v. Maricopa County Medical Society, 457 U.S. 332, 348 (1982). The District Court provided a vivid example of this system in practice:

"A clear example of the failure of the rights fees paid to respond to market forces occurred in the fall of 1981. On one weekend of that year, Oklahoma was scheduled to play a football game with the University of Southern California. Both Oklahoma and USC have long had outstanding football programs, and indeed, both teams were ranked among the top five teams in the country by the wire service polls. ABC chose to televise the game along with several others on a regional basis. A game between two schools which are not well-known for their football programs, Citadel and Appalachian State, was carried on four of ABC's local affiliated stations. The USC–Oklahoma contest was carried on over 200 stations. Yet, incredibly, all four of these teams received exactly the same amount of

money for the right to televise their games." 546 F.Supp., at 1291.

54. As the District Court observed:

"Perhaps the most pernicious aspect is that under the controls, the market is not responsive to viewer preference. Every witness who testified on the matter confirmed that the consumers, the viewers of college football television, receive absolutely no benefit from the controls. Many games for which there is a large viewer demand are kept from the viewers, and many games for which there is little if any demand are nonetheless televised." 546 F.Supp., at 1319.

55. The impact on competitors is thus analogous to the effect of block booking in the motion picture industry that we concluded violated the Sherman Act.

"In the first place, they eliminate the possibility of bidding for films theater by theater. In that way they eliminate the opportunity for the small competitor to obtain the choice first runs, and put a premium on the size of the circuit." United States v. Paramount Pictures, Inc., 334 U.S. 131, 154 (1948).

56. Market power is the ability to raise prices above those that would be charged in a competitive market. Jefferson Parish Hosp.

As a matter of law, the absence of proof of market power does not justify a naked restriction on price or output. To the contrary, when there is an agreement not to compete in terms of price or output, "no elaborate industry analysis is required to demonstrate the anticompetitive character of such an agreement." *Professional Engineers*, 435 U.S., at 692.[57] Petitioner does not quarrel with the District Court's finding that price and output are not responsive to demand. Thus the plan is inconsistent with the Sherman Act's command that price and supply be responsive to consumer preference.[58] We have never required proof of market power in such a case.[59] This naked restraint on price and output requires some competitive justification even in the absence of a detailed market analysis.[60]

Dist. No. 2 v. Hyde, 466 U.S. 2, 27 n. 46 (1984); United States Steel Corp. v. Fortner Enterprises, 429 U.S. 610, 620 (1977); United States v. E.I. Du Pont de Nemours & Co., 351 U.S. 377, 391 (1956).

57. "The fact that a practice is not categorically unlawful in all or most of its manifestations certainly does not mean that it is universally lawful. For example, joint buying or selling arrangements are not unlawful *per se*, but a court would not hesitate in enjoining a domestic selling arrangement by which, say, Ford and General Motors distributed their automobiles nationally through a single selling agent. Even without a trial, the judge will know that these two large firms are major factors in the automobile market, that such joint selling would eliminate important price competition between them, that they are quite substantial enough to distribute their products independently, and that one can hardly imagine a pro-competitive justification actually probable in fact or strong enough in principle to make this particular joint selling arrangement 'reasonable' under Sherman Act § 1. The essential point is that the rule of reason can sometimes be applied in the twinkling of an eye." P. Areeda, The "Rule of Reason" in Antitrust Analysis: General Issues 37–38 (Federal Judicial Center June 1981) (parenthetical omitted).

58. Moreover, because under the plan member institutions may not compete in terms of price and output, it is manifest that significant forms of competition are eliminated. See Catalano, Inc. v. Target Sales, Inc., 446 U.S. 643, 648–649 (1980) (per curiam); Professional Engineers, 435 U.S., at 692–695; Paramount Famous Lasky Corp. v. United States, 282 U.S. 30, 43–44 (1930).

59. See United States v. McKesson & Robbins, Inc., 351 U.S. 305, 309–310 (1956); United States v. Socony–Vacuum Oil Co., 310 U.S. 150, 221 (1940). See also Klor's, Inc. v. Broadway–Hale Stores, Inc., 359 U.S. 207, 213 (1959).

60. The Solicitor General correctly observes:

"There was no need for the respondents to establish monopoly power in any precisely defined market for television programming in order to prove the restraint unreasonable. Both lower courts found not only that NCAA has power over the market for intercollegiate sports, but also that in the market for television programming—no matter how broadly or narrowly the market is defined—the NCAA television restrictions have reduced output, subverted viewer choice, and distorted pricing. Consequently, unless the controls have some countervailing procompetitive justification, they should be deemed unlawful regardless of whether petitioner has substantial market power over advertising dollars. While the 'reasonableness' of a particular alleged restraint often depends on the market power of the parties involved, because a judgment about market power is the means by which the effects of the conduct on the market place can be assessed, market power is only one test of 'reasonableness.' And where the anticompetitive effects of conduct can be ascertained through means short of extensive market analysis, and where no countervailing competitive virtues are evident, a lengthy analysis of market power is not necessary." Brief for United States as Amicus Curiae 19–20 (footnote and citation omitted).

As a factual matter, it is evident that petitioner does possess market power. The District Court employed the correct test for determining whether college football broadcasts constitute a separate market—whether there are other products that are reasonably substitutable for televised NCAA football games.[61] Petitioner's argument that it cannot obtain supra-competitive prices from broadcasters since advertisers, and hence broadcasters, can switch from college football to other types of programming simply ignores the findings of the District Court. It found that intercollegiate football telecasts generate an audience uniquely attractive to advertisers and that competitors are unable to offer programming that can attract a similar audience.[62] These findings amply support its conclusion that the NCAA possesses market power. Indeed, the District Court's subsidiary finding that advertisers will pay a premium price per viewer to reach audiences watching college football because of their demographic characteristics is vivid evidence of the uniqueness of this product.[63] Moreover, the District Court's market analysis is firmly supported by our decision in International Boxing Club v. United States, 358 U.S. 242 (1958), that championship boxing events are uniquely attractive to fans[64] and hence constitute a market separate from that for non-championship events.[65] Thus, respondents have demonstrated that there is a separate market for telecasts of college football which "rest[s] on generic qualities differentiating" viewers. Times–Picayune Publishing Co. v. United States, 345 U.S. 594, 613 (1953). It inexorably follows that if college football broadcasts be defined as a separate market—and we are convinced they are—then the NCAA's complete control over those broadcasts provides a solid basis for the District Court's conclusion that the NCAA possesses market power with respect to those broadcasts. "When a product is controlled by one interest, without substitutes available in the market, there is monopoly

---

61. *See, e.g.*, United States v. Grinnell Corp., 384 U.S. 563, 571 (1966); United States v. E.I. Du Pont de Nemours & Co., 351 U.S. 377, 394–395 (1956); Times–Picayune Publishing Co. v. United States, 345 U.S. 594, 612, n. 31 (1953).

62. See 546 F.Supp. at 1297–1300. See also Hochberg & Horowitz, Broadcasting and CATV: The Beauty and the Bane of Major College Football. Law & Contemp. Probs., Winter–Spring 1973, at 118–120.

63. As the District Court observed, 546 F.Supp., at 1297, the most analogous programming in terms of the demographic characteristics of its audience is professional football, and as a condition of its limited exemption from the antitrust laws the professional football leagues are prohibited from telecasting games at times that conflict with intercollegiate football. See 15 U.S.C. § 1293.

64. We approved of the District Court's reliance on the greater revenue-producing potential and higher television ratings of championship events as opposed to other events to support its market definition. See 358 U.S., at 250–251.

65. For the same reasons, it is also apparent that the unique appeal of NCAA football telecasts for viewers means that "from the standpoint of the consumer—whose interests the statute was especially intended to serve," Jefferson Parish Hosp. Dist. No. 2 v. Hyde, 466 U.S. 2, 15 (1984), there can be no doubt that college football constitutes a separate market for which there is no reasonable substitute. Thus we agree with the District Court that it makes no difference whether the market is defined from the standpoint of broadcasters, advertisers, or viewers.

power." United States v. E.I. Du Pont de Nemours & Co., 351 U.S., 377, 394 (1956).

Thus, the NCAA television plan on its face constitutes a restraint upon the operation of a free market, and the findings of the District Court establish that it has operated to raise price and reduce output. Under the Rule of Reason, these hallmarks of anticompetitive behavior place upon petitioner a heavy burden of establishing an affirmative defense which competitively justifies this apparent deviation from the operations of a free market. See *Professional Engineers,* 435 U.S., at 692–696. We turn now to the NCAA's proffered justifications.

IV

Relying on *Broadcast Music,* petitioner argues that its television plan constitutes a cooperative "joint venture" which assists in the marketing of broadcast rights and hence is procompetitive. While joint ventures have no immunity from the antitrust laws, as *Broadcast Music* indicates, a joint selling arrangement may "mak[e] possible a new product by reaping otherwise unattainable efficiencies." Arizona v. Maricopa County Medical Society, 457 U.S. 332, 365 (1982) (Powell, J., dissenting) (footnote omitted). The essential contribution made by the NCAA's arrangement is to define the number of games that may be televised, to establish the price for each exposure, and to define the basic terms of each contract between the network and a home team. The NCAA does not, however, act as a selling agent for any school or for any conference of schools. The selection of individual games, and the negotiation of particular agreements, is a matter left to the networks and the individual schools. Thus, the effect of the network plan is not to eliminate individual sales of broadcasts, since these still occur, albeit subject to fixed prices and output limitations. Unlike *Broadcast Music's* blanket license covering broadcast rights to a large number of individual compositions, here the same rights are still sold on an individual basis, only in a noncompetitive market.

The District Court did not find that the NCAA's television plan produced any procompetitive efficiencies which enhanced the competitiveness of college football television rights; to the contrary it concluded that NCAA football could be marketed just as effectively without the television plan. There is therefore no predicate in the findings for petitioner's efficiency justification. Indeed, petitioner's argument is refuted by the District Court's finding concerning price and output. If the NCAA's television plan produced procompetitive efficiencies, the plan would increase output and reduce the price of televised games. The District Court's contrary findings accordingly undermine petitioner's position. In light of these findings, it cannot be said that "the agreement on price is necessary to market the product at all." *Broadcast Music,* 441 U.S., at 23.[66] In

66. Compare 546 F.Supp., at 1307–1308 ("The colleges are clearly able to negotiate agreements with whatever broadcasters they choose. We are not dealing with tens of thousands of relatively brief musical works, but with three-hour football games played eleven times each year.") with Broadcast Music, 441 U.S., at 22–23 (footnotes omitted) ("[T]o the

Broadcast Music, the availability of a package product that no individual could offer enhanced the total volume of music that was sold. Unlike this case, there was no limit of any kind placed on the volume that might be sold in the entire market and each individual remained free to sell his own music without restraint. Here production has been limited, not enhanced.[67] No individual school is free to televise its own games without restraint. The NCAA's efficiency justification is not supported by the record.

Neither is the NCAA's television plan necessary to enable the NCAA to penetrate the market through an attractive package sale. Since broadcasting rights to college football constitute a unique product for which there is no ready substitute, there is no need for collective action in order to enable the product to compete against its nonexistent competitors.[68] This is borne out by the District Court's finding that the NCAA's television *reduces* the volume of television rights sold.

V

Throughout the history of its regulation of intercollegiate football telecasts, the NCAA has indicated its concern with protecting live attendance. This concern, it should be noted, is not with protecting live attendance at games which *are* shown on television; that type of interest is not at issue in this case. Rather, the concern is that fan interest in a televised game may adversely affect ticket sales for games that will not appear on television.[69]

Although the NORC studies in the 1950's provided some support for the thesis that live attendance would suffer if unlimited television were permitted,[70] the District Court found that there was no evidence to support

extent the blanket license is a different product, ASCAP is not really a joint sales agency offering the individual goods of many sellers, but is a separate seller offering its blanket license, of which the individual compositions are raw material. ASCAP, in short, made a market in which individual composers are inherently unable to compete fully effectively.").

67. Ensuring that individual members of a joint venture are free to increase output has been viewed as central in evaluating the competitive character of joint ventures. See Brodley, Joint Ventures and Antitrust Policy, 95 Harv.L.Rev. 1523, 1550–1552, 1555–1560 (1982). See also Note, United Charities and the Sherman Act, 91 Yale L.J. 1593 (1982).

68. If the NCAA faced "interbrand" competition from available substitutes, then certain forms of collective action might be appropriate in order to enhance its ability to compete. See Continental T.V., Inc., 433 U.S., at 54–57. Our conclusion concerning the availability of substitutes in Part III, supra,

forecloses such a justification in this case, however.

69. The NCAA's plan is not even arguably related to a desire to protect live attendance by ensuring that a game is not televised in the area where it is to be played. No cooperative action is necessary for that kind of "blackout." The home team can always refuse to sell the right to telecast its game to stations in the immediate area. The NCAA does not now and never has justified its television plan by an interest in assisting schools in "blacking out" their home games in the areas in which they are played.

70. During this period, the NCAA also expressed its concern to Congress in urging it to limit the antitrust exemption professional football obtained for telecasting its games to contests not held on Friday or Saturday when such telecasts might interfere with attendance at intercollegiate games. See H.R.Rep. No. 1178, 87th Cong., 1st Sess., 3–4 (1961); 107 Cong.Rec. 20060–20061 (1961) (remarks

that theory in today's market. Moreover, as the District Court found, the television plan has evolved in a manner inconsistent with its original design to protect gate attendance. Under the current plan, games are shown on television during all hours that college football games are played. The plan simply does not protect live attendance by ensuring that games will not be shown on television at the same time as live events.[71]

There is, however, a more fundamental reason for rejecting this defense. The NCAA's argument that its television plan is necessary to protect live attendance is not based on a desire to maintain the integrity of college football as a distinct and attractive product, but rather on a fear that the product will not prove sufficiently attractive to draw live attendance when faced with competition from televised games. At bottom the NCAA's position is that ticket sales for most college games are unable to compete in a free market.[72] The television plan protects ticket sales by limiting output—just as any monopolist increases revenues by reducing output. By seeking to insulate live ticket sales from the full spectrum of competition because of its assumption that the product itself is insufficiently attractive to consumers, petitioner forwards a justification that is inconsistent with the basic policy of the Sherman Act. "[T]he Rule of Reason does not support a defense based on the assumption that competition itself is unreasonable." *Professional Engineers*, 435 U.S., at 696.

VI

Petitioner argues that the interest in maintaining a competitive balance among amateur athletic teams is legitimate and important and that it justifies the regulations challenged in this case. We agree with the first part of the argument but not the second.

Our decision not to apply a *per se* rule to this case rests in large part on our recognition that a certain degree of cooperation is necessary if the type of competition that petitioner and its member institutions seek to market is to be preserved. It is reasonable to assume that most of the regulatory controls of the NCAA are justifiable means of fostering competition among amateur athletic teams and therefore procompetitive because they enhance

---

of Rep. Celler); id., at 20062; Hearings, supra n. 28, at 66–68 (statement of William R. Reed). The provision enacted as a result is now found in 15 U.S.C. § 1293.

71. "[T]he greatest flaw in the NCAA's argument is that it is manifest that the new plan for football television does not limit televised football in order to protect gate attendance. The evidence shows that under the new plan, many areas of the country will have access to nine hours of college football television on several Saturdays in the coming season. Because the 'ground rules' eliminate head-to-head programming, a full nine hours of college football will have to be shown on television during a nine-to-twelve hour period

on almost every Saturday of the football season in most of the major television markets in the country. It can hardly be said that such a plan is devised in order to protect gate attendance." 546 F.Supp., at 1296.

72. Ironically, to the extent that the NCAA's position has merit, it rests on the assumption that football telecasts are a unique product. If, as the NCAA argues, all television programming is essentially fungible, it would not be possible to protect attendance without banning all television during the hours at which intercollegiate football games are held.

public interest in intercollegiate athletics. The specific restraints on football telecasts that are challenged in this case do not, however, fit into the same mold as do rules defining the conditions of the contest, the eligibility of participants, or the manner in which members of a joint enterprise shall share the responsibilities and the benefits of the total venture.

The NCAA does not claim that its television plan has equalized or is intended to equalize competition within any one league.[73] The plan is nationwide in scope and there is no single league or tournament in which all college football teams compete. There is no evidence of any intent to equalize the strength of teams in Division I–A with those in Division II or Division III, and not even a colorable basis for giving colleges that have no football program at all a voice in the management of the revenues generated by the football programs at other schools.[74] The interest in maintaining a competitive balance that is asserted by the NCAA as a justification for regulating all television of intercollegiate football is not related to any neutral standard or to any readily identifiable group of competitors.

The television plan is not even arguably tailored to serve such an interest. It does not regulate the amount of money that any college may spend on its football program, nor the way in which the colleges may use the revenues that are generated by their football programs, whether derived from the sale of television rights, the sale of tickets, or the sale of concessions or program advertising.[75] The plan simply imposes a restriction on one source of revenue that is more important to some colleges than to others. There is no evidence that this restriction produces any greater

---

73. It seems unlikely, for example, that there would have been a greater disparity between the football prowess of Ohio State University and that of Northwestern University in recent years without the NCAA's television plan. The District Court found that in fact the NCAA has been strikingly unsuccessful if it has indeed attempted to prevent the emergence of a "power elite" in intercollegiate football. See 546 F.Supp., at 1310–1311. Moreover, the District Court's finding that there would be more local and regional telecasts without the NCAA controls means that Northwestern could well have generated more television income in a free market than was obtained under the NCAA regime.

74. Indeed, the District Court found that the basic reason the television plan has endured is that the NCAA is in effect controlled by schools that are not restrained by the plan:

"The plaintiffs and other CFA members attempted to persuade the majority of NCAA members that NCAA had gone far beyond its legitimate role in football television. Not surprisingly, none of the CFA proposals were adopted. Instead the membership uniformly adopted the proposals of the NCAA administration which 'legitimized' NCAA's exercises of power. The result was not surprising in light of the makeup of the voting membership. Of approximately 800 voting members of the NCAA, 500 or so are in Divisions II and III and are not subjected to NCAA television controls. Of the 275 Division I members, only 187 play football, and only 135 were members of Division I–A at the time of the January Convention. Division I–A was made up of the most prominent football-playing schools, and those schools account for most of the football games shown on network television. Therefore, of some 850 voting members, less than 150 suffer any direct restriction on their right to sell football games to television." 546 F.Supp., at 1317.

75. Moreover, the District Court found that those schools which would realize increased revenues in a free market would not funnel those revenues into their football programs. See 546 F.Supp., at 1310.

measure of equality throughout the NCAA than would a restriction on alumni donations, tuition rates, or any other revenue producing activity. At the same time, as the District Court found, the NCAA imposes a variety of other restrictions designed to preserve amateurism which are much better tailored to the goal of competitive balance than is the television plan, and which are "clearly sufficient" to preserve competitive balance to the extent it is within the NCAA's power to do so. And much more than speculation supported the District Court's findings on this score. No other NCAA sport employs a similar plan, and in particular the court found that in the most closely analogous sport, college basketball, competitive balance has been maintained without resort to a restrictive television plan.

Perhaps the most important reason for rejecting the argument that the interest in competitive balance is served by the television plan is the District Court's unambiguous and well supported finding that many more games would be televised in a free market than under the NCAA plan. The hypothesis that legitimates the maintenance of competitive balance as a procompetitive justification under the Rule of Reason is that equal competition will maximize consumer demand for the product. The finding that consumption will materially increase if the controls are removed is a compelling demonstration that they do not in fact serve any such legitimate purpose.[76]

VII

The NCAA plays a critical role in the maintenance of a revered tradition of amateurism in college sports. There can be no question but that it needs ample latitude to play that role, or that the preservation of the student-athlete in higher education adds richness and diversity to intercollegiate athletics and is entirely consistent with the goals of the Sherman Act. But consistent with the Sherman Act, the role of the NCAA must be to *preserve* a tradition that might otherwise die; rules that restrict output are hardly consistent with this role. Today we hold only that the record supports the District Court's conclusion that by curtailing output and blunting the ability of member institutions to respond to consumer preference, the NCAA has restricted rather than enhanced the place of intercollegiate athletics in the Nation's life. Accordingly, the judgment of the Court of Appeals is affirmed.

■ WHITE, J., with whom REHNQUIST, J., joined, dissented. The dissenters agreed with the majority that the NCAA television plan should be viewed under a rule of reason rather than a *per se* approach, emphasizing to a greater extent than the majority that the plan was "non-commercial" in character. They concluded, however, that the plan should have been declared legal under a rule of reason. They noted that there were many

76. This is true not only for television viewers, but also for athletes. The District Court's finding that the television exposure of all schools would increase in the absence of the NCAA's television plan means that smaller institutions appealing to essentially local or regional markets would get more exposure if the plan is enjoined, enhancing their ability to compete for student athletes.

NCAA enforced rules limiting competition—for example, rules restricting compensation of student athletes, restricting the number of athletic scholarships that may be awarded, and establishing minimum academic standards—which would be condemned as anticompetitive in a more traditional business setting. The NCAA plan was reasonable in their view because (1) college football should be viewed as part of a broad entertainment market and hence collective action was an appropriate procompetitive response to existing competition, and (2) it was reasonably ancillary to the legitimate non-economic goal of fostering amateurism "by spreading revenues among various schools and reducing the financial incentives towards professionalism."

NOTES AND QUESTIONS

1. Are the Supreme Court decisions in *BMI* and *NCAA* reconcilable? On what theory? Can the decisions be aligned on the basis of differences in market share, nature and extent of efficiencies, or presence or absence of actual integration of resources? Are there other factors that the Court might have taken into account? How would you formulate the *"per se* rule" of *Socony Vacuum* in light of these more recent decisions?

2. What exactly was the role of the NCAA in negotiating with the networks on behalf of colleges? Did the NCAA negotiate actual fees with the various networks, or did it simply establish parameters within which the colleges and networks could bargain? If individual bargaining still had to occur, then what "efficiencies" were generated as a result of the NCAA contract?

United States v. Brown University

United States Court of Appeals, Third Circuit, 1993.
5 F.3d 658.

[In 1958, MIT and eight Ivy League schools formed the "Ivy Overlap Group" to collectively determine the amount of financial assistance to be awarded to students who had been admitted to more than one of the schools. The Overlap Group agreed that each school would award financial aid only on the basis of demonstrated need. To ensure that aid packages would be comparable, the Overlap Group agreed to share financial information concerning admitted students and to jointly develop and apply a "uniform needs analysis" for assessing family contributions.

Although each school employed the same analysis to compute need, "discrepancies" arose. To eliminate these discrepancies, Overlap Group members would meet in early April each year to jointly determine the amount of "family contribution" (*i.e.*, in determining need) for each commonly admitted student. In 1991, the Antitrust Division brought this civil action against MIT and the eight Ivy League schools.]

■ COWEN, J ... [The Antitrust Division] brought this civil suit alleging that the Ivy Overlap Group unlawfully conspired to restrain trade in violation of section one of the Sherman Act by (1) agreeing to award financial aid exclusively on the basis of need; (2) agreeing to utilize a common formula to calculate need; and (3) collectively setting, with only insignificant discrepancies, each commonly admitted students' family contribution toward the price of tuition. The Division sought only injunctive relief. All of the Ivy League institutions signed a consent decree with the United States, and only MIT proceeded to trial. After a ten-day bench trial, the district court held that the Ivy Overlap Group's conduct constituted "trade or commerce" under section one of the Sherman Act. Rejecting MIT's argument that financial aid is pure charity and thus exempt from the dictates of the Sherman Act, the district court characterized the Overlap Agreement as setting a selective discount off the price of educational services.

The district court found that the Overlap Agreement constituted price fixing. Due to the nonprofit status and educational mission of the alleged conspirators, however, the court declined to apply the *per se* rule of illegality that summarily invalidates most horizontal price fixing agreements. Because the conflicting and complex expert testimony left the court unsure that the economic effect of Overlap could be accurately measured, it assumed without deciding MIT's premise that the Overlap Agreement was revenue neutral, *i.e.,* did not increase or decrease the *average* tuition payment made by students. Nevertheless, the court was quick to point out that assuming the fact of revenue neutrality, without more, offers no insight into any alleged procompetitive virtue of a restraint. Hence, despite this assumption of revenue neutrality, the court found the Agreement plainly anticompetitive because it eliminated price competition for outstanding students among the participating schools. Because the harm was tampering with free market forces, the court deemed it irrelevant whether the total amount of tuition payments collected from all students increased, decreased or remained the same.

Faced with what it believed was a plainly anticompetitive agreement, the district court applied an abbreviated version of the rule of reason and took only a "quick look" to determine if MIT presented any plausible procompetitive affirmative defenses that justified the Overlap Agreement. MIT argued that Overlap widened the pool of applicants to Overlap institutions by providing needy students with the ability to enroll if accepted. This, MIT asserted, increased consumer choice and enhanced the quality of the education provided to all students by opening the doors of the most elite colleges in the nation to diversely gifted students of varied socioeconomic backgrounds. The district court deemed these explanations to be social welfare justifications and flatly rejected the contention that the elimination of competition may be justified by non-economic considerations . . .

As a threshold matter, we must decide whether section one of the Sherman Act applies to the challenged conduct—MIT's agreement with the other Overlap institutions to award financial aid only to needy students and to set the amount of family contribution from commonly admitted students. Section one, by its terms, does not apply to all conspiracies, but only to those which restrain "trade or commerce." 15 U.S.C. § 1. MIT characterizes its conduct as disbursing charitable funds to achieve the twin objectives of advancing equality of access to higher education and promoting socio-economic and racial diversity within the nation's most elite universities. This alleged pure charity, MIT argues, does not implicate trade or commerce, and is thus exempt from antitrust scrutiny.

It is axiomatic that section one of the Sherman Act regulates only transactions that are commercial in nature. Congress, however, intended this statute to embrace the widest array of conduct possible. Goldfarb v. Virginia State Bar, 421 U.S. 773, 787–88 (1975). Section one's scope thus reaches the activities of nonprofit organizations, including institutions of higher learning. NCAA v. Board of Regents of the Univ. of Oklahoma, 468 U.S. 85, 100 n. 22 (1984) ("There is no doubt that the sweeping language of § 1 applies to non-profit entities.")....

Although nonprofit organizations are not entitled to a class exemption from the Sherman Act, when they perform acts that are the antithesis of commercial activity, they are immune from antitrust regulation. Cf. Apex Hosiery Co. v. Leader, 310 U.S. 469 (1940) (labor union strike does not implicate commerce under Sherman Act); National Org. For Women, Inc. v. Scheidler, 968 F.2d 612 (7th Cir.1992) (violent pro-life protests that successfully closed abortion clinics do not implicate commerce), *cert. granted in part,* 113 S.Ct. 2958 (1993). This immunity, however, is narrowly circumscribed. It does not extend to commercial transactions with a "public-service aspect." *Goldfarb,* 421 U.S. at 787–88. Courts classify a transaction as commercial or noncommercial based on the nature of the conduct in light of the totality of surrounding circumstances.

The exchange of money for services, even by a nonprofit organization, is a quintessential commercial transaction. Therefore, the payment of tuition in return for educational services constitutes commerce. MIT concedes as much by acknowledging that its determination of the full tuition amount is a commercial decision.

We thus come to the crux of the issue—is providing financial assistance solely to needy students a selective reduction or "discount" from the full tuition amount, or a charitable gift? If this financial aid is a component of the process of setting tuition prices, it is commerce. See Catalano, Inc. v. Target Sales, Inc., 446 U.S. 643, 648 (1980) (agreement to eliminate discounts violates section one). If it is pure charity, it is not.[77]

When MIT admits an affluent student, that student must pay approximately $25,000 annually (tuition plus room, board, and incidental expenses) if he or she wishes to enroll at MIT. If MIT accepts a needy student and calculates that it will extend $10,000 in financial aid to that student, the student must pay approximately $15,000 to attend MIT. The student

---

77. The district court commenced its analysis by noting that MIT is a significant economic entity, controlling substantial assets and operating a billion dollar budget. We agree with MIT that the extent of its resources is not probative of whether its financial aid is commerce.

certainly is not free to take the $10,000 and apply it toward attendance at a different college. The assistance package is only available in conjunction with a complemented payment of approximately $15,000 to MIT. The amount of financial aid not only impacts, but directly determines the amount that a needy student must pay to receive an education at MIT. The financial aid, therefore, is part of the commercial process of setting tuition.

MIT suggests that providing aid exclusively to needy students and setting the amount of that aid is not commercial because the price needy students are charged is substantially below the marginal cost of supplying a year of education to an undergraduate student. Because profit maximizing companies would not engage in such economically abnormal behavior, MIT concludes that such activity must be noncommercial. MIT's concession, however, that setting the full tuition amount is a commercial decision subject to antitrust scrutiny undermines this argument. The full tuition figure, like the varying amounts charged to needy students, is significantly below MIT's marginal cost. Therefore, whether the price charged for educational services is below marginal cost is not probative of the commercial or noncommercial nature of the methodology utilized to determine financial aid packages.

The fact that MIT is not obligated to provide any financial aid does not transform that aid to charity. Similarly, discounting the price of educational services for needy students is not charity when a university receives tangible benefits in exchange. Regardless of whether MIT's motive is altruism, self-enhancement or a combination of the two,[78] MIT benefits from providing financial aid. MIT admits that it competes with other Overlap members for outstanding students. By distributing aid, MIT en-

78. The district court did not make a factual finding with respect to MIT's motivation for joining the Overlap Agreement. There is ample evidence that MIT's indirect objective was to promote equal access to higher education and diversity within the student body. We cannot overlook, however, that MIT also desired to attract the most talented students at the least expense to itself, a result which would also flow directly from the elimination of price competition among the Ivy Overlap member institutions. In fact, we could conjecture a number of self-serving reasons why MIT might have entered the Overlap Agreement, not the least of which might have been the market power which typically accompanies combinations. The higher than competitive tuition prices which MIT and the other Overlap members were able to charge, absent tuition competition, enhances "revenues," if not "profits," which can be allocated to any conceivable internal institutional purpose.

In any event, to determine whether trade or commerce is implicated, motive plays a much less important role when the nature of the activity, as here, is plainly commercial. An anticompetitive motive may trigger antitrust scrutiny of otherwise noncommercial conduct. See Marjorie Webster Junior College, Inc. v. Middle States Ass'n of Colleges and Secondary Schools, Inc., 423 F.2d 650, 654–55 (D.C.Cir.), cert. denied, 400 U.S. 965 (1970). The opposite, however, is not also true. A beneficent objective does not excuse commercial activities from compliance with the Sherman Act. In Goldfarb, the Supreme Court held that a minimum fee schedule for attorneys published by a county bar association violated section one of the Sherman Act. 421 U.S. at 781–87. The bar association argued that the goal of professions, in contrast to businesses, "is to provide services necessary to the community." The Supreme Court discounted the significance of this purported motive, finding that motive arguments lose force when used to justify an obviously commercial endeavor.

ables exceptional students to attend its school who otherwise could not afford to attend. The resulting expansion in MIT's pool of exceptional applicants increases the quality of MIT's student body. MIT then enjoys enhanced prestige by virtue of its ability to attract a greater portion of the "cream of the crop." The Supreme Court has recognized that nonprofit organizations derive significant benefit from increased prestige and influence. See American Society of Mechanical Engineers, Inc. v. Hydrolevel Corp., 456 U.S. 556, 576 (1982). Although MIT could fill its class with students able to pay the full tuition, the caliber of its student body, and consequently the institution's reputation, obviously would suffer. Overlap affords MIT the benefit of an overrepresentation of high caliber students, with the concomitant institutional prestige, without forcing MIT to be responsive to market forces in terms of its tuition costs. By immunizing itself through the Overlap from competition for students based on a price/quality ratio, MIT achieves certain institutional benefits at a bargain. . . .

We hold that financial assistance to students is part and parcel of the process of setting tuition and thus a commercial transaction. Although MIT's status as a nonprofit educational organization and its advancement of congressionally-recognized and important social welfare goals does not remove its conduct from the realm of trade or commerce, these factors will influence whether this conduct violates the Sherman Act. . . .

In addition to the traditional rule of reason and the *per se* rule, courts sometimes apply what amounts to an abbreviated or "quick look" rule of reason analysis. The abbreviated rule of reason is an intermediate standard. It applies in cases where *per se* condemnation is inappropriate, but where "no elaborate industry analysis is required to demonstrate the anticompetitive character" of an inherently suspect restraint. See *NCAA*, 468 U.S. at 109 (quoting *Professional Engineers*, 435 U.S. at 692); *Indiana Dentists*, 476 U.S. at 459 (same). Because competitive harm is presumed, the defendant must promulgate "some competitive justification" for the restraint, "even in the absence of detailed market analysis" indicating actual profit maximization or increased costs to the consumer resulting from the restraint. . . . If the defendant offers sound procompetitive justifications, however, the court must proceed to weigh the overall reasonableness of the restraint using a full-scale rule of reason analysis.

In the present case, the district court applied the abbreviated rule of reason analysis. Emphasizing that its decision to apply this analysis did "not stem from a reluctance to characterize the Ivy Overlap process as the type of price fixing which is ordinarily *per se* unreasonable," the court nevertheless adopted the more cautious approach in deference to Supreme Court precedents counseling special scrutiny of restraints involving professional associations. Accordingly, rather than immediately condemning the Overlap because of its apparent quintessentially anticompetitive nature, the court afforded MIT an opportunity to proffer a procompetitive affirmative defense—an acknowledged "heavy burden."

MIT first claims that the district court erred by applying an abbreviated rather than a full-scale rule of reason analysis. The Division, on the other hand, argues that the district court erred by failing to declare Overlap illegal *per se.* In the alternative, the Division argues that if the *per se* rule is inapplicable, the district court correctly applied the abbreviated rule of reason. . . .

[The Supreme] Court has been . . . hesitant to condemn agreements by professional associations as unreasonable *per se,* or to apply a *per se* rejection to competitive restraints imposed in contexts where the economic impact of such practices is neither one with which the Court has dealt previously, nor immediately apparent. In *Indiana Dentists,* the Court once again reaffirmed *Goldfarb* and *Professional Engineers.* . . .

As a qualified charitable organization under 26 U.S.C. § 501(c)(3), MIT deviates even further from the profit-maximizing prototype than do professional associations. While non-profit professional associations advance the commercial interests of their for-profit constituents, MIT is, as its § 501(c)(3) status suggests, an organization "operated exclusively for . . . educational purposes . . . no part of the net earnings of which inures to the benefit of any private shareholder or individual." This does not mean, of course, that MIT and other bona fide charitable organizations lack incentives to increase revenues. Nor does it necessarily mean that commercially motivated conduct of such organizations should be immune from *per se* treatment. Like the defendant associations in *Indiana Dentists* and *Professional Engineers,* however, MIT vigorously maintains that Overlap was the product of a concern for the public interest, here the undisputed public interest in equality of educational access and opportunity, and alleges the absence of any revenue maximizing purpose.

This alleged pure altruistic motive and alleged absence of a revenue maximizing purpose contribute to our uncertainty with regard to Overlap's anticompetitiveness, and thus prompts us to give careful scrutiny to the nature of Overlap, and to refrain from declaring Overlap *per se* unreasonable. We thus agree with the district court that Overlap must be judged under the rule of reason. . . .

MIT does not dispute that the stated purpose of Overlap is to eliminate price competition for talented students among member institutions. Indeed, the intent to eliminate price competition among the Overlap schools for commonly admitted students appears on the face of the Agreement itself. In addition to agreeing to offer financial aid solely on the basis of need and to develop a common system of needs analysis, the Overlap members agreed to meet each spring to compare data and to conform one another's aid packages to the greatest possible extent. Because the Overlap Agreement aims to restrain "competitive bidding" and deprive prospective students of "the ability to utilize and compare prices" in selecting among schools, it is anticompetitive "on its face." *Professional Engineers,* 435 U.S. at 693. Price is "the central nervous system of the economy," *Socony–Vacuum Oil,* 310 U.S. at 224 n. 59, and "[t]he heart of our national economic policy long has been faith in the value of competition," *Standard*

Oil Co. v. FTC, 340 U.S. 231, 248 (1951). We therefore agree that Overlap initially "requires some competitive justification even in the absence of a detailed market analysis." *Indiana Dentists,* 476 U.S. at 460 (quoting *NCAA,* 468 U.S. at 109–10); see *Professional Engineers,* 435 U.S. at 695.

MIT's principal counterargument is that an abbreviated rule of reason analysis is appropriate only where economic harm to consumers may fairly be presumed; and such harm may be presumed only when evidence establishes that "the challenged practice, unlike Overlap, manifestly has an adverse effect on price, output, or quality." As the Division aptly points out, however, if an abbreviated rule of reason analysis always required a clear evidentiary showing of a detrimental effect on price, output, or quality, it would no longer be abbreviated.... This is because proof of actual adverse effects generally will require the elaborate, threshold industry analysis that an abbreviated inquiry is designed to obviate.

MIT's position also is contradicted by Supreme Court precedent. Without any mention of actual effects on price, output, or quality, the Court in *Professional Engineers* required the association of engineers to affirmatively defend an ethics rule prohibiting members from discussing fees with prospective customers prior to being selected for a project. 435 U.S. at 692–96. The Court reasoned that the "anticompetitive character" of the agreement could be presumed because the ban on competitive bidding, like price fixing, "impede[d] the ordinary give and take of the market place." ...

MIT claims that even if the district court properly decided to apply an abbreviated rule of reason analysis, the court applied it incorrectly by failing to adequately consider the economic and social welfare justifications proffered by MIT. We will address MIT's claims with respect to economic and social welfare justifications separately.

At trial, MIT maintained that Overlap had the following procompetitive effects: (1) it improved the quality of the educational program at the Overlap schools; (2) it increased consumer choice by making an Overlap education more accessible to a greater number of students; and (3) it promoted competition for students among Overlap schools in areas other than price. The district court rejected each of these alleged competitive virtues, summarily concluding that they amounted to no more than noneconomic social welfare justifications....

MIT next claims that beyond ignoring the procompetitive effects of Overlap, the district court erroneously refused to consider compelling social welfare justifications. MIT argues that by enabling member schools to maintain a steadfast policy of need—blind admissions and full need-based aid, Overlap promoted the social ideal of equality of educational access and opportunity....

Both the public safety justification rejected by the Supreme Court in *Professional Engineers* and the public health justification rejected by the Court in *Indiana Dentists* were based on the defendants' faulty premise that consumer choices made under competitive market conditions are "unwise" or "dangerous." Here MIT argues that participation in the

Overlap arrangement provided some consumers, the needy, with additional choices which an entirely free market would deny them. The facts and arguments before us may suggest some significant areas of distinction from those in *Professional Engineers* and *Indiana Dentists* in that MIT is asserting that Overlap not only serves a social benefit, but actually enhances consumer choice. Overlap is not an attempt to withhold a particular desirable service from customers, as was the professional combination in *Indiana Dentists,* but rather it purports only to seek to extend a service to qualified students who are financially "needy" and would not otherwise be able to afford the high cost of education at MIT. Further, while Overlap resembles the ban on competitive bidding at issue in *Professional Engineers,* MIT alleges that Overlap enhances competition by broadening the socio-economic sphere of its potential student body. Thus, rather than suppress competition, Overlap may in fact merely regulate competition in order to enhance it, while also deriving certain social benefits. If the rule of reason analysis leads to this conclusion, then indeed Overlap will be beyond the scope of the prohibitions of the Sherman Act.

We note the unfortunate fact that financial aid resources are limited even at the Ivy League schools. A trade-off may need to be made between providing some financial aid to a large number of the most needy students or allowing the free market to bestow the limited financial aid on the very few most talented who may not need financial aid to attain their academic goals. Under such circumstances, if this trade-off is proven to be worthy in terms of obtaining a more diverse student body (or other legitimate institutional goals), the limitations on the choices of the most talented students might not be so egregious as to trigger the obvious concerns which led the Court to reject the "public interest" justifications in *Professional Engineers* and *Indiana Dentists.* However, we leave it for the district court to decide whether full funding of need may be continued on an individual institutional basis, absent Overlap, whether tuition could be lowered as a way to compete for qualified "needy" students, or whether there are other imaginable creative alternatives to implement MIT's professed social welfare goal.

We note too, however, that another aspect of the agreements condemned in *Professional Engineers* and *Indiana Dentists* was that those agreements embodied a strong economic self-interest of the parties to them. In *Professional Engineers,* the undisputed objective of the ban on competitive bidding was to maintain higher prices for engineering services than a free competitive market would sustain. The engineers' public safety justification "rest[ed] on the assumption that the agreement [would] tend to maintain price level; if it had no such effect, it would not serve its intended purpose." *Id.* Likewise, the Court in *Indiana Dentists* characterized the dentists' agreement to withhold x-rays as an "attempt to thwart" the goal of "choosing the least expensive adequate course of dental treatment." *Indiana Dentists,* 476 U.S. at 461. Though not singled out by the Court in these two cases, the nature of the agreements made any public interest argument greatly suspect. To the extent that economic self-interest or revenue maximization is operative in Overlap, it too renders MIT's public interest justification suspect.

The role that economic self-interest plays in evaluating affirmative defenses to a Sherman Act claim was made clear by the Court in FTC v. Superior Court Trial Lawyers Ass'n, 493 U.S. 411 (1990), where the Court condemned as *per se* illegal the trial lawyers' concerted refusal to accept further assignments to defend indigents until they receive an increase in compensation.... In the case *sub judice,* the quest for economic self-interest is professed to be absent, as it is alleged that the Overlap agreement was intended, not to obtain an economic profit in the form of greater revenue for the participating schools, but rather to benefit talented but needy prospective students who otherwise could not attend the school of their choice.

The nature of higher education, and the asserted procompetitive and pro-consumer features of the Overlap, convince us that a full rule of reason analysis is in order here. It may be that institutions of higher education "require that a particular practice, which could properly be viewed as a violation of the Sherman Act in another context, be treated differently." Goldfarb v. Virginia, 421 U.S. 773, 788 n. 17 (1975). See also Klor's Inc. v. Broadway–Hale Stores, Inc., 359 U.S. 207, 213 n. 7 (1959) ("[t]he Act is aimed primarily at combinations having commercial objectives and is applied only to a very limited extent to organizations ... which normally have other objectives").

It is most desirable that schools achieve equality of educational access and opportunity in order that more people enjoy the benefits of a worthy higher education. There is no doubt, too, that enhancing the quality of our educational system redounds to the general good. To the extent that higher education endeavors to foster vitality of the mind, to promote free exchange between bodies of thought and truths, and better communication among a broad spectrum of individuals, as well as prepares individuals for the intellectual demands of responsible citizenship, it is a common good that should be extended to as wide a range of individuals from as broad a range of socio-economic backgrounds as possible. It is with this in mind that the Overlap Agreement should be submitted to the rule of reason scrutiny under the Sherman Act.

We conclude that the district court was obliged to more fully investigate the procompetitive and noneconomic justifications proffered by MIT than it did when it performed the truncated rule of reason analysis. Accordingly, we will remand this case to the district court with instructions to evaluate Overlap using the full-scale rule of reason analysis outlined above.

The final step of the rule of reason involves determining whether the challenged agreement is necessary to achieve its purported goals. The district court alternatively rejected MIT's social welfare justifications because it "questioned" whether Overlap was necessary to achieve egalitarian educational access. Even if an anticompetitive restraint is intended to achieve a legitimate objective, the restraint only survives a rule of reason analysis if it is reasonably necessary to achieve the legitimate objectives proffered by the defendant.... To determine if a restraint is reasonably necessary, courts must examine first whether the restraint furthers the legitimate objectives, and then whether comparable benefits could be achieved through a substantially less restrictive alternative. 7 P. Areeda, supra ¶ 1505, at 388. Once a defendant demonstrates that its conduct promotes a legitimate goal, the plaintiff, in order to prevail, bears the burden of proving that there exists a viable less restrictive alternative....

The district court "questioned" whether the Overlap Agreement was "a necessary ingredient" to achieve the social welfare objectives offered by MIT. *Brown University,* 806 F.Supp. at 306. The district court implicitly concluded, and we agree, that to some extent the Overlap Agreement promoted equality of access to higher education and economic and cultural diversity. It thus turned directly to the second inquiry—whether a substantially less restrictive alternative, the free market coupled with MIT's institutional resolve, could achieve the same benefits. In a conclusory statement, the court found "no evidence supporting MIT's fatalistic prediction that the end of the Ivy Overlap Group necessarily would sound the death knell of need-blind admissions or need-based aid." Although the district court acknowledged that the end of Overlap could herald the end of full need-based aid at MIT, it also observed that this was not an inevitability if indeed MIT counted full need-based aid among its priority institutional goals.

On remand if the district court, under a full scale rule of reason analysis, finds that MIT has proffered a persuasive justification for the Overlap Agreement, then the Antitrust Division of the Justice Department, the plaintiff in this case, must prove that a reasonable less restrictive alternative exists. The district court should consider, if and when the issue arises, whether the Antitrust Division has shown, by a preponderance of the evidence, that another viable option, perhaps the free market, can achieve the same benefits as Overlap.

■ WEIS, J., dissenting. Although the century that has passed since the enactment of the Sherman Act may make reliance upon legislative history somewhat hazardous, it is a fair assumption that the drafters of the statute would have been quite astounded at the government's contention that the student aid program at issue here is covered by the antitrust laws....

Glossing over the policy articulated in this bit of legislative history, the government has rushed into discussions of economic theory using pejorative terms such as "price fixing" and illegal "discounts." But before such considerations have any relevance, a formidable threshold must be crossed in this case—the applicability of the Sherman Act to agreements on need-blind admission policies and student aid. It is premature to analyze activities in the business world that violate antitrust law until it has been established that the Sherman Act does, in fact, govern the conduct in the circumstances present here.

The challenged practices, designed to provide high quality education to those who have demonstrated academic talent without regard to their financial status, do not instinctively conjure up images of reprehensible business dealings. Quite to the contrary, the initial reaction is to question why the heavy artillery of antitrust has been wheeled into position to shoot down practices that so obviously advance the public interest.

Practices that might be illegal in the commercial area do not transform a charitable activity into a business one. To the extent that the government pursues that course, its argument is simply a non sequitur.... My view that the antitrust laws do not apply to student aid activities in the circumstances of this case is not meant to convey any opinion on the desirability or necessity of all of the Overlap procedures....

NOTES AND QUESTIONS

1. If MIT and the Ivy League schools had agreed on tuition, would the Third Circuit have applied the *per se* rule?

2. On December 22, 1993, MIT and the Department of Justice settled their litigation. The Department of Justice's press release said the following:

> Under today's settlement, MIT acknowledges that it is obliged in its dealings with the Ivy League colleges to act in accordance with a 1991 consent decree in which Brown, Columbia, Cornell, Dartmouth, Harvard, Princeton, the University of Pennsylvania, and Yale agreed not to fix tuition, faculty salaries, or the payments needy students would be expected to make on their own.

> MIT has further promised that in its dealings with other schools it will abide by standards of conduct, agreed upon today, that prohibit any discussion or agreement on the contribution expected to be made by students receiving financial aid. The standards also prohibit any discussion or agreement on the composition of financial aid packages....

> Under today's settlement, MIT may agree with other colleges on general principles for determining financial aid, to award aid solely on the basis of financial need, and to exchange limited data about applicants' financial profiles.

> In order to do this, MIT and other participating schools must commit to need-blind admissions and to meet the full financial need of their undergraduate students....

If you were in charge of the Antitrust Division, would you have agreed to the settlement? What is likely to have happened if the case had reached the Supreme Court?

3. On June 27, 1995, the Antitrust Division and the ABA "resolved charges that the ABA process for accrediting law schools had been misused to inflate faculty salaries and benefits." The Department of Justice's press release indicated that the settlement (filed in the D.C. District Court) prohibited: (i) "fixing faculty salaries;" (ii) "refusing to accredit schools simply because they are for-profit;" and (iii) "refusing to allow ABA-approved law schools to accept credits for classes at schools that are state-accredited but not ABA-approved." The settlement also established "a special committee to determine if ABA accreditation requirements in six other areas should be revised—student to faculty ratios, teaching loads, sabbaticals, bar

preparation courses, facilities, and other resources." The head of the Antitrust Division commented:

> The powerful status of the ABA does not insulate it from the antitrust laws. The Antitrust Division has sued many professional trade associations, which, like the ABA, have violated the antitrust laws. Lawyers must keep their own house in order as well.

4. In Dedication and Everlasting Love to Animals v. The Humane Society, 50 F.3d 710 (9th Cir.1995), the Ninth Circuit held that the solicitation of donations by the Humane Society was not "trade or commerce" under the Sherman Act. Do you agree?

California Dental Assn. v. Federal Trade Commission

Supreme Court of the United States, 1999.
526 U.S. 756, 119 S.Ct. 1604, 143 L.Ed.2d 935.

■ SOUTER, J. There are two issues in this case: whether the jurisdiction of the Federal Trade Commission extends to the California Dental Association (CDA), a nonprofit professional association, and whether a "quick look" sufficed to justify finding that certain advertising restrictions adopted by the CDA violated the antitrust laws. We hold that the Commission's jurisdiction under the Federal Trade Commission Act (FTC Act) extends to an association that, like the CDA, provides substantial economic benefit to its for-profit members, but that where, as here, any anticompetitive effects of given restraints are far from intuitively obvious, the rule of reason demands a more thorough enquiry into the consequences of those restraints than the Court of Appeals performed.

I

The CDA is a voluntary nonprofit association of local dental societies to which some 19,000 dentists belong, including about three-quarters of those practicing in the State. In re California Dental Assn., 121 F.T.C. 190, 196–197 (1996). The CDA is exempt from federal income tax under 26 U.S.C. § 501(c)(6), covering "business leagues, chambers of commerce, real-estate boards, [and] boards of trade," although it has for-profit subsidiaries that give its members advantageous access to various sorts of insurance, including liability coverage, and to financing for their real estate, equipment, cars, and patients' bills. The CDA lobbies and litigates in its members' interests, and conducts marketing and public relations campaigns for their benefit.

The dentists who belong to the CDA through these associations agree to abide by a Code of Ethics (Code) including the following 10:

> "Although any dentist may advertise, no dentist shall advertise or solicit patients in any form of communication in a manner that is false or misleading in any material respect. In order to properly serve the public, dentists should represent themselves in a manner that contributes to the esteem of the public. Dentists

should not misrepresent their training and competence in any way that would be false or misleading in any material respect."

The CDA has issued a number of advisory opinions interpreting this section, and through separate advertising guidelines intended to help members comply with the Code and with state law the CDA has advised its dentists of disclosures they must make under state law when engaging in discount advertising.[79]

Responsibility for enforcing the Code rests in the first instance with the local dental societies, to which applicants for CDA membership must submit copies of their own advertisements and those of their employers or referral services to assure compliance with the Code. The local societies also actively seek information about potential Code violations by applicants or CDA members. Applicants who refuse to withdraw or revise objectionable advertisements may be denied membership; and members who, after a hearing, remain similarly recalcitrant are subject to censure, suspension, or expulsion from the CDA. 128 F.3d at 724.

The Commission brought a complaint against the CDA, alleging that it applied its guidelines so as to restrict truthful, nondeceptive advertising, and so violated § 5 of the FTC Act, 38 Stat. 717, 15 U.S.C. § 45.[80] The complaint alleged that the CDA had unreasonably restricted two types of advertising: price advertising, particularly discounted fees, and advertising relating to the quality of dental services. An Administrative Law Judge (ALJ) held the Commission to have jurisdiction over the CDA, which, the ALJ noted, had itself "stated that a selection of its programs and services has a potential value to members of between $22,739 and $65,127," 121 F.T.C. at 207. He found that, although there had been no proof that the CDA exerted market power, no such proof was required to establish an antitrust violation under In re Mass. Bd. of Registration in Optometry, 110 F.T.C. 549 (1988), since the CDA had unreasonably prevented members and potential members from using truthful, nondeceptive advertising, all to the detriment of both dentists and consumers of dental services. He accordingly found a violation of § 5 of the FTC Act.

The Commission adopted the factual findings of the ALJ except for his conclusion that the CDA lacked market power, with which the Commission disagreed. The Commission treated the CDA's restrictions on discount

---

79. The disclosures include:

"1. The dollar amount of the nondiscounted fee for the service[.]

"2. Either the dollar amount of the discount fee or the percentage of the discount for the specific service[.]

"3. The length of time that the discount will be offered[.]

"4. Verifiable fees[.]

"5. [The identity of] specific groups who qualify for the discount or any other terms

and conditions or restrictions for qualifying for the discount." Id., at 724.

80. The FTC Act's prohibition of unfair competition and deceptive acts or practices, 15 U.S.C. § 45(a)(1), overlaps the scope of § 1 of the Sherman Act, 15 U.S.C. § 1, aimed at prohibiting restraint of trade, FTC v. Indiana Federation of Dentists, 476 U.S. 447, 454–455 (1986), and the Commission relied upon Sherman Act law in adjudicating this case, In re California Dental Assn., 121 F.T.C. 190, 292, n. 5 (1996).

advertising as illegal *per se*. 128 F.3d at 725. In the alternative, the Commission held the price advertising (as well as the nonprice) restrictions to be violations of the Sherman and FTC Acts under an abbreviated rule-of-reason analysis....

The Court of Appeals for the Ninth Circuit affirmed, sustaining the Commission's assertion of jurisdiction over the CDA and its ultimate conclusion on the merits. Id. at 730. The court thought it error for the Commission to have applied *per se* analysis to the price advertising restrictions, finding analysis under the rule of reason required for all the restrictions. But the Court of Appeals went on to explain that the Commission had properly

> "applied an abbreviated, or 'quick look,' rule of reason analysis designed for restraints that are not *per se* unlawful but are sufficiently anticompetitive on their face that they do not require a full-blown rule of reason inquiry. See [National Collegiate Athletic Assn. v. Board of Regents of Univ. of Okla., 468 U.S. 85 and n. 39 (1984)] ('The essential point is that the rule of reason can sometimes be applied in the twinkling of an eye.') [Ibid. citing P. Areeda, The "Rule of Reason" in Antitrust Analysis: General Issues 37–38 (Federal Judicial Center, June 1981) (parenthetical omitted).] It allows the condemnation of a 'naked restraint' on price or output without an 'elaborate industry analysis.' Id. at 109." Id., at 727.

The Court of Appeals thought truncated rule-of-reason analysis to be in order for several reasons. As for the restrictions on discount advertising, they "amounted in practice to a fairly 'naked' restraint on price competition itself," ibid. The CDA's procompetitive justification, that the restrictions encouraged disclosure and prevented false and misleading advertising, carried little weight because "it is simply infeasible to disclose all of the information that is required," id., at 728, and "the record provides no evidence that the rule has in fact led to increased disclosure and transparency of dental pricing," ibid. As to non-price advertising restrictions, the court said that

> "[t]hese restrictions are in effect a form of output limitation, as they restrict the supply of information about individual dentists' services. *See* Areeda & Hovenkamp, Antitrust Law ¶ 1505 at 693–694 (Supp. 1997).... The restrictions may also affect output more directly, as quality and comfort advertising may induce some customers to obtain nonemergency care when they might not otherwise do so.... Under these circumstances, we think that the restriction is a sufficiently naked restraint on output to justify quick look analysis." Ibid.

The Court of Appeals went on to hold that the Commission's findings with respect to the CDA's agreement and intent to restrain trade, as well as on the effect of the restrictions and the existence of market power, were all supported by substantial evidence. *Id.*, at 728–730. In dissent, Judge Real took the position that the Commission's jurisdiction did not cover the

CDA as a nonprofit professional association engaging in no commercial operations. But even assuming jurisdiction, he argued, full-bore rule-of-reason analysis was called for, since the disclosure requirements were not naked restraints and neither fixed prices nor banned nondeceptive advertising.

We granted certiorari to resolve conflicts among the Circuits on the Commission's jurisdiction over a nonprofit professional association and the occasions for abbreviated rule-of-reason analysis. We now vacate the judgment of the Court of Appeals and remand.

II

The FTC Act gives the Commission authority over "persons, partnerships, or corporations," 15 U.S.C. § 45(a)(2), and defines "corporation" to include "any company . . . or association, incorporated or unincorporated, without shares of capital or capital stock or certificates of interest, except partnerships, which is organized to carry on business for its own profit or that of its members," § 44. Although the Circuits have not agreed on the precise extent of this definition, the Commission has long held that some circumstances give it jurisdiction over an entity that seeks no profit for itself. While the Commission has claimed to have jurisdiction over a nonprofit entity if a substantial part of its total activities provide pecuniary benefits to its members, see In re American Medical Assn., 94 F.T.C. 701, 983–984 (1980), respondent now advances the slightly different formulation that the Commission has jurisdiction "over anticompetitive practices by nonprofit associations whose activities provide substantial economic benefits to their for-profit members' businesses." Brief for Respondent 20. . . .

Just as the FTC Act does not require that a supporting organization must devote itself entirely to its members' profits, neither does the Act say anything about how much of the entity's activities must go to raising the members' bottom lines. There is accordingly no apparent reason to let the statute's application turn on meeting some threshold percentage of activity for this purpose, or even satisfying a softer formulation calling for a substantial part of the nonprofit entity's total activities to be aimed at its members' pecuniary benefit. To be sure, proximate relation to lucre must appear; the FTC Act does not cover all membership organizations of profit-making corporations without more, and an organization devoted solely to professional education may lie outside the FTC Act's jurisdictional reach, even though the quality of professional services ultimately affects the profits of those who deliver them.

There is no line drawing exercise in this case, however, where the CDA's contributions to the profits of its individual members are proximate and apparent. Through for-profit subsidiaries, the CDA provides advantageous insurance and preferential financing arrangements for its members, and it engages in lobbying, litigation, marketing, and public relations for the benefit of its members' interests. This congeries of activities confers far more than de minimis or merely presumed economic benefits on CDA members; the economic benefits conferred upon the CDA's profit-seeking professionals plainly fall within the object of enhancing its members' "profit,"[81] which the FTC Act makes the jurisdictional touchstone. There is no difficulty in concluding that the Commission has jurisdiction over the CDA. . . .

III

The Court of Appeals treated as distinct questions the sufficiency of the analysis of anticompetitive effects and the substantiality of the evidence supporting the Commission's conclusions. Because we decide that the Court of Appeals erred when it held as a matter of law that quick-look analysis was appropriate (with the consequence that the Commission's abbreviated analysis and conclusion were sustainable), we do not reach the question of the substantiality of the evidence supporting the Commission's conclusion.[82]

In National Collegiate Athletic Assn. v. Board of Regents of Univ. of Okla., 468 U.S. 85 (1984), we held that a "naked restraint on price and output requires some competitive justification even in the absence of a detailed market analysis." *Id.*, at 110. Elsewhere, we held that "no elaborate industry analysis is required to demonstrate the anticompetitive character of "horizontal agreements among competitors to refuse to discuss prices, National Soc. of Professional Engineers v. United States, 435 U.S. 679, 692 (1978), or to withhold a particular desired service, FTC v. Indiana Federation of Dentists, 476 U.S. 447, 459, (1986) (quoting National Soc. of Professional Engineers, supra, at 692). In each of these cases, which have formed the basis for what has come to be called abbreviated or "quick-look" analysis under the rule of reason, an observer with even a rudimentary understanding of economics could conclude that the arrangements in question would have an anticompetitive effect on customers and markets. In National Collegiate Athletic Assn., the league's television plan expressly limited output (the number of games that could be televised) and fixed a minimum price. 468 U.S. at 99–100. In National Soc. of Professional Engineers, the restraint was "an absolute ban on competitive bidding." 435 U.S. at 692. In Indiana Federation of Dentists, the restraint was "a horizontal agreement among the participating dentists to withhold from their customers a particular service that they desire." 476 U.S. at 459. As

---

81. .... (It should go without saying that the FTC Act does not require for Commission jurisdiction that members of an entity turn a profit on their membership, but only that the entity be organized to carry on business for members' profit.) Nonetheless, we do not, and indeed, on the facts here, could not, decide today whether the Commission has jurisdiction over nonprofit organizations that do not confer profit on for-profit members but do, for example, show annual income surpluses, engage in significant commerce, or compete in relevant markets with for-profit players. We therefore do not foreclose the possibility that various paradigms of profit might fall within the ambit of the FTC Act. Nor do we decide whether a purpose of contributing to profit only in a presumed sense, as by enhancing professional educational efforts, would implicate the Commission's jurisdiction.

82. We leave to the Court of Appeals the question whether on remand it can effectively assess the Commission's decision for substantial evidence on the record, or whether it must remand to the Commission for a more extensive rule-of-reason analysis on the basis of an enhanced record.

in such cases, quick-look analysis carries the day when the great likelihood of anticompetitive effects can easily be ascertained. See Law v. National Collegiate Athletic Assn., 134 F.3d 1010, 1020 (C.A.10 1998) (explaining that quick-look analysis applies "where a practice has obvious anticompetitive effects"); Chicago Professional Sports Limited Partnership v. National Basketball Assn., 961 F.2d 667, 674–676 (C.A.7 1992) (finding quick-look analysis adequate after assessing and rejecting logic of proffered procompetitive justifications); cf. United States v. Brown University, 5 F.3d 658, 677–678 (C.A.3 1993) (finding full rule-of-reason analysis required where universities sought to provide financial aid to needy students and noting by way of contrast that the agreements in *National Soc. of Professional Engineers* and *Indiana Federation of Dentists* "embodied a strong economic self-interest of the parties to them").

The case before us, however, fails to present a situation in which the likelihood of anticompetitive effects is comparably obvious. Even on JUSTICE BREYER's view that bars on truthful and verifiable price and quality advertising are prima facie anticompetitive, and place the burden of procompetitive justification on those who agree to adopt them, the very issue at the threshold of this case is whether professional price and quality advertising is sufficiently verifiable in theory and in fact to fall within such a general rule. Ultimately our disagreement with JUSTICE BREYER turns on our different responses to this issue. Whereas he accepts, as the Ninth Circuit seems to have done, that the restrictions here were like restrictions on advertisement of price and quality generally, it seems to us that the CDA's advertising restrictions might plausibly be thought to have a net procompetitive effect, or possibly no effect at all on competition. The restrictions on both discount and nondiscount advertising are, at least on their face, designed to avoid false or deceptive advertising[83] in a market characterized by striking disparities between the information available to the professional and the patient.[84] Cf. Carr & Mathewson, The Economics of Law Firms: A Study in the Legal Organization of the Firm, 33 J. Law & Econ. 307, 309 (1990) (explaining that in a market for complex professional services, "inherent asymmetry of knowledge about the product" arises because "professionals supplying the good are knowledgeable [whereas] consumers demanding the good are uninformed"); Akerlof, The Market for 'Lemons': Quality Uncertainty and the Market Mechanism, 84 Q. J. Econ. 488 (1970) (pointing out quality problems in market characterized by

83. That false or misleading advertising has an anticompetitive effect, as that term is customarily used, has been long established. Cf. FTC v. Algoma Lumber Co., 291 U.S. 67, 79–80 (1934) (finding a false advertisement to be unfair competition).

84. "The fact that a restraint operates upon a profession as distinguished from a business is, of course, relevant in determining whether that particular restraint violates the Sherman Act. It would be unrealistic to view the practice of professions as interchangeable with other business activities, and automatically to apply to the professions antitrust concepts which originated in other areas. The public service aspect, and other features of the professions, may require that a particular practice, which could properly be viewed as a violation of the Sherman Act in another context, be treated differently." Goldfarb v. Virginia State Bar, 421 U.S. 773, 788–789 and n. 17 (1975).

asymmetrical information). In a market for professional services, in which advertising is relatively rare and the comparability of service packages not easily established, the difficulty for customers or potential competitors to get and verify information about the price and availability of services magnifies the dangers to competition associated with misleading advertising. What is more, the quality of professional services tends to resist either calibration or monitoring by individual patients or clients, partly because of the specialized knowledge required to evaluate the services, and partly because of the difficulty in determining whether, and the degree to which, an outcome is attributable to the quality of services (like a poor job of tooth-filling) or to something else (like a very tough walnut). . . . Patients' attachments to particular professionals, the rationality of which is difficult to assess, complicate the picture even further. Cf. Evans, Professionals and the Production Function: Can Competition Policy Improve Efficiency in the Licensed Professions?, in Occupational Licensure and Regulation 235–236 (S. Rottenberg ed. 1980) (describing long-term relationship between professional and client not as "a series of spot contracts" but rather as "a long-term agreement, often implicit, to deal with each other in a set of future unspecified or incompletely specified circumstances according to certain rules," and adding that "it is not clear how or if these [implicit contracts] can be reconciled with the promotion of effective price competition in individual spot markets for particular services"). The existence of such significant challenges to informed decisionmaking by the customer for professional services immediately suggests that advertising restrictions arguably protecting patients from misleading or irrelevant advertising call for more than cursory treatment as obviously comparable to classic horizontal agreements to limit output or price competition.

The explanation proffered by the Court of Appeals for the likely anticompetitive effect of the CDA's restrictions on discount advertising began with the unexceptionable statements that "price advertising is fundamental to price competition," 128 F.3d at 727, and that "restrictions on the ability to advertise prices normally make it more difficult for consumers to find a lower price and for dentists to compete on the basis of price," ibid. (citing Bates v. State Bar of Ariz., 433 U.S. 350, 364, (1977); Morales v. Trans World Airlines, Inc., 504 U.S. 374, 388 (1992)). The court then acknowledged that, according to the CDA, the restrictions nonetheless furthered the "legitimate, indeed procompetitive, goal of preventing false and misleading price advertising." 128 F.3d at 728. The Court of Appeals might, at this juncture, have recognized that the restrictions at issue here are very far from a total ban on price or discount advertising, and might have considered the possibility that the particular restrictions on professional advertising could have different effects from those "normally" found in the commercial world, even to the point of promoting competition by reducing the occurrence of unverifiable and misleading across-the-board discount advertising.[85] Instead, the Court of Appeals confined itself to the

---

85. JUSTICE BREYER claims that "the Court of Appeals did consider the rele- vant differences." But the language he cites says nothing more than that *per se* analysis is

brief assertion that the "CDA's disclosure requirements appear to prohibit across-the-board discounts because it is simply infeasible to disclose all of the information that is required," ibid., followed by the observation that "the record provides no evidence that the rule has in fact led to increased disclosure and transparency of dental pricing," ibid.

But these observations brush over the professional context and describe no anticompetitive effects. Assuming that the record in fact supports the conclusion that the CDA disclosure rules essentially bar advertisement of across-the-board discounts, it does not obviously follow that such a ban would have a net anticompetitive effect here. Whether advertisements that announced discounts for, say, first-time customers, would be less effective at conveying information relevant to competition if they listed the original and discounted prices for checkups, X-rays, and fillings, than they would be if they simply specified a percentage discount across the board, seems to us a question susceptible to empirical but not a priori analysis. In a suspicious world, the discipline of specific example may well be a necessary condition of plausibility for professional claims that for all practical purposes defy comparison shopping. It is also possible in principle that, even if across-the-board discount advertisements were more effective in drawing customers in the short run, the recurrence of some measure of intentional or accidental misstatement due to the breadth of their claims might leak out over time to make potential patients skeptical of any such across-the-board advertising, so undercutting the method's effectiveness.... It might be, too, that across-the-board discount advertisements would continue to attract business indefinitely, but might work precisely because they were misleading customers, and thus just because their effect would be anticompetitive, not procompetitive. Put another way, the CDA's rule appears to reflect the prediction that any costs to competition associated with the elimination of across-the-board advertising will be outweighed by gains to consumer information (and hence competition) created by discount advertising that is exact, accurate, and more easily verifiable (at least by regulators). As a matter of economics this view may or may not be correct, but it is not implausible, and neither a court nor the Commission may initially dismiss it as presumptively wrong.[86]

inappropriate here and that "some caution" was appropriate where restrictions purported to restrict false advertising, see 128 F.3d at 726–727. Caution was of course appropriate, but this statement by the Court of Appeals does not constitute a consideration of the possible differences between these and other advertising restrictions.

86. JUSTICE BREYER suggests that our analysis is "of limited relevance," because "the basic question is whether this ... theoretically redeeming virtue in fact offsets the restrictions' anticompetitive effects in this case." He thinks that the Commission and the Court of Appeals "adequately an-

swered that question," but the absence of any empirical evidence on this point indicates that the question was not answered, merely avoided by implicit burden-shifting of the kind accepted by JUSTICE BREYER. The point is that before a theoretical claim of anticompetitive effects can justify shifting to a defendant the burden to show empirical evidence of procompetitive effects, as quick-look analysis in effect requires, there must be some indication that the court making the decision has properly identified the theoretical basis for the anticompetitive effects and considered whether the effects actually are anticompetitive. Where, as here, the circum-

In theory, it is true, the Court of Appeals neither ruled out the plausibility of some procompetitive support for the CDA's requirements nor foreclosed the utility of an evidentiary discussion on the point. The court indirectly acknowledged the plausibility of procompetitive justifications for the CDA's position when it stated that "the record provides no evidence that the rule has in fact led to increased disclosure and transparency of dental pricing," 128 F.3d at 728. But because petitioner alone would have had the incentive to introduce such evidence, the statement sounds as though the Court of Appeals may have thought it was justified without further analysis to shift a burden to the CDA to adduce hard evidence of the procompetitive nature of its policy; the court's adversion to empirical evidence at the moment of this implicit burden-shifting underscores the leniency of its enquiry into evidence of the restrictions' anticompetitive effects.

The Court of Appeals was comparably tolerant in accepting the sufficiency of abbreviated rule-of-reason analysis as to the nonprice advertising restrictions. The court began with the argument that "[t]hese restrictions are in effect a form of output limitation, as they restrict the supply of information about individual dentists' services." Ibid. (citing P. Areeda & H. Hovenkamp, Antitrust Law ¶ 1505, pp. 693–694 (1997 Supp.)). Although this sentence does indeed appear as cited, it is puzzling, given that the relevant output for antitrust purposes here is presumably not information or advertising, but dental services themselves. The question is not whether the universe of possible advertisements has been limited (as assuredly it has), but whether the limitation on advertisements obviously tends to limit the total delivery of dental services. The court came closest to addressing this latter question when it went on to assert that limiting advertisements regarding quality and safety "prevents dentists from fully describing the package of services they offer," 128 F.3d at 728, adding that "the restrictions may also affect output more directly, as quality and comfort advertising may induce some customers to obtain nonemergency care when they might not otherwise do so," ibid. This suggestion about output is also puzzling. If quality advertising actually induces some patients to obtain more care than they would in its absence, then restricting such advertising would reduce the demand for dental services, not the supply; and it is of course the producers' supply of a good in relation to demand that is normally relevant in determining whether a producer-imposed output limitation has the anticompetitive effect of artificially raising prices,[87] see

---

stances of the restriction are somewhat complex, assumption alone will not do.

87. JUSTICE BREYER wonders if we "mea[n] this statement as an argument against the anticompetitive tendencies that flow from an agreement not to advertise service quality." But as the preceding sentence shows, we intend simply to question the logic of the Court of Appeals's suggestion that the restrictions are anticompetitive because they

somehow "affect output," 128 F.3d at 728, presumably with the intent to raise prices by limiting supply while demand remains constant. We do not mean to deny that an agreement not to advertise service quality might have anticompetitive effects. We merely mean that, absent further analysis of the kind JUSTICE BREYER undertakes, it is not possible to conclude that the net effect of this particular restriction is anticompetitive.

General Leaseways, Inc. v. National Truck Leasing Assn., 744 F.2d 588, 594–595 (C.A.7 1984) ("An agreement on output also equates to a price-fixing agreement. If firms raise price, the market's demand for their product will fall, so the amount supplied will fall too—in other words, output will be restricted. If instead the firms restrict output directly, price will as mentioned rise in order to limit demand to the reduced supply. Thus, with exceptions not relevant here, raising price, reducing output, and dividing markets have the same anticompetitive effects").

Although the Court of Appeals acknowledged the CDA's view that "claims about quality are inherently unverifiable and therefore misleading," 128 F.3d at 728, it responded that this concern "does not justify banning all quality claims without regard to whether they are, in fact, false or misleading," *ibid.* As a result, the court said, "the restriction is a sufficiently naked restraint on output to justify quick look analysis." *Ibid.* The court assumed, in these words, that some dental quality claims may escape justifiable censure, because they are both verifiable and true. But its implicit assumption fails to explain why it gave no weight to the counter-vailing, and at least equally plausible, suggestion that restricting difficult-to-verify claims about quality or patient comfort would have a procompetitive effect by preventing misleading or false claims that distort the market. It is, indeed, entirely possible to understand the CDA's restrictions on unverifiable quality and comfort advertising as nothing more than a procompetitive ban on puffery, cf. Bates, 433 U.S. at 366 (claims relating to the quality of legal services "probably are not susceptible of precise measurement or verification and, under some circumstances, might well be deceptive or misleading to the public, or even false"); *id.* at 383–384 ("[A]dvertising claims as to the quality of services ... are not susceptible of measurement or verification; accordingly, such claims may be so likely to be misleading as to warrant restriction"), notwithstanding JUSTICE BREYER's citation (to a Commission discussion that never faces the issue of the unverifiability of professional quality claims, raised in Bates), post, at 5.[88]

The point is not that the CDA's restrictions necessarily have the procompetitive effect claimed by the CDA; it is possible that banning quality claims might have no effect at all on competitiveness if, for example, many dentists made very much the same sort of claims. And it is also of course possible that the restrictions might in the final analysis be anticompetitive. The point, rather, is that the plausibility of competing claims about the effects of the professional advertising restrictions rules out the indulgently abbreviated review to which the Commission's order was treated. The obvious anticompetitive effect that triggers abbreviated analysis has not been shown.

88. The Commission said only that "'mere puffing' deceives no one and has never been subject to regulation.'" 121 F.T.C. at 318. The question here, of course, is not whether puffery may be subject to governmental regulation, but whether a professional organization may ban it.

In light of our focus on the adequacy of the Court of Appeals's analysis, JUSTICE BREYER's thorough-going, *de novo* antitrust analysis contains much to impress on its own merits but little to demonstrate the sufficiency of the Court of Appeals's review. The obligation to give a more deliberate look than a quick one does not arise at the door of this Court and should not be satisfied here in the first instance. Had the Court of Appeals engaged in a painstaking discussion in a league with JUSTICE BREYER's (compare his 14 pages with the Ninth Circuit's 8), and had it confronted the comparability of these restrictions to bars on clearly verifiable advertising, its reasoning might have sufficed to justify its conclusion. Certainly JUSTICE BREYER's treatment of the antitrust issues here is no "quick look." Lingering is more like it, and indeed JUSTICE BREYER, not surprisingly, stops short of endorsing the Court of Appeals's discussion as adequate to the task at hand.

Saying here that the Court of Appeals's conclusion at least required a more extended examination of the possible factual underpinnings than it received is not, of course, necessarily to call for the fullest market analysis. Although we have said that a challenge to a "naked restraint on price and output" need not be supported by "a detailed market analysis" in order to "requir[e] some competitive justification," National Collegiate Athletic Assn., 468 U.S. at 110, it does not follow that every case attacking a less obviously anticompetitive restraint (like this one) is a candidate for plenary market examination. The truth is that our categories of analysis of anti-competitive effect are less fixed than terms like "*per se*," "quick look," and "rule of reason" tend to make them appear. We have recognized, for example, that "there is often no bright line separating *per se* from Rule of Reason analysis," since "considerable inquiry into market conditions" may be required before the application of any so-called "*per se*" condemnation is justified. *Id.*, at 104, n. 26. "[W]hether the ultimate finding is the product of a presumption or actual market analysis, the essential inquiry remains the same—whether or not the challenged restraint enhances competition." *Id.*, at 104. Indeed, the scholar who enriched antitrust law with the metaphor of "the twinkling of an eye" for the most condensed rule-of-reason analysis himself cautioned against the risk of misleading even in speaking of a "spectrum" of adequate reasonableness analysis for passing upon antitrust claims: "There is always something of a sliding scale in appraising reasonableness, but the sliding scale formula deceptively suggests greater precision than we can hope for.... Nevertheless, the quality of proof required should vary with the circumstances." P. Areeda, Antitrust Law ¶ 1507, p. 402 (1986).[89] At the same time, Professor Areeda also

---

89. Other commentators have expressed similar views. *See, e.g.*, Kolasky, Counterpoint: The Department of Justice's "Stepwise" Approach Imposes Too Heavy a Burden on Parties to Horizontal Agreements, Antitrust 41, 43 (Spring 1998) ("[I]n applying the rule of reason, the courts, as with any balancing test, use a sliding scale to determine how much proof to require"); Piraino, Making Sense of the Rule of Reason: A New Standard for Section 1 of the Sherman Act, 47 Vand. L. Rev. 1753, 1771 (1994) ("[C]ourts will have to undertake varying degrees of inquiry depending upon the type of restraint at issue. The legality of certain restraints will be easy to determine because

emphasized the necessity, particularly great in the quasi-common law realm of antitrust, that courts explain the logic of their conclusions. "By exposing their reasoning, judges . . . are subjected to others' critical analyses, which in turn can lead to better understanding for the future." *Id.* ¶ 1500, at 364. As the circumstances here demonstrate, there is generally no categorical line to be drawn between restraints that give rise to an intuitively obvious inference of anticompetitive effect and those that call for more detailed treatment. What is required, rather, is an enquiry meet for the case, looking to the circumstances, details, and logic of a restraint. The object is to see whether the experience of the market has been so clear, or necessarily will be, that a confident conclusion about the principal tendency of a restriction will follow from a quick (or at least quicker) look, in place of a more sedulous one. And of course what we see may vary over time, if rule-of-reason analyses in case after case reach identical conclusions. For now, at least, a less quick look was required for the initial assessment of the tendency of these professional advertising restrictions. Because the Court of Appeals did not scrutinize the assumption of relative anticompetitive tendencies, we vacate the judgment and remand the case for a fuller consideration of the issue.

■ BREYER, J., with whom STEVENS, KENNEDY, and GINSBURG, JJ., join, concurring in part and dissenting in part.

I agree with the Court that the Federal Trade Commission has jurisdiction over petitioner, and I join Parts I and II of its opinion. I also agree that in a "rule of reason" antitrust case "the quality of proof required should vary with the circumstances," that "[w]hat is required . . . is an enquiry meet for the case," and that the object is a "confident conclusion about the principal tendency of a restriction." But I do not agree that the Court has properly applied those unobjectionable principles here. In my view, a traditional application of the rule of reason to the facts as found by the Commission requires affirming the Commission—just as the Court of Appeals did below.

I

The Commission's conclusion is lawful if its "factual findings," insofar as they are supported by "substantial evidence," "make out a violation of Sherman Act § 1." FTC v. Indiana Federation of Dentists, 476 U.S. 447, 454–455 (1986). To determine whether that is so, I would not simply ask whether the restraints at issue are anticompetitive overall. Rather, like the Court of Appeals (and the Commission), I would break that question down into four classical, subsidiary antitrust questions: (1) What is the specific restraint at issue? (2) What are its likely anticompetitive effects? (3) Are

their competitive effects are obvious. Other restrictions will require a more detailed analysis because their competitive impact is more ambiguous"). But see Klein, A "Stepwise" Approach for Analyzing Horizontal Agreements Will Provide a Much Needed Structure for Antitrust Review, Antitrust 41, 42 (Spring 1990) (examination of procompetitive justifications "is by no means a full scrutiny of the proffered efficiency justification. It is, rather, a hard look at the justification to determine if it meets the defendant's burden of coming forward with—but not establishing—a valid efficiency justification").

there offsetting procompetitive justifications? (4) Do the parties have sufficient market power to make a difference?

A

The most important question is the first: What are the specific restraints at issue? . . . Those restraints do not include merely the agreement
to which the California Dental Association's (Dental Association or Association) ethical rule literally refers, namely, a promise to refrain from advertising that is " 'false or misleading in any material respect.' " Instead, the
Commission found a set of restraints arising out of the way the Dental
Association implemented this innocent-sounding ethical rule in practice,
through advisory opinions, guidelines, enforcement policies, and review of
membership applications. In re California Dental Assn., 121 F.T.C. 190
(1996). As implemented, the ethical rule reached beyond its nominal target,
to prevent truthful and nondeceptive advertising. In particular, the Commission determined that the rule, in practice:

> (1) "precluded advertising that characterized a dentist's fees as
> being low, reasonable, or affordable," *Id.*, at 301.

> (2) "precluded advertising . . . of across the board discounts,"
> ibid.; and

> (3) "prohibited all quality claims," *id.*, at 308.

Whether the Dental Association's basic rule as *implemented* actually
restrained the truthful and nondeceptive advertising of low prices, across-
the-board discounts, and quality service are questions of fact. The Administrative Law Judge (ALJ) and the Commission may have found those
questions difficult ones. But both the ALJ and the Commission ultimately
found against the Dental Association in respect to these facts. And the
question for us—whether those agency findings are supported by substantial evidence, see Indiana Federation, supra, is not difficult.

The Court of Appeals referred explicitly to some of the evidence that it
found adequate to support the Commission's conclusions. It pointed out, for
example, that the Dental Association's "advisory opinions and guidelines
indicate that . . . descriptions of prices as 'reasonable' or 'low' do not
comply" with the Association's rule; that in "numerous cases" the Association "advised members of objections to special offers, senior citizen discounts, and new patient discounts, apparently without regard to their
truth"; and that one advisory opinion "expressly states that claims as to
the quality of services are inherently likely to be false or misleading," all
"without any particular consideration of whether" such statements were
"true or false." 128 F.3d 720, 729 (C.A.9 1997).

The Commission itself had before it far more evidence. It referred to
instances in which the Association, without regard for the truthfulness of
the statements at issue, recommended denial of membership to dentists
wishing to advertise, for example, "reasonable fees quoted in advance,"
"major savings," or "making teeth cleaning . . . inexpensive." 121 F.T.C. at
301. It referred to testimony that "across-the-board discount advertising in

literal compliance with the requirements 'would probably take two pages in the telephone book' and 'nobody is going to really advertise in that fashion.' " *Id.* at 302. And it pointed to many instances in which the Dental Association suppressed such advertising claims as "we guarantee all dental work for 1 year," "latest in cosmetic dentistry," and "gentle dentistry in a caring environment." *Id.* at 308–310.

I need not review the evidence further, for this Court has said that "substantial evidence" is a matter for the courts of appeals, and that it "will intervene only in what ought to be the rare instance when the standard appears to have been misapprehended or grossly misapplied." Universal Camera Corp. v. NLRB, 340 U.S. 474, 490–491 (1951). I have said enough to make clear that this is not a case warranting our intervention. Consequently, we must decide only the basic legal question whether the three restraints described above unreasonably restrict competition.

B

Do each of the three restrictions mentioned have "the potential for genuine adverse effects on competition"? Indiana Federation, 476 U.S. at 460; 7 P. Areeda, Antitrust Law ¶ 1503a, pp. 372–377 (1986) (hereinafter Areeda). I should have thought that the anticompetitive tendencies of the three restrictions were obvious. An agreement not to advertise that a fee is reasonable, that service is inexpensive, or that a customer will receive a discount makes it more difficult for a dentist to inform customers that he charges a lower price. If the customer does not know about a lower price, he will find it more difficult to buy lower price service. That fact, in turn, makes it less likely that a dentist will obtain more customers by offering lower prices. And that likelihood means that dentists will prove less likely to offer lower prices. But why should I have to spell out the obvious? To restrain truthful advertising about lower prices is likely to restrict competition in respect to price—"the central nervous system of the economy." United States v. Socony–Vacuum Oil Co., 310 U.S. 150, 226, n. 59 (1940); cf., *e.g.*, Bates v. State Bar of Ariz., 433 U.S. 350, 364 (1977) (price advertising plays an "indispensable role in the allocation of resources in a free enterprise system"); Virginia Bd. of Pharmacy v. Virginia Citizens Consumer Council, Inc., 425 U.S. 748, 765 (1976). The Commission thought this fact sufficient to hold (in the alternative) that the price advertising restrictions were unlawful *per se*. See 121 F.T.C. at 307; cf. Socony–Vacuum, supra, at 222–228 (finding agreement among competitors to buy "spot-market oil" unlawful *per se* because of its tendency to restrict price competition). For present purposes, I need not decide whether the Commission was right in applying a *per se* rule. I need only assume a rule of reason applies, and note the serious anticompetitive tendencies of the price advertising restraints.

The restrictions on the advertising of service quality also have serious anticompetitive tendencies. This is not a case of "mere puffing," as the FTC recognized. The days of my youth, when the billboards near Emeryville, California, home of AAA baseball's Oakland Oaks, displayed the name of "Painless" Parker, Dentist, are long gone—along with the Oakland Oaks. But some parents may still want to know that a particular dentist makes a point of "gentle care." Others may want to know about 1–year dental work guarantees. To restrict that kind of service quality advertisement is to restrict competition over the quality of service itself, for, unless consumers know, they may not purchase, and dentists may not compete to supply that which will make little difference to the demand for their services. That, at any rate, is the theory of the Sherman Act. And it is rather late in the day for anyone to deny the significant anticompetitive tendencies of an agreement that restricts competition in any legitimate respect, see, *e.g.*, Paramount Famous Lasky Corp. v. United States, 282 U.S. 30, 43 (1930); United States v. First Nat. Pictures, Inc., 282 U.S. 44, 54–55 (1930), let alone one that inhibits customers from learning about the quality of a dentist's service.

Nor did the Commission rely solely on the unobjectionable proposition that a restriction on the ability of dentists to advertise on quality is likely to limit their incentive to compete on quality. Rather, the Commission pointed to record evidence affirmatively establishing that quality-based competition is important to dental consumers in California. Unsurprisingly, these consumers choose dental services based at least in part on "information about the type and quality of service." Similarly, as the Commission noted, the ALJ credited testimony to the effect that "advertising the comfort of services will 'absolutely' bring in more patients," and, conversely, that restraining the ability to advertise based on quality would decrease the number of patients that a dentist could attract. Finally, the Commission looked to the testimony of dentists who themselves had suffered adverse effects on their business when forced by petitioner to discontinue advertising quality of care.

The FTC found that the price advertising restrictions amounted to a "naked attempt to eliminate price competition." *Id.* at 300. It found that the service quality advertising restrictions "deprive consumers of information they value and of healthy competition for their patronage." *Id.*, at 311. It added that the "anticompetitive nature of these restrictions" was "plain." *Ibid.* The Court of Appeals agreed. I do not believe it possible to deny the anticompetitive tendencies I have mentioned.

C

We must also ask whether, despite their anticompetitive tendencies, these restrictions might be justified by other procompetitive tendencies or redeeming virtues. See 7 Areeda, ¶ 1504, at 377–383. This is a closer question—at least in theory. The Dental Association argues that the three relevant restrictions are inextricably tied to a legitimate Association effort to restrict false or misleading advertising. The Association, the argument goes, had to prevent dentists from engaging in the kind of truthful, nondeceptive advertising that it banned in order effectively to stop dentists from making unverifiable claims about price or service quality, which claims would mislead the consumer.

The problem with this or any similar argument is an empirical one. Notwithstanding its theoretical plausibility, the record does not bear out such a claim. The Commission, which is expert in the area of false and misleading advertising, was uncertain whether petitioner had even *made* the claim. It characterized petitioner's efficiencies argument as rooted in the (unproved) factual assertion that its ethical rule "challenges *only* advertising that is false or misleading." 121 F.T.C. at 316 (emphasis added). Regardless, the Court of Appeals wrote, in respect to the price restrictions, that "the record provides no evidence that the rule has in fact led to increased disclosure and transparency of dental pricing." 128 F.3d at 728. With respect to quality advertising, the Commission stressed that the Association "offered no convincing argument, let alone evidence, that consumers of dental services have been, or are likely to be, harmed by the broad categories of advertising it restricts." 121 F.T.C. at 319. Nor did the Court of Appeals think that the Association's unsubstantiated contention that "claims about quality are inherently unverifiable and therefore misleading" could "justify banning all quality claims without regard to whether they are, in fact, false or misleading." 128 F.3d at 728.

With one exception, my own review of the record reveals no significant evidentiary support for the proposition that the Association's members must agree to ban truthful price and quality advertising in order to stop untruthful claims. The one exception is the obvious fact that one can stop untruthful advertising if one prohibits all advertising. But since the Association made virtually no effort to sift the false from the true, *see* 121 F.T.C. at 316–317, that fact does not make out a valid antitrust defense. See *NCAA*, 468 U.S. at 119; 7 Areeda, ¶ 1505, at 383–384.

In the usual Sherman Act § 1 case, the defendant bears the burden of establishing a procompetitive justification. See National Soc. of Professional Engineers v. United States, 435 U.S. 679, 695 (1978); 7 Areeda, ¶ 1507b, at 397; 11 H. Hovenkamp, Antitrust Law ¶ 1914c, pp. 313–315 (1998); see also Law v. National Collegiate Athletic Assn., 134 F.3d 1010, 1019 (C.A.10), cert. denied, 525 U.S. ___ (1998); United States v. Brown Univ., 5 F.3d 658, 669 (C.A.3 1993).... And the Court of Appeals was correct when it concluded that no such justification had been established here.

D

I shall assume that the Commission must prove one additional circumstance, namely, that the Association's restraints would likely have made a real difference in the marketplace. See 7 Areeda, ¶ 1503, at 376–377. The Commission, disagreeing with the ALJ on this single point, found that the Association did possess enough market power to make a difference. In at least one region of California, the mid-Peninsula, its members accounted for more than 90% of the marketplace; on average they accounted for 75%. See 121 F.T.C. at 314. In addition, entry by new dentists into the market place is fairly difficult. Dental education is expensive (leaving graduates of dental school with $50,000–$100,000 of debt), as is opening a new dentistry office (which costs $75,000–$100,000). And Dental Association members believe membership in the Association is important, valuable, and recognized as such by the public.

These facts, in the Court of Appeals' view, were sufficient to show "enough market power to harm competition through [the Association's] standard setting in the area of advertising." 128 F.3d at 730. And that conclusion is correct. Restrictions on advertising price discounts in Palo Alto may make a difference because potential patients may not respond readily to discount advertising by the handful (10%) of dentists who are not members of the Association. And that fact, in turn, means that the remaining 90% will prove less likely to engage in price competition. Facts such as these have previously led this Court to find market power—unless the defendant has overcome the showing with strong contrary evidence. *See, e.g.,* Indiana Federation, 476 U.S. at 456–457; cf. United States v. Loew's Inc., 371 U.S. 38, 45 (1962); Brown Shoe Co. v. United States, 370 U.S. 294, 341–344 (1962); accord, United States v. Aluminum Co. of America, 148 F.2d 416, 424 (C.A.2 1945). I can find no reason for departing from that precedent here.

II

In the Court's view, the legal analysis conducted by the Court of Appeals was insufficient, and the Court remands the case for a more thorough application of the rule of reason. But in what way did the Court of Appeals fail? I find the Court's answers to this question unsatisfactory—when one divides the overall Sherman Act question into its traditional component parts and adheres to traditional judicial practice for allocating the burdens of persuasion in an antitrust case.

Did the Court of Appeals misconceive the anticompetitive tendencies of the restrictions? After all, the object of the rule of reason is to separate those restraints that "may suppress or even destroy competition" from those that "merely regulat[e] and perhaps thereby promot[e] competition." Board of Trade of Chicago v. United States, 246 U.S. 231, 238 (1918). The majority says that the Association's "advertising restrictions might plausibly be thought to have a net procompetitive effect, or possibly no effect at all on competition." It adds that

> "advertising restrictions arguably protecting patients from misleading or irrelevant advertising call for more than cursory treatment as obviously comparable to classic horizontal agreements to limit output or price competition."

And it criticizes the Court of Appeals for failing to recognize that "the restrictions at issue here are very far from a total ban on price or discount advertising" and that "the particular restrictions on professional advertising could have different effects from those 'normally' found in the commercial world, even to the point of promoting competition. . . ."

The problem with these statements is that the Court of Appeals did consider the relevant differences. It *rejected* the legal "treatment" customarily applied "to classic horizontal agreements to limit output or price competition"—*i.e.*, the FTC's (alternative) *per se* approach. See 128 F.3d at 726–727. It did so because the Association's "policies do not, on their face, ban truthful nondeceptive ads"; instead, they "have been enforced in a way that restricts truthful advertising." *Id.*, at 727. It added that "[t]he value of restricting false advertising ... counsels some caution in attacking rules that purport to do so but merely sweep too broadly." *Ibid.*

Did the Court of Appeals misunderstand the nature of an anticompetitive effect? The Court says:

> "If quality advertising actually induces some patients to obtain more care than they would in its absence, then restricting such advertising would reduce the demand for dental services, not the supply; and ... the producers' supply ... is normally relevant in determining whether a ... limitation has the anticompetitive effect of artificially raising prices."

But if the Court means this statement as an argument against the anticompetitive tendencies that flow from an agreement not to advertise service quality, I believe it is the majority, and not the Court of Appeals, that is mistaken. An agreement not to advertise, say, "gentle care" is anticompetitive because it imposes an artificial barrier against each dentist's independent decision to advertise gentle care. That barrier, in turn, tends to inhibit those dentists who want to supply gentle care from getting together with those customers who want to buy gentle care. See P. Areeda & H. Hovenkamp, Antitrust Law ¶ 1505, p. 404 (Supp. 1998). There is adequate reason to believe that tendency present in this case.

Did the Court of Appeals inadequately consider possible procompetitive justifications? The Court seems to think so, for it says:

> "[T]he [Association's] rule appears to reflect the prediction that any costs to competition associated with the elimination of across-the-board advertising will be outweighed by gains to consumer information (and hence competition) created by discount advertising that is exact, accurate, and more easily verifiable (at least by regulators)."

That may or may not be an accurate assessment of the Association's motives in adopting its rule, but it is of limited relevance. Cf. *Chicago Board of Trade*, supra, at 238. The basic question is whether this, or some other, theoretically redeeming virtue in fact offsets the restrictions' anticompetitive effects in this case. Both court and Commission adequately answered that question.

The Commission found that the defendant did not make the necessary showing that a redeeming virtue existed in practice. The Court of Appeals, asking whether the rules, as enforced, "augmented competition and increased market efficiency," found the Commission's conclusion supported by substantial evidence. 128 F.3d at 728. That is why the court said that "the record provides no evidence that the rule has in fact led to increased disclosure and transparency of dental pricing"—which is to say that the record provides no evidence that the effects, though anticompetitive, are nonetheless redeemed or justified. *Ibid.*

The majority correctly points out that "petitioner alone would have had the incentive to introduce such evidence" of procompetitive justification. (Indeed, that is one of the reasons defendants normally bear the burden of persuasion about redeeming virtues.) But despite this incentive, petitioner's brief in this Court offers nothing concrete to counter the Commission's conclusion that the record does not support the claim of justification. Petitioner's failure to produce such evidence itself "explain[s] why [the lower court] gave no weight to the . . . suggestion that restricting difficult-to-verify claims about quality or patient comfort would have a procompetitive effect by preventing misleading or false claims that distort the market."

With respect to the restraint on advertising across-the-board discounts, the majority summarizes its concerns as follows: "Assuming that the record in fact supports the conclusion that the [Association's] disclosure rules essentially bar advertisement of [such] discounts, it does not obviously follow that such a ban would have a net anticompetitive effect here." I accept, rather than assume, the premise: The FTC found that the disclosure rules did bar advertisement of across-the-board discounts, and that finding is supported by substantial evidence. And I accept as *literally* true the conclusion that the Court says follows from that premise, namely, that "net anticompetitive effects" do not "*obviously*" follow from that premise. But obviousness is not the point. With respect to any of the three restraints found by the Commission, whether "net anticompetitive effects" follow is a matter of how the Commission, and, here, the Court of Appeals, have answered the questions I laid out at the beginning. Has the Commission shown that the restriction has anticompetitive tendencies? It has. Has the Association nonetheless shown offsetting virtues? It has not. Has the Commission shown market power sufficient for it to believe that the restrictions will likely make a real world difference? It has.

The upshot, in my view, is that the Court of Appeals, applying ordinary antitrust principles, reached an unexceptional conclusion. It is the same legal conclusion that this Court itself reached in Indiana Federation—a much closer case than this one. There the Court found that an agreement by dentists not to submit dental X-rays to insurers violated the rule of reason. The anticompetitive tendency of that agreement was to reduce competition among dentists in respect to their willingness to submit X-rays to insurers, see 476 U.S. at 456—a matter in respect to which consumers are relatively indifferent, as compared to advertising of price discounts and service quality, the matters at issue here. The redeeming virtue in *Indiana Federation* was the alleged undesirability of having insurers consider a range of matters when deciding whether treatment was justified—a virtue no less plausible, and no less proved, than the virtue offered here. See *id.*, at 462–464. The "power" of the dentists to enforce their agreement was no greater than that at issue here (control of 75% to 90% of the relevant markets). See *id.,* at 460. It is difficult to see how the two cases can be reconciled.

. . .

I would note that the form of analysis I have followed is not rigid; it admits of some variation according to the circumstances. The important point, however, is that its allocation of the burdens of persuasion reflects a gradual evolution within the courts over a period of many years. That evolution represents an effort carefully to blend the procompetitive objectives of the law of antitrust with administrative necessity. It represents a considerable advance, both from the days when the Commission had to present and/or refute every possible fact and theory, and from antitrust theories so abbreviated as to prevent proper analysis. The former prevented cases from ever reaching a conclusion, cf. Bok, Section 7 of the Clayton Act and the Merging of Law and Economics, 74 Harv. L. Rev. 226, 266 (1960), and the latter called forth the criticism that the "Government always wins," United States v. Von's Grocery Co., 384 U.S. 270, 301 (1966) (Stewart, J., dissenting). I hope that this case does not represent an abandonment of that basic, and important, form of analysis.

For these reasons, I respectfully dissent from Part III of the Court's opinion.

NOTES

1. In September 2000, after *California Dental* was remanded, the Ninth Circuit held that the FTC had failed to carry its burden of proving that the restrictions on price and quality advertising had a net anticompetitive effect. The FTC, according to the Ninth Circuit, made a tactical decision to try to win the case on a *per se* or abbreviated rule-of-reason theory, and under these circumstances, the CDA was found correct in arguing that "further factfinding would give the FTC an unwarranted second bite at the apple." California Dental Assn. v. FTC, 224 F.3d 942 (9th Cir.2000).

2. Professor Timothy J. Muris (now chairman of the FTC) provided the following conclusion with respect to *California Dental*:

> Many antitrust lawyers read *CDA* without proper focus on its professional advertising context. Although new as an antitrust issue, for over two decades the Court has struggled with the extent to which the First Amendment protects professional advertising. *CDA*, like *WFI* [Florida Bar v. Went For It, 515 U.S. 618 (1995)] decided by the same Court four years before, is a victory for those who seek to restrict such advertising. The Court is closely divided, however, and resolution of this struggle is not in sight.

> Thus, this article asserts that had some other group, such as car repairers, restrained advertising, the Court would have had little difficulty applying truncated analysis to condemn the restraint. Although defense lawyers would try to read *CDA* expansively, even a cautious judge should have little difficulty with the car repair case. *CDA* should be read to require

all plaintiffs to have an empirical basis for why the restraint harms consumers, but not more. The literature discussed in ... this article provides such evidence regarding restraints on professional advertising. The few studies of advertising restraints among non-professionals are consistent with the studies of professionals. At a minimum, the existing evidence should establish the plaintiffs' *prima facie* case and force the defendants to produce evidence of their own about the positive benefits of restraining advertising. Muris, California Dental Association v. Federal Trade Commission: The Revenge of Footnote 17, 8 S.Ct. Econ. Rev. 265, 309–10 (2000).

3. What does the Supreme Court mean when it seeks empirical evidence of effect in the marketplace? The record showed that virtually every dentist in California went along with the Dental Association's ban on price advertising. Is that the requisite effect? Or, must the plaintiff prove that the price of filling a cavity in Los Angeles is higher than in Oregon or Nevada, or higher than it otherwise would have been, but for the ban on price advertising? Is there non-price empirical evidence that could or should be considered?

PROBLEM 3

SALES AGENCY FOR MONUMENTAL PICTURES

Monumental Pictures recently found itself in the following quandary: it had a substantial library of motion picture films suitable for showing on television; its market investigations revealed that the greatest return could be derived by releasing films in small packages for showing on individual stations throughout the country; but it had no sales organization adapted to such marketing and the cost of establishing such an organization would be high in relation to returns to be derived from Monumental's films alone.

At the same time, Zenith Epics was also having problems. It had embarked much earlier in distributing its feature films to television stations, using the method contemplated by Monumental; it had established a nationwide sales organization for the purpose; but now, having marketed many of its own films, it was having difficulty finding sufficient material to cover the overhead of its marketing organization.

Monumental's search for a distributor and Zenith's search for material led to an arrangement between the two companies under which:

(a) Zenith agreed to distribute Monumental's films for a commission.

(b) Monumental gave Zenith complete freedom of action in establishing the terms and conditions of distribution of Monumental films, including the price to be charged, subject to the following limitations.

(c) Zenith agreed not to market Monumental films at less than their fair market value.

(d) Zenith was obligated not to discriminate against Monumental films; Monumental films were not to be released at rates less than the rates being charged contemporaneously for comparable Zenith films.

(e) For purposes of applying the anti-discrimination provision, and for dividing the proceeds of any sales of mixed packages of Zenith and Monumental films, individual films would be classified by a committee of Monumental and Zenith officials, and any disputes resolved by arbitration.

Pointing out that the arrangement would give Zenith control of 40% of all feature films in this country available for television, the Antitrust Division seeks to enjoin the arrangement. What result?

PROBLEM 4

PRICE ADVERTISING BY LAWYERS

A new private legal clinic opened recently in a large city. It ran a series of ads on radio and in local community newspapers, one of which was along the following lines:

> Marriage getting you down? More and more people are finding that divorce is cheaper and less of a hassle than they thought.

> We can handle your divorce for the lowest prices in town. As little as $10 down, $300 complete for an uncontested divorce. That's $100 less than any other clinic or firm in the area. We'll have you back in action, take care of any problems presented if there are children, and ensure no legal problems.

> Call the Modern Law Clinic today.

The local bar association petitioned the state court to commence disciplinary proceedings against lawyers working in Modern citing the ABA Code of Professional Responsibility (which is in effect in Modern's state) to the effect that information disclosed by a lawyer in any publication or broadcast may not be "false, fraudulent, or misleading," DR 2–101(A), and must be "presented in a dignified manner." DR 2–101(B). The bar noted that the ad (1) improperly and fraudulently understates the seriousness and complexity of divorce proceedings, and (2) implies that all legal services are comparable, regardless of the quality of work done. Modern says the bar is really up in arms because of low prices offered on divorces, which are 33% below the average in the community. It also claims that divorce work is simple and represents a high profit line of work for many specialty lawyers.

Modern's lawyers file suit in federal district court under the antitrust laws, alleging a price-fixing conspiracy, and seek an order enjoining the local bar from any further disciplinary proceedings, claiming the bar action violates Section 1 of the Sherman Act. The local bar association moves to dismiss the complaint. What result?

SECTION 4.   DIVISION OF TERRITORIES AND SOME OTHER HORIZONTAL RESTRAINTS

NOTE ON MARKET SHARING

Competitors, fearful of the consequences of unrestricted price competition and eager to establish competitive stability, may seek to accomplish their purpose by sharing markets rather than by resorting to direct price fixing. Sharing the market may consist of allocating fixed percentages of the available business to each producer, dividing sales territory on a geographical basis or allotting customers to each seller. Techniques for market sharing vary; for example, by restricting the hours of plant operation, markets may be shared on the basis of productive capacity. Business may also be channeled through a common sales agency which may have the power either to impose production quotas on its members or apportion orders among them.

Though price fixing, of course, suppresses competition, such agreements do not of themselves guarantee that each competitor will receive a satisfactory share of the business. Especially when products are not fungible, as when they are built to specifications or possess brand names of differing attractiveness, price control alone may be insufficient and market division may be the only practicable means of "regulating" competition. Whether or not prices are fixed, each competitor will then receive his share of the business and no more. The policy is essentially one of "live and let live." The effect of any agreement for sharing the markets is manifestly to eliminate competition.

Even if not fixed by agreement, prices tend to be uniform when markets are shared, except as products differ or are marketed under conditions permitting differences in prices without disturbing the desired allocation of business. Flexibility and freedom in the response of prices to economic changes are lost. Markets may be shared at any level of prices and the tendency is for prices to be higher than when competition is left unrestrained.

Market sharing necessarily constricts firms capable of expansion and thus increases costs. The least efficient producers are often protected and the advantages of a less costly method of distribution and production are lost to the public.

The regulation of production may suppress competition as effectively as direct price fixing—or even more so—and may, in fact, be one of the methods by which prices are regulated. The essence of successful production control is the equation of industry supply with probable demand. As demand may vary with price, establishment of a definite price or price range reduces uncertainties as to probable demand and the production necessary to meet such demand. It is, therefore, not surprising that price-fixing agreements frequently accompany production controls.

Output control sometimes has for its object not the regulation of prices or the creation of artificial scarcity but the solution of problems created by excess capacity. Moreover, the regulation of output does not necessarily imply its curtailment. Production may be maintained at an agreed level or provision may even be made to increase production. Whatever the terms or object of the agreement, the evil of market sharing flows from its definite tendency to eliminate competition and to displace the normal operation of market forces by concerted and cooperative action of competitors.

National Association of Window Glass Manufacturers v. United States

Supreme Court of the United States, 1923.
263 U.S. 403, 44 S.Ct. 148, 68 L.Ed. 358.

■ HOLMES, J. This is a proceeding brought by the United States ... to prevent an alleged violation of section 1 [of the Sherman Act] which forbids combinations in restraint of trade among the States. The defendants are all the manufacturers of handblown window glass, with certain of their officers, and the National Window Glass Workers, a voluntary association, its officers and members, embracing all the labor to be had for this work in the United States. The defendants established a wage scale to be in effect from September 25, 1922, to January 27, 1923, and from January 29, 1923, to

June 11, 1923; and the feature that is the object of the present attack is that this scale would be issued to one set of factories for the first period and to another for the second, but that no factory could get it for both, and without it they could not get labor and therefore must stop work. After a hearing a final decree was entered enjoining the defendants from carrying out the above or any similar agreements so far as they might limit and prescribe the time during which the defendant manufacturers should operate their factories for handblown window glass. 287 F. 228.

This agreement does not concern sales or distribution, it is directed only to the way in which union labor, the only labor obtainable it is true, shall be employed in production. If such an agreement can be within the Sherman Act at least it is not necessarily so. To determine its legality requires a consideration of the particular facts. Board of Trade of Chicago v. United States, 246 U.S. 231.

The dominant fact in this case is that in the last quarter of a century machines have been brought into use that dispense with the employment of the highly trained blowers . . . and in that and other ways have enabled the factories using machines to produce window glass at half the cost of the handmade. The price for the two kinds is the same. It has followed of course that the companies using machines fix the price, that they make much the greater part of the glass in the market, and probably, as was testified for the defendants, that the handmakers are able to keep on only by the sufferance of the others and by working longer hours. The defendants say, and it is altogether likely, that the conditions thus brought about and the nature of the work have driven many laborers away and made it impossible to get new ones. For the work is very trying, requires considerable training, and is always liable to a reduction of wages if the machine industry lowers the price. The only chance for the handworkers has been when and where they could get cheap fuel and therefore their tendency has been to follow the discoveries of natural gas. The defendants contend with a good deal of force that it is absurd to speak of their arrangements as possibly having any effect upon commerce among the States, when manufacturers of this kind obviously are not able to do more than struggle to survive a little longer before they disappear, as human effort always disappears when it is not needed to direct the force than can be got more cheaply from water or coal.

But that is not all of the defendants' case. There are not twenty-five hundred men at present in the industry. The Government says that this is the fault of the union; the defendants with much greater probability that it is the inevitable coming to pass. But wherever the fault, if there is any, that is the fact with which the defendants had to deal. There were not men enough to enable the factories to run continuously during the working season, leaving out the two or three summer months in which the heat makes it impossible to go on. To work undermanned costs the same in fuel and overhead expenses as to work fully manned, and therefore means a serious loss. On the other hand the men are less well off with the uncertainties that such a situation brings. The purpose of the arrangement is to secure employment for all the men during the whole of the two seasons, thus to give all the labor available to the factories, and to divide it equally among them. From the view that we take we think it unnecessary to explain how the present system sprang from experience during the war when the Government restricted production to one-half of what it had been and an accident was found to work well, or to do more than advert to the defendants' contention that with the means available the production is increased. It is enough that we see no combination in unreasonable restraint of trade in the arrangements made to meet the short supply of men.

Decree reversed. Petition dismissed.

NOTES AND QUESTIONS

1. 1 HOLMES–POLLOCK LETTERS 163 (1941); April 23, 1910: "I don't disguise my belief that the Sherman Act is a humbug based on economic ignorance and incompetence."

2. The *Window Glass* facts are more elaborately set forth in the opinion of the lower court, 287 Fed. 228 (N.D.Ohio 1923). The district judge saw the arrangement as an attempt by the manufacturers to curtail production. The court points out that the arrangement favors the inefficient plants at the expense of the more efficient and suggests that the labor agreement was designed, not so much to spread employment, as to curb production. It is asserted that the members of the union, in August 1922, voted four to one in favor of abandoning the two period system of operation. The adverse effects of the plan upon the workers as well as the industry are stressed. Does Holmes or the district judge get the best of their debate?

3. LOCAL UNION NO. 189 v. JEWEL TEA CO., 381 U.S. 676, 85 S.Ct. 1596, 14 L.Ed.2d 640 (1965): "Judicial pronouncements regarding the reasonableness of restraints on hours of business are relatively few. Some cases appear to have viewed such restraints as tantamount to limits on hours of work and thus reasonable, even though contained in agreements among competitors." Thus in Chicago Board of Trade v. United States, 246 U.S. 231 (1918), the Court upheld a rule of a grain exchange that had the form of a restriction on prices of transactions outside regular trading hours but was characterized by the Court as a rule designed to shift transactions to the regular trading period, *i.e.*, to limit hours of operation.... Other cases have upheld operating hours restraints in factual circumstances that make it seem likely that the agreement affected hours of operation and hours of work in equal measure but without stressing that fact.

"Kold Kist, Inc. v. Amalgamated Meat Cutters, Local No. 421, 99 Cal.App.2d 191, 221 P.2d 724 (1950), held unreasonable a union-employer agreement limiting night sales of frozen poultry, which had previously been obtained from the plaintiff-distributor. The plaintiff alleged, however, that he had been severely affected, since many stores had stopped carrying its products entirely due to the lack of storage facilities in which to keep the poultry during hours in which sale was prohibited, and such effects may be atypical. The decided cases thus do not appear to offer any easy answer to the question whether in a particular case an operating hours restraint is unreasonable." (White, J., 381 U.S. at 693–94 n. 6.)

"If ... employers alone agreed not to sell meat from 6 p.m. to 9 a.m., they would be guilty of an anticompetitive practice, barred by the antitrust laws." (Douglas, J., dissenting, 381 U.S. at 736, 85 S.Ct. at 1606.)

4. Most restraints on hours today would arise in the context of labor negotiations and would be exempt from antitrust scrutiny under the statutory or nonstatutory labor exemptions. See p. 125 supra. A recent case, In re Detroit Auto Dealers Ass'n., Inc. v. FTC, 955 F.2d 457 (6th Cir.1992), elaborates on the scope of the nonstatutory labor exemption and supports Justice Douglas' sense in *Jewel Tea* that restraints on hours, if not covered by the labor exemptions, can be vulnerable.

In 1984, the FTC challenged an agreement by 90 automobile dealers to keep their showrooms closed all day Saturdays and on three weekday evenings. The Sixth Circuit affirmed the FTC's finding of unreasonable restraint of trade, reasoning as follows:

> We adopted the standards set out in *Mackey* in analyzing ... [a] professional sport controversy between a hockey player and the National Hockey League. Those standards deemed to be proper in *Mackey* were reiterated in McCourt v. California Sports, Inc., 600 F.2d 1193 (6th Cir.1979):
>
>> First, the labor policy favoring collective bargaining may potentially be given preeminence over the antitrust laws where the restraint on trade primarily affects only the parties to the collective bargaining relationship. Second, federal labor policy is implicated sufficiently to prevail only where the agreement sought to be exempted concerns a mandatory subject of collective bargaining. Finally, the policy favoring collective bargaining is furthered to the degree necessary to override the antitrust laws only where the agreement sought to be exempted is the product of bona fide arm's-length bargaining. . . .
>
> The FTC argues that because the agreement at issue was among dealers, not involving unions or employees, there was a direct antitrust violation through restraint of trade by means of closing of showrooms and foreclosing availability of new cars to the public. FTC adds that the purpose of the dealers' agreement was "to avoid collective bargaining and to obtain the benefits of reduced competition ... [and to avoid] arm's-length good faith bargaining." Petitioners respond that they were forced, through union and collective salesperson pressure, to reach agreement on standardized and uniform—and limited—showroom hours. We must decide whether the agreement should be subject to the nonstatutory labor exemption and therefore be immunized from antitrust scrutiny. . . .
>
> The statutory labor exemption from antitrust laws specifically provides for labor unions and labor organizations. This exemption may only be asserted by a labor organization itself, not by employers.
>
> The nonstatutory labor exemption is not so narrowly limited; it extends antitrust immunity to both labor unions, employees, and to non-labor parties; those who have engaged in bona fide labor negotiations. . . .
>
> We are ... satisfied that the Commission analyzed and set out in its opinion the legal precedent and rationale for its decision. We find no error in the following specific legal conclusions of the Commission:

1.   To say that collective bargaining is at the heart of the [nonstatutory labor] exemption, however, is not to say that the exemption applies only to collective bargaining agreements.

2.   [T]he cases also demonstrate that concerted conduct does not automatically qualify for the exemption simply because it is motivated by labor concerns ... motivation by labor concerns is only a necessary and not a sufficient condition for application of the nonstatutory exemption.

3.   The vast majority of nonstatutory labor exemption cases involve some sort of concerted activity or agreement between a union and an employer.

4.   [T]hose few cases [involving only employers] clearly show that the nonstatutory labor exemption protects employer agreements only when those agreements are part of the give-and-take of a negotiation process.

5.   [T]he agreement ... was designed to *prevent* collective bargaining ... to *avoid* arm's-length negotiation.

6.   The mere fact that sales employees benefit from the hours restraint also cannot justify granting an exemption ... since they have the same incentive to reduce competition as the dealers.

7.   *Jewel Tea* [381 U.S. at 676] and the present case have superficial similarities. Both involve a restriction on marketing hours and efforts by labor unions to obtain shorter working hours. But in *Jewel Tea,* unlike the case before us, the agreement was one to which the employees and employers were parties. Moreover, there was no question in *Jewel Tea* that the restrictive agreement had been reached through bona fide, arm's-length bargaining.

8.   Respondents [petitioners here as a group] have agreed among themselves, not with their employees....

We agree with the Commission that the process generally was not.... a direct product of employer collective bargaining, nor of arm's-length dealing with salespersons. 955 F.2d at 463–67.[90]

90. Ed. See Brown v. Pro Football, Inc., 518 U.S. 231 (1996), where the Supreme Court held that football club owners who had agreed among themselves—but not with the football players' union—to implement the terms of their last best bargaining offer (*i.e.,* a $1,000 weekly salary for "development squad" players) after an impasse in negotiations were protected by the nonstatutory labor exemption. Justice Breyer wrote for the Court:

As a matter of logic, it would be difficult, if not impossible, to require groups of employers and employees to bargain together, but at the same time to forbid them to make among themselves or with each other any of the competition-restricting agreements potentially

necessary to make the process work or its results mutually acceptable. Thus, the implicit exemption recognizes that, to give effect to federal labor laws and policies and to allow meaningful collective bargaining to take place, some restraints on competition imposed through the bargaining process must be shielded from antitrust sanctions. See Connell (federal labor law's "goals" could "never" be achieved if ordinary anticompetitive effects of collective bargaining were held to violate the antitrust laws); Jewel Tea (national labor law scheme would be "virtually destroyed" by the routine imposition of antitrust penalties upon parties engaged in collective bargaining); Pennington (implicit exemption neces-

As to the reasonableness of the restraint, which the FTC viewed as "inherently suspect," the Sixth Circuit concluded:

> While we do not agree in all respects with the Commission's rationale, we find some legal basis and support for its conclusions in an area that is murky and unclear. Limitation of hours has been held to be an anticompetitive restraint although relief in that case was limited and the damages to users or customers was found to be "entirely speculative." Tennessee, ex rel. Leech v. Highland Memorial Cemetery, Inc., 489 F.Supp. 65, 68 (E.D.Tenn.1980). We do not equate limitation of hours to price-fixing, but we do not find error in the Commission's conclusion that hours of operation in this business is a means of competition, and that such limitation may be an unreasonable restraint of trade.[91]

955 F.2d at 472.

5. Although restraints on hours may be analyzed as unreasonable, they clearly are not as competitively dangerous as horizontal agreements to fix prices, divide markets, and regulate production. Do horizontal agreements to fix prices, divide markets, and regulate production necessarily have the same effect upon competition? Are each of them pernicious enough to be declared illegal *per se?* Assuming that different types of market sharing arrangements and production regulations may have differing effects on competition, and may be adopted for different business reasons, does it follow that they should all be governed by different rules of law?

sary to harmonize Sherman Act with "national policy ... of promoting 'the peaceful settlement of industrial disputes by subjecting labor-management controversies to the mediatory influence of negotiation' " ...) Consequently, the question before us is one of determining the exemption's scope: Does it apply to an agreement among several employers bargaining together to implement after impasse the terms of their last best good-faith wage offer? We assume that such conduct, as practiced in this case, is unobjectionable as a matter of labor law and policy. On that assumption, we conclude that the exemption applies....

[W]e hold that the implicit ("nonstatutory") antitrust exemption applies to the employer conduct at issue here. That conduct took place during and immediately after a collective-bargaining negotiation. It grew out of, and was directly related to, the lawful operation of the bargaining process. It involved a matter that the parties were required to negotiate collectively. And it concerned only the parties to the collective-bargaining relationship.

Our holding is not intended to insulate from antitrust review every joint

imposition of terms by employers, for an agreement among employers could be sufficiently distant in time and in circumstances from the collective-bargaining process that a rule permitting antitrust intervention would not significantly interfere with that process. *See, e.g.,* 50 F.3d at 1057 (suggesting that exemption lasts until collapse of the collective-bargaining relationship, as evidenced by decertification of the union); El Cerrito Mill & Lumber Co., 316 N.L.R.B., at 1006–1007 (suggesting that "extremely long" impasse, accompanied by "instability" or "defunctness" of multiemployer unit, might justify union withdrawal from group bargaining). We need not decide in this case whether, or where, within these extreme outer boundaries to draw that line.

91. Neither do we necessarily agree that "the parties' focus on retail prices misses the point in this case." Under a Rule of Reason analysis effect on prices, output and market forces in a competitive market of a particular practice is frequently relevant and may be determinative. The special factors noted in this case support the Commission's conclusion on restraint of trade despite lack of evidence of increased prices.

NOTE ON *TIMKEN, GENERAL MOTORS,* AND *SEALY*

1.   TIMKEN ROLLER BEARING CO. v. UNITED STATES, 341 U.S. 593, 71 S.Ct. 971, 95 L.Ed. 1199 (1951). In this civil action the government charged that Timken had combined, conspired and acted with British Timken, Ltd. and Societe Anonyme Francaise Timken (French Timken) to restrain interstate and foreign commerce in the manufacture and sale of antifriction bearings throughout the world in violation of §§ 1 and 3 of the Sherman Act.

In 1927, Timken and an English businessman, Dewar, purchased all the stock of British Timken. At the time of the suit, Timken controlled 30% of the outstanding stock and Dewar 24%. In 1928, Timken and Dewar organized French Timken; all of the stock was still owned by them when this action was commenced. Since 1928, the three companies had been parties to agreements regulating the manufacture and sale of antifriction bearings and providing for the use by the British and French corporations of the "Timken" trademark. "Under these agreements the contracting parties have (1) allocated trade territories among themselves; (2) fixed prices on products of one sold in the territory of the others; (3) cooperated to protect each other's markets and to eliminate outside competition; and (4) participated in cartels to restrict imports to, and exports from, the United States." Timken contended that the restraints were reasonable, and therefore, not in violation of the Sherman Act because they were ancillary to a joint venture between Timken and Dewar and to an exercise of Timken's right to license its trademark.

The Supreme Court held that, regardless of the purpose of the restrictive agreements, "agreements providing for an aggregation of trade restraints such as those existing in this case are illegal under the Act."

The Court also held that the restrictions went beyond the trademark's purpose of "merely afford[ing] protection to a name." A majority of the Court also rejected Timken's argument that tariffs, quotas and the like had made restrictive agreements necessary to sell products abroad.

Justice Jackson dissented and raised the question whether the antitrust laws should be interpreted with respect to foreign trade in the same way they are interpreted when applied to domestic transactions, thus raising in 1951 an issue that is hotly debated today.

2.   UNITED STATES v. GENERAL MOTORS CORP., 384 U.S. 127, 86 S.Ct. 1321, 16 L.Ed.2d 415 (1966). Civil action by the Government for injunctive relief. General Motors distributes Chevrolets through independent franchised dealers. Although the franchise agreement contains no limitations on the customers to whom or the territories in which the dealers may sell, it does contain a "location clause" which prohibits the dealer from moving to or establishing "a new or different location, branch sales office, branch service station, or place of business" without Chevrolet's consent. Starting in the late 1950's, discount houses began to sell Chevrolets at alleged bargain prices either by referral of the customer to a dealer (who sold at a lower than usual price, paying the discounter a commission) or by purchasing the car from the dealer at less than the retail price and reselling it to the customer. An association of dealers formally complained to General Motors, after which General Motors' personnel discussed the matter with every dealer in the area, eliciting a promise not to do business with discounters. Various associations policed the situation and, at General Motors' request, supplied it with information concerning dealers continuing to do business with discounters. *Held,* for plaintiff. "We do not decide whether the 'location clause' may be construed to prohibit a dealer, party to it, from selling through discounters, or whether General Motors could by unilateral

action enforce the clause, so construed.[92] We have here a classic conspiracy in restraint of trade: joint, collaborative action by dealers, the appellee associations, and General Motors to eliminate a class of competitors by terminating business dealings between them and a minority of Chevrolet dealers and to deprive franchised dealers of their freedom to deal through discounters if they so choose.... Whatever General Motors might or might not lawfully have done to enforce individual Dealer Selling Agreements by action within the borders of those agreements and the relationship which each defines, is beside the point. And, because the action taken constitutes a combination or conspiracy, it is not necessary to consider what might be the legitimate interest of a dealer in securing compliance by others with the 'location clause,' or the lawfulness of action a dealer might individually take to vindicate this interest." (Fortas, J.)

3. UNITED STATES v. SEALY, INC., 388 U.S. 350, 87 S.Ct. 1847, 18 L.Ed.2d 1238 (1967). Sealy licensed manufacturers of mattresses and bedding products to make and sell such products under the Sealy name and trademarks. Its 30 licensees owned substantially all of its stock. Each director was a stockholder or a stockholder-licensee's nominee. The Government charged that Sealy had violated Section 1 of the Sherman Act by conspiring with its licensees to fix prices at which the licensees' customers could resell bedding products bearing the Sealy name and to allocate exclusive territories among the manufacturers.

The district court's finding of price fixing was not appealed. The Supreme Court reversed the district court's holding that the territorial restraints had not been shown to be "unreasonable." The Court concluded that the "territorial arrangements must be regarded as the creature of horizontal action by the licensees. It would violate reality to treat them as equivalent to territorial limitations imposed by a manufacturer upon independent dealers as incident to the sale of a trademarked product. Sealy, Inc., is an instrumentality of the licensees for purposes of the horizontal territorial allocation. It is not the principal." The Court declared the territorial restraints unlawful, because "they gave to each licensee an enclave in which it could and did zealously and effectively maintain resale prices, free from the danger of outside incursions."

This "aggregation of trade restraints including unlawful price-fixing and policing" was "unlawful under Section 1 of the Sherman Act without the necessity for an inquiry in each particular case as to their business or economic justification, their impact in the marketplace, or their reasonableness." (Fortas, J.)

United States v. Topco Associates, Inc.

Supreme Court of the United States, 1972.
405 U.S. 596, 92 S.Ct. 1126, 31 L.Ed.2d 515.

■ MARSHALL, J. The United States brought this action for injunctive relief against Topco Associates, Inc.'s (Topco) alleged violation of § 1 of the Sherman Act. Following a trial on the merits, the United States District Court for the Northern District of Illinois entered judgment for Topco, 319 F.Supp. 1031, and the United States appealed directly to this Court pursuant to § 2 of the Expediting Act, 32 Stat. 823, as amended, 15 U.S.C.A. § 29. We noted probable jurisdiction, 402 U.S. 905 (1971), and we now reverse the judgment of the District Court.

92. Ed. For a discussion of this point, see Chapter 7 infra.

I

Topco is a cooperative association of approximately 25 small and medium-sized regional supermarket chains which operate stores in some 33 States. Each of the member chains operates independently; there is no pooling of earnings, profits, capital, management, or advertising resources. No grocery business is conducted under the Topco name. Its basic function is to serve as a purchasing agent for its members. In this capacity, it procures and distributes to the members more than 1,000 different food and related nonfood items, most of which are distributed under brand names owned by Topco. The association does not itself own any manufacturing, processing, or warehousing facilities, and the items that it procures for members are usually shipped directly from the packer or manufacturer to the members. Payment is made either to Topco or directly to the manufacturer at a cost that is virtually the same for the members as for Topco itself.

All of the stock in Topco is owned by the members, with the common stock, the only stock having voting rights, being equally distributed. The board of directors, which controls the operation of the association, is drawn from the members and is normally composed of high-ranking executive officers of member chains. It is the board that elects the association's officers and appoints committee members, and it is from the board that the principal executive officers of Topco must be drawn. Restrictions on the alienation of stock and the procedure for selecting all important officials of the association from within the ranks of its members give the members complete and unfettered control over the operations of the association.

Topco was founded in the 1940s by a group of small, local grocery chains, independently owned and operated, which desired to cooperate to obtain high quality merchandise under private labels in order to compete more effectively with larger national and regional chains.[93] With a line of

93. The founding members of Topco were having difficulty competing with larger chains. This difficulty was attributable in some degree to the fact that the larger chains were capable of developing their own private-label programs.

Private-label products differ from other brand-name products in that they are sold at a limited number of easily ascertainable stores. A & P, for example, was a pioneer in developing a series of products that were sold under an A & P label and that were only available in A & P stores. It is obvious that by using private-label products, a chain can achieve significant cost economies in purchasing, transportation, warehousing, promotion, and advertising. These economies may afford the chain opportunities for offering private-label products at lower prices than other brand-name products. This, in turn, provides many advantages of which some of the more important are: a store can offer national-brand products at the same price as other stores, while simultaneously offering a desirable, lower priced alternative; or, if the profit margin is sufficiently high on private-brand goods, national-brand products may be sold at reduced price. Other advantages include: enabling a chain to bargain more favorably with national-brand manufacturers by creating a broader supply base of manufacturers, thereby decreasing dependence on a few, large national-brand manufacturers; enabling a chain to create a "price-mix" whereby prices on special items can be lowered to attract customers while profits are maintained on other items; and creating of general goodwill by offering lower priced, higher quality goods.

canned, dairy, and other products, the association began. It added frozen foods in 1950, fresh produce in 1958, more general merchandise equipment and supplies in 1960, and a branded bacon and carcass beef selection program in 1966. By 1964, Topco's members had combined retail sales of more than $2 billion; by 1967, their sales totaled more than $2.3 billion, a figure exceeded by only three national grocery chains.

Members of the association vary in the degree of market share that they possess in their respective areas. The range is from 1.5% to 16%, with the average being approximately 6%. While it is more difficult to compare these figures with the market shares of larger regional and national chains because of the absence in the record of accurate statistics for these chains, there is much evidence in the record that Topco members are frequently in as strong a competitive position in their respective areas as any other chain. The strength of this competitive position is due, in some measure, to the success of Topco-brand products. Although only 10% of the total goods sold by Topco members bear the association's brand names, the profit on these goods is substantial and their very existence has improved the competitive potential of Topco members with respect to other large and powerful chains.

It is apparent that from meager beginnings approximately a quarter of a century ago, Topco has developed into a purchasing association wholly owned and operated by member chains, which possess much economic muscle, individually as well as cooperatively.

II

... The United States charged that, beginning at least as early as 1960 and continuing up to the time that the complaint was filed, Topco had combined and conspired with its members to violate § 1 in two respects. First, the Government alleged that there existed:

> "a continuing agreement, understanding and concert of action among the co-conspirator member firms acting through Topco, the substantial terms of which have been and are that each co-conspirator member firm will sell Topco-controlled brands only within the marketing territory allocated to it, and will refrain from selling Topco-controlled brands outside such marketing territory."

... Membership must first be approved by the board of directors, and thereafter by an affirmative vote of 75% of the association's members. If, however, the member whose operations are closest to those of the applicant, or any member whose operations are located within 100 miles of the applicant, votes against approval, an affirmative vote of 85% of the members is required for approval. Bylaws, Art. I, § 5. Because, as indicated by the record, members cooperate in accommodating each other's wishes, the procedure for approval provides, in essence, that members have a veto of sorts over actual or potential competition in the territorial areas in which they are concerned.

Following approval, each new member signs an agreement with Topco designating the territory in which that member may sell Topco-brand products. No member may sell these products outside the territory in which it is licensed. Most licenses are exclusive, and even those denominated "coextensive" or "non-exclusive" prove to be *de facto* exclusive. Exclusive territorial areas are often allocated to members who do no actual business in those areas on the theory that they may wish to expand at some indefinite future time and that expansion would likely be in the direction of the allocated territory. When combined with each member's veto power over new members, provisions for exclusivity work effectively to insulate members from competition in Topco-brand goods. Should a member violate its license agreement and sell in areas other than those in which it is licensed, its membership can be terminated under Art. IV, §§ 2(a) and 2(b) of the bylaws. Once a territory is classified as exclusive, either formally or *de facto,* it is extremely unlikely that the classification will ever be changed. See Bylaws, Art. IX.

The Government maintains that this scheme of dividing markets violates the Sherman Act because it operates to prohibit competition in Topco-brand products among grocery chains engaged in retail operations. The Government also makes a subsidiary challenge to Topco's practices regarding licensing members to sell at wholesale. Under the bylaws, members are not permitted to sell any products supplied by the association at wholesale, whether trademarked or not, without first applying for and receiving special permission from the association to do so. Before permission is granted, other licensees (usually retailers), whose interests may potentially be affected by wholesale operations, are consulted as to their wishes in the matter. If permission is obtained, the member must agree to restrict the sale of Topco products to a specific geographic area and to sell under any conditions imposed by the association. Permission to wholesale has often been sought by members, only to be denied by the association. The Government contends that this amounts not only to a territorial restriction violative of the Sherman Act, but also to a restriction on customers which in itself is violative of the Act.

From the inception of this lawsuit, Topco accepted as true most of the Government's allegations regarding territorial divisions and restrictions on wholesaling, although it differed greatly with the Government on the conclusions, both factual and legal, to be drawn from these facts.

Topco's answer to the complaint is illustrative of its posture in the District Court and before this Court:

> "Private label merchandising is a way of economic life in the food retailing industry, and exclusivity is the essence of a private label program; without exclusivity, a private label would not be private. Each national and large regional chain has its own exclusive private label products in addition to the nationally advertised brands which all chains sell. Each such chain relies upon the exclusivity of its own private label line to differentiate its private label products from those of its competitors and to attract and

retain the repeat business and loyalty of consumers. Smaller retail grocery stores and chains are unable to compete effectively with the national and large regional chains without also offering their own exclusive private label products.

. . .

"The only feasible method by which Topco can procure private label products and assure the exclusivity thereof is through trademark licenses specifying the territory in which each member may sell such trademarked products." Answer, App. 11.

Topco essentially maintains that it needs territorial divisions to compete with larger chains; that the association could not exist if the territorial divisions were anything but exclusive; and that by restricting competition in the sale of Topco-brand goods, the association actually increases competition by enabling its members to compete successfully with larger regional and national chains.

The District Court, considering all these things relevant to its decision, agreed with Topco. It recognized that the panoply of restraints that Topco imposed on its members worked to prevent competition in Topco-brand products, but concluded that

"[w]hatever anti-competitive effect these practices may have on competition in the sale of Topco private label brands is far outweighed by the increased ability of Topco members to compete both with the national chains and other supermarkets operating in their respective territories." 319 F.Supp. 1031, 1043 (1970).

The court held that Topco's practices were pro-competitive and, therefore, consistent with the purposes of the antitrust laws. But we conclude that the District Court used an improper analysis in reaching its result.

. . . It is only after considerable experience with certain business relationships that courts classify them as *per se* violations of the Sherman Act. See generally Van Cise, The Future of *per se* in Antitrust Law, 50 Va.L.Rev. 1165 (1964). One of the classic examples of a *per se* violation of § 1 is an agreement between competitors at the same level of the market structure to allocate territories in order to minimize competition. Such concerted action is usually termed a "horizontal" restraint, in contradistinction to combinations of persons at different levels of the market structure, *e.g.*, manufacturers and distributors, which are termed "vertical" restraints. This Court has reiterated time and time again that "[h]orizontal territorial limitations . . . are naked restraints of trade with no purpose except stifling of competition." White Motor Co. v. United States, 372 U.S. 253, 263 (1963). Such limitations are *per se* violations of the Sherman Act. See Addyston Pipe & Steel Co. v. United States, 175 F. 211 (1899), aff'g 85 F. 271 (C.A.6 1898) (Taft, J.); United States v. National Lead Co., 332 U.S. 319 (1947); Timken Roller Bearing Co. v. United States, 341 U.S. 593 (1951); Northern Pacific R. Co. v. United States, supra; Citizen Publishing Co. v. United States, 394 U.S. 131 (1969); United States v. Sealy, Inc., 388 U.S. 350 (1967); United States v. Arnold, Schwinn & Co.,

388 U.S. 365, 390 (1967) (Stewart, J., concurring in part and dissenting in part); Serta Associates, Inc. v. United States, 393 U.S. 534 (1969), aff'g 296 F.Supp. 1121, 1128 (N.D.Ill.1968).

We think that it is clear that the restraint in this case is a horizontal one, and, therefore, a *per se* violation of § 1. The District Court failed to make any determination as to whether there were *per se* horizontal territorial restraints in this case and simply applied a rule of reason in reaching its conclusions that the restraints were not illegal. *See, e.g.,* Comment, Horizontal Territorial Restraints and the *per se* Rule, 28 Wash. & Lee L.Rev. 457, 469 (1971). In so doing, the District Court erred. . . .

Whether or not we would decide this case the same way under the rule of reason used by the District Court is irrelevant to the issue before us. The fact is that courts are of limited utility in examining difficult economic problems.[94] Our inability to weigh, in any meaningful sense, destruction of competition in one sector of the economy against promotion of competition in another sector is one important reason we have formulated *per se* rules.

In applying these rigid rules, the Court has consistently rejected the notion that naked restraints of trade are to be tolerated because they are well intended or because they are allegedly developed to increase competition. . . .

Antitrust laws in general, and the Sherman Act in particular, are the Magna Carta of free enterprise. They are as important to the preservation of economic freedom and our free-enterprise system as the Bill of Rights is to the protection of our fundamental personal freedoms. And the freedom guaranteed each and every business, no matter how small, is the freedom to compete—to assert with vigor, imagination, devotion, and ingenuity whatever economic muscle it can muster. Implicit in such freedom is the notion that it cannot be foreclosed with respect to one sector of the economy because certain private citizens or groups believe that such foreclosure might promote greater competition in a more important sector of the economy. Cf. United States v. Philadelphia National Bank, 374 U.S. 321, 371 (1963).

The District Court determined that by limiting the freedom of its individual members to compete with each other, Topco was doing a greater good by fostering competition between members and other large supermarket chains. But, the fallacy in this is that Topco has no authority under the Sherman Act to determine the respective values of competition in various sectors of the economy. On the contrary, the Sherman Act gives to each Topco member and to each prospective member the right to ascertain for itself whether or not competition with other supermarket chains is more

---

94. There has been much recent commentary on the wisdom of *per se* rules. . . . Without the *per se* rules, businessmen would be left with little to aid them in predicting in any particular case what courts will find to be legal and illegal under the Sherman Act. Should Congress ultimately determine that predictability is unimportant in this area of the law, it can, of course, make *per se* rules inapplicable in some or all cases, and leave courts free to ramble through the wilds of economic theory in order to maintain a flexible approach.

desirable than competition in the sale of Topco-brand products. Without territorial restrictions, Topco members may indeed "[cut] each other's throats." Cf. *White Motor Co., supra,* at 278 (Clark, J., dissenting). But, we have never found this possibility sufficient to warrant condoning horizontal restraints of trade. . . .

There have been tremendous departures from the notion of a free-enterprise system as it was originally conceived in this country. These departures have been the product of congressional action and the will of the people. If a decision is to be made to sacrifice competition in one portion of the economy for greater competition in another portion, this too is a decision that must be made by Congress and not by private forces or by the courts. Private forces are too keenly aware of their own interests in making such decisions and courts are ill-equipped and ill-situated for such decisionmaking. To analyze, interpret, and evaluate the myriad of competing interests and the endless data that would surely be brought to bear on such decisions, and to make the delicate judgment on the relative values to society of competitive areas of the economy, the judgment of the elected representatives of the people is required.

Just as the territorial restrictions on retailing Topco-brand products must fall, so must the territorial restrictions on wholesaling. The considerations are the same, and the Sherman Act requires identical results.

We also strike down Topco's other restrictions on the rights of its members to wholesale goods. These restrictions amount to regulation of the customers to whom members of Topco may sell Topco-brand goods. Like territorial restrictions, limitations on customers are intended to limit intra-brand competition and to promote inter-brand competition. For the reasons previously discussed, the arena in which Topco members compete must be left to their unfettered choice absent a contrary congressional determination.

We reverse the judgment of the District Court and remand the case for entry of an appropriate decree.

It is so ordered.

■ POWELL and REHNQUIST, JJ., took no part in the consideration or decision of this case.

■ BLACKMUN, J., concurring in the result.

The conclusion the Court reaches has its anomalous aspects for surely, as the District Court's findings make clear, today's decision in the Government's favor will tend to stultify Topco members' competition with the great and larger chains. The bigs, therefore, should find it easier to get bigger and, as a consequence, reality seems at odds with the public interest. The *per se* rule, however, now appears to be so firmly established by the Court that, at this late date, I could not oppose it. Relief, if any is to be forthcoming, apparently must be by way of legislation.

■ BURGER, C.J., dissenting.

This case does not involve restraints on interbrand competition or an allocation of markets by an association with monopoly or near-monopoly control of the sources of supply of one or more varieties of staple goods. Rather, we have here an agreement among several small grocery chains to join in a cooperative endeavor which, in my view, has an unquestionably lawful principal purpose; in pursuit of that purpose they have mutually agreed to certain minimal ancillary restraints that are fully reasonable in view of the principal purpose and that have never before today been held by this Court to be *per se* violations of the Sherman Act.

In joining in this cooperative endeavor, these small chains did not agree to the restraints here at issue in order to make it possible for them to exploit an already established line of products through non-competitive pricing. There was no such thing as a Topco line of products until this cooperative was formed. The restraints to which the cooperative's members have agreed deal only with the marketing of the products in the Topco line, and the only function of those restraints is to permit each member chain to establish, within its own geographical area and through its own local advertising and marketing efforts, a local consumer awareness of the trademarked family of products as that member's "private label" line. The goal sought was the enhancement of the individual members' abilities to compete, albeit to a modest degree, with the large national chains which had been successfully marketing private-label lines for several years. The sole reason for a cooperative endeavor was to make economically feasible such things as quality control, large quantity purchases at bulk prices, the development of attractively printed labels, and the ability to offer a number of different lines of trademarked products. All these things, of course, are feasible for the large national chains operating individually, but they are beyond the reach of the small operators proceeding alone.[95]

After a careful review of the economic considerations bearing upon this case, the District Court determined that "the relief which the government here seeks would not increase competition in Topco private label brands"; on the contrary, such relief "would substantially diminish competition in the supermarket field." 319 F.Supp. 1031, 1043. This Court has not today determined, on the basis of an examination of the underlying economic realities, that the District Court's conclusions are incorrect. Rather, the majority holds that the District Court had no business examining Topco's practices under the "rule of reason"; it should not have sought to determine whether Topco's practices did in fact restrain trade or commerce within the meaning of § 1 of the Sherman Act; it should have found no more than that those practices involve a "horizontal division of markets" and are, by that very fact, *per se* violations of the Act.

---

95. The District Court's findings of fact include the following:

"33. A competitively effective private label program to be independently undertaken by a single retailer or chain would require an annual sales volume of $250 million or more and in order to achieve optimum efficiency, the volume required would probably have to be twice that amount." 319 F.Supp. 1031, 1036.

I do not believe that our prior decisions justify the result reached by the majority. Nor do I believe that a new *per se* rule should be established in disposing of this case, for the judicial convenience and ready predictability that are made possible by *per se* rules are not such overriding considerations in antitrust law as to justify their promulgation without careful prior consideration of the relevant economic realities in the light of the basic policy and goals of the Sherman Act.

I

I deal first with the cases upon which the majority relies in stating that "[t]his Court has reiterated time and time again that '[h]orizontal territorial limitations ... are naked restraints of trade with no purpose except stifling of competition.' White Motor Co. v. United States, 372 U.S. 253, 263 (1963)." *White Motor,* of course, laid down no *per se* rule; nor were any horizontal territorial limitations involved in that case....

Having quoted this dictum from *White Motor,* the Court then cites eight cases for the proposition that horizontal territorial limitations are *per se* violations of the Sherman Act. One of these cases, Northern Pacific R. Co. v. United States, 356 U.S. 1 (1958), dealt exclusively with a prohibited tying arrangement and is improperly cited as a case concerned with a division of markets.[96] Of the remaining seven cases, four involved an aggregation of trade restraints that included price-fixing agreements. Timken Roller Bearing Co. v. United States, 341 U.S. 593 (1951); United States v. Sealy, Inc., 388 U.S. 350 (1967); Serta Associates, Inc. v. United States, 393 U.S. 534 (1969), aff'g 296 F.Supp. 1121 (N.D.Ill.1968). Price-fixing is, of course, not a factor in the instant case.

Another of the cases relied upon by the Court, United States v. National Lead Co., 332 U.S. 319 (1947), involved a worldwide arrangement for dividing territories, pooling patents, and exchanging technological information. The arrangement was found illegal by the District Court without any reliance on a *per se* rule; this Court, in affirming, was concerned almost exclusively with the remedies ordered by the District Court and made no attempt to declare a *per se* rule to govern the merits of the case.

In still another case on which the majority relies, United States v. Arnold, Schwinn & Co., 388 U.S. 365 (1967), the District Court had, indeed, held that the agreements between the manufacturer and certain of its distributors, providing the latter with exclusive territories, were horizontal in nature and that they were, as such, *per se* violations of the Act. 237 F.Supp. 323, 342–343. Since no appeal was taken from this part of the District Court's order, that issue was not before this Court in its review of the case....

96. There is dictum in the case to the effect that United States v. Addyston Pipe & Steel Co., 85 F. 271 (C.A.6 1898), aff'd, 175 U.S. 211 (1899), established a "division of markets" as unlawful in and of itself. 356 U.S., at 5. As I will show, however, Addyston Pipe established no such thing; it was primarily a price-fixing case.

Finally, there remains the eighth of the cases relied upon by the Court—actually, the first in its list of "authorities" for the purported *per se* rule. Circuit Judge (later Chief Justice) Taft's opinion for the court in United States v. Addyston Pipe & Steel Co., 85 F. 271 (C.A.6 1898), aff'd, 175 U.S. 211 (1899), has generally been recognized—and properly so—as a fully authoritative exposition of antitrust law. But neither he, nor this Court in affirming, made any pretense of establishing a *per se* rule against all agreements involving horizontal territorial limitations.... Although the case has frequently—and quite properly—been cited as a horizontal allocation-of-markets case, the sole purpose of the secret customer allocations was to enable the members of the association to fix prices charged to the public at non-competitive levels. Judge Taft rejected the defendants' argument that the prices actually charged were "reasonable"; he held that it was sufficient for a finding of a Sherman Act violation that the combination and agreement of the defendants gave them such monopoly power that they, rather than market forces, fixed the prices of all cast-iron pipe in three-fourths of the Nation's territory. The case unquestionably laid important groundwork for the subsequent establishment of *per se* rule against price fixing. It did not, however, establish that a horizontal division of markets is, without more, a *per se* violation of the Sherman Act.

II

The foregoing analysis of the cases relied upon by the majority indicates to me that the Court is not merely following prior holdings; on the contrary, it is establishing a new *per se* rule. In the face of the District Court's well supported findings that the effects of such a rule in this case will be adverse to the public welfare,[97] the Court lays down that rule without regard to the impact that the condemned practices may have on competition. In doing so, the Court virtually invites Congress to undertake to determine that impact. I question whether the Court is fulfilling the role assigned to it under the statute when it declines to make this determination; in any event, if the Court is unwilling on this record to assess the economic impact, it surely should not proceed to make a new rule to govern the economic activity. White Motor Co. v. United States, 372 U.S., at 263....

In formulating a new *per se* rule today, the Court does not tell us what "pernicious effect on competition" the practices here outlawed are perceived to have; nor does it attempt to show that those practices "lack ...

---

97. Among the facts found by the District Court are the following: private label brand merchandising, which is beyond the reach of the small chains acting independently and which by definition depends upon local exclusivity, permits the merchandiser to offer the public "lower consumer prices on products of high quality" and "to bargain more favorably with national brand manufacturers"; such merchandising fosters "the estab-lishment of a broader supply base of manufacturers, thereby decreasing dependence upon a relatively few, large national brand manufacturers"; it also enables "[s]maller manufacturers, the most common source of private label products, who are generally unable to develop national brand name recognition for their products, [to] benefit ... by the assurance of a substantial market for their products".... 319 F.Supp., at 1035.

any redeeming virtue." Rather, it emphasizes only the importance of predictability, asserting that "courts are of limited utility in examining difficult economic problems" and have not yet been left free by Congress to "ramble through the wilds of economic theory in order to maintain a flexible approach."

With all respect, I believe that there are two basic fallacies in the Court's approach here. First, while I would not characterize our role under the Sherman Act as one of "rambl[ing] through the wilds," it is indeed one that requires our "examin[ation of] difficult economic problems." We can undoubtedly ease our task, but we should not abdicate that role by formulation of *per se* rules with no justification other than the enhancement of predictability and the reduction of judicial investigation. Second, from the general proposition that *per se* rules play a necessary role in antitrust law, it does not follow that the particular *per se* rule promulgated today is an appropriate one. Although it might well be desirable in a proper case for this Court to formulate a *per se* rule dealing with horizontal territorial limitations, it would not necessarily be appropriate for such a rule to amount to a blanket prohibition against all such limitations. More specifically, it is far from clear to me why such a rule should cover those division-of-market agreements which involve no price fixing and which are concerned only with trademarked products that are not in a monopoly or near-monopoly position with respect to competing brands. The instant case presents such an agreement; I would not decide it upon the basis of a *per se* rule.[98]

The District Court specifically found that the horizontal restraints involved here tend positively to promote competition in the supermarket field and to produce lower costs for the consumer. The Court seems implicitly to accept this determination, but says that the Sherman Act does not give Topco the authority to determine for itself "whether or not competition with other supermarket chains is more desirable than competition in the sale of Topco-brand products." Ante, at 611. But the majority overlooks a further specific determination of the District Court, namely, that the invalidation of the restraints here at issue "would not increase competition in Topco private label brands." 319 F.Supp., at 1043. Indeed, the District Court seemed to believe that it would, on the contrary, lead to the likely demise of those brands in time. And the evidence before the District Court would appear to justify that conclusion.

---

98. The national chains market their own private-label products, and these products are available nowhere else than in the stores of those chains. The stores of any one chain, of course, do not engage in price competition with each other with respect to their chain's private-label brands, and no serious suggestion could be made that the Sherman Act requires otherwise. I fail to see any difference whatsoever in the economic effect of the Topco arrangement for the marketing of Topco-brand products and the methods used by the national chains in marketing their private-label brands. True, the Topco arrangement involves a "combination," while each of the national chains is a single integrated corporation. The controlling consideration, however, should be that in neither case is the policy of the Sherman Act offended, for the practices in both cases work to the benefit, and not to the detriment, of the consuming public.

There is no national demand for Topco brands, nor has there ever been any national advertising of those brands. It would be impracticable for Topco, with its limited financial resources, to convert itself into a national brand distributor in competition with distributors of existing national brands. Furthermore, without the right to grant exclusive licenses, it could not attract and hold new members as replacements for those of its present members who, following the pattern of the past, eventually grow sufficiently in size to be able to leave the cooperative organization and develop their own individual private-label brands. Moreover, Topco's present members, once today's decision has had its full impact over the course of time, will have no more reason to promote Topco products through local advertising and merchandising efforts than they will have such reason to promote any other generally available brands.

The issue presented by the antitrust cases reaching this Court are rarely simple to resolve under the rule of reason; they do indeed frequently require us to make difficult economic determinations. We should not for that reason alone, however, be overly zealous in formulating new *per se* rules, for an excess of zeal in that regard is both contrary to the policy of the Sherman Act and detrimental to the welfare of consumers generally. Indeed, the economic effect of the new rule laid down by the Court today seems clear: unless Congress intervenes, grocery staples marketed under private-label brands with their lower consumer prices will soon be available only to those who patronize the large national chains.

General Leaseways Inc. v. National Truck Leasing Association

United States Court of Appeals, Seventh Circuit, 1984.
744 F.2d 588.

Defendant National Truck Leasing Association (NTLA) was a league of 130 companies that leased trucks to businesses, occasionally on a "full service" basis. Under those arrangements, the members of NTLA were responsible for maintaining the trucks and for repairing them at locations throughout the country. Members of the Association were small local companies, however, without nation-wide service facilities. The Association was created to establish a reciprocal service arrangement enabling each member to lease trucks on a full service basis and thus compete with national truck leasing companies which owned and operated service facilities throughout the United States. Each Association member was required to provide other members with prompt and efficient repair services.

As a condition of membership, each member accepted a franchise from NTLA designating a particular location at which it could conduct its business, and forbidding operations as a franchisee of NTLA at any other location. Members were also forbidden from affiliating with any other full service truck leasing enterprise such as Hertz or Avis. As a practical matter, lessees invariably dealt with firms having an outlet within a few miles of their place of business to insure the convenience of picking up trucks nearby and facilitating regular (as opposed to emergency repair) maintenance. The Association's policy was to space franchises at least 10 or 20 miles apart. Members of NTLA could open up outlets at unauthorized locations, but in those circumstances, the member would not be entitled to reciprocal service.

General Leaseways elected to defy the location and nonaffiliation restrictions and successfully obtained a preliminary injunction from the district court preventing it from being expelled from the Association pending trial on the merits. The Court of Appeals' discussion on appeal includes the following:

■ POSNER, J....

Until a few years ago it would have been possible to opine confidently ... that when firms in the same line of business agree not to enter each other's territories they violate section 1 of the Sherman Act even if they might be able to show that dividing markets had yielded economic benefits greater than any plausible estimate of the costs in diminished competition; that, in short, horizontal market divisions are illegal *per se. See, e.g.,* United States v. Topco Associates, Inc., 405 U.S. 596, 608; United States v. Sealy, Inc., 388 U.S. 350, 356–57; Timken Roller Bearing Co. v. United States, 341 U.S. 593, 598; United States v. Nationwide Trailer Rental System, Inc., 156 F.Supp. 800 (D.Kan.), aff'd without opinion, 355 U.S. 10.

In both *Sealy* and *Topco,* a group of small competitors had divided markets on geographic lines as an incident to the sharing of a trademark, and the group argued that its market share was too small to make cartelization a palpable danger to competition or a plausible explanation of what it was doing. Apparently each group was just trying to prevent members from taking a free ride on other members' efforts to promote the trademark. And yet in both cases the market division was held to be a *per se* violation of section 1. In *Sealy* (as in *Timken*) the division of markets was coupled with price fixing, against which antitrust law has long come down very hard—though, as we shall see, price fixing and division of markets have identical competitive effects. But *Topco* held that horizontal market division is illegal *per se* even if price fixing is not present. 405 U.S. 609 at n. 9.

This case is even stronger for condemnation, because the free-rider argument made by National Truck Leasing Association is much weaker than the free-rider arguments in *Sealy* and *Topco.* A member of the Sealy group who promoted the Sealy trademark in his sales area by extensive (and expensive) advertising could not recoup his expenses by charging the people who saw his ads for the privilege of seeing them; virtually no one will pay to consume advertising. He could recoup only by selling his mattresses at a price that covered those expenses along with all his other costs. It is this form of recoupment that the free rider—in *Sealy,* a manufacturer of mattresses under the same trademark who has not borne the expense of promoting the mark—thwarts by invading the territory of the advertising manufacturer: by seeking, in other words, to reap where he has not sown. But members of National Truck Leasing Association charge each other for emergency repair service.

The Association argues that they do not charge the full price: that is, do not charge the premium—indeed, the extortionate—price they could get in an unregulated market for providing the prompt service to which members of the Association are entitled by its rules. When a truck breaks down, the owner is pretty much at the mercy of the nearest repair service. Unless he owns the service or has a contract with the owner or the sort of reciprocal-service arrangement that the Association has created for its members, he will not have access to a competitive market in repairs. (The salvage of ships in distress involves surprisingly similar problems, on which see Gilmore & Black, The Law of Admiralty 578–81 (2d ed. 1975).) Therefore, if one member of the Association—General Leaseways, say—grew so large relative to the others that it was consistently demanding more repairs on its trucks than it was performing on its fellow members' trucks, it would be exploiting the "underpricing" of repair service by the other members.

This argument is terribly speculative, though. As a member of the Association grows, he puts himself in a position to expect more service calls on himself (because he is serving a larger area) as well as to demand more service from others. Moreover, there is no evidence that the Association seeks to limit the growth of its members so that all remain about the same size. Also the Association does not limit repair prices, and it has not explained why its members do not (has not even shown they do not) charge fully remunerative prices for the repair services they provide each other. Even if they do refrain from gouging one another, such forbearance would be a burden or cost of repairing a fellow member's truck only if that repair job made it impossible to do another repair job that would fetch a higher price. The Association put in no evidence that this has ever happened.

It is not repairs that sellers find hard to charge for directly. It is *information-* in the form of advertising, showroom display, sales demonstrations, courteous and informed salesmen, and other presale services—that free riders in previous cases were able to take advantage of because the information was being "given away" by a seller who could recover his cost only by selling the product to the consumer who used the information. Repairing is not informing. And National's franchisees do little advertising or other promotion of the NationaLease trademark. They are selling to businesses, not consumers, and advertising usually is less important in selling to businessmen than to consumers. But whatever the reason for the lack of promotional effort, the division of markets cannot (on this record) be justified as a measure for promoting the NationaLease mark. . . .

Broadcast Music upheld the blanket licenses by which associations of composers sell musical performance rights to radio stations and other performance outlets. Since the blanket license gives the licensee, for a fixed fee, the right to play any composition in the association's library, it eliminates price competition among the composers belonging to the association. Nevertheless the Supreme Court held that the blanket license was not a *per se* violation of section 1 of the Sherman Act. National Truck Leasing Association argues in effect that after *Broadcast Music* no reasonable cartel agreement can be a *per se* violation of section 1. We hesitate to read the decision so broadly. Access to a repertoire of thousands of songs is not something the individual composer can give, so what the performing-rights associations are engaged in is not (or not just) the suppression of price competition among composers. It is the provision of a distinctive product—access to a vast musical repertoire. Each association is the "producer," and is entitled to price its "product" as it wants as long as it does not collude with the other association. So viewed, *Broadcast Music* was not a cartel case.

There is nothing distinctive about the product involved in this case. Many firms offer full-service over-the-road commercial truck leasing; the Association merely makes it easier for small firms to offer it, by providing a reciprocal service arrangement that enables each member to provide his customers with emergency repair service anywhere in the nation. Unlike the composers' associations in the *Broadcast Music* case, this association sells nothing.

If this analysis is too formalistic—if *Broadcast Music* is more realistically described as a case where the Supreme Court, though aware that an exclusive sales agency normally is a method of cartelization ... upheld exclusive sales agencies of composers because of the enormous efficiency of selling musical performing rights jointly (see NCAA v. Board of Regents, supra, 104 S.Ct. at 2961, where *Broadcast Music* is so described)—National Truck Leasing Association still loses. ASCAP and BMI could not provide ready access to their entire repertoires if each radio station had to negotiate separately with each composer over the price of each song. But National's members could—were it not for the territorial restrictions—compete in each other's territories while continuing to provide each other emergency repair services of a specified quality at a specified price. Of course this would make the members each other's competitors in leasing and customers in repairs. But firms often have both a competitive and a supply relationship with one another. A manufacturer of aluminum might both sell aluminum to fabricators and do its own fabrication in competition with its customers. Airlines compete but also feed passengers to each other. Railroads compete but also join in offering through routes and joint rates. Oil companies compete in some markets and are joint venturers in others. It does not follow that because two firms sometimes have a cooperative relationship there are no competitive gains from forbidding them to cooperate in ways that yield no economies but simply limit competition....

After argument in this case, the Supreme Court decided the *NCAA* case, supra, and again refused to hold that an agreement between competitors not to compete was illegal *per se* under the Sherman Act. The agreement was among the college football teams that belong to the NCAA, and limited the number of football games that each team could license for television broadcast. The Supreme Court described this agreement as one to limit output. That is the equivalent of a division of markets. A firm that is free from effective competition will reduce its output below the competitive level (whether directly or, as we shall see in a moment, indirectly by raising price). Consumers will pay more when supply is scarcer, yet it will cost the firm less to produce a smaller supply—so the firm's profits will be greater at the reduced output. One way the firm can free itself from competition is by agreeing with sellers of the same product that they will not enter each other's markets; such an agreement will create a series of regional or local (sometimes, as in *Timken,* national) monopolies. An agreement on output also equates to a price-fixing agreement. If firms raise price, the market's demand for their product will fall, so the amount supplied will fall too—in other words, output will be restricted. If instead the firms restrict output directly, price will as mentioned rise in order to limit demand to the reduced supply. Thus, with exceptions not relevant here, raising price, reducing output, and dividing markets have the same anticompetitive effects.

The Court held nevertheless that the NCAA's agreement to limit output had to be tested under the Rule of Reason, because organized athletic competition is "an industry in which horizontal restraints on competition are essential if the product is to be available at all." The essence of successful league competition is maintaining a balance of power among the competitors—a goal antithetic to the goals of competition in a conventional economic market. *NCAA* may seem to go a step beyond *Broadcast Music* toward a regime in which only unreasonable horizontal restraints are illegal, because the Court in *NCAA* did not condition the applicability of the Rule of Reason on proof that the particular restriction that had been challenged was necessary if the product was to be brought to market at all. There was, however, a plausible connection between the specific restriction and the essential character of the product. Since the balance of power among the teams in the NCAA might be disturbed by disparities in team wealth, limiting the ability of the more popular teams to cash in on their popularity through unrestricted televising of their games might have promoted the NCAA's essential lawful objectives. It was arguable, in other words, that the television output restriction was "ancillary" to a lawful main purpose. See United States v. Addyston Pipe & Steel Co., 85 F. 271, 281–82 (6th Cir.1898), aff'd as modified, 175 U.S. 211, Bork, The Antitrust Paradox 29–30 (1978). But in this case the organic connection between the restraint and the cooperative needs of the enterprise that would allow us to call the restraint a merely ancillary one is missing. Although some degree of cooperation among members of National Truck Leasing Association in providing reciprocal services may well promote competition in the truck-leasing industry, no reason has been suggested why that cooperation requires that members be forbidden to compete with each other in leasing trucks.

The *per se* rule would collapse if every claim of economies from restricting competition, however implausible, could be used to move a horizontal agreement not to compete from the *per se* to the Rule of Reason category. We are told, therefore, to apply the *per se* rule when "the practice facially appears to be one that would always or almost always tend to restrict competition and decrease output." Broadcast Music, Inc. v. Columbia Broadcasting System, Inc., supra, 442 U.S. at 19–20, quoted in National Collegiate Athletic Ass'n v. Board of Regents, supra, 104 S.Ct. at 2960. In other words, if the elimination of competition is apparent on a quick look, without undertaking the kind of searching inquiry that would make the case a Rule of Reason case in fact if not in name, the practice is illegal *per se*.

Taking a quick look here, we conclude, on the basis of the record compiled in the preliminary-injunction hearing, that the division of markets among National Truck Leasing Association's members is a *per se* violation of section 1 of the Sherman Act. It is a horizontal market division that does not appear to be ancillary to the reciprocal provision of service or any other lawful activity. . . .

[The Court went on to examine the arrangement under a rule of reason and concluded that, despite the modest market power of defendants, the arrangement was unreasonable largely because "the Association's attempted justification based on free-rider problems is unpersuasive." As a result, the district court's award of a preliminary injunction was affirmed.]

Palmer v. BRG of Georgia, Inc.

Supreme Court of the United States, 1990.
498 U.S. 46, 111 S.Ct. 401, 112 L.Ed.2d 349.

■ PER CURIAM. . . . HBJ began offering a Georgia bar review course on a limited basis in 1976, and was in direct, and often intense, competition with BRG during the period from 1977–1979. BRG and HBJ were two main providers of bar review courses in Georgia during this time period. In early 1980, they entered into an agreement that gave BRG an exclusive license to market HBJ's material in Georgia and to use its trade name "Bar/Bri." The parties agreed that HBJ would not compete with BRG in Georgia and that BRG would not compete with HBJ outside Georgia.[1] Under the agreement, HBJ received $100 per student enrolled by BRG and 40% of all revenues over $350. Immediately after the 1980 agreement, the price of BRG's course was increased from $150 to over $400.

---

1. The 1980 agreement contained two provisions, one called a "Covenant Not to Compete" and the other called "Other Ventures." The former required HBJ not to "directly or indirectly own, manage, operate, join, invest, control, or participate in or be connected as an officer, employee, partner, director, independent contractor or otherwise with any business which is operating or participating in the preparation of candidates for the Georgia State Bar Examination." Plaintiffs' Motion for Partial Summary Judgment, Attachment E, at 10. The latter required BRG not to compete against HBJ in states in which HBJ currently operated outside the State of Georgia.

On petitioners' motion for partial summary judgment as to the § 1 counts in the complaint and respondents' motion for summary judgment, the District Court held that the agreement was lawful. The United States Court of Appeals for the Eleventh Circuit, with one judge dissenting, agreed with the District Court that *per se* unlawful horizontal price fixing required an explicit agreement on prices to be charged or that one party have the right to be consulted about the other's prices. The Court of Appeals also agreed with the District Court that to prove a *per se* violation under a geographic market allocation theory, petitioners had to show that respondents had subdivided some relevant market in which they had previously competed. 874 F.2d 1417 (1989).[2] The Court of Appeals denied a petition for rehearing en banc that had been supported by the United States. 893 F.2d 293 (1990).

In United States v. Socony–Vacuum Oil Co., 310 U.S. 150 (1940), we held that an agreement among competitors to engage in a program of buying surplus gasoline on the spot market in order to prevent prices from falling sharply was unlawful, even though there was no direct agreement on the actual prices to be maintained. We explained that "under the Sherman Act a combination formed for the purpose and with the effect of raising, depressing, fixing, pegging, or stabilizing the price of a commodity in interstate or foreign commerce is illegal *per se*." *Id.*, at 223. See also Catalano, Inc. v. Target Sales, Inc., 446 U.S. 643 (1980) (per curiam); National Society of Professional Engineers v. United States, 435 U.S. 679 (1978).

The revenue-sharing formula in the 1980 agreement between BRG and HBJ, coupled with the price increase that took place immediately after this agreement was "formed for the purpose and with the effect of raising" the price of the bar review course. It was, therefore, plainly incorrect for the

---

2. In dissent, Judge Clark explained that in his view HBJ and BRG were capable of engaging in *per se* horizontal restraints because they had competed against each other, and then had joined forces. He believed the District Court's analysis was flawed because it had failed to recognize that the agreements could be price-fixing agreements even without explicit reference to price and because it had failed to recognize the allocation, rather than subdivision, of markets could also constitute a *per se* antitrust violation.

District Court to enter summary judgment in respondents' favor. Moreover, it is equally clear that the District Court and the Court of Appeals erred when they assumed that an allocation of markets or submarkets by competitors is not unlawful unless the market in which the two previously competed is divided between them.

In United States v. Topco Associates, Inc., 405 U.S. 596 (1972), we held that agreements between competitors to allocate territories to minimize competition are illegal:

> One of the classic examples of a *per se* violation of § 1 is an agreement between competitors at the same level of the market structure to allocate territories in order to minimize competition.... This Court has reiterated time and time again that "horizontal territorial limitations ... are naked restraints of trade with no purpose except stifling of competition." Such limitations are *per se* violations of the Sherman Act. Id., at 608 (citations omitted).

The defendants in *Topco* had never competed in the same market, but had simply agreed to allocate markets. Here, HBJ and BRG had previously competed in the Georgia market; under their allocation agreement, BRG received that market, while HBJ received the remainder of the United States. Each agreed not to compete in the other's territories. Such agreements are anticompetitive regardless of whether the parties split a market within which both do business or whether they merely reserve one market for one and another for the other. Thus, the 1980 agreement between HBJ and BRG was unlawful on its face.

The petition for writ of certiorari is granted, the judgment of the Court of Appeals is reversed, and the case is remanded for further proceedings consistent with this opinion.

NOTES AND QUESTIONS

1. Can you justify Justice Marshall's refusal in *Topco* to "ramble through the wilds of economic theory"? Would the Court's result have changed if a "reasonableness" analysis had been used?

2. Do you agree with Chief Justice Burger (who could cite many Supreme Court decisions which support his view) that a *per se* rule should be promulgated only when a practice has a "pernicious effect on competition" and lacks "any redeeming virtue"? When practices are likely to have a pernicious effect, how heavily should matters like (i) enforcement difficulties and limited resources, (ii) administrative and court time, and (iii) certainty weigh on the pro *per se* side of the scale?[3]

3. For commentaries on *per se* rules, see Goldschmid, Is Antitrust Antagonistic to American Competitiveness, 93 Colum.L.Rev. 1572 (1993); Horizontal Territorial Restraints and the *per se* Rule, 28 Wash. & Lee L.Rev. 457 (1971); Elman, "Petrified Opinions" and Competitive Realities, 66 Colum.L.Rev. 625 (1966); Bork, The Rule of Reason and the *Per se* Concept: Price Fixing

3. Chief Justice Burger's prediction, that "unless Congress intervenes ... private-label brands with their lower consumer prices will soon be available only to those who patronize the large national chains," should be evaluated in the context of the final judgment in *Topco* which was issued on remand below. The judgment contained provisions for both "areas of primary responsibility" (allowing for termination of those who did not adequately promote Topco's products) and "pass-overs." The "pass-over" clause would preclude "cream-skimming"—*i.e.*, selling in another's "primary area" absent the payment of a pro rata share for legitimate advertising and service expenditures. United States v. Topco Associates, 1973 Trade Cas. ¶ 74,485 (N.D.Ill.1973), affirmed per curiam, 414 U.S. 801 (1973). Arguably, these "less restrictive alternatives" indicate that Topco need not be seriously affected by the Supreme Court's adverse ruling. "Primary responsibility" and "pass-over" clauses are, of course, vulnerable to abuse; "pass-over" agreements, for example, may be set artificially high and thus create, in practice, an exclusive territory. Courts will closely scrutinize their use.[4]

4. Does anything in the Supreme Court's decision prevent Topco from acting as a "purchasing agent" or achieving cost economies related to transportation, warehousing, or promotion?

5. Judge Posner in *General Leaseways* suggests that arrangements designed to eliminate "free riders" reflect the kind of efficiencies that justify rule of reason rather than *per se* treatment. If that is correct, does it follow that *Topco* and *Sealy* were wrongly decided, or at least decided on the basis of an incorrect theory?

Consider *General Leaseways* an introduction to the "free rider" debate. The issue usually arises in connection with vertical rather than horizontal arrangements, and its implications will be examined more extensively in Chapter 7 infra.

6. Can Justice Blackmun's "relief must come from the legislature" approach in *Topco* be reconciled with over 100 years of practice or the legislative history of the Sherman Act?

7. In Polk Brothers, Inc. v. Forest City Enterprises, Inc., 776 F.2d 185 (7th Cir.1985), Polk Brothers, which sold appliances and home furnishings, and Forest City, which sold lumber, tools and building materials, entered into an agreement to own and operate their respective businesses out of a single building in Burbank, Illinois. Each party agreed, with minor exceptions, not to sell products which constituted the principal lines of the other. Seven years later, Forest City asked to be relieved of its covenant and, when Polk refused, advised Polk that it considered the covenant invalid; Polk responded by seeking an injunction.

The district court held the covenant invalid and the Seventh Circuit reversed. One theory of the Court of Appeals' opinion was that the parties would not have entered into the arrangement without assurances of noncompetition; hence, but for the covenant, there would not have been any joint arrangement. Cf. Broadcast Music Inc. v. CBS, p. 233 supra. A broader theme touched on by the Court distinguished between "naked" restraints, where a restraint on competition is unaccompanied by new production or products (and therefore a *per se* rule applies), and "ancillary" restraints which are part of a larger endeavor and deserve "rule of

and Market Division, 74 Yale L.J. 775 (1965) and 75 Yale L.J. 373 (1966).

4. See Sherman v. British Leyland Motors Ltd., 601 F.2d 429, 449 (9th Cir.1979);

Hobart Bros. Co. v. Gilliland, Inc., 471 F.2d 894, 900 (5th Cir.), cert. denied, 412 U.S. 923 (1973).

reason" treatment. That concept was related back to United States v. Addyston Pipe & Steel Co., p. 56 supra:

> A restraint is ancillary when it may contribute to the success of a cooperative venture that promises greater productivity and output. If the restraint, viewed at the time it was adopted, may promote the success of this more extensive cooperation, then the court must scrutinize things carefully under the Rule of Reason. Only when a quick look reveals that "the practice facially appears to be one that always or almost always tends to restrict competition and decrease output" should a court cut off further inquiry.

What are the limits of an "ancillary defense?" Suppose three companies in a distressed industry, all producing a long line of products, agreed that each would specialize in one-third of their previous product line. If that arrangement would allow each company to cut costs (by operating at higher levels of capacity on one-third of their line and dismantling the rest), lower prices, and increase output, would the arrangement be "ancillary" to an efficient, cooperative venture? Would that mean there is an efficiency defense to horizontal market division? Should there be?

8. If BRG and HBJ in *Palmer* could have shown that their 1980 agreement would achieve significant efficiencies, would the Supreme Court have considered the efficiencies an adequate justification? Would the Supreme Court have considered an efficiency justification to be relevant to the issues before it? Is the agreement in *Palmer* a horizontal price-fixing arrangement, a territorial division, or both? Does it matter?

COMPARATIVE NOTE ON CRISIS CARTELS

As we have seen, the law in the United States has not always expressed as firm a prohibition against cartels as the Supreme Court articulated in *Socony–Vacuum*. Before that case, we saw *Appalachian Coals*, supra p. 211, and since then we have learned from *BMI*, supra p. 233, that a sophisticated characterization process is necessary before something can be labeled a *per se* illegal cartel. It should not be surprising, therefore, to learn that differences of opinion exist from country to country about the advisability of making exceptions to the prohibition against cartels for industries facing structural crises or other severe adjustment problems. Indeed, one author in the United States has urged, using the tools of real options theory, that our own approach should be more accommodating. See Shubha Ghosh, Relaxing Antitrust During Economic Downturns: A Real Options Analysis of Appalachian Coals and the Failing Firm Defense, 68 Antitrust L.J. 111 (2000). Two of the most important economies in the world, that of the European Union and that of Japan, provide for a safety valve in their competition laws. This is not inconsistent with the OECD's Recommendation Concerning Effective Action Against Hard Core Cartels, OECD Doc. C(98)35/Final (adopted by the Council on 25 March 1998), which carefully defines the term "hard core cartel" to exclude agreements "excluded directly or indirectly from the coverage of a Member country's own laws, or . . . authorized in accordance with those laws." *Id.* ¶ 2(b). The Recommendation merely calls for transparency for such exclusions and authorizations, and urges member states to consider eliminating or reducing them. *Id.* ¶ 3.

The Japanese Antimonopoly Law (AMA), Law No. 54, 1947, as amended through Law No. 63, 1977, contains a number of provisions that allow the Japanese Fair Trade Commission (JFTC) to authorize cartels. In addition (as is the case in virtually every other country as well, including the United States), other laws provide for exemptions from the general prohibitions of the AMA. Professor Mitsuo Matsushita, a leading expert on Japanese competition law, suggests that the following six exemptions are the most significant: (1) Article 24–3, which permits enterprises to obtain authorization from the JFTC for a "depression cartel," (2) specific laws, such as the Medium and Small Business Organizations Law, the Environmental Sanitation Law, and the Liquor Tax and Liquor Association Law, which permit joint activities for the purpose of "stabilizing operations," (3) the Medium and Small Business Cooperatives Law, which permits enterprises to associate in order to obtain countervailing power against larger suppliers or purchasers, (4) Article 24–4 of the AMA and certain other specific statutes that permit enterprises to agree on terms of business to promote "rationalization" of operations (*i.e.* standard-setting, specialization), (5) the Insurance Business Law, the Aviation Law, and the Marine Transportation Law, which permit associations to limit price and terms of business, and (6) the Export and Import Transactions Law, which authorizes agreements to implement voluntary export restraints. See Matsushita, Cartels Under the Japanese Antimonopoly Law, in Chih–Kang Wang et al. (eds.), International Harmonization of Competition Laws 65–66 (1995).

The European Community also has the legal authority to exempt companies from the cartel prohibitions of Article 81 (ex Article 85) of the Treaty of Rome, under strictly limited circumstances. See generally Andre Fiebig, Crisis Cartels and the Triumph of Industrial Policy over Competition Law in Europe, 25 Brook. J. Int'l L. 607 (1999). For example, in the Synthetic Fibres decision, Commission decision 84/380, O.J. 207/17 (Aug. 2, 1984), the Commission approved a limited, short-term agreement to reduce excess capacity among the major European producers of synthetic fibers. The agreement was a narrow one; the Commission did not authorize the companies to agree on sensitive terms such as price, market sharing, or production or sales quotas. In its Twelfth Report on Competition Policy[5], the Commission had the following comment on structural adjustment arrangements:

> ... within a given crisis-struck industry, economic circumstances do not necessarily guarantee a reduction of the least profitable surplus capacity. Undertakings which have failed to make the necessary adjustments may have their losses offset within their groups.... Against this background, and in order to combat the structural problems of individual sectors, the Commission may be able to condone agreements in restraint of competition which relate to a sector as a whole....

The Commission has also exempted agreements designed to reduce overcapacity and to lower costs by increased specialization, in circumstances where the "crisis" element does not enter the picture.[6]

Do the Japanese and European systems introduce necessary flexibility into the general prohibition against cartels, or do they invite political undercutting of the market mechanism and industrial policy-style protectionism on behalf of unsuccessful companies or industries? Which provides the more reliable adjustment mecha-

---

5. Commission of the European Communities, Twelfth Report on Competition Policy 43 (1983). See also George and Jacquemin, Competition Policy in the European Community, in Comanor et al. (eds.), Competition Policy in Europe and North America: Economic Issues and Institutions 215–16 (1990).

6. *See, e.g.,* Enichem/ICI, Commission Decision 88/87, O.J. 50/18 (Feb. 24, 1988), described in the Seventeenth Report on Competition Policy 73 (1988).

nism: administrative review of cartel arrangements, or market devices such as mergers, bankruptcies, and reorganizations?[7]

Whatever the correct answer may be for domestic antitrust policy, is there any justification for taking a different approach when we consider the role of international competition? Should cartels or mergers that would otherwise be unlawful under the U.S. antitrust laws be permitted as a way of helping U.S. companies compete globally?[8]

PROBLEM 5

THE TRANSOCEAN VENTURE FOR MARINE PAINT

Transocean was an organization created by agreement among 18 manufacturers of marine paint, each located in a different country. The parties agreed to develop, manufacture, and sell identical paint under an identical "Transocean" trademark. The "Transocean Venture," as it was called, spent large sums to develop a new and highly effective paint composition. In addition to economies in research, development, advertising, promotion, and service, the arrangement offered a special technical benefit in that paint applied over identical paint is more durable. Thus, a standardized paint available throughout the world was of particular value. The common trademark provided an efficient way to convey the idea that the paint offered by each member was identical.

The arrangement included prohibitions against establishing manufacturing facilities by a participant in the home territory of another. It also prohibited a member from selling in the home territory of another without its consent (supposedly routinely given), and then only on the payment of a commission in an unspecified amount. Alternatively, if an order were received by a member for sale outside its own country, it could turn that over to a local concern and a commission would be paid to the firm securing the order.

The arrangement has been in effect for about five years. During the first several years, members occasionally asked permission to make sales in the home territories of others and such requests were sometimes granted and sometimes denied. The United States member of the arrangement turned down three requests and granted two during the past two years. In general, in the great bulk of instances, members are content to accept a commission for referring sales.

The Antitrust Division has initiated an investigation of the legality of the arrangement under Section 1. Is there a violation?

SELECTIVE BIBLIOGRAPHY

Hovenkamp, Federal Antitrust Policy: The Law of Competition and Its Practice Chs. 4–5 (2d ed. 1999).

FTC Staff, Anticipating the 21st Century: Competition Policy in the New High–Tech, Global Marketplace Chs. 1, 3, 4, 9, and 10 (1996).

7. See Pitofsky, Antitrust and Problems of Adjustment in Distressed Industries, 55 Antitrust L.J. 21 (1986).

8. See, e.g., FTC Staff, Anticipating the 21st Century: Competition Policy in the New High–Tech, Global Marketplace (1996); Pitofsky, Proposals for Revised United States Merger Enforcement in a Global Economy, 81 Geo. L. J. 195 (1992); First, Structural Antitrust Rules and International Competition: The Case of Distressed Industries, 62 N.Y.U. L. Rev. 1054 (1987).

Scherer & Ross, Industrial Market Structure and Economic Performance Ch. 9 (1990).

6–7 Areeda & Turner, Antitrust Law: An Analysis of Antitrust Principles and Their Application (1986 & Supp. 2001).

Muris, California Dental Association v. Federal Trade Commission: The Revenge of Footnote 17, 8 S.Ct. Econ. Rev. 265 (2000).

Hovenkamp, Competitor Collaboration After California Dental Association, 2000 U. Chi. Legal F. 149 (2000).

Calkins, California Dental Association: Not a Quick Look But Not the Full Monty, 67 Antitrust L.J. 495 (2000).

Sullivan, The Viability of the Current Law on Horizontal Restraints, 75 Cal.L.Rev. 835 (1987).

Goldschmid, Horizontal Restraints in Antitrust: Current Treatment and Future Needs, 75 Cal.L.Rev. 925 (1987).

CHAPTER 5

GROUP REFUSALS TO DEAL AND JOINT VENTURES

INTRODUCTION

In Chapter 4, we began our consideration of agreements among competing firms. Despite the fact that one can find language in many opinions that indicates that all such agreements are banned, the actual situation has always been far more complex. *BMI* was a case in which actual or potential competitors in the market for the sale of copyrighted music were permitted to band together and authorize a common selling agent to act for them. The Supreme Court recognized that the product made possible by this collaboration—the package license—would not have been possible in the absence of the agreement. Moreover, the collective product was better than the sum of its parts: it reduced costs for buyers and sellers alike, and it therefore enhanced output. In another case from Chapter 4, *NCAA*, the Court ultimately condemned the agreement among the competing colleges and universities before it. Nevertheless, it treated the NCAA as a joint venture and evaluated the television contract under the rule of reason. In the present chapter, we continue our consideration of collaborative arrangements among competitors. Which arrangements are legal? What ancillary restrictions on competition among the members will pass muster? How should actions that affect third parties, such as refusals to deal or group boycotts, be evaluated? Here as elsewhere, the trend has been toward increased use of the rule of reason and an increased need to consider the economic purpose and effect of the arrangement.

SECTION 1. REFUSALS TO DEAL

Early Decisions

1. MONTAGUE & CO. V. LOWRY, 193 U.S. 38, 24 S.Ct. 307, 48 L.Ed. 608 (1904). Defendants were an association of wholesale dealers of tiles, mantels, and grates in and around San Francisco and of manufacturers of such products (located in other states) who sold to dealer-members in the San Francisco area, the members of the association, and its officers. The bylaws of the association provided:

> Sec. 7. No dealer and active member of this association shall purchase, directly or indirectly, any tile or fireplace fixtures from any manufacturer or resident or traveling agent of any manufacturer not a member of this association, neither shall they sell or dispose of, directly or indirectly, any unset tile for less than list prices to any person or persons not a member of this association, under penalty of expulsion from the association.

329

Sec. 8. Manufacturers of tile or fireplace fixtures or resident or traveling agents or manufacturers selling or disposing, directly or indirectly, their products or wares to any person or persons not members of the Tile, Mantel and Grate Association of California, shall forfeit their membership in the association.

The term "list prices" referred to in Section 7, above, pertained to prices on the sale of tiles. The "list price" rule had the effect of forcing non-members of the association to pay more than 50 per cent more for their tiles than members did. Plaintiff Lowry was a dealer in tiles, mantels, and grates in San Francisco and a competitor of certain members of the association, but did not itself belong to the association. It alleged that a unanimous vote was necessary to become a member, and that there were several members of the association who were antagonistic to it and who would not have permitted it to join if it applied. In addition, the constitution of the association provided that firms engaged in the tile, mantel, or grate business in the San Francisco area could join only if they carried not less than $3,000 worth of stock, and Lowry alleged that membership was therefore not an option for it because it did not at all times carry that much stock.

Prior to the formation of the association, Lowry had purchased tiles from manufacturers in eastern states, but afterwards, it was unable to purchase tiles from the same sources because those manufacturers joined the association. Worse, Lowry found that it could obtain product from dealers in San Francisco only at the inflated "list prices" established by the association.

The case went to trial before a jury, which returned a verdict for Lowry. The Supreme Court affirmed, finding that the association "constituted or amounted to an agreement or combination in restraint of trade" under the Sherman Act. Defendants tried to argue that the arrangement failed to satisfy the interstate commerce requirement of the statute, but the Court was unpersuaded. The Court also rejected the defendants' contention that Lowry could have avoided damage to its business simply by applying for membership in the association. It pointed out that any such application was subject to arbitrary rejection by the association, and also that it might have been doomed because Lowry did not fulfill the condition provided for eligibility (*i.e.*, maintenance of stock valued at $3,000). The Court concluded:

> ... The case stands, therefore, that the plaintiffs had not been asked to join the association at its formation; that they did not fill the condition provided for in its constitution as to eligibility, and that if they had applied their application was subject to arbitrary rejection.
>
> The plaintiffs, however, could not, by virtue of any agreement contained in such association, be legally put under obligation to become members in order to enable them to transact their business as they had theretofore done, and to purchase tiles as they had been accustomed to do before the association was formed.

2. PARAMOUNT FAMOUS LASKY CORP. v. UNITED STATES, 282 U.S. 30, 51 S.Ct. 42, 75 L.Ed. 145 (1930). Members of the Motion Picture Producers and Distributors of America agreed that they would do business with some 25,000 theater owners and exhibitors for the display of films only through a standard contract requiring that exhibitors submit all disputes to arbitration or post $500 security with each distributor. The arbitration would be conducted before members of the regional film board of trade and other industry members. An exhibitor's failure to comply with any lease provision or arbitration award would be grounds for all distributors to suspend all contracts with that exhibitor.

Noting that the arrangement was unusual at the time (consider how it would be regarded today, in light of the Supreme Court's far greater receptivity to arbitration) and tended to suppress normal competition, the Supreme Court concluded that it violated Section 1. The Court reasoned that it "may be that arbitration is well adapted to the needs of the motion picture industry; but when under the guise of arbitration parties enter into unusual arrangements which unreasonably suppress normal competition their action becomes illegal." The fact that the challenged arrangement did not suppress all competition between the parties was regarded as irrelevant.

In a companion case, United States v. First National Pictures, Inc., 282 U.S. 44, 51 S.Ct. 45, 75 L.Ed. 151 (1930), the Court reached the same result with respect to an arrangement by the same association requiring each exhibitor to set aside cash security in amounts determined by credit committee members of the association, or run the risk of suspension of all contracts.

Fashion Originators' Guild of America v. Federal Trade Commission

Supreme Court of the United States, 1941.
312 U.S. 457, 61 S.Ct. 703, 85 L.Ed. 949.

■ BLACK, J. The Circuit Court of Appeals, with modifications not here challenged, affirmed a Federal Trade Commission decree ordering petitioners to cease and desist from certain practices found to have been done in combination and to constitute "unfair methods of competition" tending to monopoly. . . .

Some of the members of the combination design, manufacture, sell and distribute women's garments—chiefly dresses. Others are manufacturers, converters or dyers of textiles from which these garments are made. Fashion Originators' Guild of America (FOGA), an organization controlled by these groups, is the instrument through which petitioners work to accomplish the purposes condemned by the Commission. The garment manufacturers claim to be creators of original and distinctive designs of fashionable clothes for women, and the textile manufacturers claim to be creators of similar original fabric designs. After these designs enter the channels of trade, other manufacturers systematically make and sell copies of them, the copies usually selling at prices lower than the garments copied. Petitioners call this practice of copying unethical and immoral, and give it the name of "style piracy." And although they admit that their "original creations" are neither copyrighted nor patented, and indeed assert that existing legislation affords them no protection against copyists, they nevertheless urge that sale of copied designs constitutes an unfair trade practice and a tortious invasion of their rights. Because of these alleged wrongs, petitioners, while continuing to compete with one another in many respects, combined among themselves to combat and, if possible, destroy all competition from the sale of garments which are copies of their "original creations." They admit that to destroy such competition they have in combination purposely boycotted and declined to sell their products to retailers who follow a policy of selling garments copied by other manufacturers from designs put out by Guild members. As a result of their efforts, approximately 12,000 retailers throughout the country have signed agreements to "cooperate" with the Guild's boycott program, but more than half of these signed the agreements only because constrained by threats that Guild members would not sell to retailers who failed to yield to their demands—threats that have been carried out by the Guild practice of placing on red cards the names of non-cooperators (to whom no sales are to be made), placing on white cards the names of cooperators (to whom sales are to be made), and then distributing both sets of cards to the manufacturers.

The one hundred and seventy-six manufacturers of women's garments who are members of the Guild occupy a commanding position in their line of business. In 1936, they sold in the United States more than 38% of all women's garments wholesaling at $6.75 and up, and more than 60% of those at $10.75 and above. The power of the combination is great; competition and the demand of the consuming public make it necessary for most retail dealers to stock some of the products of these manufacturers. And the power of the combination is made even greater by reason of the affiliation of some members of the National Federation of Textiles, Inc.— that being an organization composed of about one hundred textile manufacturers, converters, dyers and printers of silk and rayon used in making women's garments. Those members of the Federation who are affiliated with the Guild have agreed to sell their products only to those garment manufacturers who have in turn agreed to sell only to cooperating retailers.

The Guild maintains a Design Registration Bureau for garments, and the Textile Federation maintains a similar Bureau for textiles. The Guild employs "shoppers" to visit the stores of both cooperating and non-cooperating retailers, "for the purpose of examining their stocks, to determine and report as to whether they contain ... copies of registered designs. . . ." An elaborate system of trial and appellate tribunals exists, for the determination of whether a given garment is in fact a copy of a Guild member's design. In order to assure the success of its plan of registration and restraint, and to ascertain whether Guild regulations are being violated, the Guild audits its members' books. And if violations of Guild requirements are discovered, as for example, sales to red-carded retailers, the violators are subject to heavy fines.

In addition to the elements of the agreement set out above, all of which relate more or less closely to competition by so-called style copyists, the Guild has undertaken to do many things apparently independent of and distinct from the fight against copying. Among them are the following: the combination prohibits its members from participating in retail advertising; regulates the discount they may allow; prohibits their selling at retail; cooperates with local guilds in regulating days upon which special sales shall be held; prohibits its members from selling women's garments to persons who conduct businesses in residences, residential quarters, hotels or apartment houses; and denies the benefits of membership to retailers who participate with dress manufacturers in promoting fashion shows unless the merchandise used is actually purchased and delivered.

If the purpose and practice of the combination of garment manufacturers and their affiliates runs counter to the public policy declared in the Sherman and Clayton Acts, the Federal Trade Commission has the power to suppress it as an unfair method of competition. From its findings the Commission concluded that the petitioners, "pursuant to understandings, arrangements, agreements, combinations and conspiracies entered into jointly and severally," had prevented sales in interstate commerce, had "substantially lessened, hindered and suppressed" competition, and had tended "to create in themselves a monopoly." ... The relevance of ... section [3] of the Clayton Act to petitioners' scheme is shown by the fact that the scheme is bottomed upon a system of sale under which (1) textiles shall be sold to garment manufacturers only upon the condition and understanding that the buyers will not use or deal in textiles which are copied from the designs of textile manufacturing Guild members; (2) garment manufacturers shall sell to retailers only upon the condition and understanding that the retailers shall not use or deal in such copied designs. And the Federal Trade Commission concluded in the language of the Clayton Act that these understandings substantially lessened competition and tended to create a monopoly. We hold that the Commission, upon adequate and unchallenged findings, correctly concluded that this practice constituted an unfair method of competition.

Not only does the plan in the respects above discussed thus conflict with the principles of the Clayton Act; the findings of the Commission bring petitioners' combination in its entirety well within the inhibition of the policies declared by the Sherman Act itself. ... Under the Sherman Act "competition, not combination, should be the law of trade." National Cotton Oil Co. v. Texas, 197 U.S. 115, 129. And among the many respects in which the Guild's plan runs contrary to the policy of the Sherman Act are these: it narrows the outlets to which garment and textile manufacturers can sell and the sources from which retailers can buy (Montague & Co. v. Lowry, 193 U.S. 38, 45; Standard Sanitary Manufacturing Co. v. United States, 226 U.S. 20, 48, 49); subjects all retailers and manufacturers who decline to comply with the Guild's program to an organized boycott

(Eastern States Retail Lumber Dealers' Association v. United States, 234 U.S. 600, 609–611); takes away the freedom of action of members by requiring each to reveal to the Guild the intimate details of their individual affairs (United States v. American Linseed Oil Co., 262 U.S. 371, 389); and has both as its necessary tendency and as its purpose and effect the direct suppression of competition from the sale of unregistered textiles and copied designs (United States v. American Linseed Oil Co., supra, 262 U.S. at 389). In addition to all this, the combination is in reality an extra-governmental agency, which prescribes rules for the regulation and re-straint of interstate commerce, and provides extra-judicial tribunals for determination and punishment of violations, and thus "trenches upon the power of the national legislature and violates the statute." Addyston Pipe & Steel Co. v. United States, 175 U.S. 211, 242.

Nor is it determinative in considering the policy of the Sherman Act that petitioners may not yet have achieved a complete monopoly. For "it is sufficient if it really tends to that end, and to deprive the public of the advantages which flow from free competition." United States v. E.C. Knight Co., 156 U.S. 1, 16; Addyston Pipe & Steel Co. v. United States, 175 U.S. 211, 237. It was, in fact, one of the hopes of those who sponsored the Federal Trade Commission Act that its effect might be prophylactic and that through it attempts to bring about complete monopolization of an industry might be stopped in their incipiency.

Petitioners, however, argue that the combination cannot be contrary to the policy of the Sherman and Clayton Acts, since the Federal Trade Commission did not find that the combination fixed or regulated prices, parceled out or limited production, or brought about a deterioration in quality. But action falling into these three categories does not exhaust the types of conduct banned by the Sherman and Clayton Acts. And as previously pointed out, it was the object of the Federal Trade Commission Act to reach not merely in their fruition but also in their incipiency combinations which could lead to these and other trade restraints and practices deemed undesirable. In this case, the Commission found that the combination exercised sufficient control and power in the women's gar-ments and textile businesses "to exclude from the industry those manufac-turers and distributors who do not conform to the rules and regulations of said respondents, and thus tend to create in themselves a monopoly in the said industries." While a conspiracy to fix prices is illegal, an intent to increase prices is not an ever-present essential of conduct amounting to a violation of the policy of the Sherman and Clayton Acts; a monopoly contrary to their policies can exist even though a combination may tempo-rarily or even permanently reduce the price of the articles manufactured or sold. . . .

But petitioners further argue that their boycott and restraint of interstate trade is not within the ban of the policies of the Sherman and Clayton Acts because "the practices of FOGA were reasonable and neces-sary to protect the manufacturer, laborer, retailer and consumer against the devastating evils growing from the pirating of original designs and had in fact benefited all four." The Commission declined to hear much of the evidence that petitioners desired to offer on this subject. As we have pointed out, however, the aim of petitioners' combination was the intentional destruction of one type of manufacture and sale which competed with Guild members. The purpose and object of this combination, its potential power, its tendency to monopoly, the coercion it could and did practice upon a rival method of competition, all brought it within the policy of the prohibition declared by the Sherman and Clayton Acts. For this reason, the principles announced in Appalachian Coals, Inc. v. United States, 288 U.S. 344, and Sugar Institute v. United States, 297 U.S. 553, have no application here. Under these circumstances it was not error to refuse to hear the evidence offered, for the reasonableness of the methods pursued by the combination to accomplish its unlawful object is no more material than would be the reasonableness of the prices fixed by unlawful combination. Nor can the unlawful combination be justified upon the argument that systematic copying of dress designs is itself tortious, or should now be declared so by us. In the first place, whether or not given conduct is tortious is a question of state law, under our decision in Erie Railroad Co. v. Tompkins, 304 U.S. 64. In the second place, even if copying were an acknowledged tort under the law of every state, that situation would not justify petitioners in combining together to regulate and restrain interstate commerce in violation of federal law.... The decision below is accordingly

Affirmed.

NOTES AND QUESTIONS

1.   Is *FOGA* still good law after *BMI?* Suppose the defendants in *FOGA* argued that it is very costly to prepare original designs for the fashion trade, and that design houses will eventually be driven out of business or at least severely hampered in their activities if they cannot control free riding "style pirates." Should a court today feel it had a responsibility under *BMI* to examine the merits of that contention before "characterizing" the arrangement as a boycott?

2.   Would it be legal under *Paramount Famous Lasky* and *FOGA* for all insurance companies in a state to establish a committee to pass upon the creditworthiness of applicants for insurance pursuant to guidelines jointly established? Suppose that all the committee did was to establish criteria (*i.e.*, no coverage for "environmental damage" discovered more than 12 months after the termination date of the policy), but left it to each insurance company to implement the policy? Lastly, suppose the committee only recommended standards for "acceptable insurance risks" and then left it to each insurance company to adopt or reject its proposals; all insurance companies in the state can be shown to have adopted the proposal? What are the differences among these three fact situations?

3.   To what extent can the actions of the Guild members be explained as a private system for the protection of their intellectual property in their designs? Can this be done collectively, or must each holder of a trademarked or copyrighted design act individually? Companies might try to use intellectual property to obtain

or extend market power, thereby attempting to reap monopoly profits beyond what the protected property itself would command. (Note that the soundness of this theory has been challenged; see the discussion of tying arrangements, at Chapter 8, Section 3, infra.) But the question may be somewhat different if the degree of protection to which the intellectual property is entitled is less than complete. For example, companies today are testing the limits of patent law by obtaining broad "business method" patents. State Street Bank & Trust Co. v. Signature Financial Group, Inc., 149 F.3d 1368, 1375 (Fed.Cir.1998) (squarely holding that there is no "business methods" exception to general rules of patentability, and upholding a patent for a data processing system).

Klor's, Inc. v. Broadway–Hale Stores, Inc.

Supreme Court of the United States, 1959.
359 U.S. 207, 79 S.Ct. 705, 3 L.Ed.2d 741.

■ BLACK, J. Klor's, Inc., operates a retail store on Mission Street, San Francisco, California; Broadway–Hale Stores, Inc., a chain of department stores, operates one of its stores next door. The two stores compete in the sale of radios, television sets, refrigerators and other household appliances. Claiming that Broadway–Hale and 10 national manufacturers and their distributors have conspired to restrain and monopolize commerce in violation of §§ 1 and 2 of the Sherman Act, 26 Stat. 209, as amended, 15 U.S.C. §§ 1, 2, Klor's brought this action for treble damages and injunction in the United States District Court.

In support of its claim Klor's made the following allegations: George Klor started an appliance store some years before 1952 and has operated it ever since either individually or as Klor's, Inc. Klor's is as well equipped as Broadway–Hale to handle all brands of appliances. Nevertheless, manufacturers and distributors of such well-known brands as General Electric, RCA, Admiral, Zenith, Emerson and others have conspired among themselves and with Broadway–Hale either not to sell to Klor's or to sell to it only at discriminatory prices and highly unfavorable terms. Broadway–Hale has used its "monopolistic" buying power to bring about this situation. The business of manufacturing, distributing and selling household appliances is in interstate commerce. The concerted refusal to deal with Klor's has seriously handicapped its ability to compete and has already caused it a great loss of profits, goodwill, reputation and prestige.

The defendants did not dispute these allegations, but sought summary judgment and dismissal of the complaint for failure to state a cause of action. They submitted unchallenged affidavits which showed that there were hundreds of other household appliance retailers, some within a few blocks of Klor's who sold many competing brands of appliances, including those the defendants refused to sell to Klor's. From the allegations of the complaint, and from the affidavits supporting the motion for summary judgment, the District Court concluded that the controversy was a "purely private quarrel" between Klor's and Broadway–Hale, which did not amount to a "public wrong proscribed by the [Sherman] Act." On this ground the complaint was dismissed and summary judgment was entered for the defendants. The Court of Appeals for the Ninth Circuit affirmed the summary judgment. 255 F.2d 214. It stated that "a violation of the Sherman Act requires conduct of defendants by which the public is or conceivably may be ultimately injured." 255 F.2d at page 233. It held that here the required public injury was missing since "there was no charge or proof that by any act of defendants the price, quantity, or quality offered the public was affected, nor that there was any intent or purpose to effect a change in, or an influence on, prices, quantity or quality." Id., at page 230. The holding, if correct, means that unless the opportunities for customers to buy in a competitive market are reduced, a group of powerful business-men may act in concert to deprive a single merchant, like Klor, of the goods he needs to compete effectively. We granted certiorari to consider this important question in the administration of the Sherman Act. 358 U.S. 809.

We think Klor's allegations clearly show one type of trade restraint and public harm the Sherman Act forbids, and that defendants' affidavits provide no defense to the charges. Section 1 of the Sherman Act makes illegal any contract, combination or conspiracy in restraint of trade, and § 2 forbids any person or combination from monopolizing or attempting to monopolize any part of interstate commerce. In the landmark case of Standard Oil Co. of New Jersey v. United States, 221 U.S. 1, this Court read § 1 to prohibit those classes of contracts or acts which the common law had deemed to be undue restraints of trade and those which new times and economic conditions would make unreasonable. Id., 59–60. The Court construed § 2 as making "the prohibitions of the act all the more complete and perfect by embracing all attempts to reach the end prohibited by the 1st section, that is, restraints of trade, by any attempt to monopolize or monopolization thereof...." Id., at 61. The effect of both sections, the Court said, was to adopt the common-law proscription of all "contracts or acts which it was considered had a monopolistic tendency ..." and which interfered with the "natural flow" of an appreciable amount of interstate commerce. Id., at 57, 61; Eastern States Retail Lumber Dealers' Ass'n v. United States, 234 U.S. 600, 609. The Court recognized that there were some agreements whose validity depended on the surrounding circum-stances. It emphasized, however, that there were classes of restraints which from their "nature or character" were unduly restrictive, and hence forbidden by both the common law and the statute. 221 U.S. at 58, 65.[1] As to these classes of restraints, the Court noted, Congress had determined its own criteria of public harm and it was not for the courts to decide whether in an individual case injury had actually occurred. Id., at 63–68.[2]

1. See also United States v. American Tobacco Co., 221 U.S. 106, 179, where the Court noted that the statute forbade all "acts or contracts or agreements or combinations ... which, either because of their inherent nature or effect or because of the evident purpose of the acts, etc., injuriously re-strained trade...."

2. In this regard the Sherman Act should be contrasted with § 5 of the Federal Trade Commission Act, 38 Stat. 719, as amended, 15 U.S.C. § 45(b), which requires that the Commission find "that a proceeding by it ... be to the interest of the public" before it issues a complaint for unfair compe-tition.

Group boycotts, or concerted refusals by traders to deal with other traders, have long been held to be in the forbidden category.[3] They have not been saved by allegations that they were reasonable in the specific circumstances, nor by a failure to show that they "fixed or regulated prices, parcelled out or limited production, or brought about a deterioration in quality." Fashion Originators' Guild v. Federal Trade Commission, 312 U.S. 457, 466, 467–468. Cf. United States v. Trenton Potteries Co., 273 U.S. 392. Even when they operated to lower prices or temporarily to stimulate competition they were banned. For, as this Court said in Kiefer–Stewart Co. v. Joseph E. Seagram & Sons, 340 U.S. 211, 213, "such agreements, no less than those to fix minimum prices, cripple the freedom of traders and thereby restrain their ability to sell in accordance with their own judgment." Cf. United States v. Patten, 226 U.S. 525, 542.

Plainly the allegations of this complaint disclose such a boycott. This is not a case of a single trader refusing to deal with another,[4] nor even of a manufacturer and a dealer agreeing to an exclusive distributorship. Alleged in this complaint is a wide combination consisting of manufacturers, distributors and a retailer. This combination takes from Klor's its freedom to buy appliances in an open competitive market and drives it out of business as a dealer in the defendants' products. It deprives the manufacturers and distributors of their freedom to sell to Klor's at the same prices and conditions made available to Broadway–Hale and in some instances forbids them from selling to it on any terms whatsoever. It interferes with the natural flow of interstate commerce. It clearly has, by its "nature" and "character," a "monopolistic tendency." As such it is not to be tolerated merely because the victim is just one merchant whose business is so small that his destruction makes little difference to the economy.[5] Monopoly can as surely thrive by the elimination of such small businessmen, one at a time, as it can by driving them out in large groups. In recognition of this fact the Sherman Act has consistently been read to forbid all contracts and combinations "which 'tend to create a monopoly,'" whether "the business-men, one at a time, as it can by driving them out in large groups. In recognition of this fact the Sherman Act has consistently been read to

---

3. *See, e.g.*, Eastern States Retail Lumber Dealers' Association v. United States, 234 U.S. 600.

4. Compare United States v. Colgate & Co., 250 U.S. 300, with United States v. Schrader's Son, Inc., 252 U.S. 85; United States v. Bausch & Lomb Optical Co., 321 U.S. 707, 719–723; Lorain Journal Co. v. United States, 342 U.S. 143.

5. The court below relied heavily on Apex Hosiery Co. v. Leader, 310 U.S. 469, in reaching its conclusion. While some language in that case can be read as supporting the position that no restraint on trade is prohibited by § 1 of the Sherman Act unless it has or is intended to have an effect on market prices, such statements must be considered in the light of the fact that the defendant in that case was a labor union. The Court in Apex recognized that the Act is aimed primarily at combinations having commercial objectives and is applied only to a very limited extent to organizations, like labor unions, which normally have other objectives. See United States v. Hutcheson, 312 U.S. 219; Allen Bradley Co. v. Local Union No. 3, International Brotherhood of Electrical Workers, 325 U.S. 797. Moreover, cases subsequent to Apex have made clear that an effect on prices is not essential to a Sherman Act violation. *See, e.g.*, Fashion Originators' Guild v. Federal Trade Commission, 312 U.S. 457, 466.

whether "the tendency is a creeping one" or "one that proceeds at full gallop." International Salt Co. v. United States, 332 U.S. 392, 396.

The judgment of the Court of Appeals is reversed and the cause is remanded to the District Court for trial.

NYNEX Corp. v. Discon, Inc.

Supreme Court of the United States, 1998.
525 U.S. 128, 119 S.Ct. 493, 142 L.Ed.2d 510.

■ BREYER, J. In this case we ask whether the antitrust rule that group boycotts are illegal *per se* as set forth in Klor's, Inc. v. Broadway–Hale Stores, Inc., 359 U.S. 207, 212 (1959), applies to a buyer's decision to buy from one seller rather than another, when that decision cannot be justified in terms of ordinary competitive objectives. We hold that the *per se* group boycott rule does not apply.

I

Before 1984 American Telephone and Telegraph Company (AT & T) supplied most of the Nation's telephone service and, through wholly owned subsidiaries such as Western Electric, it also supplied much of the Nation's telephone equipment. In 1984 an antitrust consent decree took AT & T out of the local telephone service business and left AT & T a *long-distance* telephone service provider, competing with such firms as MCI and Sprint. See M. Kellogg, J. Thorne, & P. Huber, Federal Telecommunications Law § 4.6, p. 221 (1992). The decree transformed AT & T's formerly owned local telephone companies into independent firms. At the same time, the decree insisted that those local firms help assure competitive long-distance service by guaranteeing long-distance companies physical access to their systems and to their local customers. See United States v. American Telephone & Telegraph Co., 552 F. Supp. 131, 225, 227 (DDC 1982), aff'd *sub nom*. Maryland v. United States, 460 U.S. 1001 (1983). To guarantee that physical access, some local telephone firms had to install new call-switching equipment; and to install new call-switching equipment, they often had to remove old call-switching equipment. This case involves the business of removing that old switching equipment (and other obsolete telephone equipment)—a business called *"removal services."*

Discon, Inc., the respondent, sold removal services used by New York Telephone Company, a firm supplying local telephone service in much of New York State and parts of Connecticut. New York Telephone is a subsidiary of NYNEX Corporation. NYNEX also owns Materiel Enterprises Company, a purchasing entity that bought removal services for New York Telephone. Discon, in a lengthy detailed complaint, alleged that the NYNEX defendants (namely, NYNEX, New York Telephone, Materiel Enterprises, and several NYNEX related individuals) engaged in unfair, improper, and anticompetitive activities in order to hurt Discon and to benefit Discon's removal services competitor, AT & T Technologies, a lineal descendant of Western Electric. The Federal District Court dismissed Discon's complaint for failure to state a claim. The Court of Appeals for the Second Circuit affirmed that dismissal with an exception, and that exception is before us for consideration.

The Second Circuit focused on one of Discon's specific claims, a claim that Materiel Enterprises had switched its purchases from Discon to Discon's competitor, AT & T Technologies, as part of an attempt to defraud local telephone service customers by hoodwinking regulators. According to Discon, Materiel Enterprises would pay AT & T Technologies more than Discon would have charged for similar removal services. It did so because it could pass the higher prices on to New York Telephone, which in turn could pass those prices on to telephone consumers in the form of higher regulatory-agency-approved telephone service charges. At the end of the year, Materiel Enterprises would receive a special rebate from AT & T Technologies, which Materiel Enterprises would share with its parent, NYNEX. Discon added that it refused to participate in this fraudulent scheme, with the result that Materiel Enterprises would not buy from Discon, and Discon went out of business.

These allegations, the Second Circuit said, state a cause of action under § 1 of the Sherman Act, though under a "different legal theory" from the one articulated by Discon. The Second Circuit conceded that ordinarily "the decision to discriminate in favor of one supplier over another will have a pro-competitive intent and effect." But, it added, in this case, "no such pro-competitive rationale appears on the face of the complaint." Rather, the complaint alleges Materiel Enterprises' decision to buy from AT & T Technologies, rather than from Discon, was intended to be, and was, "anti-competitive." Hence, "Discon has alleged a cause of action under, at least, the rule of reason, and possibly under the *per se* rule applied to group boycotts in *Klor's*, if the restraint of trade 'has no purpose except stifling competition.'" (Quoting Oreck Corp. v. Whirlpool Corp., 579 F.2d 126, 131 (C.A.2) (en banc) (in turn quoting White Motor Co. v. United States, 372 U.S. 253, 263 (1963)), cert. denied, 439 U.S. 946 (1978)). For somewhat similar reasons the Second Circuit believed the complaint stated a valid claim of conspiracy to monopolize under § 2 of the Sherman Act. See 93 F.3d at 1061–1062.

The Second Circuit noted that the Courts of Appeals are uncertain as to whether, or when, the *per se* group boycott rule applies to a decision by a purchaser to favor one supplier over another (which the Second Circuit called a "two-firm group boycott"). Compare Com–Tel, Inc. v. DuKane Corp., 669 F.2d 404, 411–413, and nn. 13, 16 (C.A.6 1982); Cascade Cabinet Co. v. Western Cabinet & Millwork Inc., 710 F.2d 1366, 1370–1371 (C.A.9 1983), with Construction Aggregate Transport, Inc. v. Florida Rock Industries, Inc., 710 F.2d 752, 776–778 (C.A.11 1983). We granted certiorari in order to consider the applicability of the *per se* group boycott rule where a single buyer favors one seller over another, albeit for an improper reason.

II

As this Court has made clear, the Sherman Act's prohibition of "[e]very" agreement in "restraint of trade," prohibits only agreements that *unreasonably* restrain trade. See Business Electronics Corp. v. Sharp Electronics Corp., 485 U.S. 717, 723 (1988) (citing National Collegiate Athletic Assn. v. Board of Regents of Univ. of Okla., 468 U.S. 85, 98 (1984)); Standard Oil Co. of N. J. v. United States, 221 U.S. 1, 59–62 (1911); 2 P. Areeda & H. Hovenkamp, Antitrust Law ¶ 320b, p. 49 (1995). Yet certain kinds of agreements will so often prove so harmful to competition and so rarely prove justified that the antitrust laws do not require proof that an agreement of that kind is, in fact, anticompetitive in the particular circumstances. See State Oil Co. v. Khan, 522 U.S. 3, 10 (1997); Northwest Wholesale Stationers, Inc. v. Pacific Stationery & Printing Co., 472 U.S. 284, 289–290 (1985); supra 2 Areeda & Hovenkamp, ¶ 320b, at 49–52. An agreement of such a kind is unlawful *per se*. *See, e.g.*, United States v. Socony–Vacuum Oil Co., 310 U.S. 150, 218 (1940) (finding horizontal price-fixing agreement *per se* illegal); Dr. Miles Medical Co. v. John D. Park & Sons Co., 220 U.S. 373, 408 (1911) (finding vertical price-fixing agreement *per se* illegal); Palmer v. BRG of Ga., Inc., 498 U.S. 46, 49–50 (1990) (per curiam) (finding horizontal market division *per se* illegal).

The Court has found the *per se* rule applicable in certain group boycott cases. Thus, in Fashion Originators' Guild of America, Inc. v. FTC, 312 U.S. 457 (1941), this Court considered a group boycott created by an agreement among a group of clothing designers, manufacturers, suppliers, and retailers. The defendant designers, manufacturers, and suppliers had promised not to sell their clothes to retailers who bought clothes from competing manufacturers and suppliers. The defendants wanted to present evidence that would show their agreement was justified because the boycotted competitors used "pira[ted]" fashion designs. But the Court wrote that "it was not error to refuse to hear the evidence offered"—evidence that the agreement was reasonable and necessary to "protect . . . against the devastating evils" of design pirating—for that evidence "is no more material than would be the reasonableness of the prices fixed" by a price-fixing agreement.

In *Klor's* the Court also applied the *per se* rule. The Court considered a boycott created when a retail store, Broadway–Hale, and 10 household appliance manufacturers and their distributors agreed that the distributors would not sell, or would sell only at discriminatory prices, household appliances to Broadway–Hale's small, nearby competitor, namely, Klor's. 359 U.S. at 208–209. The defendants had submitted undisputed evidence that their agreement hurt only one competitor (Klor's) and that so many other nearby appliance-selling competitors remained that competition in the marketplace continued to thrive. *Id.* at 209–210. The Court held that this evidence was beside the point. The conspiracy was "not to be tolerated merely because the victim is just one merchant." The Court thereby inferred injury to the competitive process itself from the nature of the boycott agreement. And it forbade, as a matter of law, a defense based upon a claim that only one small firm, not competition itself, had suffered injury.

The case before us involves *Klor's*. The Second Circuit did not forbid the defendants to introduce evidence of "justification." To the contrary, it invited the defendants to do so, for it said that the *"per se* rule" would apply only if no "pro-competitive justification" were to be found. 93 F.3d at 1061; cf. 7 P. Areeda & H. Hovenkamp, Antitrust Law ¶ 1510, p. 416 (1986) ("Boycotts are said to be unlawful *per se* but justifications are routinely considered in defining the forbidden category"). Thus, the specific legal question before us is whether an antitrust court considering an agreement by a buyer to purchase goods or services from one supplier rather than another should (after examining the buyer's reasons or justifications) apply the *per se* rule if it finds no legitimate business reason for that purchasing decision. We conclude no boycott-related *per se* rule applies and that the plaintiff here must allege and prove harm, not just to a single competitor, but to the competitive process, *i.e.*, to competition itself.

Our conclusion rests in large part upon precedent, for precedent limits the *per se* rule in the boycott context to cases involving horizontal agreements among direct competitors. The agreement in *Fashion Originators' Guild* involved what may be called a group boycott in the strongest sense: A group of competitors threatened to withhold business from third parties unless those third parties would help them injure their directly competing rivals. Although *Klor's* involved a threat made by a *single* powerful firm, it also involved a horizontal agreement among those threatened, namely, the appliance suppliers, to hurt a competitor of the retailer who made the threat. See 359 U.S. at 208–209; see also P. Areeda & L. Kaplow, Antitrust Analysis: Problems, Text, and Cases 333 (5th ed. 1997) (defining paradigmatic boycott as "collective action among a group of competitors that may inhibit the competitive vitality of rivals"); 11 H. Hovenkamp, Antitrust Law ¶ 1901e, pp. 189–190 (1998). This Court emphasized in *Klor's* that the agreement at issue was

> "not a case of a single trader refusing to deal with another, nor even of a manufacturer and a dealer agreeing to an exclusive distributorship. Alleged in this complaint is a wide combination consisting of manufacturers, distributors and a retailer." 359 U.S. at 212–213 (footnote omitted).

This Court subsequently pointed out specifically that *Klor's* was a case involving not simply a "vertical" agreement between supplier and customer, but a case that also involved a "horizontal" agreement among competitors. See Business Electronics, 485 U.S. at 734. And in doing so, the Court held that a "vertical restraint is not illegal *per se* unless it includes some agreement on price or price levels." This precedent makes the *per se* rule inapplicable, for the case before us concerns only a vertical agreement and a vertical restraint, a restraint that takes the form of depriving a supplier of a potential customer. See 11 Hovenkamp, supra, ¶ 1902d, at 198.

Nor have we found any special feature of this case that could distinguish it from the precedent we have just discussed. We concede Discon's claim that the petitioners' behavior hurt consumers by raising telephone service rates. But that consumer injury naturally flowed not so much from a less competitive market for removal services, as from the exercise of market power that is *lawfully* in the hands of a monopolist, namely, New York Telephone, combined with a deception worked upon the regulatory agency that prevented the agency from controlling New York Telephone's exercise of its monopoly power.

To apply the *per se* rule here—where the buyer's decision, though not made for competitive reasons, composes part of a regulatory fraud—would transform cases involving business behavior that is improper for various reasons, say, cases involving nepotism or personal pique, into treble-damages antitrust cases. And that *per se* rule would discourage firms from changing suppliers—even where the competitive process itself does not suffer harm. Cf. Poller v. Columbia Broadcasting System, Inc., 368 U.S. 464, 484 (1962) (Harlan, J., dissenting) (citing Packard Motor Car Co. v. Webster Motor Car Co., 243 F.2d 418, 421 (C.A.D.C.1957)).

The freedom to switch suppliers lies close to the heart of the competitive process that the antitrust laws seek to encourage. Cf. Standard Oil, 221 U.S., at 62 (noting "the freedom of the individual right to contract when not unduly or improperly exercised [is] the most efficient means for the prevention of monopoly"). At the same time, other laws, for example, "unfair competition" laws, business tort laws, or regulatory laws, provide remedies for various "competitive practices thought to be offensive to proper standards of business morality." 3 P. Areeda & H. Hovenkamp, Antitrust Law ¶ 651d, p. 78 (1996). Thus, this Court has refused to apply *per se* reasoning in cases involving that kind of activity. See Brooke Group Ltd. v. Brown & Williamson Tobacco Corp., 509 U.S. 209, 225 (1993) ("Even an act of pure malice by one business competitor against another does not, without more, state a claim under the federal antitrust laws"); 3 Areeda & Hovenkamp, supra, ¶ 651d, at 80 ("[I]n the presence of substantial market power, some kinds of tortious behavior could anticompetitively create or sustain a monopoly, [but] it is wrong categorically to condemn such practices . . . or categorically to excuse them").

Discon points to another special feature of its complaint, namely, its claim that Materiel Enterprises hoped to drive Discon from the market lest Discon reveal its behavior to New York Telephone or to the relevant regulatory agency. That hope, says Discon, amounts to a special anticompetitive motive.

We do not see how the presence of this special motive, however, could make a significant difference. That motive does not turn Materiel Enterprises' actions into a "boycott" within the meaning of this Court's precedents. Nor, for that matter, do we understand how Discon believes the motive affected Materiel Enterprises' behavior. Why would Discon's demise have made Discon's employees less likely, rather than more likely, to report the overcharge/rebate scheme to telephone regulators? Regardless, a *per se* rule that would turn upon a showing that a defendant not only knew about but also hoped for a firm's demise would create a legal distinction—

between corporate knowledge and corporate motive—that does not necessarily correspond to behavioral differences and which would be difficult to prove, making the resolution of already complex antitrust cases yet more difficult. We cannot find a convincing reason why the presence of this special motive should lead to the application of the *per se* rule.

Finally, we shall consider an argument that is related tangentially to Discon's *per se* claims. The complaint alleges that New York Telephone (through Materiel Enterprises) was the largest buyer of removal services in New York State, and that only AT & T Technologies competed for New York Telephone's business. We might ask whether these accompanying allegations are sufficient to warrant application of a *Klor's*-type presumption of consequent harm to the competitive process itself.

We believe that these allegations do not do so, for, as we have said, antitrust law does not permit the application of the *per se* rule in the boycott context in the absence of a horizontal agreement. (Though in other contexts, say, vertical price fixing, conduct may fall within the scope of a *per se* rule not at issue here. *See, e.g.*, Dr. Miles Medical Co., 220 U.S. at 408.) The complaint itself explains why any such presumption would be particularly inappropriate here, for it suggests the presence of other potential or actual competitors, which fact, in the circumstances, could argue against the likelihood of anticompetitive harm. The complaint says, for example, that New York Telephone itself was a potential competitor in that New York Telephone considered removing its equipment by itself, and in fact did perform a few jobs itself. The complaint also suggests that other nearby small local telephone companies needing removal services must have worked out some way to supply them. The complaint's description of the removal business suggests that entry was easy, perhaps to the point where other firms, employing workers who knew how to remove a switch and sell it for scrap, might have entered that business almost at will. To that extent, the complaint suggests other actual or potential competitors might have provided roughly similar checks upon "equipment removal" prices and services with or without Discon. At the least, the complaint provides no sound basis for assuming the contrary. Its simple allegation of harm to Discon does not automatically show injury to competition.

III

The Court of Appeals also upheld the complaint's charge of a conspiracy to monopolize in violation of § 2 of the Sherman Act. It did so, however, on the understanding that the conspiracy in question consisted of the very same purchasing practices that we have previously discussed. Unless those agreements harmed the competitive process, they did not amount to a conspiracy to monopolize. We do not see, on the basis of the facts alleged, how Discon could succeed on this claim without prevailing on its § 1 claim. See 3 Areeda & Hovenkamp, supra. Given our conclusion that Discon has not alleged a § 1 *per se* violation, we think it prudent to vacate this portion of the Court of Appeals' decision and allow the court to reconsider its finding of a § 2 claim.

IV

Petitioners ask us to reach beyond the *"per se"* issues and to hold that Discon's complaint does not allege anywhere that their purchasing decisions harmed the competitive process itself and, for this reason, it should be dismissed. They note that Discon has not pointed to any paragraph of the complaint that alleges harm to the competitive process. This matter, however, lies outside the questions presented for certiorari. Those questions were limited to the application of the *per se* rule. For that reason, we believe petitioners cannot raise that argument in this Court.

V

For these reasons, the judgment of the Court of Appeals is vacated, and the case is remanded for further proceedings consistent with this opinion.

Toys "R" Us, Inc. v. Federal Trade Commission

United States Court of Appeals, Seventh Circuit, 2000.
221 F.3d 928.

[Reprinted p. 505, infra.]

NOTES AND QUESTIONS

1. Does *Klor's* recognize the possibility that all boycotts or group refusals to deal might not fall within the illegal *per se* approach taken in the opinion? Would somewhat different facts have compelled application of the rule of reason? What if the appliance manufacturers had a convincing rationale for refusing to deal with Klor's, such as a collective complaint that Klor's discount prices were undercutting Broadway–Hale's ability to maintain an extensive service department to the detriment of the manufacturers' reputations?

2. Was the refusal to deal in *Klor's* horizontal, vertical, or both? If it was both, should that make a difference? Compare Business Electronics Corp. v. Sharp Electronics Corp., 485 U.S. 717 (1988), Chapter 7, p. 696 infra. How does *NYNEX* affect your answer to this question?

3. Is it important that *Klor's* came up on a motion to dismiss, and hence that the allegations of the complaint—particularly that the refusal to sell was instigated by Broadway–Hale to impair Klor's ability to compete—were not disputed by defendants?

4. In the years following *Klor's,* lower courts struggled mightily trying to decide what conduct to characterize as a "group boycott" and how far the *Klor's per se* ruling should extend. The problem they encountered was that the phrases "concerted refusal to deal" or "boycott" cover an extremely wide range of business behavior. Some courts simply applied a *per se* rule without extended discussion of its potential reach. *See, e.g.*, Com–Tel Inc. v. D.U. Kane Corp., 669 F.2d 404 (6th Cir.1982); Williams v. St. Joseph Hospital, 629 F.2d 448, 452 (7th Cir.1980).

Other courts struggled for alternative formulations. In Larry V. Muko Inc. v. Southwestern Pennsylvania Building and Construction Trades Council, 670 F.2d

421, 429–431 (3d Cir.1982), two groups of labor unions and the corporation that operated Long John Silver's were charged with conspiring to award construction contracts for new Silver's restaurants in the Pittsburgh area only to union contractors. Plaintiff, a general contractor, had built several restaurants for Silver's in the past and claimed the arrangement was a boycott in violation of Section 1. In response to special interrogatories, a jury found that the agreement did not follow from agreements concerning wage rates and working conditions and thus was not immune from the antitrust laws because of any labor exemption. The jury further found, however, that the arrangement was not an unreasonable restraint of trade. Plaintiff appealed on grounds, *inter alia,* that a *per se* rule should have applied.

The court affirmed the application of the rule of reason:

> Though *Klor's* appears flatly to proscribe group boycotts, whatever their form or function, courts and commentators alike continue to resist the notion that all concerted refusals to deal fall automatically as *per se* violations of the antitrust laws. Generally, the application of the *per se* rule has been limited to those "classic" boycotts in which a group of business competitors seek to benefit economically by excluding other competitors from the marketplace. "The crucial element" in such boycotts, according to Professor Sullivan, "is an effort to exclude or cause disadvantage to one or more competitors by cutting them off from trade relationships which are necessary to any firm trying to compete. The classic boycott ... also usually entails an effort to induce two or more suppliers or customers not to deal with firms being excluded from the protected level. ..."

> [We have outlined previously] a "core group of situations" in which group boycotts have been deemed illegal *per se:* (1) horizontal combinations of traders at one level of distribution having the purpose of excluding direct competitors from the market [citing *Associated Press*]; (2) vertical combinations, designed to exclude from the market direct competitors of some members of the combination [citing *Klor's*], and (3) coercive combinations aimed at influencing the trade practice of boycott victims [citing *FOGA*].

Noting that the case before it did not fall comfortably into any of those "core group situations," the court concluded that a rule of reason should apply. No market place price fixing was involved. Silver's goal was not adversely to affect Muko's business, but rather to prevent labor strife; the labor organization's goal was to ensure payment of the prevailing union wage to local construction workers. Also, there was no clear anticompetitive effect. Muko remained in the construction business and its profits increased. The Court of Appeals concluded that the trial court was correct in charging the jury under a rule of reason and that the jury was justified in finding no antitrust violation.

5. *Boycotts and Professional Sports.* Because professional sports leagues traditionally have been composed of a number of different entities, they often find their rules challenged under a group boycott theory. Their first line of defense has typically been to try to portray themselves as a single entity, rather than a group of competing firms, but those efforts have met with little success. See Fraser v. Major League Soccer, L.L.C., 284 F.3d 47 (1st Cir.2002); compare Chicago Professional Sports Ltd. v. National Basketball Ass'n, 95 F.3d 593 (7th Cir.1996). The courts have recognized, however, that some collaboration must be accepted within leagues, and the Supreme Court's decision in the *NCAA* case, supra, ch. 4, p. 249, makes it clear that horizontal restraints on competition within sports leagues will not be treated under the *per se* rule. The question is how much collaboration is too much.

Many associations of professional athletic teams use a standard player contract containing provisions which effectively prohibit a player from negotiating freely for his services with other teams in the league. Sometimes there is an absolute ban on negotiations without the consent of the team holding the contract; more frequently in recent years, the team that acquires the player's contract must "compensate" the original team for the loss of services. In addition, some of these associations use a player selection system, commonly called the "draft," in which negotiating rights to graduating college players are allocated among the clubs. Finally, most leagues have bylaws regulating movement of franchises from city to city, and controlling admission to the league of new franchises. Should professional athletes be deprived of the opportunity to take advantage of the kind of lively bidding for services that occurs with respect to outstanding scientists, film stars, or corporate vice-presidents? Should communities be denied the opportunity to compete for sports franchises, as they do for other industrial enterprises?

What restrictions are reasonable under the special circumstances of sports competition has produced some perplexing questions for the courts. In Mid–South Grizzlies v. National Football League, 720 F.2d 772 (3d Cir.1983), a former member of the defunct World Football League (WFL) sued the National Football League (NFL) and its president for refusal to grant a franchise for a team in Memphis, Tennessee. The Grizzlies were rejected pursuant to a league rule, common in professional sports, that requires new franchises to be approved by at least three-fourths of existing members. Plaintiff charged that the exclusion was an illegal boycott under Section 1, motivated by a desire to punish the Grizzlies for participating in the WFL, which had challenged the NFL. The Third Circuit affirmed a grant of summary judgment, noting that an additional franchise would not enhance competition since the Memphis team would have a monopoly (and would compete with no other NFL team) in its home territory, and might actually diminish competition by depriving a future league that might challenge the NFL monopoly of an attractive site for a franchise. In Los Angeles Memorial Coliseum Commission v. NFL, 726 F.2d 1381 (9th Cir.1984), a Court of Appeals was faced with another antitrust challenge to the three-fourths rule concerning franchise changes. The Oakland Raiders, an established franchise in the NFL, was denied permission by League members to move from Oakland to Los Angeles. The Los Angeles stadium sued, claiming that the League rule was a violation of Section 1 of the Sherman Act. The Court of Appeals sustained a jury verdict in favor of plaintiffs. It accepted at the outset the now-conventional approach that rule of reason treatment was justified because of the special economic and competitive attributes of league sports, but noted that the three-fourths rule had an anticompetitive effect in permitting maintenance of local monopolies and preventing competition among stadia to seek tenants. In response to NFL arguments that the rule, and the conditional exclusivity it provided, helped induce teams to invest in football franchises, preserve traditional rivalries between cities, and satisfy TV viewers by ensuring a wide geographic dispersion of teams, the Ninth Circuit noted that the availability of less restrictive alternatives—for example, guidelines to NFL members about voting procedures and standards—may have led the jury justifiably to find a violation. Can you reconcile these two decisions? On what theory?

Other examples of cases involving application of the antitrust laws to sports competition include Law v. National Collegiate Athletic Ass'n, 134 F.3d 1010 (10th Cir.1998) (upholding summary judgment and an injunction against the NCAA's rule limiting compensation for certain Division I entry-level coaches to $16,000 per year; using "quick look" rule of reason analysis); Chicago Professional Sports, Ltd. Partnership v. National Basketball Association, 961 F.2d 667 (7th Cir.1992) (NBA's rule of limiting superstation broadcasts to no more than 20 per season held illegal under a rule of reason analysis); Brenner v. World Boxing Council, 675 F.2d 445 (2d Cir.), cert. denied, 459 U.S. 835 (1982) (suspension of prize fight promoter not *per se* illegal); Smith v. Pro Football, Inc., 593 F.2d 1173, 1178 (D.C.Cir.1978) (player "draft" system declared illegal under rule of reason); Mackey v. National Football League, 543 F.2d 606, 618–20 (8th Cir.1976), cert. dismissed, 434 U.S. 801 (1977) ("Rozelle Rule," which essentially provided that when a player's contract with a team expired and he signed with a different club the signing club must compensate that player's former team, held under a rule of reason analysis to be in violation of § 1 of the Sherman Act). See also Deesen v. Professional Golfers' Association of America, 358 F.2d 165 (9th Cir.1966), cert. denied, 385 U.S. 846 (PGA golf tournament eligibility rule that ensured tournament play without large numbers of players of inferior quality upheld against antitrust challenge); United States Trotting Association v. Chicago Downs Association, 665 F.2d 781 (7th Cir.1981) (en banc) (USTA rules disciplining members who race horses at non-Association meets upheld under rule of reason, because of "need for self-regulation of sporting activities" and as necessary to avoid "free ride" otherwise enjoyed by outsiders benefiting from Association's regulatory activities); North American Soccer League v. National Football League, 670 F.2d 1249 (2d Cir.1982) (proposed NFL by-law to prohibit club owners from acquiring any other professional sports league team unreasonable restraint, because it unnecessarily deprives NASL teams of access to "sports capital and skill," thus limiting their ability to compete with NFL teams for fans and TV revenue).

Has *Professional Engineers,* p. 230 supra, made it more difficult to accord organized sports special antitrust treatment where the principal justification for the rule is noneconomic? See Law v. NCAA, 134 F.3d 1010, supra; Neeld v. National Hockey League, 594 F.2d 1297, 1300 (9th Cir.1979) (by-law barring persons with one eye from playing professional hockey upheld on the basis of safety considerations).

Baseball, of course, is different. The Supreme Court has adhered to a 1922 holding (despite all later developments in both antitrust and constitutional law) that baseball is not "trade or commerce" within the meaning of the Sherman Act. See Federal Baseball Club of Baltimore, Inc. v. National League of Professional Base Ball Clubs, 259 U.S. 200 (1922); Toolson v. New York Yankees, Inc., 346 U.S. 356 (1953); Flood v. Kuhn, 407 U.S. 258 (1972). Other sports do not benefit from any comparable "exemption" from the antitrust laws. See Radovich v. National Football League, 352 U.S. 445 (1957). The scope of baseball's exemption is, however, unclear. Compare Piazza v. Major League Baseball, 831 F.Supp. 420, 436 (E.D.Pa.1993) (exemption limited to the reserve system, which bound a player to negotiate his contract for the current year with the team that held his contract in the prior year); Butterworth v. National League of Professional Baseball Clubs, 644 So.2d 1021 (Fla.1994) (following *Piazza*) with Charles O. Finley & Co. v. Kuhn, 569 F.2d 527, 541 (7th Cir.1978) (the antitrust exemption extends to "the business of baseball, not any particular facet of that business").

6. *Non-commercial Boycotts.* The Supreme Court noted in *Klor's* that the Sherman Act "is aimed primarily at combinations having commercial objectives and is applied only to a very limited extent to organizations ... which normally have other objectives." The current status, scope, and application of this principle presents difficult problems. The D.C. Court of Appeals noted in Marjorie Webster Junior College v. Middle States Association of Colleges and Secondary Schools, 432 F.2d 650 (D.C.Cir.1970), cert. denied, 400 U.S. 965, that

the proscriptions of the Sherman Act were "tailored ... for the business world," not for the noncommercial aspects of the liberal arts and the learned professions. In these contexts, an incidental restraint of trade, absent an intent or purpose to affect the commercial aspects of the profession, is not sufficient to warrant application of the antitrust laws.

Id. at 654. See also NAACP v. Claiborne Hardware Co., 458 U.S. 886 (1982) (holding that NAACP could not be held liable for business losses that resulted from a boycott organized by the NAACP against white merchants, to the extent that the losses arose from nonviolent, protected expressive activity).

The Middle States Association, a nonprofit corporation whose principal business was accrediting member schools, refused to accredit Marjorie Webster since it considered only nonprofit institutions for accreditation, and Marjorie Webster was proprietary. The court held that the process of accreditation by a nonprofit educational corporation was an activity "distinct from the sphere of commerce"; instead it was one going to the "heart of the concept of education itself." The court tempered its finding that the antitrust laws are not applicable to noncommercial associations by noting that "the extent to which deference is due the professional judgment of the association will vary both with the subject matter at issue and with the degree of harm resulting from the association's action." Id. at 655–56. The court's conclusion that Middle States Association had not committed an antitrust violation rested in part on Marjorie Webster's ability to operate successfully for over 20 years without accreditation, and the possibility of setting up an accrediting association for proprietary schools. The court stressed that the situation is not analogous to that of an individual denied membership in or certification by a professional society, who might suffer greater injury, and who would lack the ability to set up an alternative group. See Massachusetts School of Law at Andover, Inc. v. American Bar Association, 855 F.Supp. 108 (E.D.Pa.1994); compare United States v. Brown University, 5 F.3d 658 (3d Cir.1993), ch. 4, p. 265 supra.

Some of the most difficult problems in the refusal to deal area arise where a commercial boycott is used to coerce or induce others to adopt certain lines of conduct for reasons that do not relate directly to commercial considerations. For example, would the rule announced in *Klor's* apply in the following situations:

(a) Where a union and its affiliates refuse to load ships trading with the Soviet Union as a means of discouraging such trade? See Allied International, Inc. v. International Longshoremen's Association, AFL–CIO, 640 F.2d 1368 (1st Cir.1981);

(b) Where a patriotic organization attempts to persuade retail distributors not to handle publications which oppose specific aspects of American foreign policy? See Council of Defense of State of New Mexico v. International Magazine Co., 267 F. 390 (8th Cir.1920);

(c) Where organizations in a southern city agree that their members will not patronize stores within the city until the stores abandon policies of refusing to hire blacks? See Henry v. First National Bank of Clarksdale, 595 F.2d 291 (5th Cir.1979), cert. denied, 444 U.S. 1074 (1980);

(d) Where a women's group urges organizations holding conventions to boycott states that have not ratified the Equal Rights Amendment? See Missouri v. National Organization of Women, 620 F.2d 1301 (8th Cir.1980).

(e) Where real estate brokers in all-white communities agree not to rent homes to blacks? See Bratcher v. Akron Area Board of Realtors, 381 F.2d 723 (6th Cir.1967);

(f) Where a religious organization exhorts its members, under threat of punishment in an afterlife, to shun certain salacious books and movies? See Konecky v. Jewish Press, 288 F. 179 (8th Cir.1923).

Can it be said that the activities described above are strictly noncommercial? May questions of economics be so inextricably interwoven with social justice as to make inadvisable any effort to restrict the group boycott rule to purely economic phenomena? Did Congress in 1890 have in mind that the Sherman Act might be applied in situations like those described above? Is that relevant? Of what relevance are First Amendment considerations? See NAACP v. Claiborne Hardware Co., 458 U.S. 886 (1982).

7.   In Hamilton Chapter of Alpha Delta Phi, Inc. v. Hamilton College, 128 F.3d 59 (2d Cir.1997), four Hamilton College fraternities challenged the College's new policy forcing all students to live in college-owned housing for their entire time in college. The College's stated purpose for the policy was to eliminate the disparity in social opportunities created by fraternities, which in turn was allegedly causing the most talented prospective female students to seek education elsewhere.

The District Court granted summary judgment to Hamilton College on jurisdictional grounds, finding that the provision of room and board to Hamilton College students is not "trade or commerce" and therefore jurisdiction was lacking under Section 2 of the Sherman Act. The Second Circuit reversed, finding that the "trade or commerce" requirement of Section 2 is not jurisdictional.

The fraternities alleged that "Hamilton adopted the residential policy for the commercial purpose of raising revenues by (1) forcing all students to purchase residential services from Hamilton; (2) allowing Hamilton to raise its prices for such services and (3) attempting to purchase the fraternity houses at below-market prices." The Second Circuit found these allegations were enough to require further proceedings. It declined, however, to reach the question whether a failure to prove a commercial motive would be fatal to plaintiff's claim.

8.   In private antitrust suits, a plaintiff must prove actual injury in order to recover damages. In Malcolm v. Marathon Oil Co., 642 F.2d 845 (5th Cir.1981), a discount gasoline retailer who went out of business after his supplies were cut off sued his suppliers alleging Section 1 violations. The lower court directed a verdict against Malcolm since he had not shown that his failure was caused by the refusal to deal. The defendants, Marathon and four other gasoline wholesalers, argued that since Malcolm had failed to contact all alternate suppliers, their refusal had not caused his demise.

The Court of Appeals reversed. In holding that the case should not have been taken from the jury, the court said, "in a refusal to deal case a plaintiff who bypasses an obviously adequate alternative supplier should not recover for the loss of his business. But we do not agree that a plaintiff, seeking to recover damages because of an unlawful refusal to deal, must show a lack of an alternative supply." Id. at 863. But cf. Elder–Beerman Stores Corp. v. Federated Department Stores, Inc., 459 F.2d 138 (6th Cir.1972). In that case, after holding that Beerman's allegation of a conspiracy between his major competitor and several manufacturers to cut him off from several brand name products was not supported by the evidence, the Sixth Circuit noted that even if there was a conspiracy, Beerman was not entitled to damages because he had not shown the lack of "alternative comparable substitutes" for the defendants' products. Id. at 148.

9.   As we will see, the Supreme Court in 1985 and 1986 addressed the problem of general chaos in the lower courts in boycott decisions in its opinions in *Northwest*

Stationers (p. 354 infra) and *Indiana Federation of Dentists* (p. 362 infra). Before turning to those two decisions, we need to examine another line of "boycott" cases—those in which trade associations and other private groups establish standards or provide certification which may result directly or indirectly in the exclusion of competitors' products from the market.

10.   Does *NYNEX* suggest that the rule respecting individual firm boycotts is analytically different from the group boycott rule, or is the Supreme Court developing a general jurisprudence with respect to this business practice? After *NYNEX*, can there ever be a *per se* illegal group boycott in the absence of a proven horizontal conspiracy at one of the relevant levels of the market?

11.   A group refusal to deal, even if it is injurious to the plaintiff, may not be sufficient to sustain an antitrust claim. In Levine v. Central Florida Medical Affiliates, 72 F.3d 1538 (11th Cir.1996), the court sustained summary judgment for the defendants. Although the plaintiff-physician's allegations were enough to create an issue of fact on the question whether a concerted refusal to deal had occurred, the district court ruled against the plaintiff "because he had failed to establish that his suspension resulted in any antitrust injury." The Eleventh Circuit affirmed, but not on antitrust injury grounds. It found that there was no threat to competition from the alleged refusal to deal, and thus that no violation of the antitrust laws could be proven. Is this result consistent with *Klor's*?

Radiant Burners, Inc. v. Peoples Gas Light & Coke Co.

Supreme Court of the United States, 1961.
364 U.S. 656, 81 S.Ct. 365, 5 L.Ed.2d 358.

■ PER CURIAM.

The question here is whether petitioner's complaint stated a claim upon which relief could be granted. Petitioner is engaged at Lombard, Illinois, in the manufacture and sale in interstate commerce of a ceramic gas burner, known as the "Radiant Burner," for the heating of houses and other buildings. Claiming that American Gas Association, Inc. (AGA), a membership corporation doing business in the Northern District of Illinois and in other States, and 10 of its numerous members who also are doing business in the Northern District of Illinois, combined and conspired to restrain interstate commerce in the manufacture, sale and use of gas burners in violation of § 1 of the Sherman Act, petitioner brought this action against those parties for treble damages and an injunction in the United States District Court for the Northern District of Illinois.

The complaint included the following allegations: American Gas Association operates testing laboratories wherein it purports to determine the safety, utility and durability of gas burners. It has adopted a "seal of approval" which it affixes on such gas burners as it determines have passed its tests. Its tests are not based on "objective standards," but are influenced by respondents, some of whom are in competition with petitioner, and thus its determinations can be made "arbitrarily and capriciously." Petitioner has twice submitted its Radiant Burner to AGA for approval but it has not been approved, although it is safer and more efficient than, and just as durable as, gas burners which AGA has approved. "[B]ecause AGA and its Utility members, including Peoples and Northern, effectuate the plan and purpose of the unlawful combination and conspiracy alleged herein by ... refusing to provide gas for use in the plaintiff's Radiant Burner[s] ... which are not approved by AGA," petitioner's gas burners have been effectively excluded from the market, as its potential customers will not buy gas burners for which they cannot obtain gas, and in consequence petitioner has suffered and is suffering the loss of substantial profits.

Respondents moved to dismiss for failure of the complaint to state a claim upon which relief could be granted. The District Court granted the motions, dismissed the complaint and entered judgment for respondents. The Court of Appeals for the Seventh Circuit affirmed. 273 F.2d 196. It stated that "No boycott, conspiracy to boycott or other form of *per se* violation is established by the facts alleged" (id., at page 199), and that "[i]n the absence of a *per se* violation the Sherman Act protects the individual injured competitor and affords him relief, but only under circumstances where there is such general injury to the competitive process that the public at large suffers economic harm." Id., at page 200. It held that public injury was not alleged since "[t]he allegations of [the] plaintiff's complaint fail to establish that there has been any appreciable lessening in the sale of conversion gas burners or gas furnaces or that the public has been deprived of a product of overall superiority." Id., at page 200. Because of petitioner's claim that this holding is contrary to controlling decisions of this Court, we granted certiorari. 363 U.S. 809.

We think the decision of the Court of Appeals does not accord with our recent decision in Klor's, Inc. v. Broadway–Hale Stores, 359 U.S. 207. The allegation in the complaint that "AGA and its Utility members, including Peoples and Northern, effectuate the plan and purpose of the unlawful combination and conspiracy ... by ... refusing to provide gas for use in the plaintiff's Radiant Burner[s]" because they "are not approved by AGA" clearly shows "one type of trade restraint and public harm the Sherman Act forbids".... Id., 359 U.S. at 210. It is obvious that petitioner cannot sell its gas burners, whatever may be their virtues, if, because of the alleged conspiracy, the purchasers cannot buy gas for use in those burners. The conspiratorial refusal "to provide gas for use in the plaintiff's Radiant Burner[s] [because they] are not approved by AGA" therefore falls within one of the "classes of restraints which from their 'nature or character' [are] unduly restrictive, and hence forbidden by both the common law and the statute.... As to these classes of restraints ... Congress [has] determined its own criteria of public harm and it [is] not for the courts to decide whether in an individual case injury [has] actually occurred." Id., 359 U.S. at 211. The alleged conspiratorial refusal to provide gas for use in plaintiff's Radiant Burners "interferes with the natural flow of interstate commerce [and] clearly has, by its 'nature' and 'character,' a 'monopolistic tendency.' As such it is not to be tolerated merely because the victim is just one [manufacturer] whose business is so small that his destruction makes little difference to the economy." Id., 359 U.S. at 213.

By § 1, Congress has made illegal: "Every contract, combination ... or conspiracy," in restraint of trade or commerce among the several States.... Standard Oil Co. of New Jersey v. United States, 221 U.S. 1. Congress having thus prescribed the criteria of the prohibitions, the courts may not expand them. Therefore, to state a claim upon which relief can be granted under that section, allegations adequate to show a violation and, in a private treble damage action, that plaintiff was damaged thereby are all the law requires.

The judgment of the Court of Appeals is reversed and the cause is remanded to the District Court for further proceedings not inconsistent with this opinion.

NOTES AND QUESTIONS

1.   STRUCTURAL LAMINATES, INC. v. DOUGLAS FIR PLYWOOD ASSOCIATION, 261 F.Supp. 154 (D.Or.1966), affirmed, 399 F.2d 155 (9th Cir.1968). A plywood manufacturer brought a treble damage action against a trade association whose members accounted for 82 to 89 percent of the plywood produced in the United States, charging that defendant's quality control program blocked plaintiff's access to the market and, eventually, drove plaintiff out of business. After inspection and testing of members' products, the association permitted members whose products were approved to use its stamp and a certificate. In addition, quality standards adopted by 75 percent of the producers of a product automatically were published by the Department of Commerce, and producers with products meeting these standards usually indicated the fact of conformity with the standards on the product. Plywood not bearing a mark indicating conformity was more difficult to sell and brought a lower price.

The association played a dominant role in proposing standards and soliciting approval by members of this industry. One quality standard that defendant had succeeded in having accepted as early as 1948 had the effect of excluding plywood composed of relatively thick veneers, apparently because of bonding difficulties. Plaintiff believed it had solved these technical problems and, after constructing a plywood mill in 1957, sought a modification in this quality standard. Defendant conducted a series of tests over a substantial period of time and finally, in 1963, recommended that the quality standard be revised, but plaintiff had gone out of business in November, 1960.

The district court found that "mere adoption of a standard which discriminates between products cannot be ... a *per se* violation of the Sherman Act—particularly where, as here, the standard is the product of a Congressionally sanctioned scheme." The court went on to find that the plaintiff had failed to show that the quality standard that adversely affected plaintiff's business "was either unreasonable or done with an evil intent," although the court recognized that some of defendant's members were competitors of plaintiff and had "a real economic motive" in opposing widespread use of plaintiff's product.

2.   The same result as in *Structural Laminates* was reached in Eliason Corp. v. National Sanitation Foundation, 614 F.2d 126 (6th Cir.1980), where the independent, nonprofit, standard-setting organization (1) was not shown to have any relationship to the Department of Commerce or any governmental agency; (2)

promulgated uniform health and product standards directly to local governments and buyers and encouraged their adoption; but (3) was not shown to be under the control of industry leaders or other competitors of plaintiff, or to discriminate against it in testing or applying standards.

The court held that, absent discrimination or "manifestly anticompetitive and unreasonable conduct," alleged boycotts arising from "standard-making or even industry self-regulation" did not give rise to Sherman Act problems. It noted that it did "not intend to foreclose the possibility that some standards may be so unreasonable in content that their net effect injures competition even though some policies of uniformity are served." Nationwide uniformity of standards, however, was seen to promote competition, enabling "manufacturers who elect to comply ... to be reasonably sure they will not have to modify their product in order to meet the different requirements of many jurisdictions."

Plaintiff had argued that the testing program gave large competitors an unfair competitive advantage over smaller manufacturers of functionally equivalent products and created barriers to entry for innovative manufacturers. One commentator speculates that the Foundation was "created and maintained by larger manufacturers ... to eliminate the need to innovate and to curtail competition by price-cutters ..." and that many states which adopted the uniform standards did so "only in response to the foundations' activities." J. Ponsoldt, The Application of Sherman Act Antiboycott Law to Industry Self–Regulation, 55 So.Cal.L.Rev. 1 (1981).

Can the theories of *Structural Laminates* and *Eliason* be reconciled with *Fashion Originators'* and *Radiant Burners*? Does *NYNEX* prove that these standard-setting cases were correctly decided, or is it unhelpful as an essentially vertical case?

3.   How real is the "barrier to entry" problem if standard-fixing agencies win nationwide acceptance of their criteria or seal of approval? How would one prove that such an agency is (or is not) in fact totally independent and impartial? Would it be relevant that the agency is supported by industry members, perhaps proportionately to their volume of business, rather than exclusively by fees for testing and other services rendered? Should the agency, rather than the plaintiff, bear the burden of establishing that procedures it followed were adequate and standards it adopted were reasonable? Cf. *Allied Tube & Conduit Corp. v. Indian Head*, p. 421 infra.

Northwest Wholesale Stationers, Inc. v. Pacific Stationery & Printing Co.

Supreme Court of the United States, 1985.
472 U.S. 284, 105 S.Ct. 2613, 86 L.Ed.2d 202.

■ BRENNAN, J.... This case requires that we decide whether a *per se* violation of § 1 of the Sherman Act, 15 U.S.C. § 1, occurs when a cooperative buying agency comprising various retailers expels a member without providing any procedural means for challenging the expulsion. This case also raises broader questions as to when *per se* antitrust analysis is appropriately applied to joint activity that is susceptible of being characterized as a concerted refusal to deal.

I

Because the District Court ruled on cross-motions for summary judgment after only limited discovery, this case comes to us on a sparse record. Certain background facts are undisputed. Petitioner Northwest Wholesale Stationers is a purchasing cooperative made up of approximately 100 office supply retailers in the Pacific Northwest States. The cooperative acts as the primary wholesaler for the retailers. Retailers that are not members of the cooperative can purchase wholesale supplies from Northwest at the same price as members. At the end of each year, however, Northwest distributes its profits to members in the form of a percentage rebate on purchases. Members therefore effectively purchase supplies at a price significantly lower than do nonmembers.[6] Northwest also provides certain warehousing facilities. The cooperative arrangement thus permits the participating retailers to achieve economies of scale in purchasing and warehousing that would otherwise be unavailable to them. In fiscal 1978 Northwest had $5.8 million in sales.

Respondent Pacific Stationery, Inc. sells office supplies at both the retail and wholesale levels. Its total sales in fiscal 1978 were approximately $7.6 million; the record does not indicate what percentage of revenue is attributable to retail and what percentage is attributable to wholesale. Pacific became a member of Northwest in 1958. In 1974 Northwest amended its bylaws to prohibit members from engaging in both retail and wholesale operations. A grandfather clause preserved Pacific's membership rights. In 1977 ownership of a controlling share of the stock of Pacific changed hands, and the new owners did not officially bring this change to the attention of the directors of Northwest. This failure to notify apparently violated another of Northwest's bylaws.

In 1978 the membership of Northwest voted to expel Pacific. Most factual matters relevant to the expulsion are in dispute. No explanation for the expulsion was advanced at the time and Pacific was given neither notice, a hearing, nor any other opportunity to challenge the decision. Pacific argues that the expulsion resulted from Pacific's decision to maintain a wholesale operation. Northwest contends that the expulsion resulted from Pacific's failure to notify the cooperative members of the change in stock ownership. The minutes of the meeting of Northwest's directors do not definitively indicate the motive for the expulsion. It is undisputed that Pacific received approximately $10,000 in rebates from Northwest in 1978, Pacific's last year of membership. Beyond a possible inference of loss from

---

6. Although this patronage rebate policy is a form of price discrimination, § 4 of the Robinson–Patman Act specifically sanctions such activity by cooperatives.

"Nothing in this Act shall prevent a cooperative association from returning to its members, producers, or consumers the whole, or any part of, the net earn-ings or surplus resulting from its trading operations, in proportion to their purchases or sales from, to, or through the association." 49 Stat. 1528, 15 U.S.C. § 13b.

A relevant state-law provision provides analogous protection. Ore.Rev.Stat. 646.030 (1983).

this fact, however, the record is devoid of allegations indicating the nature and extent of competitive injury the expulsion caused Pacific to suffer.

Pacific brought suit in 1980 in the United States District Court for the District of Oregon alleging a violation of § 1 of the Sherman Act. The gravamen of the action was that Northwest's expulsion of Pacific from the cooperative without procedural protections was a group boycott that limited Pacific's ability to compete and should be considered *per se* violative of § 1. On cross-motions for summary judgment the District Court rejected application of the *per se* rule and held instead that rule-of-reason analysis should govern the case. Finding no anticompetitive effect on the basis of the record as presented, the court granted summary judgment for Northwest.

The Court of Appeals for the Ninth Circuit reversed, holding "that the uncontroverted facts of this case support a finding of *per se* liability." 715 F.2d 1393, 1395 (1983). The court reasoned that the cooperative's expulsion of Pacific was an anticompetitive concerted refusal to deal with Pacific on equal footing, which would be a *per se* violation of § 1 in the absence of any specific legislative mandate for self-regulation sanctioning the expulsion. The court noted that § 4 of the Robinson–Patman Act, 15 U.S.C. § 13b, specifically approves the price discrimination occasioned by such expulsion and concluded that § 4 therefore provided a mandate for self-regulation. Such a legislative mandate, according to the court, would ordinarily result in evaluation of the challenged practice under the rule of reason. But, drawing on Silver v. New York Stock Exchange, 373 U.S. 341, 348–349 (1963), the court decided that rule-of-reason analysis was appropriate only on the condition that the cooperative had provided procedural safeguards sufficient to prevent arbitrary expulsion and to furnish a basis for judicial review. Because Northwest had not provided any procedural safeguards, the court held that the expulsion of Pacific was not shielded by Robinson–Patman immunity and therefore constituted a *per se* group boycott in violation of § 1 of the Sherman Act. 715 F.2d, at 1395–1398.

We granted certiorari to examine this application of Silver v. New York Stock Exchange, supra, in an area of antitrust law that has not been free of confusion. 469 U.S. 814 (1984). We reverse.

II

The decision of the cooperative members to expel Pacific was certainly a restraint of trade in the sense that every commercial agreement restrains trade. Chicago Board of Trade v. United States, 246 U.S. 231, 238 (1918). Whether this action violates § 1 of the Sherman Act depends on whether it is adjudged an unreasonable restraint. Rule-of-reason analysis guides the inquiry, see Standard Oil Co. v. United States, 221 U.S. 1 (1911), unless the challenged action falls into the category of "agreements or practices which because of their pernicious effect on competition and lack of any redeeming virtue are conclusively presumed to be unreasonable and therefore illegal without elaborate inquiry as to the precise harm they have caused or the business excuse for their use." Northern Pacific R. Co. v. United States, 356 U.S. 1, 5 (1958).

This *per se* approach permits categorical judgments with respect to certain business practices that have proved to be predominantly anticompetitive. Courts can thereby avoid the "significant costs" in "business certainty and litigation efficiency" that a full-fledged rule-of-reason inquiry entails. Arizona v. Maricopa County Medical Society, 457 U.S. 332, 343–344 (1982). See also United States v. Topco Associates, Inc., 405 U.S. 596, 609–610 (1972). . . .

This Court has long held that certain concerted refusals to deal or group boycotts are so likely to restrict competition without any offsetting efficiency gains that they should be condemned as *per se* violations of § 1 of the Sherman Act. See Klor's, Inc. v. Broadway Hale Stores, Inc., 359 U.S. 207 (1959); United States v. General Motors Corp., 384 U.S. 127 (1966); Radiant Burners, Inc. v. Peoples Gas Light & Coke Co., 364 U.S. 656 (1961); Associated Press v. United States, 326 U.S. 1 (1945); Fashion Originators' Guild of America, Inc. v. FTC, 312 U.S. 457 (1941); Eastern States Retail Lumber Dealers' Assn. v. United States, 234 U.S. 600 (1914). The question presented in this case is whether Northwest's decision to expel Pacific should fall within this category of activity that is conclusively presumed to be anticompetitive. The Court of Appeals held that the exclusion of Pacific from the cooperative should conclusively be presumed unreasonable on the ground that Northwest provided no procedural protections to Pacific. Even if the lack of procedural protections does not justify a conclusive presumption of predominantly anticompetitive effect, the mere act of expulsion of a competitor from a wholesale cooperative might be argued to be sufficiently likely to have such effects under the present circumstances and therefore to justify application of the *per se* rule. These possibilities will be analyzed separately.

A

The Court of Appeals drew from Silver v. New York Stock Exchange, supra, a broad rule that the conduct of a cooperative venture—including a concerted refusal to deal—undertaken pursuant to a legislative mandate for self-regulation is immune from *per se* scrutiny and subject to rule of reason analysis only if adequate procedural safeguards accompany self-regulation. We disagree and conclude that the approach of the Court in *Silver* has no proper application to the present controversy.

The Court in *Silver* framed the issue as follows:

"[W]hether the New York Stock Exchange is to be held liable to a nonmember broker-dealer under the antitrust laws or regarded as impliedly immune therefrom when, pursuant to rules the Exchange has adopted under the Securities Exchange Act of 1934, it orders a number of its members to remove private direct telephone wire connections previously in operation between their offices and those of the nonmember, without giving the nonmember notice, assigning him any reason for the action, or affording him an opportunity to be heard." 373 U.S., at 343.

Because the New York Stock Exchange occupied such a dominant position in the securities trading markets that the boycott would devastate the nonmember, the Court concluded that the refusal to deal with the non-member would amount to a *per se* violation of § 1 unless the Securities Exchange Act provided an immunity. The question for the Court thus was whether effectuation of the policies of the Securities Exchange Act required partial repeal of the Sherman Act insofar as it proscribed this aspect of exchange self-regulation.

Finding exchange self-regulation—including the power to expel members and limit dealings with nonmembers—to be an essential policy of the Securities Exchange Act, the Court held that the Sherman Act should be construed as having been partially repealed to permit the type of exchange activity at issue. But the interpretive maxim disfavoring repeals by implication led the Court to narrow permissible self-policing to situations in which adequate procedural safeguards had been provided.

> "Congress . . . cannot be thought to have sanctioned and protected self-regulative activity when carried out in a fundamentally unfair manner. The point is not that the antitrust laws impose the requirement of notice and a hearing here, but rather that, in acting without according petitioners these safeguards in response to their request, the Exchange has plainly exceeded the scope of its authority under the Securities Exchange Act to engage in self-regulation."

Thus it was the specific need to accommodate the important national policy of promoting effective exchange self-regulation, tempered by the principle that the Sherman Act should be narrowed only to the extent necessary to effectuate that policy, that dictated the result in *Silver*.

Section 4 of the Robinson–Patman Act is not comparable to the self-policing provisions of the Securities Exchange Act. That section is no more than a narrow immunity from the price discrimination prohibitions of the Robinson–Patman Act itself. . . .

[T]here can be no argument that § 4 of the Robinson–Patman Act should be viewed as a broad mandate for industry self-regulation. No need exists, therefore, to narrow the Sherman Act in order to accommodate any competing congressional policy requiring discretionary self-policing. Indeed, Congress would appear to have taken some care to make clear that no constriction of the Sherman Act was intended. In any event, the absence of procedural safeguards can in no sense determine the anti-trust analysis. If the challenged concerted activity of Northwest's members would amount to a *per se* violation of § 1 of the Sherman Act, no amount of procedural protection would save it. If the challenged action would not amount to a violation of § 1, no lack of procedural protections would convert it into a *per se* violation because the antitrust laws do not themselves impose on joint ventures a requirement of process.

B

This case therefore turns not on the lack of procedural protections but on whether the decision to expel Pacific is properly viewed as a group boycott or concerted refusal to deal mandating *per se* invalidation. "Group boycotts" are often listed among the classes of economic activity that merit *per se* invalidation under § 1. See Klor's, Inc. v. Broadway–Hale Stores, Inc., 359 U.S., at 212; Northern Pacific Railway Co. v. United States, 356 U.S., at 5; Silver v. New York Stock Exchange, 373 U.S., at 348; White Motor Co. v. United States, 372 U.S. 253, 259–260 (1963). Exactly what types of activity fall within the forbidden category is, however, far from certain. "[T]here is more confusion about the scope and operation of the *per se* rule against group boycotts than in reference to any other aspect of the *per se* doctrine." L. Sullivan, Law of Antitrust 229–230 (1977). Some care is therefore necessary in defining the category of concerted refusals to deal that mandate *per se* condemnation. See St. Paul Fire & Marine Ins. Co. v. Barry, 438 U.S. 531, 543 (1978) (concerted refusals to deal "are not a unitary phenomenon"). Cf. Broadcast Music, Inc. v. Columbia Broadcasting System, Inc., 441 U.S., at 9.

Cases to which this Court has applied the *per se* approach have generally involved joint efforts by a firm or firms to disadvantage competitors by "either directly denying or persuading or coercing suppliers or customers to deny relationships the competitors need in the competitive struggle." Sullivan, supra, at 261–262. *See, e.g., Silver,* supra (denial of necessary access to exchange members); Radiant Burners, Inc. v. Peoples Gas Light & Coke Co., 364 U.S. 656 (1961) (denial of necessary certification of product); Associated Press v. United States, 326 U.S. 1 (1945) (denial of important sources of news); *Klor's, Inc.,* supra (denial of wholesale supplies). In these cases, the boycott often cut off access to a supply, facility, or market necessary to enable the boycotted firm to compete, *Silver,* supra; *Radiant Burners, Inc.,* supra, and frequently the boycotting firms possessed a dominant position in the relevant market. *E.g., Silver,* supra; *Associated Press,* supra; Fashion Originators Guild of America, Inc. v. FTC, 312 U.S. 457 (1941). See generally Brodley, Joint Ventures and Antitrust Policy, 95 Harv.L.Rev. 1523, 1533, 1563–1565 (1982). In addition, the practices were generally not justified by plausible arguments that they were intended to enhance overall efficiency and make markets more competitive. Under such circumstances the likelihood of anticompetitive effects is clear and the possibility of countervailing procompetitive effects is remote.

Although a concerted refusal to deal need not necessarily possess all of these traits to merit *per se* treatment, not every cooperative activity involving a restraint or exclusion will share with the *per se* forbidden boycotts the likelihood of predominantly anticompetitive consequences. For example, we recognized last Term in National Collegiate Athletic Assn. v. Board of Regents of University of Oklahoma that *per se* treatment of the NCAA's restrictions on the marketing of televised college football was inappropriate—despite the obvious restraint on output—because the "case involves an industry in which horizontal restraints on competition are essential if the product is to be available at all."

Wholesale purchasing cooperatives such as Northwest are not a form of concerted activity characteristically likely to result in predominantly anti-competitive effects. Rather, such cooperative arrangements would seem to be "designed to increase economic efficiency and render markets more, rather than less, competitive." Broadcast Music, Inc. v. Columbia Broadcasting System, Inc. The arrangement permits the participating retailers to achieve economies of scale in both the purchase and warehousing of wholesale supplies, and also ensures ready access to a stock of goods that might otherwise be unavailable on short notice. The cost savings and order-filling guarantees enable smaller retailers to reduce prices and maintain their retail stock so as to compete more effectively with larger retailers.

Pacific, of course, does not object to the existence of the cooperative arrangement, but rather raises an antitrust challenge to Northwest's decision to bar Pacific from continued membership.[7] It is therefore the action of expulsion that must be evaluated to determine whether *per se* treatment is appropriate. The act of expulsion from a wholesale cooperative does not necessarily imply anticompetitive animus and thereby raise a probability of anticompetitive effect. See Broadcast Music, Inc. v. Columbia Broadcasting System, Inc. Wholesale purchasing cooperatives must establish and enforce reasonable rules in order to function effectively. Disclosure rules, such as the one on which Northwest relies, may well provide the cooperative with a needed means for monitoring the creditworthiness of its members.[8] Nor would the expulsion characteristically be likely to result in predominantly anticompetitive effects, at least in the type of situation this case presents. Unless the cooperative possesses market power or exclusive access to an element essential to effective competition, the conclusion that expulsion is virtually always likely to have an anticompetitive effect is not warranted. See L. Sullivan, Law of Antitrust 292–293 (1977); Brodley, 95 Harv.L.Rev., at 1563–1565. Cf. Jefferson Parish Hospital Dist. v. Hyde, 466 U.S. 212–15 (1984) (absent indication of market power, tying arrangement does not warrant *per se* invalidation). See generally NCAA v. Board of Regents of University of Oklahoma, 468 U.S., at 104, n. 26 ("*Per se* rules

7. Because Pacific has not been wholly excluded from access to Northwest's wholesale operations, there is perhaps some question whether the challenged activity is properly characterized a concerted refusal to deal. To be precise, Northwest's activity is a concerted refusal to deal with Pacific on substantially equal terms. Such activity might justify *per se* invalidation if it placed a competing firm at a severe competitive disadvantage. See generally Brodley, Joint Ventures and Antitrust Policy, 95 Harv.L.Rev. 1521, 1532 (1982) ("Even if the joint venture does deal with outside firms, it may place them at a severe competitive disadvantage by treating them less favorably than it treats the [participants in the joint venture]").

8. Pacific argues, however, that this justification for expulsion was a pretext because the members of Northwest were fully aware of the change in ownership despite lack of formal notice. According to Pacific, Northwest's motive in the expulsion was to place Pacific at a competitive disadvantage to retaliate for Pacific's decision to engage in an independent wholesale operation. Such a motive might be more troubling. If Northwest's action were not substantially related to the efficiency-enhancing or procompetitive purposes that otherwise justify the cooperative's practices, an inference of anticompetitive animus might be appropriate. But such an argument is appropriately evaluated under the rule of reason analysis.

may require considerable inquiry into market conditions before the evidence justifies a presumption of anticompetitive conduct''). Absent such a showing with respect to a cooperative buying arrangement, courts should apply a rule-of-reason analysis. At no time has Pacific made a threshold showing that these structural characteristics are present in this case.[9]

The District Court appears to have followed the correct path of analysis—recognizing that not all concerted refusals to deal should be accorded *per se* treatment and deciding this one should not. The foregoing discussion suggests, however, that a satisfactory threshold determination whether anticompetitive effects would be likely might require a more detailed factual picture of market structure than the District Court had before it. Nonetheless, in our judgment the District Court's rejection of *per se* analysis in this case was correct. A plaintiff seeking application of the *per se* rule must present a threshold case that the challenged activity falls into a category likely to have predominantly anticompetitive effects. The mere allegation of a concerted refusal to deal does not suffice because not all concerted refusals to deal are predominantly anticompetitive. When the plaintiff challenges expulsion from a joint buying cooperative, some showing must be made that the cooperative possesses market power or unique access to a business element necessary for effective competition. Focusing on the argument that the lack of procedural safeguards required *per se* liability, Pacific did not allege any such facts. Because the Court of Appeals applied an erroneous *per se* analysis in this case, the court never evaluated the District Court's rule-of-reason analysis rejecting Pacific's claim. A remand is therefore appropriate for the limited purpose of permitting appellate review of that determination.

III

"The *per se* rule is a valid and useful tool of antitrust policy and enforcement." Broadcast Music, Inc. v. Columbia Broadcasting System, Inc., 441 U.S., at 8. It does not denigrate the *per se* approach to suggest care in application. In this case, the Court of Appeals failed to exercise the requisite care and applied *per se* analysis inappropriately. The judgment of the Court of Appeals is therefore reversed, and the case is remanded for further proceedings consistent with this opinion.

■ MARSHALL, J., and POWELL, J., took no part in the decision of this case.

NOTES AND QUESTIONS

1. Can *Northwest Stationers* and *Klor's* be reconciled? What is the maximum and minimum reading that can be given to *Klor's* after *Northwest Stationers?*

---

9. Given the state of this record it is difficult to understand how the court of appeals could have concluded that Pacific "loses the ability to use Northwest's superior warehousing and expedited order-filling facilities, as well as any competitive advantages that may flow simply from being known in the industry as a member of an established cooperative." 715 F.2d 1393, 1395 (1983). The District Court had specifically found no anticompetitive effect....

2. What are the factors that *Northwest Stationers* requires be examined before concluding that a collaborative arrangement is a "boycott" meriting *per se* treatment? Are these the same factors that the Supreme Court examined in the "characterization" phase of *BMI?* Are they the same as the ones the Court consulted in *NYNEX?*

3. According to *Northwest Stationers,* is market power a precondition to application of *per se* rules in all boycott cases or only in buying and selling co-ops? If a precondition in all cases, what remains of *Klor's?*

FTC v. Indiana Federation of Dentists

Supreme Court of the United States, 1986.
476 U.S. 447, 106 S.Ct. 2009, 90 L.Ed.2d 445.

■ WHITE, J. . . . This case concerns commercial relations among certain Indiana dentists, their patients, and the patients' dental health care insurers. The question presented is whether the Federal Trade Commission correctly concluded that a conspiracy among dentists to refuse to submit x-rays to dental insurers for use in benefits determinations constituted an "unfair method of competition" in violation of § 5 of the Federal Trade Commission Act.

I

Since the 1970s, dental health insurers, responding to the demands of their policyholders, have attempted to contain the cost of dental treatment by, among other devices, limiting payment of benefits to the cost of the "least expensive yet adequate treatment" suitable to the needs of individual patients. Implementation of such cost-containment measures, known as "alternative benefits" plans, requires evaluation by the insurer of the diagnosis and recommendation of the treating dentist, either in advance of or following the provision of care. In order to carry out such evaluation, insurers frequently request dentists to submit, along with insurance claim forms requesting payment of benefits, any dental x-rays that have been used by the dentist in examining the patient as well as other information concerning their diagnoses and treatment recommendations. Typically, claim forms and accompanying x-rays are reviewed by lay claims examiners, who either approve payment of claims or, if the materials submitted raise a question whether the recommended course of treatment is in fact necessary, refer claims to dental consultants, who are licensed dentists, for further review. On the basis of the materials available, supplemented where appropriate by further diagnostic aids, the dental consultant may recommend that the insurer approve a claim, deny it, or pay only for a less expensive course of treatment.

Such review of diagnostic and treatment decisions has been viewed by some dentists as a threat to their professional independence and economic well-being. In the early 1970s, the Indiana Dental Association, a professional organization comprising some 85% of practicing dentists in the State of Indiana, initiated an aggressive effort to hinder insurers' efforts to implement alternative benefits plans by enlisting member dentists to pledge not to submit x-rays in conjunction with claim forms.[10] The Association's efforts met considerable success: large numbers of dentists signed the pledge, and insurers operating in Indiana found it difficult to obtain compliance with their requests for x-rays and accordingly had to choose either to employ more expensive means of making alternative benefits determinations (for example, visiting the office of the treating dentist or conducting an independent oral examination) or to abandon such efforts altogether.

By the mid–1970s, fears of possible antitrust liability had dampened the Association's enthusiasm for opposing the submission of x-rays to insurers. In 1979, the Association and a number of its constituent societies consented to a Federal Trade Commission order requiring them to cease and desist from further efforts to prevent member dentists from submitting x-rays. In re Indiana Dental Assn., 93 F.T.C. 392 (1979). Not all Indiana dentists were content to leave the matter of submitting x-rays to the individual dentist. In 1976, a group of such dentists formed the Indiana Federation of Dentists, respondent in this case, in order to continue to pursue the Association's policy of resisting insurers' requests for x-rays. The Federation, which styled itself a "union" in the belief that this label would stave off antitrust liability, immediately promulgated a "work rule" forbidding its members to submit x-rays to dental insurers in conjunction with claim forms. Although the Federation's membership was small, numbering less than 100, its members were highly concentrated in and around three Indiana communities: Anderson, Lafayette, and Fort Wayne. The Federation succeeded in enlisting nearly 100% of the dental specialists in the Anderson area, and approximately 67% of the dentists in and around Lafayette. In the areas of its strength, the Federation was successful in continuing to enforce the Association's prior policy of refusal to submit x-rays to dental insurers.

10. A presentation made in 1974 by Dr. David McClure, an Association official and later one of the founders of respondent Indiana Federation of Dentists, is revealing as to the motives underlying the dentists' resistance to the provision of x-rays for use by insurers in making alternative benefits determinations:

> The problems associated with third party programs are many, but I believe the "Indiana Plan" [i.e., the policy of refusing to submit x-rays] to be sound and if we work together, we can win this battle. We are fighting an economic war where the very survival of our profession is at stake.

> "How long can some of the leaders of dentistry in other states be so complacent and willing to fall into the trap that

is being set for us. If only they would take the time, to see from whence come the arrows that are heading in our direction. The Delta Dental Plans have bedded down with the unions and have been a party to setting up the greatest controls that any profession has ever known in a free society....

> "The name of the game is money. The government and labor are determined to reduce the cost of the dental health dollar at the expense of the dentist. There is no way a dental service can be rendered cheaper when the third party has to have its share of the dollar.

> "Already we are locked into a fee freeze that could completely control the quality of dental care, if left on long enough."

In 1978, the Federal Trade Commission issued a complaint against the Federation, alleging in substance that its efforts to prevent its members from complying with insurers' requests for x-rays constituted an unfair method of competition in violation of § 5 of the Federal Trade Commission Act. . . .

The Federation sought judicial review of the Commission's order in the United States Court of Appeals for the Seventh Circuit, which vacated the order on the ground that it was not supported by substantial evidence. Accepting the Federation's characterization of its rule against submission of x-rays as merely an ethical and moral policy designed to enhance the welfare of dental patients, the majority concluded that the Commission's findings that the policy was anticompetitive were erroneous. According to the majority, the evidence did not support the finding that in the absence of restraint dentists would compete for patients by offering cooperation with the requests of the patients' insurers, nor, even accepting that finding, was there evidence that the Federation's efforts had prevented such competition. Further, the court held that the Commission's findings were inadequate because of its failure both to offer a precise definition of the market in which the Federation was alleged to have restrained competition and to establish that the Federation had the power to restrain competition in that market. Finally, the majority faulted the Commission for not finding that the alleged restraint on competition among dentists had actually resulted in higher dental costs to patients and insurers. The third member of the Court of Appeals panel concurred in the judgment solely on the ground that there was insufficient proof that cooperation with insurers was an element of dental services as to which dentists would tend to compete. . . .

III

The relevant factual findings are that the members of the Federation conspired among themselves to withhold x-rays requested by dental insurers for use in evaluating claims for benefits, and that this conspiracy had the effect of suppressing competition among dentists with respect to cooperation with the requests of the insurance companies. As to the first of these findings there can be no serious dispute: abundant evidence in the record reveals that one of the primary reasons—if not the primary reason—for the Federation's existence was the promulgation and enforcement of the so-called "work rule" against submission of x-rays in conjunction with insurance claim forms.

As for the second crucial finding—that competition was actually suppressed—the Seventh Circuit held it to be unsupported by the evidence, on two theories. First, the court stated that the evidence did not establish that cooperation with requests for information by patients' insurance companies was an aspect of the provision of dental services with respect to which dentists would, in the absence of some restraint, compete. Second, the court found that even assuming that dentists would otherwise compete with respect to policies of cooperating or not cooperating with insurance companies, the Federation's policy did not impair that competition, for the member dentists continued to allow insurance companies to use other means of evaluating their diagnoses when reviewing claims for benefits: specifically, "the IFD member dentists allowed insurers to visit the dental office to review and examine the patient's x-rays along with all of the other diagnostic and clinical aids used in formulating a proper course of dental treatment."

Neither of these criticisms of the Commission's findings is well founded. The Commission's finding that "[i]n the absence of ... concerted behavior, individual dentists would have been subject to market forces of competition, creating incentives for them to ... comply with the requests of patients' third-party insurers," finds support not only in common sense and economic theory, upon both of which the FTC may reasonably rely, but also in record documents, including newsletters circulated among Indiana dentists, revealing that Indiana dentists themselves perceived that unrestrained competition tended to lead their colleagues to comply with insurers' requests for x-rays. Moreover, there was evidence that outside of Indiana, in States where dentists had not collectively refused to submit x-rays, insurance companies found little difficulty in obtaining compliance by dentists with their requests. A "reasonable mind" could conclude on the basis of this evidence that competition for patients, who have obvious incentives for seeking dentists who will cooperate with their insurers, would tend to lead dentists in Indiana (and elsewhere) to cooperate with requests for information by their patients' insurers.

The Commission's finding that such competition was actually diminished where the Federation held sway also finds adequate support in the record. The Commission found that in the areas where Federation membership among dentists was most significant (that is, in the vicinity of Anderson and Lafayette) insurance companies were unable to obtain compliance with their requests for submission of x-rays in conjunction with claim forms and were forced to resort to other, more costly, means of reviewing diagnoses for the purpose of benefit determination. Neither the opinion of the Court of Appeals nor the brief of respondent identifies any evidence suggesting that the Commission's finding that the Federation's policy had an actual impact on the ability of insurers to obtain the x-rays they requested was incorrect. The lower court's conclusion that this evidence is to be discounted because Federation members continued to cooperate with insurers by allowing them to use more costly—indeed, prohibitively costly—methods of reviewing treatment decisions is unpersuasive. The fact remains that the dentists' customers (that is, the patients and their insurers) sought a particular service: cooperation with the insurers' pretreatment review through the forwarding of x-rays in conjunction with claim forms. The Federation's collective activities resulted in the denial of the information the customers requested in the form that they requested it, and forced them to choose between acquiring that information in a more costly manner or forgoing it altogether. To this extent, at least, competition among dentists with respect to cooperation with the requests of insurers was restrained.

IV

The question remains whether these findings are legally sufficient to establish a violation of § 1 of the Sherman Act—that is, whether the Federation's collective refusal to cooperate with insurers' requests for x-rays constitutes an "unreasonable" restraint of trade. Under our precedents, a restraint may be adjudged unreasonable either because it fits within a class of restraints that has been held to be *"per se "*unreasonable, or because it violates what has come to be known as the "Rule of Reason," under which the "test of legality is whether the restraint imposed is such as merely regulates and perhaps thereby promotes competition or whether it is such as may suppress or even destroy competition." Chicago Board of Trade v. United States, 246 U.S., at 238.

The policy of the Federation with respect to its members' dealings with third-party insurers resembles practices that have been labeled "group boycotts": the policy constitutes a concerted refusal to deal on particular terms with patients covered by group dental insurance. Cf. St. Paul Fire & Marine Insurance Co. v. Barry, 438 U.S. 531 (1978); Paramount Famous Lasky Corp. v. United States, 282 U.S. 30 (1930). Although this Court has in the past stated that group boycotts are unlawful *per se,* see United States v. General Motors Corp., 384 U.S. 127 (1966); Klor's, Inc. v. Broadway–Hale Stores, Inc., 359 U.S. 207 (1959), we decline to resolve this case by forcing the Federation's policy into the "boycott" pigeonhole and invoking the *per se* rule. As we observed last Term in Northwest Wholesale Stationers, Inc. v. Pacific Stationery and Printing Co., 472 U.S. 284 (1985), the category of restraints classed as group boycotts is not to be expanded indiscriminately, and the *per se* approach has generally been limited to cases in which firms with market power boycott suppliers or customers in order to discourage them from doing business with a competitor—a situation obviously not present here. Moreover, we have been slow to condemn rules adopted by professional associations as unreasonable *per se,* see National Society of Professional Engineers v. United States, 435 U.S. 679 (1978), and, in general, to extend *per se* analysis to restraints imposed in the context of business relationships where the economic impact of certain practices is not immediately obvious, see Broadcast Music, Inc. v. CBS, 441 U.S. 1 (1979). Thus, as did the FTC, we evaluate the restraint at issue in this case under the Rule of Reason rather than a rule of *per se* illegality.

Application of the Rule of Reason to these facts is not a matter of any great difficulty. The Federation's policy takes the form of a horizontal agreement among the participating dentists to withhold from their customers a particular service that they desire—the forwarding of x-rays to insurance companies along with claim forms. "While this is not price fixing as such, no elaborate industry analysis is required to demonstrate the anticompetitive character of such an agreement." *Society of Professional Engineers,* supra, 435 U.S. at 692. A refusal to compete with respect to the package of services offered to customers, no less than a refusal to compete with respect to the price term of an agreement, impairs the ability of the market to advance social welfare by ensuring the provision of desired goods and services to consumers at a price approximating the marginal cost of providing them. Absent some countervailing procompetitive virtue—such as, for example, the creation of efficiencies in the operation of a market or the provision of goods and services, see Broadcast Music, Inc. v. CBS, supra; Chicago Board of Trade, supra; cf. NCAA v. Board of Regents of Univ. of Okla., 468 U.S. 85 (1984)—such an agreement limiting consumer choice by impeding the "ordinary give and take of the market place," Society of Professional Engineers, supra, 435 U.S. at 692, cannot be sustained under the Rule of Reason. No credible argument has been advanced for the proposition that making it more costly for the insurers and patients who are the dentists' customers to obtain information needed for evaluating the dentists' diagnoses has any such procompetitive effect.

The Federation advances three principal arguments for the proposition that, notwithstanding its lack of competitive virtue, the Federation's policy of withholding x-rays should not be deemed an unreasonable restraint of trade. First, as did the Court of Appeals, the Federation suggests that in the absence of specific findings by the Commission concerning the definition of the market in which the Federation allegedly restrained trade and the power of the Federation's members in that market, the conclusion that the Federation unreasonably restrained trade is erroneous as a matter of law, regardless of whether the challenged practices might be impermissibly anticompetitive if engaged in by persons who together possessed power in a specifically defined market. This contention, however, runs counter to the Court's holding in *NCAA v. Board of Regents,* supra, that "[a]s a matter of law, the absence of proof of market power does not justify a naked restriction on price or output," and that such a restriction "requires some competitive justification even in the absence of a detailed market analysis." 468 U.S., at 109–110. Moreover, even if the restriction imposed by the Federation is not sufficiently "naked" to call this principle into play, the Commission's failure to engage in detailed market analysis is not fatal to its finding of a violation of the Rule of Reason. The Commission found that in two localities in the State of Indiana (the Anderson and Lafayette areas), Federation dentists constituted heavy majorities of the practicing dentists and that as a result of the efforts of the Federation, insurers in those areas were, over a period of years, actually unable to obtain compliance with their requests for submission of x rays. Since the purpose of the inquiries into market definition and market power is to determine whether an arrangement has the potential for genuine adverse effects on competition, "proof of actual detrimental effects, such as a reduction of output" can obviate the need for an inquiry into market power, which is but a "surrogate for detrimental effects." 7 P. Areeda, Antitrust Law ¶ 1511, p. 429 (1986). In this case, we conclude that the finding of actual, sustained adverse effects on competition in those areas where IFD dentists predominated, viewed in light of the reality that markets for dental services tend to be relatively localized, is legally sufficient to support a finding that the challenged restraint was unreasonable even in the absence of elaborate market analysis.[11]

Second, the Federation, again following the lead of the Court of Appeals, argues that a holding that its policy of withholding x-rays constituted an unreasonable restraint of trade is precluded by the Commission's failure to make any finding that the policy resulted in the provision of dental services that were more costly than those that the patients and their insurers would have chosen were they able to evaluate x-rays in conjunction with claim forms. This argument, too, is unpersuasive. Although it is true that the goal of the insurers in seeking submission of x-rays for use in their review of benefits claims was to minimize costs by choosing the least expensive adequate course of dental treatment, a showing that this goal was actually achieved through the means chosen is not an essential step in establishing that the dentists' attempt to thwart its achievement by collectively refusing to supply the requested information was an unreasonable restraint of trade. A concerted and effective effort to withhold (or make more costly) information desired by consumers for the purpose of determining whether a particular purchase is cost-justified is likely enough to disrupt the proper functioning of the price-setting mechanism of the market that it may be condemned even absent proof that it resulted in higher prices or, as here, the purchase of higher-priced services, than would occur in its absence. *Society of Professional Engineers,* supra. Moreover, even if the desired information were in fact completely useless to the insurers and their patients in making an informed choice regarding the least costly adequate course of treatment—or, to put it another way, if the costs of evaluating the information were far greater than the cost savings resulting from its use—the Federation would still not be justified in deciding on behalf of its members' customers that they did not need the information: presumably, if that were the case, the discipline of the market would itself soon result in the insurers' abandoning their requests for x-rays. The Federation is not entitled to pre-empt the working of the market by deciding for itself that its customers do not need that which they demand.

Third, the Federation complains that the Commission erred in failing to consider, as relevant to its Rule of Reason analysis, noncompetitive "quality of care" justifications for the prohibition on provision of x-rays to insurers in conjunction with claim forms. This claim reflects the Court of Appeals' repeated characterization of the Federation's policy as a "legal, moral, and ethical policy of quality dental care, requiring that insurers examine and review all diagnostic and clinical aids before formulating a proper course of dental treatment." The gist of the claim is that x-rays, standing alone, are not adequate bases for diagnosis of dental problems or for the formulation of an acceptable course of treatment. Accordingly, if

---

11. Because we find that the Commission's findings can be sustained on this basis, we do not address the Commission's contention that the Federation's activities can be condemned regardless of market power or actual effect merely because they constitute a continuation of the restraints formerly imposed by the Indiana Dental Association, which allegedly had market power throughout the State of Indiana.

insurance companies are permitted to determine whether they will pay a claim for dental treatment on the basis of x-rays as opposed to a full examination of all the diagnostic aids available to the examining dentist, there is a danger that they will erroneously decline to pay for treatment that is in fact in the interest of the patient, and that the patient will as a result be deprived of fully adequate care.

The Federation's argument is flawed both legally and factually. The premise of the argument is that, far from having no effect on the cost of dental services chosen by patients and their insurers, the provision of x-rays will have too great an impact: it will lead to the reduction of costs through the selection of inadequate treatment. Precisely such a justification for withholding information from customers was rejected as illegitimate in the *Society of Professional Engineers* case. The argument is, in essence, that an unrestrained market in which consumers are given access to the information they believe to be relevant to their choices will lead them to make unwise and even dangerous choices. Such an argument amounts to "nothing less than a frontal assault on the basic policy of the Sherman Act." *Society of Professional Engineers*, supra, 435 U.S. at 695. Moreover, there is no particular reason to believe that the provision of information will be more harmful to consumers in the market for dental services than in other markets. Insurers deciding what level of care to pay for are not themselves the recipients of those services, but it is by no means clear that they lack incentives to consider the welfare of the patient as well as the minimization of costs. They are themselves in competition for the patronage of the patients—or, in most cases, the unions or businesses that contract on their behalf for group insurance coverage—and must satisfy their potential customers not only that they will provide coverage at a reasonable cost, but also that that coverage will be adequate to meet their customers' dental needs. There is thus no more reason to expect dental insurance companies to sacrifice quality in return for cost savings than to believe this of consumers in, say, the market for engineering services. Accordingly, if noncompetitive quality-of-service justifications are inadmissible to justify the denial of information to consumers in the latter market, there is little reason to credit such justifications here.

In any event, the Commission did not, as the Federation suggests, refuse even to consider the quality of care justification for the withholding of x-rays. Rather, the Commission held that the Federation had failed to introduce sufficient evidence to establish such a justification: "IFD has not pointed to any evidence—or even argued—that any consumers have in fact been harmed by alternative benefits determinations, or that actual determinations have been medically erroneous." 101 F.T.C., at 177. The evidence before the Administrative Law Judge on this issue appears to have consisted entirely of expert opinion testimony, with the Federation's experts arguing that x-rays generally provide an insufficient basis, standing alone, for dental diagnosis, and the Commission's experts testifying that x-rays may be useful in assessing diagnosis of and appropriate treatment for a variety of dental complaints. Id., 384 U.S. at 128–132. The Commission was amply justified in concluding on the basis of this conflicting evidence that even if concern for the quality of patient care could under some circumstances serve as a justification for a restraint of the sort imposed here, the evidence did not support a finding that the careful use of x-rays as a basis for evaluating insurance claims is in fact destructive of proper standards of dental care.

In addition to arguing that its conspiracy did not effect an unreasonable restraint of trade, the Federation appears to renew its argument, pressed before both the Commission and the Court of Appeals, that the conspiracy to withhold x-rays is immunized from antitrust scrutiny by virtue of a supposed policy of the State of Indiana against the evaluation of dental x-rays by lay employees of insurance companies. See Brief for Respondent 25–26, and n. 10. Allegedly, such use of x-rays by insurance companies—even where no claim was actually denied without examination of an x-ray by a licensed dentist—would constitute unauthorized practice of dentistry by the insurance company and its employees. The Commission found that this claim had no basis in any authoritative source of Indiana law, and the Federation has not identified any adequate reason for rejecting the Commission's conclusion. Even if the Commission were incorrect in its reading of the law, however, the Federation's claim of immunity would fail. That a particular practice may be unlawful is not, in itself, a sufficient justification for collusion among competitors to prevent it. See Fashion Originators' Guild of America, Inc. v. FTC, 312 U.S. 457, 468 (1941). Anticompetitive collusion among private actors, even when its goal is consistent with state policy, acquires antitrust immunity only when it is actively supervised by the State. See Southern Motor Carriers Rate Conference, Inc. v. United States, 471 U.S. 48 (1985). There is no suggestion of "any" such active supervision here; accordingly, whether or not the policy that Federation has taken upon itself to advance is consistent with the policy of the State of Indiana, the Federation's activities are subject to Sherman Act condemnation. . . . Reversed.

NOTES AND QUESTIONS

1. ROTHERY STORAGE AND VAN CO. V. ATLAS VAN LINES, 792 F.2d 210 (D.C.Cir. 1986), was decided before several of the Supreme Court cases we have considered, but Judge Bork's opinion was ahead of its time. In that case, defendant Atlas was a nationwide common carrier of household goods. Like most national moving companies, it employed independent moving companies throughout the country as its agents to find customers and handle packing, loading, hauling and storage. Atlas set the rates for shipment, chose routes, arranged back-hauls, collected revenues, and paid the agents for their services. Atlas also conducted national advertising, established uniform rules for appearance and quality, maintained insurance and handled claims. In 1982, it announced that it would terminate agency arrangements with any affiliated company that handled interstate carriage on its own account as well as for Atlas. Agent carriers could compete in the interstate market by setting up separate corporations with new names, but could not use the facilities or services of Atlas. Atlas stood sixth in 1981 national market share for interstate van lines with

5.86%. The market itself was far from concentrated, with the top 15 firms accounting for less than 70%. Plaintiff carrier agents challenged the arrangement as a group boycott and illegal *per se*.

Writing a few months before *Indiana Federation of Dentists* was decided, Judge Bork upheld the arrangements on several grounds, including (1) that the challenged restraint was ancillary to the economic integration of the Atlas enterprise, (2) that the non-compete policy was a reasonable response to the problem of agent carriers taking a free ride on Atlas' name and investments, and (3) that Atlas' market share was far too small for the restraint to threaten competition.

On the market power point, the opinion had this to say:

Analysis might begin and end with the observation that Atlas and its agents command between 5.1% and 6.0% of the relevant market, which is the interstate carriage of used household goods. It is impossible to believe that an agreement to eliminate competition within a group of that size can produce any of the evils of monopoly. . . . A monopolist (or those acting together to achieve monopoly results) enhances its revenues by raising the market price. It can do that only if its share of the market is so large that by reducing its output of goods and services the amount offered by the industry is substantially reduced so that the price is bid up. If a group of Atlas' size reduced its output of services, there would be no effect upon market price because firms making up the other 94% of the market would simply take over the abandoned business. The only effect would be a loss of revenues to Atlas. Indeed, so impotent to raise prices is a firm with a market share of 5% or 6% that any attempt by it to engage in monopolistic restriction of output would be little short of suicidal.

At a later point in the opinion, Judge Bork explicitly used market power as a screen for liability, despite the "boycott" label that had been used:

We might well rest, therefore, upon the absence of market power as demonstrated both by Atlas' 6% national market share and by the structure of the market. If it is clear that Atlas and its agents by eliminating competition among themselves are not attempting to restrict industry output, then their agreement must be designed to make the conduct of their business more effective. No third possibility suggests itself.

Chief Judge Wald concurred in the result, largely on grounds that the challenged arrangements appeared to enhance efficiency of the van lines and clearly overbalanced any possible anticompetitive evils. On the question of market power, Judge Wald wrote:

The panel concludes that no balancing was required here since the defendant lacking significant market power cannot act anticompetitively by reducing output and increasing prices. If, as the panel assumes, the *only* legitimate purpose of the antitrust laws is this concern with the potential for decrease in output and rise in prices, reliance on market power alone might be appropriate. But I do not believe that the debate over the purposes of antitrust laws has yet been settled. Until the Supreme Court provides more definitive instruction in this regard, I think it premature to construct an antitrust test that ignores all other potential concerns of the antitrust laws except for restriction of output and price raising.

2.   What difference did it make in *Indiana Federation of Dentists* that the Court applied a "rule of reason" rather than a *per se* rule? What evidence did the Court take into account that would have been precluded by a *per se* analysis?

3. Is it correct to argue (as the majority did in *Rothery*) that its market power test followed from Supreme Court decisions in *BMI, NCAA,* and *Northwest Wholesale Stationers?* If so, does it follow that *Topco* must have been overruled, *sub silentio,* by those three cases? Is the *Rothery* majority's view that a finding of substantial market power is a necessary prerequisite to any finding of an antitrust violation consistent with the Supreme Court's decision, handed down several months later, in *Indiana Federation of Dentists?* Should the Government ever bother to challenge practices by companies or groups of companies with modest market shares? Which ones (if any)? Why?

Federal Trade Commission v. Superior Court Trial Lawyers Association

Supreme Court of the United States, 1990.
493 U.S. 411, 110 S.Ct. 768, 107 L.Ed.2d 851.

[In 1983, a group of lawyers in the District of Columbia, all members of the Superior Court Trial Lawyers Association (SCTLA), agreed not to accept appointment under the District of Columbia Criminal Justice Act to represent indigent criminal defendants in the Superior Court unless the D.C. city government agreed to increase their compensation. Many bar association and city officials agreed that compensation to court-appointed lawyers was low, but the Mayor insisted that no money was available for a fee increase.

The refusal to accept appointment was well publicized and was accompanied by successful efforts to secure press and public support for the pay increase. Within ten days, city officials recognized that the criminal justice system "was on the brink of collapse because of the refusal of CJA lawyers to take on new cases," and the Mayor and the SCTLA lawyers negotiated and eventually agreed to a modest fee increase.

The FTC filed a complaint against SCTLA and four of its officers for conspiring to fix prices and to conduct a boycott which it characterized as an unfair method of competition in violation of Section 5 of the FTC Act. The Commission eventually found a *per se* violation. The D.C. Court of Appeals rejected SCTLA's argument that the boycott was justified because it was designed to improve the quality of representation for indigent defendants. It noted, however, that boycotts historically have been used as a dramatic means of expression and that the lawyers intended to convey a political message to the public, and concluded that a boycott with such an expressive component warranted First Amendment protection, including a finding that the restriction was no greater than essential to an important government interest. The Court of Appeals concluded that such boycotts ought not to be found to be an antitrust violation unless there was a serious risk of competitive harm, and that required a determination whether respondents possessed "significant market power." Such a finding was impossible under a *per se* rule, and accordingly, the Court of Appeals remanded the case for further proceedings on that point.

The Supreme Court reinstated the Commission's finding of a violation. It concluded that the horizontal arrangement was a "naked restraint," constricting supply in order to raise price. The *Noerr* case (p. 410 infra) was distinguished on grounds that it was the desired legislation in that case that would have created the restraint on truckers' competition, while in the instant case, the means by which respondents sought favorable legislation was itself the source of the competitive injury.]

■ STEVENS, J.... The lawyers' association argues that if its conduct would otherwise be prohibited by the Sherman Act and the Federal Trade Act, it is nonetheless protected by the First Amendment rights recognized in NAACP v. Claiborne Hardware, 458 U.S. 886 (1982). That case arose after black citizens boycotted white merchants in Claiborne County, Miss. The white merchants sued under state law to recover losses from the boycott. We found that the "right of the States to regulate economic activity could not justify a complete prohibition against a nonviolent, politically motivated boycott designed to force governmental and economic change and to effectuate rights guaranteed by the Constitution itself." We accordingly held that "the nonviolent elements of petitioners' activities are entitled to the protection of the First Amendment."

The lawyers' association contends that because it, like the boycotters in *Claiborne Hardware,* sought to vindicate constitutional rights, it should enjoy a similar First Amendment protection....

The activity that the FTC order prohibits is a concerted refusal by CJA lawyers to accept any further assignments until they receive an increase in their compensation; the undenied objective of their boycott was an economic advantage for those who agreed to participate. It is true that the *Claiborne Hardware* case also involved a boycott. That boycott, however, differs in a decisive respect. Those who joined the *Claiborne Hardware* boycott sought no special advantage for themselves. They were black citizens in Port Gibson, Mississippi, who had been the victims of political, social, and economic discrimination for many years. They sought only the equal respect and equal treatment to which they were constitutionally entitled. They struggled "to change a social order that had consistently treated them as second class citizens." 458 U.S., at 912. As we observed, the campaign was not intended "to destroy legitimate competition." Id., at 914. Equality and freedom are preconditions of the free market, and not commodities to be haggled over within it.

The same cannot be said of attorney's fees. As we recently pointed out, our reasoning in *Claiborne Hardware* is not applicable to a boycott conducted by business competitors who "stand to profit financially from a lessening of competition in the boycotted market." Allied Tube Corp. v. Indian Head....

The Court of Appeals, however, crafted a new exception to the *per se* rules, and it is this exception which provoked the FTC's petition to this Court. The Court of Appeals derived its exception from United States v. O'Brien, 391 U.S. 367 (1968). In that case O'Brien had burned his Selective Service registration certificate on the steps of the South Boston Courthouse. He did so before a sizable crowd and with the purpose of advocating his antiwar beliefs. We affirmed his conviction. We held that the governmental interest in regulating the "nonspeech element" of his conduct adequately justified the incidental restriction on First Amendment freedoms. Specifically, we concluded that the statute's incidental restriction on O'Brien's freedom of expression was no greater than necessary to further the Government's interest in requiring registrants to have valid certificates continually available.

However, the Court of Appeals held that, in light of *O'Brien*, the expressive component of respondents' boycott compelled courts to apply the antitrust laws "prudently and with sensitivity," 856 F.2d, at 233–234, with a "special solicitude for the First Amendment rights" of respondents. The Court of Appeals concluded that the governmental interest in prohibiting boycotts is not sufficient to justify a restriction on the communicative element of the boycott unless the FTC can prove, and not merely presume, that the boycotters have market power. Because the Court of Appeals imposed this special requirement upon the Government, it ruled that *per se* antitrust analysis was inapplicable to boycotts having an expressive component.

There are at least two critical flaws in the Court of Appeals' antitrust analysis: it exaggerates the significance of the expressive component in respondents' boycott and it denigrates the importance of the rule of law that respondents violated. Implicit in the conclusion of the Court of Appeals are unstated assumptions that most economic boycotts do not have an expressive component, and that the categorical prohibitions against price fixing and boycotts are merely rules of "administrative convenience" that do not serve any substantial governmental interest unless the price-fixing competitors actually possess market power.

It would not much matter to the outcome of this case if these flawed assumptions were sound. *O'Brien* would offer respondents no protection even if their boycott were uniquely expressive and even if the purpose of the *per se* rules were purely that of administrative efficiency. We have recognized that the Government's interest in adhering to a uniform rule may sometimes satisfy the *O'Brien* test even if making an exception to the rule in a particular case might cause no serious damage. United States v. Albertini, 472 U.S. 675, 688 (1985) ("The First Amendment does not bar application of a neutral regulation that incidentally burdens speech merely because a party contends that allowing an exception in the particular case will not threaten important government interests"). The administrative efficiency interests in antitrust regulation are unusually compelling. The *per se* rules avoid "the necessity for an incredibly complicated and prolonged economic investigation into the entire history of the industry involved, as well as related industries, in an effort to determine at large whether a particular restraint has been unreasonable." Northern Pac. R. Co. v. United States, 356 U.S. 1, 5 (1958). If small parties "were allowed to prove lack of market power, all parties would have that right, thus introducing the enormous complexities of market definition into every price-fixing case." R. Bork, The Antitrust Paradox 269 (1978). For these reasons, it is at least possible that the *Claiborne Hardware* doctrine, which itself rests in part upon *O'Brien,* exhausts *O'Brien's* application to the antitrust statutes.

In any event, however, we cannot accept the Court of Appeals' characterization of this boycott or the antitrust laws. Every concerted refusal to do business with a potential customer or supplier has an expressive component. At one level, the competitors must exchange their views about their objectives and the means of obtaining them. The most blatant, naked price-fixing agreement is a product of communication, but that is surely not a reason for viewing it with special solicitude. At another level, after the terms of the boycotters' demands have been agreed upon, they must be communicated to its target: "we will not do business until you do what we ask." That expressive component of the boycott conducted by these respondents is surely not unique. On the contrary, it is the hallmark of every effective boycott.

At a third level, the boycotters may communicate with third parties to enlist public support for their objectives; to the extent that the boycott is newsworthy, it will facilitate the expression of the boycotters' ideas. But this level of expression is not an element of the boycott. Publicity may be generated by any other activity that is sufficiently newsworthy. Some activities, including the boycott here, may be newsworthy precisely for the reasons that they are prohibited: the harms they produce are matters of public concern. Certainly that is no reason for removing the prohibition.

In sum, there is thus nothing unique about the "expressive component" of respondents' boycott. A rule that requires courts to apply the antitrust laws "prudently and with sensitivity" whenever an economic boycott has an "expressive component" would create a gaping hole in the fabric of those laws. Respondents' boycott thus has no special characteristics meriting an exemption from the *per se* rules of antitrust law.

Equally important is the second error implicit in respondents' claim to immunity from the *per se* rules. In its opinion, the Court of Appeals assumed that the antitrust laws permit, but do not require, the condemnation of price fixing and boycotts without proof of market power. The opinion further assumed that the *per se* rule prohibiting such activity "is only a rule of 'administrative convenience and efficiency,' not a statutory command." 856 F.2d, at 249. This statement contains two errors. The *per se* rules are, of course, the product of judicial interpretations of the Sherman Act, but the rules nevertheless have the same force and effect as any other statutory commands. Moreover, while the *per se* rule against price fixing and boycotts is indeed justified in part by "administrative convenience," the Court of Appeals erred in describing the prohibition as justified only by such concerns. The *per se* rules also reflect a long-standing judgment that the prohibited practices by their nature have "a substantial potential for impact on competition." *Jefferson Parish Hospital District,* 466 U.S., at 16. . . .

The *per se* rules in antitrust law serve purposes analogous to *per se* restrictions upon, for example, stunt flying in congested areas or speeding. Laws prohibiting stunt flying or setting speed limits are justified by the State's interest in protecting human life and property. Perhaps most violations of such rules actually cause no harm. No doubt many experienced drivers and pilots can operate much more safely, even at prohibited speeds, than the average citizen.

If the especially skilled drivers and pilots were to paint messages on their cars, or attach streamers to their planes, their conduct would have an expressive component. High speeds and unusual maneuvers would help to draw attention to their messages. Yet the laws may nonetheless be enforced against these skilled persons without proof that their conduct was actually harmful or dangerous.

In part, the justification for these *per se* rules is rooted in administrative convenience. They are also supported, however, by the observation that every speeder and every stunt pilot poses some threat to the community. An unpredictable event may overwhelm the skills of the best driver or pilot, even if the proposed course of action was entirely prudent when initiated. A bad driver going slowly may be more dangerous than a good driver going quickly, but a good driver who obeys the law is safer still.

So it is with boycotts and price fixing. Every such horizontal arrangement among competitors poses some threat to the free market. A small participant in the market is, obviously, less likely to cause persistent damage than a large participant. Other participants in the market may act quickly and effectively to take the small participant's place. For reasons including market inertia and information failures, however, a small conspirator may be able to impede competition over some period of time. Given an appropriate set of circumstances and some luck, the period can be long enough to inflict real injury upon particular consumers or competitors. . . .

Of course, some boycotts and some price-fixing agreements are more pernicious than others; some are only partly successful, and some may only succeed when they are buttressed by other causative factors, such as political influence. But an assumption that, absent proof of market power, the boycott disclosed by this record was totally harmless—when overwhelming testimony demonstrated that it almost produced a crisis in the administration of criminal justice in the District and when it achieved its economic goal—is flatly inconsistent with the clear course of our antitrust jurisprudence. Conspirators need not achieve the dimensions of a monopoly, or even a degree of market power any greater than that already disclosed by this record, to warrant condemnation under the antitrust laws.

The judgment of the Court of Appeals is accordingly reversed insofar as that court held the *per se* rules inapplicable to the lawyers' boycott.[12]

---

12. In response to the dissent, and particularly to its observation that some concerted arrangements that might be characterized as "group boycotts" may not merit *per se* condemnation, we emphasize that this case involves not only a boycott but also a horizontal price-fixing arrangement—a type of conspiracy that has been consistently analyzed as a *per se* violation for many decades. . . .

■ [BRENNAN, J., joined by BLACKMUN and MARSHALL, JJ., dissented on grounds that an expressive boycott—*i.e.*, one that appears to operate on a political rather than economic level—ought not to be condemned under a *per se* rule. Historically, such boycotts have been essential to the "poorly financed causes of little people," who often cannot use established organizational techniques to advance their political interests.]

NOTE ON HARTFORD FIRE INSURANCE CO. v. CALIFORNIA

In 1993, the Supreme Court decided Hartford Fire Insurance Co. v. California, 509 U.S. 764, 113 S.Ct. 2891, 125 L.Ed.2d 612 (1993). Plaintiffs (for the most part, state attorneys general) alleged that certain domestic and foreign insurance companies and re-insurance companies had violated the Sherman Act by conspiring to change commercial general insurance policies from "occurrence based" policies to "claims made" policies and to cease underwriting certain environmental risks. At the center of their claims was an allegation that the domestic insurers, acting with the foreign re-insurers, had agreed to boycott any company that did not abide by the new rules. Justice Scalia, writing for a five-person majority on this aspect of the case, concluded that the term "boycott" should not be so broadly construed. This was important because of the McCarran–Ferguson Act, 15 U.S.C. § 1011 *et seq.*, which exempts insurance companies from the antitrust laws to the extent that they are regulated by the states (and in this instance, arguably, by foreign governments). An exception to that exemption exists, under section 3(b) of the McCarran–Ferguson Act, 15 U.S.C. § 1013(b), for boycotts. Justice Scalia thought it important to distinguish between a "conditional boycott and a concerted agreement to seek particular terms in particular transactions." 509 U.S. at 801–02. Only the former qualified as a true boycott. Here, he wrote, it was "obviously not a 'boycott' for the reinsurers to 'refus[e] to reinsure coverages written on the ISO CGL forms until the desired changes were made,' . . . because the terms of the primary coverages are central elements of the reinsurance contract—they are *what* is reinsured." *Id.* at 806 (emphasis in original). Notwithstanding this narrow definition of boycott, the Court went on to find that there were sufficient allegations of a true conditional boycott in the complaints to survive a motion to dismiss. For example, there was an allegation that primary insurers who wrote insurance on disfavored forms would be refused all reinsurance, even as to risks written on other forms. *Id.* at 810.

The dissenters, led by Justice Souter, believed that the majority had adopted an overly narrow definition of the term "boycott" as it was used in section 3(b) of the McCarran–Ferguson Act. They saw no reason to confine the concept of "boycott" to refusals to deal that are unrelated or collateral to the objective sought by those refusing to deal. Justice Souter also pointed out certain common ground between the majority and the dissenters: (1) only those refusals to deal involving the coordinated action of multiple actors fall within the scope of § 3(b); (2) a § 3(b) boycott need not involve an absolute refusal to deal; (3) such a boycott need not entail unequal treatment of the targets of the boycott and its instigators, and (4) concerted activity, while a necessary element of a § 3(b) boycott, is not by itself sufficient. The dissenters' view would have preserved far more of the complaint for further proceedings.

PROBLEM 6

INVESTIGATION AGENCY FOR KANSAS CITY BANKS

In Kansas City, all the local banks decided to eliminate duplication of effort and expense by setting up a common agency to investigate local applicants for loans to determine if they are creditworthy. Upon the request of a bank, the joint agency investigated any person or concern and circulated to all banks a resume of information supporting its conclusions as to whether the party involved was a good or bad risk under general criteria established by the local bankers' association.

The plaintiff owned a tavern in Kansas City and applied for a loan. The joint agency, however, determined that plaintiff should be disqualified because its tavern was located in a "crime-ridden" section of town and therefore subject to constant risk of robbery. Plaintiff claimed that the refusal was racially motivated, since almost all of the establishments in the part of town designated as "crime-ridden" were patronized by blacks. Attempts to obtain loans from banks in nearby cities proved unavailing when the plaintiff explained why it had been refused by the Kansas City banks.

Plaintiff eventually received a loan from an out-of-state bank at higher interest rates than available earlier to businesses in Kansas City, and then sued for treble damages under Section 1 of the Sherman Act. Should the plaintiff recover?

SECTION 2.   JOINT VENTURES REVISITED: ISSUES OF MEMBERSHIP AND ACCESS

NOTE ON THE ANTITRUST STATUS OF JOINT VENTURES

1. Almost any collaborative activity among business firms can be referred to as a joint venture, since the designation is not a technical "term of art" in antitrust law. In common usage, however, a joint venture carries the positive connotation of cooperation among firms, usually accompanied by some actual integration of managerial or production resources, to achieve some useful business objective more efficiently than either (or any) could alone. It is thus distinguished from a cartel or price-fixing arrangement, for example.

A joint venture often takes the form of a new jointly owned corporate subsidiary, in which case the asset and share transfers involved may invoke the antitrust law dealing with mergers, Section 7 of the Clayton Act. Thus, we will deal with joint ventures more fully in Chapter 9 infra.

But frequently joint ventures are contractual in form or a kind of partnership among firms for a limited purpose, and only Sherman Act questions are raised. Since joint venture agreements may result in the exclusion of competitors from access to the jointly created new product, technology, or facility, thus placing them at a competitive disadvantage, it has some characteristics of a group boycott. Thus the subject was introduced in Chapter 4 and will be discussed again here.

2. Joint ventures raise in a particularly significant way the question of the proper standard for evaluating injury under the antitrust laws. In a static sense, monopoly (or cartel) pricing has two effects. First, the monopoly overcharge transfers wealth from the consumer to the monopolist. Second, the higher price chokes off demand. Some consumers would be willing to buy the monopolist's

product at a price less than the monopoly price but more than monopolist's cost of producing the product. The monopolist, assuming it cannot price discriminate, will not produce these units.

While everyone agrees that monopoly pricing has these effects, commentators disagree over whether both pose antitrust problems. Some commentators view the antitrust laws as consumer welfare statutes. They contend that the laws must be used to prevent both types of harm. Other commentators insist that the antitrust laws are social welfare statutes. These commentators are indifferent to wealth transfers and focus solely on the deadweight loss.

To see why this disagreement becomes acute with joint ventures, consider an industry wide joint venture that has two effects: (1) it creates efficiencies in production that lowers production costs and (2) it creates monopoly power by erecting barriers to entry and eliminating competition, allowing the participants to raise prices to the monopoly level. If the cost savings of the joint venture exceed the deadweight efficiency loss associated with the new monopoly pricing, should the antitrust laws applaud or condemn the arrangement?

The problem becomes even more complicated when posed in dynamic rather than static terms. The prospect of raising prices to the monopoly level gives firms incentives to expend resources to become monopolists. The way firms choose to expend these resources has important implications for social and consumer welfare.

Firms can attempt to create or maintain monopoly profits in a myriad of ways. They might attempt to deter rivals from entering their industries or to raise their rivals' costs. Economists refer to such behavior as "rent-seeking." It includes lobbying legislatures to create exclusionary regulations, licensing boards or tariffs. According to some commentators, it includes hoarding scarce inputs in order to deny them to rivals. See Krattenmaker & Salop, Anticompetitive Exclusion: Raising Rivals' Costs to Achieve Power Over Price, 96 Yale L.J. 209 (1986). Whatever its form, "rent-seeking" behavior does not increase productive efficiency. On the other hand, firms might pursue monopoly profits through research and development. R & D might allow firms to reduce their costs of production or allow them to offer new and better products. R & D, although motivated by the same monopoly profits that drive "rent-seeking," may benefit consumers.

Note, however, that a pure consumer welfare standard would find a joint venture devoted to research and development problematic. Suppose the industry wide joint venture introduced above developed a production technology that reduced costs industry-wide. From the pure consumer welfare standpoint, such a combination would be unacceptable unless competition among the participating firms ensured that lower costs would be passed on to consumers in the form of lower prices.

Suppose the joint venture reduced production costs and created monopoly power. Suppose, also, that the post-development price was equal to (or less than) the pre-development price. Would the pure consumer welfare standard have a problem with this arrangement? Should it?

3. UNITED STATES v. TERMINAL RAILROAD ASSOCIATION, 224 U.S. 383, 32 S.Ct. 507, 56 L.Ed. 810 (1912). At the turn of the century, 24 railroads converged at the east and west banks of the Mississippi near St. Louis. About one half of the lines terminated (had their "termini") on the Illinois side of the river; others, coming from the west and north of St. Louis, terminated either in the city itself or on its northern edge. By 1890, as the system of car ferry transfer across the river became inadequate to meet the growing demands of the railroads, railroad bridges were

built. Three independent terminal companies operated the connections of the ferry and the two bridges with the various railroad termini on each side of the Mississippi. Described by Justice Lurton in his opinion for the Court,

> [t]his resulted in some cases in an unnecessary duplication of facilities, but it at least gave to carriers and shippers some choice, a condition which, if it [did] not lead to competition in charges, [did] insure competition in service.... [T]heir independence of one another served to keep open the means for the entrance of new lines to [St. Louis], and was an obstacle to united opposition from existing lines.

224 U.S. at 393.

In 1899, 14 of the railroads, under the leadership of Jay Gould, formed the Terminal Railroad Association of St. Louis to acquire the terminal companies and operate them as a unified system. By their original agreement, the "proprietary companies" bound themselves to use the Association facilities exclusively and required unanimous consent for the admission of new roads to the Association or use of the facility by non-member roads. The Court noted in its opinion that

> [t]he result of the geographical and topographical situation [was] that it [was], as a practical matter, impossible for any railroad company to pass through, or even enter St. Louis, so as to be within reach of its industries or commerce, without using the facilities entirely controlled by the Terminal Company.

Id. at 397.

The Supreme Court concluded that the combination constituted a restraint of trade in violation of the Sherman Act, and regarded it as no defense that the proprietary companies had not availed themselves of their power to impede free competition by excluding all non-proprietary companies or charging exorbitant rates:

> ... [I]n ordinary circumstances, a number of independent companies [may lawfully] combine for the purpose of controlling or acquiring terminals for their common but exclusive use. In such cases other companies [may lawfully] be admitted upon terms or excluded altogether. If such term were too onerous, there would ordinarily remain the right and power to construct their own terminals. *But the situation at St. Louis is most extraordinary, and we base our conclusion in this case, in a large measure, upon that fact.* The "physical or topographical condition peculiar to the locality," which is advanced as a prime justification for a unified system of terminals, constitutes a most obvious reason why such a unified system is an obstacle, a hindrance and a restriction upon interstate commerce, unless it is the impartial agent of all who, owing to conditions, are under such compulsion as here exists, to use its facilities....

Id. at 405 (emphasis added).

The Court then pointed out various practices that did not meet the "impartial agency" standard it imposed on the Association:

> There are certain practices of this Terminal Company which operate to the disadvantage of the commerce which must cross the river at St. Louis, and of non-proprietary railroad lines compelled to use its facilities. One of them grows out of the fact that the Terminal Company is a terminal company and something more. It does not confine itself to supplying and operating mere facilities for the interchange of traffic between railroads

and to assistance in the collecting and distributing of traffic for the carrier companies.... This Terminal Company, in addition ... [sets and charges rates] for the transportation of every class of merchandise from the termini of the railroads on the Illinois side of the river to destinations across the river.... [An] exception to the rule imposing this arbitrary [rate] is that it does not apply to traffic which originates in East St. Louis [on the east bank of the Mississippi], whether it is destined to cross the river or not.... Another practice which marks this terminal Company as a transportation company which interposed itself between railroads having their termini on opposite sides of the river, and between [St. Louis] itself and the roads terminating on the east side of the river, is that all traffic destined to cross the river at St. Louis, whether bound east or west, or destined for the city if coming from the east, is billed only to East St. Louis, and there rebilled to destination.

Id. at 406–8.

The Court considered that the effect of the "arbitrary discrimination" in rates as "obviously injurious to the commerce and manufacturers of St. Louis," and that the billing practices were only justifiable at a time when the eastern lines had no terminals in St. Louis. Id. at 408.

The Court rejected the Government's petition for dissolution of the Association, and instead provided that it must: (1) provide for admission to proprietary status or use of the terminal facilities by all railroads on reasonable and non-discriminating terms; and (2) abolish the Company's discriminatory charges and billing practices.

Associated Press v. United States

Supreme Court of the United States, 1945.
326 U.S. 1, 65 S.Ct. 1416, 89 L.Ed. 2013.

■ BLACK, J. The publishers of more than 1200 newspapers are members of the Associated Press (AP), a cooperative association incorporated under the Membership Corporations Law of the State of New York, Consol. Laws c. 35. Its business is the collection, assembly and distribution of news. The news it distributes is originally obtained by direct employees of the Association, employees of the member newspapers, and the employees of foreign independent news agencies with which AP has contractual relations, such as the Canadian Press. Distribution of the news is made through interstate channels of communication to the various newspaper members of the Association, who pay for it under an assessment plan which contemplates no profit to AP.

The United States filed a bill in a Federal District Court for an injunction against AP and other defendants charging that they had violated the Sherman Anti–Trust Act, 26 Stat. 209, 15 U.S.C.A. §§ 1–7, 15 note, in that their acts and conduct constituted (1) a combination and conspiracy in restraint of trade and commerce in news among the states, and (2) an attempt to monopolize a part of that trade.

The heart of the government's charge was that appellants had by concerted action set up a system of By–Laws which prohibited all AP members from selling news to non-members, and which granted each member powers to block its non-member competitors from membership. These By–Laws, to which all AP members had assented, were, in the context of the admitted facts, charged to be in violation of the Sherman Act.... The District Court, composed of three judges, held that the By–Laws unlawfully restricted admission to AP membership, and violated the Sherman Act insofar as the By–Laws' provisions clothed a member with powers to impose or dispense with conditions upon the admission of his business competitor. Continued observance of these By–Laws was enjoined.... The government's motion for summary judgment, under Rule 56 of the Rules of Civil Procedure, was granted and its prayer for relief was granted in part and denied in part. 52 F.Supp. 362. Both sides have brought the case to us on direct appeal. 15 U.S.C., Sec. 29; 28 U.S.C., Sec. 345....

To put the issue into proper focus, it becomes necessary at this juncture to examine the By–Laws.

All members must consent to be bound by them. They impose upon members certain duties and restrictions in the conduct of their separate businesses. For a violation of the By–Laws severe disciplinary action may be taken by the Association. The Board of Directors may impose a fine of $1000.00 or suspend a member and such "action ... shall be final and conclusive. No member shall have any right to question the same." ...

These By–Laws, for a violation of which members may be thus fined, suspended, or expelled, require that each newspaper member publish the AP news regularly in whole or in part, and that each shall "promptly furnish to the corporation, through its agents or employees, all the news of such member's district, the area of which shall be determined by the Board of Directors." All members are prohibited from selling or furnishing their spontaneous news to any agency or publisher except to AP. Other By–Laws require each newspaper member to conduct his or its business in such manner that the news furnished by the corporations shall not be made available to any non-member in advance of publication. The joint effect of these By–Laws is to block all newspaper non-members from any opportunity to buy news from AP or any of its publisher members. Admission to membership in AP thereby becomes a prerequisite to obtaining AP news or buying news from any one of its more than twelve hundred publishers. The erection of obstacles to the acquisition of membership consequently can make it difficult, if not impossible for non-members to get any of the news furnished by AP or any of the individual members of this combination of American newspaper publishers.[13] The District Court found that the By–Laws in and of themselves were contracts in restraint of commerce in that they contained provisions designed to stifle competition in the newspaper publishing field. The court also found that AP's restrictive By–Laws had hindered and impeded the growth of competing newspapers. This latter

13. The [District] Court found that out of the 1803 daily English language newspapers published in the United States, with a total circulation of 42,080,391, 1179 of them, with a circulation of 34,762,120, were under joint contractual obligations not to supply either AP or their own "spontaneous" news to any nonmember of AP.

finding, as to the *past* effect of the restrictions, is challenged. We are inclined to think that it is supported by undisputed evidence, but we do not stop to labor the point. For the court below found, and we think correctly, that the By–Laws on their face, and without regard to their past effect, constitute restraints of trade. Combinations are no less unlawful because they have not as yet resulted in restraint. An agreement or combination to follow a course of conduct which will necessarily restrain or monopolize a part of trade or commerce may violate the Sherman Act, whether it be "wholly nascent or abortive on the one hand, or successful on the other." [United States v. Socony–Vacuum Oil Co., 310 U.S. 150, 225 (1940).] For these reasons the argument, repeated here in various forms, that AP had not yet achieved a complete monopoly is wholly irrelevant. Undisputed evidence did show, however, that its By–Laws had tied the hands of all of its numerous publishers, to the extent that they could not and did not sell any part of their news so that it could reach any of their non-member competitors. In this respect the Court did find, and that finding cannot possibly be challenged, that AP's By–Laws had hindered and restrained the sale of interstate news to non-members who competed with members. Inability to buy news from the largest news agency, or any one of its multitude of members, can have most serious effects on the publication of competitive newspapers, both those presently published and those which but for these restrictions, might be published in the future. This is illustrated by the District Court's finding that in 26 cities of the United States, existing newspapers already have contracts for AP news and the same newspapers have contracts with United Press and International News Service under which new newspapers would be required to pay the contract holders large sums to enter the field.[14] The net effect is seriously to limit the opportunity of any new paper to enter these cities. Trade restraints of this character, aimed at the destruction of competition, tend to block the initiative which brings newcomers into a field of business and to frustrate the free enterprise system which it was the purpose of the Sherman Act to protect. . . .

Nor can we treat this case as though it merely involved a reporter's contract to deliver his news reports exclusively to a single newspaper, or an exclusive agreement as to news between two newspapers in different cities. For such trade restraints might well be "reasonable," and therefore not in violation of the Sherman Act. Standard Oil Co. v. United States, 221 U.S. 1. But however innocent such agreements might be, standing alone, they would assume quite a different aspect if utilized as essential features of a program to hamper or destroy competition. It is in this light that we must view this case.

It has been argued that the restrictive By–Laws should be treated as beyond the prohibitions of the Sherman Act, since the owner of the property can choose his associates and can, as to that which he has

---

14. INS and UP make so-called "asset value" contracts under which if another newspaper wishes to obtain their press services, the newcomer shall pay to the competitor holding the UP or INS contract the stipulated "asset value."

produced by his own enterprise and sagacity, efforts or ingenuity, decide for himself whether and to whom to sell or not to sell. While it is true in a very general sense that one can dispose of his property as he pleases, he cannot "go beyond the exercise of this right, and by contracts or combinations, express or implied, unduly hinder or obstruct the free and natural flow of commerce in the channels of interstate trade." United States v. Bausch & Lomb Co., 321 U.S. 707, 722. The Sherman Act was specifically intended to prohibit independent businesses from becoming "associates" in a common plan which is bound to reduce their competitor's opportunity to buy or sell the things in which the groups compete. Victory of a member of such a combination over its business rivals achieved by such collective means cannot consistently with the Sherman Act or with practical, everyday knowledge be attributed to *individual* "enterprise and sagacity"; such hampering of business rivals can only be attributed to that which really makes it possible—the collective power of an unlawful combination. That the object of sale is the creation or product of a man's ingenuity does not alter this principle. Fashion Originators' Guild, Inc. v. Federal Trade Commission, 312 U.S. 457. It is obviously fallacious to view the By–Laws here in issue as instituting a program to encourage and permit full freedom of sale and disposal of property by its owners. Rather, these publishers have, by concerted arrangements, pooled their power to acquire, to purchase, and to dispose of news reports through the channels of commerce. They have also pooled their economic and news control power and, in exerting that power, have entered into agreements which the District Court found to be "plainly designed in the interest of preventing competition."[15]

It is further contended that since there are other news agencies which sell news, it is not a violation of the Act for an overwhelming majority of American publishers to combine to decline to sell their news to the minority. But the fact that an agreement to restrain trade does not inhibit competition in all of the objects of that trade cannot save it from the condemnation of the Sherman Act. It is apparent that the exclusive right to publish news in a given field, furnished by AP and all of its members gives many newspapers a competitive advantage over their rivals.[16] Conversely, a

---

15. Even if additional purposes were involved, it would not justify the combination, since the Sherman Act cannot "be evaded by good motives. The law is its own measure of right and wrong, of what it permits, or forbids, and the judgment of the courts cannot be set up against it in a supposed accommodation of its policy with the good intention of parties, and, it may be, of some good results." Standard Sanitary Mfg. Co. v. United States, 226 U.S. 20, 49.

16. The District Court pointed out that, "monopoly is a relative word. If one means by it the possession of something absolutely necessary to the conduct of an activity, there are few except the exclusive possession of some natural resource without which the ac-

tivity is impossible. Most monopolies, like most patents, give control over only some means of production for which there is a substitute; the possessor enjoys an advantage over his competitors, but he can seldom shut them out altogether; his monopoly is measured by the handicap he can impose.... And yet that advantage alone may make a monopoly unlawful. It would be possible, for instance, to conduct some kind of a newspaper without any news service whatever; but nobody will maintain that, if AP were the only news service in existence, the members could keep it wholly to themselves and reduce all other papers to such news as they could gather by their own efforts." United States v. Associated Press, D.C., 52 F.Supp. 362, 371.

newspaper without AP service is more than likely to be at a competitive disadvantage. The District Court stated that it was to secure this advantage over rivals that the By–Laws existed. It is true that the record shows that some competing papers have gotten along without AP news, but morning newspapers, which control 96% of the total circulation in the United States, have AP news service. And the District Court's unchallenged finding was that "AP is a vast, intricately reticulated organization, the largest of its kind, gathering news from all over the world, the chief single source of news for the American press, universally agreed to be of great consequence."

Nevertheless, we are asked to reverse these judgments on the ground that the evidence failed to show that AP reports, which might be attributable to their own "enterprise and sagacity," are clothed "in the robes of indispensability." The absence of "indispensability" is said to have been established under the following chain of reasoning: AP has made its news generally available to the people by supplying it to a limited and select group of publishers in the various cities; therefore, it is said, AP and its member publishers have not deprived the reading public of AP news; all local readers have an "adequate access" to AP news, since all they need do in any city to get it is to buy, on whatever terms they can in a protected market, the particular newspaper selected for the public by AP and its members. We reject these contentions. The proposed "indispensability" test would fly in the face of the language of the Sherman Act and all of our previous interpretations of it. Moreover, it would make that law a dead letter in all fields of business, a law which Congress has consistently maintained to be an essential safeguard to the kind of private competitive business economy this country has sought to maintain.

The restraints on trade in news here were no less than those held to fall within the ban of the Sherman Act with reference to combinations to restrain trade outlets in the sale of tiles, Montague & Co. v. Lowry, 193 U.S. 38.... By the restrictive By–Laws each of the publishers in the combination has, in effect, "surrendered himself completely to the control of the association," Anderson v. Shipowners' Ass'n, 272 U.S. 359, 362, in respect to the disposition of news in interstate commerce. Therefore this contractual restraint of interstate trade, "designed in the interest of preventing competition," cannot be one of the "normal and usual agreements in aid of trade and commerce which may be found not to be within the [Sherman] Act...." Eastern States Lumber Dealers' Ass'n v. United States, 234 U.S. 612, 613. It is further said that we reach our conclusion by application of the "public utility" concept to the newspaper business. This is not correct. We merely hold that arrangements or combinations designed to stifle competition cannot be immunized by adopting a membership device accomplishing that purpose....

We now turn to the decree. Having adjudged the By–Laws imposing restrictions on applications for membership to be illegal, the court enjoined the defendants from observing them, or agreeing to observe any new or amended By–Law having a like purpose or effect. It further provided that nothing in the decree should prevent the adoption by the Associated Press of new or amended By–Laws "which will restrict admission, provided that members in the same city and in the same 'field' (morning, evening or Sunday), as an applicant published in a newspaper in the United States of America or its Territories, shall not have power to impose, or dispense with, any conditions upon his admission and that the By–Laws shall affirmatively declare that the effect of admission upon the ability of such applicant to compete with members in the same city and 'field' shall not be taken into consideration in passing upon its application." Some of appellants argue that this decree is vague and indefinite. They argue that it will be impossible for the Association to know whether or not its members took into consideration the competitive situation in passing upon applications for membership. We cannot agree that the decree is ambiguous. We assume, with the court below, that AP will faithfully carry out its purpose. Interpreting the decree to mean that AP news is to be furnished to competitors of old members without discrimination through By–Laws controlling membership, or otherwise, we approve it. . . .

The judgment in all three cases is affirmed.[17]

SCFC ILC, Inc. v. Visa USA, Inc.

United States Court of Appeals, Tenth Circuit, 1994.
36 F.3d 958.

■ MOORE, J. . . . Visa USA provides payment services to its 6,000 members which individually issue credit cards to consumers. Sears, Roebuck and Company, a competitor offering its own credit card, the Discover Card, wanted to become a Visa USA member and also issue Visa cards. The question presented by this case is whether Visa USA's refusal to admit Sears to its joint venture restrains trade in violation of section 1 of the Sherman Act, 15 U.S.C. § 1. Rejecting Visa USA's legal and factual challenges to the jury's adverse verdict, the district court found the evidence of exclusion constituted antitrust injury and harm to competition. SCFC ILC, Inc. v. Visa U.S.A., Inc., 819 F.Supp. 956, 990 (D.Utah 1993). We conclude, however, the exclusion does not trigger section 1 liability and reverse.

I. Background

As set forth more extensively in the district court's order, the factual background of this dispute encompasses the history of the general purpose credit card industry. What is known today "everywhere you want to be" as Visa has evolved over the last forty years from direct extensions of credit for a single purpose; for example, oil company or department store credit

---

17. Ed. Jackson, J., did not participate in the decision. The concurring opinions of Douglas and Frankfurter, JJ., the dissenting opinion of Roberts, J., in which Stone, C.J., joined, and the dissenting opinion of Murphy, J., are omitted.

cards, to a "charge card which could be used for general purposes at a wide variety of retail establishments." *Id.* at 963 n. 2. The resulting card was offered without geographic restrictions under the neutral trademark, Visa.

Now to its approximately 6,000 associates Visa USA,[18] the umbrella organization, provides technology to process credit card transactions and regulates and coordinates the individual programs through rules and by-laws proposed by management and adopted by a board of directors (the Board).[19] The bylaws cover a range of issues: members' liability, termination, and confidentiality, to name a few. However, since its inception, each Visa USA member independently decides the terms and conditions of credit extensions, the number of cards issued, and the interest rates charged. That is, individual banks establish, operate, and promote their own credit card programs under the Visa aegis, while Visa USA serves as a clearinghouse for the ultimate transaction between issuer, consumer, and merchant. The fees members pay to Visa USA for its services vary according to a formula established by the association.

Any financial institution which is eligible for federal deposit insurance may become a Visa USA member. Among its current membership are Citicorp, Ford Motor Company, General Electric, and ITT. Although the membership was originally restricted to exclusively issuing Visa cards, a challenge to the bylaw prohibiting members from issuing MasterCard forced Visa USA to withdraw the rule.... Consequently, Visa USA members now generally offer both Visa and MasterCard, a practice referred to in the industry as *duality*.

Prior to its entry into the general credit card arena, Sears mustered a bankcard steering committee to investigate the alternatives of developing its own general-purpose charge card or joining the Visa USA/MasterCard association. In 1985, Sears introduced the Discover Card, its own proprietary card, one "owned and distributed solely by a single business entity," 819 F.Supp. at 963 n. 3, to be marketed and issued nationally. This entry was intended to compete with Visa, MasterCard, American Express and Citibank's Diners' Club/Carte Blanche, the only other national proprietary cards. Despite Visa USA's aggressive efforts to thwart its new rival, *id.* at 963, Discover succeeded with such innovations as preapproved, no fee cards offering cash back bonuses to cardholders and deeper discounts to merchants. In fact, at the time of this litigation, Sears was the largest individual issuer of credit cards in terms of the number of cards distributed and the second largest, following Citicorp in credit card receivables vol-

18. In this opinion, Visa USA designates the joint venture named as the defendant. We refer to its credit cards simply as Visa.

19. The Visa USA Board draws its members from twelve designated regions, each electing a representative, generally a bank's chief executive officer or chief operating officer. Based on a formula, larger regions may have a second board seat. Seven directors are elected nationally, and a separate seat is reserved for a director who represents small banks. Citicorp has it own seat on the board based on the rule of automatic appointment to any member with more than ten percent of the total volume of outstanding cards. MasterCard board members are not permitted to sit on the Visa USA Board.

ume.[20] To compete with the Visa Gold Card and American Express Optima Card, Sears also introduced an upscale Discover Card called Prime Issue. Another Sears' entity, Sears Payment Services (SPS), assists other companies in operating their credit card programs.

In 1988, Greenwood Trust Company, a Sears-owned Delaware bank which issues Discover Card, applied for membership in Visa USA, prompting the Board to adopt the bylaw which is the genesis of this antitrust litigation. The amendment to the Board rule, Bylaw 2.06, stated:

> Notwithstanding (a) above, if permitted by applicable law, the corporation shall not accept for membership any applicant which is issuing, directly or indirectly, Discover cards or American Express cards, or any other cards deemed competitive by the Board of Directors; an applicant shall be deemed to be issuing such cards if its parent, subsidiary or affiliate issues such cards.

Subsequently, the Board denied Greenwood Trust's application to Visa USA.

In 1990, the Resolution Trust Corporation sold Sears the assets, including the Visa USA membership, of MountainWest Savings and Loan Association, a bankrupt savings and loan in Sandy, Utah. Sears then created a new entity, SCFC ILC Inc., doing business as MountainWest Financial, by merging the Sandy bank with Basin Loans, a Utah Industrial Loan Company.

Through this vehicle, Sears was poised to inaugurate a national Visa program it dubbed the Prime Option card, a charge card featuring a two-tiered interest rate, 9.9% for the first two months and 15.9% thereafter. To this end, Sears moved Discover's top executives to Prime Option and ordered an initial printing of 1.5 million Prime Option Visa cards. However, upon inadvertently discovering the plan, Visa USA canceled the printing and invoked Bylaw 2.06 to exclude Sears from the association. Sears then instituted this antitrust litigation.

II.   Fed.R.Civ.P. 50(b) Review

In this appeal, Visa USA contends Sears has failed to carry its burden of showing Visa USA's conduct was harmful to competition in violation of section 1. Indeed, Visa USA underscores, the district court conceded had it tried the facts, it "would have concluded that the harm to competition from letting Sears into the Visa system is greater than any harm from keeping Sears out." 819 F.Supp. at 983. Sears, however, urges this fact-intensive case persuaded the jury that preventing consumers access to the Prime Option card and destroying rivals' incentives to develop new proprietary cards harmed competition.

Nonetheless, we focus only on those relevant antitrust facts, which, when viewed most favorably to Sears, underpin our plenary review under

---

20. In 1991, approximately 24 million Discover cards had been issued, while Citi-corp had approximately 21 million cards in the market.

Fed.R.Civ.P. 50(b). In the context of this case, if there is evidence upon which a jury could properly find Visa USA restrained trade, we must affirm. . . .

III. Joint Ventures and Section 1

Section 1 forbids agreements in restraint of trade. Read costively, section 1 might prohibit "every conceivable contract or combination . . . anywhere in the whole field of human activity." Standard Oil Co. of N.J. v. United States, 221 U.S. 1, 60 (1911). However, "the 'rule of reason' limits the Act's literal words by forbidding only those arrangements the anticompetitive consequences of which outweigh their legitimate business justifications." . . .

Of course, reasonability is of no consequence when certain practices, for example, price fixing, are entirely void of redeeming competitive rationales. These we deem *per se* illegal under section 1, no offsetting economic or efficiency justifications salvaging them. . . .

The sharp line between *per se* and rule of reason analysis, however, especially blurs under section 1 when the actors change. In the case of a joint venture, present here in the Visa USA association, competitive incentives between independent firms are intentionally restrained and their functions and operations integrated to achieve efficiencies and increase output. See Joseph F. Brodley, Joint Venture and Antitrust Policy, 94 Harv.L.Rev. 1523, 1524 (1982). Although virtually any collaborative activity among business firms may be called a joint venture, joint ventures differ from mergers and cartels

> by the extent to which they integrate the resources of their partners. A cartel constitutes a naked agreement among competitors unaccompanied by any integration of resources. In a joint venture, partners contribute assets, such as capital, technology, or production facilities to a common endeavor. This integration of resources creates economic efficiencies that cannot be achieved by naked agreements among competitors. Indeed, the efficiencies created by joint ventures are similar to those resulting from mergers—risk-sharing, economies of scale, access to complementary resources and the elimination of duplication and waste. Joint ventures, however, differ from mergers in a critical way: because they are less integrated than mergers, *they allow their partners to continue to compete with each other in the relevant market.*

Thomas A. Piraino, Jr. Beyond *per se*, Rule of Reason or Merger Analysis: A New Antitrust Standard for Joint Ventures, 76 Minn.L.Rev. 1, 7 (1991) (italics added). The whole becomes greater than the sum of its parts. However, at its center remains an agreement among competitors to eliminate competition in some way.

The Supreme Court has recognized this tension in its evolving treatment of allegedly anticompetitive agreements by joint ventures. In Broadcast Music, Inc. v. Columbia Broadcasting, Inc., 441 U.S. 1 (1979) (BMI), the Court refused to condemn under a *per se* analysis blanket licenses which amounted to price fixing among the participants....

[I]n Northwest Wholesale Stationers, 472 U.S. at 284, the Court looked at the economic efficiency justifications of a joint purchasing cooperative to determine the anticompetitive effect of its expelling a member who did not comply with one of the cooperative's rules. Rejecting *per se* condemnation, the Court suggested the disclosure rule which excluded plaintiff from membership might be necessary to monitor the creditworthiness of the cooperative's members....

In rejecting automatic *per se* treatment in these joint venture cases,[21] the Court directs us instead to look at the challenged agreement to judge whether it represents the essential reason for the competitors' cooperation or reflects a matter merely ancillary to the venture's operation; whether it has the effect of decreasing output; and whether it affects price. Underlying these cases is an effort to appreciate the economic reality of the particular business behavior to assure that the procompetitive goals, in fact, are neither undervalued nor mask a reduction in competition....

We do not read the Court's precedent involving joint ventures to imply any special treatment or differing antitrust analysis. Indeed, aside from clarifying the inappropriateness of automatically invoking *per se* scrutiny of a joint venture's alleged antitrust violation, the Court has not articulated a different rule of reason approach. Thus, under the Court's precedent, cooperative business activity in one setting may permit its participants to achieve market efficiencies or economies of scale, while in another, a similar activity might run afoul under rule of reason review....

IV. Market Power

Rule of reason analysis first asks whether the offending competitor, here Visa USA, possesses market power in the relevant market where the alleged anticompetitive activity occurs. The answer to that question may end the suit or permit an abbreviated rule of reason inquiry.

Broadly, market power is the ability to raise price by restricting output. "[I]n economic terms [it] is the ability to raise price without a total loss of sales." 2 P. Areeda & D. Turner, Antitrust Law at 322 (1978). Without market power, consumers shop around to find a rival offering a better deal. Indeed,

> if we accept the notion that the point of antitrust is promoting consumer welfare, then it is clear why the concept of market power plays such a prominent role in antitrust analysis. If the structure of the market is such that there is little potential for consumers to be harmed, we need not be especially concerned with how firms behave because the presence of effective competition will provide a powerful antidote to any effort to exploit consumers.

---

21. *BMI, NCAA,* and *Northwest Wholesale Stationers* are emblematic and not intended to be all-inclusive or exhaustive of the extant Supreme Court precedent on joint venture under section 1.

George A. Hay, Market Power in Antitrust, 60 Antitrust L.J. 807, 808 (1992) [hereinafter Market Power].

Consequently, whether a firm possesses market power may facilitate the determination that the practice harms competition and not simply a single competitor. Proof of market power, then, for many courts is a critical first step, or "screen," or "filter,"[22] which is often dispositive of the case. Valley Liquors, Inc. v. Renfield Importers, Ltd., 822 F.2d 656, 666–667 (7th Cir.), cert. denied, 484 U.S. 977 (1987). If market power is found, the court may then proceed under rule of reason analysis to assess the procompetitive justifications of the alleged anticompetitive conduct. National Bancard Corp. (NaBanco) v. VISA U.S.A., 779 F.2d 592, 603 (11th Cir.), cert. denied, 479 U.S. 923 (1986). . . .

The market power inquiry begins with the determination of the relevant market, "that is, a market relevant to the legal issue before the court." P. Areeda & H. Hovenkamp, Antitrust Law ¶ 518.1, at 535 (Supp.1993) [hereinafter 1993 Supplement]. "The 'market' which one must study to determine when a producer has monopoly power will vary with the part of commerce under consideration. The tests are constant. That market is composed of products that have reasonable interchangeability for the purposes for which they are produced—price, use and qualities considered." United States v. E.I. du Pont de Nemours & Co., 351 U.S. 377, 404 (1956). We also look to the geographic reach of the group of sales or sellers to determine the relevant market. . . . By defining the relevant market . . . we identify the firms that compete with each other. Plugged into the market power inquiry, we may then determine whether the alleged anticompetitive activity restrained trade, that is, raised price or reduced output.

V.   Issuer Market

This case illustrates both the utility and difficulties of the market power tool. In this lawsuit, Sears and Visa USA stipulated "the relevant market is the general purpose charge card market in the United States." 819 F.Supp. at 966. Presently, the only participants in this market are Visa USA, MasterCard, American Express, Citibank (Diners Club and Carte Blanche), and Sears (Discover Card). Competition among these five firms to place their individual credit cards into a consumer's pocket is called *intersystem* . . . .

In its complaint, Sears alleged the amendment to Bylaw 2.06 represented a concerted refusal to deal which unreasonably restrained trade in the general purpose charge card market. The parties agreed, and the testimony clearly established that in this relevant market competition occurs only at the issuer level. That is, to the extent that Visa USA is in the

22. These screens or filters are presumptions in antitrust analysis. They "help to screen out cases in which the risk of loss to consumers and the economy is sufficiently small that there is no need of extended inquiry and significant risk that inquiry would lead to wrongful condemnation or to the deterrence of competitive activity as firms try to steer clear of the danger zone." Frank H. Easterbrook, The Limits of Antitrust, 63 Tex. L.Rev. 1, 17 (1984). . . .

market, it operates in the *systems* market, not the *issuer* market. Its *members* issue cards, competing with each other to offer better terms or more attractive features for their individual credit card programs. This is *intrasystem* competition.

The issuer market, thus, remains atomistic, each issuer financial institution, bank, or other entity being independent from another.[23] Although Sears does not dispute this characterization of the market, it contends it attempted to launch its Prime Option program under the Visa aegis to "compete more effectively" at the issuer level. By offering multiple credit cards, Discover and Prime Option Visa, Sears contended it would then "strengthen competition."

If the general credit card issuer market is the relevant market, however, the evidence the district court relied upon to deny the Rule 50(b) motion belies Sears' contention and calls into question the definition of relevant market the court apparently adopted. First, the district court recounted the market shares of each intersystem competitor: "Visa was estimated to possess 45.6% of the nation-wide general purpose charge card market; MasterCard, 26.4%; American Express, 20.5%; Discover Card, 5.5%; and Diners Club, 2.0%." 819 F.Supp. at 966 (footnote omitted). Within Visa USA's intersystem share, aggregated to include MasterCard issues as well, the district court noted the evidence showed "in 1991 the ten largest issuers of Visa and MasterCard accounted for approximately 48% of the total Visa/MasterCard charge volume. The top-ten issuers were Citicorp, First Chicago, AT & T, Chase Manhattan, MBNA America, Bank of America, Nationsbank, Chemical Bank, Banc One, and Wells Fargo Bank. The largest issuer, Citicorp, accounted for approximately $42.5 billion in charge volume in 1991, representing approximately 15.8% of the Visa/MasterCard market and 11.4% of the entire general purpose charge card market." *Id.* at 966 n. 8.

While these raw figures may suggest Visa USA possesses market power in the intersystem market, the parties have established a different paradigm. By their agreement, the context of this case was intended to focus on the issuance of credit cards as the relevant market. Indeed, that is the market the district court defined for the jury. To determine, therefore, whether Visa USA possesses market power, we must compare *issuers,* the point where both Sears and Visa USA agreed they compete. At that level, testimony from both Sears and Visa experts established Discover Card is the second largest issuer preceded only by Citicorp in terms of charge volume, that is, what consumers owe on their credit cards.

Based on the district court's figures, Citicorp's charge volume represented about 15.8% of the Visa/MasterCard market share, aggregated at 72% of the general-purpose credit card market. If we compare issuers'

---

23. Although approximately 6,000 financial institutions separately are issuers in the association, setting fees, interest rates, and other conditions, approximately 19,000 "participating members" offer cards under their own names and utilize the services of their issuing bank. Litan, Consumers, Competition, and Choice, The Impact of Price Controls on the Credit Card Industry, March 1992.

charge volume, our calculations demonstrate Citicorp's is 21.9% in the relevant market, while that of Sears' Discover Card is 5%. Neither figure reflects *at the issuer* level that Visa USA through its members possesses market power.

Nevertheless, Sears' expert, Dr. James Kearl, upon whom the district court relied to conclude the evidence was sufficient to establish Visa USA's market power, explained he looked at the collective, aggregated shares of Visa and MasterCard, because "we have a collective rule, bylaw 2.06 . . . I found that the collective share was very large, and as a consequence my conclusion was that the collective rule was an *exercise of market power.*" (italics added). Dr. Kearl opined that the association members:

> have both incentive and the ability to exercise that market power. They have the incentive because this market share was large and they want to protect that market share. And they also had the incentive because since this is large, *if they can keep prices up or from falling they can make a lot of money.* (italics added).

Second, despite the stipulation on the relevant market, "the market relevant to the legal issue before the court," the testimony reflects that Sears, in fact, sought to expand its competition not specifically in the general purpose credit card market but in a segment of that market represented by financial institutions or banks. For example, Sears' executive, William O'Hara, stated, "We were trying to compete *in that segment* of the general purpose credit card market called the bank association segment." (Emphasis added.) Visa USA's witness Richard Rosenberg, explained he voted for Bylaw 2.06, believing that because a non-bank like Dean Witter did not have to comply with certain requirements imposed on banks like the Community Reinvestment Act, Sears would have a competitive advantage over its bank rivals.

Indeed, albeit the stipulation, as the trial progressed, the "relevant market" devolved into *Visa USA's share* of the defined market. Thus, the legal issue was transformed, equating exclusion from Visa USA to exclusion from the market. The evidence, however, does not support this mutation. The district court recognized five active rivals presently compete at the intersystem level. Of that market, for example, Citicorp represents 21.9%, American Express 20.5%, and Sears 5%. At the issuer level, where intrasystem competition occurs, the court found, and the parties' expert agreed, the market is remarkably unconcentrated.[24] Given the wide range of interest rates and terms offered by various issuers and Sears' recognized intersys-

---

24. Ironically, the district court rejected Visa USA's argument that the present market is highly concentrated, such that admitting Sears would constitute a violation of section 7 of the Clayton Act. After discussing the Herfindahl–Hirschman Index (HHI), which is used to determine market concentration, the district court rejected Visa USA's aggregation of market shares, stating "the court agrees with Visa's expert Professor Schmalensee that each individual issuer of Visa and MasterCard cards should be included in the HHI analysis, resulting in a system HHI of below 500." SCFC ILC, Inc. v. Visa U.S.A., Inc., 819 F.Supp. 956, 994 (D.Utah 1993). This figure represents an unconcentrated market.

tem strength, we are at a loss to find the evidence to support the district court's contrary conclusion.

From this standpoint, even if Visa USA possesses market power, Dr. Kearl's testimony that Visa USA exercised that market power in *its ability* to make collective rules misses the point in the context of joint ventures. "A joint venture made more efficient by ancillary restraints, is a fusion of the productive capacities of the members of the venture." *Rothery Storage*, 792 F.2d at 230. The very existence of a joint venture in the first instance is premised on a pooling of resources to affect competition in some manner and is made functional through some form of cooperative behavior or rule-making. However, the Court has made clear, as previously discussed, cooperative conduct alone is not prohibited.

Hence, it is not the rule-making *per se* that should be the focus of the market power analysis, but the effect of those rules—whether they increase price, decrease output, or otherwise capitalize on barriers to entry that potential rivals cannot overcome. Although Dr. Kearl testified "if they can keep prices up or from falling they can make a lot of money" to support his conclusion Visa USA possesses market power, there was no evidence that price had been increased, output had decreased, or other indicia of anticompetitive activity had occurred.

Thus, without any eye on effect, the very exercise of rule-making became the factual basis of rule of reason condemnation of By-law 2.06. Consequently, rule-making was not only divorced from its functional analysis but also from the facts of the case. "When an expert opinion is not supported by sufficient facts to validate it in the eyes of the law, or when indisputable record facts contradict or otherwise render the opinion unreasonable, it cannot support a jury's verdict." Brooke Group, Ltd. v. Brown & Williamson Tobacco Corp., 113 S.Ct. 2578, 2598 (1993). In this complex area, the Court cautioned, "Expert testimony is useful as a guide to interpreting market facts, but it is not a substitute for them." *Id.*

We believe the evidence cited by the district court to conclude Visa USA possessed market power is insufficient as a matter of law. Although the district court did not end its rule of reason inquiry upon that finding, the conclusion set the path for its uncharted journey upon a landscape of speculation, conjecture, and theoretical harm. The consequence is the finding of liability based on tendentious and conclusory statements, none of which amounts to evidence of restraint of trade.[25]

VI.   Efficiency Justifications

We therefore return to the two-step analysis previously discussed to assess the procompetitive justification of Bylaw 2.06 to counteract Sears' allegation the restraint is unreasonable. Visa USA maintained it instituted

---

25. In particular, Sears' disincentive argument provides the widest array of speculation and raises concerns about its standing to represent the supposed injury of others hoping to start up proprietary charge cards. Nevertheless, the parties each shared in charting the court's terrain.

Bylaw 2.06 to protect its property from intersystem competitors who otherwise would enjoy a free ride at this time of entry. Its general counsel, Bennett Katz, described technological advancement Visa USA achieved and incentives for innovation to system-wide competition generated. In a letter informing Sears of the Board's action, he stated, "As I indicated to you by phone, we believe that intersystem competition should be preserved and enhanced; membership by Greenwood Trust Co. would have the opposite effect." Describing the industry as small, "we only have three basic competitors ... Visa and MasterCard ... American Express and Discover," Katz expressed concern about government regulation if the existing competition diminished or Visa USA became too large.[26] In addition, there was testimony that after duality was permitted, MasterCard and Visa competed less aggressively, consumers regarding the two cards often as interchangeable. Other witnesses expressed concern, for example, about Sears' threat to their own profits; the effect a big player like Sears would have on the many small banks that compete in the Visa USA association; and Sears' likely ability to become a Board member and privy to confidential information.

Against these justifications, Sears offered testimony about a two-stage strategy in which it had always planned to enter the market first with its Discover Card and then with a low-cost Visa card; that marketing the Prime Option card as a Discover Card program would not meet the objectives of "Sears' branding strategy," and that consumers would be harmed by being denied the opportunity to select a Prime Option Visa card from the possible choices in the general charge card market. Broadly, Sears promised a low-cost, competitive alternative to the existing market's cards and elicited, through expert testimony, the prospect of other similarly situated potential intersystem competitors being excluded and discouraged from offering new rival cards because of Bylaw 2.06.

Most of this evidence relied upon by the district court is irrelevant to the central antitrust question posed, however. First, intent to harm a rival, protect and maximize profits, or "do all the business if they can," *Ball Memorial Hosp.*, 784 F.2d at 1325, is neither actionable nor sanctioned by the antitrust laws. "Competition, which is always deliberate, has never been a tort, intentional or otherwise." Olympia Equip. Leasing Co. v. Western Union Tel. Co., 797 F.2d 370, 379 (7th Cir.1986), *cert. denied*, 480 U.S. 934 (1987). "Most businessmen don't like their competitors or for that matter competition. They want to make as much money as possible and getting a monopoly is one way of making a lot of money." *Id.* Thus, evidence that a Board member voted for Bylaw 2.06 to discourage price competition, within Visa USA may reveal a mental state but is not an objective basis upon which section 1 liability may be found. If Bylaws 2.06 is not "objectively anticompetitive the fact that this was motivated by hostility to competitors ... is irrelevant." *Id.* (citation omitted).

---

26. In testimony, Katz explained, not only was Justice Department scrutiny a concern, but also "attorneys general around the country who had been looking at Visa and deciding whether it is too large."

What we ask under section 1 is whether the alleged restraint is reasonably related to Visa USA's operation and no broader than necessary to effectuate the association's business. *NaBanco*, 779 F.2d at 592, 601. That is, is Bylaw 2.06 ancillary, "subordinate and collateral ... [making] the main transaction more effective in accomplishing its purpose," which is to provide credit card services to its members? *Rothery Storage*, 792 F.2d at 224. If it is not ancillary, does it restrain trade in a manner which alters the structure of the general purpose credit card market and, thus, harms consumers?

We think the analysis in *Rothery Storage* helps us resolve this question.... After a thorough and well-reasoned analysis, the D.C. Circuit rejected plaintiffs' claim, based not simply on the evidence Atlas did not possess market power in the market for the interstate carriage of used household goods, but also on the conclusion the new rule was ancillary to Atlas' main enterprise, enhancing consumer welfare by creating efficiency. *Id.* at 223. What improved the company's efficiency, the court found, was the elimination of the free ride:

> The restraints preserve the efficiencies of the nationwide van line by eliminating the problem of the free ride. There is, on the other hand, no possibility that the restraints can suppress market competition and so decrease output.

Id. at 229. This conclusion was built on the foundation of *BMI, NCAA,* and *Northwest Wholesale Stationers.*

Similarly, Visa USA urges its concern about protecting the property it has created over the years and preventing Sears and American Express, successful rivals, from profiting by a free ride does not represent a refusal to deal or group boycott but is reasonably necessary to ensure the effective operation of its credit card services. It urges Bylaw 2.06 avoids "free-riding, an unlevel playing field, and the added costs that Sears would impose on VISA members by taking advantage of a brand and operating systems that it not only had done nothing to create but had chosen to compete against." Visa USA contends Sears does not need Visa USA to compete in the relevant market and cannot demonstrate that it can only issue a low-cost card with Visa USA's help.

Sears urges the justification is pretext. "In this case, the issue is whether the selective exclusion imposed by Visa's Bylaws 2.06 is ancillary to Visa's legitimate purposes as an open industry association." Sears contends Visa USA is a network joint venture, one whose integrative efficiencies actually grow as its membership increases. To accept Visa USA's analogy to a research venture, one expending individual talent and resources in a small laboratory only to be forced to include rival researchers, Sears argues, is naive. It protests everyone gets into Visa USA except Sears itself. In support Sears relies on the bulwark of exclusionary conduct cases.

We do not believe either precedent or policy compels Sears' position however. For example, United States v. Terminal R.R. Ass'n of St. Louis,

224 U.S. 383 (1912) (joint venture railroad companies that acquired Terminal Company, which controlled bridge across Mississippi River, approaches, and terminal at St. Louis must admit rivals to permit use of facilities on nondiscriminatory terms), involved a "most extraordinary" situation in St. Louis "and we base our conclusion in the case, in a large measure, upon the fact." *Id.* at 405. In that setting, mandating the combined railroad companies admit their competitors merely permitted joint ownership of common facilities. "The defendants had not built or created anything except a combination to take over existing facilities." 1993 Supplement ¶ 736.1, at 841.

Similarly, *Associated Press v. United States,* 326 U.S. 1 (1945) (joint venture news gathering agency must provide reasonable access to excluded firms), never stated a joint venture cannot exclude anyone. The Court's prohibition of the membership restriction was focused particularly on the operation of the rule itself, where an individual Associated Press member could singly veto a rival's access to its local market. More importantly, the joint venture, "the largest news agency," was factually unique: its news gathering and dissemination capacity could not be duplicated and represented in and of itself a limitation on nonmembers. *Id.* at 13.[27] . . . . Bylaw 2.06 did not alter the character of the general purpose credit card market or change any present pattern of distribution. Nor did it bar Sears from access to this market. There was no evidence that Sears could only introduce a Prime Option card with Visa USA's help or that Visa USA's exclusion from its joint venture disabled Sears from developing its new card under the Discover mantle. More importantly, there was no evidence the bylaw harms consumers, the focus of the alleged violation. Indeed, the evidence established the current market in general purpose credit cards is structurally competitive, issuers targeting different consumer groups and consumer needs. In this market, Sears already competes vigorously. Surely, if its goal is to compete *more effectively* in that market, we do not believe this objective constitutes the proverbial sparrow the Sherman Act protects. "[A] producer's loss is no concern of the antitrust laws, which protect consumers from suppliers rather than suppliers from each other." *Stamatakis Indus.,* 965 F.2d at 471.[28]

---

27. *Terminal Railroad* and *Associated Press* are the roots of the essential facility analysis in antitrust. See Phillip E. Areeda, Essential Facilities: An Epithet in Need of Limiting Principles, 58 Antitrust L.J. 841 (1990).

28. Indeed, when the question becomes whether the restraint is reasonably necessary to achieve the joint venture's goals, "[e]xclusivity of venture membership will not generally be regarded as suspect." The Department of Justice made the following statement in 1988:

[S]electivity in the membership of a joint venture often enhances a joint venture's

procompetitive potential. Forcing joint ventures to open membership to all competitors (or to licenses) would decrease the incentives to form joint ventures. . . . For example, the inability to exclude those who would bring little or nothing to the joint venture, or those who would fail to share fully in the risk, would decrease the efficiency of the joint venture's mission. An enforcement policy that denied a joint venture the ability to select its members might also encourage firms to forego risky endeavors in the hope of being able to gain access through antitrust litigation to the fruits of the

Given Visa USA's justification the bylaw is necessary to prevent free-riding in a market in which there was no evidence price was raised or output decreased or Sears needed Visa USA to develop the new card, we are left with a vast sea of commercial policy into which Sears would have us wade. To impose liability on Visa USA for refusing to admit Sears or revise the bylaw to open its membership to intersystem rivals, we think, sucks the judiciary into an economic riptide of contrived market forces. Whatever currents Sears imagines Visa USA wrongly created, we believe can be better corrected by the marketplace itself. The Sherman Act ultimately must protect competition, not a competitor, and were we tempted to collapse the distinction, we would distort its continuing viability to safeguard consumer welfare. . . .

NOTES AND QUESTIONS

1. The Tenth Circuit's opinion was not the only time a court had considered the question whether the Visa/Mastercard system violated the antitrust laws. In United States v. Visa U.S.A., Inc., 163 F.Supp.2d 322 (S.D.N.Y.2001), the district court ruled that the government failed to prove that the governance structures of the Visa and MasterCard associations had resulted in a significant adverse effect on competition or consumer welfare, but that the government's proof "clearly show[ed] that the exclusionary rules and practices of the defendants [had] resulted in such adverse effect and should be abolished." Specifically, it found objectionable the Visa and MasterCard rules forbidding members of the associations from issuing credit cards on competing networks. It found that general purpose credit cards constituted a relevant product market; that general purpose card network services also constituted a relevant product market; that the United States was the relevant geographic market; and that the defendants had market power in the network market. The defendants' exclusionary rules made American Express and Discover unable to convince U.S. banks to issue cards over their networks, and thus it prevented them from competing in the network services market for the business of bank issuers. The existence of multiple bank issuers, it found, would significantly enhance network-level competition; non-bank issuers were not an adequate substitute for banks. Finally, the court found that Visa and MasterCard had not offered a legitimate pro-competitive justification for their exclusionary rules, rejecting arguments that the rules enhanced loyalty and network cohesion.

2. Can *MountainWest* and the district court's opinion in the government's Visa case be reconciled?

3. If the "joint venture" involved in the *Associated Press* case were declared illegal under the antitrust laws, could the substantial economies of scale and other

successful endeavors of others. Thus, the Department [of Justice] generally will be concerned about a joint venture's policy of excluding others only if (i) an excluded firm cannot compete in a related market or markets . . . in which the joint venture members are currently exercising market power without having access to the joint venture and (ii) there is no reasonable basis related to the efficient operation of the joint venture for excluding other firms.

Justice Department International Operations Antitrust Enforcement Policy 42 (Nov. 10, 1988) (CCH Supp.).

beneficial results achieved by Associated Press and other cooperative news agencies be obtained by any alternative arrangement? Does it follow that joint ventures that produce economies that could not otherwise be achieved should be permitted under the antitrust laws, even where they generate substantial market power?

The Supreme Court seems to answer with a qualified yes, even in price-fixing cases. Cf. Broadcast Music, Inc. v. Columbia Broadcasting System, Inc., 441 U.S. 1 (1979), p. 233 supra ("joint ventures and other cooperative arrangements are also not usually unlawful, at least not as price-fixing schemes, where the agreement on price is necessary to market the product at all").

4. In WORTHEN BANK AND TRUST CO. v. NATIONAL BANKAMERICARD, INC., 485 F.2d 119 (8th Cir.1973), cert. denied, 415 U.S. 918 (1974), plaintiff on behalf of itself and other small banks sued National BankAmericard (NBI), claiming that a bylaw precluding member banks in the NBI system from participating as credit card issuers in the Master Charge system constituted a group boycott in violation of Section 1. BankAmericard and Master Card constituted the two principal nation-wide bank credit cards, each comprised of numerous member banks. For purposes of summary judgment, Worthen Bank conceded that the bylaw promoted competition between the two national systems, and that absent the provision there would be a "substantial lessening of competition." The District Court found that the bylaw restricting membership in a competing credit card system was a group boycott and therefore illegal *per se*.

The Court of Appeals reversed. It noted that bylaw provisions in credit card systems involved questions of some novelty and importance and that courts should be slow to apply *per se* rules in such situations. Moreover, Worthen had conceded that member banks, acting alone, could not issue and support a national credit card arrangement. The Court concluded that there was here an economic justification in terms of "productive capacity," whereas in *Klor's* and some other similar cases, the proscribed conduct had no redeeming virtue. It remanded the case, asking the district court to consider various proffered justifications for the rule.

Eventually, NBI (now Visa USA) amended the bylaw to allow member banks to issue the MasterCard.

What accounts for the different outcomes in *Visa* and *Worthen?* Did the *Worthen Bank* court err by characterizing the case as a group boycott? Did the *SCFC* court underestimate Visa USA's power to exclude Sears from the relevant market? Are there practices short of exclusion that would allow Visa USA to avoid the free riding problem? Should this have affected the *SCFC* court's analysis?

5. It has been asserted that if joint ventures confer significant competitive advantages, those advantages must be made available to all on reasonable terms—a kind of public utility concept of regulation. See Kaysen & Turner, Antitrust Policy 137 (1959). How far can this concept be carried? Would the American Medical Association be required to accept faith healers? Cf. American Medical Association v. United States, 317 U.S. 519 (1943).

6. Is there any reason to treat a joint venture that dominates a relevant market differently under the antitrust laws than a single firm monopoly? If not, does it follow that the limitations on permissible conduct by a single firm monopolist, set forth in *Alcoa* (p. 130 supra), apply equally to a dominant joint venture? Should even more stringent limitations apply in the joint venture situation?

7.a. In BLUE CROSS & BLUE SHIELD UNITED OF WISCONSIN v. MARSHFIELD CLINIC, 65 F.3d 1406 (7th Cir.1995), Blue Cross and its subsidiary health maintenance organization (HMO), Compcare, sued the Marshfield Clinic of north central Wisconsin and its subsidiary HMO, Security Health Plan. Compcare complained that the Marshfield Clinic maintained a monopoly in north Central Wisconsin, excluding Compcare from the HMO "market" in the region. Blue Cross complained that the Marshfield clinic charged supra-competitive prices to patients covered by Blue Cross. A jury returned a verdict of $20 million against the defendants, after remittitur, trebling and attorney's fees.

The Seventh Circuit, in an opinion authored by Judge Posner, reversed Compcare's portion of the judgment. The court refused to find that HMOs always constitute a separate market. It explained that HMOs are simply one more means of pricing medical services. In the court's view, HMOs simply compete with other types of fee-for-service pricing mechanisms, including preferred provider plans. As for the market for all physicians' services in north central Wisconsin, the court declined to treat the Marshfield clinic as anything more than the alliance of 400 physicians. It noted that the 900 physicians who affiliated with Marshfield through Security did not have exclusive arrangements with the clinic or its HMO. The court also pointed out that those physicians, on average, earned only 6% of their total income from their affiliation with Security. Based on the facts, the court found that Security, despite its membership base of 90% of all HMO subscribers in the region, was not a monopolist.

The court then addressed Compcare's argument that the Marshfield Clinic should be forced to contract with HMOs other than Security. Compcare argued, citing *Terminal Railroad Ass'n,* p. 379 supra, that the clinic was an essential facility. The court dismissed this argument, explaining:

We are mindful that a concept of essential or bottleneck facilities has been used from time to time to require a natural monopolist to cooperate with would-be competitors.... The principal case remains the old St. Louis terminal case.... The decision, along with the rest of the decisions in the essential facilities line, has been criticized as having nothing to do with antitrust law.... Had the terminal facilities been owned by a firm unaffiliated with any railroad, the firm could have charged whatever prices it wanted, including prices that discriminated against some of the users (monopolists frequently price discriminate), because the antitrust laws do not regulate the prices of natural monopolists. A natural monopolist that acquired and maintained its monopoly without excluding competitors by improper means is not guilty of "monopolizing" in violation of the Sherman Act, ... for the antitrust laws are not a price-control statute or a public-utility or common-carrier rate-regulation statute.

And the charging of a high price is, so far as potential competitors are concerned, an attracting rather than an excluding practice. Consumers are not better off if the natural monopolist is forced to share some of his profits with potential competitors, as required by *Terminal Railroad Ass'n.* Similarly, if the practice of medicine in some sparsely populated county of north central Wisconsin is a natural monopoly, consumers will not be helped by our forcing the handful of physicians there to affiliate with multiple HMOs. Those physicians will still charge fees reflecting their monopoly.

We are not authorized to abrogate doctrines that have been endorsed and not yet rejected by the Supreme Court.... To be an essential facility, however, a facility must be essential. The terminal association controlled 100 percent of a market, assumed to be properly defined, consisting of terminal services at St. Louis. The Clinic does not control 100 percent—or even 50 percent—of any properly defined market.

Id. at 1412–13. The court thus rejected Compcare's essential facility argument.

b. Judge Posner, in his analysis of the antitrust problem posed by Security's physician network, identified one factor as conclusive—the lack of exclusive contracts between Security and the 900 physicians outside the clinic. The FTC and the Antitrust Division proposed a more flexible analysis in their Statement of Department of Justice and Federal Trade Commission Analytical Principles Relating to Multiprovider Networks. See Statements of Antitrust Enforcement Policy in Health Care (Aug. 28, 1996), 71 BNA ATRR 1777 (Sp. Supp. 8/29/96). The Guidelines suggest that exclusiveness would be looked at as one important factor among many. They also highlight economic integration among providers (sharing financial risk through shared capitation or through a bonus formula based on utilization review) as an important factor in assessing the legality of provider networks. They go so far as to say that significant economic integration would bring joint pricing and service allocation by otherwise competing providers within rule of reason analysis.

8. In UNITED STATES v. REALTY MULTI-LIST INC., 629 F.2d 1351 (5th Cir.1980), the United States challenged certain bylaws of Realty Multi-List, controlling membership in the organization, as constituting a boycott under Section 1 of the Sherman Act. A real estate multiple listing service is a joint venture in which members attempt to obtain from real estate sellers "exclusive" listings which they then pool among other members. The system produces a variety of efficiencies: buyers have access to a broader range of listings; sellers have access to a wider range of potential buyers; and as a result price is more in line with supply and demand.

A key element of the Realty Multi-List arrangement provided that members may not allow non-members access to listing pool information. Membership criteria for RML included findings that the prospective member: (1) had a favorable credit report and business reputation; and (2) maintained a real estate office open during customary business hours. Also, each member was required to pay an initiation fee set by the RML Board of Directors. At the time of suit, RML was the sole multiple listing service in Muskogee County, Georgia, and its members constituted the majority of the active real estate brokers there.

The Court of Appeals rejected the United States' request for *per se* treatment of the multi-list system, noting that the arrangement arguably improved the efficient operation of the real estate market. The government had next argued that the specific bylaws arbitrarily excluded prospective members and therefore were "facially unreasonable"—an approach the Court of Appeals interpreted as a version of the rule of reason.

Under a rule of reason approach, the Court first concluded that RML had substantial market power and that membership was a competitive advantage and perhaps a competitive necessity. As a result, its membership regulations needed to be fair and reasonable, and they were not. With respect to the "favorable credit report and business reputation" requirement, the Court noted that Georgia state law already regulated real estate brokers extensively. While such state regulation did not preclude self-regulation rules, the RML rule seemed unreasonable in the absence of a showing by RML that state regulation was inadequate, and because its "credit report" and "business reputation" rules were unduly broad and vague. The Court found the requirement that a member maintain an office during customary business hours similarly unreasonable. Although a prospective member might be required to be "actively engaged in the business," the hours requirement unreasonably discriminated against brokers who operated primarily on weekends or evenings, times particularly convenient for many customers. As to the third membership requirement—the membership fee—the Court found that fees based on start-up costs and a pro-rata contribution toward maintenance and development of the list would be reasonable, but that a sizeable membership fee bearing no relationship to those cost factors created a strong inference of an anticompetitive intent. The case was remanded for further proceedings.

9.   In shopping center leases, it is common for the developer to grant to major (or "anchor") tenants approval rights over admission to the shopping center of various other commercial enterprises. These lease provisions have been defended on grounds that the developer is unlikely to be able to secure financing until long-term leases have been signed with anchor tenants (see The Antitrust Implications of Restrictive Covenants in Shopping Center Leases, 86 Harv.L.Rev. 1201 (1973)), and the anchor tenants have a legitimate interest in participating in the decision to include or exclude would-be entrants.

Could the series of agreements between the developer and major tenants be viewed as a joint venture? If the shopping center were in an isolated area or of unusual commercial prominence, might access constitute a significant competitive advantage under *Associated Press*? In Tyson's Corner Regional Shopping Center, FTC Docket 886, ATRR No. 722, p. E–1 (FTC 1975), the FTC declared illegal *per se* under Section 5 of the FTCA lease clauses that gave to an anchor tenant a blanket veto over would-be entrants. It noted that such broad lease provisions would permit the anchor tenant to exclude later entrants because they were discounters or because they competed with the anchor tenant. The Commission went on to say that more carefully tailored provisions, such as those which would preclude subsequent entrants who were not financially sound or would require the developer to consider the objective of maintaining a balanced and diversified grouping of retail stores, would be permissible.

NOTE ON RESEARCH AND PRODUCTION JOINT VENTURES

In many high-tech industries, and increasingly in modern economies generally, successful innovation is the key to commercial success. Innovation may allow a company to cut cost or furnish a new and better product and thereby achieve greater market share, higher profits or both. Often, there are powerful reasons why research is best undertaken on a collaborative basis.

In 1984, responding to complaints by domestic companies that the antitrust laws were a threat to cooperative joint research, Congress enacted the National Cooperative Research Act. The NCRA provided that collaborative "joint research and development" activities, as defined in the NCRA, would be judged on the basis of a rule of reason. The NCRA also provided a limited "safe harbor" for joint R & D ventures. Under the NCRA, anyone filing a notification of the organization of a joint R & D venture with the Department of Justice and the FTC would limit their antitrust exposure to single damages and reasonable attorney's fees. Finally, the NCRA provided that defendants who prevail in a challenge to an R & D joint venture may recover costs and attorney's fees from the challenger if the claim or the claimant's conduct is found to be "frivolous, unreasonable, without foundation, or in bad faith."

The NCRA defined "joint research and development" as:

[A]ny group of activities, including attempting to make, making or performing a contract, by two or more persons for the purpose of—

(A) theoretical analysis, experimentation, or systematic study of phenomena or observable facts,

(B) the development or testing of basic engineering techniques,

(C) the extension of investigative findings or theory of a scientific or technical nature into practical application for experimental and demonstration purposes, including the experimental production and testing of models, prototypes, equipment, materials, and processes,

(D) the collection, exchange and analysis of research information, or

(E) any combination of the purposes specified in subparagraphs (A), (B), (C), and (D),

and may include the establishment and operation of facilities for the conducting of research....

In 1993, Congress amended the meaning of "joint venture" to include:

(D) the production of a product, process, or service,

(E) the testing in connection with the production of a product, process, or service by such venture.

Joint research and development is specifically defined to exclude: exchanging information relating to cost, sales, profitability, pricing, etc.; agreements relating to marketing; agreements relating to the sale, licensing or sharing of inventions; and agreements that restrict or require participation in other research and development activities—unless those restrictions are reasonably required to prevent misappropriation of proprietary information contributed by any person who is a party to such venture or the results of the venture. Conduct excluded from the protection of the NCRA is not necessarily unlawful, but would be subject to a rule of reason.

Further guidance on the antitrust treatment of research and production joint ventures appears in the following Business Review Letter from the Antitrust Division of the Department of Justice. It concerns a possible patent pool in which the manufacturers of DVD's and DVD ROM's wished to participate, so that they could license all of the more than 100 patents required for these processes at once. The letter follows:

June 10, 1999

You have requested a statement of the Department of Justice's antitrust enforcement intentions with respect to a proposed arrangement pursuant to which Toshiba will assemble and offer a package license under the Licensors' patents that are "essential," as defined below, to manufacturing products in compliance with the DVD–ROM and DVD–Video formats and will distribute royalty income to the other Licensors.

A.   The patents to be licensed

The Licensors commit to license each other and third parties to make, use and sell DVD Products under their present and future patents that are "essential" to doing so. The Licensors agree to two separate means of carrying out this obligation. First, they agree to grant Toshiba the right to sublicense third parties under their present and future "essential" patents for these purposes, and Toshiba agrees in turn to sublicense those patents, along with its own such patents, in the DVD Patent Licenses. Second, each Licensor agrees to "offer to license its essential DVD patents on a non-exclusive basis to interested third-party licensees pursuant to separate negotiations on fair, reasonable and non-discriminatory terms, whether or not said third-party licensees intend to make, use and sell DVD products that are in conformity with the Specifications."

A Licensor's patent is "essential," and thus subject to the commitments in the MOU, if it is "necessarily infringed," or "there is no realistic alternative" to it, "in implementing the DVD Standard Specifications." Initially, each Licensor will identify its own "essential" patents in an attachment to its Authorization Agreement with Toshiba. Toshiba will then incorporate those patents in a list attached to the DVD Patent License. Shortly, however, an expert individual or panel, with "full and sufficient knowledge and skill in the relevant technology," will complete a review of the patents each Licensor has designated as "essential" in order to determine whether they satisfy the MOU criteria. MOU, ¶ 8; Expert Agreement, preamble. At that time, any patent initially designated by a Licensor for inclusion in the DVD Patent License that the expert determines is not "essential" will be excluded from subsequent DVD Patent Licenses, although current licensees will have the option to retain it in their existing licenses.

B.   The joint licensing arrangement

In the Authorization Agreement, each Licensor grants Toshiba the non-exclusive right to grant: (1) sublicenses, "substantially on the terms contained in the form of the DVD Patent License," on its "essential" patents to third parties to "make, have made, use, sell or otherwise dispose of DVD Products"; and (2) releases to the same third parties from liability for pre-license infringement of the licensed patents. Toshiba assumes the obligation to grant such sublicenses and releases "to all interested third party licensees," to collect royalties from licensees, and to distribute royalty income to other Licensors.

Consistent with the MOU, the Authorization Agreement preserves the Licensors' right to license their "essential" patents independently for any application. While the Licensors agree to provide each other with notification of "infringement [of the portfolio patents] or other misuse or unauthorized use" and to cooperate "in taking such steps as may be reasonably necessary to prevent any such unauthorized uses," each Licensor remains "solely responsible" for enforcing its own patent rights against infringement.

III.   Analysis

As with any aggregation of patent rights for the purpose of joint package licensing, commonly known as a patent pool, an antitrust analysis of this proposed licensing program must examine both the pool's expected competitive benefits and its potential restraints on competition. The potential benefit of a patent pool is that it "may provide competitive benefits by integrating complementary technologies, reducing transaction costs, clearing blocking positions, and avoiding costly infringement litigation." At the same time, "some patent pools can restrict competition, whether among intellectual property rights within the pool or downstream products incorporating the pooled patents or in innovation among parties to the pool." Accordingly, the following analysis addresses (1) whether the proposed licensing program here at issue is likely to integrate complementary patent rights and (2), if so, whether the resulting competitive benefits are likely to be outweighed by competitive harm posed by other aspects of the program.

A. Integration of Complementary Patent Rights

If the Licensors owned patent rights that could be licensed and used in competition with each other, they might have an economic incentive to utilize a patent pool to eliminate competition among them. A pool that served that purpose "would raise serious competitive concerns." In combining such substitute patents, the pool could serve as a price-fixing mechanism, ultimately raising the price of products and services that utilize the pooled patents. If, on the other hand, the pool were to bring together complementary patent rights, it could be "an efficient and pro-competitive method of disseminating those rights to would-be users." By reducing what would otherwise be six licensing transactions to one, the pool would reduce transactions costs for Licensors and licensees alike. By ensuring that each Licensor's patents will not be blocked by those of the other five, the pool would enhance the value of all six Licensors' patents.

One way to ensure that the proposed pool will integrate only complementary patent rights is to limit the pool to patents that are essential to compliance with the Standard Specifications. Essential patents by definition have no substitutes; one needs licenses to each of them in order to comply with the standard. At the same time, they are complementary to each other; a license to one essential patent is more valuable if the licensee also has licenses to use other essential patents.

An inclusion criterion broader than "essentiality" carries with it two anticompetitive risks, both arising from the possibility that the pool might include patents that are substitutes for one another and not just complements. Consider, for example, a situation in which there are several patented methods for placing DVD–ROMs into packaging—each a useful complement to DVD–ROM manufacturing technology, but not essential to the standard. A DVD–ROM maker would need to license only one of them; they would be substitutes for each other. Inclusion in the pool of two or more such patents would risk turning the pool into a price-fixing mechanism. Inclusion in the pool of only one of the competing non-essential patents, which the pool would convey along with the essential patents, could in certain cases unreasonably foreclose the non-included competing patents from use by manufacturers; because the manufacturers would obtain a license to the one patent with the pool, they might choose not to license any of the competing patents, even if they otherwise would regard the competitive patents as superior. Limiting a pool to essential patents ensures that neither of these concerns will arise; rivalry is foreclosed neither among patents within the pool nor between patents in the pool and patents outside it.

From the information you have provided us, it appears reasonably likely that the pool will combine only complementary patents for which there are no substitutes for the purpose of compliance with the Standard Specifications. To be sure, the definition of "essential" contained in the MOU and the Authorization Agreement introduces some uncertainty. By asking the expert to identify not only those patents that are literally essential to compliance with the DVD–ROM and DVD–Video standards, but also those for which there is no "realistic" alternative, the definition introduces a degree of subjectivity into the selection process. Based on your representations, however, it appears that the expert will interpret "realistic" to mean economically feasible. So long as the patent expert applies this criterion scrupulously and independently, it is reasonable to expect that the Portfolio will combine only complementary patent rights, and not limit competition between them and other patent rights for purposes of the licensed applications. If, however, the expert over time interprets "realistic" more broadly, so as to include patents for which economically feasible alternatives exist, there would be serious questions as to whether the pool might injure competition by including such substitutes.

The retention of the expert by the Licensors creates some initial concern about the expert's ability to apply the essentiality criterion entirely independent of the Licensors. While the Licensors have agreed that the expert must be free from any substantial business relationship with any individual Licensor, the Licensors as a group, to which the expert answers, have an economic incentive to do the opposite of what they have retained the expert to do—to combine in the pool their competing DVD-related patents and to foreclose others' competing patents. Without more, there would be justifiable skepticism that the expert can be counted on to undertake a disinterested review of the "essentiality" of the patent rights put forward.

B.   Foreclosure of Competition in Related Markets

As mentioned above, the Licensors are competitors in markets vertically related to the licensed technology—not only in "downstream" markets such as the manufacture of DVD discs and players, but also in the creation of content that is incorporated in DVD discs. Consequently, the question arises whether the pool is likely to impede competition in any of those markets, not only between any Licensor and licensees or other third parties, but also among the Licensors themselves.

Based on what you have told us, the proposed licensing program does not appear to have any such anticompetitive potential in the markets in which the licensed technology will be used. First, the agreed royalty is sufficiently small relative to the total costs of manufacture that it is unlikely to enable collusion among sellers of DVD discs, decoders or players. Second, the proposed program should enhance rather than limit access to the Licensors' "essential" patents. Because Toshiba, the joint licensor, must license on a non-discriminatory basis to all interested parties, it cannot impose disadvantageous terms on competitors, let alone refuse to license to them altogether. Third, the extent of Toshiba's access to proprietary licensee information, either through information provided directly to its licensing employees or through audits conducted by independent accountants, is unlikely to afford it anticompetitive access to competitively sensitive proprietary information, such as cost data. The other Licensors' similarly limited right to an annual audit of Toshiba's conduct as joint licensor should not increase the likelihood of collusion. Nor does there seem to be any facet of the proposed program that would facilitate collusion or dampen competition among the Licensors in the creation of content for software.

C.   Effect on Innovation

The proposed licensing program would require Licensors and licensees alike to agree to license to each other not only their present "essential" patents, but also any ones they obtain in the future. The procompetitive benefits of such a requirement are clear. It ensures that no party to the pool will be able to benefit from the pool while blocking other parties from utilizing the Standard Specifications. Further, by bringing other "essential" patents into the portfolio, the requirement lowers licensees' costs in assembling the patent rights they need to comply with the Standard Specifications. And while it is unclear whether any future "essential" patent will emerge absent an amendment of the Standard Specifications, the requirement as to future patents reduces the possibility that a future patent will block licensees from practicing a technology in which they may already have invested in heavily. Reducing this uncertainty may be a significant benefit to licensees.

The question arises, nevertheless, whether these procompetitive benefits are likely to be outweighed by significant discouragement of research and development relating to the Standard Specifications. Licensors and licensees might have greater incentives to invest in research and development in the field were they free to refuse to license other users of the Standard Specifications under any patent that resulted.

IV. Conclusion

For these reasons, the Department is not presently inclined to initiate antitrust enforcement action against the conduct you have described. This letter, however, expresses the Department's current enforcement intention. In accordance with our normal practices, the Department reserves the right to bring an enforcement action in the future if the actual operation of the proposed conduct proves to be anticompetitive in purpose or effect.

* * *

Comment: Compare the patent pool justifications accepted by the Justice Department in this letter with the justification accepted by the Court in Broadcast Music, Inc. v. Columbia Broadcasting System, Inc., supra, p. 233.

NOTE ON THE U.S. DEPARTMENT OF JUSTICE AND FTC ANTITRUST GUIDELINES FOR COLLABORATIONS AMONG COMPETITORS, 2000

In recent years, the antitrust enforcement agencies have issued guidelines with respect to enforcement intentions involving joint ventures in particular sections of the economy such as healthcare (p. 401, note 7b) and the licensing of intellectual property. In April 2000, they issued guidelines that endeavored to set forth a comprehensive analytical approach to all horizontal collaborations. The Competitor Collaboration Guidelines, as we will call them here, define the term "competitor collaboration" as "a set of one or more agreements, other than merger agreements, between or among competitors to engage in economic activity, and the economic activity resulting therefrom." The term "competitors" encompasses both actual and potential competitors. The Guidelines do not expressly take into account the possible effects of competitor collaborations in foreclosing or limiting competition by rivals not participating in a collaboration, or the possible anticompetitive effects of standard setting in the context of competitor collaborations, but the agencies reserve the right to take appropriate actions if such effects are present. Competitor collaborations may involve one or more business activities, such as research and development ("R & D"), production, marketing, distribution, sales or purchasing.

Information sharing and various trade association activities also may take place through competitor collaborations.

The Guidelines go on to set forth the usual distinction between agreements that are *per se* illegal, such as those between competitors to fix prices, rig bids, or divide markets, and agreements that are analyzed under the rule of reason. Rule of reason analysis, they state, focuses on the state of competition with, as compared to without, the relevant agreement. The central question is whether the relevant agreement is likely to harm competition by increasing the ability or incentive profitably to raise price above or reduce output, quality, service, or innovation below what likely would prevail in the absence of the relevant agreement.

The remainder of the Guidelines presents a useful description of a classic rule of reason analysis. The first step is to look at the business purpose of the agreement and the question whether the agreement, if already in operation, has caused anticompetitive harm. If the initial examination of the nature of the agreement indicates possible competitive concerns, then it is necessary to analyze the agreement in greater depth. That process begins with a definition of relevant markets and the calculation of market shares and concentration, to see if it is likely that the agreement may create or increase market power or facilitate its exercise. The Agencies also take into account the extent to which the participants and the collaboration have the ability and incentive to compete independently and other market circumstances, such as entry, that may foster or prevent anticompetitive harms. The examination will stop there if those factors indicate that there is no potential for anticompetitive harm. If such a potential exists, then the analysis goes on to consider whether the relevant agreement is reasonably necessary to achieve procompetitive benefits that likely would offset anticompetitive harms.

The Guidelines spell out a number of factors that are considered to be relevant to the ability and incentive of the participants in a competitor collaboration either to compete or to collude. Six such factors are highlighted in the Guidelines: "(a) the extent to which the relevant agreement is non-exclusive in that participants are likely to continue to compete independently outside the collaboration in the market in which the collaboration operates; (b) the extent to which participants retain independent control of assets necessary to compete; (c) the nature and extent of participants' financial interests in the collaboration or in each other; (d) the control of the collaboration's competitively significant decision making; (e) the likelihood of anticompetitive information sharing; and (f) the duration of the collaboration." Competitor Collaboration Guidelines, § 3.34.

Not long after the Competitor Collaboration Guidelines were issued, the Federal Trade Commission hosted a public workshop on the topic of "Competition Policy in the World of B2B Electronic Marketplaces," on June 29 and 30, 2000. The term "B2B" refers to business-to-business electronic marketplaces that use the internet to connect businesses to one another electronically. Their growth can only be described as explosive, from practically nothing in the mid–1990s to billions of dollars at present. The results of the workshop were summarized and discussed in a report prepared by the staff of the FTC in October 2000, entitled "Entering the 21st Century: Competition Policy in the World of B2B Marketplaces." The report touches on subjects including the potential efficiencies that B2B marketplaces may generate, the kinds of antitrust issues B2Bs may raise (both in the markets for goods and services traded on B2Bs at both the seller and buyer level, and in the market for the marketplaces themselves), and the particular issues posed by information-sharing agreements, joint purchasing agreements, and new forms of exclusionary practices that can occur in the B2B world. The overall message of the report, which is also reflected in the many public statements both from FTC members and from Department of Justice enforcers, is that the form of business arrangements may be new, but the antitrust principles and analysis that have evolved over the years remain pertinent and adequate to the task of policing these new markets.

On January 6, 2001, the Commission of the European Union issued a set of guidelines on horizontal arrangements comparable to those issued by the Department of Justice and FTC. The official title was the "Guidelines on the applicability of Article 81 of the EC Treaty to horizontal cooperation agreements." See Official Journal C 3/02, 6.1.2001. These guidelines cover agreements on research and development, production, marketing, purchasing, standardization, and environmental matters. The introductory section describes the purpose and scope of the guidelines. It is followed by a discussion of the basic principles for the assessment of these kinds of arrangements first under Article 81(1) (which prohibits agreements with the object or effect of preventing, restricting, or distorting competition) and then under Article 81(3) (which allows for exemptions of agreements with potentially beneficial effects). Particular attention is paid to the way in which market power and market structure are analyzed and how economic benefits are assessed. After this initial section, the remainder of the guidelines are devoted to more particular discussion of different kinds of agreements, with brief case examples that are analyzed.

PROBLEM 7

JOINT RESEARCH AND PRODUCTION OF CHEMICAL RESEARCH ASSOCIATES

In order to counter the research laboratories of larger chemical companies, seven small manufacturers of industrial chemicals formed Chemical Research Associates, a partnership. Each of the seven manufacturers contributed $100,000 in cash and agreed to furnish up to $15,000 per year to meet the partnership's expenses. Chemical Research began by studying the techniques of the member corporations. After its study was complete, it took the following actions: (1) it recommended adoption of desirable techniques being used by some but not all of the seven constituent companies; (2) it recommended adoption of new techniques discovered by its own research, patenting them where appropriate and otherwise maintaining them as trade secrets; and (3) it licensed to members for a fee (and sometimes to non-members) major improvements which would not redound to the benefit of all constituent corporations equally. One such improvement, made available only to members, involved a secret manufacturing process that greatly reduced costs of a major product, Zap, produced by all the participating companies and most smaller producers.

Satisfied with Phase I of Chemical Research's work, the member companies met and decided that they would expand their cooperation to joint production of Zap. In order to organize the Zap production optimally, all the members agreed to produce Zap only through Chemical Research. They continued to compete as before on all other products that they manufactured, and each company marketed Zap independently.

There were four other small chemical manufacturers of about the same size as the seven above. One of these, Bluster, sought to participate in the Chemical Research venture and offered to pay its pro rata share of capital contribution and operating expenses. The offer was declined by Chemical Research and by its seven constituent members. They charged (a) that Bluster was a spy for the large chemical companies; (b) that Bluster was in poor condition financially and could not be relied on to meet its obligations under the arrangement; and (c) that some of Bluster's personnel were so untrustworthy that Chemical Research's trade secrets would not be safe with them. Bluster replied that the obvious reason for its exclusion was its record as a price-cutter. Furthermore, even though not admitted, Bluster sought a license at a reasonable royalty for the new secret process and admission to the joint production consortium.

Can Bluster obtain relief under the antitrust laws if the contentions of the Chemical Research group are accepted? What if Bluster is right as to the basis for exclusion?

SECTION 3. GOVERNMENT ACTION

A. EFFORTS TO INFLUENCE GOVERNMENT

Eastern Railroad Presidents Conference v. Noerr Motor Freight Co.

Supreme Court of the United States, 1961.
365 U.S. 127, 81 S.Ct. 523, 5 L.Ed.2d 464.

■ BLACK, J. American railroads have always largely depended upon income from the long-distance transportation of heavy freight for economic surviv-al. During the early years of their existence, they had virtually no competi-tion in this aspect of their business, but, as early as the 1920s, the growth of the trucking industry in this country began to bring about changes in this situation. For the truckers found, just as the railroads had learned earlier, that a very profitable part of the transportation business was the long hauling of heavy freight. As the trucking industry became more and more powerful, the competition between it and the railroads for this business became increasingly intense until, during the period following the conclusion of World War II, at least the railroads, if not both of the competing groups, came to view the struggle as one of economic life or death for their method of transportation. The present litigation is an outgrowth of one part of that struggle.

The case was commenced by a complaint filed in the United States District Court in Pennsylvania on behalf of 41 Pennsylvania truck opera-tors and their trade association, the Pennsylvania Motor Truck Association. This complaint, which named as defendants 24 Eastern railroads, an association of the presidents of those railroads known as the Eastern Railroad Presidents Conference, and a public relations firm, Carl Byoir & Associates, Inc., charged that the defendants had conspired to restrain trade in and monopolize the long-distance freight business in violation of §§ 1 and 2 of the Sherman Act. The gist of the conspiracy alleged was that the railroads had engaged Byoir to conduct a publicity campaign against the truckers designed to foster the adoption and retention of laws and law enforcement practices destructive of the trucking business, to create an atmosphere of distaste for the truckers among the general public, and to impair the relationships existing between the truckers and their customers. The campaign so conducted was described in the complaint as "vicious, corrupt, and fraudulent," first, in that the sole motivation behind it was the desire on the part of the railroads to injure the truckers and eventually to destroy them as competitors in the long-distance freight business, and, secondly, in that the defendants utilized the so-called third-party technique, that is, the publicity matter circulated in the campaign was made to appear as spontaneously expressed views of independent persons and civic groups when, in fact, it was largely prepared and produced by Byoir and paid for by the railroads. The complaint then went on to supplement these more or less general allegations with specific charges as to particular instances in which the railroads had attempted to influence legislation by means of their publicity campaign. One of several such charges was that the defendants had succeeded in persuading the Governor of Pennsylvania to veto a measure known as the "Fair Truck Bill," which would have permitted truckers to carry heavier loads over Pennsylvania roads.

The prayer of the complaint was for treble damages under § 4 of the Clayton Act and an injunction restraining the defendants from further acts in pursuance of the conspiracy. Insofar as the prayer for damages was concerned, a stipulation was entered that the only damages suffered by the individual truck operators was the loss of business that resulted from the veto of the "Fair Truck Bill" by the Governor of Pennsylvania, and accordingly the claim for damages was limited to an amount based upon the loss of profits as a result of this veto plus the expenses incurred by the truckers' trade association for the purpose of combatting the railroads' publicity campaign. The prayer for injunctive relief was much broader, however, asking that the defendants be restrained from disseminating any disparaging information about the truckers without disclosing railroad participation, from attempting to exert any pressure upon the legislature or Governor of Pennsylvania through the medium of front organizations, from paying any private or public organizations to propagate the arguments of the railroads against the truckers or their business, and from doing "any other act or thing to further ... the objects and purposes" of the conspiracy.

In their answer to this complaint, the railroads admitted that they had conducted a publicity campaign designed to influence the passage of state laws relating to truck weight limits and tax rates on heavy trucks, and to encourage a more rigid enforcement of state laws penalizing trucks for overweight loads and other traffic violations, but they denied that their campaign was motivated either by a desire to destroy the trucking business as a competitor or to interfere with the relationships between the truckers and their customers. Rather, they insisted, the campaign was conducted in furtherance of their rights "to inform the public and the legislatures of the several states of the truth with regard to the enormous damage done to the roads by the operators of heavy and especially of overweight trucks, with regard to their repeated and deliberate violations of the law limiting the weight and speed of big trucks, with regard to their failure to pay their fair share of the cost of constructing, maintaining and repairing the roads, and with regard to the driving hazards they create.... Such a campaign, the defendants maintained, did not constitute a violation of the Sherman Act, presumably because that Act could not properly be interpreted to apply either to restraints of trade or monopolizations that result from the passage or enforcement of laws or to efforts of individuals to bring about the passage or enforcement of the laws."[29]

Subsequently, defendants broadened the scope of the litigation by filing a counterclaim in which they charged that the truckers had themselves violated §§ 1 and 2 of the Sherman Act by conspiring to destroy the railroads' competition in the long-distance freight business and to monopolize that business for heavy trucks. The means of the conspiracy alleged in the counterclaim were much the same as those with which the truckers had charged the railroads in the original complaint, including allegations of the conduct of a malicious publicity campaign designed to destroy the railroads' business by law, to create an atmosphere hostile to the railroads among the general public, and to interfere with relationships existing between the railroads and their customers. The prayer for relief of the counterclaim, like that of the truckers' original complaint, was for treble damages and an injunction restraining continuance of the allegedly unlawful practices. In their reply to this counterclaim, the truckers denied each of the allegations that charged a violation of the Sherman Act and, in addition, interposed a number of affirmative defenses, none of which are relevant here.

In this posture, the case went to trial. After hearings, the trial court entered a judgment, based upon extensive findings of fact and conclusions of law, that the railroads' publicity campaign had violated the Sherman Act while that of the truckers had not. In reaching this conclusion, the trial court expressly disclaimed any purpose to condemn as illegal mere efforts on the part of the railroads to influence the passage of new legislation or the enforcement of existing law. Instead, it rested its judgment upon findings, first, that the railroads' publicity campaign, insofar as it was actually directed at lawmaking and law enforcement authorities, was malicious and fraudulent—malicious in that its only purpose was to destroy the truckers as competitors, and fraudulent in that it was predicated upon the deceiving of those authorities through the use of the third-party technique; and, secondly, that the railroads' campaign also had as an important, if not overriding, purpose the destruction of the truckers' goodwill, among both the general public and the truckers' existing customers, and thus injured the truckers in ways unrelated to the passage or enforcement of law. In line with its theory that restraints of trade and monopolizations resulting from valid laws are not actionable under the Sherman Act, however, the trial

---

29. The answer to the truckers' complaint also interposed a number of other defenses, including the contention that the activities complained of were constitutionally protected under the First Amendment and the contention that the truckers were barred from prosecuting this suit by reason of the fact that they had themselves engaged in conduct identical to that about which they were complaining with regard to the railroads and were thus *in pari delicto*. Because of the view we take of the proper construction of the Sherman Act, we find it unnecessary to consider any of these other defenses.

court awarded only nominal damages to the individual truckers, holding that no damages were recoverable for loss of business due to the veto of the Pennsylvania "Fair Truck Bill." The judgment did, however, award substantial damages to the truckers' trade association as well as the broad injunction asked for in the complaint.[30]

The conclusion that the truckers' publicity campaign had not violated the Sherman Act was reached despite findings that the truckers also had engaged in a publicity campaign designed to influence legislation, as charged in the counterclaim, and despite findings that the truckers had utilized the third-party technique in this campaign. Resting largely upon the fact that the efforts of the truckers were directed, at least for the most part, at trying to get legislation passed that was beneficial to them rather than harmful to the railroads, the trial court found that the truckers' campaign was purely defensive in purpose and concluded that the truckers' campaign differed from that of the railroads in that the truckers were not trying to destroy a competitor. Accordingly, it held that the truckers' campaign, though technically in restraint of trade, was well within the rule of reason which governs the interpretation of §§ 1 and 2 of the Sherman Act and consequently dismissed the counterclaim. . . .

We accept, as the starting point for our consideration of the case, the same basic construction of the Sherman Act adopted . . . below—that no violation of the Act can be predicated upon mere attempts to influence the passage or enforcement of laws. It has been recognized, at least since the landmark decision of this Court in Standard Oil Co. v. United States, that the Sherman Act forbids only those trade restraints and monopolizations that are created, or attempted, by the acts of "individuals or combinations of individuals or corporations." [221 U.S. 1, 57] Accordingly, it has been held that where a restraint upon trade or monopolization is the result of valid governmental action, as opposed to private action, no violation of the Act can be made out.[31] These decisions rest upon the fact that under our form of government the question whether a law of that kind should pass, or if passed be enforced, is the responsibility of the appropriate legislative or executive branch of government so long as the law itself does not violate some provision of the Constitution.

We think it equally clear that the Sherman Act does not prohibit two or more persons from associating together in an attempt to persuade the legislature or the executive to take particular action with respect to a law that would produce a restraint or a monopoly. Although such associations could perhaps, through a process of expansive construction, be brought within the general proscription of "combination[s] . . . in restraint of trade," they bear very little if any resemblance to the combinations normally held violative of the Sherman Act, combinations ordinarily char-

---

30. If anything, the injunction was even broader than had been requested in the complaint for it effectively enjoined the defendants from any publicity activities against the truckers whether or not the third-party technique was used. See 166 F.Supp., at 172–173.

31. United States v. Rock Royal Co-op., 307 U.S. 533; Parker v. Brown, 317 U.S. 341.

acterized by an express or implied agreement or understanding that the participants will jointly give up their trade freedom, or help one another to take away the trade freedom of others through the use of such devices as price-fixing agreements, boycotts, market-division agreements, and other similar arrangements.[32] This essential dissimilarity between an agreement jointly to seek legislation or law enforcement and the agreements traditionally condemned by § 1 of the Act, even if not itself conclusive on the question of the applicability of the Act, does constitute a warning against treating the defendants' conduct as though it amounted to a common-law trade restraint. And we do think that the question is conclusively settled, against the application of the Act, when this factor of essential dissimilarity is considered along with the other difficulties that would be presented by a holding that the Sherman Act forbids associations for the purpose of influencing the passage or enforcement of laws.

In the first place, such a holding would substantially impair the power of government to take actions through its legislature and executive that operate to restrain trade. In a representative democracy such as this, these branches of government act on behalf of the people and, to a very large extent, the whole concept of representation depends upon the ability of the people to make their wishes known to their representatives. To hold that the government retains the power to act in this representative capacity and yet hold, at the same time, that the people cannot freely inform the government of their wishes would impute to the Sherman Act a purpose to regulate, not business activity, but political activity, a purpose which would have no basis whatever in the legislative history of that Act. Secondly, and of at least equal significance, such a construction of the Sherman Act would raise important constitutional questions. The right of petition is one of the freedoms protected by the Bill of Rights, and we cannot, of course, lightly impute to Congress an intent to invade these freedoms. Indeed, such an imputation would be particularly unjustified in this case in view of all the countervailing considerations enumerated above. For these reasons, we think it clear that the Sherman Act does not apply to the activities of the railroads at least insofar as those activities comprised mere solicitation of governmental action with respect to the passage and enforcement of laws. We are thus called upon to consider whether the courts below were correct in holding that, notwithstanding this principle, the Act was violated here because of the presence in the railroads' publicity campaign of additional factors sufficient to take the case out of the area in which the principle is controlling.

The first such factor relied upon was the fact, established by the finding of the District Court, that the railroads' sole purpose in seeking to influence the passage and enforcement of laws was to destroy the truckers as competitors for the long-distance freight business. But we do not see how this fact, even if adequately supported in the record, could transform conduct otherwise lawful into a violation of the Sherman Act. All of the considerations that have led us to the conclusion that the Act does not

---

32.   See Apex Hosiery Co. v. Leader, 310 U.S. 469, 491–493.

apply to mere group solicitation of governmental action are equally applicable in spite of the addition of this factor. The right of the people to inform their representatives in government of their desires with respect to the passage or enforcement of laws cannot properly be made to depend upon their intent in doing so. It is neither unusual nor illegal for people to seek action on laws in the hope that they may bring about an advantage to themselves and a disadvantage to their competitors. This Court has expressly recognized this fact in its opinion in United States v. Rock Royal Co-op., where it was said: "If ulterior motives of corporate aggrandizement stimulated their activities, their efforts were not thereby rendered unlawful." If the Act and Order are otherwise valid, the fact that their effect would be to give cooperatives a monopoly of the market would not violate the Sherman Act. . . .[33] Indeed, it is quite probably people with just such a hope of personal advantage who provide much of the information upon which governments must act. A construction of the Sherman Act that would disqualify people from taking a public position on matters in which they are financially interested would thus deprive the government of a valuable source of information and, at the same time, deprive the people of their right to petition in the very instances in which that right may be of the most importance to them. We reject such a construction of the Act and hold that, at least insofar as the railroads' campaign was directed toward obtaining governmental action, its legality was not at all affected by any anticompetitive purpose it may have had.

The second factor relied upon by the courts below to justify the application of the Sherman Act to the railroads' publicity campaign was the use in the campaign of the so-called third-party technique. The theory under which this factor was related to the proscriptions of the Sherman Act, though not entirely clear from any of the opinions below, was apparently that it involved unethical business conduct on the part of the railroads. As pointed out above, the third-party technique, which was aptly characterized by the District Court as involving "deception of the public, manufacture of bogus sources of reference, [and] distortion of public sources of information," depends upon giving propaganda actually circulated by a party in interest the appearance of being spontaneous declarations of independent groups. We can certainly agree with the courts below that this technique, though in widespread use among practitioners of the art of public relations, is one which falls far short of the ethical standards generally approved in this country. It does not follow, however, that the use of the technique in a publicity campaign designed to influence governmental action constitutes a violation of the Sherman Act. Insofar as that Act sets up a code of ethics at all, it is a code that condemns trade restraints, not political activity, and, as we have already pointed out, a publicity campaign to influence governmental action falls clearly into the category of political activity. The proscriptions of the Act, tailored as they are for the business world, are not at all appropriate for application in the political arena. Congress has traditionally exercised extreme caution in legislating

33. 307 U.S. 533, 560.

with respect to problems relating to the conduct of political activities, a caution which has been reflected in the decisions of this Court interpreting such legislation. All of this caution would go for naught if we permitted an extension of the Sherman Act to regulate activities of that nature simply because those activities have a commercial impact and involve conduct that can be termed unethical.

Moreover, we think the courts below themselves recognized this fact to some extent for their disposition of the case is inconsistent with the position that the use of the third-party technique alone could constitute a violation of the Sherman Act. This much is apparent from the fact that the railroads' counterclaim against the truckers was not allowed. Since it is undisputed that the truckers were as guilty as the railroads of the use of the technique, this factor could not have been in any sense controlling of the holding against the railroads. Rather, it appears to have been relied upon primarily as an indication of the vicious nature of the campaign against the truckers. But whatever its purpose, we have come to the conclusion that the reliance of the lower courts upon this factor was misplaced and that the railroads' use of the third-party technique was, so far as the Sherman Act is concerned, legally irrelevant.

In addition to the foregoing factors, both of which relate to the intent and methods of the railroads in seeking governmental action, the courts below rested their holding that the Sherman Act had been violated upon a finding that the purpose of the railroads was "more than merely an attempt to obtain legislation. *It was the purpose and intent . . . to hurt the truckers in every way possible even though they secured no legislation.*" (Emphasis in original.) Specifically, the District Court found that the purpose of the railroads was to destroy the goodwill of the truckers among the public generally and among the truckers' customers particularly, in the hope that by doing so the over-all competitive position of the truckers would be weakened, and that the railroads were successful in these efforts to the extent that such injury was actually inflicted. The apparent effect of these findings is to take this case out of the category of those that involve restraints through governmental action and thus render inapplicable the principles announced above. But this effect is only apparent and cannot stand under close scrutiny. There are no specific findings that the railroads attempted directly to persuade anyone not to deal with the truckers. Moreover, all of the evidence in the record, both oral and documentary, deals with the railroads' efforts to influence the passage and enforcement of laws. Circulars, speeches, newspaper articles, editorials, magazine articles, memoranda and all other documents discuss in one way or another the railroads' charges that heavy trucks injure the roads, violate the laws and create traffic hazards, and urge that truckers should be forced to pay a fair share of the costs of rebuilding the roads, that they should be compelled to obey the laws, and that limits should be placed upon the weight of the loads they are permitted to carry. In the light of this, the findings of the District Court that the railroads' campaign was intended to and did in fact injure the truckers in their relationships with the public and with their customers can mean no more than that the truckers sustained some direct injury as an incidental effect of the railroads' campaign to influence governmental action and that the railroads were hopeful that this might happen.[34] Thus, the issue presented by the lower courts' conclusion of a violation of the Sherman Act on the basis of this injury is no different than the issue presented by the factors already discussed. It is inevitable, whenever an attempt is made to influence legislation by a campaign of publicity, that an incidental effect of that campaign may be the infliction of some direct injury upon the interests of the party against whom the campaign is directed. And it seems equally inevitable that those conducting the campaign would be aware of, and possibly even pleased by, the prospect of such injury. To hold that the knowing infliction of such injury renders the campaign itself illegal would thus be tantamount to outlawing all such campaigns. We have already discussed the reasons which have led us to the conclusion that this has not been done by anything in the Sherman Act.

There may be situations in which a publicity campaign, ostensibly directed toward influencing governmental action, is a mere sham to cover what is actually nothing more than an attempt to interfere directly with the business relationships of a competitor and the application of the Sherman Act would be justified. But this certainly is not the case here. No one denies that the railroads were making a genuine effort to influence legislation and law enforcement practices. Indeed, if the version of the facts set forth in the truckers' complaint is fully credited, as it was by the courts below, that effort was not only genuine but also highly successful. Under these circumstances, we conclude that no attempt to interfere with business relationships in a manner proscribed by the Sherman Act is involved in this case.

In rejecting each of the grounds relied upon by the courts below to justify application of the Sherman Act to the campaign of the railroads, we have rejected the very grounds upon which those courts relied to distinguish the campaign conducted by the truckers. In doing so, we have restored what appears to be the true nature of the case—a "no-holds-barred fight" between two industries both of which are seeking control of a profitable source of income. Inherent in such fights, which are commonplace in the halls of legislative bodies, is the possibility, and in many instances even the probability, that one group or the other will get hurt by the arguments that are made. In this particular instance, each group appears to have utilized all the political powers it could muster in an attempt to bring about the passage of laws that would help it or injure the other. But the contest itself appears to have been conducted along lines

34. Here again, the petitioners have leveled a vigorous attack upon the trial court's findings. As a part of this attack, they urge that there is no basis in reason for the finding that some shippers quit doing business with the truckers as a result of the railroads' publicity campaign. Their contention is that since the theme of the campaign was that the truckers had an unfair competitive advantage and could consequently charge unfairly low prices, the campaign would have encouraged, rather than discouraged, shippers who availed themselves of the truckers' services. This argument has considerable appeal but, as before, we find it unnecessary to pass upon the validity of these findings for we think the conclusion must be the same whether they are allowed to stand or not.

normally accepted in our political system, except to the extent that each group has deliberately deceived the public and public officials. And that deception, reprehensible as it is, can be of no consequence so far as the Sherman Act is concerned. . . .

Reversed.

———

CALIFORNIA MOTOR TRANSPORT CO. v. TRUCKING UNLIMITED, 404 U.S. 508, 92 S.Ct. 609, 30 L.Ed.2d 642 (1972). A group of highway truckers sued another group of highway carriers seeking injunctive relief and damages, and charged that they had conspired to institute actions and federal agency proceedings to delay and defeat applications for operating rights. Defendants claimed that their resort to administrative agencies was protected by *Noerr.*

The Court began by observing that while *Noerr* involved attempts to influence passage of laws before the legislative branch and enforcement by the executive, "the same philosophy governs the approach of citizens or groups of them to administrative agencies . . . and to courts . . ." Emphasizing the "mere sham" exception in *Noerr,* however, the Court asserted that actions were not protected when designed "to harass and deter respondents in their use of administrative and judicial proceedings." Thus, defendants in this case were not seeking to influence public officials but rather "to bar their competitors from meaningful access to adjudicatory tribunals and to usurp that decision-making process."

After observing that the political campaign in *Noerr* employed deception and misrepresentation and used unethical tactics, the Court noted:

Yet unethical conduct in the setting of the adjudicatory process often results in sanctions. Perjury of witnesses is one example. Use of a patent obtained by fraud to exclude a competitor from the market may involve a violation of the antitrust laws, as we held in Walker Process Equipment Inc. v. Food Machinery & Chemical Corp. . . . Conspiracy with a licensing authority to eliminate a competitor may also result in an antitrust transgression. Continental Ore Co. v. Union Carbide & Carbite Corp. . . . Similarly, bribery of a public purchasing agent may constitute a violation of Section 2(c) of the Clayton Act as amended by the Robinson–Patman Act. . . .

There are many other forms of illegal and reprehensible practices which may corrupt the administrative or judicial processes and which may result in antitrust violations. Misrepresentations, condoned in the political arena, are not immunized when used in the adjudicatory process. Opponents before agencies or courts often think poorly of the other's tactics, motions, or defenses and may readily call them baseless. One claim, which a court or agency may think baseless, may go unnoticed; but a pattern of baseless repetitive claims may emerge which leads the fact finder to conclude that the administrative and judicial processes have been abused.

The Court concluded that a combination "to harass and deter" competitors from access to agencies and courts could not be protected under the First Amendment.

NOTES AND QUESTIONS

1. What is the import of Justice Black's remarks in *Noerr* that the exemption from Sherman Act coverage will not apply if a campaign is a mere "sham" to cover an attempt "to interfere directly with the business relationships of a competitor...." Would the sham exception permit a court to take into account the very factors considered irrelevant in *Noerr*?

2. Assuming the truth of information submitted is irrelevant in deciding whether the *Noerr* doctrine applies, should it follow that the means of communicating information is also an irrelevant factor? Note that the "third-party technique" discussed in *Noerr* arguably only serves to confuse proper lines of communication between government officials and the public and yet the court in *Noerr* apparently did not regard that as important in reaching its decision.

3. In WOODS EXPLORATION AND PRODUCING CO. v. ALUMINUM CO. OF AMERICA, 438 F.2d 1286 (5th Cir.1971), the *Noerr* doctrine was held inapplicable where competitive injury occurred because of false production forecasts filed by defendants with the Texas Railroad Commission, which allegedly led the Commission to reduce plaintiffs' allowable production. The earlier case of Okefenokee Rural Electric Membership Corp. v. Florida Power & Light Co., 214 F.2d 413 (5th Cir.1954), was distinguished on grounds that the defendants there may have submitted exaggerated and misleading arguments to a state regulatory agency, but submitted no false factual data.

4. In MISSOURI v. NATIONAL ORGANIZATION FOR WOMEN, 620 F.2d 1301 (8th Cir.), cert. denied, 449 U.S. 842 (1980) the National Organization for Women (NOW) organized a convention boycott against all states that had not ratified the proposed Equal Rights Amendment (ERA). The state of Missouri sought an injunction claiming that its economy, and specifically Missouri motels and restaurants, were suffering revenue losses. The District Court denied relief and the Court of Appeals affirmed. Relying on *Noerr,* the Court noted that the boycott was an attempt to influence ratification by the Missouri legislature of the proposed ERA. With respect to the argument that the injury to economic interests in Missouri did not result from legislation, but rather as a direct consequence of the boycott designed to achieve that legislation, the Court concluded that was an incidental effect of NOW's campaign to influence government action. The Court appeared to be influenced by the fact that the legislation sought had social or political rather than commercial goals, and that the members of NOW were not competitors or potential competitors of the victims of the boycott.

5. *California Motor Transport's* approach to the *Noerr* doctrine's "sham" exception raises the issue of whether litigation must be repetitive before it becomes a "sham?" Can a single lawsuit ever be a "sham?" See Vendo Co. v. Lektro-Vend Corp., 433 U.S. 623, 644 (1977) (Blackmun, J., concurring in result). See also Fischel, Antitrust Liability for Attempts to Influence Government Action: The Basis and Limits of the Noerr–Pennington Doctrine, 45 U.Chi.L.Rev. 80 (1977).

   a. In OTTER TAIL POWER CO. v. UNITED STATES, 410 U.S. 366 (1973), p. 735 infra, plaintiff alleged that Otter Tail, an electric utility company, had sponsored litigation against certain municipal electric systems, in part to hamper the marketing of necessary bonds to finance municipal systems. The Supreme Court remanded for consideration in light of *California Motor Transport,* and the District Court found that repetitive litigation was designed to prevent establishment of competitive systems and therefore fell within the "sham" exception. United States v. Otter Tail

Power Co., 360 F.Supp. 451 (D.Minn.1973), affirmed per curiam, 417 U.S. 901 (1974).

b. In MCI COMMUNICATIONS CORP. v. AT & T CO., 708 F.2d 1081 (7th Cir.), cert. denied, 464 U.S. 891 (1983), the Seventh Circuit held that the filing of tariffs with numerous state utilities commissions, while defendant believed or knew that the state commissions lacked jurisdiction to approve them (by reason of exclusive FCC jurisdiction), provided a strong basis for a claim of "sham." The Court quoted with approval the view that "the requisite motive for the sham exception is the intent to harm one's competitors not by the *result* of the litigation, but by the simple fact of the *institution* of the litigation," citing Gainesville v. Florida Power & Light Co., 488 F.Supp. 1258 (S.D.Fla.1980). AT & T's filings were found to have injured MCI by (1) imposing litigation costs in 49 different forums, (2) increasing the risk of disruption of MCI's plans if even only one commission were to take jurisdiction, and (3) adding additional months of costly delay in MCI's efforts to implement its plans.

c. In CLIPPER EXXPRESS v. ROCKY MOUNTAIN MOTOR TARIFF BUREAU, INC., 674 F.2d 1252 (9th Cir.1982), cert. denied, 459 U.S. 1227 (1983), plaintiff alleged that defendant trucking companies violated the Sherman Act by conspiring to prosecute deliberate false protests before the ICC, against plaintiff's lower rate tariffs, to enforce and protect their illegal price fixing and customer allocations. The District Court granted summary judgment for defendants on grounds, among others, that the ICC protests were protected under *Noerr,* but the Ninth Circuit reversed. The language of *California Motor Transport* was held to make it clear that multiple suits or protests were not required to support a claim of "sham"; in any event, defendants here had allegedly agreed to protest all plaintiff's tariff modifications without regard to their merit, during the course of a single ICC proceeding. "Abuse of administration process may injure competition by something less than complete blockage of access—as here, by delaying effectiveness of new rates, imposing litigation costs, or by injuring relationships with customers."

Is it a sensible policy to subject parties seeking relief in court to antitrust liabilities (including possible treble damages) if it turns out that the lawsuit was lacking in merit? Is this an undue burden on the right to seek redress in court?

d. IN RE BURLINGTON NORTHERN INC., 822 F.2d 518 (5th Cir.1987), grew out of Energy Transportation System, Inc.'s unsuccessful attempt to build a coal slurry pipeline from Wyoming to Arkansas. ETSI claimed that a host of railroads conspired to prevent ETSI from completing the project and brought an antitrust claim against them. In particular, ETSI complained about two groups of lawsuits. The first group of lawsuits, the Andrews litigation, were brought by various railroads to void a contract between the United States Department of the Interior and ETSI for water for the pipeline. The second group of lawsuits, the Windows litigation, arose from ETSI's attempt to secure rights to cross the railroads' rights of way. ETSI wanted to show that both groups of lawsuits were shams and tried to obtain documents prepared in connection with the allegedly sham litigation. The district court allowed ETSI to proceed with its discovery.

The railroads petitioned the Fifth Circuit for mandamus to block the discovery. They claimed the protection of the Noerr–Pennington doctrine for their litigation efforts. They argued that a finding of sham was precluded because they had been partially successful in one lawsuit, the Andrews litigation, and defendants in the other, the Windows litigation. The Fifth Circuit rejected both arguments. It held that partial success on the merits is no substitute for the Noerr–Pennington inquiry into the antitrust defendant's reasons for bringing the underlying lawsuit. It also held that a defendant's conduct in a suit might be proved a sham for Noerr–

Pennington purposes. The court, however, did find error in the district court's decision to allow discovery to proceed without first considering whether the railroads' litigation efforts had been driven by a genuine desire for judicial relief.

Allied Tube & Conduit Corp. v. Indian Head, Inc.

Supreme Court of the United States, 1988.
486 U.S. 492, 108 S.Ct. 1931, 100 L.Ed.2d 497.

■ BRENNAN, J. Petitioner contends that its efforts to affect the product standard-setting process of a private association are immune from antitrust liability under the *Noerr* doctrine primarily because the association's standards are widely adopted into law by state and local governments. Eastern Railroad Presidents Conference v. Noerr Motor Freight, Inc., 365 U.S. 127 (1961). The United States Court of Appeals for the Second Circuit held that *Noerr* immunity did not apply. We affirm.

I

The National Fire Protection Association (Association) is a private, voluntary organization with more than 31,500 individual and group members representing industry, labor, academia, insurers, organized medicine, firefighters, and government. The Association, among other things, publishes product standards and codes related to fire protection through a process known as "consensus standard making." One of the codes it publishes is the National Electrical Code, which establishes product and performance requirements for the design and installation of electrical wiring systems. Revised every three years, the National Electric Code (Code) is the most influential electrical code in the nation. A substantial number of state and local governments routinely adopt the Code into law with little or no change; private certification laboratories, such as Underwriters Laboratories, normally will not list and label an electrical product that does not meet Code standards; many underwriters will refuse to insure structures that are not built in conformity with the Code; and many electrical inspectors, contractors, and distributors will not use a product that falls outside the Code.

Among the electrical products covered by the Code is electrical conduit, the hollow tubing used as a raceway to carry electrical wires through the walls and floors of buildings. Throughout the relevant period, the Code permitted using electrical conduit made of steel, and almost all conduit sold was in fact steel conduit. Starting in 1980, respondent began to offer plastic conduit made of polyvinyl chloride. Respondent claims its plastic conduit offers significant competitive advantages over steel conduit, including pliability, lower installed cost, and lower susceptibility to short circuiting. In 1980, however, there was also a scientific basis for concern that, during fires in high-rise buildings, polyvinyl chloride conduit might burn and emit toxic fumes.

Respondent initiated a proposal to include polyvinyl chloride conduit as an approved type of electrical conduit in the 1981 edition of the Code.

Following approval by one of the Association's professional panels, this proposal was scheduled for consideration at the 1980 annual meeting, where it could be adopted or rejected by a simple majority of the members present. Alarmed that, if approved, respondent's product might pose a competitive threat to steel conduit, petitioner, the nation's largest producer of steel conduit, met to plan strategy with, among others, members of the steel industry, other steel conduit manufacturers, and its independent sales agents. They collectively agreed to exclude respondent's product from the 1981 Code by packing the upcoming annual meeting with new Association members whose only function would be to vote against the polyvinyl chloride proposal.

Combined, the steel interests recruited 230 persons to join the Association and to attend the annual meeting to vote against the proposal. Petitioner alone recruited 155 persons—including employees, executives, sales agents, the agents' employees, employees from two divisions that did not sell electrical products, and the wife of a national sales director. Petitioner and the other steel interests also paid over $100,000 for the membership, registration, and attendance expenses of these voters. At the annual meeting, the steel group voters were instructed where to sit and how and when to vote by group leaders who used walkie-talkies and hand signals to facilitate communication. Few of the steel group voters had any of the technical documentation necessary to follow the meeting. None of them spoke at the meeting to give their reasons for opposing the proposal to approve polyvinyl chloride conduit. Nonetheless, with their solid vote in opposition, the proposal was rejected and returned to committee by a vote of 394 to 390. Respondent appealed the membership's vote to the Association's Board of Directors, but the Board denied the appeal on the ground that, although the Association's rules had been circumvented, they had not been violated.[35]

In October 1981, respondent brought this suit in Federal District Court, alleging that petitioner and others had unreasonably restrained trade in the electrical conduit market in violation of § 1 of the Sherman Act. A bifurcated jury trial began in March 1985. Petitioner conceded that it had conspired with the other steel interests to exclude respondent's product from the Code and that it had a pecuniary interest to do so. The jury, instructed under the rule of reason that respondent carried the burden of showing that the anticompetitive effects of petitioner's actions outweighed any procompetitive benefits of standard setting, found petitioner liable. In answers to special interrogatories, the jury found that petitioner did not violate any rules of the Association and acted, at least in part, based on a genuine belief that plastic conduit was unsafe, but that petitioner nonetheless did "subvert" the consensus standard making process of the Association. The jury also made special findings that petitioner's actions

---

35. Respondent also sought a tentative interim amendment to the Code, but that was denied on the ground that there was not sufficient exigency to merit an interim amendment. The Association subsequently approved use of polyvinyl chloride conduit for buildings of less than four stories in the 1984 Code, and for all buildings in the 1987 Code.

had an adverse impact on competition, were not the least restrictive means of expressing petitioner's opposition to the use of polyvinyl chloride conduit in the marketplace, and unreasonably restrained trade in violation of the antitrust laws. The jury then awarded respondent damages, to be trebled, of $3.8 million for lost profits resulting from the effect that excluding polyvinyl chloride conduit from the 1981 Code had of its own force in the marketplace. No damages were awarded for injuries stemming from the adoption of the 1981 Code by governmental entities.[36]

The District Court then granted a judgment n.o.v. for petitioner, reasoning that *Noerr* immunity applied because the Association was "akin to a legislature" and because petitioner, "by the use of methods consistent with acceptable standards of political action, genuinely intended to influence the [Association] with respect to the National Electrical Code, and to thereby influence the various state and local legislative bodies which adopt the [Code]." The Court of Appeals reversed, rejecting both the argument that the Association should be treated as a "quasi-legislative" body because legislatures routinely adopt the Code and the argument that efforts to influence the Code were immune under *Noerr* as indirect attempts to influence state and local governments. 817 F.2d 938 (C.A.2 1987). We granted certiorari to address important issues regarding the application of *Noerr* immunity to private standard-setting associations.

II

Concerted efforts to restrain or monopolize trade by petitioning government officials are protected from antitrust liability under the doctrine established by *Noerr*, 365 U.S. 127 (1961); Mine Workers v. Pennington, 381 U.S. 657, 669–672 (1965); and California Motor Transport Co. v. Trucking Unlimited, 404 U.S. 508 (1972). The scope of this protection depends, however, on the source, context, and nature of the anticompetitive restraint at issue. "[W]here a restraint upon trade or monopolization is the result of valid governmental action, as opposed to private action," those urging the governmental action enjoy absolute immunity from antitrust liability for the anticompetitive restraint. *Noerr*, supra, at 136; see also *Pennington*, supra, at 671. In addition, where, independent of any government action, the anticompetitive restraint results directly from private action, the restraint cannot form the basis for antitrust liability if it is "incidental" to a valid effort to influence governmental action. *Noerr*, supra, at 365 U.S. at 143. The validity of such efforts, and thus the

---

36. Although the District Court was of the view that at trial respondent relied solely on the theory that its injury "flowed from legislative action," the Court of Appeals determined that respondent was awarded damages only on the theory "that the stigma of not obtaining [Code] approval of its products and [petitioner's] 'marketing' of that stigma caused independent marketplace harm to [respondent] in those jurisdictions permitting use of [polyvinyl chloride] conduit, as well as those which later adopted the 1984 [Code], which permitted use of [polyvinyl chloride] conduit in buildings less than three stories high. [Respondent] did not seek redress for any injury arising from the adopting of the [Code] by the various governments." 817 F.2d 938, 941, n. 3 (1987) (emphasis added). We decide the case as it was framed by the Court of Appeals.

applicability of *Noerr* immunity, varies with the context and nature of the activity. A publicity campaign directed at the general public, seeking legislation or executive action, enjoys antitrust immunity even when the campaign employs unethical and deceptive methods. *Noerr, supra,* 365 U.S. at 140–41. But in less political arenas, unethical and deceptive practices can constitute abuses of administrative or judicial processes that may result in antitrust violations.[37] *California Motor Transport, supra,* 404 U.S. at 512–13.

In this case, the restraint of trade on which liability was predicated was the Association's exclusion of respondent's product from the Code, and no damages were imposed for the incorporation of that Code by any government. The relevant context is thus the standard-setting process of a private association. Typically, private standard-setting associations, like the Association in this case, include members having horizontal and vertical business relations. See generally 7 P. Areeda, Antitrust Law ¶ 1477, p. 343 (1986) (trade and standard-setting associations routinely treated as continuing conspiracies of their members). There is no doubt that the members of such associations often have economic incentives to restrain competition and that the product standards set by such associations have a serious potential for anticompetitive harm.[38] See American Society of Mechanical Engineers, Inc. v. Hydrolevel Corp., 456 U.S. 556, 571 (1982). Agreement on a product standard is, after all, implicitly an agreement not to manufacture, distribute, or purchase certain types of products. Accordingly, private standard-setting associations have traditionally been objects of antitrust scrutiny. *See, e.g.,* ibid.; Radiant Burners, Inc. v. Peoples Gas Light & Coke Co., 364 U.S. 656 (1961). See also FTC v. Indiana Federation of Dentists, 476 U.S. 447 (1986). When, however, private associations promulgate safety standards based on the merits of objective expert judgments and through procedures that prevent the standard-setting process from being biased by members with economic interests in stifling product competition, compare *Hydrolevel* (noting absence of "meaningful safeguards"), those private standards can have significant procompetitive advantages. It is this potential for procompetitive benefits that has led most lower courts to apply rule of reason analysis to product standard-setting by private associations.[39]

37. Of course, in whatever forum, private action that is not genuinely aimed at procuring favorable government action is a mere sham that cannot be deemed a valid effort to influence government action. Noerr, 365 U.S., at 144; California Motor Transport, 404 U.S., at 511.

38. "Product standardization might impair competition in several ways.... [It] might deprive some consumers of a desired product, eliminate quality competition, exclude rival producers, or facilitate oligopolistic pricing by easing rivals' ability to monitor each other's prices." 7 P. Areeda, Antitrust Law ¶ 1503, p. 373 (1986).

39. See 2 J. von Kalinowski, Antitrust Laws and Trade Regulation §§ 6I.01[3], 6I.03, 6I.04, pp. 6I–6 to 6I–7, 6I–18 to 6I–29 (1981) (collecting cases). Concerted efforts to enforce (rather than just agree upon) private product standards face more rigorous antitrust scrutiny. See Radiant Burners, 364 U.S., at 659–660. See also Fashion Originators' Guild of America, Inc. v. FTC, 312 U.S. 457 (1941).

Given this context, petitioner does not enjoy the immunity accorded those who merely urge the government to restrain trade. We agree with the Court of Appeals that the Association cannot be treated as a "quasi-legislative" body simply because legislatures routinely adopt the Code the Association publishes. Whatever *de facto* authority the Association enjoys, no official authority has been conferred on it by any government, and the decisionmaking body of the Association is composed, at least in part, of persons with economic incentives to restrain trade. See Continental Ore Co. v. Union Carbide & Carbon Corp., 370 U.S. 690, 707–708 (1962). See also id., at 706–707; Goldfarb v. Virginia State Bar, 421 U.S. 773, 791–792 (1975). "We may presume, absent a showing to the contrary, that [a government] acts in the public interest. A private party, on the other hand, may be presumed to be acting primarily on his or its own behalf." Hallie v. Eau Claire, 471 U.S. 34, 45 (1985). The dividing line between restraints resulting from governmental action and those resulting from private action may not always be obvious.[40] But where, as here, the restraint is imposed by persons unaccountable to the public and without official authority, many of whom have personal financial interests in restraining competition, we have no difficulty concluding that the restraint has resulted from private action.

Noerr immunity might still apply, however, if, as petitioner argues, the exclusion of polyvinyl chloride conduit from the Code, and the effect that exclusion had of its own force in the marketplace, were incidental to a valid effort to influence governmental action. Petitioner notes that the lion's share of the anticompetitive effect in this case came from the predictable adoption of the Code into law by a large number of state and local governments. Indeed, petitioner argues that, because state and local governments rely so heavily on the Code and lack the resources or technical expertise to second-guess it, efforts to influence the Association's standard-setting process are the most effective means of influencing legislation regulating electrical conduit. This claim to *Noerr* immunity has some force. The effort to influence governmental action in this case certainly cannot be characterized as a sham given the actual adoption of the 1981 Code into a number of statutes and local ordinances. Nor can we quarrel with petitioner's contention that, given the widespread adoption of the Code into law, any effect the 1981 Code had in the marketplace of its own force was, in the main, incidental to petitioner's genuine effort to influence governmental action.[41] And, as petitioner persuasively argues, the claim of *Noerr* immuni-

40. *See, e.g.,* California Motor Transport, 404 U.S., at 513 (stating in dicta that "[c]onspiracy with a licensing authority to eliminate a competitor" or "bribery of a public purchasing agent" may violate the antitrust laws); Mine Workers v. Pennington, 381 U.S. 657, 671, and n. 4 (1965) (holding that immunity applied but noting that the trade restraint at issue "was the act of a public official who is not claimed to be a co-conspirator" and contrasting *Continental Ore*); Continental Ore Co. v. Union Carbide & Carbon Corp., 370 U.S. 690, 707–708 (1962); 1 P. Areeda & D. Turner, Antitrust Law ¶ 206 (1978) (discussing the extent to which Noerr immunity should apply to commercial transactions involving the government). See also Goldfarb v. Virginia State Bar, 421 U.S. 773, 791–792 (1975); *Continental Ore,* supra, 370 U.S. at 706–707.

41. The effect, independent of government action, that the 1981 Code had in the

ty cannot be dismissed on the ground that the conduct at issue involved no "direct" petitioning of government officials, for *Noerr* itself immunized a form of "indirect" petitioning. See *Noerr*, 365 U.S. 127 (1961) (immunizing a publicity campaign directed at the general public on the ground that it was part of an effort to influence legislative and executive action).

Nonetheless, the validity of petitioner's actions remains an issue. We cannot agree with petitioner's absolutist position that the *Noerr* doctrine immunizes every concerted effort that is genuinely intended to influence governmental action. If all such conduct were immunized then, for example, competitors would be free to enter into horizontal price agreements as long as they wished to propose that price as an appropriate level for governmental ratemaking or price supports. But see Georgia v. Pennsylvania R. Co., 324 U.S. 439, 456–463 (1945). Horizontal conspiracies or boycotts designed to exact higher prices or other economic advantages from the government would be immunized on the ground that they are genuinely intended to influence the government to agree to the conspirators' terms. But see Georgia v. Evans, 316 U.S. 159 (1942). Firms could claim immunity for boycotts or horizontal output restrictions on the ground that they are intended to dramatize the plight of their industry and spur legislative action. Immunity might even be claimed for anticompetitive mergers on the theory that they give the merging corporations added political clout. Nor is it necessarily dispositive that packing the Association's meeting may have been the most effective means of securing government action, for one could imagine situations where the most effective means of influencing government officials is bribery, and we have never suggested that that kind of attempt to influence the government merits protection. We thus conclude that the *Noerr* immunity of anticompetitive activity intended to influence the government depends not only on its impact, but also on the context and nature of the activity.

Here petitioner's actions took place within the context of the standard-setting process of a private association. Having concluded that the Association is not a "quasi-legislative" body, we reject petitioner's argument that any efforts to influence the Association must be treated as efforts to influence a "quasi-legislature" and given the same wide berth accorded legislative lobbying. That rounding up supporters is an acceptable and constitutionally protected method of influencing elections does not mean that rounding up economically interested persons to set private standards must also be protected. Nor do we agree with petitioner's contention that, regardless of the Association's nonlegislative status, the effort to influence the Code should receive the same wide latitude given ethically dubious efforts to influence legislative action in the political arena, see *Noerr*, supra,

marketplace may to some extent have been exacerbated by petitioner's efforts to "market" the stigma respondent's product suffered by being excluded from the Code. See 817 F.2d, at 941, n. 3. Given our disposition infra, we need not decide whether, or to what extent, these "marketing" efforts alter the incidental status of the resulting anticompetitive harm. See generally Noerr, 365 U.S., at 142 (noting that in that case there were "no specific findings that the railroads attempted directly to persuade anyone not to deal with the truckers").

365 U.S. at 140–141, simply because the ultimate aim of the effort to influence the private standard-setting process was (principally) legislative action. The ultimate aim is not dispositive. A misrepresentation to a court would not necessarily be entitled to the same antitrust immunity allowed deceptive practices in the political arena simply because the odds were very good that the court's decision would be codified—nor for that matter would misrepresentations made under oath at a legislative committee hearing in the hopes of spurring legislative action.

What distinguishes this case from *Noerr* and its progeny is that the context and nature of petitioner's activity make it the type of commercial activity that has traditionally had its validity determined by the antitrust laws themselves. True, in *Noerr* we immunized conduct that could be characterized as a conspiracy among railroads to destroy business relations between truckers and their customers. *Noerr,* supra, 365 U.S. at 142. But we noted there that:

> There are no specific findings that the railroads attempted directly to persuade anyone not to deal with the truckers. Moreover, all the evidence in the record, both oral and documentary, deals with the railroads' efforts to influence the passage and enforcement of laws. Circulars, speeches, newspaper articles, editorials, magazine articles, memoranda and all other documents discuss in one way or another the railroads' charges that heavy trucks injure the roads, violate the laws and create traffic hazards, and urge that truckers should be forced to pay a fair share of the costs of rebuilding the roads, that they should be compelled to obey the laws, and that limits should be placed upon the weight of the loads they are permitted to carry. 365 U.S., at 142–143.

In light of those findings, we characterized the railroads' activity as a classic "attempt ... to influence legislation by a campaign of publicity," an "inevitable" and "incidental" effect of which was "the infliction of some direct injury upon the interests of the party against whom the campaign is directed." Id., at 143. The essential character of such a publicity campaign was, we concluded, political, and could not be segregated from the activity's impact on business. Rather, the plaintiff's cause of action simply embraced the inherent possibility in such political fights "that one group or the other will get hurt by the arguments that are made." As a political activity, special factors counseled against regulating the publicity campaign under the antitrust laws:

> Insofar as [the Sherman] Act sets up a code of ethics at all, it is a code that condemns trade restraints, not political activity, and, as we have already pointed out, a publicity campaign to influence governmental action falls clearly into the category of political activity. The proscriptions of the Act, tailored as they are for the business world, are not at all appropriate for application in the political arena. Congress has traditionally exercised extreme caution in legislating with respect to problems relating to the conduct of political activities, a caution which has been reflected in the

decisions of this Court interpreting such legislation. All of this caution would go for naught if we permitted an extension of the Sherman Act to regulate activities of that nature simply because those activities have a commercial impact and involve conduct that can be termed unethical. (footnote omitted).

In *Noerr,* then, the political context and nature of the activity precluded inquiry into its antitrust validity.[42]

Here the context and nature of the activity do not counsel against inquiry into its validity. Unlike the publicity campaign in *Noerr,* the activity at issue here did not take place in the open political arena, where partisanship is the hallmark of decisionmaking, but within the confines of a private standard-setting process. The validity of conduct within that process has long been defined and circumscribed by the antitrust laws without regard to whether the private standards are likely to be adopted into law. Indeed, because private standard-setting by associations comprising firms with horizontal and vertical business relations is permitted at all under the antitrust laws only on the understanding that it will be conducted in a nonpartisan manner offering procompetitive benefits, the standards of conduct in this context are, at least in some respects, more rigorous than the standards of conduct prevailing in the partisan political arena or in the adversarial process of adjudication. The activity at issue here thus cannot, as in *Noerr,* be characterized as an activity that has traditionally been regulated with extreme caution, see *Noerr,* or as an activity that "bear[s] little if any resemblance to the combinations normally held violative of the Sherman Act," 365 U.S., at 136. And petitioner did not confine itself to efforts to persuade an independent decisionmaker, compare id., at 138, 139 (describing the immunized conduct as "mere solicitation"); rather, it organized and orchestrated the actual exercise of the Association's decisionmaking authority in setting a standard. Nor can the setting of the Association's Code be characterized as merely an exercise of the power of persuasion, for it in part involves the exercise of market power. The Association's members, after all, include consumers, distributors, and manufacturers of electrical conduit, and any agreement to exclude polyvinyl chloride conduit from the Code is in part an implicit agreement not to trade in that type of electrical conduit. Although one could reason backwards from the legislative impact of the Code to the conclusion that the conduct at issue here is "political," we think that, given the context and nature of the conduct, it can more aptly be characterized as commercial activity with a political impact. Just as the antitrust laws should not regulate political activities "simply because those activities have a commercial impact," so the antitrust laws should not necessarily immunize what are in essence commercial activities simply because they have a political impact.[43]

---

42. Similarly in *California Motor Transport* any antitrust review of the validity of the activity at issue was limited and structured by the fact that there the antitrust defendants were "us[ing] the channels and procedures of state and federal agencies and courts." 404 U.S., at 511; see also id., at 512–513.

43. It is admittedly difficult to draw the precise lines separating anticompetitive polit-

NAACP v. Claiborne Hardware Co., 458 U.S. 886 (1982), is not to the contrary. In that case we held that the First Amendment protected the nonviolent elements of a boycott of white merchants organized by the National Association for the Advancement of Colored People and designed to make white government and business leaders comply with a list of demands for equality and racial justice. Although the boycotters intended to inflict economic injury on the merchants, the boycott was not motivated by any desire to lessen competition or to reap economic benefits but by the aim of vindicating rights of equality and freedom lying at the heart of the Constitution, and the boycotters were consumers who did not stand to profit financially from a lessening of competition in the boycotted market. Here, in contrast, petitioner was at least partially motivated by the desire to lessen competition, and, because of petitioner's line of business, stood to reap substantial economic benefits from making it difficult for respondent to compete.[44]

Thus in this case the context and nature of petitioner's efforts to influence the Code persuade us that the validity of those efforts must, despite their political impact, be evaluated under the standards of conduct set forth by the antitrust laws that govern the private standard-setting process. The antitrust validity of these efforts is not established, without more, by petitioner's literal compliance with the rules of the Association, for the hope of procompetitive benefits depends upon the existence of

ical activity that is immunized despite its commercial impact from anticompetitive commercial activity that is unprotected despite its political impact, and this is itself a case close to the line. For that reason we caution that our decision today depends on the context and nature of the activity. Although criticizing the uncertainty of such a particularized inquiry, the dissent does not dispute that the types of activity we describe, could not be immune under Noerr and fails to offer an intelligible alternative for distinguishing those non-immune activities from the activity at issue in this case. Rather, the dissent states without elaboration that the sham exception "is enough to guard against flagrant abuse," apparently embracing the conclusion of the United States Court of Appeals for the Ninth Circuit that the sham exception covers the activity of a defendant who "genuinely seeks to achieve his governmental result, but does so *through* improper means." Sessions Tank Liners, Inc. v. Joor Mfg., 827 F.2d 458, 465, n. 5 (1987) (emphasis in original). Such a use of the word "sham" distorts its meaning and bears little relation to the sham exception Noerr described to cover activity that was not genuinely intended to influence governmental action. 365 U.S., at 144. See also P. Areeda & H. Hovenkamp, Antitrust Law ¶ 203.1a, p. 13–14 (1987 Supp.). More

importantly, the Ninth Circuit's approach renders "sham" no more than a label courts could apply to activity they deem unworthy of antitrust immunity (probably based on unarticulated consideration of the nature and context of the activity), thus providing a certain superficial certainty but no real "intelligible guidance" to courts or litigants. Indeed, the Ninth Circuit concluded that the very activity the dissent deems protected was an unprotected "sham."

44. Although the absence of such anticompetitive motives and incentives is relevant to determining whether petitioner's restraint of trade is protected under *Claiborne Hardware*, we do not suggest that the absence of anticompetitive purpose is necessary for *Noerr* immunity. As the dissent points out, in *Noerr* itself the major purpose of the activity at issue was anticompetitive. Our statement that the "ultimate aim" of petitioner "is not dispositive," stands only for the proposition that, at least outside the political context, the mere fact that an anticompetitive activity is also intended to influence governmental action is not alone *sufficient* to render that activity immune from antitrust liability.

safeguards sufficient to prevent the standard-setting process from being biased by members with economic interests in restraining competition. An association cannot validate the anticompetitive activities of its members simply by adopting rules that fail to provide such safeguards.[45] The issue of immunity in this case thus collapses into the issue of antitrust liability. Although we do not here set forth the rules of antitrust liability governing the private standard-setting process, we hold that at least where, as here, an economically interested party exercises decisionmaking authority in formulating a product standard for a private association that comprises market participants, that party enjoys no *Noerr* immunity from any antitrust liability flowing from the effect the standard has of its own force in the marketplace.

This conclusion does not deprive state and local governments of input and information from interested individuals or organizations or leave petitioner without ample means to petition those governments. Cf. *Noerr,* supra. See also *California Motor Transport,* 404 U.S., at 510. Petitioner, and others concerned about the safety or competitive threat of polyvinyl chloride conduit, can, with full antitrust immunity, engage in concerted efforts to influence those governments through direct lobbying, publicity campaigns, and other traditional avenues of political expression. To the extent state and local governments are more difficult to persuade through these other avenues, that no doubt reflects their preference for and confidence in the nonpartisan consensus process that petitioner has undermined. Petitioner remains free to take advantage of the forum provided by the standard-setting process by presenting and vigorously arguing accurate scientific evidence before a nonpartisan private standard-setting body.[46] And petitioner can avoid the strictures of the private standard-setting process by attempting to influence legislatures through other forums. What petitioner may not do (without exposing itself to possible antitrust liability for direct injuries) is bias the process by, as in this case, stacking the private standard-setting body with decisionmakers sharing their economic interest in restraining competition.

The judgment of the Court of Appeals is *Affirmed.*

■ WHITE, J., with whom O'CONNOR J. joins, dissenting.

---

45. Even petitioner's counsel concedes, for example, that *Noerr* would not apply if the Association had a rule giving the steel conduit manufacturers a veto over changes in the Code. Tr. of Oral Arg. 41–42.

46. The dissent mistakenly asserts that we today hold that Noerr immunity does not apply to mere efforts to persuade others to exclude a competitor's product from a private code. . . . Our holding is expressly limited to cases where an "economically interested party exercises decisionmaking authority in formulating a product standard for a private association that comprises market partici-

pants." Supra this page (emphasis added); (relying in part on the distinction between activity involving the exercise of decision-making authority and market power and activity involving mere attempts to persuade an independent decisionmaker). Compare *Noerr,* 365 U.S., at 136. The dissent also mistakenly asserts that this description encompasses all private standard-setting associations. In fact, many such associations are composed of members with expertise but no economic interest in suppressing competition. *See, e.g., Sessions,* 827 F.2d, at 460, and n. 2.

Eastern Railroad Presidents Conference v. Noerr Motor Freight, Inc., 365 U.S. 127 (1961), held that the Sherman Act should not be construed to forbid joint efforts by railway companies seeking legislation that would disadvantage the trucking industry. These efforts for the most part involved a public relations campaign rather than direct lobbying of the lawmakers and were held not subject to antitrust challenge because of the fundamental importance of maintaining the free flow of information to the government and the right of the people to seek legislative relief, directly or indirectly. United Mine Workers v. Pennington, 381 U.S. 657 (1965), and California Motor Transport Co. v. Trucking Unlimited, 404 U.S. 508 (1972), applied the rule to efforts to seek executive action and to administrative and adjudicative proceedings.

The Court now refuses to apply the rule of these cases to the participants in those private organizations, such as National Fire Protection Association (NFPA), that regularly propound and publish health and safety standards for a variety of products and industries and then present these codes to state and local authorities for the purpose of having them enacted into law. The NFPA and those participating in the code-writing process will now be subject to antitrust liability if their efforts have anti-competitive effects and do not withstand scrutiny under the rule of reason. Believing that this result is a misapplication of the *Noerr* decision and an improvident construction of the Sherman Act, I respectfully dissent.

This case presents an even stronger argument for immunity than did *Noerr* itself. That decision turned on whether the design or purpose of the conduct was to obtain or influence the passage or enforcement of laws. The Court concedes that petitioner's actions in this case constituted a "genuine effort to influence governmental action," and that this was its "ultimate aim." In *Noerr,* the publicity campaign was dispersed widely among the public in a broad but necessarily diluted attempt to move public opinion in hopes that government officials would take note and respond accordingly. The campaign apparently had some influence on the passage of tax laws and other legislation favorable to the railroads in New Jersey, New York, and Ohio, and procured the governor's veto of a bill that had been passed in Pennsylvania. See 365 U.S., at 130; see also 155 F.Supp. 768, 777–801 (E.D.Pa.1957). Here, NFPA actually drafted proposed legislation in the form of the National Electrical Code (NEC) and presented it countrywide. Not only were petitioner's efforts in this case designed to influence the passage of state laws, but there was also a much greater likelihood that they would be successful than was the case in *Noerr.* This is germane because it establishes a much greater likelihood that the "purpose" and "design" of petitioner's actions in this case was the "solicitation of governmental action with respect to the passage and enforcement of laws," 365 U.S., at 138.

Rather than directly confronting the severe damage that today's decision does to the *Noerr* doctrine, the majority asserts that the "ultimate aim" of petitioner's efforts "is not dispositive." That statement cannot be reconciled with the statements quoted earlier from *Noerr,* where it was held that even if one of the major purposes, or even the *sole* purpose, of the publicity campaign was "to destroy the truckers as competitors," 365 U.S., at 138, those actions were immunized from antitrust liability because ultimately they were "directed toward obtaining governmental action," id., at 140. The majority later doubles back on this statement, and suggests that it is important in this case that "petitioner was at least partially motivated by the desire to lessen competition, and ... stood to reap substantial economic benefits from making it difficult for respondent to compete." It need hardly be said that all of this was also true in *Noerr*. Nobody condones fraud, bribery, or misrepresentation in any form, and other state and federal laws ensure that such conduct is punishable. But the point here is that conduct otherwise punishable under the antitrust laws either becomes immune from the operation of those laws when it is part of a larger design to influence the passage and enforcement of laws, or it does not. No workable boundaries to the *Noerr* doctrine are established by declaring, and then repeating at every turn, that everything depends on "the context and nature of" the activity, if we are unable to offer any further guidance about what this vague reference is supposed to mean, especially when the result here is so clearly wrong as long as *Noerr* itself is reputed to remain good law. One unfortunate consequence of today's decision, therefore, is that district courts and courts of appeals will be obliged to puzzle over claims raised under the doctrine without any intelligible guidance about when and why to apply it.

If there were no private code-writing organizations, and state legislatures themselves held the necessary hearing and wrote codes from scratch, then business concerns like Allied, together with their friends, could jointly testify with impunity about the safety of various products, even though they had anti-competitive motives in doing so. This much the majority concedes, as it does that the major purpose of the code-writing organizations is to influence legislative action. These days it is almost a foregone conclusion that the vast majority of the states will adopt these codes with little or no change. It is untenable to consider the code-writing process by such organizations as NFPA as too far removed from the legislative process to warrant application of the doctrine announced in *Noerr* and faithfully applied in other cases. This was the view of Judge Sneed and his colleagues on the Ninth Circuit in Sessions Tank Liners, Inc. v. Joor Mfg., Inc., 827 F.2d 458 (1987), and the reasons they gave for applying *Noerr* in this context are much more persuasive than anything to the contrary the majority now has to offer.

The Court's decision is unfortunate for another reason. There are now over 400 private organizations preparing and publishing an enormous variety of codes and standards. State and local governments necessarily, and as a matter of course, turn to these proposed codes in the process of legislating to further the health and safety of their citizens. The code that is at issue in this case, for example, was adopted verbatim by 25 states and the District of Columbia; 19 others adopted it with only minor changes. It is the most widely disseminated and adopted model code in the world today. There is no doubt that the work of these private organizations contributes enormously to the public interest and that participation in their work by those who have the technical competence and experience to do so should not be discouraged.

The Court's decision today will surely do just that. It must inevitably be the case that codes such as NEC will set standards that some products cannot satisfy and hence in the name of health and safety will reduce or prevent competition, as was the case here. Yet, putative competitors of the producer of such products will now think twice before urging in the course of the code-making process that those products not be approved; for if they are successful (or even if they are not), they may well become antitrust defendants facing treble-damages liability unless they can prove to a court and a jury that they had no evil motives but were merely "presenting and vigorously arguing accurate scientific evidence before a nonpartisan private standard-setting body," ante at 15, (though with the knowing and inevitable result of eliminating competition). In this case, for example, even if Allied had not resorted to the tactics it employed, but had done no more than successfully argue in good faith the hazards of using respondent's products, it would have inflicted the same damage on respondent and would have risked facing the same antitrust suit, with a jury ultimately deciding the health and safety implications of the products at issue.

The Court's suggestion that its decision will not affect the ability of these organizations to assist state and local governments is surely wrong. The Court's holding is "that at least where, as here, an economically interested party exercises decisionmaking authority in formulating a product standard for a private association that comprises market participants, that party enjoys no *Noerr* immunity from any antitrust liability flowing from the effects the standard has of its own force in the marketplace." This description encompasses the structure and work of all such organizations as we now know them. The Court is saying, in effect, that where a private organization sets standards, the participants can be sued under the antitrust laws for *any* effects those standards have in the marketplace *other than* those flowing from their adoption into law. But the standards will have *some* effect in the marketplace even where they are also adopted into law, through publicity and other means, thus exposing the participants to liability. Henceforth, therefore, any private organization offers such standards at its peril, and without any of the breathing room enjoyed by other participants in the political process.

The alternative apparently envisioned by the Court is that an organization can gain the protection of the *Noerr* doctrine as long as nobody with any economic interest in the product is permitted to "exercis[e] decision-making authority" (*i.e.*, vote) on its recommendations as to particular product standards. Insisting that organizations like NFPA conduct themselves like courts of law will have perverse effects. Legislatures are willing to rely on such organizations precisely because their standards are being set by those who possess an expert understanding of the products and their uses, which are primarily if not entirely those who design, manufacture, sell, and distribute them. Sanitizing such bodies by discouraging the active participation of those with economic interests in the subject matter undermines their utility.

I fear that exposing organizations like NFPA to antitrust liability will impair their usefulness by inhibiting frank and open discussion of the health and safety characteristics of new or old products that will be affected by their codes. The Court focuses on the tactics of petitioner that are thought to have subverted the entire process. But it is not suggested that if there are abuses, they are anything more than occasional happenings. The Court does speculate about the terrible practices that applying *Noerr* in this context could lead us to condone in future cases, but these are no more than fantasies, since nothing of the sort occurred in the wake of *Noerr* itself. It seems to me that today's decision is therefore an unfortunate case of overkill.

Of course, the *Noerr* immunity is not unlimited and by its terms is unavailable where the alleged efforts to influence legislation are nothing but a sham. As the Ninth Circuit held, this limitation is enough to guard against flagrant abuse. In any event, occasional abuse is insufficient ground to render the entire process less useful and reliable. I would reverse the judgment below and remand for further proceedings.

NOTE

1. In SESSIONS TANK LINERS, INC. v. JOOR MANUFACTURING INC., 17 F.3d 295 (9th Cir.1994), the president of Joor, a manufacturer of underground storage tanks, persuaded the Western Fire Chiefs Association to insert a provision into the Uniform Fire Code requiring the removal of leaking underground storage tanks. Sessions sued Joor for violating the antitrust laws. The Ninth Circuit ruled that Joor was shielded from antitrust liability by *Noerr–Pennington*. It distinguished *Allied Tube & Conduit,* pointing out that the plaintiff in *Allied* had been awarded damages on the theory that banishment from a uniform code had caused the product independent harm in the marketplace. Sessions, on the other hand, had suffered its injuries when municipal governments enacted the Uniform Fire Code.

Massachusetts School of Law at Andover, Inc. v. American Bar Association

United States Court of Appeals, Third Circuit, 1997.
107 F.3d 1026.

■ GREENBERG, CIRCUIT JUDGE. This case is before this court on appeal from an order of the district court granting summary judgment on all counts to the appellees in this antitrust action brought against them by the Massachusetts School of Law at Andover, Inc. ("MSL").

I.   FACTUAL AND PROCEDURAL HISTORY

A.   The Parties

MSL has been operating a law school in Massachusetts since 1988. The Board of Regents of Massachusetts authorized MSL to grant the J.D.

degree in 1990. This authority allowed MSL's graduates to take several bar examinations, including that in Massachusetts. MSL has the stated policy of providing low-cost but high-quality legal education and attracting mid-life, working class, and minority students. MSL facilitates this policy with its admissions procedure and a tuition of $9,000 per year. Many of MSL's policies and practices conflict with American Bar Association ("ABA") accreditation standards, and MSL aggressively has sought changes in those standards.

The ABA, a national professional organization of attorneys whose membership is open to members of any bar in the United States, has been concerned with legal education and bar admissions throughout its history. In 1921, through its Section of Legal Education and Admissions to the Bar (the "Section"), the ABA first developed standards of accreditation for legal education programs. The ABA petitioned state supreme courts to rely on its accreditation decisions in connection with bar admission decisions. Now, all 50 states and the District of Columbia consider graduation from an ABA-accredited law school sufficient for the legal education requirement of bar admission. The United States Secretary of Education considers the Council of the Section to be the national agency for accreditation of professional schools of law and a reliable authority concerning the quality of legal education. The ABA informs the states of its accreditation decisions and annually sends them the Review of Legal Education in the United States, the ABA accreditation standards, and any proposed revisions of the standards. During the period at issue, there were 177 ABA-accredited law schools in the United States and over 50 unaccredited schools with some form of state approval such as MSL enjoys. The ABA consistently has opposed attempts to change or waive bar admission rules to allow graduates of schools not accredited by the ABA to take the bar examination.

Many states have methods of satisfying the legal education requirement other than graduation from an ABA-accredited school. These methods include legal apprenticeship, practice in another state, and graduation from a school approved by the American Association of Law Schools ("AALS") or a state agency. The AALS is an association of 160 law schools which serves as a learned society for law schools and legal faculty and as a representative of the law school community with the federal government and other education organizations. Furthermore, in every state, a bar applicant or law school can petition the bar admission authority for revision or waiver of the rules. MSL won a waiver of New Hampshire's rules to allow its graduates to take the bar in 1995, and has filed petitions seeking similar relief in Connecticut, Maine, New York, and Rhode Island. Maryland and Washington, D.C. have granted petitions of graduates of MSL to take the bar. MSL graduates can take the bar examination immediately after graduation in California, Massachusetts, New Hampshire, Vermont and West Virginia, and in 12 other states after practicing in another state first.

The ABA allows graduates of non-accredited schools to join the ABA once they are admitted to a bar and does not prohibit its members from hiring or otherwise dealing with graduates of such schools. The ABA does not prevent its members from teaching at non-ABA-accredited schools, but it does not allow its accredited schools to let students transfer credits from unaccredited schools or to accept graduates of unaccredited schools into graduate programs.

ABA accreditation is open to any law school that applies and meets the ABA standards. The ABA grants provisional accreditation to schools that substantially comply with its standards and promise to comply fully within three years. An Accreditation Committee makes an initial evaluation of a school for provisional accreditation and gives a recommendation to the Council of the Section. The Council then makes a recommendation to the ABA House of Delegates, which has the ultimate decisionmaking authority.

A law school must have been teaching students for five years and graduated three classes to be eligible for AALS membership. The AALS holds an annual meeting, professional conferences and workshops, and publishes the Journal of Legal Education. All of its current members are ABA-accredited, but accreditation is neither necessary nor sufficient for membership approval. The AALS accredits schools in the sense that it determines whether a school meets its membership requirements, but it has accreditation standards and procedures separate from those of the ABA. The AALS conducts a site visit, independently of the ABA, when a school applies for membership, and it conducts periodic visits after membership, usually jointly with the ABA if the school is ABA-accredited. The AALS is not involved with site inspections for provisional ABA accreditation, such as the one the ABA undertook at MSL.

The Law School Admissions Council, Inc. ("LSAC") is the successor organization to the Law School Admission Council and Law School Admission Services, Inc. The LSAC, as have its predecessors, administers the Law School Admissions Test ("LSAT"). The LSAC is not affiliated formally with either the ABA or the AALS and does not participate in the ABA accreditation process. Membership in the LSAC is open to any United States law school that (1) requires that "substantially all of its applicants for admission take the Law School Admission Test," and (2) is ABA-accredited or an AALS member. MSL does not require the LSAT, never has applied for AALS membership, and is not ABA-accredited, so thus is not eligible for LSAC membership.

In addition to administering the LSAT, the LSAC performs a number of other services. The Candidate Referral Service ("CRS") provides lists of names and addresses of people who have taken the LSAT. Use of the CRS is open to any school which has degree granting authority from a state, regardless of LSAC membership or ABA accreditation, and MSL has made use of this service. The Law School Data Assembly Service ("LSDAS") provides a summary of a law school applicant's college record and LSAT score. LSDAS is also open to all schools and has been used by MSL. The LSAC publishes a handbook, The Official Guide to U.S. Law Schools, with a two-page description of each United States LSAC member school, and two appendices with the names and addresses of Canadian LSAC members and unaccredited United States law schools, including MSL, known to the

LSAC. The LSAC also sponsors regional recruiting forums for law school applicants and conferences of pre-law advisors which are only open to LSAC members.

B.   The Complaint

MSL applied for provisional ABA accreditation during the fall of 1992 and early 1993. MSL never claimed it was or would be in compliance with ABA standards, but instead asked for a waiver under Standard 802 which allows the Council to grant variances from the standards. Following the established process, a seven-member site evaluation team appointed by and representing only the ABA visited MSL and then prepared a 76–page report which was sent to MSL. MSL sent a 90–page response to the site team report.

The Accreditation Committee, after reviewing the site report and the MSL materials, and hearing a presentation from six MSL representatives, recommended denial of MSL's accreditation application because it did not meet the ABA requirements. The Committee also recommended denial of the waiver request. In a letter to MSL explaining its denial recommendation, the Committee listed 11 areas where MSL failed to comply with ABA standards. These areas included the high student/faculty ratio, over reliance on part-time faculty, the heavy teaching load of full-time faculty, the lack of adequate sabbaticals for faculty, the use of a for-credit bar review class, the failure to limit the hours students may be employed, and the failure to use the LSAT or give evidence validating its own admission test. The body of the letter discussed the inadequacy of MSL's law library, but the letter did not cite that inadequacy as one of the reasons for the denial recommendation. The letter did not discuss the salaries of MSL's faculty. Invoking ABA procedures, MSL appealed but, after a full review at which MSL had the opportunity to make a presentation, the denial of accreditation was upheld on February 8, 1994.

MSL filed this action on November 23, 1993, alleging that the ABA, AALS, LSAC, and 22 individuals combined and conspired to organize and enforce a group boycott in violation of section 1 of the Sherman Act and conspired to monopolize legal education, law school accreditation, and the licensing of lawyers, in violation of section 2 of the Sherman Act. 15 U.S.C. §§ 1–2. The complaint basically alleged that the appellees conspired to enforce the ABA's anticompetitive accreditation standards by: (1) fixing the price of faculty salaries; (2) requiring reduced teaching hours and non-teaching duties; (3) requiring paid sabbaticals; (4) forcing the hiring of more professors in order to lower student/faculty ratios; (5) limiting the use of adjunct professors; (6) prohibiting the use of required or for-credit bar review courses; (7) forcing schools to limit the number of hours students could work; (8) prohibiting ABA-accredited schools from accepting credit transfers from unaccredited schools and from enrolling graduates of unaccredited schools in graduate programs; (9) requiring more expensive and elaborate physical and library facilities; and (10) requiring schools to use the LSAT. MSL alleged that enforcement of these anticompetitive criteria led to the denial of its application for provisional accreditation and caused MSL to suffer a "loss of prestige" and direct economic damage in the form of declining enrollments and tuition revenue. [Enrollments allegedly declined to 40% of the level they had attained prior to the denial of accreditation.]

After MSL filed its complaint, the Antitrust Division of the United States Department of Justice ("DOJ") began an investigation of the ABA's accreditation process and on June 27, 1995, filed suit against the ABA in the United States District Court for the District of Columbia alleging violations of section 1 of the Sherman Act. The ABA entered into a consent decree with the DOJ on June 25, 1996, settling that case.

[The District Court granted summary judgment for the appellees. MSL appealed from that order.]

II.   DISCUSSION

C.   Summary Judgment

MSL asserts three types of injury resulting from the ABA's allegedly anticompetitive conduct. The first is that MSL is at a competitive disadvantage in recruiting students because graduates of unaccredited schools cannot take the bar examination in most states. Second, MSL says that denial of accreditation creates a stigma, independent of the bar examination issue. Finally, MSL contends that the ABA's enforcement of its accreditation standards injures it directly by increasing the cost of faculty salaries and creating a boycott of unaccredited schools.

In granting summary judgment to the appellees, the district court held that they were not subject to antitrust liability for MSL's principal alleged injury, a competitive disadvantage in recruiting students, to the extent that the decisions of the individual states to prohibit graduates of unaccredited schools from taking their bar examinations caused the injury. The court based this holding on the principles of *Noerr*, 365 U.S. 127. MSL argues on appeal that the *Noerr* principles do not apply here because private anti-competitive conduct is immunized only where it is (1) clearly and affirmatively authorized by state policy, and (2) actively supervised by the state. California Retail Liquor Dealers Ass'n v. Midcal Aluminum, Inc., 445 U.S. 97 (1980). See also FTC v. Ticor Title Ins. Co., 504 U.S. 621 (1992); Patrick v. Burget, 486 U.S. 94(1988).

In Parker v. Brown the Supreme Court held that the Sherman Act does not prohibit an anticompetitive restraint imposed by a state as an act of government. 317 U.S. 341, 352(1943). The decision in *Noerr* reaffirmed the *Parker* doctrine in stating "where a restraint upon trade or monopolization is the result of valid governmental action, as opposed to private action, no violation of the Act can be made out." 365 U.S. at 136. *Noerr* went on to hold that any attempt to petition or influence the government to impose an anticompetitive restraint is immune from antitrust action. Id. Further, even if the anticompetitive restraint results directly from private action, it is still immune if it is an "incidental effect" of a legitimate attempt to influence governmental action. Id. at 143–44. As the Supreme Court put it, *"Parker* and *Noerr* are complementary expressions of the principle that the antitrust laws regulate business, not politics; the former decision protects the States' acts of governing, and the latter the citizens' participation in government." City of Columbia v. Omni Outdoor Advertising, Inc., 499 U.S. 365, 383(1991). Thus, the initial substantive issues on this appeal are whether state or private conduct caused the injury MSL alleges it suffered because its graduates could not take the bar examination in most states, and whether, if MSL suffered an injury as a result of the ABA's conduct, the injury was an incidental effect of the ABA's attempt to influence the states with respect to establishing criteria for bar admission. We will discuss each alleged injury separately

1. Injury from bar examination requirements

Each state retains the authority to decide what applicants may take its bar examination and may be admitted to the bar. Accordingly, MSL's argument that the ABA received "carte-blanche delegated authority to decide who can take bar exams," is simply wrong. Many, but not all, states consider the accreditation decisions of the ABA in their legal education requirement (one of many requirements) for taking the bar examination. Yet, every state retains the final authority to set all the bar admission rules, and individual applicants or law schools can petition the states for waivers or changes.

To the extent that MSL's alleged injury arises from the inability of its graduates to take the bar examination in most states, the injury is the result of state action and thus is immune from antitrust action under the doctrine of Parker v. Brown, 317 U.S. at 352. The ABA does not decide who can take the bar examinations. Rather, it makes an accreditation decision which it conveys to the states, but the states make the decisions as to bar admissions. Without state action, the ABA's accreditation decisions would not affect state bar admissions requirements. Because the states are sovereign in imposing the bar admission requirements, the clear articulation and active supervision requirements urged by MSL are inapplicable. In short, this case does not involve a delegation of state authority. To the contrary, the states use the ABA to assist them in their decision-making processes. Thus, we have here a government action case.

Our holding is consistent with current antitrust jurisprudence. The Supreme Court held in a challenge to Arizona's bar admissions policies that the conduct in question "was in reality that of the Arizona Supreme Court," and thus immune under *Parker.* Hoover v. Ronwin, 466 U.S. 558, 573–74,(1984). Further, the Supreme Court has held that when a state supreme court adopts a state bar rule banning legal advertising, and retains final enforcement authority over it, *Parker* immunity applies. Bates v. State Bar of Arizona, 433 U.S. 350, 361 (1977) ("The Arizona Supreme Court is the real party in interest; it adopted the rules, and it is the ultimate trier of fact and law in the enforcement process."). This case is entirely analogous. The states do not adopt the ABA's accreditation processes, but they do adopt and give effect to the results. Thus, the cases cited by MSL (*Midcal, Patrick*, and *Ticor*) are inapplicable because they dealt with situations where private parties were engaging in conduct, whether price-fixing (*Midcal* and *Ticor*) or denying hospital privileges (*Patrick*), which led directly to the alleged antitrust injury. Here, the state action setting the bar examination requirements led to the alleged injury.

[The court distinguished the Supreme Court's opinion in Allied Tube & Conduit Corp. v. Indian Head, Inc., 486 U.S. 492 (1988), because that case specifically did not reach the question of any injury caused by the adoption of the challenged standards by a governmental body. It then discussed several additional lower court decisions applying the principles of Noerr and rejected MSL's claim that the ABA's conduct injured it because its graduates could not take the bar examination in most states.]

2.   Stigma Injury

MSL also alleges that independent of any bar examination require-ments, it was injured by the stigmatic effect in the market place of the denial of accreditation. MSL claims that the ABA has conducted a cam-paign to convey the idea that ABA accreditation is the sine qua non of quality and that the ABA is the most, or only, competent organization to judge law schools. There is enough evidence to create a genuine dispute of material fact on this issue. Nevertheless, the district court ruled that this injury could not form the basis for antitrust liability because it was "incidental to the primary, protected injury," and thus immune under *Noerr*. MSL challenges this holding on the grounds that there was no petitioning of government here, and therefore *Noerr* does not apply. We hold that there was sufficient petitioning to invoke *Noerr* immunity.

MSL relies extensively on the Supreme Court's decision in Allied Tube & Conduit Corp. v. Indian Head, Inc., 486 U.S. 492, 108 S.Ct. 1931, 100 L.Ed.2d 497 (1988). [After further describing Allied Tube, the court applied it to MSL's claim.]

The conduct of which MSL complains here is basically the ABA's justification of its accreditation decisions and MSL is asserting a loss of prestige resulting from it. This conduct is neither normal commercial activity nor the type of restraint of trade involved in Allied Tube, and thus that case is not controlling. A loss of prestige resulting from a refusal to approve a product or service does not alone make out an antitrust claim.

Noerr immunity is proper in this case because the ABA engaged in petitioning activity, and the stigma injury which MSL suffered was inciden-tal to that activity. [Citing Omni Outdoor Advertising, the court flatly rejected the concept of a "conspiracy" exception to either *Noerr* or *Parker* immunity] MSL admits that in the past, "from the 1920's to approximately the mid 1970's," the ABA petitioned the states in a campaign to prohibit graduates from unaccredited schools from taking bar examinations. This campaign was obviously successful as now most states require graduation from an ABA-accredited school for admission to the bar. The ABA's current conduct surely would be considered petitioning if it took place during the past campaign. The fact that the ABA was successful in lobbying the states does not weaken its position. The ABA continues to communicate its accreditation decisions to the states, and it desires that they continue to give them credence. Discussing the quality and competence of its decisions is a legitimate, although somewhat indirect, way of petitioning the states to continue to follow its guidance. Yet, such activity is no more indirect than the public relations campaign held to be petitioning in *Noerr*.

There is an exception to *Noerr* immunity that would apply if the ABA "attempted directly to persuade anyone not to deal with" MSL. There is no evidence that the ABA made such an attempt (there was such evidence in *Allied Tube*), nor is there any other evidence suggesting that *Noerr* immunity should not apply here. In a supplemental filing of information after oral argument, MSL produced two instances where it claims the ABA directly mentioned MSL. The first is a Boston Globe article about the denial of accreditation to MSL in which an ABA governor defended the ABA standards as providing "a minimum level of quality and consumer protection assurance to the public." John H. Kennedy, "Andover Law School Loses Appeal for Accreditation," Boston Globe, February 9, 1994, at 42. The second proffered piece of evidence is a transcript of the ABA House of Delegates debate of MSL's accreditation application, where one member urged the denial of MSL's application and stated that the standards with which MSL did not comply "lie at the heart of a quality institution."

Both of these statements do nothing more than defend the ABA standards. As we discuss above, this is valid, if indirect, petitioning activity. The ABA is not saying directly that MSL is a bad institution, or that a particular student should not go there. MSL's attempts to characterize all the ABA's comments about the quality of its accreditation process as direct attacks on MSL does not make them direct attacks. We also point out that if a claim for stigma injury could be advanced in circumstances like those here, *Noerr* immunity would be confined severely; a petitioner for governmental action is likely to urge that the action is needed to ensure that standards are met, thereby suggesting that some entities do not meet appropriate standards.

3.   Direct injury from ABA standards

MSL alleges a third injury which occurs directly from the ABA's enforcement of its standards, independent of both the bar examination and stigma issues. The challenged standards relate to faculty salaries (MSL charges price-fixing) and limitations on accredited schools accepting transfers or graduate students from unaccredited schools (MSL charges a boycott). Although the ABA is immune from liability attributable to the state action in requiring applicants for the bar examination to have graduated from an ABA-accredited law school and from any stigma injury resulting from the denial of accreditation under the *Noerr* petitioning doctrine, the ABA is not immune in the actual enforcement of its standards. The state action relates to the use of the results of the accreditation process, not the process itself. The process is entirely private conduct which has not been approved or supervised explicitly by any state. Thus, the ABA's enforcement of an anticompetitive standard which injures MSL would not be immune from possible antitrust liability. Extending *Noerr* immunity to this type of private activity would run counter to *Allied Tube*.

[MSL failed to show sufficient evidence that it was denied accreditation because it did not comply with the salary standard.]

MSL alleges that the faculty salary standards injured it in two ways. First, MSL asserts that it raised its salaries in an attempt to get accreditation. This claim is in direct conflict to its consistent assertion that it refused to comply with the ABA's anticompetitive standards and for that reason was denied accreditation. The claim also is remarkable because MSL made it clear that it would not comply with ABA standards to obtain certification. The only other related evidence shows that MSL acted independently to increase its salaries, and then later found that this action might help it get accreditation. There has not been sufficient explanation of the contradiction to create a genuine issue of material fact and justify reversing the summary judgment.

MSL's second contention that the ABA's salary standards injured it is that the standards inflated the market cost of law professors, thereby increasing the salaries MSL must pay its faculty. This market price argument is equally unavailing. MSL's stated policy was to rely on adjunct faculty. MSL did not produce evidence that any of its faculty other than its dean ever had been employed at another law school. In effect, MSL was hiring faculty from a different market, one unaffected by the ABA's conduct, or at least a different provider in the same market (teachers who never taught at ABA-accredited schools).

MSL also alleges a boycott in that the ABA prevented its accredited schools from accepting transfers or graduate students from unaccredited schools. The district court held that MSL had not produced any evidence that it was injured by either of these rules. This holding is correct. MSL has done nothing more than state the standards and allege that they injured MSL. There is no factual support for these allegations. Further, the evidence shows that MSL actively opposed its students transferring, both in policy and practice. MSL therefore cannot claim that the ABA's prohibition on transfers with credit injured it.

MSL also alleges that the AALS boycotted MSL by refusing membership and that the LSAC boycotted MSL by refusing to allow it to attend certain recruiting conferences. The allegations regarding the AALS are simply incorrect. AALS membership is independent of ABA accreditation, and MSL never has applied for such membership. Even though it is not a member, MSL can attend AALS conferences and has done so. Therefore MSL has not suffered any injury at the hands of the AALS.

The LSAC's failure to invite MSL to its conferences does not constitute a boycott. Under the fact-pattern here, to demonstrate a boycott MSL has to show that these conferences are an essential facility for recruiting students, as there is no other potential basis for the boycott claim. Such an essential facility or claim fails whenever a plaintiff (1) cannot show that the defendant has a monopoly over the alleged essential facility; (2) the facility cannot be duplicated in a reasonable manner; and (3) the plaintiff has been denied its use. Ideal Dairy Farms, Inc. v. John Labatt, Ltd., 90 F.3d 737, 748 (3d Cir.1996). MSL has shown only that the LSAC denies it participation. There is no evidence suggesting that the LSAC has a monopoly over access to law students or pre-law advisors, or even over recruiting fairs. The LSAC does not hinder MSL's recruiting in any way, it just does not aid it by allowing MSL to attend its conferences. Such activity is not required by the antitrust laws, and its absence does not constitute antitrust injury.

Further, MSL has not shown that the LSAC injured it.

III. CONCLUSION

The order of the district court entered August 29, 1996, granting the appellees summary judgment and the other orders on appeal will be affirmed.

Professional Real Estate Investors v. Columbia Pictures

Supreme Court of the United States, 1993.
508 U.S. 49, 113 S.Ct. 1920, 123 L.Ed.2d 611.

■ JUSTICE THOMAS delivered the opinion of the Court.

This case requires us to define the "sham" exception to the doctrine of antitrust immunity first identified in Eastern R. Presidents Conference v. Noerr Motor Freight, Inc., 365 U.S. 127 (1961), as the doctrine applies in the litigation context. Under the sham exception, activity "ostensibly directed toward influencing governmental action" does not qualify for *Noerr* immunity if it "is a mere sham to cover ... an attempt to interfere directly with the business relationships of a competitor." We hold that litigation cannot be deprived of immunity as a sham unless the litigation is objectively baseless. The Court of Appeals for the Ninth Circuit refused to characterize as sham a lawsuit that the antitrust defendant admittedly had probable cause to institute. We affirm.

I

Petitioners Professional Real Estate Investors, Inc., and Kenneth F. Irwin (collectively, PRE) operated La Mancha Private Club and Villas, a resort hotel in Palm Springs, California. Having installed videodisc players in the resort's hotel rooms and assembled a library of more than 200 motion picture titles, PRE rented videodiscs to guests for in-room viewing. PRE also sought to develop a market for the sale of videodisc players to other hotels wishing to offer in-room viewing of prerecorded material. Respondents, Columbia Pictures Industries, Inc., and seven other major motion picture studios (collectively, Columbia), held copyrights to the motion pictures recorded on the videodiscs that PRE purchased. Columbia also licensed the transmission of copyrighted motion pictures to hotel rooms through a wired cable system called Spectradyne. PRE therefore competed with Columbia not only for the viewing market at La Mancha but also for the broader market for in-room entertainment services in hotels.

In 1983, Columbia sued PRE for alleged copyright infringement through the rental of videodiscs for viewing in hotel rooms. PRE counterclaimed, charging Columbia with violations of §§ 1 and 2 of the Sherman Act, 26 Stat. 209, as amended, 15 U.S.C. §§ 1–2 and various state law infractions. In particular, PRE alleged that Columbia's copyright action was a mere sham that cloaked underlying acts of monopolization and conspiracy to restrain trade. . . .

PRE contends that "the Ninth Circuit erred in holding that an antitrust plaintiff must, as a threshold prerequisite . . . , establish that a sham lawsuit is baseless as a matter of law." Brief for Petitioners 14. It invites us to adopt an approach under which either "indifference to . . . outcome," *ibid.*, or failure to prove that a petition for redress of grievances "would . . . have been brought but for [a] predatory motive," Tr. of Oral Arg. 10, would expose a defendant to antitrust liability under the sham exception. We decline PRE's invitation. . . .

In *California Motor Transport Co. v. Trucking Unlimited*, 404 U.S. 508 (1972), we elaborated on *Noerr* in two relevant respects. First, we extended *Noerr* to "the approach of citizens . . . to administrative agencies . . . and to courts." 404 U.S., at 510. Second, we held that the complaint showed a sham not entitled to immunity when it contained allegations that one group of highway carriers "sought to bar . . . competitors from meaningful access to adjudicatory tribunals and so to usurp that decisionmaking process" by "institut[ing] . . . proceedings and actions . . . with or without probable cause, and regardless of the merits of the cases." *Id.*, at 512 (internal quotation marks omitted). We left unresolved the question presented by this case—whether litigation may be sham merely because a subjective expectation of success does not motivate the litigant. We now answer this question in the negative and hold that an objectively reasonable effort to litigate cannot be sham regardless of subjective intent.[47]

Our original formulation of antitrust petitioning immunity required that unprotected activity lack objective reasonableness. *Noerr* rejected the contention that an attempt "to influence the passage and enforcement of laws" might lose immunity merely because the lobbyists' "sole purpose . . . was to destroy [their] competitors." 365 U.S., at 138. Nor were we persuaded by a showing that a publicity campaign "was intended to and did in fact injure [competitors] in their relationships with the public and with their

---

47. *California Motor Transportation* did refer to the antitrust defendants' "purpose to deprive . . . competitors of meaningful access to the . . . courts." 404 U.S., at 512. See also *id.*, at 515 (noting a "purpose to eliminate . . . a competitor by denying him free and meaningful access to the agencies and courts"); *id.*, at 518 (Stewart, J., concurring in judgment) (agreeing that the antitrust laws could punish acts intended "to discourage and ultimately to prevent [a competitor] from invoking" administrative and judicial process). That a sham depends on the existence of anticompetitive intent, however, does not transform the sham inquiry into a purely subjective investigation.

customers," since such "direct injury" was merely "an incidental effect of the ... campaign to influence governmental action." *Id.*, at 143. We reasoned that "[t]he right of the people to inform their representatives in government of their desires with respect to the passage or enforcement of laws cannot properly be made to depend upon their intent in doing so." *Id.*, at 139. In short, "*Noerr* shields from the Sherman Act a concerted effort to influence public officials regardless of intent or purpose." *Pennington*, 381 U.S. at 670.

Nothing in *California Motor Transport* retreated from these principles. Indeed, we recognized that recourse to agencies and courts should not be condemned as sham until a reviewing court has "discern[ed] and draw[n]" the "difficult line" separating objectively reasonable claims from "a pattern of baseless, repetitive claims ... which leads the factfinder to conclude that the administrative and judicial processes have been abused." 404 U.S., at 513. Our recognition of a sham in that case signifies that the institution of legal proceedings "without probable cause" will give rise to a sham if such activity effectively "bar[s] ... competitors from meaningful access to adjudicatory tribunals and so ... usurp[s] th[e] decisionmaking process." *Id.* at 512.

Since *California Motor Transport,* we have consistently assumed that the sham exception contains an indispensable objective component. We have described a sham as "evidenced by repetitive lawsuits carrying the hallmark of *insubstantial* claims." Otter Tail Power Co. v. United States, 410 U.S. 366, 380 (1973) (emphasis added). We regard as sham "private action that is not genuinely aimed at procuring favorable government action," as opposed to "a valid effort to influence government action." Allied Tube & Conduit Corp. v. Indian Head, Inc., 486 U.S. 492, 500 n. 4 (1988). "And government action ... certainly cannot be characterized as a sham." *Id.*, at 502. See also Vendo Co. v. Lektro–Vend Corp., 433 U.S. 623, 645 (1977) (Blackmun, J., concurring in result) (describing a successful lawsuit as a "genuine attemp[t] to use the ... adjudicative process legitimately" rather than " 'a pattern of baseless, repetitive claims' "). Whether applying *Noerr* as an antitrust doctrine or invoking it in other contexts, we have repeatedly reaffirmed that evidence of anticompetitive intent or purpose alone cannot transform otherwise legitimate activity into a sham. *See, e.g.,* FTC v. Superior Court Trial Lawyers Assn., 493 U.S. 411, 424 (1990); NAACP v. Claiborne Hardware Co., 458 U.S. 886, 913–914 (1982). Cf. *Vendo, supra,* at 635–636, n. 639, n. 9 (plurality opinion of Rehnquist, J.); *id.*, at 644, n. 645 (Blackmun, J., concurring in result). Indeed, by analogy to *Noerr's* sham exception, we held that even an "improperly motivated" lawsuit may not be enjoined under the National Labor Relations Act as an unfair labor practice unless such litigation is "baseless." Bill Johnson's Restaurants, Inc. v. NLRB, 461 U.S. 731, 743–744 (1983). Our decisions therefore establish that the legality of objectively reasonable petitioning "directed toward obtaining governmental action" is "not at all affected by an anticompetitive purpose [the actor] may have had." *Noerr,* 365 U.S., at 140, quoted in *Pennington*, supra at 669.

Our most recent applications of *Noerr* immunity further demonstrate that neither *Noerr* immunity nor its sham exception turns on subjective intent alone. In *Allied Tube,* 486 U.S., at 503, and *FTC v. Trial Lawyers, supra,* at 424, 427, and n. 11, we refused to let antitrust defendants immunize otherwise unlawful restraints of trade by pleading a subjective intent to seek favorable legislation or to influence governmental action. Cf. National Collegiate Athletic Assn. v. Board of Regents of Univ. of Okla., 468 U.S. 85, 101, n. 23 (1984) ("[G]ood motives will not validate an otherwise anticompetitive practice"). In Columbia v. Omni Outdoor Advertising, Inc., 499 U.S. 365 (1991), we similarly held that challenges to allegedly sham petitioning activity must be resolved according to objective criteria. We dispelled the notion that an antitrust plaintiff could prove a sham merely by showing that its competitor's "purposes were to delay [the plaintiff's] entry into the market and even to deny it a meaningful access to the appropriate . . . administrative and legislative fora." *Id.,* at 381 (internal quotation marks omitted). We reasoned that such inimical intent "may render the manner of lobbying improper or even unlawful, but does not necessarily render it a 'sham.'" *Ibid.,* Accord, *id.,* at 398 (Stevens, J., dissenting).

In sum, fidelity to precedent compels us to reject a purely subjective definition of "sham." The sham exception so construed would undermine, if not vitiate, *Noerr.* And despite whatever "superficial certainty" it might provide, a subjective standard would utterly fail to supply "real 'intelligible guidance.'" *Allied Tube, supra,* at 508, n. 10.

III

We now outline a two-part definition of "sham" litigation. First, the lawsuit must be objectively baseless in the sense that no reasonable litigant could realistically expect success on the merits. If an objective litigant could conclude that the suit is reasonably calculated to elicit a favorable outcome, the suit is immunized under *Noerr,* and an antitrust claim premised on the sham exception must fail.[48] Only if challenged litigation is objectively meritless may a court examine the litigant's subjective motivation. Under this second part of our definition of sham, the court should focus on whether the baseless lawsuit conceals "an attempt to interfere *directly* with the business relationships of a competitor," *Noerr, supra,* at 144 (emphasis added), through the "use [of] the governmental *process*—as opposed to the *outcome* of that process—as an anticompetitive weapon," *Omni,* 499 U.S., at 380 (emphasis in original). This two-tiered process requires the plaintiff

---

48. A winning lawsuit is by definition a reasonable effort at petitioning for redress and therefore not a sham. On the other hand, when the antitrust defendant has lost the underlying litigation, a court must "resist the understandable temptation to engage in *post hoc* reasoning by concluding" that an ultimately unsuccessful "action must have been unreasonable or without foundation." Chris-tiansburg Garment Co. v. EEOC, 434 U.S. 412, 421–422 (1978). Accord, Hughes v. Rowe, 449 U.S. 5, 114–15 (1980) (*per curiam*). The court must remember that "[e]ven when the law or the facts appear questionable or unfavorable at the outset, a party may have an entirely reasonable ground for bringing suit." *Christiansburg, supra,* at 422.

to disprove the challenged lawsuit's *legal* viability before the court will entertain evidence of the suit's *economic* viability. Of course, even a plaintiff who defeats the defendant's claim to *Noerr* immunity by demonstrating both the objective and the subjective components of a sham must still prove a substantive antitrust violation. Proof of a sham merely deprives the defendant of immunity; it does not relieve the plaintiff of the obligation to establish all other elements of his claim.

Some of the apparent confusion over the meaning of "sham" may stem from our use of the word "genuine" to denote the opposite of "sham." See *Omni, supra,* at 380; *Allied Tube, supra,* at 500, n. 4; *Noerr, supra,* at 144; *Vendo Co. v. Lektro–Vend Corp.,* supra at 645 (Blackmun, J., concurring in result). The word "genuine" has both objective and subjective connotations. On one hand, "genuine" means "actually having the reputed or apparent qualities or character." Webster's Third New International Dictionary 948 (1986). "Genuine" in this sense governs Federal Rule of Civil Procedure 56, under which a "genuine issue" is one "that properly can be resolved only by a finder of fact because [it] may *reasonably* be resolved in favor of either party." Anderson v. Liberty Lobby, Inc., 477 U.S. 242, 250 (1986) (emphasis added). On the other hand, "genuine" also means "sincerely and honestly felt or experienced." Webster's Dictionary, supra, at 948. To be sham, therefore, litigation must fail to be "genuine" in all senses of the word.[49]

IV

... The existence of probable cause to institute legal proceedings precludes a finding that an antitrust defendant has engaged in sham litigation. The notion of probable cause, as understood and applied in the common law tort of wrongful civil proceedings,[50] requires the plaintiff to prove that the defendant lacked probable cause to institute an unsuccessful civil lawsuit and that the defendant pressed the action for an improper, malicious purpose.... Because the absence of probable cause is an essential element of the tort, the existence of probable cause is an absolute

49. In surveying the "forms of illegal and reprehensible practice which may corrupt the administrative or judicial processes and which may result in antitrust violations," we have noted that "unethical conduct in the setting of the adjudicatory process often results in sanctions" and that "misrepresentations, condoned in the political arena, are not immunized when used in the adjudicatory process." California Motor Transport, 404 U.S., at 512–513. We need not decide here whether and, if so, to what extent *Noerr* permits the imposition of antitrust liability for a litigant's fraud or other misrepresentations. Cf. Fed.Rule Civ.Proc. 60(b)(3) (allowing a federal court to "relieve a party ... from a final judgment" for "fraud ..., mis-representation, or other misconduct of an adverse party"); Walker Process Equipment, Inc. v. Food Machinery & Chemical Corp., 382 U.S. 172, 176–177 (1965), *id.,* at 179–180 (Harlan, J., concurring).

50. This tort is frequently called "malicious prosecution," which (strictly speaking) governs the malicious pursuit of *criminal* proceedings without probable cause. See W. Keeton, D. Dobbs, R. Keeton, & D. Owen, Prosser and Keeton on Torts § 120, p. 892 (5th ed. 1984). The threshold for showing probable cause is no higher in the civil context than in the criminal. See Restatement (Second) of Torts § 674, Comment *e,* pp. 454–455 (1977).

defense. . . . Just as evidence of anticompetitive intent cannot affect the objective prong of *Noerr's* sham exception, a showing of malice alone will neither entitle the wrongful civil proceedings plaintiff to prevail nor permit the factfinder to infer the absence of probable cause. *Stewart, supra,* at 194; *Wheeler, supra,* at 551; 2 C. Addison, Law of Torts § 1, ¶ 853, pp. 67–68 (1876); *T. Cooley, supra,* at 184. When a court has found that an antitrust defendant claiming *Noerr* immunity had probable cause to sue, that finding compels the conclusion that a reasonable litigant in the defendant's position could realistically expect success on the merits of the challenged lawsuit. Under our decision today, therefore, a proper probable cause determination irrefutably demonstrates that an antitrust plaintiff has not proved the objective prong of the sham exception and that the defendant is accordingly entitled to *Noerr* immunity.

The District Court and the Court of Appeals correctly found that Columbia had probable cause to sue PRE for copyright infringement. . . .

■ Justice Stevens, with whom Justice O'Connor joins, concurring in the judgment.

While I agree with the Court's disposition of this case and with its holding that an "objectively reasonable effort to litigate cannot be sham regardless of subjective intent," *ante,* at 7, I write separately to disassociate myself from some of the unnecessarily broad dicta in the Court's opinion. Specifically, I disagree with the Court's equation of "objectively baseless" with the answer to the question whether any "reasonable litigant could realistically expect success on the merits." There might well be lawsuits that fit the latter definition but can be shown to be objectively *unreasonable,* and thus shams. It might not be objectively reasonable to bring a lawsuit just because some form of success on the merits—no matter how insignificant—could be expected.[51] With that possibility in mind, the Court should avoid an unnecessarily broad holding that it might regret when confronted with a more complicated case.

As the Court recently explained, a "sham" is the use of "the governmental *process-* as opposed to the *outcome* of that process—as an anticompetitive weapon." Columbia v. Omni Outdoor Advertising, Inc., 499 U.S. 365, 381 (1991). The distinction between abusing the judicial process to restrain competition, and prosecuting a lawsuit that, if successful, will restrain competition, must guide any court's decision whether a particular filing, or series of filings, is a sham. The label "sham" is appropriately applied to a case, or series of cases, in which the plaintiff is indifferent to the outcome of the litigation itself, but has nevertheless sought to impose a collateral harm on the defendant by, for example, impairing his credit, abusing the discovery process, or interfering with his access to governmental agencies. It might also apply to a plaintiff who had some reason to expect success on the merits but because of its tremendous cost would not

---

51. The Court's recent decision in Farrar v. Hobby, 506 U.S. 103 (1992) makes me wonder whether "10 years of litigation and two trips to the Court of Appeals" to recover "one dollar from one defendant," (O'Connor, J., concurring), would qualify as a reasonable expectation of "favorable relief" under today's opinion.

bother to achieve that result without the benefit of collateral injuries imposed on its competitor by the legal process alone. Litigation filed or pursued for such collateral purposes is fundamentally different from a case in which the relief sought in the litigation itself would give the plaintiff a competitive advantage or, perhaps, exclude a potential competitor from entering a market with a product that either infringes the plaintiff's patent or copyright or violates an exclusive franchise granted by a governmental body.

The case before us today is in the latter, obviously legitimate, category. There was no unethical or other improper use of the judicial system; instead, respondents invoked the federal court's jurisdiction to determine whether they could lawfully restrain competition with petitioners. The relief they sought in their original action, if granted, would have had the anticompetitive consequences authorized by federal copyright law. Given that the original copyright infringement action was objectively reasonable—and the District Court, the Court of Appeals, and this Court all agree that it was—neither the respondents' own measure of their chances of success nor an alleged goal of harming petitioners provides a sufficient basis for treating it as a sham. We may presume that every litigant intends harm to his adversary; moreover, uncertainty about the possible resolution of unsettled questions of law is characteristic of the adversary process. Access to the courts is far too precious a right for us to infer wrongdoing from nothing more than using the judicial process to seek a competitive advantage in a doubtful case. Thus, the Court's disposition in this case is unquestionably correct....

NOTES AND QUESTIONS

1. Could an expensive lawsuit with very small potential damages and little chance of success be considered a sham? Might such a lawsuit be considered a sham under Justice Stevens' approach in his concurrence?

2. What is the difference (if any) between the following standards:

   a. "no reasonable litigant could realistically expect success on the merits";

   b. "an objective litigant could conclude that the suit is reasonably calculated to elicit a favorable outcome";

   c. "the existence of probable cause to institute legal proceedings"; and

   d. Fed.Rule Civ.Proc. 11.

   Which standard does the Court adopt?

3. How does Justice Stevens' objective standard of baselessness differ from the standard in the majority opinion? According to Justice Stevens, what must a "reasonable litigant" expect in addition to "success on the merits."

4. Would bringing a sham lawsuit against a competitor violate the antitrust laws?

PROBLEM 8

THE STRUGGLE FOR STONEFORD'S CABLE TV FRANCHISE

In 1988, Stone Cable Co. obtained from the City of Stoneford, Illinois, an exclusive ten-year franchise to install and operate a cable TV transmission system in that city. Illinois and federal law and regulations left cable TV franchising decisions to the discretion of local authorities, and the Stoneford city council recommended and the mayor approved grant of the franchise.

While Stone was undertaking studies and preparing to subcontract installation work, a regular city election was held, and the incumbent mayor and three of the five incumbent city council members were replaced. Prior to the election, the two principal shareholders of Stoneford's local regular television station, Able and Baker, and one of the successful city council candidates, Charlie, had formed CATV Stoneford, Inc., with the purpose of securing the exclusive franchise earlier issued to Stone. Able and Baker each made substantial campaign contributions to Charlie and other council candidates on the successful ticket. Stone alleges that their television station's coverage of the election was biased in favor of the same candidates.

After the election, CATV and its affiliated local TV station filed an unfair competition complaint in a state court in Stoneford alleging that Stone had within the previous year hired several employees from the affiliated local TV station to obtain trade secrets with respect to the Stoneford television advertising market. Plaintiffs claimed damages and sought an injunction prohibiting Stone from proceeding with any activity to carry out plans to implement its Stoneford cable TV franchise. Extensive discovery procedures failed to disclose facts sufficient to support the allegations and defendant's motion for summary judgment was eventually granted.

Shortly thereafter, at Charlie's behest, the city council invited Able and Baker to appear before it. They testified that Stone was both technically and financially unqualified to implement the franchise. After some discussion, but no public hearing or other opportunity for Stone to dispute the charges, the council exercised a revocation clause in the franchise agreement and transferred the exclusive franchise to CATV.

Stone charged a conspiracy in restraint of trade among Able, Baker, Charlie, and CATV. It alleged, *inter alia,* that CATV's lawsuit was brought in bad faith and for harassment, the statements of Able and Baker before the council were false and motivated solely by their interest in CATV's obtaining the franchise, and that the decision of the council was tainted as a result of Able and Baker's campaign contributions. Defendants moved to dismiss on the grounds that their conduct was protected under the *Noerr* doctrine. What result?

B.   "State Action" and Tensions With Federalism

Parker v. Brown

Supreme Court of the United States, 1943.
317 U.S. 341, 63 S.Ct. 307, 87 L.Ed. 315.

[Action brought by a producer and packer of raisins to enjoin various state officials charged with the administration of a marketing program under the California Agricultural Prorate Act. In order to "prevent economic waste in the marketing of agricultural products," and to "conserve the agricultural wealth of the State" the Act authorized the establishment of marketing programs which would "restrict competition among the growers and maintain prices" of certain agricultural products. The Act further authorized the establishment of a Commission which was to hold public hearings and make findings to the effect that the institution of a program would "prevent agricultural waste ... without permitting unreasonable profits to producers." The Commission could then select a program committee principally from nominees chosen by producers in the area, and the program committee was required to formulate a marketing program which the Commission, after public hearings, was authorized to approve. The program would be instituted if consented to by 65 per cent of the producers in the zone owning 5 per cent of the acreage devoted to production of the particular crop.

The proration marketing program for raisins provided for classification of raisins as "standard," "substandard," and "inferior." Inferior raisins were unfit for human consumption and were to be disposed of by the committee for by-product and other diversion purposes. Substandard raisins and at least 20 per cent of total standard and substandard raisins were to be placed in a "surplus pool" to be disposed of for by-product and other diversion purposes with the producers receiving from $25 to $27.50 per ton. Of the remainder of the raisin crop, 50 percent was to be placed in a "stabilization pool" and disposed of by the committee "in such manner as to obtain stability in the market" with the producers receiving from $50 to $55 per ton; the other 30 per cent was denominated "free tonnage" and could be sold through ordinary commercial channels if the producer paid a fee of $2.50 per ton.

Plaintiff-producer had challenged the marketing program as invalid under both the "dormant" Commerce Clause of the Constitution and the Sherman Act.]

■ STONE, C.J.... We may assume for present purposes that the California prorate program would violate the Sherman Act if it were organized and made effective solely by virtue of a contract, combination or conspiracy of private persons, individual or corporate. We may assume also, without deciding, that Congress could, in the exercise of its commerce power, prohibit a state from maintaining a stabilization program like the present because of its effect on interstate commerce....

But it is plain that the prorate program here was never intended to operate by force of individual agreement or combination. It derived its authority and its efficacy from the legislative command of the state and was not intended to operate or become effective without that command. We find nothing in the language of the Sherman Act or in its history which suggests that its purpose was to restrain a state or its officers or agents from activities directed by its legislature. In a dual system of government in which, under the Constitution, the states are sovereign, save only as Congress may constitutionally subtract from their authority, an unexpressed purpose to nullify a state's control over its officers and agents is not lightly to be attributed to Congress.

The Sherman Act makes no mention of the state as such, and gives no hint that it was intended to restrain state action or official action directed by a state. The Act is applicable to "persons" including corporations, and it authorizes suits under it by persons and corporations. A state may maintain a suit for damages under it, . . . but the United States may not . . . — conclusions derived not from the literal meaning of the words "person" and "corporation" but from the purpose, the subject matter, the context and the legislative history of the statute.

There is no suggestion of a purpose to restrain state action in the Act's legislative history. The sponsor of the bill which was ultimately enacted as the Sherman Act declared that it prevented only "business combinations." 21 Cong.Rec. 2562, 2457; see also at 2459, 2461. That its purpose was to suppress combinations to restrain competition and attempts to monopolize by individuals and corporations, abundantly appears from its legislative history. See Apex Hosiery Co. v. Leader, 310 U.S. 469, 492–93 and n. 15; United States v. Addyston Pipe & Steel Co., 85 F. 271, affirmed, 175 U.S. 211; Standard Oil Co. v. United States, 221 U.S. 1, 54–58.

True, a state does not give immunity to those who violate the Sherman Act by authorizing them to violate it, or by declaring that their action is lawful, Northern Securities Co. v. United States, 193 U.S. 197, 332, 344–47; and we have no question of the state or its municipality becoming a participant in a private agreement or combination by others for restraint of trade, cf. Union Pacific R. Co. v. United States, 313 U.S. 450. Here the state command to the Commission and to the program committee of the California Prorate Act is not rendered unlawful by the Sherman Act since, in view of the latter's words and history, it must be taken to be a prohibition of individual and not state action. It is the state which has created the machinery for establishing the prorate program. Although the organization of a prorate zone is proposed by producers, and a prorate program, approved by the Commission, must also be approved by referendum of producers, it is the state, acting through the Commission, which adopts the program and which enforces it with penal sanctions, in the execution of a governmental policy. The prerequisite approval of the program upon referendum by a prescribed number of producers is not the imposition by them of their will upon the minority by force of agreement or combination which the Sherman Act prohibits. The state itself exercises its legislative authority in making the regulation and in prescribing the conditions of its application. The required vote on the referendum is one of these conditions. . . .

The state in adopting and enforcing the prorate program made no contract or agreement and entered into no conspiracy in restraint of trade or to establish monopoly but, as sovereign, imposed the restraint as an act of government which the Sherman Act did not undertake to prohibit. . . .

SCHWEGMANN BROS. V. CALVERT DISTILLERS CORP., 341 U.S. 384, 71 S.Ct. 745, 95 L.Ed. 1035 (1951). Plaintiff liquor distributors entered into agreements with retailers in Louisiana under which the latter agreed to maintain stipulated resale prices. Such agreements were authorized by Louisiana law and, under the Miller–Tydings Act, they did not contravene the Sherman Act. Defendant was a Louisiana liquor retailer who refused to enter into such a resale price maintenance contract. Plaintiffs sought an injunction against sales by defendant at less than the prices stipulated in the agreements with conforming Louisiana retailers, relying on a Louisiana statute making sales under such circumstances "unfair competition." In refusing plaintiffs the injunctive relief sought against the non-signing and nonconforming retailer, the Supreme Court reasoned:

1. "The fact that a state authorizes the price fixing does not, of course, give immunity to the scheme, absent approval by Congress."

2. The Miller–Tydings Act does not immunize the imposition of minimum resale prices upon retailers who have not agreed to such prices.

3. Because the Sherman Act prohibits "horizontal" price fixing by competitors, a prohibition the Miller–Tydings Act recognizes, "when a state compels retailers to follow a parallel price policy, it demands private conduct which the Sherman Act forbids. See Parker v. Brown.... [W]hen retailers are *forced* to abandon price competition, they are driven into a compact in violation of the spirit of the [Miller–Tydings] proviso which forbids 'horizontal' price fixing."

GOLDFARB V. VIRGINIA STATE BAR, 421 U.S. 773, 95 S.Ct. 2004, 44 L.Ed.2d 572 (1975). Chief Justice Burger rendered the following opinion on "state action" for a unanimous Court:[52]

In Parker v. Brown, 317 U.S. 341 (1943), the Court held that an anticompetitive marketing program which "derived its authority and its efficacy from the legislative command of the state" was not a violation of the Sherman Act because the Act was intended to regulate private practices and not to prohibit a State from imposing a restraint as an act of government....

Through its legislature Virginia has authorized its highest court to regulate the practice of law. That court has adopted ethical codes which deal in part with fees, and far from exercising state power to authorize binding price fixing, explicitly directed lawyers not "to be controlled" by fee schedules.[53] The State Bar, a state agency by law, argues that in issuing

52. For a discussion of Chief Justice Burger's opinion, see pp. 121–122, supra.

53. In 1938 the Supreme Court of Virginia adopted Rules for the Integration of the Virginia State Bar, and Rule II, § 12 dealt with the procedure for setting fees. Among six factors that court directed to be considered in setting a fee were "the customary charges of the Bar for similar services." The court also directed that

"[i]n determining the customary charges of the Bar for similar services, it is proper for a lawyer to consider a schedule of minimum fees adopted by a Bar Association, but *no lawyer should permit himself to be controlled* thereby or to follow it as his sole guide in determining the amount of his fee." Rules for Integration of the Virginia State Bar, 171 Va. xvii, xxiii. (Emphasis supplied.)

fee schedule reports and ethical opinions dealing with fee schedules it was merely implementing the fee provisions of the ethical codes. The County Bar, although it is a voluntary association and not a state agency, claims that the ethical codes and the activities of the State Bar "prompted" it to issue fee schedules and thus its actions, too, are state action for Sherman Act purposes.

The threshold inquiry in determining if an anticompetitive activity is state action of the type the Sherman Act was not meant to proscribe is whether the activity is required by the State acting as sovereign. Parker v. Brown, 317 U.S., at 350–352; Continental Co. v. Union Carbide, 370 U.S. 690, 706–707 (1962). Here we need not inquire further into the state-action question because it cannot fairly be said that the State of Virginia through its Supreme Court Rules required the anticompetitive activities of either respondent. Respondents have pointed to no Virginia statute requiring their activities; state law simply does not refer to fees, leaving regulation of the profession to the Virginia Supreme Court; although the Supreme Court's ethical codes mention advisory fee schedules they do not direct either respondent to supply them, or require the type of price floor which arose from respondents' activities. Although the State Bar apparently has been granted the power to issue ethical opinions, there is no indication in this record that the Virginia Supreme Court approves the opinions. Respondents' arguments, at most, constitute the contention that their activities complemented the objective of the ethical codes. In our view that is not state action for Sherman Act purposes. It is not enough that, as the County Bar puts it, anticompetitive conduct is "prompted" by state action; rather, anticompetitive activities must be compelled by direction of the State acting as a sovereign.

The fact that the State Bar is a state agency for some limited purposes does not create an antitrust shield that allows it to foster anticompetitive practices for the benefit of its members. The State Bar, by providing that deviation from County Bar minimum fees may lead to disciplinary action, has voluntarily joined in what is essentially a private anticompetitive activity, and in that posture cannot claim it is beyond the reach of the Sherman Act. Parker v. Brown, supra. Its activities resulted in a rigid price floor from which petitioners, as consumers, could not escape if they wished to borrow money to buy a home.

We recognize that the States have a compelling interest in the practice of professions within their boundaries, and that as part of their power to protect the public health, safety, and other valid interests they have broad power to establish standards for licensing practitioners and regulating the practice of professions. We also recognize that in some instances the State may decide that "forms of competition usual in the business world may be

---

In 1970 the Virginia Supreme Court amended the 1938 rules in part, and adopted the Code of Professional Responsibility, effective January 1, 1971. 211 Va. 295 (1970). Certain of its provisions also dealt with the fee-setting procedure. In EC 2–18 lawyers were told again that fees vary according to many factors, but that "[s]uggested fee schedules and economic reports of state and local bar associations provide some guidance on the subject of reasonable fees." Id., at 302. In DR 2–106(B), which detailed eight factors that should be considered in avoiding an excessive fee, one of the factors was "[t]he fee customarily charged in the locality for similar legal services." DR 2–106(B)(3). 211 Va., at 313.

demoralizing to the ethical standards of a profession." United States v. Oregon State Medical Society, 343 U.S. 326, 336 (1952). The interest of the States in regulating lawyers is especially great since lawyers are essential to the primary governmental function of administering justice, and have historically been "officers of the courts." ... In holding that certain anticompetitive conduct by lawyers is within the reach of the Sherman Act we intend no diminution of the authority of the State to regulate its professions.[54]

NOTES AND QUESTIONS

1. In *Parker,* the benefit to the participants was clear, but note also that 90% of all raisins were produced in California for export. This would give the State of California an additional reason to establish the cartel—its residents would benefit as producers very much more than they would pay as consumers. Check your Constitutional Law authorities to find out why the commerce clause wasn't offended by this apparent exploitation of out-of-state consumers in dealing with local resources. The answer may, in part, lie in the fact that Congress had affirmatively exercised its commerce power in general legislation supporting cartelization of agricultural products as national policy to combat the depression in the 1930s.

2. What are the important differences in the form and degree of state involvement between *Parker* and *Schwegmann?*

3. Note that the Miller–Tydings Act, referred to in *Schwegmann* as immunizing some forms of state "fair trade" laws from the Sherman Act (and the severe rule of *Dr. Miles,* p. 624, infra), was passed before *Parker* was decided. Was it necessary, in retrospect, in light of *Parker?* If it had not been enacted, might *Schwegmann* have been decided differently?

4. Note that the *Goldfarb* formulation leaves open such questions as: (a) When does the state "act as sovereign," and through what instrumentalities may it act? (b) If action is through courts, regulatory agencies, or municipalities, must standards be set by the legislature? (c) Who may supervise? (d) Why is the "mandatory" nature of the state action crucial? These are but a few of the technical questions raised by the Court's approach, and the questions will be addressed, in large part, by later Supreme Court decisions in this Section. But what are the policy considerations motivating the Court? In this area in particular, understanding the underlying policy issues may be the only way to understand the Court's decisions.

"STATE ACTION" BETWEEN *GOLDFARB* AND *MIDCAL*

1. CANTOR V. DETROIT EDISON CO., 428 U.S. 579, 96 S.Ct. 3110, 49 L.Ed.2d 1141 (1976). Defendant Detroit Edison, an electric utility, distributed light bulbs to its residential customers without additional charge, including the cost in its state-regulated electricity rates. Cantor, a light bulb retailer, brought suit, claiming that the utility was using its monopoly power in the distribution of electricity to foreclose competition in the sale of light bulbs. The Court held that the utility could not immunize itself from an action challenging the tying arrangement under the "state action" doctrine by embodying the practice in a tariff routinely approved by the state public utility commission. Michigan had no independent regulatory inter-

---

54. Ed. Since *Goldfarb* there has been considerable antitrust activity directed to- wards the professions. See Chapter 4, pp. 230–233 supra.

est in the market for light bulbs, and the light-bulb program was instigated by the utility. It was never independently considered by the commission.

2. BATES V. STATE BAR OF ARIZONA, 433 U.S. 350, 97 S.Ct. 2691, 53 L.Ed.2d 810 (1977). Two Phoenix attorneys challenged disciplinary rules prohibiting a lawyer from publicizing himself or others in his firm through any form of advertising or "commercial publicity." The attorneys published a newspaper advertisement showing fees for the services of their "legal clinic," and for this, were suspended from practice for a short period after a disciplinary proceeding by the State Bar Association. The Supreme Court unanimously held the disciplinary rules immune from Sherman Act challenge:

> In Parker v. Brown, 317 U.S. 341 (1943), this Court held that the Sherman Act was not intended to apply against certain state action.... Appellee argues, and the Arizona Supreme Court held, that the *Parker* exemption also bars the instant Sherman Act claim. We agree....

> In *Goldfarb* we held that § 1 of the Sherman Act was violated by the publication of a minimum-fee schedule by a county bar association and by its enforcement by the State Bar. The schedule and its enforcement mechanism operated to create a rigid price floor for services and thus constituted a classic example of price fixing. Both bar associations argued that their activity was shielded by the state-action exemption. This Court concluded that the action was not protected, emphasizing that "we need not inquire further into the state-action question because it cannot fairly be said that the State of Virginia through its Supreme Court Rules required the anticompetitive activities of either respondent." 421 U.S., at 790. In the instant case, by contrast, the challenged restraint is the affirmative command of the Arizona Supreme Court under its Rules 27(a) and 29(a) and its Disciplinary Rule 2–10(B). That court is the ultimate body wielding the State's power over the practice of law ... and, thus, the restraint is "compelled by direction of the State acting as a sovereign." 421 U.S., at 791.[55]

> Appellants seek to draw solace from *Cantor*.... Since the disciplinary rule at issue here is derived from the Code of Professional Responsibility of the American Bar Association, appellants argue by analogy to *Cantor* that no immunity should result from the bar's success in having the Code adopted by the State. They also assert that the interest embodied in the Sherman Act must prevail over the state interest in regulating the bar. Particularly is this the case, they claim, because the advertising ban is not tailored so as to intrude upon the federal interest to the minimum extent necessary.

> We believe, however, that the context in which *Cantor* arose is critical.... [T]he Court emphasized in *Cantor* that the State had no independent regulatory interest in the market for light bulbs.... There was no suggestion that the bulb program was justified by flaws in the competitive market or was a response to health or safety concerns. And an exemption for the program was not essential to the State's regulation of electric

---

55. We note, moreover, that the Court's opinion in *Goldfarb* concluded with the observation that "[i]n holding that certain anticompetitive conduct by lawyers is within the reach of the Sherman Act we intend no diminution of the authority of the State to regulate its professions." 421 U.S., at 793. Allowing the instant Sherman Act challenge to the disciplinary rule would have precisely that undesired effect.

utilities. In contrast, the regulation of the activities of the bar is at the core of the State's power to protect the public. Indeed, this Court in *Goldfarb* acknowledged that "[t]he interest of the States in regulating lawyers is especially great since lawyers are essential to the primary governmental function of administering justice, and have historically been 'officers of the courts.' " 421 U.S., at 792.... More specifically, controls over solicitation and advertising by attorneys have long been subject to the State's oversight.[56] Federal interference with a State's traditional regulation of a profession is entirely unlike the intrusion the Court sanctions in *Cantor*.[57]

Finally, the light-bulb program in *Cantor* was instigated by the utility with only the acquiescence of the state regulatory commission. The State's incorporation of the program into the tariff reflected its conclusion that the utility was authorized to employ the practice if it so desired.... The situation now before us is entirely different. The disciplinary rules reflect a clear articulation of the State's policy with regard to professional behavior. Moreover, as the instant case shows, the rules are subject to pointed reexamination by the policymaker—the Arizona Supreme Court—in enforcement proceedings. Our concern that federal policy is being unnecessarily and inappropriately subordinated to state policy is reduced in such a situation; we deem it significant that the state policy is so clearly and affirmatively expressed and that the State's supervision is so active.

Writing for a majority of five justices, Justice Blackmun then held that the First Amendment protects an attorney truthfully advertising the prices at which certain routine services may be performed. He reasoned:

In holding that advertising by attorneys may not be subjected to blanket suppression, and that the advertisement at issue is protected, we, of course, do not hold that advertising by attorneys may not be regulated in any way.... [W]e recognize that many of the problems in defining the boundary between deceptive and nondeceptive advertising remain to be resolved, and we expect that the bar will have a special role to play in assuring that advertising by attorneys flows both freely and cleanly.

3. NEW MOTOR VEHICLE BOARD OF CALIFORNIA v. ORRIN W. FOX CO., 439 U.S. 96, 109–111, 99 S.Ct. 403, 411–413, 58 L.Ed.2d 361 (1978). Under the California Automobile Franchise Act a motor vehicle manufacturer was required to secure the approval of the New Motor Vehicle Board before opening a dealership within the market area of an existing franchisee. The Supreme Court dealt with plaintiff's claim that the Automobile Franchise Act conflicted with the Sherman Act as follows:

The dispositive answer is that the ... Act's regulatory scheme is a system of regulation, clearly articulated and affirmatively expressed, designed to displace unfettered business freedom in the matter of the establishment and relocation of automobile dealerships. The regulation is

56. The limitation on advertising by attorneys in Arizona seems to have commenced in 1919 with the incorporation by reference of the American Bar Association's 1908 Canons of Professional Ethics into Arizona's statutory law.

57. Indeed, our decision today on the Sherman Act issue was presaged in Virginia Pharmacy Board v. Virginia Consumer Council, 425 U.S. 748, 770 (1976). We noted there: "Virginia is free to require whatever professional standards it wishes of its pharmacists; it may subsidize them or protect them from competition in other ways. Cf. Parker v. Brown, 317 U.S. 341 (1943)."

therefore outside the reach of the antitrust laws under the "state action" exemption. . . .

The Act does not lose this exemption simply because, as part of its regulatory framework, it accords existing dealers notice and an opportunity to be heard before their franchisor is permitted to locate a dealership likely to subject them to injurious and possibly illegal competition. Protests serve only to trigger Board action. They do not mandate significant delay. On the contrary, the Board has the authority to order an immediate hearing on a dealer protest if it concludes that the public interest so requires. The duration of interim restraint is subject to on-going regulatory supervision.

Appellee's reliance upon Schwegmann Bros. v. Calvert Distillers is misplaced. In *Schwegmann,* the State attempted to authorize and immunize private conduct violative of the antitrust laws. California has not done that here. Protesting dealers who invoke in good faith their statutory right to governmental action in the form of a Board determination that there is good cause for not permitting a proposed dealership do not violate the Sherman Act, Eastern Railroad Presidents Conference v. Noerr Motor Freight, Inc., 365 U.S. 127 (1961); and United Mine Workers v. Pennington, 381 U.S. 657, 670 (1965).

Appellees also argue conflict with the Sherman Act because the Automobile Franchise Act permits auto dealers to invoke state power for the purpose of restraining intrabrand competition. "This is merely another way of stating that the . . . statute will have an anticompetitive effect. In this sense, there is a conflict between the statute and the central policy of the Sherman Act—'our charter of economic liberty.' . . . Nevertheless, this sort of conflict cannot itself constitute a sufficient reason for invalidating the . . . statute. For if an adverse effect on competition were, in and of itself, enough to render a state statute invalid, the States' power to engage in economic regulation would be effectively destroyed." Exxon Corp. v. Governor of Maryland, 437 U.S. 117, 133 (1978).

California Retail Liquor Dealers Association v. Midcal Aluminum, Inc.

Supreme Court of the United States, 1980.
445 U.S. 97, 100 S.Ct. 937, 63 L.Ed.2d 233.

■ POWELL, J., . . . Under § 24866(b) of the California Business and Professions Code, all wine producers, wholesalers, and rectifiers must file fair trade contracts or price schedules with the State.[58] If a wine producer has not set prices through a fair trade contract, wholesalers must post a resale price schedule for that producer's brands. No state-licensed wine merchant

---

58. The statute provides:

"Each wine grower, wholesaler licensed to sell wine, wine rectifier, and rectifier shall:

"(a) Post a schedule of selling prices of wine to retailers or consumers for which his resale price is not governed by a fair trade contract made by the person who owns or controls the brand.

"(b) Make and file a fair trade contract and file a schedule of resale prices, if he owns or controls a brand of wine resold to retailers or consumers." Cal.Bus. & Prof.Code Ann. § 24866 (West 1964).

may sell wine to a retailer at other than the price set "either in an effective price schedule or in an effective fair trade contract. . . ."

The State is divided into three trading areas for administration of the wine pricing program. A single fair trade contract or schedule for each brand sets the terms for all wholesale transactions in that brand within a given trading area. Similarly, state regulations provide that the wine prices posted by a single wholesaler within a trading area bind all wholesalers in that area. . . . A licensee selling below the established prices faces fines, license suspension, or outright license revocation.[59] The State has no direct control over wine prices, and it does not review the reasonableness of the prices set by wine dealers.

Midcal Aluminum, Inc., is a wholesale distributor of wine in southern California. In July 1978, the Department of Alcoholic Beverage Control charged Midcal with selling 27 cases of wine for less than the prices set by the effective price schedule of the E. & J. Gallo Winery. The Department also alleged that Midcal sold wines for which no fair trade contract or schedule had been filed. Midcal stipulated that the allegations were true and that the State could fine it or suspend its license for those transgressions. Midcal then filed a writ of mandate in the California Court of Appeal for the Third Appellate District asking for an injunction against the State's wine pricing system.

The Court of Appeal ruled that the wine pricing scheme restrains trade in violation of the Sherman Act. . . . An appeal was brought by the California Retail Liquor Dealers Association, an intervenor.[60] The California Supreme Court declined to hear the case, and the Dealers Association sought certiorari from this Court. We granted the writ, 444 U.S. 824 (1979), and now affirm the decision of the state court.

The threshold question is whether California's plan for wine pricing violates the Sherman Act. This Court has ruled consistently that resale price maintenance illegally restrains trade. In Dr. Miles Medical Co. v. John D. Park & Sons Co., 220 U.S. 373, 407 (1911), the Court observed that such arrangements are "designed to maintain prices . . . , and to prevent competition among those who trade in [competing goods]." For many years, however, the Miller–Tydings Act of 1937 permitted the States to authorize resale price maintenance. The goal of that statute was to allow the States to protect small retail establishments that Congress thought might otherwise be driven from the market place by large-volume discounters. But in 1975 that congressional permission was rescinded. The Consumer Goods Pricing Act of 1975, 89 Stat. 801, repealed the Miller–Tydings Act and related legislation. Consequently, the Sherman Act's ban on resale price maintenance now applies to fair trade contracts unless an industry or program enjoys a special antitrust immunity.

---

59. Licensees that sell wine below the prices specified in fair trade contracts or schedules also may be subject to private damage suits for unfair competition.

60. The California Retail Liquor Dealers Association, a trade association of independent retail liquor dealers in California, claims over 3,000 members.

California's system for wine pricing plainly constitutes resale price maintenance in violation of the Sherman Act. The wine producer holds the power to prevent price competition by dictating the prices charged by wholesalers. As Mr. Justice Hughes pointed out in *Dr. Miles,* such vertical control destroys horizontal competition as effectively as if wholesalers "formed a combination and endeavored to establish the same restrictions ... by agreement with each other." 220 U.S., at 408. Moreover, there can be no claim that the California program is simply intrastate regulation beyond the reach of the Sherman Act. See Schwegmann Bros. v. Calvert Corp., supra; Burke v. Ford, 389 U.S. 320 (1967) (per curiam).

Thus, we must consider whether the State's involvement in the price-setting program is sufficient to establish antitrust immunity under Parker v. Brown, 317 U.S. 341 (1943). That immunity for state regulatory programs is grounded in our federal structure. "In a dual system of government in which, under the Constitution, the states are sovereign, save only as Congress may constitutionally subtract from their authority, an unexpressed purpose to nullify a state's control over its officers and agents is not lightly to be attributed to Congress." Id., at 351. In Parker v. Brown, this Court found in the Sherman Act no purpose to nullify state powers. Because the Act is directed against "individual and not state action," the Court concluded that state regulatory programs could not violate it. Id., at 352.

Under the program challenged in *Parker,* the State Agricultural Prorate Advisory Commission authorized the organization of local cooperatives to develop marketing policies for the raisin crop. The Court emphasized that the Advisory Commission, which was appointed by the Governor, had to approve cooperative policies following public hearings: "It is the state which has created the machinery for establishing the prorate program.... [I]t is the state, acting through the Commission, which adopts the program and enforces it...." Ibid. In view of this extensive official oversight, the Court wrote, the Sherman Act did not apply. Without such oversight, the result could have been different. The Court expressly noted that "a state does not give immunity to those who violate the Sherman Act by authorizing them to violate it, or by declaring that their action is lawful...." Id., at 351.

Several recent decisions have applied *Parker*'s analysis....[61] These decisions establish two standards for antitrust immunity under Parker v. Brown. First, the challenged restraint must be "one clearly articulated and affirmatively expressed as state policy"; second, the policy must be "actively supervised" by the State itself. City of Lafayette v. Louisiana Power & Light Co., 435 U.S. 389, 410 (1978) (opinion of Brennan, J.). The California system for wine pricing satisfies the first standard. The legislative policy is forthrightly stated and clear in its purpose to permit resale price maintenance. The program, however, does not meet the second requirement for

61. Ed. The Court then discussed the *Goldfarb, Cantor,* and *New Motor Vehicle* *Board* cases.

Parker immunity. The State simply authorizes price-setting and enforces the prices established by private parties. The State neither establishes prices nor reviews the reasonableness of the price schedules; nor does it regulate the terms of fair trade contracts. The State does not monitor market conditions or engage in any "pointed reexamination" of the program. The national policy in favor of competition cannot be thwarted by casting such a gauzy cloak of state involvement over what is essentially a private price-fixing arrangement. As *Parker* teaches, "a state does not give immunity to those who violate the Sherman Act by authorizing them to violate it, or by declaring that their action is lawful.... 317 U.S., at 351.

NOTE: ELABORATIONS ON *MIDCAL*

1. SOUTHERN MOTOR CARRIERS RATE CONFERENCE v. UNITED STATES, 471 U.S. 48 (1985). In this case, the United States brought an antitrust action against certain rate bureaus composed of private motor carriers operating in four southeastern states, each of which engaged in collective rate-setting for intrastate transactions (*i.e.*, price-fixing, in the Government's opinion). The respective states authorized, but did not compel, that activity. The rate bureaus, on behalf of their members, submitted joint rate proposals to the Public Service Commissions in each State for approval or rejection. This collective ratemaking was authorized, but not compelled, by the States in which the rate bureaus operate. The lower courts ruled against the rate bureaus, and the Supreme Court "granted certiorari to decide whether petitioners' collective ratemaking activities, though not compelled by the States in which they operate, are entitled to *Parker* immunity."

It decided that the answer to that question was yes. It began by noting that although *Parker* involved an action against a state official, the reasoning of that case extended to suits against private parties. This was because *Parker* was premised on the assumption that Congress, in enacting the Sherman Act, did not intend to compromise the States' ability to regulate their domestic commerce. Later, in *Midcal*, the Court adopted the two-part test under which *Parker* immunity follows if (1) the restraint is one that is clearly articulated and affirmatively established as state policy, and (2) the policy is actively supervised by the state itself.

The first part of that test was at issue in *Southern Motor Carriers*. The Court rejected the Government's argument that only actual compulsion by the state would be sufficient to constitute "clear articulation" and "affirmative establishment" of the state policy. It explained "[t]his type of analysis ignores the manner in which the States in this case clearly have intended their permissive policies to work. Most common carriers probably will engage in collective ratemaking, as that will allow them to share the cost of preparing rate proposals. If the joint rates are viewed as too high, however, carriers individually may submit lower proposed rates to the commission in order to obtain a larger share of the market. Thus, through the self-interested actions of private common carriers, the States may achieve the desired balance between the efficiency of collective ratemaking and the competition fostered by individual submissions. Construing the Sherman Act to prohibit collective rate proposals eliminates the free choice necessary to ensure that these policies function in the manner intended by the States. The federal antitrust laws do not forbid the States to adopt policies that permit, but do not compel, anticompetitive conduct by *regulated* private parties. As long as the State clearly articulates its intent to adopt a permissive policy, the first prong of the *Midcal* test is satisfied...."

It went on to explain its holding as follows:

The *Parker* doctrine represents an attempt to resolve conflicts that may arise between principles of federalism and the goal of the antitrust laws, unfettered competition in the marketplace. A compulsion requirement is inconsistent with both values. It reduces the range of regulatory alternatives available to the State. At the same time, insofar as it encourages States to require, rather than merely permit, anticompetitive conduct, a compulsion requirement may result in *greater* restraints on trade. We do not believe that Congress intended to resolve conflicts between two competing interests by impairing both more than necessary.

In summary, we hold *Midcal's* two-pronged test applicable to private parties' claims of state action immunity. Moreover, a state policy that expressly *permits,* but does not compel, anticompetitive conduct may be "clearly articulated" within the meaning of *Midcal.* Our holding today does not suggest, however, that compulsion is irrelevant. To the contrary, compulsion often is the best evidence that the State has a clearly articulated and affirmatively expressed policy to displace competition. See *Town of Hallie v. City of Eau Claire....* Nevertheless, when other evidence conclusively shows that a State intends to adopt a permissive policy, the absence of compulsion should not prove fatal to a claim of *Parker* immunity....

Our holding that there is no inflexible "compulsion requirement" does not suggest necessarily that petitioners' collective ratemaking activities are shielded from the federal antitrust laws. A private party may claim state action immunity only if both prongs of the *Midcal* test are satisfied. Here the Court of Appeals found, and the Government concedes, that the State Public Service Commissions actively supervise the collective ratemaking activities of the rate bureaus. Therefore, the only issue left to resolve is whether the petitioners' challenged conduct was taken pursuant to a clearly articulated state policy....

The Court found the latter requirement satisfied, and thus ruled for the petitioners.

2. TOWN OF HALLIE v. CITY OF EAU CLAIRE, 471 U.S. 34 (1985). This case examined the other half of the *Midcal* test—what is enough to constitute active supervision—in the special context of municipal regulations. Specifically, it presented the question whether a municipality's anticompetitive activities are protected by the state action exemption to the federal antitrust laws established by Parker v. Brown, 317 U.S. 341 (1943), when the activities are authorized, but not compelled, by the State, and the State does not actively supervise the anticompetitive conduct.

The plaintiffs were four unincorporated townships in Wisconsin who were suing the City of Eau Claire, alleging that the City violated the Sherman Act by acquiring a monopoly over the provision of sewage treatment services in Eau Claire and Chippewa Counties, and by tying the provision of such services to the provision of sewage collection and transportation services. Under the Federal Water Pollution Control Act, the City had obtained federal funds to help build a sewage treatment facility within the Eau Claire Service Area, that included the Towns; the facility was the only one in the market available to the Towns. The City had refused to supply sewage treatment services to the Towns, although it did supply the services to individual landowners located within the Towns if the people living in that area voted in favor of annexation by the City and use of its sewage collection and transportation services.

Alleging that they were potential competitors of the City in the collection and transportation of sewage, the Towns argued in the district court that the City used its monopoly over sewage treatment to gain an unlawful monopoly over the provision of sewage collection and transportation services, in violation of the Sherman Act. They also contended that the City's actions constituted an illegal tying arrangement and an unlawful refusal to deal with the Towns. Both the district court and the Court of Appeals for the Seventh Circuit ruled in favor of the City.

The Supreme Court began its discussion of the *Parker* doctrine by noting that municipalities are not "the state" for purposes of the antitrust laws, because they are not themselves sovereign, citing City of Lafayette v. Louisiana Power & Light Co., 435 U.S. 389 (1978). Rather, to obtain an exemption, municipalities (like the private parties in *Southern Motor Carriers*) must demonstrate that their anticompetitive activities were authorized by the State "pursuant to state policy to displace competition with regulation or monopoly public service." The Court then summarized the rule pertaining to municipalities:

"It is therefore clear from our cases that before a municipality will be entitled to the protection of the state action exemption from the antitrust laws, it must demonstrate that it is engaging in the challenged activity pursuant to a clearly expressed state policy. We have never fully considered, however, how clearly a state policy must be articulated for a municipality to be able to establish that its anticompetitive activity constitutes state action. Moreover, we have expressly left open the question whether action by a municipality—like action by a private party—must satisfy the "active state supervision" requirement. *City of Boulder,* supra. We consider both of those issues below."

After a detailed examination of the provisions of Wisconsin law that allegedly authorized the City's activities, the Court concluded that the statutes clearly contemplated that a city might engage in anticompetitive conduct. Such conduct is a foreseeable result of empowering the City to refuse to serve unannexed areas. It was not necessary for the state legislature to have stated explicitly that it expected the City to engage in conduct that would have anticompetitive effects. It was sufficient, instead, that the statutes authorized the City to provide sewage services and also to determine the areas to be served. The Court further rejected the Towns' argument that the statutes at issue were neutral on state policy, more like the Home Rule Amendment involved in *City of Boulder.* "The Towns' argument amounts to a contention that to pass the 'clear articulation' test, a legislature must expressly state in a statute or its legislative history that it intends for the delegated action to have anticompetitive effects. This contention embodies an unrealistic view of how legislatures work and of how statutes are written. No legislature can be expected to catalog all of the anticipated effects of a statute of this kind."

In sum, said the Court, "we conclude that the Wisconsin statutes evidence a 'clearly articulated and affirmatively expressed' state policy to displace competition with regulation in the area of municipal provision of sewerage services. These statutory provisions plainly show that " 'the legislature contemplated the kind of action complained of.' " *City of Lafayette,* supra. This is sufficient to satisfy the clear articulation requirement of the state action test."

Finally, the Court held that the "active state supervision" requirement of the Midcal test should not be imposed in cases in which the actor is a municipality.

That element served only an evidentiary function: it furnished one way of ensuring that the actor is engaging in the challenged conduct pursuant to state policy. The danger perceived in *Midcal* of a state's circumventing the Sherman Act's proscriptions "by casting ... a gauzy cloak of state involvement over what is essentially a private price-fixing arrangement," 445 U.S. at 10, might be a real one where a private party is engaging in the anticompetitive activity. "Where the actor is a municipality, there is little or no danger that it is involved in a *private* price-fixing arrangement. The only real danger is that it will seek to further purely parochial public interests at the expense of more overriding state goals. This danger is minimal, however, because of the requirement that the municipality act pursuant to a clearly articulated state policy. Once it is clear that state authorization exists, there is no need to require the State to supervise actively the municipality's execution of what is a properly delegated function."

3. FTC v. TICOR TITLE INSURANCE CO., 504 U.S. 621 (1992). This was a case brought by the Federal Trade Commission against six of the nation's largest title insurance companies, alleging horizontal price fixing in their fees for title searches and title examinations. One company settled by consent decree, while five other firms continue to contest the matter. A key issue was whether *Parker* immunity protected them. The Commission thought not; the Court of Appeals for the Third Circuit disagreed and held that state-action immunity was available. The Supreme Court reversed and remanded the case to the Commission for further proceedings.

The title insurance companies performed a variety of services for their customers, including the insurance of real property titles, and searching the chain of title to alert the prospective buyer to any defects or risks. The insured is protected from some losses resulting from title defects not discoverable from a search of the public records, such as forgery, missing heirs, previous marriages, impersonation, or confusion in names. He or she is also protected against errors or mistakes in the search and examination. Negligence need not be proved in order to recover. Title insurance also includes the obligation to defend in the event that an insured is sued by reason of some defect within the scope of the policy's guarantee. The respondents accounted for 57 percent of the $1.35 billion in gross revenues that the industry had reaped in 1982. In 1985, the Commission issued an administrative complaint in which it charged classic horizontal price-fixing: "Respondents have agreed on the price to be charged for title search and examination services or settlement services through rating bureaus in various states...." The companies defended on several grounds: McCarran–Ferguson Act exemption, *Noerr-Pennington* exemption, and state-action immunity. The ALJ rejected all three, and the Commission accepted his findings and conclusions.

Most importantly for the *Parker* argument, the Commission (and ALJ) found that the rating bureaus were not pooling risk information or otherwise setting insurance rates according to actuarial loss experience. Instead, they were looking simply at profitability studies. Each of the four States in question used what has come to be called a "negative option" system to approve rate filings by the bureaus. This meant in practice that the rating bureau filed rates for title searches and title examinations with the state insurance office, and the rates became effective unless the state rejected them within a specified period, such as 30 days. Although the negative option system provided a theoretical mechanism for substantive review, the ALJ determined that the rate filings were subject to minimal scrutiny by state regulators.

This was not enough, in the Commission's opinion, to rise to the level of "active supervision" for *Parker* and *Midcal* purposes. The court of appeals (agreeing here with the First Circuit's decision in New England Motor Rate Bureau, Inc. v. FTC, 908 F.2d 1064 (1st Cir.1990)), held that it was enough if a state regulatory program existed, was staffed, funded, and empowered by law to supervise the private actions. The Supreme Court disagreed with that standard, with the following explanation:

The principle of freedom of action for the States, adopted to foster and preserve the federal system, explains the later evolution and application of the *Parker* doctrine in our decisions in *Midcal, supra,* and Patrick v. Burget, 486 U.S. 94 (1988).... *Midcal* confirms that while a State may not confer antitrust immunity on private persons by fiat, it may displace competition with active state supervision if the displacement is both intended by the State and implemented in its specific details. Actual state involvement, not deference to private price-fixing arrangements under the general auspices of state law, is the precondition for immunity from federal law. Immunity is conferred out of respect for ongoing regulation by the State, not out of respect for the economics of price restraint. In *Midcal* we found that the intent to restrain prices was expressed with sufficient precision so that the first part of the test was met, but that the absence of state participation in the mechanics of the price posting was so apparent that the requirement of active supervision had not been met.

The rationale was further elaborated in *Patrick v. Burget* [described p. 468, note 5]. Because the particular anticompetitive conduct at issue in *Patrick* had not been supervised by governmental actors, we decided that the actions of the peer review committee were not entitled to state-action immunity.

Our decisions make clear that the purpose of the active supervision inquiry is not to determine whether the State has met some normative standard, such as efficiency, in its regulatory practices. Its purpose is to determine whether the State has exercised sufficient independent judgment and control so that the details of the rates or prices have been established as a product of deliberate state intervention, not simply by agreement among private parties. Much as in causation inquiries, the analysis asks whether the State has played a substantial role in determining the specifics of the economic policy. The question is not how well state regulation works but whether the anticompetitive scheme is the State's own.

Although the point bears but brief mention, we observe that our prior cases considered state-action immunity against actions brought under the Sherman Act, and this case arises under the Federal Trade Commission Act. The Commission has argued at other times that state-action immunity does not apply to Commission action under § 5 of the Federal Trade Commission Act.... We need not determine whether the antitrust statutes can be distinguished on this basis, because the Commission does not assert any superior pre-emption authority in the instant matter. We apply our prior cases to the one before us....

If the States must act in the shadow of state-action immunity whenever they enter the realm of economic regulation, then our doctrine will impede their freedom of action, not advance it. The fact of the matter is that the States regulate their economies in many ways not inconsistent with the antitrust laws. For example, Oregon may provide for peer review by its physicians without approving anticompetitive conduct by them.... Or Michigan may regulate its public utilities without authorizing monopolization in the market for electric light bulbs. See Cantor v. Detroit Edison Co., 428 U.S. 579, 596 (1976). So we have held that state-action immunity is disfavored, much as are repeals by implication. Lafayette v. Louisiana Power & Light Co., 435 U.S. 389, 398–399 (1978). By adhering in most cases to fundamental and accepted assumptions about the benefits of competition within the framework of the antitrust laws, we increase the States' regulatory flexibility. . . .

The respondents contend that these concerns are better addressed by the requirement that the States articulate a clear policy to displace the antitrust laws with their own forms of economic regulation. This contention misapprehends the close relation between *Midcal's* two elements. Both are directed at ensuring that particular anticompetitive mechanisms operate because of a deliberate and intended state policy. In the usual case, *Midcal's* requirement that the State articulate a clear policy shows little more than that the State has not acted through inadvertence; it cannot alone ensure, as required by our precedents, that particular anticompetitive conduct has been approved by the State. It seems plain, moreover, in light of the *amici curiae* brief to which we have referred, that sole reliance on the requirement of clear articulation will not allow the regulatory flexibility that these States deem necessary. For States whose object it is to benefit their citizens through regulation, a broad doctrine of state-action immunity may serve as nothing more than an attractive nuisance in the economic sphere. To oppose these pressures, sole reliance on the requirement of clear articulation could become a rather meaningless formal constraint.

The Court found that the standard used by the courts of appeals, under which it was enough to have a program "in place, staffed, funded," under which the state officials had sufficient authority to regulate, was "insufficient to establish the requisite level of active supervision." Instead, the party claiming the immunity must show that state officials have undertaken the necessary steps to determine the specifics of the price-fixing or rate-setting scheme. The Court distinguished between the mere potential for state supervision and an actual decision by the State. Under those standards, it concluded that there was no active supervision in either Wisconsin or Montana:

This case involves horizontal price fixing under a vague imprimatur in form and agency inaction in fact. No antitrust offense is more pernicious than price fixing. FTC v. Superior Court Trial Lawyers Assn., 493 U.S. 411, 434, n. 16 (1990). In this context, we decline to formulate a rule that would lead to a finding of active state supervision where in fact there was none. Our decision should be read in light of the gravity of the antitrust offense, the involvement of private actors throughout, and the clear absence of state supervision. We do not imply that some particular form of state or local regulation is required to achieve ends other than the establishment of uniform prices. Cf. Columbia v. Omni Outdoor Advertising, Inc., 499 U.S. 365 (1991) (city billboard zoning ordinance entitled to state-action immunity). We do not have before us a case in which governmental actors made unilateral decisions without participation by private actors. Cf. Fisher v. Berkeley, 475 U.S. 260 (1986) (private actors not liable without private action). And we do not here call into question a regulatory regime in which sampling techniques or a specified rate of return allow state regulators to provide comprehensive supervision without complete control, or in which there was an infrequent lapse of state supervision. Cf. 324 Liquor Corp. v.

Duffy, 479 U.S. 335, 344, n. 6 (1987) (a statute specifying the margin between wholesale and retail prices may satisfy the active supervision requirement). In the circumstances of this case, however, we conclude that the acts of the respondents in the States of Montana and Wisconsin are not immune from antitrust liability.

The Court remanded for further findings on the actual extent of state supervision. Justice Scalia concurred, commenting that while the Court's standard was faithful to what prior cases had said about active supervision, it was troubling in its vagueness. He also noted that he was "skeptical about the *Parker v. Brown* exemption for state-programmed private collusion in the first place." Chief Justice Rehnquist (with Justices O'Connor and Thomas joining him) dissented, finding that the Court's standard was neither warranted by earlier cases nor sound as a matter of policy. He expressed concern about the way in which the courts were to decide whether a state had played a substantial enough role in determining the specifics of a policy to justify the immunity. Because, in the States at issue in the *Ticor* case itself, the particular conduct was approved by a state agency when it raised no objection, he would have found enough to satisfy the "active supervision" requirement.

NOTES AND QUESTIONS

1.   After *Southern Motor Carriers,* how clearly articulated and affirmatively expressed must a state decision be to replace competition with regulation? May any institution, agency, or part of state government—other than the legislature or the state's highest court—provide state authorization for regulation rather than competition? *See, e.g.,* Hoover v. Ronwin, 466 U.S. 558 (1984); Hardy v. City Optical Inc., 39 F.3d 765 (7th Cir.1994); Hovenkamp, Federal Antitrust Policy: The Law of Competition and Its Practice 678–81 (1994). Why was not the filing of tariffs in the *Ticor* case considered petitioning protected by *Noerr?*

2.   Was there adequate state supervision in the *Parker* case? After *Ticor,* how far may (or must) federal courts now go in reviewing the effectiveness of state supervision? What if a state commission is tilted towards—or corrupted by—a regulated group? Against what policy objectives should active supervision by the state be measured? Why do municipalities get a free pass, if they really are nothing more than corporate creations of the state?

3.   What if, altering the facts of *Goldfarb,* the Supreme Court of Virginia, without specific legislative authority, had mandated minimum fee schedules and authorized each county bar to establish local levels of fees? Would complying associations, or their members, be subject to Sherman Act scrutiny? Would it make a difference if the Virginia Supreme Court reviewed each such schedule for reasonableness prior to its adoption?

What if the Virginia Supreme Court (or the legislature) actually set mandatory minimum fee schedules itself?

4.   In 324 LIQUOR CORP. V. DUFFY, 479 U.S. 335 (1987), the State of New York required retailers to charge at least 112 percent of the "posted" wholesale price for liquor, but permitted wholesalers to sell to retailers at less than the "posted" price. Justice Powell, writing for seven members of the Supreme Court, declared the legislation invalid and reasoned as follows:

> Section 101–bb directly restricts retail prices, and retailers are subject
> to penalties for failure to adhere to the resale price schedules. The New

York statute, moreover, applies to *all* wholesalers and retailers of liquor. We have noted that industry wide resale price maintenance also may facilitate cartelization.... Mandatory industry wide resale price fixing is virtually certain to reduce interbrand competition as well as intrabrand competition, because it prevents manufacturers and wholesalers from allowing or requiring retail price competition. The New York statute specifically forbids retailers from reducing the minimum prices set by wholesalers....

Our decisions have established a two-part test for determining immunity under *Parker v. Brown*.... New York's liquor pricing system meets the first requirement. The state legislature clearly has adopted a policy of resale price maintenance. Just as clearly, however, New York's liquor pricing system is not actively supervised by the State. As in *Midcal*, the State "simply authorizes price setting and enforces the prices established by private parties."[62] New York "neither establishes prices nor reviews the reasonableness of the price schedules." New York "does not monitor market conditions or engage in any 'pointed reexamination' of the program." ... [63]The State has displaced competition among liquor retailers without substituting an adequate system of regulation.

5. In PATRICK V. BURGET, 486 U.S. 94 (1988), an independent surgeon brought suit against medical practitioners who were partners in a private group-medical clinic in a small Oregon community. The partners made up a majority of the staff members of the only hospital in town. Dr. Patrick's Sherman Act claim was that the clinic partners had initiated and participated in hospital peer-review proceedings to reduce competition by excluding him.

62. A simple "minimum markup" statute requiring retailers to charge 112 percent of their actual wholesale cost may satisfy the "active supervision" requirement, and so be exempt from the antitrust laws under Parker v. Brown, 317 U.S. 341 (1943). See Morgan v. Division of Liquor Control, 664 F.2d 353 (C.A.2 1981) (upholding a simple markup statute). Section 101–bb, however, is not a simple minimum markup statute because it imposes a markup on the "posted bottle price," a price that may greatly exceed what the retailer actually paid for the liquor. As we have explained, Bulletin 471 permits wholesalers to reduce the case price—the price actually paid by most retailers—without reducing the bottle price. The New York Court of Appeals expressly held that Bulletin 471 "is consistent with Alcoholic Beverage Control Law § 101–b(3) which does not mandate any price ratio between scheduled case and bottle prices." ... We thus have no occasion to consider whether a simple minimum markup statute would be entitled to antitrust immunity under *Parker v. Brown*.

Some States completely control the distribution of liquor within their boundaries. *E.g.,* Va.Code §§ 4–15, 4–28 (1983). Such comprehensive regulation is immune under *Parker v. Brown* because the State substitutes its own power for "unfettered business freedom." See New Motor Vehicle Bd. of Cal. v. Orrin W. Fox Co., 439 U.S. 96, 109 (1978).

63. In a concurring opinion, Judge Jasen argued that the State actively supervises the liquor pricing system.... Judge Jasen noted that the SLA can respond to market conditions by permitting individual wholesalers to depart from their posted prices, and by permitting individual retailers to sell below the statutory definition of "cost," ABC Law, § 101–bb(3), "for good cause shown." Bulletin 471 itself was issued by the SLA in response to market conditions. Moreover, the State Legislature frequently considers proposals to alter the liquor pricing system. Neither the "monitoring" by the SLA, nor the periodic reexaminations by the State Legislature, exerts any significant control over retail liquor prices or mark-ups. Thus, the State's involvement does not satisfy the second requirement of *Midcal*.

There was extensive evidence of other harassment by partners in the clinic after plaintiff had refused an invitation to become a member, which doubtless played a role in the jury's substantial verdict, and the Court of Appeal's opinion characterizing defendants' conduct as "shabby, unprincipled and unprofessional." However, the Court of Appeals reversed the judgment for plaintiff and held that since Oregon had articulated a policy in favor of peer review, and actively supervised the process, "state action" immunity was applicable. The Supreme Court, per Marshall, J., reversed and reasoned:

> In this case, we need not consider the "clear articulation" prong of the *Midcal* test, because the "active supervision" requirement is not satisfied.... The requirement is designed to ensure that the state action doctrine will shelter only the particular anticompetitive acts of private parties that, in the judgment of the State, actually further state regulatory policies. To accomplish this purpose, the active supervision requirement mandates that the State exercise ultimate control over the challenged anticompetitive conduct.... The mere presence of some state involvement or monitoring does not suffice.... The active supervision prong of the *Midcal* test requires that state officials have and exercise power to review particular anticompetitive acts of private parties and disapprove those that fail to accord with state policy. Absent such a program of supervision, there is no realistic assurance that a private party's anticompetitive conduct promotes state policy, rather than merely the party's individual interests.

> Respondents in this case contend that the State of Oregon actively supervises the peer-review process through the state Health Division, the [state Board of Medical Examiner (BOME)], and the state judicial system. The Court of Appeals, in finding the active supervision requirement satisfied, also relied primarily on the powers and responsibilities of these state actors. Neither the Court of Appeals nor respondents, however, have succeeded in showing that any of these actors review—or even could review—private decisions regarding hospital privileges to determine whether such decisions comport with state regulatory policy and to correct abuses.

> [U]nder the statutory scheme, the Health Division has no power to review private peer-review decisions and overturn a decision that fails to accord with state policy. Thus, the activities of the Health Division under Oregon law cannot satisfy the active supervision requirement of the state action doctrine. Similarly, the BOME does not engage in active supervision over private peer-review decisions.... Certainly, respondents have not shown that the BOME in practice reviews privilege decisions or that it ever has asserted the authority to reverse them.

> The only remaining alleged supervisory authority in this case is the state judiciary. Respondents claim, and the Court of Appeals agreed, that Oregon's courts directly review privilege-termination decisions and that this judicial review constitutes active state supervision. This Court has not previously considered whether state courts, acting in their judicial capacity, can adequately supervise private conduct for purposes of the state action doctrine. All of our prior cases concerning state supervision over private parties have involved administrative agencies, *see, e.g.*, [*Southern Motor Carriers*], or state supreme courts with agency-like responsibilities over the organized bar, see [*Bates*]. This case, however, does not require us to decide the broad question whether judicial review of private conduct ever can

constitute active supervision, because judicial review of privilege-termination decisions in Oregon, if such review exists at all, falls far short of satisfying the active supervision requirement.

As an initial matter, it is not clear that Oregon law affords any direct judicial review of private peer-review decisions. Oregon has no statute expressly providing for judicial review of privilege terminations. Moreover, we are aware of no case in which an Oregon court has held that judicial review of peer-review decisions is available.

Moreover, the Oregon courts have indicated that even if they were to provide judicial review of hospital peer-review proceedings, the review would be of a very limited nature. The Oregon Supreme Court, in its most recent decision addressing this matter, stated that a court "should [not] decide the merits of plaintiff's dismissal" and that "[i]t would be unwise for a court to do more than to make sure that some sort of reasonable procedure was afforded and that there was evidence from which it could be found that plaintiff's conduct posed a threat to patient care." Straube v. Emmanuel Lutheran Charity Board, supra, at 384, 600 P.2d, at 386. This kind of review would fail to satisfy the state action doctrine's requirement of active supervision. Under the standard suggested by the Oregon Supreme Court, a state court would not review the merits of a privilege-termination decision to determine whether it accorded with state regulatory policy. Such constricted review does not convert the action of a private party in terminating a physician's privileges into the action of the State for purposes of the state action doctrine. In so holding, we are not unmindful of the policy argument that respondents and their amici have advanced for reaching the opposite conclusion. They contend that effective peer review is essential to the provision of quality medical care and that any threat of antitrust liability will prevent physicians from participating openly and actively in peer-review proceedings. This argument, however, essentially challenges the wisdom of applying the antitrust laws to the sphere of medical care, and as such is properly directed to the legislative branch. To the extent that Congress has declined to exempt medical peer review from the reach of the antitrust laws, peer review is immune from antitrust scrutiny only if the State effectively has made this conduct its own. The State of Oregon has not done so.

6. Should the *Parker* exemption to the Sherman Act apply—or apply in precisely the same way—to violations of the Clayton Act? To proceedings brought by the Federal Trade Commission under § 5 of the FTC Act? Notice that the Supreme Court was able to avoid resolving the issue in *Ticor.* See p. 464 supra.

7. After the *City of Lafayette* and *City of Boulder* decisions, but before *Town of Hallie,* Congress responded to lower court treble damage awards against municipalities and municipal officials, and a widespread fear of a deluge of such suits, by passage of the Local Government Antitrust Act of 1984.[64] The Act prohibits plaintiffs from recovering monetary damages "from any local government, or official or employee thereof acting in an official capacity." The Act also provides that no damages may be recovered from any person "based on any official action directed by a local government, or official or employee thereof acting in an official capacity."[65]

---

64. 15 U.S.C. §§ 34–36.

65. *See, e.g.,* Cohn v. Wilkes General Hospital, 767 F.Supp. 111 (W.D.N.C.), aff'd

sub. nom., Cohn v. Bond, 953 F.2d 154 (4th Cir.1991), cert. denied, 505 U.S. 1230 (1992) (rejecting claim that the Act does not protect

The Act leaves intact the possibility of obtaining injunctive relief against local governments or other persons. In light of *Town of Hallie* and *Omni Outdoor* (p. 472 infra), should the Act now be repealed?

8. In CITY OF LAFAYETTE V. LOUISIANA POWER & LIGHT CO., 435 U.S. 389 (1978), discussed in *Town of Hallie,* two Louisiana cities sued several privately owned utilities, alleging that utility systems owned and operated by plaintiff cities had been injured as a result of defendants' conspiracy to restrain trade in the generation, transmission, and distribution of electric power in the region. Louisiana Power counterclaimed, alleging that, among other things, plaintiffs required that customers located outside city limits purchase electricity from their utilities as a condition of continued water and gas service, *i.e.,* employed tie-ins which deprived the private utilities of customers.

The Supreme Court rejected the cities' "state action" defense, noting in a plurality opinion: (1) that municipalities must be distinguished from the states from which they derive their existence; (2) that they did not "exercise the sovereign power of the state" for "state action" purposes, since their interests are necessarily more parochial than, and might even conflict with, the broader interest of the states recognized in the *Parker* case; (3) that redress through political action did not protect those injured by municipalities' conduct outside their borders; and (4) that if the "62,437 different units of local government in this country ... were free to make economic choices without regard to anticompetitive effects" the national policy embodied in antitrust laws would be seriously subverted.

The plurality asserted that municipalities could claim "state action" exemption only "pursuant to state policy to displace competition with regulation or monopoly public service"; this need not be "a specific, detailed legislative authorization," but rather a sufficient basis for concluding that the legislature contemplated the kind of action complained of.

Applying the later *Town of Hallie* formulation, should the "state action" claim in the *Lafayette* case have been sustained? What further information would you need?

9. COMMUNITY COMMUNICATIONS CO. V. CITY OF BOULDER, 455 U.S. 40 (1982), also discussed in *Town of Hallie,* involved a claim that the City's "emergency" ordinance prohibiting plaintiff from expanding service under its cable TV franchise constituted an antitrust violation. The City of Boulder, organized as a "home rule" municipality under Colorado's state constitution, claimed that this status justified its assertion of a "state action" exemption.

The Supreme Court rejected this claim, stating that the general authority to act provided by "home rule" status was not sufficiently particularized to satisfy the requirement announced in *City of Lafayette.* The criterion of "clear articulation and affirmative expression is not satisfied when the State's position is one of mere *neutrality* respecting the municipal actions challenged as anticompetitive."

10. School districts and "authorities" established by state law to operate highways, bridges, airports, seaports, stadiums, convention halls, and the like, sometimes compete with private business, and often enter into exclusive contracts or other arrangements which foreclose others from access to the facility or are

private physician defendants, at a municipal hospital, if they use their official capacity "as a cloak for advancing their private economic interests" because the Act does not require consideration of the actors' intentions but rather grants immunity for acts undertaken in an official capacity).

otherwise anticompetitive. Such entities are usually created with explicit or implicit authority to enter into all necessary contracts. As *Town of Hallie* recognizes, at least as to municipalities, "state action" requirements of clearly articulated policy to displace competition and continuing surveillance by the state are not entirely appropriate. Is this also the case as to special-purpose "authorities"? They are usually chartered as monopolies and they can hardly act as if they were operating in a competitive market. They also usually have no direct accountability to the electorate. Should they be subject to no greater requirement of surveillance than municipalities?

Columbia v. Omni Outdoor Advertising, Inc.

Supreme Court of the United States, 1991.
499 U.S. 365, 111 S.Ct. 1344, 113 L.Ed.2d 382.

■ SCALIA, J. This case requires us to clarify the application of the Sherman Act to municipal governments and to the citizens who seek action from them.

I

Petitioner Columbia Outdoor Advertising, Inc. (COA), a South Carolina corporation, entered the billboard business in the city of Columbia, South Carolina (also a petitioner here), in the 1940s. By 1981 it controlled more than 95% of what has been conceded to be the relevant market. COA was a local business owned by a family with deep roots in the community, and enjoyed close relations with the city's political leaders. The mayor and other members of the city council were personal friends of COA's majority owner, and the company and its officers occasionally contributed funds and free billboard space to their campaigns. According to respondent, these beneficiaries were part of a "longstanding" "secret anticompetitive agreement" whereby "the City and COA would each use their [*sic*] respective power and resources to protect . . . COA's monopoly position," in return for which "City Council members received advantages made possible by COA's monopoly."

In 1981, respondent Omni Outdoor Advertising, Inc., a Georgia corporation, began erecting billboards in and around the city. COA responded to this competition in several ways. First, it redoubled its own billboard construction efforts and modernized its existing stock. Second—according to Omni—it took a number of anticompetitive private actions, such as offering artificially low rates, spreading untrue and malicious rumors about Omni, and attempting to induce Omni's customers to break their contracts. Finally (and this is what gives rise to the issue we address today), COA executives met with city officials to seek the enactment of zoning ordinances that would restrict billboard construction. COA was not alone in urging this course; a number of citizens concerned about the city's recent explosion of billboards advocated restrictions, including writers of articles and editorials in local newspapers.

In the spring of 1982, the city council passed an ordinance requiring the council's approval for every billboard constructed in downtown Columbia. This was later amended to impose a 180–day moratorium on the construction of billboards throughout the city, except as specifically authorized by the council. A state court invalidated this ordinance on the ground that its conferral of unconstrained discretion upon the city council violated both the South Carolina and Federal Constitutions. The city then requested the State's regional planning authority to conduct a comprehensive analysis of the local billboard situation as a basis for developing a final, constitutionally valid, ordinance. In September 1982, after a series of public hearings and numerous meetings involving city officials, Omni, and COA (in all of which, according to Omni, positions contrary to COA's were not genuinely considered), the city council passed a new ordinance restricting the size, location, and spacing of billboards. These restrictions, particularly those on spacing, obviously benefitted COA, which already had its billboards in place; they severely hindered Omni's ability to compete.

In November 1982, Omni filed suit against COA and the city in Federal District Court, charging that they had violated §§ 1 and 2 of the Sherman Act, as well as South Carolina's Unfair Trade Practices Act, S.C.Code § 39–5–140 (1976). Omni contended, in particular, that the city's billboard ordinances were the result of an anticompetitive conspiracy between city officials and COA that stripped both parties of any immunity they might otherwise enjoy from the federal antitrust laws. In January 1986, after more than two weeks of trial, a jury returned general verdicts against the city and COA on both the federal and state claims. It awarded damages, before trebling, of $600,000 on the § 1 Sherman Act claim, and $400,000 on the § 2 claim.[66] The jury also answered two special interrogatories, finding specifically that the city and COA had conspired both to restrain trade and to monopolize the market. Petitioners moved for judgment notwithstanding the verdict, contending among other things that their activities were outside the scope of the federal antitrust laws. In November 1988, the District Court granted the motion.

A divided panel of the United States Court of Appeals for the Fourth Circuit reversed the judgment of the District Court and reinstated the jury verdict on all counts. 891 F.2d 1127 (1989). We granted certiorari.

II

In the landmark case of Parker v. Brown, 317 U.S. 341 (1943), we rejected the contention that a program restricting the marketing of privately produced raisins, adopted pursuant to California's Agricultural Prorate

---

66. The monetary damages in this case were assessed entirely against COA, the District Court having ruled that the city was immunized by the Local Government Antitrust Act of 1984, which exempts local governments from paying damages for violations of the federal antitrust laws. Although enacted in 1984, after the events at issue in this case, the Act specifically provides that it may be applied retroactively if "the defendant establishes and the court determines, in light of all the circumstances ... that it would be inequitable not to apply this subsection to a pending case." 15 U.S.C. § 35(b). The District Court determined that it would be, and the Court of Appeals refused to disturb that judgment. Respondent has not challenged that determination in this Court, and we express no view on the matter.

Act, violated the Sherman Act. Relying on principles of federalism and state sovereignty, we held that the Sherman Act did not apply to anticompetitive restraints imposed by the States "as an act of government."

Since *Parker* emphasized the role of sovereign States in a federal system, it was initially unclear whether the governmental actions of political subdivisions enjoyed similar protection. In recent years, we have held that *Parker* immunity does not apply directly to local governments, see Hallie v. Eau Claire, 471 U.S. 34, 38 (1985). We have recognized, however, that a municipality's restriction of competition may sometimes be an authorized implementation of state policy, and have accorded *Parker* immunity where that is the case.

The South Carolina statutes under which the city acted in the present case authorize municipalities to regulate the use of land and the construction of buildings and other structures within their boundaries.[67] It is undisputed that, as a matter of state law, these statutes authorize the city to regulate the size, location, and spacing of billboards. It could be argued, however, that a municipality acts beyond its delegated authority, for *Parker* purposes, whenever the nature of its regulation is substantively or even procedurally defective. On such an analysis it could be contended, for example, that the city's regulation in the present case was not "authorized" by S.C.Code § 5–23–10 (1976), if it was not, as that statute requires, adopted "for the purpose of promoting health, safety, morals or the general welfare of the community." As scholarly commentary has noted, such an expansive interpretation of the *Parker*–defense authorization requirement would have unacceptable consequences.

> "To be sure, state law 'authorizes' only agency decisions that are substantively and procedurally correct. Errors of fact, law, or judgment by the agency are not 'authorized.' Erroneous acts or decisions are subject to reversal by superior tribunals because unauthorized. If the antitrust court demands unqualified 'authority' in this sense, it inevitably becomes the standard reviewer not only of federal agency activity but also of state and local activity whenever it is alleged that the governmental body, though possessing the power to engage in the challenged conduct, has actually exercised its power in a manner not authorized by state law. We should not lightly assume that *Lafayette's* authorization requirement dictates transformation of state administrative review into a federal antitrust job. Yet that would be the consequence of making antitrust liability depend on an undiscriminating and mechanical demand for 'authority' in the full administrative law sense." P. Areeda & H. Hovenkamp, Antitrust Law para. 212.3b, p. 145 (Supp. 1989).

---

67. S.C.Code § 5–23–10 (1976) ("Building and zoning regulations authorized") provides that "[f]or the purpose of promoting health, safety, morals or the general welfare of the community, the legislative body of cities and incorporated towns may by ordinance regulate and restrict the height, number of stories and size of buildings and other structures." . . .

We agree with that assessment, and believe that in order to prevent *Parker* from undermining the very interests of federalism it is designed to protect, it is necessary to adopt a concept of authority broader than what is applied to determine the legality of the municipality's action under state law. We have adopted an approach that is similar in principle, though not necessarily in precise application, elsewhere. See Stump v. Sparkman, 435 U.S. 349 (1978). It suffices for the present to conclude that here no more is needed to establish, for *Parker* purposes, the city's authority to regulate than its unquestioned zoning power over the size, location, and spacing of billboards.

Besides authority to regulate, however, the *Parker* defense also requires authority to suppress competition—more specifically, "clear articulation of a state policy to authorize anticompetitive conduct" by the municipality in connection with its regulation. *Hallie,* 471 U.S., at 40 (internal quotation omitted). We have rejected the contention that this requirement can be met only if the delegating statute explicitly permits the displacement of competition. It is enough, we have held, if suppression of competition is the "foreseeable result" of what the statute authorizes, *id.,* at 42. That condition is amply met here. The very purpose of zoning regulation is to displace unfettered business freedom in a manner that regularly has the effect of preventing normal acts of competition, particularly on the part of new entrants. A municipal ordinance restricting the size, location, and spacing of billboards (surely a common form of zoning) necessarily protects existing billboards against some competition from newcomers.[68]

---

68. The dissent contends that, in order successfully to delegate its *Parker* immunity to a municipality, a State must expressly authorize the municipality to engage (1) in specifically "economic regulation," (2) of a specific industry. These dual specificities are without support in our precedents, for the good reason that they defy rational implementation.

If, by authority to engage in specifically "economic" regulation, the dissent means authority specifically to regulate competition, we squarely rejected that in *Hallie,* as discussed in text. Seemingly, however, the dissent means only that the State authorization must specify that sort of regulation whereunder *decisions* about prices and output are not made by individual firms, but rather by a public body. But why is not the restriction of billboards in a city a restriction on the "output" of the local billboard industry? It assuredly *is*- and that is indeed the very gravamen of Omni's complaint. It seems to us that the dissent's concession that "it is often difficult to differentiate economic regulation from municipal regulation of health, safety, and welfare" is a gross understatement. Loose talk about a "regulated industry" may suffice for what the dissent calls "antitrust parlance," but it is not a definition upon which the criminal liability of public officials ought to depend.

Under the dissent's second requirement for a valid delegation of *Parker* immunity— that the authorization to regulate pertain to a specific industry—the problem with the South Carolina statute is that it used the generic term "structures," instead of conferring its regulatory authority industry-by-industry (presumably "billboards," "movie houses," "mobile homes," "TV antennas," and every other conceivable object of zoning regulation that can be the subject of a relevant "market" for purposes of antitrust analysis). To describe this is to refute it. Our precedents not only fail to suggest but positively reject such an approach. "The municipality need not 'be able to point to a specific, detailed legislative authorization' in order to assert a successful *Parker* defense to an antitrust suit." *Hallie,* 471 U.S., at 39 (quoting *Lafayette,* 435 U.S., at 415).

The Court of Appeals was therefore correct in its conclusion that the city's restriction of billboard construction was prima facie entitled to *Parker* immunity. The Court of Appeals upheld the jury verdict, however, by invoking a "conspiracy" exception to *Parker* that has been recognized by several Courts of Appeals. That exception is thought to be supported by two of our statements in *Parker:* "[W]e have no question of the state or its municipality becoming a *participant in a private agreement* or combination by others for restraint of trade." "The state in adopting and enforcing the prorate program made no contract or agreement *and entered into no conspiracy in restraint of trade or to establish monopoly* but, as sovereign, imposed the restraint as an act of government which the Sherman Act did not undertake to prohibit." *Id.,* at 352 (emphasis added). *Parker* does not apply, according to the Fourth Circuit, "where politicians or political entities are involved as conspirators" with private actors in the restraint of trade. 891 F.2d, at 1134.

There is no such conspiracy exception. The rationale of *Parker* was that, in light of our national commitment to federalism, the general language of the Sherman Act should not be interpreted to prohibit anticompetitive actions by the States in their governmental capacities as sovereign regulators. The sentences from the opinion quoted above simply clarify that this immunity does not necessarily obtain where the State acts not in a regulatory capacity but as a commercial participant in a given market.... These sentences should not be read to suggest the general proposition that even governmental *regulatory* action may be deemed private—and therefore subject to antitrust liability—when it is taken pursuant to a conspiracy with private parties. The impracticality of such a principle is evident if, for purposes of the exception, "conspiracy" means nothing more than an agreement to impose the regulation in question. Since it is both inevitable and desirable that public officials often agree to do what one or another group of private citizens urge upon them, such an exception would virtually swallow up the *Parker* rule: All anticompetitive regulation would be vulnerable to a "conspiracy" charge. See Areeda & Hovenkamp, supra, para. 203.3b, at 34, and n. 1; Elhauge, The Scope of Antitrust Process, 104 Harv.L.Rev. 667, 704–705 (1991).[69]

69. The dissent is confident that a jury composed of citizens of the vicinage will be able to tell the difference between "independent municipal action and action taken for the sole purpose of carrying out an anticompetitive agreement for the private party." No doubt. But those are merely the polar extremes, which like the geographic poles will rarely be seen by jurors of the vicinage. Ordinarily the allegation will merely be (and the dissent says this is enough) that the municipal action was not prompted *"exclusively* by a concern for the general public interest" (emphasis added). Thus, the real question is whether a jury can tell the difference— whether Solomon can tell the difference— between municipal-action-not-entirely-independent-because-based-partly-on-agreement-with-private-parties that is *lawful* and municipal-action-not-entirely-independent-because-based-partly-on-agreement-with-private-parties that is *unlawful.* The dissent does not tell us how to put this question coherently, much less how to answer it intelligently. *"Independent* municipal action" is unobjectionable, "action taken for the *sole* purpose of carrying out an anticompetitive agreement for the private party" is unlawful, and everything else (that is, the known world between the two poles) is unaddressed....

Omni suggests, however, that "conspiracy" might be limited to instances of governmental "corruption," defined variously as "abandonment of public responsibilities to private interests," "corrupt or bad faith decisions," and "selfish or corrupt motives." Ultimately, Omni asks us not to define "corruption" at all, but simply to leave that task to the jury: "[a]t bottom, however, it was within the jury's province to determine what constituted corruption of the governmental process in their community." Omni's amicus eschews this emphasis on "corruption," instead urging us to define the conspiracy exception as encompassing any governmental act "not in the public interest."

A conspiracy exception narrowed along such vague lines is similarly impractical. Few governmental actions are immune from the charge that they are "not in the public interest" or in some sense "corrupt." The California marketing scheme at issue in *Parker* itself, for example, can readily be viewed as the result of a "conspiracy" to put the "private" interest of the State's raisin growers above the "public" interest of the State's consumers. The fact is that virtually all regulation benefits some segments of the society and harms others; and that it is not universally considered contrary to the public good if the net economic loss to the losers exceeds the net economic gain to the winners. *Parker* was not written in ignorance of the reality that determination of "the public interest" in the manifold areas of government regulation entails not merely economic and mathematical analysis but value judgment, and it was not meant to shift that judgment from elected officials to judges and juries. If the city of Columbia's decision to regulate what one local newspaper called "billboard jungles" is made subject to *ex post facto* judicial assessment of "the public interest," with personal liability of city officials a possible consequence, we will have gone far to "compromise the States' ability to regulate their domestic commerce," Southern Motor Carriers Rate Conference, Inc. v. United States, 471 U.S. 48, 56 (1985). The situation would not be better, but arguably even worse, if the courts were to apply a subjective test: not whether the action was in the public interest, but whether the officials

The dissent contends, moreover, that "the instructions in this case, fairly read, told the jury that the plaintiff should not prevail *unless* the ordinance was enacted for the sole purpose of interfering with access to the market" (emphasis added). That is not so. The sum and substance of the jury's instructions here was that anticompetitive municipal action is not lawful when taken as part of a conspiracy, and that a conspiracy is "an agreement between two or more persons to violate the law, or to accomplish an otherwise lawful result in an unlawful manner." Although the District Court explained that "it is perfectly lawful for any and all persons to petition their government," the court immediately added, "but they may not do so as a part or as the object of a conspiracy." These instructions, then, are entirely circular: an anticompetitive agreement becomes unlawful if it is part of a conspiracy, and a conspiracy is an agreement to do something unlawful. The District Court's observation, upon which the dissent places so much weight, that "if by the evidence you find that [COA] procured and brought about the passage of ordinances solely for the purpose of hindering, delaying or otherwise interfering with the access of [Omni] to the marketing area involved in this case ... and thereby conspired, then, of course, their conduct would not be excused under the antitrust laws" is in no way tantamount to an instruction that this was the only theory upon which the jury could find an immunity-destroying "conspiracy."

involved thought it to be so. This would require the sort of deconstruction of the governmental process and probing of the official "intent" that we have consistently sought to avoid.[70] "[W]here the action complained of ... was that of the State itself, the action is exempt from antitrust liability regardless of the State's motives in taking the action." Hoover v. Ronwin, 466 U.S. 558, 579–580 (1984).

The foregoing approach to establishing a "conspiracy" exception at least seeks (however impractically) to draw the line of impermissible action in a manner relevant to the purposes of the Sherman Act and of *Parker:* prohibiting the restriction of competition for private gain but permitting the restriction of competition in the public interest. Another approach is possible, which has the virtue of practicality but the vice of being unrelated to those purposes. That is the approach which would consider *Parker* inapplicable only if, in connection with the governmental action in question, bribery or some other violation of state or federal law has been established. Such unlawful activity has no necessary relationship to whether the governmental action is in the public interest. A mayor is guilty of accepting a bribe even if he would and should have taken, in the public interest, the same action for which the bribe was paid. (That is frequently the defense asserted to a criminal bribery charge—and though it is never valid in law, *see, e.g.,* United States v. Jannotti, 673 F.2d 578, 601 (CA3) (en banc), cert. denied, 457 U.S. 1106 (1982), it is often plausible in fact.) When, moreover, the regulatory body is not a single individual but a state legislature or city council, there is even less reason to believe that violation of the law (by bribing a minority of the decisionmakers) establishes that the regulation has no valid public purpose. To use unlawful political influence as the test of legality of state regulation undoubtedly vindicates (in a rather blunt way) principles of good government. But the statute we are construing is not directed to that end. Congress has passed other laws aimed at combatting corruption in state and local governments. "Insofar as [the Sherman Act] sets up a code of ethics at all, it is a code that condemns trade restraints, not political activity." Eastern Railroad Presidents Conference v. Noerr Motor Freight, Inc., 365 U.S. 127, 140 (1961).

For these reasons, we reaffirm our rejection of any interpretation of the Sherman Act that would allow plaintiffs to look behind the actions of state sovereigns to base their claims on "perceived conspiracies to restrain trade," *Hoover,* 466 U.S., at 580. We reiterate that, with the possible market participant exception, any action that qualifies as state action is *"ipso facto ...* exempt from the operation of the antitrust laws," *id.,* at 568. This does not mean, of course, that the States may exempt private action from the scope of the Sherman Act; we in no way qualify the well established principle that "a state does not give immunity to those who

---

70. We have proceeded otherwise only in the "very limited and well-defined class of cases where the very nature of the constitutional question requires [this] inquiry." United States v. O'Brien, 391 U.S. 367, 383, n. 30 (1968) (bill of attainder). See also Arlington Heights v. Metropolitan Housing Development Corp., 429 U.S. 252, 268, n. 18 (1977) (race-based motivation).

violate the Sherman Act by authorizing them to violate it, or by declaring that their action is lawful." *Parker,* 317 U.S., at 351 (citing Northern Securities Co. v. United States, 193 U.S. 197, 332, 344–347 (1904)). See also Schwegmann Brothers v. Calvert Distillers Corp., 341 U.S. 384 (1951).

III

While *Parker* recognized the States' freedom to engage in anticompetitive regulation, it did not purport to immunize from antitrust liability the private parties who urge them to engage in anticompetitive regulation. However, it is obviously peculiar in a democracy, and perhaps in derogation of the constitutional right "to petition the Government for a redress of grievances," U.S. Const., Amdt. 1, to establish a category of lawful state action that citizens are not permitted to urge. Thus, beginning with Eastern Railroad Presidents Conference v. Noerr Motor Freight, Inc., supra, we have developed a corollary to *Parker:* the federal antitrust laws also do not regulate the conduct of private individuals in seeking anticompetitive action from the government. This doctrine, like *Parker,* rests ultimately upon a recognition that the antitrust laws, "tailored as they are for the business world, are not at all appropriate for application in the political arena." *Noerr, supra,* at 141. That a private party's political motives are selfish is irrelevant: "*Noerr* shields from the Sherman Act a concerted effort to influence public officials regardless of intent or purpose." United Mine Workers of America v. Pennington, 381 U.S. 657, 670 (1965).

Noerr recognized, however, what has come to be known as the "sham" exception to its rule: "There may be situations in which a publicity campaign, ostensibly directed toward influencing governmental action, is a mere sham to cover what is actually nothing more than an attempt to interfere directly with the business relationships of a competitor and the application of the Sherman Act would be justified." 365 U.S., at 144. The Court of Appeals concluded that the jury in this case could have found that COA's activities on behalf of the restrictive billboard ordinances fell within this exception. In our view that was error.

The "sham" exception to *Noerr* encompasses situations in which persons use the governmental *process*—as opposed to the *outcome* of that process—as an anticompetitive weapon. A classic example is the filing of frivolous objections to the license application of a competitor, with no expectation of achieving denial of the license but simply in order to impose expense and delay. See California Motor Transport Co. v. Trucking Unlimited, 404 U.S. 508 (1972). A "sham" situation involves a defendant whose activities are "not genuinely aimed at procuring favorable government action" at all, Allied Tube & Conduit Corp. v. Indian Head, Inc., 486 U.S. 492, 500, n. 4 (1988), not one "who 'genuinely seeks to achieve his governmental result, but does so *through improper means,*'" *id.,* at 508, n. 10 (quoting Sessions Tank Liners, Inc. v. Joor Mfg., Inc., 827 F.2d 458, 465, n. 5 (C.A.9 1987)).

Neither of the Court of Appeals' theories for application of the "sham" exception to the facts of the present case is sound. The court reasoned, first, that the jury could have concluded that COA's interaction with city officials "was 'actually nothing more than an attempt to interfere directly with the business relations [sic] of a competitor.'" 891 F.2d, at 1139 (quoting *Noerr, supra,* at 144). This analysis relies upon language from *Noerr,* but ignores the import of the critical word "directly." Although COA indisputably set out to disrupt Omni's business relationships, it sought to do so not through the very process of lobbying, or of causing the city council to consider zoning measures, but rather through the ultimate *product* of that lobbying and consideration, viz., the zoning ordinances. The Court of Appeals' second theory was that the jury could have found "that COA's purposes were to delay Omni's entry into the market and even to deny it a meaningful access to the appropriate city administrative and legislative fora." But the purpose of delaying a competitor's entry into the market does not render lobbying activity a "sham," unless (as no evidence suggested was true here) the delay is sought to be achieved only by the lobbying process itself, and not by the governmental action that the lobbying seeks. "If *Noerr* teaches anything it is that an intent to restrain trade as a result of government action sought ... does not foreclose protection." Sullivan, Developments in the Noerr Doctrine, 56 Antitrust L.J. 361, 362 (1987). As for "denying ... meaningful access to the appropriate city administrative and legislative fora," that may render the manner of lobbying improper or even unlawful, but does not necessarily render it a "sham." We did hold in *California Motor Transport, supra,* that a conspiracy among private parties to monopolize trade by excluding a competitor from participation in the regulatory process did not enjoy *Noerr* protection. But *California Motor Transport* involved a context in which the conspirators' participation in the governmental process was itself claimed to be a "sham," employed as a means of imposing cost and delay. ("It is alleged that petitioners 'instituted the proceedings and actions ... with or without probable cause, and regardless of the merits of the cases.'" 404 U.S., at 512.) The holding of the case is limited to that situation. To extend it to a context in which the regulatory process is being invoked genuinely, and not in a "sham" fashion, would produce precisely that conversion of antitrust law into regulation of the political process that we have sought to avoid. Any lobbyist or applicant, in addition to getting himself heard, seeks by procedural and other means to get his opponent ignored. Policing the legitimate boundaries of such defensive strategies, when they are conducted in the context of a genuine attempt to influence governmental action, is not the role of the Sherman Act. In the present case, of course, any denial to Omni of "meaningful access to the appropriate city administrative and legislative fora" was achieved by COA in the course of an attempt to influence governmental action that, far from being a "sham," was if anything more in earnest than it should have been. If the denial was wrongful there may be other remedies, but as for the Sherman Act, the *Noerr* exemption applies.

Omni urges that if, as we have concluded, the "sham" exception is inapplicable, we should use this case to recognize another exception to *Noerr* immunity—a "conspiracy" exception, which would apply when government officials conspire with a private party to employ government action as a means of stifling competition. We have left open the possibility of such an exception, *see, e.g., Allied Tube*, supra, at 502 n. 7, as have a number of Courts of Appeals. . . .

Giving full consideration to this matter for the first time, we conclude that a "conspiracy" exception to *Noerr* must be rejected. We need not describe our reasons at length, since they are largely the same as those set forth in Part II above for rejecting a "conspiracy" exception to *Parker*. As we have described, *Parker* and *Noerr* are complementary expressions of the principle that the antitrust laws regulate business, not politics; the former decision protects the States' acts of governing, and the latter the citizens' participation in government. Insofar as the identification of an immunity-destroying "conspiracy" is concerned, *Parker* and *Noerr* generally present two faces of the same coin. The *Noerr*-invalidating conspiracy alleged here is just the *Parker*-invalidating conspiracy viewed from the standpoint of the private-sector participants rather than the governmental participants. The same factors which, as we have described above, make it impracticable or beyond the purpose of the antitrust laws to identify and invalidate lawmaking that has been infected by selfishly motivated agreement with private interests likewise make it impracticable or beyond that scope to identify and invalidate lobbying that has produced selfishly motivated agreement with public officials. "It would be unlikely that any effort to influence legislative action could succeed unless one or more members of the legislative body became . . . 'coconspirators' " in some sense with the private party urging such action, Metro Cable Co. v. CATV of Rockford, Inc., 516 F.2d 220, 230 (C.A.7 1975). And if the invalidating "conspiracy" is limited to one that involves some element of unlawfulness (beyond mere anticompetitive motivation), the invalidation would have nothing to do with the policies of the antitrust laws. In *Noerr* itself, where the private party "deliberately deceived the public and public officials" in its successful lobbying campaign, we said that "deception, reprehensible as it is, can be of no consequence so far as the Sherman Act is concerned." 365 U.S., at 145.

IV

Under *Parker* and *Noerr*, therefore, both the city and COA are entitled to immunity from the federal antitrust laws for their activities relating to enactment of the ordinances. This determination does not entirely resolve the dispute before us, since other activities are at issue in the case with respect to COA. Omni asserts that COA engaged in private anticompetitive actions such as trade libel, the setting of artificially low rates, and inducement to breach of contract. Thus, although the jury's general verdict against COA cannot be permitted to stand (since it was based on instructions that erroneously permitted liability for seeking the ordinances) if the evidence was sufficient to sustain a verdict on the basis of these other actions alone, and if this theory of liability has been properly preserved, Omni would be entitled to a new trial.

There also remains to be considered the effect of our judgment upon Omni's claim against COA under the South Carolina Unfair Trade Practices Act. . . . We leave these remaining questions for determination by the Court of Appeals on remand. The judgment of the Court of Appeals is reversed, and the case is remanded for further proceedings consistent with this opinion.

■ STEVENS, J., with whom WHITE and MARSHALL, JJ., join, dissenting. . . . Today the Court adopts a significant enlargement of the state action exemption. The South Carolina statutes that confer zoning authority on municipalities in the State do not articulate any state policy to displace competition with economic regulation in any line of commerce or in any specific industry. As the Court notes, the state statutes were expressly adopted to promote the " 'health, safety, morals or the general welfare of the community.' " Like Colorado's grant of "home rule" powers to the city of Boulder, they are simply neutral on the question whether the municipality should displace competition with economic regulation in any industry. There is not even an arguable basis for concluding that the State authorized the city of Columbia to enter into exclusive agreements with any person, or to use the zoning power to protect favored citizens from competition. Nevertheless, under the guise of acting pursuant to a state legislative grant to regulate health, safety, and welfare, the city of Columbia in this case enacted an ordinance that amounted to economic regulation of the billboard market; as the Court recognizes, the ordinance "obviously benefitted COA, which already had its billboards in place . . . [and] severely hindered Omni's ability to compete." . . .

In this case, the jury found that the city's ordinance—ostensibly one promoting health, safety, and welfare—was in fact enacted pursuant to an agreement between city officials and a private party to restrict competition. In my opinion such a finding necessarily leads to the conclusion that the city's ordinance was fundamentally a form of economic regulation of the billboard market rather than a general welfare regulation having incidental anticompetitive effects. Because I believe our cases have wisely held that the decision to embark upon economic regulation is a nondelegable one that must expressly be made by the State in the context of a specific industry in order to qualify for state action immunity, I would hold that the city of Columbia's economic regulation of the billboard market pursuant to a general state grant of zoning power is not exempt from antitrust scrutiny. . . .

Just as I am convinced that municipal "lawmaking that has been infected by selfishly motivated agreement with private interests" is not authorized by a grant of zoning authority, and therefore not within the state action exemption, so am I persuaded that a private party's agreement with selfishly motivated public officials is sufficient to remove the antitrust immunity that protects private lobbying under Eastern Railroad Presidents Conference v. Noerr Motor Freight, Inc., 365 U.S. 127 (1961), and Mine

Workers v. Pennington, 381 U.S. 657 (1965). Although I agree that the "sham" exception to the *Noerr–Pennington* rule exempting lobbying activities from the antitrust laws does not apply to the private petitioner's conduct in this case for the reasons stated by the Court in Part III of its opinion, I am satisfied that the evidence in the record is sufficient to support the jury's finding that a conspiracy existed between the private party and the municipal officials in this case so as to remove the private petitioner's conduct from the scope of *Noerr–Pennington* antitrust immunity. Accordingly, I would affirm the judgment of the Court of Appeals as to both the city of Columbia and Columbia Outdoor Advertising.

NOTES AND QUESTIONS

1. Is the *Omni* opinion consistent with—or does it significantly broaden—*Town of Hallie's* "clearly articulated" test? After *Omni,* under what circumstances, if any, would bribing public officials be considered unprotected by the *Noerr–Pennington* doctrine? Is bribery really "petitioning"? If bribery is not protected by the First Amendment, should it be protected by *Noerr?* If a company is able to achieve monopoly power by means of bribery, is the "means" used irrelevant for Sherman Act purposes? Why not *presume* that the monopoly power improperly resulted from such unlawful conduct? Is private action entitled to *Noerr–Pennington* immunity when the defendants engage in anticompetitive conduct with the intent of achieving the ultimate end and of deterring competition through the process?

2. *Parker* immunity rests on the principles of state sovereignty and government accountability. How do these concepts apply to the City of Columbia's action in this case? Would antitrust sanctions (*e.g.,* treble damages and attorney's fees) add to the deterrence of unlawful activity provided by state law? Would private parties have more incentive to bring actions if antitrust sanctions were available?

3. In FISHER v. CITY OF BERKELEY, 475 U.S. 260 (1986), the Court considered yet another permutation of the immunity theme, when it decided whether a rent control ordinance enacted by the City of Berkeley, California, pursuant to popular initiative was unconstitutional because pre-empted by the Sherman Act. The Ordinance placed strict rent controls on all real property that "is being rented or is available for rent for residential use in whole or in part"; it made exceptions for government-owned units, transient units, cooperatives, hospitals, certain small owner-occupied buildings, and all newly constructed buildings. For the remaining units, numbering approximately 23,000, the Ordinance establishes a base rent ceiling reflecting the rents in effect at the end of May 1980 and made provisions for rent increases only upon the approval of a Rent Stabilization Board. Violators were subject to fines by the Board, suit by the tenants, rent withholding, and (for willful violations) criminal penalties.

This suit was brought in California Superior Court by a group of landlords owning rental property in Berkeley. They claimed that the Ordinance violated their rights under the Due Process and Equal Protection Clauses of the Fourteenth Amendment, and sought declaratory and injunctive relief. The Superior Court upheld the Ordinance on its face, but was reversed by the Court of Appeal. While that appeal was pending, the Supreme Court's decision in Community Communications Co. v. City of Boulder, 455 U.S. 40 (1982), raised the possibility of a federal preemption challenge to the ordinance. Although this had not been raised earlier, the California Supreme Court opted to consider the pre-emption claim along with the other properly preserved arguments. It found no conflict between the Rent Stabilization Ordinance and either § 1 or § 2 of the Sherman Act. The Supreme Court of the United States then noted probable jurisdiction limited to the antitrust pre-emption question. It affirmed the judgment of the California courts, but on different grounds, finding that "traditional antitrust analysis" was adequate to resolve the issue presented.

The problem for the Court was whether the regulatory scheme established by Berkeley conflicted with the Sherman Act and was therefore pre-empted. In *Rice v. Norman Williams Co.,* the Court had held that a "state statute is not pre-empted by the federal antitrust laws simply because the state scheme may have an anticompetitive effect," 458 U.S. at 659. See Exxon Corp. v. Governor of Maryland, 437 U.S. 117, 133 (1978). A state statute must be invalidated on pre-emption grounds "only if it mandates or authorizes conduct that necessarily constitutes a violation of the antitrust laws in all cases, or if it places irresistible pressure on a private party to violate the antitrust laws in order to comply with the statute." 458 U.S., at 661. The same rule, the Court observed, applied to municipal ordinances. Furthermore, legislation that would otherwise be pre-empted under *Rice* may nonetheless survive if it is found to be state action immune from antitrust scrutiny under Parker v. Brown, 317 U.S. 341 (1943). The ultimate source of that immunity can be only the State, not its subdivisions.

The Court agreed that if the owners of residential rental property in Berkeley had voluntarily banded together to stabilize rents in the city, their activities would not be saved from antitrust attack by claims that they had set reasonable prices out of solicitude for the welfare of their tenants. See National Society of Professional Engineers v. United States, 435 U.S., at 695; United States v. Trans–Missouri Freight Assn., 166 U.S. 290 (1897). It also conceded that the ordinance would affect the residential housing rental market in much the same way as would the philanthropic activities of this hypothetical trade association. What distinguished the operation of Berkeley's Ordinance from the activities of a benevolent landlords' cartel was not that the Ordinance will necessarily have a different economic effect, but that the rent ceilings imposed by the Ordinance and maintained by the Stabilization Board were unilaterally imposed by government upon landlords to the exclusion of private control.

As we have repeatedly seen, here too the distinction between unilateral and concerted action was critical. See Copperweld, Chapter 6, infra at p. 613. Applying that principle if the Berkeley Ordinance stabilized rents without the element of concerted action, the program it established by definition could not violate § 1. The Court rejected the landlords' argument that concerted action could be found in a combination between the City and its officials, on the one hand, and the property owners, on the other. This, it held, "misconstrue[d] the concerted action requirement of § 1. A restraint imposed unilaterally by government does not become concerted action within the meaning of the statute simply because it has a coercive effect upon parties who must obey the law. The ordinary relationship between the government and those who must obey its regulatory commands whether they wish to or not is not enough to establish a conspiracy. Similarly, the mere fact that all competing property owners must comply with the same provisions of the Ordinance is not enough to establish a conspiracy among landlords."

The Court then distinguished so-called hybrid restraints, in which private actors have some degree of private regulatory power, citing as examples Rice v. Norman Williams Co., 458 U.S., at 665 (Stevens, J., concurring in the judgment), Schwegmann Bros. v. Calvert Distillers Corp., 341 U.S. 384 (1951); and California Retail Liquor Dealers Assn. v. Midcal Aluminum, Inc., 445 U.S. 97 (1980). It acknowledged that "[t]here may be cases in which what appears to be a state-or municipality-administered price stabilization scheme is really a private price-fixing conspiracy, concealed under a "gauzy cloak of state involvement," *Midcal,* supra, at 106. This might occur even where prices are ostensibly under the absolute control of government officials. The Berkeley ordinance did not present such case, however. The Court concluded:

> Because under settled principles of antitrust law, the rent controls established by Berkeley's Ordinance lack the element of concerted action needed before they can be characterized as a *per se* violation of § 1 of the Sherman Act, we cannot say that the Ordinance is facially inconsistent with the federal antitrust laws. See *Rice v. Norman Williams Co.,* supra, 458 U.S., at 661. We therefore need not address whether, even if the controls were to mandate § 1 violations, they would be exempt under the state-action doctrine from antitrust scrutiny. See Town of Hallie v. City of Eau Claire, 471 U.S. 34 (1985).

Justice Powell concurred and argued that the Supreme Court should not have decided "a difficult pre-emption question," but instead should have found a state-action exemption. Justice Brennan dissented "because the Ordinance has the force of law" and compels "landlords to do what the Sherman Act plainly forbids—to fix prices for rental units in Berkeley." The Ordinance, Brennan continued, precluded the possibility that the city and the landlords were acting independently; the Ordinance eliminated "price competition more effectively than any private 'agreement' ever could, and is therefore pre-empted by the Sherman Act."

4. Is *Fisher* consistent with *Midcal?* Was there an "agreement" in *Midcal* between the producers and the retailers with respect to resale prices? After *Fisher,* how do you distinguish unilateral acts of government from concerted activities or "hybrid restraints"? If, for example, tenant representatives had sat on Berkeley's Rent Stabilization Board would this have changed the *Fisher* case? What if landlord representatives dominated the Rent Stabilization Board? What if landlords had lobbied hard for what purported to be a rent stabilization program?

5. In HERTZ CORP. v. CITY OF NEW YORK, 1 F.3d 121 (2d Cir.1993), the City of New York passed a local law to prevent Hertz from charging higher rates to residents of different parts of the city. Hertz brought suit claiming that the law controlled an aspect of Hertz' pricing process and thus violated the Sherman Act. On the issue of whether the city ordinance was a "contract, combination, or conspiracy," the Second Circuit distinguished *Fisher* as follows:

> First, the law is not a "pure regulatory scheme," [citing *Fisher*] because it is not a "scheme" at all; the law is simply a directive for all rental-car companies doing business in New York City to remove one factor from their competitive-pricing structures. Second, the law lacks the independent, quasi-judicial board that in *Berkeley* could adjust rates and provide relief in individual circumstances. Finally, the City of Berkeley was operating in an area vital to its municipal authority—housing; less vital is the rental-car industry in New York City.

Nor does the Hertz law easily fit the fact pattern of the cases held to involve "hybrid" restraints—those that restrain trade through some combination of governmental and private conduct. The three Supreme Court cases in this category involved the pricing of liquor [citing *324 Liquor, Midcal,* and *Schwegmann*]. Each involved classic price-setting that was delegated by statute or regulation to private industry but was left unsupervised by the state legislature. The Hertz law, in contrast, does not purport to authorize price-setting by private industry; it simply eliminates an element of price competition among industry members.

We reject the city's suggestion to apply *Fisher* expansively so as to view Local Law No. 21 as a unilateral action that lacks the degree of private-governmental agreement required to be a contract, combination, or conspiracy in restraint of trade. To do so would remove from the reach of the antitrust laws all local governmental actions not fitting the precise fact pattern of the liquor cases. 1 F.3d at 127.

Regardless of the differences between the *Hertz* case and *324 Liquor, Midcal,* and *Schwegmann,* the Second Circuit held that the New York City law was to be characterized as a "hybrid" situation, where the law called for "anticompetitive private conduct in setting rental rates and making rental decisions." Thus, it was a contract, combination, or conspiracy that would have to be evaluated—because no state action was found—under the Sherman Act. 1 F.3d at 127.

The Second Circuit remanded the *Hertz* case to the district court and asked it to make a broad rule of reason analysis (including consideration of such factors as the city's concern about not unfairly burdening "minorities and the working poor") of the restraint. Cf. Chapter 4, p. ___ supra. The Second Circuit (quoting *City of Boulder*) noted that "*per se* treatment may not be well tailored to assessing municipal antitrust liability, and 'certain activities which might appear anticompetitive when engaged in by private parties, take on a different complexion when adopted by a local government.'" 1 F.3d at 129.

PROBLEM 9

BOLDEN'S AIRPORT INDEPENDENT AUTHORITY

Kent's state constitution, like that of Colorado, provides for the "home rule" of cities of a certain size, delegating to them all powers of legislation, independent of the state legislature, in matters of primarily local concern. Kent's state legislature has adopted a general "Airport Independent Authorities" statute which provides for the incorporation of local "independent authorities" to build, own, and operate municipal airports after approval of plans by the appropriate municipal authorities. The first board of directors of each independent authority is selected by the state and municipal governments, and then becomes a self-perpetuating board with no governmental involvement in the selection of new board members.

The state Airport Independent authorities statute includes a provision which "authorizes and directs" any authority's board of directors "to enter into such contractual arrangements which in its judgment are necessary and proper to provide airport related commercial services." The statute also states that the board of directors "should act in the public interest by maximizing revenues and by providing the most cost-effective services to air travelers."

One year ago, the City Council of Bolden approved a plan for operating Bolden's new airport, which included a provision authorizing the Independent Authority's "board of directors to enter into commercial contracts of all types."

Last month, the board of directors of Bolden's Independent Authority entered into two car rental contracts—one with Hurts, a national organization, and the other with Boldencars, a locally owned rental car company. Included in the contracts, which were exclusive and were to last for ten years, was a provision for setting rates by the Independent Authority on local rentals; the first rental rates set were at rates substantially in excess of the rates at other comparable airports. For car rentals that would not result in a car being returned in the Bolden area, Hurts (the sole supplier of such cars) was instructed to "charge what the market would bear." The Independent Authority will receive a percentage of Hurts' net revenues on such rentals.

Several excluded national and local car rental companies, and a local consumer group, have joined forces to seek to enjoin the implementation of the two rental contracts as violations of Sections 1 and 2 of the Sherman Act. They can prove that almost all airports of comparable size across the country provide four to six facilities for separate rental car companies, have much shorter contractual terms, and have no provision for the setting of rental rates.

How would the "state action" issues be argued and decided? Would it make any difference if plaintiffs could prove that Boldencars received its contract as a result of pressure placed on the Independent Authority by the president of the City Council of Bolden, who was "paying off" a political debt? In addition, would it make any difference if the rental rates that the Independent Authority set were based on intentionally erroneous projections of costs and revenues provided by Boldencars and Hurts? Finally, would it make any difference if plaintiffs could prove that the contract with Hurts (which at most would have been one of three national companies to receive a contract) resulted from bribes paid to the board members of the Independent Authority?

NOTE: STATE VIOLATION OF ANTITRUST LAWS

Whether a state's regulatory scheme is protected from a Sherman Act challenge was litigated in the recent case of TFWS, Inc. v. Schaefer, 242 F.3d 198 (4th Cir.2001). The Maryland state government instituted a number of restrictions on the liquor market. One of these restrictions was the post-and-hold system, which required the state's Comptroller and Administrator of the Alcohol and Tobacco Tax Unit to establish a price posting system. The price posting system required liquor manufacturers and wholesalers to file price schedules and proposed price changes. The price schedules and proposed price changes were then made available to competitors. Another restriction involved a prohibition on volume discounts. Liquor wholesalers were prohibited from offering any type of discount to its retailers. The purpose of the post-and-hold system and the volume discount ban was to foster and promote temperance by maintaining wholesale liquor prices at stable, higher levels.

The plaintiff, a liquor retailer, claimed that the post-and-hold system and the volume discount ban violated the Sherman Act because it restricted trade in two ways. First, it allowed wholesalers to match each other's prices at artificially high levels. Second, it allowed wholesalers to maintain those artificially higher prices. The Maryland Comptroller argued that the suit was barred by the state action doctrine.

The court articulated a three-step analysis to decide whether a state's liquor pricing regulations could be challenged under the antitrust laws. First, the court must decide whether the state's pricing regulations are violative of the Sherman Act. This requires the court to consider whether the pricing regulations were a unilateral or a hybrid restraint. A unilateral restraint is one that is undertaken solely by the state, whereas a hybrid restraint is one in which the government is enforcing private marketing decisions. If the regulations are a hybrid restraint, the court must then consider whether it involves a *per se* violation of section 1 of the Sherman Act. Second, the court must decide whether the regulations are shielded from the Sherman Act under the "state action" doctrine. Lastly, the court had to decide whether there was a constitutional provision (such as the 11th Amendment) that trumped the Sherman Act.

In finding that the state pricing regulations were illegal, the court stated:

> Again, Maryland's post-and-hold pricing scheme mandates the exchange of price information by wholesalers through public posting and dissemination, and it requires adherence to the publicly announced prices. The Maryland system thus mandates activity that is essentially a form of horizontal price fixing, which has been called "the paradigm of an unreasonable restraint of trade." *N.C.A.A. v. Board of Regents of the University of Oklahoma*, 468 U.S. 85, 100, 104 S.Ct. 2948, 82 L.Ed.2d 70 (1984). Maryland's post-and-hold regime is subject to § 1 as a hybrid restraint, and we hold that it is illegal *per se*.

The court also found that the volume discount ban was illegal *per se*, as other courts had held that the elimination of volume discounts is a *per se* violation of § 1 of the Sherman Act. In short, this case shows courts' unwillingness to sanction state regulations that compel activity that is *per se* illegal.

SELECTIVE BIBLIOGRAPHY

1. Group Boycotts and Refusals to Deal

Bauer, *per se* Illegality of Concerted Refusals to Deal: A Rule Ripe for Reexamination, 79 Colum.L.Rev. 685 (1979).

Jones, Concerted Refusals to Deal and the Producer Interest in Antitrust, 50 Ohio St.L.J. 73 (1989).

Minda, The Law and Metaphor of Boycott, 41 Buff.L.Rev. 807 (1993).

Note, *NOW* or Never: Is There Antitrust Liability for Noncommercial Boycotts, 80 Colum.L.Rev. 1317 (1980).

Ponsoldt, The Application of Sherman Act Antiboycott Law to Industry Self–Regulation: An Analysis Integrating Non-boycott Sherman Act Principles, 55 S.Cal.L.Rev. 1 (1981).

Werden, The Law and Economics of the Essential Facility Doctrine, 32 St. Louis U.L.J. 433 (1987).

2. Joint Ventures

Balto, Access Demands to Payment Systems Joint Ventures, 18 Harv.J.L. & Pub.Pol'y 623 (1995).

Baker: Compulsory Access to Network Joint Ventures Under the Sherman Act: Rules or Roulette?, 1993 Utah L. Rev. 999.

Brodley, Joint Ventures and Antitrust Policy, 95 Harv.L.Rev. 1521 (1982).

Carlton & Frankel, The Antitrust Economics of Credit Card Networks, 63 Antitrust L.J. 643 (1995).

Chang, Evans & Schmalensee, Some Economic Principles for Guiding Antitrust Policy Towards Joint Ventures, 1998 Colum. Bus. L. Rev. 223 (1998).

Hovenkamp, Exclusive Joint Ventures and Antitrust Policy, 1995 Colum.Bus.L.Rev. 1 (1995).

Makar, The Essential Facility Doctrine and the Health Care Industry, 21 Fla.St.U.L.Rev. 913 (1994).

McFalls, The Role and Assessment of Classical Market Power in Joint Venture Analysis, 66 Antitrust L. J. 651 (1998).

Piraino, The Antitrust Analysis of Network Joint Ventures, 47 Hastings L.J. 5 (1995).

Pitofsky, Joint Ventures Under the Antitrust Laws: Some Reflections on the Significance of *Penn–Olin,* 82 Harv.L.Rev. 1007 (1969).

Werden, Antitrust Analysis of Joint Ventures: an Overview, 66 Antitrust L. J. 701 (1998).

3. *Noerr–Pennington* Doctrine

Bien, Litigation as an Antitrust Violation: Conflict Between the First Amendment and the Supreme Court, 16 U.S.F.L. Rev. 41 (1981).

Calkins, 1988 Developments in Antitrust and the First Amendment: The Disaggregation of Noerr, 57 Antitrust L.J. 327 (1988).

Fischel, Antitrust Liability for Attempts to Influence Government Action: The Basis and Limits of the *Noerr–Pennington* Doctrine, 45 U.Chi.L.Rev. 80 (1977).

Garland: Antitrust and State Action: Economic Efficiency and the Political Process, 96 Yale L.J. 486 (1987).

Hurwitz, Abuse of Governmental Processes, the First Amendment, and the Boundaries of Noerr, 74 Geo.L.J. 65 (1985).

Temple Lang, the European Community Competition Law and Member State Action, 10 Northwestern J. Law & Bus. 114 (1989).

Meyer, A Standard for Tailoring Noerr–Pennington Immunity More Closely to the First Amendment Mandate, 95 Yale L.J. 832 (1986).

Page, Interest Groups, Antitrust, and State Regulation: Parker v. Brown in the Economic Theory of Legislation, 1987 Duke L.J. 618.

Wrona, A Clash of Titans: The First Amendment Right to Petition vs. The Antitrust Laws, 28 New Eng.L.Rev. 637 (1994).

CHAPTER 6

MARKET CONCENTRATION, CONSPIRACY, AND THE ANTITRUST LAWS

SECTION 1. NOTE ON OLIGOPOLY

An oligopolistic market is one in which there is a small number of dominant sellers, each with a large market share.[1] A seller in such a market, unlike a monopolist, realizes that if it raises its price above the competitive level, its rivals will undercut its price.[2] In contrast to firms in a competitive market, however, the seller in an oligopolistic market realizes that initiating a round of price competition will make all rivals worse off.[3] This means that sellers in an oligopolistic market have an incentive to avoid rigorous competition and instead to collude with one another. The small number of firms in the market facilitates collusion, and in many instances, firms need not even reach express agreements with each other. The challenge for antitrust law lies in detecting tacit collusion and in improving the competitive structure of the market, so as to avoid such collusion.

Robert H. Lande and Howard P. Marvel write that there are three types of collusion: (1) collusion to raise prices, (2) collusion to disadvantage rivals, and (3) collusion to manipulate the rules under which competition takes place.[4] Firms in an oligopolistic market can collude to raise prices by either fixing prices directly, dividing the market into competition-free segments assigned to individual cartel members, or by bid rigging. The goal of the first type of collusion is to mimic the result that a monopolist could obtain in the marketplace. The second type of collusion consists of agreements to take action jointly to harm existing or potential rivals that are not party to the collusion. Colluding firms may attempt to harm rivals by boycotts, predatory pricing, or by raising their rivals' costs. These practices can cause rivals to exit the market or to compete less aggressively. The goal of the third type of collusion is to change the rules of competition so as to

1. Excerpts from Report of the White House Task Force on Antitrust Policy (1968), 2 Antitrust Law & Econ. Rev. 11, 22–30 (Win. 1968–69).

2. Hay, "Oligopoly, Shared Monopoly, and Antitrust Law," 67 Cornell L. Rev. 439 (March 1982).

3. Ibid.

4. Lande and Marvel, "The Three Types of Collusion: Fixing Prices, Rivals, and Rules," 2000 Wis. L. Rev. 941.

decrease the price competition among members. Examples of this last type of collusion include restrictions on advertising, especially price advertising, restrictions on the information that can be made available to consumers, agreements to restrict affiliations, and agreements not to solicit customers of rivals. The third type of collusion often takes place within the context of a professional association. Many real world arrangements among firms will fit into more than one category of collusion.

Collusion is more likely to be successful in concentrated industries with homogenous, fungible products. On the other hand, as F.M. Scherer writes:

> ... [C]ooperation to hold prices above the competitive level is less likely to be successful, the less concentrated an industry is; the larger the competitive fringe is, the more heterogeneous, complex, and changing the products supplied are; the higher the ratio of fixed or overhead to total costs is, the more depressed business conditions are; the more dependent the industry is on large, infrequent orders, the more opportunities there are for under-the-counter price shading, and the more relations among company executives are marred by distrust and animosity.[5]

None of these characteristics alone, however, unambiguously points to the existence of collusion among sellers. The difficulty for practitioners lies in determining which factors are probative in each situation. This is further complicated by the fact that a concentrated market structure will not automatically lead to a situation where prices are substantially above competitive levels for extended periods of time.[6]

Other challenges to antitrust practitioners lie in the changing global economy and the expansion of the high technology sector. Because U.S. companies must now compete with foreign firms, both domestically and abroad, competition increasingly occurs over more than just the selling price. Firms today also compete on the variety and speed of production, development, and innovation.[7] As an FTC staff report put it:

> ... [w]hen innovation is the mark of competition of the day, antitrust faces new challenges in analyzing the competitive effects of single and multi-firm transactions and strategies, as well as acting affirmatively while protecting incentives and the property of pioneers. The importance of these issues is only enhanced with the growth in communications networks and the increasing demand for compatibility among producers that are to present viable alternatives for consumers.

5. Scherer, "Industrial Market Structure and Economics Performance," 151, 227, 266 (2d. ed. 1980)

6. Ibid.

7. "Excerpts from Staff Report of the FTC on Anticipating the 21st Century: Competition Policy in the New High–Tech, Global Marketplace," 70 Antitrust & Trade Reg. Rep. 1765 (1996).

SECTION 2. INFERENCE OF AGREEMENT AS A LEGAL BUILDING BLOCK

INTRODUCTORY NOTE

The Sherman Act, at least as interpreted and applied to date, has been inadequate to deal effectively with the oligopoly pricing or price leadership associated with concentrated industries. This is partly because of difficulties created by the Act's apparent "bi-polar" structure. Section 1 deals explicitly with conduct by more than a single firm, and it reaches only "contract, combination ... or conspiracy." Section 2 deals with the single firm, but its proscriptions of "monopolization" and "attempts to monopolize" do not seem to encompass parallel conduct by firms of less than monopoly dimension. This produces the apparent paradox that joint action (not agreed upon) by an oligopoly group may legally achieve noncompetitive prices which would be illegal if set by a cartel enjoying the same or even a lesser degree of market dominance. If protecting consumers and others from market power is a central objective of antitrust, here is an obvious flaw.

Antitrust enforcers and others have argued occasionally that the antitrust laws are capable of reaching such oligopoly pricing. Legal building blocks to bring about this result would have to be found, of course, in the language of these laws and the cases interpreting them.

One approach would be to infer agreement from consciously parallel conduct. This step would enable action to be taken under Section 1 of the Sherman Act, which requires some kind of agreement, or the "conspiracy to monopolize" subpart of Section 2. For a variety of reasons that will be explored in this chapter, the courts have resisted that approach.

If conscious parallelism alone is not an appropriate basis for antitrust liability, what is? One possibility is to take a cumulative approach and look for "other circumstances" which, if considered along with the consciously parallel conduct, add up to something from which agreement legitimately can be inferred. But on what principled basis does one determine what additional circumstances should produce this result? One suggestion is that when oligopolists independently engage in parallel practices that facilitate price uniformity—making it more likely, more complete, or more durable—the inference of conspiracy should be permissible. Short of that, perhaps such "facilitating practices" are properly characterized as an "unfair method of competition" under Section 5 of the Federal Trade Commission Act, which does not explicitly require direct or inferred agreement. Does or should Section 5 go beyond the Sherman and Clayton Acts to reach techniques to achieve oligopoly pricing?

Another approach, which has been taken in the European Union, is to entertain the possibility of shared monopoly (called "joint dominance" in EU terminology). If firms acting together as a group mimic the results that would be expected from a single dominant firm, then the EU has the legal tools with which to address the situation. Efforts in the United States to develop a shared monopoly doctrine have been notoriously unsuccessful, but the reasons for those failures help us to understand both the possibilities and the limits of antitrust law.

Finally, there was a time when it was thought that the necessary agreement for Section 1 liability could be found within a single firm (either a monopolist or one with less than monopoly power) through the so-called intra-enterprise conspiracy doctrine. That entailed treating the firm and (1) its officers or other employees, (2) its operating divisions, (3) its wholly-owned subsidiaries or (4) controlled (but not wholly-owned) subsidiaries, as separate entities for purposes of agreement, conspiracy or combination, *i.e.*, satisfying Section 1's plurality requirement? Although that idea undoubtedly permitted review of pricing (and other competitive behavior) by large firms falling short of monopoly power, it also risked intrusive government regulation of virtually all internal company decisions. Recognizing the importance of the distinction between genuinely unilateral action and concerted action, in 1984 the Supreme Court rejected the intra-enterprise conspiracy doctrine as applied to firms and their wholly owned subsidiaries. We discuss in this chapter what still may remain of it.

A closely related procedural problem is important: when should the ultimate questions of fact as to "contract, combination or conspiracy" go to the jury or be withdrawn by the court at or prior to trial? Is there a special rule for antitrust cases, or do they follow general rules with respect to devices such as summary judgment? Should antitrust policy dictate some degree of encouragement of private actions, or do the hazards of treble damages and class actions to sensible business decisionmaking suggest a restrained approach?

These are some of the major questions with which the remainder of this chapter deals.

Interstate Circuit v. United States

Supreme Court of the United States, 1939.
306 U.S. 208, 59 S.Ct. 467, 83 L.Ed. 610.

■ STONE, J. This case is here on appeal ... from a final decree of the District Court for Northern Texas restraining appellants from continuing in a combination and conspiracy condemned by the court as a violation of § 1 of the Sherman Antitrust Act ... and from enforcing or renewing certain contracts found by the court to have been entered into in pursuance of the conspiracy. 20 F.Supp. 868.... The case is now before us on findings of the District Court specifically stating that appellants did in fact agree with each other to enter into and carry out the contracts, which the court found to result in unreasonable and therefore unlawful restraints of interstate commerce.

Appellants comprise the two groups of defendants in the District Court.... The distributor appellants are engaged in the business of distributing in interstate commerce motion picture films, copyrights on which they own or control, for exhibition in theatres throughout the United States. They distribute about 75 per cent of all first-class feature films exhibited in the United States. They solicit from motion picture theatre owners and managers in Texas and other states applications for licenses to exhibit films, and forward the applications when received from such exhibitors, to their respective New York offices, where they are accepted or rejected. If the applications are accepted, the distributors ship the films from points outside the states of exhibition to their exchanges within those states, from which, pursuant to the license agreements, the films are delivered to the local theatres for exhibition. After exhibition the films are reshipped to the distributors at points outside the state.

The exhibitor group of appellants consists of Interstate Circuit, Inc., and Texas Consolidated Theatres, Inc., and Hoblitzelle and O'Donnell, who are respectively president and general manager of both and in active charge of their business operations. The two corporations are affiliated with each other and with Paramount Pictures Distributing Co., Inc., one of the distributor appellants.

Interstate operates forty-three first-run and second-run motion picture theatres, located in six Texas cities. It has a complete monopoly of first-run theatres in these cities, except for one in Houston operated by one distributor's Texas agent. In most of these theatres the admission price for adults for the better seats at night is 40 cents or more. Interstate also operates several subsequent-run theatres in each of these cities, twenty-two in all, but in all but Galveston there are other subsequent-run theatres which compete with both its first-and subsequent-run theatres in those cities.

Texas Consolidated operates sixty-six theatres, some first-and some subsequent-run houses, in various cities and towns in the Rio Grande Valley and elsewhere in Texas and in New Mexico. In some of these cities there are no competing theatres, and in six leading cities there are no competing first-run theatres. It has no theatres in the six Texas cities in which Interstate operates. That Interstate and Texas Consolidated dominate the motion picture business in the cities where their theatres are located is indicated by the fact that at the time of the contracts in question Interstate and Consolidated each contributed more than 74 per cent of all the license fees paid by the motion picture theatres in their respective territories to the distributor appellants.

On July 11, 1934, following a previous communication on the subject to the eight branch managers of the distributor appellants, O'Donnell, the manager of Interstate and Consolidated, sent to each of them a letter on the letterhead of Interstate, each letter naming all of them as addressees, in which he asked compliance with two demands as a condition of Interstate's continued exhibition of the distributors' films in its "A" or first-run theatres at a night admission of 40 cents or more. One demand was that the distributors "agree that in selling their product to subsequent runs, that this 'A' product will never be exhibited at any time or in any theatre at a smaller admission price than 25 for adults in the evening." The other was that "on 'A' pictures which are exhibited at a night admission of 40 or more-they shall never be exhibited in conjunction with another feature picture under the so-called policy of double features." The letter added that with respect to the "Rio Grande Valley situation," with which Consolidated alone was concerned, "We must insist that all pictures exhibited in our 'A' theatres at a maximum night admission price of 35 must also be restricted to subsequent runs in the Valley at 25¢."

The admission price customarily charged for preferred seats at night in independently operated subsequent-run theatres in Texas at the time of these letters was less than 25 cents. In seventeen of the eighteen independent theatres of this kind whose operations were described by witnesses the admission price was less than 25 cents. In one only was it 25 cents. In most of them the admission was 15 cents or less. It was also the general practice in those theatres to provide double bills either on certain days of the week or with any feature picture which was weak in drawing power. The distributor appellants had generally provided in their license contracts for a minimum admission price of 10 or 15 cents, and three of them had included provisions restricting double-billing. But none was at any time previously subject to contractual compulsion to continue the restrictions. The trial court found that the proposed restrictions constituted an important departure from prior practice.

The local representatives of the distributors, having no authority to enter into the proposed agreements, communicated the proposal to their home offices. Conferences followed between Hoblitzelle and O'Donnell, acting for Interstate and Consolidated, and the representatives of the various distributors. In these conferences each distributor was represented by its local branch manager and by one or more superior officials from outside the state of Texas. In the course of them each distributor agreed with Interstate for the 1934–35 season to impose both the demanded restrictions upon their subsequent-run licensees in the six Texas cities served by Interstate, except Austin and Galveston. While only two of the distributors incorporated the agreement to impose the restrictions in their license contracts with Interstate, the evidence establishes, and it is not denied, that all joined in the agreement, four of them after some delay in negotiating terms other than the restrictions and not now material. These agreements for the restrictions-with the immaterial exceptions noted-were carried into effect by each of the distributors' imposing them on their subsequent-run licensees in the four Texas cities during the 1934–35 season. One agreement, that of Metro–Goldwyn–Mayer Distributing Corporation, was for three years. The others were renewed in the two following seasons and all were in force when the present suit was begun.

None of the distributors yielded to the demand that subsequent runs in towns in the Rio Grande Valley served by Consolidated should be restricted. One distributor, Paramount, which was affiliated with Consolidated, agreed to impose the restrictions in certain other Texas and New Mexico cities.

The trial court found that the distributor appellants agreed and conspired among themselves to take uniform action upon the proposals made by Interstate, and that they agreed and conspired with each other and with Interstate to impose the demanded restrictions upon all subsequent-run exhibitors in Dallas, Forth Worth, Houston and San Antonio; that they carried out the agreement by imposing the restrictions upon their subsequent-run licensees in those cities, causing some of them to increase their admission price to 25 cents, either generally or when restricted pictures were shown, and to abandon double-billing of all such pictures, and causing the other subsequent-run exhibitors, who were either unable or unwilling to accept the restrictions, to be deprived of any opportunity to exhibit the restricted pictures, which were the best and most popular of all new feature pictures; that the effect of the restrictions upon "low-income members of the community" patronizing the theatres of these exhibitors was to withhold from them altogether the "best entertainment furnished by the motion picture industry"; and that the restrictions operated to increase the income of the distributors and of Interstate and to deflect attendance from later-run exhibitors who yielded to the restrictions to the first-run theatres of Interstate.

The court concluded as matters of law that the agreement of the distributors with each other and those with Interstate to impose the restrictions upon subsequent-run exhibitors and the carrying of the agreements into effect, with the aid and participation of Hoblitzelle and O'Donnell, constituted a combination and conspiracy in restraint of interstate commerce in violation of the Sherman Act. It also concluded that each separate agreement between Interstate and a distributor that Interstate should subject itself to the restrictions in its subsequent-run theatres and that the distributors should impose the restrictions on all subsequent-run theatres in the Texas cities as a condition of supplying them with its feature pictures, was likewise a violation of the Act.

It accordingly enjoined the conspiracy and restrained the distributors from enforcing the restrictions in their license agreements with subsequent-run exhibitors and from enforcing the contracts or any of them. This included both the contracts of Interstate with the distributors and the contract between Consolidated and Paramount, whereby the latter agreed to impose the restrictions upon subsequent-run theatres in Texas and New Mexico served by it.

Appellants assail the decree of the District Court upon three principal grounds: (a) that the finding of agreement and conspiracy among the distributor appellants to impose the restrictions upon later-run exhibitors is not supported by the court's subsidiary findings or by the evidence; (b) that the several separate contracts entered into by Interstate with the distributors are within the protection of the Copyright Act and consequently are not violations of the Sherman Act; and (c) that the restrictions do not unreasonably restrain interstate commerce within the provisions of the Sherman Act.

Although the films were copyrighted, appellants do not deny that the conspiracy charge is established if the distributors agreed among themselves to impose the restrictions upon subsequent-run exhibitors. Straus v. American Publishers' Association, 231 U.S. 222; Paramount Famous Lasky Corp. v. United States, 282 U.S. 30. As is usual in cases of alleged unlawful agreements to restrain commerce, the government is without the aid of direct testimony that the distributors entered into any agreement with each other to impose the restrictions upon subsequent-run exhibitors. In order to establish agreement it is compelled to rely on inferences drawn from the course of conduct of the alleged conspirators.

The trial court drew the inference of agreement from the nature of the proposals made on behalf of Interstate and Consolidated; from the manner in which they were made; from the substantial unanimity of action taken upon them by the distributors; and from the fact that appellants did not call as witnesses any of the superior officials who negotiated the contracts with Interstate or any official who, in the normal course of business, would have had knowledge of the existence or non-existence of such an agreement among the distributors. This conclusion is challenged by appellants because not supported by subsidiary findings or by the evidence. We think this inference of the trial court was rightly drawn from the evidence. In the view we take of the legal effect of the cooperative action of the distributor appellants in carrying into effect the restrictions imposed upon subsequent-run theatres in the four Texas cities and of the legal effect of the separate agreements for the imposition of those restrictions entered into between Interstate and each of the distributors, it is unnecessary to discuss in great detail the evidence concerning this aspect of the case.

The O'Donnell letter named on its face as addressees the eight local representatives of the distributors, and so from the beginning each of the distributors knew that the proposals were under consideration by the others. Each was aware that all were in active competition and that without substantially unanimous action with respect to the restrictions for any given territory there was risk of a substantial loss of the business and good will of the subsequent-run and independent exhibitors, but that with it there was the prospect of increased profits. There was, therefore, strong motive for concerted action, full advantage of which was taken by Interstate and Consolidated in presenting their demands to all in a single document.

There was risk, too, that without agreement diversity of action would follow. Compliance with the proposals involved a radical departure from the previous business practices of the industry and a drastic increase in admission prices of most of the subsequent-run theatres. Acceptance of the proposals was discouraged by at least three of the distributors' local managers. Independent exhibitors met and organized a futile protest which they presented to the representatives of Interstate and Consolidated. While as a result of independent negotiations either of the two restrictions without the other could have been put into effect by any one or more of the distributors and in any one or more of the Texas cities served by Interstate, the negotiations which ensued and which in fact did result in modifications of the proposals resulted in substantially unanimous action of the distributors, both as to the terms of the restrictions and in the selection of the four cities where they were to operate. . . .

But we are unable to find in the record any persuasive explanation other than agreed concert of action, of the singular unanimity of action on the part of the distributors by which the proposals were carried into effect as written in four Texas cities but not in a fifth or in the Rio Grande Valley. Numerous variations in the form of the provisions in the distributors' license agreements and the fact that in later years two of them extended the restrictions into all six cities, do not weaken the significance or force of the nature of the response to the proposals made by all the distributor appellants. It taxes credulity to believe that the several distributors would, in the circumstances, have accepted and put into operation with substantial unanimity such far-reaching changes in their business methods without some understanding that all were to join, and we reject as beyond the range of probability that it was the result of mere chance.

Appellants present an elaborate argument, based on the minutiae of the evidence, that other inferences are to be drawn which explain, at least in some respects, the unanimity of action both in accepting the restrictions for some territories and rejecting them for others.... Taken together, the circumstances of the case which we have mentioned, when uncontradicted and with no more explanation than the record affords, justify the inference that the distributors acted in concert and in common agreement in imposing the restrictions upon their licensees in the four Texas cities.

This inference was supported and strengthened when the distributors, with like unanimity, failed to tender the testimony, at their command, of any officer or agent of a distributor who knew, or was in a position to know, whether in fact an agreement had been reached among them for concerted action. When the proof supported, as we think it did, the inference of such concert, the burden rested on appellants of going forward with the evidence to explain away or contradict it. They undertook to carry that burden by calling upon local managers of the distributors to testify that they had acted independently of the other distributors, and that they did not have conferences with or reach agreements with the other distributors or their representatives. The failure under the circumstances to call as witnesses those officers who did have authority to act for the distributors and who were in a position to know whether they had acted in pursuance of agreement is itself persuasive that their testimony, if given, would have been unfavorable to appellants. The production of weak evidence when strong is available can lead only to the conclusion that the strong would have been adverse. Clifton v. United States, 4 How. 242, 247. Silence then becomes evidence of the most convincing character.

While the District Court's finding of an agreement of the distributors among themselves is supported by the evidence, we think that in the circumstances of this case such agreement for the imposition of the restrictions upon subsequent-run exhibitors was not a prerequisite to an unlawful conspiracy. It was enough that, knowing that concerted action was contemplated and invited, the distributors gave their adherence to the scheme and participated in it. Each distributor was advised that the others were asked to participate; each knew that cooperation was essential to successful operation of the plan. They knew that the plan, if carried out, would result in a restraint of commerce, which ... was unreasonable within the meaning of the Sherman Act, and knowing it, all participated in the plan. The evidence is persuasive that each distributor early became aware that the others had joined. With that knowledge they renewed the arrangement and carried it into effect for the two successive years.

It is elementary that an unlawful conspiracy may be and often is formed without simultaneous action or agreement on the part of the conspirators. United States v. Schenck, D.C., 253 F. 212, 213, affirmed 249 U.S. 47; Levey v. United States, 9 Cir., 92 F.2d 688, 691. Acceptance by competitors, without previous agreement, of an invitation to participate in a plan, the necessary consequence of which, if carried out, is restraint of interstate commerce, is sufficient to establish an unlawful conspiracy under the Sherman Act.[8] . . .

We think the conclusion is unavoidable that the conspiracy and each contract between Interstate and the distributors by which those consequences were effected are violations of the Sherman Act and that the District Court rightly enjoined enforcement and renewal of these agreements, as well as of the conspiracy among the distributors.[9]

Affirmed.

NOTES

1. IN RE BABY FOOD ANTITRUST LITIGATION, 166 F.3d 112 (3d Cir.1999). In this case, plaintiffs were direct purchasers of baby food from the defendant manufacturers, including such well-known firms as Gerber, Heinz, and Beech–Nut. They claimed that the defendants were conspiring to create and maintain high prices for baby food in the United States. The district court granted summary judgment for the defendants, and the Court of Appeals for the Third Circuit affirmed. After it found no direct evidence of agreement, it discussed conscious parallelism and oligopoly pricing, with the following comments:

> Because the evidence of conscious parallelism is circumstantial in nature, courts are concerned that they do not punish unilateral, independent conduct of competitors. They therefore require that evidence of a defendant's parallel pricing be supplemented with "plus factors." The simple term "plus factors" refers to "the additional facts or factors required to be proved as a prerequisite to finding that parallel action amounts to a conspiracy." They are necessary conditions for the conspiracy inference.... The plus factors may include, and often do, evidence demonstrating that the defendants: (1) acted contrary to their economic interests, and (2) were motivated to enter into a price fixing conspiracy.

166 F.3d at 122. The court found that evidence showing (1) a pattern of parallel price increases during the certified time period, (2) documentary and testimonial evidence indicating that each company was deliberately matching the other's prices or pegging their prices to another competitor's level, (3) certain reciprocal exchanges of price information, and (4) evidence showing parallel list and transaction pricing, was insufficient to allow the agreement issue to reach the jury.

2. C-O-TWO FIRE EQUIPMENT CO. v. UNITED STATES, 197 F.2d 489, 497 (9th Cir.1952), cert. denied, 344 U.S. 892, 73 S.Ct. 211, 97 L.Ed. 690 (1952). "Here,

---

8. Ed. The omission is of the Court's discussion, and rejection, of the argument that the restrictions as to admission prices and double billing were sheltered by the copyright laws and did not violate the Sherman Act.

9. Ed. Frankfurter, J., did not participate. The dissenting opinion of Roberts, J., in which McReynolds and Butler, JJ., joined, is omitted.

however, we have in addition to price uniformity, the other so-called plus factors hereinbefore treated. They include a background of illegal licensing agreements containing minimum price maintenance provisions, an artificial standardization of product, a raising of prices at a time when a surplus existed in the industry, and a policing of dealers to effectuate the maintenance of minimum price provisions in accordance with price lists published and distributed by the corporate defendants, including appellant, C–O–Two. Other factors which convinced the trial court, beyond a reasonable doubt, that the conspiracy did in fact exist, as charged, were the use of a delivered price system which resulted in price identity to the customer for the products sold, regardless of where they were manufactured, and the submitting of identical bids to public agencies. We think that the facts are not only consistent with the guilt of appellants, but also inconsistent with any other reasonable hypothesis.''

3.   BAILEY v. ALLGAS, INC., 284 F.3d 1237, 1251 (11th Cir.2002). This case involved the Robinson–Patman Act, 15 U.S.C. § 13(a), but in the course of evaluating that claim, the court found it necessary to consider whether the seller had market power. This led it to discuss both the possibility of monopoly power and the possibility of an oligopoly. In the latter context, it remarked that ''[t]he most reliable method of proving an oligopoly may be through extensive analysis of the historical price and output data for all the competitors within a relevant market. By examining such data, and even comparing data with similar retailers operating in non-oligopolistic markets, it may be possible to discern whether there is an interdependence in price and output between leading retailers in the market.''

4.   In ESCO CORP. v. UNITED STATES, 340 F.2d 1000, 1007 (9th Cir.1965), the court of appeals discussed the following hypothetical in an effort to clarify some of the problems in this area:

> Let us suppose five competitors meet on several occasions, discuss their problems, and one finally states ''I won't fix prices with any of you, but here is what I am going to do—put the price of my gidget at X dollars; now you all do what you want.'' He then leaves the meeting. Competitor number two says ''I don't care whether number one does what he says he's going to do or not; nor do I care what the rest of you do, but I am going to price my gidget at X dollars.'' Number three makes a similar statement— ''My price is X dollars.'' Number four says not one word. All leave and fix ''their'' prices at ''X'' dollars.

> We do not say the foregoing illustration compels an inference in this case that the competitors' conduct constituted a price-fixing conspiracy, including an agreement to so conspire, but neither can we say, as a matter of law, that an inference of no agreement is compelled. As in so many other instances, it remains a question for the trier of fact to consider and determine what inference appeals to it (the jury) as most logical and persuasive, after it has heard all the evidence as to what these competitors had done before such meeting, and what actions they took thereafter, or what actions they did not take.

Theatre Enterprises v. Paramount Film Distributing Corp.

Supreme Court of the United States, 1954.
346 U.S. 537, 74 S.Ct. 257, 98 L.Ed. 273.

■ CLARK, J. Petitioner brought this suit for treble damages and an injunction under §§ 4 and 16 of the Clayton Act, alleging that respondent motion picture producers and distributors had violated the antitrust laws by conspiring to restrict "first-run"[10] pictures to downtown Baltimore theatres, thus confining its suburban theatre to subsequent runs and unreasonable "clearances."[11] After hearing the evidence a jury returned a general verdict for respondents. The Court of Appeals for the Fourth Circuit affirmed the judgment based on the verdict. 201 F.2d 306. We granted certiorari. 345 U.S. 963.

Petitioner now urges, as it did in the Court of Appeals, that the trial judge should have directed a verdict in its favor and submitted to the jury only the question of the amount of damages. . . .

The opinion of the Court of Appeals contains a complete summary of the evidence presented to the jury. We need not recite that evidence again. It is sufficient to note that petitioner owns and operates the Crest Theatre, located in a neighborhood shopping district some six miles from the downtown shopping center in Baltimore, Maryland. The Crest, possessing the most modern improvements and appointments, opened on February 26, 1949. Before and after the opening, petitioner, through its president, repeatedly sought to obtain first-run features for the theatre. Petitioner approached each respondent separately, initially requesting exclusive first-runs, later asking for first-runs on a "day and date" basis.[12] But respondents uniformly rebuffed petitioner's efforts and adhered to an established policy of restricting first-runs in Baltimore to the eight downtown theatres. Admittedly there is no direct evidence of illegal agreement between the respondents and no conspiracy is charged as to the independent exhibitors in Baltimore, who account for 63% of first-run exhibitions. The various respondents advanced much the same reasons for denying petitioner's offers. Among other reasons they asserted that day and date first-runs are normally granted only to noncompeting theatres. Since the Crest is in "substantial competition" with the downtown theatres, a day and date arrangement would be economically unfeasible. And even if respondents wished to grant petitioner such a license, no downtown exhibitor would waive his clearance rights over the Crest and agree to a simultaneous showing. As a result, if petitioner were to receive first-runs, the license would have to be an exclusive one. However, an exclusive license would be economically unsound because the Crest is a suburban theatre, located in a small shopping center, and served by limited public transportation facilities; and, with a drawing area of less than one-tenth that of a downtown theatre, it cannot compare with those easily accessible theatres in the power to draw patrons. Hence the downtown theatres offer far greater

10. "Runs are successive exhibitions of a feature in a given area, first-run being the first exhibition in that area, second-run being the next subsequent, and so on. . . ." United States v. Paramount Pictures, Inc., 334 U.S. 131, 144–145, n. 6 (1948).

11. "A clearance is the period of time, usually stipulated in license contracts, which must elapse between runs of the same fea-

ture within a particular area or in specified theatres." United States v. Paramount Pictures, Inc., 334 U.S. 131, 144, n. 6 (1948).

12. A first-run "day-and-date" means that two theatres exhibit a first-run at the same time. Had petitioner's request for a day and date first-run been granted, the Crest and a downtown theatre would have exhibited the same features simultaneously.

opportunities for the widespread advertisement and exploitation of newly released features, which is thought necessary to maximize the overall return from subsequent runs as well as first-runs. The respondents, in the light of these conditions, attacked the guaranteed offers of petitioner, one of which occurred during the trial, as not being made in good faith. Respondents Loew's and Warner refused petitioner an exclusive license because they owned the three downtown theatres receiving their first-run product.

The crucial question is whether respondents' conduct toward petitioner stemmed from independent decision or from an agreement, tacit or express. To be sure, business behavior is admissible circumstantial evidence from which the fact finder may infer agreement. But this Court has never held that proof of parallel business behavior conclusively establishes agreement or, phrased differently, that such behavior itself constitutes a Sherman Act offense. Circumstantial evidence of consciously parallel behavior may have made heavy inroads into the traditional judicial attitude toward conspiracy; but "conscious parallelism" has not yet read conspiracy out of the Sherman Act entirely. Realizing this, petitioner attempts to bolster its argument for a directed verdict by urging that the conscious unanimity of action by respondents should be "measured against the background and findings in the Paramount case." In other words, since the same respondents had conspired in the Paramount case to impose a uniform system of runs and clearances without adequate explanation to sustain them as reasonable restraints of trade, use of the same device in the present case should be legally equated to conspiracy. But the Paramount decrees, even if admissible, were only prima facie evidence of a conspiracy covering the area and existing during the period there involved. Alone or in conjunction with the other proof of the petitioner, they would form no basis for a directed verdict. Here each of the respondents had denied the existence of any collaboration and in addition had introduced evidence of the local conditions surrounding the Crest operation which, they contended, precluded it from being a successful first-run house. They also attacked the good faith of the guaranteed offers of the petitioner for first-run pictures and attributed uniform action to individual business judgment motivated by the desire for maximum revenue. This evidence, together with other testimony of an explanatory nature, raised fact issues requiring the trial judge to submit the issue of conspiracy to the jury....

Affirmed.[13]

NOTES AND QUESTIONS

1. BROOKE GROUP V. BROWN & WILLIAMSON TOBACCO, 509 U.S. 209, 113 S.Ct. 2578, 125 L.Ed.2d 168 (1993), infra Chapter 8, page 847, the Supreme Court had

13. Ed. Douglas, J., did not participate in the decision. Black, J., dissented in a memorandum stating that the charge to the jury as to the burden of proof resting on plaintiff (which is omitted here) deprived it of a large part of the benefits intended to be afforded by the prima facie evidence provision of § 5 of the Clayton Act.

the occasion to comment on oligpolistic behavior. There, in the context of considering a claim that the respondent had engaged in predatory pricing, the Court said that "[e]ven in an oligpolistic market, when a firm drops its prices to a competitive level to demonstrate to a maverick the unprofitability of straying from the group, it would be illogical to condemn the price cut: The antitrust laws then would be an obstacle to the chain of events most conducive to a breakdown of oligopoly pricing and the onset of competition." Does this imply that the Court believes that oligopoly pricing issues are simply beyond the reach—and should be beyond the reach—of the antitrust laws?

2. The Supreme Court's conclusion in Theatre Enterprises that "parallel business behavior" did not "conclusively" establish an agreement—*i.e.*, a contract, combination, or conspiracy under Section 1 of the Sherman Act—was unexceptional. This proposition was relatively well settled in the lower courts prior to Theatre Enterprises and has been uniformly acknowledged since 1954.[14]

A far more difficult issue was posed for the lower courts by the following question: Assuming uniformity of action, without any "plus" factor, is a court warranted in submitting the question of conspiracy to the jury? In general, the lower courts have concluded that consciously parallel business behavior cannot support a submission to the jury (or a conspiracy finding) unless the conduct is inconsistent with independent, non-concerted action. See Mitchael v. Intracorp, Inc., 179 F.3d 847, 858 (10th Cir.1999); Winchester Theatre Co. v. Paramount Film Distributing Corp., 324 F.2d 652 (1st Cir.1963). See generally Matsushita Elec. Indus. Co., Ltd. v. Zenith Radio Corp., 475 U.S. 574, 588 (1986).

3. Of course, traditional evidence of conspiratorial activity—*e.g.*, clandestine meetings, secret exchanges of information—when combined with consciously parallel business conduct will support a jury's finding of conspiracy. U.S. v. Andreas, 216 F.3d 645 (7th Cir.2000), for example, involved an appeal from a conviction for conspiring to fix the global price and allocate sales volume of lysine among top producers. Throughout the early 1990s, executives from American and foreign firms met to fix prices and allocate sales volume amongst themselves. In order to avoid liability for their actions, they fabricated aliases and front organizations to hide their activities, hired prostitutes to gather information from competitors, lied, cheated, embezzled, extorted and obstructed justice.

4. Please consider at this time the interrelation between the oligopoly theory set forth in Section 1, supra, and the quality and quantum of evidence of conspiracy that one would expect to find in a case involving a concentrated industry. In other words, are the structural characteristics of a market of any legal importance in an oligopoly case? Would conspirators in a concentrated or unconcentrated industry be more likely to leave a well-marked trail? Should courts be more willing to sustain a jury's finding of conspiracy on limited evidence in a case involving a concentrated industry?

5. The most difficult cases after Theatre Enterprises have involved situations in which traditional conspiratorial conduct was not shown, but defendants' "consciously parallel" conduct appeared to be inconsistent with each defendant's economic self-interest.

In Bogosian v. Gulf Oil Corp., 561 F.2d 434, 440, 445–46 (3d Cir.1977), cert. denied, 434 U.S. 1086 (1978), operators of service stations brought antitrust class

---

14. *See, e.g.*, Bogosian v. Gulf Oil Corp., 561 F.2d 434 (3d Cir.1977), cert. denied, 434 U.S. 1086 (1978); Modern Home Institute, Inc. v. Hartford Accident & Indemnity Co., 513 F.2d 102 (2d Cir.1975).

actions against major oil companies, alleging concerted action unlawfully to tie the leasing of gas station sites to the purchase of gasoline supplied by each operator's lessor. Each defendant was alleged to have required its station lessees, through "a course of interdependent consciously parallel action" with other defendants, to handle its brand of gasoline exclusively. The district court granted motions for summary judgment made by all defendants with no business dealings with the named plaintiffs because "the allegation of 'interdependent consciously parallel action' in a complaint is an insufficient statement of the concerted action necessary to state a claim under § 1."

In a 2–1 decision, the Third Circuit reversed. The court first observed that plaintiffs' complaint alleged "an unlawful combination" and we "perceive no distinction between the terms combination and conspiracy.... Our reading of § 1 cases indicates that the two terms are used interchangeably."[15] The court then said:

> The law is settled that proof of consciously parallel business behavior is circumstantial evidence from which an agreement, tacit or express, can be inferred but that such evidence, without more, is insufficient unless the circumstances under which it occurred make the inference of rational, independent choice less attractive than that of concerted action.... We recently articulated those circumstances in Venzie Corp. v. United States Mineral Products Co., 521 F.2d 1309 (3d Cir.1975);

> "(1) a showing of acts by defendants in contradiction of their own economic interests ..., and

> "(2) satisfactory demonstration of a motivation to enter an agreement ..."

> Plaintiffs argue that, given an opportunity to conduct discovery, they will prove that both of these circumstances are present. They contend that independent self-interest would indicate that each oil company seeks to market gasoline to their competitors' lessees, and that the failure to so compete can be explained only by a mutual understanding, tacit or expressed, that gasoline be marketed to lessee-dealers on an exclusive basis. The motivation to participate in such an agreement, of course, is the elimination of price competition among oil companies at the wholesale level.... We conclude that the ruling that the specific allegation of interdependent consciously parallel action made here fails to state a claim should be vacated....

Some years later, in Petruzzi's IGA Supermarkets, Inc. v. Darling–Delaware Company, Inc., 998 F.2d 1224 (3d Cir.1993), the Third Circuit revisited this issue. In that case, a supermarket brought an action against fat and bone rendering companies for restraint of trade in violation of the Sherman Act. The defendants were alleged to have conspired to allocate existing accounts in parts of the Northeast. The court said:

> "To establish a conspiracy based on consciously parallel behavior, a plaintiff must show:

> that the defendants' behavior was parallel;

> that the defendants were conscious of each other's conduct and that this awareness was an element in their decision-making processes; and

> certain "plus" factors ...

15. Ed. Compare the Supreme Court's analysis of "combination" and "conspiracy" at pp. 684–685 infra.

. . . However, even without this evidence [the "plus" factors] purporting to show a traditional agreement, we have stated that a plaintiff can survive summary judgment if it shows that the defendants had a motive to conspire and acted contrary to their self-interest."

Under the Third Circuit's approach, if defendants' conduct is parallel, conscious, and interdependent should a case go to the jury? Can a defendant's decision be "unilateral" and "interdependent" at the same time? What does the Third Circuit's focus on "motivation" and economic self-interest add to the "interdependence" analysis? Should a defendant's "motive" to profit from consciously parallel and interdependent activity provide a sufficient "plus factor" to permit a plaintiff to get to a jury? What does the Third Circuit mean by "contradiction of their own economic interests"? It is difficult to understand why a company would join in a decision against its economic interests. Furthermore, as we have already noted, it is in the oligopolist's independent interest to go along with pricing decisions its competitors have made. Do these words, as used by the Third Circuit, merely mean that a company should ignore the likely decisions of its competitors? Would ignoring the likely decisions of competitors (*e.g.*, refraining from marketing gasoline to their competitors' lessees or adopting a practice resulting in high entry barriers and high profits) truly be in furtherance of a company's "own economic interests"?

Toys "R" Us, Inc. v. F.T.C.

United States Court of Appeals, Seventh Circuit, 2000.
221 F.3d 928.

■ DIANE P. WOOD, CIRCUIT JUDGE. The antitrust laws, which aim to preserve and protect competition in economically sensible markets, have long drawn a sharp distinction between contractual restrictions that occur up and down a distribution chain—so-called vertical restraints—and restrictions that come about as a result of agreements among competitors, or horizontal restraints. Sometimes, however, it can be hard as a matter of fact to be sure what kind of agreement is at issue. This was the problem facing the Federal Trade Commission ("the Commission") when it brought under its antitrust microscope the large toy retailer Toys "R" Us (TRU).

The Commission concluded, upon an extensive administrative record, that TRU had acted as the coordinator of a horizontal agreement among a number of toy manufacturers. The agreements took the form of a network of vertical agreements between TRU and the individual manufacturers, in each of which the manufacturer promised to restrict the distribution of its products to low-priced warehouse club stores, on the condition that other manufacturers would do the same. This practice, the Commission found, violated § 5 of the Federal Trade Commission Act, 15 U.S.C. § 45. It also found that TRU had entered into a series of vertical agreements that flunked scrutiny under antitrust's rule of reason. TRU appealed that decision to us. It attacks both the sufficiency of the evidence supporting the Commission's conclusions and the scope of the Commission's remedial order. It is hard to prevail on either type of challenge: the former is fact-intensive and faces the hurdle of the substantial evidence standard of review, while the latter calls into question the Commission's exercise of its discretion to remedy an established violation of the law. We conclude that, while reasonable people could differ on the facts in this voluminous record, the Commission's decisions pass muster, and we therefore affirm.

I

TRU is a giant in the toy retailing industry. The Commission found that it sells approximately 20% of all the toys sold in the United States, and that in some metropolitan areas its share of toy sales ranges between 35% and 49%. The variety of toys it sells is staggering: over the course of a year, it offers about 11,000 individual toy items, far more than any of its competitors. As one might suspect from these figures alone, TRU is a critical outlet for toy manufacturers. It buys about 30% of the large, traditional toy companies' total output and it is usually their most important customer. According to evidence before the Commission's administrative law judge, or ALJ, even a company as large as Hasbro felt that it could not find other retailers to replace TRU—and Hasbro, along with Mattel, is one of the two largest toy manufacturers in the country, accounting for approximately 12% of the market for traditional toys and 10% of a market that includes video games. Similar opinions were offered by Mattel and smaller manufacturers.

Toys are sold in a number of different kinds of stores. At the high end are traditional toy stores and department stores, both of which typically sell toys for 40 to 50% above their cost. Next are the specialized discount stores—a category virtually monopolized by TRU today—that sell at an average 30% mark-up. General discounters like Wal–Mart, K–Mart, and Target are next, with a 22% mark-up, and last are the stores that are the focus of this case, the warehouse clubs like Costco and Pace. The clubs sell toys at a slender mark-up of 9% or so.

The toys customers seek in all these stores are highly differentiated products. The little girl who wants Malibu Barbie is not likely to be satisfied with My First Barbie, and she certainly does not want Ken or Skipper. The boy who has his heart set on a figure of Anakin Skywalker will be disappointed if he receives Jar–Jar Binks, or a truck, or a baseball bat instead. Toy retailers naturally want to have available for their customers the season's hottest items, because toys are also a very faddish product, as those old enough to recall the mania over Cabbage Patch kids or Tickle Me Elmo dolls will attest.

What happened in this case, according to the Commission, was fairly simple. For a long time, TRU had enjoyed a strong position at the low price end for toy sales, because its only competition came from traditional toy stores who could not or did not wish to meet its prices, or from general discounters like Wal–Mart or K–Mart, which could not offer anything like the variety of items TRU had and whose prices were not too far off TRU's mark.

The advent of the warehouse clubs changed all that. They were a retail innovation of the late 1970s: the first one opened in 1976, and by 1992 there were some 600 individual club stores around the country. Rather than earning all of their money from their mark-up on products, the clubs sell only to their members, and they charge a modest annual membership fee, often about $30. As the word "warehouse" in the name suggests, the clubs emphasize price competition over service amenities. Nevertheless, the Commission found that the clubs seek to offer name-brand merchandise, including toys. During the late 1980s and early 1990s, warehouse clubs selected and purchased from the toy manufacturers' full array of products, just like everyone else. In some instances they bought specialized packs assembled for the "club" trade, but they normally preferred stocking conventional products so that their customers could readily compare the price of an item at the club against the price of the same item at a competing store.

To the extent this strategy was successful, however, TRU did not welcome it. By 1989, its senior executives were concerned that the clubs were a threat to TRU's low-price image and, more importantly, to its profits. A little legwork revealed that as of that year the clubs carried approximately 120–240 items in direct competition with TRU, priced as much as 25 to 30% below TRU's own price levels.

TRU put its President of Merchandising, a Mr. Goddu, to work to see what could be done. The response Goddu and other TRU executives formulated to beat back the challenge from the clubs began with TRU's decision to contact some of its suppliers, including toy manufacturing heavyweights Mattel, Hasbro, and Fisher Price. At the Toy Fair in 1992 (a major event at which the next Christmas season's orders are placed), Goddu informed the manufacturers of a new TRU policy, which was reflected in a memo of January 29, 1992. The policy set forth the following conditions and privileges for TRU:

- The clubs could have no new or promoted product unless they carried the entire line.
- All specials and exclusives to be sold to the clubs had to be shown first to TRU to see if TRU wanted the item.
- Old and basic product had to be in special packs.
- Clearance and closeout items were permissible provided that TRU was given the first opportunity to buy the product.
- There would be no discussion about prices.

TRU was careful to meet individually with each of its suppliers to explain its new policy. Afterwards, it then asked each one what it intended to do. Negotiations between TRU and the manufacturers followed, as a result of which each manufacturer eventually agreed that it would sell to the clubs only highly-differentiated products (either unique individual items or combo packs) that were not offered to anything but a club (and thus of course not to TRU). As the Commission put it, "through its announced policy and the related agreements discussed below, TRU sought to eliminate the competitive threat the clubs posed by denying them merchandise, forcing the clubs' customers to buy products they did not want, and frustrating customers' ability to make direct price comparisons of club prices and TRU prices."

The agreements between TRU and the various manufacturers were, of course, vertical agreements, because they ran individually from the supplier/manufacturer to the purchaser/retailer. The Commission found that TRU reached about 10 of these agreements. After the agreements were concluded, TRU then supervised and enforced each toy company's compliance with its commitment.

But TRU was not content to stop with vertical agreements. Instead, the Commission found, it decided to go further. It worked for over a year and a half to put the vertical agreements in place, but "the biggest hindrance TRU had to overcome was the major toy companies' reluctance to give up a new, fast-growing, and profitable channel of distribution." The manufacturers were also concerned that any of their rivals who broke ranks and sold to the clubs might gain sales at their expense, given the widespread and increasing popularity of the club format. To address this problem, the Commission found, TRU orchestrated a horizontal agreement among its key suppliers to boycott the clubs. The evidence on which the Commission relied showed that, at a minimum, Mattel, Hasbro, Fisher Price, Tyco, Little Tikes, Today's Kids, and Tiger Electronics agreed to join in the boycott "on the condition that their competitors would do the same."

The Commission first noted that internal documents from the manufacturers revealed that they were trying to expand, not to restrict, the number of their major retail outlets and to reduce their dependence on TRU. They were specifically interested in cultivating a relationship with the warehouse clubs and increasing sales there. Thus, the sudden adoption of measures under which they decreased sales to the clubs ran against their independent economic self-interest. Second, the Commission cited evidence that the manufacturers were unwilling to limit sales to the clubs without assurances that their competitors would do likewise. Goddu himself testified that TRU communicated the message "I'll stop if they stop" from manufacturer to competing manufacturer. He specifically mentioned having such conversations with Mattel and Hasbro, and he said more generally "We communicated to our vendors that we were communicating with all our key suppliers, and we did that I believe at Toy Fair 1992. We made a point to tell each of the vendors that we spoke to that we would be talking to our other key suppliers."

Evidence from the manufacturers corroborated Goddu's account. A Mattel executive said that it would not sell the clubs the same items it was selling to TRU, and that this decision was "based on the fact that competition would do the same." A Hasbro executive said much the same thing: "because our competitors had agreed not to sell loaded [that is, promoted] product to the clubs, that we would ... go along with this." TRU went so far as to assure individual manufacturers that no one would be singled out.

Once the special warehouse club policy (or, in the Commission's more pejorative language, boycott) was underway, TRU served as the central clearinghouse for complaints about breaches in the agreement. The Commission gave numerous examples of this conduct in its opinion.

Last, the Commission found that TRU's policies had bite. In the year before the boycott began, the clubs' share of all toy sales in the United States grew from 1.5% in 1991 to 1.9% in 1992. After the boycott took hold, that percentage slipped back by 1995 to 1.4%. Local numbers were more impressive. Costco, for example, experienced overall growth on sales of all products during the period 1991 to 1993 of 25%. Its toy sales increased during [the] same period by 51%. But, after the boycott took hold in 1993, its toy sales decreased by 1.6% even while its overall sales were still growing by 19.5%. The evidence indicated that this was because TRU had succeeded in cutting off its access to the popular toys it needed. In 1989, over 90% of the Mattel toys Costco and other clubs purchased were regular (*i.e.* easily comparable) items, but by 1993 that percentage was zero. Once again, the Commission's opinion is chock full of similar statistics.

The Commission also considered the question whether TRU might have been trying to protect itself against free riding, at least with respect to its vertical agreements. It acknowledged that TRU provided several services that might be important to consumers, including "advertising, carrying an inventory of goods early in the year, and supporting a full line of products." Nevertheless, it found that the manufacturers compensated TRU directly for advertising toys, storing toys made early in the year, and stocking a broad line of each manufacturer's toys under one roof. A 1993 TRU memorandum confirms that advertising is manufacturer-funded and is "essentially free." In 1994, TRU's net cost of advertising was a tiny 0.02% of sales, or $750,000, out of a total of $199 million it spent on advertising that year. As the Commission saw it, "advertising . . . was a service the toy manufacturers provided for TRU and not the other way around." Id. (emphasis in original). TRU records also showed that manufacturers routinely paid TRU credits for warehousing services, and that they compensated it for full line stocking. In short, the Commission found, there was no evidence that club competition without comparable services threatened to drive TRU services out of the market or to harm customers. Manufacturers paid each retailer directly for the services they wanted the retailer to furnish.

Based on this record, the Commission drew three central conclusions of law: (1) the TRU-led manufacturer boycott of the warehouse clubs was illegal *per se* under the rule enunciated in Northwest Wholesale Stationers, Inc. v. Pacific Stationery & Printing Co., 472 U.S. 284, 86 L. Ed. 2d 202, 105 S. Ct. 2613 (1985); (2) the boycott was illegal under a full rule of reason analysis because its anticompetitive effects "clearly outweighed any possible business justification"; and (3) the vertical agreements between TRU and the individual toy manufacturers, "entered into seriatim with clear anticompetitive effect, violate section 1 of the Sherman Act." These antitrust violations in turn were enough to prove a violation of FTC Act § 5, which for present purposes tracks the prohibitions of the Sherman and Clayton Acts. After offering a detailed explanation of these conclusions (spanning 42 pages in its slip opinion), it turned to the question of remedy and affirmed the order the ALJ had entered.

In the Commission's words, its order:

> . . . prohibits TRU from continuing, entering into, or attempting to enter into, vertical agreements with its suppliers to limit the supply of, or refuse to sell, toys to a toy discounter. See para. II.A. The order also prohibits TRU from facilitating, or attempting to facilitate, an agreement between or among its suppliers relating to the sale of toys to any retailer. See para. II.D. Additionally, TRU is enjoined from requesting information from suppliers about their sales to any toy discounter, and from urging or coercing suppliers to restrict sales to any toy discounter. See para. II.B, C. These four elements of relief are narrowly tailored to stop, and prevent the repetition of, TRU's illegal conduct.

TRU complained that the order trampled on its ability to exercise its rights under United States v. Colgate & Co., 250 U.S. 300, 63 L. Ed. 992, 39 S. Ct. 465 (1919), to choose unilaterally the companies with which it wanted to deal. The Commission rejected the point, because it found that TRU had repeatedly crossed the line from unilateral to concerted behavior in illegal ways, and that it was entitled to include remedial provisions that were necessary to prevent recurrence of the illegal behavior, citing FTC v. National Lead Co., 352 U.S. 419, 430, 1 L. Ed. 2d 438, 77 S. Ct. 502 (1957).

Commissioner Swindle concurred in part and dissented in part. He agreed with the majority's determination that TRU had engaged in a series of anticompetitive vertical agreements, and he thus agreed with the remedial provisions designed to proscribe those practices and their effects. He was unconvinced, however, that TRU had orchestrated a horizontal combination as well, believing that the evidence was too thin to support that conclusion. TRU appealed from the Commission's final order of October 13, 1998, to this court, under 15 U.S.C. § 45(c), as it carries on business in this circuit (as well as every other circuit, to the best of our knowledge).

II

On appeal, TRU makes four principal arguments: (1) the Commission's finding of a horizontal conspiracy is contrary to the facts and impermissibly confuses the law of vertical restraints with the law of horizontal restraints; (2) whether the restrictions were vertical or horizontal, they were not unlawful because TRU has no market power, and thus the conduct can have no significant anticompetitive effect; (3) the TRU policy was a legitimate response to free riding; and (4) the relief ordered by the Commission goes too far. We review the Commission's legal conclusions *de novo*, but we must accept its findings of fact if they are supported by such relevant evidence as a reasonable mind might accept as adequate to support a conclusion. FTC v. Indiana Fed'n of Dentists, 476 U.S. 447, 454, 90 L. Ed. 2d 445, 106 S. Ct. 2009 (1986).

A. Horizontal Conspiracy

As TRU correctly points out, the critical question here is whether substantial evidence supported the Commission's finding that there was a horizontal agreement among the toy manufacturers, with TRU in the center as the ringmaster, to boycott the warehouse clubs. It acknowledges that such an agreement may be proved by either direct or circumstantial evidence, under cases such as Matsushita Electric Indus. Co. v. Zenith Radio Corp., 475 U.S. 574, 89 L. Ed. 2d 538, 106 S. Ct. 1348 (1986) (horizontal agreements), Monsanto Co. v. Spray–Rite Service Corp., 465 U.S. 752, 79 L. Ed. 2d 775, 104 S. Ct. 1464 (1984) (vertical agreements), and Interstate Circuit, Inc. v. United States, 306 U.S. 208, 83 L. Ed. 610, 59 S. Ct. 467 (1939). When circumstantial evidence is used, there must be some evidence that "tends to exclude the possibility" that the alleged conspirators acted independently. Monsanto, 465 U.S. at 764, quoted in Matsushita, 475 U.S. at 588. This does not mean, however, that the Commission had to exclude all possibility that the manufacturers acted independently. As we pointed out in In re Brand Name Prescription Drugs Antitrust Litigation, 186 F.3d 781 (7th Cir.1999), that would amount to an absurd and legally unfounded burden to prove with 100% certainty that an antitrust violation occurred. Id. at 787. The test states only that there must be some evidence which, if believed, would support a finding of concerted behavior. In the context of an appeal from the Commission, the question is whether substantial evidence supports its conclusion that it is more likely than not that the manufacturers acted collusively.

In TRU's opinion, this record shows nothing more than a series of separate, similar vertical agreements between itself and various toy manufacturers. It believes that each manufacturer in its independent self-interest had an incentive to limit sales to the clubs, because TRU's policy provided strong unilateral incentives for the manufacturer to reduce its sales to the clubs. Why gain a few sales at the clubs, it asks, when it would have much more to gain by maintaining a good relationship with the 100-pound gorilla of the industry, TRU, and make far more sales?

We do not disagree that there was some evidence in the record that would bear TRU's interpretation. But that is not the standard we apply when we review decisions of the Federal Trade Commission. Instead, we apply the substantial evidence test, which we described as follows in another case in which the Commission's decision to stop a hospital merger was at issue:

> Our only function is to determine whether the Commission's analysis of the probable effects of these acquisitions on hospital competition in Chattanooga is so implausible, so feebly supported by the record, that it flunks even the deferential test of substantial evidence.

Hospital Corp. of America v. F.T.C., 807 F.2d 1381, 1385 (7th Cir.1986). There, as here, the Commission painstakingly explained in a long opinion exactly what evidence in the record supported its conclusion. We need only decide whether the inference the Commission drew of horizontal agreement was a permissible one from that evidence, not if it was the only possible one.

The Commission's theory, stripped to its essentials, is that this case is a modern equivalent of the old Interstate Circuit decision. That case too involved actors at two levels of the distribution chain, distributors of motion pictures and exhibitors. Interstate Circuit was one of the exhibitors; it had a stranglehold on the exhibition of movies in a number of Texas cities. The antitrust violation occurred when Interstate's manager, O'Don-nell, sent an identical letter to the eight branch managers of the distributor companies, with each letter naming all eight as addressees, in which he asked them to comply with two demands: a minimum price for first-run theaters, and a policy against double features at night. The trial court there drew an inference of agreement from the nature of the proposals, from the manner in which they were made, from the substantial unanimity of action taken, and from the lack of evidence of a benign motive; the Supreme Court affirmed. The new policies represented a radical shift from the industry's prior business practices, and the Court rejected as beyond the range of probability that such unanimity of action was explainable only by chance.

The Commission is right. Indeed, as it argues in its brief, the TRU case if anything presents a more compelling case for inferring horizontal agree-ment than did Interstate Circuit, because not only was the manufacturers' decision to stop dealing with the warehouse clubs an abrupt shift from the past, and not only is it suspicious for a manufacturer to deprive itself of a profitable sales outlet, but the record here included the direct evidence of communications that was missing in Interstate Circuit. Just as in Inter-state Circuit, TRU tries to avoid this result by hypothesizing independent motives. 306 U.S. at 223–24. If there were no evidence in the record tending to support concerted behavior, then we agree that Matsushita would require a ruling in TRU's favor. But there is. The evidence showed that the companies wanted to diversify from TRU, not to become more dependent upon it; it showed that each manufacturer was afraid to curb its sales to the warehouse clubs alone, because it was afraid its rivals would cheat and gain a special advantage in that popular new market niche. The Commission was not required to disbelieve the testimony of the different toy company executives and TRU itself to the effect that the only condition on which each toy manufacturer would agree to TRU's demands was if it could be sure its competitors were doing the same thing.

That is a horizontal agreement. As we explain further below in discussing TRU's free rider argument, it has nothing to do with enhancing efficiencies of distribution from the manufacturer's point of view. The typical story of a legitimate vertical transaction would have the manufac-turer going to TRU and asking it to be the exclusive carrier of the manufacturer's goods; in exchange for that exclusivity, the manufacturer would hope to receive more effective promotion of its goods, and TRU would have a large enough profit margin to do the job well. But not all manufacturers think that exclusive dealing arrangements will maximize their profits. Some think, and are entitled to think, that using the greatest number of retailers possible is a better strategy. These manufacturers were in effect being asked by TRU to reduce their output (especially of the popular toys), and as is classically true in such cartels, they were willing to do so only if TRU could protect them against cheaters.

Northwest Stationers also demonstrates why the facts the Commission found support its conclusion that the essence of the agreement network TRU supervised was horizontal. There the Court described the cases that had condemned boycotts as "per se" illegal as those involving "joint efforts by a firm or firms to disadvantage competitors by either directly denying or persuading or coercing suppliers or customers to deny relationships the competitors need in the competitive struggle." 472 U.S. at 294 (internal citations omitted). The boycotters had to have some market power, though the Court did not suggest that the level had to be as high as it would require in a case under Sherman Act § 2. Here, TRU was trying to disadvantage the warehouse clubs, its competitors, by coercing suppliers to deny the clubs the products they needed. It accomplished this goal by inducing the suppliers to collude, rather than to compete independently for shelf space in the different toy retail stores. See also NYNEX Corp. v. Discon, Inc., 525 U.S. 128, 142 L. Ed. 2d 510, 119 S. Ct. 493 (1998); Klor's, Inc. v. Broadway–Hale Stores, Inc., 359 U.S. 207, 3 L. Ed. 2d 741, 79 S. Ct. 705 (1959).

B.   Degree of TRU's Market Power

TRU's efforts to deflate the Commission's finding of market power are pertinent only if we had agreed with its argument that the Commission's finding of a horizontal agreement was without support. Horizontal agreements among competitors, including group boycotts, remain illegal *per se* in the sense the Court used the term in Northwest Stationers. We have found that this case satisfies the criteria the Court used in Northwest Stationers for condemnation without an extensive inquiry into market power and economic pros and cons: (1) the boycotting firm has cut off access to a supply, facility or market necessary for the boycotted firm (*i.e.* the clubs) to compete; (2) the boycotting firm possesses a "dominant" position in the market (where "dominant" is an undefined term, but plainly chosen to stand for something different from antitrust's term of art "monopoly"); and (3) the boycott, as we explain further below, cannot be justified by plausible arguments that it was designed to enhance overall efficiency. 472 U.S. at 294. We address the market power point here, therefore, only in the alternative.

TRU seems to think that anticompetitive effects in a market cannot be shown unless the plaintiff, or here the Commission, first proves that it has a large market share. This, however, has things backwards. As we have explained elsewhere, the share a firm has in a properly defined relevant market is only a way of estimating market power, which is the ultimate consideration. Ball Memorial Hospital, Inc. v. Mutual Hospital Insurance, 784 F.2d 1325, 1336 (7th Cir.1986). The Supreme Court has made it clear that there are two ways of proving market power. One is through direct evidence of anticompetitive effects. See FTC v. Indiana Fed'n of Dentists, 476 U.S. 447, 460–61, 90 L. Ed. 2d 445, 106 S. Ct. 2009 (1986) ("the finding of actual, sustained adverse effects on competition in those areas where IFD dentists predominated, viewed in light of the reality that markets for dental services tend to be relatively localized, is legally sufficient to support a finding that the challenged restraint was unreasonable even in the absence of elaborate market analysis."). The other, more conventional way, is by proving relevant product and geographic markets and by showing that the defendant's share exceeds whatever threshold is important for the practice in the case. *See, e.g.,* United States v. E.I. du Pont de Nemours & Co., 351 U.S. 377, 100 L. Ed. 1264, 76 S. Ct. 994 (1956); United States v. Grinnell Corp., 384 U.S. 563, 16 L. Ed. 2d 778, 86 S. Ct. 1698 (1966); United States v. Aluminum Co. of America, 148 F.2d 416 (2d Cir.1945) (suggesting that more than 90% is enough to constitute a monopoly for purposes of Sherman Act § 2 and 33% is not); Jefferson Parish Hospital Dist. No. 2 v. Hyde, 466 U.S. 2, 80 L. Ed. 2d 2, 104 S. Ct. 1551 (1984) (indicating that something more than 30% would be needed to show the kind of power over a tying product necessary for a violation of Sherman Act § 1).

The Commission found here that, however TRU's market power as a toy retailer was measured, it was clear that its boycott was having an effect in the market. It was remarkably successful in causing the 10 major toy manufacturers to reduce output of toys to the warehouse clubs, and that reduction in output protected TRU from having to lower its prices to meet the clubs' price levels. Price competition from conventional discounters like Wal–Mart and K–Mart, in contrast, imposed no such constraint on it, or so the Commission found. In addition, the Commission showed that the affected manufacturers accounted for some 40% of the traditional toy market, and that TRU had 20% of the national wholesale market and up to 49% of some local wholesale markets. Taking steps to prevent a price collapse through coordination of action among competitors has been illegal at least since United States v. Socony–Vacuum Oil Co., 310 U.S. 150, 84 L. Ed. 1129, 60 S. Ct. 811 (1940). Proof that this is what TRU was doing is sufficient proof of actual anticompetitive effects that no more elaborate market analysis was necessary.

C.   Free Riding Explanation

TRU next urges that its policy was a legitimate business response to combat free riding by the warehouse clubs. We think, however, that it has fundamentally misunderstood the theory of free riding. Briefly, that theory is as follows. The manufacturer of a product, say widgets, has an incentive to distribute as many widgets as it can, while keeping its costs of distribution down as low as possible. In many instances, this means that the manufacturer will want to sell its widgets for a particular wholesale price and it will want its retailer to apply as low a mark-up as possible (*i.e.,* put the product on the market for as little extra expense as possible). Sometimes, however, the manufacturer will want the retailer to provide special services or amenities that cost money, such as attractive premises, trained salespeople, long business hours, full-line stocking, or fast warranty service. But the costs of providing some of those amenities (usually pre-sale services) are hard to pass on to customers unless some form of restricted distribution is available. What the manufacturer does not want is for the shopper to visit the attractive store with highly paid, intelligent sales help, learn all about the product, and then go home and order it from a discount warehouse or (today) on-line discounters. The shopper in that situation has taken a "free ride" on the retailer's efforts; the retailer never gets paid for them, and eventually it stops offering the services. If those services were genuinely useful, in the sense that the product plus service package resulted in greater sales for the manufacturer than the product alone would have enjoyed, there is a loss both for the manufacturer and the consumer. Hence, antitrust law permits nonprice vertical restraints that are designed to facilitate the provision of extra services, recognizing that a manufacturer in a competitive market who has guessed wrong will eventually be forced by the market to abandon the restrictions. See Business Electronics Corp. v. Sharp Electronics Corp., 485 U.S. 717, 724, 99 L. Ed. 2d 808, 108 S. Ct. 1515 (1988), quoting Continental T.V., Inc. v. GTE Sylvania Inc., 433 U.S. 36, 52 n. 19, 53 L. Ed. 2d 568, 97 S. Ct. 2549 (1977).

Here, the evidence shows that the free-riding story is inverted. The manufacturers wanted a business strategy under which they distributed their toys to as many different kinds of outlets as would accept them: exclusive toy shops, TRU, discount department stores, and warehouse clubs. Rightly or wrongly, this was the distribution strategy that each one believed would maximize its individual output and profits. The manufacturers did not think that the alleged "extra services" TRU might have been providing were necessary. This is crucial, because the most important insight behind the free rider concept is the fact that, with respect to the cost of distribution services, the interests of the manufacturer and the consumer are aligned, and are basically adverse to the interests of the retailer (who would presumably like to charge as much as possible for its part in the process). See Premier Electrical Construction Co. v. Nat'l Electrical Contractors Ass'n, 814 F.2d 358, 369–70 (7th Cir.1987) ("[the rationale for permitting restricted distribution policies] depends on the alignment of interests between consumers and manufacturers. Destroy that alignment and you destroy the power of the argument.").

What TRU wanted or did not want is neither here nor there for purposes of the free rider argument. Its economic interest was in maximizing its own profits, not in keeping down its suppliers' cost of doing business. Furthermore, we note that the Commission made a plausible argument for the proposition that there was little or no opportunity to "free" ride on anything here in any event. The consumer is not taking a free ride if the cost of the service can be captured in the price of the item. As our earlier review of the facts demonstrated, the manufacturers were paying for the services TRU furnished, such as advertising, full-line product stocking, and extensive inventories. These expenses, we may assume, were folded into the price of the goods the manufacturers charged to TRU, and thus these services were not susceptible to free riding. On this record, in short, TRU cannot prevail on the basis that its practices were designed to combat free riding.

D. Remedy

Last, we consider TRU's challenge to the remedial provisions the Commission ordered. TRU's basic point here is that the Commission has commanded it to do things that it would have been free to refuse, and conversely to refrain from actions it would have been free to take, in the absence of its violation of FTC Act § 5. So that its arguments can be fully understood, we set forth Section II of the decree in its entirety here:

> IT IS ORDERED that respondent, directly or indirectly, through any corporation, subsidiary, division or other device, in connection with the actual or potential purchase or distribution of toys and related products, in or affecting commerce, as "commerce" is defined in the Federal Trade Commission Act, forthwith cease and desist from:
>
> A.   Continuing, maintaining, entering into, and attempting to enter into any agreement or understanding with any supplier to limit supply or to refuse to sell toys and related products to any toy discounter.
>
> B.   Urging, inducing, coercing, or pressuring, or attempting to urge, induce, coerce, or pressure, any supplier to limit supply or to refuse to sell toys and related products to any toy discounter.
>
> C.   Requiring, soliciting, requesting or encouraging any supplier to furnish information to respondent relating to any supplier's sales or actual or intended shipments to any toy discounter.
>
> D.   Facilitating or attempting to facilitate agreements or under-standings between or among suppliers relating to limiting the sale of toys and related products to any retailer(s) by, among other things, transmitting or conveying complaints, intentions, plans, actions, or other similar information from one supplier to another supplier relating to sales to such retailer(s).
>
> E.   For a period of five years, (1) announcing or communicating that respondent will or may discontinue purchasing or refuse to purchase toys and related products from any supplier because that supplier intends to sell or sells toys and related products to any toy discounter, or (2) refusing to purchase toys and related products from a supplier because, in whole or in part, that supplier offered to sell or sold toys and related products to any toy discounter.
>
> PROVIDED, however, that nothing in this order shall prevent respondent from seeking or entering into exclusive arrangements with suppliers with respect to particular toys.

TRU makes a perfunctory, one-paragraph argument that paragraphs II(B), II(C), II(D), and II(E)(1) impose a "gag order" that contravenes the Supreme Court's recognition in Monsanto Co. v. Spray–Rite Corp., supra, that manufacturers and distributors have a legitimate need for a free flow of information between them. This order, they claim, will create an irrational dislocation in the market to the detriment of toy suppliers, retailers, and consumers. With respect to paragraph II(E)(2), it argues that the five-year restriction on refusals to deal impermissibly cabins its Colgate rights to choose the suppliers with which it wants to deal. In effect, it claims, the decree will force it to purchase all toys that are offered to anyone, unless it can somehow prove that its refusal was because of a safety defect or other similar flaw.

We consider first TRU's challenges to parts II(B) through II(D) of the order. (It has not mentioned II(A) in its brief, and thus it has waived any challenge to that part of the order.) In general, if a retailer had some kind of restricted distribution arrangement with a manufacturer, Monsanto holds that it is permissible for the retailer to urge the manufacturer to respect the limits of that agreement. The retailer may communicate complaints about the provision of product to discounters, if that runs afoul of the promises in the distribution agreement. Colgate indicates that the retailer would also be within its rights to tell the manufacturer that it will no longer stock the manufacturer's product, if it is unhappy with the company it is keeping (*i.e.*, if the manufacturer is sending too many goods to discounters, stores with a reputation for rude and sloppy service, or other undesirables).

Two facts distinguish these general rules from the situation in which TRU finds itself. First, unilateral actions of the sort protected by Monsanto and Colgate are not the same thing as a retailer's request to the manufacturer to change the latter's business practice. Under paragraph II(B) of the decree, TRU must not tell the manufacturer what to do; it is still permitted to decide which toys it wants to carry and which ones to drop, based on business considerations such as the expected popularity of the item. Second, to the extent paragraph II(B) might indirectly inhibit TRU from exercising its unilateral judgment, TRU must confront the fact that the FTC is not limited to restating the law in its remedial orders. Such orders can restrict the options for a company that has violated § 5, to ensure that the violation will cease and competition will be restored. See National Lead Co., supra, 352 U.S. at 430; FTC v. Cement Institute, 333 U.S. 683, 726–27, 92 L. Ed. 1010, 68 S. Ct. 793 (1948); Corning Glass Works v. FTC, 509 F.2d 293, 303 (7th Cir.1975). See also FTC v. Colgate–Palmolive Co., 380 U.S. 374, 392, 13 L. Ed. 2d 904, 85 S. Ct. 1035 (1965) (making the same point, in context of the Commission's deceptive practices authority).

The second point also applies to TRU's objections to paragraphs II(C) and II(D). In addition, we note that the retailer should not have any reason to obtain its suppliers' business records about shipments to the retailer's competitors. That is the supplier's concern. TRU is protected as long as it can ensure that it receives what was promised to it. Also, of course, the decree preserves TRU's right to enter into exclusive arrangements with respect to particular toys. In so doing, it also implicitly allows TRU to engage in communications that are necessary for the implementation and enforcement of such agreements. Paragraph II(D) directly addresses the Commission's finding of a horizontal agreement, and it orders TRU not to go out and create a new one. The Commission was certainly acting within the bounds of its discretion when it included these provisions.

Paragraph II(E) appears to be the one that causes the greatest concern to TRU. This strikes us as a closer call, but in this connection the standard of review becomes important. The Commission has represented in its brief to this court that the decree "leaves [TRU] free to make stocking decisions based on a wide range of business reasons; it must simply make those decisions—for a period of five years—independent of whether clubs or other discounters are carrying the same item." FTC Brief at 58. The attempt to use its market clout to harm the warehouse clubs lies at the heart of this case, and so it is easy to see why the Commission chose to prohibit reliance on the supplier's practices vis .. vis the clubs as a reason for TRU's own purchasing decisions. At bottom, TRU is really just worried that it will be difficult to prove that any particular purchasing decision was free from the prohibited taint. It will be easy to refrain from announcements or communications about refusals to deal, which is what II(E)(1) prohibits. With respect to II(E)(2), if TRU implements adequate internal procedural safeguards, it should be possible to demonstrate that its buying decisions were not influenced by anything the manufacturers were doing with discounters like the clubs. These refusals to deal were the means TRU used to accomplish the unlawful result, and as such, they are subject to regulation by the Commission. See National Lead, 352 U.S. at 425. Under the abuse of discretion standard that governs our review of the Commission's choice of remedy, see Siegel Co. v. FTC, 327 U.S. 608, 612–13, 90 L. Ed. 888, 66 S. Ct. 758 (1946), this does not appear to be a remedy that "has no reasonable relation to the unlawful practices found to exist." We therefore have no warrant to set it aside. If, however, it becomes clear in practice that this provision is unworkable, TRU is free to return to the Commission to petition for a modification of the order.

III

We conclude that the Commission's decision is supported by substantial evidence on the record, and that its remedial decree falls within the broad discretion it has been granted under the FTC Act. The decision is hereby Affirmed.

NOTE ON SUMMARY DISPOSITION IN ANTITRUST CASES

As a practical matter, the likelihood that a plaintiff can prove "agreement" on the basis of conscious parallelism and other circumstantial evidence is affected by whether the decision is made by judge or jury. Especially where large corporate defendants are involved, the theory is that a jury is more likely to infer "agreement" from ambiguous evidence.

In the 1960s, many commentators and courts believed that summary disposition (summary judgment or a motion to dismiss) was particularly inappropriate in antitrust cases. To a large extent, the source of this view was some language in Poller v. Columbia Broadcasting System, 368 U.S. 464 (1962) where Justice Clark wrote:

> ... [s]ummary procedures should be used sparingly in complex antitrust litigation where motive and intent play leading roles, the proof is largely in the hands of the alleged conspirators, and hostile witnesses thicken the plot.... It is only when the witnesses are present and subject to cross-examination that their credibility and the weight to be given their testimony can be appraised. Trial by affidavit is no substitute for trial by jury which so long has been the hallmark of "even handed justice." 368 U.S. at 473.

Many commentators criticized the *Poller* language, and several studies showed that summary judgment or motions to dismiss were granted, if not as often, then *almost* as often in antitrust cases as in general civil litigation.[16] Moreover, there appeared to be a general trend toward granting summary disposition, especially to defendants, more frequently.

In 1986, the approach in *Poller* to the question of summary judgment in antitrust cases was changed dramatically in Matsushita Electric Industrial Co. v. Zenith Radio Corp., 475 U.S. 574 (1986). Some courts of appeals have interpreted Matsushita as effectively overruling that part of *Poller*. See, *e.g.*, Wallace v. SMC Pneumatics, Inc., 103 F.3d 1394, 1396 (7th Cir.1997) ("[I]n antitrust law ... early decisions pronouncing it a field inapt for summary judgment were later repudiated"); Ideal Dairy Farms, Inc. v. John Labatt, Ltd., 90 F.3d 737, 747 (3d Cir.1996) ("At one time, the Supreme Court endorsed a slightly stricter standard of review when a summary judgment order was challenged in an antitrust case.... However, that 'special standard' was abandoned in Eastman Kodak Co. v. Image Technical Servs., Inc., 504 U.S. 451, 468–69 (1992)...."). Other courts continue to cite *Poller*, even as they affirm grants of summary judgment for defendants. *See, e.g.*, Dickson v. Microsoft Corp., 309 F.3d 193, 212 (4th Cir.2002); Toscano v. Professional Golfers Ass'n, 258 F.3d 978, 982–83 (9th Cir.2001). Indeed, some courts thought that Matsushita imposed a special burden on plaintiffs to show that their claims made economic sense, but the Supreme Court rejected that theory in Eastman Kodak, 504 U.S. at 468–69. The Matsushita case and its significance are discussed in Calkins, Summary Judgment, Motions to Dismiss and Other Examples of Equilibrating Tendencies in the Antitrust System, 74 Geo.L.J. 1065, 1122–27 (1986).

In 1986, a comprehensive study of treble damage litigation—the "Georgetown Study of Private Antitrust Litigation"—included statistics on the likelihood that motions for summary disposition would be filed and what the rates of grants and denial were. The study found that motions for summary disposition were frequent in antitrust-perhaps because the financial stakes were so high. Nevertheless, plaintiffs rarely succeeded in obtaining summary judgment, even in relatively simple *per se* cases. Thus, summary judgment motions by plaintiff were successful in less than 1% of all cases filed during the period under review.

In contrast, the study found that defendants were more successful in winning summary judgments in the 1980's than previously. For example, defendants won

---

16. Commentary and statistics are gathered in Calkins, "Summary Judgment, Motions to Dismiss, and Other Examples of Equilibrating Tendencies in the Antitrust System," 74 Geo.L.J. 1065, 1120–22 (1986).

summary disposition in about 6% of all antitrust cases in 1983 and 8.3% in 1984. This worked out to about a 50% success rate where summary disposition was sought. Presumably, the success rate will continue to climb as the effect of the Matsushita opinion is felt. Professor Calkins concluded his review of the data with the following comments:

> The most important finding in this article is that summary judgments and dismissals for failure to state a claim appear to be ordered as frequently in antitrust cases as in other cases, and they may be ordered even more frequently. . . .

> This unexpected finding can be explained, at least in part, by the treble damages remedy. A number of courts recently have suggested that the in *terrorem* effect of the treble damages remedy makes summary procedures particularly appropriate in antitrust cases. The Supreme Court's [decision in *Matsushita* is] consistent with this suggestion. The empirical findings that use of summary procedures remains constant or rises with increasing damages requests, and is as great or greater in class action suits as in other ones, also supports this conclusion. Conventional wisdom would predict a decline with increasing complexity, and complexity should be associated with high damage requests and class status. Apparently, some courts want to prevent finders of fact from deciding high-stakes cases.

Donald F. Turner, The Definition of Agreement Under The Sherman Act[17]

75 Harv.L.Rev. 655, 663–666 (1962).

. . . [C]onscious parallelism is devoid of anything that might reasonably be called agreement when it involves simply the independent responses of a group of competitors to the same set of economic facts—independent in the sense that each would have made the same decision for himself even though his competitors decided otherwise. But the consciously parallel decisions of oligopolists in setting their basic prices, which are interdependent in that they depend on competitors setting the same price, are not nearly so easily disposed of on the ground that no agreement is involved.

One can pose an extreme hypothetical case in which it might be conceded that no element that could properly be called "agreement" is present. If there were an industry consisting of only two or three sellers, where the sellers were of identical size and had identical costs, where the products of the sellers were completely indistinguishable, where conditions of demand and supply were completely static, and where sellers and buyers were completely aware of all relevant facts—then the "best" price for each seller would be precisely the same, would be known to be the same by all, and would be charged without hesitation in absolute certainty that the others would price likewise. To be sure, the decisions would be interdependent in the sense that the best price for each depends on the others charging that same price, but this, under the assumed facts, would be so completely certain that hardly a shade of even a "meeting of minds" could be said to be involved.[18]

But the hypothetical case has no counterpart in reality. There are indeed many cases of completely or almost completely standardized products; but sellers will always have some differences in cost structures, face somewhat different demand conditions, and be in ignorance of some relevant market facts. Moreover, conditions are not static, they change; and change breeds uncertainty. In short, in real life the "best" price for each seller in even the oligopolistic market will never be the same; and even if it were, individual calculations by each seller based on imperfect and usually different information would normally lead, in the absence of fully recognized interdependence, to different decisions as to price. For a pattern of noncompetitive pricing to emerge in such a situation requires something which we could, not unreasonably, call a "meeting of minds," or to use Professor Kaysen's phrase, an "agreement to agree...."[19]

Even if some explicit communication at some time was not involved, though in reality it probably always has been, explicit communication seems hardly a logically necessary ingredient of the kind of agreement that is an element in the legal concept of conspiracy. Considered purely as a problem in linguistic definition, there is no reason to exclude oligopolistic behavior from the scope of the term agreement simply because the circumstances make it possible to communicate without speech. It is not novel conspiracy doctrine to say that agreement can be signified by action as well as by words. And of course if there is agreement in the legal sense, the agreement seems inescapably an unlawful conspiracy in restraint of trade because a price-fixing agreement is unlawful *per se*.

Yet another look at the behavior involved points to a different conclusion. In a significant sense, the behavior of the rational oligopolist in setting his price is precisely the same as that of the rational seller in an industry consisting of a very large number of competitors. Both are pricing their product and determining their output so as to make the highest profit, or suffer the least loss, that can be obtained in the market conditions facing them. The rational oligopolist simply takes one more factor into account-the reactions of his competitors to any price change that he makes. He must take them into account because his competitors will inevitably react. They will inevitably react, for example, to a price cut on his part because otherwise the price cut will make a substantial inroad on their sales; if, for example, there are only three producers of equal size and a price cut by one doubles his sales, the sales of each of his two competitors will be cut in half. The rational seller in an industry with a very large number of competitors does not calculate their reactions to a price cut by him, because they are not likely to be sufficiently affected by the price cut

---

18. There is also no "agreement" in those cases of price leadership where the price leader is the dominant and the low-cost firm. See generally "Markham, The Nature and Significance of Price Leadership," in Readings in Industrial Organization and Public Policy 176 Heflebower & Stocking ed. (1958).

19. Kaysen, "Collusion Under the Sherman Act," 65 Q.J.Econ. 263, 268 (1951).

to react; if, for example, there are one hundred producers of equal size, a doubling of sales by one, evenly drawn from his competitors, would cut their sales by only one ninety-ninth. To repeat, it can fairly be said that the rational oligopolist is behaving in exactly the same way as is the rational seller in a competitively structured industry; he is simply taking another factor into account, which he has to take into account because the situation in which he finds himself puts it there.

In this light, several comments may be made. First, there is fair ground for argument that oligopoly price behavior can be described as individual behavior-rational individual decision in the light of relevant economic facts-as well as it can be described as "agreement." It can readily be said that each seller in this situation, in refraining from price competition, is not agreeing with his competitors but simply throwing their probable decisions into his price calculus as impersonal market facts. . . .

Second, it seems questionable to call the behavior of oligopolists in setting their prices unlawful when the behavior in essence is identical to that of sellers in a competitive industry. Particularly is this so when the behavior involved, setting the "profit-maximizing" price in light of all market facts, is not only legally acceptable but vitally necessary to make competitive markets function as they are supposed to function.

NOTES

1. After having served as Assistant Attorney General in charge of the Antitrust Division, Professor Turner wrote an article in which he modified his views concerning the applicability of the antitrust laws to oligopolies. See Turner, "The Scope of Antitrust and Other Economic Regulatory Policies," 82 Harv. L. Rev. 1207 (1969). As to individual monopolists, he concluded that Section 2 could be read to apply whenever significant monopoly power "has persisted over a long enough time to indicate relatively impervious barriers to entry, regardless of how it [the monopoly] was obtained or maintained, excepting only monopoly based on economies of scale or on the same unexpired patents that gave it birth."

Turner next focused on oligopolistic conduct, noting that an "attack on shared monopoly is a highly important aspect of any effective competition policy." He reasserted his position that consciously parallel non-competitive pricing by oligopolists could not reasonably be attacked as a conspiracy to fix prices, or as a conspiracy or combination to monopolize, but argued that other "exclusionary behavior without adequate business justification" by oligopolists could be deemed an unlawful attempt to monopolize under Section 2. Thus a lease-only policy, or packaging machines and service at a single price, was viewed as having a sufficiently substantial anticompetitive effect to justify a finding of illegality if each oligopolist engaged in similar conduct.

> . . . I believe that the law on shared monopoly may be brought virtually in line with the law on individual monopoly, and divestiture where feasible invoked as a remedy, whenever it appears that injunctive relief would not adequate dissipate the power within a reasonable time. Where oligopolists sharing monopoly power have engaged in restrictive

conduct lacking any substantial justification, they may appropriately be said to have unlawfully attempted to monopolize. Where it appears that their decisions to carry on particular exclusionary practices are interdependent, where one would not have carried on the practice unless the others had gone along, they may also be charged with a conspiracy or combination to monopolize. Finally, where each of the companies effectively sharing monopoly power has engaged in possibly justifiable conduct that nevertheless has unnecessary exclusionary effects, it seems logical and appropriate to me to charge each with having individually "monopolized" in violation of Section 2. Each has obtained and maintained monopoly power—real, though shared—to which factors other than skill, foresight, industry, and the like have contributed.

The remaining question is whether one can fairly apply to shared monopoly power the prohibition of individual monopoly suggested by Alcoa that, barring economies of scale or power still based on the unexpired patents that created it, monopoly becomes subject to judicial relief when retained over a sufficient period of time to indicate that it is substantially impervious to erosion by market forces. I would conclude that it is appropriate to do so if one accepts the Alcoa principle in the first place, because there is not enough difference between individual and shared monopoly to warrant different treatment.

2. Turner's view that consciously parallel pricing is nothing more than rational competitive behavior was challenged by many, including Professor (now Judge) Richard A. Posner, who argued that while noncompetitive pricing by oligopolists is made easier by market structure, it is not compelled. Structure may eliminate the need for explicit agreement, but coordinated pricing still requires action from which tacit agreement may be inferred. A showing of concentrated market structure and voluntary pricing conduct—such as signaling and response, systematic price discrimination, price leadership, or filing of identical sealed bids for sale of nonstandard items—could support an inference of tacit conspiracy. Other relevant factors would be oligopoly firms' refusal to offer discounts in the presence of prolonged excess capacity, market shares fixed over time, infrequent price changes, and abnormally high profits. Since Posner's emphasis is on conduct, he argues that injunctive relief can be effective in dealing with the problem of oligopoly pricing. Posner, "Oligopoly and the Antitrust Laws: A Suggested Approach," 21 Stan.L.Rev. 1562 (1969). See also Kauper, "New Approaches to the Old Problem," 46 Antitrust L.J. 435 (1977).

3. Consider, in connection with the previous note, the Seventh Circuit's opinion in In re High Fructose Corn Syrup Antitrust Litigation, 295 F.3d 651 (7th Cir.2002). There, writing for the court in a case charging that the principal manufacturers of high fructose corn syrup (HFCS) had unlawfully fixed prices, Judge Posner took the occasion to revisit the agreement requirement of section 1 of the Sherman Act, in the following passage:

> Section 1 of the Sherman Act forbids contracts, combinations, and conspiracies in restraint of trade. This statutory language is broad enough, as we noted in JTC Petroleum Co. v. Piasa Motor Fuels, Inc., 190 F.3d 775, 780 (7th Cir.1999), to encompass a purely tacit agreement to fix prices, that is, an agreement made without any actual communication among the parties to the agreement. If a firm raises price in the expectation that its competitors will do likewise, and they do, the firm's behavior can be conceptualized as the offer of a unilateral contract that the offerees accept

by raising their prices. Or as the creation of a contract implied in fact. "Suppose a person walks into a store and takes a newspaper that is for sale there, intending to pay for it. The circumstances would create a contract implied in fact" even though there was no communication between the parties. A.E.I. Music Network, Inc. v. Business Computers, Inc., 290 F.3d 952, 956 (7th Cir.1992). Nevertheless it is generally believed, and the plaintiffs implicitly accept, that an express, manifested agreement, and thus an agreement involving actual, verbalized communication, must be proved in order for a price-fixing conspiracy to be actionable under the Sherman Act. 295 F.3d at 654.

Going on, Judge Posner discussed the kind of evidence that would permit an inference of agreement, assuming that the plaintiffs (as is usually the case) had no direct proof. The necessary evidence would be of two types, economic and non-economic. The economic evidence in turn typically takes two forms: evidence that the structure of the market was conducive to secret price-fixing, and evidence that the market was behaving in a non-competitive manner. *Id.* at 655. In weighing this economic evidence at the summary judgment stage, the court warned against falling into any of three possible traps. The first trap is the temptation to weigh conflicting economic testimony. The second is to assume that if no single item of evidence points unequivocally to conspiracy, then the plaintiffs must lose. The key word here is "unequivocally": the court stressed that most evidence is susceptible to competing interpretations, and that can be enough. Finally, the third trap is "failing to distinguish between the existence of a conspiracy and its efficacy." *Id.* at 656. In the case before it, after considering both the economic evidence and the non-economic evidence tending to show explicit agreement (party statements, damaging comments in documents, and the like), the court concluded that the district court should not have granted summary judgment for the defendants and it remanded the case for trial.

4. The concept of shared or collective dominance has received a warmer welcome in the competition law of the European Union. When such a position exists, the conduct of the companies is evaluated under Article 82 (ex Art. 86) of the Treaty; on a similar theory, the creation of a position of collective dominance is grounds for refusing to permit a merger. The first important case under what is now Article 82 was Società Italiano Vetro SpA (SIV) & Ors v. Commission of the European Communities (Joined Cases T-68/89, T-77/89 and T-78/89), CFI [1992] 2 CEC at 33 (CCH Europe). In that case, the Commission had proceeded against three Italian flat glass manufacturers under both Articles 85 and 86 of the Treaty of Rome. It found that the companies had infringed Article 85(1) through a number of agreements and arrangements affecting two markets: the automotive market and the non-automotive market. It also concluded that they abused their collective dominant position by depriving customers of the opportunity to get suppliers to compete on prices and terms of sales, and, by means of a quota system, limiting the outlets for glass. The Court of First Instance decided that there was "nothing, in principle, to prevent two or more independent economic entities from being, on a specific market, united by such economic links that, by virtue of that fact, together they hold a dominant position vis-à-vis the other operators on the same market." Opinion at ¶ 358. It cautioned, however, that the Commission could not simply "recycle" the facts of an alleged Article 85 violation through Article 86 and come up with a violation based on the joint dominance theory. It pointed out that Article 86 presupposes that a market has been defined, and that the firm or firms holds a dominant position in that market-criteria that may not necessarily be present in an

Article 85 case. Here the Commission failed, in the court's view, to justify its position that there was a single market for flat glass for Article 86 purposes. Given the failure of proof, it annulled the Commission's finding of an Article 86 violation.

More recently, the European Court of Justice affirmed a decision of the Commission finding that the members of a liner conference that provided shipping services between two African countries and the North Sea area had violated Article 86 (now Art. 82). See Cie Maritime Belge Transports SA and others v. European Commission and others, ECJ (5th Chamber) [2000] All ER (EC) 385, 14 May, 29 Oct. 1998, 16 Mar. 2000. In the merger context, however, the Court of First Instance in 2002 reversed a decision by the Commission to prohibit a merger on the grounds of the creation of a situation of collective dominance among the remaining three providers of certain holiday packages. See Airtours plc v. European Commission (Case T–342/99) CFI (5th Chamber) [2002] All ER (EC) 783, 11 Oct. 2001, 6 June 2002. The court's decision was based on the Commission's failure to present sufficient evidence; it was not a rejection of the collective dominance idea in general.

The theory of shared or collective dominance thus seems clearly established as a matter of theory in Europe. Cases in which it is actually used either as a basis of liability under Article 82 or as a reason to block a merger exist, but they are very rare. Is the collective dominance, shared monopoly, or conscious parallelism problem a conundrum that antitrust law is simply incapable of solving, or do you see a place for enforcement against oligopoly?

PROBLEM 10

PROBLEM: AIRLINE PRICING

Seven airlines own the Airline Fare Finder Company (AFFC). AFFC is a database that collects and disseminates fare information for most of the domestic airlines in the United States. AFFC provides fare information to its subscribers, which include its seven owners, and to computer reservation systems.

Each airline supplies AFFC with fare information, including fare codes (*e.g.*, "F" is first class), fare amounts, restrictions, and routings. An airline can attach footnotes to any fare in the AFFC database. Footnotes can include information such as first and last ticket dates. The first ticket date is the future date at which a fare is supposed to become available for purchase by travelers. A last ticket date is the date at which a current fare ends.

Ameri–World Airlines (AWA) decided to offer discount fares between Dallas and San Francisco, two of its hubs, on a few flights. Gamma, through the AFFC database, observed the AWA-discounted fares and decided to offer the discount fare on all of its flights between the same cities. AWA responded by lowering its prices on flights between Gamma's hubs, Dallas and New York's Kennedy Airport, to the same fare level as the Dallas–San Francisco flights. AWA's Dallas–Kennedy fares on the AFFC system included the same footnote designator and last ticket date as the Dallas–San Francisco fares.

The Department of Justice believes that AFFC makes coordination more likely because it is effective and easy to punish deviations from coordinated fares. Can the government prove coordinated action? Would the system be any better, or any worse, if all first and last ticket dates were freely available over the Internet to users of on-line travel services?

SECTION 3. DELIVERED PRICING SYSTEMS AND OTHER "FACILITATING PRACTICES"—USEFUL BUILDING BLOCKS?

NOTE ON PRICE COORDINATION AMONG OLIGOPOLISTS[20]

I. The Difficulties of Price Coordination

In order to coordinate their prices successfully, oligopolists must (1) *agree* on the cooperative outcome, (2) *achieve* that outcome, and (3) *maintain* the outcome over time, in the face of changing conditions and incentives of the participants to deviate from the oligopolistic outcome. All three conditions are difficult to satisfy.

Firms will find it difficult to agree on a particular outcome because their interests are not perfectly aligned. To be sure, raising prices may increase joint profits among the participants in a cartel. But firms may not agree on how the oligopoly should distribute those joint profits. Some participants might prefer distribution based on market share in last period before the oligopoly was imposed. Others might favor distribution based on market share after the oligopoly has been formed. Still others might propose that distribution be tied to capital investment. Non-price variables complicate the matter even further. Oligopolists must coordinate product design, delivery schedules, transportation methods and customer service. The desire to indulge in price discrimination adds an additional layer of complexity. Also, any agreement, in order to allow participants to respond to changing market conditions, must predict and plan for contingencies or allow the parties to renegotiate.

The difficulties are compounded because parties may not negotiate these agreements openly. They must signal their understandings through newspaper interviews and at meetings of trade associations, clearly enough to inform conspirators of their intentions yet subtly enough to avoid discovery by the ever vigilant enforcers of the antitrust laws. Once the parties have surmounted these hurdles, they must implement their agreements. While this is a simple matter for legal cartels, which can rely on courts to enforce their agreements, illegal cartels must devise self-enforcing agreements. Otherwise, the hoped-for oligopoly will not materialize.

To see why this might be difficult, consider a two firm industry composed of Bart Inc. and Homer Co. In each period, Bart and Homer independently set their price either "high" or "low." Each firm's profits are determined, in part, by the price the other has chosen. Profits are given by the following matrix with Homer's on the left and Bart's price on the right (the numbers are merely illustrative):

		Bart's Price	
		High	Low
	High	*(100, 100)*	*(–10, 140)*
Homer's Price			
	Low	*(140, –10)*	*(70, 70)*

---

20. Adapted from notes prepared by Professor Stephen C. Salop.

Bart and Homer face a variant of the "prisoner's dilemma." Obviously, Bart and Homer, would like to coordinate their behavior, pick the high price level and maximize joint profits. But, since combination is barred, it will be difficult for them to achieve their desired outcome. If Bart implements the high price strategy and Homer does not, Bart's profits plunge to–10 while Homer's soar to 140. Both Bart and Homer, therefore, have an incentive to deviate from the joint profit maximizing outcome, keeping prices at the competitive (low/low) level. Their dilemma does not dissolve once they achieve the cooperative outcome. Even if they manage to coordinate their behavior in one period, they will face the same incentive to deviate from the cooperative outcome in the next period.

Bart and Homer may do better if they recognize that their long term interests lie in cooperation. If they recognize that their "game" will be repeated in the future, they might be able to reach an equilibrium at the joint profit maximizing level by adopting a strategy where each threatens to match immediately a price cut by the other. In order for such a strategy to be effective, there must be almost no lag time between a price cut by one and a retaliatory cut by the other. If lag time is sufficiently long, both will have reason to cheat, making the cooperative outcome, even in a repeated game, unstable. Thus, Bart and Homer's likelihood of successfully imposing a cartel on their industry depends on: (i) the short term benefits from cheating, relative to, (ii) the longer term loss from not cooperating, and (iii) the detection lag, that is, the likelihood that cheating will be discovered and punished.

II. Structural Factors That Facilitate or Complicate Price Coordination

Certain structural factors in the market will make it easier for oligopolists to coordinate their behavior. These factors affect the relative payoffs from cooperating, cheating and competing. They also impede or facilitate the participants' ability to detect and to retaliate against cheating. Where these factors coincide, successful collusion (tacit or express) will be more likely.

1. *High Concentration*. When there are only a small number of competitors, coordination is more likely to succeed. An agreement is easier to reach because there are fewer firms that must agree. A few firms with large market shares also are more likely to recognize their interdependence. They have more to gain from collusion and more to lose from cheating because they will earn the higher collusive price on more sales.

2. *Barriers to Entry*. When barriers to entry are high, a cartel is more stable because it need not add new members to maintain control over the market. Coordinated pricing is more profitable and more likely to occur.

3. *Open Sales*. When sales are public and prices are known to all market participants (buyers and sellers), firms can detect cheating more easily. If cheating is easy to detect, an agreement or tacit understanding is easier to enforce, making such agreements more likely.

4. *Homogeneous Products*. When rivals sell identical products, the number of variables for which an agreement must account is reduced, again facilitating agreement and making cheating more difficult to hide.

5. *Lumpy Sales*. Lumpy sales refers to markets where large buyers or long term contracts account for a large share of sales (*e.g.*, the market for commercial airplanes). Lumpy sales increase the incentives for firms to cheat on the cartel, making collusion less likely in the first place.

6. *Excess Capacity.* Excess capacity cuts both ways. When firms have excess capacity, it is less costly for them to cheat. But, where demand is fixed or falling, firms have the incentive to collude to maintain higher profits.

7. *Static Demand.* When demand is fixed, rivals can detect cheating by looking at their own sales, making retaliation more likely.

8. *Similarity.* When rivals are similarly situated, they are more likely to have similar preferences regarding prices and output. Agreements are easier to negotiate and achieve than if firms have much different preferences.

III.   Facilitating Practices

Oligopolists also might adopt "facilitating practices" to increase the likelihood of successful collusion. "Facilitating practices" like structural conditions in the market make collusion more likely by altering the incentives of market participants (*i.e.*, breaking the prisoner's dilemma). There are two distinct effects of facilitating practices—*information exchange* and *incentive management*. Although particular practices often combine elements of both roles, it is useful to distinguish between them. Because the information exchange effect is better understood, we will discuss it only briefly and focus instead on incentive management.

1. *Information exchange.* Information exchange facilitates both explicit and tacit coordination by eliminating uncertainty about rivals' actions. Classic examples of information exchanges are interseller verification of price quotations and advance notice of price changes. In each case, the exchange of information shortens or eliminates detection lags by competitors. By decreasing the transitional losses from price rises (*i.e.*, losses to the price leader before rivals follow) and the transitional gains from price discounts (gains to the initiator of the discount before rivals follow), incentives are altered in such a way as to make the joint profit outcome easier to achieve and maintain.

2. *Incentive management.* The incentive management role of facilitating practices functions by *directly* altering payoffs rather than working through the medium of information exchange. By restructuring payoffs, the incentives for a firm to offer price discounts or raise prices may be directly affected. Similarly, a firm may change its own incentives to match price changes initiated by its rivals, thereby affecting its rivals' incentives to initiate such price changes. In this way, adoption of facilitating practices can convert competitive oligopoly outcomes into cooperative ones.

Perhaps the purest example of an incentive management device is a monetary penalty on price discounts. For example, suppose in a two-firm industry, each seller agrees to pay a third party a monetary penalty equal to 50 percent of its price if either charges any of its customers a price below "list," and that price is not matched by the rival seller. Under those circumstances, price cuts by either seller become self-defeating, and a high oligopoly price is insured.

Incentive management devices can also be created by provisions of purchase contracts between an oligopolist and its customers. Embedding an incentive management device in a sales contract has a number of advantages. First, use of a contract with a purchaser allows the oligopolist to make a binding commitment to transform its incentives. If necessary, a court will enforce the contract, so that the credibility of the promised behavior is increased. Moreover, the ability to collect damages gives the buyer an incentive to ensure performance and to bear the costs of enforcing the contract. If the buyer is better situated than rivals or third parties to detect price discounts, this can increase the efficiency of enforcement. Of course, more efficient enforcement increases the credibility of a promise.

3. *"Stampede" effect.* The obvious question is why rational buyers would be willing to act as accomplices in achieving this possibly anticompetitive conduct by their suppliers. To the extent that the contractual provision makes discounting less desirable or price increases less risky, it is difficult to see why buyers would agree to clauses that have such an effect. The answer lies in the possibility of designing contractual provisions that are valued by each buyer individually even as they create an external cost to all other buyers. If such clauses can be developed, they create a type of stampede. Each buyer willingly accepts (indeed, rushes to purchase) the clause. Yet the collective acceptance by all buyers eliminates the individual benefit by stabilizing the sellers' joint profit outcome.

We now turn to a number of examples of practices that can transform incentives so as to stabilize an agreement. It should be noted that these practices sometimes have procompetitive and efficiency benefits as well as potential anticompetitive effects, although in this note we focus on the latter.

4. *Most-favored-nation clauses.* A *most-favored-nation* (MFN) clause in a sales contract provides the buyer with insurance protection against the contingency that the seller offers a lower price to another customer. These clauses may prevent price discrimination when the seller offers a discount price to another buyer, either in the future (a "retroactive" MFN) or in the present (a "contemporaneous" MFN). Although all MFN change the seller's incentives in the same general way, it is clearer to illustrate some issues with the case of a retroactive MFN and others with a contemporaneous MFN.

Consider an industry in which public utility customers contract for the purchase of custom manufactured generators. Because delivery occurs many months after the contract is made, increased competition, reduced demand, or reduced costs during the intervening time period may reduce the average price paid by later buyers for comparable generators. By placing the following retroactive MFN clause in the sales agreement, early buyers may share that price decrease:

> If at any time before [buyer] takes delivery of said generator, [seller] offers a lower price for a comparable size and quality generator to any other purchaser, [seller] will also offer that lower price to [buyer].

That is, any future price decreases must be rebated to the buyer.[21] The MFN requires the seller to pay a monetary penalty if it lowers its price.[22] Because price decreases are penalized, they are discouraged. Thus, if all rivals provide all buyers with MFN protection, a high oligopoly price can be stabilized, once it is achieved.[23]

Provision of an MFN *by even just one rival* may be advantageous to all sellers, including the one that institutes the MFN. This may be surprising, because a seller's unilateral adoption of an MFN also places it at a competitive disadvantage— it is deterred from matching selective discounts offered by its rivals. However, this

---

21. Compare the GE–Westinghouse decree, discussed at pp. 550–551 infra. Variants of this contract could provide for a rebate of price cuts made even after delivery is taken, or for a partial rather than a full rebate. The contract might also ease enforcement of the clause by providing the buyer with the right to inspect the seller's books.

22. The total penalty equals the price decrease times the number of outstanding orders. It is paid even if the discount is matched.

23. Of course, the MFN makes it more difficult to achieve a lower price cooperative outcome, if changed conditions warrant a lower price. This is a cost to the oligopolists of adopting such a plan. In contrast, the penalty scheme discussed earlier does not share this problem because only *unmatched* price cuts are penalized.

competitive disadvantage may be more than offset by the effect of the clause in stabilizing a higher price.

Most-favored-nation clauses are also found in long-term requirements contracts governing the sale of repeatedly purchased industrial supplies. These clauses insure buyers against contemporaneous price discrimination in favor of other buyers who may or may not be rivals. Consider the following standard form:

> If [seller] should, during the term of this contract, offer or sell goods of equal quality and quantity to any other buyer at a price lower than that provided for herein, [buyer] shall receive the benefit of such lower price on all shipments made hereunder for which such lower price is effective.

This contemporaneous MFN clause differs somewhat from the retroactive MFN. Whereas the retroactive MFN penalizes all price decreases made after some date, this clause penalizes and deters only *selective discounts*, that is, price cuts that are restricted to a limited number of customers. General price cuts are not penalized or deterred. Thus, selective discounts are made relatively less profitable than general price cuts. In that oligopoly competition (*i.e.*, "cheating" on a cartel) usually takes the form of selective discounts, the MFN may serve to stabilize the cooperative outcome.

Since general price cuts are not penalized by a contemporaneous MFN, adjustments to a lower price *cooperative* outcome are not deterred if they become necessary, for example, if costs fall. Similarly, the ability to retaliate with a general price reduction against rivals' secret discounts is not constrained. Only selective discounts are penalized.

Following this analysis, a contemporaneous MFN constrains the oligopolist's response in the same way as would its inability to identify the customers offered discounts. For example, suppose Company A offers a selective discount to a limited number of Company B's customers. Suppose Company B can identify these customers. However, due to the MFN, suppose Company B can only feasibly respond with a general price cut to all its customers. In this case, it will compare the profit reduction from this customer loss to the alternative of offering a general price cut to all its customers, including those not approached by Company A. The deeper is Company A's discount and the fewer customers that are approached, the relatively more costly is a matching response by Company B. Hence, the more likely it is that Company B will accommodate the discounts rather than respond with a general price cut. In short, if Company A restricts its secret discounting, it is more profitable for Company B to accommodate rather than touch off a price war.

In spite of this anticompetitive effect, buyers may be willing to "purchase" the "protection" of an MFN for two reasons. First, insurance protection against price reductions may have value to risk-averse buyers. The MFN provides this insurance. Of course, broad MFN protection reduces the probability that a lower price will ever materialize because it induces an adverse incentive in sellers who provide it. However, for any individual buyer, this effect may be small relative to the insurance benefit. Instead, the adverse incentive is mainly an "externality" that injures buyers other than the one that negotiates for the clause. The profit-maximizing purchaser does not reckon this external effect into its calculus. This creates the stampede mentality discussed earlier. In fact, the more buyers there are in the market, the more likely that the price stabilizing effect will be ignored by buyers.

In addition, a buyer who does add this potential injury to other buyers into its profit calculus may count that injury as a benefit, not as a cost. If rival buyers are also his downstream product market competitors, then his profitability is enhanced when his rivals' costs rise. Looking at the problem in this way, a buyer even may be willing to pay more for an MFN, because the MFN acts as a type of bribe to the seller to forgo deeper discounts to rival buyers.

5. *Meeting competition clauses.* A *meeting competition* clause (MCC) in a long-term supply contract or advertisement provides the buyer with insurance protection against a lost opportunity in the contingency that the buyer is offered a lower price by some other seller. The economic effects of an MCC depend on the exact form the provision takes. One common variant is the *meet or release* (MOR) clause, as illustrated by the following example:

> If the [buyer] should be offered by a responsible manufacturer [product] of equal quality and in a quantity equivalent to or less than that remaining as a commitment hereunder, at a lower delivered cost to the [buyer], and [buyer] gives [seller] satisfactory evidence thereof before the date on which any shipment is required, [seller] shall either supply such quantity of [product] at the lower cost or permit [buyer] to purchase elsewhere. Any quantity so purchased shall be deducted from the quantity deliverable under this contract.

The MOR clause serves mainly as an information exchange device. If the buyer discovers a lower price elsewhere, it cannot escape its obligation to purchase from its original supplier without informing that supplier of the lower price. By requiring this flow of information, the clause eliminates any detection lag. Thus, the seller is protected against the possibility of losing sales to a rival offering an undetected discount to a current customer. In this way, an MOR facilitates selective matching of an otherwise secret discount.

It is unlikely that a seller would choose to *meet* rather than *release* in all cases. For example, if a rival offers a price below the seller's marginal cost, the seller has no obvious incentive to match. Likewise, the seller has no incentive to match a discount he suspects the buyer will reject. For example, if the rival's product is of lower quality or otherwise unsuitable, the buyer might be suspected of using the lower bid simply as a bluff in order to obtain a better deal.

In these cases, an MOR clause offers no protection to the buyer. The buyer prefers, all things being equal, a contractual provision that allows the seller no escape. This can be accomplished by deleting the *release* language from the provision. Of course, such a *no-release* MCC may lead to allocative inefficiencies if the seller, as a result of the clause, must provide units at a below-cost price. However, if the seller's primary interest is in deterring rivals' discounts, the losses entailed by this inefficiency may be small relative to the anticompetitive benefit of the clause. For, by deleting the *release* option, the clause is made a more credible deterrent. Now, the seller must meet all rivals' offers.

An MCC also facilitates successful *achievement* of the cooperative outcome. For example, a seller who provides a *no-release* MCC to current customers can raise price without losing any sales to a lower pricing rival. Buyers are automatically given the rival's lower price until all firms raise their prices. This eliminates the transitional losses that might otherwise deter price rises. It also eliminates the rival's transitional gains and, with it, the incentive to delay a matching price increase. In this sense, when a duopoly seller who has an MCC raises his price, his rival is automatically transformed into a *de facto* price leader, with the ability to set prices for both firms.

6. *Entry deterrence.* To this point, the focus of this analysis has been oligopoly coordination. It has been assumed throughout that the industry is protected by

insurmountable barriers to entry. As noted in the text, meeting competition clauses can also facilitate entry deterrence.

By providing a *no-release* MCC, an incumbent can add needed credibility to its threat to cut price in the event entry occurs. Even if the incumbent would otherwise prefer to accommodate a rational entrant, the MCC requires it to match the entrant's price. Similarly, even if below-cost pricing is unprofitable, it must be carried out. Knowing that the threat will be carried out, a rational entrant will be deterred. Although the exact effect of the MCC depends on the wording of the clause and the structure of the industry, the potential benefit of the MCC to the incumbent is clear. An MCC can deter entry by allowing the incumbent to make credible threats to lower its price in the event of entry, even to a below-cost, "predatory" level.

Boise Cascade Corp. v. Federal Trade Commission

United States Court of Appeals, Ninth Circuit, 1980.
637 F.2d 573.

■ WALLACE, J.: Petitioners in these consolidated actions seek reversal of a Federal Trade Commission (Commission) order finding that each violated section 5 of the Federal Trade Commission Act, by adopting and maintaining a system of delivered pricing which utilized the computation of rail freight charges from the Pacific Northwest in determining the price of southern plywood. Boise Cascade Corp., 91 F.T.C. 1 (1978). We decline to enforce the order.

I

Petitioners are manufacturers of softwood plywood with mills located in the southern part of the United States. Until 1947 all plywood was manufactured from Douglas Fir and was produced in the states of Washington and Oregon. By 1963, technological advances had made possible the fabrication of plywood from various species of southern pine, leading to the development of the southern plywood industry. By 1974 the South produced 32.3 percent of all plywood marketed in the United States and 45.7 percent of plywood sheathing, the subject of this controversy. Petitioners accounted for more than 50 percent of southern production of plywood sheathing.

Because the product is considered to be fungible, price is the main factor of competition in the marketing of southern plywood sheathing. Prior to the development of the southern plywood industry, West Coast plywood manufacturers typically quoted a "delivered price," which consisted of a "mill price" plus the amount for rail freight from the West Coast (West Coast freight). This freight factor was computed by reference to concentric bands or freight zones running from north to south and radiating eastward from a Portland, Oregon zone. Although the rate for shipping plywood increases as a shipment enters new freight zones going east, freight rates are identical within any given zone.

The southern plywood industry has from its inception used West Coast freight in calculating and quoting prices to buyers across the country. The parties agree that this practice was a natural development and reflected the fact that in the early years of southern production, western mills remained the dominant supplier of plywood even in the South. Since southern plywood was widely viewed as inferior in quality to western plywood, it was necessary to sell southern plywood at a slightly lower price. The use of West Coast freight made possible ready comparison between western and southern plywood prices,[24] encouraged expansion of southern mills, and probably prevented southern prices from dropping so low as to create a disincentive to ship western plywood into the South at a time when southern mills lacked the capacity to meet southern needs.

The Commission found, however, that these original justifications dissipated as the southern plywood industry developed to the point where southern and western plywood no longer competed in the South. It concluded that the industry-wide practice of continuing to utilize West Coast freight has had the tendency and effect of inhibiting competition over the freight factor in the price of southern plywood. On the other hand, petitioners contend that use of the West Coast freight factor is merely a matter of form that has no effect on price in the "highly competitive" plywood industry, and that West Coast freight is justified as a convenience to buyers when comparing the price of plywood in regions where there is western and southern plywood competition.[25]

II

The hallmark of challenged delivered pricing systems has been the industry-wide use of an artificial freight factor as a "freight equalizer." Since in many industries freight is one of the important variables in the price-setting process, there is a natural tendency toward price cutting based on locational advantages, especially when production capacity exceeds demand. One way of eliminating such price competition is to create a pricing system that eliminates freight differentials as a bargaining subject. See Turner, The Definition of Agreement under the Sherman Act: Conscious Parallelism and Refusals to Deal, 75 Harv.L.Rev. 655, 674–75 (1962) [hereinafter cited as Agreement under the Sherman Act] ... Comment, Price Systems and Competition: The Basing–Point Issues, 58 Yale L.J. 426, 430–34 (1949) [hereinafter cited as *The Basing–Point Issues*]. Typical of such systems are so-called basing-point pricing systems, in which one or

---

24. The use of West Coast freight enabled buyers to compare western and southern plywood prices by reference to a single mill or index price, knowing that the precise difference would be reflected in a total delivered price. Without West Coast freight, comparison would also have been more cumbersome because southern freight rates are point-to-point rather than zone rates and vary according to the weight of the load. Ironically, the greater ease with which price quotations are compared when based on West Coast freight is the basis not only of petitioners' business justification for the practice, but also of the Commission's conclusion that it serves as an influence to eliminate potential bargaining and thereby reduces price competition.

25. When this opinion makes reference to the use of West Coast freight, there is no intention to answer thereby the critical question whether its use involves the adding of an anti-competitive premium or merely one way of stating a competitive delivered price.

more locations are established as centers for the computing of a delivered price. A non-basing-point producer calculates his freight charge as though his plant were located at the basing point, either "absorbing" or gaining the difference between his basing-point freight charge and the actual freight charge. While various differences in operation might be described, "the multiple and single [basing-point pricing] systems function in the same general manner and produce the same consequences-identity of prices and diversity of net returns." FTC v. Cement Institute, 333 U.S. 683, 699 (1948).

Petitioners' West Coast freight is not a true basing-point pricing system.[26] Nevertheless, being a delivered pricing system, it has the same potential to stabilize prices as basing-point systems. When combined with the standardization of delivery methods, service extras, and discounts, any delivered pricing system can become a potent tool for assuring that competitors are able to match prices and avoid the rigors of price competition. The Commission typically has challenged delivered pricing systems under a theory of conspiracy to eliminate price competition by adherence to a formula which has the effect of making their prices identical. Frequently the finding of concerted action has been based on direct evidence of explicit agreement, *e.g.*, American Chain & Cable Co. v. FTC, 139 F.2d 622 (4th Cir.1944), or, as in the *Cement Institute* case, on circumstantial evidence of "collective methods" used to assure compliance with the pricing formula- including boycotts, discharge of employees, retaliatory price-cutting against recalcitrants, and preparation and distribution of freight rate books. In addition, reviewing courts and the commission have relied in varying degrees on the inferences to be drawn from identical prices, particularly when independent evidence suggests that the identities are unusually rigid and that the price structure as a whole is unusually stable (as when demand is falling). See Bond Crown & Cork Co. v. FTC, 176 F.2d 974, 978– 79 (4th Cir.1949) (price identity and rigidity); Cement Institute v. FTC, supra, 333 U.S. at 715–16 (uniform pricing); Triangle Conduit & Cable Co. v. FTC, 168 F.2d 175, 180 (7th Cir.1948), aff'd by an equally divided Supreme Court sub nom., Clayton Mark & Co. v. FTC, 336 U.S. 956 (1949) (matching prices and inability of local buyers to obtain better prices); United States Maltsters Ass'n v. FTC, 152 F.2d 161, 164 (7th Cir.1945) (identical prices).

The tension in the law of delivered pricing stems from the fact that, notwithstanding their potential for abuse as a price-fixing device, Congress has repeatedly refused to require the exclusive use of f.o.b. pricing or to

---

26. One is tempted to describe the challenged pricing system here as a "single basing-point" system. Certainly the West Coast serves as a "basing point" for southern mills in that West Coast freight is used to calculate a delivered price; but the classic example of single basing-point pricing is the "Pittsburgh Plus" system utilized in the Steel industry, which rigidly required all sellers to use not only the rail freight charge from Pittsburgh to the point of delivery, but also "the Pittsburgh base price." See FTC v. Cement Institute, supra, 333 U.S. at 697–98. Petitioners here contend that varying index prices in the southern plywood industry rebut any inference that this pricing system operates in the classic fashion.

prohibit freight equalization. Cement Institute v. FTC, supra, 333 U.S. at 737–38 & n. 11 (Burton, J., dissenting). Thus, there appears to be little doubt that the independent decision of an individual seller to absorb freight in order to match a distant competitor's price is legal under the antitrust laws. . . .

A more doubtful issue concerns the legal status of the industry-wide use of an artificial freight factor under circumstances which provide no ready evidence of any actual collusion. At least as of 1948, the Commission adopted the view that the "conscious parallelism" involved in the industry-wide adoption of a basing-point pricing system, although lacking the traditional ingredients of Sherman Act conspiracy, may constitute grounds for proceeding under section 5. Indeed, the Commission utilized the conscious parallelism theory in Count Two of its complaint in Triangle Conduit & Cable Co. v. FTC, supra, 168 F.2d 175. In *Triangle Conduit*, the Seventh Circuit sustained a conspiracy count as well as the count which charged that the concurrent use of an elaborate basing point pricing system by individual competitors constituted a section 5 violation.

The combined effect of the Supreme Court opinion in Cement Institute and the Seventh Circuit decision in *Triangle Conduit* was to set off a storm of protest from Congress and industry. Many expressed the belief that the Commission was bent on making freight equalization practices illegal *per se*, and the Commission's conscious parallelism theory met strong opposition.[27]

Under the pressure of the situation, the Commission appeared to back away from its conscious parallelism theory. In response to written questions submitted by a Senate subcommittee investigating the Commission's pricing policies, a majority of the commissioners agreed that *Cement Institute* and *Triangle Conduit* applied only to "conspiracy situations." The *Interim Report* of the committee concluded that "the commission appears to have written off the theory that 'conscious parallel action,' absent conspiracy, constitutes an unfair method of competition under the [FTCA]." Id. at 62. See also Herbert, Delivered Pricing as Conspiracy and as Discrimination: the Legal Status, 15 Law & Contemp.Prob. 181, 198–99 (1950). Subsequent Commission decisions appear to have been grounded in findings of collusion, and this is the first case since *Triangle Conduit* in which the Commission has grounded its ruling on a finding of conscious parallelism. In at least one delivered pricing case, the Commission has dismissed the action for failure to demonstrate concerted action. In re Crouse–Hinds Co., 46 F.T.C. 1114 (1950). See P. Areeda, Antitrust Analysis 318 (1974); In re Virginia–Carolina Peanut Ass'n, 51 F.T.C. 1156, 1184–86 (1955) (dictum). . . .

It is important to stress that the weight of the case law and the Commission's own policy statement make it clear that we are looking for at

---

27. For scholarly examples of such opposition, see Kittelle & Lamb, "The Implied Conspiracy Doctrine and Delivered Pricing," 15 Law & Contemp.Prob. 227 (1950); Hilder, "The Attack upon Delivered Price Systems," 14 Geo.Wash.L.Rev. 397 (1946).

least tacit agreement to use a formula which has the effect of fixing prices. Indeed, none of the delivered pricing cases support a finding of a section 5 violation for the bare existence of an industry-wide artificial freight factor. In each case, the system had been utilized, tacitly or overtly, to match prices and avoid price competition. We thus hold that in the absence of evidence of overt agreement to utilize a pricing system to avoid price competition, the Commission must demonstrate that the challenged pricing system has actually had the effect of fixing or stabilizing prices. Without such effect, a mere showing of parallel action will not establish a section 5 violation.

III

We are thus faced with the issue whether the Commission's finding that the challenged practice had the effect of undermining price competition is supported by substantial evidence in the record, considered as a whole. . . .

The case before us bears certain resemblances to classic basing-point cases. The Commission found that the plywood industry is a relatively concentrated industry in which the freight factor is an important element of price competition. Although there was no evidence to support a finding of overt collusion to adopt a pricing system which utilized West Coast freight in calculating prices, there is no doubt that it is the dominant industry-wide practice. In addition to the use of West Coast freight, the Commission found that other common practices had the effect of reducing uncertainty in industry pricing. It is an industry-wide practice, for example, to use certain estimated figures (called "association weights") for calculating the shipping weight of varying quantities of plywood sheathing. The Commission found that the use of universal association weights, based on prior experience with West Coast plywood rather than the actual experience of individual southern mills, also tended to reduce potential uncertainties in plywood pricing. In addition, industry members commonly rely on commercial price reporters, *Crow's* and *Randomlengths*, as the basis for setting the index price to which West Coast freight is added.

Despite these similarities, neither the Commission nor the administrative law judge (ALJ) purported to find that the pricing system here was used with the price-stabilizing purpose and effect of a classic basing-point system. Not only was there the lack of any overt collusion, but the ALJ specifically found that the complaint counsel had failed to prove that any of the practices engaged in by respondents resulted in exactly matching price offers to any customers. The ALJ acknowledged that, in spite of the practices described above, the range of available prices was sufficiently important that buyers expended time and effort probing the market by telephone for the most favorable price. Over the long run, the price for plywood sheathing rises or falls in response to market factors affecting supply and demand: housing starts, weather conditions, box car shortages and strikes. We have found no evidence in the record suggesting that the price of plywood has been unresponsive to market conditions.

Despite the evidence of bargaining over price and the apparent flexibility of price levels over time, the Commission found that the challenged practices had the tendency and effect of narrowing the range of transactional prices and stabilizing the price of plywood at higher than competitive levels. It reached these conclusions indirectly, largely by relying on indicators that West Coast freight operated as something more than a purely formal feature in a competitive price. These indicators included industry memos and statements characterizing West Coast freight "pick-up" as a source of income; the tendency of southern plywood mills to prefer eastward shipments which reap additional freight pick-up; invoices showing identical prices for shipments to different localities within the same West Coast freight zone, despite their varying distance from the production mill; and the use of West Coast freight in intra-corporate transfers. The Commission also emphasized that prices were computed on the basis of a rail freight factor when most southern plywood is delivered by truck and that buyers were unable to obtain a true f.o.b. mill price quotation.

Although the Commission acknowledged that it is impossible to know with any certainty what prices would have been without West Coast freight, it reasoned that the uniform addition of an artificial price factor would inevitably produce a higher-than-normal price. In light of this logic and its own findings that the freight factor was not a mere matter of form, the Commission held that the burden shifted to petitioners to show that the low, bargainable prices for southern plywood "systematically dissipate[d]" the effects of West Coast freight. When the petitioners failed to make such a showing, the Commission concluded that proof of the "extreme artificiality" of the West Coast freight pricing method was sufficient to establish an unfair method of competition.

Petitioners, on the other hand, contend that the evidence of competition in the index price of plywood, price fluctuations over time, and the consistently lower price of southern plywood, rebut any inference that West Coast freight has actually had the effect of stabilizing the price level for southern plywood at noncompetitive levels. In addition, they argue that the preference for eastward shipments reflects their locational advantage over western mills and the tendency to ship away from "surplus production areas," rather than the seeking of an artificial price gain; that the Commission's finding of identical prices charged for shipment to varying distances within the same freight zone was based on an exaggerated estimate of the supporting evidence and the disregard of substantial rebuttal evidence showing that such prices do vary according to the actual freight costs; and that the Commission's reliance on the use of West Coast freight in intracompany transfer prices ignored the reality that market prices determine petitioners' wholesaler prices, not petitioners' accounting procedures. Petitioners also deny that f.o.b. prices are unobtainable. They argue that their cost discounts and the subtracting of actual freight costs provide a mill price based on a competitive delivered price despite the inclusion of West Coast freight.

Finally, by way of affirmative justification, petitioners observe that the record demonstrates that buyers generally prefer the form of delivered price quotations used in the industry. A closely related business justification for the continuation of the practice, according to petitioners, is the fact that southern plywood continues to compete with western plywood in many areas of the country. Buyers in these areas are particularly likely to prefer the ready price comparison between western and southern plywood made possible by the use of the West Coast index price.

We need not discuss all the evidentiary disputes between the parties to determine that there is not substantial evidence in the record, considered as a whole, to sustain the Commission's finding that petitioners' delivered pricing methods stabilized prices in the plywood industry at supra-normal levels. In truth, the Commission has provided us with little more than a theory of the likely effect of the challenged pricing practices. While this general observation perhaps summarizes all that follows, we offer the following specific points in support of our conclusion.

There is a complete absence of meaningful evidence in the record that price levels in the southern plywood industry reflect an anticompetitive effect. Surely the evidence here falls far short of the evidence presented in virtually all of the classic basing-point cases. In the past the Commission has placed great stress on the inferences to be drawn from the "systematic matching" of prices. . . .

It is no real answer to this problem for the Commission to rely on its finding that the challenged pricing method had narrowed the range of quoted prices. The Commission makes the critical assumption that West Coast freight contributed substantially to pricing certainty over and above the unchallenged use of industry pricing reporters and was, therefore, responsible for the narrow range of prices for southern plywood. But the Commission offers no evidence to suggest that this narrow range resulted from the use of West Coast freight or was itself an appropriate ground for suspicion. One commentator on delivered pricing has stated that "[w]ith any standardized commodity, identity [of price] tends to be the rule, for no seller can set a price higher than his competitors' and hope to make sales." Comment, The Basing Point Issues, supra, 58 Yale L.J. at 454. It is thus "an identity which is *unbroken* by hidden or open price-cutting over a variety of market conditions . . . which deserve suspicion." Id. (emphasis in original).

As we have seen, anticompetitive delivered pricing systems generally developed as a means of resisting market pressures for price cuts that might lead to feared price wars; they tend to reinforce rather than cause an anticompetitive market. Where market forces are not artificially harnessed by an elaborate pricing formula, the normal assumption is that prices will tend to be driven to competitive levels. Systematic matching of prices, unbroken by hidden or open price cutting, thus becomes the signal that market pressures are being artificially restrained. . . .

We are aware that it is theoretically possible that prices could vary over time, as well as within some individual transactions, even when a monopolistic price is being charged. But such a theoretical possibility is not evidence that an anticompetitive price is being charged in the plywood industry. In light of the precedents and the statements of leading authorities on delivered pricing, including the Commission itself, the existence of substantial bargaining in the base price of plywood provides at least a prima facie inference that competition has not been affected by the use of West Coast freight. The Commission has provided no substantial evidence to rebut that inference.

. . . The Commission has cited no evidence that tends to disprove the common-sense proposition that southern producers would simply adjust the index price upwards if they were quoting delivered prices in terms of actual freight. The ability of buyers to find different prices suggests that the converse is also true-the sellers vary the index price in accordance with locational or other trade advantages.

Similarly, we place some significance on the complete lack of buyer testimony objecting to the practice. Indeed, buyers not only expressed the belief that the system had no effect on prices, but also frequently expressed a preference for receiving quotations in terms of West Coast freight. Although we recognize that plywood middlemen arguably would have little stake in an artificially imposed but uniform addition to price that could readily be passed on to the consumer, we believe, nevertheless, that the complete lack of objection to the practice is another indicator pointing away from anticompetitive effect.

Finally, we do not find that the record data on costs and profits lends any additional support to the Commission's thesis. There is no question that the South's shipping advantage has been a source of profit to southern mills in competing with the West, with the net effect of attracting new entrants into the southern market until very recently. While the Commission acknowledged that this profit base was not only legitimate but essential in the early years of the southern industry, it concluded that the use of West Coast freight in calculating price had impeded natural forces that would have tended to drive prices and profits down. Again, however, the conclusion is largely a deduction from the Commission's reasoning about the tendencies of the challenged practice. The southern plywood industry is still relatively young and the most recent figures on costs and profits were equivocal at best.[28] The Commission itself acknowledged that because of the "numerous uncertainties and inadequacies in the cost and profit information available in this record" and the inherent uncertainties in-

---

28. While both the Commission and the ALJ found that southern mills have consistently yielded higher profits than western mills, petitioners observe that the company focused on by the ALJ, Georgia–Pacific, earned approximately equal profits in its southern and western mills between 1973 and 1975. The ALJ attributed the declining profit figures for southern plywood in 1974– 1975 to the nation's economic recession and strikes against southern mills. Without attempting to speculate on what would have occurred under normal circumstances, the data show that profits for western plywood were also affected by the recession but that the 1973 figures reflected a lower profit gap between western and southern plywood than that of most prior years.

volved in profit analysis, 91 F.T.C. at 109, it "placed little reliance upon such data in [the] disposition of the appeal." Id. at 97.

In light of these observations, we agree with petitioners that the Commission's approach had the effect of requiring them to prove that the challenged practices had no effect on the level of prices in the plywood industry. The Commission justified this approach on grounds that it is impossible to know what prices would have been without the challenged practices. While we are sympathetic with the difficulties of proof in a case such as this, we are unable to sustain an approach that finds a non-collusive pricing method to be illegal despite the absence of some reliable indicator that the practice had an effect on overall price levels.

IV

We discuss, finally, the Commission arguments suggesting that we should sustain the order on the basis of something less than substantial evidence that West Coast freight has produced an anticompetitive effect. First, we decline to follow the Commission's suggestion that industry-wide adoption of an artificial method of price-quoting should be deemed a *per se* violation of section 5 by analogy to section 1 price-tampering cases. *E.g.*, United States v. Socony–Vacuum Oil Co., 310 U.S. 150, 221–23 (1940); Plymouth Dealers Ass'n v. United States, 279 F.2d 128, 132 (9th Cir.1960); Allied Paper Mills v. FTC, 168 F.2d 600, 607 (7th Cir.1948), cert. denied, 336 U.S. 918 (1949). *Per se* analysis is justified by the inherent danger to our competitive system posed by agreements to fix prices. We thus refuse to allow parties to show the reasonableness or ineffectiveness of their efforts to tamper with "the central nervous system of the economy." United States v. Socony–Vacuum Oil Co., supra, 310 U.S. at 224 n. 59.

In *Allied Paper Mills*, for example, the Seventh Circuit utilized a *per se* analysis in sustaining the Commission's order, based on the Commission's finding of overt agreement as to all aspects of pricing, including "uniform base prices." Although the court found evidence in the record of uniform sealed bidding, petitioners in that case pointed to conflicting evidence that prices had not been invariably matching. The Seventh Circuit responded that "[t]he petitioners' temporary departure from their system or temporary inability to carry through their purpose does not affect its illegality." Id.

The Commission asks us to find that the industry-wide use of West Coast freight constitutes a form of private control over the pricing process equivalent to conspiracy for purposes of *per se* analysis under section 5. We believe, however, that parallel behavior, without more, does not trigger the *per se* treatment which is given to overt agreement. Under our antitrust laws, we begin with the assumption that decisions are made independently and competitively. The debate over conscious parallelism comes down to whether it is ever appropriate for evidence of the anticompetitive effect of certain types of parallel conduct to serve as a substitute for the Sherman Act requirement of agreement. Without reaching that broader issue, we believe that to apply *per se* analysis to these facts would be to assume what must be proven, namely, that the use of West Coast freight by southern plywood producers is not a natural competitive response to buyer preference for traditional forms of price quotation, but rather is a deliberate restraint on competition. Without proof that the practice exerts an anticompetitive effect on the price of plywood, we have no reason to make such an assumption. Cf. Turner, Agreement under the Sherman Act, supra, 75 Harv.L.Rev. at 658–59 (conscious parallelism is evidence of agreement only if additional facts indicate that the decisions are inexplicable as ordinary competitive decisions).

Second, we are not persuaded that a different result is warranted by the unique features of the FTCA. It is often repeated that the Commission was set up as an expert body with power "to restrain practices ... which, although not yet having grown into Sherman Act dimensions, would most likely do so if left unrestrained." The policies calling for deference to the Commission are, of course, in tension with the acknowledged responsibility of the courts to interpret section 5. Moreover, the law of delivered pricing is well forged, having been developed by the Commission and courts over years of litigation. As we concluded in part II, the weight of the case law, as well as the practices and statements of the Commission, establish the rule that the Commission must find either collusion or actual effect on competition to make out a section 5 violation for use of delivered pricing. In this setting at least, where the parties agree that the practice was a natural and competitive development in the emergence of the southern plywood industry, and where there is a complete absence of evidence implying overt conspiracy, to allow a finding of a section 5 violation on the theory that the mere widespread use of the practice makes it an incipient threat to competition would be to blur the distinction between guilty and innocent commercial behavior. Since we have found that there is not substantial evidence in the record to support the Commission's finding of anticompetitive effect, it follows that the Commission's order may not be enforced.

NOTES AND QUESTIONS

1. After this *Boise Cascade* decision, several classes of plywood purchasers and users succeeded in private damage actions based on the same underlying facts. Plaintiffs in those cases, however, introduced direct evidence of conspiracy, as well as expert testimony on injury caused plaintiffs by "phantom freight" and other practices. On appeal, the Fifth Circuit held that there was plainly enough evidence to permit the jury finding of collusion. In re Plywood Antitrust Litigation, 655 F.2d 627, 636 (5th Cir.1981), cert. granted sub nom., Weyerhaeuser Co. v. Lyman Lamb Co., 456 U.S. 971 (1982), later dismissed (after settlement), 462 U.S. 1125 (1983). Was the Fifth Circuit's result correct?

2. Consider carefully the facts in *Cement Institute*, summarized at p. 600. Why was the basing point system in *Cement* more anticompetitive than the delivered price system in *Boise*?

Ethyl Corp. v. FTC

United States Circuit Court of Appeals, Second Circuit, 1984.
729 F.2d 128.

■ MANSFIELD, J. . . . From the 1920s until 1948, Ethyl was the sole domestic producer of antiknock compounds. Demand for the compounds increased with the increase in gasoline use, however, and in 1948 Du Pont entered the industry and captured a substantial market share. In 1961 PPG (then known as Houston Chemical Company) began to manufacture and sell the compounds; and in 1964 Nalco followed suit. By 1974, Du Pont had 38.4% of the market; Ethyl 33.5%; PPG 16.2%; and Nalco 11.8%. During 1974–1979, the period of the alleged violations, these were the only four domestic producers and sellers of the compounds. No other firm has ever made or sold the compounds in this country. Thus the industry has always been highly concentrated. However, there are no technological or financial barriers to new entries.

The only purchasers of lead antiknocks are the gasoline refining companies which are large, aggressive and sophisticated buyers. Indeed, several are among the largest industrial corporations in the world. If prospective profits from the sale of antiknock compounds were sufficiently attractive, nothing would prevent them from integrating backwards into the antiknock industry. Of the 154 refiners who purchase the product, the ten largest buy about 30% of the total amount produced in this country.

The steady increase in demand for antiknock compounds during the 1960s allowed PPG and Nalco to enter the market. From August 1971 to January 1974, however, federal controls froze the price of the compounds and beginning in 1973 the federal government initiated steps that were to lead to a drastic reduction in demand. At that time the Environmental Protection Agency ("EPA") required that all automobiles made in the United States, beginning in 1975, be equipped with catalytic converters; since the lead in antiknock compounds fouls such converters, almost all new cars produced since 1975 require unleaded gasoline. At about the same time, in order to reduce the amount of lead in the atmosphere the EPA imposed severe limitations on the amount of lead that could be used in gasoline. As a result of these two measures the use of lead antiknock compounds sharply declined from more than one billion pounds in 1974 to approximately 400 million pounds in 1980, leaving manufacturers with excess capacity. Additional EPA regulations are likely to cause a further decline in the use of the product from an estimated 260 million pounds in 1985 to an estimated 90 million pounds in 1990.

Thus, even though there are no technological or financial constraints barring new entries into the industry and there were two new entrants during the 1960s, the cost of staying in production in a dying industry has made it unlikely that there will be new entrants in the future. The problem confronted by existing producers is the same as that faced by potentially new entrants. Indeed, PPG has recently ceased production of lead antiknock compounds, leaving only three manufacturers in this evaporating line of business. . . .

   . . .

These characteristics of the industry-high concentration, small likelihood of new entries because of a sharply declining market, inelastic demand, and homogeneity of product-led to a natural oligopoly with a high degree of pricing interdependence in which there was far less incentive to engage in price competition than if there had been many sellers in an expanding market. . . . [D]uring the 1970s, profits in the industry-particularly Du Pont's and Ethyl's were substantially greater than what is described as the benchmark in the chemical industry, which in this case is 150% of the average rate of return in that industry. During the 1974–1979 period under investigation by the FTC, the returns of Ethyl and Du Pont on investment substantially exceeded the 150% benchmark in each year; although PPG's and Nalco's returns on investment also exceeded the 150% benchmark in four of the five years, PPG operated at a loss in 1979 and in 1983 ceased production.

Notwithstanding the highly concentrated structure of the industry, there was substantial price and non-price competition during the 1974–1979 period that is the subject of the complaint. More than 80% of Nalco's sales during that period were at discounts off its list price, and more than one-third of PPG's sales during the same period were at discounts, rising to 58% of its sales in 1979. Despite the fact that the compounds were sold by all four firms on a delivered price basis, the record reveals that, because of the variations in secret discounts granted by Nalco to its customers, the other 3 producers were uncertain as to Nalco's strategy and the net prices actually received by it. Du Pont, for example, was unclear whether Nalco always followed price increases or even had a price list. Ethyl was unsure whether Nalco sometimes sold to certain customers on an f.o.b. basis. . . .

Ethyl and Du Pont, apparently recognizing the futility of meeting price discounts in an inelastic, declining market, each individually chose to meet this price competition on the part of PPG and Nalco not by price discounts but by various forms of non-price competition. These included late billing and "advance buying," the latter of which permitted customers to order extra volume at the old price before a price increase went into effect. Du Pont and Ethyl also provided valuable "free" services, including (1) provision of free equipment, (2) education on how to use the product more efficiently, (3) assistance in building and monitoring facilities for the storage and blending of antiknock compounds, (4) computer programming assistance, (5) training of refiners' employees, (6) payment for consultant services, and (7) favorable credit terms. These competitive practices, according to the ALJ, "played a significant role in the competitive rivalry between the antiknock suppliers" and were responsible for a 35% increase in sales by one respondent to 10 sizeable customers in 1975 over the previous year. . . .

On May 30, 1979, the FTC filed a complaint against the four manufacturers, alleging that each of the companies had engaged in "unfair methods of competition" and "unfair acts and practices" in violation of § 5 of the Act. The complaint attacked the following non-collusive practices: (1) the sale of lead antiknock additives by each respondent only on the basis of a delivered price that included the cost of transportation; (2) the use by Du Pont and Ethyl of "most favored nation" clauses in their standard form sales contracts and the use of such clauses by Nalco in a substantial number of its sales contracts; (3) the use by each company of contract clauses requiring at least 30 days advance notice to customers of changes in price; and (4) providing advance notice of price increases to the press. The complaint did not claim that the practices were the result of any agreement, express or tacit, among the manufacturers or that the practices had been undertaken for other than legitimate business purposes. It simply alleged that the practices "individually and in combination had the effect of reducing uncertainty about competitors' prices of lead-based antiknock compounds," and that such reduced uncertainty "unfairly facilitated the maintenance of substantial, uniform price levels and the reduction or elimination of price competition in the lead-based antiknock market."

Each of the challenged practices was initiated by Ethyl during the period prior to 1948 when it was the sole producer in the industry. There is no suggestion that the practices constituted unfair methods of competition at that time. For example, Ethyl began quoting prices on a delivered basis in 1937 in response to customer demand. Each of the three subsequent manufacturers, upon entry into the market, followed that practice. There is no evidence that the practice was adopted by any of the respondents for other than legitimate business reasons, the principal of which were tradition and customer demand. Customers demanded a delivered price because it would require the manufacturers to retain title to and responsibility for the dangerously volatile compounds during transit to the refiner's plant and in at least some cases would result in savings on state transportation and inventory taxes which the customer would pay if title passed prior to delivery. It is undisputed that, as the ALJ found, the delivery charge is a very small factor in relation to the sales price of the compounds. In 1979, for instance, average delivery costs to respondents' customers amounted to $1.53 cents per pound or less than 2% of list price, hardly a substantial competitive factor.

At trial the FTC offered no expert freight witnesses or other proof regarding the effect of delivered pricing on price competition. Du Pont's expert witness, who had extensive experience in f.o.b. pricing and who was the only witness to testify on the subject, stated that even without uniform delivered pricing (*i.e.*, if antiknocks were sold f.o.b.) published freight tariffs would allow each manufacturer easily to determine any other manufacturer's freight prices to each customer and to match those prices to the penny.

Similarly, Ethyl adopted the "most favored nation" contractual clause more than fifty years ago when it was the sole producer of antiknocks as a guarantee against price discrimination between its own customers who competed against each other in the sale of gasoline containing antiknock compounds. The clause assured the smaller refiners that they would not be placed at a competitive disadvantage on account of price discounts to giants such as Standard Oil, Texaco and Gulf. For the same legitimate business reason Du Pont adopted the same contractual clause when it later entered the industry. Even though such clauses arguably reduce price discounting, they comport with the requirements of the Robinson–Patman Act, which prohibits price discrimination between customers. There is no evidence that Ethyl or Du Pont adopted or continued to use the most favored nation clause for the purpose of influencing the price discounting policies of other producers or of facilitating their adoption of or adherence to uniform prices. Indeed, PPG did not include the clause in its standard contract with customers and the complaint did not charge it with engaging in this practice. Nalco made only limited use of the clause.

Finally, the issuance of advance notice of price increases both to buyers and to the press, a common practice in the chemical industry, was initiated by Ethyl, well before the entry of Du Pont or the other two manufacturers into the market, as a means of aiding buyers in their financial and purchase planning. The contract clause used by two producers (Ethyl and Nalco) required them to give 30 days notice to the customer of price changes, while the clause used by the others (Du Pont and PPG) was limited to price increases. Du Pont and Ethyl gave customers a few days additional notice of their price increases (sometimes called a "grace period") but Nalco did not do so and PPG did not do so in any price increase that it initiated. Although the advance noticing had the indirect effect of informing competitors as to the producer's price increases, the record, not surprisingly, contains considerable proof that in such a small industry manufacturers quickly learn of competitors' price changes, usually within hours, regardless of the advance public notice. Typically, when one producer changed its price and communicated that change to its buyers, those buyers would immediately call the other producers to secure the best price. Moreover, the giving of 30 or more days advance notice of a price increase did not preclude the initiator, upon finding that competitors did not follow, from rescinding or modifying the increase or extending its effective date at any time prior to the end of the 30–day period.[29]

. . .

The Commission concluded from its examination of the record that the structure of the antiknock industry-high concentration, high barriers to entry, a homogeneous product, and inelastic demand-rendered it susceptible to unilateral but interdependent conduct which lessened competition. The Commission further decided that the record contained substantial evidence of noncompetitive performance in the industry: highly uniform

---

29. An example was Du Pont's giving of a 30–day notice of a price increase in August 1977 without any additional advance, or grace period, notice. When Ethyl thereafter undercut Du Pont's increase by adopting a lesser increase Du Pont rolled back its increase to the lesser competitive amount rather than sell at its proposed higher price.

prices and price changes, limited price discounting, stable market shares, relatively high profits, prices in excess of marginal cost, and rising prices despite excess capacity and sluggish demand. On such a record, the FTC held that unilateral but interdependent practices engaged in by the petitioners constituted an unfair method of competition in violation of § 5....

The essential question is whether, given the characteristics of the antiknock industry, the Commission erred in holding that the challenged business practices constitute "unfair methods of competition" in violation of § 5 simply because they "facilitate" consciously parallel pricing at identical levels....

The Commission here asks us ... to hold that the "unfair methods of competition" provision of § 5 can be violated by non-collusive, non-predatory and independent conduct of a non-artificial nature, at least when it results in a substantial lessening of competition. We recognize that § 5 invests the Commission with broad powers designed to enable it to cope with new threats to competition as they arise.... However, ... appropriate standards must be adopted and applied to protect a respondent against abuse of power. As the Commission moves away from attacking conduct that is either a violation of the antitrust laws or collusive, coercive, predatory, restrictive or deceitful, and seeks to break new ground by enjoining otherwise legitimate practices, the closer must be our scrutiny upon judicial review. A test based solely upon restraint of competition, even if qualified by the requirement that the conduct be "analogous" to an antitrust violation, is so vague as to permit arbitrary or undue government interference with the reasonable freedom of action that has marked our country's competitive system.

The term "unfair" is an elusive concept, often dependent upon the eye of the beholder.[30] A line must therefore be drawn between conduct that is

---

30. Two decisions heavily relied on by the Commission, *Triangle Conduit & Cable Co. v. FTC,* 168 F.2d 175 (7th Cir.1948), aff'd by an equally divided court sub nom., *Clayton Mark & Co. v. FTC,* 336 U.S. 956 (1949), and *Boise Cascade Corp. v. FTC,* 637 F.2d 573 (9th Cir.1980), are not of assistance in resolving the issue before us. In *Triangle Conduit* the FTC had found that the use of a mathematical formula by members of a trade association to compute delivered price amounted to both a conspiracy to fix prices and an unfair method of competition in violation of § 5. Upon appeal the Seventh Circuit held that the conspiracy had been proved by circumstantial evidence. 168 F.2d at 180. Although it went on to state in reliance on *FTC v. Cement Institute,* supra, that it could not "say the Commission was wrong in concluding that the individual use of the basing point method ... does constitute an unfair method of competition," id. at 181, the finding of a

conspiracy sheds doubt on the significance of the latter statement. Indeed, a majority of the Commission took the view that *Cement Institute* and *Triangle Conduit* apply only to "conspiracy situations." Interim Report on the Study of the Federal Trade Commission Pricing Policies, S.Doc. No. 27, 81st Cong., 1st Sess. 62–63 (1949). The Commission's failure thereafter for over 30 years to seek to apply § 5 to consciously parallel behavior not involving collusion, coercion or restrictive conduct indicates that it believed it has no power to curb otherwise legitimate behavior allegedly facilitating conscious price parallelism.

Boise Cascade Corp. is at best ambiguous. There the FTC alleged that plywood manufacturers, acting individually, had adopted a freight pricing scheme that lessened competition in the industry. The pricing scheme, use of a West Coast freight factor for

anticompetitive and legitimate conduct that has an impact on competition. Lessening of competition is not the substantial equivalent of "unfair methods" of competition. Section 5 is aimed at conduct, not at the result of such conduct, even though the latter is usually a relevant factor in determining whether the challenged conduct is "unfair." Nor does the statute obligate a business to engage in competition; if that were the case, many acceptable pricing and market decisions would be barred. A manufacturer, for instance, would be prevented from making a concededly lawful change in its distribution system, designed to increase sales efficiency, by unilaterally reducing the number of its wholesalers, since the effect would be to diminish substantial competition at the wholesaler level. Similarly, if anticompetitive impact were the sole test, the admittedly lawful unilateral closing of a plant or refusal to expand capacity could be found to be "unfair." The holder of a valid product patent could be prevented from exercising its lawful monopoly to charge whatever the traffic would bear, even though "a monopolist, as long as he has no purpose to restrain competition or to enhance or expand his monopoly, and does not act coercively, retains [the right to trade with whom he wishes]." Official Airline Guides, Inc. v. FTC, 630 F.2d 920, 927–28 (2d Cir.1980), cert. denied, 450 U.S. 917 (1981); see United States v. Colgate & Co., 250 U.S. 300, 307 (1919).

When a business practice is challenged by the Commission, even though, as here, it does not violate the antitrust or other laws and is not collusive, coercive, predatory or exclusionary in character, standards for determining whether it is "unfair" within the meaning of § 5 must be formulated to discriminate between normally acceptable business behavior and conduct that is unreasonable or unacceptable. Otherwise the door

determining freight prices from southern shipping points, was alleged to have resulted in an "artificial" method of calculating freight prices, contributing to pricing uniformity of southern plywood. The FTC argued that even though there was no agreement, there was liability because of the anticompetitive effect. The Ninth Circuit set aside the FTC order, finding no anticompetitive effect. The FTC in the instant case relies upon the following statement by the court:

"We thus hold that in the absence of evidence of overt agreement to utilize a pricing system to avoid price competition, the Commission must demonstrate that the challenged pricing system has actually had the effect of fixing or stabilizing prices. Without such effect, a mere showing of parallel action will not establish a section 5 violation." 637 F.2d at 577.

Standing alone, the statement tends to support the Commission's position here, particularly since a finding of price conspiracy would obviate the necessity of proving that it had the effect of fixing or stabilizing prices. But earlier in the same paragraph the court stated:

"It is important to stress that the weight of the case law and the Commission's own policy statement make it clear that we are looking for at least tacit agreement to use a formula which has the effect of fixing prices. Indeed, none of the delivered pricing cases support a finding of a section 5 violation for the bare existence of an industry-wide artificial freight factor. In each case, the system had been utilized, tacitly or overtly, to match prices and avoid price competition." Id. at 576–77.

In view of this statement we cannot place much reliance on Boise Cascade as support for the Commission's position here.

would be open to arbitrary or capricious administration of § 5; the FTC could, whenever it believed that an industry was not achieving its maximum competitive potential, ban certain practices in the hope that its action would increase competition. The mere existence of an oligopolistic market structure in which a small group of manufacturers engage in consciously parallel pricing of an identical product does not violate the antitrust laws. Theatre Enterprises, Inc. v. Paramount Film Distributing Corp., 346 U.S. 537 (1954). It represents a condition, not a "method;" indeed it could be consistent with intense competition. Labeling one producer's price change in such a market as a "signal," parallel price changes as "lock-step," or prices as "supracompetitive," hardly converts its pricing into an "unfair" method of competition. To so hold would be to condemn any such price increase or moves, however independent; yet the FTC has not suggested that § 5 authorizes it to ban all price increases in an oligopolistic market. On the contrary, it states that "Section 5 should not prohibit oligopolistic *pricing* alone, even supracompetitive parallel prices, in the absence of specific conduct which promotes such a result." (Emphasis in original). This fine distinction creates doubt as to the types of otherwise legitimate conduct that are lawful and those that are not. The doubt is increased by the Commission's concession that price uniformity is normal in a market with few sellers and homogeneous products, such as that in the antiknock compound industry.

In view of this patent uncertainty the Commission owes a duty to define the conditions under which conduct claimed to facilitate price uniformity would be unfair so that businesses will have an inkling as to what they can lawfully do rather than be left in a state of complete unpredictability. The Commission's decision in the present case does not provide any guidelines; it would require each producer not only to assess the general conduct of the antiknock business but also that of each of its competitors and the reaction of each to the other, which would be virtually impossible. Some idea of the fickleness and uncertainty of the FTC's position in the present case can be gathered from its ambivalent view towards some of the practices which it attacks. Certain otherwise-legitimate practices were declared unlawful only when used cumulatively with other practices. Others were found unfair when used by certain producers (Du Pont and Ethyl) but not when used by others (PPG and Nalco). Press announcements of price increases and contractual 30–day price increase notice requirements were held permissible but giving buyers a few days additional notice was found to be unfair even though there was no proof that the extra days made any competitive difference. Indeed, with or without the additional days' notice the initiator of a price increase was not precluded from withdrawing or modifying it within the 30–day period or from extending the 30–day notice period itself. Thus the FTC's rulings and order appear to represent uncertain guesswork rather than workable rules of law.

In our view, before business conduct in an oligopolistic industry may be labeled "unfair" within the meaning of § 5 a minimum standard demands that, absent a tacit agreement, at least some indicia of oppressiveness must exist such as (1) evidence of anticompetitive intent or purpose on the part of the producer charged, or (2) the absence of an independent legitimate business reason for its conduct.[31] If, for instance, a seller's conduct, even absent identical behavior on the part of its competitors, is contrary to its independent self-interest, that circumstance would indicate that the business practice is "unfair" within the meaning of § 5. In short, in the absence of proof of a violation of the antitrust laws or evidence of collusive, coercive, predatory, or exclusionary conduct, business practices are not "unfair" in violation of § 5 unless those practices either have an anticompetitive purpose or cannot be supported by an independent legitimate reason. To suggest, as does the Commission in its opinion, that the defendant can escape violating § 5 only by showing that there are "countervailing procompetitive justifications" for the challenged business practices goes too far. . . .

The tenuousness of the Commission's finding that the challenged practices are "unfair" is illustrated by the fact that it does not tell us when the practices became unlawful: at the time of their original adoption by Ethyl when it was the sole manufacturer of antiknock compounds, when Du Pont entered the market in 1948, when PPG entered in 1961, when Nalco appeared on the scene in 1964, or at some other time. . . .

In the first place, price uniformity and parallelism was much more limited than the FTC would have it. During the relevant period (1974–1979) Nalco extended price discounts on more than 80% of its sales and PPG on more than one-third of its sales, the latter increasing to 58% of its sales in 1979 as the sellers competed for fewer buyers in a diminishing market. Although there was for the most part price parallelism on the part of Du Pont and Ethyl, they effectively met the price discounts of the other two producers by providing competition in the form of extensive services which had the effect of retaining old customers or luring away new ones. Thus the total package, including free valuable services and discounts,

31. The requirement is comparable to the principle that there must be a "plus factor" before conscious parallelism may be found to be conspiratorial in violation of the Sherman Act. *See, e.g.,* Naumkeag Theatres Co. v. New England Theatres, Inc., 345 F.2d 910, 911–12 (1st Cir.), cert. denied, 382 U.S. 906 (1965) (parallel clearances and run schedules by motion picture distributors); Modern Home Inst. Inc. v. Hartford Accident & Indemn. Co., 513 F.2d 102 (2d Cir.1975) (defendant insurers had independent reasons for refusing to buy plaintiff's list of customers). The "plus factor" may be conduct that is contrary to the defendants' independent self-interest, Morton Salt Co. v. United States, 235 F.2d 573, 578–79 (10th Cir.1956), the presence or absence of a strong motive on a defendants' part to enter an alleged conspiracy, First National Bank of Arizona v. Cities Service Co., 391 U.S. 253, 286–88 (1968); Interstate Circuit, Inc. v. United States, 306 U.S. 208, 222–23 (1939), or the artificial standardization of products, C–O–Two Fire Equip. Co. v. United States, 197 F.2d 489, 493 (9th Cir.), cert. denied, 344 U.S. 892 (1952). In United States v. General Electric Co., et al., 565 F.2d 208 [1977–2] Trade Cas. & 61,659, at 72,715 (E.D.Pa. 1977), for instance, General Electric in addition to announcing that it would adhere to its published prices and grant no discounts, adopted a "price-protection" policy under which, if it offered a discount to a customer, it obligated itself to give the same discount retroactively to all other customers who had bought the product within the previous six months, thus voluntarily penalizing itself for price-discounting.

presents a picture of a competitive market in which large, sophisticated and aggressive buyers were making demands and were satisfied with the results. To the extent that there was price uniformity, that condition is as consistent with competitive as with anticompetitive behavior.

The problems faced by anyone thinking of entering the market were not "barriers" in the usual sense used by economists, such as requirements for high capital investment or advanced technological know-how. The main problem has been that market demand, due to factors uncontrolled by petitioners, is sharply declining. A dying market, which will soon dry up altogether, does not attract new entries. Absent some reasonable prospect that a price reduction would increase demand-and there is none-it is not surprising that existing producers have not engaged in as much price competition as might exist under other conditions. To suggest that industry-wide use of delivered instead of f.o.b. pricing restrained price competition in such a market ignores the de minimis part freight charges played in the price paid by customers. It also overlooks the fact that f.o.b. pricing is not necessarily more competitive than delivered pricing.

In short, we do not find substantial evidence in this record as a whole that the challenged practices significantly lessened competition in the antiknock industry or that the elimination of those practices would improve competition.

The FTC's order is vacated.

[Judge Lumbard concurred in the conclusion of the majority that the "record does not support the FTC's finding of substantial [anticompetitive] effect," but stated that it was unnecessary to reach the "broader question" of whether "§ 5 is limited to conduct that is either *per se* pernicious (*i.e.*, collusive, coercive, predatory, or exclusionary) or could not have been adopted for other than pernicious reasons; or whether, as the FTC now argues, it extends also to conduct that may be acceptable in some situations but not in others, in light of poor industry structure and performance, substantial anticompetitive effects, and lack of offsetting procompetitive justification."]

NOTE ON GE/WESTINGHOUSE

A number of electrical equipment manufacturers and many of their employees were indicted in 1960 for a conspiracy to fix prices and allocate business in various heavy electrical equipment product lines. Most of the defendants pleaded guilty and some individuals went to jail, substantial fines were paid, an order was entered against the manufacturers and some 1,800 private treble damage lawsuits were filed. In many respects, it was the biggest cartel "bust" in the history of Sherman Act enforcement.

For a time, vigorous competition flourished, but after a time, only GE and Westinghouse remained as active competitors in the market for sale of large turbine generators. In 1972, the government undertook an investigation and concluded that beginning in 1963, price competition between the two had been eliminated. As we noted in Chapter 4, the government contended that this had been accomplished in the following ways: (1) each company published a similar and unusually extensive price book which would allow the other to predict the price each would bid on a particular type and size of machine; (2) both companies adopted a "price protection plan" whereby if the manufacturer lowered a price to a customer, any other customer purchasing within the previous six-month period would be given an identical retroactive discount; and (3) each company published a list of outstanding bids whenever there was a price change, so that customers (and the other seller) would not be confused as to who was entitled to a particular price.

The government did not claim any of these practices were adopted by agreement, but rather that these consciously parallel policies had led to identical prices.

GE and Westinghouse denied that any violation had occurred, but agreed to a modification in the order that had been entered after the 1960 price-fixing conspiracy was uncovered. As a result of the order, the two companies were enjoined, among other things, from: (1) "offering a price protection policy or entering into any agreement whereby the price of a large turbine-generator to any customer would be retroactively reduced ..." and (2) publishing any price book or price list relating to large turbine-generators, except one "based on the defendant's own individually determined criteria and costs...."

Consider the following questions with respect to GE/Westinghouse:

1.   Can you reconcile the government's view in GE/Westinghouse that consciously parallel adoption of price protection plans was illegal with the Second Circuit's conclusion in *Ethyl* that the most favored customer clauses adopted by several of the lead additive manufacturers created no antitrust problems? In that connection, see note 40 of the Second Circuit's opinion, where the Court attempts to distinguish the GE/Westinghouse arrangement. Did the Second Circuit adequately consider the type of economic concerns raised by Professor Salop?

2.   Suppose two competing department stores announce publicly that each will not be undersold by the other on any item carried in both stores. Each tells customers that if they will bring in an ad or sales slip from the other store showing a lower price, each will meet that price. Is that different from the price protection plan? Should it be illegal?

3.   Suppose members of a trade association agree that trade association dues and support for the association's public welfare activities would be computed according to the number of successful bids by each member; can you imagine a set of circumstances in which that might be regarded as a "facilitating practice"?

Todd v. Exxon Corporation

United States Court of Appeals, Second Circuit, 2001.
275 F.3d 191.

■ SOTOMAYOR, CIRCUIT JUDGE: Plaintiff-appellant Roberta Todd appeals from an order of the United States District Court for the Southern District of New York (Sprizzo, J.) granting defendants-appellees' motion to dismiss the complaint for failure to state a claim pursuant to Fed. R. Civ. P. 12(b)(6). We hold that plaintiff adequately alleges a § 1 Sherman Act violation for an unlawful information exchange. Plaintiff's complaint alleges a plausible product market, a market structure that is susceptible to collusive activity, a data exchange with anticompetitive potential, and antitrust injury. We therefore vacate and remand.

Background

Plaintiff brought this action against fourteen major companies in the integrated oil and petrochemical industry, collectively accounting for 80–90% of the industry's revenues and employing approximately the same percentage of the industry's workforce. Todd v. Exxon Corp., 126 F. Supp. 2d 321, 323 (S.D.N.Y.2000). On behalf of herself and all other similarly situated current and former Exxon employees (the putative class), plaintiff alleges that defendants violated § 1 of the Sherman Act by regularly sharing detailed information regarding compensation paid to nonunion managerial, professional, and technical ("MPT") employees and using this information in setting the salaries of these employees at artificially low levels. Plaintiff seeks money damages and equitable relief pursuant to § 1 of the Sherman Act.

Accepting the allegations in the complaint as true, as we must on this motion to dismiss, the facts of this case are as follows. Defendants instituted a system whereby they periodically conducted surveys comparing past and current MPT salary information and participated in regular meetings at which current and future salary budgets were discussed. The data exchanges were also accompanied by assurances that the information would be used in setting the salaries of MPT employees. Defendants' "Job Match Survey" created a common denominator to facilitate the comparison of MPT salaries. The survey used certain jobs at defendant Chevron as benchmarks. The other defendants would submit detailed information regarding the jobs at their companies that were most comparable to the Chevron benchmark jobs so that they could be matched. The survey compared the responsibilities and compensation packages offered by defendants for certain jobs and job types against those of the benchmark positions at Chevron. This survey was coordinated by defendants Unocal and Chevron. Chevron and Unocal each would meet with half of the other companies involved to develop matches to the benchmarks, and then would gather the information before submitting it to a third-party consultant, Towers Perrin. Towers Perrin compiled the information, then analyzed, refined, and distributed it to the defendants on diskettes and in the form of hard copies. Since not all jobs could be matched precisely, defendants agreed upon certain percentage "offsets" to facilitate the comparison. The Job Match Survey was performed every two years and was supplemented in the "off years" by the "Grade Average Update," which would calculate the change in grade average salaries since the last Job Match Survey and then adjust the salary level from the previous year's survey by the amount of the change.

Defendants' "Job Family Survey" provided the most current account of the compensation being paid in the industry. Each company submitted information on salaries actually paid in thirty different categories of jobs, or "job families," classified according to the nature of the work. The information exchanged for each family was broken down by the job level classification, experience level, and academic background of the MPT employee. This survey was coordinated by Exxon, and again the information was submitted to and compiled by Towers Perrin. Each participating company received the information from Towers Perrin in hard copy and disk form. The information gathered in the survey was updated and distributed to the participants several times per year.

Furthermore, each company was entitled to receive subsets of Job Family Survey data, consisting of salary information from as few as three companies at a time. Plaintiff alleges that Exxon used these subsets to compare its own salaries with those of six particular competitors, referred to as the "Six Majors." These periodically updated data sets were used by each defendant to determine whether the announced budgets of its competitors had been implemented so that each could consider what adjustments should be made to coordinate salary levels.

Although these were the primary forms of salary information exchange, defendants supplemented this information with data from other sources. Defendants' "Advancement Guides" established requirements for advancement within a given salary grade of employee. These guides were used by defendants to slow the rates of advancement for MPT employees in defendants' companies. The "ABC," "B–1" and "B–2" surveys collected additional data regarding bonuses and other non-standard payments above base compensation that were not captured in the Job Match and Job Family Surveys. The "Long–Term Incentive Survey" refined the comparison further by accounting for the economic value of certain non-cash benefits paid to MPT employees. The "Starting Salary Survey," in which only the Six Majors apparently participated, measured starting salaries of college graduates entering MPT positions. In addition to the data exchange surveys, human resource personnel at defendant companies held regular meetings—at least three times per year—to discuss and exchange salary and salary-related information. These meetings included discussions of individual defendants' current and future salary budgets for MPT employees.

Plaintiff contends that defendants' arrangement violated § 1 of the Sherman Act. According to the complaint, these violations had the purpose and effect of depressing MPT salaries paid by defendants. The arrangement reduced the incentive for defendants to bid up salaries in order to attract experienced MPT employees or to retain employees who might be lured to other firms. As a result, the plaintiffs in the putative class received compensation that was materially lower than what they would have received but for defendants' anticompetitive practices.

Plaintiff alleges that Exxon, in particular, used this data to maintain a market position slightly above the so-called "Six Majors" and below three higher-paying competitors referred to as the "High Three." Exxon capitalized on the shared data to decrease its "competitive factor"—the percentage by which Exxon would have to adjust its salary levels in order to maintain alignment with the salaries offered by its competitors. Exxon's competitive factor dropped from 6.5% in 1991 to 0% in 1995, and its salaries decreased 4.1% between 1987 and 1994 in comparison to the Six Majors. The various information exchanges also allowed Exxon to reduce its overall salary index versus the competition from 110.7% in 1987 to 107.0% in 1993.

The district court granted defendants' motion to dismiss the complaint for failure to state a claim pursuant to Fed. R. Civ. P. 12(b)(6). The court held that (1) plaintiff failed to plead a plausible product market, undermining the claim that defendants control 80–90% of the relevant market; (2) even if the alleged market were plausible, plaintiff failed to allege that the market structure is susceptible to collusive activity; (3) plaintiff failed to allege facts supporting an agreement to fix salary levels; and (4) plaintiff failed to show detrimental effects on competition. Plaintiff appeals the dismissal.

Discussion

I.   [In this section, the court noted that its standard of review was *de novo*; that the complaint would be reviewed in the light most favorable to the plaintiff; and that there is no heightened pleading requirements applicable to antitrust cases.]

II.   The Rule of Reason

Section 1 of the Sherman Act prohibits "every contract, combination in the form of trust or otherwise, or conspiracy, in restraint of trade or commerce among the several States, or with foreign nations." 15 U.S.C. § 1. Traditional "hard-core" price fixing remains *per se* unlawful under the seminal case United States v. Socony–Vacuum Oil Co., 310 U.S. 150, 212–24, 84 L. Ed. 1129, 60 S. Ct. 811 (1940), and its progeny. If the plaintiff in this case could allege that defendants actually formed an agreement to fix MPT salaries, this *per se* rule would likely apply. Furthermore, even in the absence of direct "smoking gun" evidence, a horizontal price-fixing agreement may be inferred on the basis of conscious parallelism, when such interdependent conduct is accompanied by circumstantial evidence and plus factors such as defendants' use of facilitating practices. *See, e.g.*, Interstate Circuit, Inc. v. United States, 306 U.S. 208, 226–27, 83 L. Ed. 610, 59 S. Ct. 467 (1939); Ambook Enters. v. Time Inc., 612 F.2d 604, 614–18 (2d Cir.1979). Information exchange is an example of a facilitating practice that can help support an inference of a price-fixing agreement.

There is a closely related but analytically distinct type of claim, also based on § 1 of the Sherman Act, where the violation lies in the information exchange itself—as opposed to merely using the information exchange as evidence upon which to infer a price-fixing agreement. This exchange of information is not illegal *per se*, but can be found unlawful under a rule of reason analysis. . . . The state of the law on this issue was not always so clear . . . . . In *United States v. Container Corp. of America*, the Supreme Court held that information exchange itself could constitute a § 1 violation, upholding the sufficiency of a complaint charging "an exchange of price information but no agreement to adhere to a price schedule." 393 U.S. 333, 334, 89 S. Ct. 510, 21 L. Ed. 2d 526 (1969). The Court found that under the market conditions present in that case, and in light of the nature of the information disseminated, the data exchange caused a stabilization of prices and thus had an anticompetitive effect on the market for corrugated containers. *See id.* 393 U.S. at 337. Unclear in the wake of Container Corp. was whether such exchanges were *per se* unlawful or subject to a rule of reason. The Court used some of the language of the Court's *per se* jurisprudence, yet conducted a market analysis that suggested a rule of reason. *See id.* 393 U.S. at 336–38.

The Supreme Court resolved the confusion in *United States v. Citizens & Southern National Bank*, clarifying that "the dissemination of price information is not itself a *per se* violation of the Sherman Act." 422 U.S. 86, 113, 95 S. Ct. 2099, 45 L. Ed. 2d 41 (1975). In *United States v. United States Gypsum Co.*, the Court explained its reasoning: "The exchange of price data and other information among competitors does not invariably have anticompetitive effects; indeed such practices can in certain circumstances increase economic efficiency and render markets more, rather than less, competitive." 438 U.S. 422, 441 n. 16, 98 S. Ct. 2864, 57 L. Ed. 2d 854 (1978). The Court then set out the basic framework for the rule of reason inquiry in this context: "A number of factors including most prominently the structure of the industry involved and the nature of the information exchanged are generally considered in divining the procompetitive or anticompetitive effects of this type of interseller communication." *Id.*

As plaintiff does not allege an actual agreement among defendants to fix salaries, we analyze plaintiff's complaint solely as to whether it alleges unlawful information exchange pursuant to this rule of reason.

III.   Market Power

A.   The Relevant Market

. . . Plaintiff argues that the relevant market in this case is the market for "the services of experienced, salaried, non-union, managerial, professional and technical (MPT) employees in the oil and petrochemical industry, in the continental United States and various submarkets thereof." If the market is defined in this way, defendants would have a substantial market share of 80–90%. If the market cannot be limited in this way, defendants' percentage market share would drop substantially. . . .

[The district court rejected the plaintiff's proposed market, on the grounds that it was both over-inclusive (because it had failed to explain why a variety of professional jobs in the oil industry were interchangeable with one another) and under-inclusive (because it was skeptical about the existence of industry-specific expertise). The court of appeals disagreed on both counts. It agreed with plaintiffs that the proper focus was on the commonality and interchangeability of the buyers, not the sellers, and that employees indeed did acquire industry-specific expertise.]

In sum, plaintiff's complaint alleges a plausible product market. The district court erred by requiring that the different MPT jobs be interchangeable with one another, by rejecting plaintiff's allegation about industry-specific experience on a Rule 12(b)(6) motion to dismiss, and by failing to consider allegations about industry recognition.

B. Anticompetitive Effect As an Indication of Market Power

Plaintiff's alleged product market would support the 80–90% market share figure for defendants. Market power defined as a percentage market share, however, is not the only way to demonstrate defendants' ability to depress salaries. If a plaintiff can show that a defendant's conduct exerted an actual adverse effect on competition, this is a strong indicator of market power. In fact, this arguably is more direct evidence of market power than calculations of elusive market share figures.

In this Circuit, a threshold showing of market share is not a prerequisite for bringing a § 1 claim. If, for example, the plaintiff in this case could prove that (1) defendants engaged in information exchanges that would be deemed anticompetitive under *Gypsum* and (2) such activities did in fact have an anticompetitive effect on the market for MPT labor in the oil and petrochemical industry, we would not deny relief on the basis of market share figures. On remand, therefore, the court should consider whether plaintiff has demonstrated anticompetitive effects as part of the court's assessment of defendants' market power.

Defendants mistake this approach for the "quick look" or "truncated" rule of reason inquiry that the Supreme Court has endorsed in certain contexts. Defendants are correct to assert that in *California Dental Ass'n v. FTC* the Supreme Court limited the use of the "quick look" to cases in which the probable anticompetitive effects of the alleged conduct would be "intuitively obvious" and "easily ... ascertained" with "even a rudimentary understanding of economics." 526 U.S. 756, 759, 770, 119 S. Ct. 1604, 143 L. Ed. 2d 935 (1999).... The alleged conduct in this case—the exchange of information—is not so inherently or intuitively anticompetitive. The Supreme Court has said as much and specifically prescribed a full rule of reason. *See Gypsum*, 438 U.S. at 441 n.16.... We do not suggest that the district court can avoid conducting a full analysis of the pro-and anticompetitive characteristics of the arrangement in this case.

The use of anticompetitive effects to demonstrate market power, however, is not limited to "quick look" or "truncated" rule of reason cases. This Court's precedents discussed above were not "quick look" cases; they merely accepted alternative ways of demonstrating market power. The question of whether plaintiff has alleged adverse effects on competition and antitrust injury sufficient to survive a Rule 12(b)(6) motion is addressed infra Part VI.

IV. Susceptibility of the Market

The Supreme Court in *Gypsum* explained that one of the two "most prominent[]" factors in the rule of reason analysis of a data exchange is "the structure of the industry involved." 438 U.S. at 441 n.16. Therefore, once the relevant market is defined, a court must analyze the structure of that market to determine whether it is "susceptible to the exercise of market power through tacit coordination." As the district court explained, "susceptible markets tend to be highly concentrated—that is, oligopolistic—and to have fungible products subject to inelastic demand." These factors are addressed in turn.

A. Concentration

Generally speaking, the possibility of anticompetitive collusive practices is most realistic in concentrated industries. If the relevant market in this case is defined as the plaintiff contends, the defendants would control collectively a 80–90% market share. While this is an extremely high market share by any measure, the district court contends that the alleged market "is not, as plaintiff contends, so clearly oligopolistic." The district court points out that there are fourteen defendants in this case, and that this is not a concentrated market under the Department of Justice Merger Guidelines. That the market would not be deemed highly concentrated by this measure, however, does not preclude the possibility of collusive activity. . . .

The Supreme Court has found that data exchange can be unlawful despite a relatively large number of sellers. In *Container Corp.*, the Court used the oft-cited language that the industry was "dominated by relatively few sellers." 393 U.S. at 337. But in fact, the defendants in *Container Corp.* were eighteen firms controlling 90% of the market, defined as the sale of cardboard cartons in the Southeast. Id. 393 U.S. at 342 (Marshall, J., dissenting). The Court nonetheless found the market sufficiently concentrated to support the finding of a violation. Id. 393 U.S. at 334–38. It is fairly clear that the reason the Court reached its holding despite the multiplicity of sellers was the specific anticompetitive characteristics of the information exchange. Given that the market concentration in this case is not radically different from that in *Container Corp.*, and given that concentration is part of a rule of reason inquiry that also emphasizes the nature of the information exchanged, we do not think that fourteen companies sharing an 80–90% market share is so unconcentrated as to warrant a Rule 12(b)(6) dismissal where the nature of the exchanges appears anticompetitive. We also find it unsurprising that data exchange cases may involve a number of participants that begins to push the boundaries of oligopoly. These players are most in need of such data exchange arrangements in order to facilitate price coordination; a very small handful of firms in a more highly concentrated market may be less likely to require the kind of sophisticated data dissemination alleged in this case.

B. Fungibility

The district court also asserted that "even if the proposed market were oligopolistic, plaintiff still could not establish its susceptibility to the exercise of market power through tacit coordination. The 'products' in her proposed market are, as discussed above, far from fungible." The district court apparently refers to its previous discussion of interchangeability, wherein it argued that the various types of jobs included in the MPT category are vastly different from one another.

It is important to bear in mind the context in which the fungibility question arises. The inquiry is one part of the question of whether the market is susceptible to the exercise of market power though tacit coordination. Fungibility is relevant on this point because it is less realistic for a cartel to establish and police a price conspiracy where it is difficult to compare the products being sold. In contrast, "fungible products facilitate coordination of pricing in a concentrated industry because it is easier to determine and monitor a consensus on some competitive variable." Therefore, fungibility plays a significant role in evaluating the anticompetitive potential of an information exchange.

The question in this case is whether jobs at the various oil and petrochemical companies were comparable, or fungible enough so that the defendants could have used the exchanged information as part of a tacit conspiracy to depress salaries. . . .

As an initial matter, the district court's discussion about the clear differences among the various types of MPT jobs is inapposite. Plaintiff alleges that the information exchanged by defendants related to specific job categories—not to MPT employment in general. Therefore, the fact that a job as an attorney and one as a geologist are not comparable does not bear on the ability of defendants to coordinate salaries. Rather, the relevant question is whether jobs *within* each category are fungible enough across the oil and petrochemical industry to allow for such coordination.

One might argue that the jobs still are not fungible—even within each category of MPT employee. Varied jobs in a complex industry are far less fungible than, say, a product such as corrugated containers. Services generally tend not to be fungible or susceptible to standardization, and it is unlikely that these fourteen different companies would have positions with job descriptions that precisely match one another. Even this argument, however, is complicated by the specific facts of this case, coupled with the policy rationale behind the fungibility inquiry.

Plaintiff's complaint alleges in detail the sophisticated techniques defendants used to "achieve a common denominator" with respect to the compensation paid to their MPT employees. Defendants developed the Job Match Survey because they "realized it was not functionally efficient simply to know what each others' employees were being paid unless they were able to horizontally match the various job classifications." The survey revolved around certain benchmark jobs provided by Chevron. The defendants would submit detailed information relating to the jobs most nearly comparable to the benchmark jobs so that they could be matched. "A 'match' is defined as a similar job in a similar organization whose combined reporting functions and scope adjustments are not more than two survey salary grades above or below the benchmarked job." Plaintiff alleges that, during the relevant time period, Exxon was able to match 70–80% of its jobs to the 155 Chevron benchmark positions. Furthermore, because not all jobs could be matched precisely, the defendants agreed upon certain "off-sets" reflecting the specific differences between jobs as a percentage figure. For purposes of the survey, each grade level was assumed to have a salary difference of 14% at its midpoint. The offset factor assigned to each job was thus stated as a fraction of 14%—a positive fraction for jobs with greater responsibilities than the Chevron benchmark job and a negative fraction for jobs with lesser responsibilities. Defendants even devised a formula to enhance the comparability of non-cash benefits afforded to MPT employees in their Long Term Incentive Survey.

Plaintiff is thus on solid ground when she argues that defendants "made their own employees' positions 'fungible' for comparison purposes with those of their competitors." The jobs in question may not be inherently fungible, but since the purpose of the fungibility inquiry is to test whether defendants would be able to compare the positions for coordination purposes, the sophisticated techniques employed by defendants to account for the differences among jobs are extremely telling.

C. Inelastic Demand

Concluding its discussion of the susceptibility of the market to tacit coordination, the district court stated that "plaintiff has pleaded no facts tending to establish that the demand for these 'products' is inelastic." We disagree. This part of the inquiry, easily confused with the cross-elasticity and interchangeability analysis that is used to define the relevant market, traditionally asks whether demand is inelastic because "buyers place orders only for immediate, short-run needs." In other words, the question is whether it is economically feasible for buyers to abstain from purchasing the product for some period of time.

Here again, we reverse the equation in the context of an oligopsony. Where market power is exercised by buyers, it is the elasticity of the sellers' *supply* that is at issue. Sellers' supply could be elastic if, for example, they have "the option of withholding some output from the market in hopes of higher prices in future years." If, however, the goods are perishable, short-run supply may be quite inelastic. In this case, the supply at issue is the labor of the MPT employees. "Labor is an extremely perishable commodity—an hour not worked today can never be recovered." As a result, "collusion among employers can drive the wage down to the individual's reservation wage." As labor is a classic example of inelastic supply flow, it is unclear what additional facts plaintiffs would have to allege with regard to this aspect of the inquiry.

In sum, the pleadings support the contention that the market was susceptible to tacit coordination by the defendant companies: The market is sufficiently concentrated under *Container Corp.*; the defendants have in effect manufactured a form of fungibility through sophisticated comparison techniques; and the supply of labor has an inherently inelastic quality.

V. The Nature of the Information Exchanged

Alongside the "structure of the industry involved," the other major factor for courts to consider in a data exchange case is the "nature of the information exchanged." There are certain well-established criteria used to help ascertain the anticompetitive potential of information exchanges. As part of the analysis, a court should consider, "broadly speaking, whether it was of the sort in *American Column & Lumber Co. v. United States* . . . or of that in *Maple Flooring Manufacturers Ass'n v. United States.*" Applying the relevant criteria reveals anticompetitive potential in this case.

The first factor to consider is the time frame of the data. The Supreme Court has made clear that "exchanges of current price information, of course, have the greatest potential for generating anti-competitive effects and although not *per se* unlawful have consistently been held to violate the Sherman Act." The exchange of past price data is greatly preferred because current data have greater potential to affect future prices and facilitate price conspiracies. By the same reasoning, exchanges of future price information are considered especially anticompetitive.

Plaintiff's complaint alleges that defendants exchanged past and current salary information, as well as future salary budget information. It claims that there has been an:

> exchange among Defendants of massive amounts of extremely detailed information concerning job classifications, salaries, bonuses, and benefits paid, or to be paid, to categories of employees within the different job classifications; starting salaries of new employees; "signing bonuses"; relocation expenses, stock options; and related information.... Updated information on salaries is exchanged in oral and written communications throughout the year.

Most prominently, the Job Family Survey coordinated by Exxon gathered information regarding the salaries paid for specific types of work to employees with particular experience levels and academic backgrounds. This survey sought and obtained current data on the actual compensation paid by defendants to employees in various "job families." The information gathered was distributed to the survey participants several times a year. Meanwhile, the Starting Salary Survey gathered information from the Six Majors measuring starting salaries of college graduates entering MPT positions. Defendants also attended meetings at least three times per year at which various types of salary information were discussed. Among the information exchanged at these meetings [were] current and future increases in Defendants' salary budgets.

In addition to the time frame, another factor courts look to is the specificity of the information. Price exchanges that identify particular parties, transactions, and prices are seen as potentially anticompetitive because they may be used to police a secret or tacit conspiracy to stabilize prices. Courts prefer that information be aggregated in the form of industry averages, thus avoiding transactional specificity.

Two aspects of the information exchange at issue are problematic in this regard. First, although the salary information was aggregated and distributed by a third-party consulting firm, companies participating in the

Job Family Survey received compensation data broken down to subsets consisting of as few as three competitors. Plaintiff alleges that these periodically updated data sets were used by each defendant to determine whether the announced budgets of its competitors had in fact been implemented so that each could consider what adjustments should be made to coordinate salaries.... This practice, plaintiff argues on appeal, made deviations from previously announced salary levels easily and quickly detectable. Second, at their meetings defendants discussed current and future salary budgets, including "company-specific" information, such that all participants learn where each other participant is going with its salary budget for the upcoming year or, if a participant's salary year had only recently begun, for that new year.

Another important factor to consider in evaluating an information exchange is whether the data are made publicly available. Public dissemination is a primary way for data exchange to realize its procompetitive potential. For example, in the traditional oligopoly (seller-side) context, access to information may better equip buyers to compare products, rendering the market more efficient while diminishing the anticompetitive effects of the exchange. A court is therefore more likely to approve a data exchange where the information is made public.

In the instant case, dissemination of the information to the employees could have helped mitigate any anticompetitive effects of the exchange and possibly enhanced market efficiency by making employees more sensitive to salary increases. No such dissemination occurred, however. The information was not disclosed to the public nor to the employees whose salaries were the subject of the exchange. Plaintiff alleges that the confidential treatment of the information exchanged impedes the ability of employees to bargain intelligently and competitively with the members of the information exchange.

A final troubling aspect of the arrangement at issue is the fact that the defendants allegedly participated in frequent meetings to discuss the salary information, accompanied by assurances that the participants would primarily use the exchanged data in setting their MPT salaries. Meetings, of course, are not inherently unlawful but in this context they have the potential to enhance the anticompetitive effects and "likelihood of ... uniformity" caused by information exchange. Meanwhile, the frequency of the meetings is itself problematic for the same reason that the exchange of current price data is suspect: It tends to facilitate the policing of price conspiracies.

In sum, the "nature of the information exchanged" weighs against the motion to dismiss. The characteristics of the data exchange in this case are precisely those that arouse suspicion of anticompetitive activity under the rule of reason.

VI. Effect on Competition and Antitrust Injury

An antitrust plaintiff must allege not only cognizable harm to herself, but an adverse effect on competition market-wide. In the traditional oligopoly case, horizontal coordination may inflate prices to supracompetitive levels. In an oligopsony, the risk is that buyers will collude to depress prices, causing harm to sellers. However, information exchange is not always anticompetitive and can enhance competition by making competitors more sensitive to each other's price changes, enhancing rivalry among them.

The complaint in this case, however, points to anticompetitive effects the exchanges have had on MPT salaries market-wide, most particularly with respect to Exxon. Plaintiff specifically alleges that salary levels across the integrated oil and petrochemical industry have been artificially depressed because the information exchange has reduced competitive incentives. Moreover, Exxon has supposedly used the information to reduce its competitive factor from 6.5% in 1991 to 0% in 1995, to reduce its salaries 4.1% between 1987 and 1994 in comparison to the Six Majors, and to reduce its salary index in relation to the competition from 110.7% in 1987 to 107.0% in 1993. In her claim for relief, plaintiff again alleges that she received compensation ''materially below'' what she would have received in an ''uncontaminated marketplace.''

The district court found that the pleadings support, if anything, an inference that ''each defendant oil company used the information exchanged to stake out an optimal competitive level for its MPT salaries.'' The district court interprets the decrease in the competitive factor as ''indicating that Exxon was *raising* its salaries to meet the competition.'' *Id.* The court concludes that ''raising salary levels to meet the competition and attract highly qualified employees is certainly not evidence of a conspiracy to restrain trade.'' *Id.* We read the complaint differently. The fact that Exxon increased its salaries each year would not defeat an allegation that those increases were lower than they would have been but for a conspiracy to stabilize prices. We understand the complaint as alleging a market where Exxon's salaries and those of the Six Majors continue to increase, but where the difference grows gradually smaller—a portrait of market stabilization.

Plaintiff further claims that information exchanged at the meetings among defendants and in the ''Advancement Guides'' created by defendants were used by Exxon ''to 'slow down' its employee advancement rates, reduce the payments made to the uppermost members of some of its employee classifications, and lower the top classification levels for most of its job families.'' According to the complaint, ''the result has slowed the advancement rate at Exxon by two to eight years.''

In all, plaintiff alleges that with Exxon's total salary budget at $800 million, the conduct described in the complaint had the effect of lowering Exxon's MPT salaries by a total of $20 million per year. Whether this is so is a question of fact that cannot be resolved on this Rule 12(b)(6) motion. Plaintiff will have to make a substantial presentation of evidence to support her claim that salaries would have been higher without the information exchange. Furthermore, we agree with plaintiff that the economic effects of the arrangement with respect to the other defendants is an appropriate matter for discovery.

CONCLUSION

For the reasons stated, we vacate the district court's grant of defendants' Rule 12(b)(6) motion to dismiss and remand for proceedings consistent with this opinion.

Blomkest Fertilizer, Inc. v. Potash Corp. of Sask., Inc.

United States Court of Appeals, Eighth Circuit (en banc), 2000.
203 F.3d 1028.

■ BEAM, CIRCUIT JUDGE. A certified class of potash consumers appeals the district court's grant of summary judgment in favor of defendants (collectively "the producers") in this action for conspiracy in restraint of trade under section 1 of the Sherman Act. We affirm.

I. BACKGROUND

This case involves the production and sale of potash, a mineral essential to plant growth and therefore used in fertilizer. The certified class includes all of those persons who directly purchased potash from one of the producers between April 1987 and July 1994. The class named six Canadian potash companies and two American companies.

Both parties agree that the North American potash industry is an oligopoly. Prices in an oligopolistic market tend to be higher than those in purely competitive markets, and will fluctuate independently of supply and demand. Furthermore, price uniformity is normal in a market with few sellers and homogeneous products. This is because all producers in an oligopoly must charge roughly the same price or risk losing market share. The Canadian province of Saskatchewan is the source of most potash consumed in the United States. The province founded defendant Potash Corporation of Saskatchewan (PCS), which holds thirty-eight percent of the North American potash production capacity. As a governmental company, PCS had no mandate to maximize profits and was not accountable to private owners. Instead, the company was primarily concerned with maintaining employment and generating money for the local economy. Not surprisingly, PCS suffered huge losses as it mined potash in quantities that far outstripped global demand. These policies impacted the entire potash industry: during the 1980s, the price of potash fell to an historic low. In 1986, Saskatchewan voters elected a provincial government which had promised to privatize PCS. New management was appointed to PCS after the elections. Thereafter, PCS significantly reduced its output and raised its price.

Also in 1986, New Mexico Potash Corporation (NMPC) and another American potash producer (who is not a named defendant) filed a complaint with the United States Department of Commerce. Frustrated with low potash prices, the petitioners alleged that Canadian producers had been dumping their product in the United States at prices below fair market value. In 1987, the Department issued a preliminary determination that the Canadian producers were dumping potash and ordered the companies to post bonds on all exports to the United States. These bonds were set according to each firm's calculated "dumping margin." Eventually, the Department negotiated a Suspension Agreement with each of the Canadian producers. The agreement raised the price of Canadian potash in the United States by setting a minimum price at which each Canadian producer could sell in the United States. That agreement remains in effect today. When the Canadian producers entered into the Suspension Agreement, PCS announced that it was raising its prices by eighteen dollars per ton. Other producers quickly followed suit. The price of potash has remained markedly higher after the Suspension Agreement, although prices have slowly but steadily declined for the most part since the agreement was signed by the producers on January 8, 1988.

The class alleges that between April 1987 and July 1994 the producers colluded to increase the price of potash. The producers, in turn, maintain that the price increase was the product of the interdependent nature of the industry and its reaction to the privatization of PCS and the Suspension Agreement. The district court granted the producers' motions for summary judgment and the class appeals.

II. DISCUSSION

The class asserts that if we affirm the district court, we will "stand alone in holding that circumstantial evidence, even if overwhelming, cannot be used to defeat a summary judgment motion in anti-trust cases." We make no such legal history here, however, because the class's proffered evidence, far from overwhelming, fails to establish the elements of a prima facie case.

[The court reviewed the familiar test for finding an agreement covered by section 1, stating that the "plaintiffs must present evidence that 'tends to exclude the possibility of independent action' by the defendants."] Applied in this case, the standard requires that if it is as reasonable to infer from the evidence a price-fixing conspiracy as it is to infer permissible activity, then the plaintiffs' claim, without more, fails on summary judgment.

The class's price-fixing claim is based on a theory of conscious parallelism. Conscious parallelism is the process "not in itself unlawful, by which firms in a concentrated market might in effect share monopoly power, setting their prices at a profit-maximizing, supracompetitive level by recognizing their shared economic interests." Brooke Group Ltd. v. Brown & Williamson Tobacco Corp., 509 U.S. 209, 227, 125 L. Ed. 2d 168, 113 S. Ct. 2578 (1993). The class points out that the producers' prices were roughly equivalent during the alleged conspiracy, despite differing production costs. It further points out that price changes by one producer were quickly met by the others. This establishes only that the producers consciously paralleled each other's prices.

Evidence that a business consciously met the pricing of its competitors does not prove a violation of the antitrust laws. See Theatre Enter., Inc. v. Paramount Film Distrib. Corp., 346 U.S. 537, 540–41, 98 L. Ed. 273, 74 S. Ct. 257 (1954). Particularly when the product in question is fungible, as potash is, courts have noted that parallel pricing lacks probative significance. An agreement is properly inferred from conscious parallelism only when certain "plus factors" exist. A plus factor refers to " 'the additional facts or factors required to be proved as a prerequisite to finding that parallel [price] action amounts to a conspiracy.' "

A plaintiff has the burden to present evidence of consciously paralleled pricing *supplemented with* one or more plus factors. However, even if a plaintiff carries its initial burden, a court must still find, based upon all the evidence before it, that the plaintiff's evidence tends to exclude the possibility of independent action. As noted, the class identified parallel pricing. The class also asserts that it has established the existence of three plus factors: (1) interfirm communications between the producers; (2) the producers's acts against self-interest; and (3) econometric models which purport to prove that the price of potash would have been substantially lower in the absence of collusion. The evidence underlying these assertions, however, does not bear the weight the class places upon it.

A.   Interfirm Communications

The class alleges a high level of interfirm communications between the producers and complains most vociferously about price verification information. Courts have held that a high level of communications among competitors can constitute a plus factor which, when combined with parallel behavior, supports an inference of conspiracy. However, the evidence presented by the class here is far too ambiguous to support such an inference. Considering the proof as a whole, the evidence of interfirm communications does not tend to exclude the possibility of independent action, as required under *Monsanto* and *Matsushita*, since other significant events strongly suggest independent behavior. The fundamental difficulty with the class's argument regarding price verifications is that it assumes a conspiracy first, and then sets out to "prove" it. However, a litigant may not proceed by first assuming a conspiracy and then explaining the evidence accordingly.

The class's evidence shows that the communications include meetings at trade shows and conventions, price verification calls, discussions regarding a Canadian potash export association, and the like. Taking the class's evidence as true, roughly three dozen price verifications occurred between employees, including high-level sales employees, of different companies, over at least a seven-year period. In large part, these contacts involved the verification of prices the companies had already charged on particular sales. The impotence of this circumstantial evidence is that it bears no relationship to the price increases most in question because it lacks the logical link necessary to infer such a relationship.

The class alleges that the price-fixing conspiracy began at least as early as April, 1987. In 1987, the price for potash was at historically low levels, such that producers were losing millions of dollars. Then, a sudden and dramatic increase in price by PCS occurred on September 4, 1987, and approximately a week later the remaining producers followed suit. The class argues that the large and parallel price increases together with nearly simultaneous price verifications create an inference sufficient to survive summary judgment.

The problem with this theory, as indicated, is that the price verification communications only concerned charges on particular completed sales, not future market prices. There is no evidence to support the inference that the verifications had an impact on price increases. The only evidence is that prices were possibly cut as a result. "To survive summary judgment, there must be evidence that the exchanges of information had an impact on pricing decisions." There is no evidence here that price increases resulted from any price verification or any specific communication of any kind. *Subsequent* price verification evidence on particular sales cannot support a conspiracy for the setting of a broad market price on September 4, 1987.

Even if we were to find the price verification evidence relevant, when considered with all the facts, it does not tend to exclude the possibility of independent action. To the contrary, there is strong evidence of independent action. Just before and concurrent with the suspect price increases, the following occurred: the price of potash was at historic lows and the producers were losing millions; potash companies in the United States complained to the United States Department of Commerce that the Canadian producers were dumping potash at well-below market value; the Department of Commerce made a preliminary determination that the Canadian producers were dumping and required expensive bonds for all imports; the industry leader, the government-founded PCS, hired new management and began privatization with the goal of becoming profitable; legislation was passed in the province of Saskatchewan—the source of nearly all United States potash—that provided for the setting and prorating of potash production; potash producers reached a Suspension Agreement with the Department of Commerce that set price floors for potash; and PCS was finally privatized and significantly reduced its output. In the face of these circumstances and with the price leadership of PCS in this oligopolistic industry, it would have been ridiculous for the remaining companies to not also raise their prices in a parallel fashion. Thus, we find the class's weak circumstantial evidence that the dramatic increases were the result of a price-fixing agreement is not sufficient to survive summary judgment.

This leaves only the question whether there is sufficient evidence to support an agreement to stabilize and maintain prices in violation of section 1 of the Sherman Act. The class's evidence of an agreement to maintain the price of potash at an artificially high level after the initial price increases is again the parallel pricing and price verifications. Parallel pricing has been conceded, leaving the burden once again on the verifications. Common sense dictates that a conspiracy to fix a price would involve one company communicating with another company *before* the price quotation to the customer. Here, however, the class's evidence consists solely of communications to verify a price on a *completed* sale. The price verifications relied upon were sporadic and testimony suggests that price verifications were not always given. The fact that there were several dozen communications is not so significant considering the communications occurred over at least a seven-year period in which there would have been tens of thousands of transactions. Furthermore, one would expect companies to verify prices considering that this is an oligopolistic industry and accounts are often very large. We find the evidence falls far short of excluding the possibility of independent action.

In re Baby Food, 166 F.3d 112, aptly illustrates why the communications complained about here are inadequate to exclude the possibility of independent action by the producers. The defendants, nationally prominent corporations with ninety-eight percent of the baby food business, were Gerber, H.J. Heinz, and Beech–Nut. It is true that the numerous intercompany pricing communications found by the Third Circuit to be *insufficient* to support a section 1 violation were characterized in one part of the opinion as price discussions among low-level employees. However, deposition testimony in that case revealed that district sales employees and district sales managers of Heinz were required to submit competitive activity reports to their superiors concerning baby food sales from information they picked up from competitor sales representatives. This same line of testimony revealed that supervising managers for Heinz informed district managers "on a regular basis before any announcement to the trade as to when Heinz's competitors were going to increase [their] wholesale list prices." The president of Beech–Nut "testified that it was [Beech–Nut's] policy for sales representatives to gather *and report* pricing information of [Beech–Nut's] competitors." Indeed, the In re Baby Food case is replete with evidence that pricing information was systematically obtained and directed to high-level executives of Gerber (including Gerber's vice president of sales), Beech–Nut and Heinz, the principal national competitors in the baby food industry.

The evidence in the case shows that a carefully conceived and effective system of price information gathering for the benefit of corporate executives was at all relevant times alive and well in the baby food industry. Notwithstanding communications that far surpassed any information exchanges established in this case, the Third Circuit applied *Matsushita* and granted summary judgment to the defendants, in large part because there was no evidence that the exchanges of information had an impact on pricing decisions. As earlier stated, there likewise is absolutely no such evidence in this litigation, only speculation.

The class directs our attention to In re Brand Name Prescription Drugs Antitrust Litigation, 123 F.3d 599, 614 (7th Cir.), cert. denied, 118 S. Ct. 1178 (1998), in which the plaintiffs, like the class, searched through an enormous quantity of discovery material and culled out a number of suspicious interfirm communications. The court in Brand Name described these documents produced as "smoking guns." By contrast, the communications here are facially innocent contacts which are, at most, ambiguous on the question of whether the producers schemed to set prices.

The class argues that a memorandum issued by Canpotex, a lawful Canadian cartel that sets prices for potash sold outside of the United States, is the class's "smoking gun." This memorandum, dated January 8, 1988, and directed to its "agents and offices" reads in pertinent part:

> FYI Canadian potash producers have reached agreement with the United States Department of Commerce and all dumping action has been suspended for minimum 5 years. It is rumoured that the USD 35.00 per metric ton increase posted by Canadian producers in 1987 to cover possible tariff payments to the U.S. Govt will be refunded in full or part. In the meantime new price lists are being issued on Monday Jan. 11 at:
>
> Standard Grade USD 80.00
>
> Coarse Grade USD 84.00
>
> Granular Grade USD 86.00

The class asserts that this memorandum establishes an agreement to fix prices. The class argues that the people who received the January 8, 1988, memorandum were all high-ranking officials in the producers' companies who were on the Board of Directors of Canpotex, and therefore, the memorandum is evidence that tends to exclude an inference that the producers acted independently.

The magistrate judge disagreed that this memorandum was sufficient evidence to exclude the possibility that the producers acted independently. The magistrate judge first noted that PCS had also announced the same prices in a telex to its customers on January 8, 1988, and thus the possibility that Canpotex learned of the price list from a customer of PCS could not be excluded. Further, the magistrate judge discovered that while most of the Canadian defendants had matched the prices in the memorandum by January 22, 1988, they did not uniformly issue price lists matching those prices on January 11, 1988, and one producer, Kalium, did not match those prices at all. However, as the magistrate judge pointed out, "evidence that the alleged conspirators were aware of each other's prices, before announcing their own prices, 'is nothing more than a restatement of conscious parallelism, 'which is not enough to show an antitrust conspiracy.' "

We agree with the magistrate judge's finding that this document was not sufficient evidence to exclude an inference that the producers acted independently. First, the memorandum was written by R.J. Ford and directed to "agents and offices." It is not at all clear who this memorandum was sent to or received by, and a thorough review of the appellants' voluminous joint appendix has not clarified this point. Dozens of these high-ranking officials were deposed during pretrial discovery, and according to the documents submitted by the class in its joint appendix, only one person, Dave Benusa, was asked if he received "any document dated the

8th of January 1988 concerning pricing." Benusa was manager of marketing for Cominco American in 1988. Benusa stated in his deposition that he did not receive any document dated January 8, 1988, concerning pricing. The class apparently did not depose the author of the memorandum, R.J. Ford, nor did they make any further attempt that we can find to identify who received this "smoking gun" piece of evidence. Another document produced by Canpotex, an inter-office memorandum dated September 8, 1993, is actually directed to "Members of the Board of Directors of Canpotex Limited." We assume that had the January 8, 1988, memorandum been intended for the members of the board of directors, it likewise would have so stated.

Furthermore, even if, as the class asserts, the memorandum had been received by high-ranking officials in the producers' companies, we agree with the magistrate judge's reasoning that the memorandum does not assist the class in proving the existence of a conspiracy. As the magistrate judge pointed out, the producers did not uniformly increase prices to match the memorandum on January 11, 1988, and furthermore, one producer, Kalium, did not match the memorandum price at all. The fact that most of the producers did increase prices to match the PCS price increase of January 11, 1988, is not surprising in a market where conscious parallelism is the norm. Despite submitting a five-volume joint appendix, the class has failed to present evidence about this memorandum which tends to exclude the possibility of independent action by the producers. As it turns out, the "smoke" from this gun is barely, if at all, discernible.

Finally, the class asserts that the producers signaled pricing intentions to each other through advance price announcements and price lists. The Supreme Court has held, however, that "the dissemination of price information is not itself a *per se* violation of the Sherman Act." United States v. Citizens & S. Nat'l Bank, 422 U.S. 86, 113, 45 L. Ed. 2d 41, 95 S. Ct. 2099 (1975).

As we noted at the outset, the class may not proceed by first assuming a conspiracy and then setting out to prove it. If the class were to present independent evidence tending to exclude an inference that the producers acted independently, then, and only then, could it use these communications for whatever additional evidence of conspiracy they may provide. As the record stands, we find these contacts far too ambiguous to defeat summary judgment.

B. Actions Against Self-interest

Evidence that defendants have acted against their economic interest can also constitute a plus factor. However, where there is an independent business justification for the defendants' behavior, no inference of conspiracy can be drawn.

The only evidence of actions against interest that the class has identified is the producers' uniform participation in the Suspension Agreement. The class argues that those producers with low dumping margins could have undercut other producers' prices and gained market share while still maintaining prices at profitable levels. Instead, the low tariff producers joined the Suspension Agreement. The class further posits that NMPC's failure to object to the agreement was an action against self-interest.

In response, the producers point out that Department of Commerce investigations are unpredictable, and participation in the agreement reduced uncertainty. Furthermore, without the Suspension Agreement, even low tariff producers would have been required to post substantial bonds which would have caused considerable capital drain on corporate coffers. Like the Canadian producers, NMPC was uncertain about the ultimate outcome of the Department of Commerce's investigation. Under the Suspension Agreement, NMPC obtained certainty and a higher price for potash sold in the American market. This is the relief NMPC initially sought, and it is unsurprising that NMPC would not oppose such an outcome.

The class has thus failed to carry its burden to rebut the producers' independent business justification for their actions. There is nothing in this record that contradicts the conclusion that ending the dumping investigation with a settlement that required unreasonably low potash prices to rise was a legitimate business decision for the low tariff producers. They benefited from increased revenues, while avoiding the cost of litigation and the risk of penalties. This cannot be construed as an act against self-interest.

C.   Expert Testimony

Finally, the class argues that its expert's econometric model provided crucial confirmation that the prevailing potash prices during the alleged conspiracy were above those expected in the absence of collusion. While their expert concedes that the prices have primarily steadily decreased since January 8, 1988, he asserts that prices would have been much lower absent an agreement to fix prices. We need not decide whether such evidence, in a proper case, could constitute a plus factor, because we find the report in this case is not probative of collusion.

The class's expert evidence is lacking in two crucial respects. First, the expert admits that his model fails to take into account the dramatic events of 1986. In his deposition, the class's expert confirmed that his model considers neither the privatization of PCS nor the anti-dumping proceedings. It is beyond dispute that even without collusion, those events would have led to higher potash prices. A model that does no more than report that prices did, indeed, rise after these events tells us nothing about the existence of industry collusion.

A second flaw in the expert's report, as the magistrate judge noted, is that it relies almost exclusively on evidence (such as the producers' common membership in trade associations and their publication of price lists to customers) that is not probative of collusion as a matter of law. Under Federal Rule of Evidence 703, the facts underlying an expert's opinion need not be admissible if they are "of a type reasonably relied upon by experts in a particular field." The rule, however, contemplates that there will be sufficient facts already in evidence or disclosed by the witness as a result of his or her investigation to take such expert opinion testimony out of the realm of guesswork and speculation. In this case, the expert's model is fundamentally unreliable because of his heavy (if not exclusive) reliance on evidence that is not probative of conspiracy, coupled with his failure to consider significant external forces that served to raise the price of potash.

III.   CONCLUSION

We have carefully considered each of the class's other arguments and find them to be without merit. The class has failed to present evidence of collusion sufficient to create a genuine issue of material fact. The producers are therefore entitled to summary judgment. For the foregoing reasons, the decision of the district court is affirmed.

■ JOHN R. GIBSON, Circuit Judge, dissenting, with whom Heaney, McMillian, Richard S. Arnold, and Murphy, Circuit Judges, join.

I dissent.

The Court today rejects circumstantial evidence of conspiracy and requires direct evidence to withstand summary judgment in an antitrust case. The court's requirement of direct evidence is contrary to Monsanto v. Spray–Rite Service Corp., 465 U.S. 752, 768, 79 L. Ed. 2d 775, 104 S. Ct. 1464 (1984), which only required "direct or circumstantial evidence that reasonably tends to prove ... a conscious commitment to a common scheme designed to achieve an unlawful objective." Because conspirators cannot be relied upon either to confess or to preserve signed agreements memorializing their conspiracies, the court's requirement for direct evidence will substantially eliminate antitrust conspiracy as a ground for recovery in our circuit.

The potash industry is an oligopoly in which the producers ended a price war and raised prices dramatically. The question is whether the class has shown that the new prices resulted from an agreement among the producers to raise and stabilize prices, rather than from independent reactions to market conditions combined with actions of the United States and Canadian governments. I believe that the class has satisfied the existing standards for circumstantial proof that the prices resulted from collusion.

The market for potash in the United States is dominated by Canadian firms. In 1986, 84.3 per cent of the potash consumed in the United States was imported from Canada. The principal Canadian potash producers are defendants in this case: Potash Corporation of Saskatchewan Incorporated (PCS); Potash Corporation of America (PCA); IMC Fertilizer Group, Inc.; Kalium; Noranda Minerals, Inc.; and Cominco. These Canadian firms are allied in Canpotex, a cartel that exists to sell potash outside the United States.

Potash is a mineral that is an essential ingredient in fertilizer. Because potash is an essential ingredient, the demand for potash is "inelastic," meaning that people will continue to buy it even if the price goes up, and they will not buy much more, even if the price goes down. The effect of this inelastic demand is that low prices are bad for the producers because the low price does not result in greater sales, except insofar as one producer can take sales away from other producers. Conversely, producers benefit from high prices, because they can sell about as much potash and keep the extra money. Newcomers cannot enter the market without first gaining control of a potash mine, which is a significant entry barrier preventing new sellers from entering the market.

The biggest of the Canadian producers, PCS, was originally owned by the province of Saskatchewan and was run as a governmental company for the avowed purposes of providing jobs and promoting the local Saskatchewan economy. Unfortunately for the potash industry, due to a slump in agriculture, potash demand fell tremendously in the 1980s, resulting in oversupply. The effect of the oversupply was a potash price war, with prices bottoming in 1986 when PCS charged C$45.36 per ton FOB mine. The industry was in crisis. PCS alone lost $103 million in 1986. The president of PCS Sales wrote in an internal memorandum that the industry would not be able to end the price war without "joint action":

> It is not possible for a single producer to affect [sic] a turn-around; however, joint action by a group of producers or governments could achieve this.

> Given the competitive nature of the business, joint action in North America is not possible except through a vehicle such as Canpotex.

> Canpotex by itself cannot achieve the objectives unless there is tacit approval and support on the part of other potash exporters. The danger inherent in multilateral decisions by Canpotex (or PCS Sales) is that the world will again see us as a residual supplier.... PCS Sales' past support of price with a view to achieve stability is proof of the fallacy of such attempts.

In fact, Noranda, Kalium, PCA, and PCS had each tried to increase prices unilaterally during 1986 and were forced to rescind the increases when the other producers undercut them.

In 1986, the province of Saskatchewan elected a government which promised to privatize PCS. In preparation for privatizing the company, PCS replaced its management with Charles Childers, CEO, and William Doyle, sales chief, who came to PCS from rival company IMC. Childers was quoted in a trade publication as saying that it was incumbent on PCS "to lead" in order to "straighten out our own company and hopefully give some strength to the potash industry as a whole."

Also in 1986, two American producers filed a complaint with the United States Department of Commerce alleging that the Canadian companies were dumping potash in the United States at less than fair value (which can mean below prices charged for exports to a third country, below domestic prices in the country where the product is produced, or below a reconstructed cost of production). The Department investigated the claim and in August 1987 issued a preliminary determination that the Canadian producers were dumping potash. The Department ordered the Canadian companies to post bonds on all exports to the United States, which would be payable to the United States as a duty if there were a final determination of dumping and injury to American producers. The amount of the bond varied for each firm according to the firm's "dumping margin," that is, the average amount by which the firm's United States sale price fell below the foreign market value in the cases examined by the Department. The dumping margins varied wildly, from 9.14 percent for IMC up to a crippling 85.2 percent for Noranda.

The Saskatchewan government responded to the United States action by adopting legislation which would give the province the power to limit and prorate production among Saskatchewan producers. Within days of the introduction of the Saskatchewan legislation, on September 4, 1987, PCS announced that it would increase its prices by $35 per ton (from $58 to $93 per short ton for coarse grade FOB mine) to account for the bond expense. PCS's dumping margin was set at 51.9 per cent. PCS chose to raise its price only by $35, the amount necessary to pay duties on the industry average dumping margin of 36.62 per cent, rather than by the amount necessary to pay its own duty of 51.9 percent. It is undisputed that PCS chose the industry average figure in an attempt to pick a figure that other producers would follow. On September 11, 1987, the other Canadian producer defendants all announced either a $35 price increase or a new price of $93, rather than simply increasing the price by the amount necessary to cover their individual duty costs.

On January 8, 1988, the Canadian producers reached an agreement with the Department of Commerce, suspending the earlier order. The suspension agreement imposed a minimum price on Canadian producers selling in the United States market, but oddly, the minimum price chosen was still less than the "foreign market value": the Canadians were only forbidden from undercutting "foreign market value" by more than fifteen percent of the producer's dumping margin. The literal terms of the suspension agreement made each producer's minimum price vary with its own foreign market value (which was arrived at by different methodologies for different firms) and with its own dumping margin; as the producers' expert William Barringer opined, the "uncertainties" in such a calculation make it impossible to predict with accuracy what price for any particular transaction would be in compliance with the agreement. However, correspondence from the Department of Commerce, which had responsibility for monitoring compliance with the suspension agreement, indicates that the Department used an industry average figure in assessing compliance.

As soon as the suspension agreement was in place, PCS again led the way in determining industry pricing, announcing it would rebate the earlier $35 surcharge, and on January 11, 1988, publishing its new price list at $86 per ton for granular grade, a net increase of $28 over the $58 it charged before the Department of Commerce imposed the bond requirement. The other Canadian producers matched PCS's increase within 11 days, and Kalium raised its price to $87. The Department of Commerce, in monitoring compliance with the agreement, noted that the agreement imposed an average floor price of $60.67, and that in the five months following the agreement the average price charged was $79.28.

The class's expert, Professor Gordon Rausser, opined and presented data purporting to show that the industry average prices for potash were higher than would be expected based on market factors during the 1988–1993 period (*i.e.*, prices were "supra-competitive"). Perhaps more to the point, prices remained significantly higher than the minimum prices imposed by the suspension agreement from 1988 to 1992, with the exception of a short period in 1990 after PCS cut its prices drastically (and temporarily) for the avowed purpose of stabilizing prices within the industry. Only in January and February 1990, in the wake of this "market correction," did prices briefly dip below the suspension agreement price floor.

I.

This is a circumstantial evidence case based on parallel pricing, an example of the economic phenomenon called "conscious parallelism," in which competitors act alike. Conscious parallelism is never meaningful by itself, but always assumes whatever significance it might have from additional facts. The threshold question in deciding whether parallelism could be evidence of an agreement is whether the parallelism is "interdependent," meaning that the sellers would only take the course of action they took if they expected the others to behave the same way. In this case interdependence is obvious; no producer would have been able to raise prices and keep them high unless the others did.

According to accepted economic theory, oligopolies are characterized by interdependent behavior because each seller is a big enough player to affect the market by price cuts; as a result, in raising or lowering prices or output, each seller must take into account his competitors' responses to his action. In an oligopoly, price rises are not sustainable as long as one major seller continues to undercut the price leader and steal his customers. When one seller raises his price, no buyers will buy his product unless the other sellers follow the price leader and raise their prices. The other oligopolists know that if they keep their prices low, the brave price leader will simply cut his prices and the battle will resume. On the other hand, if they raise their prices in turn, all sellers will receive higher prices and end up with more money in their pockets. The loser will be the consumer, who benefits from competition, not peaceful coexistence between suppliers.

Even though oligopoly pricing harms the consumer in the same way monopoly does, interdependent pricing that occurs with no actual agreement does not violate the Sherman Act, for the very good reason that we cannot order sellers to make their decisions without taking into account the reactions of their competitors. As then-Judge Breyer explained:

> Courts have noted that the Sherman Act prohibits agreements, and they have almost uniformly held, at least in the pricing area, that such individual pricing decisions (even when each firm rests its own decision upon its belief that competitors will do the same) do not constitute an unlawful agreement under section 1 of the

Sherman Act. That is not because such pricing is desirable (it is not), but because it is close to impossible to devise a judicially enforceable remedy for "interdependent" pricing. How does one order a firm to set its prices without regard to the likely reactions of its competitors?

Clamp–All, 851 F.2d at 484 (citations omitted).

Although interdependent pricing tends to happen naturally in an oligopoly, there are good reasons for competitors to enter into an actual agreement to fix prices. First, successful price coordination requires accurate predictions about what other competitors will do; it is easier to predict what people mean to do if they tell you. In the absence of express agreements, oligopolists must rely on uncertain and ambiguous signals to achieve concerted action. The signals are subject to misinterpretation and are a blunt and imprecise means of ensuring smooth cooperation, especially in the context of changing or unprecedented market circumstances. This anticompetitive minuet is most difficult to compose and to perform, even for a disciplined oligopoly.

Brooke Group Ltd. v. Brown & Williamson Tobacco Corp., 509 U.S. 209, 227–28, 125 L. Ed. 2d 168, 113 S. Ct. 2578 (1993). Second, competitors may have different preferences on decisions such as pricing and therefore may not be willing just to follow a leader's decision; words (or word substitutes) may be necessary to negotiate a common course of action. Third, some oligopoly markets are more conducive than others to supracompetitive pricing. Market traits that make oligopoly pricing more likely to succeed include a standardized product and publicly announced prices, which make it easier for sellers to keep track of each others' prices. Actual agreement allows competitors to modify their market to facilitate collusion, particularly by setting up procedures for detecting and punishing price-cutting.

While the oligopoly market structure naturally facilitates supra-competitive pricing, that same market structure also makes cooperative arrangements unstable, for this reason: It is in the best interest of each individual competitor for his competitors to charge high prices, while he charges somewhat less when that will help him steal customers from his competitors. The temptation to shade prices secretly is just as inherent in the oligopoly market structure as the temptation to collude to raise prices. Of course, if the competitors know about the undercutting, they will match it. Therefore, price-shading and secrecy must go hand in hand. While publicly announced prices discourage the sellers from cutting prices because they know that their price cuts will be matched, thus eliminating any competitive advantage, conversely, secretly negotiated discounts encourage price-cutting, since each seller hopes to steal customers without suffering retaliation from its competitors. As a result, a cartel can only succeed for any period of time if it has the ability to detect cheating and punish it effectively.

If the oligopolists agree, either tacitly or expressly, to coordinate price increases, they have committed a *per se* violation of section 1 of the

Sherman Act. From the outside, however, the conspirators' actions may look the same as innocent oligopoly pricing. Although parallel pricing evidence is consistent with illegal conduct, it is equally consistent with lawful conduct, and thus does not tend to exclude the possibility of independent action, as required by Monsanto. Therefore, parallel pricing in a concentrated market cannot make a submissible section one case, although it may set the groundwork for such a case.

In a rather primitive way, the "plus factors" test incorporates the economic principles outlined above as a way to distinguish between innocent interdependence and illegal conspiracy. Under this test, plaintiffs can establish a prima facie case of conspiracy by showing parallel prices together with "plus factors" that increase the likelihood that the parallel prices resulted from conspiracy.

We must, of course, take care to interpret the "plus factors" test in a way that is consistent with Monsanto. With Monsanto in mind, it is useful to distinguish between "plus factors" that establish a background making conspiracy likely and "plus factors" that tend to exclude the possibility that the defendants acted without agreement. For instance, "motive to conspire" and "high level of interfirm communications," are often cited as "plus factors" because they make conspiracy possible. Background facts showing a situation conducive to collusion do not tend to exclude the possibility of independent action, but they nevertheless form an essential foundation for a circumstantial case. In Matsushita Electric Industrial Co. v. Zenith Radio Corp., 475 U.S. 574, 593–98, 89 L. Ed. 2d 538, 106 S. Ct. 1348 (1986), the Supreme Court held that a conspiracy case based on circumstantial evidence must be economically plausible. The background "plus factors" of market structure, motivation and opportunity play an important role in establishing such plausibility. Generally, these background "plus factors" are necessary but not sufficient to prove conspiracy.

On the other hand, acts that would be irrational or contrary to the defendant's economic interest if no conspiracy existed, but which would be rational if the alleged agreement existed, do tend to exclude the possibility of innocence.

A.

Of the "plus factors" that merely make conspiracy possible, such as motive and opportunity to conspire, the class has adduced abundant evidence. Within this category some "plus factors" are purely situational, involving no action on the part of the defendant, and some are volitional; while the former are important, the latter begin to make the required showing of collusion.

The purely situational factors in this case are the market structure and the crisis in the potash industry. The structure of the potash market was conducive to collusion, featuring an oligopoly, barriers to new sellers entering the market, inelastic demand, and a standardized product. However, there was excess production capacity, which spurs competition, and a price war, which shows the producers had not been able to achieve a stable interdependent equilibrium. Individual attempts in 1986 by Noranda, Kalium, PCA, and PCS to initiate a price rise had failed. The producers were losing millions of dollars. The producers had good reason to wish for a truce.

The volitional background "plus factors" are also very strong in this case. At least one of the defendants actively considered the possibility of joint action, as is stated in the PCS "Corporate Plan" document dated September 25, 1986: "It is not possible for a single producer to affect [sic] a turn-around; however, joint action by a group of producers or governments could achieve this." Then there was a break in pattern, as the market went from price-war to profitability.

The class has introduced significant evidence of solicitations to enter a price-fixing agreement. Most, but not all, of the solicitations were by PCS. For instance, PCS freely complained to Kalium about Kalium's failure to adhere to pricing cut-offs. It was the custom in the industry to give lower prices at times of year when there was no immediate need for fertilizer, but to raise prices during high-use periods. Kalium published price lists announcing the pricing cut-off pattern, but in fact often shipped at the lower price after the cut-off date when it did not get orders filled before the cut-off date. PCS sales chief William Doyle repeatedly upbraided Kalium's vice president Robert Turner for shipping at the lower price after the cut-off date. Turner responded "something to the effect" that he would run his own business. Another time, Doyle called Turner and advised him that neither PCS, IMC, nor Cominco planned to accede to a certain customer's request to delay filling an order-that is, to ship at the old price after the cut-off. Turner answered that Kalium would try to ship by a certain date, as it had already said it would do in a letter to its customers. In the same vein, Doyle approached Turner about a certain bid and told Turner that Kalium's action was "wrong." John Ripperger, vice president of PCA, also testified that Doyle asked him if PCA was going to institute a price increase and not carry over product at the old price; Ripperger interpreted this question to mean that Doyle "would prefer that we don't make sales at the old price." Also, Doyle complained to Ripperger that PCA's pricing was undermining prices in Florida. Ripperger reported a conversation in which Gary Snyder of PCS asked a PCA salesman if he had sold at a certain price, and then said, "We [PCS] will take it [price] down and bury you [PCA] if that's what you want."

In 1988, after the sale of Kalium, Charles Childers, the CEO of PCS, called on Jay Proops, one of Kalium's new owners, armed with a chart showing that PCS was losing market share and that Kalium and other producers were gaining. Childers said Kalium was undercutting the price. Proops did some research and concluded that the chart had incorrect information and that Kalium was not undercutting. Therefore, Proops took no action in response to Childers's visit. In August 1990, Childers telephoned Joseph Sullivan, the other owner of Kalium. Childers told Sullivan that PCS's "price leadership was not working, despite major efforts" and that Childers "wanted to discuss this issue" with Sullivan. Sullivan declined to discuss prices.

Another time, a PCS employee took advantage of a trade meeting to apologize to Kalium's Turner about a low bid PCS had made by mistake. The PCS employee testified that he explained the mistake to Turner because he had "some concern that [the low price] may spread in the marketplace," and that he "was hopeful that it wouldn't go any darn further." Turner testified that Kalium matched the bid, but the reaction was "pretty much confined to that account. It did not go beyond that."

Though PCS made most of these overtures, on isolated occasions others did the same. Kalium's Turner called Ripperger of PCA to complain about a salesman who was cutting prices in Wisconsin. Similarly, Kip Williams of IMC complained to Ripperger about price-cutting in Florida.

Despite evidence that various defendants invited others to join in stabilizing prices, the class was not able to adduce direct evidence that the people on the receiving end of these solicitations accepted them and formed a deal. The evidence of solicitation is relevant, however, because it shows conspiratorial state of mind on the part of the solicitor and may also indicate that the solicitor was acting upon an earlier agreement.

B.

The stage was clearly set for conspiracy in this case. The question is whether the additional evidence tends to exclude the possibility that the producers acted independently. I believe that it does.

First, the class has produced evidence that the producers cooperated in disclosing prices they had charged on particular sales. The industry practice was that each producer published a price list stating its price, the dates for which that price would be available, and any discounts that the producer would extend. The price lists were widely distributed to customers and certainly were no secret. However, actual prices sometimes deviated from the lists. When Childers and Doyle came to PCS, a key aspect of their program to raise industry prices was to insist on the list price. Doyle stated in an industry publication: "When I first came on board in the spring of 1987, the first word I put out to our sales force was that the price list was our price, stick to that price and no bending. Anybody who bends was out of here." Despite published price lists with the high follow-the-leader price, the producers continued to undercut each other in privately negotiated deals. When word of the discounting got around to PCS, PCS executives, particularly sales chief Doyle, were quite active in contacting the discounter and asking for verification of the rumored price. Significantly, Doyle testified that he never made any such price verification calls before 1987. The number of these verification communications is difficult to pin down, but Doyle estimated he initiated or received three to four calls per year with PCA, five to six per year with IMC, three to four per year with Cominco, five to six total with Kalium, "a few" with NMPC, and one to two total with Noranda. Doyle was by no means the only person making such calls on behalf of PCS, and there is evidence that the other defendants called each other as well (except that there is no evidence of others calling Noranda).

These exchanges were often between high-level executives who were responsible for pricing decisions for their companies or who conveyed the price information to those who did set prices. For instance, Dale Massie, vice president of marketing for Cominco, testified that he had price verification communications with Doyle, head of sales at PCS. Massie testified that he made up the Cominco price lists, and the evidence shows that Doyle had a key role in determining PCS pricing policy. Charles Hoffman at IMC reported price information from Doyle to his superiors to inform them that "we would have to meet" PCS's price. Similarly, John Ripperger, vice president of PCA, had price verification discussions with Doyle, and Doyle said he had obtained price information from John Huber, Kalium's vice president of sales.

Price verification communications can either violate section 1 directly or they can be evidence of a violation. An agreement to exchange such communications can constitute an unreasonable restraint of trade under the rule of reason if the anticompetitive effect of the agreement outweighs its beneficial effects. In price fixing cases, the exchange of sensitive price information can sometimes be circumstantial evidence of the existence of a *per se* violation. It is this second theory that the class pursues in this case.

Again, acts that would be contrary to the actor's self-interest in the absence of a conspiracy, but which make economic sense as part of a conspiracy, provide the crucial type of "plus factor" evidence necessary to exclude the possibility of independent action. The class contends that "the price verification calls were inconsistent with the 'pricing secrecy' sought by participants in oligopolistic industries because in such industries 'each producer would like to secretly "shade" prices, thereby gaining sales and avoiding retaliation.' " The class's argument finds support in the reasoning of United States v. United States Gypsum Co., 438 U.S. 422, 57 L. Ed. 2d 854, 98 S. Ct. 2864 (1978), which stated:

> Price concessions by oligopolists generally yield competitive advantages only if secrecy can be maintained; when the terms of the concession are made publicly known, other competitors are likely to follow and any advantage to the initiator is lost in the process. Thus, if one seller offers a price concession for the purpose of winning over one of his competitor's customers, it is unlikely that the same seller will freely inform its competitors the details of the concession so that it can be promptly matched and diffused.

Id. at 456 (citations omitted). Therefore, if there were no reciprocal agreement to share prices (and the producers certainly do not argue that there was), an individual seller who revealed to his competitors the amount of his privately negotiated discounts would have been shooting himself in the foot. On the other hand, if there were a cartel, it would be crucial for the cartel members to cooperate in telling each other about actual prices charged in order to prevent the sort of widespread discounting that would eventually sink the cartel.

Nor is there any legitimate business purpose which would make it desirable for the producers to reveal their pricing concessions notwithstanding the disadvantage of helping their competitors compete more effectively. These private communications between competitors had no redeeming effect of informing customers of prices ... To the contrary, the prices stated here were discounts from the published price lists that reflected the prices the producers wanted to charge. The producers had no interest in publicizing these discounts to the market as a whole. Nor is there any evidence of special necessity for horizontal price communications, such as the customer fraud which justified the producers' practices in Cement Manufacturers Protective Ass'n v. United States, 268 U.S. 588, 595–96, 69 L. Ed. 1104, 45 S. Ct. 586 (1925). The price communications in this case are more like those in In re Coordinated Pretrial Proceedings, 906 F.2d at 448, which served "little purpose" other than facilitating price coordination.

The Court today concludes that voluntarily revealing secret price-cutting to one's competitors is not probative of conspiracy, for three reasons, each of which is unsound. First, the price verification communications involved completed sales, not future sales. The Court states: "Common sense dictates that a conspiracy to fix a price would involve one company communicating with another company before the price quotation to the customer." This misconceives the purpose for which the price communications are being offered. The communications are not supposed to be direct evidence of a one-time mini-conspiracy to fix the price on one sale. Rather, they are circumstantial evidence of a type of behavior one would not expect in the absence of an agreement to cooperate. If no cartel was in place, each competitor would seek to benefit from high prices generally, while secretly shading prices when it would gain a customer without provoking retaliation. Confessing price-cutting when one needn't do so would only invite retaliation and guarantee that one's competitors could match the discounted price exactly next time. This is contrary to self-interest. On the other hand, if the producers were cooperating in a cartel, a necessary feature of their arrangement would be some way to determine who was discounting. Thus, confessing price-cutting to competitors makes no economic sense for independent actors, but makes perfect economic sense for cartel members. The Court has rejected circumstantial evidence of an agreement because it is not direct evidence.

The Court's second reason for dismissing the price verification evidence is that "there is no evidence to support the inference that the verifications had an impact on price increases." The class points to the price verifications as circumstantial evidence of a broader conspiracy. Parallel price increases are the starting point for the class's case, so that if the conspiracy is proved, effect on prices has been proved at the first step. The Court argues that prices eventually went down, but this glosses over the fact that they first rose dramatically, then remained above both the forecasted price based on market factors and the suspension agreement price until 1992 (with the exception of the two-month dip caused by the PCS "market correction program"). If, to prove collusion, a plaintiff has to prove that there was no cheating, thus no downward pressure on prices, cartels will be quite safe from the Sherman Act.

To support its proposition that there is nothing suspicious about oligopolists exchanging non-public price information, the Court relies on In re Baby Food Antitrust Litigation, where the Third Circuit stated: "No evidence . . . shows that any executive of any defendant exchanged price or market information with any other executive." 166 F.3d at 135. The court held that price discussions among low level employees did not show a conspiracy. Id. at 137. This reasoning implies that if high-level executives had been involved, it would have constituted evidence of conspiracy (if, indeed, the plaintiffs had been able to prove parallel pricing, which they did not in In re Baby Food, 166 F.3d at 128–32). In our case there is a wealth of evidence that high level executives, who were in a position to respond to what they learned, were directly involved in exchanging secret price information. Citing In re Baby Food in a case with this kind of evidence vitiates the distinction on which the Third Circuit relied.

The Court ignores the Third Circuit's articulated rationale in *In re Baby Food* because the Court thinks the rationale is belied by facts in that case showing that high level executives used information gathered by low-level employees. The Third Circuit apparently saw a crucial difference between gathering information to use to one's own advantage and giving out information for one's competitors to use to their advantage (and one's own detriment). However gladly the baby food executives used information relayed to them, the facts of *In re Baby Food* recited by the Third Circuit do not show that the executives were giving away their firms' secrets. The Third Circuit expressly stated that Anderson, a salesman who testified that he gathered information for his superiors, was not instructed to go around giving out advance pricing information about his own company. In this case, it is the potash producers' pattern of giving their competitors valuable information that we identify as an act contrary to the producers' self-interest unless there was an agreement.

The Court's third reason for dismissing the price verifications is that the verifications were "sporadic." The evidence indicates that the producers called each other when they had reason to think their competitors were cutting prices, and that they responded to each other's inquiries. The total number of such inquiries is difficult to set, but the defendants characterize it as "no more than several dozen"—surely more than a scintilla.

This "sporadic" argument seems to be directed to the quantum of proof, rather than the quality of it. In other words, it is an argument that more proof should exist, rather than an argument that the existing proof is not probative. If the plaintiff adduces evidence of the kind that tends to prove the existence of a conspiracy, I do not believe that *Monsanto* and *Matsushita* give a justification for rejecting it. *Monsanto* and *Matsushita* lay out a test for the kind of proof necessary in antitrust cases, not the quantity of it. There is no heightened "clear and convincing" standard of proof in civil antitrust conspiracy cases, requiring a greater quantum of proof than the ordinary "preponderance of the evidence" standard. The plaintiff's evidence must amount to more than a scintilla, but the plaintiff does not have to outweigh the defendant's evidence item by item.

The Ninth Circuit, in its recent decision of In re Citric Acid Litigation, dismissed evidence of price discussions as "sporadic," but it is not clear whether the court rejected the evidence qualitatively under Monsanto or because it was not quantitatively sufficient to create a material issue of fact. In *Citric Acid* the existence of a price-fixing conspiracy was conceded, but the question remained whether one defendant, Cargill, had been a party to the conspiracy. See 191 F.3d at 1093. Cargill received summary judgment despite testimony that a competitor had discussions regarding the bidding price of citric acid with someone from Cargill. The Ninth Circuit cited *In re Baby Foods* and dismissed the evidence as "sporadic price discussions with one individual at Cargill." The testimony in question was vague, with no specific evidence of what was said, and there were other qualitative reasons for rejecting it, including the fact that the timing of the alleged discussions was inconsistent with the plaintiff's theory of the case. The court also concluded the case by saying that there was no more than a scintilla of evidence that Cargill participated in the conspiracy. *In re Citric Acid* is therefore consistent with the ordinary summary judgment standard in cases requiring a preponderance of evidence, and it does not stand for the proposition that a heightened quantum of proof is necessary to survive summary judgment in antitrust cases.

The Court states in this case that the fact that there were "several dozen communications" among competitors is not "significant." I would hold that evidence of several dozen communications of the type that tends to prove conspiracy creates a genuine issue of material fact.

In addition to the price verification practices, evidence concerning PCS's "market correction program" in December 1989 also tends to exclude the hypothesis of independent action. On December 18, 1989, PCS cut its prices by $18 a ton for five days. PCS's Carlos Smith stated that the purpose (and effect) of the program was to stabilize prices in the industry:

Q.   Was it an attempt to stabilize prices?

A.   Yes. . . .

Q.   And did it work?

A.   It leveled them.

A high-level Kalium executive, John Huber, wrote the following notes: "Program was a market correction. Weren't trying to teach other people— only got tired of people who kept chipping away. Program was reasonable one—checked with people. . . . People started cheating. . . . We wanted to get their attention. Program to be short, very specific." Huber said he did not recall to whom he had been talking when he made these notes, but the use of the phrase, "We wanted to get their attention," suggests he was taking dictation from someone at PCS.

The wording of Huber's notes implies that the "market correction" program was a way of disciplining producers who had breached an earlier agreement. In plain English, the use of the word "cheating" denotes the breach of an agreement or convention, not independent action. Without an agreement, price cutting would be called "competing," not "cheating."

Moreover, the Huber notes suggest PCS's action was not lonely price leadership, but rather that PCS "checked with people" before cutting prices. Apparently, PCS did not want to risk sparking another price war by letting other producers misunderstand the intent behind the "market correction program." These notes illustrate a situation in which smoke signals were just too ambiguous and dangerous to be trusted, so that competitors had to resort to explicit communications to coordinate prices. The notes, taken together with the successful "market correction" program, tend to exclude the possibility of independent action.

The class also points to another piece of evidence that tends to exclude the hypothesis of independent action. This is the Canpotex memorandum of Friday, January 8, 1988, which stated:

> FYI Canadian potash producers have reached agreement with the United States Department of Commerce and all dumping action has been suspended for a minimum of 5 years. It is rumored that the USD per metric ton increase posted by Canadian producers in 1987 to cover possible tariff payments to the U.S. Govt will be refunded in full or part. In the meantime new price lists are being issued on Monday Jan. 11 at: Standard Grade USD 80.00; Coarse Grade USD 84.00; Granular Grade USD 86.00.

Canpotex is the Canadian producers' cartel organized for sales outside the United States.

Again, the Court misconceives the import of this evidence, rejecting it as direct evidence of an attempt to reach an agreement, when the class offers it as circumstantial evidence of an agreement that already existed. The Court considers it crucial to establish who received the Canpotex memorandum, apparently reasoning that if the memorandum was meant to negotiate an agreement, only people who got the memorandum could respond to it. Instead, the class offers this memorandum as circumstantial evidence tending to show that Canpotex knew on Friday, January 8, of an existing agreement to raise prices. The prophecy by Canpotex that its members would issue new "price lists" with particular prices does indeed tend to show the price increase was coordinated, because otherwise it would have been impossible to know in advance what the individual producers would do.

In sum, the class has adduced evidence of a market structure ripe for collusion, a sudden change from price war to supra-competitive pricing, price-fixing overtures from one competitor to another, voluntary disclosure of secret price concessions, an explicitly discussed cheater punishment program, and advance knowledge of other producers' price moves. Taken together, this list of "plus factors" adds up to evidence that satisfies the Monsanto standard.

II.

As I understand our previous cases, it is still necessary to take into account the producers' explanation of their conduct in order to ascertain whether their theory deprives the plaintiffs' case of its probative value. In this case, the producers' theory is that the price rises are explained entirely by the suspension agreement and the spectre of Saskatchewan prorationing legislation. In light of the evidence adduced by Professor Rausser and the Commerce Department correspondence indicating that the industry price far exceeded the price floors set by the suspension agreement, I cannot see that the producers' explanation deflates the class's price-fixing theory. I fully understand that the producers dispute Rausser's understanding of the suspension agreement price levels. Moreover, there is absolutely no dispute that prices had to rise above the price-war levels to comply with the suspension agreement. However, the producers make no attempt to identify a price floor required by the suspension agreement or to show that the producers actually set their prices, for instance the January 11 price of $86.00 for granular grade, by reference to the suspension agreement floor. Indeed, their expert William Barringer argued that it was actually impossible to ascertain whether a given price would satisfy the agreement. Instead, the producers' expert Andrew Rosenfield opined that the defendants needed only to set their prices "well above" suspension agreement floor prices. Under these experts' testimony, the suspension agreement did not dictate the actual prices charged; therefore, the existence of the suspension agreement does not explain away the facts supporting the class's theory that the actual prices were set by illegal collusion.

Not only were the January 1988 prices higher than the prices required by the suspension agreement, but there is evidence tending to prove that the producers felt free to dip below the suspension agreement prices when it served their purposes. Professor Rausser's price chart shows that during PCS's "market correction" program in January and February 1990, prices dipped below the suspension agreement floor. Deliberately taking prices below the suspension agreement floor to punish price-cutters is not a convincing sign of industry devotion to the suspension agreement, and the fact that it happened discredits the producers' argument that their prices were compelled by the suspension agreement.

The producers have not made a showing that the governmental intervention so explains their actual behavior as to take away the probative power of the class's case. This case should therefore proceed to trial. Accordingly, I dissent.

NOTE: THE EUROPEAN APPROACH TO THE OLIGOPOLY PROBLEM

As noted in Chapter 1 at pp. 19–20, Article 81 (ex Article 85) of the Treaty establishing the European Community prohibits "all agreements between undertakings, decisions by associations of undertakings and concerted practices which may affect trade between Member States, and which have as their object or effect the prevention, restriction, or distortion of competition within the common market. . . ." Article 82 (ex Article 86) prohibits "abuse by one or more undertakings of a dominant position."

Although the language of the EC Treaty is similar to the language of the first two sections of the Sherman Act, the European Commission's approach to the problem of tacit collusion differs slightly from that of the American antitrust enforcement agencies and courts. In contrast to the law in the United States, the European regime is more concerned with the ability of dominant firms to exert market power than with the possibility of market-wide collusion. The law is violated whenever such an exertion of market power amounts to an "abuse of a dominant position." As a result of its somewhat different focus, the Commission's analysis tends to emphasize the merger's impact upon competitors. Kauper, Merger Control in the United States and the European Union: Some Observations, 74 St. John's L. Rev. 305, 346 (Spring 2000). Some criticize the European antitrust regulators' emphasis on "abuse of a dominant position." The critics believe that the abuse concept may serve to control "excesses and concentration" in oligopolistic markets, but that it is ineffective in dealing with issues such as conscious parallelism. Raffaelli, Oligopolies and Antitrust Law, 19 Fordham Int'l L.J. 915, 932 (Feb. 1996). In large part, just as in the United States, the difficulty in tackling conscious parallelism is attributable to the fact that European law also requires (under Article 81) a finding of concerted practices.

Though analogous to the American theory of conscious parallelism, the theory of concerted practices is not the same. In the *Wood Pulp* decision, an Article 81 case, the Commission challenged the practices of 40 wood pulp producers from the United States, Canada, and Finland and three of their trade associations. The European Court of Justice held that the practice of issuing quarterly price announcements in dollar terms did not infringe Article 81(1). It also analyzed whether the price announcements constituted evidence of "concertation." The Court held that "parallel conduct cannot be regarded as furnishing proof of concertation unless concertation constituted the only plausible explanation for such conduct." The Court found that the system of price announcements, the simultaneity of the price announcements, and the parallelism of the announced prices could be explained by reasons other than consciously coordinated behavior, such as common business practices, rapid means of communication, and the transparency of the market. *A. Ahlstrom Osakeyhtio v. Commission*, Cases C–89, 104, 114, 116–117, 125–129/85 (1992) ECR I–1307; Rodger, The Oligopoly Problem and the Concept of Collective Dominance, 2 Colum. J. Euro. L. 25, 38–39 (Winter 1996). In the Italian Flat Glass decision, 1989 O.J. (L 33), 1990 C.M.L.R. 535, the Court of First Instance's dicta stated that abuse of a dominant position through concerted practices could only be established by the presence of "economic links" between the dominant parties. Id. at 45.

As Raffaelli puts it:

"Based on this case law, a concerted practice exists when the following conditions are met: (1) there must be a form of coordination or practical cooperation between undertakings that replaces their independent action; (2) this coordination needs to be achieved through direct or indirect contact; and (3) the aim must be to remove, in advance, any uncertainty as to the future conduct of their competitors. On the other hand, conscious parallelism results from undertakings' experience in an oligopolistic market, which by its very nature restricts competition, especially with respect to price. The comparison of concerted practices to conscious parallelism is problematic because it may lead to the repression of individual conduct by oligopolistic undertakings, such as the decision to make one's prices uniform with the others. Furthermore, this repression may occur even in the absence of the abuses that trigger the application of antitrust provisions against a monopolistic or dominant undertaking."

Raffaelli, supra, 19 Fordham Int'l L.J. at 932. In contrast to the conscious parallelism theory, the "concertation" theory places a higher burden of proof on the antitrust authorities.

PROBLEM 11

PRICING PRACTICES OF GLUCOSE MANUFACTURERS

Glucose is manufactured in 50 mills in the United States, owned by 30 different companies. About half of the productive capacity is owned by 6 companies. Relatively little glucose is imported.

Over at least the last ten years, prices for glucose have followed this pattern: X Company, the largest in the industry, would announce a change in "base price," to take effect in 48 hours; all other companies would then make similar announcements within 48 hours, and by the time X Company's price change went into effect identical price changes had been made by all other producers. The price to glucose purchasers was a "delivered price"—the "base price" plus the cost of rail shipment to the station nearest the point of use. If the price was quoted by the nearest mill, the rail shipment costs equaled the freight actually paid; if the price was quoted by a more distant mill, the rail shipment costs added were the expenses incurred by the *nearest* glucose producer (*i.e.*, the additional freight costs were absorbed by the more distant seller). As a result, a purchaser at any point would receive, from every glucose manufacturer solicited, identical delivered prices to the nearest railroad station. Discounts for cash, sales warranties, and other terms of sale were the same for all manufacturers. Glucose producers also uniformly refused to quote prices on other than a delivered basis or to use other than rail transportation. The Government has been unable to show that the glucose manufacturers have ever conferred about price or any of these sales practices.

Have the glucose manufacturers engaged in any "contract, combination or conspiracy" to restrain trade? Has any of them engaged in an "unfair method of competition"?

SECTION 4. THE ROLE OF TRADE ASSOCIATIONS AND INFORMATION DISSEMINATION

NOTE

"People of the same trade seldom meet together, even for merriment and diversion, but the conversation ends in a conspiracy against the public, or in some contrivance to raise prices. It is impossible indeed to prevent such meetings, by any law which either could be executed, or would be consistent with liberty and justice. But though the law cannot hinder people of the same trade from sometimes assembling together, it ought to do nothing to facilitate such assemblies, much less to render them necessary." Adam Smith, The Wealth of Nations, Bk. I, Ch. X (1776).

INTRODUCTION

Trade associations engage in a broad variety of activities, many of which are beneficial from a commercial point of view and raise little or no threat of anticompetitive effects. Such activities include joint insurance arrangements, arbitration services to consumers, lobbying activities and publication of journals relating to the businesses of its members.

Another function performed by a trade association for the benefit of its members is dissemination of information about price, terms of sale, output, and other industrial statistics. Such exchanges characteristically occur pursuant to agreement (often in the bylaws of the trade association), and questions may arise whether the data exchanged in a particular market setting will have an anticompetitive effect.

In one sense, information can be procompetitive in assisting enterprises to know at what levels they must price in order to compete effectively. Arguably a stock exchange is an example of perfect data dissemination in that each seller and each buyer knows almost instantaneously the price and quantity of each previous transaction. On the other hand, where sellers and buyers are fewer in number, too much information or the wrong kind of information may impair the operation of an effective competitive market. In the following line of cases, the courts addressed the question of what kinds of information exchanges may demonstrate a purpose or effect of restraining competition.

American Column & Lumber Co. v. United States

Supreme Court of the United States, 1921.
257 U.S. 377, 42 S.Ct. 114, 66 L.Ed. 284.

■ CLARKE, J. The unincorporated "American Hardwood Manufacturers' Association" was formed in December, 1918, by the consolidation of two similar associations, from one of which it took over a department of activity designated the "Open Competition Plan," and hereinafter referred to as the "Plan."

Participation in the "Plan" was optional with the members of the Association, but, at the time this suit was commenced, of its 400 members, 365, operating 465 mills, were members of the "Plan." The importance and strength of the Association are shown by the admission in the joint answer that while the defendants operated only five per cent of the number of mills engaged in hardwood manufacture in the country, they produced one-third of the total production of the United States. The places of business of the corporations and partnerships, members of the "Plan," were located in many States from New York to Texas, but chiefly in the hardwood producing territory of the Southwest. The defendants are the members of the "Plan," their personal representatives, and F.R. Gadd, its "Manager of Statistics."

The bill alleged, in substance, that the "Plan" constituted a combination and conspiracy to restrain interstate commerce in hardwood lumber by restricting competition and maintaining and increasing prices, in violation of the Antitrust Act of 1890, c. 647, 26 Stat. 209.

The answer denied that the "Plan" had any such purpose and effect as charged, and averred that it promoted competition, especially among its own members.

A temporary injunction, granted by the District Court, restricting the activities of the "Plan" in specified respects, by consent of the parties was made permanent and a direct appeal brings the case here for review.

The activities which we shall see were comprehended within the "Open Competition Plan" (which is sometimes called "The New Competition") have come to be widely adopted in our country, and as this is the first time their legality has been before this Court for decision, some detail of statement with respect to them is necessary.

There is very little dispute as to the facts. The testimony of the Government consists of various documents and excerpts from others, obtained from the files of the "Plan," and the testimony of the defendants consists of like documents and excerpts from other documents, also from the same files, supplemented by affidavits of a number of persons, members and non-members, chiefly to the point that the confessedly great increases of prices during 1919 were due to natural trade and weather conditions and not to the influence of the "Plan."

The record shows that the "Plan" was evolved by a committee, which, in recommending its adoption, said:

> "The purpose of this plan is to disseminate among members accurate knowledge of production and market conditions so that each member may gauge the market intelligently instead of guessing at it; to make competition open and above board instead of secret and concealed; to substitute, in estimated market conditions, frank and full statements of our competitors for the frequently misleading and colored statements of the buyer." ...

... [A] further explanation of the objects and purposes of the "Plan" was made in an appeal to members to join it, in which it is said:

> "The theoretical proposition at the basis of the Open Competition plan is that,
>
> "Knowledge regarding prices actually made is all that is necessary to keep prices at reasonably stable and normal levels.
>
> "The Open Competition plan is a central clearing house for information on prices, trade statistics and practices. By keeping all members fully and quickly informed of what the others have done, the work of the plan results in a certain uniformity of trade practice. There is no agreement to follow the practice of others, although members do naturally follow their most intelligent competitors, if they know what these competitors have been actually doing.
>
> "The monthly meetings held in various sections of the country each month have improved the human relations existing between the members before the organization of this plan." ...

Thus, the "Plan" proposed a system of cooperation among the members, consisting of the interchange of reports of sales, prices, production and practices, and in meetings of the members for discussion, for the avowed purpose of substituting "Cooperative Competition" for "Cut-throat Competition," of keeping "prices at reasonably stable and normal levels," and of improving the "human relations" among the members. But the purpose to agree upon prices or production was always disclaimed.

Coming now to the fully worked out paper plan as adopted.

It required each member to make six reports to the Secretary, viz.:

1. A *daily* report of all sales actually made, with the name and address of the purchaser, the kind, grade and quality of lumber sold and all special agreements of every kind, verbal or written with respect thereto. "These reports are to be exact copies of orders taken."

2. A *daily* shipping report, with exact copies of the invoices, all special agreements as to terms, grade, etc. The classification shall be the same as with sales.

3. A *monthly* production report, showing the production of the member reporting during the previous month, with the grades and thickness classified as prescribed in the "Plan."

4. A *monthly* stock report by each member, showing the stock on hand on the first day of the month, sold and unsold, green and dry, with the total of each kind, grade and thickness.

5. Price lists. Members must file at the beginning of each month price lists showing prices f.o.b. shipping point, which shall be stated. New prices must be filed with the association as soon as made.

6. Inspection reports. These reports are to be made to the association by a service of its own, established for the purpose of checking up grades of the various members and the "Plan" provides for a chief inspector and sufficient assistants to inspect the stocks of all members from time to time.

The declared purpose of the inspection service is not to change any member's grading except with his consent, but to furnish each member a basis on which he can compare his prices with those of other members, thereby making all members' reports more intelligible and accurate.

All of these reports by members are subject to complete audit by representatives of the association. Any member who fails to report *shall not receive the reports* of the secretary, and failure to report for twelve days in six months shall cause the member failing to be dropped from membership. . . .

But, since such voluminous disclosures to the secretary would be valueless unless communicated to the members in a condensed and interpreted form, provision is made for this, as follows:

The secretary is required to send to each member:

1. A *monthly* summary showing the production of each member for the previous month, "subdivided as to grade, kind, thickness," etc.

2. A *weekly* report, not later than Saturday, of all sales, to and including the preceding Tuesday, giving each sale and the price, and the name of the purchaser.

3. On Tuesday of each week the secretary must send to each member a report of each shipment by each member, complete up to the evening of the preceding Thursday.

4. He must send a *monthly* report, showing the individual stock on hand of each member and a summary of all stocks, green and dry, sold and unsold. This report is very aptly referred to by the managing statistician as a monthly inventory of the stock of each member.

5. Not later than the 10th of each month the secretary shall send a summary of the price lists furnished by members, showing the prices asked by each, and any changes made therein must be immediately transmitted to all the members.

6. A market report letter shall be sent to each member of the association (whether participating in the "Plan" or not) pointing "out changes in conditions both in the producing and consuming sections, giving a comparison of production and sales and in general an analysis of the market conditions."

7. Meetings shall be held once a month at Cincinnati "or at points to be agreed upon by the members." "It is intended that the regular meetings shall afford opportunity for the discussion of all subjects of interest to the members."

"The 'Plan' also requires the selection of a man to take charge of the gathering and dissemination of data, with necessary assistants," and the defendant F.R. Gadd was selected and given the title of "Manager of Statistics." . . .

Such, in outline, was the paper plan adopted by the association, but elaborate though it was, in practice three important additions were made to it.

First of all, the southwestern territory for meeting purposes was divided into four districts, and instead of the monthly meeting provided for in the "Plan," "in order that members could more conveniently attend," the record shows that forty-nine of these meetings were held between January 31, 1919, and February 19, 1920,—approximately one for each week, in some part of the territory.

Second. Before each of these meetings a questionnaire was sent out to the members, and from the replies received, supplementing the other reports, the statistician compiled an estimate of the condition of the market, actual and prospective, which was distributed to the members attending each meeting, and was mailed to those not present. There were eleven questions on this list of which the most important were:

"4th. What was your total production of hardwoods during the last month? What do you estimate your production will probably be for the next two months?"

"10th. Do you expect to shut down within the next few months on account of shortage of logs or for any other reason? If so, please state how long mill will be idle."

"11th. What is your view of market conditions for the next few months? What is the general outlook for business? State all reasons for your conclusions."

The "Plan" on paper provided only for reports of past transactions and much is made of this in the record and in argument—that reporting to one another past transactions cannot fix prices for the future. But each of these three questions plainly invited an estimate and discussion of future market conditions by each member, and a coordination of them by an expert analyst could readily evolve an attractive basis for cooperative, even if unexpressed, "harmony" with respect to future prices.

Third. The "Plan" provided for a monthly "market report letter" to go to all members of the association. In practice this market report letter was prepared by F.R. Gadd, Manager of Statistics, but his review of the market and forecast for the future were contained, almost from the beginning, not only in these market letters but also in the weekly sales reports, so that they were sent out to all of the members nineteen times between February 1 and December 6, 1919, and they were discussed at all but one or two of the forty-nine meetings which were held. All the activities of the "Plan" plainly culminated in the counsels contained in these letters and reports.

This elaborate plan for the interchange of reports does not simply supply to each member the amount of stock held, the sales made and the prices received, by every other member of the group, thereby furnishing the data for judging the market, on the basis of supply and demand and current prices. It goes much farther. It not only furnishes such information, with respect to stock, sales and prices, but also reports, giving the views of each member as to "market conditions for the next few months," what the production of each will be for the next "two months;" frequent analyses of the reports by an expert, with, we shall see, significant suggestions as to both future prices and production; and opportunities for future meetings for the interchange of views, which the record shows were very important. It is plain that the only element lacking in this scheme to make it a familiar type of the competition suppressing organization is a definite agreement as to production and prices. But this is supplied: by the disposition of men "to follow their most intelligent competitors," especially when powerful; by the inherent disposition to make all the money possible, joined with the steady cultivation of the value of "harmony" of action; and by the system of reports, which makes the discovery of price reductions inevitable and immediate. The sanctions of the plan obviously are, financial interest, intimate personal contact, and business honor, all operating under the restraint of exposure of what would be deemed bad faith and of trade punishment by powerful rivals. . . .

Obviously the organization of the defendants constitutes a combination and confessedly they are engaged in a large way in the transportation and sale of lumber in interstate commerce so that there remains for decision only the question whether the system of doing business adopted resulted in that direct and undue restraint of interstate commerce which is condemned by this Antitrust statute.

It has been repeatedly held by this court that the purpose of the statute is to maintain free competition in interstate commerce and that any concerted action by any combination of men or corporations to cause, or which in fact does cause, direct and undue restraint of competition in such commerce falls within the condemnation of the act and is unlawful. . . .

With this rule of law and the details of the "Plan" in mind, we come to consider what the record shows as to the purpose of this combination and as to its effect upon interstate commerce. . . .

The record shows that the lumber market was inactive in the months of January and February and the first part of March of 1919. It grew better late in March and progressively stronger until in July, when it became very active, with prices high, and so continued until the end of the year we are considering.

In the first quarter of the year the problem was to maintain the war prices then prevailing rather than to advance them, and although the minutes of the various meetings were kept in barest outline, we find that beginning within a month of the consolidation of the two associations, the members of the "Plan" began actively to co-operate, through the meetings, to suppress competition by restricting production. This is very clearly shown by the excerpts following from the minutes of meetings and from the market letters and sales reports distributed at them.

Thus, at the meeting held at Cincinnati, on January 21, 1919, in the discussion of business conditions, the chairman said:

> "If there is no increase in production, particularly in oak, there is going to be good business." "No man is safe in increasing his production. If he does, he will be in bad shape, as the demand won't come." . . .

Again, a week later, at a meeting at Shreveport, Louisiana, in the discussion of market conditions, one of the members declared: that in his opinion it was "suicidal to run mills night and day; that the pine mills had done it, but he hoped they [we] would profit by their past experience and not do it this year."

Much more of like purport appears in the minutes of the meetings throughout the year, but this is sufficient to convincingly show that one of the prime purposes of the meetings, held in every part of the lumber district, and of the various reports, was to induce members to cooperate in restricting production, thereby keeping the supply low and the prices high, and that whenever there was any suggestion of running the mills to an extent which would bring up the supply to a point which might affect prices, the advice against operations which might lead to such result was put in the strongest possible terms. The cooperation is palpable and avowed, its purpose is clear, and we shall see that it was completely realized.

Next, the record shows clearly that the members of the combination were not satisfied to secure, each for himself, the price which might be obtainable even as the result of cooperative restriction of production, but that throughout the year they assiduously cultivated, through the letters of Gadd, speaking for them all, and through the discussions at the meetings, the general conviction that higher and higher prices were obtainable and a disposition on the part of all to demand them. . . .

To this we must add that constantly throughout the minutes of the various meetings there is shown discussion of the stock and production reports in which the shortage of supply was continually emphasized, with the implication, not disguised, that higher prices must result. Men in general are so easily persuaded to do that which will obviously prove profitable that this reiterated opinion from the analyst of their association, with all obtainable data before him, that higher prices were justified and could easily be obtained must, inevitably, have resulted, as it did result, in concert of action in demanding them.

But not only does the record thus show a persistent purpose to encourage members to unite in pressing for higher and higher prices without regard to cost, but there are many admissions by members, not only that this was the purpose of the "Plan," but that it was fully realized. . . .

As to the price conditions during the year. Without going into detail the record shows that the prices of the grades of hardwood in most general use were increased to an unprecedented extent during the year. Thus, the increases in prices of varieties of oak, range from 33.3 per cent to 296 per cent during the year; of gum, 60 per cent to 343 per cent, and of ash, from 55 per cent to 181 per cent. While it is true that 1919 was a year of high and increasing prices generally and that wet weather may have restricted production to some extent, we cannot but agree with the members of the "Plan" themselves, as we have quoted them, and with the District Court in the conclusion that the united action of this large and influential membership of dealers contributed greatly to this extraordinary price increase.

Such close cooperation, between many persons, firms, and corporations controlling a large volume of interstate commerce, as is provided for in this "Plan," is plainly in theory, as it proved to be in fact, inconsistent with that free and unrestricted trade which the statute contemplates shall be maintained. . . .

To call the activities of the defendants, as they are proved in this record, an "Open Competition Plan" of action is plainly a misleading misnomer.

Genuine competitors do not make daily, weekly and monthly reports of the minutest details of their business to their rivals, as the defendants did; they do not contract, as was done here, to submit their books to the discretionary audit and their stocks to the discretionary inspection of their rivals for the purpose of successfully competing with them; and they do not submit the details of their business to the analysis of an expert, jointly employed, and obtain from him a "harmonized" estimate of the market as it is and as, in his specially and confidentially informed judgment, it promises to be. This is not the conduct of competitors but is so clearly that of men united in an agreement, express or implied, to act together and pursue a common purpose under a common guide that, if it did not stand confessed a combination to restrict production and increase prices in interstate commerce and as, therefore, a direct restraint upon that commerce as we have seen that it is, that conclusion must inevitably have been inferred from the facts which were proved. To pronounce such abnormal conduct on the part of 365 natural competitors, controlling one-third of the trade of the country in an article of prime necessity, a "new form of competition" and not an old form of combination in restraint of trade, as it so plainly is, would be for this Court to confess itself blinded by words and forms to realities which men in general very plainly see and understand and condemn as an old evil in a new dress and with a new name.

The "Plan" is, essentially, simply an expansion of the gentlemen's agreement of former days, skillfully devised to evade the law. To call it open competition because the meetings were nominally open to the public, or because some voluminous reports were transmitted to the Department of Justice, or because no specific agreement to restrict trade or fix prices is proved, cannot conceal the fact that the fundamental purpose of the "Plan" was to procure "harmonious" individual action among a large number of naturally competing dealers with respect to the volume of production and prices, without having any specific agreement with respect to them, and to rely for maintenance of concerted action in both respects, not upon fines and forfeitures as in earlier days, but upon what experience has shown to be the more potent and dependable restraints, of business honor and social penalties—cautiously reinforced by many and elaborate reports, which would promptly expose to his associates any disposition in any member to deviate from the tacit understanding that all were to act together under the subtle direction of a single interpreter of their common purposes, as evidenced in the minute reports of what they had done and in their expressed purposes as to what they intended to do.

In the presence of this record it is futile to argue that the purpose of the "Plan" was simply to furnish those engaged in this industry, with widely scattered units, the equivalent of such information as is contained in the newspaper and government publications with respect to the market for commodities sold on boards of trade or stock exchanges. One distinguishing and sufficient difference is that the published reports go to both seller and buyer, but these reports go to the seller only; and another is that there is no skilled interpreter of the published reports, such as we have in this case, to insistently recommend harmony of action likely to prove profitable in proportion as it is unitedly pursued.

Convinced, as we are, that the purpose and effect of the activities of the "Open Competition Plan," here under discussion, were to restrict competition and thereby restrain interstate commerce in the manufacture and sale of hardwood lumber by concerted action in curtailing production and in increasing prices, we agree with the District Court that it constituted a combination and conspiracy in restraint of interstate commerce within the meaning of the Antitrust Act of 1890 (26 Stat. 209) and the decree of that court must be

Affirmed.

■ Holmes, J., dissenting.

When there are competing sellers of a class of goods, knowledge of the total stock on hand, of the probable total demand, and of the prices paid, of course will tend to equalize the prices asked. But I should have supposed that the Sherman Act did not set itself against knowledge—did not aim at a transitory cheapness unprofitable to the community as a whole because not corresponding to the actual conditions of the country. I should have thought that the ideal of commerce was an intelligent interchange made with full knowledge of the facts as a basis for a forecast of the future on both sides. A combination to get and distribute such knowledge, notwithstanding its tendency to equalize, not necessarily to raise, prices, is very far from a combination in unreasonable restraint of trade. It is true that it is a combination of sellers only, but the knowledge acquired is not secret, it is public, and the buyers, I think I may assume, are not less active in their efforts to know the facts. A combination in unreasonable restraint of trade imports an attempt to override normal market conditions. An attempt to conform to them seems to me the most reasonable thing in the world. I see nothing in the conduct of the appellants that binds the members even by merely social sanctions to anything that would not be practised, if we could imagine it, by an allwise socialistic government acting for the benefit of the community as a whole. The parties to the combination are free to do as they will.

I must add that the decree as it stands seems to me surprising in a country of free speech that affects to regard education and knowledge as desirable. It prohibits the distribution of stock, production, or sales reports, the discussion of prices at association meetings, and the exchange of predictions of high prices. It is true that these acts are the main evidence of the supposed conspiracy, but that to my mind only shows the weakness of the Government's case. I cannot believe that the fact, if it be assumed, that the acts have been done with a sinister purpose, justifies excluding mills in the backwoods from information, in order to enable centralized purchasers to take advantage of their ignorance of the facts....

■ Brandeis, J., dissenting, with whom McKenna, J., concurs.

... Restraint of trade may be exerted upon rivals; upon buyers or upon sellers; upon employers or upon employed. Restraint may be exerted through force or fraud or agreement. It may be exerted through moral or through legal obligations; through fear or through hope. It may exist although it is not manifested in any overt act and even though there is no intent to restrain. Words of advice seemingly innocent and perhaps benevolent, may restrain, when uttered under circumstances that make advice equivalent to command. For the essence of restraint is powers; and power may arise merely out of position. Wherever a dominant position has been attained, restraint necessarily arises. And when dominance is attained, or is sought, through combination—however good the motives or the manners of those participating—the Sherman Law is violated; provided, of course, that the restraint be what is called unreasonable.

In the case before us there was clearly no coercion. There is no claim that a monopoly was sought or created. There is no claim that a division of territory was planned or secured. There is no claim that uniform prices were established or desired. There is no claim that by agreement, force, or fraud, any producer, dealer or consumer was to be or has in fact been controlled or coerced. The Plan is a voluntary system for collecting from these independent concerns detailed information concerning the business operations of each, and its opinions as to trade conditions, prospects and policy; and of collating, interpreting, and distributing the data so received among the members of the association and others. No information gathered under the Plan was kept secret from any producer, any buyer or the public....

It is claimed that the purpose of the "Open Competition Plan" was to lessen competition. Competition among members was contemplated and was in vigorous operation. The Sherman Law does not prohibit every lessening of competition; and it certainly does not command that competition shall be pursued blindly, that business rivals shall remain ignorant of trade facts or be denied aid in weighing their significance. It is lawful to regulate competition in some degree. Chicago Board of Trade v. United States, 246 U.S. 231. But it was neither the aim of the plan, nor the practice under it, to regulate competition in any way. Its purpose was to make rational competition possible by supplying data not otherwise available and without which most of those engaged in the trade would be unable to trade intelligently.

The hardwood lumber mills are widely scattered. The principal area of production is the Southern States. But there are mills in Minnesota, New York, New England and the Middle States. Most plants are located near the sources of supply; isolated, remote from the larger cities and from the principal markets. No official, or other public, means have been established for collecting from these mills and from dealers data as to current production, stocks on hand and market prices. Concerning grain, cotton, coal and oil, the Government collects and publishes regularly, at frequent intervals, current information on production, consumption and stocks on hand; and boards of trade furnish freely to the public details of current market prices of those commodities, the volume of sales, and even individual sales, as recorded in daily transactions. Persons interested in such commodities are enabled through this information to deal with one another on an equal footing. The absence of such information in the hardwood lumber trade enables dealers in the large centers more readily to secure advantage over the isolated producer. And the large concerns, which are able to establish their own bureaus of statistics, secure an advantage over smaller concerns. Surely it is not against the public interest to distribute knowledge of trade facts, however detailed. Nor are the other features of the Plan—the market letters and the regional conferences, an unreasonable interference with freedom in trade. Intelligent conduct of business implies not only knowledge of trade facts, but an understanding of them. To this understanding editorial comment and free discussion by those engaged in the business and by others interested are aids. Opinions expressed may be unsound; predictions may be unfounded; but there is nothing in the Sherman Law which should limit freedom of discussion, even among traders.

. . . The illegality of a combination under the Sherman Law lies not in its effect upon the price level, but in the coercion thereby effected. It is the limitation of freedom, by agreements which narrow a market, as in Addyston Pipe & Steel Co. v. United States, 175 U.S. 211, and Montague & Co. v. Lowry, 193 U.S. 38, or by organized boycott, as in Loewe v. Lawlor, 208 U.S. 274, and Eastern States Retail Lumber Dealers' Association v. United States, 234 U.S. 600, or by the coercive power of rebates, as in Thomsen v. Cayser, 243 U.S. 66, which constitutes the unlawful restraint.

The co-operation which is incident to this Plan does not suppress competition. On the contrary it tends to promote all in competition which is desirable. By substituting knowledge for ignorance, rumor, guess and suspicion, it tends also to substitute research and reasoning for gambling and piracy, without closing the door to adventure or lessening the value of prophetic wisdom. In making such knowledge available to the smallest concern it creates among producers equality of opportunity. In making it available also to purchasers and the general public it does all that can actually be done to protect the community from extortion. If, as is alleged, the Plan tends to substitute stability in prices for violent fluctuations, its influence, in this respect, is not against the public interest. The evidence in this case, far from establishing an illegal restraint of trade, presents, in my opinion, an instance of commendable effort by concerns engaged in a chaotic industry to make possible its intelligent conduct under competitive conditions.

The refusal to permit a multitude of small rivals to co-operate, as they have done here, in order to protect themselves and the public from the chaos and havoc wrought in their trade by ignorance, may result in suppressing competition in the hardwood industry. These keen business rivals, who sought through cooperative exchange of trade information to create conditions under which alone rational competition is possible, produce in the aggregate about one-third of the hardwood lumber of the country. This Court held in United States v. United States Steel Corporation, 251 U.S. 417, that it was not unlawful to vest in a single corporation control of 50 per cent of the steel industry of the country; and in United States v. United Shoe Machinery Co., 247 U.S. 32, the Court held that it was not unlawful to vest in a single corporation control of practically the whole shoe machinery industry. May not these hardwood lumber concerns, frustrated in their efforts to rationalize competition, be led to enter the inviting field of consolidation? And if they do, may not another huge trust with highly centralized control over vast resources, natural, manufacturing and financial, become so powerful as to dominate competitors, wholesalers, retailers, consumers, employees and, in large measure, the community?[32]

NOTES

1. MAPLE FLOORING MANUFACTURERS' ASSOCIATION v. UNITED STATES, 268 U.S. 563, 45 S.Ct. 578, 69 L.Ed. 1093 (1925). The Maple Flooring Association consisted of producers of rough lumber and manufacturers of finished flooring. While the manufacturing capacity of the defendants was much less than that of non-members, their output was about 70 per cent of the total production of the types of flooring produced by them. The association engaged in many activities which were not questioned by the Government, such as cooperative advertising, and standardization and improvement of their products. The Government complained of the following activities: (1) the computation and distribution of the average cost of all grades and dimensions of flooring to members; (2) the compilation and distribution of a freight book showing rates from Cadillac, Mich., to about 6,000 points in the United States; (3) the gathering of information by the association as to prices, stocks on hand and the kind and quantity of flooring sold by members, which information was summarized and circulated in tabular form without disclosing the identity of the members regarding the information summarized; and (4) the meetings held to discuss the conditions of the industry. There was no proof nor was it alleged that any agreements had been made affecting prices or production. In preparing the cost data, the association statisticians made use of various arbitrary cost accounting conventions as, for example, in allocating the costs of the rough lumber to the various grades and types of flooring which were produced. Since prices were determined on a delivered basis, it was imperative for the sellers to have ready access to information revealing the pertinent freight rates. The rates from Cadillac, Mich., to most places of shipment approximated that from the various places of manufacture of the association members and the freight book was compiled for purposes of convenience. The Government contended the association had under a previous plan used the freight book as a cloak for price-fixing activities and that the present plan was used for the same purpose. Under the earlier plan, the association fixed a minimum price consisting of cost plus 10 per cent profit, to which the arbitrary freight rate was added. It was contended that under the present plan, price uniformity could be attained by adding the freight rates to the average costs as determined by the secretary from the data submitted by members. The earlier

---

32. Ed. On the dissemination of statistics, see Lamb & Shields, Trade Association Law and Practice Ch. 3 (1971).

plan had been abandoned after the failure of the association to obtain the approval of the FTC and defendants denied that the present plan was being used to fix prices. The Court sustained the contention of the defendants, pointing out, however, that the Sherman Law forbade price fixing and that if defendants used the cost and price data plus an arbitrary percentage of profit as the basis of fixing prices, the statute would be violated.

The trade statistics related to past and closed transactions and the association before suit had abandoned the practice of identifying the information of members in its reports to them. The data compiled by the association were submitted to the Department of Commerce and the Federal Reserve Board. The statistics did not include present price quotations or details as to new or unfilled orders. There was no discussion of prices at the meetings of the association. The district court granted an injunction at the request of the Government. This was reversed by the Supreme Court. The Court pointed out that defendants had not attempted to monopolize their industry and that they had not limited by agreement their freedom of action regarding prices and production. The Sherman Law, it was said, did not inhibit the intelligent conduct of business operations:

> Persons who unite in gathering and disseminating information in trade journals and statistical reports on industry; who gather and publish statistics as to the amount of production of commodities in interstate commerce, and who report market prices, are not engaged in unlawful conspiracies in restraint of trade merely because the ultimate result of their efforts may be to stabilize prices or limit production through a better understanding of economic laws and a more general ability to conform to them, for the simple reason that the Sherman Law neither repeals economic laws nor prohibits the gathering and dissemination of information. . . .

> We realize that such information, gathered and disseminated among the members of a trade or business, may be the basis of agreement or concerted action to lessen production arbitrarily or to raise prices beyond the levels of production and price which would prevail if no such agreement or concerted action ensued and those engaged in commerce were left free to base individual initiative on full information of the essential elements of their business. Such concerted action constitutes a restraint of commerce and is illegal and may be enjoined as may any other combination or activity necessarily resulting in such concerted action as was the subject of consideration in American Column & Lumber Co. v. United States, supra, and United States v. American Linseed Oil Co., supra. But in the absence of proof of such agreement or concerted action having been actually reached or actually attempted, under the present plan of operation of defendants we can find no basis in the gathering and dissemination of such information by them or in their activities under their present organization for the inference that such concerted action will necessarily result within the rule laid down in those cases.

> We decide only that trade associations or combinations of persons or corporations which openly and fairly gather and disseminate information as to the cost of their product, the volume of production, the actual price which the product has brought in past transactions, stocks of merchandise on hand, approximate cost of transportation from the principal point of shipment to the points of consumption, as did these defendants, and who, as they did, meet and discuss such information and statistics without however reaching or attempting to reach any agreement or any concerted

action with respect to prices or production or restraining competition, do not thereby engage in unlawful restraint of commerce. (Stone, J.; Taft, C.J., Sanford and McReynolds, JJ., dissented.)[33]

2.   CEMENT MANUFACTURERS' PROTECTIVE ASSOCIATION v. UNITED STATES, 268 U.S. 588, 45 S.Ct. 586, 69 L.Ed. 1104 (1925). The Government made no charge that the association had placed any limitations upon prices or production. Prices of cement were found in fact to have advanced less than in other fields. The Government challenged the statistical and credit activities of the association. Members submitted to the association a monthly statement of their production, shipments and stocks on hand, and semi-monthly statements of their shipments. These were distributed to members without change or comment, each member thus receiving full information as to the available supply of cement and by whom it was held. The Court does not indicate the precise nature of the shipment reports. It is customary in this industry for manufacturers to make specific job contracts whereby cement is sold for future delivery for use in specific construction jobs. The contract is really an option which does not bind the purchaser but insures him of necessary supplies for the particular construction project. In a rising market, purchasers entered into numerous contracts with manufacturers for the same construction project and thus were able to obtain cement much in excess of their requirements for that job. As they were not bound themselves, they could refuse to accept delivery if the market fell and obtain more than they were entitled to receive when prices rose. To avoid the abuses that had occurred, the manufacturers exchanged detailed information as to all their specific job contracts and employed checkers to inspect and ascertain the exact amounts of cement required on specific jobs. The buyers were thus prevented from obtaining greater supplies than they were entitled to receive under these one-sided agreements. Extensive credit information, including detailed reports concerning delinquent accounts, was also exchanged. "The evidence falls far short of establishing any understanding on the basis of which credit was to be extended to customers or that any cooperation resulted from the distribution of this information, or that there were any consequences from it other than such as would naturally ensue from the exercise of the individual judgment of manufacturers in determining, on the basis of available information, whether to extend credit or to require cash or security from any given customer." A freight book, involving a basing point system, was distributed by the association to its members. Periodic meetings were held at which minor subjects, such as return of bags, bag reports, and trade acceptances were discussed, but not current or future prices, or production or market conditions. There was no proof that these meetings resulted in any agreement or in any uniformity of trade practice. Following its decision in the companion case of the *Maple Flooring Association*, the Court per Stone, J., denied the Government's prayer for an injunction, Taft, C.J., Sanford and McReynolds, JJ., dissenting. See L.C.L. Theatres, Inc. v. Columbia Pictures Inc., 421 F.Supp. 1090 (N.D.Tex.1976), reversed on other grounds, 566 F.2d 494 (5th Cir.1978) (no violation where exchange of information designed to prevent fraudulent reporting).

3.   SUGAR INSTITUTE v. UNITED STATES, 297 U.S. 553, 56 S.Ct. 629, 80 L.Ed. 859 (1936). The defendant sugar refining companies, which supplied 70 to 80 per cent of the sugar consumed in the United States, organized The Sugar Institute in 1927 to cope with the widespread practice of giving largely arbitrary secret price concessions. The members of the Institute agreed in its "Code of Ethics" to sell only upon

---

33. See Phillips, Market Structure, Organization and Performance Ch. VII (1962), discussing the *Hardwood* litigation. See also Wire Mesh Products, Inc. v. Wire Belting Association, 520 F.Supp. 1004 (E.D.Pa.1981).

prices and terms openly announced. The trade practice was to sell on "moves," *i.e.*, price changes were publicly announced in advance and buyers, according to the long-standing custom, were permitted a grace period in which to purchase at a lower price. The change brought on by the Institute was the replacement of an uncertain period of grace with a definite one. There was no agreement to maintain prices or to follow an advance in price, no comment on circulated price changes, and no discussions of prices at meetings.

"The distinctive feature of the 'basic agreement' was not the advance announcements of prices, or a concert to maintain any particular basis price for any period, but a requirement of adherence, without deviation, to the prices and terms publicly announced." Among the practices designed to support the basic agreement were preventing the combination of distribution functions by brokers and warehousemen; concertedly maintaining a system of delivered, rather than f.o.b. refinery, prices; concertedly reducing consignment points from which sugar was distributed; concertedly prohibiting long-term contracts; concertedly refusing to grant quantity discounts, though cost justified; and disseminating statistics—which were withheld from purchasers—relating to production and deliveries of individual refiners, to deliveries by states, to deliveries by states by important differential routes, and to consigned and in-transit stocks by states, while other statistics on total production and deliveries were also supplied to purchasers. The Court held:

> The restraints, found to be unreasonable, were the offspring of the basic agreement. The vice in that agreement was not in the mere open announcement of prices and terms in accordance with the custom of the trade. That practice which had grown out of the special character of the industry did not restrain competition. The trial court did not hold that practice to be illegal and we see no reason for condemning it. The unreasonable restraints which defendants imposed lay not in advance announcements, but in the steps taken to secure adherence, without deviation, to prices and terms thus announced. It was that concerted undertaking which cut off opportunities for variation in the course of competition however fair and appropriate they might be. But, in ending that restraint, the beneficial and curative agency of publicity should not be unnecessarily hampered. The trial court left defendants free to provide for immediate publicity as to prices and terms in all closed transactions. We think that a limitation to that sort of publicity fails to take proper account of the practice of the trade in selling on "moves," as already described, a practice in accordance with which the court found that "the great bulk of sugar always was and is purchased." That custom involves advance announcements, and it does not appear that arrangements merely to circulate or relay such announcements threaten competitive opportunities. On the other hand, such provision for publicity may be helpful in promoting fair competition. If the requirement that there must be adherence to prices and terms openly announced in advance is abrogated and the restraints which followed that requirement are removed, the just interests of competition will be safeguarded and the trade will still be left with whatever advantage may be incidental to its established practice.

The defendants were also ordered to make statistical information relating to production, sales, deliveries, stocks on hand, on consignment or in transit, transportation, and new business, fully and fairly available to the purchasing and distributing trade, as well as to refiners. (Hughes, C.J.; Sutherland and Stone, JJ., not participating).

4.   Compare the legality of the following price reporting plans:

I	II	III
1. Detailed reports to Association of all closed transactions.	1. Filing current and future prices.	1. Detailed reports of all closed transactions and filing current and future prices.
2. Circulation of abstract, statistical summaries.	2. Circulation of prices of individual sellers.	2. Circulation of abstract, statistical summaries.
3. Availability of reports to customers and the public.	3. Non-disclosure of reports to customers and the public.	3. Availability of reports to customers and the public.
4. No agreement affecting freedom of price action.	4. Agreement not to deviate from filed prices without notification of change to Association.	4. No agreement affecting freedom of price action.
	5. Immediate report to the Association of all price changes.	5. Use of impartial statistical agency.
	6. Waiting period.	6. No waiting period.
	7. Circulation of interpretative comments.	7. No interpretative comments.
	8. Penalties for noncompliance with plan.	8. Penalties for not furnishing accurate information.

Would the validity of Plan I be affected by the full disclosure of all the terms of sale, including the names of buyers and sellers? Would the validity of Plan II be affected by the use of an impartial statistical agency and the disclosure of statistical reports to customers and the public? How much would the validity of each plan be affected by a finding that the companies involved were in a highly or moderately concentrated market?[34]

United States v. Container Corporation of America

Supreme Court of the United States, 1969.
393 U.S. 333, 89 S.Ct. 510, 21 L.Ed.2d 526.

■ DOUGLAS, J. This is a civil antitrust action charging a price-fixing agreement in violation of § 1 of the Sherman Act. The District Court dismissed the complaint. 273 F.Supp. 18. The case is here on appeal, 15 U.S.C.A. § 29; and we noted probable jurisdiction. 390 U.S. 1022.

---

34. See Sullivan, Handbook of the Law of Antitrust 265–73 (1977). Lamb & Shields, Trade Association Law and Practice Pt. I (1971), presents a most helpful summary and analysis of the antitrust laws as they affect trade association activities, and ABA Antitrust Section, Antitrust Law Developments 35–37 (2d ed. 1984) contains a useful summary of recent cases. See also Symposium on Trade Associations, 27 ABA Antitrust Section 127 (1965); 1955 Att'y Gen.Rep. 17; Kemker, "Legality of Trade Association Statistical Reporting under the Antitrust Laws," 11 Vand. L.Rev. 361 (1958); Kern, "Price Reporting by Trade Associations," 6 ABA Antitrust Section 62 (1955); Jacobs, "Statistical Standardization and Research Activities," 6 ABA Antitrust Section 80 (1955).

The case as proved is unlike any other price decisions we have rendered. There was here an exchange of price information but no agreement to adhere to a price schedule as in Sugar Institute v. United States, 297 U.S. 553, or United States v. Socony–Vacuum Oil Co., 310 U.S. 150. There was here an exchange of information concerning specific sales to identified customers, not a statistical report on the average cost to all members, without identifying the parties to specific transactions, as in Maple Flooring Mfrs. Ass'n v. United States, 268 U.S. 563. While there was present here, as in Cement Mfrs. Protective Ass'n v. United States, 268 U.S. 588, an exchange of prices to specific customers, there was absent the controlling circumstances, viz., that cement manufacturers, to protect themselves from delivering to contractors more cement than was needed for a specific job and thus receiving a lower price, exchanged price information as a means of protecting their legal rights from fraudulent inducements to deliver more cement than needed for a specific job.

Here all that was present was a request by each defendant of its competitor for information as to the most recent price charged or quoted, whenever it needed such information and whenever it was not available from another source. Each defendant on receiving that request usually furnished the data with the expectation that he would be furnished reciprocal information when he wanted it.[35] That concerted action is of course sufficient to establish the combination or conspiracy, the initial ingredient of a violation of § 1 of the Sherman Act.

There was of course freedom to withdraw from the agreement. But the fact remains that when a defendant requested and received price information, it was affirming its willingness to furnish such information in return.

There was to be sure an infrequency and irregularity of price exchanges between the defendants; and often the data was available from the records of the defendants or from the customers themselves. Yet the essence of the agreement was to furnish price information whenever requested.

Moreover, although the most recent price charged or quoted was sometimes fragmentary, each defendant had the manuals with which it could compute the price charged by a competitor on a specific order to a specific customer.

Further, the price quoted was the current price which a customer would need to pay in order to obtain products from the defendant furnishing the data.

The defendants account for about 90% of the shipment of corrugated containers from plants in the southeastern United States. While containers vary as to dimensions, weight, color, and so on, they are substantially identical, no matter who produces them, when made to particular specifications. The prices paid depend on price alternatives. Suppliers when seeking new or additional business or keeping old customers, do not exceed a

---

35. This is obviously quite different from the parallel business behavior condoned in Theatre Enterprises, Inc. v. Paramount Film Distributing Corp., 346 U.S. 537.

competitor's price. It is common for purchasers to buy from two or more suppliers concurrently. A defendant supplying a customer with containers would usually quote the same price on additional orders, unless costs had changed. Yet where a competitor was charging a particular price, a defendant would normally quote the same price or even a lower price.

The exchange of price information seemed to have the effect of keeping prices within a fairly narrow ambit. Capacity has exceeded the demand from 1955 to 1963, the period covered by the complaint, and the trend of corrugated container prices has been downward. Yet despite this excess capacity and the downward trend of prices, the industry has expanded in the Southeast from 30 manufacturers with 49 plants to 51 manufacturers with 98 plants. An abundance of raw materials and machinery makes entry into the industry easy with an investment of $50,000 to $75,000.

The result of this reciprocal exchange of prices was to stabilize prices though at a downward level. Knowledge of a competitor's price usually meant matching that price. The continuation of some price competition is not fatal to the Government's case. The limitation or reduction of price competition brings the case within the ban, for as we held in United States v. Socony–Vacuum Oil Co., supra, 310 U.S. at 224, n. 59, interference with the setting of price by free market forces is unlawful *per se*. Price information exchanged in some markets may have no effect on a truly competitive price. But the corrugated container industry is dominated by relatively few sellers. The product is fungible and the competition for sales is price. The demand is inelastic, as buyers place orders only for immediate, short-run needs. The exchange of price data tends toward price uniformity. For a lower price does not mean a larger share of the available business but a sharing of the existing business at a lower return. Stabilizing prices as well as raising them is within the ban of § 1 of the Sherman Act. As we said in United States v. Socony–Vacuum Oil Co., "in terms of market operations, stabilization is but one form of manipulation." The inferences are irresistible that the exchange of price information has had an anticompetitive effect in the industry, chilling the vigor of price competition. The agreement in the present case, though somewhat casual, is analogous to American Column & Lumber Co. v. United States, 257 U.S. 377; United States v. American Linseed Oil Co., 262 U.S. 371.[36]

Price is too critical, too sensitive a control to allow it to be used even in an informal manner to restrain competition.[37]

---

36. The *American Column* case was a sophisticated and well supervised plan for the exchange of price information between competitors with the idea of keeping prices reasonably stable and of putting an end to cut-throat competition. There were no sanctions except financial interest and business honor. But the purpose of the plan being to increase prices, it was held to fall within the ban of the Sherman Act.

Another elaborate plan for the exchange of price data among competitors was involved in *American Linseed Oil;* and informal sanctions were used to establish "modern cooperative business methods." The arrangement was declared illegal because its "necessary tendency" was to suppress competition. 262 U.S. at 389.

37. Thorstein Veblen in The Theory of Business Enterprise (1904) makes clear how the overabundance of a commodity creates a

Reversed.

■ FORTAS, J., concurring. I join in the judgment and opinion of the Court. I do not understand the Court's opinion to hold that the exchange of specific information among sellers as to price charged to individual customers, pursuant to mutual arrangement, is a *per se* violation of the Sherman Act.

Absent *per se* violation, proof is essential that the practice resulted in an unreasonable restraint of trade. There is no single test to determine when the record adequately shows an "unreasonable restraint of trade"; but a practice such as that here involved, which is adopted for the purpose of arriving at determination of prices to be quoted to individual customers, inevitably suggests the probability that it so materially interfered with the operation of the price mechanism of the marketplace as to bring it within the condemnation of this Court's decisions. [Citing cases]

Theoretical probability, however, is not enough unless we are to regard mere exchange of current price information as so akin to price fixing by combination or conspiracy as to deserve the *per se* classification. I am not prepared to do this, nor is it necessary here. In this case, the probability that the exchange of specific price information led to an unlawful effect upon prices is adequately buttressed by evidence in the record. This evidence, although not overwhelming, is sufficient in the special circumstances of this case to show an actual effect on pricing and to compel us to hold that the court below erred in dismissing the Government's complaint.

In summary, the record shows that the defendants sought and obtained from competitors who were part of the arrangement information about the competitors' prices to specific customers. "[I]n the majority of instances," the District Court found, once a defendant had this information he quoted substantially the same price as the competitor, although a higher or lower price would "occasionally" be quoted. Thus the exchange of prices made it possible for individual defendants confidently to name a price equal to that which their competitors were asking. The obvious effect was to "stabilize" prices by joint arrangement-at least to limit any price cuts to the minimum necessary to meet competition. In addition, there was evidence that, in some instances, during periods when various defendants ceased exchanging prices exceptionally sharp and vigorous price reductions resulted.

On this record, taking into account the specially sensitive function of the price term in the antitrust equation, I cannot see that we would be justified in reaching any conclusion other than that defendants' tacit

business appetite to regulate or control prices or output or both. Measures short of monopoly may have "a salutary effect," as for example a degree of control or supervision over prices not obtainable while the parties "stood on their old footing of severalty." But that relief is apt to be "only transient," for as the costs of production decline and growth of the industry "catches up with the gain in econo-

my," the need for further controls or restraints increase. And so the restless, never-ending search for price control and other types of restraint.

We held in United States v. Socony–Vacuum Oil Co., 310 U.S. 150, that all forms of price fixing are *per se* violations of the Sherman Act....

agreement to exchange information about current prices to specific customers did in fact substantially limit the amount of price competition in the industry. That being so, there is no need to consider the possibility of a *per se* violation.

■ MARSHALL, J., with whom HARLAN, J., and STEWART, J., join, dissenting.

I agree with the Court's holding that there existed an agreement among the defendants to exchange price information whenever requested. However, I cannot agree that that agreement should be condemned, either as illegal *per se*, or as having had the purpose or effect of restricting price competition in the corrugated container industry in the Southeastern United States.

Under the antitrust laws, numerous practices have been held to be illegal *per se* without regard to their precise purpose or harm.... This Court has refused to apply a *per se* rule to exchanges of price and market information in the past.... I believe we should follow the same course in the present case.

Per se rules always contain a degree of arbitrariness. They are justified on the assumption that the gains from imposition of the rule will far outweigh the losses and that significant administrative advantages will result. In other words, the potential competitive harm plus the administrative costs of determining in what particular situations the practice may be harmful must far outweigh the benefits that may result. If the potential benefits in the aggregate are outweighed to this degree, then they are simply not worth identifying in individual cases.

I do not believe that the agreement in the present case is so devoid of potential benefit or so inherently harmful that we are justified in condemning it without proof that it was entered into for the purpose of restraining price competition or that it actually had that effect....

Complete market knowledge is certainly not an evil in perfectly competitive markets. This is not, however, such a market, and there is admittedly some danger that price information will be used for anticompetitive purposes, particularly the maintenance of prices at a high level. If the danger that price information will be so used is particularly high in a given situation, then perhaps exchange of information should be condemned.

I do not think the danger is sufficiently high in the present case. Defendants are only 18 of the 51 producers of corrugated containers in the Southeastern United States. Together, they do make up 90% of the market and the six largest defendants do control 60% of the market. But entry is easy; an investment of $50,000 to $75,000 is ordinarily all that is necessary. In fact, the number of sellers has increased from 30 to the present 51 in the eight-year period covered by the complaint. The size of the market has almost doubled because of increased demand for corrugated containers. Nevertheless, some excess capacity is present. The products produced by defendants are undifferentiated. Industry demand is inelastic, so that price changes will not, up to a certain point, affect the total amount purchased.

The only effect of price changes will to be to reallocate market shares among sellers.

In a competitive situation, each seller will cut his price in order to increase his share of the market, and prices will ultimately stabilize at a competitive level—*i.e.*, price will equal cost, including a reasonable return on capital. Obviously, it would be to everyone's benefit to avoid such price competition and maintain prices at a higher level, with a corresponding increase in profit. In a market with very few sellers, and detailed knowledge of each other's price, such action is possible. However, I do not think it can be concluded that this particular market is sufficiently oligopolistic, especially in light of the ease of entry, to justify the inference that price information will necessarily be used to stabilize prices. Nor do I think that the danger of such a result is sufficiently high to justify imposing a *per se* rule without actual proof.

In this market, we have a few sellers presently controlling a substantial share of the market. We have a large number competing for the remainder of the market, also quite substantial. And total demand is increasing. In such a case, I think it just as logical to assume that the sellers, especially the smaller and newer ones[38] will desire to capture a larger market share by cutting prices as it is that they will acquiesce in oligopolistic behavior. The likelihood that prices will be cut and that those lower prices will have to be met acts as a deterrent to setting prices at an artificially high level in the first place. Given the uncertainty about the probable effect of an exchange of price information in this context, I would require that the Government prove that the exchange was entered into for the purpose of or that it had the effect of restraining price competition.

I do not find the inference that the exchange of price information has had an anticompetitive effect as "irresistible" as does the Court. Like my Brother Fortas, I would prefer that a finding of anticompetitive effect be supported by "evidence in the record." I cannot agree that the evidence in this case was sufficient to prove such an effect. The Government has simply not proved its case.

The Court does not hold that the agreement in the present case was a purposeful attempt to stabilize prices. The evidence in the case, largely the result of stipulation, would not support such a holding. The Government points to a few isolated statements found in the depositions of industry witnesses, but I find these few fragmentary references totally insufficient. The weight of the evidence in the present case indicates that the price information was employed by each defendant on an individual basis, and was used by the defendant to set his prices for a specific customer; ultimately each seller wanted to obtain all or part of that customer's business at the expense of a competitor. The District Court found that there was no explicit agreement among defendants to stabilize prices and I

---

38. The record does not indicate whether all manufacturers engaged in exchange of price information, or whether the practice was limited to defendants. There is no indica- tion that other manufacturers would not have been given price information had they requested it.

do not believe that the desire of a few industry witnesses to use the information to minimize price cuts supports the conclusion that such an agreement was implicit. On the contrary, the evidence establishes that the information was used by defendants as each pleased and was actually employed for the purpose of engaging in active price competition.

Nor do I believe that the Government has proved that the exchange of price information has in this case had the necessary effect of restraining price competition.[39] In its brief before this Court, the Government relies very largely on one finding of the District Court and upon economic theory. The Government has presented a convincing argument in theoretical terms. However, the evidence simply does not square with that theory. And, this is not a case in which it would be unduly difficult to demonstrate anticompetitive effects.

The record indicates that defendants have offered voluminous evidence concerning price trends and competitive behavior in the corrugated container market. Their exhibits indicate a downward trend in prices, with substantial price variations among defendants and among their different plants. There was also a great deal of shifting of accounts. The District Court specifically found that the corrugated container market was highly competitive and that each defendant engaged in active price competition. The Government would have us ignore this evidence and these findings, and assume that because we are dealing with an industry with overcapacity and yet continued entry, the new entrants must have been attracted by high profits. The Government then argues that high profits can only result from stabilization of prices at an unduly high level. Yet the Government did not introduce any evidence about the level of profits in this industry, and no evidence about price levels. Not one customer was called, although the Government surely had ample access to defendants' customers. The Government admits that the price trend was down, but asks the Court to assume that the trend would have been accelerated with less informed, and hence more vigorous, price competition.[40] In the absence of any proof whatsoever, I cannot make such an assumption. It is just as likely that price competition was furthered by the exchange as is it that it was depressed.

Finally, the Government focuses on the finding of the District Court that in a majority of instances a defendant, when it received what it considered reliable price information, would quote or charge substantially the same price.[41] The Court and my Brother Fortas also focus on this

---

39. Here, it is relevant to note again that the evidence was largely the result of stipulation, with the Government admittedly introducing very little evidence on the actual effect of the allegedly illegal practice.

40. There was no effort to demonstrate that the price behavior of those manufacturers who didn't exchange price information, if any, varied significantly from the price be-

havior of those who did. In fact, several of the District Court's findings indicate that when certain defendants stopped exchanging price information, their price behavior remained essentially the same, and, in some cases, prices actually increased.

41. It should be noted that, in most cases, this information was obtained from a

finding. Such an approach ignores, however, the remainder of the District Court's findings. The trial judge found that price decisions were individual decisions, and that defendants frequently did cut prices in order to obtain a particular order.[42] And, the absence of any price parallelism or price uniformity and the downward trend in the industry undercuts the conclusion that price information was used to stabilize prices.[43]

The Government is ultimately forced to fall back on the theoretical argument that prices would have been more unstable and would have fallen faster without price information. As I said earlier, I cannot make this assumption on the basis of the evidence in this record.... Rather the record indicates that, while each defendant occasionally received price information from a competitor, that information was used in the same manner as other reliable market information—*i.e.*, to reach an individual price decision based upon all available information. The District Court's findings that this was a competitive industry, lacking any price parallelism or uniformity, effectively refute the Government's assertion that the result of those decisions was to maintain or tend to maintain prices at other than a competitive level. Accordingly, I would affirm the decision of the court below.

United States v. United States Gypsum Co.

Supreme Court of the United States, 1978.
438 U.S. 422, 98 S.Ct. 2864, 57 L.Ed.2d 854.

In a footnote that was omitted from the *Gypsum* opinion, as noted at p. 246 supra, the Supreme Court said:

> The exchange of price data and other information among competitors does not invariably have anti-competitive effects; indeed such practices can in certain circumstances increase economic efficiency and render markets more rather than less competitive. For this reason, we have held that such exchanges of information do not constitute a *per se* violation of the Sherman Act. *See, e.g.*, United States v. Citizens & Southern National Bank, 422 U.S. 86, 113; United States v. Container Corp., 393 U.S. 333, 338 (Fortas, J., concurring). A number of factors including most prominently the structure of the industry involved and the nature of the information exchanged are generally considered in divining the pro-or anti-competitive effects of this type of interseller communication. See United States v. Container Corp., supra. See generally

customer rather than a competitor, a practice the Government does not condemn.

42. Immediately following the particular sentence emphasized by the Government, there appears the finding that "[i]n many instances, however, depending upon particular circumstances, each defendant quoted lower or higher prices, and in all instances the determination as to the price to be charged or quoted was its individual decision." Other findings of fact are to the same effect.

43. As mentioned above, no evidence was introduced that would indicate that more than minimal price cuts were economically feasible.

Sullivan, Law of Antitrust, 265–274 (1977). Exchanges of current price information, of course, have the greatest potential for generating anti-competitive effects and although not *per se* unlawful have consistently been held to violate the Sherman Act. See American Column & Lumber Co. v. United States, 257 U.S. 377 (1921); United States v. American Linseed Oil Co., 262 U.S. 371 (1923); United States v. Container Corp., supra.

NOTE ON INFORMATION DISSEMINATION

1. Richard A. Posner, in "Information and Antitrust: Reflections on the *Gypsum* and *Engineers* Decisions," 67 Geo.L.J. 1187, 1197, 1199 (1979), proposes the following with respect to exchanges of price data and other information:

> I want to suggest an approach that would dispel this uncertainty in a manner consistent with the fundamental spirit, if not the specific results and narrow holdings, of the series of price exchange cases from *Hardwood* [*i.e., American Column & Lumber*, p. 548] to *Gypsum*. The heart of my proposal is that an agreement simply to exchange price information should not be regarded as a violation of the antitrust laws. Such an agreement should only be admissible as evidence of an agreement to fix prices, which would be, in my view, unlawful whether express or tacit. If the trier of fact is satisfied that a group of firms has agreed to exchange price information but has not directly or indirectly, tacitly or explicitly, formally or informally, agreed to fix prices, there should be no finding of a Sherman Act violation.... If the only thing that a group of competitors does is exchange price information—no matter how detailed the information is, how frequently it is exchanged, or whether it pertains to past or current prices—the price level will be unaffected. Some firms will discover that their prices are too high, others that their prices are too low, but the average price should be unchanged. Narrowing the dispersion of prices will have none of the bad effects associated with monopoly or price fixing; on the contrary, it will bring the pricing in the market more closely in line with the conditions that would prevail under perfect competition.... A pure agreement to exchange price information should always be considered lawful. Market structure becomes relevant only when the Government or a private plaintiff argues, as it is always free to do, that the existence of the agreement to exchange information provides circumstantial evidence of an underlying agreement to fix prices. Suppose, for example, that there were only two firms in a market, selling a completely homogeneous product to knowledgeable buyers, and that the two firms agreed on a very detailed exchange of current and future prices.... There would thus be a strong basis for an inference that the agreement was a mask for something more sinister....

What are the advantages, if any, of forcing the Government or a private plaintiff to prove a conspiracy to fix prices rather than treating an agreement to exchange information as a contract, combination, or conspiracy that may be an unreasonable restraint of trade? What are the disadvantages? Why not allow the Government or a private plaintiff to use the exchange of information to prove either a conspiracy to fix prices or an unreasonable restraint of trade? Do you read the *Container* and *Gypsum* decisions as consistent or inconsistent with Posner's view?

2.   A consent decree between the Government and GE and Westinghouse[44] summarized at pp. 550 to 551 supra, addressed the situation postulated by Posner as to two firms in a market. As noted earlier, the consent decree prohibited GE and Westinghouse, producers of large turbine generators, from: (i) disseminating price lists or price-related information from which a general pricing policy can be inferred; (ii) using or retaining "price books" of the other; (iii) publicly announcing price changes or examining the bid that the other manufacturer had made to a customer; and (iv) granting retroactive price cuts on previously concluded transactions. GE had previously announced a retroactive discount program that guaranteed that if GE cut a price it would pay a retroactive discount to all customers who had purchased similar equipment in a prior period. Assistant Attorney General Donald I. Baker explained:

> Essentially, the Government's allegations were that GE and Westinghouse engaged in indirect price communication and signaling. Information was communicated, in public, which established a body of public data sufficient to identify the appropriate price of a given turbine generator. At the same time certain policy positions were adopted which had the effect, and we contend the purpose, of assuring each seller that the other would adhere to a formula price based on the book. Rather than simply a case of unavoidable conscious parallelism, the Government views this as a case of "avoidable cooperation."

> We drafted relief designed to eliminate those artificially-created conditions which made it possible for two companies jointly to control prices and market conditions—to create certainty where uncertainty should have existed.... Some of the specific provisions will illustrate our efforts to ensure independent pricing in the future. For example ... by limiting the distribution of such individually prepared price books, and prohibiting the companies from announcing their pricing policies, we hope to have broken the parallel pricing pattern of the past thirteen years. In the event the companies rely upon formulas, multipliers or pricing policies internally, they may not communicate such formulas or policies outside the company. The publication of such factors facilitates the communication of prices and changes in prices.[45]

3.   The federal government has taken a similar position with regard to the sharing of information in the health care industry. Three of the nine statements released by the FTC and the Antitrust Division in September 1994 on antitrust and the health care industry deal with information sharing and gathering by competing providers. All three of the statements related to information recognize that information sharing among providers provides some benefit to consumers. The Guidelines suggest that allowing providers to collect and to share information with health care purchasers (particularly third-party payers) should help consumers decide what procedures to cover and how much to pay and that allowing providers to participate in market surveys of current and past fees, reimbursement and costs should help individual providers to set prices more competitively. To ensure that the sharing of fee information does not diminish competition, the Guidelines establish an antitrust safety zone. Three conditions must be met to remain within the safety zone: (i) a third-party (*e.g.*, the government, a purchaser, a consultant or an academic institu-

44. United States v. General Electric Co., 1977–2 Trade Cases ¶ 72,717 (E.D.Pa. 1977).

45. Baker, Monopoly: Problems & Progress, address at the Association of the Bar of the City of New York (Jan. 18, 1977)

tion) must collect the information; (ii) the information available to competing providers (but not to consumers) must be more than three months old; and (iii) at least five providers must supply information, with no individual provider's data representing more than 25% of a given statistic on a weighted basis. The sharing of information about prospective fees is outside the safety zone. According to the Guidelines, prospective fee information poses a more significant risk to competition. As a result, the Guidelines provide that any agreement to share information about future fees will be evaluated on a case-by-case basis.

NOTE: TRADE MEETINGS

Should a trade association be liable when its members use its meetings as the planning grounds for the conspiracy? In a recent case, two metal building insulation suppliers faced with an increase in the price of fiberglass, a major metal building insulation component, adopted uniform pricing policies. The purpose of the uniform price was to ensure that neither company would quote or sell under the other's prices. At a laminators' trade association meeting, the two suppliers discussed the plan to adopt uniform prices with other members, and solicited additional competitors to participate in the conspiracy. The two suppliers were successful in their recruitment scheme, and at the criminal appeal, a representative from another supplier testified that he agreed to the proposal to fix prices and to publish a common or substantially identical price list. United States v. Maloof, 205 F.3d 819 (5th Cir.2000). In this case, the trade association's liability was not litigated, implying that the trade association must take affirmative action in order to be liable under the antitrust laws.

PROBLEM 12

STATISTICAL REPORTING OF TAG MFRS. INSTITUTE

The Tag Manufacturers Institute is a trade association of the producers of 95 per cent of the tag products sold in the United States; the four largest manufacturers share 55 per cent of the business. The Institute engages in the collection and dissemination of statistics; the participation of members is defined in the Institute's by-laws and reinforced by provisions for liquidated damages in the event members are derelict in performing their duties.

Members provide the Institute with a complete list of their products, including specifications, and with a complete list of prices, including terms of sale. By the close of business on the day following the event, members are obliged to sell to the Institute complete details concerning: (1) changes in their price lists or specifications; (2) sales at other than list prices, which the members retain complete freedom to make; and (3) sales at list prices. The Institute then sends to its members, within a few days and without commentary, (1) revisions in the Institute's compilation of the price lists of all members, (2) complete details concerning off-list sales (except for the identity of the buyer), and (3) summaries of volume and value of list-price sales of various categories of tags, without indicating either seller or buyer identity. These materials are available to members of the public desiring to pay the expense of the service; there is but one such subscriber. The materials are also examined occasionally by members of the public at the Institute's offices in New York City.

No fixed patterns have emerged with respect to pricing policies under the Institute's arrangements. Some 25 per cent of sales are made at off-list prices, scattered without regard to size or location of buyer or seller. Prices on some products are more uniform than on others, but no increase or decrease in price uniformity is discernible since the beginning of the Institute's operations. Off-list prices consist largely of responses by other members to non-uniform competitive offers by two or three members of the Institute.

Are any of the Institute's activities violative of the antitrust laws?

PROBLEM 13

INFORMATION ON THE INTERNET

A trade association maintains a website that serves as a discussion board for its members. Mindful of the antitrust case law, the trade association clearly states that its members are not to explicitly nor implicitly agree to fix prices, boycott suppliers or customers, or violate the laws against collusion in any other manner. The members, ably aided by antitrust counsel, restrict their discussions to matters of technical import.

One of the member companies, Company A, lays off its Marketing and Business Development Manager. The Manager, in a fit of anger, posts his company's price list, including current prices and expected price changes. Shortly thereafter, the other member companies begin to raise their prices to match those of Company A. Their prices do not rise above the level charged by Company A, and Company A does not lower its price levels in an attempt to attract more customers.

Are the member companies liable under the antitrust laws?

Section 5.   Intra-Enterprise Conspiracy—A Building Block Largely Abandoned

In Copperweld Corp. v. Independence Tube Corp., 467 U.S. 752 (1984), the Supreme Court swept aside the largely lamented intra-enterprise conspiracy doctrine. Prior to *Copperweld*, plaintiffs could pursue § 1 Sherman Act claims against companies and their wholly-owned subsidiaries because, according to United States v. Yellow Cab Co., 332 U.S. 218 (1947), "common ownership and control ... are impotent to liberate [an] alleged combination and conspiracy from the impact of the Act." *Id.* at 227. In *Copperweld*, the Court reexamined the intra-enterprise conspiracy doctrine started by Yellow Cab and found it wanting. The Court explained that the unity of purpose between parent and subsidiary makes conspiracy for § 1 purposes impossible. It held that "the coordinated conduct of a parent and its wholly owned subsidiary must be viewed as that of a single enterprise for purposes of § 1 of the Sherman Act." 467 U.S. at 772. *Copperweld* has spawned nearly as many questions as it answered. See Calkins, *Copperweld* in the Courts: The Road to Caribe, 63 Antitrust L.J. 345 (1995).

1.   While the Supreme Court rejected the intra-enterprise conspiracy doctrine for parents and their wholly-owned subsidiaries, it carefully left open the question at what point below full ownership such protection would cease. Courts agree that *de minimis* departures from 100% ownership fall within the rule. But once that threshold is crossed courts are all over the map. *Copperweld* has been applied where the parent held 91.9, 85,

82, 80, and 51 percent of its subsidiary's stock but not to holdings of 79, 74, and 54 percent. For a sense of the confusion, compare Viacom International, Inc. v. Time, Inc., 785 F.Supp. 371 (S.D.N.Y.1992) (sufficient unity of interest with 82% of the stock and 93% of the voting power) with Aspen Title & Escrow, Inc. v. Jeld–Wen, Inc., 677 F.Supp. 1477 (D.Or.1987) (75% insufficient to fall within *Copperweld*).

On this issue, there is also a split of authority in agencies and in the academy. The Justice Department has advocated at least two different positions. The Solicitor General, in his brief to the Supreme Court in *Copperweld*, suggested that ownership levels between 50 percent and 100 percent should create a presumption that two companies are insufficiently independent to conspire. However, in the 1988 International Guidelines, the Antitrust Division adopted a majority-stockholding test. The Division dropped this test from the most recent revision of the International Guidelines. As for the academy, Professor (now Judge) Diane Wood suggested that courts should extend *Copperweld* to reach 51–99 percent subsidiaries, because they do not pose a risk to competition. Diane Wood (Hutchinson), Antitrust 1984: Five Decisions in Search of a Theory, 1984 Sup.Ct.Rev. 69, 96. Other commentators have suggested that partially owned subsidiaries and affiliates should be distinguished from their wholly-owned cousins. Stewart, Comment, The Intra–Enterprise Conspiracy Doctrine After *Copperweld Corp. v. Independence Tube Corp.*, 86 Colum.L.Rev. 198 (1986).

2. *Copperweld* problems arise when companies (and shareholders) have contemplated but not consummated a merger (or a transfer of a controlling interest). Should intra-enterprise immunity apply once two companies have agreed to merge? If so, at what point in the merger negotiations should the suitors be outside § 1? The Eighth Circuit has concluded that once a merger agreement has been announced, the parties to the agreement are beyond the reach of § 1. International Travel Arrangers v. NWA, Inc., 991 F.2d 1389, 1398 (8th Cir.1993), cert. denied, 510 U.S. 932. Do you agree? Consider the planned 1996 merger of two large drugstore chains, Rite Aid and Revco. The FTC opposed the deal, and, eventually, it collapsed. Should the companies be beyond the reach of § 1 for any joint decision made during their engagement? Until the merger is completed, aren't companies distinct enough to have divergent economic interests?

3. Another variant of this problem arises when companies have common owners. The Fifth Circuit rejected a § 1 claim against two companies that were owned in common by three people, two of whom each owned 30% and the other 40% of both companies. Century Oil Tool, Inc. v. Production Specialties, Inc., 737 F.2d 1316, 1317 (5th Cir.1984). Should this rule apply when ownership groups only partially overlap or when the interests are not identical? Is there a sufficient "unity of purpose" among the two companies? What if the companies had been integrated in the past? What if control was all in the family, such that a mother controlled one company and her daughter the other? In Fishman v. Estate of Wirtz, 807

F.2d 520, 542 n. 19 (7th Cir.1986), the Seventh Circuit suggested that control, even if all in the family, would not create the "complete unity of interest" necessary to fall within *Copperweld*. Judge Easterbrook, dissenting, disagreed. He emphasized that the two companies allegedly conspiring—the company that owned the Chicago Stadium and a group of investors put together to buy the Chicago Bulls, which included the stadium owner's son—had never operated independently. Id. at 576–77.

4. *Copperweld* also crops up when antitrust conspiracies are alleged between a corporation and its agents. Even before *Copperweld*, courts had recognized that agents ordinarily cannot conspire with their principals for § 1 purposes. Courts had created, as the Supreme Court recognized in *Copperweld*, an exception to this general rule "for corporate officers acting on their own behalf." 467 U.S. at 770 n. 15. Courts have stated (and restated) this exception in different ways. In Siegel Transfer, Inc. v. Carrier Express, Inc., 54 F.3d 1125, 1136–37 (3d Cir.1995), the court explained it as follows:

> [I]n order for the concept of a conspiracy between a principal and an agent to apply in the antitrust context, the exception to the general rule should arise only where an agent acts to further his own economic interest in a marketplace actor which benefits from the alleged restraint, and cause his principal to take the anticompetitive actions about which the plaintiff complains. In this way, the exception captures agreements that bring together the economic power of actors which were previously pursuing divergent interests and goals, the type of activity that § 1 was intended to overcome.

a. While other courts have put a different spin on the exception, the trick is not in reconciling competing verbal formulae but in deciding whether an agent has an interest independent of its principal sufficiently related to the alleged conspiracy. In St. Joseph's Hosp. v. Hospital Corp. of America, 795 F.2d 948 (11th Cir.1986), St. Joseph's sought approval from a state regulatory body to provide cardiac surgery. A competing hospital managed by a wholly-owned subsidiary of HCA asked the state to deny the request. When the state did, St. Joseph's sued HCA and the hospital, alleging that they had conspired to prevent St. Joseph's from competing in the cardiac surgery market. The district court granted HCA's motion to dismiss the complaint on the ground that HCA and the hospital were incapable of conspiring with one another for § 1 purposes.

The Eleventh Circuit reversed. It explained that HCA's relationship with the hospital was more complicated than the usual employee/employer relationship. It noted that HCA and the hospital were separate corporate entities and that HCA, because it owned and managed hundreds of hospitals around the country, could have its own reasons for opposing St. Joseph's expansion. The court pointed out, however, that St. Joseph's had not alleged facts to support an inference that HCA had any reason, independent of its employee relationship with the hospital, to oppose St.

Joseph's petition. The court remanded the case to the district court to give St. Joseph's the opportunity to allege the missing facts.

b. The issue of independent interest frequently arises when hospitals deny (or revoke) admitting privileges to physicians. As traditionally organized, hospitals grant certain doctors the right to admit patients to their facilities based on the recommendations of "staff physicians" (*i.e.*, the physicians that already have admitting privileges). The doctors market their practices independently of the hospitals but draw on the resources of the hospital to care for their patients. Physicians denied admitting privileges or whose privileges the hospital has revoked often sue the hospital and the staff physicians, alleging violations of § 1 of the Sherman Act. See generally, Havighurst, Doctors and Hospitals: An Antitrust Perspective on Traditional Relationships, 1984 Duke L.J. 1071.

Post *Copperweld*, courts have tread an uncertain path in deciding whether these decisions can be challenged under § 1. In Oksanen v. Page Memorial Hosp., 945 F.2d 696, 703 (4th Cir.1991) (en banc), cert. denied, 502 U.S. 1074 (1992), the court, after examining the relationship between the staff and the hospital, concluded that "[f]ar from being a competitor with the hospital, the medical staff was in fact a natural component of the hospital's management structure." It explained that the hospital's by-laws left it in complete control over the peer review process and that this control would enable it to bend the process to its, rather than its staff's, interest. The court held that intra-corporate immunity shields a hospital and its medical staff from antitrust liability for decisions made by the staff in the peer review process. However, in Bolt v. Halifax Hospital Medical Center, 851 F.2d 1273, 1280 (11th Cir.1988), cert. denied, 495 U.S. 924 (1990), the court "perceive[d] no basis ... for holding that the members of a medical staff are legally incapable of conspiring with one another" or the hospital. It explained that "each [physician] is a separate economic entity potentially in competition with other physicians." Id. It likewise found the hospital distinct from the staff, declining to draw an analogy to the company/officer cases.

5. Other "untraditional" business relationships also raise the unity of economic purpose issue. In Williams v. I.B. Fischer Nevada, 999 F.2d 445 (9th Cir.1993) (per curiam), the manager of a Jack-in-the-Box fast food restaurant in Las Vegas, Nevada, sued the owner of his franchise, Fischbein, and several others when Fischbein refused to grant him permission to manage a Jack-in-the-Box opening up in Bullhead City, Nevada. The manager alleged that a provision in the contract between the franchisor and the franchisees violated § 1. The provision at issue required him to get the permission of the owner of one franchise in order to take a job at another franchise. The district court found that the franchisor and franchisee shared such a unity of economic purpose that they could not conspire within the meaning of § 1. The court noted, among other things: that all franchises serve the same food; that all share the same logo; that all benefit from advertising created and approved by the franchisor; that employees of every franchise wear the same uniform; and that every contract provides

for an exclusive geographic area. The court also noted that franchisors strive to prevent competition among franchises. The Ninth Circuit affirmed.

Are you persuaded? Do any of the facts noted by the district court justify treating a franchisor and a franchisee the same for § 1 purposes as a parent and its wholly-owned subsidiary? Can you think of any relevant differences overlooked by the district court? If this contractual relationship is immune from § 1 scrutiny, should all contractual relationships be similarly immune as long as the alleged conspiracy falls within the ambit of the contract? See generally Williamson, Markets and Hierarchies: Analysis and Antitrust Implications (1975); Leibenstein, Inside the Firm: The Inefficiencies of Hierarchy (1988). Wouldn't that practically read § 1 out of the statute?

6.   Joint ventures also pose *Copperweld* problems. As noted in Chapter 5, professional sports leagues have argued unsuccessfully that they should be treated as single economic units for the purposes of § 1. In fact, the new Major League Soccer was designed, at least in part, to circumvent this problem. In the MLS, the league owns all the teams while individual investors, in addition to owning shares in the league, own the rights to operate the teams. The new league's backers hope that this structure will allow them to avoid the antitrust problems that have plagued the NBA and NFL. (As an aside: given the Supreme Court's decision in *Brown v. Pro Football, Inc.*, p. 302 n. 90 supra, will future sports leagues likely choose a similar ownership structure?)

At least one admitted joint venture, however, has been held to be a single economic unit for § 1 purposes. In City of Mt. Pleasant, Iowa v. Associated Elec. Co-op., 838 F.2d 268 (8th Cir.1988), the City sued a three-tier rural electrical cooperative, alleging a "price-squeeze" (*i.e.*, that the organization's prices left the city with little room to buy or resell power). At the top of the pyramid sat the Associated Electric Cooperative. The Cooperative owned the organization's transmission grid and most of its electrical generating capacity. It controlled the production and distribution of electricity for the organization. Beneath the Cooperative stood six generation-and-transmission cooperatives (G & Ts). The G & Ts owned a small portion of the transmission grid (mostly smaller lines) and were responsible for selling and transporting power to the next tier, 43 local distribution companies. The 43 distribution companies sold power to 425,000 retail customers. Each customer owned a share of its distribution company, which owned a share of its G & T, which owned the Cooperative. The Eighth Circuit found that the organization was a "single enterprise pursuing a common goal-the provision of low-cost electricity to its rural consumer-members." Id. at 276. The court found "no evidence that any defendant ever pursued interests antithetical to those of the cooperative as a whole." Id. It held that the organization was shielded from § 1 liability by *Copperweld*.

Do you agree that the entire organization was a "single enterprise?" If not, could the organization be structured differently and yet still be owned by the retail consumers (and so retain eligibility for financial assistance from the federal government through the Rural Electrification Administration)? Can this organization be distinguished from other joint ventures, particularly production joint ventures?

SELECTIVE BIBLIOGRAPHY

1. General

FTC Staff, Anticipating the 21st Century: Competition Policy in the New High–Tech, Global Marketplace (1996).

3 Areeda & Turner, Antitrust Law: An Analysis of Antitrust Principles and Their Application 359–90 (1978 & Supp.1996).

Baumol, Panzar & Willig, Contestable Markets and the Theory of Industry Structure (1988 ed.).

Bork, The Antitrust Paradox 163–97 (1978).

Goldschmid, Mann & Weston (eds.), Industrial Concentration: The New Learning (1974).

Posner, Antitrust Law: An Economic Perspective (2d ed. 2001).

Scherer, Competition Policy, Domestic and International (Economists of the Twentieth Century) (2001 ed.).

Stigler, A Theory of Price Ch. 12 (4th ed. 1987).

Stigler, The Organization of Industry (reprinted 1983).

Viscusi, Vernon, and Harrington, Economics of Regulation and Antitrust, (3d ed. 2000).

Williamson, Markets and Hierarchies: Analysis and Antitrust Implications (1983).

Bernheim and Whinston, Multimarket Contact and Collusive Behavior, RAND J Econ. 1990, 21 (1), 1–26.

Calkins, Copperweld in the Courts: The Road to Caribe, 63 Antitrust L.J. 345 (1995).

Duquette, Regulating the National Pastime: Baseball and Antitrust (Jan. 2000).

Hay, Oligopoly, Shared Monopoly, and Antitrust Law, 67 Cornell L.Rev. 439 (1982).

Kwoka, White, eds., The Antitrust Revolution: Economics, Competition and Policy (3d ed. 1998).

Posner, Information and Antitrust: Reflections on the Gypsum and Engineers Decisions, 67 Geo. L.J. 1187 (1979).

Posner, Oligopoly and the Antitrust Laws: A Suggested Approach, 21 Stan. L.Rev. 1562 (1969).

Salop, Strategic Entry Deterrence, 69 Am. Economic Rev. 335 (1979).

Raffaelli, Oligopolies and Antitrust Law, 19 Fordham Int'l L.J. 915 (1996).

Stigler, A Theory of Oligopoly, 72 J.Pol.Econ. 44 (1964).

Turner, The Scope of Antitrust and Other Economic Regulatory Policies, 82 Harv. L. Rev. 1207 (Apr. 1969).

2. The Problem of Oligopoly

Blair, Economic Concentration: Structure, Behavior and Public Policy (1972).

Chamberlin, The Theory of Monopolistic Competition (8th ed. 1962).

Galbraith, American Capitalism—The Concept of Countervailing Power (1993 ed., Classics in Economics Series).

Shepherd, The Economics of Industrial Organization (4th ed. 1999).

Symeonidis, The Effect of Competition: Cartel Policy and the Evolution of Strategy and Structure in British Industry (February 1, 2002).

Mueller, Sources of Monopoly Power: A Phenomenon Called "Product Differentiation," 18 Am.U.L.Rev. (1968).

Raffaelli, Oligopolies and Antitrust Law, 19 Fordham Int'l L.J. 915 (Feb. 1996).

Rodger, The Oligopoly Problem and the Concept of Collective Dominance: EC Developments in Light of U.S. Trends in Antitrust Law and Policy, 2 Colum. J. Eur. L. 25 (Winter 1996).

Salop, Strategic Entry Deterrence, 69 Am.Economic Rev. 335 (1979).

Vives, Oligopoly Pricing: Old Ideas and New Tools (September 2001).

3. Facilitating Mechanisms

Carlton, A Reexamination of Delivered Pricing Systems, 26 J.L. & Econ. 51 (1983).

Clark, Price–Fixing Without Collusion: An Antitrust Analysis of Facilitating Practices After Ethyl Corp, 1983 Wis.L.Rev. 887 (1983).

Crocker, What Do "Facilitating Practices" Facilitate? An Empirical Investigation of Most–Favored–Nation Clauses in Natural Gas Contracts, 37 J.L. & Econ. 297 (1994).

DeSanti, and Nagata, Competitor Communications: Facilitating Practices or Invitations to Collude? An Application of Theories to Proposed Horizontal Agreements Submitted for Antitrust Review, 63 Antitrust L.J. 93 (Fall, 1994).

Havighurst, Doctors and Hospitals: An Antitrust Perspective on Traditional Relationships, 1984 Duke L.J. 1071 (1984).

Henry, Benchmarking and Antitrust, 62 Antitrust L.J. 483 (Winter 1994).

Kattan, Beyond Facilitating Practices: Price Signaling and Price Protection Clauses in the New Antitrust Environment, 63 Antitrust L.J. 133 (1994).

Turner, The Definition of Agreement Under the Sherman Act: Conscious Parallelism and Refusals to Deal, 75 Harv.L.Rev. 665 (1962).

Vita, Fifteen Years After Ethyl: The Past and Future of Facilitating Practices, 68 Antitrust L.J. 991 (2001).

Willis & Pitofsky, Antitrust Consequences of Using Corporate Subsidiaries, 43 N.Y.U.L.Rev. 20 (1968).

4. Trade Associations

Lande and Marvel, The Three Types of Collusion: Fixing Prices, Rivals, and Rules, 2000 Wis. L. Rev. 941 (2000).

CHAPTER 7

VERTICAL RESTRAINTS ON COMPETITION

SECTION 1. THE ECONOMICS OF VERTICAL RESTRAINTS

INTRODUCTORY NOTE ON VERTICAL RESTRAINTS

Manufacturers usually decide not to sell products to consumers directly or through agents, but rather to develop a network of independent intermediate distributors and retail outlets. When their product is a trademarked commodity or line of goods, they frequently enter into continuing contractual relations, sometimes designating the distributors as "franchisees." They may find it in their interests to limit the degree and nature of competition among their dealers or classes of dealers. Such so-called "vertical" restraints on competition in distribution produce a host of antitrust problems.

The most important vertical restraints relate to the prices at which distributors sell, the geographic territories or classes of customers to which they sell, or the degree of exclusivity the manufacturer or the distributor can count on from the other.

Vertical *price fixing* can involve the fixing of either maximum or minimum prices at which dealers can resell. Effects on price can also be achieved indirectly through lesser restraints—for example, an agreement between the supplier and intermediate dealers that does not limit the price at which they sell, but provides that they will not do business with "known discounters."

Vertical *market allocation* usually establishes the territories in which dealers may sell or the classes of customers to whom they may sell. Territorial restraints may be "air-tight" in the sense that each dealer has an exclusive territory, or they may create a system in which several dealers service the same geographic area but are bound not to sell outside it. An example of customer allocation would be a distribution system in which one set of dealers agrees to service only wholesalers or industrial users, and another set of dealers agrees to service only retailers.

Less pronounced market allocation effects can be achieved in other ways. For example, a "location clause" specifies the site of a distributor's place of business and may provide that the distributor cannot sell the manufacturer's product, without permission, from any other location. Unlike "air-tight" territorial alloca- tion, however, a location clause permits the distributor to sell to any customer whose business it can obtain wherever the customer is located. A "primary responsibility" clause constitutes an agreement by a distributor to use its best effort to achieve an agreed-upon sales target within a specified geographic area or to a specified class of customers. After it has achieved that target (for example, a sales quota of at least 75% of the previous year's annual sales), it is free to sell anywhere or to any class of customers it chooses. A "profit passover" clause provides that the distributor may sell into territories or to classes of customers not assigned to it, provided that it pays over a portion of the profit attributable to such sales to the distributor whose assigned territory or class of customers is "invaded." The amount of profit "passed over" is often designed to compensate the recipient for past expenses incurred in advertising or pre-sale marketing efforts that may have been instrumental in the sale.

A third general class of vertical restrictions involves *exclusive dealership* agreements, in which the manufacturer itself agrees not to sell in competition with the dealer and not to establish another dealership in the assigned area. The legality of exclusive dealerships will be examined in Chapter 8. They need to be mentioned here, however, because of the way they relate to vertical territorial and customer restraints. Promises of "air-tight" exclusivity by a manufacturer can usually be made effective only if territorial or customer restraints, location clauses, or other vertical restrictions effectively prevent the manufacturer's other distributors from intruding. In effect, exclusive distributional systems require that each dealer accept at least some limitations on its own freedom to compete in favor of others.

Arguments with respect to the pro-and anticompetitive effects of vertical price fixing and vertical territorial and customer allocation are similar but not identical. We will examine first arguments concerning the effects of minimum vertical price fixing.

1. Anticompetitive Effect Of Vertical Price Fixing

The essential argument supporting antitrust illegality of vertical minimum price fixing (or "resale price maintenance") is that such agreements produce the same effects as horizontal price fixing among dealers. The manufacturer may be induced to act as organizer of a dealers' cartel by the dealers' threat to turn elsewhere or because it expects in return some "payment" from the dealers in terms of preferred treatment (such as shelf space), or more aggressive marketing of the manufacturer's product.

Another possible anticompetitive effect of resale price maintenance is that it tends to stabilize prices at the manufacturers' level. Cartels, as we have learned, are often unstable because of the tendency of members to "cheat." Manufacturers in a cartel—especially one that generates high monopoly profits by sharply curtailing output—will be tempted to offer price concessions to some buyers in order to increase their volume at least in part at the expense of fellow cartel members. If resale price maintenance eliminates distributor price-cutting, one important pressure for manufacturer price concessions is diminished and the manufacturers' cartel is stabilized. Detection of "cheating" at the manufacturer level is also more readily accomplished where resale prices are generally maintained. All this does not mean that there can be no price competition among manufacturers where there is industry-wide resale price maintenance. Manufacturers still might offer lower prices in order to compete for dealers, as opposed to seeking additional sales volume by competing through dealers for a larger share of purchases by consumers. But resale price maintenance does change and arguably diminishes the incentives to cut price at the manufacturers' level, and in that sense may be viewed as a "facilitating device" for a manufacturers' cartel.

2. Possible Justifications

Despite the plausibility of the argument that vertical price fixing may have horizontal effects at either the dealer or the manufacturer level, it does not follow that it has the *same* anticompetitive impact as horizontal price fixing and should therefore, by analogy, be treated as illegal *per se*. Set out below are some of the arguments that have been advanced to distinguish vertical from horizontal price fixing, and some questions with respect to each. To a large extent, the answer to the policy questions about how to treat vertical price-fixing and other vertical restraints under the antitrust laws depends on the relative weight that you attach to these contentions.

a. *Differing Incentives*

Once a manufacturer has sold a product to one of its dealers, it has extracted all the profit it can take from that particular sale. If the dealer raises or lowers the resale price, that will raise or lower the dealer's profit margin but have no effect on the manufacturer's profit on that particular item. On the other hand, generally higher distributor markups, with resulting higher prices to consumers, will (all other things being equal) tend to lower sales volume.

Thus if the manufacturer is acting to further its own interests—*i.e.*, if it is not simply acting on behalf of a dealer cartel—the resale price it establishes is almost certain to be different from the resale price that would be set by a dealer cartel. The main argument against treating vertical price fixing as the equivalent of horizontal price fixing (and thus as illegal *per se*) is that the manufacturer, concerned about prevailing in interbrand competition with other brands, can be depended upon to set the minimum resale price at a reasonable (or "efficient") level.

Are you satisfied that the manufacturer will act as an effective surrogate for consumers' interests? Suppose the manufacturer has a relatively high market share or its products can successfully be differentiated from those of interbrand rivals by advertising? Or suppose the rivals also engage in resale price maintenance? In those circumstances is interbrand competition an adequate assurance that appropriate competitive prices will be charged? Also, is it an accurate reflection of actual markets to depict the manufacturer as either fully controlling distributional processes for its own interests, on the one hand, or simply serving as an agent for its dealers, on the other? Are there plausible intermediate relationships between those two extremes? For example, might the manufacturers and dealers sometimes best be viewed as joint venturers, seeking over the long run to achieve higher prices and greater profits for all at the expense of consumers?

b. *Attracting Dealers*

Resale price maintenance may assure substantial distributor profits and thereby induce dealers to stock and promote the supplier's brand. This might be particularly important where taking on a new brand requires a substantial investment. But is this defense consistent with the argument that vertical price fixing is different from horizontal price fixing because of the manufacturer's interest in maintaining a high-volume, low-markup sales policy? Are there ways to secure and hold dealers that do not have the adverse competitive impact of resale price maintenance?

c. *Inducing Desired Services*

A manufacturer may independently conclude that a particular mix of price and service competition will be the optimum strategy for selling its product in competition with other brands. For example, suppose marketing studies show that point of sale advertising, elaborate dealer demonstrations and post-sale warranty programs are highly prized by consumers and will help to sell the manufacturer's product. Distributors may not respond to these competitive incentives on their own because of so-called "free rider" and "cream-skimming" problems. Thus, dealers will hesitate to make investments in those kinds of services if other dealers, without being burdened by comparable costs, can offer the same product at lower prices.

As an example of a "free ride," consider the situation in which one dealer maintains an attractive showroom and provides salesperson demonstrations of complicated products while a dealer across the street sells the same product in a no-frills discount operation. Customers may take advantage of the free demonstrations and then buy from the second dealer at a lower price. The "free rider" argument posits that unless the manufacturer can prevent the latter type of operation, services essential to its competitive success will be provided by no one. Similarly, other distributors might seek out only low-cost repeat or high volume business, "skimming the cream" from a market and leaving the less profitable, more difficult sales to the regular outlet.

Is this a persuasive justification for resale price maintenance? If higher mark-ups are assured to dealers, does it follow that they will undertake outlays on non-price competition up to the level of extra profits made available through the vertical restriction? If competition is less than perfect, will not the dealers pocket at least a part of the additional profit? Also, if some purchasers truly want service competition, why can the market not be depended upon to solve this problem by producing some outlets that sell the product at a low price without services and other outlets that charge a higher price but provide more advertising, explanations, and post-sale guarantees? Is there no less anticompetitive way in which any "market failure" can be remedied? Is resale price maintenance the only or even the most likely technique a manufacturer would use to deliver these services to consumers? Why cannot the manufacturer deliver the services itself or separately contract with the dealer to pay all or part of the costs of the services that are desired? Can you think of any services that can *only* be provided through vertical price fixing?

d. *Product Image and "Loss Leaders"*

In an earlier day, advocates of vertical price fixing relied heavily on the argument that it was unfair to the manufacturer to allow dealers to sell its product, against the manufacturer's wishes, at discount prices. The argument is most persuasive when a manufacturer invests resources to create a product image of "quality," or if the product is of a type (perfume, wines) where price reductions may actually reduce sales volume. Some manufacturers dislike seeing their product used as a "loss leader" to induce customers to come into a store and stay to buy other products.

Is it frequently the case that a manufacturer's prospects for profits will be injured by a dealer's offering its product at an extremely low price? Are there some limits on how low that price can be?

e. *Preservation of Small Business*

At various times intense political pressure has been exercised to legalize or even mandate vertical price fixing (see pp. 643–645 infra). In many states, statutes have been enacted declaring "sales below cost" illegal. Most of the political pressure has been generated by the small business community, apparently because many have been apprehensive that aggressive national chains or discount operations would eventually drive small or local merchants out of business. Associations of retail druggists and grocers have been most active historically in advocating resale price maintenance.

In the long run, is resale price maintenance likely to enable an otherwise inefficient retailer to stay in business? Are such attitudes favoring "soft competition" defensible in the public interest?

3. Vertical Restraints Induced By A Policy Of Refusals To Deal

Restraints of the kind here discussed can be implemented either by agreements (express or tacit) between a manufacturer and individual distributors, which are clearly reached by § 1 of the Sherman Act, or by a manufacturer's refusal to deal with distributors who do not comply with suggested prices or other distributional restraints. The materials that follow also deal with the extent to which the antitrust laws reach the latter mode of implementation. In terms of economic effect, are there any reasons why the two should be treated differently?

SECTION 2. THE INTERPLAY OF COMMON LAW AND ANTITRUST LAWS

A. VERTICAL PRICE FIXING

Dr. Miles Medical Co. v. John D. Park & Sons Co.

Supreme Court of the United States, 1911.
220 U.S. 373, 31 S.Ct. 376, 55 L.Ed. 502.

■ HUGHES, J. This is a writ of certiorari to review a judgment of the Circuit Court of Appeals for the Sixth Circuit which affirmed a judgment of the Circuit Court, dismissing, on demurrer, the bill of complaint for want of equity. 164 Fed. 803.

The complainant, a manufacturer of proprietary medicines which are prepared in accordance with secret formulas, presents by its bill a system, carefully devised, by which it seeks to maintain certain prices fixed by it for all the sales of its products both at wholesale and retail. Its purpose is to establish minimum prices at which sales shall be made by its vendees and by all subsequent purchasers who traffic in its remedies. Its plan is thus to govern directly the entire trade in the medicines it manufactures, embracing interstate commerce as well as commerce within the States respectively. To accomplish this result it has adopted two forms of restrictive agreements limiting trade in the articles to those who become parties to one or the other. The one sort of contract, known as "Consignment Contract—Wholesale," has been made with over four hundred jobbers and wholesale dealers, and the other, described as "Retail Agency Contract," with twenty-five thousand retail dealers in the United States.

The defendant is a wholesale drug concern which has refused to enter into the required contract, and is charged with procuring medicines for sale at "cut prices" by inducing those who have made the contracts to violate the restrictions. The complainant invokes the established doctrine that an actionable wrong is committed by one who maliciously interferes with a contract between two parties, and induces one of them to break that contract to the injury of the other and that, in the absence of an adequate remedy at law, equitable relief will be granted.

The principal question is as to the validity of the restrictive agreements.

Preliminarily there are opposing contentions as to the construction of the agreements, or at least of that made with jobbers and wholesale dealers. The complainant insists that the "consignment contract" contemplates a true consignment for sale for account of the complainant, and that those who make sales under it are the complainant's agents and not its vendees. The court below did not so construe the agreement and considered it an effort "to disguise the wholesale dealers in the mask of agency upon the theory that in that character one link in the system for the suppression of the 'cut rate' business might be regarded as valid," and that under this agreement "the jobber must be regarded as the general owner and engaged in selling for himself and not as a mere agent of another."

There are certain allegations in the bill which do not accord with the complainant's argument. Thus it is alleged that it "has been and is the uniform custom" of the complainant "to sell said medicines, remedies and cures to jobbers and wholesale druggists, who in turn sell and dispose of the same to retail druggists for sale and distribution to the ultimate purchaser or consumer." And in setting forth the form of the agreement in question it is alleged that it was "required to be executed by all jobbers and wholesale druggists to whom your orator sold its aforesaid remedies, medicines and cures." It is further stated that as a means of maintaining "said list of prices," cards bearing serial identifying numbers are placed in each package of remedies "sold to jobbers and wholesale druggists." But it is also alleged in the bill that under the provisions of the contract the title to the medicines remained in the complainant "until actual sale in good faith to retail dealers, as therein provided." . . .

If, however, we consider the "consignment contract" as one which in legal effect provides for consignments of goods to be sold by an agent for his principal's account, and that the tenor of the agreement as set forth must be taken to override the inconsistent general allegations to which we have referred, this alone would not be sufficient to support the bill.

The bill charges that the defendant has unlawfully and fraudulently procured the proprietary medicines from the complainant's "wholesale and retail agents" in violation of their contracts. But it does not allege that the goods procured by the defendant from "wholesale agents" were goods consigned to the latter for sale. The description "wholesale agent" refers to those who have signed the "consignment contract." This contract, however, permits one "wholesale agent" to sell to another "wholesale agent." For all that appears, the goods procured by the defendant may have been purchased by the defendant's vendors from other wholesale agents. The bill avers that prior to the introduction of the described system the defendant, a wholesale house, had dealt in the remedies and had purchased them from the complainant and from "wholesale druggists and jobbers." There is nothing in the bill which is inconsistent with such an actual course of dealing, permitted by the agreement itself, with respect to the wholesale dealers who have signed it. But the goods which one wholesale agent purchased from another wholesale agent would not be held for sale as consigned goods belonging to the complainant and to be accounted for as such; and their sale by the wholesale dealer, who had acquired title, would be made for his own account and not for that of the complainant. The allegations of the bill and the plain purpose of the system of contracts do not permit the conclusion that it was intended that wholesale dealers purchasing goods in this way should be free to sell to any one at any price. Evidently it was not contemplated that the restrictions of the system should be escaped in such a simple manner. But if the restrictions of the "consignment contract," as to prices and vendees, are to be deemed to apply to the sale of goods which one wholesale dealer has purchased from another, it is evident that the validity of the restrictions in this aspect must be supported on some other ground than that such sale is made by the wholesale dealer as the agent of the complainant. The case presented by the bill cannot properly be regarded as one for inducing breach of trust by an agent.

The other form of contract, adopted by the complainant, while described as a "retail agency contract," is clearly an agreement looking to sale and not to agency. The so-called "retail agents" are not agents at all, either of the complainant or of its consignees, but are contemplated purchasers who buy to sell again, that is, retail dealers. It is agreed that they may purchase the medicines manufactured by the complainant at stated prices. . . .

The bill asserts complainant's "right to maintain and preserve the aforesaid system and method of contracts and sales adopted and established by it." It is, as we have seen, a system of interlocking restrictions by which the complainant seeks to control not merely the prices at which its agents may sell its products, but the prices for all sales by all dealers at wholesale or retail, whether purchasers or sub-purchasers, and thus to fix the amount which the consumer shall pay, eliminating all competition. The essential features of such a system are thus described by Mr. Justice Lurton (then Circuit Judge), in the opinion of the Circuit Court of Appeals in the case of *John D. Park & Sons Co. v. Samuel B. Hartman*, 153 Fed. 24: "The contracting wholesalers or jobbers covenant that they will sell to no one who does not come with complainant's license to buy, and that they will not sell below a minimum price dictated by complainant. Next, all competition between retailers is destroyed, for each such retailer can obtain his supply only by signing one of the uniform contracts prepared for retailers, whereby he covenants not to sell to anyone who proposes to sell again unless the buyer is authorized in writing by the complainant, and not to sell at less than a standard price named in the agreement. Thus, all room for competition between retailers, who supply the public, is made impossible. If these contracts leave any room at any point of the line for the usual play of competition between the dealers in the product marketed by complainant, it is not discoverable. Thus, a combination between the manufacturer, the wholesalers, and the retailers to maintain prices and stifle competition has been brought about."

That these agreements restrain trade is obvious. That, having been made, as the bill alleges, with "most of the jobbers and wholesale druggists and a majority of the retail druggists of the country" and having for their purpose the control of the entire trade, they relate directly to interstate as well as intrastate trade, and operate to restrain trade or commerce among the several States, is also clear.

But it is insisted that the restrictions are not invalid either at common law or under the [Sherman Act] . . . upon the following grounds, which may be taken to embrace the fundamental contentions for the complainant: (1) That the restrictions are valid because they relate to proprietary medicines manufactured under a secret process; and (2) that, apart from this, a manufacturer is entitled to control the prices on all sales of his own products.

First. The first inquiry is whether there is any distinction, with respect to such restrictions as are here presented, between the case of an article manufactured by the owner of a secret process and that of one produced under ordinary conditions. The complainant urges an analogy to rights secured by letters patent. *E. Bement & Sons v. National Harrow Co.*, 186 U.S. 70. In the case cited, there were licenses for the manufacture and sale of articles covered by letters patent with stipulations as to the prices at which the licensee should sell. The court said, referring to the act of July 2, 1890 (p. 92): "But that statute clearly does not refer to that kind of restraint of interstate commerce which may arise from reasonable and legal conditions imposed upon the assignee or licensee of a patent by the owner thereof, restricting the terms upon which the article may be used and the price to be demanded therefor. . . ."

But whatever rights the patentee may enjoy are derived from statutory grant under the authority conferred by the Constitution. This grant is based upon public considerations. The purpose of the patent law is to stimulate invention by protecting inventors for a fixed time in the advantages that may be derived from exclusive manufacture, use and sale. . . .

The complainant has no statutory grant. So far as appears, there are no letters patent relating to the remedies in question. The complainant has not seen fit to make the disclosure required by the statute and thus to secure the privileges it confers. Its case lies outside the policy of the patent law, and the extent of the right which that law secures is not here involved or determined.

The complainant relies upon the ownership of its secret process and its rights are to be determined accordingly. . . .

Here, however, the question concerns not the process of manufacture, but the manufactured product, an article of commerce. The complainant has not communicated its process in trust, or under contract, or executed a license for the use of the process with restrictions as to the manufacture and sale by the licensee to whom the communication is made. The complaintant has retained its secret which apparently it believes to be undiscoverable. Whether its remedies are sold or unsold, whether the restrictions as to future sales are valid or invalid, the complainant's secret remains intact. That the complainant may rightfully object to attempts to discover it by fraudulent means, or to a breach of trust or contract relating to the process, does not require the conclusion that it is entitled to establish restrictions with respect to future sales by those who purchase its manufactured product. It is said that the remedies "embody" the secret. It would be more correct to say that they are manufactured according to the secret process and do not constitute a communication of it. It is also urged that as the process is secret no one else can manufacture the article. But this argument rests on monopoly of production, and not on the secrecy of the process or the particular fact that may confer that monopoly. It implies that, if for any reason monopoly of production exists, it carries with it the right to control the entire trade of the produced article and to prevent any competition that otherwise might arise between wholesale and retail dealers. The principle would not be limited to secret processes, but would extend to goods manufactured by anyone who secured control of the source of supply of a necessary raw material or ingredient. But, because there is monopoly of production, it certainly cannot be said that there is no public interest in maintaining freedom of trade with respect to future sales after the article has been placed on the market and the producer has parted with his title. Moreover, every manufacturer, before sale, controls the articles he makes. With respect to these, he has the rights of ownership and his dominion does not depend upon whether the process of manufacture is known or unknown, or upon any special advantage he may possess by reason of location, materials or efficiency. The fact that the market may not be supplied with the particular article, unless he produces it, is a practical consequence which does not enlarge his right of property in what he does produce.

If a manufacturer, in the absence of statutory privilege, has the control over the sales of the manufactured article, for which the complainant here contends, it is not because the process of manufacture is kept secret. . . .

Second. We come, then, to the second question, whether the complainant, irrespective of the secrecy of its process, is entitled to maintain the restrictions by virtue of the fact that they relate to products of its own manufacture.

The basis of the argument appears to be that, as the manufacturer may make and sell, or not, as he chooses, he may affix conditions as to the use of the article or as to the prices at which purchasers may dispose of it. The propriety of the restraint is sought to be derived from the liberty of the producer.

But because a manufacturer is not bound to make or sell, it does not follow in case of sales actually made he may impose upon purchasers every sort of restriction. Thus a general restraint upon alienation is ordinarily invalid. "The right of alienation is one of the essential incidents of a right of general property in movables, and restraints upon alienation have been generally regarded as obnoxious to public policy, which is best subserved by great freedom of traffic in such things as pass from hand to hand. General restraint in the alienation of articles, things, chattels, except when a very special kind of property is involved, such as a slave or an heirloom, have been generally held void. 'If a man,' says Lord Coke, in Coke on Littleton, section 360, 'be possessed of a horse or any other chattel, real or personal, and give his whole interest or property therein, upon condition that the donee or vendee shall not alien the same, the same is void, because his whole interest and property is out of him, so as he hath no possibility of reverter; and it is against trade and traffic and bargaining and contracting between man and man.' " *Park v. Hartman*, supra. See also Gray on Restraints on Alienation, §§ 27, 28.

Nor can the manufacturer by rule and notice, in the absence of contract or statutory right, even though the restriction be known to purchasers, fix prices for future sales. It has been held by this court that no such privilege exists under the copyright statutes, although the owner of the copyright has the sole right to vend copies of the copyrighted production. *Bobbs–Merrill Co. v. Straus*, 210 U.S. 339. It will hardly be contended, with respect to such a matter, that the manufacturer of an article of commerce, not protected by any statutory grant is in any better case. [Citing cases.] Whatever right the manufacturer may have to project his control beyond his own sales must depend not upon an inherent power incident to production and original ownership, but upon agreement.

With respect to contracts in restraint of trade, the earlier doctrine of the common law has been substantially modified in adaptation to modern conditions. But the public interest is still the first consideration. To sustain the restraint, it must be found to be reasonable both with respect to the public and to the parties and that it is limited to what is fairly necessary, in the circumstances of the particular case, for the protection of the convenantee. Otherwise restraints of trade are void as against public policy. . . .

The present case is not analogous to that of a sale of good will, or of an interest in a business, or of the grant of a right to use a process of manufacture. The complainant has not parted with any interest in its business or instrumentalities of production. It has conferred no right by virtue of which purchasers of its products may compete with it. It retains complete control over the business in which it is engaged, manufacturing what it pleases and fixing such prices for its own sales as it may desire. Nor are we dealing with a single transaction, conceivably unrelated to the public interest. The agreements are designed to maintain prices after the complainant has parted with the title to the articles, and to prevent competition among those who trade in them.

The bill asserts the importance of a standard retail price and alleges generally that confusion and damage have resulted from sales at less than the prices fixed. But the advantage of established retail prices primarily concerns the dealers. The enlarged profits which would result from adherence to the established rates would go to them and not to the complainant. It is through the inability of the favored dealers to realize these profits, on account of the described competition, that the complainant works out its alleged injury. If there be an advantage to a manufacturer in the maintenance of fixed retail prices, the question remains whether it is one which he is entitled to secure by agreements restricting the freedom of trade on the part of dealers who own what they sell. As to this, the complainant can fare no better with its plan of identical contracts than could the dealers themselves if they formed a combination and endeavored to establish the same restrictions, and thus to achieve the same result, by agreement with each other. If the immediate advantage they would thus obtain would not be sufficient to sustain such a direct agreement, the asserted ulterior benefit to the complainant cannot be regarded as sufficient to support its system.

But agreements or combinations between dealers, having for their sole purpose the destruction of competition and the fixing of prices, are injurious to the public interest and void. They are not saved by the advantages which the participants expect to derive from the enhanced price to the consumer.

The complainant's plan falls within the principle which condemns contracts of this class. It, in effect, creates a combination for the prohibited purposes. No distinction can properly be made by reason of the particular character of the commodity in question. It is not entitled to special privilege or immunity. It is an article of commerce, and the rules concerning the freedom of trade must be held to apply to it. Nor does the fact that the margin of freedom is reduced by the control of production make the protection of what remains, in such a case, a negligible matter. And where commodities have passed into the channels of trade and are owned by dealers, the validity of agreements to prevent competition and to maintain prices is not to be determined by the circumstance whether they were produced by several manufacturers or by one, or whether they were previously owned by one or by many. The complainant having sold its product at prices satisfactory to itself, the public is entitled to whatever advantage may be derived from competition in the subsequent traffic....

Judgment affirmed.

■ Holmes, J., dissenting.... I think that we greatly exaggerate the value and importance to the public of competition in the production or distribution of an article (here it is only distribution), as fixing a fair price. What really fixes that is the competition of conflicting desires. We, none of us, can have as much as we want of all the things that we want. Therefore, we have to choose. As soon as the price of something that we want goes above the point at which we are willing to give up other things to have that, we cease to buy it and buy something else. Of course, I am speaking of things that we can get along without. There may be necessaries that sooner or later must be dealt with like short rations in a shipwreck, but they are not Dr. Miles's medicines. With regard to things like the latter it seems to me that the point of most profitable returns marks the equilibrium of social desires and determines the fair price in the only sense in which I can find meaning in those words. The Dr. Miles Medical Company knows better than we do what will enable it to do the best business. We must assume its retail price to be reasonable, for it is so alleged and the case is here on demurrer; so I see nothing to warrant my assuming that the public will not be served best by the company being allowed to carry out its plan. I cannot believe that in the long run the public will profit by this court permitting knaves to cut reasonable prices for some ulterior purpose of their own and thus to impair, if not to destroy, the production and sale of articles which it is assumed to be desirable that the public should be able to get....

NOTES AND QUESTIONS

1. Dr. Miles' initial argument was that the price restrictions were valid because they related to proprietary medicines manufactured under a secret process. Since no one else could manufacture them, Dr. Miles had the legal right to keep them from reaching the market; price restrictions in licenses, it was argued, are less restrictive than no distribution at all. If the more restrictive course of conduct is protected, the less restrictive cannot logically be illegal. This kind of argument—sometimes called the "inherency" or "divisibility theory"[1]—had been successful for patent owners engaging in resale price maintenance. *E. Bement & Sons v. National Harrow Co.*, 186 U.S. 70 (1902). Dr. Miles unsuccessfully urged that the owner of a secret process be accorded the same treatment. What is wrong with this line of argument? The *Bement* case is no longer good law and price maintenance of a patented[2] or copyrighted[3] article is no more protected than price maintenance of any other. Is this the correct rule for any kind of product protected by intellectual property?

2. How essential to the outcome and opinion is the Court's reliance on the common law rule against general restraints on the alienability of chattels, for which Coke on Littleton is cited? What was the policy underlying that rule? What relevance does it have to maintaining resale prices? Were such restraints on alienability always unlawful at common law, or only when unreasonable?

3. What does it mean to say that vertical price fixing "falls within the same principle which condemns" horizontal price fixing? Would an *Interstate Circuit* type of inference of agreement among the retailers be supportable? When retailers go along with a resale price maintenance scheme, is their conduct, according to Professor Turner's analysis (see p. 520 supra), independent or interdependent?

4. Are manufacturers or their distributors most likely to be initiators of resale price maintenance programs? Consider the following:

> ... [R]esale price maintenance is a method used by organized dealers to force unwilling manufacturers to work for them to protect dealer profit

1. See Adelman and Juenger, Patent–Antitrust: Patent Dynamics and Field of Use Licensing, 50 N.Y.U.L.Rev. 273 (1975); Buxbaum, Restrictions Inherent in the Patent Monopoly: A Comparative Critique, 113 U.Pa.L.Rev. 633 (1965).

2. See *United States v. Univis Lens Co.*, 316 U.S. 241 (1942); *Ethyl Gasoline Corp. v. United States*, 309 U.S. 436 (1940); *Straus v. Victor Talking Machine Co.*, 243 U.S. 490 (1917); *Boston Store v. American Graphophone Co.*, 246 U.S. 8 (1918); *Bauer & Cie. v. O'Donnell*, 229 U.S. 1 (1913).

3. See *Bobbs–Merrill Co. v. Straus*, 210 U.S. 339 (1908).

margins. This is a simple, plausible explanation of resale price maintenance, and probably explains much of its recent as well as its early use.
This explanation is supported by the very high proportion of "fair-trade"
cases involving products the dealers of which have been organized in
effective trade associations, for example, drugs, cosmetics and liquor.

Bowman, The Prerequisites and Effect of Resale Price Maintenance, 22 U.Chi.
L.Rev. 825, 830–31 (1955).

In litigation, is it likely that dealer initiated resale price maintenance will be
exposed? Cf. *United States v. General Motors Corp.*, p. 304 supra.

5.   Studies by the Antitrust Division of the Department of Justice and others
indicate that resale price maintenance does result in increased retail prices. For
example, see Hearings on S. 408 Before the Subcommittee on Antitrust and
Monopoly of the Senate Judiciary Committee, 94th Cong., 1st Sess., 174 (1975).
That should not be surprising, however, since the arguments in favor of resale price
maintenance assume that it is imposed in order to generate high profit margins that
in turn will be used to subsidize pre-sale and post-sale services. How would you
devise a study to see whether consumers were getting a better package of product
plus service under RPM?

6.   In Simpson v. Union Oil Co., 377 U.S. 13 (1964), the Supreme Court
extended the prohibition on resale price maintenance to strike down a retail-dealer
consignment agreement. Under the terms of the agreement struck down in
Simpson, Union Oil set the retail price of gasoline and retained "title" to the
gasoline until it passed into the consumer's tanks. While Union Oil paid property
taxes on the gasoline consigned to its dealers, the dealers were liable for any
gasoline lost, except for losses caused by certain acts of God. Simpson received a
commission on each sale. The Court described Union Oil's consignment agreement
as a "clever" attempt to avoid "the end result of *United States v. Socony–Vacuum
Co.*" *Id.* at 21–22. It held "that resale price maintenance through the present,
coercive type of 'consignment' agreement is illegal under the antitrust laws." *Id.* at
24.

Justice Stewart dissented. He explained:

I think upon remand there should be a full trial of all the issues in this
litigation, because I completely disagree with the Court that whenever a
bona fide consignor, employing numerous agents, sets the price at which
his property is to be sold "the antitrust laws prevent calling the 'consignment' an agency," and transform the consignment into a sale. In the
present posture of this case, such a determination, overruling as it does a
doctrine which has stood unquestioned for almost 40 years, is unwarranted, unnecessary and premature.

Id. at 28.

7.   In MORRISON V. MURRAY BISCUIT CO., 797 F.2d 1430 (7th Cir.1986), Morrison,
a wholesale distributor of cookies and crackers, sued the Murray Biscuit Co. on
grounds that Murray had agreed with Feldman, a competitor of Morrison, to
terminate Morrison because it had ignored certain supplier-imposed restrictions on
customers to whom it could sell. One defense was that Murray Biscuit and Feldman
could not conspire because Feldman was a broker/agent and therefore had no
discretion in the sales policies it followed.

Feldman took orders from grocery stores and forwarded them to Murray
Biscuit, which then shipped the goods directly to the stores. It maintained no

inventory. Murray Biscuit set the price and after it received payment, remitted to Feldman 5% as compensation. In analyzing whether the arrangement was a legitimate "agency" or "consignment" under the antitrust laws, the Seventh Circuit (Posner, J.) wrote the following:

> The challenge is to reconcile *Simpson* with the proposition that a homeowner does not violate section 1 of the Sherman Act when he tells his broker at what price to sell his home. The courts' travails in meeting this challenge, well discussed in 7 Areeda, Antitrust Law ¶ 1473 (1986), included such ingenious metaphoric flights as asking whether the agent and his principal constitute "a unified economic consciousness incapable of conspiring with itself." *Pink Supply Corp. v. Hiebert, Inc.*, 788 F.2d 1313, 1317 (8th Cir.1986). We think the key to reconciliation is to be found by asking whether the agency relationship has a function other than to circumvent the rule against price fixing. The consignment arrangement in *Simpson* was described by the Court as "a so-called retail dealer 'consignment' agreement," a "clever manipulation of words," a "wooden formula for administering prices on a vast scale," an "easy manipulation," and a product of "clever draftsmanship." There is no suggestion that the brokerage arrangement between Murray Biscuit and Feldman is artificial or unnatural. Feldman really is just an order taker for Murray Biscuit and other suppliers. He has no interest in or capacity for setting the retail prices of the goods he brokers.

> To answer a question about antitrust as about any other field of law it is always helpful and often essential to consider what the purpose of the law is. The purpose of antitrust law, at least as articulated in the modern cases, is to protect the competitive process as a means of promoting economic efficiency.... Efficiency would not be promoted by a rule that forbade principals to tell their agents at what price to sell the principal's product unless the agent was an employee. Principals would either convert their sales agents from independent contractors to employees or give their sales agents a discretion over price that the agents, for lack of information and expertise, would not be in a position to exercise intelligently.... Brokerage is no more a device for evading the Sherman Act than is telling one's sales clerk what price to mark on a bag of sugar rather than letting him decide for himself.

8.   Largely because of academic criticism of the *Dr. Miles per se* rule covering minimum resale price maintenance, mostly from the economic wing of the profession, enforcement at the federal level was non-existent in the 1980s. A few tentative enforcement efforts were launched during the first Bush Administration, and federal enforcement was substantially restored during the Clinton Administration, mostly in complaints issued by the Federal Trade Commission. All complaints were settled with entry of consent orders.

An interesting case involved a variation on outright RSPM—Minimum Advertised Price policies ("MAP")—adopted by the Big Five prerecorded music distributors (Warner, Universal, EMI, Sony and Bertelsmann). These five firms collectively accounted for about 85% of the market for prerecorded music. Retail margins of 40% were common in the 1980s, but were slashed in the 1990s as a result of a retail price war largely initiated by new entrants such as Best Buy and Circuit City.

Over a period of eleven months in 1995 and 1996, the majors adopted seriatum nearly identical policies providing that minimum prices be identified in all advertising, including ads funded solely by the retailer, as a prerequisite for obtaining any cooperative advertising funds from each music company. The policy also applied to all in-store advertising other than non-promotional stickers on the product (*i.e.*, small and not brightly colored). Severe penalties were imposed for violations, usually involving the loss of all promotional support for six to nine months.

The Federal Trade Commission issued complaints challenging MAP as a "facilitating practice" supporting horizontal price fixing (see discussion in Chapter 6, Section 2), and charging vertical minimum price restraints against each defendant. The vertical cases were based on a rule of reason rather than the *Dr. Miles per se* rule because the Commission's experience with programs like MAP was limited. Supporting a rule of reason challenge were the following factors: sizable market shares, high barriers to entry, and evidence that services provided by the price cutters were as good or better than services provided by smaller stores (*i.e.*, no significant free rider problem). In addition, the Commission's complaint indicated it was prepared to prove that MAP was adopted not only to preserve retail profit margins, but because it was becoming increasingly clear to the music companies that if the price war was not stopped, wholesale margins would eventually be affected. As to the last allegation, consider it in light of the argument that the upstream seller, once it has sold a product to a dealer, has no incentive other than to insure that dealer mark-ups are at the appropriate level (see discussion of "differing incentives" at p. 622, supra).

The consent order imposed the standard cease and desist provisions, with the unusual addition that the companies were denied their *Colgate* right, see p. 679, infra, for a period of five years to facilitate the restoration of competition in the industry. (FTC file No. 971 0070 (May 10, 2000)).

State Oil Co. v. Khan

Supreme Court of the United States, 1997.
522 U.S. 3, 118 S.Ct. 275, 139 L.Ed.2d 199.

■ O'CONNOR, J. Under § 1 of the Sherman Act, 26 Stat. 209, as amended, 15 U.S.C. § 1, "[e]very contract, combination . . . ., or conspiracy, in restraint of trade" is illegal. In *Albrecht v. Herald Co.*, 390 U.S. 145, 88 S.Ct. 869, 19 L.Ed.2d 998 (1968), this Court held that vertical maximum price fixing is a *per se* violation of that statute. In this case, we are asked to reconsider that decision in light of subsequent decisions of this Court. We conclude that Albrecht should be overruled.

I

Respondents, Barkat U. Khan and his corporation, entered into an agreement with petitioner, State Oil Company, to lease and operate a gas station and convenience store owned by State Oil. The agreement provided that respondents would obtain the station's gasoline supply from State Oil at a price equal to a suggested retail price set by State Oil, less a margin of 3.25 cents per gallon. Under the agreement, respondents could charge any amount for gasoline sold to the station's customers, but if the price charged was higher than State Oil's suggested retail price, the excess was to be rebated to State Oil. Respondents could sell gasoline for less than State Oil's suggested retail price, but any such decrease would reduce their 3.25 cents-per-gallon margin.

About a year after respondents began operating the gas station, they fell behind in lease payments. State Oil then gave notice of its intent to terminate the agreement and commenced a state court proceeding to evict respondents. At State Oil's request, the state court appointed a receiver to operate the gas station. The receiver operated the station for several months without being subject to the price restraints in respondents' agreement with State Oil. According to respondents, the receiver obtained an overall profit margin in excess of 3.25 cents per gallon by lowering the price of regular-grade gasoline and raising the price of premium grades.

Respondents sued State Oil in the United States District Court for the Northern District of Illinois, alleging in part that State Oil had engaged in price fixing in violation of § 1 of the Sherman Act by preventing respondents from raising or lowering retail gas prices. According to the complaint, but for the agreement with State Oil, respondents could have charged different prices based on the grades of gasoline, in the same way that the receiver had, thereby achieving increased sales and profits. State Oil responded that the agreement did not actually prevent respondents from setting gasoline prices, and that, in substance, respondents did not allege a violation of antitrust laws by their claim that State Oil's suggested retail price was not optimal.

The District Court found that the allegations in the complaint did not state a *per se* violation of the Sherman Act because they did not establish the sort of "manifestly anticompetitive implications or pernicious effect on competition" that would justify *per se* prohibition of State Oil's conduct. Subsequently, in ruling on cross-motions for summary judgment, the District Court concluded that respondents had failed to demonstrate antitrust injury or harm to competition. The District Court held that respondents had not shown that a difference in gasoline pricing would have increased the station's sales; nor had they shown that State Oil had market power or that its pricing provisions affected competition in a relevant market. Accordingly, the District Court entered summary judgment for State Oil on respondents' Sherman Act claim.

The Court of Appeals for the Seventh Circuit reversed. 93 F.3d 1358 (1996). The court first noted that the agreement between respondents and State Oil did indeed fix maximum gasoline prices by making it "worthless" for respondents to exceed the suggested retail prices. *Id.*, at 1360. After reviewing legal and economic aspects of price fixing, the court concluded that State Oil's pricing scheme was a *per se* antitrust violation under *Albrecht v. Herald Co.*, supra. Although the Court of Appeals characterized Albrecht as "unsound when decided" and "inconsistent with later decisions" of this Court, it felt constrained to follow that decision. 93 F.3d, at 1363. In light of *Albrecht* and *Atlantic Richfield Co. v. USA Petroleum Co.*, 495 U.S. 328 (1990) (ARCO), the court found that respondents could have suffered antitrust injury from not being able to adjust gasoline prices.

We granted certiorari to consider two questions, whether State Oil's conduct constitutes a *per se* violation of the Sherman Act and whether respondents are entitled to recover damages based on that conduct.

II

A

Although the Sherman Act, by its terms, prohibits every agreement "in restraint of trade," this Court has long recognized that Congress intended to outlaw only unreasonable restraints. See, *e.g.*, *Arizona v. Maricopa County Medical Soc.*, 457 U.S. 332, 342–343 (1982) (citing *United States v. Joint Traffic Assn.*, 171 U.S. 505 (1898)). As a consequence, most antitrust claims are analyzed under a "rule of reason," according to which the finder of fact must decide whether the questioned practice imposes an unreasonable restraint on competition, taking into account a variety of factors, including specific information about the relevant business, its condition before and after the restraint was imposed, and the restraint's history, nature, and effect. 457 U.S., at 343, and n. 13 (citing *Board of Trade of Chicago v. United States*, 246 U.S. 231, 238 (1918)).

Some types of restraints, however, have such predictable and pernicious anticompetitive effect, and such limited potential for procompetitive benefit, that they are deemed unlawful *per se. Northern Pacific R. Co. v. United States*, 356 U.S. 1, 5 (1958). *Per se* treatment is appropriate "[o]nce experience with a particular kind of restraint enables the Court to predict with confidence that the rule of reason will condemn it." *Maricopa County*, supra, at 344; *see also Broadcast Music, Inc. v. Columbia Broadcasting System, Inc.*, 441 U.S. 1, 19, n. 33 (1979). Thus, we have expressed reluctance to adopt *per se* rules with regard to "restraints imposed in the context of business relationships where the economic impact of certain practices is not immediately obvious." *FTC v. Indiana Federation of Dentists*, 476 U.S. 447, 458–459 (1986).

A review of this Court's decisions leading up to and beyond Albrecht is relevant to our assessment of the continuing validity of the *per se* rule established in Albrecht. Beginning with *Dr. Miles Medical Co. v. John D. Park & Sons Co.*, 220 U.S. 373 (1911), the Court recognized the illegality of agreements under which manufacturers or suppliers set the minimum resale prices to be charged by their distributors. By 1940, the Court broadly declared all business combinations "formed for the purpose and with the effect of raising, depressing, fixing, pegging, or stabilizing the price of a commodity in interstate or foreign commerce" illegal *per se. United States v. Socony–Vacuum Oil Co.*, 310 U.S. 150, 223 (1940). Accordingly, the Court condemned an agreement between two affiliated liquor distillers to limit the maximum price charged by retailers in *Kiefer-Stewart Co. v. Joseph E. Seagram & Sons, Inc.*, 340 U.S. 211 (1951), noting that agreements to fix maximum prices, "no less than those to fix minimum prices, cripple the freedom of traders and thereby restrain their ability to sell in accordance with their own judgment." *Id.*, at 213.

In subsequent cases, the Court's attention turned to arrangements through which suppliers imposed restrictions on dealers with respect to matters other than resale price. In *White Motor Co. v. United States*, 372 U.S. 253 (1963), the Court considered the validity of a manufacturer's assignment of exclusive territories to its distributors and dealers. The Court determined that too little was known about the competitive impact of such vertical limitations to warrant treating them as *per se* unlawful. *Id.*, at 263, 83 S.Ct., at 702. Four years later, in *United States v. Arnold, Schwinn & Co.*, 388 U.S. 365 (1967), the Court reconsidered the status of exclusive dealer territories and held that, upon the transfer of title to goods to a distributor, a supplier's imposition of territorial restrictions on the distributor was "so obviously destructive of competition" as to constitute a *per se* violation of the Sherman Act. *Id.*, at 379. In *Schwinn*, the Court acknowledged that some vertical restrictions, such as the conferral of territorial rights or franchises, could have procompetitive benefits by allowing smaller enterprises to compete, and that such restrictions might avert vertical integration in the distribution process. *Id.*, at 379–380. The Court drew the line, however, at permitting manufacturers to control product marketing once dominion over the goods had passed to dealers. *Id.*, at 380.

Albrecht, decided the following Term, involved a newspaper publisher who had granted exclusive territories to independent carriers subject to their adherence to a maximum price on resale of the newspapers to the public. Influenced by its decisions in *Socony-Vacuum*, *Kiefer-Stewart*, and *Schwinn*, the Court concluded that it was *per se* unlawful for the publisher to fix the maximum resale price of its newspapers. 390 U.S., at 152–154. The Court acknowledged that "[m]aximum and minimum price fixing may have different consequences in many situations," but nonetheless condemned maximum price fixing for "substituting the perhaps erroneous judgment of a seller for the forces of the competitive market." *Id.*, at 152.

Albrecht was animated in part by the fear that vertical maximum price fixing could allow suppliers to discriminate against certain dealers, restrict the services that dealers could afford to offer customers, or disguise minimum price fixing schemes. *Id.*, at 152–153. The Court rejected the notion (both on the record of that case and in the abstract) that, because the newspaper publisher "granted exclusive territories, a price ceiling was necessary to protect the public from price gouging by dealers who had monopoly power in their own territories." *Id.*, at 153.

In a vigorous dissent, Justice Harlan asserted that the majority had erred in equating the effects of maximum and minimum price fixing. *Id.*, at 156–168 (Harlan, J., dissenting). Justice Harlan pointed out that, because the majority was establishing a *per se* rule, the proper inquiry was "not whether dictation of maximum prices is ever illegal, but whether it is always illegal." *Id.*, at 165–166. He also faulted the majority for conclusively listing "certain unfortunate consequences that maximum price dictation might have in other cases," even as it rejected evidence that the publisher's practice of fixing maximum prices counteracted potentially anticompetitive actions by its distributors. *Id.*, at 165. Justice Stewart also dissented, asserting that the publisher's maximum price fixing scheme should be properly viewed as promoting competition, because it protected consumers from dealers such as Albrecht, who, as "the only person who could sell for home delivery the city's only daily morning newspaper," was "a monopolist within his own territory." *Id.*, at 168 (Stewart, J., dissenting).

Nine years later, in *Continental T.V., Inc. v. GTE Sylvania Inc.*, 433 U.S. 36 (1977), the Court overruled *Schwinn*, thereby rejecting application of a *per se* rule in the context of vertical nonprice restrictions. The Court acknowledged the principle of *stare decisis*, but explained that the need for clarification in the law justified reconsideration of *Schwinn*:

> Since its announcement, *Schwinn* has been the subject of continu- ing controversy and confusion, both in the scholarly journals and in the federal courts. The great weight of scholarly opinion has been critical of the decision, and a number of the federal courts confronted with analogous vertical restrictions have sought to limit its reach. In our view, the experience of the past 10 years should be brought to bear on this subject of considerable commer- cial importance. 433 U.S., at 47–49 (footnotes omitted).

The Court considered the historical context of Schwinn, noting that Schwinn's *per se* rule against vertical nonprice restrictions came only four years after the Court had refused to endorse a similar rule in *White Motor Co.*, and that the decision neither explained the "sudden change in posi- tion," nor referred to the accepted requirements for *per se* violations set forth in *Northern Pacific R. Co.*, 433 U.S., at 51–52. The Court then reviewed scholarly works supporting the economic utility of vertical non- price restraints. See *id.*, at 54–57 (citing, *e.g.*, Posner, Antitrust Policy and the Supreme Court: An Analysis of the Restricted Distribution, Horizontal Merger and Potential Competition Decisions, 75 Colum. L. Rev. 282 (1975); Preston, Restrictive Distribution Arrangements: Economic Analysis and Public Policy Standards, 30 Law & Contemp. Prob. 506 (1965)). The Court concluded that, because "departure from the rule of reason standard must be based upon demonstrable economic effect rather than as in *Schwinn* upon formalistic line drawing," the appropriate course would be "to return to the rule of reason that governed vertical restrictions prior to *Schwinn*." *GTE Sylvania*, supra, at 58–59.

In *GTE Sylvania*, the Court declined to comment on *Albrecht's per se* treatment of vertical maximum price restrictions, noting that the issue "involve[d] significantly different questions of analysis and policy." 433 U.S., at 51, n. 18. Subsequent decisions of the Court, however, have hinted that the analytical underpinnings of *Albrecht* were substantially weakened by *GTE Sylvania*. We noted in *Maricopa County* that vertical restraints are generally more defensible than horizontal restraints. See 457 U.S., at 348, n. 18. And we explained in 324 Liquor Corp. v. Duffy, 479 U.S. 335, 341– 342 (1987), that decisions such as *GTE Sylvania* "recognize the possibility that a vertical restraint imposed by a single manufacturer or wholesaler may stimulate interbrand competition even as it reduces intrabrand compe- tition."

Most recently, in *ARCO*, 495 U.S. 328 (1990), although *Albrecht's* continuing validity was not squarely before the Court, some disfavor with that decision was signaled by our statement that we would "assume, arguendo, that *Albrecht* correctly held that vertical, maximum price fixing is subject to the *per se* rule." 495 U.S., at 335, n. 5. More significantly, we specifically acknowledged that vertical maximum price fixing "may have procompetitive interbrand effects," and pointed out that, in the wake of GTE Sylvania, "[t]he procompetitive potential of a vertical maximum price restraint is more evident ... than it was when *Albrecht* was decided, because exclusive territorial arrangements and other nonprice restrictions were unlawful *per se* in 1968." 495 U.S., at 344, n. 13 (citing several commentators identifying procompetitive effects of vertical maximum price fixing, including, *e.g.*, P. Areeda & H. Hovenkamp, Antitrust Law ¶ 340.30b, p. 378, n. 24 (1988 Supp.); Blair & Harrison, Rethinking Antitrust Injury, 42 Vand. L.Rev. 1539, 1553 (1989); Easterbrook, Maximum Price Fixing, 48 U. Chi. L.Rev. 886, 887–890 (1981)).

B

Thus, our reconsideration of *Albrecht's* continuing validity is informed by several of our decisions, as well as a considerable body of scholarship discussing the effects of vertical restraints. Our analysis is also guided by our general view that the primary purpose of the antitrust laws is to protect interbrand competition. *See, e.g., Business Electronics Corp. v. Sharp Electronics Corp.*, 485 U.S. 717, 726 (1988). "Low prices," we have explained, "benefit consumers regardless of how those prices are set, and so long as they are above predatory levels, they do not threaten competition." *ARCO*, supra, at 340. Our interpretation of the Sherman Act also incorporates the notion that condemnation of practices resulting in lower prices to consumers is "especially costly" because "cutting prices in order to increase business often is the very essence of competition." *Matsushita Elec. Industrial Co. v. Zenith Radio Corp.*, 475 U.S. 574, 594 (1986).

So informed, we find it difficult to maintain that vertically-imposed maximum prices could harm consumers or competition to the extent necessary to justify their *per se* invalidation. As Chief Judge Posner wrote for the Court of Appeals in this case:

> As for maximum resale price fixing, unless the supplier is a monopsonist he cannot squeeze his dealers' margins below a competitive level; the attempt to do so would just drive the dealers into the arms of a competing supplier. A supplier might, however, fix a maximum resale price in order to prevent his dealers from exploiting a monopoly position.... [S]uppose that State Oil, perhaps to encourage ... dealer services ... has spaced its dealers sufficiently far apart to limit competition among them (or even given each of them an exclusive territory); and suppose further that Union 76 is a sufficiently distinctive and popular brand to give the dealers in it at least a modicum of monopoly power. Then State Oil might want to place a ceiling on the dealers' resale prices in order to prevent them from exploiting that monopoly power fully. It would do this not out of disinterested malice, but in its

commercial self-interest. The higher the price at which gasoline is resold, the smaller the volume sold, and so the lower the profit to the supplier if the higher profit per gallon at the higher price is being snared by the dealer. 93 F.3d, at 1362.

See also R. Bork, The Antitrust Paradox 281–282 (1978) ("There could, of course, be no anticonsumer effect from [the type of price fixing considered in *Albrecht*], and one suspects that the paper has a legitimate interest in keeping subscriber prices down in order to increase circulation and maximize revenues from advertising").

We recognize that the *Albrecht* decision presented a number of theoretical justifications for a *per se* rule against vertical maximum price fixing. But criticism of those premises abounds. The *Albrecht* decision was grounded in the fear that maximum price fixing by suppliers could interfere with dealer freedom. 390 U.S., at 152. In response, as one commentator has pointed out, "the ban on maximum resale price limitations declared in *Albrecht* in the name of 'dealer freedom' has actually prompted many suppliers to integrate forward into distribution, thus eliminating the very independent trader for whom *Albrecht* professed solicitude." 7 P. Areeda, Antitrust Law, ¶ 1635, p. 395 (1989). For example, integration in the newspaper industry since *Albrecht* has given rise to litigation between independent distributors and publishers. See P. Areeda & H. Hovenkamp, Antitrust Law ¶ 729.7, pp. 599–614 (1996 Supp.).

The Albrecht Court also expressed the concern that maximum prices may be set too low for dealers to offer consumers essential or desired services. 390 U.S., at 152–153. But such conduct, by driving away customers, would seem likely to harm manufacturers as well as dealers and consumers, making it unlikely that a supplier would set such a price as a matter of business judgment. See, *e.g.*, Lopatka, Stephen Breyer and Modern Antitrust: A Snug Fit, 40 Antitrust Bull. 1, 60 (1995); Blair & Lang, Albrecht After ARCO: Maximum Resale Price Fixing Moves Toward the Rule of Reason, 44 Vand. L.Rev. 1007, 1034 (1991). In addition, *Albrecht* noted that vertical maximum price fixing could effectively channel distribution through large or specially-advantaged dealers. 390 U.S., at 153. It is unclear, however, that a supplier would profit from limiting its market by excluding potential dealers. See, *e.g.*, *Easterbrook*, supra, at 905–908. Further, although vertical maximum price fixing might limit the viability of inefficient dealers, that consequence is not necessarily harmful to competition and consumers. See, *e.g.*, *Easterbrook*, supra, at 907; Lopatka, supra, at 60.

Finally, *Albrecht* reflected the Court's fear that maximum price fixing could be used to disguise arrangements to fix minimum prices, 390 U.S. at 153, which remain illegal *per se*. Although we have acknowledged the possibility that maximum pricing might mask minimum pricing, *see Maricopa County*, 457 U.S., at 348, we believe that such conduct as with the other concerns articulated in *Albrecht* can be appropriately recognized and punished under the rule of reason. See, *e.g.*, *Easterbrook*, 48 U. Chi. L.Rev., at 901–904; *see also* Pitofsky, In Defense of Discounters: The No–Frills

Case for a *Per Se* Rule Against Vertical Price Fixing, 71 Geo. L.J. 1487, 1490, n. 17 (1983).

Not only are the potential injuries cited in *Albrecht* less serious than the Court imagined, the *per se* rule established therein could in fact exacerbate problems related to the unrestrained exercise of market power by monopolist-dealers. Indeed, both courts and antitrust scholars have noted that *Albrecht's* rule may actually harm consumers and manufacturers. *See, e.g., Caribe BMW, Inc. v. Bayerische Motoren Werke Aktiengesellschaft,* 19 F.3d 745, 753 (CA1 1994) (Breyer, C. J.); Areeda, supra, ¶ 1636a, at 395; G. Mathewson & R. Winter, Competition Policy and Vertical Exchange 13–14 (1985). Other commentators have also explained that *Albrecht's per se* rule has even more potential for deleterious effect on competition after our decision in *GTE Sylvania,* because, now that vertical nonprice restrictions are not unlawful *per se,* the likelihood of dealer monopoly power is increased. *See, e.g., Easterbrook,* supra, at 890, n. 20; *see also ARCO,* 495 U.S., at 343, n. 13. We do not intend to suggest that dealers generally possess sufficient market power to exploit a monopoly situation. Such retail market power may in fact be uncommon. *See, e.g., Business Electronics,* 485 U.S., at 727, n. 2; *GTE Sylvania,* 433 U.S. at 54. Nor do we hold that a ban on vertical maximum price fixing inevitably has anticompetitive consequences in the exclusive dealer context.

After reconsidering *Albrecht's* rationale and the substantial criticism the decision has received, however, we conclude that there is insufficient economic justification for *per se* invalidation of vertical maximum price fixing. That is so not only because it is difficult to accept the assumptions underlying *Albrecht,* but also because *Albrecht* has little or no relevance to ongoing enforcement of the Sherman Act. *See Copperweld Corp. v. Independence Tube Corp.,* 467 U.S. 752, 777, and n. 25 (1984). Moreover, neither the parties nor any of the *amici curiae* have called our attention to any cases in which enforcement efforts have been directed solely against the conduct encompassed by *Albrecht's per se* rule.

Respondents argue that reconsideration of *Albrecht* should require "persuasive, expert testimony establishing that the *per se* rule has distorted the market." Their reasoning ignores the fact that *Albrecht* itself relied solely upon hypothetical effects of vertical maximum price fixing. Further, *Albrecht's* dire predictions have not been borne out, even though manufacturers and suppliers appear to have fashioned schemes to get around the *per se* rule against vertical maximum price fixing. In these circumstances, it is the retention of the rule of *Albrecht,* and not, as respondents would have it, the rule's elimination, that lacks adequate justification. *See, e.g., GTE Sylvania,* supra, at 58–59.

Respondents' reliance on *Toolson v. New York Yankees, Inc.,* 346 U.S. 356 (1953) (*per curiam*), and *Flood v. Kuhn,* 407 U.S. 258 (1972), is similarly misplaced, because those decisions are clearly inapposite, having to do with the antitrust exemption for professional baseball, which this Court has described as "an aberration ... rest[ing] on a recognition and an acceptance of baseball's unique characteristics and needs," *id.,* at 282. In the context of this case, we infer little meaning from the fact that Congress has not reacted legislatively to *Albrecht*. In any event, the history of various legislative proposals regarding price fixing seems neither clearly to support nor to denounce the *per se* rule of *Albrecht*. Respondents are of course free to seek legislative protection from gasoline suppliers of the sort embodied in the Petroleum Marketing Practices Act, 92 Stat. 322, 15 U.S.C. § 2801 et seq. For the reasons we have noted, however, the remedy for respondents' dispute with State Oil should not come in the form of a *per se* rule affecting the conduct of the entire marketplace.

C

Despite what Chief Judge Posner aptly described as *Albrecht's* "infirmities, [and] its increasingly wobbly, moth-eaten foundations," 93 F.3d, at 1363, there remains the question whether *Albrecht* deserves continuing respect under the doctrine of *stare decisis*. The Court of Appeals was correct in applying that principle despite disagreement with *Albrecht*, for it is this Court's prerogative alone to overrule one of its precedents.

We approach the reconsideration of decisions of this Court with the utmost caution. Stare decisis reflects "a policy judgment that 'in most matters it is more important that the applicable rule of law be settled than that it be settled right.'" *Agostini v. Felton*, 117 S.Ct. 1997, 2016 (1997) (quoting *Burnet v. Coronado Oil & Gas Co.*, 285 U.S. 393, 406 (1932) (Brandeis, J., dissenting)). It "is the preferred course because it promotes the evenhanded, predictable, and consistent development of legal principles, fosters reliance on judicial decisions, and contributes to the actual and perceived integrity of the judicial process." *Payne v. Tennessee*, 501 U.S. 808, 827 (1991). This Court has expressed its reluctance to overrule decisions involving statutory interpretation, *see, e.g., Illinois Brick Co. v. Illinois*, 431 U.S. 720, 736 (1977), and has acknowledged that *stare decisis* concerns are at their acme in cases involving property and contract rights, *see, e.g., Payne*, 501 U.S., at 828. Both of those concerns are arguably relevant in this case.

But "*[s]tare decisis* is not an inexorable command." *Ibid.* In the area of antitrust law, there is a competing interest, well-represented in this Court's decisions, in recognizing and adapting to changed circumstances and the lessons of accumulated experience. Thus, the general presumption that legislative changes should be left to Congress has less force with respect to the Sherman Act in light of the accepted view that Congress "expected the courts to give shape to the statute's broad mandate by drawing on common-law tradition." *National Soc. of Professional Engineers v. United States*, 435 U.S. 679, 688 (1978). As we have explained, the term "restraint of trade," as used in § 1, also "invokes the common law itself, and not merely the static content that the common law had assigned to the term in 1890." *Business Electronics*, 485 U.S., at 732; *see also GTE Sylvania*, 433 U.S., at 53, n. 21; *McNally v. United States*, 483 U.S. 350, 372–373 (1987) (Stevens, J., dissenting). Accordingly, this Court has reconsidered its decisions construing the Sherman Act when the theoretical underpinnings of those decisions are called into serious question. *See, e.g., Copperweld Corp.*, supra, at 777; *GTE Sylvania*, supra, at 47–49; *Tigner v. Texas*, 310 U.S. 141, 147 (1940).

Although we do not "lightly assume that the economic realities underlying earlier decisions have changed, or that earlier judicial perceptions of those realities were in error," we have noted that "different sorts of agreements" may amount to restraints of trade "in varying times and circumstances," and "[i]t would make no sense to create out of the single term 'restraint of trade' a chronologically schizoid statute, in which a 'rule of reason' evolves with new circumstances and new wisdom, but a line of *per se* illegality remains forever fixed where it was." *Business Electronics*, supra, at 731–732. Just as *Schwinn* was "the subject of continuing controversy and confusion" under the "great weight" of scholarly criticism, *GTE Sylvania*, supra, at 47–48, *Albrecht* has been widely criticized since its inception. With the views underlying *Albrecht* eroded by this Court's precedent, there is not much of that decision to salvage. *See, e.g., Neal v. United States*, 516 U.S. 284, 295 (1996); *Patterson v. McLean Credit Union*, 491 U.S. 164, 173 (1989); *Rodriguez de Quijas v. Shearson/ American Express, Inc.*, 490 U.S. 477, 480–481 (1989).

Although the rule of *Albrecht* has been in effect for some time, the inquiry we must undertake requires considering " 'the effect of the antitrust laws upon vertical distributional restraints in the American economy today.' " *GTE Sylvania*, supra, at 53, n. 21, (quoting *Schwinn*, 388 U.S., at 392 (Stewart, J., concurring in part and dissenting in part)). As the Court noted in *ARCO*, 495 U.S., at 336, n. 6, there has not been another case since *Albrecht* in which this Court has "confronted an unadulterated vertical, maximum-price-fixing arrangement." Now that we confront *Albrecht* directly, we find its conceptual foundations gravely weakened.

In overruling *Albrecht*, we of course do not hold that all vertical maximum price fixing is *per se* lawful. Instead, vertical maximum price fixing, like the majority of commercial arrangements subject to the antitrust laws, should be evaluated under the rule of reason. In our view, rule-of-reason analysis will effectively identify those situations in which vertical maximum price fixing amounts to anticompetitive conduct.

There remains the question whether respondents are entitled to recover damages based on State Oil's conduct. Although the Court of Appeals noted that "the district judge was right to conclude that if the rule of reason is applicable, Khan loses," 93 F.3d, at 1362, its consideration of this case was necessarily premised on *Albrecht's per se* rule. Under the circumstances, the matter should be reviewed by the Court of Appeals in the first instance. We therefore vacate the judgment of the Court of Appeals and remand the case for further proceedings consistent with this opinion.

It is so ordered.

NOTE ON RESALE PRICE MAINTENANCE

Resale price maintenance was not a substantial problem until the post–1890 development of complex distributional systems.[4] Although the Supreme Court in

Dr. Miles did not explicitly state that vertical price-fixing agreements are *per se* illegal under the Sherman Act, its reasoning supports that conclusion. In later cases the Court has either held or clearly indicated that minimum vertical price fixing contravenes the Sherman Act regardless of the nature of the commodity involved[5] and regardless of the market position of the seller.[6] Resale price maintenance has also been held to be an unfair method of competition within the meaning of the Federal Trade Commission Act.[7] *Dr. Miles* was reaffirmed in the 1980's.[8]

In response to the condemnation of vertical price fixing in *Dr. Miles*, wholesaler and retailer groups lobbied to secure state and Federal "fair trade" laws.[9] In 1937, the Sherman Act was amended by the Miller–Tydings Act to exempt "agreements prescribing minimum prices for the resale of a [branded or trademarked] commodity which . . . is in free and open competition with commodities of the same general class produced or distributed by others" where such agreements were lawful in the state of resale. Most states passed "fair trade" laws making such agreements lawful.[10] Still, many retailers preferred not to sign "fair trade" agreements, relying on a higher volume of (discount) sales to generate profits. To compel all retailers to comply with manufacturers' minimum prices, most states added "non-signer" provisions to their "fair trade" laws. "Non-signer" statutes made it "unfair competition" for any merchant to sell a "fair traded" product at less than the established price whether or not he had so agreed with the manufacturer. However, in *Schwegmann Brothers v. Calvert Distillers Corp.*, 341 U.S. 384 (1951), the Supreme Court interpreted the Miller–Tydings exemption not to extend to "non-signer" statutes. Enforcement of "fair trade" statutes thus became virtually impossible, since non-signers could not be bound by established minimum prices. In 1952, Congress acted to strengthen state "fair trade" policies by passing the McGuire Act (66 Stat. 632, 15 U.S.C.A. § 45) which in effect overruled *Schwegmann* and sanctioned state laws' non-signer provisions.

"Fair trade" still did not flourish. A number of state courts struck down non-signer provisions, often as unconstitutional delegations of state legislative power. Shoppers in "fair trade" states could order by mail or otherwise arrange major

---

4. The English cases upheld such agreements. Grether, Resale Price Maintenance in Great Britain (1935). *See Dunlop Pneumatic Tyre Co. v. New Garage & Motor Co.*, [1915] A.C. 79; *Dunlop Pneumatic Tyre Co. v. Selfridge & Co.*, [1915] A.C. 847; *cf. Chloride Electric Storage Co. v. Silvia Wireless Stores*, 48 R.P.C. 468 (1931). *See also* 44 L.Q.Rev. 278 (1928); 3 Camb.L.J. 434 (1929).

5. *See United States v. Line Material Co.*, 333 U.S. 287, 307 (1948); *United States v. Bausch & Lomb Optical Co,*, 321 U.S. 707 (1944); *United States v. Univis Lens Co.*, 316 U.S. 241 (1942); *Ethyl Gasoline Corp. v. United States*, 309 U.S. 436 (1940); *Straus v. Victor Talking Machine Co.*, 243 U.S. 490 (1917). *Cf. Purity Stores, Inc. v. Blue Chip Stamp Co.*, 1963 Trade Cas. ¶ 70,895 (N.D.Cal.1963).

6. *See United States v. McKesson & Robbins, Inc.*, 351 U.S. 305 (1956); *United*

States v. Bausch & Lomb Optical Co., 321 U.S. 707, 721 (1944).

7. *See FTC v. Beech–Nut Packing Co.*, 257 U.S. 441 (1922).

8. *See, e.g., Business Electronics Corp. v. Sharp Electronics Corp.*, p. 696 infra; *324 Liquor Corp. v. Duffy*, 479 U.S. 335 (1987); *California Retail Liquor Dealers Association v. Midcal Aluminum, Inc.*, p. 458 supra.

9. "Fair trade" laws provided in substance that there be nothing illegal about a contract specifying the resale price of a trade-marked or similarly identified commodity and that willfully and knowingly advertising or selling such commodity at less than the specified price is unfair competition permitting suit by any injured party.

10. By 1941, every state but Texas, Missouri, and Vermont, had enacted its own statute authorizing "fair trade."

purchases in "non-fair trade" states, where prices were lower. Manufacturers who also engaged in distribution could not under Fair Trade fix the resale prices of distributors with whom they competed.[11] As "discount house" merchandising grew more substantial, many manufacturers grew unenthusiastic about devoting substantial resources, or any at all, to the extensive litigation against violators necessary to make the "fair trade" system function.

Finally, after abortive efforts by retreating "fair traders" to get a mandatory federal "fair trade" law, the Ford Administration, as part of a "free market" anti-inflation program, proposed repeal of the McGuire Act. Congress responded promptly and the Consumer Goods Pricing Act of 1975 was enacted.[12]

Thus, state "fair trade" laws have been superseded by the restored supremacy of the Sherman Act as interpreted in *Dr. Miles* and later decisions.

PROBLEM 14

SOUSCHEF PURSUES THE AFFLUENT HOME CHEF

For some time, SousChef has manufactured and sold a mixer to restaurants and caterers. The SousChef mixer is generally recognized as the best in the field. Its stylish design—white or black enamel with chrome highlights and a stainless steel bowl—and powerful motor have made it one of the more successful commercial kitchen products of all time. In 1995, sensing that Americans, particularly affluent Americans, have less time to cook but more money to spend on kitchen gadgets, SousChef decided to create a mixer designed for the home cook. After designing the home mixer—a slightly smaller version of the original but now available in five colors, the original black and white and blue, green and red—but before marketing it, SousChef conducted some market research. The market research suggested that, in order for the product to succeed, SousChef had to build an upscale "brand image." Marketing consultants recommended that SousChef limit distribution to high-end specialty stores and sell the mixer at a price between $150 and $200 for five years. The consultants projected that SousChef would then be able to expand its distribution network to include traditional department stores and, possibly, consumer appliance stores. SousChef followed these recommendations and solicited information from kitchen appliance stores around the country. One month ago, SousChef signed contracts with 10 up-scale retail chains. In the contracts, the retailers agreed not to sell the SousChef home mixer for less than $150 but got the option to sell the mixers back to SousChef after six months for $110 (the wholesale price plus $5). SousChef began shipping the mixer to the authorized dealers two weeks ago. Last week, it learned that one of its retailers has violated the agreement by reselling the mixer to Electric Brands, a national consumer appliance store, which plans to sell it for $120. What can SousChef do?

COMPARATIVE NOTE ON RESALE PRICE MAINTENANCE

Most other countries with competition laws continue to prohibit resale price maintenance, without regard to the existence of possible efficiencies in a particular case. Thus, for example, in the European Union, Article 81(1)(a) (ex Article 85(1)(a)) of the Treaty of Rome expressly prohibits agreements that "directly or

---

11. *United States v. McKesson & Robbins,* 351 U.S. 305 (1956).

12. Consumer Goods Pricing Act of 1975, Pub.L. No. 94–145, 89 Stat. 801; 15 U.S.C.A. §§ 1, 45(a) (1982).

indirectly fix purchase or selling prices or any other trading conditions." The Commission construes this broadly to cover not only retail price fixing, but also the setting of minimum profit margins, maximum discounts, or minimum wholesale price fixing. *See, e.g.,* GERO-Fabriek, Com. Dec., 1977 O.J. L 16/8, 11 (Dec. 11, 1976); Centraal Bureau voor de Rijwielhandel, Com. Dec., 1978 O.J. L 20/18, 24 (Dec. 2, 1977); Flemish Travel Agents, ECJ Oct. 10, 1987, 1987 ECR 3801, 3827–28, 1989–4 CMLR 213, 234 (¶ 17). Both minimum and maximum resale price fixing are included within the prohibition. On the other hand, some European countries have permitted resale price maintenance under national laws, either in general or for particular sectors. The Commission will respect these preferences if it can find that there is no effect on trade between Member States. Furthermore, as is the case with all restrictions under Article 81, one must bear in mind that parties to the agreement can always try to obtain an exemption under Article 81(3), if the efficiency case is strong enough. Finally, through the Commission's Notice on Agreements of Minor Importance, Official Journal C 368, 22.12.2001, pages 13–15, the Commission has effectively exempted from Article 81 agreements between enterprises that do not represent more than 10 or 15% (depending on whether the agreements are concluded among competitors or not) of the total market for the goods or services in question. The Notice, in addition, provides that small or medium-size enterprises (enterprises having fewer than 250 employees and either an annual turnover not exceeding EUR 40 million or an annual balance sheet total not exceeding EUR 27 million) are rarely capable of appreciably affecting trade between member states. In U.S. terms, this would be the equivalent of a minimum market power threshold for the RPM prohibition.

Most of the most important trading partners of the United States continue to prohibit RPM as a matter of national law as well. Canada, for example, has long had a strict prohibition against RPM, which now appears in the Competition Act 1986, § 61. One of the most important differences between the Canadian prohibition and U.S. law, as it now stands, is the lack of any agreement requirement under the Canadian law. The language of the Canadian law is also more sweeping than the U.S. prohibition: § 61(a) prohibits any person from directly or indirectly "by agreement, threat, promise or any like means, attempt[ing] to influence upward, or to discourage the reduction of, the price at which any other person engaged in a business in Canada supplies or offers to supply or advertises a product within Canada...." Section 61(b) prohibits refusing to deal or discriminating against anyone because of the latter's low pricing policy.

The United Kingdom, which modernized its competition law in 1998, now follows rules comparable to those used by the EU. See Competition Act 1998, Ch. 1, sec. 2(2) (prohibiting agreements that directly or indirectly fix purchase or selling prices or any other trading conditions; this includes RPM). (See generally the Website of the Office of Fair Trading, http://www.oft.gov.uk.) In France, under the 1986 Competition Law (Ordonnance No. 86–1243 du 1er decembre, 1986, relative à la liberté des prix et de la concurrence), resale price maintenance is prohibited *per se.* Enforcement of the prohibition, interestingly, takes place in the regular courts, rather than before the Conseil de la Concurrence, which handles cartel and abuse of dominance cases, or before the Economics Ministry, which handles merger cases (referring them when appropriate to the Conseil for a recommendation). In Germany, section 15 of the Act against Restraints on Competition (1957), as amended, makes RPM agreements imposed by producers on wholesalers and retailers null and void. This section applies to both legal and economic restraints, such as those where a dealer receives a smaller rebate if her price system departs from the producer's suggested prices.

In light of the extensive economic literature suggesting that RPM may not be all bad, and in fact may enhance efficient distribution in some circumstances, the Mexican Federal Economic Competition Law is especially interesting. This law was passed in December 1992 and became effective in June 1993 at a time when Mexico was engaged in a comprehensive program of economic reforms. Ley Federal de Competencia Económica, D.O. Dec. 24, 1992 at 9 (LFCE). It distinguishes between "absolute monopolistic practices," which have no legitimate procompetitive purpose and are illegal *per se,* and "relative monopolistic practices," which are subject to a rule of reason-type analysis. Resale price maintenance, along with all other vertical restraints, appears only in the relative monopolistic practices section, LFCE art. 10. According to LFCE art. 11, before a relative monopolistic practice can be considered a violation of the law, the Federal Competition Commission must prove that the actor has "substantial power" in the relevant market, and that market power is being exercised with respect to the practices in question. The LFCE is being studied carefully by a number of other Latin American countries interested in strengthening their own competition laws, or in adopting such a law for the first time.

In the European Union important developments have occurred recently with respect to the law of vertical restraints. The current reform is part of the wider review undertaken by the Commission to simplify the rules and reduce the regulatory burden for companies (especially for small and medium-size enterprises), while ensuring a more effective control of restraints implemented by companies holding significant market power. The reforms will allow the Commission to concentrate on important cases. Member States will play an increased role in the application of Community competition rules.

The new competition rules concerning vertical arrangements consist of a new Block Exemption Regulation ("BER")[13] that entered into force in the year 2000, and a set of Guidelines on Vertical Restraints[14] that implements the BER. Replacing three previous block exemption regulations applicable to exclusive distribution, exclusive purchasing and franchising agreements, the new Regulation and Guidelines together form the basis for a new competition policy towards vertical agreements. The texts of the BER and of the Guidelines are available on the Internet.[15]

The BER defines vertical agreements in Article 2(1) as "agreements or concerted practices entered into between two or more undertakings each of which operates, for the purposes of the agreement, at a different level of the production or distribution chain, and relating to the conditions under which the parties may purchase, sell or resell certain goods or services." The BER allows companies whose market share is below 30% to benefit from a safe harbor, provided their vertical arrangements are in accordance with the provisions of the BER.

Perhaps the most important change the new BER makes is its explicitly economic approach to the analysis of this type of restriction. Paragraph 7 of the Guidelines puts the point as follows:

> The protection of competition is the primary objective of EC competition policy, as this enhances consumer welfare and creates an efficient allocation of resources. In applying the EC competition rules, the Commission will adopt an economic approach which is based on the effects on the

---

13. Regulation (EC) No. 2790/1999 of 22 December 1999 on the Application of Article 81(3) (ex Article 85(3)) of the Treaty to categories of vertical agreements and market practices. See OJ L 336, 29.12.1999, p. 21.

14. *See* Official Journal C 291 of 13.10.2000, page 1.

15. *See* <http://europa.eu.int/comm/competition/index_en.html>.

market; vertical agreements have to be analysed in their legal and economic context. However, in the case of restrictions by object as listed in Article
4 of the BER, the Commission is not required to assess the actual effects on
the market. Market integration is an additional goal of EC competition
policy. Market integration enhances competition in the Community. Companies should not be allowed to recreate private barriers between Member
States where State barriers have been successfully abolished.

The "restrictions by object" in Article 4 to which this refers are the blacklisted
clauses that will lead the entire agreement to be excluded from the scope of the
BER. The Commission further warns that individual exemption of such agreements
is also unlikely (although it is legally possible). The prohibited clauses include
things like the fixing of minimum resale prices, either directly or indirectly, and
agreements that have as their direct or indirect object the restriction of sales by the
buyer, insofar as those restrictions relate to the territory in which the customers
are located (maintaining the Community's traditional distinction between active
and passive sales for this purpose).

The Commission does not, however, apply these rules to arrangements that will
have a *de minimis* effect in the Community. It defines that term for vertical
agreements to include those "agreements entered into by undertakings whose
market share on the relevant market does not exceed 10%." The Commission
reserves the right to apply Article 81(1) to the "hardcore" restrictions of firms
below that 10% threshold, if the arrangement nonetheless has an appreciable effect
on trade between Member States and on competition. It also indicates that agreements between small and medium-sized enterprises will rarely be of concern.

The last point to make about the BER is that it is more comprehensive than
prior block exemptions in the vertical restraints area. Instead of treating separately
the question of vertical restraints in intellectual property licenses, franchises,
distribution agreements, etc., the Commission has put forth a single block exemption that applies across-the-board. Having said that, however, it is important to note
that specific block exemptions continue to exist in certain areas, including technology transfer, car distribution, and certain vertical agreements concluded in connection with horizontal agreements.

B.   CUSTOMER AND TERRITORIAL RESTRAINTS

SCOPE NOTE

During the 1960's, the Department of Justice sought to clarify the law dealing
with vertical territorial and customer restraints. It was reasonably clear that
horizontal agreements among manufacturers, among wholesalers, or among retailers (or other classes of distributors) were subject to a rule of *per se* illegality, subject
to the usual difficulties of demonstrating "contract, combination or conspiracy." By
analogy with vertical price-fixing, as treated in *Dr. Miles,* it seemed reasonable to
expect that these other forms of vertical restraints might also be *per se* illegal. But
the Supreme Court had never so decided. Its difficulties in reaching a decision are
demonstrated by a sequence of three decisions from 1963 to 1977 dealing with the
problem, each in a different way:

1. WHITE MOTOR CO. v. UNITED STATES, 372 U.S. 253, 83 S.Ct. 696, 9 L.Ed.2d
738 (1963). White Motor manufactured trucks and truck components. It sold
directly to large users and dealers, and through distributors to dealers and individu-

al users. Its contracts limited distributors to developing an assigned territory and to selling only to dealers and users there. These contracts also prohibited distributors and their dealers from making sales to federal or state governmental units.

The district court, in granting summary judgment, held these territorial and customer restrictions to be *per se* violations of the Sherman Act. The Supreme Court (per Douglas, J.) reversed, and reasoned:

> We are asked to extend the holding in *Timken Roller Bearing Co. v. United States*, (which banned *horizontal* arrangements among competitors to divide territory), to a *vertical* arrangement by one manufacturer restricting the territory of his distributors or dealers. We intimate no view one way or the other on the legality of such an arrangement, for we believe that the applicable rule of law should be designed after a trial.

> This is the first case involving a territorial restriction in a *vertical* arrangement; and we know too little of the actual impact of both that restriction and the one respecting customers to reach a conclusion on the bare bones of the documentary evidence before us. . . .

> Horizontal territorial limitations . . . are naked restraints of trade with no purpose except stifling of competition. A vertical territorial limitation may or may not have that purpose or effect. We do not know enough of the economic and business stuff out of which these arrangements emerge to be certain. They may be too dangerous to sanction or they may be allowable protections against aggressive competitors or the only practicable means a small company has for breaking into or staying in business and within the "rule of reason." We need to know more than we do about the actual impact of these arrangements on competition to decide whether they . . . should be classified as *per se* violations of the Sherman Act.

Clark, J. (with Warren and Black) dissented, stating that White Motor's distribution system was "one of the most brazen violations of the Sherman Act that I have experienced in a quarter of a century." White, J., did not participate.

Shortly after remand for development of a trial record in *White Motor,* the defendant agreed to a consent decree, and the Department of Justice discontinued the action. Trade Reg.Rep., 1964 Trade Cas., ¶ 79,762 (N.D.Ohio). The decree enjoined White Motor from agreeing with any distributor, dealer, or any other person to limit, allocate or restrict the territories in which, or the persons or classes of persons to whom, any distributor, dealer or other person may sell trucks.

2. UNITED STATES V. ARNOLD, SCHWINN & CO., 388 U.S. 365, 87 S.Ct. 1856, 18 L.Ed.2d 1249 (1967). The facts are set forth in *GTE Sylvania* p. 651, infra. The majority distinguished *White Motor,* holding that vertical customer and territorial restraints after sale of a product to a wholesaler or retailer were illegal *per se:* " . . . Such restraints are so obviously destructive of competition that their mere existence is enough." Similar restraints imposed on *bona fide* agents or consignees, however, were held subject to a rule of reason, and were upheld as reasonable.

As to the latter the Court noted:

> . . . [A]s indicated in *White Motor,* we are not prepared to introduce the inflexibility which a *per se* rule might bring if it were applied to prohibit all vertical restrictions of territory and all franchising, in the sense of designating specified distributors and retailers as the chosen instruments through which the manufacturer, retaining ownership of the goods, will distribute them to the public. Such a rule might severely hamper smaller

enterprises resorting to reasonable methods of meeting the competition of giants and of merchandising through independent dealers, and it might sharply accelerate the trend towards vertical integration of the distribution process. But to allow this freedom where the manufacturer has parted with dominion over the goods—the usual marketing situation—would violate the ancient rule against restraints on alienation and open the door to exclusivity of outlets and limitation of territory further than prudence permits.

The Government does not here contend for a *per se* rule as to agency, consignment, or Schwinn Plan transactions even though these may be used—as they are here—to implement a scheme of confining distribution outlets as in this case. Where the manufacturer retains title, dominion, and risk with respect to the product and the position and function of the dealer in question is, in fact, indistinguishable from that of an agent or salesman of the manufacturer, it is only if the impact of the confinement is "unreasonably" restrictive of competition that a violation of § 1 results from such confinement, unencumbered by culpable price fixing. *Simpson v. Union Oil Co.*, 377 U.S. 13 (1964). As the District Court found, *Schwinn* adopted the challenged distribution programs in a competitive situation dominated by mass merchandisers which command access to large-scale advertising and promotion, choice of retail outlets, both owned and franchised, and adequate sources of supply. It is not claimed that Schwinn's practices or other circumstances resulted in an inadequate competitive situation with respect to the bicycle market; and there is nothing in this record—after elimination of the price-fixing issue—to lead us to conclude that Schwinn's program exceeded the limits reasonably necessary to meet the competitive problems posed by its more powerful competitors. In these circumstances, the rule of reason is satisfied.

We do not suggest that the unilateral adoption by a single manufacturer of an agency or consignment pattern and the Schwinn type of restrictive distribution system would be justified in any and all circumstances by the presence of the competition of mass merchandisers and by the demonstrated need of the franchise system to meet that competition. . . .

. . . [C]ritical in this respect are the facts: (1) that other competitive bicycles are available to distributors and retailers in the marketplace, and there is no showing that they are not in all respects reasonably interchangeable as articles of competitive commerce with the Schwinn product; (2) that Schwinn distributors and retailers handle other brands of bicycles as well as Schwinn's; (3) in the present posture of the case we cannot rule that the vertical restraints are unreasonable because of their intermixture with price fixing; and (4) we cannot disagree with the findings of the trial court that competition made necessary the challenged program; that it was justified by, and went no further than required by, competitive pressures; and that its net effect is to preserve and not to damage competition in the bicycle market. Application of the rule of reason here cannot be confined to intrabrand competition. When we look to the product market as a whole, we cannot conclude that Schwinn's franchise system with respect to products as to which it retains ownership and risk constitutes an unreasonable restraint of trade.

3.   The third Supreme Court decision is *Continental T.V., Inc. v. GTE Sylvania Inc.*, which follows immediately.

Continental T.V., Inc. v. GTE Sylvania Inc.

Supreme Court of the United States, 1977.
433 U.S. 36, 97 S.Ct. 2549, 53 L.Ed.2d 568.

■ POWELL, J. Franchise agreements between manufacturers and retailers frequently include provisions barring the retailers from selling franchised products from locations other than those specified in the agreements. This case presents important questions concerning the appropriate antitrust analysis of these restrictions under § 1 of the Sherman Act, 15 U.S.C.A. § 1, and the Court's decision in *United States v. Arnold, Schwinn & Co.,* 388 U.S. 365 (1967).

I.

Respondent GTE Sylvania Inc. (Sylvania) manufactures and sells television sets through its Home Entertainment Products Division. Prior to 1962, like most other television manufacturers, Sylvania sold its televisions to independent or company-owned distributors who in turn resold to a large and diverse group of retailers. Prompted by a decline in its market share to a relatively insignificant 1% to 2% of national television sales,[16] Sylvania conducted an intensive reassessment of its marketing strategy, and in 1962 adopted the franchise plan challenged here. Sylvania phased out its wholesale distributors and began to sell its televisions directly to a smaller and more select group of franchised retailers. An acknowledged purpose of the change was to decrease the number of competing Sylvania retailers in the hope of attracting the more aggressive and competent retailers thought necessary to the improvement of the company's market position.[17] To this end, Sylvania limited the number of franchises granted for any given area and required each franchisee to sell his Sylvania products only from the location or locations at which he was franchised.[18] A franchise did not constitute an exclusive territory, and Sylvania retained sole discretion to increase the number of retailers in an area in light of the success or failure of existing retailers in developing their market. The revised marketing strategy appears to have been successful during the period at issue here, for by 1965 Sylvania's share of national television sales had increased to approximately 5%, and the company ranked as the Nation's eighth largest manufacturer of color television sets.

This suit is the result of the rupture of a franchisor-franchisee relationship that had previously prospered under the revised Sylvania plan. Dissatisfied with its sales in the city of San Francisco,[19] Sylvania decided in the spring of 1965 to franchise Young Brothers, an established San Francis-

---

16. RCA at that time was the dominant firm with as much as 60 to 70% of national television sales in an industry with more than 100 manufacturers.

17. The number of retailers selling Sylvania products declined significantly as a result of the change, but in 1965 there were at least two franchised Sylvania retailers in each metropolitan center of more than 100,000 population.

18. Sylvania imposed no restrictions on the right of the franchisee to sell the products of competing manufacturers.

19. Sylvania's market share in San Francisco was approximately 2.5%—half its national and Northern California average.

co retailer of televisions, as an additional San Francisco retailer. The proposed location of the new franchise was approximately a mile from a retail outlet operated by petitioner Continental T.V., Inc. (Continental), one of the most successful Sylvania franchisees. Continental protested that the location of the new franchise violated Sylvania's marketing policy, but Sylvania persisted in its plans. Continental then cancelled a large Sylvania order and placed a large order with Phillips, one of Sylvania's competitors.

During this same period, Continental expressed a desire to open a store in Sacramento, Cal., a desire Sylvania attributed at least in part to Continental's displeasure over the Young Brothers decision. Sylvania believed that the Sacramento market was adequately served by the existing Sylvania retailers and denied the request.[20] In the face of this denial, Continental advised Sylvania in early September 1965, that it was in the process of moving Sylvania merchandise from its San Jose, Cal., warehouse to a new retail location that it had leased in Sacramento. Two weeks later, allegedly for unrelated reasons, Sylvania's credit department reduced Continental's credit line from $300,000 to $50,000.[21] In response to the reduction in credit and the generally deteriorating relations with Sylvania, Continental withheld all payments owed to John P. Maguire & Co., Inc. (Maguire), the finance company that handled the credit arrangements between Sylvania and its retailers. Shortly thereafter, Sylvania terminated Continental's franchises, and Maguire filed this diversity action in the United States District Court for the Northern District of California seeking recovery of money owed and of secured merchandise held by Continental.

The antitrust issues before us originated in cross-claims brought by Continental against Sylvania and Maguire. Most important for our purposes was the claim that Sylvania had violated § 1 of the Sherman Act by entering into and enforcing franchise agreements that prohibited the sale of Sylvania products other than from specified locations.[22] At the close of evidence in the jury trial of Continental's claims, Sylvania requested the District Court to instruct the jury that its location restriction was illegal only if it unreasonably restrained or suppressed competition.... Relying on this Court's decision in *United States v. Arnold, Schwinn & Co.*, supra, the District Court rejected the proffered instruction in favor of the following one:

> "Therefore, if you find by a preponderance of the evidence that Sylvania entered into a contract, combination or conspiracy with one or more of its dealers pursuant to which Sylvania exercised dominion or control over the products sold to the dealer, after

20. Sylvania had achieved exceptional results in Sacramento, where its market share exceeded 15 percent in 1965.

21. In its findings of fact made in conjunction with Continental's plea for injunctive relief, the District Court rejected Sylvania's claim that its actions were prompted by independent concerns over Continental's credit. The jury's verdict is ambiguous on this point. In any event, we do not consider it relevant to the issue before us.

22. Although Sylvania contended in the District Court that its policy was unilaterally enforced, it now concedes that its location restriction involved understandings or agreements with the retailers.

having parted with title and risk to the products, you must find any effort thereafter to restrict outlets or store locations from which its dealers resold the merchandise which they had purchased from Sylvania to be a violation of Section 1 of the Sherman Act, regardless of the reasonableness of the location restrictions.''

. . .

In answers to special interrogatories, the jury found that Sylvania had engaged "in a contract, combination or conspiracy in restraint of trade in violation of the antitrust laws with respect to location restrictions alone," and assessed Continental's damages at $591,505, which was trebled....

On appeal, the Court of Appeals for the Ninth Circuit, sitting en banc, reversed by a divided vote.... The court acknowledged that there is language in *Schwinn* that could be read to support the District Court's instruction but concluded that *Schwinn* was distinguishable on several grounds. Contrasting the nature of the restrictions, their competitive impact, and the market shares of the franchisors in the two cases, the court concluded that Sylvania's location restriction had less potential for competitive harm than the restrictions invalidated in *Schwinn* and thus should be judged under the "rule of reason" rather than the *per se* rule stated in *Schwinn*. The court found support for its position in the policies of the Sherman Act and in the decisions of other federal courts involving nonprice vertical restrictions.[23]

II.

A.

We turn first to Continental's contention that Sylvania's restriction on retail locations is a *per se* violation of § 1 of the Sherman Act as interpreted in *Schwinn*. The restrictions at issue in *Schwinn* were part of a three-tier distribution system comprising, in addition to Arnold, Schwinn & Co. (Schwinn), 22 intermediate distributors and a network of franchised retailers. Each distributor had a defined geographic area in which it had the exclusive right to supply franchised retailers. Sales to the public were made only through franchised retailers, who were authorized to sell Schwinn bicycles only from specified locations. In support of this limitation, Schwinn prohibited both distributors and retailers from selling Schwinn bicycles to non-franchised retailers. At the retail level, therefore, Schwinn was able to control the number of retailers of its bicycles in any given area according to its view of the needs of that market.

As of 1967 approximately 75% of Schwinn's total sales were made under the "Schwinn Plan." Acting essentially as a manufacturer's repre-

---

23. This Court has never given plenary consideration to the question of the proper antitrust analysis of location restrictions. Before Schwinn such restrictions had been sustained in *Boro Hall Corp. v. General Motors Corp.*, 124 F.2d 822 (C.A.2 1942). Since the decision in *Schwinn*, location restrictions have been sustained by three Courts of Appeals, including the decision below. *Salco Corp. v. General Motors Corp.*, 517 F.2d 567 (C.A.10 1975); *Kaiser v. General Motors Corp.*, 396 F.Supp. 33 (E.D.Pa.1975), *affirmed without opinion*, 530 F.2d 964 (C.A.3 1976).

sentative or sales agent, a distributor participating in this plan forwarded orders from retailers to the factory. Schwinn then shipped the ordered bicycles directly to the retailer, billed the retailer, bore the credit risk, and paid the distributor a commission on the sale. Under the Schwinn Plan, the distributor never had title to or possession of the bicycles. The remainder of the bicycles moved to the retailers through the hands of the distributors. For the most part, the distributors functioned as traditional wholesalers with respect to these sales, stocking an inventory of bicycles owned by them to supply retailers with emergency and "fill-in" requirements. A smaller part of the bicycles that were physically distributed by the distributors were covered by consignment and agency arrangements that had been developed to deal with particular problems of certain distributors. Distributors acquired title only to those bicycles that they purchased as wholesalers; retailers, of course, acquired title to all of the bicycles sold by them.

In the District Court, the United States charged a continuing conspiracy by Schwinn and other alleged co-conspirators to fix prices, allocate exclusive territories to distributors, and confine Schwinn bicycles to franchised retailers. Relying on *United States v. Bausch & Lomb Co.*, 321 U.S. 707 (1944), the Government argued that the non-price restrictions were *per se* illegal as part of a scheme for fixing the retail prices of Schwinn bicycles. The District Court rejected the price-fixing allegation because of a failure of proof and held that Schwinn's limitation of retail bicycle sales to franchised retailers was permissible under § 1. The court found a § 1 violation, however, in "a conspiracy to divide certain borderline or overlapping counties in the territories served by four Midwestern cycle distributors." ... The court described the violation as a "division of territory by agreement between the distributors ... horizontal in nature," and held that Schwinn's participation did not change that basic characteristic.... The District Court limited its injunction to apply only to the territorial restrictions on the resale of bicycles purchased by the distributors in their roles as wholesalers....

Schwinn came to this Court on appeal by the United States from the District Court's decision. Abandoning its *per se* theories, the Government argued that Schwinn's prohibition against distributors and retailers selling Schwinn bicycles to nonfranchised retailers was unreasonable under § 1 and that the District Court's injunction against exclusive distributor territories should extend to all such restrictions regardless of the form of the transaction. The Government did not challenge the District Court's decision on price-fixing, and Schwinn did not challenge the decision on exclusive distributor territories.

The Court acknowledged the Government's abandonment of its *per se* theories and stated that the resolution of the case would require an examination of "the specifics of the challenged practices and their impact upon the marketplace in order to make a judgment as to whether the restraint is or is not 'reasonable' in the special sense in which § 1 of the Sherman Act must be read for purposes of this type of inquiry." ... Despite this description of its task, the Court proceeded to articulate the following "bright line" *per se* rule of illegality for vertical restrictions: "Under the Sherman Act, it is unreasonable without more for a manufacturer to seek to restrict and confine areas or persons with whom an article may be traded after the manufacturer has parted with dominion over it." ... But the Court expressly stated that the rule of reason governs when "the manufacturer retains title, dominion, and risk with respect to the product and the position and function of the dealer in question are, in fact, indistinguishable from those of an agent or salesman of the manufacturer."

. . .

Application of these principles to the facts of *Schwinn* produced sharply contrasting results depending upon the role played by the distributor in the distribution system. With respect to that portion of Schwinn's sales for which the distributors acted as ordinary wholesalers, buying and reselling Schwinn bicycles, the Court held that the territorial and customer restrictions challenged by the Government were *per se* illegal. But, with respect to that larger portion of Schwinn's sales in which the distributors functioned under the Schwinn Plan and under the less common consignment and agency arrangements, the Court held that the same restrictions should be judged under the rule of reason. The only retail restriction challenged by the Government prevented franchised retailers from supplying nonfranchised retailers. . . . The Court apparently perceived no material distinction between the restrictions on distributors and retailers, for it held that:

> "The principle is, of course, equally applicable to sales to retailers, and the decree should similarly enjoin the making of any sales to retailers upon any condition, agreement or understanding limiting the retailer's freedom as to where and to whom it will resell the products." . . .

Applying the rule of reason to the restrictions that were not imposed in conjunction with the sale of bicycles, the Court had little difficulty finding them all reasonable in light of the competitive situation in "the product market as a whole." . . .

B.

In the present case, it is undisputed that title to the televisions passed from Sylvania to Continental. Thus, the *Schwinn per se* rule applies unless Sylvania's restriction on locations falls outside *Schwinn's* prohibition against a manufacturer attempting to restrict a "retailer's freedom as to where and to whom it will resell the products." ... As the Court of Appeals conceded, the language of *Schwinn* is clearly broad enough to apply to the present case. Unlike the Court of Appeals, however, we are unable to find a principled basis for distinguishing *Schwinn* from the case now before us.

Both Schwinn and Sylvania sought to reduce but not to eliminate competition among their respective retailers through the adoption of a franchise system. Although it was not one of the issues addressed by the District Court or presented on appeal by the Government, the Schwinn franchise plan included a location restriction similar to the one challenged here. These restrictions allowed Schwinn and Sylvania to regulate the amount of competition among their retailers by preventing a franchisee from selling franchised products from outlets other than the one covered by the franchise agreement. To exactly the same end, the Schwinn franchise plan included a companion restriction, apparently not found in the Sylvania plan, that prohibited franchised retailers from selling Schwinn products to nonfranchised retailers. In *Schwinn* the Court expressly held that this restriction was impermissible under the broad principle stated there. In intent and competitive impact, the retail customer restriction in *Schwinn* is indistinguishable from the location restriction in the present case. In both cases the restrictions limited the freedom of the retailer to dispose of the purchased products as he desired. The fact that one restriction was addressed to territory and the other to customers is irrelevant to functional antitrust analysis and, indeed, to the language and broad thrust of the opinion in *Schwinn*.[24] As Chief Justice Hughes stated in *Appalachian Coals, Inc. v. United States*, 288 U.S. 344, 360, 377 (1933): "Realities must dominate the judgment.... The Anti–Trust Act aims at substance."

III.

Sylvania argues that if *Schwinn* cannot be distinguished, it should be reconsidered. Although *Schwinn* is supported by the principle of *stare decisis, Illinois Brick Co. v. Illinois*, ... we are convinced that the need for clarification of the law in this area justifies reconsideration. *Schwinn* itself was an abrupt and largely unexplained departure from *White Motor Co. v. United States*, 372 U.S. 253 (1963), where only four years earlier the Court had refused to endorse a *per se* rule for vertical restrictions. Since its announcement, *Schwinn* has been the subject of continuing controversy and confusion, both in the scholarly journals and in the federal courts. The great weight of scholarly opinion has been critical of the decision,[25] and a

24. The distinctions drawn by the Court of Appeals and endorsed in Mr. Justice White's separate opinion have no basis in *Schwinn*. The intrabrand competitive impact of the restrictions at issue in *Schwinn* ranged from complete elimination to mere reduction; yet, the Court did not even hint at any distinction on this ground. Similarly, there is no suggestion that the *per se* rule was applied because of Schwinn's prominent position in its industry. That position was the same whether the bicycles were sold or consigned, but the Court's analysis was quite different. In light of Mr. Justice White's emphasis on the "superior consumer acceptance" enjoyed by the Schwinn brand name, ... we note that the Court rejected precisely that premise in *Schwinn*. Applying the rule of reason to the restrictions imposed in nonsale transactions, the Court stressed that there was "no showing that [competitive bicycles were] not in all respects reasonably interchangeable as

articles of competitive commerce with the Schwinn product" and that it did "not regard Schwinn's claim of product excellence as establishing the contrary." ... Although Schwinn did hint at preferential treatment for new entrants and failing firms, the District Court below did not even submit Sylvania's claim that it was failing to the jury. Accordingly, Mr. Justice White's position appears to reflect an extension of Schwinn in this regard. Having crossed the "failing firm" line, Mr. Justice White neither attempts to draw a new one nor to explain why one should be drawn at all.

25. A former Assistant Attorney General for Antitrust has described *Schwinn* as "an exercise in barren formalism" that is "artificial and unresponsive to the competitive needs of the real world." Baker, Vertical Restraints in Times of Change: From White to Schwinn to Where?, 44 Antitrust L.J. 537

number of the federal courts confronted with analogous vertical restrictions have sought to limit its reach.[26] In our view, the experience of the past 10 years should be brought to bear on this subject of considerable commercial importance.

. . . Since the early years of this century a judicial gloss on [Section 1] has established the "rule of reason" as the prevailing standard of analysis. *Standard Oil Co. v. United States*, 221 U.S. 1 (1911). Under this rule, the factfinder weighs all of the circumstances of a case in deciding whether a restrictive practice should be prohibited as imposing an unreasonable restraint on competition.[27] *Per se* rules of illegality are appropriate only

(1975). *See, e.g.*, Handler, The Twentieth Annual Antitrust Review—1967, 53 Va.L.Rev. 1667 (1967); McLaren, Territorial and Customer Restrictions, Consignments, Suggested Retail Prices and Refusals to Deal, 37 Antitrust L.J. 137 (1968); Pollock, Alternative Distribution Methods After Schwinn, 63 Nw. U.L.Rev. 595 (1968); Posner, Antitrust Policy and the Supreme Court: An Analysis of the Restricted Distribution, Horizontal Merger and Potential Competition Decisions, 75 Colum.L.Rev. 282 (1975); Robinson, Recent Antitrust Developments; 1974, 75 Colum.L.Rev. 243 (1975); Note, Vertical Territorial and Customer Restrictions in the Franchising Industry, 10 Colum.J.L. & Soc.Prob. 497 (1974); Note, Territorial and Customer Restrictions: A Trend Toward a Broader Rule of Reason?, 40 Geo.Wash.L.Rev. 123 (1971); Note, Territorial Restrictions and *per se* Rules—A Reevaluation of the Schwinn and Sealy Doctrines, 70 Mich.L.Rev. 616 (1972). But see Louis, Vertical Distributional Restraints Under Schwinn and Sylvania: An Argument for the Continuing Use of a Partial *per se* Approach, 75 Mich.L.Rev. 275 (1976); Zimmerman, Distribution Restrictions After *Sealy* and *Schwinn*, 12 Antitrust Bull. 1181 (1967). For a more inclusive list of articles and comments, see 537 F.2d, at 988 n. 13.

26. Indeed, as one commentator has observed, many courts "have struggled to distinguish or limit *Schwinn* in ways that are a tribute to judicial ingenuity." *Robinson*, supra, n. 14. Thus, the statement in *Schwinn* that post-sale vertical restrictions as to customers or territories are "unreasonable without more," 388 U.S., at 379, has been interpreted to allow an exception to the *per se* rule where the manufacturer proves "more" by showing that the restraints will protect consumers against injury and the manufacturer against product liability claims. *See, e.g., Tripoli Co. v. Wella Corp.*, 425 F.2d 932, 936–

938 (C.A.3 1970) (en banc). Similarly, the statement that Schwinn's enforcement of its restrictions had been "firm and resolute," 388 U.S., at 372, has been relied upon to distinguish cases lacking that element. *See, e.g., Janel Sales Corp. v. Lanvin Parfums, Inc.*, 396 F.2d 398, 406 (C.A.2 1968). Other factual distinctions have been drawn to justify upholding territorial restrictions that would seem to fall within the scope of the *Schwinn per se* rule. *See, e.g., Carter–Wallace, Inc. v. United States*, 449 F.2d 1379–1380 (Ct.Cl.1971) (*per se* rule inapplicable when a purchaser can avoid the restraints by electing to buy the product at a higher price); *Colorado Pump & Supply Co. v. Febco, Inc.*, 472 F.2d 637 (C.A.10 1973) (apparent territorial restriction characterized as primary responsibility clause). One Court of Appeals has expressly urged us to consider the need in this area for greater flexibility. *Adolph Coors Co. v. FTC*, 497 F.2d 1178, 1187 (C.A.10 1974). . . .

27. One of the most frequently cited statements of the rule of reason is that of Justice Brandeis in *Chicago Board of Trade v. United States*, 246 U.S. 231, 238 (1918):

"The true test of legality is whether the restraint imposed is such as merely regulates and perhaps thereby promotes competition or whether it is such as may suppress or even destroy competition. To determine that question the court must ordinarily consider the facts peculiar to the business to which the restraint is applied; its condition before and after the restraint was imposed; the nature of the restraint and its effect, actual or probable. The history of the restraint, the evil believed to exist, the reason for adopting the particular remedy, the purpose or end sought to be attained, are all rele-

when they relate to conduct that is manifestly anti-competitive. As the Court explained in *Northern Pac. R. Co. v. United States*, 356 U.S. 1, 5 (1958), "there are certain agreements or practices which because of their pernicious effect on competition and lack of any redeeming virtue are conclusively presumed to be unreasonable and therefore illegal without elaborate inquiry as to the precise harm they have caused or the business excuse for their use."[28]

In essence, the issue before us is whether *Schwinn's per se* rule can be justified under the demanding standards of *Northern Pac. R. Co.* The Court's refusal to endorse a *per se* rule in *White Motor Co.* was based on its uncertainty as to whether vertical restrictions satisfied those standards. Addressing this question for the first time, the Court stated:

> "We need to know more than we do about the actual impact of these arrangements on competition to decide whether they have such a 'pernicious effect on competition and lack ... any redeeming virtue' (*Northern Pac. R. Co. v. United States*, supra) and therefore should be classified as *per se* violations of the Sherman Act."

Only four years later the Court in *Schwinn* announced its sweeping *per se* rule without even a reference to *Northern Pac. R. Co.* and with no explanation of its sudden change in position.[29] We turn now to consider *Schwinn* in light of *Northern Pac. R. Co.*

The market impact of vertical restrictions[30] is complex because of their potential for a simultaneous reduction of intrabrand competition and

---

vant facts. This is not because a good intention will save an otherwise objectionable regulation or the reverse; but because knowledge of the intent may help the court to interpret facts and to predict consequences."

28. *Per se* rules thus require the Court to make broad generalizations about the social utility of particular commercial practices. The probability that anticompetitive consequences will result from a practice and the severity of those consequences must be balanced against its procompetitive consequences. Cases that do not fit the generalization may arise, but a *per se* rule reflects the judgment that such cases are not sufficiently common or important to justify the time and expense necessary to identify them. Once established, *per se* rules tend to provide guidance to the business community and to minimize the burdens on litigants and the judicial system of the more complex rule of reason trials, *see Northern Pac. R. Co. v. United States*, 356 U.S. 1, 5 (1958); *United States v. Topco Associates*, 405 U.S. 596, 609–610 (1972), but those advantages are not suffi-

cient in themselves to justify the creation of *per se* rules. If it were otherwise, all of antitrust law would be reduced to *per se* rules, thus introducing an unintended and undesirable rigidity in the law.

29. After *White Motor Co.*, the courts of appeals continued to evaluate territorial restrictions according to the rule of reason. *Sandura Co. v. FTC*, 339 F.2d 847 (C.A.6 1964); *Snap–On Tools Corp. v. FTC*, 321 F.2d 825 (C.A.7 1963)....

30. As in *Schwinn*, we are concerned here only with nonprice vertical restrictions. The *per se* illegality of price restrictions has been established firmly for many years and involves significantly different questions of analysis and policy. As Mr. Justice White notes, some commentators have argued that the manufacturer's motivation for imposing vertical price restrictions may be the same as for non-price restrictions. There are, however, significant differences that could easily justify different treatment. In his concurring opinion in *White Motor Co.*, Mr. Justice Brennan noted that, unlike nonprice restrictions,

stimulation of interbrand competition.[31] Significantly, the Court in *Schwinn* did not distinguish among the challenged restrictions on the basis of their individual potential for intrabrand harm or interbrand benefit. Restrictions that completely eliminated intrabrand competition among Schwinn distributors were analyzed no differently than those that merely moderated intrabrand competition among retailers. The pivotal factor was the passage of title: All restrictions were held to be *per se* illegal where title had passed, and all were evaluated and sustained under the rule of reason where it had not. The location restriction at issue here would be subject to the same pattern of analysis under *Schwinn*.

It appears that this distinction between sale and nonsale transactions resulted from the Court's effort to accommodate the perceived intrabrand harm and interbrand benefit of vertical restrictions. The *per se* rule for sale transactions reflected the view that vertical restrictions are "so obviously destructive" of intrabrand competition[32] that their use would "open the door to exclusivity of outlets and limitation of territory further than prudence permits." ...[33] Conversely, the continued adherence to the tradi-

---

"[r]esale price maintenance is not designed to, but almost invariably does in fact, reduce price competition not only among sellers of the affected product, but quite as much between that product and competing brands." 372 U.S., at 268. Judge Posner also recognized that "industry-wide resale price maintenance might facilitate cartelizing." *Posner*, supra, n. 22, at 294 (footnote omitted); *see* Posner, Antitrust: Cases, Economic Notes and Other Materials 134 (1974); Gellhorn, Antitrust Law and Economics 252 (1976); Note, 10 Colum.J.L. & Soc.Prob., supra, n. 22, at 498 n. 12. Furthermore, Congress recently has expressed its approval of a *per se* analysis of vertical price restrictions by repealing those provisions of the Miller–Tydings and McGuire Acts allowing fair trade pricing at the option of the individual States.... No similar expression of congressional intent exists for nonprice restrictions.

31. Interbrand competition is the competition among the manufacturers of the same generic product—television sets in this case—and is the primary concern of antitrust law. The extreme example of a deficiency of interbrand competition is monopoly, where there is only one manufacturer. In contrast, intrabrand competition is the competition between the distributors—wholesale or retail—of the product of a particular manufacturer.

The degree of intrabrand competition is wholly independent of the level of interbrand competition confronting the manufacturer. Thus, there may be fierce intrabrand compe-

tition among the distributors of a product produced by a monopolist and no intrabrand competition among the distributors of a product produced by a firm in a highly competitive industry. But when interbrand competition exists, as it does among television manufacturers, it provides a significant check on the exploitation of intrabrand market power because of the ability of consumers to substitute a different brand of the same product.

32. The Court did not specifically refer to intrabrand competition, but this meaning is clear from the context.

33. The Court also stated that to impose vertical restrictions in sale transactions would "violate the ancient rule against restraints on alienation." 388 U.S., at 380. This isolated reference has provoked sharp criticism from virtually all of the commentators on the decision, most of whom have regarded the Court's apparent reliance on the "ancient rule" as both a misreading of legal history and a perversion of antitrust analysis. *See, e.g., Handler*, supra, n. 22, at 1684–1686; *Posner*, supra, n. 22, at 295–296; *Robinson*, supra, n. 22, at 270–271; but *see Louis*, supra, n. 22, at 276 n. 6. We quite agree with Mr. Justice Stewart's dissenting comment in *Schwinn* that "the state of the common law 400 or even 100 years ago is irrelevant to the issue before us: the effect of the antitrust laws upon vertical distributional restraints in the American economy today." 388 U.S., at 392.

tional rule of reason for nonsale transactions reflected the view that the restrictions have too great a potential for the promotion of interbrand competition to justify complete prohibition.[34] The Court's opinion provides no analytical support for these contrasting positions. Nor is there even an assertion in the opinion that the competitive impact of vertical restrictions is significantly affected by the form of the transaction. Nonsale transactions appear to be excluded from the *per se* rule, not because of a greater danger of intrabrand harm or a greater promise of interbrand benefit, but rather because of the Court's unexplained belief that a complete *per se* prohibition would be too "inflexible." ...

Vertical restrictions reduce intrabrand competition by limiting the number of sellers of a particular product competing for the business of a given group of buyers. Location restrictions have this effect because of practical constraints on the effective marketing area of retail outlets. Although intrabrand competition may be reduced, the ability of retailers to exploit the resulting market may be limited both by the ability of consumers to travel to other franchised locations and, perhaps more importantly, to purchase the competing products of other manufacturers. None of these key variables, however, is affected by the form of the transaction by which a manufacturer conveys his products to the retailers.

Vertical restrictions promote interbrand competition by allowing the manufacturer to achieve certain efficiencies in the distribution of his products. These "redeeming virtues" are implicit in every decision sustaining vertical restrictions under the rule of reason. Economists have identified a number of ways in which manufacturers can use such restrictions to

We are similarly unable to accept Judge Browning's interpretation of *Schwinn*. In his dissent below he argued that the decision reflects the view that the Sherman Act was intended to prohibit restrictions on the autonomy of independent businessmen even though they have no impact on "price, quality, and quantity of goods and services," .... This view is certainly not explicit in *Schwinn*, which purports to be based on an examination of the "impact [of the restrictions] upon the marketplace." ... Competitive economies have social and political as well as economic advantages, *see, e.g., Northern Pac. R. Co. v. United States*, 356 U.S., at 4, but an antitrust policy divorced from market considerations would lack any objective benchmarks. As Justice Brandeis reminded us, "Every agreement concerning trade, every regulation of trade, restrains. To bind, to restrain is of their very essence." *Chicago Board of Trade v. United States*, 246 U.S., at 238. Although Mr. Justice White's opinion endorses Judge Browning's interpretation, it purports to distinguish *Schwinn* on grounds inconsistent with that interpretation.

34. In that regard, the Court specifically stated that a more complete prohibition "might severely hamper smaller enterprises resorting to reasonable methods of meeting the competition of giants and of merchandising through independent dealers." ... The Court also broadly hinted that it would recognize additional exceptions to the *per se* rule for new entrants in an industry and for failing firms, both of which were mentioned in *White Motor* as candidates for such exceptions.... The Court might have limited the exceptions to the *per se* rule to these situations, which present the strongest arguments for the sacrifice of intrabrand competition for interbrand competition. Significantly, it chose instead to create the more extensive exception for nonsale transactions which is available to all businesses, regardless of their size, financial health, or market share. This broader exception demonstrates even more clearly the Court's awareness of the "redeeming virtues" of vertical restrictions.

compete more effectively against other manufacturers. *See, e.g.,* Preston, Restrictive Distribution Arrangements: Economic Analysis and Public Policy Standards, 30 Law & Contemp.Prob. 506, 511 (1965).[35] For example, new manufacturers and manufacturers entering new markets can use the restrictions in order to induce competent and aggressive retailers to make the kind of investment of capital and labor that is often required in the distribution of products unknown to the consumer. Established manufacturers can use them to induce retailers to engage in promotional activities or to provide service and repair facilities necessary to the efficient marketing of their products. Service and repair are vital for many products, such as automobiles and major household appliances. The availability and quality of such services affect a manufacturer's goodwill and the competitiveness of his product. Because of market imperfections such as the so-called "free rider" effect, these services might not be provided by retailers in a purely competitive situation, despite the fact that each retailer's benefit would be greater if all provided the services than if none did. Posner, supra, n. 22, at 285; cf. P. Samuelson, Economics 506–507 (10th ed. 1976).

Economists also have argued that manufacturers have an economic interest in maintaining as much intrabrand competition as is consistent with the efficient distribution of their products. Bork, The Rule of Reason and the *Per se* Concept: Price Fixing and Market Division II, 75 Yale L.J. 373, 403 (1966); Posner, supra, n. 22, at 283, 287–288.[36] Although the view that the manufacturer's interest necessarily corresponds with that of the public is not universally shared, even the leading critic of vertical restrictions concedes that *Schwinn's* distinction between sale and nonsale transactions is essentially unrelated to any relevant economic impact. Comanor, Vertical Territorial and Customer Restrictions: White Motor and Its Aftermath, 81 Harv.L.Rev. 1419, 1422 (1968).[37] Indeed, to the extent that the

35.   Marketing efficiency is not the only legitimate reason for a manufacturer's desire to exert control over the manner in which his products are sold and serviced. As a result of statutory and common law developments, society increasingly demands that manufacturers assume direct responsibility for the safety and quality of their products. For example, at the federal level, apart from more specialized requirements, manufacturers of consumer products have safety responsibilities under the Consumer Product Safety Act, . . . and obligations for warranties under the Consumer Product Warranties Act, . . . Similar obligations are imposed by state law. . . . The legitimacy of these concerns has been recognized in cases involving vertical restrictions. *See, e.g., Tripoli Co. v. Wella Corp.,* supra, n. 23.

36.   "Generally a manufacturer would prefer the lowest retail price possible, once its price to dealers has been set, because a lower retail price means increased sales and higher manufacturer revenues." Note, 88 Harv. L.Rev. 636, 641 (1975). In this context, a manufacturer is likely to view the difference between the price at which it sells to its retailers and their price to the consumer as his "cost of distribution," which it would prefer to minimize. *Posner,* supra, n. 22, at 283.

37.   Professor Comanor argues that the promotional activities encouraged by vertical restrictions result in product differentiation and, therefore, a decrease in interbrand competition. This argument is flawed by its necessary assumption that a large part of the promotional efforts resulting from vertical restrictions will not convey socially desirable information about product availability, price, quality and services. Nor is it clear that a *per se* rule would result in anything more than a shift to less efficient methods of obtaining the same promotional effects.

form of the transaction is related to interbrand benefits, the Court's distinction is inconsistent with its articulated concern for the ability of smaller firms to compete effectively with larger ones. Capital requirements and administrative expenses may prevent smaller firms from using the exception for nonsale transactions.[38]

We conclude that the distinction drawn in *Schwinn* between sale and nonsale transactions is not sufficient to justify the application of a *per se* rule in one situation and a rule of reason in the other. The question remains whether the *per se* rule stated in *Schwinn* should be expanded to include nonsale transactions or abandoned in favor of a return to the rule of reason. We have found no persuasive support for expanding the rule. As noted above, the *Schwinn* Court recognized the undesirability of "prohibit[ing] all vertical restrictions of territory and all franchising...."[39] And even Continental does not urge us to hold that all such restrictions are *per se* illegal.

We revert to the standard articulated in *Northern Pac. R. Co.*, and reiterated in *White Motor*, for determining whether vertical restrictions must be "conclusively presumed to be unreasonable and therefore illegal without elaborate inquiry as to the precise harm they have caused or the business excuse for their use." Such restrictions, in varying forms, are widely used in our free market economy. As indicated above, there is substantial scholarly and judicial authority supporting their economic utility. There is relatively little authority to the contrary.[40] Certainly, there has been no showing in this case, either generally or with respect to Sylvania's agreements, that vertical restrictions have or are likely to have a "pernicious effect on competition" or that they "lack ... any redeeming virtue." *Ibid.*[41] Accordingly, we conclude that the *per se* rule stated in *Schwinn*

---

38. We also note that *per se* rules in this area may work to the ultimate detriment of the small businessmen who operate as franchisees. To the extent that a *per se* rule prevents a firm from using the franchise system to achieve efficiencies that it perceives as important to its successful operation, the rule creates an incentive for vertical integration into the distribution system, thereby eliminating to that extent the role of independent businessmen. *See, e.g.,* Keck, The Schwinn case, 23 Bus.Law. 669 (1968); Pollock, supra, n. 22, at 608–610.

39. Continental's contention that balancing intrabrand and interbrand competitive effects of vertical restrictions is not a "proper part of the judicial function," Petitioner Brief, at 52, is refuted by Schwinn itself. *United States v. Topco Associates, Inc.,* 405 U.S. 596 (1972), is not to the contrary, for it involved a horizontal restriction among ostensible competitors. 405 U.S., at 608.

40. There may be occasional problems in differentiating vertical restrictions from horizontal restrictions originating in agreements among the retailers. There is no doubt that restrictions in the latter category would be illegal *per se, see, e.g., United States v. General Motors Corp.,* 384 U.S. 127 (1966); *United States v. Topco Associates, Inc.,* supra, but we do not regard the problems of proof as sufficiently great to justify a *per se* rule.

41. The location restriction used by Sylvania was neither the least nor the most restrictive provision that it could have used.... But we agree with the implicit judgment in *Schwinn* that a *per se* rule based on the nature of the restriction is, in general, undesirable. Although distinctions can be drawn among the frequently used restrictions, we are inclined to view them as differences of degree and form. *See Robinson,* supra, n. 22, at 279–280; *Averill, Sealy, Schwinn* and Sherman One: An Analysis and

must be overruled. In so holding we do not foreclose the possibility that particular applications of vertical restrictions might justify *per se* prohibition under *Northern Pac. R. Co.* But we do make clear that departure from the rule of reason standard must be based upon demonstrable economic effect rather than—as in *Schwinn*—upon formalistic line drawing.

In sum, we conclude that the appropriate decision is to return to the rule of reason that governed vertical restrictions prior to *Schwinn*. When anticompetitive effects are shown to result from particular vertical restrictions they can be adequately policed under the rule of reason, the standard traditionally applied for the majority of anticompetitive practices challenged under § 1 of the Act. Accordingly, the decision of the Court of Appeals is affirmed.

■ REHNQUIST, J., took no part in the consideration or decision of this case.

■ WHITE, J., concurring. Although I agree with the majority that the location clause at issue in this case is not a *per se* violation of the Sherman Act and should be judged under the rule of reason, I cannot agree that this result requires the overruling of *United States v. Arnold, Schwinn & Co.*, 388 U.S. 365 (1967). In my view this case is distinguishable from *Schwinn* because there is less potential for restraint of intrabrand competition and more potential for stimulating interbrand competition. As to intrabrand competition, Sylvania, unlike Schwinn, did not restrict the customers to whom or the territories where its purchasers could sell. As to interbrand competition, Sylvania, unlike Schwinn, had an insignificant market share at the time it adopted its challenged distribution practice and enjoyed no consumer preference that would allow its retailers to charge a premium over other brands. In two short paragraphs, the majority disposes of the view, adopted after careful analysis by the Ninth Circuit en banc below, that these differences provide a "principled basis for distinguishing *Schwinn*," . . . despite holdings by three Courts of Appeals and the District Court on remand in *Schwinn* that the *per se* rule established in that case does not apply to location clauses such as Sylvania's. To reach out to overrule one of this Court's recent interpretations of the Sherman Act, after such a cursory examination of the necessity for doing so, is surely an affront to the principle that considerations of *stare decisis* are to be given particularly strong weight in the area of statutory construction. *Illinois Brick Co. v. Illinois*, 431 U.S. 720 (1977); *Runyon v. McCrary*, 427 U.S. 160, 175 (1976); *Edelman v. Jordan*, 415 U.S. 651, 671 (1974).

One element of the system of interrelated vertical restraints invalidated in *Schwinn* was a retail customer restriction prohibiting franchised retailers from selling Schwinn products to nonfranchised retailers. The Court rests its inability to distinguish *Schwinn* entirely on this retail customer restriction, finding it "[i]n intent and competitive impact . . .

Prognosis, 15 N.Y.L.F. 39, 65 (1969). We are unable to perceive significant social gain from channeling transactions into one form or another. Finally, we agree with the Court in *Schwinn* that the advantages of vertical re-

strictions should not be limited to the categories of new entrants and failing firms. Sylvania was faltering, if not failing and we think it would be unduly artificial to deny it the use of valuable competitive tools.

indistinguishable from the location restriction in the present case," because "[i]n both cases the restrictions limited the freedom of the retailer to dispose of the purchased products as he desired." ... The customer restriction may well have, however, a very different "intent and competitive impact" than the location restriction: it prevents discount stores from getting the manufacturer's product and thus prevents intrabrand price competition. Suppose, for example, that interbrand competition is sufficiently weak that the franchised retailers are able to charge a price substantially above wholesale. Under a location restriction, these franchisers are free to sell to discount stores seeking to exploit the potential for sales at prices below the prevailing retail level. One of the franchised retailers may be tempted to lower its price and act in effect as a wholesaler for the discount house in order to share in the profits to be had from lowering prices and expanding volume.[42]

Under a retail customer restriction, on the other hand, the franchised dealers cannot sell to discounters, who are cut off altogether from the manufacturer's product and the opportunity for intrabrand price competition. This was precisely the theory on which the Government successfully challenged Schwinn's customer restrictions in this Court. The District Court in that case found that "[e]ach one of [Schwinn's franchised retailers] knows also that he is not a wholesaler and that he cannot sell as a wholesaler or act as an agent for some other unfranchised dealer, such as a discount house retailer who has not been franchised as a dealer by Schwinn." ... The Government argued on appeal, with extensive citations to the record, that the effect of this restriction was "to keep Schwinn products out of the hands of discount houses and other price cutters so as to discourage price competition in retailing...."[43]

It is true that as the majority states, Sylvania's location restriction inhibited to some degree "the freedom of the retailer to dispose of the purchased products" by requiring the retailer to sell from one particular place of business. But the retailer is still free to sell to any type of customer—including discounters and other unfranchised dealers—from any area. I think this freedom implies a significant difference for the effect of a location clause on intrabrand competition. The District Court on remand in *Schwinn* evidently thought so as well, for after enjoining Schwinn's customer restriction as directed by this Court it expressly sanctioned location clauses, permitting Schwinn to "designat[e] in its retailer franchise agree-

42. The franchised retailers would be prevented from engaging in discounting themselves if, under the Colgate doctrine, ... the manufacturer could lawfully terminate dealers who did not adhere to its suggested retail price.

43. Given the Government's emphasis on the inhibiting effect of the *Schwinn* restrictions on discounting activities, the Court may well have been referring to this effect

when it condemned the restrictions as "obviously destructive of competition." ... But the Court was also heavily influenced by its concern for the freedom of dealers to control the disposition of products they purchased from Schwinn.... In any event, the record in *Schwinn* illustrates the potentially greater threat to intrabrand competition posed by customer as opposed to location restrictions.

ments the location of the place or places of business for which the franchise is issued." ...

An additional basis for finding less restraint of intrabrand competition in this case, emphasized by the Ninth Circuit en banc, is that *Schwinn* involved restrictions on competition among distributors at the wholesale level. As Judge Ely wrote for the seven-member majority below:

> "[Schwinn] had created exclusive geographical sales territories for each of its 22 wholesale bicycle distributors and had made each distributor the sole Schwinn outlet for the distributor's designated area. Each distributor was prohibited from selling to any retailers located outside its territory....
>
> "Schwinn's territorial restrictions requiring dealers to confine their sales to exclusive territories prescribed by Schwinn prevented a dealer from competing for customers outside his territory.... Schwinn's restrictions guaranteed each wholesaler distributor that it would be absolutely isolated from all competition from other Schwinn wholesalers." ...

Moreover, like its franchised retailers, Schwinn's distributors were absolutely barred from selling to nonfranchised retailers, further limiting the possibilities of intrabrand price competition.

The majority apparently gives no weight to the Court of Appeals' reliance on the difference between the competitive effects of Sylvania's location clause and Schwinn's interlocking "system of vertical restraints affecting both wholesale and retail distribution...." It also ignores post–*Schwinn* decisions of the Third and Tenth Circuits upholding the validity of location clauses similar to Sylvania's here. *Salco Corp. v. General Motors Corp., Buick Motor Division*, 517 F.2d 567 (C.A.10 1975); *Kaiser v. General Motors Corp.*, 530 F.2d 964 (C.A.3 1976), *aff'g* 396 F.Supp. 33 (E.D.Pa. 1975). Finally, many of the scholarly authorities the majority cites in support of its overruling of *Schwinn* have not had to strain to distinguish location clauses from the restrictions invalidated there. *E.g.*, Robinson, Recent Antitrust Developments: 1974, 75 Colum.L.Rev. 243, 278 (1975) (outcome in *Sylvania* not preordained by *Schwinn* because of marked differences in the vertical restraints in the two cases); McLaren, Territorial and Customer Restrictions, Consignments, Suggested Retail Prices and Refusals to Deal, 37 Antitrust L.J. 137, 144–145 (1968) (by implication *Schwinn* exempts location clauses from its *per se* rule); Pollack, Alternative Distribution Methods After *Schwinn*, 63 N.W.U.L.Rev. 595, 603 (1968) ("Nor does the *Schwinn* doctrine outlaw the use of a so-called 'location clause' ... ").

Just as there are significant differences between *Schwinn* and this case with respect to intrabrand competition, there are also significant differences with respect to interbrand competition. Unlike Schwinn, Sylvania clearly had no economic power in the generic product market. At the time they instituted their respective distribution policies, Schwinn was "the leading bicycle producer in the Nation," with a national market share of

22.5%, ... whereas Sylvania was a "faltering, if not failing" producer of television sets, with "a relatively insignificant 1 to 2%" share of the national market in which the dominant manufacturer had a 60 to 70% share.... Moreover, the Schwinn brand name enjoyed superior consumer acceptance and commanded a premium price as, in the District Court's words, "the Cadillac of the bicycle industry." ... This premium gave Schwinn dealers a margin of protection from interbrand competition and created the possibilities for price cutting by discounters that the Government argued were forestalled by Schwinn's customer restrictions.[44] Thus, judged by the criteria economists use to measure market power—product differentiation and market share[45]—Schwinn enjoyed a substantially stronger position in the bicycle market than did Sylvania in the television market. This Court relied on Schwinn's market position as one reason not to apply the rule of reason to the vertical restraints challenged there. "Schwinn was not a newcomer, seeking to break into or stay in the bicycle business. It was not a 'failing company.' On the contrary, at the initiation of these practices, it was the leading bicycle producer in the Nation...." And the Court of Appeals below found "another significant distinction between our case and *Schwinn*" in Sylvania's "precarious market share," which "was so small when it adopted its locations practice that it was threatened with expulsion from the television market." ... [46]

In my view there are at least two considerations, both relied upon by the majority to justify overruling *Schwinn,* that would provide a "principled basis" for instead refusing to extend *Schwinn* to a vertical restraint that is imposed by a "faltering" manufacturer with a "precarious" position in a generic product market dominated by another firm. The first is that, as the majority puts it, "when interbrand competition exists, as it does among television manufacturers, it provides a significant check on the exploitation of intrabrand market power because of the ability of consumers to substitute a different brand of the same product." ... Second is the view, argued forcefully in the economic literature cited by the majority, that the potential benefits of vertical restraints in promoting interbrand competition are particularly strong where the manufacturer imposing the restraints is

44. Relying on the finding of the District Court, the Government argued in its brief, at 36:

"[T]he declared purpose of the Schwinn franchising system [was] to establish and exploit a distinctive identity and superior consumer acceptance for the Schwinn brand name as the Cadillac of bicycles, thereby enabling the charging of a premium price.... This scheme could not possibly succeed, and doubtless would long ago have been abandoned, if in the consumer's mind other bicycles were just as good as Schwinn's."

45. *See, e.g.,* Scherer, Industrial Market Structure and Economic Performance 10–11

(1970); Samuelson, Economics 485–491 (10th ed. 1976).

46. Schwinn's national market share declined to 12.8% in the 10 years following the institution of its distribution program, at which time it ranked second behind a firm with a 22.8% share.... In the three years following the adoption of its locations practice, Sylvania's national market share increased to 5%, placing it eighth among manufacturers of color television sets.... At this time Sylvania's shares of the San Francisco, Sacramento, and Northern California markets were respectively 2.5%, 15%, and 5%.... The District Court made no findings as to Schwinn's shares of local bicycle markets.

seeking to enter a new market or to expand a small market share.[47] The majority even recognizes that *Schwinn* "hinted" at an exception for new entrants and failing firms from its *per se* rule. . . .

In other areas of the antitrust law, this Court has not hesitated to base its rules of *per se* illegality in part on the defendant's market power. Indeed, in the very case from which the majority draws its standard for *per se* rules, *Northern Pac. R. Co. v. United States*, 356 U.S. 1, 5 (1958), the Court stated the reach of the *per se* rule against tie-ins under § 1 of the Sherman Act as extending to all defendants with "sufficient economic power with respect to the tying product to appreciably restrain free competition in the market for the tied product. . . ." And the Court subsequently approved an exception to this *per se* rule for "infant industries" marketing a new product. *United States v. Jerrold Electronics Corp.*, 187 F.Supp. 545 (E.D.Pa.1960), *aff'd per curiam*, 365 U.S. 567 (1961). *See also United States v. Philadelphia National Bank*, 374 U.S. 321, 363 (1963), where the Court held presumptively illegal a merger "which produces a firm controlling an undue percentage share of the relevant market. . . ." I see no doctrinal obstacle to excluding firms with such minimal market power as Sylvania's from the reach of the *Schwinn* rule.[48]

I have, moreover, substantial misgivings about the approach the majority takes to overruling *Schwinn*. The reason for the distinction in *Schwinn* between sale and nonsale transactions was not as the majority would have it, "the Court's effort to accommodate the perceived intrabrand harm and interbrand benefit of vertical restrictions," . . . the reason was rather, as Judge Browning argued in dissent below, the notion in many of our cases involving vertical restraints that independent businessmen should have the freedom to dispose of the goods they own as they see fit. Thus the first case cited by the Court in *Schwinn* for the proposition that "restraints upon alienation . . . are beyond the power of the manufacturer to impose upon its vendees and . . . are violations of § 1 of the Sherman Act," 388 U.S., at 377, was this Court's seminal decision holding a series of resale price-maintenance agreements *per se* illegal, *Dr. Miles Medical Co. v. John D. Park & Sons Co.*, 220 U.S. 373 (1911). In *Dr. Miles* the Court stated that

47. Preston, Restrictive Distribution Arrangements: Economic Analysis and Public Policy Standards, 30 Law & Contemp.Prob. 506, 511 (1965); Posner, Antitrust Policy and the Supreme Court: An Analysis of the Restricted Distribution, Horizontal Merger, and Potential Competition Decisions, 75 Colum.L.Rev. 282, 293 (1975); Scherer, supra, at 510.

48. *Cf. Sandura Co. v. FTC*, 339 F.2d 847, 850 (C.A.6 1964)(territorial restrictions on distributors imposed by small manufacturer "competing with and losing ground to the 'giants' of the floor-covering industry" is not *per se* illegal); Baker, Vertical Restraints in Times of Change: From White to Schwinn to

Where?, 44 Antitrust L.J. 537, 545–547 (1975) (presumptive illegality of territorial restrictions imposed by manufacturer with "any degree of market power"). The majority's failure to use the market share of Schwinn and Sylvania as a basis for distinguishing these cases is the more anomalous for its reliance, . . ., on the economic analysis of those who distinguish the anticompetitive effects of distribution restraints on the basis of the market shares of the distributors. *See* Posner, supra, at 299; Bork, The Rule of Reason and the *Per se* Concept: Price Fixing and Market Division II, 75 Yale L.J. 373, 391–429 (1966).

"a general restraint on alienation is ordinarily invalid," citing Coke on Littleton, and emphasized that the case involved "agreements restricting the freedom of trade on the part of dealers who own what they sell...." Mr. Justice Holmes stated in dissent, "If [the manufacturer] should make the retail dealers agent in law as well as in name and retain the title until the goods left their hands I cannot conceive that even the present enthusiasm for regulating the prices to be charged by other people would deny that the owner was acting within his rights." ...

After summarily rejecting this concern, reflected in our interpretations of the Sherman Act, for "the autonomy of independent businessmen," ... the majority not surprisingly finds "no justification" for *Schwinn's* distinction between sale and nonsale transactions because the distinction is "essentially unrelated to any relevant economic impact." ... But while according some weight to the businessman's interest in controlling the terms on which he trades in his own goods may be anathema to those who view the Sherman Act as directed solely to economic efficiency,[49] this principle is without question more deeply embedded in our cases than the notions of "free rider" effects and distributional efficiencies borrowed by the majority from the "new economics of vertical relationships." ... Perhaps the Court is right in partially abandoning this principle and in judging the instant nonprice vertical restraints solely by their "relevant economic impact"; but the precedents which reflect this principle should not be so lightly rejected by the Court. The rationale of *Schwinn* is no doubt difficult to discern from the opinion, and it may be wrong; it is not, however, the aberration the majority makes it out to be here.

I have a further reservation about the majority's reliance on "relevant economic impact" as the test for retaining *per se* rules regarding vertical restraints. It is common ground among the leading advocates of a purely economic approach to the question of distribution restraints that the economic arguments in favor of allowing vertical nonprice restraints generally apply to vertical price restraints as well.[50] Although the majority asserts that "the *per se* illegality of price restrictions ... involves significantly different questions of analysis and policy," ... I suspect this purported distinction may be as difficult to justify as that of *Schwinn* under

---

49. *E.g.*, Bork, Legislative Intent and the Policy of the Sherman Act, 9 J.Law & Econ. 7 (1966); Bork, The Rule of Reason and the *Per se* Concept: Price Fixing and Market Division I, 74 Yale L.J. 775 (1965).

50. Professor Posner writes, for example,

"There is no basis for choosing between [price fixing and market division] on social grounds. If resale price maintenance is like dealer price fixing, and therefore bad, a manufacturer's assignment of exclusive territories is like market division, and therefore bad too...."

"[If helping new entrants break into a market] is a good justification for exclusive territories, it is an equally good justification for resale price maintenance, which as we have seen is simply another method of dealing with the free rider problem.... In fact, *any* argument that can be made on behalf of exclusive territories can be made on behalf of resale price maintenance." Posner, supra, at 292–293. (Footnote omitted.)

See Bork, supra, n. 37, at 391–464.

the terms of the majority's analysis. Thus Professor Posner, in an article cited five times by the majority, concludes, "I believe the law should treat price and nonprice restrictions the same and that it should make no distinction between the imposition of restrictions in a sale contract and their imposition in an agency contract." Antitrust Policy and the Supreme Court: An Analysis of the Restricted Distribution, Horizontal Merger and Potential Competition Decisions, 75 Colum.L.Rev. 282, 298 (1975). Indeed, the Court has already recognized that resale price maintenance may increase output by inducing "demand-creating activity" by dealers (such as additional retail outlets, advertising and promotion, and product servicing) that outweighs the additional sales that would result from lower prices brought about by dealer price competition. *Albrecht v. Herald Co.*, 390 U.S. 145, 151 n. 7 (1968). These same output-enhancing possibilities of nonprice vertical restraints are relied upon by the majority as evidence of their "social utility and economic soundness," and as a justification for judging them under the rule of reason. The effect, if not the intention, of the Court's opinion is necessarily to call into question the firmly established *per se* rule against price restraints.... In order to decide this case, the Court need only hold that a location clause imposed by a manufacturer with negligible economic power in the product market has a competitive impact sufficiently less restrictive than the *Schwinn* restraints to justify a rule of reason standard, even if the same weight is given here as in *Schwinn* to dealer autonomy. I therefore concur in the judgment.

BRENNAN, J., with whom MARSHALL, J., joins, dissenting. I would not overrule the *per se* rule stated in *United States v. Arnold, Schwinn & Co.*, 388 U.S. 365 (1967), and would therefore reverse the decision of the Court of Appeals for the Ninth Circuit.

NOTES AND QUESTIONS

1. On remand, the Ninth Circuit Court of Appeals affirmed a grant of summary judgment for Sylvania. It started out by noting that the burden of proof was on Continental T.V. to prove that the location clause arrangement was unreasonable, and then noted the following points in concluding that it had not discharged that burden:

a. The distribution arrangement was adopted unilaterally by Sylvania, with no indication that any distributor had influenced that judgment;

b. A location clause (unlike more extreme distribution arrangements like airtight territorial restrictions) has only a modest impact on intrabrand competition; and

c. At the interbrand level, there were many competitors of Sylvania who could have supplied Continental if it sought to open an outlet in a location not acceptable to Sylvania. *Continental T.V., Inc. v. GTE Sylvania, Inc.*, 694 F.2d 1132 (9th Cir.1982).

2. Note how difficult it is to distinguish the competitive effect of minimum resale price fixing, on the one hand, from territorial and customer allocation, on the

other, where a "free rider" justification is advanced. In both instances, the supplier claims that it terminated, or otherwise restricted the freedom of, a "price cutter" in order to ensure the availability of services in the market. Are these vertical distribution techniques only different ways of achieving the same result? If you had to make the legal rules consistent, would you make both *per se* illegal, both subject to the rule of reason, or both *per se* legal?

In footnote 30 of *Sylvania,* the Supreme Court distinguishes price from nonprice restrictions on two grounds: (1) that resale price maintenance "almost invariably" has an effect on interbrand competition among suppliers while nonprice vertical restrictions do not, and (2) that Congress in repealing fair trade in 1975 should be understood as expressing "its approval of a *per se* analysis of vertical price restrictions...." Why exactly is the interbrand effect at the manufacturer's level different with respect to price and nonprice restrictions? And is it fair to infer from Congress' repeal of fair trade that it had in mind approval of the *per se* rule against minimum price fixing?

3.   In adopting a rule of reason approach for nonprice vertical restrictions, the principal guidance the Court offered in *Sylvania* was a reference to the famous statement of Justice Brandeis in *Chicago Board of Trade v. United States*:

> The true test of legality is whether the restraint imposed is such as merely regulates and perhaps thereby promotes competition or whether it is such as may suppress or even destroy competition. To determine that question, the Court must ordinarily consider the facts peculiar to the business to which the restraint is applied; its condition before and after the restraint was imposed; the nature of the restraint and its effect, actual or probable. The history of the restraint, the evil believed to exist, the reason for adopting the particular remedy, the purpose or end sought to be attained, are all relevant facts. 246 U.S. 231, 238 (1918).

Is this a helpful guideline for deciding cases? What priority and relative weight does the Court expect will be accorded to each factor? Note the odd fact that market share, usually regarded as critical in a rule of reason analysis, is not listed among this array of factors.

Several courts and commentators have summarized the rule of reason approach by asking three questions: (1) what are the anticompetitive effects of the arrangement, (2) what are its beneficial purposes and effects, and (3) is the restraint reasonably necessary for the achievement of the legitimate objective. *See, e.g., Eiberger v. Sony Corp. of America*, 622 F.2d 1068, 1076 (2d Cir.1980); *Donald B. Rice Tire Co. v. Michelin Tire Corp.*, 483 F.Supp. 750 (D.Md.1980), *aff'd*, 638 F.2d 15 (4th Cir.), *cert. denied*, 454 U.S. 864 (1981); P. Areeda, Antitrust Law 371 (1986).

Does this formulation capture the relevant issues? Who should have the burden of proof on each of these elements?

4.   *Sylvania* apparently concluded that vertical territorial allocation in some circumstances is justifiable as an effort to curtail the activities of "free riders." But, as we have seen, participants in a horizontal market division scheme could similarly argue that they adopted the arrangement to prevent free riding. Is the anticompetitive effect or business justification of vertical territorial allocation different from a horizontal territorial allocation? Despite the approving reference to *Topco,* in note 40 of *Sylvania,* can it be argued that *Sylvania* overruled *Topco*?

5.   In EASTERN SCIENTIFIC CO. V. WILD HEERBRUGG INSTRUMENTS INC., 572 F.2d 883 (1st Cir.), *cert. denied*, 439 U.S. 833 (1978), plaintiff, Eastern, distributed the products of defendant Wild, an importer and distributor of scientific equipment.

Eastern agreed not to sell Wild's products outside its assigned area of Rhode Island at less than list price. Within Rhode Island, Wild imposed no price restrictions upon Eastern. In upholding the price restraint under the rule of reason, the Court of Appeals argued:

> It may be true that defendant's policies here appear in *form* to resemble resale price maintenance agreements. However, we are unable to conceive of how the resale price restrictions used to enforce the assigned territories in the present case can possibly have a greater anticompetitive *effect* than a pure policy of territorial restrictions....
>
> Thus the resale price restriction in the present case produces the same anti-competitive effect as pure territorial restrictions but to a lesser degree. If the Supreme Court holds that pure territorial restrictions should be analyzed under the rule of reason, we can see no reason based on substantive economic effect why a similar but less anti-competitive scheme should be treated differently.

6. In *Eiberger v. Sony Corp. of America*, 459 F.Supp. 1276 (S.D.N.Y.1978), rev'd in part, 622 F.2d 1068 (2d Cir.1980), Sony Corporation of America (Sonam) sold dictation equipment through a network of authorized Sony retail dealerships, franchised in various locations. Prior to 1975, its agreements with dealers provided that each would "primarily devote and otherwise concentrate its operations in the retail sale" of Sony products in the dealer's area. Each dealer was responsible for providing warranty service on all Sony machines sold by the dealer. The agreement stated, however, that it was not intended to restrict dealers to sales within their territories which were "non-exclusive." Dealers who sold outside their territories could retain warranty responsibility or transfer it to the dealer in whose territory the machine was sold by paying a fee according to a schedule devised by Sonam.

In 1974, ABP, a wholly owned subsidiary of Eiberger, began selling outside its territory "wholesale quantities" of Sony machines to a former business associate in Florida who sold them at retail and performed the warranty services for ABP. After complaints by Florida authorized dealers, Sonam changed its warranty system. Dealers who sold outside their territory were now required to pay a warranty fee to Sonam, which in turn would credit the account of the authorized dealer in that territory. Sonam began to keep written records of the serial numbers of its dictation machines and relied upon authorized dealers to discover and report unauthorized sales. Sonam would compare serial numbers to determine which dealer had sold each reported machine and automatically debit its account for the warranty fees and credit the account of the reporting dealer.

The new warranty fee was charged whether or not the machine required service, even while the machine was still in the hands of an "unauthorized dealer." The fee approximated the dealer's average profit on a machine.

The trial court held that the new warranty system was a vertical restraint of trade in violation of Section 1 of the Sherman Act. The court stated:

> Judged as it must be, by the rule of reason ... these territorial restraints imposed by Sony upon its authorized dealers cannot be justified as having a valid business purpose. Whatever slight benefits the plan may have had in stimulating interbrand competition, these were far outweighed by its adverse effect upon intrabrand competition....
>
> Defendant asserts that the program's purpose and effect was to assure that the use of Sony dictation equipment would be provided with the warranty coverage necessary to make Sony product competitive in the market. This espoused purpose was simply not borne out by the evi-

dence. . . . The object of the conspiracy was the elimination of unauthorized dealers in Sony dictation equipment from the market. 459 F.Supp. at 1282.

The court concluded that a violation of Section 1 existed without analyzing the relevant market or the effect of the restraint in that market.

On appeal, Sonam argued that ABP should have been required to show that Sonam's anticompetitive activities had some impact on interbrand competition in the dictation machine market. But the Second Circuit rejected the argument, affirming the trial court's analysis:

> [T]he primary purpose of the new warranty plan was to . . . eliminate competition. . . . [T]he warranty fees were such as to eliminate any profit. . . . [T]he system had the effect of stifling intrabrand competition. . . . 622 F.2d at 1075. Unless we are to conclude that an anticompetitive impact on intrabrand competition cannot alone support a finding that Section 1 has been violated . . . we must conclude that ABP has proven such a violation here. Id. at 1081.

The Second Circuit noted that the legitimate purpose of ensuring that users receive needed warranty service "could have been achieved with but a slight change in the pre–1975 system: the introduction of a requirement that a selling dealer pay a non-selling dealer for warranty services actually performed. . . ." Id. at 1076 n. 11. *See also Ohio–Sealy Mattress Manufacturing Co. v. Sealy*, 585 F.2d 821 (7th Cir.1978), *cert. denied*, 440 U.S. 930 (1979) (jury may find that payover requirement of 3.2% to 12% of revenues on out-of-territory sales to "reimburse" for cost of servicing goods unreasonable where service seldom required and usually performed by seller); *Response of Carolina v. Leasco Response*, 537 F.2d 1307 (5th Cir.1976) (jury question whether provision that franchisee pay 15% royalty on sales within its area of primary responsibility but 70% on sales outside constitutes an illegal territorial restriction).

Eiberger is one of the very few instances since *Sylvania* in which a plaintiff prevailed in challenging a nonprice vertical restriction. Another instance was *Graphic Products Distributors v. Itek Corp.*, 717 F.2d 1560 (11th Cir.1983). In scores of other cases, however, the defendant has prevailed since a rule of reason analysis was introduced.

7.   One reason plaintiffs find successful challenges to nonprice vertical restrictions so difficult is the development of a rule in several circuits that the plaintiff, as a preliminary matter, must show that the party instituting the nonprice restraint had substantial market power. *See, e.g., Assam Drug Co. v. Miller Brewing Co.*, 624 F.Supp. 411 (D.S.D.1985), *aff'd*, 798 F.2d 311 (8th Cir.1986) (19% market share not enough to avoid summary judgment); *JBL Enterprises Inc. v. Jhirmack Enterprises, Inc.*, 698 F.2d 1011 (9th Cir.1983) (4.2% share in the market for beauty products was insufficient to enable a customer restriction to affect interbrand competition substantially); *Donald B. Rice Tire Co. v. Michelin Tire Corp.*, 483 F.Supp. 750 (D.Md.), *aff'd*, 638 F.2d 15 (4th Cir.), *cert. denied*, 454 U.S. 864 (1981) (market shares of 7.9% of passenger radial tire market and 20–25% of the truck radial tire market not sufficient to demonstrate anticompetitive effect); *cf. Valley Liquors, Inc. v. Renfield Importers, Limited*, 678 F.2d 742 (7th Cir.1982). Why should market power be a "screening device" in the area of vertical nonprice restrictions? Would your analysis be different if other manufacturers in the same market adopted the same or similar distributional restraints?

8.   The question whether a nonprice restraint was more restrictive than necessary to achieve legitimate business purposes was addressed in *American Motor*

Inns, Inc. v. Holiday Inns Inc., 521 F.2d 1230 (3d Cir.1975). American Motor Inns Inc. (AMI), the largest franchisee of Holiday Inns, Inc. (HI), sought a license from HI to open a Holiday Inn on property it had purchased for this purpose. HI rejected the application. Pursuant to the terms of HI's standard licensing agreement, AMI was foreclosed from building any other hotel on the property, since under the "non–Holiday Inn" clause, each franchisee agreed not to own, directly or indirectly, any hotel, motel, or motor inn which was not a Holiday Inn. An antitrust action was brought by AMI, which claimed *inter alia,* that the "non–Holiday Inn" franchising practice was an exclusive dealing arrangement violating Section 3 of the Clayton Act and Section 1 of the Sherman Act.

HI claimed that the clause permitted it to enforce another franchise requirement that licensees refer their customers only to other Holiday Inns if possible—a practice which, facilitated by a computerized national reservation system, contributed to the commercial success of the Holiday Inn system.

The trial court found that the effect of the "non–Holiday Inn" clauses was "the intended one of reducing and preventing competition among Holiday Inn franchisees." Protection of the reservation-referral system "was and is available through other provisions of its contract . . ., and through less restrictive provisions of the type utilized by other national hostelers." The court concluded that the "non–Holiday Inn" clause was an unreasonable restraint of trade.

The Court of Appeals for the Third Circuit reversed:

> Although relevant to ascertaining the reasonableness of the non–Holiday Inn clause, it is not determinative that the Holidex system could, as the district court found, be "protected adequately" by less restrictive alternatives. In a rule of reason case, the test is not whether the defendant deployed the least restrictive alternative. . . .

> Because the district court opinion does not demonstrate that in making his rule of reason analysis the trial judge took into account many of the relevant conditions in the industry, . . . the judgment regarding the reasonableness of the non–Holiday Inn clause must be vacated.

> *Chicago Board of Trade* remains the crucible for assaying the legality of a restraint under section 1.

> . . . [T]he issue is whether the restriction actually implemented is "fairly necessary" in the circumstances of the particular case, or whether the restriction "exceed(s) the outer limits of restraint reasonably necessary to protect the defendant."

> Application of the rigid "no less restrictive alternative" test in cases such as this one would place an undue burden on the ordinary conduct of business. Entrepreneurs such as HI would then be made guarantors that the imaginations of lawyers could not conjure up some method of achieving the business purpose in question that would result in a somewhat lesser restriction of trade. And the courts would be placed in the position of second-guessing business judgments as to what arrangements would or would not provide "adequate" protection for legitimate commercial interests. 521 F.2d at 1249–1250.

The Third Circuit rejected cases from other circuits using a "least restrictive alternative" analysis, distinguishing them on the basis that the restraints involved were *per se* unlawful. *Siegel v. Chicken Delight, Inc.*, 448 F.2d 43, 51 (9th Cir.1971), *cert. denied,* 405 U.S. 955 (1972); *Copper Liquor, Inc. v. Adolph Coors Co.,* 506 F.2d 934, 942–43 (5th Cir.1975).

Would the *Eiberger* court have decided *American Motor Inns* differently? Vice versa? Is the Third Circuit's concern about "second-guessing" a disabling problem when, as in *Eiberger,* the defendant itself grew and flourished under a less restrictive arrangement? Or where successful competitors do so?

9. In 1978, the Federal Trade Commission concluded that agreements between Coca Cola and its bottlers that the bottlers would not sell outside assigned territories was an unreasonable restraint. The bottlers then turned to Congress for relief. In special legislation enacted in 1980, an exemption was created from the antitrust laws covering a "trademark soft drink" license granting a manufacturing licensee "the sole and exclusive right to manufacture, distribute and sell ... in a defined geographic area" or permitting such a licensee to sell "only for ultimate resale to consumers within a defined geographic area." The exemption applies only to a soft drink that is "in substantial and effective competition with other products of the same general class in the relevant market or markets." *See* 94 Stat. 939 (1980).

Thereafter, other industries, including particularly the beer industry, sought a similar exemption claiming, quite plausibly, that any justification for a soft drink bottlers bill applied to them equally as well. So far no other special exemptions have been enacted.

10. After the roller coaster ride from *White Motor* to *Schwinn* to *Sylvania,* one can't help considering where the law will go from here. Professor (now Judge) Richard A. Posner and others assert that unilateral vertical restraints that divert dealers' efforts from price competition to service competition "are usually and perhaps always procompetitive and thus should be *per se* legal."[51] Resulting higher prices for the product will be kept in bounds by the competition of interbrand substitutes. They argue further that *Dr. Miles* was wrong in asserting that vertically imposed price restraints have the same economic effect as horizontal price-fixing among dealers. They feel that the manufacturer's self-interest acts as a sort of "surrogate" for consumers' interests, since the manufacturer is unlikely to set the same resale price (or markup) as would dealers acting collusively. He will instead determine the optimum price/service mix in response to consumer preferences. Posner argues that applying a rule of reason to vertical non-price restraints (*GTE Sylvania*) and a rule of *per se* illegality to vertical price restraints (*Dr. Miles*) "warps" the judicial approach by requiring courts to make distinctions where none exists. If anything, he argues, vertical non-price restraints have more potential for injury to intrabrand competition than vertical price controls, since territorial restrictions effect both price *and* service competition. Since a "rule of reason" is too diffuse and cumbersome a standard of decision, Posner argues, qualified *per se* legality is preferable.[52]

Posner avoids the "rule of reason" by a test based on whether the vertical restriction caused the firm's output to rise or fall. If output increased, the restraint must have made the firm's new mix of physical product plus "image" and services more attractive to consumers. If output falls, the defendant would have the burden of proving the decrease was not due to the restriction on competition.

51. R. Posner, The Rule of Reason and the Economic Approach: Reflections on the *Sylvania* Decision, 45 U.Chi.L.Rev. 1, 17–19 (1977).

52. R. Posner, The Next Step in the Antitrust Treatment of Restricted Distribution: *Per Se* Legality, 48 U.Chi.L.Rev. 6, 9 (1981).

Does Judge Posner's output rule protect the interests of those consumers who are interested in a no-frills product at the lowest possible price? Is output a reliable indicator of the purpose and effect of an arrangement? Might not output increase for a score of reasons unrelated to the distributional restraint, such as product improvement or changes in consumer taste?

11. An "exclusive dealership" involves a promise by a manufacturer that it will not sell or authorize others to sell the product in an assigned territory. This was not the arrangement in either *Schwinn* or *Sylvania*, but will be introduced by suppliers (frequently in the form of a "franchise") in distribution systems.

To implement the promise of complete exclusivity, the supplier arguably *must* impose territorial restraints on others in order to insure the promised exclusivity.

Cases dealing with exclusive dealerships will be examined in Chapter 8, pp. 931–962 infra. For now, it is enough to note that even during the *Schwinn* era, courts almost uniformly held that exclusive dealership arrangements were governed by a rule of reason. Absent evidence of horizontal collusion or an exceptionally large market share on the part of the supplier granting the exclusive, and assuming the duration is reasonable, it will frequently be upheld.

Does it follow that a rule of *per se* illegality for "air-tight" territorial exclusivity cannot be maintained in the face of a rule that treats exclusive dealerships in many circumstances as legal? Perhaps the most a supplier ought to be able to promise is that it will not compete with its own distributor and won't appoint another distributor in the same area.

PROBLEM 15

DISTRIBUTION OF BRECHT BEER

Brecht is the third largest of six U.S. brewers with national distribution. Bosch and Muller stand first and second with a combined market share in the U.S. of over 60%. Brecht accounts for 12% of the U.S. market and its share has been declining.

Prior to *Sylvania*, all brewers either made no effort to control areas in which customers sold or imposed primary responsibility obligations which were often unenforced. In California, wholesale beer prices varied as much as 10% in different parts of the state because of the location of breweries, distribution patterns, and consumer preferences. As a result, wholesale distributors, especially when they had excess capacity, would ship to retailers in other parts of the state to take advantage of temporarily attractive price conditions.

A few years after *Sylvania* was decided, Bosch and later Muller changed their distribution systems, established franchises for their wholesalers, and required each to sell within a designated territory (usually, in California, the size of a county or two). Brecht wholesalers soon began clamoring for a similar arrangement, and two or three of its most efficient distributors threatened to switch and become distributors for the market leaders. Brecht had about 20 independent distributors in California (some were the only distributor in an area and others had non-exclusive franchises), and decided to introduce into its revised distributor agreement the following provision:

> Distributor will serve as Brecht's distributor within the described geographic area. Distributor may not sell or supply Brecht's products to any retail location in an area assigned to another Brecht distributor without prior written approval by Brecht, nor sell to any person the distributor has

reason to believe will sell or supply to a retail location in another dealer's territory.

Documents in Brecht's files show that the provision was introduced for the following reasons: (1) to insure that able distributors would not switch to another brand of beer; (2) to eliminate the "chaotic conditions" in which distributors were shipping to all parts of the state; and (3) because Brecht felt that a requirement that distributors concentrate on a local territory would make the distributors more aggressive in marketing and promotional efforts, including sponsorship of local clubs and sporting events and attentiveness to quality control such as removal from retailer shelves of "stale beer."

Last year, Brecht became aware that one of its wholesale dealers, without asking permission, was selling in vast quantities to a retailer which in turn was shipping its beer throughout the state. At first it ignored the practice, but after several other wholesalers brought the matter to its attention, it terminated the offending wholesaler. Has Brecht violated the antitrust laws?

COMPARATIVE NOTE ON EXCLUSIVE TERRITORIAL ARRANGEMENTS

An overriding objective of the Treaty of Rome, establishing the European Economic Community, was to eliminate the divisive economic effects of tariffs, quotas, and other attributes of the national boundary lines of the Member States. Horizontal agreements dividing territories among competitors could result in similar insulation of geographic markets, and Article 81 (ex Article 85) of the Treaty has been implemented largely to eliminate such horizontal restraints, as well as other restrictive practices cartels frequently seek to implement.

Vertical agreements establishing exclusive territories may have similar effects on competition. Thus the Commission from its earliest days has devoted substantial efforts to formulating procedures and rules to deal with territorial exclusives, particularly where their limits coincide with national boundaries. The Commission's regulations and decisions treat "exclusive dealing agreements" as a generic term, with subcategories (1) territorial restrictions—limiting in geographic terms a purchaser's freedom to resell; (2) exclusive supply arrangements—limiting the supplier's freedom to sell, such as by creating an exclusive dealer or franchise in a designated territory; (3) exclusive dealing—agreement by a distributor to purchase largely or exclusively from one supplier (dealt with in Chapter 8 infra); and (4) customer restrictions—limiting a purchaser's freedom to resell to designated classes of customers, frequently other resellers or large users reserved to the producer of the product.

The EC competition rules were first defined in connection with exclusive dealerships, in part because of the large number that were notified when Regulation 17, establishing and defining powers of the Commission in the competition field, first went into effect. The first test of the law in the European Court, *Consten & Grundig v. Commission*, Comm.Mkt.Rep. (CCH) ¶ 8046 (ECCJ 1966), also involved an exclusive dealership. A year later the Commission issued Regulation 67/67, which granted a "block" exemption to certain classes of such agreements. This Regulation, as noted at pp. 647–648 supra, has been replaced by the new 2000 Block Exemption Regulation and the Guidelines on Vertical Restraints, and Regulation 17 itself will be obsolete as of May 2004, see supra at p. 20.

In the *Consten–Grundig* case, the Court of Justice affirmed the Commission's determination that an exclusive distributorship agreement between Grundig, a German manufacturer of radio, television and electronic office equipment, and Consten, a French wholesaler, violated Article 85(1) [now Article 81(1)] of the Treaty of Rome. In 1957 Grundig made Consten its exclusive distributor for France. Consten agreed to advertise Grundig's products, to maintain a repair service and a stock of spare parts, to carry out repairs required by sales warranties, and not to sell competing product lines. There was a secondary agreement which entitled Consten to use and enforce Grundig's "GINT" trademark which had been devised by Grundig to enable its foreign distributors to register a trademark in their respective countries while permitting Grundig to retain exclusive control over its own trademark. The distributors were thus able to maintain trademark infringement suits against nonauthorized importers of Grundig products. Grundig agreed not to allow any of its other distributors to deliver to retailers in France, and Consten agreed not to make any direct or indirect deliveries outside of France.

The Commission had found that intrabrand competition, *i.e.*, competition between wholesalers or distributors of a manufacturer's product, was of crucial importance in the case. Without such competition, consumers and retailers in an area would be forced to buy the brand product at an excessive mark-up because no competition would exist in the distribution of the product.

The Court of Justice concurred in the Commission's emphasis on *intra*-brand competition and rejected Grundig's argument that the agreement was valid because it increased *inter*-brand competition even though *intra*-brand competition might have been impaired:

> The principle of freedom of competition applies to all economic levels and all aspects of competition. Competition between producers is generally more apparent than competition between distributors of the same brand. This does not, however, mean that an agreement that restricts competition between distributors should escape the prohibition of Article 85, paragraph 1, because it might strengthen competition between producers.

The Court found that Grundig, by agreeing not to permit its other distributors to deliver Grundig products to France and by prohibiting Consten from re-exporting Grundig products to other countries, had established absolute territorial protection for Consten. The Court held that these provisions, including the provision providing for Consten's registration of the "GINT" trademark, which enabled Consten to eliminate parallel imports, violated Article 85(1) of the Treaty:

> The situation found to exist ... results in isolating the French market and makes it possible to apply to the products in question prices in which there is no effective competition. Furthermore, competition between producers generally loses its effectiveness as producers become more successful in their efforts to clearly differentiate their brands from other brands. Because distribution costs account for a substantial part of the total cost price, it appears important that competition between dealers should also be promoted....

Grundig's argument that the agreement came within the exemption of Article 85(3) was rejected by the Commission. There was no indication from the evidence that consumers would "share in an equitable part of the profit." In fact, the Commission found that wholesale prices for Grundig products in France ranged between 23 and 44 percent higher than those in Germany, net of customs duties and taxes and after taking discounts into consideration. As far as any "improvement in ... production or distribution" was concerned, the Commission noted that Consten's advertising and repair facility costs constituted approximately two percent of the 53 to 89 percent mark-ups that Consten received. The Commission stated further that even if some improvement in distribution were to exist, absolute territorial protection was not "indispensable" to the improvement; these functions could be suitably performed even though other French wholesalers were permitted to buy Grundig products elsewhere.

The Court agreed with the Commission's rejection of Grundig's contention that the agreement came within the exemption provided by Article 85(3).

As to Grundig's argument that the reputation of its products depended on the proper performance of warranty and repair service, the Court said:

> ... [A] buyer can ordinarily claim his right to such a guarantee only from his supplier and then only under the conditions agreed upon.... The fears concerning any possible harm to the reputation of Grundig products due to insufficient guarantee service do not, in these circumstances, appear to be justified. In fact, the UNEF company, Consten's chief competitor, which started selling Grundig products in France more recently than Consten and had to incur fairly substantial risks nevertheless furnishes free guarantee and paid after-sale services under conditions that on the whole do not appear to have harmed the reputation of the Grundig brand. Furthermore, there is nothing to prevent the plaintiffs from informing consumers, through suitable advertising, of the services and the other advantages that may be offered by the official distribution network for Grundig products. It is therefore not true that the advertising done by Consten would be of equal benefit to parallel importers.

The Commission has often granted individual exemptions to distribution arrangements containing dealer location clauses, on grounds that they improve distribution by "consolidating sales efforts." Goodyear Italiana S.A., Comm. Mkt.Rep. (CCH) ¶ 9708 (Comm'n 1974); Gebruder Junghans GmbH, Comm. Mkt.Rep. (CCH) ¶ 9912 (Comm'n 1976); SABA, Comm.Mkt.Rep. (CCH) ¶ 9802 (Comm'n 1975), aff'd sub nom. Metro SB–Grossmarkte GmbH & Co. v. Comm'n, Comm.Mkt.Rep. (CCH) ¶ 8435 (ECCJ 1977). "Area of primary responsibility" clauses have also been present in exempted arrangements. Bayerische Motoren Werke (BMW) AG, Comm.Mkt.Rep. (CCH) ¶ 9701 (Comm'n 1974).[53]

Nonprice vertical restraints in Europe continue to be regulated more closely than they are in the United States. In order to accomplish this task within the resources it has, the Commission relies heavily on its Block Exemption Regulation entered into force in the year 2000. As noted above, the Block Exemption Regulation, complemented by a set of Guidelines on "Vertical Restraints" replaces three old Block Exemption Regulations applicable to exclusive distribution, exclusive purchasing and franchising agreements and applies more generally to all categories of vertical agreements and concerted practices. The Block Exemption Regulation establishes definitional criteria, coverage criteria, and specifies particular clauses

53. While the Commission in general has been more inclined in recent years to treat vertical restrictions under a flexible rule of reason, it appears not to have abandoned its position to treat severely those territorial restrictions that result in preventing dealers from selling into non-authorized territories. For example, see, Pronuptia de Paris GmbH v. Irmgard Schillgallis, Case 161/84, 1986 ERC 353, Comm.Mkt.Rep. (CCH) ¶ 14,-245.

that are permissible and particular clauses that are prohibited (if one wants the benefit of the block exemption).

The prohibitions are interesting for what they reveal about the Commission's vertical restraints policy. The Block Exemption Regulation excludes reciprocal exclusive distribution arrangements between competitors; it excludes even non-reciprocal exclusive distribution agreements between competitors unless (a) the buyer has a total annual turnover not exceeding EUR 100 million, or (b) the supplier is a manufacturer and a distributor of goods, while the buyer is a distributor not manufacturing goods competing with the contract goods, or (c) the supplier is a provider of services at several levels of trade, while the buyer does not provide competing services at the level of trade where it purchases the contract services. In addition, following *Consten & Grundig*, it prohibits clauses restricting the territory into which the buyer may sell, except for the restriction of active sales, where such a restriction does not limit sales by the customers of the buyer. Subject to a limited number of permissible exceptions, the Regulation also excludes clauses that restrict the customers to whom the buyer may sell.

The Commission also has a concept called "selective distribution," which refers to a distribution network in which only selected dealers have the right to distribute a certain brand, and they are prohibited from reselling to dealers outside the system. The selection criteria must be objective, such as technical qualifications or expertise of the reseller's staff, particularly where high quality or complex consumer durable goods are being distributed. *Metro SB–Grossmarkte GmbH & Co. (SABA) v. Commission*, Comm.Mkt.Rep. (CCH) ¶ 8435 (ECJ 1977). In that case, the Court noted the importance of strengthening competition in factors other than price in a selective distribution system. It also approved prohibitions against wholesalers' reselling to large institutional customers. Here, as with other vertical arrangements, it is particularly sensitive to arrangements that tend to wall off one Member State from another. It also monitors the strength of intra-brand competition both within and across national boundaries carefully. The exemptions shall apply on condition that the market share held by the supplier does not exceed 30 percent.

C.   VERTICAL RESTRAINTS AND REFUSAL TO DEAL

United States v. Colgate & Co.

Supreme Court of the United States, 1919.
250 U.S. 300, 39 S.Ct. 465, 63 L.Ed. 992.

■ McREYNOLDS, J. [The Court explained that, on writs of error challenging a district court's decision to quash an indictment, it was bound to accept the district court's interpretation of the indictment and could review only the lower court's interpretation of the statute.]

We are confronted by an uncertain interpretation of an indictment itself couched in rather vague and general language. Counsel differ radically concerning the meaning of the opinion below and there is much room for the controversy between them.

The indictment runs only against Colgate & Co., a corporation engaged in manufacturing soap and toilet articles and selling them throughout the Union. It makes no reference to monopoly, and proceeds solely upon the theory of an unlawful combination. After setting out defendant's organization, place and character of business, and general methods of selling and distributing products through wholesale and retail merchants, it alleges:

> During the aforesaid period of time, within the said Eastern district of Virginia and throughout the United States, the defendant knowingly and unlawfully created and engaged in a combination with said wholesale and retail dealers, in the Eastern district of Virginia and throughout the United States, for the purpose and with the effect of procuring adherence on the part of such dealers (in reselling such products sold to them aforesaid) to resale prices fixed by the defendant, and of preventing such dealers from reselling such products at lower prices, thus suppressing competition amongst such wholesale dealers, and amongst such retail dealers, in restraint of the aforesaid trade and commerce among the several States, in violation of the act entitled "an act to protect trade and commerce against unlawful restraints and monopolies," approved July 2, 1890.

Following this is a summary of things done to carry out the purposes of the combination: distribution among dealers of letters, telegrams, circulars and lists showing uniform prices to be charged; urging them to adhere to such prices and notices, stating that no sales would be made to those who did not; requests, often complied with, for information concerning dealers who had departed from specified prices; investigation and discovery of those not adhering thereto and placing their names upon "suspended lists;" requests to offending dealers for assurances and promises of future adherence to prices, which were often given; uniform refusals to sell to any who failed to give the same; sales to those who did; similar assurances and promises required of, and given by, other dealers followed by sales to them; unrestricted sales to dealers with established accounts who had observed specified prices, etc.

Immediately thereafter comes this paragraph:

> By reason of the foregoing, wholesale dealers in the aforesaid products of the defendant in the Eastern district of Virginia and throughout the United States, with few exceptions, resold, at uniform prices fixed by the defendant, the aforesaid products, sold to them by the defendant, and refused to resell such products at lower prices to retail dealers in the state where the respective wholesale dealers did business and in other states. For the same reason retail dealers in the aforesaid products of the defendant in the Eastern district of Virginia and throughout the United States resold, at uniform prices fixed by the defendant, the aforesaid products, sold to them by the defendant and by the aforesaid wholesale dealers, and refused to sell such products at lower prices to the consuming public in the states where the respective retail dealers did business and in other states. Thus competition in the sale of such products, by wholesale dealers to retail dealers, and by retail dealers to the consuming public, was suppressed, and the prices of such products to the retail dealers and to the consuming public in the Eastern district of Virginia and throughout the United States were maintained and enhanced.

In the course of its opinion the trial court said:

No charge is made that any contract was entered into by and on the part of the defendant, and any of its retail customers, in restraint of interstate trade and commerce, the averment being, in effect, that it knowingly and unlawfully created and engaged in a combination with certain of its wholesale and retail customers, to procure adherence on their part, in the sale of its products sold to them, to resale prices fixed by the defendant, and that, in connection therewith, such wholesale and retail customers gave assurances and promises, which resulted in the enhancement and maintenance of such prices, and in the suppression of competition by wholesale dealers and retail dealers, and by the latter to the consuming public.

* * *

In the view taken by the court, the indictment here fairly presents the question of whether a manufacturer of products shipped in interstate trade, is subject to criminal prosecution under the Sherman Act, for entering into a combination in restraint of such trade and commerce, because he agrees with his wholesale and retail customers, upon prices claimed by them to be fair and reasonable, at which the same may be resold, and declines to sell his products to those who will not thus stipulate as to prices. This, at the threshold, presents for the determination of the court, how far one may control and dispose of his own property; that is to say, whether there is any limitation thereon, if he proceeds in respect thereto in a lawful and bona fide manner. That he may not do so, fraudulently, collusively, and in unlawful combination with others, may be conceded. *Eastern States Retail Lumber Dealers' Association v. United States*, 234 U.S. 600, 614. But it by no means follows that being a manufacturer of a given article, he may not, without incurring any criminal liability, refuse absolutely to sell the same at any price, or to sell at a named sum to a customer, with the understanding that such customer will resell only at an agreed price between them, and should the customer not observe the understanding as to retail prices, exercise his undoubted right to decline further to deal with such person.

* * *

The pregnant fact should never be lost sight of that no averment is made of any contract or agreement having been entered into whereby the defendant, the manufacturer, and his customers, bound themselves to enhance and maintain prices, further than is involved in the circumstances that the manufacturer, the defendant here, refused to sell to persons who would not resell at indicated prices, and that certain retailers made purchases on this condition, whereas, inferentially, others declined so to do. No suggestion is made that the defendant, the manufacturer, attempted to reserve or retain any interest in the goods sold, or to restrain the vendee in his right to barter and sell the same without restriction. The retailer, after buying, could, if he chose, give away his purchase or sell it at any price he saw fit, or not sell it at all, his course in these respects being affected only by the fact that he might by his action incur the displeasure of the manufacturer who could refuse to make further sales to him, as he had the undoubted right to do. There is no charge that the retailers themselves entered into any combination or agreement with each other, or that the defendant acted other than with his customers individually.

Our problem is to ascertain, as accurately as may be, what interpretation the trial court placed upon the indictment—not to interpret it ourselves; and then to determine whether, so construed, it fairly charges violation of the Sherman Act. Counsel for the government maintain, in effect, that, as so interpreted, the indictment adequately charges an unlawful combination (within the doctrine of *Dr. Miles Medical Co. v. Park & Sons Co.*, 220 U.S. 373) resulting from restrictive agreements between defendant and sundry dealers whereby the latter obligated themselves not to resell except at agreed prices, and to support this position they specifically rely upon the above-quoted sentence in the opinion which begins, "In the view taken by the court," etc. On the other hand, defendant maintains that looking at the whole opinion it plainly construes the indictment as alleging only recognition of the manufacturer's undoubted right to specify resale prices and refuse to deal with any one who failed to maintain the same.

Considering all said in the opinion (notwithstanding some serious doubts) we are unable to accept the construction placed upon it by the government. We cannot, *e.g.*, wholly disregard the statement that "The retailer, after buying, could, if he chose, give away his purchase or sell it at any price he saw fit, or not sell it at all, his course in these respects being affected only by the fact that he might by his action incur the displeasure of the manufacturer who could refuse to make further sales to him, as he had the undoubted right to do." And we must conclude that, as interpreted below, the indictment does not charge Colgate & Co. with selling its products to dealers under agreements which obligated the latter not to resell except at prices fixed by the company.

The position of the defendant is more nearly in accord with the whole opinion and must be accepted. And as counsel for the Government were careful to state on the argument that this conclusion would require affirmation of the judgment below, an extended discussion of the principles involved is unnecessary.

The purpose of the Sherman Act is to prohibit monopolies, contracts and combinations which probably would unduly interfere with the free exercise of their rights by those engaged, or who wish to engage, in trade and commerce—in a word to preserve the right of freedom to trade. In the absence of any purpose to create or maintain a monopoly, the act does not restrict the long recognized right of trader or manufacturer engaged in an entirely private business, freely to exercise his own independent discretion as to parties with whom he will deal; and, of course, he may announce in advance the circumstances under which he will refuse to sell. "The trader or manufacturer, on the other hand, carries on an entirely private business, and can sell to whom he pleases." *United States v. Trans–Missouri Freight Association*, 166 U.S. 290, 320. "A retail dealer has the unquestioned right to stop dealing with a wholesaler for reasons sufficient to himself, and may do so because he thinks such dealer is acting unfairly in trying to undermine his trade." *Eastern States Retail Lumber Dealers' Association v. United States*, 234 U.S. 600, 614.... In *Dr. Miles Medical Co. v. Park & Sons Co.*, supra, the unlawful combination was effected through contracts which undertook to prevent dealers from freely exercising the right to sell.

The judgment of the District Court must be affirmed.

NOTES AND QUESTIONS

1. UNITED STATES V. PARKE, DAVIS & CO., 362 U.S. 29, 80 S.Ct. 503, 4 L.Ed.2d 505 (1960). In this case, the Government sought an injunction against the drug manufacturer Parke, Davis & Company on complaint. It claimed that Parke, Davis had conspired with retail and wholesale druggists to maintain wholesale and retail prices of its pharmaceutical products. The United States District Court entered a judgment dismissing the complaint. The Supreme Court reversed. It recognized that Parke, Davis was trying to implement a program to promote general compliance with its suggested retail prices. Nevertheless, the company had not contented itself with merely announcing a policy of refusing to do business with any retailers who disregarded its pricing policy, but instead it went further and refused to deal with wholesalers in order to elicit their willingness to deny its products to retailers. Furthermore, retailers who disregarded the price policy were promptly cut off when Parke, Davis supplied wholesalers with their names. The net result was that Parke, Davis was the organizer of a retail price maintenance conspiracy in violation of Sherman Act. The Court did not repudiate the rule that a simple refusal to sell to customers who will not resell at prices suggested by seller is permissible under the *Colgate* doctrine. On the other hand, when the manufacturer's actions go beyond mere announcement of its policy and a simple refusal to deal with retailers, it becomes guilty of participating in a combination in violation of the Sherman Act. In his dissent, Justice Harlan asserted that "scrutiny of the [majority] opinion will reveal that the Court has done no less than send to its demise the Colgate doctrine which has been a basic part of antitrust law concepts since it was first announced in 1919...."[54]

2. DART DRUG CORP. V. PARKE, DAVIS & CO., 221 F.Supp. 948 (D.D.C.1963), *affirmed*, 344 F.2d 173 (D.C.Cir.1965). Upon learning that Dart Drug was selling at prices considerably below manufacturer's list price, Parke, Davis informed the retail drug chain that it no longer wished to have any further business relations with Dart Drug and that "effective immediately" it was "permanently" closing Dart Drug's

---

54. The decision is discussed in 1 Handler, Twenty–Five Years of Antitrust 444–48 (1973); Dam and Pitofsky, Debate: Is the *Colgate* Doctrine Dead? 37 ABA Antitrust L.J. 772 (1968); Levi, The *Parke Davis–Colgate* Doctrine: The Ban on Resale Price Maintenance, 1960 Sup.Ct.Rev. 258 (1960).

account. Parke, Davis made no attempt to prevent wholesalers or distributors from selling Parke, Davis' products to Dart Drug, and Dart Drug in fact was still able to buy these products from such distributors, though at a higher price than from Parke, Davis directly. Dart Drug thereupon brought a treble damage action. On cross-motions for summary judgment, *held* summary judgment for defendant granted.

Parke, Davis' action was but "a simple refusal on the part of the manufacturer to sell his goods to a specific retailer. No effort is being made to cut off other sources of supply to the retailer." The Supreme Court's view in the *Parke, Davis* case that "the *Colgate* doctrine still applied ... to a simple refusal to sell to a customer who will not resell at prices suggested by the seller," established the principle that "a simple refusal to sell to an individual customer for any purpose or for any reason is permissible, provided there is no attempt to induce others to follow that course." (Holtzoff, J.)

3. If a supplier says to its distributor "sell at not less than $1.00 or I will cut you off," and the dealer then sells at $1.00, in what sense is that, or is it not, an "agreement?" Should it matter that the dealer would be happy to adopt the $1.00 price for reasons of its own, unrelated to the threat? Compare Restatement (Second) of Contracts, §§ 19(2), (3); 32; 50 (all recognizing acceptance of contract by performance). If each of several dealers goes along with the $1.00 price as a result of the threat, knowing that a similar threat had been made to other competing dealers, might that be viewed as a horizontal agreement among the dealers? In that respect, reconsider the question of "agreement" in the horizontal line where a group of dealers, knowing that concerted action was invited, uniformly adhere to a scheme. *See Interstate Circuit, Inc. v. United States*, at p. 493 supra.

Whatever the theoretical merits of the debate about "agreement" in the vertical line, the Supreme Court, when dealing with the problem in the 1960's and 1970's, chose not to overrule *Colgate,* but it did create exceptions that made it extremely difficult for suppliers to rely on *Colgate* to impose vertical restrictions. Where a supplier set up a policing mechanism to discover violators, it was said to lose its *Colgate* defense. If the supplier distributed through both wholesalers and retailers, and somehow drew the wholesalers into assisting in the policing of its vertical price arrangements, the *Parke, Davis* decision indicated that *Colgate* protection would be lost. It was even suggested that if a supplier solicited reports from retailers about pricing policies of other retailers with whom they competed, that could move the supplier outside the protective confines of *Colgate. See Girardi v. Gates Rubber Co. Sales Division, Inc.*, 325 F.2d 196 (9th Cir.1963); but *see Klein v. American Luggage Works, Inc.*, 323 F.2d 787 (3d Cir.1963). In 1960, one circuit court summarized the situation as follows:

> [t]he Supreme Court has left a narrow channel through which a manufacturer may pass even though the facts would have to be of such Doric simplicity as to be somewhat rare in this day of complex business enterprise.[55]

4. ALBRECHT V. HERALD CO., 390 U.S. 145 (1968) (overruled with respect to maximum resale price maintenance by *State Oil v. Khan*, supra p. 634), probably represents the high point of Supreme Court hostility to *Colgate*. In that case,

---

55. *George W. Warner & Co. v. Black & Decker Mfg. Co.*, 277 F.2d 787, 790 (2d Cir. 1960).

Herald Co., publisher of the St. Louis Globe–Democrat, told independent distributors, each with an exclusive territory, that they would be terminated if their delivered prices for the paper exceeded a suggested maximum. When Albrecht nevertheless exceeded the maximum price, Herald informed subscribers that it would provide the paper at a lower price itself. Milne was hired to solicit readers for the newspaper and about 25% of Albrecht's customers switched to direct delivery; Kroner, another carrier, was induced to take over Albrecht's route "knowing that respondent would not tolerate over-charging and understanding that he might have to return the route if [Albrecht] discontinued his pricing practice."

The Supreme Court considered two issues: (1) was there a "combination or conspiracy" in restraint of trade; and (2) does a *per se* rule apply to vertical maximum resale price maintenance.

On the first question, the Court wrote:

> If a combination arose when Parke, Davis threatened its wholesalers with termination unless they put pressure on their retail customers, then there can be no doubt that a combination arose between respondent, Milne and Kroner to force petitioners to conform to the advertised retail price.

In a footnote, the court offered the following comments about the ways in which an "illegal combination" could arise under Section 1 of the Sherman Act:

> ... Under Parke, Davis, petitioner could have claimed a combination between respondent and himself, at least as of the day he unwillingly complied with respondent's advertised price. Likewise he might successfully have claimed that respondent had combined with other carriers because the firmly enforced price policy applied to all carriers, most of whom acquiesced in it....

> Petitioner's amended complaint did allege a combination between respondent and petitioner's customers. Because of our disposition of this case it is unnecessary to pass on this claim. It was not, however, a frivolous contention.

Later decisions of the Supreme Court, especially *Monsanto Co. v. Spray–Rite Corp.*, infra p. 686, take a far narrower approach to the agreement issue. As for the second question—whether maximum resale price maintenance should continue to be treated as illegal *per se*— the Albrecht Court decided that the rules should be the same for maximum and minimum resale price fixing. Justice Harlan dissented on that point. As we have seen, he was later vindicated in *State Oil*.

5. Part of the reason for confusion in the *Colgate* area is that neither the government nor any private party ever asked the Supreme Court to overrule *Colgate;* rather, in each case, the anti-*Colgate* party pointed to facts which would lead the Court to conclude that the *Colgate* doctrine had been overstepped, and therefore waived. The Federal Trade Commission attempted to remedy the situation by directly challenging the validity of the *Colgate* doctrine in *Russell Stover Candies, Inc. v. Federal Trade Commission*, 718 F.2d 256 (8th Cir.1983).

Russell Stover was one of at least seven major manufacturers of boxed chocolates and candies in the United States selling through over 18,000 retailers. It designated minimum resale prices for all of its products and ceased selling to retailers when they sold its products at less than designated prices. A survey showed that 97.4% of Stover's products were sold at or above the designated resale price, and it was stipulated that certain retailers would have sold for less except for fear of termination. A Commission majority held that Stover had illegally combined with those retailers who "unwillingly complied" with designated resale prices, interpreting *Colgate* to protect only a manufacturer's right to initially select customers.

The Eighth Circuit reversed:

> The Commission notes that in vertical restraint cases, courts continue to require the existence of "plus factors" to take the case beyond *Colgate*. The Commission believes, however, that the search for "plus factors" is illogical and in fact unnecessary. The Commission's view finds support in commentary critical of *Colgate*. Professor Sullivan has stated:
>
> > "Like the *Colgate* doctrine itself, the cases drawing these laborious distinctions between their own facts and those of *Colgate* are infused with anomaly; many of them require nothing which in any realistic sense can be said to enhance the degree of concert involved in the price maintenance; yet, because of some added fact which is logically unrelated to whether or not an agreement is being reached, they hold that the manufacturer has exceeded the scope of the *Colgate* defense."
>
> ... It may be that ... *Albrecht* foreshadows the Supreme Court's overruling of *Colgate* or it may be, as the Commission suggests, that the Court has already confined *Colgate* to willing compliance with suggested prices and to initial customer selection. However, courts continue to cite *Colgate*. As was stated by the Second Circuit in 1960 and applicable today, " '[w]hen a leading case is beset by qualifications and then atrophied by lack of use, its final demise may be difficult to detect. Perhaps the *Colgate* case is dead, despite frequent citation.' " ... In this case, the Commission has presented ... a case of "Doric simplicity." There are no "plus factors" to take the case beyond *Colgate*.... If *Colgate* no longer stands for the proposition that a "simple refusal to sell to customers who will not sell at prices suggested by the seller is permissible under the Sherman Act," *United States v. Parke, Davis & Co.*, 362 U.S. at 43, it is for the Supreme Court, not this court, to so declare.

Any thought that the Supreme Court might have an opportunity in reviewing *Russell Stover* to clarify the standing of the *Colgate* doctrine was frustrated when, after a change of Administrations, a new Federal Trade Commission elected not to seek Supreme Court review of the Eighth Circuit decision.

Monsanto Co. v. Spray–Rite Service Corp.

Supreme Court of the United States, 1984.
465 U.S. 752, 104 S.Ct. 1464, 79 L.Ed.2d 775.

■ POWELL, J. .... This case presents a question as to the standard of proof required to find a vertical price-fixing conspiracy in violation of Section 1 of the Sherman Act.

I

Petitioner Monsanto Company manufactures chemical products, including agricultural herbicides. By the late 1960's, the time at issue in this case, its sales accounted for approximately 15% of the corn herbicide market and 3% of the soybean herbicide market. In the corn herbicide market, the market leader commanded a 70% share. In the soybean herbicide market, two other competitors each had between 30% and 40% of the market. Respondent Spray–Rite Service Corporation was engaged in the wholesale distribution of agricultural chemicals from 1955 to 1972. Spray–Rite was essentially a family business, whose owner and president, Donald Yapp, was also its sole salaried salesman. Spray–Rite was a discount operation, buying in large quantities and selling at a low margin.

Spray–Rite was an authorized distributor of Monsanto herbicides from 1957 to 1968. In October 1967, Monsanto announced that it would appoint distributors for one-year terms, and that it would renew distributorships according to several new criteria. Among the criteria were: (i) whether the distributor's primary activity was soliciting sales to retail dealers; (ii) whether the distributor employed trained salesmen capable of educating its customers on the technical aspects of Monsanto's herbicides; and (iii) whether the distributor could be expected "to exploit fully" the market in its geographical area of primary responsibility. Shortly thereafter, Monsanto also introduced a number of incentive programs, such as making cash payments to distributors that sent salesmen to training classes, and providing free deliveries of products to customers within a distributor's area of primary responsibility.[56]

In October 1968, Monsanto declined to renew Spray–Rite's distributorship. At that time, Spray–Rite was the tenth largest out of approximately 100 distributors of Monsanto's primary corn herbicide. Ninety percent of Spray–Rite's sales volume was devoted to herbicides sales, and 16% of its sales were of Monsanto's products. After Monsanto's termination, Spray–Rite continued as a herbicide dealer until 1972. It was able to purchase some of Monsanto's products from other distributors, but not as much as it desired or as early in the season as it needed. Monsanto introduced a new corn herbicide in 1969. By 1972, its share of the corn herbicide market had increased to approximately 28%. Its share of the soybean herbicide market had grown to approximately 19%.

Spray–Rite brought this action under Section 1 of the Sherman Act. It alleged that Monsanto and some of its distributors conspired to fix the resale prices of Monsanto herbicides. Its complaint further alleged that Monsanto terminated Spray–Rite's distributorship, adopted compensation programs and shipping policies, and encouraged distributors to boycott Spray–Rite in furtherance of this conspiracy. Monsanto denied the allegations of conspiracy, and asserted that Spray–Rite's distributorship had been terminated because of its failure to hire trained salesmen and promote sales to dealers adequately.

The case was tried to a jury. The District Court instructed the jury that Monsanto's conduct was *per se* unlawful if it was in furtherance of a conspiracy to fix prices. In answers to special interrogatories, the jury found that (i) the termination of Spray–Rite was pursuant to a conspiracy

---

56. These areas of primary responsibility were not exclusive territorial restrictions. Approximately ten to twenty distributors were assigned to each area, and distributors were permitted to sell outside their assigned area.

between Monsanto and one or more of its distributors to set resale prices, (ii) the compensation programs, areas of primary responsibility, and/or shipping policies were created by Monsanto pursuant to such a conspiracy, and (iii) Monsanto conspired with one or more distributors to limit Spray–Rite's access to Monsanto herbicides after 1968.[57] The jury awarded $3.5 million in damages, which was trebled to $10.5 million. Only the first of the jury's findings is before us today.[58]

The Court of Appeals for the Seventh Circuit affirmed. 684 F.2d 1226 (1982). It held that there was sufficient evidence to satisfy Spray–Rite's burden of proving a conspiracy to set resale prices. The court stated that "proof of termination following competitor complaints is sufficient to support an inference of concerted action." *Id.*, at 1238.[59] Canvassing the testimony and exhibits that were before the jury, the court found evidence of numerous complaints from competing Monsanto distributors about Spray–Rite's price-cutting practices. It also noted that there was testimony that a Monsanto official had said that Spray–Rite was terminated because of the price complaints.

In substance, the Court of Appeals held that an antitrust plaintiff can survive a motion for a directed verdict if it shows that a manufacturer terminated a price-cutting distributor in response to or following complaints by other distributors. This view brought the Seventh Circuit into direct conflict with a number of other Courts of Appeals.[60] We granted certiorari to resolve the conflict. 460 U.S. 1010 (1983). We reject the statement by the Court of Appeals for the Seventh Circuit of the standard of proof required to submit a case to the jury in distributor-termination

---

57. The three special interrogatories were as follows:

"1. Was the decision by Monsanto not to offer a new contract to plaintiff for 1969 made by Monsanto pursuant to conspiracy or combination with one or more of its distributors to fix, maintain or stabilize resale prices of Monsanto herbicides?"

"2. Were the compensation programs and/or areas of primary responsibility, and/or shipping policy created by Monsanto pursuant to a conspiracy to fix, maintain or stabilize resale prices of Monsanto herbicides?"

"3. Did Monsanto conspire or combine with one or more of its distributors so that one or more of those distributors would limit plaintiff's access to Monsanto herbicides?" 684 F.2d 1226, 1233 (C.A.7 1982).

The jury answered "Yes" to each of the interrogatories.

58. *See* note 61, infra.

59. The court later in the same paragraph restated the standard of sufficiency as follows: "Proof of distributorship termination in response to competing distributors' complaints about the terminated distributor's pricing policies is sufficient to raise an inference of concerted action." 684 F.2d at 1239 (emphasis added). It may be argued that this standard is different from the one quoted in text in that this one requires a showing of a minimal causal connection between the complaints and the termination of the plaintiff, while the textual standard requires only that the one "follow" the other. As we explain infra, the difference is not ultimately significant in our analysis.

60. The court below recognized that its standard was in conflict with that articulated in *Edward J. Sweeney & Sons, Inc. v. Texaco, Inc.*, 637 F.2d 105, 110–111 (C.A.3 1980), *cert. denied*, 451 U.S. 911 (1981). Other circuit courts also have rejected the standard adopted by the Court of Appeals for the Seventh Circuit....

litigation, but affirm the judgment under the standard we announce today.[61]

II

This court had drawn two important distinctions that are at the center of this and any other distributor-termination case. First, there is the basic distinction between concerted and independent action—a distinction not always clearly drawn by parties and courts. Section 1 of the Sherman Act requires that there be a "contract, combination ... or conspiracy" between the manufacturer and other distributors in order to establish a violation. Independent action is not proscribed. A manufacturer of course generally has a right to deal, or refuse to deal, with whomever it likes, as long as it does so independently. *United States v. Colgate & Co.*, 250 U.S. 300, 307 (1919); *cf. United States v. Parke, Davis & Co.*, 362 U.S. 29 (1960). Under *Colgate*, the manufacturer can announce its resale prices in advance and

---

61. Monsanto also challenges another part of the Court of Appeals' opinion. It argues that the court held that the nonprice restrictions in the case—the compensation and shipping policies—would be judged under a rule of reason rather than a *per se* rule "only if there is no allegation that the [nonprice] restrictions are part of a conspiracy to fix prices." Brief for Petitioner 15 (quoting 684 F.2d, at 1237). Monsanto asserts that under this holding a mere allegation that nonprice restrictions were part of a price conspiracy would subject them to *per se* treatment. Monsanto contends that this view undermines our decision in *Continental T.V., Inc. v. GTE Sylvania Inc.*, 433 U.S. 36 (1977), that such restrictions are subject to the rule of reason.

If this were what the Court of Appeals held, it would present an arguable conflict. We think, however, that Monsanto misreads the court's opinion. Read in context, the court's somewhat broad language fairly may be read to say that a plaintiff must prove, as well as allege, that the nonprice restrictions were in fact a part of a price conspiracy. Thus, later in its opinion the court notes that the District Court properly instructed the jury "that Monsanto's otherwise lawful compensation programs and shipping policies were *per se* unlawful *if undertaken as part of an illegal scheme to fix prices.*" 684 F.2d, at 1237 (emphasis added). The court cited *White Motor Co. v. United States*, 372 U.S. 253, 260 (1963), in which this Court wrote that restrictive practices ancillary to a price-fixing agreement would be restrained only if there was a finding that the two were sufficiently

linked. And the Court of Appeals elsewhere noted the jury's finding that the nonprice practices here were "created by Monsanto pursuant to a conspiracy to fix ... resale prices." 684 F.2d, at 1233.

Monsanto does not dispute Spray–Rite's view that if the nonprice practices were proven to have been instituted as part of a price-fixing conspiracy, they would be subject to *per se* treatment. See Brief for Petitioner 23–27. Instead, Monsanto argues that there was insufficient evidence to support the jury's finding that the nonprice practices were "created by Monsanto pursuant" to a price-fixing conspiracy. Monsanto failed to make its sufficiency-of-the-evidence argument in the Court of Appeals with respect to this finding, *see* Brief for Defendant–Appellant Monsanto Company in No. 80–2232 (CA7), pp. 27–34, and the court did not address the point. We therefore decline to reach it. *See, e.g., Adickes v. S.H. Kress & Co.*, 398 U.S. 144, 147, n. 2 (1970); *Duignan v. United States*, 274 U.S. 195, 200 (1927).

In view of Monsanto's concession that a proper finding that nonprice practices were part of a price-fixing conspiracy would suffice to subject the entire conspiracy to *per se* treatment, *Sylvania* is not applicable to this case. In that case only a nonprice restriction was challenged. *See* 433 U.S., at 51, n. 18. Nothing in our decision today undercuts the holding of *Sylvania* that nonprice restrictions are to be judged under the rule of reason. In fact, the need to ensure the viability of *Sylvania* is an important consideration in our rejection of the Court of Appeals' standard of sufficiency of the evidence.

refuse to deal with those who fail to comply. And a distributor is free to acquiesce in the manufacturer's demand in order to avoid termination.

The second important distinction in distributor-termination cases is that between concerted action to set prices and concerted action on non-price restrictions. The former have been *per se* illegal since the early years of national antitrust enforcement. *See Dr. Miles Medical Co. v. John D. Park & Sons Co.*, 220 U.S. 373, 404–409 (1911). The latter are judged under the rule of reason, which requires a weighing of the relevant circumstances of a case to decide whether a restrictive practice constitutes an unreasonable restraint on competition. *See Continental T.V., Inc. v. GTE Sylvania Inc.*, 433 U.S. 36 (1977).[62]

While these distinctions in theory are reasonably clear, often they are difficult to apply in practice. In *Sylvania* we emphasized that the legality of arguably anticompetitive conduct should be judged primarily by its "market impact." But the economic effect of all of the conduct described above—unilateral and concerted vertical price-setting, agreements on price and nonprice restrictions—is in many, but not all, cases similar or identical. *See, e.g., Parke, Davis*, supra. And judged from a distance, the conduct of the parties in the various situations can be indistinguishable. For example, the fact that a manufacturer and its distributors are in constant communication about prices and marketing strategy does not alone show that the distributors are not making independent pricing decisions. A manufacturer and its distributors have legitimate reasons to exchange information about the prices and the reception of their products in the market. Moreover, it is precisely in cases in which the manufacturer attempts to further a particular marketing strategy by means of agreements on often costly nonprice restrictions that it will have the most interest in the distributors' resale prices. The manufacturer often will want to ensure that its distributors earn sufficient profit to pay for programs such as hiring and training additional salesmen or demonstrating the technical features of the product, and will want to see that "free-riders" do not interfere. *See Sylvania*, supra. Thus, the manufacturer's strongly felt concern about resale prices

---

62. The Solicitor General (by brief only) and several other amici suggest that we take this opportunity to reconsider whether "contract[s], combination[s] . . . or conspirac[ies]" to fix resale prices should always be unlawful. They argue that the economic effect of resale price maintenance is little different from agreements on nonprice restrictions. *See generally Continental T.V., Inc. v. GTE Sylvania Inc.*, 433 U.S. 36, 69–70 (1977) (White, J., concurring in the judgment) (citing sources); Baker, Interconnected Problems of Doctrine and Economics in the Section One Labyrinth: Is *Sylvania* a Way Out?, 67 Va.L.Rev. 1457, 1465–1466 (1981). They say that the economic objections to resale price maintenance that we discussed in *Sylvania*, supra,—such as that it facilitates horizontal cartels—can be met easily in the context of rule of reason analysis. Certainly in this case we have no occasion to consider the merits of this argument. This case was tried on *per se* instructions to the jury. Neither party argued in the District Court that the rule of reason should apply to a vertical price-fixing conspiracy, nor raised the point on appeal. In fact, neither party before this Court presses the argument advanced by amici. We therefore decline to reach the question, and we decide the case in the context in which it was decided below and argued here.

does not necessarily mean that it has done more than the *Colgate* doctrine allows.

Nevertheless, it is of considerable importance that the independent action by the manufacturer, and concerted action on nonprice restrictions, be distinguished from price-fixing agreements, since under present law the latter are subject to *per se* treatment and treble damages. On a claim of concerted price-fixing, the antitrust plaintiff must present evidence sufficient to carry its burden of proving that there was such an agreement. If an inference of such an agreement may be drawn from highly ambiguous evidence, there is a considerable danger that the doctrines enunciated in *Sylvania,* and *Colgate* will be seriously eroded.

The flaw in the evidentiary standard adopted by the Court of Appeals in this case is that it disregards this danger. Permitting an agreement to be inferred merely from the existence of complaints, or even from the fact that termination came about "in response to" complaints, could deter or penalize perfectly legitimate conduct. As Monsanto points out, complaints about price-cutters "are natural—and from the manufacturer's perspective, unavoidable—reactions by distributors to the activities of their rivals." Such complaints, particularly where the manufacturer has imposed a costly set of nonprice restrictions, "arise in the normal course of business and do not indicate illegal concerted action." *Roesch, Inc. v. Star Cooler Corp.,* 671 F.2d 1168, 1172 (C.A.8 1982), *on rehearing en banc,* 712 F.2d 1235 (C.A.8 1983) (*affirming* District Court judgment by an equally divided court). Moreover, distributors are an important source of information for manufacturers. In order to assure an efficient distribution system, manufacturers and distributors constantly must coordinate their activities to assure their product will reach the consumer persuasively and efficiently. To bar a manufacturer from acting solely because the information upon which it acts originated as a price complaint would create an irrational dislocation in the market. *See* F. Warren–Boulton, Vertical Control of Markets 13, 164 (1978). In sum, "[t]o permit the inference of concerted action on the basis of receiving complaints alone and thus to expose the defendant to treble damage liability would both inhibit management's exercise of independent business judgment and emasculate the terms of the statute." *Edward J. Sweeney & Sons, Inc. v. Texaco, Inc.,* 637 F.2d 105, 111, n. 2 (C.A.3 1980), *cert. denied,* 451 U.S. 911 (1981).[63]

Thus, something more than evidence of complaints is needed. There must be evidence that tends to exclude the possibility that the manufacturer and nonterminated distributors were acting independently. As Judge Aldisert has written, the antitrust plaintiff should present direct or circumstantial evidence that reasonably tends to prove that the manufacturer and others "had a conscious commitment to a common scheme designed to achieve an unlawful objective." *Edward J. Sweeney & Sons,* supra, at 111;

---

63. We do not suggest that evidence of complaints has no probative value at all, but only that the burden remains on the antitrust plaintiff to introduce additional evidence sufficient to support a finding of an unlawful contract, combination, or conspiracy.

accord H.L. Moore Drug Exchange v. Eli Lilly & Co., 662 F.2d 935, 941 (C.A.2 1981), *cert. denied*, 459 U.S. 880 (1982); *cf. American Tobacco Co. v. United States*, 328 U.S. 781, 810 (1946) (Circumstances must reveal "a unity of purpose or a common design and understanding, or a meeting of minds in an unlawful arrangement").[64]

III

A

Applying this standard to the facts of this case we believe there was sufficient evidence for the jury reasonably to have concluded that Monsanto and some of its distributors were parties to an "agreement" or "conspiracy" to maintain resale prices and terminate price-cutters. In fact there was substantial direct evidence of agreements to maintain prices. There was testimony from a Monsanto district manager, for example, that Monsanto on at least two occasions in early 1969, about five months after Spray–Rite was terminated, approached price-cutting distributors and advised that if they did not maintain the suggested resale price, they would not receive adequate supplies of Monsanto's new corn herbicide. When one of the distributors did not assent, this information was referred to the Monsanto regional office, and it complained to the distributor's parent company. There was evidence that the parent instructed its subsidiary to comply, and the distributor informed Monsanto that it would charge the suggested price. Evidence of this kind plainly is relevant and persuasive as to a meeting of minds.[65]

An arguably more ambiguous example is a newsletter from one of the distributors to his dealer-customers. The newsletter is dated October 1, 1968, just four weeks before Spray–Rite was terminated. It was written after a meeting between the author and several Monsanto officials, and discusses Monsanto's efforts to "get[ ] the 'market place in order'." The newsletter reviews some of Monsanto's incentive and shipping policies, and then states that in addition "every effort will be made to maintain a minimum market price level." The newsletter relates these efforts as follows:

> "In other words, we are assured that Monsanto's company-owned outlets will not retail at less than their suggested retail price to the trade as a whole. Furthermore, those of us on the

---

64. The concept of "a meeting of the minds" or "a common scheme" in a distributor-termination case includes more than a showing that the distributor conformed to the suggested price. It means as well that evidence must be presented both that the distributor communicated its acquiescence or agreement, and that this was sought by the manufacturer.

65. In addition, there was circumstantial evidence that Monsanto sought agreement from the distributor to conform to the resale price. The threat to cut off the distributor's supply came during Monsanto's "shipping season" when herbicide was in short supply. The jury could have concluded that Monsanto sought this agreement at a time when it was able to use supply as a lever to force compliance.

distributor level are not likely to deviate downward on price to anyone as the idea is implied that doing this possibly could discolor the outlook for continuity as one of the approved distributors during the future upcoming seasons. So, none interested in the retention of this arrangement is likely to risk being deleted from this customer service opportunity. Also, so far as the national accounts are concerned, they are sure to recognize the desirability of retaining Monsanto's favor on a continuing basis by respecting the wisdom of participating in the suggested program in a manner assuring order on the retail level 'playground' throughout the entire country. It is elementary that harmony can only come from following the rules of the game and that in case of dispute, the decision of the umpire is final."

It is reasonable to interpret this newsletter as referring to an agreement or understanding that distributors and retailers would maintain prices, and Monsanto would not undercut those prices on the retail level and would terminate competitors who sold at prices below those of complying distributors; these were "the rules of the game."[66]

B

If, as the courts below reasonably could have found, there was evidence of an agreement with one or more distributors to maintain prices, the remaining question is whether the termination of Spray–Rite was part of or pursuant to that agreement. It would be reasonable to find that it was, since it is necessary for competing distributors contemplating compliance with suggested prices to know that those who do not comply will be terminated. Moreover, there is some circumstantial evidence of such a link. Following the termination, there was a meeting between Spray–Rite's president and a Monsanto official. There was testimony that the first thing the official mentioned was the many complaints Monsanto had received about Spray–Rite's prices.[67] In addition, there was reliable testimony that Monsanto never discussed with Spray–Rite prior to the termination the distributorship criteria that were the alleged basis for the action. *See* 684 F.2d, at 1239. By contrast, a former Monsanto salesman for Spray–Rite's

---

66. The newsletter also is subject to the interpretation that the distributor was merely describing the likely reaction to unilateral Monsanto pronouncements. But Monsanto itself appears to have construed the flyer as reporting a price-fixing understanding. Six weeks after the newsletter was written, a Monsanto official wrote its author a letter urging him to "correct immediately any misconceptions about Monsanto's marketing policies." App. 98. The letter disavowed any intent to enter into an agreement on resale prices. The interpretation of these documents and the testimony surrounding them properly was left to the jury.

67. Monsanto argues that the reference could have been to complaints by Monsanto employees rather than distributors, suggesting that the price controls were merely unilateral action, rather than accession to the demands of the distributors. The choice between two reasonable interpretations of the testimony properly was left for the jury. *See also* Tr. 1298 (identifying source of one complaint as a distributor).

area testified that Monsanto representatives on several occasions in 1965–1966 approached Spray–Rite, informed the distributor of complaints from other distributors—including one major and influential one, and requested that prices be maintained. Later that same year, Spray–Rite's president testified, Monsanto officials made explicit threats to terminate Spray–Rite unless it raised its prices.[68]

IV

We conclude that the Court of Appeals applied an incorrect standard to the evidence in this case. The correct standard is that there must be evidence that tends to exclude the possibility of independent action by the manufacturer and distributor. That is, there must be direct or circumstantial evidence that reasonably tends to prove that the manufacturer and others had a conscious commitment to a common scheme designed to achieve an unlawful objective. Under this standard, the evidence in this case created a jury issue as to whether Spray–Rite was terminated pursuant to a price-fixing conspiracy between Monsanto and its distributors.[69] The judgment of the court below is affirmed.

■ White, J. took no part in the consideration or decision of this case.

■ Brennan, J. concurring. As the Court notes, the Solicitor General has filed a brief in this Court as amicus curiae urging us to overrule the Court's decision in *Dr. Miles Medical Co. v. John D. Park & Sons Co.*, 220 U.S. 373 (1911). That decision has stood for 73 years, and Congress has certainly been aware of its existence throughout that time. Yet Congress has never enacted legislation to overrule the interpretation of the Sherman Act adopted in that case. Under these circumstances, I see no reason for us to depart from our longstanding interpretation of the Act. Because the Court adheres to that rule and, in my view, properly applies *Dr. Miles* to this case, I join the opinion and judgment of the Court.

68. The existence of the illegal joint boycott after Spray–Rite's termination, a finding that the Court of Appeals affirmed and that is not before us, is further evidence that Monsanto and its distributors had an understanding that prices would be maintained, and that price-cutters would be terminated. This last, however, is also consistent with termination for other reasons, and is probative only of the ability of Monsanto and its distributors to act in concert.

69. Monsanto's contrary evidence has force, but we agree with the courts below that it was insufficient to take the issue from the jury. It is true that there was no testimony of any complaints about Spray–Rite's pricing for the fifteen months prior to termination. But it was permissible for the jury to conclude that there were complaints during that period from the evidence that they were mentioned at Spray–Rite's post-termination meeting with Monsanto. There is also evidence that resale prices in fact did not stabilize after 1968. On the other hand, the former Monsanto salesman testified that prices were more stable in 1969–1970 than in his earlier stint in 1965–1966. Tr. 217. And, given the evidence that Monsanto took active measures to stabilize prices, it may be that distributors did not assent in sufficient numbers, or broke their promises. In any event, we cannot say that the courts below erred in finding that Spray–Rite produced substantial evidence of the concerted action required by Section 1 of Sherman Act, and that—despite the sharp conflict in evidence—the case properly was submitted to the jury.

NOTES AND QUESTIONS

1. In GARMENT DISTRICT, INC. V. BELK STORES SERVICES INC., 799 F.2d 905 (4th Cir.1986), plaintiff Garment District was a single outlet discounter in Gastonia, North Carolina, which sold a full line of Jantzen clothing at a markup of about 30–35% over the wholesale price. It was the only discounter of Jantzen clothing in Gastonia. Belk operated 400 stores in the Southeastern United States and also carried a full line of Jantzen clothing in its Gastonia store, commonly selling at a 100% markup.

Belk pressured Jantzen to stop supplying Garment District, and at one point, placed its Jantzen line in the "budget basement" and sold the product at discount prices. After meetings with Belk officials, Jantzen terminated Garment District on what the District Court found was the "pretext" that the store did not present a suitable image for a Jantzen retailer. In fact, the relationship was terminated because of the pressure exerted by Belk to stop Garment District's price cutting. After termination, Jantzen wrote to Belk stating that "the situation that exists in Gastonia is a mistake on our part and . . . we intend to rectify this situation. Thank you for bringing this problem to my attention."

The District Court entered a directed verdict against Garment District and the Court of Appeals affirmed. It concluded that Jantzen terminated the single outlet Garment District in order to retain the vastly more valuable business of Belk, and the fact that it did so after complaints and coercion by Belk did not satisfy the *Monsanto* requirement that there "must be evidence that tends to exclude the possibility that the manufacturer and non-terminated distributors were acting independently."

Is *Belk* a fair interpretation of *Monsanto*? If it is, how will a plaintiff ever get to a jury with a claim that it was terminated as a result of an agreement between a complaining competitor and the supplier?

2. *Monsanto* confirms *Sylvania*'s reliance on a "free rider" explanation for some vertical distribution restraints. But there is some reason to believe that the "free-rider" explanation does not account for many vertical distribution restraints. For example, in the years when fair trade was legal, products that tended frequently to be "fair traded" were over-the-counter drugs (*e.g.*, toothpaste, mouthwash, shaving cream), and cosmetics (cold cream, underarm deodorant). *See* Overstreet, Resale Price Maintenance: Economic Theories and Empirical Evidence, Bureau of Economics Staff Report, 177–98 (1983). What are the services that are so essential to the manufacturer in the retail sale of those products? Similarly, products involved in cases in which the Federal Trade Commission attacked resale price maintenance agreements—*e.g.*, blue jeans, pet food, ammunition, boxed candy, and men's underwear—are not typically "service-added" retail items. What were the services the manufacturer was concerned about in insisting on resale price maintenance for blue jeans and men's underwear?

3. Would the *Monsanto* court have found a violation on the facts in *Beech-Nut, Parke, Davis,* and *Albrecht*? If the *Colgate* doctrine was almost dead before *Monsanto*, that obviously is no longer the case. *See also Copperweld Corp. v. Independence Tube Corp.*, 467 U.S. 752 (1984), stressing the importance of distinguishing between single-firm behavior and agreements between independent entities. What are the limits now on a manufacturer setting resale prices by the *Colgate* technique?

4. *Monsanto* makes clear that termination following complaints, without more, is not enough to get to a jury on the question of "agreement." That is correct, is it not, since the complaints may have been nothing more than a source of

information which then led the manufacturer to take a step entirely in its own interest. Suppose the rule were that termination following complaints is enough to get to a jury if the complaints constitute "the major contributing cause of such termination or refusal to supply." That was the approach of several bills in Congress including the Consumer Protection against Price Fixing Act of 1989, S. 865, seeking to "clarify" *Monsanto*. Is that what the Supreme Court had in mind in *Monsanto?* Would it change the result in a case like *Belk?* Is it a workable standard? None of those bills ever passed, and it appears that the momentum behind them has largely faded away.

Business Electronics Corporation v. Sharp Electronics Corporation

Supreme Court of the United States, 1988.
485 U.S. 717, 108 S.Ct. 1515, 99 L.Ed.2d 808.

■ SCALIA, J. Petitioner Business Electronics Corporation seeks review of a decision of the United States Court of Appeals for the Fifth Circuit holding that a vertical restraint is *per se* illegal under § 1 of the Sherman Act, only if there is an express or implied agreement to set resale prices at some level. We granted certiorari to resolve a conflict in the Courts of Appeals regarding the proper dividing line between the rule that vertical price restraints are illegal *per se* and the rule that vertical nonprice restraints are to be judged under the rule of reason.

I

In 1968, petitioner became the exclusive retailer in the Houston, Texas area of electronic calculators manufactured by respondent Sharp Electronics Corporation. In 1972, respondent appointed Gilbert Hartwell as a second retailer in the Houston area. During the relevant period, electronic calculators were primarily sold to business customers for prices up to $1000. While much of the evidence in this case was conflicting—in particular, concerning whether petitioner was "free riding" on Hartwell's provision of presale educational and promotional services by providing inadequate services itself—a few facts are undisputed. Respondent published a list of suggested minimum retail prices, but its written dealership agreements with petitioner and Hartwell did not obligate either to observe them, or to charge any other specific price. Petitioner's retail prices were often below respondent's suggested retail prices and generally below Hartwell's retail prices, even though Hartwell too sometimes priced below respondent's suggested retail prices. Hartwell complained to respondent on a number of occasions about petitioner's prices. In June 1973, Hartwell gave respondent the ultimatum that Hartwell would terminate his dealership unless respondent ended its relationship with petitioner within 30 days. Respondent terminated petitioner's dealership in July 1973.

Petitioner brought suit in the United States District Court for the Southern District of Texas, alleging that respondent and Hartwell had conspired to terminate petitioner and that such conspiracy was illegal *per se* under § 1 of the Sherman Act. The case was tried to a jury. The District

Court submitted a liability interrogatory to the jury that asked whether "there was an agreement or understanding between Sharp Electronics Corporation and Hartwell to terminate Business Electronics as a Sharp dealer because of Business Electronics' price cutting." Record, Doc. No. 241. The District Court instructed the jury at length about this question:

"The Sherman Act is violated when a seller enters into an agreement or understanding with one of its dealers to terminate another dealer because of the other dealer's price cutting. Plaintiff contends that Sharp terminated Business Electronics in further-ance of Hartwell's desire to eliminate Business Electronics as a price-cutting rival.

"If you find that there was an agreement between Sharp and Hartwell to terminate Business Electronics because of Business Electronics' price cutting, you should answer yes to Question Number 1.

. . .

"A combination, agreement or understanding to terminate a dealer because of his price cutting unreasonably restrains trade and cannot be justified for any reason. Therefore, even though the combination, agreement or understanding may have been formed or engaged in . . . to eliminate any alleged evils of price cutting, it is still unlawful. . . .

"If a dealer demands that a manufacturer terminate a price cutting dealer, and the manufacturer agrees to do so, the agree-ment is illegal if the manufacturer's purpose is to eliminate the price cutting." App. 18–19.

The jury answered Question 1 affirmatively and awarded $600,000 in damages. The District Court. . . . entered judgment for petitioner for treble damages plus attorney's fees.

The Fifth Circuit reversed, holding that the jury interrogatory and instructions were erroneous, and remanded for a new trial. It held that, to render illegal *per se* a vertical agreement between a manufacturer and a dealer to terminate a second dealer, the first dealer "must expressly or impliedly agree to set its prices at some level, though not a specific one. The distributor cannot retain complete freedom to set whatever price it chooses." 780 F.2d, at 1218.

II

A

. . .

Although vertical agreements on resale prices have been illegal *per se* since *Dr. Miles Medical Co. v. John D. Park & Sons Co.*, 220 U.S. 373 (1911), we have recognized that the scope of *per se* illegality should be narrow in the context of vertical restraints. In *Continental T.V., Inc. v. GTE Sylvania Inc.*, we refused to extend *per se* illegality to vertical nonprice restraints, specifically to a manufacturer's termination of one dealer pursuant to an exclusive territory agreement with another. We noted that especially in the vertical restraint context "departure from the rule-of-reason standard must be based on demonstrable economic effect rather than ... upon formalistic line drawing." We concluded that vertical nonprice restraints had not been shown to have such a " 'pernicious effect on competition' " and to be so " 'lack[ing] [in] ... redeeming value' " as to justify *per se* illegality.... Rather, we found, they had real potential to stimulate inter-brand competition, "the primary concern of antitrust law", 433 U.S., at 52, n. 19:

> "[N]ew manufacturers and manufacturers entering new markets can use the restrictions in order to induce competent and aggressive retailers to make the kind of investment of capital and labor that is often required in the distribution of products unknown to the consumer. Established manufacturers can use them to induce retailers to engage in promotional activities or to provide service and repair facilities necessary to the efficient marketing of their products. Service and repair are vital for many products.... The availability and quality of such services affect a manufacturer's goodwill and the competitiveness of his product. Because of market imperfections such as the so-called 'free-rider' effect, these services might not be provided by retailers in a purely competitive situation, despite the fact that each retailer's benefit would be greater if all provided the services than if none did." *Id.*, at 55.

Moreover, we observed that a rule of *per se* illegality for vertical nonprice restraints was not needed or effective to protect *intra* brand competition. First, so long as interbrand competition existed, that would provide a "significant check" on any attempt to exploit intrabrand market power. In fact, in order to meet that interbrand competition, a manufacturer's dominant incentive is to lower resale prices. Second, the *per se* illegality of vertical restraints would create a perverse incentive for manufacturers to integrate vertically into distribution, an outcome hardly conducive to fostering the creation and maintenance of small businesses.

Finally, our opinion in *GTE Sylvania* noted a significant distinction between vertical nonprice and vertical price restraints. That is, there was support for the proposition that vertical price restraints reduce *inter* brand price competition because they " 'facilitate cartelizing.' " Posner, Antitrust Policy and the Supreme Court: An Analysis of the Restricted Distribution, Horizontal Merger and Potential Competition Decisions, 75 Colum.L.Rev. 282, 294 (1975). The authorities cited by the Court suggested how vertical price agreements might assist horizontal price fixing at the manufacturer level (by reducing the manufacturer's incentive to cheat on a cartel, since its retailers could not pass on lower prices to consumers) or might be used to organize cartels at the retailer level. *See* R. Posner, Antitrust: Cases, Economic Notes and Other Materials 134 (1974); E. Gellhorn, Antitrust Law and Economics 252, 256 (1976); Note, Vertical Territorial and Customer Restrictions in the Franchising Industry, 10 Colum.J.L. & Soc.Prob. 497,

498, n. 12 (1974). Similar support for the cartel-facilitating effect of vertical non-price restraints was and remains lacking.

We have been solicitous to assure that the market-freeing effect of our decision in *GTE Sylvania* is not frustrated by related legal rules. In *Monsanto Co. v. Spray–Rite Service Corp.*, which addressed the evidentiary showing necessary to establish vertical concerted action, we expressed concern that "[i]f an inference of such an agreement may be drawn from highly ambiguous evidence, there is considerable danger that the doctrin[e] enunciated in *Sylvania* . . . will be seriously eroded." We eschewed adoption of an evidentiary standard that "could deter or penalize perfectly legitimate conduct" or "would create an irrational dislocation in the market" by preventing legitimate communication between a manufacturer and its distributors.

Our approach to the question presented in the present case is guided by the premises of *GTE Sylvania* and *Monsanto:* that there is a presumption in favor of a rule-of-reason standard; that departure from that standard must be justified by demonstrable economic effect, such as the facilitation of cartelizing, rather than formalistic distinctions; that interbrand competition is the primary concern of the antitrust laws; and that rules in this area should be formulated with a view towards protecting the doctrine of *GTE Sylvania*. These premises lead us to conclude that the line drawn by the Fifth Circuit is the most appropriate one.

There has been no showing here that an agreement between a manufacturer and a dealer to terminate a "price cutter," without a further agreement on the price or price levels to be charged by the remaining dealer, almost always tends to restrict competition and reduce output. Any assistance to cartelizing that such an agreement might provide cannot be distinguished from the sort of minimal assistance that might be provided by vertical nonprice agreements like the exclusive territory agreement in *GTE Sylvania,* and is insufficient to justify a *per se* rule. Cartels are neither easy to form nor easy to maintain. Uncertainty over the terms of the cartel, particularly the prices to be charged in the future, obstructs both formation and adherence by making cheating easier. *Cf. Maple Flooring Mfrs. Assn. v. United States*, 268 U.S. 563 (1925); *Cement Mfrs. Protective Assn. v. United States*, 268 U.S. 588 (1925); *see generally Matsushita Elec. Indus. Co. v. Zenith Radio Corp.*, 475 U.S. 574, 590 (1986). Without an agreement with the remaining dealer on price, the manufacturer both retains its incentive to cheat on any manufacturer-level cartel (since lower prices can still be passed on to consumers) and cannot as easily be used to organize and hold together a retailer-level cartel.[70]

---

70. The dissent's principal fear appears to be not cartelization at either level, but Hartwell's assertion of dominant retail power. This fear does not possibly justify adopting a rule of *per se* illegality. Retail market power is rare, because of the usual presence of interbrand competition and other dealers, *see Continental T.V., Inc. v. GTE Sylvania Inc.*, 433 U.S. 36, 54 (1977), and it should therefore not be assumed but rather must be proved. *Cf.* Baxter, The Viability of Vertical Restraints Doctrine, 75 Calif.L.Rev. 933, 948–949 (1987). Of course this case was not prosecuted on the theory, and therefore the jury

The District Court's rule on the scope of *per se* illegality for vertical restraints would threaten to dismantle the doctrine of *GTE Sylvania.* Any agreement between a manufacturer and a dealer to terminate another dealer who happens to have charged lower prices can be alleged to have been directed against the terminated dealer's "price cutting." In the vast majority of cases, it will be extremely difficult for the manufacturer to convince a jury that its motivation was to ensure adequate services, since price cutting and some measure of service cutting usually go hand in hand. Accordingly, a manufacturer that agrees to give one dealer an exclusive territory and terminates another dealer pursuant to that agreement, or even a manufacturer that agrees with one dealer to terminate another for failure to provide contractually-obligated services, exposes itself to the highly plausible claim that its real motivation was to terminate a price cutter. Moreover, even vertical restraints that do not result in dealer termination, such as the initial granting of an exclusive territory or the requirement that certain services be provided, can be attacked as designed to allow existing dealers to charge higher prices. Manufacturers would be likely to forgo legitimate and competitively useful conduct rather than risk treble damages and perhaps even criminal penalties.

We cannot avoid this difficulty by invalidating as illegal *per se* only those agreements imposing vertical restraints that contain the word "price," or that affect the "prices" charged by dealers. Such formalism was explicitly rejected in *GTE Sylvania.* As the above discussion indicates, all vertical restraints, including the exclusive territory agreement held not to be *per se* illegal in *GTE Sylvania,* have the potential to allow dealers to increase "prices" and can be characterized as intended to achieve just that. In fact, vertical nonprice restraints only accomplish the benefits identified in *GTE Sylvania* because they reduce intrabrand price competition to the point where the dealer's profit margin permits provision of the desired services. As we described it in *Monsanto:* "The manufacturer often will want to ensure that its distributors earn sufficient profit to pay for programs such as hiring and training additional salesmen or demonstrating the technical features of the product, and will want to see that 'free-riders' do not interfere." *See also GTE Sylvania,* 433 U.S., at 55.

The dissent erects a much more complex analytic structure, which ultimately rests, however, upon the same discredited premise that the only function this nonprice vertical restriction can serve is restraint of dealer-level competition. Specifically, the dissent's reasoning hinges upon its perception that the agreement between Sharp and Hartwell was a "naked" restraint—that is, it was not "ancillary" to any other agreement between Sharp and Hartwell. But that is not true, unless one assumes, contrary to *GTE Sylvania* and *Monsanto,* and contrary to our earlier discussion, that it is not a quite plausible purpose of the restriction to enable Hartwell to provide better services under the sales franchise agreement.[71] From its

---

was not asked to find, that Hartwell possessed such market power.

71. The conclusion of "naked" restraint could also be sustained on another

faulty conclusion that what we have before us is a "naked" restraint, the dissent proceeds, by reasoning we do not entirely follow, to the further conclusion that it is therefore a horizontal rather than a vertical restraint. We pause over this only to note that in addition to producing what we think the wrong result in the present case, it introduces needless confusion into antitrust terminology. Restraints imposed by agreement between competitors have traditionally been denominated as horizontal restraints, and those imposed by agreement between firms at different levels of distribution as vertical restraints.[72]

Finally, we do not agree with petitioner's contention that an agreement on the remaining dealer's price or price levels will so often follow from terminating another dealer "because of [its] price cutting" that prophylaxis against resale price maintenance warrants the District Court's *per se* rule. Petitioner has provided no support for the proposition that vertical price agreements generally underlie agreements to terminate a

assumption, namely that an agreement is not "ancillary" unless it is designed to enforce a contractual obligation of one of the parties to the contract. The dissent appears to accept this assumption. It is plainly wrong. The classic "ancillary" restraint is an agreement by the seller of a business not to compete within the market. *See Mitchel v. Reynolds*, 1 P.Wms. 181, 24 Eng.Rep. 347 (1711); Restatement (Second) of Contracts § 188(2)(a) (1981). That is not ancillary to any other contractual obligation, but, like the restraint here, merely enhances the value of the contract, or permits the "enjoyment of [its] fruits." *United States v. Addyston Pipe & Steel Co.*, 85 F. 271, 282 (C.A.6 1898), *aff'd*, 175 U.S. 211 (1899); *cf.* Restatement (Second) of Contracts §§ 187, 188 (1981) (restraint may be ancillary to a "transaction or relationship") (emphasis added); R. Bork, The Antitrust Paradox 29 (1978) (hereinafter Bork) (vertical arrangements are ancillary to the "transaction of supplying and purchasing").

More important than the erroneousness of the dissent's common-law analysis of "naked" and "ancillary" restraints are the perverse economic consequences of permitting nonprice vertical restraints to avoid *per se* invalidity only through attachment to an express contractual obligation. Such an approach is contrary to the express views of the principal scholar on whom the dissent relies. *See* 7 P. Areeda, Antitrust Law § 1457c, p. 170 (1986) (hereinafter Areeda) (legality of terminating price cutter should not depend upon formal adoption of service obligations that termination is assertedly designed to

protect). In the precise case of a vertical agreement to terminate other dealers, for example, there is no conceivable reason why the existence of an exclusivity commitment by the manufacturer to the one remaining dealer would render anticompetitive effects less likely, or the procompetitive effects on services more likely—so that the dissent's line for *per se* illegality fails to meet the requirement of *Continental T.V., Inc. v. GTE Sylvania Inc.*, supra, 433 U.S., at 59, 97 S.Ct., at 2562, that it be based on "demonstrable economic effect." If anything, the economic effect of the dissent's approach is perverse, encouraging manufacturers to agree to otherwise inefficient contractual provisions for the sole purpose of attaching to them efficient nonprice vertical restraints which, only by reason of such attachment, can avoid *per se* invalidity as "naked" restraints. The dissent's approach would therefore create precisely the kind of "irrational dislocation in the market" that legal rules in this area should be designed to avoid. *Monsanto Co. v. Spray–Rite Service Corp.*, 465 U.S. 752, 764 (1984).

72. The dissent apparently believes that whether a restraint is horizontal depends upon whether its anticompetitive effects are horizontal, and not upon whether it is the product of a horizontal agreement. That is of course a conceivable way of talking, but if it were the language of antitrust analysis there would be no such thing as an unlawful vertical restraint, since all anticompetitive effects are by definition horizontal effects....

price cutter. That proposition is simply incompatible with the conclusion of *GTE Sylvania* and *Monsanto* that manufacturers are often motivated by a legitimate desire to have dealers provide services, combined with the reality that price cutting is frequently made possible by "free riding" on the services provided by other dealers. The District Court's *per se* rule would therefore discourage conduct recognized by *GTE Sylvania* and *Monsanto* as beneficial to consumers.

B

In resting our decision upon the foregoing economic analysis, we do not ignore common-law precedent concerning what constituted "restraint of trade" at the time the Sherman Act was adopted. But neither do we give that pre–1890 precedent the dispositive effect some would. The term "restraint of trade" in the statute, like the term at common law, refers not to a particular list of agreements, but to a particular economic consequence, which may be produced by quite different sorts of agreements in varying times and circumstances. The changing content of the term "restraint of trade" was well recognized at the time the Sherman Act was enacted. . . .

The Sherman Act adopted the term "restraint of trade" along with its dynamic potential. It invokes the common law itself, and not merely the static content that the common law had assigned to the term in 1890. . . . If it were otherwise, not only would the line of *per se* illegality have to be drawn today precisely where it was in 1890, but also case-by-case evaluation of legality (conducted where *per se* rules do not apply) would have to be governed by 19th–century notions of reasonableness. It would make no sense to create out of the single term "restraint of trade" a chronologically schizoid statute, in which a "rule of reason" evolves with new circumstances and new wisdom, but a line of *per se* illegality remains forever fixed where it was.

Of course the common law, both in general and as embodied in the Sherman Act, does not lightly assume that the economic realities underlying earlier decisions have changed, or that earlier judicial perceptions of those realities were in error. It is relevant, therefore, whether the common law of restraint of trade ever prohibited as illegal *per se* an agreement of the sort made here, and whether our decisions under § 1 of the Sherman Act have ever expressed or necessarily implied such a prohibition.

With respect to this Court's understanding of pre-Sherman Act common law, petitioner refers to our decision in *Dr. Miles Medical Co. v. John D. Park & Sons Co.*, supra. Though that was an early Sherman Act case, its holding that a resale price maintenance agreement was *per se* illegal was based largely on the perception that such an agreement was categorically impermissible at common law. As the opinion made plain, however, the basis for that common-law judgment was that the resale restriction was an unlawful restraint on alienation. As we explained in *Boston Store of Chicago v. American Graphophone Co.*, 246 U.S. 8, 21–22 (1918), "*Dr. Miles* . . . decided that under the general law the owner of movables . . . could not sell the movables and lawfully by contract fix a price at which the product should afterwards be sold, because to do so would be at one and the same time to sell and retain, to part with and yet to hold, to project the will of the seller so as to cause it to control the movable parted with when it was not subject to his will because owned by another." In the present case, of course, no agreement on resale price or price level, and hence no restraint on alienation, was found by the jury, so the common-law rationale of *Dr. Miles* does not apply. *Cf. United States v. General Electric Co.*, 272 U.S. 476, 486–488 (1926) (*Dr. Miles* does not apply to restrictions on price to be charged by one who is in reality an agent of, not a buyer from, the manufacturer).

Petitioner's principal contention has been that the District Court's rule on *per se* illegality is compelled not by the old common law, but by our more recent Sherman Act precedents. First, petitioner contends that since certain horizontal agreements have been held to constitute price fixing (and thus to be *per se* illegal) though they did not set prices or price levels, *see, e.g., Catalano, Inc. v. Target Sales, Inc.*, 446 U.S. 643, 647–650 (1980) (*per curiam*), it is improper to require that a vertical agreement set prices or price levels before it can suffer the same fate. This notion of equivalence between the scope of horizontal *per se* illegality and that of vertical *per se* illegality was explicitly rejected in *GTE Sylvania*, see 433 U.S., at 57, n. 27—as it had to be, since a horizontal agreement to divide territories is *per se* illegal, *see United States v. Topco Assocs., Inc.*, 405 U.S. 596, 608 (1972), while *GTE Sylvania* held that a vertical agreement to do so is not. *See also United States v. Arnold, Schwinn & Co.*, 388 U.S. 365, 390–391 (1967) (Stewart, J., joined by Harlan, J., concurring in part and dissenting in part); *White Motor Co. v. United States*, 372 U.S. 253, 263 (1963).

Second, petitioner contends that *per se* illegality here follows from our two cases holding *per se* illegal a group boycott of a dealer because of its price cutting. *See United States v. General Motors Corp.*, 384 U.S. 127 (1966); *Klor's, Inc. v. Broadway–Hale Stores, Inc.*, 359 U.S. 207 (1959). This second contention is merely a restatement of the first, since both cases involved horizontal combinations—*General Motors*, supra, 384 U.S., at 140, 143–145, at the dealer level,[73] and *Klor's*, supra, 359 U.S., at 213, at the manufacturer and wholesaler levels. . . .

Third, petitioner contends, relying on *Albrecht v. Herald Co.*, 390 U.S. 145 (1968), and *United States v. Parke, Davis & Co.*, 362 U.S. 29, (1960), that our vertical price-fixing cases have already rejected the proposition that *per se* illegality requires setting a price or a price level. We disagree. In *Albrecht*, the maker of the product formed a combination to force a retailer to charge the maker's advertised retail price. *See* 390 U.S., at 149. This combination had two aspects. Initially, the maker hired a third party to solicit customers away from the noncomplying retailer. This solicitor "was aware that the aim of the solicitation campaign was to force [the noncom-

---

73. Contrary to the dissent, *General Motors* does not differ from the present case merely in that it involved a three-party rather than a two-party agreement. The agree-ment was among competitors in *General Motors;* it was between noncompetitors here. *Cf.* Bork 330 (defining "boycotts" as "agree-ments among competitors to refuse to deal").

plying retailer] to lower his price" to the suggested retail price. *Id.*, at 150. Next, the maker engaged another retailer who "undertook to deliver [products] at the suggested price" to the noncomplying retailer's customers obtained by the solicitor. *Ibid.* This combination of maker, solicitor, and new retailer was held to be *per se* illegal. *Id.*, at 150, 153. It is plain that the combination involved both an explicit agreement on resale price and an agreement to force another to adhere to the specified price.

In *Parke, Davis,* a manufacturer combined first with wholesalers and then with retailers in order to gain "the retailers' adherence to its suggested minimum retail prices." 362 U.S., at 45–46, and n. 6. The manufacturer also brokered an agreement among its retailers not to advertise prices below its suggested retail prices, which agreement was held to be part of the *per se* illegal combination. This holding also does not support a rule that an agreement on price or price level is not required for a vertical restraint to be *per se* illegal—first, because the agreement not to advertise prices was part and parcel of the combination that contained the price agreement, and second because the agreement among retailers that the manufacturer organized was a *horizontal* conspiracy among competitors. Id., at 46–47.

. . .

In sum, economic analysis supports the view, and no precedent opposes it, that a vertical restraint is not illegal *per se* unless it includes some agreement on price or price levels. Accordingly, the judgment of the Fifth Circuit is affirmed.

■ KENNEDY, J., took no part in the consideration or decision of this case.

■ STEVENS, J., with whom WHITE, J., joins, dissenting.

In its opinion the majority assumes, without analysis, that the question presented by this case concerns the legality of a "vertical nonprice restraint." As I shall demonstrate, the restraint that results when one or more dealers threatens to boycott a manufacturer unless it terminates its relationship with a price-cutting retailer is more properly viewed as a "horizontal restraint." Moreover, an agreement to terminate a dealer because of its price cutting is most certainly not a "nonprice restraint." The distinction between "vertical nonprice restraints" and "vertical price restraints," on which the majority focuses its attention, is therefore quite irrelevant to the outcome of this case. Of much greater importance is the distinction between "naked restraints" and "ancillary restraints" that has been a part of our law since the landmark opinion written by Judge (later Chief Justice) Taft in *United States v. Addyston Pipe & Steel Co.*, 85 F. 271 (C.A.6 1898), *aff'd*, 175 U.S. 211 (1899). . . .

It may be helpful to begin by explaining why the agreement in this case does not fit into certain categories of agreement that are frequently found in antitrust litigation. First, despite the contrary implications in the majority opinion, this is not a case in which the manufacturer is alleged to have imposed any vertical nonprice restraints on any of its dealers. The term "vertical nonprice restraint," as used in *Continental T.V., Inc. v. GTE*

Sylvania, Inc., 433 U.S. 36 (1977), and similar cases, refers to a contractual term that a dealer must accept in order to qualify for a franchise. Typically, the dealer must agree to meet certain standards in its advertising, promotion, product display, and provision of repair and maintenance services in order to protect the goodwill of the manufacturer's product. Sometimes a dealer must agree to sell only to certain classes of customers—for example, wholesalers generally may only sell to retailers and may be required not to sell directly to consumers. In *Sylvania,* to take another example, we examined agreements between a manufacturer and its dealers that included "provisions barring the retailers from selling franchised products from locations other than those specified in agreements." *Id.,* 433 U.S., at 37. Restrictions of that kind, which are a part of, or ancillary to, the basic franchise agreement, are perfectly lawful unless the "rule of reason" is violated. Although vertical nonprice restraints may have some adverse effect on competition, as long as they serve the main purpose of a procompetitive distribution agreement, the ancillary restraints may be defended under the rule of reason. And, of course, a dealer who violates such a restraint may properly be terminated by the manufacturer.

In this case, it does not appear that respondent imposed any vertical nonprice restraints upon either petitioner or Hartwell. Specifically, respondent did not enter into any "exclusive" agreement, as did the defendant in *Sylvania.* It is true that before Hartwell was appointed and after petitioner was terminated, the manufacturer was represented by only one retailer in the Houston market, but there is no evidence that respondent ever made any contractual commitment to give either of them any exclusive rights. This therefore is not a case in which a manufacturer's right to grant exclusive territories, or to change the identity of the dealer in an established exclusive territory, is implicated. The case is one in which one of two competing dealers entered into an agreement with the manufacturer to terminate a particular competitor without making any promise to provide better or more efficient services and without receiving any guarantee of exclusivity in the future. The contractual relationship between respondent and Hartwell was exactly the same after petitioner's termination as it had been before that termination.

Second, this case does not involve a typical vertical price restraint. As the Court of Appeals noted, there is some evidence in the record that may support the conclusion that respondent and Hartwell implicitly agreed that Hartwell's prices would be maintained at a level somewhat higher than petitioner had been charging before petitioner was terminated. 780 F.2d 1212, 1219 (C.A.5 1986). The illegality of the agreement found by the jury does not, however, depend on such evidence. For purposes of analysis, we should assume that no such agreement existed and that respondent was perfectly willing to allow its dealers to set prices at levels that would maximize their profits. That seems to have been the situation during the period when petitioner was the only dealer in Houston. Moreover, after respondent appointed Hartwell as its second dealer, it was Hartwell, rather than respondent, who objected to petitioner's pricing policies.

Third, this is not a case in which the manufacturer acted independent-ly. Indeed, given the jury's verdict, it is not even a case in which the termination can be explained as having been based on the violation of any distribution policy adopted by respondent. The termination was motivated by the ultimatum that respondent received from Hartwell and that ultima-tum, in turn, was the culmination of Hartwell's complaints about petition-er's competitive price cutting. The termination was plainly the product of coercion by the stronger of two dealers rather than an attempt to maintain an orderly and efficient system of distribution.[74]

In sum, this case does not involve the reasonableness of any vertical restraint imposed on one or more dealers by a manufacturer in its basic franchise agreement. What the jury found was a simple and naked " 'agree-ment between Sharp and Hartwell to terminate Business Electronics be-cause of Business Electronics' price cutting.' "

Because naked agreements to restrain the trade of third parties are seldom identified with such stark clarity as in this case, there appears to be no exact precedent that determines the outcome here. There are, however, perfectly clear rules that would be decisive if the facts were changed only slightly.

Thus, on the one hand, if it were clear that respondent had acted independently and decided to terminate petitioner because respondent, for reasons of its own, objected to petitioner's pricing policies, the termination would be lawful. *See United States v. Parke, Davis & Co.*, 362 U.S. 29, 43–45 (1960). On the other hand, it is equally clear that if respondent had been represented by three dealers in the Houston market instead of only two, and if two of them had threatened to terminate their dealerships "unless respondent ended its relationship with petitioner within 30 days," an agreement to comply with the ultimatum would be an obvious violation of the Sherman Act. *See, e.g., United States v. General Motors Corp.*, 384 U.S. 127 (1966); *Klor's, Inc. v. Broadway–Hale Stores, Inc.*, 359 U.S. 207 (1959). The question then is whether the two-party agreement involved in this case is more like an illegal three-party agreement or a legal independent decision. For me, the answer is plain.

The distinction between independent action and joint action is funda-mental in antitrust jurisprudence.[75] Any attempt to define the boundaries

74. "When a manufacturer acts on its own, in pursuing its own market strategy, it is seeking to compete with other manufactur-ers by imposing what may be defended as reasonable vertical restraints. This would ap-pear to be the rationale of the GTE Sylvania decision. However, if the action of a manufac-turer or other supplier is taken at the di-rection of its customer, the restraint becomes primarily horizontal in nature in that one customer is seeking to suppress its competi-tion by utilizing the power of a common supplier. Therefore, although the termination in such a situation is, itself, a vertical re-straint, the desired impact is horizontal and on the dealer, not the manufacturer, level." *Cernuto, Inc. v. United Cabinet Corp.*, 595 F.2d 164, 168 (C.A.3 1979).

75. *See United States v. Colgate & Co.*, 250 U.S. 300, 307–308 (1919). In *Monsanto Co. v. Spray–Rite Service Corp.*, 465 U.S. 752, 761 (1984), we noted that "the basic distinc-tion between concerted and independent ac-tion" was "not always clearly drawn by par-ties and courts." In its opinion today the

of *per se* illegality by the number of parties to different agreements with the same anticompetitive consequences can only breed uncertainty in the law and confusion for the businessman.

More importantly, if instead of speculating about irrelevant vertical nonprice restraints, we focus on the precise character of the agreement before us, we can readily identify its anticompetitive nature. Before the agreement was made, there was price competition in the Houston retail market for respondent's products. The stronger of the two competitors was unhappy about that competition; it wanted to have the power to set the price level in the market and therefore it "complained to respondent on a number of occasions about petitioner's prices." Quite obviously, if petitioner had agreed with either Hartwell or respondent to discontinue its competitive pricing, there would have been no ultimatum from Hartwell and no termination by respondent. It is equally obvious that either of those agreements would have been illegal *per se*. Moreover, it is also reasonable to assume that if respondent were to replace petitioner with another price-cutting dealer, there would soon be more complaints and another ultimatum from Hartwell. Although respondent has not granted Hartwell an exclusive dealership—it retains the right to appoint multiple dealers—its agreement has protected Hartwell from price competition. Indeed, given the jury's finding and the evidence in the record, that is the *sole function* of the agreement found by the jury in this case. It therefore fits squarely within the category of "naked restraints of trade with no purpose except stifling of competition." *White Motor Co. v. United States*, 372 U.S. 253, 263 (1963)....

Indeed, since the economic consequences of Hartwell's ultimatum to respondent are identical to those that would result from a comparable ultimatum by two of three dealers in a market—and since a two-party price-fixing agreement is just as unlawful as a three-party price-fixing agreement—it is appropriate to employ the term "boycott" to characterize this agreement. In my judgment the case is therefore controlled by our decision in *United States v. General Motors Corp.*, 384 U.S. 127 (1966).

The majority disposes quickly of both *General Motors* and *Klor's Inc. v. Broadway–Hale Stores, Inc.*, 359 U.S. 207 (1959), by concluding that "both cases involved horizontal combinations." But this distinction plainly will not suffice. In *General Motors*, a group of Chevrolet dealers conspired with General Motors to eliminate sales from the manufacturer to discounting dealers. We held that "[e]limination, by joint collaborative action, of discounters from access to the market is a *per se* violation of the Act," 384 U.S., at 145, and explained that "inherent in the success of the combina-

majority virtually ignores that basic distinction. Thus, ... the majority discusses the manufacturer's risks arising out of its agreement "with one dealer to terminate another for failure to provide contractually obligated services." But if such a breach of contract has occurred, the manufacturer should have an independent motivation for acting and need not enter into any agreement with a dealer to do so. As we held in *Monsanto*, the mere fact that the breach of contract may have been called to the manufacturer's attention by another dealer does not make the manufacturer's independent decision to terminate a price-cutting dealer unlawful.

tion in this case was a substantial restraint upon price competition—a goal unlawful *per se* when sought to be effected by combination or conspiracy." Id., at 147. Precisely the same goal was sought and effected in this case— the elimination of price competition at the dealer level. Moreover, the method of achieving that goal was precisely the same in both cases—the manufacturer's refusal to sell to discounting dealers. The difference between the two cases is not a difference between horizontal and vertical agreements—in both cases the critical agreement was between market actors at the retail level on the one hand and the manufacturer level on the other. Rather, the difference is simply a difference in the number of conspirators. Hartwell's coercion of respondent in order to eliminate petitioner because of its same-level price competition is not different in kind from the Chevrolet dealers' coercion of General Motors in order to eliminate other, price-cutting dealers; the only difference between the two cases—one dealer seeking a naked price-based restraint in today's case, many dealers seeking the same end in *General Motors*—is merely a difference in degree. Both boycotts lack any efficiency justification—they are simply naked restraints on price competition, rather than integral, or ancillary, parts of the manufacturers' predetermined distribution policies.

What is most troubling about the majority's opinion is its failure to attach any weight to the value of intrabrand competition. In *Continental T.V., Inc. v. GTE Sylvania Inc.*, 433 U.S. 36 (1977), we correctly held that a demonstrable benefit to interbrand competition will outweigh the harm to intrabrand competition that is caused by the imposition of vertical nonprice restrictions on dealers. But we also expressly reaffirmed earlier cases in which the illegal conspiracy affected only intrabrand competition.[76] Not a word in the *Sylvania* opinion implied that the elimination of intrabrand competition could be justified as reasonable without any evidence of a purpose to improve interbrand competition.

In the case before us today, the relevant economic market was the sale at retail in the Houston area of calculators manufactured by respondent.[77]

76. *See* 433 U.S., at 58, n. 28 (citing *United States v. General Motors Corp.*, 384 U.S. 127 (1966), and *United States v. Topco Associates, Inc.*, 405 U.S. 596 (1972)).

77. It might be helpful to note at this point that although the majority mentions only the reduction of inter brand competition as a justification for a *per se* rule against vertical price restraints, our opinion in Sylvania was quite different. As we stated then:

"The market impact of vertical restrictions is complex because of their potential for a simultaneous reduction of intrabrand competition and stimulation of interbrand competition. Significantly, the Court in *Schwinn* did not distinguish among the challenged restrictions on the basis of their individual potential for intrabrand harm or interbrand benefit. Restrictions that completely eliminated intrabrand competition among Schwinn distributors were analyzed no differently from those that merely moderated intrabrand competition among retailers." 433 U.S., at 51–52 (footnotes omitted).

In the following pages, we pointed out that because vertical nonprice restrictions imposed by manufacturers may serve to advance interbrand competition, the restriction on intrabrand competition should be subject only to a rule of reason analysis. Along these same lines, we explained that "[e]conomists also have argued that manufacturers have an economic interest in maintaining as much intrabrand competition as is

There is no dispute that an agreement to fix prices in that market, either horizontally between petitioner and Hartwell or vertically between respondent and either or both of the two dealers, would violate the Sherman Act. The "quite plausible" assumption, see ante, at 1522, that such an agreement might enable the retailers to provide better services to their customers would not have avoided the strict rule against price fixing that this Court has consistently enforced in the past.

Under petitioner's theory of the case, an agreement between respondent and Hartwell to terminate petitioner because of its price cutting was just as indefensible as any of those price-fixing agreements. At trial the jury found the existence of such an agreement to eliminate petitioner's price competition. Respondent had denied that any agreement had been made and asked the jury to find that it had independently decided to terminate petitioner because of its poor sales performance,[78] but after hearing several days of testimony, the jury concluded that this defense was pretextual.

Neither the Court of Appeals nor the majority questions the accuracy of the jury's resolution of the factual issues in this case. Nevertheless, the rule the majority fashions today is based largely on its concern that in other cases juries will be unable to tell the difference between truthful and pretextual defenses. Thus, it opines that "even a manufacturer that agrees with one dealer to terminate another for failure to provide contractually-obligated services, exposes itself to the highly plausible claim that its real motivation was to terminate a price cutter." But such a "plausible" concern in a hypothetical case that is so different from this one should not be given greater weight than facts that can be established by hard evidence. If a dealer has, in fact, failed to provide contractually obligated services, and if the manufacturer has, in fact, terminated the dealer for that reason, both of those objective facts should be provable by admissible evidence.

consistent with the efficient distribution of their products." Id., at 56. Thus, although the majority neglects to mention it, fostering intrabrand competition has been recognized as an important goal of antitrust law, and although a manufacturer's efficiency-enhancing vertical nonprice restraints may subject a reduction of intrabrand competition only to a rule of reason analysis, a similar reduction without the procompetitive "redeeming virtues" of manufacturer-imposed vertical nonprice restraints, id., 433 U.S., at 54, causes nothing but economic harm. As one commentator has recently stated:

"Intrabrand competition can benefit the consumer, and it is therefore important to insure that a manufacturer's motive for a vertical restriction is not simply to acquiesce in his distributors' desires to limit competition among themselves. The Supreme Court has rec-

ognized that restrictions on intrabrand competition can only be tolerated because of the countervailing positive impact on interbrand competition." Piraino, The Case for Presuming the Legality of Quality Motivated Restrictions on Distribution, 63 Notre Dame L.Rev. 1, 17 (1988) (footnotes omitted).

78. The court instructed the jury:

"Sharp, on the other hand, contends that it terminated Business Electronics unilaterally, not as a result of any agreement or understanding with Hartwell, but because of Business Electronics' sales performance. If you find that Sharp did not terminate Business Electronics pursuant to an agreement or understanding with Hartwell to eliminate price cutting by Business Electronics, then you should answer 'no' to question number 1." 22 Record 1587.

Both in its disposition of this case and in its attempt to justify a new approach to agreements to eliminate price competition, the majority exhibits little confidence in the judicial process as a means of ascertaining the truth.

The majority fails to consider that manufacturers such as respondent will only be held liable in the rare case in which the following can be proved: First, the terminated dealer must overcome the high hurdle of *Monsanto Co. v. Spray–Rite Service Corp.*, 465 U.S. 752 (1984). A terminated dealer must introduce "evidence that tends to exclude the possibility that the manufacturer and nonterminated distributors were acting independently." Requiring judges to adhere to the strict test for agreement laid down in *Monsanto,* in their jury instructions or own findings of fact, goes a long way toward ensuring that many legitimate dealer termination decisions do not succumb improperly to antitrust liability.[79]

Second, the terminated dealer must prove that the agreement was based on a purpose to terminate it because of its price cutting. Proof of motivation is another commonplace in antitrust litigation of which the majority appears apprehensive, but as we have explained or demonstrated many times ... in antitrust, as in many other areas of the law, motivation matters and factfinders are able to distinguish bad from good intent.

Third, the manufacturer may rebut the evidence tending to prove that the sole purpose of the agreement was to eliminate a price cutter by offering evidence that it entered the agreement for legitimate, nonprice-related reasons.

Although in this case the jury found a naked agreement to terminate a dealer because of its price cutting, the majority boldly characterizes the same agreement as "this nonprice vertical restriction." That characterization is surely an oxymoron when applied to the agreement the jury actually found. Nevertheless, the majority proceeds to justify it as "ancillary" to a "quite plausible purpose ... to enable Hartwell to provide better services under the sales franchise agreement." There are two significant reasons why that justification is unacceptable.

---

79. Although at trial respondent had asked the jury to find that it had acted independently, respondent has not disputed, either in the Court of Appeals or here, the jury's finding of an agreement. (Respondent has, of course, contended that no agreement was reached requiring some level of resale price maintenance. As I have argued, though, such an agreement is not needed to invoke the *per se* rule in a case such as this.) Respondent did argue before the District Court for an instruction explaining that "it must be shown that the manufacturer agreed with the complaining dealer to terminate the existing dealer and that, in so agreeing, the manufac- turer shared with the complaining dealer the same desire of eliminating price competition for the complaining dealer." 1 Record 151. Respondent later objected to the court's decision not to give this instruction, 1 Record 54, 22 Record 1599, but the court in fact had quite carefully explained to the jury that "[w]hat a preponderance ... of the evidence in the case must show in order to establish the existence of the required combination, agreement, or understanding is that Sharp and Hartwell knowingly came to a common and mutual understanding to accomplish or to attempt to accomplish an unlawful pur- pose." Id., at 1584–1585.

First, it is not supported by the jury's verdict. Although it did not do so with precision, the District Court did instruct the jury that in order to hold respondent liable it had to find that the agreement's purpose was to eliminate petitioner because of its price cutting and that no valid vertical nonprice restriction existed to which the motivation to eliminate price competition at the dealership level was merely ancillary.

Second, the "quite plausible purpose" the majority hypothesizes as salvation for the otherwise anticompetitive elimination of price competition—"to enable Hartwell to provide better services under the sales franchise agreement,"—is simply not the type of concern we sought to protect in *Continental T.V. Inc. v. GTE Sylvania Inc.*, 433 U.S. 36 (1977). I have emphasized in this dissent the difference between restrictions imposed in pursuit of a manufacturer's structuring of its product distribution, and those imposed at the behest of retailers who care less about the general efficiency of a product's promotion than their own profit margins. *Sylvania* stressed the importance of the former, not the latter; we referred to the use that *manufacturers* can make of vertical nonprice restraints, *see id.*, at 54–57, and nowhere did we discuss the benefits of permitting dealers to structure intrabrand competition at the retail level by coercing manufacturers into essentially anticompetitive agreements. Thus, while Hartwell may indeed be able to provide better services under the sales franchise agreement with petitioner out of the way, one would not have thought, until today, that the mere possibility of such a result—at the expense of the elimination of price competition and absent the salutary overlay of a manufacturer's distribution decision with the entire product line in mind—would be sufficient to legitimate an otherwise purely anticompetitive restraint. In fact, given the majority's total reliance on "economic analysis," it is hard to understand why, if such a purpose were sufficient to avoid the application of a *per se* rule in this context, the same purpose should not also be sufficient to trump the *per se* rule in all other price-fixing cases that arguably permit cartel members to "provide better services." . . .

NOTES AND QUESTIONS

1. As the dissent in *Sharp* points out, there was no evidence that Sharp ever sought or that Business Electronics ever failed to provide relevant services. In effect, does the majority presume that the termination occurred because Sharp was a "free rider?" Is there any justification for such a presumption in this case? Generally, in distribution situations?

2. In effect, the anti-*Dr. Miles* contingent has succeeded in part by successfully describing discounters with the epithet "free riders"—calling forth images of lazy cheats who take advantage of honest businessmen by selling at low prices without accompanying services. Consider a different model. Assume ten dealers of the same branded product, nine of whom are selling at roughly the same high price. The tenth dealer works longer and harder, is more aggressive, handles purchasing, inventory and sales more efficiently—and seeks to pass those efficiencies on to consumers in the form of lower prices in order to expand its sales. Under the

analysis of the majority in *Sharp,* would a termination of the price cutter in that situation be permissible—assuming the other nine dealers separately complained, but the manufacturer and the dealers never agreed as to a specific resale price? Should it be?

Although cases in which vertical price-fixing claims are recognized are relatively rare, consider the following decision from the Third Circuit. Do you think it is consistent with *Business Electronics* and *Monsanto*?

Pace Electronics, Inc. v. Canon Computer Systems, Inc.

United States Court of Appeals, Third Circuit, 2000.
213 F.3d 118.

■ Before McKee, Rendell, AND Rosenn, Circuit Judges.

■ ROSENN, J. The issue in this appeal is whether the termination of a wholesale dealer's contract for its refusal to acquiesce in an alleged vertical minimum price fixing conspiracy constitutes an antitrust injury that will support an action for damages under section 4 of the Clayton Act. The United States District Court for the District of New Jersey reasoned that a dealer terminated under these circumstances does not suffer an antitrust injury unless it can demonstrate that its termination had an actual, adverse economic effect on a relevant market. After concluding that the plaintiff's complaint in the instant case failed to allege such an effect, the District Court dismissed the complaint for failure to state a claim upon which relief may be granted. Because we believe the court misconstrued the antitrust injury requirement, we will reverse.

I

The plaintiff, Pace Electronics, Inc. ("Pace"), a New Jersey corporation, is engaged in the business of distributing various electronic products, including computer printers and related accessories. Pace purchases these products from manufacturers and wholesale distributors and then resells them to smaller retailers, who operate in the New Jersey and New York region.

In April of 1996, Pace entered into a nonexclusive dealer agreement with defendant Canon Computer Systems, Inc. ("Canon"), a California corporation. Under this agreement, Pace obtained the right to purchase Canon-brand ink-jet printers and related accessories from Canon at "dealer prices." In consideration for the right to purchase these products at "dealer prices," Pace agreed to purchase certain minimum quantities of the products.

The dealer agreement between Pace and Canon remained in effect for approximately one year and three months. Thereafter, on July 1, 1997, Canon terminated the agreement with Pace on the stated ground that Pace failed to purchase the minimum quantities of Canon-brand products required of it under the dealer agreement. Although Pace concedes that it did not purchase the amount of Canon-brand products called for under the dealer agreement, Pace contends that it was unable to do so because Canon ignored its purchase orders. Pace further contends that Canon ignored its purchase orders because Pace refused to acquiesce in a vertical minimum price fixing agreement designed and implemented by Canon and defendant Laguna Corporation ("Laguna"), Pace's direct competitor in the New Jersey and New York region.

In this connection, Pace alleges that, prior to the time it entered its dealer agreement with Canon, Laguna had entered into a similar dealer agreement with Canon. Additionally, Pace alleges that the agreement between Canon and Laguna contemplated the maintenance of a minimum resale price below which Laguna would not sell Canon-brand ink-jet printers. In support of its allegation, Pace asserts that after it entered into its dealer agreement with Canon, the president of Canon repeatedly instructed Pace's president not to sell to past or existing customers of Laguna and not to sell Canon brand ink-jet printers at prices less than those at which Laguna was selling its products.

Pace alleges that it has suffered financial losses as a result of its termination as an authorized Canon-brand dealer. Specifically, Pace avers that "[a]s a direct and proximate result of the actions of Defendants ... Pace has suffered significant financial detriment, consisting of, but not necessarily limited to, lost profits. Pace's losses result directly and proximately from the efforts of Canon and Laguna to limit price competition in the market ... for which both Laguna and Pace were competing." ... Although these allegations of loss appear somewhat vague and conclusory, we accept them as true, as we must, for the purposes of this appeal.

Pace also alleges that its termination as an authorized dealer of Canon-brand products has harmed competition in two respects. First, it contends that its termination as a dealer has reduced price competition in the wholesale market for Canon-brand ink-jet printers (an intrabrand market) because Laguna no longer faces price competition from Pace in selling these products to smaller retailers. Second, Pace asserts that its termination as a dealer has reduced price competition in the wholesale market for all brands of ink-jet printers (an interbrand market). In this connection, Pace alleges that: (1) Canon-brand ink-jet printers enjoy an inherent competitive price advantage over the ink-jet printers of other manufacturers; (2) until Canon permits its distributors to take advantage of this price advantage, other manufacturers will not attempt to reduce their production costs; and, (3) until an unrestrained free competitive market requires other manufacturers to reduce their production costs, the price of all brands of ink-jet printers will remain at an artificially high level.

II

To state a claim for damages under section 4 of the Clayton Act, 15 U.S.C. § 15, a plaintiff must allege more than that it has suffered an injury causally linked to a violation of the antitrust laws. *See Brunswick Corp. v. Pueblo Bowl–O–Mat, Inc.,* 429 U.S. 477, 489 (1977). In addition, it must allege antitrust injury, "which is to say injury of the type the antitrust laws were intended to prevent and that flows from that which makes defendants' acts unlawful." *Id.* This is so even where, as in the instant case, the alleged acts of the defendants constitute a *per se* violation of the antitrust laws. *See also Atlantic Richfield Co. v. USA Petroleum Co.,* 495 U.S. 328, 341 (1990). In applying the antitrust injury requirement, the Supreme Court has inquired whether the injury alleged by the plaintiff "resembles any of the potential dangers" which led the Court to label the defendants' alleged conduct violative of the antitrust laws in the first instance. *Id.* at 336. . . .

For example, in *Atlantic Richfield,* the plaintiff, an independent retail marketer of gasoline, brought suit against ARCO, an integrated oil company which sold gasoline to consumers through its own stations and indirectly through ARCO-brand dealers, claiming that ARCO violated section 1 of the Sherman Act by conspiring with its dealers to fix the maximum resale price of gasoline at an artificially low level. *Id.* at 331. Although the plaintiff conceded that the fixed prices were not predatory, it nevertheless maintained that it suffered antitrust injury, in the form of lost profits, as a result of the vertical maximum price fixing agreement between ARCO and its dealers. *See id.* at 334–35. The Supreme Court disagreed, noting that the plaintiff's alleged injury did not resemble any of the dangers which caused the Court to label vertical maximum price fixing *per se* illegal in *Albrecht v. Herald Co.,* 390 U.S. 145 (1968).[80] *See id.* at 336.

[The court then reviewed the reasons why *Albrecht* had condemned vertical maximum price arrangements: replacement of the manufacturer's judgment of market conditions with that of the dealer; prices too low for essential services; limitation on non-price competition; and transformation of a fixed maximum price into a fixed minimum.]

Having identified the potential dangers which led it to condemn categorically vertical maximum price fixing agreements, the Supreme Court had little difficulty determining that the plaintiff in *Atlantic Richfield* had not suffered an antitrust injury. The Court noted that the dangers identified in the *Albrecht* decision focused on the potential adverse effects of vertical maximum price fixing agreements on *dealers and consumers,* not competitors of dealers subject to such agreements. *See id.* The Court explained: "[i]ndeed, the gravamen of [the plaintiff's] complaint—that the price fixing scheme between[the defendant] and its dealers enabled those dealers to increase their sales—amounts to an assertion that the dangers with which we were concerned in *Albrecht* have not materialized in the instant case." *Id.* at 337. In sum, the Court concluded that the plaintiff had not suffered antitrust injury because its losses did not flow from those aspects of vertical maximum pricing that rendered it illegal. *Id.* at 337.

---

80. *Albrecht's* specific holding—that vertical maximum price fixing is *per se* illegal—has since been overruled. *See State Oil Co. v. Khan,* 522 U.S. 3, 7 (1997). However, *Atlantic Richfield's* approach—*i.e.,* discerning the reasons that led the Supreme Court to label certain conduct a *per se* violation, and determining whether the harm suffered by the plaintiff is consistent with the rationale for labeling the defendant's conduct *per se* illegitimate—remains valid and is clearly applicable to the case before us.

Turning now to the instant case, we think it appropriate to ask whether Pace's alleged injury resembles any of the dangers which have led the Supreme Court to condemn vertical minimum price fixing agreements under the antitrust laws. Pace alleges that it has suffered antitrust injury because it was terminated as a wholesale dealer after it sold Canon-brand products at prices below the minimum resale price allegedly fixed by Canon and Laguna. Pace further alleges that its termination as a wholesale dealer has caused it to suffer lost profits because it may no longer obtain profits from selling Canon-brand products at "dealer prices." Under the Supreme Court's jurisprudence, these allegations suffice to establish antitrust injury.

On this point, *Simpson v. Union Oil*, 377 U.S. 13 (1964) is instructive. In *Simpson*, the plaintiff entered into a year-to-year "consignment" agreement with Union Oil. *See id.* at 14. Under the agreement, which was terminable by either party at the end of any one-year term, Union Oil required the plaintiff to charge a minimum retail price for gasoline. *See id.* Contrary to the terms of the agreement with Union Oil, the plaintiff sold gasoline below the minimum retail price. *See id.* at 15. Because he did so, Union Oil terminated its "consignment" agreement with the plaintiff at the end of the first one-year term. *See id.*

Sometime thereafter, the plaintiff brought suit against Union Oil seeking damages under section 4 of the Clayton Act. *See id.* After two pretrial hearings, the District Court granted summary judgment in favor of Union Oil, holding that the plaintiff failed to establish a violation of section 1 of the Sherman Act and that, even assuming the plaintiff had established a violation, the plaintiff suffered no actionable damage. *See id.* at 15–16. The Court of Appeals affirmed on the ground that the plaintiff suffered no actionable wrong or damage. *See id.* at 16. The Supreme Court granted certiorari and reversed.

In reversing, the Court placed primary focus on the consignment agreement's restriction on the ability of dealers such as the plaintiff to make independent, competitive pricing decisions. For example, the Court explained:

> We disagree with the Court of Appeals that there is no actionable wrong or damage if a Sherman Act violation is assumed. If the "consignment" agreement achieves resale price maintenance in violation of the Sherman Act, it and the lease are being used to injure interstate commerce *by depriving independent dealers of the exercise of free judgment* whether to become consignees at all, or remain consignees, and, in any event, to sell at competitive prices. *Id.* (emphasis added).

The Court also stated:

> Dealers, like [the plaintiff], are independent businessmen; and they have all or most of the indicia of entrepreneurs, except for price fixing.... Their return is affected by the rise and fall in the market price, their commissions declining as retail prices drop. *Practically the only power they have to be wholly independent*

> *businessmen, whose service depends on their own initiative and enterprise, is taken from them by the proviso that they must sell their gasoline at prices fixed by Union Oil....* The evil of the resale price maintenance program ... is its inexorable potentiality for and even certainty in destroying competition in retail sales of gasoline by these nominal 'consignees' who are in reality small struggling competitors seeking retail gas customers.

Id. at 21 (emphasis added) (footnote and citations omitted).

Thus, the Supreme Court considered a restriction on dealer independence with respect to pricing decisions to be an anticompetitive aspect of vertical minimum price fixing agreements, and one that the antitrust laws have an interest in forestalling.... Accordingly, we think that a maverick dealer, such as Pace, which is terminated for charging prices less than those set under a vertical minimum price fixing agreement, suffers the type of injury which the antitrust laws are designed to prevent and may recover damages, such as lost profits, which flow from that termination....

Naturally, the defendants argue that the above analysis misses the mark. In essence, they contend that *Simpson* is no longer good law in light of the Supreme Court's decision in *Atlantic Richfield*. Furthermore, they urge, and the district court agreed, that a terminated dealer seeking to establish that it has suffered antitrust injury must allege facts demonstrating that its termination as an authorized dealer resulted in an actual, adverse economic effect on competition in a relevant interbrand market. In support of their position, the defendants primarily rely on the Supreme Court's statement in *Atlantic Richfield* that a plaintiff can recover damages under section 4 of the Clayton Act "only if [its] loss[es] stem[ ] from a competition-reducing aspect or effect of the defendant's behavior." *Atlantic Richfield,* 495 U.S. at 344. On the basis of this brief statement, the defendants then argue that to be "competition-reducing" a defendant's challenged conduct must have had an actual adverse effect on a relevant interbrand market. Although the defendants' syllogism may have some allure, we decline to construe the antitrust injury requirement as suggested by the defendants for the following reasons.

First, we believe that requiring a plaintiff to demonstrate that an injury stemming from a *per se* violation of the antitrust laws caused an actual, adverse effect on a relevant market in order to satisfy the antitrust injury requirement comes dangerously close to transforming a *per se* violation into a case to be judged under the rule of reason. The *per se* standard is reserved for certain categories of conduct which experience has shown to be "manifestly anticompetitive." *Continental T.V., Inc. v. GTE Sylvania Inc.,* 433 U.S. 36, 39 (1977). That standard, which is based on considerations of "business certainty and litigation efficiency," *Arizona v. Maricopa County Med. Society,* 457 U.S. 332, 344 (1982), allows a court to presume that certain limited classes of conduct have an anticompetitive effect without engaging in the type of involved, market-specific analysis ordinarily necessary to reach such a conclusion. *See Business Electronics*

Corp. v. Sharp Electronics Corp., 485 U.S. 717, 723 (1988) ("Certain categories of agreements, however, have been held to be *per se* illegal, dispensing with the need for case-by-case evaluation."). Were we to accept the defendants' construction of the antitrust injury requirement, we would, in substance, be removing the presumption of anticompetitive effect implicit in the *per se* standard under the guise of the antitrust injury requirement.[81]

Second, we do not believe that the Supreme Court's statement in *Atlantic Richfield* that a plaintiff can recover for losses only if they stem "from a competition-reducing aspect or effect of the defendant's behavior," *Atlantic Richfield,* 495 U.S. at 344, when viewed in the context of the Court's entire opinion, can be fairly read to require a terminated dealer to prove that its termination caused an actual, adverse economic effect on a relevant market. In this connection, we note that in determining that the plaintiff in *Atlantic Richfield* failed to satisfy the antitrust injury requirement, the Supreme Court simply did not focus on whether the challenged conduct of the defendant had an actual, adverse economic effect on a relevant market. Rather, as outlined above, the Court focused on whether the plaintiff's injury stemmed from any of the potential anticompetitive dangers which led the Court to label vertical maximum price fixing unlawful in the first instance. Implicit in the Court's approach is that a plaintiff who had suffered loss as a result of an anticompetitive aspect of a *per se* restraint of trade agreement would have suffered antitrust injury, without demonstrating that the challenged practice had an actual, adverse economic effect on a relevant market.... The issue, thus, is not whether the plaintiff's alleged injury produced an anticompetitive result, but, rather, whether the injury claimed resulted from the anticompetitive aspect of the challenged conduct.

Finally, we point out that our holding—that a dealer terminated for its refusal to abide by a vertical minimum price fixing agreement suffers antitrust injury and may recover losses flowing from that termination—is consistent with the decisions of those courts which have explored the issue thus far. *See, e.g., Sterling Interiors Group, Inc. v. Haworth, Inc.,* No. 94–9216, 1996 WL 426379 at *18–*19 (S.D.N.Y. July 30, 1996) ("The anticompetitive dangers of minimum price arrangements flow to both customers who purchase at prices set higher than competitive levels, and to dealers who are effectively foreclosed from competing in the marketplace.").

III

For the reasons set forth above, the district court's order dismissing Pace's complaint will be reversed and the case remanded to the district

---

81. We recognize that various scholars have taken issue with the Supreme Court's *per se* treatment of vertical minimum price fixing agreements and argued that these agreements may have significant, procompetitive attributes. *See, e.g.,* Antitrust Policy, 75 Colum. L.Rev. at 283. But, academic commentary, even if persuasive, does not permit us to expand the antitrust injury requirement to a point which undermines the Court's categorical disapproval of vertical minimum price fixing

court for further proceedings consistent with this opinion. Costs taxed against the appellees.

NOTES AND QUESTIONS

1. The court in *Pace* approaches the vertical restraint before it—an alleged minimum price-fixing conspiracy—through the lens of the "antitrust injury" doctrine, aspects of which are discussed in Chapter 2, pp. 99–106, and in Chapter 9, pp. 1024–1026. This brings to mind the famous observation of the English legal scholar Henry Sumner Maine, who wrote that "substantive law has at first the look of being gradually secreted in the interstices of procedure." Maine, Dissertations on Early Law and Custom 389 (Arno Press 1975) (1886). Much of antitrust law has also been secreted in the interstices of procedure: the antitrust standing doctrines, the antitrust injury idea, summary judgment rules, and the like. The district court here found that the allegations of a vertical price-fixing conspiracy failed to describe "antitrust injury," which as the court says is "injury of the type the antitrust laws were intended to prevent and that flows from that which makes the defendants' acts unlawful." *Brunswick Corp. v. Pueblo Bowl–O–Mat, Inc.*, 429 U.S. 477, 489 (1977). The court of appeals, of course, disagreed. The important point for present purposes is that the court of appeals thought that the theory the plaintiff was presenting, which we have been exploring in this section, was plausible enough as an antitrust violation that the plaintiff was entitled to have a decision on the merits. In reaching that decision, the court was necessarily making substantive choices about how far the antitrust laws go in regulating vertical arrangements. Compare this to *Cargill, Inc. v. Monfort of Colorado, Inc.*, 479 U.S. 104 (1986), Chapter 9, *infra* p. 1026, which also made important contributions to the substantive law of merger regulation under the guise of deciding whether the plaintiff had suffered antitrust injury.

2. Note the comment in the majority opinion in *Business Electronics* that "interbrand competition is the primary concern of the antitrust laws," p. 698 supra. Is such a principle fairly deduced from the Court's analysis of non-price vertical restrictions in *Sylvania* and other cases? If that dictum is the law, does it follow that *Topco* has been overruled? Note, however, that the majority opinion in *Sharp* cited *Topco* favorably. See p. 703 supra.

3. The dissenters in *Business Electronics* raised the concern that the dominant dealer in the market had coerced Sharp into terminating the other dealer in order to consolidate market power. The majority dismissed this concern, remarking that dominant retailer power is unlikely to occur and that the plaintiff did not allege it. While the majority may have been right with respect to the record before it, its suggestion that competition in the retail market will prevent dominant retailers from wielding market power is far less certain. To be sure, most of the cases in this chapter (and the next) arose as small retailers challenged the policies imposed on them by manufacturers. While these cases sometimes explore whether the challenged policies were forged by the manufacturer or produced by horizontal agreements of various dealers, they operate from the general assumption that manufacturers have more power than retailers. Is this still a valid premise? In the past 10 years, retailing in America has changed dramatically. Over the span of just a few years, super-sized retail chains, such as Wal–Mart, Home Depot and Toys "R" Us, have grown up to dominate the industry in a way never before seen. Might the

volume of sales these chains control enable them to wring special concessions or contract terms from manufacturers and might some of these contract terms be open to attack as "vertical restraints on competition"?

With this in mind, reconsider *Toys "R" Us,* supra p. 505. Recall that the Commission condemned the arrangement both under the horizontal and vertical theories. Some critics derided the FTC for overreaching since Toys "R" Us controls only 20% of the retail market. Skipping over the market power question, isn't the FTC's real problem distinguishing these special arrangements from volume discounts? Is the FTC's action justified as a way to get manufacturers and retailers to compete on price? Along these lines, see also the opinion of the court-appointed expert in *State of New York v. Kraft General Foods,* expressing concerns about the emphasis on non-price competition in the ready–to–eat cereal industry. 926 F.Supp. 321, 351, 1995–1 Trade Cases (CCH) ¶ 70,911 (S.D.N.Y.1995).

PROBLEM 16

DISTRIBUTION ARRANGEMENTS FOR GLORY HAIR RINSE

Glory Hair Rinse is one of the ten leading preparations in the United States for tinting hair; there are no others of consequence. Glory accounts for about 15% of the U.S. market.

The product is marketed primarily through wholesalers who sell to retail druggists. Each wholesaler buys the product for $5.60 per bottle. Glory suggests a wholesale price of $7.00 and a retail price of $9.50. Glory advertises heavily in fashion magazines and other media, aiming to create the image of a prestige product. Consistent with that advertising campaign, it asks its wholesalers not to sell to discount druggists and other discount outlets.

To assure that its recommended prices are followed, Glory has notified all retailers of its product as follows:

> If you are disturbed by retail sales by others of Glory Hair Rinse at less than the suggested retail price, you should notify your wholesaler of the facts surrounding the cut-rate sales.

Wholesalers have been informed that:

> It is Glory's policy to maintain suggested retail prices. However, you must not under any circumstances consult with retailers selling at less than the suggested price. Action speaks louder than words.

Wholesalers are expected to warehouse and deliver the product promptly to retailers on order. Retailers are asked but not required to display Glory's product prominently. No other services are required or requested.

A pattern has developed whereby, if a retailer sells Glory products at less than the suggested resale price, the wholesaler fills the particular order but refuses to honor future orders. The wholesaler also refuses to discuss the matter with the retailer that has been cut off. At some later date, usually after a year or 18 months, the wholesaler may offer to fill orders of the retailer; the wholesaler will again refuse to discuss the retailer's practices. Where wholesalers have not followed this practice promptly upon receiving complaints of cut-rate sales, Glory has cut off the wholesaler and performed its own wholesaling function, including the temporary suspension of sales to price-cutting retailers. Six of the other nine hair rinse manufacturers follow similar distribution practices. Their prices to wholesalers are identical with Glory's and they suggest the same wholesale and retail price. The other three manufacturers aggressively market their products to all outlets.

Last year, Able Drug complained to its wholesaler and Glory that Baker Drug, a direct rival, was purchasing Glory Hair Rinse in vast quantities, not for sale to customers, but for transshipment to discount drug stores in the area. After investigating the matter, the wholesaler cut off Baker without ever discussing the matter with Glory. Has Glory violated the antitrust laws?

SELECTIVE BIBLIOGRAPHY

1. **Resale Price Maintenance**

    Blair & Lopotka, The Albrecht Rule After Khan: Death Becomes Her, 74 Notre Dame L. Rev. 123 (1998).

    Comanor, Vertical Price Fixing, Vertical Market Restrictions, and the New Antitrust Policy, Harvard L. Rev. 983 (1985).

    Denger, Resale Pricing Issues in Distribution and Franchisor Operations, 60 Antitrust L.J. 419 (1992).

    Easterbrook, Vertical Arrangements and the Rule of Reason, 53 Antitrust L.J. 135 (1984).

    Edlin, Do Guaranteed–Low–Price Policies Guarantee High Prices, and Can Antitrust Rise to the Challenge, 111 Harvard L. Rev. 528 (1997).

    Fulda, Resale Price Maintenance, 21 U.Chi.L.Rev. 175 (1954).

    Grimes, The Seven Myths of Vertical Price Fixing: The Politics and Economics of a Century–Long Debate, 21 Southwestern U. L. Rev. 1285 (1992).

    Grimes, et al., Vertical Price Fixing Revisited, 80 Cal.L.Rev. 815 (1992).

    Kessler & Wheeler, How to Price Without being a Price Signaler, 7 Antitrust 26 (Summer 1993).

    Klein & Murphy, Vertical Restraints as Contract Enforcement Mechanisms, 31 J.Law & Econ. 265 (1988).

    Marvel, The Resale Price Maintenance Controversy: Beyond Conventional Wisdom, 63 Antitrust L.J. 59 (1994).

    Pitofsky, In Defense of Discounters: The No–Frills Case for a *per se* Rule Against Vertical Price Fixing, 71 Geo.L.J. 1487 (1983).

    Scherer, The Economics of Vertical Restraints, 52 Antitrust L.J. 687 (1983).

    Telser, Why Should Manufacturers Want Fair Trade?, 3 J.Law Econ. 86 (1960).

    Telser, Abusive Trade Practices: An Economic Analysis, 30 Law and Contemp.Probs. 488 (1965).

2. **Other Vertical Restraints and Distribution**

    6 & 7 Areeda, Antitrust Law (1986 & Supp.1994).

    Baxter, The Viability of Vertical Restraints Doctrine, 75 Cal.L.Rev. 933 (1987).

    Bork, Vertical Restraints: Schwinn Overruled, 1977 Sup.Ct.Rev. 171 (1977).

    Bohling, A Simplified Rule of Reason for Vertical Restraints: Integrating Social Goals, Economic Analysis, and Sylvania, 64 Iowa L.Rev. 461 (1979).

    Ginsburg, Vertical Restraints: De Facto Legality Under the Rule of Reason, 60 Antitrust L.J. 67 (1991).

Posner, The Next Step in the Antitrust Treatment of Restricted Distribution: *per se* Legality, 48 U.Chi.L.Rev. 6 (1980).

Posner, Antitrust Policy and The Supreme Court: An Analysis of the Restricted Distribution, Horizontal Merger, and Potential Competition Decisions, 75 Colum.L.Rev. 282 (1975).

Steiner, Manufacturers' Promotional Allowances, Free Riders and Vertical Restraints, 36 Antitrust Bull. 383 (1991).

Stewart & Roberts, Viability of the Antitrust *per se* Illegality Rule: Schwinn Down, How Many To Go?, 58 Wash.U.L.Q. 727 (1980).

3. Inferring Combination and Conspiracy

6 Areeda, Antitrust Law (1986 and Supp.1994).

Kattan, Beyond Facilitating Practices: Price Signals and Price Protection In The New Antitrust Environment, 63 Antitrust L.J. 133 (1995).

Turner, Definition of Agreement Under the Sherman Act: Conscious Parallelism and Refusals to Deal, 75 Harv.L.Rev. 655 (1962).

4. Comparative Material

Covey, Vertical Restraints Under Japanese Law: The Antimonopoly Law Study Group Report, 14 Law in Japan 49 (1981).

Van Fleet, Mexico's Federal Economic Competition Law: The Dawn of a New Antitrust Era, 64 Antitrust L.J. 183 (1995).

Mastromanolis, Insights From U.S. Antitrust Law on Exclusive and Restricted Territorial Distribution: The Creation of a New Legal Standard for European Union Competition Law, 15 U.Pa.J.Int'l.Bus.L. 559 (1995).

Paulweber, The End of a Success Story? The European Commission's White Paper on the Modernisation of the European Competition Law, 23 J. World Comp. 3 (No. 3 2000).

Pigassou, Oligopoly and Antitrust Law: A Comparison of United States, European Community, West German, and French Law, 19 Geo.Wash.J.Int'l.L. & Econ. 633 (1985).

Subiotto & Amato, The Reform of the European Competition Policy Concerning Vertical Restraints, 69 Antitrust L.J. 147 (2001).

Terhorst, The Reformation of the EC Competition Policy on Vertical Restraints, 21 Nw. J. Int'l L. & Bus. 343 (2000).

Website of the European Commission at http://europa.eu.int/comm/competition.

CHAPTER 8

ADDITIONAL LIMITATIONS ON A SINGLE FIRM EXERCISING MARKET POWER

INTRODUCTORY NOTE

As we first noted in Chapter 3, much of the law limiting conduct by single firms exercising market power has developed around the words "exclusionary" and "predatory." Chapter 8 will now deal with a wide range of possible predatory and exclusionary strategies, which may, for example, involve blocking entry or expansion, "disciplining" competitors, diminishing a rival's revenues, or adding more to a competitor's costs than to the costs of a dominant firm. In each of the cases reviewed in this Chapter, the basic need is to separate those acts to be condemned from legitimate competitive conduct. Throughout the Chapter, please keep a careful eye on how the courts define "predatory" and "exclusionary," and how they distinguish legitimate competition from anticompetitive activity.

Illegal predatory or exclusionary conduct by a firm will arise most dramatically under Section 2 of the Sherman Act (where this Chapter begins), but such conduct can arise in a number of other contexts. It can involve: an "agreement" in violation of Section 1 of the Sherman Act; a substantial lessening of competition under Section 3 of the Clayton Act; an "unfair method of competition" under Section 5 of the FTC Act; or an element of an illegal price discrimination in violation of the Robinson–Patman Act.

The District of Columbia Circuit's recent *Microsoft* decision (p. 765 infra) is a landmark because of Microsoft's economic importance and the Circuit's Section 2 analysis. But the decision also covers Section 1 issues and Clayton Act Section 3 issues like tying and exclusive dealing. While the major part of the *Microsoft* decision is set forth in Section 1 of this Chapter—"Section 2 Revisited"—its non-Section 2 implications are cross-referenced and discussed throughout Chapter 8.

SECTION 1.   SECTION 2 REVISITED: SPECIAL LIMITS ON SINGLE FIRM MARKET POWER BY MONOPOLISTS AND WOULD-BE MONOPOLISTS

A.   MONOPOLY CONDUCT REVISITED

United States v. Aluminum Co. of America

United States Circuit Court of Appeals, Second Circuit, 1945.
148 F.2d 416.

[Reprinted p. 130 supra]

United States v. Grinnell Corp.

Supreme Court of the United States, 1966.
384 U.S. 563, 86 S.Ct. 1698, 16 L.Ed.2d 778.

[Reprinted p. 172 supra]

NOTE ON MARKET POWER

1.   BROADWAY DELIVERY CORP. v. UNITED PARCEL SERVICE OF AMERICA, INC., 651 F.2d 122 (2d Cir.), cert. denied, 454 U.S. 968 (1981). A group of small New York transport firms brought a treble damage action against United Parcel Service and its subsidiary, United Parcel Service of New York, alleging that by predatory pricing defendants had attempted to monopolize and had monopolized the delivery of small packages sent by wholesalers in the New York garment district. The jury found for defendants; on appeal, plaintiffs challenged the trial court's jury instruction that plaintiffs could not prevail on a monopolization claim "unless they proved that during the relevant period the defendants controlled at least 50% of the relevant market."

The Court of Appeals assumed that the relevant market, as alleged by plaintiffs, was the pick-up and delivery in metropolitan New York of wholesale packages weighing less than 50 pounds. As to market share, plaintiffs proved that United's share sharply increased during the relevant period but never established exactly what market share was held. On the question of what percentage of market share is required to support a finding of monopoly power, the Second Circuit wrote:

The significance of particular market shares has evoked varied comment in antitrust law. The cases have considered many different percentages, and the Courts' observations cannot readily be compared because they were made in contexts that ranged from a fact-finder's assessment of the evidence, *e.g.*, United States v. United Shoe Machinery Corp., 110 F.Supp. 295 (D.Mass.1953), aff'd, 347 U.S. 521 (1954), to a legal determination of the sufficiency of a claim, *e.g.*, Brager & Co., Inc. v. Leumi Securities Corp., 429 F.Supp. 1341 (S.D.N.Y.1977). Several decisions cast doubt on whether monopoly power can be possessed by a company enjoying less than a 50% market share. In the early case of United States v. United States Steel Corp., 251 U.S. 417 (1920), the Supreme Court stated that it was "certain" that the defendant had not achieved a monopoly, reasoning that although "the power [it] attained was much greater than that possessed by any one competitor—it was not greater than that possessed by all of them." Id. at 444. It has frequently been observed, moreover, that the leading cases upholding monopolization claims involved defendants who controlled well over half the relevant market, with market shares ranging from 70 to 100%. *See, e.g.,* Hiland Dairy Inc. v. Kroger Co., 402 F.2d 968, 974 n. 6 (8th Cir.1968) (collecting cases). And an occasional statement can be found labeling a 50% market share a "prerequisite for a finding of monopoly." Cliff Food Stores, Inc. v. Kroger, Inc., 417 F.2d 203, 207 n. 2 (5th Cir.1969). In most instances, however, the courts seem to be assessing only the significance of the share possessed by a particular defendant in a particular market, rather than endeavoring to extrapolate a general rule. In United States v. Aluminum Co. of America, 148 F.2d 416 (2d Cir.1945), for example, Judge Learned Hand considered Alcoa's share under three possible market definitions and thought it "doubtful" whether a share of 60–64%, yielded by one of the definitions, would constitute a monopoly. Id. at 424. It seems unlikely that Judge Hand was doubting that any defendant with a 60–64% share of any market, regardless of its structure, could ever be found to possess monopoly power. Even if his doubts ranged beyond the case he was considering, it is significant that he expressed a doubt, not a rule of preclusion. . . .

The trend of guidance from the Supreme Court and the practice of most courts endeavoring to follow that guidance has been to give only weight and not conclusiveness to market share evidence. In United States v. Columbia Steel Co., 334 U.S. 495 (1948), the Supreme Court recognized that exclusive focus on market share percentages can produce a distorted picture of market power because "the relative effect of percentage command of a market varies with the setting in which that factor is placed." Id. at 528. The Court said that a true picture emerges only from consideration of additional market characteristics, among them, the strength of the competition, the probable development of the industry, and customer demand. Id. at 527. . . .

The extent to which market characteristics should be explained to the jury in a particular case will vary with the nature of the underlying facts and the expert testimony. Sometimes, but not inevitably, it will be useful to suggest that a market share below 50% is rarely evidence of monopoly power, a share between 50% and 70% can occasionally show monopoly power, and a share above 70% is usually strong evidence of monopoly power. But when the evidence presents a fair jury issue of monopoly power, the jury should not be told that it must find monopoly power lacking below a specified share or existing above a specified share. . . .

The Court of Appeals concluded that the trial court instruction precluding a finding of monopoly power where defendants' market share was less than 50% was in error, but the error was harmless because plaintiff had not submitted sufficient evidence to put the market power question to the jury in the first place. In the absence of conventional market share data, plaintiffs "must produce unambiguous evidence that the defendant has the power to control prices or exclude competition." That had not occurred because it was undisputed that the U.S. Postal Service, defendant's principal competitor, could not be driven out of business and that entry barriers for new competitors were low. Finally, plaintiffs' claim that United had operated consistently below cost and that below-cost selling was itself evidence of market power failed because of a lack of proof that below-cost sales had actually occurred.

2. United States v. Eastman Kodak Co., 63 F.3d 95 (2d Cir.1995). Eastman Kodak Co. ("Kodak") had moved successfully in the district court to terminate two antitrust consent decrees. The first decree, entered in 1921, imposed several restrictions on Kodak including a provision preventing it from selling "private label" film. The second decree, entered in 1954, prevented Kodak from selling its film in a "bundle" with its photo finishing services. Prior to entry of the 1954 decree, the sales price of Kodak color film included photo finishing. Since Kodak sold approximately 90% of the color film in the United States, the practice allowed Kodak to maintain a 90% share of the photo finishing market. The district court had found that Kodak no longer possessed market power over the sale of films and, therefore, termination of the 1921 decree provisions would benefit consumers. It further found that the purpose of the 1954 decree—creation of a competitive photo finishing market—had been accomplished and that neither Kodak nor its affiliates had market power in either the photo finishing or film market.

The Second Circuit affirmed. In its decision, the court first explained that the marketplace for film has changed considerably in the last 80 years. Today there is a world market, in which five companies manufacture all of the amateur color negative film sold in the United States: Kodak, Fuji, Konica, Agfa and 3M. On that worldwide basis, Kodak has 36% market-share, Fuji 34%, Konica 16%, Agfa 10%, and 3M 4%. In the United States, Kodak is still by far the leading seller of film. Its market share is 67% if measured in unit terms and 75% if measured in dollar terms. Notwithstanding Kodak's success in the United States, experts agreed that there is very little difference in quality among the various brands of film. As far as the photo-finishing market is concerned, in the last ten years, Kodak has reclaimed a large market share through acquisitions. The most important was a joint venture to establish Qualex, Inc., a company that accounts for about 30% of the U.S. photo-finishing market.

The court of appeals agreed that the case turned on the proper market definition (which is, of course, a question of fact, and thus was subject only to review for clear error). The district court had found that the relevant geographic market for film is worldwide. The government contended that this determination was erroneous and that the relevant geographic market should have been limited to the United States. The court of appeals affirmed the district court's market definition. It first noted that film sellers operate on a world-wide basis, the flow of imported film to the United States has been continuous and systematic, and there was no evidence of significant transportation costs or tariffs that put imported film at a significant cost disadvantage. Under those conditions, foreign film producers could act as a check on Kodak's ability to raise prices. The fact that film purchasers had been shown to be price sensitive and willing to shift among Fuji, Kodak, and private label film on the basis of changes in price indicated that the foreign film would be a real constraint. (In this regard, the government contended that, by relying on the significant cross-elasticity of demand between Kodak film and other brands, the district court fell victim to the so-called *Cellophane* fallacy. The government contended that because Kodak is already pricing its products at monopolistic levels in the United States, consumers' willingness to switch to other brands of film when the market price of Kodak film rises actually demonstrates that Kodak possesses market power in the United States. The economic error allegedly committed by the court in *Cellophane* was in failing to recognize that a high cross-elasticity of demand may, in some cases, be the product of monopoly power rather than a belief on the part of the consumers that the products are good substitutes for one another. The court of appeals disagreed with this argument on grounds that unlike *Cellophane*, this case did not involve a comparison of two highly differentiated products like cellophane and wax-paper: the films produced by Kodak and its competitors were of comparable quality.)

Next, the court considered the empirical challenges to the worldwide market raised by the government. In particular, the government relied on the following facts to establish that Kodak had market power in the United States: (1) Kodak's ability to engage in price discrimination against United States consumers; (2) Kodak's ability to sell the same quality of film at a substantial price premium compared to its rivals; and (3) Kodak's excessive profits, evidenced by an "own elasticity of demand" of two.

First, with regard to geographic price discrimination, the court held that even if the government's theory was correct, there was no probative evidence in the record to support the assertion that Kodak engaged in geographic price discrimination. Evidence that Kodak film sells for different prices in different parts of the world is insufficient to establish price discrimination without proof that Kodak's costs are uniform throughout the world. Second, as far as premium pricing is concerned, the court again rejected the government's contentions and attributed the price difference to the fact that Kodak has historically earned consumer's trust. The court also noted that the small price differences (an average of 4.5%) resulted from Fuji's policy of undercutting Kodak's price in order to make its product more attractive. Further, the court pointed out that there was evidence in the record showing that the amount of price premium was shrinking.

Finally, the court addressed the issue of Kodak's "own elasticity of demand". The economic concept of "own elasticity of demand" expresses the change in quantity of goods a firm will sell in response to a change in the price it charges for the goods. For a firm operating with an own elasticity of two (as Kodak purportedly does), a price increase of the firm would result in its sales dropping by twice the percentage of the price change; that is, Kodak would lose ten percent of film sales if it were to raise the price of its film by five percent. The significance of an own elasticity of two is that (in the government's view) it indicates that the sales price of Kodak film is twice Kodak's short-run marginal cost. (This conclusion comes from the "Lerner index", a mathematical formula expressing the relationship between a firm's own elasticity and the marginal cost of the goods sold.) From this, the government concluded that Kodak is earning monopolistic profits. The court found these arguments unpersuasive. Most importantly, it concluded that even accepting the government's contention that Kodak's short-run marginal costs equal one-half of the product's sales price, it does not necessarily follow that Kodak is earning monopolistic profits. Certain deviations between marginal cost and price, such as those resulting from high fixed costs, are not evidence of market power. In this case, there was sufficient evidence that Kodak's film business is subject to enormous fixed costs (in particular, R & D expenses and cost to build Hi-tech production plants) that are not reflected in the short-run marginal costs.

Once the court of appeals accepted the worldwide geographic market, it was an easy step to concluding that Kodak lacked market power over film. On a worldwide basis, Kodak has only a 36% share of the market for film. This low market share, in connection with the other factors, supported the court's finding that Kodak no longer possessed market power. Given that Kodak lacks market power, the court of appeals upheld the district court's decision to terminate the 1921 and 1954 decrees.

NOTE ON MARKET POWER FROM THE TRADE LAW PERSPECTIVE: THE KODAK–FUJI DISPUTE

At almost the same time that Kodak was successfully working for the termination of the 1921 and 1954 consent decrees discussed above in United States v.

Eastman Kodak, 63 F.3d 95 (2d Cir.1995), it was launching an all-out attack on alleged barriers in the consumer photographic film and consumer photographic paper markets in Japan. On May 18, 1995, Kodak filed a petition with the Office of the U.S. Trade Representative (USTR), pursuant to Section 301 of the Trade Act of 1974, as amended, claiming that a variety of acts, policies, and practices of the Japanese government, including notably its alleged failure to enforce the Antimonopoly Act, amounted to unreasonable burdens or restrictions on U.S. commerce. USTR responded on July 3, 1995, by initiating an investigation under Section 301. Eleven months later, on June 13, 1996, the Acting U.S. Trade Representative formally decided that the government of Japan had "established and tolerated a market structure that impedes U.S. exports of consumer photographic materials to Japan," and that practices were in fact occurring that impede U.S. exports of those products to Japan, "thereby denying fair and equitable market opportunities." 61 Fed.Reg. 30,929 (June 13, 1996). Finally, USTR alleged that certain measures adopted by the Japanese government violated a variety of international agreements to which Japan is a signatory, and, crucially, "nullified and impaired" benefits accruing to the United States under the World Trade Organization (WTO) agreements. The United States therefore invoked the dispute settlement provisions of the WTO with respect to the measures in question and their application. Id.

At first glance, Fuji's position in the Japanese market looks remarkably like Kodak's position in the United States, as described in the Second Circuit's opinion. According to Kodak's memorandum in support of its Section 301 petition, entitled Privatizing Protection: Japanese Market Barriers in Consumer Photographic Film and Consumer Photographic Paper (May 1995) (hereinafter *Privatizing Protection*), Fuji has consistently held roughly a 70% share of Japan's consumer photographic film market and a 56% share of the paper market. *Privatizing Protection* at 9. Kodak, in contrast, despite its efforts to invest in Japan, has only about 15% of the film market. Id. at 7. The key private anticompetitive practices that were alleged to constitute market access barriers were the following: (1) a closed distribution system for film, which tied up existing distribution channels for Fuji's benefit and made them unavailable for foreign competitors; (2) a rebate system that gave distributors an incentive to favor Fuji products; (3) Fuji's requirement of a large security deposit from its primary film wholesalers, which enabled it to control the distributors; and (4) a variety of practices designed to keep Kodak film off the shelves of the smaller distributors and to impede access to the large-scale retail stores that are the most common outlet for foreign film.

In addition to these private restraints, however, the Section 301 petition and the case the USTR referred to the WTO allege various governmental actions that created or reinforced the barriers to market access. Thus, for example, when the Japanese government gradually withdrew its formal restrictions on imports and inward investment beginning in the late 1960's, it simultaneously implemented countermeasures designed to restrict access to the market. The consumer photographic materials sector was among the last to be liberalized. During the transition period, Japan's powerful Ministry for International Trade and Industry (MITI) took steps to restructure film distribution, such as the promulgation of distribution guidelines for film. Japan's restrictive Large Scale Retail Stores Act has made it difficult for new retail channels to develop that might be more willing to carry a new manufacturer's product. Premiums and other promotional devices are tightly regulated by the Japan Fair Trade Commission (JFTC), which again makes it hard for newcomers to make their products known to consumers.

In a report commissioned by Fuji to examine whether the practices alleged would (hypothetically) amount to a violation of the U.S. antitrust laws, Donald I.

Baker, W. Todd Miller, and Rebecca L. Margulies concluded that they would not. They offered the following support for this conclusion. First, Fuji did not have any explicit exclusive dealing arrangements with its four principal retailers, and thus a challenge to these practices would necessarily be based on the far more difficult *de facto* exclusive theory. See p. 948 infra. Second, even if one assumed that Fuji has exclusive control of those retailers, one would need to show that Kodak's lack of access to them amounted to foreclosure from the relevant market. Kodak, they pointed out, had a subsidiary wholesaler in Japan, and it concededly had relatively unimpeded access to retailers in the Tokyo and Osaka areas. The 301 action thus focused only on access to the remainder of Japan, but this raised problems for an antitrust foreclosure theory. Kodak's claim that the four Fuji retailers were, collectively, an "essential facility" for competing in Japan was also novel from an antitrust standpoint. See p. 754 infra. To the extent that Fuji's distribution system was having the effect of keeping prices for Fuji film high, as Kodak alleged, it was not clear how that in itself could harm Kodak. Kodak noted, however, that its consistently lower prices for film should have translated into higher market shares, over the many years it had been in Japan. The fact that this did not happen indicated, according to Kodak, that something was certainly amiss.

1.   How do the practices that Kodak asserted amount to barriers to market access in the Japanese photographic film and paper markets compare to Kodak's own practices in the United States?

2.   Do you see any inconsistency between Kodak's argument, which was accepted by the Second Circuit, that the market for photographic film is global in the U.S. antitrust case, and its argument in the Section 301 petition that the market should be limited to Japan only? If so, is this inconsistency explained by: (a) the different purposes that lie behind Section 301, a market-access trade statute, and the antitrust laws; (b) the presence of additional, governmentally based barriers to entry; or (c) self-interest? Can you explain how geographic markets in antitrust (or antitrust-like) cases can be global and country-specific at the same time?

3.   On December 5, 1997 the WTO ruled in favor of Fuji and Japan against Kodak and the United States. The WTO concluded that it had found no evidence that Japan influenced its domestic markets to favor Fuji over Kodak. As was shown above, in essence, Kodak claimed that Japan's photographic market and distribution structure denied Kodak fair and equitable market opportunities. Kodak and the United States authorities were arguing that Kodak could not penetrate the Japanese market beyond a certain level due to structural restraints and government intervention that favored Fuji. On the other hand, Fuji and the Japanese government contended that Kodak's lack of success in Japan was due to its own insufficient marketing, management, and investment efforts in the Japanese market.

The debate between Kodak and Fuji illustrates the problems in assessing issues of fairness in international trade. On one hand, Kodak may have had a point: Japan has been historically slow in liberalizing its markets to allow market forces to work. On the other hand, it is hard to understand how Kodak could claim unfair treatment when another American firm, Polaroid, dominates an entire sector of the Japanese photography industry: Polaroid enjoys a 70% market share in Japan for instant photo film. Do you agree with the WTO decision? Is Kodak's Japanese failure a case of denied access or one that is due to Kodak's own inefficiency?

Fuji argued that it has only 12% of the US market share for film and photographic paper sales. This is in line with Kodak's 10% market share in Japan. What, if anything, does the fact that both firms maintain similar market shares in each others' domestic markets prove? Is there some sort of equity or reciprocity at work, since the market shares of the two companies are almost the exact mirror image of each other? Is the Kodak–Fuji WTO Dispute nothing more than a story of two corporations, each of which dominates its home market and finds it difficult to gain market share in its rival's home market, largely due to cultural and historical reasons? Was this a weak case for Kodak to begin with? Or is there more to it? Can it be that the concept of fair trade is a relative one? Or can you make the case that Kodak's failure to succeed in Japan was a result of government barriers to trade and lax enforcement of Japan's antitrust laws, while Fuji's low market shares in the United States were simply the result of the competitive battle?

4.   Once the WTO ruled against Kodak, should American lawmakers have continued the Kodak–Fuji battle by imposing unilateral sanctions on Japan? For example, what if they had capped Fuji's market share, through a system of tariffs, at 10% in order to mirror Kodak's position in Japan? Would any such renewed action have been a legitimate attempt to remedy a trade dispute that has possibly been unfairly settled? Or would it have been viewed from the outside world as just an instance of arbitrary, unilateral US trade policy? What, if anything, can Kodak and the United States now do to help open up the Japanese market?

NOTE ON TELEX AND AT&T

The *Telex*[1] and *AT&T*[2] litigations, during the 1970s and early 1980s, dealt with complex monopolization issues in the context of the enormously important and dynamic computer and telecommunications markets.

1.   *Telex.* During the late 1960s and early 1970s IBM was the world's largest supplier of computers. Organizationally, the center of a computer system is referred to as the central processing unit ("CPU"); other hardware in the system is called "peripheral equipment." This includes memory or storage units, tape drives, disks, printers, etc. and, during the relevant years, constituted 50% to 75% of the total price of a hardware system.

Telex was principally in the business of selling peripheral equipment to owners or lessees of IBM CPUs, and, in the period prior to 1970, was able to offer prices or rentals lower than those offered by IBM. Telex along with its fellow peripheral manufacturers, had, for example, managed to cut IBM's share of the disk market by about 32%. An IBM Management Committee studying the "market erosion" problem estimated that IBM could lose "over one-half of its lease base in the disk drive market and could lose up to 20% of its tape lease business to its competitors." 510 F.2d at 903.

Telex peripheral equipment was compatible with IBM's CPUs, but because of relatively slight differences in design, usually was not compatible with the CPUs of other manufacturers such as Sperry Rand, Burroughs, and Control Data. Similarly, the relatively few peripherals manufactured by Telex and its fellow peripheral manufacturers for interconnection with the systems of full-line companies other than IBM were not compatible for immediate connection with IBM systems.

During the period 1968–71, IBM reacted to the substantial business inroads by Telex and the other peripheral manufacturers. First, it cut its price on certain disk

1.   Telex Corp. v. IBM, 367 F.Supp. 258 (N.D.Okl.1973), reversed per curiam, 510 F.2d 894 (10th Cir.), cert. dism'd, 423 U.S. 802 (1975).

2.   United States v. AT&T, 524 F.Supp. 1331 (D.D.C.1981).

units to a level below that being offered by Telex and other peripheral manufacturers. There was some evidence that at the time IBM cut rates on peripherals, it raised its rates on CPUs in order to recoup lost profits. IBM's prices were not below its own costs, however, and in fact, IBM earned a 20% pretax margin at the lower prices. Telex and the other peripheral manufacturers responded by cutting their own prices below the new IBM levels. Second, IBM offered a series of "long-term" lease plans (for one or two years) which gave customers substantial direct and indirect price concessions, with stiff termination charges to customers who canceled before the end of a lease. Telex and the other peripheral manufacturers had similar lease plans, but at IBM's lowered rental rates they lost considerable business to IBM. Finally, IBM countered increasing competition for "memory" peripherals by integrating the previously separate memory component into the IBM CPU, and by lowering the price of other memory units. IBM justified these actions on grounds that the integrated memory was a technological improvement and that the lowered prices on the memory units still returned to IBM a 20% profit margin.

The parties agreed that the relevant geographic market was the United States. The trial court ruled that the relevant product market was "peripheral equipment plug-compatible to IBM CPUs" and subcategories (*e.g.*, printers, disks, tape drives) of this peripheral equipment. Since IBM manufactured most of the peripheral equipment used in its own systems, this market definition produced market shares for IBM in the 80%–90% range. Relying on *Alcoa* and *Grinnell*, the district court found a violation of Section 2 because IBM had raised prices on CPUs and lowered prices on peripheral products where competition was more intense, and because of the long-term leases with punitive termination provisions which cut into new order rates of plug-compatible competitors. IBM was ordered to pay $259.5 million in treble damages, and a variety of injunctive provisions were imposed, including a requirement that IBM enter into no lease agreement longer than 90 days that included a penalty clause.

The Court of Appeals reversed. As to relevant market, it pointed out that some peripheral equipment not plug-compatible with IBM equipment could easily and cheaply be modified for interconnection. IBM had claimed that the cost of such modification amounted to less than 1% of the product's purchase price. The court also noted that Telex had in fact modified a peripheral unit designed for interconnection with IBM equipment when a marketing opportunity arose for connection with some RCA CPUs.

The Tenth Circuit held:

[R]easonable interchangeability is proven in the case at bar and hence the market should include not only peripheral products plug compatible with IBM CPUs, but all peripheral products, those compatible not only with IBM CPUs but those compatible with non-IBM systems. This is wholly justifiable because the record shows that these products, although not fungible, are fully interchangeable and may be interchanged with minimal financial outlay, and so cross-elasticity exists within meaning of the *DuPont* decision. 510 F.2d at 919.

Insofar as the Tenth Circuit included in the relevant product market peripheral products plug-compatible with systems other than IBM whose interfaces could not easily and cheaply be modified, it apparently did so because IBM's discretion over price was limited by the fact that peripheral equipment comprised the costliest part of a computer hardware system (50% to 75%) and IBM faced competition from its full-line competitors on a system-by-system basis. Compare the Supreme Court's subsequent switching costs discussion in *Kodak*, p. 903 infra.

The Court of Appeals also rejected the trial court's finding that IBM's business conduct represented monopolizing behavior. Citing *Alcoa* and *Grinnell,* the court below had indicated that the applicable rule was that a company with monopoly power violates Section 2 where there is:

> willful acquisition or maintenance of ... [monopoly] power with intent to monopolize, which intent need not be evidenced by predatory practices but which is not to be gathered merely from growth or development as a consequence of a superior product. 510 F.2d at 925.

At another point, the trial court indicated that "it is sufficient that monopoly power is willfully acquired or maintained as distinct from the growth or development as a consequence of a superior product, business acumen or historic accident." 510 F.2d at 925.

The Tenth Circuit found that these tests were inappropriately applied in that the district court failed to take into account two relevant factors—(i) whether or not the acts were ordinary business practices typical of those used in a competitive market; and (ii) whether or not the acts derive from *use* by a monopolist of its power or size. Making the "monopoly thrust upon" defense available only to involuntary conduct would deny to a company achieving monopoly power legally—for example, by research and technological innovations—the ability to defend its market share against inroads by those who market copies of its products. The court indicated that a more expansive view of the "monopoly thrust upon" exception, and the requirement that illegal behavior reflect a "use" of monopoly power, is particularly appropriate where the alleged monopolist has achieved its market position legally, and the charge is that it is maintaining that position by illegal means.

As to IBM's direct and indirect price cuts (including the lease terms), the court noted that these were ordinary business practices and were not exclusively available to IBM because of its monopoly position. The price cuts resulted in prices which were "reasonable in that they yielded a reasonable profit" and at no time were they below IBM's costs. Thus, each of IBM's products stood on its own base and did not rely for marketing on IBM's financial reserves. Finally, the conclusion of the court below that IBM's various marketing maneuvers were "predatory" in that they were specifically aimed at particular challengers was rejected as inconsistent with the record. Apparently because of this finding that IBM's activities were not predatory but simply the actions of a vigorous, aggressive competitor, the Tenth Circuit rejected without discussion the lower court finding of an attempt to monopolize.

In a portion of the opinion not involving antitrust claims, the Court of Appeals affirmed the trial court's award to IBM of damages against Telex for misappropriation of trade secrets, though it reduced the damage award on the counterclaim from almost $22 million to $17.5 million. It also affirmed the award of $1 million as punitive damages.

Telex petitioned the Supreme Court for certiorari, but shortly before the decision on certiorari was to be announced, Telex and IBM settled the case. In return for Telex abandoning its antitrust charges, it was released from any obligation to pay damages under IBM's unfair competition counterclaim.

a. Is the Tenth Circuit's gloss in *Telex* on the definition of monopolizing conduct consistent with the tests in *Grinnell* and *Alcoa?* For example, under the *Telex* approach, would a lease-only policy by a company with monopoly power be legal under Section 2 as long as small companies in the same market followed that practice? Compare the conduct discussions in the *Aspen Skiing* (p. 736 infra) and *Kodak* (pp. 813 and 903 infra) cases.

b. Can a company which legally acquires a patent that turns out to be the basis of monopoly power refuse to license all applicants regardless of terms offered? In SCM Corp. v. Xerox Corp., 463 F.Supp. 983 (D.Conn.1978), affirmed, 645 F.2d 1195 (2d Cir.1981), cert. denied, 455 U.S. 1016 (1982), a rejected applicant sued Xerox for refusing to license patents for the manufacture and sale of plain-paper copiers—that is, machines which allow images to be reproduced on plain paper without the preliminary creation of a "master copy." Chester Carlson, the original inventor of the xerography process, had licensed his patent to Battelle, a nonprofit research organization, and Battelle in a series of agreements had licensed those patents, in return for financing and research help, to Xerox. The key agreement was executed in 1956 and granted Xerox an exclusive license on the Carlson–Battelle patents with no obligation to sublicense. While Xerox had some success in selling early generation plain-paper copiers prior to 1956, its real commercial breakthrough occurred in 1960. Two years earlier—in 1958—IBM had notified Xerox that it was not interested in manufacturing or marketing its machines because they were bad business risks. After 1960, copier sales soared and that led eventually to the creation of a new relevant product market—plain-paper copiers—which the jury found came into existence sometime between 1964 and 1969.

A jury awarded SCM $37.3 million in damages (before trebling) on grounds, among others, that the failure to license by Xerox subsequent to 1956 constituted a violation of Section 2. The trial judge, trying to harmonize the purposes of the patent laws and the antitrust laws, ruled that SCM could not recover damages:

> To deny treble damage liability for a monopolist's unilateral refusal to license patents places no limitation on the utility of the private treble damage action to deter any exclusionary conduct that is not grounded in the very structure of the patent laws. To impose such liability poses a threat to the progress of science and the useful arts not warranted by a reasonable accommodation of the patent and antitrust laws. 463 F.Supp. at 1014.

The Court of Appeals affirmed. It reasoned that while an acquisition by a dominant competitor in a market of a patent affording monopoly power in the same market would violate Section 2, that rule does not apply where the acquisition occurs prior to the commercialization of the patented art and prior to the time that that art had led to the existence of the relevant market itself. SCM had argued that commercial success and the existence of an economic market were reasonably foreseeable at the time the patents were acquired. The Second Circuit accepted the factual assertions, but rejected the argument that such foreseeability should pro-duce a different result:

> ... Xerox contributed in a very substantial way to the development of an automatic plain-paper copier by investing in research and development not only after 1956 but also for almost a decade before the agreement. Moreover, the party from whom Xerox purchased the patent under the 1956 agreement was not a potential competitor. We believe that, under the circumstances presented here, to impose antitrust liability upon Xerox would severely trample upon the incentives provided by our patent laws and thus undermine the entire patent system. Therefore ... Xerox was lawfully entitled to purchase the patents it did pursuant to the agreement it made with Battelle [in 1956].

With respect to Xerox's subsequent unilateral refusal to license the Carlson and Battelle patents, which we have held were lawfully acquired, that conduct was permissible under the patent laws and, therefore, did not give rise to any liability under § 2. 645 F.2d at 1209.[3]

c.   In United States v. Standard Oil Co. of California, 362 F.Supp. 1331 (N.D.Cal.1972), affirmed, 412 U.S. 924 (1973), a conspiracy to monopolize in violation of Section 2 was found where a dominant company entered into long-term supply contracts with key customers which operated to preclude entry by potential rivals. Socal was "virtually the only supplier and distributor of petroleum products in the territory of American Samoa," selling diesel fuel, aviation gasoline and jet fuel, gasoline, and other petroleum products. It entered into 10–year requirements contracts with certain large customers, including the two largest tuna canners and processors in Samoa, calling for delivery of from 60% to 100% of operational requirements of petroleum products. As a result, it supplied 100% of the fuel for all tuna fleets operating in the area, preventing competitors from obtaining a commercial foothold in the market. The requirements contracts were found to be illegal under Section 3 and to be part of a conspiracy to monopolize distribution and sale of petroleum products in American Samoa. Why were IBM's long-term lease plans, with their stiff termination charges, less vulnerable than the Socal supply contracts?

d.   In *Alcoa,* p. 130 supra, Judge Hand justified a tough antimonopoly rule for political as well as economic reasons. He wrote:

> [Congress] did not condone "good trusts" and condemn "bad" ones; it forbad all. Moreover, in so doing it was not necessarily actuated by economic motives alone. It is possible, because of its indirect social or moral effect, to prefer a system of small producers, each dependent for his success upon his own skill and character, to one in which the great mass of those engaged must accept the direction of a few. 148 F.2d at 427.

Most monopoly opinions, like the Tenth Circuit's *Telex* opinion, address Section 2 issues exclusively in economic terms. If you wanted to introduce considerations like those described by Judge Hand into the question of defining predation or exclusionary behavior, how would you do it? Is it true, as economically oriented critics often charge, that the *Alcoa* language reflects nothing more than a political prejudice against big business?

2.   *AT&T.*[4] The government charged that AT&T, and two of its subsidiaries, the Western Electric Company (Western) and Bell Telephone Laboratories, Inc. (Bell Labs), had monopolized various telecommunications markets in the United States. Twenty-two Bell operating companies (BOCs) which operate local telephone facilities were named as co-conspirators. The government essentially identified three relevant product markets: (1) local telecommunications service; (2) intercity telecommunication service (long-distance lines, WATS lines, telex service, etc.); and (3) telecommunications equipment. Defendants did not seriously challenge the contention that they possessed monopoly power in the first two markets.

In the various proposed relevant markets, the government alleged four major lines of monopolizing conduct:

---

3.   See Data General Corp. v. Grumman Systems Support Corp., 36 F.3d 1147 (1st Cir.1994); for important further discussion of recent anticompetitive issues raised in the context of patents, copyrights, and other forms of intellectual property, see pp. 812–31 infra.

4.   United States v. AT&T, 524 F.Supp. 1331 (D.D.C.1981).

a. *Unreasonable interference with interconnection by customer-provided equipment.* In 1968, the FCC held in the *Carterfone* decision, 13 F.C.C.2d 420 (1968), that AT&T could only prevent connection of privately owned equipment with its system if use of the devices would actually cause harm to the system, and it was authorized to establish "reasonable standards to be met by interconnection devices." AT&T then filed a tariff providing that equipment could be connected only through a protective connecting arrangement (PCA) leased to customers for a fee by the Bell System.

The government alleged that Bell unreasonably prevented interconnection with its local monopoly systems in order to preserve its monopoly in the supply of telecommunications equipment. Government evidence indicated that PCAs were unnecessary, that they were "over-engineered" so that their cost made it difficult for independent manufacturers to compete with Western, and that they were often unavailable, incompatible with non-Bell equipment, or slow to be delivered. The court appeared to accept that a PCA requirement would not have been anticompetitive if necessary to protect the quality of service of the network, but concluded that the government's evidence of intentional impairment of interconnection opportunity was adequate to bar a motion to dismiss.

b. *Unreasonable prevention of interconnection by competitive long-distance services.* It was assumed that the Bell System (with the BOCs) had monopoly power with respect to local telecommunications services. This was regarded by the court as an "essential facility" or "strategic bottleneck"—citing, *inter alia, Terminal Railways* (p. 379 supra) and *Otter Tail* (p. 735 infra)—so that failure to make access to that facility available to competitors on fair and reasonable terms, with the result that AT & T's Long Lines long-distance monopoly was maintained, would be an antitrust violation. The government offered a variety of evidence of this alleged arbitrary policy. For example, AT & T was alleged to have priced access to its local monopoly services discriminatorily when long-distance competitors were involved, and to have negotiated in bad faith, stringing competitors along for groundless reasons. It was also alleged to have been slow to implement FCC decisions authorizing interconnection by intercity competitors.

On the question of what standards should govern access to essential facilities, the government argued that the Bell System is required to afford interconnections to non-Bell carriers on terms of "parity," while defendants contended that they need make those facilities available only on a "reasonable basis." The court concluded that problems of feasibility and practicability might be taken into account, and that therefore absolute parity was not essential. Nevertheless, the court did not dismiss the government's charge since there was adequate evidence of unreasonable and discriminatory treatment of non-Bell carriers with regard to access to the BOC facilities.

c. *Intercity pricing.* The government charged that the Bell System set prices high with respect to services where it had no competition, and low, though not necessarily below cost, in product line areas where it faced competition, in order to exclude existing competition and deter entry. Specifically, the government contended that Bell priced "without regard to their costs" and indeed did not even accurately calculate costs.

Defendants argued that prices above average variable cost are presumptively legal, but the court rejected that contention on the following grounds: (1) the cases have not established that a relationship between price and marginal or average variable cost is the sole criterion in identifying predatory pricing; (2) predation through cross-subsidization of product lines, even in the absence of the "low cost" pricing, is particularly likely to occur, and is particularly in need of regulation, where the alleged predator (as here) is a multi-product firm subject to rate-of-return regulation; and (3) the government's novel "pricing in disregard of cost" theory is warranted by the uniqueness of AT&T and the fact that its cost data are "apparently impenetrable even to its own regulators."

If that theory resulted in a shift of burden of proof to AT&T to establish that their prices were reasonable, the court concluded, that would not necessarily be an unacceptable result. For a further discussion of predatory price cutting, see Section 2 infra.

d. *Bell procurement of equipment.* The government claimed that the BOCs, as a result of Bell System stock control, exhibited a bias towards purchasing equipment from Western. This was implemented through joint establishment of technical standards which favored Western, counseling of the BOCs in their procurement decisions, and pursuing crash programs to develop Western products to meet competition so that the BOCs could buy within the corporate family.

On the government's allegation that Bell failed to release technical data or compatibility specifications, defendants cited *Berkey* (p. 143 supra) in support of the argument that no such disclosure was required by the antitrust laws. The court distinguished *Berkey* on two grounds: first, that the entity in *Berkey* failing to disclose information to the industry was different from the buyers of the service to whom the information was useful (in this case AT&T both refuses to release the information and purchases the equipment which cannot be properly designed without it) and, second, that the inability to obtain technical information/compatibility data was an absolute barrier to entry, and not just an additional inconvenience or expense as was the case in *Berkey*. The court concluded that the evidence sustained the government's contentions, and observed that the "burden is on defendants to refute the factual showings made in the government's case-in-chief."

About four months later, the government and AT&T entered into a settlement providing, among other things, that AT&T divest itself completely of BOCs.

———

OTTER TAIL POWER CO. v. UNITED STATES, 410 U.S. 366, 93 S.Ct. 1022, 35 L.Ed.2d 359 (1973). In an action under § 2 of the Sherman Act against Otter Tail Power Company, the following facts were shown:

Otter Tail sold electric power at retail in 465 towns in Minnesota, North Dakota and South Dakota. There also were 45 towns in its territory served by municipal systems. Where Otter Tail provided service, it did so pursuant to municipally granted franchises, which were limited to from 10 to 20 years. When such franchises expired in various towns served by Otter Tail, proposals sometimes were made to supplant Otter Tail with municipal systems. However, the municipal systems required a source of power and, when requested to sell power at wholesale to municipal systems, Otter Tail refused. Otter Tail also refused to transfer power to the municipalities from other wholesaler suppliers over its lines. The results were as follows: Colman and Aurora, two towns in South Dakota, had access to transmission facilities not controlled by Otter Tail and were able to proceed despite Otter Tail's actions. Elbow Lake, Minnesota, constructed its own generating plant. But Hankinson, North Dakota, without access to other transmission facilities, renewed Otter Tail's retail franchise.

Each town in Otter Tail's territory generally could accommodate only one distribution system, making each such town a "natural monopoly" market for the sale and distribution of electric power at retail. Competition for the right to serve an entire retail market within the limits of a particular town generally was between Otter Tail and a prospective or existing municipal system. Between 1947 and 1970, Otter Tail acquired six municipal systems. In 12 towns, including the four mentioned above, there were contests between Otter Tail and a proposed municipal system, and in only three of these—Aurora, Elbow Lake, and Colman—were municipal systems established. In many areas of its territory, the only transmission lines available were those of Otter Tail, and the latter refused to sell or transfer power to municipal systems despite the absence of engineering or capacity obstacles to such sale or transfer. Otter Tail's position was that development of municipal systems would so erode the earnings it derived from selling electric power at retail that the viability of its total operation would be jeopardized.

Otter Tail obtained some of its power from the Bureau of Reclamation. When towns such as Elbow Lake and Hankinson requested the Bureau of Reclamation and various electric cooperatives to furnish them with wholesale power, the latter were willing to supply it; but Otter Tail refused to "wheel" the power, relying on provisions in its contracts which barred the use of its lines for wheeling power to towns which it served at retail.

The Supreme Court held that Otter Tail's conduct violated § 2 of the Sherman Act, and was not immunized from antitrust prosecution by the regulatory provisions of the Federal Power Act.

... The District Court determined that Otter Tail has "a strategic dominance in the transmission of power in most of its service area" and that it used this dominance to foreclose potential entrants into the retail arena from obtaining electric power from outside sources of supply.... Use of monopoly power "to destroy threatened competition" is a violation of the "attempt to monopolize" clause of § 2 of the Sherman Act.... There were no engineering factors that prevented Otter Tail from selling power at wholesale to those towns that wanted municipal plants nor wheeling the power. The District Court found—and its findings are supported—that Otter Tail's refusals to sell at wholesale or to wheel were solely to prevent municipal power systems from eroding its monopolistic position.

Otter Tail's wheeling contracts with the Bureau of Reclamation were held unlawful as "territorial allocation schemes," denying defendant's competitors access to fenced-off markets. Otter Tail's argument that its overall system would go downhill if more and more municipalities turned to public power was rejected; the Sherman Act "assumes that an enterprise will protect itself against loss by operating with superior service, lower costs, and improved efficiency. Otter Tail's theory collides with the Sherman Act as it sought to substitute for competition anticompetitive uses of its dominant economic power." However, the Court also observed that Otter Tail's pessimistic "erosion study" was not supported by the record, and that Bureau of Reclamation power was not a serious threat to Otter Tail.

Aspen Skiing Co. v. Aspen Highlands Skiing Corp.

Supreme Court of the United States, 1985.
472 U.S. 585, 105 S.Ct. 2847, 86 L.Ed.2d 467.

■ STEVENS, J.... In a private treble damages action, the jury found that petitioner Aspen Skiing Company (Ski Co.) had monopolized the market for downhill skiing services in Aspen, Colorado. The question presented is whether that finding is erroneous as a matter of law because it rests on an assumption that a firm with monopoly power has a duty to cooperate with its smaller rivals in a marketing arrangement in order to avoid violating § 2 of the Sherman Act.

I

Aspen is a destination ski resort with a reputation for "super powder," "a wide range of runs," and an "active night life," including "some of the best restaurants in North America." Between 1945 and 1960, private investors independently developed three major facilities for downhill skiing: Aspen Mountain (Ajax), Aspen Highlands (Highlands), and Buttermilk. A fourth mountain, Snowmass, opened in 1967.

The development of any major additional facilities is hindered by practical considerations and regulatory obstacles. The identification of appropriate topographical conditions for a new site and substantial financing are both essential. Most of the terrain in the vicinity of Aspen that is suitable for downhill skiing cannot be used for that purpose without the approval of the United States Forest Service. That approval is contingent, in part, on environmental concerns. Moreover, the county government must also approve the project, and in recent years it has followed a policy of limiting growth.

Between 1958 and 1964, three independent companies operated Ajax, Highlands, and Buttermilk. In the early years, each company offered its own day or half-day tickets for use of its mountain. In 1962, however, the three competitors also introduced an interchangeable ticket.[5] The 6–day, all-Aspen ticket provided convenience to the vast majority of skiers who visited the resort for weekly periods, but preferred to remain flexible about what mountain they might ski each day during the visit. It also emphasized the unusual variety in ski mountains available in Aspen.

As initially designed, the all-Aspen ticket program consisted of booklets containing six coupons, each redeemable for a daily lift ticket at Ajax, Highlands, or Buttermilk. The price of the booklet was often discounted from the price of six daily tickets, but all six coupons had to be used within a limited period of time—seven days, for example. The revenues from the sale of the 3area coupon books were distributed in accordance with the number of coupons collected at each mountain.

In 1964, Buttermilk was purchased by Ski Co., but the interchangeable ticket program continued. In most seasons after it acquired Buttermilk, Ski Co. offered 2–area, 6–or 7–day tickets featuring Ajax and Buttermilk in competition with the 3–area, 6–coupon booklet. Although it sold briskly,

5. Friedl Pfeiffer, one of the developers of Buttermilk, initiated the idea of an all-Aspen ticket at a luncheon with the owner of Highlands and the President of Ski Co. Pfeiffer, a native of Austria, informed his competitors that " '[i]n St. Anton, we have a mountain that has three different lift companies—lifts owned by three different lift companies ... We sell a ticket that is interchangeable.' It was good on any of those lifts; and he said, 'I think we should do the same thing here.' " Id., at 153.

the all-Aspen ticket did not sell as well as Ski Co.'s multi-area ticket until Ski Co. opened Snowmass in 1967. Thereafter, the all-Aspen coupon booklet began to outsell Ski Co.'s ticket featuring only its mountains.

In the 1971–1972 season, the coupon booklets were discontinued and an "around the neck" all-Aspen ticket was developed. This refinement on the interchangeable ticket was advantageous to the skier, who no longer found it necessary to visit the ticket window every morning before gaining access to the slopes. Lift operators at Highlands monitored usage of the ticket in the 1971–1972 season by recording the ticket numbers of persons going onto the slopes of that mountain. Highlands officials periodically met with Ski Co. officials to review the figures recorded at Highlands, and to distribute revenues based on that count.

There was some concern that usage of the all-Aspen ticket should be monitored by a more scientific method than the one used in the 1971–1972 season. After a one-season absence, the 4–area ticket returned in the 1973–1974 season with a new method of allocating revenues based on usage. Like the 1971–1972 ticket, the 1973–1974 4–area ticket consisted of a badge worn around the skier's neck. Lift operators punched the ticket when the skier first sought access to the mountain each day. A random-sample survey was commissioned to determine how many skiers with the 4–area ticket used each mountain, and the parties allocated revenues from the ticket sales in accordance with the survey's results.

In the next four seasons, Ski Co. and Highlands used such surveys to allocate the revenues from the 4–area, 6–day ticket. Highlands' share of the revenues from the ticket was 17.5% in 1973–1974, 18.5% in 1974–1975, 16.8% in 1975–1976, and 13.2% in 1976–1977.[6] During these four seasons, Ski Co. did not offer its own 3–area, multi-day ticket in competition with the all-Aspen ticket.[7] By 1977, multi-area tickets accounted for nearly 35% of the total market. Holders of multi-area passes also accounted for additional daily ticket sales to persons skiing with them.

Between 1962 and 1977, Ski Co. and Highlands had independently offered various mixes of 1–day, 3–day and 6–day passes at their own mountains.[8] In every season except one, however, they had also offered some form of all-Aspen, 6–day ticket, and divided the revenues from those sales on the basis of usage. Nevertheless, for the 1977–1978 season, Ski Co.

6. Highlands' share of the total market during those seasons, as measured in skier visits was 15.8% in 1973–1974, 17.1% in 1974–1975, 17.4% in 1975–1976, and 20.5% in 1976–1977.

7. In 1975, the Colorado Attorney General filed a complaint against Ski Co. and Highlands alleging, in part, that the negotiations over the 4–area ticket had provided them with a forum for price-fixing in violation of § 1 of the Sherman Act and that they had attempted to monopolize the market for downhill skiing services in Aspen in violation

of § 2. Record Ex. X. In 1977, the case was settled by a consent decree that permitted the parties to continue to offer the 4–area ticket provided that they set their own ticket prices unilaterally before negotiating its terms. Tr. 229–231.

8. About 15–20% of each company's ticket revenues were derived from sales to tour operators at a wholesale discount of 10–15%, while 80–85% of the ticket revenues were derived from sales to skiers in Aspen.

offered to continue the all-Aspen ticket only if Highlands would accept a 13.2% fixed share of the ticket's revenues.

Although that had been Highlands' share of the ticket revenues in 1976–1977, Highlands contended that that season was an inaccurate measure of its market performance since it had been marked by unfavorable weather and an unusually low number of visiting skiers. Moreover, Highlands wanted to continue to divide revenues on the basis of actual usage, as that method of distribution allowed it to compete for the daily loyalties of the skiers who had purchased the tickets. Fearing that the alternative might be no interchangeable ticket at all, and hoping to persuade Ski Co. to reinstate the usage division of revenues, Highlands eventually accepted a fixed percentage of 15% for the 1977–1978 season. No survey was made during that season of actual usage of the 4–area ticket at the two competitors' mountains.

In the 1970s the management of Ski Co. increasingly expressed their dislike for the all-Aspen ticket. They complained that a coupon method of monitoring usage was administratively cumbersome. They doubted the accuracy of the survey and decried the "appearance, deportment, [and] attitude" of the college students who were conducting it. In addition, Ski Co.'s President had expressed the view that the 4–area ticket was siphoning off revenues that could be recaptured by Ski Co. if the ticket was discontinued. In fact, Ski Co. had reinstated its 3–area, 6–day ticket during the 1977–1978 season, but that ticket had been outsold by the 4–area, 6–day ticket nearly two to one.

In March 1978, the Ski Co. management recommended to the Board of Directors that the 4–area ticket be discontinued for the 1978–1979 season. The Board decided to offer Highlands a 4–area ticket provided that Highlands would agree to receive a 12.5% fixed percentage of the revenue—considerably below Highlands' historical average based on usage. Later in the 1978–1979 season, a member of Ski Co.'s Board of Directors candidly informed a Highlands official that he had advocated making Highlands "an offer that [it] could not accept."

Finding the proposal unacceptable, Highlands suggested a distribution of the revenues based on usage to be monitored by coupons, electronic counting or random sample surveys. If Ski Co. was concerned about who was to conduct the survey, Highlands proposed to hire disinterested ticket counters at its own expense-" somebody like Price Waterhouse"—to count or survey usage of the 4–area ticket at Highlands. Ski Co. refused to consider any counterproposals, and Highlands finally rejected the offer of the fixed percentage.

As far as Ski Co. was concerned, the all-Aspen ticket was dead. In its place Ski Co. offered the 3–area, 6–day ticket featuring only its mountains. In an effort to promote this ticket, Ski Co. embarked on a national advertising campaign that strongly implied to people who were unfamiliar with Aspen that Ajax, Buttermilk, and Snowmass were the only ski mountains in the area. For example, Ski Co. had a sign changed in the Aspen Airways waiting room at Stapleton Airport in Denver. The old sign had a picture of the four mountains in Aspen touting "Four Big Mountains" whereas the new sign retained the picture but referred only to three.

Ski Co. took additional actions that made it extremely difficult for Highlands to market its own multi-area package to replace the joint offering. Ski Co. discontinued the 3–day, 3–area pass for the 1978–1979 season,[9] and also refused to sell Highlands any lift tickets, either at the tour operator's discount or at retail.[10] Highlands finally developed an alternative product, the "Adventure Pack," which consisted of a 3–day pass at Highlands and three vouchers, each equal to the price of a daily lift ticket at a Ski Co. mountain. The vouchers were guaranteed by funds on deposit in an Aspen bank, and were redeemed by Aspen merchants at full value. Ski Co., however, refused to accept them.

Later, Highlands redesigned the Adventure Pack to contain American Express Traveler's checks or money orders instead of vouchers. Ski Co. eventually accepted these negotiable instruments in exchange for daily lift tickets.[11] Despite some strengths of the product, the Adventure Pack met considerable resistance from tour operators and consumers who had grown accustomed to the convenience and flexibility provided by the all-Aspen ticket.

Without a convenient all-Aspen ticket, Highlands basically "becomes a day ski area in a destination resort." Highlands' share of the market for downhill skiing services in Aspen declined steadily after the 4–area ticket based on usage was abolished in 1977: from 20.5% in 1976–1977, to 15.7% in 1977–1978, to 13.1% in 1978–1979, to 12.5% in 1979–1980, to 11% in 1980–1981.[12] Highlands' revenues from associated skiing services like the ski school, ski rentals, amateur racing events, and restaurant facilities declined sharply as well.

9. Highlands' owner explained that there was a key difference between the 3–day, 3–area ticket and the 6–day, 3–area ticket: "with the three day ticket, a person could ski on the ... Aspen Skiing Corporation mountains for three days and then there would be three days in which he could ski on our mountain; but with the six-day ticket, we are absolutely locked out of those people." As a result of "tremendous consumer demand" for a 3–day ticket, Ski Co. reinstated it late in the 1978–1979 season, but without publicity or a discount off the daily rate. Id., at 622.

10. In the 1977–1978 negotiations, Ski Co. previously had refused to consider the sale of any tickets to Highlands noting that it was "obviously not interested in helping sell" a package competitive with the 3–area ticket. Later, in the 1978–1979 negotiations, Ski Co.'s Vice President of Finance told a Highlands official that "We will not have anything to do with a four-area ticket sponsored by the Aspen Highlands Skiing Corporation." When the Highlands official inquired why Ski Co. was taking this position considering that Highlands was willing to pay full retail value for the daily lift tickets, the Ski Co. official answered tersely: "we will not support our competition."

11. Of course, there was nothing to identify Highlands as the source of these instruments, unless someone saw the skier "taking it out of an Adventure Pack envelope." Id., at 505. For the 1981–1982 season, Ski Co. set its single ticket price at $22 and discounted the 3–area, 6–day ticket to $114. According to Highlands, this price structure made the Adventure Pack unprofitable.

12. In these seasons, Buttermilk Mountain, in particular, substantially increased its market share at the expense of Highlands.

II

In 1979, Highlands filed a complaint in the United States District Court for the District of Colorado naming Ski Co. as a defendant. Among various claims, the complaint alleged that Ski Co. had monopolized the market for downhill skiing services at Aspen in violation of § 2 of the Sherman Act, and prayed for treble damages. The case was tried to a jury which rendered a verdict finding Ski Co. guilty of the § 2 violation and calculating Highlands' actual damages at $2.5 million.

In her instructions to the jury, the District Judge explained that the offense of monopolization under § 2 of the Sherman Act has two elements: (1) the possession of monopoly power in a relevant market, and (2) the willful acquisition, maintenance, or use of that power by anticompetitive or exclusionary means or for anticompetitive or exclusionary purposes.[13] Although the first element was vigorously disputed at the trial and in the Court of Appeals, in this Court Ski Co. does not challenge the jury's special verdict finding that it possessed monopoly power.[14] Nor does Ski Co. criticize the trial court's instructions to the jury concerning the second element of the § 2 offense.

On this element, the jury was instructed that it had to consider whether "Aspen Skiing Corporation willfully acquired, maintained, or used that power by anti-competitive or exclusionary means or for anti-competitive or exclusionary purposes." The instructions elaborated:

"In considering whether the means or purposes were anti-competitive or exclusionary, you must draw a distinction here between practices which tend to exclude or restrict competition on the one hand and the success of a business which reflects only a superior product, a well-run business, or luck, on the other. The line between legitimately gained monopoly, its proper use and maintenance, and improper conduct has been described in various ways. It has been said that obtaining or maintaining monopoly power cannot represent monopolization if the power was gained and maintained by conduct that was honestly industrial. Or it is said that monopoly power which is thrust upon a firm due to its superior business ability and efficiency does not constitute monopolization.

"For example, a firm that has lawfully acquired a monopoly position is not barred from taking advantage of scale economies by constructing a large and efficient factory. These benefits are a consequence of size and not

13. In United States v. Grinnell Corp., 384 U.S. 563, 570–571 (1966), we explained:

"The offense of monopoly under § 2 of the Sherman Act has two elements: (1) the possession of monopoly power in the relevant market and (2) the willful acquisition or maintenance of that power as distinguished from growth or development as a consequence of a superior product, business acumen, or historic accident."

14. The jury found that the relevant product market was "[d]ownhill skiing at destination ski resorts," that the "Aspen area" was a relevant geographic submarket, and that during the years 1977–1981, Ski Co. possessed monopoly power, defined as the power to control prices in the relevant market or to exclude competitors.

an exercise of monopoly power. Nor is a corporation which possesses monopoly power under a duty to cooperate with its business rivals. Also a company which possesses monopoly power and which refuses to enter into a joint operating agreement with a competitor or otherwise refuses to deal with a competitor in some manner does not violate Section 2 if valid business reasons exist for that refusal.

"In other words, if there were legitimate business reasons for the refusal, then the defendant, even if he is found to possess monopoly power in a relevant market, has not violated the law. We are concerned with conduct which unnecessarily excludes or handicaps competitors. This is conduct which does not benefit consumers by making a better product or service available—or in other ways—and instead has the effect of impairing competition.

"To sum up, you must determine whether Aspen Skiing Corporation gained, maintained, or used monopoly power in a relevant market by arrangements and policies which rather than being a consequence of a superior product, superior business sense, or historic element, were designed primarily to further any domination of the relevant market or submarket." Id., at 181–182.

The jury answered a specific interrogatory finding the second element of the offense as defined in these instructions.[15]

Ski Co. filed a motion for judgment notwithstanding the verdict, contending that the evidence was insufficient to support a § 2 violation as a matter of law. In support of that motion, Ski Co. incorporated the arguments that it had advanced in support of its motion for a directed verdict, at which time it had primarily contested the sufficiency of the evidence on the issue of monopoly power. Counsel had, however, in the course of the argument at that time, stated: "Now, we also think, Judge, that there clearly cannot be a requirement of cooperation between competitors."[16] The

15. It answered this interrogatory affirmatively:

"Willful Acquisition, Maintenance or Use of Monopoly Power: Do you find by a preponderance of the evidence that the defendants willfully acquired, maintained or used monopoly power by anticompetitive or exclusionary means or for anticompetitive or exclusionary purposes, rather than primarily as a consequence of a superior product, superior business sense, or historic accident?"

16. Counsel also appears to have argued that it was under a legal obligation to refuse to participate in any joint marketing arrangement with Highlands:

"Aspen Skiing Corporation is required to compete. It is required to make

independent decisions. It is required to price its own product. It is required to make its own determination of the ticket that it chooses to offer and the tickets that it chooses not to offer." Tr. 1454.

In this Court, Ski Co. does not question the validity of the joint marketing arrangement under § 1 of the Sherman Act. Thus, we have no occasion to consider the circumstances that might permit such combinations in the skiing industry. See generally NCAA v. Board of Regents of Univ. of Okla., 468 U.S. 85, 113–115 (1984); Broadcast Music, Inc. v. CBS, 441 U.S. 1, 18–23 (1979); Continental T.V., Inc. v. GTE Sylvania, Inc., 433 U.S. 36, 51–57 (1977).

District Court denied Ski Co.'s motion and entered a judgment awarding Highlands treble damages of $7,500,000, costs and attorney's fees.[17]

The Court of Appeals affirmed in all respects. 738 F.2d 1509 (C.A.10 1984). The court advanced two reasons for rejecting Ski Co.'s argument that " 'there was insufficient evidence to present a jury issue of monopolization because, as a matter of law, the conduct at issue was pro-competitive conduct that a monopolist could lawfully engage in.' " First, relying on United States v. Terminal Railroad Assn. of St. Louis, 224 U.S. 383 (1912), the Court of Appeals held that the multi-day, multi-area ticket could be characterized as an "essential facility" that Ski Co. had a duty to market jointly with Highlands. Second, it held that there was sufficient evidence to support a finding that Ski Co.'s intent in refusing to market the 4–area ticket, "considered together with its other conduct," was to create or maintain a monopoly. Id., at 1522.

In its review of the evidence on the question of intent, the Court of Appeals considered the record "as a whole" and concluded that it was not necessary for Highlands to prove that each allegedly anticompetitive act was itself sufficient to demonstrate an abuse of monopoly power. Id., at 1522, n. 18.[18] The court noted that by "refusing to cooperate" with Highlands, Ski Co. "became the only business in Aspen that could offer a multi-day multi-mountain skiing experience;" that the refusal to offer a 4–mountain ticket resulted in "skiers' frustration over its unavailability;" that there was apparently no valid business reason for refusing to accept the coupons in Highlands' Adventure Pack; and that after Highlands had modified its Adventure Pack to meet Ski Co.'s objections, Ski Co. had increased its single ticket price to $22 "thereby making it unprofitable . . . to market [the] Adventure Pack." Id., at 1522. In reviewing Ski Co.'s argument that it was entitled to a directed verdict, the Court of Appeals assumed that the jury had resolved all contested questions of fact in Highlands' favor.

III

In this Court, Ski Co. contends that even a firm with monopoly power has no duty to engage in joint marketing with a competitor, that a violation of § 2 cannot be established without evidence of substantial exclusionary conduct, and that none of its activities can be characterized as exclusionary. It also contends that the Court of Appeals incorrectly relied on the "essential facilities" doctrine and that an "anticompetitive intent" does not transform nonexclusionary conduct into monopolization. In response, High-

---

17. The District Court also entered an injunction requiring the parties to offer jointly a 4–area, 6–out-of-7 day coupon booklet substantially identical to the "Ski the Summit" booklet accepted by Ski Co. at its Breckenridge resort in Summit County, Colorado. The injunction was initially for a 30–month period, but was later extended through the 1984–1985 season by stipulation of the parties. Highlands represents that "it will not seek an extension of the injunction." No question is raised concerning the character of the injunctive relief ordered by the District Court.

18. See Continental Ore Co. v. Union Carbide & Carbon Corp., 370 U.S. 690, 699 (1962); Associated Press v. United States, 326 U.S. 1, 14 (1945).

lands submits that, given the evidence in the record, it is not necessary to rely on the "essential facilities" doctrine in order to affirm the judgment.

"The central message of the Sherman Act is that a business entity must find new customers and higher profits through internal expansion—that is, by competing successfully rather than by arranging treaties with its competitors." United States v. Citizens & Southern National Bank, 422 U.S. 86, 116 (1975). Ski Co., therefore, is surely correct in submitting that even a firm with monopoly power has no general duty to engage in a joint marketing program with a competitor. Ski Co. is quite wrong, however, in suggesting that the judgment in this case rests on any such proposition of law. For the trial court unambiguously instructed the jury that a firm possessing monopoly power has no duty to cooperate with its business rivals.

The absence of an unqualified duty to cooperate does not mean that every time a firm declines to participate in a particular cooperative venture, that decision may not have evidentiary significance, or that it may not give rise to liability in certain circumstances. The absence of a duty to transact business with another firm is, in some respects, merely the counterpart of the independent businessman's cherished right to select his customers and his associates. The high value that we have placed on the right to refuse to deal with other firms does not mean that the right is unqualified.[19]

In Lorain Journal v. United States, 342 U.S. 143 (1951), we squarely held that this right was not unqualified. Between 1933 and 1948 the publisher of the Lorain Journal, a newspaper, was the only local business disseminating news and advertising in that Ohio town. In 1948, a small radio station was established in a nearby community. In an effort to destroy its small competitor, and thereby regain its "pre–1948 substantial monopoly over the mass dissemination of all news and advertising," the Journal refused to sell advertising to persons that patronized the radio station.

In holding that this conduct violated § 2 of the Sherman Act, the Court dispatched the same argument raised by the monopolist here:

> "The publisher claims a right as a private business concern to select its customers and to refuse to accept advertisements from whomever it pleases. We do not dispute that general right. 'But the word 'right' is one of the most deceptive of pitfalls; it is so easy to slip from a qualified meaning in the premise to an unqualified one in the conclusion. Most rights are qualified.' American Bank & Trust Co. v. Federal Bank, 256 U.S. 350, 358. The right claimed by the publisher is neither absolute nor exempt from regulation. Its exercise as a purposeful means of monopolizing interstate commerce is prohibited by the Sherman Act. The operator of the radio

---

19. Under § 1 of the Sherman Act, a business "generally has a right to deal, or refuse to deal, with whomever it likes, as long as it does so independently." Monsanto Co. v. Spray–Rite Service Corp., 465 U.S. 752, 761 (1984); United States v. Colgate & Co., 250 U.S. 300, 307 (1919).

station, equally with the publisher of the newspaper, is entitled to the protection of that Act. *'In the absence of any purpose to create or maintain a monopoly,* the act does not restrict the long recognized right of trader or manufacturer engaged in an entirely private business, freely to exercise his own independent discretion as to parties with whom he will deal.' (Emphasis supplied.) United States v. Colgate & Co., 250 U.S. 300, 307. See Associated Press v. United States, 326 U.S. 1, 15; United States v. Bausch & Lomb Co., 321 U.S. 707, 721–723." 342 U.S., at 155.

The Court approved the entry of an injunction ordering the Journal to print the advertisements of the customers of its small competitor.

In *Lorain Journal,* the violation of § 2 was an "attempt to monopolize," rather than monopolization, but the question of intent is relevant to both offenses. In the former case it is necessary to prove a "specific intent" to accomplish the forbidden objective—as Judge Hand explained, "an intent which goes beyond the mere intent to do the act." United States v. Aluminum Co. of America, 148 F.2d 416, 432 (C.A.2 1945). In the latter case evidence of intent is merely relevant to the question whether the challenged conduct is fairly characterized as "exclusionary" or "anticompetitive"—to use the words in the trial court's instructions—or "predatory," to use a word that scholars seem to favor. Whichever label is used, there is agreement on the proposition that "no monopolist monopolizes unconscious of what he is doing."[20] As Judge Bork stated more recently: "Improper exclusion (exclusion not the result of superior efficiency) is always deliberately intended."[21]

The qualification on the right of a monopolist to deal with whom he pleases is not so narrow that it encompasses no more than the circumstances of *Lorain Journal.* In the actual case that we must decide, the monopolist did not merely reject a novel offer to participate in a cooperative venture that had been proposed by a competitor. Rather, the monopolist elected to make an important change in a pattern of distribution that had originated in a competitive market and had persisted for several years. The all-Aspen, 6–day ticket with revenues allocated on the basis of usage was first developed when three independent companies operated three different ski mountains in the Aspen area. It continued to provide a desirable option for skiers when the market was enlarged to include four mountains, and when the character of the market was changed by Ski Co.'s acquisition of monopoly power. Moreover, since the record discloses that interchangeable tickets are used in other multi-mountain areas which apparently are

20. "In order to fall within § 2, the monopolist must have both the power to monopolize, and the intent to monopolize. To read the passage as demanding any 'specific' intent, makes nonsense of it, for no monopolist monopolizes unconscious of what he is doing. So here, 'Alcoa' meant to keep, and did keep, that complete and exclusive hold upon the ingot market with which it started. That was to 'monopolize' that market, however innocently it otherwise proceeded." United States v. Aluminum Co. of America, 148 F.2d at 432.

21. R. Bork, The Antitrust Paradox 160 (1978) (hereinafter Bork).

competitive, it seems appropriate to infer that such tickets satisfy consumer demand in free competitive markets.

Ski Co.'s decision to terminate the all-Aspen ticket was thus a decision by a monopolist to make an important change in the character of the market.[22] Such a decision is not necessarily anticompetitive, and Ski Co. contends that neither its decision, nor the conduct in which it engaged to implement that decision, can fairly be characterized as exclusionary in this case. It recognizes, however, that as the case is presented to us, we must interpret the entire record in the light most favorable to Highlands and give to it the benefit of all inferences which the evidence fairly supports, even though contrary inferences might reasonably be drawn.

Moreover, we must assume that the jury followed the court's instructions. The jury must, therefore, have drawn a distinction "between practices which tend to exclude or restrict competition on the one hand, and the success of a business which reflects only a superior product, a well-run business, or luck, on the other." Since the jury was unambiguously instructed that Ski Co.'s refusal to deal with Highlands "does not violate § 2 if valid business reasons exist for that refusal," we must assume that the jury concluded that there were no valid business reasons for the refusal. The question then is whether that conclusion finds support in the record.

IV

The question whether Ski Co.'s conduct may properly be characterized as exclusionary cannot be answered by simply considering its effect on Highlands. In addition, it is relevant to consider its impact on consumers and whether it has impaired competition in an unnecessarily restrictive way.[23] If a firm has been "attempting to exclude rivals on some basis other than efficiency," it is fair to characterize its behavior as predatory. It is, accordingly, appropriate to examine the effect of the challenged pattern of conduct on consumers, on Ski Co.'s smaller rival, and on Ski Co. itself.

Superior Quality of the All–Aspen Ticket

The average Aspen visitor "is a well-educated, relatively affluent, experienced skier who has skied a number of times in the past.... Tr. 764.

---

22. "In any business, patterns of distribution develop over time; these may reasonably be thought to be more efficient than alternative patterns of distribution that do not develop. The patterns that do develop and persist we may call the optimal patterns. By disturbing optimal distribution patterns one rival can impose costs upon another, that is, force the other to accept higher costs." Bork 156.

In § 1 cases where this Court has applied the *per se* approach to invalidity to concerted refusals to deal, "the boycott often cut off access to a supply, facility or market necessary to enable the boycotted firm to compete, ... and frequently the boycotting firms possessed a dominant position in the relevant market." Northwest Wholesale Stationers, Inc. v. Pacific Stationery & Printing Co.

23. "Thus, 'exclusionary' comprehends at the most behavior that not only (1) tends to impair the opportunities of rivals, but also (2) either does not further competition on the merits or does so in an unnecessarily restrictive way." 3 P. Areeda & D. Turner, Antitrust Law 78 (1978).

Over 80% of the skiers visiting the resort each year have been there before—40% of these repeat visitors have skied Aspen at least five times. Over the years, they developed a strong demand for the 6–day, all-Aspen ticket in its various refinements. Most experienced skiers quite logically prefer to purchase their tickets at once for the whole period that they will spend at the resort; they can then spend more time on the slopes and enjoying apres-ski amenities and less time standing in ticket lines. The 4–area attribute of the ticket allowed the skier to purchase his 6–day ticket in advance while reserving the right to decide in his own time and for his own reasons which mountain he would ski on each day. It provided convenience and flexibility, and expanded the vistas and the number of challenging runs available to him during the week's vacation.

While the 3–area, 6–day ticket offered by Ski Co. possessed some of these attributes, the evidence supports a conclusion that consumers were adversely affected by the elimination of the 4–area ticket. In the first place, the actual record of competition between a 3–area ticket and the all-Aspen ticket in the years after 1967 indicated that skiers demonstrably preferred four mountains to three. Highlands' expert marketing witness testified that many of the skiers who come to Aspen want to ski the four mountains, and the abolition of the 4–area pass made it more difficult to satisfy that ambition. A consumer survey undertaken in the 1979–1980 season indicated that 53.7% of the respondents wanted to ski Highlands, but would not; 39.9% said that they would not be skiing at the mountain of their choice because their ticket would not permit it.

Expert testimony and anecdotal evidence supported these statistical measures of consumer preference. A major wholesale tour operator asserted that he would not even consider marketing a 3–area ticket if a 4–area ticket were available. During the 1977–1978 and 1978–1979 seasons, people with Ski Co.'s 3–area ticket came to Highlands "on a very regular basis" and attempted to board the lifts or join the ski school. Highlands officials were left to explain to angry skiers that they could only ski at Highlands or join its ski school by paying for a 1–day lift ticket. Even for the affluent, this was an irritating situation because it left the skier the option of either wasting one day of the 6–day, 3–area pass or obtaining a refund which could take all morning and entailed the forfeit of the 6–day discount. An active officer in the Atlanta Ski Club testified that the elimination of the 4–area pass "infuriated" him.

Highlands' Ability to Compete

The adverse impact of Ski Co.'s pattern of conduct on Highlands is not disputed in this Court. Expert testimony described the extent of its pecuniary injury. The evidence concerning its attempt to develop a substitute product either by buying Ski Co.'s daily tickets in bulk, or by marketing its own Adventure Pack, demonstrates that it tried to protect itself from the loss of its share of the patrons of the all-Aspen ticket. The development of a new distribution system for providing the experience that skiers had learned to expect in Aspen proved to be prohibitively expensive. As a result,

Highlands' share of the relevant market steadily declined after the 4–area ticket was terminated. The size of the damages award also confirms the substantial character of the effect of Ski Co.'s conduct upon Highlands.[24]

Ski Co.'s Business Justification

Perhaps most significant, however, is the evidence relating to Ski Co. itself, for Ski Co. did not persuade the jury that its conduct was justified by any normal business purpose. Ski Co. was apparently willing to forgo daily ticket sales both to skiers who sought to exchange the coupons contained in Highlands' Adventure Pack, and to those who would have purchased Ski Co. daily lift tickets from Highlands if Highlands had been permitted to purchase them in bulk. The jury may well have concluded that Ski Co. elected to forgo these short run benefits because it was more interested in reducing competition in the Aspen market over the long run by harming its smaller competitor.

That conclusion is strongly supported by Ski Co.'s failure to offer any efficiency justification whatever for its pattern of conduct.[25] In defending the decision to terminate the jointly offered ticket, Ski Co. claimed that usage could not be properly monitored. The evidence, however, established that Ski Co. itself monitored the use of the 3–area passes based on a count taken by lift operators, and distributed the revenues among its mountains on that basis.[26] Ski Co. contended that coupons were administratively cumbersome, and that the survey takers had been disruptive and their work inaccurate. Coupons, however, were no more burdensome than the credit cards accepted at Ski Co. ticket windows. Moreover, in other markets Ski Co. itself participated in interchangeable lift tickets using coupons. As for the survey, its own manager testified that the problems were much

---

24. In considering the competitive effect of Ski Co.'s refusal to deal or cooperate with Highlands, it is not irrelevant to note that similar conduct carried out by the concerted action of three independent rivals with a similar share of the market would constitute a *per se* violation of § 1 of the Sherman Act. See Northwest Wholesale Stationers, Inc. v. Pacific Stationery & Printing Co. Cf. Lorain Journal Co. v. United States, 342 U.S. 143, 154 (1951).

25. "The law can usefully attack this form of predation only when there is evidence of specific intent to drive others from the market by means other than superior efficiency and when the predator has overwhelming market size, perhaps 80 or 90 percent. Proof of specific intent to engage in predation may be in the form of statements made by the officers or agents of the company, evidence that the conduct was used threateningly and did not continue when a rival capitulated, or *evidence that the conduct*

was not related to any apparent efficiency. These matters are not so difficult of proof as to render the test overly hard to meet." Bork 157 (emphasis added).

26. Under the Ski Co. system, each skier's ticket, whether a daily or weekly ticket, is punched before he goes out on the slopes for the day. Revenues are distributed between the mountains on the basis of this count. Ski Co.'s Vice President for Finance testified that Ski Co. "would never consider" a system like that for monitoring usage on a 4–area ticket: "it's fine to approximate within your own company." Tr. 599. The U.S. Forest Service, however, required the submission of financial information on a mountain-by-mountain basis as a condition of the permits issued for each mountain. Tr. 643, 945. A lift operator at Ajax conceded that the survey count during the years of the 4–area ticket was "generally pretty close" to the count made by Ski Co.'s staff. Id., at 1627.

overemphasized by Ski Co. officials, and were mostly resolved as they arose. Ski Co.'s explanation for the rejection of Highlands' offer to hire—at its own expense—a reputable national accounting firm to audit usage of the 4-area tickets at Highlands' mountain, was that there was no way to "control" the audit.

In the end, Ski Co. was pressed to justify its pattern of conduct on a desire to disassociate itself from—what it considered—the inferior skiing services offered at Highlands. The all-Aspen ticket based on usage, however, allowed consumers to make their own choice on these matters of quality. Ski Co.'s purported concern for the relative quality of Highlands' product was supported in the record by little more than vague insinuations, and was sharply contested by numerous witnesses. Moreover, Ski Co. admitted that it was willing to associate with what it considered to be inferior products in other markets.

Although Ski Co.'s pattern of conduct may not have been as " 'bold, relentless, and predatory' " as the publisher's actions in *Lorain Journal,* the record in this case comfortably supports an inference that the monopolist made a deliberate effort to discourage its customers from doing business with its smaller rival. The sale of its 3–area, 6–day ticket, particularly when it was discounted below the daily ticket price, deterred the ticket holders from skiing at Highlands.[27] The refusal to accept the Adventure Pack coupons in exchange for daily tickets was apparently motivated entirely by a decision to avoid providing any benefit to Highlands even though accepting the coupons would have entailed no cost to Ski Co. itself, would have provided it with immediate benefits, and would have satisfied its potential customers. Thus the evidence supports an inference that Ski Co. was not motivated by efficiency concerns and that it was willing to sacrifice short-run benefits and consumer good will in exchange for a perceived long-run impact on its smaller rival.[28]

Because we are satisfied that the evidence in the record,[29] construed most favorably in support of Highlands' position, is adequate to support the

---

27. "[W]hy didn't they buy an individual daily lift ticket at Aspen Highlands? ... For those who had bought six-day tickets, I think despite the fact that they are all relatively affluent—a lot of them are relatively affluent when they go to Aspen—they are all sort of managerial types and they seem to be pretty cautious. Certainly the comments that I have had from individual skiers and from the tour operators, club people that I have talked to—they are pretty careful with their money and they would feel—these are the people who will buy the six-day, three-area ticket that giving up one of those days and going over to ski at Aspen Highlands would mean spending extra money." Tr. 777.

28. The Ski Co. advertising that conveyed the impression that there were only three skiing mountains in Aspen is consistent with this conclusion, even though this evidence would not be sufficient in itself to sustain the judgment.

29. Given our conclusion that the evidence amply supports the verdict under the instructions as given by the trial court, we find it unnecessary to consider the possible relevance of the "essential facilities" doctrine, or the somewhat hypothetical question whether nonexclusionary conduct could ever constitute an abuse of monopoly power if motivated by an anticompetitive purpose. If, as we have assumed, no monopolist monopolizes unconscious of what he is doing, that case is unlikely to arise.

verdict under the instructions given by the trial court, the judgment of the Court of Appeals is

Affirmed.

■ WHITE, J., took no part in the decision of this case.

Eastman Kodak Co. v. Image Technical Services, Inc.

Supreme Court of the United States, 1992.
504 U.S. 451, 112 S.Ct. 2072, 119 L.Ed.2d 265.

[Reprinted p. 903 infra]

NOTES AND QUESTIONS

1. *Aspen Skiing* was the first significant monopolization case to be decided by the Supreme Court since *Grinnell* (p. 172 supra) in 1966. One way of looking at the case is to analyze Ski Co.'s conduct as involving the strategic raising of a rival's cost. As Professors Krattenmaker, Lande and Salop put it:

> A single firm or group of firms that is not constrained by competition from a sufficient number of equally efficient existing and potential competitors can profitably raise price or prevent price from falling in two ways.

> First, the firm or group of firms may raise or maintain price above the competitive level directly by restraining its own output ("control price"). The power to control price by restraining one's own output is the usual focus of Chicago School antitrust analysts....

> Second, the firm or group of firms may raise price above the competitive level or prevent it from falling to a lower competitive level by raising its rivals' costs and thereby causing them to restrain their output ("exclude competition"). Such allegations are at the bottom of most antitrust cases in which one firm or group of firms is claimed to have harmed competition by foreclosing or excluding its competitors.[30]

Ski Co.'s decision to terminate the all-Aspen ticket may have disadvantaged Ski Co., but may have been even more costly to Highlands. Should such "strategic behavior" violate the conduct requirement of Section 2? Notice that consumer welfare losses result from "controlling price" and from "excluding competition" by "strategic behavior." In both situations, output will be restrained below the efficient competitive level and consumers will be denied products they value. In addition, excluding competition by strategic behavior reduces production efficiency. What if the firm with monopoly power helps induce costly new regulatory requirements or, if it is capital intensive as compared to rivals, agrees to costly labor settlements?

2. What if Ski Co. had justified its conduct with the following explanation:

30. Krattenmaker, Lande & Salop, Monopoly Power and Market Power in Antitrust Law, 76 Geo.L.J. 241, 249 (1987).

Ski Company may have sought to make the transition from competitor in a local ski-resort market to competitor in the national market. To do that, one must advertise nationally. But a ticketing arrangement that divides any resulting increase in revenue with a local competitor saps that incentive to go forward with the marketing strategy. If Ski Company invests in advertising to bring more skiers from across the nation to Aspen, Highlands will reap a part of the return on that investment.[31]

Even if this "free-rider" explanation were accurate, were there no less restrictive alternatives available to Ski Co.? Could it not, for example, have asked Highlands to contribute a fair share of the advertising cost? Should such less restrictive alternatives be relevant in an analysis under Section 2?

3. In Data General Corp. v. Grumman Systems Support Corp., 36 F.3d 1147 (1st Cir.1994), the First Circuit analyzed the *Aspen Skiing* and *Kodak* cases as follows:

> [A] monopolist's unilateral refusal to deal with its competitors (as long as the refusal harms the competitive process) may constitute prima facie evidence of exclusionary conduct in the context of a Section 2 claim. See *Kodak*, [p. 917 n. 24] (citing Aspen Skiing Co. v. Aspen Highlands Skiing Corp., 472 U.S. 585, 602–05 (1985)). A monopolist may nevertheless rebut such evidence by establishing a valid business justification for its conduct. See *Kodak*, [p. 917 n. 24] (suggesting that monopolist may rebut an inference of exclusionary conduct by establishing "legitimate competitive reasons for the refusal"); Aspen Skiing, 472 U.S. at 608 (suggesting that sufficient evidence of harm to consumers and competitors triggers further inquiry as to whether the monopolist has "persuaded the jury that its [harmful] conduct was justified by [a] normal business purpose"). In general, a business justification is valid if it relates directly or indirectly to the enhancement of consumer welfare. Thus, pursuit of efficiency and quality control might be legitimate competitive reasons for an otherwise exclusionary refusal to deal, while the desire to maintain a monopoly market share or thwart the entry of competitors would not. See Kodak, 112 S.Ct. at 2091 (discussing the validity and sufficiency of various business justifications); Aspen Skiing, 472 U.S. at 608–11 (same); see generally 7 Areeda & Turner, at 377–83; 9 Areeda & Turner, at 148–61, 185–239. In essence, a unilateral refusal to deal is prima facie exclusionary if there is evidence of harm to the competitive process; a valid business justification requires proof of countervailing benefits to the competitive process.

36 F.3d at 1183.

The First Circuit went on to conclude that Data General's refusal to license copyrighted material (a sophisticated computer program) was not a Section 2 violation because "an author's desire to exclude others from use of its copyrighted work is a presumptively valid business justification for any immediate harm to consumers." The Court noted: "Wary of undermining the Sherman Act ... we do not hold that an antitrust plaintiff can never rebut this presumption, for there may be rare cases in which imposing liability is unlikely to frustrate the objectives of the Copyright Act." 36 F.3d at 1187, n. 64; see *SCM Corp. v. Xerox Corp.*, p. 732 supra; FTC Staff, Anticipating the 21st Century: Competition Policy in the New High–

---

31. Wiley, "After Chicago": An Exaggerated Demise?, Duke L.J. 1003, 1005 (1986).

Tech, Global Marketplace Ch. 8 (1996) (concluding that "antitrust should pay close attention to unilateral and joint business conduct involving intellectual property"); Note on Issues at the Intersection of Antitrust and Intellectual Property, p. 812 infra.

4. In Official Airline Guides, Inc. v. FTC, 630 F.2d 920 (2d Cir.1980), cert. denied, 450 U.S. 917 (1981), the Second Circuit considered whether a "monopolist publisher of flight schedules not itself an air carrier" had a duty under Section 5 of the FTC Act not to discriminate unjustifiably between certified air carriers and commuter airlines so as to place the latter at a significant competitive disadvantage. The Court of Appeals concluded:

> Conceding in effect that there is no case precisely in point, the Commission suggested in oral argument that it was but a "small step" that we would be taking were we to uphold their decision. Of course we are reminded by the line of cases including FTC v. Cement Institute, 333 U.S. 683, 692–93 (1948) and Atlantic Refining Co. v. FTC, 381 U.S. 357, 367–68 (1965), that "[w]hile the final word is left to the courts, necessarily 'we give great weight to the Commission's conclusion'" ... as to what is an "unfair method of competition" or "an unfair act or practice" within the meaning of section 5 of the FTC Act. We note that the FTC with some justification states that the arbitrary refusal of a monopolist to deal leaves the disadvantaged competitor, even though in another field, with no recourse to overcome the disadvantage, and the Commission wants us to take the "small step" in terms of "the fundamental goals of antitrust." Reuben H. Donnelley Corp., [1980] 3 Trade Reg.Rep. (CCH) ¶ 21,650, at 21,818.
>
> But we think enforcement of the FTC's order here would give the FTC too much power to substitute its own business judgment for that of the monopolist in any decision that arguably affects competition in another industry. Such a decision would permit the FTC to delve into, as the Commission itself put the extreme case, "social, political, or personal reasons" for a monopolist's refusal to deal. Professors Areeda and Turner give examples of a monopolist theater which refuses to admit men with long hair or a monopolist newspaper which refuses to publish advertising from cigarette manufacturers. 3 P. Areeda & D. Turner, supra, at 270–71. The Commission says that neither of these examples would trigger antitrust scrutiny because there is no competition among persons who attend movies, and refusing to publish advertisements for all cigarette companies would not place any of them at a disadvantage vis-a-vis a competitor. See [1980] 3 Trade Reg.Rep. (CCH) ¶ 21,650, at 21,818. Nevertheless, the Commission's own example in footnote 38 of its opinion of a monopolist newspaper refusing to take advertisements from a particular cigarette company because of the style of prior advertisements or the political views of its president shows just how far the Commission's opinion could lead us. What we are doing, as the Commission itself recognized, is weighing benefits to competition in the other field against the detrimental effect of allowing the Commission to pass judgment on many business decisions of the monopolist that arguably discriminate among customers in some way. Thus, if the only supermarket in town decides to stock Birdseye vegetables but not Green Giant vegetables, the FTC would be able to require it to stock Green Giant vegetables if it were to find Green Giant competitively disadvantaged.

We do not think that the *Colgate* doctrine is as dead as the Commission would have it.... We think that even a monopolist, as long as he has no purpose to restrain competition or to enhance or expand his monopoly, and does not act coercively, retains this right. Absent enlightenment from above, or clarification from Congress, this is our decision on the merits.

Section 5 of the FTC Act might be given a broader sweep than Section 2 of the Sherman Act because it is prospective only, has no criminal enforcement potential, and cannot be the basis of a private action. Should this have made a difference in the *Official Airline Guides* case? What if, making the Second Circuit's illustration more appropriate, there was only one supermarket chain in the nation, it decided to stock Birdseye vegetables and not Green Giant, and it offered no plausible justifications?

5. In OLYMPIA EQUIPMENT LEASING CO. v. WESTERN UNION TELEGRAPH CO., 797 F.2d 370, 376–78 (7th Cir.1986), Western Union was found guilty of monopolization under Section 2 because it abruptly stopped assisting some customers that it had helped to enter the telex service business. The Seventh Circuit distinguished *Aspen Skiing* and found a business justification for Western Union's conduct in the following discussion:

If a monopolist does extend a helping hand, though not required to do so, and later withdraws it as happened in this case, does he incur antitrust liability? We think not.... Since Western Union had no duty to encourage the entry of new firms into the equipment market, the law would be perverse if it made Western Union's encouraging gestures the fulcrum of an antitrust violation. Then no firm would dare to attempt a graceful exit from a market in which it was a major seller. We can imagine, though with difficulty, an argument that a monopolist might decide to entice new firms into its market only to destroy them and so deter other firms from trying to enter. But no such diabolical scheme is ascribed to Western Union, which undoubtedly was sincere in inviting new vendors into the market and in wanting to leave the market as soon as it liquidated its inventory of terminals bought from Teletype Corporation and leased to its subscribers.

Some cases hold, however, that a firm which controls a facility essential to its competitors may be guilty of monopolization if it refuses to allow them access to the facility. We accept the authority of these cases absolutely. They are well illustrated by Otter Tail Power Co. v. United States, 410 U.S. 366 (1973), where a wholesale supplier of electricity refused to supply electric power to a power system that competed with it in the retail electrical power market and had no other source of supply. It might seem that if a monopolist's refusal to sell his products or services to a competitor can thus be actionable under antitrust law, it must mean that monopolists sometimes do have a duty to help their competitors and that the cases which deny this proposition are wrong. But the monopolistic-refusal-to-deal cases qualify rather than refute the no-duty-to-help-competitors cases....

The present case would be an essential-facility case if Western Union had refused to supply telex service to a customer who got his terminal equipment from Olympia rather than from it, or if Olympia were a competing supplier of telex service who, like the specialized common carriers in the long-distance telephone market, depended on the owner of the local exchanges (here Western Union) to complete its service. Neither condition is satisfied. The essential feature of the refusal-to-deal cases—a monopoly supplier's discriminating against a customer because the customer has decided to compete with it—is missing here....

Aspen Skiing Co. v. Aspen Highlands Skiing Corp., supra, goes the furthest of any case we know toward imposing (more precisely, allowing a jury to impose) a duty under antitrust law to help a competitor; and as a recent decision by the Supreme Court it requires our most careful and respectful consideration.... *Aspen Highlands* is not a conventional monopoly refusal-to-deal case like *Otter Tail* because Aspen Highlands was never a customer of Aspen Skiing Company; the skiers are the customers. But it is like the essential-facility cases in that the plaintiff could not compete with the defendant without being able to offer its customers access to the defendant's larger facilities.

Olympia analogizes access to all the major mountains at Aspen to Western Union's vendor list, and argues that just as Aspen Highlands could not survive without access to the mountains so Olympia could not survive without the list. The analogy lacks not only plausibility but also evidentiary support....

Aspen Highlands could not acquire three more mountains in the Aspen area in order to be able to compete more effectively with the Aspen Skiing Company but Olympia could and did hire salesmen to substitute for the Western Union sales force that had been helping it. If Western Union had tried to prevent Olympia from making the substitution it would have been guilty of exclusionary conduct. But Olympia had no right under antitrust law to take a free ride on its competitor's sales force. You cannot conscript your competitor's salesmen to sell your product even if the competitor has monopoly power and you are a struggling new entrant....

Olympia cites *Aspen Highlands* for the proposition that if a firm with monopoly power cannot give a good business justification for not cooperating with a competitor, its refusal to cooperate violates antitrust law. Conjoined with other evidence, lack of business justification may indicate probable anticompetitive effect. But there is a clear business justification in this case: Western Union wanted to liquidate its supply of telex terminals faster, so it stopped promoting a competitor's supply....

6. In *Aspen Skiing* (n. 29 supra) the Supreme Court found it "unnecessary to consider the possible relevance of the 'essential facilities' doctrine." In the *Olympia* case, the Seventh Circuit appeared to accept a narrow version of the doctrine. A critical commentary[32] on the doctrine sets forth the following analysis:

The bottleneck doctrine, a supposed rule expressed as a metaphor, is also described more plainly as the "essential facilities" doctrine. A recent and fairly typical formulation appears in *United States v. AT & T,*[33] where Judge Greene stated:

It may be helpful at the outset to state the applicable legal standard. Any company which controls an "essential facility" or a "strategic bottleneck" in the market violates the antitrust laws if it fails to make access to that facility available to its competitors on fair and reasonable terms that do not disadvantage them.

32. Boudin, Antitrust Doctrine and the Sway of Metaphor, 75 Geo.L.J. 395, 397–401 (1986).

33. 524 F.Supp. 1336 (D.D.C.1981).

The opinion cited a number of Supreme Court and lower court decisions for this proposition.[34]

This bottleneck doctrine, couched in similar terms by other courts of appeals and district courts, is not an idle fancy but is intended as a rule of decision. Among other applications, it has been employed against a football team with an exclusive lease on a Washington stadium,[35] petroleum storage facilities in American Samoa,[36] a gas pipeline,[37] an electric power grid,[38] a distribution system for newspapers,[39] a realty listing service,[40] and a Colorado ski resort.[41] Courts often state the doctrine in the confident and unqualified terms used by Judge Greene. The bottleneck doctrine is also a favorite in pleadings filed by the Justice Department's Antitrust Division with courts and administrative agencies, usually accompanied by a reference to *United States v. Terminal Railroad Association* and *Associated Press v. United States*....

Yet when one examines the Supreme Court decisions commonly cited for the doctrine by lower courts, they do not offer much support.... The final case in the quartet, *Otter Tail Power Co. v. United States,* offers more harm than help to the bottleneck doctrine. In *Otter Tail,* an integrated electric power system refused to allow its intercity distribution network to be used to provide power to municipal systems which Otter Tail itself wanted to supply. The district court had no difficulty in bringing the bottleneck doctrine to bear in condemning this action. Largely affirming the result, Justice Douglas ignored the bottleneck rhetoric and emphasized Otter Tail's intent to destroy competition.[42] In implicating intent, the *Otter Tail* decision remains in the mainstream of section 2 doctrine.[43]

34. Judge Greene cited United States v. Terminal R.R. Ass'n, 224 U.S. 383 (1912), and Otter Tail Power Co. v. United States, 410 U.S. 366 (1973). Although these are the Supreme Court decisions most commonly cited, Associated Press v. United States, 326 U.S. 1 (1945), and United States v. Griffith, 334 U.S. 100 (1948), are, among others, invoked by lower courts in support of the doctrine from time to time.

35. Hecht v. Pro–Football, Inc., 570 F.2d 982 (D.C.Cir.1977), cert. denied, 436 U.S. 956 (1978).

36. United States v. Standard Oil Co., 362 F.Supp. 1331, 1341 (N.D.Cal.1972), aff'd mem., 412 U.S. 924 (1973).

37. Venture Technology, Inc. v. National Fuel Gas Distribution Corp., 1980–81 Trade Cas. (CCH) ¶ 63,780, at 78,169 (W.D.N.Y.1981), rev'd on other grounds, 685 F.2d 41 (2d Cir.), cert. denied, 459 U.S. 1007 (1982).

38. United States v. Otter Tail Power Co., 331 F.Supp. 54 (D.Minn.1971), aff'd in pertinent part, 410 U.S. 366 (1973).

39. Byars v. Bluff City News Co., 609 F.2d 843 (6th Cir.1979).

40. United States v. Realty Multi–List, 629 F.2d 1351 (5th Cir.1980).

41. Aspen Highlands Skiing Corp. v. Aspen Skiing Co., 738 F.2d 1509 (10th Cir. 1984), aff'd on other grounds, 472 U.S. 585 (1985).

42. *Otter Tail,* 410 U.S. at 377. This emphasis on intent predominates in the reasoning of this decision. Id. at 377–79. There are a few references to Otter Tail's "strategic dominance," but any monopoly refusing to deal with competitors could be so described. The point is that Justice Douglas did not stop with that description and infer an obligation to deal; instead, he repeatedly referred to the defendant's malign intent, citing ample evidence to support that finding. Id. at 369–72.

43. *Otter Tail*'s approach was anticipated by an earlier Supreme Court case sometimes cited in connection with the bottleneck doctrine, Eastman Kodak Co. v. Southern Photo Materials Co., 273 U.S. 359 (1927). There, Kodak's refusal to supply a competing distributor was condemned as part of a pattern evidencing a deliberate intent to secure a monopoly for Kodak. The jury was charged that refusal to deal might be justified for

Only recently the Supreme Court gave new evidence that it is not yet willing to endorse the bottleneck concept. In *Aspen Skiing Co. v. Aspen Highlands Skiing Corp.*, the Court reviewed a decision of the Tenth Circuit that relied directly on the essential facility doctrine to condemn a ski resort under section 2 of the Sherman Act after it terminated a joint ticketing arrangement with a dependent competitor. Affirming the decision below on more conventional grounds—the improper intent of the defendant to harm the competitor—the Supreme Court observed that "we find it unnecessary to consider the possible relevance of the 'essential facilities' doctrine."

A lack of Supreme Court support for the bottleneck doctrine is only the first warning signal. Doubts multiply as one ponders the implications of a general obligation for a monopolist to "share" its essential facility with its competitors. Is it truly the case that the dominant producer in an industry, having skillfully designed a plant of unique efficiency, has to let competitors use its factory at night so that they too can enjoy the benefits of this "essential facility"? If a soft drink company supplies most of the market because its secret formula produces a widely liked beverage, does section 2 require it to supply distributors even though it wishes to do all its own wholesale distribution? As the permutations pass in review, it is apparent that there are no easy answers to the problem of a monopolist dealing or refusing to deal with competitors.

Indeed, the "problem" itself is not unitary. The source of the monopoly power varies, from a natural monopoly due to economies of scale, or acquired by skill and foresight, to one granted by government franchise or patent, to one illegally acquired. The conduct may be a refusal to provide facilities, services, or supplies to a competitor or merely a discrimination in supply, price, or information. The competitor may be trying to compete in the monopolized market, a geographically adjacent one, or one vertically related. Within each class of cases, facts vary as to intent, administrative regulation, feasibility of remedies, and the economic (or other) justifications offered for denying access, refusing to deal, or discrimination. It would be amazing if this collection of concerns and variables could all be reduced to order by a one-sentence doctrine asserting that a monopolist controlling an essential facility has a duty to deal with competitors.

7.   Judge Boudin's reservations (in note 6) about the validity and scope of the essential facilities doctrine characterize much of the academic literature on the subject. If U.S. scholarship were the last word, one would expect that the essential facilities would be circumscribed narrowly or even fully abandoned. *See, e.g.*, 3A Areeda & Hovenkamp, Antitrust Law ¶ 771c (2d ed. 2002); Areeda, Essential Facilities: An Epithet in Need of Limiting Principles, 58 Antitrust L.J. 841, 852 (1989).

While acknowledging Judge Boudin's point that the essential facilities doctrine needs to be limited in application, a recent commentary on the doctrine treats it more sympathetically. See Pitofsky, Patterson & Hooks, The Essential Facilities Doctrine Under U.S. Antitrust Law, 70 Antitrust L.J. 443 (2002). The authors note that the essential facilities doctrine has a long and respected history, tracing back at the Supreme Court level to United States v. Terminal Railroad Ass'n, 224 U.S. 383 (1912) and Associated Press v. United States, 326 U.S. 1 (1945). See pp. 379 and

purposes of "improving" Kodak's own business but not if the jury found that the purpose was "strangling and destroying" a competitor.

381 supra. Interestingly, there are literally scores of lower court cases acknowledging the legitimacy of the doctrine and occasionally mandating access, generally reflecting a view that if the facility is truly essential and controlled by a monopolist, mandated access is necessary if competition is ever to flourish. The authors note with approval cases that have established stringent conditions before the doctrine may apply. These conditions include: (1) control of the essential facility must be by a monopolist; (2) a competitor would not be able practically or reasonably to duplicate the essential facility; (3) access to the facility was denied to a competitor; and (4) it would have been feasible to provide the facility to competitors. See MCI Communications v. AT & T, 708 F.2d 1081, 1132–33 (7th Cir.1983). Among many cases adopting similar limits, see City of Chanute v. Williams Natural Gas Co., 955 F.2d 641 (10th Cir.1992). The last factor has occasionally been expanded into a broad business justification, allowing a monopolist to deny access if there is a legitimate business or technological justification. City of Anaheim v. Southern Cal. Edison Co., 955 F.2d 1373, 1380 (9th Cir.1992).

One reason courts are cautious in mandating access even to an essential facility controlled by a monopolist is that the court's obligation does not stop with a simple order. To make access a reality, the court must also specify the price of access (*i.e.*, reasonable royalty), priority, and other relevant terms. That kind of continuing supervision is difficult for courts to manage (as opposed to regulatory agencies that have an ongoing mandate) with the result that mandated access is usually a last resort, imposed when the facility is truly essential and when there is no other way to preserve or restore competition.

In the Ninth Circuit, what difference, if any, would there be between a claim that a monopolist violated Section 2 because it refused to deal without legitimate competitive reasons for the refusal (under *Aspen Skiing* and *Kodak*), and an essential facilities claim? Would the business justification need to be more compelling if an essential facility were being denied?

How should an "essential facility" be defined? In general, probably the clearest case for application of the essential facilities doctrine is where the essential facility is owned or subsidized by government or is a public utility with an exclusive right created by government. Should the doctrine be applied to any natural monopoly cutting a competitor or potential competitor off from customers? Where else should the doctrine apply? What role should intent play?

8. In Conwood Co. v. United States Tobacco Co., 290 F.3d 768 (6th Cir.2002), a seller of moist snuff with about a 13% national market share sued United States Tobacco ("UST"), the dominant firm in the field with 77% of the market (down from 97% since the 1980s) for violations of Section 2 of the Sherman Act. Moist snuff is a finely chopped smokeless tobacco. The Sixth Circuit Court of Appeals affirmed a jury verdict that resulted in a damage award of $1.05 billion, the largest award in the history of antitrust.

The case revolved around the growing marketing arrangement called "category management" in which suppliers of products compete for assignment as the category captain. In that role, the category captain supplies data to the retailer about which brand, including its own, should be given advantageous shelf space and advertising prominence, and sometimes designs and services the product rack or shelf space area. Conwood alleged that U.S.T bid for and often won the category captain position (Conwood itself did not compete), and then provided false information that induced some retailers to prefer U.S.T. and removed Conwood's display racks and advertising without retailer consent. Final decisions on shelf space and display remain with the retailer, but there was extensive evidence that U.S.T.'s purpose and effect in becoming category captain was to take advantage of negligent retail employees and to eliminate or control the display of competitive products including particularly cut rate or discount offerings.

U.S.T.'s principal defenses were that its behavior amounted at worst to sporadic business torts and should not qualify as exclusionary behavior under *Aspen Ski*, and that its behavior could not have resulted in substantial market foreclosure since the collective market share of its competitors nearly doubled during the period of the alleged violation. The Court of Appeals concluded that while business torts should not casually be treated as exclusionary conduct under Section 2, U.S.T.'s orchestrated campaign to use its category manager position to disadvantage competitors, which the chairman of U.S.T. testified should not have happened and caused him some embarrassment, was exclusionary conduct lacking any business justification. As to the growth of U.S.T.'s competitors during the period of alleged violation, the Sixth Circuit simply concluded that they might have grown even more but for U.S.T.'s anticompetitive conduct.

If the antitrust laws regard business torts by a monopolist as exclusionary conduct, may that have the result of discouraging aggressive competitive programs? On the other hand, when a monopolist succeeds in becoming category manager, should it have an obligation to treat competitors and potential competitors in a particularly fair and scrupulous manner?

NOTE ON RECENT LOWER COURT CASES ON ESSENTIAL FACILITIES, LEVERAGING, AND PRICE SQUEEZE

1. Recent Court of Appeals cases demonstrate the complications that arise when plaintiffs assert causes of action depending on essential facility, leveraging, or price squeeze. In Alaska Airlines, Inc. v. United Airlines, Inc., 948 F.2d 536 (9th Cir.1991), the Ninth Circuit examined both leveraging and essential facilities as forms of exclusionary conduct under Section 2 of the Sherman Act. In *Alaska Airlines,* the defendant airlines established computerized reservations systems ("CRS") which provide flight information to travel agents who subscribe to their systems. American Airlines and United Airlines established the SABRE and Apollo systems, respectively. Airlines generally subscribe to every CRS because CRSs charge airlines per booking, generally $1.75 per booking. The plaintiff airlines brought suit against American and United Airlines, contending that each had violated Section 2 of the Sherman Act by: (1) denying plaintiffs reasonable access to the CRS services which were allegedly "essential facilities"; and (2) "leveraging" their dominance over CRS services to gain a competitive edge in the downstream air transportation market. The district court granted summary judgment for the defendants on both claims.

The Ninth Circuit stated that the "essential facilities doctrine imposes liability when one firm, which controls an essential facility, denies a second firm reasonable access to a product or service that the second firm must obtain in order to compete with the first." The Court of Appeals then observed:

> *Otter Tail,* the foundation of the essential facilities doctrine in the single firm context, was an extreme case. Otter Tail Power, an "upstream" monopolist, baldly refused to deal with its potential "downstream" competitors. Given the difficulty of duplicating Otter Tail's facilities, this refusal did more than merely impose some handicap on potential competitors; it eliminated all possibility of competition in the downstream market. As the Supreme Court indicated, Otter Tail Power had both attempted to monopo-

lize and had succeeded in monopolizing the downstream market for "retail" electric services. . . .

Weider [2d Cir.], *Olympia* and *MCI* [7th Cir.] share a concern that transcends their fact-based differences. A facility that is controlled by a single firm will be considered "essential" only if control of the facility carries with it the power to *eliminate* competition in the downstream market.

As to the essential facilities doctrine, the Ninth Circuit concluded:

In the instant case, it is clear that defendants' control of their CRSs did not give them power to eliminate competition in the downstream air transportation market. Basic economic theory tells us that plaintiffs will withdraw from SABRE or Apollo if the cost of using either CRS causes the cost to the airline of providing a flight booked on a CRS to exceed the revenue that the airline gains by providing the flight. It is difficult to imagine that a travel agent would subscribe to a CRS if it only contained information about 12–14% of available flights. Because the parties agree that neither United nor American controlled more than 12–14% of the air transportation market, SABRE and Apollo would contain information concerning approximately 12–14% of available flights if competitors withdrew from either SABRE or Apollo. Thus, the ability of United or American to abuse their downstream competitors by manipulating their CRSs is severely limited.

Moreover, United and American have never refused any of the plaintiffs access to their respective CRSs. See *Otter Tail,* 410 U.S. at 378 (outright refusal); *MCI,* 708 F.2d at 1132 (same). Rather, United and American have always given all of their competitors in the air transportation market such access for a fee. Neither United nor American have ever set this fee at a level that would drive their competitors away. As noted above, it is unlikely that defendants would set their fee at such a level, for if they did, they would destroy their CRSs rather than their competition.

Plaintiffs claim that each defendant's CRS was an "essential" facility because each defendant's control of its CRS gave it power to redistribute a portion of its rivals' revenues to itself. Plaintiffs make this claim even though they concede that each defendant's control of its CRS did not create a dangerous probability of monopolization in the downstream air transportation market. Although each defendant may have gained some leverage over its competitors through control of its CRS, each defendant's power fell far short of the power to *eliminate* competition seen in *Otter Tail* and *MCI.* At most, defendants gained a monetary profit at their rivals' expense. The exercise of this limited power is not actionable under Section 2.

Our view of the essential facilities doctrine does not render the doctrine superfluous or otherwise inappropriately curtail its reach. When a firm's power to exclude rivals from a facility gives the firm the power to *eliminate* competition in a market downstream from the facility, and the firm excludes at least some of its competitors, the danger that the firm will monopolize the downstream market is clear. In this circumstance, a finding of monopolization, or at least attempted monopolization, is appropriate, and there is little need to engage in the usual lengthy analysis of factors such as intent. We hold that neither defendant denied plaintiffs an "essential" facility in violation of the antitrust laws.

As to "monopoly leveraging," the Ninth Circuit concluded:

Plaintiffs next allege that each defendant violated Section 2 by "leveraging" its monopoly power over its competitors in the CRS market to gain a competitive advantage over these airlines in the downstream air transportation market. Plaintiffs admit that, because there was no dangerous probability that either defendant would monopolize the downstream air transportation market, they have no claim under the traditional Section 2 doctrine of attempted monopolization. This circuit expressly declined to decide whether "monopoly leveraging is a distinct Section 2 violation" in Catlin v. Washington Energy Co., 791 F.2d 1343, 1348 (9th Cir.1986).

The origin of the notion that a single firm may be liable for "monopoly leveraging," even in the absence of a threat that the "leveraged" market will be monopolized, is Berkey Photo, Inc. v. Eastman Kodak Co., 603 F.2d 263 (2d Cir.1979), cert. denied 444 U.S. 1093 (1980). In Berkey Photo, Kodak possessed a monopoly in the film and camera markets. Berkey Photo argued that Kodak had "leveraged" its dominant position in these areas to gain a "competitive advantage" in the photofinishing equipment and services markets. Berkey Photo conceded that there was no dangerous probability that Kodak could monopolize either of these markets.

The Berkey Photo court announced and applied the rule that "a firm violates § 2 by using its monopoly power in one market to gain a competitive advantage in another, albeit without an attempt to monopolize the second market." Id. In contrast to the traditional actions for monopoly and attempted monopoly, Berkey Photo's "monopoly leveraging" doctrine has only two rather loose elements: 1) there must be monopoly power in some market, and 2) such power must be "exercised ... to the detriment of competition" in another market....

We now reject Berkey's monopoly leveraging doctrine as an independent theory of liability under Section 2. Even in the two-market situation, a plaintiff cannot establish a violation of Section 2 without proving that the defendant used its monopoly power in one market to obtain, or attempt to attain, a monopoly in the downstream, or leveraged, market. We believe that Berkey Photo misapplied the elements to Section 2 by concluding that a firm violates Section 2 merely by obtaining a competitive advantage in the second market, even in the absence of an attempt to monopolize the leveraged market.... The anticompetitive dangers that implicate the Sherman Act are not present when a monopolist had a lawful monopoly in one market and uses its power to gain a competitive advantage in the second market. By definition, the monopolist has failed to gain, or attempt to gain, a monopoly in the second market. Thus, such activity fails to meet the second element necessary to establish a violation of Section 2. Unless the monopolist uses its power in the first market to acquire and maintain a monopoly in the second market, or to attempt to do so, there is no Section 2 violation.

Monopoly leveraging is just one of a number of ways that a monopolist can permissibly benefit from its position. This does not mean, however, that such conduct is anticompetitive. Both "monopoly leveraging" in an adjacent market, and setting high prices in the original "monopoly" market, represent the cost that we incur when we permit efficient and natural monopolies. See Berkey Photo, 603 F.2d at 294 ("setting a high price may be use of monopoly power, but it is not in itself anticompetitive"). The Supreme Court has consistently held that there must be "predatory" conduct to attain or perpetuate a monopoly for a monopolist to be liable under Section 2. *Aspen Skiing Co.*, 472 U.S. at 596 n. 19, 602; *Grinnell Corp.*, 384 U.S. at 570–71; see also *Syufy Enterprises*, 903 F.2d at 669 ("fostering an environment where businesses fight it out using the weapon of efficiency and consumer goodwill is what the antitrust laws are meant to champion."). We hesitate to disregard this settled rule in the absence of any meaningful substantive distinction between monopoly leveraging and other consequences of lawful monopoly.

The danger that lawful monopoly will either create a new monopoly or unduly perpetuate itself is no more evident when a lawful monopoly is leveraged than when a lawful monopolist reaps its monopoly profit solely from price increases in the monopoly market. Indeed, leveraging activity may tend to *undermine* monopoly power, just like monopoly pricing. Every time the monopolist asserts its market dominance on a firm in the leveraged market, the leveraged firm has more incentive to find an alternative supplier, which in turn gives alternate suppliers more reason to think that they can compete with the monopolist. Every act exploiting monopoly power to the disadvantage of the monopoly's customers hastens the monopoly's end by making the potential competition more attractive.

Berkey Photo errs by straying from the Sherman Act's focus on the problem of the *creation, or attempted creation, of a monopoly* through monopoly leveraging. The antitrust laws seek to punish only the willful attainment and maintenance of a monopoly, or the attempt to attain such a monopoly. If there is a dangerous probability that a monopoly will be created by leveraging conduct, then the conduct will be reached under the doctrine of attempted monopoly.

For a discussion of attempt to monopolize, see Section B, p. 832 infra.

2. In Paddock Publications, Inc. v. Chicago Tribune Co., 103 F.3d 42 (7th Cir.), cert. denied, 520 U.S. 1265 (1997), the Chicago Daily Herald, the third largest general interest newspaper in the Chicago area with 6.7% of average weekly readership, challenged a series of contracts under which various sellers of news services committed exclusive rights to news and other services (*e.g.*, comic strips) to larger newspapers in the Chicago metropolitan area. For example, the New York Times might commit exclusively to the Chicago Tribune while the Los Angeles Times–Washington Post news service might commit to the Chicago–Sun Times. As a result, smaller newspaper were consigned to lesser news services.

The Seventh Circuit noted at the outset that there were many companies that supplied news and related services and the market appeared to be quite competitive. It also noted two features of the arrangement which indicated that the contracts were not anticompetitive. First, the contracts were relatively short in duration, in some cases terminable at will. Plaintiff responded that regardless of the language of the contracts, the arrangements were renewed year-after-year so that the contracts should be treated as perpetual. The Seventh Circuit responded as follows:

> As long as the arrangement served the interests of both parties, they will continue, whether that means signing another in a series of one-year contracts or declining to exercise an annual option to cancel the contract. [All that is required is] ... that someone else could come along with a better deal and get the business. Likewise someone with a better offer can get or sell news on short notice. The Herald has never tried to make a

better offer, and we conclude that it has come to the wrong forum. It should try to outbid the Tribune and the Sun–Times in the marketplace rather than to out maneuver them in court.

The Seventh Circuit also noted that competition to become the exclusive supplier is procompetitive:

> Competition-for-the-contract is a form of competition that antitrust laws protect rather than proscribe, and it is common. Every year or two General Motors, Ford and Chrysler invite tire manufacturers to bid for exclusive rights to have their tires used in the manufacturers' cars. Exclusive contracts make the market hard to enter in mid-year but cannot stifle competition over the longer run, and competition of this kind drives down the prices of tires, to the ultimate benefit of consumers. Just so in the news business. . . .

3. Does a price squeeze constitute exclusionary conduct sufficient to satisfy the second prong of the *Grinnell* test? The First Circuit discussed price squeezes in Town of Concord, Massachusetts v. Boston Edison Co., 915 F.2d 17 (1st Cir.1990), and suggested that different standards apply to regulated and non-regulated industries.

Chief Judge (now Justice) Breyer reasoned as follows:

> We shall assume for now that Edison has monopoly power in a relevant market and begin by examining whether Edison's pricing practices amount to exclusionary conduct. Traditional antitrust principles will guide our analysis. We shall compare the challenged practice's likely anticompetitive effects with its potentially legitimate business justifications. In doing so, we shall bear in mind that a practice is not "anticompetitive" simply because it harms competitors. After all, almost all business activity, desirable and undesirable alike, seeks to advance a firm's fortunes at the expense of its competitors. Rather, a practice is "anticompetitive" only if it harms the competitive process. It harms that process when it obstructs the achievement of competition's basic goals—lower prices, better products, and more efficient production methods. . . .

> For reasons we shall now set out, these principles lead us to conclude that a price squeeze of the sort at issue here does not ordinarily violate Sherman Act § 2 where the defendant's prices are regulated at both the primary and secondary levels. In so holding, we *are not* saying either that the antitrust laws do not apply in this regulatory context, or that they somehow apply less stringently here than elsewhere. Rather, we are saying that, in light of regulatory rules, constraints, and practices, the price squeeze at issue here is not ordinarily exclusionary, and, for that reason, it does not violate the Sherman Act. We reach this conclusion by (1) analyzing the ordinary price squeeze, (2) comparing it to the "regulatory" price squeeze, and (3) noting that regulation makes a critical difference in terms of antitrust harms, benefits, and administrative considerations.

> To explain our conclusion, we must first discuss the ordinary price squeeze case, the case of an unregulated monopolist whose prices (at, say, the wholesale and retail levels) leave inadequate room for an independent competitor (at say, the retail level) to survive. Only if the reader understands the major antitrust harms, benefits, and administrative considerations in that ordinary case, and sees how they are rather evenly balanced, will he understand why price regulation tips that balance so significantly

toward legality.... What difference does it make, one might ask, whether the monopolist obtains this "maximum monopoly profit" by controlling two industry levels or just one?

At least two arguments have been made in answer to this question. The first is that a monopolist who extends his monopoly to a second industry level raises "entry barriers," thereby fortifying his monopoly position. Assume, for example, that Alcoa has monopolized only ingot production and has raised its prices somewhat above the competitive level. Alcoa's monopoly position in ingot will no doubt deter some new firms from entering ingot production, but it might also attract some new firms hoping to obtain a share of Alcoa's supercompetitive profits. Now assume Alcoa extends its monopoly to sheet production as well, the industry level, say, that consumes most of Alcoa's ingot. New firms might now be more reluctant to enter ingot production, fearing that Alcoa, in its capacity as "sheet fabricator-monopolist," would refuse to buy *ingot* from the new ingot producer, or that it would drop its own ingot prices and take the industry's entire "single monopoly profit" from the sale of sheet. The new firm might conclude that the only prudent way to challenge Alcoa would be to enter the industry at *both* levels at once. Insofar as it is more difficult for a firm to enter an industry at two levels than at one, the monopolist, by expanding its monopoly power, has made entry by new firms more difficult. And insofar as the monopolist previously set prices cautiously to avoid attracting a competitive challenge, the added security of a two-level monopoly could even lead that monopolist to raise its prices....

The second argument against permitting extension of monopoly power concerns "non-price" competition. The existence of competitors at a second "level," irrespective of their effects upon price, provides an added incentive for the monopolist to develop better products and better, more efficient ways to produce the product. Indeed, a "second-level" independent firm that develops better products or more efficient production methods may thereby obtain the strength needed to challenge the monopolist at the "primary level."

There are, however, at least two traditional circumstances in which prices that create a squeeze might simultaneously bring about economic benefits. First, the primary-level monopolist might carry out its second-level activities more efficiently than its independent competitors. If so, prices that squeeze the less efficient second-level competitors, even to the point of forcing them from the business, could (by lowering costs) lower prices, or, in any event, save economic resources.

Second, prices that squeeze a "second-level" firm will benefit consumers whenever the "second-level" firm *is itself* a monopolist....

Finally, we note that it is not easy for courts to administer Judge Hand's price squeeze test. That test makes it unlawful for a monopolist to charge more than a "fair price" for the primary product while simultaneously charging so little for the secondary product that its second-level competitors cannot make a "living profit." See *Alcoa,* 148 F.2d at 437–38. But how is a judge or jury to determine a "fair price?" Is it the price charged by other suppliers of the primary product? None exist. Is it the price that competition "would have set" were the primary level not monopolized? How can the court determine this price without examining costs and demands, indeed without acting like a rate-setting regulatory agency, the rate-setting proceedings of which often last for several years? Further, how is the court to decide the proper size of the price "gap?" Must it be large enough for all independent competing firms to make a "living profit," no matter how inefficient they may be? If not, how does one identify the "inefficient" firms? And how should the court respond when costs or demands change over time, as they inevitably will?

We do not say that these questions are unanswerable, but we have said enough to show why antitrust courts normally avoid direct price administration, relying on rules and remedies (such as structural remedies, *e.g.,* prohibiting certain vertical mergers) that are easier to administer....

Full price regulation dramatically alters the calculus of antitrust harms and benefits. First, regulation significantly diminishes the likelihood of major antitrust harm. In particular, it diminishes the likelihood of "entry barrier" harm, namely the risk that (1) prices will rise because (2) new firms will hesitate to enter a market and compete after (3) a squeeze has driven pre-existing independent competitors from the marketplace. All three propositions are made doubtful by regulation. For one thing, in a regulated industry, regulators control prices directly. Statutes typically require regulators to maintain prices at "reasonable" levels.

For another thing, factors related to regulation, such as the economic ability of a market to support new entry, or the legal requirement that a firm secure permission to enter, are likelier to determine new entry into a regulated industry than is a new entrant's fear of a two-level monopolist's enhanced retaliatory power. After all, should the regulator decide that new entry is warranted, it typically has the legal authority to prevent an existing "two-level" monopolist from improperly disadvantaging a new "second-level" competitor by, say, refusing to deal with it or by charging unreasonably high prices.

Finally, regulation in the electricity industry makes it less likely that a price squeeze will actually drive independent distributors from the marketplace. Local electricity distribution, after all, is itself considered a "natural monopoly" with service typically provided by a single franchised company to relatively immobile customers. Higher wholesale electricity prices (or lower retail prices elsewhere) will not lead the entire towns of Wellesley and Concord to pull up stakes and move to Dover. And the record lacks convincing evidence that competition between Edison and the plaintiff towns for customers living on the towns' borders, or for mobile high-energy-consuming industrial customers, is sufficiently important to threaten the plaintiffs with bankruptcy should such user switch to Edison. Even if an integrated utility such as Edison managed to set prices that severely squeezed a distributor, it could not take over the municipality's distribution area without regulator's permission.

Second, regulators try to set prices that reflect costs. To the extent that they succeed, an integrated utility's prices are likely to squeeze independent distributors who buy from it at wholesale only if those distributors operate less efficiently, *i.e.,* at higher cost. Consequently, a rule preventing prices that create a squeeze will more likely discourage efficient operations and deprive consumers of prices that reflect lower costs.

Third, for institutional reasons, an antitrust rule making the price squeeze illegal threatens consumers. The plaintiffs say that Edison violated the antitrust laws by asking for rates (*i.e.,* filing rate proposals) that would produce for Edison a "higher return" on its "wholesale sales than ... on its retail sales." ... A rule that penalizes the filing of wholesale rate increases would not necessarily lead firms to abandon wholesale rate increases; it could, instead, simply lead them to seek a retail rate increase whenever they seek a wholesale rate increase.... [T]he rule would encourage Edison to seek a retail rate increase so high that a jury could not find the wholesale/retail gap too narrow....

[A]nd finally, a distributor who disagrees with the utility's, or the commission's, cost-allocation methods or with its rates, or who believes that a price squeeze will harm it (whether or not the price squeeze also harms the competitive process), has an administrative remedy. It can challenge a utility's rates and practices before the Commission as unjust, unreasonable, or "discriminatory." If FERC permits the rates to take effect after suspension and later determines that a price squeeze exists, it can order an appropriate refund.

In sum, the relevant antitrust considerations differ significantly, in degree and in kind, when a price squeeze occurs in a fully regulated as opposed to an unregulated industry. Indeed, these considerations, which are closely balanced in the ordinary price squeeze, change so significantly when the squeeze takes place in a fully regulated industry that, in our opinion, the legal consequences of the squeeze change as well. That is to say, a price squeeze in a fully regulated industry such as electricity will not normally constitute "exclusionary conduct" under the Sherman Act § 2.

See 3A Areeda & Hovenkamp, Antitrust Law: An Analysis of Antitrust Principles and Their Application 123–38 (2002).

United States v. Microsoft Corp.

United States Court of Appeals, District of Columbia Circuit, 2001.
253 F.3d 34.

■ Before: EDWARDS, CHIEF JUDGE, WILLIAMS, GINSBURG, SENTELLE, RANDOLPH, ROGERS, and TATEL, CIRCUIT JUDGES.

■ PER CURIAM. Microsoft Corporation appeals from judgments of the District Court finding the company in violation of §§ 1 and 2 of the Sherman Act and ordering various remedies.

The action against Microsoft arose pursuant to a complaint filed by the United States and separate complaints filed by individual States. The District Court determined that Microsoft had maintained a monopoly in the market for Intel-compatible PC operating systems in violation of § 2; attempted to gain a monopoly in the market for internet browsers in violation of § 2; and illegally tied two purportedly separate products, Windows and Internet Explorer ("IE"), in violation of § 1. *United States v. Microsoft Corp.,* 87 F. Supp. 2d 30 (D.D.C. 2000) ("Conclusions of Law"). The District Court then found that the same facts that established liability under §§ 1 and 2 of the Sherman Act mandated findings of liability under analogous state law antitrust provisions. Id. To remedy the Sherman Act violations, the District Court issued a Final Judgment requiring Microsoft to submit a proposed plan of divestiture, with the company to be split into an operating systems business and an applications business. *United States v. Microsoft Corp.*, 97 F. Supp. 2d 59, 64–65 (D.D.C.2000) ("Final Judgment"). The District Court's remedial order also contains a number of interim restrictions on Microsoft's conduct. *Id. at 66–69.*

Microsoft's appeal contests both the legal conclusions and the resulting remedial order. There are three principal aspects of this appeal. First, Microsoft challenges the District Court's legal conclusions as to all three alleged antitrust violations and also a number of the procedural and factual foundations on which they rest. Second, Microsoft argues that the remedial order must be set aside, because the District Court failed to afford the company an evidentiary hearing on disputed facts and, also, because the substantive provisions of the order are flawed. Finally, Microsoft asserts that the trial judge committed ethical violations by engaging in impermissible ex parte contacts and making inappropriate public comments on the merits of the case while it was pending. Microsoft argues that these ethical violations compromised the District Judge's appearance of impartiality, thereby necessitating his disqualification and vacatur of his Findings of Fact, Conclusions of Law, and Final Judgment.

After carefully considering the voluminous record on appeal—including the District Court's Findings of Fact and Conclusions of Law, the testimony and exhibits submitted at trial, the parties' briefs, and the oral arguments before this court—we find that some but not all of Microsoft's liability challenges have merit. Accordingly, we affirm in part and reverse in part the District Court's judgment that Microsoft violated § 2 of the Sherman Act by employing anticompetitive means to maintain a monopoly in the operating system market; we reverse the District Court's determination that Microsoft violated § 2 of the Sherman Act by illegally attempting to monopolize the internet browser market; and we remand the District Court's finding that Microsoft violated § 1 of the Sherman Act by unlawfully tying its browser to its operating system. Our judgment extends to the District Court's findings with respect to the state law counterparts of the plaintiffs' Sherman Act claims.

We also find merit in Microsoft's challenge to the Final Judgment embracing the District Court's remedial order. There are several reasons supporting this conclusion. First, the District Court's Final Judgment rests on a number of liability determinations that do not survive appellate review; therefore, the remedial order as currently fashioned cannot stand. Furthermore, we would vacate and remand the remedial order even were we to uphold the District Court's liability determinations in their entirety, because the District Court failed to hold an evidentiary hearing to address remedies-specific factual disputes.

Finally, we vacate the Final Judgment on remedies, because the trial judge engaged in impermissible ex parte contacts by holding secret interviews with members of the media and made numerous offensive comments about Microsoft officials in public statements outside of the courtroom, giving rise to an appearance of partiality. Although we find no evidence of actual bias, we hold that the actions of the trial judge seriously tainted the proceedings before the District Court and called into question the integrity of the judicial process. We are therefore constrained to vacate the Final Judgment on remedies, remand the case for reconsideration of the remedial order, and require that the case be assigned to a different trial judge on remand. We believe that this disposition will be adequate to cure the cited improprieties.

In sum, for reasons more fully explained below, we affirm in part, reverse in part, and remand in part the District Court's judgment assessing liability. We vacate in full the Final Judgment embodying the remedial order and remand the case to a different trial judge for further proceedings consistent with this opinion.

I. INTRODUCTION

A. Background

In July 1994, officials at the Department of Justice ("DOJ"), on behalf of the United States, filed suit against Microsoft, charging the company with, among other things, unlawfully maintaining a monopoly in the operating system market through anticompetitive terms in its licensing and software developer agreements. The parties subsequently entered into a consent decree, thus avoiding a trial on the merits. See *United States v. Microsoft Corp.*, 56 F.3d 1448 (D.C.Cir.1995) (*"Microsoft I"*). Three years later, the Justice Department filed a civil contempt action against Microsoft for allegedly violating one of the decree's provisions. On appeal from a grant of a preliminary injunction, this court held that Microsoft's technological bundling of IE 3.0 and 4.0 with Windows 95 did not violate the relevant provision of the consent decree. *United States v. Microsoft Corp.*, 147 F.3d 935 (D.C.Cir.1998) (*"Microsoft II"*). We expressly reserved the question whether such bundling might independently violate §§ 1 or 2 of the *Sherman Act.* 147 F.3d at 950 n.14.

On May 18, 1998, shortly before issuance of the Microsoft II decision, the United States and a group of State plaintiffs filed separate (and soon thereafter consolidated) complaints, asserting antitrust violations by Microsoft and seeking preliminary and permanent injunctions against the company's allegedly unlawful conduct. The complaints also sought any "other preliminary and permanent relief as is necessary and appropriate to restore competitive conditions in the markets affected by Microsoft's unlawful conduct." Gov't Compl. at 53, *United States v. Microsoft Corp.*, 84 F. Supp. 2d 9, 19 (D.D.C.1999). Relying almost exclusively on Microsoft's varied efforts to unseat Netscape Navigator as the preeminent internet browser, plaintiffs charged four distinct violations of the Sherman Act: (1) unlawful exclusive dealing arrangements in violation of § 1; (2) unlawful tying of IE to Windows 95 and Windows 98 in violation of § 1; (3) unlawful maintenance of a monopoly in the PC operating system market in violation of § 2; and (4) unlawful attempted monopolization of the internet browser market in violation of § 2. The States also brought pendent claims charging Microsoft with violations of various State antitrust laws.

The District Court scheduled the case on a "fast track." The hearing on the preliminary injunction and the trial on the merits were consolidated pursuant to FED. R. CIV. P. 65(a)(2). The trial was then scheduled to commence on September 8, 1998, less than four months after the complaints had been filed. In a series of pretrial orders, the District Court limited each side to a maximum of 12 trial witnesses plus two rebuttal witnesses. It required that all trial witnesses' direct testimony be submitted to the court in the form of written declarations. The District Court also made allowances for the use of deposition testimony at trial to prove subordinate or predicate issues. Following the grant of three brief continuances, the trial started on October 19, 1998.

After a 76–day bench trial, the District Court issued its Findings of Fact. *United States v. Microsoft Corp.*, 84 F. Supp. 2d 9 (D.D.C.1999) ("Findings of Fact"). This triggered two independent courses of action. First, the District Court established a schedule for briefing on possible legal conclusions, inviting Professor Lawrence Lessig to participate as amicus curiae. Second, the District Court referred the case to mediation to afford the parties an opportunity to settle their differences. The Honorable Richard A. Posner, Chief Judge of the United States Court of Appeals for the Seventh Circuit, was appointed to serve as mediator. The parties concurred in the referral to mediation and in the choice of mediator.

Mediation failed after nearly four months of settlement talks between the parties. On April 3, 2000, with the parties' briefs having been submitted and considered, the District Court issued its conclusions of law. . . .

B. Overview

Before turning to the merits of Microsoft's various arguments, we pause to reflect briefly on two matters of note, one practical and one theoretical.

The practical matter relates to the temporal dimension of this case. The litigation timeline in this case is hardly problematic. Indeed, it is noteworthy that a case of this magnitude and complexity has proceeded from the filing of complaints through trial to appellate decision in a mere three years. *See, e.g.*, Data Gen. Corp. v. Grumman Sys. Support Corp., 36 F.3d 1147, 1155 (1st Cir.1994) (six years from filing of complaint to appellate decision); Transamerica Computer Co., Inc. v. IBM, 698 F.2d 1377, 1381 (9th Cir.1983) (over four years from start of trial to appellate decision); United States v. United Shoe Mach. Corp., 110 F. Supp. 295, 298 (D.Mass.1953) (over five years from filing of complaint to trial court decision).

What is somewhat problematic, however, is that just over six years have passed since Microsoft engaged in the first conduct plaintiffs allege to be anticompetitive. As the record in this case indicates, six years seems like an eternity in the computer industry. By the time a court can assess liability, firms, products, and the marketplace are likely to have changed dramatically. This, in turn, threatens enormous practical difficulties for courts considering the appropriate measure of relief in equitable enforcement actions, both in crafting injunctive remedies in the first instance and reviewing those remedies in the second. Conduct remedies may be unavailing in such cases, because innovation to a large degree has already rendered the anticompetitive conduct obsolete (although by no means harmless). And broader structural remedies present their own set of problems, including how a court goes about restoring competition to a dramatically changed, and constantly changing, marketplace. That is just one reason why we find the District Court's refusal in the present case to hold an evidentiary hearing on remedies—to update and flesh out the available information before seriously entertaining the possibility of dramatic structural relief—so problematic. See infra Section V.

We do not mean to say that enforcement actions will no longer play an important role in curbing infringements of the antitrust laws in technologically dynamic markets, nor do we assume this in assessing the merits of this case. Even in those cases where forward-looking remedies appear limited, the Government will continue to have an interest in defining the contours of the antitrust laws so that law-abiding firms will have a clear sense of what is permissible and what is not. And the threat of private damage actions will remain to deter those firms inclined to test the limits of the law.

The second matter of note is more theoretical in nature. We decide this case against a backdrop of significant debate amongst academics and practitioners over the extent to which "old economy" § 2 monopolization doctrines should apply to firms competing in dynamic technological markets characterized by network effects. In markets characterized by network effects, one product or standard tends towards dominance, because "the utility that a user derives from consumption of the good increases with the number of other agents consuming the good." Michael L. Katz & Carl Shapiro, Network Externalities, Competition, and Compatibility, 75 AM. ECON. REV. 424, 424 (1985). For example, "an individual consumer's demand to use (and hence her benefit from) the telephone network . . . increases with the number of other users on the network whom she can call or from whom she can receive calls." Howard A. Shelanski & J. Gregory Sidak, Antitrust Divestiture in Network Industries, 68 U. CHI. L. REV. 1, 8 (2001). Once a product or standard achieves wide acceptance, it becomes more or less entrenched. Competition in such industries is "for the field" rather than "within the field." See Harold Demsetz, Why Regulate Utilities?, 11 J.L. & ECON. 55, 57 & n.7 (1968) (emphasis omitted).

In technologically dynamic markets, however, such entrenchment may be temporary, because innovation may alter the field altogether. See JOSEPH A. SCHUMPETER, CAPITALISM, SOCIALISM AND DEMOCRACY 81–90 (Harper Perennial 1976) (1942). Rapid technological change leads to markets in which "firms compete through innovation for temporary market dominance, from which they may be displaced by the next wave of product advancements." Shelanski & Sidak, at 11–12 (discussing Schumpeterian competition, which proceeds "sequentially over time rather than simultaneously across a market"). Microsoft argues that the operating system market is just such a market.

Whether or not Microsoft's characterization of the operating system market is correct does not appreciably alter our mission in assessing the alleged antitrust violations in the present case. As an initial matter, we note that there is no consensus among commentators on the question of whether, and to what extent, current monopolization doctrine should be amended to account for competition in technologically dynamic markets characterized by network effects. Compare Steven C. Salop & R. Craig Romaine, Preserving Monopoly: Economic Analysis, Legal Standards, and Microsoft, 7 GEO. MASON L. REV. 617, 654–55, 663–64 (1999) (arguing that exclusionary conduct in high-tech networked industries deserves heightened antitrust scrutiny in part because it may threaten to deter innovation), with Ronald A. Cass & Keith N. Hylton, Preserving Competition: Economic Analysis, Legal Standards and Microsoft, 8 GEO. MASON L. REV. 1, 36–39 (1999) (equivocating on the antitrust implications of network effects and noting that the presence of network externalities may actually encourage innovation by guaranteeing more durable monopolies to innovating winners). Indeed, there is some suggestion that the economic consequences of network effects and technological dynamism act to offset one another, thereby making it difficult to formulate categorical antitrust rules absent a particularized analysis of a given market. See Shelanski & Sidak, at 6–7 ("High profit margins might appear to be the benign and necessary recovery of legitimate investment returns in a Schumpeterian framework, but they might represent exploitation of customer lock-in and monopoly power when viewed through the lens of network economics.... The issue is particularly complex because, in network industries characterized by rapid innovation, both forces may be operating and can be difficult to isolate.").

Moreover, it should be clear that Microsoft makes no claim that anticompetitive conduct should be assessed differently in technologically dynamic markets. It claims only that the measure of monopoly power should be different. For reasons fully discussed below, we reject Microsoft's monopoly power argument. See infra Section II.A.

With this backdrop in mind, we turn to the specific challenges raised in Microsoft's appeal.

II.   MONOPOLIZATION

Section 2 of the Sherman Act makes it unlawful for a firm to "monopolize." 15 U.S.C. § 2. The offense of monopolization has two elements: "(1) the possession of monopoly power in the relevant market and (2) the willful acquisition or maintenance of that power as distinguished from growth or development as a consequence of a superior product, business acumen, or historic accident." United States v. Grinnell Corp., 384 U.S. 563, 570–71 (1966). The District Court applied this test and found that Microsoft possesses monopoly power in the market for Intel-compatible PC operating systems. Focusing primarily on Microsoft's efforts to suppress Netscape

Navigator's threat to its operating system monopoly, the court also found that Microsoft maintained its power not through competition on the merits, but through unlawful means. Microsoft challenges both conclusions. We defer to the District Court's findings of fact, setting them aside only if clearly erroneous. We review legal questions de novo.

We begin by considering whether Microsoft possesses monopoly power, see infra Section II.A, and finding that it does, we turn to the question whether it maintained this power through anticompetitive means. Agreeing with the District Court that the company behaved anticompetitively, see infra Section II.B, and that these actions contributed to the maintenance of its monopoly power, see infra Section II.C, we affirm the court's finding of liability for monopolization.

A. Monopoly Power

While merely possessing monopoly power is not itself an antitrust violation, see *Northeastern Tel. Co. v. AT & T, 651 F.2d 76, 84–85 (2d Cir.1981)*, it is a necessary element of a monopolization charge, see *Grinnell, 384 U.S. at 570*. The Supreme Court defines monopoly power as "the power to control prices or exclude competition." *United States v. E.I. du Pont de Nemours & Co., 351 U.S. 377, 391 (1956)*. More precisely, a firm is a monopolist if it can profitably raise prices substantially above the competitive level.... Where evidence indicates that a firm has in fact profitably done so, the existence of monopoly power is clear. See *Rebel Oil Co. v. Atl. Richfield Co., 51 F.3d 1421, 1434 (9th Cir.1995)*; see also *FTC v. Indiana Fed'n of Dentists, 476 U.S. 447 (1986)* (using direct proof to show market power in Sherman Act § 1 unreasonable restraint of trade action). Because such direct proof is only rarely available, courts more typically examine market structure in search of circumstantial evidence of monopoly power. Under this structural approach, monopoly power may be inferred from a firm's possession of a dominant share of a relevant market that is protected by entry barriers. See *Rebel Oil, 51 F.3d at 1434*. "Entry barriers" are factors (such as certain regulatory requirements) that prevent new rivals from timely responding to an increase in price above the competitive level.

The District Court considered these structural factors and concluded that Microsoft possesses monopoly power in a relevant market. Defining the market as Intel-compatible PC operating systems, the District Court found that Microsoft has a greater than 95% share. It also found the company's market position protected by a substantial entry barrier. Conclusions of Law, at 36.

Microsoft argues that the District Court incorrectly defined the relevant market. It also claims that there is no barrier to entry in that market. Alternatively, Microsoft argues that because the software industry is uniquely dynamic, direct proof, rather than circumstantial evidence, more appropriately indicates whether it possesses monopoly power. Rejecting each argument, we uphold the District Court's finding of monopoly power in its entirety....

[The D.C. Circuit's analysis of market structure is set forth in Chapter 3, p. 167 supra. As indicated, the Court of Appeals affirmed the finding of an "Intel-compatible PC operating systems" market.]

b.   Market power

Having thus properly defined the relevant market, the District Court found that Windows accounts for a greater than 95% share. Findings of Fact p 35. The court also found that even if Mac OS were included, Microsoft's share would exceed 80%. Id. Microsoft challenges neither finding, nor does it argue that such a market share is not predominant. Cf. *Grinnell, 384 U.S. at 571* (87% is predominant); *Eastman Kodak Co. v. Image Technical Servs., Inc., 504 U.S. 451 (1992)* (80%); *du Pont, 351 U.S. at 379, 391* (75%).

Instead, Microsoft claims that even a predominant market share does not by itself indicate monopoly power. Although the "existence of [monopoly] power ordinarily may be inferred from the predominant share of the market," *Grinnell, 384 U.S. at 571*, we agree with Microsoft that because of the possibility of competition from new entrants, see *Ball Mem'l Hosp., Inc., 784 F.2d at 1336*, looking to current market share alone can be "misleading." *Hunt-Wesson Foods, Inc. v. Ragu Foods, Inc., 627 F.2d 919, 924 (9th Cir.1980)*; see also *Ball Mem'l Hosp., Inc., 784 F.2d at 1336* ("Market share reflects current sales, but today's sales do not always indicate power over sales and price tomorrow.") In this case, however, the District Court was not misled. Considering the possibility of new rivals, the court focused not only on Microsoft's present market share, but also on the structural barrier that protects the company's future position. Conclusions of Law, at 36. That barrier—the "applications barrier to entry"—stems from two characteristics of the software market: (1) most consumers prefer operating systems for which a large number of applications have already been written; and (2) most developers prefer to write for operating systems that already have a substantial consumer base. See Findings of Fact, pp. 30, 36. This "chicken-and-egg" situation ensures that applications will continue to be written for the already dominant Windows, which in turn ensures that consumers will continue to prefer it over other operating systems. Id. . . .

Having sustained the District Court's conclusion that circumstantial evidence proves that Microsoft possesses monopoly power, we turn to Microsoft's alternative argument that it does not behave like a monopolist. Claiming that software competition is uniquely "dynamic," Appellant's Opening Br. at 84 (quoting Findings of Fact p 59), the company suggests a new rule: that monopoly power in the software industry should be proven directly, that is, by examining a company's actual behavior to determine if it reveals the existence of monopoly power. According to Microsoft, not only does no such proof of its power exist, but record evidence demonstrates the absence of monopoly power. The company claims that it invests heavily in research and development, id. at 88–89 (citing Direct Testimony of Paul Maritz p 155, reprinted in 6 J.A. at 3698) (testifying that Microsoft invests approximately 17% of its revenue in R & D)), and charges a low price for

Windows (a small percentage of the price of an Intel-compatible PC system and less than the price of its rivals, id. at 90.

Microsoft's argument fails because, even assuming that the software market is uniquely dynamic in the long term, the District Court correctly applied the structural approach to determine if the company faces competition in the short term. Structural market power analyses are meant to determine whether potential substitutes constrain a firm's ability to raise prices above the competitive level; only threats that are likely to materialize in the relatively near future perform this function to any significant degree. . . . The District Court expressly considered and rejected Microsoft's claims that innovations such as handheld devices and portal websites would soon expand the relevant market beyond Intel-compatible PC operating systems. Because the company does not challenge these findings, we have no reason to believe that prompt substitutes are available. The structural approach, as applied by the District Court, is thus capable of fulfilling its purpose even in a changing market. Microsoft cites no case, nor are we aware of one, requiring direct evidence to show monopoly power in any market. We decline to adopt such a rule now.

Even if we were to require direct proof, moreover, Microsoft's behavior may well be sufficient to show the existence of monopoly power. Certainly, none of the conduct Microsoft points to—its investment in R & D and the relatively low price of Windows—is inconsistent with the possession of such power. Conclusions of Law, at 37. The R & D expenditures Microsoft points to are not simply for Windows, but for its entire company, which most likely does not possess a monopoly for all of its products. Moreover, because innovation can increase an already dominant market share and further delay the emergence of competition, even monopolists have reason to invest in R & D. Findings of Fact p. 61. Microsoft's pricing behavior is similarly equivocal. The company claims only that it never charged the short-term profit-maximizing price for Windows. Faced with conflicting expert testimony, the District Court found that it could not accurately determine what this price would be. Id. p. 65. In any event, the court found, a price lower than the short-term profit-maximizing price is not inconsistent with possession or improper use of monopoly power. Id. pp. 65–66. Cf. *Berkey Photo, Inc. v. Eastman Kodak Co., 603 F.2d 263, 274 (2d Cir.1979)* ("If monopoly power has been acquired or maintained through improper means, the fact that the power has not been used to extract [a monopoly price] provides no succor to the monopolist."). Microsoft never claims that it did not charge the longterm monopoly price. Micosoft does argue that the price of Windows is a fraction of the price of an Intel-compatible PC system and lower than that of rival operating systems, but these facts are not inconsistent with the District Court's finding that Microsoft has monopoly power. See Findings of Fact p. 36 ("Intel-compatible PC operating systems other than Windows [would not] attract[ ] significant demand . . . even if Microsoft held its prices substantially above the competitive level.").

More telling, the District Court found that some aspects of Microsoft's behavior are difficult to explain unless Windows is a monopoly product. For instance, according to the District Court, the company set the price of Windows without considering rivals' prices, Findings of Fact p. 62, something a firm without a monopoly would have been unable to do. The District Court also found that Microsoft's pattern of exclusionary conduct could only be rational "if the firm knew that it possessed monopoly power." Conclusions of Law, at 37. It is to that conduct that we now turn.

B. Anticompetitive Conduct

As discussed above, having a monopoly does not by itself violate § 2. A firm violates § 2 only when it acquires or maintains, or attempts to acquire or maintain, a monopoly by engaging in exclusionary conduct "as distinguished from growth or development as a consequence of a superior product, business acumen, or historic accident." *Grinnell, 384 U.S. at 571;* see also *United States v. Aluminum Co. of Am., 148 F.2d 416, 430 (2d Cir.1945)* (Hand, J.) ("The successful competitor, having been urged to compete, must not be turned upon when he wins.").

In this case, after concluding that Microsoft had monopoly power, the District Court held that Microsoft had violated § 2 by engaging in a variety of exclusionary acts (not including predatory pricing), to maintain its monopoly by preventing the effective distribution and use of products that might threaten that monopoly. Specifically, the District Court held Microsoft liable for: (1) the way in which it integrated IE into Windows; (2) its various dealings with Original Equipment Manufacturers ("OEMs"), Internet Access Providers ("IAPs"), Internet Content Providers ("ICPs"), Independent Software Vendors ("ISVs"), and Apple Computer; (3) its efforts to contain and to subvert Java technologies; and (4) its course of conduct as a whole. Upon appeal, Microsoft argues that it did not engage in any exclusionary conduct.

Whether any particular act of a monopolist is exclusionary, rather than merely a form of vigorous competition, can be difficult to discern: the means of illicit exclusion, like the means of legitimate competition, are myriad. The challenge for an antitrust court lies in stating a general rule for distinguishing between exclusionary acts, which reduce social welfare, and competitive acts, which increase it.

From a century of case law on monopolization under § 2, however, several principles do emerge. First, to be condemned as exclusionary, a monopolist's act must have an "anticompetitive effect." That is, it must harm the competitive process and thereby harm consumers. In contrast, harm to one or more competitors will not suffice. "The [Sherman Act] directs itself not against conduct which is competitive, even severely so, but against conduct which unfairly tends to destroy competition itself." *Spectrum Sports, Inc. v. McQuillan, 506 U.S. 447, (1993);* see also *Brooke Group Ltd. v. Brown & Williamson Tobacco Corp., 509 U.S. 209, 225 (1993)* ("Even an act of pure malice by one business competitor against another does not, without more, state a claim under the federal antitrust laws....").

Second, the plaintiff, on whom the burden of proof of course rests, must demonstrate that the monopolist's conduct indeed has the requisite anticompetitive effect. See generally *Brooke Group, 509 U.S. at 225–26.* In a case brought by a private plaintiff, the plaintiff must show that its injury is "of 'the type that the statute was intended to forestall,' " *Brunswick Corp. v. Pueblo Bowl–O–Mat, Inc., 429 U.S. 477, 487–88 (1977)*; no less in a case brought by the Government, it must demonstrate that the monopolist's conduct harmed competition, not just a competitor.

Third, if a plaintiff successfully establishes a prima facie case under § 2 by demonstrating anticompetitive effect, then the monopolist may proffer a "procompetitive justification" for its conduct. See *Eastman Kodak, 504 U.S. at 483.* If the monopolist asserts a procompetitive justification—a nonpretextual claim that its conduct is indeed a form of competition on the merits because it involves, for example, greater efficiency or enhanced consumer appeal—then the burden shifts back to the plaintiff to rebut that claim. Cf. *Capital Imaging Assocs., P.C. v. Mohawk Valley Med. Assocs., Inc., 996 F.2d 537, 543 (2d Cir.1993).*

Fourth, if the monopolist's procompetitive justification stands unrebutted, then the plaintiff must demonstrate that the anticompetitive harm of the conduct outweighs the procompetitive benefit. In cases arising under § 1 of the Sherman Act, the courts routinely apply a similar balancing approach under the rubric of the "rule of reason." The source of the rule of reason is *Standard Oil Co. v. United States, 221 U.S. 1 (1911),* in which the Supreme Court used that term to describe the proper inquiry under both sections of the Act. See *id. at 61–62* ("When the second section [of the Sherman Act] is thus harmonized with ... the first, it becomes obvious that the criteria to be resorted to in any given case for the purpose of ascertaining whether violations of the section have been committed, is the rule of reason guided by the established law....") As the Fifth Circuit more recently explained, "it is clear ... that the analysis under section 2 is similar to that under section 1 regardless whether the rule of reason label is applied.... *Mid-Texas Communications Sys., Inc. v. AT & T, 615 F.2d 1372, 1389 n. 13 (5th Cir.1980)* (citing *Byars v. Bluff City News Co., 609 F.2d 843, 860 (6th Cir.1979))*; see also *Cal. Computer Prods., Inc. v. IBM Corp., 613 F.2d 727, 737 (9th Cir.1979).*

Finally, in considering whether the monopolist's conduct on balance harms competition and is therefore condemned as exclusionary for purposes of § 2, our focus is upon the effect of that conduct, not upon the intent behind it. Evidence of the intent behind the conduct of a monopolist is relevant only to the extent it helps us understand the likely effect of the monopolist's conduct. *See, e.g., Chicago Bd. of Trade v. United States, 246 U.S. 231, 238 (1918)* ("knowledge of intent may help the court to interpret facts and to predict consequences"); *Aspen Skiing Co. v. Aspen Highlands Skiing Corp., 472 U.S. 585, 603 (1985).*

With these principles in mind, we now consider Microsoft's objections to the District Court's holding that Microsoft violated § 2 of the Sherman Act in a variety of ways.

1. Licenses Issued to Original Equipment Manufacturers

The District Court condemned a number of provisions in Microsoft's agreements licensing Windows to OEMs, because it found that Microsoft's imposition of those provisions (like many of Microsoft's other actions at issue in this case) serves to reduce usage share of Netscape's browser and, hence, protect Microsoft's operating system monopoly. The reason market share in the browser market affects market power in the operating system market is complex, and warrants some explanation.

Browser usage share is important because, as we explained in Section II.A above, a browser (or any middleware product, for that matter) must have a critical mass of users in order to attract software developers to write applications relying upon the APIs it exposes, and away from the APIs exposed by Windows. Applications written to a particular browser's APIs, however, would run on any computer with that browser, regardless of the underlying operating system. "The overwhelming majority of consumers will only use a PC operating system for which there already exists a large and varied set of . . . applications, and for which it seems relatively certain that new types of applications and new versions of existing applications will continue to be marketed. . . ." Findings of Fact p. 30. If a consumer could have access to the applications he desired—regardless of the operating system he uses—simply by installing a particular browser on his computer, then he would no longer feel compelled to select Windows in order to have access to those applications; he could select an operating system other than Windows based solely upon its quality and price. In other words, the market for operating systems would be competitive.

Therefore, Microsoft's efforts to gain market share in one market (browsers) served to meet the threat to Microsoft's monopoly in another market (operating systems) by keeping rival browsers from gaining the critical mass of users necessary to attract developer attention away from Windows as the platform for software development. Plaintiffs also argue that Microsoft's actions injured competition in the browser market—an argument we will examine below in relation to their specific claims that Microsoft attempted to monopolize the browser market and unlawfully tied its browser to its operating system so as to foreclose competition in the browser market. In evaluating the § 2 monopoly maintenance claim, however, our immediate concern is with the anticompetitive effect of Microsoft's conduct in preserving its monopoly in the operating system market.

In evaluating the restrictions in Microsoft's agreements licensing Windows to OEMs, we first consider whether plaintiffs have made out a prima facie case by demonstrating that the restrictions have an anticompetitive effect. In the next subsection, we conclude that plaintiffs have met this burden as to all the restrictions. We then consider Microsoft's proffered justifications for the restrictions and, for the most part, hold those justifications insufficient.

a. Anticompetitive effect of the license restrictions

The restrictions Microsoft places upon Original Equipment Manufacturers are of particular importance in determining browser usage share because having an OEM pre-install a browser on a computer is one of the two most cost-effective methods by far of distributing browsing software. (The other is bundling the browser with internet access software distributed by an IAP.) Findings of Fact p. 145. The District Court found that the restrictions Microsoft imposed in licensing Windows to OEMs prevented many OEMs from distributing browsers other than IE. Conclusions of Law, at 39–40. In particular, the District Court condemned the license provisions prohibiting the OEMs from: (1) removing any desktop icons, folders, or "Start" menu entries; (2) altering the initial boot sequence; and (3) otherwise altering the appearance of the Windows desktop. Findings of Fact p. 213.

The District Court concluded that the first license restriction—the prohibition upon the removal of desktop icons, folders, and Start menu entries—thwarts the distribution of a rival browser by preventing OEMs from removing visible means of user access to IE. Id. p. 203. The OEMs cannot practically install a second browser in addition to IE, the court found, in part because "pre-installing more than one product in a given category . . . can significantly increase an OEM's support costs, for the redundancy can lead to confusion among novice users." Id. p. 159; see also id. p. 217. That is, a certain number of novice computer users, seeing two browser icons, will wonder which to use when and will call the OEM's support line. Support calls are extremely expensive and, in the highly competitive original equipment market, firms have a strong incentive to minimize costs. Id. p. 210.

Microsoft denies the "consumer confusion" story; it observes that some OEMs do install multiple browsers and that executives from two OEMs that do so denied any knowledge of consumers being confused by multiple icons. . . .

Other testimony, however, supports the District Court's finding that fear of such confusion deters many OEMs from pre-installing multiple browsers. . . . Most telling, in presentations to OEMs, Microsoft itself represented that having only one icon in a particular category would be "less confusing for endusers." See Government's Trial Exhibit ("GX") 319 at MS98 0109453. Accordingly, we reject Microsoft's argument that we should vacate the District Court's Finding of Fact p. 159 as it relates to consumer confusion.

As noted above, the OEM channel is one of the two primary channels for distribution of browsers. By preventing OEMs from removing visible means of user access to IE, the license restriction prevents many OEMs from pre-installing a rival browser and, therefore, protects Microsoft's monopoly from the competition that middleware might otherwise present. Therefore, we conclude that the license restriction at issue is anticompetitive. We defer for the moment the question whether that anticompetitive effect is outweighed by Microsoft's proffered justifications.

The second license provision at issue prohibits OEMs from modifying the initial boot sequence—the process that occurs the first time a consumer turns on the computer. Prior to the imposition of that restriction, "among the programs that many OEMs inserted into the boot sequence were Internet sign-up procedures that encouraged users to choose from a list of IAPs assembled by the OEM." Findings of Fact p. 210. Microsoft's prohibition on any alteration of the boot sequence thus prevents OEMs from using that process to promote the services of IAPs, many of which—at least at the time Microsoft imposed the restriction—used Navigator rather than IE in their internet access software. See id. p. 212; GX 295, reprinted in 12 J.A. at 14533 (Upon learning of OEM practices including boot sequence modification, Microsoft's Chairman, Bill Gates, wrote: "Apparently a lot of OEMs are bundling non-Microsoft browsers and coming up with offerings together with [IAPs] that get displayed on their machines in a FAR more prominent way than MSN or our Internet browser."). Microsoft does not deny that the prohibition on modifying the boot sequence has the effect of decreasing competition against IE by preventing OEMs from promoting rivals' browsers. Because this prohibition has a substantial effect in protecting Microsoft's market power, and does so through a means other than competition on the merits, it is anticompetitive. Again the question whether the provision is nonetheless justified awaits later treatment.

Finally, Microsoft imposes several additional provisions that, like the prohibition on removal of icons, prevent OEMs from making various alterations to the desktop: Microsoft prohibits OEMs from causing any user interface other than the Windows desktop to launch automatically, from adding icons or folders different in size or shape from those supplied by Microsoft, and from using the "Active Desktop" feature to promote third-party brands. These restrictions impose significant costs upon the OEMs; prior to Microsoft's prohibiting the practice, many OEMs would change the appearance of the desktop in ways they found beneficial. . . .

The dissatisfaction of the OEM customers does not, of course, mean the restrictions are anticompetitive. The anticompetitive effect of the license restrictions is, as Microsoft itself recognizes, that OEMs are not able to promote rival browsers, which keeps developers focused upon the APIs in Windows. Findings of Fact p. 212 (quoting Microsoft's Gates as writing, "winning Internet browser share is a very very important goal for us," and emphasizing the need to prevent OEMs from promoting both rival browsers and IAPs that might use rivals' browsers); see also 01/13/99 Tr. at 305–06 (excerpts from deposition of James Von Holle of Gateway) (prior to restriction Gateway had pre-installed non-IE internet registration icon that was larger than other desktop icons). This kind of promotion is not a zero-sum game; but for the restrictions in their licenses to use Windows, OEMs could promote multiple IAPs and browsers. By preventing the OEMs from doing so, this type of license restriction, like the first two restrictions, is anticompetitive: Microsoft reduced rival browsers' usage share not by improving its own product but, rather, by preventing OEMs from taking actions that could increase rivals' share of usage.

b. Microsoft's justifications for the license restrictions

Microsoft argues that the license restrictions are legally justified because, in imposing them, Microsoft is simply "exercising its rights as the holder of valid copyrights." Appellant's Opening Br. at 102. Microsoft also argues that the licenses "do not unduly restrict the opportunities of Netscape to distribute Navigator in any event." Id.

Microsoft's primary copyright argument borders upon the frivolous. The company claims an absolute and unfettered right to use its intellectual property as it wishes: "If intellectual property rights have been lawfully acquired," it says, then "their subsequent exercise cannot give rise to antitrust liability. Appellant's Opening Br. at 105. That is no more correct than the proposition that use of one's personal property, such as a baseball bat, cannot give rise to tort liability. As the Federal Circuit succinctly stated: "Intellectual property rights do not confer a privilege to violate the antitrust laws." *In re Indep. Serv. Orgs. Antitrust Litig.*, 203 F.3d 1322, 1325 (Fed.Cir.2000).

Although Microsoft never overtly retreats from its bold and incorrect position on the law, it also makes two arguments to the effect that it is not exercising its copyright in an unreasonable manner, despite the anticompetitive consequences of the license restrictions discussed above. In the first variation upon its unqualified copyright defense, Microsoft cites two cases indicating that a copyright holder may limit a licensee's ability to engage in significant and deleterious alterations of a copyrighted work. See *Gilliam v. ABC*, 538 F.2d 14, 21 (2d Cir.1976), *WGN Cont'l Broad. Co. v. United Video, Inc.*, 693 F.2d 622, 625 (7th Cir.1982). The relevance of those two cases for the present one is limited, however, both because those cases involved substantial alterations of a copyrighted work, see *Gilliam, 538 F.2d at 18,* and because in neither case was there any claim that the copyright holder was, in asserting its rights, violating the antitrust laws, see *WGN Cont'l Broad., 693 F.2d at 626;* see also *Cmty. for Creative Non–Violence v. Reid, 846 F.2d 1485, 1498 (D.C.Cir.1988)* (noting, again in a context free of any antitrust concern, that "an author [ ] may have rights against" a licensee that "excessively mutilated or altered" the copyrighted work).

The only license restriction Microsoft seriously defends as necessary to prevent a "substantial alteration" of its copyrighted work is the prohibition on OEMs automatically launching a substitute user interface upon completion of the boot process. See Findings of Fact p. 211 ("[A] few large OEMs developed programs that ran automatically at the conclusion of a new PC system's first boot sequence. These programs replaced the Windows desktop either with a user interface designed by the OEM or with Navigator's user interface."). We agree that a shell that automatically prevents the Windows desktop from ever being seen by the user is a drastic alteration of Microsoft's copyrighted work, and outweighs the marginal anticompetitive effect of prohibiting the OEMs from substituting a different interface automatically upon completion of the initial boot process. We therefore hold that this particular restriction is not an exclusionary practice that violates § 2 of the Sherman Act.

In a second variation upon its copyright defense, Microsoft argues that the license restrictions merely prevent OEMs from taking actions that would reduce substantially the value of Microsoft's copyrighted work: that is, Microsoft claims each license restriction in question is necessary to prevent OEMs from so altering Windows as to undermine "the principal value of Windows as a stable and consistent platform that supports a broad range of applications and that is familiar to users." Appellant's Opening Br. at 102. Microsoft, however, never substantiates this claim, and, because an OEM's altering the appearance of the desktop or promoting programs in the boot sequence does not affect the code already in the product, the practice does not self-evidently affect either the "stability" or the "consistency" of the platform. See Conclusions of Law, at 41; Findings of Fact p. 227. Microsoft cites only one item of evidence in support of its claim that the OEMs' alterations were decreasing the value of Windows. Defendant's Trial Exhibit ("DX") 2395 at MSV0009378A, reprinted in 19 J.A. at 12575. That document, prepared by Microsoft itself, states: "there are quality issues created by OEMs who are too liberal with the pre-install process," referring to the OEMs' installation of Windows and additional software on their PCs, which the document says may result in "user concerns and confusion." To the extent the OEMs' modifications cause consumer confusion, of course, the OEMs bear the additional support costs. See Findings of Fact p. 159. Therefore, we conclude Microsoft has not shown that the OEMs' liberality reduces the value of Windows except in the sense that their promotion of rival browsers undermines Microsoft's monopoly—and that is not a permissible justification for the license restrictions.

Apart from copyright, Microsoft raises one other defense of the OEM license agreements: It argues that, despite the restrictions in the OEM license, Netscape is not completely blocked from distributing its product. That claim is insufficient to shield Microsoft from liability for those restrictions because, although Microsoft did not bar its rivals from all means of distribution, it did bar them from the cost-efficient ones.

In sum, we hold that with the exception of the one restriction, all the OEM license restrictions at issue represent uses of Microsoft's market power to protect its monopoly, unredeemed by any legitimate justification. The restrictions therefore violate § 2 of the Sherman Act.

2. Integration of IE and Windows

Although Microsoft's license restrictions have a significant effect in closing rival browsers out of one of the two primary channels of distribution, the District Court found that "Microsoft's executives believed ... its contractual restrictions placed on OEMs would not be sufficient in themselves to reverse the direction of Navigator's usage share. Consequently, in late 1995 or early 1996, Microsoft set out to bind [IE] more tightly to Windows 95 as a technical matter." Findings of Fact p. 160.

Technologically binding IE to Windows, the District Court found, both prevented OEMs from pre-installing other browsers and deterred consumers from using them. In particular, having the IE software code as an irremovable part of Windows meant that pre-installing a second browser would "increase an OEM's product testing costs," because an OEM must test and train its support staff to answer calls related to every software product preinstalled on the machine; moreover, pre-installing a browser in addition to IE would to many OEMs be "a questionable use of the scarce and valuable space on a PC's hard drive." Id. p. 159.

Although the District Court, in its Conclusions of Law, broadly condemned Microsoft's decision to bind "Internet Explorer to Windows with . . . technological shackles," Conclusions of Law, at 39, its findings of fact in support of that conclusion center upon three specific actions Microsoft took to weld IE to Windows: excluding IE from the "Add/Remove Programs" utility; designing Windows so as in certain circumstances to override the user's choice of a default browser other than IE; and commingling code related to browsing and other code in the same files, so that any attempt to delete the files containing IE would, at the same time, cripple the operating system. As with the license restrictions, we consider first whether the suspect actions had an anticompetitive effect, and then whether Microsoft has provided a procompetitive justification for them.

a. Anticompetitive effect of integration

As a general rule, courts are properly very skeptical about claims that competition has been harmed by a dominant firm's product design changes. *See, e.g., Foremost Pro Color, Inc. v. Eastman Kodak Co., 703 F.2d 534, 544–45 (9th Cir.1983).* In a competitive market, firms routinely innovate in the hope of appealing to consumers, sometimes in the process making their products incompatible with those of rivals; the imposition of liability when a monopolist does the same thing will inevitably deter a certain amount of innovation. This is all the more true in a market, such as this one, in which the product itself is rapidly changing. See Findings of Fact p 59. Judicial deference to product innovation, however, does not mean that a monopolist's product design decisions are *per se* lawful. See *Foremost Pro Color, 703 F.2d at 545;* see also *Cal. Computer Prods., 613 F.2d at 739, 744; In re IBM Peripheral EDP Devices Antitrust Litig., 481 F. Supp. 965, 1007–08 (N.D.Cal.1979).*

The District Court first condemned as anticompetitive Microsoft's decision to exclude IE from the "Add/Remove Programs" utility in Windows 98. Findings of Fact p. 170. Microsoft had included IE in the Add/Remove Programs utility in Windows 95, see id. pp. 175–76, but when it modified Windows 95 to produce Windows 98, it took IE out of the Add/Remove Programs utility. This change reduces the usage share of rival browsers not by making Microsoft's own browser more attractive to consumers but, rather, by discouraging OEMs from distributing rival products. See id. p 159. Because Microsoft's conduct, through something other than competition on the merits, has the effect of significantly reducing usage of rivals' products and hence protecting its own operating system monopoly, it is anticompetitive; we defer for the moment the question whether it is nonetheless justified.

Second, the District Court found that Microsoft designed Windows 98 "so that using Navigator on Windows 98 would have unpleasant consequences for users" by, in some circumstances, overriding the user's choice of a browser other than IE as his or her default browser. Id. pp. 171–72.

Plaintiffs argue that this override harms the competitive process by deterring consumers from using a browser other than IE even though they might prefer to do so, thereby reducing rival browsers' usage share and, hence, the ability of rival browsers to draw developer attention away from the APIs exposed by Windows. Microsoft does not deny, of course, that overriding the user's preference prevents some people from using other browsers. Because the override reduces rivals' usage share and protects Microsoft's monopoly, it too is anticompetitive.

Finally, the District Court condemned Microsoft's decision to bind IE to Windows 98 "by placing code specific to Web browsing in the same files as code that provided operating system functions." Id. p. 161; see also id. pp. 174, 192. Putting code supplying browsing functionality into a file with code supplying operating system functionality "ensures that the deletion of any file containing browsing-specific routines would also delete vital operating system routines and thus cripple Windows...." Id. p. 164. As noted above, preventing an OEM from removing IE deters it from installing a second browser because doing so increases the OEM's product testing and support costs; by contrast, had OEMs been able to remove IE, they might have chosen to pre-install Navigator alone. See id. p. 159.

Microsoft denies, as a factual matter, that it commingled browsing and non-browsing code, and it maintains the District Court's findings to the contrary are clearly erroneous. According to Microsoft, its expert "testified without contradiction that 'the very same code in Windows 98 that provides Web browsing functionality' also performs essential operating system functions—not code in the same files, but the very same software code." Appellant's Opening Br. at 79 (citing 5 J.A. 3291–92).

Microsoft's expert did not testify to that effect "without contradiction," however. A Government expert, Glenn Weadock, testified that Microsoft "designed [IE] so that some of the code that it uses co-resides in the same library files as other code needed for Windows." Direct Testimony p 30. Another Government expert likewise testified that one library file, SHDOCVW.DLL, "is really a bundle of separate functions. It contains some functions that have to do specifically with Web browsing, and it contains some general user interface functions as well." 12/14/98 am Tr. at 60–61 (trial testimony of Edward Felten), reprinted in 11 J.A. at 6953–54. One of Microsoft's own documents suggests as much. See Plaintiffs' Proposed Findings of Fact p. 131.2.vii (citing GX 1686 (under seal) (Microsoft document indicating some functions in SHDOCVW.DLL can be described as "IE only," others can be described as "shell only" and still others can be described as providing both "IE" and "shell" functions)).

In view of the contradictory testimony in the record, some of which supports the District Court's finding that Microsoft commingled browsing and non-browsing code, we cannot conclude that the finding was clearly erroneous. See *Anderson v. City of Bessemer City, 470 U.S. 564, 573–74 (1985)* ("If the district court's account of the evidence is plausible in light of the record viewed in its entirety, the court of appeals may not reverse it even though convinced that had it been sitting as the trier of fact, it would have weighed the evidence differently."). Accordingly, we reject Microsoft's argument that we should vacate Finding of Fact 159 as it relates to the commingling of code, and we conclude that such commingling has an anticompetitive effect; as noted above, the commingling deters OEMs from pre-installing rival browsers, thereby reducing the rivals' usage share and, hence, developers' interest in rivals' APIs as an alternative to the API set exposed by Microsoft's operating system.

b.   Microsoft's justifications for integration

Microsoft proffers no justification for two of the three challenged actions that it took in integrating IE into Windows—excluding IE from the Add/Remove Programs utility and commingling browser and operating system code. Although Microsoft does make some general claims regarding the benefits of integrating the browser and the operating system, *see, e.g.,* Direct Testimony of James Allchin p. 94, reprinted in 5 J.A. at 3321 ("Our vision of deeper levels of technical integration is highly efficient and provides substantial benefits to customers and developers."), it neither specifies nor substantiates those claims. Nor does it argue that either excluding IE from the Add/Remove Programs utility or commingling code achieves any integrative benefit. Plaintiffs plainly made out a prima facie case of harm to competition in the operating system market by demonstrating that Microsoft's actions increased its browser usage share and thus protected its operating system monopoly from a middleware threat and, for its part, Microsoft failed to meet its burden of showing that its conduct serves a purpose other than protecting its operating system monopoly. Accordingly, we hold that Microsoft's exclusion of IE from the Add/Remove Programs utility and its commingling of browser and operating system code constitute exclusionary conduct, in violation of § 2.

As for the other challenged act that Microsoft took in integrating IE into Windows—causing Windows to override the user's choice of a default browser in certain circumstances—Microsoft argues that it has "valid technical reasons." Specifically, Microsoft claims that it was necessary to design Windows to override the user's preferences when he or she invokes one of "a few" out "of the nearly 30 means of accessing the Internet." Appellant's Opening Br. at 82. According to Microsoft:

The Windows 98 Help system and Windows Update feature depend on ActiveX controls not supported by Navigator, and the now-discontinued Channel Bar utilized Microsoft's Channel Definition Format, which Navigator also did not support. Lastly, Windows 98 does not invoke Navigator if a user accesses the Internet through "My Computer" or "Windows Explorer" because doing so would defeat one of the purposes of those features— enabling users to move seamlessly from local storage devices to the Web in the same browsing window. Id. (internal citations omitted). The plaintiff bears the burden not only of rebutting a proffered justification but also of demonstrating that the anticompetitive effect of the challenged action outweighs it. In the District Court, plaintiffs appear to have done neither, let alone both; in any event, upon appeal, plaintiffs offer no rebuttal whatsoever. Accordingly, Microsoft may not be held liable for this aspect of its product design.

3.   Agreements with Internet Access Providers

The District Court also condemned as exclusionary Microsoft's agreements with various IAPs. The IAPs include both Internet Service Providers, which offer consumers internet access, and Online Services ("OLSs") such as America Online ("AOL"), which offer proprietary content in addition to internet access and other services. Findings of Fact p. 15. The District Court deemed Microsoft's agreements with the IAPs unlawful because:

> Microsoft licensed [IE] and the [IE] Access Kit [(of which, more below)] to hundreds of IAPs for no charge. [Findings of Fact] pp. 250–51. Then, Microsoft extended valuable promotional treatment to the ten most important IAPs in exchange for their commitment to promote and distribute [IE] and to exile Navigator from the desktop. Id. pp. 255–58, 261, 272, 288–90, 305–06. Finally, in exchange for efforts to upgrade existing subscribers to client software that came bundled with [IE] instead of Navigator, Microsoft granted rebates—and in some cases made outright payments—to those same IAPs. Id. pp. 259–60, 295. Conclusions of Law, at 41.

The District Court condemned Microsoft's actions in (1) offering IE free of charge to IAPs and (2) offering IAPs a bounty for each customer the IAP signs up for service using the IE browser. In effect, the court concluded that Microsoft is acting to preserve its monopoly by offering IE to IAPs at an attractive price. Similarly, the District Court held Microsoft liable for (3) developing the IE Access Kit ("IEAK"), a software package that allows an IAP to "create a distinctive identity for its service in as little as a few hours by customizing the [IE] title bar, icon, start and search pages," Findings of Fact p. 249, and (4) offering the IEAK to IAPs free of charge, on the ground that those acts, too, helped Microsoft preserve its monopoly. Conclusions of Law, at 41–42. Finally, the District Court found that (5) Microsoft agreed to provide easy access to IAPs' services from the Windows desktop in return for the IAPs' agreement to promote IE exclusively and to keep shipments of internet access software using Navigator under a specific percentage, typically 25%. See Conclusions of Law, at 42 (citing Findings of Fact pp. 258, 262, 289). We address the first four items—Microsoft's inducements—and then its exclusive agreements with IAPs.

Although offering a customer an attractive deal is the hallmark of competition, the Supreme Court has indicated that in very rare circumstances a price may be unlawfully low, or "predatory." See generally *Brooke Group, 509 U.S. at 220–27.* Plaintiffs argued before the District Court that Microsoft's pricing was indeed predatory; but instead of making the usual predatory pricing argument—that the predator would drive out its rivals by pricing below cost on a particular product and then, sometime in the future, raise its prices on that product above the competitive level in order to recoup its earlier losses—plaintiffs argued that by pricing below cost on IE (indeed, even paying people to take it), Microsoft was able simultaneously to preserve its stream of monopoly profits on Windows, thereby more than recouping its investment in below-cost pricing on IE. The District Court did not assign liability for predatory pricing, however, and plaintiffs do not press this theory on appeal.

The rare case of price predation aside, the antitrust laws do not condemn even a monopolist for offering its product at an attractive price, and we therefore have no warrant to condemn Microsoft for offering either IE or the IEAK free of charge or even at a negative price. Likewise, as we said above, a monopolist does not violate the Sherman Act simply by developing an attractive product. See *Grinnell, 384 U.S. at 571* ("Growth or development as a consequence of a superior product [or] business acumen" is no violation.). Therefore, Microsoft's development of the IEAK does not violate the Sherman Act.

We turn now to Microsoft's deals with IAPs concerning desktop placement. Microsoft concluded these exclusive agreements with all "the leading IAPs," Findings of Fact p. 244, including the major OLSs. Id. p. 245; see also id. pp. 305, 306. The most significant of the OLS deals is with AOL, which, when the deal was reached, "accounted for a substantial portion of all existing Internet access subscriptions and ... attracted a very large percentage of new IAP subscribers." Id. p. 272. Under that agreement Microsoft puts the AOL icon in the OLS folder on the Windows desktop and AOL does not promote any non-Microsoft browser, nor provide software using any non-Microsoft browser except at the customer's request, and even then AOL will not supply more than 15% of its subscribers with a browser other than IE. Id. p. 289.

The Supreme Court most recently considered an antitrust challenge to an exclusive contract in *Tampa Electric Co. v. Nashville Coal Co., 365 U.S. 320 (1961)*. That case, which involved a challenge to a requirements contract, was brought under § 3 of the Clayton Act and §§ 1 and 2 of the Sherman Act. The Court held that an exclusive contract does not violate the Clayton Act unless its probable effect is to "foreclose competition in a substantial share of the line of commerce affected." *Id. at 327*. The share of the market foreclosed is important because, for the contract to have an adverse effect upon competition, "the opportunities for other traders to enter into or remain in that market must be significantly limited." *Id. at 328*. Although "neither the Court of Appeals nor the District Court [had] considered in detail the question of the relevant market," *id. at 330*, the Court in Tampa Electric examined the record and, after defining the relevant market, determined that the contract affected less than one percent of that market. *Id. at 333*. After concluding, under the Clayton Act, that this share was "conservatively speaking, quite insubstantial," id., the Court went on summarily to reject the Sherman Act claims. *Id. at 335* ("If [the contract] does not fall within the broader prescription of § 3 of the Clayton Act it follows that it is not forbidden by those of the [Sherman Act].").

Following Tampa Electric, courts considering antitrust challenges to exclusive contracts have taken care to identify the share of the market foreclosed. Some courts have indicated that § 3 of the Clayton Act and § 1 of the Sherman Act require an equal degree of foreclosure before prohibiting exclusive contracts. *See, e.g., Roland Mach. Co. v. Dresser Indus., Inc., 749 F.2d 380, 393 (7th Cir.1984)* (Posner, J.). Other courts, however, have held that a higher market share must be foreclosed in order to establish a violation of the Sherman Act as compared to the Clayton Act. *See, e.g., Barr Labs. v. Abbott Labs., 978 F.2d 98, 110 (3d Cir.1992);* 11 HERBERT HOVENKAMP, ANTITRUST LAW ¶ 1800c4 (1998) ("The cases are divided, with a likely majority stating that the Clayton Act requires a smaller showing of anticompetitive effects.").

Though what is "significant" may vary depending upon the antitrust provision under which an exclusive deal is challenged, it is clear that in all cases the plaintiff must both define the relevant market and prove the degree of foreclosure. This is a prudential requirement; exclusivity provisions in contracts may serve many useful purposes. *See, e.g., Omega Envtl., Inc. v. Gilbarco, Inc., 127 F.3d 1157, 1162 (9th Cir.1997)* ("There are, however, well-recognized economic benefits to exclusive dealing arrangements, including the enhancement of interbrand competition."); *Barry Wright Corp. v. ITT Grinnell Corp., 724 F.2d 227, 236 (1st Cir.1983)* (Breyer, J.) ("Virtually every contract to buy 'forecloses' or 'excludes' alternative sellers from some portion of the market, namely the portion consisting of what was bought."). Permitting an antitrust action to proceed any time a firm enters into an exclusive deal would both discourage a presumptively legitimate business practice and encourage costly antitrust actions. Because an exclusive deal affecting a small fraction of a market clearly cannot have the requisite harmful effect upon competition, the requirement of a significant degree of foreclosure serves a useful screening function. Cf. Frank H. Easterbrook, The Limits of Antitrust, *63 TEX. L. REV. 1, 21–23 (1984)* (discussing use of presumptions in antitrust law to screen out cases in which loss to consumers and economy is likely outweighed by cost of inquiry and risk of deterring procompetitive behavior).

In this case, plaintiffs challenged Microsoft's exclusive dealing arrangements with the IAPs under both §§ 1 and 2 of the Sherman Act. The District Court, in analyzing the § 1 claim, stated, "unless the evidence demonstrates that Microsoft's agreements excluded Netscape altogether from access to roughly forty percent of the browser market, the Court should decline to find such agreements in violation of § 1." Conclusions of Law, at 52. The court recognized that Microsoft had substantially excluded Netscape from "the most efficient channels for Navigator to achieve browser usage share," *id. at 53;* see also Findings of Fact p. 145 ("No other distribution channel for browsing software even approaches the efficiency of OEM pre-installation and IAP bundling."), and had relegated it to more costly and less effective methods (such as mass mailing its browser on a disk or offering it for download over the internet); but because Microsoft has not "completely excluded Netscape" from reaching any potential user by some means of distribution, however ineffective, the court concluded the agreements do not violate § 1. Conclusions of Law, at 53. Plaintiffs did not cross-appeal this holding.

Turning to § 2, the court stated: "the fact that Microsoft's arrangements with various [IAPs and other] firms did not foreclose enough of the relevant market to constitute a § 1 violation in no way detracts from the Court's assignment of liability for the same arrangements under § 2. . . . All of Microsoft's agreements, including the non-exclusive ones, severely restricted Netscape's access to those distribution channels leading most efficiently to the acquisition of browser usage share." Conclusions of Law, at 53.

On appeal Microsoft argues that "courts have applied the same standard to alleged exclusive dealing agreements under both Section 1 and Section 2," Appellant's Opening Br. at 109, and it argues that the District Court's holding of no liability under § 1 necessarily precludes holding it liable under § 2. The District Court appears to have based its holding with respect to § 1 upon a "total exclusion test" rather than the 40% standard drawn from the caselaw. Even assuming the holding is correct, however, we nonetheless reject Microsoft's contention.

The basic prudential concerns relevant to §§ 1 and 2 are admittedly the same: exclusive contracts are commonplace-particularly in the field of distribution—in our competitive, market economy, and imposing upon a firm with market power the risk of an antitrust suit every time it enters into such a contract, no matter how small the effect, would create an unacceptable and unjustified burden upon any such firm. At the same time, however, we agree with plaintiffs that a monopolist's use of exclusive contracts, in certain circumstances, may give rise to a § 2 violation even though the contracts foreclose less than the roughly 40% or 50% share usually required in order to establish a § 1 violation. See generally Dennis W. Carlton, A General Analysis of Exclusionary Conduct and Refusal to Deal—Why Aspen and Kodak Are Misguided, *68 ANTITRUST L.J. 659 (2001)* (explaining various scenarios under which exclusive dealing, particularly by a dominant firm, may raise legitimate concerns about harm to competition).

In this case, plaintiffs allege that, by closing to rivals a substantial percentage of the available opportunities for browser distribution, Microsoft managed to preserve its monopoly in the market for operating systems. The IAPs constitute one of the two major channels by which browsers can be distributed. Findings of Fact p. 242. Microsoft has exclusive deals with "fourteen of the top fifteen access providers in North America[, which] account for a large majority of all Internet access subscriptions in this part of the world." Id. p. 308. By ensuring that the "majority" of all IAP subscribers are offered IE either as the default browser or as the only browser, Microsoft's deals with the IAPs clearly have a significant effect in preserving its monopoly; they help keep usage of Navigator below the critical level necessary for Navigator or any other rival to pose a real threat to Microsoft's monopoly. *See, e.g.*, id. p. 143 (Microsoft sought to "divert enough browser usage from Navigator to neutralize it as a platform.''); see also Carlton, at 670.

Plaintiffs having demonstrated a harm to competition, the burden falls upon Microsoft to defend its exclusive dealing contracts with IAPs by providing a procompetitive justification for them. Significantly, Microsoft's only explanation for its exclusive dealing is that it wants to keep developers focused upon its APIs—which is to say, it wants to preserve its power in the operating system market. 02/26/01 Ct. Appeals Tr. at 45–47. That is not an unlawful end, but neither is it a procompetitive justification for the specific means here in question, namely exclusive dealing contracts with IAPs. Accordingly, we affirm the District Court's decision holding that Microsoft's exclusive contracts with IAPs are exclusionary devices, in violation of § 2 of the Sherman Act.

4.   Dealings with Internet Content Providers, Independent Software Vendors, and Apple Computer

The District Court held that Microsoft engages in exclusionary conduct in its dealings with ICPs, which develop websites; ISVs, which develop software; and Apple, which is both an OEM and a software developer. See Conclusions of Law, at 42–43 (deals with ICPs, ISVs, and Apple "supplemented Microsoft's efforts in the OEM and IAP channels"). The District Court condemned Microsoft's deals with ICPs and ISVs, stating: "By granting ICPs and ISVs free licenses to bundle [IE] with their offerings, and by exchanging other valuable inducements for their agreement to distribute, promote[,] and rely on [IE] rather than Navigator, Microsoft directly induced developers to focus on its own APIs rather than ones exposed by Navigator." Id. (citing Findings of Fact pp. 334–35, 340).

With respect to the deals with ICPs, the District Court's findings do not support liability. After reviewing the ICP agreements, the District Court specifically stated that "there is not sufficient evidence to support a finding that Microsoft's promotional restrictions actually had a substantial, deleterious impact on Navigator's usage share." Findings of Fact p. 332. Because plaintiffs failed to demonstrate that Microsoft's deals with the ICPs have a substantial effect upon competition, they have not proved the violation of the Sherman Act.

As for Microsoft's ISV agreements, however, the District Court did not enter a similar finding of no substantial effect. The District Court described Microsoft's deals with ISVs as follows:

> In dozens of "First Wave" agreements signed between the fall of 1997 and the spring of 1998, Microsoft has promised to give preferential support, in the form of early Windows 98 and Windows NT betas, other technical information, and the right to use certain Microsoft seals of approval, to important ISVs that agree to certain conditions. One of these conditions is that the ISVs use Internet Explorer as the default browsing software for any software they develop with a hypertext-based user interface. Another condition is that the ISVs use Microsoft's "HTML Help," which is

accessible only with Internet Explorer, to implement their applications' help systems.

Id. p. 339. The District Court further found that the effect of these deals is to "ensure [ ] that many of the most popular Web-centric applications will rely on browsing technologies found only in Windows," id. p 340, and that Microsoft's deals with ISVs therefore "increase[ ] the likelihood that the millions of consumers using [applications designed by ISVs that entered into agreements with Microsoft] will use Internet Explorer rather than Navigator." Id. p. 340.

The District Court did not specifically identify what share of the market for browser distribution the exclusive deals with the ISVs foreclose. Although the ISVs are a relatively small channel for browser distribution, they take on greater significance because, [as discussed above, Microsoft] had largely foreclosed the two primary channels to its rivals. In that light, one can tell from the record that by affecting the applications used by "millions" of consumers, Microsoft's exclusive deals with the ISVs had a substantial effect in further foreclosing rival browsers from the market. (Data introduced by Microsoft, see Direct Testimony of Cameron Myhrvold p 84, reprinted in 6 J.A. at 3922–23, and subsequently relied upon by the District Court in its findings, *see, e.g.*, Findings of Fact p. 270, indicate that over the two-year period 1997–98, when Microsoft entered into the First Wave agreements, there were 40 million new users of the internet.) Because, by keeping rival browsers from gaining widespread distribution (and potentially attracting the attention of developers away from the APIs in Windows), the deals have a substantial effect in preserving Microsoft's monopoly, we hold that plaintiffs have made a prima facie showing that the deals have an anticompetitive effect.

Of course, that Microsoft's exclusive deals have the anticompetitive effect of preserving Microsoft's monopoly does not, in itself, make them unlawful. A monopolist, like a competitive firm, may have a perfectly legitimate reason for wanting an exclusive arrangement with its distributors. Accordingly, Microsoft had an opportunity to, but did not, present the District Court with evidence demonstrating that the exclusivity provisions have some such procompetitive justification. See Conclusions of Law, at 43 (citing Findings of Fact pp. 339–40) ("With respect to the ISV agreements, Microsoft has put forward no procompetitive business ends whatsoever to justify their exclusionary terms."). On appeal Microsoft likewise does not claim that the exclusivity required by the deals serves any legitimate purpose; instead, it states only that its ISV agreements reflect an attempt "to persuade ISVs to utilize Internet-related system services in Windows rather than Navigator." Appellant's Opening Br. at 114. As we explained before, however, keeping developers focused upon Windows—that is, preserving the Windows monopoly-is a competitively neutral goal. Microsoft having offered no procompetitive justification for its exclusive dealing arrangements with the ISVs, we hold that those arrangements violate § 2 of the Sherman Act.

Finally, the District Court held that Microsoft's dealings with Apple violated the Sherman Act. See Conclusions of Law, at 42–43. Apple is vertically integrated: it makes both software (including an operating system, Mac OS), and hardware (the Macintosh line of computers). Microsoft primarily makes software, including, in addition to its operating system, a number of popular applications. One, called "Office," is a suite of business productivity applications that Microsoft has ported to Mac OS. The District Court found that "ninety percent of Mac OS users running a suite of office productivity applications [use] Microsoft's Mac Office." Findings of Fact p. 344. Further, the District Court found that:

> In 1997, Apple's business was in steep decline, and many doubted that the company would survive much longer.... Many ISVs questioned the wisdom of continuing to spend time and money developing applications for the Mac OS. Had Microsoft announced in the midst of this atmosphere that it was ceasing to develop new versions of Mac Office, a great number of ISVs, customers, developers, and investors would have interpreted the announcement as Apple's death notice.

Id. p. 344. Microsoft recognized the importance to Apple of its continued support of Mac Office. See id. p. 347 (quoting internal Microsoft e-mail) ("[We] need a way to push these guys[, *i.e.*, Apple] and [threatening to cancel Mac Office] is the only one that seems to make them move."); see also id. ("[Microsoft Chairman Bill] Gates asked whether Microsoft could conceal from Apple in the coming month the fact that Microsoft was almost finished developing Mac Office 97."); id. at p. 354 ("I think ... Apple should be using [IE] everywhere and if they don't do it, then we can use Office as a club.").

In June 1997 Microsoft Chairman Bill Gates determined that the company's negotiations with Apple " 'have not been going well at all.... Apple let us down on the browser by making Netscape the standard install.' Gates then reported that he had already called Apple's CEO ... to ask 'how we should announce the cancellation of Mac Office....' " Id. at p. 349. The District Court further found that, within a month of Gates' call, Apple and Microsoft had reached an agreement pursuant to which

> Microsoft's primary obligation is to continue releasing up-to-date versions of Mac Office for at least five years.... [and] Apple has agreed ... to "bundle the most current version of [IE] ... with [Mac OS]" ... [and to] "make [IE] the default [browser]." ... Navigator is not installed on the computer hard drive during the default installation, which is the type of installation most users elect to employ.... [The] Agreement further provides that ... Apple may not position icons for non-Microsoft browsing software on the desktop of new Macintosh PC systems or Mac OS upgrades.

Id. pp. 350–52. The agreement also prohibits Apple from encouraging users to substitute another browser for IE, and states that Apple will "encourage its employees to use [IE]." Id. p. 352.

This exclusive deal between Microsoft and Apple has a substantial effect upon the distribution of rival browsers. If a browser developer ports its product to a second operating system, such as the Mac OS, it can continue to display a common set of APIs. Thus, usage share, not the underlying operating system, is the primary determinant of the platform challenge a browser may pose. Pre-installation of a browser [which can be accomplished either by including the browser with the operating system or by the OEM installing] (the browser) is one of the two most important methods of browser distribution, and Apple had a not insignificant share of worldwide sales of operating systems. See id. p. 35 (Microsoft has 95% of the market not counting Apple and "well above" 80% with Apple included in the relevant market). Because Microsoft's exclusive contract with Apple has a substantial effect in restricting distribution of rival browsers, and because (as we have described several times above) reducing usage share of rival browsers serves to protect Microsoft's monopoly, its deal with Apple must be regarded as anticompetitive. See Conclusions of Law, at 42 (citing Findings of Fact p. 356) ("By extracting from Apple terms that significantly diminished the usage of Navigator on the Mac OS, Microsoft helped to ensure that developers would not view Navigator as truly cross-platform middleware.").

Microsoft offers no procompetitive justification for the exclusive dealing arrangement. It makes only the irrelevant claim that the IE-for-Mac Office deal is part of a multifaceted set of agreements between itself and Apple, see Appellant's Opening Br. at 61 ("Apple's 'browsing software' obligation was [not] the quid pro quo for Microsoft's Mac Office obligation[;] ... all of the various obligations ... were part of one 'overall agreement' between the two companies."); that does not mean it has any procompetitive justification. Accordingly, we hold that the exclusive deal with Apple is exclusionary, in violation of § 2 of the Sherman Act.

5. Java

Java, a set of technologies developed by Sun Microsystems, is another type of middleware posing a potential threat to Windows' position as the ubiquitous platform for software development. Findings of Fact p. 28. The Java technologies include: (1) a programming language; (2) a set of programs written in that language, called the "Java class libraries," which expose APIs; (3) a compiler, which translates code written by a developer into "bytecode"; and (4) a Java Virtual Machine ("JVM"), which translates bytecode into instructions to the operating system. Id. p. 73. Programs calling upon the Java APIs will run on any machine with a "Java runtime environment," that is, Java class libraries and a JVM. Id. pp. 73, 74.

In May 1995 Netscape agreed with Sun to distribute a copy of the Java runtime environment with every copy of Navigator, and "Navigator quickly became the principal vehicle by which Sun placed copies of its Java runtime environment on the PC systems of Windows users." Id. p. 76. Microsoft, too, agreed to promote the Java technologies—or so it seemed. For at the same time, Microsoft took steps "to maximize the difficulty with which applications written in Java could be ported from Windows to other platforms, and vice versa." Conclusions of Law, at 43. Specifically, the District Court found that Microsoft took four steps to exclude Java from developing as a viable cross-platform threat: (a) designing a JVM incompatible with the one developed by Sun; (b) entering into contracts, the so-called "First Wave Agreements," requiring major ISVs to promote Microsoft's JVM exclusively; (c) deceiving Java developers about the Windows-specific nature of the tools it distributed to them; and (d) coercing Intel to stop aiding Sun in improving the Java technologies.

a. The incompatible JVM

The District Court held that Microsoft engaged in exclusionary conduct by developing and promoting its own JVM. Conclusions of Law, at 43–44. Sun had already developed a JVM for the Windows operating system when Microsoft began work on its version. The JVM developed by Microsoft allows Java applications to run faster on Windows than does Sun's JVM, Findings of Fact p. 389, but a Java application designed to work with Microsoft's JVM does not work with Sun's JVM and vice versa. Id. p. 390. The District Court found that Microsoft "made a large investment of engineering resources to develop a high-performance Windows JVM," id. p 396, and, "by bundling its ... JVM with every copy of [IE] ... Microsoft endowed its Java runtime environment with the unique attribute of guaranteed, enduring ubiquity across the enormous Windows installed base," id. p. 397. As explained above, however, a monopolist does not violate the antitrust laws simply by developing a product that is incompatible with those of its rivals. See supra Section II.B.1. In order to violate the antitrust laws, the incompatible product must have an anticompetitive effect that outweighs any procompetitive justification for the design. Microsoft's JVM is not only incompatible with Sun's, it allows Java applications to run faster on Windows than does Sun's JVM. Microsoft's faster JVM lured Java developers into using Microsoft's developer tools, and Microsoft offered those tools deceptively, as we discuss below. The JVM, however, does allow applications to run more swiftly and does not itself have any anticompetitive effect. Therefore, we reverse the District Court's imposition of liability for Microsoft's development and promotion of its JVM.

b. The First Wave Agreements

The District Court also found that Microsoft entered into First Wave Agreements with dozens of ISVs to use Microsoft's JVM. See Findings of Fact p. 401 ("In exchange for costly technical support and other blandishments, Microsoft induced dozens of important ISVs to make their Java applications reliant on Windows-specific technologies and to refrain from distributing to Windows users JVMs that complied with Sun's standards."). Again, we reject the District Court's condemnation of low but non-predatory pricing by Microsoft.

To the extent Microsoft's First Wave Agreements with the ISVs conditioned receipt of Windows technical information upon the ISVs' agreement to promote Microsoft's JVM exclusively, they raise a different competitive concern. The District Court found that, although not literally exclusive, the deals were exclusive in practice because they required developers to make Microsoft's JVM the default in the software they developed. Id. p. 401.

While the District Court did not enter precise findings as to the effect of the First Wave Agreements upon the overall distribution of rival JVMs, the record indicates that Microsoft's deals with the major ISVs had a significant effect upon JVM promotion. As discussed above, the products of First Wave ISVs reached millions of consumers. Id. p. 340. The First Wave ISVs included such prominent developers as Rational Software, see GX 970, reprinted in 15 J.A. at 9994–10000, "a world leader" in software development tools, see Direct Testimony of Michael Devlin p. 2, reprinted in 5 J.A. at 3520, and Symantec, see GX 2071, reprinted in 22 J.A. at 14960–66 (sealed), which, according to Microsoft itself, is "the leading supplier of utilities such as anti-virus software," Defendant's Proposed Findings of Fact p. 276, reprinted in 3 J.A. at 1689. Moreover, Microsoft's exclusive deals with the leading ISVs took place against a backdrop of foreclosure: the District Court found that "when Netscape announced in May 1995 [prior to Microsoft's execution of the First Wave Agreements] that it would include with every copy of Navigator a copy of a Windows JVM that complied with Sun's standards, it appeared that Sun's Java implementation would achieve the necessary ubiquity on Windows." Findings of Fact p. 394. As discussed above, however, Microsoft undertook a number of anti-competitive actions that seriously reduced the distribution of Navigator, and the District Court found that those actions thereby seriously impeded distribution of Sun's JVM. Conclusions of Law, at 43–44. Because Microsoft's agreements foreclosed a substantial portion of the field for JVM distribution and because, in so doing, they protected Microsoft's monopoly from a middleware threat, they are anticompetitive.

Microsoft offered no procompetitive justification for the default clause that made the First Wave Agreements exclusive as a practical matter. See Findings of Fact p. 401. Because the cumulative effect of the deals is anticompetitive and because Microsoft has no procompetitive justification for them, we hold that the provisions in the First Wave Agreements requiring use of Microsoft's JVM as the default are exclusionary, in violation of the Sherman Act.

c. Deception of Java developers

Microsoft's "Java implementation" included, in addition to a JVM, a set of software development tools it created to assist ISVs in designing Java applications. The District Court found that, not only were these tools incompatible with Sun's cross-platform aspirations for Java—no violation, to be sure-but Microsoft deceived Java developers regarding the Windows-specific nature of the tools. Microsoft's tools included "certain 'keywords' and 'compiler directives' that could only be executed properly by Microsoft's version of the Java runtime environment for Windows." Id. p. 394; see also Direct Testimony of James Gosling p. 58, reprinted in 21 J.A. at 13959 (Microsoft added "programming instructions ... that alter the behavior of the code."). As a result, even Java "developers who were opting for portability over performance ... unwittingly [wrote] Java applications that [ran] only on Windows." Conclusions of Law, at 43. That is, developers who relied upon Microsoft's public commitment to cooperate with Sun and who used Microsoft's tools to develop what Microsoft led them to believe were [cross-platform] applications ended up producing applications that would run only on the Windows operating system.

When specifically accused by a PC Week reporter of fragmenting Java standards so as to prevent cross-platform uses, Microsoft denied the accusation and indicated it was only "adding rich platform support" to what remained a crossplatform implementation. An e-mail message internal to Microsoft, written shortly after the conversation with the reporter, shows otherwise:

> Ok, i just did a followup call.... [The reporter] liked that i kept pointing customers to w3c standards [(commonly observed internet protocols)].... [but] he accused us of being schizo with this vs. our java approach, i said he misunderstood [—] that [with Java] we are merely trying to add rich platform support to an interop layer.... this plays well.... at this point its [sic] not good to create MORE noise around our win32 java classes. instead we should just quietly grow j [(Microsoft's development tools)] share and assume that people will take more advantage of our classes without ever realizing they are building win 32–only java apps.

GX 1332, reprinted in 22 J.A. at 14922–23.

Finally, other Microsoft documents confirm that Microsoft intended to deceive Java developers, and predicted that the effect of its actions would be to generate Windows-dependent Java applications that their developers believed would be cross-platform; these documents also indicate that Microsoft's ultimate objective was to thwart Java's threat to Microsoft's monopoly in the market for operating systems. One Microsoft document, for example, states as a strategic goal: "Kill cross-platform Java by growing the polluted Java market." GX 259, reprinted in 22 J.A. at 14514; see also id. ("Cross-platform capability is by far the number one reason for choosing/using Java.") (emphasis in original).

Microsoft's conduct related to its Java developer tools served to protect its monopoly of the operating system in a manner not attributable either to the superiority of the operating system or to the acumen of its makers, and therefore was anticompetitive. Unsurprisingly, Microsoft offers no procompetitive explanation for its campaign to deceive developers. Accordingly, we conclude this conduct is exclusionary, in violation of § 2 of the Sherman Act.

   d.   The threat to Intel

The District Court held that Microsoft also acted unlawfully with respect to Java by using its "monopoly power to prevent firms such as Intel from aiding in the creation of cross-platform interfaces." Conclusions of Law, at 43. In 1995 Intel was in the process of developing a highperformance, Windows-compatible JVM. Microsoft wanted Intel to abandon that effort because a fast, cross-platform JVM would threaten Microsoft's monopoly in the operating system market. At an August 1995 meeting, Microsoft's Gates told Intel that its "cooperation with Sun and Netscape to develop a Java runtime environment ... was one of the issues threatening to undermine cooperation between Intel and Microsoft." Findings of Fact p 396. Three months later, "Microsoft's Paul Maritz told a senior Intel executive that Intel's [adaptation of its multimedia software to comply with] Sun's Java standards was as inimical to Microsoft as Microsoft's support for non-Intel microprocessors would be to Intel." Id. p. 405.

Intel nonetheless continued to undertake initiatives related to Java. By 1996 "Intel had developed a JVM designed to run well ... while complying with Sun's cross-platform standards." Id. p. 396. In April of that year, Microsoft again urged Intel not to help Sun by distributing Intel's fast, Suncompliant JVM. Id. And Microsoft threatened Intel that if it did not stop aiding Sun on the multimedia front, then Microsoft would refuse to distribute Intel technologies bundled with Windows. Id. p. 404.

Intel finally capitulated in 1997, after Microsoft delivered the coup de grace.

One of Intel's competitors, called AMD, solicited support from Microsoft for its "3DX" technology.... Microsoft's Allchin asked Gates whether Microsoft should support 3DX, despite the fact that Intel would oppose it. Gates responded: "If Intel has a real problem with us supporting this then they will have to stop supporting Java Multimedia the way they are. I would gladly give up supporting this if they would back off from their work on JAVA." Id. p. 406.

Microsoft's internal documents and deposition testimony confirm both the anticompetitive effect and intent of its actions. *See, e.g.,* GX 235, reprinted in 22 J.A. at 14502 (Microsoft executive, Eric Engstrom, included among Microsoft's goals for Intel: "Intel to stop helping Sun create Java Multimedia APIs, especially ones that run well ... on Windows."); Deposition of Eric Engstrom at 179 ("We were successful [in convincing Intel to stop aiding Sun] for some period of time.").

Microsoft does not deny the facts found by the District Court, nor does it offer any procompetitive justification for pressuring Intel not to support cross-platform Java. Microsoft lamely characterizes its threat to Intel as "advice." The District Court, however, found that Microsoft's "advice" to Intel to stop aiding cross-platform Java was backed by the threat of retaliation, and this conclusion is supported by the evidence cited above. Therefore we affirm the conclusion that Microsoft's threats to Intel were exclusionary, in violation of § 2 of the Sherman Act.

6.   Course of Conduct

The District Court held that, apart from Microsoft's specific acts, Microsoft was liable under § 2 based upon its general "course of conduct." In reaching this conclusion the court relied upon *Continental Ore Co. v. Union Carbide & Carbon Corp., 370 U.S. 690, 699 (1962),* where the Supreme Court stated, "in [Sherman Act cases], plaintiffs should be given the full benefit of their proof without tightly compartmentalizing the various factual components and wiping the slate clean after scrutiny of each.''

Microsoft points out that Continental Ore and the other cases cited by plaintiffs in support of "course of conduct" liability all involve conspiracies among multiple firms, not the conduct of a single firm; in that setting the "course of conduct" is the conspiracy itself, for which all the participants may be held liable. Plaintiffs respond that, as a policy matter, a monopolist's unilateral "campaign of [acts intended to exclude a rival] that in the aggregate has the requisite impact" warrants liability even if the acts viewed individually would be lawful for want of a significant effect upon competition.

We need not pass upon plaintiffs' argument, however, because the District Court did not point to any series of acts, each of which harms competition only slightly but the cumulative effect of which is significant enough to form an independent basis for liability. The "course of conduct" section of the District Court's opinion contains, with one exception, only broad, summarizing conclusions. *See, e.g.,* Conclusions of Law, at 44 ("Microsoft placed an oppressive thumb on the scale of competitive fortune. . . .") The only specific acts to which the court refers are Microsoft's expenditures in promoting its browser, see id. ("Microsoft has expended wealth and foresworn opportunities to realize more. . . ."), which we have explained are not in themselves unlawful. Because the District Court identifies no other specific acts as a basis for "course of conduct" liability, we reverse its conclusion that Microsoft's course of conduct separately violates § 2 of the Sherman Act.

C. Causation

As a final parry, Microsoft urges this court to reverse on the monopoly maintenance claim, because plaintiffs never established a causal link between Microsoft's anticompetitive conduct, in particular its foreclosure of Netscape's and Java's distribution channels, and the maintenance of Microsoft's operating system monopoly. See Findings of Fact p. 411 ("There is insufficient evidence to find that, absent Microsoft's actions, Navigator and Java already would have ignited genuine competition in the market for Intel-compatible PC operating systems."). This is the flip side of Microsoft's earlier argument that the District Court should have included middleware in the relevant market. According to Microsoft, the District Court cannot simultaneously find that middleware is not a reasonable substitute and that Microsoft's exclusionary conduct contributed to the maintenance of monopoly power in the operating system market. Microsoft claims that the first finding depended on the court's view that middleware does not pose a serious threat to Windows, see supra Section II.A, while the second finding required the court to find that Navigator and Java would have developed into serious enough cross-platform threats to erode the applications barrier to entry. We disagree.

Microsoft points to no case, and we can find none, standing for the proposition that, as to § 2 liability in an equitable enforcement action, plaintiffs must present direct proof that a defendant's continued monopoly power is precisely attributable to its anticompetitive conduct. As its lone authority, Microsoft cites the following passage from Professor Areeda's antitrust treatise: "The plaintiff has the burden of pleading, introducing evidence, and presumably proving by a preponderance of the evidence that reprehensible behavior has contributed significantly to the ... maintenance of the monopoly." 3 PHILLIP E. AREEDA & HERBERT HOVEN-KAMP, ANTITRUST LAW ¶ 650c, at 69 (1996) (emphasis added).

But, with respect to actions seeking injunctive relief, the authors of that treatise also recognize the need for courts to infer "causation" from the fact that a defendant has engaged in anticompetitive conduct that "reasonably appears capable of making a significant contribution to ... maintaining monopoly power." Id. p. 651c, at 78; see also *Morgan v. Ponder, 892 F.2d 1355, 1363 (8th Cir.1989); Barry Wright, 724 F.2d at 230.* To require that § 2 liability turn on a plaintiff's ability or inability to reconstruct the hypothetical marketplace absent a defendant's anticompetitive conduct would only encourage monopolists to take more and earlier anticompetitive action.

We may infer causation when exclusionary conduct is aimed at producers of nascent competitive technologies as well as when it is aimed at producers of established substitutes. Admittedly, in the former case there is added uncertainty, inasmuch as nascent threats are merely potential substitutes. But the underlying proof problem is the same—neither plaintiffs nor the court can confidently reconstruct a product's hypothetical technological development in a world absent the defendant's exclusionary conduct. To some degree, "the defendant is made to suffer the uncertain consequences of its own undesirable conduct." 3 AREEDA & HOVENKAMP, ANTITRUST LAW ¶ 651c, at 78.

Given this rather edentulous test for causation, the question in this case is not whether Java or Navigator would actually have developed into viable platform substitutes, but (1) whether as a general matter the exclusion of nascent threats is the type of conduct that is reasonably capable of contributing significantly to a defendant's continued monopoly power and (2) whether Java and Navigator reasonably constituted nascent threats at the time Microsoft engaged in the anticompetitive conduct at issue. As to the first, suffice it to say that it would be inimical to the purpose of the Sherman Act to allow monopolists free reign to squash nascent, albeit unproven, competitors at will—particularly in industries marked by rapid technological advance and frequent paradigm shifts. Findings of Fact pp. 59–60. As to the second, the District Court made ample findings that both Navigator and Java showed potential as middleware platform threats. Findings of Fact pp. 68–77. Counsel for Microsoft admitted as much at oral argument. 02/26/01 Ct. Appeals Tr. at 27 ("There are no constraints on output. Marginal costs are essentially zero. And there are to some extent network effects. So a company like Netscape founded in 1994 can be by the middle of 1995 clearly a potentially lethal competitor to Windows because it can supplant its position in the market because of the characteristics of these markets.").

Microsoft's concerns over causation have more purchase in connection with the appropriate remedy issue, *i.e.*, whether the court should impose a structural remedy or merely enjoin the offensive conduct at issue. As we point out later in this opinion, divestiture is a remedy that is imposed only with great caution, in part because its long-term efficacy is rarely certain. See infra Section V.E. Absent some measure of confidence that there has been an actual loss to competition that needs to be restored, wisdom counsels against adopting radical structural relief. See 3 AREEDA & HOVENKAMP, ANTITRUST LAW p. 653b, at 91–92 ("More extensive equitable relief, particularly remedies such as divestiture designed to eliminate the monopoly altogether, raise more serious questions and require a clearer indication of a significant causal connection between the conduct and creation or maintenance of the market power."). But these queries go to questions of remedy, not liability. In short, causation affords Microsoft no defense to liability for its unlawful actions undertaken to maintain its monopoly in the operating system market.

III. ATTEMPTED MONOPOLIZATION

Microsoft further challenges the District Court's determination of liability for "attempting to monopolize . . . any part of the trade or commerce among the several States." 15 U.S.C. § 2 (1997). To establish a § 2 violation for attempted monopolization, "a plaintiff must prove . . . a dangerous probability of achieving monopoly power." *Spectrum Sports, Inc. v. McQuillan, 506 U.S. 447, 456 (1993)*. . . .

[T]he District Court concluded that "Netscape's assent to Microsoft's market division proposal would have, instanter, resulted in Microsoft's attainment of monopoly power in a second market," and that "the proposal itself created a dangerous probability of that result." Conclusions of Law, at 46 (citation omitted). The District Court further concluded that "the predatory course of conduct Microsoft has pursued since June of 1995 has revived the dangerous probability that Microsoft will attain monopoly power in a second market." Id.

At the outset we note a pervasive flaw in the District Court's and plaintiffs' discussion of attempted monopolization. Simply put, plaintiffs have made the same argument under two different headings—monopoly maintenance and attempted monopolization. They have relied upon Microsoft's § 2 liability for monopolization of the operating system market as a presumptive indicator of attempted monopolization of an entirely different market. The District Court implicitly accepted this approach: It agreed with plaintiffs that the events that formed the basis for the § 2 monopolization claim "warranted additional liability as an illegal attempt to amass monopoly power in 'the browser market.'" Id. at 45 (emphasis added). Thus, plaintiffs and the District Court failed to recognize the need for an analysis wholly independent of the conclusions and findings on monopoly maintenance.

To establish a dangerous probability of success, plaintiffs must as a threshold matter show that the browser market can be monopolized, *i.e.*, that a hypothetical monopolist in that market could enjoy market power. This, in turn, requires plaintiffs (1) to define the relevant market and (2) to demonstrate that substantial barriers to entry protect that market. Because plaintiffs have not carried their burden on either prong, we reverse without remand.

A.   Relevant Market....

Defining a market for an attempted monopolization claim involves the same steps as defining a market for a monopoly maintenance claim, namely a detailed description of the purpose of a browser—what functions may be included and what are not—and an examination of the substitutes that are part of the market and those that are not. The District Court never engaged in such an analysis nor entered detailed findings defining what a browser is or what products might constitute substitutes. In the Findings of Fact, the District Court (in a section on whether IE and Windows are separate products) stated only that "a Web browser provides the ability for the end user to select, retrieve, and perceive resources on the Web." Findings of Fact p. 150. Furthermore, in discussing attempted monopolization in its Conclusions of Law, the District Court failed to demonstrate analytical rigor when it employed varying and imprecise references to the "market for browsing technology for Windows," "the browser market," and "platform-level browsing software." Conclusions of Law, at 45....

B.   Barriers to Entry

Because a firm cannot possess monopoly power in a market unless that market is also protected by significant barriers to entry, see supra Section II.A, it follows that a firm cannot threaten to achieve monopoly power in a market unless that market is, or will be, similarly protected. See *Spectrum Sports, 506 U.S. at 456*....

Giving plaintiffs and the District Court the benefit of the doubt, we might remand if the possible existence of entry barriers resulting from the possible creation and exploitation of network effects in the browser market were the only concern. That is not enough to carry the day, however, because the District Court did not make two key findings: (1) that network effects were a necessary or even probable, rather than merely possible, consequence of high market share in the browser market and (2) that a barrier to entry resulting from network effects would be "significant" enough to confer monopoly power. Again, these deficiencies are in large part traceable to plaintiffs' own failings....

IV.   TYING

Microsoft also contests the District Court's determination of liability under § 1 of the Sherman Act. The District Court concluded that Microsoft's contractual and technological bundling of the IE web browser (the "tied" product) with its Windows operating system ("OS") (the "tying" product) resulted in a tying arrangement that was *per se* unlawful. Conclusions of Law, at 47–51. We hold that the rule of reason, rather than *per se* analysis, should govern the legality of tying arrangements involving platform software products. The Supreme Court has warned that " 'it is only after considerable experience with certain business relationships that courts classify them as *per se* violations. . . .' " *Broad. Music, Inc. v. CBS, 441 U.S. 1, 9, (1979)* (quoting *United States v. Topco Assocs., 405 U.S. 596, 607–08 (1972))* While every "business relationship" will in some sense have unique features, some represent entire, novel categories of dealings. As we shall explain, the arrangement before us is an example of the latter, offering the first up-close look at the technological integration of added functionality into software that serves as a platform for third-party applications. There being no close parallel in prior antitrust cases, simplistic application of *per se* tying rules carries a serious risk of harm. Accordingly, we vacate the District Court's finding of a *per se* tying violation and remand the case. Plaintiffs may on remand pursue their tying claim under the rule of reason.

The facts underlying the tying allegation substantially overlap with those set forth in Section II.B in connection with the § 2 monopoly maintenance claim. The key District Court findings are that (1) Microsoft required licensees of Windows 95 and 98 also to license IE as a bundle at a single price, Findings of Fact pp. 137, 155, 158; (2) Microsoft refused to allow OEMs to uninstall or remove IE from the Windows desktop, id. pp 158, 203, 213; (3) Microsoft designed Windows 98 in a way that withheld from consumers the ability to remove IE by use of the Add/Remove Programs utility, id. p 170; cf. id. p. 165 (stating that IE was subject to Add/Remove Programs utility in Windows 95); and (4) Microsoft designed Windows 98 to override the user's choice of default web browser in certain circumstances, id. pp. 171, 172. The court found that these acts constituted a *per se* tying violation. Conclusions of Law, at 47–51. Although the District Court also found that Microsoft commingled operating system-only and browser-only routines in the same library files, Findings of Fact pp. 161, 164, it did not include this as a basis for tying liability despite plaintiffs' request that it do so.

There are four elements to a *per se* tying violation: (1) the tying and tied goods are two separate products; (2) the defendant has market power in the tying product market; (3) the defendant affords consumers no choice but to purchase the tied product from it; and (4) the tying arrangement forecloses a substantial volume of commerce. See *Eastman Kodak Co. v. Image Tech. Servs., Inc., 504 U.S. 451, 461–62 (1992); Jefferson Parish Hosp. Dist. No. 2 v. Hyde, 466 U.S. 2, 12–18 (1984).* [In general, see Chapter 8, Section 3, infra.]

Microsoft does not dispute that it bound Windows and IE in the four ways the District Court cited. Instead it argues that Windows (the tying good) and IE browsers (the tied good) are not "separate products," Appellant's Opening Br. at 69–79, and that it did not substantially foreclose competing browsers from the tied product market, *id. at 79–83.* (Microsoft also contends that it does not have monopoly power in the tying product market, *id. at 84–96,* but, for reasons given in Section II.A, we uphold the District Court's finding to the contrary.)

We first address the separate-products inquiry, a source of much argument between the parties and of confusion in the cases. Our purpose is to highlight the poor fit between the separate-products test and the facts of this case. We then offer further reasons for carving an exception to the *per se* rule when the tying product is platform software. In the final section we discuss the District Court's inquiry if plaintiffs pursue a rule of reason claim on remand.

A. Separate–Products Inquiry Under the *per se* Test

The requirement that a practice involve two separate products before being condemned as an illegal tie started as a purely linguistic requirement: unless products are separate, one cannot be "tied" to the other. Indeed, the nature of the products involved in early tying cases—intuitively distinct items such as a movie projector and a film, *Motion Picture Patents Co. v. Universal Film Mfg. Co., 243 U.S. 502 (1917)*—led courts either to disregard the separate-products question. . . . It was not until *Times-Picayune Publishing Co. v. United States, 345 U.S. 594 (1953)*, that the separate-products issue became a distinct element of the test for an illegal tie. *Id. at 614.* Even that case engaged in a rather cursory inquiry into whether ads sold in the morning edition of a paper were a separate product from ads sold in the evening edition.

The first case to give content to the separate-products test was *Jefferson Parish, 466 U.S. 2.* That case addressed a tying arrangement in which a hospital conditioned surgical care at its facility on the purchase of anesthesiological services from an affiliated medical group. The facts were a challenge for casual separate-products analysis because the tied service—anesthesia—was neither intuitively distinct from nor intuitively contained within the tying service—surgical care. A further complication was that, soon after the Court enunciated the *per se* rule for tying liability in *International Salt Co. v. United States, 332 U.S. 392, 396 (1947)*, new economic research began to cast doubt on the assumption, voiced by the Court when it established the rule, that " 'tying agreements serve hardly any purpose beyond the suppression of competition. . . .' "

The Jefferson Parish Court resolved the matter in two steps. First, it clarified that "the answer to the question whether one or two products are involved" does not turn "on the functional relation between them. . . ." *Jefferson Parish, 466 U.S. at 19;* see also *466 U.S. at 19 n.30.* In other words, the mere fact that two items are complements, that "one . . . is useless without the other," id., does not make them a single "product" for purposes of tying law. Accord *Eastman Kodak, 504 U.S. at 463.* Second, reasoning that the "definitional question [whether two distinguishable products are involved] depends on whether the arrangement may have the type of competitive consequences addressed by the rule [against tying]," *Jefferson Parish, 466 U.S. at 21,* the Court decreed that "no tying arrangement can exist unless there is a sufficient demand for the purchase of anesthesiological services separate from hospital services to identify a distinct product market in which it is efficient to offer anesthesiological services separately from hospital service," *id. at 21–22* (emphasis added); accord *Eastman Kodak, 504 U.S. at 462. . . .*

To understand the logic behind the Court's consumer demand test, consider first the postulated harms from tying. The core concern is that tying prevents goods from competing directly for consumer choice on their merits, *i.e.*, being selected as a result of "buyers' independent judgment," *id. at 13* (internal quotes omitted). With a tie, a buyer's "freedom to select the best bargain in the second market [could be] impaired by his need to purchase the tying product, and perhaps by an inability to evaluate the true cost of either product. . . ." *Id. at 15.* Direct competition on the merits of the tied product is foreclosed when the tying product either is sold only in a bundle with the tied product or, though offered separately, is sold at a bundled price, so that the buyer pays the same price whether he takes the tied product or not. In both cases, a consumer buying the tying product becomes entitled to the tied product; he will therefore likely be unwilling to buy a competitor's version of the tied product even if, making his own price/quality assessment, that is what he would prefer.

But not all ties are bad. Bundling obviously saves distribution and consumer transaction costs. 9 PHILLIP E. AREEDA, ANTITRUST LAW p. 1703g2, at 51–52 (1991). This is likely to be true, to take some examples from the computer industry, with the integration of math co-processors and memory into microprocessor chips and the inclusion of spell checkers in word processors. . . . Bundling can also capitalize on certain economies of scope. A possible example is the "shared" library files that perform OS and browser functions with the very same lines of code and thus may save drive space from the clutter of redundant routines and memory when consumers use both the OS and browser simultaneously. . . . Indeed, if there were no efficiencies from a tie (including economizing on consumer transaction costs such as the time and effort involved in choice), we would expect distinct consumer demand for each individual component of every good. In a competitive market with zero transaction costs, the computers on which this opinion was written would only be sold piecemeal—keyboard, monitor, mouse, central processing unit, disk drive, and memory all sold in separate transactions and likely by different manufacturers.

Recognizing the potential benefits from tying, see *Jefferson Parish, 466 U.S. at 21 n.33*, the Court in Jefferson Parish forged a separate-products test that, like those of market power and substantial foreclosure, attempts to screen out false positives under *per se* analysis. The consumer demand test is a rough proxy for whether a tying arrangement may, on balance, be welfare-enhancing, and unsuited to *per se* condemnation. In the abstract, of course, there is always direct separate demand for products: assuming choice is available at zero cost, consumers will prefer it to no choice. Only when the efficiencies from bundling are dominated by the benefits to choice for enough consumers, however, will we actually observe consumers making independent purchases. In other words, perceptible separate demand is inversely proportional to net efficiencies. On the supply side, firms without market power will bundle two goods only when the cost savings from joint sale outweigh the value consumers place on separate choice. So bundling by all competitive firms implies strong net efficiencies. If a court finds either that there is no noticeable separate demand for the tied product or, there being no convincing direct evidence of separate demand, that the entire "competitive fringe" engages in the same behavior as the defendant, 10 AREEDA ET AL., ANTITRUST LAW p. 1744c4, at 200, then the tying and tied products should be declared one product and *per se* liability should be rejected.

Before concluding our exegesis of Jefferson Parish's separate-products test, we should clarify two things. First, Jefferson Parish does not endorse a direct inquiry into the efficiencies of a bundle. Rather, it proposes easy-to administer proxies for net efficiency. In describing the separate-products test we discuss efficiencies only to explain the rationale behind the consumer demand inquiry. To allow the separate-products test to become a detailed inquiry into possible welfare consequences would turn a screening test into the very process it is expected to render unnecessary. 10 AREEDA ET AL., ANTITRUST LAW pp. 1741b & c, at 180–85; see also *Jefferson Parish, 466 U.S. at 34–35* (O'Connor, J., concurring).

Second, the separate-products test is not a one-sided inquiry into the cost savings from a bundle. Although Jefferson Parish acknowledged that prior lower court cases looked at cost-savings to decide separate products, see *id. at 22 n.35,* the Court conspicuously did not adopt that approach in its disposition of tying arrangement before it. Instead it chose proxies that balance costs savings against reduction in consumer choice.

With this background, we now turn to the separate products inquiry before us. The District Court found that many consumers, if given the option, would choose their browser separately from the OS. Findings of Fact p. 151 (noting that "corporate consumers . . . prefer to standardize on the same browser across different [OSs]" at the workplace). Turning to industry custom, the court found that, although all major OS vendors bundled browsers with their OSs, these companies either sold versions without a browser, or allowed OEMs or end-users either not to install the bundled browser or in any event to "uninstall" it. Id. p. 153. The court did not discuss the record evidence as to whether OS vendors other than Microsoft sold at a bundled price, with no discount for a browserless OS, perhaps because the record evidence on the issue was in conflict. Compare, *e.g.*, Direct Testimony of Richard Schmalensee p. 241, reprinted in 7 J.A. at 4315 ("All major operating system vendors do in fact include Web-browsing software with the operating system at no extra charge.") (emphasis added), with, *e.g.*, 1/6/99 pm Tr. at 42 (trial testimony of Franklin Fisher of MIT) (suggesting all OSs but Microsoft offer discounts).

Microsoft does not dispute that many consumers demand alternative browsers. But on industry custom Microsoft contends that no other firm requires non-removal because no other firm has invested the resources to integrate web browsing as deeply into its OS as Microsoft has. . . . Microsoft contends not only that its integration of IE into Windows is innovative and beneficial but also that it requires non-removal of IE. In our discussion of monopoly maintenance we find that these claims fail the efficiency balancing applicable in that context. But the separate-products analysis is supposed to perform its function as a proxy without embarking on any direct analysis of efficiency. Accordingly, Microsoft's implicit argument—that in this case looking to a competitive fringe is inadequate to evaluate fully its potentially innovative technological integration, that such a comparison is between apples and oranges—poses a legitimate objection to the operation of Jefferson Parish's separate-products test for the *per se* rule.

In fact there is merit to Microsoft's broader argument that Jefferson Parish's consumer demand test would "chill innovation to the detriment of consumers by preventing firms from integrating into their products new functionality previously provided by standalone products—and hence, by definition, subject to separate consumer demand." Appellant's Opening Br. at 69. The *per se* rule's direct consumer demand and indirect industry custom inquiries are, as a general matter, backward-looking and therefore systematically poor proxies for overall efficiency in the presence of new and innovative integration. See 10 AREEDA ET AL., ANTITRUST LAW p 1746, at 224–29; Amicus Brief of Lawrence Lessig at 24–25, and sources cited therein (brief submitted regarding Conclusions of Law). The direct consumer demand test focuses on historic consumer behavior, likely before integration, and the indirect industry custom test looks at firms that, unlike the defendant, may not have integrated the tying and tied goods. Both tests compare incomparables—the defendant's decision to bundle in the presence of integration, on the one hand, and consumer and competitor calculations in its absence, on the other. If integration has efficiency benefits, these may be ignored by the Jefferson Parish proxies. Because one cannot be sure beneficial integration will be protected by the other elements of the *per se* rule, simple application of that rule's separate-products test may make consumers worse off.

In light of the monopoly maintenance section, obviously, we do not find that Microsoft's integration is welfare-enhancing or that it should be absolved of tying liability. Rather, we heed Microsoft's warning that the separate-products element of the *per se* rule may not give newly integrated products a fair shake.

B.   *Per se* Analysis Inappropriate for this Case.

We now address directly the larger question as we see it: whether standard *per se* analysis should be applied "off the shelf" to evaluate the defendant's tying arrangement, one which involves software that serves as a platform for thirdparty applications. There is no doubt that "it is far too late in the history of our antitrust jurisprudence to question the proposition that certain tying arrangements pose an unacceptable risk of stifling competition and therefore are unreasonable 'per se.' " *Jefferson Parish, 466 U.S. at 9* (emphasis added). But there are strong reasons to doubt that the integration of additional software functionality into an OS falls among these arrangements. Applying *per se* analysis to such an amalgamation creates undue risks of error and of deterring welfare-enhancing innovation . . . .

In none of these [Supreme Court] cases was the tied good physically and technologically integrated with the tying good. Nor did the defendants ever argue that their tie improved the value of the tying product to users and to makers of complementary goods. In those cases where the defendant claimed that use of the tied good made the tying good more valuable to users, the Court ruled that the same result could be achieved via quality standards for substitutes of the tied good. *See, e.g., Int'l Salt, 332 U.S. at 397–98; IBM, 298 U.S. at 138–40.* Here Microsoft argues that IE and Windows are an integrated physical product and that the bundling of IE APIs with Windows makes the latter a better applications platform for third-party software. It is unclear how the benefits from IE APIs could be achieved by quality standards for different browser manufacturers. We do not pass judgment on Microsoft's claims regarding the benefits from integration of its APIs. We merely note that these and other novel, purported efficiencies suggest that judicial "experience" provides little basis for believing that, "because of their pernicious effect on competition and lack of any redeeming virtue," a software firm's decisions to sell multiple functionalities as a package should be "conclusively presumed to be unreasonable and therefore illegal without elaborate inquiry as to the precise harm they have caused or the business excuse for their use." *N. Pac. Ry., 356 U.S. at 5* (emphasis added). Nor have we found much insight into software integration among the decisions of lower federal courts....

While the paucity of cases examining software bundling suggests a high risk that *per se* analysis may produce inaccurate results, the nature of the platform software market affirmatively suggests that *per se* rules might stunt valuable innovation. We have in mind two reasons.

First, as we explained in the previous section, the separate products test is a poor proxy for net efficiency from newly integrated products. Under *per se* analysis the first firm to merge previously distinct functionalities (*e.g.*, the inclusion of starter motors in automobiles) or to eliminate entirely the need for a second function (*e.g.*, the invention of the stain resistant carpet) risks being condemned as having tied two separate products because at the moment of integration there will appear to be a robust "distinct" market for the tied product. Rule of reason analysis, however, affords the first mover an opportunity to demonstrate that an efficiency gain from its "tie" adequately offsets any distortion of consumer choice....

The failure of the separate-products test to screen out certain cases of productive integration is particularly troubling in platform software markets such as that in which the defendant competes. Not only is integration common in such markets, but it is common among firms without market power. We have already reviewed evidence that nearly all competitive OS vendors also bundle browsers. Moreover, plaintiffs do not dispute that OS vendors can and do incorporate basic internet plumbing and other useful functionality into their Oss.... Firms without market power have no incentive to package different pieces of software together unless there are efficiency gains from doing so. The ubiquity of bundling in competitive platform software markets should give courts reason to pause before condemning such behavior in less competitive markets.

Second, because of the pervasively innovative character of platform software markets, tying in such markets may produce efficiencies that courts have not previously encountered and thus the Supreme Court had not factored into the *per se* rule as originally conceived. For example, the bundling of a browser with OSs enables an independent software developer to count on the presence of the browser's APIs, if any, on consumers' machines and thus to omit them from its own package.... It is true that software developers can bundle the browser APIs they need with their own products, see id. p 193, but that may force consumers to pay twice for the same API if it is bundled with two different software programs. It is also true that OEMs can include APIs with the computers they sell, id., but diffusion of uniform APIs by that route may be inferior....

These arguments all point to one conclusion: we cannot comfortably say that bundling in platform software markets has so little "redeeming virtue," *N. Pac. Ry., 356 U.S. at 5,* and that there would be so "very little loss to society" from its ban, that "an inquiry into its costs in the individual case [can be] considered [ ] unnecessary." *Jefferson Parish, 466 U.S. at 33–34* (O'Connor, J., concurring). We do not have enough empirical evidence regarding the effect of Microsoft's practice on the amount of consumer surplus created or consumer choice foreclosed by the integration of added functionality into platform software to exercise sensible judgment regarding that entire class of behavior. (For some issues we have no data.) "We need to know more than we do about the actual impact of these arrangements on competition to decide whether they ... should be classified as *per se* violations of the Sherman Act." *White Motor, 372 U.S. at 263.* Until then, we will heed the wisdom that "easy labels do not always supply ready answers," *Broad. Music, 441 U.S. at 8,* and vacate the District Court's finding of *per se* tying liability under Sherman Act § 1. We remand the case for evaluation of Microsoft's tying arrangements under the rule of reason....

Our judgment regarding the comparative merits of the *per se* rule and the rule of reason is confined to the tying arrangement before us, where the tying product is software whose major purpose is to serve as a platform for third-party applications and the tied product is complementary software functionality. While our reasoning may at times appear to have broader force, we do not have the confidence to speak to facts outside the record, which contains scant discussion of software integration generally. Microsoft's primary justification for bundling IE APIs is that their inclusion with Windows increases the value of third-party software (and Windows) to consumers. See Appellant's Opening Br. at 41–43. Because this claim applies with distinct force when the tying product is platform software, we have no present basis for finding the *per se* rule inapplicable to software markets generally. Nor should we be interpreted as setting a precedent for switching to the rule of reason every time a court identifies an efficiency justification for a tying arrangement. Our reading of the record suggests merely that integration of new functionality into platform software is a common practice and that wooden application of *per se* rules in this litigation may cast a cloud over platform innovation in the market for PCs, network computers and information appliances. . . .

V. TRIAL PROCEEDINGS AND REMEDY

Microsoft additionally challenges the District Court's procedural rulings on two fronts. First, with respect to the trial phase, Microsoft proposes that the court mismanaged its docket by adopting an expedited trial schedule and receiving evidence through summary witnesses. Second, with respect to the remedies decree, Microsoft argues that the court improperly ordered that it be divided into two separate companies. Only the latter claim will long detain us. The District Court's trial-phase procedures were comfortably within the bounds of its broad discretion to conduct trials as it sees fit. We conclude, however, that the District Court's remedies decree must be vacated for three independent reasons: (1) the court failed to hold a remedies-specific evidentiary hearing when there were disputed facts; (2) the court failed to provide adequate reasons for its decreed remedies; and (3) this Court has revised the scope of Microsoft's liability and it is impossible to determine to what extent that should affect the remedies provisions. . . .

Microsoft's first contention—that the District Court erred by adopting an expedited trial schedule and receiving evidence through summary witnesses—is easily disposed of. Trial courts have extraordinarily broad discretion to determine the manner in which they will conduct trials. . . . Although the company claims that setting an early trial date inhibited its ability to conduct discovery, it never identified a specific deposition or document it was unable to obtain. And while Microsoft now argues that the use of summary witnesses made inevitable the improper introduction of hearsay evidence, the company actually agreed to the District Court's proposal to limit each side to 12 summary witnesses. . . . Even absent Microsoft's agreement, the company's challenge fails to show that this use of summary witnesses falls outside the trial court's wide latitude to receive evidence as it sees fit. . . .

The District Court's remedies-phase proceedings are a different matter. It is a cardinal principle of our system of justice that factual disputes must be heard in open court and resolved through trial-like evidentiary proceedings. Any other course would be contrary "to the spirit which imbues our judicial tribunals prohibiting decision without hearing." *Sims v. Greene, 161 F.2d 87, 88 (3d Cir.1947)*.

A party has the right to judicial resolution of disputed facts not just as to the liability phase, but also as to appropriate relief. "Normally, an evidentiary hearing is required before an injunction may be granted." *United States v. McGee, 714 F.2d 607, 613 (6th Cir.1983)*. . . . Other than a temporary restraining order, no injunctive relief may be entered without a hearing. See generally FED. R. CIV. P. 65. A hearing on the merits—*i.e.*, a trial on liability—does not substitute for a relief-specific evidentiary hearing unless the matter of relief was part of the trial on liability, or unless there are no disputed factual issues regarding the matter of relief....

Despite plaintiffs' protestations, there can be no serious doubt that the parties disputed a number of facts during the remedies phase. In two separate offers of proof, Microsoft identified 23 witnesses who, had they been permitted to testify, would have challenged a wide range of plaintiffs' factual representations, including the feasibility of dividing Microsoft, the likely impact on consumers, and the effect of divestiture on shareholders. To take but two examples, where plaintiffs' economists testified that splitting Microsoft in two would be socially beneficial, the company offered to prove that the proposed remedy would "cause substantial social harm by raising software prices, lowering rates of innovation and disrupting the evolution of Windows as a software development platform." Defendant's Offer of Proof at 6, reprinted in 4 J.A. at 2747. And where plaintiffs' investment banking experts proposed that divestiture might actually increase shareholder value, Microsoft proffered evidence that structural relief "would inevitably result in a significant loss of shareholder value," a loss that could reach "tens—possibly hundreds—of billions of dollars." Id. at 19, reprinted in 4 J.A. at 2760....

We vacate the District Court's remedies decree for the additional reason that the court has failed to provide an adequate explanation for the relief it ordered. The Supreme Court has explained that a remedies decree in an antitrust case must seek to "unfetter a market from anticompetitive conduct," *Ford Motor Co., 405 U.S. at 577,* to "terminate the illegal monopoly, deny to the defendant the fruits of its statutory violation, and ensure that there remain no practices likely to result in monopolization in the future," *United States v. United Shoe Mach. Corp., 391 U.S. 244, 250 (1968);* see also *United States v. Grinnell Corp., 384 U.S. 563, 577 (1966).*

The District Court has not explained how its remedies decree would accomplish those objectives. Indeed, the court devoted a mere four paragraphs of its order to explaining its reasons for the remedy. They are: (1) Microsoft "does not yet concede that any of its business practices violated the Sherman Act"; (2) Microsoft "continues to do business as it has in the past"; (3) Microsoft "has proved untrustworthy in the past"; and (4) the Government, whose officials "are by reason of office obliged and expected to consider—and to act in—the public interest," won the case, "and for that reason alone have some entitlement to a remedy of their choice." Final Judgment, at 62–63. Nowhere did the District Court discuss the objectives the Supreme Court deems relevant....

[We must also vacate the remedies decree because this] court has drastically altered the District Court's conclusions on liability. On remand, the District Court, after affording the parties a proper opportunity to be heard, can fashion an appropriate remedy for Microsoft's antitrust violations. In particular, the court should consider which of the decree's conduct restrictions remain viable in light of our modification of the original liability decision. While the task of drafting the remedies decree is for the District Court in the first instance, because of the unusually convoluted nature of the proceedings thus far, and a desire to advance the ultimate resolution of this important controversy, we offer some further guidance for the exercise of that discretion.

As a general matter, a district court is afforded broad discretion to enter that relief it calculates will best remedy the conduct it has found to be unlawful.... And divestiture is a common form of relief in successful antitrust prosecutions: it is indeed "the most important of antitrust remedies." *See, e.g., United States v. E.I. du Pont de Nemours & Co., 366 U.S. 316, 331 (1961).*

On remand, the District Court must reconsider whether the use of the structural remedy of divestiture is appropriate with respect to Microsoft, which argues that it is a unitary company. By and large, cases upon which plaintiffs rely in arguing for the split of Microsoft have involved the dissolution of entities formed by mergers and acquisitions. On the contrary, the Supreme Court has clarified that divestiture "has traditionally been the remedy for Sherman Act violations whose heart is intercorporate combination and control," *du Pont, 366 U.S. at 329* (emphasis added), and that "complete divestiture is particularly appropriate where asset or stock acquisitions violate the antitrust laws," *Ford Motor Co., 405 U.S. at 573.*

One apparent reason why courts have not ordered the dissolution of unitary companies is logistical difficulty. As the court explained in *United States v. ALCOA, 91 F. Supp. 333, 416 (S.D.N.Y.1950)*, a "corporation, designed to operate effectively as a single entity, cannot readily be dismembered of parts of its various operations without a marked loss of efficiency." A corporation that has expanded by acquiring its competitors often has preexisting internal lines of division along which it may more easily be split than a corporation that has expanded from natural growth. Although time and corporate modifications and developments may eventually fade those lines, at least the identifiable entities preexisted to create a template for such division as the court might later decree. With reference to those corporations that are not acquired by merger and acquisition, Judge Wyzanski accurately opined in United Shoe:

> United conducts all machine manufacture at one plant in Beverly, with one set of jigs and tools, one foundry, one laboratory for machinery problems, one managerial staff, and one labor force. It takes no Solomon to see that this organism cannot be cut into three equal and viable parts.

United States v. United Shoe Machine Co., 110 F. Supp. 295, 348 (D.Mass. 1953).

Depending upon the evidence, the District Court may find in a remedies proceeding that it would be no easier to split Microsoft in two than United Shoe in three. Microsoft's Offer of Proof in response to the court's denial of an evidentiary hearing included proffered testimony from its President and CEO Steve Ballmer that the company "is, and always has been, a unified company without free-standing business units. Microsoft is not the result of mergers or acquisitions." Microsoft further offered evidence that it is "not organized along product lines," but rather is housed in a single corporate headquarters and that it has

> only one sales and marketing organization which is responsible for selling all of the company's products, one basic research organization, one product support organization, one operations department, one information technology department, one facilities department, one purchasing department, one human resources department, one finance department, one legal department and one public relations department.

Defendant's Offer of Proof at 23–26, reprinted in 4 J.A. at 2764–67. If indeed Microsoft is a unitary company, division might very well require Microsoft to reproduce each of these departments in each new entity rather than simply allocate the differing departments among them.

In devising an appropriate remedy, the District Court also should consider whether plaintiffs have established a sufficient causal connection between Microsoft's anticompetitive conduct and its dominant position in the OS market. "Mere existence of an exclusionary act does not itself justify full feasible relief against the monopolist to create maximum competition." 3 AREEDA & HOVENKAMP, ANTITRUST LAW p. 650a, at 67. Rather, structural relief, which is "designed to eliminate the monopoly altogether ... requires a clearer indication of a significant causal connection between the conduct and creation or maintenance of the market power." Id. p. 653b, at 91–92 (emphasis added). Absent such causation, the antitrust defendant's unlawful behavior should be remedied by "an injunction against continuation of that conduct." Id. p. 650a, at 67.

As noted above, see supra Section II.C, we have found a causal connection between Microsoft's exclusionary conduct and its continuing position in the operating systems market only through inference. See 3 AREEDA & HOVENKAMP, ANTITRUST LAW p. 653(b), at 91–92 (suggesting that "more extensive equitable relief, particularly remedies such as divestiture designed to eliminate the monopoly altogether, ... require a clearer indication of significant causal connection between the conduct and creation or maintenance of the market power"). Indeed, the District Court expressly did not adopt the position that Microsoft would have lost its position in the OS market but for its anticompetitive behavior. Findings of Fact p. 411 ("There is insufficient evidence to find that, absent Microsoft's actions, Navigator and Java already would have ignited genuine competition in the market for Intel-compatible PC operating systems."). If the court on remand is unconvinced of the causal connection between Microsoft's exclusionary conduct and the company's position in the OS market, it may well conclude that divestiture is not an appropriate remedy.

While we do not undertake to dictate to the District Court the precise form that relief should take on remand, we note again that it should be tailored to fit the wrong creating the occasion for the remedy....

VI.   JUDICIAL MISCONDUCT

Canon 3A(6) of the Code of Conduct for United States Judges requires federal judges to "avoid public comment on the merits of [ ] pending or impending" cases. Canon 2 tells judges to "avoid impropriety and the appearance of impropriety in all activities," on the bench and off. Canon 3A(4) forbids judges to initiate or consider ex parte communications on the merits of pending or impending proceedings. Section 455(a) of the Judicial Code requires judges to recuse themselves when their "impartiality might reasonably be questioned." 28 U.S.C. § 455(a).

All indications are that the District Judge violated each of these ethical precepts by talking about the case with reporters. The violations were deliberate, repeated, egregious, and flagrant. The only serious question is what consequences should follow. Microsoft urges us to disqualify the District Judge, vacate the judgment in its entirety and toss out the findings of fact, and remand for a new trial before a different District Judge. At the other extreme, plaintiffs ask us to do nothing. We agree with neither position. [The D.C. Circuit concluded that the district judge should be disqualified retroactively only with respect to the imposition of the remedy, and remanded the case for reassignment to a different trial judge.]

NOTES AND QUESTIONS

1.   Both the government and Microsoft claimed victory after the D.C. Circuit rendered its decision. Which side was closer to correct? Please consider when reading Chapter 8, Section 3, whether the D.C. Circuit's tying discussion is consistent with the Supreme Court's decisions. Could the D.C. Circuit have avoided fashioning a special rule of reason when the "tying product is platform software" by focusing its analysis on the special "one product" or "two products" issue, and if two products were found, retaining a *per se* analysis? Would there be any greater antitrust problem to selling two products together at a lower price than would be the case when each is purchased separately if the lower price were the result of efficiency gains from bundling the two together?

2.   Compare the D.C. Circuit's rejection, as bordering "upon the frivolous," of Microsoft's claim that it has "an absolute and unfettered right to use its intellectual property as it wishes" with the Federal Circuit's *Xerox* opinion infra. The D.C. Circuit acknowledged that in technologically dynamic markets conduct remedies may be unavailing "because innovation to a large degree has already rendered the anticompetitive conduct obsolete (although by no means harmless)." What should be the standard for the awarding of structural relief in such a situation? On remand, the government and various states settled with Microsoft for conduct relief (*i.e.*, injunctive provisions). A lively debate continues as to whether these injunctive provisions provide effective—or even meaningful—relief.

3.   The Supreme Court recently granted *certiorari* in *Verizon Commmunications, Inc. v. Law Offices of Trinko*, 123 S.Ct. 1480 (2003). The Solicitor General's brief for the government in *Trinko* argues that there can be no exclusionary behavior under Section 2 if the monopolist has any business justification. Is such an

approach consistent with the balancing test in *Microsoft*? With the approach in *Aspen Skiing*? Is it good policy?

NOTE ON ISSUES AT THE INTERSECTION OF ANTITRUST AND INTELLECTUAL PROPERTY

An emerging area of interest in recent years concerns issues that arise at the intersection of intellectual property rights (mainly patent and copyright) and antitrust. Values underlying the two systems can be reconciled: IP rights subsidize investments in innovation by conferring time-limited market power on the innovator; antitrust seeks to ensure that markets remain open and firms compete to find new paths to innovation. But there are times when the systems are in conflict—for example, patents can be enforced so as to create market power outside the legitimate scope of the patent—and reconciliation in a way that rewards, but does not over-reward, incentives to innovate can be difficult.

These issues are particularly important because products that are the embodiment of ideas, and therefore candidates for intellectual property protection, are found in the most dynamic and fastest growing sectors of the U.S. economy, including computer software, internet services, biotechnology, new forms of communications, and others. Some have suggested that IP is just another form of property and deserves no special treatment under the antitrust laws. The United States Department of Justice and FTC Antitrust Guidelines for the Licensing of Intellectual Property 1995 says as much at § 2.1, but the Guidelines later go on to identify characteristics, such as ease of misappropriation, that distinguish IP from any other forms of property. Others have suggested that sectors of the economy characterized by IP are so dynamic that antitrust has little or no useful role to play. See Teece & Coleman, The Meaning of Monopoly: Antitrust Analysis in High–Technology Industries, 43 Antitrust Bull. 801, 843, 846 (1998). Are there differences between IP and other forms of property? Several, although not uniquely limited to IP, are noteworthy:

1. Differences in Fundamental Economics

Products and services based on IP are more often characterized by large initial investments ("fixed costs") and low cost to produce individual items ("variable costs"). For example, compare the cost of developing a new line of computer code with duplicating the code and making it available to others. As a result, producers at least in the short run tend to expand sales rapidly to maximize market share and therefore prices in early stages often decline.

Moreover, there is a tendency for IP markets to drift towards single-firm dominance and even monopoly. Market power can be protected by patent or copyright law. Most IP does not confer a monopoly—there are substitute products outside the scope of the IP—but it often confers significant market power. Also, some IP products and services exhibit "network effects," *i.e.*, each individual's demand for a particular company's product or service is positively related to its wide-spread use by others. Examples include fax machines and email which become more valuable to users as more people use the service. There also can be indirect network effects such as where producers of complementary goods design and manufacture complements to work with the goods of a single dominant firm. In sum, the economics of IP can both enhance and restrain innovation and competition.

2. Importance of Innovation in a Dynamic Economy

In a dynamic economy, the major concern need not be with ensuring maximum output and minimum consumer cost but rather with protecting incentives to innovate. On the other hand, it is important not to allow abusive market behavior which impairs the ability of other firms to challenge the technology incumbent, and to promote both price and innovation competition.

3. Uncertain Durability of Market Power

The most frequently cited reason for treating IP products and services more leniently under the antitrust laws is that those markets are characterized by an increased rate of innovation, relative ease of entry, and instability of market shares. As a result, it is argued that cartels and monopoly power in IP markets will necessarily be short-lived and, in any event, will be defeated more quickly and efficiently by market forces such as new entry and innovation than by government enforcement. See Shapiro & Varian, Information Rules 305 (1999) ("Certain high-tech industries are highly dynamic, making any monopoly power transitory"). While conceding that market power on average is less durable with respect to some sectors of the economy characterized by IP, it has also been noted that some IP giants (think of Microsoft and Intel) have retained their dominant position for substantial periods of time. That would suggest that the question whether market power is durable or ephemeral is fact specific and needs to be addressed on a market-by-market and product-by-product basis.

The following two cases, which reviewed very similar conduct but reached substantially different results, nicely frame the antitrust-IP controversy. Before turning to the two cases, you might reread the "Overview" section of the unanimous Court of Appeals decision in Microsoft about whether " 'old economy' Section 2 monopolization doctrines should apply to firms competing in dynamic technology markets...." see p. 769 supra. The D.C. Circuit concluded that the dynamic aspect of the market in which Microsoft operates "does not appreciably alter our mission." See pp. 760–70 supra. Note also the Court's treatment of Microsoft's argument that its challenged license restrictions were legally justified because it was simply "exercising its rights as the holder of valid copyrights." The Court concluded that the claim that the company has an unfettered right to use its intellectual property as it wishes "borders upon the frivolous." See p. 779 supra.

Oddly, the *Eastman Kodak* case that is printed below is a remand from a Supreme Court decision that is set out in Section 3 of this Chapter. When the case was first in the Supreme Court, the plaintiffs' principal charges related to alleged tie-in sales and other forms of leverage. The plaintiffs won and the case was remanded for trial. At the trial, the plaintiffs withdrew their tie-in claims and focused on their attempted monopolization and monopolization charges based on refusals to deal, and were met with a defense that the refusal related to patented and copyrighted materials and therefore was legitimate. The plaintiffs won again at the trial level, and we turn now to the Ninth Circuit's review of that decision.

After a brief discussion of monopoly leveraging and essential facilities theory (see note pp. 758–65 supra), the Ninth Circuit turns to a defense based on intellectual property.

Image Technical Services, Inc. v. Eastman Kodak Co.

United States Court of Appeals, Ninth Circuit, 1997.
125 F.3d 1195.

■ Beezer, J. Plaintiffs–Appellees Image Technical Services, and ten other independent service organizations ("ISOs") that service Kodak photocopiers and micrographic equipment sued the Eastman Kodak Co. ("Kodak") for violations of the Sherman Act. The ISOs alleged that Kodak used its monopoly in the market for Kodak photocopier and micrographic parts to create a second monopoly in the equipment service markets. A jury verdict awarded treble damages totaling $71.8 million. The district court denied Kodak's post trial motions and entered a ten-year permanent injunction requiring Kodak to sell "all parts" to ISOs. . . .

This appeal raises questions relating to the application of antitrust principles upon a finding that a monopolist unilaterally refused to deal with competitors. We also address overlapping patent and copyright issues and their significance in the antitrust context. . . .

I

Kodak manufactures, sells and services high volume photocopiers and micrographic (or microfilm) equipment. Competition in these markets is strong. In the photocopier market Kodak's competitors include Xerox, IBM and Canon. Kodak's competitors in the micrographics market include Minolta, Bell & Howell and 3M. Despite comparable products in these markets, Kodak's equipment is distinctive. Although Kodak equipment may perform similar functions to that of its competitors, Kodak's parts are not interchangeable with parts used in other manufacturers' equipment.

Kodak sells and installs replacement parts for its equipment. Kodak competes with ISOs in these markets. Kodak has ready access to all parts necessary for repair services because it manufactures many of the parts used in its equipment and purchases the remaining necessary parts from independent original-equipment manufacturers. ISOs began servicing Kodak equipment in the early 1980s, and have provided cheaper and better service at times, according to some customers. ISOs obtain parts for repair service from a variety of sources, including, at one time, Kodak.

As ISOs grew more competitive, Kodak began restricting access to its photocopiers and micrographic parts. In 1985, Kodak stopped selling copier parts to ISOs and in 1986, Kodak halted sales of micrographic parts to ISOs. Additionally, Kodak secured agreements from their contracted original-equipment manufacturers not to sell parts to ISOs. These parts restrictions limited the ISOs' ability to compete in the service market for Kodak machines. Competition in the service market requires that service providers have ready access to all parts.

Kodak offers annual or multi-year service contracts to its customers. Service providers generally contract with equipment owners through multi-year service contracts. ISOs claim that they were unable to provide similar contracts because they lack a reliable supply of parts. Some ISOs contend that the parts shortage forced them out of business. . . .

After remand [from the Supreme Court], the case proceeded to trial in the district court. Before closing arguments, the ISOs withdrew their § 1 tying and conspiracy claims. The remaining § 2 attempted monopolization and monopolization claims were submitted to the jury. A unanimous verdict awarded damages to the ISOs totaling $71.8 million after trebling. Ten ISOs were awarded damages covering lost service profits in the amount of $12,172,900 (before trebling) and six ISOs were awarded damages covering lost profits for used equipment sales totaling $11,775,400 (before trebling).

After accepting the verdict, the district court crafted a ten year injunction requiring Kodak to sell all parts to ISOs on "reasonable and nondiscriminatory terms and prices. . . ."

II

Section 2 of the Sherman Act prohibits monopolies, attempts to form monopolies, as well as combinations and conspiracies to do so. The ISOs presented evidence in support of two § 2 theories: attempted monopolization and monopolization. They alleged, and the jury concluded, that Kodak used its monopoly over Kodak photocopier and micrographic parts to attempt to create and actually create a second monopoly over the service markets. . . .

Kodak primarily attacks the ISOs' monopoly claim because success would likely upset the "attempt" verdict as well. We now address Kodak's appeal against the background of the Supreme Court's opinion in Kodak and the extensive record developed at trial. . . .

[The Ninth Circuit concluded that Kodak had monopoly power in "all Kodak parts" markets for photocopiers and micrographics equipment.]

The second element of a § 2 monopoly claim, the "conduct" element, is the use of monopoly power "to foreclose competition, to gain a competitive advantage, or to destroy a competitor." Kodak, 504 U.S. at 482–83 (quoting United States v. Griffith, 334 U.S. 100 (1948)). The ISOs proceeded under a "monopoly leveraging" theory, alleging that Kodak used its monopoly over Kodak parts to gain or attempt to gain a monopoly over the service of Kodak equipment. The Supreme Court endorsed this theory in Kodak noting: "If Kodak adopted its parts and service policies as part of a scheme of willful acquisition or maintenance of monopoly power, it will have violated § 2." Id. (citations omitted). "Willful acquisition" or "maintenance of monopoly power" involves "exclusionary conduct," not power gained "from growth or development as a consequence of a superior product, business acumen, or historic accident." Grinnell, 384 U.S. at 570–71.

Kodak attacks the district court's monopoly conduct jury instructions as well as the ISOs' evidence establishing Kodak's exclusionary conduct. A challenge to a jury instruction on the grounds that it misstates the relevant elements is a question of law reviewed de novo. Caballero v. Concord, 956 F.2d 204, 206 (9th Cir.1992). As noted, the jury's verdict will stand if supported by substantial evidence.

1. Kodak's chief complaint with the monopoly power jury instructions lies with Jury Instruction No. 29. That Instruction, entitled "Monopolization–Monopoly Conduct," states in relevant part:

> [a] company with monopoly power in a relevant market has no general duty to cooperate with its business rivals and may refuse to deal with them or with their customers if valid business reasons exist for such refusal. It is unlawful, however, for a monopolist to engage in conduct, including refusals to deal, that unnecessarily excludes or handicaps competitors in order to maintain a monopoly.

Kodak argues that this instruction lacks objective standards and improperly includes within the prohibited activities a lawful monopolist's "aggressive" competition.

Specifically, Kodak challenges Instruction No. 29's "unnecessarily excludes or handicaps competitors" language. Kodak says that this language is based on a form of "monopoly leveraging" that we previously rejected in *Alaska Airlines, Inc. v. United Airlines, Inc.* 948 F.2d 536, 543 (9th Cir.1991). In *Alaska Airlines* we did reject the Second circuit's holding in *Berkey Photo, Inc. v. Eastman Kodak Co.*, 603 F.2d 263 (2d Cir.1979). *Berkey Photo* recognized liability under § 2 of the Sherman Act on a theory of monopoly leveraging involving a firm which used "its monopoly power in one market to gain a competitive advantage in another, albeit without an attempt to monopolize the second market." 603 F.2d at 275. In *Alaska Airlines*, we held that "monopoly leveraging" could not exist as a basis for § 2 liability in the absence of the defendant using its monopoly in one market to monopolize or attempt to monopolize the downstream market. 948 F.2d at 547. We characterized Berkey Photo's downstream monopoly requirement—"to gain a competitive advantage"—as too "loose." *Alaska Airlines*, 948 F.2d at 546.

Kodak accuses the district court of incorporating Berkey Photo's repudiated language into the court's instructions. We disagree. Instruction No. 29 required the jury to find that Kodak's monopoly conduct be undertaken "in order to maintain a monopoly" in the downstream market. Berkey Photo's watered-down standard does not go this far. Instruction No. 29 makes clear that the monopolies at issue are Kodak's alleged service monopolies and the Instruction required the jury to find that Kodak acted in furtherance of maintaining its service monopolies. Instruction No. 29's "unnecessarily excludes or handicaps competitors" language does not come from *Berkey Photo*, but from the jury instruction endorsed by the Supreme Court in *Aspen Skiing Co. v. Aspen Highlands Skiing Corp.*, 472 U.S. 585, 597, 611 (1985).

2.   Kodak also objects to the attempted monopolization and monopolization jury instructions on the grounds that they fail to describe adequately the "essential facilities" doctrine, which Kodak contends is the controlling law in unilateral refusal to deal cases. Kodak asserts that this doctrine is the sole legal theory which could require Kodak to sell "all parts." Kodak argues that the essential facilities doctrine required the jury to find that Kodak's parts monopoly carries "the power to eliminate competition."

Kodak's challenge raises a novel issue: whether a monopolist is liable under § 2 of the Sherman Act for an anticompetitive refusal to deal only under an "essential facilities" theory, that is, only when the refusal involves something "essential" to the survival of competitors. As noted, Kodak would answer affirmatively; we reject this theory. Instead, relying on *Kodak and Aspen Skiing*, we endorse the ISOs' theory that § 2 of the Sherman Act prohibits a monopolist from refusing to deal in order to create or maintain a monopoly absent a legitimate business justification. We need not apply the essential facilities doctrine. . . .

III

Our conclusion that the ISOs have shown that Kodak has both attained monopoly power and exercised exclusionary conduct does not end our inquiry. Kodak's conduct may not be actionable if supported by a legitimate business justification. When a legitimate business justification supports a monopolist's exclusionary conduct, that conduct does not violate § 2 of the Sherman Act. See Kodak, 504 U.S. at 483; Oahu Gas, 838 F.2d at 368. A plaintiff may rebut an asserted business justification by demonstrating either that the justification does not legitimately promote competition or that the justification is pretextual. See Kodak, 504 U.S. at 483–84 (citing Kodak, 903 F.2d at 618). Kodak asserts that the protection of its patented and copyrighted parts is a valid business justification for its anticompetitive conduct and argues that the district court's erroneous jury instructions made it impossible for the jury to properly consider this justification. Kodak attacks the district court's failure both to provide a "less restrictive alternatives" instruction, and to instruct as to Kodak's intellectual property rights. . . .

A. Least Restrictive Alternatives

Kodak argues that the district court erred by failing to instruct the jury that it was not to consider whether Kodak could have accomplished its business objectives through less restrictive alternatives. Kodak also questions the sufficiency of the ISOs' pretext evidence. . . .

Kodak argues that monopolization, unlike tying, does not require considerations of whether the defendant could have achieved its aims through less restrictive alternatives. Kodak, however, cites no authority mandating an instruction requirement that the jury not consider "less restrictive alternatives." Kodak's argument rests on the combination of the district court's refusal to use Kodak's requested language and Kodak's disagreement with the "unnecessarily excludes or handicaps competitors" language of Jury Instructions Nos. 29 and 34. As a result of this combination, Kodak argues, the ISOs were able to argue a "necessity" standard and ask the jury to weigh what Kodak did "against the alternatives."

As discussed above, the "unnecessarily excluded or handicaps" language was permissible under *Aspen Skiing*. Moreover, the district court's instruction here, Instruction No. 28, was very similar to both the language proposed by Kodak and the language endorsed by the Supreme Court in Aspen Skiing, 472 U.S. at 597. Jury Instruction No. 28 defines "exclusionary conduct" as impairing "the efforts of others to compete for customers in an unnecessarily restrictive way." The district court also instructed that:

(1) Kodak could refuse to deal if valid business reasons existed and (2) the jury could not "second guess whether Kodak's business judgment was wise or correct in retrospect." Under these instructions the jury could not consider "less restrictive alternatives" without "second guessing" Kodak and thus violating the jury instructions. We presume that the jury followed the court's instructions. United States v. Alston, 974 F.2d 1206, 1210 (9th Cir.1992).

Kodak next argues that the ISOs' primary arguments refuting Kodak's business justifications were "less restrictive alternative" arguments. Kodak focuses on the ISOs' attack on Kodak's quality control justification as one such "less restrictive alternative" argument. Kodak argues that because "the legitimacy of quality control is beyond reproach," the ISOs were forced to establish this justification, and others, were pretextual. The ISOs did establish pretext: they attacked Kodak's quality control justification on the grounds that it was pretextual, not because it was the least restrictive alternative. Counsel for the ISOs argued that Kodak's quality control justification was "a joke" because ISOs do not interfere with the quality of Kodak's service. We hold that the district court did not err in its instructions.

... The ISOs' evidence suffices to support the jury's rejection of Kodak's business justifications, as the record reflects evidence of pretext. The ISOs presented evidence that: (1) Kodak adopted its parts policy only after an ISO won a contract with the State of California; (2) Kodak allowed its own customers to service their machines; (3) Kodak customers could distinguish breakdowns due to poor service from breakdowns due to parts; and (4) many customers preferred ISO service.

B.   Intellectual Property Rights

Kodak also attacks the district court's business justifications instructions for their failure to properly detail Kodak's intellectual property rights. Kodak argues that the court failed to instruct the jury that Kodak's numerous patents and copyrights provide a legitimate business justification for Kodak alleged exclusionary conduct. Kodak holds 220 valid United States patents covering 65 parts for its high volume photocopiers and micrographics equipment, and all Kodak diagnostic software and service software are copyrighted. The jury instructions do not afford Kodak any "rights" or "privileges" based on its patents and copyrights: all parts are treated the same. In Jury Instruction No. 37, the court told the jury:

> if you find that Kodak engaged in monopolization or attempted monopolization by misuse of its alleged parts monopoly ... then the fact that some of the replacement parts are patented or copyrighted does not provide Kodak with a defense against any of those antitrust claims.

In Jury Instruction No. 28, the court stated, over Kodak's objection, that:

> such [exclusionary] conduct does not refer to ordinary means of competition, like offering better products or services, exercising

superior skills or business judgment, utilizing more efficient technology, or exercising natural competitive advantages.

Kodak proposed to include "exercising lawful patents and copyrights" amongst the list of non-exclusionary conduct in Instruction No. 28, but the district court rejected that language.

Kodak's challenge raises unresolved questions concerning the relationship between federal antitrust, copyright and patent laws. In particular we must determine the significance of a monopolist's unilateral refusal to sell or license a patented or copyrighted product in the context of a § 2 monopolization claim based upon monopoly leveraging. This is a question of first impression.

1.   We first identify the general principles of antitrust, copyright and patent law as we must ultimately harmonize these statutory schemes in responding to Kodak's challenge.

Antitrust law seeks to promote and protect a competitive marketplace for the benefit of the public. See Standard Oil Co. v. United States, 221 U.S. 1, 58 (1911); SCM Corp. v. Xerox Corp., 645 F.2d 1195, 1203 (2d Cir.1981). The Sherman Act, the relevant antitrust law here, prohibits efforts both to restrain trade by combination or conspiracy and the acquisition or maintenance of a monopoly by exclusionary conduct.

Patent law seeks to protect inventions, while inducing their introduction into the market for public benefit. SCM Corp., 645 F.2d at 1203. Patent laws "reward the inventor with the power to exclude others from making, using or selling [a patented] invention through the United States." Id. Meanwhile, the public benefits both from the faster introduction of inventions, and the resulting increase in market competition. Legally, a patent amounts to a permissible monopoly over the protected work. See Zenith Radio Corp. v. Hazeltine Research, Inc., 395 U.S. 100 (1969). Patent laws "are in pari materia with the antitrust laws and modify them pro tanto (as far as the patent laws go)." Simpson v. Union Oil Co., 377 U.S. 13, 24 (1964).

Federal copyright laws "secures a fair return for an author's creative labor" in the short run, while ultimately seeking "to stimulate artistic creativity for the general public good." Twentieth Century Music Corp. v. Aiken 422 U.S. 151, 156 (1975) (internal quotations omitted). The Copyright Act grants to the copyright owner the exclusive right to distribute the protected work. 17 U.S.C. § 106. This right encompasses the right to "refrain from vending or licensing," as the owner may "content [itself] with simply exercising the right to exclude others from using [its] property." Data General, 36 F.3d at 1186 (quoting Fox Film Corp. v. Doyal, 286 U.S. 123, 127 (1932)); see Stewart v. Abend, 495 U.S. 207, 228–29 (1990) ("nothing in the copyright statute would prevent an author from hoarding all of his works during the term of the copyright.").

Clearly the antitrust, copyright and patent laws both overlap and, in certain situations, seem to conflict. This is not a new revelation. We have previously noted the "obvious tension" between the patent and antitrust laws: "one body of law creates and protects monopoly power while the other seeks to proscribe it." United States v. Westinghouse Electric Corp., 648 F.2d 642, 646 (9th Cir.1981) (citations omitted). Similarly, tension exists between the antitrust and copyright laws. See Data General, 36 F.3d at 1187.

Two principles have emerged regarding the interplay between these laws: (1) neither patent nor copyright holders are immune from antitrust liability, and (2) patent and copyright holders may refuse to sell or license protected work. First, as to antitrust liability, case law supports the proposition that a holder of a patent or copyright violates the antitrust laws by "concerted and contractual behavior that threatens competition." Id. at 1185 n. 63 (citation omitted). In Kodak, the Supreme Court noted:

> [we have] held many times that power gained through some natural advantage such as a patent, copyright, or business acumen can give rise to liability if "a seller exploits his dominant position in one market to expand his empire into the next."

504 U.S. at 480 n. 29.

Case law also supports the right of a patent or copyright holder to refuse to sell or license protected work. See Westinghouse, 648 F.2d at 647. In United States v. Westinghouse Electric Corp., we held that "the right to license [a] patent, exclusively or otherwise, or to refuse to license at all, is the 'untrammeled right' of the patentee." Id.

2.   Next we lay out the problem presented here. The Supreme Court touched on this question in Kodak, *i.e.*, the effect to be given a monopolist's unilateral refusal to sell or license a patented or copyrighted product in the context of a § 2 monopoly leveraging claim.... [T]he Supreme Court in Kodak refutes the argument that the possession by a manufacturer of "inherent power" in the market for its parts "should immunize [that manufacturer] from the antitrust laws in another market." 504 U.S. at 480 n. 29. The Court stated that a monopolist who acquires a dominant position in one market through patents and copyrights may violate § 2 if the monopolist exploits that dominant position to enhance a monopoly in another market. Although footnote 29 appears in the Court's discussion of the § 1 tying claims, the § 2 discussion frequently refers back to the § 1 discussion, and the Court's statement that "exploiting [a] dominant position in one market to expand [the] empire into the next" is broad enough to cover monopoly leveraging under § 2. Id. By responding in this fashion, the Court in *Kodak* supposed that intellectual property rights do not confer an absolute immunity from antitrust claims.

The *Kodak* Court, however, did not specifically address the question of antitrust liability based upon a unilateral refusal to deal in a patented or copyrighted product. Kodak and its amicus correctly indicate that the right of exclusive dealing is reserved from antitrust liability. We find no reported case in which a court has imposed antitrust liability for a unilateral refusal to sell or license a patent or copyright. Courts do not generally view a monopolist's unilateral refusal to license a patent as "exclusionary conduct." See Data General, 36 F.3d at 1186 (citing Miller Insituform, Inc. v. Insituform of North America, 830 F.2d 606, 609 (6th Cir.1987) ("A patent holder who lawfully acquires a patent cannot be held liable under Section 2 of the Sherman Act for maintaining the monopoly power he lawfully acquired by refusing to license the patent to others.")); Westinghouse, 648 F.2d at 647 (finding no antitrust violation because "Westinghouse has done no more than to license some of its patents and refuse to license others"); SCM Corp., 645 F.2d at 1206 ("where a patent has been lawfully acquired, subsequent conduct permissible under the patent laws cannot trigger any liability under the antitrust laws.").

This basic exclusion does have limits. For example, a patent offers no protection if it was unlawfully acquired. Data General, 36 F.3d at 1186 (citing SCM Corp., 645 F.2d at 1208–09). Nor does the right of exclusion protect an attempt to extend a lawful monopoly beyond the grant of a patent. See Mercoid, 320 U.S. at 665. Section 2 of the Sherman Act condemns exclusionary conduct that extend natural monopolies into separate markets. Much depends, therefore, on the definition of the patent grant and the relevant market.

The relevant market for determining the patent or copyright grant is determined under patent or copyright law. *See, e.g.*, id. at 666 (the patent's grant "is limited to the invention which it defines."). The relevant markets for antitrust purposes are determined by examining economic conditions. See Kodak, 504 U.S. at 462. . . .

Parts and service here have been proven separate markets in the antitrust context, but this does not resolve the question whether the service market falls "reasonably within the patent [or copyright] grant" for the purpose of determining the extent of the exclusive rights conveyed. Mallinckrodt, Inc. v. Medipart, Inc., 976 F.2d 700, 708–09 (Fed.Cir.1992). These are separate questions, which may result in contrary answers. At the border of intellectual property monopolies and antitrust markets lies a field of dissonance yet to be harmonized by statute or the Supreme Court.

When an owner of intellectual property takes concerted action in violation of § 1, this dissonance does not threaten his core right of exclusion. See Brownell v. Ketcham Wire & Manufacturing Co., 211 F.2d 121, 129 (9th Cir.1954) (listing acts giving rise to antitrust liability). Contrary to the ISOs' arguments, there is an important difference between § 1 tying and § 2 monopoly leveraging: the limiting principles of § 1 restrain those claims from making the impact on intellectual property rights threatened by § 2 monopoly leveraging claims. Where, as here, the claim involves a failure to act that is at the heart of the property right, liability depends largely on market definition and lacks the limiting principles of § 1. Under § 2, "behavior that might otherwise not be of concern to the antitrust laws—or that might even be viewed as procompetitive—can take on exclusionary connotations when practiced by a monopolist." Kodak, 504 U.S. at 488 (Scalia, J. dissenting) (citing 3 Areeda & Turner, Par. 813, at 300–302); see also Greyhound Computer v. International Business Machines, 559 F.2d 488, 498 (9th Cir.1977) (otherwise lawful conduct may be exclusionary when practiced by a monopolist). Harmonizing antitrust monopoly theory with the monopolies granted by intellectual property law requires that some weight be given to the intellectual property rights of the monopolist.

The effect of claims based upon unilateral conduct on the value of intellectual property rights is a cause for serious concern. Unilateral conduct is the most common conduct in the economy. After *Kodak*, unilateral conduct by a manufacturer in its own aftermarkets may give rise to liability and, in one-brand markets, monopoly power created by patents and copyrights will frequently be found. Under current law the defense of monopolization claims will rest largely on the legitimacy of the asserted business justifications, as evidenced by the jury instructions approved in *Aspen Skiing*....

3.   We now resolve the question detailed above. Under the fact-based approaches of *Aspen Skiing* and *Kodak*, some measure must guarantee that the jury account for the procompetitive effects and statutory rights extended by the intellectual property laws. To assure such consideration, we adopt a modified version of the rebuttable presumption created by the First Circuit in *Data General*, and hold that "while exclusionary conduct can include a monopolist's unilateral refusal to license a [patent or] copyright," or to sell its patented or copyrighted work, a monopolist's "desire to exclude others from its [protected] work is a presumptively valid business justification for any immediate harm to consumers." Data General, 36 F.3d at 1187.

This presumption does not "rest on formalistic distinctions" which "are generally disfavored in antitrust laws;" rather it is based on "actual market realities." Kodak, 504 U.S. at 466 67. This presumption harmonizes the goals of the relevant statutes and takes into account the long term effects of regulation on these purposes. The presumption should act to focus the factfinder on the primary interest of both intellectual property and antitrust laws: public interest. Mercoid, 320 U.S. at 665 (citation omitted) ("It is the public interest which is dominant in the patent system."); Standard Oil, 221 U.S. at 58 (antitrust laws serve the public interest by encouraging effective competition).

Given this presumption, the district court's failure to give any weight to Kodak's intellectual property rights in the jury instructions constitutes an abuse of discretion. This error was, however, harmless. The ISOs maintain that Kodak argued protection of intellectual property as a business justification to the jury, which rejected this justification as pretextual. An error in instructing the jury in a civil case does not require reversal if it is more probably than not harmless. Jenkins v. Union Pacific R. Co., 22 F.3d 206, 210 (9th Cir.1994)....

Phrased in these broad terms, Kodak's argument repeats the "free-riding" justification rejected, as a matter of law, by the Supreme Court. Kodak, 504 U.S. at 485. The Supreme Court held that preventing the ISOs from "exploiting the investment Kodak has made in product development, manufacturing and equipment sales" does not suffice as a business justification. Id. ("This understanding of free-riding has no support in our case law.").

Given the interplay of the antitrust and intellectual property laws discussed above, Kodak's contention that its refusal to sell its parts to ISOs was based on its reluctance to sell its patented or copyrighted parts was a presumptively legitimate business justification. See Data General, 36 F.3d at 1187. Kodak may assert that its desire to profit from its intellectual property rights justifies its conduct, and the jury should presume that this justification is legitimately procompetitive.

Nevertheless, this presumption is rebuttable. See id. at 1188. In Data General, the First Circuit reasoned that the plaintiff did not rebut the presumption by drawing an analogy to *Aspen Skiing*, where a monopolist made an important change in its practices, which had both originated in a competitive market and persisted for several years. See Data General, 36 F.3d at 1188. Because competitive conditions had never prevailed in the service market, the First Circuit concluded that it would be inappropriate to infer "from [defendant's] change of heart that its former policies 'satisfy consumer demand in free competitive markets.' " Id. at 1188 (quoting Aspen Skiing, 472 U.S. at 603). As in Data General, we are not faced here with a simple comparison between the monopolist's market and the established competitive market found in *Aspen Skiing*.

The *Data General* court noted that the presumption of legitimacy can be rebutted by evidence that the monopolist acquired the protection of the intellectual property laws in an unlawful manner. See 36 F.3d at 1188 (citation omitted). The presumption may also be rebutted by evidence of pretext. Neither the aims of intellectual property law, nor the antitrust laws justify allowing a monopolist to rely upon a pretextual business justification to mask anticompetitive conduct. See Kodak, 504 U.S. at 484 (Because "Kodak's willingness to allow self-service casts doubt on its quality claim ... a reasonable tier of fact could conclude that [this justification] is pretextual.") (citation omitted).

Kodak defends its intellectual property rights "justification" against claims of pretext. Kodak argues that its subjective motivation is irrelevant. Kodak also contends, citing Olympia Equipment Leasing Co. v. Western Union Telegraphic Co., 797 F.2d 370, 379 (7th Cir.), reh'g denied, (7th Cir. 1986), that a desire to best the competition does not prove pretext, nor does hostility to competitors. Kodak's argument and its accompanying authority stands for nothing more than the proposition that a desire to compete does not demonstrate pretext.

Evidence regarding the state of mind of Kodak employees may show pretext, when such evidence suggests that the proffered business justification played no part in the decision to act. Kodak's parts manager testified that patents "did not cross [his] mind" at the time Kodak began the parts policy. Further, no distinction was made by Kodak between "proprietary" parts covered by tooling or engineering clauses and patented or copyrighted products. In denying Kodak's motion for a new trial, the district court commented that Kodak was not actually motivated by protecting its intellectual property rights. Kodak argues that the district court should have allowed the jury to reach this conclusion.

Kodak photocopy and micrographics equipment requires thousands of parts, of which only 65 were patented. Unlike the other cases involving refusals to license patents, this case concerns a blanket refusal that included protected and unprotected products. Cf. Westinghouse, 648 F.2d at 647 (refusal to license patents); SCM Corp., 645 F.2d at 1197 (same); Miller Instituform, 830 F.2d at 607 (claim based on termination of license agreement). From this evidence, it is more probably than not that the jury would have found Kodak's presumptively valid business justification rebutted on the grounds of pretext.

Kodak argues that the existence of some patented and copyrighted products undermines ISOs "all parts" theory. To the contrary, as discussed above, the "all parts market" reflect the "commercial realities" of the marketplace and the lack of identifiable separate markets for individual parts. The fact that Kodak did not differentiate between patented and nonpatented parts lends further support to the existence of these commercial realities. The jury accepted the "all parts" theory and found a scheme of monopolize the service market through Kodak's conduct. We hold that the district court's failure to instruct on Kodak's intellectual property rights was harmless. . . . [44]

In re Independent Service Organizations Antitrust Litigation v. Xerox Corp.

United States Court of Appeals, Federal Circuit, 2000.
203 F.3d 1322.

■ MAYER, J. CSU appeals the judgment of the United States District Court for the District of Kansas, dismissing on summary judgment CSU's claims that Xerox's refusal to sell patented parts and copyrighted manuals and to license copyrighted software violate the antitrust laws. . . . Because we agree with the district court that CSU has not raised a genuine issue as to any material fact and that Xerox is entitled to judgment as a matter of law, we affirm.

Background

Xerox manufactures, sells, and services high-volume copiers. Beginning in 1984, it established a policy of not selling parts unique to its series 10 copiers to independent service organizations ("ISOs"), including CSU, unless they were also end-users of the copiers. In 1987, the policy was expanded to include all new products as well as existing series 9 copiers. Enforcement of this policy was tightened in 1989, and Xerox cut off CSU's direct purchase of restricted parts. Xerox also implemented an "on-site end-user verification" procedure to confirm that the parts ordered by certain ISOs or their customers were actually for their end-user use.

---

44. The Court then affirmed the findings below on all liability issues, revised and remanded specific damage awards, and affirmed various damage awards.

Initially this procedure applied to only the six most successful ISOs, which included CSU.

To maintain its existing business of servicing Xerox equipment, CSU used parts cannibalized from used Xerox equipment, parts obtained from other ISOs, and parts purchased through a limited number of its customers. For approximately one year, CSU also obtained parts from Rank Xerox, a majority-owed European affiliate of Xerox, until Xerox forced Rank Xerox to stop selling parts to CSU and other ISOs. In 1994, Xerox settled an antitrust lawsuit with a class of ISOs by which it agreed to suspend its restrictive parts policy for six and one-half years and to license its diagnostic software for four and one-half years. CSU opted out of that settlement filed this suit alleging that Xerox violated the Sherman Act by setting the prices on its patented parts much higher for ISOs than for end-users to force ISOs to raise their prices. This would eliminate ISOs in general and CSU in particular as competitors in the relevant service markets for high speed copiers and printers.

Xerox counterclaimed for patent and copyright infringement and contested CSU's antitrust claims as relying on injury solely caused by Xerox's lawful refusal to sell or license patented parts and copyrighted software. Xerox also claimed that CSU could not assert a patent or copyright misuse defense to Xerox's infringement counterclaims based on Xerox's refusal to deal.

The district court granted summary judgment to Xerox dismissing CSU's antitrust claims and holding that if a patent or copyright is lawfully acquired, the patent or copyright holder's unilateral refusal to sell or license its patented invention or copyrighted expression is not unlawful exclusionary conduct under the antitrust laws, even if the refusal to deal impacts competition in more than one market. The court also held, in both the patent and copyright contexts, that the right holder's intent in refusing to deal and any other alleged exclusionary acts committed by the right holder are irrelevant to antitrust law. This appeal followed.

Discussion

... As a general proposition, when reviewing a district court's judgment involving federal antitrust law, we are guided by the law of the regional circuit in which that district court sits, in this case the Tenth Circuit. We apply our own law, not regional circuit law, to resolve issues that clearly involve our exclusive jurisdiction. "Whether conduct in procuring or enforcing a patent is sufficient to strip a patentee of its immunity from the antitrust laws is to be decided as a question of Federal Circuit law." ... The district court's grant of summary judgment as to CSU's antitrust claims arising from Xerox's refusal to sell its patented parts is therefore reviewed as a matter of Federal Circuit law, while consideration of the antitrust claim based on Xerox's refusal to sell or license its copyrighted manuals and software is under Tenth Circuit law.

A.

Intellectual property rights do not confer a privilege to violate the antitrust laws. See Intergraph Corp. v. Intel Corp., 195 F.3d 1346, 1362 (Fed.Cir.1999). "But it is also correct that the antitrust laws do not negate the patentee's right to exclude others from patent property." Id. "The commercial advantage gained by new technology and its statutory protection by patent do not convert the possessor thereof into a prohibited monopolist." Abbott Lab. v. Brennan, 952 F.2d 1346, 1354 (Fed.Cir.1991). "The patent right must be 'coupled with violations of § 2,' and the elements of violation of 15 U.S.C. § 2 must be met." Id. "Determination of whether the patentee meets the Sherman Act elements of monopolization or attempt to monopolize is governed by the rules of application of the antitrust laws to market participants, with due consideration to the exclusivity that inheres in the patent grant." Id. at 1354–55.

A patent alone does not demonstrate market power. The United States Department of Justice and Federal Trade Commission have issued guidance that, even where it exists, such "market power does not 'impose on the intellectual property owner an obligation to license the use of that property to others.'" Intergraph, 195 F.3d at 1362 (citing United States Department of Justice and Federal Trade Comm'n Antitrust Guidelines for the Licensing of Intellectual Property 4 (1995)). There is "no reported case in which a court has imposed antitrust liability for a unilateral refusal to sell or license a patent...." Id. The patentee's right to exclude is further supported by section 271(d) of the Patent Act which states, in pertinent part, that "no patent owner otherwise entitled to relief ... shall be denied relief or deemed guilty of misuse or illegal extension of the patent right by reason of his having ... (4) refused to license or use any rights to the patent ..." 35 U.S.C. § 271(d) (1999).

The patentee's right to exclude, however, is not without limit. As we recently observed in Glass Equipment Development Inc. v. Besten, Inc., a patent owner who brings suit to enforce the statutory right to exclude others from making, using, or selling the claimed invention is exempt from the antitrust laws, even though such a suit may have an anticompetitive effect, unless the infringement defendant proves one of two conditions. First, he may prove that the asserted patent was obtained through knowing and willful fraud within the meaning of Walker Process Equipment, Inc. v. Food Machinery & Chemical Corp., 382 U.S. 172, 177 (1965). See Glass Equip. Dev., 174 F.3d at 1343. Or he may demonstrate that the infringement suit was a mere sham to cover what is actually no more than an attempt to interfere directly with the business relationships of a competitor. See id. (citing Eastern R.R. Presidents Conference v. Noerr Motor Freight, Inc., 365 U.S. 127, 144 (1961)). Here, CSU makes no claim that Xerox obtained its patents through fraud in the Patent and Trademark Office; the *Walker Process* analysis is not implicated.

"Irrespective of the patent applicant's conduct before the [Patent and Trademark Office], an antitrust claim can also be based on [an] allegation that a suit is baseless; in order to prove that a suit was within *Noerr's* 'sham' exception to immunity, see Noerr, 365 U.S. at 144, an antitrust plaintiff must prove that the suit was both objectively baseless and subjectively motivated by a desire to impose collateral, anti-competitive injury rather than to obtain a justifiable legal remedy." Nobelpharma, 141 F.3d at 1071. "Accordingly, if a suit is not objectively baseless, an antitrust defendant's subjective motivation is immaterial." Id. at 1072. CSU has alleged that Xerox misused its patents but has not claimed that Xerox's patent infringement counterclaims were shams.

To support its argument that Xerox illegally sought to leverage its presumably legitimate dominance in the equipment and parts market into dominance in the service market, CSU relies on a footnote in Eastman Kodak Co. v. Image Technical Services, Inc., 504 U.S. 451, 480 n. 29 (1992), that "the Court has held many times that power gained through some natural and legal advantage such as a patent, . . . can give rise to liability if 'a seller exploits his dominant position in one market to expand his empire into the next.' " Notably, *Kodak* was a tying case when it came before the Supreme Court, and no patents had been asserted in defense of the antitrust claims against Kodak. Conversely, there are no claims in this case of illegally tying the sale of Xerox's patented parts to unpatented products. Therefore, the issue was not resolved by the *Kodak* language cited by CSU. Properly viewed within the framework of a tying case, the footnote can be interpreted as restating the undisputed premise that the patent holder cannot use his statutory right to refuse to sell patented parts to gain a monopoly in a market beyond the scope of the patent. . . .

The cited language from *Kodak* does nothing to limit the right of the patentee to refuse to sell or license in markets within the scope of the statutory patent grant. In fact, we have expressly held that, absent exceptional circumstances, a patent may confer the right to exclude competition altogether in more than one antitrust market. See B. Braun Med., Inc. v. Abbott Lab., 124 F.3d 1419, 1427 n. 4 (Fed.Cir.1997) (patentee had right to exclude competition in both the market for patented valves and the market for extension sets incorporating patented valves).

CSU further relies on the Ninth Circuit's holding on remand in *Image Technical Services* that "while exclusionary conduct can include a monopolist's unilateral refusal to license a [patent] or to sell its patented . . . work, a monopolist's 'desire to exclude others from its [protected] work is a presumptively valid business justification for any immediate harm to consumers.' " 125 F.3d at 1218 (citing Data General Corp. v. Grumman Sys. Support Corp., 36 F.3d 1147, 1187 (1st Cir.1994)). By that case, the Ninth Circuit adopted a rebuttable presumption that the exercise of the statutory right to exclude provides a valid business justification for consumer harm, but then excused as harmless the district court's error in failing to give any instruction on the effect of intellectual property rights on the application of the antitrust laws. It concluded that the jury must have rejected the presumptively valid business justification as pretextual. This logic requires an evaluation of the patentee's subjective motivation for refusing to sell or license its patented products for pretext. We decline to follow *Image Technical Services*.

We have held that "if a [patent infringement] suit is not objectively baseless, an antitrust defendant's subjective motivation is immaterial." Nobelpharma, 141 F.3d at 1072. We see no more reason to inquire into the subjective motivation of *Xerox* in refusing to sell or license its patented works than we found in evaluating the subjective motivation of a patentee in bringing suit to enforce that same right. In the absence of any indication of illegal tying, fraud in the Patent and Trademark Office, or sham litigation, the patent holder may enforce the statutory right to exclude others from making using, or selling the claimed invention free from liability under the antitrust laws. We therefore will not inquire into his subjective motivation for exerting his statutory rights, even though his refusal to sell or license his patented invention may have an anticompetitive effect, so long as that anticompetitive effect is not illegally extended beyond the statutory patent grant. It is the infringement defendant and not the patentee that bears the burden to show that one of these exceptional situations exists and, in the absence of such proof, we will not inquire into the patentee's motivations for asserting his statutory right to exclude. Even in cases where the infringement defendant has met this burden, which CSU has not, he must then also prove the elements of the Sherman Act violation.

We answer the threshold question of whether Xerox's refusal to sell its patented parts exceeds the scope of the patent grant in the negative.[45] Therefore, our inquiry is at an end. Xerox was under no obligation to sell or license its patented parts and did not violate the antitrust laws by refusing to do so.

B.

The Copyright Act expressly grants a copyright owner the exclusive right to distribute the protected work by "transfer of ownership, or by rental, lease, or lending." 17 U.S.C. § 106(3) (1996). "The owner of the copyright, if [it] pleases, may refrain from vending or licensing and content [itself] with simply exercising the right to exclude others from using [its] property." Data General, 36 F.3d at 1186.

The Supreme Court has made clear that the property right granted by copyright law cannot be used with impunity to extend power in the marketplace beyond what Congress intended. See United States v. Loew's, Inc., 371 U.S. 38, 47–48 (1962) (block booking of copyrighted motion pictures is illegal tying in violation of the Sherman Act). The Court has not, however, directly addressed the antitrust implications of a unilateral refusal to sell or license copyrighted expression.

The Tenth Circuit has not addressed in any published opinion the extent to which the unilateral refusal to sell or license copyrighted expres-

---

45. Having concluded that Xerox's actions fell within the statutory patent grant, we need not separately consider CSU's allegations of patent misuse and they are rejected.

sion can form the basis of a violation of the Sherman Act. We are therefore left to determine how that circuit would likely resolve the issue; the precedent of other circuits is instructive in that consideration. The Fourth Circuit has rejected a claim of illegal tying, supported only by evidence of a unilateral decision to license copyrighted diagnostic software to some but not to others. See Service & Training, Inc. v. Data General Corp., 963 F.2d 680, 686 (4th Cir.1992). In reaching this conclusion, the court recognized the copyright owner's exclusive right to "sell, rent, lease, lend, or otherwise distribute copies of a copyrighted work," id. and concluded that "Section 1 of the Sherman Act does not entitle 'a purchaser . . . to buy a product that the seller does not wish to offer for sale.' " Id.

Perhaps the most extensive analysis of the effect of a unilateral refusal to license copyrighted expression was conducted by the First Circuit in Data General Corp. v. Grumman Systems Support Corp., 36 F.3d 1147. There, the court noted that the limited copyright monopoly is based on Congress' empirical assumption that the right to "exclude others from using their works creates a system of incentives that promotes consumder welfare in the long term by encouraging investment in the creation of desirable artistic and functional works of expression. . . . We cannot require antitrust defendants to prove and reprove the merits of this legislative assumption in every case where a refusal to license a copyrighted work comes under attack." Id. at 1186–87. The court went on to establish as a legal standard that "while exclusionary conduct can include a monopolist's unilateral refusal to license a copyright, an author's desire to exclude others from use of its copyrighted work is a presumptively valid business justification for any immediate harm to consumers." See id. at 1187. The burden to overcome this presumption was firmly placed on the antitrust plaintiff. The court gave no weight to evidence showing knowledge that developing a proprietary position would help to maintain a monopoly in the service market in the face of contrary evidence of the defendant's desire to develop state-of-the-art diagnostic software to enhance its service and consumer benefit.

As discussed above, the Ninth Circuit adopted a modified version of this *Data General* standard. Both courts agreed that the presumption could be rebutted by evidence that "the monopolist acquired the protection of the intellectual property laws in an unlawful manner." Image Technical Servs., 125 F.3d at 1219. The Ninth Circuit, however, extended the possible means of rebutting the presumption to include evidence that the defense and exploitation of the copyright grant was merely a pretextual business justification to mask anticompetitive conduct. The hazards of this approach are evidence in both the path taken and the outcome reached. The jury in that case was instructed to examine each proffered business justification for pretext, and no weight was given to the intellectual property rights in the instructions. This permitted the jury to second guess the subjective motivation of the copyright holder in asserting its statutory rights to exclude under the copyright laws without properly weighing the presumption of legitimacy in asserting its rights under the copyright laws. While concluding that the failure to weigh the intellectual property rights was an abuse of discretion, the Ninth Circuit nevertheless held the error harmless because it thought the jury must have rejected the presumptive validity of asserting the copyrights as pretextual. This is in reality a significant departure from the First Circuit's central premise that rebutting the presumption would be an uphill battle and would only be appropriate in those rare cases in which imposing antitrust liability is unlikely to frustrate the objectives of the Copyright Act. See Data General, 36 F.3d at 1187 n. 64.

We believe the First Circuit's approach is more consistent with both the antitrust and the copyright laws and is the standard that would most likely be followed by the Tenth Circuit in considering the effects of Xerox's unilateral right to refuse to license or sell copyrighted manuals and diagnostic software on liability under the antitrust laws. We therefore reject CSU's invitation to examine Xerox's subjective motivation in asserting its right to exclude under the copyright laws for pretext, in the absence of any evidence that the copyrights were obtained by unlawful means or were used to gain monopoly power beyond the statutory copyright granted by Congress. In the absence of such definitive rebuttal evidence, Xerox's refusal to sell or license its copyrighted works was squarely within the rights granted by Congress to the copyright holder and did not constitute a violation of the antitrust laws.

NOTES AND QUESTIONS

1. Can the *Kodak* and *Xerox* opinions be reconciled? If not, which is right? Should the existence of an antitrust violation turn on the alleged violators' state of mind as appeared to be the case in *Kodak*? How would the "sham exception" work in *Xerox*?

2. The law is reasonably clear that a party owning intellectual property—even a monopolist—is not required to license that property in the first instance, regardless of intent or effect on competition, see SCM Corp. v. Xerox Corp., 645 F.2d 1195, 1204 (2d Cir.), cert. denied, 455 U.S. 1016 (1982). Problems arise however as to how antitrust should treat situations where the legitimate holder of a patent or copyright conditions its license on what would be an antitrust violation if intellectual property were not involved. In the *Xerox* case, the federal circuit appeared to conclude that any conditioning of a license is exempt from the antitrust laws unless the IP was obtained by fraud, the infringement claim is a sham to cover an attempt to injure a competitor, or the refusal is part of a tie-in sales strategy. Does that mean it would be acceptable to license a patent on condition that the licensee agrees not to deal with a competitor of the licensor? That would be illegal if non-IP were involved. See Lorain Journal Co. v. United States, p. 832 infra. Is there reason to believe that more lenient treatment of IP in that context would have a positive effect on incentives to innovate? What about the incentives of the rival of the patent holder who is precluded from dealing with the licensee?

3. See Townshend v. Rockwell Int'l Corp., 2000 WL 433505 (N.D.Cal.2000) illustrating how some lower courts are interpreting the federal circuit's Xerox opinion. In that case, the owner of basic patents underlying the 56K modem

technology sued for patent infringement. The co-defendant, Rockwell, asserted antitrust counterclaims alleging that the patents on which the suit was based were invalid, the technology covered by the patents had been adopted as part of an industry standard through fraud, and the patents were made available to competitors only on the condition that they cross-license their technology to the patent holder. The district court dismissed all antitrust counterclaims. "Because a patent owner has the legal right to refuse to license his or her patent on any terms, the existence of a predicate condition to a license agreement cannot state the antitrust violation." Does this mean that the undeniable premise that an intellectual property holder does not have to license anyone in the first instance leads to a conclusion that it can select among licensees or condition a license in any way it chooses to achieve an anticompetitive effect?

4. Does the Federal Circuit's decision cast doubt on the FTC's complaint against Intel, subsequently settled by consent order, that it is an antitrust violation for a monopolist to deny copyrighted technical information and advance samples to those customers and competitors who sue the monopolist for infringing on their intellectual property? See pp. 146–47 supra.

5. The D.C. Court of Appeals in *Microsoft* addressed the question of whether antitrust analysis must be modified when antitrust rules are applied to high-tech industries. For relevant comments in the *Microsoft* case, see pp. 769–70 *supra*.

PROBLEM 17

THE BATTLE FOR SAWVILLE: ROUND 2

Referring to the facts of Problem 1 (p. 191 supra), assume that the product market is exhibition of films in "art houses" and the geographic market is Sawville.

After being rebuffed in previous efforts to enter the market, Read Theaters, the largest chain of art houses on the East Coast, purchased the Bramble Bush, one of the three motion picture theaters previously devoted to "regular" films, and converted it to art films. Since the Bramble Bush was uniquely well-located, Read was willing to take the risk that it could challenge the entrenched Frolic.

The new Bramble Bush, ultramodern in decor and comfort, has been operating for two years. Read used its extensive bargaining power, partly derived from the fact that it is the only art house in some of the towns in which it operates, to bring the best art films to Sawville simultaneously with their New York City runs. The films were made available to Read on an exclusive basis, and could not be shown elsewhere until 90 days after they stopped being shown by Read. Furthermore, it reduced admission charges from the $9.00 level formerly set by the Frolic, requiring the Frolic to lower prices as well. It also engaged in extensive and costly promotion and advertising—tripling its newspaper ad budget. The net result was that the Bramble Bush, unlike any of Read's other art houses, operated at a net loss during its first two years as an art house. However, because many expenses of a movie theater are fixed rather than variable, it managed to stay barely above average variable costs.

At the end of the first year, the Bramble Bush had won a large share of the Frolic's clientele, causing the Frolic to suffer losses for the first time in its history. At the end of the second year, it had achieved near full-capacity attendance and was comfortably in the black. The Frolic then went out of business. As soon as that happened, the Bramble Bush raised its prices to $11.00, $2.00 more than the Frolic had charged before the Bramble Bush entered the market.

Is Read a monopolist and has it violated Section 2? If so, what remedy would you impose?

B. ATTEMPT TO MONOPOLIZE

INTRODUCTORY NOTE

In attempt to monopolize cases under Section 2 of the Sherman Act the courts have generally examined three elements: (1) intent; (2) the nature of the conduct; and (3) a dangerous probability that, if the conduct that constitutes the attempt is allowed to proceed unchecked, it will result in monopoly power. The classic statement of the "attempt" rule is by Justice Holmes in Swift & Co. v. United States, 196 U.S. 375, 396 (1905):

> Where acts are not sufficient in themselves to produce a result which the law seeks to prevent—for instance, the monopoly—but require further acts in addition to the mere forces of nature to bring that result to pass, an intent to bring it to pass is necessary in order to produce a dangerous probability that it will happen.... But when that intent and the consequent dangerous probability exists, this statute, like many others and like the common law in some cases, directs itself against that dangerous probability as well as against the completed result.

The conduct challenged in attempt cases ranges across a broad spectrum of allegedly anticompetitive behavior; indeed, an attempt count often parallels and duplicates monopolization or restraint of trade charges in a complaint. In recent years, questions about the proper scope of the attempt to monopolize provision have been coming up frequently in the lower federal courts, particularly in private treble damage actions, and there is a good deal of confusion as to what the law is and what it ought to be. To some extent the debate reflects the pros and cons of filling a gap in antitrust coverage. We have already seen that violations of Section 1 require more than one party. Violations of the monopolization provision of Section 2 can be charged against single-firm conduct, but the firm must be found to have monopoly power in a properly defined relevant market. However, anticompetitive market behavior—that is, conduct that has severe anticompetitive consequences and no significant economic or social redeeming virtues—can be engaged in by single firms with relatively little market power.

In part, the debate over what sort of intent, conduct, or dangerous probability needs to be proved concerns the issue of how important it is to fill the gap between Section 1 and the monopolization provisions of Section 2. In the recently decided *Spectrum Sports* case,[46] however, the Supreme Court made clear that proof of dangerous probability—*i.e.*, the "realistic probability that the defendants could achieve monopoly power" in a market—is a prerequisite to finding a violation in an attempt to monopolize case.

Lorain Journal Co. v. United States

Supreme Court of the United States, 1951.
342 U.S. 143, 72 S.Ct. 181, 96 L.Ed. 162.

■ BURTON, J. The principal question here is whether a newspaper publisher's conduct constituted an attempt to monopolize interstate commerce,

---

46. Spectrum Sports, Inc. v. McQuillan, 506 U.S. 447 (1993), p. 837 infra.

justifying the injunction issued against it under §§ 2 and 4 of the Sherman Antitrust Act. For the reasons hereafter stated, we hold that the injunction was justified.

This is a civil action, instituted by the United States in the District Court for the Northern District of Ohio, against The Lorain Journal Company, an Ohio corporation, publishing, daily except Sunday, in the City of Lorain, Ohio, a newspaper here called the Journal.... The District Court declined to issue a temporary injunction but, after trial, found that the parties were engaging in an attempt to monopolize as charged. Confining itself to that issue, the court enjoined them from continuing the attempt. 92 F.Supp. 794....

The appellant corporation, here called the publisher, has published the Journal in the City of Lorain since before 1932. In that year it, with others, purchased the Times–Herald which was the only competing daily paper published in that city. Later, without success, it sought a license to establish and operate a radio broadcasting station in Lorain....

The court below describes the position of the Journal, since 1933, as "a commanding and an overpowering one. It has a daily circulation in Lorain of over 13,000 copies and it reaches ninety-nine per cent of the families in the city." 92 F.Supp. at 796. Lorain is an industrial city on Lake Erie with a population of about 52,000 occupying 11,325 dwelling units. The Sunday News, appearing only on Sundays, is the only other newspaper published there....

From 1933 to 1948 the publisher enjoyed a substantial monopoly in Lorain of the mass dissemination of news and advertising, both of a local and national character. However, in 1948 the Elyria–Lorain Broadcasting Company, a corporation independent of the publisher, was licensed by the Federal Communications Commission to establish and operate in Elyria, Ohio, eight miles south of Lorain, a radio station whose call letters, WEOL, stand for Elyria, Oberlin and Lorain. Since then it has operated its principal studio in Elyria and a branch studio in Lorain. Lorain has about twice the population as Elyria and is by far the largest community in the station's immediate area. Oberlin is much smaller than Elyria and eight miles south of it....

The court below found that appellants knew that a substantial number of Journal advertisers wished to use the facilities of the radio station as well. For some of them it found that advertising in the Journal was essential for the promotion of their sales in Lorain County. It found that at all times since WEOL commenced broadcasting, appellants had executed a plan conceived to eliminate the threat of competition from the station. Under this plan the publisher refused to accept local advertisements in the Journal from any Lorain County advertiser who advertised or who appellants believed to be about to advertise over WEOL. The court found expressly that the purpose and intent of this procedure was to destroy the broadcasting company.

The court characterized all this as "bold, relentless, and predatory commercial behavior." 92 F.Supp. at 796. To carry out appellants' plan, the publisher monitored WEOL programs to determine the identity of the station's local Lorain advertisers. Those using the station's facilities had their contracts with the publisher terminated and were able to renew them only after ceasing to advertise through WEOL. The program was effective. Numerous Lorain County merchants testified that as a result of the publisher's policy, they either ceased or abandoned their plans to advertise over WEOL. . . .

1. *The conduct complained of was an attempt to monopolize interstate commerce.* It consisted of the publisher's practice of refusing to accept local Lorain advertising from parties using WEOL for local advertising. Because of the Journal's complete daily newspaper monopoly of local advertising in Lorain and its practically indispensable coverage of 99% of the Lorain families, this practice forced numerous advertisers to refrain from using WEOL for local advertising. That result not only reduced the number of customers available to WEOL in the field of local Lorain advertising and strengthened the Journal's monopoly in that field, but more significantly tended to destroy and eliminate WEOL altogether. Attainment of that sought-for elimination would automatically restore to the publisher of the Journal its substantial monopoly in Lorain of the mass dissemination of all news and advertising, interstate and national, as well as local. It would deprive not merely Lorain but Elyria and all surrounding communities of their only nearby radio station. . . .

2. *The publisher's attempt to regain its monopoly of interstate commerce by forcing advertisers to boycott a competing radio station violated § 2.* The findings and opinion of the trial court describe the conduct of the publisher upon which the Government relies. The surrounding circumstances are important. The most illuminating of these is the substantial monopoly which was enjoyed in Lorain by the publisher from 1933 to 1948, together with a 99% coverage of Lorain families. Those factors made the Journal an indispensable medium of advertising for many Lorain concerns. Accordingly, its publisher's refusals to print Lorain advertising for those using WEOL for like advertising often amounted to an effective prohibition of the use of WEOL for that purpose. Numerous Lorain advertisers wished to supplement their local newspaper advertising with local radio advertising but could not afford to discontinue their newspaper advertising in order to use the radio.

WEOL's greatest potential source of income was local Lorain advertising. Loss of that was a major threat to its existence. The court below found unequivocally that appellants' conduct amounted to an attempt by the publisher to destroy WEOL and, at the same time, to regain the publisher's pre–1948 substantial monopoly over the mass dissemination of all news and advertising. . . .

Assuming the interstate character of the commerce involved, it seems clear that if all the newspapers in a city, in order to monopolize the dissemination of news and advertising by eliminating a competing radio station, conspired to accept no advertisements from anyone who advertised over that station, they would violate §§ 1 and 2 of the Sherman Act. It is consistent with that result to hold here that a single newspaper, already enjoying a substantial monopoly in its area, violates the "attempt to monopolize" clause of § 2 when it uses its monopoly to destroy threatened competition.[47]

The publisher claims a right as a private business concern to select its customers and to refuse to accept advertisements from whomever it pleases. We do not dispute that general right. "But the word 'right' is one of the most deceptive of pitfalls; it is so easy to slip from a qualified meaning in the premise to an unqualified one in the conclusion. Most rights are qualified." American Bank & Trust Co. v. Federal Reserve Bank, 256 U.S. 350, 358. The right claimed by the publisher is neither absolute nor exempt from regulation. Its exercise of a purposeful means of monopolizing interstate commerce is prohibited by the Sherman Act. The operator of the radio station, equally with the publisher of the newspaper, is entitled to the protection of that Act. "*In the absence of any purpose to create or maintain a monopoly,* the act does not restrict the long recognized right of trader or manufacturer engaged in an entirely private business, freely to exercise his own independent discretion as to parties with whom he will deal." (Emphasis supplied.) United States v. Colgate & Co., 250 U.S. 300, 307.

Affirmed.[48]

NOTES AND QUESTIONS

1. FEDERAL TRADE COMMISSION v. RAYMOND BROS.-CLARK CO., 263 U.S. 565, 44 S.Ct. 162, 68 L.Ed. 448 (1924). Raymond was a grocery wholesaler who purchased from Snider at the wholesale price. Basket Stores was a wholesaler competitor of Raymond (doing about 10% of its business this way) who also operated a chain of retail stores. Raymond protested "against the sale direct to Basket Stores" by Snider and asked "for the allowance of a jobber's profit on such sale." When Snider refused to raise prices to Basket Stores or to grant a jobber's profit to Raymond, Raymond discontinued purchases. The FTC found that Raymond had engaged in an unfair method of competition and ordered it to cease attempting to influence

47. Appellants have sought to justify their conduct on the ground that it was part of the publisher's program for the protection of the Lorain market from outside competition. The publisher claimed to have refused advertising from Elyria or other out-of-town advertisers for the reason that such advertisers might compete with Lorain concerns. The publisher then classified WEOL as the publisher's own competitor from Elyria and asked its Lorain advertisers to refuse to employ WEOL as an advertising medium in competition with the Journal. We find no principle of law which required Lorain advertisers thus to boycott an Elyria advertising medium merely because the publisher of a Lorain advertising medium had chosen to boycott some Elyria advertisers who might compete for business in the Lorain market. Nor do we find any principle of law which permitted this publisher to dictate to prospective advertisers that they might advertise either by newspaper or by radio but that they might not use both facilities.

48. Clark and Minton, JJ., did not participate.

selection of customers or direct dealing between manufacturers and purchasers of groceries.

The Supreme Court reversed, noting that Raymond had acted unilaterally. In threatening to withdraw and then withdrawing its trade from Snider, Raymond was exercising its lawful right to deal with whomever it chose—leaving it to the manufacturer to decide which customer it desired to retain. How would you distinguish *Raymond Bros.–Clark* from *Lorain Journal?* Are you helped by the Supreme Court's observation that Raymond did not have monopoly power?

2. A.H. COX & CO. v. STAR MACHINERY CO., 653 F.2d 1302 (9th Cir.1981). Plaintiff Cox had been the sole distributor of heavy equipment, including truck mounted hydraulic cranes, for R.O. Products, Inc., one of four domestic manufacturers of the product line. Star succeeded in persuading R.O. Products to allow Star to carry its line exclusively instead of Cox; as a result, Cox was driven into bankruptcy and sued, charging a concerted refusal to deal in violation of Section 1 and an attempt to monopolize in violation of Section 2 of the Sherman Act.

The Ninth Circuit affirmed summary judgment against Cox. As to the alleged concerted refusal to deal, it noted that there was no horizontality at the manufacturer level since R.O. Products, in deciding to switch from Cox to Star, engaged in no concerted action with the other manufacturers. As to the attempt charge, the Court found no anticompetitive intent or effect since the result of the behavior challenged by Cox was simply to replace one distributor with another in marketing a particular manufacturer's line of products.

> Where each distributor has only one line, it is particularly appropriate to recognize the right of a distributor to initiate changes; otherwise, a weak distributor could continue ineffective promotion of a good brand, while a strong distributor could be forced to continue representing a manufacturer with whom it has poor relations. 653 F.2d at 1307.

3. SIX TWENTY-NINE PRODUCTIONS, INC. v. ROLLINS TELECASTING, INC., 365 F.2d 478 (5th Cir.1966). Appeal from a district court decision granting summary judgment to the defendant. Plaintiff was a general advertising agency in Pensacola, Florida, while defendant was licensed by the Federal Communications Commission to operate the only television station broadcasting from Pensacola. In 1963, plaintiff added to its services the preparation of television advertising and in 1964, obtained the account of Crestview Mobile Homes, Inc. Crestview had not previously employed an agency. Its advertising had been handled by various news media, including the defendant. The complaint charged that when plaintiff attempted to place advertising material with defendant, it was informed that defendant refused to grant the customary fifteen percent commission to plaintiff, which it granted as a matter of course to the three other advertising agencies active in Pensacola. Defendant's manager informed Crestview that plaintiff was not a qualified agency and that Crestview's advertising rates would be higher if Crestview retained the plaintiff as its agency. Crestview was persuaded to drop plaintiff as its agent and accept the services of another agency. Plaintiff thereupon brought this suit seeking treble damages and an injunction, alleging violations of Sections 1 and 2 of the Sherman Act.

The Court of Appeals held that summary judgment for the defendant was improperly granted, rejecting defendant's contention that it had an unrestricted right to refuse to purchase advertising from the plaintiff. Citing *Lorain Journal,* the Court noted that the Supreme Court had firmly established the principle that Section 2 prohibits an enterprise from refusing to deal with another business entity when the refusal is in furtherance of a plan to monopolize a relevant market. Packaged Programs, Inc. v. Westinghouse Broadcasting Co., 255 F.2d 708 (3d Cir.1958), was cited as a case similar to the one before the Fifth Circuit. In that case, Westinghouse Broadcasting Company, also a television station, produced filmed programs for sale to advertisers for broadcasting over its station. Packaged Programs, Inc., charged that Westinghouse refused to schedule any of its films. The district court dismissed the action but the Third Circuit reversed. The Fifth Circuit observed that in both cases the defendants were engaged in advertising production on the side in competition with other advertising agencies, and noted: "The theory of both cases is that the television stations used their legal monopoly power to create monopoly power in a separate but related field in which a monopolistic regulated industry is not the national policy."

4. For recent cases dealing with monopolization and attempt to monopolize claims, see Note on Recent Lower Court Cases on Essential Facilities, Leveraging, and Price Squeeze, p. 758 supra. Discussion of attempt to monopolize in the *Microsoft* case is found at pp. 798–99.

PROBLEM 18

A DISTRIBUTOR COMPETES WITH CLEARY

Cleary Linen is the sole manufacturer in the United States of linen rugs. These rugs are durable, reversible, easy to clean, and are especially desirable in hotels and office buildings. Linen rugs are 50% more expensive than comparable cotton and wool rugs, and account for only one percent of total rugs sold in the United States. Cleary sells through about 50 wholesale distributors located throughout the United States, except that it has always reserved exclusively to itself the right to bid for sales to the United States Government. Linen rugs have been in increasing demand and Cleary has often been unable to satisfy the full needs of its distributors.

Last year, Cleary's distributor in Chicago—Rugs Unlimited—submitted a bid on a sale to the Government without Cleary's knowledge or permission, which was 4% below the Cleary figure. Cleary asked Rugs to withdraw the bid and, when it failed to do so, refused to supply the order, claiming that linen rugs were in short supply and that it doubted that Rugs could satisfactorily service the Government's purchase order since delivery would have to occur at many locations throughout the United States. Rugs claimed that Cleary was anxious to cut off competitive challenges because high volume sales to the Government were extremely profitable. In support of that assertion, Rugs pointed out that it could underbid Cleary by 4% and make a profit, paying Cleary the usual wholesale price. When Cleary's other distributors also declined to supply linen rugs to fulfill the contract, Rugs was forced to withdraw its bid.

Rugs sues for treble damages for lost profits on the transaction. What result? Does your answer depend on whether Cleary is a monopolist?

Spectrum Sports, Inc. v. McQuillan

Supreme Court of the United States, 1993.
506 U.S. 447, 113 S.Ct. 884, 122 L.Ed.2d 247.

■ WHITE, J. Section 2 of the Sherman Act makes it an offense for any person to "monopolize, or attempt to monopolize, or combine or conspire with any other person or persons, to monopolize any part of the trade or commerce among the several States." The jury in this case returned a verdict finding that petitioners had monopolized, attempted to monopolize, and/or conspired to monopolize. The District Court entered a judgment ruling that petitioners had violated § 2, and the Court of Appeals affirmed on the ground that petitioners had attempted to monopolize. The issue we have before us is whether the District Court and the Court of Appeals correctly defined the elements of that offense.

I

Sorbothane is a patented elastic polymer whose shock-absorbing characteristics make it useful in a variety of medical, athletic, and equestrian products. BTR, Inc. (BTR), owns the patent rights to sorbothane, and its wholly owned subsidiaries manufacture the product in the United States and Britain. Hamilton–Kent Manufacturing Company (Hamilton–Kent) and Sorbothane, Inc. (S. I.) were at all relevant times owned by BTR. S. I. was formed in 1982 to take over Hamilton–Kent's sorbothane business. Respondents Shirley and Larry McQuillan, doing business as Sorboturf Enterprises, were regional distributors of sorbothane products from 1981 to 1983. Petitioner Spectrum Sports, Inc. (Spectrum), was also a distributor of sorbothane products. Petitioner Kenneth B. Leighton, Jr., is a co-owner of Spectrum. Kenneth Leighton, Jr., is the son of Kenneth Leighton, Sr., the president of Hamilton–Kent and S. I. at all relevant times.

In 1980, respondents Shirley and Larry McQuillan signed a letter of intent with Hamilton–Kent, which then owned all manufacturing and distribution rights to sorbothane. The letter of intent granted the McQuillans exclusive rights to purchase sorbothane for use in equestrian products. Respondents were designing a horseshoe pad using sorbothane.

In 1981, Hamilton–Kent decided to establish five regional distributorships for sorbothane. Respondents were selected to be distributors of all sorbothane products, including medical products and shoe inserts, in the Southwest. Spectrum was selected as distributor for another region.

In January 1982, Hamilton–Kent shifted responsibility for selling medical products from five regional distributors to a single national distributor. In April 1982, Hamilton–Kent told respondents that it wanted them to relinquish their athletic shoe distributorship as a condition for retaining the right to develop and distribute equestrian products. As of May 1982, BTR had moved the sorbothane business from Hamilton–Kent to S. I. In May, the marketing manager of S. I. again made clear that respondents had to sell their athletic distributorship to keep their equestrian distribution rights. At a meeting scheduled to discuss the sale of respondents' athletic distributorship to petitioner Leighton, Jr., Leighton, Jr., informed Shirley McQuillan that if she did not come to agreement with him she would be " 'looking for work.' " Respondents refused to sell and continued to distribute athletic shoe inserts.

In the fall of 1982, Leighton, Sr., informed respondents that another concern had been appointed as the national equestrian distributor, and that they were "no longer involved in equestrian products." In January 1983, S.

I. began marketing through a national distributor a sorbothane horseshoe pad allegedly indistinguishable from the one designed by respondents. In August 1983, S. I. informed respondents that it would no longer accept their orders. Spectrum thereupon became national distributor of sorbothane athletic shoe inserts. Respondents sought to obtain sorbothane from the BTR's British subsidiary, but were informed by that subsidiary that it would not sell sorbothane in the United States. Respondents' business failed. . . .

The case was tried to a jury, which returned a verdict against one or more of the defendants on each of the 11 alleged violations on which it was to return a verdict. All of the defendants were found to have violated § 2 by, in the words of the verdict sheet, "monopolizing, attempting to monopolize, and/or conspiring to monopolize." Petitioners were also found to have violated civil RICO and the California unfair practices law, but not § 1 of the Sherman Act. The jury awarded $1,743,000 in compensatory damages on each of the violations found to have occurred. This amount was trebled under § 4 of the Clayton Act. The District Court also awarded nearly $1 million in attorneys' fees and denied motions for judgment notwithstanding the verdict and for a new trial.

The Court of Appeals for the Ninth Circuit affirmed the judgment in an unpublished opinion. The court expressly ruled that the trial court had properly instructed the jury on the Sherman Act claims and found that the evidence supported the liability verdicts as well as the damages awards on these claims. The court then affirmed the judgment of the District Court, finding it unnecessary to rule on challenges to other violations found by the jury. On the § 2 issue that petitioners present here, the Court of Appeals, noting that the jury had found that petitioners had violated § 2 without specifying whether they had monopolized, attempted to monopolize, or conspired to monopolize, held that the verdict would stand if the evidence supported any one of the three possible violations of § 2. The court went on to conclude that a case of attempted monopolization had been established. The court rejected petitioners' argument that attempted monopolization had not been established because respondents had failed to prove that petitioners had a specific intent to monopolize a relevant market. The court also held that in order to show that respondents' attempt to monopolize was likely to succeed it was not necessary to present evidence of the relevant market or of the defendants' market power. In so doing, the Ninth Circuit relied on Lessig v. Tidewater Oil Co., 327 F.2d 459 (CA9), cert. denied, 377 U.S. 993 (1964), and its progeny. The Court of Appeals noted that these cases, in dealing with attempt to monopolize claims, had ruled that "if evidence of unfair or predatory conduct is presented, it may satisfy both the specific intent and dangerous probability elements of the offense, without any proof of relevant market or the defendant's marketpower [*sic*]." If, however, there is insufficient evidence of unfair or predatory conduct, there must be a showing of "relevant market or the defendant's marketpower [*sic*]." The court went on to find:

> "There is sufficient evidence from which the jury could conclude
> that the S. I. Group and Spectrum Group engaged in unfair or
> predatory conduct and thus inferred that they had the specific
> intent and the dangerous probability of success and, therefore,
> McQuillan did not have to prove relevant market or the defen-
> dant's marketing power."

The decision below, and the *Lessig* line of decisions on which it relies,
conflicts with holdings of courts in other Circuits. Every other Court of
Appeals has indicated that proving an attempt to monopolize requires proof
of a dangerous probability of monopolization of a relevant market. We
granted certiorari to resolve this conflict among the Circuits. We reverse.

II

While § 1 of the Sherman Act forbids contracts or conspiracies in
restraint of trade or commerce, § 2 addresses the actions of single firms
that monopolize or attempt to monopolize, as well as conspiracies and
combinations to monopolize. Section 2 does not define the elements of the
offense of attempted monopolization. Nor is there much guidance to be had
in the scant legislative history of that provision, which was added late in
the legislative process. See 1 E. Kintner, Legislative History of the Federal
Antitrust Laws and Related Statutes 23–25 (1978); 3 P. Areeda & D.
Turner, Antitrust Law ¶ 617, pp. 39–41 (1978). The legislative history does
indicate that much of the interpretation of the necessarily broad principles
of the Act was to be left for the courts in particular cases. *See, e.g.*, 21
Cong.Rec. 2460 (1890) (statement of Sen. Sherman). See also I Kintner,
supra, at 19; 3 Areeda & Turner, supra, at ¶ 617, p. 40.

This Court first addressed the meaning of attempt to monopolize under
§ 2 in Swift & Co. v. United States, 196 U.S. 375 (1905). The Court's
opinion, written by Justice Holmes, contained the following passage:

> "Where acts are not sufficient in themselves to produce a result
> which the law seeks to prevent—for instance, the monopoly—but
> require further acts in addition to the mere forces of nature to
> bring that result to pass, an intent to bring it to pass is necessary
> in order to produce a dangerous probability that it will happen.
> But when that intent and the consequent dangerous probability
> exist, this statute, like many others and like the common law in
> some cases, directs itself against that dangerous probability as well
> as against the completed result." Id., at 396.

The Court went on to explain, however, that not every act done with
intent to produce an unlawful result constitutes an attempt. "It is a
question of proximity and degree." *Id.*, at 402. *Swift* thus indicated that
intent is necessary, but alone is not sufficient, to establish the dangerous
probability of success that is the object of § 2's prohibition of attempts.

The Court's decisions since *Swift* have reflected the view that the
plaintiff charging attempted monopolization must prove a dangerous probability of actual monopolization, which has generally required a definition of
the relevant market and examination of market power. In Walker Process
Equipment, Inc. v. Food Machinery & Chemical Corp., 382 U.S. 172, 177

(1965), we found that enforcement of a fraudulently obtained patent claim could violate the Sherman Act. We stated that, to establish monopolization or attempt to monopolize under § 2 of the Sherman Act, it would be necessary to appraise the exclusionary power of the illegal patent claim in terms of the relevant market for the product involved. The reason was that "without a definition of that market there is no way to measure [the defendant's] ability to lessen or destroy competition." *Ibid.*

Similarly, this Court reaffirmed in Copperweld Corp. v. Independence Tube Corp., 467 U.S. 752 (1984), that "Congress authorized Sherman Act scrutiny of single firms only when they pose a danger of monopolization. Judging unilateral conduct in this manner reduces the risk that the antitrust laws will dampen the competitive zeal of a single aggressive entrepreneur." *Id.,* at 768. Thus, the conduct of a single firm, governed by § 2, "is unlawful only when it threatens actual monopolization." *Id.,* at 767. See also Lorain Journal Co. v. United States, 342 U.S. 143, 154 (1951); United States v. Griffith, 334 U.S. 100 (1948); American Tobacco Co. v. United States, 328 U.S. 781, 785 (1946).

The Courts of Appeals other than the Ninth Circuit have followed this approach. Consistent with our cases, it is generally required that to demonstrate attempted monopolization a plaintiff must prove (1) that the defendant has engaged in predatory or anticompetitive conduct with (2) a specific intent to monopolize and (3) a dangerous probability of achieving monopoly power. In order to determine whether there is a dangerous probability of monopolization, courts have found it necessary to consider the relevant market and the defendant's ability to lessen or destroy competition in that market.

Notwithstanding the array of authority contrary to *Lessig,* the Court of Appeals in this case reaffirmed its prior holdings; indeed, it did not mention either this Court's decisions discussed above or the many decisions of other Courts of Appeals reaching contrary results. Respondents urge us to affirm the decision below. We are not at all inclined, however, to embrace *Lessig's* interpretation of § 2, for there is little if any support for it in the statute or the case law, and the notion that proof of unfair or predatory conduct alone is sufficient to make out the offense of attempted monopolization is contrary to the purpose and policy of the Sherman Act.

The *Lessig* opinion claimed support from the language of § 2, which prohibits attempts to monopolize "any part" of commerce, and therefore forbids attempts to monopolize any appreciable segment of interstate sales of the relevant product. The "any part" clause, however, applies to charges of monopolization as well as to attempts to monopolize, and it is beyond doubt that the former requires proof of market power in a relevant market. United States v. Grinnell Corp., 384 U.S. 563, 570–571 (1966).

In support of its determination that an inference of dangerous probability was permissible from a showing of intent, the *Lessig* opinion cited, and added emphasis to, this Court's reference in its opinion in *Swift* to "intent and the *consequent* dangerous probability." 327 F.2d, at 474, n. 46, quoting 196 U.S., at 396. But any question whether dangerous probability of success requires proof of more than intent alone should have been removed by the subsequent passage in *Swift* which stated that "not every act that may be done with an intent to produce an unlawful result ... constitutes an attempt. It is a question of proximity and degree." ...

It is also our view that *Lessig* and later Ninth Circuit decisions refining and applying it are inconsistent with the policy of the Sherman Act. The purpose of the Act is not to protect businesses from the working of the market; it is to protect the public from the failure of the market. The law directs itself not against conduct which is competitive, even severely so, but against conduct which unfairly tends to destroy competition itself. It does so not out of solicitude for private concerns but out of concern for the public interest. Thus, this Court and other courts have been careful to avoid constructions of § 2 which might chill competition, rather than foster it. It is sometimes difficult to distinguish robust competition from conduct with long-term anticompetitive effects; moreover, single-firm activity is unlike concerted activity covered by § 1, which "inherently is fraught with anticompetitive risk." *Copperweld*, 467 U.S., at 767–769. For these reasons, § 2 makes the conduct of a single firm unlawful only when it actually monopolizes or dangerously threatens to do so. The concern that § 2 might be applied so as to further anticompetitive ends is plainly not met by inquiring only whether the defendant has engaged in "unfair" or "predatory" tactics. Such conduct may be sufficient to prove the necessary intent to monopolize, which is something more than an intent to compete vigorously, but demonstrating the dangerous probability of monopolization in an attempt case also requires inquiry into the relevant product and geographic market and the defendant's economic power in that market.

III

We hold that petitioners may not be liable for attempted monopolization under § 2 of the Sherman Act absent proof of a dangerous probability that they would monopolize a particular market and specific intent to monopolize. In this case, the trial instructions allowed the jury to infer specific intent and dangerous probability of success from the defendants' predatory conduct, without any proof of the relevant market or of a realistic probability that the defendants could achieve monopoly power in that market. In this respect, the instructions misconstrued § 2, as did the Court of Appeals in affirming the judgment of the District Court. Since the affirmance of the § 2 judgment against petitioners rested solely on the legally erroneous conclusion that petitioners had attempted to monopolize in violation of § 2 and since the jury's verdict did not negate the possibility that the § 2 verdict rested on the attempt to monopolize ground alone, the judgment of the Court of Appeals is reversed, and the case is remanded for further proceedings consistent with this opinion.

NOTES AND QUESTIONS

1. Does the Supreme Court in *Spectrum Sports* give any indication as to how much market power is required for there to be a dangerous probability of successful

monopolization? After *Spectrum Sports,* what is the difference between monopolization and attempted monopolization?

2.   After *Spectrum Sports,* may the Ninth Circuit still use "unfair or predatory conduct" as a factor in proving dangerous probability of success, as long as some evidence of the defendant's market power is also considered?

3.   UNITED STATES v. EMPIRE GAS CORP., 537 F.2d 296 (8th Cir.1976), cert. denied, 429 U.S. 1122 (1977). Empire was a large wholesaler and retailer of liquified petroleum (LP), a generic term for gas fuels such as propane and butane sold to consumers for heating and cooking. Empire operated in twenty-four states, but the competitive behavior challenged by the government largely had occurred in connection with retail sales of LP in areas surrounding Lebanon and Wheaton, Missouri.

On several occasions, Empire had invited competitors to raise retail prices to higher levels, equal to prices charged by an Empire subsidiary. If the competitor refused, Empire threatened to price the company out of business; if it still refused, Empire began selling gas in the rival's territory at drastically lowered prices. Salesmen solicitors of Empire told customers that the rival company was going out of business. In these price wars, Empire occasionally acquired the source of supply of gas of a competitor, and then raised the price at which it sold LP at wholesale so that the competitor could not retail the product at a price equal to Empire and still make a profit. In one such competitive episode, Empire also limited the credit of a retailer competitor to two loads of gas and then failed to mail invoices to the competitor. As a result, the competitor could not pay previous bills and on that pretense, Empire refused to sell needed supplies. In at least one instance in the record, a coerced competitor of Empire capitulated to its pressure and a compromise was worked out whereby Empire and the competitor sold at retail at a uniform higher price.

The Court of Appeals recited the familiar rule with respect to attempts to monopolize: proof is required of "specific intent" and "dangerous probability of success." The Court further found that Empire's price cuts and threats to price cut established a specific intent to monopolize. On the second element, the Court accepted plaintiff's contentions that the product market was LP gas, and that the geographic markets were Lebanon and Wheaton, Missouri, where the Court assumed (despite doubt about the government's proof) that Empire had 50 percent and 47 percent respectively, and some 11 other local marketing areas. The Eighth Circuit found no attempt to monopolize in Lebanon and Wheaton because in those areas there was no evidence that competitors of Empire raised or fixed prices because of Empire's threats or pricing actions. Presumably in other market areas where Empire's conduct had an effect on its competitors, Empire's market share was too small, and thus the company was too remote from monopoly power, to indicate any dangerous probability of achieving monopoly power. Finally, the Eighth Circuit found that the prices of LP gas in market areas spotlighted by the government were only slightly higher than in other areas, and in any event, the reasons for the difference were a matter of speculation, and that Empire's profits, averaging 11.1 percent from 1963 to 1973, were not so high as to require a conclusion that Empire was successful in controlling prices or competition in the relevant market areas. Accordingly, the Court of Appeals affirmed the district court's decision in favor of Empire. Was *Empire Gas* correctly decided?

4.   IN INTERNATIONAL DISTRIBUTION CENTERS, INC. v. WALSH TRUCKING CO., INC., 812 F.2d 786, 791–93 (2d Cir.), cert. denied, 482 U.S. 915 (1987), the Second Circuit rejected removal of the "dangerous probability" element and provided the following reasoning:

Eliminating the dangerous probability element from attempted monopolization would have the effect of extending the coverage of section 2 of the Sherman Act to similar behavior already covered by state and federal law. The Federal Trade Commission Act § 5, regulatory statutes and state business tort law all reach anticompetitive behavior by firms that lack market power. Civil RICO may have also expanded into this area.... There is no unmet need calling for judicial expansion of section 2 to reach similar behavior.

Furthermore, any significant reduction in the antitrust plaintiff's burden of proving that the defendant has a dangerous probability of monopolizing the market might discourage the healthy competition that section 2 is intended to nurture and deter businesses from aggressively expanding into new markets. Existing firms that lost market share to a newcomer could seize upon some hiring or marketing tactic, label it "anticompetitive" and then recover treble damages and attorneys' fees. *See, e.g.,* Gerber Products Co. v. Beech–Nut Life Savers, 160 F.Supp. 916, 918 (S.D.N.Y.1958) (plaintiff with 73% share of relevant market for baby food sued defendant with 4.3% share for attempted monopolization, alleging that "puffing" of baby food in glass jars and price reduction to meet plaintiff's price were anticompetitive acts). Surely the potential liability from such a suit would cast a long shadow over business planning.

We, therefore, adhere to the traditional rule that an action under section 2 of the Sherman Act for attempting to monopolize a market will lie only where there is anticompetitive conduct, a specific intent to monopolize *and* a dangerous probability that monopoly will be achieved. A dangerous probability of monopoly may exist where the defendant firm possesses a significant market share when it undertakes the challenged anticompetitive conduct.

We note that market share analysis, while essential, is not necessarily determinative in the calculation of monopoly power under this standard. Other market characteristics must also be considered in determining whether a given firm has monopoly power or has a dangerous probability of acquiring monopoly power.... Among these characteristics are the strength of the competition, the probable development of the industry, the barriers to entry, the nature of the anticompetitive conduct and the elasticity of consumer demand....

Applying this standard, NRT was entitled to a judgment notwithstanding the verdict.... One year after entering the market, NRT had no more than a seventeen percent share of the carriage of garments on hangers in the Pennsylvania Corridor. Even if NRT drove IDC out of business and took over *all* of IDC's accounts, NRT would still have a market share of no more than fifty percent. It is unlikely that even with a fifty percent market share NRT could raise prices without losing business to the several other trucking firms that had been unaffected by NRT's employee raids or alleged predatory pricing. The evidence at trial indicated that NRT's 1983 tariffs were already above those of at least three of its other competitors in the Pennsylvania Corridor.

Assuming *arguendo* that NRT could have cannibalized IDC, appropriated *all* of its customers and obtained sufficient power to raise prices in the market temporarily, the competitors from outside the market could easily have surmounted any barriers to entry and competed with NRT for business in the Pennsylvania Corridor....

Under the conditions in the market for the carriage of garments on hangers in the Pennsylvania Corridor, therefore, NRT's market share was not sufficiently significant to give rise to a dangerous probability that it would monopolize the market even when its anticompetitive conduct is taken into account. A jury could not reasonably find that such a probability existed without engaging in speculation concerning matters not in evidence.

Thus, we conclude that IDC failed as a matter of law to establish that NRT, which had at most a seventeen percent market share one year after it entered an intensely competitive market with low entry barriers, had a dangerous probability of successfully monopolizing that market. Our conclusion is supported by the majority of cases with similar facts finding no dangerous probability of a monopoly. Lektro–Vend Corp. v. Vendo Co., 660 F.2d 255, 270–71 (7th Cir.1981) (30% market share, no significant barriers to entry), cert. denied, 455 U.S. 921 (1982); Nifty Foods Corp. v. Great Atlantic & Pacific Tea Co., 614 F.2d 832, 841 (2d Cir.1980) (33% market share, defendant's share continuously declining); Yoder Brothers, Inc. v. California–Florida Plant Corp., 537 F.2d 1347, 1368–69 (5th Cir.1976) (20% market share in highly competitive market with low barriers to entry), cert. denied, 429 U.S. 1094 (1977); Hiland Dairy, Inc. v. Kroger Co., 402 F.2d 968, 971–72, 974–75 (8th Cir.1968) (20% market share in highly competitive market)....

See Tops Markets, Inc. v. Quality Markets, Inc., 142 F.3d 90, 100–01 (2d Cir.1998).

5.   Could the legitimate concern with chilling aggressive competitive behavior be dealt with by some sort of sliding scale? Thus, in situations where conduct was particularly anticompetitive and lacking in redeeming virtues, a finding of less significant market power might suffice. Would such an approach be consistent with *Spectrum Sports*? The National Commission for Review of Antitrust Laws and Procedures recommended the following:

> RECOMMENDATION 1: The "dangerous probability of success" necessary to establish an attempt to monopolize under Section 2 of the Sherman Act should not be interpreted as requiring proof of a high probability of actual monopoly, but rather a determination of whether the defendant has significantly threatened competition. Such determination should be based on the weighing of various factors including the defendant's intent, market power, and conduct. Additionally, evidence regarding the relationship of price to marginal cost properly should be considered in assessing pricing practices alleged to form the basis of an attempt, but proof that such prices were below marginal cost should not be a prerequisite to proof of a violation. In order to ensure uniform adoption of these standards, the Sherman Act should be amended to incorporate them.

National Commission, Report to the President and the Attorney General vii–viii (1979).

6.   The conduct element in many attempt cases involves business torts of the sort traditionally covered by state law—for example, false advertising, tortious interference with contract relations, and misappropriation of trade secrets. Thus, in Albert Pick–Barth Co. v. Mitchell Woodbury Corp., 57 F.2d 96 (1st Cir.), cert. denied, 286 U.S. 552 (1932), the Third Circuit found that a conspiracy to injure

intentionally the business of a competitor through tortious behavior—in that case hiring plaintiff's employees to obtain access to customer lists, cost records, and other confidential data—would be illegal *per se* under the antitrust laws.

Is that kind of conduct a serious threat to the competitive process, as opposed to the victim of the business tort? While such conduct often lacks business justification, would it often contribute significantly to the establishment of a monopoly position? Is it wise, as the Second Circuit suggests in *Walsh Trucking* (note 4 supra), to depend on state business tort law or civil RICO to remedy anticompetitive conduct? The best vehicle for dealing with predatory single-firm conduct (other than Section 2) may be Section 5 of the Federal Trade Commission Act, outlawing unfair methods of competition, since there is no criminal exposure or potential for private treble damage action. Or should the law simply leave the victim of this conduct to its common-law and other non-antitrust remedies? Would that unduly weaken deterrence?

PROBLEM 19

PASTA SUPREME TAKES ON A NEWCOMER

National Foods sells Pasta Supreme, the leading prepared spaghetti sauce in the United States, with 40% of annual sales. It distributes nationally along with its two principal competitors; they account for 12% and 10% of sales respectively, while the rest of the market consists of sales by a large number of regional manufacturers and private-label sales by large supermarket chains. There has been no new entry by companies selling on a national basis for many years.

About a year ago, Lunt–Dresson, an established packaged food producer with no previous presence in the spaghetti sauce market, introduced Prima Sauce, a thicker and spicier spaghetti sauce differentiated from existing products by additional and expensive processing. It announced plans to introduce its new product in several test markets (the New York metropolitan area, Syracuse, Buffalo, and Cincinnati–Dayton) with vigorous local advertising campaigns, low introductory prices, and special discounts to supermarkets. It also initiated market studies to see what kind of advertising was effective, and whether the product was perceived by consumers as different and better than existing spaghetti sauces.

Two months later, National Foods introduced Pasta Premium, a spaghetti sauce described on the label as "Extra Thick and Zesty," which also was different because of additional processing. It immediately introduced the product in six test markets (including the New York metropolitan area, Syracuse, and Cincinnati–Dayton). It offered special discounts to retailers in all test markets (though not so great as to drive the price below average variable costs) on condition that it was granted preferred shelf space in the stores.

Lunt–Dresson claimed that National Foods' business behavior amounted to an attempt to monopolize. It alleges that Pasta Premium was introduced "precipitously" before the product had been fully tested within the company. The name of the new product and the label design allegedly were meant to confuse people as to the source of this new kind of spaghetti sauce, and the special discounts were intended to deny Prima Sauce access to shelf space. Since supermarkets rarely carry more than two brands of spaghetti sauce, the aggressive sales in test markets by National Foods had two effects. It denied Prima Sauce access to markets and kept its sales volume low, and interfered with Lunt–Dresson's efforts to run a test program to determine whether the product and its marketing were effective. The choice by

National Foods of test markets which largely duplicated the major test markets of Lunt–Dresson was cited as evidence of exclusionary intent.

Lunt–Dresson sued, charging an attempt to monopolize under Section 2, and National Foods moved to dismiss on grounds that the plaintiff had failed to state a cause of action. What result? Would the result be different if a memorandum were introduced in evidence in which a mid-level marketing executive for National Foods reported to a Vice President of the company that aggressive marketing of the new thick and zesty sauce had "stopped Lunt–Dresson in its tracks"? Would it make a difference if an important reason for the absence of large-scale entry was that successful national distribution required extensive advertising in national media?

Section 2.   Predatory Price Cutting

Characterizing a price cut as predatory or nonpredatory in a particular case is often not easy. The same observable conduct—reducing the price of a product to consumers—may be either a necessary and desirable response to competitive forces or undesirable conduct which injures competition. Furthermore, "intent" is an uncertain indicator in these cases since the price cut is motivated in all instances by the same immediate objective—winning sales from competitors and occupying a larger share of the market—even though this may make it unprofitable for one or more competitors to remain in the market. Finding workable criteria to identify predatory pricing and other forms of predatory conduct thus becomes critical.

Brooke Group v. Brown & Williamson Tobacco

Supreme Court of the United States, 1993.
509 U.S. 209, 113 S.Ct. 2578, 125 L.Ed.2d 168.

■ KENNEDY, J. This case stems from a market struggle that erupted in the domestic cigarette industry in the mid–1980s. Petitioner Brooke Group, Inc., whom we, like the parties to the case, refer to as Liggett because of its former corporate name, charges that to counter its innovative development of generic cigarettes, respondent Brown & Williamson Tobacco Corporation introduced its own line of generic cigarettes in an unlawful effort to stifle price competition in the economy segment of the national cigarette market. Liggett contends that Brown & Williamson cut prices on generic cigarettes below cost and offered discriminatory volume rebates to wholesalers to force Liggett to raise its own generic cigarette prices and introduce oligopoly pricing in the economy segment. We hold that Brown & Williamson is entitled to judgment as a matter of law.

I

In 1980, Liggett pioneered the development of the economy segment of the national cigarette market by introducing a line of "black and white" generic cigarettes. The economy segment of the market, sometimes called the generic segment, is characterized by its bargain prices and comprises a variety of different products: black and whites, which are true generics sold in plain white packages with simple black lettering describing their contents; private label generics, which carry the trade dress of a specific purchaser, usually a retail chain; branded generics, which carry a brand name but which, like black and whites and private label generics, are sold at a deep discount and with little or no advertising; and "Value–25s," packages of 25 cigarettes that are sold to the consumer some 12.5% below the cost of a normal 20–cigarette pack. By 1984, when Brown & Williamson entered the generic segment and set in motion the series of events giving rise to this suit, Liggett's black and whites represented 97% of the generic segment, which in turn accounted for a little more than 4% of domestic cigarette sales. Prior to Liggett's introduction of black and whites in 1980, sales of generic cigarettes amounted to less than 1% of the domestic cigarette market.

Because of the procedural posture of this case, we view the evidence in the light most favorable to Liggett. The parties are in basic agreement, however, regarding the central, historical facts. Cigarette manufacturing has long been one of America's most concentrated industries, see F. Scherer & D. Ross, Industrial Market Structure and Economic Performance 250 (3d ed. 1990) (hereinafter Scherer & Ross), and for decades, production has been dominated by six firms: R.J. Reynolds, Philip Morris, American Brands, Lorillard, and the two litigants involved here, Liggett and Brown & Williamson. R.J. Reynolds and Philip Morris, the two industry leaders, enjoyed respective market shares of about 28% and 40% at the time of trial. Brown & Williamson ran a distant third, its market share never exceeding 12% at any time relevant to this dispute. Liggett's share of the market was even less, from a low of just over 2% in 1980 to a high of just over 5% in 1984.

The cigarette industry also has long been one of America's most profitable, in part because for many years there was no significant price competition among the rival firms. See Scherer & Ross 250–251; R. Tennant, American Cigarette Industry 86–87 (1950). List prices for cigarettes increased in lock-step, twice a year, for a number of years, irrespective of the rate of inflation, changes in the costs of production, or shifts in consumer demand. Substantial evidence suggests that in recent decades, the industry reaped the benefits of prices above a competitive level, though not through unlawful conduct of the type that once characterized the industry. See Tennant, supra, at 275, 342; cf. American Tobacco Co. v. United States, 328 U.S. 781 (1946); United States v. American Tobacco Co., 221 U.S. 106 (1911); Scherer & Ross 451.

By 1980, however, broad market trends were working against the industry. Overall demand for cigarettes in the United States was declining, and no immediate prospect of recovery existed. As industry volume shrank, all firms developed substantial excess capacity. This decline in demand, coupled with the effects of nonprice competition, had a severe negative impact on Liggett. Once a major force in the industry, with market shares in excess of 20%, Liggett's market share had declined by 1980 to a little over 2%. With this meager share of the market, Liggett was on the verge of going out of business.

At the urging of a distributor, Liggett took an unusual step to revive its prospects: It developed a line of black and white generic cigarettes. When introduced in 1980, black and whites were offered to consumers at a list price roughly 30% lower than the list price of full-priced, branded cigarettes. They were also promoted at the wholesale level by means of rebates that increased with the volume of cigarettes ordered. Black and white cigarettes thus represented a new marketing category. The category's principal competitive characteristic was low price. Liggett's black and whites were an immediate and considerable success, growing from a fraction of a percent of the market at their introduction to over 4% of the total cigarette market by early 1984.

As the market for Liggett's generic cigarettes expanded, the other cigarette companies found themselves unable to ignore the economy segment. In general, the growth of generics came at the expense of the other firms' profitable sales of branded cigarettes. Brown & Williamson was hardest hit, because many of Brown & Williamson's brands were favored by consumers who were sensitive to changes in cigarette prices. Although Brown & Williamson sold only 11.4% of the market's branded cigarettes, 20% of the converts to Liggett's black and whites had switched from a Brown & Williamson brand. Losing volume and profits in its branded products, Brown & Williamson determined to enter the generic segment of the cigarette market. In July 1983, Brown & Williamson had begun selling Value–25s, and in the spring of 1984, it introduced its own black and white cigarette.

Brown & Williamson was neither the first nor the only cigarette company to recognize the threat posed by Liggett's black and whites and to respond in the economy segment. R.J. Reynolds had also introduced a Value–25 in 1983. And before Brown & Williamson introduced its own black and whites, R.J. Reynolds had repriced its "Doral" branded cigarette at generic levels. To compete with Liggett's black and whites, R.J. Reynolds dropped its list price on Doral about 30% and used volume rebates to wholesalers as an incentive to spur orders. Doral was the first competition at Liggett's price level.

Brown & Williamson's entry was an even graver threat to Liggett's dominance of the generic category. Unlike R.J. Reynolds' Doral, Brown & Williamson's product was also a black and white and so would be in direct competition with Liggett's product at the wholesale level and on the retail shelf. Because Liggett's and Brown & Williamson's black and whites were more or less fungible, wholesalers had little incentive to carry more than one line. And unlike R.J. Reynolds, Brown & Williamson not only matched Liggett's prices but beat them. At the retail level, the suggested list price of Brown & Williamson's black and whites was the same as Liggett's, but Brown & Williamson's volume discounts to wholesalers were larger. Brown & Williamson's rebate structure also encompassed a greater number of volume categories than Liggett's, with the highest categories carrying special rebates for orders of very substantial size. Brown & Williamson marketed its black and whites to Liggett's existing distributors as well as to its own full list of buyers, which included a thousand wholesalers who had not yet carried any generic products.

Liggett responded to Brown & Williamson's introduction of black and whites in two ways. First, Liggett increased its own wholesale rebates. This precipitated a price war at the wholesale level, in which Liggett five times attempted to beat the rebates offered by Brown & Williamson. At the end of each round, Brown & Williamson maintained a real advantage over Liggett's prices. Although it is undisputed that Brown & Williamson's original net price for its black and whites was above its costs, Liggett contends that by the end of the rebate war, Brown & Williamson was selling its black and whites at a loss. This rebate war occurred before Brown & Williamson had sold a single black and white cigarette.

Liggett's second response was to file a lawsuit. . . . These claims were either dismissed on summary judgment or rejected by the jury. They were not appealed.

Liggett also amended its complaint to add a second Robinson–Patman Act claim, which is the subject of the present controversy. Liggett alleged that Brown & Williamson's volume rebates to wholesalers amounted to price discrimination that had a reasonable possibility of injuring competition, in violation of § 2(a) [of the Robinson–Patman Act]. Liggett claimed that Brown & Williamson's discriminatory volume rebates were integral to a scheme of predatory pricing, in which Brown & Williamson reduced its net prices for generic cigarettes below average variable costs. According to Liggett, these below-cost prices were not promotional but were intended to pressure it to raise its list prices on generic cigarettes, so that the percentage price difference between generic and branded cigarettes would narrow. Liggett explained that it would have been unable to reduce its wholesale rebates without losing substantial market share to Brown & Williamson; its only choice, if it wished to avoid prolonged losses on its principal product line, was to raise retail prices. The resulting reduction in the list price gap, it was said, would restrain the growth of the economy segment and preserve Brown & Williamson's supracompetitive profits on its branded cigarettes.

The trial began in the fall of 1989. By that time, all six cigarette companies had entered the economy segment. The economy segment was the fastest growing segment of the cigarette market, having increased from about 4% of the market in 1984, when the rebate war in generics began, to about 15% in 1989. Black and white generics had declined as a force in the economy segment as consumer interest shifted toward branded generics, but Liggett's overall volume had increased steadily to 9 billion generic cigarettes sold. Overall, the 2.8 billion generic cigarettes sold in 1981 had become 80 billion by 1989.

The consumer price of generics had increased along with output. For a year, the list prices for generic cigarettes established at the end of the rebate war remained stable. But in June of 1985, Liggett raised its list price, and the other firms followed several months later. The precise effect of the list price increase is difficult to assess, because all of the cigarette firms offered a variety of discounts, coupons, and other promotions directly to consumers on both generic and branded cigarettes. Nonetheless, at least some portion of the list price increase was reflected in a higher net price to the consumer.

In December 1985, Brown & Williamson attempted to increase its list prices, but retracted the announced increase when the other firms adhered to their existing prices. Thus, after Liggett's June 1985 increase, list prices on generics did not change again until the summer of 1986, when a pattern of twice yearly increases in tandem with the full-priced branded cigarettes was established. The dollar amount of these increases was the same for generic and full-priced cigarettes, which resulted in a greater percentage price increase in the less expensive generic cigarettes and a narrowing of the percentage gap between the list price of branded and black and white cigarettes, from approximately 38% at the time Brown & Williamson entered the segment, to approximately 27% at the time of trial. Also by the time of trial, five of the six manufacturers, including Liggett, had introduced so-called "subgenerics," a category of branded generic cigarette that sold at a discount of 50% or more off the list price of full-priced branded cigarettes.

After a 115–day trial involving almost 3,000 exhibits and over a score of witnesses, the jury returned a verdict in favor of Liggett, finding on the special verdict form that Brown & Williamson had engaged in price discrimination that had a reasonable possibility of injuring competition in the domestic cigarette market as a whole. The jury awarded Liggett $49.6 million in damages, which the District Court trebled to $148.8 million. After reviewing the record, however, the District Court held that Brown & Williamson was entitled to judgment as a matter of law on three separate grounds: lack of injury to competition, lack of antitrust injury to Liggett, and lack of a causal link between the discriminatory rebates and Liggett's alleged injury. Liggett Group, Inc. v. Brown & Williamson Tobacco Corp., 748 F.Supp. 344 (M.D.N.C.1990). With respect to the first issue, which is the only one before us, the District Court found that no slowing of the growth rate of generics, and thus no injury to competition, was possible unless there had been tacit coordination of prices in the economy segment of the cigarette market by the various manufacturers. The District Court held that a reasonable jury could come to but one conclusion about the existence of such coordination among the firms contending for shares of the economy segment: it did not exist, and Brown & Williamson therefore had no reasonable possibility of limiting the growth of the segment.

The United States Court of Appeals for the Fourth Circuit affirmed. Liggett Group, Inc. v. Brown & Williamson Tobacco Corp., 964 F.2d 335 (1992). The Court of Appeals held that the dynamic of conscious parallelism among oligopolists could not produce competitive injury in a predatory pricing setting, which necessarily involves a price cut by one of the oligopolists. In the Court of Appeals' view, "[t]o rely on the characteristics of an oligopoly to assure recoupment of losses from a predatory pricing scheme after one oligopolist has made a competitive move is ... economically irrational."

II

A

Price discrimination is made unlawful by § 2(a) of the Clayton Act, as amended by the Robinson–Patman Act....

Although we have reiterated that " 'a price discrimination within the meaning of [this] provision is merely a price difference,' " Texaco Inc. v. Hasbrouck, 496 U.S. 543, 558 (1990) (quoting FTC v. Anheuser–Busch, Inc., 363 U.S. 536, 549 (1960)), the statute as a practical matter could not, and does not, ban all price differences charged to "different purchasers of commodities of like grade and quality." Instead, the statute contains a number of important limitations, one of which is central to evaluating Liggett's claim: By its terms, the Robinson–Patman Act condemns price discrimination only to the extent that it threatens to injure competition. The availability of statutory defenses permitting price discrimination when it is based on differences in costs, § 13(a), "changing conditions affecting the market for or the marketability of the goods concerned," *ibid.*, or conduct undertaken "in good faith to meet an equally low price of a competitor," § 13(b); Standard Oil Co. v. FTC, 340 U.S. 231, 250 (1951), confirms that Congress did not intend to outlaw price differences that result from or further the forces of competition. Thus, "the Robinson–Patman Act should be construed consistently with broader policies of the antitrust laws." Great Atlantic & Pacific Tea Co., Inc. v. FTC, 440 U.S. 69, 80, n. 13 (1979). See also Automatic Canteen Co. of America v. FTC, 346 U.S. 61, 63, 74 (1953).

Liggett contends that Brown & Williamson's discriminatory volume rebates to wholesalers threatened substantial competitive injury by furthering a predatory pricing scheme designed to purge competition from the economy segment of the cigarette market. This type of injury, which harms direct competitors of the discriminating seller, is known as primary-line injury. See FTC v. Anheuser–Busch, Inc., supra, at 538. We last addressed primary line injury over 25 years ago, in Utah Pie Co. v. Continental Baking Co., 386 U.S. 685 (1967). In *Utah Pie,* we reviewed the sufficiency of the evidence supporting jury verdicts against three national pie companies that had engaged in a variety of predatory practices in the market for frozen pies in Salt Lake City, with the intent to drive a local pie manufacturer out of business. We reversed the Court of Appeals and held that the evidence presented was adequate to permit a jury to find a likelihood of injury to competition.

Utah Pie has often been interpreted to permit liability for primary-line price discrimination on a mere showing that the defendant intended to harm competition or produced a declining price structure. The case has been criticized on the grounds that such low standards of competitive injury are at odds with the antitrust laws' traditional concern for consumer welfare and price competition.... We do not regard the *Utah Pie* case itself as having the full significance attributed to it by its detractors. *Utah Pie* was an early judicial inquiry in this area and did not purport to set forth explicit, general standards for establishing a violation of the Robinson–Patman Act. As the law has been explored since *Utah Pie*, it has become evident that primary-line competitive injury under the Robinson–Patman Act is of the same general character as the injury inflicted by predatory pricing schemes actionable under § 2 of the Sherman Act.... There are, to be sure, differences between the two statutes. For example, we interpret § 2 of the Sherman Act to condemn predatory pricing when it poses "a dangerous probability of actual monopolization," Spectrum Sports, Inc. v. McQuillan, 506 U.S. 447, 455 (1993), whereas the Robinson–Patman Act requires only that there be "a reasonable possibility" of substantial injury to competition before its protections are triggered. Falls City Industries, Inc. v. Vanco Beverage, Inc., 460 U.S. 428, 434 (1983). But whatever additional flexibility the Robinson–Patman Act standard may imply, the essence of the claim under either statute is the same: A business rival has priced its products in an unfair manner with an object to eliminate or retard competition and thereby gain and exercise control over prices in the relevant market.

Accordingly, whether the claim alleges predatory pricing under § 2 of the Sherman Act or primary-line price discrimination under the Robinson–Patman Act, the two prerequisites to recovery remain the same. First, a plaintiff seeking to establish competitive injury resulting from a rival's low prices must prove that the prices complained of are below an appropriate measure of its rival's costs.[49] *See, e.g.,* Cargill, Inc. v. Monfort of Colorado, Inc., 479 U.S. 104, 117 (1986); Matsushita Electric Industrial Co. v. Zenith Radio Corp., 475 U.S. 574, 585, n. 8 (1986); Utah Pie, 386 U.S., at 698, 701, 702–703, n. 14. Although *Cargill* and *Matsushita* reserved as a formal matter the question " 'whether recovery should *ever* be available ... when the pricing in question is above some measure of incremental cost,' " the reasoning in both opinions suggests that only below-cost prices should suffice, and we have rejected elsewhere the notion that above-cost prices that are below general market levels or the costs of a firm's competitors inflict injury to competition cognizable under the antitrust laws. See Atlantic Richfield Co. v. USA Petroleum Co., 495 U.S. 328, 340 (1990). "Low prices benefit consumers regardless of how those prices are set, and so long as they are above predatory levels, they do not threaten competition.... We have adhered to this principle regardless of the type of antitrust claim involved." As a general rule, the exclusionary effect of prices above a relevant measure of cost either reflects the lower cost structure of the alleged predator, and so represents competition on the merits, or is beyond the practical ability of a judicial tribunal to control without courting intolerable risks of chilling legitimate price-cutting. See

---

49. Because the parties in this case agree that the relevant measure of cost is average variable cost, however, we again decline to resolve the conflict among the lower courts over the appropriate measure of cost. See *Cargill, supra,* at 117–118, n. 12; *Matsushita, supra,* at 585, n. 8.

Areeda & Hovenkamp ¶¶ 714.2, 714.3. "To hold that the antitrust laws protect competitors from the loss of profits due to such price competition would, in effect, render illegal any decision by a firm to cut prices in order to increase market share. The antitrust laws require no such perverse result." *Cargill, supra,* at 116.

Even in an oligopolistic market, when a firm drops its prices to a competitive level to demonstrate to a maverick the unprofitability of straying from the group, it would be illogical to condemn the price cut: The antitrust laws then would be an obstacle to the chain of events most conducive to a breakdown of oligopoly pricing and the onset of competition. Even if the ultimate effect of the cut is to induce or reestablish supracompetitive pricing, discouraging a price cut and forcing firms to maintain supracompetitive prices, thus depriving consumers of the benefits of lower prices in the interim, does not constitute sound antitrust policy.

The second prerequisite to holding a competitor liable under the antitrust laws for charging low prices is a demonstration that the competitor had a reasonable prospect, or, under § 2 of the Sherman Act, a dangerous probability, of recouping its investment in below-cost prices. See *Matsushita, supra,* at 589; *Cargill, supra,* at 119, n. 15. "For the investment to be rational, the [predator] must have a reasonable expectation of recovering, in the form of later monopoly profits, more than the losses suffered." *Matsushita, supra,* at 588–589. Recoupment is the ultimate object of an unlawful predatory pricing scheme; it is the means by which a predator profits from predation. Without it, predatory pricing produces lower aggregate prices in the market, and consumer welfare is enhanced. Although unsuccessful predatory pricing may encourage some inefficient substitution toward the product being sold at less than its cost, unsuccessful predation is in general a boon to consumers.

That below-cost pricing may impose painful losses on its target is of no moment to the antitrust laws if competition is not injured: It is axiomatic that the antitrust laws were passed for "the protection of *competition,* not *competitors.*" Brown Shoe Co. v. United States, 370 U.S. 294, 320 (1962). Earlier this Term, we held in the Sherman Act § 2 context that it was not enough to inquire "whether the defendant has engaged in 'unfair' or 'predatory' tactics"; rather, we insisted that the plaintiff prove "a dangerous probability that [the defendant] would monopolize a particular market." *Spectrum Sports.* Even an act of pure malice by one business competitor against another does not, without more, state a claim under the federal antitrust laws; those laws do not create a federal law of unfair competition or "purport to afford remedies for all torts committed by or against persons engaged in interstate commerce." Hunt v. Crumboch, 325 U.S. 821, 826 (1945).

For recoupment to occur, below-cost pricing must be capable, as a threshold matter, of producing the intended effects on the firm's rivals, whether driving them from the market, or, as was alleged to be the goal here, causing them to raise their prices to supracompetitive levels within a disciplined oligopoly. This requires an understanding of the extent and duration of the alleged predation, the relative financial strength of the predator and its intended victim, and their respective incentives and will. The inquiry is whether, given the aggregate losses caused by the below-cost pricing, the intended target would likely succumb.

If circumstances indicate that below-cost pricing could likely produce its intended effect on the target, there is still the further question whether it would likely injure competition in the relevant market. The plaintiff must demonstrate that there is a likelihood that the predatory scheme alleged would cause a rise in prices above a competitive level that would be sufficient to compensate for the amounts expended on the predation, including the time value of the money invested in it. As we have observed on a prior occasion, "[i]n order to recoup their losses, [predators] must obtain enough market power to set higher than competitive prices, and then must sustain those prices long enough to earn in excess profits what they earlier gave up in below-cost prices." *Matsushita*, 475 U.S., at 590–591.

Evidence of below-cost pricing is not alone sufficient to permit an inference of probable recoupment and injury to competition. Determining whether recoupment of predatory losses is likely requires an estimate of the cost of the alleged predation and a close analysis of both the scheme alleged by the plaintiff and the structure and conditions of the relevant market. Cf. *e.g.*, Elzinga & Mills, Testing for Predation: Is Recoupment Feasible?, 34 Antitrust Bull. 869 (1989) (constructing one possible model for evaluating recoupment). If market circumstances or deficiencies in proof would bar a reasonable jury from finding that the scheme alleged would likely result in sustained supracompetitive pricing, the plaintiff's case has failed. In certain situations—for example, where the market is highly diffuse and competitive, or where new entry is easy, or the defendant lacks adequate excess capacity to absorb the market shares of his rivals and cannot quickly create or purchase new capacity—summary disposition of the case is appropriate. *See, e.g., Cargill*, 479 U.S., at 119–120, n. 15.

These prerequisites to recovery are not easy to establish, but they are not artificial obstacles to recovery; rather, they are essential components of real market injury. As we have said in the Sherman Act context, "predatory pricing schemes are rarely tried, and even more rarely successful," *Matsushita, supra*, at 589, and the costs of an erroneous finding of liability are high. "[T]he mechanism by which a firm engages in predatory pricing—lowering prices—is the same mechanism by which a firm stimulates competition; because 'cutting prices in order to increase business often is the very essence of competition . . . [;] mistaken inferences . . . are especially costly, because they chill the very conduct the antitrust laws are designed to protect.' " *Cargill, supra*, at 122, n. 17 (quoting *Matsushita, supra*, at 594). It would be ironic indeed if the standards for predatory pricing liability were so low that antitrust suits themselves became a tool for keeping prices high.

B

Liggett does not allege that Brown & Williamson sought to drive it from the market but that Brown & Williamson sought to preserve supracompetitive profits on branded cigarettes by pressuring Liggett to raise its generic cigarette prices through a process of tacit collusion with the other cigarette companies. Tacit collusion, sometimes called oligopolistic price coordination or conscious parallelism, describes the process, not in itself unlawful, by which firms in a concentrated market might in effect share monopoly power, setting their prices at a profit-maximizing, supracompetitive level by recognizing their shared economic interests and their interdependence with respect to price and output decisions. See 2 Areeda & Turner ¶ 404; Scherer & Ross 199–208.

In *Matsushita*, we remarked upon the general implausibility of predatory pricing. See 475 U.S., at 588–590. *Matsushita* observed that such schemes are even more improbable when they require coordinated action among several firms. *Matsushita* involved an allegation of an express conspiracy to engage in predatory pricing. The Court noted that in addition to the usual difficulties that face a single firm attempting to recoup predatory losses, other problems render a conspiracy "incalculably more difficult to execute." *Ibid.* In order to succeed, the conspirators must agree on how to allocate present losses and future gains among the firms involved, and each firm must resist powerful incentives to cheat on whatever agreement is reached. *Ibid.*

However unlikely predatory pricing by multiple firms may be when they conspire, it is even less likely when, as here, there is no express coordination. Firms that seek to recoup predatory losses through the conscious parallelism of oligopoly must rely on uncertain and ambiguous signals to achieve concerted action. The signals are subject to misinterpretation and are a blunt and imprecise means of ensuring smooth cooperation, especially in the context of changing or unprecedented market circumstances. This anticompetitive minuet is most difficult to compose and to perform, even for a disciplined oligopoly.

From one standpoint, recoupment through oligopolistic price coordination could be thought more feasible than recoupment through monopoly: In the oligopoly setting, the victim itself has an economic incentive to acquiesce in the scheme. If forced to choose between cutting prices and sustaining losses, maintaining prices and losing market share, or raising prices and enjoying a share of supracompetitive profits, a firm may yield to the last alternative. Yet on the whole, tacit cooperation among oligopolists must be considered the least likely means of recouping predatory losses. In addition to the difficulty of achieving effective tacit coordination and the high likelihood that any attempt to discipline will produce an outbreak of competition, the predator's present losses in a case like this fall on it alone, while the later supracompetitive profits must be shared with every other oligopolist in proportion to its market share, including the intended victim. In this case, for example, Brown & Williamson, with its 11–12% share of the cigarette market, would have had to generate around $9 in supracompetitive profits for each $1 invested in predation; the remaining $8 would belong to its competitors, who had taken no risk. . . .

To the extent that the Court of Appeals may have held that the interdependent pricing of an oligopoly may never provide a means for achieving recoupment and so may not form the basis of a primary-line injury claim, we disagree. A predatory pricing scheme designed to preserve or create a stable oligopoly, if successful, can injure consumers in the same way, and to the same extent, as one designed to bring about a monopoly. However unlikely that possibility may be as a general matter, when the realities of the market and the record facts indicate that it has occurred and was likely to have succeeded, theory will not stand in the way of liability. See Eastman Kodak Co. v. Image Technical Services, Inc., 504 U.S. 451 (1992).

The Robinson–Patman Act, which amended § 2 of the original Clayton Act, suggests no exclusion from coverage when primary-line injury occurs in an oligopoly setting. Unlike the provisions of the Sherman Act, which speak only of various forms of express agreement and monopoly, the Robinson–Patman Act is phrased in broader, disjunctive terms, prohibiting price discrimination "where the effect of such discrimination may be substantially to lessen competition or tend to create a monopoly." 15 U.S.C. § 13(a). For all the words of the Act to carry adequate meaning, competitive injury under the Act must extend beyond the monopoly setting. Cf. Reiter v. Sonotone Corp., 442 U.S. 330, 339 (1979) ("Canons of construction ordinarily suggest that terms connected by a disjunctive be given separate meanings, unless the context dictates otherwise."). The language referring to a substantial lessening of competition was part of the original Clayton Act § 2, see Act of October 15, 1914, ch. 322, 38 Stat. 730, and the same phrasing appears in § 7 of that Act. In the § 7 context, it has long been settled that excessive concentration, and the oligopolistic price coordination it portends, may be the injury to competition the Act prohibits. *See, e.g.,* United States v. Philadelphia National Bank, 374 U.S. 321 (1963). We adhere to "the normal rule of statutory construction that identical words used in different parts of the same act are intended to have the same meaning." We decline to create a *per se* rule of nonliability for predatory price discrimination when recoupment is alleged to take place through supracompetitive oligopoly pricing. Cf. *Cargill,* 479 U.S., at 121.

III

Although Liggett's theory of liability, as an abstract matter, is within the reach of the statute, we agree with the Court of Appeals and the District Court that Liggett was not entitled to submit its case to the jury. It is not customary for this Court to review the sufficiency of the evidence, but we will do so when the issue is properly before us and the benefits of providing guidance concerning the proper application of a legal standard and avoiding the systemic costs associated with further proceedings justify the required expenditure of judicial resources. The record in this case demonstrates that the anticompetitive scheme Liggett alleged, when judged against the realities of the market, does not provide an adequate basis for a finding of liability.

A

Liggett's theory of competitive injury through oligopolistic price coordination depends upon a complex chain of cause and effect: Brown & Williamson would enter the generic segment with list prices matching Liggett's but with massive, discriminatory volume rebates directed at Liggett's biggest wholesalers; as a result, the net price of Brown & Williamson's generics would be below its costs; Liggett would suffer losses trying to defend its market share and wholesale customer base by matching Brown & Williamson's rebates; to avoid further losses, Liggett would raise its list prices on generics or acquiesce in price leadership by Brown & Williamson; higher list prices to consumers would shrink the percentage gap in retail price between generic and branded cigarettes; and this narrowing of the gap would make generics less appealing to the consumer, thus slowing the growth of the economy segment and reducing cannibalization of branded sales and their associated supracompetitive profits.

Although Brown & Williamson's entry into the generic segment could be regarded as procompetitive in intent as well as effect, the record contains sufficient evidence from which a reasonable jury could conclude that Brown & Williamson envisioned or intended this anticompetitive course of events. There is also sufficient evidence in the record from which a reasonable jury could conclude that for a period of approximately 18 months, Brown & Williamson's prices on its generic cigarettes were below its costs, and that this below-cost pricing imposed losses on Liggett that Liggett was unwilling to sustain, given its corporate parent's effort to locate a buyer for the company. Liggett has failed to demonstrate competitive injury as a matter of law, however, because its proof is flawed in a critical respect: The evidence is inadequate to show that in pursuing this scheme, Brown & Williamson had a reasonable prospect of recovering its losses from below-cost pricing through slowing the growth of generics. As we have noted, "[t]he success of any predatory scheme depends on maintaining monopoly power for long enough both to recoup the predator's losses and to harvest some additional gain." *Matsushita,* 475 U.S., at 589 (emphasis omitted).

No inference of recoupment is sustainable on this record, because no evidence suggests that Brown & Williamson—whatever its intent in introducing black and whites may have been—was likely to obtain the power to raise the prices for generic cigarettes above a competitive level. Recoupment through supracompetitive pricing in the economy segment of the cigarette market is an indispensable aspect of Liggett's own proffered theory, because a slowing of growth in the economy segment, even if it results from an increase in generic prices, is not itself anticompetitive. Only if those higher prices are a product of nonmarket forces has competition suffered. If prices rise in response to an excess of demand over supply, or segment growth slows as patterns of consumer preference become stable, the market is functioning in a competitive manner. Consumers are not injured from the perspective of the antitrust laws by the price increases; they are in fact causing them. Thus, the linchpin of the predatory scheme alleged by Liggett is Brown & Williamson's ability, with the other oligopolists, to raise prices above a competitive level in the generic segment of the market. Because relying on tacit coordination among oligopolists as a means of recouping losses from predatory pricing is "highly speculative," Areeda & Hovenkamp ¶ 711.2c, at 647, competent evidence is necessary to allow a reasonable inference that it poses an authentic threat to competition. The evidence in this case is insufficient to demonstrate the danger of Brown & Williamson's alleged scheme.

B

Based on Liggett's theory of the case and the record it created, there are two means by which one might infer that Brown & Williamson had a reasonable prospect of producing sustained supracompetitive pricing in the generic segment adequate to recoup its predatory losses: first, if generic output or price information indicates that oligopolistic price coordination in fact produced supracompetitive prices in the generic segment; or second, if evidence about the market and Brown & Williamson's conduct indicate that the alleged scheme was likely to have brought about tacit coordination and oligopoly pricing in the generic segment, even if it did not actually do so.

In this case, the price and output data do not support a reasonable inference that Brown & Williamson and the other cigarette companies elevated prices above a competitive level for generic cigarettes. Supracompetitive pricing entails a restriction in output. In the present setting, in which output expanded at a rapid rate following Brown & Williamson's alleged predation, output in the generic segment can only have been restricted in the sense that it expanded at a slower rate than it would have absent Brown & Williamson's intervention. Such a counterfactual proposition is difficult to prove in the best of circumstances; here, the record evidence does not permit a reasonable inference that output would have been greater without Brown & Williamson's entry into the generic segment.

Following Brown & Williamson's entry, the rate at which generic cigarettes were capturing market share did not slow; indeed, the average rate of growth doubled. During the four years from 1980 to 1984 in which Liggett was alone in the generic segment, the segment gained market share at an average rate of 1% of the overall market per year, from .4% in 1980 to slightly more than 4% of the cigarette market in 1984. In the next five years, following the alleged predation, the generic segment expanded from 4% to more than 15% of the domestic cigarette market, or greater than 2% per year.

While this evidence tends to show that Brown & Williamson's participation in the economy segment did not restrict output, it is not dispositive. One could speculate, for example, that the rate of segment growth would have tripled, instead of doubled, without Brown & Williamson's alleged predation. But there is no concrete evidence of this. Indeed, the only industry projection in the record estimating what the segment's growth would have been without Brown & Williamson's entry supports the opposite inference. In 1984, Brown & Williamson forecast in an important planning document that the economy segment would account for 10% of the total cigarette market by 1988 if it did not enter the segment. In fact, in 1988, after what Liggett alleges was a sustained and dangerous anticompetitive campaign by Brown & Williamson, the generic segment accounted for over 12% of the total market. Thus the segment's output expanded more robustly than Brown & Williamson had estimated it would had Brown & Williamson never entered.

Brown & Williamson did note in 1985, a year after introducing its black and whites, that its presence within the generic segment "appears to have resulted in ... a slowing in the segment's growth rate." *Id.,* at 257. But this statement was made in early 1985, when Liggett itself contends the below-cost pricing was still in effect and before any anticompetitive contraction in output is alleged to have occurred. Whatever it may mean,[50] this statement has little value in evaluating the competitive implications of Brown & Williamson's later conduct, which was alleged to provide the basis for recouping predatory losses.

In arguing that Brown & Williamson was able to exert market power and raise generic prices above a competitive level in the generic category through tacit price coordination with the other cigarette manufacturers, Liggett places its principal reliance on direct evidence of price behavior. This evidence demonstrates that the list prices on all cigarettes, generic and branded alike, rose to a significant degree during the late 1980s. From 1986 to 1989, list prices on both generic and branded cigarettes increased twice a year by similar amounts. Liggett's economic expert testified that these price increases outpaced increases in costs, taxes, and promotional expenditures. The list prices of generics, moreover, rose at a faster rate than the prices of branded cigarettes, thus narrowing the list price differential between branded and generic products. Liggett argues that this would permit a reasonable jury to find that Brown & Williamson succeeded in bringing about oligopolistic price coordination and supracompetitive prices in the generic category sufficient to slow its growth, thereby preserving supracompetitive branded profits and recouping its predatory losses.

A reasonable jury, however, could not have drawn the inferences Liggett proposes. All of Liggett's data is based upon the list prices of various categories of cigarettes. Yet the jury had before it undisputed evidence that during the period in question, list prices were not the actual prices paid by consumers. As the market became unsettled in the mid–1980s, the cigarette companies invested substantial sums in promotional schemes, including coupons, stickers, and giveaways, that reduced the actual cost of cigarettes to consumers below list prices. This promotional

---

50. This statement could well have referred to the rate at which the segment was growing relative to prior years' generic volume; this "internal" rate of growth would inevitably slow as the base volume against which it was measured grew.

activity accelerated as the decade progressed. Many wholesalers also passed portions of their volume rebates on to the consumer, which had the effect of further undermining the significance of the retail list prices. Especially in an oligopoly setting, in which price competition is most likely to take place through less observable and less regulatable means than list prices, it would be unreasonable to draw conclusions about the existence of tacit coordination or supracompetitive pricing from data that reflects only list prices.

Even on its own terms, the list price data relied upon by Liggett to demonstrate a narrowing of the price differential between generic and full-priced branded cigarettes could not support the conclusion that supracompetitive pricing had been introduced into the generic segment. Liggett's gap data ignores the effect of "subgeneric" cigarettes, which were priced at discounts of 50% or more from the list prices of normal branded cigarettes. Liggett itself, while supposedly under the sway of oligopoly power, pioneered this development in 1988 with the introduction of its "Pyramid" brand. By the time of trial, five of the six major manufacturers offered a cigarette in this category at a discount from the full list price of at least 50%. Thus, the priced difference between the highest priced branded cigarette and the lowest price cigarettes in the economy segment, instead of narrowing over the course of the period of alleged predation as Liggett would argue, grew to a substantial extent. In June 1984, before Brown & Williamson entered the generic segment, a consumer could obtain a carton of black and white generic cigarettes from Liggett at a 38% discount from the list price of a leading brand; after the conduct Liggett complains of, consumers could obtain a branded generic from Liggett for 52% off the list price of a leading brand.

It may be that a reasonable jury could conclude that the cumulative discounts attributable to subgenerics and the various consumer promotions did not cancel out the full effect of the increases in list prices, and that actual prices to the consumer did indeed rise, but rising prices do not themselves permit an inference of a collusive market dynamic. Even in a concentrated market, the occurrence of a price increase does not in itself permit a rational inference of conscious parallelism or supracompetitive pricing. Where, as here, output is expanding at the same time prices are increasing, rising prices are equally consistent with growing product demand. Under these conditions, a jury may not infer competitive injury from price and output data absent some evidence that tends to prove that output was restricted or prices were above a competitive level. Cf. *Monsanto*, 465 U.S., at 763.

Quite apart from the absence of any evidence of that sort, an inference of supracompetitive pricing would be particularly anomalous in this case, as the very party alleged to have been coerced into pricing through oligopolistic coordination denied that such coordination existed: Liggett's own officers and directors consistently denied that they or other firms in the industry priced their cigarettes through tacit collusion or reaped supracompetitive profits. Liggett seeks to explain away this testimony by arguing that its officers and directors are businesspeople who do not ascribe the same meaning to words like "competitive" and "collusion" that an economist would. This explanation is entitled to little, if any, weight. As the District Court found:

> "This argument was considered at the summary judgment stage since these executives gave basically the same testimony at their depositions. The court allowed the case to go to trial in part because the Liggett executives were not economists and in part because of affidavits from the Liggett executives stating that they were confused by the questions asked by B[rown] & W[illiamson] lawyers' and did not mean to contradict the testimony of [their economic expert] Burnett. However, at trial, despite having consulted extensively with Burnett and having had adequate time to familiarize themselves with concepts such as tacit collusion, oligopoly, and monopoly profits, these Liggett executives again contradicted Burnett's theory." 748 F.Supp., at 356.

Not only does the evidence fail to show actual supracompetitive pricing in the generic segment, it also does not demonstrate its likelihood. At the time Brown & Williamson entered the generic segment, the cigarette industry as a whole faced declining demand and possessed substantial excess capacity. These circumstances tend to break down patterns of oligopoly pricing and produce price competition. See Scherer & Ross 294, 315; 2 Areeda & Turner ¶ 404b2, at 275–276; 6 P. Areeda, Antitrust Law ¶ 1430e, at 181 (1986). The only means by which Brown & Williamson is alleged to have established oligopoly pricing in the face of these unusual competitive pressures is through tacit price coordination with the other cigarette firms.

Yet the situation facing the cigarette companies in the 1980's would have made such tacit coordination unmanageable. Tacit coordination is facilitated by a stable market environment, fungible products, and a small number of variables upon which the firms seeking to coordinate their pricing may focus. Uncertainty is an oligopoly's greatest enemy. By 1984, however, the cigarette market was in an obvious state of flux. The introduction of generic cigarettes in 1980 represented the first serious price competition in the cigarette market since the 1930's. See Scherer & Ross 250–251; App. 128. This development was bound to unsettle previous expectations and patterns of market conduct and to reduce the cigarette firms' ability to predict each other's behavior.

The larger number of product types and pricing variables also decreased the probability of effective parallel pricing.... In addition, R.J. Reynolds had incentives that, in some respects, ran counter to those of the other cigarette companies. It is implausible that without a shared interest in retarding the growth of the economy segment, Brown & Williamson and its fellow oligopolists could have engaged in parallel pricing and raised generic prices above a competitive level. "[C]oordination will not be possible when any significant firm chooses, for any reason, to 'go it alone.' " 2 Areeda and Turner ¶ 404b2, at 276. It is undisputed—indeed it was conceded by Liggett's expert—that R.J. Reynolds acted without regard to the supposed benefits of oligopolistic coordination when it repriced Doral at generic levels in the spring of 1984 and that the natural and probable consequence of its entry into the generic segment was procompetitive. Indeed, Reynolds' apparent objective in entering the segment was to capture a significant amount of volume in order to regain its number one sales position in the cigarette industry from Philip Morris. There is no evidence that R.J. Reynolds accomplished this goal during the period relevant to this case, or that its commitment to achieving that goal changed. Indeed, R.J. Reynolds refused to follow Brown & Williamson's attempt to raise generic prices in June 1985. The jury thus had before it undisputed evidence that contradicts the suggestion that the major cigarette companies shared a goal of limiting the growth of the economy segment; one of the industry's two major players concededly entered the segment to expand volume and compete.

Even if all the cigarette companies were willing to participate in a scheme to restrain the growth of the generic segment, they would not have been able to coordinate their actions and raise prices above a competitive level unless they understood that Brown & Williamson's entry into the segment was not a genuine effort to compete with Liggett. If even one other firm misinterpreted Brown & Williamson's entry as an effort to expand market share, a chain reaction of competitive responses would almost certainly have resulted, and oligopoly discipline would have broken down, perhaps irretrievably. "[O]nce the trust among rivals breaks down, it is as hard to put back together again as was Humpty–Dumpty, and non-collusive behavior is likely to take over." Samuelson & Nordhaus, Economics, at 534.

Liggett argues that the means by which Brown & Williamson signaled its anticompetitive intent to its rivals was through its pricing structure. According to Liggett, maintaining existing list prices while offering substantial rebates to wholesalers was a signal to the other cigarette firms that Brown & Williamson did not intend to attract additional smokers to the generic segment by its entry. But a reasonable jury could not conclude that this pricing structure eliminated or rendered insignificant the risk that the other firms might misunderstand Brown & Williamson's entry as a competitive move. The likelihood that Brown & Williamson's rivals would have regarded its pricing structure as an important signal is low, given that Liggett itself, the purported target of the predation, was already using similar rebates, as was R.J. Reynolds in marketing its Doral branded generic. A Reynolds executive responsible for Doral testified that given its and Liggett's use of wholesaler rebates, Brown & Williamson could not have competed effectively without them. And despite extensive discovery of the corporate records of R.J. Reynolds and Philip Morris, no documents appeared that indicated any awareness of Brown & Williamson's supposed signal by its principal rivals. Without effective signaling, it is difficult to see how the alleged predation could have had a reasonable chance of success through oligopoly pricing.

Finally, although some of Brown & Williamson's corporate planning documents speak of a desire to slow the growth of the segment, no objective evidence of its conduct permits a reasonable inference that it had any real prospect of doing so through anticompetitive means. It is undisputed that when Brown & Williamson introduced its generic cigarettes, it offered them to a thousand wholesalers who had never before purchased generic cigarettes. The inevitable effect of this marketing effort was to expand the segment, as the new wholesalers recruited retail outlets to carry generic cigarettes. Even with respect to wholesalers already carrying generics, Brown & Williamson's unprecedented volume rebates had a similar expansionary effect. Unlike many branded cigarettes, generics came with no sales guarantee to the wholesaler; any unsold stock represented pure loss to the wholesaler. By providing substantial incentives for wholesalers to place large orders, Brown & Williamson created strong pressure for them to sell more generic cigarettes. In addition, as we have already observed, many wholesalers passed portions of the rebates about which Liggett complains on to consumers, thus dropping the retail price of generics and further stimulating demand. Brown & Williamson provided a further, direct stimulus, through some $10 million it spent during the period of alleged predation placing discount stickers on its generic cartons to reduce prices to the ultimate consumer. In light of these uncontested facts about Brown & Williamson's conduct, it is not reasonable to conclude that Brown & Williamson threatened in a serious way to restrict output, raise prices above a competitive level, and artificially slow the growth of the economy segment of the national cigarette market.

To be sure, Liggett's economic expert explained Liggett's theory of predatory price discrimination and testified that he believed it created a reasonable possibility that Brown & Williamson could injure competition in the United States cigarette market as a whole. But this does not alter our analysis. When an expert opinion is not supported by sufficient facts to validate it in the eyes of the law, or when indisputable record facts contradict or otherwise render the opinion unreasonable, it cannot support a jury's verdict. . . .

IV

We understand that the chain of reasoning by which we have concluded that Brown & Williamson is entitled to judgment as a matter of law is demanding. But a reasonable jury is presumed to know and understand the law, the facts of the case, and the realities of the market. We hold that the evidence cannot support a finding that Brown & Williamson's alleged scheme was likely to result in oligopolistic price coordination and sustained supracompetitive pricing in the generic segment of the national cigarette market. Without this, Brown & Williamson had no reasonable prospect of recouping its predatory losses and could not inflict the injury to competition the antitrust laws prohibit. The judgment of the Court of Appeals is affirmed.

■ STEVENS J., with whom WHITE and BLACKMAN, JJ., joined, dissented. [The dissenters divided the period under review into three phases: *phase 1,* prior to July 1984, when it was generally agreed that cigarette prices increased in lock step and produced unusually large industry profits; *phase 2,* during the period July 1984 to the end of 1985, when Brown & Williamson (B & W) initiated a price war that clearly put its prices below its average variable cost; and *phase 3,* covering the period after the price war, when prices of generic brands and black and whites increased so as to narrow the profit between products in the economy market and branded cigarettes. Thereafter, the prices of all cigarettes—branded and unbranded—increased in lock step as they had prior to the price war.]

The dissent emphasized that the Robinson–Patman Act required only a "reasonable probability" of harm and cited documents that clearly would have indicated to a jury that B & W's intention was to "manage up the prices of branded generics" and "manage down generic volume." In their view, it was reasonable for the jury to assume that B & W had embarked on a strategy with a reasonable probability of success and, to the extent cooperation from other cigarette companies was necessary, B & W could signal its intention and goals to the other companies and expect them to respond cooperatively.

With respect to the majority's dismissal of evidence that prices in the post-price war period were supracompetitive because list prices were not an accurate indicator of competitive conditions without taking promotional activities into account, the dissent noted that the promotions related primarily to branded cigarettes, and accordingly, did not reduce the consumer price of black and whites. The dissent suggested that the majority's conclusion was speculative in light of record evidence that semiannual list price increases offset consumer promotions. Justice Stevens concluded:]

As a matter of economics, the Court reminds us that price-cutting is generally pro-competitive, and hence a "boon to consumers." This is true, however, only so long as reduced prices do not fall below cost, as the cases cited by the majority make clear. When a predator deliberately engages in below-cost pricing targeted at a particular competitor over a sustained period of time, then price-cutting raises a credible inference that harm to competition is likely to ensue. None of our cases disputes that proposition.

Also as a matter of economics, the Court insists that a predatory pricing program in an oligopoly is unlikely to succeed absent actual conspiracy. Though it has rejected a somewhat stronger version of this proposition as a rule of decision, the Court comes back to the same economic theory, relying on the supposition that an "anticompetitive minuet is most difficult to compose and to perform, even for a disciplined oligopoly" (implausibility of tacit coordination among cigarette oligopolists in 1980's). I would suppose, however, that the professional performers who had danced the minuet for 40 to 50 years would be better able to predict whether their favorite partners would follow them in the future than would an outsider, who might not know the difference between Haydn and Mozart. In any event, the jury was surely entitled to infer that at the time of the price war itself, B & W reasonably believed that it could signal its intentions to its fellow oligopolists assuring their continued cooperation.

Perhaps the Court's most significant error is the assumption that seems to pervade much of the final sections of its opinion: that Liggett had the burden of proving either the actuality of supracompetitive pricing, or the actuality of tacit collusion.... In my opinion, the jury was entitled to infer from the succession of price increases after 1985—when the prices for branded and generic cigarettes increased every six months from $33.15 and $19.75, respectively, to $46.15 and $33.75—that B & W's below-cost pricing actually produced supracompetitive prices, with the help of tacit collusion among the players. But even if that were not so clear, the jury would surely be entitled to infer that B & W's predatory plan, in which it invested millions of dollars for the purpose of achieving an admittedly anticompetitive result, carried a "reasonable possibility" of injuring competition.

NOTES AND QUESTIONS

1.   What is the difference between a primary line competitive injury case under the Robinson–Patman Act and a predatory pricing scheme under Section 2 of the Sherman Act? In what respect, if any, would it be easier for the plaintiff to win under the Robinson–Patman Act?

2.   Is the idea that predatory pricing by a firm could lead to tacit collusion or "conscious parallelism" economically irrational? In emphasizing that prices declined and output increased during the price war, was the majority in the *Brooke Group* case confusing the first phase of a predatory strategy with the entire game plan? Is it not usually the case that prices will decline and output increase during the first phase of a predatory scheme?

3.   Prior to the Supreme Court's decision in *Brooke Group,* much of the debate regarding predatory pricing revolved around the issue of the measure of cost to be used in judging whether a defendant's price was predatory. In *Brooke Group,* as it had done in two earlier cases (*i.e., Cargill* and *Matsushita*), the Supreme Court deferred consideration of the measure of cost issue until another day. See p. 853 n. 49 supra. Nevertheless, the issue remains of great consequence. The writings of Professors Areeda and Turner have been particularly prominent in measure of cost debates. They developed a series of cost-based rules to distinguish legal from illegal pricing. They defined "alternative measures of cost" in the following way:

The economic costs facing a firm differ in an important respect: some are "fixed," and others are "variable." *Fixed costs* are costs that do not vary with changes in output. They typically include some management expenses, interest on bonded debt, depreciation (to the extent that equipment is not consumed by using it), property taxes, and other irreducible overhead. And though not an accounting cost, fixed costs should be deemed to include the return on investment that would currently be necessary to attract capital to the firm—what the economist refers to as the *opportunity cost* to the owners of the firm. In short, it is reasonably accurate to say that fixed costs are costs that would continue even if the firm produced no output at all.

Variable costs, as the name implies, are costs that vary with changes in output. They typically include such items as materials, fuel, labor directly used to produce the product, indirect labor such as foremen, clerks, and custodial help, use-depreciation, repair and maintenance, and per unit royalties and license fees. The average variable cost is the sum of all variable costs divided by output.

Marginal cost is the increment to total cost that results from producing an additional increment of output. It is a function solely of variable costs, since fixed costs, by definition, are costs unaffected by changes in output. Marginal cost usually decreases over low levels of output and increases as production approaches plant capacity.

Total cost is the sum of fixed cost and total variable cost. That total divided by output is *average cost* or, to use the layman's synonym, *full cost.* It is, by definition, higher than average variable cost at all outputs, but will typically be below marginal cost at very high levels of output, when the plant is strained beyond efficient operating capacity.

Which costs are fixed and which are variable (and hence marginal) is a function of both (1) the magnitude of the contemplated change in output, and (2) time. Virtually all costs are variable when a firm, operating at capacity, plans to double its output by constructing new plants and purchasing new equipment. Moreover, more costs become variable as the time period increases. The variable costs described above are those incurred in what is usually termed the "short run," namely, the period in which the firm cannot replace or increase plant or equipment. Conversely, in the "long run" the firm can vary quantities of *all* inputs (plant and equipment as well as short run variable inputs); thus, all costs are variable over the long run. Accordingly, *long-run marginal cost* approximates anticipated average total cost (full cost) for various levels of output.

In order to determine which of these various costs is relevant to predatory, "below-cost" selling, we must first ask what costs are relevant to the firm which is seeking to maximize profits or minimize losses, since a firm which seeks to do so is normally responding to acceptable economic incentives and thus is not engaging in predatory behavior. The profit-maximizing or loss-minimizing output for any firm, whether competitive or monopolistic, is that where any increase in output would add more to costs than to revenues and any decrease in output would reduce revenues more than costs. In short, in deciding whether it would increase or decrease output, the firm looks to the *incremental* effects on revenues and costs. Thus, the relevant cost is marginal cost.

Although Areeda and Turner believed "marginal-cost pricing is the economically sound division between acceptable, competitive behavior and 'below-cost' predation," they concluded that "average variable cost" is a reasonable proxy for marginal cost and more satisfactory as a test because of the extreme difficulty of ascertaining marginal cost. For prices below average variable cost a "presumption of illegality" exists and this presumption will usually prove conclusive. Conversely, prices above average variable cost are "presumptively lawful" and this presumption will usually prove conclusive. Areeda and Turner also pointed out that the legality of price levels should be based on "reasonably anticipated" costs, so that prices may be cut without antitrust consequences in anticipation of lower costs in the future. 3 Areeda & Turner, Antitrust Law ¶¶ 712–15 (1978); see 3 Areeda & Hovenkamp, Antitrust Law ¶¶ 722–24, 735–41 (2d ed. 2002).

4. The Areeda and Turner proposals have not lacked critics. A number of alternative approaches have been offered (mostly by economists):

(a) *Scherer.* Professor Frederic M. Scherer was an early critic of the Areeda and Turner proposals, arguing that rigid cost-based rules were simplistic and overly generous to predators and would-be monopolists. He urged that the focus be on "long-term economic welfare," which involved a determination of:

> [T]he relative cost positions of the monopolist and fringe firms, the scale of entry required to secure minimum costs, whether fringe firms are driven out entirely or merely suppressed, whether the monopolist expands its output to replace the output of excluded rivals or restricts supply again when the rivals withdraw, and whether any long-run compensatory expansion by the monopolist entails investment in scale economy-embodying new plant.

Scherer, Predatory Pricing and the Sherman Act: A Comment, 89 Harv.L.Rev. 869, 890 (1976). Are the factors cited by Scherer relevant after *Brooke Group*? Is his approach administratively feasible?

(b) *Baumol.* A recurrent criticism of Areeda and Turner is that their cost-based rules failed to take "timing" into account. Professor William J. Baumol has suggested that a seller be permitted to reduce its price to whatever level it chooses, but it would then be prevented for a period of time from raising its price unless it could show necessity as a result of marketplace cost changes. Baumol, Quasi–Permanence of Price Reductions: A Policy for Prevention of Predatory Pricing, 89 Yale L.J. 1 (1979).

(c) *Posner.* Viewing the Areeda and Turner rule as somewhat too permissive, Chief Judge Richard A. Posner defined the level of predatory pricing as the "level calculated to exclude from the market an equally or more efficient competitor." He suggests that predatory pricing occurs not only on sales below average variable costs but also, at least presumptively, where there are sales at less than long-run marginal costs (ordinarily higher than short-run marginal costs) accompanied by intent to exclude an equally or more efficient competitor. This approach recognizes that new entrants may have short-run costs—such as expenditures to build "image" or create research capacity—which have long since become fixed costs to the established firm. Posner, Antitrust Law 215 (2d ed. 2001).

(d) *Joskow & Klevorick.* In an effort to simplify predatory pricing litigation (with similarities to the approach later used in *Brooke Group*), Professors Paul Joskow and Richard A. Klevorick proposed a "two-tier" approach. In a preliminary inquiry, courts would determine whether the market in question was conducive to predation; if so, behavioral considerations would then be examined. The central inquiries of a first-tier analysis would look to number and size distribution of firms, entry barriers, and profit levels of the alleged predator. In a second stage inquiry, prices below average variable cost would establish predation while prices above average total cost would be presumed legal unless withdrawn within two years. In that event, the burden of proof would shift to the dominant firm to show that the increase was justified (*i.e.*, the Baumol proposal). Prices between average variable cost and average total cost would be presumed predatory unless the dominant firm could show that the strategy was justified because it maximized short-run profits (essentially, that substantial excess capacity was unused by the price cutter). Finally, documentary evidence about "intent" would also be admissible. Joskow & Klevorick, A Framework For Analyzing Predatory Pricing Policy, 89 Yale L.J. 213 (1979).

(e) *Bolton, Brodley, and Riordan.* Recent criticism of the Areeda & Turner rule focuses on its static as opposed to dynamic approach to predatory pricing issues, and specifically on its assumption that predatory pricing is rare and usually does not have severe market consequences. More recent literature asserts that when strategic considerations are incorporated, and particularly in light of modern game theory, predatory pricing is a rational and often-used strategy.

In connection with easing various elements that plaintiff must prove to establish predatory pricing, the authors offer several examples of low pricing that would be rational if strategic factors were taken into account. These include: (1) *Financial Market Predation.* Low prices by a dominant incumbent can cut off access to financial markets for its victim by undermining the relationship between the victim and its investors. Given that new ventures will often offer disappointing initial results, a predator may use cost-cutting to make initial performance poor and thus cut off a competitor's access to capital. (2) *Signaling Strategies.* A predator may cut costs in one market to establish a reputation as a price-cutter in other markets where new entry is threatened. (A "reputation for predation" issue is presented by the Department of Justice's recent complaint against American Airlines, see p. 873 infra.) (3) *Test Market Predation.* The predator may cut prices in a potential entrant's test market to skew results as to demand for new products. The victim, lacking knowledge and experience in the market, is prevented from discovering whether demand is sufficiently strong to justify entry or continued presence in the test market. (4) *Cost Signalling.* A predator attempts to establish a reputation for low cost by cutting its price below its short-run profit-maximizing level. The target of the cost-cutting, particularly when it is a company considering entry, is persuaded to seek some other market which seems more likely to be profitable and less threatening. Bolton, Brodley & Riordan, Predatory Pricing: Strategic Theory and Legal Policy, 88 Geo. L.J. 2239 (2000); see Elzinga & Mills, Predatory Pricing and Strategic Theory, 89 Geo. L.J. 2475 (2001); Bolton, Brodley & Riordan, Predatory Pricing: Response to Critique and Further Elaboration, 89 Geo. L.J. 2495 (2001).

5. In the courts, the Areeda and Turner cost proposals have had a mixed reception. In McGahee v. Northern Propane Gas Co., 858 F.2d 1487 (11th Cir.1988), cert. denied, 490 U.S. 1084 (1989), for example, the Eleventh Circuit concluded:

> The Areeda and Turner test is like the Venus de Milo: it is much admired and often discussed, but rarely embraced. Perhaps this reluctance to embrace is due to the substance from which it is formed. The Areeda and Turner test is carved from economic assumptions, not from antitrust statutes and judicial precedents. Perhaps this reluctance is due to attacks upon it. The Areeda and Turner test has been criticized for being impractical, for using static short-run analysis, and for being too permissive of predatory activity; these criticisms break any notion that economists agree that the Areeda and Turner test is best. We ... decline to embrace the Areeda and Turner test.

A recent commentary[51] concluded that the circuits "applying the anticipated average variable cost standard (or a substantially equivalent formulation) include the First,[52] Second,[53] Fifth,[54] and Eighth.[55]" The commentary went on to observe:

> In various circuits, courts have held, as *Brooke Group* suggested, that prices above average total cost are *per se* lawful. These courts have also held that prices below average total cost may be unlawful, placing different burdens on plaintiff and defendant when the price is above average variable cost but below average total cost. Such circuits include the Sixth,[56] Eighth,[57] Ninth,[58] Tenth,[59] and Eleventh.[60] Moreover, the Fifth Circuit permits evidence of pricing above average variable cost in some cases when entry barriers are high and where the defendant has charged a price below its short-run, profit-maximizing price.... Circuits that have not articulated a cost standard for determining predatory pricing include the Third, Fourth, Seventh, and the District of Columbia.[61]

To date, the Supreme Court has permitted the measure of cost debate to rage in the lower courts and has kept its options open. See *Brooke Group,* p. 853 n. 49 supra. If you were on the Supreme Court, how would you cast your vote?

6.   Judgments about the formulation of legal rules for predatory pricing turn largely on estimates as to three uncertain factual matters: first, how often does predatory pricing actually occur and how likely is it to be destructive of competition absent legal intervention; second, the degree of difficulty courts will have in administering cost-based rules; and third, the capacity of courts to distinguish

51. Denger & Herfort, Predatory Pricing Claims After *Brooke Group,* 62 Antitrust L.J. 541, 548 (1994).

52. Clamp–All Corp. v. Cast Iron Soil Pipe Inst., 851 F.2d 478, 483 (1st Cir.1988) (below "incremental cost"), cert. denied, 488 U.S. 1007 (1989).

53. Northeastern Tel. Co. v. AT & T Co., 651 F.2d 76, 88 (2d Cir.1981) (below "reasonably anticipated marginal cost" conclusively predatory), cert. denied, 455 U.S. 943 (1982).

54. International Air Indus., Inc. v. American Excelsior Co., 517 F.2d 714, 724 (5th Cir.1975) (below average variable cost or below short-run, profit-maximizing price with high barriers to entry permitting recoupment), cert. denied, 424 U.S. 943 (1976).

55. *E.g.,* Henry v. Chloride, 809 F.2d 1334, 1346 (8th Cir.1987) (prices above average variable cost have a rebuttable presumption of legality and those below average variable costs have a rebuttable presumption of illegality).

56. D.E. Rogers Assocs., Inc. v. Gardner–Denver Co., 718 F.2d 1431, 1436 (6th Cir.1983) (plaintiff bears burden of showing prices between average variable cost and average total cost are predatory), cert. denied, 467 U.S. 1242 (1984).

57. Morgan v. Ponder, 892 F.2d 1355, 1360 (8th Cir.1989) (prices above average variable cost have "strong presumption" of legality).

58. William Inglis & Sons Baking Co. v. ITT Continental Baking Co., 668 F.2d 1014, 1035–36 (9th Cir.1981) (plaintiff bears burden of proving pricing was predatory if above average variable cost but below average total cost), cert. denied, 459 U.S. 825 (1982).

59. Pacific Eng'g & Prod. Co. of Nevada v. Kerr–McGee Corp., 551 F.2d 790 (10th Cir.1977) (prices above average variable cost but below average total cost lawful absent other evidence indicating anticompetitive behavior), cert. denied, 434 U.S. 879.

60. McGahee v. Northern Propane Gas Co., 858 F.2d 1487, 1503–04 (11th Cir.1988) (prices below average total cost and above average variable cost constitute "circumstantial evidence of predatory intent"; the closer the price to average total cost, the stronger plaintiff's other evidence of predatory intent must be to avoid summary judgment), cert. denied, 490 U.S. 1084 (1989).

61. Denger & Herfort, supra note 4, at 548–50.

accurately between—and the utility of distinguishing—long-term and short-term costs and fixed and variable costs.

With respect to the first issue, there is much theoretical justification (although not much empirical proof) for concluding that predatory pricing may be more prevalent than the Supreme Court majority in *Brooke Group* seemed to suggest. In addition to Bolton, Brodley and Riordan (note 4(e) supra), Jonathan Baker[62] recently provided the following hypothetical example of how multimarket recoupment might work:

> Suppose a chain store faces a non-chain rival in each of a large number of towns. The chain cuts its prices drastically in a few towns. When the chain's rivals in those towns either exit or begin to compete less aggressively with the chain, the price war ends and high prices are restored. In addition, the chain store's rivals in all the other towns, in which the chain did not cut prices, also respond by avoiding aggressive competition with the chain. As a result, prices also increase in the towns in which predation did not occur.

> In this hypothetical example of price predation with multimarket recoupment, the firm developed a reputation as a predator by reducing price in a small number of markets.[63] It in effect engaged in selective predation. The rivals in the markets in which predation occurred may have ended up crippled or destroyed, as the traditional predatory pricing story would have it. But rivals competing against the predator in markets in which predation did not occur were not injured directly. Most of the victimized rivals never experienced a price war but were merely intimidated by the threat of a price war into engaging in less aggressive behavior than they would otherwise have found most profitable.[64]

The hypothetical demonstrates that a dynamic analysis—taking into account possible strategic uses of predatory behavior—indicates that predatory pricing may be more prevalent than had earlier been believed.

Some of the difficulties courts have in administering cost-based rules—and the problem of distinguishing between fixed and variable costs—are illustrated by the Second Circuit's opinion in Kelco Disposal, Inc. v. Browning–Ferris Industries of Vermont, Inc., 845 F.2d 404 (2d Cir.1988). The Second Circuit, in affirming the award of damages for predatory pricing,[65] dealt with fixed and variable cost distinctions as follows:

> Kelco claims that defendants' anticompetitive or exclusionary conduct consisted of predatory pricing, and introduced evidence that defendants' price of $65 per roll-off haul was below its average variable cost of roughly $104 per haul. Defendants argue that Kelco's $104 figure was inflated

62. Baker, Predatory Pricing After *Brooke Group*: An Economic Perspective, 62 Antitrust L.J. 585, 590–91 (1994).

63. In the example, the other markets involved different geographic areas; a similar story could be told involving different product markets.

64. In the hypothetical example, these firms refrained from cutting price below the price the predator preferred, and they refrained from taking a larger market share

than the predator permitted them to have. In other cases, the indirectly victimized rivals might refrain from soliciting the predator's customers, not expand into other markets, or agree to be acquired at a low price.

65. The predatory pricing was found to be an attempt to monopolize under Section 2 of the Sherman Act. For a discussion of attempt to monopolize, see Section 4 B infra.

because Kelco's expert witness mistakenly characterized certain fixed costs as variable in making his computations. Asserting that depreciation of equipment, selling and administrative costs, and national overhead should have been considered fixed costs, defendants contend that their true average variable cost was less than $50 per haul, well below their $65 haul charge. . . .

Prices that are below reasonably anticipated marginal cost, and its surrogate, reasonably anticipated average variable cost, see *Northeastern Telephone,* 651 F.2d at 88, are presumed predatory. Id. By definition variable costs are dependent on the firm's output, while fixed costs are not. The characterization of certain costs as either variable or fixed frequently becomes a battleground where the plaintiff proceeds on a predatory pricing theory. The reason is obvious: the higher a party's average variable cost, the more likely it is that the party has priced below that cost.

Defendants argue that equipment depreciation should have been considered a fixed cost because defendants' accountants have always treated it so. Passing, for the moment, the bootstrap feature of this argument, the general legal rule is that depreciation caused by use is a variable cost, while depreciation through obsolescence is a fixed cost. See id. The characterization of legitimately disputed costs is a question of fact for the jury. The jury may consider, but obviously cannot be bound by, a party's characterization of its own costs.

In this case, we conclude that the jury could have reasonably characterized equipment depreciation as a variable cost. The waste disposal industry makes intensive use of heavy equipment. There was no evidence presented that defendants' trucks, compactors, or containers became obsolete; rather, the picture painted was one of constant wear, tear, and damage due to use.

Defendants do not challenge the characterization of disposal fees and drivers' salaries as variable costs. Adding equipment depreciation costs to these other costs yields an average variable cost of roughly $81 per haul, well above defendants' $65 fee. Based on these figures alone, we conclude that the jury could have found that defendants engaged in predatory pricing.

7. Must market power and specific intent (*i.e.,* in an attempt to monopolize case) be shown in predatory pricing cases under Section 2 of the Sherman Act? *See, e.g.,* Rebel Oil Co. v. Atlantic Richfield Co., 51 F.3d 1421 (9th Cir.), cert. denied, 516 U.S. 987 (1995) (plaintiff failed to establish a "genuine issue of material fact on market power"); Advo, Inc. v. Philadelphia Newspapers, Inc., 51 F.3d 1191 (3d Cir.1995) (summary judgment where no specific intent in an attempt to monopolize case); U.S. Anchor Manufacturing v. Rule Industries, 7 F.3d 986 (11th Cir.1993), cert. denied, 512 U.S. 1221 (1994); Chapter 8, Section 1B, supra. Would market power or specific intent have to be shown in a Robinson–Patman case? See Chapter 11 infra.

8. A recent commentary concluded:

Brooke Group unquestionably sends a chilling message to potential predatory pricing plaintiffs. The recoupment standard is rigorous and, as explained by the Court, invites lower courts to scrutinize the record before trial to find facts that mitigate against a likelihood of effective supracompetitive pricing or output restriction. This "screen," as well as the Court's list of factors warranting "summary disposition," doubtless will be used to strengthen pretrial summary judgment motions. In non-Robinson–Patman Act cases, focus on the defendant's market share alone—as in the Eleventh Circuit's decision in *U.S. Anchor* may also serve as a filtering mechanism.[66]

Is this analysis consistent with your reading of *Brooke Group?* Does it apply equally to single firm monopoly situations and to concentrated industries? How, if at all, would you modify or supplement the Supreme Court's *Brooke Group* opinion? Please note that since *Brooke Group* was decided, no plaintiff has succeeded on the merits of a predatory pricing claim in federal court. If the possibility of recoupment is found to be likely, why not presume any price below average total cost is predatory?

9. In United States v. AMR Corp., American Airlines, Inc., 140 F.Supp.2d 1141 (D.Kan.2001), American Airlines, the dominant airline on routes into and out of Dallas–Fort Worth, during the period from 1995–97, was often challenged by small carriers charging substantially lower fares. The government charged that American Airlines violated Section 2 of the Sherman Act when it responded by cutting fares below its costs to the level of its challengers and adding to the number of its flights per day, thereby taking passenger business away from challengers. The result, intended according to American Airlines' documents, was that the low-price carriers abandoned their challenges on these particular routes or went out of business altogether.

The Antitrust Division charged that American Airlines priced below cost to drive low-price carriers out of business and with the intent subsequently to recoup its investment through higher airline prices. It further claimed that even on routes where American Airlines was not directly challenged, American Airlines' aggressive behavior earned the company a "reputation for predation" which deterred other challengers on other routes from taking on the company.

The district court granted American Airlines motion for summary judgment. It followed those courts and commentators that have adopted the rule that predatory pricing requires pricing below average variable costs, and found that American Airlines' pricing never reached so low a level. It also found that American's prices were not predatory because it met but did not beat prices offered by smaller challengers, and that it was implausible that American Airlines could recoup its lower prices through subsequent high prices, a requirement to show predation, because there continued to be a substantial number of competitors into and out of Dallas–Fort Worth.

With respect to predation by reputation, the court found that the theory was unprecedented, and was dependent on a finding of underlying predatory pricing behavior which the court concluded was not present. In any event, any such reputation is almost an inevitable consequence of hard-nosed competition which the law does not preclude. The district court's approach on the central policy question of what constitutes predation is summarized in the following italicized portion of its opinion:

> *Antitrust begins with the premise that all firms, even dominant firms, are permitted to compete aggressively, and that hard competition is a desidera-*

66. Denger & Herfort, Predatory Pricing Claims After *Brooke Group,* 62 Antitrust L.J. 541, 556–57 (1994).

tum rather than an evil. Thus prices above the relevant measure of costs become an absolute safe harbor.

But if American Airlines had sufficient cost or non-cost advantages—at least in the short run—to force new or smaller carriers from the field, will its customers truly be better off in the long run? Is "average variable cost," presumably low for an established airline with extra capacity on flights, the right test, particularly when applied to dramatic price cutting against new or smaller carriers who have not yet been able to build their goodwill or reputations? Was the district court correct in summarily brushing aside the government's "reputation for predation" claim? What if the Antitrust Division could prove that both equally efficient and higher cost rivals have, in fact, been deterred from competing because of American's reputation? What if the government could show that American raised price substantially when it forced rivals from the field? See Edlin, Stopping Above–Cost Predatory Pricing, 111 Yale L.J. 941 (2002).

COMPARATIVE NOTE: PREDATORY PRICING IN THE EUROPEAN UNION

EU competition law takes a somewhat more critical view of predatory pricing than its American counterpart now does. In AKZO CHEMIE BV v. COMMISSION, Case C–62/86, [1991] ECR I–3359, the Court of Justice had before it a case in which Akzo, a large Dutch multinational firm, was accused of holding a dominant position in benzoyl peroxide, which is used as a bleaching agent for flour and as a catalyst in the production of certain plastics. One of Akzo's tactics involved the alleged use of predatory pricing. In that connection, the Court of Justice said that "[p]rices below average variable costs (that is to say, those which vary depending on the quantities produced) by means of which a dominant undertaking seeks to eliminate a competitor must be regarded as abusive." Id., ¶ 71. The Court focused there on the intent of the dominant firm to eliminate a competitor by means of such pricing. In a later decision given by the Court of First Instance in TETRA PAK INTERNATIONAL SA v. COMMISSION, Case T–83/91, [1994] ECR II–755, the CFI held that the intent to eliminate a competitor was crucial, but it implied that prices would be predatory only if recoupment could occur. The Court of Justice disagreed with the CFI on this point. It described the rules for predatory pricing as follows:

> In *AKZO* this court did indeed sanction the existence of two different methods of analysis for determining whether an undertaking has practised predatory pricing. First, prices below average variable costs must always be considered abusive.... Secondly, prices below total costs but above average variable costs are only to be considered abusive if an intention to eliminate can be shown.

> ... Furthermore, it would not be appropriate, in the circumstances of the present case, to require in addition proof that Tetra Pak had a realistic chance of recouping its losses. It must be possible to penalise predatory pricing whenever there is a risk that competitors will be eliminated.

Case C–333/94P, [1996] ECR I–5951, ¶¶ 41, 44. It is plain from this language, therefore, that at present the United States and Europe have two different views on the type of pricing that should be condemned as "predatory" and hence abusive. See also "North Atlantic Competition Policy: Converging Toward What?", Address by William J. Kolasky, Deputy Assistant Attorney General, Antitrust Division, U.S. Dept. of Justice, Before the BIICL Second Annual Int'l and Comp. Law Conference, London, May 17, 2002, at http://www.usdoj.gov/atr/public/speeches/ 11153.htm.

PROBLEM 20

AMERICAN FOODS EXPANDS ITS MARKET SHARE

American Foods is one of the largest manufacturers and distributors of household products in the United States. Its sales last year were in excess of $5 billion and its profits were $500 million. It is the third largest general advertiser and second largest TV advertiser in the United States.

One of its relatively minor product lines is potato chips. Last year it accounted for 28% of sales and stood first in the market, but it has been losing market share. Its high water mark occurred five years ago when it accounted for 39% of sales, which contributed about $10 million to the company's profits. Two other diversified national food companies—Jones & Turner and National Mills—stand second and third respectively with 18% and 15%; and their market shares have also been down in the last five years. All other potato chip sales are by regional and local companies or are accounted for by private label sales. Several regional companies have enjoyed great success in recent years and have cut into the market leaders' market shares.

An American Foods strategic planning task force reported that American's potato chip plants were obsolete and that an aggressive expansion program would require modernization of existing plants and construction of two new plants on the east and west coasts. Despite the decline in the company's market share, its total volume of potato chip sales had fallen only slightly in the last five years so that there was little unused capacity in the American Foods system.

To justify a modernization and expansion program, the strategic planning group proposed and implemented a three-pronged promotional program to expand the company's sales base and respond to the effective competition of the regionals. The advertising budget, currently the largest in the potato chip industry, was doubled with emphasis on national spot TV. New types and brands were introduced (*i.e.*, Bar–B–Que chips, low calorie chips), as well as more package sizes. Finally, selective wholesale price cuts were offered in major cities where regional companies had made their most extensive in-roads. The combination of advertising expenditures and price cuts has placed American Foods' national average price well below average total cost, but about 4% above average variable cost. In eight key cities, price was above but within 1% of average variable cost and in a ninth city—Rochester, New York—American Foods' price last year was below average variable cost. This occurred because of a delivery strike which cut sales for the year below anticipated volume. The wholesale price in other cities would have been below average variable cost if advertising expenditures had been expensed in the year in which they were made. American Foods follows an allocation program, however, which treats advertising in part as current expense and in part as a future "investment," and allocates only 60% in the year in which the ads are run, 30% the following year, and 10% the third year. This accounting formula was adopted by American Foods two years before implementation of the expansion program.

American Foods' market share is up to 41% this year and it anticipates that it will be 45% next year if it continues its marketing program. The two other national firms have met American Foods' price cuts and maintained their market shares, but several regionals are losing money and either have been or will be driven out of business unless American Foods' promotional program is discontinued.

The Federal Trade Commission has challenged the program, charging an attempt to monopolize under Section 2 and an unfair method of competition under Section 5. What result? If the Commission prevails in court, what remedy should be imposed?

SECTION 3.   TYING ARRANGEMENTS

Clayton Act, Section 3[67]

> That it shall be unlawful for any person engaged in commerce, in the course of such commerce, to lease or make a sale or contract for sale of goods, wares, merchandise, machinery, supplies or other commodities, whether patented or unpatented, for use, consumption or resale within the United States or any Territory thereof or the District of Columbia or any insular possession or other place under the jurisdiction of the United States, or fix a price charged therefor or discount from or rebate upon, such price, on the condition, agreement or understanding that the lessee or purchaser thereof shall not use or deal in the goods, wares, merchandise, machinery, supplies, or other commodities of a competitor or competitors of the lessor or seller, where the effect of such lease, sale, or contract for sale or such condition, agreement or understanding may be to substantially lessen competition or tend to create a monopoly in any line of commerce.

UNITED SHOE MACHINERY CORP. v. UNITED STATES, 258 U.S. 451, 42 S.Ct. 363, 66 L.Ed. 708 (1922). This was a suit to enjoin the defendants from making leases containing clauses and conditions alleged to violate Section 3 of the Clayton Act. The United Shoe Machinery Corporation controlled more than ninety-five percent of the shoe machinery business in this country. Its machines were protected by patents. The district court had enjoined the use of

> (1) the restricted use clause, which provides that the leased machinery shall not ... be used upon shoes, etc., or portions thereof, upon which certain other operations have not been performed on other machines of the defendants; (2) the exclusive use clause, which provides that if the lessee fails to use exclusively machinery of certain kinds made by the lessor, the lessor shall have the right to cancel the right to use all such machinery so leased; (3) the supplies clause, which provides that the lessee shall purchase supplies exclusively from the lessor; (4) the patent insole clause, which provides that the lessee shall only use machinery leased on shoes which have had certain other operations performed upon them by the defendant's machines; (5) the additional machinery clause, which provides that the lessee shall take all additional machinery for certain kinds of work from the lessor or lose his right to retain the machines which he has already leased; (6) the factory output clause, which requires the payment of

---

67.   38 Stat. 731 (1914), 15 U.S.C.A.
§ 14.

a royalty on shoes operated upon by machines made by competitors; (7) the discriminatory royalty clause, providing lower royalty for lessees who agree not to use certain machinery on shoes lasted on machines other than those leased from the lessor. The defendant's restrictive form of lease embraces the right of the lessor to cancel a lease for the breach of a provision in such lease, or in any other lease or license agreement between the lessor and the lessee. The lessor in such case is given the right, by notice in writing to the lessee, to terminate any and all leases or licenses then in force to use the machinery and this notwithstanding previous breaches or defaults may have been unnoticed, waived, or condoned by or on behalf of the lessor.

The Supreme Court (Day, J.) affirmed:

While the clauses enjoined do not contain specific agreements not to use the machinery of a competitor of the lessor, the practical effect of these drastic provisions is to prevent such use. We can entertain no doubt that such provisions as were enjoined are embraced in the broad terms of the Clayton Act which cover all conditions, agreements, or understandings of this nature. That such restrictive and tying agreements must necessarily lessen competition and tend to monopoly is, we believe, equally apparent. When it is considered that the United Company occupies a dominating position in supplying shoe machinery of the classes involved, these covenants signed by the lessee and binding upon him effectually prevent him from acquiring the machinery of a competitor of the lessor except at the risk of forfeiting the right to use the machines furnished by the United Company which may be absolutely essential to the prosecution and success of his business.

This system of "tying" restrictions is quite as effective as express covenants could be and practically compels the use of the machinery of the lessor except upon risks which manufacturers will not willingly incur. It is true that the record discloses that in many instances these provisions were not enforced. . . . The fact that the lessor in many instances forbore to enforce these provisions does not make them any the less agreements within the condemnation of the Clayton Act.

It is contended that the decree in favor of the defendants affirmed in the former suit [brought by] the Government under the Sherman Act . . . is res judicata [as to] the present issues. . . .

The Sherman Act suit had for its object the dissolution of the United Company, which had been formed by the union of other shoe machinery companies. It also attacked and sought to enjoin the use of the restrictive and tying clauses contained in the leases as being in themselves contracts in violation of the Sherman Act. The Sherman Act and the Clayton Act provide different tests of liability.

The previous litigation merely concerned the validity of the leases under the Sherman law. The restrictions in the defendant's leases are specifically forbidden by the Clayton Act.

International Salt Co. v. United States

Supreme Court of the United States, 1947.
332 U.S. 392, 68 S.Ct. 12, 92 L.Ed. 20.

■ JACKSON, J. The Government brought this civil action to enjoin the International Salt Company, appellant here, from carrying out provisions of the leases of its patented machines to the effect that lessees would use therein only International's salt products. The restriction is alleged to violate § 1 of the Sherman Act, and § 3 of the Clayton Act. Upon appellant's answer and admissions of fact, the Government moved for summary judgment under Rule 56 of the Rules of Civil Procedure [28 U.S.C.A. following section 723c], upon the ground that no issue as to a material fact was presented and that, on the admissions, judgment followed as a matter of law. Neither party submitted affidavits. Judgment was granted and appeal was taken directly to this Court.

It was established by pleadings or admissions that the International Salt Company is engaged in interstate commerce in salt, of which it is the country's largest producer for industrial uses. It also owns patents on two machines for utilization of salt products. One, the "Lixator," dissolves rock salt into a brine used in various industrial processes. The other, the "Saltomat," injects salt, in tablet form, into canned products during the canning process. The principal distribution of each of these machines is under leases which, among other things, require the lessees to purchase from appellant all unpatented salt and salt tablets consumed in the leased machines.

Appellant had outstanding 790 leases of an equal number of "Lixators," all of which leases were on appellant's standard form containing the tying clause and other standard provisions; of 50 other leases which somewhat varied the terms, all but 4 contained the tying clause. It also had in effect 73 leases of 96 "Saltomats," all containing the restrictive clause. In 1944, appellant sold approximately 119,000 tons of salt, for about $500,000, for use in these machines.

The appellant's patents confer a limited monopoly of the invention they reward. From them appellant derives a right to restrain others from making, vending or using the patented machines. But the patents confer no right to restrain use of, or trade in, unpatented salt. By contracting to close this market for salt against competition, International has engaged in a restraint of trade for which its patents afford no immunity from the antitrust laws. [Citing cases.]

Appellant contends, however, that summary judgment was unauthorized because it precluded trial of alleged issues of fact as to whether the restraint was unreasonable within the Sherman Act or substantially lessened competition or tended to create a monopoly in salt within the Clayton Act. We think the admitted facts left no genuine issue. Not only is price-fixing unreasonable, *per se*, United States v. Socony–Vacuum Oil Co., 310 U.S. 150; United States v. Trenton Potteries Co., 273 U.S. 392, but also it is unreasonable, *per se*, to foreclose competitors from any substantial market. Fashion Originators' Guild of America v. Federal Trade Commission, 114 F.2d 80, affirmed 312 U.S. 457. The volume of business affected by these contracts cannot be said to be insignificant or insubstantial and the tendency of the arrangement to accomplishment of monopoly seems obvious. Under the law, agreements are forbidden which "tend to create a monopoly," and it is immaterial that the tendency is a creeping one rather than one that proceeds at full gallop; nor does the law await arrival at the goal before condemning the direction of the movement.

Appellant contends, however, that the "Lixator" contracts are saved from unreasonableness and from the tendency to monopoly because they provided that if any competitor offered salt of equal grade at a lower price, the lessee should be free to buy in the open market, unless appellant would furnish the salt at an equal price; and the "Saltomat" agreements provided that the lessee was entitled to the benefit of any general price reduction in lessor's salt tablets. The "Lixator" provision does, of course, afford a measure of protection to the lessee, but it does not avoid the stifling effect of the agreement on competition. The appellant had at all times a priority on the business at equal prices. A competitor would have to undercut appellant's price to have any hope of capturing the market, while appellant could hold that market by merely meeting competition. We do not think this concession relieves the contract of being a restraint of trade, albeit a less harsh one than would result in the absence of such a provision. The "Saltomat" provision obviously has no effect of legal significance since it gives the lessee nothing more than a right to buy appellant's salt tablets at appellant's going price. All purchases must in any event be of appellant's product.

Appellant also urges that since under the leases it remained under an obligation to repair and maintain the machines, it was reasonable to confine their use to its own salt because its high quality assured satisfactory functioning and low maintenance cost. The appellant's rock salt is alleged to have an average sodium chloride content of 98.2%. Rock salt of other producers, it is said, "does not run consistent in sodium chloride content and in many instances runs as low as 95% of sodium chloride." This greater percentage of insoluble impurities allegedly disturbs the functioning of the "Lixator" machine. A somewhat similar claim is pleaded as to the "Saltomat."

Of course, a lessor may impose on a lessee reasonable restrictions designed in good faith to minimize maintenance burdens and to assure satisfactory operation. We may assume, as matter of argument, that if the "Lixator" functions best on rock salt of average sodium chloride content of 98.2%, the lessee might be required to use only salt meeting such a specification of quality. But it is not pleaded, nor is it argued, that the machine is allergic to salt of equal quality produced by anyone except International. If others cannot produce salt equal to reasonable specifications for machine use, it is one thing; but it is admitted that, at times, at least, competitors do offer such a product. They are, however, shut out of the market by a provision that limits it, not in terms of quality, but in terms of a particular vendor. Rules for use of leased machinery must not be disguised restraints of free competition, though they may set reasonable standards which all suppliers must meet. Cf. International Business Machines Corporation v. United States, 298 U.S. 131....

Judgment affirmed.[68]

NOTES AND QUESTIONS

International Salt suggests that antitrust enforcement against tie-in sales rests on the assumption that firms with market power with respect to a tying product will distort competition as to a second or tied product by insisting that the two products be purchased jointly. A question to keep in mind in thinking about *International Salt* and the following tie-in cases is what kind of incentives—legitimate or illegitimate—lead the seller to insist on a tie-in arrangement. Consider the following questions when reviewing the cases and materials in the remainder of this section.

1. Suppose the seller has no discernable market power with respect to the tying product, but nevertheless offers that product for sale only if purchased in conjunction with a second independent product. Why would any seller follow such a marketing strategy? Would it be likely to succeed?

2. At the other extreme, consider a situation in which a seller has an absolute monopoly of a tying product and offers it for sale only in conjunction with purchase of a second, independent product. What are the possible incentives for tie-in sales in that situation? Will a tie-in strategy succeed, or are there limits on its effectiveness? Is it necessarily the case that the seller will earn greater profits from this linked sale of the tying and tied products than it could earn by selling the monopolized tying product at the highest possible price and reducing the price on the tied product or giving the tied product away?

3. Suppose instead of an outright tie-in, the seller offers the tying product with or without the tied product, but offers the two products at a lower combined price than could be obtained if they were purchased separately. That situation is covered by Section 3 which deals not only with a "lease or . . . sale" of a commodity but also with a "discount from or rebate upon" a sales price. Is that kind of offer significantly less anticompetitive than an outright tie-in sale? What is the difference in competitive effect?

4. Are there explanations for tie-in sales other than an intention on the part of the seller to increase sales and thereby profits on the tied product? What are these other possible justifications and do they reflect legitimate business considerations?

5. In TIMES-PICAYUNE PUBLISHING CO. v. UNITED STATES, 345 U.S. 594, 73 S.Ct. 872, 97 L.Ed. 1277 (1953), the Supreme Court considered the legality of a plan under which a company that owned the sole morning newspaper in New Orleans and one of two afternoon papers required advertisers to buy space in both, if they wanted to advertise in either. The Court found that this so-called "unit plan" did not violate Sherman Act § 1. Before a tying arrangement would violate § 1, the government would have had to prove (1) that the seller enjoyed a monopolistic position in the market for the tying product, and (2) that a substantial volume of commerce in the tied product was restrained. (Either one of those showings, the Court said, would have been enough to make out a violation of Clayton Act § 3.)

68. The Court's rejection of defendant's objections to the decree is omitted. Also omitted is the opinion of Frankfurter, J., in which Reed and Burton, JJ., joined, dissenting from the refusal to modify the decree.

The government's proof failed on both counts: the paper had only about 40% of the market for advertising sales, and the unit plan did not have a substantial adverse effect on competition.

———

NORTHERN PACIFIC RAILWAY v. UNITED STATES, 356 U.S. 1, 78 S.Ct. 514, 2 L.Ed.2d 545 (1958). In 1864 and 1870, Congress granted the predecessor of the Northern Pacific Railway Company approximately 40 million acres of land in several Northwestern States and Territories to facilitate its construction of a railroad from Lake Superior to Puget Sound. By 1949, the Northern Pacific had sold about 37 million acres of its holdings. In a large number of its sales contracts and most of its lease agreements Northern Pacific had inserted "preferential routing" clauses which compelled the transferee to ship over Northern Pacific lines all commodities produced or manufactured on the land, provided that its rates (and in some instances its services) were equal to those of competing carriers. There were alternative means of transportation available, including two major railroad systems.

The government, in a suit alleging violations of § 1 of the Sherman Act, moved for summary judgment which was granted by the district court. In affirming the grant of summary judgment, the Supreme Court, per Black, J., wrote:

> For our purposes a tying arrangement may be defined as an agreement by a party to sell one product but only on the condition that the buyer also purchases a different (or tied) product, or at least agrees that he will not purchase that product from any other supplier.[69] Where such conditions are successfully exacted competition on the merits with respect to the tied product is inevitably curbed. Indeed "tying agreements serve hardly any purpose beyond the suppression of competition." ... They deny competitors free access to the market for the tied product, not because the party imposing the tying requirements has a better product or a lower price but because of his power or leverage in another market. At the same time buyers are forced to forego their free choice between competing products. For these reasons "tying agreements fare harshly under the laws forbidding restraints of trade." Times–Picayune Publishing Co. v. United States. They are unreasonable in and of themselves whenever a party has sufficient economic power with respect to the tying product to appreciably restrain free competition in the market for the tied product and a "not insubstantial" amount of interstate commerce is affected. International Salt Co. v. United States.... Of course where the seller has no control or dominance over the tying product so that it does not represent an effectual weapon to pressure buyers into taking the tied item any restraint of trade attributable to such tying arrangements would obviously be insignificant at most. As a simple example, if one of a dozen food stores in a community were to refuse to sell flour unless the buyer also took sugar it would hardly tend to restrain competition in sugar if its competitors were ready and able to sell flour by itself.

The Court explained that requisite market power in the tying "product" was clearly present.

69. Of course, when the buyer is free to take either product by itself, there is no tying problem even though the seller may also offer the two items as a unit at a single price.

We wholly agree that the undisputed facts established beyond any genuine question that the defendant possessed substantial economic power by virtue of its extensive landholdings which it used as leverage to induce large numbers of purchasers and lessees to give it preference, to the exclusion of its competitors, in carrying goods or produce from the land transferred to them.... This land was strategically located ... amid private holdings and within economic distance of transportation facilities.... [C]ommon sense makes it evident that this particular land was often prized by those who purchased or leased it and was frequently essential to their business activities.

The Court went on to explain:

The very existence of this host of tying arrangements is itself compelling evidence of the defendant's great power, at least where, as here, no other explanation has been offered for the existence of these restraints.

The Court conceded that there was language in *Times-Picayune* which referred to "monopoly power" or "dominance" over the tying product as being a precondition for application of the *per se* rule to tying arrangements, but declined to construe the requirement as anything more than "sufficient economic power to impose an appreciable restraint on free competition in the tied product (assuming all the time, of course, that a 'not insubstantial' amount of interstate commerce is affected)."[70]

NOTES CONCERNING TYING LAW PRIOR TO THE JEFFERSON PARISH CASE AND QUESTIONS

1. The Supreme Court in *Northern Pacific* came down heavily on the point that the tying arrangements were suspect because of the failure of the defendant to offer any legitimate business justification for their existence. On the question of possible justifications, consider the following excerpt from Scherer, Industrial Market Structure and Economic Performance 582–83 (2d ed. 1980):

Businesses have diverse reasons for attempting to tie the sale of one product to that of another. First, a firm may have monopoly power over one product by virtue of patent protection, strong product differentiation, or scale economies; and it may try to exploit this leverage in a second market where, without the tie, it could earn no more than a normal return. Thus, it adds to its monopoly profits in the tying good market the profits it can realize by exercising power over price in at least part of the tied good market. The economics of such ties are similar to those of downstream integration by a firm to obtain control over the purchase of inputs complementary in production to the input on which the firm enjoys monopoly power. Second and closely related, the profits attainable from coordinated monopoly pricing of two goods which, for example, are complements in use, will generally be higher than those realized by setting a monopoly price for each commodity separately. This is so because, by ignoring interdependence between the demand functions of complementary products, a producer in effect fails to adjust for all the variables affecting its profit maximum, just as oligopolists producing the same product maximize joint profits only when they take into account fully the interdependence

70. Clark, J., did not participate. The dissenting opinion of Harlan, J., with whom Frankfurter, J., and Whittaker, J., joined, is omitted. See U.S. v. Northern Pacific Railway Co., 1959 Trade Cas. ¶ 69,256 (W.D.Wash. 1959) (consent decree).

of their demand functions. Third, tying is sometimes a convenient way of discriminating in price according to intensity of demand. Suppose, for instance, that one copying machine user makes 3,000 copies per month, while another makes 10,000 copies per month. It would be difficult for a company selling only copying machines to price its machines in such a way as to extract more revenue from the more intensive user. But if the machine maker can tie the purchase of special copying paper to the purchase of its machine, and if it can wield sufficient leverage in the paper market to realize a supranormal profit margin there, it will be able to secure additional profits from the high-volume user. An analogous but more complex variant occurs when firms sell related but separable products only at a single package or bundled price. Fourth, the producer of a technically complex machine may engage in tying to control the quality of materials and supplies used with its machine, so that the reputation of its product is not sullied by breakdowns caused through the use of faulty supplies. Fifth, certain economies may be realized by producing or distributing the tied and tying goods together. For example, supplies of special copying machine paper or ink may be delivered by maintenance personnel in the course of routine service visits, saving separate delivery costs. It is doubtful, however, whether the savings realized in this way could be very substantial. Finally, tying contracts may be employed to evade governmental price controls—*e.g.*, when a firm supplying some commodity such as gas or telephone service whose price is regulated requires customers to buy from it fixtures and attachments whose prices are not effectively controlled.

In studying the remaining cases in this section, you should consider whether any of these explanations for tying are applicable. Which, if any, explanations should be treated as a legitimate defense?

2.   Note that the purchaser or lessee of Northern Pacific's land had to ship over the Northern Pacific line only if its rates were no higher than competing carriers. Does it follow that Northern Pacific could not have been using the tie-in to increase sales and profits on the tied product? If you accept that, then what was Northern Pacific up to? It has been suggested that Northern Pacific's contracts and leases compelled a shipper to disclose the lower rates or better sales service available elsewhere and that therefore the traffic clauses may have been designed to help Northern Pacific detect lower rates and service standards on competing railroads. See Cummings and Ruhter, The Northern Pacific Case, 22 J.L. & Econ. 329 (1979). Do you find that persuasive?

3.   In UNITED STATES v. LOEW'S INC., 371 U.S. 38, 45–47 (1962), the Supreme Court concluded that even "absent a showing of market dominance, the crucial economic power may be inferred from the tying product's desirability to consumers or from uniqueness in its attributes." The Court added: "when the tying product is patented or copyrighted . . . sufficiency of economic power is presumed."

4.   In FORTNER ENTERPRISES, INC. v. UNITED STATES STEEL CORP., 394 U.S. 495 (1969) (*Fortner I*) and 429 U.S. 610 (1977) (*Fortner II*), cases discussed at some length in *Hyde* infra, the Court spoke in terms of "appreciable economic power." How would you describe the degree of power a seller should have, stemming from the tying product, to raise a Sherman Act claim? Should it make a difference if Section 3 of the Clayton Act or Section 1 of the Sherman Act applies? Can you infer market power with respect to the tying product, as suggested in *Northern Pacific*, from the fact that the tie-in offer is accepted? Should tie-in sales ever be illegal if

competitors, acting singly or in combination, can offer a comparable package? If that were the law, what would a plaintiff have to prove in order to successfully challenge a tie?

5.   Where a tie is not part of a contract or other formal agreement, difficult questions arise as to whether the tied product was accepted by the buyer because of coercion or just because the combined offer was an attractive deal. In FTC v. Texaco, Inc., 393 U.S. 223 (1968), the Federal Trade Commission sued Texaco under Section 5 of the Federal Trade Commission Act charging that it improperly induced independent Texaco dealers to purchase Goodrich TBA (tires, batteries, and accessories). In return, Goodrich paid Texaco a 10% commission. In related proceedings, the Commission had sued Atlantic Refining for a similar arrangement with Goodyear, and Shell for a similar arrangement with Firestone.

All three arrangements were struck down by the Commission on grounds that the sales commission arrangement was the equivalent of a tie-in sale and the decisions against Atlantic Refining—Goodyear and Shell—Firestone were affirmed on appeal (Atlantic Refining Co. v. FTC, 381 U.S. 357 (1965); Shell Oil Co. v. FTC, 360 F.2d 470 (5th Cir.1966), cert. denied, 385 U.S. 1002 (1967)).

The Supreme Court acknowledged that in the case involving Texaco–Goodrich, there was no evidence of threats of cancellation, establishment of quotas, or other requirements that dealers purchase TBA from sponsored sources, with the result that the evidence of coercion was less substantial than in the other TBA cases. Nevertheless, it pointed out that Texaco enjoyed dominant economic power over its dealers, largely because most of them held one year leases for their stations subject to termination at the end of the year on ten days' notice, and because their supply contract on gasoline and other petroleum products also was renewable year to year and terminable on 30 days' notice. The majority quoted Judge Wisdom in the *Shell* case: "A man operating a gas station is bound to be overawed by the great corporation that is his supplier, his banker, and his landlord."

As to the exercise of that power, the Court noted Texaco's constant recommendations to dealers of favored brands of TBA, promotion of Goodrich products by Texaco salesmen, occasional joint visits to dealers by Texaco and Goodrich salesmen, and Texaco arrangements to receive regular reports on the amount of sponsored TBA purchased by each dealer. The Court concluded that the sales commission system was "inherently coercive," observing that there would be little point in Goodrich paying 10% to Texaco if they did not think Texaco could effectively assert some influence over dealers.

Interestingly, when Texaco dealers brought private treble damage actions against Texaco charging illegal tie-in sales, the Court of Appeals ruled that TBA sponsorship was illegal *per se* only in a suit under Section 5 of the FTC Act. It found no evidence of economic coercion and accordingly, a jury verdict for the dealers was set aside. Belliston v. Texaco, Inc., 455 F.2d 175 (10th Cir.), cert. denied, 408 U.S. 928 (1972).

6.   The coercion question can arise in other contexts. For example, we have seen in previous cases that a seller cannot insist upon the purchase of a tied product if its goodwill or the efficiency of the tying product can be adequately protected either by indicating minimum specifications or a list of approved sources for the tied product. (Cf. *International Salt,* p. 877 supra.) Plaintiffs have argued that a coercive tie-in effect exists where the seller issues unreasonably demanding specifications or unreasonably withholds approval for alternative sources. In Kentucky Fried Chicken Corp. v. Diversified Packaging Corp., 549 F.2d 368 (5th Cir.1977), Kentucky

Fried Chicken successfully defended against such charges by showing that it had approved ten sources for the alleged tied products (cartons), only one of the ten was affiliated with Kentucky Fried; the franchise agreement provided that Kentucky Fried's approval would "not be unreasonably withheld," and Kentucky Fried had never withheld approval from a supplier where it had been requested.

Compare Photovest Corp. v. Fotomat Corp., 606 F.2d 704 (7th Cir.1979), cert. denied, 445 U.S. 917 (1980), where failure of a franchisor of film processing outlets to provide a list of approved film processors was not regarded as the equivalent of a tie, at least where the franchisor expressly communicated that processing could be done at non-franchisor sources and the franchisee never submitted a processor for approval. On the other hand, an illegal tie-in was found during a later period of time when the franchisee sought approval of an alternative source and approval was granted only on condition that the franchisee perform costly additional services (pickup and delivery of the film from the outside processor) which under the franchise agreement were supposed to be provided by the franchisor. After reading the *Jefferson Parish* and *Kodak* cases infra, consider whether these "franchise" cases would—and should—come out the same way today?

7.   In ADVANCE BUSINESS SYSTEMS & SUPPLY CO. V. SCM CORP., 415 F.2d 55 (4th Cir.1969), cert. denied, 397 U.S. 920 (1970), the Court of Appeals held that a discount tying arrangement was illegal because it effectively deprived customers of their freedom of choice. One of the practices at issue involved SCM's marketing of a copying machine on a so-called "copy service" basis. Under the plan SCM customers were charged a single price per copy for the rental of the machine, supplies and service. The district court concluded that the arrangement constituted an illegal tie-in, and the Court of Appeals affirmed.

SCM had argued that the plan was not illegal because both the machine and the supplies were separately available to customers. The Court of Appeals, however, concluded that this alleged separate availability was essentially a sham. While customers could buy the copying machine separately: "Purchase of a copying machine for $4250 . . . is clearly not the economic equivalent of rental at a charge of approximately $.035 per copy."

Accordingly, the Fourth Circuit concluded that the machine and supplies "cannot realistically be regarded as separately available to SCM's customers." In the Court's view, such a tie-in was: "non-coercive, and therefore legal, only if the components are separately available to the customer on a basis as favorable as the tie-in arrangement." 415 F.2d at 62.

8.   It was commonly said that tie-in sales are illegal *per se* if certain preconditions are satisfied (*e.g.*, sufficient or appreciable economic power with respect to the tying product, not insubstantial amount of commerce in the tied product, etc.). Consider the following cases in light of this qualified *per se* rule covering tie-in sales:

(a) UNITED STATES v. JERROLD ELECTRONICS CORP., 187 F.Supp. 545 (E.D.Pa.1960), affirmed per curiam, 365 U.S. 567 (1961). Defendant, which had pioneered the community television antenna industry, sold various items of equipment, including cable, amplifiers, converters and electronic units only as components of a single system, and also required purchasers to secure servicing solely from Jerrold. The arrangement was attacked as a Sherman Act violation. Finding that the scheme constituted a tie-in, the court nevertheless upheld the arrangement as justified during the development period of this new industry. At least at that time, the arrangement assured Jerrold's profits, reputation, and future, upon which the success and orderly growth of the industry depended.

Unrestricted sales would have resulted in much of this equipment going into systems where prospects of success were at best extremely doubtful. Jerrold's short and long-term well-being depended on the success of these first systems. It could not afford to permit some of its limited equipment to be used in such a way that it would work against its interest. A wave of system failures at the start would have greatly retarded, if not destroyed, this new industry.... [But] as the industry took root and grew, the reasons for the blanket insistence on a service contract disappeared.... [A]t some time during its use, Jerrold's tie-in of services to equipment became unreasonable.[71]

(b) DEHYDRATING PROCESS CO. v. A.O. SMITH CORP., 292 F.2d 653 (1st Cir.), cert. denied, 368 U.S. 931 (1961). Defendant was a manufacturer of patented glass-lined silos used for the storage of fish meal and also of a patented unloading device installed in the bottom of the silo for the unloading of the meal. Defendant had originally sold the two products separately. Many buyers of unloaders who did not use its silos complained about the performance of the unloader. Eighteen customers made claims against A.O. Smith, and six unloaders were taken back for refund. As a result, defendant adopted a policy of selling unloaders only to those purchasing or already owning the silos. Plaintiff argued that the sales policy established a tying arrangement that violated Section 3 of the Clayton Act. *Held*, directed verdict for defendant affirmed. Although finding the products separable, the Court found that "a proper business reason may justify what might otherwise be an unlawful tie-in." Since about half of the persons who had bought the unloaders separately had been dissatisfied, the "tie-in" was justified.

(c) BAKER v. SIMMONS CO., 307 F.2d 458 (1st Cir.1962). The Simmons Company had established a program whereby it leased to qualifying motels signs bearing the legend "Sleep Best on Beautyrest by Simmons," or "Ask for Beautyrest by Simmons," as well as roadside signs bearing the trademark "Beautyrest" and the name of the motel. Simmons required that motels receiving the signs be fully equipped with Simmons "Beautyrest" mattresses. Baker argued that the program unlawfully tied the mattresses to the signs in violation of the Clayton and Sherman Acts. *Held*, for Simmons. The First Circuit observed that such a tying arrangement:

> might be exculpated from the reach of the antitrust laws if the arrangement was actuated by or could be explained on the basis of a legitimate business justification as opposed to an improper motive, *e.g.*, desire to increase market control through the economic leverage supplied by the tying arrangement.... [W]hile the instant arrangement might technically be deemed a tie-in, we do not believe that it is an illegal one nor one which presents the evils at which the antitrust statutes were aimed.... [I]f the motel in fact did not have the Beautyrest mattress in its rooms but rather had an inferior brand, then the Simmons name, reputation and good will predictably might well suffer.

Jefferson Parish Hospital District No. 2 v. Hyde

Supreme Court of the United States, 1984.
466 U.S. 2, 104 S.Ct. 1551, 80 L.Ed.2d 2.

■ STEVENS, J.... At issue in this case is the validity of an exclusive contract between a hospital and a firm of anesthesiologists. We must decide whether

---

71. For the private action side, see Jerrold Electronics Corp. v. Wescoast Broadcast-ing Co., Inc., 341 F.2d 653 (9th Cir.), cert. denied, 382 U.S. 817 (1965).

the contract gives rise to a *per se* violation of § 1 of the Sherman Act because every patient undergoing surgery at the hospital must use the services of one firm of anesthesiologists, and, if not, whether the contract is nevertheless illegal because it unreasonably restrains competition among anesthesiologists.

In July 1977, respondent Edwin G. Hyde, a board certified anesthesiologist, applied for admission to the medical staff of East Jefferson Hospital. The credentials committee and the medical staff executive committee recommended approval, but the hospital board denied the application because the hospital was a party to a contract providing that all anesthesiological services required by the hospital's patients would be performed by Roux & Associates, a professional medical corporation. Respondent then commenced this action seeking a declaratory judgment that the contract is unlawful and an injunction ordering petitioners to appoint him to the hospital staff. After trial, the District Court denied relief, finding that the anticompetitive consequences of the Roux contract were minimal and outweighed by benefits in the form of improved patient care. 513 F.Supp. 532 (E.D.La.1981). The Court of Appeals reversed because it was persuaded that the contract was illegal "per se." 686 F.2d 286 (5th Cir.1982). We granted certiorari, 460 U.S. 1021, and now reverse.

I

In February 1971, shortly before East Jefferson Hospital opened, it entered into an "Anesthesiology Agreement" with Roux & Associates ("Roux"), a firm that had recently been organized by Dr. Kermit Roux. The contract provided that any anesthesiologist designated by Roux would be admitted to the hospital's medical staff. The hospital agreed to provide the space, equipment, maintenance, and other supporting services necessary to operate the anesthesiology department. It also agreed to purchase all necessary drugs and other supplies. All nursing personnel required by the anesthesia department were to be supplied by the hospital, but Roux had the right to approve their selection and retention.[72] The hospital agreed to "restrict the use of its anesthesia department to Roux & Associates and [that] no other persons, parties or entities shall perform such services within the Hospital for the term of this contract."[73]

The 1971 contract provided for a one-year term automatically renewable for successive one-year periods unless either party elected to terminate.

---

72. The contract required all of the physicians employed by Roux to confine their practice of anesthesiology to East Jefferson.

73. Originally Roux agreed to provide at least two full time anesthesiologists acceptable to the hospital's credentials committee. Roux agreed to furnish additional anesthesiologists as necessary. The contract also provided that Roux would designate one of its qualified anesthesiologists to serve as the head of the hospital's department of anesthesia.

The fees for anesthesiological services are billed separately to the patients by the hospital. They cover the hospital's costs and the professional services provided by Roux. After a deduction of eight per cent to provide a reserve for uncollectible accounts, the fees are divided equally between Roux and the hospital.

In 1976, a second written contract was executed containing most of the provisions of the 1971 agreement. Its term was five years and the clause excluding other anesthesiologists from the hospital was deleted;[74] the hospital nevertheless continued to regard itself as committed to a closed anesthesiology department. Only Roux was permitted to practice anesthesiology at the hospital. At the time of trial the department included four anesthesiologists. The hospital usually employed 13 or 14 certified registered nurse anesthetists.[75]

The exclusive contract had an impact on two different segments of the economy: consumers of medical services, and providers of anesthesiological services. Any consumer of medical services who elects to have an operation performed at East Jefferson Hospital may not employ any anesthesiologist not associated with Roux. No anesthesiologists except those employed by Roux may practice at East Jefferson.

There are at least 20 hospitals in the New Orleans metropolitan area and about 70 percent of the patients living in Jefferson Parish go to hospitals other than East Jefferson. Because it regarded the entire New Orleans metropolitan area as the relevant geographic market in which hospitals compete, this evidence convinced the District Court that East Jefferson does not possess any significant "market power"; therefore it concluded that petitioners could not use the Roux contract to anticompetitive ends. The same evidence led the Court of Appeals to draw a different conclusion. Noting that 30 percent of the residents of the Parish go to East Jefferson Hospital, and that in fact "patients tend to choose hospitals by location rather than price or quality," the Court of Appeals concluded that the relevant geographic market was the East Bank of Jefferson Parish. The conclusion that East Jefferson Hospital possessed market power in that area was buttressed by the facts that the prevalence of health insurance eliminates a patient's incentive to compare costs, that the patient is not sufficiently informed to compare quality, and that family convenience tends to magnify the importance of location.

The Court of Appeals held that the case involves a "tying arrangement" because the "users of the hospital's operating rooms (the tying product) are also compelled to purchase the hospital's chosen anesthesia service (the tied product)." 686 F.2d at 289. Having defined the relevant geographic market for the tying product as the East Bank of Jefferson Parish, the court held that the hospital possessed "sufficient market power in the tying market to coerce purchasers of the tied product." 686 F.2d, at 291. Since the purchase of the tied product constituted a "not insubstantial amount of interstate commerce," under the Court of Appeals' reading of

74. "Roux testified that he requested the omission of the exclusive language in his 1976 contract because he believes a surgeon or patient is entitled to the services of the anesthesiologist of his choice. He admitted that he and others in his group did work outside East Jefferson following the 1976 contract but felt he was not in violation of the contract in light of the changes made in it." 513 F.Supp., at 537.

75. Approximately 875 operations are performed at the hospital each month; as many as 12 or 13 operating rooms may be in use at one time.

our decision in Northern Pac. R. Co. v. United States, 356 U.S. 1, 11 (1958), the tying arrangement was therefore illegal "per se."[76]

II

... It is far too late in the history of our antitrust jurisprudence to question the proposition that certain tying arrangements pose an unacceptable risk of stifling competition and therefore are unreasonable "per se." The rule was first enunciated in International Salt Co. v. United States, 332 U.S. 392, 396 (1947), and has been endorsed by this Court many times since. The rule also reflects congressional policies underlying the antitrust laws. In enacting section 3 of the Clayton Act, 15 U.S.C. 14, Congress expressed great concern about the anticompetitive character of tying arrangements. While this case does not arise under the Clayton Act, the congressional finding made therein concerning the competitive consequences of tying is illuminating, and must be respected.

It is clear, however, that every refusal to sell two products separately cannot be said to restrain competition. If each of the products may be purchased separately in a competitive market, one seller's decision to sell the two in a single package imposes no unreasonable restraint on either market, particularly if competing suppliers are free to sell either the entire package or its several parts.[77] For example, we have written that "if one of a dozen food stores in a community were to refuse to sell flour unless the buyer also took sugar it would hardly tend to restrain competition if its competitors were ready and able to sell flour by itself." Northern Pac. R. Co. v. United States, 356 U.S. 1, 7 (1958).[78] Buyers often find package sales attractive; a seller's decision to offer such packages can merely be an attempt to compete effectively—conduct that is entirely consistent with the Sherman Act. See Fortner Enterprises v. United States Steel Corp. (*Fortner I*), 394 U.S. 495, 517–518 (1969) (White, J., dissenting); id. at 524–525 (Fortas, J., dissenting).

Our cases have concluded that the essential characteristic of an invalid tying arrangement lies in the seller's exploitation of its control over the tying product to force the buyer into the purchase of a tied product that the buyer either did not want at all, or might have preferred to purchase elsewhere on different terms. When such "forcing" is present, competition on the merits in the market for the tied item is restrained and the Sherman Act is violated.

76. The Court of Appeals rejected as "clearly erroneous" the District Court's finding that the exclusive contract was justified by quality considerations. See 686 F.2d, at 292.

77. "Of course where the buyer is free to take either product by itself there is no tying problem even though the seller may also offer the two items as a unit at a single price." Northern Pac. R. Co. v. United States, 356 U.S. 1, 6, n. 4 (1958).

78. Thus, we have held that a seller who ties the sale of houses to the provision of credit simply as a way of effectively competing in a competitive market does not violate the antitrust laws. "The unusual credit bargain offered to Fortner proves nothing more than a willingness to provide cheap financing to sell expensive houses." United States Steel Corp. v. Fortner Enterprises, 429 U.S. 610, 622 (1977) (footnote omitted).

"Basic to the faith that a free economy best promotes the public weal is that goods must stand the cold test of competition; that the public, acting through the market's impersonal judgment, shall allocate the Nation's resources and thus direct the course its economic development will take.... By conditioning his sale of one commodity on the purchase of another, a seller coerces the abdication of buyers' independent judgment as to the 'tied' product's merits and insulates it from the competitive stresses of the open market. But any intrinsic superiority of the 'tied' product would convince freely choosing buyers to select it over others anyway." Times–Picayune Publishing Co. v. United States, 345 U.S. 594, 605 (1953) (footnote omitted).

Accordingly, we have condemned tying arrangements when the seller has some special ability—usually called "market power"—to force a purchaser to do something that he would not do in a competitive market.... When "forcing" occurs, our cases have found the tying arrangement to be unlawful.

Thus, the law draws a distinction between the exploitation of market power by merely enhancing the price of the tying product, on the one hand, and by attempting to impose restraints on competition in the market for a tied product, on the other. When the seller's power is just used to maximize its return in the tying product market, where presumably its product enjoys some justifiable advantage over its competitors, the competitive ideal of the Sherman Act is not necessarily compromised. But if that power is used to impair competition on the merits in another market, a potentially inferior product may be insulated from competitive pressures. This impairment could either harm existing competitors or create barriers to entry of new competitors in the market for the tied product, *Fortner I*, 394 U.S., at 509, and can increase the social costs of market power by facilitating price discrimination, thereby increasing monopoly profits over what they would be absent the tie, *Fortner II*, 429 U.S., at 617.[79] And from the standpoint of the consumer—whose interests the statute was especially intended to serve—the freedom to select the best bargain in the second market is impaired by his need to purchase the tying product, and perhaps by an inability to evaluate the true cost of either product when they are available only as a package.[80] In sum, to permit restraint of competition on the merits through tying arrangements would be, as we observed in *Fortner II*, to condone "the existence of power that a free market would not tolerate." 429 U.S., at 617 (footnote omitted).

Per se condemnation—condemnation without inquiry into actual market conditions—is only appropriate if the existence of forcing is probable.[81]

---

79. Sales of the tied item can be used to measure demand for the tying item; purchasers with greater needs for the tied item make larger purchases and in effect must pay a higher price to obtain the tying item....

80. Especially where market imperfections exist, purchasers may not be fully sensi-tive to the price or quality implications of a tying arrangement, and hence it may impede competition on the merits.

81. The rationale for *per se* rules in part is to avoid a burdensome inquiry into actual market conditions in situations where

Thus, application of the *per se* rule focuses on the probability of anticompetitive consequences. Of course, as a threshold matter there must be a substantial potential for impact on competition in order to justify *per se* condemnation. If only a single purchaser were "forced" with respect to the purchase of a tied item, the resultant impact on competition would not be sufficient to warrant the concern of antitrust law. It is for this reason that we have refused to condemn tying arrangements unless a substantial volume of commerce is foreclosed thereby. See *Fortner I, . . . International Salt*, 332 U.S., at 396. Similarly, when a purchaser is "forced" to buy a product he would not have otherwise bought even from another seller in the tied product market, there can be no adverse impact on competition because no portion of the market which would otherwise have been available to other sellers has been foreclosed.

Once this threshold is surmounted, *per se* prohibition is appropriate if anticompetitive forcing is likely. For example, if the government has granted the seller a patent or similar monopoly over a product, it is fair to presume that the inability to buy the product elsewhere gives the seller market power. . . . Any effort to enlarge the scope of the patent monopoly by using the market power it confers to restrain competition in the market for a second product will undermine competition on the merits in that second market. Thus, the sale or lease of a patented item on condition that the buyer make all his purchases of a separate tied product from the patentee is unlawful. . . .

The same strict rule is appropriate in other situations in which the existence of market power is probable. When the seller's share of the market is high, see Times–Picayune Publishing Co. v. United States, 345 U.S. 594, 611–613 (1953), or when the seller offers a unique product that competitors are not able to offer, see *Fortner I*, the Court has held that the likelihood that market power exists and is being used to restrain competition in a separate market is sufficient to make *per se* condemnation appropriate. Thus, in Northern Pac. R. Co. v. United States, 356 U.S. 1 (1958), we held that the railroad's control over vast tracts of western real estate, although not itself unlawful, gave the railroad a unique kind of bargaining power that enabled it to tie the sales of that land to exclusive, long term commitments that fenced out competition in the transportation market over a protracted period. When, however, the seller does not have either the degree or the kind of market power that enables him to force customers to purchase a second, unwanted product in order to obtain the tying product, an antitrust violation can be established only by evidence of an unreasonable restraint on competition in the relevant market. See *Fortner I*, 394 U.S., at 499–500; Times–Picayune Publishing Co. v. United States, 345 U.S. 594, 614–615 (1953).

In sum, any inquiry into the validity of a tying arrangement must focus on the market or markets in which the two products are sold, for that

the likelihood of anticompetitive conduct is so great as to render unjustified the costs of determining whether the particular case at bar involves anticompetitive conduct. *See, e.g.*, Arizona v. Maricopa County Medical Society, 457 U.S. 332, 350–351 (1982).

is where the anticompetitive forcing has its impact. Thus, in this case our analysis of the tying issue must focus on the hospital's sale of services to its patients, rather than its contractual arrangements with the providers of anesthesiological services. In making that analysis, we must consider whether petitioners are selling two separate products that may be tied together, and, if so, whether they have used their market power to force their patients to accept the tying arrangement.

III

The hospital has provided its patients with a package that includes the range of facilities and services required for a variety of surgical operations.[82] At East Jefferson Hospital the package includes the services of the anesthesiologist.[83] Petitioners argue that the package does not involve a tying arrangement at all—they are merely providing a functionally integrated package of services. Therefore, petitioners contend that it is inappropriate to apply principles concerning tying arrangements to this case.

Our cases indicate, however, that the answer to the question whether one or two products are involved turns not on the functional relation between them, but rather on the character of the demand for the two items.[84] In Times–Picayune Publishing Co. v. United States, 345 U.S. 594 (1953), the Court held that a tying arrangement was not present because the arrangement did not link two distinct markets for products that were distinguishable in the eyes of buyers. In *Fortner I*, the Court concluded that a sale involving two independent transactions, separately priced and purchased from the buyer's perspective, was a tying arrangement. These cases make it clear that a tying arrangement cannot exist unless two separate product markets have been linked.

The requirement that two distinguishable product markets be involved follows from the underlying rationale of the rule against tying. The definitional question depends on whether the arrangement may have the type of competitive consequences addressed by the rule.[85] The answer to

---

82. The physical facilities include the operating room, the recovery room, and the hospital room where the patient stays before and after the operation. The services include those provided by staff physicians, such as radiologists or pathologists, and interns, nurses, dietitians, pharmacists and laboratory technicians.

83. It is essential to differentiate between the Roux contract and the legality of the contract between the hospital and its patients. The Roux contract is nothing more than an arrangement whereby Roux supplies all of the hospital's needs for anesthesiological services. That contract raised only an exclusive dealing question. The issue here is whether the hospital's insistence that its patients purchase anesthesiological services from Roux creates a tying arrangement.

84. The fact that anesthesiological services are functionally linked to the other services provided by the hospital is not in itself sufficient to remove the Roux contract from the realm of tying arrangements. We have often found arrangements involving functionally linked products at least one of which is useless without the other to be prohibited tying devices.... In fact, in some situations the functional link between the two items may enable the seller to maximize its monopoly return on the tying item as a means of charging a higher rent or purchase price to a larger user of the tying item.

85. Professor Dam has pointed out that the *per se* rule against tying can be coherent only if tying is defined by reference to the economic effect of the arrangement.

the question whether petitioners have utilized a tying arrangement must be based on whether there is a possibility that the economic effect of the arrangement is that condemned by the rule against tying that petitioners have foreclosed competition on the merits in a product market distinct from the market for the tying item.[86] Thus, in this case no tying arrangement can exist unless there is a sufficient demand for the purchase of anesthesiological services separate from hospital services to identify a distinct product market in which it is efficient to offer anesthesiological services separately from hospital services.

Unquestionably, the anesthesiological component of the package offered by the hospital could be provided separately and could be selected either by the individual patient or by one of the patient's doctors if the hospital did not insist on including anesthesiological services in the package it offers to its customers. As a matter of actual practice, anesthesiological services are billed separately from the hospital services petitioners provide. There was ample and uncontroverted testimony that patients or surgeons often request specific anesthesiologists to come to a hospital and provide anesthesia, and that the choice of an individual anesthesiologist separate from the choice of a hospital is particularly frequent in respondent's specialty, obstetric anesthesiology. The District Court found that "[t]he provision of anesthesia services is a medical service separate from the other services provided by the hospital." 513 F.Supp., at 540. The Court of Appeals agreed with this finding, and went on to observe that "an anesthesiologist is normally selected by the surgeon, rather than the patient, based on familiarity gained through a working relationship. Obviously, the surgeons who practice at East Jefferson Hospital do not gain familiarity with any anesthesiologists other than Roux and Associates." 686 F.2d, at 291. The record amply supports the conclusion that consumers differentiate between anesthesiological services and other hospital services provided by petitioners.[87]

"[T]he definitional question is hard to separate from the question when tie-ins are harmful. Yet the decisions, in adopting the *per se* rule, have been attempting to flee from that economic question by ruling that tying arrangements are presumptively harmful, at least whenever certain nominal threshold standards on power and foreclosure are met. The weakness of the *per se* methodology is that it places crucial importance on the definition of the practice. Once an arrangement falls within the defined limits, no justification will be heard. But the *per se* rule gives no economic standards for defining the practice. To treat the definitional question as an abstract inquiry into whether one or two products is involved is thus to compound the weakness of the *per se* approach." Dam,

[Fortner Enterprises v. United States Steel: "Neither a Borrower Nor a Lender Be," 1969 Sup.Ct.Rev. 19].

86. Of course, the Sherman Act does not prohibit "tying," it prohibits "contracts ... in restraint of trade." Thus, in a sense the question whether this case involves "tying" is beside the point. The legality of petitioners' conduct depends on its competitive consequences, not whether it can be labeled "tying." If the competitive consequences of this arrangement are not those to which the *per se* rule is addressed, then it should not be condemned irrespective of its label.

87. One of the most frequently cited statements on this subject was made by Judge Van Dusen in United States v. Jerrold Electronics Corp., 187 F.Supp. 545 (E.D.Pa. 1960), affirmed, 365 U.S. 567 (1961) (per

Thus, the hospital's requirement that its patients obtain necessary anesthesiological services from Roux combined the purchase of two distinguishable services in a single transaction.[88] Nevertheless, the fact that this case involved a required purchase of two services that would otherwise be purchased separately does not make the Roux contract illegal. As noted above, there is nothing inherently anticompetitive about packaged sales. Only if patients are forced to purchase Roux's services as a result of the hospital's market power would the arrangement have anticompetitive consequences. If no forcing is present, patients are free to enter a competing hospital and to use another anesthesiologist instead of Roux.[89] The fact

curiam). While this statement was specifically made with respect to § 3 of the Clayton Act, 15 U.S.C. § 14, its analysis is also applicable to § 1 of the Sherman Act, since with respect to the definition of tying the standards used by the two statutes are the same. See Times–Picayune, 345 U.S., at 608–609.

"There are several facts presented in this record which tend to show that a community television antenna system cannot properly be characterized as a single product. Others who entered the community antenna field offered all the equipment necessary for a complete system, but none of them sold their gear exclusively as a single package as did Jerrold. The record also establishes that the number of pieces in each system varied considerably so that hardly any two versions of the alleged product were the same. Furthermore, the customer was charged for each item of equipment and not a lump sum for total payment. Finally, while Jerrold had cable and antennas to sell which were manufactured by other concerns, it required that the electronic equipment in the system be bought from it." 187 F.Supp., at 559.

The record here shows that other hospitals often permit anesthesiological services to be purchased separately, that anesthesiologists are not fungible in that the services provided by each are not precisely the same, that anesthesiological services are billed separately, and that the hospital required purchases from Roux even though other anesthesiologists were available and Roux had no objection to their receiving staff privileges at East Jefferson. Therefore, the *Jerrold* analysis indicates that there was a tying arrangement here. *Jerrold* also indicates that tying may be permissible when necessary to enable a new business to break into the market. See

id., at 555–558. Assuming this defense exists, and assuming it justified the 1971 Roux contract in order to give Roux an incentive to go to work at a new hospital with an uncertain future, that justification is inapplicable to the 1976 contract, since by then Roux was willing to continue to service the hospital without a tying arrangement.

88. This is not to say that § 1 of the Sherman Act gives a purchaser the right to buy a product that the seller does not wish to offer for sale. A grocer may decide to carry four brands of cookies and no more. If the customer wants a fifth brand, he may go elsewhere but he cannot sue the grocer even if there is no other in town. However, in such a case the customer is free to purchase no cookies at all, while buying other needed food. If the grocer required the customer to buy an unwanted brand of cookies in order to buy other items which the customer needs and cannot readily obtain elsewhere, then a tying question arises. Cf. Northern Pac. R. Co. v. United States, 356 U.S. 1, 7 (1958) (grocer selling flour can require customers to also buy sugar only "if its competitors were ready and able to sell flour by itself"). Here, the question is whether patients are forced to use an unwanted anesthesiologist in order to obtain needed hospital services.

89. An examination of the reason or reasons why petitioners denied respondent staff privileges will not provide the answer to the question whether the package of services they offered to their patients is an illegal tying arrangement. As a matter of antitrust law, petitioners may give their anesthesiology business to Roux because he is the best doctor available, because he is willing to work long hours, or because he is the son-in-law of the hospital administrator without violating the *per se* rule against tying. Without evidence that petitioners are using market pow-

that petitioners' patients are required to purchase two separate items is only the beginning of the appropriate inquiry.[90]

IV

The question remains whether this arrangement involves the use of market power to force patients to buy services they would not otherwise purchase. Respondent's only basis for invoking the *per se* rule against tying and thereby avoiding analysis of actual market conditions is by relying on the preference of persons residing in Jefferson Parish to go to East Jefferson, the closest hospital. A preference of this kind, however, is not necessarily probative of significant market power.

Seventy per cent of the patients residing in Jefferson Parish enter hospitals other than East Jefferson. 513 F.Supp., at 539. Thus East Jefferson's "dominance" over persons residing in Jefferson Parish is far from overwhelming.[91] The fact that a substantial majority of the parish's residents elect not to enter East Jefferson means that the geographic data does not establish the kind of dominant market position that obviates the need for further inquiry into actual competitive conditions. The Court of Appeals acknowledged as much; it recognized that East Jefferson's market share alone was insufficient as a basis to infer market power, and buttressed its conclusion by relying on "market imperfections" that permit petitioners to charge noncompetitive prices for hospital services: the preva-

---

er to force Roux upon patients there is no basis to view the arrangement as unreasonably restraining competition whatever the reasons for its creation. Conversely, with such evidence, the *per se* rule against tying may apply. Thus, we reject the view of the District Court that the legality of an arrangement of this kind turns on whether it was adopted for the purpose of improving patient care.

90. Petitioners argue and the District Court found that the exclusive contract had what it characterized as procompetitive justifications in that an exclusive contract ensures 24–hour anesthesiology coverage, enables flexible scheduling, and facilitates work routine, professional standards and maintenance of equipment. The Court of Appeals held these findings to be clearly erroneous since the exclusive contract was not necessary to achieve these ends. Roux was willing to provide 24–hour coverage even without an exclusive contract and the credentials committee of the hospital could impose standards for staff privileges that would ensure staff would comply with the demands of scheduling, maintenance, and professional standards. 686 F.2d, at 292. In the past, we have refused to tolerate manifestly anticompetitive conduct

simply because the health care industry is involved. See Arizona v. Maricopa Medical Society, 457 U.S. 332, 348–351 (1982); National Gerimedical Hospital v. Blue Cross, 452 U.S. 378 (1981); American Medical Assn. v. United States, 317 U.S. 519, 528–529 (1943). Petitioners seek no special solicitude. We have also uniformly rejected similar "goodwill" defenses for tying arrangements, finding that the use of contractual quality specifications are generally sufficient to protect quality without the use of a tying arrangement.... Since the District Court made no finding as to why contractual quality specifications would not protect the hospital, there is no basis for departing from our prior cases here.

91. In fact its position in this market is not dissimilar from the market share at issue in *Times-Picayune*, which the Court found insufficient as a basis for inferring market power. See 345 U.S., at 611–613. Moreover, in other antitrust contexts this Court has found that market shares comparable to that present here do not create an unacceptable likelihood of anticompetitive conduct. See United States v. Connecticut National Bank, 418 U.S. 656 (1974); United States v. Du Pont & Co., 351 U.S. 377 (1956).

lence of third party payment for health care costs reduces price competition, and a lack of adequate information renders consumers unable to evaluate the quality of the medical care provided by competing hospitals. 686 F.2d, at 290. While these factors may generate "market power" in some abstract sense,[92] they do not generate the kind of market power that justifies condemnation of tying.

Tying arrangements need only be condemned if they restrain competition on the merits by forcing purchases that would not otherwise be made. A lack of price or quality competition does not create this type of forcing. If consumers lack price consciousness, that fact will not force them to take an anesthesiologist whose services they do not want—their indifference to price will have no impact on their willingness or ability to go to another hospital where they can utilize the services of the anesthesiologist of their choice. Similarly, if consumers cannot evaluate the quality of anesthesiological services, it follows that they are indifferent between certified anesthesiologists even in the absence of a tying arrangement—such an arrangement cannot be said to have foreclosed a choice that would have otherwise been made "on the merits."

Thus, neither of the "market imperfections" relied upon by the Court of Appeals forces consumers to take anesthesiological services they would not select in the absence of a tie. It is safe to assume that every patient undergoing a surgical operation needs the services of an anesthesiologist; at least this record contains no evidence that the hospital "forced" any such services on unwilling patients.[93] The record therefore does not provide a basis for applying the *per se* rule against tying to this arrangement.

92. As an economic matter, market power exists whenever prices can be raised above the levels that would be charged in a competitive market. See *Fortner II*, 429 U.S., at 620; *Fortner I*, 394 U.S., at 503–504.

93. Nor is there an indication in the record that respondents' practices have increased the social costs of its market power. Since patients' anesthesiological needs are fixed by medical judgment, respondent does not argue that the tying arrangement facilitates price discrimination. Where variable-quantity purchasing is unavailable as a means to enable price discrimination, commentators have seen less justification for condemning tying. See Dam, supra, at 15–17; Turner, supra, at 67–72. While tying arrangements like the one at issue here are unlikely to be used to facilitate price discrimination, they could have the similar effect of enabling hospitals "to evade price control in the tying product through clandestine transfer of the profit to the tied product...." *Fortner I*, 394 U.S., at 513 (White, J., dissenting). Insurance companies are the principal source of price restraint in the hospital industry; they place

some limitations on the ability of hospitals to exploit their market power. Through this arrangement, petitioners may be able to evade the restraint by obtaining a portion of the anesthesiologists' fees and therefore realize a greater return than they could in the absence of the arrangement. This could also have an adverse effect on the anesthesiology market since it is possible that only less able anesthesiologists would be willing to give up part of their fees in return for the security of an exclusive contract. However, there are no findings of either the District Court or the Court of Appeals which indicate that this type of exploitation of market power has occurred here. The Court of Appeals found only that Roux's use of nurse anesthetists increased its and the hospital's profits, but there was no finding that nurse anesthetists might not be used with equal frequency absent the exclusive contract. Indeed, the District Court found that nurse anesthetists are utilized in all hospitals in the area. 513 F.Supp., at 537, 543. Moreover, there is nothing in the record which details whether this arrangement has enhanced the value of East

V

In order to prevail in the absence of *per se* liability, respondent has the burden of proving that the Roux contract violated the Sherman Act because it unreasonably restrained competition. That burden necessarily involves an inquiry into the actual effect of the exclusive contract on competition among anesthesiologists. This competition takes place in offering services to patients; it may encompass competition among anesthesiologists for exclusive contracts such as the Roux contract and might be statewide or merely local.[94] There is, however, insufficient evidence in this record to provide a basis for finding that the Roux contract, as it actually operates in the market, has unreasonably restrained competition. The record sheds little light on how this arrangement affected consumer demand for separate arrangements with a specific anesthesiologist. The evidence indicates that some surgeons and patients preferred respondent's services to those of Roux, but there is no evidence that any patient who was sophisticated enough to know the difference between two anesthesiologists was not also able to go to a hospital that would provide him with the anesthesiologist of his choice.[95]

In sum, all that the record establishes is that the choice of anesthesiologists at East Jefferson has been limited to one of the four doctors who are associated with Roux and therefore have staff privileges.[96] Even if Roux did not have an exclusive contract, the range of alternatives open to the patient would be severely limited by the nature of the transaction and the hospital's unquestioned right to exercise some control over the identity and the number of doctors to whom it accords staff privileges. If respondent is admitted to the staff of East Jefferson, the range of choice will be enlarged from four to five doctors, but the most significant restraints on the patient's freedom to select a specific anesthesiologist will nevertheless

Jefferson's market power or harmed quality competition in the anesthesiology market.

94. While there was some rather impressionistic testimony that the prevalence of exclusive contracts tended to discourage young doctors from entering the market, the evidence was equivocal and neither the District Court nor the Court of Appeals made any findings concerning the contract's effect on entry barriers. Respondent does not press the point before this Court. It is possible that under some circumstances an exclusive contract could raise entry barriers since anesthesiologists could not compete for the contract without raising the capital necessary to run a hospital-wide operation. However, since the hospital has provided most of the capital for the exclusive contractor in this case, that problem does not appear to be present.

95. If, as is likely, it is the patient's doctor and not the patient who selects an anesthesiologist, the doctor can simply take the patient elsewhere if he is dissatisfied with Roux. The District Court found that most doctors in the area have staff privileges at more than one hospital. 513 F.Supp., at 541.

96. The effect of the contract has, of course, been to remove the East Jefferson Hospital from the market open to Roux's competitors. Like any exclusive requirements contract, this contract could be unlawful if it foreclosed so much of the market from penetration by Roux's competitors as to unreasonably restrain competition in the affected market, the market for anesthesiological services. See generally Tampa Electric Co. v. Nashville Coal Co., 365 U.S. 320 (1961); United States v. Standard Oil Co., 337 U.S. 293 (1949). However, respondent has not attempted to make this showing.

remain.[97] Without a showing of actual adverse effect on competition, respondent cannot make out a case under the antitrust laws, and no such showing has been made.

VI

Petitioners' closed policy may raise questions of medical ethics, and may have inconvenienced some patients who would prefer to have their anesthesia administered by someone other than a member of Roux & Associates, but it does not have the obviously unreasonable impact on purchasers that has characterized the tying arrangements that this Court has branded unlawful. There is no evidence that the price, the quality, or the supply or demand for either the "tying product" or the "tied product" involved in this case has been adversely affected by the exclusive contract between Roux and the hospital. It may well be true that the contract made it necessary for Dr. Hyde and others to practice elsewhere, rather than at East Jefferson. But there has been no showing that the market as a whole has been affected at all by the contract. Indeed, as we previously noted, the record tells us very little about the market for the services of anesthesiologists. Yet that is the market in which the exclusive contract has had its principal impact. There is simply no showing here of the kind of restraint on competition that is prohibited by the Sherman Act. Accordingly, the judgment of the Court of Appeals is reversed and the case is remanded to that court for further proceedings consistent with this opinion.

■ Brennan, J., with whom Marshall, J., joins, concurring. As the opinion for the Court demonstrates, we have long held that tying arrangements are subject to evaluation for *per se* illegality under § 1 of the Sherman Act. Whatever merit the policy arguments against this longstanding construction of the Act might have, Congress, presumably aware of our decision, has never changed the rule by amending the Act. In such circumstances, our practice usually has been to stand by a settled statutory interpretation and leave the task of modifying the statute's reach to Congress.... I see no reason to depart from the principle in this case and therefore join the opinion and judgment of the Court.

■ O'Connor, J., with whom Burger, J., Powell, J., and Rehnquist, J., join, concurring in the judgment.... Under the usual logic of the *per se* rule, a restraint on trade that rarely serves any purposes other than to restrain competition is illegal without proof of market power or anticompetitive effect.... Some of our earlier cases did indeed declare that tying arrangements serve "hardly any purpose beyond the suppression of competition."

---

97. The record simply tells us little if anything about the effect of this arrangement on price or quality of anesthesiological services. As to price, the arrangement did not lead to an increase in the price charged to the patient. 686 F.2d, at 291. As to quality, the record indicates little more than that there have never been any complaints about the quality of Roux's services, and no contention that his services are in any respect inferior to those of respondent. Moreover, the self interest of the hospital, as well as the ethical and professional norms under which it operates, presumably protects the quality of anesthesiological services. See Joint Commission on Accreditation of Hospitals, Accreditation Manual for Hospitals 3–10, 151–154 (1983).

Standard Oil Co. of California v. United States, 337 U.S. 293, 305–306 (1949) (dictum). However, this declaration was not taken literally even by the cases that purported to rely upon it. In practice, a tie has been illegal only if the seller is shown to have "sufficient economic power with respect to the tying product to appreciably restrain free competition in the market for the tied product...." *Northern Pacific R.* Co., supra. Without "control or dominance over the tying product" the seller could not use the tying product as "an effectual weapon to pressure buyers into taking the tied item," so that any restraint of trade would be "insignificant." Ibid. The Court has never been willing to say of tying arrangements, as it has of price-fixing, division of markets and other agreements subject to *per se* analysis, that they are always illegal, without proof of market power or anticompetitive effect.

The "per se" doctrine in tying cases has thus always required an elaborate inquiry into the economic effects of the tying arrangement.[98] As a result, tying doctrine incurs the costs of a rule of reason approach without achieving its benefits: the doctrine calls for the extensive and time-consuming economic analysis characteristic of the rule of reason, but then may be interpreted to prohibit arrangements that economic analysis would show to be beneficial. Moreover, the *per se* label in the tying context has generated more confusion than coherent law because it appears to invite lower courts to omit the analysis of economic circumstances of the tie that has always been a necessary element of tying analysis.

The time has therefore come to abandon the "per se" label and refocus the inquiry on the adverse economic effects, and the potential economic benefits, that the tie may have. The law of tie-ins will thus be brought into accord with the law applicable to all other allegedly anticompetitive economic arrangements, except those few horizontal or quasi-horizontal restraints that can be said to have no economic justification whatsoever.[99] This change will rationalize rather than abandon tie-in doctrine as it is already applied.

Our prior opinions indicate that the purpose of tying law has been to identify and control those tie-ins that have a demonstrably exclusionary impact in the tied product market, see Times–Picayune Publishing Co. v.

---

98. This inquiry has been required in analyzing both the prima facie case and affirmative defenses. Most notably, United States v. Jerrold Electronics Corp., 187 F.Supp. 545, 599–560 (E.D.Pa.1960), affirmed per curiam 365 U.S. 567 (1961), upheld a requirement that buyers of television systems purchase the complete system, as well as installation and repair service, on the grounds that the tie assured that the systems would operate and thereby protected the seller's business reputation.

99. Tying law is particularly anomalous in this respect because arrangements largely indistinguishable from tie-ins are generally analyzed under the rule of reason. For example, the "per se" analysis of tie-ins subjects restrictions on a franchisee's freedom to purchase supplies to a more searching scrutiny than restrictions on his freedom to sell his products. *Compare, e.g.,* Siegel v. Chicken Delight, Inc., 448 F.2d 43 (C.A.9 1971), cert. denied, 405 U.S. 955 (1972), with Continental T.V., Inc. v. GTE Sylvania Inc., 433 U.S. 36 (1977). And exclusive contracts, that, like tie-ins, require the buyer to purchase a product from one seller, are subject only to the rule of reason.

United States, 345 U.S. 594, 605 (1953), or that abet the harmful exercise of market power that the seller possesses in the tying product market. Under the rule of reason tying arrangements should be disapproved only in such instances.

Market power in the tying product may be acquired legitimately (*e.g.*, through the grant of a patent) or illegitimately (*e.g.*, as a result of unlawful monopolization). In either event, exploitation of consumers in the market for the tying product is a possibility that exists and that may be regulated under § 2 of the Sherman Act without reference to any tying arrangements that the seller may have developed. The existence of a tied product normally does not increase the profit that the seller with market power can extract from sales of the *tying* product. A seller with a monopoly on flour, for example, cannot increase the profit it can extract from flour consumers simply by forcing them to buy sugar along with their flour. Counterintuitive though that assertion may seem, it is easily demonstrated and widely accepted. *See, e.g.,* R. Bork, The Antitrust Paradox 372–374 (1978); P. Areeda, Antitrust Analysis 735 (3d ed. 1981).

Tying may be economically harmful primarily in the rare cases where power in the market for the tying product is used to create *additional* market power in the market for the *tied* product.[1] The antitrust law is properly concerned with tying when, for example, the flour monopolist threatens to use its market power to acquire additional power in the sugar market, perhaps by driving out competing sellers of sugar, or by making it more difficult for new sellers to enter the sugar market....

These three conditions—market power in the tying product, a substantial threat of market power in the tied product, and a coherent economic basis for treating the products as distinct—are only threshold requirements. Under the Rule of Reason a tie-in may prove acceptable even when all three are met. Tie-ins may entail economic benefits as well as economic harms, and if the threshold requirements are met these benefits should enter the Rule of Reason balance.

"Tie-ins ... may facilitate new entry into fields where established sellers have wedded their customers to them by ties of habit and

---

1. Tying might be undesirable in two other instances, but the Hospital–Roux arrangement involves neither one.

In a regulated industry a firm with market power may be unable to extract a supercompetitive profit because it lacks control over the prices it charges for regulated products or services. Tying may then be used to extract that profit from sale of the unregulated, tied products or services. See Fortner Enterprises, Inc. v. United States Steel Corp., 394 U.S. 495, 513 (1969) (White, J., dissenting).

Tying may also help the seller engage in price discrimination by "metering" the buy-er's use of the tying product.... Price discrimination may be independently unlawful, see 15 U.S.C. § 13. Price discrimination may, however, *decrease* rather than increase the economic costs of a seller's market power.... [*Fortner II*] did not hold that price discrimination in the form of a tie-in is always economically harmful; that case indicated only that price discrimination may indicate market power in the tying product market. But there is no need in this case to address the problem of price discrimination facilitated by tying. The discussion herein is aimed only at tying arrangements as to which no price discrimination is alleged.

custom. Brown Shoe Co. v. United States, 370 U.S. 294, 330 (1962).... They may permit clandestine price cutting in products which otherwise would have no price competition at all because of fear of retaliation from the few other producers dealing in the market. They may protect the reputation of the tying product if failure to use the tied product in conjunction with it may cause it to misfunction: [citing Pick Mfg. Co. v. General Motors Corp., 80 F.2d 641 (C.A.7 1935), affirmed 299 U.S. 3 (1936)].... And, if the tied and tying products are functionally related, they may reduce costs through economies of joint production and distribution." *Fortner I*, 394 U.S., at 514 n. 9 (WHITE, J., dissenting).

The ultimate decision whether a tie-in is illegal under the antitrust laws should depend upon the demonstrated economic effects of the challenged agreement. It may, for example, be entirely innocuous that the seller exploits its control over the tying product to "force" the buyer to purchase the tied product. For when the seller exerts market power only in the tying product market, it makes no difference to him or his customers whether he exploits that power by raising the price of the tying product or by "forcing" customers to buy a tied product.... On the other hand, tying may make the provision of packages of goods and services more efficient. A tie-in should be condemned only when its anticompetitive impact outweighs its contribution to efficiency.

Application of these criteria to the case at hand is straightforward.

Although the issue is in doubt, we may assume that the Hospital does have market power in the provision of hospital services in its area....

Second, in light of the Hospital's presumed market power, we may also assume that there is a substantial threat that East Jefferson will acquire market power over the provision of anesthesiological services in its market. By tying the sale of anesthesia to the sale of other hospital services the Hospital can drive out other sellers of those services who might otherwise operate in the local market. The Hospital may thus gain local market power in the provision of anesthesiology: anesthesiological services offered in the Hospital's market, narrowly defined, will be purchased only from Roux, under the Hospital's auspices.

But the third threshold condition for giving closer scrutiny to a tying arrangement is not satisfied here: there is no sound economic reason for treating surgery and anesthesia as separate services. Patients are interested in purchasing anesthesia only in conjunction with hospital services, so the Hospital can acquire no *additional* market power by selling the two services together. Accordingly, the link between the Hospital's services and anesthesia administered by Roux will affect neither the amount of anesthesia provided nor the combined price of anesthesia and surgery for those who choose to become the Hospital's patients. In these circumstances, anesthesia and surgical services should probably not be characterized as distinct products for tying purposes.

Even if they are, the tying should not be considered a violation of § 1 of the Sherman Act because tying here cannot increase the seller's already absolute power over the volume of production of the tied product, which is an inevitable consequence of the fact that very few patients will choose to undergo surgery without receiving anesthesia. The Hospital–Roux contract therefore has little potential to harm the patients. On the other side of the balance, the District Court found, and the Court of Appeals did not dispute, that the tie-in conferred significant benefits upon the hospital and the patients that it served.

The tie-in improves patient care and permits more efficient hospital operation in a number of ways. From the viewpoint of hospital management, the tie-in ensures 24 hour anesthesiology coverage, aids in standardization of procedures and efficient use of equipment, facilitates flexible scheduling of operations, and permits the hospital more effectively to monitor the quality of anesthesiological services. Further, the tying arrangement is advantageous to patients because, as the District Court found, the closed anesthesiology department places upon the hospital, rather than the individual patient, responsibility to select the physician who is to provide anesthesiological services. The hospital also assumes the responsibility that the anesthesiologist will be available, will be acceptable to the surgeon, and will provide suitable care to the patient. In assuming these responsibilities—responsibilities that a seriously ill patient frequently may be unable to discharge—the hospital provides a valuable service to its patients. And there is no indication that patients were dissatisfied with the quality of anesthesiology that was provided at the hospital or that patients wished to enjoy the services of anesthesiologists other than those that the hospital employed. Given this evidence of the advantages and effectiveness of the closed anesthesiology department, it is not surprising that, as the District Court found, such arrangements are accepted practice in the majority of hospitals of New Orleans and in the health care industry generally. Such an arrangement, that has little anti-competitive effect and achieves substantial benefits in the provision of care to patients, is hardly one that the antitrust law should condemn. This conclusion reaffirms our threshold determination that the joint provision of hospital services and anesthesiology should not be viewed as involving a tie between distinct products, and therefore should require no additional scrutiny under the antitrust law.

Whether or not the Hospital–Roux contract is characterized as a tie between distinct products, the contract unquestionably does constitute exclusive dealing.... The Hospital–Roux arrangement could conceivably have an adverse effect on horizontal competition among anesthesiologists, or among hospitals. Dr. Hyde, who competes with the Roux anesthesiologists, and other hospitals in the area, who compete with East Jefferson, may have grounds to complain that the exclusive contract stifles horizontal competition and therefore has an adverse, albeit indirect, impact on consumer welfare even if it is not a tie....

At issue here is an exclusive dealing arrangement between a firm of four anesthesiologists and one relatively small hospital. There is no suggestion that East Jefferson Hospital is likely to create a "bottleneck" in the availability of anesthesiologists that might deprive other hospitals of access to needed anesthesiological services, or that the Roux associates have unreasonably narrowed the range of choices available to other anesthesiologists in search of a hospital or patients that will buy their services. Contrast Associated Press v. United States, 326 U.S. 1 (1945). A firm of four anesthesiologists represents only a very small fraction of the total number of anesthesiologists whose services are available for hire by other hospitals, and East Jefferson is one among numerous hospitals buying such services. Even without engaging in a detailed analysis of the size of the relevant markets we may readily conclude that there is no likelihood that the exclusive dealing arrangement challenged here will either unreasonably enhance the Hospital's market position relative to other hospitals, or unreasonably permit Roux to acquire power relative to other anesthesiologists. Accordingly, this exclusive dealing arrangement must be sustained under the Rule of Reason. . . .

Eastman Kodak Co. v. Image Technical Services, Inc.

Supreme Court of the United States, 1992.
504 U.S. 451, 112 S.Ct. 2072, 119 L.Ed.2d 265.

■ BLACKMUN, J. This is yet another case that concerns the standard for summary judgment in an antitrust controversy. The principal issue here is whether a defendant's lack of market power in the primary equipment market precludes—as a matter of law—the possibility of market power in derivative aftermarkets.

Petitioner Eastman Kodak Company manufactures and sells photocopiers and micrographic equipment. Kodak also sells service and replacement parts for its equipment. Respondents are 18 independent service organizations (ISOs) that in the early 1980s began servicing Kodak copying and micrographic equipment. Kodak subsequently adopted policies to limit the availability of parts to ISOs and to make it more difficult for ISOs to compete with Kodak in servicing Kodak equipment.

Respondents instituted this action in the United States District Court for the Northern District of California alleging that Kodak's policies were unlawful under both 1 and 2 of the Sherman Act. After truncated discovery, the District Court granted summary judgment for Kodak. The Court of Appeals for the Ninth Circuit reversed. The appellate court found that respondents had presented sufficient evidence to raise a genuine issue concerning Kodak's market power in the service and parts markets. It rejected Kodak's contention that lack of market power in service and parts must be assumed when such power is absent in the equipment market. Because of the importance of the issue, we granted certiorari.

I

A

Because this case comes to us on petitioner Kodak's motion for summary judgment, "the evidence of [respondents] is to be believed, and all justifiable inferences are to be drawn in [their] favor...." Kodak manufactures and sells complex business machines—as relevant here, high-volume photocopier and micrographic equipments.[2] Kodak equipment is unique; micrographic software programs that operate on Kodak machines, for example, are not compatible with competitors' machines. Kodak parts are not compatible with other manufacturers' equipment, and vice versa. Kodak equipment, although expensive when new, has little resale value.

Kodak provides service and parts for its machines to its customers. It produces some of the parts itself; the rest are made to order for Kodak by independent original-equipment manufacturers (OEMs). Kodak does not sell a complete system of original equipment, lifetime service, and lifetime parts for a single price. Instead, Kodak provides service after the initial warranty period either through annual service contracts, which include all necessary parts, or on a per-call basis. It charges, through negotiations and bidding, different prices for equipment, service, and parts for different customers. Kodak provides 80% to 95% of the service for Kodak machines.

Beginning in the early 1980s, ISOs began repairing and servicing Kodak equipment. They also sold parts and reconditioned and sold used Kodak equipment. Their customers were federal, state, and local government agencies, banks, insurance companies, industrial enterprises, and providers of specialized copy and microfilming services. ISOs provide service at a price substantially lower than Kodak does. Some customers found that the ISO service was of higher quality.

Some of the ISOs' customers purchase their own parts and hire ISOs only for service. Others choose ISOs to supply both service and parts. ISOs keep an inventory of parts, purchased from Kodak or other sources, primarily the OEMs.[3]

In 1985 and 1986, Kodak implemented a policy of selling replacement parts for micrographic and copying machines only to buyers of Kodak equipment who use Kodak service or repair their own machines. As part of the same policy, Kodak sought to limit ISO access to other sources of Kodak parts. Kodak and the OEMs agreed that the OEMs would not sell

2. Kodak's micrographic equipment includes four different product areas. The first is capture products such as microfilmers and electronic scanners, which compact an image and capture it on microfilm. The second is equipment such as microfilm viewers and viewer/printers. This equipment is used to retrieve the images. The third is Computer Output Microform (COM) recorders, which are data-processing peripherals that record computer-generated data onto microfilm. The fourth is Computer Assisted Retrieval (CAR) systems, which utilize computers to locate and retrieve micrographic images.

3. In addition to the OEMs, other sources of Kodak parts include (1) brokers who would buy parts from Kodak, or strip used Kodak equipment to obtain the useful parts and resell them, (2) customers who buy parts from Kodak and make them available to ISOs, and (3) used equipment to be stripped for parts.

parts that fit Kodak equipment to anyone other than Kodak. Kodak also pressured Kodak equipment owners and independent parts distributors not to sell Kodak parts to ISOs. In addition, Kodak took steps to restrict the availability of used machines.

Kodak intended, through these policies, to make it more difficult for ISOs to sell service for Kodak machines. It succeeded. ISOs were unable to obtain parts from reliable sources, and many were forced out of business, while others lost substantial revenue. Customers were forced to switch to Kodak service even though they preferred ISO service.

B

In 1987, the ISOs filed the present action in the District Court, alleging, *inter alia*, that Kodak had unlawfully tied the sale of service for Kodak machines to the sale of parts, in violation of § 1 of the Sherman Act, and had unlawfully monopolized and attempted to monopolize the sale of service for Kodak machines, in violation of § 2 of that Act.

Kodak filed a motion for summary judgment before respondents had initiated discovery. The District Court permitted respondents to file one set of interrogatories and one set of requests for production of documents, and to take six depositions. Without a hearing, the District Court granted summary judgment in favor of Kodak.... The Court of Appeals for the Ninth Circuit, by a divided vote, reversed. 903 F.2d 612 (1990)....

II

A tying arrangement is "an agreement by a party to sell one product but only on the condition that the buyer also purchases a different (or tied) product, or at least agrees that he will not purchase that product from any other supplier." Northern Pacific R. Co. v. United States, 356 U.S. 1, 5–6 (1958). Such an arrangement violates § 1 of the Sherman Act if the seller has "appreciable economic power" in the tying product market and if the arrangement affects a substantial volume of commerce in the tied market. Fortner Enterprises, Inc. v. United States Steel Corp., 394 U.S. 495, 503 (1969).

Kodak did not dispute that its arrangement affects a substantial volume of interstate commerce. It, however, did challenge whether its activities constituted a "tying arrangement" and whether Kodak exercised "appreciable economic power" in the tying market. We consider these issues in turn.

A

For the respondents to defeat a motion for summary judgment on their claim of a tying arrangement, a reasonable trier of fact must be able to find, first, that service and parts are two distinct products, and, second, that Kodak has tied the sale of the two products.

For service and parts to be considered two distinct products, there must be sufficient consumer demand so that it is efficient for a firm to provide service separately from parts. Jefferson Parish Hospital Dist. No. 2 v. Hyde, 466 U.S. 2, 21–22 (1984). Evidence in the record indicates that service and parts have been sold separately in the past and still are sold separately to self-service equipment owners.[4] Indeed, the development of the entire high-technology service industry is evidence of the efficiency of a separate market for service.

Kodak insists that because there is no demand for parts separate from service, there cannot be separate markets for service and parts. By that logic, we would be forced to conclude that there can never be separate markets, for example, for cameras and film, computers and software, or automobiles and tires. That is an assumption we are unwilling to make. "We have often found arrangements involving functionally linked products at least one of which is useless without the other to be prohibited tying devices." *Jefferson Parish*, 466 U.S., at 19, n. 30.

Kodak's assertion also appears to be incorrect as a factual matter. At least some consumers would purchase service without parts, because some service does not require parts, and some consumers, those who self-service for example, would purchase parts without service.[5] Enough doubt is cast on Kodak's claim of a unified market that it should be resolved by the trier of fact.

Finally, respondents have presented sufficient evidence of a tie between service and parts. The record indicates that Kodak would sell parts to third parties only if they agreed not to buy service from ISOs.[6]

B

Having found sufficient evidence of a tying arrangement, we consider the other necessary feature of an illegal tying arrangement: appreciable economic power in the tying market. Market power is the power "to force a purchaser to do something that he would not do in a competitive market." *Jefferson Parish*, 466 U.S., at 14. It has been defined as "the ability of a single seller to raise price and restrict output." *Fortner*, 394 U.S., at 503. The existence of such power ordinarily is inferred from the seller's possession of a predominant share of the market. *Jefferson Parish*, 466 U.S., at 17; United States v. Grinnell Corp., 384 U.S. 563, 571 (1966); Times–Picayune Publishing Co. v. United States, 345 U.S. 594, 611–613 (1953).

4. The Court of Appeals found: "Kodak's policy of allowing customers to purchase parts on condition that they agree to service their own machines suggests that the demand for parts can be separated from the demand for service."

5. The dissent suggests that parts and service are not separate products for tying purposes because all service may involve installation of parts. Because the record does not support this factual assertion, under the approach of both the Court and the concurrence in Jefferson Parish Hospital Dist. No. 2 v. Hyde, 466 U.S. 1 (1984), Kodak is not entitled to summary judgment on whether parts and service are distinct markets.

6. In a footnote, Kodak contends that this practice is only a unilateral refusal to deal, which does not violate the antitrust laws. Assuming, *arguendo*, that Kodak's refusal to sell parts to any company providing service can be characterized as a unilateral refusal to deal, its alleged sale of parts to third parties on condition that they buy service from Kodak is not. See 903 F.2d at 619.

1

Respondents contend that Kodak has more than sufficient power in the parts market to force unwanted purchases of the tied market service. Respondents provide evidence that certain parts are available exclusively through Kodak. Respondents also assert that Kodak has control over the availability of parts it does not manufacture. According to respondents' evidence, Kodak has prohibited independent manufacturers from selling Kodak parts to ISOs, pressured Kodak equipment owners and independent parts distributors to deny ISOs the purchase of Kodak parts, and taken steps to restrict the availability of used machines.

Respondents also allege that Kodak's control over the parts market has excluded service competition, boosted service prices, and forced unwilling consumption of Kodak service. Respondents offer evidence that consumers have switched to Kodak service even though they preferred ISO service, that Kodak service was of higher price and lower quality than the preferred ISO service, and that ISOs were driven out of business by Kodak's policies. Under our prior precedents, this evidence would be sufficient to entitle respondents to a trial on their claim of market power.

2

Kodak counters that even if it concedes monopoly share of the relevant parts market, it cannot actually exercise the necessary market power for a Sherman Act violation. This is so, according to Kodak, because competition exists in the equipment market.[7] Kodak argues that it could not have the ability to raise prices of service and parts above the level that would be charged in a competitive market because any increase in profits from a higher price in the aftermarkets at least would be offset by a corresponding loss in profits from lower equipment sales as consumers began purchasing equipment with more attractive service costs.

Kodak does not present any actual data on the equipment, service, or parts markets. Instead, it urges the adoption of a substantive legal rule that "equipment competition precludes any finding of monopoly power in derivative aftermarkets." Kodak argues that such a rule would satisfy its

---

7. In their brief and at oral argument, respondents argued that Kodak's market share figures for high-volume copy machines, computer-assisted retrieval systems, and micrographic-capture equipment demonstrate Kodak's market power in the equipment market.

In the Court of Appeals, however, respondents did not contest Kodak's assertion that its market shares indicated a competitive equipment market. The Court of Appeals believed that respondents "do not dispute Kodak's assertion that it lacks market power in the [equipment] markets." 903 F.2d, at 616, n. 3. Nor did respondents question Kodak's asserted lack of market power in their Brief in Opposition to the Petition for Certiorari, although they acknowledged that Kodak's entire case rested on its understanding that respondents were not disputing the existence of competition in the equipment market.... Because respondents failed to bring their objections to the premise underlying the questions presented to our attention in their opposition to the petition for certiorari, we decide those questions based on the same premise as the Court of Appeals, namely, that competition exists in the equipment market.

burden as the moving party of showing "that there is no genuine issue as to any material fact" on the market power issue.[8]

Legal presumptions that rest on formalistic distinctions rather than actual market realities are generally disfavored in antitrust law. This Court has preferred to resolve antitrust claims on a case-by-case basis, focusing on the "particular facts disclosed by the record." In determining the existence of market power, and specifically the "responsiveness of the sales of one product to price changes of the other," *du Pont*, 351 U.S., at 400, this Court has examined closely the economic reality of the market at issue.[9]

Kodak contends that there is no need to examine the facts when the issue is market power in the aftermarkets. A legal presumption against a finding of market power is warranted in this situation, according to Kodak, because the existence of market power in the service and parts markets absent power in the equipment market "simply makes no economic sense," and the absence of a legal presumption would deter procompetitive behavior.

Kodak analogizes this case to *Matsushita* where a group of American corporations that manufactured or sold consumer electronic products alleged that their 21 Japanese counterparts were engaging in a 20–year conspiracy to price below cost in the United States in the hope of expanding their market share sometime in the future. After several years of detailed discovery, the defendants moved for summary judgment. Because the defendants had every incentive not to engage in the alleged conduct which required them to sustain losses for decades with no foreseeable profits, the Court found an "absence of any rational motive to conspire." In that context, the Court determined that the plaintiffs' theory of predatory pricing makes no practical sense, was "speculative" and was not "reasonable." Accordingly, the Court held that a reasonable jury could not return a verdict for the plaintiffs and that summary judgment would be appropriate against them unless they came forward with more persuasive evidence to support their theory.

The Court's requirement in *Matsushita* that the plaintiffs' claims make economic sense did not introduce a special burden on plaintiffs facing summary judgment in antitrust cases. The Court did not hold that if the moving party enunciates any economic theory supporting its behavior, regardless of its accuracy in reflecting the actual market, it is entitled to summary judgment. *Matsushita* demands only that the nonmoving party's inferences be reasonable in order to reach the jury, a requirement that was

---

8. Kodak argues that such a rule would be *per se*, with no opportunity for respondents to rebut the conclusion that market power is lacking in the parts market....

9. *See, e.g., Jefferson Parish*, 466 U.S., at 26–29; United States v. Connecticut National Bank, 418 U.S. 656, 661–666 (1974); United States v. Grinnell Corp., 384 U.S.

563, 571–576 (1966); International Boxing Club of New York, Inc. v. United States, 358 U.S. 242, 250–251 (1959); see also *Jefferson Parish*, 466 U.S., at 37, n. 6 (O'Connor, J., concurring) (citing cases and describing the careful consideration the Court gives to the particular facts when determining market power).

not invented, but merely articulated, in that decision. If the plaintiff's theory is economically senseless, no reasonable jury could find in its favor, and summary judgment should be granted.

Kodak, then, bears a substantial burden in showing that it is entitled to summary judgment. It must show that despite evidence of increased prices and excluded competition, an inference of market power is unreasonable. To determine whether Kodak has met that burden, we must unravel the factual assumptions underlying its proposed rule that lack of power in the equipment market necessarily precludes power in the aftermarkets.

The extent to which one market prevents exploitation of another market depends on the extent to which consumers will change their consumption of one product in response to a price change in another, *i.e.*, the "cross-elasticity of demand." See *du Pont*, 351 U.S., at 400; P. Areeda & L. Kaplow, Antitrust Analysis 342(c) (4th ed. 1988).[10] Kodak's proposed rule rests on a factual assumption about the cross-elasticity of demand in the equipment and aftermarkets: "If Kodak raised its parts or service prices above competitive levels, potential customers would simply stop buying Kodak equipment. Perhaps Kodak would be able to increase short term profits through such a strategy, but at a devastating cost to its long term interests."[11] Kodak argues that the Court should accept, as a matter of law, this "basic economic realit[y]" that competition in the equipment market necessarily prevents market power in the aftermarkets.[12]

Even if Kodak could not raise the price of service and parts one cent without losing equipment sales, that fact would not disprove market power in the aftermarkets. The sales of even a monopolist are reduced when it sells goods at a monopoly price, but the higher price more than compensates for the loss in sales. Areeda & Kaplow, at ¶¶ 112 and 340(a). Kodak's claim that charging more for service and parts would be a "short-run

10. Courts usually have considered the relationship between price in one market and demand in another in defining the relevant market. Because market power is often inferred from market share, market definition generally determines the result of the case. Pitofsky, New Definitions of Relevant Market and the Assault on Antitrust, 90 Colum.L.Rev. 1805, 1806–1813 (1990). Kodak chose to focus on market power directly rather than arguing that the relationship between equipment and service and parts is such that the three should be included in the same market definition. Whether considered in the conceptual category of "market definition" or "market power," the ultimate inquiry is the same—whether competition in the equipment market will significantly restrain power in the service and parts markets.

11. The United States as Amicus Curiae in support of Kodak echoes this argument:

"The ISOs' claims are implausible because Kodak lacks market power in the markets for its copier and micrographic equipment. Buyers of such equipment regard an increase in the price of parts or service as an increase in the price of the equipment, and sellers recognize that the revenues from sales of parts and service are attributable to sales of the equipment. In such circumstances, it is not apparent how an equipment manufacturer such as Kodak could exercise power in the aftermarkets for parts and service."

12. It is clearly true, as the United States claims, that Kodak "cannot set service or parts prices without regard to the impact on the market for equipment." The fact that the cross-elasticity of demand is not zero proves nothing; the disputed issue is how much of an impact an increase in parts and service prices has on equipment sales and on Kodak's profits.

game'' is based on the false dichotomy that there are only two prices that can be charged—a competitive price or a ruinous one. But there could easily be a middle, optimum price at which the increased revenues from the higher-priced sales of service and parts would more than compensate for the lower revenues from lost equipment sales. The fact that the equipment market imposes a restraint on prices in the aftermarkets by no means disproves the existence of power in those markets. See Areeda & Kaplow, at ¶ 340(b) (''[T]he existence of significant substitution in the event of *further* price increases or even at the *current* price does not tell us whether the defendant *already* exercises significant market power'') (emphasis in original). Thus, contrary to Kodak's assertion, there is no immutable physical law—no ''basic economic reality''—insisting that competition in the equipment market cannot coexist with market power in the aftermarkets.

We next consider the more narrowly drawn question: Does Kodak's theory describe actual market behavior so accurately that respondents' assertion of Kodak market power in the aftermarkets, if not impossible, is at least unreasonable?[13]

To review Kodak's theory, it contends that higher service prices will lead to a disastrous drop in equipment sales. Presumably, the theory's corollary is to the effect that low service prices lead to a dramatic increase in equipment sales. According to the theory, one would have expected Kodak to take advantage of lower-priced ISO service as an opportunity to expand equipment sales. Instead, Kodak adopted a restrictive sales policy consciously designed to eliminate the lower-priced ISO service, an act that would be expected to devastate either Kodak's equipment sales or Kodak's faith in its theory. Yet, according to the record, it has done neither. Service prices have risen for Kodak customers, but there is no evidence or assertion that Kodak equipment sales have dropped.

Kodak and the United States attempt to reconcile Kodak's theory with the contrary actual results by describing a ''marketing strategy of spreading over time the total cost to the buyer of Kodak equipment.'' In other words, Kodak could charge subcompetitive prices for equipment and make up the difference with supracompetitive prices for service, resulting in an overall competitive price. This pricing strategy would provide an explana-

13. Although Kodak repeatedly relies on *Continental T.V.* as support for its factual assertion that the equipment market will prevent exploitation of the service and parts markets, the case is inapposite. In *Continental T.V.*, the Court found that a manufacturer's policy restricting the number of retailers that were permitted to sell its product could have a procompetitive effect. See 433 U.S., at 55. The Court also noted that any negative effect of exploitation of the intrabrand market (the competition between retailers of the same product) would be checked by competition in the interbrand market (competition over the same generic product) because con- sumers would substitute a different brand of the same product. Unlike *Continental T.V.*, this case does not concern vertical relationships between parties at different levels of the same distribution chain. In the relevant market, service, Kodak and the ISOs are direct competitors; their relationship is horizontal. The interbrand competition at issue here is competition over the provision of service. Despite petitioner's best effort, repeating the mantra ''interbrand competition'' does not transform this case into one over an agreement the manufacturer has with its dealers that would fall under the rubric of *Continental T.V.*

tion for the theory's descriptive failings—if Kodak in fact had adopted it. But Kodak never has asserted that it prices its equipment or parts subcompetitively and recoups its profits through service. Instead, it claims that it prices its equipment comparably to its competitors, and intends that both its equipment sales and service divisions be profitable. Moreover, this hypothetical pricing strategy is inconsistent with Kodak's policy toward its self-service customers. If Kodak were underpricing its equipment, hoping to lock in customers and recover its losses in the service market, it could not afford to sell customers parts without service. In sum, Kodak's theory does not explain the actual market behavior revealed in the record.

Respondents offer a forceful reason why Kodak's theory, although perhaps intuitively appealing, may not accurately explain the behavior of the primary and derivative markets for complex durable goods: the existence of significant information and switching costs. These costs could create a less responsive connection between service and parts prices and equipment sales.

For the service-market price to affect equipment demand, consumers must inform themselves of the total cost of the "package"—equipment, service and parts—at the time of purchase; that is, consumers must engage in accurate lifecycle pricing.[14] Lifecycle pricing of complex, durable equipment is difficult and costly. In order to arrive at an accurate price, a consumer must acquire a substantial amount of raw data and undertake sophisticated analysis. The necessary information would include data on price, quality, and availability of products needed to operate, upgrade, or enhance the initial equipment, as well as service and repair costs, including estimates of breakdown frequency, nature of repairs, price of service and parts, length of "down-time" and losses incurred from down-time.[15]

Much of this information is difficult—some of it impossible—to acquire at the time of purchase. During the life of a product, companies may change the service and parts prices, and develop products with more advanced features, a decreased need for repair, or new warranties. In addition, the information is likely to be customer-specific: lifecycle costs will vary from customer to customer with the type of equipment, degrees of equipment use, and costs of down-time.

Kodak acknowledges the cost of information, but suggests, again without evidentiary support, that customer information needs will be satisfied by competitors in the equipment markets. It is a question of fact, however, whether competitors would provide the necessary information. A competitor in the equipment market may not have reliable information about the

---

14. See Craswell, Tying Requirements in Competitive Markets: The Consumer Protection Issues, 62 B.U.L.Rev. 661, 676 (1982); Beales, Craswell, & Salop, The Efficient Regulation of Consumer Information, 24 J.Law & Econ. 491, 509–511 (1981); *Jefferson Parish*, 466 U.S., at 15.

15. In addition, of course, in order to price accurately the equipment, a consumer would need initial purchase information such as prices, features, quality, and available warranties, for different machinery with different capabilities, and residual value information such as the longevity of product use and its potential resale or trade-in value.

lifecycle costs of complex equipment it does not service or the needs of customers it does not serve. Even if competitors had the relevant information, it is not clear that their interests would be advanced by providing such information to consumers. See 2 P. Areeda & D. Turner, Antitrust Law, ¶ 404b1 (1978).[16]

Moreover, even if consumers were capable of acquiring and processing the complex body of information, they may choose not to do so. Acquiring the information is expensive. If the costs of service are small relative to the equipment price, or if consumers are more concerned about equipment capabilities than service costs, they may not find it cost-efficient to compile the information. Similarly, some consumers, such as the Federal Government, have purchasing systems that make it difficult to consider the complete cost of the "package" at the time of purchase. State and local governments often treat service as an operating expense and equipment as a capital expense, delegating each to a different department. These governmental entities do not lifecycle price, but rather choose the lowest price in each market.

As Kodak notes, there likely will be some large-volume, sophisticated purchasers who will undertake the comparative studies and insist, in return for their patronage, that Kodak charge them competitive lifecycle prices. Kodak contends that these knowledgeable customers will hold down the package price for all other customers. There are reasons, however, to doubt that sophisticated purchasers will ensure that competitive prices are charged to unsophisticated purchasers, too. As an initial matter, if the number of sophisticated customers is relatively small, the amount of profits to be gained by supracompetitive pricing in the service market could make it profitable to let the knowledgeable consumers take their business elsewhere. More importantly, if a company is able to price-discriminate between sophisticated and unsophisticated consumers, the sophisticated will be unable to prevent the exploitation of the uninformed. A seller could easily price-discriminate by varying the equipment/parts/service package, developing different warranties, or offering price discounts on different components.

Given the potentially high cost of information and the possibility a seller may be able to price-discriminate between knowledgeable and unsophisticated consumers, it makes little sense to assume, in the absence of

---

16. To inform consumers about Kodak, the competitor must be willing to forgo the opportunity to reap supracompetitive prices in its own service and parts markets. The competitor may anticipate that charging lower service and parts prices and informing consumers about Kodak in the hopes of gaining future equipment sales will cause Kodak to lower the price on its service and parts, canceling any gains in equipment sales to the competitor and leaving both worse off. Thus, in an equipment market with relatively few sellers, competitors may find it more profitable to adopt Kodak's service and parts policy than to inform the consumers. See 2 P. Areeda & D. Turner, Antitrust Law ¶ 404b1 (1978); App. 177 (Kodak, Xerox, and IBM together have nearly 100% of relevant market). Even in a market with many sellers, any one competitor may not have sufficient incentive to inform consumers because the increased patronage attributable to the corrected consumer beliefs will be

any evidentiary support, that equipment-purchasing decisions are based on an accurate assessment of the total cost of equipment, service, and parts over the lifetime of the machine.

Indeed, respondents have presented evidence that Kodak practices price-discrimination by selling parts to customers who service their own equipment, but refusing to sell parts to customers who hire third-party service companies. Companies that have their own service staff are likely to be high-volume users, the same companies for whom it is most likely to be economically worthwhile to acquire the complex information needed for comparative lifecycle pricing.

A second factor undermining Kodak's claim that supracompetitive prices in the service market lead to ruinous losses in equipment sales is the cost to current owners of switching to a different product. See Areeda & Turner, at ¶ 519a.[17] If the cost of switching is high, consumers who already have purchased the equipment, and are thus "locked-in," will tolerate some level of service-price increases before changing equipment brands. Under this scenario, a seller profitably could maintain supracompetitive prices in the aftermarket if the switching costs were high relative to the increase in service prices, and the number of locked-in customers were high relative to the number of new purchasers.

Moreover, if the seller can price-discriminate between its locked-in customers and potential new customers, this strategy is even more likely to prove profitable. The seller could simply charge new customers below-marginal cost on the equipment and recoup the charges in service, or offer packages with lifetime warranties or long-term service agreements that are not available to locked-in customers.

Respondents have offered evidence that the heavy initial outlay for Kodak equipment, combined with the required support material that works only with Kodak equipment, makes switching costs very high for existing Kodak customers. And Kodak's own evidence confirms that it varies the package price of equipment/parts/service for different customers.

In sum, there is a question of fact whether information costs and switching costs foil the simple assumption that the equipment and service markets act as pure complements to one another.[18]

We conclude, then, that Kodak has failed to demonstrate that respondents' inference of market power in the service and parts markets is

---

17. A firm can exact leverage whenever other equipment is not a ready substitute. F.M. Scherer & D. Ross, Industrial Market Structure and Economic Performance 16–17 (3d ed. 1990).

18. The dissent disagrees based on its hypothetical case of a tie between equipment and service. "The only thing lacking" to bring this case within the hypothetical case, states the dissent, "is concrete evidence that the restrictive parts policy was ... generally known." But the dissent's "only thing lack-

ing" is the crucial thing lacking—evidence. Whether a tie between parts and service should be treated identically to a tie between equipment and service, as the dissent and Kodak argue, depends on whether the equipment market prevents the exertion of market power in the parts market. Far from being "anomalous," requiring Kodak to provide evidence on this factual question is completely consistent with our prior precedent.

unreasonable, and that, consequently, Kodak is entitled to summary judgment. It is clearly reasonable to infer that Kodak has market power to raise prices and drive out competition in the aftermarkets, since respondents offer direct evidence that Kodak did so. It is also plausible, as discussed above, to infer that Kodak chose to gain immediate profits by exerting that market power where locked-in customers, high information costs, and discriminatory pricing limited and perhaps eliminated any long-term loss. Viewing the evidence in the light most favorable to respondents, their allegations of market power "make ... economic sense." Cf. *Matsushita*, 475 U.S., at 587.

Nor are we persuaded by Kodak's contention that it is entitled to a legal presumption on the lack of market power because, as in *Matsushita*, there is a significant risk of deterring procompetitive conduct. Plaintiffs in *Matsushita* attempted to prove the antitrust conspiracy "through evidence of rebates and other price-cutting activities." Because cutting prices to increase business is "the very essence of competition," the Court was concerned that mistaken inferences would be "especially costly," and would "chill the very conduct the antitrust laws are designed to protect." *Id.*, at 594. See also Monsanto Co. v. Spray–Rite Service Corp., 465 U.S. 752, 763 (1984) (permitting inference of concerted action would "deter or penalize perfectly legitimate conduct"). But the facts in this case are just the opposite. The alleged conduct—higher service prices and market foreclosure—is facially anticompetitive and exactly the harm that antitrust laws aim to prevent. In this situation, *Matsushita* does not create any presumption in favor of summary judgment for the defendant.

Kodak contends that, despite the appearance of anticompetitiveness, its behavior actually favors competition because its ability to pursue innovative marketing plans will allow it to compete more effectively in the equipment market. A pricing strategy based on lower equipment prices and higher aftermarket prices could enhance equipment sales by making it easier for the buyer to finance the initial purchase.[19] It is undisputed that competition is enhanced when a firm is able to offer various marketing options, including bundling of support and maintenance service with the sale of equipment. Nor do such actions run afoul of the antitrust laws.[20] But the procompetitive effect of the specific conduct challenged here, eliminating all consumer parts and service options, is far less clear.

We need not decide whether Kodak's behavior has any procompetitive effects and, if so, whether they outweigh the anticompetitive effects. We note only that Kodak's service and parts policy is simply not one that

19. It bears repeating that in this case Kodak has never claimed that it is in fact pursuing such a pricing strategy.

20. See *Jefferson Parish*, 466 U.S., at 12 ("Buyers often find package sales attractive; a seller's decision to offer such packages can merely be an attempt to compete effectively—conduct that is entirely consistent with the Sherman Act"). See also Yates & DiResta, Software Support and Hardware, Maintenance Practices: Tying Considerations, 8 The Computer Lawyer 17 (1991) (describing various service and parts policies that enhance quality and sales but do not violate the antitrust laws).

appears always or almost always to enhance competition, and therefore to warrant a legal presumption without any evidence of its actual economic impact. In this case, when we weigh the risk of deterring procompetitive behavior by proceeding to trial against the risk that illegal behavior go unpunished, the balance tips against summary judgment.

For the foregoing reasons, we hold that Kodak has not met the requirements of Fed.Rule Civ.Proc. 56(c). We therefore affirm the denial of summary judgment on respondents' § 1 claim.[21]

III

Respondents also claim that they have presented genuine issues for trial as to whether Kodak has monopolized or attempted to monopolize the service and parts markets in violation of § 2 of the Sherman Act. "The offense of monopoly under § 2 of the Sherman Act has two elements: (1) the possession of monopoly power in the relevant market and (2) the willful acquisition or maintenance of that power as distinguished from growth or

---

21. The dissent urges a radical departure in this Court's antitrust law. It argues that because Kodak has only an "inherent" monopoly in parts for its equipment the antitrust laws do not apply to its efforts to expand that power into other markets. The dissent's proposal to grant *per se* immunity to manufacturers competing in the service market would exempt a vast and growing sector of the economy from antitrust laws. Leaving aside the question whether the Court has the authority to make such a policy decision, there is no support for it in our jurisprudence or the evidence in this case.

Even assuming, despite the absence of any proof from the dissent, that all manufacturers possess some inherent market power in the parts market, it is not clear why that should immunize them from the antitrust laws in another market. The Court has held many times that power gained through some natural and legal advantage such as a patent, copyright, or business acumen can give rise to liability if "a seller exploits his dominant position in one market to expand his empire into the next." Times–Picayune Publishing Co. v. United States, 345 U.S. 594, 611 (1953); *see, e.g.*, Northern Pacific R. Co. v. United States, 356 U.S. 1 (1958). Moreover, on the occasions when the Court has considered tying in derivative aftermarkets by manufacturers, it has not adopted any exception to the usual antitrust analysis, treating derivative aftermarkets as it has every other separate market. See International Salt Co. v. United States, 332 U.S. 392 (1947); International Business Machines Corp. v. United States, 298 U.S. 131 (1936); United Shoe Machinery Co. v. United States, 258 U.S. 451 (1922). Our past decisions are reason enough to reject the dissent's proposal....

Nor does the record in this case support the dissent's proposed exemption for aftermarkets. The dissent urges its exemption because the tie here "does not permit the manufacturer to project power over a class of consumers distinct from that which it is already able to exploit (and fully) without the inconvenience of the tie." Beyond the dissent's obvious difficulty in explaining why Kodak would adopt this expensive tying policy if it could achieve the same profits more conveniently through some other means, respondents offer an alternative theory, supported by the record, that suggests Kodak is able to exploit some customers who in the absence of the tie would be protected from increases in parts prices by knowledgeable customers.

At bottom, whatever the ultimate merits of the dissent's theory, at this point it is mere conjecture. Neither Kodak nor the dissent have provided any evidence refuting respondents' theory of forced unwanted purchases at higher prices and price discrimination. While it may be, as the dissent predicts, that the equipment market will prevent any harms to consumers in the aftermarkets, the dissent never makes plain why the Court should accept that theory on faith rather than requiring the usual evidence needed to win a summary judgment motion.

development as a consequence of a superior product, business acumen, or historic accident." United States v. Grinnell Corp., 384 U.S., at 570–571.

A

The existence of the first element, possession of monopoly power, is easily resolved. As has been noted, respondents have presented a triable claim that service and parts are separate markets, and that Kodak has the "power to control prices or exclude competition" in service and parts. *du Pont*, 351 U.S., at 391. Monopoly power under § 2 requires, of course, something greater than market power under § 1. See Fortner, 394 U.S., at 502. Respondents' evidence that Kodak controls nearly 100% of the parts market and 80% to 95% of the service market, with no readily available substitutes, is, however, sufficient to survive summary judgment under the more stringent monopoly standard of § 2. . . .

Kodak also contends that, as a matter of law, a single brand of a product or service can never be a relevant market under the Sherman Act. We disagree. The relevant market for antitrust purposes is determined by the choices available to Kodak equipment owners. See *Jefferson Parish*, 466 U.S., at 19. Because service and parts for Kodak equipment are not interchangeable with other manufacturers' service and parts, the relevant market from the Kodak-equipment owner's perspective is composed of only those companies that service Kodak machines. See *du Pont*, 351 U.S., at 404 (the "market is composed of products that have reasonable inter-changeability").[22] This Court's prior cases support the proposition that in some instances one brand of a product can constitute a separate market. See National Collegiate Athletic Assn., 468 U.S., at 101–102, 111–112 (1984); International Boxing Club of New York, Inc. v. United States, 358 U.S. 242, 249–252 (1959); International Business Machines Corp. v. United States, 298 U.S. 131 (1936).[23] The proper market definition in this case can be determined only after a factual inquiry into the "commercial realities" faced by consumers. United States v. Grinnell Corp., 384 U.S., at 572.

B

The second element of a § 2 claim is the use of monopoly power "to foreclose competition, to gain a competitive advantage, or to destroy a

---

22. Kodak erroneously contends that this Court in *du Pont* rejected the notion that a relevant market could be limited to one brand. The Court simply held in *du Pont* that one brand does not necessarily constitute a relevant market if substitutes are available. 351 U.S., at 393. See also *Boxing Club, 358 U.S.,* at 249–250. Here respondents contend there are no substitutes.

23. Other courts have limited the market to parts for a particular brand of equipment. *See e.g.,* International Logistics Group, Ltd. v. Chrysler Corp. 884 F.2d 904, 905, 908 (C.A.6 1989) (parts for Chrysler cars is the

relevant market), cert. denied, 494 U.S. 1066 (1990); Dimidowich v. Bell & Howell, 803 F.2d 1473, 1480–1481, n. 3 (C.A.9 1986), modified, 810 F.2d 1517 (1987) (service for Bell & Howell equipment is the relevant market); In re General Motors Corp., 99 F.T.C. 464, 554, 584 (1982) (crash parts for General Motors cars is the relevant market); Heatransfer Corp. v. Volkswagenwerk A.G., 553 F.2d 964 (CAS 1977), cert. denied, 434 U.S. 1087 (1978) (air conditioners for Volkswagons is the relevant market).

competitor." United States v. Griffith, 334 U.S. 100, 107 (1948). If Kodak adopted its parts and service policies as part of a scheme of willful acquisition or maintenance of monopoly power, it will have violated § 2. Grinnell Corp., 384 U.S., at 570–571; United States v. Aluminum Co. of America, 148 F.2d 416, 432 (C.A.2 1945); Aspen Skiing Co. v. Aspen Highlands Skiing Corp., 472 U.S. 585, 600–605 (1985).[24]

As recounted at length above, respondents have presented evidence that Kodak took exclusionary action to maintain its parts monopoly and used its control over parts to strengthen its monopoly share of the Kodak service market. Liability turns, then, on whether "valid business reasons" can explain Kodak's actions. *Aspen Skiing Co.*, 472 U.S., at 605; United States v. Aluminum Co. of America, 148 F.2d, at 432. Kodak contends that it has three valid business justifications for its actions: "(1) to promote interbrand equipment competition by allowing Kodak to stress the quality of its service; (2) to improve asset management by reducing Kodak's inventory costs; and (3) to prevent ISOs from free riding on Kodak's capital investment in equipment, parts and service." Factual questions exist, however, about the validity and sufficiency of each claimed justification, making summary judgment inappropriate.

Kodak first asserts that by preventing customers from using ISOs, "it [can] best maintain high quality service for its sophisticated equipment" and avoid being "blamed for an equipment malfunction, even if the problem is the result of improper diagnosis, maintenance or repair by an ISO." Respondents have offered evidence that ISOs provide quality service and are preferred by some Kodak equipment owners. This is sufficient to raise a genuine issue of fact. See International Business Machines Corp. v. United States, 298 U.S., at 139–140 (rejecting IBM's claim that it had to control the cards used in its machines to avoid "injury to the reputation of the machines and the good will of" IBM in the absence of proof that other companies could not make quality cards); International Salt Co. v. United States, 332 U.S. 392, 397–398 (1947) (rejecting International Salt's claim that it had to control the supply of salt to protect its leased machines in the absence of proof that competitors could not supply salt of equal quality).

Moreover, there are other reasons to question Kodak's proffered motive of commitment to quality service; its quality justification appears inconsistent with its thesis that consumers are knowledgeable enough to lifecycle price, and its self-service policy. Kodak claims the exclusive-service contract is warranted because customers would otherwise blame Kodak equipment for breakdowns resulting from inferior ISO service. Thus, Kodak simultaneously claims that its customers are sophisticated enough to make complex and subtle lifecycle-pricing decisions, and yet too obtuse to distinguish which breakdowns are due to bad equipment and which are due to bad service. Kodak has failed to offer any reason why informational

---

24. It is true that as a general matter a firm can refuse to deal with its competitors. But such a right is not absolute; it exists only if there are legitimate competitive reasons for the refusal. See Aspen Skiing Co. v. Aspen Highlands Skiing Corp., 472 U.S. 585, 602–605 (1985).

sophistication should be present in one circumstance and absent in the other. In addition, because self-service customers are just as likely as others to blame Kodak equipment for breakdowns resulting from (their own) inferior service, Kodak's willingness to allow self-service casts doubt on its quality claim. In sum, we agree with the Court of Appeals that respondents "have presented evidence from which a reasonable trier of fact could conclude that Kodak's first reason is pretextual." 903 F.2d, at 618.

There is also a triable issue of fact on Kodak's second justification—controlling inventory costs. As respondents argue, Kodak's actions appear inconsistent with any need to control inventory costs. Presumably, the inventory of parts needed to repair Kodak machines turns only on breakdown rates, and those rates should be the same whether Kodak or ISOs perform the repair. More importantly, the justification fails to explain respondents' evidence that Kodak forced OEMs, equipment owners, and parts brokers not to sell parts to ISOs, actions that would have no effect on Kodak's inventory costs.

Nor does Kodak's final justification entitle it to summary judgment on respondents' § 2 claim. Kodak claims that its policies prevent ISOs from "exploit[ing] the investment Kodak has made in product development, manufacturing and equipment sales in order to take away Kodak's service revenues." Kodak does not dispute that respondents invest substantially in the service market, with training of repair workers and investment in parts inventory. Instead, according to Kodak, the ISOs are free-riding because they have failed to enter the equipment and parts markets. This understanding of free-riding has no support in our case law.[25] To the contrary, as the Court of Appeals noted, one of the evils proscribed by the antitrust laws is the creation of entry barriers to potential competitors by requiring them to enter two markets simultaneously. *Jefferson Parish*, 466 U.S., at 14; *Fortner*, 394 U.S., at 509.

None of Kodak's asserted business justifications, then, are sufficient to prove that Kodak is "entitled to a judgment as a matter of law" on respondents' § 2 claim. Fed.Rule.Civ.Proc. 56(c).

IV

In the end, of course, Kodak's arguments may prove to be correct. It may be that its parts, service, and equipment are components of one unified market, or that the equipment market does discipline the aftermarkets so that all three are priced competitively overall, or that any anticom-

---

25. Kodak claims that both *Continental T.V.* and *Monsanto* support its free-rider argument. Neither is applicable. In both *Continental T.V.*, 433 U.S., at 55, and *Monsanto*, 465 U.S., at 762–763, the Court accepted free-riding as a justification because without restrictions a manufacturer would not be able to induce competent and aggressive retailers to make the kind of investment of capital and labor necessary to distribute the product. In *Continental T.V.* the relevant market level was retail sale of televisions and in *Monsanto* retail sales of herbicides. Some retailers were investing in those markets; others were not, relying, instead, on the investment of the other retailers. To be applicable to this case, the ISOs would have to be relying on Kodak's investment in the service market; that, however, is not Kodak's argument.

petitive effects of Kodak's behavior are outweighed by its competitive effects. But we cannot reach these conclusions as a matter of law on a record this sparse. Accordingly, the judgment of the Court of Appeals denying summary judgment is affirmed.

■ SCALIA, J., with whom O'CONNOR and THOMAS, JJ., join, dissenting. This is not, as the Court describes it, just "another case that concerns the standard for summary judgment in an antitrust controversy." Rather, the case presents a very narrow—but extremely important—question of substantive antitrust law: Whether, for purposes of applying our *per se* rule condemning "ties," and for purposes of applying our exacting rules governing the behavior of would-be monopolists, a manufacturer's conceded lack of power in the interbrand market for its equipment is somehow consistent with its possession of "market," or even "monopoly," power in wholly derivative aftermarkets for that equipment. In my view, the Court supplies an erroneous answer to this question, and I dissent.

Per se rules of antitrust illegality are reserved for those situations where logic and experience show that the risk of injury to competition from the defendant's behavior is so pronounced that it is needless and wasteful to conduct the usual judicial inquiry into the balance between the behavior's procompetitive benefits and its anticompetitive costs.... The *per se* rule against tying is just such a rule: Where the conditions precedent to application of the rule are met, *i.e.*, where the tying arrangement is backed up by the defendant's market power in the "tying" product, the arrangement is adjudged in violation of § 1 of the Sherman Act without any inquiry into the practice's actual effect on competition and consumer welfare. But see United States v. Jerrold Electronics Corp., 187 F.Supp. 545, 560 (E.D.Pa.1960), aff'd *per curiam*, 365 U.S. 567 (1961) (accepting affirmative defense to *per se* tying allegation).

Despite intense criticism of the tying doctrine in academic circles, *see, e.g.*, R. Bork, The Antitrust Paradox 365–381 (1978), the stated rationale for our *per se* rule has varied little over the years. When the defendant has genuine "market power" in the tying product—the power to raise price by reducing output—the tie potentially enables him to extend that power into a second distinct market, enhancing barriers to entry in each....

Our Section 2 monopolization doctrines are similarly directed to discrete situations in which a defendant's possession of substantial market power, combined with his exclusionary or anticompetitive behavior, threatens to defeat or forestall the corrective forces of competition and thereby sustain or extend the defendant's agglomeration of power. See United States v. Grinnell Corp., 384 U.S. 563, 570–571 (1966). Where a defendant maintains substantial market power, his activities are examined through a special lens: Behavior that might otherwise not be of concern to the antitrust laws—or that might even be viewed as procompetitive—can take on exclusionary connotations when practiced by a monopolist. 3 P. Areeda & D. Turner, Antitrust Law ¶ 813, pp. 300–302 (1978) (hereinafter 3 Areeda & Turner).

The concerns, however, that have led the courts to heightened scrutiny both of the "exclusionary conduct" practiced by a monopolist and of tying arrangements subject to *per se* prohibition, are completely without force when the participants lack market power.... The Court today finds in the typical manufacturer's inherent power over its own brand of equipment— over the sale of distinctive repair parts for that equipment, for example— the sort of "monopoly power" sufficient to bring the sledgehammer of § 2 into play. And, not surprisingly in light of that insight, it readily labels single-brand power over aftermarket products "market power" sufficient to permit an antitrust plaintiff to invoke the *per se* rule against tying. In my opinion, this makes no economic sense. The holding that market power can be found on the present record causes these venerable rules of selective proscription to extend well beyond the point where the reasoning that supports them leaves off. Moreover, because the sort of power condemned by the Court today is possessed by every manufacturer of durable goods with distinctive parts, the Court's opinion threatens to release a torrent of litigation and a flood of commercial intimidation that will do much more harm than good to enforcement of the antitrust laws and to genuine competition....

[Justice Scalia, in Parts II and III of his dissent, explained at length how "neither logic nor experience" warranted application of "the *per se* tying prohibition and the monopolization doctrine" to Kodak's behavior in its single-branded aftermarket, "when the seller is without power at the interbrand level."]

NOTES AND QUESTIONS

1. Note that both the majority and the dissent in *Kodak* appeared to discuss tying arrangements under a *per se* rule. What does that suggest about the staying power of Justice O'Connor's concurrence in *Jefferson Parish*? Contrast the treatment of tying in United States v. Microsoft Corp., supra pp. 799 to 807. Would the *per se* treatment have been different if the *Kodak* case had not been before the Court on summary judgment?

2. With respect to the analysis of market power, carefully note the majority's insistence in *Kodak* on examining "economic reality" (including information costs and switching costs), and its unwillingness to rely on theoretical economic arguments about why Kodak could not have market power in the aftermarkets when there is interbrand competition in the equipment market.

3. Does *Kodak* mean that virtually every manufacturer has monopoly power in parts and service aftermarkets? Is Justice Scalia correct in arguing that the majority decision "threatens to release a torrent of litigation?" On remand of the *Kodak* case, a jury returned a verdict against *Kodak* and awarded damages totaling $24 million; the district court issued an injunction which included a broad compulsory licensing provision. The Ninth Circuit affirmed. See Image Technical Services, Inc. v. Eastman Kodak Co., 125 F.3d 1195 (9th Cir.1997); see also Note on Issues at the Intersection of Antitrust and Intellectual Property, *supra* p. 812. The court of appeals agreed that the ISOs had satisfactorily demonstrated both that Kodak had

attained monopoly power in a market for Kodak photocopiers and micrographic parts and that it had engaged in exclusionary conduct to gain or attempt to gain a monopoly over the servicing of Kodak equipment. The court rejected Kodak's asserted business justifications for its conduct, which centered principally on its alleged right to protect its patented and copyrighted parts. The Court of Appeals for the Federal Circuit issued an opinion in substantial tension with the Ninth Circuit's decision on remand in *Kodak*, in In re Independent Service Organizations Antitrust Litigation (Xerox), 203 F.3d 1322 (Fed.Cir.2000), p. 824, supra.

4.   In Mozart Co. v. Mercedes-Benz of North America, Inc., 833 F.2d 1342 (9th Cir.1987), cert. denied, 488 U.S. 870 (1988), the Ninth Circuit accepted a district court's finding that Mercedes passenger cars and their replacement parts are separate products. Similarly, in Multistate Legal Studies, Inc. v. Harcourt Brace Jovanovich Legal and Professional Publications, Inc., 63 F.3d 1540 (10th Cir.1995), cert. denied, 516 U.S. 1044 (1996), the Court had to decide whether a bar examination course focused on the Multistate Bar Exam (MBE) was the same product as a "full-service course," which prepared students for all components of Colorado's bar examination. The Tenth Circuit concluded that two products were involved and reasoned as follows:

> The elements, then, of a *per se* violation, are (1) two separate products, (2) a tie—or conditioning of the sale of one product on the purchase of another, (3) sufficient economic power in the tying product market, and (4) substantial volume of commerce affected in the tied product market.... [Defendants] argue that their actions involved nothing more than the improvement of a single product—their full-service course. PMBR argues on appeal that the district court failed to apply the proper test to determine whether two products exist. We agree. The court focused on PMBR's stipulation that the purpose of a full-service course includes preparing bar applicants for the MBE as well as for the other parts of the bar exam. From this, the court appears to have concluded that any effort to improve the full-service course by adding elements to it could not possibly constitute the bundling of a second product, at least where those added elements related to the MBE. In this the court erred.

> The Supreme Court has made clear that the test for determining whether two components are separate products turns not on their function, but on the nature of any consumer demand for them. For two items at issue to be considered distinct products, "there must be sufficient consumer demand so that it is efficient for a firm to provide [one] separate from [the other]." *Kodak.... Jefferson Parish....* See also Service & Training, Inc. v. Data Gen. Corp., 963 F.2d 680, 684–85 (4th Cir.1992) (district court erred in reasoning that since customers' only legitimate purpose for using defendant's diagnostic software was to repair computers, defendant was providing only a single integrated product of computer servicing, rather than a package of service and diagnostic software)....

> PMBR maintains that by incorporating BAR/BRI and Gilbert into a package, the Defendants have "linked two distinct markets for products that were distinguishable in the eyes of buyers." Jefferson Parish, 466 U.S. at 19.

> PMBR's evidence includes the following: ...

Defendants have marketed their full-service course and their supplemental workshop as separate products, for separate fees, for over a decade and still offer Gilbert separately.

In Kansas, Ohio and Hawaii, HBJL and/or its licensees still offer the full-service course unbundled from Gilbert.

Prior to Defendants' bundling, not every full-service course customer chose to purchase a supplemental workshop; in Colorado, only one-third to one-half did so.

In the past, HBJL officials worked to keep their external Gilbert workshop separate and distinct in customers' minds from the HarBrace workshop within the full-service course, because many customers preferred to buy from two different companies to get multiple providers' perspectives on the MBE.

Defendants have not consolidated the operation of the full-service and supplemental courses; Gilbert continues to be administered and marketed separately....

Other bar review industry participants view full-service and supplemental MBE courses as separate products.

This evidence is sufficient to create a material factual dispute over whether there is enough consumer demand in Colorado for full-service courses without supplemental MBE workshops to make it efficient to sell the two separately. If there is, then the BAR/BRI–Gilbert package should be viewed as two products.

Does the Tenth Circuit's opinion suggest that new, improved product development—*i.e.*, when two products are combined—may be vulnerable? Should the nature and efficiency of the product integration matter? How would you formulate a rule for distinguishing one product from two separate products for purposes of the tying doctrine? Should courts give weight, as a number have, to the fact that at times selling what are two products together results in manufacturing savings or other cost savings? Should this tip a close case to a single-product conclusion, or is it better to recognize both the reality of two products and the cost savings by encouraging manufacturers to sell the two products together at a cost-justified lower price?

5. Is it likely that the usual franchisor will be found to have sufficient or appreciable economic power in the tying product? In GRAPPONE, INC. v. SUBARU OF NEW ENGLAND, INC., 858 F.2d 792 (1st Cir.1988), the First Circuit dealt with the "market power" concept as follows:

The majority and concurrence [in *Jefferson Parish*] recognized that a Seller, possessing significant market power with respect to Product A, may cause anticompetitive harm by tying as follows: by reducing the price of Product A slightly (or by otherwise not fully exploiting its power with respect to Product A), the Seller may induce the Buyer to accept the tie; by doing so, the Seller may build a strong market position in Product B; and *that position* in Product B, in turn, may increase its power to charge high prices in respect to Product A. If a monopolist of patented can-closing machinery, for example, insists, as a condition of selling his machines, that its purchasers buy his cans, he will likely soon have a monopoly in cans as well as machines. And, that fact—the fact that he controls *both* cans and machines—may make his monopoly safer from competitive attack when his patent on the can-closing machinery expires. A new competitor would then have to enter *both* levels of the business (cans and machines) to deprive him of monopoly profits. And, this added security may enable the machinery monopolist to charge higher prices. The tie, by permitting the Seller to extend its market power from one level to two, may thereby raise entry barriers, providing security that helps a monopolist-seller further harm the consumer....

[Plaintiffs, however, were not able to meet the "market power" requirement of *Jefferson Parish* because they] have not provided evidence that SNE could raise prices significantly above the competitive level; in fact, the evidence in the record indicates the contrary. For one thing, Subaru's market share, whether measured in terms of sales of all autos or of imports or in any other reasonable way, is miniscule.... National sales of Subarus during the relevant years (as suggested by the import figures in the record) were likely about a fraction of 1 percent of all autos sold. Subaru at most accounted for 3.4 percent of auto imports sold in New Hampshire in 1974.... The record shows that Subaru was but one of many automobile franchisors, and that Grappone itself held not only Subaru, but also AMC, Pontiac, Jeep, Toyota, and Peugeot franchises....

Finally, plaintiff has made no showing that Subarus had any special or unique features, such as patents or copyrights, that might demonstrate market power. See Digidyne Corp. v. Data General Corp., 734 F.2d 1336, 1341–42 (9th Cir.1984), cert. denied, 473 U.S. 908 (1985); cf. Jefferson Parish, 466 U.S. at 16–17. The most one can say is that Subaru has a brand name and sells through "authorized" Subaru dealers. But, we find no Supreme Court case law suggesting that such features by themselves are sufficient to show "market power." They do not automatically demonstrate any "economic" or "cost advantage" or any other advantage "not shared by ... competitors," *Fortner II*, 429 U.S. at 620–21 (quoting in part *Fortner I*, 394 U.S. at 505 n. 2), particularly in an industry where many larger competing firms all do business in this way. *Will*, 776 F.2d at 672 (no uniqueness argument unless plaintiff shows barrier preventing rivals from offering same package at same cost); cf. Ungar v. Dunkin' Donuts of America, Inc., 531 F.2d 1211, 1224–25 (3d Cir.1976) (proof of coercion needed, otherwise factors "inherent" in voluntary franchise agreement would suffice to show tie), cert. denied, 429 U.S. 823 (1976). Grappone points to *Digidyne*, supra, as contrary authority, but in that case the Ninth Circuit found a tying product, a computer operating system, "unique" because (1) it was copyrighted, and (2) many of its buyers had previously invested millions of dollars in software design that worked only with that system. We find no directly analogous circumstances here. Grappone does not offer similar evidence of such large dealer investments in Subaru dealerships by those who protested the tie; Grappone's multiple brand representation suggests the contrary, at least for some significant number of franchisees....

For discussions of market power in other lower court cases, *see, e.g.*, Allen–Myland, Inc. v. IBM, 33 F.3d 194 (3d Cir.), cert. denied, 513 U.S. 1066 (1994) (vacating a district court finding that IBM lacked sufficient market power in large-scale mainframe computers); Breaux Bros. Farms Inc. v. Teche Sugar Co., 21 F.3d 83 (5th Cir.1994), cert. denied, 513 U.S. 963 (1994); (manufacturer of sugar held at most 17.5% of the tying market, and thus lacked sufficient market power).

6. Did the majority opinions in *Jefferson Parish* and *Kodak* bless a "business justification" defense? If so, what is the breadth of the defense? If a broad business

justification defense exists, would it leave any substance in the *per se* tying rule? How would you narrowly define business justifications? See pp. 885–86, supra.

7. Plaintiffs have challenged so-called "technological ties"—that is, situations in which a seller is alleged to have designed a product so as to integrate it, or make it compatible, with a second product which it exclusively sells. For example, in TELEX CORP. v. IBM, 367 F.Supp. 258 (N.D.Okl.1973), reversed on other grounds, 510 F.2d 894 (10th Cir.), cert. dismissed, 423 U.S. 802 (1975), a manufacturer of "memory units" sued IBM on grounds, among others, that it had contrived to integrate "memory capacity" into its central processing units (CPUs) so as to preclude effective competition from competitors offering compatible memory units. Computers consisted of a group of electronically interconnected "boxes" (called "hardware") operating under the control of a set of electronic instructions (called "software"). Organizationally, the center of a hardware system was the CPU and the rest of the hardware in the system (such as memory units, printers, tape drives, etc.) was called peripheral equipment. By putting memory units into the CPU "box," purchasers desiring to purchase IBM CPUs, in effect, were denied a choice as to the source of memory equipment. The district court found that IBM's main incentive in integrating memory into CPUs was to reduce costs and improve performance, and that competitors of IBM accept increasing integration as an objective of good engineering design. The court indicated that it was influenced in its determination that no violation had occurred by a recognition that a finding of a tie-in under the antitrust laws could "preclude or discourage the utilization of advancing technology...." 367 F.Supp. at 306. How would you distinguish the *Telex* case from the Tenth Circuit's *Multistate Legal Studies* case discussed in Note 4 supra?

8. Price discrimination is a very controversial issue in antitrust. Courts and commentators disagree over whether or not it usually harms consumers. It is easy to construct examples where price discrimination either raises or lowers total output. Notice the concern about "metering" and other forms of price discrimination indicated in the majority opinions in *Jefferson Parish* and *Kodak* (see pp. 886, 903 supra), and the more ambiguous attitude of Justice O'Connor in her *Jefferson Parish* concurrence (p. 900 n. 1 supra).

9. The Supreme Court in *Kodak* retreated from language in *Matsushita* (see p. 514 supra) that suggested a special standard for summary judgment in antitrust cases. Is this of any concern?

United States v. Microsoft Corp.

United States Court of Appeals, District of Columbia Circuit, 2001.
253 F.3d 34, cert. denied, 534 U.S. 952.

[Among other contributions it made to antitrust law, the decision of the D.C. Court of Appeals with respect to the government's allegations of illegal tying marked a potentially important step in the development of tying doctrine. The tie-in portion of the opinion is printed at pp. 799–807, supra.]

NOTES AND QUESTIONS

1. Did the D.C. Circuit go too far in this case when it decided to apply the rule of reason to the tying arrangements before it? How can you reconcile this step with

the fact that the majority in *Jefferson Parish* expressly refused to take it, over the explicit invitation of Justice O'Connor's concurring opinion. On the other hand, how can you explain the fact that the Supreme Court denied certiorari in *Microsoft*, apart from the usual fact that a denial of review carries no substantive implications one way or the other?

2.   With respect to the court's comments on price bundling, see the Note on Package Discounts, infra.

3.   Do you agree that *Jefferson Parish* adopted consumer demand as the sole determinant of whether one is faced with one product (or service) or two? Does it open the door as widely as the D.C. Circuit suggests to a consideration of the efficiencies of a bundle?

NOTE ON PACKAGE DISCOUNTS

An increasingly popular marketing approach (and frequent subject of private litigation in the lower courts) is the offer of a package of two or more products at a discount. The offer does not represent a tie-in sale because each product is available separately at a specified price. If the buyer takes all items in the package, however, the combined price is lower than the total of prices if all items were purchased separately.

Some have suggested that package discounts can never be illegal, citing a footnote in *Northern Pacific* stating that: "Of course, when the buyer is free to take either product by itself, there is no tying problem even though the seller may also offer the two items as a unit at a single price." The Supreme Court probably only meant to suggest by that footnote that the harsh rules against tie-in sales—in *Northern Pacific* a rule of *per se* illegality was adopted—might be relaxed with respect to package discounts. In support of that view, note that a rule of complete immunity would mean that the seller could charge a very high price for the tying product and a trivial price for the tied product and, as a result of that strategy, induce purchase of the tied product and yet avoid any challenge under traditional tie-in restrictions. At the other extreme, others have argued that package discounts are the equivalent of outright tie-in sales because consumers are "coerced" into taking the various items in the package if offered at a substantial discount. *See Advance Business Systems & Supply Co. v. SCM Corp.*, 415 F.2d 55 (4th Cir.1969), cert. denied, 397 U.S. 920 (1970) declaring illegal a plan to rent machines, supplies and service in a single package because it effectively deprived customers of freedom of choice. These extreme positions are summarized and criticized in 10 Areeda, Elhauge & Hovenkamp, Antitrust Law: An Analysis of Antitrust Principles and Their Application, 341–43 (1996).

In seeking a more nuanced approach, courts have recognized that package discounts are a way of waging competition and usually result in lower prices to purchasers. Also, the seller's goal might be to increase total sales through a promotional discount, and then pass the efficiencies on to consumers in the form of lower prices. Finally, a rule that discourages package pricing might discourage aggressive competition by efficient firms and hold a price umbrella over their less efficient rivals. On the other hand, there can be circumstances in which package discounts can be anticompetitive. Two sorts of challenges have emerged in the cases: (1) charges that one or more of the items in the package, as a result of the discount, are sold at "predatory prices" (see section 2 of this chapter) or (2) that the exclusionary effect of the package discount is much the same as a conventional tie-in sale.

With respect to predatory pricing, we have already seen that price on a product can only be "predatory" if it is below some appropriate measure of cost, *see Brooke Group v. Brown & Williamson Tobacco*, supra, p. 897—widely regarded in the lower courts and in treatises as below average variable cost (see note at pp. 866–74, supra). In that connection, consider a marketing plan in which ten items are included in a package. Each item can be purchased separately but, if a customer takes the entire package, it receives a three percent discount on each of the ten items. Assuming each product in the package is purchased in equal quantities, the competitor on item ten might complain that in effect it must lower its price by 30% to induce the customer to buy its product in place of packaged item 10. In effect, the complainant would be asking that the entire value of the discount be allocated to each of the products in the package. *See Ortho Diagnostic Systems v. Abbott Laboratories*, 926 F.Supp. 371 (S.D.N.Y.1996) (accepting the concept of allocating the entire discount to each product but finding no predation on the record before it). An alternative to allocating the entire discount to one product would be to require that the price of the entire package remain above the standard for predatory pricing. Note that if the approach of allocating the discount to each product were adopted, many package discounts, especially with a considerable number of items in the package, would be illegal. Perhaps it would even be illegal to add an eleventh item to the package without increasing the price of the package—essentially an offer of a free good—as a reward or bonus for taking the first ten items.

The second line of attack on package discounts is the charge that they often are identical in effect to outright tie-in sales. Thus a package discount could be illegal if the package price is so attractive that all or nearly all customers would accept it because it would be economically irrational to pay the higher price for the separate products. *See T. Harris Young & Assoc. v. Marquette Electr., Inc.*, 931 F.2d 816, 822 (11th Cir.1991). With regard to that charge, the lower courts appear to be moving generally in the direction of a common rule of law—*i.e.*, that no antitrust violation can be found where a significant number of purchasers offered the package decline the offer and buy the product separately. *See Nobel Scientific Indus. v. Beckman Instruments*, 670 F.Supp. 1313, 1324 (D.Md.1986) (no *de facto* tie because 50–55% of the tied product sales were separate); Ways & Means v. IVAC Corp., 506 F.Supp. 697, 701 (N.D.Cal.1979), affirmed, 638 F.2d 143 (9th Cir.1981) (no *de facto* tie because 25% of the time product sales were separate.) But *see LaPage's Inc. v. 3M*, 324 F.3d 141 (3d Cir.2003) where the 3rd Circuit in an *en banc* opinion found that 3M, the leading supplier of transparent tape in the United States through its Scotch Tape brand, offered rebates to a number of its customers on condition that they purchase unrelated 3M product lines; the Court did not examine whether all or most customers that were offered rebates accepted the deal.

Should the law be less or more concerned about package discounts than outright ties? Are any of the defenses that have progressively developed in the area of tie-in sales irrelevant or inappropriate to package ties? Should we be concerned about the plight of the rival on product ten—a single item manufacturer—losing out to the diversified company even though its product is of equal or better quality and price?

PROBLEM 21

SERVICE CONTRACTS FOR BURGLAR ALARM SYSTEMS

In 1990, Berger Co. invented a new and highly complicated electronic burglar alarm system. Included in the system is a device containing a new, secret conductive alloy which makes for more reliable performance. Because of dissatisfaction with existing systems, Berger had no difficulty in selling its product to numerous industrial and commercial establishments throughout the country. From a negligible share of burglar systems installed in 1990, Berger installed 2% in 1991, 8% in 1992, 43% in 1994, and 78% in 1995. A competitive system went on the market at the end of 1995, and in 1996 reduced Berger's share to 66% of new installations. During these same years, Berger accounted for the following shares of systems in use: 1991, 0.5%; 1992, 2%; 1994, 12%; 1995, 21%; and 1996, 29%.

Throughout the period 1990–1996, Berger refused to sell its system except on the condition that the system be serviced exclusively by Berger's technicians. Among other reasons, Berger does not want repairmen not in its employ to have access to the secret feature of its system. In the first two years, while the system was relatively unknown and unused, any notoriety about failures of the system would have been disastrous to Berger. On the other hand, Berger's services have always been expensive and it is conceded that, without the compulsory service contract, many purchasers of the system would have made other servicing arrangements.

Has Berger violated the antitrust laws?

NOTE ON RECIPROCITY

A variation on the characteristic tie-in occurs when firm A (producing Product A) agrees with firm B (producing Product B) that it will buy Product B only on condition that firm B buys Product A. Arguably, one or both companies are using their purchasing power with respect to one product to "distort competition on the merits" with respect to sale of another product.

Reciprocity antitrust problems can arise in two ways. First, there can be formal or informal agreements, consensual or coerced, which lead to reciprocal dealings. Second, a merger can be challenged on grounds that it puts the combined company in a position to exercise reciprocity pressures, when the combined firm both buys from and sells to intermediate enterprises. The company is thus in a position to suggest that it will initiate or continue purchases only if the supplier agrees to buy from its newly acquired subsidiary. During the 1960s, there was much discussion of reciprocity. See Handler, Emerging Antitrust Issues: Reciprocity, Diversification and Joint Ventures, 49 Va.L.Rev. 433 (1963); Hausman, Reciprocal Dealing and the Antitrust Laws, 77 Harv.L.Rev. 873 (1964). In United States v. General Dynamics Corp., Trade Reg.Rep. (CCH) ¶ 71,870 (S.D.N.Y. 1966), a merger was found invalid under Section 7 of the Clayton Act because actual and potential resort to reciprocity pressures, made possible by the merger, led to a substantial lessening of competition. In general, there has been little further litigation involving reciprocity; the issue has been raised in a few merger cases, and we will deal with reciprocity issues again, in the merger context in Chapter 9.

Betaseed, Inc. v. U & I Inc., 681 F.2d 1203 (9th Cir.1982) is a rare exception to the paucity of caselaw in the reciprocity area. Betaseed, which sold seeds to sugarbeet farmers, alleged that U & I, a company which competed in the sale of seeds and also purchased sugarbeets for processing sugar, used its purchasing power with respect to sugarbeets to induce growers to buy its seeds. U & I had considerable purchasing power as the only processor of sugarbeets in the relevant geographic area. Beginning in 1975, U & I included a clause in its sugarbeet purchase contracts providing that it would be obligated to buy beets only from those purchasers who accepted its seeds or "such other seed as has been established by tests satisfactory to the COMPANY to produce beets having substantially the same characteristics...."

Betaseed claimed that the equivalency clause was a sham in that U & I never established objective standards to determine when seeds possessed "substantially the same characteristics," and in fact, never accepted as a satisfactory substitute any seeds offered by other sellers.

Betaseed alleged, among other antitrust claims, that the contractual arrangement and the course of dealing constituted coercive reciprocal dealing in violation of Section 1 of the Sherman Act. The Court of Appeals reversed a grant of summary judgment for U & I, concluding that the cause of action was valid and that there were legitimate issues of fact that needed to be tried.

After a review of the history of reciprocity enforcement, the Court of Appeals concluded that coercive reciprocity should be treated as illegal *per se*, but under the same kind of modified *per se* approach applied in tie-in cases. Specifically, the Court noted that there needed to be two distinct products or services, some "modicum of coercion," sufficient economic power in the market for the tying product to impose significant restrictions in the tied market, and a not insubstantial amount of commerce:

"In our view, the malevolent economic results of market foreclosure and raising of artificial entry barriers in a market tinged with coercive reciprocity evinces the anticompetitive and predatory nature of the practice. The similarity between coercive reciprocity and tying arrangements, both in form and in anticompetitive consequences, leads to the conclusion that the two practices should be judged by similar standards. Coercive reciprocity, in our view, is a form of tying and hence 'fits' this category."

The Court noted that there was no serious dispute about the fact that U & I had significant economic power and that a not insubstantial amount of commerce was affected. As to whether coercion had occurred, that was an issue of fact turning on whether an appreciable number of buyers had been induced not to purchase Betaseed's products because of U & I's contractual provision conditioning its purchase of sugarbeets on its sale of sugarbeet seeds.

Finally, the Court of Appeals noted that even if the U & I contractual arrangement did not deserve *per se* treatment, it might nevertheless be illegal under a rule of reason analysis. In either event a full trial would be necessary to explore those issues and therefore the grant of summary judgment was improper.

It is interesting to speculate why there have been so few reciprocity cases since the 1960s. One explanation is that the antitrust enforcement agencies have come to doubt that reciprocity is as anticompetitive as earlier thought. Can you think of any "business justifications" for coercive reciprocity? What if the reciprocity comes about because of non-coercive voluntary purchasing? Should the antitrust laws be concerned about non-coercive, consensual reciprocity?

COMPARATIVE NOTE: TYING IN THE EUROPEAN UNION

As discussed above on pages [192 to 193] in Chapter 3,[26] Article 82 (ex Article 86) of the Rome Treaty prohibits abuses of a dominant position.[27] The article

---

26. For the text of Article 82, see p. 22 supra.

27. Id.

provides a non-exclusive list of what may constitute such an abuse. The list includes, in paragraph (d), "making the conclusion of contracts subject to acceptance by the other parties of supplementary obligations which, by their nature or according to commercial usage, have no connection with the subject of such contracts."

A company with market power may resort to tying in order to identify and extract a higher price from those who put the tying product to heavier use and therefore are able and willing to pay more. By putting a premium on the tied product, the seller is able to charge more to heavy users and less to light users. See Hilti v. Commission, Case C–53/92, [1994] ECR I–667. Companies with market power in the tying product may also use tying to strengthen their position in the market for the tied product. One of the leading tying cases in the European Union is Tetra Pak International S.A. v. Commission.[28] The case involves what is called the problem of "associated product markets" in the European Union and "monopoly leveraging" in the United States. While reading the following case summary, watch out for the differences in approach on the two sides of the Atlantic.

Tetra Pak was a Swiss-based group that made packaging machines and containers for liquid and semi-liquid food, especially for milk. It operated in the aseptic, as well as in the non-aseptic sector. It accounted for 78% of both sectors combined, which was seven times more than the market share of its leading competitor. The structure of the market for aseptic packaging was quasi-monopolistic, with Tetra Pak holding 90% to 95% of the Community market. In the non-aseptic sector, the market was oligopolistic. Tetra Pak held 50% to 55% and the Norwegian group Elopak held 27%. The third largest player on the market was PKL with 11%. Non-aseptic packaging requires less sterility and less sophisticated equipment than aseptic packaging.

The Commission charged Tetra Pak with both tying and predatory practices. The Commission distinguished between four different markets: aseptic cartons, aseptic filling machines, non-aseptic cartons and non-aseptic filling machines. In terms of tying, the Commission found that Tetra Pak had a dominant position on the aseptic markets and abused its dominance by requiring buyers of its non-aseptic machines to use Tetra Pak cartons for the non-aseptic machines in the UK. The Court of First Instance (CFI) upheld the Commission decision.

Tetra Pak argued that the marketing of complete packaging systems was objectively justified by public health concerns, as well as its reputation through exclusive control of the entire packaging process. The CFI, however, found these points unpersuasive. Citing to Hilti v. EC Commission, it noted that it was "clearly not the task of an undertaking in a dominant position to take steps on its own initiative to eliminate products which, rightly or wrongly, it regards as dangerous or at least as inferior in quality to its own products." The CFI found that compliance with standards of hygiene could be ensured by requiring the users of Tetra Pak machines to adhere to all the technical specifications concerning the cartons to be used on those systems. Under those circumstances, the court thought it was clear that the tied-sale clauses went beyond their purpose and were intended to strength-

28. See Case T–83/91, [1994] ECR II–755, aff'd, Case C–333/94P, [1996] ECR I–5951.

en Tetra Pak's dominant position by reinforcing its customers' economic dependence on it.

On appeal to the European Court of Justice (ECJ), Tetra Pak argued that Article 86 (now Article 82) was inapplicable because the tie-in neither strengthened its dominant position in the tying market, nor threatened to create a new dominant position in the market of the tied product. The ECJ, referring extensively to the judgment of the CFI, rejected Tetra Pak's arguments. The ECJ acknowledged that "Article 86 presupposes a link between the dominant position and the alleged abusive conduct, which is normally not present where conduct on the market distinct from the dominated market produces effects on the distinct market." The Court went on to say that "[i]n the case of distinct, but associated markets, as in the present case, application of art. 86 to conduct found on the associated, non-dominated market can only be justified by special circumstances." The Court then reviewed the circumstances of the case and concluded that such special circumstances did, in fact, exist.

Following a summary of the findings of the CFI regarding markets shares, the Court emphasized that application of art. 86 was justified by the situation on the different markets and the close associative links between them. The Court stated that "[t]he fact that the various materials involved are used for packaging the same basic liquid products shows that Tetra Pak's customers in one sector are also potential customers in the other.... Given its almost complete domination of the aseptic markets, Tetra Pak could also count on favored status on the non-aseptic markets.... The circumstances thus ... justified the Court of First Instance, without any need to show that the undertaking was dominant on the non-aseptic markets, in finding that Tetra Pak enjoyed freedom of conduct compared with other economic operators on those markets." Accordingly, the Court concluded that "the Court of First Instance was right to accept the application of art. 86 of the Treaty in this case, given that the quasi-monopoly enjoyed by Tetra Pak on the aseptic markets, and its leading position on the distinct, though closely associated, non-aseptic markets placed it in a situation comparable to that of holding a dominant position on the markets in question as a whole."

In his Address before the BIICL Second Annual International and Comparative Law Conference in London, on May 17, 2002, William J. Kolasky, Deputy Assistant Attorney General, Antitrust Division, U.S. Department of Justice compared the U.S. and E.U. approaches on monopoly leveraging as follows:[29]

> The final area of divergence is what we call monopoly leveraging in the United States—that is, using a dominant position in one market to gain a competitive advantage in another. Most U.S. courts have held that it is not unlawful for a firm with a monopoly in one market to use its monopoly power in that market to gain a competitive advantage in neighboring markets, unless by so doing it serves either to maintain its existing monopoly or to create a dangerous probability of gaining a monopoly in the adjacent market as well.[30] My understanding is that under EU law, by contrast, it is an abuse of dominance for a firm that is dominant in one

29. See North Atlantic Competition Policy: Converging Toward What? Address by William J. Kolasky, Deputy Assistant Attorney General, Antitrust Division, U.S. Department of Justice Before the BIICL Second Annual International and Comparative Law Conference, London, England on May 17, 2002, retrieved from http://www.usdoj.gov/atr/public/speeches/ 11153.htm

30. See ABA Section of Antitrust Law, I Antitrust Developments 282–85 (4th ed. 1997).

market to use that position to gain a competitive advantage in a neighboring market in which it is not dominant even if the conduct is not shown to be likely to create a dominant position in the second market unless the dominant firm can show a legitimate business justification for its conduct.[31]

Our view, by contrast, is that, "so long as we allow a firm to compete in several markets, we must expect it to seek the competitive advantages of its broad-based activity—more efficient production, greater ability to develop complementary products, reduced transactions costs, and so forth,"[32] and that allowing it to do so ultimately benefits consumers. Again, this is an area that would benefit from a constructive transatlantic dialog over our differing approaches.

SECTION 4. PARTIAL VERTICAL INTEGRATION BY CONTRACT: EXCLUSIVE SELLING AND EXCLUSIVE DEALING ARRANGEMENTS

A. EXCLUSIVE SELLING

INTRODUCTORY NOTE

An "exclusive selling arrangement," also termed an "exclusive dealership" and a "sole outlet," usually comes about through a contractual arrangement under which all but one seller is eliminated or, in a start-up context, only one seller is appointed. Typically, the supplier of the product agrees not to appoint another seller and to do all its business through the single outlet. The basic antitrust issue raised by exclusive selling is whether the agreement—which by definition precludes other sellers from entering the market—may violate Section 1 of the Sherman Act and, if so, under what circumstances? Since the manufacturer is agreeing to restrict its own freedom, and in a pure case, not limiting the seller, Section 3 of the Clayton Act is not applicable.

In general, courts have been quite permissive in dealing with exclusive selling arrangements. For example, in Packard Motor Car Co. v. Webster Motor Car Co., 243 F.2d 418, 420–21 (D.C.Cir.1957), the Court of Appeals quoted with approval the following language: "When an exclusive dealership 'is not part and parcel of a scheme to monopolize, and effective competition exists at both the seller and buyer levels, the arrangement has invariably been upheld as a reasonable restraint of trade.'" In the *Packard* case, the Court of Appeals overturned a jury award for Webster Motor, one of three dealers in Packard cars in Baltimore. Packard terminated Webster Motor because Zell Motor, Packard's largest dealer in Baltimore, demanded an exclusive contract.

The Court rejected Webster Motor's claim under Section 2 of the Sherman Act because there were many other cars "reasonably interchangeable" with Packard cars and therefore "an exclusive contract for marketing Packards does not create a monopoly." As to Section 1, the Court, quoting language indicating "the rule was virtually one of *per se* legality," brushed aside the "fact that Zell asked for the

31. *See, e.g.*, Tetra Pack Rausing SA v. Comm'n, C–333/94P, [1996] ECR I–5951 (1996).

32. Berkey Photo v. Eastman Kodak Co., 603 F.2d 263 (2d Cir.1979).

arrangement," since "the immediate object of an exclusive dealership is to protect the dealer from competition in the manufacturer's product, it is likely to be the dealer who asks for it."

Packard was a small manufacturer. The Court observed that it would be "advantageous [for Packard] to retain its largest dealer in Baltimore," and to "penalize the small manufacturer for competing in this way not only fails to promote the policy of the antitrust laws but defeats it."

In evaluating exclusive selling arrangements, please note that many of the efficiency incentives, for both manufacturer and dealer, discussed in Chapter 7 are applicable. Are such arrangements as "dangerous" to competition, intrabrand and interbrand, as some of the arrangements (*e.g.*, resale price maintenance, airtight territorial arrangements) considered in Chapter 7? Are they likely to be "harmless" in all circumstances? What if the manufacturer was dominant? What if the surviving dealer was also the sole outlet for all or most other manufacturers selling in the area?

Also, as the *Renfield* case (infra) indicates, often at issue in these cases is whether the exclusive or semi-exclusive selling arrangement comes about because of a horizontal conspiracy to set price or a vertical resale price maintenance agreement. Please review Chapters 4 and 7 as to these aspects of the *Renfield* case, and ask yourself whether Judge Posner's reasoning is consistent with the cases in those Chapters.

Valley Liquors, Inc. v. Renfield Importers, Ltd.

United States Court of Appeals, Seventh Circuit, 1982.
678 F.2d 742.

■ POSNER, J. Valley Liquors, Inc., is a wholesale wine and liquor distributor in northern Illinois, and Renfield Importers, Ltd., is one of its suppliers. Effective November 1, 1981, Renfield terminated Valley as a distributor of Renfield products (which include such popular brands as Gordon's and Martini & Rossi) in two counties, McHenry and Du Page (and part of a third, which we shall ignore to simplify this opinion). Valley sued, charging that Renfield had violated section 1 of the Sherman Act. . . .

Until November 1, Renfield generally sold its products to several wholesalers in the same county. But its sales had not been growing as rapidly in Illinois as in the rest of the country, and it decided to adopt a system of restricted distribution whereby it would sell to one, or at most two, wholesalers in each county. (In some instances, however, the plan resulted in an increase in the number of wholesalers from one to two.) Although Valley was Renfield's largest wholesaler in McHenry and Du Page Counties, accounting for some 50 percent of Renfield's total sales there, the new plan terminated Valley and all of Renfield's other distributors in the two counties except Continental and Romano; they were, however, terminated in some other areas. There is unrebutted evidence that Valley had been selling Renfield products at prices five percent below those charged by Renfield's other distributors in McHenry and Du Page Counties and that Valley's termination followed discussions between Renfield and Continental and between Renfield and Romano in which Continental and Romano had expressed unhappiness at Renfield's terminating them in other areas. There is virtually no evidence concerning Renfield's motivation for the adoption of a more restricted distribution system and the concomitant realignment of wholesaler territories, except that it was a reaction to Renfield's disappointing sales in Illinois.

Valley contends that two distinct restraints of trade can be inferred from these facts. The first is a conspiracy among Renfield, Continental, and Romano to increase the wholesale prices of Renfield products in McHenry and Du Page Counties by cutting off Valley—Valley's termination being a concession demanded by Continental and Romano in exchange for consenting to the proposed realignment, under which they lost some of their territories. This is alleged to be a "horizontal" conspiracy, unlawful without more ("per se") under section 1 of the Sherman Act. The second alleged restraint of trade is the exclusion of Valley, pursuant to its distribution agreement with Renfield, from McHenry and Du Page Counties. Valley argues that this "vertical" restriction is unreasonable and hence unlawful under section 1's "Rule of Reason."

The district judge denied a preliminary injunction against Renfield's termination of Valley because he did not think that Valley had demonstrated that it was likely to win the case if tried in full. If the judge was right in his estimation of Valley's chances of success, he was right to deny a preliminary injunction, regardless of other considerations relevant to the exercise of his equitable powers.

If Continental and Romano had agreed to raise the prices of Renfield products in McHenry and Du Page Counties and to that end had persuaded Renfield (perhaps by threatening to discontinue carrying its products if it did not cooperate with them) to terminate Valley, their pesky low-price competitor, then they and their cat's paw Renfield would be guilty of a *per se* unlawful restraint of trade. Although there was no direct evidence of such a chain of events—in particular no evidence that Continental and Romano ever communicated with each other about Valley—we are asked to infer from the fact that Continental and Romano (separately) expressed unhappiness at being terminated in some of their sales areas that they demanded and received, as a quid pro quo, the termination of their major competitor in the two counties, Valley. However, this hypothesis is too speculative to compel a trier of fact to infer conspiracy, at least if Renfield may have had independent reasons for wanting to terminate Valley. We are asked to exclude that possibility because Valley was Renfield's largest and lowest-priced wholesaler in McHenry and Du Page Counties, and therefore its best. We follow the argument until "therefore." If Renfield had been content with a policy of maximizing wholesaler price competition, it would not have changed to a system of exclusive and dual wholesalers; it would have thought that the more competing wholesalers it had the better off it was. The adoption of a restricted distribution system implies a decision to emphasize nonprice competition over price competition, which such a system tends to suppress. This does not make restricted distribution good, or even lawful; we shall get to that question in a moment. Right now we are just concerned with whether Renfield may have had reasons for terminating Valley that were independent of the desires of Continental and

Romano to be rid of the competition of a price cutter. It may have. That possibility is enough to rebut an inference of collusion with those distributors based solely on the termination of Valley. . . .

There is, we admit, a certain unreality in the careful parsing of motives that *Cernuto* [595 F.2d 164 (3d Cir.1979)] seems to require. If a supplier wants his distributors to emphasize nonprice rather than price competition, which as we said is the usual reason why he would restrict his distribution, he will be hostile to price cutters because they will make it harder for his other distributors to recoup the expenditures that he wants them to make on pre-sale services to consumers and on other forms of nonprice competition, and of course the undersold distributors will be equally or more hostile. The motive of supplier and distributors alike could thus be described as wanting to eliminate price cutters yet there would be no *per se* illegality so long as the supplier was not just knuckling under to the distributors' desire for less competition. It is difficult to see how a court could distinguish empirically between such a case and the pure antipathy to price competition envisaged by *Cernuto*. But the unraveling of this skein can be left for another occasion. It is enough that in this case the plaintiff did not prove an improper motive by its supplier.

We turn to the vertical aspect of the case. If we accept, as on the state of the record we must, that Valley sold at lower prices than the other distributors in McHenry and Du Page Counties, then the territorial restriction pursuant to which it was terminated in those two counties has reduced price competition among wholesalers of the brands supplied by Renfield ("intrabrand price competition"). Valley contends that this reduction establishes a prima facie case of unreasonable restraint of trade which shifts to Renfield the burden of showing an offsetting increase in competition between brands supplied by Renfield on the one hand and brands supplied by other importers or national distributors of alcoholic beverages on the other hand ("interbrand competition").

We reject the casual equation of intrabrand price competition with interbrand competition. The elimination of a price cutter who is taking a free ride on the promotional efforts of competing distributors will tend to stimulate nonprice competition among the distributors at the same time that it dampens price competition among them, so that the net effect on intrabrand competition need not be negative. In any event, the suggestion that proof of a reduction in intrabrand competition creates a presumption of illegality is inconsistent with the test that the courts apply in restricted distribution cases. Building from a suggestive footnote in Continental T.V., Inc. v. GTE Sylvania Inc., 433 U.S. 36, 57 n. 27 (1976), the courts have held that the effects on intrabrand and on interbrand competition must be balanced in deciding whether a challenged restriction on distribution is unreasonable. And it is not generally true of balancing tests that the plaintiff, in order to make out a prima facie case, has only to show that if you put something on his side of the empty balance the balance will tilt his way. The plaintiff in a restricted distribution case must show that the restriction he is complaining of was unreasonable because, weighing effects on both intrabrand and interbrand competition, it made consumers worse off.

Admittedly, this test of illegality is easier to state than to apply, the effects to be weighed being so difficult to measure or even estimate by the methods of litigation. The courts have therefore looked for shortcuts. A popular one is to say that the balance tips in the defendant's favor if the plaintiff fails to show that the defendant has significant market power (that is, power to raise prices significantly above the competitive level without losing all of one's business). That is the approach of the Fifth and Ninth Circuits. *See, e.g.*, Muenster Butane, supra, 651 F.2d at 298; Cowley v. Braden Indus., Inc., 613 F.2d 751, 755 (9th Cir.1980). The Second Circuit seems divided on the question. Compare Oreck Corp. v. Whirlpool Corp., 579 F.2d 126, 130 n. 5 (2d Cir.1978) (*en banc*), with Eiberger, supra, 622 F.2d at 1081. We agree with the Fifth and Ninth Circuits. A firm that has no market power is unlikely to adopt policies that disserve its consumers; it cannot afford to. And if it blunders and does adopt such a policy, market retribution will be swift. Thus its mistakes do not seriously threaten consumer welfare, which is the objective that we are told should guide us in interpreting the Sherman Act. *See, e.g.*, Reiter v. Sonotone Corp., 442 U.S. 330, 343 (1979). Even if there is some possibility that the distribution practices of a powerless firm will have a substantial anticompetitive effect, it is too small a possibility to warrant trundling out the great machinery of antitrust enforcement.

Since market power can rarely be measured directly by the methods of litigation, it is normally inferred from possession of a substantial percentage of the sales in a market carefully defined in terms of both product and geography. In this case no evidence of market share was presented. In fact, no market was defined, either in product or in geographical terms, so that we do not have even a rough idea whether Renfield was a big firm in its market or a small firm. Nor did Valley seek to establish Renfield's market power by some alternative route, not involving proof of relevant market and market share.

On this as on all the other issues in this case our comments on the weight of the evidence have reference only to the evidence introduced in support of and in opposition to Valley's motion for a preliminary injunction. We are not prejudging Valley's right to a permanent injunction at the end of the trial. That right depends on the evidence introduced at trial, which for all we know may cure the deficiencies in Valley's proof that require us to order that the denial of its motion for a preliminary injunction be, and it hereby is, affirmed.[33]

B.   EXCLUSIVE DEALING

Clayton Act, Section 3

[Reprinted p. 876 supra]

---

33. On remand, the district court granted summary judgment for defendant Renfield and the Seventh Circuit affirmed. 822 F.2d 656 (7th Cir.1987).

Standard Fashion Co. v. Magrane–Houston Co.

Supreme Court of the United States, 1922.
258 U.S. 346, 42 S.Ct. 360, 66 L.Ed. 653.

■ DAY, J. Petitioner brought suit in the United States District Court for the District of Massachusetts to restrain the respondent from violating a certain contract concerning the sale of patterns for garments worn by women and children, called Standard Patterns. The bill was dismissed by the District Court and its decree was affirmed by the Circuit Court of Appeals. 259 F. 793....

Petitioner is a New York corporation engaged in the manufacture and distribution of patterns. Respondent conducted a retail dry goods business at the corner of Washington Street and Temple Place in the City of Boston. On November 25, 1914, the parties entered into a contract by which the petitioner granted to the respondent an agency for the sale of Standard Patterns at respondent's store, for a term of two years from the date of the contract, and from term to term thereafter until the agreement should be terminated as thereinafter provided.... Respondent agreed not to assign or transfer the agency, or to remove it from its original location without the written consent of the petitioner, and not to sell or permit to be sold on its premises during the term of the contract any other make of patterns, and not to sell Standard Patterns except at labeled prices....

The contract contains an agreement that the respondent shall not sell or permit to be sold on its premises during the term of the contract any other make of patterns. It is shown that on or about July 1, 1917, the respondent discontinued the sale of the petitioner's patterns and placed on sale in its store patterns of a rival company known as the McCall Company....

The contract required the purchaser not to deal in goods of competitors of the seller. It is idle to say that the covenant was limited to the premises of the purchaser, and that sales might be made by it elsewhere. The contract should have a reasonable construction. The purchaser kept a retail store in Boston. It was not contemplated that it would make sales elsewhere. The covenant, read in the light of the circumstances in which it was made, is one by which the purchaser agreed not to sell any other make of patterns while the contract was in force. The real question is: Does the contract of sale come within the third section of the Clayton Act because the covenant not to sell the patterns of others "may be to substantially lessen competition or tend to create a monopoly." ...

The Clayton Act sought to reach the agreements embraced within its sphere in their incipiency, and in the section under consideration to determine their legality by specific tests of its own which declared illegal contracts of sale made upon the agreement or understanding that the purchaser shall not deal in the goods of a competitor or competitors of the seller, which may "substantially lessen competition or tend to create a monopoly."

Much is said in the briefs concerning the Reports of Committees concerned with the enactment of this legislation, but the words of the act are plain and their meaning is apparent without the necessity of resorting to the extraneous statements and often unsatisfactory aid of such reports. . . .

Section 3 condemns sales or agreements where the effect of such sale or contract of sale "may" be to substantially lessen competition or tend to create monopoly. It thus deals with consequences to follow the making of the restrictive covenant limiting the right of the purchaser to deal in the goods of the seller only. But we do not think that the purpose in using the word "may" was to prohibit the mere possibility of the consequences described. It was intended to prevent such agreements as would under the circumstances disclosed probably lessen competition, or create an actual tendency to monopoly. That it was not intended to reach every remote lessening of competition is shown in the requirement that such lessening must be substantial.

Both courts below found that the contract interpreted in the light of the circumstances surrounding the making of it was within the provisions of the Clayton Act as one which substantially lessened competition and tended to create monopoly. These courts put special stress upon the fact found that, of 52,000 so-called pattern agencies in the entire country, the petitioner, or a holding company controlling it and two other pattern companies, approximately controlled two-fifths of such agencies. As the Circuit Court of Appeals summarizing the matter pertinently observed:

> The restriction of each merchant to one pattern manufacturer must in hundreds, perhaps in thousands of small communities amount to giving such single pattern manufacturer a monopoly of the business in such community. Even in the larger cities, to limit to a single pattern maker the pattern business of dealers most resorted to by customers whose purchases tend to give fashions their vogue, may tend to facilitate further combinations; so that the plaintiff, or some other aggressive concern, instead of controlling two-fifths, will shortly have almost, if not quite, all the pattern business.

We agree with these conclusions, and have no doubt that the contract, properly interpreted, with its restrictive covenant, brings it fairly within the section of the Clayton Act under consideration.

Affirmed.

NOTES

1. STANDARD OIL CO. OF CALIFORNIA v. UNITED STATES, 337 U.S. 293, 69 S.Ct. 1051, 93 L.Ed. 1371 (1949). Standard Oil Company of California and its wholly owned subsidiary, Standard Stations, Inc., entered into exclusive supply contracts with independent service stations. Standard Oil was the largest seller of gasoline in

the market with 23% of the total taxable gallonage. Sales by company-owned service stations constituted 6.8% of the total, and sales under exclusive dealing contracts with independent service stations constituted 6.7%. Standard Oil had entered into exclusive supply contracts with about 16% of the independent service stations in the market. Justice Frankfurter, writing for the Court, trying to narrow the scope of the inquiry under Section 3 of the Clayton Act, held:

> We conclude, therefore, that the qualifying clause of § 3 is satisfied by proof that competition has been foreclosed in a substantial share of the line of commerce affected. It cannot be gainsaid that observance by a dealer of his requirements contract with Standard does effectively foreclose whatever opportunity there might be for competing suppliers to attract his patronage, and it is clear that the affected proportion of retail sales of petroleum products is substantial. In view of the widespread adoption of such contracts by Standard's competitors and the availability of alternative ways of obtaining an assured market, evidence that competitive activity has not actually declined is inconclusive. Standard's use of the contracts creates just such a potential clog on competition as it was the purpose of § 3 to remove wherever, were it to become actual, it would impede a substantial amount of competitive activity.[34]

2. FEDERAL TRADE COMMISSION v. MOTION PICTURE ADVERTISING SERVICE CO., 344 U.S. 392, 73 S.Ct. 361, 97 L.Ed. 426 (1953). Motion Picture Advertising's exclusive contracts were alleged to be an "unfair method of competition" in violation of § 5 of the Federal Trade Commission Act. Respondent produced and distributed advertising motion pictures which depict commodities offered for sale by commercial establishments. Its contracts with theatre owners for the display of such films provide that the theatre owner will display only advertising films supplied by the respondent, with certain exceptions. These contracts run for terms up to five years, although most are for one or two years. They covered almost forty percent of the theatres in the 27–state area in which it operated. Motion Picture and three other firms (against which proceedings were also brought) together had exclusive arrangements with approximately three-fourths of the total number of theatres in the United States showing such films.

The Court of Appeals reversed the Commission's holding that the exclusive contracts were unduly restrictive of competition when they extended for periods in excess of one year.

The Supreme Court upheld the Commission:

> This is not a situation where by the nature of the market there is room for newcomers, irrespective of the existing restrictive practices. The number of outlets for the films is quite limited. And due to the exclusive contracts, respondent and the three other major companies have foreclosed to competitors 75 percent of all available outlets for this business throughout the United States. It is, we think, plain ... that a device which has sewed up a market so tightly for the benefit of a few falls within the prohibitions of the Sherman Act and is therefore an "unfair method of competition" within the meaning of § 5(a) of the Federal Trade Commission Act.

The Court noted that "unfair methods of competition" were not confined to those condemned by the Sherman Act or illegal at common law. The Court also

---

34. 337 U.S. at 314.

affirmed the Commission's finding that, in light of the compelling business reasons for some exclusive arrangement, exclusive contracts limited to one year would not unduly restrain competition:

> The precise impact of a particular practice on the trade is for the Commission, not the courts, to determine. The point where a method of competition becomes "unfair" within the meaning of the Act will often turn on the exigencies of a particular situation, trade practices, or the practical requirements of the business in question.

Tampa Electric Co. v. Nashville Coal Co.

Supreme Court of the United States, 1961.
365 U.S. 320, 81 S.Ct. 623, 5 L.Ed.2d 580.

■ CLARK, J. We granted certiorari to review a declaratory judgment holding illegal under § 3 of the Clayton Act a requirements contract between the parties providing for the purchase by petitioner of all the coal it would require as boiler fuel at its Gannon Station in Tampa, Florida, over a 20–year period. 363 U.S. 836. Both the District Court, 168 F.Supp. 456, and the Court of Appeals, 276 F.2d 766, Judge Weick dissenting, agreed with respondents that the contract fell within the proscription of § 3 and therefore was illegal and unenforceable. We cannot agree that the contract suffers the claimed antitrust illegality and, therefore, do not find it necessary to consider respondents' additional argument that such illegality is a defense to the action and a bar to enforceability.

Petitioner Tampa Electric Company is a public utility located in Tampa, Florida. It produces and sells electric energy to a service area, including the city, extending from Tampa Bay eastward 60 miles to the center of the State, and some 30 miles in width. As of 1954 petitioner operated two electrical generating plants comprising a total of 11 individual generating units, all of which consumed oil in their burners. In 1955 Tampa Electric decided to expand its facilities by the construction of an additional generating plant to be comprised ultimately of six generating units, and to be known as the "Francis J. Gannon Station." Although every electrical generating plant in peninsular Florida burned oil at that time, Tampa Electric decided to try coal as boiler fuel in the first two units constructed at the Gannon Station. Accordingly, it contracted with the respondents to furnish the expected coal requirements for the units. The agreement, dated May 23, 1955, embraced Tampa Electric's "total requirements of fuel ... for the operation of its first two units to be installed at the Gannon Station ... not less than 225,000 tons of coal per unit per year," for a period of 20 years. The contract further provided that "if during the first 10 years of the term ... the Buyer constructs additional units [at Gannon] in which coal is used as the fuel, it shall give the Seller notice thereof two years prior to the completion of such unit or units and upon completion of same the fuel requirements thereof shall be added to this contract." It was understood and agreed, however, that "the Buyer has the option to be exercised two years prior to completion of said unit or units of determining whether coal or some other fuel shall be used in same." Tampa Electric had the further option of reducing, up to 15%, the amount of its coal purchases covered by the contract after giving six months' notice of an intention to use as fuel a by-product of any of its local customers. The minimum price was set at $6.40 per ton delivered, subject to an escalation clause based on labor cost and other factors. Deliveries were originally expected to begin in March 1957, for the first unit, and for the second unit at the completion of its construction.

In April 1957, soon before the first coal was actually to be delivered and after Tampa Electric, in order to equip its first two Gannon units for the use of coal, had expended some $3,000,000 more than the cost of constructing oil-burning units, and after respondents had expended approximately $7,500,000 readying themselves to perform the contract, the latter advised petitioner that the contract was illegal under the antitrust laws, would therefore not be performed, and no coal would be delivered. This turn of events required Tampa Electric to look elsewhere for its coal requirements. The first unit at Gannon began operating August 1, 1957, using coal purchased on a temporary basis, but on December 23, 1957, a purchase order contract for the total coal requirements of the Gannon Station was made with Love and Amos Coal Company. It was for an indefinite period cancellable on 12 months' notice by either party, or immediately upon tender of performance by respondents under the contract sued upon here. The maximum price was $8.80 per ton, depending upon the freight rate. In its purchase order to the Love and Amos Company, Tampa estimated that its requirements at the Gannon Station would be 350,000 tons in 1958; 700,000 tons in 1959 and 1960; 1,000,000 tons in 1961; and would increase thereafter, as required, to "about 2,250,000 tons per year." The second unit at Gannon Station commenced operation 14 months after the first, *i.e.*, October 1958. Construction of a third unit, the coal for which was to have been provided under the original contract, was also begun.

The record indicates that the total consumption of coal in peninsular Florida, as of 1958, aside from Gannon Station, was approximately 700,000 tons annually. It further shows that there were some 700 coal suppliers in the producing area where respondents operated, and that Tampa Electric's anticipated maximum requirements at Gannon Station, *i.e.*, 2,250,000 tons annually, would approximate 1% of the total coal of the same type produced and marketed from respondents' producing area.

Petitioner brought this suit in the District Court pursuant to 28 U.S.C. § 2201, 28 U.S.C.A. § 2201, for a declaration that its contract with respondents was valid, and for enforcement according to its terms.... The District Court ... granted respondents' motion for summary judgment on the sole ground that the undisputed facts, recited above, showed the contract to be a violation of § 3 of the Clayton Act. The Court of Appeals agreed....

Both courts admitted that the contract "does not expressly contain the 'condition' " [276 F.2d 771] that Tampa Electric would not use or deal in the coal of respondents' competitors. Nonetheless, they reasoned, the "total requirements" provision had the same practical effect, for it prevented Tampa Electric for a period of 20 years from buying coal from any other source for use at that station. Each court cast aside as "irrelevant" arguments citing the use of oil as boiler fuel by Tampa Electric at its other stations, and by other utilities in peninsular Florida, because oil was not in fact used at Gannon Station, and the possibility of exercise by Tampa Electric of the option reserved to it to build oil-burning units at Gannon was too remote. Found to be equally remote was the possibility of Tampa's conversion of existing oil-burning units at its other stations to the use of coal which would not be covered by the contract with respondents. It followed, both courts found, that the "line of commerce" [168 F.Supp. 460] on which the restraint was to be tested was coal—not boiler fuels. Both courts compared the estimated coal tonnage as to which the contract pre-empted competition for 20 years, namely, 1,000,000 tons a year by 1961, with the previous annual consumption of peninsular Florida, 700,000 tons. Emphasizing that fact as well as the contract value of the coal covered by the 20–year term, i.e., $128,000,000, they held that such volume was not "insignificant or insubstantial" and that the effect of the contract would "be to substantially lessen competition," in violation of the Act. Both courts were of the opinion that in view of the executory nature of the contract, judicial enforcement of any portion of it could not be granted without directing a violation of the Act itself, and enforcement was, therefore, denied. . . .

. . . Following the guidelines of earlier decisions, certain considerations must be taken. *First,* the line of commerce, *i.e.,* the type of goods, wares, or merchandise, etc., involved must be determined, where it is in controversy, on the basis of the facts peculiar to the case. *Second,* the area of effective competition in the known line of commerce must be charted by careful selection of the market area in which the seller operates, and to which the purchaser can practically turn for supplies. In short, the threatened foreclosure of competition must be in relation to the market affected. . . .

. . . In [Standard Oil Co. v. United States, 337 U.S. 293 (1949)], the area of effective competition—the relevant market—was found to be where the seller and some 75 of its competitors sold petroleum products. Conveniently identified as the Western Area, it included Arizona, California, Idaho, Nevada, Oregon, Utah and Washington. Similarly, in United States v. Columbia Steel Co., 1948, 334 U.S. 495, a § 1 Sherman Act case, this Court decided the relevant market to be the competitive area in which Consolidated marketed its products, i.e., 11 Western States. The Court found Consolidated's share of the nationwide market for the relevant line of commerce, rolled steel products, to be less than ½ of 1%, an "insignificant fraction of the total market," 334 U.S. at page 508; and its share of the more narrow but only relevant market, 3%, was described as "a small part," 334 U.S. at page 511, not sufficient to injure any competitor of United States Steel in that area or elsewhere.

Third, and last, the competition foreclosed by the contract must be found to constitute a substantial share of the relevant market. That is to say, the opportunities for other traders to enter into or remain in that market must be significantly limited as was pointed out in Standard Oil Co. v. United States, supra. There the impact of the requirements contracts was studied in the setting of the large number of gasoline stations—5,937 or 16% of the retail outlets in the relevant market—and the large number of contracts, over 8,000, together with the great volume of products involved. This combination dictated a finding that "Standard's use of the contracts [created] just such a potential clog on competition as it was the purpose of § 3 to remove" where, as there, the affected proportion of retail sales was substantial. 337 U.S. at page 314. As we noted above, in United States v. Columbia Steel Co., supra, substantiality was judged on a comparative basis, i.e., Consolidated's use of rolled steel was "a small part" when weighed against the total volume of that product in the relevant market.

To determine substantiality in a given case, it is necessary to weigh the probable effect of the contract on the relevant area of effective competition, taking into account the relative strength of the parties, the proportionate volume of commerce involved in relation to the total volume of commerce in the relevant market area, and the probable immediate and future effects which pre-emption of that share of the market might have on effective competition therein. It follows that a mere showing that the contract itself involves a substantial number of dollars is ordinarily of little consequence.

In applying these considerations to the facts of the case before us, it appears clear that both the Court of Appeals and the District Court have not given the required effect to a controlling factor in the case—the relevant competitive market area. This omission, by itself, requires reversal, for, as we have pointed out, the relevant market is the prime factor in relation to which the ultimate question, whether the contract forecloses competition in a substantial share of the line of commerce involved, must be decided. For the purposes of this case, therefore, we need not decide two threshold questions pressed by Tampa Electric. They are whether the contract in fact satisfies the initial requirement of § 3, i.e., whether it is truly an exclusive-dealing one, and, secondly, whether the line of commerce is boiler fuels, including coal, oil and gas, rather than coal alone. We, therefore, for the purposes of this case, assume, but do not decide, that the contract is an exclusive-dealing arrangement within the compass of § 3, and that the line of commerce is bituminous coal.

Neither the Court of Appeals nor the District Court considered in detail the question of the relevant market. They do seem, however, to have been satisfied with inquiring only as to competition within "Peninsular Florida." It was noted that the total consumption of peninsular Florida was 700,000 tons of coal per year, about equal to the estimated 1959 requirements of Tampa Electric. It was also pointed out that coal accounted for less than 6% of the fuel consumed in the entire State. The District Court concluded that though the respondents were only one of 700 coal producers who could serve the same market, peninsular Florida, the contract for a period of 20 years excluded competitors from a substantial amount of trade. Respondents contend that the coal tonnage covered by the contract must be weighed against either the total consumption of coal in peninsular Florida, or all of Florida, or the Bituminous Coal Act area comprising peninsular Florida and the Georgia "finger," or, at most, all of Florida and Georgia. If the latter area were considered the relevant market, Tampa Electric's proposed requirements would be 18% of the tonnage sold therein. Tampa Electric says that both courts and respondents are in error, because the "700 coal producers who could serve" it, as recognized by the trial court and admitted by respondents, operated in the Appalachian coal area and that its contract requirements were less than 1% of the total marketed production of these producers; that the relevant effective area of competition was the area in which these producers operated, and in which they were willing to compete for the consumer potential.

We are persuaded that on the record in this case, neither peninsular Florida, nor the entire State of Florida, nor Florida and Georgia combined constituted the relevant market of effective competition. We do not believe that the pie will slice so thinly. By far the bulk of the overwhelming tonnage marketed from the same producing area as serves Tampa is sold outside of Georgia and Florida, and the producers were "eager" to sell more coal in those States. While the relevant competitive market is not ordinarily susceptible to a "metes and bounds" definition, cf. Times–Picayune Pub. Co. v. United States, 345 U.S. 594, 611, it is of course the area in which respondents and the other 700 producers effectively compete. Standard Oil Co. v. United States, supra. The record shows that, like the respondents, they sold bituminous coal "suitable for [Tampa's] requirements," mined in parts of Pennsylvania, Virginia, West Virginia, Kentucky, Tennessee, Alabama, Ohio and Illinois. We take notice of the fact that the approximate total bituminous coal (and lignite) product in the year 1954 from the districts in which these 700 producers are located was 359,289,000 tons, of which some 290,567,000 tons were sold on the open market. Of the latter amount some 78,716,000 tons were sold to electric utilities. We also note that in 1954 Florida and Georgia combined consumed at least 2,304,-000 tons, 1,100,000 of which were used by electric utilities, and the sources of which were mines located in no less than seven States. We take further notice that the production and marketing of bituminous coal (and lignite) from the same districts, and assumedly equally available to Tampa on a commercially feasible basis, is currently on a par with prior years. In point of statistical fact, coal consumption in the combined Florida–Georgia area has increased significantly since 1954. In 1959 more than 3,775,000 tons were there consumed, 2,913,000 being used by electric utilities including, presumably, the coal used by the petitioner.

The coal continued to come from at least seven States. From these statistics it clearly appears that the proportionate volume of the total relevant coal product as to which the challenged contract pre-empted competition, less than 1%, is, conservatively speaking, quite insubstantial. A more accurate figure, even assuming pre-emption to the extent of the maximum anticipated total requirements, 2,250,000 tons a year, would be .77%.

It may well be that in the context of antitrust legislation protracted requirements contracts are suspect, but they have not been declared illegal *per se*. Even though a single contract between single traders may fall within the initial broad proscription of the section, it must also suffer the qualifying disability, tendency to work a substantial—not remote—lessening of competition in the relevant competitive market. It is urged that the present contract pre-empts competition to the extent of purchases worth perhaps $128,000,000, and that this "is, of course, not insignificant or insubstantial." While $128,000,000 is a considerable sum of money, even in these days, the dollar volume, by itself, is not the test, as we have already pointed out.

The remaining determination, therefore, is whether the pre-emption of competition to the extent of the tonnage involved tends to substantially foreclose competition in the relevant coal market. We think not. That market sees an annual trade in excess of 250,000,000 tons of coal and over a billion dollars—multiplied by 20 years it runs into astronomical figures. There is here neither a seller with a dominant position in the market as in Standard Fashions, supra; nor myriad outlets with substantial sales volume, coupled with an industry-wide practice of relying upon exclusive contracts, as in Standard Oil, supra; nor a plainly restrictive tying arrangement as in International Salt, supra. On the contrary, we seem to have only that type of contract which "may well be of economic advantage to buyers as well as to sellers." Standard Oil v. United States, supra, 337 U.S. at 306. In the case of the buyer it "may assure supply," while on the part of the seller it "may make possible the substantial reduction of selling expenses, give protection against price fluctuations, and . . . offer the possibility of a predictable market." Id., 337 U.S. at 306–307. The 20–year period of the contract is singled out as the principal vice, but at least in the case of public utilities the assurance of a steady and ample supply of fuel is necessary in the public interest. Otherwise consumers are left unprotected against service failures owing to shutdowns; and increasingly unjustified costs might result in more burdensome rate structures eventually to be reflected in the consumer's bill. The compelling validity of such considerations has been recognized fully in the natural gas public utility field. This is not to say that utilities are immunized from Clayton Act proscriptions, but merely that, in judging the term of a requirements contract in relation to the substantiality of the foreclosure of competition, particularized considerations of the parties' operations are not irrelevant. In weighing the various factors, we have decided that in the competitive bituminous coal marketing area involved here the contract sued upon does not tend to foreclose a substantial volume of competition. . . .

The judgment is reversed and the case remanded to the District Court for further proceedings not inconsistent with this opinion.[35]

---

35. Ed. Black and Douglas, JJ., dissented without opinion, stating that the lower courts "correctly decided this case."

NOTES AND QUESTIONS

1. CURLY'S DAIRY, INC. v. DAIRY COOPERATIVE ASSOCIATION, 202 F.Supp. 481 (D.Or.1962), was a private action for damages and an injunction brought against a wholesaler of dairy products by a competing wholesaler. Plaintiff has alleged that defendant granted loans to retail stores and restaurants on condition that the borrower agree to purchase its complete dairy requirements from defendant as long as the debt remained outstanding. After defining the relevant market for sale of dairy products at wholesale to include most of the states of Washington and Oregon, the district court concluded that the challenged agreements covered less than 1% of sales in that market, and dismissed the complaint under authority of *Tampa Electric*. With respect to the *Standard Oil* decision, the court wrote:

> The Court in *Tampa* made it perfectly clear that neither comparative quantitative substantiality (*i.e.*, the market share foreclosed) nor absolute quantitative substantiality (*i.e.*, the dollar volume foreclosed) (as defined in *Standard*) should be the controlling factor. 202 F.Supp. at 484–85.

2. How greatly do the approaches in *Tampa Electric* and *Standard Oil* (p. 937 supra) differ? Is the more complex economic analysis suggested by *Tampa Electric* likely to provide enhanced accuracy in gauging anticompetitive effect? Will it increase certainty or be easily administrable in courts? What factors beyond market power, extent of foreclosure, ease of replicating the distribution scheme, and duration should be considered in determining whether there has been a substantial lessening of competition? How about the level of, and trends with respect to, concentration and the use of exclusive dealing arrangements by other competitors? Barriers to entry and history of entry? Justifications for the exclusive dealing arrangement? Which of these, and other factors you might think of, are likely to be truly important in a given case?

3. As the *Jefferson Parish* case (p. 886 supra) demonstrates, the Supreme Court is now approaching tying more cautiously and this may have implications for exclusive dealing too. Indeed, one commentary concluded:

> *Jefferson Parish Hospital District No. 2 v. Hyde* teetered on the brink between characterization as a tying case and characterization as an exclusive dealing case, as evidenced by the four-vote concurring opinion which would have treated the arrangement as exclusive dealing. Because of this, the decision is important to the law of exclusive dealing as well as to the law of tying. Justice O'Connor wrote:
>
> > A firm of four anesthesiologists represents only a very small fraction of the total number of anesthesiologists whose services are available for hire by other hospitals, and East Jefferson is one among numerous hospitals buying such services. Even without engaging in a detailed analysis of the size of the relevant markets we may readily conclude that there is no likelihood that the exclusive dealing arrangement challenged here will either unreasonably enhance the hospital's market position relative to other hospitals, or unreasonably permit Roux [the holder of the exclusive contract] to acquire power relative to other anesthesiologists. Accordingly, this exclusive dealing arrangement must be sustained under the rule of reason.

Justice O'Connor was correct, of course, in pointing out that the defendant hospital was only one of many hospitals admitting patients in New Orleans, so the foreclosure effect on other anesthesiologists was limited. At the same time, however, that hospital did account for fully thirty percent of the patients in the area. If a thirty percent foreclosure is not significant, we now know considerably more about where to draw the line than we did after *Tampa Electric* (the Supreme Court's last statement on exclusive dealing), where less than one percent of the market was foreclosed.[36]

Review Justice Stevens' majority opinion in *Jefferson Parish* and Justice O'Connor's concurrence; is it true that thirty percent of the market for anesthesiological services was foreclosed? For exclusive dealing purposes, what is the relevance of the fact that thirty percent of the patients living in Jefferson Parish went to East Jefferson Hospital and seventy percent went elsewhere—most to the "at least 20 hospitals in the New Orleans metropolitan area"?

4. IN ROLAND MACHINERY CO. v. DRESSER INDUSTRIES, INC., 749 F.2d 380 (7th Cir.1984), Judge Posner, in reversing the grant of a preliminary injunction, set forth his view of the current state of exclusive dealing law:

[Defendant Dresser signed a dealership agreement with Roland, a dealer in construction equipment and related items.] The agreement provided that it could be terminated by either party, without cause, on 90 days' notice. It did not contain an exclusive-dealing clause (that is, a clause forbidding the dealer to sell any competing manufacturer's construction equipment). Eight months after signing the agreement Roland signed a similar agreement with Komatsu, a Japanese manufacturer of construction equipment. Several months after discovering that Roland had done this, Dresser gave notice that it would exercise its contract right to terminate its dealership agreement with Roland without cause. Roland brought this suit shortly before the end of the 90–day notice period, charging that Dresser had violated section 3 of the Clayton Act and other provisions of federal and state law. The district judge granted Roland a preliminary injunction based solely on the section 3 charges, and Dresser has appealed....

In order to prevail on its section 3 claim, Roland will have to show both that there was an agreement, though not necessarily an explicit agreement (see *Tire Sales Corp. v. Cities Service Oil Co.*, 637 F.2d 467, 474 (7th Cir.1980); *McElhenney Co. v. Western Auto Supply Co.*, 269 F.2d 332, 338 (4th Cir.1959)), between it and Dresser that it not carry a line of construction equipment competitive with Dresser's, and that the agreement was likely to have a substantial though not necessarily an immediate anticompetitive effect. Regarding the first of these required showings, the record of the preliminary-injunction proceeding contains no evidence that either Roland or any other Dresser dealer agreed with Dresser not to carry a competing manufacturer's line. Nothing in the dealership agreement even hints at a requirement of exclusive dealing, and the fact that after signing the agreement with Dresser, Roland applied for a Komatsu dealership is evidence that Roland itself did not think it had made an implied commitment to exclusive dealing. True, Dresser prefers exclusive dealers— so much so as to be willing to terminate its only dealer in a large marketing area. The district judge believed that evidence of this preference, coupled with the absence of any reason for Dresser's having terminated Roland other than Roland's having taken on an additional line of construc-

36. Steuer, Exclusive Dealing After Jefferson Parish, 54 Antitrust L.J. 1229, 1232 (1985).

tion equipment, established a prima facie case of agreement. But an agreement requires a meeting of minds, and there is no evidence that Roland ever thought itself bound to carry only the Dresser line. Indeed, at argument Roland disclaimed any knowledge of what it describes as the implied exclusive-dealing term in the contract; it called it a "secret" term, echoing the district judge's description of exclusive dealing as something "in the mind of" Dresser. One mind is not enough for a meeting of minds. The fact that Dresser was hostile to dealers who would not live and die by its product (as the district judge put it), and acted on its hostility by canceling a dealer who did the thing to which it was hostile, does not establish an agreement, but if anything the opposite: a failure to agree on a point critical to one of the parties.

Actually, it is not important whether Dresser's antipathy to nonexclusive dealing was secret. Assume that Dresser made clear to Roland and its other dealers that it wanted only exclusive dealers and would exercise its contract right to terminate, immediately and without cause, any dealer who took on a competing line. The mere announcement of such a policy, and the carrying out of it by canceling Roland or any other noncomplying dealer, would not establish an agreement. It would be a classic example of the conduct permitted by United States v. Colgate & Co., 250 U.S. 300 (1919).... True, there is some evidence that Dresser, fearing the competition of Komatsu, made efforts to discover which of its dealers were considering dealing with Komatsu. Surveillance could in some circumstances intimidate—could be the stick that forced dealers into a tacit understanding not to handle a competitor's goods. See Yentsch v. Texaco, Inc., 630 F.2d 46, 54 (2d Cir.1980). But there is no evidence that it was such here, when Roland within months after signing a dealership agreement with Dresser went and signed another one with Komatsu. The district judge did not rely on evidence of surveillance in concluding that there was an implicit exclusive-dealing agreement.

Dresser's preference for exclusive dealers, its efforts to find out whether its dealers were exclusive dealers, and its terminating Roland when it found out that Roland no longer was its exclusive dealer do not support an inference "both that the distributor communicated its acquiescence or agreement" to exclusive dealing "and that this was sought by the manufacturer." Monsanto Co. v. Spray–Rite Service Corp., supra, 465 U.S. at 764, n. 9. But even if Roland can prove at trial that there was an exclusive-dealing agreement, it will have grave difficulty—we infer from this record—in proving that the agreement is anticompetitive. The objection to exclusive-dealing agreements is that they deny outlets to a competitor during the term of the agreement. At one time it was thought that this effect alone would condemn exclusive-dealing agreements under section 3 of the Clayton Act, provided that the agreements covered a large fraction of the market. See Standard Oil Co. v. United States, 337 U.S. 293 (1949) ("Standard Stations"). Although the Supreme Court has not decided an exclusive-dealing case in many years, it now appears most unlikely that such agreements, whether challenged under section 3 of the Clayton Act or section 1 of the Sherman Act, will be judged by the simple and strict test of *Standard Stations*. They will be judged under the Rule of Reason, and thus condemned only if found to restrain trade unreasonably. *See, e.g.,* Jefferson Parish Hospital District No. 2 v. Hyde, 466 U.S. 2 (1984) (concurring opinion); Tampa Elec. Co. v. Nashville Coal Co., 365 U.S. 320, 333–35 (1961)....

The exclusion of competitors is cause for antitrust concern only if it impairs the health of the competitive process itself. Hence a plaintiff must prove two things to show that an exclusive-dealing agreement is unreasonable. First, he must prove that it is likely to keep at least one significant competitor of the defendant from doing business in a relevant market. If there is no exclusion of a significant competitor, the agreement cannot possibly harm competition. Second, he must prove that the probable (not certain) effect of the exclusion will be to raise prices above (and therefore reduce output below) the competitive level, or otherwise injure competition; he must show in other words that the anticompetitive effects (if any) of the exclusion outweigh any benefits to competition from it. Roland has as yet made very little effort to establish either of these two things.

5. The 90–days' notice provision—exercisable by either party—in *Roland* helped greatly in the defense of the implied exclusive dealing arrangement. But does either *Tampa Electric* or *Jefferson Parish* stand for the proposition that a plaintiff "must prove that ... [the exclusive dealing arrangement] is likely to keep at least one significant competitor ... from doing business in a relevant market" *and* that price will probably rise above "the competitive level"? Has not the Supreme Court since *Standard Fashion* (p. 936 supra) spoken in terms of "probability" and "incipiency" in this area?

The willingness of courts to imply an exclusive dealing arrangement—as Judge Posner was willing to do in *Roland* if proper evidence had been presented—varies. Compare Alles Corp. v. Senco Products, Inc., 329 F.2d 567 (6th Cir.1964) (exclusive dealing arrangements can be "implied," in part, from a refusal to deal with a distributor who handles competitors' products) with Nelson Radio and Supply Co. v. Motorola, Inc., 200 F.2d 911 (5th Cir.1952), cert. denied, 345 U.S. 925 (1953) ("there is nothing whatever in [Section 3] to suggest that it covers a situation where the manufacturer refuses to make a sale or enter into a contract.... There is a real difference between the act of refusing to deal and the execution of a contract which prevents a person from dealing with another").

Although Dresser's distributors were free to switch to another supplier on 90–days' notice, they apparently could not carry two lines of construction equipment from different manufacturers simultaneously. Might that arrangement have anticompetitive effects?

6. Should vertical integration by exclusive dealing contracts be treated in the same way—or more permissively or more harshly—as vertical integration by merger? In which circumstance would the foreclosure be more permanent and complete? See Chapter 9, Section 4, infra.

Federal Trade Commission v. Brown Shoe Co.

Supreme Court of the United States, 1966.
384 U.S. 316, 86 S.Ct. 1501, 16 L.Ed.2d 587.

■ BLACK, J. Section 5(a)(6) of the Federal Trade Commission Act empowers and directs the Commission "to prevent persons, partnerships, or corporations ... from using unfair methods of competition in commerce and unfair or deceptive acts or practices in commerce." Proceeding under the authority of § 5, the Federal Trade Commission filed a complaint against the Brown Shoe Co., Inc., one of the world's largest manufacturers of shoes with total sales of $236,946,078 for the year ending October 31, 1957. The unfair practices charged against Brown revolve around the "Brown Franchise Stores' Program" through which Brown sells its shoes to some 650 retail stores. The complaint alleged that under this plan Brown, a corporation engaged in interstate commerce, had "entered into contracts or franchises with a substantial number of its independent retail shoe store operator customers which require said customers to restrict their purchases of shoes for resale to the Brown lines and which prohibit them from purchasing, stocking or reselling shoes manufactured by competitors of Brown." Brown's customers who entered into these restrictive franchise agreements, so the complaint charged, were given in return special treatment and valuable benefits which were not granted to Brown's customers who did not enter into the agreements. In its answer to the Commission's complaint Brown admitted that approximately 259 of its retail customers had executed written franchise agreements and that over 400 others had entered into its franchise program without execution of the franchise agreement. Also in its answer Brown attached as an exhibit an unexecuted copy of the "Franchise Agreement" which, when executed by Brown's representative and a retail shoe dealer, obligates Brown to give to the dealer but not to other customers certain valuable services, including among others, architectural plans, costly merchandising records, services of a Brown field representative, and a right to participate in group insurance at lower rates than the dealer could obtain individually. In return, according to the franchise agreement set out in Brown's answer, the retailer must make this promise:

"In return I will:

"1. Concentrate my business within the grades and price lines of shoes representing Brown Shoe Company Franchises of the Brown Division and will have no lines conflicting with Brown Division Brands of the Brown Shoe Company."

Brown's answer further admitted that the operators of "such Brown Franchise Stores in individually varying degrees accept the benefits and perform the obligations contained in such franchise agreements or implicit in such Program," and that Brown refuses to grant these benefits "to dealers who are dropped or voluntarily withdraw from the Brown Franchise Program...." The foregoing admissions of Brown as to the existence and operation of the franchise program were buttressed by many separate detailed fact findings of a trial examiner, one of which findings was that the franchise program effectively foreclosed Brown's competitors from selling to a substantial number of retail shoe dealers.[37] Based on these findings

---

37. In its opinion the Commission found that the services provided by Brown in its franchise program were the "prime motivation" for dealers to join and remain in the program; that the program resulted in franchised stores purchasing 75% of their total shoe requirements from Brown—the remainder being for the most part shoes which were not "conflicting" lines, as provided by the agreement; that the effect of the plan was to

and on Brown's admissions the Commission concluded that the restrictive contract program was an unfair method of competition within the meaning of § 5 and ordered Brown to cease and desist from its use.

On review the Court of Appeals set aside the Commission's order. In doing so the court said:

> "By passage of the Federal Trade Commission Act, particularly § 5 thereof, we do not believe that Congress meant to prohibit or limit sales programs such as Brown Shoe engaged in in this case.... The custom of giving free service to those who will buy their shoes is widespread, and we cannot agree with the Commission that it is an unfair method of competition in commerce." 339 F.2d 45, 56.

In addition the Court of Appeals held that there was a "complete failure to prove an exclusive dealing agreement which might be held violative of Section 5 of the Act." We are asked to treat this general conclusionary statement as though the court intended it to be a rejection of the Commission's findings of fact. We cannot do this. Neither this statement of the court nor any other statement in the opinion indicates a purpose to hold that the evidence failed to show an agreement between Brown and more than 650 franchise dealers which restrained the dealers from buying competing lines of shoes from Brown's competitors. Indeed, in view of the crucial admissions in Brown's formal answer to the complaint we cannot attribute to the Court of Appeals a purpose to set aside the Commission's findings that these restrictive agreements existed and that Brown and most of the franchised dealers in varying degrees lived up to their obligations. Thus the question we have for decision is whether the Federal Trade Commission can declare it to be an unfair practice for Brown, the second largest manufacturer of shoes in the Nation, to pay a valuable consideration to hundreds of retail shoe purchasers in order to secure a contractual promise from them that they will deal primarily with Brown and will not purchase conflicting lines of shoes from Brown's competitors. We hold that the Commission has power to find, on the record here, such an anticompetitive practice unfair, subject of course to judicial review. See Atlantic Rfg. Co. v. FTC, 381 U.S. 357, 367.

In holding that the Federal Trade Commission lacked the power to declare Brown's program to be unfair the Court of Appeals was much influenced by and quoted at length from this Court's opinion in Federal Trade Comm'n v. Gratz, 253 U.S. 421. That case, decided shortly after the Federal Trade Commission Act was passed, construed the Act over a strong dissent by Mr. Justice Brandeis as giving the Commission very little power to declare any trade practice unfair. Later cases of this Court, however, have rejected the *Gratz* view and it is now recognized in line with the

---

foreclose retail outlets to Brown's competitors, particularly small manufacturers; and that enforcement of the plan was effected by teams of field men who called upon the shoe stores, urged the elimination of other manu-facturers' conflicting lines and reported deviations to Brown who then cancelled under a provision of the agreement. Compare Brown Shoe Co. v. United States, 370 U.S. 294, 296.

dissent of Mr. Justice Brandeis in *Gratz* that the Commission has broad powers to declare trade practices unfair. This broad power of the Commission is particularly well established with regard to trade practices which conflict with the basic policies of the Sherman and Clayton Acts even though such practices may not actually violate these laws. The record in this case shows beyond doubt that Brown, the country's second largest manufacturer of shoes, has a program, which requires shoe retailers, unless faithless to their contractual obligations with Brown, substantially to limit their trade with Brown's competitors. This program obviously conflicts with the central policy of both § 1 of the Sherman Act and § 3 of the Clayton Act against contracts which take away freedom of purchasers to buy in an open market. Brown nevertheless contends that the Commission had no power to declare the franchise program unfair without proof that its effect "may be to substantially lessen competition or tend to create a monopoly" which of course would have to be proved if the Government were proceeding against Brown under § 3 of the Clayton Act rather than § 5 of the Federal Trade Commission Act. We reject the argument that proof of this § 3 element must be made for as we pointed out above our cases hold that the Commission has power under § 5 to arrest trade restraints in their incipiency without proof that they amount to an outright violation of § 3 of the Clayton Act or other provisions of the antitrust laws. This power of the Commission was emphatically stated in F.T.C. v. Motion Picture Adv. Co., 344 U.S. 392, at 394–395:

> "It is ... clear that the Federal Trade Commission Act was designed to supplement and bolster the Sherman Act and the Clayton Act ... to stop in their incipiency acts and practices which, when full blown, would violate those Acts ... as well as to condemn as 'unfair methods of competition' existing violations of them."

We hold that the Commission acted well within its authority in declaring the Brown franchise program unfair whether it was completely full blown or not.

Reversed.

NOTES AND QUESTIONS

1. Note 37 in the Supreme Court's *Brown Shoe* opinion indicates that if Brown Shoe's franchised outlets did not abide by the terms of the agreement, they were cancelled as franchisees. In the Commission opinion, it is clear that many of the franchise arrangements were oral and terminable at any time, and written franchise contracts contained a clause saying the dealer could terminate at will. Brown Shoe Co., 62 F.T.C. 679 (1963). Given those facts, what was the duration and consequent anticompetitive effect of the franchise agreements? What sort of competitor of Brown Shoe would be disadvantaged by the franchise arrangements? Is *Brown Shoe* really a tying case in which availability of services is conditioned upon acceptance of shoes? There is a suggestion to that effect in the Commission opinion,

62 F.T.C. at 715, but it was not picked up by the Supreme Court. Would the arrangement be illegal under *Jefferson Parish, Kodak,* and other tying cases?

2.   Characterization questions about what constitutes an "exclusive dealing contract" occasionally arise. For example, in Magnus Petroleum Co. v. Skelly Oil Co., 599 F.2d 196 (7th Cir.), cert. denied, 444 U.S. 916 (1979) the Seventh Circuit reversed jury verdicts for plaintiff based on findings of violation of Section 1 of the Sherman Act and Section 3 of the Clayton Act. Magnus Petroleum was a wholesaler and retailer of gasoline and fuel oil in Sheboygan, Wisconsin. It entered into a series of franchise sales agreements and lease agreements with Skelly Oil calling for Skelly to sell and Magnus to buy specified quantities of gasoline each year. The agreements were terminable by either party on 60 days' notice at the end of a five-year "primary term" and year to year thereafter. Plaintiff charged that the contracts in effect made it impossible for it to distribute branded products of other oil companies and thus were illegal exclusive dealing contracts.

The Court of Appeals reversed on two grounds. First, it noted that the specified quantity (for example, 810,000 gallons in 1976) amounted to less than 60%–80% of plaintiff's total requirements and that plaintiff regularly purchased the remainder of its requirements from competitors of Skelly. The Seventh Circuit concluded that there was no "exclusive dealing" or "total requirements" contract. Second, even if the franchise sales agreements amounted to exclusive dealing contracts, the Court noted that Magnus accounted for less than 1% of all purchases of gasoline in the 13 county area surrounding Sheboygan which it regarded as the relevant geographic market.

Compare United States v. Richfield Oil Corp., 99 F.Supp. 280 (S.D.Cal.1951), affirmed per curiam, 343 U.S. 922 (1952), where the government charged that Richfield's contracts with leased and owned retail gasoline stations amounted to exclusive dealing contracts violative of Section 1 of the Sherman Act and Section 3 of the Clayton Act. Richfield had entered into a sales contract with all its gas stations calling for purchase of specified quantities of gasoline, lubricating oil and greases per month which were intended to cover 80% of each station's estimated requirements. If lessees failed to achieve the indicated quotas, their lease could be terminated on as little as 24 hours' notice. As to owned stations, Richfield entered into "painting agreements" whereby Richfield agreed to paint the station in its own colors and insignia. If those station owners failed to purchase and sell specified quotas, the agreement was breached and the dealer became liable to Richfield for the cost of painting. In addition, Richfield sales representatives urged all dealers to sell Richfield products exclusively, terminated dealers who located competitive pumps on their station property ("split-pump operators"), and ceased dealing with those stations who showed signs advertising competitive products. The court found that the intent of the arrangements was to exclude *all* competition, that the stations in fact sold only Richfield products, and that the dealings constituted *de facto* exclusive dealing contracts.

3.   Please note that the opinion in *Brown Shoe* is the most explicit authority we have seen for the proposition that the Commission's authority under Section 5 to prevent unfair methods of competition extends beyond the reach of the Sherman and Clayton Acts. Questions arise as to what the Supreme Court intended to cover under "trade practices which conflict with the basic policies of the Sherman and Clayton Acts, even though such practices may not actually violate these laws." One set of applications would involve practices which slip through the relatively intricate language of the Clayton Act, and particularly the Robinson–Patman amendments to that statute, which are indistinguishable in purpose and effect from practices which

are clearly covered. That coverage is relatively non-controversial, and we will see some examples when we take up the Robinson–Patman Act in Chapter 11. The opinion in *Brown Shoe* seems to go further, however, and may be understood to interpret Section 5 to reach practices which lack anticompetitive effects necessary to make out violations of the Sherman and Clayton Acts. By definition, those practices do not violate the basic antitrust laws; when that is the case, what standards are available to define this Commission authority?

There is no criminal exposure under Section 5, and the statute cannot be used as a basis for private treble damage actions. Do these differences indicate any guidelines for limiting the reach of Section 5? Could Section 5 be used successfully by the Commission to challenge monopolies without evidence of illegal conduct (*i.e.*, the no-fault monopoly concept, see p. 184 supra), or to declare consciously parallel pricing illegal? (see p. 542 supra.) Is it likely that Congress intended to place such a broad grant of authority with respect to major policy questions in the hands of a regulatory agency? Or is the development of new law at the frontiers of antitrust— without criminal sanctions or treble damage exposure—a role Congress had in mind when it created a second agency to enforce the antitrust laws?

U.S. Healthcare, Inc. v. Healthsource, Inc.

United States Court of Appeals, First Circuit, 1993.
986 F.2d 589.

■ BOUDIN, J. U.S. Healthcare and two related companies (collectively "U.S. Healthcare") brought this antitrust case in the district court against Healthsource, Inc., its founder and one of its subsidiaries. Both sides are engaged in providing medical services through health maintenance organizations ("HMOs") in New Hampshire. In its suit U.S. Healthcare challenged an exclusive dealing clause in the contracts between the Healthsource HMO and doctors who provide primary care for it in New Hampshire. After a trial in district court, the magistrate judge found no violation, and U.S. Healthcare appealed. We affirm.

I. BACKGROUND

Healthsource New Hampshire is an HMO founded in 1985 by Dr. Norman Payson and a group of doctors in Concord, N.H. Its parent company, Healthsource, Inc., is headed by Dr. Payson, and it manages or has interests in HMOs in a number of states. We refer to both the parent company and its New Hampshire HMO as "Healthsource."

In simpler days, health care comprised a doctor, a patient and sometimes a hospital, but the Norman Rockwell era of medicine has given way to a new world of diverse and complex insurance and provider arrangements. One of the more successful innovations is the HMO, which acts both as a health insurer and provider, charging employers a fixed premium for each employee who subscribes. To provide medical care to subscribers, an HMO of Healthsource's type—sometimes called an individual practice association or "IPA" model HMO—contracts with independent doctors. These doctors continue to treat other patients, in contrast to a "staff" model HMO whose doctors would normally be full-time employees of the HMO.

HMOs often can provide health care at lower cost by stressing preventative care, controlling costs, and driving hard bargains with doctors or hospitals (who thereby obtain more patients in exchange for a reduced charge). Healthsource, like other HMOs, uses primary care physicians—usually internists but sometimes pediatricians or others—as "gatekeepers" who direct the patients to specialists only when necessary and who monitor hospital stays. Typically, the contracting primary care physicians do not charge by the visit but are paid "capitations" by the HMO, a fixed amount per month for each patient who selects the doctor as the patient's primary care physician. Unlike a patient with ordinary health insurance, the HMO patient is limited to the panel of doctors who have contracted with the HMO.

There are familiar alternatives to HMOs. At the "financing" end, these include traditional insurance company policies that reimburse patients for doctor or hospital bills without limiting the patient's choice of doctor, as well as Blue Cross/Blue Shield plans of various types and Medicare and Medicaid programs. At the "provider" end, there is also diversity. Doctors may now form so-called preferred provider organizations, which may include peer review and other joint activities, and contract together to provide medical services to large buyers like Blue Cross or to "network" model HMOs. There are also ordinary group medical practices. And, of course, there are still doctors engaged solely in independent practice on a fee-for-service basis.

Healthsource's HMO operations in New Hampshire were a success. At the time of suit, Healthsource was the only non-staff HMO in the state with 47,000 patients (some in nearby areas of Massachusetts), representing about 5 percent of New Hampshire's population. Stringent controls gave it low costs, including a low hospital utilization rate; and it sought and obtained favorable rates from hospitals and specialists. Giving doctors a further stake in Healthsource's success and incentive to contain costs, Dr. Payson apparently encouraged doctors to become stockholders as well, and at least 400 did so. By 1989 Dr. Payson was proposing to make Healthsource a publicly traded company, in part to permit greater liquidity for its doctor shareholders.

U.S. Healthcare is also in the business of operating HMOs. U.S. Healthcare, Inc., the parent of the other two plaintiff companies—U.S. Healthcare, Inc. (Massachusetts) and U.S. Healthcare of New Hampshire, Inc.—may be the largest publicly held provider of HMO services in the country, serving over one million patients and having total 1990 revenues of well over a billion dollars.... In 1989, U.S. Healthcare had a substantial interest in expanding into New Hampshire.

Dr. Payson was aware in the fall of 1989 that HMOs operating in other states were thinking about offering their services in New Hampshire. He was also concerned that, when Healthsource went public, many of its doctor-shareholders would sell their stock, decreasing their interest in

Healthsource and their incentive to control its costs. After considering alternative incentives, Dr. Payson and the HMO's chief operating officer conceived the exclusivity clause that has prompted this litigation. Shortly after the Healthsource public offering in November 1989, Healthsource notified its panel doctors that they would receive greater compensation if they agreed not to serve any other HMO.

The new contract term, effective January 26, 1990, provided for an increase in the standard monthly capitation paid to each primary care physician, for each Healthsource HMO patient cared for by that doctor, if the doctor agreed to the following *optional* paragraph in the basic doctor-Healthsource agreement:

> 11.01 *Exclusive Services of Physicians.* Physician agrees during the term of this Agreement not to serve as a participating physician for any other HMO plan; this shall not, however, preclude Physician from providing professional courtesy coverage arrangements for brief periods of time or emergency services to members of other HMO plans.

A doctor who adopted the option remained free to serve non-HMO patients under ordinary indemnity insurance policies, under Blue Cross/Blue Shield plans, or under preferred provider arrangements. A doctor who accepted the option could also return to non-exclusive status by giving notice.[38]

Although Healthsource capitation amounts varied, a doctor who accepted the exclusivity option generally increased his or her capitation payments by a little more than $1 per patient per month; the magistrate judge put the amount at $1.16 and said that it represented an average increase of about 14 percent as compared with non-exclusive status. The dollar benefit of exclusivity for an individual doctor obviously varies with the number of HMO patients handled by the doctor. Many of the doctors had less than 100 Healthsource patients while about 50 of them had 200 or more. About 250 doctors, or 87 percent of Healthsource's primary care physicians, opted for exclusivity. . . .

II. DISCUSSION

In this court, U.S. Healthcare attacks the exclusivity clause primarily as a *per se* or near *per se* violation of section 1; accordingly we begin by examining the case through the *per se* or "quick look" lenses urged by U.S. Healthcare. We then consider the claim recast in the more conventional framework of Tampa Electric Co. v. Nashville Coal Co., 365 U.S. 320 (1961), the Supreme Court's latest word on exclusivity contracts, appraising them under section 1's rule of reason. Finally, we address U.S. Healthcare's claims of section 2 violation and its attacks on the market-definition findings of the magistrate judge.

---

38. The original notice period was 180 days. This was reduced to 30 days in March or April 1991. It appears, at least in practice, that a doctor could switch to non-exclusive status more rapidly by returning some of the extra compensation previously paid.

The per se *and "Quick Look" Claims.* U.S. Healthcare's challenge to the exclusivity clause, calling it first a *per se* violation and later a monopolization offense, invokes a signal aspect of antitrust analysis: the same competitive practice may be reviewed under several different rubrics and a plaintiff may prevail by establishing a claim under any one of them. Thus, while an exclusivity arrangement is often considered under section 1's rule of reason, it might in theory play a role in a *per se* violation of section 1 or as an element in attempted or actual monopolization, United States v. United Shoe Machinery Corp., 110 F.Supp. 295 (D.Mass.1953), *aff'd per curiam*, 347 U.S. 521 (1954). But each rubric has its own conditions and requirements of proof.

We begin, as U.S. Healthcare does, with the *per se* rules of section 1 of the Sherman Act. It is a familiar story that Congress left the development of the Sherman Act largely to the courts and they in turn responded by classifying certain practices as *per se* violations under section 1. Today, the only serious candidates for this label are price (or output) fixing agreements and *certain* group boycotts or concerted refusals to deal.[39] The advantage to a plaintiff is that given a *per se* violation, proof of the defendant's power, of illicit purpose and of anticompetitive effect are all said to be irrelevant, see United States v. Socony–Vacuum Oil Co., 310 U.S. 150 (1940); the disadvantage is the difficulty of squeezing a practice into the ever narrowing *per se* niche.

U.S. Healthcare's main argument for *per se* treatment is to describe the exclusivity clause as a group boycott. To understand why the claim ultimately fails one must begin by recognizing that *per se* condemnation is not visited on every arrangement that might, as a matter of language, be called a group boycott or concerted refusal to deal. Rather, today that designation is principally reserved for cases in which competitors agree with each other not to deal with a supplier or distributor if it continues to serve a competitor whom they seek to injure. . . .

We doubt that the modern Supreme Court would use the boycott label to describe, or the rubric to condemn, a joint venture among competitors in which participation was allowed to some but not all, compare Northwest Wholesale Stationers, Inc. v. Pacific Stationery & Printing Co., 472 U.S. 284 (1985), with Associated Press v. United States, 326 U.S. 1 (1945), although such a restriction might well fall after a more complete analysis under the rule of reason. What is even more clear is that a purely vertical arrangement, by which (for example) a supplier or dealer makes an agreement exclusively to supply or serve a manufacturer, is not a group boycott. Were the law otherwise, every distributor or retailer who agreed with a manufacturer to handle only one brand of television or bicycle would be engaged in a group boycott of other manufacturers.

39. Tying is sometimes also described as a *per se* offense but, since some element of power must be shown and defenses are effectively available, "quasi" *per se* might be a better label. *See* Eastman Kodak Co. v. Image Technical Services, Inc., 112 S.Ct. 2072 (1992).

There are multiple reasons why the law permits (or, more accurately, does not condemn *per se*) vertical exclusivity; it is enough to say here that the incentives for and effects of such arrangements are usually more benign than a horizontal arrangement among competitors that none of them will supply a company that deals with one of their competitors. No one would think twice about a doctor agreeing to work full time for a staff HMO, an extreme case of vertical exclusivity. Imagine, by contrast, the motives and effects of a horizontal agreement by all of the doctors in a town not to work at a hospital that serves a staff HMO which competes with the doctors.

In this case, the exclusivity arrangements challenged by U.S. Health-care are vertical in form, that is, they comprise individual promises to Healthsource made by each doctor selecting the option not to offer his or her services to another HMO. The closest that U.S. Healthcare gets to a possible horizontal case is this: it suggests that the exclusivity clause in question, although vertical in form, is in substance an implicit horizontal agreement by the doctors involved. U.S. Healthcare appears to argue that stockholder-doctors dominate Healthsource and, in order to protect their individual interests (as stockholders in Healthsource), they agreed (in their capacity as doctors) not to deal with any other HMO that might compete with Healthsource. We agree that such a horizontal arrangement, if devoid of joint venture efficiencies, might warrant *per se* condemnation.

The difficulty is that there is no evidence of such a horizontal agreement in this case. Although U.S. Healthcare notes that doctor-stockholders predominate on the Healthsource board that adopted the option, there is nothing to show that the clause was devised or encouraged by the panel doctors. On the contrary, the record indicates that Dr. Payson and Health-source's chief operating officer developed the option to serve Healthsource's own interests. Formally vertical arrangements used to disguise horizontal ones are not unknown, see Interstate Circuit, Inc. v. United States, 306 U.S. 208 (1939), but U.S. Healthcare has supplied us with no evidence of such a masquerade in this case.

There is less to be said for U.S. Healthcare's alternative argument that, if *per se* treatment is not proper, then at least the exclusivity clause can be condemned almost as swiftly based on "a quick look." Citing FTC v. Indiana Federation of Dentists, 476 U.S. 447 (1986), and NCAA v. Board of Regents, 468 U.S. 85 (1984), U.S. Healthcare argues that the exclusivity clause is so patently bad that even a brief glance at its impact, lack of business benefit and anticompetitive intent suffice to condemn it. The cases relied on provide little help to U.S. Healthcare and, even on its own version of those cases, the facts would not conceivably justify a "quick look" condemnation of the clause.

In the cited cases, the Supreme Court actually contracted the *per se* rule by refusing to apply it to horizontal agreements that involved price and output fixing (television rights by NCAA members) or the setting of other terms of trade (refusal of dentists by agreement to provide x-rays to insurers). Given the unusual contexts (an interdependent sports league in one case; medical care in the other), the Court declined to condemn the arrangements *per se*, without at least weighing the alleged justifications. At the same time it required only the briefest inspection (the cited "quick look") for the Court to reject the excuses and strike down the agreements. Accord, National Society of Professional Engineers v. United States, 435 U.S. 679 (1978).

In any event, no "quick look" would ever suffice to condemn the exclusivity clause at issue in this case. Exclusive dealing arrangements come with the imprimatur of two leading Supreme Court decisions describing the potential virtues of such arrangements. *Tampa;* Standard Oil Co. of California v. United States, 337 U.S. 293 (1949) (Standard Stations); see also Jefferson Parish Hospital District No. 2 v. Hyde, 466 U.S. 2, 46 (1984) (O'Connor, J., concurring). To condemn such arrangements after *Tampa* requires a detailed depiction of circumstances and the most careful weighing of alleged dangers and potential benefits, which is to say the normal treatment afforded by the rule of reason. To that subject we now turn.

Rule of Reason. Exclusive dealing arrangements, like information exchanges or standard settings, come in a variety of forms and serve a range of objectives. Many of the purposes are benign, such as assurance of supply or outlets, enhanced ability to plan, reduced transaction costs, creation of dealer loyalty, and the like. *See Standard Stations,* 337 U.S. at 307. But there is one common danger for competition: an exclusive arrangement may "foreclose" so much of the available supply or outlet capacity that existing competitors or new entrants may be limited or excluded and, under certain circumstances, this may reinforce market power and raise prices for consumers.

Although the Supreme Court once said that a "substantial" percentage foreclosure of suppliers or outlets would violate section 1, *Standard Stations,* the Court's *Tampa* decision effectively replaced any such quantitative test by an open-ended inquiry into competitive impact. What is required under *Tampa* is to determine "the probable effect of the [exclusive] contract on the relevant area of effective competition, taking into account . . . [various factors including] the probable immediate and future effects which pre-emption of that share of the market might have on effective competition therein." 365 U.S. at 329. The lower courts have followed *Tampa* and under this standard judgments for plaintiffs are not easily obtained.

On this appeal we are handicapped in appraising the extent and impact of the foreclosure wrought by Healthsource because U.S. Healthcare has not chosen to present its argument in these traditional terms. *Tampa* is not even cited in the opening or reply briefs. Some useful facts pertaining to the extent of the foreclosure are adverted to in U.S. Healthcare's opening "statement of the case" but never seriously developed in the argument section of its brief. Since the brief itself also describes countervailing evidence of Healthsource, something more is assuredly needed. In the two paragraphs of its "quick look" formulation addressed to "anticompetitive impact," U.S. Healthcare simply asserts that competitive impact has already been discussed and that the exclusivity clause has completely foreclosed U.S. Healthcare and any other non-staff HMO from operation in New Hampshire.

This is not a persuasive treatment of a difficult issue or, rather, a host of issues. First, the extent to which the clause operated economically to restrict doctors is a serious question.[40] True, most doctors signed up for it; but who would not take the extra compensation when no competing non-staff HMO was yet operating? The extent of the financial incentive to remain in an exclusive status is unclear, since it varies with patient load, and the least loaded (and thus least constrained by the clause) doctors would normally be the best candidates for a competing HMO. Healthsource suggests that by relatively modest amounts, U.S. Healthcare could offset the exclusivity bonus for a substantial number of Healthsource doctors. U.S. Healthcare's reply brief offers no response.

Second, along with the economic inducement is the issue of duration. Normally an exclusivity clause terminable on 30 days' notice would be close to a *de minimus* constraint (*Tampa* involved a 20–year contract, and one year is sometimes taken as the trigger for close scrutiny). On the other hand, it may be that the original 180–day clause did frustrate U.S. Healthcare's initial efforts to enlist panel doctors, without whom it would be hard to sign up employers. Perhaps even a 30–day clause would have this effect, especially if a reimbursement penalty were visited on doctors switching back to non-exclusive status. Once again, U.S. Healthcare's brief offers conclusions and a few record references, but neither the precise operation of the clause nor its effects on individual doctors are clearly settled.

Third, even assuming that the financial incentive and duration of the exclusivity clause did remove many of the Healthsource doctors from the reach of new HMOs, it is unclear how much this foreclosure impairs the ability of new HMOs to operate. Certainly the number of primary care physicians tied to Healthsource was significant—one figure suggested is 25 percent or more of all such primary care physicians in New Hampshire—but this still leaves a much larger number not tied to Healthsource. It may be, as U.S. Healthcare urges, that many of the remaining "available" doctors cannot fairly be counted (*e.g.*, those employed full time elsewhere, or reaching retirement, or unwilling to serve HMOs at all). But the dimensions of this limitation were disputed and, by the same token, new doctors are constantly entering the market with an immediate need for patients.

U.S. Healthcare lays great stress upon claims, supported by some meeting notes of Healthsource staff members, that the latter was aware of new HMO entry and conscious that new HMOs like U.S. Healthcare could

---

40. Even with no notice period, Health-source's differential pricing policy—paying more to those who exclusively serve Health-source—would disadvantage competing HMOs. Some courts hesitate to apply the exclusivity label to such arrangements because there is no continuing promise not to deal, but the differential pricing plan is unquestionably part of a contract and so subject to section 1, whatever label may be applied.

be adversely affected by the exclusivity clause.[41] Healthsource in turn says that these were notes made in the absence of policy-making officers and that its real motivation for the clause was to bolster loyalty and cost-cutting incentives. Motive can, of course, be a guide to expected effects, but effects are still the central concern of the antitrust laws, and motive is mainly a clue, see Barry Wright Corp. v. ITT Grinnell Corp., 724 F.2d 227 (1st Cir.1983). This case itself suggests how far motives in business arrangement may be mixed, ambiguous, and subject to dispute. In any event, under *Tampa* the ultimate issue in exclusivity cases remains the issue of foreclosure and its consequences.

Absent a compelling showing of foreclosure of substantial dimensions, we think there is no need for us to pursue any inquiry into Healthsource's precise motives for the clause, the existence and measure of any claimed benefits from exclusivity, the balance between harms and benefits, or the possible existence and relevance of any less restrictive means of achieving the benefits. We are similarly spared the difficulty of assessing the fact that the clause is limited to HMOs, a fact from which more than one inference may be drawn. The point is that proof of substantial foreclosure and of "probable immediate and future effects" is the essential basis under *Tampa* for an attack on an exclusivity clause. U.S. Healthcare has not supplied that basis. . . .

United States v. Microsoft Corp.

United States Court of Appeals, District of Columbia Circuit, 2001.
253 F.3d 34.

[The extensive discussion of exclusive dealing contracts in general, and then legality of such contracts when the seller has monopoly power, can be found at pp. 776–88, supra.]

NOTES AND QUESTIONS

1. In CONCORD BOAT CORP. v. BRUNSWICK CORP., 207 F.3d 1039 (8th Cir.2000), Brunswick Corporation, accounting for 75% or more of the stern drive boat engine market, offered an array of discounts to certain boat builders for committing to its engines. These discounts included a market share discount (*e.g.*, 3% off if the builder bought 80% of its engines from Brunswick), and quantity discounts depending on the quantity of engines purchased.

The Eighth Circuit summarized modern exclusive dealing law by stating that antitrust analysis proceeds through a rule of reason, and requires proof of a substantial portion of the market foreclosed (including definition of relevant product and geographic market), barriers to entry, and evidence that the contracts

41. Two examples of these staff notes give their flavor: "Looking at '90 rates—and a deterent [sic] to joining other HMOs (like Healthcare)"; and "amend contract (sending this or next week) based on exclusivity. HMOs only (careful about restraint of trade) will be sent to even those in Healthcare already. . . ."

persisted for a substantial period of time. Even if those elements were demonstrated, defendants could still avoid liability by showing good business reasons that motivated the arrangements. The court found that the discount program lacked duration because buyers were free to accept or reject the various discounts and switch at any time to Brunswick's rivals and there were few if any barriers to entry. Finally, the court saw the aggressive pricing by Brunswick as a way of waging competition:

> Because cutting prices in order to increase business often is the very essence of competition, which antitrust laws were designed to encourage, it "is beyond the practical ability of a judicial tribunal to control [above cost discounting] without courting intolerable risks of chilling legitimate price cutting."

2. In UNITED STATES V. DENTSPLY INTERNATIONAL INC., 2001–1 Trade Cases 73,247 (D.Del.2001), the United States sued Dentsply, the leading manufacturer and seller of artificial teeth, for monopolization under Section 2 of the Sherman Act and for unreasonable exclusive dealing under Section 1 of the Sherman Act, and Section 3 of the Clayton Act. Several class action plaintiff suits had been filed and were consolidated with the government action.

We deal here only with the government case which alleged that Dentsply accounted for 70–80% of the sales of artificial teeth for the previous ten years, distributing primarily to dental laboratories, either directly or through about 30 dental laboratory dealers. There was no agreement between Dentsply and its dealers relating to exclusivity, but Dentsply did publish "dealer criteria" indicating that dealers could remain Dentsply distributors only if they did not add competitive lines to their product offerings. In a few instances in which dealers did add a second line, Dentsply terminated its relationship with the dealer; the dealer then backed off carrying a second line and was promptly reinstated. Dentsply defended on grounds that nothing prevented its competitors from selling direct to the laboratories noting that smaller competitors did indeed sell on occasion directly to dental labs, and in any event, the exclusive dealing contracts had no duration—*i.e.*, dealers could switch at any time but could not carry a second line. It also argued that its exclusive dealing policy had procompetitive effects in that it allowed Dentsply to recoup expenses for national advertising, sales calls by its sales representatives, and training and education programs.

The District Court rejected Dentsply's motion for summary judgment, noting that it was not clear on a preliminary record that direct sale was a viable option and that under a rule of reason the foreclosure effect may outweigh the purported business justifications.

What are the anticompetitive effects of an arrangement in which dealers can switch at any time, but cannot carry a second or third line? Are dealers likely to give up access to a dominant established brand in order to take on a far smaller manufacturer with little market acceptance? On the other hand, if a second or third line is carried, is the dominant firm in effect "subsidizing" its competitors by making an efficient and successful distribution network available?

PROBLEM 22

GILBERT'S ARRANGEMENTS WITH GAS PUMP DISTRIBUTORS

Gilbert is the largest of five U.S. manufacturers of petroleum dispensing equipment (*i.e.*, gas pumps) accounting for 55% of U.S. sales. U.S. manufacturers sell directly to major oil companies, but sell through distributors to regional oil companies, independent retail stations, and convenience store chains. Although the major oil companies buy direct from the five manufacturers, smaller companies buy through some 500 authorized dealers—each restricted to selling only one manufacturer's equipment. Competition at the dealer level is intense.

Gilbert follows the trend of most of its competitors and sells one-third of its equipment direct and two-thirds through dealers. Gilbert has signed up 220 dealers as exclusive distributors of its equipment. Each initial agreement is for a three-year term, and thereafter agreements can be cancelled without cause and without penalty on 90–days' notice. The other four manufacturers insist on the same terms with respect to exclusivity and duration. Sigma attempted to enter the petroleum dispensing equipment market, initially by purchasing six of Gilbert's largest dealers. Its business plan was to offer to sell all manufacturers' products and related equipment (credit card readers, underground tanks, etc.) as a form of one-stop shopping. Gilbert learned of the business plan and, after 60–days' notice, terminated the Sigma dealers as distributors of Gilbert products.

Occasionally companies that service dispensing equipment, of which there are thousands, go into the business of selling equipment, but because of inadequate finances, lack of sales ability or absence of existing customer relations, they are not as effective as authorized dealers. Only 40 of the 500 existing dealers migrated from the service company sector of the market.

Sigma sues under Sections 1 and 2 of the Sherman Act and Section 3 of the Clayton Act, claiming it was foreclosed from the ability to compete in the relevant market. It is prepared to prove at trial that two foreign manufacturers of petroleum dispensing equipment made initial efforts to enter the U.S. market, but were discouraged and eventually withdrew because of what they regarded as the absence of distribution opportunities.

SELECTIVE BIBLIOGRAPHY

1. General

3, 3A Areeda & Hovenkamp, Antitrust Law: An Analysis of Antitrust Principles and Their Application (2d ed. 2002).

Posner, Antitrust Law (2d ed. 2001).

Hovenkamp, Federal Antitrust Policy: The Law of Competition and Its Practice (2d ed. 1999).

FTC Staff, Anticipating the 21st Century: Competition Policy in the New High–Tech, Global Marketplace (1996).

Ross, Principles of Antitrust Law (1993).

Letwin, Law and Economic Policy in America: The Evolution of the Sherman Antitrust Act Ch. 7 (1965).

2. Predatory Pricing And Attempts To Monopolize

3 Areeda & Hovenkamp, Antitrust Law: An Analysis of Antitrust Principles and Their Application ¶ ¶ 722–24, 735–41 (2d ed. 2002).

Posner, Antitrust Law 215 (2d ed. 2001).

Hovenkamp, Federal Antitrust Policy: The Law of Competition and Its Practice Chs. 6–8 (2d. ed. 1999).

Scherer & Ross, Industrial Market Structure and Economic Performance Ch. 12 (3d ed. 1990).

Edlin, Stopping Above–Cost Predatory Pricing, 111 Yale L.J. 941 (2002).

Bolton, Brodley & Riordan, Predatory Pricing: Strategic Theory and Legal Policy, 88 Geo.L.J. 2239 (2000).

Denger & Herfort, Predatory Pricing Claims After *Brook Group*, 62 Antitrust L.J. 541 (1994).

Krattenmaker, Lande & Salop, Monopoly Power and Market Power in Antitrust Law, 76 Geo.L.J. 241 (1987).

Campbell, Predation and Competition in Antitrust: The Case of Nonfungible Goods, 87 Colum.L.Rev. 1625 (1987).

Krattenmaker & Salop, Anticompetitive Exclusion: Raising Rivals' Costs to Achieve Power Over Price, 96 Yale L.J. 209 (1986).

Handler & Steuer, Attempts to Monopolize and No–Fault Monopolization, 129 U.Pa.L.Rev. 125 (1980).

Areeda & Turner, Predatory Pricing and Related Practices under Section 2 of the Sherman Act, 88 Harv.L.Rev. 697 (1975).

Cooper, Attempts and Monopolization: A Mildly Expansionary Answer to the Prophylactic Riddle of Section 2, 72 Mich.L.Rev. 375 (1974).

3. Tie–In Sales

Sullivan & Grimes, The Law of Antitrust: An Integrated Handbook (2000).

Hovenkamp, Federal Antitrust Policy: The Law of Competition and Its Practice Ch. 10 (2d ed. 1999).

Hylton & Salinger, Tying Law and Policy: A Decision–Theoretic Approach, 69 Antitrust L.J. 469 (2001).

Feldman, Defensive Leveraging in Antitrust, 87 Georgetown L. J. 2079 (1999).

Piraino, An Antitrust Remedy for Monopoly Leveraging by Electronic Networks, 93 Northwestern U. L. Rev. 1 (1998).

Bauer, A Simplified Approach to Tying Arrangements: A Legal and Economic Analysis, 33 Vand.L.Rev. 283 (1980).

Jones, The Two Faces of *Fortner* : Comment on a Recent Antitrust Opinion, 78 Colum.L.Rev. 39 (1978).

[Materials relating to monopolization are found in the Selective Bibliography following Chapter 3, and materials relating to discriminatory pricing will be found in the Selective Bibliography following Chapter 11.]

CHAPTER 9

MERGERS

SECTION 1. BACKGROUND ON EARLY MERGER LAW AND THE AMENDMENT OF SECTION 7 OF THE CLAYTON ACT IN 1950

Chapters 1 (see pp. 1–69), and 6 (see pp. 490–619), discussed the ebb and flow of merger enforcement during the first fifty years of this century and, in many instances, the discussions of "market power" throughout the casebook illustrate the negative consequences of periods of lax or permissive merger enforcement. Where a market has grown concentrated, for example, there is reason to monitor more closely the conduct of firms in that market. Although, as Chapter 6 indicates, prices above competitive levels do not automatically result from a concentrated market structure, one must be concerned about interdependent pricing and other parallel anticompetitive practices. Even those in the Chicago School recognize that concentrated markets facilitate collusion.

In the United States, the basic alternative to intensive governmental monitoring or regulation has been an effective merger policy. The goal is both to maintain efficiency and to keep market structures fragmented enough to allow competitive pressures to work. As Professor F.M. Scherer put it,

> Unless one believes that noncompetitive conduct is naturally rare and fleeting in duration, [effective merger policy] is the less interventionist of the alternatives, since minimal monitoring is required and, if intervention proves warranted, it can be episodic. It is not too far fetched to say that merger policy is to price conduct policy as surgery is to continuing drug therapy.[1]

UNITED STATES v. COLUMBIA STEEL CO., 334 U.S. 495 (1948), provides an excellent illustration of the type of case which concerned Congress when it enacted the Celler–Kefauver Act of 1950, amending Section 7 of the Clayton Act. In *Columbia Steel*, the government sued under Sections 1 and 2 of the Sherman Act to enjoin the acquisition by United States Steel Company of Consolidated Steel, a West Coast manufacturer of fabricated steel plates and shapes (*e.g.*, building framework, bridges, tanks, welded pipe). The acquisition was to be accomplished through United States Steel's wholly owned subsidiary, Columbia Steel.

Rolled steel products, made from ingots at rolling mills, consist of plates, shapes, bars and other unfinished steel products, which in turn are used in various types of steel fabrication. United States Steel was the

---

1. Scherer, Merger Policy in the 1970s and 1980s 1 (1988).

largest producer of rolled steel products in the United States, accounting for about one-third of the market with annual sales of about $1 billion. Columbia Steel was the largest producer of rolled steel on the Pacific Coast, and also acted as sales agent for two other subsidiaries of United States Steel that were engaged in structural fabrication. In addition, United States Steel had acquired after World War II a government-owned rolled steel plant at Geneva, Utah; this occurred after the War Assets Administration had received an opinion from the Attorney General that the sale of the Geneva facilities to United States Steel would not violate the antitrust laws.

The government challenged the acquisition of Consolidated principally on the grounds that: (1) it would lessen actual and potential horizontal competition between Consolidated and United States Steel in the sale of structural fabricated products, and (2) it would exclude all sellers except United States Steel from supplying Consolidated's requirements of rolled steel.

As to the charge of lessening competition in sales of rolled steel, the government contended that the relevant market included the purchase of all rolled steel in the eleven western states in which Consolidated marketed (Consolidated accounting for about 3% in that market), and that it could be further refined to include the consumption in that area of rolled steel only by structural and plate fabricators (in which case, Consolidated would account for about 13%).

The Supreme Court majority adopted as the relevant market "total demand for rolled steel products in the eleven-state area." The government argued that because vertical integration excludes other producers of rolled steel from the opportunity to sell to the acquired company, any vertical integration involving an appreciable amount of interstate commerce should be illegal *per se*. Justice Reed responded:

> The legality of the acquisition by United States Steel of a market outlet for its rolled steel through the purchase of the manufacturing facilities of Consolidated depends not merely upon the fact of that acquired control but also upon many other factors. Exclusive dealings for rolled steel between Consolidated and United States Steel, brought about by vertical integration or otherwise, are not illegal, at any rate until the effect of such control is to unreasonably restrict the opportunities of competitors to market their product. . . .
>
> It seems clear to us that vertical integration, as such without more, cannot be held violative of the Sherman Act. It is an indefinite term without explicit meaning. Even in the iron industry, where could a line be drawn-at the end of mining the ore, the production of the pig-iron or steel ingots, when the rolling mill operation is completed, fabrication on order or at some stage of manufacture into standard merchandise? No answer would be possible and therefore the extent of permissible integration must

be governed, as other factors in Sherman Act violations, by the other circumstances of individual cases.

As to the alleged lessening of horizontal competition, the majority concluded that while United States Steel accounted for 13% of the fabricating business in the eleven-state area and Consolidated for 11%, the merger did not violate Section 1—principally because the relevant geographic market was viewed as nationwide. In addition, the Court took account of developments then taking place in the western steel industry and concluded that it was unlikely that the companies would continue to account for 11% and 13%, even if the geographic market were more narrowly defined.

The Court held that the same tests were to be applied in judging the legality of both vertical and horizontal integration. The approach for measuring the legality of a corporate fusion under the Sherman Act was described as follows:

> It is first necessary to delimit the market in which the concerns compete and then determine the extent to which the concerns are in competition in that market. If such acquisition results in or is aimed at unreasonable restraint, then the purchase is forbidden by the Sherman Act. In determining what constitutes unreasonable restraint, we do not think the dollar volume is in itself of compelling significance; we look rather to the percentage of business controlled, the strength of the remaining competition, whether the action springs from business requirements or purpose to monopolize, the probable development of the industry, consumer demands, and other characteristics of the market.

Douglas, J., with whom Black, Murphy and Rutledge, JJ., joined, dissented. He stated that the majority had failed to heed the lesson about, as Brandeis put it, the "curse of bigness." The lesson, in Douglas' opinion, was forgotten by the Supreme Court in the United States Steel and similar cases; the vice of the majority opinion was that it was in the tradition of discredited precedents.

Congress had been holding hearings throughout most of the 1940's on proposals for stricter merger laws. The Columbia Steel decision provided fuel for those efforts. Another problem to be addressed was the fact that the original version of Section 7 of the Clayton Act, as enacted in 1914, contained some gaping loopholes. Thus, the original Clayton Act[2] applied to stock but not asset acquisitions. It was of little significance to the acquiring company, however, whether it obtained stock or assets, and the result was increasing numbers of merger transactions were accomplished through asset acquisitions to avoid application of the statute. A second loophole in the statute arose because of language which required that the anticompeti-

---

2. The original version of Section 7 provided: "That no corporation engaged in commerce shall acquire, directly or indirectly, the whole or any part of the stock or other share capital of another corporation engaged also in commerce, where the effect of such acquisition may be to substantially lessen competition between the corporation whose stock is so acquired and the corporation making the acquisition, or to restrain such commerce in any section or community, or tend to create a monopoly of any line of commerce . . ."

tive effect be between the acquiring and the acquired company. Since the effect of a vertical merger is not on the merging parties, but on a third party foreclosed or otherwise injured as a result of the merger, several courts interpreted the statute as not covering vertical mergers. The result was a significantly amended Section 7, enacted in 1950.

BROWN SHOE CO. v. UNITED STATES, 370 U.S. 294, 315–23 (1962) was the first merger case that came before the Supreme Court after Section 7 was amended in 1950. The opinion is a good indication of how Congress and the Court thought about merger issues in the several decades after the Act was revised. The case involved alleged anticompetitive effects in both the horizontal and vertical lines, and its discussion on the merits will be examined at pages 1140 to 1145, infra. We set out here the Court's review of the legislative history of the Celler–Kefauver Act:

> The dominant theme pervading congressional consideration of the 1950 amendments was a fear of what was considered to be a rising tide of economic concentration in the American economy. Apprehension in this regard was bolstered by the publication in 1948 of the Federal Trade Commission's study on corporate mergers. Statistics from this and other current studies were cited as evidence of the danger to the American economy in unchecked corporate expansions through mergers. Other considerations cited in support of the bill were the desirability of retaining "local control" over industry and the protection of small businesses. Throughout the recorded discussion may be found examples of Congress' fear not only of accelerated concentration of economic power on economic grounds, but also of the threat to other values a trend toward concentration was thought to pose.

> What were some of the factors, relevant to a judgment as to the validity of a given merger, specifically discussed by Congress in redrafting § 7?

> First, there is no doubt that Congress did wish to "plug the loophole" and to include within the coverage of the Act the acquisition of assets no less than the acquisition of stock.[3]

> Second, by the deletion of the "acquiring-acquired" language in the original text, it hoped to make plain that § 7 applied not only to mergers between actual competitors, but also to vertical and conglomerate mergers whose effect may tend to lessen competition in any line of commerce in any section of the country.

> Third, it is apparent that a keystone in the erection of a barrier to what Congress saw was the rising tide of economic concentration was its provision of authority for arresting mergers at a time when the trend to a lessening of competition in a line of commerce was still in its incipiency. Congress saw the process of concentration in American business as a dynamic force; it sought

---

3. Virtually every member of Congress who spoke in support of the amendments indicated that this aspect of the legislation was its salient characteristic. . . .

to assure the Federal Trade Commission and the courts the power to brake this force at its outset and before it gathered momentum.[4]

Fourth, and closely related to the third, Congress rejected, as inappropriate to the problem it sought to remedy, the application to § 7 cases of the standards for judging the legality of business combinations adopted by the courts in dealing with cases arising under the Sherman Act, and which may have been applied to some early cases arising under original § 7.[5]

Fifth, at the same time that it sought to create an effective tool for preventing all mergers having demonstrable anticompetitive effects, Congress recognized the stimulation to competition that might flow from particular mergers. When concern as to the Act's breadth was expressed, supporters of the amendments indicated that it would not impede, for example, a merger between two small companies to enable the combination to compete more effectively with larger corporations dominating the relevant market, nor a merger between a corporation which is financially healthy and a failing one which no longer can be a vital competi-

---

4. That § 7 of the Clayton Act was intended to reach incipient monopolies and trade restraints outside the scope of the Sherman Act was explicitly stated in the Senate Report on the original Act. S.Rep. No. 698, 63d Cong., 2d Sess. 1. See United States v. E.I. du Pont de Nemours & Co., 353 U.S. 586, 589. This theme was reiterated in congressional consideration of the amendments adopted in 1950, and found expression in the final House and Senate Reports on the measure. H.R.Rep. No. 1191, 81st Cong., 1st Sess. 8 ("Acquisitions of stock or assets have a cumulative effect, and control of the market ... may be achieved not in a single acquisition but as the result of a series of acquisitions. The bill is intended to permit intervention in such a cumulative process when the effect of an acquisition may be a significant reduction in the vigor of competition."); S.Rep. No. 1775, 81st Cong., 2d Sess. 4–5, U.S.Code Cong. and Adm.News, 1950, p. 4296 ("The intent here ... is to cope with monopolistic tendencies in their incipiency and well before they have attained such effects as would justify a Sherman Act proceeding."). And see F.T.C., The Merger Movement: A Summary Report 6–7.

5. The Report of the House Judiciary Committee on H.R. 515 recommended the adoption of tests more stringent than those in the Sherman Act. 15 U.S.C.A. §§1–7, 15 note H.R.Rep. No. 596, 80th Cong., 1st Sess. 7. A vigorous minority thought no new legis-

lation was needed. Id., at 11–18. Between the issuance of this Report and the Committee's subsequent consideration of H.R. 2734, this Court had decided United States v. Columbia Steel Co., 334 U.S. 495, which some understood to indicate that existing law might be inadequate to prevent mergers that had substantially lessened competition in a section of the country, but which, nevertheless, had not risen to the level of those restraints of trade or monopoly prohibited by the Sherman Act. See 96 Cong.Rec. 16502 (remarks of Senator Kefauver); H.R.Rep. No. 1191, 81st Cong., 1st Sess. 10–11. Numerous other statements by Congressmen and Senators and by representatives of the Federal Trade Commission, the Department of Justice and the President's Council of Economic Advisors were made to the Congress suggesting that a standard of illegality stricter than that imposed by the Sherman Act was needed. The House Judiciary Committee's 1949 Report supported this concept unanimously although five of the nine members who had dissented two years earlier in H.R.Rep. No. 596 were still serving on the Committee. H.R.Rep. No. 1191, 81st Cong., 1st Sess. 7–8. The Senate Report was explicit: "The committee wish to make it clear that the bill is not intended to revert to the Sherman Act test. The intent here ... is to cope with monopolistic tendencies in their incipiency and well before they have attained such effects as would justify a Sherman Act proceeding...."

tive factor in the market. The deletion of the word "community" in the original Act's description of the relevant geographic market is another illustration of Congress' desire to indicate that its concern was with the adverse effects of a given merger on competition only in an economically significant "section" of the country.[6] Taken as a whole, the legislative history illuminates congressional concern with the protection of competition, not competitors, and its desire to restrain mergers only to the extent that such combinations may tend to lessen competition.

Sixth, Congress neither adopted nor rejected specifically any particular tests for measuring the relevant markets, either as defined in terms of product or in terms of geographic locus of competition, within which the anticompetitive effects of a merger were to be judged. Nor did it adopt a definition of the word "substantially," whether in quantitative terms of sales or assets or market shares or in designated qualitative terms, by which a merger's effects on competition were to be measured.[7]

Seventh, while providing no definite quantitative or qualitative tests by which enforcement agencies could gauge the effects of

6. The Federal Trade Commission's amendment, included the phrase "where . . . in any section, community, or trade area, there is reasonable probability that the effect of such acquisition may be to substantially lessen competition." Congressman Kefauver urged deletion of the word "community" on the ground that it might suggest, for example, that a merger between two small filling stations in a section of a city was proscribed. The fear of literal prohibition of all but de minimis mergers through the use of the word "community" was also cited by the Senate Report as the basis for its retention solely of the word "section." S.Rep. No. 1775, 81st Cong., 2d Sess. 4. The reference to "trade area" was deleted as redundant, when it became clear that the "section" of the country to which the Act was to apply, referred not to a definite geographic area of the country, but rather the geographic area of effective competition in the relevant line of commerce . . . The Senate Report cited with approval the definition of the market employed by the Court in Standard Oil Co. of California v. United States, 337 U.S. 293, 299 n. 5 (1949).

7. The House Report on H.R. 2734 stated that two tests of illegality were included in the proposed Act: whether the merger substantially lessened competition or tended to create a monopoly. It stated that such effects could be perceived through findings, for example, that a whole or material part of the competitive activity of an enterprise, which had been a substantial factor in competition, had been eliminated; that the relative size of the acquiring corporation had increased to such a point that its advantage over competitors threatened to be "decisive"; that an "undue" number of competing enterprises had been eliminated; or that buyers and sellers in the relevant market had established relationships depriving their rivals of a fair opportunity to compete. H.R.Rep. No. 1191, 81st Cong., 1st Sess. 8. Each of these standards, couched in general language, reflects a conscious avoidance of exclusively mathematical tests even though the case of Standard Oil Co. of California v. United States, 337 U.S. 293 (1949), said to have created a "quantitative substantiality" test for suits arising under § 3 of the Clayton Act, was decided while Congress was considering H.R. 2734. Some discussion of the applicability of this test to § 7 cases ensued, but this aspect of the *Standard Oil* decision was neither specifically endorsed nor impugned by the bill's supporters. However, the House Judiciary Committee's Report, issued two months after *Standard Oil* had been decided, remarked that the tests of illegality under the new Act were intended to be "similar to those which the courts have applied in interpreting the same language as used in other sections of the Clayton Act." H.R.Rep. No. 1191, 81st Cong., 1st Sess. 8.

a given merger to determine whether it may "substantially" lessen competition or tend toward monopoly, Congress indicated plainly that a merger had to be functionally viewed, in the context of its particular industry.[8] That is, whether the consolidation was to take place in an industry that was fragmented rather than concentrated, that had seen a recent trend toward domination by a few leaders or had remained fairly consistent in its distribution of market shares among the participating companies, that had experienced easy access to markets by suppliers and easy access to suppliers by buyers or had witnessed foreclosure of business, that had witnessed the ready entry of new competition or the erection of barriers to prospective entrants, all were aspects, varying in importance with the merger under consideration, which would properly be taken into account.

Eighth, Congress used the words "may be substantially to lessen competition" (emphasis supplied), to indicate that its concern was with probabilities, not certainties.[9] Statutes existed for dealing with clear-cut menaces to competition; no statute was sought for dealing with ephemeral possibilities. Mergers with a probable anticompetitive effect were to be proscribed by this Act.

Clayton Act, Section 7

That no person engaged in commerce or in any activity affecting commerce shall acquire, directly or indirectly, the whole or any part of the stock or other share capital and no person subject to the jurisdiction of the Federal Trade Commission shall acquire the whole or any part of

8. A number of the supporters of the amendments voiced their concern that passage of the bill would amount to locking the barn door after most of the horses had been stolen, but urged approval of the measure to prevent the theft of those still in the barn. Which was to say that, if particular industries had not yet been subject to the congressionally perceived trend toward concentration, adoption of the amendments was urged as a way of preventing the trend from reaching those industries as yet unaffected. . . .

9. In the course of both the Committee hearings and floor debate, attention was occasionally focused on the issue of whether "possible," "probable" or "certain" anticompetitive effects of a proposed merger would have to be proven to establish a violation of the Act. Language was quoted from prior decisions of the Court in antitrust cases in which each of these interpretations of the

word "may" was suggested as appropriate. The final Senate Report on the question was explicit on the point:

"The use of these words ["may be"] means that the bill, if enacted, would not apply to the mere possibility but only to the reasonable probability of the prescribed [sic] effect. . . . The words 'may be' have been in section 7 of the Clayton Act since 1914. The concept of reasonable probability conveyed by these words is a necessary element in any statute which seeks to arrest restraints of trade in their incipiency and before they develop into full-fledged restraints violative of the Sherman Act. A requirement of certainty and actuality of injury to competition is incompatible with any effort to supplement the Sherman Act by reaching incipient restraints." S.Rep. No. 1775, 81st Cong., 2d Sess. 6. . . .

the assets of another person engaged also in commerce or in any activity affecting commerce, where in any line of commerce or in any activity affecting commerce in any section of the country, the effect of such acquisition may be substantially to lessen competition, or to tend to create monopoly. . . .

This section shall not apply to persons purchasing such stock solely for investment and not using the same by voting or otherwise to bring about, or in attempting to bring about, the substantial lessening of competition. Nor shall anything contained in this section prevent a corporation engaged in commerce or in any activity affecting commerce from causing the formation of subsidiary corporations for the actual carrying on of their immediate lawful business, or the natural and legitimate branches or extensions thereof, or from owning and holding all or a part of the stock of such subsidiary corporations, when the effect of such formation is not to substantially lessen competition. . . .

SECTION 2.   PROSCRIBED EFFECT IN HORIZONTAL MERGERS

F.M. Scherer & D. Ross, Industrial Market Structure and Economic Performance

159–67 (3d ed. 1990).

The Motives for Merger

Mergers occur for a myriad of reasons, and in any given case, several different motives may simultaneously influence the merging parties' behavior. Still it is useful to attempt a preliminary sorting-out of the diverse motivating forces.

The Monopoly Motive

In horizontal mergers, and especially in the massive consolidations that took place around the turn of the century, the desire to achieve or strengthen monopoly power played a prominent role. Some 1887–1904 consolidations gained monopoly power by creating firms that dominated their industries. Others fell short of dominance, but transformed market structures sufficiently to curb the tendencies toward price competition toward which sellers gravitated in the rapidly changing market conditions of the time. As Thomas Edison remarked to a reporter concerning reasons for the formation of the General Electric Company in 1892:

Recently there has been sharp rivalry between [Thomson–Houston and Edison General Electric], and prices have been cut so that there has been little profit in the manufacture of electrical machinery for anybody. The consolidation of the companies ... will do away with a competition which has become so sharp that the product of the factories has been worth little more than ordinary hardware.[10] ...

Those were days when businesspeople were not yet intimidated by the wrath of trustbusters or public opinion. Now they are more circumspect, and evidence of monopoly-creating intent is harder to find....

Speculative Motives

Monopoly and speculative motives interacted to propel the great merger wave of 1887–1904. The value of a company's common stock depends upon investor expectations regarding future profits. If competition can be eliminated or reduced through merger, profits will presumably rise, making the new consolidated firm's shares worth more than the sum of the previously competing companies' share values. Entrepreneurs sought to achieve such capital value transformations by arranging competition-reducing mergers. However, many went farther. Because investors were captivated by the prospect of pursuing this road to fortune, and because there were no effective controls on the quality of information disseminated in connection with new stock flotations, promoters arranged mergers with little chance of securing appreciable monopoly power, but simultaneously issued prospectuses, planted rumors, and primed the market to convince investors otherwise. By exciting false expectations, the promoters were able to sell the stocks of newly consolidated firms at prices far exceeding their true economic value—a practice known at the time as stock watering. As in honestly monopolistic consolidations, the promoters were paid in newly issued stock for their contribution. Only in this case, the merger makers hastened to sell their shares to unwary outsiders before the bubble burst....

Alarm over such abuses led to passage of the Securities Act of 1933 and the Securities Exchange Act of 1934, establishing federal regulation of securities issue information and other promotional practices. They and the antitrust laws made it difficult for promoters to repeat the experiences of the 1890s and 1920s....

Normal Business Motives

Any explanation of mergers that ignores such speculative inducements is likely to miss the mark. Yet it must be recognized that there are many normal, wholesome business motives for merger. These compel careful examination.

It is widely believed that mergers serve as an efficient, humane escape route for companies that are otherwise about to fail. This is true, but not very important quantitatively. As a rule, merger makers seek healthy acquisition targets, not basket cases. Among 698 sizable manufacturing

10. *New York Times,* February 21, 1892, p. 2, cited in H.C. Passer, *The Electrical Manufacturers: 1875–1900* (Cambridge: Harvard University Press, 1953), p. 326. See also p. 54 of Passer on the motives for several earlier Thomson–Houston mergers.

companies acquired between 1948 and 1968, only 4.8 percent had negative profits in the year before acquisition occurred.[11] In a 634–company sample including a cross section of both small and large acquisition targets, 5.8 percent had negative operating income (before deduction of interest charges) in the year before acquisition.[12]

Small companies are often acquired because their owner-managers are aging or weary of business pressures and lack heirs or other successors to take their place. Interacting with this motive is the desire of family company owners to diversify their investment portfolios, thereby reducing their risk exposure, and to raise funds for paying the sometimes substantial estate taxes levied when an owner-manager dies.[13]

Tax considerations also affect the urge to merge in a variety of more complex ways. When an acquisition premium is paid above the values at which a company's depreciable assets are recorded in tax accounts, the acquired assets can under U.S. law be stepped up and subjected to higher depreciation charges, shielding the acquirer from tax liabilities. Until reforms were enacted in 1986, acquiring companies making such step-ups could normally escape immediate capital gains taxation. Such tax advantages appear to have been an important consideration in many merger decisions, but not critical enough to determine whether merger would or would not occur.[14] Under the structure of U.S. and many other nations' tax laws, corporate profits are taxed directly when realized by the corporation and again at the personal level when they are distributed as dividends to individual (but not institutional) stockholders. To avoid this double taxation, corporations are tempted to reinvest their profits in merger-making rather than paying them out as dividends. When capital gains are taxed more lightly than dividend income, as was true in the United States until 1989, successful reinvestment increased the value of the company's stock, permitting shareholders to sell some of their shares and realize their gains under the more lightly-taxed capital gains provisions. Expanding upon this theme, Oliver Williamson argued that conglomerate firms achieved efficiencies by reinvesting earnings in internal capital markets better able than

11. Stanley E. Boyle, "Pre–Merger Growth and Profit Characteristics of Large Conglomerate Mergers in the United States, 1948–1968," *St. John's Law Review,* vol. 44 (Spring 1970, special edition), pp. 152–170.

12. Ravenscraft and Scherer, *Mergers,* p. 60.

13. Studies showing the importance of estate tax considerations to the sale of small firms include J.K. Butters, John M. Lintner, and W.L. Cary, *Effects of Taxation on Corporate Mergers* (Boston: Harvard Business School Division of Research, 1951), Chapter 8; and C.C. Bosland, "Has Estate Taxation Induced Recent Mergers?" *National Tax Journal,* vol. 16 (June 1963), pp. 159–168. In 1976 the tax law was changed to give small business heirs up to ten years to settle federal estate tax liabilities, lessening the incentive to merge for estate tax reasons.

14. See Alan J. Auerbach and David Reishus, "The Impact of Taxation on Mergers and Acquisitions," in Auerbach, ed., *Mergers and Acquisitions,* pp. 69–88; and Ronald J. Gilson, Myron S. Scholes, and Mark A. Wolfson, "Taxation and the Dynamics of Corporate Control," in John C. Coffee, Louis Lowenstein, and Susan Rose–Ackerman, eds., *Knights, Raiders, and Targets: The Impact of the Hostile Takeover* (New York: Oxford University Press, 1988), pp. 271–299.

external markets to assimilate information on investment opportunities.[15] However, intracompany capital markets are often highly bureaucratic and politicized, and it is unclear whether they actually do a better job allocating capital than is achieved in the give-and-take between a firm and its outside investors. . . .[16]

Other merger-based economies of scale are even more difficult to evaluate. Distinctions must be made inter alia between horizontal mergers, in which the merging firms produce and sell similar products, and conglomerates, in which the product lines differ, perhaps greatly.

Economies of scale in production are much more likely to be achieved following horizontal (or perhaps vertical) mergers than when unrelated operations are combined. Even then, problems arise.

When firms that make the same products merge, their plants are already built; not much can be done in the short run to unbuild them and achieve the principal plant-specific economies of scale. Exceptions are most likely to be found in declining or severely depressed industries. When multiple plants are combined, the least efficient units can be shut down and the most efficient units retained or even expanded. . . .

Mergers may also confer advantages in marketing—for example, through the pooling and streamlining of field sales forces, the ability to offer distributors a broader product line, the use of common advertising themes, and (to the extent they exist) the sharing of advertising media quantity discounts. In a survey of sixty-nine U.S. acquisitions, mostly conglomerate, John Kitching found marketing complementarities to be much more important than production economies, and second only in importance to capital-cost economies.[17] However, conflicting evidence emerged from analyses by the Federal Trade Commission, the Economic Council of Canada, and (for the United Kingdom) Gerald Newbould, all of whom found post-merger marketing economies to be relatively unimportant.[18] The Canadian study showed marketing economies to emerge even less frequently than production economies, which were reported in 6.5 percent of the 1,826 surveyed acquisitions and 15.2 percent of the horizontal manufacturing industry mergers.

15. Oliver E. Williamson, *Corporate Control and Business Behavior* (Englewood Cliffs, NJ: Prentice–Hall, 1970), pp. 121–130, 163–164, and 176–177.

16. Ravenscraft and Scherer, *Mergers,* supra note 32, pp. 213–214; and Joseph L. Bower, *Managing the Resource Allocation Process* (Boston: Harvard Business School Division of Research, 1970), especially Chapter 9.

17. John Kitching, "Why Do Mergers Miscarry?" *Harvard Business Review,* vol. 45 (November–December 1967), pp. 87–90.

18. Gerald D. Newbould, *Management and Merger Activity* (Liverpool: Guthstead, 1970), p. 178; Eonomic Council of Canada, *Interim Report on Competition Policy* (Ottawa: Queen's Printer, July 1969), pp. 213–218; and Federal Trade Commission staff report, *Conglomerate Merger Performance: An Empirical Analysis of Nine Corporations* (Washington: Government Printing Office, 1972), pp. 37, 41, and 47–49.

Complementarities also exist in research and development. One firm may have two or three unusually creative engineers but lack the distribution network needed to derive full commercial benefit from the new products they turn out. Another may have superb marketing channels but find its laboratories populated by unimaginative clods. Together they can make beautiful music. Ideas and money can also be brought together through merger. There is reason to believe that such motives have influenced an appreciable number of mergers, especially those in which small research-based enterprises were acquired.[19] Once such creative individuals are ensconced in the larger, more bureaucratic R & D organizations of large acquirers, however, they often become frustrated. A study by super-computer specialist Control Data Corporation revealed that fewer than 15 percent of the innovative engineers and scientists recruited through acquisitions over a period of twenty-two years remained with the company.[20] More generally, a statistical analysis covering 2,955 lines of business showed that having all of a line's assets stemming from conglomerate mergers was associated with R & D/sales ratios 18 percent lower on average than those prevailing generally in the industry in which the unit operated.[21]

Finally, there is the possibility that mergers infuse superior new management into companies suffering from talent or motivational deficiencies. Or they may permit managerial overhead streamlining.

U.S. Department of Justice and Federal Trade Commission Horizontal Merger Guidelines, 1992.

[Ed. The reasons for concern about anticompetitive effects of mergers and the structure of the analysis under which they are reviewed are summarized in the introduction to the joint Department of Justice–FTC merger guidelines.]

1. Purpose and Underlying Policy Assumptions of the Guidelines

Mergers are motivated by the prospect of financial gains. The possible sources of the financial gains from mergers are many, and the Guidelines

---

19. See Murray N. Friedman, *The Research and Development Factor in Mergers and Acquisitions,* Study No. 16, U.S. Senate Committee on the Judiciary; Subcommittee on Patents, Trademarks, and Copyrights (Washington: USGPO, 1958). In a survey of venture capital institutions, Robert Premus found that approximately 42 percent of the new high-technology companies in which the funds invested were expected to "go public" with their own stock exchange listings, 26 percent would merge with larger firms, 19 percent would "just survive," and 13 per-

cent would fail outright. *Venture Capital and Innovation,* study prepared for the Joint Economic Committee, U.S. Congress (Washington: USGPO, 1985), p. 35. Premus' percentages for three size categories were weighted to yield the overall averages reported here.

20. William C. Norris, "The Social Costs of Takeovers," *Corporate Report,* September 1983, p. 47.

21. Ravenscraft and Scherer, *Mergers,* supra note 32, pp. 120–121.

do not attempt to identify all possible sources of gain in every merger. Instead, the Guidelines focus on the one potential source of gain that is of concern under the antitrust laws: market power.

The unifying theme of the Guidelines is that mergers should not be permitted to create or enhance market power or to facilitate its exercise. Market power to a seller is the ability profitably to maintain prices above competitive levels for a significant period of time.[22] In some circumstances, a sole seller (a "monopolist") of a product with no good substitutes can maintain a selling price that is above the level that would prevail if the market were competitive. Similarly, in some circumstances, where only a few firms account for most of the sales of a product, those firms can exercise market power, perhaps even approximating the performance of a monopolist, by either explicitly or implicitly coordinating their actions. Circumstances also may permit a single firm, not a monopolist, to exercise market power through unilateral or non-coordinated conduct—conduct the success of which does not rely on the concurrence of other firms in the market or on coordinated responses by those firms. In any case, the result of the exercise of market power is a transfer of wealth from buyers to sellers or a misallocation of resources.

Market power also encompasses the ability of a single buyer (a "monopsonist"), a coordinating group of buyers, or a single buyer, not a monopsonist, to depress the price paid for a product to a level that is below the competitive price and thereby depress output. The exercise of market power by buyers ("monopsony power") has adverse effects comparable to those associated with the exercise of market power by sellers. In order to assess potential monopsony concerns, the Agency will apply an analytical framework analogous to the framework of these Guidelines.

While challenging competitively harmful mergers, the Agency seeks to avoid unnecessary interference with the larger universe of mergers that are either competitively beneficial or neutral. In implementing this objective, however, the Guidelines reflect the congressional intent that merger enforcement should interdict competitive problems in their incipiency.

2. Overview

The Guidelines describe the analytical process that the Agency will employ in determining whether to challenge a horizontal merger. First, the Agency assesses whether the merger would significantly increase concentration and result in a concentrated market, properly defined and measured. Second, the Agency assesses whether the merger, in light of market concentration and other factors that characterize the market, raises concern about potential adverse competitive effects. Third, the Agency assesses whether entry would be timely, likely and sufficient either to deter or to counteract the competitive effects of concern. Fourth, the Agency assesses any efficiency gains that reasonably cannot be achieved by the parties

---

22. Sellers with market power also may lessen competition on dimensions other than price, such as product quality, service, or innovation.

through other means. Finally the Agency assesses whether, but for the merger, either party to the transaction would be likely to fail, causing its assets to exit the market. The process of assessing market concentration, potential adverse competitive effects, entry, efficiency and failure is a tool that allows the Agency to answer the ultimate inquiry in merger analysis: whether the merger is likely to create or enhance market power or to facilitate its exercise.

NOTES

1. As Chapter 6 indicates, the state of economic knowledge about the consequences of industrial concentration is still relatively rudimentary, subject to substantial debate, and somewhat in flux. Traditional economic theory emphasizes that the "fewness" of firms in a market is a "necessary" but not "sufficient" prerequisite to higher prices and profits, lower output, and generally poor performance. During the past two decades in particular, however, "revisionist" economists have argued that high concentration most often results from efficiency considerations and that concentrated markets often work well.

This led Professors Scherer and Ross to conclude:

> Economists have developed literally dozens of oligopoly pricing theories—some simple, some marvels of mathematical complexity. Recognizing the wide range of behavioral and theoretical predictions, some economists have asserted that the oligopoly problem is indeterminate. This is correct in the narrow sense that one cannot forge unique and compelling mechanistic links from cost and demand conditions to price equilibria. But a more constructive interpretation is this: To make workable predictions, we need a theory much richer than the received theories of pure competition and monopoly—a theory that includes variables irrelevant to these polar cases. We must not expect too much, however. The most that can be hoped for is a kind of soft determinism: an understanding of broad tendencies and predictions correct on the average, but subject to occasional substantial errors.[23]

Some economic studies have found that high market shares of the leading firm or the two leading firms in a market are a more significant determinant of excessive profitability than concentration.[24] The reasons for the reported significance of high market share are still being debated. But there appears to be no doubt that many firms are acting on the assumption that high market share will, at least in the long run, lead to high profitability.

2. Largely influenced by economic analysis, there is an increased level of skepticism that mergers that leave a significant number of firms in the market—for example, that reduce the number of significant firms to seven or eight—have much of an impact on competition. Also, there is an increasing awareness that some

23. Scherer & Ross, Industrial Market Structure and Economic Performance 199–200 (3d ed. 1990).

24. *See, e.g.*, Kwoka & Ravenscraft, Collusion vs. Rivalry: Price–Cost Margins by Line of Business, 53 Economica 642 (1986); Kwoka, Does the Choice of Concentration Measure Really Matter?, 29 J. Industrial Economics 445 (1981); Pautler, A Review of the Economic Basis for Broad–Based Horizontal Merger Policy 63–87 (1981).

mergers might be competitively beneficial, at least as long as the number of firms did not become too few. *Cf.* Weiss, "The Structure–Conduct—Performance Paradigm and Antitrust," 127 U.Pa. L.Rev. 1004, 1119 (1979).

As you read the cases set out in Section 2, consider what effect, if any, these continuing dialogues among industrial organization economists should have on horizontal merger policy. Given the limits as to what economists now know or can agree upon, should we be cautious about erring on the side of a permissive horizontal merger policy? What are the costs of a relatively restrictive merger policy? If major markets become too concentrated and this results in poor economic performance, do we have the "tools" to undo the harm?

3. Recent economic studies also have emphasized the existence of barriers to entry as a crucial determinent of noncompetitive pricing and performance. At this point, it might be useful to review the "Note on Barriers to Entry" in Chapter 4, page 199, supra. As you read the cases in Section 2, consider whether courts have paid sufficient attention or excessive attention to barriers to entry.

United States v. Philadelphia National Bank

Supreme Court of the United States, 1963.
374 U.S. 321, 83 S.Ct. 1715, 10 L.Ed.2d 915.

■ BRENNAN, J. The United States, appellant here, brought this civil action . . . to enjoin a proposed merger of The Philadelphia National Bank (PNB) and Girard Trust Corn Exchange Bank (Girard), appellees here. . . . We reverse the judgment of the District Court [upholding the merger]. We hold that the merger of appellees is forbidden by § 7 of the Clayton Act and so must be enjoined; we need not, and therefore do not, reach the further question of alleged violation of § 1 of the Sherman Act.

I. The Facts and Proceedings Below

A. *The Background: Commercial Banking in the United States*

Because this is the first case which has required this Court to consider the application of the antitrust laws to the commercial banking industry, and because aspects of the industry and of the degree of governmental regulation of it will recur throughout our discussion, we deem it appropriate to begin with a brief background description.

Commercial banking in this country is primarily unit banking. That is, control of commercial banking is diffused throughout a very large number of independent, local banks—13,460 of them in 1960—rather than concentrated in a handful of nationwide banks, as, for example, in England and Germany. There are, to be sure, in addition to the independent banks, some 10,000 branch banks; but branching, which is controlled largely by state law—and prohibited altogether by some States—enables a bank to extend itself only to state lines and often not that far.[25] It is also the case,

---

25. In addition, there is a certain amount of bank holding company activity. The Bank Holding Company Act of 1956, 12 U.S.C. §§ 1841–1848, brought bank holding companies under stringent federal regulation. As of 1958, the 43 registered bank holding companies controlled 5.7% of all banking offices and 7.4% of all deposits. Lent, The

of course, that many banks place loans and solicit deposits outside their home area. But with these qualifications, it remains true that ours is essentially a decentralized system of community banks. Recent years, however, have witnessed a definite trend toward concentration. Thus, during the decade ending in 1960 the number of commercial banks in the United States declined by 714, despite the chartering of 887 new banks and a very substantial increase in the Nation's credit needs during the period. Of the 1,601 independent banks which thus disappeared, 1,503, with combined total resources of well over $25,000,000,000, disappeared as the result of mergers.

Commercial banks are unique among financial institutions in that they alone are permitted by law to accept demand deposits. This distinctive power gives commercial banking a key role in the national economy. For banks do not merely deal in but are actually a source of money and credit; when a bank makes a loan by crediting the borrower's demand deposit account, it augments the Nation's credit supply. Furthermore, the power to accept demand deposits makes banks the intermediaries in most financial transactions (since transfers of substantial moneys are almost always by check rather than by cash) and, concomitantly, the repositories of very substantial individual and corporate funds. The banks' use of these funds is conditioned by the fact that their working capital consists very largely of demand deposits, which makes liquidity the guiding principle of bank lending and investing policies; thus it is that banks are the chief source of the country's short-term business credit.

Banking operations are varied and complex; "commercial banking" describes a congeries of services and credit devices.[26] But among them the creation of additional money and credit, the management of the checking-account system, and the furnishing of short-term business loans, would appear to be the most important. For the proper discharge of these functions is indispensable to a healthy national economy, as the role of bank failures in depression periods attests. It is therefore not surprising that commercial banking in the United States is subject to a variety of governmental controls, state and federal.

Changing Structure of Commercial Banking (1960).

26. The principal banking "products" are of course various types of credit, for example: unsecured personal and business loans, mortgage loans, loans secured by securities or accounts receivable, automobile installment and consumer goods installment loans, tuition financing, bank credit cards, revolving credit funds. Banking services include: acceptance of demand deposits from individuals, corporations, governmental agencies, and other banks; acceptance of time and savings deposits; estate and trust planning and trusteeship services; lock boxes and safe-ty deposit boxes; account reconciliation services; foreign department services (acceptances and letters of credit); correspondent services; investment advice. It should be noted that many other institutions are in the business of supplying credit, and so more or less in competition with commercial banks ..., for example: mutual savings banks, savings and loan associations, credit unions, personal-finance companies, sales-finance companies, private businessmen (through the furnishing of trade credit), factors, direct-lending government agencies, the Post Office, Small Business Investment Corporations, life insurance companies.

Federal supervision of banking has been called "[p]robably the outstanding example in the federal government of regulation of an entire industry through methods of supervision. . . . The system may be one of the most successful [systems of economic regulation], if not the most successful." . . . To the efficacy of this system we may owe, in part, the virtual disappearance of bank failures from the American economic scene.[27]

B. *The Proposed Merger of PNB and Girard*

The Philadelphia National Bank and Girard Trust Corn Exchange Bank are, respectively, the second and third largest of the 42 commercial banks with head offices in the Philadelphia metropolitan area, which consists of the City of Philadelphia and its three contiguous counties in Pennsylvania. The home county of both banks is the city itself; Pennsylvania law, however, permits branching into the counties contiguous to the home county, Pa.Stat.Ann. (1961 Supp.), Tit. 7, §§ 819–204.1, and both banks have offices throughout the four-county area. PNB, a national bank, has assets of over $1,000,000,000, making it (as of 1959) the twenty-first largest bank in the Nation. Girard, a state bank, is a member of the FRS and is insured by the FDIC; it has assets of about $750,000,000. Were the proposed merger to be consummated, the resulting bank would be the largest in the four-county area, with (approximately) 36% of the area banks' total assets, 36% of deposits, and 34% of net loans. It and the second largest (First Pennsylvania Bank and Trust Company, now the largest) would have between them 59% of the total assets, 58% of deposits, and 58% of the net loans, while after the merger the four largest banks in the area would have 78% of total assets, 77% of deposits, and 78% of net loans.

The present size of both PNB and Girard is in part the result of mergers. Indeed, the trend toward concentration is noticeable in the Philadelphia area generally, in which the number of commercial banks has declined from 108 in 1947 to the present 42. Since 1950, PNB has acquired nine formerly independent banks and Girard six; and these acquisitions have accounted for 59% and 85% of the respective banks' asset growth during the period, 63% and 91% of their deposit growth, and 12% and 37% of their loan growth. During this period, the seven largest banks in the area increased their combined share of the area's total commercial bank resources from about 61% to about 90%.

In November 1960 the boards of directors of the two banks approved a proposed agreement for their consolidation, under the PNB charter. . . . Such a consolidation is authorized, subject to the approval of the Comptroller of the Currency, by 12 U.S.C.A. (1958 ed., Supp.IV) § 215. But under the Bank Merger Act of 1960, 12 U.S.C.A. (1963 ed., Supp.IV) § 1828(c),

27. In 1957, for example, there were three bank suspensions in the entire country by reason of financial difficulties, in 1960, two, and in 1961, nine. Of these nine, four involved state banks which were neither members of the FRS nor insured by the FDIC. 1961 Annual Report of the Comptroller of the Currency 286. In a typical year in the 1920's, roughly 600 banks failed throughout the country, about 100 of them national banks. See S.Rep. No. 196, Regulation of Bank Mergers, 86th Cong., 1st Sess., 17–18.

the Comptroller may not give his approval until he has received reports from the other two banking agencies and the Attorney General respecting the probable effects of the proposed transaction on competition. All three reports advised that the proposed merger would have substantial anticompetitive effects in the Philadelphia metropolitan area. However, on February 24, 1961, the Comptroller approved the merger. No opinion was rendered at that time. But as required by § 1828(c), the Comptroller explained the basis for his decision to approve the merger in a statement to be included in his annual report to Congress. As to effect upon competition, he reasoned that "[s]ince there will remain an adequate number of alternative sources of banking service in Philadelphia, and in view of the beneficial effects of this consolidation upon international and national competition it was concluded that the overall effect upon competition would not be unfavorable." He also stated that the consolidated bank "would be far better able to serve the convenience and needs of its community by being of material assistance to its city and state in their efforts to attract new industry and to retain existing industry." The day after the Comptroller approved the merger, the United States commenced the present action. No steps have been taken to consummate the merger pending the outcome of this litigation.

C. *The Trial and the District Court's Decision*

The Government's case in the District Court relied chiefly on statistical evidence bearing upon market structure and on testimony by economists and bankers to the effect that, notwithstanding the intensive governmental regulation of banking, there was a substantial area for the free play of competitive forces; that concentration of commercial banking, which the proposed merger would increase was inimical to that free play; that the principal anticompetitive effect of the merger would be felt in the area in which the banks had their offices, thus making the four-county metropolitan area the relevant geographical market; and that commercial banking was the relevant product market. The defendants, in addition to offering contrary evidence on these points, attempted to show business justifications for the merger. They conceded that both banks were economically strong and had sound management, but offered the testimony of bankers to show that the resulting bank, with its greater prestige and increased lending limit,[28] would be better able to compete with large out-of-state (particularly New York) banks, would attract new business to Philadelphia, and in general would promote the economic development of the metropolitan area.[29]

---

28. See 12 U.S.C.A § 84. The resulting bank would have a lending limit of $15,000,000, of which $1,000,000 would not be attributable to the merger but to unrelated accounting factors.

29. There was evidence that Philadelphia, although it ranks fourth or fifth among the Nation's urban areas in terms of general commercial activity, ranks only ninth in terms of the size of its largest bank, and that some large business firms which have their head offices in Philadelphia must seek elsewhere to satisfy their banking needs because of the inadequate lending limits of Philadelphia's banks; First Pennsylvania and PNB, currently the two largest banks in Philadel-

... [The Court next explained its reasons for (1) affirming the district court's holding that the passage of the Bank Merger Act of 1960 did not repeal by implication the antitrust laws insofar as they might apply to bank mergers, and (2) reversing the district court's holding that § 7 of the Clayton Act is inapplicable to bank mergers.]

III.   The Lawfulness of the Proposed Merger Under Section 7

The statutory test is whether the effect of the merger "may be substantially to lessen competition" "in any line of commerce in any section of the country." We analyzed the test in detail in *Brown Shoe Co. v. United States*, 370 U.S. 294, and that analysis need not be repeated or extended here, for the instant case presents only a straightforward problem of application to particular facts.

We have no difficulty in determining the "line of commerce" (relevant product or services market) and "section of the country" (relevant geographical market) in which to appraise the probable competitive effects of appellees' proposed merger. We agree with the District Court that the cluster of products (various kinds of credit) and services (such as checking accounts and trust administration) denoted by the term "commercial banking," *see* note [26], supra, composes a distinct line of commerce. Some commercial banking products or services are so distinctive that they are entirely free of effective competition from products or services of other financial institutions; the checking account is in this category. Others enjoy such cost advantages as to be insulated within a broad range from substitutes furnished by other institutions. For example, commercial banks compete with small-loan companies in the personal-loan market; but the small-loan companies' rates are invariably much higher than the banks', in part, it seems, because the companies' working capital consists in substantial part of bank loans.[30] Finally, there are banking facilities which, although in terms of cost and price they are freely competitive with the facilities provided by other financial institutions, nevertheless enjoy a settled consumer preference, insulating them, to a marked degree, from competition; this seems to be the case with savings deposits.[31] In sum, it is

phia, each have a lending limit of $8,000,000. Girard's is $6,000,000.

Appellees offered testimony that the merger would enable certain economies of scale, specifically, that it would enable the formation of a more elaborate foreign department than either bank is presently able to maintain. But this attempted justification, which was not mentioned by the District Court in its opinion and has not been developed with any fullness before this Court, we consider abandoned.

30. Cf. United States v. Aluminum Co. of America, 148 F.2d 416, 425 (C.A.2d Cir.,1945). In the instant case, unlike *Aluminum Co.*, there is virtually no time lag be-

tween the banks' furnishing competing financial institutions (small-loan companies, for example) with the raw material, *i.e.*, money, and the institutions' selling the finished product, *i.e.*, loans; hence the instant case, compared with *Aluminum Co.* in this respect, is *a fortiori*. . . .

31. As one witness for the defendants testified:

"We have had in Philadelphia for 50 years or more the mutual savings banks offering ½ per cent and in some instances more than ½ per cent higher interest than the commercial banks. Nevertheless, the rate of increase in savings accounts in commercial banks has kept

clear that commercial banking is a market "sufficiently inclusive to be meaningful in terms of trade realities." *Crown Zellerbach Corp. v. Federal Trade Comm'n*, 296 F.2d 800, 811 (C.A.9th Cir.1961).

We part company with the District Court on the determination of the appropriate "section of the country." The proper question to be asked in this case is not where the parties to the merger do business or even where they compete, but where, within the area of competitive overlap, the effect of the merger on competition will be direct and immediate. *See* Bock, Mergers and Markets (1960), 42. This depends upon "the geographic structure of supplier-customer relations." Kaysen and Turner, Anti-trust Policy (1959), 102. In banking, as in most service industries, convenience of location is essential to effective competition. Individuals and corporations typically confer the bulk of their patronage on banks in their local community; they find it impractical to conduct their banking business at a distance.[32] *See Transamerica Corp. v. Board of Govs. of Fed.Res.Sys.*, 206 F.2d 163, 169 (C.A.3d Cir., 1953). The factor of inconvenience localizes banking competition as effectively as high transportation costs in other industries. *See, e.g., American Crystal–Sugar Co. v. Cuban–American Sugar Co.*, 152 F.Supp. 387, 398 (S.D.N.Y.1957), *affirmed* 259 F.2d 524 (C.A.2d Cir., 1958). Therefore, since as we recently said in a related context the "area of effective competition in the known line of commerce must be charted by careful selection of the market area in which the seller operates, and to which the purchaser can practicably turn for supplies," *Tampa Elec. Co. v. Nashville Coal Co.*, 365 U.S. 320, 327 (emphasis supplied); *see Standard Oil Co. v. United States*, 337 U.S. 293, 299 and 300, n. 5, the four-county area in which appellees' offices are located would seem to be the relevant geographical market. *Cf. Brown Shoe Co.*, supra, 370 U.S. at 338–339. In fact, the vast bulk of appellees' business originates in the four-county area. Theoretically, we should be concerned with the possibility that bank offices on the perimeter of the area may be in effective competition

---

pace with and in many of the banks exceeded the rate of increase of the mutual banks paying 3½ per cent. . . .

"I have made some inquiries. There are four banks on the corner of Broad and Chestnut. Three of them are commercial banks all offering 3 per cent, and one is a mutual savings bank offering 3½. As far as I have been able to discover, there isn't anybody in Philadelphia who will take the trouble to walk across Broad Street to get ½ of 1 percent more interest. If you ask me why, I will say I do not know. Habit, custom, personal relationships, convenience, doing all your banking under one roof appear to be factors superior to changes in the interest rate level." (R. 1388–1389.)

32. As far as the customer for a bank loan is concerned, "the size of his market is somewhat dependent upon his own size, how well he is known, and so on. For example, for small business concerns known primarily locally, they may consider that their market is a strictly local one, and they may be forced by circumstances to do business with banks in a nearby geographic relationship to them. On the other hand, as businesses increase in size, the scope of their business activities, their national reputation, the alternatives, they have available to them will be spread again over a very large area, possibly as large as the entire United States." (R. 1372.) (Defendants' testimony on direct examination.)

with bank offices within; actually, this seems to be a factor of little significance.[33]

We recognize that the area in which appellees have their offices does not delineate with perfect accuracy an appropriate "section of the country" in which to appraise the effect of the merger upon competition. Large borrowers and large depositors, the record shows, may find it practical to do a large part of their banking business outside their home community; very small borrowers and depositors may, as a practical matter, be confined to bank offices in their immediate neighborhood; and customers of intermediate size, it would appear, deal with banks within an area intermediate between these extremes. *See* note [33], supra. So also, some banking services are evidently more local in nature than others. But that in banking the relevant geographical market is a function of each separate customer's economic scale means simply that a workable compromise must be found: some fair intermediate delineation which avoids the indefensible extremes of drawing the market either so expansively as to make the effect of the merger upon competition seem insignificant, because only the very largest bank customers are taken into account in defining the market, or so narrowly as to place appellees in different markets, because only the smallest customers are considered. We think that the four-county Philadelphia metropolitan area, which state law apparently recognizes as a meaningful banking community in allowing Philadelphia banks to branch within it, and which would seem roughly to delineate the area in which bank customers that are neither very large nor very small find it practical to do their banking business, is a more appropriate "section of the country" in which to appraise the instant merger than any larger or smaller or different area. *Cf.* Hale and Hale, Market Power: Size and Shape Under the Sherman Act (1958), 119. We are helped to this conclusion by the fact that the three federal banking agencies regard the area in which banks have their offices as an "area of effective competition." Not only did the FDIC and FRB, in the reports they submitted to the Comptroller of the Currency in connection with appellees' application for permission to merge, so hold,

---

33. Appellees suggest not that bank offices skirting the four-county area provide meaningful alternatives to bank customers within the area, but that such alternatives are provided by large banks, from New York and elsewhere, which solicit business in the Philadelphia area. There is no evidence of the amount of business done in the area by banks with offices outside the area; it may be that such figures are unobtainable. In any event, it would seem from the local orientation of banking insofar as smaller customers are concerned, see note [21], supra, that competition from outside the area would only be important to the larger borrowers and depositors. If so, the four-county area remains a valid geographical market in which to assess the anticompetitive effect of the proposed merger upon the banking facilities available to the smaller customer—a perfectly good "line of commerce," in light of Congress' evident concern, in enacting the 1950 amendments to § 7, with preserving small business. See Brown Shoe Co., supra, 370 U.S., at 315–316. As a practical matter the small businessman can only satisfy his credit needs at local banks. To be sure, there is still some artificiality in deeming the four-county area the relevant "section of the country" so far as businessmen located near the perimeter are concerned. But such fuzziness would seem inherent in any attempt to delineate relevant geographical market. Note, 52 Colum.L.Rev. 766, 778–779, n. 77 (1952). And it is notable that outside the four-county area, appellees' business rapidly thins out....

but the Comptroller, in his statement approving the merger, agreed: "With respect to the effect upon competition, there are three separate levels and effective areas of competition involved. These are the national level for national accounts, the regional or sectional area, and the local area of the City of Philadelphia and the immediately surrounding area."

Having determined the relevant market, we come to the ultimate question under § 7: whether the effect of the merger "may be substantially to lessen competition" in the relevant market. Clearly, this is not the kind of question which is susceptible of a ready and precise answer in most cases. It requires not merely an appraisal of the immediate impact of the merger upon competition, but a prediction of its impact upon competitive conditions in the future; this is what is meant when it is said that the amended § 7 was intended to arrest anticompetitive tendencies in their "incipiency." *See Brown Shoe Co.*, supra, 370 U.S., at 317, 322. Such a prediction is sound only if it is based upon a firm understanding of the structure of the relevant market; yet the relevant economic data are both complex and elusive. *See generally* Bok, Section 7 of the Clayton Act and the Merging of Law and Economics, 74 Harv.L.Rev. 226 (1960). And unless businessmen can assess the legal consequences of a merger with some confidence, sound business planning is retarded.... So also, we must be alert to the danger of subverting congressional intent by permitting a too-broad economic investigation. *Standard Oil Co. of Cal. v. United States*, 337 U.S. 293. And so in any case in which it is possible, without doing violence to the congressional objective embodied in § 7, to simplify the test of illegality, the courts ought to do so in the interest of sound and practical judicial administration.... This is such a case.

We noted in *Brown Shoe Co.*, supra, 370 U.S., at 315, that "[t]he dominant theme pervading congressional consideration of the 1950 amendments [to § 7] was a fear of what was considered to be a rising tide of economic concentration in the American economy." This intense congressional concern with the trend toward concentration warrants dispensing, in certain cases, with elaborate proof of market structure, market behavior, or probable anticompetitive effects. Specifically, we think that a merger which produces a firm controlling an undue percentage share of the relevant market, and results in a significant increase in the concentration of firms in that market is so inherently likely to lessen competition substantially that it must be enjoined in the absence of evidence clearly showing that the merger is not likely to have such anticompetitive effects....

Such a test lightens the burden of proving illegality only with respect to mergers whose size makes them inherently suspect in light of Congress' design in § 7 to prevent undue concentration. Furthermore, the test is fully consonant with economic theory.[34] That "[c]ompetition is likely to be greatest when there are many sellers, none of which has any significant

---

34. See Kaysen and Turner, Antitrust Policy (1959), 133; Stigler, Mergers and Preventive Antitrust Policy, 104 U. of Pa.L.Rev. 176, 182 (1955); Bok, supra, at 308–316, 328.

Cf. Markham, Merger Policy Under the New Section 7: A Six–Year Appraisal, 43 Va.L.Rev. 489, 521–522 (1957).

market share," is common ground among most economists, and was undoubtedly a premise of congressional reasoning about the antimerger statute.

The merger of appellees will result in a single bank's controlling at least 30% of the commercial banking business in the four-county Philadelphia metropolitan area.[35] Without attempting to specify the smallest market share which would still be considered to threaten undue concentration, we are clear that 30% presents that threat.[36] Further, whereas presently the two largest banks in the area (First Pennsylvania and PNB) control between them approximately 44% of the area's commercial banking business, the two largest after the merger (PNB–Girard and First Pennsylvania) will control 59%. Plainly, we think, this increase of more than 33% in concentration must be regarded as significant.[37]

Our conclusion that these percentages raise an inference that the effect of the contemplated merger of appellees may be substantially to lessen

35. We note three factors that cause us to shade the percentages given earlier in this opinion, in seeking to calculate market share. (1) The percentages took no account of banks which do business in the four-county area but have no offices there; however, this seems to be a factor of little importance, at least insofar as smaller customers are concerned, (2) The percentages took no account of banks which have offices in the four-county area but not their home offices there; however, there seem to be only two such offices and appellees in this Court make no reference to this omission. (3) There are no percentages for the amount of business of banks located in the area, other than appellees, which originates in the area. Appellees contend that since most of the 40 other banks are smaller, they do a more concentratedly local business than appellees, and hence account for a relatively larger proportion of such business. If so, we doubt much correction is needed. The five largest banks in the four-county area at present control some 78% of the area banks' assets. Thus, even if the small banks have a somewhat different pattern of business, it is difficult to see how that would substantially diminish the appellees' share of the local banking business.

No evidence was introduced as to the quantitative significance of these three factors, and appellees do not contend that as a practical matter such evidence could have been obtained. Under the circumstances, we think a downward correction of the percentages to 30% produces a conservative estimate of appellees' market share.

36. Kaysen and Turner, supra, note [34], suggest that 20% should be the line of prima facie unlawfulness; Stigler suggests that any acquisition by a firm controlling 20% of the market after the merger is presumptively unlawful; Markham mentions 25%. Bok's principal test is increase in market concentration, and he suggests a figure of 7% or 8%. [And consider the *Columbia Steel* case, a prime target of the amendment of § 7, which in its horizontal aspect resulted in the creation of a firm with 24% of the market.] We intimate no view on the validity of such tests for we have no need to consider percentages smaller than those in the case at bar, but we note that such tests are more rigorous than is required to dispose of the instant case. Needless to say, the fact that a merger results in a less-than–30% market share, or in a less substantial increase in concentration than in the instant case, does not raise an inference that the merger is *not* violative of § 7. *See, e.g.*, Brown Shoe Co., supra.

37. It is no answer that, among the three presently largest firms (First Pennsylvania, PNB, and Girard), there will be no increase in concentration. If this argument were valid, then once a market had become unduly concentrated, further concentration would be legally privileged. On the contrary, if concentration is already great, the importance of preventing even slight increases in concentration and so preserving the possibility of eventual deconcentration is correspondingly great....

competition is not an arbitrary one, although neither the terms of § 7 nor the legislative history suggests that any particular percentage share was deemed critical. The House Report states that the tests of illegality under amended § 7 "are intended to be similar to those which the courts have applied in interpreting the same language as used in other sections of the Clayton Act." H.R.Rep. No. 1191, 81st Cong., 1st Sess. 8. Accordingly, we have relied upon decisions under these other sections in applying § 7. *See Brown Shoe Co., supra, passim; cf. United States v. E.I. Du Pont De Nemours & Co.*, 353 U.S. 586, 595, and n. 15. In *Standard Oil Co. of Cal. v. United States*, 337 U.S. 293, cited in S.Rep. No. 1775, 81st Cong., 2d Sess. 6, this Court held violative of § 3 of the Clayton Act exclusive contracts whereby the defendant company, which accounted for 23% of the sales in the relevant market and, together with six other firms, accounted for 65% of such sales, maintained control over outlets through which approximately 7% of the sales were made. In *Federal Trade Comm'n v. Motion Picture Adv. Serv. Co.*, 344 U.S. 392, we held unlawful, under § 1 of the Sherman Act and § 5 of the Federal Trade Commission Act, rather than under § 3 of the Clayton Act, exclusive arrangements whereby the four major firms in the industry had foreclosed 75% of the relevant market; the respondent's market share, evidently, was 20%. Kessler and Stern, Competition, Contract, and Vertical Integration, 69 Yale L.J. 1, 53 n. 231 (1959). In the instant case, by way of comparison, the four largest banks after the merger will foreclose 78% of the relevant market.... And in *Standard Fashion Co. v. Magrane–Houston Co.*, 258 U.S. 346, the Court held violative of § 3 a series of exclusive contracts whereby a single manufacturer controlled 40% of the industry's retail outlets. Doubtless these cases turned to some extent upon whether "by the nature of the market there is room for newcomers." *Federal Trade Com'n v. Motion Picture Adv. Serv. Co.*, supra, 344 U.S., at 395. But they remain highly suggestive in the present context, for as we noted in *Brown Shoe Co.*, supra, integration by merger is more suspect than integration by contract, because of the greater permanence of the former. The market share and market concentration figures in the contract-integration cases, taken together with scholarly opinion, ... support, we believe, the inference we draw in the instant case from the figure disclosed by the record.

There is nothing in the record of this case to rebut the inherently anticompetitive tendency manifested by these percentages. There was, to be sure, testimony by bank officers to the effect that competition among banks in Philadelphia was vigorous and would continue to be vigorous after the merger. We think, however, that the District Court's reliance on such evidence was misplaced. This lay evidence on so complex an economic-legal problem as the substantiality of the effect of this merger upon competition was entitled to little weight, in view of the witnesses' failure to give concrete reasons for their conclusions.[38]

38. The fact that some of the bank officers who testified represented small banks in competition with appellees does not substantially enhance the probative value of their testimony. The test of a competitive market is not only whether small competitors flour-

Of equally little value, we think, are the assurances offered by appellees' witnesses that customers dissatisfied with the services of the resulting bank may readily turn to the 40 other banks in the Philadelphia area. In every case short of outright monopoly, the disgruntled customer has alternatives; even in tightly oligopolistic markets, there may be small firms operating. A fundamental purpose of amending § 7 was to arrest the trend toward concentration, the tendency to monopoly, before the customer's alternatives disappeared through merger, and that purpose would be ill served if the law stayed its hand until 10, or 20, or 30 more Philadelphia banks were absorbed. This is not a fanciful eventuality, in view of the strong trend toward mergers evident in the area, . . . and we might note also that entry of new competitors into the banking field is far from easy.[39]

So also, we reject the position that commercial banking, because it is subject to a high degree of governmental regulation, or because it deals in the intangibles of credit and services rather than in the manufacture or sale of tangible commodities, is somehow immune from the anticompetitive effects of undue concentration. Competition among banks exists at every level?price, variety of credit arrangements, convenience of location, attractiveness of physical surroundings, credit information, investment advice, service charges, personal accommodations, advertising, miscellaneous special and extra services—and it is keen; on this appellees' own witnesses were emphatic. There is no reason to think that concentration is less inimical to the free play of competition in banking than in other service industries. On the contrary, it is in all probability more inimical. For example, banks compete to fill the credit needs of businessmen. Small businessmen especially are, as a practical matter, confined to their locality for the satisfaction of their credit needs . . . If the number of banks in the locality is reduced, the vigor of competition for filling the marginal small business borrower's needs is likely to diminish. At the same time, his concomitantly greater difficulty in obtaining credit is likely to put him at a disadvantage *vis-à-vis* larger businesses with which he competes. In this fashion, concentration in banking accelerates concentration generally.

We turn now to three affirmative justifications which appellees offer for the proposed merger. The first is that only through mergers can banks follow their customers to the suburbs and retain their business. This justification does not seem particularly related to the instant merger, but in any event it has no merit. There is an alternative to the merger route: the opening of new branches in the areas to which the customers have moved—

ish but also whether consumers are well served. See United States v. Bethlehem Steel Corp., 168 F.Supp. 576, 588, 592 (S.D.N.Y. 1958). "[C]ongressional concern [was] with the protection of *competition,* not *competitors.*" Brown Shoe Co., supra, 370 U.S. at 320. In an oligopolistic market, small companies may be perfectly content to follow the high prices set by the dominant firms, yet the market may be profoundly anticompetitive.

39. Entry is, of course, wholly a matter of governmental grace. . . . In the 10–year period ending in 1961, only one new bank opened in the Philadelphia four-county area. That was in 1951. At the end of 10 years, the new bank controlled only one-third of 1% of the area's deposits.

so-called de novo branching. Appellees do not contend that they are unable to expand thus, by opening new offices rather than acquiring existing ones, and surely one premise of an antimerger statute such as § 7 is that corporate growth by internal expansion is socially preferable to growth by acquisition.

Second, it is suggested that the increased lending limit of the resulting bank will enable it to compete with the large out-of-state bank, particularly the New York banks, for very large loans. We reject this application of the concept of "countervailing power." *Cf. Kiefer–Stewart Co. v. Joseph E. Seagram & Sons*, 340 U.S. 211. If anticompetitive effects in one market could be justified by procompetitive consequences in another, the logical upshot would be that every firm in an industry could, without violating § 7, embark on a series of mergers that would make it in the end as large as the industry leader. For if all the commercial banks in the Philadelphia area merged into one, it would be smaller than the largest bank in New York City. This is not a case, plainly, where two small firms in a market propose to merge in order to be able to compete more successfully with the leading firms in that market. Nor is it a case in which lack of adequate banking facilities is causing hardships to individuals or businesses in the community. The present two largest banks in Philadelphia have lending limits of $8,000,000 each. The only businesses located in the Philadelphia area which find such limits inadequate are large enough readily to obtain bank credit in other cities.

This brings us to appellees' final contention, that Philadelphia needs a bank larger than it now has in order to bring business to the area and stimulate its economic development.... We are clear, however, that a merger the effect of which "may be substantially to lessen competition" is not saved because, on some ultimate reckoning of social or economic debits and credits, it may be deemed beneficial. A value choice of such magnitude is beyond the ordinary limits of judicial competence, and in any event has been made for us already, by Congress when it enacted the amended § 7. Congress determined to preserve our traditionally competitive economy. It therefore proscribed anticompetitive mergers, the benign and the malignant alike, fully aware, we must assume, that some price might have to be paid.

In holding as we do that the merger of appellees would violate § 7 and must therefore be enjoined, we reject appellees' pervasive suggestion that application of the procompetitive policy of § 7 to the banking industry will have dire, although unspecified, consequences for the national economy. Concededly, PNB and Girard are healthy and strong; they are not undercapitalized or overloaned; they have no management problems; the Philadelphia area is not overbanked; ruinous competition is not in the offing. Section 7 does not mandate cutthroat competition in the banking industry, and does not exclude defenses based on dangers to liquidity or solvency, if to avert them a merger is necessary.[40] It does require, however, that the

---

40. Thus, arguably, the so-called failing-company defense, see International Shoe Co. v. Federal Trade Comm'n, 280 U.S. 291, 299–303, might have somewhat larger con-

forces of competition be allowed to operate within the broad framework of governmental regulation of the industry. . . .

Reversed and remanded with direction.[41]

NOTE ON MERGER CASES DURING THE 1960S

After Philadelphia National Bank, a relatively large number of merger cases reached the Supreme Court during the 1960s. The Court's decisions almost always favored those opposing a merger. Critics of the Court's decisions pointed to lack of precision in its analysis, alleged "gerrymandering" of market definitions to produce results favorable to the government, overly aggressive use of the "incipiency" concept, and inadequate concern for the efficiency-enhancing aspects of proposed mergers. As Justice Stewart put it in dissenting in *Von's Grocery* (p. 993 infra): "The Court has substituted bare conjecture for the statutory standard of a reasonable probability that competition may be lessened. . . . The sole consistency that I can find [in the Court's decisions] is that in litigation under § 7, the Government always wins." The following cases—some easier to defend than others—are representative of the Court's merger jurisprudence during the 1960s.

1. UNITED STATES V. ALUMINUM CO. OF AMERICA, 377 U.S. 271, 84 S.Ct. 1283, 12 L.Ed.2d, 314 (1964). There is a long history of the enforcement agencies and the courts taking into account whether one of the parties to a merger, usually the acquired firm, is a "maverick"—*i.e.*, a firm that, as a result of aggressive pricing or innovation, makes it difficult for other firms in the market to achieve coordinated results. *See* J. Baker, "Mavericks, Mergers and Exclusion: Providing Coordinated Competitive Effects Under the Antitrust Laws," 77 NYU L.Rev. 135 (2002). An extreme example involved a successful challenge to Alcoa, the leading producer in several lines of aluminum wire and cable, when it attempted in 1964 to acquire Rome Cable, a company principally in the copper wire and cable line, but with some production in aluminum wire and cable. Rome Cable was a small company that added little to Alcoa's existing market share; Rome accounted for 0.3% of total industry production of bare aluminum conductor, 4.7% of insulated aluminum conductor, and 1.3% of the broader aluminum conductor line.

The Supreme Court acknowledged that acquisition of a company with such small market shares would rarely result in a finding of a violation, but observed that Rome was an aggressive, independent competitor that had been a pioneer in aluminum insulation and continued to have an active and efficient research and sales organization; and Rome had a broad line of quality copper wire and cable products and special aptitudes and skill in insulation. The Court concluded: "Preservation of Rome, rather than its absorption by one of the giants, will keep it as an 'important competitive factor.' . . . Rome seems to us the prototype of the small independent that Congress aimed to preserve by § 7."

tours as applied to bank mergers because of the greater public impact of a bank failure compared with ordinary business failures. But the question what defenses in § 7 actions must be allowed in order to avert unsound banking conditions is not before us, and we intimate no view upon it.

41. White, J., did not participate in the decision of this case. The dissenting opinion of Harlan, J., in which Stewart, J., joined, is omitted.

2. UNITED STATES V. CONTINENTAL CAN CO., 378 U.S. 441, 84 S.Ct. 1738, 12 L.Ed.2d 953 (1964). In 1956, Continental Can, the second largest producer of metal containers, acquired Hazel–Atlas, the third largest producer of glass containers. Continental, which was itself a result of mergers in 1913, had acquired 21 domestic metal container companies as well as a number of others in the packaging business. Just before its acquisition of Hazel–Atlas, it shipped about 33% of all metal containers. American Can shipped about 38% and the remainder of the market was divided among about 75 to 90 other firms, none holding more than 5%. Hazel–Atlas accounted for about 9.6% of glass container shipments and followed Owens–Illinois which had 34.2% and Anchor–Hocking with 11.6%. The remainder was divided among 39 other firms.

All agreed that the relevant geographic market was the United States. With respect to relevant product market, all agreed that the can industry and the glass container industry were relevant lines of commerce. In the district court, the government had urged market definitions largely defined in terms of end uses of the product. Thus it sought market definitions which would segregate containers for the beer, soft drink, canning, toiletries and cosmetics, medicine and health, and household and chemical industries. The district court accepted only the proposed market definition for containers for the beer industry, and in relevant markets so defined, found no violation of Section 7.

Observing that "we must recognize meaningful competition where it is found to exist ...," the Supreme Court rejected the district court's product market definitions. It recognized that machinery to pack in glass is different from that employed for cans, that particular users may pack in one or the other and not consider shifts from day to day as price and other factors make them desirable, and that glass and metal containers have different characteristics that may disqualify one or the other for particular uses. There were situations, however, in which one type of container had supplanted the other. Baby food for a time had been packed entirely in cans, but Hazel–Atlas had succeeded in inducing a shift to glass as the dominant container. In the soft drink business, strenuous efforts were being made to promote use of cans for carbonated beverages. In summary, on the inter-industry competition point, the Court, per White, J., wrote:

> In our view there is and has been a rather general confrontation between metal and glass containers and competition between them for the same end uses which is insistent, continuous, effective and quantitywise very substantial. Metal has replaced glass and glass has replaced metal as the leading container for some important uses; both are used for other purposes; each is trying to expand its share of the market at the expense of the other; and each is attempting to preempt for itself every use for which its product is physically suitable, even though some such uses have traditionally been regarded as the exclusive domain of the competing industry. In differing degrees for different end uses manufacturers in each industry take into consideration the price of the containers of the opposing industry in formulating their own pricing policy. Thus, though the interchangeability of use may not be so complete and the cross-elasticity of demand not so immediate as in the case of most intraindustry mergers, there is over the long run the kind of customer response to innovation and other competitive stimuli that brings the competition between these two industries within § 7's competition-preserving proscriptions.

On the evidence already on the record, the Supreme Court concluded that inter-industry competition between glass and metal containers warranted treating as a relevant product market the combined glass and metal container industries and all end uses for which they compete. The Court recognized the possibility that there might be broader or different market configurations if plastic, paper, foil and other materials were considered, but concluded nevertheless that glass and metal container submarkets would exist in any broader market definition.

Turning to the question of possible anticompetitive effects, the Court noted that of the 59 billion containers shipped in 1955 by the metal (39¾ billion) and glass (19⅕ billion) industries, Continental shipped 21.9%. In terms of total containers shipped, Hazel–Atlas shipped about 3.1% of the product market. In the combined metal and glass container industries, 6 firms dominated with 70.1% of the business; Continental ranked second and Hazel–Atlas sixth. The resulting combined percentage of the firms was observed by the Court to approach that held presumptively illegal in Philadelphia National Bank, and to be almost the same as that involved in Alcoa–Rome Cable.

Finally, the lack of current competition between Continental and Hazel–Atlas for some important end uses of metal and glass containers was not viewed as diminishing the adverse effects of the merger on competition. Thus, the Court was prepared to assume that each would be less innovative in areas that would adversely affect the business fortunes of the other:

> It would make little sense for one entity within the Continental empire to be busily engaged in persuading the public of metal's superiority over glass for a given end use, while the other is making plans to increase the Nation's total glass container output for that same end use.

Justice Goldberg concurred, while Justices Harlan and Stewart dissented. Justice Harlan's dissent noted: "The Court's spurious market-share analysis should not obscure the fact that the Court is, in effect, laying down a 'per se' rule that mergers between two large companies in related industries are presumptively unlawful...."

3. UNITED STATES v. PABST BREWING CO., 384 U.S. 546, 86 S.Ct. 1665, 16 L.Ed.2d 765 (1966). In 1958, the Pabst Brewing Co., the nation's tenth largest brewer, acquired the Blatz Brewing Company, the eighteenth largest. The two companies competed against each other in 40 states, and in 1957, had combined sales of 23.95% of beer sales in Wisconsin, 11.32% of sales in the three-state area of Wisconsin, Illinois and Michigan, and 4.49% of sales throughout the country. By 1961, three years after the merger, Pabst had increased its share of the national beer market to 5.83% and ranked third in the country. The district court dismissed the government's complaint, holding that it failed to show that Wisconsin or the three-state area were proper relevant geographic markets, and had not shown substantial anticompetitive effects in a national market. The Supreme Court reversed. On the relevant geographic market question, Justice Black wrote:

> Apparently the District Court thought that in order to show a violation of § 7 it was essential for the Government to show a "relevant geographic market" in the same way the corpus delicti must be proved to establish a crime. But when the Government brings an action under § 7 it must, according to the language of the statute, prove no more than that there has been a merger between two corporations engaged in commerce and that the effect of the merger may be substantially to lessen competition or tend to create a monopoly in any line of commerce "in any section of the country." (Emphasis supplied.) The language of this section requires merely that the Government prove the merger has a substantial anti-competitive effect

somewhere in the United States—"in any section" of the United States. This phrase does not call for the delineation of a "section of the country" by metes and bounds as a surveyor would lay off a plot of ground. The Government may introduce evidence which shows that as a result of a merger competition may be substantially lessened throughout the country, or on the other hand it may prove that competition may be substantially lessened only in one or more sections of the country. In either event a violation of § 7 would be proved. Certainly the failure of the Government to prove by an army of expert witnesses what constitutes a relevant "economic" or "geographic" market is not an adequate ground on which to dismiss a § 7 case....

On the question of anticompetitive effect, the majority opinion noted that the number of breweries in the United States had declined from 714 in 1934 to 229 in 1961, and the total number of different competitors had fallen from 206 in 1957 to 162 in 1961. There had also been a sharp rise in the percentage share of the market controlled by the leading brewers. Viewing the respective market shares of Pabst and Blatz against that background, the majority found a proscribed effect on competition in Wisconsin, the three-state area, and the nation.

Justice Fortas concurred in the result, noting his view, contrary to statements in the majority opinion, that it continues to be the government's duty to prove the relevant market or "section of the country" in which the alleged anticompetitive effect had occurred.

Harlan and Stewart, JJ., concurred in the result, expressing similar misgivings about that part of the majority opinion which "appears to emasculate the statutory phrase 'in any section of the country.'"

4. UNITED STATES V. VON'S GROCERY CO., 384 U.S. 270, 86 S.Ct. 1478, 16 L.Ed.2d 555 (1966). In 1960, Von's—ranked third in retail grocery sales in the Los Angeles area—acquired Shopping Bag Food stores, sixth in rank, to make them, combined, the second largest chain in the area. Before the merger, in 1958, the largest firm had 8% of sales; in that same year, Von's had 4.7% and Shopping Bag had 4.2%. In 1958, the top four firms had accounted for 24.4%, the top eight for 40.9%, and the top twelve for 48.8% of the Los Angeles retail grocery market. Ten years earlier, the four-firm share was 25.9%, the eight-firm share was 33.7%, and the twelve-firm share was 38.8%. During those ten years, the top ten firms had gained market share, and remained quite stable in identity. Both Von's and Shopping Bag had increased market share. After the merger, their combined share of the market was 7.5%.

The Supreme Court reversed the district court's judgment for defendants and ordered prompt divestiture. The majority pointed to the fact that the number of owners operating a single store had "decreased from 5,365 in 1950 to 3,818 in 1961," while the number and size of chains was increasing, largely as a result of "absorptions." The Court held that "these facts alone are enough to cause us to conclude ... that the ... merger did violate § 7." Justice Black's review of the legislative history of the 1950 amendments that "revitalized § 7" led him to conclude that the Von's Grocery facts "present exactly the threatening trend toward concentration which Congress wanted to halt."

Fortas, J., did not participate, while White, J., concurred on the basis of the market share data. Justice White observed that after the "merger the four largest firms had 28.8%, the eight largest had 44%, and the twelve largest had 50%. The merger not only disposed of a substantial competitor but increased the concentration in the leading firms." Justice White noted that he did not read the Court's opinion to declare illegal every merger where the resulting firm had 7.5% of the market even "in any industry exhibiting a decided trend toward concentration."

Stewart, J., and Harlan, J., in dissent, anticipated the strong criticisms which would be leveled at the majority opinion and termed the Court's ruling "a startling *per se* rule based not on analysis of market concentration or effect on competition but a simple exercise in sums." They questioned whether a decline in the total number of sellers in the market was relevant for purposes of antitrust enforcement (as opposed to concentration among the largest sellers), and noted that a nationwide "supermarket revolution" had been taking place, adding to the intensity of competition in Los Angeles, as well as elsewhere, by replacing stodgy "mom and pop" stores with more efficient chains. They also pointed out that ease of entry with "modest initial investment" assured that vigorous competition would continue.

5. In *Philadelphia National Bank*, the Supreme Court rejected as justification for anticompetitive effects in a "local" market that the "increased lending limit of the resulting bank will enable it to compete with the large out-of-state bank." Would this rejection of "countervailing power" be as persuasive if the claim related to the need to compete in a global market with foreign companies? The Court also dismissed the allegation that the resulting bank would contribute to the economic development of Philadelphia by observing that Congress "proscribed anticompetitive mergers, the benign and malignant alike" and by noting that a "value choice" of this type "is beyond the ordinary limits of judicial competence." Do you agree with the Court's reasoning? With the rejection of this claim on the facts of the *Philadelphia National Bank* case?

6. It was against the background of very aggressive enforcement, supported consistently by the Supreme Court, that the government in 1974 finally lost a merger case in the Supreme Court. In *General Dynamics*, set out below, the Court not only rejected the government's contentions in that particular case, but signaled the beginning of a significant change in attitude toward antitrust limits on mergers.

United States v. General Dynamics Corp.

Supreme Court of the United States, 1974.
415 U.S. 486, 94 S.Ct. 1186, 39 L.Ed.2d 530.

■ STEWART, J. On September 22, 1967, the Government commenced this suit in the United States District Court for the Northern District of Illinois, challenging as violative of § 7 of the Clayton Act, 15 U.S.C. 18, the acquisition of the stock of United Electric Coal Companies by Material Service Corp. and its successor, General Dynamics Corp. After lengthy discovery proceedings, a trial was held from March 30 to April 22, 1970, and on April 13, 1972, the District Court issued an opinion and judgment finding no violation of the Clayton Act. . . .

I

At the time of the acquisition involved here, Material Service Corp. was a large midwest producer and supplier of building materials, concrete, limestone, and coal. All of its coal production was from deep-shaft mines operated by it or its affiliate, appellee Freeman Coal Mining Corp., and production from these operations amounted to 6.9 million tons of coal in

1959 and 8.4 million tons in 1967. In 1954, Material Service began to acquire the stock of United Electric Coal Companies. United Electric at all relevant times operated only strip or open pit mines in Illinois and Kentucky; at the time of trial in 1970 a number of its mines had closed and its operations had been reduced to four mines in Illinois and none in Kentucky.[42] In 1959, it produced 3.6 million tons of coal, and by 1967, it had increased this output to 5.7 million tons. Material Service's purchase of United Electric stock continued until 1959. At this point Material's holdings amounted to more than 34% of United Electric's outstanding shares and—all parties are now agreed on this point—Material had effective control of United Electric. The president of Freeman was elected chairman of United Electric's Executive Committee, and other changes in the corporate structure of United Electric were made at the behest of Material Service.

Some months after this takeover, Material Service was itself acquired by the appellee General Dynamics Corp. General Dynamics is a large diversified corporation, much of its revenues coming from sales of aircraft, communications, and marine products to government agencies. The trial court found that its purchase of Material Service was part of a broad diversification program aimed at expanding General Dynamics into commercial nondefense business. As a result of the purchase of Material Service, and through it, of Freeman and United Electric, General Dynamics became the Nation's fifth largest commercial coal producer. During the early 1960s General Dynamics increased its equity in United Electric by direct purchases of United Electric stock, and by 1966 it held or controlled 66.15% of United Electric's outstanding shares. In September 1966 the Board of Directors of General Dynamics authorized a tender offer to holders of the remaining United Electric stock. This offer was successful, and United Electric shortly thereafter became a wholly-owned subsidiary of General Dynamics.

The thrust of the Government's complaint was that the acquisition of United Electric by Freeman and Material Service in 1959 violated § 7 of the Clayton Act because the takeover substantially lessened competition in the production and sale of coal in either or both of two geographical markets. It contended that a relevant "section of the country" within the meaning of § 7 was, alternatively, the State of Illinois or the Eastern Interior Coal Province Sales Area, the latter being one of four major coal distribution areas recognized by the coal industry and comprising Illinois and Indiana, and parts of Kentucky, Tennessee, Iowa, Minnesota, Wisconsin, and Missouri.[43]

---

42. United Electric also had coal mining operations in Utah and other western States. The Government has not contended, however, that these holdings are of any relevance in this case.

43. Testimony at trial indicated that the Eastern Interior Coal Province—the area of coal production upon which the Eastern Coal Province Sales Area was based—was originally named by United States Geological Survey maps of the coalfields in the United States and described one portion of a sequence of coal-bearing rock formations known geologically as the Pennsylvania Sys-

At trial controversy focused on three basic issues: the propriety of coal as a "line of commerce," the definition of Illinois or the Eastern Interior Coal Province Sales Area as a relevant "section of the country," and the probability of a lessening of competition within these or any other product and geographic markets resulting from the acquisition. The District Court decided against the Government on each of these issues.

As to the relevant product market, the court found that coal faced strong and direct competition from other sources of energy such as oil, natural gas, nuclear energy, and geothermal power which created a cross-elasticity of demand among those various fuels. As a result, it concluded that coal, by itself, was not a permissible product market and that the "energy market" was the sole "line of commerce" in which anticompetitive effects could properly be canvassed.

Similarly, the District Court rejected the Government's proposed geographic markets on the ground that they were "based essentially on past and present production statistics and do not relate to actual coal consumption patterns." The court found that a realistic geographic market should be defined in terms of transportation arteries and freight charges that determined the cost of delivered coal to purchasers and thus the competitive position of various coal producers. In particular, it found that Freight Rate Districts, designated by the Interstate Commerce Commission for determining rail transportation rates, of which there were four in the area served by the respondent companies, were the prime determinants for the geographic competitive patterns among coal producers. In addition, the court concluded that two large and specialized coal consumption units were sufficiently differentiable in their coal use patterns to be included as relevant geographic areas.[44] In lieu of the State of Illinois or the Eastern Interior Coal Province Sales Area, the court accordingly found the relevant geographic market to be 10 smaller areas, comprising the two unique consumers together with four utility sales areas and four non-utility sales areas based on the ICC freight rate districts.

Finally, and, for purposes of this appeal most significantly, the District Court found that the evidence did not support the Government's contention that the 1959 acquisition of United Electric substantially lessened

tem. The Sales Area of the Eastern Interior Coal Province was derived from the assumption, acknowledged in the trial court's opinion, that the high costs of transporting coal—which may amount to 40% of the price of delivered coal—will inevitably give producers of coal a clear competitive advantage in sales in the immediate areas of the mines.

44. The trial court found that Commonwealth Edison, a large private electric utility with generation facilities in many parts of Illinois, and the Metropolitan Chicago Interstate Air Quality Control Region constituted separate and unique geographic regions. Commonwealth Edison was found to have unique attributes because of the great size of its coal consumption requirements, its distinctive distribution patterns, and its extensive commitment to air pollution programs and the development of nuclear energy. The Chicago Control Region, a congressionally designated area consisting of six counties in Illinois and two in Indiana, was distinguished from other geographic markets because of the impact of existing and anticipated air pollution regulations which would create special problems in the competition for coal sales contracts.

competition in any product or geographic market. This conclusion was based on four determinations made in the court's opinion. First, the court noted that while the number of coal producers in the Eastern Interior Coal Province declined from 144 to 39 during the period of 1957–1967, this reduction "occurred not because small producers have been acquired by others, but as the inevitable result of the change in the nature of demand for coal." Consequently, the court found, "this litigation presents a very different situation from that in such cases as *United States v. Philadelphia National Bank*, 374 U.S. 321 (1963), and *United States v. Von's Grocery Co.*, 384 U.S. 270 (1966) where the Supreme Court was concerned with 'preventing even slight increases in concentration.'" Second, the court noted that United Electric and Freeman were "predominantly complementary in nature" since "United Electric is a strip mining company with no experience in deep mining nor likelihood of acquiring it [and] Freeman is a deep mining company with no experience or expertise in strip mining." *Ibid.* Third, the court found that if Commonwealth Edison, a large investor-owned public utility, were excluded, "none of the sales by United Electric in the period 1965 to 1967, the years chosen by the Government for analysis, would have or could have been competitive with Freeman, had the two companies been independent," because of relative distances from potential consumers and the resultant impact on relative competitive position. *Ibid.* Finally, the court found that United Electric's coal reserves were so low that its potential to compete with other coal producers in the future was far weaker than the aggregate production statistics relied on by the Government might otherwise have indicated. In particular, the court found that virtually all of United Electric's proven coal reserves were either depleted or already committed by long-term contracts with large customers, and that United Electric's power to affect the price of coal was thus severely limited and steadily diminishing. On the basis of these considerations, the court concluded: "Under these circumstances, continuation of the affiliation between United Electric and Freeman is not adverse to competition, nor would divestiture benefit competition even were this court to accept the Government's unrealistic product and geographic market definitions." *Id.*, at 560.

II

The Government sought to prove a violation of § 7 of the Clayton Act principally through statistics showing that within certain geographic markets the coal industry was concentrated among a small number of large producers; that this concentration was increasing; and that the acquisition of United Electric would materially enlarge the market share of the acquiring company and thereby contribute to the trend toward concentration.

The concentration of the coal market in Illinois and, alternatively, in the Eastern Interior Coal Province was demonstrated by a table of the shares of the largest two, four, and 10 coal producing firms in each of these areas and for both 1957 and 1967 that revealed the following:[45]

	Eastern Interior Coal Province		Illinois	
	1957	1967	1957	1967
Top 2 firms	29.6	48.6	37.8	52.9
Top 4 firms	43.0	62.9	54.5	75.2
Top 10 firms	65.5	91.4	84.0	98.0

These statistics, the Government argued, showed not only that the coal industry was concentrated among a small number of leading producers, but that the trend had been toward increasing concentration.[46] Furthermore, the undisputed fact that the number of coal-producing firms in Illinois decreased almost 73% during the period of 1957 to 1967 from 144 to 39 was claimed to be indicative of the same trend. The acquisition of United Electric by Freeman resulted in increased concentration of coal sales among the leading producers in the areas chosen by the Government, as shown by the following table:[47]

	1959			1967		
	Share of top 2 but for merger	Share of top 2 given merger	Percent increase	Share of top 2 but for merger	Share of top 2 given merger	Percent increase
Province	33.1	37.9	14.5	45.0	48.6	8.0
Illinois	36.6	44.3	22.4	44.0	52.9	20.2

Finally, the Government's statistics indicated that the acquisition increased the share of the merged company in the Illinois and Eastern Interior Coal Province coal markets by significant degrees:[48]

45. The figures for 1967 reflect the impact on market concentration of the acquisition involved here.

46. The figures demonstrating the degree of concentration in the two coal markets chosen by the Government were roughly comparable to those in United States v. Von's Grocery Co., 384 U.S. 270, where the top four firms in the market controlled 24.4% of the sales, the top eight 40.9%, and the top 12, 48.8%. See, id., at 281 (White, J., concurring). See also United States v. Pabst Brewing Co., 384 U.S. 546, 551, where the top four producers of beer in Wisconsin were found to control 47.74% of the market, and the top 10 in the Nation and the local three-state area to control 45.06% and 58.93%, respectively. The statistics in the present case appear to represent a less advanced state of concentration than those involved in United States v. Aluminum Co. of America, 377 U.S. 271, 279, where the two largest firms held 50% of the

market, and the top five and the top nine controlled, respectively, 76% and 95.7%; and in United States v. Philadelphia National Bank, 374 U.S. 321, 363, where the two largest banks controlled 44% of the pre-merger market.

47. The percentage increase in concentration asserted here was thus analogous to that found in Von's Grocery, supra, where the concentration among the top four, eight, and 12 firms was increased, respectively, by 18.0%, 7.6%, and 2.5% as a result of the merger invalidated there. In Philadelphia Bank, supra, the 34% increase in concentration in the two largest firms from 44% to 59% was found to be clearly significant. 374 U.S., at 365.

48. The 1959 Illinois figure of 23.2% was asserted by the Government to be comparable to the 23.94% share of the Wisconsin beer market found to be significant in Pabst, supra, and the 25% share controlled by the

	Province		Illinois	
	Rank	Share (percent)	Rank	Share (percent)
1959				
Freeman		7.6		15.1
United Electric		4.8		8.1
Combined		12.4		23.2
1967				
Freeman		6.5		12.9
United Electric		4.4		8.9
Combined		10.9		21.8

In prior decisions involving horizontal mergers between competitors, this Court has found prima facie violations of § 7 of the Clayton Act from aggregate statistics of the sort relied on by the United States in this case. In *Brown Shoe Co. v. United States*, 370 U.S. 294, the Court reviewed the legislative history of the most recent amendments to the Act and found that "[t]he dominant theme pervading congressional consideration of the 1950 amendment was a fear of what was considered to be a rising tide of economic concentration in the American economy." *Id.*, at 315. A year later, in *United States v. Philadelphia National Bank*, 374 U.S. 321, the Court clarified the relevance of a statistical demonstration of concentration in a particular industry and of the effects thereupon of a merger or acquisition with the following language:

> This intense congressional concern with the trend toward concentration warrants dispensing, in certain cases, with elaborate proof of market structure, market behavior, or probable anticompetitive effects. Specifically, we think that a merger which produces a firm controlling an undue percentage share of the relevant market, and results in a significant increase in the concentration of firms in that market, is so inherently likely to lessen competition substantially that it must be enjoined in the absence of evidence clearly showing that the merger is not likely to have such anticompetitive effects. Id., at 363.

See also United States v. Continental Can Co., 378 U.S. 441, 458; *United States v. Von's Grocery Co.*, 384 U.S. 270, 277; *United States v. Pabst Brewing Co.*, 384 U.S. 546, 550–552.

The effect of adopting this approach to a determination of a "substantial" lessening of competition is to allow the Government to rest its case on a showing of even small increases of market share or market concentration in those industries or markets where concentration is already great or has been recently increasing, since "if concentration is already great, the importance of preventing even slight increases in concentration and so

merged company in United States v. Continental Can Co., 378 U.S. 441, 461. The Province figure of 12.4% was compared with the shares held by the merged companies in *Von's Grocery* (7.5%), and in the *Pabst* national (4.49%) and three-state (11.32%) markets.

preserving the possibility of eventual deconcentration is correspondingly great." *United States v. Aluminum Co. of America*, 377 U.S. 271, 279, *citing United States v. Philadelphia National Bank*, supra, 374 U.S., at 365, n. 42.

While the statistical showing proffered by the Government in this case, the accuracy of which was not discredited by the District Court or contested by the respondents, would under this approach have sufficed to support a finding of "undue concentration" in the absence of other considerations, the question before us is whether the District Court was justified in finding that other pertinent factors affecting the coal industry and the business of the respondents mandated a conclusion that no substantial lessening of competition occurred or was threatened by the acquisition of United Electric. We are satisfied that the court's ultimate finding was not in error.

In *Brown Shoe v. United States*, supra, we cautioned that statistics concerning market share and concentration, while of great significance, were not conclusive indicators of anticompetitive effects:

> Congress indicated plainly that a merger had to be functionally viewed, in the context of its particular industry. 370 U.S., at 321–322.

> Statistics reflecting the shares of the market controlled by the industry leaders and the parties to the merger are, of course, the primary index of market power; but only a further examination of the particular market—its structure, history and probable future—can provide the appropriate setting for judging the probable anticompetitive effect of the merger. Id., at 322 n. 38.

See also United States v. Continental Can Co., supra, 378 U.S. at 458. In this case, the District Court assessed the evidence of the "structure, history and probable future" of the coal industry, and on the basis of this assessment found no substantial probability of anticompetitive effects from the merger.

Much of the District Court's opinion was devoted to a description of the changes that have affected the coal industry since World War II. On the basis of more than three weeks of testimony and a voluminous record, the court discerned a number of clear and significant developments in the industry. First, it found that coal had become increasingly less able to compete with other sources of energy in many segments of the energy market. Following the War the industry entirely lost its largest single purchaser of coal—the railroads—and faced increasingly stiffer competition from oil and natural gas as sources of energy for industrial and residential uses. Because of these changes in consumption patterns, coal's share of the energy resources consumed in this country fell from 78.4% in 1920 to 21.4% in 1968. The court reviewed evidence attributing this decline not only to the changing relative economics of alternative fuels and to new distribution and consumption patterns, but also to more recent concern with the effect of coal use on the environment and consequent regulation of the extent and means of much coal consumption.

Second, the court found that to a growing extent since 1954, the electric utility industry has become the mainstay of coal consumption. While electric utilities consumed only 15.76% of the coal produced nationally in 1947, their share of total consumption increased every year thereafter, and in 1968 amounted to more than 59% of all the coal consumed throughout the Nation.[49]

Third, and most significantly, the court found that to an increasing degree, nearly all coal sold to utilities is transferred under long-term requirements contracts, under which coal producers promise to meet utilities' coal consumption requirements for a fixed period of time, and at predetermined prices.... These developments in the patterns of coal distribution and consumption, the District Court found, have limited the amounts of coal immediately available for "spot" purchases on the open market, since "[t]he growing practice by coal producers of expanding mine capacity only to meet long-term contractual commitments and the gradual disappearance of the small truck mines has tended to limit the production capacity available for spot sales." *Ibid.*

Because of these fundamental changes in the structure of the market for coal, the District Court was justified in viewing the statistics relied on by the Government as insufficient to sustain its case. Evidence of past production does not, as a matter of logic, necessarily give a proper picture of a company's future ability to compete. In most situations, of course, the unstated assumption is that a company that has maintained a certain share of a market in the recent past will be in a position to do so in the immediate future. Thus, companies that have controlled sufficiently large shares of a concentrated market are barred from merger by § 7 not because of their past acts, but because their past performances imply an ability to continue to dominate with at least equal vigor. In markets involving groceries or beer, as in *Von's Market,* supra, and *Pabst,* supra, statistics involving annual sales naturally indicate the power of each company to compete in the future. Evidence of the amount of annual sales is relevant as a prediction of future competitive strength, since in most markets distribution systems and brand recognition are such significant factors that one may reasonably suppose that a company which has attracted a given number of sales will retain that competitive strength.

In the coal market, as analyzed by the District Court, however, statistical evidence of coal production was of considerably less significance. The bulk of the coal produced is delivered under long-term requirements contracts, and such sales thus do not represent the exercise of competitive power but rather the obligation to fulfill previously negotiated contracts at a previously fixed price. The focus of competition in a given time-frame is not on the disposition of coal already produced but on the procurement of new long-term supply contracts. In this situation, a company's past ability to produce is of limited significance, since it is in a position to offer for sale

---

49. In 1968, electric utilities accounted for 59.09% of United States coal consumption, coke plants 18.20%, cement mills 1.88%, other manufacturing (including steel and rolling mills) 17.70%, and retail and miscellaneous consumers 3.14%.

neither its past production nor the bulk of the coal it is presently capable of producing, which is typically already committed under a long-term supply contract. A more significant indicator of a company's power effectively to compete with other companies lies in the state of a company's uncommitted reserves of recoverable coal. A company with relatively large supplies of coal which are not already under contract to a consumer will have a more important influence upon competition in the contemporaneous negotiation of supply contracts than a firm with small reserves, even though the latter may presently produce a greater tonnage of coal. In a market where the availability and price for coal are set by long-term contracts rather than immediate or short-term purchases and sales, reserves rather than past production are the best measure of a company's ability to compete.

The testimony and exhibits in the District Court revealed that United Electric's coal reserve prospects were "unpromising." *Id.*, at 559. United's relative position of strength in reserves was considerably weaker than its past and current ability to produce. While United ranked fifth among Illinois coal producers in terms of annual production, it was 10th in reserve holdings, and controlled less than 1% of the reserves held by coal producers in Illinois, Indiana, and western Kentucky. *Id.*, at 538. Many of the reserves held by United had already been depleted, at the time of trial, forcing the closing of some of United's midwest mines.[50] Even more significantly, the District Court found that of the 52,033,304 tons of currently mineable reserves in Illinois, Indiana, and Kentucky controlled by United, only four million tons had not already been committed under long-term contracts. United was found to be facing the future with relatively depleted resources at its disposal, and with the vast majority of those resources already committed under contracts allowing no further adjustment in price. In addition, the District Court found that "United Electric has neither the possibility of acquiring more [reserves] nor the ability to develop deep coal reserves," and thus was not in a position to increase its reserves to replace those already depleted or committed. *Id.*, at 560.

Viewed in terms of present and future reserve prospects—and thus in terms of probable future ability to compete—rather than in terms of past production, the District Court held that United Electric was a far less significant factor in the coal market than the Government contended or the production statistics seemed to indicate. While the company had been and remained a "highly profitable" and efficient producer of relatively large amounts of coal, its current and future power to compete for subsequent long-term contracts was severely limited by its scarce uncommitted resources.[51] Irrespective of the company's size when viewed as a producer, its

50. The District Court found that while United Electric held six mines operating in the midwest in 1948, it had opened only three new ones since then and four had closed because of exhaustion of reserves. The court found that the evidence showed that reserves in two other mines would soon be depleted, and the respondents inform us in their briefs that these events have already occurred.

51. As an example of the impact of depleted or committed reserves on a company's ability to compete for long-term contracts, the District Court noted that a number of requirements contracts signed by United

weakness as a competitor was properly analyzed by the District Court and fully substantiated that court's conclusion that its acquisition by Material Service would not "substantially ... lessen competition...." The validity of this conclusion is not undermined, we think, by the three-faceted attack made upon it by the Government in this Court—to which we now turn.

III

First, the Government urges that the court committed legal error by giving undue consideration to facts occurring after the effective acquisition in 1959.[52] In *FTC v. Consolidated Foods Corp.*, 380 U.S. 592, 598, this Court stated that post-acquisition evidence tending to diminish the probability or impact of anticompetitive effects might be considered in a § 7 case. *See also United States v. E.I. du Pont de Nemours & Co.*, 353 U.S. 586, 597 *et seq.*, 602 *et seq.* But in *Consolidated Foods and in United States v. Continental Can Co.*, 378 U.S. 441, 463, the probative value of such evidence was found to be extremely limited, and judgments against the Government were in each instance reversed in part because "too much weight" had been given to post-acquisition events. The need for such a limitation is obvious. If a demonstration that no anticompetitive effects had occurred at the time of trial or of judgment constituted a permissible defense to a § 7 divestiture suit, violators could stave off such actions merely by refraining from aggressive or anticompetitive behavior when such a suit was threatened or pending.[53]

Electric to supply coal to electric utilities were backed up by reserves belonging to Freeman and *"could not have been obtained without that guarantee"* because of the utilities' fear that the contract obligation could not otherwise be fulfilled. 341 F.Supp. at 599 (emphasis in original).

52. The court's reliance on such facts and the absence of specific findings of fact concerning the competitive situation in 1959, at which point both sides now agree the acquisition took place, may have been engendered by the Government's apparent inconsistency in its position concerning the critical date. Certain of the respondents' proposed findings of fact concerning its resources in 1959 and its attempts to increase its depleted holdings were termed "irrelevant" by the Government at the trial.

53. The mere nonoccurrence of anticompetitive effects from a merger would, of course, merely postpone rather than preclude a divestiture suit. This Court indicated in United States v. E.I. du Pont de Nemours & Co., 353 U.S. 586, 597, that a merger may be attacked *ab initio* long after its culmination if

effect on competition not apparent immediately after the merger subsequently appears, since § 7 was designed to arrest the creation of monopolies "in their incipiency" and " 'incipiency' ... denotes not the time the stock was acquired but any time when the acquisition threatens to ripen into a prohibited effect...."See also FTC v. Consolidated Foods Corp., 380 U.S. 592, 598. The scope this "time of suit" concept gives to the Government in attacking mergers under § 7 is discussed in Orrick, The Clayton Act: Then and Now, 24 ABA Antitrust Section 44 (1964); Subcommittee on Section 7, The Backward Sweep Theory and the Oligopoly Problem, 32 ABA Antitrust L.J. 306 (1966). In the context of the present case, the "time of suit" rule coupled with the limited weight given to post-merger evidence of no anticompetitive impact tends to give the Government a "Heads–I-win, Tails-you-lose" advantage over a § 7 defendant: post-merger evidence showing a lessening of competition may constitute an "incipiency" on which to base a divestiture suit, but evidence showing that such lessening has not, in fact, occurred cannot be accorded "too much weight."

Furthermore, the fact that no concrete anticompetitive symptoms have occurred does not itself imply that competition has not already been affected, "for once the two companies are united no one knows what the fate of the acquired company and its competitors would have been but for the merger." *FTC v. Consolidated Foods*, supra, 380 U.S. 592, 598. And, most significantly, § 7 deals in "probabilities, not certainties," *Brown Shoe v. United States*, supra, 370 U.S., at 323, and the mere nonoccurrence of a substantial lessening of competition in the interval between acquisition and trial does not mean that no substantial lessening will develop thereafter; the essential question remains whether the probability of such future impact exists at the time of trial.

In this case, the District Court relied on evidence relating to changes in the patterns and structure of the coal industry and in United Electric's coal reserve situation after the time of acquisition in 1959. Such evidence could not reflect a positive decision on the part of the merged companies to deliberately but temporarily refrain from anticompetitive actions, nor could it reasonably be thought to reflect less active competition than that which might have occurred had there not been an acquisition in 1959. As the District Court convincingly found, the trend toward increased dependence on utilities as consumers of coal and toward the near-exclusive use of long-term contracts were the products of inevitable pressures on the coal industry in all parts of the country. And unlike evidence showing only that no lessening of competition has yet occurred, the demonstration of weak coal resources necessarily and logically implied that United Electric was not merely disinclined but unable to compete effectively for future contracts. Such evidence went directly to the question of whether future lessening of competition was probable, and the District Court was fully justified in using it.

Second, the Government contends that reliance on depleted and committed resources is essentially a failing company defense which must meet the strict limits placed on that defense by this Court's decisions in *United States v. Third National Bank of Nashville*, 390 U.S. 171; *Citizen Publishing Co. v. United States*, 394 U.S. 131; and *United States v. Greater Buffalo Press, Inc.*, 402 U.S. 549. The failing company doctrine, recognized as a valid defense to a § 7 suit in *Brown Shoe*, supra, 370 U.S., at 346, was first announced by this Court in *International Shoe Co. v. FTC*, 280 U.S. 291, and was preserved by explicit references in the legislative history of the modern amendments to § 7. H.R.Rep. No. 1191, 81st Cong., 1st Sess., 6 (1949); S.Rep. No. 1775, 81st Cong., 2d Sess., 7 (1950). A company invoking the defense has the burden[54] of showing that its "resources [were] so depleted and the prospect of rehabilitation so remote that it faced the grave probability of a business failure ...," *International Shoe*, supra, 280 U.S., at 302, and further that it tried and failed to merge with a company other

---

54. In Citizen Publishing Co. v. United States, 394 U.S. 131, 138–139, "[t]he burden of proving that the conditions of the failing company doctrine have been satisfied" was found to be "on those who seek refuge under it."

than the acquiring one, *Citizen Publishing Co.*, supra, 394 U.S., at 138; *Greater Buffalo Press*, supra, 402 U.S., at 555.

The Government asserts that United Electric was a healthy and thriving company at the time of the acquisition and could not be considered on the brink of failure, and also that the respondents have not shown that Material Service was the only available acquiring company. These considerations would be significant if the District Court had found no violation of § 7 by reason of United Electric's being a failing company, but the District Court's conclusion was not, as the Government suggests, identical with or even analogous to such a finding. The failing company defense presupposes that the effect on competition and the "loss to [the company's] stockholders and injury to the communities where its plants were operated," International Shoe, supra, 280 U.S., at 302, will be less if a company continues to exist even as a party to a merger than if it disappears entirely from the market. It is, in a sense, a "lesser of two evils" approach, in which the possible threat to competition resulting from an acquisition is deemed preferable to the adverse impact on competition and other losses if the company goes out of business. The respondents' demonstration of United's weak reserves position, however, proved an entirely different point. Rather than showing that United would have gone out of business but for the merger with Material Service, the finding of inadequate reserves went to the heart of the Government's statistical prima facie case based on production figures and substantiated the District Court's conclusion that United Electric, even if it remained on the market, did not have sufficient reserves to compete effectively for long-term contracts. The failing company defense is simply inapposite to this finding and the failure of the respondents to meet the prerequisites of that doctrine did not detract from the validity of the court's analysis.

Finally, the Government contends that the factual underpinning of the District Court's opinion was not supported by the evidence contained in the record, and should be reevaluated by this Court.... Suffice it to say that we find the controlling findings and conclusions contained in the District Court's careful and lengthy opinion to be supported by the evidence in the record and not clearly erroneous.

One factual claim by the Government, however, goes to the heart of the reasoning of the District Court and thus is worthy of explicit note here. The Government asserts that the paucity of United Electric's coal reserves could not have the significance perceived by the District Court, since all companies engaged in extracting minerals at some point deplete their reserves and then acquire new reserves or the new technology required to extract more minerals from their existing holdings. United Electric, the Government suggests, could at any point either purchase new strip reserves or acquire the expertise to recover currently held deep reserves.

But the District Court specifically found new strip reserves not to be available: "Evidence was presented at trial by experts, by state officials, by industry witnesses and by the Government itself indicating that economically mineable strip reserves that would permit United Electric to continue operations beyond the life of its present mines are not available. The Government failed to come forward with any evidence that such reserves are presently available." 341 F. Supp., at 559. In addition, there was considerable testimony at trial, apparently credited by the District Court, indicating that United Electric and others had tried to find additional strip reserves not already held for coal production, and had been largely unable to do so.

Moreover, the hypothetical possibility that United Electric might in the future acquire the expertise to mine deep reserves proves nothing—or too much. As the Government pointed out in its brief and at oral argument, in recent years a number of companies with no prior experience in extracting coal have purchased coal reserves and entered the coal production business in order to diversify and complement their current operations. The mere possibility that United Electric, in common with all other companies with the inclination and the corporate treasury to do so, could someday expand into an essentially new line of business does not depreciate the validity of the conclusion that United Electric at the time of the trial did not have the power to compete on a significant scale for the procurement of future long-term contracts, nor does it vest in the production statistics relied on by the Government more significance than ascribed to them by the District Court.

IV

In addition to contending that the District Court erred in finding that the acquisition of United Electric would not substantially lessen competition, the Government urges us to review the court's determinations of the proper product and geographic markets. The Government suggests that while the "energy market" might have been an appropriate "line of commerce," coal also had sufficient "practical indicia" as a separate "line of commerce" to qualify as an independent and consistent submarket. *Cf. United States v. Continental Can Co.*, 378 U.S. 441, 456–457. It also suggests that irrespective of the validity of the criteria adopted by the District Court in selecting its 10 geographic markets, competition between United Electric and Material Service within the larger alternative geographic markets claimed by the Government established those areas as a permissible "section of the country" within the meaning of § 7.

While under normal circumstances a delineation of proper geographic and product markets is a necessary precondition to assessment of the probabilities of a substantial effect on competition within them, in this case we nevertheless affirm the District Court's judgment without reaching these questions. By determining that the amount and availability of usable reserves, and not the past annual production figures relied on by the Government, were the proper indicators of future ability to compete, the District Court wholly rejected the Government's *prima facie* case. Irrespective of the markets within which the acquiring and the acquired company might be viewed as competitors for purposes of this § 7 suit, the Government's statistical presentation simply did not establish that a substantial lessening of competition was likely to occur in any market. By concluding that "divestiture [would not] benefit competition even were this court to accept the Government's unrealistic product and geographic market definitions," 341 F.Supp., at 560, the District Court rendered superfluous its further determinations that the Government also erred in its choice of relevant markets. Since we agree with the District Court that the Government's reliance on production statistics in the context of this case was insufficient, it follows that the judgment before us may be affirmed without reaching the issues of geographic and product markets.

The judgment of the District Court is affirmed.

■ DOUGLAS, J., with whom BRENNAN, WHITE, and MARSHALL, JJ., concur, dissenting.

In this case the United States appeals from a district court decision upholding the acquisition of stock in United Electric Coal Companies by Material Service Corporation and its successor, General Dynamics Corporation, against a challenge that the acquisition violated § 7 of the Clayton Act. The United States instituted this civil antitrust action on the claim that the acquisition may substantially lessen competition in the Illinois and Eastern Interior Coal Province sales area coal markets. After trial on the merits the District Court rejected the Government's proposed product and geographic markets and dismissed the action, concluding that the Government had failed to show a substantial lessening of competition in the markets the court deemed relevant.

I

The combination here challenged is the union of two major Illinois coal producers—Freeman Coal Mining Corporation and United Electric Coal Companies—under the ultimate corporate control of General Dynamics Corporation.

[Ed. In Sections II and III, the dissenting justices argued against the district court's findings that the relevant product market was all energy and the relevant geographic market was ICC Freight Rate Districts, localized producing areas grouped for ICC ratemaking purposes.

On the product market question, the dissenters argued that coal should be a relevant submarket, relying on its substantial price advantages over other energy sources and operational disadvantages for certain purposes, *i.e.*, the virtual requirement of liquid fuel for highway and air transportation. As a result of these factors, the market for coal had become limited for the most part to large industrial energy consumers such as electric utilities and certain manufacturers. For example, in the years under review coal accounted for over 90% of energy consumed by steam electric utility plants. Finally, since coal using facilities are not easily adaptable to alternative energy sources, there was little inter-fuel price sensitivity.

As to the narrow geographic market categories—which had the effect of putting Freeman and United Electric in different markets—the dissenters argued that they did not correspond to "commercial realities," noting in that connection, that Freeman and United Electric sold one half of their output to the same customers at the same facilities.]

IV

The court further found that United Electric, standing alone, would not contribute meaningfully to further competition since virtually all its economically mineable strip reserves were committed under long-term contracts and it possessed neither the capability to obtain more strip reserves nor the expertise to develop its deep reserves. Although the doctrine was not invoked by name, this appears to be an application of the "failing company" defense. *See Citizen Publishing Co. v. United States*, 394 U.S. 131 (1969). If it is, the court proceeded on an analysis made at the wrong point in time and failed to discuss the legal standards employed in finding the defense to be established. The finding that 48 of United's 52 million tons of strip reserves were committed related to the time of trial. But, since the rationale of the failing company defense is the lack of anticompetitive consequence if one of the combining companies was about to disappear from the market at any rate, the viability of the "failing company" must be assessed as of the time of the merger. *United States v. Greater Buffalo Press, Inc.*, 402 U.S. 549, 555 (1971); *Citizen Publishing Co. v. United States*, supra, at 138.

The Court urges that United's weak reserve position, rather than establishing a failing company defense "went to the heart of the Government's prima facie case based on production figures." Under this view United's weak reserve position at the time of trial constitutes postacquisition evidence which diminishes the possibility of anticompetitive impact and thus directly affects the strength of time-of-acquisition findings. The problem with this analysis is that the District Court made no time-of-acquisition findings which such postacquisition evidence could affect. The majority concedes the obvious need for a limitation on the weight given postacquisition evidence and notes that we have reversed cases where "too much weight" has been given. Here the postacquisition events were given all the weight because all the District Court's findings were made as of the time of the trial. While findings made as of the time of the merger could concededly be tempered to a limited degree by postacquisition events, no such findings were ever made.

Many of the commitments here which reduced United's available reserves occurred after the acquisition; 21 million tons for example were committed in 1968. Similarly, though the District Court found further mineable strip reserves unavailable at the time of trial, there is no finding that they were unavailable in 1959 or 1967. To the contrary, the record demonstrates that other coal producers did acquire new strip reserves during the 1960s. United's 1959 viability is further supported by the fact that it possessed 27 million tons of deep reserves. While we do not know if all these reserves were economically mineable at the time of the acquisition, there was no finding that they would not become so in the near future with advances in technology or changes in the price structure of the coal market.[55] Further there was no contention nor finding that further deep reserves were not available for acquisition.[56] The District Court merely concluded that United had no "ability to develop deep coal reserves."[57]

While it is true that United is a strip mining company which has not extracted deep reserves since 1954, this does not mean that United would not develop deep mining expertise if deep reserves were all it had left or that it could not sell the reserves to some company which poses less of a threat to increased concentration in the coal market than does Freeman. United Electric was not, as the Court suggests, merely one of many companies with the possible "inclination and corporate treasury" to allow expansion into "an essentially new line of business." United was a coal company with a thriving coal marketing structure. At the time of the merger it had access to at least 27 million tons of deep reserves and it had operated a deep mine only five years previously. While deep coal mining may have been an essentially new line of business for many, it was for United merely a matter of regaining the expertise it once had to extract reserves it already owned for sale in a market where it already had a good name.

V

Thus, from product and geographic markets to market share and industry concentration analysis to the failing company defense, the findings below are based on legal standards which are either incorrect or not disclosed. While the court did gratuitously state that no § 7 violation would be found "even were this court to accept the Government's unrealistic product and market definitions," this conclusory statement is supported by no analysis sufficient to allow review in this Court. The majority notes that production figures are of limited significance because they include deliveries under long-term contracts entered into in prior years. It is true that uncommitted reserves or sales of previously uncommitted coal would be preferable indicia of competitive strength, but the District Court made no

55. Research into new methods of extraction or a rise in the price of coal could make reserves which are uneconomical to mine at any given point in time economically mineable in the future.

56. To the contrary, United Electric acquired substantial new deep reserves since the time of the acquisition since it now owns about 44 million tons of deep reserves and controls by location another 40 to 50 million tons. Reserves are controlled by location if, in order to be mined at all, they must be mined by those who control, by ownership, lease or option, the contiguous reserves.

57. If that conclusion is to lend support to the combination on the ground that United "standing alone, cannot contribute meaningfully to competition," it must be made in light of the stringent standards applicable to the failing company defense. In Citizen Publishing Co. v. United States, 394 U.S. 131, 139, we said that defense is one of "narrow scope" and that the burden of proving the defense is "on those who seek refuge under it." We also stated that the prospects of continued independent existence must be "dim or nonexistent" and that it must be established that the acquiring company is the only available purchaser. See also United States v. Greater Buffalo Press, Inc., 402 U.S. 549, 555–556 (1971), and United States v. Third National Bank of Nashville, 390 U.S. 171, 189 (1968).

findings as to United's or Freeman's respective market shares at the time of the acquisition under either of these standards.[58]

On the basis of a record so devoid of findings based on correct legal standards, the judgment may not be affirmed except on a deep-seated judicial bias against § 7 of the Clayton Act. We should remand the case to the District Court with directions to assess the impact of the Freeman–United Electric combination on the Illinois and Eastern Interior Coal Province sales area coal markets as of 1959.[59] We should direct the court to make findings of respective market shares, and further to evaluate United Electric's viability as an independent producer or as the possible "acquiree" of a company other than General Dynamics as of 1959, in light of the strict standards applicable to the failing company defense. Since we abdicate our duty for responsible review and accept the mere conclusion that no § 7 violation is established on the basis of a record with none of these necessary findings, I dissent from the affirmance of the District Court's judgment.

———

CITIZEN PUBLISHING CO. v. UNITED STATES, 394 U.S. 131, 89 S.Ct. 927, 22 L.Ed.2d 148 (1969). The Star and the Citizen were the only two daily newspapers of general circulation in Tucson, Arizona. Prior to 1940, they competed vigorously and while their circulation was equal, the Star sold 50% more advertising space than the Citizen and operated at a slight profit while the Citizen sustained losses. The

58. The District Court did find that, as of 1968, Freeman controlled 6.5% of the total coal reserves dedicated to existing mines in the EICP. At the same point in time, United Electric controlled 2.5% of that total, but almost all of this was contractually committed. If market shares are to be determined by percentage of total reserves, what is necessary is a finding as to each company's 1959 share of uncommitted Illinois and EICP reserves—including reserves which were economically mineable or which might have become so in the reasonably near future and further including an estimate as to uncontrolled reserves which might have been acquired by either company in the reasonably near future.

The District Court also found that, as of 1968, the two companies together accounted for 10.9% of the EICP coal production, and that this figure represented more than a 10% decrease from the combined production for 1959. Combined 1959 production by the companies was thus at least 12.1% of the EICP total. If market shares are to be determined by percentage of industry sales, this figure is in excess of percentages found illegal in markets with a trend toward concentration (see, e.g., United States v. Von's Grocery Co., 384 U.S. 270 (1966) (7.5%), and United States v. Pabst Brewing Co., 384 U.S. 546 (1966) (4.49%)), and the court below recognized an increase in concentration in the coal market. It might be argued, however, that, if market share is to be determined by sales, the production figures found by the court below are not the relevant ones for they include production which goes to meet obligations incurred in long-term contracts entered into in prior years. In terms of competition, if sales are the relevant criteria, what is needed is a finding of "new" sales (sales of previously uncommitted coal) as a percentage of total industry new sales in Illinois and the EICP at the time of the acquisition.

59. Common control of the two companies was achieved in 1959 and the combination was completed in 1967; at oral argument both parties conceded that the merger "took place" in 1959.

Citizen was not about to go out of business, however, nor had its owners sought to sell the paper to others.

In 1940, a joint operating agreement was negotiated providing for the establishment of a 50–50 joint venture which would manage all departments of the newspapers' business except news and editorial policy. Subscription and advertising rates were set jointly, profits were pooled and distributed to the Star and Citizen pursuant to an agreed ratio, and it was further agreed that neither the Star nor the Citizen nor any of its stockholders, officers and executives would engage in any other business in metropolitan Tucson in conflict with the agreement.

The government challenged the joint venture agreement under Sections 1 and 2 of the Sherman Act on grounds that it involved price fixing and division of markets, and under Section 7 of the Clayton Act on the ground that the joint venture constituted an illegal acquisition.

The Supreme Court affirmed the district court's holding for the government, noting that the newspapers' only real defense depended upon the "failing company" doctrine—a judicially created defense (see International Shoe Co. v. FTC, 280 U.S. 291 (1930)), referred to with approval in the legislative history of the 1950 amendments to Section 7 of the Clayton Act.

The Court gave a narrow scope to the failing company defense, emphasizing that International Shoe was a case where the evidence showed that the resources of the acquired company were so depleted and its prospects for rehabilitation so remote that "it faced the grave probability of a business failure," and that there was no other prospective purchaser available. The failing company defense on behalf of the Citizen was rejected because there was no evidence that "the joint operating agreement was the last straw" nor that the acquiring company was "the only available purchaser." The Court also noted: " ... no effort was made to sell the Citizen; its properties and franchise were not put in the hands of a broker; and the record is silent on what the market, if any, for the Citizen might have been." The burden of proof to demonstrate a failing company defense was placed on defendants, and the Court concluded they had not satisfied that burden. Justice Stewart, who later wrote the majority opinion in General Dynamics touching on failing company considerations, dissented.

NOTE ON FAILING COMPANIES, FLAILING COMPANIES, AND DISTRESSED INDUSTRIES

The legislative history of revised Section 7 does not squarely address a failing company defense for mergers but rather refers in approving language to an older case—*International Shoe Co. v. FTC*, 280 U.S. 291 (1930). That decision arguably justifies only a very limited failing company exception since the evidence there showed that the resources of the acquired company were so depleted and its prospects for rehabilitation so remote that "it faced the grave probability of a business failure" and there were no other prospective purchasers available.

By addressing the failing company issue simply by an approving reference to an old case, the legislation provides little guidance as to what constitutes a "failing company," whether the defense is absolute or qualified, or the reasons underlying the exemption. Derek Bok, in his 1960 article, Section 7 of the Clayton Act and the Merging of Law and Economics, 74 Harv.L.Rev. 226, 339–47 (1960), cites three possible sets of considerations that might have motivated Congress: (1) efficiency considerations, since a failing company might be improved by a change in management (regarded as unlikely in light of Congress' general lack of concern in the legislative debates and reports with efficiency considerations); (2) a view that the disappearance from competitive markets of the failing company would not lessen competition; and (3) legislative concern with the interests of creditors, owners, and employees who would be interested in avoiding a total collapse and realizing the highest selling price possible.

The second argument—disappearance of a failing firm cannot affect competition in a significant way—is weak. A failing firm's assets could be of immense competitive significance since the ability of a large firm to extract higher than competitive profits can be augmented by acquisition of those assets. To take an obvious example, the failing firm may be a more aggressive price-cutting competitor or a more innovative designer than its rivals, and its disruptive influence may be extinguished if a large competitor acquires its assets.

But what of the other factors? Might some sort of antitrust approach to failing firms be grounded on the theory that a merger might produce a more efficient firm, or help pay off creditors, owners or employees?

United States antitrust law and policy with respect to failing firms and distressed industries falls into three categories:

1.   *Failing Firm/Absolute Defense.* If a company (or one of its divisions) is truly failing, it may be sold to any purchaser without any antitrust consequence. We have already noted, however, that "failing firm" is defined narrowly and in effect, firms must be virtually on the steps of a bankruptcy court before they can assert a failing firm or failing division defense, and a few courts seem to have insisted on present insolvency before they would permit the defense. *See United States v. Pabst Brewing Co.*, 296 F.Supp. 994, 1000–01 (E.D.Wis.1969); *United States v. Reed Roller Bit Co.*, 274 F.Supp. 573, 584 (W.D.Okl.1967). Also, there must be no other prospective purchaser available that poses a less severe danger to competition than does the proposed merger. *Citizen Publishing Co. v. United States*, p. 1010 supra.

The 1992 DOJ/FTC Horizontal Merger Guidelines adopt this restrictive approach to the defense and in addition provide that it is available only if the allegedly failing firm would not be able to reorganize successfully through bankruptcy proceedings, and only if, absent the merger, the assets of the failing firm would exit from the market. *See* Merger Guidelines, p. 964–65 infra.

One reason for a rigorous approach to a failing firm exemption involves the difficulty of determining if a business failure really is imminent. Is the company unalterably in decline? Are its problems permanent or temporary (for example, where a decline in demand is cyclical)? Could efficiency be restored by the sale or elimination of excess capacity? It is partly because of a lack of confidence in judges' ability to weigh such factors accurately, and fairly balance private and public (*i.e.*, competitive) interests that American law insists that this absolute defense be available only where the qualifying conditions are demonstrated by clear proof.

There is, however, one important exception to the rule that firms must be in a condition of actual failure rather than likely failure to take advantage of the defense. In 1970, Congress passed the Newspaper Preservation Act, 15 U.S.C.A. 1801–04, which eased the law with respect to joint publishing ventures involving one or more failing newspapers, allowing them to merge their business functions if they kept their editorial functions separate. The Act defined a failing newspaper as a newspaper that, regardless of its ownership or affiliations, was in "probable danger of financial failure." 15 U.S.C.A. 1802(5). The standard providing that one of the two newspapers in the joint agreement need only be suffering losses that probably could not be reversed was sustained by an equally divided Supreme Court in Michigan Citizens for an *Independent Press v. Thornburgh*, 493 U.S. 38 (1989).

Why not adopt the Newspaper Preservation Act across the board? Admittedly, it is easier to ascertain that a firm is presently insolvent than that it will become insolvent as a result of prevailing conditions. But if uncertainty of proof is the concern, why not simply require clear proof of probable failure, rather than waiting until actual failure (and its attendant waste and dislocations) occurs?

2. *Flailing Firm/Qualified Defense.* Even if a firm is not on the brink of bankruptcy, its financial position may be so weak or its capacity to compete so diminished (for example, because of depleted financial resources, lack of access to an essential raw material, or weakened distribution) that its market share measured by percentage of past sales may overstate its competitive significance. In *United States v. International Harvester Co.*, 564 F.2d 769, 773 (7th Cir.1977), the Seventh Circuit appeared to accept a "weak competitor" defense when it stated:

> This showing, which has been called the "General Dynamics defense," establishes that the Government's past market statistics are really insufficient to constitute a prima facie case because Steiger's weak financial reserves (like United Electric's weak coal reserves in General Dynamics) would not allow it to be as strong a competitor as the bald statistical projections indicate.[60]

Professors Areeda and Turner offered the following critique of International Harvester and similar "weak competitor" cases:

> We conclude that financial difficulties should be disregarded unless it is reasonably clear that (1) if unresolved, they would cause the firm's market share to decline to a level that would make the merger permissible, and (2) there is no competitively preferable alternative for resolving them.

> Such a showing is likely to be rare, at least in other than marginal cases. Financial difficulties peculiar to one of the merging firms would normally have already been reflected in declining market shares, which would be taken into account without regard to specific cause. Indeed, the cause-and-effect relationship would usually run the other way-low or declining sales causing the financial difficulties, rather than vice versa. And even if it were established that financial difficulties would cause the requisite further sales decline—as, for example, inability to obtain capital for expansion in a growing market—it would be a rare case where there would be no competitively preferable alternative solutions. . . .

> All that we have said concerning financial difficulties applies to claims of management weaknesses, and more. Any inability to revamp management would in all likelihood simply be a derivative of financial difficulties. Moreover, it seems highly implausible that a presumptively unlawful merger would be the only suitable avenue for replacing poor management.[61]

60. *See, e.g.,* FTC v. University Health Inc., 938 F.2d 1206, 1221 (11th Cir.1991) (financial weakness just one factor among many); Lektro–Vend Corp. v. Vendo Co., 660 F.2d 255, 277 n. 22 (7th Cir.1981) (financial weakness alone cannot justify a merger but may be a relevant factor); FTC v. National Tea Co., 603 F.2d 694 (8th Cir.1979).

61. 4 Areeda & Turner, Antitrust Law: An Analysis of Antitrust Principles and Their Application 141–42 (1980).

In *Kaiser Aluminum & Chemical Corp. v. FTC*, 652 F.2d 1324 (7th Cir.1981), the Seventh Circuit explained its present position:

> It should be emphasized that *International Harvester* does not rely solely on the acquired firm's weak financial condition as a defense to § 7. The case instead considers the firm's weak condition as one relevant economic factor among many. It is therefore a mischaracterization to view *International Harvester* as adopting a weakened company doctrine as a *per se* defense to § 7 liability.... Financial weakness, while perhaps relevant in some cases, is probably the weakest ground of all for justifying a merger. The acquisition of a financially weak company in effect hands over its customers to the financially strong, thereby deterring competition by preventing others from acquiring those customers, making entry into the market more difficult. Moreover, a weak company defense would extend the failing company doctrine, a defense which the Supreme Court in *General Dynamics* observed has strict limits.[62]

If courts permit "weak financial condition" (or similar factors that are easily manipulatable and correctable) to override market share statistics, how much will be left of Section 7?

3. *Distressed Industries*. There is nothing in Section 7, its legislative history, or the case law that would modify antitrust enforcement when all or most firms in an industry are barely breaking even (though not in imminent danger of failure) and long-term excess capacity is growing worse. The fact that an industry is under economic siege because of chronic excess capacity and too high unit costs is irrelevant.

We saw earlier that the Supreme Court did take distressed industry conditions into account in the 1930s when much of the American economy was made up of "distressed industries." In *Appalachian Coals v. United States*, p. 211 supra, a joint sales venture of producers of bituminous coal was upheld, in part because of distressed conditions in the production and distribution of coal. *Appalachian Coals* was more of a cartel than a merger and put together firms with a very large market share, so that its lenient approach might not have been justified. In any event, after World War II when prosperity followed, the concept of distressed industry was discarded by the enforcement agencies and the courts.

To date, the problem of distressed industries has been left for the market to solve—a "survival of the fittest" approach. The orthodox economic view is if there is capacity underutilization combined with financial problems and declining demand, eventually the appropriate number of firms will exit from the market—presumably the least efficient—and in that way capacity will be brought in line with demand. Exit can occur abruptly through bankruptcy or more slowly through downsizing of facilities and staff.

But is it always predictable that the less efficient firms are most likely to leave the market? Conceivably, the more efficient firm will exit first and the less efficient firm with better access to capital will remain.

Presumably, special treatment for firms in a distressed industry would only occur in moderately concentrated markets where the merger is borderline in terms of illegality. But who is to say that after the merger, the lower costs or higher

---

62. 652 F.2d at 1339.

profits resulting from the merger will be devoted to addressing problems of chronic structural weakness? How might a "distressed industry" be defined so as to avoid a gaping hole in antitrust enforcement?

Hospital Corporation of America v. FTC

United States Court of Appeals, Seventh Circuit, 1986.
807 F.2d 1381.

■ POSNER, J. Hospital Corporation of America, the largest proprietary hospital chain in the United States, asks us to set aside the decision by the Federal Trade Commission that it violated section 7 of the Clayton Act by the acquisition in 1981 and 1982 of two corporations, Hospital Affiliates International, Inc. and Health Care Corporation. Before these acquisitions (which cost Hospital Corporation almost $700 million), Hospital Corporation had owned one hospital in Chattanooga, Tennessee. The acquisitions gave it ownership of two more. In addition, pursuant to the terms of the acquisitions it assumed contracts, both with four-year terms, that Hospital Affiliates International had made to manage two other Chattanooga-area hospitals. So after the acquisitions Hospital Corporation owned or managed 5 of the 11 hospitals in the area. Later one of the management contracts was cancelled; and one of the lesser issues raised by Hospital Corporation, which we might as well dispose of right now, is whether the Commission should have disregarded the assumption of that contract. We agree with the Commission that it was not required to take account of a post-acquisition transaction that may have been made to improve Hospital Corporation's litigating position. The contract was cancelled after the Commission began investigating Hospital Corporation's acquisition of Hospital Affiliates, and while the initiative in cancelling was taken by the managed hospital, Hospital Corporation reacted with unaccustomed mildness by allowing the hospital to withdraw from the contract. For it had sued three other hospitals that tried to get out of their management contracts with Hospital Affiliates when Hospital Corporation assumed the contracts—only none of these hospitals was in a market where Hospital Corporation's acquisition of Hospital Affiliates was likely to be challenged. Post-acquisition evidence that is subject to manipulation by the party seeking to use it is entitled to little or no weight. Cf. *Lektro-Vend Corp. v. Vendo Co.*, 660 F.2d 255, 276 (7th Cir.1981). The Commission was entitled to give it no weight in this case, both to simplify the adjudication of merger cases generally and because excluding this one hospital would not have altered the market share figures significantly.

If all the hospitals brought under common ownership or control by the two challenged acquisitions are treated as a single entity, the acquisitions raised Hospital Corporation's market share in the Chattanooga area from 14 percent to 26 percent. This made it the second largest provider of hospital services in a highly concentrated market where the four largest firms together had a 91 percent market share compared to 79 percent before the acquisitions. These are the FTC's figures, and Hospital Corporation thinks they are slightly too high (quite apart from the question what to do with either or both management contracts); but the discrepancy is too slight to make a legal difference. Nor would expressing the market shares in terms of the Herfindahl index alter the impression of a highly concentrated market....

The Clayton Act allows Hospital Corporation to seek judicial review of the Commission's order in any circuit in which it does business and for unexplained reasons it has chosen this circuit. It makes three arguments to us: there is no reasonable probability that its acquisitions in Chattanooga will lessen competition substantially; anyway the Federal Trade Commission has no constitutional power to bring an enforcement action, because the members of the Commission do not serve at the pleasure of the President; failing all else, Hospital Corporation should at least not be required to give the Commission advance notice of all future acquisitions....

The Commission's detailed analysis of [the] effects [of the acquisitions] fills most of a 117–page opinion that, whatever its substantive merits or demerits, is a model of lucidity. The Commission may have made its task harder (and opinion longer) than strictly necessary, however, by studiously avoiding reliance on any of the Supreme Court's section 7 decisions from the 1960s except *United States v. Philadelphia Nat'l Bank*, 374 U.S. 321, 83 S.Ct. 1715, 10 L.Ed.2d 915 (1963), which took an explicitly economic approach to the interpretation of the statute. The other decisions in that decade—in particular *Brown Shoe Co. v. United States*, 370 U.S. 294, 82 S.Ct. 1502, 8 L.Ed.2d 510 (1962); *United States v. Aluminum Co. of America*, 377 U.S. 271, 84 S.Ct. 1283, 12 L.Ed.2d 314 (1964); *United States v. Von's Grocery Co.*, 384 U.S. 270, 86 S.Ct. 1478, 16 L.Ed.2d 555 (1966), and *United States v. Pabst Brewing Co.*, 384 U.S. 546, 86 S.Ct. 1665, 16 L.Ed.2d 765 (1966)—seemed, taken as a group, to establish the illegality of any nontrivial acquisition of a competitor, whether or not the acquisition was likely either to bring about or shore up collusive or oligopoly pricing. The elimination of a significant rival was thought by itself to infringe the complex of social and economic values conceived by a majority of the Court to inform the statutory words "may ... substantially ... lessen competition."

None of these decisions has been overruled. Although both *United States v. General Dynamics Corp.*, 415 U.S. 486, 94 S.Ct. 1186, 39 L.Ed.2d 530 (1974), and *United States v. Citizens & Southern Nat'l Bank*, 422 U.S. 86, 95 S.Ct. 2099, 45 L.Ed.2d 41 (1975) refused to equate the possession of a significant market share with a significant threat to competition, these cases involved highly unusual facts, having no counterpart in this case, that required discounting large market shares. In General Dynamics the shares were of current sales (of coal) made pursuant to long-term contracts entered into a long time ago; future sales would depend on uncommitted reserves, and one of the acquired firms had no uncommitted reserves. In *Citizens & Southern* the acquired banks were already under the effective control of the acquirer (they were its "*de facto* branches"), so that the formal merger had little competitive significance.

These cases show that market share figures are not always decisive in a section 7 case, but it can be argued that the cases themselves carve only limited exceptions to the broad holdings of some of the merger decisions of the 1960s. General Dynamics was like a failing-company case; in *Citizens & Southern* the merger was a mere formality—like a marriage ceremony between common law spouses. The most important developments that cast doubt on the continued vitality of such cases as *Brown Shoe* and *Von's* are found in other cases, where the Supreme Court, echoed by the lower courts, has said repeatedly that the economic concept of competition, rather than any desire to preserve rivals as such, is the lodestar that shall guide the contemporary application of the antitrust laws, not excluding the Clayton Act.... Applied to cases brought under section 7, this principle requires the district court (in this case, the Commission) to make a judgment whether the challenged acquisition is likely to hurt consumers, as by making it easier for the firms in the market to collude, expressly or tacitly, and thereby force price above or farther above the competitive level. So it was prudent for the Commission, rather than resting on the very strict merger decisions of the 1960s, to inquire into the probability of harm to consumers. In any event, even if we thought those decisions still authoritative, we could not uphold the Commission's decision on a rationale different from its own.

When an economic approach is taken in a section 7 case, the ultimate issue is whether the challenged acquisition is likely to facilitate collusion. In this perspective the acquisition of a competitor has no economic significance in itself; the worry is that it may enable the acquiring firm to cooperate (or cooperate better) with other leading competitors on reducing or limiting output, thereby pushing up the market price. Hospital Corporation calls the issue whether an acquisition is likely to have such an effect "economic," which of course it is. But for purposes of judicial review, as we have said, it is a factual issue subject to the substantial evidence rule, not a legal issue on which review usually is plenary and invariably is much less deferential than is the review of findings of fact. One of the main reasons for creating the Federal Trade Commission and giving it concurrent jurisdiction to enforce the Clayton Act was that Congress distrusted judicial determination of antitrust questions. It thought the assistance of an administrative body would be helpful in resolving such questions and indeed expected the FTC to take the leading role in enforcing the Clayton Act, which was passed at the same time as the statute creating the Commission. See Henderson, The Federal Trade Commission, ch. 1 (1924). In the present case the underlying facts are, as Hospital Corporation asserts, largely undisputed. The dispute is over the inferences of competitive consequence to be drawn from them. But the drawing of those inferences is a matter within the Commission's primary responsibility too. There is plenty of evidence to support the Commission's prediction of adverse competitive effect in this case; whether we might have come up with a different prediction on our own is irrelevant.

The acquisitions reduced the number of competing hospitals in the Chattanooga market from 11 to 7. True, this calculation assumes that the hospitals that came under the management although not ownership of Hospital Corporation should be considered allies rather than competitors of Hospital Corporation; but the Commission was entitled to so conclude. The manager (Hospital Corporation) sets the prices charged by the managed hospitals, just as it sets its own prices. Although the pricing and other decisions that it makes in its management role are subject to the ultimate control of the board of directors of the managed hospital, there is substantial evidence that the board usually defers to the manager's decisions. If it were not inclined to defer, it would not have a management contract; it would do its own managing, through officers hired by it. A hospital managed by Hospital Corporation is therefore unlikely to engage in vigorous or perhaps in any price competition with Hospital Corporation—or so at least the Commission was entitled to conclude.

The reduction in the number of competitors is significant in assessing the competitive vitality of the Chattanooga hospital market. The fewer competitors there are in a market, the easier it is for them to coordinate their pricing without committing detectable violations of section 1 of the Sherman Act, which forbids price fixing. This would not be very important if the four competitors eliminated by the acquisitions in this case had been insignificant, but they were not; they accounted in the aggregate for 12 percent of the sales of the market. As a result of the acquisitions the four largest firms came to control virtually the whole market, and the problem of coordination was therefore reduced to one of coordination among these four.

Moreover, both the ability of the remaining firms to expand their output should the big four reduce their own output in order to raise the market price (and, by expanding, to offset the leading firms' restriction of their own output), and the ability of outsiders to come in and build completely new hospitals, are reduced by Tennessee's certificate-of-need law. Any addition to hospital capacity must be approved by a state agency. The parties disagree over whether this law, as actually enforced, inhibits the expansion of hospital capacity. The law may indeed be laxly enforced. Not only is there little evidence that it has ever prevented a hospital in Chattanooga from making a capacity addition it wanted to make, but empirical studies of certificate of need regulation nationwide have found little effect on hospital expenditures. *See* Joskow, Controlling Hospital Costs: The Role of Government Regulation, ch. 7 (1981). Yet the Tennessee law might have some effect under the conditions that would obtain if the challenged acquisitions enabled collusive pricing of hospital services. Should the leading hospitals in Chattanooga collude, a natural consequence would be the creation of excess hospital capacity, for the higher prices resulting from collusion would drive some patients to shorten their hospital stays and others to postpone or reject elective surgery. If a noncolluding hospital wanted to expand its capacity so that it could serve patients driven off by the high prices charged by the colluding hospitals, the colluders would have not only a strong incentive to oppose the grant of a certificate of need but also substantial evidence with which to oppose it—the excess capacity (in the market considered as a whole) created by their own collusive efforts. At least the certificate of need law would enable them to delay any competitive sally by a noncolluding competitor. Or so the Commission could conclude (a refrain we shall now stop repeating). We add that at the very least a certificate of need law forces hospitals to give public notice, well in advance, of any plans to add capacity. The requirement of notice makes it harder for the member of a hospital cartel to "cheat" on the cartel by adding capacity in advance of other members; its attempt to cheat will be known in advance, and countermeasures taken.

All this would be of little moment if, in the event that hospital prices in Chattanooga rose above the competitive level, persons desiring hospital services in Chattanooga would switch to hospitals in other cities, or to nonhospital providers of medical care. But this would mean that the Chattanooga hospital market, which is to say the set of hospital-services providers to which consumers in Chattanooga can feasibly turn, *see United States v. Philadelphia Nat'l Bank*, supra, 374 U.S. at 358–61, 83 S.Ct. at 1738–40; *Tampa Elec. Co. v. Nashville Coal Co.*, 365 U.S. 320, 327–28, 81 S.Ct. 623, 627–29, 5 L.Ed.2d 580 (1961), includes hospitals in other cities plus non-hospital providers both in Chattanooga and elsewhere; and we do not understand Hospital Corporation to be challenging the Commission's market definition, which is limited to hospital providers in Chattanooga. Anyway, these competitive alternatives are not important enough to deprive the market shares statistics of competitive significance. Going to another city is out of the question in medical emergencies; and even when an operation or some other hospital service can be deferred, the patient's doctor will not (at least not for reasons of price) send the patient to another city, where the doctor is unlikely to have hospital privileges. Finally, although hospitals increasingly are providing services on an out-patient basis, thus competing with nonhospital providers of the same services (tests, minor surgical procedures, etc.), most hospital services cannot be provided by nonhospital providers; as to these, hospitals have no competition from other providers of medical care.

In showing that the challenged acquisitions gave four firms control over an entire market so that they would have little reason to fear a competitive reaction if they raised prices above the competitive level, the Commission went far to justify its prediction of probable anticompetitive effects. Maybe it need have gone no further. *See United States v. Philadelphia Nat'l Bank*, supra, 374 U.S. at 362–63, 83 S.Ct. at 1740–41; *Monfort of Colorado, Inc. v. Cargill, Inc.*, 761 F.2d 570, 580 (10th Cir.1985), rev'd on other grounds, 479 U.S. 104, 107 S.Ct. 484, 93 L.Ed.2d 427 (1986). But it did. First it pointed out that the demand for hospital services by patients and their doctors is highly inelastic under competitive conditions. This is not only because people place a high value on their safety and comfort and because many of their treatment decisions are made for them by their doctor, who doesn't pay their hospital bills; it is also because most hospital bills are paid largely by insurance companies or the federal government rather than by the patient. The less elastic the demand for a good or service is, the greater are the profits that providers can make by raising price through collusion. A low elasticity of demand means that raising price will cause a relatively slight fall in demand, with the result that total revenues will rise sharply. For example, if the price elasticity of demand throughout the relevant portion of the demand curve is-.2, meaning that within that area every 1 percent increase in price will result in a two-tenths of 1 percent decrease in the quantity demanded, then a 10 percent increase in price will cause only a 2 percent reduction in quantity sold, and hence an almost 8 percent increase in total revenue. And since less is being produced, costs will fall at the same time that revenue is rising, resulting in an even greater percentage increase in profit than in revenue.

Second, there is a tradition, well documented in the Commission's opinion, of cooperation between competing hospitals in Chattanooga. Of course, not all forms of cooperation between competitors are bad. *See, e.g., Broadcast Music, Inc. v. Columbia Broadcasting System, Inc.*, 441 U.S. 1, 99 S.Ct. 1551, 60 L.Ed.2d 1 (1979). But a market in which competitors are unusually disposed to cooperate is a market prone to collusion. The history of successful cooperation establishes a precondition to effective collusion-mutual trust and forbearance, without which an informal collusive arrangement is unlikely to overcome the temptation to steal a march on a fellow colluder by undercutting him slightly. That temptation is great. A seller who makes a profit of $10 on each sale at the cartel price, and then cuts price by $1 and thereby (let us suppose) doubles his output, will increase his total profits by 180 percent.

The management contracts between Hospital Affiliates (itself an owner as well as manager of hospitals) and two other hospitals in Chattanooga— contracts that when taken over by Hospital Corporation gave it virtual control over the pricing and other decisions of two of its competitors, at least for a time—illustrate the unusual degree of cooperation in this industry; imagine Ford's signing a management contract with General Motors whereby General Motors installed one of its officers (who would remain an officer of GM) as Ford's manager. Hospitals routinely exchange intimate information on prices and costs in connection with making joint applications to insurers for higher reimbursement schedules. Such cooperation may be salutary but it facilitates collusion and therefore entitles the Commission to worry even more about large horizontal acquisitions in this industry than in industries where competitors deal with each other at arm's length.

Third, hospitals are under great pressure from the federal government and the insurance companies to cut costs. One way of resisting this pressure is by presenting a united front in negotiations with the third-party payors—which indeed, as we have just said, hospitals in Chattanooga have done. *See also United States v. North Dakota Hospital Ass'n*, 640 F.Supp. 1028 (D.N.D.1986). The fewer the independent competitors in a hospital market, the easier they will find it, by presenting an unbroken phalanx of representations and requests, to frustrate efforts to control hospital costs. This too is a form of collusion that the antitrust laws seek to discourage, though within the limitations of the Noerr–Pennington doctrine, which insulates some cooperative efforts to obtain government benefits from attack under antitrust law. Not all third-party payors, however, are governmental; not all cooperative efforts to influence government are immunized by the doctrine, *see, e.g., California Motor Transport Co. v. Trucking Unlimited*, 404 U.S. 508, 92 S.Ct. 609, 30 L.Ed.2d 642 (1972); most important, the doctrine does not forbid enforcement efforts designed to make such efforts less effective by preserving a substantial number of competitors.

All these considerations, taken together, supported—we do not say they compelled—the Commission's conclusion that the challenged acquisitions are likely to foster collusive practices, harmful to consumers, in the Chattanooga hospital market. Section 7 does not require proof that a merger or other acquisition has caused higher prices in the affected market. All that is necessary is that the merger create an appreciable danger of such consequences in the future. A predictive judgment, necessarily probabilistic and judgmental rather than demonstrable (*see United States v. Philadelphia Nat'l Bank*, supra, 374 U.S. at 362, 83 S.Ct. at 1740), is called for. Considering the concentration of the market, the absence of competitive alternatives, the regulatory barrier to entry (the certificate of need law), the low elasticity of demand, the exceptionally severe cost pressures under which American hospitals labor today, the history of collusion in the industry, and the sharp reduction in the number of substantial competitors in this market brought about by the acquisition of four hospitals in a city with only eleven (one already owned by Hospital Corporation), we cannot say that the Commission's prediction is not supported by substantial evidence.

But of course we cannot just consider the evidence that supports the Commission's prediction. We must consider all the evidence in the record. We must therefore consider the significance of the facts, pressed on us by Hospital Corporation, that hospital services are complex and heterogeneous, that the sellers in this market are themselves heterogeneous because of differences in the services provided by the different hospitals and differences in the corporate character of the hospitals (some are publicly owned, some are proprietary, and some are private but nonprofit), that the hospital industry is undergoing rapid technological and economic change, that the payors for most hospital services (Blue Cross and other insurance companies, and the federal government) are large and knowledgeable, and that the FTC's investigation which led to this proceeding was touched off by a complaint from a competitor of Hospital Corporation. Most of these facts do detract from a conclusion that collusion in this market is a serious danger, but it was for the Commission—it is not for us—to determine their weight.

The first fact is the least impressive. It is true that hospitals provide a variety of different services many of which are "customized" for the individual patient, but the degree to which this is true seems no greater than in other markets. Although collusion is more difficult the more heterogeneous the output of the colluding firms, there is no established threshold of complexity beyond which it is infeasible and Hospital Corporation made no serious effort to show that hospital services are more complex than products and services in other markets, such as steel, building materials, and transportation, where collusion has been frequent.

The heterogeneity of the sellers has two aspects: the hospitals in Chattanooga offer different mixtures of services; and they have different types of ownership—private for-profit ("proprietary"), private not-for-profit, public. The significance of these features is unclear. Concerning the first, if one assumes that collusion is practiced on a service-by-service basis, the fact that hospitals provide different mixtures of service seems irrelevant to the feasibility of collusion. True, since different types of service may not be substitutable—open-heart surgery is not a substitute for setting a broken leg—specialized hospitals might not compete with one another. But that is not Hospital Corporation's argument. Its argument is that the different mixture of services in the different hospitals would make it difficult for their owners to fix prices of competing services, and this we don't understand.

Different ownership structures might reduce the likelihood of collusion but this possibility is conjectural and the Commission was not required to give it conclusive weight. The adoption of the nonprofit form does not change human nature, *see* Clark, *Does the Nonprofit Form Fit the Hospital Industry?*, 93 Harv.L.Rev. 1416, 1447, 1465 (1980), as the courts have recognized in rejecting an implicit antitrust exemption for nonprofit enterprises. *National Collegiate Athletic Ass'n v. Board of Regents*, 468 U.S. 85, 100 n. 22, 104 S.Ct. 2948, 2960 n. 22, 82 L.Ed.2d 70 (1984). (There is a possible gap in the FTC's jurisdiction over acquisitions involving nonprofit corporations, compare 15 U.S.C. § 18 with 15 U.S.C. §§ 44, 45(a)(2), but it doesn't affect this case, since the acquired and acquiring firms are all proprietary.) Nonprofit status affects the method of financing the enterprise (substituting a combination of gift and debt financing for equity and debt financing) and the form in which profits (in the sense of the difference between revenue and costs) are distributed, and it may make management somewhat less beady-eyed in trying to control costs, *see* Clarkson, *Some Implications of Property Rights in Hospital Management*, 15 J. Law & Econ. 363 (1972). But no one has shown that it makes the enterprise unwilling to cooperate in reducing competition (some contrary evidence is presented in Hersch, Competition and the Performance of Hospital Markets, 1 Rev.Ind.Org. 324 (1984))—which most enterprises dislike and which nonprofit enterprises may dislike on ideological as well as selfish grounds. "Nonprofit hospitals, in fact, make rather sizable profits and these profits have been growing over time." True, nonprofit hospitals, private and public, harbor considerable antipathy toward proprietary hospitals, regarding them as "cream skimmers" who lure away the affluent patients that nonproprietary hospitals need to defray the costs of serving the less affluent. This antipathy may retard the emergence of the mutual trust and forbearance that informal collusive schemes depend on for their effectiveness. But the other side of this coin is that the nonproprietaries fear the competition of the proprietaries (that is the source, or a source, of their antipathy to them)—and what better foundation for a collusive arrangement than fear of competition?

Political pressures might inhibit publicly owned hospitals from raising prices. But similar pressures might inhibit them from expanding capacity to take on additional patients attracted by lower prices. A seller's refusal to join a cartel is significant only insofar as the seller can expand output if and when the cartel, by raising prices, drives consumers to search for sellers who are not part of the cartel and are willing to undersell it. A public hospital that in order to expand its capacity must seek governmental appropriations is in a poor position to take advantage of the competitive opportunities created by the presence of a cartel in its market. Moreover, compelled as they are to treat charity cases while minimizing the cost to the taxpayers of supporting the hospital, public hospitals are under added pressure to charge high prices to their paying (or insured) patients, which may make collusion particularly attractive to these hospitals.

The economic and technological ferment in the hospital industry may make collusion more difficult, but also more urgent, since risk-averse managers may be strongly inclined to stabilize, if necessary through collusion, whatever features of an uncertain environment they are able to bring under their control. Regarding the weighing of such imponderables as this, much must be left to the judgment of the Commission.

The concentration of the buying side of a market does inhibit collusion. The bigger a buyer is, the more easily and lucratively a member of the cartel can cheat on his fellows; for with a single transaction, he may be able to increase his sales and hence profits dramatically. But with all the members thus vying for the large orders of big buyers, the cartel will erode. *See* Stigler, *A Theory of Oligopoly*, in Stigler, The Organization of Industry 39, 43–44 (1968). Hospital Corporation argues that the effective buyers of most hospital services are large and knowledgeable institutions rather than the patients who are the nominal buyers. But the role of the third-party payor is not quite that of a large buyer. The explicit contract between the insurance companies and their patients, and the statutory and regulatory obligations of government to Medicare and Medicaid recipients, require reimbursing patients for hospital services. Of course the insurer is not required to, and no insurer does, reimburse the insured for whatever services are consumed, regardless of price. But as a practical matter Blue Cross could not tell its subscribers in Chattanooga that it will not reimburse them for any hospital services there because prices are too high. As a practical matter it could not, if the four major hospital owners in the city, controlling more than 90 percent of the city's hospital capacity, raised their prices, tell its subscribers that they must use the remaining hospitals—whose aggregate capacity would be completely inadequate and, for reasons discussed earlier, could not readily, or at least rapidly, be expanded—if they want to be reimbursed. The insurers are in a better position to detect violations of the Sherman Act than the patients are but if the challenged acquisitions enable the major hospital owners in Chattanooga to collude without violating the Sherman Act, that is, collude tacitly rather than expressly, there would be no violations to detect and report.

Hospital Corporation's most telling point is that the impetus for the Commission's complaint came from a competitor—a large nonprofit hospital in Chattanooga. A rational competitor would not complain just because it thought that Hospital Corporation's acquisitions would facilitate collusion. Whether the competitor chose to join a cartel or stay out of it, it would be better off if the cartel were formed than if it were not formed. For the cartel would enable this seller to raise its price, whether or not to the cartel level. By staying out of the cartel and by pricing just below the cartel price, the competitor might, as we noted earlier, do even better than by joining the cartel.

The hospital that complained to the Commission must have thought that the acquisitions would lead to lower rather than high prices—which would benefit consumers, and hence, under contemporary principles of antitrust law, would support the view that the acquisitions were lawful. But this is just one firm's opinion. It was not binding on the Commission, which having weighed all the relevant facts concluded that the acquisitions had made collusion in this market significantly more likely than before. Since, moreover, the complainant was a nonprofit hospital, in attributing the complaint to fear of lower prices Hospital Corporation is contradicting its argument that the non-profit sector of the hospital industry does not obey the laws of economic self-interest.

[In the remaining portions of its opinion, the Court found unpersuasive the argument that the Federal Trade Commission was unconstitutional because it exercised executive (*i.e.*, prosecutorial) authority and yet the members could not be removed by the President except for cause. It also rejected a challenge to that portion of the Commission's order requiring that Hospital Corporation of America provide the Commission with advance notification of future acquisitions, noting earlier decisions to the effect that the Commission operated like a court of equity and had broad discretion to fence in respondents found guilty of violating the law.]

The Commission's order is affirmed and enforced.

NOTE ON "ANTITRUST INJURY," PRIVATE ENFORCEMENT, AND REMEDIES UNDER SECTION 7

1. BRUNSWICK CORP. v. PUEBLO BOWL-O-MAT, INC., 429 U.S. 477, 97 S.Ct. 690, 50 L.Ed.2d 701 (1977). Defendant Brunswick was one of the two largest manufacturers of bowling equipment in the United States. Plaintiffs were three bowling centers. Beginning in 1965, Brunswick had acquired and operated a large number of bowling centers. It had done so because most of its sales of bowling equipment had been on credit, and when the bowling industry went into sharp decline in the early 1960s, attempts to sell or lease repossessed equipment from delinquent purchasers met with only limited success. The acquisitions made Brunswick by far the largest

operator of bowling centers in the United States, but it controlled only 2% of the national total.

Plaintiffs contended that Brunswick's acquisitions in three local markets violated Section 7 of the Clayton Act. They attempted to establish damages by showing that if Brunswick had allowed certain defaulting centers to close, plaintiffs' profits would have increased. A jury returned a verdict of $2,358,030 for plaintiffs and, with some modification, this figure was trebled.

The Court of Appeals for the Third Circuit found that a properly instructed jury could have concluded that Brunswick was a "giant" whose entry into a "market of pygmies" might lessen horizontal retail competition. The Court also said that there was sufficient evidence to permit a jury to find that but for Brunswick's actions the acquired centers would have gone out of business, and if such a finding were made, plaintiffs would be entitled to treble damages. After reviewing the trial judge's instructions, however, the Court decided that the jury had been improperly charged. The Third Circuit reversed the judgment and remanded for a new trial.

The Supreme Court granted defendant judgment notwithstanding the verdict and reasoned:

> Every merger of two existing entities into one, whether lawful or unlawful, has the potential for producing economic readjustments that adversely affect some persons. But Congress has not condemned mergers on that account; it has condemned them only when they may produce anticompetitive effects. Yet under the Court of Appeals' holding, once a merger is found to violate § 7, all dislocations caused by the merger are actionable, regardless of whether those dislocations have anything to do with the reason the merger was condemned. This holding would make § 4 recovery entirely fortuitous, and would authorize damages for losses which are of no concern to the antitrust laws.

> Both of these consequences are well illustrated by the facts of this case. If the acquisitions here were unlawful, it is because they brought a "deep pocket" parent into a market of "pygmies." Yet respondents' injury—the loss of income that would have accrued had the acquired centers gone bankrupt—bears no relationship to the size of either the acquiring company or its competitors. Respondents would have suffered the identical "loss"—but no compensable injury—had the acquired centers instead obtained refinancing or been purchased by "shallow pocket" parents as the Court of Appeals itself acknowledged, 523 F.2d at 279. Thus, respondents' injury was not of "the type that the statute was intended to forestall," *Wyandotte Co. v. United States*, 389 U.S. 191, 202 (1967).

> But the antitrust laws are not merely indifferent to the injury claimed here. At base, respondents complain that by acquiring the failing centers petitioner preserved competition, thereby depriving respondents of the benefits of increased concentration. The damages respondents obtained are designed to provide them with the profits they would have realized had competition been reduced. The antitrust laws, however, were enacted for "the protection of *competition* not *competitors*," *Brown Shoe Co. v. United States*, 370 U.S. 294, 320 (1962). It is inimical to the purposes of these laws to award damages for the type of injury claimed here....

> We therefore hold that for the plaintiffs to recover treble damages on account of § 7 violations, they must prove more than injury causally linked to an illegal presence in the market. Plaintiffs must prove *antitrust* injury,

which is to say injury of the type the antitrust laws were intended to prevent and that flows from that which makes defendants' acts unlawful. The injury should reflect the anticompetitive effect either of the violation or of anticompetitive acts made possible by the violation. It should, in short, be "the type of loss that the claimed violations ... would be likely to cause." *Zenith Radio Corp. v. Hazeltine Research, Inc.*, supra, 395 U.S., at 125.

See Chapter 2 (pp. 99–106 supra) for a discussion of how lower courts have, at times, wrenched the "antitrust injury" concept free of these sensible Section 7 moorings.

2.   CARGILL, INC. v. MONFORT OF COLORADO, INC., 479 U.S. 104, 107 S.Ct. 484, 93 L.Ed.2d 427 (1986). Monfort, the nation's fifth largest beef packer, brought an action under the Clayton Act to enjoin a merger between the second and third largest beef packers. After a trial, a district court enjoined the proposed merger, and held that Monfort's allegation of a "price-cost squeeze" that would severely narrow its profit margins constituted an allegation of antitrust injury. The Tenth Circuit affirmed. Justice Brennan, writing for six members of the Supreme Court, reversed and reasoned as follows:

This case requires us to decide, at the outset, a question we have not previously addressed: whether a private plaintiff seeking an injunction under § 16 of the Clayton Act must show a threat of antitrust injury. To decide the question, we must look first to the source of the antitrust injury requirement, which lies in a related provision of the Clayton Act, § 4, 15 U.S.C. § 15.... In *Brunswick Corp. v. Pueblo Bowl–O–Mat, Inc.*, supra, we held that plaintiffs seeking treble damages under § 4 must show more than simply an "injury causally linked" to a particular merger; instead, "plaintiffs must prove antitrust injury, which is to say injury of the type the antitrust laws were intended to prevent and that flows from that which makes the defendants' acts unlawful." ...

Section 16 of the Clayton Act provides in part that "[a]ny person, firm, corporation, or association shall be entitled to sue for and have injunctive relief ... against threatened loss or damage by a violation of the antitrust laws...." 15 U.S.C. § 26. It is plain that § 16 and § 4 do differ in various ways. For example, § 4 requires a plaintiff to show actual injury, but § 16 requires a showing only of "threatened" loss or damage; similarly, § 4 requires a showing of injury to "business or property," cf. *Hawaii v. Standard Oil Co.*, 405 U.S. 251 (1972), while § 16 contains no such limitation.[63] Although these differences do affect the nature of the injury

63. Standing analysis under § 16 will not always be identical to standing analysis under § 4. For example, the difference in the remedy each section provides means that certain considerations relevant to a determination of standing under § 4 are not relevant under § 16. The treble-damage remedy, if afforded to "every person tangentially affected by an antitrust violation," *McCready*, 457 U.S., at 476–477, or for "all injuries that might conceivably be traced to an antitrust violation," Hawaii v. Standard Oil Co., 405 U.S., at 263, n. 14 would "open the door to duplicative recoveries," id., at 264, and to multiple lawsuits. In order to protect against multiple lawsuits and duplicative recoveries, courts should examine other factors in addition to antitrust injury, such as the potential for duplicative recovery, the complexity of apportioning damages, and the existence of other parties that have been more directly harmed, to determine whether a party is a proper plaintiff under § 4. See *Associated General Contractors*, supra, at 544–545; Illinois Brick Co. v. Illinois, 431 U.S. 720 (1977). Conversely, under § 16, the only remedy available is equitable in nature, and, as we recognized in *Hawaii v. Standard Oil Co.*,

cognizable under each section, the lower courts, including the courts below, have found that under both § 16 and § 4 the plaintiff must still allege an injury of the type the antitrust laws were designed to prevent. We agree.

The wording concerning the relationship of the injury to the violation of the antitrust laws in each section is comparable. Section 4 requires proof of injury "by reason of anything forbidden in the antitrust laws"; § 16 requires proof of "threatened loss or damage by a violation of the antitrust laws." It would be anomalous, we think, to read the Clayton Act to authorize a private plaintiff to secure an injunction against a threatened injury for which he would not be entitled to compensation if the injury actually occurred. . . .

Sections 4 and 16 are thus best understood as providing complementary remedies for a single set of injuries. Accordingly, we conclude that in order to seek injunctive relief under § 16, a private plaintiff must allege threatened loss or damage "of the type the antitrust laws were designed to prevent and that flows from that which makes defendants' acts unlawful." Brunswick, 429 U.S., at 489. We therefore turn to the question of whether the proposed merger in this case threatened respondent with antitrust injury. . . .

Monfort's first claim is that after the merger, Excel would lower its prices to some level at or slightly above its costs in order to compete with other packers for market share. Excel would be in a position to do this because of the multiplant efficiencies its acquisition of Spencer would provide. To remain competitive, Monfort would have to lower its prices; as a result, Monfort would suffer a loss in profitability, but would not be driven out of business. The question is whether Monfort's loss of profits in such circumstances constitutes antitrust injury. . . .

We find respondent's proposed construction of § 7 too broad, for reasons that *Brunswick* illustrates. *Brunswick* holds that the antitrust laws do not require the courts to protect small businesses from the loss of profits due to continued competition, but only against the loss of profits from practices forbidden by the antitrust laws. The kind of competition that Monfort alleges here, competition for increased market share, is not activity forbidden by the antitrust laws. It is simply, as petitioners claim, vigorous competition. To hold that the antitrust laws protect competitors from the loss of profits due to such price competition would, in effect, render illegal any decision by a firm to cut prices in order to increase market share. The antitrust laws require no such perverse result, for "[i]t is in the interest of competition to permit dominant firms to engage in vigorous competition, including price competition." . . . The logic of *Brunswick* compels the conclusion that the threat of loss of profits due to possible price competition following a merger does not constitute a threat of antitrust injury.

The second theory of injury argued here is that after the merger Excel would attempt to drive Monfort out of business by engaging in sustained

"the fact is that one injunction is as effective as 100, and concomitantly, that 100 injunctions are no more effective than one." 405 U.S., at 261. Thus, because standing under § 16 raises no threat of multiple lawsuits or duplicative recoveries, some of the factors other than antitrust injury that are appropriate to a determination of standing under § 4 are not relevant under § 16.

predatory pricing. Predatory pricing may be defined as pricing below an appropriate measure of cost for the purpose of eliminating competitors in the short run and reducing competition in the long run. It is a practice that harms both competitors and competition. In contrast to price cutting aimed simply at increasing market share, predatory pricing has as its aim the elimination of competition. Predatory pricing is thus a practice "inimical to the purposes of [the antitrust] laws," *Brunswick*, 429 U.S., at 488, and one capable of inflicting antitrust injury....

[T]he Court of Appeals can be understood to mean that Monfort had shown a credible threat of injury from below-cost pricing. To the extent the judgment rests on this ground, however, it must also be reversed, because Monfort did not allege injury from below-cost pricing before the District Court....

In its *amicus* brief, the United States argues that the "danger of allowing a competitor to challenge an acquisition on the basis of necessarily speculative claims of post-acquisition predatory pricing far outweighs the danger that any anticompetitive merger will go unchallenged." Brief for United States as *Amicus Curiae* 25. On this basis, the United States invites the Court to adopt in effect a *per se* rule "denying competitors standing to challenge acquisitions on the basis of predatory pricing theories."

We decline the invitation. As the foregoing discussion makes plain, predatory pricing is an anticompetitive practice forbidden by the antitrust laws. While firms may engage in the practice only infrequently, there is ample evidence suggesting that the practice does occur. It would be novel indeed for a court to deny standing to a party seeking an injunction against threatened injury merely because such injuries rarely occur. In any case, nothing in the language or legislative history of the Clayton Act suggests that Congress intended this Court to ignore injuries caused by such anticompetitive practices as predatory pricing....

In dissent, Justice Stevens, joined by Justice White, argued as follows:

In Brunswick, we began our analysis by acknowledging the difficulty of meshing § 7, "a statutory prohibition against acts that have a potential to cause certain harms," with § 4, a "damages action intended to remedy those harms." We concluded that a plaintiff must prove more than a violation of § 7 to recover damages, "since such proof establishes only that injury may result." Beyond the special nature of an action for treble damages, § 16 differs from § 4 because by its terms it requires only that the antitrust violation threaten that a competitor of the merging firms will suffer some corresponding harm in due course. In my opinion, that reasonable probability gives the competitor an interest in the proceeding adequate to confer standing to challenge the merger. To hold otherwise is to frustrate § 7 and to read § 16 far too restrictively.

It would be a strange antitrust statute indeed which defined a violation enforceable by no private party. Effective enforcement of the antitrust laws has always depended largely on the work of private attorney generals, for whom Congress made special provision in the Clayton Act itself. As recently as 1976, Congress specifically indicated its intent to encourage private enforcement of § 16 by authorizing recovery of a reasonable attorney's fee by a plaintiff in an action for injunctive relief. The Hart–Scott–Rodino Antitrust Improvements Act of 1976.

The Court misunderstands the message that Congress conveyed in 1914 and emphasized in 1950. If, as the District Court and the Court of Appeals held, the merger is illegal, it should be set aside.

3. The 1980s was a period of minimal enforcement of the anti-merger laws by the federal enforcement agencies. Until the Supreme Court's decision in *Cargill*, private plaintiffs had enjoyed significant success in obtaining preliminary injunctive relief against proposed transactions.[64] Many of the acquisitions found to be likely to violate Section 7 by the courts had been "cleared" by the Department of Justice or the FTC.

Although there was great fear in 1986 that *Cargill* would sharply curtail—or eliminate—private actions in the merger area, this appears to be much less the case than originally feared.

For example, in *R.C. Bigelow, Inc. v. Unilever N.V.*, 867 F.2d 102 (2d Cir.), *cert. denied*, 493 U.S. 815 (1989), the FTC had "cleared" a merger between two herbal tea manufacturers that would have given the merger combination 84 percent of the national herbal tea market. The FTC apparently thought the relevant market included, at least, "all tea" and that entry was easy. The Second Circuit, on the assumption that the relevant market was in fact limited to herbal teas, reversed a district court's grant of summary judgment for defendants and concluded:

> Although we must be wary of competitors attempting to obtain antitrust standing based upon prospective loss or damage due to competition for increased market share, *cf. Cargill*, 479 U.S. at 116 & 122, we have little doubt that antitrust injury to a competitor can be found when the market share of the merging firms threatens to be decisive.

Similarly, in *Consolidated Gold Fields PLC v. Minorco, S.A.*, 871 F.2d 252 (2d Cir.1989), the FTC had "cleared" a hostile tender offer by foreign gold-mining interests seeking to acquire a foreign corporation with gold-mining interests in the United States. Consummation of the transaction would have given the combined entity 32 percent of the market. Although several courts and commentators have argued that a "target company" has no standing because after the takeover it would benefit from a "super-competitive advantage,"[65] the Second Circuit rejected this analysis:

> This Circuit has previously upheld target standing to challenge take-overs alleged to violate section 7, and we reaffirm that position today. In our view, Gold Fields has demonstrated a threat of "antitrust injury." If the acquisition is permitted to go forward, Gold Fields will lose its ability to compete independently in the gold production market. Its wholly owned United States mining subsidiary, GFMC, is threatened with curtailment of its production, much like Newmont. Surely Gold Fields' loss of independence is causally linked to the injury occurring in the marketplace, where the acquisition threatens to diminish competitive forces. Though what happens to Gold Fields and what happens to competition may not be precisely the same type of injury, there is a common element in that the independent existence of a major competitor is being eliminated. It is not a

64. *See, e.g.*, Christian Schmidt Brewing Co. v. G. Heileman Brewing Co., 600 F.Supp. 1326 (E.D.Mich.), aff'd, 753 F.2d 1354 (6th Cir.1985); Cia. Petrolera Caribe, Inc. v. Arco Caribbean, Inc., 754 F.2d 404 (1st Cir.1985).

65. *See, e.g.*, Central Nat'l Bank v. Rainbolt, 720 F.2d 1183 (10th Cir.1983); but see Marathon Oil Co. v. Mobil Corp., 669 F.2d 378 (6th Cir.1981).

sufficient answer to say that even though competition is diminished, Gold Fields is not injured because of its absorption into the Minorco group. The enlarged entity that emerges from the takeover may benefit from the acquisition, but Gold Fields will have lost one of the vital components of competition—the power of independent decision-making as to price and output. It is hard to imagine an injury to competition more clearly "of the type the antitrust laws were intended to prevent," *Brunswick Corp. v. Pueblo Bowl–O–Mat, Inc.*, supra 429 U.S. at 489, than the elimination of a major competitor's power to determine its prices and output. It is precisely the loss of this power that makes a section 1 conspiracy so pernicious. For this reason, a member of a section 1 conspiracy has standing to challenge the restraint upon its freedom to compete, even though, in the long run, it may enjoy the benefits of the cartel....

It is possible, of course, that Gold Fields, if it remains a distinct corporation within the enlarged Minorco combination, will ultimately derive some economic benefit from the enhanced power of its corporate parent. But Gold Fields is entitled to prefer to take its chances on its capacity to prosper as an independent entity. Whether in the long run more profits will enter its corporate treasury as an independent company than as a subsidiary of Minorco is a speculative matter that need not concern us. The antitrust laws ensure the right to compete. That is what Gold Fields wishes to do, and that is what it will not be able to do if the threatened takeover succeeds.

The Second Circuit then asserted that the Supreme Court decision in *Cargill* did not require a different result since in that case the Supreme Court held only that a claim by a competitor that it would be hurt by *increased* competition resulting from the acquisition did not constitute "antitrust injury." Here, the injury alleged would result from the new parent's decision to *reduce* competition by eliminating the target as a competitor.

The Second Circuit also upheld the district court's findings: (1) that the 32 percent market share which would result from the takeover triggered a presumption of Section 7 illegality under *Philadelphia Bank*; (2) that eastern bloc gold sources were properly excluded from the market definition, since there was evidence that sales of eastern bloc gold did not increase when the price of western gold rose over substantial periods; and (3) that a preliminary injunction was appropriate relief.

Since 1988, federal enforcement of antimerger legislation has increased substantially and, as a consequence, challenges by state attorneys general and private parties have declined. Nevertheless, there are still occasional instances when the federal agencies clear a transaction that is subsequently challenged. *See State of New York v. Kraft General Foods, Inc.*, 926 F.Supp. 321 (S.D.N.Y.1995), where a district court found that the acquisition by Kraft (owner of Post cereals with 11.7% of sales in the ready-to-eat cereal market) of Nabisco (with 2.8% of sales—primarily of shredded wheat cereals), previously cleared by the Federal Trade Commission, did not violate Section 7 of the antitrust laws.

4. Problems related to designing appropriate remedies are often of central importance to the effective enforcement of Section 7. The guiding principle is that equitable decrees should restore effective competition. *United States v. Crescent Amusement Co.*, 323 U.S. 173 (1944); see Chapter 2, p. 90 supra. In the remedy phase of the *du Pont–GM* case, p. 1134 infra, the Supreme Court noted that equitable relief may not go beyond what is necessary to restore effective competi-

tion. But possible economic hardship, however severe, is relevant only if a court has a choice between two effective remedies; an effective remedy cannot be defeated because it would entail harsh consequences. The Court concluded: " ... complete divestiture is particularly appropriate in cases of stock acquisitions which violate Section 7.... It is simple, relatively easy to administer and sure. It should always be in the forefront of a Court's mind when a violation of Section 7 has been found." 366 U.S. at 331.

5.   A dispute arose in lower federal courts as to the availability of divestiture as a remedy in private actions under the Sherman and Clayton Acts. In *ITT v. General Telephone & Electronics Corp.*, 518 F.2d 913 (9th Cir.1975), the Court of Appeals heard GTE's appeal from a district court's ruling that "equitable remedies are available to private plaintiffs under Section 16." 351 F.Supp. at 1207. The district court had held that GTE's acquisition of telephone operating companies had foreclosed manufacturing competitors of GTE from selling equipment and supplies to the operating companies in violation of Sections 1 and 2 of the Sherman Act and Section 7 of the Clayton Act.

The Ninth Circuit held that the remedy of divestiture was not available in private actions. The Court noted that the reference in Section 16 of the Clayton Act to "injunctive relief" is ambiguous; "while some courts have viewed divestiture as a subspecies of 'injunctive relief,' others have held that injunctive remedies and divestiture are distinct categories of equitable relief" and that Section 16 "is not broad enough to include divestiture." 518 F.2d at 921. After a review of the Clayton Act's legislative history, the Court concluded that Congressional intent precluded the use of divestiture as a remedy in private cases. Injunctive relief was chosen as a substitute for divestiture, the Court suggested, because the latter was too harsh and potent a remedy to be entrusted to private hands. The Court reasoned:

> In holding that the remedy of divestiture is not available we do not jeopardize the district court's ability to restrain GTE effectively from violating the antitrust laws. Injunctive remedies under § 16 may be as broad as necessary to ensure that "threatened loss or damage" does not materialize or that prior violations do not recur.

518 F.2d at 924–25, *see, e.g., Calnetics Corp. v. Volkswagen of America, Inc.*, 532 F.2d 674 (9th Cir.), *cert. denied*, 429 U.S. 940 (1976); *Venner v. Pennsylvania Steel Co.*, 250 F. 292 (D.N.J.1918).

A contrary view was taken by the Court of Appeals for the Third Circuit in *NBO Industries Treadway Co. v. Brunswick Corp.*, 523 F.2d 262 (3d Cir.1975), cert. denied on this issue, 429 U.S. 1090 (1977). In *dictum*, the Third Circuit questioned the Ninth Circuit's legislative history and perceived:

> danger in permitting the pronouncements of statesmen long deceased to control the contemporary meaning of statutes which are almost an economic constitution for our complex national economy. 523 F.2d at 279.[66]

In 1990, the Supreme Court resolved the conflict in the circuits in *California v. American Stores Co.*[67] The Court held that divestiture is a form of injunctive relief within the meaning of Section 16 of the Clayton Act.

---

66.   *See, e.g.,* Cia. Petrolera Caribe, Inc. v. Arco Caribbean, Inc., 754 F.2d 404 (1st Cir.1985); Julius Nasso Concrete Corp. v. DIC Concrete Corp., 467 F.Supp. 1016 (S.D.N.Y.1979); Fuchs Sugars & Syrups, Inc. v. Amstar Corp., 402 F.Supp. 636 (S.D.N.Y. 1975); Julius M. Ames Co. v. Bostitch Inc., 240 F.Supp. 521 (S.D.N.Y.1965).

67.   495 U.S. 271 (1990).

The history of the *American Stores* case provides important insights into the usefulness of private actions—or state attorneys general acting in an analogous capacity—under Section 7. The FTC had challenged the merger but settled for a consent decree that California's Attorney General found inadequate, and he challenged the acquisition on behalf of himself and as *parens patriae* for consumers in California.

The district court, using the geographic market defined by American Stores, found American Stores' average post-merger share of the market to be 24 percent, with a range from 15 to 38 percent in individual areas. After considering concentration ratios and entry barriers, the Ninth Circuit concluded that "the district court's holding that American Stores did not satisfy its burden of rebutting California's prima facie showing of a violation of section 7 was not an abuse of discretion." The Ninth Circuit, however, modified the district judge's grant of relief because "divestiture, whether direct or indirect, is not an available form of relief under section 16...."[68]

Justice Stevens, writing for a unanimous Supreme Court, reversed the Ninth Circuit and reasoned:

> If we assume that the merger violated the antitrust laws, and if we agree with the District Court's finding that the conduct of the merged enterprise threatens economic harm to California consumers, the literal text of § 16 is plainly sufficient to authorize injunctive relief, including an order of divestiture, that will prohibit that conduct from causing that harm. This interpretation is consistent with our precedents, which have upheld injunctions issued pursuant to § 16 regardless of whether they were mandatory or prohibitory in character.... We have recognized when construing § 16 that it was enacted "not merely to provide private relief, but ... to serve as well the high purpose of enforcing the antitrust laws." *Zenith Radio Corp.*, 395 U.S., at 130–131. We have accordingly applied the section "with this purpose in mind, and with the knowledge that the remedy it affords, like other equitable remedies, is flexible and capable of nice 'adjustment and reconciliation between the public interest and private needs as well as between competing private claims.' " *Ibid.*, quoting *Hecht Co. v. Bowles*, 321 U.S. 321, 329–330 (1944).
>
> Finally, by construing § 16 to encompass divestiture decrees we are better able than is American to harmonize the section with its statutory context. The Act's other provisions manifest a clear intent to encourage vigorous private litigation against anticompetitive mergers. Section 7 itself creates a relatively expansive definition of antitrust liability: to show that a merger is unlawful, a plaintiff need only prove that its effect "*may* be substantially to lessen competition." Clayton Act § 7, 38 Stat. 731, 15 U.S.C. § 18 (emphasis supplied). *See Brown Shoe Co. v. United States*, 370 U.S. 294, 323 (1962). In addition, § 5 of the Act provided that during the pendency of a government action, the statute of limitations for private actions would be tolled. The section also permitted plaintiffs to use the final judgment in a government antitrust suit as prima facie evidence of liability in a later civil suit. Private enforcement of the Act was in no sense an afterthought; it was an integral part of the congressional plan for protecting competition. *See Minnesota Mining & Mfg. Co. v. New Jersey Wood Finishing Co.*, 381 U.S. 311, 318 (1965). Congress also made express

68. 872 F.2d 837 (9th Cir.1989).

its view that divestiture was the most suitable remedy in a suit for relief from a § 7 violation: in § 11 of the Act, Congress directed the Federal Trade Commission to issue orders requiring that a violator of § 7 "cease and desist from the violation," and, specifically, that the violator "divest itself of the stock held" in violation of the Act. Section 16, construed to authorize a private divestiture remedy when appropriate in light of equitable principles, fits well in a statutory scheme that favors private enforcement, subjects mergers to searching scrutiny, and regards divestiture as the remedy best suited to redress the ills of an anticompetitive merger. . . .

[I]n *Weinberger v. Romero–Barcelo*, 456 U.S. 305, 313 (1982), we observed that when Congress endows the federal courts with equitable jurisdiction, Congress acts aware of this longstanding tradition of flexibility. " 'Unless a statute in so many words, or by a necessary and inescapable inference, restricts the court's jurisdiction in equity, the full scope of that jurisdiction is to be recognized and applied.' " *Id.*, quoting *Porter v. Warner Holding Co.*, 328 U.S. 395, 398 (1946). These principles unquestionably support a construction of the statute that will enable a chancellor to impose the most effective, usual and straightforward remedy to rescind an unlawful purchase of stock or assets. The fact that the term "divestiture" is used to describe what is typically nothing more than the familiar remedy of rescission does not place the remedy beyond the normal reach of the chancellor.

Our conclusion that a district court has the power to order divestiture in appropriate cases brought under § 16 of the Clayton Act does not, of course, mean that such power should be exercised in every situation in which the Government would be entitled to such relief under § 15. In a Government case the proof of the violation of law may itself establish sufficient public injury to warrant relief. *See Du Pont*, 366 U.S., at 319–321; *see also Virginia R. Co. v. Railway Employees*, 300 U.S. 515, 552 (1937) ("Courts of equity may, and frequently do, go much farther both to give and withhold relief in furtherance of the public interest than they are accustomed to go when only private interests are involved"); *United States v. San Francisco*, 310 U.S. 16, 30–31 (1940) (authorizing issuance of injunction at Government's request without balancing of the equities). A private litigant, however, must have standing—in the words of § 16, he must prove "threatened loss or damage" to his own interests in order to obtain relief. *See Cargill, Inc. v. Montfort of Colorado, Inc.*, 479 U.S. 104 (1986). Moreover, equitable defenses such as laches, or perhaps "unclean hands," may protect consummated transactions from belated attacks by private parties when it would not be too late for the Government to vindicate the public interest.

Such questions, however, are not presented in this case. We are merely confronted with the naked question whether the District Court had the power to divest American of any part of its ownership interests in the acquired Lucky Stores, either by forbidding the exercise of the owner's normal right to integrate the operations of the two previously separate companies, or by requiring it to sell certain assets located in California. We hold that such a remedy is a form of "injunctive relief" within the meaning of § 16 of the Clayton Act. Accordingly, the judgment of the Court of Appeals is reversed and the case is remanded for further proceedings consistent with this opinion.[69]

69. 495 U.S. 271, 283–85, 295–96 (1990).

U.S. Department of Justice and FTC Joint Horizontal Merger Guidelines, 1992

[Introduction. Federal merger enforcement has largely become a matter of administrative action.

If the government elects not to sue, the transaction usually goes forward. It is relatively rare that private parties or state attorneys general will elect to challenge. If the government believes the transaction violates Section 7, the parties often attempt to negotiate a settlement (frequently spinning off a portion of the acquired assets in order to allow the rest of the deal to go through), or they abandon the deal. There was a slight uptick in government merger litigation in the mid–1990s—*see FTC v. Staples*, infra, p. 1062, and *FTC v. Beechnut–Heinz*, infra, p. 1067, but they were still very much the exception to the rule of administrative treatment.

In order to advise businesses of enforcement intentions, the Justice Department issued merger guidelines in 1968, 1982 and 1984. In 1992, the Federal Trade Commission and the Department of Justice issued joint horizontal merger guidelines, amended in 1997 to introduce an expanded section 4 dealing with claims of efficiency. Vertical and conglomerate mergers continue to be examined under the now rather dated 1984 guidelines.

In general, the guidelines have tended to become more lenient with each iteration and also more detailed, specific, and economically sophisticated.

These guidelines are designed to help people predict the enforcement intentions of the federal agencies. They have no binding effect on courts, although a few courts have taken the guidelines and their analytical approaches into account. Although not binding, the guidelines have had an enormous impact on merger policy in the United States. Particularly because the Supreme Court has not accepted review of the merits of a merger since its General Dynamics opinion in 1974, the guidelines have been the principal source of new thinking about merger policy.

The joint FTC–DOJ 1992 horizontal merger guidelines (including the 1997 revisions) are set out below and the 1984 vertical and conglomerate guidelines in subsequent sections of this chapter.]

1. MARKET DEFINITION, MEASUREMENT AND CONCENTRATION

1.0 Overview

A merger is unlikely to create or enhance market power or to facilitate its exercise unless it significantly increases concentration and results in a concentrated market, properly defined and measured. Mergers that either do not significantly increase concentration or do not result in a concentrated market ordinarily require no further analysis.

The analytic process described in this section ensures that the Agency evaluates the likely competitive impact of a merger within the context of economically meaningful markets—*i.e.*, markets that could be subject to the exercise of market power. Accordingly, for each product or service (hereafter "product") of each merging firm, the Agency seeks to define a market in which firms could effectively exercise market power if they were able to coordinate their actions.

Market definition focuses solely on demand substitution factors—*i.e.*, possible consumer responses. Supply substitution factors—*i.e.*, possible production responses—are considered elsewhere in the Guidelines in the identification of firms that participate in the relevant market and the analysis of entry. *See* Sections 1.3 and 3. A market is defined as a product or group of products and a geographic area in which it is produced or sold such that a hypothetical profit-maximizing firm, not subject to price regulation, that was the only present and future producer or seller of those products in that area likely would impose at least a "small but significant and nontransitory" increase in price, assuming the terms of sale of all other products are held constant. A relevant market is a group of products and a geographic area that is no bigger than necessary to satisfy this test. The "small but significant and nontransitory" increase in price is employed solely as a methodological tool for the analysis of mergers: it is not a tolerance level for price increases.

Absent price discrimination, a relevant market is described by a product or group of products and a geographic area. In determining whether a hypothetical monopolist would be in a position to exercise market power, it is necessary to evaluate the likely demand responses of consumers to a price increase. A price increase could be made unprofitable by consumers either switching to other products or switching to the same product produced by firms at other locations. The nature and magnitude of these two types of demand responses respectively determine the scope of the product market and the geographic market.

In contrast, where a hypothetical monopolist likely would discriminate in prices charged to different groups of buyers, distinguished, for example, by their uses or locations, the Agency may delineate different relevant markets corresponding to each such buyer group. Competition for sales to each such group may be affected differently by a particular merger and markets are delineated by evaluating the demand response of each such buyer group. A relevant market of this kind is described by a collection of products for sale to a given group of buyers.

Once defined, a relevant market must be measured in terms of its participants and concentration. Participants include firms currently producing or selling the market's products in the market's geographic area. In addition, participants may include other firms depending on their likely supply responses to a "small but significant and nontransitory" price increase. A firm is viewed as a participant if, in response to a "small but significant and nontransitory" price increase, it likely would enter rapidly into production or sale of a market product in the market's area, without incurring significant sunk costs of entry and exit. Firms likely to make any of these supply responses are considered to be "uncommitted" entrants because their supply response would create new production or sale in the relevant market and because that production or sale could be quickly terminated without significant loss.[70] Uncommitted entrants are capable of making such quick and uncommitted supply responses that they likely influenced the market pre-merger, would influence it post-merger, and accordingly are considered as market participants at both times. This analysis of market definition and market measurement applies equally to foreign and domestic firms.

If the process of market definition and market measurement identifies one or more relevant markets in which the merging firms are both participants, then the merger is considered to be horizontal. Sections 1.1 through 1.5 describe in greater detail how product and geographic markets will be defined, how market shares will be calculated and how market concentration will be assessed.

1.1   Product Market Definition

The Agency will first define the relevant product market with respect to each of the products of each of the merging firms.[71]

1.11   General Standards

Absent price discrimination, the Agency will delineate the product market to be a product or group of products such that a hypothetical profitmaximizing firm that was the only present and future seller of those products ("monopolist") likely would impose at least a "small but significant and nontransitory" increase in price. That is, assuming that buyers likely would respond to an increase in price for a tentatively identified product group only by shifting to other products, what would happen? If the alternatives were, in the aggregate, sufficiently attractive at their existing terms of sale, an attempt to raise prices would result in a reduction of sales large enough that the price increase would not prove profitable, and the tentatively identified product group would prove to be too narrow.

Specifically, the Agency will begin with each product (narrowly defined) produced or sold by each merging firm and ask what would happen if a hypothetical monopolist of that product imposed at least a "small but significant and nontransitory" increase in price, but the terms of sale of all other products remained constant. If, in response to the price increase, the

---

70. Probable supply responses that require the entrant to incur significant sunk costs of entry and exit are not part of market measurement, but are included in the analysis of the significance of entry. See Section 3. Entrants that must commit substantial sunk costs are regarded as "committed" entrants because those sunk costs make entry irreversible in the short term without foregoing that investment; thus the likelihood of their entry must be evaluated with regard to their long-term profitability.

71. Although discussed separately, product market definition and geographic market definition are interrelated. In particular, the extent to which buyers of a particular product would shift to other products in the event of a "small but significant and nontransitory" increase in price must be evaluated in the context of the relevant geographic market.

reduction in sales of the product would be large enough that a hypothetical monopolist would not find it profitable to impose such an increase in price, then the Agency will add to the product group the product that is the next best substitute for the merging firm's product.[72]

In considering the likely reaction of buyers to a price increase, the Agency will take into account all relevant evidence, including, but not limited to, the following:

(1) evidence that buyers have shifted or have considered shifting purchases between products in response to relative changes in price or other competitive variables;

(2) evidence that sellers base business decisions on the prospect of buyer substitution between products in response to relative changes in price or other competitive variables;

(3) the influence of downstream competition faced by buyers in their output markets; and

(4) the timing and costs of switching products.

The price increase question is then asked for a hypothetical monopolist controlling the expanded product group. In performing successive iterations of the price increase test, the hypothetical monopolist will be assumed to pursue maximum profits in deciding whether to raise the prices of any or all of the additional products under its control. This process will continue until a group of products is identified such that a hypothetical monopolist over that group of products would profitably impose at least a "small but significant and nontransitory" increase, including the price of a product of one of the merging firms. The Agency generally will consider the relevant product market to be the smallest group of products that satisfies this test.

In the above analysis, the Agency will use prevailing prices of the products of the merging firms and possible substitutes for such products, unless premerger circumstances are strongly suggestive of coordinated interaction, in which case the Agency will use a price more reflective of the competitive price.[73] However, the Agency may use likely future prices, absent the merger, when changes in the prevailing prices can be predicted with reasonable reliability. Changes in price may be predicted on the basis of, for example, changes in regulation which affect price either directly or indirectly by affecting costs or demand.

In general, the price for which an increase will be postulated will be whatever is considered to be the price of the product at the stage of the

72. Throughout the Guidelines, the term "next best substitute" refers to the alternative which, if available in unlimited quantities at constant prices, would account for the greatest value of diversion of demand in response to a "small but significant and nontransitory" price increase.

73. The terms of sale of all other products are held constant in order to focus market definition on the behavior of consumers. Movements in the terms of sale for other products, as may result from the behavior of producers of those products, are accounted for in the analysis of competitive effects and entry. See Sections 2 and 3.

industry being examined.[74] In attempting to determine objectively the effect of a "small but significant and nontransitory" increase in price, the Agency, in most contexts, will use a price increase of five percent lasting for the foreseeable future. However, what constitutes a "small but significant and nontransitory" increase in price will depend on the nature of the industry, and the Agency at times may use a price increase that is larger or smaller than five percent.

1.12   Product Market Definition in the Presence of Price Discrimination

The analysis of product market definition to this point has assumed that price discrimination—charging different buyers different prices for the same product, for example—would not be profitable for a hypothetical monopolist. A different analysis applies where price discrimination would be profitable for a hypothetical monopolist.

Existing buyers sometimes will differ significantly in their likelihood of switching to other products in response to a "small but significant and nontransitory" price increase. If a hypothetical monopolist can identify and price differently to those buyers ("targeted buyers") who would not defeat the targeted price increase by substituting to other products in response to a "small but significant and nontransitory" price increase for the relevant product, and if other buyers likely would not purchase the relevant product and resell to targeted buyers, then a hypothetical monopolist would profitably impose a discriminatory price increase on sales to targeted buyers. This is true regardless of whether a general increase in price would cause such significant substitution that the price increase would not be profitable. The Agency will consider additional relevant product markets consisting of a particular use or uses by groups of buyers of the product for which a hypothetical monopolist would profitably and separately impose at least a "small but significant and nontransitory" increase in price.

1.2   Geographic Market Definition

For each product market in which both merging firms participate, the Agency will determine the geographic market or markets in which the firms produce or sell. A single firm may operate in a number of different geographic markets.

1.21   General Standards

Absent price discrimination, the Agency will delineate the geographic market to be a region such that a hypothetical monopolist that was the only present or future producer of the relevant product at locations in that region would profitably impose at least a "small but significant and nontransitory" increase in price, holding constant the terms of sale for all products produced elsewhere. That is, assuming that buyers likely would respond to a price increase on products produced within the tentatively

---

74. For example, in a merger between retailers, the relevant price would be the retail price of a product to consumers. In the case of a merger among oil pipelines, the relevant price would be the tariff—the price of the transportation service.

identified region only by shifting to products produced at locations of production outside the region, what would happen? If those locations of production outside the region were, in the aggregate, sufficiently attractive at their existing terms of sale, an attempt to raise price would result in a reduction in sales large enough that the price increase would not prove profitable, and the tentatively identified geographic area would prove to be too narrow.

In defining the geographic market or markets affected by a merger, the Agency will begin with the location of each merging firm (or each plant of a multiplant firm) and ask what would happen if a hypothetical monopolist of the relevant product at that point imposed at least a "small but significant and nontransitory" increase in price, but the terms of sale at all other locations remained constant. If, in response to the price increase, the reduction in sales of the product at that location would be large enough that a hypothetical monopolist producing or selling the relevant product at the merging firm's location would not find it profitable to impose such an increase in price, then the Agency will add the location from which production is the next-best substitute for production at the merging firm's location.

In considering the likely reaction of buyers to a price increase, the Agency will take into account all relevant evidence, including, but not limited to, the following:

(1) evidence that buyers have shifted or have considered shifting purchases between different geographic locations in response to relative changes in price or other competitive variables;

(2) evidence that sellers base business decisions on the prospect of buyer substitution between geographic locations in response to relative changes in price or other competitive variables;

(3) the influence of downstream competition faced by buyers in their output markets; and

(4) the timing and costs of switching suppliers.

The price increase question is then asked for a hypothetical monopolist controlling the expanded group of locations. In performing successive iterations of the price increase test, the hypothetical monopolist will be assumed to pursue maximum profits in deciding whether to raise the price at any or all of the additional locations under its control. This process will continue until a group of locations is identified such that a hypothetical monopolist over that group of locations would profitably impose at least a "small but significant and nontransitory" increase, including the price charged at a location of one of the merging firms.

The "smallest market" principle will be applied as it is in product market definition. The price for which an increase will be postulated, what constitutes a "small but significant and nontransitory" increase in price, and the substitution decisions of consumers all will be determined in the same way in which they are determined in product market definition.

1.22   Geographic Market Definition in the Presence of Price Discrimination

The analysis of geographic market definition to this point has assumed that geographic price discrimination—charging different prices net of transportation costs for the same product to buyers in different areas, for example—would not be profitable for a hypothetical monopolist. However, if a hypothetical monopolist can identify and price differently to buyers in certain areas ("targeted buyers") who would not defeat the targeted price increase by substituting to more distant sellers in response to a "small but significant and nontransitory" price increase for the relevant product, and if other buyers likely would not purchase the relevant product and resell to targeted buyers,[75] then a hypothetical monopolist would profitably impose a discriminatory price increase. This is true even where a general price increase would cause such significant substitution that the price increase would not be profitable. The Agency will consider additional geographic markets consisting of particular locations of buyers for which a hypothetical monopolist would profitably and separately impose at least a "small but significant and nontransitory" increase in price.

1.3   Identification of Firms That Participate in the Relevant Market

1.31   Current Producers or Sellers

The Agency's identification of firms that participate in the relevant market begins with all firms that currently produce or sell in the relevant market. This includes vertically integrated firms to the extent that such inclusion accurately reflects their competitive significance in the relevant market prior to the merger. To the extent that the analysis under Section 1.1 indicates that used, reconditioned or recycled goods are included in the relevant market, market participants will include firms that produce or sell such goods and that likely would offer those goods in competition with other relevant products.

1.32   Firms That Participate Through Supply Response

In addition, the Agency will identify other firms not currently producing or selling the relevant product in the relevant area as participating in the relevant market if their inclusion would more accurately reflect probable supply responses. These firms are termed "uncommitted." These supply responses must be likely to occur within one year and without the expenditure of significant sunk costs of entry and exit, in response to a "small but significant and nontransitory" price increase. If a firm has the technological capability to achieve such an uncommitted supply response, but likely would not (*e.g.*, because difficulties in achieving product acceptance, distribution, or production would render such a response unprofitable), that firm will not be considered to be a market participant. The competitive significance of supply responses that require more time or that require firms to

---

75. This arbitrage is inherently impossible for many services and is particularly difficult where the product is sold on a delivered basis and where transportation costs are a significant percentage of the final cost.

incur significant sunk costs of entry and exit will be considered in entry analysis. *See* Section 3.[76]

Sunk costs are the acquisition costs of tangible and intangible assets that cannot be recovered through the redeployment of these assets outside the relevant market, *i.e.*, costs uniquely incurred to supply the relevant product and geographic market. Examples of sunk costs may include market-specific investments in production facilities, technologies, marketing (including product acceptance), research and development, regulatory approvals, and testing. A significant sunk cost is one which would not be recouped within one year of the commencement of the supply response, assuming a "small but significant and nontransitory" price increase in the relevant market. In this context, a "small but significant and nontransitory" price increase will be determined in the same way in which it is determined in product market definition, except the price increase will be assumed to last one year. In some instances, it may be difficult to calculate sunk costs with precision. Accordingly, when necessary, the Agency will make an overall assessment of the extent of sunk costs for firms likely to participate through supply responses.

These supply responses may give rise to new production of products in the relevant product market or new sources of supply in the relevant geographic market. Alternatively, where price discrimination is likely so that the relevant market is defined in terms of a targeted group of buyers, these supply responses serve to identify new sellers to the targeted buyers. Uncommitted supply responses may occur in several different ways: by the switching or extension of existing assets to production or sale in the relevant market; or by the construction or acquisition of assets that enable production or sale in the relevant market.

1.321 Production Substitution and Extension: The Switching or Extension of Existing Assets to Production or Sale in the Relevant Market

The productive and distributive assets of a firm sometimes can be used to produce and sell either the relevant products or products that buyers do not regard as good substitutes. Production substitution refers to the shift by a firm in the use of assets from producing and selling one product to producing and selling another. Production extension refers to the use of those assets, for example, existing brand names and reputation, both for their current production and for production of the relevant product. Depending upon the speed of that shift and the extent of sunk costs incurred in the shift or extension, the potential for production substitution or extension may necessitate treating as market participants firms that do not currently produce the relevant product.[77]

---

76. If uncommitted entrants likely would also remain in the market and would meet the entry tests of timeliness, likelihood and sufficiency, and thus would likely deter anticompetitive mergers or deter or counter-act the competitive effects of concern (see Section 3, infra), the Agency will consider the impact of those firms in the entry analysis.

77. Under other analytical approaches, production substitution sometimes has been

If a firm has existing assets that likely would be shifted or extended into production and sale of the relevant product within one year, and without incurring significant sunk costs of entry and exit, in response to a "small but significant and nontransitory" increase in price for only the relevant product, the Agency will treat that firm as a market participant. In assessing whether a firm is such a market participant, the Agency will take into account the costs of substitution or extension relative to the profitability of sales at the elevated price, and whether the firm's capacity is elsewhere committed or elsewhere so profitably employed that such capacity likely would not be available to respond to an increase in price in the market.

1.322 Obtaining New Assets for Production or Sale of the Relevant Product

A firm may also be able to enter into production or sale in the relevant market within one year and without the expenditure of significant sunk costs of entry and exit, in response to a "small but significant and nontransitory" increase in price for only the relevant product, even if the firm is newly organized or is an existing firm without products or productive assets closely related to the relevant market. If new firms, or existing firms without closely related products or productive assets, likely would enter into production or sale in the relevant market within one year without the expenditure of significant sunk costs of entry and exit, the Agency will treat those firms as market participants.

1.4   Calculating Market Shares

1.41   General Approach

The Agency normally will calculate market shares for all firms (or plants) identified as market participants in Section 1.3 based on the total sales or capacity currently devoted to the relevant market together with that which likely would be devoted to the relevant market in response to a "small but significant and nontransitory" price increase. Market shares can be expressed either in dollar terms through measurement of sales, shipments, or production, or in physical terms through measurement of sales, shipments, production, capacity, or reserves.

Market shares will be calculated using the best indicator of firms' future competitive significance. Dollar sales or shipments generally will be used if firms are distinguished primarily by differentiation of their products. Unit sales generally will be used if firms are distinguished primarily on the basis of their relative advantages in serving different buyers or

reflected in the description of the product market. For example, the product market for stamped metal products such as automobile hub caps might be described as "light metal stamping," a production process rather than a product. The Agency believes that the approach described in the text provides a more clearly focused method of incorporating this factor in merger analysis. If production substitution among a group of products is nearly universal along the firms selling one or more of those products, however, the Agency may use an aggregate description of those markets as a matter of convenience.

groups of buyers. Physical capacity or reserves generally will be used if it is these measures that most effectively distinguish firms.[78] Typically, annual data are used, but where individual sales are large and infrequent so that annual data may be unrepresentative, the Agency may measure market shares over a longer period of time.

In measuring a firm's market share, the Agency will not include its sales or capacity to the extent that the firm's capacity is committed or so profitably employed outside the relevant market that it would not be able to increase price in the market.

1.42   Price Discrimination Markets

When markets are defined on the basis of price discrimination (Sections 1.12 and 1.22), the Agency will include only sales likely to be made into, or capacity likely to be used to supply, the relevant market in response to a "small but significant and nontransitory" price increase.

1.43   Special Factors Affecting Foreign Firms

Market shares will be assigned to foreign competitors in the same way in which they are assigned to domestic competitors. However, if exchange rates fluctuate significantly, so that comparable dollar calculations on an annual basis may be unrepresentative, the Agency may measure market shares over a period longer than one year.

If shipments from a particular country to the United States are subject to a quota, the market shares assigned to firms in that country will not exceed the amount of shipments by such firms allowed under the quota.[79] In the case of restraints that limit imports to some percentage of the total amount of the product sold in the United States (*i.e.*, percentage quotas), a domestic price increase that reduced domestic consumption also would reduce the volume of imports into the United States. Accordingly, actual import sales and capacity data will be reduced for purposes of calculating market shares. Finally, a single market share may be assigned to a country or group of countries if firms in that country or group of countries act in coordination.

1.5   Concentration and Market Shares

Market concentration is a function of the number of firms in a market and their respective market shares. As an aid to the interpretation of market data, the Agency will use the Herfindahl–Hirschman Index ("HHI") of market concentration. The HHI is calculated by summing the squares of the individual market shares of all the participants.[80] Unlike the

---

78. Where all firms have, on a forward-looking basis, an equal likelihood of securing sales, the Agency will assign firms equal shares.

79. The constraining effect of the quota on the importer's ability to expand sales is relevant to the evaluation of potential adverse competitive effects. See Section 2.

80. For example, a market consisting of four firms with market shares of 30 percent, 30 percent, 20 percent and 20 percent has an HHI of 2600 ($30^2 + 30^2 + 20^2 + 20^2 =$

four-firm concentration ratio, the HHI reflects both the distribution of the market shares of the top four firms and the composition of the market outside the top four firms. It also gives proportionately greater weight to the market shares of the larger firms, in accord with their relative importance in competitive interactions.

The Agency divides the spectrum of market concentration as measured by the HHI into three regions that can be broadly characterized as unconcentrated (HHI below 1000), moderately concentrated (HHI between 1000 and 1800), and highly concentrated (HHI above 1800). Although the resulting regions provide a useful framework for merger analysis, the numerical divisions suggest greater precision than is possible with the available economic tools and information. Other things being equal, cases falling just above and just below a threshold present comparable competitive issues.

1.51   General Standards

In evaluating horizontal mergers, the Agency will consider both the post-merger market concentration and the increase in concentration resulting from the merger.[81] Market concentration is a useful indicator of the likely potential competitive effect of a merger. The general standards for horizontal mergers are as follows:

a) Post–Merger HHI Below 1000. The Agency regards markets in this region to be unconcentrated. Mergers resulting in unconcentrated markets are unlikely to have adverse competitive effects and ordinarily require no further analysis.

b) Post–Merger HHI Between 1000 and 1800. The Agency regards markets in this region to be moderately concentrated. Mergers producing an increase in the HHI of less than 100 points in moderately concentrated markets post-merger are unlikely to have adverse competitive consequences and ordinarily require no further analysis. Mergers producing an increase in the HHI of more than 100 points in moderately concentrated markets postmerger potentially raise significant competitive concerns depending on the factors set forth in Sections 2–5 of the Guidelines.

c) Post–Merger HHI Above 1800. The Agency regards markets in this region to be highly concentrated. Mergers producing an increase in the

2600). The HHI ranges from 10,000 (in the case of a pure monopoly) to a number approaching zero (in the case of an atomistic market). Although it is desirable to include all firms in the calculation, lack of information about small firms is not critical because such firms do not affect the HHI significantly.

81. The increase in concentration as measured by the HHI can be calculated independently of the overall market concentration by doubling the product of the market shares of the merging firms. For example, the merger of firms with shares of 5 percent and 10 percent of the market would increase the HHI by 100 (5 x 10 x 2 = 100). The explanation for this technique is as follows: In calculating the HHI before the merger, the market shares of the merging firms are squared individually: $(a)^2 + (b)^2$. After the merger, the sum of those shares would be squared: $(a + b)^2$, which equals $a^2 + 2ab + b^2$. The increase in the HHI therefore is represented by $2ab$.

HHI of less than 50 points, even in highly concentrated markets post-merger, are unlikely to have adverse competitive consequences and ordinarily require no further analysis. Mergers producing an increase in the HHI of more than 50 points in highly concentrated markets post-merger potentially raise significant competitive concerns, depending on the factors set forth in Sections 2–5 of the Guidelines. Where the post-merger HHI exceeds 1800, it will be presumed that mergers producing an increase in the HHI of more than 100 points are likely to create or enhance market power or facilitate its exercise. The presumption may be overcome by a showing that factors set forth in Sections 2–5 of the Guidelines make it unlikely that the merger will create or enhance market power or facilitate its exercise, in light of market concentration and market shares.

1.52   Factors Affecting the Significance of Market Shares and Concentration

The post-merger level of market concentration and the change in concentration resulting from a merger affect the degree to which a merger raises competitive concerns. However, in some situations, market share and market concentration data may either understate or overstate the likely future competitive significance of a firm or firms in the market or the impact of a merger. The following are examples of such situations.

1.521   Changing Market Conditions

Market concentration and market share data of necessity are based on historical evidence. However, recent or ongoing changes in the market may indicate that the current market share of a particular firm either understates or overstates the firm's future competitive significance. For example, if a new technology that is important to long-term competitive viability is available to other firms in the market, but is not available to a particular firm, the Agency may conclude that the historical market share of that firm overstates its future competitive significance. The Agency will consider reasonably predictable effects of recent or ongoing changes in market conditions in interpreting market concentration and market share data.

1.522   Degree of Difference Between the Products and Locations in the Market and Substitutes Outside the Market

All else equal, the magnitude of potential competitive harm from a merger is greater if a hypothetical monopolist would raise price within the relevant market by substantially more than a "small but significant and nontransitory" amount. This may occur when the demand substitutes outside the relevant market, as a group, are not close substitutes for the products and locations within the relevant market. There thus may be a wide gap in the chain of demand substitutes at the edge of the product and geographic market. Under such circumstances, more market power is at stake in the relevant market than in a market in which a hypothetical monopolist would raise price by exactly five percent.

2. THE POTENTIAL ADVERSE COMPETITIVE EFFECTS OF MERGERS

2.0   Overview

Other things being equal, market concentration affects the likelihood that one firm, or a small group of firms, could successfully exercise market power. The smaller the percentage of total supply that a firm controls, the more severely it must restrict its own output in order to produce a given price increase, and the less likely it is that an output restriction will be profitable. If collective action is necessary for the exercise of market power, as the number of firms necessary to control a given percentage of total supply decreases, the difficulties and costs of reaching and enforcing an understanding with respect to the control of that supply might be reduced. However, market share and concentration data provide only the starting point for analyzing the competitive impact of a merger. Before determining whether to challenge a merger, the Agency also will assess the other market factors that pertain to competitive effects, as well as entry, efficiencies and failure.

This section considers some of the potential adverse competitive effects of mergers and the factors in addition to market concentration relevant to each. Because an individual merger may threaten to harm competition through more than one of these effects, mergers will be analyzed in terms of as many potential adverse competitive effects as are appropriate. Entry, efficiencies, and failure are treated in Sections 3–5.

2.1   Lessening of Competition Through Coordinated Interaction

A merger may diminish competition by enabling the firms selling in the relevant market more likely, more successfully, or more completely to engage in coordinated interaction that harms consumers. Coordinated interaction is comprised of actions by a group of firms that are profitable for each of them only as a result of the accommodating reactions of the others. This behavior includes tacit or express collusion, and may or may not be lawful in and of itself.

Successful coordinated interaction entails reaching terms of coordination that are profitable to the firms involved and an ability to detect and punish deviations that would undermine the coordinated interaction. Detection and punishment of deviations ensure that coordinating firms will find it more profitable to adhere to the terms of coordination than to pursue short-term profits from deviating, given the costs of reprisal. In this phase of the analysis, the Agency will examine the extent to which post-merger market conditions are conducive to reaching terms of coordination, detecting deviations from those terms, and punishing such deviations. Depending upon the circumstances, the following market factors, among others, may be relevant: the availability of key information concerning market conditions, transactions and individual competitors; the extent of firm and product heterogeneity; pricing or marketing practices typically employed by firms in the market; the characteristics of buyers and sellers; and the characteristics of typical transactions.

Certain market conditions that are conducive to reaching terms of coordination also may be conducive to detecting or punishing deviations from those terms. For example, the extent of information available to firms in the market, or the extent of homogeneity, may be relevant to both the ability to reach terms of coordination and to detect or punish deviations from those terms. The extent to which any specific market condition will be relevant to one or more of the conditions necessary for coordinated interaction will depend on the circumstances of the particular case.

It is likely that market conditions are conducive to coordinated interaction when the firms in the market previously have engaged in express collusion and when the salient characteristics of the market have not changed appreciably the most recent such incident. Previous express collusion in another geographic market will have the same weight when the salient characteristics of that other market at the time of the collusion are comparable to those in the relevant market.

In analyzing the effect of a particular merger on coordinated interaction, the Agency is mindful of the difficulties of predicting likely future behavior based on the types of incomplete and sometimes contradictory information typically generated in merger investigations. Whether a merger is likely to diminish competition by enabling firms more likely, more successfully or more completely to engage in coordinated interaction depends on whether market conditions, on the whole, are conducive to reaching terms of coordination and detecting and punishing deviations from those terms.

2.11   Conditions Conducive to Reaching Terms of Coordination

Firms coordinating their interactions need not reach complex terms concerning the allocation of the market output across firms or the level of the market prices but may, instead, follow simple terms such as a common price, fixed price differentials, stable market shares, or customer or territorial restrictions. Terms of coordination need not perfectly achieve the monopoly outcome in order to be harmful to consumers. Instead, the terms of coordination may be imperfect and incomplete—inasmuch as they omit some market participants, omit some dimensions of competition, omit some customers, yield elevated prices short of monopoly levels, or lapse into episodic price wars—and still result in significant competitive harm. At some point, however, imperfections cause the profitability of abiding by the terms of coordination to decrease and, depending on their extent, may make coordinated interaction unlikely in the first instance.

Market conditions may be conducive to or hinder reaching terms of coordination. For example, reaching terms of coordination may be facilitated by product or firm homogeneity and by existing practices among firms, practices not necessarily themselves antitrust violations, such as standardization of pricing or product variables on which firms could compete. Key information about rival firms and the market may also facilitate reaching terms of coordination. Conversely, reaching terms of coordination may be limited or impeded by product heterogeneity or by firms having substantially incomplete information about the conditions and prospects of their rivals' businesses, perhaps because of important differences among their current business operations. In addition, reaching terms of coordination may be limited or impeded by firm heterogeneity, for example, differences in vertical integration or the production of another product that tends to be used together with the relevant product.

2.12   Conditions Conducive to Detecting and Punishing Deviations

Where market conditions are conducive to timely detection and punishment of significant deviations, a firm will find it more profitable to abide by the terms of coordination than to deviate from them. Deviation from the terms of coordination will be deterred where the threat of punishment is credible. Credible punishment, however, may not need to be any more complex than temporary abandonment of the terms of coordination by other firms in the market.

Where detection and punishment likely would be rapid, incentives to deviate are diminished and coordination is likely to be successful. The detection and punishment of deviations may be facilitated by existing practices among firms, themselves not necessarily antitrust violations, and by the characteristics of typical transactions. For example, if key information about specific transactions or individual price or output levels is available routinely to competitors, it may be difficult for a firm to deviate secretly. If orders for the relevant product are frequent, regular and small relative to the total output of a firm in a market, it may be difficult for the firm to deviate in a substantial way without the knowledge of rivals and without the opportunity for rivals to react. If demand or cost fluctuations are relatively infrequent and small, deviations may be relatively easy to deter.

By contrast, where detection or punishment is likely to be slow, incentives to deviate are enhanced and coordinated interaction is unlikely to be successful. If demand or cost fluctuations are relatively frequent and large, deviations may be relatively difficult to distinguish from these other sources of market price fluctuations, and, in consequence, deviations may be relatively difficult to deter.

In certain circumstances, buyer characteristics and the nature of the procurement process may affect the incentives to deviate from terms of coordination. Buyer size alone is not the determining characteristic. Where large buyers likely would engage in long-term contracting, so that the sales covered by such contracts can be large relative to the total output of a firm in the market, firms may have the incentive to deviate. However, this only can be accomplished where the duration, volume and profitability of the business covered by such contracts are sufficiently large as to make deviation more profitable in the long term than honoring the terms of coordination, and buyers likely would switch suppliers.

In some circumstances, coordinated interaction can be effectively prevented or limited by maverick firms—firms that have a greater economic incentive to deviate from the terms of coordination than do most of their rivals (*e.g.*, firms that are unusually disruptive and competitive influences in the market). Consequently, acquisition of a maverick firm is one way in which a merger may make coordinated interaction more likely, more successful, or more complete. For example, in a market where capacity constraints are significant for many competitors, a firm is more likely to be a maverick the greater its excess or divertable capacity in relation to its sales or its total capacity, and the lower its direct and opportunity costs are of expanding sales in the relevant market.[82] This is so because a firm's incentive to deviate from price-elevating and output-limiting terms of coordination is greater the more the firm is able profitably to expand its output as a proportion of the sales it would obtain if it adhered to the terms of coordination and the smaller is the base of sales on which it enjoys elevated profits prior to the price cutting deviation.[83] A firm also may be a maverick if it has an unusual ability secretly to expand its sales in relation to the sales it would obtain if it adhered to the terms of coordination. This ability might arise from opportunities to expand captive production for a downstream affiliate.

2.2   Lessening of Competition Through Unilateral Effects

A merger may diminish competition even if it does not lead to increased likelihood of successful coordinated interaction, because merging firms may find it profitable to alter their behavior unilaterally following the acquisition by elevating price and suppressing output. Unilateral competitive effects can arise in a variety of different settings. In each setting, particular other factors describing the relevant market affect the likelihood of unilateral competitive effects. The settings differ by the primary characteristics that distinguish firms and shape the nature of their competition.

2.21   Firms Distinguished Primarily by Differentiated Products

In some markets the products are differentiated, so that products sold by different participants in the market are not perfect substitutes for one another. Moreover, different products in the market may vary in the degree of their substitutability for one another. In this setting, competition may be non-uniform (*i.e.*, localized), so that individual sellers compete more directly with those rivals selling closer substitutes.[84]

---

82. But excess capacity in the hands of non-maverick firms may be a potent weapon with which to punish deviations from the terms of coordination.

83. Similarly, in a market where product design or quality is significant, a firm is more likely to be an effective maverick the greater the sales potential of its products are among customers of its rivals, in relation to the sales it would obtain if it adhered to the terms of coordination. The likelihood of expansion responses by a maverick will be analyzed in the same fashion as uncommitted entry or committed entry (see Sections 1.3

and 3) depending on the significance of the sunk costs entailed in expansion.

84. Similarly, in some markets sellers are primarily distinguished by their relative advantages in serving different buyers or groups of buyers, and buyers negotiate individually with sellers. Here, for example, sellers may formally bid against one another for the business of a buyer, or each buyer may elicit individual price quotes from multiple sellers. A seller may find it relatively inexpensive to meet the demands of particular buyers or types of buyers, and relatively expensive to meet others' demands. Competi-

A merger between firms in a market for differentiated products may diminish competition by enabling the merged firm to profit by unilaterally raising the price of one or both products above the premerger level. Some of the sales loss due to the price rise merely will be diverted to the product of the merger partner and, depending on relative margins, capturing such sales loss through merger may make the price increase profitable even though it would not have been profitable premerger. Substantial unilateral price elevation in a market for differentiated products requires that there be a significant share of sales in the market accounted for by consumers who regard the products of the merging firms as their first and second choices, and that repositioning of the non-parties' product lines to replace the localized competition lost through the merger be unlikely. The price rise will be greater the closer substitutes are to the products of the merging firms, *i.e.,* the more the buyers of one product consider the other product to be their next choice.

2.211   Closeness of the Products of the Merging Firms

The market concentration measures articulated in Section 1 may help assess the extent of the likely competitive effect from a unilateral price elevation by the merged firm notwithstanding the fact that the affected products are differentiated. The market concentration measures provide a measure of this effect if each product's market share is reflective of not only its relative appeal as a first choice to consumers of the merging firms' products but also its relative appeal as a second choice, and hence as a competitive constraint to the first choice.[85] Where this circumstance holds, market concentration data fall outside the safeharbor regions of Section 1.5, and the merging firms have a combined market share of at least thirty-five percent, the Agency will presume that a significant share of sales in the market are accounted for by consumers who regard the products of the merging firms as their first and second choices.

Purchasers of one of the merging firms' products may be more or less likely to make the other their second choice than market shares alone would indicate. The market shares of the merging firms' products may understate the competitive effect of concern, when, for example, the products of the merging firms are relatively more similar in their various attributes to one another than to other products in the relevant market. On the other hand, the market shares alone may overstate the competitive effects of concern when, for example, the relevant products are less similar

tion, again, may be localized: sellers compete more directly with those rivals having similar relative advantages in serving particular buyers or groups of buyers. For example, in open outcry auctions, price is determined by the cost of the second lowest-cost seller. A merger involving the first and second lowest-cost sellers could cause prices to rise to the constraining level of the next lowest-cost seller.

85. Information about consumers' actual first and second product choices may be provided by marketing surveys, information from bidding structures, or normal course of business documents from industry participants.

in their attributes to one another than to other products in the relevant market.

Where market concentration data fall outside the safeharbor regions of Section 1.5, the merging firms have a combined market share of at least thirty-five percent, and where data on product attributes and relative product appeal show that a significant share of purchasers of one merging firm's product regard the other as their second choice, then market share data may be relied upon to demonstrate that there is a significant share of sales in the market accounted for by consumers who would be adversely affected by the merger.

2.212   Ability of Rival Sellers to Replace Lost Competition

A merger is not likely to lead to unilateral elevation of prices of differentiated products if, in response to such an effect, rival sellers likely would replace any localized competition lost through the merger by repositioning their product lines.[86]

In markets where it is costly for buyers to evaluate product quality, buyers who consider purchasing from both merging parties may limit the total number of sellers they consider. If either of the merging firms would be replaced in such buyers' consideration by an equally competitive seller not formerly considered, then the merger is not likely to lead to a unilateral elevation of prices.

2.22   Firms Distinguished Primarily by Their Capacities

Where products are relatively undifferentiated and capacity primarily distinguishes firms and shapes the nature of their competition, the merged firm may find it profitable unilaterally to raise price and suppress output. The merger provides the merged firm a larger base of sales on which to enjoy the resulting price rise and also eliminates a competitor to which customers otherwise would have diverted their sales. Where the merging firms have a combined market share of at least thirty-five percent, merged firms may find it profitable to raise price and reduce joint output below the sum of their premerger outputs because the lost markups on the foregone sales may be outweighed by the resulting price increase on the merged base of sales.

This unilateral effect is unlikely unless a sufficiently large number of the merged firm's customers would not be able to find economical alternative sources of supply, *i.e.,* competitors of the merged firm likely would not respond to the price increase and output reduction by the merged firm with increases in their own outputs sufficient in the aggregate to make the unilateral action of the merged firm unprofitable. Such non-party expansion is unlikely if those firms face binding capacity constraints that could

---

86. The timeliness and likelihood of re-positioning responses will be analyzed using the same methodology as used in analyzing uncommitted entry or committed entry (see Sections 1.3 and 3), depending on the significance of the sunk costs entailed in reposition-ing.

not be economically relaxed within two years or if existing excess capacity is significantly more costly to operate than capacity currently in use.[87]

3. ENTRY ANALYSIS

3.0 Overview

A merger is not likely to create or enhance market power or to facilitate its exercise, if entry into the market is so easy that market participants, after the merger, either collectively or unilaterally could not profitably maintain a price increase above premerger levels. Such entry likely will deter an anticompetitive merger in its incipiency, or deter or counteract the competitive effects of concern.

Entry is that easy if entry would be timely, likely, and sufficient in its magnitude, character and scope to deter or counteract the competitive effects of concern. In markets where entry is that easy (*i.e.*, where entry passes these tests of timeliness, likelihood, and sufficiency), the merger raises no antitrust concern and ordinarily requires no further analysis.

The committed entry treated in this Section is defined as new competition that requires expenditure of significant sunk costs of entry and exit.[88] The Agency employs a three step methodology to assess whether committed entry would deter or counteract a competitive effect of concern.

The first step assesses whether entry can achieve significant market impact within a timely period. If significant market impact would require a longer period, entry will not deter or counteract the competitive effect of concern.

The second step assesses whether committed entry would be a profitable and, hence, a likely response to a merger having competitive effects of concern. Firms considering entry that requires significant sunk costs must evaluate the profitability of the entry on the basis of long term participation in the market, because the underlying assets will be committed to the market until they are economically depreciated. Entry that is sufficient to counteract the competitive effects of concern will cause prices to fall to their premerger levels or lower. Thus, the profitability of such committed entry must be determined on the basis of premerger market prices over the long-term.

A merger having anticompetitive effects can attract committed entry, profitable at premerger prices, that would not have occurred premerger at these same prices. But following the merger, the reduction in industry output and increase in prices associated with the competitive effect of concern may allow the same entry to occur without driving market prices below premerger levels. After a merger that results in decreased output and

---

87. The timeliness and likelihood of non-party expansion will be analyzed using the same methodology as used in analyzing uncommitted or committed entry (*see* Sections 1.3 and 3) depending on the significance of the sunk costs entailed in expansion.

88. Supply responses that require less than one year and insignificant sunk costs to effectuate are analyzed as uncommitted entry in Section 1.3.

increased prices, the likely sales opportunities available to entrants at premerger prices will be larger than they were premerger, larger by the output reduction caused by the merger. If entry could be profitable at premerger prices without exceeding the likely sales opportunities—opportunities that include pre-existing pertinent factors as well as the merger-induced output reduction—then such entry is likely in response to the merger.

The third step assesses whether timely and likely entry would be sufficient to return market prices to their premerger levels. This end may be accomplished either through multiple entry or individual entry at a sufficient scale. Entry may not be sufficient, even though timely and likely, where the constraints on availability of essential assets, due to incumbent control, make it impossible for entry profitably to achieve the necessary level of sales. Also, the character and scope of entrants' products might not be fully responsive to the localized sales opportunities created by the removal of direct competition among sellers of differentiated products. In assessing whether entry will be timely, likely, and sufficient, the Agency recognizes that precise and detailed information may be difficult or impossible to obtain. In such instances, the Agency will rely on all available evidence bearing on whether entry will satisfy the conditions of timeliness, likelihood, and sufficiency.

3.1 Entry Alternatives

The Agency will examine the timeliness, likelihood, and sufficiency of the means of entry (entry alternatives) a potential entrant might practically employ, without attempting to identify who might be potential entrants. An entry alternative is defined by the actions the firm must take in order to produce and sell in the market. All phases of the entry effort will be considered, including, where relevant, planning, design, and management; permitting, licensing, and other approvals; construction, debugging, and operation of production facilities; and promotion (including necessary introductory discounts), marketing, distribution, and satisfaction of customer testing and qualification requirements.[89] Recent examples of entry, whether successful or unsuccessful, may provide a useful starting point for identifying the necessary actions, time requirements, and characteristics of possible entry alternatives.

3.2 Timeliness of Entry

In order to deter or counteract the competitive effects of concern, entrants quickly must achieve a significant impact on price in the relevant market. The Agency generally will consider timely only those committed entry alternatives that can be achieved within two years from initial planning to significant market impact.[90] Where the relevant product is a

---

89. Many of these phases may be undertaken simultaneously.

90. Firms which have committed to entering the market prior to the merger gener- ally will be included in the measurement of the market. Only committed entry or adjustments to pre-existing entry plans that are induced by the merger will be considered as

durable good, consumers, in response to a significant commitment to entry, may defer purchases by making additional investments to extend the useful life of previously purchased goods and in this way deter or counteract for a time the competitive effects of concern. In these circumstances, if entry only can occur outside of the two year period, the Agency will consider entry to be timely so long as it would deter or counteract the competitive effects of concern within the two year period and subsequently.

3.3   Likelihood of Entry

An entry alternative is likely if it would be profitable at premerger prices, and if such prices could be secured by the entrant.[91] The committed entrant will be unable to secure prices at premerger levels if its output is too large for the market to absorb without depressing prices further. Thus, entry is unlikely if the minimum viable scale is larger than the likely sales opportunity available to entrants.

Minimum viable scale is the smallest average annual level of sales that the committed entrant must persistently achieve for profitability at premerger prices.[92] Minimum viable scale is a function of expected revenues, based upon premerger prices,[93] and all categories of costs associated with the entry alternative, including an appropriate rate of return on invested capital given that entry could fail and sunk costs, if any, will be lost.[94]

Sources of sales opportunities available to entrants include: (a) the output reduction associated with the competitive effect of concern,[95] (b) entrants' ability to capture a share of reasonably expected growth in market demand,[96] (c) entrants' ability securely to divert sales from incumbents, for example, through vertical integration or through forward contracting, and (d) any additional anticipated contraction in incumbents' output in response to entry.[97] Factors that reduce the sales opportunities

possibly deterring or counteracting the competitive effects of concern.

91. Where conditions indicate that entry may be profitable at prices below premerger levels, the Agency will assess the likelihood of entry at the lowest price at which such entry would be profitable.

92. The concept of minimum viable scale ("MVS") differs from the concept of minimum efficient scale ("MES"). While MES is the smallest scale at which average costs are minimized, MVS is the smallest scale at which average costs equal the premerger price.

93. The expected path of future prices, absent the merger, may be used if future price changes can be predicted with reasonable reliability.

94. The minimum viable scale of an entry alternative will be relatively large when the fixed costs of entry are large, when the fixed costs of entry are largely sunk, when the marginal costs of production are high at low levels of output, and when a plant is underutilized for a long time because of delays in achieving market acceptance.

95. Five percent of total market sales typically is used because where a monopolist profitably would raise price by five percent or more across the entire relevant market, it is likely that the accompanying reduction in sales would be no less than five percent.

96. Entrants' anticipated share of growth in demand depends on incumbents' capacity constraints and irreversible investments in capacity expansion, as well as on the relative appeal, acceptability and reputation of incumbents' and entrants' products to the new demand.

97. For example, in a bidding market where all bidders are on equal footing, the market share of incumbents will contract as a result of entry.

available to entrants include: (a) the prospect that an entrant will share in a reasonably expected decline in market demand, (b) the exclusion of an entrant from a portion of the market over the long term because of vertical integration or forward contracting by incumbents, and (c) any anticipated sales expansion by incumbents in reaction to entry, either generalized or targeted at customers approached by the entrant, that utilizes prior irreversible investments in excess production capacity. Demand growth or decline will be viewed as relevant only if total market demand is projected to experience long-lasting change during at least the two year period following the competitive effect of concern.

3.4   Sufficiency of Entry

Inasmuch as multiple entry generally is possible and individual entrants may flexibly choose their scale, committed entry generally will be sufficient to deter or counteract the competitive effects of concern whenever entry is likely under the analysis of Section 3.3. However, entry, although likely, will not be sufficient if, as a result of incumbent control, the tangible and intangible assets required for entry are not adequately available for entrants to respond fully to their opportunities. In addition, where the competitive effect of concern is not uniform across the relevant market, in order for entry to be sufficient, the character and scope of entrants' products must be responsive to the localized sales opportunities that include the output reduction associated with the competitive effect of concern. For example, where the concern is unilateral price elevation as a result of a merger between producers of differentiated products, entry, in order to be sufficient, must involve a product so close to the products of the merging firms that the merged firm will be unable to internalize enough of the sales loss due to the price rise, rendering the price increase unprofitable.

4.   EFFICIENCIES

Competition usually spurs firms to achieve efficiencies internally. Nevertheless, mergers have the potential to generate significant efficiencies by permitting a better utilization of existing assets, enabling the combined firm to achieve lower costs in producing a given quantity and quality than either firm could have achieved without the proposed transaction. Indeed, the primary benefit of mergers to the economy is their potential to generate such efficiencies.

Efficiencies generated through merger can enhance the merged firm's ability and incentive to compete, which may result in lower prices, improved quality, enhanced service, or new products. For example, merger-generated efficiencies may enhance competition by permitting two ineffective (*e.g.*, high cost) competitors to become one effective (*e.g.*, lower cost) competitor. In a coordinated interaction context (see Section 2.1), marginal cost reductions may make coordination less likely or effective by enhancing the incentive of a maverick to lower price or by creating a new maverick firm. In a unilateral effects context (see Section 2.2), marginal cost reductions may reduce the merged firm's incentive to elevate price. Efficiencies also may result in benefits in the form of new or improved products, and efficiencies may result in benefits even when price is not immediately and directly affected. Even when efficiencies generated through merger enhance a firm's ability to compete, however, a merger may have other effects that may lessen competition and ultimately may make the merger anticompetitive.

The Agency will consider only those efficiencies likely to be accomplished with the proposed merger and unlikely to be accomplished in the absence of either the proposed merger or another means having comparable anticompetitive effects. These are termed merger-specific efficiencies.[98] Only alternatives that are practical in the business situation faced by the merging firms will be considered in making this determination; the Agency will not insist upon a less restrictive alternative that is merely theoretical.

Efficiencies are difficult to verify and quantify, in part because much of the information relating to efficiencies is uniquely in the possession of the merging firms. Moreover, efficiencies projected reasonably and in good faith by the merging firms may not be realized. Therefore, the merging firms must substantiate efficiency claims so that the Agency can verify by reasonable means the likelihood and magnitude of each asserted efficiency, how and when each would be achieved (and any costs of doing so), how each would enhance the merged firm's ability and incentive to compete, and why each would be merger-specific. Efficiency claims will not be considered if they are vague or speculative or otherwise cannot be verified by reasonable means.

Cognizable efficiencies are merger-specific efficiencies that have been verified and do not arise from anticompetitive reductions in output or service. Cognizable efficiencies are assessed net of costs produced by the merger or incurred in achieving those efficiencies.

The Agency will not challenge a merger if cognizable efficiencies are of a character and magnitude such that the merger is not likely to be anticompetitive in any relevant market.[99] To make the requisite determination, the Agency considers whether cognizable efficiencies likely would be sufficient to reverse the merger's potential to harm consumers in the

---

98. The Agency will not deem efficiencies to be merger-specific if they could be preserved by practical alternatives that mitigate competitive concerns, such as divestiture or licensing. If a merger affects not whether but only when an efficiency would be achieved, only the timing advantage is a merger-specific efficiency.

99. Section 7 of the Clayton Act prohibits mergers that may substantially lessen competition "in any line of commerce . . . in any section of the country." Accordingly, the Agency normally assesses competition in each relevant market affected by a merger independently and normally will challenge the

merger if it is likely to be anticompetitive in any relevant market. In some cases, however, the Agency in its prosecutorial discretion will consider efficiencies not strictly in the relevant market, but so inextricably linked with it that a partial divestiture or other remedy could not feasibly eliminate the anticompetitive effect in the relevant market without sacrificing the efficiencies in the other market(s). Inextricably linked efficiencies rarely are a significant factor in the Agency's determination not to challenge a merger. They are most likely to make a difference when they are great and the likely anticompetitive effect in the relevant market(s) is small.

relevant market, *e.g.*, by preventing price increases in that market. In conducting this analysis,[1] the Agency will not simply compare the magnitude of the cognizable efficiencies with the magnitude of the likely harm to competition absent the efficiencies. The greater the potential adverse competitive effect of a merger—as indicated by the increase in the HHI and post-merger HHI from Section 1, the analysis of potential adverse competitive effects from Section 2, and the timeliness, likelihood, and sufficiency of entry from Section 3—the greater must be cognizable efficiencies in order for the Agency to conclude that the merger will not have an anticompetitive effect in the relevant market. When the potential adverse competitive effect of a merger is likely to be particularly large, extraordinarily great cognizable efficiencies would be necessary to prevent the merger from being anticompetitive.

In the Agency's experience, efficiencies are most likely to make a difference in merger analysis when the likely adverse competitive effects, absent the efficiencies, are not great. Efficiencies almost never justify a merger to monopoly or near-monopoly.

The Agency has found that certain types of efficiencies are more likely to be cognizable and substantial than others. For example, efficiencies resulting from shifting production among facilities formerly owned separately, which enable the merging firms to reduce the marginal cost of production, are more likely to be susceptible to verification, merger-specific, and substantial, and are less likely to result from anticompetitive reductions in output. Other efficiencies, such as those relating to research and development, are potentially substantial but are generally less susceptible to verification and may be the result of anticompetitive output reductions. Yet others, such as those relating to procurement, management, or capital cost are less likely to be merger-specific or substantial, or may not be cognizable for other reasons.

5. FAILURE AND EXITING ASSETS

5.0 Overview

Notwithstanding the analysis of Sections 1–4 of the Guidelines, a merger is not likely to create or enhance market power or to facilitate its exercise, if imminent failure, as defined below, of one of the merging firms would cause the assets of that firm to exit the relevant market. In such circumstances, post-merger performance in the relevant market may be no worse than market performance had the merger been blocked and the assets left the market.

1. The result of this analysis over the short term will determine the Agency's enforcement decision in most cases. The Agency also will consider the effects of cognizable efficiencies with no short-term, direct effect on prices in the relevant market. Delayed benefits from efficiencies (due to delay in the achievement of, or the realization of consumer benefits from the efficiencies) will be given less weight because they are less proximate and more difficult to predict.

5.1   Failing Firm

A merger is not likely to create or enhance market power or facilitate its exercise if the following circumstances are met: 1) the allegedly failing firm would be unable to meet its financial obligations in the near future; 2) it would not be able to reorganize successfully under Chapter 11 of the Bankruptcy Act;[2] 3) it has made unsuccessful good-faith efforts to elicit reasonable alternative offers of acquisition of the assets of the failing firm[3] that would both keep its tangible and intangible assets in the relevant market and pose a less severe danger to competition than does the proposed merger; and 4) absent the acquisition, the assets of the failing firm would exit the relevant market.

5.2   Failing Division

A similar argument can be made for "failing" divisions as for failing firms. First, upon applying appropriate cost allocation rules, the division must have a negative cash flow on an operating basis. Second, absent the acquisition, it must be that the assets of the division would exit the relevant market in the near future if not sold. Due to the ability of the parent firm to allocate costs, revenues, and intracompany transactions among itself and its subsidiaries and divisions, the Agency will require evidence, not based solely on management plans that could be prepared solely for the purpose of demonstrating negative cash flow or the prospect of exit from the relevant market. Third, the owner of the failing division also must have complied with the competitively-preferable purchaser requirement of Section 5.1.

NOTES

1.   The introduction to the Guidelines indicated that the "Department hopes to reduce uncertainty associated with enforcement of the antitrust laws in this area." Are the Guidelines likely to reduce uncertainty? Are the various "what if" hypotheticals (e.g., the 5% test) likely to enhance predictability?

2.   What are the advantages and disadvantages of the Herfindahl–Hirschman Index (HHI)? Is, for example, the extra emphasis that the HHI will put on dominant firms (*i.e.*, as opposed to four-firm and eight-firm concentration ratios) helpful? Donald I. Baker, a former chief of the Antitrust Division, prepared the following chart to indicate the impact of the HHI on some leading horizontal merger cases:

2.   11 U.S.C. §§1101–1174 (1988).

3.   Any offer to purchase the assets of the failing firm for a price above the liquidation value of those assets—the highest valued use outside the relevant market or equivalent offer to purchase the stock of the failing firm—will be regarded as a reasonable alternative offer.

CASE	MARKET SHARES	HHI TOTAL*	INCREASE
U.S. v. Bethlehem Steel (1957)	16.3% + 4.6%	1,429	150
U.S. v. Philadelphia National Bank (1963)	21.3% + 14.5%	1,337	618
U.S. v. ALCOA–Rome (1964)	27.8% + 1.3%	2,354	72
U.S. v. Continental Can (1964)	21.9% + 3.1%	1,494	136
U.S. v. Pabst (1966): Wisconsin	10.7% + 13.0%	N.A.	275
Three States	5.5% + 5.6%	N.A.	64
National	2.7% + 2.0%	N.A.	11
U.S. v. Von's Grocery Co. (1966)	4.7% + 4.2%	257	39

* In various instances, this is understated because of incomplete data. (The understatement may be as much as 150 in some cases).[4]

3. Note that the Guidelines appear studiously to avoid reference to "trends towards concentration" as a factor in the evaluation of mergers. How would you explain this neglect of a factor that played a large role in the enactment of the Celler–Kefauver amendments to Section 7 in 1950 and weighed heavily in many key cases? Might the answer be that a trend to concentration indicates no more than that a particular line of mergers makes sense to participants in the industry, probably because there are substantial efficiencies to be achieved by the mergers? Even if that generalization were true, is that an interpretation that properly should be made only by Congress? Similarly, the Guidelines state that a merger in a market falling below 1,000 on the HHI will not be challenged "except in extraordinary circumstances." Should mergers in markets below 1,000 on the HHI be in a "safe harbor"? How would you deal with a merger between two firms with 14% and 15% of a market where all of the other competitors were minnows too small to count in terms of HHI?

4. The 1992 Guidelines preserve the generally successful analytical approach to relevant market definition of the earlier guidelines. In particular, they preserve the government's hostility to the use of submarkets. This hostility is not consistent with Supreme Court analyses in *United States v. Philadelphia National Bank* (p. 978 supra), and *United States v. Pabst Brewing Co.* (p. 992 supra). As a matter of policy, is the free and easy use of submarket analysis best discarded?

5. In the 1980s, challenges to mergers were often defeated even where post-merger market shares were 40% or more on grounds that if the parties tried to raise price after the merger, they would be swamped by new entry. For example, *see United States v. Waste Management Inc.*, 743 F.2d 976 (2d Cir.1984); *United States v. Calmar Inc.*, 612 F.Supp. 1298 (D.N.J.1985). Many of these cases treated entry as relevant if a firm *could* enter a market (*i.e.*, there were no insurmountable or even serious barriers to entry), apparently on the theory that firms that *could* enter *would* do so if profitable opportunities were created by price increases after the merger. Section 3 of the 1992 Guidelines ("Entry Analysis") takes a much tougher stand on the question of entry, noting that entry is easy only if it "would be timely, likely and sufficient in its magnitude, character and scope to deter or counteract the competitive acts of concern."

Consider the various policies reasons that argue in favor of a restrictive or a permissive standard on the question of entry.

6. Do the Guidelines deal adequately with foreign competition? In recent years, increasing attention has been paid to the question of whether there can or should be international or global markets in antitrust enforcement. Economists, members of the business community, and others have raised the question whether

---

4. Baker, Justice Dept. Merger Guidelines Contribute a Dose of Rationality, National L.J., June 28, 1982, at 16. Mr. Baker's chart was addressed to the original 1982 version of the Guidelines, but the analysis would not change under the 1992 Guidelines.

competition limited to a national market is realistic in many industries (*e.g.*, automobiles, steel and textiles). *See* 2 Areeda & Turner, Antitrust Law 362–63 (1978). Of course, even if a market is defined as national, current imports (along with domestic production) would be taken into account. But should not a defendant in a merger case be permitted to prove, for example, that production by a foreign company that sells to the United States, when that production is currently sold to purchasers abroad, is relevant in determining the probable consequences of a merger? In effect, the argument would be that production already committed to export by the foreign firm could easily and quickly be diverted to the U.S. if post-merger prices increased. When should such foreign production not be taken into account?

7.   A new and complicated concept introduced in these guidelines relates to "sunk costs"—*i.e.* the acquisition costs of tangible and intangible assets incurred in order to participate in a relevant product and geographic market. Certain firms will be regarded as "in the market" if through supply responses or geographic diversion, they can switch production and sales into a market. Firms that will be so regarded are called "uncommitted entrants," designated as those firms that do not have significant sunk costs. A firm has no significant sunk costs and therefore is an "uncommitted entrant" if there are no such investments or if they are sufficiently modest that they can be recouped within one year. If a firm has sunk costs, and therefore is a "committed" entrant, its competitive potential will only be taken into account if it satisfies the requirements of "new entry."

As a practical matter, will firms often have no significant sunk costs in order to be characterized as "uncommitted" entrants? How often will a firm enter a market with no costs, or make sufficient money in the first year to recoup its entire investment? The people who drafted the new guidelines obviously believe that concepts of supply substitution, geographic diversion and new entry were too lax under the former guidelines—but have they tightened up too much?

8.   The 1992 guidelines retain the market concentration analysis and use of the Herfindahl–Hirschman index of concentration. In some respects however, treatment varies from the earlier guidelines:

a.   Mergers resulting in concentrations below 1,000 on the HHI scale are still in a "safe harbor."

b.   In the HHI zone between 1,000 and 1,800, the 1984 guidelines indicated that the Department was "likely to challenge" if there was an increase of 100 points. Now the guidelines only say that in that concentration zone, mergers "potentially raise significant competitive concerns" and will be analyzed in terms of other factors. In fact, the Department of Justice and FTC brought almost no cases in the 1,000–1,800 range in the period from 1981 to 2000. Cases that were brought in the below 1800 range were invariably challenges to mergers where anticompetitive effects occurred in a number of different markets. Some markets were above 1800 and others below that mark. For example, in oil industry mergers such as the combination of Exxon and Mobil and British Petroleum's acquisition of Amoco, the parties were required to sell off company-owned stations in concentrated local markets, including some local markets where the HHI numbers were well below 1800. Might the explanation be that gasoline sold at retail is a largely homogeneous product, and price increases and decreases at retail are public and therefore prices often tend to be identical?

c. In the over 1,800 HHI range, the earlier guidelines indicated that the government was likely to challenge mergers if they added 50 points on the Herfindahl scale, and would challenge mergers that added 100 points except in "extraordinary circumstances." The 1992 guidelines establish a presumption that mergers that result in an HHI of over 1,800 will only be challenged if there is an increase of more than 100 points, and indicate that even that presumption can be overcome by a showing based on other factors. The indication that a failure to sue in the over 1,800 zone would only occur in "extraordinary circumstances" is dropped.

9. The Guidelines add a new qualification to the failing company defense. Aside from the preconditions that previously had to be satisfied, the Guidelines add that the firm claiming a failing company status must demonstrate that its assets, but for the merger, would probably leave the market. Why tighten up on the failing company defense?

10. Section 4 of the Guidelines, revised in 1997, opened the door to an efficiency defense and reflects a remarkable turnaround in United States antitrust law. In *United States v. Brown Shoe*, the first Supreme Court case to interpret revised Section 7, the Court held efficiencies against the legality of the merger. In that portion of the opinion that addressed the competitive effect of vertical integration between a shoe manufacturer and retail shoe outlets (p. 1140, *infra*), the Court concluded as follows:

[Another] significant aspect of this merger is that it creates a large national chain which is integrated with a manufacturing operation. The retail outlets of integrated companies, by eliminating wholesalers and by increasing the volume of purchases from the manufacturing division of the enterprise, can market their own brands at prices below those of competing independent retailers. Of course, some of the results of large integrated or chain operations are beneficial to consumers.... But, we cannot fail to recognize Congress' desire to promote competition through the protection of viable, small, locally owned business. Congress appreciated that occasionally higher costs and prices might result from the maintenance of fragmented industries and markets.

The Supreme Court soon retreated from the position that efficiencies were anticompetitive and moved on to the view that they were not a defense, but were essentially neutral, in evaluating the competitive effects of the merger. *See FTC v. Procter & Gamble Co.*, p. 1093, infra. To the extent that earlier Merger Guidelines mentioned efficiency claims, they were addressed to prosecutorial discretion.

The 1997 revisions now allow efficiency claims addressed to prosecutorial discretion *and* in courts. Note that the efficiency defense in the Guidelines is circumscribed in various ways, and some have criticized Section 4 on grounds that the defense is unduly narrow and grudging. The efficiencies must be merger specific (*i.e.*, they could not be achieved in some less anticompetitive way), substantial, verifiable, and will almost never justify mergers to monopoly or near monopoly. In addition, a successful efficiency defense requires proof that the claimed efficiency likely would be sufficient to reverse the merger's potential to harm consumers in the relevant market. So far, no party has successfully asserted an efficiency defense in court, but it is said that mergers that might otherwise have been challenged were allowed to proceed as a matter of prosecutorial discretion because of the presence of significant efficiencies.

Finally recall that in *Philadelphia National Bank* (supra, p. 978), the Supreme Court concluded it was not permissible to justify anticompetitive effects in one market by pointing to redeeming virtues in another market. Note 99 of the 1997 Guideline revision recognizes that precedent, but goes on to say that the enforcement agencies, as a matter of prosecutorial discretion, will consider efficiencies in a different market if they are "inextricably linked." Can you imagine a set of facts that would satisfy the "inextricably linked" standard?

MERGER ACTIVITY AND ENFORCEMENT IN THE 1990s

The decade of the 1990s witnessed probably the greatest merger wave in the history of the country—certainly the greatest since the end of the 19th Century. The number of mergers filed with the government under the Hart–Scott–Rodino Act, the statute requiring that mergers and joint ventures with acquired assets valued at more than $15 million be prefiled with the government, increased from 1529 filings in 1991 to 4642 in 1999.[5] Total assets acquired by merger increased from $169 billion in 1991 to almost $2 trillion in 1999—about an 11–fold increase.

About 97% of mergers that were large enough to require filing were neither challenged nor extensively investigated, roughly the same percentage as in the 1980s. The difference, however, was that of the 3% investigated, over 60% resulted in enforcement actions. Some very large mergers were restructured and then allowed to proceed. These included Exxon–Mobil, British Petroleum–Amoco, Bell Atlantic–Nynex (now "Verizon"), AT & T–Media One, Ciba Geigy–Sandoz, and two of the largest mergers of the decade—Time Warner–Turner and then AOL–Time Warner. There were substantially more government challenges than in the 1980s. Most resulted in the deals being abandoned or restructured, but a few government challenges were litigated. Important aspects of merger analysis during the decade are illustrated in the next three cases—two leading to court opinions and one settled with an elaborate consent order.

1. FEDERAL TRADE COMMISSION V. STAPLES, INC., 970 F.Supp. 1066 (D.D.C.1997), Staples, the second largest office supply superstore in the United States with 550 retail stores, sought to acquire Office Depot, the largest office supply superstore chain, with over 500 outlets. The office supply superstore market was defined to include superstores selling "consumable" office products—*e.g.,* paper, pens, file folders, computer discs and toner cartridges, but "consumable" did not include capital goods such as computers and office furniture. Defendants argued that the proper product market was all outlets selling office supply products, and in any such market, Staples and Office Depot accounted for only 5.5 percent of total North American sales. They also argued that the efficiencies of the transaction would lead to lower consumer prices and outweigh any possible anticompetitive effect. In that connection the parties emphasized a long record of office supply superstores cutting prices in order to increase market share, and claimed that track record showed that efficiencies would be passed along to consumers.

The proposed merger was the last of a series that had reduced the superstore category from 23 to 3. Office Max was third after Staples and Office Depot. Efforts by chains selling other products to expand into office supplies had not been successful.

5. R. Parker, Report from the Bureau of Competition (April 7, 2000); HTTP:// www.FTC.gov/os.

The key question was whether office supply superstores constituted, as alleged by the government, an appropriate market or submarket, since functionally interchangeable products could be purchased at many outlets, including chains that did not emphasize office supplies but carried some items, and also at small stationery stores.

In seeking a preliminary injunction, the FTC had offered econometric evidence—more extensive than in previous cases—about prices in cities where a company owned the only superstore in town compared to cities where there were two or three competing superstores. In all cities reviewed, non-superstore outlets were present. The court summarized the Commission's approach as follows:

> First, the FTC presented evidence comparing Staples' prices in geographic markets where Staples is the only office superstore to markets where Staples competes with Office Depot or Office Max, or both. Based on the FTC's calculations, in markets where Staples faces no office superstore competition at all, something which was termed a one-firm market during the hearing, prices are 13% higher than in three firm markets where it competes with both Office Depot and Office Max.

* * *

> The evidence all suggests that office superstore prices are affected primarily by other office superstores and not by non-superstore competitors such as mass merchandisers like Wal–Mart, K–Mart or Target, wholesale clubs such as BJ's, Sam's and Price Costco, computer or electronic stores such as Computer City and Best Buy, independent retail office supply stores, mail-order firms like Quill and Viking, and contract stationers.

Staples' and Office Depot's internal documents confirmed the differences in price in one, two, and three superstore cities. In addition, upon request, District Judge Hogan visited and viewed many of the different types of retail formats and found that office superstores were very different in appearance, physical size, format, the number and variety of products offered, and the type of customers targeted and served than other sellers of office supplies.

Assuming an office supply superstore market, concentration statistics showed the merged company would have a dominant market share in 42 geographic markets across the country, with 100 percent in 15 metropolitan areas. In 27 other areas, post-merger market share would range from 45 percent to 94 percent. The average increase in HHI caused by the merger would be 2,715 points.

With respect to efficiency claims in defense of the merger, the court acknowledged that the government had changed its merger guidelines to allow the offer of an efficiency defense, but also noted that the Supreme Court, in *Procter & Gamble* (*see, infra,* p. 1097), concluded that "possible economies cannot be used as a defense to illegality in Section 7 merger cases." Despite the *Procter & Gamble* language, the district court assumed that efficiencies could be offered as a viable defense. Nevertheless, the court rejected the efficiency claims on grounds that those proffered were speculative and conjectural. The court noted the defendant claims of $5 billion dollar cost savings over 5 years, but observed that most of these alleged savings were undocumented, lacking backup sources and calculations. It further noted that the $5 billion figure exceeded by almost 500 percent the figures presented to the boards of directors of the companies when they were asked to approve the transaction, and were substantially greater than claims in the joint proxy statement/prospectus which was said to reflect the best currently available estimate of savings by management and was submitted to the Securities and Exchange Commission.

The court concluded that the Commission had shown a likelihood it would succeed after a full administrative trial and granted a preliminary injunction.

2. IN RE AMERICA ONLINE INC., No. C 3989 (2000). America Online, the largest internet service provider ("ISP") in the United States with 25 million subscribers (about 50 percent of all subscribers) and 70 percent of total ISP revenues, sought to acquire Time Warner, a leading entertainment conglomerate with major holdings in magazines (Time, People, Sports Illustrated), copyrighted music (Warner Records), film and film libraries (Warner Brothers and New Line Cinema), and national network broadcasting (WB Network). Time Warner also was the second largest cable system in the United States with 12.6 million cable subscribers or approximately 20 percent of all U.S. cable television households. Time Warner was virtually the only cable provider in several major cities in the United States, including New York and Los Angeles. At the time the merger was announced in January 2000, it was valued at $183 billion, the largest merger in U.S. corporate history.

The merger raised significant competitive issues because the technology of internet connection was in the process of changing. Almost all residential users accessed the internet through a "narrowband" connection over standard telephone lines. "Broadband" internet access, offering faster service, a greater range of data, and more sophisticated programming through computers (including movies on demand and other entertainment), was expected to displace much of narrowband access in the several years after 2000. The vast majority of broadband access at the time of the merger was over cable, with upgraded telephone lines ("DSL") gaining ground but still a distant second. Long term, it is anticipated that wireless and satellite connections also would offer broadband services.

Time Warner was a majority owner of Roadrunner, the second largest provider of cable broadband ISP service in the United States, with about one million subscribers, while AOL with its enormous installed base in narrowband, and a small but developing base in broadband, was the most likely and most formidable future ISP presence in the broadband market. To the extent that AOL was in the broadband market, it provided access through DSL, but after the merger, would be expected to move aggressively into cable broadband connections.

The FTC approved the merger, but with extensive and somewhat unusual conditions. According to the "Analysis of Proposed Consent Order to Aid Public Comment," the Commission was concerned principally with two theories of possible anticompetitive effects: (1) the combination of Roadrunner with its cable broadband connections, and AOL with its DSL broadband connections, would have anticompetitive horizontal effects, particularly in areas of the country where Time Warner cable was dominant, and (2) the merger would decrease the incentives of AOL to promote and market access over DSL, the closest competitor to cable, particularly in Time Warner cable areas. With respect to both theories, the Commission was prepared to prove that wireless and satellite connections were not a sufficiently timely new entrant to curb AOL–Time Warner's post-merger market power.

A third theory related to interactive tv (ITV), an innovative technology at the time which combined television programming over computer connections with the ability of viewers to control the content of programs they see (*e.g.*, adding statistics or camera angles to sports events). Cable has distinct competitive advantages over DSL in providing ITV services, and AOL had recently launched AOL TV, a first generation ITV service. The concern was that after the merger, AOL–Time Warner would have incentives to discriminate against other ITV providers (*i.e.*, competitors of Time Warner content) from competing over cable with AOL's ITV service.

Under the terms of the antitrust consent order, which permitted the merger to be consummated, the combined companies were required to make cable broadband service available to an identified ISP (it turned out to be Earthlink) pursuant to terms and conditions evaluated and approved by the Commission. Within 90 days of making AOL broadband ISP service available over Time Warner cable to subscribers, Time Warner was required to enter into agreements to carry at least two additional non-affiliated broadband ISPs over its cable system on terms comparable to Earthlink. If Time Warner failed to enter into agreements within the time period, the Commission had the power to appoint a trustee with authority to enter into such agreements on Time Warner's behalf. Extensive ancillary provisions were designed to ensure that the contracts would not discriminate against competing ISPs and required that disputes be submitted to binding arbitration. In addition to the three ISPs that were required, the consent order permitted the combined company to decline to enter into agreements with other cable broadband ISPs because of technical limitations on the system or other good business considerations, but could not exclude or discriminate against other ISPs simply because adding competition over its cable systems would have an impact on the merged company's profits.

With respect to DSL, the order required AOL to market and promote DSL services in Time Warner cable areas at a comparable level and in the same manner as it promoted DSL services in non-Time Warner cable areas and not to discriminate in price between Time Warner and non-Time Warner cable areas.

Finally, as to ITV, the order prohibited Time Warner from interfering with an ISP competitor from making interactive features available when program content is delivered to viewers over Time Warner cable systems. Because the merger occurred in an exceptionally dynamic sector of the economy, the duration of the order was limited to five years from the time a final consent agreement was signed—the shortest duration of an antitrust consent order in the history of the FTC.

At the time the proposed merger was under review, the press reported great concern on the part of competitors of Time Warner, particularly other movie and music companies, that their content delivered over AOL would not be treated on fair and equal terms with Time Warner material, and they sought anti-discrimination provisions. Given the size and market power of Time Warner at the content level and AOL at the ISP delivery level, such "vertical concerns" were understandable. Nevertheless, despite Time Warner's formidable market presence, it did not account in any segment of the entertainment industry (*i.e.*, movies, music, print) for more than about 20 percent of the market and faced powerful competitors (*e.g.*, Disney in movies, Bertelsmann in music) with products and artists that enjoyed strong consumer allegiance. Excluding such companies from the AOL system arguably would dissatisfy AOL users and therefore would not be likely to occur. In addition, the Commission apparently felt that content provisions precluding discrimination would not be necessary as long as competitors of Time Warner could reach viewers through Earthlink and the other ISPs on Time Warner cable as required by the consent order.

NOTES

1. The consent order entered into between AOL–Time Warner and the FTC is an extreme example of a decree that puts an agency in a position where it must, in

effect, supervise business activities in a particular industry. Earlier examples include decrees in patent cases that have, at times, led the Department of Justice to participate extensively in subsequent negotiations of contracts between licensors and licensees. Also, the district judge in *United States v. AT&T*, supra p. 733, had a very significant and continuing role in implementing the settlement breaking up AT&T.

Questions have been raised about whether this kind of economic regulation—in effect continuing supervision—is a wise use of the time and efforts of the Antitrust Division, the FTC and the judiciary. Are judges or bureaucrats equipped to supervise business activities in this way? Is it likely that the wide range of information necessary for courts to carry out this supervisory function effectively will be made available by the parties in these proceedings? On the other hand, if close judicial and administrative supervision does not follow upon the entry of antitrust decrees, is there a danger that the decrees will fail to restore competitive conditions?

Perhaps because of discomfort with the supervisory role (as well as the rapid changes in the nature of competition in high-tech industries like provision of internet service), the AOL–Time Warner decree was limited to five years—a short duration that was unprecedented.

2. During the 1990s, the Department of Justice and the Federal Trade Commission had a remarkable string of successes in challenging proposed mergers in court. An exception to that general level of success related to hospital mergers. In that sector of the economy, the contrast was striking with the federal enforcement agencies losing most of the merger challenges that were mounted.

An example of judicial reaction to government enforcement in this area is *Federal Trade Commission v. Tenet Health Care*, 186 F.3d 1045 (8th Cir.1999) where the Commission challenged the acquisition by Tenet of the only other acute care hospital in Popular Bluff, Missouri. Hospital customers, including health insurance providers such as employers, health plans and network providers, unanimously opposed the merger, arguing that they had played the two hospitals—Lucy Lee and Doctors' Regional—against each other and obtained significant discounts. The controlling issue related to definition of relevant geographic market. The Commission alleged that the market was the city of Popular Bluff and eight surrounding counties, an area covering approximately a 50–mile radius. Other hospitals in that area were small rural operations. The Commission charged that the Lucy Lee and Doctors' Regional between them drew 90% of their patients from zip codes within the 50–mile radius and accounted for a post-merger market share of 84%. The hospitals responded that the relevant market should be slightly larger—roughly an area with a radius of 65 miles from Popular Bluff (thereby including additional hospitals), and, more important, that many patients living at the outer edges of the proposed geographic market already traveled to hospitals outside the radius. In a "critical loss" analysis—*i.e.*, an investigation of whether enough patients would abandon the Popular Bluff hospitals if prices were increased so as to defeat that increase—defendants contended that even with respect to services offered at the Popular Bluff hospitals, 22% to 70% of potential patients were already dealing with hospitals outside the proposed geographic area.

The Court of Appeals reversed a District Court decision to issue an injunction blocking the merger, finding that the Commission had failed to discharge its burden of establishing a plausible relevant geographic market. It appeared also to be influenced by the claims of the sponsors of the merger that the combined hospitals would result in enhanced efficiency, and that it might be that Popular Bluff was such a small market as not to be able to sustain two high quality hospitals.

As this book goes to press, the Bureau of Economics of the Federal Trade Commission is revisiting the various hospital mergers cleared by the agencies and the courts during the 1990s, investigating whether claims by the sponsors of the mergers that they would not lead to enhanced prices, but would lead to improved efficiency, have turned out as predicted.

Federal Trade Commission v. H.J. Heinz Co.

United States Court of Appeals, D.C. Circuit 2001.
246 F.3d 708.

■ HENDERSON, J. On February 28, 2000 H.J. Heinz Company (Heinz) and Milnot Holding Corporation (Beech–Nut) entered into a merger agreement. The Federal Trade Commission (Commission or FTC) sought a preliminary injunction pursuant to section 13(b) of the Federal Trade Commission Act, to enjoin the consummation of the merger. . . . The district court denied the preliminary injunction and the FTC appealed to this court. For the reasons set forth below, we reverse the district court and remand for entry of a preliminary injunction against Heinz and Beech–Nut.

I. Background

Four million infants in the United States consume 80 million cases of jarred baby food annually, representing a domestic market of $865 million to $1 billion. The baby food market is dominated by three firms, Gerber Products Company (Gerber), Heinz and Beech–Nut. Gerber, the industry leader, enjoys a 65 per cent market share while Heinz and Beech–Nut come in second and third, with a 17.4 per cent and a 15.4 per cent share respectively. The district court found that Gerber enjoys unparalleled brand recognition with a brand loyalty greater than any other product sold in the United States. Gerber's products are found in over 90 per cent of all American supermarkets.[6]

By contrast, Heinz is sold in approximately 40 per cent of all supermarkets. Its sales are nationwide but concentrated in northern New England, the Southeast and Deep South and the Midwest. Despite its second-place domestic market share, Heinz is the largest producer of baby food in the world with $1 billion in sales worldwide. Its domestic baby food products with annual net sales of $103 million are manufactured at its Pittsburgh, Pennsylvania plant, which was updated in 1991 at a cost of $120 million. The plant operates at 40 per cent of its production capacity and produces 12 million cases of baby food annually. Its baby food line includes about 130 SKUs (stock keeping units), that is, product varieties (*e.g.*, strained carrots, apple sauce, etc.). Heinz lacks Gerber's brand recognition; it markets itself as a "value brand" with a shelf price several cents below Gerber's.

---

6. Product volume in retail stores throughout the country is measured by the product's All Commodity Volume (ACV). Gerber's near 100 per cent ACV is impressive because virtually all supermarkets stock at most two brands of baby food. In at least one area of the country as many as 80 per cent of supermarket retailers stock only Gerber.

Beech–Nut has a market share (15.4%) comparable to that of Heinz (17.4%), with $138.7 million in annual sales of baby food, of which 72 per cent is jarred baby food. Its jarred baby food line consists of 128 SKUs. Beech–Nut manufactures all of its baby food in Canajoharie, New York at a manufacturing plant that was built in 1907 and began manufacturing baby food in 1931. Beech–Nut maintains price parity with Gerber, selling at about one penny less. It markets its product as a premium brand. Consumers generally view its product as comparable in quality to Gerber's. Beech–Nut is carried in approximately 45 per cent of all grocery stores. Although its sales are nationwide, they are concentrated in New York, New Jersey, California and Florida.[7]

At the wholesale level Heinz and Beech–Nut both make lump-sum payments called "fixed trade spending" (also known as "slotting fees" or "pay-to-stay" arrangements) to grocery stores to obtain shelf placement. Gerber, with its strong name recognition and brand loyalty, does not make such pay-to-stay payments. The other type of wholesale trade spending is "variable trade spending," which typically consists of manufacturers' discounts and allowances to supermarkets to create retail price differentials that entice the consumer to purchase their product instead of a competitor's.

Under the terms of their merger agreement, Heinz would acquire 100 per cent of Beech–Nut's voting securities for $185 million. . . .

II. Analysis

A. Standard of Review

We review a district court order denying preliminary injunctive relief for abuse of discretion, *National Wildlife Fed'n v. Burford*, 835 F.2d 305, 319 (D.C.Cir.1987), and will set aside the court's factual findings only if they are "clearly erroneous." . . .

B. Section 7 of the Clayton Act

Section 7 of the Clayton Act prohibits acquisitions, including mergers, "where in any line of commerce or in any activity affecting commerce in any section of the country, the effect of such acquisition may be substantially to lessen competition, or to tend to create a monopoly." See United States v. Philadelphia Nat'l Bank, 374 U.S. 321, 355 (1963) ("The statutory test is whether the effect of the merger 'may be substantially to lessen competition' 'in any line of commerce in any section of the country.' "). The "Congress used the words 'may be substantially to lessen competition', to indicate that its concern was with probabilities, not certainties." Brown Shoe Co. v. United States, 370 U.S. 294, 323 (1962) (emphasis original); see S. Rep. No. 1775, at 6 (1950) ("The use of these words ["may be"] means

7. Although Heinz and Beech–Nut introduced evidence showing that in areas that account for 80% of Beech–Nut sales, Heinz has a market share of about 2% and in areas that account for about 72% of Heinz sales, Beech–Nut's share is about 4%, the FTC introduced evidence that Heinz and Beech–Nut are locked in an intense battle at the wholesale level to gain (and maintain) position as the second brand on retail shelves.

that the bill, if enacted, would not apply to the mere possibility but only to the reasonable probability of the proscribed effect....''). "Merger enforcement, like other areas of antitrust, is directed at market power. It shares with the law of monopolization a degree of schizophrenia: an aversion to potent power that heightens risk of abuse; and tolerance of that degree of power required to attain economic benefits." Lawrence A. Sullivan & Warren S. Grimes, The Law of Antitrust § 9.1, at 511 (2000). The Congress has empowered the FTC, inter alia, to weed out those mergers whose effect "may be substantially to lessen competition" from those that enhance competition. See H.R. Rep. No. 1142, at 18–19 (1914). In section 13(b) of the FTCA, the Congress provided a mechanism whereby the FTC may seek preliminary injunctive relief preventing the merging parties from consummating the merger until the Commission has had an opportunity to investigate and, if necessary, adjudicate the matter.

C. Section 13(b) of the Federal Trade Commission Act

"Whenever the Commission has reason to believe that a corporation is violating, or is about to violate, Section 7 of the Clayton Act, the FTC may seek a preliminary injunction to prevent a merger pending the Commission's administrative adjudication of the merger's legality." *FTC v. Staples, Inc.*, 970 F. Supp. 1066, 1070 (D.D.C.1997)....

1. Likelihood of Success

To determine likelihood of success on the merits we measure the probability that, after an administrative hearing on the merits, the Commission will succeed in proving that the effect of the Heinz/Beech–Nut merger "may be substantially to lessen competition, or to tend to create a monopoly" in violation of section 7 of the Clayton Act. This court and others have suggested that the standard for likelihood of success on the merits is met if the FTC "has raised questions going to the merits so serious, substantial, difficult and doubtful as to make them fair ground for thorough investigation, study, deliberation and determination by the FTC in the first instance and ultimately by the Court of Appeals." ...

In *United States v. Baker Hughes Inc.*, 908 F.2d 981, 982–83 (D.C.Cir. 1990), we explained the analytical approach by which the government establishes a section 7 violation. First the government must show that the merger would produce "a firm controlling an undue percentage share of the relevant market, and [would] result in a significant increase in the concentration of firms in that market." *Philadelphia Nat'l Bank*, 374 U.S. at 363. Such a showing establishes a "presumption" that the merger will substantially lessen competition. To rebut the presumption, the defendants must produce evidence that "shows that the market-share statistics [give] an inaccurate account of the [merger's] probable effects on competition" in the relevant market. *United States v. Citizens & S. Nat'l Bank*, 422 U.S. 86, 120 (1975).[8] "If the defendant successfully rebuts the presumption [of

---

8. To rebut the defendants may rely on "nonstatistical evidence which casts doubt on the persuasive quality of the statistics to predict future anticompetitive consequences"

illegality], the burden of producing additional evidence of anticompetitive effect shifts to the government, and merges with the ultimate burden of persuasion, which remains with the government at all times." *Baker Hughes Inc.*, 908 F.2d at 983; *see also Kaiser Aluminum & Chemical Corp. v. FTC*, 652 F.2d 1324 at 1340 & n. 12. Although *Baker Hughes* was decided at the merits stage as opposed to the preliminary injunctive relief stage, we can nonetheless use its analytical approach in evaluating the Commission's showing of likelihood of success. Accordingly, we look at the FTC's *prima facie* case and the defendants' rebuttal evidence.

a.   Prima Facie Case

Merger law "rests upon the theory that, where rivals are few, firms will be able to coordinate their behavior, either by overt collusion or implicit understanding, in order to restrict output and achieve profits above competitive levels." FTC v. PPG Indus., 798 F.2d 1500, 1503 (D.C.Cir. 1986). Increases in concentration above certain levels are thought to "raise a likelihood of 'interdependent anticompetitive conduct.' " Id. (quoting General Dynamics, 415 U.S. at 497); see FTC v. Elders Grain, 868 F.2d 901, 905 (7th Cir.1989). Market concentration, or the lack thereof, is often measured by the Herfindahl–Hirschmann Index (HHI).[9]

Sufficiently large HHI figures establish the FTC's prima facie case that a merger is anti-competitive. The district court found that the pre-merger HHI "score for the baby food industry is 4775"—indicative of a highly concentrated industry.[10] The merger of Heinz and Beech–Nut will increase the HHI by 510 points. This creates, by a wide margin, a presumption that the merger will lessen competition in the domestic jarred baby food market. See Horizontal Merger Guidelines, supra, § 1.51 (stating that HHI increase of more than 100 points, where post-merger HHI exceeds 1800, is "presumed ... likely to create or enhance market power or facilitate its exercise"); *see also Baker Hughes*, 908 F.2d at 982–83 & n.3; PPG, 798 F.2d

---

such as "ease of entry into the market, the trend of the market either toward or away from concentration, and the continuation of active price competition." Kaiser Aluminum & Chem. Corp. v. FTC, 652 F.2d 1324, 1341 (7th Cir.1981). In addition, the defendants may demonstrate unique economic circumstances that undermine the predictive value of the government's statistics. See United States v. General Dynamics Corp., 415 U.S. 486, 506–10 (1974) (fundamental changes in structure of coal market made market concentration statistics inaccurate predictors of anticompetitive effect); see also University Health, 938 F.2d at 1218.

9.   The FTC and the Department of Justice, as well as most economists, consider the measure superior to such cruder measures as

the four-or eight-firm concentration ratios which merely sum up the market shares of the largest four or eight firms. PPG, 798 F.2d at 1503. The Department of Justice and the FTC rely on the HHI in evaluating proposed horizontal mergers. See United States Dep't of Justice & Federal Trade Comm'n, Horizontal Merger Guidelines §§ 1.5, 1.51 (1992), as revised (1997). Although the Merger Guidelines are not binding on the court, they provide "a useful illustration of the application of the HHI." PPG, 798 F.2d at 1503 n.4.

10.   To determine the HHI score the district court first had to define the relevant market. The court defined the product market as jarred baby food and the geographic market as the United States. H.J. Heinz, 116 F. Supp. 2d at 195. The parties do not challenge the court's definition.

at 1503.[11] Here, the FTC's market concentration statistics[12] are bolstered by the indisputable fact that the merger will eliminate competition between the two merging parties at the wholesale level, where they are currently the only competitors for what the district court described as the "second position on the supermarket shelves." Heinz's own documents recognize the wholesale competition and anticipate that the merger will end it. Indeed, those documents disclose that Heinz considered three options to end the vigorous wholesale competition with Beech–Nut: two involved innovative measures while the third entailed the acquisition of Beech–Nut. Heinz chose the third, and least pro-competitive, of the options.

Finally, the anticompetitive effect of the merger is further enhanced by high barriers to market entry.[13] The district court found that there had been no significant entries in the baby food market in decades and that new

11. The FTC argues that this finding alone—that it is certain to establish a prima facie case—entitles it to preliminary injunctive relief under PPG. We disagree with the Commission's reading of PPG. In PPG, the Commission appealed the district court's denial of its request for a preliminary injunction to prevent PPG Industries, the world's largest producer of glass aircraft transparencies, from acquiring Swedlow, Inc., the world's largest manufacturer of acrylic aircraft transparencies. 798 F.2d at 1502. After defining the relevant market and determining market share, the district court found that the merger would significantly increase the concentration in an already highly concentrated market. It also "found high market-entry barriers that would prolong high market concentration." Id. at 1503. On appeal, this court stated: "There is no doubt that the pre-and post-acquisition HHI's and market shares found in this case entitle the Commission to some preliminary relief." Id. This statement came, however, in the context of a case in which the appellants offered no rebuttal (other than the observation of rapid and continuing technological changes in the industry) to the presumption generated by the market concentration data on which the FTC based its prima facie showing. Id. at 1506. The court then noted the rule established in Weyerhaeuser that the FTC is entitled to a "presumption in favor of a preliminary injunction when [it] establishes a strong likelihood of success on the merits." Id. at 1507.

12. The Supreme Court has cautioned that statistics reflecting market share and concentration, while of great significance, are not conclusive indicators of anticompetitive effects. See General Dynamics, 415 U.S. at 498.

13. Barriers to entry are important in evaluating whether market concentration statistics accurately reflect the pre-and likely post-merger competitive picture. Cf. Baker Hughes, 908 F.2d at 987. If entry barriers are low, the threat of outside entry can significantly alter the anticompetitive effects of the merger by deterring the remaining entities from colluding or exercising market power. See United States v. Falstaff Brewing Corp., 410 U.S. 526, 532–33 (1973); Baker Hughes, 908 F.2d at 987 ("In the absence of significant barriers, a company probably cannot maintain supracompetitive pricing for any length of time."); Horizontal Merger Guidelines, supra, § 3.0 ("A merger is not likely to create or enhance market power or to facilitate its exercise, if entry into the market is so easy that market participants, after the merger, either collectively or unilaterally could not profitably maintain a price increase above premerger levels."). Low barriers to entry enable a potential competitor to deter anticompetitive behavior by firms within the market simply by its ability to enter the market. FTC v. Procter & Gamble Co., 386 U.S. 568, 581 (1967) ("It is clear that the existence of Procter at the edge of the industry exerted considerable influence on the market."). Existing firms know that if they collude or exercise market power to charge supracompetitive prices, entry by firms currently not competing in the market becomes likely, thereby increasing the pressure on them to act competitively. See Baker Hughes, 908 F.2d at 988; Byars v. Bluff City News Co., 609 F.2d 843, 851 n. 19 (6th Cir.1979).

entry was "difficult and improbable." This finding largely eliminates the possibility that the reduced competition caused by the merger will be ameliorated by new competition from outsiders and further strengthens the FTC's case.

As far as we can determine, no court has ever approved a merger to duopoly under similar circumstances.

b. Rebuttal Arguments

In response to the FTC's prima facie showing, the appellees make three rebuttal arguments, which the district court accepted in reaching its conclusion that the merger was not likely to lessen competition substantially. For the reasons discussed below, these arguments fail and thus were not a proper basis for denying the FTC injunctive relief.

1. Extent of Pre–Merger Competition

The appellees first contend, and the district court agreed, that Heinz and Beech–Nut do not really compete against each other at the retail level. Consumers do not regard the products of the two companies as substitutes, the appellees claim, and generally only one of the two brands is available on any given store's shelves. Hence, they argue, there is little competitive loss from the merger.

This argument has a number of flaws that render clearly erroneous the court's finding that Heinz and Beech–Nut have not engaged in significant pre-merger competition. First, in accepting the appellees' argument that Heinz and Beech–Nut do not compete, the district court failed to address the record evidence that the two do in fact price against each other, and that, where both are present in the same areas,[14] they depress each other's prices as well as those of Gerber even though they are virtually never all found in the same store. This evidence undermines the district court's factual finding.

Second, the district court's finding is inconsistent with its conclusion that there is a single, national market for jarred baby food in the United States. The Supreme Court has explained that "the outer boundaries of a product market are determined by the reasonable interchangeability of use [by consumers] or the cross-elasticity of demand between the product itself and substitutes for it." *Brown Shoe,* 370 U.S. at 325; *see also United States v. E.I. du Pont de Nemours & Co.,* 351 U.S. 377, 395 (1956).[15] The definition of product market thus "focuses solely on demand substitution factors," *i.e.,* that consumers regard the products as substitutes. *Horizontal Merger Guidelines,* supra, § 1.0; *Sullivan & Grimes,* supra, § 11.2b1, at 579. By defining the relevant product market generically as jarred baby

---

14. There are at least ten metropolitan areas in which Heinz and Beech–Nut both have more than a 10 per cent market share and their combined share exceeds 35 per cent. PX 781 at Ex. 1B.

15. Interchangeability of use and cross-elasticity of demand look to the availability of products that are similar in nature or use and the degree to which buyers are willing to substitute those similar products for one another. See E.I. du Pont de Nemours, 351 U.S. at 393.

food, the district court concluded that in areas where Heinz's and Beech–Nut's products are both sold, consumers will switch between them in response to a "small but significant and nontransitory increase in price (SSNIP)." *Horizontal Merger Guidelines*, supra, § 1.11. The district court never explained this inherent inconsistency in its logic nor could counsel for the appellees explain it at oral argument.

Third, and perhaps most important, the court's conclusion concerning pre-merger competition does not take into account the indisputable fact that the merger will eliminate competition at the wholesale level between the only two competitors for the "second shelf" position. Competition between Heinz and Beech–Nut to gain accounts at the wholesale level is fierce with each contest concluding in a winner-take-all result. The district court regarded this loss of competition as irrelevant because the FTC did not establish to its satisfaction that wholesale competition ultimately benefited consumers through lower retail prices. The district court concluded that fixed trade spending did not affect consumer prices and that "the FTC's assertion that the proposed merger will affect variable trade spending levels and consumer prices is ... at best, inconclusive."[16] *H.J. Heinz,* 116 F. Supp. 2d at 197. Although the court noted the FTC's examples of consumer benefit through couponing initiatives, the court held that it was "impossible to conclude with any certainty that the consumer benefit from such couponing initiatives would be lost in the merger." *Id.*

In rejecting the FTC's argument regarding the loss of wholesale competition, the court committed two legal errors. First, as the appellees conceded at oral argument, no court has ever held that a reduction in competition for wholesale purchasers is not relevant unless the plaintiff can prove impact at the consumer level. *See Hospital Corp. of Am. v. FTC,* 807 F.2d 1381, 1389 (7th Cir.1986) ("Section 7 does not require proof that a merger or other acquisition has caused higher prices in the affected market. All that is necessary is that the merger create an appreciable danger of [collusive practices] in the future. A predictive judgment, necessarily probabilistic and judgmental rather than demonstrable, is called for.") Second, it is, in any event, not the FTC's burden to prove such an impact with "certainty." To the contrary, the antitrust laws assume that a retailer faced with an increase in the cost of one of its inventory items "will try so far as competition allows to pass that cost on to its customers in the form of a higher price for its product." *In re Brand Name Prescription Drugs Antitrust Litig.,* 123 F.3d 599, 605 (7th Cir.1997). Section 7 is, after all, concerned with probabilities, not certainties. *United States v. El Paso Natural Gas Co.,* 376 U.S. 651, 658 (1964); *Brown Shoe,* 370 U.S. at 323; *Baker Hughes,* 908 F.2d at 984.[17]

16. Fixed trade spending consists of "slotting fees," "pay-to-stay" arrangements, new store allowances and other payments to retailers in exchange for shelf space and desired product display. Variable trade spending includes payments to retailers tied to sales volume and intended to insure a specific sales volume and lower shelf price.

17. Although the merger's effects on the wholesale market for baby food are important to a determination of whether the merger is likely to reduce competition in the

2.   Post–Merger Efficiencies

The appellees' second attempt to rebut the FTC's prima facie showing is their contention that the anticompetitive effects of the merger will be offset by efficiencies resulting from the union of the two companies, efficiencies which they assert will be used to compete more effectively against Gerber. It is true that a merger's primary benefit to the economy is its potential to generate efficiencies. *See generally* 4A Phillip E. Areeda, Herbert Hovenkamp & John L. Solow, Antitrust Law p. 970 at 22–25 (1998). As the Merger Guidelines now recognize, efficiencies "can enhance the merged firm's ability and incentive to compete, which may result in lower prices, improved quality, or new products." Horizontal Merger Guidelines, supra, § 4.

Although the Supreme Court has not sanctioned the use of the efficiencies defense in a section 7 case, *see Procter & Gamble Co.*, 386 U.S. at 580,[18] the trend among lower courts is to recognize the defense. *See, e.g., FTC v. Tenet Health Care Corp.*, 186 F.3d 1045, 1054 (8th Cir.1999); *University Health*, 938 F.2d at 1222; *FTC v. Cardinal Health, Inc.*, 12 F. Supp. 2d 34, 61 (D.D.C.1998); *Staples*, 970 F. Supp. at 1088–89; *see also* ABA Antitrust Section, Mergers and Acquisitions: Understanding the Antitrust Issues 152 (2000) ("The majority of courts have considered efficiencies as a means to rebut the government's prima facie case that a merger will lead to restricted output or increased prices. These courts, however, generally have found inadequate proof of efficiencies to sustain a rebuttal of the government's case."). In 1997 the Department of Justice and the FTC revised their Horizontal Merger Guidelines to recognize that "mergers have the poten-

---

baby food market overall, we reject the FTC's argument here that the "wholesale competition" between Heinz and Beech–Nut is an entirely distinct "line of commerce" within the meaning of section 7 of the Clayton Act such that it must be analyzed independently from "retail competition." The Congress amended section 7 in 1950 "to make the measure of anticompetitive acquisitions the extent to which they lessened competition 'in any line of commerce,' rather than the extent to which they lessened competition 'between' the two companies." *Citizen Publishing Co. v. United States*, 394 U.S. 131, 137 n. 3, (1969). Courts interpret "line of commerce" as synonymous with the relevant product market. See *General Dynamics*, 415 U.S. at 510; *Falstaff Brewing*, 410 U.S. at 531–32. The district court defined only one market—jarred baby food sold throughout the line of commerce in the United States. Thus, the proper "line of commerce" for analysis in this case is the overall market for jarred baby food, which includes both retail and wholesale levels. At this point in the proceedings, the

wholesale market cannot be separated out for analysis without regard to the merger's effect on other levels of competition.

18. In Procter & Gamble Co., 386 U.S. at 580, the Supreme Court stated that "possible economies cannot be used as a defense to illegality" in section 7 merger cases. The issue is, however, not a closed book. See Staples, 970 F. Supp. at 1088 (collecting cases). Areeda and Turner explain that "in interpreting the Clorox language, moreover, observe that the court referred only to 'possible' economies and to economies that 'may' result from mergers that lessen competition. To reject an economies defense based on mere possibilities does not mean that one should reject such a defense based on more convincing proof." 4 Phillip Areeda & Donald Turner, Antitrust Law p 941b, at 154 (1980). They conclude that "the Court's brief and unelaborated language [in Clorox] cannot reasonably be taken as a definitive disposition of so important and complex an issue as the role of economies in analyzing legality of a merger." *Id.*

tial to generate significant efficiencies by permitting a better utilization of existing assets, enabling the combined firm to achieve lower costs in producing a given quantity and quality than either firm could have achieved without the proposed transaction." Horizontal Merger Guidelines, supra, § 4.

Nevertheless, the high market concentration levels present in this case require, in rebuttal, proof of extraordinary efficiencies, which the appellees failed to supply. *See University Health*, 938 F.2d at 1223 ("[A] defendant who seeks to overcome a presumption that a proposed acquisition would substantially lessen competition must demonstrate that the intended acquisition would result in significant economies and that these economies ultimately would benefit competition and, hence, consumers."); Horizontal Merger Guidelines, supra, § 4 (stating that "efficiencies almost never justify a merger to monopoly or near-monopoly"); 4A Areeda, et al., Antitrust Law p. 971f, at 44 (requiring "extraordinary" efficiencies where the "HHI is well above 1800 and the HHI increase is well above 100"). Moreover, given the high concentration levels, the court must undertake a rigorous analysis of the kinds of efficiencies being urged by the parties in order to ensure that those "efficiencies" represent more than mere speculation and promises about post-merger behavior. The district court did not undertake that analysis here.

In support of its conclusion that post-merger efficiencies will outweigh the merger's anticompetitive effects, the district court found that the consolidation of baby food production in Heinz's under-utilized Pittsburgh plant "will achieve substantial cost savings in salaries and operating costs." The court also credited the appellees' promise of improved product quality as a result of recipe consolidation.[19] The only cost reduction the court quantified as a percentage of pre-merger costs, however, was the so-called "variable conversion cost": the cost of processing the volume of baby food now processed by Beech–Nut. The court accepted the appellees' claim that this cost would be reduced by 43% if the Beech–Nut production were shifted to Heinz's plant, a reduction the appellees' expert characterized as "extraordinary."

The district court's analysis falls short of the findings necessary for a successful efficiencies defense in the circumstances of this case. We mention only three of the most important deficiencies here. First, "variable conversion cost" is only a percentage of the total variable manufacturing cost. A large percentage reduction in only a small portion of the company's overall variable manufacturing cost does not necessarily translate into a significant cost advantage to the merger. Thus, for cost reduction to be

19. In addition, the district court described Heinz's distribution network as much more efficient than Beech–Nut's. It failed to find, however, a significant diseconomy of scale in distribution from which either Heinz or Beech–Nut suffers. 4A Areeda, et al., supra, p. 975e1, at 73. In other words, although Beech–Nut has an inefficient distribution system, it can make that system more efficient without merger. Heinz's own efficient distribution network illustrates that a firm the size of Beech–Nut does not need to merge in order to attain an efficient distribution system.

relevant, we must at least consider the percentage of Beech–Nut's total variable manufacturing cost that would be reduced as a consequence of the merger. At oral argument, the appellees' counsel agreed. This correction immediately cuts the asserted efficiency gain in half since, according to the appellees' evidence, using total variable manufacturing cost as the measure cuts the cost savings from 43% to 22.3%.

Second, the percentage reduction in Beech–Nut's cost is still not the relevant figure. After the merger, the two entities will be combined, and to determine whether the merged entity will be a significantly more efficient competitor, cost reductions must be measured across the new entity's combined production—not just across the pre-merger output of Beech–Nut. The district court, however, did not consider the cost reduction over the merged firm's combined output. At oral argument the appellees' counsel was unable to suggest a formula that could be used for determining that cost reduction.

Finally, and as the district court recognized, the asserted efficiencies must be "merger-specific" to be cognizable as a defense. That is, they must be efficiencies that cannot be achieved by either company alone because, if they can, the merger's asserted benefits can be achieved without the concomitant loss of a competitor. *See generally* 4A Areeda, et al., supra, p. 973. Yet the district court never explained why Heinz could not achieve the kind of efficiencies urged without merger. As noted, the principal merger benefit asserted for Heinz is the acquisition of Beech–Nut's better recipes, which will allegedly make its product more attractive and permit expanded sales at prices lower than those charged by Beech–Nut, which produces at an inefficient plant. Yet, neither the district court nor the appellees addressed the question whether Heinz could obtain the benefit of better recipes by investing more money in product development and promotion—say, by an amount less than the amount Heinz would spend to acquire Beech–Nut. At oral argument, Heinz's counsel agreed that the taste of Heinz's products was not so bad that no amount of money could improve the brand's consumer appeal. That being the case, the question is how much Heinz would have to spend to make its product equivalent to the Beech–Nut product and hence whether Heinz could achieve the efficiencies of merger without eliminating Beech–Nut as a competitor. The district court, however, undertook no inquiry in this regard. In short, the district court failed to make the kind of factual determinations necessary to render the appellees' efficiency defense sufficiently concrete to offset the FTC's prima facie showing.

3. Innovation

The appellees claim next that the merger is required to enable Heinz to innovate, and thus to improve its competitive position against Gerber. Heinz and Beech–Nut asserted, and the district court found, that without the merger the two firms are unable to launch new products to compete with Gerber because they lack a sufficient shelf presence or ACV. This kind of defense is often a speculative proposition. See 4A Areeda, et al., supra, p.

975g (noting "truly formidable" proof problems in determining innovation economies). In this case, given the old-economy nature of the industry as well as Heinz's position as the world's largest baby food manufacturer, it is a particularly difficult defense to prove. The court below accepted the appellees' argument principally on the basis of their expert's testimony that new product launches are cost-effective only when a firm's ACV is 70% or greater (Heinz's is presently 40%; Beech–Nut's is 45%). That testimony, in turn, was based on a graph that plotted revenue against ACV. According to the expert, the graph showed that only four out of 27 new products launched in 1995 had been successful—all for companies with an ACV of 70% or greater.

The chart, however, does not establish this proposition and the court's consequent finding that the merger is necessary for innovation is thus unsupported and clearly erroneous. All the chart plotted was revenue against ACV and hence all it showed was the unsurprising fact that the greater a company's ACV, the greater the revenue it received. Because the graph did not plot the profitability (or any measure of "cost-effectiveness"), there is no way to know whether the expert's claim—that a 70% ACV is required for a launch to be "successful" in an economic sense—is true.[20] Moreover, the number of data points on the chart were few; they were limited to launches in a single year; and they involved launches of all new grocery products rather than of baby food alone. Assessing such data's statistical significance in establishing the proposition at issue, *i.e.*, the necessity of 70% ACV penetration, is thus highly speculative. The district court did not even address the question of the data's statistical significance and the appellees' counsel could offer no help at oral argument. ("I'm not aware of the statistical significance of the underlying study.").[21] In the absence of reliable and significant evidence that the merger will permit innovation that otherwise could not be accomplished, the district court had no basis to conclude that the FTC's showing was rebutted by an innovation defense....

4. Structural Barriers to Collusion

In a footnote the district court dismissed the likelihood of collusion derived from the FTC's market concentration data. "Structural market

---

20. For example, a 5 cent piece of bubble gum introduced with a 90 ACV could appear as a failure on the graph because of low revenue but nonetheless be profitable. On the other hand, a high priced grocery product introduced with the same ACV could generate a lot of revenue (and thus appear as a "success" on the graph) yet be unprofitable.

21. The graph evidence is also not useful unless we know the "sunk" costs in bringing the product to market and the manufacturer's fixed and variable costs in producing the product. Sunk costs are costs that have already been incurred such as research

and development and promotional expenses, including brand name development. *See* Henry N. Butler, *Economic Analysis for Lawyers* 935 (1998). Fixed costs refer to those expenses that do not vary with output and will be incurred as long as the firm continues in business. Variable costs are those that change with the rate of output such as wages paid to workers and payments for raw materials. See *id.* at 920, 936; E. Thomas Sullivan & Jeffrey L. Harrison, *Understanding Antitrust and its Economic Implications* 19–21 (3d ed. 1998).

barriers to collusion" in the retail market for jarred baby food, the court said, rebut the normal presumption that increases in concentration will increase the likelihood of tacit collusion. The court's sole citation, however, was to testimony by the appellees' expert, Jonathan B. Baker, a former Director of the Bureau of Economics at the FTC, who testified that in order to coordinate successfully, firms must solve "cartel problems" such as reaching a consensus on price and market share and deterring each other from deviating from that consensus by either lowering price or increasing production. He opined that after the merger the merged entity would want to expand its market share at Gerber's expense, thereby decreasing the likelihood of consensus on price and market share. In his report, Baker elaborated on his theory, explaining that the efficiencies created by the merger will give the merged firm the ability and incentive to take on Gerber in price and product improvements. He also predicted that policing and monitoring of any agreement would be more difficult than it is now, due in part to a time lag in the ability of one firm to detect price cuts by another. But the district court made no finding that any of these "cartel problems" are so much greater in the baby food industry than in other industries that they rebut the normal presumption. In fact, Baker's testimony about "time lag" is refuted by the record that reflects that supermarket prices are available from industry-wide scanner data within 4–8 weeks. His testimony is further undermined by the record evidence of past price leadership in the baby food industry.[22]

The combination of a concentrated market and barriers to entry is a recipe for price coordination. *See University Health*, 938 F.2d at 1218 n.24 ("Significant market concentration makes it 'easier for firms in the market to collude, expressly or tacitly, and thereby force price above or farther above the competitive level.' " (citation omitted)). "Where rivals are few, firms will be able to coordinate their behavior, either by overt collusion or implicit understanding, in order to restrict output and achieve profits above competitive levels." PPG, 798 F.2d at 1503. The creation of a durable duopoly affords both the opportunity and incentive for both firms to coordinate to increase prices. The district court recognized this when it questioned Baker on whether the merged entity will, up to a point, expand its market share but "then [with Gerber will] find a nice equilibrium and they'll all get along together." 9/8/2000 Tr. 1014. Tacit coordination

> is feared by antitrust policy even more than express collusion, for tacit coordination, even when observed, cannot easily be controlled directly by the antitrust laws. It is a central object of merger policy to obstruct the creation or reinforcement by merger of such oligopolistic market structures in which tacit coordination can occur.

22. In an oligopolistic market characterized by few producers, price leadership occurs when firms engage in interdependent pricing, setting their prices at a profit-maximizing, supracompetitive level by recognizing their shared economic interests with respect to price and output decisions. See Brooke Group Ltd. v. Brown & Williamson Tobacco Corp., 509 U.S. 209, 227 (1993).

4 Phillip E. Areeda, Herbert Hovenkamp & John L. Solow, Antitrust Law p
901b2, at 9 (rev. ed. 1998). Because the district court failed to specify any
"structural market barriers to collusion" that are unique to the baby food
industry, its conclusion that the ordinary presumption of collusion in a
merger to duopoly was rebutted is clearly erroneous.

* * *

Although we recognize that, post-hearing, the FTC may accept the
rebuttal arguments proffered by the appellees, including their efficiencies
defense, and permit the merger to proceed, we conclude that the FTC
succeeded in "raising questions going to the merits so serious, substantial,
difficult and doubtful as to make them fair ground for thorough investigation, study, deliberation and determination by the FTC." *Warner Communications*, 742 F.2d at 1162. The FTC demonstrated that the merger to
duopoly will increase the concentration in an already highly concentrated
market; that entry barriers in the market make it unlikely that any
anticompetitive effects will be avoided; that pre-merger competition is
vigorous at the wholesale level nationwide and present at the retail level in
some metropolitan areas; and that post-merger competition may be lessened substantially. These substantial questions have not been sufficiently
answered by the appellees. As we said in *Baker Hughes,* "the more
compelling the prima facie case, the more evidence the defendant must
present to rebut it successfully." 908 F.2d at 991. In concluding that the
FTC failed to make the requisite showing, the district court erred in a
number of respects. Regarding the contention of lack of pre-merger competition, it made a clearly erroneous factual finding and misunderstood the
law with respect to the import of competition at the wholesale level.
Regarding the proffered efficiencies defense, the court failed to make the
kind of factual findings required to render that defense sufficiently concrete
to rebut the government's prima facie showing. Finally, as to the contention that the merger is necessary for innovation, the court clearly erred in
relying on evidence that does not support its conclusion. Because the
district court incorrectly assessed the merits of the appellees' rebuttal
arguments, it improperly discounted the FTC's showing of likelihood of
success....

[In a concluding section, the Court of Appeals "weighed the equities."
On the government's side, it cited legislative history and prior cases to the
effect that denial of an injunction might prevent the government from ever
undoing the anticompetitive effects of the merger. It assumed that the
Beech–Nut manufacturing facility would be closed and its distribution
channels closed. On the defendants' side, it recognized that the parties
might abandon the proposed merger if they had to await full administrative
litigation before the FTC and a possible appeal. The D.C. Circuit came
down in favor of the government, noting that the alleged efficiencies would
still be available after litigation.]

III. Conclusion

It is important to emphasize the posture of this case. We do not decide
whether the FTC will ultimately prove its case or whether the defendants'

claimed efficiencies will carry the day.[23] Our task is to review the district court's order to determine whether, under section 13(b), preliminary injunctive relief would be in the public interest. We have considered the FTC's likelihood of success on the merits. We have weighed the equities. We conclude that the FTC has raised serious and substantial questions. We also conclude that the public equities weigh in favor of preliminary injunctive relief and therefore that a preliminary injunction would be in the public interest. Accordingly, we reverse the district court's denial of preliminary injunctive relief and remand the case for entry of a preliminary injunction pursuant to section 13(b) of the Federal Trade Commission Act.[24]

PROBLEM 23

MERGERS AT CEDAR LAKE

Cedar Lake, Colorado is the site of a major winter sports resort, similar but 100 miles distant from Aspen, Colorado (see Aspen Skiing, p. 736 supra). Its main attraction lies in downhill skiing offered on the high slopes of Mount Cedar. Five companies run the major ski operations, each offering daily and weekly lift tickets. The companies and their ticket revenues for last season were as follows: Colorado Ski Resorts, $30 million; Mount Cedar Ski, $30 million; Big Sky, $20 million; High Sky, $8 million; and Ski America, $5 million.

Cedar Lake is one of three major destination ski resorts in Colorado (a destination ski resort is one where most of the patrons come from elsewhere; in the case of Cedar Lake, 80% come from distant locations and 20% are local residents). Two other ski areas, totaling $4 million in revenues, are located 10 to 15 miles south of the town of Cedar Lake. These are primarily used by local residents, although they could be expanded to offer more destination resort competition with the Cedar Lake group. Expansion could occur within one year and would allow ski slopes in these adjacent areas to double the number of skiers they could handle. Constructing a hotel at the base of the slope would increase the potential of these areas even more, though hotel construction would take at least three years.

Ski America and High Sky, located adjacent to each other on the southern slopes of Mount Cedar, have proposed a merger. All three other Mount Cedar ski operations are on the northern slope. Skiers using the southern slope find it convenient if they are staying at one of the hotels nearby at the base of the mountain. About 50% of skiers on Ski America and High Sky use only the southern slopes, while the rest occasionally migrate to the northern side during an average stay.

Until three or four years ago, Ski America and High Sky offered a weekly joint ticket that allowed the skier to use the slopes of either company, but that joint ticket was eliminated following a series of squabbles between the two companies over the proper division of revenues. The companies anticipate a number of benefits from the merger, including new and better trails that combine the two facilities and

---

23. "The most difficult mergers to assess may be those that combine both negative and positive effects: creating market power that increases the risk of oligopolistic pricing while at the same time creating efficiencies that reduce production or marketing costs." Sullivan & Grimes, supra, § 9.1, at 511.

24. Ed. The parties abandoned the merger shortly after the D.C. Circuit's decision was issued.

can be developed at a lower cost, a better and more highly utilized ski school, and the ability to offer a joint weekly ticket as well as to offer package tours in conjunction with the hotels on the southern slope.

New ski resorts could be opened in Colorado, Utah, and Wyoming. The cost of laying out slopes and constructing lifts amounts to approximately $4 million, and the cost of land can range from $5 million to $15 million. Additional operations could be profitably constructed if new operations could achieve the equivalent of 10% of current total Cedar Lake ski revenues. It would take about three years to complete a new operation.

All of the ski operations at Cedar Lake except High Sky have been exceptionally profitable. High Sky is saddled with obsolete equipment and has shown small deficits in four of the last five years. As a result, High Sky is the least aggressive of the five in offering discounts on bulk sales of lift tickets or in creating package tours. Before closing the deal, the owners of High Sky made a conscientious effort to find a purchaser completely outside its ski area. It received an offer from Aspen Ski at a price 30% below the amount offered by Ski America, but well above scrap value. Because of the special expertise necessary in running a ski operation, other business enterprises shied away from the investment.

Would the proposed merger violate the antitrust laws?

SECTION 3. JOINT VENTURES, POTENTIAL COMPETITION, AND CONGLOMERATE MERGERS

UNITED STATES V. EL PASO NATURAL GAS CO., 376 U.S. 651, 84 S.Ct. 1044, 12 L.Ed.2d 12 (1964). Suit by the government for violation of Section 7 by reason of the acquisition of the stock and assets of Pacific Northwest Pipeline Corp. by El Paso Natural Gas Co. El Paso was the "sole out of state supplier" of natural gas in California, with a pre-acquisition share exceeding 50%. Pacific Northwest was "the only other important interstate pipeline west of the Rocky Mountains." Although Pacific, prior to the acquisition, sold no gas in California, it had "proximity to the California market" by virtue of its facilities and "enormous reserves" in surrounding areas. In addition, it had "adequate ... managerial skill" and "was so strong and militant that it was viewed with concern, and coveted, by El Paso." Pacific's pre-acquisition attempts to sell natural gas in California had been unsuccessful. Its efforts to obtain a contract from a large California utility were fought "to the last ditch" by El Paso, which ultimately closed the deal, only after reducing its original offer from 40¢ per million cubic feet to 30¢. Moreover, the Federal Power Commission rejected Pacific's proposal to pipe gas into that state and refused to issue the necessary certification. Held, for the government. Pacific Northwest was a "substantial factor in the California market at the time it was acquired by El Paso." The Court viewed the merger in the context of a regulated industry, rather than in a "field where merchants are in a continuous daily struggle to hold old customers and to win new ones over from their rivals." Competition in natural gas "is for the new increments of demand that may emerge with an expanding population and with an expanding industrial or household use of gas." Accordingly, in the natural gas field, the merger foreclosed Pacific from competing for new contracts for the incremental gas demand. (Douglas, J.)

United States v. Penn–Olin Chemical Co.

Supreme Court of the United States, 1964.
378 U.S. 158, 84 S.Ct. 1710, 12 L.Ed.2d 775.

■ CLARK, J. Pennsalt Chemicals Corporation and Olin Mathieson Chemical Corporation jointly formed Penn–Olin Chemical Company to produce and sell sodium chlorate in the southeastern United States. The Government seeks to dissolve this joint venture as violative of both § 7 of the Clayton Act and § 1 of the Sherman Act. . . .

Pennsalt is engaged solely in the production and sale of chemicals and chemical products throughout the United States. Its assets are around a hundred million dollars and its sales are about the same amount. Its sodium chlorate production is located at Portland, Oregon, with a capacity of some 15,000 tons as of 1959. It occupied 57.8% of the market west of the Rocky Mountains. It has marketed sodium chlorate in the southeastern United States to some extent since 1957. Its shipments into that territory in 1960 were 4,186 tons of which Olin sold 3,202 tons on its sales agency contract.

Olin is a large diversified corporation, the result of a merger of Olin Industries, Inc., and Mathieson Chemical Corporation in 1954. One of its seven divisions operates plants in 15 States and produces a wide range of chemicals and chemical products accounting for about 30% of Olin's revenues. Olin's sales in 1960 grossed some $690,000,000 and its total assets were $860,000,000.

Penn–Olin was organized in 1960 as a joint venture of Olin and Pennsalt. Each owns 50% of its stock and the officers and directors are divided equally between the parents. Its plant at Calvert City, Kentucky, was built by equal contribution of the two parents and cost $6,500,000. It has a capacity to produce 26,500 tons of sodium chlorate annually and began operations in 1961. Pennsalt operates the plant and Olin handles the sales. Penn–Olin deals in no other chemicals.

Prior to 1961 the sodium chlorate industry in the United States was made up of three producing companies. The largest producer, Hooker Chemical Corporation, entered the industry in 1956 when it acquired Oldbury Electro Chemical Company, which had been producing sodium chlorate for over half a century. Hooker now has two plants, one in the relevant marketing area at Columbus, Mississippi, which originally had a capacity of 16,000 tons but which was doubled in 1962. The other plant is at Niagara Falls, New York, with a capacity of 18,000 tons. Hooker has assets of almost $200,000,000. American Potash & Chemical Corporation entered the industry in 1955 by the acquisition of Western Electro Chemical Company. American Potash also has two plants, one located at Henderson, Nevada, with a 27,000–ton capacity and the other at Aberdeen,

Mississippi (built in 1957), the capacity of which was 15,000 tons. Its assets are almost $100,000,000. The trial court found that these two corporations "had a virtual monopoly" in the relevant southeast market, holding over 90% of the market.

A third company in the industry was Pennsalt which had a 15,392–ton plant at Portland, Oregon. It entered seriously into the relevant marketing area through a sales arrangement with Olin dated December 1957 and finalized in 1958, which was aimed at testing the availability of the southeastern market. Olin as an exclusive seller was to undertake the sale of 2,000 tons of sodium chlorate per year to pulp and paper mills in the southeast (except for Buckeye Cellulose Co., at Foley, Florida, which Pennsalt reserved to serve directly). In 1960, 4,186 tons of sodium chlorate were marketed in the relevant market with the aid of this agreement. This accounted for 8.9% of the sales in that market.

During the previous decade no new firms had entered the sodium chlorate industry, and little effort had been made by existing companies to expand their facilities prior to 1957. In 1953 Olin had made available to Pennsalt its Mathieson patented process for bleaching pulp with chlorine dioxide and the latter had installed it 100% in all of the western paper mills. This process uses sodium chlorate. At about the same time the process was likewise made available, royalty free, to the entire pulp and paper industry. By 1960 most of the chlorine dioxide generated by paper manufacturers was being produced under the Olin controlled process. This created an expanding demand for sodium chlorate and by 1960 the heaviest concentration of purchasers was located in the relevant southeastern territory. By 1957 Hooker began increasing the capacity of its Columbus plant and by 1960 it had been almost doubled. American Potash sensed the need of a plant in Mississippi to compete with Hooker and began its Aberdeen plant in 1957. It was completed to a 15,000–ton capacity in 1959, and this capacity was expanded 50% by 1961.

The sales arrangement between Pennsalt and Olin, previously mentioned, was superseded by the joint venture agreement on February 11, 1960, and the Penn–Olin plant operations at Calvert City, Kentucky, began in 1961. In the same year Pittsburgh Plate Glass Company announced that it would build a plant at Lake Charles, Louisiana, with a capacity of 15,000 tons. Pittsburgh Plate Glass had operated a sodium chlorate plant in Canada.

As a result of these expansions and new entries into the southeastern market, the projected production of sodium chlorate there more than doubled. By 1962 Hooker had 32,000 tons; American Potash, 22,500 tons; Penn–Olin, 26,500 tons; and Pittsburgh Glass, 15,000 tons—a total of 96,000 tons as contrasted to 41,150 in 1959. Penn–Olin's share of the expanded relevant market was about 27.6% . . . .

As early as 1951 Pennsalt had considered building a plant at Calvert City and starting in 1955 it initiated several cost and market studies for a sodium chlorate plant in the southeast. Three different proposals from within its own organization were rejected prior to 1957, apparently because the rate of return was so unattractive that "the expense of refining these figures further would be unwarranted." When Hooker announced in December 1956 that it was going to increase the capacity of its Columbus plant, the interest of Pennsalt management was reactivated. It appointed a "task force" to evaluate the company's future in the eastern market; it retained management consultants to study that market and its chief engineer prepared cost estimates. However, in December 1957 the management decided that the estimated rate of return was unattractive and considered it "unlikely" that Pennsalt would go it alone. It was suggested that Olin would be a "logical partner" in a joint venture and might in the interim be interested in distributing in the East 2,000 tons of the Portland sodium chlorate production. The sales agreement with Olin, heretofore mentioned, was eventually made. In the final draft the parties agreed that "neither ... should move in the chlorate or perchlorate field without keeping the other party informed ..." and that one would "bring to the attention of the other any unusual aspects of this business which might make it desirable to proceed further with production plans." Pennsalt claims that it finally decided, prior to this agreement, that it should not build a plant itself and that this decision was never reconsidered or changed. But the District Court found to the contrary.

During this same period—beginning slightly earlier—Olin began investigating the possibility of entering the sodium chlorate industry. It had never produced sodium chlorate commercially, although its predecessor had done so years before. However, the electrolytic process used in making sodium chlorate is intimately related to other operations of Olin and required the same general knowledge. Olin also possessed extensive experience in the technical aspects of bleaching pulp and paper and was intimate with the pulp and paper mills of the southeast. In April 1958 Olin's chemical division wrote and circulated to the management a "Whither Report" which stated in part:

> We have an unparalleled opportunity to move sodium chlorate into the paper industry as the result of our work on the installation of chlorine dioxide generators. We have a captive consumption for sodium chlorate.

And Olin's engineering supervisor concluded that entry into sodium chlorate production was "an attractive venture" since it "represents a logical expansion of the product line of the Industrial Chemicals Division ..." with respect to "one of the major markets, pulp and paper bleaching, [with which] we have a favorable marketing position, particularly in the southeast."

The staff, however, did not agree with the engineering supervisor or the "Whither Report" and concluded "that they didn't feel that this particular project showed any merit worthy of serious consideration by the corporation at that time." They were dubious of the cost estimates and felt the need to temper their scientists' enthusiasm for new products with the uncertainties of plant construction and operation. But, as the trial court found, the testimony indicated that Olin's decision to enter the joint venture was made without determining that Olin could not or would not be an independent competitor. That question, "never reached the point of final decision."

This led the District Court to find that the president of Penn–Olin testified, "[t]he possibility of individual entry into the southeastern market had not been completely rejected by either Pennsalt or Olin before they decided upon the joint venture." 217 F.Supp. 110, 128–129.

Appellees argue that § 7 applies only where the acquired company is "engaged" in commerce and that it would not apply to a newly formed corporation, such as Penn–Olin. The test, they say, is whether the enterprise to be acquired is engaged in commerce—not whether a corporation formed as the instrumentality for the acquisition is itself engaged in commerce at the moment of its formation. We believe that this logic fails in the light of the wording of the section and its legislative background. The test of the section is the effect of the acquisition. Certainly the formation of a joint venture and purchase by the organizers of its stock would substantially lessen competition—indeed foreclose it—as between them, both being engaged in commerce. This would be true whether they were in actual or potential competition with each other and even though the new corporation was formed to create a wholly new enterprise. Realistically, the parents would not compete with their progeny. Moreover, in this case the progeny was organized to further the business of its parents, already in commerce, and the fact that it was organized specifically to engage in commerce should bring it within the coverage of § 7. In addition, long prior to trial Penn–Olin was actually engaged in commerce. To hold that it was not "would be illogical and disrespectful of the plain congressional purpose in amending § 7 ... [for] it would create a large loophole in a statute designed to close a loophole." *United States v. Philadelphia National Bank,* 374 U.S. 321, 343 (1963). In any event, Penn–Olin was engaged in commerce at the time of suit and the economic effects of an acquisition are to be measured at that point rather than at the time of acquisition. *United States v. E.I. du Pont de Nemours & Co.,* 353 U.S. 586, 607 (1957). The technicality could, therefore, be averted by merely refiling an amended complaint at the time of trial. This would be a useless requirement.

This is the first case reaching this Court and on which we have written that directly involves the validity under § 7 of the joint participation of two corporations in the creation of a third as a new domestic producing organization. We are, therefore, plowing new ground. It is true, however, that some aspects of the problem might be found in *United States v. Terminal R. Assn.,* 224 U.S. 383 (1912), and *Associated Press v. United States,* 326 U.S. 1 (1945), where joint ventures with great market power were subjected to control, even prior to the amendment to § 7....

The District Court found that "Pennsalt and Olin each possessed the resources and general capability needed to build its own plant in the southeast and to compete with Hooker and [American Potash] in that market. Each could have done so if it had wished." 217 F.Supp. 110, 129.[25] In addition, the District Court found that, contrary to the position of the management of Olin and Pennsalt, "the forecasts of each company indicated that a plant could be operated with profit."

The District Court held, however, that these considerations had no controlling significance, except "as a factor in determining whether as a matter of probability both companies would have entered the market as individual competitors if Penn–Olin had not been formed. Only in this event would potential competition between the two companies have been foreclosed by the joint venture." *Id.*, at 130. In this regard the court found it "impossible to conclude that as a matter of reasonable probability both Pennsalt and Olin would have built plants in the southeast if Penn–Olin had not been created." *Ibid.* The court made no decision concerning the probability that one would have built "while the other continued to ponder." It found that this "hypothesized situation affords no basis for concluding that Penn–Olin had the effect of substantially lessening competition." *Ibid.* That would depend, the court said, "upon the competitive impact which Penn–Olin will have as against that which might have resulted if Pennsalt or Olin had been an individual market entrant." *Ibid.* The court found that this impact could not be determined from the record in this case. "Solely as a matter of theory," it said, " ... no reason exists to suppose that Penn–Olin will be a less effective competitor than Pennsalt or Olin would have been. The contrary conclusion is the more reasonable." *Id.*, at 131.

We believe that the court erred in this regard. Certainly the sole test would not be the probability that both companies would have entered the market. Nor would the consideration be limited to the probability that one entered alone. There still remained for consideration the fact that Penn–Olin eliminated the potential competition of the corporation that might have remained at the edge of the market, continually threatening to enter. Just as a merger eliminates actual competition, this joint venture may well foreclose any prospect of competition between Olin and Pennsalt in the relevant sodium chlorate market. The difference, of course, is that the merger's foreclosure is present while the joint venture's is prospective. Nevertheless, "[p]otential competition ... as a substitute for ... [actual competition] may restrain producers from overcharging those to whom they sell or underpaying those from whom they buy.... Potential competition,

---

25. The court explained further: "At the time when the joint venture was agreed upon Pennsalt and Olin each had an extensive background in sodium chlorate. Pennsalt had years of experience in manufacturing and selling it. Although Olin had never been a commercial manufacturer, it possessed a substantially developed manufacturing technique of its own, and also had available to it a process developed by Vickers–Krebs with whom it had been negotiating to construct a plant. Olin had contacts among the southeastern pulp and paper mills which Pennsalt lacked, but Pennsalt's own estimates indicate that in a reasonable time it would develop adequate business to support a plant if it decided to build. A suitable location for a plant was available to each company—Calvert City, Kentucky for Pennsalt, and the TVA area around Chattanooga, Tennessee for Olin. The financing required would not have been a problem for either company." Ibid.

insofar as the threat survives [as it would have here in the absence of Penn–Olin], may compensate in part for the imperfection characteristic of actual competition in the great majority of competitive markets." Wilcox, Competition and Monopoly in American Industry, TNEC Monograph No. 21 (1940) 7–8. Potential competition cannot be put to a subjective test. It is not "susceptible of a ready and precise answer." As we found in *United States v. El Paso Natural Gas Co.*, supra, 376 U.S. at 660, the "effect on competition ... is determined by the nature or extent of that market and by the nearness of the absorbed company to it, that company's eagerness to enter that market, its resourcefulness, and so on." The position of a company "as a competitive factor ... was not disproved by the fact that it had never sold ... there.... [I]t is irrelevant in a market ... where incremental needs are booming." The existence of an aggressive, well equipped and well financed corporation engaged in the same or related lines of commerce waiting anxiously to enter an oligopolistic market would be a substantial incentive to competition which cannot be underestimated. Witness the expansion undertaken by Hooker and American Potash as soon as they heard of the interest of Olin Mathieson and of Pennsalt in southeast territory. This same situation might well have come about had either Olin or Pennsalt entered the relevant market alone and the other remained aloof watching developments.

Here the evidence shows beyond question that the industry was rapidly expanding; the relevant southeast market was requiring about one-half of the national production of sodium chlorate; few corporations had the inclination, resources and know-how to enter this market; both parent corporations of Penn–Olin had great resources; each had long been identified with the industry, one owning valuable patent rights while the other had engaged in sodium chlorate production for years; each had other chemicals, the production of which required the use of sodium chlorate; right up to the creation of Penn–Olin, each had evidenced a long-sustained and strong interest in entering the relevant market area; each enjoyed good reputation and business connections with the major consumers of sodium chlorate in the relevant market, *i.e.*, the pulp and paper mills; and, finally, each had the know-how and the capacity to enter that market and could have done so individually at a reasonable profit. Moreover, each company had compelling reasons for entering the southeast market. Pennsalt needed to expand its sales to the southeast, which it could not do economically without a plant in that area. Olin was motivated by "the fact that [it was] already buying and using a fair quantity [of sodium chlorate] for the production of sodium chlorite and that [it was] promoting the Mathieson process of the generation of chlorine dioxide which uses sodium chlorate." Unless we are going to require subjective evidence, this array of probability certainly reaches the prima facie stage. As we have indicated, to require more would be to read the statutory requirement of reasonable probability into a requirement of certainty. This we will not do.

However, despite these strong circumstances, we are not disposed to disturb the court's finding that there was not a reasonable probability that both Pennsalt and Olin would have built a plant in the relevant market area. But we have concluded that a finding should have been made as to the reasonable probability that either one of the corporations would have entered the market by building a plant, while the other would have remained a significant potential competitor. . . .

We note generally the following criteria which the trial court might take into account in assessing the probability of a substantial lessening of competition: the number and power of the competitors in the relevant market; the background of their growth; the power of the joint venturers; the relationship of their lines of commerce; the competition existing between them and the power of each in dealing with the competitors of the other; the setting in which the joint venture was created; the reasons and necessities for its existence; the joint venture's line of commerce and the relationship thereof to that of its parents; the adaptability of its line of commerce to non-competitive practices; the potential power of the joint venture in the relevant market; an appraisal of what the competition in the relevant market would have been if one of the joint venturers had entered it alone instead of through Penn–Olin; the effect, in the event of this occurrence, of the other joint venturer's potential competition; and such other factors as might indicate potential risk to competition in the relevant market. In weighing these factors the court should remember that the mandate of the Congress is in terms of the probability of a lessening of substantial competition, not in terms of tangible present restraint. . . .

Vacated and remanded.[26]

NOTES AND QUESTIONS

1. On remand, the district court in *Penn–Olin* took additional evidence and then entered a finding that neither Pennsalt nor Olin Mathieson would have entered the southeastern market on its own. On the basis of that finding, it dismissed the government's action, 246 F.Supp. 917 (D.Del.1965). The Supreme Court affirmed *per curiam* by an equally divided court, 389 U.S. 308 (1967). Does it necessarily follow that where none of the parents of a joint venture would have entered the market on its own, the formation of the joint venture cannot violate Section 7? Even if none of the joint venture parents would have entered alone, might not the venture constitute a dangerous aggregation of market power?

2. GENERAL MOTORS CORP., 103 FTC 374 (1984). A majority of the Federal Trade Commission approved, as modified pursuant to Commission order, a joint venture between GM and Toyota to manufacture subcompact cars in the United States. Plans for the design of the car were contributed by Toyota and construction would occur at an underutilized GM plant in California. Ownership of the joint venture was on a 50–50 basis, with Toyota's representative serving as chief of management.

At the time of the venture, GM stood first in automobile sales in the U.S. market with 44% and Toyota stood fourth; in the subcompact portion of the U.S. market, Ford stood first with over 19%, Toyota second with a little over 16% and GM third with 14.4%. The duration of the joint venture was 12 years, with a maximum production per year of 250,000 cars. Distribution of the new car was to be

---

26. White, J. dissented. The dissenting opinion of Douglas, J., with whom Black, J., agreed, and the dissenting opinion of Harlan, J., are omitted.

handled entirely by GM in the United States, with Toyota and GM free to compete in all respects with the joint venture. A key provision of the arrangement related to the price charged GM by the joint venture. This was to be determined and then adjusted according to a complicated formula which took into account market prices of ten other best selling models in the U.S., with special weight given to the wholesale price of Toyota's Corolla model. In effect, the joint venture car price would rise or fall depending on price changes on the ten leading subcompact cars in the previous model year, weighting the Corolla at 30% of the total market price.

The Commission majority saw three significant procompetitive effects resulting from the joint venture: (1) it would allow introduction into the U.S. of a new small car, an addition to competition that was unlikely to be achieved by Toyota alone because Voluntary Restrictive Agreements instituted by the Japanese government put a ceiling on the number of imports per year from Japan to the U.S.; (2) the joint venture car could be produced efficiently and therefore would cost consumers less; and (3) the joint venture offered an opportunity for GM to learn about more efficient Japanese manufacturing and management techniques.

Two dissenting Commissioners concluded that these advantages could have been achieved through less restrictive alternatives than a joint venture between two of the largest automobile companies in the world, and noted that there were two important anticompetitive aspects to the joint venture. First, the dissenters argued that the pricing formula for sale of joint venture cars to GM, based heavily on the sales prices of Toyota's Corolla, would have a market-wide impact on price. Toyota might be induced to raise the price on its Corolla model, knowing this would inevitably lead to price increases on the joint venture model and give it greater profits; also, GM would be led to raise the prices on its more expensive cars to maintain margins between the joint venture subcompact and the rest of the GM line. The majority regarded these pricing effects as speculative and uncertain. Second, the dissenters were concerned that the inevitable exchange of information between GM and Toyota, in the operation of the joint venture, would lead to anticompetitive effects in other portions of the GM/Toyota line. The majority noted that the Commission staff had required modifications in the original joint venture arrangement prohibiting the exchange of information with respect to future prices, and requiring that extensive records be maintained on all other sensitive competitive information that was exchanged.

Is it troublesome that the wholesale price of the joint venture car was influenced to a great extent by the price of cars sold by Toyota? Chrysler intervened in the proceeding and argued that any pricing formula should be triggered "by a cost index which is not under Toyota's control yet is highly correlated to Toyota's costs" and urged that the inclusion of Corolla prices in the equation was grounds to strike down the entire joint venture. Do you find convincing GM's claim that the joint venture was competitively valuable as a device to help GM learn about highly successful Japanese manufacturing and marketing techniques? Would Toyota be likely to sell that kind of information and experience to a competitor like GM, without an equity arrangement that allowed it to share in profits? Is that kind of learning advantage a factor the antitrust laws should take into account?

3. Suppose two or more parents of a joint venture were about to enter a market separately, but agreed to join forces in a joint undertaking on the eve of entry. Are there any circumstances in which such a joint venture should survive a challenge under Section 7? Suppose the parents are already in the market and then join forces to market a new improved or modified product to compete with products sold by each of the parents. Was not that the situation with respect to G.M. and Toyota? Did the Commission correctly measure the procompetitive and anticompetitive aspects of that deal?

4. Should joint research and joint exploration ventures be treated differently than joint sales agencies with respect to legality under Section 7? Why? In this connection, see Chapter 5, pp. 402–403 supra; Pitofsky, A Framework for Antitrust Analysis of Joint Ventures, 74 Geo.L.J. 1605 (1986).

5. Penn–Olin recognized that a joint venture that precludes future market entry can be the basis of a violation of Section 7. It examined only in a very general way what the necessary elements would be to prove future entry. Subsequent case law indicates that the essential elements are capacity, interest, and economic incentive. *See, e.g., Yamaha Motor Co. v. FTC*, 657 F.2d 971 (8th Cir.1981). A determination of what a company would have done had it not entered the joint venture—would it have proceeded alone or jointly in a less anticompetitive partnership—has proven to be an extremely difficult piece of analysis. See Brodley, Potential Competition Mergers: A Structural Synthesis, 87 Yale L.J. 1 (1977). Even if entry by one or both members of a joint venture is likely, should not the government still have to prove a probable substantial lessening of competition as a result of the venture? How would you make that showing?

6. In 1986, Professor Pitofsky commented on developments in the law since the Penn–Olin case:

> The likelihood of a successful antitrust challenge in the "one-in, one-out" situation has declined radically in the 20 years since Penn–Olin was decided because of the array of conditions that the courts require to be satisfied before an "in the wings" competitive effect can be shown. Assuming it is clear that the first parent was either in the market or had the capacity, interest, and economic incentive to enter, the plaintiff must further show the following: (1) the market in which the joint venture would operate is not competitive, so that an "in the wings" entrant could have some significant effects on levels of competition (generally requiring proof of high levels of concentration and of substantial barriers to entry); (2) other competitors in the market served by the joint venture would have perceived the nonentering parent as a likely potential entrant; (3) the nonentering parent was one of a few (probably two or three) most likely potential entrants so that the loss of in the wings potential competition was a substantial loss; and (4) the in the wings entrant would have a substantial likely procompetitive effect on the market. It is possible to challenge a joint venture on the basis of loss of potential competition, but the plaintiff's burden is a formidable one. Where it is clear that only one parent was in the market or would have entered and that substantial efficiencies are really generated by the joint arrangement, it would be an exceptional case in which the joint venture could be struck down because of the loss of potential competition. As a result, the central question in joint venture analysis has become whether both parents were in the market or about to enter. Without that preliminary finding, the likelihood that a violation will be found on the basis of a loss of potential competition declines sharply.[27]

PROBLEM 24

THE BZT THREE–WAY VENTURE

General Circuits Co. and Electro, Inc. have dominated the United States electrical industry for decades. Each has been independently working on the

---

27. Pitofsky, A Framework for Antitrust Analysis of Joint Ventures, 74 Geo.L.J. 1605, 1609–10 (1986).

development of a new kind of circuit breaker for high voltage power. This device would use a vacuum to interrupt electric power instead of conventional systems based on use of oil, compressed air, or inert gas. A vacuum circuit breaker would produce extremely rapid cut-off of power, have less risk of fire, and dramatically increase the durability of working parts. Both General Circuits and Electro have perfected small-sized vacuum circuit breakers, but neither has been able to solve a number of difficult problems in applying that technology to high voltages. The same is true for Brits, Ltd., a British company, ZAF, a German company, and Toyo, Inc., a Japanese company, all of which manufacture circuit breakers and are the world's only other significant electrical concerns. If a vacuum circuit breaker for high voltage power is developed, the market would be very sizeable.

Breakers, Inc., a United States company, is a very small but highly successful, aggressive, technology-oriented firm in the electrical industry. Rather than offering a full range of electrical products, Breakers sells only a few products which it can produce at lower prices or which are technologically superior to those produced by the industry giants. Breakers is the only other United States manufacturer of circuit breakers using conventional technology and is interested in producing high voltage vacuum circuit breakers.

Breakers is about to enter a "research joint venture" with ZAF and Toyo. BZT, Inc. will be formed, in a three-way venture, to conduct research on and develop a high voltage vacuum circuit breaker. The terms of the joint venture provide that: (1) each of the three venturers will receive equal access to the research; (2) profits will be shared equally; (3) sale of high voltage vacuum circuit breakers in the United States will be made only by Breakers; (4) sale of high voltage vacuum breakers in Germany will be made only by ZAF and in Japan only by Toyo; and (5) all other world-wide sales of high voltage vacuum breakers will be made only by BZT.

Breakers' president has explained the venture as follows:

> Although ZAF and Toyo have been working on similar ideas, we are well ahead of them. Indeed, in the absence of the joint venture, it is almost certain that Toyo would have given up on its vacuum circuit breaker research and possible that ZAF also would have done so. But the resource supplementation (particularly by ZAF) and the manufacturing and distribution skills of Toyo will cut several years off the time it would otherwise take us to get the high voltage vacuum breakers to the market. ZAF and Toyo now have about 4% of the United States market for conventional circuit breakers (Breakers has 3%) and have competition only from General Circuits and Electro in their own countries. This will be a wonderful relationship for all concerned. Our attorneys have advised that "any antitrust challenge to the venture stands near zero chance of success."

Do you agree with the legal advice provided by Breakers' attorneys? If you have problems, can you suggest more viable alternatives?

INTRODUCTION TO QUESTIONS RELATING TO CONGLOMERATE MERGERS

Section 7 covers some mergers that do not involve firms in either a horizontal or vertical relationship. If the firms don't compete, and don't buy or sell to each other, what is the problem?

The legislative history of Section 7 establishes that Congress intended to cover "conglomerate" mergers as well as horizontal and vertical mergers, but said almost nothing about possible theories. Several have been developed by the courts. We saw in *Penn-Olin,* a joint venture case but in many ways related to conglomerate theory, that a firm that enters a market by acquisition is no longer "in the wings" and threatening to enter, and the elimination of that perceived threat may substantially lessen competition by relieving incumbents of the need to keep prices low or the quality of service high to deter entry. The theory can easily be applied to mergers as well as joint ventures. A related but more straightforward theory concerns the firm that enters the market by acquisition, but was reasonably likely to enter by internal expansion (so called "actual potential entry"), or by acquisition of a much smaller firm and expansion from the smaller base (so called "toe hold" acquisition)—with the result that the path it did take may substantially lessen competition. Beyond these "potential competition" theories, questions have been raised as a result of "bigness" and "diversification"—how might the concentration of industrial assets by merger produce anticompetitive effects (or even political or social effects) that are undesirable and deserve to be blocked.

One such theory is that a large firm with "deep pockets" can focus its aggressive actions on a smaller local rival and put that rival out of business, or persuade the rival to be a docile follower, without any danger of retaliation by the smaller rival against the extensive resources of the larger corporation. An increase in size can also produce "opportunities for self-sufficiency." See G Stocking, Comment on C. Edwards "Conglomerate Bigness as a Source of Power" Business Concentration and Price Policy, 353–57 (1957). The large firm can effectively bargain with its suppliers and customers by threatening to integrate into their line of business. Also, large diversified conglomerate firms that meet each other in many product and geographic markets may engage in "mutual forbearance"—that is one conglomerate will not compete as aggressively in a particular market for fear that a rival conglomerate will respond aggressively in a different market. Some studies suggest that prices and profits are higher where conglomerate firms have high levels of multimarket contacts. See Scott, Multimarket Contact and Economic Performance, 64 Rev. Econ. Stat. 368–75 (1982) and Feinberg, "Sales at Risk": A Test of the Mutual Forbearance Theory of Conglomerate Behavior, 58 J. Bus. 225–41 (1985). Lastly, it has been suggested that heavy advertising is a characteristic marketing approach of very large firms, and that advertising expenditures raise barriers to entry by new but smaller competitors.

Beyond traditional competition theory, it has been suggested that there are some political consequences to high levels of concentration of market power. For example, it has been suggested that firms with scores of production facilities and distributors in different states and congressional districts will have more clout in the federal legislature than smaller rivals. One response might be that associations of small businesses (gasoline dealers, funeral directors, even doctors and lawyers) have demonstrated time and again their ability to influence the political process. Another "political" theory, less potent in recent years, is that firms may become "too big to fail"—that is the consequences on employees, suppliers and the economy in general may be so disastrous that federal or state legislatures will bail the firm out rather than allow it to proceed into bankruptcy. Bail outs have occurred infrequently in recent years.

Balanced against these concerns is the fact that many conglomerate mergers are extremely efficient, placing resources in the hands of experienced and capable management or integrating related economic functions in a single corporate institution. How should claims of efficiency be treated in the context of conglomerate mergers? Recall the 1997 amendments to the FTC horizontal merger guidelines, expressly providing that the government "will not challenge a merger if efficiencies are of a character and magnitude such that the merger is not likely to be anticompetitive" . . . supra, at 1056. Is there any reason to treat efficiencies in the conglomerate context any different than in the horizontal merger context?

We begin with the Supreme Court's 1967 decision in *Procter & Gamble,* addressing many of the issues that have arisen in connection with conglomerate acquisitions.

Federal Trade Commission v. Procter & Gamble Co.

Supreme Court of the United States, 1967.
386 U.S. 568, 87 S.Ct. 1224, 18 L.Ed.2d 303.

■ DOUGLAS, J. This is a proceeding initiated by the Federal Trade Commission charging that respondent, Procter & Gamble Co., had acquired the assets of Clorox Chemical Co. in violation of § 7 of the Clayton Act. . . . The charge was that Procter's acquisition of Clorox may substantially lessen competition or tend to create a monopoly in the production and sale of household liquid bleaches.

. . .

As indicated by the Commission in its painstaking and illuminating report, it does not particularly aid analysis to talk of this merger in conventional terms, namely, horizontal or vertical or conglomerate. This merger may most appropriately be described as a "product-extension merger," as the Commission stated. The facts are not disputed, and a summary will demonstrate the correctness of the Commission's decision.

At the time of the merger, Clorox was the leading manufacturer in the heavily concentrated household liquid bleach industry. It is agreed that household liquid bleach is the relevant line of commerce. The product is used in the home as a germicide and disinfectant, and, more importantly, as a whitening agent in washing clothes and fabrics. It is a distinctive product with no close substitutes. Liquid bleach is a low-price, high-turnover consumer product sold mainly through grocery stores and supermarkets. The relevant geographical market is the Nation and a series of regional markets. Because of high shipping costs and low sales price, it is not feasible to ship the product more than 300 miles from its point of manufacture. Most manufacturers are limited to competition within a single region since they have but one plant. Clorox is the only firm selling nationally; it has 13 plants distributed throughout the Nation. Purex, Clorox's closest competitor in size, does not distribute its bleach in the northeast or middle-Atlantic States; in 1957, Purex's bleach was available in less than 50% of the national market.

At the time of the acquisition, Clorox was the leading manufacturer of household liquid bleach, with 48.8% of the national sales—annual sales of slightly less than $40,000,000. Its market share had been steadily increasing for the five years prior to the merger. Its nearest rival was Purex, which manufactures a number of products other than household liquid bleaches, including abrasive cleaners, toilet soap, and detergents. Purex accounted for 15.7% of the household liquid bleach market. The industry is highly concentrated; in 1957, Clorox and Purex accounted for almost 65% of the Nation's household liquid bleach sales, and, together with four other firms, for almost 80%. The remaining 20% was divided among over 200 small producers. Clorox had total assets of $12,000,000; only eight producers had assets in excess of $1,000,000 and very few had assets of more than $75,000.

In light of the territorial limitations on distribution, national figures do not give an accurate picture of Clorox's dominance in the various regions. Thus, Clorox's seven principal competitors did no business in New England, the mid-Atlantic States, or metropolitan New York. Clorox's share of the sales in those areas was 56%, 72%, and 64% respectively. Even in regions where its principal competitors were active, Clorox maintained a dominant position. Except in metropolitan Chicago and the west-central States Clorox accounted for at least 39%, and often a much higher percentage, of liquid bleach sales.

Since all liquid bleach is chemically identical, advertising and sales promotion is vital. In 1957 Clorox spent almost $3,700,000 on advertising, imprinting the value of its bleach in the mind of the consumer. In addition, it spent $1,700,000 for other promotional activities. The Commission found that these heavy expenditures went far to explain why Clorox maintained so high a market share despite the fact that its brand, though chemically indistinguishable from rival brands, retailed for a price equal to or, in many instances, higher than its competitors.

Procter is a large, diversified manufacturer of low-price, high-turnover household products sold through grocery, drug, and department stores. Prior to its acquisition of Clorox, it did not produce household liquid bleach. Its 1957 sales were in excess of $1,100,000,000 from which it realized profits of more than $67,000,000; its assets were over $500,000,000. Procter has been marked by rapid growth and diversification. It has successfully developed and introduced a number of new products. Its primary activity is in the general area of soaps, detergents, and cleansers; in 1957, of total domestic sales, more than one-half (over $500,000,000) were in this field. Procter was the dominant factor in this area. It accounted for 54.4% of all packaged detergent sales. The industry is heavily concentrated—Procter and its nearest competitors, Colgate–Palmolive and Lever Brothers, account for 80% of the market.

In the marketing of soaps, detergents, and cleansers, as in the marketing of household liquid bleach, advertising and sales promotion are vital. In 1957, Procter was the Nation's largest advertiser, spending more than $80,000,000 on advertising and an additional $47,000,000 on sales promotion. Due to its tremendous volume, Procter receives substantial discounts from the media. As a multi-product producer Procter enjoys substantial advantages in advertising and sales promotion. Thus, it can and does feature several products in its promotions, reducing the printing, mailing, and other costs for each product. It also purchases network programs on behalf of several products, enabling it to give each product network exposure at a fraction of the cost per product that a firm with only one product to advertise would incur.

Prior to the acquisition, Procter was in the course of diversifying into product lines related to its basic detergent-soap-cleanser business. Liquid bleach was a distinct possibility since packaged detergents–Procter's primary product line—and liquid bleach are used complementarily in washing clothes and fabrics, and in general household clothing. . . .

. . .

The decision to acquire Clorox was the result of a study conducted by Procter's promotion department designed to determine the advisability of entering the liquid bleach industry. The initial report noted the ascendancy of liquid bleach in the large and expanding household bleach market, and recommended that Procter purchase Clorox rather than enter independently. Since a large investment would be needed to obtain a satisfactory market share, acquisition of the industry's leading firm was attractive. "Taking over the Clorox business ... could be a way of achieving a dominant position in the liquid bleach market quickly, which would pay out reasonably well." The initial report predicted that Procter's "sales, distribution and manufacturing setup" could increase Clorox's share of the markets in areas where it was low. The final report confirmed the conclusions of the initial report and emphasized that Procter could make more effective use of Clorox's advertising budget and that the merger would facilitate advertising economies. A few months later, Procter acquired the assets of Clorox in the name of a wholly owned subsidiary, the Clorox Company, in exchange for Procter stock.

... The Commission found that the substitution of Procter with its huge assets and advertising advantages for the already dominant Clorox would dissuade new entrants and discourage active competition from the firms already in the industry due to fear of retaliation by Procter. The Commission thought it relevant that retailers might be induced to give Clorox preferred shelf space since it would be manufactured by Procter, which also produced a number of other products marketed by the retailers. There was also the danger that Procter might underprice Clorox in order to drive out competition, and subsidize the underpricing with revenue from other products. The Commission carefully reviewed the effect of the acquisition on the structure of the industry, noting that "the practical tendency of the ... merger ... is to transform the liquid bleach industry into an arena of big business competition only, with the few small firms falling by the wayside, unable to compete with their giant rivals." Further, the merger would seriously diminish potential competition by eliminating Procter as a potential entrant into the industry. Prior to the merger, the Commission found that Procter was the most likely prospective entrant, and absent the merger would have remained on the periphery, restraining Clorox from exercising its market power. If Procter had actually entered, Clorox's dominant position would have been eroded and the concentration of the industry reduced. The Commission stated that it had not placed reliance on post-acquisition evidence in holding the merger unlawful.

. . .

The anticompetitive effects with which this product-extension merger is fraught can easily be seen: (1) the substitution of the powerful acquiring firm for the smaller, but already dominant, firm may substantially reduce the competitive structure of the industry by raising entry barriers, and by dissuading the smaller firms from aggressively competing; (2) the acquisition eliminates the potential competition of the acquiring firm.

The liquid bleach industry was already oligopolistic before the acquisition, and price competition was certainly not as vigorous as it would have been if the industry were competitive. Clorox enjoyed a dominant position nationally, and its position approached monopoly proportions in certain areas. The existence of some 200 fringe firms certainly does not belie that fact. Nor does the fact, relied upon by the court below, that after the merger, producers other than Clorox "were selling more bleach for more money than ever before." 358 F.2d at 80. In the same period, Clorox increased its share from 48.8% to 52%. The interjection of Procter into the market considerably changed the situation. There is every reason to assume that the smaller firms would become more cautious in competing due to their fear of retaliation by Procter. It is probable that Procter would become the price leader and that oligopoly would become more rigid.

The acquisition may also have the tendency of raising the barriers to new entry. The major competitive weapon in the successful marketing of bleach is advertising. Clorox was limited in this area by its relatively small budget and its inability to obtain substantial discounts. By contrast, Procter's budget was much larger; and, although it would not devote its entire budget to advertising Clorox, it could divert a large portion to meet the short-term threat of a new entrant. Procter would be able to use its volume discounts to advantage in advertising Clorox. Thus, a new entrant would be much more reluctant to face the giant Procter than it would have been to face the smaller Clorox.[28]

28. The barriers to entry have been raised both for entry by new firms and for entry into new geographical markets by established firms. The latter aspect is demonstrated by Purex's lesson in Erie, Pennsylvania. In October 1957, Purex selected Erie, Pennsylvania—where it had not sold previously—as an area in which to test the salability, under competitive conditions, of a new bleach. The leading brands in Erie were Clorox, with 52%, and the "101" brand, sold by Gardner Manufacturing Company, with 29% of the market. Purex launched an advertising and promotional campaign to obtain a broad distribution in a short time, and, in five months captured 33% of the Erie market.

Clorox's share dropped to 35% and 101's to 17%. Clorox responded by offering its bleach at reduced prices, and then added an offer of a $1–value ironing board cover for 50 cents with each purchase of Clorox at the reduced price. It also increased its advertising with television spots. The result was to restore Clorox's lost market share and, indeed, to increase it slightly. Purex's share fell to 7%.

Since the merger Purex has acquired the fourth largest producer of bleach, John Paul Products Company, which owned and marketed "Fleecy White" brand in geographic markets which Purex was anxious to enter. One of the reasons for this acquisition, according to Purex's president, was that:

Possible economies cannot be used as a defense to illegality. Congress was aware that some mergers which lessen competition may also result in economies but it struck the balance in favor of protecting competition. *See Brown Shoe Co. v. United States*, 370 U.S. at 344.

The Commission also found that the acquisition of Clorox by Procter eliminated Procter as a potential competitor. The Court of Appeals declared that this finding was not supported by evidence because there was no evidence that Procter's management had ever intended to enter the industry independently and that Procter had never attempted to enter. The evidence, however, clearly shows that Procter was the most likely entrant. Procter had recently launched a new abrasive cleaner in an industry similar to the liquid bleach industry, and had wrested leadership from a brand that had enjoyed even a larger market share than had Clorox. Procter was engaged in a vigorous program of diversifying into product lines closely related to its basic products. Liquid bleach was a natural avenue of diversification since it is complementary to Procter's products, is sold to the same customers through the same channels, and is advertised and merchandised in the same manner. Procter had substantial advantages in advertising and sales promotions, which, as we have seen, are vital to the success of liquid bleach. No manufacturer had a patent on the product or its manufacture, necessary information relating to manufacturing methods and processes was readily available, there was no shortage of raw material, and the machinery and equipment required for a plant of efficient capacity were available at reasonable cost. Procter's management was experienced in producing and marketing goods similar to liquid bleach. Procter had considered the possibility of independently entering but decided against it because the acquisition of Clorox would enable Procter to capture a more commanding share of the market.

It is clear that the existence of Procter at the edge of the industry exerted considerable influence on the market. First, the market behavior of the liquid bleach industry was influenced by each firm's predictions of the market behavior of its competitors, actual and potential. Second, the barriers to entry by a firm of Procter's size and with its advantages were not significant. There is no indication that the barriers were so high that the price Procter would have to charge would be above the price that would maximize the profits of the existing firms. Third, the number of potential entrants was not so large that the elimination of one would be insignificant. Few firms would have the temerity to challenge a firm as solidly entrenched as Clorox. Fourth, Procter was found by the Commission to be the most likely entrant. These findings of the Commission were amply supported by the evidence.

"Purex had been unsuccessful in expanding its market position geographically on Purex liquid bleach. The economics of the bleach business, and the strong competitive factors as illustrated by our experience in Erie, Pennsylvania, make it impossible, in our judgment for us to expand our market on liquid bleach."

■ STEWART, J., and FORTAS, J., took no part in the consideration or decision of this case.

■ HARLAN, J., concurring. I agree that the Commission's order should be sustained, but I do not share the majority opinion's view that a mere "summary will demonstrate the correctness of the Commission's decision" nor that "[t]he anticompetitive effects with which this product-extension merger is fraught can easily be seen." I consider the case difficult within its own four corners, and beyond that, its portents for future administrative and judicial application of § 7 of the Clayton Act to this kind of merger important and far reaching. . . .

At the outset, it seems to me that there is a serious question whether the state of our economic knowledge is sufficiently advanced to enable a sure-footed administrative or judicial determination to be made a priori of substantial anticompetitive effect in mergers of this kind. It is clear enough that Congress desired that conglomerate and product-extension mergers be brought under § 7 scrutiny, but well versed economists have argued that such scrutiny can never lead to a valid finding of illegality.

> "Where a business concern buys out a firm producing . . . [a product] which is neither competing, nor a raw material for its own product . . . there is no competition between them to be extinguished, nor the possibility of fewer alternatives for any customer or supplier anywhere. . . . Perhaps Congress intended to stop conglomerate mergers but their act does not." Adelman, quoted in Blair, supra. . . .

Lending strength to this position is the fact that such mergers do provide significant economic benefits which argue against excessive controls being imposed on them. The ability to merge brings large firms into the market for capital assets and encourages economic development by holding out the incentive of easy and profitable liquidation to others. Here, for example, the owners of Clorox who had built the business, were able to liquify their capital on profitable terms without dismantling the enterprise they had created. Also merger allows an active management to move rapidly into new markets bringing with its intervention competitive stimulation and innovation. It permits a large corporation to protect its shareholders from business fluctuation through diversification, and may facilitate the introduction of capital resources, allowing significant economies of scale, into a stagnating market.

At the other end of the spectrum, it has been argued that the entry of a large conglomerate enterprise may have a destructive effect on competition in any market. Edwards, Conglomerate Bigness as a Source of Power, in National Bureau of Economic Research, Business Concentration and Price Policy 331. . . . [W]hile fully agreeing that mergers of this kind are not to be regarded as something entirely set apart from scrutiny under § 7, I am of the view that when this Court does undertake to establish the standards for judging their legality, it should proceed with utmost circumspection. Meanwhile with this case before us, I cannot escape the necessity of venturing my own views as to some of the governing standards. . . .

[T]he Commission noted that dependence on post-merger evidence would allow controls to be evaded by the dissimulation of market power during the period of observation. For example, Procter had been aware of the § 7 challenge almost from the date of the merger, and it would be unrealistic, so reasoned the Commission, to assume that market power would be used adversely to competition during the pendency of the proceeding.

The Commission also emphasized the difficulty of unscrambling a completed merger, and the need for businessmen to be able to make at least some predictions as to the legality of their actions when formulating future market plans. Finally, the Commission pointed to the strain which would be placed upon its limited enforcement resources by a requirement to assemble large amounts of post-merger data.

The Sixth Circuit was in disagreement with the ... Commission's view. It held that "[a]ny relevant evidence must be considered in a Section 7 case.... The extent to which inquiry may be made into post-merger conditions may well depend on the facts of the case and where the evidence is obtained it should not be ignored." 358 F.2d at p. 83. The court characterized as "pure conjecture" the finding that Procter's behavior might have been influenced by the pendency of the proceeding.

If § 7 is to serve the purposes Congress intended for it, we must, I think, stand with the Commission on this issue. Only by focusing on market structure can we begin to formulate standards which will allow the responsible agencies to give proper consideration to such mergers and allow businessmen to plan their actions with a fair degree of certainty.... The value of post-merger evidence seems more than offset by the difficulties encountered in obtaining it. And the post-merger evidence before us in this proceeding is at best inconclusive.

Deciding that § 7 inquiry in conglomerate or product-extension merger cases should be directed toward reasonably probable changes in market structure does not, however, decide how that inquiry should be narrowed and focused. The Commission and the Court isolate two separate structural elements, the degree of concentration in the existing market and the "condition of entry." The interplay of these two factors is said to determine the existence and extent of market power, since the "condition of entry" determines the limits potential competition places on the existing market. It must be noted, however, that economic theory teaches that potential competition will have no effect on the market behavior of existing firms unless present market power is sufficient to drive the market price to the point where entry would become a real possibility. So long as existing competition is sufficient to keep the market price below that point, potential competition is of marginal significance as a market regulator. Thus in a conglomerate or product-extension case, where the effects on market structure which are easiest to discover are generally effects on the "condition of entry," an understanding of the workings of the premerger market cannot be ignored, and, indeed, is critical to a determination whether the visible effects on "condition of entry" have any competitive significance.

The Commission pinned its analysis of the premerger market exclusively on its concentration, the large market share enjoyed by the leading firms. In so doing the Commission was following the path taken by this Court in judging more conventional merger cases, *e.g., United States v. Philadelphia Nat'l Bank*, supra, and taking the position favored by the great weight of economic authority. *See, e.g.*, Bain, Industrial Organization. The Sixth Circuit discounted the Commission's analysis because of the presence of some 200 small competitors in the market. The Court bases its agreement with the Commission and its rejection of the Court of Appeals' position on Clorox's alleged domination of the market. But domination is an elusive term, for dominance in terms of percentage of sales is not the equivalent of dominance in terms of control over price or other aspects of market behavior. Just as the total number of sellers in the market is not determinative of its operation, the percentage of sales made by any group of sellers is similarly not conclusive. The determinative issue is, instead, how the sellers interact and establish the pattern of market behavior. The significance of concentration analysis is that it allows measurement of one easily determined variable to serve as an opening key to the pattern of market behavior.

I think that the Commission, on this record, was entitled to regard the market as "oligopolistic" and that it could properly ignore the impact of the smaller firms. I hasten to add, however, that there are significant "economic dissents" from oligopoly analysis in general and stronger arguments that if its principles are justified in some cases, they are not justified in all cases.... Brodley, supra. In adjudicating § 7 questions in a conglomerate or product-extension merger context where the pattern of behavior in the existing market is apt to be crucial, I would, therefore, allow the introduction by a defendant of evidence designed to show that the actual operation of the market did not accord with oligopoly theory, or whatever other theory the Commission desires to apply. In other words, I believe that defendants in § 7 proceedings are entitled, in the case of conglomerate or product-extension mergers, to build their own economic case for the proposition that the merger will not substantially impair competition.

For example, had Procter desired to go beyond demonstrating the mere presence of small competitors and attempted to show that the prices of unadvertised bleaches which were cost-determined set an effective ceiling on market price through the mechanism of an acceptable differential, I think that the Commission would have been obliged to receive and evaluate the proof. But to challenge effectively the presumption which the Commission is entitled to draw from general economic theory, a defendant must present, in my opinion, not only contradictory facts but a more cogent explanation of the pattern of market behavior.

If the proof as a whole establishes that pricing power may be exercised by a firm or firms in the market—that prices may be raised in the long run over competitive prices—then the Commission may legitimately focus on the role of potential competition and the "condition of entry." See Bain, Barriers to New Competition 5, 27. In so doing, however, a new difficulty is encountered. The threat of potential competition merely affects the range over which price power extends. Potential competition does not compel more vigorous striving in the market, nor advance any other social goal which Congress might be said to have favored in passing § 7.[29] Thus it may legitimately be questioned whether even a substantial increase in entry barriers creates a substantial lessening of competition or tendency to monopoly as required by § 7.

Two justifications for the use of entry barriers as a determinant under § 7 can be given. The first is that an increased range over which pricing power may be exercised is contrary to the mandate of § 7 because Congress' use of the word "competition" was a shorthand for the invocation of the benefits of a competitive market, one of which is a price close to average cost. Such an approach leads also to the conclusion that economic efficiencies produced by the merger must be weighed against anticompetitive consequences in the final determination whether the net effect on competition is substantially adverse. See Bork & Bowman, The Crisis in Antitrust, 65 Col.L.Rev. 363. The second justification is found in the tendency to monopoly clause of § 7. Certainly the clearest evil of monopoly is the excessive power the monopolist has over price. Since "antitrust operates to forestall concentrations of economic power which, if allowed to develop unhindered, would call for much more intrusive government supervision of the economy," Blake & Jones, In Defense of Antitrust, 65 Col.L.Rev. 377, 383, increased power over price should be attackable under § 7. Cf. S.Rep. No. 1775, 81st Cong., 2d Sess., 4–5. For these reasons I conclude that the Commission may properly find a conglomerate or product-extension merger illegal under § 7 because it substantially increases pricing power in the relevant market.

. . .

To summarize then, four important guides to the adjudication of conglomerate or product-extension mergers under § 7 seem to come forward. First, the decision can rest on analysis of market structure without resort to evidence of post-merger anticompetitive behavior. Second, the operation of the premerger market must be understood as the foundation of successful analysis. The responsible agency may presume that the market operates in accord with generally accepted principles of economic theory, but the presumption must be open to the challenge of alternative operational formulations. Third, if it is reasonably probable that there will be a change in market structure which will allow the exercise of substantially greater market power, then a *prima facie* case has been made out under § 7. Fourth, where the case against the merger rests on the probability of increased market power, the merging companies may attempt to

---

29. Potential entry does not keep "a large number of small competitors in business," United States v. Von's Grocery Co., 384 U.S. 270, 275, even if that goal could be considered desirable. In fact, by placing a ceiling market price it may serve to drive out small competitors who may be relatively inefficient producers. Potential entry does not control the market share of dominant firms or prevent them from expanding their power to force others to accede to their practices.

prove that there are countervailing economies reasonably probable which should be weighed against the adverse effects.

The Commission's decision did, I think, conform to this analysis. . . . To hold the merger unlawful, the Commission relied on five factors which taken together convinced it that "substantial" anticompetitive conse-quences could be expected. A "substantial" impact was said to be "signifi-cant and real, and discernible not merely to theorists or scholars but to practical hard-headed businessmen." The relevant factors were (1) the excessive concentration in the industry at the time of the merger and the commanding market position of Clorox, (2) the relative disparity in size and strength as between Procter and the firms in the liquid bleach industry, (3) the position of Procter in other markets, (4) the elimination of Procter as a potential competitor, and (5) the nature of the "economies" expected from the merger. The net of these factors was to establish a substantial effect on the market structure variable involved, condition of entry.

. . .

I do not think . . . that on the record presented Procter has shown any true efficiencies in advertising. Procter has merely shown that it is able to command equivalent resources at a lower dollar cost than other bleach producers. No peculiarly efficient marketing techniques have been demon-strated, nor does the record show that a smaller net advertising expendi-ture could be expected. Economies cannot be premised solely on dollar figures, lest accounting controversies dominate § 7 proceedings. Economies employed in defense of a merger must be shown in what economists label "real" terms, that is in terms of resources applied to the accomplishment of the objective. For this reason, the Commission, I think, was justified in discounting Procter's efficiency defense. . . .

NOTES AND QUESTIONS

1. In *Procter & Gamble*, the majority relied in part on a finding that the combined firm could drive smaller liquid bleach rivals out of the market, or render those firms more cautious because of fear of retaliation through predatory or otherwise low pricing. But a strategy of predation or even aggressively low pricing does not follow inevitably from the entry by merger of a large firm into a market populated by smaller rivals. Was there evidence cited by the majority or concurring justice that Procter would follow a predatory strategy or was it simply assumed from the size of the combined parties?

2. A second theory in *Procter* was that the merger raised barriers to entry by making available to the combined company volume discounts in advertising previ-ously only available to Procter with its enormous advertising budget. Suppose the efficiencies did not relate to advertising—for, example, suppose the merger lowered distribution costs for two non-competing products sold to the same outlets. Would that be a reason for blocking the merger? In effect, would that amount to holding efficiencies against the legality of the transaction? Is it likely that the Department of Justice or the FTC would challenge a conglomerate merger on any such theory,

given the amendments in 1997 which clarify and allow more scope to efficiencies claims?

3. It has been suggested that advertising efficiencies be treated differently from other forms of efficiencies because they are characteristically a marketing tool of very large companies, quantity discounts are not available to smaller firms, and high levels of advertising appear to be associated systematically with high levels of concentration and high barriers to entry. See Turner, Advertising and Competition, speech delivered in Washington, D.C. before the briefing Conference on Federal Controls of Advertising and Promotion (June 2, 1966). Even severe critics of advertising acknowledge that it can serve a pro-competitive purpose by making potential customers aware of new, improved or superior products. On the other hand, extremely heavy advertising may create consumer preferences that cannot be broken down except by comparable counter-advertising, but is often wasteful in a sense that it does not provide information that consumers can use to make sensible choices between products. Does hostility to advertising makes sense in competitive terms, or is it just an anti-Madison Avenue reaction?

4. In *Procter*, and more clearly in the *Falstaff* opinion summarized immediately following, we begin to see a difference between the two forms of lessening of potential competition. If the anticompetitive effect of the merger is the elimination of a perceived potential entrant ("in the wings"), the analysis focuses on the question of whether that elimination would make a competitive difference. If the theory is that the consequence of the merger is that the acquiring firm would have entered the market if the acquisition were blocked ("actual potential entry") and by that entry improved competition, that could be seen as an argument that competition was not necessarily lessened, but rather that it was not improved as much as it would have been through entry by internal expansion. Can you argue that a failure to improve competition is a violation of Section 7? Consider whether that question is the reason why the Supreme Court in *Falstaff* and elsewhere has left open the question of whether the elimination of actual potential entry is a legitimate theory under Section 7.

UNITED STATES V. FALSTAFF BREWING CORP., 410 U.S. 526, 93 S.Ct. 1096, 35 L.Ed.2d 475 (1973). The government charged that the 1965 acquisition of Narragansett Brewing Co. by Falstaff Brewing Corp. violated Section 7. The district court held that there was no violation. The Supreme Court reversed and remanded the proceeding for further consideration by the district court.

The parties stipulated that the relevant product market was the production and sale of beer, and that the relevant geographic market was the six New England states. Within this market, the eight largest sellers accounted for 81.2% of sales in 1965, up from 74% in 1960; the four largest accounted for 61.3% in 1965, up from 50% in 1960; Narragansett, the largest seller in 1965, accounted for approximately 20% of sales. The number of brewers operating plants in New England declined from 11 in 1957 to 6 in 1964.

Falstaff was the fourth largest producer of beer in the United States with 5.9% of national production. However, Falstaff did not distribute beer nationally, and, of the nation's ten largest brewers, Falstaff was the largest of three that did not sell beer in New England. In relation to the New England market, Falstaff's sales in western Ohio and in Washington, D.C., were the closest of these three firms.

Falstaff had been interested in entering the New England market for some time, had made public statements to that effect, and had commissioned studies on the subject. "National brewers possess competitive advantages since they are able to advertise on a nationwide basis, their beers have greater prestige than regional or local beers, and they are less affected by the weather or labor problems in a particular region." Thus, Falstaff wished to move from regional to national status. A 1958 study recommended entry de novo into the New England market rather than entry by acquisition. However, Falstaff decided to enter by acquisition because such an approach would be more profitable and would provide an existing distributorship arrangement which Falstaff considered essential to successful entry. After negotiations with other firms, the acquisition of Narragansett was consummated. Falstaff's management maintained that they would not enter the New England market by any means other than the acquisition of Narragansett. The government contended that entry by Falstaff would be both feasible and profitable if Falstaff entered de novo or made a "toehold acquisition" of one of the small brewers in the New England market.

The district court accepted the position of Falstaff and held that, since Falstaff would not have entered the New England market by any means other than the acquisition of Narragansett, such acquisition did not have an anticompetitive effect. Competition in the market was found to be vigorous at the time of the acquisition and not to have diminished subsequent to the acquisition. Narragansett's market share dropped from 21.5% in 1964 to 15.5% in 1969, while the shares of the two leading national brewers increased from 16.5% to 35.8%.

The Supreme Court reversed, writing four separate opinions. The opinion of the Court, by Justice White, in which Chief Justice Burger and Justice Blackmun concurred in full, and Justice Douglas concurred in part, held that the district court erred in assuming "that because Falstaff, as a matter of fact, would never have entered the market de novo, it could in no sense be considered a potential competitor. More specifically, the district court failed to give separate consideration to whether Falstaff was a potential competitor in the sense that it was so positioned on the edge of the market that it exerted beneficial influence on competitive conditions in that market." The Court continued:

> The specific question with respect to this phase of the case is not what Falstaff's internal company decisions were but whether, given its financial capabilities and conditions in the New England market, it would be reasonable to consider it a potential entrant into that market. Surely, it could not be said on this record that Falstaff's general interest in the New England market was unknown; and if it would appear to rational beer merchants in New England that Falstaff might well build a new brewery to supply the northeastern market then its entry by merger becomes suspect under § 7. The District Court should therefore have appraised the economic facts about Falstaff and the New England market in order to determine whether in any realistic sense Falstaff could be said to be a potential competitor on the fringe of the market with likely influence on existing competition. This does not mean that the testimony of company officials about actual intentions of the company is irrelevant or is to be looked upon with suspicion; but it does mean that theirs is not necessarily the last word in arriving at a conclusion about how Falstaff should be considered in terms of its status as a potential entrant into the market in issue.

> Since it appears that the District Court entertained too narrow a view of Falstaff as a potential competitor and since it appears that the District

Court's conclusion that the merger posed no probable threat to competition followed automatically from the finding that Falstaff had no intent to enter de novo, we remand this case for the District Court to make the proper assessment of Falstaff as a potential competitor. . . .

Because we remand for proper assessment of Falstaff as an on-the-fringe potential competitor, it is not necessary to reach the question of whether § 7 bars a market-extension merger by a company whose entry into the market would have no influence whatsoever on the present state of competition in the market—that is, the entrant will not be a dominant force in the market and has no current influence in the marketplace. We leave for another day the question of the applicability of § 7 to a merger that will leave competition in the marketplace exactly as it was, neither hurt nor helped, and that is challengeable under § 7 only on grounds that the company could, but did not, enter de novo or through "toe-hold" acquisition and that there is less competition than there would have been had entry been in such a manner. There are traces of this view in our cases, *see Ford Motor Co. v. United States,* 405 U.S. 562, 567 (1972); id., at 587 (Burger, C.J., concurring in part and dissenting in part); *FTC v. Procter & Gamble Co.,* 386 U.S., at 580; *id.,* at 586 (Harlan, J., concurring); *United States v. Penn–Olin Chemical Co.,* 378 U.S., at 173, but the Court has not squarely faced the question, if for no other reason than because there has been no necessity to consider it. *See Ford Motor Co. v. United States, supra; FTC v. Procter & Gamble Co., supra; United States v. Penn–Olin Chemical Co., supra; United States v. El Paso Natural Gas Co.,* 376 U.S. 651 (1964).

Justices Brennan and Powell did not participate in the decision. Justice Douglas concurred for the most part in the Court's opinion, but inclined to the view that the question left open should be resolved in favor of the government.

Justice Marshall disagreed with the basis of the Court's remand because the government had not claimed that Falstaff was exerting a present pro-competitive influence and had introduced no evidence to support this view; Justices Rehnquist and Stewart dissented.

On remand, the district court found that Falstaff had not been perceived as a potential competitor. It dismissed the complaint and the government did not appeal. *See United States v. Falstaff Brewing Corp.,* 383 F.Supp. 1020 (D.R.I.1974).

———

United States v. Marine Bancorporation, 418 U.S. 602, 94 S.Ct. 2856, 41 L.Ed.2d 978 (1974). The government challenged the merger of two commercial banks under Section 7. National Bank of Commerce ("NBC") was a national bank with its principal office in Seattle and with 107 branch offices in Seattle and elsewhere in the western part of the State of Washington (but not in Spokane). The acquired bank, Washington Trust Bank ("WTB") was a state bank with seven branch offices, all in Spokane or its immediate vicinity. There was no claim that significant actual competition existed between NBC and WTB. The government's contention rather was that the merger would eliminate each bank as a potential competitor of the other, and specifically that NBC would be eliminated as a potential competitor into commercial banking in the Spokane metropolitan area.

The Court framed the question as follows:

Two essential pre-conditions must exist before it is possible to resolve whether the government's theory, if proved, establishes a violation of § 7. It must be determined: (i) that in fact NBC has available feasible means for entering the Spokane market other than by acquiring WTB; and (ii) that those means offer a substantial likelihood of ultimately producing decon-centration of that market or other significant procompetitive effects.

Under state law, NBC was prohibited from establishing de novo branches in Spokane even if it could get around that state law restriction by "sponsoring" and then acquiring the sponsored bank. State law would then provide that NBC could not branch from a sponsored bank after it was acquired. In effect, NBC would be frozen at the level of its initial acquisition. As a result of these state law restrictions, NBC was not likely to enter the Spokane market in a way that would offer a reasonable prospect of procompetitive benefits. Moreover, rational bankers in Spokane presumably would be aware of regulatory barriers and therefore, the Court concluded "It is improbable that NBC exerts any meaningful procompetitive influence over Spokane banks by standing 'in the wings' . . . ."

Justices White, Brennan, and Marshall dissented.

———

BOC International Ltd. v. FTC, 557 F.2d 24 (2d Cir.1977). British Oxygen, the world's second largest producer of industrial gases, acquired a controlling interest in Airco, the third largest industrial gas producer in the United States with approximately 16% of the national market. British Oxygen had never sold industrial gases in the United States.

The FTC found that the acquisition constituted a violation of Section 7 under the "actual potential entrant" theory—that is, if the acquisition were blocked, British Oxygen would have entered the market de novo or by a toe-hold acquisition and such entry would have had pro-competitive effects. The Commission specifically found that there was no evidence that British Oxygen, prior to the acquisition, exerted any "in the wings" pro-competitive effect. As a result, the legal issue presented was one the Supreme Court had twice declined to pass upon: Whether the "actual potential entrant" doctrine was a valid form of Section 7 enforcement?

As to the likelihood of independent entry but for the acquisition, the FTC found:

> [A]s of December 1973, there was a "reasonable probability" that [British Oxygen] would have eventually entered the U.S. industrial gases market by internal expansion, or its equivalent, but for the acquisition of Airco. . . .

The Second Circuit approved the Commission's adoption of a "reasonable probability" test, but set aside the Commission order finding a violation because the Commission's reference to "eventual entry" makes the overall FTC test one based largely on "ephemeral possibilities." At oral argument, Commission counsel had conceded that the "eventually" standard contained no time estimate or time limitation whatsoever, but rather involved "long-range considerations" that might take decades to come to pass. The Court of Appeals reacted as follows:

> We hold that such uncabined speculation cannot be the basis of a finding that Section 7 has been violated. . . . While it is not clear—and we need not decide—whether the probable entry of the acquiring firm must be "immi-

nent" in an actual potential entrant situation, it seems necessary under Section 7 that the finding of probable entry at least contain some reasonable temporal estimate relating to the near future, with "near" defined in terms of the entry barriers and lead time necessary for entry in the particular industry, and that the finding be supported by substantial evidence in the record.

We emphasize that we are not requiring any exact, precisely calibrated assessment of time of entry. . . . But here there was no finding regarding a reasonable probability of entry in the near future, nor is there any evidence in the record on which such a finding might be based.

The Court of Appeals declined to pass upon, and like the Supreme Court decided to "leave for another day," the issue of the basic validity of the "actual potential entrant" doctrine.

————

UNITED STATES V. CITIZENS & SOUTHERN NATIONAL BANK, 422 U.S. 86, 95 S.Ct. 2099, 45 L.Ed.2d 41 (1975). The government challenged Citizens & Southern's acquisition of five so-called "5–percent banks." For many years, Georgia had restricted banks located in cities from operating branches in suburban areas. To circumvent these restrictions, Citizens & Southern embarked on a program of forming de facto branch banks. According to the Court:

This program involved, among other features, ownership by C & S Holding of 5 percent of the stock of each of the suburban banks (the maximum allowed by state law), ownership of much of the remaining stock by parties friendly to C & S, use by the suburban banks of the C & S logogram and of all of C & S's banking services, and close C & S oversight of the operation and governance of the suburban banks. The expectation on all sides—by C & S, by the suburban banks, and by state and federal bank regulators—was that C & S would acquire these "5–percent banks" outright, and convert them into de jure branches, as soon as state law, or the Atlanta city limits, were altered so as to permit the accomplishment of this end.

In 1970, Georgia amended its banking law and C & S attempted to acquire formally the five banks. The Court affirmed the district court's holding that neither the Sherman Act nor Clayton Act was violated. As to the Clayton Act claim, the Court reasoned:

As to present and past competition, the Government agrees there is and has been none. If this state of affairs were the result of violations of the Sherman Act, we agree with the Government that making the evil permanent through acquisition or merger would offend the Clayton Act. *See Citizen Publishing Co. v. United States*, 394 U.S. 131, 135. But we have already concluded that C & S's program of founding and maintaining new de facto branches in the face of Georgia's antibranching law did not violate the Sherman Act, and the de facto branches which C & S proposes to acquire were all founded ab initio with C & S sponsorship. It thus indisputably follows that the proposed acquisitions will extinguish no present competitive conduct or relationships. . . .

As for future competition, neither the District Court nor the FDIC could find any realistic prospect that denial of these acquisitions would lead the defendant banks to compete against each other. The 5–percent banks theoretically could break their ties with C & S and its correspondent associate program, for these banks are each independently owned, but the record shows that none of the shareholders, directors, or officers of the 5–percent banks expressed any inclination to do so, and there was no evidence that the program has been other than beneficial and profitable for both C & S and the 5–percent banks. The Clayton Act is concerned with "probable" effects on competition, not with "ephemeral possibilities." *Brown Shoe Co. v. United States*, 370 U.S. 294, 323.

———

FTC v. CONSOLIDATED FOODS CORP., 380 U.S. 592, 85 S.Ct. 1220, 14 L.Ed.2d 95 (1965), raises in the merger context "reciprocity" issues examined in Chapter 8. Consolidated Foods Corporation owned "food processing plants and a network of wholesale and retail food stores." In 1951 it acquired Gentry, Inc., a manufacturer of dehydrated onion and garlic. The FTC found this to be a violation of Section 7 because it gave Consolidated the opportunity for reciprocal dealing as well as "the power to foreclose competition from a substantial share of the markets for dehydrated onion and garlic." The Court of Appeals for the Seventh Circuit set aside the Commission's order of divestiture, relying on post-acquisition experience to conclude that the Commission had failed to prove a probability that the acquisition would substantially lessen competition. *Consolidated Foods Corp. v. FTC*, 329 F.2d 623 (7th Cir.1964). The Supreme Court reversed in an opinion written by Justice Douglas.

As a wholesaler and retailer Consolidated purchased goods from food processors. As a manufacturer, Gentry sold its products to many of these same food processors and could potentially sell to still more. There was evidence presented that the food processors who sold to Consolidated "would give their onion and garlic business to Gentry for reciprocity reasons if it could meet the price and quality of its competitors' products."

The dehydrated onion and garlic industry was highly concentrated at the time of the merger, with Gentry and Basic, its principal competitor, accounting for about 90% of sales. The Commission found:

> If it is desirable to prevent a trend toward oligopoly it is a fortiori desirable to remove, so far as possible, obstacles to the creation of genuinely competitive conditions in an oligopolistic industry. Respondent's reciprocal buying power, obtained through acquisition of Gentry, is just such an anticompetitive obstacle. 380 U.S. at 597.

The Supreme Court accepted the Commission's findings. It disagreed with the analysis made by the Court of Appeals of post-acquisition evidence. Justice Douglas found that "the post-acquisition evidence ... tended to confirm rather than cast doubt upon, the probable anticompetitive effect which the Commission found the merger would have." He concluded:

> We do not go so far as to say that any acquisition, no matter how small, violates § 7 if there is a probability of reciprocal buying. Some situations may amount only to de minimis. But where, as here, the acquisition is of a company that commands a substantial share of a market,

a finding of probability of reciprocal buying by the Commission, whose expertise the Congress trusts, should be honored, if there is substantial evidence to support it. 380 U.S. at 600.[30]

In considering the implications of this decision, note the following questions:

1. If Consolidated Foods did attempt to pressure food processors into buying from Gentry, and those processors found it disadvantageous to purchase from Gentry (because Gentry could not compete as to price, quality, or service), why would not the processors simply shift their purchases to Basic or some other supplier and shift their sales to a competitor of Consolidated Foods?

2. Is it likely that Consolidated Foods, owner of a network of wholesale and retail food outlets, would be willing to forego handling a brand with established consumer acceptance solely because the seller of that brand would not purchase from Gentry? At a minimum, would not Consolidated Foods have to balance the loss of profit resulting from discontinuance of the national brand against possible profits that might be earned by Gentry if it succeeded in selling to the coerced food processor? Would food processors realize this and therefore assume they could buy or refrain from buying from Gentry without any threat to continued sales relations with Consolidated Foods?

NOTE ANALYZING ENFORCEMENT AGAINST CONGLOMERATE MERGERS SINCE *PROCTER & GAMBLE* AND THE ECONOMIC IMPACT OF A VERY PERMISSIVE PERIOD

The United States witnessed a great surge of conglomerate merger activity from 1965 through 1968.[31] Although during this period the Supreme Court and FTC decided a number of cases in which conglomerate mergers were declared illegal under Section 7 (*e.g., Procter & Gamble*, p. 1093 *supra; Consolidated Foods*, p. 1108 *supra*), the conglomerate merger movement continued to accelerate.

During the first few months of the Nixon Administration, in 1969, the Antitrust Division filed five major conglomerate merger cases containing allegations raising various economic and policy considerations underlying the wave of conglomerate mergers.[32] For example, a complaint against the ITT–Grinnell merger charged that if the court were to allow the merger:

30. Ed. Since *Consolidated Foods*, the courts have struggled with reciprocity problems in several merger cases, including Allis-Chalmers Manufacturing Co. v. White Consolidated Industries Inc., 414 F.2d 506 (3d Cir.1969), cert. denied, 396 U.S. 1009 (1970); United States v. International Telephone & Telegraph Corp., 306 F.Supp. 766 (D.Conn. 1969), appeal dismissed, 404 U.S. 801 (1971); United States v. Northwest Industries, Inc., 301 F.Supp. 1066 (N.D.Ill.1969).

31. FTC Bureau of Economics, Current Trends in Merger Activity, 1971, Table 6 (1972).

32. United States v. Ling–Temco–Vought, Inc., 315 F.Supp. 1301 (W.D.Pa. 1970), consent judgment entered, 1970 Trade Cas. (CCH) ¶ 73,105 (W.D.Pa.1970); United States v. Northwest Industries, Inc., 301 F.Supp. 1066 (N.D.Ill.1969); United States v. International Tel. & Tel. Corp. (Canteen), 1971 Trade Cas. (CCH) P73,619 (N.D.Ill. 1971), consent judgment entered, 1971 Trade Cas. (CCH) ¶ 73,667 (N.D.Ill.1971); United States v. International Tel. & Tel. Corp. (Hartford, Grinnell), 306 F.Supp. 766 (D.Conn.1969), 324 F.Supp. 19 (D.Conn.1970) (Grinnell), appeal dismissed per stipulation, 404 U.S. 801 (1971), consent judgments entered, 1971 Trade Cas. (CCH) ¶ 73,665 (D.Conn.1971) (Grinnell), 1971 Trade Cas. (CCH) P 73,666 (D.Conn.1971) (Hartford), 1972 Trade Cas. (CCH) ¶ 74,093 (D.Conn. 1971).

. . . the current trend of acquisitions of dominant firms in concentrated markets by large companies [would] be furthered and encouraged, thereby (i) increasing the concentration of control of manufacturing assets, (ii) increasing the barriers to entry in concentrated markets, and (iii) diminishing the vigor of competition by increasing actual and potential customer-supplier relationships among leading firms in concentrated markets.[33]

However, all five of these cases were settled before they could be appealed to the Supreme Court.[34]

In the late 1970s, a new and even more dramatic conglomerate merger wave took shape. This time, as opposed to the 1960s where most significant acquisitions were by "glamour" firms using highly leveraged stock, the acquiring firms included the nation's largest and most established corporations (*e.g.*, American Express, Exxon, GE, Grace, Kraft, Mobil, RCA, R.J. Reynolds, and United Technologies). A prominent characteristic of the new conglomerate merger wave was the increase in very large acquisitions. For example, the number of acquisitions valued at $100 million or more rose from forty-one in 1977, to eighty in 1978, to eighty-three in 1979, and to ninety-four in 1980.[35]

This conglomerate merger activity may have been stimulated, in part, by the permissive approach taken to conglomerate acquisitions (*i.e.*, certainly as compared to the relatively strict approach taken to horizontal mergers) in the courts. To paraphrase Justice Stewart's dissent in the *Von's Grocery* case, the only consistency in conglomerate merger litigation since the late 1960s has been that the government almost never wins. The *Falstaff* case, p. 1103 supra, stands for this proposition and a number of lower court decisions may also be cited.[36]

Two Court of Appeals cases,[37] offer evidence that the government must travel a very rough road in potential competition cases in the courts. In the *Yamaha Motor* case, Brunswick, a diversified manufacturer, was the second largest seller of outboard motors in the United States and had somewhere between 19.8% and 26% of a highly concentrated market. Brunswick entered into a joint venture with

---

33. Complaint § 24(f), United States v. International Tel. & Tel. Corp. (Grinnell).

34. After the consent decrees were entered, Ralph Nader unsuccessfully moved to have the Hartford settlement set aside on grounds of fraud and misrepresentation. United States v. International Tel. & Tel. Corp. (Hartford), 349 F.Supp. 22 (D.Conn. 1972), aff'd sub nom., Nader v. United States, 410 U.S. 919 (1973) (per curiam).

For discussions of consent decrees, *see, e.g.,* United States v. AT & T, ATRR No. 1077, p. S–1 (D.D.C. 1982); Buxbaum, Public Participation in the Enforcement of the Antitrust Laws, 59 Calif.L.Rev. 1113 (1971); Posner, A Statistical Study of Antitrust Enforcement, 13 J.Law & Econ. 365 (1970); Turner, Antitrust Consent Decrees: Some Basic Policy Questions, 23 Record of N.Y.C.B.A. 118 (1968); Zimmerman, Procedure for Settling with the Antitrust Division, 37 ABA Antitrust Section 212 (1968); Note, The ITT Dividend: Reform of Department of Justice Consent Decree Procedures, 73 Colum.L.Rev. 594 (1973). See generally, Hearings on S. 782 (Administrative Procedures and Penalties Act) Before the Subcomm. on Antitrust and Monopoly of the Senate Comm. on the Judiciary, 93d Cong., 1st Sess. (1973).

35. See Davidson, Looking at the Strategic Impacts of Mergers, 2 J. of Business Strategy 13, 18 (1981).

36. *See, e.g.,* Tenneco, Inc. v. FTC, 689 F.2d 346 (2d Cir.1982), discussed p. 1111 infra; United States v. Siemens Corp., 621 F.2d 499 (2d Cir.1980); BOC Int'l Ltd. v. FTC, p. 1106 supra; FTC v. Atlantic Richfield Co., 549 F.2d 289 (4th Cir.1977). But see Yamaha Motor Co. v. FTC, 657 F.2d 971 (8th Cir.1981), discussed in text, above.

37. Yamaha Motor Co. v. FTC, 657 F.2d 971 (8th Cir.1981), cert. denied, 456 U.S. 915 (1982), and Tenneco, Inc. v. FTC, 689 F.2d 346 (2d Cir.1982).

Yamaha, a Japanese corporation which manufactured outboard motors but did not sell them in the United States, to produce outboard motors. The Eighth Circuit, after evaluating both objective and subjective evidence, affirmed the FTC's finding of a violation of Section 7 and reasoned:

> The Commission's first ground [for finding a Section 7 violation] involves application of a theory known as the "actual potential entrant doctrine." In essence the doctrine, under the circumstances of this case, would bar under § 7 acquisitions by a large firm in an oligopolistic market, if the acquisition eliminated the acquired firm as a potential competitor, and if the acquired firm would otherwise have been expected to enter the relevant market de novo. To put the question in terms applicable to the present case, would Yamaha, absent the joint venture, probably have entered the U.S. outboard-motor market independently, and would this new entry probably have increased competition more than the joint venture did? We stress the word "probably" in this formulation of the issue, because the question under Section 7 is not whether competition was actually lessened, but whether it "may be" lessened substantially. The question arises here, of course, not in the perhaps more common context of an outright acquisition of a competitor that might otherwise have entered, but in the form of acquisition of stock in a jointly owned company, an acquisition that necessarily foreclosed (for the duration of the joint venture) the independent entry of Yamaha, the other joint venturer.
>
> Although the Supreme Court has yet to rule specifically on the validity of the actual-potential-entrant doctrine, it has delineated two pre-conditions that must be present, prior to any resolution of the issue. First, it must be shown that the alleged potential entrant had "available feasible means" for entering the relevant market, and second, "that those means offer[ed] a substantial likelihood of ultimately producing deconcentration of that market or other significant procompetitive effects." *United States v. Marine Bancorporation*, supra, 418 U.S. at 633. On this basis the Commission's decision is amply supported by the evidence.[38]

In the *Tenneco* case, the Second Circuit held the FTC to a very high standard of proof of potential entry. In a 2–1 decision, the Court placed heavy emphasis on a lack of evidence of Tenneco's subjective intent to enter the market, in the near future, either de novo or through a toehold acquisition; the Court set aside the FTC's order reasoning as follows:

> [Even though the market was oligopolistic] we reject the Commission's finding that Tenneco was an actual potential entrant likely to increase competition in the market for replacement shock absorbers....
>
> The record contains abundant evidence that Tenneco had both the interest and the incentive to enter the market for replacement shock absorbers.... In addition, uncontradicted evidence revealed that Tenneco had negotiated with major European shock absorber manufacturers regarding possible acquisitions or license arrangements and had actually acquired a small manufacturing company that held a patent on a new shock absorber design. The record strongly supports the conclusion that Tenneco was actively considering entry into the market and was pursuing all leads to that end at least since the late 1960s or early 1970s. Moreover, Tenneco clearly possessed adequate financial resources to make the large initial

---

38. 657 F.2d at 977–78.

investment needed to attempt to penetrate the market. The record, however, is deficient in evidence that there were viable toehold options available to Tenneco or that Tenneco would have entered the market *de novo*.

The Commission conceded in its opinion that Tenneco never expressed any interest in entering the market for replacement shock absorbers "on a completely *de novo* basis." However, the Commission found that Tenneco had expressed interest in entering the market essentially *de novo*, building the required production facilities from scratch and acquiring the necessary technology via a license from an established foreign shock absorber producer. The Commission concluded that Tenneco would likely have done so absent its acquisition of Monroe.

The Commission's reasoning is flawed. It ignores Tenneco's decision not to enter the market during the 1960s and early 1970s, a period of high profitability for shock absorber manufacturers, because of anticipated inadequate earnings during early years. The record is devoid of evidentiary support for the Commission's assertion that in the period relevant to this case, when industry earnings were in decline, Tenneco would have been willing to suffer the "cost disadvantage" inherent in the building of an efficient scale plant that would remain underutilized "for a number of years." The Commission's conclusion that Tenneco would have entered the market *de novo* with the aid of a license absent its acquisition of Monroe is based on the kind of unsupported speculation that the Supreme Court condemned when it warned that we should "remember that § 7 deals in 'probabilities,' not 'ephemeral possibilities.'" *Marine Bancorporation*....

The Commission's conclusion that Tenneco would likely have entered the replacement shock absorber market through toehold acquisition is similarly flawed....

We also conclude that the record contains inadequate evidence to support the Commission's conclusion that Tenneco's acquisition of Monroe violated section 7 by eliminating Tenneco as a perceived potential competitor in the market for replacement shock absorbers.[39]

Judge Mansfield dissented and noted that the majority opinion "flies in the face of the record" and "violates well-established rules" of judicial review of administrative proceedings.

Partly because of generally relaxed attitudes towards antitrust enforcement in the 1980s, but also because of widespread doubts about the validity of theories used earlier to attack conglomerate mergers, there was virtually no conglomerate merger enforcement in the 1980s and little in the 1990s. In the few cases in which government challenges were mounted, the parties either settled with the government or abandoned the transaction. The only conglomerate merger case brought in court during the period of the Clinton Administration was an FTC challenge to an acquisition in the natural gas pipeline industry, *FTC v. Questar*, file no. 961 001 (D.Utah 1995). After suit was filed, the parties abandoned the transaction. Thus, there have been no judicial opinions in the area for many years. Note also that in the 1984 Department of Justice merger guidelines, the controversial theories underlying decisions like *Procter & Gamble* and *Consolidated Foods* were simply ignored, and the only theories of challenge to conglomerate mergers were based on elimination of perceived or actual potential competition.

---

39. 689 F.2d at 353–55.

In economic terms, the 1980s and 1990s was a period of manic merger and acquisition activity. In 1980, the total reported value of U.S. corporate acquisitions and takeovers was $33 billion; by 1986 that figure had risen to $190 billion. ATRR No. 1305, p. 451 (1987). The level of merger activity was still modest when compared to the merger wave that swamped the country in the 1990s. Much of that merger activity was conglomerate. Although precise data for measurement are not yet available, it appears that the impact of the merger wave on the conglomerate area has been mixed.

Some huge conglomerate mergers, with significant potential competition attributes (*e.g.*, GE and RCA, BellAtlantic–Nynex), have been consummated, but many of the acquisitions have, in fact, been correcting the excesses of the 1960s and 1970s. The so-called "bust up" takeover (or corporate restructuring done under takeover threat) often has reflected a widely shared view in the 1980s and 1990s that the conglomerate merger waves of the 1960s and 1970s had, on balance, efficiency-reducing effects. After the most comprehensive study to date, Professors Ravenscraft and Scherer[40] reached the following conclusions:

> ... How successful have manufacturing mergers of the 1960s and early 1970s been? Did they serve the economy well by increasing the efficiency of resource allocation and utilization? ...

> One important insight is that corporate acquirers of the 1960s and 1970s began by selecting good material. They sought promising, well-managed acquisition targets, and on average, they succeeded in finding them. The typical acquired company reported operating returns on assets well above the norms for all manufacturing industry in the last year before surrendering its independence. The typical acquiree was also small, and the target selection process had a size bias: the smaller the target, the more its profitability tended to surpass peer industry norms. Yet even the larger acquired firms had good records....

> After merger, the acquired entities sooner or later divided into two groups—the sell-offs and the survivors....

> [R]oughly a third of all acquisitions were eventually divested, with an average lag of nearly ten years.

> For the divested entities, the story from an efficiency perspective is overwhelmingly one of failure. Operating income fell, turning negative on average in the year preceding divestiture. The reasons for this decline are not rooted simply in industry-specific problems.... Our case studies illuminate the reasons. The targets were often acquired at or near a profit peak, and some subsequent disappointment was virtually inevitable. Bad luck struck frequently. But the fault was not only in the stars. The acquired entities often coped poorly with adversity because the new and more complex organizational structures imposed upon them slowed corrective responses and sapped motivation. Crises aggravated the organizational mismatch between parent and subsidiary and impaired constructive problem-solving. [T]he evidence points strongly toward a conclusion that the loss of control was worse under merger than it would have been in the simpler organizational structure of an independent entity. And in a smaller set of cases, organizational complexity and incentive breakdowns actively

40. Ravenscraft & Scherer, Mergers, Sell–Offs and Economic Efficiency 192–227 (1987).

precipitated new problems, rather than merely impeding the solution of exogenously generated problems.

For the more numerous acquisitions that were survivors, the evidence on efficiency effects ... suggests a post-merger profitability decline of roughly one-half percentage point per year.... Although some of the decline is attributable to the unsustainably high level of pre-merger profits, an appreciable fraction appears to be a scaled-down manifestation of the control loss problems that led to sell-off in more extreme cases. Not surprisingly, the problems were most serious following pure conglomerate acquisitions, in which the parent's managerial experience was least well-suited to crisis problem-solving. Even for the "related business" and horizontal acquisitions, however, post-acquisition profitability was depressed relative to the levels identified in our pre-merger analysis ...

There are surely more opinions on why mergers are made than there are economists who have written on the subject. This may be inevitable, since merger motives are complex, and multiple motives may be at work in any given decision. Despite the difficulties, it is useful to see what light our research sheds on the question. Among other things, we must attempt to explain what motives led companies to make so many acquisitions that on average yielded such modest returns.

There are many broad (but not necessarily mutually exclusive) theories of merger motivation. The efficiency theory says that mergers occur because they improve the combined firms' operations—for example, by letting superior managers assume control, by exploiting cost-reducing "synergies" or complementarities in the partners' operations, or by taking fuller advantage of scale economies and risk-spreading opportunities, among other things in securing capital. The monopoly theory stresses the price-raising opportunities arising from consolidated market control, especially following horizontal mergers, or the possibility of buying inputs more cheaply owing to enhanced monopsony power. Undervalued-assets and bargain theories point to the opportunity for perceived mutual gain when a potential acquirer values a company's anticipated earnings stream more highly than current shareholders do. Empire-building theories propose that managers make acquisitions because they seek the power, prestige, and perquisites of controlling a large organization, even if shareholders' wealth is reduced in the process. Mergers can also be effected to secure tax advantages or to avoid investment strategy constraints imposed by the tax laws. And to round out what must necessarily be an incomplete list, we include the speculative or "bubble" theories, which imply that firms can persuade investors to support intensive merger activity through accounting manipulations, clever public relations, and the like.

None of these theories can be rejected flatly on the basis of our evidence. The most we can do is suggest degrees of plausibility and importance.... Our finding that, on average, profitability declined and efficiency losses resulted from mergers of the 1960s and early 1970s casts doubt on the widespread applicability of an efficiency theory of merger motives....

Pure conglomerate acquisitions were the least successful members of our sample, in terms of both subsequent sell-off rates and the profitability of the survivors. The movement away from such acquisitions is, as indicated already, a good sign. Our sample included 96 tender offer acquisitions or their "white knight" alternatives, so unless managers have become considerably more adept at making hostile unions turn out favorably, our findings continue to have relevance. . . .

Our historical research suggests a skeptical public policy stance toward mergers. This is not to say that all mergers are bad, which is most assuredly not true. Some mergers are clearly efficiency-increasing. Prominent among them are the second-order mergers that move units being sold off by a previous acquirer to a new, more knowledgeable, less organizationally complex parent. Other mergers are so equivocal in their effects that there is little cause for tilting the instruments of policy one way or another to influence them. But that mergers on average can lead to efficiency losses is reason for concern.

If the conclusions of Professors Ravenscraft and Scherer are assumed to be correct, what impact, if any, should they have on the judicial treatment of conglomerate mergers? Should courts, for example, be more cautious and less permissive when considering a potential competition case? If you assume that the odds were less than even that the merger would be efficiency enhancing, which way would you vote in the *Falstaff*, *BOC International*, and *Tenneco* cases?

Department of Justice Merger Guidelines, 1984[41]

4. HORIZONTAL EFFECT FROM NON–HORIZONTAL MERGERS

4.0 By definition, non-horizontal mergers involve firms that do not operate in the same market. It necessarily follows that such mergers produce no immediate change in the level of concentration in any relevant market as defined in Section 2 of these Guidelines. Although non-horizontal mergers are less likely than horizontal mergers to create competitive problems, they are not invariably innocuous. This section describes the principal theories under which the Department is likely to challenge non-horizontal mergers.

4.1 Elimination of Specific Potential Entrants

4.11 The Theory of Potential Competition

In some circumstances, the non-horizontal merger[42] of a firm already in a market (the "acquired firm") with a potential entrant to that market (the "acquiring firm")[43] may adversely affect competition in the market. If the merger effectively removes the acquiring firm from the edge of the market, it could have either of the following effects:

41. See pp. 1034–1056 supra and pp. 1156–1159 infra for other sections of the Guidelines. As noted earlier, these Guidelines were not modified in 1992, when new horizontal merger guidelines were published, nor in 1997 when the horizontal merger guidelines were revised.

42. Under traditional usage, such a merger could be characterized as either "ver-

tical" or "conglomerate," but the label adds nothing to the analysis.

43. The terms "acquired" and "acquiring" refer to the relationship of the firms to the market of interest, not to the way the particular transaction is formally structured.

4.111   Harm to "Perceived Potential Competition"

By eliminating a significant present competitive threat that constrains the behavior of the firms already in the market, the merger could result in an immediate deterioration in market performance. The economic theory of limit pricing suggests that monopolists and groups of colluding firms may find it profitable to restrain their pricing in order to deter new entry that is likely to push prices even lower by adding capacity to the market. If the acquiring firm had unique advantages in entering the market, the firms in the market might be able to set a new and higher price after the threat of entry by the acquiring firm was eliminated by the merger.

4.112   Harm to "Actual Potential Competition"

By eliminating the possibility of entry by the acquiring firm in a more procompetitive manner, the merger could result in a lost opportunity for improvement in market performance resulting from the addition of a significant competitor. The more procompetitive alternatives include both new entry and entry through a "toehold" acquisition of a present small competitor.

4.12   Relation Between Perceived and Actual Competition

If it were always profit-maximizing for incumbent firms to set price in such a way that all entry was deterred and if information and coordination were sufficient to implement this strategy, harm to perceived potential competition would be the only competitive problem to address. In practice, however, actual potential competition has independent importance. Firms already in the market may not find it optimal to set price low enough to deter all entry; moreover, those firms may misjudge the entry advantages of a particular firm and, therefore, the price necessary to deter its entry.[44]

4.13   Enforcement Standards

Because of the close relationship between perceived potential competition and actual potential competition, the Department will evaluate mergers that raise either type of potential competition concern under a single structural analysis analogous to that applied to horizontal mergers. The Department first will consider a set of objective factors designed to identify cases in which harmful effects are plausible. In such cases, the Department then will conduct a more focused inquiry to determine whether the likelihood and magnitude of the possible harm justify a challenge to the merger. In this context, the Department will consider any specific evidence presented by the merging parties to show that the inferences of competitive harm drawn from the objective factors are unreliable.

The factors that the Department will consider are as follows:

4.131   Market Concentration

Barriers to entry are unlikely to affect market performance if the structure of the market is otherwise not conducive to monopolization or

---

44. When collusion is only tacit, the problem of arriving at and enforcing the cor- rect limit price is likely to be particularly difficult.

collusion. Adverse competitive effects are likely only if overall concentration, or the largest firm's market share, is high. The Department is unlikely to challenge a potential competition merger unless overall concentration of the acquired firm's market is above 1800 HHI (a somewhat lower concentration will suffice if one or more of the factors discussed in Section 3.4 indicate that effective collusion in the market is particularly likely). Other things being equal, the Department is increasingly likely to challenge a merger as this threshold is exceeded.

4.132   Conditions of Entry Generally

If entry to the market is generally easy, the fact that entry is marginally easier for one or more firms is unlikely to affect the behavior of the firms in the market. The Department is unlikely to challenge a potential competition merger when new entry into the acquired firm's market can be accomplished by firms without any specific entry advantages under the conditions stated in Section 3.3. Other things being equal, the Department is increasingly likely to challenge a merger as the difficulty of entry increases above that threshold.

4.133   The Acquiring Firm's Entry Advantage

If more than a few firms have the same or a comparable advantage in entering the acquired firm's market, the elimination of one firm is unlikely to have any adverse competitive effect. The other similarly situated firm(s) would continue to exert a present restraining influence, or, if entry would be profitable, would recognize the opportunity and enter. The Department is unlikely to challenge a potential competition merger if the entry advantage ascribed to the acquiring firm (or another advantage of comparable importance) is also possessed by three or more other firms. Other things being equal, the Department is increasingly likely to challenge a merger as the number of other similarly situated firms decreases below three and as the extent of the entry advantage over non-advantaged firms increases.

If the evidence of likely actual entry by the acquiring firm is particularly strong,[45] however, the Department may challenge a potential competition merger, notwithstanding the presence of three or more firms that are objectively similarly situated. In such cases, the Department will determine the likely scale of entry, using either the firm's own documents or the minimum efficient scale in the industry. The Department will then evaluate the merger much as it would a horizontal merger between a firm the size of the likely scale of entry and the acquired firm.

4.134   The Market Share of the Acquired Firm

Entry through the acquisition of a relatively small firm in the market may have a competitive effect comparable to new entry. Small firms frequently play peripheral roles in collusive interactions, and the particular advantages of the acquiring firm may convert a fringe firm into a signifi-

---

45. For example, the firm already may have moved beyond the stage of consideration and have made significant investments demonstrating an actual decision to enter.

cant factor in the market.[46] The Department is unlikely to challenge a potential competition merger when the acquired firm has a market share of five percent or less. Other things being equal, the Department is increasingly likely to challenge a merger as the market share of the acquired firm increases above that threshold. The Department is likely to challenge any merger satisfying the other conditions in which the acquired firm has a market share of 20 percent or more.

4.135   Efficiencies

As in the case of horizontal mergers, the Department will consider expected efficiencies in determining whether to challenge a potential competition merger. See Section 3.5 (Efficiencies).

PROBLEM 25

MERGER OF NATIONAL FOODS WITH PERFECT PAPER

National Foods, with annual sales of $3 billion, manufactures a wide variety of food products, and is the country's largest producer of packaged food. Competitive conditions in the various product markets in which National competes vary, but those markets generally exhibit a high degree of price rigidity and fairly high profit margins. National is one of the country's largest advertisers, with an annual advertising budget of $445 million. The company takes advantage of the maximum bulk rate discounts offered by the various media to large advertisers. This merger will constitute its second recent entry into a non-food market. The merger represents an early fruit of a diversification program under which National "is entering a number of new markets either through acquisitions or by de novo expansion."

Perfect Paper Products manufactures paper napkins and other household paper products, but does not produce containers. It also owns large tracts of timber in Canada, and mills and other facilities for the conversion of this timber into paper. It produces considerably more paper than it uses for the manufacture of paper products, and sells the rest to fabricators. Perfect is the second largest competitor in the household paper products market, which is dominated by four large producers having 80% of the market among them, but which also contains about ten smaller firms.

For the four large producers, the household paper products market is extremely profitable. The ten smaller firms are not, however, very profitable, and entry and exit for the smaller firms appears relatively easy; four smaller firms have entered and six have departed from the market in the past five years. No paper products company spends more than $30 million per year in advertising, with Perfect spending about $29 million.

The paper and cardboard container industry consists of five large, integrated firms, each owning its own timberland, paper mills, etc., and over thirty smaller, non-integrated firms. These latter firms must purchase their raw paper from other companies. The integrated and non-integrated firms each account for about 50% of the market.

---

46. Although a similar effect is possible with the acquisition of larger firms, there is an increased danger that the acquiring firm will choose to acquiesce in monopolization or collusion because of the enhanced profits that would result from its own disappearance from the edge of the market.

National has never been a purchaser of paper napkins or other household paper products, but is a large purchaser of paper and cardboard containers, accounting for 6% of the industrial market. Presently, it buys half of its requirements from integrated and half from non-integrated companies.

The merger of National and Perfect will result in cost savings in the distribution and promotion of paper products of about 3%, about half of which will come from savings in advertising costs directly related to Perfect's newly created ability to take advantage of the bulk rate discounts presently allowed by the media to National.

Another cost saving will result from the fact that Perfect will be able to participate in the sponsorship of the "National Food Hour," a popular network television program. (It is generally considered that the sponsorship of a network program is a more efficient utilization of advertising dollars for those who are able to afford it than the purchase of "spot" time. Companies spending less than $34 million per year on advertising cannot generally become sponsors.) Other less important efficiency savings will arise in the warehousing and distribution of Perfect's products through National channels. In connection with the proposed merger, the president of Perfect publicly stated the following:

> We thought that any one of four other companies might enter the household paper products market, but we never thought National would want to come in. Nevertheless, National made a very tempting offer and we are all delighted with the serendipitous result.

Does this proposed merger violate Section 7?

COMPARATIVE NOTES ON CONGLOMERATE MERGERS, PORTFOLIO EFFECTS, AND OTHER DIFFERENCES BETWEEN US AND EC MERGER ENFORCEMENT

1. *Introduction to the theory of portfolio effects.* The term "portfolio effects" or "range effects" refers to the potential anticompetitive effects of conglomerate mergers between manufacturers of complementary products. In such mergers some have argued that there may be a potential threat that an already dominant firm may extend power from one product market to another complementary product market. This is, in part, explained by the tendency of purchasers to prefer buying a full line of complementary products from a single supplier, instead of purchasing each product separately from different suppliers who do not offer a full line of products. Therefore, if a company with market power acquires a fuller line, the idea is that the acquisition may enable the firm to foreclose market access to firms that do not offer a full line.

2. *Approach to portfolio theory in the United States.* As noted above at page 1109, during the ten-year period from 1965 to 1975, the United States experienced a wave of conglomerate mergers. During this period, the courts and the antitrust agencies experimented with a number of theories of competitive harm from conglomerate mergers, including the entrenchment theory, which bears some similarity to the "portfolio effects" or "range effects" theories. Under the entrenchment doctrine, as embodied in the U.S. Supreme Court's decision in *FTC v. Procter & Gamble,*[47] mergers could be prohibited if they strengthened an already dominant firm through greater efficiencies or gave the acquired firm access to a broader line

---

47. See page 1093, supra.

of products or greater financial resources, thereby as a practical matter foreclosing participation in the market by smaller rivals. Although the Supreme Court has never taken the occasion to revisit its *Procter & Gamble* entrenchment theory, the U.S. antitrust agencies eliminated entrenchment as a basis for challenging non-horizontal mergers in 1982 when the Department issued its new Merger Guidelines and the Federal Trade Commission issued its Statement on Horizontal Mergers. According to the current approach of both federal authorities, a close scrutiny of conglomerate mergers on the basis of portfolio effects would place the interests of competitors ahead of those of consumers and runs the risk of blocking or deterring pro-competitive, efficiency-enhancing mergers. Because efficiencies are likely to benefit consumers, such mergers are to be encouraged, even if they may strengthen a particular firm at the expense of its competitors.

3. *European approach to portfolio theory.* In Europe, up until the middle of 2002 at least, the Commission was willing to undertake much more severe scrutiny of conglomerate mergers. A series of recent decisions of the Court of First Instance, however, have rejected decisions of the Commission that were based on portfolio effects, and thus it is possible that an approach that gives greater weight to the positive effects of efficiencies and less to the harm to competitors—in short, a less interventionist approach—might be the future trend in Europe as well.

The term "portfolio effects" came into use in Europe in connection with the merger of the hard liquor subsidiaries of *Guinness* and *Grand Metropolitan*,[48] although the concept itself had been used in earlier cases, including in *de Havilland* and in *Boeing*.[49]

In *Guinness*, the Commission found that there were some product and geographic markets in Europe in which the merging firms had direct horizontal overlaps. In the Greek market, however, the problem was different. There was no competitive overlap, but the merged firm would have had the advantages of a full portfolio. The Commission accepted the merger, but set conditions to address both the problems of horizontal overlap and the portfolio problem. Among other things, the Commission ordered spin-offs of competing brands and termination of certain distribution agreements. The Commission justified the relief relating to the non-overlapping markets on the grounds that a wide portfolio of leading brands "confers considerable price flexibility and marketing opportunities" and gives the merged firm "the possibility of bundling sales or increasing the sales volume of one category by tying it to the sale of another category."

In the *Boeing/McDonnell–Douglas* merger, the Commission again predicted that the merger had a substantial chance of resulting in enhanced dominance by the merged firm: "Where a large fleet in service is combined with a broad product range, the existing fleet in service can be a key factor which may often determine decisions of airlines on fleet planning or acquisitions. Cost savings arising from commonality benefits, such as engineering, spares, inventory and flight crew qualifications, are very influential in an airline's decision-making process for aircraft type selections and may frequently lead to the acquisition of a certain type of aircraft even if the price of competing products is lower."

48. See Guinness/Grand Metropolitan, Commission Decision, Case IV/M. 938, O.J. L 288/24 (Oct. 27, 1998).

49. See Aerospatiale–Alenia/de Havilland, Commission Decision 91/619, O.J. L 334/42 (Dec. 5, 1991) and Boeing/McDonell Douglas, Commission Decision, Case IV/M877, O.J. L. 336/16 (Dec. 8, 1997).

In addition, the Commission feared that the sheer size and scope of the merged firm would lead to a strengthening of Boeing's dominant position in commercial airframe manufacture: "The doubling of governmental-funded military R & D and the tripling of Boeing's general revenues generated in the defense and space sector will increase the scope of cross-subsidization of Boeing's sales in commercial aircraft in cases where Boeing wants to meet specific competition.... It is clear that, as already stated, the addition of products from McDonnell–Douglas (in particular the small-segment MD–95) and the large increase in its overall resources would enhance Boeing's opportunities to engage in such pricing practices, especially in view of its strong, and increasingly strengthening, cash-flow position as outlined above." The net result was that, as in *Guinness*, it cleared the merger (after substantial trans-Atlantic consultations), but only on certain conditions.

4. *General Electric/Honeywell, Commission Decision.*[50] The case that has brought the most attention to portfolio effects is the Commission's decision blocking the merger of General Electric and Honeywell. The proposed takeover of Honeywell by the U.S. conglomerate General Electric became the focus for intensifying trade antagonisms between the European Union and the United States.

General Electric, one of the world's largest companies, is also the world's largest maker of jet engines. Honeywell manufactures products for the aerospace industry, in particular industrial automation and control systems, and it is also a supplier to the automotive sector. General Electric and Honeywell agreed to GE's planned takeover of Honeywell in October 2000; the acquisition would at the time have been the largest in industrial history, increasing GE's size by nearly a third. The U.S. Department of Justice Antitrust Division indicated that it would not seek to stop the GE/Honeywell deal in May 2001, on the minor condition that the merged group had to sell off a helicopter engine business. The European Commission, however, blocked the merger in July of the same year, on the stated ground that the integration of Honeywell's avionics and GE's strength in jet engines might lead to dominance of the market. The theory on which the Commission relied was fundamentally different from anything in the U.S. authorities' own merger guidelines. Moreover, this was the first time that a proposed merger between two U.S. companies was vetoed solely by European regulators. It is instructive to use the *GE/Honeywell* matter as a case study on portfolio effects because the two antitrust agencies reached fundamentally different conclusions despite analyzing the identical product and geographic markets, considering the same theories of competitive harm, and largely having access to the same set of facts.

In adopting its decision, the Commission concluded that the merger would create or strengthen dominant positions on several markets and that the remedies proposed by GE were insufficient to resolve the competitive concerns. The Commission's investigation concluded that GE alone already had a dominant position in the markets for jet engines for large commercial and large regional aircraft. Its strong market position combined with its financial strength and vertical integration into aircraft leasing was a key reason for the finding of GE's dominance in these markets. The investigation also showed that Honeywell was the leading supplier of avionics and non-avionics products, as well as of engines for corporate jets and of engine starters (which are a key input in the manufacturing of engines).

According to the Commission's findings, the combination of the two companies' activities would have resulted in the creation of dominant positions in the markets

---

50. See   General   Electric/Honeywell,   July 3, 2001, app. to Court of First Instance
Case COMP/M.2220, Commission Decision of   pending.

for the supply of avionics, non-avionics and corporate jet engines, as well as to the strengthening of GE's existing dominant positions in jet engines for large commercial and large regional jets. The dominance would have been strengthened as a result of horizontal overlaps in some markets as well as through the extension of GE's financial power and vertical integration to Honeywell's activities and of the combination of their respective complementary products. Such integration would enable the merged entity to leverage the respective market power of the two companies into the products of one another. This would have the effect of foreclosing competitors, thereby eliminating competition in these markets, ultimately affecting adversely product quality, service and increasing prices.

More specifically, the Commission's decision focused on the following anticompetitive effects: (i) that the merger would create opportunities for the merged firm to offer low-priced bundles of aircraft engines and systems to which narrow-line competitors would be unable to respond effectively; (ii) that GE would leverage its existing dominance in aircraft engines into avionics and non-avionics systems markets by, among other things, bringing its "enormous financial means" to bear; (iii) that GE's aircraft leasing arm (GECAS) would buy only (or at least would heavily favor) Honeywell products, which would lead airframe manufacturers to prefer Honeywell products in the hope that this would induce GE to buy their airframes, and thus would help create a dominant position for the merged firm in avionics and non-avionics systems markets in which Honeywell is currently active. The Commission concluded that as result of these actions, revenue streams for GE and Honeywell competitors in both engines and avionics/non-avionics systems markets would shrink, leading to a reduction in their future investment and their competitiveness.

Working with largely the same facts and analyzing identical problems, the Antitrust Division of the U.S. Department of Justice came to a different conclusion. First, in terms of GE's market power, it concluded that while GE currently enjoys a large market share, the market for large aircraft engines is a bid market with three strong competitors–GE, Rolls Royce, and Pratt & Whitney. In such a market, historic market shares are only weakly indicative of future success, as illustrated by the fact that recent contract awards have been quite evenly divided among the three firms, with GE winning 42%, Pratt & Whitney 32%, and Rolls Royce 27%. The Antitrust Division therefore saw no basis for finding that GE would be able to impose restrictions on its engines customers (for example, by tying Honeywell avionics to its engine sales) without disadvantaging itself in its battle against Pratt & Whitney and Rolls Royce to have its engines selected on future platforms.

The Antitrust Division was also unpersuaded that GE would be able to leverage its strong position in engines to gain a decisive competitive advantage in the markets for avionics and non-avionics systems through either mixed bundling or technological tying. The mixed bundling theory of competitive harm used the so-called "Cournot effect" to predict that the merged firm would lower the price of complementary goods because it would internalize the external effects of its prices on sales of the complementary goods it now controls. That is, the firm adjusts its pricing to reflect the fact that if it lowers the price of its product A, it will stimulate sales of product B, if B is a complement of A. The agency pointed out that this theory predicts that the merged firm's prices will go down post-merger, at least in the short run. Harm occurs only if competitors lose profits *and* are forced to withdraw from the market. Thus, while the benefits are certain and immediate, the predicted harm is much more distant and speculative.

The Antitrust Division also examined the claim that GE had used its aircraft leasing arm, GE Capital Aviation Services ("GECAS"), to gain an advantage in engine competitions and would be likely, post-merger, to use GECAS similarly to expand Honeywell's market share for avionics and non-avionics systems. The Antitrust Division concluded that GECAS's share of aircraft purchases—less than 10% of all planes worldwide—was too small to give rise to a significant foreclosure effect. To the extent GECAS was offering more attractive financing terms than its competitors, GE was simply discounting its engines.

In summary, the Antitrust Division found no factual support for any of the key elements of portfolio effects theory, even assuming that in principle the theory was a sound one. To the contrary, it concluded that to the extent those elements were based on the argument that the merged firm would have the ability and incentive to offer customers lower prices and better products, that meant the merger should benefit customers both directly—through the lower prices and better products offered by the merged firm—and indirectly—by inducing rivals to respond with their own lower prices and product improvements. In other words, in the U.S. view, there were good reasons to welcome the merger, not to condemn it.

General Electric and Honeywell have appealed against the European Commission's decision to reject their merger plans. A court decision is not expected before the end of 2003. Please read the summaries of three recent decisions of the European courts below. In light of these recent decisions, would you expect the Commission's decision in *Honeywell* to be reversed or upheld?

5. *Airtours v. Commission* (June 6, 2002). In June 2002, the European Court of First Instance reversed the Commission's decision to stop travel group AirTours from buying rival First Choice. According to the Commission decision, the merger would have created a collective dominant position, as a result of which effective competition would have been significantly impeded. The court held that the conditions for collective dominance have not been met.

The merger was between two of the four largest tour operators in the United Kingdom. The relevant market was the so-called "short-haul" package holidays from the UK; the market shares of the four largest tour operators were as follows: Thomson 27%, Airtours 21%, Thomas Cook 20% and First Choice 11%. All other operators had under 5%. So far the Commission and the court agreed. The Commission found that the merger would create a collective dominant position in which the three leading tour operators would restrict capacity, that is, would reduce the numbers of holidays they sold. This would lead to a tightening of the market with a corresponding increase in prices and profits.

Collective dominance, as we have noted earlier, pages 524–525 supra, arises where the structure of the market is such that the few players may tacitly adopt a common policy and can act independently of competitors, without having to enter into an agreement or resort to a concerted practice.[51] Characteristics of the market include, most importantly, market concentration, transparency and product homogeneity. Assuming there is a market structure conducive to collective dominance, what other conditions need to be met before antitrust law enforcement can step in and prohibit a merger? The Commission and the court agreed that the three key elements of collective dominance are transparency, deterrence, and the reaction of customers and competitors. Transparency stands for the requirement that each

---

51. See Gencor Ltd. v. Commission, Case T–102/96, [1999] ECR II–753, p. 970, 988.

member of the group in question must have a means of knowing whether the other operators are adopting the same strategy and whether they are maintaining it. The deterrence requirement means that adequate deterrents must be in place to ensure that each participant has a long-term incentive not to depart from the common policy. Third, the Commission must establish that the foreseeable reaction of current and potential competitors, as well as of consumers, would not jeopardize the results expected from the common policy.

The Commission had found that the market showed a high degree of transparency: (i) tour operators planned the next year's holidays by simply adjusting capacity by a fixed percentage from the year before, (ii) major tour operators used the same hotels, and (iii) capacity expansions could not be kept secret (because of the need to charter new planes). The court, in contrast, found that (i) capacity decisions were taken on a package-by-package basis; (ii) the major tour operators did not in general use the same hotels, and (iii) decisions about airline seats were taken after the capacity planning stage and so would not increase transparency. The court found that the Commission had wrongly concluded that the high degree of transparency made the market conducive to collective dominance.

As far as deterrence is concerned, although the court did not suggest that a specific punishment mechanism was required, it is clear from the judgment that the court will insist upon an effective deterrent. The court rejected the mechanisms proposed by the Commissions as insufficient. The mere threat of returning to a situation of oversupply was insufficient.

With respect to the third element of collective dominance, the court found that the Commission should also have established that the foreseeable reactions of current and future competitors and consumers would not jeopardize the results expected from the large tour operators' common policy. Although in this case all fringe competitors were small, the court nevertheless held that this did not matter. The court found that small competitors could nevertheless counteract the creation of collective dominance. The court also found that foreign tour operators could enter the UK market if capacity was artificially reduced. The same point was made with respect to customers: although individual customers have no buyer power, the question was whether customers would be able to react to the price increases caused by the oligopoly's restriction of capacity. The Commission, therefore, in the opinion of the court, had underestimated the reaction of competitors and consumers as a countervailing force capable of counteracting the effects of collective dominance.

Although the case involves a horizontal rather than a conglomerate merger and did not implicate the "portfolio effects" theory, it was a landmark in the development of the role of judicial review in EU merger control: *Airtours* is the first case in which the Court of First Instance overturned a Commission decision to block a major merger.

6. *Schneider Electric SA v. Commission.* Within just a couple of months of the *Airtours* decision, the European Court of First Instance overturned yet another European Commission decision to block a merger. The court annulled the Commission's prohibition on essentially two grounds: (i) substantial errors in the economic analysis and (ii) failure to respect the rights of defense. The case, once again, confirms the increased importance of judicial review in the European Union.

In October 2001, the Commission prohibited a merger between Schneider Electric and Legrand, two French-based electrical equipment manufacturers, on the ground that it would considerably weaken competition on a large number of electrical equipment markets both at a wholesale and retail level.

The court's main criticism has been that after the Commission had cited the purely national dimensions of the various electrical product markets, it proceeded to take into account the European and global positions of the merging parties without demonstrating their relevance to competition at the national level. The court was of the view that this led the Commission to overestimate the power of the merged entity on each of the national markets. In addition, the court rejected the conclusion that the merged entity would have power because of portfolio effects, on grounds that the facts did not support such an assertion. Finally, the court found fault with the Commission's estimates of market shares of competitors (which had not included internal sales by certain suppliers to their specialized subsidiaries) and concluded that there were further mistakes arising out of its analysis of the figures and data on the Italian and Danish markets.

The court accepted that in relation to the various product markets in France where the two companies had considerable market shares, there was an elimination of competition. However, the court took the view that the Commission violated the parties' rights of defense (essentially because the decision was based on reasoning not previously presented to the parties in the earlier statements of objections to the merger) and so, even with respect of the French markets, the decision could not be upheld.

Observers of the EU believe that the *Schneider/Legrand* decision supports renewed criticism of the Commission's performance in investigating mergers. At the same time, Commission officials have argued that the court's more active approach demonstrates that there is indeed an effective judicial review procedure attached to the EC's regulation of mergers. It is notable in that connection that Schneider successfully appealed to the court using the court's new "fast track procedure" that allows urgent cases to be dealt with on an accelerated basis. As a result, the Court of First Instance reached a judgment after only twelve months (as opposed to two or three years—see *Airtours*, for example). By way of comparison, this is roughly the same amount of time it would take for a U.S. trial court to pass on a government request to block a merger with a preliminary injunction.

7. *Tetra Laval BV v. Commission.*[52] The *Schneider/Legrand* decision was followed by yet another defeat for the Commission in the Court of First Instance in a merger case. *Tetra Laval* marks the third consecutive time in the year 2002 that the court reversed a Commission decision blocking a merger. In March 2001, Tetra Laval SA (part of the group including Tetra Pak, the world leader in liquid food carton packaging) made an unconditional bid (as required under French law) for Sidel SA (active in producing a particular form of plastic bottles ("PETs") and filling machines). Despite Tetra's offering two separate sets of undertakings to remedy competition problems, the Commission prohibited the transaction on 30 October 2001. The Commission based its prohibition on three kinds of anti-competitive effects: horizontal (overlaps in the relevant markets), vertical (the creation of a vertically integrated structure as a result of the merger) and conglomerate (the ability of the merged party to leverage its position into related markets, eliminate potential competition and strengthen its overall position).

Looking first at the horizontal overlaps, the court noted that in markets where the merged company would combine the businesses of both Tetra and Sidel, the resulting firm's market share would be between 0% and 20%. Following by then

52. Tetra Laval BV v. Commission, cases T–5/02 and T–80/02, Judgments of the Court of First Instance of 25 October 2002.

well-established caselaw, the court found that this would be extremely unlikely to indicate a dominant position. In one market the court pointed out that the Commission referred to Sidel's market share as between 60% and 70%, although this figure actually referred to the combined market shares of both Tetra and Sidel; moreover, the Commission failed to take account of the fact that Tetra undertook to divest itself of its business altogether, thereby eliminating any horizontal overlap. With respect to the alleged vertical issues, the court held that Tetra's undertakings would be sufficient to ensure that the market remained highly competitive.

The court accepted the Commission's view that conglomerate mergers could properly be prohibited under the merger regulation, but it made a number of critical observations. The court stated: " ... the Commission's analysis of a merger producing a conglomerate effect is conditioned by requirements similar to those defined by the court with regard to the creation of a situation of collective dominance. Thus the Commission's analysis of a merger transaction which is expected to have an anti-competitive conglomerate effect calls for a particularly close examination of the circumstances which are relevant for an assessment of that effect on the conditions of competition in the reference market." On the facts, the court found that carton users would switch to PET products only in response to a price rise of 20% or more and that competition on the aseptic carton market was driven mainly by consumer-led innovation and not PET products. The court also held that the Commission had grossly overestimated future growth trends in the relevant markets and the potential convergence between aseptic cartons and PETs. Therefore, it concluded that, in relation to its competitors, Tetra's position on the aseptic carton market would not be strengthened by purchasing Sidel.

The court has yet to hand down its opinion in the *GE/Honeywell* appeal, but one thing is certain: the Court of First Instance has unequivocally, in this series of three decisions, demonstrated just how closely it will now scrutinize the Commission's rationale for its decision—both from the standpoint of economic analysis and from the standpoint of other factual support. From a theoretical standpoint, however, the court has not yet signaled a retreat from the more distinctly European theories. In *Tetra Pak,* it approved the application of the "associative links" theory to merger decisions, even though it held at the same time that the theory was not relevant to the case. "Associative links" first arose in a case against Tetra Pak for an abuse of a dominant position under Article 82 of the EC Treaty where it was held that its conduct (tying and predatory pricing) on the non-aseptic carton market (where Tetra was not dominant) constituted an abuse of its dominant position on the aseptic market since the two were closely associated and it was placed in a situation comparable to that of holding a dominant position on the markets in question as a whole.

In its analysis, the court distinguished between a situation where the conglomerate effect immediately changes the conditions of competition on the market to result in the creation or strengthening of a dominant position and that where such creation or strengthening will occur only after a certain time and as a result of the future conduct of the merged entity. The court held that in the second category the Commission may take account of incentives for the merged party to engage in future conduct which would, in itself, be anti-competitive (and separately prohibited by Articles 81 and/or 82 EC), but held that the Commission: "must also consider the extent to which those incentives would be reduced, or even eliminated owing to the illegality of the conduct in question, the likelihood of its detection, action taken by the competent authorities, both at Community and national level, and the financial penalties which could ensue." In the present case, the court held that because the MTF had not undertaken such assessment, it could only take into account future behavior, which "at least probably" did not constitute an abuse of Tetra's dominant position.

SECTION 4. INTEGRATION THROUGH VERTICAL MERGER

Robert H. Bork, The Antitrust Paradox: A Policy at War with Itself

225–233 (1978)

Vertical Mergers

Antitrust has been concerned about the effects of vertical mergers upon competition for over sixty years, but it has never evolved a satisfactory theory of the ways in which such integration could be harmful. The predominant fear has been that the acquisition of a customer or supplier would "foreclose" a market or source of supply to rivals and thereby fence out competition. That theory appeared in the 1911 *American Tobacco* decision, which supposed that the acquisition of suppliers was a means of gaining or maintaining monopoly in tobacco manufacture. . . .

Antitrust's concern with vertical mergers is mistaken. Vertical mergers are means of creating efficiency, not of injuring competition. There is a faint theoretical case, hardly worth mentioning, that vertical mergers can be used by very large firms for purposes of predation under exceptional circumstances, but it is highly doubtful that that narrow possibility has any application to reality. In any event, the vertical mergers attacked by the law do not contain even that possibility. The vertical mergers the law currently outlaws have no effect other than the creation of efficiency.

It is conventional and useful to say, as Morris Adelman does, that vertical integration exists when a firm "transmits from one of its departments to another a good or service which could, without major adaptation, be sold in a market." This definition calls attention to the choice of the firm to bypass a market transaction in favor of internal control. But the definition may lead us to overlook the ubiquity of such integration in our economy. Often there is no outside market for a good or service transmitted within a firm precisely because the efficiencies of vertical integration are so great that no firm would think of selling or buying at that stage. Every firm in the economy is vertically integrated in the sense that goods and services are transmitted within it and not offered on any market. This fact is important because it shows the vertical integration is indispensable to the realization of productive efficiencies. One can imagine the chaos and costs that would arise if the law were logically to extend its aversion to vertical integration by requiring, for example, an open market transaction every time goods moved from one worker or department to another or, indeed, by forbidding individuals to perform more than one task in the productive chain before selling. This is entirely fanciful, of course, but it is worth stressing that all economic activity displays vertical integration, because that tends to remove some of the sinister coloration this essential form of integration has undeservedly acquired.

The word "integration" means only that administrative direction rather than a market transaction organizes the cooperation of two or more persons engaged in a productive or distributive activity. The firm chooses between modes of organization according to their relative costs. On this basis, it chooses to perform particular tasks itself, to subtract them to others, or to sell a finished or semifinished product to other firms which perform further functions in bringing a finished product to the final market. The firm itself is best defined for purposes of economic analysis as the area of operations within which administration, rather than market processes, coordinates work.

What antitrust law perceives as vertical merger, and therefore as a suspect and probably traumatic event, is merely an instance of replacing a market transaction with administrative direction because the latter is believed to be a more efficient method of coordination. Vertical mergers may cut sales and distribution costs, facilitate the flow of information between levels of the industry (for example, marketing possibilities may be transmitted more effectively from the retail to the manufacturing level, new product possibilities may be transmitted in the other direction, better inventory control may be attained, and better planning of production runs may be achieved), create economies of scale in management, and so on. When such possibilities become apparent throughout an industry, a trend toward vertical integration will develop, as it did in shoe manufacturing and retailing, and as it has done in many other industries. Such trends are merely the responses of businessmen to changing circumstances. They are essentially no different from, and certainly no more cause for alarm than, countless other trends in product styles, types of outlets, automation, prices, and the like. What is incipient in any such trend is not the lessening of competition but the attainment of new efficiency, and it is the latter result at which amended Section 7 of the Clayton Act is actually striking in vertical merger cases.

It is thoroughly naïve of the law to suppose that vertical merger affects resource allocation adversely while vertical growth affects it not at all. The only difference between vertical merger and vertical growth is that in a specific situation at a particular moment one or the other will be the lower-cost way of achieving the efficiencies of integration. In fact, the sole difference between vertical merger and existing vertical integration within all firms is historical. In the latter case the efficiencies of integration have been present, recognized, and realized in firm structures for some time, while in the case of merger the efficiencies are either just becoming possible or are just being recognized, and firms are seeking to realize them through structural change.

Vertical integration is often believed somehow to cause or permit a firm to behave differently than it would in the absence of integration. Aside from the efficiency effect, however, it is clear that vertical integration does not affect the firm's pricing and output policies. If, for example, a firm operates at both the manufacturing and retailing levels of an industry, it maximizes overall profit by setting the output at each level as though the units were independent of one another. The firm will not, as is frequently suggested, sell to its own retail subsidiary for less than it sells to outsiders, unless the efficiencies of integration lower the cost of selling to its own retail unit.

The reasons for this are obvious. It is impossible for a firm actually to sell to itself for less than it sells to outside firms because the real cost of any transfer from the manufacturing unit to the retailing unit includes the return that could have been made on a sale to an outsider. No matter what the bookkeeper writes down as the transfer price, the real cost is always the opportunity foregone. (If a garment manufacturer spends $50 to make a dress, could sell it for $100, but chooses to give it to his wife, the cost to him is $100, not $50, and the fact cannot be altered by any number he chooses to put in his books.) Nor would there be any point in the firm's subsidizing its retail level by transfers at artificially low prices. Such a policy would merely entail the sacrifice of return at the manufacturing level, and the self-deception as to true costs would cause the retailing subsidiary to operate at an uneconomical rate. If the marginal costs of retailing are rising—as they certainly are, unless the retailer is a natural monopolist—the artificially low price would result in an increased output at higher costs. The integrated firm would be paying more for the performance of the retailing function than it would if it recognized real costs and operated at a smaller scale on the retail level.

These principles may usefully be applied to varying industry structures. Where the firm is competitive at both levels, it maximizes by equating marginal cost and price at each level, and each level makes a competitive rate of return. Should the firm enjoy a monopoly at the manufacturing level but face competition in retailing, it will of course exact a monopoly profit in manufacturing; but, for the reasons discussed, it will sell to the retail level at the same monopoly price it asks of independent retailers.

If the integrated firm has monopoly positions in both manufacturing and retailing, however, the levels will not maximize independently. This is true because vertically related monopolies can take only one monopoly profit. If each level tries to maximize by restricting output, the result will be a price higher than the monopoly price and an output smaller, the result being less than a full monopoly return. The reason for this is easily seen. Suppose the firm starts as a manufacturing monopoly selling to a competitive retail level. The manufacturer would set his output and price so that the appropriate monopoly price would be charged consumers after retailers had added their costs, including a competitive return. The monopolist must allow the retailers a competitive return, and he will not want to allow them more than that. If he allowed them less, the level of investment and operation in retailing would decline to the manufacturer's detriment. If he allowed them more, the level of investment and operation would rise above the optimal, and the manufacturer would be paying for retailing services he did not want.

We may suppose that the manufacturer purchases all of the retailers, converting that level of the industry to a second monopoly held by him. This will not change his price and output decisions at all. Though he now holds both manufacturing and retailing, the monopolist is still facing the same consumer demand and the same costs at both levels. The maximizing price to consumers, therefore, remains the same. The new retail subsidiary will not be permitted to act independently and restrict output further than the manufacturing level had already restricted it, since that would result in an output lower and a price higher than the maximizing level.

The case under discussion is, in any event, a very rare one: the acquisition by a monopolist of a second vertically-related monopoly. Much of the theoretical case against vertical integration begins by trying to establish some possibility of competitive hard from the joining of two vertically related monopolies, and then proceeds on the unstated assumption that a case has been made which is applicable to all vertical mergers. The point here is that no case has been made against the vertical acquisition by a monopolist of a second monopoly; moreover, even if such a case could be made, it would be largely an academic exercise and would have no force in the broader context of the vertical mergers the law is actually preventing.

The argument so far holds, of course, whether vertical integration is created by growth or merger. Vertical merger does not create or increase the firm's power to restrict output. The ability to restrict output depends upon the share of the market occupied by the firm. Horizontal mergers increase market share, but vertical mergers do not.

These observations indicate that vertical mergers are merely one means of creating a valuable form of integration and that there is no reason for the law to oppose such mergers. Adherence to an economic fallacy almost as old as antitrust policy, however, has caused the law to take an entirely different course.

"Foreclosure": The Law's Objection to Vertical Merger

The law developed under amended Section 7 of the Clayton Act assumes that vertical mergers may sometimes be beneficial or neutral but that their dominant effect is so heavily deleterious as to merit the prohibition of almost all such integrations. The law's current theory of the way in which vertical mergers injure competition is contained in the concept of "foreclosure." It is supposed that, for instance, a manufacturer may acquire a retailer, force the retail subsidiary to sell the manufacturer parent's products, and thus "foreclose" rival manufacturers from the market represented by the captive retailer. This thought to be a means by which the competitive process may be injured.

In analyzing the *Brown Shoe* case we have seen the extremes to which this theory can be carried, but once an erroneous idea is let loose in antitrust it tends to run riot. Even before *Brown Shoe* the Federal Trade Commission had ingeniously devised what was, apparently, a doctrine of reciprocal foreclosure. This theory, whose sole merit is that it establishes a new high in preposterousness, is illustrated by the Commission's refusal to permit the acquisition by A.G. Spalding & Bros. of another full-line sporting goods company, Rawling Manufacturing Co. The case was decided primarily as a horizontal merger, but the Commission objected to possible vertical foreclosure as well.

A fair sample of the *Spalding* opinion's foreclosure reasoning runs this way: before the merger Spalding did not manufacture baseball gloves but bought its requirements from others. Rawlings, on the other hand, made gloves and sold them to others. The merger might therefore wreak havoc on competition at both manufacturing and selling levels, for as the Commission saw it "by acquiring Rawlings, Spalding can not only prevent competitors from purchasing [baseball gloves] from Rawlings but can also foreclose manufacturers of [gloves] from access to Spalding as a purchaser thereof."

A two-edge sword indeed! The Commission's opinion does not inform us why the people who formerly made gloves for Spalding could not sell them to the people who formerly bought gloves from Rawlings. Instead, we are left to imagine eager suppliers and hungry customers, unable to find each other, forever foreclosed and left to languish. It would appear the Commission could have cured this aspect of the situation by throwing an industry social mixer.

M.H. Riordan & S.C. Salop, Evaluating Vertical Mergers: A Post–Chicago Approach

63 Antitrust L.J. 516–19 (1995).

THE POST–CHICAGO ANALYSIS OF VERTICAL MERGERS

The permissive policy toward vertical mergers, derived from the Chicago School, is premised on a simple economic model. In contrast, the post-Chicago approach relies on more realistic and complex economic analysis that facilitates the identification of anticompetitive concerns that have less importance in the Chicago School approach.

A. The Chicago School Critique of 1960s Vertical Merger Law

The Chicago School critique . . . is based on two main tenets. First, the mere fact that a vertical merger forecloses rival firms' access to the supply of inputs produced by one input supplier does not mean that the net supply of inputs available to those rival firms has been reduced. When the rivals lose access to the input supplies produced by one firm, they are likely to gain access to the input suppliers that previously supplied the merging supplier's downstream merger partner. In that case, according to Chicago School theory, the vertical merger does not reduce the net supply available to rivals. Instead, it merely realigns purchase patterns among competing firms.[53]

Second, the Chicago School utilizes an oversimplified microeconomic model to conclude that vertical mergers carried out by a monopolist cannot enhance monopoly power. The idea is that there is only a "single monopoly profit" that can be earned by the monopolist, whether or not the monopolist is vertically integrated.[54] Instead of enhancing monopoly power, the only economic motive for vertical merger is to reduce costs by achieving synergies.

Post–Chicago industrial organization economics accepts, as a starting point, these criticisms of pre-Chicago foreclosure theory. However, it has extended the economic models to more realistic assumptions that reach a more refined understanding of foreclosure. The modern industrial organization literature has formulated models of vertical integration in which vertical mergers lead to real foreclosure in which the net supply of inputs available to rivals is decreased. Models have been formulated in which monopoly power may be created or enhanced—and monopoly profits thereby increased—by vertical mergers that have little or no efficiency benefits. In these post-Chicago models, some vertical mergers can be anticompetitive, although others are procompetitive.

Post–Chicago analysis also relaxes the restrictive assumptions upon which the single monopoly profit theory is based. In particular, the single monopoly profit theory relies on the following four assumptions:[55]

(1) there is a monopoly input supplier, whose monopoly is protected by prohibitive barriers to entry;

(2) the monopoly is unregulated;

(3) there is perfect competition in the downstream output market; and

(4) the technology for producing output involves usage of all inputs in fixed proportions.

In the absence of these four assumptions, the single monopoly profit result no longer holds. Instead, vertical mergers may be motivated by either monopoly power, economic efficiency concerns, or both.

When the input market is not a monopoly, the analysis of vertical mergers is altered. Vertical mergers in these circumstances can have anticompetitive or procompetitive effects through a number of mechanisms. A vertical merger can create barriers to entry or expansion by foreclosing

---

53. As Bork points out, the cure for such naive allegations of foreclosure could be "an industry social mixer" to facilitate the realignment, supra, p. 1131.

54. Ed. The "single monopoly profit" theory traces most notably to the scholarship of Robert Bork: "... vertically related monopolies can take only one monopoly profit...." supra, p. 1129.

55. An analogous version would center the monopoly in the output market and perfect competition in the input market. Relaxing those assumptions alters the results analogously to the results discussed in the text below.

or disadvantaging unintegrated rivals. A vertical merger also can facilitate tacit or express pricing coordination among the competing input suppliers. In either case, a vertical merger may lead to a reduction in net input supply to rivals, not just a supply realignment.

Further, even if there is an input monopolist but that monopolist's price is regulated, a vertical merger can be used to evade price control regulations. A vertical merger also can be used to facilitate price discrimination, where price discrimination by an unintegrated monopolist would be constrained by regulation or a competitive output market.

By contrast, when there is not perfect competition in the output market, a vertical merger has the potential to reduce costs and increase efficiency by eliminating a double monopoly markup on input costs. When the output technology is not in fixed proportions, a vertical merger also has the potential to reduce costs by eliminating distortions in efficient input usage that arise from noncompetitive input prices.

Although the original Chicago School commentators focused primarily on the efficiency benefits of vertical mergers, they did identify some competitive concerns. For example, they paid close attention to the potential for collusion and recognized evasion of regulation as a potential concern. Nevertheless, the original Chicago School approach placed little credence in the harm from foreclosure. This rejection of foreclosure as a competitive concern has two sources in addition to those identified earlier. First, the Chicago School approach is based on an assumption that barriers to entry generally are low. Second, the Chicago approach pre-dated the recent interest among economists in game theory and strategic behavior. Along with other advances in economic theory, the game theoretic analysis of strategic behavior forms the core of what has been termed the post-Chicago approach.[56] The strategic behavior models study the decisions of firms that take rivals' likely reactions to their conduct into account when making their decisions. These involve models of strategic oligopoly conduct rather than the models of simple monopoly and perfect competition that form the foundations of the traditional Chicago School approach.[57]

These more realistic models of competitive behavior form the basis for a richer analysis of vertical mergers and their potential anticompetitive or procompetitive effects. In such a light, vertical mergers should be neither universally condemned nor universally applauded.

56. See Oliver Williamson, Antitrust Enforcement: Where It's Been, Where It's Going, 27 St. Louis U.L.J. 289 (1983); Herbert Hovenkamp, Antitrust Policy After Chicago, 84 Mich.L.Rev. 213, 274–80 (1985); Carl Shapiro, The Theory of Business Strategy, 20 Rand J.Econ. 125 (1989).

57. Chicago School economist George Stigler was a pioneer in the modern analysis of oligopoly theory. George J. Stigler, A Theory of Oligopoly, 72 J.Pol.Econ. 44 (1964). However, that work had little impact on the Chicago School approach to monopoly conduct or vertical relationships. Cf. Carl Shapiro & David J. Teece, Systems Competition and Aftermarkets: An Economic Analysis of Kodak, 39 Antitrust Bull. 135 (1994).

United States v. E.I. du Pont de Nemours & Co.

Supreme Court of the United States, 1957.
353 U.S. 586, 77 S.Ct. 872, 1 L.Ed.2d 1057.

■ BRENNAN, J. This is a direct appeal under § 2 of the Expediting Act from a judgment of the District Court for the Northern District of Illinois, dismissing the Government's action brought in 1949 under § 15 of the Clayton Act. The complaint alleged a violation of § 7 of the Act[58] resulting from the purchase by E.I. du Pont de Nemours and Company in 1917–1919 of a 23% stock interest in General Motors Corporation. This appeal is from the dismissal of the action as to du Pont, General Motors and the corporate holders of large amounts of du Pont stock, Christiana Securities Corporation and Delaware Realty & Investment Company.[59]

The primary issue is whether du Pont's commanding position as General Motors' supplier of automotive finishes and fabrics was achieved on competitive merit alone, or because its acquisition of the General Motors' stock, and the consequent close intercompany relationship, led to the insulation of most of the General Motors' market from free competition, with the resultant likelihood, at the time of suit, of the creation of a monopoly of a line of commerce. . . .

Section 7 is designed to arrest in its incipiency not only the substantial lessening of competition from the acquisition by one corporation of the whole or any part of the stock of a competing corporation, but also to arrest in their incipiency restraints or monopolies in a relevant market which, as a reasonable probability, appear at the time of suit likely to result from the acquisition by one corporation of all or any part of the stock of any other corporation. The section is violated whether or not actual restraints or monopolies, or the substantial lessening of competition, have occurred or are intended. Acquisitions solely for investment are excepted, but only if, and so long as, the stock is not used by voting or otherwise to bring about, or in attempting to bring about, the substantial lessening of competition.

We are met at the threshold with the argument that § 7 before its amendment applied only to an acquisition of the stock of a competing corporation, and not to an acquisition by a supplier corporation of the stock of a customer corporation—in other words, that the statute applied only to horizontal and not to vertical acquisitions. . . .

We hold that any acquisition by one corporation of all or any part of the stock of another corporation, competitor or not, is within the reach of the section whenever the reasonable likelihood appears that the acquisition

---

58. This action is governed by the Clayton Act as it was before the 1950 amendments, which by their terms are inapplicable to acquisitions prior to 1950. 64 Stat. 1125, 15 U.S.C. § 18, 15 U.S.C.A. § 18.

59. The amended complaint also alleged violation of §§ 1 and 2 of the Sherman Act, 26 Stat. 209, as amended, 50 Stat. 693, 15 U.S.C. §§ 1, 2, 15 U.S.C.A. §§ 1, 2. In view of our determination of the case, we are not deciding the Government's appeal from the dismissal of the action under the Sherman Act.

will result in a restraint of commerce or in the creation of a monopoly of any line of commerce. Thus, although du Pont and General Motors are not competitors, a violation of the section has occurred if, as a result of the acquisition, there was at the time of suit a reasonable likelihood of a monopoly of any line of commerce. . . .

Appellees argue that there exists no basis for a finding of a probable restraint or monopoly within the meaning of § 7 because the total General Motors market for finishes and fabrics constituted only a negligible percentage of the total market for these materials for all uses, including automotive uses. It is stated in the General Motors brief that in 1947 du Pont's finish sales to General Motors constituted 3.5% of all sales of finishes to industrial users, and that its fabrics sales to General Motors comprised 1.6% of the total market for the type of fabric used by the automobile industry.

Determination of the relevant market is a necessary predicate to a finding of a violation of the Clayton Act because the threatened monopoly must be one which will substantially lessen competition "within the area of effective competition."[60] Substantiality can be determined only in terms of the market affected. The record shows that automobile finishes and fabrics have sufficient peculiar characteristics and uses to constitute them products sufficiently distinct from all other finishes and fabrics[61] to make them

60. Standard Oil Co. of California v. United States, 337 U.S. 293, 299, note 5. Section 3 of the Act, with which the Court was concerned in *Standard Oil,* makes unlawful certain agreements " . . . where the effect . . . may be to substantially lessen competition or tend to create a monopoly *in any line of commerce.*" 38 Stat. 731, 15 U.S.C. (1946 ed.) § 14, 15 U.S.C.A. § 14. (Emphasis added.)

61. For example, the following is said as to finishes in the du Pont brief:

"The largest single finish item which du Pont sells to General Motors is a low-viscosity nitrocellulose lacquer, discovered and patented by du Pont and for which its trademark is 'Duco'.

" . . .

"The invention and development of 'Duco' represented a truly significant advance in the art of paint making and in the production of automobiles; without 'Duco' mass production of automobiles would not have been possible.

"By the early 1920's the need for better finishing materials for automobiles had become urgent. . . . The varnish method then used in finishing automo-

biles was described in detail at the trial by automobile pioneers. . . . Finishing an automobile with varnish required an intolerably long time—up to 3 or 4 weeks—to apply the numerous coats needed. When the finish was complete, its longest life expectancy was less than a year, and often it began to peel off before the car was delivered. . . ."

Du Pont's Director of Sales since 1944, Nickowitz, testified as to fabrics sold to automobile manufacturers as follows:

"Q. Now, over the years, isn't it true that speaking generally du Pont has followed the policy in selling its fabrics to the automobile field of undercutting its competitors in price? You don't try to sell it on a lower price than that quoted by any other competitor, do you?

"A. Well, we don't know. We go in and we bid based on our costs. *Now, in the automotive industry, we have a different situation than you do in the furniture trade, for example, where you have an established price.*

"You see, in the automobile industry, each manufacturer uses a different construction. They all have their own peculiar ideas of what they want about these

a "line of commerce" within the meaning of the Clayton Act. *Cf. Van Camp & Sons Co. v. American Can Co.*, 278 U.S. 245.[62] Thus, the bounds of the relevant market for the purposes of this case are not coextensive with the total market for finishes and fabrics, but are coextensive with the automobile industry, the relevant market for automotive finishes and fabrics.[63]

The market affected must be substantial. *Standard Fashion Co. v. Magrane–Houston Co.*, 258 U.S. 346, 357. Moreover, in order to establish a violation of § 7 the Government must prove a likelihood that competition may be "foreclosed in a substantial share of ... [that market]."[64] Both requirements are satisfied in this case. The substantiality of a relevant market comprising the automobile industry is undisputed. The substantiality of General Motors' share of that market is fully established in the evidence.

General Motors is the colossus of the giant automobile industry. It accounts annually for upwards of two fifths of the total sales of automotive vehicles in the nation. In 1955 General Motors ranked first in sales and second in assets among all United States industrial corporations and became the first corporation to earn over a billion dollars in annual net income. In 1947 General Motors' total purchases of all products from du Pont were $26,628,274, of which $18,938,229 (71%) represented purchases from du Pont's Finishes Division. Of the latter amount purchases of "Duco"[65] and the thinner used to apply "Duco" totaled $12,224,798 (65%), and "Dulux"[66] purchases totaled $3,179,225. Purchases by General Motors of du Pont fabrics in 1948 amounted to $3,700,000, making it the largest account of du Pont's Fabrics Division. Expressed in percentages, du Pont supplied 67% of General Motors' requirements for finishes in 1946 and 68% in 1947. In fabrics du Pont supplied 52.3% of requirements in 1946, and 38.5% in 1947. Because General Motors accounts for almost one-half of the automobile industry's annual sales, its requirements for automotive finishes and fabrics must represent approximately one-half of the relevant market for these materials. Because the record clearly shows that quantitatively and percentagewise du Pont supplies the largest part of General Motors' requirements, we must conclude that du Pont has a substantial share of the relevant market.

fabrics. Some want dyed backs, and some want different finishes, so you don't have any standard prices in the automobile industry." (Emphasis added.) ...

62. "The phrase ['in any line of commerce'] is comprehensive and means that if the forbidden effect or tendency is produced in *one* out of *all* the various lines of commerce, the words 'in *any* line of commerce' literally are satisfied." 278 U.S. at 253.

63. The General Motors brief states:

"If the market for these products were solely or mainly the General Motors Corporation, or the automobile industry as a whole, General Motors' volume and present share of the automobile industry might constitute a market large enough for the Government to rely on."

64. Standard Oil Co. of California v. United States, 337 U.S. 293, at 314.

65. A finish developed specially by du Pont and General Motors for use as an automotive finish.

66. A synthetic enamel developed by du Pont which is used on refrigerators, also manufactured by General Motors.

The appellees argue that the Government could not maintain this action in 1949 because § 7 is applicable only to the acquisition of stock and not to the holding or subsequent use of the stock. This argument misconceives the objective toward which § 7 is directed. The Clayton Act was intended to supplement the Sherman Act. Its aim was primarily to arrest apprehended consequences of inter-corporate relationships before those relationships could work their evil, which may be at or any time after the acquisition, depending upon the circumstances of the particular case. The Senate declared the objective of the Clayton Act to be as follows:

> ... Broadly stated, the bill, in its treatment of unlawful restraints and monopolies, seeks to prohibit and make unlawful certain trade practices which, as a rule, singly and in themselves, are not covered by the Act of July 2, 1890 [the Sherman Act], or other existing antitrust acts, and thus, by making these practices illegal, to arrest the creation of trusts, conspiracies, and monopolies *in their incipiency and before consummatio....* S.Rep. No. 698, 63d Cong., 2d Sess. 1. (Emphasis added.)

"Incipiency" in this context denotes not the time the stock was acquired, but any time when the acquisition threatens to ripen into a prohibited effect. *See Transamerica Corp. v. Board of Governors*, 3 Cir., 206 F.2d 163, 166. To accomplish the congressional aim, the Government may proceed at any time that an acquisition may be said with reasonable probability to contain a threat that it may lead to a restraint of commerce or tend to create a monopoly of a line of commerce. Even when the purchase is solely for investment, the plain language of § 7 contemplates an action at any time the stock is used to bring about or in attempting to bring about the substantial lessening of competition....

Related to this argument is the District Court's conclusion that 30 years of nonrestraint negated "any reasonable probability of such a restraint" at the time of the suit. While it is, of course, true that proof of a mere possibility of a prohibited restraint or tendency to monopoly will not establish the statutory requirement that the effect of an acquisition "may be" such restraint or tendency, the basic facts found by the District Court demonstrate the error of its conclusion.[67]

The du Pont Company's commanding position as a General Motors supplier was not achieved until shortly after its purchase of a sizeable block of General Motors stock in 1917. At that time its production for the automobile industry and its sales to General Motors were relatively insignificant. General Motors then produced only about 11% of the total automobile production and its requirements, while relatively substantial, were far short of the proportions they assumed as it forged ahead to its present place in the industry....

---

67. There is no significant dispute as to the basic facts pertinent to the decision. We are thus not confronted here with the provi-sion of Fed.Rules Civ.Proc. 52(a), 28 U.S.C.A., that findings of fact shall not be set aside unless clearly erroneous.

This background of the acquisition, particularly the plain implications of the contemporaneous documents, destroys any basis for a conclusion that the purchase was made "solely for investment." Moreover, immediately after the acquisition, du Pont's influence growing out of it was brought to bear within General Motors to achieve primacy for du Pont as General Motors' supplier of automotive fabrics and finishes....

The fact that sticks out in this voluminous record is that the bulk of du Pont's production has always supplied the largest part of the requirements of the one customer in the automobile industry connected to du Pont by a stock interest. The inference is overwhelming that du Pont's commanding position was promoted by its stock interest and was not gained solely on competitive merit.

We agree with the trial court that considerations of price, quality and service were not overlooked by either du Pont or General Motors. Pride in its product and its high financial stake in General Motors' success would naturally lead du Pont to try to supply the best. But the wisdom of this business judgment cannot obscure the fact, plainly revealed by the record, that du Pont purposely employed its stock to pry open the General Motors market to entrench itself as the primary supplier of General Motors' requirements for automotive finishes and fabrics.

Similarly, the fact that all concerned in high executive posts in both companies acted honorably and fairly, each in the honest conviction that his actions were in the best interests of his own company and without any design to overreach anyone, including du Pont's competitors, does not defeat the Government's right to relief. It is not requisite to the proof of a violation of § 7 to show that restraint or monopoly was intended.

The statutory policy of fostering free competition is obviously furthered when no supplier has an advantage over his competitors from an acquisition of his customer's stock likely to have the effects condemned by the statute. We repeat, that the test of a violation of § 7 is whether at the time of suit there is a reasonable probability that the acquisition is likely to result in the condemned restraints. The conclusion upon this record is inescapable that such likelihood was proved as to this acquisition. The fire that was kindled in 1917 continues to smolder. It burned briskly to forge the ties that bind the General Motors market to du Pont, and if it has quieted down, it remains hot, and, from past performance, is likely at any time to blaze and make the fusion complete.[68]

The judgment must therefore be reversed and the cause remanded to the District Court for a determination after further hearing of the equitable relief necessary and appropriate in the public interest to eliminate the

68. The potency of the influence of du Pont's 23% stock interest is greater today because of the diffusion of the remaining shares which, in 1947, were held by 436,510 stockholders; 92% owned no more than 100 shares each, and 60% owned no more than 25 shares each. 126 F.Supp. at page 244.

effects of the acquisition offensive to the statute. The District Courts, in the framing of equitable decrees, are clothed "with large discretion to model their judgments to fit the exigencies of the particular case." *International Salt Co. v. United States*, 332 U.S. 392, 400–401....[69]

69. Clark, Harlan and Whittaker, JJ., did not participate.

The dissenting opinion of Burton, J., with whom Frankfurter, J., concurred, is omitted. In the course of his dissent, Justice Burton stated:

"I agree with the Court that § 7 does not require findings and conclusions of actual anticompetitive effects. Unlike the Sherman Act, § 7 merely requires proof of a reasonable probability of a substantial lessening of competition, restraint of commerce, or tendency toward monopoly. International Shoe Co. v. Federal Trade Commission, 280 U.S. 291; Transamerica Corp. v. Board of Governors, 3 Cir., 206 F.2d 163. When a vertical acquisition is involved, its legality thus turns on whether there is a reasonable probability that it will foreclose competition from a substantial share of the market, either by significantly restricting access to needed supplies or by significantly limiting the market for any product. See Report of the Attorney General's National Committee to Study the Antitrust Laws (1955) 122–127. The determination of such probable economic consequences requires study of the markets affected, of the companies involved in relation to those markets, and of the probable immediate and future effects on competition. A mere showing that a substantial dollar volume of sales is involved cannot suffice. As the Court says, 'The market affected must be substantial,' 77 S.Ct. 877 and 'Substantiality can be determined only in terms of the market affected,' 77 S.Ct. 877. Section 7 thus requires a case-by-case analysis of the relevant economic factors....

"The remaining issues are factual: (1) whether the record establishes the existence of a reasonable probability that du Pont's competitors will be foreclosed from securing General Motors' trade, and (2) whether the record establishes that such foreclosure, if probable, in-volves a substantial share of the relevant market and significantly limits the competitive opportunities of others trading in that market....

"The burden was on the Government to prove that a substantial share of the relevant market would, in all probability, be affected by du Pont's 23% stock interest in General Motors. The Government proved only that du Pont's sales of finishes and fabrics to General Motors were large in volume, and that General Motors was the leading manufacturer of automobiles during the later years covered by the record. The Government did not show that the identical products were not used on a large scale for many other purposes in many other industries. Nor did the Government show that the automobile industry in general or General Motors in particular, comprised a large or substantial share of the total market. What evidence there is in the record affirmatively indicates that the products involved do have wide use in many industries, and that an insubstantial portion of this total market would be affected even if an unlawful preference existed or were probable.

"For the reasons stated, I conclude that § 7 of the Clayton Act, prior to its amendment in 1950, did not apply to vertical acquisitions; that the Government failed to prove that there was a reasonable probability at the time of the stock acquisition (1917–1919) of a restraint of commerce or a tendency toward monopoly; and that, in any event, the District Court was not clearly in error in concluding that the Government failed to prove that du Pont's competitors have been or may be foreclosed from a substantial share of the relevant market."

The Supreme Court's opinion in *du Pont–General Motors* engendered a host of comment in the legal journals. See Handler, Annual Review of Recent Antitrust Developments, 12 Record of the N.Y.C.B.A. 411, 415

NOTE AND QUESTIONS

In considering the majority's decision in the *du Pont–GM* case to analyze legality under Section 7 as of the time of trial—rather than as of the time of the acquisition—determine the probable outcome of the following hypothetical suits instituted in 2003. Assume in each case that company A is the leading producer of goods used by company B, the leading customer for those goods.

(a) In 1920, A purchases all the assets of B. A becomes exclusive supplier of B, but both are newcomers to the field. As B grows, however, A—as exclusive supplier—grows with it so that both are dominant in their fields at the time of suit.

(b) In 1920, A purchases a controlling stock interest in B. A produces goods that are wholly unrelated to B's needs, but in 1940, A begins producing a line of goods used by B and gradually thereafter becomes B's exclusive supplier.

Notice that the *du Pont–GM* case, if broadly read, would appear to give the government power under existing law to radically restructure large parts of the nation's industry. What would prevent the Antitrust Division, for example, from challenging the asset acquisition in "(a)" above under Section 1 of the Sherman Act? *See, e.g., United States v. First National Bank & Trust Co. of Lexington*, 376 U.S. 665 (1964), citing with approval the rigorous merger standard set forth by the Supreme Court in four (pre–1914) railroad consolidation cases.

Why not challenge mergers consummated before and after 1914 under either Section 7 of the Clayton Act and/or Section 1 of the Sherman Act? Many of the mergers that occurred at the turn of the century and in the second great merger wave in the 1920s would violate current antitrust standards.

Obviously, one must consider arguments about whether it is fair to challenge half century old transactions, legal when originally consummated, on the basis of anticompetitive consequences that probably could not have been foreseen at the time. Also, many have argued that no such radical restructuring should occur—certainly not on the basis of imprecise language in judicial opinions unconcerned with broad policy questions—without authorization from Congress in the form of a specific deconcentration statute.

Brown Shoe Co. v. United States

Supreme Court of the United States, 1962.
370 U.S. 294, 82 S.Ct. 1502, 8 L.Ed.2d 510.

[In 1955, the government brought suit to enjoin the acquisition by Brown Shoe, the nation's third largest seller of shoes, of G.R. Kinney Company, Inc. ("Kinney"), the eighth largest seller. The district court enjoined the merger and the Supreme Court affirmed.[70] Kinney's 350 retail outlets accounted for less than 2% of the nation's retail sales, but it was the largest distributor to handle brands other than its own. Brown Shoe distributed its own brands through an even larger retail network consisting

(1957), and Antitrust in Perspective 49 (1957); Blake, Mergers and the United States Antitrust Law, 6 Int. and Comp.L.Q.Supp. 78 (1963).

70. The merger had several horizontal aspects, which have been deleted from the

case by the editors. Chief Justice Warren's important and illuminating discussion of the Celler–Kefauver amendments is set forth at pp. 967–970 supra.

of 1,230 outlets (470 were owned by Brown Shoe and 760 were "controlled," franchised independents). Prior to the merger, Brown Shoe manufactured about 4% of the nation's shoes, and after the merger, the 24 largest manufacturers produced approximately 35% of the nation's shoes, with the top 4 (including Brown Shoe) producing 23%.

The public purchased shoes through about 70,000 retail outlets, but only 22,000 of these derived 50% of their gross receipts from the sale of shoes and were classified as "shoe stores." The district court had "found a 'definite trend' among shoe manufacturers to acquire retail outlets." Between "1950 and 1956 nine independent shoe store chains, operating 1,114 retail shoe stores, were found to have become subsidiaries of these large firms and to have ceased their independent operations." The district court also "found there was a 'definite trend' for the parent-manufacturers to supply an ever increasing percentage of the retail outlets' needs thereby foreclosing other manufacturers from effectively competing for the retail accounts. Manufacturer-dominated stores were found to be 'drying up' the available outlets for independent producers."]

■ WARREN, C.J.... [T]he Clayton Act does not render unlawful all ... vertical arrangements, but forbids only those whose effect "may be substantially to lessen competition, or to tend to create a monopoly" "in any line of commerce in any section of the country." Thus, as we have previously noted,

> [d]etermination of the relevant market is a necessary predicate to a finding of a violation of the Clayton Act because the threatened monopoly must be one which will substantially lessen competition "within the area of effective competition." Substantiality can be determined only in terms of the market affected.[71]

The "area of effective competition" must be determined by reference to a product market (the "line of commerce") and a geographic market (the "section of the country").

The outer boundaries of a product market are determined by the reasonable interchangeability of use or the cross-elasticity of demand between the product itself and substitutes for it.[72] However, within this broad market, well-defined submarkets may exist which, in themselves, constitute product markets for antitrust purposes. *United States v. E.I. du Pont de Nemours & Co.*, 353 U.S. 586, 593–595. The boundaries of such a submarket may be determined by examining such practical indicia as industry or public recognition of the submarket as a separate economic entity, the product's peculiar characteristics and uses, unique production

---

71. United States v. E.I. du Pont de Nemours & Co., 353 U.S. 586, 593.

72. The cross-elasticity of production facilities may also be an important factor in defining a product market within which a vertical merger is to be viewed. Cf. United States v. Columbia Steel Co., 334 U.S. 495; United States v. Bethlehem Steel Corp., 168 F.Supp. 576, 592 (S.D.N.Y.). However, the District Court made but limited findings concerning the feasibility of interchanging equipment in the manufacture of nonrubber footwear. At the same time, the record supports the court's conclusion that individual plants generally produced shoes in only one of the product lines the court found relevant.

facilities, distinct customers, distinct prices, sensitivity to price changes, and specialized vendors. Because § 7 of the Clayton Act prohibits any merger which may substantially lessen competition "in *any* line of commerce" (emphasis supplied), it is necessary to examine the effects of a merger in each such economically significant submarket to determine if there is a reasonable probability that the merger will substantially lessen competition. If such a probability is found to exist, the merger is proscribed.

Applying these considerations to the present case, we conclude that the record supports the District Court's finding that the relevant lines of commerce are men's, women's, and children's shoes. These product lines are recognized by the public; each line is manufactured in separate plants; each has characteristics peculiar to itself rendering it generally noncompetitive with the others; and each is, of course, directed toward a distinct class of customers. . . .

This is not to say, however, that "price/quality" differences, where they exist, are unimportant in analyzing a merger; they may be of importance in determining the likely effect of a merger. But the boundaries of the relevant market must be drawn with sufficient breadth to include the competing products of each of the merging companies and to recognize competition where, in fact, competition exists. Thus we agree with the District Court that in this case a further division of product lines based on "price/quality" differences would be "unrealistic." . . .

We agree with the parties and the District Court that insofar as the vertical aspect of this merger is concerned, the relevant geographic market is the entire Nation. The relationships of product value, bulk, weight and consumer demand enable manufacturers to distribute their shoes on a nationwide basis, as Brown and Kinney, in fact, do. The anticompetitive effects of the merger are to be measured within this range of distribution. . . .

Once the area of the effective competition affected by a vertical arrangement has been defined, an analysis must be made to determine if the effect of the arrangement "may be substantially to lessen competition, or to tend to create a monopoly" in this market.

Since the diminution of the vigor of competition which may stem from a vertical arrangement results primarily from a foreclosure of a share of the market otherwise open to competitors, an important consideration in determining whether the effect of a vertical arrangement "may be substantially to lessen competition, or to tend to create a monopoly" is the size of the share of the market foreclosed. However, this factor will seldom be determinative. If the share of the market foreclosed is so large that it approaches monopoly proportions, the Clayton Act will, of course, have been violated; but the arrangement will also have run afoul of the Sherman Act. And the legislative history of § 7 indicates clearly that the tests for measuring the legality of any particular economic arrangement under the Clayton Act are to be less stringent than those used in applying the

Sherman Act. On the other hand, foreclosure of a *de minimis* share of the market will not tend "substantially to lessen competition."

Between these extremes, in cases such as the one before us, in which the foreclosure is neither of monopoly nor *de minimis* proportions, the percentage of the market foreclosed by the vertical arrangement cannot itself be decisive. In such cases, it becomes necessary to undertake an examination of various economic and historical factors in order to determine whether the arrangement under review is of the type Congress sought to proscribe.

A most important such factor to examine is the very nature and purpose of the arrangement.[73] Congress not only indicated that "the tests of illegality [under § 7] are intended to be similar to those which the courts have applied in interpreting the same language as used in other sections of the Clayton Act," but also chose for § 7 language virtually identical to that of § 3 of the Clayton Act, 15 U.S.C. §§ 14, 15 U.S.C.A. § 14, which had been interpreted by this Court to require an examination of the interdependence of the market share foreclosed by, and the economic purpose of, the vertical arrangement. Thus, for example, if a particular vertical arrangement, considered under § 3, appears to be a limited term exclusive-dealing contract, the market foreclosure must generally be significantly greater than if the arrangement is a tying contract before the arrangement will be held to have violated the Act....

The importance which Congress attached to economic purpose is further demonstrated by the Senate and House Reports on H.R. 2734, which evince an intention to preserve the "failing company" doctrine of *International Shoe Co. v. Federal Trade Comm.*, 280 U.S. 291. Similarly, Congress foresaw that the merger of two large companies or a large and a small company might violate the Clayton Act while the merger of two small companies might not, although the share of the market foreclosed be identical, if the purpose of the small companies is to enable them in combination to compete with larger corporations dominating the market.

The present merger involved neither small companies nor failing companies.... [I]n this industry, no merger between a manufacturer and an independent retailer could involve a larger potential market foreclosure. Moreover, it is apparent both from past behavior of Brown and from the testimony of Brown's President, that Brown would use its ownership of Kinney to force Brown shoes into Kinney stores. Thus, in operation this vertical arrangement would be quite analogous to one involving a tying clause.[74]

---

73. Although it is "unnecessary for the Government to speculate as to what is in the 'back of the minds' of those who promote a merger," H.R.Rep. No. 1191, 81st Cong., 1st Sess. 8, evidence indicating the purpose of the merging parties, where available, is an aid in predicting the probable future conduct of the parties and thus the probable effects of the merger....

74. Moreover, ownership integration is a more permanent and irreversible tie than is contract integration. See Kessler and Stern, Competition, Contract, and Vertical Integration, 69 Yale L.J. 1, 78 (1959).

Another important factor to consider is the trend toward concentration in the industry. It is true, of course, that the statute prohibits a given merger only if the effect of that merger may be substantially to lessen competition. But the very wording of § 7 requires a prognosis of the probable future effect of the merger.

The existence of a trend toward vertical integration, which the District Court found, is well substantiated by the record. Moreover, the court found a tendency of the acquiring manufacturers to become increasingly important sources of supply for their acquired outlets. The necessary corollary of these trends is the foreclosure of independent manufacturers from markets otherwise open to them. And because these trends are not the product of accident but are rather the result of deliberate policies of Brown and other leading shoe manufacturers, account must be taken of these facts in order to predict the probable future consequences of this merger. It is against this background of continuing concentration that the present merger must be viewed.

Brown argues, however, that the shoe industry is at present composed of a large number of manufacturers and retailers, and that the industry is dynamically competitive. But remaining vigor cannot immunize a merger if the trend in that industry is toward oligopoly. *See Pillsbury Mills, Inc.*, 50 F.T.C. 555, 573. It is the probable effect of the merger upon the future as well as the present which the Clayton Act commands the courts and the Commission to examine.

Moreover, as we have remarked above, not only must we consider the probable effects of the merger upon the economics of the particular markets affected but also we must consider its probable effects upon the economic way of life sought to be preserved by Congress. Congress was desirous of preventing the formation of future oligopolies with their attendant adverse effects upon local control of industry and upon small business. Where an industry was composed of numerous units, Congress appeared anxious to preserve this structure. . . .

The District Court's findings, and the record facts, . . . convince us that the shoe industry is being subjected to . . . a cumulative series of vertical mergers which, if left unchecked, will be likely "substantially to lessen competition."

We reach this conclusion because the trend toward vertical integration in the shoe industry, when combined with Brown's avowed policy of forcing its own shoes upon its retail subsidiaries, may foreclose competition from a substantial share of the markets for men's, women's, and children's shoes, without producing any countervailing competitive, economic, or social advantages. . . .

[Another] significant aspect of this merger is that it creates a large national chain which is integrated with a manufacturing operation. The retail outlets of integrated companies, by eliminating wholesalers and by increasing the volume of purchases from the manufacturing division of the enterprise, can market their own brands at prices below those of competing independent retailers. Of course, some of the results of large integrated or chain operations are beneficial to consumers. Their expansion is not rendered unlawful by the mere fact that small independent stores may be adversely affected. It is competition, not competitors, which the Act protects. But we cannot fail to recognize Congress' desire to promote competition through the protection of viable, small, locally-owned businesses. Congress appreciated that occasional higher costs and prices might result from the maintenance of fragmented industries and markets. It resolved these competing considerations in favor of decentralization. We must give effect to that decision.[75]

NOTES AND QUESTIONS

1.   Most of the shoe stores attributed to Brown Shoe for purposes of computing its market share in the retail sale of shoes were owned by others. In assigning these shoe stores to Brown Shoe's control, Chief Justice Warren referred, *inter alia*, to the fact that Brown Shoe provided substantial assistance in the form of merchandising and advertising aids, granted loans, and sold to the stores under short-term franchise agreements. Also, Brown Shoe required retailers to deal "almost exclusively" in its products. In that connection, consider the facts and discussion in *FTC v. Brown Shoe*, p. 948 supra, where the Commission successfully challenged these arrangements under Section 5 of the FTC Act. Does the relationship between Brown Shoe and these retailers, as described in the Supreme Court opinions in the two Brown Shoe cases, persuasively demonstrate that the outlets were subject to Brown Shoe's "control"? *Cf. Standard Oil Co. of California v. United States*, p. 937 supra. What standard of "control" ought to apply for purposes of measuring market shares under Section 7?

2.   In his concurring opinion, Justice Harlan noted the following facts with respect to the effects of the Brown Shoe–Kinney merger in the vertical line:

> . . . While Kinney was making only about 1.2% of the total retail dollar sales in the United States in 1955, that percentage can hardly be deemed an accurate reflection of its proportion of nationwide shoe *purchases* by retailers since the retail sales figure is based on a computation that includes all retail stores, whether or not they were vertically integrated or otherwise affiliated. In terms of available markets for independent shoe manufacturers, the percentage of Kinney's purchases must have been substantially larger—though the precise figure is unavailable on the record before us.

The implication of these remarks seems to be that for purposes of computing market shares foreclosed by the merger, captive sales in the industry ought to be excluded. Does this make sense since shoe manufacturers that had supplied Kinney and were displaced by the merger could not turn to captive outlets of other shoe manufacturers and expect to compete on an equal footing? On the other hand, recall Section 1.31 of the DOJ–FTC Horizontal Merger Guidelines which proposes to include in the market the production of "vertically integrated firms to the extent

---

75.   Frankfurter, J., took no part in the decision of the case and White, J., took no part in the consideration or decision of the case. The concurring opinion of Clark, J., is omitted, as is the opinion of Harlan, J., dissenting in part and concurring in part.

that such inclusion accurately reflects their competitive significance in the relevant market prior to the merger." That suggests that captive production is in the market unless there is a special reason (for example, commitment of capacity under long-term supply contracts) why the captive production could not flow into the market in response to a post-merger price increase. That formulation seems to buy into the Bork notion (supra page 1129) that an upstream firm is likely to abandon its downstream subsidiary and sell in the open market (unless prevented by contract or some other reason) if it can obtain a better price in the open market. Which approach seems more realistic?

3. According to the majority opinion, Brown Shoe, by 1957, supplied 7.9 percent of Kinney's shoe needs, and Kinney accounted for 1.6 percent of national pairage of non-rubber shoes. Does this mean that the Supreme Court found a violation of Section 7 where a merger resulted in the foreclosure of 7.9 percent of 1.6 percent?

4. Also, the Court concluded that a principal purpose of the merger was to "force Brown Shoes into Kinney stores," p. 1144 supra. How could Brown Shoe profit from forcing Kinney to purchase its shoes? Would advantages to Brown Shoe be offset by equivalent disadvantages to Kinney?

5. After the merger, it will almost certainly be true that Brown Shoe will continue to supply independent, unintegrated shoe stores that compete with Kinney. To what extent is it predictable that Brown Shoe will discriminate in favor of Kinney as opposed to the unaffiliated outlets? In price? Quality? Reliability of service? Should the fact that a vertically integrated firm is likely to follow a preferential policy in favor of itself be a major consideration in developing standards to test the legality of vertical mergers under Section 7? Or would it be wiser to wait until some sort of "price squeeze" or "discrimination" results in injury to competition before intervention under the antitrust laws is attempted?

6. Professors Blake and Jones defended the Supreme Court's decision in the *Brown Shoe* case by spotlighting the remarkable trend toward vertical integration between major shoe manufacturers and large chain operations (for example, of 3534 stores in large chain operations, 1114 had become subsidiaries of the major shoe manufacturers), and the fact that the "incipiency" aspect of Section 7 justified government intervention at an early point when there was a marked trend toward concentration. Blake & Jones, Towards a Three–Dimensional Antitrust Policy, 65 Colum. L.Rev. 422, 453–57 (1965). Again, recall that the DOJ–FTC Horizontal Merger Guidelines omit any mention of industry trend as a factor in analyzing mergers even though it was so clearly a part of Congress' thinking when it revised Section 7 in 1950 (*see* note 4, supra page 968).

7. Professors Areeda and Turner reached the following conclusion about the *Brown Shoe* case:

> Both the reasoning and the result in *Brown Shoe* seem indefensible. As a Supreme Court precedent never subsequently repudiated, the decision was undoubtedly responsible in large part for those subsequent court and Federal Trade Commission decisions invalidating vertical mergers involving relatively small "foreclosures" and no substantial threats to competition. Accordingly, those subsequent decisions do not "add" to the weight of precedent or impose any significant obstacle to those courts willing to think hard about the competitive implications of vertical mergers while confining *Brown Shoe* to its particular facts as perceived by the 1962 Court.

4 Areeda & Turner, Antitrust Law 314 (1980).

Do you agree with Areeda and Turner? How much weight would you put on the trend towards vertical integration described by Professors Blake and Jones? Although the Supreme Court's decision points in both directions, would your view of the *Brown Shoe* case be influenced by solid evidence that the merger had no "countervailing competitive, economic, or social advantages"? Do you think the *Ford Motor* case (discussed in note 8 below) falls into the Areeda and Turner category of "vertical mergers involving relatively small 'foreclosures' and no substantial threats to competition"?

8.   FORD MOTOR CO. v. UNITED STATES, 405 U.S. 562, 92 S.Ct. 1142, 31 L.Ed.2d 492 (1972). Ford Motor Company, the nation's second largest producer of automobiles, in 1961 acquired from Electric Autolite Co. the following assets: the Autolite trade name, Autolite's only spark plug plant in this country (located in New Fostoria, Ohio), a battery plant, and extensive rights to Autolite's nationwide distribution organization for spark plugs and batteries. Electric Autolite continued in business, and in 1962 began manufacturing spark plugs under the brand name Prestolite, capturing 1.6% of the market by 1964. The district court ruled that Ford's acquisition of the Autolite assets violated Section 7 of the Clayton Act, and the Supreme Court affirmed, the issues on appeal being limited to the spark plug business.

The three leading automobile manufacturers, General Motors, Ford and Chrysler (accounting for 90% of the nation's automobile production), were matched by three leading spark plug manufacturers. General Motors manufactured spark plugs under its AC brand for its own automobiles; Ford purchased spark plugs from Champion for its automobiles; and Chrysler purchased spark plugs from Autolite for its automobiles. By custom in the repair trade, mechanics used the same plugs as the original equipment. This "OE tie" was of significance, leading Champion and Autolite to sell spark plugs at less than cost to Ford and Chrysler in order to assure their participation in the profitable "aftermarket." In 1961, Autolite's share of the spark plug market was 15%, Champion's share was 50%, and AC's share was 30%. Subsequently, Champion's share declined to 33%. Other small manufacturers of spark plugs had no important share of the market. Ford was interested in participating in the profitable spark plug aftermarket, and, in order to avoid the 5–to–8–year delay that would be incident to internal expansion, it acquired the designated assets of Autolite.

The merger was held to be unlawful on two grounds. First, Ford was a potential entrant into the spark plug industry and exerted a moderating influence on Champion and the other spark plug companies, because it was both a prime candidate for entry and because it was a major customer of Champion. Also, Ford might someday have entered by internal expansion and set the stage for noticeable deconcentration. Second, the acquisition of the Autolite assets resulted in the foreclosure of Ford as a purchaser of about 10% of spark plug output. Considered with the General Motors ownership of AC, the acquisition tended to transmit to the spark plug industry the rigidity of the automobile industry, reducing the chances for future deconcentration of the spark plug industry and raising barriers to entry.

The Court rejected as not material the argument that the acquisition would make Autolite a more vigorous and effective competitor against Champion and AC than Autolite had been as an independent. Ford was seeking a foothold in the aftermarket. Once established, it would have every incentive to perpetuate the "OE tie" and thus maintain the virtually insurmountable barriers to entry to the aftermarket. The major possibility for deconcentration of the aftermarket was the development of private brands by mass merchandisers. To the extent that spark plug manufacturers were not owned by the auto makers, they would be more favorably disposed toward private-brand sales and would compete more vigorously for such sales. It would be in the interest of OE plug manufacturers to discourage private-brand sales and to encourage the "OE tie."

In addition to ordering divestiture, the district court's decree:

(1) enjoined Ford for 10 years from manufacturing spark plugs,

(2) ordered Ford for five years to purchase one-half of its total annual requirements of spark plugs from the divested plant under the "Autolite" name,

(3) prohibited Ford for the same period from using its own trade names on spark plugs, and

(4) required Ford for 10 years to continue its policy of selling spark plugs to its dealers at prices no less than its prevailing minimum suggested jobbers' selling price.

The latter provision, designed to assemble an adequate distribution system for the aftermarket by permitting service stations and independent jobbers to compete with franchised car dealers, was not challenged before the Supreme Court. The first three provisions were challenged but were sustained by a divided Court. The majority opinion reasoned: "The ancillary measures ordered by the District Court are designed to allow Autolite to re-establish itself in the OE and replacement markets and to maintain it as a viable competitor until such time as forces within the market place weaken the OE tie." Ford argued that the 10–year prohibition on its manufacture of spark plugs would lessen competition because it would remove a potential competitor from the marketplace. Recalling the 5–to–8 years estimated as required for Ford to establish a spark plug division internally, the Court observed:

> The five-year prohibition on the use of its own name and the 10–year limitation on its own manufacturing mesh neatly to allow Ford to establish itself in the aftermarket prior to becoming a manufacturer.... Thus, the District Court's decree delays for only two to five years the date on which Ford may become a manufacturer with an established share of the aftermarket. Given the normal five-to-eight year lead time on entry through internal expansion, the District Court's decree does not significantly lessen Ford's moderating influence as a potential entrant on the edge of the market.

Justices Powell and Rehnquist did not participate in the decision. Justice Stewart concurred in the result in a separate opinion not markedly different from the majority opinion. Chief Justice Burger and Justice Blackmun dissented on the ancillary injunctive provisions.

Fruehauf Corp. v. FTC

United States Court of Appeals, Second Circuit, 1979.
603 F.2d 345.

[Fruehauf, the nation's largest manufacturer of truck trailers, acquired Kelsey, which made heavy duty wheels ("HDW"), an "essential component" of truck trailers. It was "undisputed" that the relevant geographic market in which to judge the acquisition was the United States and that the product markets were truck trailers and HDW.[76] The total value of truck trailer shipments in the United States was approximately $1 billion per year. Fruehauf accounted for about 25% of sales; the top four firms accounted for about 49% and the top eight firms for about 64%. In the HDW market, Kelsey accounted for 15% of the market sales. The top four HDW producers accounted for between 65% and 71% of the market and the top eight firms had 93% to 95% of the market. HDW were used for either trucks (or similar vehicles) or truck trailers.

The FTC found a violation of Section 7 of the Clayton Act. The Second Circuit reversed and denied enforcement.]

■ MANSFIELD, J. . . .

As the Supreme Court recognized in *Brown Shoe*, supra, the fountainhead of § 7 analysis of vertical mergers, the competitive significance of a vertical merger results primarily from the degree, if any, to which it may increase barriers to entry into the market or reduce competition by (1) foreclosing competitors of the purchasing firm in the merger from access to a potential source of supply, or from access on competitive terms, (2) by foreclosing competitors of the selling firm (in this case other HDW . . . manufacturers) from access to the market or a substantial portion of it, or (3) by forcing actual or potential competitors to enter or continue in the market only on a vertically integrated basis because of advantages unrelated to economies attributable solely to integration. The ultimate objective, however, is to determine whether and how the particular merger in issue may lessen competition, *i.e.*, what its anticompetitive effect on the market, if any, is likely to be. . . .

In *Brown Shoe* the Court described some of the factors to be considered in "predicting the probable future conduct of the parties and thus the probable effects of the merger." Most important among the factors are the nature and economic purpose of the arrangement, the likelihood and size of any market foreclosure, the extent of concentration of sellers and buyers in the industry, the capital cost required to enter the market, the market share needed by a buyer or seller to achieve a profitable level of production (sometimes referred to as "scale economy"), the existence of a trend toward vertical concentration or oligopoly in the industry, and whether the merger will eliminate potential competition by one of the merging parties. To these factors may be added the degree of market power that would be possessed by the merged enterprise and the number and strength of competing suppliers and purchasers, which might indicate whether the merger would increase the risk that prices or terms would cease to be competitive. This

76. Ed. Kelsey also made antiskid brake devices ("ASBD") and accounted for 32% of sales by unit and 28.6% of sales by dollar volume in this market. Fruehauf's purchases amounted to 4.7% of the market. But the ASBD were purchased only to satisfy certain government regulations which had been withdrawn as to truck trailers. Therefore, Fruehauf was unlikely to purchase a significant volume of these devices in the future, and the Second Circuit set aside the FTC's conclusions "without prejudice to its right to renew its proceeding if future developments should prove that the predicted demise of the ASBD market is greatly exaggerated." 603 F.2d at 356.

list, with some variations, has been the standard framework for analysis of the legality of a vertical merger.... Application of these factors may reveal that a vertical merger poses no threat to competition at all, resulting merely in a realignment of sales as a result of "in-house" transactions within the merged enterprise but leaving the number of competing sellers and their market shares unchanged, or that it poses a threatened lessening of competition that may be *de minimis*, may be of monopoly proportions, or may lie somewhere in between the two, 370 U.S. at 328–29.

As the Supreme Court made clear in *Brown Shoe*, there are no precise formulas for determining whether a vertical merger may probably lessen competition. Rather, the objective of discerning what, if any, anticompetitive effects the merger may have can be achieved only by examining the foregoing market factors as they exist for the particular merger in issue. It is true that the Department of Justice has for many years issued "Merger Guidelines" for the purpose of indicating to the business community, legal profession and the public generally when the Department may question the legality of a merger. *See* U.S. Dept. of Justice Merger Guidelines, 1 Trade Reg.Rep. (CCH) ¶ 4510.[77] But just as these guidelines do not preclude governmental challenge to a merger which does not fall within all the terms of the guidelines, *see Atlantic Richfield*, supra, 297 F.Supp. at 1073, so the guidelines do not establish the illegality of a merger which does fit the criteria used by the Justice Department in deciding whether to challenge a merger. The guidelines, therefore, simply reflect the considered view of the Justice Department as to which mergers are most likely to create a reasonable probability of substantially lessening competition and which may therefore warrant the institution of legal action. *See* Guidelines ¶ 1, supra, at 6882. Accordingly, whether or not the degree of market concentration, the height of entry barriers, the size of the merging firms, and the extent of foreclosure match or exceed the benchmarks incorporated into the Justice Department's guidelines, the Commission still bears the burden of showing the likelihood that the future effect of "*that* merger [of Kelsey and Fruehauf] may be substantially to lessen competition." *Brown Shoe*, supra, 370 U.S. at 332 (emphasis in original).

With these basic principles in mind we proceed to review the Commission's findings and conclusions with respect to the Fruehauf–Kelsey merger.

The Truck Trailer Market

The Commission concluded that the merger violated § 7 with respect to the truck trailer market solely on the theory that in the event of a shortage of HDWs Kelsey would give Fruehauf a substantial competitive advantage over other trailer manufacturers by diverting to Fruehauf

---

77. The Guidelines [of 1968] state that the Department may be expected to challenge "a merger or series of mergers between a supplying firm, accounting for approximately 10% or more of the sales in its market, and one or more purchasing firms, accounting *in toto* for approximately 6% or more of the total purchases in that market, unless it clearly appears that there are no significant barriers to entry into the business of the purchasing firm or firms." Guidelines ¶ 12.

wheels that would otherwise go to Kelsey's other customers, some of which are trailer manufacturers.[78] This conclusion rests upon several assumptions, having no appreciable evidentiary support. One assumption is that Kelsey is a significant and substantial supplier of HDWs to Fruehauf's competitors. The record reveals that, on the contrary, trailer manufacturers have in the past purchased almost all of their HDWs from other suppliers, with Kelsey's sales of wheels to trailer manufacturers other than Fruehauf amounting to approximately $1.4 million per year out of total average annual HDW market sales amounting to $200 million per year during the three-year period prior to the merger. In the years 1970–72, sales to trailer manufacturers, including Fruehauf, accounted for only about 7% of Kelsey's HDW output. Thus Kelsey, while a large manufacturer of HDWs, has hardly been a substantial supplier of HDWs to trailer manufacturers.

The second unsupported assumption is that Kelsey would, in the event of an HDW shortage, divert to Fruehauf HDW sales that would otherwise be made to other customers. There is no evidence, and it is not alleged, that Fruehauf contemplated such a stratagem when it entered the merger with Kelsey. More important, there is no credible evidence that another shortage is reasonably foreseeable. Even if it were, the evidence that Kelsey would give priority to Fruehauf's needs is insubstantial. As to the likelihood of a shortage, the record indicates that the combined capacity of wheel producers was considerably expanded after the 1973–74 shortage and that, even when conservatively estimated, this capacity exceeds a liberal estimate of anticipated demand during the next five or ten years.

During past shortages Kelsey, like other wheel producers, has allocated its production pro rata among its customers in accordance with their regular volume of purchases. Appellant insists that Kelsey will follow this precedent in the future, notwithstanding Fruehauf's ownership of the company. The Commission cites no evidence shedding doubt upon this representation. On the contrary a spokesman from Trailmobile Corp., Fruehauf largest competitor, testified that his company believed that the merger would not affect Kelsey's policy in favor of pro rata distribution in the event of a shortage.

One might reasonably question the weight to be given to appellant's self-serving assurances that Kelsey would allocate pro rata if the need arose, as well as the significance of Kelsey's pro rata distribution of wheels during the 1973–74 shortage, which took place after the merger but at a time when appellant could have anticipated a challenge to its legality. However Kelsey's policy in favor of pro rata allocation need not rest upon some philosophical commitment to egalitarianism since it could also make sound business sense. If Kelsey deprived its regular customers of a propor-

---

78. Fruehauf would enjoy an unfair advantage over its competitors if Kelsey diverted sales to Fruehauf from customers who do not build trailers, but the relative advantage would not be as great. Moreover, Kelsey's non-trailer customers, including Ford and General Motors, exercise the greatest leverage over Kelsey with the threat of retaliatory withdrawal of patronage.

tionate share of HDWs in times of shortage it would risk their retaliating by shifting to competing suppliers not only their purchases of HDWs but of other products presently bought from Kelsey, which could cause it greater economic harm. In addition, by granting priority to Fruehauf over other trailer manufacturers who purchase wheels from Kelsey, Kelsey would invite antitrust damage actions against it by these trailer firms. Under the circumstances, it appears highly unlikely that Kelsey would take such risks.

Thus the Commission's finding that the merger violates § 7 with respect to the truck trailer market is based on speculation rather than fact. It assumes in the face of contrary evidence that a shortage will recur in the reasonably proximate future. Upon this unsupported basis it infers that in the event of a shortage Kelsey would give priority to Fruehauf to the detriment of its competitors. Although neither of these assumptions is by any means beyond the realm of the possible, here they run counter to the actual evidence in the record. We cannot therefore say that they add up to a reasonable probability that the merger will substantially lessen competition. Accordingly, the finding of a § 7 violation based upon the effect of the merger on the truck trailer market must be set aside as unsupported by substantial evidence. . . .

We accept at the outset the Commission's findings that the HDW market is significantly concentrated, based on evidence that the top four producers account for 65–71% of the market, the top eight for 93–95%, and Kelsey, the third largest producer, 15%. Moreover, the Commission's determination that barriers to entry into HDW production are substantial is supported by evidence that the initial capital outlay required to enter production at an efficient level is $10–$20 million. . . .

There is, therefore, substantial evidence, albeit not uncontroverted, supporting the Commission's conclusion that the capital cost barrier is substantial and significant, whatever the minimum level of efficient production might be. For this reason we do not reject the Commission's decision on this issue.

The Commission further concluded that the amount of market foreclosure likely to result from the merger would range from "a weak 3.9" [actually 3.3%] to a "strong 5.8" of the market production of HDWs, depending upon whether one limits the calculation of Fruehauf's purchases of cast spoke HDWs, which are made by Kelsey and accounted for 3.3% of the market during the three-year premerger period, or also includes Fruehauf's purchases of heavy duty disc wheels, not presently manufactured by Kelsey, which accounted for 2.5% of the total HDW market during the same period. Since Kelsey does make discs for light-weight trucks and could produce heavy duty discs, the Commission was entitled to infer that Fruehauf, with its tradition of in-house purchasing, could expand Kelsey's disc wheel facilities to furnish at least the major part of Fruehauf's disc needs except possibly for nonintegral hubs. However, there is no evidence that competing purchasers of these products would be foreclosed from continuing to obtain all or part of their cast spoke needs from Kelsey or its competitors at competitive prices. Nor was there proof that removal from the market of up to 5.8% of its HDW sales would preclude any existing competitor from continuing to operate economically or any potential competitor from entering the market.

The Commission further found that there had been periodic HDW shortages within the 12 years prior to the merger (*i.e.*, in 1966, 1968–69, 1973–74) and that, although Fruehauf was not itself a potential competitor in the production of HDWs prior to the merger, it had engaged in certain pro-competitive activities, consisting of experiments with new types of fabricated aluminum and steel wheels and encouragement of one foundry, McConway and Torley, to produce cast spoke wheels.

From the foregoing the Commission concluded that the merger

"runs afoul of Section 7 by foreclosing Fruehauf as a source of patronage of heavy duty wheels in a market setting in which such foreclosure is likely to increase barriers to entry, make new entry more difficult and less likely, and thereby enhance the market power conferred by a highly concentrated market structure into which entry was previously difficult to begin with. Additionally we believe that the merger is likely to lessen competition substantially by foreclosing Kelsey–Hayes as a source of supply to truck trailer manufacturers should shortages of supply recur." 91 F.T.C. at 236.

With due respect for the Commission's expertise, we fail to find any logical basis in the evidence for this conclusion, even when the record is viewed most favorably to the Commission. Not only is the conclusion a *non sequitur* but it flies in the face of undisputed contrary evidence.

There is no evidence in the record that existing barriers to entry into the HDW market or the existing concentration of producers in it, both admittedly substantial, have been or would be increased by the merger. There is no reason to believe that the merger will adversely affect scale economies for HDW production, thereby increasing the cost of entry. Nor does the Commission suggest that as a result of the merger a firm could successfully enter the HDW or the trailer market only by simultaneously entering at both levels. As to the effect of the merger on the concentration of the HDW industry, since Fruehauf's principal supplier of spoke wheels has been Dayton?Walther, the largest producers of spokes and second largest wheel producer, any shifting of patronage from Dayton to Kelsey will tend to even out the market shares of the three largest sellers of HDWs, but not increase their aggregate market share. The ALJ expressly refused to find that the merger would entrench Kelsey as a producer, stating "I cannot conclude that Kelsey–Hayes has been 'entrenched' as that term has heretofore been used in Section 7 cases."

Moreover, there is no allegation that the merger of Fruehauf and Kelsey is part of an existing or prospective trend toward vertical integration, such as existed in *Brown Shoe*, supra, and in other cases.[79] There

---

79. See Brown Shoe, supra, 370 U.S. at 332–33, 334; United States Steel Corp. v. FTC, 426 F.2d 592, 603 (6th Cir.1970); United States v. Ford Motor Co., 315 F.Supp. 372,

is no suggestion, much less evidence, that the merger was motivated by a desire to restrain competition. On the contrary, the evidence is undisputed that Kelsey, whose stock was selling substantially below book value, sought out Fruehauf in order to avoid takeover efforts on the part of others. Nor is there any evidence that the merger might impair competition by conferring upon one of the merging partners a "deep pocket" or financial clout not enjoyed by its rivals. It is true that some market foreclosure may ensue from the merger, but not one that deprives rivals from major channels of distribution, much less one that excludes them from the market altogether. Even if Fruehauf were to switch its purchase of its entire HDW wheel needs, amounting to 5.8% of the market, from others to Kelsey (which would require Kelsey to enter heavy duty disc production), there would merely be a realignment of existing market sales without any likelihood of a diminution in competition.

The only theory suggested by the Commission as to how the merger might impair competition in the HDW market is that, assuming Kelsey supplied all of Fruehauf's HDW needs, amounting to 5.8% of the market or slightly less than the minimum Department of Justice Guideline figure, this foreclosure would be sufficient alone in such a setting to significantly lessen the likelihood that a new firm would enter this market or, what amounts to the same thing for our purposes, to lessen the chance that an existing small competitor would substantially increase its capacity and compete on a wider scale. According to the Commission, although it found that Fruehauf itself was not a potential entrant into the HDW market, Fruehauf had a pro-competitive effect on the market through its collaborative efforts to develop new types of heavy duty wheels and by virtue of its ability to draw new entrants into production of conventional wheels by offering to deliver its patronage.[80]

375 (E.D.Mich.1970), aff'd, 405 U.S. 562 (1972); United States v. Kennecott Copper Corp., 231 F.Supp. 95, 103–05 (S.D.N.Y. 1964), aff'd per curiam, 381 U.S. 414 (1965); Ash Grove Cement Co., 85 F.T.C. 1123, 1165–66 (1975), aff'd, 577 F.2d 1368 (9th Cir.1978).

80. In the late 1960s and early 1970s Fruehauf experimented with a fabricated aluminum wheel and a fabricated steel wheel for production in Fruehauf's own facilities. Fruehauf abandoned the steel wheel project in early 1970 in order to concentrate its efforts on the aluminum wheel, which seemed more promising. This project was abandoned in 1971 when Fruehauf determined that under existing market conditions production of fabricated aluminum wheels was not economically feasible. Following the termination of these efforts to develop a wheel for in-house production, Fruehauf explored with U.S. Steel the development of a fabricated steel wheel to be designed by an outside engineer-

ing firm and produced by U.S. Steel. The prototype turned out to be unacceptable for commercial use, and the project ended in September 1973.

In 1967–68, when a strike halted wheel production at Dayton–Walther, the leading producer of cast spoke wheels and Fruehauf's traditional principal supplier, Fruehauf favorably responded to an inquiry from McConway and Torley, a leading producer of cast steel components used by the railroad industry, about the possibility of it producing wheels for Fruehauf. Eager to cultivate an alternate source of supply, Fruehauf provided McConway with necessary drawings and helped finance the purchase of patterns and equipment. For a few years, McConway sold cast spokes to Fruehauf. Fruehauf stopped buying from McConway in late 1973, and shortly thereafter McConway, which had experienced greater than anticipated production problems, exited from the market....

In light of the record evidence, this theory is too ephemeral to sustain the Commission's decision. Although Fruehauf did experiment in the development of new kinds of wheels and assisted one foundry in temporary production of HDWs, both adventures proved to be complete failures and there is no evidence that, if the merger were disapproved, Fruehauf would engage in similar activities. Moreover, the Commission has presented no evidence suggesting that Fruehauf was unique in its ability to elicit new competition, and there is no reason to believe that other firms patronizing the HDW market, particularly the automotive and trucking giants, will not encourage firms in the wings to enter that market, should they be dissatisfied with the quality of the existing competition.

NOTES AND QUESTIONS

1. Is the *Fruehauf* case consistent with *Brown Shoe* in approach? In level of concern about the dangers of vertical integration? If, for example, you were a manufacturer of truck trailers (or another purchaser of HDW) would you feel more vulnerable after the Fruehauf–Kelsey acquisition? How could you protect yourself in terms of supply and price?

2. In its *Fruehauf* opinion, the Second Circuit states that the merger was not motivated by "a desire to restrain competition" but rather Kelsey sought out Fruehauf "in order to avoid takeover efforts on the part of others." In this regard, a report by the Congressional Research Service concluded:

> In the current hostile atmosphere, few companies faced with an unsolicited tender offer survive as independent companies even though companies are employing a variety of defensive tactics to thwart raiders. Often the only possibility is to secure the protection of a "white knight," a company willing to purchase the target on terms arguably more favorable to it and usually with a provision to retain existing management.... But the spectacle of large Fortune 500 companies attacking each other, counter-attacking and maneuvering as if engaged in war games has raised public policy questions which go beyond the traditional antitrust and economic concentration questions raised in prior merger periods.

> In a somewhat skewed notion of the survival of the fittest, it is the well-managed firms which are frequently the targets. At a time of concern over the competitive position and the rate of investment of U.S. industry, some cash-rich firms are moving to acquire in order to avoid being acquired.[81]

When a vertical (or other) merger comes about in this "war games" atmosphere, is it as likely to be efficiency enhancing? Should such a consideration be relevant to the analysis of mergers under Section 7?

3. The reference in the *Fruehauf* case to Department of Justice Merger Guidelines is to a set of guidelines issued in 1968. As you know, the latest version of the Guidelines covering vertical mergers was issued in 1984, and that portion of the

81. Congressional Research Service, (March 1982).
Merger Tactics and Public Policy 24–25

Guidelines is printed directly below. Do you agree with the Second Circuit's treatment of the legal effect of the old guidelines? Are the new Guidelines consistent with *Brown Shoe*? With *Fruehauf*? With sound public policy?

Department of Justice Merger Guidelines, 1984[82]

June 14, 1984.

4.2   Competitive Problems from Vertical Mergers

4.21   Barriers to Entry from Vertical Mergers

In certain circumstances, the vertical integration resulting from vertical mergers could create competitively objectionable barriers to entry. Stated generally, three conditions are necessary (but not sufficient) for this problem to exist. First, the degree of vertical integration between the two markets must be so extensive that entrants to one market (the "primary market") also would have to enter the other market (the "secondary market")[83] simultaneously. Second, the requirement of entry at the secondary level must make entry at the primary level significantly more difficult and less likely to occur. Finally, the structure and other characteristics of the primary market must be otherwise so conducive to non-competitive performance that the increased difficulty of entry is likely to affect its performance. The following standards state the criteria by which the Department will determine whether these conditions are satisfied.

4.211   Need for Two–Level Entry

If there is sufficient unintegrated capacity[84] in the secondary market, new entrants to the primary market would not have to enter both markets simultaneously. The Department is unlikely to challenge a merger on this ground where post-merger sales (purchases) by unintegrated firms in the secondary market would be sufficient to service two minimum-efficient-scale plants in the primary market. When the other conditions are satisfied, the Department is increasingly likely to challenge a merger as the unintegrated capacity declines below this level.

---

82. See p. 1115 and p. 1034 supra for other sections of the Guidelines.

83. This competitive problem could result from either upstream or downstream integration, and could affect competition in either the upstream market or the downstream market. In the text, the term "primary market" refers to the market in which the competitive concerns are being considered, and the term "secondary market" refers to the adjacent market.

84. Ownership integration does not necessarily mandate two-level entry by new entrants to the primary market. Such entry is most likely to be necessary where the primary and secondary markets are completely

integrated by ownership and each firm in the primary market uses all of the capacity of its associated firm in the secondary market. In many cases of ownership integration, however, the functional fit between vertically integrated firms is not perfect, and an outside market exists for the sales (purchases) of the firms in the secondary market. If that market is sufficiently large and diverse, new entrants to the primary market may be able to participate without simultaneous entry to the secondary market. In considering the adequacy of this alternative, the Department will consider the likelihood of predatory price or supply "squeezes" by the integrated firms against their unintegrated rivals.

4.212 Increased Difficulty of Simultaneous Entry to Both Markets

The relevant question is whether the need for simultaneous entry to the secondary market gives rise to a substantial incremental difficulty as compared to entry into the primary market alone. If entry at the secondary level is easy in absolute terms, the requirement of simultaneous entry to that market is unlikely adversely to affect entry to the primary market. Whatever the difficulties of entry into the primary market may be, the Department is unlikely to challenge a merger on this ground if new entry into the secondary market can be accomplished under the conditions stated in Section 3.3.[85] When entry is not possible under those conditions, the Department is increasingly concerned about vertical mergers as the difficulty of entering the secondary market increases. The Department, however, will invoke this theory only where the need for secondary market entry significantly increases the costs (which may take the form of risks) of primary market entry.

More capital is necessary to enter two markets than to enter one. Standing alone, however, this additional capital requirement does not constitute a barrier to entry to the primary market. If the necessary funds were available at a cost commensurate with the level of risk in the secondary market, there would be no adverse effect. In some cases, however, lenders may doubt that would-be entrants to the primary market have the necessary skills and knowledge to succeed in the secondary market and, therefore, in the primary market. In order to compensate for this risk of failure, lenders might charge a higher rate for the necessary capital. This problem becomes increasingly significant as a higher percentage of the capital assets in the secondary market are long-lived and specialized to that market and, therefore, difficult to recover in the event of failure. In evaluating the likelihood of increased barriers to entry resulting from increased cost of capital, therefore, the Department will consider both the degree of similarity in the essential skills in the primary and secondary markets and the economic life and degree of specialization of the capital assets in the secondary market.

Economies of scale in the secondary market may constitute an additional barrier to entry to the primary market in some situations requiring two-level entry. The problem could arise if the capacities of minimum-efficient-scale plants in the primary and secondary markets differ significantly. For example, if the capacity of a minimum-efficient-scale plant in the secondary market were significantly greater than the needs of a minimum-efficient-scale plant in the primary market, entrants would have to choose between inefficient operation at the secondary level (because of operating an efficient plant at an inefficient output or because of operating an inefficiently small plant) or a larger than necessary scale at the primary level. Either of these effects could cause a significant increase in the operating costs of the entering firm.[86]

---

85. Entry into the secondary market may be greatly facilitated in that an assured supplier (customer) is provided by the primary market entry.

86. It is important to note, however,

4.213 Structure and Performance of the Primary Market

Barriers to entry are unlikely to affect performance if the structure of the primary market is otherwise not conducive to monopolization or collusion. The Department is unlikely to challenge a merger on this ground unless overall concentration of the primary market is above 1800 HHI (a somewhat lower concentration will suffice if one or more of the factors discussed in Section 3.4 indicate that effective collusion is particularly likely). Above that threshold, the Department is increasingly likely to challenge a merger that meets the other criteria set forth above as the concentration increases.

4.22 Facilitating Collusion Through Vertical Mergers

4.221 Vertical Integration to the Retail Level

A high level of vertical integration by upstream firms into the associated retail market may facilitate collusion in the upstream market by making it easier to monitor price. Retail prices are generally more visible than prices in upstream markets, and vertical mergers may increase the level of vertical integration to the point at which the monitoring effect becomes significant. Adverse competitive consequences are unlikely unless the upstream market is generally conducive to collusion and a large percentage of the products produced there are sold through vertically integrated retail outlets.

The Department is unlikely to challenge a merger on this ground unless 1) overall concentration of the upstream market is above 1800 HHI (a somewhat lower concentration will suffice if one or more of the factors discussed in Section 3.4 indicate that effective collusion is particularly likely), and 2) a large percentage of the upstream product would be sold through vertically integrated retail outlets after the merger. Where the stated thresholds are met or exceeded, the Department's decision whether to challenge a merger on this ground will depend upon an individual evaluation of its likely competitive effect.

4.222 Elimination of a Disruptive Buyer

The elimination by vertical merger of a particularly disruptive buyer in a downstream market may facilitate collusion in the upstream market. If upstream firms view sales to a particular buyer as sufficiently important, they may deviate from the terms of a collusive agreement in an effort to secure that business, thereby disrupting the operation of the agreement. The merger of such a buyer with an upstream firm may eliminate that rivalry, making it easier for the upstream firms to collude effectively. Adverse competitive consequences are unlikely unless the upstream market is generally conducive to collusion and the disruptive firm is significantly more attractive to sellers than the other firms in its market.

that this problem would not exist if a significant outside market exists at the secondary level. In that case, entrants could enter with the appropriately scaled plants at both levels, and sell or buy in the market as necessary.

The Department is unlikely to challenge a merger on this ground unless 1) overall concentration of the upstream market is 1800 HHI or above (a somewhat lower concentration will suffice if one or more of the factors discussed in Section 3.4 indicate that effective collusion is particularly likely), and 2) the allegedly disruptive firm differs substantially in volume of purchases or other relevant characteristics from the other firms in its market. Where the stated thresholds are met or exceeded, the Department's decision whether to challenge a merger on this ground will depend upon an individual evaluation of its likely competitive effect.

4.23 Evasion of Rate Regulation

Non-horizontal mergers may be used by monopoly public utilities subject to rate regulation as a tool for circumventing that regulation. The clearest example is the acquisition by a regulated utility of a supplier of its fixed or variable inputs. After the merger, the utility would be selling to itself and might be able arbitrarily to inflate the prices of internal transactions. Regulators may have great difficulty in policing these practices, particularly if there is no independent market for the product (or service) purchased from the affiliate. As a result, inflated prices could be passed along to consumers as "legitimate" costs. In extreme cases, the regulated firm may effectively preempt the adjacent market, perhaps for the purpose of suppressing observable market transactions, and may distort resource allocation in that adjacent market as well as in the regulated market. In such cases, however, the Department recognizes that genuine economies of integration may be involved. The Department will consider challenging mergers that create substantial opportunities for such abuses.

4.24 Efficiencies

As in the case of horizontal mergers, the Department will consider expected efficiencies in determining whether to challenge a vertical merger. *See* Section 3.5 (Efficiencies) [ed: now Section 4]. An extensive pattern of vertical integration may constitute evidence that substantial economies are afforded by vertical integration. Therefore, the Department will give relatively more weight to expected efficiencies in determining whether to challenge a vertical merger than in determining whether to challenge a horizontal merger.

NOTES AND QUESTIONS

1. The Department of Justice Vertical Merger Guidelines were adopted in 1982 and revised in 1984; arguably they still represent Department of Justice views on the subject. In neither instance did the Federal Trade Commission join in adoption of the Guidelines.

2. The Vertical Merger Guidelines, which purport to introduce new economic learning into conventional antitrust enforcement, have been controversial. Note that they do not mention the concept of "foreclosure" as a relevant competitive effect. Rather they suggest that the only challenges the Department of Justice

would support involve vertical mergers that have horizontal effects—either by raising barriers to entry at the primary or secondary level, or by contributing to the feasibility of collusion. Does that mean the Department of Justice, at least in the 1980s, believed that *Ford–Autolite* was wrongly decided?

Restoration of Federal Enforcement Against Vertical Mergers in the 1990s

During the 1980s and early 1990s, influenced by conservative scholarship like the excerpt from Robert Bork (page 1127, supra) and the permissive 1984 Department of Justice Merger Guidelines, there was no enforcement against vertical mergers at the federal level. In addition, there was widespread rejection of the views expressed by the Supreme Court in *Brown Shoe* that made vertical mergers between relatively small firms, with low barriers to entry, a violation of revised Section 7. The enforcement situation changed in the 1990s when a series of vertical mergers were either blocked or substantially restructured as a condition of government approval. Enforcement activity that was exclusively or primarily addressed to vertical aspects of a merger occurred for the most part at the Federal Trade Commission. Three examples of vertical challenges are described below:

1. *In re Silicon Graphics, Inc.*, 120 FTC 928 (1995). (5 Trade Reg. Rep. ¶ 23,838 (1995)). Silicon Graphics ("SGI") was the dominant provider of entertainment graphics workstations with a 90% market share, and proposed to acquire Alias and Wavefront, two of the three dominant developers of entertainment graphics and animation software. The workstation and software created 3–D computer graphics special effects used in film and video, television and interactive computer games. The Commission indicated concern about vertical foreclosure in both directions. Workstation manufacturers that were rivals to SGI would not be able to compete effectively if Alias and Wavefront were to design their software to be compatible only with SGI, and at the same time rival graphic software manufacturers would be foreclosed from 90% of the market if SGI were to close its previously open software interface so that only Alias and Wavefront would be able to design compatible software. On the other hand, there were very strong indications that the combination of SGI, Alias and Wavefront's complementary capacities was efficient and would lead to important innovation. To allow the merger to proceed, SGI signed a consent order providing that SGI would use best efforts to ensure optimal interoperation of Alias' leading software programs with competitor workstations, and that SGI would maintain an open architecture and publish its application programming interface for its workstations so that it did not discriminate against software rivals of Alias and Wavefront.

2. In *Time Warner–Turner*, 5 Trade Reg. Rep. ¶ 24,104 (1996), the Commission examined the potential competitive effects of a merger of Time Warner, a dominant programmer in movies, magazines, music, and network broadcasting (and also the second largest cable company in the U.S.)

with Turner, another major television programmer. Concern was expressed both with respect to upstream and downstream foreclosure effects. Programming competitors of Turner feared that they would be denied equal access to Time Warner cable as a result of the merger, and competitors of Time Warner cable (including particularly companies delivering programming through satellite systems) feared that they would be denied equal access to Turner's valuable news, sports and movie programming. The merger was allowed to proceed pursuant to a consent order that imposed an elaborate set of restrictions on the complying companies preserving access to competitors and banning unjustified discrimination.

The blockbuster sequel to *Time Warner–Turner* was *AOL-Time Warner*, a merger that involved both horizontal and vertical effects and is discussed at p. 1064, supra. Again, the merger was allowed to proceed, but only after acceptance of some unusually regulatory provisions designed to keep access open to new broadband technology and thereby allow programming competitors of Time Warner and internet service provider competitors of AOL to compete effectively after the merger.

3. *Barnes & Noble–Ingram.* In 1999, Barnes & Noble, the largest retail bookseller in the United States with 34% of national sales, proposed to acquire Ingram, the largest book wholesaler in the United States with 23% of national sales. The Commission investigated primarily on the theory that smaller bookstores competing with Barnes & Noble, after the merger, would not receive from the Ingram subsidiary comparable discounts, terms of sale, delivery dates, or marketing specials since their source of supply would be owned by a direct competitor. Another theory, explored but not emphasized, is that new entrants who wanted to come into the market for sale of books on the internet (and compete with such powerful early entrants as Amazon and Barnes & Noble's electronic subsidiary) would be denied a source of supply and arguably would have to enter not just internet retailing but become their own wholesaler. After the Commission staff indicated its intention to propose challenging the deal, the merger was abandoned. See Labaton, "Book Chain Gives In; Barnes and Noble Won't Seek $600 Million Deal," N.Y. Times, June 3, 1999.

4. Consider whether any or all of these transactions could be successfully challenged under the 1984 Department of Justice Merger Guidelines.

PROBLEM 26

PHILIPS PAPER ACQUIRES SOME PULP SOURCES

Five years ago, Philips Paper was the third largest manufacturer in the United States of paper products including toilet tissue, facial tissue, paper napkins, paper towels, and a full line of other specialty items. Philips sells directly to retail stores, grocery chains and supermarkets, and to wholesalers for distribution to industrial plants, offices, and hotels. Before the mergers here challenged, it accounted for 8% of total sales; National was first with 28% of sales, Wells second with 11%, and six other full-line companies averaged about 5% each. The remainder of the market was accounted for by about 30 small companies, each specializing in some particular paper product. Entry barriers into the business are moderate for full-line companies, involving a minimum investment of about $50 million, but low for specialty outlets.

Traditionally all full-line companies owned some timberland and paper pulp mills, but none was fully integrated. On the average, these companies including Philips supplied about 50% of their own needs; the captive share of the market was stable, however, and there had been no sizable vertical mergers in recent years. After several years of careful study, Philips decided to make itself independent of pulp suppliers and converters by acquiring three companies, each of which had extensive timber holdings and pulp converting facilities. The three together accounted for only about 2½% of all pulp sold, but 13% of the type of semi-processed materials suitable for conversion into Philips products. The acquisition involved an enormous outlay of cash and securities by Philips, since the acquired companies were valued at nearly $500 million. As a result of the acquisitions, Philips could not only satisfy all of its own needs but became a seller of semi-processed pulp to some of the specialty companies in the business. Soon after this acquisition, Philips embarked on a program of replacement or improvement of pulp conversion equipment in the acquired companies. The improvement program and full integration have led to substantial efficiencies of operation, with the result that Philips has become an aggressive competitor on sales of semi-processed pulp to specialty paper producers and on sales of its own finished paper products to retail and industrial users. With respect to the latter, Philips now accounts for 12% of total sales of paper products, is second in the industry, and continues to grow. Several news and business magazines have done feature stories on the remarkable recent success engineered by Philips' management, and its stock is highly prized by institutional investors.

Early last year, labor troubles led to a temporary period of short supply of pulp suitable for conversion to products other than newsprint. Philips used its supply of processed pulp to keep its own conversion operation going and delayed deliveries to independent converters. As soon as the shortages eased, Philips went back to supplying the independents at better prices than anyone else in the industry. Too late, however, because the independents had already complained to the FTC, and, as a result, a complaint will soon be filed.

Has Philips violated the antitrust laws?

NOTE ON FOREIGN MERGER REGULATION

Over the last twenty-five to thirty years, there has been a virtual explosion of merger regulation legislation around the world. It began in 1973 with the addition of merger control provisions to the German Law Against Restraints of Competition. In that same year, the Commission of the European Community first began serious discussions of its proposal for a new Council Regulation on the subject of mergers— a discussion that did not culminate in the enactment of the Merger Regulation until December 21, 1989, when the Council adopted Regulation 4064/89, O.J. L 395/1 (Dec. 30, 1989), corrected, O.J. L 257/14 (Sept. 21, 1990), with an effective date of September 21, 1990. In the United Kingdom, the Secretary of State for Trade and Industry was given the discretionary power to refer certain mergers to the Monopolies and Mergers Commission (MMC) under the Fair Trading Act 1973, for the MMC to investigate their effect on "the public interest." Merger regulation in its current form became part of the French and Canadian competition laws in 1986. For an excellent, in-depth comparative presentation of the major merger laws of the world, see Rowley & Baker (eds.), International Mergers: The Antitrust Process (1996).

Perhaps because few subjects in antitrust law cut more closely at the basic industrial or economic policy of a country, there is considerable variation in the substantive standards of the different merger regimes. In the United States, of course, mergers and acquisitions can be enjoined only if their effect would be substantially to lessen competition in a particular, defined market. The European Merger Regulation also uses criteria derived from competition law, as opposed to other fields of economic or social policy. Article 2(1) of the Regulation instructs the Commission to take into account "the need to maintain and develop effective competition within the common market," and familiar factors such as the market position of the companies, alternatives available to suppliers and users, their access to supplies or markets, barriers to entry, supply and demand trends, and "the development of technical and economic progress provided that it is to consumers' advantage and does not form an obstacle to competition." Article 2(2) provides that "a concentration which does not create or strengthen a dominant position as a result of which effective competition would be significantly impeded in the common market or in a substantial part of it shall be declared compatible with the common market." Article 2(3) states the converse: if the concentration creates or strengthens a dominant position, it must be declared incompatible with the common market.

Some merger laws are based on competition criteria, but they contain a political safety valve for the extraordinary case. The German law is a good case in point. The Federal Cartel Office reviews mergers for compliance with the German competition law, but its decisions are subject to review by the Economics and Technology Minister, who can override a decision to prohibit a merger for compelling reasons of public policy. Grounds for giving ministerial authorization can include rationalization advantages, the wish to preserve jobs or secure the supply of energy or raw materials. Merger review is organized in two stages: the Federal Cartel Office is exclusively responsible for review of the merger from the perspective of competition law. Any political grounds for the justification of the merger can only be taken into account in the second stage, in the form of a ministerial authorization. This power is exercised quite rarely: over a 20 years period, a ministerial authorization was granted only in 6 cases.[87]

The same possibility also appears to exist in the French system under the new merger control rules that came into effect in the spring of 2002. As in Germany, the French merger control procedure comprises two phases. In the first phase, the Minister for Economy, acting through the Director General for Competition, Consumer Protection, and Repression of Fraud (DGCCRF), decides whether the transaction should be approved (possibly subject to conditions), or whether the transaction is likely to harm competition so as to trigger the second phase of the procedure. If the Minister decides to enter into phase II, he must request a formal opinion from the Competition Council (Conseil de la Concurrence). If a transaction has been brought before the Council, the Council must examine whether it is likely to jeopardize competition, particularly by creating or strengthening a dominant position or by creating or strengthening buying power that places suppliers in a state of economic dependence. It must also assess whether the operation makes a great enough contribution to economic progress that the damage to competition will be offset. The Council is obliged to take into account the competitiveness of the undertaking in question with respect to international competition.[88] Following

---

87. See generally http://www.internationalcompetitionnetwork.org/.

88. See generally Article L430–6 of the French Commercial Code.

receipt of the Council's opinion, the Minister of Economy may either prohibit or approve the transaction, with or without conditions. The Minister is not bound by the opinions of the Competition Council. Although in a majority of cases the final decision of the Minister essentially reiterates the Council's formal opinion, there are cases in which the Minister did not follow the analysis or the solutions suggested by the Council.[89]

At the other extreme is the "public interest" standard applied under the law of the United Kingdom. Although some governments have chosen to interpret the public interest as referring exclusively, or almost exclusively, to competition criteria, nothing in the statutes requires this kind of self-restraint. Like France or Germany, the U.K. operates under a system of divided powers for mergers. Any mergers involving U.K. companies which do not fall under the regulation, and which meet the jurisdictional tests in the Fair Trading Act 1973, fall to three UK authorities: Office of Fair Trading (OFT), Competition Commission (CC) and the Secretary of State for Trade and Industry (SoS).[90] The OFT investigates all mergers in the first instance and recommends to the SoS whether or not they should be referred to the CC for further investigation. The then -SoS announced in October 2000 that he would follow the advice of the OFT on reference decisions, save in exceptional circumstances. At this stage there are three ways in which a merger may be treated: it may be referred to the CC for further investigation; it may be cleared; or undertakings may be sought in lieu of a reference to the CC. Where a merger is referred to the CC, they are required to report to the SoS whether or not the merger would be against the public interest. If the CC concludes that the merger would be against the public interest, the SoS may decide to prohibit the merger, to allow it to proceed subject to certain conditions, or to take no action. If the CC concludes that the merger would not operate against the public interest the SoS can take no action in respect of the merger. Any undertakings required following an adverse report by the CC are negotiated by the OFT.[91]

Systems vary almost as much procedurally as they do substantively. Some countries and regions, such as the United States, Canada, the EU, Mexico, Japan, Germany, (more recently) France and others, have a system of mandatory pre-merger notification in place. These systems usually rely on quantitative criteria to establish who must notify. In the EU, the Merger Regulation itself applies only to very large transactions, where the combined aggregate worldwide turnover of all the undertakings concerned is more than EUR 5 billion (more than $5 billion), and where the aggregate Community-wide turnover of each of at least two of the undertakings concerned is more than EUR 250 million, unless each of the undertakings concerned achieves more than two-thirds of its turnover in one and the same Member State. In the United States, in contrast, notification under the Hart–Scott–Rodino Antitrust Improvements Act of 1976, as amended, must normally take place if one party has total assets or net annual sales of $200 million or more (a number that is now indexed), or if one party has $10 million and the other $100 million (also indexed numbers). Timetables are also different, ranging from the EU's

---

89. See the DGCCRF website at http://www.finances.gouv.fr/DGCCRF/concurrence/index.html, and the links to the applicable part of the French Commercial Code.

90. See EC Merger.

91. Note that the competition White Paper "Productivity and Enterprise: A World Class Competition Regime" (published July 2001) included proposals to reform the merger and monopoly regimes with decisions taken by independent competition authorities, new duties for OFT to promote competition, and criminal penalties for those involved in cartels. Therefore, all of this may be subject to further changes soon.

currently rigid maximum of five months, if the case must be studied beyond the "first stage" one-month period, to the U.S. open-ended period that depends on a party's compliance with requests for information from the government, to an utterly open-ended time to study the deal in some countries.

As multinational activities increase, difficulties for firms can also increase if their mergers are subject to review in more than one country. The problems are well illustrated by the first case in which the EC blocked a merger, Aerospatiale–Alenia/de Havilland, Com.Dec. 91/619, O.J. L 334/42 (Dec. 5, 1991). The case arose when the United States aircraft manufacturer, Boeing, decided to sell its Canadian aircraft subsidiary, de Havilland, to a joint venture (ATR) of two European firms, Aerospatiale (France) and Alenia e Selenia (Italy). ATR was the world's leading manufacturer of commuter aircraft, and de Havilland was the number two firm. Boeing's decision to sell de Havilland meant that it was exiting this market. Few other competitors existed: British Aerospace and Fokker in Europe were smaller factors in the market; Indonesian and East European companies were unable to compete effectively due to a combination of financial and quality problems. From the Canadian perspective, however, de Havilland was a "failing firm," and the Canadians therefore affirmatively wanted the deal to go through. The Commission concluded that the proposed concentration would create a dominant position that was "incompatible" with the common market. The GE/Honeywell case, discussed at page [1121] above in connection with portfolio effects is another, more recent example of the problems that may arise in a global economy with multiple, conflicting notifications systems.

More commonly, the Commission, like other authorities with responsibility for mergers, imposes conditions on mergers that appear troublesome but allows the overall transaction to be completed. The business community has begun to express concern that conflicting conditions from a variety of merger authorities may (at best) impose unwarranted transaction costs on them, or (at worst) subject them to conflicting legal requirements. In any event, many concede that consistency in enforcement policy in different jurisdictions and elimination of unnecessary or duplicative procedural burdens would benefit consumers and businesses around the globe. See the Report of the Special Committee on International Antitrust of the American Bar Association Section of Antitrust Law, September 1, 1991. See also OECD, Merger Cases in the Real World: A Study of Merger Control Procedures (1994). Is there a need for harmonized procedural rules for mergers? What about harmonized substantive standards? Can or should merger rules be the same regardless of the size of national markets? Would you expect merger standards to be the same between the EC and Brazil, or between the United States and Mexico? Why or why not? How can jurisdiction best be allocated among countries when a transnational merger is simultaneously being considered by as many as 10 or 15 authorities?

Although "hard" harmonization may not be on the agenda of the day (except, notably, in regional arrangements such as within the European Union), there are a growing number of initiatives for soft harmonization, including an increasing number of global fora for discussions. The OECD Competition Committee has for decades been the leading forum for regular policy dialogue among the world's leading competition officials. The Competition Committee has also identified voluntary "best practices" and created substantial analytical convergence.[92] Recently,

---

92. See, for example, documents entitled Portfolio Effects in Conglomerate Merg-

ers; Airline Mergers and Alliances; Efficiency Claims in Mergers and Other Horizontal

OECD created a "Global Forum on Competition". This Forum comprises an expanded network of high-level officials from 55 or more economies who meet regularly (in principle twice a year) to share experiences on competition issues.

Other initiatives are also underway. For example, the International Competition Network (ICN) has recently been created as an additional global forum. ICN's goal is to provide antitrust agencies from developed and developing countries with a network for addressing practical antitrust enforcement and policy issues of common concern. Its stated aim is to facilitate procedural and substantive convergence in antitrust enforcement. By enhancing convergence and cooperation, ICN wishes to promote more efficient, effective antitrust enforcement worldwide. ICN's recent work products[93] include the "Guiding Principles for Merger Notification and Review", as well as "Recommended Practices for Merger Notification Procedures."

In addition, the European Commission, the Department of Justice and the Federal Trade Commission, the competition authorities of the world's two most significant antitrust regulatory systems, have been cooperating closely for the past two decades in an attempt to minimize the risk of divergent outcomes in cases that involve both jurisdictions. The basis for the cooperation was the conclusion of the original version of the EU–US Agreement on the Application of their Competition Laws Competition Laws in 1991. In October, 2002, the EU and the US jointly issued a set of best practices for cooperation in reviewing mergers that require approval on both sides of the Atlantic. The best practices recognize that cooperation is most effective when the investigation timetables of the reviewing agencies run in parallel. Merging companies will therefore be offered the possibility of meeting at an early stage with the agencies to discuss timing issues. Companies are also encouraged to permit the agencies to exchange information, which they have submitted and, where appropriate, to allow joint EU/US interviews of the companies concerned. The practices also designate key points in the investigations when it may be appropriate for direct contacts to occur between senior officials on both sides.

Clayton Act, Section 8

> **No person at the same time shall be a director in any two or more corporations, any one of which has capital, surplus, and undivided profits aggregating more than $10,000,000, engaged in whole or in part in commerce, ... if such corporations are or shall have been theretofore, by virtue of their business and location of operation, competitors, so that the elimination of competition by agreement between them would constitute a violation of any of the provisions of any of the antitrust laws**....

Agreements; Failing Firm Defense. Long extracts of these documents are available online at OECD's website at http://www.oecd.org.

93. Available at the ICN website at http://www.internationalcompetitionnetwork.org.

NOTES AND QUESTIONS

1. UNITED STATES V. SEARS, ROEBUCK & CO., 111 F.Supp. 614 (S.D.N.Y.1953). Motion for summary judgment by the government in an action seeking the resignation of Sidney J. Weinberg as a director of Sears, Roebuck & Co. or The B.F. Goodrich Co. because of an alleged violation of Section 8 of the Clayton Act. Defendants admit that the corporations are of the required size; that Weinberg is a director of both corporations; that each corporation is engaged in commerce; and that they compete in the sale of seven categories of items at retail in commerce. They also admit that Sears and Goodrich compete in the sale of these items in 97 communities, in 31 states, and that Sears' sales of these items in such communities exceeded $65 million and Goodrich's exceeded $16 million. Held, for the government. Defendants argue that Section 8 does not prohibit Weinberg's directorship on both Boards, absent a showing that the effect of an assumed consolidation of Sears and Goodrich would be to violate Section 7 of the Clayton Act. The vital distinction between Section 7 and Section 8, however, is that Section 8 promulgates its own substantiality standard in the form of the $1 million size requirement. Were the defendants' construction to be adopted, it would require the application of a test which Congress appears deliberately to have omitted. Further, defendants' construction would denude of meaning the phrase "any of the provisions of any of the antitrust laws." There is no logical basis upon which to infer that this all-inclusive language was intended to exclude methods other than merger or acquisition from the reach of Section 8. "Since Sears and Goodrich are competitors, since a price fixing or division of territory agreement would eliminate competition between them, and since such an agreement would *per se* violate at least one 'of the provisions of . . . the antitrust laws,' namely § 1 of the Sherman Act, it follows that § 8 forbids defendant Weinberg to be a director of both corporations." (Weinfeld, J.).[94]

94. See United States v. Sears, Roebuck & Co., 165 F.Supp. 356 (S.D.N.Y.1958), holding that the decree barred Weinberg from serving as a trustee of the Sears Savings and Profit Sharing Pension Fund, which held 26% of the total Sears shares outstanding, while he continued as a director of Goodrich.

In United States v. W.T. Grant Co., 345 U.S. 629 (1953), the Court noted, in passing, that Section 8 has not been systematically enforced and held that the director's resignation from the board of one of the competing corporations rendered injunctive relief unnecessary. See also Paramount Pictures Corp. v. Baldwin–Montrose Chemical Co., 1966 Trade Cas. (CCH) ¶ 71,678 (S.D.N.Y. 1966), holding that: (1) Section 8 does not apply to: (1) vertical relationships, or (2) *de minimis* competition.

On June 21, 1973, the FTC accepted consent orders from Alcoa and Armco Steel, and from Alcoa and Kennecott Copper involving interlocking directorates under Section 8 of the Clayton Act and Section 5 of the FTC Act. In Aluminum Co. of America, [1973–76 Transfer Binder] Trade Reg.Rep. (CCH) ¶ 20,382 (1973) Alcoa and Armco were regarded as competitors under Section 8 because of the interchangeability of aluminum and steel for such uses as industrial siding and roofing and automobile bumpers and trim, and Alcoa and Kennecott Copper were regarded as competitors because of the interchangeability of aluminum and copper for electrical conductors and heat exchange components. In each case, an individual who was a director of the two companies resigned from one of the companies as part of the consent agreement. See In re Aluminum Company of America and Kennecott Copper, Dkt. No. 731-0014, [1970–1973 Transfer Binder] Trade Reg.Rep. (CCH) ¶ 20,331 and In re Aluminum Company of America and Armco Steel, Dkt. No. 721-0055 [1970–1973 Transfer Binder] Trade Reg.Rep. (CCH) ¶ 20,127.

In United States v. Cleveland Trust Co., 392 F.Supp. 699 (N.D.Ohio 1974), affirmed mem., 513 F.2d 633 (6th Cir.1975), the government argued that a corporation could be the interlocking director. Cleveland held substantial stock of two competing companies, and had an executive acting as a director for

CHAPTER 9 MERGERS

2. In 1990, Congress amended Section 8 to raise the threshold level from $1 million to $10 million dollars each in capital surplus and undivided profits. The same 1990 amendments provided for certain safe harbors even when the $10 million dollar minimum was met. These exceptions applied where the sales of either corporation in competition with the other were less than $1 million dollars, where the sales of either corporation in competition with the other were less than 2% of that corporation's total sales, or where sales of each corporation in competition with the other were less than 4% of that corporation's sales.

The statute is not enforced aggressively or systematically. In those rare instances where an illegal interlocking arrangement is found, the remedy is for the director to resign from one board or the other.

SELECTIVE BIBLIOGRAPHY

1. Horizontal and Conglomerate Mergers

FTC Staff, Anticipating the 21st Century: Competition Policy in the New High–Tech, Global Marketplace (1996).

Sullivan & Grimes, The Law of Antitrust, An Integrated Handbook (2000), Chapters IX–X.

4–5 Areeda & Hovenkamp, Antitrust Law: An Analysis of Antitrust Principles and Their Application Chs. 9–11 (2nd ed. 2000).

Hovenkamp, Federal Antitrust Policy: The Law of Competition and Its Practice Chs. 9, 12, and 13 (1994).

Gellhorn & Kovacic, Antitrust Law and Economics in a Nutshell (4th ed. 1994).

Kwoka & White (ed.), The Antitrust Revolution 1–119 (1989).

Scherer, Industrial Market Structure and Economic Performance Chs. 12 and 20 (3d ed. 1990).

Bork, The Antitrust Paradox 217–24, 246–62 (1978).

Sullivan, Handbook of the Law of Antitrust 600–57 (1977).

Kaysen & Turner, Antitrust Policy Ch. 3 (1959).

Baker, Mavericks, Mergers and Exclusion: Proving Coordinated Competitive Effects Under the Antitrust Laws, 77 NYU L.Rev. 135, 177–88 (2002).

each of the companies. The government advanced the theory that the two men were merely acting as deputies of Cleveland and thus Cleveland was a director of both companies. The government's motion for summary judgment was denied, but its theory was not dismissed. However, it must be shown that there is a true principal-agent relationship between the corporation and the directors. This might be shown if the directors were actual employees of the corporation as in Cleveland, and not just outside directors of both who might act merely out of good will instead of for an anticompetitive purpose. This theory was strengthened by SCM Corp. v. FTC, 565 F.2d 807 (2d Cir.1977), wherein

it was held that a corporation is a proper defendant and the proper object of an enforcement order under Section 8.

On interlocking directorates, see Reports, Accounting and Management Subcomm. Staff, Senate Governmental Affairs Comm., 95th Cong., 2d Sess., Interlocking Directorates Among the Major U.S. Corporations 7 (Comm.Print 1978); Wilson, Unlocking Interlocks: The On–Again Off–Again Saga of Section 8 of the Clayton Act, 45 Antitrust L.J. 317 (1976); Kramer, Interlocking Directorships and the Clayton Act After 35 Years, 59 Yale L.J. 1266 (1950).

Pitofsky, Proposals for Revised United States Merger Enforcement in a Global Economy, 81 Geo.L.J. 195 (1992).

Calkins, Developments in Merger Litigation: The Government Doesn't Always Win, 56 Antitrust L.J. 855 (1987).

Cirace, The Horizontal Merger Guidelines of the Department of Justice and the National Association of Attorneys General Compared, 33 Vill.L.Rev. 281 (1988).

Krattenmaker & Pitofsky, Antitrust Merger Policy and the Reagan Administration, 33 Antitrust Bull. 211 (1988).

Fisher, Lande & Vandaele, Efficiency Considerations in Merger Enforcement 71 Cal.L.Rev. 1580 (1983).

Landes & Posner, Market Power in Antitrust Cases, 94 Harv.L.Rev. 937 (1981).

Weiss, The Structure–Conduct–Performance Paradigm and Antitrust, 127 U.Pa.L.Rev. 1104 (1979).

Brodley, Potential Competition Mergers: A Structural Synthesis, 87 Yale L.J. 1 (1977).

Bok, Section 7 of the Clayton Act and the Merging of Law and Economics, 74 Harv.L.Rev. 226 (1960).

2.   Joint Ventures

Pitofsky, A Framework for Antitrust Analysis of Joint Ventures, 74 Geo.L.J. 1605 (1986).

Brodley, Potential Competition Mergers: A Structural Synthesis, 87 Yale L.J. 1 (1977).

Pitofsky, Joint Ventures Under the Antitrust Laws: Some Reflections on the Significance of Penn–Olin, 82 Harv.L.Rev. 1007 (1969).

3.   Vertical Mergers

4 Areeda & Hovenkamp, Antitrust Law: An Analysis of Antitrust Principles and Their Application Ch. 10 (2nd ed. 2000, & Supp. 2002).

Posner, Antitrust Law: An Economic Perspective 223–229 (2nd ed. 2001).

Scherer & Ross, Industrial Market Structure and Economic Performance Ch. 5 (3d ed. 1990).

Bork, The Antitrust Paradox 225–45 (1978).

Sullivan, Handbook of the Law of Antitrust 657–69 (1977).

Bain, Industrial Organization 360–62 (2d ed. 1968).

Kaysen & Turner, Antitrust Policy 130–33 (1959).

Riordan & Salop, Evaluating Vertical Mergers: A Post–Chicago Approach, 63 Antitrust L.J. 513 (1995).

Posner, The Chicago School of Antitrust Analysis, 127 U.Pa.L.Rev. 925 (1979).

Bork & Bowman, The Crisis in Antitrust, 65 Colum.L.Rev. 363 (1965).

Blake & Jones, Toward a Three–Dimensional Antitrust Policy, 65 Colum.L.Rev. 422 (1965); In Defense of Antitrust, 65 Colum.L.Rev. 377 (1965).

Bork, Contrasts in Antitrust Theory: I, 65 Colum.L.Rev. 401 (1965).

Bowman, Contrasts in Antitrust Theory: II, 65 Colum.L.Rev. 417 (1965).

4. Comparative Materials

Antitrust Division Submission for OECD Roundtable on portfolio effects in Conglomerate Mergers, Range Effects: the United States Perspective (10/12/01) available at http://www.usdoj.gov/atr/public/international/9550.htm.

Reynolds and Ordover, "Archimedean Leveraging and the GE/Honeywell Transaction," Antitrust Law Journal, Issue 1, 2002.

CHAPTER 10

FOREIGN COMMERCE AND THE U.S. ANTITRUST LAWS

SCOPE NOTE

From the day the Sherman Act was passed to the present time, it has been clear that the U.S. antitrust laws have some application to foreign trade and commerce. Sections 1 and 2 of the Sherman Act both refer explicitly to restraints or monopolization of "trade or commerce among the several States, or with foreign nations...." On the other hand, it is equally clear that the United States did not, and cannot, legislate rules of market organization or behavior for the entire world. The question of how far the U.S. antitrust laws reach beyond our borders, and how they interact with the competition laws that exist in almost every other commercially significant country in the world, is one of increasing importance.

The expansion of global commerce, particularly since the end of World War II, is an economic development of surpassing importance not only for U.S. business, but also for consumers and producers around the world. As of the end of FY 2001, the U.S. Department of Commerce reported that the U.S. gross domestic product (GDP) was a seasonally adjusted $9,214.5 billion; of that figure, exports contributed $1,076.1 billion, and imports $1,492.0 billion.[1] Taken together, international trade in goods amounted to about 25% of U.S. GDP;[2] the Commerce Department reported that international trade in services for 2001 was a little less than 30% of the level of trade in goods on the export side, and on the import side trade in services was about 15% of the total.[3] The world-wide figures are even more impressive: the World Trade Organization estimates that the value of global trade in 2001 was $5,984 billion in merchandise, and $1,458 billion in goods.[4] Finally, more and more companies are "multi-national enterprises," with affiliates, subsidiaries, plants, and customers in two or more countries around the world. When we couple these facts with the reality that nearly 100 countries now have antitrust laws, the risk of conflict and the possibilities of cooperation among antitrust authorities become plain.

The materials that follow provide an introduction to the doctrines that address the twin problems of complex international commercial activity and multiplicity of regulating sovereigns. We begin with the scope of legislative jurisdiction under U.S.

---

1. See U.S. Dept. of Commerce, Bureau of Economic Analysis, Press rel. BEA 02–35 (Nov.26, 2002), Table 3.

2. FTC Staff Report, Anticipating the 21st Century: Competition Policy in the New High–Tech, Global Marketplace, 70 ATRR at S–10 (Special Supplement) (June 6, 1996) (hereinafter FTC 21st Century Report).

3. See U.S. Dept. of Commerce report (BEA 02–35), Table 3. Total seasonally ad-

justed exports for 2001 were $1,076.1 billion, as noted; exports of services were $292.0 billion (about 27%). Total seasonally adjusted imports were $1,492.0 billion, of which $222.4 million were services (about 15%).

4. These statistics are available on the WTO's website, http://www.wto.org.

antitrust law to reach conduct that is in whole or in part located abroad–often referred to as the "extraterritoriality" question. In a more forward-looking sense we then consider some of the international agreements that address comity and cooperation issues more directly. Finally, we turn to some of the special considerations that are present when foreign sovereigns have acted, including the doctrine of foreign sovereign immunity, the act of state doctrine, and the concept of foreign sovereign compulsion.

SECTION 1. JURISDICTION OVER FOREIGN COMMERCE

The question of how far the U.S. antitrust laws may extend to regulate people, companies, and transactions whose actions affect U.S. markets has been both legally and politically sensitive. We begin here with the earliest case to give the question significant attention, with an opinion by Justice Holmes. The Justice, who was at best skeptical about the value of the antitrust laws (compare his dissenting opinion in *Dr. Miles*, supra Ch. 7, p. 630, for example) took a narrow approach both to the jurisdictional reach of the statute and to the related question of how much deference was due to the acts of a foreign authority.

A. FOREIGN COMMERCE BEFORE 1982

American Banana Co. v. United Fruit Co.

Supreme Court of the United States, 1909.
213 U.S. 347, 29 S.Ct. 511, 53 L.Ed. 826.

■ HOLMES, J. This is an action brought to recover threefold damages under the [Sherman Act]. The Circuit Court dismissed the complaint upon motion, as not setting forth a cause of action. 160 Fed.Rep. 184. This judgment was affirmed by the Circuit Court of Appeals, 166 Fed.Rep. 261, and the case then was brought to this Court by writ of error.

The allegations of the complaint may be summed up as follows: The plaintiff is an Alabama corporation, organized in 1904. The defendant is a New Jersey corporation, organized in 1899. Long before the plaintiff was formed, the defendant, with intent to prevent competition and to control and monopolize the banana trade, bought the property and business of several of its previous competitors, with provision against their resuming the trade, made contracts with others, including a majority of the most important, regulating the quantity to be purchased and the price to be paid, and acquired a controlling amount of stock in still others. For the same purpose it organized a selling company, of which it held the stock, that by agreement sold at fixed prices all the bananas of the combining parties. By this and other means it did monopolize and restrain the trade and maintained unreasonable prices. The defendant being in this ominous attitude, one McConnell in 1903 started a banana plantation in Panama, then part of the United States of Colombia, and began to build a railway (which would afford his only means of export), both in accordance with the laws of the United States of Colombia. He was notified by the defendant that he must either combine or stop. Two months later, it is believed at the defendant's instigation, the governor of Panama recommended to his national government that Costa Rica be allowed to administer the territory through which the railroad was to run, and this although that territory had been awarded to Colombia under an arbitration agreed to by treaty. The defendant, and afterwards, in September, the government of Costa Rica, it is believed by the inducement of the defendant, interfered with McConnell. In November, 1903, Panama revolted and became an independent republic, declaring its boundary to be that settled by the award. In June, 1904, the plaintiff bought out McConnell and went on with the work, as it had a right to do under the laws of Panama. But in July, Costa Rican soldiers and officials, instigated by the defendant, seized a part of the plantation and a cargo of supplies and have held them ever since, and stopped the construction and operation of the plantation and railway. In August one Astua, by ex parte proceedings, got a judgment from a Costa Rican court, declaring the plantation to be his, although, it is alleged, the proceedings were not within the jurisdiction of Costa Rica, and were contrary to its laws and void. Agents of the defendant then bought the lands from Astua. The plaintiff has tried to induce the government of Costa Rica to withdraw its soldiers, and also has tried to persuade the United States to interfere, but has been thwarted in both by the defendant and has failed. The government of Costa Rica remained in possession down to the bringing of the suit.

As a result of the defendant's acts the plaintiff has been deprived of the use of the plantation, and the railway, the plantation and supplies have been injured. The defendant also, by outbidding, has driven purchasers out of the market and has compelled producers to come to its terms, and it has prevented the plaintiff from buying for export and sale. This is the substantial damage alleged. There is thrown in a further allegation that the defendant has "sought to injure" the plaintiff's business by offering positions to its employees, and by discharging and threatening to discharge persons in its own employ who were stockholders of the plaintiff. But no particular point is made of this. It is contended, however, that, even if the main argument fails and the defendant is held not to be answerable for acts depending on the cooperation of the government of Costa Rica for their effect, a wrongful conspiracy resulting in driving the plaintiff out of business is to be gathered from the complaint and that it was entitled to go to trial upon that.

It is obvious that, however stated, the plaintiff's case depends on several rather startling propositions. In the first place the acts causing the damage were done, so far as appears, outside the jurisdiction of the United States and within that of other states. It is surprising to hear it argued that they were governed by the act of Congress.

No doubt in regions subject to no sovereign, like the high seas, or to no law that civilized countries would recognize as adequate, such countries may treat some relations between their citizens as governed by their own law, and keep, to some extent, the old notion of personal sovereignty alive.

See The Hamilton (*Old Dominion S.S. Co. v. Gilmore*), 207 U.S. 398, 403; Hart v. Gumpach, *L.R., 4 P.C. 439, 463, 464; British South Africa Co. v. Companhia de Mocambique* [1893], A.C. 602. They go further, at times, and declare that they will punish any one, subject or not, who shall do certain things, if they can catch him, as in the case of pirates on the high seas. In cases immediately affecting national interests they may go further still and may make, and, if they get the chance, execute, similar threats as to acts done within another recognized jurisdiction.... But the general and almost universal rule is that the character of an act as lawful or unlawful must be determined wholly by the law of the country where the act is done.... For another jurisdiction, if it should happen to lay hold of the actor, to treat him according to its own notions rather than those of the place where he did the acts, not only would be unjust, but would be an interference with the authority of another sovereign, contrary to the comity of nations, which the other state concerned justly might resent....

The foregoing considerations would lead in case of doubt to a construction of any statute as intended to be confined in its operation and effect to the territorial limits over which the lawmaker has general and legitimate power. "All legislation is *prima facie* territorial." ... Words having universal scope, such as "Every contract in restraint of trade," "Every person who shall monopolize," etc., will be taken as a matter of course to mean only everyone subject to such legislation, not all that the legislator subsequently may be able to catch. In the case of the present statute the improbability of the United States attempting to make acts done in Panama or Costa Rica criminal is obvious, yet the law begins by making criminal the acts for which it gives a right to sue. We think it entirely plain that what the defendant did in Panama or Costa Rica is not within the scope of the statute so far as the present suit is concerned....

For again, not only were the acts of the defendant in Panama or Costa Rica not within the Sherman Act, but they were not torts by the law of the place and therefore were not torts at all, however contrary to the ethical and economic postulates of that statute. The substance of the complaint is that, the plantation being within the *de facto* jurisdiction of Costa Rica, that state took and keeps possession of it by virtue of its sovereign power. But a seizure by a state is not a thing that can be complained of elsewhere in the courts. *Underhill v. Hernandez*, 168 U.S. 250. The fact, if it be one, that *de jure* the estate is in Panama does not matter in the least; sovereignty is pure fact. The fact has been recognized by the United States, and, by the implications of the bill is assented to by Panama.

The fundamental reason why persuading a sovereign power to do this or that cannot be a tort is not that the sovereign cannot be joined as a defendant or because it must be assumed to be acting lawfully.... The fundamental reason is that it is a contradiction in terms to say that within its jurisdiction, it is unlawful to persuade a sovereign power to bring about a result that it declares by its conduct to be desirable and proper. It does not, and foreign courts cannot, admit that the influences were improper or the results bad. It makes the persuasion lawful by its own act. The very meaning of sovereignty is that the decree of the sovereign makes law. *See Kawananakoa v. Polyblank*, 205 U.S. 349, 353. In the case of private persons it consistently may assert the freedom of the immediate parties to an injury and yet declare that certain persuasions addressed to them are wrong....

The plaintiff relied a good deal on *Rafael v. Verelst*, 2 W.Bl. 983, 1055. But in that case, although the Nabob who imprisoned the plaintiff was called a sovereign for certain purposes, he was found to be the mere tool of the defendant, an English Governor. That hardly could be listened to concerning a really independent state. But of course it is not alleged that Costa Rica stands in that relation to the United Fruit Company.

The acts of the soldiers and officials of Costa Rica are not alleged to have been without the consent of the government and must be taken to have been done by its order. It ratified them, at all events, and adopted and keeps the possession taken by them.... The injuries to the plantation and supplies seem to have been the direct effect of the acts of the Costa Rican government which is holding them under an adverse claim of right. The claim for them must fall with the claim for being deprived of the use and profits of the place. As to the buying at a high price, etc., it is enough to say that we have no ground for supposing that it was unlawful in the countries where the purchases were made. Giving to this complaint every reasonable latitude of interpretation we are of opinion that it alleges no case under the act of Congress and discloses nothing that we can suppose to have been a tort where it was done. A conspiracy in this country to do acts in another jurisdiction does not draw to itself those acts and make them unlawful, if they are permitted by the local law....

Judgment affirmed.

■ HARLAN, J., concurred in the result.

NOTES AND QUESTIONS

1.   UNITED STATES V. AMERICAN TOBACCO CO., 221 U.S. 106 (1911). It only took two years after *American Banana* was decided for the Supreme Court to begin finding reasons why jurisdiction could be asserted in foreign commerce cases notwithstanding the holding in *American Banana*. In *American Tobacco* the Supreme Court asserted subject matter jurisdiction without even spending time on discussing this issue in greater detail and held that an anticompetitive conspiracy to monopolize the tobacco industry violated the Sherman Act, despite the fact that some of the contracts leading to the violation were executed in England. *American Banana's* strict territorial doctrine was further eroded in a series of subsequent cases.

2.   UNITED STATES V. PACIFIC & ARCTIC RY., 228 U.S. 87 (1913). In this case, the Supreme Court upheld a criminal indictment charging American and Canadian corporations with conspiring to set discriminatory rates on shipping between points in the United States and Canada. The conspiracy was effectuated by control of certain wharves in American territory. This was enough, in the Supreme Court's

view, to justify applying the Sherman Act both to the U.S. side of the conspiracy and to activity taking place partially in Canada. In his opinion, Justice McKenna said that American anti-trust law applied to foreign "citizens and corporations operating in our territory."

3.   THOMSEN V. CAYSER, 243 U.S. 66 (1917). In *Thomsen*, the Supreme Court applied the Sherman Act to a combination affecting foreign commerce that was put into operation in the United States. The Court awarded treble damages in a suit against the agents of foreign shipping lines for charging discriminatory rates on shipments between New York and South Africa, pursuant to an agreement made in London; the Court held that the agents' activities within the United States were a sufficient basis for liability. The mere fact that a combination in restraint of trade was formed in a foreign country, the Court said, did not exempt it from American law so long as it "affected the foreign commerce of this country and was put into operation here." The laws were found applicable, therefore, based on reasoning that an antitrust conspiracy is subject to U.S. law even if some of the actions took place outside the borders so long as such activity also occurred within. As in the *Sisal* case which we discuss next, the Court was willing to expand, but not to entirely dispense with, the strict territorial approach.

4.   UNITED STATES V. SISAL SALES CORP., 274 U.S. 268 (1927). In *Sisal*, a conspiracy to control the American sisal market, entered into and partially carried out in the United States and implemented by legislation secured in Mexico to regulate the sources of supply, was held to violate the U.S. antitrust laws. The Supreme Court once again upheld the extraterritorial application of the Sherman Act to the conspiracy between U.S. and Mexican firms. The Court attempted to distinguish *American Banana* by noting that a few of the agreements in the conspiracy took place in the United States and that the conspiracy was funded by U.S. banks. The Court also distinguished *American Banana* as a case involving an alleged conspiracy in the United States "to do acts in another jurisdiction." Such a conspiracy, Justice McReynold said, does not violate the Sherman Act. In *Sisal*, by contrast, the conspiracy in question was "entered into by parties within the United States," and it was "made effective by acts done therein." Do you find these distinctions satisfactory?

These decisions lead us to the famous *Alcoa* decision of the Second Circuit, other parts of which you saw in Chapter 3, p. 130 supra. *Alcoa* was a final, unappealable judgment even though it was not before the United States Supreme Court. Because a quorum of the Supreme Court could not be assembled, the case was certified to the Court of Appeals for the Second Circuit, which sat in place of the Supreme Court.

United States v. Aluminum Co. of America

United States Court of Appeals, Second Circuit, 1945.
148 F.2d 416.

■ Before L. HAND, SWAN, and AUGUSTUS N. HAND, CIRCUIT JUDGES.

[As the excerpt from *Alcoa* at p. 130 supra, sets forth, this case involved Alcoa's alleged monopolization of the market for virgin aluminum ingot in violation of Sherman Act § 2. The government also claimed that Alcoa had entered into a conspiracy in restraint of commerce in aluminum, including in foreign commerce. Because much of the conduct took place outside the United States, and was undertaken by foreign companies, the

Court had to consider whether the Sherman Act even applied. Judge Hand's discussion of that issue remains, more than fifty years later, one of the leading formulations of the jurisdictional reach of the U.S. antitrust laws.

The Second Circuit divided the classes of defendants into four groups, of which the most important for present purposes were Alcoa itself, with its wholly-owned subsidiaries, directors, officers and shareholders, and Aluminum Limited (Alcoa's Canadian subsidiary), with its directors, officers and shareholders. The discussion that follows was the third part of the Court's opinion, in which it discussed whether Limited and Alcoa were in an unlawful conspiracy, and whether, if not, Limited was guilty of a conspiracy with foreign producers.]

■ L. HAND, CIRCUIT JUDGE.

III.   Limited.

Limited was incorporated in Canada on May 31, 1928, to take over those properties of Alcoa which were outside the United States. Only two were excepted: a Dutch company which owned bauxite deposits in Dutch Guiana; and a Canadian power transmission company, which supplied Alcoa's Massena plant.... At first there remained some officers common to both companies; but by the middle of 1931, this had ceased, and, formally at any rate, the separation between the two companies was complete. At the conclusion of the transfers a majority, though only a bare majority, of the common shares of Alcoa was in the hands of three persons: Andrew W. Mellon, Richard B. Mellon, his brother, and Arthur V. Davis. Richard Mellon died in 1933, and Andrew in 1937, and their shares passed to their families; but in January, 1939, the Davises, the officers and directors of Alcoa and the Mellon families—eleven individuals in all—collectively still held 48.9 per cent of Alcoa's shares, and 48.5 per cent of Limited's and ArthurV. Davis was then the largest shareholder in both companies.

The companies had a number of transactions with each other, upon which the plaintiff relies to prove that they did not deal at arms length, but that Limited was organized only as a creature of Alcoa.... Alcoa also did some fabrication for Limited from Limited's own aluminum, and did it at only mill cost without overhead. That substantially ended by 1931; but, while it lasted, it was confessedly a favor, and indeed for a short season Alcoa undoubtedly did cast a kindly eye upon its "fledgling," as Arthur V. Davis called it....

There was also some evidence that Alcoa took part in the formation of the Alliance, a foreign "cartel" which we shall describe later. This consists very largely of declarations of Arthur V. Davis, put in his mouth by other witnesses; of a cable of Edward K. Davis to one of Limited's other officers; and of the improbability that the Alliance should have been set up without the active cooperation of Arthur V. Davis, especially as he was concededly in Europe and in communication with some foreign producers at about the time that the Alliance was first bruited. Edward K. Davis was the originator of the Alliance; he gave as his reason for it that he feared that the other foreign producers who had already joined in a "cartel," would shut him out. When these producers came to Canada in 1931 to arrange for the Alliance, they visited Arthur V. Davis and made an extended visit to Alcoa's plants in the East. As anticipatory confirmation that Alcoa had had a share in forming the Alliance, the plaintiff also introduced evidence to show that before 1928 Alcoa had already had an understanding with foreigners as to prices. This consisted largely of the statements of what others had said about an agreement to keep their prices the same as Alcoa's. The plaintiff rested particularly upon the testimony of Haskell, (who testified, not only upon this point, but more generally), because, when Haskell testified, although he had been one of the important figures in the Baush company, he had made his peace with Alcoa which had employed him in some advisory capacity. It must be remembered, however, that he had already testified in the action of the Baush company against Alcoa, and that he could scarcely have repudiated what he then said.

The Davises in answer to all this evidence swore that Limited had been organized for three reasons, quite different from controlling prices in the United States. First, there was at that time a growing nationalism in the British Empire—where Alcoa sold most of its foreign aluminum—which manifested itself in the slogan: "Buy British," and which would be better satisfied, if the properties were owned by a Canadian corporation, even though its shareholders were American. Next, Alcoa had neglected its foreign properties—relatively—and they would better prosper under a management, singly devoted to them. Finally, the time was coming when Arthur V. Davis wished to take a less active part in affairs; and there would be embarrassment in choosing between Hunt and Edward K. Davis, as his successor. Both said that the separation between the companies had been actually as complete as it was in form. Arthur said that, although while in Europe shortly before the Alliance was formed, foreign producers had spoken to him, he had then and always referred all their inquiries to his brother. He had discussed little with Edward any questions of policy about Limited; they had talked for the most part only about the history, development and future of the properties. He had indeed seen a preliminary draft of the agreement, forming the Alliance, but not its final form until the time of the trial; and he had had nothing whatever to do with its formation. As for the trip of the foreign producers in the United States, it was purely social; a "good-will" excursion, so to say, in which the relations of Alcoa and foreign production was not discussed.

Upon the whole evidence the judge found that by 1935 Limited had become altogether free from any connection with Alcoa, and that Alcoa had had no part in forming the Alliance, or in any effort at any time to limit imports, to fix their price, or to intervene in price fixing "cartels" in Europe—except the early ones. In short, he again felt persuaded by the testimony against any inferences to be drawn from the conceded facts, and from the declarations put in the mouths of the Davises. As before, to do otherwise he would have had to find that both these men had deliberately perjured themselves; and we cannot see that these findings present us with anything different in substance from those on which we have already passed. Considering the interests in Limited which Arthur V. Davis and both the Mellons had, it would perhaps have taxed our credulity to the breaking point to believe that they knew nothing about the formation of the Alliance. Arthur V. Davis did not go as far as that; and that he and the Mellons should have put into the hands of Edward K. Davis the whole management of Limited, does not appear to us to pass the bounds of reasonable entertainment. Alcoa had had collisions in plenty with the plaintiff and others before 1931; the first Baush action, which challenged the "price squeeze," had been filed in April, 1928, and the second in July, 1931. It was not unreasonable to believe that Arthur V. Davis and the Mellons, seeing that some kind of "cartel" might be an inescapable incident to continuing business abroad, wished in 1931 to keep Alcoa as far removed from it as possible.

[The Court then concluded that Alcoa could not be held responsible for the Alliance's actions solely by virtue of the fact that a majority (or controlling group) of Alcoa's shareholders were also a majority (or controlling group) of Limited's shareholders.] For these reasons we conclude that Alcoa was not a party to the Alliance, and did not join in any violation of Sec. 1 of the Act, so far as concerned foreign commerce.

Whether Limited itself violated that section depends upon the character of the Alliance. It was a Swiss corporation, created in pursuance of an agreement entered into on July 3, 1931, the signatories to which were a French corporation, two German, one Swiss, a British, and Limited. The original agreement, or "cartel," provided for the formation of a corporation in Switzerland which should issue shares, to be taken up by the signatories. This corporation was from time to time to fix a quota of production for each share, and each shareholder was to be limited to the quantity measured by the number of shares it held, but was free to sell at any price it chose. The corporation fixed a price every year at which it would take off any shareholder's hands any part of its quota which it did not sell. No shareholder was to "buy, borrow, fabricate or sell" aluminum produced by anyone not a shareholder except with the consent of the board of governors, but that must not be "unreasonably withheld." Nothing was said as to whether the arrangement extended to sales in the United States; but Article X, known as the "Conversion Clause," provided that any shareholder might exceed his quota to the extent that he converted into aluminum in the United States or Canada any ores delivered to him in either of those countries by persons situated in the United States. This was confessedly put in to allow Limited to receive bauxite or alumina from Alcoa, to smelt it into aluminum and to deliver the aluminum to Alcoa.

Edward K. Davis gave as an explanation of this that Limited needed some protection against Alcoa's possible refusal to convey Alcoa Power Company, which Alcoa had never actually bound itself to transfer. Although in 1931 Alcoa had all the producing capacity which it seemed likely to need (and so the event proved, for the clause was never invoked), Davis said that he did not know whether in the future the demand might not outrun that capacity, and whether Alcoa might not therefore be tempted to hold onto the Lower Development, unless Limited would smelt its alumina. That does indeed seem a somewhat farfetched reason; but on the other hand it is hard to suppose that Alcoa really feared that it could not meet its future needs and meant to lean upon Limited. The incident may be thought to have a bearing on Alcoa's implication in the Alliance; but its only substantial importance, so far as we can see, is as showing whether the 1931 agreement was intended to cover the United States. That question arose very shortly after the agreement was made, and Edward K. Davis took the position that the United States was included, relying upon absence of any exception in the general language. His interpretation would seem to have been plainly right, not only for the reason he gave, but because otherwise there would have been no occasion for the "Conversion Clause." However, the other shareholders overruled him, and until 1936, when the new arrangement was made, imports into the United States were not included in the quotas. The issue turned out to be unimportant anyway, for the annual average of imports during the five years was in the neighborhood of only fifteen million pounds.

The agreement of 1936 abandoned the system of unconditional quotas, and substituted a system of royalties. Each shareholder was to have a fixed free quota for every share it held, but as its production exceeded the sum of its quotas, it was to pay a royalty, graduated progressively in proportion to the excess; and these royalties the Alliance divided among the shareholders in proportion to their shares. This agreement—unlike the first—did not contain an express promise that the Alliance would buy any undisposed of stocks at a fixed price, although perhaps § 3 of Subdivision A, of Part X may have impliedly recognized such an obligation. Probably, during the two years in which the shareholders operated under this agreement, that question did not arise for the demand for aluminum was very active. Nevertheless, we understand from Limited's answer to an interrogatory that the last price fixed under the agreement of 1931 was understood to remain in force. Although this agreement, like its predecessor, was silent as to imports into the United States, when that question arose during its preparation, as it did, all the shareholders agreed that such imports should be included in the quotas. The German companies were exempted from royalties—for obvious reasons—and that, it would seem, for practical purposes put them out of the "cartel" for the future, for it was scarcely possible that a German producer would be unable to dispose of all its production, at least within any future period that would be provided for. The shareholders continued this agreement unchanged until the end of March, 1938, by which time it had become plain that, at least for the time being, it was no longer of service to anyone. Nothing was, however, done to end it, although the German shareholders of course became enemies of the French, British and Canadian shareholders in 1939. The Alliance itself has apparently never been dissolved; and indeed it appeared on the "Proclaimed List of Blocked Nationals" of September 13, 1944.

Did either the agreement of 1931 or that of 1936 violate § 1 of the Act? The answer does not depend upon whether we shall recognize as a source of liability a liability imposed by another state. On the contrary we are concerned only with whether Congress chose to attach liability to the conduct outside the United States of persons not in allegiance to it. That being so, the only question open is whether Congress intended to impose the liability, and whether our own Constitution permitted it to do so: as a court of the United States, we cannot look beyond our own law. Nevertheless, it is quite true that we are not to read general words, such as those in this Act, without regard to the limitations customarily observed by nations upon the exercise of their powers; limitations which generally correspond to those fixed by the "Conflict of Laws." We should not impute to Congress an intent to punish all whom its courts can catch, for conduct which has no consequences within the United States. *American Banana Co. v. United Fruit Co.*, 213 U.S. 347, 357; *United States v. Bowman*, 260 U.S. 94, 98; *Blackmer v. United States*, 284 U.S. 421, 437. On the other hand, it is settled law—as Limited itself agrees—that any state may impose liabilities, even upon persons not within its allegiance, for conduct outside its borders that has consequences within its borders which the state reprehends; and these liabilities other states will ordinarily recognize. *Strassheim v. Daily*, 221 U.S. 280, 284, 285; *Lamar v. United States*, 240 U.S. 60, 65, 66; *Ford v. United States*, 273 U.S. 593, 620, 621; Restatement of Conflict of Laws Sec. 65.

It may be argued that this Act extends further. Two situations are possible. There may be agreements made beyond our borders not intended to affect imports, which do affect them, or which affect exports. Almost any limitation of the supply of goods in Europe, for example, or in South America, may have repercussions in the United States if there is trade between the two. Yet when one considers the international complications likely to arise from an effort in this country to treat such agreements as unlawful, it is safe to assume that Congress certainly did not intend the Act to cover them. Such agreements may on the other hand intend to include imports into the United States, and yet it may appear that they had no effect upon them. That situation might be thought to fall within the doctrine that intent may be a substitute for performance in the case of a contract made within the United States; or it might be thought to fall within the doctrine that a statute should not be interpreted to cover acts abroad which have no consequence here. We shall not choose between these alternatives; but for argument we shall assume that the Act does not cover agreements, even though intended to affect imports or exports, unless its performance is shown actually to have had some effect upon them. Where both conditions are satisfied, the situation certainly falls within such decisions as *United States v. Pacific & Arctic R. & Navigation Co.*, 228 U.S. 87; *Thomsen v. Cayser*, 243 U.S. 66; and *United States v. Sisal Sales Corporation*, 274 U.S. 268. (*United States v. Nord Deutcher Lloyd*, 223 U.S. 512, illustrates the same conception in another field.) It is true that in those cases the persons held liable had sent agents into the United States to perform part of the agreement; but an agent is merely an animate means of executing his principal's purposes, and, for the purposes of this case, he does not differ from an inanimate means; besides, only human agents can import and sell ingot.

Both agreements would clearly have been unlawful, had they been made within the United States; and it follows from what we have just said that both were unlawful, though made abroad, if they were intended to affect imports and did affect them. Since the shareholders almost at once agreed that the agreement of 1931 should not cover imports, we may ignore it and confine our discussion to that of 1936: indeed that we should have to do anyway, since it superseded the earlier agreement. The judge found that it was not the purpose of the agreement to "suppress or restrain the exportation of aluminum to the United States for sale in competition with Alcoa." By that we understand that he meant that the agreement was not specifically directed to Alcoa, because it only applied generally to the production of the shareholders. If he meant that it was not expected that the general restriction upon production would have an effect upon imports, we cannot agree, for the change made in 1936 was deliberate and was expressly made to accomplish just that. It would have been an idle gesture, unless the shareholders had supposed that it would, or at least might, have that effect. The first of the conditions which we mentioned was therefore satisfied; the intent was to set up a quota system for imports.

The judge also found that the 1936 agreement did not "materially affect the . . . foreign trade or commerce of the United States"; apparently because the imported ingot was greater in 1936 and 1937 than in earlier years. We cannot accept this finding, based as it was upon the fact that, in 1936, 1937 and the first quarter of 1938, the gross imports of ingot increased. It by no means follows from such an increase that the agreement did not restrict imports; and incidentally it so happens that in those years such inference as is possible at all, leads to the opposite conclusion. It is true that the average imports—including Alcoa's—for the years 1932–1935 inclusive were about 15 million pounds, and that for 1936, 1937 and one-fourth of 1938 they were about 33 million pounds; but the average domestic ingot manufacture in the first period was about 96 million and in the second about 262 million; so that the proportion of imports to domestic ingot was about 15.6 per cent for the first period and about 12.6 per cent for the second. We do not mean to infer from this that the quota system of 1936 did in fact restrain imports, as these figures might suggest; but we do mean that nothing is to be inferred from the gross increase of imports. We shall dispose of the matter therefore upon the assumption that, although the shareholders intended to restrict imports, it does not appear whether in fact they did so. Upon our hypothesis the plaintiff would therefore fail, if it carried the burden of proof upon this issue as upon others. We think, however, that, after the intent to affect imports was proved, the burden of proof shifted to Limited. In the first place a depressant upon production which applies generally may be assumed, ceteris paribus, to distribute its effect evenly upon all markets. Again, when the parties took the trouble specifically to make the depressant apply to a given market, there is reason to suppose that they expected that it would have some effect, which it could have only by lessening what would otherwise have been imported. If the motive they introduced was over-balanced in all instances by motives which induced the shareholders to import, if the United States market became so attractive that the royalties did not count at all and their expectations were in fact defeated, they to whom the facts were more accessible than to the plaintiff ought to prove it, for a prima facie case had been made. Moreover, there is an especial propriety in demanding this of Limited, because it was Limited which procured the inclusion in the agreement of 1936 of imports in the quotas.

There remains only the question whether this assumed restriction had any influence upon prices, *Apex Hosiery Co. v. Leader*, supra, 310 U.S. 469. To that *Socony–Vacuum Oil Co. v. United States*, supra, 310 U.S. 150, is an entire answer. It will be remembered that, when the defendants in that case protested that the prosecution had not proved that the "distress" gasoline had affected prices, the court answered that that was not necessary, because an agreement to withdraw any substantial part of the supply from a market would, if carried out, have some effect upon prices, and was as unlawful as an agreement expressly to fix prices. The underlying doctrine was that all factors which contribute to determine prices, must be kept free to operate unhampered by agreements. For these reasons we think that the agreement of 1936 violated Sec. 1 of the Act.

NOTES AND QUESTIONS

1. Justice Holmes considered the plaintiff's claim that the Sherman Act covered the foreign conduct in question in *American Banana* at least "surprising," if not "startling," while Judge Hand thought it equally clear that "any state may impose liabilities, even upon persons not within its allegiance, for conduct outside its borders that has consequences within its borders which the state reprehends." Does this reflect a difference in views about the content of international law limitations on State prescriptive jurisdiction? See generally ALI, Restatement (Third) of the Foreign Relations Law of the United States §§ 401–03 (1987). Does it suggest that international law itself had evolved between the opening years of the 20th century and the time immediately after World War II? To what extent, if at all, should or must the Sherman Act be construed to conform to norms of public international law? *See The Paquete Habana*, 175 U.S. 677 (1900); see also *Hartford Fire Insurance Co. v. California*, 509 U.S. 764 (1993) (dissenting opinion of Justice Scalia), p. 1197 infra.

2. *Alcoa* is usually cited for the proposition that the Sherman Act (as it then read) reaches the conduct of foreigners undertaken solely in their own countries, if the necessary actual and intended effects on U.S. commerce can be detected. If this is true, then where does U.S. jurisdiction stop? Judge Hand thought that principles borrowed from the field of conflicts of law would be adequate to prevent excessive assertions of U.S. jurisdiction. But given the ease with which actual effects can be proven under *Socony*, was he right? Suppose one of the foreign countries in question had an express policy that encouraged membership in the international aluminum cartel. If the company were then found guilty of an offense under U.S. law, or in private litigation it was subject to treble damages, whose law should prevail?

Continental Ore Co. v. Union Carbide and Carbon Corp.

Supreme Court of the United States, 1962.
370 U.S. 690, 82 S.Ct. 1404, 8 L.Ed.2d 777.

■ WHITE, J. This is a private treble damage action under the anti-trust laws. Continental Ore Company, a partnership, and its individual partners, who were plaintiffs in the trial court, are petitioners here. Henry J. Leir, the principal party in Continental, had engaged in the buying and selling of metals, including vanadium products, in Europe prior to 1938, in which year he immigrated to the United States. This case concerns his subsequent efforts in this country to build a successful business in the production and sale of vanadium.

Vanadium is a metal obtained from certain ores which, in this country, are mined principally on the Colorado plateau. The ore is processed at mills near the mines into a substance commonly known as vanadium oxide. The oxide is then transported to the East and converted into ferrovanadium, which is purchased chiefly by steel companies for use as an alloy in hardening steels.

The defendants named in the complaint were Vanadium Corporation of America (VCA), a fully integrated miner and manufacturer of vanadium products, Union Carbide and Carbon Corporation (Carbide), and the following four wholly owned subsidiary corporations of the latter company: United States Vanadium Corporation (USV), engaged in mining vanadium ore and processing vanadium oxide; Electro Metallurgical Company (Electro Met), engaged in making ferrovanadium; Electro Metallurgical Sales Corporation (Electro Met Sales), engaged in the sale of vanadium oxide and ferrovanadium; and Electro Metallurgical Company of Canada, Ltd. (Electro Met of Canada), engaged in selling vanadium products in Canada. . . .

The complaint alleged that, beginning in about 1933, the defendants and others acting in concert with them violated §§ 1 and 2 of the Sherman Act by conspiring to restrain, by monopolizing, and by attempting and conspiring to monopolize, trade and commerce in ferrovanadium and vanadium oxide. The defendants were charged with purchasing and acquiring control over substantially all accessible vanadium-bearing ore deposits in the United States and substantially all vanadium oxide produced by others in the United States, with refusing to sell vanadium oxide to other potential producers of ferrovanadium, including Continental and its associates, with apportioning and dividing sales of ferrovanadium and vanadium oxide among themselves in certain proportions, with fixing identical prices for the sale of ferrovanadium and vanadium oxide and for the purchase of ore, and with making certain mutual arrangements whereby one or more Carbide subsidiaries supplied VCA with substantial quantities of vanadium oxide at preferential prices to VCA. The complaint stated that between 1933 and 1949 the defendants produced over 99% of all ferrovanadium and over 90% of all vanadium oxide produced in the United States and that during the same period the defendants sold over 99% of the ferrovanadium and vanadium oxide sold in this country.[5]

According to the complaint, as a proximate consequence of defendants' monopolistic and restrictive practices, independent producers and distributors of ferrovanadium and vanadium oxide, including Continental, were eliminated from the business. Specifically, the complaint detailed several efforts which Continental made to enter and maintain itself in the vanadium business, all of which were allegedly frustrated by defendants' Sherman Act violations: (1) In 1938, Continental negotiated a contract with Apex Smelting Company of Chicago whereby Apex was to build and operate a plant for the conversion of oxide to ferrovanadium by use of the aluminothermic process. Continental and Apex were to share the profits of this venture. On its part, Continental agreed to obtain raw materials for Apex and to sell the finished product. Operations under this contract began in the spring of 1940, but Apex terminated the agreement in 1942 allegedly because the illegal activities of defendants prevented the obtaining of a sufficient supply of vanadium oxide. (2) Meanwhile, Continental itself had begun to produce a compound called "Van–Ex," composed of vanadium oxide and other materials, which was designed for direct introduction into the steel-making process without prior conversion to ferrovanadium. This venture was allegedly terminated in 1944 because of the difficulty of securing raw materials caused by defendants' unlawful practices, including the efforts of defendants to obtain ownership or control of the mines and mills of Continental's suppliers. (3) Continental had developed a business with a Canadian customer during 1942. When Electro Met Sales of Canada was appointed by the Canadian Government as the exclusive wartime agent to purchase and allocate vanadium for Canadian industries, that company, it is alleged, acting under the control and direction of its parent, Carbide, eliminated Continental entirely from the Canadian market and divided Continental's business solely between defendants. (4) Defendants in 1943, by open threats of reprisals, allegedly frustrated certain arrangements which Continental had with the Climax Molybdenum Corporation for the manufacture of ferrovanadium. (5) In January 1944, Continental contracted with Imperial Paper & Color Corporation for the processing by the latter of vanadium oxide and ferrovanadium. Continental agreed to act as sales agent for the output. The complaint charged that Imperial abandoned the contract at the end of 1944 because of the inability to secure raw materials and that Continental then left the vanadium business altogether, all as a result of the restrictive and monopolistic practices of the defendants.

[The Court next reviewed the evidence presented or offered by plaintiff relating to allegations other than that with respect to the Canadian market, holding that the trial court had erred in excluding certain items and that

---

5. The complaint alleged that VCA sold approximately two-thirds of all ferrovanadium and vanadium oxide sold by defendants (which was said to amount to approximately 99% of all ferrovanadium and vanadium oxide sold and consumed in the United States), while Electro Met Sales (a Carbide subsidiary) sold approximately one-third. According to petitioners' evidence, the Carbide group produced approximately 77% of domestic vanadium oxide, while VCA produced about 65% of ferrovanadium.

the Court of Appeals had erred in its affirmance on grounds that there was insufficient evidence to go to the jury.]

Continental's alleged elimination from the Canadian market raises different issues. At the trial Continental introduced evidence to show that beginning in March 1942, it had shipped Van–Ex to a Canadian customer each month during the remainder of that year. There was then received in evidence a letter dated January 19, 1943, from Continental to Electro Met in New York City reciting that the new allocation system in Canada[6] had eliminated Continental from the Canadian market in January, that Continental had inquired about the matter from the Metals Controller for the Canadian Government and that the latter had referred Continental to Electro Met. The court then struck this letter from the record and rejected petitioners' offer to prove that Continental was excluded from the Canadian market by Electro Met of Canada, a wholly owned subsidiary corporation of Carbide, acting as exclusive purchasing agent for the Metals Controller but allegedly operating in this connection under the control and direction of Carbide for the purpose of carrying out the overall conspiracy to restrain and monopolize the vanadium industry. To that end, Continental offered to prove that its former share of the Canadian market was divided between Carbide and VCA. Continental offered various correspondence with Electro Met of Canada and a memorandum and proposed testimony by Continental's vice president concerning his conversations with an employee of Electro Met who had communicated with Continental in response to Continental's letter of January 19, 1943, to Electro Met. The court denied the entire offer of proof "for the reason that this is a transaction wholly in the hands of the Canadian Government and that whether or not this plaintiff was permitted to sell his material to a customer in Canada was a matter wholly within the control of the Canadian Government."

The Court of Appeals agreed with the trial court and concluded that Continental was not legally entitled to recover from respondents for the destruction of its Canadian business. The court said that no vanadium oxide could be imported into Canada by anyone other than the Canadian Government's agent, Electro Met of Canada, which refused to purchase from the petitioners. Thus, according to the court, "even if we assume that Electro Metallurgical Company of Canada, Ltd. acted for the purpose of entrenching the monopoly position of the defendants in the United States, it was acting as an arm of the Canadian Government, and we do not see

6. Canada's entry into World War II prompted the Canadian Government to take extraordinary measures to assure optimum availability of strategic materials to Canadian private industries engaged in the war effort. Pursuant to these measures, the Office of Metals Controller was established and given broad powers to regulate the procurement of the materials and to allocate them to industrial users. See Order of the Governor General in Council, P.C. 3187, July 15, 1940. The Metals Controller enlisted the aid of Electro Met of Canada in early 1943, delegating to it the discretionary agency power to purchase and allocate to Canadian industries all vanadium products required by them. The validity of these wartime measures and delegations under Canadian law is not here contested. *Cf.* Reference Re Regulations (Chemicals) Under War Measures Act, 1 D.L.R. [1943] 248.

how such efforts as appellants claim defendants took to persuade and influence the Canadian Government through its agent are within the purview of the Sherman Act.'' 289 F.2d, at 94. This ruling was erroneous and we hold that Continental's offer of proof was relevant evidence of a violation of the Sherman Act as charged in the complaint and was not inadmissible on the grounds stated by the courts below.

Respondents say that *American Banana Co. v. United Fruit Co.*, 213 U.S. 347, shields them from liability. This Court there held that an antitrust plaintiff could not collect damages from a defendant who had allegedly influenced a foreign government to seize plaintiff's properties. But in the light of later cases in this Court respondents' reliance upon American Banana is misplaced. A conspiracy to monopolize or restrain the domestic or foreign commerce of the United States is not outside the reach of the Sherman Act just because part of the conduct complained of occurs in foreign countries. *United States v. American Tobacco Co.*, 221 U.S. 106; *United States v. Pacific & Arctic R. & Navigation Co.*, 228 U.S. 87; *Thomsen v. Cayser*, 243 U.S. 66; *United States v. Sisal Sales Corp.*, 274 U.S. 268. Cf. *Steele v. Bulova Watch Co.*, 344 U.S. 280; *Branch v. Federal Trade Comm'n*, 141 F.2d 31 (C.A.7th Cir.). See *United States v. Aluminum Co. of America*, 148 F.2d 416 (C.A.2d Cir.); *United States v. National Lead Co.*, 63 F. Supp. 513 (D.C.S.D.N.Y.), *affirmed* 332 U.S. 319.[7]

Furthermore, in the *Sisal* case, supra, a combination entered into within the United States to monopolize an article of commerce produced abroad was held to violate the Sherman Act even though the defendants' control of that production was aided by discriminatory legislation of the foreign country which established an official agency as the sole buyer of the product from the producers and even though one of the defendants became the exclusive selling agent of that governmental authority. Since the activities of the defendants had an impact within the United States and upon its foreign trade, *American Banana* was expressly held not to be controlling.[8]

---

7. See also Brewster, Antitrust and American Business Abroad 65–75 (1958); Fugate, Foreign Commerce and the Antitrust Laws 20–55 (1958); Atty.Gen.Nat.Comm. Antitrust Rep. 66–77 (1955); Kramer, Application of the Sherman Act to Foreign Commerce, 3 Antitrust Bull. 387 (1958); Carlston, Antitrust Policy Abroad, 49 N.W.U.L.Rev. 569 (1954).

8. "The circumstances of the present controversy are radically different from those presented in *American Banana Co. v. United Fruit Co.*, supra, and the doctrine there approved is not controlling here. . . .

"Here we have a contract, combination and conspiracy entered into by parties within the United States and made effective by acts done therein. The fundamental object was control of both importation and sales of sisal and complete monopoly of both internal and external trade and commerce therein. The United States complain of a violation of their laws within their own territory by parties subject to their jurisdiction, not merely of something done by another government at the instigation of private parties. True, the conspirators were aided by discriminating legislation, but by their own deliberate acts, here and elsewhere, they brought about forbidden results within the United States. They are within the jurisdiction of our courts and may be punished for offenses against our laws." 274 U.S., at 275–276.

Olsen v. Smith, 195 U.S. 332; *United States v. Rock Royal Co-op*, 307 U.S. 533; and *Parker v. Brown*, 317 U.S. 341, do not help respondents. These decisions, each of which sustained the validity of mandatory state or federal governmental regulations against a claim of antitrust illegality, are wide of the mark. In the present case petitioners do not question the validity of any action taken by the Canadian Government or of its Metals Controller. Nor is there left in the case any question that the Canadian Government's agent for Electro Met of Canada was not served. What the petitioners here contend is that the respondents are liable for actions which they themselves jointly took, as part of their unlawful conspiracy, to influence or to direct the elimination of Continental from the Canadian market. As in Sisal, the conspiracy was laid in the United States, was effectuated both here and abroad, and respondents are not insulated by the fact that their conspiracy involved some acts by the agent of a foreign government.

From the evidence which petitioners offered it appears that Continental complained to the Canadian Metals Controller that Continental had lost its Canadian business. The Controller referred Continental to one of the respondents. But there is no indication that the Controller or any other official within the structure of the Canadian Government approved or would have approved of joint efforts to monopolize the production and sale of vanadium or directed that purchases from Continental be stopped. The exclusion, Continental claims, resulted from the action of Electro Met of Canada, taken within the area of its discretionary powers granted by the Metals Controller and in concert with or under the direction of the respondents. The offer of proof at least presented an issue for the jury's resolution as to whether the loss of Continental's Canadian business was occasioned by respondents' activities. Respondents are afforded no defense from the fact that Electro Met of Canada, in carrying out the bare act of purchasing vanadium from respondents rather than Continental, was acting in a manner permitted by Canadian law. There is nothing to indicate that such law in any way compelled discriminatory purchasing, and it is well settled that acts which are in themselves legal lose that character when they become constituent elements of an unlawful scheme. . . .

The case of *Eastern Railroad Presidents Conf. v. Noerr Motor Freight, Inc.*, 365 U.S. 127, cited by the court below and much relied upon by respondents here, is plainly inapposite. The Court there held not cognizable under the Sherman Act a complaint charging, in essence, that the defendants had engaged in a concerted publicity campaign to foster the adoption of laws and law enforcement practices inimical to plaintiffs' business. Finding no basis for imputing to the Sherman Act a purpose to regulate political activity, a purpose which would have encountered serious constitutional barriers, the Court ruled the defendants' activities to be outside the ban of the Act "at least insofar as those activities comprised mere solicitation of governmental action with respect to the passage and enforcement of laws." 365 U.S., at 138. In this case, respondents' conduct is wholly dissimilar to that of the defendants in *Noerr*. Respondents were engaged in private commercial activity, no element of which involved seeking to procure the passage or enforcement of laws. To subject them to liability under the Sherman Act for eliminating a competitor from the Canadian market by exercise of the discretionary power conferred upon Electro Met of Canada by the Canadian Government would effectuate the purposes of the Sherman Act and would not remotely infringe upon any of the constitutionally protected freedoms spoken of in Noerr.

Since our decision concerning the alleged loss of Continental's Canadian business will in any event require a new trial of the entire case in view of the close interconnection between the Canadian and domestic issues, we shall remand the case to the District Court for further proceedings....

Judgment of Court of Appeals vacated and case remanded.

■ FRANKFURTER, J., took no part in the consideration or decision of this case.

NOTES AND QUESTIONS

1. In PFIZER, INC. V. GOVERNMENT OF INDIA, 434 U.S. 308, 98 S.Ct. 584, 54 L.Ed.2d 563 (1978), the Court held that "a foreign nation otherwise entitled to sue in our courts is entitled to sue for treble damages under the antitrust laws to the same extent as any other plaintiff. Neither the fact that respondents are foreign nor the fact that they are sovereign is reason to deny them the remedy of treble damages Congress afforded to 'any person' victimized by violation of the antitrust laws." The governments of several foreign countries, as purchasers of antibiotics, had brought antitrust treble damage suits against major pharmaceutical firms in the United States. The Court was asked to decide whether a foreign sovereign was a "person" within the meaning of Section 4 of the Clayton Act. The Court reasoned that since "the antitrust laws extend to trade 'with foreign nations as well as among the several States of the Union'.... Congress did not intend to make the treble damage remedy available only to consumers in our own country." The Court relied on its decision in *Georgia v. Evans*, 316 U.S. 159 (1942), which held that a state could sue for treble damages, to reject "the proposition that the word 'person' as used in the antitrust laws excludes all sovereign states." It also noted that depriving foreign sovereigns of standing to sue would, in some circumstances, greatly diminish the deterrent effect of the statutory treble damage provisions. A foreign sovereign remains a "person" under Section 4 of the Clayton Act, pursuant to the Antitrust Reciprocity Amendment enacted in 1982 (96 Stat. 1964 (1982)), but pursuant to 15 U.S.C. § 15(b) it may recover only actual damages.

2. Note that *Parker v. Brown*, the leading "state action" case, p. 450 supra, is cited in *Continental Ore*. How was it used by counsel, and how was it distinguished by the Court? Should "state action" cases be persuasive in deciding "extraterritorial jurisdiction" cases?

3. Do you see any difference, for purposes of determining extraterritorial coverage, between cases alleging restrictions on U.S. import commerce, such as *Alcoa*, and cases alleging restrictions on exports from the United States, such as *Continental Ore*? This distinction moved to the forefront in the late 1980's, as a result of 1982 legislation and several rounds of guidelines from the U.S. Department of Justice and the Federal Trade Commission. See p. 1246 infra. The *Canadian Radio Patent Pool* case, which is summarized in note 4, shows that the Supreme

Court was relatively unaware of the international sensitivities that would be offended by exercises of jurisdiction in export cases.

    4.   ZENITH RADIO CORP. v. HAZELTINE RESEARCH, INC., 395 U.S. 100 (1969). Zenith was a Delaware corporation that manufactured radio and television sets for sale in the United States and abroad. Hazeltine and its subsidiary HRI had the right to a number of foreign and U.S. patents that Zenith needed in its business. For a time, it licensed a package of patents from Hazeltine, but in 1959 it decided that it did not need to renew its package license. Litigation ensued in which Hazeltine tried to enforce its patent rights and Zenith resisted, eventually filing an antitrust counter-claim against Hazeltine. The district court found that Hazeltine had violated the antitrust laws, but the court of appeals reversed, principally on the ground that the U.S. courts had no jurisdiction over Hazeltine. The Supreme Court then reversed the court of appeals, finding that there was enough evidence in the record to support the district court's finding of injury to Zenith's export business from the way in which Hazeltine used its Canadian patents.

    The holder of the patents in question was a patent pool in Canada (Canadian Radio Patents, Ltd., or CRPL), which had been formed in 1926 by the Canadian subsidiaries of two U.S. companies, General Electric and Westinghouse. The Supreme Court noted that:

> The pool was made up largely of Canadian manufacturers, most of which were subsidiaries of American companies. The pool for many years had the exclusive right to sublicense the patents of its member companies and also those of Hazeltine and a number of other foreign concerns. About 5,000 patents were available to the pool for licensing, and only package licenses were granted, covering all patents in the pool and strictly limited to manufacture in Canada. No license to importers was available. The chief purpose of the pool was to protect the manufacturing members and licensees from competition by American and other foreign companies seeking to export their products into Canada.

> CRPL's efforts to prevent importation of radio and television sets from the United States were highly organized and effective.

    Zenith tried to establish itself in Canada without obtaining a license from the pool, but it was unsuccessful. It then brought an antitrust suit against several individual pool members and settled the suit in a way that gave it worldwide licenses on patents owned by the named defendants. Armed with these and other licenses, Zenith in 1958 began exporting radio and television products to Canada. CRPL immediately took steps to enforce its Canadian rights, informing Zenith that it had to sign CRPL's standard license, which did not permit importation, and that to sell in Canada it must manufacture there. Zenith refused, and this lawsuit was the result. Without so much as a nod to the fact that it was dealing with an arrangement that blocked U.S. exports into a foreign country, or any indication of concern about the legality of the arrangement in Canada, the Supreme Court found that:

> The evidence was quite sufficient to sustain a finding that competing business concerns and patentees joined together to pool their Canadian patents, granting only package licenses and refusing to license imported goods. Their clear purpose was to exclude concerns like Zenith from the Canadian market unless willing to manufacture there. Zenith, consequent-ly, was never able to obtain a license. This fact and the pool's vigorous campaign to discourage importers, distributors, dealers, and consumers

from selling, handling, or using unlicensed foreign merchandise effectively prevented Zenith from making any headway in the Canadian market until after the 1957 settlement with RCA and its codefendants. And even in 1958, when Zenith undertook in earnest to establish its distribution system in Canada and to market its merchandise, Zenith was met with further pool advertisements threatening action against imported goods and further notifications, continuing past May 22, 1959, that its products were infringing pool patents and that no license was available unless Zenith manufactured in Canada.

It was enough, in the Court's view, that "Zenith was denied a valuable license and submitted testimony that without the license it had encountered distribution difficulties which prevented its securing a share of the market comparable to that which it enjoyed in the United States, and which its business proficiency, demonstrated in the United States, dictated it should have obtained in Canada." It concluded that the district court's injunction was proper, with the following statements:

> The findings of the District Court were that HRI and CRPL were conspiring to exclude Zenith and others from the Canadian market; there was nothing indicating that this clear violation of the antitrust laws had terminated or that the threat to Zenith inherent in the conduct would cease in the foreseeable future. Neither the relative quiescence of the pool during the litigation nor claims that objectionable conduct would cease with the judgment negated the threat to Zenith's foreign trade.[9] That threat was too clear for argument, and injunctive relief against HRI with respect to the Canadian market was wholly proper.

We also reinstate the injunction entered by the District Court insofar as it more broadly barred HRI from conspiring with others to restrict or prevent Zenith from entering any other foreign market. In exercising its equitable jurisdiction, "(a) federal court has broad power to restrain acts which are of the same type or class as unlawful acts which the court has found to have been committed or whose commission in the future unless enjoined, may fairly be anticipated from the defendant's conduct in the past." *NLRB v. Express Publishing Co.*, 312 U.S. 426, 435 (1941). *See also United States v. National Lead Co.*, 332 U.S. 319, 328–335 and n. 4 (1947). Given the findings that HRI was conspiring with the Canadian pool, its purpose to exclude Zenith from Canada and its violation of the Sherman Act were clearly established. Its propensity for arrangements of this sort was also indicated by the findings revealing its participation in similar pools operating in England and

---

9. HRI informs us that Hazeltine, having obtained an early termination of its licensing agreement with CRPL, is now prepared to license any one or more of its Canadian patents "with no restrictions on imports." Since Hazeltine's abandonment of its participation in the Canadian pool occurred only after—and, apparently, in response to—the District Court's judgment and decree, we cannot agree with the suggestion that injunctive relief as to Canada has been rendered unnecessary and inappropriate. *See United States v. Oregon State Medical Society*, 343 U.S. 326, 333 (1952);

United States v. Concentrated Phosphate Export Assn., 393 U.S. 199, 202–203 (1968). Although HRI is free to attempt to demonstrate in the future that the need for injunctive relief with respect to Canada has been eliminated, or that a change of circumstances elsewhere justifies additional modification of the injunction, *see, e.g.,* United States v. W.T. Grant Co., 345 U.S. 629, 633–636 (1953), we are not willing at this time to undertake a reappraisal of the injunction in light of post-trial developments.

Australia.[10] Zenith, a company interested in expanding its foreign commerce and having suffered at the hands of HRI and its coconspirators in the Canadian market, was entitled to injunctive relief against like conduct by HRI in other world markets....

5.   Cases like *Continental Ore* and *Canadian Patent Pools* represented a sort of extraterritorial high-water mark for the U.S. antitrust laws. Several developments coincided to rein in these ambitious positions: objections from foreign governments; the development of an abstention-like doctrine of comity by the federal courts; and the enactment of legislation by Congress. We look at the comity issue in Section 2 of this chapter; here, we continue the story with the statute that currently regulates most assertions of jurisdiction in foreign commerce cases: section 6a of the Sherman Act (and its FTC Act analog), which was enacted in 1982 in the Foreign Trade Antitrust Improvements Act (FTAIA).

B.   THE FOREIGN TRADE ANTITRUST IMPROVEMENTS ACT

The FTAIA amended both the Sherman Act and the Federal Trade Commission Act to clarify the meaning of the phrase "conduct involving trade or commerce with foreign nations" in the two statutes. Because there is no pertinent different in the amendments of the two, only the Sherman Act language is reproduced here:

> Sections 1 to 7 of this title [Title 15, U.S.C.] shall not apply to conduct involving trade or commerce (other than import trade or import commerce) with foreign nations unless—
>
> > (1) such conduct has a direct, substantial, and reasonably foreseeable effect—
> >
> > > (A) on trade or commerce which is not trade or commerce with foreign nations, or on import trade or import commerce with foreign nations; or
> > >
> > > (B) on export trade or export commerce with foreign nations, of a person engaged in such trade or commerce in the United States; and
> >
> > (2) such effect gives rise to a claim under the provisions of sections 1 to 7 of this title, other than this section.
>
> If sections 1 to 7 of this title apply to such conduct only because of the operation of paragraph (1)(B), then sections 1 to 7 of this title shall apply to such conduct only for injury to export business in the United States.

---

10. Having not disturbed the District Court's findings that HRI and Hazeltine were conspiring with English and Australian patent pools which refused to license imports, the Court of Appeals in any event should have sustained the injunction with respect to the English and Australian markets. These findings, together with Zenith's demonstrated intent to expand its export business, were sufficient foundation for the conclusion that continued participation by HRI and Hazeltine in the English and Australian pools posed a significant threat of loss or damage to Zenith's business.

Although the statute may not be destined for inclusion in a manual of style, it essentially creates two categories of "foreign commerce" cases: those in which the effects of the conduct in question are felt in domestic or import commerce, and those in which the effects of the conduct are felt in the export trade of U.S. exporters.

NOTES AND QUESTIONS

1. The extent to which this statute governs applications of the U.S. antitrust laws to foreign commerce cases has not been as clear as the drafters might have hoped. Nor is it clear whether the statute creates a limitation on the subject matter jurisdiction of the federal courts, in the same way that 28 U.S.C. § 1332 allows assertions of jurisdiction only when there is "complete" diversity, or whether it addresses jurisdiction in the broader sense of international prescriptive jurisdiction or legislative jurisdiction. Which do you think it is, and why? See *United Phosphorus, Ltd. v. Angus Chem. Co.*, 322 F.3d 942 (7th Cir.2003)(en banc), in which the court held by a 5-4 vote that the statute creates a limitation on the subject matter jurisdiction of the federal courts.

2. Why do you think Congress so explicitly excluded import commerce from the statute? Is the formula "direct, substantial, and reasonably foreseeable effects" an appropriate one for import commerce cases, or should the courts use something more like the test in *Summit Health, Ltd. v. Pinhas*, 500 U.S. 322 (1991), which governs conventional jurisdictional analysis under the Sherman Act? Is there any reason to treat criminal cases differently? See *United States v. Nippon Paper Indus.*, 109 F.3d 1 (1st Cir.1997), infra p. 1203.

3. Congress specified when it passed the FTAIA that it was not taking a position one way or the other on the question whether the exercise of judicial power should also be tempered by "comity." See *Timberlane Lumber Co. v. Bank of America, N.T. & S.A.*, 549 F.2d 597 (9th Cir.1976), *cert. denied*, 472 U.S. 1032, infra p. 1233. How should the "comity" considerations of *Timberlane* interact with the statutory test for foreign commerce jurisdiction?

4. After passage of the FTAIA, a number of district courts began to dismiss cases on the grounds that the jurisdictional allegations were insufficient. *See, e.g., Eurim–Pharm GmbH v. Pfizer Inc.*, 593 F.Supp. 1102 (S.D.N.Y.1984); *Liamuiga Tours v. Travel Impressions, Ltd.*, 617 F.Supp. 920 (E.D.N.Y.1985); *The In Porters, S.A. v. Hanes Printables, Inc.*, 663 F.Supp. 494 (M.D.N.C.1987); *Optimum, S.A. v. Legent Corp.*, 926 F.Supp. 530 (W.D.Pa.1996). Occasionally, however, jurisdiction succeeds. *See, e.g., Coors Brewing Co. v. Miller Brewing Co.*, 889 F.Supp. 1394 (D.Colo.1995). The next case went all the way to the Supreme Court on the jurisdictional issue. See if you can identify the theory on which the majority based its jurisdictional ruling.

5. We now turn first to the Supreme Court's only post-FTAIA foreign commerce antitrust decision, which arose out of an elaborate alleged conspiracy in international insurance markets that limited policies written in the United States. That case is followed by some court of appeals decisions exploring other aspects of this question.

Hartford Fire Insurance Co. v. California

Supreme Court of the United States, 1993.
509 U.S. 764, 113 S.Ct. 2891, 125 L.Ed.2d 612.

[Nineteen states and many private plaintiffs sued domestic insurance companies and domestic and foreign reinsurers alleging a conspiracy to restrict the coverage of commercial general liability (CGL) insurance available in the United States. Plaintiffs alleged conspiracies to curtail insurance coverage in several respects, the most important limiting the insurer's responsibility so that it must pay only for claims made during the policy period on accidents occurring during the time period the policy was in effect, rather than claims whenever made. Other conspiracies allegedly made pollution coverage unavailable or practically unavailable in the plaintiffs' states.

The Supreme Court's review of dismissal of the complaints focused on two issues: whether the alleged conduct was immune from the antitrust laws because it constituted "the business of insurance" within the meaning of the McCarran–Ferguson Act, and whether the action against several of the foreign defendants should be dismissed because the Sherman Act should not apply to the foreign conduct at issue.

The Court found that the McCarran–Ferguson Act was no bar to Sherman Act enforcement and then turned for the first time in many years to the question of the extraterritorial reach of the Sherman Act. The majority opinion of Justice Souter and the dissenting opinion of Justice Scalia follow.]

SOUTER, J. . . . Finally, we take up the question. . . . whether certain claims against the London reinsurers should have been dismissed as improper applications of the Sherman Act to foreign conduct. The Fifth Claim for Relief of the California Complaint alleges a violation of § 1 of the Sherman Act by certain London reinsurers who conspired to coerce primary insurers in the United States to offer CGL coverage on a claims-made basis, thereby making "occurrence CGL coverage . . . unavailable in the State of California for many risks." The Sixth Claim for Relief of the California Complaint alleges that the London reinsurers violated § 1 by a conspiracy to limit coverage of pollution risks in North America, thereby rendering "pollution liability coverage . . . almost entirely unavailable for the vast majority of casualty insurance purchasers in the State of California."

At the outset, we note that the District Court undoubtedly had jurisdiction of these Sherman Act claims, as the London reinsurers apparently concede. ("Our position is not that the Sherman Act does not apply in the sense that a minimal basis for the exercise of jurisdiction doesn't exist here. Our position is that there are certain circumstances, and that this is one of them, in which the interests of another State are sufficient that the exercise of that jurisdiction should be restrained").[11] Although the proposi-

---

11. One of the London reinsurers, Sturge Reinsurance Syndicate Management   Limited, argues that the Sherman Act does not apply to its conduct in attending a single

tion was perhaps not always free from doubt, *see American Banana Co. v. United Fruit Co.*, 213 U.S. 347, 53 L.Ed. 826, 29 S.Ct. 511 (1909), it is well established by now that the Sherman Act applies to foreign conduct that was meant to produce and did in fact produce some substantial effect in the United States. *See Matsushita Elec. Industrial Co. v. Zenith Radio Corp.*, 475 U.S. 574, 582, 89 L.Ed.2d 538, 106 S.Ct. 1348, n. 6 (1986); *United States v. Aluminum Co. of America*, 148 F.2d 416, 444 (C.A.2 1945) (L. Hand, J.); Restatement (Third) of Foreign Relations Law of the United States § 415, and Reporters' Note 3 (1987) (hereinafter Restatement (Third) Foreign Relations Law); 1 P. Areeda & D. Turner, Antitrust Law ¶ 236 (1978); *cf. Continental Ore Co. v. Union Carbide & Carbon Corp.*, 370 U.S. 690, 704, 8 L.Ed.2d 777, 82 S.Ct. 1404 (1962); *Steele v. Bulova Watch Co.*, 344 U.S. 280, 288, 97 L.Ed. 319, 73 S.Ct. 252 (1952); *United States v. Sisal Sales Corp.*, 274 U.S. 268, 275–276, 71 L.Ed. 1042, 47 S.Ct. 592 (1972).[12] Such is the conduct alleged here: that the London reinsurers engaged in unlawful conspiracies to affect the market for insurance in the United States and that their conduct in fact produced substantial effect.[13] See 938 F.2d, at 933.

According to the London reinsurers, the District Court should have declined to exercise such jurisdiction under the principle of international comity.[14] The Court of Appeals agreed that courts should look to that

meeting at which it allegedly agreed to exclude all pollution coverage from its reinsurance contracts. Brief for Petitioner Sturge Reinsurance Syndicate Management Limited in No. 91–1128, p. 22. Sturge may have attended only one meeting, but the allegations, which we are bound to credit, remain that it participated in conduct that was intended to and did in fact produce a substantial effect on the American insurance market.

12. Justice Scalia believes that what is at issue in this case is prescriptive, as opposed to subject-matter, jurisdiction. The parties do not question prescriptive jurisdiction, however, and for good reason: it is well established that Congress had exercised such jurisdiction under the Sherman Act. *See* G. Born & D. Westin, International Civil Litigation in United States Courts, 542, n. 5 (2d ed. 1992) (Sherman Act is a "prime example of the simultaneous exercise of prescriptive jurisdiction and grant of subject matter jurisdiction").

13. Under § 402 of the Foreign Trade Antitrust Improvements Act of 1982 (FTAIA), 96 Stat. 1246, 15 U.S.C. § 6a, the Sherman Act does not apply to conduct involving foreign trade or commerce, other than import trade or import commerce, un-

less "such conduct has a direct, substantial, and reasonably foreseeable effect" on domestic or import commerce. 15 U.S.C. § 6a(1)(A). The FTAIA was intended to exempt from the Sherman Act export transactions that did not injure the United States economy, *see* H.R.Rep. No. 97–686, pp. 2–3, 9–10 (1982); P. Areeda & H. Hovenkamp, Antitrust Law ¶ 236'a, pp. 296–297 (Supp.1992), and it is unclear how it might apply to the conduct alleged here. Also unclear is whether the Act's "direct, substantial, and reasonably foreseeable effect" standard amends existing law or merely codifies it. See id., ¶ 236'a, p. 297. We need not address these questions here. Assuming that the FTAIA's standard affects this case, and assuming further that the standard differs from the prior law, the conduct alleged plainly meets its requirements.

14. Justice Scalia contends that comity concerns figure into the prior analysis whether jurisdiction exists under the Sherman Act. This contention is inconsistent with the general understanding that the Sherman Act covers foreign conduct producing a substantial intended effect in the United States, and that concerns of comity come into play, if at all, only after a court has determined that the acts complained of are subject to Sherman

principle in deciding whether to exercise jurisdiction under the Sherman Act. This availed the London reinsurers nothing, however. To be sure, the Court of Appeals believed that "application of [American] antitrust laws to the London reinsurance market 'would lead to significant conflict with English law and policy,'" and that "such a conflict, unless outweighed by other factors, would by itself be reason to decline exercise of jurisdiction." But other factors, in the court's view, including the London reinsurers' express purpose to affect United States commerce and the substantial nature of the effect produced, outweighed the supposed conflict and require the exercise of jurisdiction in this case.

When it enacted the Foreign Trade Antitrust Improvements Act of 1982 (FTAIA), 96 Stat. 1246, 15 U.S.C. § 6a, Congress expressed no view on the question whether a court with Sherman Act jurisdiction should ever decline to exercise such jurisdiction on grounds of international comity. *See* H.R.Rep. No. 97–686, p. 13 (1982) ("If a court determines that the requirements for subject matter jurisdiction are met, [the FTAIA] would have no effect on the court['s] ability to employ notions of comity ... or otherwise to take account of the international character of the transaction") (citing *Timberlane*). We need not decide that question here, however, for even assuming that in a proper case a court may decline to exercise Sherman Act jurisdiction over foreign conduct (or, as Justice Scalia would put it, may conclude by the employment of comity analysis in the first instance that there is no jurisdiction), international comity would not counsel against exercising jurisdiction in the circumstances alleged here.

The only substantial question in this case is whether "there is in fact a true conflict between domestic and foreign law." *Societe Nationale Industrielle Aerospatiale v. United States District Court*, 482 U.S. 522, 555, 96 L.Ed.2d 461, 107 S.Ct. 2542 (1987) (Blackmun, J., concurring in part and dissenting in part). The London reinsurers contend that applying the Act to their conduct would conflict significantly with British law, and the British Government, appearing before us as amicus curiae, concurs. They assert that Parliament has established a comprehensive regulatory regime over the London reinsurance market and that the conduct alleged here was perfectly consistent with British law and policy. But this is not to state a conflict. "[T]he fact that conduct is lawful in the state in which it took place will not, of itself, bar application of the United States antitrust laws," even where the foreign state has a strong policy to permit or encourage such conduct. Restatement (Third) Foreign Relations Law § 415, Comment

Act jurisdiction. *See United States v. Aluminum Co. of America*, 148 F.2d 416, 444 (C.A.2 1945) ("it follows from what we have ... said that [the agreements at issue] were unlawful [under the Sherman Act], though made abroad, if they were intended to affect imports and did affect them"); *Mannington Mills, Inc. v. Congoleum Corp.*, 595 F.2d 1287, 1294 (C.A.3 1979) (once court determines that jurisdiction exists under the Sher-man Act, question remains whether comity precludes its exercise); H.R.Rep. No. 97–686, p. 13 (1982). But cf. *Timberlane Lumber Co. v. Bank of America, N.T. & S.A.*, 549 F.2d 597, 613 (C.A.9 1976); 1 J. Atwood & K. Brewster, Antitrust and American Business Abroad 166 (1981). In any event, the parties conceded jurisdiction at oral argument, and we see no need to address this contention here.

j; *see Continental Ore Co.*, supra, at 706–707. No conflict exists, for these purposes, "where a person subject to regulation by two states can comply with the laws of both." Restatement (Third) Foreign Relations Law § 403, Comment e.[15] Since the London reinsurers do not argue that British law requires them to act in some fashion prohibited by the law of the United States, or claim that their compliance with the laws of both countries is otherwise impossible, we see no conflict with British law. See Restatement (Third) Foreign Relations Law § 403, Comment e, § 415, Comment j. We have no need in this case to address other considerations that might inform a decision to refrain from the exercise of jurisdiction on grounds of international comity.

■ SCALIA, J. dissenting. . . . The petitioners, . . . various British corporations and other British subjects, argue that certain of the claims against them constitute an inappropriate extraterritorial application of the Sherman Act. It is important to distinguish two distinct questions raised by this petition: whether the District Court had jurisdiction, and whether the Sherman Act reaches the extraterritorial conduct alleged here. On the first question, I believe that the District Court had subject-matter jurisdiction over the Sherman Act claims against all the defendants (personal jurisdiction is not contested). The respondents asserted nonfrivolous claims under the Sherman Act, and 28 U.S.C. § 1331 vests district courts with subject-matter jurisdiction over cases "arising under" federal statutes. As precedents such as *Lauritzen v. Larsen*, 345 U.S. 571, 97 L.Ed. 1254, 73 S.Ct. 921 (1953), make clear, that is sufficient to establish the District Court's jurisdiction over these claims. *Lauritzen* involved a Jones Act claim brought by a foreign sailor against a foreign shipowner. The shipowner contested the District Court's jurisdiction apparently on the grounds that the Jones Act did not govern the dispute between the foreign parties to the action. Though ultimately agreeing with the shipowner that the Jones Act did not apply, see discussion infra, the Court held that the District Court had jurisdiction.

> "As frequently happens, a contention that there is some barrier to granting plaintiff's claim is cast in terms of an exception to jurisdiction of subject matter. A cause of action under our law was asserted here, and the court had power to determine whether it was or was not founded in law and in fact." 345 U.S., at 575. . . .

The second question—the extraterritorial reach of the Sherman Act—has nothing to do with the jurisdiction of the courts. It is a question of substantive law turning on whether, in enacting the Sherman Act, Congress asserted regulatory power over the challenged conduct. *See EEOC v. Arabian American Oil Co.*, 449 U.S. 244 (1991) ("It is our task to determine whether Congress intended the protections of Title VII to apply to

---

15. Justice Scalia says that we put the cart before the horse in citing this authority, for he argues it may be apposite only after a determination that jurisdiction over the for-eign acts is reasonable. But whatever the order of cart and horse, conflict in this sense is the only substantial issue before the Court.

United States citizens employed by American employers outside of the United States"). If a plaintiff fails to prevail on this issue, the court does not dismiss the claim for want of subject-matter jurisdiction—want of power to adjudicate; rather, it decides the claim, ruling on the merits that the plaintiff has failed to state a cause of action under the relevant statute. *See Romero*, supra, at 384 (holding no claim available under the Jones Act); *American Banana Co. v. United Fruit Co.*, 213 U.S. 347, 359, 53 L.Ed. 826, 29 S.Ct. 511 (1909) (holding that complaint based upon foreign conduct "alleges no case under the [Sherman Act]").

There is, however, a type of "jurisdiction" relevant to determining the extraterritorial reach of a statute; it is known as "legislative jurisdiction," *Aramco*, supra at 253, Restatement (First) Conflict of Laws § 60 (1934), or "jurisdiction to prescribe," 1 Restatement (Third) of Foreign Relations Law of the United States 235 (1987) (hereinafter Restatement (Third)). This refers to "the authority of a state to make its law applicable to persons or activities," and is quite a separate matter from "jurisdiction to adjudicate." There is no doubt, of course, that Congress possesses legislative jurisdiction over the acts alleged in this complaint: Congress has broad power under Article I, § 8, cl. 3 "[t]o regulate Commerce with foreign Nations," and this Court has repeatedly upheld its power to make laws applicable to persons or activities beyond our territorial boundaries where United States interests are affected. *See Ford v. United States*, 273 U.S. 593, 621–623, 71 L.Ed. 793, 47 S.Ct. 531 (1972); *United States v. Bowman*, 260 U.S. 94, 98–99, 67 L.Ed. 149, 43 S.Ct. 39 (1922); *American Banana*, supra, at 356. But the question in this case is whether, and to what extent, Congress has exercised that undoubted legislative jurisdiction in enacting the Sherman Act.

Two canons of statutory construction are relevant in this inquiry. The first is the "long-standing principle of American law 'that legislation of Congress, unless a contrary intent appears, is meant to apply only within the territorial jurisdiction of the United States.'" *Aramco*, supra ... Applying that canon in *Aramco*, we held that the version of Title VII of the Civil Rights Act of 1964 then in force, 42 U.S.C. §§ 2000e–2000e–17 (1988 ed.), did not extend outside the territory of the United States even though the statute contained broad provisions extending its prohibitions to, for example, " 'any activity, business, or industry in commerce.' " We held such "boilerplate language" to be an insufficient indication to override the presumption against extraterritoriality. The Sherman Act contains similar "boilerplate language," and if the question were not governed by precedent, it would be worth considering whether that presumption controls the outcome here. We have, however, found the presumption to be overcome with respect to our antitrust laws; it is now well established that the Sherman Act applies extraterritorially. *See Matsushita Elec. Industrial Co. v. Zenith Radio Corp.*, 475 U.S. 574, 582, 89 L.Ed.2d 538, 106 S.Ct. 1348, n. 6 (1986); *Continental Ore Co. v. Union Carbide & Carbon Corp.*, 370 U.S. 690, 704, 8 L.Ed.2d 777, 82 S.Ct. 1404 (1962); *see also United States v. Aluminum Co. of America*, 148 F.2d 416 (C.A.2 1945).

But if the presumption against extraterritoriality has been overcome or is otherwise inapplicable, a second canon of statutory construction becomes relevant: "[A]n act of congress ought never to be construed to violate the law of nations if any other possible construction remains." *Murray v. The Charming Betsy*, 6 U.S. 64, 2 Cranch 64, 118, 2 L.Ed. 208 (1804) (Marshall, C.J.). This canon is "wholly independent" of the presumption against extraterritoriality. [citation omitted] It is relevant to determining the substantive reach of a statute because "the law of nations," or customary international law, includes limitations on a nation's exercise of its jurisdiction to prescribe. *See* Restatement (Third) §§ 401–416. Though it clearly has constitutional authority to do so, Congress is generally presumed not to have exceeded those customary international-law limits on jurisdiction to prescribe.

Consistent with that presumption, this and other courts have frequently recognized that, even where the presumption against extraterritoriality does not apply, statutes should not be interpreted to regulate foreign persons or conduct if that regulation would conflict with principles of international law. For example, in *Romero v. International Terminal Operating Co.*, 358 U.S. 354, 3 L.Ed.2d 368, 79 S.Ct. 468 (1959), the plaintiff, a Spanish sailor who had been injured while working aboard a Spanish-flag and Spanish-owned vessel, filed a Jones Act claim against his Spanish employer. The presumption against extraterritorial application of federal statutes was inapplicable to the case, as the actionable tort had occurred in American waters. *See id.*, at 383. The Court nonetheless stated that, "in the absence of contrary congressional direction," it would apply "principles of choice of law that are consonant with the needs of a general federal maritime law and with due recognition of our self-regarding respect for the relevant interests of foreign nations in the regulation of maritime commerce as part of the legitimate concern of the international community." Id., at 382–383. "The controlling considerations" in this choice-of-law analysis were "the interacting interests of the United States and of foreign countries." Id., at 383.

Romero referred to, and followed, the choice-of-law analysis set forth in *Lauritzen v. Larsen*, 345 U.S. 571, 97 L.Ed. 1254, 73 S.Ct. 921 (1953). As previously mentioned, *Lauritzen* also involved a Jones Act claim brought by a foreign sailor against a foreign employer. The Lauritzen Court recognized the basic problem: "If [the Jones Act were] read literally, Congress has conferred an American right of action which requires nothing more than that plaintiff be 'any seaman who shall suffer personal injury in the course of his employment.' " *Id.*, at 576. The solution it adopted was to construe the statute "to apply only to areas and transactions in which American law would be considered operative under prevalent doctrines of international law." *id.*, at 577. To support application of international law to limit the facial breadth of the statute, the Court relied upon—of course—Chief Justice Marshall's statement in The Charming Betsy quoted supra, at 16. It then set forth "several factors which, alone or in combination, are generally conceded to influence choice of law to govern a tort claim." [citations omitted]

Lauritzen, Romero, and *McCulloch* were maritime cases, but we have recognized the principle that the scope of generally worded statutes must be construed in light of international law in other areas as well. *See, e.g., Sale v. Haitian Centers Council, Inc.,* 509 U.S. 155, 178, n. 35 (1993); *Weinberger v. Rossi,* 456 U.S. 25, 32, 71 L.Ed.2d 715 102 S.Ct. 1510 (1982). More specifically, the principle was expressed in United States v. Aluminum Co. of America, 148 F.2d 416 (C.A.2 1945), the decision that established the extraterritorial reach of the Sherman Act. In his opinion for the court, Judge Learned Hand cautioned "we are not to read general words, such as those in [the Sherman] Act, without regard to the limitations customarily observed by nations upon the exercise of their powers; limitations which generally correspond to those fixed by the 'Conflict of Laws.'" *Id.,* at 443.

More recent lower court precedent has also tempered the extraterritorial application of the Sherman Act with considerations of "international comity." *See Timberlane Lumber Co. v. Bank of America, N.T. & S.A.,* 549 F.2d 597, 608–615 (C.A.9 1976); *Mannington Mills, Inc. v. Congoleum Corp.,* 595 F.2d 1287, 1294–1298 (C.A.3 1979); *Montreal Trading Ltd. v. Amax Inc.,* 661 F.2d 864, 869–871 (C.A.10 1981); *Laker Airways v. Sabena, Belgian World Airlines,* 235 U.S.App.D.C. 207, 236, 731 F.2d 909, and n. 109, 731 F.2d 909, 938, and n. 109 (1984); *see also Pacific Seafarers, Inc. v. Pacific Far East Line, Inc.,* 131 U.S.App.D.C. 226, 236, 404 F.2d 804, and n. 31, 404 F.2d 804, 814, and n. 31 (1968). The "comity" they refer to is not the comity of courts, whereby judges decline to exercise jurisdiction over matters more appropriately adjudged elsewhere, but rather what might be termed "prescriptive comity": the respect sovereign nations afford each other by limiting the reach of their laws. That comity is exercised by legislatures when they enact laws, and courts assume it has been exercised when they come to interpreting the scope of laws their legislatures have enacted. It is a traditional component of choice-of-law theory. *See* J. Story, Commentaries on the Conflict of Laws § 38 (1834) (distinguishing between the "comity of the courts" and the "comity of nations," and defining the latter as "the true foundation and extent of the obligation of the laws of one nation within the territories of another"). Comity in this sense includes the choice-of-law principles that, "in the absence of contrary congressional direction," are assumed to be incorporated into our substantive laws having extraterritorial reach. *Romero,* supra, at 382–383; *see also Lauritzen,* supra, at 578–579; *Hilton v. Guyot,* 159 U.S. 113, 162–166, 40 L.Ed. 95, 16 S.Ct. 139 (1895). Considering comity in this way is just part of determining whether the Sherman Act prohibits the conduct at issue.[16]

---

16. Some antitrust courts, including the Court of Appeals in the present case, have mistaken the comity at issue for the "comity of courts," which has led them to characterize the question presented as one of "abstention," that is, whether they should "exercise or decline jurisdiction." *Mannington Mills, Inc. v. Congoleum Corp.,* 595 F.2d 1287, 1294, 1296 (C.A.3 1979); *see also In re Insurance Antitrust Litigation,* 938 F.2d 919, 932 (C.A.9 1991). As I shall discuss, that seems to be the error the Court has fallen into today. Because courts are generally reluctant to refuse the exercise of conferred jurisdiction, confusion on this seemingly theoretical point can have the very practical

In sum, the practice of using international law to limit the extraterritorial reach of statutes is firmly established in our jurisprudence. In proceeding to apply that practice to the present case, I shall rely on the Restatement (Third) of Foreign Relations Law for the relevant principles of international law. Its standards appear fairly supported in the decisions of this Court construing international choice-of-law principles (*Lauritzen, Romero,* and *McCulloch*) and in the decisions of other federal courts, especially Timberlane. Whether the Restatement precisely reflects international law in every detail matters little here, as I believe this case would be resolved the same way under virtually any conceivable test that takes account of foreign regulatory interests.

Under the Restatement, a nation having some "basis" for jurisdiction to prescribe law should nonetheless refrain from exercising that jurisdiction "with respect to a person or activity having connections with another state when the exercise of such jurisdiction is unreasonable." Restatement (Third) § 403(1). The "reasonableness" inquiry turns on a number of factors including, but not limited to: "the extent to which the activity takes place within the territory [of the regulating state]," *id.,* § 403(2)(a); "the connections, such as nationality, residence, or economic activity, between the regulating state and the person principally responsible for the activity to be regulated," *id.,* § 403(2)(b); "the character of the activity to be regulated, the importance of regulation to the regulating state, the extent to which other states regulate such activities, and the degree to which the desirability of such regulation is generally accepted," *id.,* § 403(2)(c); "the extent to which another state may have an interest in regulating the activity," id., § 403(2)(g); and "the likelihood of conflict with regulation by another state," *id.,* § 403(2)(h). Rarely would these factors point more clearly against application of United States law. The activity relevant to the counts at issue here took place primarily in the United Kingdom, and the defendants in these counts are British corporations and British subjects having their principal place of business or residence outside the United States.[17] Great Britain has established a comprehensive regulatory scheme governing the London reinsurance markets, and clearly has a heavy "interest in regulating the activity," *id.,* § 403(2)(g). *See* 935 F.2d, at 932–933; *In re Insurance Antitrust Litigation,* 723 F.Supp. 464, 487–488 (N.D.Cal.1989); see also J. Butler & R. Merkin, Reinsurance Law A.1.1–02 (1992). Finally, § 2(b) of the McCarran–Ferguson Act allows state regulatory statutes to override the Sherman Act in the insurance field, subject only to the narrow "boycott" exception set forth in § 3(b)—suggesting that "the importance of regulation to the [United States]," *id.,* § 403(2)(c), is slight. Considering these factors, I think it unimaginable that an assertion of legislative jurisdiction by the United States would be considered reasonable, and

consequence of greatly expanding the extraterritorial reach of the Sherman Act.

17. Some of the British corporations are subsidiaries of American corporations, and the Court of Appeals held that "[t]he interests of Britain are at least diminished where the parties are subsidiaries of American corporations." 938 F.2d, at 933. In effect, the Court of Appeals pierced the corporate veil in weighing the interests at stake. I do not think that was proper.

therefore it is inappropriate to assume, in the absence of statutory indication to the contrary, that Congress had made such an assertion.

It is evident from what I have said that the Court's comity analysis, which proceeds as though the issue is whether the courts should "decline to exercise . . . jurisdiction," rather than whether the Sherman Act covers this conduct, is simply misdirected. I do not at all agree, moreover, with the Court's conclusion that the issue of the substantive scope of the Sherman Act is not in the case. To be sure, the parties did not make a clear distinction between adjudicative jurisdiction and the scope of the statute. Parties often do not, as we have observed (and have declined to punish with procedural default) before. See the excerpt from Lauritzen quoted supra, at 14; see also Romero, 358 U.S. 359. It is not realistic, and also not helpful, to pretend that the only really relevant issue in this case is not before us. In any event, if one erroneously chooses, as the Court does, to make adjudicative jurisdiction (or more precisely, abstention) the vehicle for taking account of the needs of prescriptive comity, the Court still gets it wrong. It concludes that no "true conflict" counseling nonapplication of United States law (or rather, as it thinks, United States judicial jurisdiction) exists unless compliance with United States law would constitute a violation of another country's law. That breathtakingly broad proposition, which contradicts the many cases discussed earlier, will bring the Sherman Act and other laws into sharp and unnecessary conflict with the legitimate interests of other countries—particularly our closest trading partners.

In the sense in which the term "conflic[t]" was used in *Lauritzen*, 345 U.S., at 582, 592, and is generally understood in the field of conflicts of laws, there is clearly a conflict in this case. The petitioners here, like the defendant in *Lauritzen*, were not compelled by any foreign law to take their allegedly wrongful actions, but that no more precludes a conflict-of-laws analysis here than it did there. *See id.*, at 575–576 (detailing the differences between foreign and United States law). Where applicable foreign and domestic law provide different substantive rules of decision to govern the parties' dispute, a conflict-of-laws analysis is necessary. *See generally* R. Weintraub, Commentary on Conflict of Laws 2–3 (1980); Restatement (First) of Conflict of Laws § 1, Comment c and Illustrations (1934).

Literally the only support that the Court adduces for its position is § 403 of the Restatement (Third) of Foreign Relations Law—or more precisely Comment e to that provision, which states:

> "Subsection (3) [which says that a state should defer to another state if that state's interest is clearly greater] applies only when one state requires what another prohibits, or where compliance with the regulations of two states exercising jurisdiction consistently with this section is otherwise impossible. It does not apply where a person subject to regulation by two states can comply with the laws of both. . . ."

The Court has completely misinterpreted this provision. Subsection (3) of § 403 (requiring one State to defer to another in the limited circumstances just described) comes into play only after subsection (1) of § 403 has been complied with—*i.e.*, after it has been determined that the exercise of jurisdiction by both of the two states is not "unreasonable." That prior question is answered by applying the factors (inter alia) set forth in subsection (2) of § 403, that is, precisely the factors that I have discussed in text and that the Court rejects.[18]

I would reverse the judgment of the Court of Appeals on this issue, and remand to the District Court with instructions to dismiss for failure to state a claim on the three counts at issue in No. 91–1128.

United States v. Nippon Paper

United States Court of Appeals, First Circuit, 1997.
109 F.3d 1.

■ Before: SELYA, CIRCUIT JUDGE, COFFIN, SENIOR CIRCUIT JUDGE, and LYNCH, CIRCUIT JUDGE.

■ SELYA, J. This case raises an important, hitherto unanswered question. In it, the United States attempts to convict a foreign corporation under the Sherman Act, a federal antitrust statute, alleging that price-fixing activities which took place entirely in Japan are prosecutable because they were intended to have, and did in fact have, substantial effects in this country. The district court, declaring that a criminal antitrust prosecution could not be based on wholly extraterritorial conduct, dismissed the indictment. *See United States v. Nippon Paper Indus. Co.*, 944 F. Supp. 55 (D.Mass.1996). We reverse.

I. JUST THE FAX

Since the district court granted the defendant's motion to dismiss for failure to state a prosecutable offense, we draw our account of the pertinent events from the well-pleaded facts in the indictment itself. *See United States v. National Dairy Prods. Corp.*, 372 U.S. 29, 33 n. 2 (1963).

In 1995, a federal grand jury handed up an indictment naming as a defendant Nippon Paper Industries Co., Ltd. (NPI), a Japanese manufacturer of facsimile paper. The indictment alleges that in 1990 NPI and certain unnamed coconspirators held a number of meetings in Japan which culminated in an agreement to fix the price of thermal fax paper throughout North America. NPI and other manufacturers who were privy to the scheme purportedly accomplished their objective by selling the paper in Japan to unaffiliated trading houses on condition that the latter charge specified (inflated) prices for the paper when they resold it in North America. The trading houses then shipped and sold the paper to their subsidiaries in the United States who in turn sold it to American consum-

---

18. The Court skips directly to subsection (3) of § 403, apparently on the authority of Comment j to § 415 of the Restatement (Third). But the preceding commentary to § 415 makes clear that "any exercise of [legislative] jurisdiction under this section is sub- ject to [a] the requirement of reasonableness" set forth in § 403(2). Restatement (Third) § 415, Comment a. Comment j refers back to the conflict analysis set forth in § 403(3) which, as noted above, comes after the reasonableness analysis of § 403(2).

ers at swollen prices. The indictment further relates that, in 1990 alone, NPI sold thermal fax paper worth approximately $6,100,000 for eventual import into the United States; and that in order to ensure the success of the venture, NPI monitored the paper trail and confirmed that the prices charged to end users were those that it had arranged. These activities, the indictment posits, had a substantial adverse effect on commerce in the United States and unreasonably restrained trade in violation of Section One of the Sherman Act, 15 U.S.C. § 1 (1994).

NPI moved to dismiss because, inter alia, if the conduct attributed to NPI occurred at all, it took place entirely in Japan, and, thus, the indictment failed to limn an offense under Section One of the Sherman Act. The government opposed this initiative on two grounds. First, it claimed that the law deserved a less grudging reading and that, properly read, Section One of the Sherman Act applied criminally to wholly foreign conduct as long as that conduct produced substantial and intended effects within the United States. Second, it claimed that the indictment, too, deserved a less grudging reading and that, properly read, the bill alleged a vertical conspiracy in restraint of trade that involved overt acts by certain coconspirators within the United States. Accepting a restrictive reading of both the statute and the indictment, the district court dismissed the case. See United States v. NPI, 944 F. Supp. at 64–66. This appeal followed.

II.   ANALYSIS

We begin—and end—with the overriding legal question. Because this question is one of statutory construction, we review de novo the holding that Section One of the Sherman Act does not cover wholly extraterritorial conduct in the criminal context. See United States v. Gifford, 17 F.3d 462, 471–72 (1st Cir.1994).

Our analysis proceeds in moieties. We first present the historical context in which this important question arises. We move next to the specifics of the case.

A.   An Historical Perspective.

Our law has long presumed that "legislation of Congress, unless a contrary intent appears, is meant to apply only within the territorial jurisdiction of the United States." EEOC v. Arabian American Oil Co., 499 U.S. 244 (1991) (citation omitted). In this context, the Supreme Court has charged inquiring courts with determining whether Congress has clearly expressed an affirmative desire to apply particular laws to conduct that occurs beyond the borders of the United States. See id.

The earliest Supreme Court case which undertook a comparable task in respect to Section One of the Sherman Act determined that the presumption against extraterritoriality had not been overcome. In American Banana Co. v. United Fruit Co., 213 U.S. 347 (1909), the Court considered the application of the Sherman Act in a civil action concerning conduct which occurred entirely in Central America and which had no discernible effect on imports to the United States. Starting with what Justice Holmes termed "the general and almost universal rule" holding "that the character of an act as lawful or unlawful must be determined wholly by the law of the country where the act is done," *id.* at 356, and the ancillary proposition that, in cases of doubt, a statute should be "confined in its operation and effect to the territorial limits over which the lawmaker has general and legitimate power," *id.* at 357, the Court held that the defendant's actions abroad were not proscribed by the Sherman Act.

Our jurisprudence is precedent-based, but it is not static. By 1945, a different court saw a very similar problem in a somewhat softer light. In *United States v. Aluminum Co. of Am.,* 148 F.2d 416 (2d Cir.1945) (Alcoa), the Second Circuit, sitting as a court of last resort, see 15 U.S.C. § 29 (authorizing designation of a court of appeals as a court of last resort for certain antitrust cases), mulled a civil action brought under Section One against a Canadian corporation for acts committed entirely abroad which, the government averred, had produced substantial anticompetitive effects within the United States. The Alcoa court read American Banana narrowly; that case, Judge Learned Hand wrote, stood only for the principle that "[w]e should not impute to Congress an intent to punish all whom its courts can catch, for conduct which has no consequences within the United States." *Id.* at 443. But a sovereign ordinarily can impose liability for conduct outside its borders that produces consequences within them, and while considerations of comity argue against applying Section One to situations in which no effect within the United States has been shown—the American Banana scenario—the statute, properly interpreted, does proscribe extraterritorial acts which were "intended to affect imports [to the United States] and did affect them." *Id.* at 444. On the facts of Alcoa, therefore, the presumption against extraterritoriality had been overcome, and the Sherman Act had been violated. *See id.* at 444–45.

Any perceived tension between American Banana and Alcoa was eased by the Supreme Court's most recent exploration of the Sherman Act's extraterritorial reach. In *Hartford Fire Ins. Co. v. California,* 509 U.S. 764 (1993), the Justices endorsed *Alcoa's* core holding, permitting civil antitrust claims under Section One to go forward despite the fact that the actions which allegedly violated Section One occurred entirely on British soil. While noting American Banana's initial disagreement with this proposition, the Hartford Fire Court deemed it "well established by now that the Sherman Act applies to foreign conduct that was meant to produce and did in fact produce some substantial effect in the United States." *Id.* at 796. The conduct alleged, a London-based conspiracy to alter the American insurance market, met that benchmark. *See id.*

To sum up, the case law now conclusively establishes that civil antitrust actions predicated on wholly foreign conduct which has an intended and substantial effect in the United States come within Section One's jurisdictional reach. In arriving at this conclusion, we take no view of the government's asseveration that the Foreign Trade Antitrust Improvements Act of 1982 (FTAIA), 15 U.S.C. § 6a (1994), makes manifest Congress' intent to apply the Sherman Act extraterritorially. The FTAIA is inelegantly phrased and the court in *Hartford Fire* declined to place any weight on it. *See Hartford Fire*, 509 U.S. at 796 n. 23. We emulate this example and do not rest our ultimate conclusion about Section One's scope upon the FTAIA.

B. The Merits.

Were this a civil case, our journey would be complete. But here the United States essays a criminal prosecution for solely extraterritorial conduct rather than a civil action. This is largely uncharted terrain; we are aware of no authority directly on point, and the parties have cited none.

Be that as it may, one datum sticks out like a sore thumb: in both criminal and civil cases, the claim that Section One applies extraterritorially is based on the same language in the same section of the same statute: "Every contract, combination in the form of trust or otherwise, or conspiracy, in restraint of trade or commerce among the several States, or with foreign nations, is declared to be illegal." 15 U.S.C. § 1. Words may sometimes be chameleons, possessing different shades of meaning in different contexts, *see, e.g., Hanover Ins. Co. v. United States*, 880 F.2d 1503, 1504 (1st Cir.1989), *cert. denied*, 493 U.S. 1023 (1990), but common sense suggests that courts should interpret the same language in the same section of the same statute uniformly, regardless of whether the impetus for interpretation is criminal or civil.

Common sense is usually a good barometer of statutory meaning. Here, however, we need not rely on common sense alone; accepted canons of statutory construction point in the same direction. It is a fundamental interpretive principle that identical words or terms used in different parts of the same act are intended to have the same meaning. *See Commissioner of Internal Revenue v. Lundy*, 116 S.Ct. 647, 655 (1996); *Gustafson v. Alloyd Co.*, 115 S.Ct. 1061, 1067 (1995). This principle—which the Court recently called "the basic canon of statutory construction," *Estate of Cowart v. Nicklos Drilling Co.*, 505 U.S. 469, 479 (1992)—operates not only when particular phrases appear in different sections of the same act, but also when they appear in different paragraphs or sentences of a single section. *See Russo v. Texaco, Inc.*, 808 F.2d 221, 227 (2d Cir.1986) ("It is a settled principle of statutory construction that [w]hen the same word or phrase is used in the same section of an act more than once, and the meaning is clear as used in one place, it will be construed to have the same meaning in the next place.") (citations and internal quotation marks omitted); *United States v. Gertz*, 249 F.2d 662, 665 (9th Cir.1957) (similar). It follows, therefore, that if the language upon which the indictment rests were the same as the language upon which civil liability rests but appeared in a different section of the Sherman Act, or in a different part of the same section, we would be under great pressure to follow the lead of the Hartford Fire Court and construe the two iterations of the language identically. Where, as here, the tie binds more tightly—that is, the text under consideration is not merely a duplicate appearing somewhere else in the statute, but is the original phrase in the original setting—the pressure escalates and the case for reading the language in a manner consonant with a prior Supreme Court interpretation is irresistible. *See United States v. Thompson/Center Arms Co.*, 504 U.S. 505, 518 n. 10, (1992) (plurality op.) (flatly rejecting the idea, while construing language from a statute with both civil and criminal implications, that a court should "refrain in criminal cases from applying statutory language that would have been held to apply if challenged in civil litigation").

[The court here discussed the Supreme Court's opinion in *Ratzlaf v. United States*, 510 U.S. 135 (1994), and its own opinions in *Strickland v. Commissioner, Me. Dep't of Human Servs.*, 48 F.3d 12, 21 (1st Cir.), cert. denied, 116 S.Ct. 145, (1995), and *Strickland v. Commissioner, Me. Dep't of Human Servs.*, 96 F.3d 542, 547 (1st Cir.1996). All three supported the proposition that the same phrase, appearing in the same portion of the same statute, cannot bear divergent interpretations in different litigation contexts.]

The shared rationale of the *Ratzlaf* and *Strickland* cases reinforces the basic canon of construction and gives us confidence that we should follow the canon here. The words of Section One have not changed since the Hartford Fire Court found that they clearly evince Congress' intent to apply the Sherman Act extraterritorially in civil actions, and it would be disingenuous for us to pretend that the words had lost their clarity simply because this is a criminal proceeding. Thus, unless some special circumstance obtains in this case, there is no principled way in which we can uphold the order of dismissal.

NPI and its amicus, the Government of Japan, urge that special reasons exist for measuring Section One's reach differently in a criminal context. We have reviewed their exhortations and found them hollow. We discuss the five most promising theses below. The rest do not require comment.

1.   Lack of Precedent. NPI and its amicus make much of the fact that this appears to be the first criminal case in which the United States endeavors to extend Section One to wholly foreign conduct. We are not impressed. There is a first time for everything, and the absence of earlier criminal actions is probably more a demonstration of the increasingly global nature of our economy than proof that Section One cannot cover wholly foreign conduct in the criminal milieu.

Moreover, this argument overstates the lack of precedent. There is, for example, solid authority for applying a state's criminal statute to conduct occurring entirely outside the state's borders. *See Strassheim v. Daily*, 221 U.S. 280 (1911) (Holmes, J.) ("Acts done outside a jurisdiction, but intended to produce and producing detrimental effects within it, justify a State in punishing the cause of the harm as if he had been present at the effect, if the State should succeed in getting him within its power."). It is not much of a stretch to apply this same principle internationally, especially in a shrinking world. *See, e.g., Chua Han Mow v. United States*, 730 F.2d 1308, 1311–12 (9th Cir.1984) (applying *Strassheim* principle to conduct in Malaysia involving drugs intended for distribution in the United States), cert.

denied, 470 U.S. 1031 (1985); *United States v. Hayes*, 653 F.2d 8, 11 (1st Cir.1981) (similar); *cf.* John Donne, Devotions Upon Emergent Occasions, no. 17 (1624) (warning that "no man is an island, entire of itself; every man is a piece of the continent, a part of the main").

2.   Difference in Strength of Presumption. The lower court and NPI both cite United States v. Bowman, 260 U.S. 94 (1922), for the proposition that the presumption against extraterritoriality operates with greater force in the criminal arena than in civil litigation. This misreads the opinion. To be sure, the Bowman Court, dealing with a charged conspiracy to defraud, warned that if the criminal law "is to be extended to include those [crimes] committed outside of the strict territorial jurisdiction, it is natural for Congress to say so in the statute, and failure to do so will negative the purpose of Congress in this regard." *Id.* at 98. But this pronouncement merely restated the presumption against extraterritoriality previously established in civil cases like *American Banana*, 213 U.S. at 357. The Bowman Court nowhere suggested that a different, more resilient presumption arises in criminal cases.

Nor does *United States v. United States Gypsum Co.*, 438 U.S. 422 (1978), offer aid and succor to NPI. Recognizing that "the behavior proscribed by the [Sherman] Act is often difficult to distinguish from the gray zone of socially acceptable and economically justifiable business conduct," id. at 440–41, the Gypsum Court held that criminal intent generally is required to convict under the Act. See id. at 443. Although this distinguishes some civil antitrust cases (in which intent need not be proven) from their criminal counterparts, the Gypsum Court made it plain that intent need not be shown to prosecute criminally "conduct regarded as *per se* illegal because of its unquestionably anticompetitive effects." *Id.* at 440. This means, of course, that defendants can be convicted of participation in price-fixing conspiracies without any demonstration of a specific criminal intent to violate the antitrust laws. *See, e.g., United States v. Brown*, 936 F.2d 1042, 1046 (9th Cir.1991); *United States v. Society of Indep. Gas. Marketers*, 624 F.2d 461, 465 (4th Cir.1980), *cert. denied*, 449 U.S. 1078 (1981); *United States v. Gillen*, 599 F.2d 541, 544–45 (3d Cir.), *cert. denied*, 444 U.S. 866 (1979). Because the instant case falls within that rubric, *Gypsum* does not help NPI.

We add that even if *Gypsum* had differentiated between civil and criminal price-fixing cases, NPI's reliance on it would still be problematic. Reduced to bare essence, *Gypsum* focuses on mens rea, noting that centuries of Anglo–American legal tradition instruct that criminal liability ordinarily should be premised on malevolent intent, *see id.* at 436–37, whereas civil liability, to which less stigma and milder consequences commonly attach, often requires a lesser showing of intent. There is simply no comparable tradition or rationale for drawing a criminal/civil distinction with regard to extraterritoriality, and neither NPI nor its amicus have alluded to any case which does so.

3.   The Restatement. NPI and the district court, 944 F. Supp. at 65, both sing the praises of the Restatement (Third) of Foreign Relations Law

(1987), claiming that it supports a distinction between civil and criminal cases on the issue of extraterritoriality. The passage to which they pin their hopes states:

> [I]n the case of regulatory statutes that may give rise to both civil and criminal liability, such as the United States antitrust and securities laws, the presence of substantial foreign elements will ordinarily weigh against application of criminal law. In such cases, legislative intent to subject conduct outside the state's territory to its criminal law should be found only on the basis of express statement or clear implication.

Id. at § 403 cmt. f. We believe that this statement merely reaffirms the classic presumption against extraterritoriality—no more, no less. After all, nothing in the text of the Restatement proper contradicts the government's interpretation of Section One. *See, e.g., id.* at § 402(1)(c) (explaining that, subject only to a general requirement of reasonableness, a state has jurisdiction to proscribe "conduct outside its territory that has or is intended to have substantial effect within its territory"); *id.* at § 415(2) ("Any agreement in restraint of United States trade that is made outside of the United States ... [is] subject to the jurisdiction to prescribe of the United States, if a principal purpose of the conduct or agreement is to interfere with the commerce of the United States, and the agreement or conduct has some effect on that commerce."). What is more, other comments indicate that a country's decision to prosecute wholly foreign conduct is discretionary. *See, e.g., id.* at § 403 rep. n. 8.

4. The Rule of Lenity. The next arrow which NPI yanks from its quiver is the rule of lenity. The rule itself is venerable; it provides that, in the course of interpreting statutes in criminal cases, a reviewing court should resolve ambiguities affecting a statute's scope in the defendant's favor.... But the rule of lenity is inapposite unless a statutory ambiguity looms, and a statute is not ambiguous for this purpose simply because some courts or commentators have questioned its proper interpretation.... Rather, "[t]he rule of lenity applies only if, after seizing everything from which aid can be derived, [a court] can make no more than a guess as to what Congress intended." *Reno [v. Koray]*, 515 U.S. [50, 64–65], (citations, internal quotation marks, and certain brackets omitted); *accord United States v. O'Neil*, 11 F.3d 292, 301 n. 10 (1st Cir.1993) (describing the rule of lenity as "a background principle that properly comes into play when, at the end of a thorough inquiry, the meaning of a criminal statute remains obscure"). Put bluntly, the rule of lenity cannot be used to create ambiguity when the meaning of a law, even if not readily apparent, is, upon inquiry, reasonably clear.

That ends the matter of lenity. In view of the fact that the Supreme Court deems it "well established" that Section One of the Sherman Act applies to wholly foreign conduct, *Hartford Fire*, 509 U.S. at 796, we effectively are foreclosed from trying to tease an ambiguity out of Section One relative to its extraterritorial application. Accordingly, the rule of lenity plays no part in the instant case.

5.   Comity. International comity is a doctrine that counsels voluntary forbearance when a sovereign which has a legitimate claim to jurisdiction concludes that a second sovereign also has a legitimate claim to jurisdiction under principles of international law. *See* Harold G. Maier, Extraterritorial Jurisdiction at a Crossroads: An Intersection Between Public and Private International Law, 76 A.J. Int'l L. 280, 281 n. 1 (1982). Comity is more an aspiration than a fixed rule, more a matter of grace than a matter of obligation. In all events, its growth in the antitrust sphere has been stunted by Hartford Fire, in which the Court suggested that comity concerns would operate to defeat the exercise of jurisdiction only in those few cases in which the law of the foreign sovereign required a defendant to act in a manner incompatible with the Sherman Act or in which full compliance with both statutory schemes was impossible. *See Hartford Fire*, 509 U.S. at 798–99, 113 S.Ct. at 2910–11; *see also Kenneth W. Dam*, Extraterritoriality in an Age of Globalization: The Hartford Fire Case, 1993 Sup.Ct.Rev. 289, 306–07 (1993). Accordingly, the Hartford Fire Court gave short shrift to the defendants' entreaty that the conduct leading to antitrust liability was perfectly legal in the United Kingdom. *See Hartford Fire*, 509 U.S. at 798–99.

In this case the defendant's comity-based argument is even more attenuated. The conduct with which NPI is charged is illegal under both Japanese and American laws, thereby alleviating any founded concern about NPI being whipsawed between separate sovereigns. And, moreover, to the extent that comity is informed by general principles of reasonableness, see Restatement (Third) of Foreign Relations Law § 403, the indictment lodged against NPI is well within the pale. In it, the government charges that the defendant orchestrated a conspiracy with the object of rigging prices in the United States. If the government can prove these charges, we see no tenable reason why principles of comity should shield NPI from prosecution. We live in an age of international commerce, where decisions reached in one corner of the world can reverberate around the globe in less time than it takes to tell the tale. Thus, a ruling in NPI's favor would create perverse incentives for those who would use nefarious means to influence markets in the United States, rewarding them for erecting as many territorial firewalls as possible between cause and effect.

We need go no further. *Hartford Fire* definitively establishes that Section One of the Sherman Act applies to wholly foreign conduct which has an intended and substantial effect in the United States. We are bound to accept that holding. Under settled principles of statutory construction, we also are bound to apply it by interpreting Section One the same way in a criminal case. The combined force of these commitments requires that we accept the government's cardinal argument, reverse the order of the district court, reinstate the indictment, and remand for further proceedings.

Reversed and remanded.

■ LYNCH, CIRCUIT JUDGE (concurring).

The question presented in this case is whether Section One of the Sherman Act authorizes criminal prosecutions of defendants for their actions committed entirely outside the United States. Judicial precedents, culminating with the Supreme Court's decision in *Hartford Fire Insurance Co. v. California*, 509 U.S. 764 (1993), conclusively establish that Section One's jurisdictional reach extends, in civil actions, to foreign conduct that is meant to produce, and does in fact produce, substantial effects in the United States. The next question to be asked is whether there is any persuasive reason to believe that, with regard to wholly foreign conduct, Section One in the criminal context is not co-extensive with Section One in the civil context.

In answering this second question, courts must be careful to determine whether this construction of Section One's criminal reach conforms with principles of international law. "It has been a maxim of statutory construction since the decision in *Murray v. The Charming Betsy*, 2 Cranch 64, 118, 2 L.Ed. 208 (1804), that 'an act of congress ought never to be construed to violate the law of nations, if any other possible construction remains.'" *Weinberger v. Rossi*, 456 U.S. 25, 32 (1982). In the *Alcoa* case, Judge Learned Hand found this canon of construction relevant to determining the substantive reach of the Sherman Act, observing that "we are not to read general words [*i.e.*, Section One] ... without regard to the limitations customarily observed by nations upon the exercise of their powers." *United States v. Aluminum Co. of Am.*, 148 F.2d 416, 443 (2d Cir.1945); *see also Hartford Fire*, 509 U.S. at 814–15 (Scalia, J., dissenting).

The task of construing Section One in this context is not the usual one of determining congressional intent by parsing the language or legislative history of the statute. The broad, general language of the federal antitrust laws and their unilluminating legislative history place a special interpretive responsibility upon the judiciary. The Supreme Court has called the Sherman Act a "charter of freedom" for the courts, with "a generality and adaptability comparable to that found ... in constitutional provisions." *Appalachian Coals, Inc. v. United States*, 288 U.S. 344, 359–60 (1933). As Professors Areeda and Turner have said, the federal courts have been invested "with a jurisdiction to create and develop an 'antitrust law' in the manner of the common law courts." I Areeda & Turner, Antitrust Law ¶ 106, at 15 (1978). The courts are aided in this task by canons of statutory construction, such as the presumption against violating international law, which serve as both guides and limits in the absence of more explicit indicia of congressional intent.

Here, we are asked to determine the substantive content of Section One's inexact jurisdictional provision, "commerce ... with foreign nations." 15 U.S.C. § 1. Because of the "compunctions against the creation of crimes by judges rather than by legislators," II Areeda & Hovenkamp, Antitrust Law ¶ 311b, at 33 (1995 rev. ed.), the constitution-like aspects of the antitrust laws must be handled particularly carefully in criminal prosecutions.

As the antitrust laws give the federal enforcement agencies a relatively blank check, the development of antitrust law has been largely shaped by the cases that the executive branch chooses—or does not choose—to bring. Accordingly it has been said that:

> novel interpretations or great departures have seldom, if ever, occurred in criminal cases, which prosecutors have usually reserved for defendants whose knowing behavior would be generally recognized as appropriate for criminal sanctions.

Id. at 34. This case does present a new interpretation. We are told this is the first instance in which the executive branch has chosen to interpret the criminal provisions of the Sherman Act as reaching conduct wholly committed outside of this country's borders.

Changing economic conditions, as well as different political agendas, mean that antitrust policies may change from administration to administration. The present administration has promulgated new Antitrust Enforcement Guidelines for International Operations which "focus primarily on situations in which the Sherman Act will grant jurisdiction and when the United States will exercise that jurisdiction" internationally. Brockbank, The 1995 International Antitrust Guidelines: The Reach of U.S. Antitrust Law Continues to Expand, 2 J. Int'l Legal Stud. 1, *22 (1996). The new Guidelines reflect a stronger enforcement stance than earlier versions of the Guidelines, and have been described as a "warning to foreign governments and enterprises that the [antitrust enforcement] Agencies intend to actively pursue restraints on trade occurring abroad that adversely affect American markets or damage American exporting opportunities." *Id.* at *21. The instant case is likely a result of this policy.

It is with this context in mind that we must determine if the exercise of jurisdiction occasioned by the decision of the executive branch of the United States is proper in this case. While courts, including this one, speak of determining congressional intent when interpreting statutes, the meaning of the antitrust laws has emerged through the relationship among all three branches of government. In this criminal case, it is our responsibility to ensure that the executive's interpretation of the Sherman Act does not conflict with other legal principles, including principles of international law.

That question requires examination beyond the language of Section One of the Sherman Act. It is, of course, generally true that, as a principle of statutory interpretation, the same language should be read the same way in all contexts to which the language applies. But this is not invariably true. New content is sometimes ascribed to statutory terms depending upon context. *Cf. Robinson v. Shell Oil Co.*, 117 S.Ct. 843, 847 (1997) (depending on context, statutory term may have different meanings in different sections of single statute); 3 Sutherland, Statutory Construction § 60.04 (5th ed. 1995) (statutes with both remedial and penal provisions may be construed liberally in remedial context and strictly in penal context). As NPI and the Government of Japan point out, the Supreme Court has held that Section One of the Sherman Act, which defines both criminal and civil violations with one general phrase, "should be construed as including intent as an element" of a criminal violation. *United States v. United States Gypsum Co.*, 438 U.S. 422, 443 (1978). Where Congress intends that our laws conform with international law, and where international law suggests that criminal enforcement and civil enforcement be viewed differently, it is at least conceivable that different content could be ascribed to the same language depending on whether the context is civil or criminal. It is then worth asking about the effect of the international law which Congress presumably also meant to respect.

The content of international law is determined "by reference 'to the customs and usages of civilized nations, and, as evidence of these, to the works of jurists and commentators.'" *Hilao v. Estate of Marcos*, 103 F.3d 789, 794 (9th Cir.1996) (quoting The Paquete Habana, 175 U.S. 677, 700 (1900)); *see also Kadic v. Karadzic*, 70 F.3d 232 (2d Cir.1995). The Restatement (Third) of the Foreign Relations Law of the United States restates international law, as derived from customary international law and from international agreements to which the United States is a party, as it applies to the United States. [Judge Lynch then concluded that the Restatement served "as a useful guide to evaluating the international interests at stake."] . . . .

Restatement Section 402(1)(c) states that "Subject to § 403," a state has jurisdiction to prescribe law to "conduct outside its territory that has or is intended to have substantial effect within its territory." Id. § 402(1)(c). Section 403(1) states that, even when Section 402 has been satisfied, jurisdiction may not be exercised if it is "unreasonable." Id. § 403(1). Section 403(2) lists factors to be evaluated in determining if jurisdiction is reasonable:

(a) the link of the activity to the territory of the regulating state, *i.e.*, the extent to which the activity takes place within the territory, or has substantial, direct, and foreseeable effect upon or in the territory;

(b) the connections, such as nationality, residence, or economic activity, between the regulating state and the person principally responsible for the activity to be regulated, or between that state and those whom the regulation is designed to protect;

(c) the character of the activity to be regulated, the importance of regulation to the regulating state, the extent to which other states regulate such activities, and the degree to which the desirability of such regulation is generally accepted;

(d) the existence of justified expectations that might be protected or hurt by the regulation;

(e) the importance of the regulation to the international political, legal, or economic system;

(f) the extent to which the regulation is consistent with the traditions of the international system;

(g) the extent to which another state may have an interest in regulating the activity; and

(h) the likelihood of conflict with regulation by another state.

Id. § 403(2).

Comment f to Section 403 states that the principles of Sections 402 and 403 "apply to criminal as well as to civil regulation." *Id.* § 403 cmt. f. But, specifically naming the United States antitrust laws, the comment also says that for statutes that give rise to both types of liability, "the presence of substantial foreign elements will ordinarily weigh against application of criminal law." *Id.* The comment argues that legislative intent to apply these laws criminally should only be found on the basis of "express statement or clear implication." *Id.*

While the majority opinion accurately states that this comment is an expression of the clear statement rule, the comment also implies that there are special concerns associated with the imposition of criminal sanctions on foreign conduct. *See also* id. § 403 n. 8 ("In applying the principle of reasonableness, the exercise of criminal (as distinguished from civil) jurisdiction in relation to acts committed in another state may be perceived as particularly intrusive."). Indeed, most people recognize a distinction between civil and criminal liability; that the law of nations should do so as well is not surprising. And while Hartford Fire and earlier judicial decisions have found that the antitrust laws do apply, in the civil context, to foreign conduct, this antitrust common law is not the express statement of legislative intent that the Restatement suggests may be appropriate in the criminal context.

Also relevant to the present inquiry is section 415(2), which states that:

> Any agreement in restraint of United States trade that is made outside of the United States, and any conduct or agreement in restraint of such trade that is carried out predominantly outside of the United States, are subject to the jurisdiction to prescribe of the United States, if a principal purpose of the conduct or agreement is to interfere with the commerce of the United States and the agreement or conduct has some effect on that commerce.

Restatement § 415(2). Comment a to Section 415 states that the reasonableness principles articulated in Section 403 must still be satisfied. *See id* cmt. a.

Application of these principles to the indictment at issue here leads to the conclusion that the exercise of jurisdiction is reasonable in this case. Here, raising prices in the United States and Canada was not only a purpose of the alleged conspiracy, it was the purpose, thus satisfying Section 415's "principal purpose" requirement. Moreover, Section 415's requirement of "some effect" on United States markets is amply met here. The indictment alleges that NPI sold $6.1 million of fax paper into the United States during 1990, approximately the period covered by the charged conspiracy. In 1990, total sales of fax paper in North America were approximately $100 million. NPI's price increases thus affected a not insignificant share of the United States market.

These same factors weigh heavily in the Section 403 reasonableness analysis. Because only North American markets were targeted, the United States' interest in combatting this activity appears to be greater than the Japanese interest, which may only be the general interest of a state in having its industries comport with foreign legal norms. Japan has no interest in protecting Japanese consumers in this case as they were unaffected by the alleged conspiracy. The United States, in contrast, has a strong interest in protecting United States consumers, who were affected by the increase in prices. In this situation, it may be that only the United States has sufficient incentive to pursue the alleged wrongdoers, thereby providing the necessary deterrent to similar anticompetitive behavior. In another case, where the consumers of the situs nation were injured as well, that state's interest in regulating anticompetitive conduct might be stronger than it is here.

Other Section 403 factors also counsel in favor of the exercise of jurisdiction here. The effects on United States markets were foreseeable and direct. The Government of Japan acknowledges that antitrust regulation is part of the international legal system, and NPI does not really assert that it has justified expectations that were hurt by the regulation. The only factor counseling against finding that the United States' antitrust laws apply to this conduct is the fact that the situs of the conduct was Japan and that the principals were Japanese corporations. This consideration is inherent in the nature of jurisdiction based on effects of conduct, where the situs of the conduct is, by definition, always a foreign country. This alone does not tip the balance against jurisdiction.

For these reasons, I agree with the majority that the district court erred in dismissing the indictment.

NOTES AND QUESTIONS

1. Does "comity" have any role to play after *Hartford*? Does the Supreme Court regard the term "comity" as a synonym for conflict (or lack thereof) with foreign laws? Compare *Timberlane*, infra p. 1233.

2. In *Hartford*, as in *Continental Ore*, the Court faced a situation where the foreign law was arguably more lenient from an antitrust point of view than the U.S. law. Thus, it was possible to say that the companies in question could comply with both by simply complying with the U.S. law. As we will see below, if the companies had faced directly conflicting commands from two sovereigns, they might have been able to take advantage of the foreign sovereign compulsion defense in any event. It is hard, therefore, to see how much content there is to this notion of conflict. More seriously, does the Court's approach give proper deference to countries that have decided to adopt a deregulatory, laissez-faire system for certain sectors of their economies? From that perspective, it was impossible for the insurance companies both to benefit from the freedom of action the U.K. wanted to extend to them and

to comply with the antitrust rules in force in the United States. How would the U.S. enforcers or courts react if they were faced with a case in which a U.S. company's non-price vertical restrictions (*e.g.*, territorial divisions), which were perfectly legal under U.S. antitrust law, were attacked in Europe as violations of Article 85, and the company had no practical way of complying with the order of the European Commission without modifying its international distributional scheme as a whole?

3.   How did the First Circuit approach the question of extraterritorial jurisdiction: as a "jurisdictional" matter, or as a question of the scope and extent of the statutory coverage of the Sherman Act (as Justice Scalia argued in *Hartford Fire*)?

4.   Should U.S. courts resort to general principles of international law when they confront questions of extraterritorial jurisdiction, as Judge Lynch did in her concurring opinion in *Nippon Paper*, or is it enough to look to conventional principles of statutory construction, as the majority did?

5.   The subject of foreign commerce enforcement took a somewhat different twist in the Ninth Circuit's decision in *Metro Industries, Inc. v. Sammi Corp.*, 82 F.3d 839 (9th Cir.1996). In that case, Metro, an importer and wholesaler of kitchenware, sued Sammi, a South Korean exporting company, and two of its U.S. subsidiaries, claiming that a Korean design registration system that gave Korean holloware producers the exclusive right to export a particular design for three years, constituted an unlawful market division that was a *per se* violation of Sherman Act § 1. The Court of Appeals, in a broadly worded opinion, held that the *per se* rule can never apply to foreign conduct, because it is always necessary in a foreign commerce case to examine the impact of the practice on commerce in the United States. The opinion also suggests, however, that the registration system was not the kind of thing that would ordinarily receive *per se* treatment. Do you agree that the substantive rules of antitrust should be different in foreign commerce cases? Why or why not? Is the necessity of examining the links to U.S. foreign commerce any different from the need to examine the interstate commerce nexus in ordinary antitrust cases? If so, what distinguishes the two? If not, then what does that imply for the *per se* rule any time the interstate or foreign commerce element is disputed?

6.   One important question remained unanswered in the FTAIA: what kind of effects count to support either jurisdiction or a finding that the statute covers the conduct in question. The circuits are currently split on this question, along the lines outlined by the majority and dissenting opinions in the next case.

Den Norske Stats Oljeselskap As v. HeereMac Vof

United States Court of Appeals, Fifth Circuit, 2001.
241 F.3d 420, cert. denied, 534 U.S. 1127 (2002).

■ Before: JOLLY, HIGGINBOTHAM and EMILIO M. GARZA, CIRCUIT JUDGES.

■ JOLLY, J. This appeal requires us to interpret the scope of the United States antitrust laws and their application to foreign conduct. The plaintiff is a Norwegian oil corporation that conducts business solely in the North Sea. It seeks redress under the United States antitrust laws against the defendants for an alleged anticompetitive conspiracy that supposedly inflated the plaintiff's operating costs in the North Sea. Supreme Court precedent makes clear as a general proposition that United States antitrust laws "do not regulate the competitive conditions of other nations' economies," *Matsushita Elec. Indus. Co. v. Zenith Radio Corp.*, 475 U.S. 574, 582,

(1986). More specifically, today we are bound by the plain language of the Foreign Trade Antitrust Improvements Act (FTAIA). Thus, even though the plaintiff alleges that the antitrust conspiracy raised prices in the United States, it fails to assert jurisdiction under the antitrust laws because the plaintiff's injury did not arise from that domestic anticompetitive effect. Accordingly, we find that the district court properly dismissed the plaintiff's antitrust claims for lack of subject matter jurisdiction. It follows that we affirm the court's determination that the plaintiff lacked antitrust standing to bring these claims in United States federal court.

I

We begin with the basics. Sections 1 and 2 of the Sherman Act prohibit restraints of trade and monopolization.... The FTAIA, enacted by Congress in 1982 to clarify the application of United States antitrust laws to foreign conduct, limits the application of such laws when non-import foreign commerce is involved. The FTAIA states that the antitrust laws will not apply to non-import commerce with foreign nations unless the conduct at issue has a "direct, substantial, and reasonably foreseeable effect" on domestic commerce and "such effect gives rise to a claim under" the antitrust laws.

II

The plaintiff, Den Norske Stats Oljeselskap As ("Statoil"), is a Norwegian oil company that owns and operates oil and gas drilling platforms exclusively in the North Sea. The defendants are providers of heavy-lift barge services in the Gulf of Mexico, the North Sea, and the Far East. Only six or seven heavy-lift barges exist in the world. These immense vessels have cranes capable of hoisting and transporting offshore oil platforms and decks weighing in excess of 4,000 tons. During the 1993–1997 time frame, which is at issue in this suit, the three defendants controlled these barges. Between 1993 and 1997, Statoil purchased heavy lift barge services from the HeereMac and Saipem defendants in the North Sea.

Statoil alleges that the defendants conspired to fix bids and allocate customers, territories, and projects between 1993 and 1997. Under the alleged arrangement, the defendants agreed that HeereMac [a Dutch company] and McDermott [an American company] would have exclusive access to heavy-lift projects in the Gulf of Mexico, while Saipem [a British company] would receive a higher allocation of North Sea projects in exchange for staying out of the Gulf. The defendants also allegedly agreed to submit embellished bids on heavy-lift projects. As a result of this conspiracy, Statoil contends that it paid inflated prices for heavy-lift barge services in the North Sea. Statoil further argues that the conspiracy compelled it to charge higher prices for the crude oil it exported to the United States. Finally, Statoil asserts that purchasers of heavy-lift services in the Gulf of Mexico were forced to pay inflated prices for those services because of the conspiracy.

III

By way of background, it should be noted that in December 1997, the United States Department of Justice filed a criminal complaint against defendants HeereMac and Jan Meek, one of HeereMac's managing directors. The complaint alleged that the defendants conspired "to suppress and eliminate competition by rigging bids for the sale of heavy-lift derrick barge and related marine construction services in the United States and elsewhere." HeereMac and Meek submitted to United States jurisdiction and pled guilty to the charges. They agreed to pay fines of $49 million and $100,000, respectively.

Following the guilty pleas, numerous companies across the globe filed suit in United States federal court seeking redress for injuries stemming from defendants' conduct. The first of these suits was filed in the Southern District of Texas in June 1998 by Phillips Petroleum Company and three of its foreign-based subsidiaries.

On January 22, 1999, the court dismissed Phillips's claims for injuries sustained by its foreign subsidiaries relating to projects in foreign waters but allowed those claims asserting injury from projects in United States waters to proceed. While the court acknowledged the worldwide nature of the alleged conspiracy in its order, it nonetheless held that subject matter jurisdiction did not exist for those claims pled by foreign-based subsidiaries for injuries allegedly sustained on foreign platforms. Specifically, the court determined that those claims did not fall within the ambit of the United States antitrust laws because the claims did not arise from a direct and substantial effect on United States commerce.

Statoil filed this suit in the same court in December 1998. The court dismissed Statoil's complaint against the defendants on July 12, 1999. In its order, the court relied heavily upon its decision in the Phillips case and found no subject matter jurisdiction over the claims because "Statoil's damages arise from its projects in the Norwegian sector of the North Sea"; thus, the FTAIA's requirement that the effect on domestic commerce "gives rise" to the antitrust claim was not satisfied. See 15 U.S.C. § 6a(2). The court also held that the defendants' conspiracy "did not have a direct, substantial, and reasonably foreseeable anticompetitive effect on United States trade or commerce" under the FTAIA. See 15 U.S.C. § 6a(1). Finally, the court determined that "Statoil lacks standing to bring a claim under United States antitrust laws because its alleged injuries are not of the type that the antitrust statute was intended to redress." Statoil timely appealed the judgment.

IV

The issue presented to us is primarily one of statutory interpretation. Specifically, this appeal requires us to interpret the relevant provisions of the FTAIA to determine whether the defendants' conduct and Statoil's injury in the North Sea presents a justiciable claim in the federal courts of the United States.

It is not helpful that the federal courts have generally disagreed as to the extraterritorial reach of the antitrust laws and have employed assorted tests to determine the scope of the Sherman Act. The history of this body of case law is confusing and unsettled. However, as far as this appeal is concerned, our work is simplified by Congress' passage in 1982 of the FTAIA, which specifically exempts certain foreign conduct from the antitrust laws. This circuit has never interpreted the relevant portions of the FTAIA as they apply to global conspiracies and resulting foreign injury. Today, we take on this task, and make no claim that it is an easy one.

V

A

* * * [The court applied a de novo standard of review.] ... We first outline Statoil's argument that United States antitrust jurisdiction encompasses the conduct and injury in its complaint.

B

Statoil argues that the FTAIA does not preclude the district court's jurisdiction over its antitrust claims. Specifically, Statoil argues that the FTAIA was enacted exclusively to ensure that the conduct providing the basis of the plaintiff's claim have the requisite domestic effects, and was not intended to preclude recovery to foreign plaintiffs based on the situs of the injury. Moreover, Statoil contends that Section 2 of the FTAIA was inserted only to ensure that the effect on United States commerce that provides jurisdiction is itself a violation of the antitrust laws; that is, the statute simply requires that there be some anticompetitive, *harmful* effect in this country—not just a positive or neutral domestic effect.

Addressing specifically the FTAIA's requirement that the domestic effect "gives rise" to its antitrust claim, Statoil primarily argues that, because the defendants operating in the Gulf of Mexico were able to maintain their monopolistic pricing only because of their overall market allocation scheme (which included agreements regarding operations in the North Sea), Statoil's injury in the North Sea was a "necessary prerequisite to" and was "the quid pro quo for" the injury suffered in the United States domestic market. Statoil alleges that the market for heavy-lift services in the world is a single, unified, global market; therefore, because the United States is a part of this worldwide market, the effect of the conspiracy, whether in the United States or in the North Sea, "gives rise" to any claim that is based upon this conspiracy.

C

We must disagree with Statoil's arguments based on our reading of the antitrust statutes. Although we are controlled by the plain language of the statutes, we also find that the legislative history of the FTAIA and applicable case law supports our determination that the district court lacked jurisdiction over Statoil's claims....

1

* * *

We begin by first noting that the Sherman Act itself applies only to conduct in "trade or commerce with foreign nations." 15 U.S.C. §§ 1, 2 (emphasis added). The commerce that gives rise to the action here—the contracting for heavy lift barge services in the North Sea—was not United States commerce with foreign nations, but commerce between or among foreign nations—that is, between or among Statoil (a Norwegian corporation), Saipem (England), and HeereMac (The Netherlands). Therefore, we doubt that foreign commercial transactions between foreign entities in foreign waters is conduct cognizable by federal courts under the Sherman Act.[19]

As we have noted, the FTAIA states that the antitrust laws will not apply to non-import foreign conduct unless (1) such conduct has a direct, substantial, and reasonably foreseeable effect on United States domestic commerce, and (2) such effect gives rise to the antitrust claim.[20] The conduct of these defendants is foreign conduct that falls within the general parameters of the FTAIA and, thus, Statoil must show that the two specific requirements of the statute are met to establish subject matter jurisdiction over its claims.

We accept the contention that Statoil has sufficiently alleged that the defendants' conduct—that is, the agreement among heavy-lift service providers to divide territory, rig bids, and fix prices—had a direct, substantial, and reasonably foreseeable effect on the United States market. Statoil alleges that the conspiracy not only forced purchasers of heavy-lift services in the Gulf of Mexico to pay inflated prices, but also that the agreement compelled Americans to pay supra-competitive prices for oil [at least $165 million in U.S. commerce from 1993 to 1997]. These allegations are sufficient to satisfy the first requirement of the FTAIA.

---

19. This interpretation is further strengthened by the limits placed on Congressional power in the Constitution. Article I, § 8 of the Constitution gives Congress the authority only to regulate interstate commerce and "commerce with foreign nations" (emphasis added). Thus, even if Congress indeed intended to regulate purely foreign commerce in the Sherman Act, it was not empowered to do so under the Commerce Clause.

20. The dissent, like Statoil, argues that Section 2 should be read to require only that the domestic effect give rise to any antitrust claim, not necessarily the plaintiff's claim. This interpretation contradicts the explicit intent of Congress to require that the effect must give rise to the particular injury claimed by the plaintiff in the suit ... The dissent asserts that reading Section 2 as requiring that the domestic effect give rise to the plaintiff's claim renders the FTAIA's proviso redundant. Although giving the statute a clear understanding is difficult, we disagree with the dissent's reading. We read Section 1(B) to provide that the export commerce covered under the exception must be conducted by a person who is engaged in that export business in the United States. Section 2 provides that the defendant's antitrust effect on this export commerce described in Section 1(B) must give rise to the plaintiff's cause of action. The proviso, in turn, states that the recovery for injuries resulting from the conduct described in Section 1(B), which gives rise to the plaintiff's antitrust claim in Section 2, is limited to injuries occurring in the United States. Therefore, we fail to see the redundancy to which the dissent refers....

However, Statoil fails to show that this effect on United States commerce in any way "gives rise" to its antitrust claim. Based on the language of Section 2 of the FTAIA, the effect on United States commerce—in this case, the higher prices paid by United States companies for heavy-lift services in the Gulf of Mexico—must give rise to the claim that Statoil asserts against the defendants. That is, Statoil's injury must stem from the effect of higher prices for heavy-lift services in the Gulf. We find no evidence that this requirement is met here. The higher prices American companies allegedly paid for services provided by the McDermott defendants in the Gulf of Mexico does not give rise to Statoil's claim that it paid inflated prices for HeereMac and Saipem's services in the North Sea. This is not to say that any antitrust injury suffered by customers or competitors of McDermott that arose from the anticompetitive effect in the Gulf of Mexico cannot be addressed. This means only that, while we recognize that there may be a connection and an interrelatedness between the high prices paid for services in the Gulf of Mexico and the high prices paid in the North Sea, the FTAIA requires more than a "close relationship" between the domestic injury and the plaintiff's claim; it demands that the domestic effect "gives rise" to the claim.

Statoil asks that we interpret the requirement of Section 2 that the domestic *"effect"* give rise to a claim under the antitrust laws as merely requiring that the defendants' domestic *"conduct"* (here, for example, agreements relating to the Gulf of Mexico) give rise to a claim. This interpretation is not true to the plain language of the FTAIA. Moreover, under such an expansive interpretation, any entities, anywhere, that were injured by any conduct that also had sufficient effect on United States commerce could flock to United States federal court for redress, even if those plaintiffs had no commercial relationship with any United States market and their injuries were unrelated to the injuries suffered in the United States. Such an expansive reading of the extraterritorial application of the antitrust laws was never intended nor contemplated by Congress. . . .

In sum, we find that the plain language of the FTAIA precludes subject matter jurisdiction over claims by foreign plaintiffs against defendants where the situs of the injury is overseas and that injury arises from effects in a non-domestic market. Although the plain language of the relevant statutes is clear and controlling, we nonetheless turn now to address briefly the legislative history of the FTAIA to illustrate how that history reinforces our interpretation of the extraterritorial reach of the antitrust laws.

2

[In this section of the opinion, the majority finds support for its conclusion that a foreign plaintiff injured in a foreign marketplace must show that a substantial domestic effect on United States commerce "gives rise" to its antitrust claim in the legislative history of the FTAIA.].

3

... To begin, we note that the only three federal courts that have addressed the narrow question before us interpreted Section 2 exactly as we have. *See Kruman v. Christie's Int'l PLC, et al.*, 129 F.Supp.2d 620 (S.D.N.Y.2001) (holding that the FTAIA permits jurisdiction "only where the conduct complained of had 'direct, substantial and reasonably foreseeable' effects in the United States and the effects giving rise to jurisdiction are the basis for the alleged injury."); *In re Microsoft Corp.*, 2001 U.S. Dist. LEXIS 305, at *37 (holding that, under the FTAIA, "foreign consumers who have not participated in any way in the U.S. market have no right to institute a Sherman Act claim."); *Sumitomo*, 117 F. Supp.2d 875, 876 (holding that "it is plain from the language of this act and bolstered by the legislative history that a private plaintiff cannot sue under the antitrust laws of the United States for injuries incurred as a result of international transactions that have an anticompetitive effect on a United States market if the domestic anticompetitive effect is not the same one that gives rise to the plaintiff's injury.").

We further note that we have found no case in which jurisdiction was found in a case like this—where a foreign plaintiff is injured in a foreign market with no injuries arising from the anticompetitive effect on a United States market. In those cases where the domestic effect on commerce did not give rise to the plaintiff's claim, courts have found subject matter jurisdiction lacking. *See, e.g., S. Megga Telecomm. Ltd. v. Lucent Technologies, Inc.*, 1997 WL 86413 (D.Del. Feb.14, 1997) (anticompetitive domestic effect of higher prices for United States consumers did not "give rise" to plaintiff's claim for lost sales to defendant); *The "In" Porters, S.A. v. Hanes Printables, Inc.*, 663 F.Supp. 494 (M.D.N.C.1987) (anticompetitive domestic effect (lost exports of United States exporters) did not "give rise" to plaintiff's claim for lost sales in France due to marketing sales agreement with defendant); *de Atucha v. Commodity Exch., Inc.*, 608 F.Supp. 510 (S.D.N.Y.1985) (conspiracy's effect on silver prices on United States exchange did not "give rise" to plaintiff's injury on London exchange).

On the other hand, in every case where jurisdiction has been found, the substantial effect on United States commerce has "give[n] rise" to the plaintiff's injury and claim under the antitrust laws. *See, e.g., Carpet Group Int'l v. Oriental Rug Importers Ass'n*, 227 F.3d 62 (3d Cir.2000) (anticompetitive effect on domestic rug market "gives rise" to plaintiff's injury); *Caribbean*, 148 F.3d 1080 (monopolization of United States market for advertising in the Caribbean "gives rise" to plaintiff's claim of being blocked from that market); *Nippon Paper*, 109 F.3d 1 (collusion amongst fax paper producers resulted in higher prices for fax paper in the United States, which "gives rise" to the United States' claim); *Hartford Fire*, 509 U.S. 764 (conspiracy's effect on the United States insurance market "gives rise" to the plaintiffs' injury, the inability to obtain certain types of coverage in that market).

Finally, we note that none of the cases cited by Statoil in support of its interpretation of the FTAIA cast doubt upon our plain language interpretation of Section 2. Statoil cites *Pfizer v. India*, 434 U.S. 308 (1978), for the proposition that antitrust jurisdiction exists over foreign conduct like the commerce between Statoil and defendants in this case. *Pfizer*, however, was decided four years before enactment of the FTAIA, and the court's holding was limited to the question of whether a foreign government qualified as a "person" under the Sherman Act. *Id.* at 320. Statoil further maintains that *Caribbean Broadcasting*, 148 F.3d 1080, requires that jurisdiction be found over its claims. Initially, that case looks similar to today's case in that both the plaintiff and the defendant were foreign, and the defendant's international conspiracy had anticompetitive effects both inside and outside the United States. The critical difference, however, is that the effect on United States commerce in that case (that is, limiting to one radio station potential advertisers in the United States who wished to advertise in the Eastern Caribbean radio market) gave rise to the injury suffered by the plaintiff, a competing radio station—that is, exclusion of the plaintiff from the market for United States advertising dollars. *Id.* at 1082, 1086. As previously explained, that is simply not true with Statoil's claims. Similarly, Statoil's reliance on *Nippon Paper*, 109 F.3d 1, is misplaced because the global conspiracy in that case had the domestic effect of raising fax paper prices in the United States, which gave rise to the government's claim under the antitrust laws. *Id.* at 2.

Simply put, Statoil has cited no case law to support an interpretation of Section 2 of the FTAIA different from the one we now adopt. This absence of such precedent, when considered with the plain language of the statute and evidence of congressional intent in enacting the FTAIA, reinforces our conclusion in this case.

VI

In sum, we find that the district court did not err when it dismissed Statoil's antitrust claims for lack of subject matter jurisdiction. Any reading of the FTAIA authorizing jurisdiction over Statoil's claims would open United States courts to global claims on a scale never intended by Congress. Without subject matter jurisdiction, United States federal courts are without power to entertain Statoil's claims. The judgment of the district court is therefore AFFIRMED.

■ HIGGINBOTHAM, J., dissenting. I agree that this is not an easy case, but I have no hesitation in concluding that the Foreign Trade and Antitrust Improvements Act does not here divest the federal courts of jurisdiction and that the plaintiff has standing. With deference to my colleagues, I am persuaded by the plain text of section 6a, as well as its statutory context, legislative history, and purpose.

The claim is that defendants allocated the market for hundreds of millions of dollars of commerce—an allocation that placed United States markets at the mercy of monopoly charges in an industry vital to national security. The charged conspiracy was no foreign cabal whose secondary effects only lapped at United States shores. The impact of the conspiracy was direct and substantial. Indeed, the participation of American business in the market allocation scheme was critical to its success. The plaintiff here is a foreign company, true enough, but it was injured by the same acts of defendants that injured American plaintiffs whose right to seek recovery of their losses the district court recognized in this litigation.

With the Foreign Trade and Antitrust Improvements Act, Congress set out to insulate United States business from its antitrust laws for certain business conducted outside the country. Its central purpose was to assist American business in competing abroad. This pass from antitrust restrictions did not extend to all conduct outside the United States. It stopped short of insulating conduct having direct and substantial effects upon American commerce and causing antitrust injury to that commerce sufficient to support a claim for treble damages.

I am not persuaded that when illegal conduct produces these domestic effects, that Congress intended to close the door to a foreign company injured by the same illegal conduct. That was not the law before this effort to assist American business abroad, and Congress did not intend to change it or do so unwittingly. I would reverse and remand for further proceedings.

I

A

Interpretation of a statute must begin with the text of the statute itself. ... Section 6a(1), p. 1192, requires an effect on (A) domestic or import commerce of the United States or (B) the export commerce of a person in the United States. Section 6a(2) requires that this effect "give[ ] rise to a claim under the provisions of sections 1 to 7 of this title, the Sherman Act, other than this section." The majority reads section 6a(2) to require that the effect "give[ ] rise to" *the plaintiff's* claim. It does not say that. It does say that the effect must "give[ ] rise to a claim." In other words, the effect on United States commerce must be sufficient to support a claim, an injury of some person in a way cognizable under the Sherman Act.

The literal text of the statute supports this conclusion. It reads, "gives rise to a claim." The word "a" has a simple and universally understood meaning. It is the indefinite article. There are many terms of art about which one can debate whether Congress uses the term as courts do, but this word is not one of them. If the drafters of the FTAIA had wished to say "the claim" instead of "a claim," they certainly would have.

The reference to "a" claim makes clear that the "effect" described by section 6a(1) must violate the Sherman Act—that is, harm competition. Section 6a(1) requires that the conspiracy have an effect on United States commerce; section 6a(2) requires that this effect either monopolize commerce or restrain trade in the United States, thereby giving rise to a Sherman Act claim. Section 6a(2) removes jurisdiction over conspiracies whose effects on United States commerce are beneficial or benign, even if they restrain competition in other parts of the world. That an injury that "gives rise to" an antitrust claim must be an injury caused by harm to competition is no light notion. It is a well established and fundamental tenet of antitrust law. Termed "antitrust injury," it is frequently encountered in enforcement action under the Clayton Act, by which Congress enlisted private enforcement in supplementation of governmental enforcement of the Sherman Act.

Thus, the literal text does not require that the effect on United States commerce give rise to the plaintiff's claim. At worst, the text is sufficiently ambiguous to allow for both the construction the majority offers and the construction I believe is correct. At the least, the majority cannot find support in a plain text argument.

Accepting that the text of the FTAIA compels neither the majority's reading or mine, we must enlist other aids in determining the meaning of the statute. In doing so, I conclude that the textual conclusion that "a" means "a" is supported by the statutory context of the FTAIA, which describes the function of the FTAIA and its animating purpose, and by the purposes of the antitrust laws in general; by the legislative history of the FTAIA; and by the sparse case law that interprets the FTAIA.

B

The FTAIA was enacted as Title IV of Public Law 97–290, entitled "Export Trading Company Act of 1982." Title I contains the congressional findings. Every single congressional finding relates to the importance of export business and the need to encourage export activity by American business. The statute then states: "It is the purpose of this Act to increase United States exports of products and services by encouraging more efficient provision of export trade services to United States producers and suppliers, in particular by . . . modifying the application of the antitrust laws to certain export trade."[21] It could not be clearer that the FTAIA serves to exempt exporting from antitrust scrutiny, not to limit the liability of participants in transnational conspiracies that affect United States commerce.

The text of the FTAIA implements this purpose perfectly. The Sherman Act, prior to the enactment of the FTAIA, applied to conduct that affected domestic, import, and export commerce. Recall that section 6a(1) limiting the reach of the Sherman Act applies to conduct that affects (1) domestic commerce; (2) import commerce; or (3) export commerce, but only to the extent that American exporters are affected. One class of conduct is excluded: conduct that affects only foreign purchasers of American exports. This is the function of the FTAIA: to protect American exporters who

---

21. § 102(b), 96 Stat. at 1234. The Third Circuit has recently cited this concluding language in that "Congress enacted the FTAIA for the purpose of facilitating the export of domestic goods by exempting export transactions that did not injure the United States economy from the Sherman Act and thereby relieving exporters from a competitive disadvantage in foreign trade." *Carpet Group Int'l v. Oriental Rug Importers Ass'n, Inc.*, 227 F.3d 62, 71 (3d Cir.2000).

monopolize or conspire to restrain export trade that does not harm United States commerce.

The purpose of the FTAIA offers no support for the majority's reading of the statute. It is undisputed that if proved, the conspiracy in this case would have direct, substantial, and reasonably foreseeable effects upon United States commerce. No American exporters are implicated by this suit. American exporting business can only be harmed by the alleged conspiracy in this case.

Indeed, interpreting the FTAIA as the majority wishes will impair the competitiveness of American exporters. Under the majority's view, an American cartel that fixes prices worldwide will be subject to Clayton Act suits by plaintiffs from around the world, but a foreign cartel that fixes prices worldwide will be subject to suit under the Clayton Act only from plaintiffs injured in American commerce. This interpretation of the FTAIA transforms a safe harbor for American exporters into a boon for foreign cartels that restrain commerce in the United States.

With respect to my colleagues, I fear that their reading of the FTAIA will hinder its purposes and reduce the effectiveness of the antitrust laws. Nothing in the text of the FTAIA, or the Export Trading Company Act of 1982 as a whole, or its legislative history, casts doubt on the importance of deterring restraints of trade that affect United States commerce. The Supreme Court has repeatedly recognized that the accent of the Sherman and the Clayton Acts is deterrence, requiring violators to pay full, treble damages, even if some plaintiffs gain a windfall or are foreigners. For example, in *Illinois Brick Co. v. Illinois*, [431 U.S. 720] the Supreme Court noted the importance of "vigorous private enforcement of the antitrust laws" and "deterring violators" and recognized that "from the deterrence standpoint, it is irrelevant to whom damages are paid, so long as some one redresses the violation." [*Id.* at 745–46.]

The Supreme Court in *Pfizer, Inc. v. Government of India* [434 U.S. 308] addressed a situation somewhat analogous to this case. The government of India sued several American pharmaceutical manufacturers under the Clayton Act for damages caused by a price-fixing conspiracy. Like Statoil, the government of India alleged a worldwide conspiracy that raised prices in the United States and abroad. Unlike in this case, in *Pfizer* the sales were made in the United States. In holding that foreign governments could recover under the Clayton Act, Justice Stewart observed: "Treble-damage suits by foreigners who have been victimized by antitrust violations clearly may contribute to the protection of American consumers.... [A]n exclusion of all foreign plaintiffs would lessen the deterrent effect of treble damages." [*Id.* at 314–15.]

The logic underlying this conclusion is straightforward. Conspirators facing antitrust liability only to plaintiffs injured by their conspiracy's effects on the United States may not be deterred from restraining trade in the United States. A worldwide price-fixing scheme could sustain monopoly prices in the United States even in the face of such liability if it could cross-subsidize its American operations with profits from abroad. Unless persons injured by the conspiracy's effects on foreign commerce could also bring antitrust suits against the conspiracy, the conspiracy could remain profitable and undeterred.

It is no rejoinder that conspirators would simply choose to exclude the United States from any price-fixing conspiracy as long as American plaintiffs could sue. In at least some cases, including the United States in a price-fixing conspiracy is necessary to generate monopoly profits. Otherwise, arbitrage would rapidly equalize unequal prices around the globe as speculators resold goods purchased in the United States to buyers in high-price regions. Thus, a cartel may find it impossible to fix prices anywhere without a worldwide conspiracy. The Sherman Act can only deter these violations if it protects all parties injured by such a conspiracy....

C

The legislative history also supports this reading of the statute and undermines the majority's interpretation of section 6a(2).... [Judge Higginbotham here argues that the Committee distinguishes between where the plaintiffs suffered economic injury and where, or whether, anticompetitive effects in the United States result from the conduct.]

D

I recognize that there is little precedent to guide our analysis of this question. Of the case law that does exist, there are no appellate court cases supporting the majority's holding. To the contrary, the majority must reconcile or distinguish the only other circuit court decisions interpreting the FTAIA, because all of them find jurisdiction present.

The majority opinion struggles, and I believe fails, to reconcile *Caribbean Broadcasting System, Ltd. v. Cable & Wireless PLC*, [148 F.3d 1080 (D.C.Cir.1998)], which involved a foreign plaintiff alleging monopolization in radio advertising in the Caribbean by a competing radio station. The defendant was also a foreign entity. Consistent with the reasoning of this dissent, the D.C. Circuit held that the FTAIA did not preclude jurisdiction, because the plaintiff showed that the foreign defendants' conduct had the effect of harming United States purchasers of advertising. It stated: "the alleged injury is to advertisers in the United States." Thus, based on the injury to advertisers in the United States, the court found jurisdiction over a suit by a radio broadcaster in the Caribbean. The D.C. Circuit did not require that the injury to American advertisers "give[ ] rise to" the plaintiff's cause of action; its determination that the injury gave rise to "a" claim was sufficient.

E

Finally, the majority's attempt to enlist the aid of the Commerce Clause and the canon of construction that creates a presumption against extraterritoriality is mistaken.... The majority is correct to note that the courts' historical willingness to apply the Sherman Act extraterritorially is not dispositive of this appeal, since the FTAIA, and not the courts' earlier interpretations of the Sherman Act, is controlling here. But precisely because the FTAIA applies here, the majority's reliance on the canon against extraterritorial application of statutes is misplaced. This canon operates when Congress has not clearly spoken on the issue of extraterritoriality. The FTAIA, however, explicitly addresses nothing other than extraterritoriality. We must be careful not to use such a canon when Congress is speaking directly to the relevant issue. Make no mistake: such canons reflect substantive presumptions about the content of laws. If courts apply substantive canons of construction against statutes that do speak to an issue, then it is the courts, not Congress, who are making the policy choices that form the content of legislation.

II

[In this section of the dissent, Judge Higginbotham explains that he would find that the plaintiff Statoil has standing.]

III

The antitrust laws have always given federal courts jurisdiction over conspiracies that adversely affect competition in the United States. The FTAIA limits that jurisdiction; but it does so by exempting American export conspiracies, not foreign conspiracies that injure American competition.

The majority opinion expresses concern that foreign litigants will flock to the United States for redress of their injuries in distant lands. The majority opinion, and the district court opinions it cites, seem to fear that the interpretation of the FTAIA that Statoil advocates makes the Sherman Act an antitrust regulation of foreign economies throughout the entire world, a paternalistic lawmaking enterprise that ignores the adequacy of foreign tribunals. But Congress has enacted no such thing. Congress enacted the FTAIA to serve the United States' narrow interest in vigorous domestic competition.

The text of the FTAIA may be inelegant, but it serves the selfish national interests of the United States: the FTAIA excludes from antitrust liability all conduct that has caused no antitrust injury to the United States economy; but it enlists all injured parties—foreign or domestic—to assist the Department of Justice in deterring conduct that does harm the forces of competition in the United States. When a conspiracy causes a direct and substantial injury to competition in the United States, the Clayton Act recruits private parties to supplement the efforts of the Department of Justice in ending the conspiracy. The FTAIA ensures that parties injured by foreign aspects of the same conspiracy that harms American commerce are part of the phalanx of enforcers brought to bear by the Clayton Act. Thus, treble damages suits by parties who suffer antitrust injury from a conspiracy that has a direct and substantial harmful impact on United States commerce serve a single function: the protection of United States commerce. The FTAIA threatens no parade of horribles—it does nothing more than zealously protect competition in the United States while sparing from the docket of American courts suits involving conspiracies that affect only foreign economies.

In sum, I believe the FTAIA does not divest the federal courts of jurisdiction over suits by plaintiffs who suffer antitrust injuries from a conspiracy that also harms competition in United States commerce. Whether the harm felt in the United States is the source of the injury to the plaintiff is irrelevant; it is the effects on the United States that creates jurisdiction. Under the facts of this case, I would conclude that the district court had jurisdiction over the suit and that Statoil had standing to sue the defendants under the Clayton Act. I respectfully dissent.

NOTES AND QUESTIONS

1. In Kruman v. Christie's Intern. PLC, 284 F.3d 384 (2d Cir.2002), the Second Circuit specifically rejected the position of the *Statoil* majority and cited Judge Higginbotham's dissenting opinion with approval. *Kruman* was a class action in which the plaintiffs claimed that the two largest auction houses in the world had entered into an agreement to fix the prices they charged their clients for auction services. Both defendants were based outside the United States. The court found that the FTAIA applied. With respect to the "effects" debate, it stated that "[w]e find that an interpretation [of the FTAIA] centered on whether the plaintiff has suffered domestic injury cannot be squared with the text of the FTAIA." *Id.* at 396.

2. Two other courts of appeals found it unnecessary squarely to confront the question that split the Fifth Circuit. In Turicentro, S.A. v. American Airlines Inc., 303 F.3d 293 (3d Cir.2002), the court considered the question whether an alleged conspiracy among four domestic U.S. airlines and their trade association to fix the commissions paid to foreign travel agents, operating outside the United States, fell within the scope of U.S. law. The court concluded that it did not. The key, in its view, was the geographic target of the alleged conspiracy; there was no allegation that this one caused any injury felt in the United States or any impact on the U.S. economy. The court went out of its way to remark that it was not reaching the issue that the Fifth Circuit had confronted in *Statoil*.

The Fourth Circuit, in Dee-K Enterprises, Inc. v. Heveafil Sdn. Bhd., 299 F.3d 281 (4th Cir.2002), hinted that it agreed with the Fifth Circuit majority, but like the Third Circuit it found no need to resolve the question definitively. *Dee-K* was a suit brought by U.S. purchasers of a type of rubber thread made by South East Asian producers. After a jury trial, the jury found that the plaintiffs had failed to prove sufficient effects on U.S. markets, and the district court entered judgment for the defendants. The court of appeals affirmed. It found that the FTAIA did not apply directly, because the commerce in question related to imports. It therefore turned to the older line of cases for guidance. Ultimately it adopted a test under which it asked if the "participants, acts, targets, and effects [challenged in the suit] are primarily foreign or primarily domestic." 299 F.3d at 294. Finding that the jury reasonably could have concluded that these factors were primarily foreign, it concluded that there was no "jurisdiction" under the Sherman Act.

3. Finally, there is Carpet Group Int'l v. Oriental Rug Importers Ass'n, Inc., 227 F.3d 62 (3d Cir.2000), in which the court considered whether the FTAIA divested the district court of jurisdiction over a case alleging a conspiracy to

monopolize the U.S. market for oriental rugs. The plaintiffs were Virginia entities selling oriental rugs to U.S. consumers; the defendants were an association of importers and wholesalers of the rugs (Oriental Rug Importers Association, Inc., or ORIA), several member companies, and some individual officers and directors of the association. The district court had found that there was no jurisdiction, but the court of appeals reversed. It noted that the defendants were claiming that the facts did not support the court's "subject matter jurisdiction," and thus that the court would need to consider the evidence supporting its power to hear the case. The complaint detailed various alleged restraints, including threats not to purchase rugs from manufacturers that participated in the plaintiffs' trade shows and other boycott-like activity, retaliatory threats, and efforts to induce export groups not to participate in the plaintiffs' trade shows.

The court of appeals concluded that ordinary Sherman Act principles applied to the case, because it involved import commerce, and import commerce is expressly excluded from the coverage of the FTAIA. The lower courts had erred, it held, when they found that the FTAIA applied. That error came about because the lower courts were looking at the brokerage function the plaintiffs played, rather than at the defendants' conduct. As for that, the court said that "the defendants intended their alleged conduct to subvert commercial activities that solely impacted domestic commerce," and that they took steps "designed to ensure that only United States importers, and not United States retailers, could bring oriental rugs manufactured abroad into the stream of American commerce." It went on to note that its conclusion that jurisdiction existed found

> even stronger support when one considers all of the evidence submitted before both the Magistrate Judge and the District Court, especially in light of Mortensen's less stringent evidentiary standard. The plaintiffs have offered evidence that defendants took steps to: (1) prevent foreign manufacturers from selling to United States retailers, (2) prevent at least one American retailer from purchasing rugs directly from foreign manufacturers, (3) prevent foreign governments and trade associations from sponsoring trade fairs at which retailers could purchase directly from foreign manufacturers, and (4) prevent an American rug retailers' trade association from sponsoring the trade fairs.

> Finally, the evidence offered by plaintiffs (including the evidence offered after the Magistrate Judge's initial report issued) reveals that the defendants' alleged conduct had its intended negative effect on CGI's trade shows and, consequently, had the effect of protecting the defendants' import and wholesale business. Accordingly, the evidence, taken as a whole, is sufficient to support the plaintiffs' allegations that the challenged conduct "involved" import trade or commerce. The crux of their case involves conduct in the United States, not conduct abroad. We hold that these activities are not the type of conduct Congress intended to remove from our antitrust jurisdiction when it enacted the FTAIA. The FTAIA therefore did not divest the District Court of subject matter jurisdiction over the plaintiffs' claims.

In the end, the court "conclud[ed] that the FTAIA is inapplicable and that the District Court erred in dismissing this case. Further, the plaintiffs have offered sufficient evidence to demonstrate that the activities of the wholesale importers were intended to and adversely did impact on domestic commerce by engaging in a course of anticompetitive conduct to ensure that only they, the importers, could bring oriental rugs manufactured abroad into the United States for distribution. We further hold that subject matter jurisdiction exists under the Sherman Act, and that the plaintiffs have antitrust standing."

NOTE ON JURISDICTION IN EXPORT CASES

As you can see from *Zenith Radio v. Hazeltine*, 395 U.S. 100 (1969), supra p. 1190, the U.S. courts from time to time entertained cases in which the alleged restriction on U.S. commerce focused on outbound trade to other countries. This became one of the most sensitive issues in the eyes of other countries, who regarded it as an impermissible extension of extraterritorial jurisdiction into their own markets. Why, for example, shouldn't the Canadian government be the one to decide whether the patent pool at issue in Zenith was consistent with its own competition policy? Why should it matter if a U.S. firm is denied access to one foreign market, if the markets of the other 180–some countries in the world are open to it? If we think the antitrust laws are principally designed to protect U.S. consumer welfare, what justifies this "market access" branch of jurisdiction? On the other hand, isn't subsection (1)(B) of the FTAIA a plain indication from Congress that it regards market access cases as something that may fall within the antitrust laws?

This area had never been the central point of U.S. enforcement activity, but there had been a steady stream of cases over the years nonetheless. For example, in *United States v. C. Itoh & Co.*, 1982–83 Trade Cas. (CCH) ¶ 65,010 (W.D.Wash. 1982), the U.S. Department of Justice obtained a consent decree against an alleged monopsonistic cartel of Japanese fish importers, who had agreed to depress the price they were willing to pay Alaskan fishermen for certain products. However, the Reagan Administration's Department of Justice announced in its 1988 Antitrust Enforcement Guidelines for International Operations, at footnote 159, that it would no longer bring export cases unless harm to U.S. consumers was also present. This position met with criticism both from Congress, which believed that its six-year old statute was being flouted, and from U.S. exporters anxious to be able to bring antitrust actions when anticompetitive behavior was barring access to foreign markets. Four years later, in 1992, footnote 159 was withdrawn by the first Bush Administration. See U.S. Department of Justice Press Release dated April 3, 1992. A diplomatic firestorm ensued. Claiming that the withdrawal of footnote 159 was a signal that antitrust had become just another retaliatory weapon for international trade problems, foreign governments argued strongly that market access cases violated international law.

Notwithstanding the controversial nature of market access jurisdiction abroad, the 1995 International Guidelines make it clear that this is one ground of jurisdiction that falls within the Agencies' competence. *See* 1995 Guidelines, § 3.122 and Illustrative Examples D and E. *See also United States v. Pilkington*, 1994–2 Trade Cas. (CCH) ¶ 70,842 (D.Ariz.1994) (dismantling restrictions on exports of glass-making technology from the United States to other countries). Unless or until Congress changes the language of the FTAIA, this is likely to remain the official enforcement position. In the meantime, the increase in the number of cooperation agreements and the spread of antitrust to the majority of countries around the world has had the effect of diminishing the importance of direct enforcement designed to protect export markets. This is because the countries to which the goods or services are sent now enforce their own laws against foreign-based restraints that harm their consumers (either on their own initiative or because of a "positive comity" request from the exporting nation).

NOTE ON THE EXPORT TRADING COMPANY ACT OF 1982

In 1982, Congress enacted the Export Trading Company Act, Pub.L. No. 97–290, 96 Stat. 1233 (1982). Its purpose was to stimulate the export trade of United States businesses by encouraging the establishment of export trading companies ("ETCs"), and by modifying the jurisdictional reach of the Sherman Act.

With respect to ETCs, the statute provides:

> The term "export trading company" means a company which does business under the laws of the United States or any state, which is exclusively engaged in activities related to international trade, and which is organized and operated principally for purposes of exporting goods or services in the United States or for purposes of facilitating the exportation of goods or services produced in the United States by unaffiliated persons by providing one or more export trade services.

The Act encourages the formation of ETCs in three ways. First, it gives ETCs greater access to financing and financial expertise by permitting bank holding companies and certain other financial institutions to invest in ETCs. Bank holding companies now may invest up to 5% of their consolidated capital and surplus in the ownership of ETCs. An investor may extend credit to an affiliated ETC, but the outstanding credit may not exceed 10% of the investor's consolidated capital and surplus. The Act also reduces limitations on export trade financing by financial institutions.

Second, the Act establishes an office in the Department of Commerce to promote the formation of ETCs and to serve as a clearing house of information for ETCs and producers of goods and services that could be exported.

Finally, and most important to our study, the Act provides ETCs with certain exemptions from the antitrust laws. It provides for issuance by the Secretary of Commerce of certificates that specifically exempt from antitrust scrutiny particular export activities by any person who applies for the certificate.

Certificate-holders are protected from the trebling of damages for any injury arising from, and from criminal liability for, conduct that is specified in, and that complies with, the terms of a certificate. For this purpose antitrust laws are: the Sherman Act (15 U.S.C.A. §§ 1 through 7), the Wilson Tariff Act (15 U.S.C.A. §§ 8 through 11), the Clayton Act (15 U.S.C.A. §§ 10, 13, 14 through 21, and 22 through 27), and all state antitrust and unfair competition laws. Notwithstanding this protection, there are three ways certificate-holders may be subject to actions for conduct subject to antitrust laws.

First, a person who is injured by the conduct of a certificate-holder who is protected from antitrust liability still may obtain injunctive relief and actual damages for violation by the certificate-holder of the standards of § 303(a) of the Act.

Second, the Attorney General may bring an action under § 15 of the Clayton Act (15 U.S.C.A. § 25) to enjoin conduct that threatens clear and irreparable harm to the national interest.

Third, certificate-holders are protected from liability under antitrust laws only to the extent they have complied with their certificates. Conduct that is not specified in a certificate therefore is fully subject to all antitrust laws, as is the conduct of any person who does not hold a valid certificate.

SECTION 2.   COMITY AND COOPERATION

A.   COMITY IN THE COURTS

Timberlane Lumber Co. v. Bank of America, N.T. & S.A.

United States Court of Appeals, Ninth Circuit, 1976.
549 F.2d 597, cert. denied, 472 U.S. 1032.

■ BROWNING and CHOY, CIRCUIT JUDGES, and GRAY, DISTRICT JUDGE.

[Timberlane Lumber Co., an Oregon partnership engaged in the purchase, importation, and distribution of lumber in the U.S., formed two Honduran corporations to acquire forest properties and operate a lumber mill in that country. Timberlane, through one of these subsidiaries, sought to acquire the Lima family mill, which had been in competition with the two largest lumber companies in Honduras, both defendants in the suit. Defendant Bank of America's Tegucigalpa branch held significant financial interests in each. The Lima mill had passed into the hands of creditors, including one of the defendant firms and certain unpaid employees, who under Honduras law had priority. From the latter Timberlane purchased the controlling assets and reactivated the Lima mill. It also sought to acquire the remaining interests in the Lima assets, to clear title, but was refused. Allegedly conspiring to eliminate plaintiff's competition, defendants placed their claims in the hands of an agent who took them to court for enforcement. The agent obtained court orders of attachment ("embargos") and appointment of a judicial officer ("intervenor"), alleged to be on the payroll of the Bank, who caused guards and "troops" to cripple and partially shut down Timberlane's milling operations. The conspirators also allegedly caused defamatory articles regarding Timberlane to be published in the press and the false arrest and imprisonment of the manager of Timberlane's operations. Plaintiffs alleged damages in excess of $5 million and a "direct and substantial" effect on U.S. foreign commerce, intended by defendants.]

■ CHOY, CIR. J. . . . This action raises important questions concerning the application of American antitrust laws to activities in another country, including actions of foreign government officials. The district court dismissed the Timberlane action under the act of state doctrine and for lack of subject matter jurisdiction. . . .

The Timberlane Action

The basic allegation of the Timberlane plaintiffs is that officials of the Bank of America and others located in both the United States and Honduras conspired to prevent Timberlane, through its Honduras subsidiaries, from milling lumber in Honduras and exporting it to the United States, thus maintaining control of the Honduran lumber export business in the hands of a few select individuals financed and controlled by the Bank. The intent and result of the conspiracy, they contend, was to interfere with the exportation to the United States, including Puerto Rico, of Honduran lumber for sale or use there by the plaintiffs, thus directly and substantially affecting the foreign commerce of the United States....

The court gave as its reason [for dismissal] "that it is prohibited under the act of state doctrine from examining the acts of a foreign sovereign state; and in any event, that there is no direct and substantial effect on United States foreign commerce," the latter apparently being deemed a prerequisite for jurisdiction. No specific findings of fact were announced, nor were any more extensive conclusions of law stated.

It is unclear whether the decision was a dismissal for lack of subject matter jurisdiction or for failure to state a claim, F.R.Civ.P. 12(b)(1) & (6), or a summary judgment under F.R.Civ.P. 56....

We will ... review the judgment ... treating it as a Rule 12(b)(6) dismissal. Accordingly, we assume the allegations of the Timberlane plaintiffs to be true....

The classic enunciation of the act of state doctrine is found in *Underhill v. Hernandez,* 168 U.S. 250, 252 (1897):

> Every sovereign State is bound to respect the independence of every other sovereign State, and the courts of one country will not sit in judgment on the acts of the government of another done within its own territory.

From the beginning, this principle has been applied in foreign trade antitrust cases. In *American Banana Co. v. United Fruit Co.,* 213 U.S. 347 (1909), the first such case of significance, the American owner of a banana plantation caught in a border dispute between Panama and Costa Rica claimed that a competitor violated the Sherman Act by persuading the Costa Rican government to seize his lands. The act complained of would have required an adjudication of the legality of the Costa Rican seizure, an action which the Supreme Court said our courts could not challenge....

The defendants argue—as the district court apparently held—that the injuries allegedly suffered by Timberlane resulted from acts of the Honduran government, principally in connection with the enforcement of the security interests in the ... plant, which American courts cannot review. Such an application of the act of state doctrine seems to us to be erroneous. Even if the *coup de grace* to Timberlane's enterprise in Honduras was applied by official authorities, we do not agree that the doctrine necessarily shelters these defendants or requires dismissal of the Timberlane action.

The leading modern statement of the act of state doctrine appears in *Banco National de Cuba v. Abating,* 376 U.S. 398 (1964). Despite contrary implications in *Underhill* and *American Banana,* the Court concluded that the doctrine was not compelled by the nature of sovereignty, by international law, or by the text of the Constitution. 376 U.S. at 421–23. Rather, it derives from the judiciary's concern for its possible interference with the conduct of foreign affairs by the political branches of the government:

The doctrine as formulated in past decisions expresses the strong sense of the Judicial Branch that its engagement in the task of passing on the validity of foreign acts of state may hinder rather than further this country's pursuit of goals both for itself and for the community of nations as a whole in the international sphere.

Id. at 423. The Court recognized that not every case is identical in its potential impact on our relations with other nations. For instance:

[S]ome aspects of international law touch much more sharply on national nerves than do others; the less important the implications of an issue are for our foreign relations, the weaker the justification for exclusivity in the political branches.

Id. at 428. Thus the Court explicitly rejected "laying down or reaffirming an inflexible and all-encompassing rule." *Id.* Whether forbearance by an American court in a given situation is advisable or appropriate depends upon the "balance of relevant considerations." *Id.*

It is apparent that the doctrine does not bestow a blank-check immunity upon all conduct blessed with some imprimatur of a foreign government. In *Continental Ore Co. v. Union Carbide & Carbon Corp.*, 370 U.S. 690 (1962), the Canadian government had made a private corporation its exclusive agent for the purchase of vanadium, a material used in steel production. The Canadian corporation, acting in concert with an affiliated American company, used its position to exclude a competitor of the American affiliate from the Canadian market. The Court held that the Canadian corporation's activity was not entitled to immunity, carefully noting that the plaintiff did not question the validity of any action taken by the Canadian government and that there was no indication that any Canadian government official "approved or would have approved" of the monopolizing efforts. *Id.* at 706.

In *Alfred Dunhill of London, Inc. v. The Republic of Cuba*, 425 U.S. 682 (1976), interventors appointed by the Cuban government to take possession of and operate nationalized Cuban cigar manufacturers had been paid large sums by importers in the United States and elsewhere for pre-nationalization shipments. These payments were found to have been made in error, since they should have been made to the prior owners of the cigar firms. The importers sought to recover the money. Counsel for the Cuban government and the interventors argued that the interventors' refusal to repay the pre-intervention sums represented a sovereign repudiation of any obligation to refund the amounts and as such an act of state not subject to challenge in American courts. The Court disagreed, refusing to conclude that "the conduct in question was the public act of those with authority to exercise sovereign authority and was entitled to respect in our courts." *Id.* at 694. There was no proof that the failure of the interventors to repay the money reached the level of an "act of state," a sovereign assertion of the Cuban government:

No statute, decree, order or resolution of the Cuban government itself was offered in evidence indicating that Cuba had repudiated her obligations in general or any class thereof or that she had as a sovereign matter determined to confiscate the amounts due three foreign importers.

Id.

A corollary to the act of state doctrine in the foreign trade antitrust field is the often-recognized principle that corporate conduct which is compelled by a foreign sovereign is also protected from antitrust liability, as if it were an act of the state itself. Thus, in *Interamerican Refining Corp. v. Texaco Maracaibo, Inc.*, 307 F.Supp. 1291 (D.Del.1970), a refusal by defendants to sell Venezuelan crude oil to plaintiff was held not to be an illegal restraint of trade because it was a complete defense that the Venezuelan government had imposed a boycott forbidding such sales. The court there observed that "[w]hen a nation compels a trade practice, firms there have no choice but to obey. Acts of business become effectively acts of the sovereign." *Id.* at 1298.

On the other hand, mere governmental approval or foreign governmental involvement which the defendants had arranged does not necessarily provide a defense. In *United States v. Sisal Sales Corp.*, 274 U.S. 268 (1927), the defendants were accused of conspiring to monopolize sales of sisal, a material used in making rope, from Mexico to the United States by inducing Mexican officials to recognize the conspirators as the exclusive traders and to impose discriminatory taxes on rival sellers. The Court rejected the defendants' claim to act of state protection, ruling that a conspiracy formed in the United States for the purpose of monopolizing sales to the United States was not protected simply because one element of the conspiracy involved securing favorable action by foreign officials. In *Continental Ore*, the Court indicated that it continued to accept the Sisal reasoning. See 370 U.S. at 705.

The distinction was recognized and relied upon in *United States v. The Watchmakers of Switzerland Information Center, Inc.*, 1963 Trade Cases ¶ 70,600 (S.D.N.Y.1962), order modified, 1965 Trade Cases ¶ 70,352 (S.D.N.Y.1965), the *"Swiss Watch"* case:

> If, of course, the defendants' activities had been required by Swiss law, this court could indeed do nothing. An American court would have under such circumstances no right to condemn the governmental activity of another sovereign nation. In the present case, however, the defendants' activities were not required by the laws of Switzerland. They were agreements formulated privately without compulsion on the part of the Swiss Government. It is clear that these private agreements were then recognized as facts of economic and industrial life by that nation's government. Nonetheless, the fact that the Swiss Government may, as a practical matter, approve of the effects of this private activity cannot convert what is essentially a vulnerable private conspiracy into an unassailable system resulting from foreign governmental mandate. . . .

The touchstone of *Sabbatino*—the potential for interference with our foreign relations—is the crucial element in determining whether deference should be accorded in any given case. We wish to avoid "passing on the validity" of foreign acts. *Sabbatino*, 376 U.S. at 423. Similarly, we do not wish to challenge the sovereignty of another nation, the wisdom of its policy, or the integrity and motivation of its action. On the other hand, repeating the terms of *Sabbatino, id.* at 428, "the less important the implications of an issue are for our foreign relations, the weaker the justification for exclusivity in the political branches."

While we do not wish to impugn or question the nobility of a foreign nation's motivation, we are necessarily interested in the depth and nature of its interest. The Restatement (Second) of Foreign Relations Law of the United States § 41 (1965) makes an important distinction on this basis in limiting the deference of American courts:

> [A] court in the United States ... will refrain from examining the validity of an act of a foreign state by which that state has exercised its jurisdiction to *give effect to its public interests.* [Emphasis added.]

The "public interest" qualification is intentional and significant in the context of Timberlane's action, as a comment to § 41 makes plain:

> *Comment d. Nature of act of state.* An "act of state" as the term is used in this Title involves the public interests of a state as a state, as distinct from its interest in providing the means of adjudicating disputes or claims that arise within its territory.... A judgment of a court may be an act of state. Usually it is not, because it involves the interests of private litigants or because court adjudication is not the usual way in which the state exercises its jurisdiction to give effect to public interests.

Id. at 127.[22]

   ... The actions of the Honduran government that are involved here—including the application by its courts and their agents of the Honduran laws concerning security interests and the protection of the underlying property against diminution are clearly distinguishable from the sovereign decree ... at issue in Occidental Petroleum.... Here, the allegedly "sovereign" acts of Honduras consisted of judicial proceedings which were initi-

---

22. Illustrations 4, 5 and 6 accompanying this comment demonstrate how a court's judgment can be, but usually is not, an act of state:

   4. In a suit in tort by X against Y, a court of state A decides that X is entitled to a specified amount of damages. This decision is not an act of state within the meaning of the rule stated in this Section.

   5. In an action to determine title to land, brought by X against Y, a court of state A decides that X is the owner of the land. This decision is not an act of state within the meaning of the rule stated in this Section.

   6. State A obtains by eminent domain proceedings title to an electric utility system in its territory. The vesting of title is an act of state within the meaning of the rule stated in this Section.

As used in this Restatement, "state" refers to a sovereign nation, not to one of the United States.

ated by ... one of the alleged co-conspirators, not by the Honduran government itself.... Timberlane does not seek to name Honduras or any Honduran officer as a defendant or co-conspirator, nor does it challenge Honduran policy or sovereignty in any fashion that appears on its face to hold any threat to relations between Honduras and the United States. In fact, there is no indication that the actions of the Honduran court and authorities reflected a sovereign decision that Timberlane's efforts should be crippled or that trade with the United States should be restrained....

Under these circumstances, it is clear that the "act of state" doctrine does not require dismissal of the Timberlane action.

Extraterritorial Reach of the United States Antitrust Laws

There is no doubt that American antitrust laws extend over some conduct in other nations.[23] There was language in the first Supreme Court case in point, *American Banana Co. v. United Fruit Co.*, 213 U.S. 347 (1909), casting doubt on the extension of the Sherman Act to acts outside United States territory. But subsequent cases have limited *American Banana* to its particular facts, and the Sherman Act—and with it other antitrust laws—has been applied to extraterritorial conduct. *See, e.g., Continental Ore Co. v. Union Carbide & Carbon Corp.*, 370 U.S. 690 (1962); *United States v. Sisal Sales Corp.*, 274 U.S. 268 (1927); *United States v. Aluminum Co. of America*, 148 F.2d 416 (2d Cir.1945) (the *"Alcoa"* case). The act may encompass the foreign activities of aliens as well as American citizens....

That American law covers some conduct beyond this nation's borders does not mean that it embraces all, however. Extraterritorial application is understandably a matter of concern for the other countries involved. Those nations have sometimes resented and protested, as excessive intrusions into their own spheres, broad assertions of authority by American courts.... Our courts have recognized this concern and have, at times, responded to it, even if not always enough to satisfy all the foreign critics.... In any event, it is evident that at some point the interests of the United States are too weak and the foreign harmony incentive for restraint too strong to justify an extraterritorial assertion of jurisdiction.

23. The subject of extraterritorial jurisdiction of American antitrust laws is one about which there has been a great deal of discussion. The commentaries cited in this opinion represent only a fraction of those discussing the subject. Worthy of special comment are K. Brewster, Antitrust and American Business Abroad (1958), and W. Fugate, Foreign Commerce and the Antitrust Laws (2d ed. 1973). There has, however, been much less action. In actual litigation, jurisdiction has not often been found lacking. Up to May 1973, the Department of Justice filed some 248 foreign trade antitrust cases; not one was lost for want of jurisdiction over the activities claimed to violate the law. W. Fugate, Foreign Commerce and the Antitrust Laws, App. B. at 498 (2d ed. 1973). The instant case is, of course, a private action, but reported dismissals of such cases also appear to be infrequent. The only case lost on appeal on this ground was *American Banana Co. v. United Fruit Co.*, 213 U.S. 347 (1909), a decision which is today considered largely obsolete. Rahl, Foreign Commerce Jurisdiction of the American Antitrust Laws, 43 Antitrust L.J. 521 (1974).

What that point is or how it is determined is not defined by international law.... Nor does the Sherman Act limit itself. In the domestic field the Sherman Act extends to the full reach of the commerce power. *United States v. South–Eastern Underwriters Assn.*, 322 U.S. 533, 558 (1944). To define it somewhat more modestly in the foreign commerce area courts have generally, and logically, fallen back on a narrower construction of congressional intent, such as expressed in Judge Learned Hand's oft-cited opinion in *Alcoa*, 148 F.2d at 443:

> [T]he only question open is whether Congress intended to impose the liability and whether our own Constitution permitted it to do so: as a court of the United States we cannot look beyond our own law. Nevertheless, it is quite true that we are not to read general words, such as those in this Act, without regard to the limitations customarily observed by nations upon the exercise of their powers; limitations which generally correspond to those fixed by the "Conflict of Laws." We should not impute to Congress an intent to punish all whom its courts can catch, for conduct which has no consequences within the United States.

It is the effect on American foreign commerce which is usually cited to support extraterritorial jurisdiction. Alcoa set the course, when Judge Hand declared, *id.*:

> [I]t is settled law ... that any state may impose liabilities, even upon persons not within its allegiance, for conduct outside its borders that has consequences within its borders which the state reprehends; and these liabilities other states will ordinarily recognize.

Despite its description as "settled law," *Alcoa's* assertion has been roundly disputed by many foreign commentators as being in conflict with international law, comity, and good judgment. Nonetheless, American courts have firmly concluded that there is some extraterritorial jurisdiction under the Sherman Act.

Even among American courts and commentators, however, there is no consensus on how far the jurisdiction should extend. The district court here concluded that a "direct and substantial effect" on United States foreign commerce was a prerequisite, without stating whether other factors were relevant or considered.... Restatement (Second) of Foreign Relations Law of the United States § 18.[24]

---

24. Restatement § 18 reads:

A state has jurisdiction to prescribe a rule of law attaching legal consequences to conduct that occurs outside its territory and causes an effect within its territory, if either

(a) the conduct and its effect are generally recognized as constituent elements of a crime or tort under the law of states that have reasonably developed legal systems, or

(b)(i) the conduct and its effect are constituent elements of activity to which the rule applies; (ii) the effect within the territory is substantial; (iii) it occurs as a direct and foreseeable result of the conduct outside the territory; and (iv) the rule is not inconsistent with the princi-

Other courts have used different expressions, however. *See e.g., Thomsen v. Cayser*, 243 U.S. 66, 88 (1917) ("the combination affected the foreign commerce of this country"); *Alcoa*, 148 F.2d at 444 ("intended to affect imports and exports [and] ... is shown actually to have had some effect on them");[25] *United States v. Imperial Chemical Industries, Ltd.*, 100 F.Supp. 504, 592 (S.D.N.Y.1951) ("a conspiracy ... which affects American commerce"); *United States v. Timken Roller Bearing Co.*, 83 F.Supp. 284, 309 (N.D.Ohio 1949), modified and affirmed, 341 U.S. 593 (1951) ("a direct and influencing effect on trade")....

Few cases have discussed the nature of the effect required for jurisdiction, perhaps because most of the litigated cases have involved relatively obvious offenses and rather significant and apparent effects on competition within the United States. It is probably in part because the standard has not often been put to a real test that it seems so poorly defined.... What the threshold of significance is, however, has not been identified. Nor is it quite clear what the "direct-indirect" distinction is supposed to mean....

The effects test by itself is incomplete because it fails to consider other nations' interests. Nor does it expressly take into account the full nature of the relationship between the actors and this country. Whether the alleged offender is an American citizen, for instance, may make a big difference; applying American laws to American citizens raises fewer problems than application to foreigners. As was observed in *Pacific Seafarers, Inc. v. Pacific Far East Line, Inc.*, 404 F.2d 804, 815 (1968), *cert. denied*, 393 U.S. 1093 (1969):

> If ... [American antitrust] policy cannot extend to the full sweep of American foreign commerce because of the international complications involved, then surely the test which determines whether United States law is applicable must focus on the nexus between the parties and their practices and the United States, not on the mechanical circumstances of effect on commodity exports or imports.

American courts have, in fact, often displayed a regard for comity and the prerogatives of other nations and considered their interests as well as other parts of the factual circumstances, even when professing to apply an effects test. To some degree, the requirement for a "substantial" effect may silently incorporate these additional considerations, with "substantial" as a

---

ples of justice generally recognized by states that have reasonably developed legal systems.

The "direct" and "substantial" requirements come from (b)(ii) and (iii). Comment a to this section specifically indicates, however, that this rule applies only to aliens, since United States citizens may be bound by nationality, and govern only where there has been no significant conduct within the United States, since otherwise territorial jurisdiction could be asserted.

25. This portion of Alcoa referred only to a combination of foreigners, specifically for whom the intent requirement may have been imposed, not American citizens or corporations. Further, Judge Hand's opinion noted that either intent or effect individually might suffice, but that both were present in that case, so that the question did not have to be faced.

flexible standard that varies with other factors. The intent requirement suggested by *Alcoa*, 148 F.2d at 443–44, is one example of an attempt to broaden the court's perspective, as is drawing a distinction between American citizens and non-citizens.

The failure to articulate these other elements in addition to the standard effects analysis is costly, however, for it is more likely that they will be overlooked or slighted in interpreting past decisions and reaching new ones. Placing emphasis on the qualification that effects be "substantial" is also risky, for the term has a meaning in the interstate antitrust context which does not encompass all the factors relevant to the foreign trade case.

Indeed, that "substantial effects" element of interstate antitrust analysis may well be responsible for the use of an effects test for foreign commerce. The Sherman Act reaches restraints directly intended to limit the flow of interstate trade or whose sole impact is on interstate commerce, but it also reaches "wholly local business restraints" if the particular restraint "substantially and adversely affects interstate commerce." *Hospital Building*, 425 U.S. at 743; *Gulf Oil Corp. v. Copp Paving Co.*, 419 U.S. 186, 195 (1974); *United States v. Employing Plasterers Assn.*, 347 U.S. 186, 189 (1954). Such a test is necessary in the interstate context to separate the restraints which fall within the federal ambit under the interstate commerce clause from those which, as purely intrastate burdens, remain the province of the states. . . . Since, however, no comparable constitutional problem exists in defining the scope of congressional power to regulate foreign commerce, it may be unwise blindly to apply the "substantiality" test to the international setting. . . . Only respect for the role of the executive and for international notions of comity and fairness limit that constitutional grant.

A tripartite analysis seems to be indicated. As acknowledged above, the antitrust laws require in the first instance that there be some effect—actual or intended—on American foreign commerce before the federal courts may legitimately exercise subject matter jurisdiction under those statutes. Second, a greater showing of burden or restraint may be necessary to demonstrate that the effect is sufficiently large to present a cognizable injury to the plaintiffs and, therefore, a civil violation of the antitrust laws. . . . Third, there is the additional question which is unique to the international setting of whether the interests of, and links to, the United States—including the magnitude of the effect on American foreign commerce—are sufficiently strong, vis-à-vis those of other nations, to justify an assertion of extraterritorial authority.

It is this final issue which is both obscured by undue reliance on the "substantiality" test and complicated to resolve. An effect on United States commerce, although necessary to the exercise of jurisdiction under the antitrust laws, is alone not a sufficient basis on which to determine whether American authority should be asserted in a given case as a matter of international comity and fairness. In some cases, the application of the direct and substantial test in the international context might open the door too widely by sanctioning jurisdiction over an action when these considerations would indicate dismissal. At other times, it may fail in the other direction, dismissing a case for which comity and fairness do not require forbearance, thus closing the jurisdictional door too tightly—for the Sherman Act does reach some restraints which do not have both a direct and substantial effect on the foreign commerce of the United States. A more comprehensive inquiry is necessary. We believe that the field of conflict of laws presents the proper approach, as was suggested, if not specifically employed, in *Alcoa* in expressing the basic limitation on application of American laws:

> [W]e are not to read general words, such as those in this Act, without regard to the limitations customarily observed by nations upon the exercise of their powers; limitations which generally correspond to those fixed by the "Conflict of Laws."

148 F.2d at 443. The same idea is reflected in Restatement (Second) of Foreign Relations Law of the United States § 40:

> Where two states have jurisdiction to prescribe and enforce rules of law and the rules they may prescribe require inconsistent conduct upon the part of a person, each state is required by international law to consider, in good faith, moderating the exercise of its enforcement jurisdiction....[26]

The act of state doctrine discussed earlier demonstrates that the judiciary is sometimes cognizant of the possible foreign implications of its action. Similar awareness should be extended to the general problems of extraterritoriality. Such acuity is especially required in private suits, like this one, for in these cases there is no opportunity for the executive branch to weigh the foreign relations impact, nor any statement implicit in the filing of the suit that that consideration has been outweighed.

What we prefer is an evaluation and balancing of the relevant considerations in each case—in the words of Kingman Brewster, a "jurisdictional rule of reason." Balancing of the foreign interests involved was the approach taken by the Supreme Court in *Continental Ore Co. v. Union Carbide & Carbon Corp.*, 370 U.S. 690 (1962), where the involvement of the Canadian government in the alleged monopolization was held not to require dismissal. The Court stressed that there was no indication that the Canadian authorities approved or would have approved of the monopolization, meaning that the Canadian interest, if any, was slight and was outweighed by the American interest in condemning the restraint....

The elements to be weighed include the degree of conflict with foreign law or policy, the nationality or allegiance of the parties and the locations or principal places of business of corporations, the extent to which enforcement by either state can be expected to achieve compliance, the relative significance of effects on the United States as compared with those else-

26. This section was obviously fashioned with trade regulation problems in mind, for all five illustrations presented in the comment to this section involve such regulation. It also indicates that "jurisdictional" forbearance in the international setting is more a question of comity and fairness than one of national power.

where, the extent to which there is explicit purpose to harm or affect American commerce, the foreseeability of such effect, and the relative importance to the violations charged of conduct within the United States as compared with conduct abroad.[27] A court evaluating these factors should identify the potential degree of conflict if American authority is asserted. A difference in law or policy is one likely sore spot, though one which may not always be present. Nationality is another; though foreign governments may have some concern for the treatment of American citizens and business residing there, they primarily care about their own nationals.[28] Having assessed the conflict, the court should then determine whether in the face of it the contacts and interests of the United States are sufficient to support the exercise of extraterritorial jurisdiction.[29]

We conclude, then, that the problem should be approached in three parts: Does the alleged restraint affect, or was it intended to affect, the foreign commerce of the United States? Is it of such a type and magnitude so as to be cognizable as a violation of the Sherman Act? As a matter of

---

27. Restatement (Second) of Foreign Relations Law of the United States § 40 states that a court should act in the light of such factors as (a) vital national interests of each of the states,

> (b) the extent and the nature of the hardship that inconsistent enforcement actions would impose upon the person,

> (c) the extent to which the required conduct is to take place in the territory of the other state,

> (d) the nationality of the person, and

> (e) the extent to which enforcement by action of either state can reasonably be expected to achieve compliance with the rule prescribed by that state.

President (then Professor) Brewster lists these variables:

> (a) the relative significance to the violations charged of conduct within the United States as compared with conduct abroad; (b) the extent to which there is explicit purpose to harm or affect American consumers or Americans' business opportunities; (c) the relative seriousness of effects on the United States compared with those abroad; (d) the nationality or allegiance of the parties or in the case of business associations, their corporate location, and the fairness of applying our law to them; (e) the degree of conflict with foreign laws and policies, and (f) the extent to which conflict can be avoided without serious impairment of the inter-

ests of the United States or the foreign country.

K. Brewster, supra at 446.

28. Some argue that a defendant's American citizenship might be enough by itself to support jurisdiction. See Restatement (Second) of Foreign Relations Law of the United States § 30.

29. In requiring district courts to assess the conflicting contacts and interests of those nations involved, we do not thereby assign them the same task which the "act of state" doctrine prohibits them from undertaking. As the quotation from comment d. to § 41 of the Restatement, Second, Foreign Relations Law of the United States (1965), see pp. 607–08, supra, makes clear, there is an important distinction between examining the validity of the "public interests" which are involved in a sovereign policy decision amounting to an "act of state" and evaluating the relative "interests" which each state may have "in providing the means of adjudicating disputes or claims that arise within its territory." Our "jurisdictional rule of reason" does not in any way require the court to question the "validity" of "foreign law or policy." Rather, the legitimacy of each nation's interests is assumed. It is merely the relative involvement and concern of each state with the suit at hand that is to be evaluated in determining whether extraterritorial jurisdiction should be exercised by American courts as a matter of comity and fairness.

international comity and fairness, should the extraterritorial jurisdiction of the United States be asserted to cover it? The district court's judgment found only that the restraint involved in the instant suit did not produce a direct and substantial effect on American foreign commerce. That holding does not satisfy any of these inquiries.

The Sherman Act is not limited to trade restraints which have both a direct and substantial effect on our foreign commerce. Timberlane has alleged that the complained of activities were intended to, and did, affect the export of lumber from Honduras to the United States—the flow of United States foreign commerce, and as such they are within the jurisdiction of the federal courts under the Sherman Act. Moreover, the magnitude of the effect alleged would appear to be sufficient to state a claim.[30]

The comity question is more complicated. From Timberlane's complaint it is evident that there are grounds for concern as to at least a few of the defendants, for some are identified as foreign citizens: Laureano Gutierrez Falla, Michael Casanova and the Casanova firms, of Honduras, and Patrick Byrne, of Canada. Moreover, it is clear that most of the activity took place in Honduras, though the conspiracy may have been directed from San Francisco, and that the most direct economic effect was probably on Honduras. However, there has been no indication of any conflict with the law or policy of the Honduran government, nor any comprehensive analysis of the relative connections and interests of Honduras and the United States. Under these circumstances, the dismissal by the district court cannot be sustained on jurisdictional grounds.

We, therefore, vacate the dismissal and remand the Timberlane action.

NOTES AND QUESTIONS

1. What foreign interests can you identify in the facts of *Timberlane*? The mere fact that the conduct in question was occurring in another country? The fact that the foreign sovereign in question had taken some positive action, if only a fairly routine court order? Is this case more or less likely to interfere with legitimate foreign regulatory interests than *Continental Ore* or *Canadian Radio Patent Pool*?

---

30. Our separation in the foreign commerce context between the degree of restraint necessary for establishing subject matter jurisdiction as opposed to that required to state a claim is, of course, not duplicated in the interstate setting, for there a "substantial" restraint is in any event necessary for the establishment of jurisdiction itself. Nevertheless, since the interstate cases provide a standard for both jurisdiction and the statement of a claim, *Hospital Building Co. v. Trustees of the Rex Hospital*, 425 U.S. 738, 742, n. 1 (1976), they thus offer some guidance for determining the degree of restraint necessary to support a claim for relief in the foreign commerce context as well.... Although the decision whether the restraint alleged in the instant case qualifies to state a claim is for the district court in the first instance, we note that the quantitative test of substantiality is a "practical, case-by-case economic judgment," not one based on "abstract or mechanistic formulae," *Rasmussen v. American Dairy Ass'n*, 472 F.2d 517, 523 (9th Cir.1972), *cert. denied* 412 U.S. 950 (1973), and that the barrier raised is not very high. *See, e.g., Hospital Building*, 425 U.S. at 743–47; *United States v. Employing Plasterers Ass'n*, 347 U.S. 186, 189 (1954).

2. *Timberlane's* "balancing" test was in part a response to long-standing criticism of Alcoa's test as insular and overly intrusive into conduct mainly of interest to other nations. One foreign observer, expressing a typical sentiment, hailed Judge Choy's approach as one that eliminated "an affront to international law occasioned by the present exercise of American antitrust jurisdiction purely on the basis of 'effects' upon American commerce." Taylor, The Extraterritoriality of Australian Antitrust Law, 13 J. Int'l L. & Econ. 273, 300 (1979).

3. The balancing test has come in for criticism as well as praise. Although at first blush it is hard to imagine defending the right to make unreasonable assertions of jurisdiction, the real question is whether jurisdictional limitations are best defined through complex balancing tests like the one adopted in *Timberlane*, or if it is better to try to confine the initial scope of jurisdiction through a clear threshold rule.

(a) The history of *Timberlane* itself casts some doubt on the efficiency and utility of the jurisdictional rule of reason. Recall that the case was filed around 1974 in the district court in California, after some years of litigation in both Honduras and in California state courts. The Ninth Circuit announced its path-breaking test in 1976. On remand, the district court (with the help of a master) allowed the parties to conduct extensive discovery, so that it would be able to evaluate the relevant factors appropriately. In 1983, the district court once again dismissed the case for lack of jurisdiction, hinting broadly that it would also have dismissed on the merits if jurisdiction were proper. 574 F.Supp. 1453 (N.D.Cal.1983). Up again on appeal to the Ninth Circuit, the Court of Appeals decided that it was not fully satisfied with the district court's application of the balancing test, and it therefore conducted yet another full-blown analysis of the factors. Finally, it concluded that jurisdiction was indeed lacking, just as the district court had initially decided nearly a decade earlier. 749 F.2d 1378 (9th Cir.1984). Ten years is a long time to spend on a "preliminary" matter like jurisdiction.

(b) Some argue that the balancing test presses judges well beyond any special competence, and perhaps authority, of the judiciary to evaluate the importance and correctness of foreign relations policies of the United States and foreign governments. Under what circumstances do you think a court would be entitled to refuse to enforce the U.S. antitrust laws where it concluded that the parties were predominantly foreign and the greater weight of the effects was felt in foreign countries, if you also assume that direct and intended effects existed in the United States and U.S. consumers were affected? Does the answer to this question depend on whether the plaintiff is a private party, the Department of Justice, or the Federal Trade Commission? What weight, if any, should the court give to a communication from the U.S. Department of State to the effect that entertaining a particular antitrust suit would have an adverse effect on U.S. foreign relations with an affected country?

(c) Whenever multiple factor tests like the *Timberlane* balancing approach exist, the point can be made that the test creates the appearance of structure without the reality of structure. The factors do not have weights attached to them; they are not capable of any kind of measurement; and there is no way to tell which ones should be able to offset which other ones. In short, virtually any result can be justified under the balancing test, no matter what facts are in the record, unless the case has such an obvious outcome that the test was unnecessary to begin with. One can always add more factors as well, as the Third Circuit did in *Mannington Mills, Inc. v. Congoleum Corp.*, 595 F.2d 1287, 1297–98 (3d Cir.1979), where it took *Timberlane* one step further and created a ten-factor test.

4. Is the *Timberlane* balancing test part of the jurisdictional inquiry, or is it more properly viewed as something like abstention? If it is the former, then what

kind of "jurisdiction" are we talking about: federal court subject matter jurisdiction, in the sense of Fed.R.Civ.P. 12(b)(1), or legislative jurisdiction, which is better addressed under Fed.R.Civ.P. 12(b)(6)? What difference does this make as a practical matter?

5.   In a case involving substantial interest to U.S. consumers, Laker Airways Ltd. v. Sabena, 731 F.2d 909 (D.C.Cir.1984), Judge Wilkey rejected the balancing approach and found in favor of U.S. jurisdiction. The liquidators of Freddie Laker's no-frills airline, Laker Airways, sued U.S. and foreign airlines—members of the International Air Transport Association, a treaty-based international cartel of air carriers which set fares that were then approved by the appropriate national authorities. Laker alleged a predatory cartel that drove his airline company out of business. At the instance of British defendants, a British court ordered Laker not to proceed against the British defendants. *British Airways v. Laker Airways Ltd.*, 1984 Q.B. 142 (C.A.1983). The injunction was later dissolved by the British House of Lords, which observed that the U.S. court was the only forum in which Laker could seek relief, *British Airways v. Laker Airways Ltd.*, 1985 A.C. 58 (1984). But before this decision, Laker brought a motion in the U.S. district court to enjoin defendants Sabena, the Belgian airline, and KLM, the Dutch airline, from trying to bring themselves under the protection of the British court's injunction. Judge Greene granted Laker's motion, holding that the district court clearly had prescriptive jurisdiction and ought to exercise it. See *Laker Airways v. Pan American World Airways*, 577 F.Supp. 348 (D.D.C.1983). The case then took a bizarre turn when, after that ruling, the plaintiffs sought an injunction that would have restrained the British airlines from petitioning Parliament for relief. After rejecting the proposition that he had no *power* to grant such an injunction, Judge Greene ultimately refused to issue it on the ground that international comity required the court to respect political processes in the U.K., and in turn required Parliament to respect the lawful jurisdiction of the U.S. court. *Laker Airways v. Pan American World Airways*, 604 F.Supp. 280 (D.D.C.1984).

B.   DEPARTMENT OF JUSTICE/FEDERAL TRADE COMMISSION INTERNATIONAL GUIDELINES

The subjects of jurisdiction and international comity are treated extensively in the 1995 Antitrust Enforcement Guidelines for International Operations, jointly issued by the U.S. Department of Justice and the Federal Trade Commission. Pertinent parts of the Guidelines (omitting the illustrative examples) are reproduced below. The full text is available on the websites of either the U.S. Department of Justice Antitrust Division, http://www.usdoj.gov/atr, or the Federal Trade Commission, http://www.ftc.gov.

U.S. Department Of Justice And Federal Trade Commission Antitrust Enforcement Guidelines For International Operations

April 1995

1.   INTRODUCTION

For more than a century, the U.S. antitrust laws have stood as the ultimate protector of the competitive process that underlies our free market economy. Through this process, which enhances consumer choice and promotes competitive prices, society as a whole benefits from the best possible allocation of resources.

Although the federal antitrust laws have always applied to foreign commerce, that application is particularly important today. Throughout the world, the importance of antitrust law as a means to ensure open and free markets, protect consumers, and prevent conduct that impedes competition is becoming more apparent. The Department of Justice ("the Department") and the Federal Trade Commission ("the Commission" or "FTC") (when referred to collectively, "the Agencies"), as the federal agencies charged with the responsibility of enforcing the antitrust laws, thus have made it a high priority to enforce the antitrust laws with respect to international operations and to cooperate wherever appropriate with foreign authorities regarding such enforcement. In furtherance of this priority, the Agencies have revised and updated the Department's 1988 Antitrust Enforcement Guidelines for International Operations, which are hereby withdrawn.[31]

The 1995 Antitrust Enforcement Guidelines for International Operations (hereinafter "Guidelines") are intended to provide antitrust guidance to businesses engaged in international operations on questions that relate specifically to the Agencies' international enforcement policy.[32] They do not, therefore, provide a complete statement of the Agencies' general enforcement policies. The topics covered include the Agencies' subject matter jurisdiction over conduct and entities outside the United States and the considerations, issues, policies, and processes that govern their decision to exercise that jurisdiction; comity; mutual assistance in international antitrust enforcement; and the effects of foreign governmental involvement on the antitrust liability of private entities. In addition, the Guidelines discuss the relationship between antitrust and international trade initiatives. Finally, to illustrate how these principles may operate in certain contexts, the Guidelines include a number of examples.

As is the case with all guidelines, users should rely on qualified counsel to assist them in evaluating the antitrust risk associated with any contemplated transaction or activity. No set of guidelines can possibly indicate how the Agencies will assess the particular facts of every case. Persons seeking more specific advance statements of enforcement intentions with respect to the matters treated in these Guidelines should use the Department's Business Review procedure,[33] the Commission's Advisory Opinion proce-

---

31. The U.S. Department of Justice and Federal Trade Commission Antitrust Guidelines for the Licensing of Intellectual Property (1995), the U.S. Department of Justice and Federal Trade Commission Horizontal Merger Guidelines (1992), and the Statements of Antitrust Enforcement Policy and Analytical Principles Relating to Health Care and Antitrust, Jointly Issued by the U.S. Department of Justice and Federal Trade Commission (1994), are not qualified, modified, or otherwise amended by the issuance of these Guidelines.

32. Readers should separately evaluate the risk of private litigation by competitors, consumers and suppliers, as well as the risk of enforcement by state prosecutors under state and federal antitrust laws.

33. 28 C.F.R. § 50.6 (1994).

dure,[34] or one of the more specific procedures described below for particular types of transactions.

2.   ANTITRUST LAWS ENFORCED BY THE AGENCIES

Foreign commerce cases can involve almost any provision of the antitrust laws. The Agencies do not discriminate in the enforcement of the antitrust laws on the basis of the nationality of the parties. Nor do the Agencies employ their statutory authority to further non-antitrust goals. Once jurisdictional requirements, comity, and doctrines of foreign governmental involvement have been considered and satisfied, the same substantive rules apply to all cases.

The following is a brief summary of the laws enforced by the Agencies that are likely to have the greatest significance for international transactions. [Sections 2.1 through 2.5 omitted.]

2.6   Webb–Pomerene Act

The Webb–Pomerene Act, 15 U.S.C. §§ 61–65, provides a limited antitrust exemption for the formation and operation of associations of otherwise competing businesses to engage in collective export sales. The exemption applies only to the export of "goods, wares, or merchandise."[35] It does not apply to conduct that has an anticompetitive effect in the United States or that injures domestic competitors of the members of an export association. Nor does it provide any immunity from prosecution under foreign antitrust laws.[36] Associations seeking an exemption under the Webb–Pomerene Act must file their articles of agreement and annual reports with the Commission, but preformation approval from the Commission is not required.

2.7   Export Trading Company Act of 1982

The Export Trading Company Act of 1982 (the "ETC Act"), Pub.L. No. 97–290, 96 Stat. 1234, is designed to increase U.S. exports of goods and services. It addresses that goal in several ways. First, in Title II, it encourages more efficient provision of export trade services to U.S. producers and suppliers by reducing restrictions on trade financing provided by financial institutions.[37] Second, in Title III, it reduces uncertainty concerning the application of the U.S. antitrust laws to export trade through the creation of a procedure by which persons engaged in U.S. export trade may obtain an export trade certificate of review ("ETCR").[38] Third, in Title IV, it clarifies the jurisdictional rules applicable to non-import cases brought under the Sherman Act and the FTC Act.[39] The Title III certificates are

---

34. 16 C.F.R. §§ 1.1–1.4 (1994).

35. 15 U.S.C. § 61 (1988).

36. See, *e.g.*, Cases 89/85, etc., *A. Ahlstrom Osakeyhtio v. Commission* ("Wood Pulp"), 1988 E.C.R. 5193, [1987–1988 Transfer Binder] Common Mkt. Rep. (CCH) ¶ 14,-491 (1988).

37. See 12 U.S.C. §§ 372, 635a–4, 1841, 1843 (1988 & Supp.1993). (Because Title II does not implicate the antitrust laws, it is not discussed further in these Guidelines.)

38. 15 U.S.C. §§ 4011–21 (1988 & Supp.1993).

39. 15 U.S.C. § 6a (1988); 15 U.S.C. § 45(a)(3) (1988).

discussed briefly here; the jurisdictional rules are treated below in Section 3.1.

Export trade certificates of review are issued by the Secretary of Commerce with the concurrence of the Attorney General. Persons named in the ETCR obtain limited immunity from suit under both state and federal antitrust laws for activities that are specified in the certificate and that comply with the terms of the certificate. To obtain an ETCR, an applicant must show that proposed export conduct will:

(1) result in neither a substantial lessening of competition or restraint of trade within the United States nor a substantial restraint of the export trade of any competitor of the applicant;

(2) not unreasonably enhance, stabilize, or depress prices in the United States of the class of goods or services covered by the application;

(3) not constitute unfair methods of competition against competitors engaged in the export of the class of goods or services exported by the applicant; and

(4) not include any act that may reasonably be expected to result in the sale for consumption or resale in the United States of such goods or services.[40]

Congress intended that these standards "encompass the full range of the antitrust laws," as defined in the ETC Act.[41]

Although an ETCR provides significant protection under the antitrust laws, it has certain limitations. First, conduct that falls outside the scope of a certificate remains fully subject to private and governmental enforcement actions. Second, an ETCR that is obtained by fraud is void from the outset and thus offers no protection under the antitrust laws. Third, any person that has been injured by certified conduct may recover actual (though not treble) damages if that conduct is found to violate any of the statutory criteria described above. In any such action, certified conduct enjoys a presumption of legality, and the prevailing party is entitled to recover costs and attorneys' fees.[42] Fourth, an ETCR does not constitute, explicitly or implicitly, an endorsement or opinion by the Secretary of Commerce or by the Attorney General concerning the legality of such business plans under the laws of any foreign country.

The Secretary of Commerce may revoke or modify an ETCR if the Secretary or the Attorney General determines that the applicant's export activities have ceased to comply with the statutory criteria for obtaining a certificate. The Attorney General may also bring suit under Section 15 of the Clayton Act to enjoin conduct that threatens "a clear and irreparable

40. 15 U.S.C. § 4013(a) (1988).

41. H.R.Rep. No. 924, 97th Cong., 2d Sess. 26 (1982). See 15 U.S.C. § 4021(6).

42. See 15 U.S.C. § 4016(b)(1) (1988) (injured party) and § 4016(b)(4) (1988) (party against whom claim is brought).

harm to the national interest,"[43] even if the conduct has been pre-approved as part of an ETCR.

The Commerce Department, in consultation with the Department, has issued guidelines setting forth the standards used in reviewing ETCR applications.[44] The ETC Guidelines contain several examples illustrating application of the certification standards to specific export trade conduct, including the use of vertical and horizontal restraints and technology licensing arrangements. In addition, the Commerce Department's Export Trading Company Guidebook[45] provides information on the functions and advantages of establishing or using an export trading company, including factors to consider in applying for an ETCR. The Commerce Department's Office of Export Trading Company Affairs provides advice and information on the formation of export trading companies and facilitates contacts between producers of exportable goods and services and firms offering export trade services.

2.8   Other Pertinent Legislation

2.81   Wilson Tariff Act

The Wilson Tariff Act, 15 U.S.C. §§ 8–11, prohibits "every combination, conspiracy, trust, agreement, or contract" made by or between two or more persons or corporations, either of whom is engaged in importing any article from a foreign country into the United States, where the agreement is intended to restrain trade or increase the market price in any part of the United States of the imported articles, or of "any manufacture into which such imported article enters or is intended to enter." Violation of the Act is a misdemeanor, punishable by a maximum fine of $5,000 or one year in prison. The Act also provides for seizure of the imported articles.[46]

2.82   Antidumping Act of 1916

The Revenue Act of 1916, better known as the Antidumping Act, 15 U.S.C. §§ 71–74, is not an antitrust statute, but its subject matter is closely related to the antitrust rules regarding predation. It is a trade statute that creates a private claim against importers who sell goods into the United States at prices substantially below the prices charged for the same goods in their home market. In order to state a claim, a plaintiff must show both that such lower prices were commonly and systematically charged, and that the importer had the specific intent to injure or destroy an industry in the United States, or to prevent the establishment of an industry. Dumping cases are more commonly brought using the administrative procedures of the Tariff Act of 1930, discussed below.

43. 15 U.S.C. § 4016(b)(5) (1988); see 15 U.S.C. § 25 (1988).

44. See Department of Commerce, International Trade Administration, Guidelines for the Issuance of Export Trade Certificates of Review (2d ed.), 50 Fed.Reg. 1786 (1985) (hereinafter "ETC Guidelines").

45. U.S. Department of Commerce, International Trade Administration, The Export Trading Company Guidebook (1984).

46. 15 U.S.C. § 11 (1988).

2.83 Tariff Act of 1930

A comprehensive discussion of the trade remedies available under the Tariff Act is beyond the scope of these Guidelines. However, because antitrust questions sometimes arise in the context of trade actions, it is appropriate to describe these laws briefly.

2.831 *Countervailing Duties*

Pursuant to Title VII.A of the Tariff Act,[47] U.S. manufacturers, producers, wholesalers, unions, and trade associations may petition for the imposition of offsetting duties on subsidized foreign imports.[48] The Department of Commerce's International Trade Administration ("ITA") must make a determination that the foreign government in question is subsidizing the imports, and in almost all cases the International Trade Commission ("ITC") must determine that a domestic industry is materially injured or threatened with material injury by reason of these imports.

2.832 *Antidumping Duties*

Pursuant to Title VII.B of the Tariff Act,[49] parties designated in the statute (the same parties as in the countervailing duties provision) may petition for antidumping duties, which must be imposed on foreign merchandise that is being, or is likely to be, sold in the United States at "less than fair value" ("LTFV"), if the U.S. industry is materially injured or threatened with material injury by imports of the foreign merchandise. The ITA makes the LTFV determination, and the ITC is responsible for the injury decision.

2.833 *Section 337*

Section 337 of the Tariff Act, 19 U.S.C. § 1337, prohibits "unfair methods of competition and unfair acts in the importation of articles into the United States," if the effect is to destroy or substantially injure a U.S. industry, or where the acts relate to importation of articles infringing U.S. patents, copyrights, trademarks, or registered mask works.[50] Complaints are filed with the ITC. The principal remedies under Section 337 are an exclusion order directing that any offending goods be excluded from entry into the United States, and a cease and desist order directed toward any offending U.S. firms and individuals.[51] The ITC is required to give the Agencies an opportunity to comment before making a final determination.[52] In addition, the Department participates in the interagency group that

---

47. See 19 U.S.C. §§ 1671 et seq. (1988 & Supp.1993), amended by Uruguay Round Agreements Act, Pub.L. No. 103–465, 108 Stat. 4809 (1994).

48. Some alternative procedures exist under Tariff Act § 701(c) for countries that have not subscribed to the World Trade Organization ("WTO") Agreement on Subsidies and Countervailing Measures or measures equivalent to it. 19 U.S.C. § 1671(c) (1988 & Supp.1993), amended by the Uruguay Round

Agreements Act, Pub.L. No. 103–465, 108 Stat. 4809 (1994).

49. See 19 U.S.C. §§ 1673 et seq. (1988).

50. 19 U.S.C. § 1337 (1988), amended by the Uruguay Round Agreements Act, Pub.L. No. 103–465, 108 Stat. 4809 (1994).

51. 19 U.S.C. §§ 1337(d), (f) (1988).

52. 19 U.S.C. § 1337(b)(2) (1988).

prepares recommendations for the President to approve, disapprove, or allow to take effect the import relief proposed by the ITC.

2.84 Trade Act of 1974

2.841 Section 201

Section 201 of the Trade Act of 1974, 19 U.S.C. §§ 2251 *et seq.*, provides that American businesses claiming serious injury due to significant increases in imports may petition the ITC for relief or modification under the so-called "escape clause." If the ITC makes a determination that "an article is being imported into the United States in such increased quantities as to be a substantial cause of serious injury, or the threat thereof, to the domestic industry producing an article like or directly competitive with the imported article," and formulates its recommendation for appropriate relief, the Department participates in the interagency committee that conducts the investigations and advises the President whether to adopt, modify, or reject the import relief recommended by the ITC.

2.842 Section 301

Section 301 of the Trade Act of 1974, 19 U.S.C. § 2411, provides that the U.S. Trade Representative ("USTR"), subject to the specific direction, if any, of the President, may take action, including restricting imports, to enforce rights of the United States under any trade agreement, to address acts inconsistent with the international legal rights of the United States, or to respond to unjustifiable, unreasonable or discriminatory practices of foreign governments that burden or restrict U.S. commerce. Interested parties may initiate such actions through petitions to the USTR, or the USTR may itself initiate proceedings.[53] Of particular interest to antitrust enforcement is Section 301(d)(3)(B)(i)(IV), which includes among the "unreasonable" practices of foreign governments that might justify a proceeding the "toleration by a foreign government of systematic anticompetitive activities by enterprises or among enterprises in the foreign country that have the effect of restricting ... access of United States goods or services to a foreign market."[54] The Department participates in the interagency committee that makes recommendations to the President on what actions, if any, should be taken.

2.9 Relevant International Agreements

To further the twin goals of promoting enforcement cooperation between the United States and foreign governments and of reducing any tensions that may arise in particular proceedings, the Agencies have developed close relationships with antitrust and competition policy officials of many different countries. In some instances, understandings have been

---

53. 19 U.S.C. § 2412(a), (b) (1988), amended by the Uruguay Round Agreements Act, Pub.L. No. 103–465, 108 Stat. 4809 (1994); see also Identification of Trade Expansion Priorities, Exec. Order No. 12,901, 59 Fed.Reg. 10,727 (1994).

54. 19 U.S.C. § 2411(d)(3)(B)(i)(IV) (1988), amended by the Uruguay Round Agreements Act, Pub.L. No. 103–465, 108 Stat. 4809 (1994), § 314(c).

reached with respect to notifications, consultations, and cooperation in antitrust matters.[55] In other instances, more general rules endorsed by multilateral organizations such as the Organization for Economic Cooperation and Development ("OECD") provide the basis for the Agencies' cooperative policies. Finally, even in the absence of specific or general international understandings or recommendations, the Agencies often seek cooperation with foreign authorities.

2.91 Bilateral Cooperation Agreements

Formal written bilateral arrangements exist between the United States and the Federal Republic of Germany, Australia, and Canada.[56] International antitrust cooperation can also occur through mutual legal assistance treaties ("MLATs"), which are treaties of general application pursuant to which the United States and a foreign country agree to assist one another in criminal law enforcement matters. MLATs currently are in force with over one dozen countries, and many more are in the process of ratification or negotiation. However, only the MLAT with Canada has been used to date to obtain assistance in antitrust investigations.[57] The Agencies also hold regular consultations with the antitrust officials of Canada, the European Commission, and Japan, and have close, informal ties with the antitrust authorities of many other countries. Since 1990, the Agencies have cooperated closely with countries in the process of establishing competition agencies, assisted by funding provided by the Agency for International Development.

On November 2, 1994, President Clinton signed into law the International Antitrust Enforcement Assistance Act of 1994,[58] which authorizes

55. Chapter 15 of the North American Free Trade Agreement ("NAFTA") addresses competition policy matters and commits the Parties to cooperate on antitrust matters. North American Free Trade Agreement Between the Government of the United States of America, the Government of Canada and the Government of the United Mexican States, 32 I.L.M. 605, 663 (1993), reprinted in H.R. Doc. No. 159, 103d Cong., 1st Sess. 712, 1170–1174 (1993).

56. See Agreement Relating to Mutual Cooperation Regarding Restrictive Business Practices, June 23, 1976, U.S.–Federal Republic of Germany, 27 U.S.T. 1956, T.I.S. No. 8291, reprinted in 4 Trade Reg.Rep. (CCH) ¶ 13,501; Agreement Between the Government of the United States of America and the Government of Australia Relating to Cooperation on Antitrust Matters, June 29, 1982, U.S.–Australia, T.I.A.S. No. 10365, reprinted in 4 Trade Reg.Rep. (CCH) ¶ 13,502; and Memorandum of Understanding as to Notification, Consultation, and Cooperation with Respect to the Application of National Antitrust Laws, March 9, 1984, U.S.–Canada, re-

printed in 4 Trade Reg.Rep. (CCH) ¶ 13,503. The Agencies also signed a similar agreement with the Commission of the European Communities in 1991. See Agreement Between the Government of the United States of America and the Commission of the European Communities Regarding the Application of Their Competition Laws, Sept. 23, 1991, 30 I.L.M. 1491 (Nov. 1991), reprinted in 4 Trade Reg.Rep. (CCH) ¶ 13,504. However, on August 9, 1994, the European Court of Justice ruled that the conclusion of the Agreement did not comply with institutional requirements of the law of the European Union ("EU"). Under the Court's decision, action by the EU Council of Ministers is necessary for this type of agreement. See French Republic v. Commission of European Communities (No. C–327/91) (Aug. 9, 1994).

57. Treaty with Canada on Mutual Legal Assistance in Criminal Matters, S. Treaty Doc. No. 28, 100th Cong., 2d Sess. (1988).

58. Pub.L. No. 103–438, 108 Stat. 4597 (1994).

the Agencies to enter into antitrust mutual assistance agreements in accordance with the legislation.

2.92   International Guidelines and Recommendations

The Agencies have agreed with respect to member countries of the OECD to consider the legitimate interests of other nations in accordance with relevant OECD recommendations.[59] Under the terms of a 1986 recommendation, the United States agency with responsibility for a particular case notifies a member country whenever an antitrust enforcement action may affect important interests of that country or its nationals.[60] Examples of potentially notifiable actions include requests for documents located outside the United States, attempts to obtain information from potential witnesses located outside the United States, and cases or investigations with significant foreign conduct or involvement of foreign persons.

3.   THRESHOLD INTERNATIONAL ENFORCEMENT ISSUES

3.1   Jurisdiction

Just as the acts of U.S. citizens in a foreign nation ordinarily are subject to the law of the country in which they occur, the acts of foreign citizens in the United States ordinarily are subject to U.S. law. The reach of the U.S. antitrust laws is not limited, however, to conduct and transactions that occur within the boundaries of the United States. Anticompetitive conduct that affects U.S. domestic or foreign commerce may violate the U.S. antitrust laws regardless of where such conduct occurs or the nationality of the parties involved.

Under the Sherman Act and the FTC Act, there are two principal tests for subject matter jurisdiction in foreign commerce cases. With respect to foreign import commerce, the Supreme Court has recently stated in *Hartford Fire Insurance Co. v. California* that "the Sherman Act applies to foreign conduct that was meant to produce and did in fact produce some substantial effect in the United States."[61] There has been no such authori-

---

59. See Revised Recommendation of the OECD Council Concerning Cooperation Between Member Countries on Restrictive Business Practices Affecting International Trade, OECD Doc. No. C(86)44 (Final) (May 21, 1986). The Recommendation also calls for countries to consult with each other in appropriate situations, with the aim of promoting enforcement cooperation and minimizing differences that may arise.

60. The OECD has 25 member countries and the European Commission takes part in its work. The OECD's membership includes many of the most advanced market economies in the world. The OECD also has several observer nations, which have made rapid progress toward open market economies. The Agencies follow recommended OECD practices with respect to all member countries.

61. 113 S.Ct. 2891, 2909 (1993). In a world in which economic transactions observe no boundaries, international recognition of the "effects doctrine" of jurisdiction has become more widespread. In the context of import trade, the "implementation" test adopted in the European Court of Justice usually produces the same outcome as the "effects" test employed in the United States. See Cases 89/85, etc., *Ahlstrom v. Commission*, supra at note 36. The merger laws of the European Union, Canada, Germany, France, Australia, and the Czech and Slovak Republics, among others, take a similar approach.

tative ruling on the scope of the FTC Act, but both Acts apply to commerce "with foreign nations" and the Commission has held that terms used by both Acts should be construed together.[62] Second, with respect to foreign commerce other than imports, the Foreign Trade Antitrust Improvements Act of 1982 ("FTAIA") applies to foreign conduct that has a direct, substantial, and reasonably foreseeable effect on U.S. commerce.[63]

3.11   Jurisdiction Over Conduct Involving Import Commerce

Imports into the United States by definition affect the U.S. domestic market directly, and will, therefore, almost invariably satisfy the intent part of the Hartford Fire test. Whether they in fact produce the requisite substantial effects will depend on the facts of each case.

3.12   Jurisdiction Over Conduct Involving Other Foreign Commerce

With respect to foreign commerce other than imports, the jurisdictional limits of the Sherman Act and the FTC Act are delineated in the FTAIA. [Text omitted; see p. 1192 supra.]

3.121   Jurisdiction in Cases Under Subsection 1(A) of the FTAIA

To the extent that conduct in foreign countries does not "involve" import commerce but does have an "effect" on either import transactions or commerce within the United States, the Agencies apply the "direct, substantial, and reasonably foreseeable" standard of the FTAIA. That standard is applied, for example, in cases in which a cartel of foreign enterprises, or a foreign monopolist, reaches the U.S. market through any mechanism that goes beyond direct sales, such as the use of an unrelated intermediary, as well as in cases in which foreign vertical restrictions or intellectual property licensing arrangements have an anticompetitive effect on U.S. commerce.

3.122   Jurisdiction in Cases Under Subsection 1(B) of the FTAIA

Two categories of "export cases" fall within the FTAIA's jurisdictional test. First, the Agencies may, in appropriate cases, take enforcement action against anticompetitive conduct, wherever occurring, that restrains U.S. exports, if (1) the conduct has a direct, substantial, and reasonably foreseeable effect on exports of goods or services from the United States, and (2) the U.S. courts can obtain jurisdiction over persons or corporations engaged in such conduct.[64] As Section 3.2 below explains more fully, if the conduct is unlawful under the importing country's antitrust laws as well, the Agencies are also prepared to work with that country's authorities if they are better situated to remedy the conduct, and if they are prepared to take action that will address the U.S. concerns, pursuant to their antitrust laws.

---

62. *In re Massachusetts Bd. of Registration in Optometry*, 110 F.T.C. 598, 609 (1988).

63. 15 U.S.C. § 6a (1988) (Sherman Act) and § 45(a)(3) (1988) (FTC Act).

64. See U.S. Department of Justice Press Release dated April 3, 1992 (announc-ing enforcement policy that would permit the Department to challenge foreign business conduct that harms U.S. exports when the conduct would have violated U.S. antitrust laws if it occurred in the United States).

Second, the Agencies may in appropriate cases take enforcement action against conduct by U.S. exporters that has a direct, substantial, and reasonably foreseeable effect on trade or commerce within the United States, or on import trade or commerce. This can arise in two principal ways. First, if U.S. supply and demand were not particularly elastic, an agreement among U.S. firms accounting for a substantial share of the relevant market, regarding the level of their exports, could reduce supply and raise prices in the United States.[65] Second, conduct ostensibly export-related could affect the price of products sold or resold in the United States. This kind of effect could occur if, for example, U.S. firms fixed the price of an input used to manufacture a product overseas for ultimate resale in the United States.

3.13   Jurisdiction When U.S. Government Finances or Purchases

The Agencies may, in appropriate cases, take enforcement action when the U.S. Government is a purchaser, or substantially funds the purchase, of goods or services for consumption or use abroad. Cases in which the effect of anticompetitive conduct with respect to the sale of these goods or services falls primarily on U.S. taxpayers may qualify for redress under the federal antitrust laws.[66] As a general matter, the Agencies consider there to be a sufficient effect on U.S. commerce to support the assertion of jurisdiction if, as a result of its payment or financing, the U.S. Government bears more than half the cost of the transaction. For purposes of this determination, the Agencies apply the standards used in certifying export conduct under the ETC Act of 1982, 15 U.S.C. §§ 4011–21 (1982).[67]

3.14   Jurisdiction Under Section 7 of the Clayton Act

Section 7 of the Clayton Act applies to mergers and acquisitions between firms that are engaged in commerce or in any activity affecting

---

65. One would need to show more than indirect price effects resulting from legitimate export efforts to support an antitrust challenge. See ETC Guidelines, supra at note 44, 50 Fed.Reg. at 1791.

66. Cf. *United States v. Concentrated Phosphate Export Ass'n*, 393 U.S. 199, 208 (1968) ("[A]lthough the fertilizer shipments were consigned to Korea and although in most cases Korea formally let the contracts, American participation was the overwhelmingly dominant feature. The burden of noncompetitive pricing fell, not on any foreign purchaser, but on the American taxpayer. The United States was, in essence, furnishing fertilizer to Korea.... The foreign elements in the transaction were, by comparison, insignificant."); *United States v. Standard Tallow Corp.*, 1988–1 Trade Cas. (CCH) ¶ 67,913 (S.D.N.Y.1988) (consent decree) (barring suppliers from fixing prices or rigging bids for the sale of tallow financed in whole or in part through grants or loans by the U.S. Govern-

ment); *United States v. Anthracite Export Ass'n*, 1970 Trade Cas. (CCH) ¶ 73,348 (M.D.Pa.1970) (consent decree) (barring price-fixing, bid-rigging, and market allocation in Army foreign aid program).

67. See ETC Guidelines, supra at note 44, 50 Fed.Reg. at 1799–1800. The requisite U.S. Government involvement could include the actual purchase of goods by the U.S. Government for shipment abroad, a U.S. Government grant to a foreign government that is specifically earmarked for the transaction, or a U.S. Government loan specifically earmarked for the transaction that is made on such generous terms that it amounts to a grant. U.S. Government interests would not be considered to be sufficiently implicated with respect to a transaction that is funded by an international agency, or a transaction in which the foreign government received non-earmarked funds from the United States as part of a general government-to-government aid program.

commerce. The Agencies would apply the same principles regarding their foreign commerce jurisdiction to Clayton Section 7 cases as they would apply in Sherman Act cases.

3.2   Comity

In enforcing the antitrust laws, the Agencies consider international comity. Comity itself reflects the broad concept of respect among co-equal sovereign nations and plays a role in determining "the recognition which one nation allows within its territory to the legislative, executive or judicial acts of another nation."[68] Thus, in determining whether to assert jurisdiction to investigate or bring an action, or to seek particular remedies in a given case, each Agency takes into account whether significant interests of any foreign sovereign would be affected.[69]

In performing a comity analysis, the Agencies take into account all relevant factors. Among others, these may include (1) the relative significance to the alleged violation of conduct within the United States, as compared to conduct abroad; (2) the nationality of the persons involved in or affected by the conduct; (3) the presence or absence of a purpose to affect U.S. consumers, markets, or exporters; (4) the relative significance and foreseeability of the effects of the conduct on the United States as compared to the effects abroad; (5) the existence of reasonable expectations that would be furthered or defeated by the action; (6) the degree of conflict with foreign law or articulated foreign economic policies; (7) the extent to which the enforcement activities of another country with respect to the same persons, including remedies resulting from those activities, may be affected; and (8) the effectiveness of foreign enforcement as compared to U.S. enforcement action.[70]

The relative weight that each factor should be given depends on the facts and circumstances of each case. With respect to the factor concerning conflict with foreign law, the Supreme Court made clear in *Hartford Fire*[71] that no conflict exists for purposes of an international comity analysis in the courts if the person subject to regulation by two states can comply with the laws of both. Bearing this in mind, the Agencies first ask what laws or policies of the arguably interested foreign jurisdictions are implicated by the conduct in question. There may be no actual conflict between the antitrust enforcement interests of the United States and the laws or policies of a foreign sovereign. This is increasingly true as more countries adopt antitrust or competition laws that are compatible with those of the United States. In these cases, the anticompetitive conduct in question may also be prohibited under the pertinent foreign laws, and thus the possible

---

68.   *Hilton v. Guyot*, 159 U.S. 113, 164 (1895).

69.   The Agencies have agreed to consider the legitimate interests of other nations in accordance with the recommendations of the OECD and various bilateral agreements, see *supra* at Section 2.9.

70.   The first six of these factors are based on previous Department Guidelines. The seventh and eighth factors are derived from considerations in the U.S.–EC Antitrust Cooperation Agreement. See supra at note 56.

71.   113 S.Ct. 2891, 2910.

conflict would relate to enforcement practices or remedy. If the laws or policies of a foreign nation are neutral, it is again possible for the parties in question to comply with the U.S. prohibition without violating foreign law.

The Agencies also take full account of comity factors beyond whether there is a conflict with foreign law. In deciding whether or not to challenge an alleged antitrust violation, the Agencies would, as part of a comity analysis, consider whether one country encourages a certain course of conduct, leaves parties free to choose among different strategies, or prohibits some of those strategies. In addition, the Agencies take into account the effect of their enforcement activities on related enforcement activities of a foreign antitrust authority. For example, the Agencies would consider whether their activities would interfere with or reinforce the objectives of the foreign proceeding, including any remedies contemplated or obtained by the foreign antitrust authority.

The Agencies also will consider whether the objectives sought to be obtained by the assertion of U.S. law would be achieved in a particular instance by foreign enforcement. In lieu of bringing an enforcement action, the Agencies may consult with interested foreign sovereigns through appropriate diplomatic channels to attempt to eliminate anticompetitive effects in the United States.

In cases where the United States decides to prosecute an antitrust action, such a decision represents a determination by the Executive Branch that the importance of antitrust enforcement outweighs any relevant foreign policy concerns.[72] The Department does not believe that it is the role of the courts to "second-guess the executive branch's judgment as to the proper role of comity concerns under these circumstances."[73] To date, no Commission cases have presented the issue of the degree of deference that courts should give to the Commission's comity decisions.[74] It is important also to note that in disputes between private parties, many courts are willing to undertake a comity analysis.[75]

3.3 Effects of Foreign Government Involvement

Foreign governments may be involved in a variety of ways in conduct that may have antitrust consequences. To address the implications of such foreign governmental involvement, Congress and the courts have developed four special doctrines: the doctrine of foreign sovereign immunity; the doctrine of foreign sovereign compulsion; the act of state doctrine; and the

---

72. Foreign policy concerns may also lead the United States not to prosecute a case. *See, e.g.,* U.S. Department of Justice Press Release dated Nov. 19, 1984 (announcing the termination, based on foreign policy concerns, of a grand jury investigation into passenger air travel between the United States and the United Kingdom).

73. *United States v. Baker Hughes, Inc.,* 731 F.Supp. 3, 6 n. 5 (D.D.C.1990), aff'd, 908 F.2d 981 (D.C.Cir.1990).

74. Like the Department, the Commission considers comity issues and consults with foreign antitrust authorities, but the Commission is not part of the Executive Branch.

75. *See, e.g., Timberlane Lumber Co. v. Bank of America,* 549 F.2d 597 (9th Cir. 1976).

application of the *Noerr–Pennington* doctrine to immunize the lobbying of foreign governments. Although these doctrines are interrelated, for purposes of discussion the Guidelines discuss each one individually.

3.31 Foreign Sovereign Immunity

The scope of immunity of a foreign government or its agencies and instrumentalities (hereinafter foreign government)[76] from the jurisdiction of the U.S. courts for all causes of action, including antitrust, is governed by the Foreign Sovereign Immunities Act of 1976 ("FSIA").[77] Subject to the treaties in place at the time of FSIA's enactment, a foreign government is immune from suit except where designated in the FSIA.[78]

Under the FSIA, a U.S. court has jurisdiction if the foreign government has:

(a) waived its immunity explicitly or by implication,

(b) engaged in commercial activity as described in the statute,

(c) expropriated property in violation of international law,

(d) acquired rights to U.S. property,

(e) committed certain torts within the United States, or agree to arbitration of a dispute.[79]

The commercial activities exception is a frequently invoked exception to sovereign immunity under the FSIA. Under the FSIA, a foreign government is not immune in any case:

in which the action is based upon a commercial activity carried on in the United States by the foreign state; or upon an act performed in the United States in connection with a commercial activity of the foreign state elsewhere; or upon an act outside the territory of the United States in connection with a commercial activity of the foreign state elsewhere and that act causes a direct effect in the United States.[80]

"Commercial activity of the foreign state" is not defined in the FSIA, but is to be determined by the "nature of the course of conduct or particular transaction or act, rather than by reference to its purpose."[81] In attempting to differentiate commercial from sovereign activity, courts have considered whether the conduct being challenged is customarily performed

---

76. Section 1603(b) of the Foreign Sovereign Immunities Act of 1976 defines an "agency or instrumentality of a foreign state" to be any entity "(1) which is a separate legal person, corporate or otherwise; and (2) which is an organ of a foreign state or political subdivision thereof, or a majority of whose shares or other ownership interest is owned by a foreign state or political subdivision thereof; and (3) which is neither a citizen of a State of the United States as defined in Section 1332(c) and (d) of [Title 28, U.S.Code], nor created under the laws of any

third country." 28 U.S.C. § 1603(b) (1988). It is not uncommon in antitrust cases to see state-owned enterprises meeting this definition.

77. 28 U.S.C. §§ 1602, et seq. (1988).

78. 28 U.S.C. § 1604 (1988 & Supp. 1993).

79. 28 U.S.C. § 1605(a)(1–6) (1988).

80. 28 U.S.C. § 1605(a)(2) (1988).

81. 28 U.S.C. § 1603(d) (1988).

for profit[82] and whether the conduct is of a type that only a sovereign government can perform.[83] As a practical matter, most activities of foreign government-owned corporations operating in the commercial marketplace will be subject to U.S. antitrust laws to the same extent as the activities of foreign privately-owned firms.

The commercial activity also must have a substantial nexus with the United States before a foreign government is subject to suit. The FSIA sets out three different standards for meeting this requirement. First, the challenged conduct by the foreign government may occur in the United States.[84] Alternatively, the challenged commercial activity may entail an act performed in the United States in connection with a commercial activity of the foreign government elsewhere.[85] Or, finally, the challenged commercial activity of a foreign government outside of the United States may produce a direct effect within the United States, *i.e.*, an effect which follows "as an immediate consequence of the defendant's . . . activity."[86]

3.32 Foreign Sovereign Compulsion

Although U.S. antitrust jurisdiction extends to conduct and parties in foreign countries whose actions have the required effects on U.S. commerce, as discussed above, those parties may find themselves subject to conflicting requirements from the other country (or countries) where they are located.[87] Under *Hartford Fire*, if it is possible for the party to comply both with the foreign law and the U.S. antitrust laws, the existence of the

82. See, *e.g., Republic of Argentina v. Weltover, Inc.*, 112 S.Ct. 2160 (1992); *Schoenberg v. Exportadora de Sal, S.A. de C.V.*, 930 F.2d 777 (9th Cir.1991); *Rush–Presbyterian–St. Luke's Medical Ctr. v. Hellenic Republic*, 877 F.2d 574, 578 n. 4 (7th Cir.), *cert. denied*, 493 U.S. 937 (1989).

83. See, *e.g., Saudi Arabia v. Nelson*, 113 S.Ct. 1471 (1993); *de Sanchez v. Banco Central de Nicaragua*, 770 F.2d 1385 (5th Cir.1985); *Letelier v. Republic of Chile*, 748 F.2d 790, 797–98 (2d Cir.1984), *cert. denied*, 471 U.S. 1125 (1985); *International Ass'n of Machinists & Aerospace Workers v. Organization of Petroleum Exporting Countries*, 477 F.Supp. 553 (C.D.Cal.1979), aff'd on other grounds, 649 F.2d 1354 (9th Cir.1981), *cert. denied*, 454 U.S. 1163 (1982).

84. 28 U.S.C. § 1603(e) (1988).

85. See H.R.Rep. No. 1487, 94th Cong., 2d Sess. 18–19 (1976), reprinted in 1976 U.S.C.C.A.N. 6604, 6617–18 (providing as an example the wrongful termination in the United States of an employee of a foreign state employed in connection with commercial activity in a third country). *But see Filus v. LOT Polish Airlines*, 907 F.2d 1328, 1333 (2d Cir.1990) (holding as too attenuated the failure to warn of a defective product sold outside of the United States in connection with an accident outside the United States.)

86. *Republic of Argentina*, 112 S.Ct. at 2168. This test is similar to proximate cause formulations adopted by other courts. See *Martin v. Republic of South Africa*, 836 F.2d 91, 95 (2d Cir.1987) (a direct effect is one with no intervening element which flows in a straight line without deviation or interruption), quoting *Upton v. Empire of Iran*, 459 F.Supp. 264, 266 (D.D.C.1978), *aff'd mem.*, 607 F.2d 494 (D.C.Cir.1979).

87. Conduct by private entities not required by law is entirely outside of the protections afforded by this defense. See *Continental Ore Co. v. Union Carbide & Carbon Corp.*, 370 U.S. 690, 706 (1962); *United States v. Watchmakers of Switzerland Info. Ctr., Inc.*, 1963 Trade Cas. (CCH) ¶ 70,600 at 77,456–57 (S.D.N.Y.1962) ("[T]he fact that the Swiss Government may, as a practical matter, approve the effects of this private activity cannot convert what is essentially a vulnerable private conspiracy into an unassailable system resulting from a foreign government mandate.") See supra at Section 3.2.

foreign law does not provide any legal excuse for actions that do not comply with U.S. law. However, a direct conflict may arise when the facts demonstrate that the foreign sovereign has compelled the very conduct that the U.S. antitrust law prohibits.

In these circumstances, at least one court has recognized a defense under the U.S. antitrust laws, and the Agencies will also recognize it.[88] There are two rationales underlying the defense of foreign sovereign compulsion. First, Congress enacted the U.S. antitrust laws against the background of well recognized principles of international law and comity among nations, pursuant to which U.S. authorities give due deference to the official acts of foreign governments. A defense for actions taken under the circumstances spelled out below serves to accommodate two equal sovereigns. Second, important considerations of fairness to the defendant require some mechanism that provides a predictable rule of decision for those seeking to conform their behavior to all pertinent laws.

Because of the limited scope of the defense, the Agencies will refrain from enforcement actions on the ground of foreign sovereign compulsion only when certain criteria are satisfied. First, the foreign government must have compelled the anticompetitive conduct under circumstances in which a refusal to comply with the foreign government's command would give rise to the imposition of penal or other severe sanctions. As a general matter, the Agencies regard the foreign government's formal representation that refusal to comply with its command would have such a result as being sufficient to establish that the conduct in question has been compelled, as long as that representation contains sufficient detail to enable the Agencies to see precisely how the compulsion would be accomplished under local law.[89] Foreign government measures short of compulsion do not suffice for this defense, although they can be relevant in a comity analysis.

Second, although there can be no strict territorial test for this defense, the defense normally applies only when the foreign government compels conduct which can be accomplished entirely within its own territory. If the compelled conduct occurs in the United States, the Agencies will not recognize the defense.[90] For example, no defense arises when a foreign

---

88. *Interamerican Refining Corp. v. Texaco Maracaibo, Inc.*, 307 F.Supp. 1291 (D.Del.1970) (defendant, having been ordered by the government of Venezuela not to sell oil to a particular refiner out of favor with the current political regime, held not subject to antitrust liability under the Sherman Act for an illegal group boycott). The defense of foreign sovereign compulsion is distinguished from the federalism-based state action doctrine. The state action doctrine applies not just to the actions of states and their subdivisions, but also to private anticompetitive conduct that is both undertaken pursuant to clearly articulated state policies, and is actively supervised by the state. See *Federal Trade Comm'n v. Ticor Title Insurance Co.*, 112 S.Ct. 2169 (1992); *California Retail Liquor Dealers Ass'n v. Midcal Aluminum, Inc.*, 445 U.S. 97, 105 (1980); *Parker v. Brown*, 317 U.S. 341 (1943).

89. For example, the Agencies may not regard as dispositive a statement that is ambiguous or that on its face appears to be internally inconsistent. The Agencies may inquire into the circumstances underlying the statement and they may also request further information if the source of the power to compel is unclear.

90. See *Linseman v. World Hockey Ass'n*, 439 F.Supp. 1315, 1325 (D.Conn.1977).

government requires the U.S. subsidiaries of several firms to organize a cartel in the United States to fix the price at which products would be sold in the United States, or when it requires its firms to fix mandatory resale prices for their U.S. distributors to use in the United States.

Third, with reference to the discussion of foreign sovereign immunity in Section 3.31 above, the order must come from the foreign government acting in its governmental capacity. The defense does not arise from conduct that would fall within the FSIA commercial activity exception.

3.33   Acts of State

The act of state doctrine is a judge-made rule of federal common law.[91] It is a doctrine of judicial abstention based on considerations of international comity and separation of powers, and applies only if the specific conduct complained of is a public act of the foreign sovereign within its territorial jurisdiction on matters pertaining to its governmental sovereignty. The act of state doctrine arises when the validity of the acts of a foreign government is an unavoidable issue in a case.[92]

Courts have refused to adjudicate claims or issues that would require the court to judge the legality (as a matter of U.S. law or international law) of the sovereign act of a foreign state.[93] Although in some cases the sovereign act in question may compel private behavior, such compulsion is not required by the doctrine.[94] While the act of state doctrine does not compel dismissal as a matter of course, judicial abstention is appropriate in a case where the court must "declare invalid, and thus ineffective as a rule of decision in the U.S. courts, ... the official act of a foreign sovereign."[95]

When a restraint on competition arises directly from the act of a foreign sovereign, such as the grant of a license, award of a contract, expropriation of property, or the like, the Agencies may refrain from bringing an enforcement action based on the act of state doctrine. For example, the Agencies will not challenge foreign acts of state if the facts and circumstances indicate that: (1) the specific conduct complained of is a public act of the sovereign, (2) the act was taken within the territorial jurisdiction of the sovereign, and (3) the matter is governmental, rather than commercial.

3.34   Petitioning of Sovereigns

Under the *Noerr–Pennington* doctrine, a genuine effort to obtain or influence action by governmental entities in the United States is immune from application of the Sherman Act, even if the intent or effect of that

---

91. *Banco Nacional de Cuba v. Sabbatino*, 376 U.S. 398, 421–22 n. 21 (1964) (noting that other countries do not adhere in any formulaic way to an act of state doctrine).

92. See *W.S. Kirkpatrick & Co. v. Environmental Tectonics Corp.*, 493 U.S. 400 (1990).

93. *International Ass'n of Machinists and Aerospace Workers v. Organization of Petroleum Exporting Countries*, 649 F.2d 1354, 1358 (9th Cir.1981), *cert. denied*, 454 U.S. 1163 (1982).

94. See *Timberlane*, supra at note 75, 549 F.2d at 606–08.

95. *Kirkpatrick*, 493 U.S. at 405, quoting *Ricaud v. American Metal Co.*, 246 U.S. 304, 310 (1918).

effort is to restrain or monopolize trade.[96] Whatever the basis asserted for *Noerr–Pennington* immunity (either as an application of the First Amendment or as a limit on the statutory reach of the Sherman Act, or both), the Agencies will apply it in the same manner to the petitioning of foreign governments and the U.S. Government.

3.4 Antitrust Enforcement and International Trade Regulation

There has always been a close relationship between the international application of the antitrust laws and the policies and rules governing the international trade of the United States. Restrictions such as tariffs or quotas on the free flow of goods affect market definition, consumer choice, and supply options for U.S. producers. In certain instances, the U.S. trade laws set forth specific procedures for settling disputes under those laws, which can involve price and quantity agreements by the foreign firms involved. When those procedures are followed, an implied antitrust immunity results.[97] However, agreements among competitors that do not comply with the law, or go beyond the measures authorized by the law, do not enjoy antitrust immunity. In the absence of legal authority, the fact, without more, that U.S. or foreign government officials were involved in or encouraged measures that would otherwise violate the antitrust laws does not immunize such arrangements.[98]

If a particular voluntary export restraint does not qualify for express or implied immunity from the antitrust laws, then the legality of the arrangement would depend upon the existence of the ordinary elements of an antitrust offense, such as whether or not a prohibited agreement exists or whether defenses such as foreign sovereign compulsion can be invoked.

96. See *Eastern R.R. Presidents Conference v. Noerr Motor Freight, Inc.*, 365 U.S. 127 (1961); *United Mine Workers of Am. v. Pennington*, 381 U.S. 657 (1965); *California Motor Transp. Co. v. Trucking Unlimited*, 404 U.S. 508 (1972) (extending protection to petitioning before "all departments of Government," including the courts); *Professional Real Estate Investors, Inc. v. Columbia Pictures Indus.*, 113 S.Ct. 1920 (1993). However, this immunity has never applied to "sham" activities, in which petitioning "ostensibly directed toward influencing governmental action, is a mere sham to cover . . . an attempt to interfere directly with the business relationships of a competitor." *Professional Real Estate Investors*, 113 S.Ct. at 1926, quoting *Noerr*, 365 U.S. at 144. See also *USS–Posco Indus. v. Contra Costa Cty. Bldg. Constr. Council, AFL–CIO*, 31 F.3d 800 (9th Cir. 1994).

97. See, *e.g.*, Letter from Charles F. Rule, Acting Assistant Attorney General, Antitrust Division, Department of Justice, to Mr. Makoto Kuroda, Vice–Minister for International Affairs, Japanese Ministry of International Trade and Industry, July 30, 1986 (concluding that a suspension agreement did not violate U.S. antitrust laws on the basis of factual representations that the agreement applied only to products under investigation, that it did not require pricing above levels needed to eliminate sales below foreign market value, and that assigning weighted-average foreign market values to exporters who were not respondents in the investigation was necessary to achieve the purpose of the antidumping law).

98. Cf. *United States v. Socony–Vacuum Oil Co.*, 310 U.S. 150, 226 (1940) ("Though employees of the government may have known of those programs and winked at them or tacitly approved them, no immunity would have thereby been obtained. For Congress had specified the precise manner and method of securing immunity [in the National Industrial Recovery Act]. None other would suffice. . . ."); see also *Otter Tail Power Co. v. United States*, 410 U.S. 366, 378–79 (1973).

4. PERSONAL JURISDICTION AND PROCEDURAL RULES

4.1 Personal Jurisdiction And Venue

The Agencies will bring suit only if they conclude that personal jurisdiction exists under the due process clause of the U.S. Constitution.[99] The Constitution requires that the defendant have affiliating or minimum contacts with the United States, such that the proceeding comports with "fair play and substantial justice."[1]

Section 12 of the Clayton Act, 15 U.S.C. § 22, provides that any suit under the antitrust laws against a corporation may be brought in the judicial district where it is an inhabitant, where it may be found, or where it transacts business. The concept of transacting business is interpreted pragmatically by the Agencies. Thus, a company may transact business in a particular district directly through an agent, or through a related corporation that is actually the "alter ego" of the foreign party.[2]

4.2 Investigatory Practice Relating to Foreign Nations

In conducting investigations that require documents that are located outside the United States, or contacts with persons located outside the United States, the Agencies first consider requests for voluntary cooperation when practical and consistent with enforcement objectives. When compulsory measures are needed, they seek whenever possible to work with the foreign government involved. U.S. law also provides authority in some circumstances for the use of compulsory measures directed to parties over whom the courts have personal jurisdiction, which the Agencies may use when other efforts to obtain information have been exhausted or would be unavailing.[3]

Conflicts can arise, however, where foreign statutes purport to prevent persons from disclosing documents or information for use in U.S. proceedings. However, the mere existence of such statutes does not excuse noncompliance with a request for information from one of the Agencies.[4] To enable

---

99. See also *International Shoe Co. v. Washington*, 326 U.S. 310 (1945); *Asahi Metal Industry Co. Ltd. v. Superior Court*, 480 U.S. 102 (1987).

1. *Go–Video, Inc. v. Akai Elec. Co., Ltd.*, 885 F.2d 1406, 1414 (9th Cir.1989); *Wells Fargo & Co. v. Wells Fargo Express Co.*, 556 F.2d 406, 418 (9th Cir.1977). To establish jurisdiction, parties must also be served in accordance with the Federal Rules of Civil Procedure or other relevant authority. Fed. R.Civ.P. 4(k); 15 U.S.C. §§ 22, 44.

2. See, *e.g.*, Letter from Donald S. Clark, Secretary of the Federal Trade Commission, to Caswell O. Hobbs, Esq., Morgan, Lewis & Bockius, Jan. 17, 1990 (Re: Petition to Quash Subpoena Nippon Sheet Glass, et al., File No. 891–0088, at page 3) ("The Commission ... may exercise jurisdiction over and serve process on, a foreign entity that has a related company in the United States acting as its agent or alter ego."); see also Fed.R.Civ.P. 4; *Volkswagenwerk AG v. Schlunk*, 486 U.S. 694, 707–708 (1988); *United States v. Scophony Corp.*, 333 U.S. 795, 810–818 (1948).

3. For example, 28 U.S.C. § 1783(a) (1988) authorizes a U.S. court to order the issuance of a subpoena "requiring the appearance as a witness before it, or before a person or body designated by it, of a national or resident of the United States who is in a foreign country, or requiring the production of a specified document or other thing by him," under circumstances spelled out in the statute.

4. See *Societe Internationale pour Participations Industrielles et Commerciales, S.A. v. Rogers,* 357 U.S. 197 (1958).

the Agencies to obtain evidence located abroad more effectively, as noted in Section 2.91 above, Congress recently has enacted legislation authorizing the Agencies to negotiate bilateral agreements with foreign governments or antitrust enforcement agencies to facilitate the exchange of documents and evidence in civil and criminal investigations.[5]

4.22   Hart–Scott–Rodino: Special Foreign Commerce Rules

[Section omitted.]

C.   ANTITRUST COOPERATION AGREEMENTS

Perhaps the most important recent development in the area of international comity has been the expansion of the cooperation agreements that exist among some of the major antitrust enforcement authorities of the world. The United States is now party to a number of such agreements.[6] In one, the Treaty with Canada on Mutual Legal Assistance in Criminal Matters (MLAT), S. Treaty Doc. No. 28, 100th Cong., 2d Sess. (1988), the U.S. Department of Justice and the Canadian Bureau of Competition Policy are empowered actually to conduct joint investigations, including the sharing of confidential information. This has been done successfully in a number of cases. The practical result of these cooperation agreements has been to reduce tensions over extraterritoriality, for the simple reason that agencies begin to feel free to call upon one another's resources rather than to try to act unilaterally. On November 2, 1994, the President signed the International Antitrust Enforcement Assistance Act (IAEAA), Pub.L. No. 103–438, 108 Stat. 4597 (1994), which authorizes the U.S. antitrust agencies to enter into antitrust mutual assistance agreements along the lines of the U.S.–Canada MLAT.

Most of the more recent cooperation agreements, such as the U.S.–EC agreement and the 1995 U.S.–Canada agreement, emphasize both traditional comity and so-called positive comity. The U.S. authorities promise, in those agreements, to take into account the interests of the foreign country in the course of their enforcement activities. In the 1995 International Guidelines, § 3.2, the Agencies list eight non-exclusive factors that they consider:

---

5. International Antitrust Enforcement Assistance Act of 1994, Pub.L. No. 103–438, 108 Stat. 4597 (1994).

6. See Agreement Relating to Mutual Cooperation Regarding Restrictive Business Practices, June 23, 1976, U.S.–Federal Republic of Germany, 27 U.S.T. 1956, T.I.S. No. 8291, reprinted in 4 Trade Reg.Rep. (CCH) ¶ 13,501; Agreement Between the Government of the United States and the Government of Australia Relating to Cooperation on Antitrust Matters, June 29, 1982, U.S.–Australia, T.I.A.S. No. 10365, reprinted in 4 Trade Reg.Rep. (CCH) ¶ 13,502; the Agreement Between the Government of The United States of America and The Government of Canada Regarding the Application of Their Competition and Deceptive Marketing Practices Laws, U.S.–Canada, reprinted in 4 Trade Reg.Rep. (CCH) ¶ 13,503; and the Agreement Between the Government of the United States of America and the Council of the European Communities Regarding the Application of Their Competition Laws, Sept. 23, 1991, 30 I.L.M. 1491 (Nov. 1991), reprinted in 4 Trade Reg.Rep. (CCH) ¶ 13,504, as amended in 1998.

(1) the relative significance to the alleged violation of conduct within the United States, as compared to conduct abroad;

(2) the nationality of the persons involved in or affected by the conduct;

(3) the presence or absence of a purpose to affect U.S. consumers, markets, or exporters;

(4) the relative significance and foreseeability of the effects of the conduct on the United States as compared to the effects abroad;

(5) the existence of reasonable expectations that would be furthered or defeated by the action;

(6) the degree of conflict with foreign law or articulated foreign economic policies;

(7) the extent to which the enforcement activities of another country with respect to the same persons, including remedies resulting from those activities, may be affected; and

(8) the effectiveness of foreign enforcement as compared to U.S. enforcement action.

The concept of positive comity builds on the last two factors. Briefly, it allows the enforcement agency to seek action from the foreign authority in whose territory the alleged anticompetitive conduct is taking place, if that conduct would also violate the foreign country's law. In its present form, positive comity has not been made mandatory either for the requesting agency or for the requested agency. Instead, it is an option that is encouraged under the cooperation agreements.

On April 17, 1997, the U.S. Department of Justice and the Federal Trade Commission announced the conclusion of the first International Antitrust Assistance Agreement made possible by the IAEAA which was concluded with Australia. After publication in the Federal Register and a lengthy period of consideration, the agreement formally entered into force on April 27, 1999. The full text can be found at <http://www.usdoj.gov/atr/public/international/docs/ usaus7.htm>.

Although the United States and the European Community have yet to conclude an agreement for direct enforcement cooperation under the auspices of the IAEAA, they have nonetheless managed to move forward under more conventional agreements. On June 4, 1998, representatives of the U.S. government and the European Community signed a new Agreement between the Government of the United States of America and the European Communities on the Application of Positive Comity Principles in the Enforcement of Their Competition Laws. The full text of the agreement can be found on the Antitrust Division's Webpage, at <http://www.usdoj.gov/atr/public/international/docs/1781.htm>. It commits both parties to greater use of the positive comity principle, under which one party may request another to take enforcement action against anticompetitive activities occurring within its territory in violation of its law, when those activities also have an effect on the other party.

Is positive comity the answer to the problem of extraterritorial jurisdiction, or is more necessary? In other areas of international law, notably the law of diplomatic protection, a State will not espouse the claim of its national unless the national has either exhausted local remedies or it can show that application of the exhaustion requirement would be futile in the circumstances. *See generally* ALI Restatement of the Law of Foreign Relations, § 703, comment d, § 713, comments b and f, and § 902(2) and comment k. Should the antitrust enforcement agencies adopt an analogous exhaustion requirement, under which they would consider bringing a market access case pursuant to § 6(1)(B)? What advantages or disadvantages would you foresee in such an approach?

* * *

PROBLEM 27

AN INTERNATIONAL CARTEL

Megafirm is a large U.S. corporation that specializes in the development and distribution of operating systems and applications software for personal computers. In the United States market, its operating systems are present in more than 60% of all such computers. It has approximately 40% of the market for office systems applications software, and only 25% of entertainment software. In Europe, the market shares are quite comparable, although Megafirm's operating systems appear in more than 75% of all personal computers. Its applications software market shares are somewhat smaller: about 30% of office systems programs, and 20% of entertainment software. Finally, in some of the more advanced developing countries, the market for computer systems has been growing rapidly. In one of them, Atlantis, the Ministry of Technology has urged its local firms not to allow foreigners to grab this lucrative and growing market for themselves. The three local computer manufacturing companies in Atlantis, with the knowledge and blessing of Atlantis antitrust authorities, accordingly entered into an agreement whereby they promised to limit imports of Megafirm software for incorporation in their products drastically. They stated in a press release that the agreement was necessary to avoid giving any one firm a competitive advantage through the use of Megafirm's popular products.

Under prevailing U.S. law, Megafirm believed itself safe from antitrust attack. It was therefore surprised when the European Commission opened a proceeding against it, issued a formal statement of objections, and demanded the immediate cessation of several of Megafirm's key licensing practices, including its insistence on appointing an exclusive company for distribution of its product in each Member State of the EU, its insistence that all improvements in the programs become the exclusive property of Megafirm, and its refusal to disclose changes in the operating systems before they reached the markets. Megafirm comes to the U.S. government and complains that the EC proceeding is an impermissible exercise of extraterritorial jurisdiction. Megafirm also urges the U.S. authorities to bring a market access case against the three companies in Atlantis, on the ground that they have practically shut down Megafirm's exports to that country.

Relying on the jurisdictional principles developed in the U.S. courts, how would you advise the U.S. authorities to react to Megafirm's two complaints? How would the case be handled if the facts were the same except that Megafirm was a Japanese company, imposing the same kinds of licensing restraints on a country-by-country basis worldwide, with 60% of the U.S. market, and customers complained to the U.S. authorities?

SECTION 3. THE EFFECT OF FOREIGN SOVEREIGN INVOLVEMENT

A number of doctrines apply when a foreign sovereign has taken some affirmative action that relates to the conduct being examined in a U.S. antitrust case. We have already seen examples of this in *American Banana*, *Continental Ore*, and *Timberlane*. This section briefly considers the three most important of these doctrines: foreign sovereign immunity, the act of state doctrine, and the defense of foreign sovereign compulsion. For a comprehensive examination of these and other special defenses, see ABA Antitrust Section, Monograph No. 20, Special Defenses in International Antitrust Litigation (1995).

A. FOREIGN SOVEREIGN IMMUNITY

Since 1976, this area has been governed by the Foreign Sovereign Immunities Act, 28 U.S.C. §§ 1330, 1602 et seq. (FSIA). The FSIA adopts what is known as the "restrictive" theory of sovereign immunity, under which "states are not immune from the jurisdiction of foreign courts insofar as their commercial activities are concerned...." 28 U.S.C. § 1602. Of importance for antitrust litigation is the breadth of the definition of the term "foreign state" in the statute. According to 28 U.S.C. § 1603(a), a foreign state includes not only the state itself, but also its political subdivisions and its agencies or instrumentalities. If the foreign state owns a majority of the shares of a corporation, that corporation is an "instrumentality" of the state for FSIA purposes. 28 U.S.C. § 1603(b)(1), (2).

An interesting sub-issue with significant practical implications involves the question of "tiering". The issue is whether, in a tiered corporate structure, indirect subsidiaries of a foreign state or political subdivision can also qualify as state instrumentalities, or if instead the statute confers "foreign state" status only on entities directly owned by the state itself. The circuits were split on that issue, but the Supreme Court recently resolved it in *Dole Food Co. v. Patrickson*, 123 S.Ct. 1655 (2003). The *Dole Food* case was brought by banana workers from various countries against Dole Food, among others, seeking damages for injuries. The defendants impleaded two Israeli chemical companies, which removed the case to federal court claiming that they were "foreign states" for purposes of the FSIA. Whether they satisfied the statutory definition or not depended on whether the FSIA contemplated "tiering." The State of Israel owned a majority of the shares of another corporation, which in turn owned a majority of the shares of the impleaded companies.

The Supreme Court decided that the FSIA extends only to instrumentalities or subsidiaries whose shares are held directly by the foreign state itself, thus rejecting the "tiering" theory. It relied on general principles of corporate law and the fact that the FSIA itself makes no mention of indirect ownership. The net result, of course, will be to restrict the applicability of the FSIA to a smaller number of entities in which foreign states have an ultimate interest.

The FSIA confers significant protections on foreign states, agencies or instrumentalities of foreign states, and companies in which foreign states hold a majority share of the ownership. Under the statute, a foreign state is presumed to be immune from suit unless one of the exceptions set forth in § 1605 applies. Some of the exceptions are unlikely to be of interest in an antitrust case, including explicit waiver (§ 1605(a)(1)), expropriations in violation of international law (§ 1605(a)(3)), disputes over gifts or succession rights (§ 1605(a)(4)), and torts committed by the foreign state or its agents in the course of their employment (§ 1605(a)(5), a rough equivalent to the Federal Tort Claims Act). The exception that is of intense interest to antitrust practitioners is the so-called commercial activity exception, found in § 1605(a)(2):

> [A foreign state shall not be immune from the jurisdiction of courts of the United States or of the States in any case—]
>
> (2) in which the action is based upon a commercial activity carried on in the United States by the foreign state; or upon an act performed in the United States in connection with a commercial activity of the foreign state elsewhere; or upon an act outside the territory of the United States in connection with a commercial activity of the foreign state elsewhere and that act causes a direct effect in the United States.

The statute instructs that whether or not something is a "commercial activity" must be determined "by reference to the nature of the course of conduct or particular transaction or act, rather than by reference to its purpose." § 1603(d). In the legislative history of the Act, Congress explained that a regular course of commercial conduct would include "the carrying on of a commercial enterprise such as a mineral extraction company, an airline or a state trading corporation.... [I]f an activity is customarily carried on for profit, its commercial nature could readily be assumed." H.Rep. No. 94–1487, 94th Cong., 2d Sess. (1976).

In Republic of Argentina v. Weltover, Inc., 504 U.S. 607 (1992), the Supreme Court gave a broad interpretation to § 1605(a)(2)'s requirement of a "direct effect" in the United States. There the Court rejected the argument that the effect had to be substantial and foreseeable, although it admitted that the effect should be more than *de minimis*. It defined a "direct effect" as one that follows "as an immediate consequence of the defendant's ... activity." 504 U.S. at 618. Note that this places the courts in the difficult position of applying three distinct tests for the degree of contact a foreign sovereign's instrumentality has with the United States: the "direct, substantial, and reasonably foreseeable" test of the FTAIA for antitrust jurisdiction; the "minimum contacts" test usually applied to questions of personal jurisdiction, and the "direct effect" test for assessing whether an exception to sovereign immunity exists. Are these tests really different, or do they merge in practice? Do the purposes of the three separate inquiries (reach of the antitrust laws, connections to the forum, and sovereign immunity) justify the separate formulations?

NOTE ON THE APPLICATION OF THE FOREIGN SOVEREIGN IMMUNITY DOCTRINE IN ANTITRUST CASES

1. Before the passage of the FSIA, U.S. courts had occasionally faced the question whether foreign sovereign immunity would apply. In *United States v. Deutsches Kalisyndikat Gesellschaft*, 31 F.2d 199 (S.D.N.Y.1929), the government charged members of a European potash cartel with conspiring to monopolize the importation of potash into the United States. The French Ambassador intervened in the suit, claiming that the French defendant, a corporation in which the French government owned an 11/15ths interest, was an instrumentality of the Republic of France and that the suit was, in effect, an impermissible action against the French sovereign.

The court held that the French corporation could be sued despite the plea of sovereign immunity, because a private corporation was an "entity distinct from its stockholders," and cannot claim immunity "on the ground that it and the government of France are identical in any respect." The court noted that the company's French charter explicitly provided that it, like any private corporation, could be sued, and that French courts did not extend immunity to commercial enterprises owned or controlled by a sovereign state. The court added that:

> A foreign sovereign cannot authorize his agents to violate the law in a foreign jurisdiction, or to perform any sovereign or governmental functions within the domain of another sovereign, without his consent. He, therefore, cannot claim as a matter of comity or otherwise that the act of the alleged agent in such case is the act of the sovereign, and that the suit against the agent is in fact a suit against the sovereign. *Id.* at 203.

2. In the 1953 grand jury investigation of the oil cartels, *In re Investigation of World Arrangements*, 13 F.R.D. 280 (D.D.C.1952), Anglo–Iranian Oil Company, Ltd., a corporation controlled by the British government, moved to quash a subpoena on the ground that the company was an instrumentality of the British crown. Although the corporation's counsel claimed only that the company could not produce the necessary documents as a result of an order of the British government, the trial court held that the corporation itself was immune from the grand jury proceedings. It distinguished the Deutsches Kalisyndikat case, relying on the fact that Anglo–Iranian performed a vital government function in supplying oil for the British navy.

Would the same justification be available today under §§ 1603(d) and 1605(a)(2)?

3. Before the collapse of most of the Communist regimes, the courts occasionally faced questions about state trading organizations from those countries. In *Outboard Marine Corp. v. Pezetel*, 461 F.Supp. 384 (D.Del.1978), the Polish government tried to assert a sovereign immunity defense in a case brought by Outboard

Marine claiming that the Polish company was attempting to monopolize the U.S. market for electric golf carts by means of sales in violation of the antidumping laws. The court was unpersuaded, finding that the type of market activity in which Pezetel was engaged (competing through low-priced sales) was subject to the jurisdiction of the U.S. courts under the commercial activity exception.

4. The most complex cases have arisen where foreign governments, either singly or in combination with other governments, have regulated the extraction, processing, and sale of natural resources. The leading case remains *International Association of Machinists v. Organization of Petroleum Exporting Countries*, 477 F.Supp. 553 (C.D.Cal.1979), *aff'd* on other grounds, 649 F.2d 1354 (9th Cir.1981), *cert. denied*, 454 U.S. 1163 (1982). At a time when gasoline pump prices were soaring in the United States due to the OPEC cartel, the Machinists' Union sued OPEC itself in federal district court in California, claiming a classic violation of Sherman Act § 1. The district court dismissed on the ground that OPEC's actions in controlling oil production were sovereign, not commercial, and that OPEC's price-fixing activities were merely incidental to its regulatory acts. As is noted in Section 2 below, the Ninth Circuit was uncomfortable with this analysis, because of the distinction drawn in the FSIA between the nature of a course of conduct and its purpose. It therefore did not rely on foreign sovereign immunity in disposing of the case, but instead it affirmed on the basis of the act of state doctrine.

Does a case like *OPEC* belong in the federal courts of the United States? Should the Executive Branch have any role in advising the court of the foreign policy implications of such litigation? Note that the government never intervened in any capacity, either formally or as amicus, to express views in the OPEC case. For contrasting views on the OPEC litigation, see Hovenkamp, Can a Foreign Sovereign Be an Antitrust Defendant? 32 Syracuse L.Rev. 879 (1981), and de Kieffer, The Foreign Sovereign Immunities Act and Antitrust: A Hollow Promise, 7 Syracuse J. Int'l L. & Com. 37 (1979).

B.   THE ACT OF STATE DOCTRINE

Timberlane contains a brief introduction to the act of state doctrine. This section adds only a few additional notes about the doctrine and its application in antitrust cases. In order to place it in perspective, it may be useful to note that there have actually been two strands of act of state cases: one in which the action of the foreign government allegedly violates international law, such as the *Sabbatino* and *Dunhill* cases discussed in *Timberlane*, and the other in which the action of the foreign government allegedly violates either its own law or U.S. law. As Justice White's dissenting opinion in Sabbatino implies, the justification for abstaining from decision when an international law violation is alleged (such as an expropriation of property without the payment of prompt, adequate, and effective compensation) is harder to find than when the problem is essentially one of choice of law.

In *W.S. Kirkpatrick & Co. v. Environmental Tectonics Corp.*, 493 U.S. 400 (1990), the Supreme Court considered the application of the act of state doctrine in a case arising under RICO and the anti-bribery provisions of the Robinson–Patman Act. The chief executive officer of Kirkpatrick & Co. had arranged with a Nigerian official to pay a bribe to other officials of the Nigerian government in order to obtain a contract for some construction work at an air force base in Nigeria. Environmental Tectonics, the unsuccessful bidder allegedly ousted from the work because of the bribes, complained to the U.S. government. After an investigation, both Kirkpatrick & Co. and its CEO pleaded guilty to violations of the Foreign Corrupt Practices Act. Tectonics then brought a civil action for damages against the company, the CEO, and the Nigerian agent.

The district court granted summary judgment against Tectonics on the ground that the claim required an inquiry into "the motivations of a sovereign act which would result in embarrassment to the sovereign or constitute interference in the conduct of foreign policy in the United States." The Third Circuit reversed, relying to a great extent on a letter from the Legal Adviser to the U.S. Department of State stating that the judicial inquiry would not produce "unique embarrassment" to the foreign policy of the United States. (Indeed, the opposite might have been true, although this does not appear on the record. The State Department had been trying for years to strengthen international rules against bribery and corrupt practices, and it may have welcomed this kind of case.)

The Supreme Court affirmed the Third Circuit's view. It noted that the "act of state" doctrine only comes into play where the relief sought or the defense interposed requires a U.S. court to declare invalid the official act of a foreign sovereign performed within its territory. Thus, the issue in this litigation was not whether the award of the contract was valid but whether, valid or not, it was secured by illegal acts of the defendants. The Supreme Court concluded:

> The Act of State doctrine does not establish an exception for cases and controversies that may embarrass foreign governments, but merely requires that in the process of deciding, the acts of foreign sovereigns taken within their own jurisdictions shall be deemed valid. That doctrine has no application to the present case because the validity of no foreign sovereign act is at issue.

If the Nigerian government's award of the contract to Kirkpatrick must be deemed valid, has Tectonics stated a claim upon which relief can be granted? What damages would be available to Tectonics if it were entitled to base liability on actions of Kirkpatrick (*e.g.*, in offering the bribes), if the court cannot look behind the government's action?

NOTES AND QUESTIONS

1. The defense of "act of state" was sufficient to defeat an antitrust claim in *Occidental Petroleum Corp. v. Buttes Gas and Oil Co.*, 331 F.Supp. 92 (C.D.Cal. 1971), *aff'd*, 461 F.2d 1261 (9th Cir.), *cert. denied*, 409 U.S. 950 (1972). There the sheik supported by the British as Ruler of Sharjah was charged with conspiring with U.S. oil companies to deprive plaintiff of the value of oil concessions granted to it by a neighboring sheikdom. This injury was caused by the Ruler's decree asserting his proprietary claim, as sovereign, to land and oil under coast waters located in an area between the two mainlands. Since few things are more traditional

acts of sovereignty than defining and defending boundaries, it was not surprising that the U.S. antitrust court, even though accepting extraterritorial jurisdiction, refused to decide the issue on "act of state" grounds.

2. HUNT V. MOBIL OIL CORP., 550 F.2d 68 (2d Cir.1977), *cert. denied*, 434 U.S. 984 (1977), involved Nelson Bunker Hunt's claim that defendant major oil companies' conspiracy caused the government of Libya to nationalize Hunt's oil production rights. The District Court had noted that this would require it to explore the sovereign's motives for the expropriation. The Second Circuit agreed that the "act of state" doctrine prohibited such judicial intrusions into sovereign decision-making. Note that Hunt's lawyers carefully did not charge Libya as a co-conspirator; on the contrary, plaintiff's position was that the oil companies' alleged conspiracy was at the expense of both Libya and Hunt. Why did they have reason to hope that this would improve their client's case?

Hunt was criticized by a divided Fifth Circuit in Industrial Investment Development Corp. v. Mitsui & Co., Ltd., 594 F.2d 48 (5th Cir.1979), *cert. denied*, 445 U.S. 903 (1980), which involved an allegation that defendants had procured the Indonesian government's cancellation of plaintiff's timber concession in an effort to monopolize the regional timber market. The majority criticized *Hunt* as encouraging the use of the "act of state" doctrine as a shield by private conspirators who are able to include some foreign governmental act in their anticompetitive scheme. The Fifth Circuit advanced a "two-step" inquiry to determine whether the alleged conspiracy afforded an independent basis for liability, and concluded that defendants' acts in the case before it were divisible from the ultimate denial of the concession by Indonesia.

3. INTERNATIONAL ASSOCIATION OF MACHINISTS V. ORGANIZATION OF PETROLEUM EXPORTING COUNTRIES, 649 F.2d 1354 (9th Cir.1981), cert. denied, 454 U.S. 1163 (1982). A labor union sued OPEC and its member nations for allegedly fixing oil prices, resulting in reduced economic activity and fewer and less well-paid jobs for the union's members. No defendant appeared, but the trial court held a full hearing as required by the Foreign Sovereign Immunities Act, then held the member states protected by it. The Ninth Circuit, however, held that the OPEC cartel fell within the Act's "commercial activity" exemption, Judge Choy again writing the opinion. Congress intended the commercial exception to be broadly read, and the trial court's characterization of defendant's acts as "the establishment by a sovereign state of the terms and conditions for the removal of a prime natural resource" contravenes the Act by looking to the "purpose" rather than the nature of the conduct, price-fixing.

However, Congress did not intend to limit the "act of state" defense:

> While the [Act] ignores the underlying purpose of a state's action, the act of state doctrine does not. This court has stated that the motivations of the sovereign must be examined for a public interest basis. [Citing *Timberlane*.] ... Because the act of state doctrine and the doctrine of sovereign immunity address different concerns and apply in different circumstances, we find that the act of state doctrine remains available when ... caution is appropriate, regardless of any commercial component of the activity involved.

Id. at 1360. The District Court's dismissal was affirmed on that ground.

Note that under this approach, which seems likely to prevail, the absolute bar to jurisdiction arising from sovereign immunity is present only in cases of purely governmental conduct. The act of state doctrine assures that non-immune conduct may also be privileged where intervention by U.S. courts would endanger foreign relations interests. Perhaps where private parties claim act of state through sovereign compulsion, fairness will also be taken into account.

C.   FOREIGN SOVEREIGN COMPULSION

Although the defense of foreign sovereign compulsion is rarely raised, and even more rarely succeeds, in litigated cases, it is nonetheless an important concept for international antitrust. If, in a case brought in a U.S. court, a defendant can show that its actions were compelled by a foreign sovereign, it may be relieved of liability. This is so both because it is inherently unfair to force a defendant to violate the law of one country or another, with no "legal" middle road, and because considerations of international comity sometimes require this kind of deference to the foreign country's laws.

The defense applies only when the foreign government has actually compelled the conduct in question. In the 1995 International Guidelines, the Agencies explain that "compulsion" exists "under circumstances in which a refusal to comply with the foreign government's command would give rise to the imposition of penal or other severe sanctions." 1995 Guidelines, § 3.32. Thus, encouragement, toleration, administrative guidance, or similar practices will not suffice. The defense also does not apply to procedural matters, such as a foreign government's command that documents located within its territory are not to be produced in response to an order of a U.S. court. In the latter cases, a more complex balancing process (ultimately informed by due process) governs how much weight the foreign government's order will be given.

There is also a territorial component to the defense, for the obvious reason that there would be no need to defer if the government of Country X told its company "we are hereby ordering you to violate the antitrust laws of Country A in your business there." From the standpoint of comity, the need to apply the defense is strongest when the actor is abiding by compulsory orders of its own government (*e.g.*, applying mandatory product standards, belonging to a compulsory association, etc.) that might raise antitrust problems elsewhere.

Only one court has applied the foreign sovereign compulsion defense in circumstances that were dispositive: the district court in *Interamerican Refining Corp. v. Texaco Maracaibo, Inc.*, 307 F.Supp. 1291 (D.Del.1970). Interamerican, the plaintiff, was a company owned by Venezuelan nationals that planned to process low-cost Venezuelan crude oil in a bonded refinery off the coast of New Jersey, and to export the product to New York. This tactic would have enabled it to avoid certain tariffs and import quotas. It took steps to implement the plan, but it found itself thwarted when its supplier of the Venezuelan crude (Amoco, and ultimately Texaco Maracaibo) refused to continue selling to it. The reason was that the Venezuelan government had flatly forbidden further sales of oil that either directly or indirectly would end up in Interamerican's hands. No other seller in

Venezuela was willing to supply oil without the express permission of the government, which was not forthcoming.

When Interamerican sued Texaco Maracaibo and others under Sherman Act §§ 1 and 2, claiming an unlawful group boycott or concerted refusal to deal, the defendants moved for summary judgment on the ground that their actions were compelled by the Venezuelan government. The district court agreed, and dismissed the case. It noted first that "sovereignty includes the right to regulate commerce within the nation. When a nation compels a trade practice, firms there have no choice but to obey...." *Id.* at 1298. It then observed:

> Anticompetitive practices compelled by foreign nations are not restrains of commerce, as commerce is understood in the Sherman Act, because refusal to comply would put an end to commerce.... Commerce may exist at the will of the [foreign] government, and to impose liability for obedience to that will would eliminate for many companies the ability to transact business in foreign lands. Were compulsion not a defense, American firms abroad faced with a government order would have to choose one country or the other in which to do business. The Sherman Act does not go so far. *Id.* at 1297.

Why, if there is so little law, has the foreign sovereign compulsion defense remained as important as it has? The answer lies not in antitrust law, but in international trade law. From time to time, either at the request of the U.S. government or on their own, foreign governments have imposed "voluntary restraints" on the export of products to the United States. In order to be effective, those restraints normally must be controlled by the foreign government just as any output-restricting cartel is controlled: an overall quantity must be set, and shares of the market must be parceled out somehow to the companies involved. This is, more or less, what happened when the Japanese government imposed a series of voluntary restraints on the export of automobiles to the U.S. market. Nervous about the antitrust consequences of the arrangement, the Government of Japan asked whether liability would result from these actions. The U.S. government advised it, on a number of occasions, that as long as the Government of Japan was actually compelling its companies to take the specified measures and otherwise conformed to the requirements of the foreign sovereign compulsion defense, it believed that a U.S. court would dismiss any action that was brought. (Remarkably, no direct attack was brought during the many years the auto restraints were in place. Compare *Hammons v. Alcan Aluminum Co.*, No. 96–CV–319, C.D.Cal., a pending case which claims that an international aluminum cartel formed under the cover of an intergovernmental agreement regarding trade in aluminum, part of which involved restrictions on exports from the Russian market.) These trade measures, with their obvious effect on competition in U.S. markets, are possible under existing U.S. antitrust laws largely because of the foreign sovereign compulsion defense.

SELECTIVE BIBLIOGRAPHY

ABA Section of Antitrust Law, Report of the Special Committee on International Antitrust (Sept. 1, 1991) (2 vol.).

ABA Section of Antitrust Law, Special Defenses in International Antitrust Litigation, Monograph 20 (1995).

Anderson, Frédéric Jenny, Convergence or Divergence? Current Developments in Competition Policy in the World Trade Organization (2001).

Atwood, Brewster & Waller, Antitrust and American Business Abroad (3d ed. 1997) (2 vol.).

Born, International Civil Litigation in United States Courts: Commentary & Materials, Chs. 7, 8, 9 (3d ed. 1996).

Dam, Extraterritoriality in an Age of Globalization: The Hartford Fire Case, 1993 Sup. Ct. Rev. 289.

Foster, While America Slept: the Harmonization of Competition Laws Based upon the European Union Model (2001).

Fox, Antitrust and Regulatory Federalism: Races Up, Down, and Sideways, 75 N.Y.U.L. Rev. 1781 (2000).

Fox, National Law, Global Markets, and Hartford: Eyes Wide Shut, 68 Antitrust L. J. 73 (2000).

Fugate, Foreign Commerce and the Antitrust Laws (5th ed. 2001) (2 vol.).

Gifford, The Draft International Antitrust Code proposed at Munich: Good Intentions Gone Awry, 6 Minnesota J. Global Trade 1 (1997).

Griffin, Extraterritoriality in U.S. and E.U. Antitrust Enforcement, 67 Antitrust L. J. 159 (1999).

Guzman, Antitrust and International Regulatory Federalism, 76 N.Y.U. L. Rev. 1142 (2001).

Hawk, United States, Common Market and International Antitrust: A Comparative Guide (2d ed. 1985 & Supp.1995).

International Competition Network website at http://www.internationalcompetitionnetwork.org.

Kennedy, Global Trade Issues in the New Millennium: Foreign Direct Investment and Competition Policy at the World Trade Organization (2001).

Klein, Time for a Global Competition Initiative? (Sept 14, 2000).

Kramer, Note: Extraterritorial Application of American Law After the Insurance Antitrust Case: A Reply to Professors Lowenfeld and Trimble, 89 Am.J.Int'l L. 750 (1995).

Lowenfeld, Conflict, Balancing of Interests, and the Exercise of Jurisdiction to Prescribe: Reflections on the Insurance Antitrust Case, 89 Am.J.Int'l L. 42 (1995).

Lowenstein, The Foreign Sovereign Immunities Act and Corporate Subsidiaries of Agencies or Instrumentalities of Foreign States, 19 Berkeley J. Int'l L. 350, 379 (2001).

Neale & Stephens, International Business and National Jurisdiction (1988).

Rosenthal & Knighton, National Laws and International Commerce: The Problem of Extraterritoriality (Chatham House Papers No. 17) (1982).

Scherer, Competition Policies for an Integrated World Economy (1994).

Shank, The Justice Department's Recent Antitrust Enforcement Policy: Toward a "Positive Comity" Solution to International Competition Problems?, Vanderbilt J. Transnational L. 155 (1996).

Trimble, The Supreme Court and International Law: The Demise of Restatement Section 403, 89 Am.J.Int'l L. 53 (1995).

U.S. Department of Justice and the Federal Trade Commission, Antitrust Enforcement Guidelines for International Operations (1995).

Waller, The Internationalization of Antitrust Enforcement, 77 B.Y.U. L. Rev. 343 (1997).

Website of the Organization for Economic Co-operation and Development (OECD) at http://www.oecd.com.

Diane P. Wood, The Impossible Dream: Real International Antitrust, 1992 U.Chi. Legal Forum 277.

Diane P. Wood, International Harmonization of Antitrust Law: the Tortoise or the Hare?, 3 Chi. J.Int'l L. 391 (Fall 2002).

CHAPTER 11

PRICE DISCRIMINATION AND THE ROBINSON–PATMAN ACT

SECTION 1. THE ECONOMICS AND POLITICS OF PRICE DISCRIMINATION LEGISLATION

Few things are more attractive to a seller with some degree of market power, even when no more than that conferred by a brand name, than to be able to structure a marketing operation in which he or she can engage in price discrimination. There is no more profitable way to sell a product than to charge each purchaser exactly that price which reflects the value of the product to him or her. (Indeed, if the product is consumed in quantity, the monopolist would like to be able to charge a different price for each unit sold even to the same buyer, to reflect the normal "diminishing incremental utility" of successive units.)

To be most profitable, the discrimination must be "systematic"—that is, not simply a "one-shot" concession, but a continuing differential reflecting different elasticities of demand for the good on the part of different users or different classes of users. The problem, in most cases, is that if a price discrimination is continuing, the buyer paying the higher price will find a way to get his supply from someone who buys at a lower price. In other words, arbitrage eliminates the differential since the different markets cannot be kept separate. With services, as opposed to discrete products, arbitrage is usually no problem—a doctor can charge each patient whatever he is thought to be willing to pay for his appendectomy, and Grinnell presumably worked out individual contracts with major users of its burglar alarm service. See United States v. Grinnell, p. 172 supra. Television networks or stations, newspapers, periodicals and other media can discriminate between large and small advertisers. See FTC v. Procter & Gamble, p. 1193 supra. Sylvania attempted to separate markets by a direct "customer restriction" on its dealers specifying locations from which they might sell. See Continental T.V., Inc. v. GTE Sylvania Inc., p. 651 supra. One way to succeed is to acquire by merger (or effectively to control through less formal means of vertical integration) the "low price, high elasticity" users, if they are not too great in number, so that the price to other "low elasticity" users may be increased, i.e., to discriminate in favor of a vertically integrated subsidiary which can be prevented from engaging in arbitrage. Often this is feasible, however, only if one's rivals share the burden, i.e., if the entire industry integrates vertically into the offending submarket.

If a cartel or oligopoly works well enough to enable the members of the group to develop parallel marketing structures and methods, as for example in the vertical integration example just discussed, the rewards of price discrimination may be even greater or the costs of policing the marketing structure reduced for each individual firm.

Many tying arrangements may be explained, in part or in whole, as "metering" devices that enable lessors to engage in price discrimination between high intensity and low intensity users, as in International Salt Co. v. United States, p. 877 supra, or in package licensing situations as devices to allow a single "package" price to effectuate profitable discriminations in the prices of unit components.

Finally, discrimination in price or through refusal to deal may be an inexpensive and potent weapon for use in protecting an existing market position or in expanding into a vertically related field.

None of these cases arose under the Robinson–Patman Act. Indeed, as we will note, if that Act is interpreted restrictively, *i.e.*, as limited to "purchasers" as opposed to lessees or consignees, and to discrete, physical "commodities," as opposed to services or goods more broadly defined, it will not apply to just those cases in which systematic price discrimination is most likely to exist and to have potent economic effects. Price discrimination, in an economic sense, pervades the marketing practices to which the Sherman Act and Clayton Act in general apply. So it is inaccurate to call the Robinson–Patman Act *the* price discrimination law. It is only one somewhat specialized aspect of the concern of antitrust law with the economic problems that arise from discriminatory treatment of suppliers or purchasers.

Section 2 of the original Clayton Act, as enacted in 1914, made it illegal "to discriminate in price between different purchasers of commodities . . ., where the effect of such discrimination may be to substantially lessen competition or tend to create a monopoly in any line of commerce. . . ." However, this prohibition was qualified to allow discrimination "on account of differences in the . . . quantity of the commodity sold . . . or discrimination in price . . . made in good faith to meet competition. . . ."

Large-scale buyers often negotiated for discounts without regard to sellers' costs, using their large orders as a bargaining weapon. They sought not only quantity discounts and special advertising and promotional allowances but to capture for themselves the brokerage commissions which had characterized traditional distributional methods. The severe economic depression of the 1930's accentuated the problems of the many small local merchants who could neither buy in large enough quantities to claim real cost savings nor exert much economic muscle in the interests of getting favored treatment. The local retailer, however, was not without political influence. Forming alliances with the wholesalers and distributors whose prosperity depended on his survival, he was able to bring pressure to bear on local and state legislative bodies.

Further relief was found in the short-lived National Industrial Recovery Act's industry-devised manufacturing, wholesaling, and retailing codes which barred or severely limited discounts and allowances to mass buyers. But even before the *Schechter* decision struck down the NIRA, the U.S. Wholesale Grocers' Association was preparing legislation that was to become the Robinson–Patman Act. Within two weeks after that decision, on June 11, 1935, Representative Wright Patman introduced a bill which drastically limited mass buyers by prohibiting all price differentials other than those based on the seller's cost savings or the distributional activities of the buyer, without regard to whether the discrimination had an adverse effect on competition. Furthermore, the cost justification proviso was extremely narrow.

The legislative history of the original bill reflects the multiple conflicts of different policy and group interests. Those legislators who envisioned a statute extending the existing antitrust laws scored an early victory in both the Senate and House committees. They succeeded in limiting the discriminations interdicted by the bill to those whose effect "may be to substantially lessen competition or tend to create a monopoly." However, a further amendment proscribed discrimination if its effect might be "to injure competition with any person who receives or grants the benefit of the discrimination, or with customers of either of them." This was a victory for those whose interest was to protect individual competitors rather than concern for the health of competition in a broader sense. The Section 2 defense that the differential was granted "in good faith to meet an equally low price of a competitor" was continued.

A second bill was pending before the Senate committee during the Robinson–Patman debate. The Borah–Van Nuys bill was not, however, an amendment to the Clayton Act, but was intended as an alternative to the Robinson–Patman bill, providing criminal penalties for the granting or receiving of any discriminatory "discount, rebate, allowance, or advertising service charge ... [on] a sale of goods of like grade, quality, and quantity." The same penalties were to attach to geographical price discriminations or the sale of goods at "unreasonably low prices ... for the purpose of destroying competition or eliminating a competitor." The Borah–Van Nuys bill was killed in committee, but was later tacked on to the Robinson–Patman bill as a floor amendment and now survives as Section 3 of the Act. The bill finally went to the Conference Committee with an additional amendment that made it unlawful for a buyer to "knowingly ... induce or receive" a prohibited seller's price discrimination.

Few significant changes were made by the committee. The conferees apparently failed to reach a consensus on the basic issue of whether the new law should be primarily an extension of the antitrust law or a measure for the protection of traditional distributional arrangements. The House discussion prior to the adoption of the Conference Committee report indicates that the conferees took the pragmatic position of compromise rather than agreement on basic policy.

Robinson–Patman Act[1]

Section 2. (a) That it shall be unlawful for any person engaged in commerce, in the course of such commerce, either directly or indirectly, to discriminate in price between different purchasers of commodities of like grade and quality, where either or any of the purchases involved in such discrimination are in commerce, where such commodities are sold for use, consumption, or resale within the United States or any Territory thereof or the District of Columbia or any insular possession or other place under the jurisdiction of the United States, and where the effect of such discrimination may be substantially to lessen competition or tend to create a monopoly in any line of commerce, or to injure, destroy, or prevent competition with any person who either grants or knowingly receives the benefit of such discrimination, or with customers of either of them: *Provided,* That nothing herein contained shall prevent differentials which make only due allowance for differences in the cost of manufacture, sale, or delivery resulting from the differing methods or quantities in which such commodities are to such purchasers sold or delivered: *Provided, however,* That the Federal Trade Commission may, after due investigation and hearing to all interested parties, fix and establish quantity limits, and revise the same as it finds necessary, as to particular commodities or classes of commodities, where it finds that available purchasers in greater quantities are so few as to render differentials on account thereof unjustly discriminatory or promotive of monopoly in any line of commerce; and the foregoing shall then not be construed to permit differentials based on differences in quantities greater than those so fixed and established: *And provided further,* That nothing herein contained shall prevent persons engaged in selling goods, wares, or merchandise in commerce from selecting their own customers in bona fide transactions and not in restraint of trade: *And provided further,* That nothing herein contained shall prevent price changes from time to time where in response to changing conditions affecting the market for or the marketability of the goods concerned, such as but not limited to actual or imminent deterioration of perishable goods, obsolescence of seasonal goods, distress sales under court process, or sales in good faith in discontinuance of business in the goods concerned.

---

1. Section 2 of the Robinson–Patman Act is Section 2 of the Clayton Act, as amended, 49 Stat. 1526 (1936), 15 U.S.C.A. § 13.

Section 3 of the Act is 49 Stat. 1528 (1936), 15 U.S.C.A. § 13a.

(b) Upon proof being made, at any hearing on a complaint under this section, that there has been discrimination in price or services or facilities furnished, the burden of rebutting the prima-facie case thus made by showing justification shall be upon the person charged with a violation of this section, and unless justification shall be affirmatively shown, the Commission is authorized to issue an order terminating the discrimination: *Provided, however,* That nothing herein contained shall prevent a seller rebutting the prima-facie case thus made by showing that his lower price or the furnishing of services or facilities to any purchaser or purchasers was made in good faith to meet an equally low price of a competitor, or the services or facilities furnished by a competitor.

(c) That it shall be unlawful for any person engaged in commerce, in the course of such commerce to pay or grant, or to receive or accept, anything of value as a commission, brokerage, or other compensation, or any allowance or discount in lieu thereof, except for services rendered in connection with the sale or purchase of goods, wares, or merchandise, either to the other party to such transaction or to an agent, representative or other intermediary therein where such intermediary is acting in fact for or in behalf, or is subject to the direct or indirect control, of any party to such transaction other than the person by whom such compensation is so granted or paid.

(d) That it shall be unlawful for any person engaged in commerce to pay or contract for the payment of anything of value to or for the benefit of a customer of such person in the course of such commerce as compensation or in consideration for any services or facilities furnished by or through such customer in connection with the processing, handling, sale, or offering for sale of any products or commodities manufactured, sold, or offered for sale by such person, unless such payment or consideration is available on proportionally equal terms to all other customers competing in the distribution of such products or commodities.

(e) That it shall be unlawful for any person to discriminate in favor of one purchaser against another purchaser or purchasers of a commodity bought for resale, with or without processing, by contracting to furnish or furnishing, or by contributing to the furnishing of, any services or facilities connected with the processing, handling, sale, or offering for sale of such commodity so purchased upon terms not accorded to all purchasers on proportionally equal terms.

(f) That it shall be unlawful for any person engaged in commerce, in the course of such commerce, knowingly to induce or receive a discrimination in price which is prohibited by this section.

Section 3. It shall be unlawful for any person engaged in commerce, in the course of such commerce, to be a party to, or assist in, any transaction of sale, or contract to sell, which discriminates to his knowledge against competitors of the purchaser, in that, any discount, rebate, allowance, or advertising service charge is granted to the purchaser over and above any discount, rebate, allowance, or advertising service charge available at the time of such transaction to said competitors in respect of a sale of goods of like grade, quality, and quantity; to sell, or contract to sell, goods in any part of the United States at prices lower than those exacted by said person elsewhere in the United States for the purpose of destroying competition, or eliminating a competitor in such part of the United States; or, to sell, or contract to sell, goods at unreasonably low prices for the purpose of destroying competition or eliminating a competitor.

Any person violating any of the provisions of this section shall, upon conviction thereof, be fined not more than $5,000 or imprisoned not more than one year, or both.

. . .[2]

---

2. Section 2 of the Clayton Act of 1914 (38 Stat. 730), provided:

"That it shall be unlawful for any person engaged in commerce, in the course of such commerce, either directly or indirectly, to discriminate in price between different purchasers of commodities, which commodities are sold for use, consumption, or resale within the United States or any Territory thereof or the District of Columbia or any insular possession or other place under the jurisdiction of the United States, where the effect of such discrimination may be to substantially lessen competition or tend to create a monopoly in any line of commerce: *Provided,* That nothing herein contained shall prevent discrimination in price between purchasers of commodities on account of differences in the grade, quality, or quantity of the commodity sold, or that makes only due allowance for difference in the cost of selling or transportation, or discrimination in price in the same or different communities made in good faith to meet competition: *And provided further,* That nothing herein contained shall prevent persons engaged in selling goods, wares, or merchandise in commerce from selecting their own customers in bona fide transactions and not in restraint of trade."

Section 4, 49 Stat. 1528 (1936), 15 U.S.C.A. § 13b, which is applicable to cooperatives, and the Non–Profit Institutions Act, 52 Stat. 446 (1938), 15 U.S.C.A. § 13c, exempting non-profit institutions, are omitted. It is likely that government purchases for use in traditional governmental functions are not covered by the Robinson–Patman Act, but government purchases for the purpose of competing with private enterprise come within the ambit of the Act. See Jefferson County Pharmaceutical Ass'n v. Abbott Laboratories, 460 U.S. 150 (1983).

On the background and history of the Robinson–Patman Act, Patman, Complete Guide to the Robinson–Patman Act Ch. I (1963) (hereafter referred to as "Patman"); Rowe, Price Discrimination Under the Robin-

SECTION 2.   SOME JURISDICTIONAL PROBLEMS AND ISSUES OF LANGUAGE

The Act starts with a series of jurisdictional provisions that a plaintiff must satisfy before moving on to the question of whether there has been an unjustified injury to competition. Many of these raise difficult issues because, as the Supreme Court observed in the *Automatic Canteen* case,[3] "precision of expression is not an outstanding characteristic of the Robinson–Patman Act."

Current law on these jurisdictional requirements is summarized below:

1. *Interstate Commerce.* Section 2(a) prevents persons "engaged in commerce" from discriminating "in the course of such commerce" where either of the purchases involved in the discrimination is "in commerce." In practice, if the third element is proven, it has been found that the other two elements must necessarily be present.[4] But one of the sales—either the high price sale or the low price sale—must cross a state line.

In Gulf Oil Corp. v. Copp Paving Co., 419 U.S. 186 (1974), plaintiffs were concrete processors who sold paving materials to California contractors engaged in building interstate highways. Plaintiffs charged that the defendant oil companies had engaged in price discrimination in sales of "asphaltic oil" produced and sold in California. Copp argued that there was a "nexus" between the sales and interstate commerce, and that Congress intended the "in commerce" language of the Robinson–Patman Act to be construed to include the full scope of Congress' commerce power. The Supreme Court rejected those arguments, noting that the distinct "in commerce" language of the Robinson–Patman Act requires that at least one of the two transactions must cross a state line. There is authority that only a small volume of sales crossing a state line is necessary to satisfy a jurisdictional requirement.[5]

Section 2(a) does not apply at all to sales for export since the provision includes the phrase "sold for use, consumption or resale within the United States ... or other place under the jurisdiction of the United States."

son–Patman Act Ch. 1 (1962 Supp. 1964) (hereafter referred to as "Rowe"); Austin, Price Discrimination Ch. I (2d rev. ed. 1959).

3. Automatic Canteen Co. v. FTC, 346 U.S. 61, 65 (1953).

4. *See, e.g.,* Lehrman v. Gulf Oil Corp., 464 F.2d 26, 36–37 (5th Cir.), cert. denied, 409 U.S. 1077 (1972); Precision Printing Co., Inc. v. Unisource Worldwide, Inc., 993 F.Supp. 338 (W.D.Pa.1998); McCallum v. City of Athens, Ga., 976 F.2d 649 (11th Cir.1992) (discussing strict interstate commerce re-

quirement under Robinson–Patman Act). See, also, Chawla v. Shell Oil Co., 75 F.Supp.2d 626 (S.D.Tex.1999) (rejecting plaintiff's reliance on defendant's interstate advertising activities and use of additives transported from out of state to refine gasoline to establish "in commerce" requirement.)

5. William Inglis & Sons Baking Co. v. ITT Continental Baking Co., 668 F.2d 1014, 1044 (9th Cir.), cert. denied, 459 U.S. 825 (1982).

2. *The Requirement of Discrimination.* The term "discrimination" as used in the Robinson–Patman Act presupposes that there is a difference in price charged by a seller to two different purchasers.[6] In computing what constitutes price, the various components of price—including discounts, surcharges, credit terms—are taken into account, and a substantial difference in these terms can produce a price difference.[7]

The majority view appears to be that where nondiscriminatory prices are *made available* to competing purchasers, any buyers paying a higher price are not victims of price discrimination.[8] Of course, the lower price must be realistically available to all customers. If a small buyer cannot take advantage of the lower price (for example, because minimum quantity purchases are required and smaller companies do not have adequate storage facilities), availability will not constitute a defense.

3. *Sales to Two Different Purchasers.* The Robinson–Patman Act only applies where goods have been sold to two different purchasers. Thus, a very early interpretation of the Act concluded that it does not apply where the seller "discriminates" by selling to one customer and refusing to sell to another.[9] Similarly, a sale at one price and nothing more than an offer to sell at a different price would not satisfy the "two purchaser requirement."[10]

Similarly, the Act does not apply to certain "non-sale transactions." For example, it has been held inapplicable to software and movie licenses[11]

---

6. *See* FTC v. Anheuser–Busch Inc., 363 U.S. 536, 549 (1960); Hoover Color Corp. v. Bayer Corp., 199 F.3d 160, 163 (4th Cir. 1999); Best Brands Beverage Inc. v. Falstaff Brewing Corp., 653 F.Supp. 47 (S.D.N.Y. 1985).

7. *See* Rose Confections, Inc. v. Ambrosia Choc. Co., 816 F.2d 381 (8th Cir.1987); Cemar, Inc. v. Nissan Motor Corp., 678 F.Supp. 1091 (D.Del.1988) (credit terms); Robbins Flooring, Inc. v. Federal Floors, Inc., 445 F.Supp. 4, 9 (E.D.Pa.1977) (credit terms); O'Connell v. Citrus Bowl Inc., 99 F.R.D. 117, 121–22 (E.D.N.Y.1983) (discounts for prompt payment and access to preferable distribution centers).

8. *See, e.g.*, Metro Ford Truck Sales v. Ford Motor Co., 145 F.3d 320, 326 (5th Cir. 1998) ("A price discount equally available to all purchasers for the same customer and product is not price discrimination"); Caribe BMW, Inc. v. Bayerische Motoren Werke, 19 F.3d 745, 751 (1st Cir.1994) ("[I]f a seller makes its favorable prices and terms available to an otherwise disfavored customer, that customer has no legal right to complain"); Edward J. Sweeney & Sons v. Texaco, Inc., 637 F.2d 105 (3d Cir.1980), cert.

denied, 451 U.S. 911 (1981); Monahan's Marine Inc. v. Boston Whaler, Inc., 676 F.Supp. 379 (D.Mass.1987).

9. In the Matter of Bird & Son, Inc., 25 F.T.C. 548 (1937); see also L & L Oil Co. v. Murphy Oil Corp., 674 F.2d 1113, 1120 (5th Cir.1982); Peter Satori of California, Inc. v. Studebaker–Packard Corp., 1964 Trade Cas. (CCH) ¶ 71,309 (S.D.Cal.1964); General United Co. v. American Honda Motor Co., 618 F.Supp. 1452, 1454 (W.D.N.C.1985).

10. Crossroads Cogeneration Corp. v. Orange & Rockland Util., Inc., 159 F.3d 129, 142 (3d Cir.1998) (offer to sell insufficient); Terry's Floor Fashions, Inc. v. Burlington Industries, Inc., 763 F.2d 604, 615 (4th Cir. 1985); Koblar Constructors and Engineers v. G.H. Dacy Associates, 1987-2 Trade Cases p 67665 (N.D.Fla.1987) (unpublished case).

11. Microsoft Corp. v. BEC Computer Co., 818 F.Supp. 1313 (C.D.Cal.1992) (computer software licenses are not sales to different purchasers); County Theatre Co. v. Paramount Film Distributing Corp., 146 F.Supp. 933 (E.D.Pa.1956) (movie licenses).

and product swaps among oil companies.[12]

Some difference of view has arisen where purported sales occur between different affiliates or subsidiaries within the same corporate family. Most courts would conclude that where a wholly owned subsidiary receives a low price, especially when fully controlled by the parent, that is not a reviewable sale that may be compared to purchases by outsiders at a higher price.[13]

Problems arise when supplier sells directly to retailers, and indirectly by selling to wholesalers who in turn sell to retailers. If the sale to the direct-buying retailers and to the wholesalers is at the same price, there are no two buyers paying different prices, and therefore there is no discrimination cognizable under the statute. Assuming the retailer who buys indirectly (*i.e.*, through wholesale channels) will end up paying more than the direct-buying retail competitor, the retailer can only obtain relief if it can somehow "attribute" the wholesale price to the manufacturer so that there are sales at two difference prices. Such attribution can only occur if the intermediary is owned or controlled by the manufacturer. See National Lead Co. v. FTC, 227 F.2d 825 (7th Cir.1955), rev'd on other grounds, 352 U.S. 419 (1957); Purolator Products Inc. v. FTC, 352 F.2d 874 (7th Cir.1965).

Finally, there is a statutory exemption to the Robinson–Patman Act that provides that it does not apply to non-profit institutions.[14]

4. *The Requirement of "Commodity."* Section 2(a) prohibits discrimination in price between different purchasers of "commodities," a condition also described in Section 2(a), apparently interchangeably, as the sale of "goods, wares or merchandise."[15] In general, the term "commodity" has been limited to tangible products and, as a result, the Act has been held not to apply to newspaper advertising,[16] services and trades on a stock ex-

---

12. Rebel Oil Co. v. Atlantic Richfield Co., 146 F.3d 1088 (9th Cir.), cert. denied, 525 U.S. 1017 (1998) (swap transactions not subject to statute); American Oil Co. v. McMullin, 508 F.2d 1345, 1353 (10th Cir. 1975).

13. Recent decisions have applied Copperweld Corp. v. Independence Tube Corp., 467 U.S. 752 (1984), to sales between corporate entities, finding that sales within a corporate structure are not subject to the Robinson–Patman Act. Caribe BMW, Inc. v. Bayerische Motoren Werke, 19 F.3d 745, 748 (1st Cir.1994); City of Mount Pleasant v. Associated Elec. Cooperative, Inc., 838 F.2d 268 (8th Cir.1988) (Robinson–Patman Act should not reach activity that has no economic consequence, such as sales between a parent and subsidiary); Russ' Kwik Car Wash, Inc. v. Marathon Petroleum Co., 772 F.2d 214 (6th Cir.1985) (per curiam) (*Cop-*

perweld applies to Robinson–Patman Act and the parent and subsidiary should be viewed as a single economic unit); Precision Printing Co. v. Unisource Worldwide, Inc., 993 F.Supp. 338 (W.D.Pa.1998) (relying on *Copperweld* and *Caribe BMW*, division of corporation could not be deemed a separate seller).

A related question concerns the "indirect purchaser" doctrine. Thus, a purchaser may bring an action against a seller even if it buys through some intermediary where the seller controls the terms on which sales are made to both purchasers.

14. 52 Stat. 446 (1938), 15 U.S.C.A. § 13C (1980).

15. 15 U.S.C.A. § 13(a) (1962).

16. Ambook Enterprises v. Time, Inc., 612 F.2d 604 (2d Cir.1979), cert. dismissed, 448 U.S. 914 (1980).

change,[17] sales of telephone pole space for cable television,[18] or the loan of money at interest[19] or medical services.[20]

In Columbia Broadcasting System v. Amana Refrigeration, Inc.,[21] Amana charged that CBS violated Section 2(a) by granting greater discounts on the basis of quantity to sponsors of evening hour programs, including competitors of Amana. The court concluded that the transaction between CBS and advertisers was not accurately characterized as a "sale" of television "time," but rather involved the purchase by Amana of the privilege of having itself identified as sponsor of a program broadcast. The court concluded that the word "commodity" in context applies to tangible products, not the privilege of sponsorship identification involved in TV broadcasting.[22]

5. *Like Grade and Quality.* Violation of Section 2(a) occurs only if the discrimination occurs with respect to commodities "of like grade and quality."

One set of questions involves application of the statute to products that are comparable in the eyes of consumers but not identical. In Atalanta Trading Corp. v. FTC,[23] a Court of Appeals rejected a Commission conclusion that canned hams, pork shoulders and precooked Canadian bacon were of like grade and quality because, as the Commission put it, "ham is ham...."The court concluded that because various products are derived from a common source, it does not follow that they all need to be marketed in an identical fashion. Other cases have concluded some "more than insubstantial" difference is required to trigger the statute.[24]

---

17. Gordon v. New York Stock Exchange, 366 F.Supp. 1261 (S.D.N.Y.1973).

18. T.V. Signal Co. v. American Tel. & Tel. Co., 462 F.2d 1256 (8th Cir.1972).

19. Bichel Optical Laboratories, Inc. v. Marquette National Bank, 336 F.Supp. 1368 (D.Minn.1971). Recent cases addressing what is covered by "commodity" have held cellular phone services and telecommunications services are not "commodities" under the Robinson–Patman Act. Metro Comm. Co. v. Ameritech Mobile Comm., Inc., 984 F.2d 739 (6th Cir.1993) (cellular telephone services); National Comm. Ass'n v. AT & T, 808 F.Supp. 1131 (S.D.N.Y.1992) (long distance voice telecommunications).

20. Ball Memorial Hospital v. Mutual Hospital Ins., 784 F.2d 1325, 1340 (7th Cir. 1986).

21. 295 F.2d 375 (7th Cir.1961), cert. denied, 369 U.S. 812 (1962).

22. See Blake & Blum, Network Television Rate Practices: A Case Study in the Failure of Social Control of Price Discrimina-

tion, 74 Yale L.J. 1339 (1965). Note Antitrust Implications of Network Television Quantity Advertising Discounts, 65 Colum.L.Rev. 12, 13 (1965).

In 1978, the Commission ruled that newspaper advertising could be a commodity, 92 F.T.C. 230 (1978), in an interlocutory order, but later dismissed the proceeding, even after the respondents offered a proposed consent order, indicating doubts whether the Robinson–Patman Act should be applied to advertising media. Times Mirror Co., 100 F.T.C. 252 (1982).

23. 258 F.2d 365 (2d Cir.1958).

24. William Inglis & Sons Baking Co. v. ITT Continental Baking Co., 461 F.Supp. 410, 421 (N.D.Cal.1978), aff'd in part and reversed in part on other grounds, 668 F.2d 1014 (9th Cir.), cert. denied, 459 U.S. 825 (1982); but see A.A. Poultry Farms v. Rose Acre Farms, 881 F.2d 1396, 1407 (7th Cir. 1989), cert. denied, 494 U.S. 1019 (1990).

It has been urged that the question of fungibility be analyzed in terms of consumer reaction. If buyers would be equally happy with one product or the other for the same amount of money, they should be determined "of like grade and quality" for purposes of the statute.[25] Manufacturing costs have occasionally been looked to as an aid in deciding "like grade and quality" questions. Where manufacturing costs are the same, that can contribute to a finding of fungibility;[26] on the other hand, if there are substantial physical differences in products which affect consumer preference or marketability, similar products will not be found to be of like grade and quality just because manufacturing costs are the same.[27]

More vexing questions arise where products are chemically identical but, because of national advertising or trade names, can be sold at different prices. In FTC v. Borden Co.,[28] Borden produced and sold evaporated milk under the Borden name as a nationally advertised, premium brand. It also marketed evaporated milk under various private brands owned by its customers. The private label milk was physically and chemically identical with the Borden brand milk, but the former was sold at both wholesale and retail levels at prices regularly below those obtained for the premium brand. The Supreme Court, in a 7–2 decision, held that Borden brand milk and the private label were of "like grade and quality" within the meaning of Section 2(a) of the Robinson–Patman Act. The majority was reluctant to read out of the reach of the statute on a jurisdictional basis price discrimination between chemically identical products, preferring to preserve for the Commission an opportunity to examine under the more flexible standards of cost justification and injury to competition whether a violation had occurred. On remand, the Court of Appeals, noting evidence of a strong consumer preference for the premium brand, concluded there had been no violation because of no injury to competition.[29]

Finally, there is a time dimension to the issue of like grade and quality. For example, in Atalanta Trading Corp. v. FTC, 258 F.2d 365 (2d Cir.1958), a court regarded the failure to provide a promotional allowance more than five months after the original transaction as not relating to a reasonably contemporaneous transaction, and hence not an actionable discrimination. It noted that a contrary determination would require sellers to hold open promotional arrangements to prospective purchasers for extended periods of time or to refuse to deal with them altogether. The nature of the product or special market conditions may affect the question of what constitutes reasonably contemporaneous sales. For example, later sales of perishable

25. F. Rowe, Price Discrimination Under the Robinson–Patman Act, 74–76 (1962).

26. See Quaker Oats Co., FTC Docket 8112, 66 F.T.C. 1190, 1192 (1964).

27. Universal–Rundle Corp., FTC Docket 8070, 65 F.T.C. 924, 955 (1964).

28. 383 U.S. 637 (1966).

29. To the same effect, see Texaco Inc. v. Hasbrouck, 496 U.S. 543, 556 (1990); International Tel. & Tel. Corp., 3 Trade Reg. Rep. (CCH) ¶ 22,188 (FTC 1984); Beatrice Foods Co., 76 FTC 719, 809 (1969), aff'd sub nom. Kroger Co. v. FTC, 438 F.2d 1372 (6th Cir.), cert. denied, 404 U.S. 871 (1971).

On the issue of like grade and quality, see Antitrust Law Developments (Second) 227–29 (1984); C. Austin, Price Discrimination 38, 128 (ALI Second Rev.Ed. 1959); Rowe, at 62.

products at lower prices may not be treated as being of like grade and quality because perishable foods may become less valuable after a short period of time.[30]

6. *Proof of Damages.* In government cases where the relief sought is an injunction, the standard for proof of damages is not very demanding. The statute itself talks about situations where the effect of a discrimination "may be substantially to lessen competition," and usually proof of a substantial discrimination in a market in which there is keen competition will be adequate to establish a base for a remedy.[31]

Where a private party sues for damages, it must proceed under Section 4 of the Clayton Act which provides such damages to "any person who *shall be injured* in his business or property by reason of anything forbidden in the antitrust laws ..." (emphasis added).[32] Prior to 1981, there was a division in the lower courts on what a plaintiff needed to prove. Some courts followed the "automatic damage theory" which allowed an inference of an injury from a showing of a substantial price discrimination,[33] while other courts insisted on evidence that the private injury complained of was directly attributable to something outlawed by the antitrust laws.[34]

The issue is important because, given the difficulty of proving the particular effect of a price discrimination, a demanding standard of evidence will restrict opportunities for private plaintiffs to bring treble damage actions under the Robinson–Patman Act. In J. Truett Payne Co. v. Chrysler Motors Corp.,[35] the Supreme Court rejected the automatic damage approach and required proof of actual injury "attributable to something the antitrust laws were designed to prevent." The Court indicated that a disfavored purchaser could show "actual" injury if it could prove that the favored purchaser lowered its resale price as a result of the discrimination and took sales away from the disfavored purchaser, or even that the disfavored purchaser was less able to compete because it had fewer funds available for advertising and capital expenditures. But in *Truett Payne* where the evidence only showed that a local market share had dropped slightly, with no indication that the decline was due to the price discrimination, the Court concluded that the fact of injury had not been proven.

---

30. Dyno Nobel, Inc. v. Amotech Corp., 63 F.Supp.2d 140, 147 (D.P.R.1999) (old blasting caps that were obsolete or approaching end of their shelf lives differed in grade and quality from new blasting caps; an essential feature of a blasting capability is to set off explosives with exact timing and as product ages, ability to do so deteriorates). Lombino & Sons, Inc. v. Standard Fruit & S.S. Co., 1975–2 Trade Cas. (CCH) ¶ 60,527 (S.D.N.Y. 1975). Similarly, see Peter Satori Inc. v. Studebaker–Packard Corp., 1964 Trade Cas. (CCH) ¶ 71,309 (S.D.Cal. 1964) (introduction of newer models influences what constitutes a contemporaneous transaction).

31. See discussion infra in Section 3.

32. 15 U.S.C.A. § 15 (Supp.1982).

33. Fowler Manufacturing Co. v. Gorlick, 415 F.2d 1248 (9th Cir.1969), cert. denied, 396 U.S. 1012 (1970); Elizabeth Arden Sales Corp. v. Gus Blass Co., 150 F.2d 988 (8th Cir.), cert. denied, 326 U.S. 773 (1945).

34. See Enterprise Industries Inc. v. Texas Co., 240 F.2d 457 (2d Cir.), cert. denied, 353 U.S. 965 (1957); Edward J. Sweeney & Sons v. Texaco, Inc., 637 F.2d 105 (3d Cir.1980).

35. 451 U.S. 557 (1981).

Lower courts have extended the *Truett Payne* decision to actions involving services and facilities under Section 2(d) and 2(e) of the Act, as well as direct price discrimination under 2(a).[36]

7. *Criminal Provisions—Section 3 of the Robinson–Patman Act.* Section 3 of the Robinson–Patman Act makes it criminal to sell goods at "unreasonably low prices for the purpose of destroying competition or eliminating a competitor." The provision can be enforced by the government but not by private parties.[37]

In United States v. National Dairy Products Corp., 372 U.S. 29 (1963), the Supreme Court sustained the statute against a claim by defendants that the phrase "unreasonably low prices" was unconstitutionally vague. The Court concluded that the Act fairly applied to sales below cost (although it did not attempt to specify what elements of cost, such as direct and indirect, needed to be taken into account), and emphasized that the additional element of predatory intent alleged in the indictment provided adequate definition of the prohibited conduct. The Court did not attempt to specify whether the intent or conduct necessary to make out a civil violation of Section 2(a) of the Act would automatically also violate Section 3, although the tenor of the opinion and its emphasis on intent would appear to indicate that a higher standard of proof would be required before a Section 3 criminal violation would be found.

Criminal enforcement of the Robinson–Patman Act has rarely been undertaken, and not at all in over 40 years.

8. *Enforcement Since 1980.* Although the target of widespread and constant criticism, the Robinson–Patman Act has been neither repealed nor significantly amended.

Largely as a result of doubts about the Act's utility, it has been virtually unenforced at the federal level in recent years. The Antitrust Division of the Department of Justice has never enforced the statute. The Federal Trade Commission brought scores of Robinson–Patman cases each year in the 1940s and the 1950s, but that situation has changed. Since 1980, the Commission has enforced the Act only twice. It sued six major U.S. book publishers for price and service discrimination, but later abandoned the actions. In 2000, the Commission brought an action against McCormick & Co. and later settled the case. For a description of the case see page 1308, *infra*.

Robinson–Patman Act enforcement continues to be a favorite of the private bar; many treble damage actions are brought each year by private plaintiffs, but their chances of prevailing have declined substantially. One reason is the widespread skepticism within the judiciary that price discrimination often leads to serious injuries to competition (as opposed to individu-

---

36. See Rutman Wine Co. v. E. & J. Gallo Winery, 829 F.2d 729 (9th Cir.1987); World of Sleep, Inc. v. La–Z–Boy Chair Co., 756 F.2d 1467 (10th Cir.1985), cert. denied, 474 U.S. 823 (1985).

37. Nashville Milk Co. v. Carnation Co., 355 U.S. 373 (1958).

al competitors). Another reason is the development of a rule of damages, discussed at pp. 99–106, supra, requiring proof of actual injury "attributable to something the antitrust law was designed to prevent." See J. Truett Payne v. Chrysler Motors Corp., 451 U.S. 557 (1981). Since it is difficult to prove that a particular price or service discrimination led to injury to competition, the rule has significantly deterred private plaintiffs from even initiating actions.

NOTE ON INTERNATIONAL PRICE DISCRIMINATION

As noted above, the Robinson–Patman Act does not apply to sales for export, nor does it apply when one sale is made in a foreign country and the other sale is in the United States. A different body of laws does apply to such sales, however: the antidumping provisions of the laws regulating international trade. Dumping, in its simplest form, is international price discrimination. It occurs when a company sells merchandise in its home country at a higher price than it sells the same merchandise in a foreign market (the importing country). The difference between the home market price and the foreign price is known as the "margin of dumping," and the sales made in the importing country are sometimes referred to as the "less than fair value" sales.

U.S. law on dumping today implements the international agreement known as the General Agreement on Tariffs and Trade (GATT), which in turn is now administered by the World Trade Organization. Article VI of the GATT 1947 recognizes dumping as an unfair trade practice, and it permits countries to impose an "antidumping" duty on goods that have been dumped, if the practice causes injury to the affected industry in the importing country. Although it is far beyond the scope of this book to provide a comprehensive discussion of antidumping law, the differences between the treatment of international price discrimination and its domestic counterpart are stark enough that a brief look is warranted.

The Tariff Act of 1930, as amended, is the principal U.S. antidumping statute today. See 19 U.S.C.A. §§ 1673 et seq.; 1677 et seq. Two different agencies administer the laws. It is the responsibility of the Department of Commerce's International Trade Administration (ITA) to determine, upon a proper petition, whether the merchandise in question is being sold at "less than fair value," or LTFV, and if so, to calculate the margin of dumping. An independent agency, the International Trade Commission, is charged with deciding whether the dumped merchandise is materially injuring, or threatening to inflict material injury, or materially retarding the establishment of, a U.S. industry. If both determinations are affirmative, the Department of Commerce issues an antidumping order requiring the collection of a duty, which must be equal to the dumping margin (regardless of whether or not the injury would be redressed with a smaller duty). The U.S. Customs Service actually collects the duty, on a company-specific basis. Both the need for duties and their amounts can be reviewed on an annual basis.

The salient differences between the dumping laws and the Robinson–Patman Act and other U.S. antitrust laws include the following. First, in an ordinary dumping case it does not matter whether the LTFV sales are made below cost or at a fully remunerative price. It is enough to show that there is a difference, and that the cheaper price (adjusted to show ex-factory equivalents for both sales being compared) is in the United States. Second, the dumping laws have no defenses analogous to the meeting competition defense or the cost-justification defense recognized under the Robinson–Patman Act. See Section 4 infra. Third, in some antidumping cases, where the ITA either has insufficient home market sales from which to derive a price, or it believes that the home market sales themselves were below the cost of production or otherwise not cost-based (as in nonmarket economy countries), it may "construct" a value. To construct a value, the ITA adds up (1) the costs of materials and fabrication, using whatever data it can gather from the country or an appropriate surrogate, (2) an amount for general expenses based on actual financial performance, which *cannot* be less than 10% of materials and fabrication, (3) an amount for profits, based on actual performance, but which *cannot* be less than 8% of the sum of (1) and (2), and (4) the costs of containers, coverings, and packing. Throughout this process, if companies in the exporting country do not wish to turn over proprietary financial information to the U.S. Department of Commerce, the ITA is entitled to rely on the "best information available," which usually comes from the complaining U.S. company or industry. These rules mean, in effect, that dumping will be found when sales below "total cost" are occurring, even though for antitrust purposes this would not suffice to show predatory pricing. See Chapter 8, Section 2 supra. Finally, the rules for injury in an antidumping cases require only a form of "but for causation"—but for the dumped imports, prices and profits would have been higher, ergo injury exists. See Wood, "Unfair" Trade Injury: A Competition–Based Approach, 41 Stanford L.Rev. 1153 (1989). This is in marked contrast to the rules for antitrust injury that have evolved since Brunswick v. Pueblo Bowl–O–Mat, 429 U.S. 477 (1977).

Since the conclusion of the Uruguay Round of Multilateral Trade Negotiations, which led to the agreements establishing the WTO, more and more people have begun to call for greater harmonization of antitrust law at a global level. Some believe that it will be enough to put mechanisms in place that will facilitate enforcement cooperation at the national level, and others urge the drafting and adoption of a WTO agreement on competition law. If discussions for such an agreement are launched, the antidumping laws could be part of the agenda. Within NAFTA, working groups are already considering the question whether antitrust law in the three countries can replace dumping laws within the free trade area, and if so, what aspects of both laws the new regime should retain. If and when international competition policy moves to the forefront of the economic agenda, we may find concepts from the Robinson–Patman Act playing a part in the debate. As you consider the materials that follow, you should therefore ask yourself how they might operate if the rules were expanded to cover international cases, either in lieu of today's antidumping laws or in addition to them.

SECTION 3. THE ANTICOMPETITIVE EFFECTS OF PRICE DISCRIMINATION
A. "PRIMARY-LINE" EFFECTS

Utah Pie Co. v. Continental Baking Co.
Supreme Court of the United States, 1967.
386 U.S. 685, 87 S.Ct. 1326, 18 L.Ed.2d 406.

[Utah Pie was a small family-owned company that baked frozen dessert pies—apple, cherry, boysenberry, peach, pumpkin and mince—in Salt Lake

City and sold in Utah and surrounding states. Defendants were Continental Baking, Carnation Company and Pet Milk—each a large company selling frozen dessert pies in one or more regions of the country. None of the defendants had a plant in Utah and for the most part supplied the Salt Lake City market from California bakeries.

During the period covered by the suit—1958, 1959, 1960 and the first 8 months of 1961—Utah Pie's share of the market was 66.5%, 34.3%, 45.5% and 45.3%, respectively. The frozen pie market itself was a rapidly expanding one and Utah Pie's sales volume steadily increased over the 4 years. Its total sales more than doubled during the period under review, although its net income remained very low, in the neighborhood of $7,000 to $12,000 per year.

For most of the period under review, Utah Pie's prices were the lowest in Salt Lake City. Price competition was extremely aggressive among the four companies, however, and there was evidence that each company in the course of a price war sold frozen pies in the Salt Lake City market at prices lower than they sold pies of like grade and quality in other markets closer to their bakeries.

Each of the defendants charged very low prices, but it is not clear from the opinion what standard the court applied to measure whether prices were "below cost." Thus, the court said with respect to Continental that its price in Salt Lake City was "less than its direct cost plus an allocation for overhead" and described Carnation's prices as "well below its costs." Pet was described as having suffered "substantial losses, greater than those incurred elsewhere." In addition, the court cited evidence from which the jury could have concluded that some of the discriminatory pricing was aimed at Utah Pie and predatory in its intent.

> Pet's own management, as early as 1959, identified Utah Pie as an "unfavorable factor," one which "dug holes in our operation" and posed a constant "check" on Pet's performance in the Salt Lake City market. Moreover, Pet candidly admitted that during the period when it was establishing its relationship with Safeway, it sent into Utah Pie's plant an industrial spy to seek information that would be of use to Pet in convincing Safeway that Utah Pie was not worthy of its custom?

386 U.S. 685, 697, 87 S.Ct. 1326, 1333. A jury found for Utah Pie on price discrimination charges, a court of appeals reversed on grounds that the evidence was not sufficient to support a finding of probable injury to competition, and the Supreme Court reinstated the jury verdict.]

■ WHITE, J.

Section 2(a) does not forbid price competition that will probably injure or lessen competition by eliminating competitors, discouraging entry into the market or enhancing the market shares of the dominant sellers. But Congress has established some ground rules for the game. Sellers may not sell like goods to different purchasers at different prices if the result may be to injure competition in either the sellers' or the buyers' market unless such discriminations are justified as permitted by the Act. This case concerns the sellers' market. In this context, the Court of Appeals placed heavy emphasis on the fact that Utah Pie constantly increased its sales volume and continued to make a profit. But we disagree with its apparent view that there is no reasonably possible injury to competition as long as the volume of sales in a particular market is expanding and at least some of the competitors in the market continue to operate at a profit. Nor do we think that the Act only comes into play to regulate the conduct of price discriminators when their discriminatory prices consistently undercut other competitors. It is true that many of the primary line cases that have reached the courts have involved blatant predatory price discriminations employed with the hope of immediate destruction of a particular competitor. On the question of injury to competition such cases present courts with no difficulty, for such pricing is clearly within the heart of the proscription of the Act. Courts and commentators alike have noted that the existence of predatory intent might bear on the likelihood of injury to competition. In this case there was some evidence of predatory intent with respect to each of these respondents.[38] There was also other evidence upon which the jury could rationally find the requisite injury to competition. The frozen pie market in Salt Lake City was highly competitive. At times Utah Pie was a leader in moving the general level of prices down, and at other times each of the respondents also bore responsibility for the downward pressure on the price structure. We believe that the Act reaches price discrimination that erodes competition as much as it does price discrimination that is intended to have immediate destructive impact. In this case, the evidence shows a drastically declining price structure which the jury could rationally attribute to continued or sporadic price discrimination. The jury was entitled to conclude that "the effect of such discrimination," by each of these respondents, "may be substantially to lessen competition . . . or to injure, destroy, or prevent competition with any person who either grants or knowingly receives the benefit of such discrimination. . . ." The statutory test is one that necessarily looks forward on the basis of proven conduct in the past. Proper application of that standard here requires reversal of the judgment of the Court of Appeals.[39]

38. It might be argued that the respondents' conduct displayed only fierce competitive instincts. Actual intent to injure another competitor does not, however, fall into that category, and neither, when viewed in the context of the Robinson–Patman Act, do persistent sales below cost and radical price cuts themselves discriminatory. Nor does the fact that a local competitor has a major share of the market make him fair game for discriminatory price cutting free of Robinson–Patman Act proscriptions. "The Clayton Act proscription as to discrimination in price is not nullified merely because of a showing that the existing competition in a particular market had a major share of the sales of the product involved." Maryland Baking Co., 52 F.T.C. 1679, aff'd, 243 F.2d 716. In that case the local competitor's share of the market when price discrimination began was 91.3%, yet the Federal Trade Commission was not impressed by the argument that the effect of the discrimination had been to terminate a monopoly and to create a competitive market.

39. Each respondent argues here that prior price discrimination cases in the courts and before the Federal Trade Commission, in which no primary line injury to competition was found, establish a standard which compels affirmance of the Court of Appeals' holding. But the cases upon which the re-

■ WARREN, C.J., took no part in the decision of this case.

■ STEWART, J., with whom HARLAN, J., joins, dissenting.

I would affirm the judgment, agreeing substantially with the reasoning of the Court of Appeals. . . .

There is only one issue in this case in its present posture: . . . did the respondents' actions have the anticompetitive effect required by the statute as an element of a cause of action?

The Court's own description of the Salt Lake City frozen pie market from 1958 through 1961 shows that the answer to that question must be no. In 1958 Utah Pie had a quasi-monopolistic 66.5% of the market. In 1961—after the alleged predations of the respondents—Utah Pie still had a commanding 45.3%, Pet had 29.4%, and the remainder of the market was divided almost equally between Continental, Carnation, and other small local bakers. Unless we disregard the lessons so laboriously learned in scores of Sherman and Clayton Act cases, the 1961 situation has to be considered more competitive than that of 1958. Thus, if we assume that the price discrimination proven against the respondents had any effect on competition, that effect must have been beneficent.

That the Court has fallen into the error of reading the Robinson–Patman Act as protecting competitors, instead of competition, can be seen from its unsuccessful attempt to distinguish cases relied upon by the respondents.[40] Those cases are said to be inapposite because they involved "no general decline in price structure," and no "lasting impact upon prices." But lower prices are the hallmark of intensified competition.

The Court of Appeals squarely identified the fallacy which the Court today embraces:

> . . . a contention that Utah Pie was entitled to hold the extraordi-nary market share percentage of 66.5, attained in 1958, falls of its own dead weight. To approve such a contention would be to hold that Utah Pie was entitled to maintain a position which ap-

spondents rely are readily distinguishable. In Anheuser–Busch, Inc. v. FTC, 289 F.2d 835, 839, there was no general decline in price structure attributable to the defendant's price discrimination, nor was there any evidence that the price discriminations were "a single lethal weapon aimed at a victim for predatory purposes." Id., at 842. In Borden Co. v. FTC, 339 F.2d 953, the court reversed the Commission's decision on price discrimination in one market for want of sufficient interstate connection, and the Commission's charge regarding the other market failed to show any lasting impact upon prices caused by the single, isolated incident of price discrimination proved. Absence of proof that the alleged injury was due to challenged price discriminations was determinative in

International Milling Co., Trade Reg.Rep.Transfer Binder, 1963–1965, ¶ ¶ 16,-494, 16,648. In Uarco, Inc., Trade Reg.Rep.Transfer Binder, 1963–1965, ¶ 16,-807, there was no evidence from which pred-atory intent could be inferred and no evi-dence of a long-term market price decline. Similar failure of proof and absence of sales below cost were evident in Quaker Oats Co., Trade Reg.Rep.Transfer Binder, 1963–1965, ¶ 17,134. Dean Milk Co., 3 Trade Reg.Rep. ¶ 17,357, is not to the contrary. There in the one market where the Commission found no primary line injury there was no evidence of a generally declining price structure.

40. See ante, n. 39.

proached, if it did not in fact amount to a monopoly, and could not exist in the face of proper and healthy competition.

349 F.2d 122, 155.

I cannot hold that Utah Pie's monopolistic position was protected by the federal antitrust laws from effective price competition, and I therefore respectfully dissent.

Anheuser–Busch, Inc. v. FTC

United States Court of Appeals, Seventh Circuit, 1961.
289 F.2d 835.

[The Seventh Circuit previously had held that certain pricing practices by Anheuser–Busch, described below, did not constitute price discrimination and the Supreme Court reversed and remanded, 363 U.S. 536 (1960).

The statement of facts in the Supreme Court included the following. Anheuser–Busch (AB) ranked first or second nationally in brewing, and sold its Budweiser label at prices higher than beers of regional and local breweries in most markets. Prices and price differentials between beers varied a good deal from market to market. In the St. Louis area, AB's principal competitors were Falstaff Brewing Corp., Griesedieck Western Brewing Co. (GW), and Griesedieck Bros. Brewery Co. (GB). In line with the prevailing price structure, these competitors normally sold their product at a price substantially lower than AB.

In late 1953, most breweries in the country introduced a price increase following renegotiation of an employee wage contract, but AB and its competitors in the St. Louis market maintained their previous prices. Thereafter, the following price moves occurred. In January 1954, AB cut its price on Budweiser in St. Louis by 25 cents per case, thereby reducing the previous differential between Budweiser and the local beers from 58 to 33 cents. In June, 1954, AB again cut its prices so as to be exactly equal to the prices of its St. Louis competitors. In March 1955, AB increased its price in St. Louis by 45 cents per case, and its competitors raised their prices by 15 cents per case which reestablished a substantial price differential. Prior to the 1954 price cut and during the period of the price war, AB prices on Budweiser were lower in the St. Louis market than in other markets around the country.

The Commission had originally held that these price cuts constituted a discrimination in that they diverted business to AB from its St. Louis competitors. In its first decision, the Court of Appeals reversed on grounds that there could be no "price discrimination" under 2(a) unless different competing purchasers bought at different prices; here all competing purchasers bought at the same price. The Supreme Court reversed and remanded, and the Court of Appeals' second opinion picks up at that point:]

■ SCHNAKENBERG, J. . . . The gains and losses in the shares of the St. Louis packaged beer market commencing before and ending after AB's price reductions of January 4, and June 21, 1954, expressed in percentages of sales as divided among AB, Griesedieck Brothers (GB), Falstaff, Griesedieck Western (GW) and "All Others," are set forth in the following tabulation:

	Dec. 31 1953	June 30 1954*	March 1 1955	July 31 1955	Jan. 31 1956[41]
AB	12.5	16.55	39.3	21.03	17.5
GB	14.4	12.58	4.8	7.36	6.2
Falstaff	29.4	32.05	29.1	36.62	43.2
GW	38.9	33.00	23.1	27.78	27.3
All Others	4.8	5.82	3.94	7.21	5.8

* The entire packaged beer sales in the St. Louis market during the six months ending June 30, 1954 increased 2.7% over the same period for 1953.

This tabulation shows that AB's overall market increase in the St. Louis market area from December 31, 1953 to February 1, 1956 was 5% of the said market, while Falstaff's was 13.8% thereof.

In 1953 AB stood in fourth place in the St. Louis market and in 1956 it was in third place, having displaced GB.[42] While GW at all dates shown in the table led AB in the St. Louis market, with the exception of March 1, 1955, its relatively low rating of 23.1% at that date is explainable by unique circumstances.[43]

At the hearing before the examiner, counsel for the Commission made it clear that no claim was made that the statutory effect on competition resulted from the January 4, 1954 drop in price by AB.

Outside of St. Louis, Falstaff had eight different breweries and grew from sixth to fourth largest brewer in the United States from 1954 to 1955; its beer was sold in 26 states in the West, Midwest, South and Southeast. GB was sold in 13 states, and, indeed, as was true with each of the other beers, it was found that more than three-quarters of its sales were outside St. Louis. GW was sold in 20 states.

While AB sells its Budweiser beer throughout the United States and has ranked first or second in national sales, it has never accounted for more

41. The trial examiner found that regardless of the cut-off date used, July 31, 1955 or January 31, 1956, competition was lessened or injured. In order to determine the actual effect on competition, a statistical period must extend a reasonable time beyond the alleged illegal price reduction in order that all factors affecting the market may come into play. The tabulation becomes more comprehensive.

42. The hearing examiner's finding reveals: GB's sales were progressively declining in the St. Louis market from a share thereof in 1950 of 18% to 14.4% in 1953. In 1953 it replaced the beer it had theretofore been selling with an entirely new product which was badly named, poorly merchandised, bitter in taste and "wild"—that is with unstabi-

lized air content. AB offered the testimony of eleven saloonkeepers and storekeepers that this new beer was disliked by the consumer with the result that consumer sales thereof dropped sharply during the latter part of 1954.

43. GW had been progressively losing sales in the St. Louis market prior to 1954. Its management had been maintaining a highly liquid cash position at the expense of renewal or replacement of productive facilities. In October 1954, GW was sold to Carling Brewing Company (a subsidiary of Canadian Brewers, Ltd., which owned 18 breweries throughout the United States and Canada), at a price which reflected the good will to be about one-fifth of realizable net worth.

than about 7% of such sales and is not first in any major market in the United States. Rather, competitors such as Falstaff, GW and GB dominate most markets, just as they dominated St. Louis with 82.7% of sales.

Although the hearing examiner found that AB's position in the St. Louis market had increased from sixth to fourth from 1945 to 1953, the fact is that at all these times AB was in *last* place in St. Louis, the number of brewers having decreased from six to four by reason of mergers, none of which involved AB.

In the fall of 1953, after an increase in costs due to a new wage contract, AB increased the price of Budweiser .15¢ a case in all markets except those in Missouri and Wisconsin. In many areas this small increase was multiplied by wholesalers' and retailers' markups to $1.20 a case at the retail level.

Despite similar cost increases due to the same new wage contracts, a number of brewers, including Falstaff and AB's other St. Louis competitors, chose to absorb the increased costs, and did not raise prices in any market in which they did business. Their right to do so is not challenged. However, as a consequence, there was a spread between the price of Budweiser and the price of other beers in markets other than in Missouri and Wisconsin. In some cases this spread was created by this increase, but in most cases a preexisting spread was increased. As a result, in November and December 1953, AB began to suffer severe sales losses in the Midwest sales area, supplied by its St. Louis brewery—losses as high as 73% in Nebraska, 53% in Oklahoma, 58% in Texas, etc. In some states AB's sales were down as much as 83% below the previous year; and while industry sales were down only 8%, AB's sales were more than 35% below the previous year.

AB contends that it was obvious that something had to be done to correct the situation. The question was *what* should be done.

AB tried to roll back its price increase in one area, Ohio. but found, as it had anticipated, that the retailers and wholesalers were unwilling to give up their total additional markup of $1.20 per case merely because AB reduced its price 15¢ per case.

The first price reduction in St. Louis went into effect on January 4, 1954 and amounted to $25 per case. This still left the price of Budweiser $33 higher than the prices of its three principal competitors in St. Louis. All St. Louis brewers sold directly to retailers, and there were no wholesalers' markups to concern them. Furthermore, AB's home office was in St. Louis, and by a direct effort it was able to convince 85% of the retailers there to pass on the price reduction to consumers. Thus the problem of wholesalers' and retailers' markups was not present in St. Louis as it was elsewhere. Moreover, from a freight standpoint, AB was one of the few brewers who attempted to sell throughout the United States from one or two brewing sites. For example, in the area served by AB's single St. Louis brewery, Falstaff had seven breweries and intensely cultivated the area within about 300 miles of each of those seven, resulting in an estimated annual saving of $1,000,000. If AB reduced its price in an area where it had no plant, it would have to pay high freight costs from St. Louis and compete with the regional brewery getting its products from a local plant. Accordingly, all four named brewers there had at least one local plant so that none of them was faced with a freight disadvantage.

While the January 4, 1954 new price was in effect, AB also increased its advertising expenditures in St. Louis, which theretofore had been a fraction of its competitors' advertising. AB also changed its method of solicitation and delivery of orders to the system used by all of its St. Louis competitors and changed the organization of its sales force.

Despite all these changes, AB's national sales continued to decline. Then, on June 21, 1954, the second price reduction of Budweiser in St. Louis was made, the new price being the same as its three competitors had been, and were then, charging for their beers, or, as the complaint states, the price of beer "exactly matched the established price charged for beer" by the St. Louis competitors. In addition AB continued its efforts to solve its sales problem. Early in 1954, it considered proposals for reducing the capacity of its containers. On March 1, 1955, it marketed a new brand of beer to be priced competitively with its dominant competitors in the various markets, but this beer proved to be a failure. It then raised the price of Budweiser 45¢ per case and the St. Louis competitors raised their price by 15¢ a case, making Budweiser 30¢ higher-priced than its competitors. The record fails to reveal the fate of a different and cheaper beer introduced by AB in August, 1955.

While it is true that AB's sales increased in St. Louis during the period of the price reductions,[44] a fact which alone surely cannot constitute a violation of § 2(a), nevertheless AB's competitors still controlled more than three-fourths of market sales in the twelve months after the price of Budweiser was voluntarily increased in St. Louis in March, 1955. While Budweiser and other premium beers were selling at the same price in St. Louis, buyers had a greater freedom of choice at the same price level and thus the contest for beer sales was intensified.

During the 1954–1955 price reductions, AB's St. Louis competitors continued to sell in St. Louis at the same price at which they had previously sold. None of them lost retail customers; each continued to sell to the same retailers to whom it had always sold; and each continued to sell at the same prices at which it had previously sold. Each continued to make profits—Falstaff, for example, earned almost $7,000,000 in 1954. Each continued to vary its competitive activities, *e.g.*, changing the formula of its products, changing its labels, varying its advertising, offering special price promotions, entering new markets, etc.

The record reveals only a temporary shift in volume of business among the competitors in the St. Louis market. Although AB did attain a monthly average of 36.6% of sales during the eight months of the second price

---

44. As indicated, ... AB's sales increase was equal to 5% of the St. Louis market between Dec. 31, 1953 and Feb. 1, 1956.

reduction, nevertheless this was not as great a share of the market as its leading competitors obtained before or after the price reduction. Whatever position AB obtained was temporary; by 1956 its sales had receded to 17.5% of the market, whereas Falstaff at that time had increased to 43% of the market from the 29.4% it had enjoyed before the price reductions.

The examiner expressly found that there was no proof that AB used income or profit from the rest of its business to stabilize losses in St. Louis, or indeed, that there were any losses by AB in St. Louis during the period of the price reductions.

AB's two price reductions were parts of an experimental program of sales promotion in the St. Louis market and the reductions were temporary and made necessary by competitive conditions. A primary result of AB's price reductions was that the consumers of beer in St. Louis enjoyed a lower price on Budweiser, since the price reductions were passed on to them by the retailers.

While AB's two price reductions undoubtedly contributed to moderate changes in the division of the beer sales in the St. Louis market, there was also a causal connection between those changes and (a) GW's and GB's special problems, . . . (b) Falstaff's gain of 13.8% of the market and (c) a 1% gain by "All Others."

Considering that the Commission relied on a percentage test, no one is able to determine from this record how much of the losses of AB's competitors were attributable to these special facts as compared to any losses resulting solely from AB's price reductions.

From these undisputed facts we find that the Commission failed to prove that AB's price reductions in 1954 caused any present, actual injury to competition. . . .

. . . [We now] consider the Commission's reliance on Corn Products Refining Co. v. Federal Trade Commission, 1945, 324 U.S. 726. In that case, 324 U.S. at page 738 the Court pointed out:

> . . . § 2(a) does not require a finding that the discriminations in price have in fact had an adverse effect on competition. . . . It is enough that they "may" have the proscribed effect. . . . The use of the word "may" was not to prohibit discriminations having "the mere possibility" of those consequences, but to reach those which would probably have the defined effect on competition.

. . . [W]e find that, there being no showing that AB had aid from its other markets and despite a decrease in its national sales,[45] AB forthrightly met its robust competition in the St. Louis market by a multiple-pronged program, which included but was not limited to a two-step reduction in its price to exactly meet that of its competitors. The record affirmatively shows that AB used restraint in its competitive efforts. Its conduct was in

45. Its total sales were off more than 1,000,000 cases in May and 1,500,000 cases in June 1954. These followed successive declines in national sales for each preceding month in 1954 and for November and December 1953.

conformity with the principle that competition is the decisive force in the market place. That conduct is the antithesis of the predatory misconduct condemned in ... territorial pricing cases relied on by the Commission. In each of those cases the motive for the price cut was vindictive and the effect was punitive. There was not even a pretense that the price change was incident to a general intensification of the sales effort, as in the case at bar. It was a single lethal weapon aimed at a victim for a predatory purpose.

The Commission relies heavily upon finding 26 in the initial decision of the examiner, which includes the following statements:

> ... we are here concerned not only with actual injury but with potential injury as well, and there is nothing in this record to show that what A.B. did in the St. Louis market could not or would not be done by it, in the future, in other markets as well.... A.B. has total assets of more than twice those of its three St. Louis brewery competitors, and, selling nation-wide as it does, is able, *although there is no proof that it did*, to use income or profit from the rest of its business to stabilize losses, if any, incurred in such a price raid. I repeat, there is *no showing that it did, but* the record shows *it could*—the potentiality is there.... (Italics supplied.)

It is true that the effects of AB's acts on competition might have been different from what they actually were and that nevertheless it could be held to account under § 2(a) for what actually happened as well as the reasonably possible effects thereof. But, to prove the *acts* themselves, the Commission was required to adduce evidence of what AB *did* and a finding of a violation cannot rest upon a conjecture as to what it *might do*. Potentiality to commit an act cannot be used as a substitute for proof of the act itself. While it has been said that every person has a little larceny in his heart, not even a cynic would attempt to procure a conviction on that ground alone. Nor are we convinced that guilt of an alleged malefactor can be proved by only its bigness.[46] The Commission's argument that the "over-all size of the interstate enterprise" of AB "is significant, for it enables a seller to engage in area price discriminations without fear of severe monetary loss to itself", is met by the examiner's finding that there was no proof that AB had employed its size to support its price reductions.

... [T]he findings of the Commission cannot, on the consideration of the whole record, be deemed to be supported by substantial evidence.

Brooke Group v. Brown & Williamson Tobacco

Supreme Court of the United States, 1993.
509 U.S. 209, 113 S.Ct. 2578, 125 L.Ed.2d 168.

[Reprinted p. 847 supra]

---

46. If bigness be a disqualification for a firm to compete, interesting collateral questions arise, such as, how small does a company have to be before it has the right to enter into price competition with its competitors? And how large does it have to be before it must stop competing in price?

NOTE

In recent years, particularly since the Supreme Court decision in *Brooke Group*, there is a tendency to define predatory pricing under the Sherman Act the same as injury to competition in primary line cases—*i.e.*, the challenged price in each situation must be "below cost." For an early indication of this change in direction, see International Air Industries Inc. v. American Excelsior Co., 517 F.2d 714 (5th Cir.1975); cert. denied, 424 U.S. 943 (1976).

Should the analysis under the Sherman Act and the Robinson–Patman Act be identical, given the "reasonable probability" standard of the Robinson–Patman Act?

PROBLEM 28

BARRY'S DAIRY v. BARDEN FARMS

Barden Farms manufactures and sells ice cream and other dairy products in California and nearby western states. In Los Angeles, it is in competition with three national producers and three local competitors, one of which is Barry's Dairy. Barry's specializes in making ice cream.

Barden's three national dairy competitors have been steadily increasing their share of the Los Angeles market, primarily by marketing aggressively to the larger chain food stores. Barden's share in the Los Angeles market had fallen from 23% in 1999 to 18% in 2002. During that same stretch, Barry's share had held steady at 2.5%.

At the end of 2002, Barden made a 15% discount available to all purchasers in the Los Angeles market, but did not grant any comparable discount to purchasers in other cities in California or nearby states. Barden's national competitors responded by offering the same localized price cut in Los Angeles. As a result of the discount, Barden was close to but slightly above short-run average variable cost. Barden's share of the Los Angeles market promptly rose to 20%. Shortly thereafter, one of Barden's competitors cut price again and, when Barden met that price, it was below its average variable cost. As a result of this "price war," Barry's lost several of its largest customers, two of them to Barden, and was forced to go out of business. The two other local competitors also encountered hard times and quit the market. Thereafter, Barden raised the prices, the national competition followed, and dairy product prices in Los Angeles were restored to levels that were maintained before the initial Barden price reduction.

Has Barry's a cause of action against Barden under the Robinson–Patman Act?

B.   "SECONDARY-LINE" EFFECTS

Federal Trade Commission v. Morton Salt Co.

Supreme Court of the United States, 1948.
334 U.S. 37, 68 S.Ct. 822, 92 L.Ed. 1196.

■ BLACK, J. The Federal Trade Commission, after a hearing, found that the respondent, which manufactures and sells table salt in interstate commerce, had discriminated in price between different purchasers of like grades and qualities, and concluded that such discriminations were in violation of § 2 of the Clayton Act, as amended by the Robinson–Patman

Act. Upon petition of the respondent the Circuit Court of Appeals, with one judge dissenting, set aside the Commission's findings and order, directed the Commission to dismiss its complaint against respondent, and denied a cross petition of the Commission for enforcement of its order. 7 Cir., 162 F.2d 949. . . .

Respondent manufactures several different brands of table salt and sells them directly to (1) wholesalers or jobbers, who in turn resell to the retail trade, and (2) large retailers, including chain store retailers. Respondent sells its finest brand of table salt, known as Blue Label, on what it terms a standard quantity discount system available to all customers. Under this system the purchasers pay a delivered price and the cost to both wholesale and retail purchasers of this brand differs according to the quantities bought. These prices are as follows, after making allowance for rebates and discounts:

	Per case
Less-than-carload purchases	$1.60
Carload purchases	1.50
5,000–case purchases in any consecutive 12 months	1.40
50,000–case purchases in any consecutive 12 months	1.35

Only five companies have ever bought sufficient quantities of respondent's salt to obtain the $1.35 per case price. These companies could buy in such quantities because they operate large chains of retail stores in various parts of the country. As a result of this low price these five companies have been able to sell Blue Label salt at retail cheaper than wholesale purchasers from respondent could reasonably sell the same brand of salt to independently operated retail stores, many of whom competed with the local outlets of the five chain stores.

Respondent's table salts, other than Blue Label, are also sold under a quantity discount system differing slightly from that used in selling Blue Label. Sales of these other brands in less-than-carload lots are made at list price plus freight from plant to destination. Carload purchasers are granted approximately a 5 per cent discount; approximately a 10 per cent discount is granted to purchasers who buy as much as $50,000 worth of all brands of salt in any consecutive twelve-month period. Respondent's quantity discounts on Blue Label and on other table salts were enjoyed by certain wholesalers and retailers who competed with other wholesalers and retailers to whom these discounts were refused.

In addition to these standard quantity discounts, special allowances were granted certain favored customers who competed with other customers to whom they were denied.

First. Respondent's basic contention, which it argues this case hinges upon, is that its "standard quantity discounts, available to all on equal terms, as contrasted for example, to hidden or special rebates, allowances, prices or discounts, are not discriminatory, within the meaning of the Robinson–Patman Act." Theoretically, these discounts are equally available to all, but functionally they are not. For as the record indicates (if reference to it on this point were necessary) no single independent retail grocery store, and probably no single wholesaler, bought as many as 50,000 cases or as much as $50,000 worth of table salt in one year. Furthermore, the record shows that, while certain purchasers were enjoying one or more of respondent's standard quantity discounts, some of their competitors made purchases in such small quantities that they could not qualify for any of respondent's discounts, even those based on carload shipments. The legislative history of the Robinson–Patman Act makes it abundantly clear that Congress considered it to be an evil that a large buyer could secure a competitive advantage over a small buyer solely because of the large buyer's quantity purchasing ability. The Robinson–Patman Act was passed to deprive a large buyer of such advantages except to the extent that a lower price could be justified by reason of a seller's diminished costs due to quantity manufacture, delivery or sale, or by reason of the seller's good faith effort to meet a competitor's equally low price.

Section 2 of the original Clayton Act had ... been construed as permitting quantity discounts, such as those here, without regard to the amount of the seller's actual savings in cost attributable to quantity sales or quantity deliveries. Goodyear Tire & Rubber Co. v. Federal Trade Comm., 6 Cir., 101 F.2d 620. The House Committee Report on the Robinson–Patman Act considered that the Clayton Act's proviso allowing quantity discounts so weakened § 2 "as to render it inadequate, if not almost a nullity." The Committee considered the present Robinson–Patman amendment to § 2 "of great importance." Its purpose was to limit "the use of quantity price differentials to the sphere of actual cost differences. Otherwise," the report continued, "such differentials would become instruments of favor and privilege and weapons of competitive oppression." The Senate Committee reporting the bill emphasized the same purpose, as did the Congressman in charge of the Conference Report when explaining it to the House just before final passage. And it was in furtherance of this avowed purpose—to protect competition from all price differentials except those based in full on cost savings—that § 2(a) of the amendment [was enacted in its present form].

The foregoing references, without regard to others that could be mentioned, establish that respondent's standard quantity discounts are discriminatory within the meaning of the Act, and are prohibited by it whenever they have the defined effect on competition. See Federal Trade Comm. v. Staley Co., 324 U.S. 746, 751.

Second. The Government interprets the opinion of the Circuit Court of Appeals as having held that in order to establish "discrimination in price" under the Act the burden rested on the Commission to prove that respondent's quantity discount differentials were not justified by its cost savings. Respondent does not so understand the Court of Appeals decision, and furthermore admits that no such burden rests on the Commission. We agree that it does not. First, the general rule of statutory construction that the burden of proving justification or exemption under a special exception to the prohibitions of a statute generally rests on one who claims its benefits, requires that respondent undertake this proof under the proviso of § 2(a). Secondly, § 2(b) of the Act specifically imposes the burden of showing justification upon one who is shown to have discriminated in prices. And the Senate committee report on the bill explained that the provisos of § 2(a) throw "upon any who claims the benefit of those exceptions the burden of showing that their case falls within them." We think that the language of the Act, and the legislative history just cited, show that Congress meant by using the words "discrimination in price" in § 2 that in a case involving competitive injury between a seller's customers the Commission need only prove that a seller had charged one purchaser a higher price for like goods than he had charged one or more of the purchaser's competitors....

Third. It is argued that the findings fail to show that respondent's discriminatory discounts had in fact caused injury to competition. There are specific findings that such injuries had resulted from respondent's discounts although the statute does not require the Commission to find that injury has actually resulted. The statute requires no more than that the effect of the prohibited price discriminations "may be substantially to lessen competition ... or to injure, destroy, or prevent competition." After a careful consideration of this provision of the Robinson–Patman Act, we have said that "the statute does not require that the discriminations must in fact have harmed competition, but only that there is a reasonable possibility that they 'may' have such an effect." Corn Products Co. v. Federal Trade Comm., 324 U.S. 726, 742. Here the Commission found what would appear to be obvious, that the competitive opportunities of certain merchants were injured when they had to pay respondent substantially more for their goods than their competitors had to pay. The findings are adequate.

Fourth. It is urged that the evidence is inadequate to support the Commission's findings of injury to competition. As we have pointed out, however, the Commission is authorized by the Act to bar discriminatory prices upon the "reasonable possibility" that different prices for like goods to competing purchasers may have the defined effect on competition. That respondent's quantity discounts did result in price differentials between competing purchasers sufficient in amount to influence their resale price of salt was shown by evidence. This showing in itself is adequate to support the Commission's appropriate findings....

The adequacy of the evidence to support the Commission's findings of reasonably possible injury to competition from respondent's price differentials between competing carload and less-than-carload purchasers is singled out for special attacks here. It is suggested that in considering the adequacy of the evidence to show injury to competition respondent's carload discounts and its other quantity discounts should not be treated alike. The argument is that there is an obvious saving to a seller who delivers goods in carload lots. Assuming this to be true, that fact would not tend to disprove injury to the merchant compelled to pay the less-than-carload price. For a ten-cent carload price differential against a merchant would injure him competitively just as much as a ten-cent differential under any other name. However relevant the separate carload argument might be to the question of justifying a differential by cost savings, it has no relevancy in determining whether the differential works an injury to a competitor. Since Congress has not seen fit to give carload discounts any favored classification we cannot do so. Such discounts, like all others, can be justified by a seller who proves that the full amount of the discount is based on his actual savings in cost. The trouble with this phase of respondent's case is that it has thus far failed to make such proof.

It is also argued that respondent's less-than-carload sales are very small in comparison with the total volume of its business and for that reason we should reject the Commission's finding that the effect of the carload discrimination may substantially lessen competition and may injure competition between purchasers who are granted and those who are denied this discriminatory discount. To support this argument, reference is made to the fact that salt is a small item in most wholesale and retail businesses and in consumers' budgets. For several reasons we cannot accept this contention.

There are many articles in a grocery store that, considered separately, are comparatively small parts of a merchant's stock. Congress intended to protect a merchant from competitive injury attributable to discriminatory prices on any or all goods sold in interstate commerce, whether the particular goods constituted a major or minor portion of his stock. Since a grocery store consists of many comparatively small articles, there is no possible way effectively to protect a grocer from discriminatory prices except by applying the prohibitions of the Act to each individual article in the store.

Furthermore, in enacting the Robinson–Patman Act Congress was especially concerned with protecting small businesses that were unable to buy in quantities, such as the merchants here who purchased in less-than-carload lots. To this end it undertook to strengthen this very phase of the old Clayton Act. The committee reports on the Robinson–Patman Act emphasized a belief that § 2 of the Clayton Act had "been too restrictive in requiring a showing of general injury to competitive conditions...." The new provision, here controlling, was intended to justify a finding of injury to competition by a showing of "injury to the competitor victimized by the discrimination." Since there was evidence sufficient to show that the less-than-carload purchasers might have been handicapped in competing with the more favored carload purchasers by the differential in price established by respondent, the Commission was justified in finding that competition might have thereby been substantially lessened or have been injured within the meaning of the Act.

Apprehension is expressed in this Court that enforcement of the Commission's order against respondent's continued violations of the Robinson–Patman Act might lead respondent to raise table salt prices to its carload purchasers. Such a conceivable, though, we think, highly improbable, contingency could afford us no reason for upsetting the Commission's findings and declining to direct compliance with a statute passed by Congress.

The Commission here went much further in receiving evidence than the statute requires. It heard testimony from many witnesses in various parts of the country to show that they had suffered actual financial losses on account of respondent's discriminatory prices. Experts were offered to prove the tendency of injury from such prices. The evidence covers about two thousand pages, largely devoted to this single issue—injury to competition. It would greatly handicap effective enforcement of the Act to require testimony to show that which we believe to be self-evident, namely, that there is a "reasonable possibility" that competition may be adversely affected by a practice under which manufacturers and producers sell their goods to some customers substantially cheaper than they sell like goods to the competitors of these customers. This showing in itself is sufficient to justify our conclusion that the Commission's findings of injury to competition were adequately supported by evidence....

The judgment of the Circuit Court of Appeals is reversed and the proceedings are remanded to that court to be disposed of in conformity with this opinion.[47]

––––––––

COASTAL FUELS OF PUERTO RICO V. CARIBBEAN PETROLEUM CORP., 79 F.3d 182 (1st Cir.1996). Carribean owned and operated a refinery in Puerto Rico and sold fuel products to resellers, including "bunker fuel" used by cruise ships and other ocean going vehicles. Coastal was a reseller and claimed a violation of Section 2(a) of the Robinson–Patman Act on grounds that Caribbean sold to two other competing resellers in San Juan harbor at a substantially lower price than to Coastal. A jury found for Coastal and assessed damages of $1.5 million, trebled to $4.5 million under the statute.

On appeal, Caribbean challenged the finding of a secondary line price discrimination on, among other grounds, an absence of competitive injury. Caribbean recognized that the *Morton Salt* rule, providing that injury to competition is established *prima facie* by proof of a substantial price discrimination between competing purchasers over time, supported Coastal's position. It asked the Court of Appeals to treat *Morton Salt* as no longer good law as a result of the Supreme Court's 1993 decision in *Brooke Group* (see p. 847, supra). It described *Brooke Group* as concluding that in primary line Robinson–Patman cases, courts must reconcile the goals of the Robinson–Patman and Sherman Acts, and that both statutes were designed to protect competition and not competitors, and argued that this same reasoning should apply in secondary line cases.

The First Circuit Court of Appeals joined two other circuits in rejecting the claim that *Morton Salt* had been overruled. The Court concluded from legislative history and the statutory language of the Robinson–Patman Act that Congress' intent in 1936 was to protect small retailers from being driven out of business by

47. The opinion of Jackson, J., with whom Frankfurter, J., joined, dissenting in part, is omitted.

large retail chains' ability to secure discriminatory discounts. The economic evil Congress intended to address did not necessarily relate to "consumer welfare *per se*" alone, but had an element of protecting small business. Noting that the *Brooke Group* opinion expressly applied only to primary line cases, the Court concluded that "given the legislative history and statutory language distinctions, we will not presume, without more guidance, that the Supreme Court intended in *Brooke Group* to alter the well established rule that it had adopted in *Morton Salt*".

IN THE MATTER OF McCORMICK & CO. In 2000, the Federal Trade Commission added yet another twist to the interpretation of *Morton Salt*. McCormick was the world's largest manufacturer and distributor of spice products sold through supermarkets and other grocery outlets, and offered substantial discounts to some large supermarket chains but not to competing stores. Typically, McCormick's discounts were in the form of upfront cash payments that resembled the payments sometimes called slotting allowances in the supermarket industry. The payments commonly required that the customer allocate to Mccormick a large portion, often as much as 90%, of the shelf space devoted to spice products.

The Commission's complaint alleged that each instance of discrimination involved a substantial price difference, over a substantial period of time, between competing purchasers in markets where profit margins were low and competition was keen—circumstances that give rise to an inference of competitive harm within the meaning of *Morton Salt*. The Commission did not rest entirely on *Morton Salt*, however, but looked at a range of other factors to examine whether there was actual injury to competition. In its Analysis to Aid Public Comment, the Commission explained:

> While [*Morton Salt*] inference may not be sufficient by itself in some circumstances to warrant bringing a case, in this instance, the inference is strengthened by McCormick's position as the largest supplier of spice and seasoning products in the United States and by the fact that McCormick typically demanded that customers allocate to McCormick the large majority of the space devoted to spice products. . . .

As alleged in the Complaint, disfavored purchasers consequently had few, if any, alternative sources from which to purchase comparable goods at prices and terms equivalent to those which McCormick provided to the favored purchasers.

C.   FUNCTIONAL DISCOUNTS—INTRODUCTORY NOTE

F. ROWE, PRICE DISCRIMINATION UNDER THE ROBINSON–PATMAN ACT 174 (1962). "In practice, the competitive effects requirement permits a supplier to quote different prices between different distributor classes—so long as those who are higher up (nearer the supplier) on the distribution ladder pay *less* than those who are further down (nearer the consumer). Put another way, wholesalers or jobbers (or their equivalent) may receive greater discounts or lower prices than retailers or dealers—so long as the wholesalers or jobbers sell only to retailers or dealers but not to consumers *in competition with* the retailers paying more. In effect, the supplier may thus reward various distributor classes with *scaled* price benefits according to their rank in the distributive hierarchy: the lowest price to the customer class nearest the seller, the highest price to the customer class nearest the consumer, with appropriate differentials to distributor classes in between."

Texaco Inc. v. Hasbrouck

Supreme Court of the United States, 1990.
496 U.S. 543, 110 S.Ct. 2535, 110 L.Ed.2d 492.

■ STEVENS, J. delivered the opinion of the Court.

Petitioner (Texaco) sold gasoline directly to respondents and several other retailers in Spokane, Washington, at its retail tank wagon prices (RTW) while it granted substantial discounts to two distributors. During the period between 1972 and 1981, the stations supplied by the two distributors increased their sales volume dramatically, while respondents' sales suffered a corresponding decline. Respondents filed an action against Texaco under the Robinson–Patman Amendment to the Clayton Act (Act) alleging that the distributor discounts violated § 2(a) of the Act. Respondents recovered treble damages, and the Court of Appeals for the Ninth Circuit affirmed the judgment. We granted certiorari to consider Texaco's contention that legitimate functional discounts do not violate the Act because a seller is not responsible for its customers' independent resale pricing decisions. While we agree with the basic thrust of Texaco's argument, we conclude that in this case it is foreclosed by the facts of record.

I

. . .

Respondents are 12 independent Texaco retailers. They displayed the Texaco trademark, accepted Texaco credit cards, and bought their gasoline products directly from Texaco. Texaco delivered the gasoline to respondents' stations.

The retail gasoline market in Spokane was highly competitive throughout the damages period, which ran from 1972 to 1981. Stations marketing the nationally advertised Texaco gasoline competed with other major brands as well as with stations featuring independent brands. Moreover, although discounted prices at a nearby Texaco station would have the most obvious impact on a respondent's trade, the cross-city traffic patterns and relatively small size of Spokane produced a city-wide competitive market. Texaco's through put sales in the Spokane market declined from a monthly volume of 569,269 gallons in 1970 to 389,557 gallons in 1975. Texaco's independent retailers' share of the market for Texaco gas declined from 76% to 49%. Seven of the respondents' stations were out of business by the end of 1978.

The respondents tried unsuccessfully to increase their ability to compete with lower priced stations. Some tried converting from full service to self-service stations. Two of the respondents sought to buy their own tank trucks and haul their gasoline from Texaco's supply point, but Texaco vetoed that proposal.

While the independent retailers struggled, two Spokane gasoline distributors supplied by Texaco prospered. Gull Oil Company (Gull) had its headquarters in Seattle and distributed petroleum products in four western

States under its own name. In Spokane it purchased its gas from Texaco at prices that ranged from six to four cents below Texaco's RTW price. Gull resold that product under its own name; the fact that it was being supplied by Texaco was not known by either the public or the respondents. In Spokane, Gull supplied about 15 stations; some were "consignment stations" and some were "commission stations." In both situations Gull retained title to the gasoline until it was pumped into a motorist's tank. In the consignment stations, the station operator set the retail prices, but in the commission stations Gull set the prices and paid the operator a commission. Its policy was to price its gasoline at a penny less than the prevailing price for major brands. Gull employed two truck drivers in Spokane who picked up product at Texaco's bulk plant and delivered it to the Gull stations. It also employed one supervisor in Spokane. Apart from its trucks and investment in retail facilities, Gull apparently owned no assets in that market. At least with respect to the commission stations, Gull is fairly characterized as a retailer of gasoline throughout the relevant period.

The Dompier Oil Company (Dompier) started business in 1954 selling Quaker State Motor Oil. In 1960 it became a full line distributor of Texaco products, and by the mid–1970's its sales of gasoline represented over three-quarters of its business. Dompier purchased Texaco gasoline at prices of 3.95 cents to 3.65 cents below the RTW price. Dompier thus paid a higher price than Gull, but Dompier, unlike Gull resold its gas under the Texaco brand names. It supplied about eight to ten Spokane retail stations. In the period prior to October 1974, two of those stations were owned by the president of Dompier but the others were independently operated. In the early 1970's, Texaco representatives encouraged Dompier to enter the retail business directly, and in 1974 and 1975 it acquired four stations. Dompier's president estimated at trial that the share of its total gasoline sales made at retail during the middle 1970's was "probably 84 to 90 percent."

Like Gull, Dompier picked up Texaco's product at the Texaco bulk plant and delivered directly to retail outlets. Unlike Gull, Dompier owned a bulk storage facility, but it was seldom used because its capacity was less than that of many retail stations. Again unlike Gull, Dompier received from Texaco the equivalent of the common carrier rate for delivering the gasoline product to the retail outlets. Thus, in addition to its discount from the RTW price, Dompier made a profit on its hauling function.

The stations supplied by Dompier regularly sold at retail at lower prices than respondents'. Even before Dompier directly entered the retail business in 1974, its customers were selling to consumers at prices barely above the RTW price. Dompier's sales volume increased continuously and substantially throughout the relevant period. Between 1970 and 1975 its monthly sales volume increased from 155,152 gallons to 462,956 gallons; this represented an increase from 20.7% to almost 50% of Texaco's sales in Spokane.

There was ample evidence that Texaco executives were well aware of Dompier's dramatic growth and believed that it was attributable to "the magnitude of the distributor discount and the hauling allowance." In response to complaints from individual respondents about Dompier's aggressive pricing, however, Texaco representatives professed that they "couldn't understand it."

II

Respondents filed suit against Texaco in July 1976. After a four-week trial, the jury awarded damages measured by the difference between the RTW price and the price paid by Dompier. As we subsequently decided in J. Truett Payne Co. v. Chrysler Motors Corp., 451 U.S. 557 (1981), this measure of damages was improper. Accordingly, although it rejected Texaco's defenses on the issue of liability, the Court of Appeals for the Ninth Circuit remanded the case for a new trial. Hasbrouck v. Texaco, Inc., 663 F.2d 930 (1981), cert. denied, 459 U.S. 828 (1982).

At the second trial, Texaco contended that the special prices to Gull and Dompier were justified by cost savings, were the product of a good faith attempt to meet competition, and were lawful "functional discounts." . . .

In Texaco's motion for judgment notwithstanding the verdict, it claimed as a matter of law that its functional discounts did not adversely affect competition within the meaning of the Act because any injury to respondents was attributable to decisions made independently by Dompier. The District Court denied the motion. . . .

III

It is appropriate to begin our consideration of the legal status of functional discounts[48] by examining the language of the Act. Section 2(a) provides in part:

"It shall be unlawful for any person engaged in commerce, in the course of such commerce, either directly or indirectly, to discriminate in price between different purchasers of commodities of like grade and quality, where either or any of the purchases involved in such discrimination are in commerce, where such commodities are sold for use, consumption, or resale within the United States or any Territory thereof or the District of Columbia or any insular possession or other place under the jurisdiction of the United States, and where the effect of such discrimination may be substantially to lessen competition or tend to create a monopoly in any line of commerce, or to injure, destroy, or prevent competition with any person who either grants or knowingly receives the benefit of such discrimination, or with customers of either of them. . . ." 15 U.S.C. § 13(a).

---

48. In their brief as amici curiae, the United States and the Federal Trade Commission suggest the following definition of "functional discount," which is adequate for our discussion: "A functional discount is one given to a purchaser based on its role in the supplier's distributive system, reflecting, at least in a generalized sense, the services performed by the purchaser for the supplier." Brief for United States et al. as Amici Curiae 10 (filed Aug. 3, 1989). . . .

The Act contains no express reference to functional discounts.[49] It does contain two affirmative defenses that provide protection for two categories of discounts—those that are justified by savings in the seller's cost of manufacture, delivery or sale, and those that represent a good faith response to the equally low prices of a competitor. Standard Oil Co. v. FTC, 340 U.S. 231, 250 (1951). As the case comes to us, neither of those defenses is available to Texaco.

In order to establish a violation of the Act, respondents had the burden of proving four facts: (1) that Texaco's sales to Gull and Dompier were made in interstate commerce; (2) that the gasoline sold to them was of the same grade and quality as that sold to respondents; (3) that Texaco discriminated in price as between Gull and Dompier on the one hand and respondents on the other; and (4) that the discrimination had a prohibited effect on competition. 15 U.S.C. § 13(a). Moreover, for each respondent to recover damages, he had the burden of proving the extent of his actual injuries. *J. Truett Payne*, 451 U.S., at 562.

The first two elements of respondents' case are not disputed in this court,[50] and we do not understand Texaco to be challenging the sufficiency of respondents' proof of damages. Texaco does argue, however, that although it charged different prices, it did not "discriminate in price" within the meaning of the Act, and that, at least to the extent that Gull and Dompier acted as wholesalers, the price differentials did not injure competition. We consider the two arguments separately.

IV

Texaco's first argument would create a blanket exemption for all functional discounts. Indeed, carried to its logical conclusion, it would exempt all price differentials except those given to competing purchasers. The primary basis for Texaco's argument is the following comment by Congressman Utterback, an active sponsor of the Act.

"In its meaning as simple English, a discrimination is more than a mere difference. Underlying the meaning of the word is the

---

49. The legislative history indicates that earlier drafts of the Act did include such a proviso. *See, e.g.,* Shniderman, "The Tyranny of Labels"—A Study of Functional Discounts Under the Robinson–Patman Act, 60 Harv.L.Rev. 571, 583–586, and nn. 40–57 (1947). The deletion of this exception for functional discounts has ambiguous significance. It may be, as one commentator has suggested, that the circumstances of the Act's passage "must have conveyed to the congressional mind the realization that the judiciary and the FTC would view what had occurred as a narrowing of the gates through which the functional classification plan of a seller had to pass to come within the law." Id., at 588. In any event, the deletion in no way detracts from the blunt direction of the statutory text, which indicates that any price discrimination substantially lessening competition will expose the discriminator to liability, regardless of whether the discriminator attempts to characterize the pricing scheme as a functional discount.

50. Texaco has not contested here the proposition that branded gas and unbranded gas are of like grade and quality. See FTC v. Borden Co., 383 U.S. 637, 645–646 (1966) ("the economic factors inherent in brand names and national advertising should not be considered in the jurisdictional inquiry under the statutory 'like grade and quality' test").

idea that some relationship exists between the parties to the discrimination which entitles them to equal treatment, whereby the difference granted to one casts some burden or disadvantage upon the other. If the two are competing in the resale of the goods concerned, that relationship exists. Where, also, the price to one is so low as to involve a sacrifice of some part of the seller's necessary costs and profit as applied to that business, it leaves that deficit inevitably to be made up in higher prices to his other customers; and there, too, a relationship may exist upon which to base the charge of discrimination. But where no such relationship exists, where the goods are sold in different markets and the conditions affecting those markets set different price levels for them, the sale to different customers at those different prices would not constitute a discrimination within the meaning of this bill." 80 Cong.Rec. 9416 (1936).

We have previously considered this excerpt from the legislative history and have refused to draw from it the conclusion which Texaco proposes. FTC v. Anheuser–Busch, Inc., 363 U.S. 536, 547–551 (1960). Although the excerpt does support Texaco's argument, we remain persuaded that the argument is foreclosed by the text of the Act itself. In the context of a statute that plainly reveals a concern with competitive consequences at different levels of distribution, and carefully defines specific affirmative defenses, it would be anomalous to assume that the Congress intended the term "discriminate" to have such a limited meaning. In *Anheuser–Busch* we rejected an argument identical to Texaco's in the context of a claim that a seller's price differential had injured its own competitors—a so called "primary line" claim.[51] The reasons we gave for our decision in *Anheuser–Busch* apply here as well. After quoting Congressman Utterback's statement in full, we wrote:

"The trouble with respondent's arguments is not that they are necessarily irrelevant in a § 2(a) proceeding, but that they are misdirected when the issue under consideration is solely whether there has been a price discrimination. We are convinced that, whatever may be said with respect to the rest of §§ 2(a) and 2(b)— and we say nothing here—there are no overtones of business buccaneering in the § 2(a) phrase 'discriminate in price.' Rather, a price discrimination within the meaning of that provision is merely a price difference." 363 U.S., at 549.

After noting that this view was consistent with our precedents, we added:

"the statute itself spells out the conditions which make a price difference illegal or legal, and we would derange this integrated statutory scheme were we to read other conditions into the law

---

51. It has proven useful in Robinson–Patman Act cases to distinguish among "the probable impact of the [price] discrimination on competitors of the seller (primary-line injury), on the favored and disfavored buyers (second-line injury), or on the customers of either of them (third-line injury)." See 3 E. Kintner & J. Bauer, Federal Antitrust Law § 20.9 p. 127 (1983).

by means of the nondirective phrase, 'discriminate in price.' Not only would such action be contrary to what we conceive to be the meaning of the statute, but, perhaps because of this, it would be thoroughly undesirable. As one commentator has succinctly put it, 'Inevitably every legal controversy over any price difference would shift from the detailed governing provisions—"injury," cost justification, "meeting competition," etc.—over into the "discrimination" concept of ad hoc resolution divorced from specifically pertinent statutory text.' Rowe, Price Differentials and Product Differentiation: The Issues Under the Robinson–Patman Act, 66 Yale L.J. 1, 38." 363 U.S., at 550–551.

Since we have already decided that a price discrimination within the meaning of § 2(a) "is merely a price difference," we must reject Texaco's first argument.

V

In FTC v. Morton Salt Co., 334 U.S. 37, 46–47 (1948), we held that an injury to competition may be inferred from evidence that some purchasers had to pay their supplier "substantially more for their goods than their competitors had to pay." See also Falls City Industries, Inc. v. Vanco Beverage, Inc., 460 U.S. 428, 435–436 (1983). Texaco, supported by the United States and the Federal Trade Commission as amici curiae, (the Government), argues that this presumption should not apply to differences between prices charged to wholesalers and those charged to retailers. Moreover, they argue that it would be inconsistent with fundamental antitrust policies to construe the Act as requiring a seller to control his customers' resale prices. The seller should not be held liable for the independent pricing decisions of his customers. As the Government correctly notes, Brief for United States et al. as Amici Curiae 21–22 (filed Aug. 3, 1989), this argument endorses the position advocated 35 years ago in the Report of the Attorney General's National Committee to Study the Antitrust Laws (1955).

After observing that suppliers ought not to be held liable for the independent pricing decisions of their buyers, and that without functional discounts distributors might go uncompensated for services they performed, the Committee wrote:

> "The Committee recommends, therefore, that suppliers granting functional discounts either to single-function or to integrated buyers should not be held responsible for any consequences of their customers' pricing tactics. Price cutting at the resale level is not in fact, and should not be held in law, 'the effect of' a differential that merely accords due recognition and reimbursement for actual marketing functions. The price cutting of a customer who receives this type of differential results from his own independent decision to lower price and operate at a lower profit margin per unit. The legality or illegality of this price cutting must

be judged by the usual legal tests. In any event, consequent injury or lack of injury should not be the supplier's legal concern.

"On the other hand, the law should tolerate no subterfuge. For instance, where a wholesaler-retailer buys only part of his goods as a wholesaler, he must not claim a functional discount on all. Only to the extent that a buyer actually performs certain functions, assuming all the risk, investment, and costs involved, should he legally qualify for a functional discount. Hence a distributor should be eligible for a discount corresponding to any part of the function he actually performs on that part of the goods for which he performs it." Id., at 208.

We generally agree with this description of the legal status of functional discounts. A supplier need not satisfy the rigorous requirements of the cost justification defense in order to prove that a particular functional discount is reasonable and accordingly did not cause any substantial lessening of competition between a wholesaler's customers and the supplier's direct customers.[52] The record in this case, however, adequately supports the finding that Texaco violated the Act.

The hypothetical predicate for the Committee's entire discussion of functional discounts is a price differential "that merely accords due recognition and reimbursement for actual marketing functions." Such a discount is not illegal. In this case, however, both the District Court and the Court

---

52. In theory, a supplier could try to defend a functional discount by invoking the Act's cost justification defense, but the burden of proof with respect to the defense is upon the supplier, and interposing the defense "has proven difficult, expensive, and often unsuccessful." 3 E. Kintner & J. Bauer, Federal Antitrust Law, § 23.19, pp. 366–367 (1983). Moreover, to establish the defense a "seller must show that the price reductions given did not exceed the actual cost savings," id., § 23.10, p. 345, and this requirement of exactitude is ill-suited to the defense of discounts set by reference to legitimate, but less precisely measured, market factors. Cf. Calvani, Functional Discounts Under the Robinson–Patman Act, 17 B.C. Ind. & Com.L.Rev. 543, 546 n. 16 (1976) (distinguishing functional discounts from cost-justified price differences); Report of the Attorney General's National Committee on the Antitrust Laws, at 171 ("the cost defense has proved largely illusory in practice").

Discounters will therefore likely find it more useful to defend against claims under the Act by negating the causation element in the case against them: a legitimate functional discount will not cause any substantial lessening of competition. The concept of sub-

stantiality permits the causation inquiry to accommodate a notion of economic reasonableness with respect to the pass-through effects of functional discounts, and so provides a latitude denied by the cost-justification defense. Cf. Shniderman, 60 Harv. L.Rev., at 603–604 (substantiality defense in functional discount cases). We thus find ourselves in substantial agreement with the view that:

"Conceived as a vehicle for allowing differential pricing to reward distributive efficiencies among customers operating at the same level, the cost justification defense focuses on narrowly defined savings to the seller derived from the different method or quantities in which goods are sold or delivered to different buyers.... Moreover, the burden of proof as to the cost justification defense is on the seller charged with violating the Act, whereas the burden of proof remains with the enforcement agency or plaintiff in circumstances involving functional discounts since functional pricing negates the probability of competitive injury, an element of a prima facie case of violation." Rill, Availability and Functional Discounts Justifying Discriminatory Pricing, 53 Antitrust L.J. 929, 935 (1985) (footnotes omitted).

of Appeals concluded that even without viewing the evidence in the light most favorable to the respondents, there was no substantial evidence indicating that the discounts to Gull and Dompier constituted a reasonable reimbursement for the value to Texaco of their actual marketing functions. 842 F.2d, at 1039; 634 F.Supp., at 37, 38. Indeed, Dompier was separately compensated for its hauling function, and neither Gull nor Dompier maintained any significant storage facilities.

. . .

As we have already observed, the "due recognition and reimbursement" concept endorsed in the Attorney General's Committee's study would not countenance a functional discount completely untethered to either the supplier's savings or the wholesaler's costs. The longstanding principle that functional discounts provide no safe harbor from the Act is likewise evident from the practice of the Federal Trade Commission, which has, while permitting legitimate functional discounts, proceeded against those discounts which appeared to be subterfuges to avoid the Act's restrictions. *See, e.g.,* In re Sherwin Williams Co., 36 F.T.C. 25, 70–71 (1943) (finding a violation of the Act by paint manufacturers who granted "functional or special discounts to some of their dealer-distributors on the purchases of such dealer-distributors which are resold by such dealer-distributors directly to the consumer through their retail departments or branch stores wholly owned by them"); In re The Ruberoid Co., 46 F.T.C. 379, 386, ¶ 5 (1950) (liability appropriate when functional designations do not always indicate accurately "the functions actually performed by such purchasers"), aff'd, 189 F.2d 893 (C.A.2 1951), rev'd on rehearing, 191 F.2d 294, aff'd, 343 U.S. 470 (1952).[53] *See also, e.g.,* In re Doubleday & Co., 52 F.T.C. 169, 209 (1955) ("the Commission should tolerate no subterfuge. Only to the extent that a buyer actually performs certain functions, assuming all the risks and costs involved, should he qualify for a compensating discount. The amount of the discount should be reasonably related to the expenses assumed by the buyer"); In re General Foods Corp., 52 F.T.C. 798, 824–825 (1956) ("a seller is not forbidden to sell at different prices to buyers in different functional classes and orders have been issued permitting lower prices to one functional class as against another, provided that injury to commerce as contemplated in the law does not result," but "[t]o hold that the rendering of special services ipso facto [creates] a separate functional classification would be to read Section 2(d) out of the

---

53. In the *Standard Oil* case, the FTC itself on remand dropped the part of its order prohibiting Standard Oil from giving functional discounts. See C. Edwards, Price Discrimination Law 309 (1959). The FTC's pre-remand theory in the *Standard Oil* case has of course been the subject of harsh criticism. *See, e.g.,* Report of the Attorney General's National Committee to Study the Antitrust Laws, at 206. Much, if not all, of this criticism rests upon the view that, under the FTC's *Standard Oil* ruling, a "supplier is charged with legal responsibility for the middlemen's pricing tactics, and hence must control their resale prices lest they undercut him to the unlawful detriment of his directly purchasing retailers. Alternatively, the seller may forego his operational freedom by matching his quotations to retailers with theirs." Ibid. Nothing in our opinion today should be read to condone or approve such a result.

Act"); In re Boise Cascade Corp., 107 F.T.C. 76, 212, 214–215 (1986) (regardless of whether the FTC has judged functional discounts by reference to the supplier's savings or the buyer's costs, the FTC has recognized that "functional discounts may usually be granted to customers who operate at different levels of trade, and thus do not compete with each other, without risk of secondary line competitive injury under the Act"), rev'd on other grounds, 267 U.S.App.D.C. 124, 837 F.2d 1127 (1988). Cf. FLM Collision Parts, Inc. v. Ford Motor Co., 543 F.2d 1019, 1027 (C.A.2 1976) ("We do not suggest or imply that, if a manufacturer grants a price discount or allowance to its wholesalers (whether or not labelled 'incentive'), which has the purpose or effect of defeating the objectives of the Act, § 2(a)'s language may not be construed to defeat it"); C. Edwards, Price Discrimination Law 286–348 (1959) (analyzing cases).

Most of these cases involve discounts made questionable because offered to "complex types of distributors" whose "functions became scrambled." *Doubleday & Co.*, 52 F.T.C., at 208. This fact is predictable: manufacturers will more likely be able to effectuate tertiary line price discrimination through functional discounts to a secondary line buyer when the favored distributor is vertically integrated. Nevertheless, this general tendency does not preclude the possibility that a seller may pursue a price discrimination strategy despite the absence of any discrete mechanism for allocating the favorable price discrepancy between secondary and tertiary line recipients.[54]

. . .

Nor should any reader of the commentary on functional discounts be much surprised by today's result. Commentators have disagreed about the extent to which functional discounts are generally or presumptively allowable under the Robinson–Patman Act. They nevertheless tend to agree that in exceptional cases what is nominally a functional discount may be an unjustifiable price discrimination entirely within the coverage of the Act. Others, like Frederick Rowe, have asserted the legitimacy of function

---

54. The seller may be willing to accept any division of the price difference so long as some significant part is passed on to the distributor's customers. Although respondents here did not need to show any benefit to Texaco from the price discrimination scheme in order to establish a violation of the Act, one possibility is indicated by the brief filed amicus curiae by the Service Station Dealers of America (SSDA), an organization representing both stations supplied by independent jobbers and stations supplied directly by sellers. See Brief for SSDA as Amicus Curiae 1–2. SSDA suggests that an indirect price discount to competitors may be used to force directly supplied franchisees out of the market, and so to circumvent federal restrictions upon the termination of franchise agreements. See 92 Stat. 324–332, 15 U.S.C. §§ 2801–2806.

One would expect that—absent a safe harbor rule making functional discounts a useful means to engage in otherwise unlawful price discrimination—excessive functional discounts of the sort in evidence here would be rare. As the Government correctly observes, "[t]his case appears to reflect rather anomalous behavior on the part of the supplier." Brief for United States et al. as Amici Curiae 17, n. 15 (filed Aug. 3, 1989). See also Brief for United States as Amicus Curiae 15 (filed May 16, 1989) ("market forces should tend to discourage a supplier from offering independent wholesalers discounts that would allow them to undercut the supplier's own retail customers").

discounts in more sweeping terms, but even Rowe concedes the existence of an "exception to the general rule." F. Rowe, Price Discrimination Under the Robinson–Patman Act 174, n. 7 (1962); id., at 195–205.

We conclude that the commentators' analysis, like the reasoning in Perkins [v. Standard Oil Co. of California, 395 U.S. 642 (1969)] and like the Federal Trade Commission's practice, renders implausible Texaco's contention that holding it liable here involves some departure from established understandings. Perhaps respondents' case against Texaco rests more squarely than do most functional discount cases upon direct evidence of the seller's intent to pass a price advantage through an intermediary. This difference, however, hardly cuts in Texaco's favor. In any event, the evidence produced by respondents also shows the scrambled functions which have more frequently signaled the illegitimacy under the Act of what is alleged to be a permissible functional discount. Both Gull and Dompier received the full discount on all their purchases even though most of their volume was resold directly to consumers. The extra margin on those sales obviously enabled them to price aggressively in both their retail and their wholesale marketing. To the extent that Dompier and Gull competed with respondents in the retail market, the presumption of adverse effect on competition recognized in the *Morton Salt* case becomes all the more appropriate. Their competitive advantage in that market also constitutes evidence tending to rebut any presumption of legality that would otherwise apply to their wholesale sales.

The evidence indicates, moreover, that Texaco affirmatively encouraged Dompier to expand its retail business and that Texaco was fully informed about the persistent and marketwide consequences of its own pricing policies. Indeed, its own executives recognized that the dramatic impact on the market was almost entirely attributable to the magnitude of the distributor discount and the hauling allowance. Yet at the same time that Texaco was encouraging Dompier to integrate downward, and supplying Dompier with a generous discount useful to such integration, Texaco was inhibiting upward integration by the respondents: two of the respondents sought permission from Texaco to haul their own fuel using their own tankwagons, but Texaco refused. The special facts of this case thus make it peculiarly difficult for Texaco to claim that it is being held liable for the independent pricing decisions of Gull or Dompier.

As we recognized in *Falls City Industries,* "the competitive injury component of a Robinson–Patman Act violation is not limited to the injury to competition between the favored and the disfavored purchaser; *it also encompasses the injury to competition between their customers." 460 U.S., at 436. This conclusion is compelled by the statutory language, which specifically encompasses not only the adverse effect of price discrimination on persons who either grant or knowingly receive the benefit of such discrimination, but also on "customers of either of them." Such indirect competitive effects surely may not be presumed automatically in every functional discount setting, and, indeed, one would expect that most functional discounts will be legitimate discounts which do not cause harm to competition. At the least, a functional discount that constitutes a reasonable reimbursement for the purchasers' actual marketing functions will not violate the Act. When a functional discount is legitimate, the inference of injury to competition recognized in the *Morton Salt* case will simply not arise. Yet it is also true that not every functional discount is entitled to a judgment of legitimacy, and that it will sometimes be possible to produce evidence showing that a particular functional discount caused a price discrimination of the sort the Act prohibits. When such anticompetitive effects are proved—as we believe they were in this case—they are covered by the Act.

. . .

■ JUSTICE WHITE, concurring in the result.

. . .

In the absence of Congressional attention to this long-standing issue involving antitrust policy, I doubt that at this late date we should attempt to set the matter right, at least not in a case that does not require us to define what a legitimate functional discount is. If the FTC now recognizes that functional discounts given by a producer who sells both to distributors and retailers are legitimate if they reflect only proper factors and are not subterfuges, I would await a case challenging such a ruling by the FTC. We would then be reviewing a construction of the Act by the FTC and its explanation of legitimate functional discount pricing.

This is obviously not such a case. This is a private action for treble damages, and the Court rules against the seller-discounter since under no definition of a legitimate functional discount do the discounts extended here qualify as a defense to a charge of price discrimination. We need do no more than the Court did in Perkins v. Standard Oil Co. of California, 395 U.S. 642 (1969). This the Court plainly recognizes, and it should stop there. Hence, I concur in the result.

. . .

D.   MORE REMOTE EFFECTS

PERKINS v. STANDARD OIL CO. OF CALIFORNIA, 395 U.S. 642, 89 S.Ct. 1871, 23 L.Ed.2d 599 (1969). Perkins, a large independent gasoline wholesaler and retailer in Washington and Oregon, sued for treble damages under §§ 2(a), (d), and (e) of the Robinson–Patman Act alleging that Standard of California had discriminated between it and Signal Oil.

Standard sold gasoline to the motoring public through its own retail stations, to independent dealers handling Standard brands ("branded dealers"), to re-brand jobbers (including Perkins) and to other integrated oil companies like Signal. Perkins purchased from Standard virtually all the gas which it distributed through numerous retail service stations and bulk storage plants. Signal also purchased from Standard, allegedly at discriminatorily low prices and at other favorable terms of sale, and in turn sold Standard gasoline to Western Highway, a corporation of which it was 60% owner, the other 40% being owned by Signal's officers. Western in turn sold to Regal, an operator of stations which competed with Perkins' stations; Western owned a 55% stock interest in Regal.

Perkins won a jury verdict of about $1.3 million based on injury to competition both with Regal stations and with Standard's branded dealers. The Court of Appeals reversed, primarily because the jury award included damages for injury to Perkins resulting from discrimination not only in favor of Standard's branded dealers but also because of competition from Regal retail stations. Noting that the statute makes liable the seller who offers discriminatorily lower prices that affect competition "with any person who ... knowingly receives the benefit of such discrimination or with customers of either of them ...," it found that Regal operated in a market "four levels removed" from that in which the discriminatory price was charged. Since Regal purchased from Western, which in turn purchased from Signal, the court concluded that damages in such remote markets were not contemplated under the statute.

The Supreme Court reversed. In an opinion by Black, J., the Court observed:

> ... We find no basis in the language or purpose of the Act for immunizing Standard's price discriminations simply because the product in question passed through an additional formal exchange before reaching the level of Perkins' actual competitor. From Perkins' point of view, the competitive harm done him by Standard is certainly no less because of the presence of an additional link in this particular distribution chain from the producer to the retailer. Here Standard discriminated in price between Perkins and Signal, and there was evidence from which the jury could conclude that Perkins was harmed competitively when Signal's price advantage was passed on to Perkins' retail competitor Regal. These facts are sufficient to give rise to recoverable damages under the Robinson–Patman Act.

> Before an injured party can recover damages under the Act, he must, of course, be able to show a causal connection between the price discrimination in violation of the Act and the injury suffered. This is true regardless of the "level" in the chain of distribution on which the injury occurs. The court below held that as a matter of law, "section 2(a) does not recognize a causal connection, essential to liability, between a supplier's price discrimination and the trade practices of a customer as far removed on the distribution ladder as Regal was from Standard." As we have noted above, we do not accept such an artificial limitation. If there is sufficient evidence in the record to support an inference of causation, the ultimate conclusion as to what that evidence proves is for the jury.

Marshall, J., concurred in part and dissented in part, in an opinion in which Stewart, J. joined. They went along with the majority on the competitive injury point because the case involved a chain of majority-owned subsidiaries and they therefore treated Signal, the beneficiary of the discriminatory price, as if it were directly competing with Perkins. They expressly left open the question what the result would be if wholly independent firms had intervened in the distribution chain.

PROBLEM 29

UNITED'S NEW DISTRIBUTIONAL SYSTEM

United is the largest manufacturer in the office product industry, producing a wide range of business forms, file cabinets, ringbinders, notebooks, etc. The industry, however, is deconcentrated with at least 1,000 manufacturers and United accounts for just under 6% of U.S. sales. Below the manufacturing level, there are two other major levels of competitive activity:

Wholesalers. There are approximately 100 wholesalers in the industry but five nationwide companies (the "Big Five") dominate the trade and account for 60 per cent of total sales. Each of the "Big Five" sells to dealers and also directly to large corporate consumers.

Dealers. There are thousands of dealers who buy from manufacturers or wholesalers and resell to consumers. Some specialize in one line of products, others are "mass marketers" who carry a full line, and others compete through mail-order catalogs.

In recent years, United has paid the Big Five wholesalers discounts ranging from 5 per cent to 33 per cent more on their purchases than other wholesalers. United justified the discounts on the ground that the Big Five performed services, particularly on sales to large customers, that benefited United and reduced its cost of doing business. Among the services were computerized inventory control, prompt delivery to customers, and inventory reports to United demonstrating the pace and volume of sales of particular products. Some of the disfavored wholesalers performed some of the services provided by the Big Five, but none provided the full range of services. On the other hand, the discounts that United paid to the Big Five on average were greater than the net profit of the smaller disfavored wholesalers.

The effect in the marketplace of the special discounts was uncertain. Often, the disfavored wholesalers sold to dealers and consumers at a lower price than the Big Five. On the other hand since the special discount was introduced the market share of the Big Five increased slightly, though most would attribute that result not to lower prices but to more aggressive advertising and marketing activities. One exception involves Thrift Mart, the largest mass marketer in the United States. Soon after United introduced its wholesaler discount, Montana Corp., the largest of the Big Five, cut its prices to Thrift Mart by twenty-five per cent and succeeded in obtaining all its business. As a result, several wholesalers not receiving the discount enjoyed by Montana Corp. lost a substantial amount of business.

Has United violated the Robinson–Patman Act?

SECTION 4. DEFENSES

A. COST JUSTIFICATION

United States v. Borden Co.

Supreme Court of the United States, 1962.
370 U.S. 460, 82 S.Ct. 1309, 8 L.Ed.2d 627.

■ CLARK, J. This is a direct appeal from a judgment dismissing the Government's Section 2(a) Clayton Act suit in which is sought an injunction against the selling of fluid milk products by the appellees, The Borden Company and Bowman Dairy Company, at prices which discriminate between independently owned grocery stores and grocery store chains. The District Court in an unreported decision found the pricing plan of each dairy to be a prima facie violation of § 2(a) but concluded that these discriminatory prices were legalized by the cost justification proviso of § 2(a), which permits price differentials as long as they "make only due allowance for differences in the cost of manufacture, sale, or delivery resulting from the differing methods or quantities in which such commodities are to such purchasers sold or delivered." To review the Government's contention that the District Court had improperly permitted cost justifications based on the *average* cost of dealing with broad groups of customers unrelated in cost-saving factors, we noted probable jurisdiction, 368 U.S. 924, and directed the parties to brief and argue the case separately as to each appellee, 368 U.S. 963. However, finding the same problem at the root of the cost justifications of each appellee, we have dealt with both in this single opinion. We have concluded that the class cost justifications submitted to the District Court by the appellees did not satisfy their burden of showing that their respective discriminatory pricing plans reflected only a "due allowance" for cost differences.

[The Court summarized the background of litigation between the parties which began in 1951, concluding that the sole question in the instant case was whether the differences in price reflected permissible allowances for variances in cost.]

In view of our disposition, we need not relate the facts in detail. Both appellees are major distributors of fluid milk products in metropolitan Chicago. The sales of both dairies to retail stores during the period in question were handled under plans which gave most of their customers—the independently owned stores—percentage discounts off list price which increased with the volume of their purchases to a specified maximum while granting a few customers—the grocery store chains—a flat discount without reference to volume and substantially greater than the maximum discount available under the volume plan offered independent stores. These discounts were made effective through schedules which appeared to cover all stores; however, the schedules were modified by private letters to the grocery chains confirming their higher discounts.[55] Although the two sets of

---

55. Borden in June of 1954 issued the following discount schedule to "be applied to all purchases of Borden's fresh milk":

Average converted points per day:	Percent of discounts
0– 24	0
25– 74	2
75–149	3
150 and over	4

At this same time, letters were sent to The Great Atlantic and Pacific Tea Company and The Jewel Food Stores granting them flat 8½% discounts. A few of the larger independents by special arrangement were given an additional 1½% discount thereby raising their total discount to 5½%.

In September 1955, Borden discontinued the above discount system and utilized a net price scheme which resulted in even greater disparities between chains and independents.

Bowman in June of 1954 operated under the following "Resale Store Discount Schedule":

discounts were never officially labeled "independent" and "chain" prices, they were treated, called, and regarded as such throughout the record.

To support their defense that the disparities in price between independents and chains were attributable to differences in the cost of dealing with the two types of customers, the appellees introduced cost studies which will be described separately because of their differing content and analytical approach.

The Borden pricing system produced two classes of customers. The two chains, A & P and Jewel, with their combined total of 254 stores constituted one class. The 1,322 independent stores, grouped in four brackets based on the volume of their purchases, made up the other. Borden's cost justification was built on comparisons of its average cost per $100 of sales to the chains in relation to the average cost of similar sales to each of the four groups of independents. The costs considered were personnel (including routemen, clerical and sales employees), truck expenses, and losses on bad debts and returned milk. Various methods of cost allocation were utilized: drivers' time spent at each store was charged directly to that store; certain clerical expenses were allocated between the two general classes; costs not susceptible of either of the foregoing were charged to the various stores on a per stop, per store, or volume basis.

Bowman's cost justification was based on differences in volume and methods of delivery. It relied heavily upon a study of the cost per minute of its routemen's time. It determined that substantial portions of this time were devoted to three operations, none of which was ever performed for the 163 stores operated by its two major chain customers. These added work steps arose from the method of collection, *i.e.*, cash on delivery and the delayed collections connected therewith, and the performance of "optional customer services." The customer services, performed with varying frequency depending upon the circumstances, included "services that the driver may be requested to do, such as deliver the order inside, place the containers in a refrigerator, rearrange containers so that any product

Average converted points per day:	*Percent of discounts*
0 to 10	3.0 to 3.4
10 to 20	3.4 to 3.8
20 to 30	3.8 to 4.2
30 to 40	4.2 to 4.6
40 to 50	4.6 to 5.0
50 to 60	5.0 to 5.2
60 to 70	5.2 to 5.4
70 to 80	5.4 to 5.6
80 to 90	5.6 to 5.8
90 to 100	5.8 to 6.0
100 to 110	6.0 to 6.2
110 to 120	6.2 to 6.4
120 to 130	6.4 to 6.6
130 to 140	6.6 to 6.8
140 to 150	6.8 to 7.0

This schedule was modified in August by the addition of the following discounts:

Average converted points per day:	*Percent of discounts*
150 to 200	7.0 to 8.0
Over 200	8.0

During this same period Bowman by letter granted The Great Atlantic and Pacific Tea Company and the Kroger Company flat 11% discounts. Goldblatt Bros., also a multi-store operation, was granted a flat 8½%.

In 1955 and again in 1956 Bowman modified the brackets and percentages of its discount schedules, but not in a manner which reduced the disparity between independents and chains.

remaining unsold from yesterday will be sold first today, leave cases of products at different spots in the store, etc." The experts conducting the study calculated as to these elements a "standard" cost per unit of product delivered: the aggregate time required to perform the services, as determined by sample time studies, was divided by the total number of units of product delivered. In essence, the Bowman justification was merely a comparison of the cost of these services in relation to the disparity between the chain and independent prices. Although it was shown that the five sample independents in the Government's prima facie case received the added services, it was not shown or found that all 2,500 independents supplied by Bowman partook of them. On the basis of its studies Bowman estimated that about two-thirds of the independent stores received the "optional customer services" on a daily basis and that "most store customers pay the driver in cash daily."

On these facts, stated here in rather summary fashion, the trial court held that appellees had met the requirements of the proviso of § 2(a) on the theory that the general cost differences between chain stores as a class and independents as a class justified the disparities in price reflected in appellees' schedules. In so doing the trial court itself found "the studies ... imperfect in some respects...." It noted the "seemingly arbitrary" nature of a classification resulting "in percentage discounts which do not bear a direct ratio to differences in volume of sales." But it found "this mode of classification is *not* wholly arbitrary—after all, most chain stores do purchase larger volumes of milk than do most independent stores."[56] We believe it was erroneous for the trial court to permit cost justifications based upon such classifications.

The burden, of course, was upon the appellees to prove that the illegal price discrimination, which the Government claimed and the trial court found present, was immunized by the cost justification proviso of § 2(a). Such is the mandate of § 2(b) as interpreted by this Court in Federal Trade Comm'n v. Morton Salt Co., 334 U.S. 37, 44–45 (1948). There can be no doubt that the § 2(a) proviso as amended by the Robinson–Patman Act contemplates, both in express wording and legislative history, a showing of actual cost differences resulting from the differing methods or quantities in which the commodities in question are sold or delivered. The only question before us is how accurate this showing must be in relation to each particular purchaser.

Although the language of the proviso, with some support in the legislative history, is literally susceptible of a construction which would require any discrepancy in price between any two purchasers to be individually justified, the proviso has not been so construed by those charged with its enforcement. The Government candidly recognizes in its briefs filed in

---

56. Even the trial court was unwilling to give its "stamp of approval to all pricing policies and practices revealed by the evidence." But it concluded that to enjoin such practices would lead to regulation and would require the court continually "to pass judgment on the pricing practices of these defendants," a matter which might better be handled by proceedings before the Federal Trade Commission.

the instant case that "[a]s a matter of practical necessity ... when a seller deals with a very large number of customers, he cannot be required to establish different cost-reflecting prices for each customer." In this same vein, the practice of grouping customers for pricing purposes has long had the approval of the Federal Trade Commission. We ourselves have noted the "elusiveness of cost data" in a Robinson–Patman Act proceeding. Automatic Canteen Co. v. Federal Trade Comm'n, 346 U.S. 61, 68 (1953). In short, to completely renounce class pricing as justified by class accounting would be to eliminate in practical effect the cost justification proviso as to sellers having a large number of purchasers, thereby preventing such sellers from passing on economies to their customers. It seems hardly necessary to say that such a result is at war with Congress' language and purpose.

But this is not to say that price differentials can be justified on the basis of arbitrary classifications or even classifications which are representative of a numerical majority of the individual members. At some point practical considerations shade into a circumvention of the proviso. A balance is struck by the use of classes for cost justification which are composed of members of such selfsameness as to make the averaging of the cost of dealing with the group a valid and reasonable indicium of the cost of dealing with any specific group member. High on the list of "musts" in the use of the average cost of customer groupings under the proviso of § 2(a) is a close resemblance of the individual members of each group on the essential point or points which determine the costs considered.

In this regard we do not find the classifications submitted by the appellees to have been shown to be of sufficient homogeneity. Certainly, the cost factors considered were not necessarily encompassed within the manner in which a customer is owned. Turning first to Borden's justification, we note that it not only failed to show that the economies relied upon were isolated within the favored class but affirmatively revealed that members of the classes utilized were substantially unlike in the cost saving aspects considered. For instance, the favorable cost comparisons between the chains and the larger independents were for the greater part controlled by the higher average volume of the chain stores in comparison to the average volume of the 80–member class to which these independents were relegated. The District Court allowed this manner of justification because "most chain stores do purchase larger volumes of milk than do most independent stores." However, such a grouping for cost justification purposes, composed as it is of some independents having volumes comparable to, and in some cases larger than, that of the chain stores, created artificial disparities between the larger independents and the chain stores. It is like averaging one horse and one rabbit. As the Federal Trade Commission said in In the Matter of Champion Spark Plug Co., 50 F.T.C. 30, 43 (1953): "A cost justification based on the difference between an estimated average cost of selling to one or two large customers and an average cost of selling to all other customers cannot be accepted as a defense to a charge of price discrimination." This volume gap between the larger independents and the chain stores was further widened by grouping together the two chains, thereby raising the average volume of the stores of the smaller of the two chains in relation to the larger independents. Nor is the vice in the Borden class justification solely in the paper volumes relied upon, for it attributed to many independents cost factors which were not true indicia of the cost of dealing with those particular consumers. To illustrate, each independent was assigned a portion of the total expenses involved in daily cash collections, although it was not shown that all independents paid cash and in fact Borden admitted that only a "large majority" did so.

Likewise the details of Bowman's cost study show a failure in classification. Only one additional point need be made. Its justification emphasized its costs for "optional customer service" and daily cash collection with the resulting "delay to collect." As shown by its study these elements were crucial to Bowman's cost justification. In the study the experts charged all independents and no chain store with these costs. Yet, it was not shown that all independents received these services daily or even on some lesser basis. Bowman's studies indicated only that a large majority of independents took these services on a daily basis. Under such circumstances the use of these cost factors across the board in calculating independent store costs is not a permissible justification for it possibly allocates costs to some independents whose mode of purchasing does not give rise to them. The burden was upon the profferer of the classification to negate this possibility and this burden has not been met here. If these factors control the cost of dealing, then their presence or absence might with more justification be the password for admission into the various price categories.[57]

The appellees argue in the alternative that their cost justifications can be sufficiently unscrambled to remove any taint the Court may find in them and still show a cost gap sufficient to justify the price disparity between the chains and any independent. This mass of underlying statistical data not considered by the trial court and now tied together by untried theories can best be evaluated on remand, and we therefore do not consider its sufficiency here.

In sum, the record here shows that price discriminations have been permitted on the basis of cost differences between broad customer groupings, apparently based on the nature of ownership but in any event not shown to be so homogeneous as to permit the joining together of these purchasers for cost allocations purposes. If this is the only justification for appellees' pricing schemes, they are illegal. We do not believe that an appropriate decree would require the trial court continuously to "pass judgment on the pricing practices of these defendants." As to the issuance of an injunction, however, the case is now 11 years old and we have no way of knowing whether equitable relief is in order. Certainly a relevant factor in such consideration would be whether the practices described above are still being followed in any form. This the record here does not show. Such

---

57. Another suspect feature is that classifications based on services received by independents were apparently frozen—making it impossible for them to obtain larger discounts by electing not to receive the cost-determinative services—with no justifiable business reason offered in support of the practice.

matters can only be ascertained upon the presently existing facts and the careful application of the principles we have enunciated. For that purpose the case is reversed and remanded.

Reversed and remanded.[58]

NOTE

Over the years the Federal Trade Commission has been demanding in its requirements that the defendant discharge its burden of demonstrating cost justification, but its standards have not always been enforced by the courts. For example in Federal Trade Commission v. Standard Motor Products, Inc., 371 F.2d 613 (2d Cir.1967), the Commission had rejected as inadequate a cost justification for retroactive annual rebates on purchases of automotive replacement parts. Standard had offered the following rebates:

Volume Class	Rebate
$0–2,999	4%
$3,000–$5,999	10%
$6,000–$9,999	13%
$10,000–$24,999	15%
$25,000–over	17%

Standard claimed it had cost justification studies showing that the rebate percentages were justified because of savings in direct selling, catalog, branch warehouse, and administrative expenses. The Federal Trade Commission rejected the defense on grounds that selling costs to individual purchasers in each category frequently deviated substantially. The Commission noted that many purchasers in each category had costs that were equal to or closer to costs of serving purchasers in other categories than purchasers in its own category.

The Second Circuit refused to enforce the Commission order, noting that the Commission had offered no substitute standard that was administrable, nor had it examined whether other sellers in the automobile replacement markets could meet the standards of classification the Commission formulated. "A careful comparison of the economic discrimination under Standard's present rebates with that under any practicable alternative system of pricing might have led to the conclusion that the present system is the best attainable...."

How strict a standard should the courts impose in order to satisfy the "cost justification" defense? Should a seller be allowed to establish a defense where it can show a reasonable estimate of cost savings, with all forms of savings being relevant? Should a court take into account that a more demanding system of classification of

---

58. Frankfurter, J., took no part in the consideration or decision of the case. A concurring opinion by Douglas, J., and a dissenting opinion by Harlan, J., are omitted.

Defendants have rarely succeeded in establishing a cost justification defense. For cases rejecting cost justification, see Allied Accessories & Auto Parts Co. v. General Motors Corp., 825 F.2d 971, 977 (6th Cir.1987); Continental Baking Co. v. Old Homestead Bread Co., 476 F.2d 97 (10th Cir.), cert. denied, 414 U.S. 975 (1973); National Dairy Products Corp. v. FTC, 395 F.2d 517 (7th Cir.1968), cert. denied 393 U.S. 977; William H. Rorer, Inc., FTC Dkt. 8599, Trade Reg. Rep. (CCH) ¶ 17,535 (1966); National Dairy Products Corp., FTC Dkt. 7018, Trade Reg. Rep. (CCH) ¶ 17,656 (1966).

savings would be so expensive as to make it impractical to assert in an administrative or judicial proceeding?

B.   Good Faith Meeting of Competition

NOTE

1. Section 2(b) provides that a seller can defend against a charge of price discrimination "by showing that his lower price . . . was made in good faith to meet an equally low price of a competitor."[59] In Standard Oil Co. v. Federal Trade Commission, 340 U.S. 231 (1951), the Supreme Court held that the defense is absolute and is not undermined or modified in any way by evidence that the lower price resulted in an injury to competition.

In 1963, the Commission sustained a meeting competition defense in a proceeding against Continental Baking Co., and summarized its view of the applicable standard of "good faith:"

At the heart of Section 2(b) is the concept of "good faith." This is a flexible and pragmatic, not a technical or doctrinaire, concept. The standard of good faith is simply the standard of the prudent businessman responding fairly to what he reasonably believes is a situation of competitive necessity.[60]

Interpretation of the meeting competition defense has varied over the years, particularly on the issues of the degree of certainty required for a seller to satisfy the defense, and the related question of how to define the defense to best reconcile the goals of the Sherman Act and the Robinson–Patman Act.

The Supreme Court in the following two decisions has done much to clarify the scope of the defense and reconcile prior conflicting doctrine.

United States v. United States Gypsum Co.

Supreme Court of the United States, 1978.
438 U.S. 422, 98 S.Ct. 2864, 57 L.Ed.2d 854.

[The *Gypsum* opinion, setting forth the consequences of an exchange of current price information, and determining that "intent" is an element of a criminal antitrust offense, is summarized at pp. 246–247 supra. In Part III of the Supreme Court's opinion, printed below, Chief Justice Burger attempted to reconcile the proscriptions of the Sherman Act with those of Section 2(b) of the Robinson–Patman Act.]

III

Our construction of the Sherman Act to require proof of intent as an element of a criminal antitrust violation leaves unresolved the question upon which the Court of Appeals focused, whether verification of price concessions with competitors for the sole purpose of taking advantage of

59. The full text of Section 2(b) of the Robinson–Patman Act is reprinted at p. 1282 supra.

60. 63 F.T.C. 2071, 2163 (1963).

the § 2(b) meeting competition defense of the Robinson–Patman Act should be treated as a "controlling circumstance" precluding liability under § 1 of the Sherman Act. We now turn to that question.[61]

A

In Cement Mfgrs. Protective Assn. v. United States, 268 U.S. 588, the Court held exempt from Sherman § 1 liability an exchange of price information among competitors because the exchange of information was necessary to protect the cement manufacturers from fraudulent behavior by contractors.[62] Over 40 years later, in United States v. Container Corp., 393 U.S. 333, 335, Mr. Justice Douglas characterized the *Cement* holding in the following terms:

> While there was present here, as in Cement Mfgrs. Protective Association v. United States, 268 U.S. 588, an exchange of prices to specific customers, there was absent the controlling circumstances, viz., that cement manufacturers, to protect themselves from delivering to contractors more cement than was needed for a specific job and thus receiving a lower price, exchanged price information as a means of protecting their legal rights from fraudulent inducements to deliver more cement than needed for a specific job.

The use of the phrase "controlling circumstance" in *Container* implied that the exception from Sherman Act liability recognized in *Cement Mfgrs.* was not necessarily limited to special circumstances of that case, although the exact scope of the exception remained largely undefined.

Since *Container*, several courts have read the controlling circumstance exception as encompassing exchanges of price information when undertaken for the purpose of compliance with § 2(b) of the Robinson–Patman Act.... The Court of Appeals in the instant case essentially adopted the same tack—albeit with some additional limitations[63]—finding such a step necessary to eliminate a perceived conflict between the Sherman Act's proscriptions regarding the exchange of price information among competitors and the claimed necessity of such exchanges to perfect the § 2(b) defense of the Robinson–Patman Act....

---

61. This question was not resolved by the prior discussion because a purpose of complying with the Robinson–Patman Act by exchanging price information is not inconsistent with knowledge that such exchanges of information will have the probable effect of fixing or stabilizing prices. Since we hold knowledge of the probable consequences of conduct to be the requisite mental state in a criminal prosecution like the instant one where an effect on prices is also alleged, a defendant's purpose in engaging in the proscribed conduct will not insulate him from liability unless it is deemed of sufficient merit to justify a general exception to the Sherman Act's proscriptions. Cf. Cement Mfrs. Protective Assn. v. United States, 268 U.S. 588.

62. Respondents maintain that their verification practices not only were for the purpose of complying with the Robinson–Patman Act, but also served to protect them from fraud on the part of their customers, and thus fall squarely within the *Cement* exception. The Court of Appeals rejected this claim, 550 F.2d, at 123 n. 9, and we find no reason to upset this determination.

63. Ed. See pp. 602–609 supra.

B

Section 2(a) of the Robinson–Patman Act, 15 U.S.C.A. § 13(a), embodies a general prohibition of price discrimination between buyers when an injury to competition is the consequence. The primary exception to the § 2(a) bar is the meeting-competition defense....

In FTC v. A.E. Staley Manufacturing Co., 324 U.S. 746 (1945), the Court provided the first and still the most complete explanation of the kind of showing which a seller must make in order to satisfy the good-faith requirement of the § 2(b) defense:

> Section 2(b) does not require the seller to justify price discriminations by showing that in fact they met a competitor's price. But it does place on the seller the burden of showing that the price was made in good faith to meet a competitor's.... We agree with the Commission that the statute at least requires the seller, who has knowingly discriminated in price, to show the existence of facts which would lead a reasonable and prudent person to believe that the granting of a lower price would in fact meet the equally low price of a competitor.

324 U.S., at 759–760.

Application of these standards to the facts in *Staley* led to the conclusion that the § 2(b) defense had not been made out. The record revealed that the lower price had been based simply on reports of salesmen, brokers, or purchasers with no efforts having been made by the seller "to investigate or verify" the reports or the character and reliability of the informants. Id., at 758. Similarly, in Corn Products v. FTC, 324 U.S. 726 (1945), decided the same day, the § 2(b) defense was not allowed because "the only evidence said to rebut the *prima facie* case ... of the price discriminations was given by witnesses who had no personal knowledge of the transactions, and was limited to statements of each witness's assumption or conclusion that the price discriminations were justified by competition." Id., at 741.

Staley's "investigate or verify" language coupled with the *Corn Products'* focus on "personal knowledge of the transactions" have apparently suggested to a number of courts that, at least in certain circumstances, direct verification of discounts between competitors may be necessary to meet the burden of proof requirements of the § 2(b) defense.... The Court of Appeals critically and perceptively analyzed these cases and concluded that only a very narrow exception to Sherman Act liability should be recognized; that exception would cover the relatively few situations where the veracity of the buyer seeking the matching discount was legitimately in doubt, other reasonable means of corroboration were unavailable to the seller, and the interseller communication was for the sole purpose of complying with the Robinson–Patman Act. Despite the court's efforts to circumscribe the scope of the exception it was constrained to recognize, we find its analysis unacceptable.

C

A good-faith belief, rather than absolute certainty, that a price concession is being offered to meet an equally low price offered by a competitor is sufficient to satisfy the Robinson–Patman's § 2(b) defense. While casual reliance on uncorroborated reports of buyers or sales representatives without further investigation may not, as we noted earlier, be sufficient to make the requisite showing of good faith, nothing in the language of § 2(b) or the gloss on that language in *Staley* and *Corn Products* indicates that direct discussions of price between competitors are required. Nor has any court, so far as we are aware, ever imposed such a requirement.[64] ... On the contrary, the § 2(b) defense has been successfully invoked in the absence of interseller verification on numerous occasions,.... And in Kroger Co. v. FTC, 438 F.2d 1372, 1376–1377 (C.A.6 1971), aff'g Beatrice Foods Co., 76 F.T.C. 719, the defense was recognized despite the fact that the price concession was ultimately found to have undercut that of the competition and thus technically to have fallen outside the "meet not beat" strictures of the defense. As these cases indicate, and as the Federal Trade Commission observed, it is the concept of good faith which lies at the core of the meeting-competition defense and good faith

> "is a flexible and pragmatic, not technical or doctrinaire, concept.... Rigid rules and inflexible absolutes are especially inappropriate in dealing with the § 2(b) defense; the facts and circumstances of the particular case, not abstract theories or remote conjectures, should govern its interpretation and application."

Continental Baking Co., 63 F.T.C. 2071, 2163 (1963).

The so-called problem of the untruthful buyer which concerned the Court of Appeals does not in our view call for a different approach to the § 2(b) defense. The good-faith standard remains the benchmark against which the seller's conduct is to be evaluated, and we agree with the government and the FTC that this standard can be satisfied by efforts falling short of interseller verification in most circumstances where the seller has only vague, generalized doubts about the reliability of its commercial adversary—the buyer.[65] Given the fact specific nature of the

---

64. In Viviano Macaroni Co. v. FTC, 411 F.2d 255 (C.A.3 1969), the § 2(b) defense was not recognized because the seller had relied solely on the report of its customer regarding other competitive offers without undertaking any investigation to corroborate the offer or the reliability of the customer. The Court of Appeals in the instant case read *Viviano* as at least suggesting, if not requiring, interseller verification when the veracity of the buyer was in doubt. As we read that case, however, it simply reaffirms the teaching of *Staley,* and does not compel the further conclusion that only interseller verification will satisfy the good-faith requirement, even

in the particular circumstances identified by the Court of Appeals. See 550 F.2d, at 135 (Weis, J., dissenting).

65. "Although a seller may take advantage of the meeting competition defense only if it has a commercially reasonable belief that its price concession is necessary to meet an equally low price of a competitor, a seller may acquire this belief, and hence perfect its defense, by doing everything reasonably feasible—short of violating some other statute, such as the Sherman Act—to determine the veracity of a customer's statement that he has been offered a lower price. If, after making reasonable, lawful, inquiries, the seller

inquiry, it is difficult to predict all the factors the FTC or a court would consider in appraising a seller's good faith in matching a competing offer in these circumstances. Certainly, evidence that a seller had received reports of similar discounts from other customers, cf. Jones v. Borden Co., [430 F.2d 568, 572–573 (5th Cir.1970)]; or was threatened with a termination of purchases if the discount were not met, cf. International Air Industries, Inc. v. American Excelsior Co., [517 F.2d 714, 726 (5th Cir.1975)], Cadigan v. Texaco, Inc., [492 F.2d 383, 386 (9th Cir.1971)], would be relevant in this regard. Efforts to corroborate the reported discount by seeking documentary evidence or by appraising its reasonableness in terms of available market data would also be probative as would the seller's past experience with the particular buyer in question.[66]

There remains the possibility that in a limited number of situations a seller may have substantial reasons to doubt the accuracy of reports of a competing offer and may be unable to corroborate such reports in any of the generally accepted ways. Thus the defense may be rendered unavailable since unanswered questions about the reliability of a buyer's representations may well be inconsistent with a good-faith belief that a competing offer had in fact been made.[67] As an abstract proposition, resort to interseller verification as a means of checking the buyer's reliability seems a possible solution to the seller's plight, but careful examination reveals serious problems with the practice.

Both economic theory and common human experience suggest that interseller verification—if undertaken on an isolated and infrequent basis with no provision for reciprocity or cooperation—will not serve its putative function of corroborating the representations of unreliable buyers regarding the existence of competing offers. Price concessions by oligopolists generally yield competitive advantages only if secrecy can be maintained; when the terms of the concession are made publicly known, other competitors are likely to follow and any advantage to the initiator is lost in the

---

cannot ascertain that the buyer is lying, the seller is entitled to make the sale. There is no need for a seller to discuss price with his competitors to take advantage of the meeting competition defense." (Citations omitted.) Brief of Petitioner, 86–87, and n. 78. See also Pet.App., 97a–99a.

66. It may also turn out that sustained enforcement of § 2(f) of the Robinson–Patman Act, which imposes liability on buyers for inducing illegal price discounts, will serve to bolster the credibility of buyer's representations and render reliance thereon by sellers a more reasonable and secure predicate for a finding of good faith under § 2(b). See generally Note, Meeting Competition Under the Robinson–Patman Act, 90 Harv.L.Rev. 1476, 1495–1496 (1977). In both Great Atlantic & Pacific Tea Co. v. FTC, 557 F.2d 971 (C.A.2 1977), and Kroger v. FTC, supra, buyers have

been held liable under § 2(f) despite the fact that the sellers were either found not to have violated the Robinson–Patman Act (Kroger) or were not charged with such a violation (A & P). Certiorari has been granted in *Great Atlantic & Pacific Tea Co.* to consider the permissibility of enforcing the Robinson–Patman Act in this manner. 435 U.S. 922 (1978).

67. We need not and do not decide that in all such circumstances the defense would be unavailable. The case by case interpretation and elaboration of the § 2(b) defense is properly left to the other federal courts and the FTC in the context of concrete fact situations. We note also that our conclusion regarding the proper interpretation of § 2(f) of the Robinson–Patman Act, see n. 66 supra, may well affect subsequent application of the § 2(b) defense.

process. . . . Thus, if one seller offers a price concession for the purpose of winning over one of his competitor's customers, it is unlikely that the same seller will freely inform its competitor of the details of the concession so that it can be promptly matched and diffused. Instead, such a seller would appear to have at least as great an incentive to misrepresent the existence or size of the discount as would the buyer who received it. Thus verification, if undertaken on a one shot basis for the sole purpose of complying with the § 2(b) defense, does not hold out much promise as a means of shoring up buyers' representations.

The other variety of interseller verification is, like the conduct charged in the instant case, undertaken pursuant to an agreement, either tacit or express, providing for reciprocity among competitors in the exchange of price information. Such an agreement would make little economic sense, in our view, if its sole purpose were to guarantee all participants the opportunity to match the secret price concessions of other participants under § 2(b) of the Robinson–Patman Act. For in such circumstances, each seller would know that his price concession could not be kept from his competitors and no seller participating in the information exchange arrangement would, therefore, have any incentive for deviating from the prevailing price level in the industry. See United States v. Container Corp., 393 U.S., at 336–337. Regardless of its putative purpose, the most likely consequence of any such agreement to exchange price information would be the stabilization of industry prices. . . . Instead of facilitating use of the § 2(b) defense, such an agreement would have the effect of eliminating the very price concessions which provide the main element of competition in oligopolistic industries and the primary occasion for resort to the meeting competition defense.

Especially in oligopolistic industries such as the gypsum board industry, the exchange of price information among competitors carries with it the added potential for the development of concerted price-fixing arrangements which lie at the core of the Sherman Act's prohibitions. The Department of Justice's 1977 Report on the Robinson–Patman Act focused on the growing use of the Act as a cover for price fixing; former Antitrust Division Assistant Attorney General Kauper discussed the mechanics of the process:

> And thus you find in some industries relatively extensive exchanges of price information for the purpose, at least the stated purpose, of complying with the Robinson–Patman Act. . . .
>
> Now, the mere exchange of price information itself may tend to stabilize prices. But I think it is also relatively common that once the exchange process begins, certain understandings go along with it—that we will exchange prices, but it will be understood, for example, you will not undercut my prices.
>
> And from there it is a rather easy step into a full-fledged price-fixing agreement. I think we have seen that from time to time, and I suspect we will continue to see it as long as there

continues to be a need to justify particular price discriminations in the terms of the Robinson–Patman Act.

United States Department of Justice, Report on the Robinson–Patman Act 58–61 (1977).

We are left, therefore, on the one hand, with doubts about both the need for and the efficacy of interseller verification as a means of facilitating compliance with § 2(b) of the Robinson–Patman Act, and, on the other, with recognition of the tendency for price discussions between competitors to contribute to the stability of oligopolistic prices and open the way for the growth of prohibited anticompetitive activity. To recognize even a limited "controlling circumstance" exception for interseller verification in such circumstances would be to remove from scrutiny under the Sherman Act conduct falling near its core with no assurance, and indeed with serious doubts, that competing antitrust policies would be served thereby. In Automatic Canteen v. FTC, 346 U.S. 61, 74 (1953), the Court suggested that as a general rule the Robinson–Patman Act should be construed so as to insure its coherence with "the broader antitrust policies that have been laid down by Congress"; that observation buttresses our conclusion that exchanges of price information—even when putatively for purposes of Robinson–Patman Act compliance—must remain subject to close scrutiny under the Sherman Act.[68]

Great Atlantic & Pacific Tea Co. v. FTC

Supreme Court of the United States, 1979.
440 U.S. 69, 99 S.Ct. 925, 59 L.Ed.2d 153.

[Printed p. 1350 infra]

Falls City Industries v. Vanco Beverage

Supreme Court of the United States, 1983.
460 U.S. 428, 103 S.Ct. 1282, 75 L.Ed.2d 174.

[Falls City sold beer to wholesalers in Indiana, Kentucky and eleven other states. Vanco was its sole wholesale distributor in Evansville, Indiana and Dawson Springs was its sole wholesale distributor in nearby Henderson, Kentucky. Because of state regulations, neither wholesaler

---

68. That the § 2(b) defense may not be available in every situation where a competing offer has in fact been made is not, in our view, a meaningful objection to our holding. The good-faith requirement of the § 2(b) defense implicitly suggests a somewhat imperfect matching between competing offers actually made and those allowed to be met. Unless this requirement is to be abandoned, it seems clear that inadequate information will in a limited number of cases, deny the defense to some who, if all the facts had been known, would have been entitled to invoke it. For reasons already discussed, interseller verification does not provide a satisfactory solution to this seemingly inevitable problem of inadequate information. Moreover, § 2(b) affords only a defense to liability and not an affirmative right under the Act. While sellers are of course entitled to take advantage of the defense when they can satisfy its requirements, efforts to increase its availability at the expense of broader, affirmative antitrust policies must be rejected.

could sell to retailers in the state served by the other, but consumers frequently crossed state lines to buy beer from retailers offering the lowest prices. Vanco sued Falls City under Section 2(a) of the Robinson–Patman Act charging that the defendant had charged 10–30% higher prices in Indiana than it charged in Kentucky. It claimed it was injured because Dawson Springs passed on the lower prices to retailers in Kentucky, and that many consumers purchased in Kentucky to obtain lower prices, thus reducing Vanco's total sales.

Justice Blackmun, writing for a unanimous Court, noted that the Robinson–Patman Act is not limited in coverage to injuries to competition between the favored and disfavored purchaser, but also applies to injuries in competition between their customers. The Court then turned to Falls City's defense that its price structure was justified because it was meeting equally low prices in Kentucky.]

. . .

III

When proved, the meeting-competition defense of § 2(b) exonerates a seller from Robinson–Patman Act liability. Standard Oil Co. v. FTC, 340 U.S. 231, 246–247 (1951). This Court consistently has held that the meeting-competition defense " 'at least requires the seller, who has knowingly discriminated in price, to show the existence of facts which would lead a reasonable and prudent person to believe that the granting of a lower price would in fact meet the equally low price of a competitor.' " United States v. United States Gypsum Co., 438 U.S. 422, 451 (1978), quoting FTC v. A.E. Staley Mfg. Co., 324 U.S. 746, 759–760 (1945); see Great A & P Tea Co. v. FTC, 440 U.S. 69, 82 (1979). The seller must show that under the circumstances it was reasonable to believe that the quoted price or a lower one was available to the favored purchaser or purchasers from the seller's competitors. See *United States Gypsum Co.*, 438 U.S., at 451. Neither the District Court nor the Court of Appeals addressed the question whether Falls City had shown information that would have led a reasonable and prudent person to believe that its lower Kentucky price would meet competitors' equally low prices there; indeed, no findings whatever were made regarding competitors' Kentucky prices, or the information available to Falls City about its competitors' Kentucky prices.

Instead, the Court of Appeals reasoned that Falls City had otherwise failed to show that its pricing "was a good faith effort" to meet competition. The Court of Appeals considered it sufficient to defeat the defense that the price difference "resulted from price increases in Indiana, not price decreases in Kentucky," and that the higher Indiana price was the result of Falls City's policy of following the Indiana prices of its larger competitors in order to enhance its profits. The Court of Appeals also suggested that Falls City's defense failed because it adopted a "general system of competition," rather than responding to "individual situations." The court believed that FTC v. A.E. Staley Mfg. Co., supra, supported this holding. 654 F.2d, at 1230.

A

On its face, § 2(b) requires more than a showing of facts that would have led a reasonable person to believe that a lower price was available to the favored purchaser from a competitor. The showing required is that the "lower price ... *was made* in good faith *to meet*" the competitor's low price. 15 U.S.C. § 13(b) (emphasis added). Thus, the defense requires that the seller offer the lower price in good faith *for the purpose* of meeting the competitor's price, that is, the lower price must actually have been a good-faith response to that competing low price. See Rowe, at 234–235. See generally Kuenzel & Schiffres, Making Sense of Robinson–Patman: The Need to Revitalize Its Affirmative Defenses, 62 Va.L.Rev. 1211, 1237–1255 (1976). In most situations, a showing of facts giving rise to a reasonable belief that equally low prices were available to the favored purchaser from a competitor will be sufficient to establish that the seller's lower price was offered in good faith to meet that price. In others, however, despite the availability from other sellers of a low price, it may be apparent that the defendant's low offer was not a good-faith response.

In *Staley,* this Court applied that principle. The Federal Trade Commission (FTC) had proceeded against Staley and six competing manufacturers of glucose, all of whom adhered to the same Chicago basing-point pricing system. Like its competitors, Staley, whose plant was located in Decatur, Ill., sold glucose to candy and syrup manufacturers at a delivered price that included the freight rate from Chicago to the point of delivery. Purchasers nearer Decatur thus were charged an element of "phantom" freight, while Staley "absorbed" an element of freight in sales to buyers nearer Chicago. Customers located near Staley's Decatur plant were harmed because, despite being located closer to the plant, they were forced to pay more for glucose than did their Chicago area competitors.

The FTC eventually charged all seven manufacturers individually with price discrimination and jointly under the Federal Trade Commission Act with price fixing. See Corn Products Refining Co., 47 F.T.C. 587 (1950). At the time of the Staley decision, both the FTC and this Court had determined that use of the pricing system by Staley's competitors was illegal under § 2(a). See Corn Products Refining Co. v. FTC, 324 U.S., at 732, 737–739. And, although neither the FTC nor this Court directly relied on the fact in finding price discrimination, Staley itself had been found to be a party to an interseller conspiracy aimed at maintaining "oppressive and uniform net delivered prices" throughout the country. See A.E. Staley Mfg. Co. v. FTC, 4 F.T.C. Stat. & Dec. 795, 805 (1943).

The Court observed that § 2(b) could exonerate Staley only if that section permitted a seller to establish "an otherwise unlawful system of discriminatory prices" in order to benefit from "a like unlawful system maintained by his competitors." Staley could not claim that its low Chicago prices were set for the purpose of meeting the equally low prices of competitors there; the Chicago prices could be seen only as part of a collusive pricing system designed to exact artificially high prices throughout the country. Since the low prices were set "in order to establish elsewhere the artificially high prices whose discriminatory effect permeates respondents' entire pricing system," the Court sustained the FTC's finding "that respondents' price discriminations were not made to meet a 'lower' price and consequently were not in good faith," id., at 758.

Thus, even had Staley been able to show that its prices throughout the country did not undercut those of its competitors, its lower price in the Chicago area was not a good-faith response to the lower prices there. Staley had not priced in response to competitors' discrete pricing decisions, but from the outset had followed an industrywide practice of setting its prices according to a single, arbitrary scheme that by its nature *precluded* independent pricing in response to normal competitive forces.

B

Almost 20 years ago, the FTC set forth the standard that governs the requirement of a "good-faith response":

> "At the heart of Section 2(b) is the concept of 'good faith'. This is a flexible and pragmatic, not a technical or doctrinaire, concept. The standard of good faith is simply the standard of the prudent businessman responding fairly to what he reasonably believes is a situation of competitive necessity." Continental Baking Co., 63 F.T.C. 2071, 2163 (1963).

Whether this standard is met depends on " 'the facts and circumstances of the particular case, not abstract theories or remote conjectures.' " United States v. United States Gypsum Co., 438 U.S., at 454, quoting Continental Baking Co., 63 F.T.C., at 2163.

The "facts and circumstances" present in *Staley* differ markedly from those present here. Although the District Court characterized the Indiana prices charged by Falls City and its competitors as "artificially high," there is no evidence that Falls City's lower prices in Kentucky were set as part of a plan to obtain artificially high profits in Indiana rather than in response to competitive conditions in Kentucky. Falls City did not adopt an illegal system of prices maintained by its competitors.[69] The District Court found that Falls City's prices rose in Indiana in response to competitors' price increases there; it did not address the crucial question whether Falls City's Kentucky prices remained lower in response to competitors' prices in that State.

Vanco attempts to liken this case to *Staley* by arguing that the existence of industrywide price discrimination within the single geographic retail market itself indicates "tacit or explicit collusion, or ... market power" inconsistent with a good-faith response. By its terms, however, the

---

69. Except through its rejected Sherman Act claim, Vanco has never attempted to prove that the competing prices Falls City claims to have met were themselves illegal, or that Falls City met those prices knowing them to be unlawful. The plaintiff bears the burden of proving that the prices met were actually illegal. Cadigan v. Texaco, Inc., 492 F.2d 383, 387 (C.A.9 1974); National Dairy Products Corp. v. FTC, 395 F.2d 517, 524 (CA7), cert. denied, 393 U.S. 977 (1968); see Standard Oil Co. v. Brown, 238 F.2d 54, 58, and n. 7 (C.A.5 1956).

meeting-competition defense requires a seller to justify only its *lower* price. See *Staley*, 324 U.S., at 753. Thus, although the Sherman Act would provide a remedy if Falls City's higher Indiana price were set collusively, collusion is relevant to Vanco's Robinson–Patman Act claim only if it affected Falls City's lower Kentucky price. If Falls City set its lower price in good faith to meet an equally low price of a competitor, it did not violate the Robinson–Patman Act.

Moreover, the collusion argument founders on a complete lack of proof. Persistent, industrywide price discrimination within a geographic market should certainly alert a court to a substantial possibility of collusion.[70] See Posner, Oliogopoly and the Antitrust Laws: A Suggested Approach, 21 Stan.L.Rev. 1562, 1578–1579 (1969). Here, however, the persistent interstate price difference could well have been attributable, not to Falls City, but to extensive state regulation of the sale of beer. Indiana required each brewer to charge a single price for its beer throughout the State, and barred direct competition between Indiana and Kentucky distributors for sales to retailers. In these unusual circumstances, the prices charged to Vanco and other wholesalers in Vanderburgh County may have been influenced more by market conditions in distant Gary and Fort Wayne than by conditions in nearby Henderson County, Ky. Moreover, wholesalers in Henderson County competed directly, and attempted to price competitively, with wholesalers in neighboring Kentucky counties. A separate pricing structure might well have evolved in the two States without collusion, notwithstanding the existence of a common retail market along the border. Thus, the sustained price discrimination does not itself demonstrate that Falls City's Kentucky prices were not a good-faith response to competitors' prices there.

C

The Court of Appeals explicitly relied on two other factors in rejecting Falls City's meeting-competition defense: the price discrimination was created by raising rather than lowering prices, and Falls City raised its prices in order to increase its profits. Neither of these factors is controlling. Nothing in § 2(b) requires a seller to *lower* its price in order to meet competition. On the contrary, § 2(b) requires the defendant to show only that its "lower price ... was made in good faith to meet an equally low

---

70. Indeed, in some circumstances there may be no other plausible explanation for persistent "economic" price discrimination. Cf. FTC v. Cement Institute, 333 U.S. 683, 715 (1948) ("the multiple basing point system of delivered prices as employed by respondents contravened accepted economic principles and could only have been maintained through collusion"); *Staley*, 324 U.S., at 756 (it "seems inescapable" that basing point system was adopted not to meet equally low prices of competitors, but to establish artificially high prices elsewhere).

"Economic" price discrimination consists in selling a product to different customers at prices that bear different ratios to the marginal costs of sales to those customers, for example, charging the same price to two customers despite the fact that the seller incurs higher costs to serve one than the other, or charging different prices to two customers despite the fact that the seller's costs of service are the same. Price discrimination under the Robinson–Patman Act, however, "is merely a price difference." FTC v. Anheuser-Busch, Inc., 363 U.S. 536, 549 (1960).

price of a competitor." A seller is required to justify a price difference by showing that it reasonably believed that an equally low price was available to the purchaser and that it offered the lower price for that reason; the seller is not required to show that the difference resulted from subtraction rather than addition.

A different rule would not only be contrary to the language of the statute, but also might stifle the only kind of legitimate price competition reasonably available in particular industries. In a period of generally rising prices, vigorous price competition for a particular customer or customers may take the form of smaller price increases rather than price cuts. Thus, a price discrimination created by selective price increases can result from a good-faith effort to meet a competitor's low price.

Nor is the good faith with which the lower price is offered impugned if the prices raised, like those kept lower, respond to competitors' prices and are set with the goal of increasing the seller's profits. A seller need not choose between "ruinously cutting its prices to all its customers to match the price offered to one, [and] refusing to meet the competition and then ruinously raising its prices to its remaining customers to cover increased unit costs." Standard Oil Co. v. FTC, 340 U.S., at 250. Nor need a seller choose between keeping all its prices ruinously low to meet the price offered to one, and ruinously raising its prices to all customers to a level significantly above that charged by its competitors. A seller is permitted "to retain a customer by realistically meeting in good faith the price offered to that customer, without necessarily changing the seller's price to its other customers." Ibid. The plain language of § 2(b) also permits a seller to retain a customer by realistically meeting in good faith the price offered to that customer, without necessarily freezing his price to his other customers.

Section 2(b) does not require a seller, meeting in good faith a competitor's lower price to certain customers, to forgo the profits that otherwise would be available in sales to its remaining customers. The very purpose of the defense is to permit a seller to treat different competitive situations differently. The prudent businessman responding fairly to what he believes in good faith is a situation of competitive necessity might well raise his prices to some customers to increase his profits, while meeting competitors' prices by keeping his prices to other customers low.

The Court in *Staley* said that the meeting-competition defense "presupposes that the person charged with violating the Act would, by his normal, non-discriminatory pricing methods, have reached a price so high that he could reduce it in order to meet the competitor's equally low price." In that case, however, the Court was not dealing with a seller whose "normal, non-discriminatory pricing methods" called for a price increase but who wished to exempt certain customers from the increase in order to meet prices, lower than the increased price, available to those customers from competitors. Of course, a seller could accomplish the same result within the guidelines the Court of Appeals would impose by instituting across-the-board price increases followed by selective reductions. But far from being flexible and pragmatic, a rule requiring such costly behavior would be nonsensical.[71]

D

Vanco also contends that Falls City did not satisfy § 2(b) because its price discrimination "was not a *defensive* response to competition." Brief for Respondent 47 (emphasis supplied). According to Vanco, the Robinson–Patman Act permits price discrimination only if its purpose is to retain a customer. We agree that a seller's response must be defensive, in the sense that the lower price must be calculated and offered in good faith to "meet not beat" the competitor's low price. See *United States Gypsum Co.,* 438 U.S., at 454. Section 2(b), however, does not distinguish between one who meets a competitor's lower price to retain an old customer and one who meets a competitor's lower price in an attempt to gain new customers.[72] See Stevens, Defense of Meeting the Lower Price of a Competitor in Summer Institute on International and Comparative Law, University of Michigan Law School, Lectures on Federal Antitrust Laws 129, 135–136 (1953). Such a distinction would be inconsistent with that section's language and logic, see Sunshine Biscuits, Inc. v. FTC, 306 F.2d 48, 51–52 (C.A.7 1962), "would not be in keeping with elementary principles of competition, and would in fact foster tight and rigid commercial relationships by insulating them from market forces." 1955 Report, at 184; see 1977 Report, at 26, 265.[73]

IV

The Court of Appeals also relied on *Staley* for the proposition that the meeting-competition defense " 'places emphasis on individual [competitive] situations, rather than upon a general system of competition' " (quoting *Staley,* 324 U.S., at 753), and "does not justify the maintenance of discriminatory pricing among classes of customers that results merely from the adoption of a competitor's discriminatory pricing structure." The Court of Appeals was apparently invoking the District Court's findings that Falls City set prices statewide rather than on a "customer to customer basis,"

71. "Section 2(b) should not require proof that the seller departed from a previously uniform price schedule. Such *previous* pricing is not relevant to evaluation of genuine responses to a *current* competitive situation." Report of the Attorney General's National Committee to Study the Antitrust Laws 182 (1955 Report) (emphasis in original).

72. At least three Courts of Appeals have held that the defense is not limited to attempts to retain customers. Cadigan v. Texaco, Inc., 492 F.2d, at 387, and n. 3; Hanson v. Pittsburgh Plate Glass Industries, Inc., 482 F.2d 220, 226–227 (C.A.5 1973), cert. denied, 414 U.S. 1136 (1974); Sunshine Biscuits, Inc. v. FTC, 306 F.2d 48, 51–52 (C.A.7 1962). But

see Standard Motor Products, Inc. v. FTC, 265 F.2d 674, 677 (CA2) (defense available only if lower price responds to individual competitive demand).

73. Standard Oil Co. v. FTC, 340 U.S. 231 (1951) is not to the contrary. The Court there referred to the defense's being available to a seller seeking to "retain" customers, id., at 242, 249, 250, simply because the petitioner had so framed its defense in that particular case. Id., at 234, 236; see 1955 Report, at 184; Kuenzel & Schiffres, Making Sense of Robinson–Patman: The Need to Revitalize its Affirmative Defenses, 62 Va.L.Rev. 1211, 1253–1254 (1976).

and the District Court's conclusion that this practice disqualified Falls City from asserting the meeting-competition defense. 1980–2 Trade Cases, at 75,817. At least two other Courts of Appeals have read *Staley* to hold that the defense is unavailable to sellers pricing on other than a customer-by-customer basis, while two Courts of Appeals have held that a customer-by-customer response is not required.[74] . . .

Section 2(b) specifically allows a "lower price . . . to any purchaser or purchasers" made in good faith to meet a competitor's equally low price. A single low price surely may be extended to numerous purchasers if the seller has a reasonable basis for believing that the competitor's lower price is available to them.[75] Beyond the requirement that the lower price be reasonably calculated to "meet not beat" the competition, Congress intended to leave it a "question of fact . . . whether the way in which the competition was met lies within the latitude allowed." 80 Cong.Rec. 9418 (1936) (remarks of Rep. Utterback). Once again, this inquiry is guided by the standard of the prudent businessman responding fairly to what he reasonably believes are the competitive necessities.

A seller may have good reason to believe that a competitor or competitors are charging lower prices throughout a particular region. See William Inglis & Sons Baking Co. v. ITT Continental Baking Co., 668 F.2d 1014, 1046 (C.A.9 1981), cert. denied, 459 U.S. 825 (1982); Balian Ice Cream Co. v. Arden Farms Co., 231 F.2d 356, 366 (C.A.9 1955), cert. denied, 350 U.S. 991 (1956); Rowe, at 235–236. In such circumstances, customer-by-customer negotiations would be unlikely to result in prices different from those set according to information relating to competitors' territorial prices. A customer-by-customer requirement might also make meaningful price competition unrealistically expensive for smaller firms such as Falls City, which was attempting to compete with larger national breweries in 13 separate States. Cf. Callaway Mills Co. v. FTC, 362 F.2d 435, 442 (C.A.5 1966) (in some circumstances, requirement of customer-by-customer pricing "would be burdensome, unreasonable, and practically unfeasible").

In *Staley*, 324 U.S., at 753, as in each of the later cases in which this Court has contrasted a "general system of competition" with "individual competitive situations," *see, e.g.,* FTC v. National Lead Co., 352 U.S. 419,

---

74. Compare Exquisite Form Brassiere, Inc. v. FTC, 360 F.2d 492, 493 (1965) (customer-by-customer response required), cert. denied, 384 U.S. 959 (1966), and Standard Motor Products, Inc. v. FTC, 265 F.2d, at 677 (same), with William Inglis & Sons Baking Co. v. ITT Continental Baking Co., 668 F.2d 1014, 1046 (C.A.9 1981) (customer-by-customer response not necessarily required), cert. denied, 459 U.S. 825 (1982), Callaway Mills Co. v. FTC, 362 F.2d 435, 442 (C.A.5 1966) (same), and Balian Ice Cream Co. v. Arden Farms Co., 231 F.2d 356, 366 (C.A.9 1955) (same), cert. denied, 350 U.S. 991 (1956).

75. See also Standard Oil Co. v. FTC, 340 U.S., at 247, n. 13, quoting statement of Herbert A. Bergson, Assistant Attorney General, at Hearings on S. 236 before a Subcommittee of the Senate Committee on Interstate and Foreign Commerce, 81st Cong., 1st Sess., 77 (1949) (" 'The section presently permits sellers to justify otherwise forbidden price discriminations on the ground that the lower prices to one set of buyers were made in good faith to meet the equally low prices of a competitor' ").

431 (1957); FTC v. Cement Institute, 333 U.S. 683, 708 (1948), the seller's lower price was quoted not *"because* of lower prices by a competitor,"but *"because* of a preconceived pricing scale which [was] operative regardless of variations in competitor's prices." Rowe, at 234 (emphasis in original). In those cases, the contested lower prices were not truly *"responsive* to rivals' competitive prices,"ibid. (emphasis in original), and therefore were not genuinely made to meet competitors' lower prices. Territorial pricing, however, can be a perfectly reasonable method—sometimes the most reasonable method—of responding to rivals' low prices.[76] We choose not to read into § 2(b) a restriction that would deny the meeting-competition defense to one whose areawide price is a well-tailored response to competitors' low prices.

Of course, a seller must limit its lower price to that group of customers reasonably believed to have the lower price available to it from competitors. A response that is not reasonably tailored to the competitive situation as known to the seller, or one that is based on inadequate verification, would not meet the standard of good faith. Similarly, the response may continue only as long as the competitive circumstances justifying it, as reasonably known by the seller, persist.[77] One choosing to price on a territorial basis, rather than on a customer-by-customer basis, must show that this decision was a genuine, reasonable response to prevailing competitive circumstances. See International Air Industries, Inc. v. American Excelsior Co., 517 F.2d 714, 725–726 (C.A.5 1975), cert. denied, 424 U.S. 943 (1976); Callaway Mills Co. v. FTC, 362 F.2d, at 441–442. See generally 1977 Report, at 265. Unless the circumstances call into question the seller's good faith, this burden will be discharged by showing that a reasonable and prudent businessman would believe that the lower price he charged was generally available from his competitors throughout the territory and throughout the period in which he made the lower price available. See William Inglis & Sons Baking Co. v. ITT Continental Baking Co., 668 F.2d, at 1045–1046.

V

[The case was remanded to give Falls City an opportunity to prove that its prices were equal to those offered by competitors in the relevant territory and throughout the period during which lower prices were offered.]

76. See Rowe, at 240 ("a seller's area-wide and blanket lower price, if made in good faith to meet competitors' lower prices, may be justified ... as responsive to an 'individual competitive situation' "). Cf. Maryland Baking Co. v. FTC, 243 F.2d 716, 719 (C.A.4 1957) (FTC permits competitive area price variations to avert placing "prices in a straightjacket throughout the country"); Anheuser–Busch, Inc., 54 F.T.C. 277, 301 (1957) (suggesting that offer of lower price throughout particular area might be responsive to "individual competitive situation"); C.E. Niehoff & Co., 51 F.T.C. 1114, 1130, 1146 (1955) (rejecting position that "showing that the seller's discriminations were temporary and localized in area is an indispensable prerequisite" to defense).

77. See Klein, Meeting Competition by Price Systems Under § 2(b) of the Robinson–Patman Act: Problems and Prospects, 16 Antitrust Bull. 213, 233–234, 238 (1971); Kuenzel & Schiffres, 62 Va.L.Rev., at 1244–1249.

SECTION 5. BROKERAGE, AD ALLOWANCES AND SERVICES

Congress recognized that the provisions of Section 2(a) of the Robinson–Patman Act, forbidding discrimination in price to favored buyers, might be circumvented by indirect forms of discrimination. It therefore set out to outlaw payments of "brokerage" in 2(c) of the Act, payments to customers as compensation for the customer providing services or facilities (for example, sales people who demonstrated a product), in 2(d) of the Act, or by direct contribution of services or facilities (such as storage or display units) in Section 2(e) of the Act.[78]

During the 1940's and 1950's, government enforcement of the provisions of 2(c), 2(d) and 2(e) represented a substantial portion of all Robinson Patman enforcement. In the past two decades, the level of enforcement actions under these sections has subsided. Nevertheless, precedent remains on the books—often quite restrictive and demanding—and most companies try to comply with the provisions of these portions of the Act even though it is burdensome and expensive and even though there have been signals in Supreme Court and lower court cases that some of the more rigid aspects of those provisions would not be enforced in the courts today.

A. Brokerage.

Section 2(c) of the Robinson–Patman Act provides as follows:

> "That it shall be unlawful for any person engaged in commerce in the course of such commerce, to pay or grant, or to receive or accept, anything of value as a commission, brokerage, or other compensation, or any allowance or discount in lieu thereof, except for services rendered in connection with the sale or purchase of goods, wares, or merchandise, either to the other party to such transaction or to an agent, representative or other intermediary therein where such intermediary is acting in fact for or on behalf, or is subject to the direct or indirect control, of any party to such transaction other than the person by whom such compensation is so granted or paid."

1. Identification of "brokerage" or "discounts in lieu thereof."

Early cases defined "brokerage" as any payment by a buyer or intermediary controlled by the buyer, or seller or intermediary controlled by the seller, i.e., a payment to any party with a relation to the opposite party to the transaction.[79] In effect, Section 2(c) which was designed to prevent

78. For Sections 2(c), 2(d) and 2(f) of the Robinson–Patman Act, see pp. 1282–1283, supra.

79. See, e.g., Southgate Brokerage Co. v. FTC, 150 F.2d 607 (4th Cir.), cert. denied,

326 U.S. 774 (1945); Great Atlantic & Pacific Tea Co. v. FTC, 106 F.2d 667 (3d Cir.1939), cert. denied, 308 U.S. 625 (1940).

discrimination through the use of "dummy brokerage" operations was interpreted to strike down all brokerage arrangements. Defenses based on absence of competitive injury or claims that valuable services had been provided—arguably triggering the clause in Section 2(c) that brokerage payments would not be illegal if made for "services rendered"—was downplayed or ignored.

Another early interpretation of Section 2(c) that extended its reach adopted as an inference that an allowance or payment to a particular buyer or a class of buyers was "brokerage" if it was the mathematical equivalent of brokerage paid in usual brokerage transactions in the industry.[80] The "mathematical correlation" approach was not unanimous, and was rejected by the court in Central–Retailer–Owned Grocers, Inc. v. FTC, 319 F.2d 410 (7th Cir.1963).

Indications in more recent judicial opinions that restrictive interpretations of 2(c) in the early cases may no longer be valid are discussed in Section 3 below.

2.   Limited availability of defenses.

The language of 2(c) and early interpretations offer little in the way of opportunity to defend brokerage allowances. The statute appears to outlaw all brokerage payments even when not discriminatory and early decisions adopted that view.[81] The Federal Trade Commission took a similar position in a 1980 proceeding, noting that " ... a general requirement that discrimination be shown cannot and should not be read into Section 2(c)."[82]

At least according to the language of Section 2(c), a violation can be found whether or not there is evidence of an adverse effect on competition.

Since the statute does permit payments "for services rendered," that provision might have been interpreted to allow payments on the basis of services provided by the buyer to the seller. In effect, the payment could be considered as comparable to a "cost justified" allowance, or could be defended on the grounds that the payment was no greater than the value of services rendered and therefore could not injure competition. That interpretation was rejected however, and the services rendered were interpreted as being provided by the buyer to itself rather than to the seller, even though the seller benefited from the provision of services. Overall, these various interpretations made it exceedingly difficult to defend against any challenge to payments that looked like brokerage.[83]

3.   The impact of *Broch* and other decisions.

It is uncertain whether the extremely grudging interpretations of 2(c) would prevail today. The only Supreme Court case directly interpreting

80.   Great Atlantic & Pacific Tea Co. v. FTC, note ___ supra; Union Maleable Manufacturing Co., 52 F.T.C. 408 (1952).

81.   FTC v. Washington Fish & Oyster Co., 282 F.2d 595 (9th Cir.1960); Southgate Brokerage Co. v. FTC, 150 F.2d 607 (4th Cir.), cert. denied, 326 U.S. 774 (1945).

82.   Herbert R. Gibson, Sr., 95 F.T.C. 553, 740 (1980), aff'd, 682 F.2d 554 (5th Cir.1982), cert. denied, 460 U.S. 1068 (1983).

83.   *See, e.g.*, Southgate Brokerage Co. v. FTC, 150 F.2d 607 (4th Cir.), cert. denied, 326 U.S. 774 (1945).

Section 2(c) was FTC v. Henry Broch & Co.[84] involving a food broker that passed along part of its brokerage commission to one of its largest purchasers. The purchaser had insisted on a five cent per gallon discount ($1.25 rather than $1.30). Broch provided that information to its supplier, and the supplier determined that it could meet the $1.25 price only if Broch would reduce its commission from 5% to 3%. The Supreme Court found that the arrangement violated 2(c), but, in reaching that result, offered explanations arguably inconsistent with the narrower early interpretations of the statute. Thus the court explained:

> "[t]here is no evidence that the buyer rendered any services to the seller or to the respondent nor that anything in its method of dealing justified its getting a discriminatory price by means of a reduced brokerage charge. We would have quite a different case if there was such evidence and we need not explore the applicability of Section 2(c) to such circumstances."[85]

At another point the Court emphasized that 2(c) was aimed at price discrimination through abuse of the brokerage function. Those two quotes suggest that brokerage would not be illegal unless there was some form of discrimination (*i.e.*, legitimate brokerage could occur) and also that there may be some substance to the "services rendered" defense as well.

Similarly, in Allen Pen Co. v. Springfield Photo Mount Co.,[86] no violation was found because the court concluded that the plaintiff was required and had failed to show that the brokerage arrangement was a sham, designed to grant favored treatment to the plaintiff's competitors and that the payments were sufficiently substantial to justify a finding of competitive injury.

4. Repeal or modification of Section 2(c).

Two presidential task forces[87] and a Department of Justice report on the Robinson–Patman Act[88] have advocated repeal of the provision. The essential point advocated in both task force reports is that any valid purpose served by Section 2(c) could be recognized by revising Section 2(a) to cover brokerage allowances. The Justice Department study notes:

> "Any legitimate concern over the use of brokerage payments as a form of indirect price discrimination can be dealt with by making clear that brokerage payments should be netted against price for the purpose of determining the existence of a discrimination under Section 2(a)."[89]

Any such reform would make it clear that violations can only be found if there is real discrimination and competitive injury. Because there has

---

84. 363 U.S. 166 (1960).

85. Id. at 173.

86. 653 F.2d 17 (1st Cir.1981).

87. White House Task Force on Antitrust Policy, 411 Antitrust and Trade Reg. Rep. (BNA) 10, 18 (1969); President's Task Force on Productivity and Competition, 5 Trade Reg.Rep. (CCH) ¶ 50,108 (1969).

88. U.S. Department of Justice Report on the Robinson–Patman Act, 267 (1976).

89. Id. at 268.

been so little enforcement of the statute in recent years, and because the *Broch* decision and lower court cases have backed away from the virtual *per se* prohibitions adopted in the early opinions, efforts at reform have subsided.

B. Allowances or Services.

Section 2(d) covers a supplier's payment for services or facilities and provides as follows:

> "That it shall be unlawful for any person engaged in commerce to pay or contract for the payment of anything of value to or for the benefit of a customer of such person in the course of such commerce as compensation or in consideration for any services or facilities furnished by or through such customer in connection with the processing, handling, sale or offering for sale of any products or commodities manufactured, sold, or offered for sale by such person, unless such payment or consideration is available on proportionally equal terms to all other customers competing in the distribution of such products or commodities."

Section 2(e) of the Act covers a supplier's furnishing of services or facilities to the customer and provides:

> "That it shall be unlawful for any person to discriminate in favor of one purchaser against another purchaser or purchasers of a commodity bought for resale, with or without processing, by contracting to furnish or furnishing, or by contributing to the furnishing of, any services or facilities connected with the processing, handling, sale, or offering for sale of such commodity so purchased upon terms not accorded to all purchasers on proportionally equal terms."[90]

In guidelines published by the Federal Trade Commission in 1969 and amended in 1972, the following were listed as examples of services for which sellers frequently pay the buyer: any kind of advertising including cooperative advertising, hand bills, window and floor displays and demonstrators and demonstrations. As examples of services or facilities frequently furnished to customers, the guidelines list the following: any kind of advertising, catalogs, demonstrators, display and storage cabinets, display materials, special packaging, accepting returns for credit, or prizes or merchandise for conducting promotional contests.

Although the language of the two sections is not identical, the case law interpreting the provisions has worked out a reconciliation so that the same statutory requirements and defenses apply to both sections.[91] As will be discussed below, the real problem is that the coverage and interpretation of 2(d) and 2(e) is sharply different from the coverage and interpretation of 2(a) of the Robinson–Patman Act.

90. 15 U.S.C.A. §§ 13(d), 13(e) (1936).

91. See Rowe, Price Discrimination Under the Robinson–Patman Act 390 (1962).

1. Definition of allowance or service.

In general, a payment in connection with the original sale of a product to a distributor is covered under 2(a) of the Robinson–Patman Act, while a payment or provision of services in connection with resale of the product is covered by 2(d) or 2(e) of the Act.[92] Thus if a supplier simply pays money to a distributor for the distributor's account, that would be covered under 2(a) of the Act, but if it pays money for a joint program in connection with the resale of the supplier's product, that would be covered under Section 2(d).

2. Available and unavailable defenses.

2(d) and 2(e) come into play only if the seller discriminates between competing buyers[93] and there is also available a meeting competition defense. For a time, the commission argued that the meeting competition defense was unavailable under Section 2(d) because the language of Section 2(b) referred only to "services or facilities" and not to allowances for services or facilities, but the court in *Exquisite Form Brassiere* rejected that interpretation.[94]

On the other hand, Sections 2(d) and 2(e) have an almost *per se* quality in the sense that allowances or services cannot be defended as "cost justified" and, more importantly, there is no requirement of a showing of competitive injury in order to establish a violation. Thus a direct and unjustified payment to a customer may be defended on grounds that the payment was not sufficiently significant to cause competitive injury, but a payment in the same amount for a service or facility would be illegal. In FTC v. Simplicity Pattern Co.,[95] the Supreme Court justified different treatment on the grounds that Congress' purpose was to deter difficult to detect payments for services or the providing of services, and force such discrimination into the form of a direct discount. Why direct discounts (pocketed by the buyer) would be easier to detect than discriminatory payments for services by the buyer was not made clear in the opinion.

3. Available on proportionally equal terms.

The text of both sections requires that services and facilities, or payments for services and facilities, be made available "on proportionally equal terms." The first requirement is that the plan be "functionally available." In Guide 9 of the FTC's 1972 guideline amendments, the Commission advised:

> "The plan should be such that all types of competing customers may participate. It should not be tailored to favor or discriminate against a particular customer or class of customers, but should in its terms be usable in a practical business sense by all competing

92. Herbert R. Gibson, Sr., 95 F.T.C. 553, 725 (1980), aff'd, 682 F.2d 554 (5th Cir.1982).

93. See Exquisite Form Brassiere v. FTC, 301 F.2d 499 (D.C.Cir.1961), cert. denied, 369 U.S. 888 (1962).

94. Exquisite Form Brassiere, supra.

95. 360 U.S. 55 (1959).

customers. This may require offering all such customers more than one way to participate in the plan ... if [the seller] offers alternative plans, all the plans offered should provide the same proportionate equality and the seller should inform competing customers of the various alternative plans. . . . ''

As interpreted, ''functional availability'' means that the allowance or service must realistically be useful to all customers, regardless of their size, location, or way of doing business.[96] Thus, all dealers must legitimately be on notice that certain services or payments are available.[97] And if the particular service provided or subsidized is not appropriate for a class of customers, the seller must offer a subsidy for alternative marketing efforts. For example, a facility that requires substantial floor space at the retail outlet would not be ''functionally available'' to small dealers and some sort of alternative marketing support would have to be offered. Thus the Commission guidelines provide: ''This may require offering all such customers more than one way to participate in the plan or offering alternative terms and conditions to customers for whom the basic plan is not usable and suitable.''[98]

Even greater complications emerge out of the provision that payments and services must be made available on ''proportionally equal terms.'' In Guide 7 of its 1979 guidelines, the Commission explained:

''This means that payments or services shall be proportionalized on some basis that is fair to all customers who compete in the resale of the sellers' products. No single way to proportionalize is prescribed by law. Any method that treats competing customers on proportionally equal terms may be used. Generally this can best be done by basing the payments made or the services furnished on the dollar volume or on the quantity of the goods purchased during a specified period. Other methods which are fair to all competing customers are also acceptable.''

If all distributors buy approximately in the same amounts, no problem arises since they can all be accorded the same payments or services. But where large and small dealers are involved, questions of proportionality are perplexing. The fact that a display in the front of a store in a mall is of much greater marketing impact—*i.e.*, the value to the seller is great—does not justify a larger payment than to an isolated store in an untravelled part of town. Plans which grant allowances or services based on the dollar amount or quantity of purchases have usually been approved, but other plans keyed to market impact—for example, payments depending on how much business increased in a period of time or the number of transactions in the store—have been rejected.[99]

The result of the Commission's interpretation is that sellers often find themselves in a position where they must subsidize forms of market

---

96. 16 C.F.R. § 240.9(a) (1982).

97. See Vanity Fair Paper Mills v. FTC, 311 F.2d 480 (2d Cir.1962).

98. 16 C.F.R. § 240.9(a) (1982).

99. Amstar Corp., 78 F.T.C. 536 (1971).

support that are not especially efficient or cost effective or be willing to give up the form of merchandising support entirely. Also, administrative expenses in seeing to it that plans and alternatives are made available to competing customers can undermine the effectiveness of the whole marketing program. In a 1966 dissent, Commissioner Elman summarized the ways in which interpretations of 2(d) and 2(e) have placed burdens on sellers:

> "He must disregard his own promotional needs and set up an intricate 'promotional program' designed to satisfy the desires of all his customers. He may be compelled to pay for 'promotional activity' which is of no benefit to him whatsoever and which indeed is wasteful as well as not beneficial ...
>
> "I do not believe that Section 2(d) was intended to have this result. As I read the Act, it provides that a seller may choose those promotional and advertising services for which he will compensate his customers; if he gives a payment to one customer who renders such services, he must give proportionally equal payments to all other customers who are ready, able and willing to provide him with the same services."[1]

4.   Direct and indirect sales to dealers: The problem of *Fred Meyer*.

Often suppliers will sell directly to some distributors (often large outlets or chains who can afford to do their own wholesaling) and indirectly (*i.e.*, through wholesalers) to smaller retailers. In *Fred Meyer*,[2] several suppliers made allowances available to a direct purchasing retailer but did not make comparable allowances available to small retailers who competed with the direct buyer. The suppliers defended on grounds that the statute only requires payment of allowances or provision of services to customers, and the indirect purchasing retailers were not "customers" of the suppliers but only of the wholesalers. The Supreme Court rejected that interpretation, noting that it would lead to the anomalous result that smaller retailers who can only afford to purchase through wholesalers would be left unprotected against discriminatory promotional allowances to the direct buyers. Incidentally, the court found that the suppliers did not have to provide comparable payments or services to the wholesalers and the direct buying retailers because they did not compete at the same functional level.

In response to the argument that suppliers may not always find it feasible to seek out and compensate retailers with whom they have no direct dealings, the Court noted that the supplier could simply compensate the wholesalers and then ensure that the wholesalers distribute payments or administer programs to the indirect buyers.

In dissent, Justice Harlan noted that compensating retailers with whom the supplier had no business relationship will be "no simple matter." In fact, that has clearly turned out to be the case. For example, it has been held that the intermediate wholesalers need only compensate those retail-

1. House of Lords, Inc., 69 F.T.C. 44 (1966).   2. FTC v. Fred Meyer, 390 U.S. 341 (1968).

ers who compete with the favored direct-buying retailer. See Motive Parts Warehouse v. Facet Enterprises, 774 F.2d 380 (10th Cir.1985). However, wholesalers may be ill-equipped to determine which of their retailers compete with the favored buyer and which do not. Furthermore, assuming the supplier must make available some allowances to some of its direct buying purchasers, it then must determine whether it has to make comparable allowances to all of its indirect buying retailers or at least those who compete with each other. Again, the administrative burdens of making "proportionally equal" services and allowances available to retailers who buy directly or indirectly through various channels of distribution may be so great as to undermine the effectiveness of the entire program.

SECTION 6. BUYER'S LIABILITY FOR INDUCING OR RECEIVING DISCRIMINATIONS IN PRICE[3]

Great Atlantic & Pacific Tea Co. v. Federal Trade Commission

Supreme Court of the United States, 1979.
440 U.S. 69, 99 S.Ct. 925, 59 L.Ed.2d 153.

■ STEWART, J. The question presented in this case is whether the petitioner, the Great Atlantic & Pacific Tea Company (A & P), violated § 2(f) of the Robinson–Patman Act, as amended, 15 U.S.C.A. § 13(f), by knowingly inducing or receiving illegal price discriminations from the Borden Company (Borden).

The alleged violation was reflected in a 1965 agreement between A & P and Borden under which Borden undertook to supply "private label" milk to more than 200 A & P stores in a Chicago area that included portions of Illinois and Indiana. This agreement resulted from an effort by A & P to achieve cost savings by switching from the sale of "brand label" milk (milk sold under the brand name of the supplying dairy) to the sale of "private label" milk (milk sold under the A & P label).

To implement this plan, A & P asked Borden, its longtime supplier, to submit an offer to supply under private label certain of A & P's milk and other dairy product requirements. After prolonged negotiations, Borden offered to grant A & P a discount for switching to private label milk provided A & P would accept limited delivery service. Borden claimed that this offer would save A & P $410,000 a year compared to what it had been paying for its dairy products. A & P, however, was not satisfied with this offer and solicited offers from other dairies. A competitor of Borden, Bowman Dairy, then submitted an offer which was lower than Borden's.[4]

---

3. For Section 2(f) of the Robinson–Patman Act, see p. 1283 supra.

4. The Bowman bid would have produced estimated annual savings of approxi-mately $737,000 for A & P as compared with the first Borden bid, which would have produced estimated annual savings of $410,000.

At this point, A & P's Chicago buyer contacted Borden's chain store sales manager and stated, "I have a bid in my pocket. You [Borden] people are so far out of line it is not even funny. You are not even in the ball park." When the Borden representative asked for more details, he was told nothing except that a $50,000 improvement in Borden's bid "would not be a drop in the bucket."

Borden was thus faced with the problem of deciding whether to rebid. A & P at the time was one of Borden's largest customers in the Chicago area. Moreover, Borden had just invested more than five million dollars in a new dairy facility in Illinois. The loss of the A & P account would result in underutilization of this new plant. Under these circumstances, Borden decided to submit a new bid which doubled the estimated annual savings to A & P, from $410,000 to $820,000. In presenting its offer, Borden emphasized to A & P that it needed to keep A & P's business and was making the new offer in order to meet Bowman's bid. A & P then accepted Borden's bid after concluding that it was substantially better than Bowman's.

I

Based on these facts, the Federal Trade Commission filed a ... complaint against A & P. Count I charged that A & P had violated § 5 of the Federal Trade Commission Act by misleading Borden in the course of negotiations for the private label contract, in that A & P had failed to inform Borden that its second offer was better than the Bowman bid. Count II involving the same conduct, charged that A & P had violated § 2(f) of the Robinson–Patman Act by knowingly inducing or receiving price discriminations from Borden....

An Administrative Law Judge found, after extended discovery and a hearing that lasted over 110 days, that A & P had acted unfairly and deceptively in accepting the second offer from Borden and had therefore violated § 5 of the Federal Trade Commission Act as charged in Count I. The Administrative Law Judge similarly found that this same conduct had violated § 2(f) of the Robinson–Patman Act....

On review, the Commission reversed the Administrative Law Judge's finding as to Count I. Pointing out that the question at issue was what amount of disclosure is required of the buyer during contract negotiations, the Commission held that the imposition of a duty of affirmative disclosure would be "contrary to normal business practice and we think, contrary to the public interest." Despite this ruling, however, the Commission held as to Count II that the identical conduct on the part of A & P had violated § 2(f) of the Robinson–Patman Act, finding that Borden had discriminated in price between A & P and its competitors, that the discrimination had been injurious to competition, and that A & P had known or should have known that it was the beneficiary of unlawful price discrimination. The

Commission rejected A & P's defenses that the Borden bid had been made to meet competition and was cost justified.[5]

A & P filed a petition for review of the Commission's order in the Court of Appeals for the Second Circuit. The court held that substantial evidence supported the findings of the Commission, and that as a matter of law A & P could not successfully assert a meeting competition defense because it, unlike Borden, had known that Borden's offer was better than Bowman's.[6] Finally, the court held that the Commission had correctly determined that A & P had no cost justification defense.

II

The Robinson–Patman Act was passed in response to the problem perceived in the increased market power and coercive practices of chain stores and other big buyers that threatened the existence of small independent retailers. Notwithstanding this concern with buyers, however, the emphasis of the Act is in § 2(a), which prohibits price discrimination by sellers. Indeed, the original Patman Bill as reported by Committees of both Houses prohibited only seller activity, with no mention of buyer liability. Section 2(f) of the Act, making buyers liable for inducing or receiving price discriminations by sellers, was the product of a belated floor amendment near the conclusion of the Senate debates.[7]

As finally enacted, § 2(f) provides:

> "That it shall be unlawful for any person engaged in commerce, in the course of such commerce, knowingly to induce or receive a discrimination in price *which is prohibited by this section*." (Emphasis added.)

Liability under § 2(f) thus is limited to situations where the price discrimination is one "which is prohibited by this section." While the phrase "this section" refers to the entire § 2 of the Act, only subsections (a) and (b) dealing with seller liability involve discriminations in price. Under the plain meaning of § 2(f), therefore, a buyer cannot be liable if a prima facie case

5. . . . With respect to the meeting competition defense, the Commission stated that even though Borden as the seller might have had a meeting competition defense, A & P as the buyer did not have such a defense because it knew that the bid offered was, in fact, better than the Bowman bid. With respect to the cost justification defense, the Commission found that Commission counsel had met the initial burden of going forward as required by this Court's decision in Automatic Canteen Co. of America v. FTC, 346 U.S. 61, and that A & P had not then satisfied its burden of showing that the prices were cost justified, or that it did not know that they were not. . . .

6. The Court of Appeals, like the Commission, relied on Kroger Co. v. FTC, 438 F.2d 1372 ([6th Cir.] 1971), for the proposition that a buyer can be liable under § 2(f) of the Act even if the seller has a meeting competition defense. The *Kroger* case involved a buyer who had made deliberate misrepresentations to a seller in order to induce price concessions. While the Court of Appeals in this case did not find that A & P had made any affirmative misrepresentations, it viewed the distinction between a "lying buyer" and a buyer who knowingly accepts the lower of two bids as without legal significance. See n. 33, infra.

7. F. Rowe, Price Discrimination Under the Robinson–Patman Act 423 (1962).

could not be established against a seller or if the seller has an affirmative defense. In either situation, there is no price discrimination "prohibited by this section." The legislative history of § 2(f) fully confirms the conclusion that buyer liability under § 2(f) is dependent on seller liability under § 2(a).

The derivative nature of liability under § 2(f) was recognized by this Court in Automatic Canteen Co. of America v. FTC, 346 U.S. 61. In that case, the Court stated that even if the Commission has established a prima facie case of price discrimination, a buyer does not violate § 2(f) if the lower prices received are either within one of the seller's defenses or not known by him not to be within one of those defenses.... The Court thus explicitly recognized that a buyer cannot be held liable under § 2(f) if the lower prices received are justified by reason of one of the seller's affirmative defenses.

III

The petitioner, relying on this plain meaning of § 2(f) and the teaching of the *Automatic Canteen* case, argues that it cannot be liable under § 2(f) if Borden had a valid meeting competition defense. The respondent, on the other hand, argues that the petitioner may be liable even assuming that Borden had such a defense. The meeting competition defense, the respondent contends, must in these circumstances be judged from the point of view of the buyer. Since A & P knew for a fact that the final Borden bid beat the Bowman bid, it was not entitled to assert the meeting competition defense even though Borden may have honestly believed that it was simply meeting competition. Recognition of a meeting competition defense for the buyer in this situation, the respondent argues, would be contrary to the basic purpose of the Robinson–Patman Act to curtail abuses by large buyers.

A

The short answer to these contentions of the respondent is that Congress did not provide in § 2(f) that a buyer can be liable even if the seller has a valid defense. The clear language of § 2(f) states that a buyer can be liable only if he receives a price discrimination "prohibited by this section." If a seller has a valid meeting competition defense, there is simply no prohibited price discrimination....

B

In the *Automatic Canteen* case, the Court warned against interpretations of the Robinson–Patman Act which "extend beyond the prohibitions of the Act and, in so doing, help give rise to a price uniformity and rigidity in open conflict with the purposes of other antitrust legislation." 346 U.S., at 63. Imposition of § 2(f) liability on the petitioner in this case would lead to just such price uniformity and rigidity.[8]

8. More than once the Court has stated that the Robinson–Patman Act should be construed consistently with broader policies of the antitrust laws. United States v. United

In a competitive market, uncertainty among sellers will cause them to compete for business by offering buyers lower prices. Because of the evils of collusive action, the Court has held that the exchange of price information by competitors violates the Sherman Act. United States v. Container Corp., 393 U.S. 333. Under the view advanced by the respondent, however, a buyer, to avoid liability, must either refuse a seller's bid or at least inform him that his bid has beaten competition. Such a duty of affirmative disclosure would almost inevitably frustrate competitive bidding and, by reducing uncertainty, lead to price matching and anticompetitive cooperation among sellers.[9]

Ironically, the Commission itself, in dismissing the charge under § 5 of the Federal Trade Commission Act in this case, recognized the dangers inherent in a duty of affirmative disclosure:

> The imposition of a duty of affirmative disclosure, applicable to a buyer whenever a seller states that his offer is intended to meet competition, is contrary to normal business practice and, we think, contrary to the public interest.
>
> . . .
>
> We fear a scenario where the seller automatically attaches a meeting competition caveat to every bid. The buyer would then state whether such bid meets, beats, or loses to another bid. The seller would then submit a second, a third, and perhaps a fourth bid until finally he is able to ascertain his competitor's bid.

The effect of the finding that the same conduct of the petitioner violated § 2(f), however, is to impose the same duty of affirmative disclosure which the Commission condemned as anticompetitive, "contrary to the public interest," and "contrary to normal business practice," in dismissing the charge under § 5 of the Federal Trade Commission Act. Neither the Commission nor the Court of Appeals offered any explanation for this apparent anomaly.

As in the *Automatic Canteen* case, we decline to adopt a construction of § 2(f) that is contrary to its plain meaning and would lead to anticompetitive results. Accordingly, we hold that a buyer who has done no more than accept the lower of two prices competitively offered does not violate § 2(f) provided the seller has a meeting competition defense.[10]

States Gypsum Co., 438 U.S. 422; Automatic Canteen Co. v. FTC, supra, 346 U.S., at 74.

9. A duty of affirmative disclosure might also be difficult to enforce. In cases where a seller offers differing quantities or a different quality product, or offers to serve the buyer in a different manner, it might be difficult for the buyer to determine when disclosure is required.

10. In Kroger Co. v. FTC, supra, the Court of Appeals for the Sixth Circuit held that a buyer who induced price concessions by a seller by making deliberate misrepresentations could be liable under § 2(f) even if the seller has a meeting competition defense.

This case does not involve a "lying buyer" situation. The complaint issued by the FTC alleged that "A & P accepted Borden's offer knowing that Borden had granted a substantially lower price than the only other

IV

Because both the Commission and the Court of Appeals proceeded on the assumption that a buyer who accepts the lower of two competitive bids can be liable under § 2(f) even if the seller has a meeting competition defense, there was not a specific finding that Borden did in fact have such a defense. But it quite clearly did.

A

The test for determining when a seller has a valid meeting competition defense is whether a seller can "show the existence of facts which would lead a reasonable and prudent person to believe that the granting of a lower price would in fact meet the equally low price of a competitor." FTC v. A.E. Staley Manufacturing Co., 324 U.S. 746. "A good faith belief, rather than absolute certainty, that a price concession is being offered to meet an equally low price offered by a competitor is sufficient to satisfy the Robinson–Patman's § 2(b) defense." United States v. United States Gypsum Co., 438 U.S. 422.[11] Since good faith, rather than absolute certainty, is the touchstone of the meeting competition defense, a seller can assert the defense even if it has unknowingly made a bid that in fact not only met but beat his competition. Id., at 453–55.

B

Under the circumstances of this case, Borden did act reasonably and in good faith when it made its second bid. The petitioner, despite its long-

competitive bidder without notifying Borden of this fact." The complaint did not allege that Borden's second bid was induced by any misrepresentation. The Court of Appeals recognized that the Kroger case involved a "lying buyer," but stated that there was no meaningful distinction between the situation where "the buyer lies or merely keeps quiet about the nature of the competing bid." 557 F.2d 971, 983.

Despite this background, the respondent argues that A & P did engage in misrepresentations and therefore can be found liable as a "lying buyer" under the rationale of the Kroger case. The misrepresentation relied upon by the respondent is a statement allegedly made by a representative of A & P to Borden after Borden made its second bid which would have resulted in annual savings to A & P of $820,000. The A & P representative allegedly told Borden to "sharpen your pencil a little bit because you are not quite there." But the Commission itself referred to this comment only to note its irrelevance, and neither the Commission nor the Court of Appeals mentioned it in considering the § 2(f) charge against A & P. This is quite

understandable, since the comment was allegedly made *after* Borden made its second bid and therefore cannot be said to have induced the bid as in the *Kroger* case.

Because A & P was not a "lying buyer," we need not decide whether such a buyer could be liable under § 2(f) even if the seller has a meeting competition defense.

11. Recognition of the right of a seller to meet a lower competitive price in good faith may be the primary means of reconciling the Robinson–Patman Act with the more general purposes of the antitrust laws of encouraging competition between sellers. As the Court stated in Standard Oil Co. v. FTC, 340 U.S. 231, 249:

"We need not now reconcile, in its entirety, the economic theory which underlies the Robinson–Patman Act with that of the Sherman and Clayton Acts. It is enough to say that Congress did not seek by the Robinson–Patman Act either to abolish competition or so radically to curtail it that a seller would have no substantial right of self-defense against a price raid by a competitor."

standing relationship with Borden, was dissatisfied with Borden's first bid and solicited offers from other dairies. The subsequent events are aptly described in the opinion of the Commission:

> Thereafter, on August 31, 1965, A & P received an offer from Bowman Dairy that was lower than Borden's August 13 offer. On or about September 1, 1965, Elmer Schmidt, A & P's Chicago unit buyer, telephoned Gordon Tarr, Borden's Chicago chain store sales manager, and stated, "I have a bid in my pocket. You [Borden] people are so far out of line it is not even funny. You are not even in the ball park." Although Tarr asked Schmidt for some details, Schmidt said that he could not tell Tarr anything except that a $50,000 improvement in Borden's bid "would not be a drop in the [bucket]." Contrary to its usual practice, A & P then offered Borden the opportunity to submit another bid. (Footnotes and record citations omitted.)

Thus Borden was informed by the petitioner that it was in danger of losing it's A & P business in the Chicago area unless it came up with a better offer. It was told that its first offer was "not even in the ball park" and that a $50,000 improvement "would not be a drop in the bucket." In light of Borden's established business relationship with the petitioner, Borden could justifiably conclude that A & P's statements were reliable and that it was necessary to make another bid offering substantial concessions to avoid losing its account with the petitioner.

Borden was unable to ascertain the details of the Bowman bid. It requested more information about the bid from the petitioner, but this request was refused. It could not then attempt to verify the existence and terms of the competing offer from Bowman without risking Sherman Act liability. United States v. United States Gypsum Co., supra. Faced with a substantial loss of business and unable to find out the precise details of the competing bid, Borden made another offer stating that it was doing so in order to meet competition. Under these circumstances, the conclusion is virtually inescapable that in making that offer Borden acted in a reasonable and good-faith effort to meet its competition, and therefore was entitled to a meeting competition defense.[12]

12. The facts of this case are thus readily distinguishable from Corn Products v. FTC, 324 U.S. 726, and FTC v. A.E. Staley Manufacturing Co., 324 U.S. 746, in both of which the Court held that a seller had failed to establish a meeting competition defense. In the *Corn Products* case, the only evidence to rebut the prima facie case of price discrimination was testimony by witnesses who had no personal knowledge of the transactions in question. Similarly, in the *Staley Manufacturing Co.* case, unsupported testimony from informants of uncertain character and reliability was insufficient to establish the defense. In the present case, by contrast, the source of the information was a person whose reliability was not questioned and who had personal knowledge of the competing bid. Moreover, Borden attempted to investigate by asking A & P for more information about the competing bid. Finally, Borden was faced with a credible threat of a termination of purchases by A & P if it did not make a second offer. All of these factors serve to show that Borden did have a valid meeting competition defense. See United States v. United States Gypsum Co., supra.

Since Borden had a meeting competition defense and thus could not be liable under § 2(b) the petitioner who did no more than accept that offer cannot be liable under § 2(f).[13]

Accordingly, the judgment is reversed.

■ STEVENS, J., took no part in the consideration or decision of this case.

■ WHITE, J., concurring in part and dissenting in part.

I concur in Parts I, II, and III of the Court's opinion but dissent from Part IV. Because it was thought the issue was irrelevant where the buyer knows that the price offered is lower than necessary to meet competition, neither the Commission nor the Court of Appeals decided whether Borden itself would have had a valid meeting-competition defense. The Court should not decide this question here but should remand to the Commission whose job it is initially to consider such matters.

For the reason stated by the Commission and the Court of Appeals, I am also convinced that the United States made a sufficient, unrebutted showing that Borden would not have had a cost-justification defense to a Robinson–Patman Act charge.[14]

NOTE

Sections 2(d) and 2(e) of the Robinson–Patman Act cover allowances and services made available by sellers, but those two provisions do not address the question of buyer liability. In *Grand Union Co. v. FTC*, 300 F.2d 92 (2d Cir.1962), the Court of Appeals sustained a Commission finding that knowing receipt of an illegal allowance could constitute an unfair method of competition under Section 5 of the Federal Trade Commission Act. This expansive interpretation of Section 5 appears to have been limited by the Court to situations in which an omission in the antitrust laws by Congress appeared to be inadvertent, and the coverage of the

13. Because we hold that the petitioner is not liable under § 2(f), we do not reach the question whether Borden might also have had a cost justification defense under § 2(a).

14. The opinion of Marshall, J., dissenting in part, is omitted. In the course of his opinion, Justice Marshall said:

I would hold that under § 2(f), the Robinson–Patman Act defenses must be available to buyers on the same basic terms as they are to sellers. To be sure, some differences in the nature of the defenses would obtain because of the different bargaining positions of sellers and buyers. With respect to the meeting-competition defense at issue here, a seller can justify a price discrimination by showing that his lower price was offered in "good faith" to meet that of a compet-

itor. . . . In my view, a buyer should be able to claim that defense—independently of the seller—if he acted in good faith to induce the seller to meet a competitor's price, regardless of whether the seller's price happens to beat the competitor's. But a buyer who induces the lower bid by misrepresentation should not escape Robinson–Patman Act liability. See Kroger Co. v. FTC, 438 F.2d 1372 (C.A.6) (Clark, J.), cert. denied, 404 U.S. 871 (1971). This definition of the meeting-competition defense both extricates buyers from an impossible dilemma and respects the congressional intent to prevent buyers from abusing their market power to gain competitive advantage. . . . In my judgment, the numerous ambiguities in the record dictate that this case be remanded to the Commission.

transaction under Section 5 was consistent with the overall purposes of the particular antitrust provision. Compare *FTC v. Brown Shoe Co.*, page 948, supra.

SELECTIVE BIBLIOGRAPHY

Hovenkamp, Federal Antitrust Policy Ch. 14 (2d ed. 1999).

ABA Antitrust Section, The Robinson–Patman Act: Policy and Law (2 vol. 1980 and 1983).

Shniderman, Price Discrimination in Perspective (2d ed. 1987).

Sullivan, Handbook of the Law of Antitrust 676–706 (1977).

United States Department of Justice, Report on the Robinson–Patman Act (1977).

Posner, The Robinson–Patman Act (1976).

Report of the White House Task Force on Antitrust Policy, 2 Antitrust Law & Econ.Rev. 11, 17–18 (Winter 1968–69).

Rowe, Price Discrimination Under the Robinson–Patman Act (1962 & Supp. 1964).

Celnicker & Seaman, Functional Discounts, Trade Discounts, Economic Price Discrimination and the Robinson–Patman Act, 1989 Utah L.Rev. 813 (1989).

Kintner & Bauer, The Robinson–Patman Act: A Look Backward, A View Forward, 31 Antitrust Bull. 571 (1986).

Rill, Availability and Functional Discounts Justifying Discriminatory Pricing, 56 Antitrust L.J. 929 (1985).

Calvani, Government Enforcement of the Robinson–Patman Act, 53 Antitrust L.J. 921 (1985).

Hovenkamp, Market Power and Secondary–Line Differential Pricing, 71 Geo. L.Rev. 1157 (1983).

PRINCIPAL ANTITRUST STATUTES

SHERMAN ACT[2]

An act to protect trade and commerce against unlawful restraints and monopolies.

That this Act may be cited as the "Sherman Act".

Sec. 1. Every contract, combination in the form of trust or otherwise, or conspiracy, in restraint of trade or commerce among the several States, or with foreign nations, is declared to be illegal. Every person who shall make any contract or engage in any combination or conspiracy hereby declared to be illegal shall be deemed guilty of a felony and, on conviction thereof, shall be punished by fine not exceeding $10,000,000 if a corporation, or, if any other person, $350,000, or by imprisonment not exceeding three years, or by both said punishments, in the discretion of the court.[3]

Sec. 2. Every person who shall monopolize, or attempt to monopolize, or combine or conspire with any other person or persons, to monopolize any part of the trade or commerce among the several States, or with foreign nations, shall be deemed guilty of a felony, and, on conviction thereof, shall be punished by fine not exceeding $10,000,000 if a corporation, or, if any other person, $350,000, or by imprisonment not exceeding three years, or by both said punishments, in the discretion of the court.

Sec. 3. (a) Every contract, combination in form of trust or otherwise, or conspiracy, in restraint of trade or commerce in any Territory of the United States or of the District of Columbia, or in restraint of trade or commerce between any such Territory and another, or between any such Territory or Territories and any State or States or the District of Columbia, or with foreign nations, or between the District of Columbia and any State or States or foreign nations, is declared illegal.

(b) Every person who shall make any such contract or engage in any such combination or conspiracy, shall be deemed guilty of a felony, and, on conviction thereof, shall be punished by fine not exceeding $10,000,000 if a

---

1. Only the principal statutes are reprinted in this Appendix.

2. The Sherman Act was the Act of July 2, 1890, c. 647, 26 Stat. 209; 15 U.S.C.A. §§ 1–7.

3. The fine for a violation was increased from $5,000 to $50,000 by Act of July 7, 1955, c. 281, 69 Stat. 282. It was raised again to $1,000,000 for corporations and $100,000 for individuals by Act of December 21, 1974, Pub.L. 93–528, 88 Stat. 1708. The latter act also redesignated violations as felonies instead of misdemeanors, and increased the maximum prison term by two years, for a total of three years. Most recently, the fine was raised to $10,000,000 for corporations and $350,000 for individuals by Act of November 16, 1990, Pub.L. 101–588, 104 Stat. 2880.

corporation, or, if any other person, $350,000, or by imprisonment not exceeding three years, or by both said punishments, in the discretion of the court.

Sec. 4. The several circuit courts of the United States are invested with jurisdiction to prevent and restrain violations of this Act; and it shall be the duty of the several United States attorneys, in their respective districts, under the direction of the Attorney–General, to institute proceedings in equity to prevent and restrain such violations. Such proceedings may be by way of petition setting forth the case and praying that such violation shall be enjoined or otherwise prohibited. When the parties complained of shall have been duly notified of such petition the court shall proceed, as soon as may be, to the hearing and determination of the case; and pending such petition and before final decree, the court may at any time make such temporary restraining order or prohibition as shall be deemed just in the premises. . . .

Sec. 6a. This Act shall not apply to conduct involving trade or commerce (other than import trade or import commerce) with foreign nations unless—

(1) such conduct has a direct, substantial, and reasonably foreseeable effect—

(A) on trade or commerce which is not trade or commerce with foreign nations, or on import trade or import commerce with foreign nations; or

(B) on export trade or export commerce with foreign nations, of a person engaged in such trade or commerce in the United States; and

(2) such effect gives rise to a claim under the provisions of this Act, other than this section.

If this Act applies to such conduct only because of the operation of paragraph (1)(B), then this Act shall apply to such conduct only for injury to export business in the United States.

Sec. 7. That the word "person," or "persons," wherever used in this Act shall be deemed to include corporations and associations existing under; or authorized by the laws of either the United States, the laws of any of the Territories, the laws of any State, or the laws of any foreign country.

CLAYTON ACT[4]

AN ACT To supplement existing laws against unlawful restraints and monopolies, and for other purposes.

Sec. 1. That (a) "antitrust laws," as used herein, includes the Act entitled "An Act to protect trade and commerce against unlawful restraints and monopolies," approved July second, eighteen hundred and ninety;

4. The Clayton Act was the Act of October 15, 1914, c. 323, 38 Stat. 730; 15 U.S.C.A. §§ 12–27.

sections seventy-three to seventy-six inclusive, of an entitled "An Act to reduce taxation, to provide revenue for the Government, and for other purposes," of August twenty-seventh, eighteen hundred and ninety-four; an Act entitled "An Act to amend sections seventy-three and seventy-six of the Act of August twenty-seventh, eighteen hundred and ninety-four, titled 'An Act to reduce taxation, to provide revenue for the Government, for other purposes,'" approved February twelfth, nineteen hundred thirteen; and also this Act.

"Commerce," as used herein, means trade or commerce among the several States and with foreign nations, or between the District of Columbia or any Territory of the United States and any State, Territory, or foreign nation, or between any insular possessions or other places under jurisdiction of the United States, or between any such possession or place and any State or Territory of the United States or the District of Columbia or any foreign nation, or within the District of Columbia or any Territory or any insular possession or other place under the jurisdiction of United States: *Provided,* That nothing in this Act contained shall apply to the Philippine Islands.

The word "person" or "persons" wherever used in this Act shall be deemed to include corporations and associations existing under or authorized by the laws of either the United States, the laws of any of the Territories, the laws of any State, or the laws of any foreign country.

(b) This Act may be cited as the "Clayton Act".

Sec. 2. (a) That it shall be unlawful for any person engaged in commerce, in the course of such commerce, either directly or indirectly, to discriminate in price between different purchasers of commodities of like grade and quality, where either or any of the purchases involved in such discrimination are in commerce, where such commodities are sold for use, consumption, or resale within the United States or any Territory thereof or the District of Columbia or any insular possession or other place under the jurisdiction of the United States, and where the effect of such discrimination be substantially to lessen competition or tend to create a monopoly in any line of commerce, or to injure, destroy, or prevent competition any person who either grants or knowingly receives the benefit of such discrimination, or with customers of either of them: *Provided,* That nothing herein contained shall prevent differentials which make only due allowance for differences in the cost of manufacture, sale, or delivery resulting from the differing methods or quantities in which such commodities are to such purchasers sold or delivered: *Provided, however,* That the Federal Trade Commission may, after due investigation and hearing to all interested parties, fix and establish quantity limits, and revise the same as it finds necessary, as to particular commodities or classes of commodities, where it finds that available purchasers in greater quantities are so few as to render differentials on account thereof unjustly discriminatory or promotive of monopoly in any line of commerce; and the foregoing shall then not be construed to permit differentials based on differences in quantities greater than those so fixed and established: *And provided further,* That nothing herein contained shall prevent persons engaged in selling goods, wares, or merchandise in commerce from selecting their own customers in bona fide transactions and not in restraint of trade: *And, provided further*, That nothing herein contained shall prevent price changes from time to time where in response to changing conditions affecting the market for or the marketability of the goods concerned, such as but not limited to actual or imminent deterioration of perishable goods, obsolescence of seasonal goods, distress sales under court process, or sales in good faith in discontinuance of business in the goods concerned.

(b) Upon proof being made, at any hearing on a complaint under this section, that there has been discrimination in price or services or facilities furnished, the burden of rebutting the prima fade case thus made by showing justification shall be upon the person charged with a violation of this section, and unless justification shall be affirmatively shown, the Commission is authorized to issue an order terminating the discrimination; *Provided, however,* That nothing herein contained shall prevent a seller rebutting the prima facie case thus made by showing that his lower price or the furnishing of services or facilities to any purchaser or purchasers was made in good faith to meet an equally low price of a competitor, or the services or facilities furnished by a competitor.

(c) That it shall be unlawful for any person engaged in comments, in the course of such commerce, to pay or grant, or to receive or accept anything of value as a commission, brokerage, or other compensation, or any allowance or discount in lieu thereof, except for services rendered in connection with the sale or purchase of goods, wares, or merchandise, either to the other party to such transaction or to an agent, representative, or other intermediary therein where such intermediary is acting in fact for or in behalf, or is subject to the direct or indirect control, of any party to such transaction other than the person by whom such compensation is so granted or paid.

(d) That it shall be unlawful for any person engaged in commerce to pay or contract for the payment of anything of value to or for the benefit of a customer of such person in the course of such commerce as compensation or in consideration for any services or facilities furnished by or through such customer in connection with the processing, handling, sale, or offering for sale of any products or commodities manufactured, sold, or offered for sale by such person, unless such payment or consideration is available on proportionally equal terms to all other customers competing in the distribution of such products or commodities.

(e) That it shall be unlawful for any person to discriminate in favor of one purchaser against another purchaser or purchasers of a commodity bought for resale, with or without processing, by contracting to furnish or furnishing, or by contributing to the furnishing of, any services or facilities connected with the processing, handling, sale, or offering for sale of such commodity so purchased upon terms not accorded to all purchasers on proportionally equal terms.

(f) That it shall be unlawful for any person engaged in commerce, in the course of such commerce, knowingly to induce or receive a discrimination in price which is prohibited by this section.

Sec. 3. That it shall be unlawful for any person engaged in commerce, in the course of such commerce, to lease or make a sale or contract for sale of goods, wares, merchandise, machinery, supplies or other commodities, whether patented or unpatented, for use, consumption or resale within the United States or any Territory thereof or the District of Columbia or any insular possession or other place under the jurisdiction of the United States, or fix a price charged therefor, or discount from, or rebate upon, such price, on the condition, agreement or understanding that the lessee or purchaser thereof shall not use or deal in the goods, wares, merchandise, machinery, supplies or other commodities of a competitor or competitors of the lessor or seller, where the effect of such lease, sale, or contract for sale or such condition, agreement or understanding may be to substantially lessen competition or tend to create a monopoly in any line of commerce.

Sec. 4. That any person who shall be injured in his business or property by reason of anything forbidden in the antitrust laws may sue therefor in any district court of the United States in the district in which the defendant resides or is found or has an agent, without respect to the amount in controversy, and shall recover threefold the damages by him sustained, and the cost of suit, including a reasonable attorney's fee. The court may award under this section, pursuant to a motion by such person promptly made, simple interest on actual damages for the period beginning on the date of service of such person's pleading setting forth a claim under the antitrust laws and ending on the date of judgment, or for any shorter period therein, if the court finds that the award of such interest for such period is just in the circumstances. In determining whether an award of interest under this section for any period is just in the circumstances, the court shall consider only—

(1) whether such person or the opposing party, or either party's representative, made motions or asserted claims or defenses so lacking in merit as to show that such party or representative acted intentionally for delay, or otherwise acted in bad faith;

(2) whether, in the course of the action involved, such person or the opposing party, or either party's representative, violated any applicable rule, statute, or court order providing for sanctions for dilatory behavior or otherwise providing for expeditious proceedings; and

(3) whether such person or the opposing party, or either party's representative, engaged in conduct primarily for the purpose of delaying the litigation or increasing the cost thereof. . . .

Sec. 4A. Whenever the United States is hereafter injured in its business or property by reason of anything forbidden in the antitrust laws it may sue therefor in the United States district court for the district in which the defendant resides or is found or has an agent, without respect to the amount in controversy, and shall recover threefold the damages by it sustained and the cost of the suit. The court may award under this section, pursuant to a motion by the United States promptly made, simple interest on threefold the damages for the period beginning on the date of service of the pleading of the United States setting forth a claim under the antitrust laws and ending on the date of judgment, or for any shorter period therein, if the court finds that the award of such interest for such period is just in the circumstances....[5]

Sec. 4B. Any action to enforce any cause of action under section 4, 4A, or 4C shall be forever barred unless commenced within four years after the cause of action accrued. No cause of action barred under existing law on the effective date of this Act shall be revived by this Act.

Sec. 4C. (a)(1) Any attorney general of a State may bring a civil action in the name of such State, as parens patriae on behalf of natural persons residing in such State, in any district court of the United States having jurisdiction of the defendant, to secure monetary relief as provided in this section for injury sustained by such natural persons to their property by reason of any violation of the Sherman Act. The court shall exclude from the amount of monetary relief awarded in such action any amount of monetary relief (A) which duplicates amounts which have been awarded for the same injury, or (B) which is properly allocable to (i) natural persons who have excluded their claims pursuant to subsection (b)(2) of this section, and (ii) any business entity.

(2) The court shall award the State as monetary relief threefold the total damage sustained as described in paragraph (1) of this subsection, and the cost of suit, including a reasonable attorney's fee. The court may award under this paragraph, pursuant to a motion by such State promptly made, simple interest on the total damage for the period beginning on the date of service of such State's pleading setting forth a claim under the antitrust laws and ending on the date of judgment, or for any shorter period therein, if the court finds that the award of such interest for such period is just in the circumstances....

(b)(1) In any action brought under subsection (a)(1) of this section, the State attorney general shall, at such times, in such manner, and with such content as the court may direct, cause notice thereof to be given by publication. If the court finds that notice given solely by publication would deny due process of law to any person or persons, the court may direct further notice to such person or persons according to the circumstances of the case.

(2) Any person on whose behalf an action is brought under subsection (a)(1) may elect to exclude from adjudication the portion of the State claim for monetary relief attributable to him by filing notice of such election with

5. Antitrust Reciprocity Amendment, Pub.L. 97–393, 96 Stat. 1964 (1982), the Clayton Act, 15 U.S.C.A. § 15(b) allows foreign government to recover in treble damage actions under certain circumstances. As amended November 16, 1990, Pub.L. 101–588, 104 Stat. 2880.

the court within such time as specified in the notice given pursuant to paragraph (1) of this subsection.

(3) The final judgment in an action under subsection (a)(1) shall be res judicata as to any claim under section 4 of this Act by any person on behalf of whom such action was brought and who fails to give such notice within the period specified in the notice given pursuant to paragraph (1) of this subsection.

(c) An action under subsection (a)(1) shall not be dismissed or compromised without the approval of the court, and notice of any proposed dismissal or compromise shall be given in such manner as the court directs.

(d) In any action under subsection (a)—

(1) the amount of the plaintiffs' attorney's fee, if any, shall be determined by the court; and

(2) the court may, in its discretion, award a reasonable attorney's fee to a prevailing defendant upon a finding that the State attorney general has acted in bad faith, vexatiously, wantonly, or for oppressive reasons.

Sec.4D. In any action under section 4C(a)(1), in which there has been a determination that a defendant agreed to fix prices in violation of the Sherman Act, damages may be proved and assessed in the aggregate by statistical or sampling methods, by the computation of illegal overcharges, or by such other reasonable system of estimating aggregate damages as the court in its discretion may permit without the necessity of separately proving the individual claim of, or amount of damage to, persons on whose behalf the suit was brought.

Sec. 4E. Monetary relief recovered in an action under section 4C(a)(1) shall—

(1) be distributed in such manner as the district court in its discretion may authorize; or

(2) be deemed a civil penalty by the court and deposited with the State as general revenues;

subject in either case to the requirement that any distribution procedure adopted afford each person a reasonable opportunity to secure his appropriate portion of the net monetary relief.

Sec. 4F. (a) Whenever the Attorney General of the United States has brought an action under the antitrust laws, and he has reason to believe that any State attorney general would be entitled to bring an action under this Act based substantially on the same alleged violation of the antitrust laws, he shall promptly give written notification thereof to such State attorney general.

(b) To assist a State attorney general in evaluating the notice or in bringing any action under this Act, the Attorney General of the United States shall, upon request by such State attorney general, make available to him, to the extent permitted by law, any investigative files or other materials which are or may be relevant or material to the actual or potential cause of action under this Act.

Sec. 4G. For the purposes of sections 4C, 4D, 4E, and 4F of this Act:

(1) The term "State attorney general" means the chief legal officer of a State, or any other person authorized by State law to bring actions under, section 4C of this Act, and includes the Corporation Counsel of the District of Columbia, except that such term does not include any person employed or retained on—

(A) a contingency fee based on a percentage of the monetary relief awarded under this section; or

(B) any other contingency fee basis, unless the amount of the award of a reasonable attorney's fee to a prevailing plaintiff is determined by the court under section 4C(d)(i).

(2) The term "State" means a State, the District of Columbia, the Commonwealth of Puerto Rico, and any other territory or possession of the United States.

(3) The term "natural persons" does not include proprietorships or partnerships.

Sec. 4H. Sections 4C, 4D, 4E, 4F, and 4G shall apply in any State, unless such State provides by law for its nonapplicability in such State.[6]

Sec. 5. (a) A final judgment or decree heretofore or hereafter rendered in any civil or criminal proceeding brought by or on behalf of the United States under the antitrust laws to the effect that a defendant has violated said laws shall be prima facie evidence against such defendant in any action or proceeding brought by any other party against such defendant under said laws as to all matters respecting which said judgment or decree would be an estoppel as between the parties thereto: *Provided,* That this section shall not apply to consent judgments or decrees entered before any testimony has been taken. Nothing contained in this section shall be construed to impose any limitation on the application of collateral estoppel, except that, in any action or proceeding brought under the antitrust laws, collateral estoppel effect shall not be given to any finding made by the Federal Trade Commission under the antitrust laws or under section 5 of the Federal Trade Commission Act which could give rise to a claim for relief under the antitrust laws.

(b) Any proposal for a consent judgment submitted by the United States for entry in any civil proceeding brought by or on behalf of the United States under the antitrust laws shall be filed with the district court before which such proceeding is pending and published by the United States in the Federal Register at least 60 days prior to the effective date of such judgment. Any written comments relating to such proposal and any

---

6. Sections 4A and 4B were added by Act of July 7, 1955, c. 283, 69 Stat. 282–83. Sections 4C through 4H were added by Act of September 30, 1976, Pub.L. 94–435, 90 Stat. 1394. Section 4, 4A, and 4C were amended to allow an award of interest to a plaintiff when equitable, by Act of September 12, 1980, Pub.L. 96–349, 94 Stat. 1156.

responses by the United States thereto, shall also be filed with such district court and published by the United States in the Federal Register within such sixty-day period. Copies of such proposal and any other materials and documents which the United States considered determinative in formulating such proposal, shall also be made available to the public at the district court and in such other districts as the court may subsequently direct. Simultaneously with the filing of such proposal, unless otherwise instructed by the court, the United States shall file with the district court, publish in the Federal Register, and thereafter furnish to any person upon request, a competitive impact statement which shall recite—

(1) the nature and purpose of the proceeding,

(2) a description of the practices or events giving rise to the alleged violation of the antitrust laws;

(3) an explanation of the proposal for a consent judgment, including an explanation of any unusual circumstances giving rise to such proposal or any provision contained therein, relief to be obtained thereby, and the anticipated effects on competition of such relief;

(4) the remedies available to potential private plaintiffs damaged by the alleged violation in the event that such proposal for the consent judgment is entered in such proceeding,

(5) a description of the procedures available for modification of such proposal; and

(6) a description and evaluation of alternatives to such proposal actually considered by the United States.

(c) The United States shall also cause to be published. . . .

(d) During the 60–day period as specified in subsection (b) of this section, and such additional time as the United States may request and the court may grant, the United States shall receive and consider any written comments relating to the proposal for the consent judgment submitted under subsection (b). The Attorney General or his designee shall establish procedures to carry out the provisions of this subsection, but such 60–day time period shall not be shortened except by order of the district court upon a showing that (1) extraordinary circumstances require such shortening and (2) such shortening is not adverse to the public interest. At the close of the period during which such comments may be received, the United States shall file with the district court and cause to be published in the Federal Register a response to such comments.

(e) Before entering any consent judgment proposed by the United States under this section, the court shall determine that the entry of such judgment is in the public interest. For the purpose of such determination, the court may consider—

(1) the competitive impact of such judgment, including termination of alleged violations, provisions for enforcement and modification, duration or relief sought, anticipated effects of alternative remedies actually consid-

ered, and any other considerations bearing upon the adequacy of such judgment;

(2) the impact of entry of such judgment upon the public generally and individuals alleging specific injury from the violations set forth in the complaint including consideration of the public benefit, if any, to be derived from a determination of the issues at trial.

(f) In making its determination under subsection (e), the court may—

(1) take testimony of Government officials or experts or such other expert witnesses, upon motion of any party or participant or upon its own motion, as the court may deem appropriate;

(2) appoint a special master and such outside consultants or expert witnesses as the court may deem appropriate; and request and obtain the views, evaluations, or advice of any individual, group or agency of government with respect to any aspects of the proposed judgment or the effect of, such judgment, in such manner as the court deems appropriate;

(3) authorize full or limited participation in proceedings before the court by interested persons or agencies, including appearance amicus curiae, intervention as a party pursuant to the Federal Rules of Civil Procedure, examination of witnesses or documentary materials, or participation in any other manner and extent which serves the public interest the court may deem appropriate;

(4) review any comments including any objections filed with the United States under subsection (d) concerning the proposed judgment and the responses of the United States to such comments and objections; and

(5) take such other action in the public interest as the court may deem appropriate.

(g) Not later than 10 days following the date for the filing of any proposal for a consent judgment under subsection (b), each defendant shall file with the district court a description of any and all written or oral communications by or on behalf of such defendant, including any and all written or oral communications on behalf of such defendant, or other person, with any officer or employee of the United States concerning or relevant to such proposal, except that any such communications made by counsel of record alone with the Attorney General or the employees of the Department of Justice alone shall be excluded from the requirements of this subsection. Prior to the entry of any consent judgment pursuant to the antitrust laws, each defendant shall certify to the district court that then requirements of this subsection have been complied with and that such filing is a true and complete description of such communications known to the defendant or which the defendant reasonably should have known.

(h) Proceedings before the district court under subsections (e) and (f) of this section, and the competitive impact statement filed under subsections (b) of this section, shall not be admissible against any defendant in any action or proceeding brought by any other party against such defendant under the antitrust laws or by the United States under section 4A of this Act nor constitute a basis for the introduction of the consent judgment as prima fade evidence against such defendant in any such action or proceeding.

(i) Whenever any civil or criminal proceeding is instituted by the United States to prevent, restrain, or punish violations of any of the antitrust laws, but not including an action under section 4A, the running of the statute of limitations in respect of every private or State right of action arising under said laws and based in whole or in part on any matter complained of in said proceeding shall be suspended during the pendency thereof and for one year thereafter: *Provided, however,* That whenever the running of the statute of limitations in respect of a cause of action arising under section 4 or 4C is suspended hereunder, any action to enforce such cause of action shall be forever barred unless commenced either within the period of suspension or within four years after the cause of action accrued.[7]

Sec. 6. That the labor of a human being is not a commodity or article of commerce. Nothing contained in the antitrust laws shall be construed to forbid the existence and operation of labor, agricultural, or horticultural organizations, instituted for the purposes of mutual help, and not having capital stock or conducted for profit, or to forbid or restrain individual members of such organizations from lawfully carrying out the legitimate objects thereof; nor shall such organizations, or the members thereof, be held or construed to be illegal combinations or conspiracies in restraint of trade, under the antitrust laws.

Sec. 7. That no person engaged in commerce or in any activity affecting commerce shall acquire, directly or indirectly the whole or any part of the stock or other share capital and no person subject to the jurisdiction of the Federal Trade Commission shall acquire the whole or any part of the assets of another person engaged also in commerce or in any activity affecting commerce, where in any line of commerce or in any activity affecting commerce in any section of the country, the effect of such acquisition may be substantially to lessen competition, or to tend to create a monopoly.

No person shall acquire, directly or indirectly, the whole or any part of the stock or other share capital and no person subject to the jurisdiction of the Federal Trade Commission shall acquire the whole or any part of the assets of one or more persons engaged in commerce or in any activity affecting commerce, where in any line of commerce or in any activity affecting commerce in any section of the country, the effect of such acquisition, of such stocks or assets, or of the use of such stock by the

7. The Clayton Act was amended by Act of July 7, 1955, c. 283, 69 Stat. 283, to provide for damage suits brought by the United States under Section 4A and to establish a statute of limitations. Subsections (b) through (h) were added by Antitrust Procedures and Penalties Act, Act of December 21, 1974, Pub.L. 93–528, 88 Stat. 1706 and former subsection () was redesignated subsection (i). Subsection (a) was amended by Act of September 12, 1980, Pub.L. 96–349, 94 Stat. 11157, to restrict the use of collateral estoppel as to findings made by the etc. Also amended was subsection (i) to expand the tolling of the statute of limitations to include state action.

voting or granting of proxies or otherwise, may be substantially to lessen competition, or to tend to create a monopoly.

This section shall not apply to persons purchasing such stock solely for investment and not using the same by voting or otherwise to bring about, or in attempting to bring about, the substantial lessening of competition. Nor shall anything contained in this section prevent a corporation engaged in commerce or in any activity affecting commerce from causing the formation of subsidiary corporations for the actual carrying on of their immediate lawful business, or the natural and legitimate branches or extensions thereof, or from owning and holding all or a part of the stock of such subsidiary corporations, when the effect of such formation is not to substantially lessen competition....

Nothing contained in this section shall be held to affect or impair any right heretofore legally acquired: *Provided,* That nothing in this section shall be held or construed to authorize or make lawful anything heretofore prohibited or made illegal by the antitrust laws, nor to exempt any person from the penal provisions thereof or the civil remedies therein provided.

Nothing contained in this section shall apply to transactions duly consummated pursuant to authority given by the Secretary of Transportation, Federal Communications Commission, Federal Power Commission, interstate Commerce Commission, the Securities and Exchange Commission in the exercise of its jurisdiction under section 79j of this Act, the United States Maritime Commission, or the Secretary of Agriculture under any statutory provision vesting such power in such Commission or Secretary.[8]

Sec. 7A.(a) Except as exempted pursuant to subsection (c), no person shall acquire, directly or indirectly, any voting securities or assets of any other person, unless both persons (or in the case of a tender offer, the acquiring person) file notification pursuant to rules under subsection (d)(1) and the waiting period described in subsection (b)(1) has expired, if-

(1) the acquiring person, or the person whose voting securities or assets are being acquired, is engaged in commerce or in any activity affecting commerce; and

(2) as a result of such acquisition, the acquiring person would hold an aggregate total amount of the voting securities and assets of the acquired person—

(A) in excess of $200,000,000 (as adjusted and published for each fiscal year beginning after September 30, 2004, in the same manner as provided in section *8(a)(5)* to reflect the percentage change in the gross national product for such fiscal year compared to the gross national product for the year ending September 30, 2003); or

---

8. Section 7 was amended by Act of September 12, 1980, Pub.L. 96–349, 94 Stat. 1157, to cover all persons, instead of just corporations, and to reach activities affecting commerce as opposed to just in commerce.

(B)(i) in excess of $50,000,000 (as so adjusted and published) but not in excess of $200,000,000 (as so adjusted and published); and (ii)

(I) any voting securities or assets of a person engaged in manufacturing which has annual net sales or total assets of $10,000,000 (as so adjusted and published) or more are being acquired by any person which has total assets or annual net sales of $100,000,000 (as so adjusted and published) or more;

(II) any voting securities or assets of a person not engaged in manufacturing which has total assets of $10,000,000 (as so adjusted and published) or more are being acquired by any person which has total assets or annual net sales of $100,000,000 (as so adjusted and published) or more; or

(III) any voting securities or assets of a person with annual net sales or total asset of $100,000,000 (as so adjusted and published) or more are being acquired by any person with total assets or annual net sales of $10,000,000 (as so adjusted and published) or more.

In the case of a tender offer, the person whose voting securities are sought to be acquired by a person required to file notification under this subsection shall file notification pursuant to rules under subsection (d).

(b)(1) The waiting period required under subsection (a) shall—

(A) begin on the date of the receipt by the Federal Trade Commission and the Assistant Attorney General in charge of the Antitrust Division of the Department of Justice (hereinafter referred to in this section as the "Assistant Attorney General") of—

(i) the completed notification required under subsection (a), or

(ii) if such notification is not completed, the notification to the extent completed and a statement of the reasons for such noncompliance, from both persons, or, in the case of a tender offer, the acquiring person; and

(B) end on the thirtieth day after the date of such receipt (or in the case of a cash tender offer, the fifteenth day), or on such later date as may be set under subsection (e)(2) or (g)(2).

(2) The Federal Trade Commission and the Assistant Attorney General may, in individual eases, terminate the waiting period specified in paragraph (1) and allow any person to proceed with any acquisition subject to this section, and promptly shall cause to be published in the Federal Register a notice that neither intends to take any action within such period with respect to such acquisition. . . .

(c) The following classes of transactions are exempt from the requirements of this section—. . . .

(9) acquisitions, solely for the purpose of investment, or voting securities, if, as a result of such acquisition, the securities acquired or held do not exceed 10 per centum of the outstanding voting securities of the issuer; . . .

(d) The Federal Trade Commission, with the concurrence of the Assistant Attorney General and by rule in accordance with section 553 of title 5, United States Code, consistent with the purposes of this section—

(1) shall require that the notification required under subsection (a) be in such form and contain such documentary material and information relevant to a proposed acquisition as is necessary and appropriate to enable the Federal Trade Commission and the Assistant Attorney General to determine whether such acquisition may, if consummated, violate the antitrust laws; and

(2) may—

(A) define the terms used in this section;

(B) exempt, from the requirements of this section, classes of persons, acquisitions, transfers, or transactions which are not likely to violate the antitrust laws; and

(C) prescribe such other rules as may be necessary and appropriate to carry out the purposes of this section.

(e)(1)(A) Federal Trade Commission or the Assistant Attorney General may, prior to the expiration of the 30–day waiting period (or in the case of a cash tender offer, the 15–day waiting period) specified in subsection (b)(1) of this section, require the submission of additional information or documentary material relevant to the proposed acquisition, from a person required to file notification with respect to such acquisition under subsection (a) of this section prior to the expiration of the waiting period specified in subsection (b)(1) of this section, or from any officer, director, partner, agent, or employee of such person.

(B)(i) The Assistant Attorney General and the Federal Trade Commission shall each designate a senior official who does not have direct responsibility for the review of any enforcement recommendation under this section concerning the transaction at issue, to hear any petition filed by such person to determine—

(I) whether the request for additional information or documentary material is unreasonably cumulative, unduly burdensome, or duplicative; or

(II) whether the request for additional information or documentary material has been substantially complied with by the petitioning person.

(ii) Internal review procedures for petitions filed pursuant to clause (i) shall include reasonable deadlines for expedited review of such petitions, after reasonable negotiations with investigative staff; in order to avoid undue delay of the merger review process.

(iii) Not later than 90 days after the date of the enactment of this Act, the Assistant Attorney General and the Federal Trade Commission shall conduct an internal review and implement reforms of the merger review process in order to eliminate unnecessary burden, remove costly duplication, and eliminate undue delay, in order to achieve a more effective and more efficient merger review process.

(iv) Not later than 120 days after the date of enactment of this Act, the Assistant Attorney General and the Federal Trade Commission shall issue or amend their respective industry guidance, regulations, operating manuals and relevant policy documents, to the extent appropriate, to implement each reform in this subparagraph.

(v) Not later than 180 days after the date the of enactment of this Act, the Assistant Attorney General and the Federal Trade Commission shall each report to Congress—

(I) which reforms each agency has adopted under this subparagraph;

(II) which steps each has taken to implement such internal reforms; and

(III) the effects of such reforms.

(2) Federal Trade Commission or the Assistant Attorney General, in its or his discretion, may extend the 30-day waiting period (or in the case of a cash tender offer, the 15-day waiting period) specified in subsection (b)(1) of this section for an additional period of not more than 30 days (or in the case of a cash tender offer, 10 days) after the date on which the Federal Trade Commission or the Assistant Attorney General, as the case may be, receives from any person to whom a request is made under paragraph (1), or in the case of tender offers, the acquiring person, (A) all the information and documentary material required to be submitted pursuant to such a request, or (B) if such request is not fully complied with, the information and documentary material submitted and a statement of the reasons for such noncompliance. Such additional period may be further extended only by the United States district court, upon an application by the Federal Trade Commission or the Assistant Attorney General pursuant to subsection (g)(2)....

(g)(1) Any person, or any officer, director, or partner thereof, who fails to comply with any provision of this section shall be liable to the United States for a civil penalty of not more than $10,000 for each day during which such person is in violation of this section. Such penalty may be ? recovered in a civil action brought by the United States.

(2) If any person, or any officer, director, partner, agent, or employee thereof, fails substantially to comply with the notification requirement under subsection (a) or any request for the submission of additional information or documentary material under subsection (e)(1) of this section within the waiting period specified in subsection (b)(1) and as may be extended under subsection (e)(2), the United States district court—

(A) may order compliance;

(B) shall extend the waiting period specified in subsection (b)(1) and as may have been extended under subsection (e)(2) until there has been substantial compliance, except that, in the case of a tender offer, the court may not extend such waiting period on the basis of a failures by the person whose stock is sought to be acquired, to comply substantially with such notification requirement or any such request; and

(C) may grant such other equitable relief as the court in its discretion determines necessary or appropriate, upon application of the Federal Trade

Commission or the Assistant Attorney General.[9]

Sec. 8

No person at the same time shall be a director in any two or more corporations, any one of which has capital, surplus, and undivided profits aggregating more than $1,000,000, engaged in whole or in part in commerce, other than banks, banking associations, trust companies, and common carriers subject to Subtitle IV of Title 49, to regulate commerce, if such corporations are or shall have been theretofore, by virtue of their business and location of operation, competitors, so that the elimination of competition by agreement between them would constitute a violation of any of the provisions of any of the anti-trust laws. The eligibility of a director under the foregoing provision shall be determined by the aggregate amount of the capital, surplus, and undivided profits, exclusive of dividends declared but not paid to stockholders, at the end of the fiscal year of said corporation next preceding the election of directors, and when a director has been elected in accordance with the provisions of this Act it shall be lawful for him to continue as such for one year thereafter.

When any person elected or chosen as a director or officer or selected as an employee of any bank or other corporation subject to the provisions of this Act is eligible at the time of his election or selection to act for such bank or other corporation in such capacity his eligibility to act in such capacity shall not be affected and he shall not become or be deemed amenable to any of the provisions hereof by reason of any change in the affairs of such bank or other corporation from whatsoever cause, whether specifically excepted by any of the provisions hereof or not, until the expiration of one year from the date of his election or employment.

Sec. 11.

(b) Whenever the Commission, Board, or Secretary vested with jurisdiction thereof shall have reason to believe that any person is violating or has violated any of the provisions of sections 2, 3, 7, and 8 of this Act, it shall issue and serve upon such person and the Attorney General a complaint stating its charges in that respect, and containing a notice of a hearing upon a day and at a place therein fixed at least thirty days after the service of said complaint. The person so complained of shall have the right to appear at the place and time so fixed and show cause why an order should not be entered by the Commission, Board, or Secretary requiring such person to cease and desist from the violation of the law so charged in said complaint. The Attorney General shall have the right to intervene and appear in said proceeding and any person may make application, and upon good cause shown may be allowed by the Commission, Board, or Secretary to intervene and appear in said proceeding by counsel or in person. The testimony in any such proceeding shall be reduced to writing and filed in the office of the Commission, Board, or Secretary. If upon such hearing the Commission, Board, or Secretary, as the case may be, shall be of the

---

9. Section 7A was added by Act of September 30, 1976, Pub.L. 94–435, 90 Stat. 1390 and amended by Act of December 21, 2000, Pub.L. 106–553, 114 Stat. 2762.

opinion that any of the provisions of said sections have been or are being violated, it shall make a report in writing, in which it shall state its findings as to the facts, and shall issue and cause to be served on such person an order requiring such person to cease and desist from such. violations, and divest itself of the stock, or other share capital, or assets, held or rid itself of the directors chosen contrary to the provisions of sections 7 and of this Act, if any there be, in the manner and within the time fixed by said order. Until the expiration of the time allowed for filing a petition for review, if no such petition has been duly filed within such time, or, if a petition for review has been filed within such time then until the record in the proceeding has been filed in a court of appeals of the United States, as hereinafter provided, the Commission, Board, or Secretary may at any time, upon such notice and in such manner as it shall deem proper, modify or set aside, in whole or in part, any report or any order made or issued by it under this section. After the expiration of the time allowed for filing a petition for review, if no such petition has been duly filed within such time, the Commission, Board, or Secretary may at any time, after notice and opportunity for hearing, reopen and alter, modify, or set aside, in whole or in part, any report or order made or issued by it under this section, whenever in the opinion of the Commission, Board, or Secretary conditions of fact or of law have so changed as to require such action or if the public interest shall so require: *Provided, however,* That the said person may, within sixty days after service upon him or it of said. report or order entered after such a reopening, obtain a review thereof in the appropriate court of appeals of the United States, in the manner provided in subsection (c) of this section.

(c) Any person required by such order of the Commission, Board, or Secretary to cease and desist from any such violation may obtain a review of such order in the court of appeals of the United States for any circuit within which such violation occurred or within which such person resides or carries on business, by filing in the court, within sixty days after the date of the service of such order, a written petition praying that the order of the Commission, Board, or Secretary be set aside. A copy of such, petition shall be forthwith transmitted by the clerk of the court to the Commission, Board, or Secretary, and thereupon the Commission, Board, or Secretary shall file in the court the record in the proceeding, as provided in section 2112 of title 28, United States Code. Upon such filing of the petition the court shall have jurisdiction of the proceeding and of the question determined therein concurrently with the Commission, Board, or Secretary until the filing of the record, and shall have power to make and enter a decree affirming, modifying, or setting aside the order of the Commission, Board, or Secretary, and enforcing the same to the extent that such order is affirmed, and to issue such writs as are ancillary to its jurisdiction or are necessary in its judgment to prevent injury to the public or to competitors pendent elite. The findings of the Commission, Board, or Secretary as to the facts, if supported by substantial evidence, shall be conclusive. To the extent that the order of the Commission, Board, or Secretary is affirmed, the court shall issue its own order commanding obedience to the terms of such order of the Commission, Board, or Secretary. If either party shall apply to the court for leave to adduce additional evidence, and shall show to the satisfaction of the court that such additional evidence is material and that there were reasonable grounds for the failure to adduce such evidence in the proceeding before the Commission, Board, or Secretary, the court may order such additional evidence to be taken before the Commission, Board, or Secretary, and to be adduced upon the hearing in such manner and upon such terms and conditions as to the court may seem proper. The Commission, Board, or Secretary may modify its findings as to the facts, or make new findings, by reason of the additional evidence so taken, and shall file such modified or new findings, which, if supported by substantial evidence, shall be conclusive, and its recommendation, if any, for the modification or setting aside of its original order, with the return of such additional evidence. The judgment and decree of the court shall be final, except that the same shall be subject to review by the Supreme Court upon certiorari, as provided in section 1254 of title 28 of the United States Code.

(d) Upon the filing of the record with it the jurisdiction of the court of appeals to affirm, enforce, modify, or set aside orders of the Commission, Board, or Secretary shall be exclusive.

(e) No order of the Commission, Board, or Secretary or judgment of the court to enforce the same shall in anywise relieve or absolve any person from any liability under the antitrust laws. . . .

(1) Any person who violates any order issued by the Commission, Board, or Secretary under subsection (b) after such order has become final, and while such order is in effect, shall forfeit and pay to the United States a civil penalty of not more than $5,000 for each violation, which shall accrue to the United States and may be recovered in a civil action brought by the United States. Each separate violation of any such order shall be a separate offense, except that in the case of a violation through continuing failure or neglect to obey a final order of the Commission, Board, or Secretary each day of continuance of such failure or neglect shall be deemed a separate offense.

Sec. 12. That any suit, action, or proceeding under the antitrust laws against a corporation may be brought not only in the judicial district whereof it is an inhabitant, but also in any district wherein it may be found or transacts business; and all process in such cases may be served in the district of which it is an inhabitant, or wherever it may be found.

Sec. 13. That in any suit, action, or proceeding brought by or on behalf of the United States subpoenas for witnesses who are required to attend a court of the United States in any judicial district in any case, civil or criminal, arising under the antitrust laws may run into any other district: *Provided,* That in civil cases no writ of subpoena shall issue for witnesses living out of the district in which the court is held at a greater distance than one hundred miles from the place of holding the same without the permission of the trial court being first had upon proper application and cause shown.

Sec. 14. That whenever a corporation shall violate any of the penal provisions of the antitrust laws, such violation shall be deemed to be that of the individual directors, officers, or agents of such corporation who shall have authorized, ordered, or done any of the acts constituting whole or in part such violation, and such violation shall be deemed a misdemeanor, and upon conviction therefor of any such director, officer or agent he shall be punished by a fine of not exceeding $5,000 or by imprisonment for not exceeding one year, or by both, in the discretion of the court.

Sec. 15. That the several district courts of the United States are invested with jurisdiction to prevent and restrain violations of this Act, and it shall be the duty of the United States attorneys, in their respective districts, under the direction of the Attorney General, to institute proceedings in equity to prevent and restrain such violations. Such proceeding may be by way of petition setting forth the case and praying that such violation shall be enjoined or otherwise prohibited. When the parties complained of shall have been duly notified of such petition, the court shall proceed, as soon as may be, to the hearing and determination of the case; and pending such petition, and before final decree, the court may at any time make such temporary restraining order or prohibition as shall be deemed just in the premises. Whenever it shall appear to the court before which any such proceeding may be pending that the ends of justice require that other parties should be brought before the court, the court may cause them to be summoned, whether they reside in the district in which the court is held or not, and subpoenas to that end may be served in any district by the marshal thereof.

Sec. 16. That any person, firm, corporation, or association shall be entitled to sue for and have injunctive relief, in any court of the United States having jurisdiction over the parties, against threatened loss or damage by a violation of the antitrust laws, including sections two, three seven and eight of this Act, when and under the same conditions and principles as injunctive relief against threatened conduct that will cause loss or damage is granted by courts of equity, under the rules governing such proceedings, and upon the execution of proper bond against damages for an injunction improvidently granted and a showing that the danger of irreparable loss or damage is immediate, a preliminary injunction may issue: *Provided,* That nothing herein contained shall be construed to entitle any person, firm, corporation, or association, except the United States, to bring suit in equity for injunctive relief against any common carrier subject to the provisions of Subtitle IV of Title 49 in respect of any matter subject to the regulation, supervision, or other jurisdiction of the Interstate Commerce Commission. In any action under this section in which the plaintiff substantially prevails, the court shall award the cost of suit, including a reasonable attorney's fee, to such plaintiff.[10]

---

10. Section 16 was amended by Act of September 30, 1976, Pub. L. 94–435, 90 Stat. 1396, to provide for an award of costs to a successful plaintiff.

FEDERAL TRADE COMMISSION ACT[11]

An Act To create a Federal Trade Commission, to define its powers and duties, and for other purposes.

Sec. 1. That a commission is hereby created and established, to be known as the Federal Trade Commission (hereinafter referred to as the Commission), which shall be composed of five commissioners, who shall be appointed by the President, by and with the advice and consent of the Senate. Not more than three of the commissioners shall be members of the same political party. The first commissioners appointed shall continue in office for terms of three, four, five, six, and seven years, respectively, from the date of the taking effect of this Act, the term of each to be designated by the President, but their successors shall be appointed for terms of seven years, except that any person chosen to fill a vacancy shall be appointed only for the unexpired term of the commissioner whom he shall succeed: *Provided, however,* That upon the expiration of his term of office a Commissioner shall continue to serve until his successor shall have been appointed and shall have qualified. The President shall choose a chairman from the Commission's membership. No Commissioner shall engage in any other business, vocation, or employment. Any Commissioner may be removed by the President for inefficiency, neglect of duty, or malfeasance in office. A vacancy in the Commission shall not impair the right of the remaining Commissioners to exercise all the powers of the Commission.

The Commission shall have an official seal, which shall be judicially noticed. . . .

Sec. 4. The words defined in this section shall have the following meaning when found in this Act, to wit:

"Commerce" means commerce among the several States or with foreign nations, or in any Territory of the United States or in the District of Columbia, or between any such Territory and another, or between any such Territory and any State or foreign nation, or between the District of Columbia and any State or Territory or foreign nation.

"Corporation" shall be deemed to include any company, trust, so-called Massachusetts trust, or association, incorporated or unincorporated, which is organized to carry on business for its own profit or that of its members, and has shares of capital or capital stock or certificates of interest, and any company, trust, so-called Massachusetts trust, or association, incorporated or unincorporated, without shares of capital or capital stock or certificates of interest, except partnerships, which is organized to carry on business for its own profit or that of its members.

"Documentary evidence" includes all documents, papers, correspondence, books of account, and financial and corporate records.

---

11. Act of September 26, 1914, c. 311, 38 Stat. 717; 15 U.S.C.A. §§ 41–61. Certain less important amendments are omitted. Most of these were made by the Wheeler–Lea Act, Act of March 21, 1938, c. 49, 52 Stat. 111.

"Acts to regulate commerce" means the Act entitled "an act to regulate commerce," approved February 14, 1887, and all Acts amendatory thereof and supplementary thereto and the Communications Act of 1934 and all Acts amendatory and supplementary thereto.

"Antitrust Acts," means the Act entitled "An Act to protect trade and commerce against unlawful restraints and monopolies," approved July 2, 1890; also sections 73 to 76, inclusive, of an Act entitled "An Act to reduce taxation, to provide revenue for the Government, and for other purposes," approved August 27, 1894; also the Act entitled "An Act to amend section 73 and 76 of the Act of August 27, 1894, entitled 'An Act to reduce taxation, to provide revenue for the Government, and for other purposes,'" approved February 12, 1913; and also the Act entitled "An Act to supplement existing laws against unlawful restraints and monopolies, and for other purposes," approved October 15, 1914.

"Banks" means the types of banks and other financial institutions referred to in section 18(f)(2).

Sec. 5. (a)(1) Unfair methods of competition in or affecting commerce, and unfair or deceptive acts or practices in or affecting commerce, are hereby declared unlawful.[12]

(2) The Commission is empowered and directed to prevent persons, partnerships, or corporations, except banks, savings and loan institutions described in section 18(f)(3), common carriers subject to the Acts to regulate commerce, air carriers and foreign air carriers subject to the Federal Aviation Act of 1958, and persons, partnerships, or corporations, insofar as they are subject to the Packers and Stockyards Act, 1921, as amended [17 U.S.C.A. § 181 et seq.], except as provided in section 406(b) of said Act, [17 U.S.C.A. § 227(a)] from using unfair methods of competition in or affecting commerce and unfair or deceptive acts or practices in or affecting commerce.[13]

(3) This subsection shall not apply to unfair methods of competition involving commerce with foreign nations (other than import commerce) unless—

(A) such methods of competition have a direct, substantial, and reasonably foreseeable effect—

(i) on commerce which is not commerce with foreign nations, or on import commerce with foreign nations; or

(ii) on export commerce with foreign nations, of a person engaged in such commerce in the United States; and

12. The phrase, "and unfair or deceptive acts or practices in commerce," was added by the Wheeler–Lea Act, 52 Stat. 111 (1938).

13. The phrase "in or affecting commerce" was added by Act of January 4 1975, Pub.L. 93–637, 88 Stat. 2193, to Sections 5 and 6.

Former subsections (a)(2) through (a)(5), added by the McGuire Fair Trade Act, Act of July 14, 1952, c.745, 66 Stat. 631, were repealed by Act of December 12, 1975, Pub.L. 94–145, 89 Stat. 801. The phrase "savings and loan institutions described in section 18(f)(3)," was added by Act of July 23 1979, Pub.L 96–37, 93 Stat. 95, to Sections 5 and 6.

(B) such effect gives rise to a claim under the provisions of this subsection, other than this paragraph.

If this subsection applies to such methods of competition only because of the operation of subparagraph (A)(ii), this subsection shall apply to such conduct only for injury to export business in the United States.

(b) Whenever the Commission shall have reason to believe that any such person, partnership, or corporation has been or is using any unfair method of competition or unfair or deceptive act or practice in or affecting commerce, and if it shall appear to the Commission that a proceeding by it in respect thereof would be to the interest of the public, it shall issue and serve upon such person, partnership, or corporation a complaint stating its charges in that respect and containing a notice of a hearing upon a day and at a place therein fixed at least thirty days after the service of said complaint. The person, partnership, or corporation so complained of shall have the right to appear at the place and time so fixed and show cause why an order should not be entered by the Commission requiring such person, partnership, or corporation to cease and desist from the violation of the law so charged in said complaint. Any person, partnership, or corporation may make application, and upon good cause shown may be allowed by the Commission to intervene and appear in said proceeding by counsel or in person. The testimony in any such proceeding shall be reduced to writing and filed in the office of the Commission. If upon such hearing the Commission shall be of the opinion that the method of competition or the act or practice in question is prohibited by this Act, it shall make a report in writing in which it shall state its findings as to the facts and shall issue and cause to be served on such person, partnership, or corporation an order requiring such person, partnership, or corporation to cease and desist from using such method of competition or such act or practice. Until the expiration of the time allowed for filing a petition for review, if no such petition has been duly filed within such time, or, if a petition for review has been filed within such time then until the record in the proceeding has been filed in a court of appeals of the United States, as hereinafter provided, the Commission may at any time, upon such notice and in such manner as it shall deem proper, modify or set aside, in whole or in part, any report or any order made or issued by it under this section. After the expiration of the time allowed for filing a petition for review, if no such petition has been duly filed within such time, the Commission may at any time, after notice and opportunity for hearing, reopen and alter, modify, or set aside, in whole or in part, any report or order made or issued by it under this section, whenever in the opinion of the Commission conditions of fact or of law have so changed as to require such action or if the public interest shall so require, except that (1) the said person, partnership, or corporation may, within sixty days after service upon him or it of said report or order entered after such a reopening, obtain a review thereof in the appropriate court of appeals of the United States, in the manner provided in subsection (c) of this section; and (2) in the case of an order, the Commission shall reopen any such order to consider whether such order (including any affirmative relief provision contained in such order) should be altered, modified, or set aside, in whole or in part, if the person, partnership, or corporation involved files a request with the Commission which makes a satisfactory showing that changed conditions of law or fact require such order to be altered, modified, or set aside, in whole or in part. The Commission shall determine whether to alter, modify, or set aside any order of the Commission in response to a request made by a person, partnership, or corporation under paragraph (2) not later than 120 days after the date of the filing of such request.[14]

(c) Any person, partnership, or corporation required by an order of the Commission to cease and desist from using any method of competition or act or practice may obtain a review of such order in the court of appeals of the United States, within any circuit where the method of competition or the act or practice in question was used or where such person, partnership, or corporation resides or carries on business, by filing in the court, within sixty days from the date of the service of such order, a written petition praying that the order of the Commission be set aside.... The findings of the Commission as to the facts, if supported by evidence, shall be conclusive. To the extent that the order of the Commission is affirmed, the court shall thereupon issue its own order commanding obedience to the terms of such order of the Commission. If either party shall apply to the court for leave to adduce additional evidence, and shall show to the satisfaction of the court that such additional evidence is material and that there were reasonable grounds for the failure to adduce such evidence in the proceeding before the Commission, the court may order such additional evidence to be taken before the Commission and to be adduced upon the hearing in such manner and upon such terms and conditions as to the court may seem proper. The Commission may modify its findings as to the facts, or make new findings, by reason of the additional evidence so taken, and it shall file such modified or new findings, which, if supported by evidence, shall be conclusive, and its recommendation, if any, for the modification or setting aside of its original order, with the return *of* such additional evidence. The judgment and decree of the court shall be final, except that the same shall be subject to review by the Supreme Court upon certiorari, as provided in section 347 of Title 28 of the Judicial Code.[15]

(d) Upon the filing of the record with it the jurisdiction of the court of appeals of the United States to affirm, enforce, modify, or set aside orders of the Commission shall be exclusive.

(e) No order of the Commission or judgment of court to enforce the same shall in anywise relieve or absolve any person, partnership, or corporation from any liability under the Antitrust Acts.

(f) Any person, partnership, or corporation who violates an order of the Commission after it has become final, and while such order is in effect,

---

14. Subsection (b)(2) was added by Act of May 28, 1980. Pub.L. 96–252, 94 Stat. 374.

15. Subsection (c) was first amended by the Wheeler–Lea Act, 52 Stat. 111 (1938). Subsections (c) and (d) were amended by Act of August 28, 1958, 72 Stat. 942–43. The substance of Section 240 of the Judicial Code, which has been repealed, may be found in 28 U.S.C.A. § 1254.

shall forfeit and pay to the United States a civil penalty of not more than $10,000 for each violation, which shall accrue to the United States and may be recovered in a civil action brought by the Attorney General of the United States. Each separate violation of such an order shall be a separate offense, except that in the case of a violation through continuing failure to obey or neglect to obey a final order of the Commission, each day of continuance of such failure or neglect shall be deemed a separate offense. In such actions, the United States district courts are empowered to grant mandatory injunctions and such other and further equitable relief as they deem appropriate in the enforcement of such final orders of the Commission.[16]

(m)(1)(A) The Commission may commence a civil action to recover a civil penalty in a district court of the United States against any person, partnership, or corporation which violates any rule under this Act respecting unfair or deceptive acts or practices (other than an interpretive rule or a rule violation of which the Commission has provided is not an unfair or deceptive act or practice in violation of subsection (a)(1)) with actual knowledge or knowledge fairly implied on the basis of objective circumstances that such act is unfair or deceptive and is prohibited by such rule. In such action, such person, partnership, or corporation shall be liable for a civil penalty of not more than $10,000 for each violation.

(B) If the Commission determines in a proceeding under subsection (b) that any act or practice is unfair or deceptive, and issues a final cease and desist order other than a consent order with respect to such act or practice, then the Commission may commence a civil action to obtain a civil penalty in a district court of the United States against any person, partnership, or corporation which engages in such act or practice—

(1) after such cease and desist order becomes final (whether or not such person, partnership, or corporation was subject to such cease and desist order), and

(2) with actual knowledge that such act or practice is unfair or deceptive and is unlawful under subsection (a)(1) of this section.

In such action, such person, partnership, or corporation shall be liable for a civil penalty of not more than $10,000 for each violation.

(C) In the case of a violation through continuing failure to comply wit! a rule or with section 5(a)(1), each day of continuance of such failure shat be treated as a separate violation, for purposes of subparagraphs (A) and (B). In determining the amount of such a civil penalty, the court shall task into account the degree of culpability, any history of such prior conduct ability to pay, effect on ability to continue to do business, and such other matters as justice may require.

Sec. 6. The Commission shall also have power—

---

16. Subsection (*l*) was generally amended by Act of November 16, 1973, Pub.L. 93–15, 87 Stat. 591, to raise the maximum penalty to $10,000 from $5,000, and to empower the district courts to grant mandatory injunctions.

(a) To gather and compile information concerning, and to investigate from time to time the organization, business, conduct, practices and management of any person, partnership, or corporation engaged in or whose business affects commerce, excepting banks, savings and loan institutions described in section 18(f)(3), and common carriers subject to the Act to regulate commerce, and its relation to other persons, partnerships, and corporations.

(b) To require, by general or special orders, persons, partnerships, and corporations engaged in or whose business affects commerce, excepting banks, savings and loan institutions described in section 18(f)(3), Federal credit unions described in section 18(f)(4), and common carriers subject to the Act to regulate commerce, or any class of them, or any of them,-respectively, to file with the Commission in such form as the Commission may prescribe annual or special, or both annual and special, reports or answers in writing to specific questions, furnishing to the Commission such information as it may require as to the organization, business, conduct, practices, management, and relation to other corporations, partnerships, and individuals of the respective persons, partnerships, and corporations filing such reports or answers in writing. Such reports and answers shall be made under oath, or otherwise, as the Commission may prescribe, and shall be filed with the Commission within such reasonable period as the Commission may prescribe, unless additional time be granted in any case by the Commission.

(c) Whenever a final decree has been entered against any defendant corporation in any suit brought by the United States to prevent and restrain any violation of the antitrust Acts, to make investigation, upon its own initiative, of the manner in which the decree has been or is being carried out, and upon the application of the Attorney General it shall be its duty to make such investigation. It shall transmit to the Attorney General a report embodying its findings and recommendations as a result of any such investigation, and the report shall be made public in the discretion of the Commission.

(d) Upon the direction of the President or either House of Congress to investigate and report the facts relating to any alleged violations of the antitrust Acts by any corporation.

(e) Upon the application of the Attorney General to investigate and make recommendations for the readjustment of the business of any corporation alleged to be violating the antitrust Acts in order that the corporation may thereafter maintain its organization, management, and conduct of business in accordance with law.

(f) To make public from time to time such portions of the information obtained by it hereunder as are in the public interest; and to make annual and special reports to the Congress and to submit therewith recommendations for additional legislation; and to provide for the publication of its reports and decisions in such form and manner as may be best adapted for public information and use: *Provided,* That the Commission shall not have any authority to make public any trade secret or any commercial or financial information which is obtained from any person and which is privileged or confidential, except that the Commission may disclose such information to officers and employees of appropriate Federal law enforcement agencies or to any officer or employee of any State law enforcement agency upon the prior certification of an officer of any such Federal or State law enforcement agency that such information will be maintained in confidence and will be used only for official law enforcement purposes.

(g) From time to time to classify corporations and (except as provided in section 18(a)(2) of this Act) to make rules and regulations for the purpose of carrying out the provisions of this Act.

(h) To investigate, from time to time, trade conditions in and with foreign countries where associations, combinations, or practices of manufacturers, merchants or traders, or other conditions, may affect the foreign trade of the United States, and to report to Congress thereon, with such recommendations as it deems advisable.

(i) With respect to the International Antitrust Enforcement Assistance Act of 1994, to conduct investigations of possible violations of foreign antitrust laws (as defined in section 12 of such Act).

Provided, That the exception of "banks, savings and loan institutions described in section 18(f)(3), Federal credit unions described in section 18(f)(3) of this Act, and common carriers subject to the Act to regulate commerce" from the Commission's powers defined in clauses (a) and (b) of this section, shall not be construed to limit the Commission's authority to gather and compile information, to investigate, or to require reports or answers from, any person, partnership, or corporation to the extent that such action is necessary to the investigation of any person, partnership, or corporation, group of persons, partnerships, or corporations, or industry which is not engaged or is engaged only incidentally in banking, in business as a savings and loan institution, in business as a Federal credit union, or in business as a common carrier subject to the Act to regulate commerce.

The Commission shall establish a plan designed to substantially reduce burdens imposed upon small businesses as a result of requirements established by the Commission under clause (b) relating to the filing of quarterly financial reports. . . .

No officer or employee of the Commission or any Commissioner may publish or disclose information to the public, or to any Federal agency; whereby any line-of-business data furnished by a particular establishment or individual can be identified. No one other than designated sworn officers and employees of the Commission may examine the line-of-business reports from individual firms, and information provided in the line-of business program administered by the Commission shall be used only for statistical purposes. Information for carrying out specific law enforcement responsibilities of the Commission shall be obtained under practices and procedures in effect on May 28, 1980, or as changed by law.

Nothing in this section (other than the provisions of clause (c) and clause (d)) shall apply to the business of insurance, except that the

Commission shall have authority to conduct studies and prepare reports relating to the business of insurance. The Commission may exercise such authority only upon receiving a request which is agreed to by a majority of the members of the Committee on Commerce, Science, and Transportation of the Senate or the Committee on Energy and Commerce of the House of Representatives. The authority to conduct any such study shall expire at the end of the Congress during which the request for such study was made.[17]

Sec. 7. In any suit in equity brought by or under the direction of the Attorney General as provided in the antitrust Acts, the court may, upon the conclusion of the testimony therein, if it shall be then of the opinion that the complainant is entitled to relief, refer said suit to the Commission, as a master in chancery, to ascertain and report an appropriate form of decree therein. The Commission shall proceed upon such notice to the parties and under such rules of procedure as the court may prescribe, and upon the coming in of such report such exceptions may be filed and such proceedings had in relation thereto as upon the report of a master in other equity causes, but the court may adopt or reject such report, in whole or in part, and enter such decree as the nature of the case may in its judgment require.

Sec. 8. The several departments and bureaus of the government when directed by the President shall furnish the Commission upon its request, all records, papers and information in their possession relating to any corporation subject to any of the provisions of this Act, and shall detail—from time to time such officials and employees to the Commission as he may direct.

Sec. 9. For the purposes of this Act the Commission, or its duly authorized agent or agents, shall at all reasonable times have access to, for the purpose of examination, and the right to copy any documentary evidence of any person, partnership, or corporation being investigated or proceeded against; and the Commission shall have power to require by subpoena the attendance and testimony of witnesses and the production of all such documentary evidence relating to any matter under investigation. Any member of the Commission may sign subpoenas, and members and examiners of the Commission may administer oaths and affirmations, examine witnesses and receive evidence.

Such attendance of witnesses, and the production of such documentary evidence, may be required from any place in the United States, at any designated place of hearing. And in case of disobedience to a subpoena the Commission may invoke the aid of any court of the United States in requiring the attendance and testimony of witnesses and the production of documentary evidence.

---

17. The proviso was added by Act of November 16, 1973, Pub.L. 93–153, 87 Stat. 592. The Act of January 4, 1975, Pub.L. 93–637, 88 Stat. 2193, amended the section by substituting "person, partnership, or corporation," for "corporation." The Act of May 28, 1980, Pub.L. 96–252, 94 Stat. 374, amended the section by adding the proviso to subsection (f), and by adding the last three undesignated paragraphs.

Any of the district courts of the United States within the jurisdiction of which such inquiry is carried on may, in case of contumacy or refusal to obey a subpoena issued to any person, partnership or corporation, issue an order requiring such person, partnership or corporation to appear before the Commission, or to produce documentary evidence if so ordered, or to give evidence touching the matter in question; and any failure to obey such order of the court may be punished by such court as a contempt thereof.

Upon the application of the Attorney General of the United States, at the request of the Commission, the district courts of the United States shall have jurisdiction to issue writs of mandamus commanding any person, partnership, or corporation to comply with the provisions of this Act or any order of the Commission made in pursuance thereof.

The Commission may order testimony to be taken by deposition in any proceeding or investigation pending under this Act at any stage of such proceeding or investigation. Such depositions may be taken before any person designated by the Commission and having power to administer oaths. Such testimony shall be reduced to writing by the person taking the deposition, or under his direction, and shall then be subscribed by the deponent. Any person may be compelled to appear and depose and to produce documentary evidence in the same manner as witnesses may be compelled to appear and testify and produce documentary evidence before the Commission as herein before provided.

Witnesses summoned before the Commission shall be paid the same fees and mileage that are paid witnesses in the courts of the United States, and witnesses whose depositions are taken and the persons taking the same shall severally be entitled to the same fees as are paid for like services in the courts of the United States.[18]

Sec. 10. Any person who shall neglect or refuse to attend and testify, or to answer any lawful inquiry, or to produce any documentary evidence, if in his power to do so, in obedience to an order of a district court of the United States directing compliance with the subpoena or lawful requirement of the Commission, shall be guilty of an offense and upon conviction thereof by a court of competent jurisdiction shall be punished by a fine of not less than $1,000 nor more than $5,000, or by imprisonment for not more than one year, or by both such fine and imprisonment.

Any person who shall wilfully make, or cause to be made, any false entry or statement of fact in any report required to be made under this Act, or who shall wilfully make, or cause to be made, any false entry in any account, record, or memorandum kept by any person, partnership, or corporation subject to this Act, or who shall wilfully neglect or fail to make or to cause to be made, full, true and correct entries in such account, records, or memoranda of all facts and transactions appertaining to the business of such person, partnership, or corporation, or who shall wilfully remove out of the jurisdiction of the United States, or wilfully mutilate,

18. Section 9 and 10 were expanded to reach person and partnerships as well as corporations by Act of January 4, 1975, Pub.L. 93–637, 88 Stat. 2198.

alter, or by any other means falsify any documentary evidence of such person, partnership, or corporation, or who shall wilfully refuse to submit to the Commission or to any of its authorized agents, for the purpose of inspection and taking copies, any documentary evidence of such person partnership, or corporation in his possession or within his control, shall be deemed guilty of an offense against the United States, and shall be subject upon conviction in any court of the United States of competent jurisdiction to a fine of not less than $1,000 nor more than $5,000, or to imprisonment for a term of not more than three years, or to both such fine and imprisonment.

If any persons, partnership, or corporation required by this Act to file any annual or special report shall fail so to do within the time fixed by the Commission for filing the same, and such failure shall continue for thirty days after notice of such default, the corporation shall forfeit to the United States the sum of $100 for each and every day of the continuance of such failure, which forfeiture shall be payable into the treasury of the United States, and shall be recoverable in a civil suit in the name of the United States brought in the case of a corporation or partnership in the district, where the corporation or partnership has its principal office or in any district in which it shall do business, and in the case of any person in the district where such person resides or has his principal place of business. It shall be the duty of the various United States attorneys, under the direction of the Attorney–General of the United States, to prosecute for the recovery of forfeitures. The costs and expenses of such prosecution shall be paid out of the appropriation for the expenses of the courts of the United States.

Any officer or employee of the Commission who shall make public any information obtained by the Commission without its authority, unless directed by a court, shall be deemed guilty of a misdemeanor, and, upon, conviction thereof, shall be punished by a fine not exceeding $5,000, or by imprisonment not exceeding one year, or by fine and imprisonment, in the discretion of the court.

Sec. 11. Nothing contained in this Act shall be construed to prevent or interfere with the enforcement of the provisions of the antitrust Acts or the Acts to regulate commerce, nor shall anything contained in the Act be construed to alter, modify, or repeal the said antitrust Acts or the Acts to regulate commerce or any part or parts thereof.

Sec. 12. (a) It shall be unlawful for any person, partnership, or corporation to disseminate, or cause to be disseminated, any false advertisement-

(1) By United States mails, or in or having an effect upon commerce by any means, for the purpose of inducing, or which is likely to induce, directly or indirectly, the purchase of food, drugs, devices, services, or cosmetics; or

(2) By any means, for the purpose of inducing, or which is likely to induce, directly or indirectly, the purchase in or having an effect upon commerce of food, drugs, devices, services, or cosmetics.

(b) The dissemination or the causing to be disseminated of any false advertisement within the provisions of subsection (a) of this section shall be an unfair or deceptive act or practice in or affecting commerce within the meaning of section 5.[19]

Sec. 13. . . .

(b) Whenever the Commission has reason to believe—

(1) that any person, partnership, or corporation is violating, or is about to violate, any provision of law enforced by the Federal Trade Commission, and

(2) that the enjoining thereof pending the issuance of a complaint by the Commission and until such complaint is dismissed by the Commission or set aside by the court on review, or until the order of the Commission made thereon has become final, would be in the interest of the public—the Commission by any of its attorneys designated by it for such purpose may bring suit in a district court of the United States to enjoin any such act or practice. Upon a proper showing that, weighing the equities and considering the Commission's likelihood of ultimate success, such action would be in the public interest, and after notice to the defendant, a temporary restraining order or a preliminary injunction may be granted without bond: *Provided, however,* That if a complaint is not filed within such period (not exceeding 20 days) as may be specified by the court after issuance of the temporary restraining order or preliminary injunction, the order or injunction shall be dissolved by the court and be of no further force and effect: *Provided further,* That in proper cases the Commission may seek, and after proper proof, the court may issue, a permanent injunction. Any suit may be brought where such person, partnership, or corporation resides or transacts business, or whenever venue is proper under section 1391 of Title 28, United States Code . . . . . [20]

(A) interpretive rules and general statements of policy with respect to unfair or deceptive acts or practices in or affecting commerce (within the meaning of section 5(a)(1) of this Act), and

(B) rules which define with specificity acts or practices which are unfair or deceptive acts or practices in or affecting commerce (within the meaning of such section 5(a)(1)), except that the Commission shall not develop or promulgate any trade rule or regulation with regard to the regulation of the development and utilization of the standards and certification activities pursuant to this section. Rules under this subparagraph may include requirements prescribed for the purpose of preventing such acts or practices.

19. Sections 12 through 18 were added by the Wheeler–Lea Act, 52 Stat. 111 (1938).

Section 12 was amended to reach activities having an effect on commerce, as well as in commerce, by Act of January 4, 1975, Pub.L. 93–637, 88 Stat. 2193.

20. Subsection (b) was added by Act of November 16, 1973, Pub.L. 93–153, 87 Stat. 592.

(2) The Commission shall have no authority under this Act, other than its authority under this section, to prescribe any rule with respect to unfair or deceptive acts or practices in or affecting commerce (within the meaning of section 5(a)(1)). The preceding sentence shall not affect any authority of the Commission to prescribe rules (including interpretive rules), and general statements of policy, with respect to unfair methods of competition in or affecting commerce.[21]

(b)(1) When prescribing a rule under subsection (a)(1)(B) of this section, the Commission shall proceed in accordance with section 553 of title 5, United States Code (without regard to any reference in such section to sections 556 and 557 of such title), and shall also (A) publish a notice of proposed rulemaking stating with particularity the text of the rule, including any alternatives, which the Commission proposes to promulgate, and the reason for the proposed rule; (B) allow interested persons to submit written data, views, and arguments, and make all such submissions publicly available; (C) provide an opportunity for an informal hearing in accordance with subsection (c); and (D) promulgate, if appropriate, a final rule based on the matter in the rulemaking record (as defined in subsection (e)(1)(B)), together with a statement of basis and purpose.

(2)(A) Prior to the publication of any notice of proposed rulemaking pursuant to paragraph (1)(A), the Commission shall publish an advance notice of proposed rulemaking in the Federal Register. Such advance notice shall—

(i) contain a brief description of the area of inquiry under consideration, the objectives which the Commission seeks to achieve, and possible regulatory alternatives under consideration by the Commission; and

(ii) invite the response of interested parties with respect to such proposed rulemaking, including any suggestions or alternative methods for achieving such objectives. . . . [22]

Sec. 19. (a)(1) If any person, partnership, or corporation violates any rule under this Act respecting unfair or deceptive acts or practices (other than an interpretive rule, or a rule violation of which the Commission has provided is not an unfair or deceptive act or practice in violation of section 5(a)), then the Commission may commence a civil action against such person, partnership, or corporation for relief under subsection (b) in a United States district court or in any court of competent jurisdiction of a State.

(2) If any person, partnership, or corporation engages in any unfair or deceptive act or practice (within the meaning of section 5(a)(1)) with respect to which the Commission has issued a final cease and desist order

21. Subsections (a) and (b) were added by Act of January 4, 1975, Pub.L. 93–637, 88 Stat. 2193.

Subsection (a) was amended by Act of May 28,1980, Pub.L. 96–252,94 Stat. 376, to restrict the FTC's power to develop rules concerning "the regulation of the development and utilization of the standards and certification activities pursuant to this section."

22. Subsection (b)(2) was added by Act of May 28,1980, Pub.L. 96–252,94 Stat. 376.

which is applicable to such person, partnership, or corporation, then the Commission may commence a civil action against such person, partnership, or corporation in a United States district court or in any court of competent jurisdiction of a State. If the Commission satisfies the court that the act or practice to which the cease and desist order relates is one which a reasonable man would have known under the circumstances was dishonest or fraudulent, the court may grant relief under subsection (b).

(b) The court in an action under subsection (a) shall have jurisdiction to grant such relief as the court finds necessary to redress injury to consumers or other persons, partnerships, and corporations resulting from the rule violation or the unfair or deceptive act or practice, as the case may be. Such relief may include, but shall not be limited to, rescission or reformation of contracts, the refund of money or return of property, the payment of damages, and public notification respecting the rule violation or the unfair or deceptive act or practice, as the case may be; except that nothing in this subsection is intended to authorize the imposition of any exemplary or punitive damages.

(c)(1) If (A) a cease and desist order issued under section 5(b) has become final under section 5(g) with respect to any person's, partnership's, or corporation's rule violation or unfair or deceptive act or practice, and (B) an action under this section is brought with respect to such person's, partnership's, or corporation's rule violation or act or practice, then the findings of the Commission as to the material facts in the proceeding under section 5(b) with respect to such person's, partnership's, or corporation's rule violation or act or practice, shall be conclusive unless (i) the terms of such cease and desist order expressly provide that the Commission's findings shall not be conclusive, or (ii) the order became final by reason of section 5(g)(1), in which case such finding shall be conclusive if supported by evidence,

(2) The court shall cause notice of an action under this section to be given in a manner which is reasonably calculated under all of the circumstances, to apprise the persons, partnerships, and corporations allegedly injured by the defendant's rule violation or act or practice of the pendency of such action. Such notice may, in the discretion of the court, be given by publication.

(d) No action may be brought by the Commission under this section more than 3 years after the rule violation to which an action under subsection (a)(1) relates, or the unfair or deceptive act or practice to which an action under subsection (a)(2) relates; except that if a cease and desist order with respect to any person's, partnership's, or corporation's rule violation or unfair or deceptive act or practice has become final and such order was issued in proceeding under section (5)(b) which was commenced not later than 3 years after the rule violation or act or practice occurred, a civil action may be commenced under this section against such person, partnership, or corporation at any time before the expiration of one year after such order becomes final.

(e) Remedies provided in this section are in addition to, and not in lieu of, any other remedy or right of action provided by State or Federal law. Nothing in this section shall be construed to affect any authority of the Commission under any other provision of law.[23]

Sec. 20. . . .

(b) For the purpose of investigations performed pursuant to this section with respect to unfair or deceptive acts or practices in or affecting commerce (within the meaning of section 5(a)(1)), all actions of the Commission taken under section 6 and section 9 shall be conducted pursuant to subsection (c).

(c)(1) Whenever the Commission has reason to believe that any person may be in possession, custody, or control of any documentary material, or may have any information, relevant to unfair or deceptive acts or practices in or affecting commerce (within the meaning of section 5(a)(1)), the Commission may, before the institution of any proceedings under this Act, issue in writing, and cause to be served upon such person, a civil investigative demand requiring such person to produce such documentary material for inspection and copying or reproduction, to file written reports or answers to questions, to give oral testimony concerning documentary material or other information, or to furnish any combination of such material, answers, or testimony . . . . . [24]

Sec. 25. This Act may be cited as the "Federal Trade Commission Act."

"ANTITRUST CIVIL PROCESS ACT"[25]

AN ACT TO authorize the Attorney General to compel the production of documentary evidence required in civil investigations for the enforcement of the antitrust laws, and for other purposes.

Sec. 1. That this Act may e cited as the "Antitrust Civil Process Act".

Sec. 2. For the purposes of this Act—

(a) The term "antitrust law" includes:

(1) Each provision of law defined as one of the antitrust laws by section 1 of the Act entitled "An Act to supplement existing laws against unlawful restraints and monopolies, and for other purposes", approved October 15, 1914 (38 Stat. 730, as amended; 15 U.S.C. 12), commonly known as the Clayton Act; and

(2) Any statute enacted on and after September 19, 1962 by the Congress which prohibits, or makes available to the United States in any court of the United States any civil remedy with respect to any restraint upon or monopolization of interstate or foreign trade or commerce;

23. Section 19 was added by Act of January 4, 1975, Pub.L. 93–637, 88 Stat. 2201.

24. Section 20 was added by Act of May 28, 1990, Pub.L. 96–252, 94 Stat. 380.

25. 76 Stat. 548 (1962), 15 U.S.C.A. §§ 1311–14.

(b) The term "antitrust order" means any final order, decree, or judgment of any court of the United States, duly entered in any case or proceeding arising under any antitrust law;

(c) The term "antitrust investigation" means any inquiry conducted by any antitrust investigator for the purpose of ascertaining whether any person is or has been engaged in any antitrust violation or in any activities in preparation for a merger, acquisition, joint venture, or similar transaction, which, if consummated, may result in an antitrust violation;

(d) The term "antitrust violation" means any act or omission in violation of any antitrust law or any antitrust order or, with respect to the International Antitrust Enforcement Act of 1944 any of the foreign anttrust laws;

(e) The term "antitrust investigator" means any attorney or investigator employed by the Department of Justice who is charged with the duty of enforcing or carrying into effect any antitrust law;

(f) The term "person" means any natural person, partnership, corporation, association, or other legal entity, including any person acting under color or authority of State law;

(g) The term "documentary material" includes the original or any copy of any book, record, report, memorandum, paper, communication, tabulation, chart, or other document, and any product of discovery;.... [26]

Sec. 3. (a) Whenever the Attorney General, *or* the Assistant Attorney General in charge of the Antitrust Division of the Department of Justice, has reason to believe that any person may be in possession, custody, or control of any documentary material, or may have any information, relevant to a civil antitrust investigation, or, with respect to the International Antitrust Enforcement Assistance Act of 1994, an investigation authorized by section 3 of such Act, he may, prior to the institution of a civil or criminal proceeding by the United States thereon, issue in writing, and cause to be served upon such person, a civil investigative demand requiring such person to produce such documentary material for inspection and copying or reproduction, to answer in writing written interrogatories, to give oral testimony concerning documentary material or information, or to furnish any combination of such material, answers, or testimony. Whenever a civil investigative demand is an express demand for any product of discovery, the Attorney General or the Assistant Attorney General in charge of the Antitrust Division shall cause to be served, in any manner authorized by this section, a copy of such demand upon the person from whom the discovery was obtained and notify the person to whom such demand is issued of the date on which such copy was served ...

Sec. 4. (a) The Assistant Attorney General in charge of the Antitrust Division of the Department of Justice shall designate an antitrust investi-

---

26. Section 2 through 6 of the Act were generally amended first by Act of September 30, 1976, Pub.L. 94–435, 90 Stat. 1389, then by Act of September 12, 1980, Pub.L. 96–349, 94 Stat. 1154, and finally by Act of November 2, 1994, Pub.L. 103–438, 108 Stat. 4598.

gator to serve as custodian of documentary material, answers to interrogatories, and transcripts of oral testimony received under this Act, and such additional antitrust investigators as he shall determine from time to time to be necessary to serve as deputies to such officer.

Sec. 5. (a) Whenever any person fails to comply with any civil investigative demand duly served upon him under section 3 or whenever satisfactory copying or reproduction of any such material cannot be done and such person refuses to surrender such material, the Attorney General, through such officers or attorneys as he may designate, may file, in the district court of the United States for any judicial district in which such person resides, is found, or transacts business, and serve upon such person a petition for an order of such court for the enforcement of this Act....

Sec. 6. (a) Section 1505, title 18, United States Code, is amended to read as follows:

"§ 1505. Obstruction of proceedings before departments, agencies, and committees

"Whoever, with intent to avoid, evade, prevent, or obstruct compliance, in whole or in part, with any civil investigative demand duly and properly made under the Antitrust Civil Process Act, willfully withholds, misrepresents, removes from any place, conceals, covers up, destroys, mutilates, alters, or by other means falsifies any documentary material, answers to written interrogatories, or oral testimony, which is the subject of such demand; or attempts to do so or solicits another to do so;

"Shall be fined not more than $5,000 or imprisoned not more than five years, or both."

(b) The analysis of chapter 73 of title 18 of United States Code is amended so that the title of section 1505 shall read therein as follows:

"1505. Obstruction of proceedings before departments, agencies, and committees."

†